GOOD NEWS
BIBLE

TODAY'S ENGLISH VERSION
SECOND EDITION

THOMAS NELSON PUBLISHERS
Nashville • Atlanta • London • Vancouver

GOOD NEWS
BIBLE

TODAY'S ENGLISH VERSION
SECOND EDITION

Quotation Rights For Today's English Version Bible

The American Bible Society is glad to grant authors and publishers the right to use up to one thousand (1,000) verses from the Today's English Version text in church, religious and other publications without the need to seek and receive written permission. However, the extent of quotation must not comprise a complete book nor should it amount to more than 50% of the work. The proper copyright notice must appear on the title or copyright page.

When quotations from TEV are used in non-saleable media, such as church bulletins, orders of service, posters, transparencies or similar media, a complete copyright notice is not required, but the initials (TEV) must appear at the end of each quotation.

Requests for quotations in excess of one thousand (1,000) verses in any publication must be directed to, and written approval received from, the American Bible Society, 1865 Broadway, New York, NY 10023.

ALPHABETICAL LIST OF
BIBLICAL BOOKS AND ABBREVIATIONS

Name	Abbrev.	Page	Name	Abbrev.	Page
Acts	Ac	145	Judges	Jg	229
Amos	Am	872	1 Kings	1 K	325
1 Chronicles	1 Ch	392	2 Kings	2 K	358
2 Chronicles	2 Ch	423	Lamentations	Lm	785
Colossians	Col	250	Leviticus	Lv	97
1 Corinthians	1 Co	209	Luke	Lk	69
2 Corinthians	2 Co	225	Malachi	Ml	912
Daniel	Dn	844	Mark	Mk	43
Deuteronomy	Dt	165	Matthew	Mt	3
Ecclesiastes	Ec	650	Micah	Mic	886
Ephesians	Eph	240	Nahum	Nh	892
Esther	Es	487	Nehemiah	Ne	470
Exodus	Ex	53	Numbers	Nu	127
Ezekiel	Ez	793	Obadiah	Ob	881
Ezra	Ezra	459	1 Peter	1 P	289
Galatians	Ga	235	2 Peter	2 P	293
Genesis	Gn	1	Philemon	Phm	270
Habakkuk	Hb	895	Philippians	Phil	246
Haggai	Hg	901	Proverbs	Pr	626
Hebrews	He	273	Psalms	Ps	534
Hosea	Ho	858	Revelation	Rev	304
Isaiah	Is	665	Romans	Ro	191
James	Jas	285	Ruth	Ru	255
Jeremiah	Jr	726	1 Samuel	1 S	260
Job	Job	498	2 Samuel	2 S	295
Joel	Jl	868	Song of Songs	Sgs	657
John	Jn	112	1 Thessalonians	1 Th	254
1 John	1 Jn	296	2 Thessalonians	2 Th	258
2 John	2 Jn	300	1 Timothy	1 Ti	260
3 John	3 Jn	301	2 Timothy	2 Ti	265
Jonah	Jon	882	Titus	Titus	268
Joshua	Js	203	Zechariah	Zec	903
Jude	Jd	302	Zephaniah	Zep	898

OTHER ABBREVIATIONS

Circa (around)	c.
Old Testament	OT
New Testament	NT
Septuagint	LXX

INDEX OF TEXTUAL STUDY AIDS

ALPHABETICAL LIST OF
BIBLICAL BOOKS AND ABBREVIATIONS

OTHER ABBREVIATIONS

Circa (around)	c.
Old Testament	OT
New Testament	NT
Septuagint	LXX

INDEX OF TEXTUAL STUDY AIDS

FOREWORD

The Bible in Today's English Version is a new translation which seeks to state clearly and accurately the meaning of the original texts in words and forms that are widely accepted by all people who use English as a means of communication. This translation does not follow the traditional vocabulary and style found in the historic English Bible versions. Rather it attempts in this century to set forth the Biblical content and message in a standard, everyday, natural form of English.

The aim of this Bible is to give today's readers maximum understanding of the content of the original texts. The Preface explains the nature of special aids for readers which are included in the volume. It also sets forth the basic principles which the translators followed in their work.

The Bible in Today's English Version was translated and published by the United Bible Societies for use throughout the world. The Bible Societies trust that people everywhere will not only find increased understanding through the reading and study of this translation, but will also find a saving hope through faith in God, who made possible this message of Good News for all people.

PREFACE

In September 1966 the American Bible Society published *The New Testament in Today's English Version,* a translation intended for people everywhere for whom English is either their mother tongue or an acquired language. Shortly thereafter the United Bible Societies requested the American Bible Society to undertake on its behalf a translation of the Old Testament following the same principles. Accordingly the American Bible Society appointed a group of translators to prepare the translation. In 1971 this group added a British consultant recommended by the British and Foreign Bible Society. The translation of the Old Testament, which was completed in 1976, was joined to the fourth edition New Testament, thus completing the first edition of the *Good News Bible.*

The basic text for the Old Testament is the Masoretic Text made available through printed editions, published by the UBS, and since 1977 under the title of *Biblia Hebraica Stuttgartensia.* In some instances the words of the printed consonantal text have been divided differently or have been read with a different set of vowels; at times a variant reading in the margin of the Hebrew text (qere) has been followed instead of the reading in the text (kethiv); and in other instances a variant reading supported by one or more Hebrew manuscripts has been adopted. Where no Hebrew source yields a satisfactory meaning in the context, the translation has either followed one or more of the ancient versions (e.g. Greek, Syriac, Latin) or has adopted a reconstructed text (technically referred to as a conjectural emendation) based on scholarly consensus; such departures from the Hebrew are indicated in footnotes.

The basic text for the translation of the New Testament is *The Greek New Testament* published by the United Bible Societies (3rd edition, 1975), but in a few instances the translation is based on a variant reading supported by one or more Greek manuscripts.

Drafts of the translation in its early stages were sent for comments and suggestions to a Review Panel consisting of prominent theologians and Biblical scholars appointed by the American Bible Society Board of Managers in its capacity as trustee for the translation. In addition, drafts were sent to major English-speaking Bible Societies throughout the world. Final approval of the translation on behalf of the United Bible Societies was given by the American Bible Society's Board of Managers upon recommendation of its Translations Committee.

The primary concern of the translators has been to provide a faithful translation of the meaning of the Hebrew, Aramaic, and Greek texts. Their first task was to understand correctly the meaning of the original. At times the original meaning cannot be precisely known, not only because the meaning of some words and phrases cannot be determined with a great degree of assurance, but also because the underlying cultural and historical context is sometimes beyond recovery. All aids available were used in this task, including the ancient versions and the modern translations in English and other languages. After ascertaining as accurately as possible the meaning of the original, the translators' next task was to express that meaning in a manner and form easily understood by the readers. Since this translation is intended for all who use English as a means of communication, the translators have tried to avoid words and forms not in current or widespread use; but no artificial limit has been set to the range of the vocabulary employed. Every effort has been made to use language that is natural, clear, simple, and unambiguous. Consequently there has been no attempt to reproduce in English the parts of speech, sentence structure, word order and grammatical devices of the original languages. Faithfulness in translation also includes a faithful representation of the cultural and historical features of the original. Certain features, however, such as the hours of the day and the measures of weight, capacity, distance, and area, are given their modern equivalents, since the information in those terms conveys more meaning to the reader than the Biblical form of those terms.

In cases where a person or place is called by two or more different names in the original, this translation has normally used only the more familiar name in all places; e.g. King Jehoiachin of Judah (Jeremiah 52.31), also called Jeconiah (Jeremiah 24.1) and Coniah (Jeremiah 37.1). Where a proper name is spelled two or more different ways in the original text, this translation has used only one spelling; e.g. Nebuchadnezzar, also spelled Nebuchadrezzar (compare Jeremiah 29.3 and 29.21), and Priscilla, also spelled Prisca (compare Acts 18.26 and Romans 16.3).

In view of the differences in vocabulary and form which exist between the American and the British use of the English language, a British edition has been published, which incorporates changes that are in keeping with British usage.

Following an ancient tradition, begun by the first translation of the Hebrew Scriptures into Greek (the Septuagint) and followed by the vast majority of English translations, the distinctive Hebrew name for God (usually transliterated *Jehovah* or *Yahweh*) is in this translation represented by "Lord." When *Adonai*, normally translated "Lord," is followed by *Yahweh*, the combination is rendered by the phrase "Sovereign Lord."

Since the appearance of the full Bible in *Today's English Version* in 1976, some minor editorial changes and corrections of printing errors have been introduced into the text in connection with various printings. The New Testament was already in its fourth edition at the time the full Bible appeared, but for the Old Testament and the Deuterocanonicals/Apocrypha there has been no revised edition. The preparation and publication of this second edition of the full TEV Bible in two formats, with and without the Deuterocanonicals/Apocrypha, is the result of a broad international process of careful review and evaluation of the TEV translation by many scholars and experts over a period of several years.

In December 1986, acting in response to a mounting perception of a need for TEV revisions, the ABS Board of Managers approved the undertaking of a revision of the TEV translation. The revision is restricted to two main areas of concern that have been raised and discussed over the years since the first appearance of *Today's English Version*: (1) passages in which the English style has been unnecessarily exclusive and inattentive to gender concerns, and (2) passages in which the translation has been seen as problematic or insensitive from either a stylistic or an exegetical viewpoint.

The process followed in preparing this revised edition was one of first inviting and collecting proposals for needed revisions from all English-language Bible Societies and English-speaking UBS translations consultants around the world, as well as numerous scholarly consultants in the USA and representatives of various American churches. The proposals received were then assembled for review and evaluation by the same broad array of experts whose specializations included translation, linguistics, English usage, literary and poetic style, biblical studies, and theology. In a series of four stages, consensus was sought on which proposals were necessary and valid, and at each of these review stages the number of proposals under consideration was reduced until widespread agreement was reached. On the recommendation of the program committee of the ABS Board of Trustees, and its Translations subcommittee, the ABS Board acted to approve the revisions for the TEV Second Edition in September, 1990. These revisions have also been adapted for use in British usage editions of the TEV.

In the decade and a half since publication of the full TEV Bible, many Bible readers have become sensitive to the negative effects of exclusive language; that is, to the ways in which the built-in linguistic biases of the ancient languages and the English language toward the masculine gender has led some Bible readers to feel excluded from being addressed by the scriptural Word. This concern has led to the revision of most major English translations during the 1980s, and, increasingly, TEV readers have written to request that the Bible Society take this concern into consideration in preparing any revision. In practical terms what this means is that, where references in particular passages are to both men and women, the revision aims at language that is not exclusively masculine-oriented. At the same time, however, great care was taken not to distort the historical situation of the ancient patriarchal culture of Bible times.

In order to make the text easier to understand, various kinds of readers' helps are supplied. The text itself has been divided into sections, and headings are provided which indicate the contents of the section. Where there are parallel accounts elsewhere in the Bible, a reference to such a passage appears within parentheses below the heading. There are, in addition, several kinds of notes which appear at the bottom of the page. (1) *Cultural or Historical Notes.* These provide information required to enable the reader to understand the meaning of the text in terms of its original setting (e.g. the explanation of *Rahab* in Psalm 89.10; the explanation of *Day of Atonement* in Acts 27.9). (2) *Textual Notes.* In the Old Testament these indicate primarily those places where the translators were compelled for a variety of reasons to base the translation on some text other than the Hebrew. Where one or more of the ancient versions were followed, the note indicates this by *One ancient translation* (e.g. Genesis 1.26) or *Some ancient translations* (e.g. Genesis 4.8); where a conjectural emendation was adopted, the note reads *Probable text* (e.g. Genesis 10.14). In the New Testament, there are textual notes indicating some of the places where there are significant differences among the ancient manuscripts. These differences may consist of additions to the text (e.g. Matthew 21.43), deletions (e.g. Matthew 24.36), or substitutions (e.g. Mark 1.41). (3) *Alternative Renderings.* In many places the precise meaning of the original text is in dispute, and there are two or more different ways in which the text may be understood. In some of the more important of such instances an alternative rendering is given (e.g. Genesis 2.9; Matthew 6.11).

There are several appendices at the end of the volume. A *Word List* identifies many objects or cultural features whose meaning may not be known to all readers. A *Chronological Chart* gives the approximate dates of the major events recorded in the Bible. The *Maps* are designed to help the reader to visualize the geographical setting of countries and localities mentioned in the Bible.

The numbering of chapters and verses in this translation follows the traditional system of major English translations of the Bible. In some instances, however, where the order of thought or events in two or more verses is more clearly represented by a rearrangement of the material, two or more verse numbers are joined (e.g. Exodus 2.15,16; Acts 1.21,22).

No one knows better than the translators how difficult has been their task. But they have performed it gladly, conscious always of the presence of the Holy Spirit and of the tremendous debt which they owe to the dedication and scholarship of those who have preceded them. The Bible is not simply great literature to be admired and revered; it is Good News for all people everywhere—a message both to be understood and to be applied in daily life. It is with the prayer that the Lord of the Scriptures will be pleased to use this translation for his sovereign purpose that the United Bible Societies has published the Bible in *Today's English Version*. And to Christ be the glory forever and ever!

CONTENTS

OLD TESTAMENT

NEW TESTAMENT

HELPS FOR THE READER

OLD TESTAMENT

THE PENTATEUCH

The Pentateuch is the first five books of the Bible, called *Torah* in the Hebrew Scriptures. Though we often call these books The Law, Torah does not mean law, but teaching. Basic to the Torah is the idea of the covenant, which is an agreement. Biblical covenants have three parts: (1) a statement about God's saving act (what God brings to the agreement); (2) a statement about what God expects from humanity in response; (3) a sign or symbol as a reminder of the covenant.

Genesis begins with the creation, setting the covenant in the context of God's rule over the entire universe. The first covenant is with Adam and Eve, representatives of all humanity, and includes the understanding that human beings will be responsible stewards of all of creation. The second covenant is with Noah, the promise that the world will never again be destroyed by flood. Then the biblical account focuses on one particular person, Abraham, who enters into covenant with God and is given the promise that he and his descendants will become a blessing to all humanity.

Exodus centers on the escape of God's people from Egypt under the leadership of Moses and the making of the great covenant at Mt. Sinai. The parts of the covenant are clear: God's gracious saving act is seen in Passover and Exodus; the expectation of human response is summarized in the Ten Commandments; and the Feast of the Passover is the great sign and reminder. Moses, Aaron, and Miriam are both the leaders of God's people and the models of struggle and faith.

Leviticus takes its name from the Latin word for *book of the Levites*. The major concern of the book is the holiness of the community of Israel. Holiness means to be set apart by God for a special purpose. Holiness is expressed in proper forms of worship and living out the love of God in the routine of daily life. The Holiness Code (chs. 17—27) is a good example of how worship and justice mingle together in the life of Israel.

Numbers is named for the census that begins the book. The narrative part of the book is the wilderness journey from Kadesh-barnea to the promised land. Included are the great accounts of the spies entering Canaan, the 40 years of wandering, and the miracles of Moses. Finally come the conquests of the Kingdoms of Sihon and Og in the Transjordan, and the story of Balaam. The book ends with Israel prepared to enter the promised land under the leadership of Joshua.

Deuteronomy is written as Moses' farewell speech before the tribes enter Canaan. It reviews God's acts of salvation and the implications of salvation for life. The book itself was apparently found in the Temple in the reign of Josiah (621 B.C.). The discovery sparked a great religious reform. One of the real concerns of Deuteronomy is how to make old traditions relevant for a new time. The most important statement of belief is the Shema, found in 6.4–5.

GENESIS

Introduction

The name Genesis means "origin." The book tells about the creation of the universe, the origin of human beings, the beginning of sin and suffering in the world, and about God's way of dealing with people. Genesis can be divided into two main parts:

1) Chapters 1–11 The creation of the world and the early history of the human race. Here are the accounts of Adam and Eve, Cain and Abel, Noah and the flood, and the Tower of Babylon.

2) Chapters 12–50 The history of the early ancestors of the Israelites. The first is Abraham, who was notable for his faith and his obedience to God. Then follow the stories of his son Isaac, and grandson Jacob (also called Israel), and of Jacob's twelve sons, the founders of the twelve tribes of Israel. Special attention is given to one of the sons, Joseph, and the events that brought Jacob and his other sons with their families to live in Egypt,

While this book tells stories about people, it is first and foremost an account of what God has done. It begins with the affirmation that God created the universe, and it ends with a promise that God will continue to show his concern for his people. Throughout the book the main character is God, who judges and punishes those who do wrong, leads and helps his people, and shapes their history. This ancient book was written to record the story of a people's faith and to help keep that faith alive.

Outline of Contents

The Story of Creation

1 In the beginning, when God created the universe,[a] 2the earth was formless and desolate. The raging ocean that covered everything was engulfed in total darkness, and the Spirit of God[b] was moving over the water. 3Then God commanded, "Let there be light"—and light appeared. 4God was pleased with what he saw. Then he separated the light from the darkness, 5and he named the light "Day" and the darkness "Night." Evening passed and morning came—that was the first day.

6-7Then God commanded, "Let there be a dome to divide the water and to keep it in two separate places"—and it was done. So God made a dome, and it sepa- rated the water under it from the water above it. 8He named the dome "Sky." Evening passed and morning came— that was the second day.

9Then God commanded, "Let the wa- ter below the sky come together in one place, so that the land will appear"—and it was done. 10He named the land "Earth," and the water which had come together he named "Sea." And God was pleased with what he saw. 11Then he commanded, "Let the earth produce all kinds of plants, those that bear grain and those that bear fruit"—and it was done. 12So the earth produced all kinds of plants, and God was pleased with what he saw. 13Evening passed and morning came—that was the third day.

14Then God commanded, "Let lights

---

a In the beginning ... the universe; or In the beginning God created the universe; or When God began to create the universe.   b the Spirit of God; or the power of God; or a wind from God; or an awesome wind.

GENESIS

appear in the sky to separate day from night and to show the time when days, years, and religious festivals[c] begin; 15they will shine in the sky to give light to the earth"—and it was done. 16So God made the two larger lights, the sun to rule over the day and the moon to rule over the night; he also made the stars. 17He placed the lights in the sky to shine on the earth, 18to rule over the day and the night, and to separate light from darkness. And God was pleased with what he saw. 19Evening passed and morning came—that was the fourth day.

20Then God commanded, "Let the water be filled with many kinds of living beings, and let the air be filled with birds." 21So God created the great sea monsters, all kinds of creatures that live in the water, and all kinds of birds. And God was pleased with what he saw. 22He blessed them all and told the creatures that live in the water to reproduce and to fill the sea, and he told the birds to increase in number. 23Evening passed and morning came—that was the fifth day.

24Then God commanded, "Let the earth produce all kinds of animal life: domestic and wild, large and small"— and it was done. 25So God made them all, and he was pleased with what he saw. 26Then God said, "And now we will make human beings; they will be like us and resemble us. They will have power over the fish, the birds, and all animals, domestic and wild,[d] large and small." 27So God created human beings, making them to be like himself. He created them male and female, 28blessed them, and said, "Have many children, so that your descendants will live all over the earth and bring it under their control. I am putting you in charge of the fish, the birds, and all the wild animals. 29I have provided all kinds of grain and all kinds of fruit for you to eat; 30but for all the wild animals and for all the birds I have provided grass and leafy plants for food"— and it was done. 31God looked at everything he had made, and he was

very pleased. Evening passed and morning came—that was the sixth day.

2 And so the whole universe was completed. 2By the seventh day God finished what he had been doing and stopped working. 3He blessed the seventh day and set it apart as a special day, because by that day he had completed his creation[e] and stopped working. 4And that is how the universe was created.

The Garden of Eden

When the LORD[f] God made the universe, 5there were no plants on the earth and no seeds had sprouted, because he had not sent any rain, and there was no one to cultivate the land; 6but water would come up from beneath the surface and water the ground.

7Then the LORD God took some soil from the ground[g] and formed a man[g] out of it; he breathed life-giving breath into his nostrils and the man began to live.

8Then the LORD God planted a garden in Eden, in the East, and there he put the man he had formed. 9He made all kinds of beautiful trees grow there and produce good fruit. In the middle of the garden stood the tree that gives life and the tree that gives knowledge of what is good and what is bad.[h]

10A stream flowed in Eden and watered the garden; beyond Eden it divided into four rivers. 11The first river is the Pishon; it flows around the country of Havilah. (12Pure gold is found there and also rare perfume and precious stones.) 13The second river is the Gihon; it flows around the country of Cush.[i] 14The third river is the Tigris, which flows east of Assyria, and the fourth river is the Euphrates.

15Then the LORD God placed the man in the Garden of Eden to cultivate it and guard it. 16He told him, "You may eat the fruit of any tree in the garden, 17except the tree that gives knowledge of what is good and what is bad.[j] You must not eat

---

c religious festivals; or seasons.   d One ancient translation animals, domestic and wild; Hebrew domestic animals and all the earth.   e by that day he had completed his creation; or on that day he completed his creation.   f THE LORD: Where the Hebrew text has Yahweh, traditionally transliterated as Jehovah, this translation employs LORD with capital letters, following a usage which is widespread in English versions.   g GROUND . . . MAN: The Hebrew words for "man" and "ground" have similar sounds.   h knowledge of what is good and what is bad; or knowledge of everything.   i Cush (of Mesopotamia); or Ethiopia.   j knowledge of what is good and what is bad; or knowledge of everything.

GENESIS

the fruit of that tree; if you do, you will die the same day."

18 Then the Lord God said, "It is not good for the man to live alone. I will make a suitable companion to help him." 19 So he took some soil from the ground and formed all the animals and all the birds. Then he brought them to the man to see what he would name them; and that is how they all got their names. 20 So the man named all the birds and all the animals; but not one of them was a suitable companion to help him.

21 Then the Lord God made the man fall into a deep sleep, and while he was sleeping, he took out one of the man's ribs and closed up the flesh. 22 He formed a woman out of the rib and brought her to him. 23 Then the man said,

"At last, here is one of my own
      kind—
Bone taken from my bone, and
      flesh from my flesh.
'Woman' is her name because she
      was taken out of man."k

24 That is why a man leaves his father and mother and is united with his wife, and they become one.

25 The man and the woman were both naked, but they were not embarrassed.

Human Disobedience

3 Now the snake was the most cunning animal that the Lord God had made. The snake asked the woman, "Did God really tell you not to eat fruit from any tree in the garden?"

2 "We may eat the fruit of any tree in the garden," the woman answered, 3 "except the tree in the middle of it. God told us not to eat the fruit of that tree or even touch it; if we do, we will die."

4 The snake replied, "That's not true; you will not die. 5 God said that because he knows that when you eat it, you will be like God l and know what is good and what is bad." m

6 The woman saw how beautiful the tree was and how good its fruit would be to eat, and she thought how wonderful it would be to become wise. So she took some of the fruit and ate it. Then she gave some to her husband, and he also ate it.

7 As soon as they had eaten it, they were given understanding and realized that they were naked; so they sewed fig leaves together and covered themselves.

8 That evening they heard the Lord God walking in the garden, and they hid from him among the trees. 9 But the Lord God called out to the man, "Where are you?"

10 He answered, "I heard you in the garden; I was afraid and hid from you, because I was naked."

11 "Who told you that you were naked?" God asked. "Did you eat the fruit that I told you not to eat?"

12 The man answered, "The woman you put here with me gave me the fruit, and I ate it."

13 The Lord God asked the woman, "Why did you do this?"

She replied, "The snake tricked me into eating it."

God Pronounces Judgment

14 Then the Lord God said to the snake, "You will be punished for this; you alone of all the animals must bear this curse: From now on you will crawl on your belly, and you will have to eat dust as long as you live. 15 I will make you and the woman hate each other; her offspring and yours will always be enemies. Her offspring will crush your head, and you will bite her offspring's n heel."

16 And he said to the woman, "I will increase your trouble in pregnancy and your pain in giving birth. In spite of this, you will still have desire for your husband, yet you will be subject to him."

17 And he said to the man, "You listened to your wife and ate the fruit which I told you not to eat. Because of what you have done, the ground will be under a curse. You will have to work hard all your life to make it produce enough food for you. 18 It will produce weeds and thorns, and you will have to eat wild plants. 19 You will have to work hard and sweat to make the soil produce anything, until you go back to the soil from which you were formed. You were made from soil, and you will become soil again."

20 Adam o named his wife Eve, p because she was the mother of all human

k WOMAN . . . MAN: The Hebrew words for "woman" and "man" have rather similar sounds.
l God; or the gods.   m know what is good and what is bad; or know everything.   n her offspring's; or their.   o ADAM: This name in Hebrew means "all human beings."   p EVE: This name sounds similar to the Hebrew word for "living," which is rendered in this context as "human beings."

GENESIS

beings. 21 And the LORD God made clothes out of animal skins for Adam and his wife, and he clothed them.

Adam and Eve Are Sent Out of the Garden

22 Then the LORD God said, "Now these human beings have become like one of us and have knowledge of what is good and what is bad.q They must not be allowed to take fruit from the tree that gives life, eat it, and live forever." 23 So the LORD God sent them out of the Garden of Eden and made them cultivate the soil from which they had been formed. 24 Then at the east side of the garden he put living creaturesr and a flaming sword which turned in all directions. This was to keep anyone from coming near the tree that gives life.

Cain and Abel

4 Then Adam had intercourse with his wife, and she became pregnant. She bore a son and said, "By the LORD's help I have gotten a son." So she named him Cain.s 2 Later she gave birth to another son, Abel. Abel became a shepherd, but Cain was a farmer. 3 After some time Cain brought some of his harvest and gave it as an offering to the LORD. 4 Then Abel brought the first lamb born to one of his sheep, killed it, and gave the best parts of it as an offering. The LORD was pleased with Abel and his offering, 5 but he rejected Cain and his offering. Cain became furious, and he scowled in anger. 6 Then the LORD said to Cain, "Why are you angry? Why that scowl on your face? 7 If you had done the right thing, you would be smiling;t but because you have done evil, sin is crouching at your door. It wants to rule you, but you must overcome it."

8 Then Cain said to his brother Abel, "Let's go out in the fields."u When they were out in the fields, Cain turned on his brother and killed him.

9 The LORD asked Cain, "Where is your brother Abel?"

He answered, "I don't know. Am I supposed to take care of my brother?"

10 Then the LORD said, "Why have you done this terrible thing? Your brother's blood is crying out to me from the ground, like a voice calling for revenge. 11 You are placed under a curse and can no longer farm the soil. It has soaked up your brother's blood as if it had opened its mouth to receive it when you killed him. 12 If you try to grow crops, the soil will not produce anything; you will be a homeless wanderer on the earth."

13 And Cain said to the LORD, "This punishment is too hard for me to bear. 14 You are driving me off the land and away from your presence. I will be a homeless wanderer on the earth, and anyone who finds me will kill me."

15 But the LORD answered, "No. If anyone kills you, seven lives will be taken in revenge." So the LORD put a mark on Cain to warn anyone who met him not to kill him. 16 And Cain went away from the LORD's presence and lived in a land called "Wandering," which is east of Eden.

The Descendants of Cain

17 Cain and his wife had a son and named him Enoch. Then Cain built a city and named it after his son. 18 Enoch had a son named Irad, who was the father of Mehujael, and Mehujael had a son named Methushael, who was the father of Lamech. 19 Lamech had two wives, Adah and Zillah. 20 Adah gave birth to Jabal, who was the ancestor of those who raise livestock and live in tents. 21 His brother was Jubal, the ancestor of all musicians who play the harp and the flute. 22 Zillah gave birth to Tubal Cain, who made all kinds of toolsv out of bronze and iron. The sister of Tubal Cain was Naamah.

23 Lamech said to his wives,

"Adah and Zillah, listen to me:
I have killed a young man because
he struck me.
24 If seven lives are taken to pay for
killing Cain,
Seventy-seven will be taken if
anyone kills me."

Seth and Enosh

25 Adam and his wife had another son. She said, "God has given me a son to

---

q knowledge of what is good and what is bad; or knowledge of everything.   r LIVING CREATURES: See Word List.   s CAIN: This name sounds like the Hebrew for "gotten."   t you would be smiling; or I would have accepted your offering.   u Some ancient translations Let's go out in the fields; Hebrew does not have these words.   v who made all kinds of tools; one ancient translation ancestor of all metalworkers.

replace Abel, whom Cain killed." So she named him Seth.[w] [26] Seth had a son whom he named Enosh. It was then that people began using the LORD's holy name in worship.

The Descendants of Adam
(1 Chronicles 1.1-4)

5 This is the list of the descendants of Adam. (When God created human beings, he made them like himself. [2] He created them male and female, blessed them, and named them "Human Beings.") [3] When Adam was 130 years old, he had a son who was like him, and he named him Seth. [4] After that, Adam lived another 800 years. He had other children [5] and died at the age of 930.

[6] When Seth was 105, he had a son, Enosh, [7] and then lived another 807 years. He had other children [8] and died at the age of 912.

[9] When Enosh was 90, he had a son, Kenan, [10] and then lived another 815 years. He had other children [11] and died at the age of 905.

[12] When Kenan was 70, he had a son, Mahalalel, [13] and then lived another 840 years. He had other children [14] and died at the age of 910.

[15] When Mahalalel was 65, he had a son, Jared, [16] and then lived another 830 years. He had other children [17] and died at the age of 895.

[18] When Jared was 162, he had a son, Enoch, [19] and then lived another 800 years. He had other children [20] and died at the age of 962.

[21] When Enoch was 65, he had a son, Methuselah. [22] After that, Enoch lived in fellowship with God for 300 years and had other children. [23] He lived to be 365 years old. [24] He spent his life in fellowship with God, and then he disappeared, because God took him away.

[25] When Methuselah was 187, he had a son, Lamech, [26] and then lived another 782 years. He had other children [27] and died at the age of 969.

[28] When Lamech was 182, he had a son [29] and said, "From the very ground on which the LORD put a curse, this child will bring us relief from all our hard work"; so he named him Noah.[x] [30] Lamech lived another 595 years. He had other children [31] and died at the age of 777.

[32] After Noah was 500 years old, he had three sons: Shem, Ham, and Japheth.

Human Wickedness

6 When people had spread all over the world, and daughters were being born, [2] some of the heavenly beings[y] saw that these young women were beautiful, so they took the ones they liked. [3] Then the LORD said, "I will not allow people to live forever; they are mortal. From now on they will live no longer than 120 years." [4] In those days, and even later, there were giants on the earth who were descendants of human women and the heavenly beings. They were the great heroes and famous men of long ago.

[5] When the LORD saw how wicked everyone on earth was and how evil their thoughts were all the time, [6] he was sorry that he had ever made them and put them on the earth. He was so filled with regret [7] that he said, "I will wipe out these people I have created, and also the animals and the birds, because I am sorry that I made any of them." [8] But the LORD was pleased with Noah.

Noah

[9-10] This is the story of Noah. He had three sons, Shem, Ham, and Japheth. Noah had no faults and was the only good man of his time. He lived in fellowship with God, [11] but everyone else was evil in God's sight, and violence had spread everywhere. [12] God looked at the world and saw that it was evil, for the people were all living evil lives.

[13] God said to Noah, "I have decided to put an end to all people. I will destroy them completely, because the world is full of their violent deeds. [14] Build a boat for yourself out of good timber; make rooms in it and cover it with tar inside and out. [15] Make it 450 feet long, 75 feet wide, and 45 feet high. [16] Make a roof[z] for the boat and leave a space of 18 inches between the roof[z] and the sides. Build it with three decks and put a door in the side. [17] I am going to send a flood on the earth to destroy every living being. Everything on the earth will die, [18] but I will make a covenant with you. Go

---

[w] SETH: *This name sounds like the Hebrew for "has given."* [x] NOAH: *This name sounds like the Hebrew for "relief."* [y] heavenly beings; *or* sons of the gods; *or* sons of God. [z] roof; *or* window.

into the boat with your wife, your sons, and their wives. 19-20 Take into the boat with you a male and a female of every kind of animal and of every kind of bird, in order to keep them alive. 21 Take along all kinds of food for you and for them." 22 Noah did everything that God commanded.

The Flood

7 The LORD said to Noah, "Go into the boat with your whole family; I have found that you are the only one in all the world who does what is right. 2 Take with you seven pairs of each kind of ritually clean animal, but only one pair of each kind of unclean animal. 3 Take also seven pairs of each kind of bird. Do this so that every kind of animal and bird will be kept alive to reproduce again on the earth. 4 Seven days from now I am going to send rain that will fall for forty days and nights, in order to destroy all the living beings that I have made." 5 And Noah did everything that the LORD commanded.

6 Noah was six hundred years old when the flood came on the earth. 7 He and his wife, and his sons and their wives, went into the boat to escape the flood. 8 A male and a female of every kind of animal and bird, whether ritually clean or unclean, 9 went into the boat with Noah, as God had commanded. 10 Seven days later the flood came.

11 When Noah was six hundred years old, on the seventeenth day of the second month all the outlets of the vast body of water beneath the earth burst open, all the floodgates of the sky were opened, 12 and rain fell on the earth for forty days and nights. 13 On that same day Noah and his wife went into the boat with their three sons, Shem, Ham, and Japheth, and their wives. 14 With them went every kind of animal, domestic and wild, large and small, and every kind of bird. 15 A male and a female of each kind of living being went into the boat with Noah, 16 as God had commanded. Then the LORD shut the door behind Noah.

17 The flood continued for forty days, and the water became deep enough for the boat to float. 18 The water became deeper, and the boat drifted on the surface. 19 It became so deep that it covered the highest mountains; 20 it went on rising until it was about twenty-five feet above the tops of the mountains. 21 Every living being on the earth died—every bird, every animal, and every person. 22 Everything on earth that breathed died. 23 The LORD destroyed all living beings on the earth—human beings, animals, and birds. The only ones left were Noah and those who were with him in the boat. 24 The water did not start going down for a hundred and fifty days.

The End of the Flood

8 God had not forgotten Noah and all the animals with him in the boat; he caused a wind to blow, and the water started going down. 2 The outlets of the water beneath the earth and the floodgates of the sky were closed. The rain stopped, 3 and the water gradually went down for 150 days. 4 On the seventeenth day of the seventh month the boat came to rest on a mountain in the Ararat range. 5 The water kept going down, and on the first day of the tenth month the tops of the mountains appeared.

6 After forty days Noah opened a window 7 and sent out a raven. It did not come back, but kept flying around until the water was completely gone. 8 Meanwhile, Noah sent out a dove to see if the water had gone down, 9 but since the water still covered all the land, the dove did not find a place to light. It flew back to the boat, and Noah reached out and took it in. 10 He waited another seven days and sent out the dove again. 11 It returned to him in the evening with a fresh olive leaf in its beak. So Noah knew that the water had gone down. 12 Then he waited another seven days and sent out the dove once more; this time it did not come back.

13 When Noah was 601 years old, on the first day of the first month, the water was gone. Noah removed the covering of the boat, looked around, and saw that the ground was getting dry. 14 By the twenty-seventh day of the second month the earth was completely dry.

15 God said to Noah, 16 "Go out of the boat with your wife, your sons, and their wives. 17 Take all the birds and animals out with you, so that they may reproduce and spread over all the earth." 18 So Noah went out of the boat with his wife, his sons, and their wives. 19 All the animals and birds went out of the boat in groups of their own kind.

Noah Offers a Sacrifice

20 Noah built an altar to the LORD; he took one of each kind of ritually clean animal and bird, and burned them whole as a sacrifice on the altar. 21 The odor of the sacrifice pleased the LORD, and he said to himself, "Never again will I put the earth under a curse because of what people do; I know that from the time they are young their thoughts are evil. Never again will I destroy all living beings, as I have done this time. 22 As long as the world exists, there will be a time for planting and a time for harvest. There will always be cold and heat, summer and winter, day and night."

God's Covenant with Noah

9 God blessed Noah and his sons and said, "Have many children, so that your descendants will live all over the earth. 2 All the animals, birds, and fish will live in fear of you. They are all placed under your power. 3 Now you can eat them, as well as green plants; I give them all to you for food. 4 The one thing you must not eat is meat with blood still in it; I forbid this because the life is in the blood. 5 If anyone takes human life, he will be punished. I will punish with death any animal that takes a human life. 6 Human beings were made like God, so whoever murders one of them will be killed by someone else.

7 "You must have many children, so that your descendants will live all over the earth."

8 God said to Noah and his sons, 9 "I am now making my covenant with you and with your descendants, 10 and with all living beings—all birds and all animals—everything that came out of the boat with you. 11 With these words I make my covenant with you: I promise that never again will all living beings be destroyed by a flood; never again will a flood destroy the earth. 12 As a sign of this everlasting covenant which I am making with you and with all living beings, 13 I am putting my bow in the clouds. It will be the sign of my covenant with the world. 14 Whenever I cover the sky with clouds and the rainbow appears, 15 I will remember my promise to you and to all the animals that a flood will never again destroy all living beings. 16 When the rainbow appears in the clouds, I will see it and remember the everlasting covenant between me and all living beings on earth. 17 That is the sign of the promise which I am making to all living beings."

Noah and His Sons

18 The sons of Noah who went out of the boat were Shem, Ham, and Japheth. (Ham was the father of Canaan.) 19 These three sons of Noah were the ancestors of all the people on earth.

20 Noah, who was a farmer, was the first man to plant a vineyard. 21 After he drank some of the wine, he became drunk, took off his clothes, and lay naked in his tent. 22 When Ham, the father of Canaan, saw that his father was naked, he went out and told his two brothers. 23 Then Shem and Japheth took a robe and held it behind them on their shoulders. They walked backward into the tent and covered their father, keeping their faces turned away so as not to see him naked. 24 When Noah sobered up and learned what his youngest son had done to him, 25 he said,

"A curse on Canaan!
He will be a slave to his brothers.
26 Give praise to the LORD, the God
   of Shem!
Canaan will be the slave of Shem.
27 May God cause Japheth a to
   increase!
May his descendants live with the
   people of Shem!
Canaan will be the slave of
   Japheth."

28 After the flood Noah lived 350 years 29 and died at the age of 950.

The Descendants of Noah's Sons

(1 Chronicles 1.5-23)

10 These are the descendants of Noah's sons, Shem, Ham, and Japheth. These three had sons after the flood.

2 The sons of Japheth—Gomer, Magog, Madai, Javan, Tubal, Meshech, and Tiras—were the ancestors of the peoples who bear their names. 3 The descendants of Gomer were the people of Ashkenaz, Riphath, and Togarmah. 4 The descendants of Javan were the people of Elishah, Spain, Cyprus, and Rhodes; 5 they were the ancestors of the people who live

---

a JAPHETH: *This name sounds like the Hebrew for "increase."*

along the coast and on the islands. These are the descendants of Japheth, living in their different tribes and countries, each group speaking its own language.

6 The sons of Ham — Cush, Egypt, Libya, and Canaan — were the ancestors of the peoples who bear their names. 7 The descendants of Cush were the people of Seba, Havilah, Sabtah, Raamah, and Sabteca. The descendants of Raamah were the people of Sheba and Dedan. 8 Cush had a son named Nimrod, who became the world's first great conqueror. 9 By the LORD's help he was a great hunter, and that is why people say, "May the LORD make you as great a hunter as Nimrod!" 10 At first his kingdom included Babylon, Erech, and Accad, all three of them in Babylonia. 11 From that land he went to Assyria and built the cities of Nineveh, Rehoboth Ir, Calah, 12 and Resen, which is between Nineveh and the great city of Calah.

13 The descendants of Egypt were the people of Lydia, Anam, Lehab, Naphtuh, 14 Pathrus, Casluh, and of Crete, from whom the Philistines are descended.b

15 Canaan's sons — Sidon, the oldest, and Heth — were the ancestors of the peoples who bear their names. 16 Canaan was also the ancestor of the Jebusites, the Amorites, the Girgashites, 17 the Hivites, the Arkites, the Sinites, 18 the Arvadites, the Zemarites, and the Hamathites. The different tribes of the Canaanites spread out, 19 until the Canaanite borders reached from Sidon southward to Gerar near Gaza, and eastward to Sodom, Gomorrah, Admah, and Zeboiim near Lasha. 20 These are the descendants of Ham, living in their different tribes and countries, each group speaking its own language.

21 Shem, the older brother of Japheth, was the ancestor of all the Hebrews. 22 Shem's sons — Elam, Asshur, Arpachshad, Lud, and Aram — were the ancestors of the peoples who bear their names. 23 The descendants of Aram were the people of Uz, Hul, Gether, and Meshek. 24 Arpachshad was the father of Shelah, who was the father of Eber. 25 Eber had two sons: one was named Peleg,c because during his time the people of the world were divided; and the other was

named Joktan. 26 The descendants of Joktan were the people of Almodad, Sheleph, Hazarmaveth, Jerah, 27 Hadoram, Uzal, Diklah, 28 Obal, Abimael, Sheba, 29 Ophir, Havilah, and Jobab. All of them were descended from Joktan. 30 The land in which they lived extended from Mesha to Sephar in the eastern hill country. 31 These are the descendants of Shem, living in their different tribes and countries, each group speaking its own language.

32 All these peoples are the descendants of Noah, nation by nation, according to their different lines of descent. After the flood all the nations of the earth were descended from the sons of Noah.

The Tower of Babylon

11 At first, the people of the whole world had only one language and used the same words. 2 As they wandered about in the East, they came to a plain in Babylonia and settled there. 3 They said to one another, "Come on! Let's make bricks and bake them hard." So they had bricks to build with and tar to hold them together. 4 They said, "Now let's build a city with a tower that reaches the sky, so that we can make a name for ourselves and not be scattered all over the earth."

5 Then the LORD came down to see the city and the tower which they had built, 6 and he said, "Now then, these are all one people and they speak one language; this is just the beginning of what they are going to do. Soon they will be able to do anything they want! 7 Let us go down and mix up their language so that they will not understand each other." 8 So the LORD scattered them all over the earth, and they stopped building the city. 9 The city was called Babylon,d because there the LORD mixed up the language of all the people, and from there he scattered them all over the earth.

The Descendants of Shem
(1 Chronicles 1.24-27)

10 These are the descendants of Shem. Two years after the flood, when Shem was 100 years old, he had a son, Arpachshad. 11 After that, he lived another 500 years and had other children.

12 When Arpachshad was 35 years old,

b *Probable text* and of Crete . . . descended; *Hebrew* from whom the Philistines are descended, and Crete.   c PELEG: *This name sounds like the Hebrew for "divide."*   d BABYLON: *This name sounds like the Hebrew for "mixed up."*

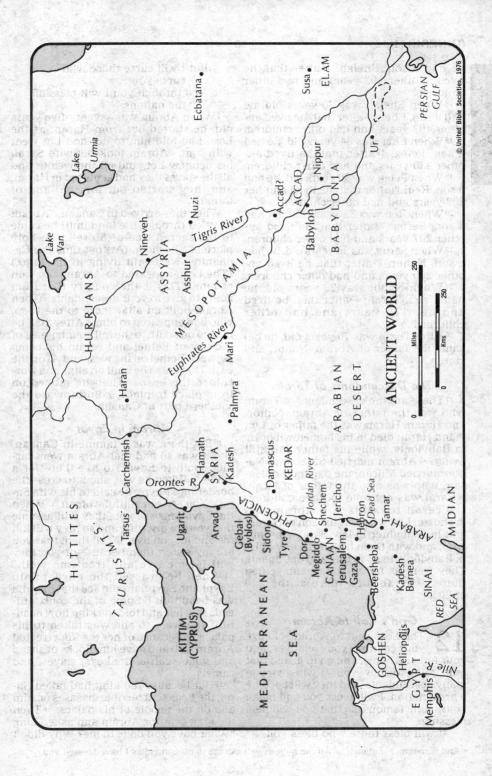

ANCIENT WORLD

PERSIAN GULF

ELAM

Susa

Ecbatana

Lake Urmia

Lake Van

Nippur

Ur

BABYLONIA

Babylon

ACCAD

Accad?

HURRIANS

Nuzi

Nineveh

ASSYRIA

Asshur

Tigris River

MESOPOTAMIA

Euphrates River

Mari

Haran

Palmyra

Miles

Kms

Hamath

Kadesh

Carchemish

HITTITES

Tarsus

TAURUS MTS.

Orontes R.

SYRIA

Kadesh

Damascus

KEDAR

Ugarit

Arvad

Gebal (Byblos)

Sidon

Tyre

Dor

Jordan River

Megiddo

Shechem

Jericho

Dead Sea

Hebron

Tamar

CANAAN

Jerusalem

Gaza

Beersheba

Kadesh Barnea

ARABIAN DESERT

ARABAH

MIDIAN

PHOENICIA

MEDITERRANEAN SEA

KITTIM (CYPRUS)

GOSHEN

Heliopolis

Memphis

Nile R.

EGYPT

SINAI

RED SEA

G
E
N
E
S
I
S

he had a son, Shelah; 13after that, he lived another 403 years and had other children.

14When Shelah was 30 years old, he had a son, Eber; 15after that, he lived another 403 years and had other children.

16When Eber was 34 years old, he had a son, Peleg; 17after that, he lived another 430 years and had other children.

18When Peleg was 30 years old, he had a son, Reu; 19after that, he lived another 209 years and had other children.

20When Reu was 32 years old, he had a son, Serug; 21after that, he lived another 207 years and had other children.

22When Serug was 30 years old, he had a son, Nahor; 23after that, he lived another 200 years and had other children.

24When Nahor was 29 years old, he had a son, Terah; 25after that, he lived another 119 years and had other children.

26After Terah was 70 years old, he became the father of Abram, Nahor, and Haran.

The Descendants of Terah

27These are the descendants of Terah, who was the father of Abram, Nahor, and Haran. Haran was the father of Lot, 28and Haran died in his hometown of Ur in Babylonia, while his father was still living. 29Abram married Sarai, and Nahor married Milcah, the daughter of Haran, who was also the father of Iscah. 30Sarai was not able to have children.

31Terah took his son Abram, his grandson Lot, who was the son of Haran, and his daughter-in-law Sarai, Abram's wife, and with them he left the city of Ur in Babylonia to go to the land of Canaan. They went as far as Haran and settled there. 32Terah died there at the age of 205.

God's Call to Abram

12 The LORD said to Abram, "Leave your country, your relatives, and your father's home, and go to a land that I am going to show you. 2I will give you many descendants, and they will become a great nation. I will bless you and make your name famous, so that you will be a blessing.

3I will bless those who bless you,

But I will curse those who
    curse you.
And through you I will bless all
    the nations."e

4When Abram was seventy-five years old, he started out from Haran, as the LORD had told him to do; and Lot went with him. 5Abram took his wife Sarai, his nephew Lot, and all the wealth and all the slaves they had acquired in Haran, and they started out for the land of Canaan.

When they arrived in Canaan, 6Abram traveled through the land until he came to the sacred tree of Moreh, the holy place at Shechem. (At that time the Canaanites were still living in the land.) 7The LORD appeared to Abram and said to him, "This is the country that I am going to give to your descendants." Then Abram built an altar there to the LORD, who had appeared to him. 8After that, he moved on to the hill country east of the city of Bethel and set up his camp between Bethel on the west and Ai on the east. There also he built an altar and worshiped the LORD. 9Then he moved on from place to place, going toward the southern part of Canaan.

Abram in Egypt

10But there was a famine in Canaan, and it was so bad that Abram went farther south to Egypt, to live there for a while. 11When he was about to cross the border into Egypt, he said to his wife Sarai, "You are a beautiful woman. 12When the Egyptians see you, they will assume that you are my wife, and so they will kill me and let you live. 13Tell them that you are my sister; then because of you they will let me live and treat me well." 14When he crossed the border into Egypt, the Egyptians did see that his wife was beautiful. 15Some of the court officials saw her and told the king how beautiful she was; so she was taken to his palace. 16Because of her the king treated Abram well and gave him flocks of sheep and goats, cattle, donkeys, slaves, and camels.

17But because the king had taken Sarai, the LORD sent terrible diseases on him and on the people of his palace. 18Then the king sent for Abram and asked him, "What have you done to me? Why didn't

e And through . . . nations; or All the nations will ask me to bless them as I have blessed you.

you tell me that she was your wife? 19 Why did you say that she was your sister, and let me take her as my wife? Here is your wife; take her and get out!" 20 The king gave orders to his men, so they took Abram and put him out of the country, together with his wife and everything he owned.

Abram and Lot Separate

13 Abram went north out of Egypt to the southern part of Canaan with his wife and everything he owned, and Lot went with him. 2 Abram was a very rich man, with sheep, goats, and cattle, as well as silver and gold. 3 Then he left there and moved from place to place, going toward Bethel. He reached the place between Bethel and Ai where he had camped before 4 and had built an altar. There he worshiped the LORD.

5 Lot also had sheep, goats, and cattle, as well as his own family and servants. 6 And so there was not enough pasture land for the two of them to stay together, because they had too many animals. 7 So quarrels broke out between the men who took care of Abram's animals and those who took care of Lot's animals. (At that time the Canaanites and the Perizzites were still living in the land.)

8 Then Abram said to Lot, "We are relatives, and your men and my men shouldn't be quarreling. 9 So let's separate. Choose any part of the land you want. You go one way, and I'll go the other."

10 Lot looked around and saw that the whole Jordan Valley, all the way to Zoar, had plenty of water, like the Garden of the LORD*f* or like the land of Egypt. (This was before the LORD had destroyed the cities of Sodom and Gomorrah.) 11 So Lot chose the whole Jordan Valley for himself and moved away toward the east. That is how the two men parted. 12 Abram stayed in the land of Canaan, and Lot settled among the cities in the valley and camped near Sodom, 13 whose people were wicked and sinned against the LORD.

Abram Moves to Hebron

14 After Lot had left, the LORD said to Abram, "From where you are, look carefully in all directions. 15 I am going to give you and your descendants all the land that you see, and it will be yours forever. 16 I am going to give you so many descendants that no one will be able to count them all; it would be as easy to count all the specks of dust on earth! 17 Now, go and look over the whole land, because I am going to give it all to you." 18 So Abram moved his camp and settled near the sacred trees of Mamre at Hebron, and there he built an altar to the LORD.

Abram Rescues Lot

14 Four kings, Amraphel of Babylonia, Arioch of Ellasar, Chedorlaomer of Elam, and Tidal of Goiim, 2 went to war against five other kings: Bera of Sodom, Birsha of Gomorrah, Shinab of Admah, Shemeber of Zeboiim, and the king of Bela (or Zoar). 3 These five kings had formed an alliance and joined forces in Siddim Valley, which is now the Dead Sea. 4 They had been under the control of Chedorlaomer for twelve years, but in the thirteenth year they rebelled against him. 5 In the fourteenth year Chedorlaomer and his allies came with their armies and defeated the Rephaim in Ashteroth Karnaim, the Zuzim in Ham, the Emim in the plain of Kiriathaim, 6 and the Horites in the mountains of Edom, pursuing them as far as Elparan on the edge of the desert. 7 Then they turned around and came back to Kadesh (then known as Enmishpat). They conquered all the land of the Amalekites and defeated the Amorites who lived in Hazazon Tamar.

8 Then the kings of Sodom, Gomorrah, Admah, Zeboiim, and Bela drew up their armies for battle in Siddim Valley and fought 9 against the kings of Elam, Goiim, Babylonia, and Ellasar, five kings against four. 10 The valley was full of tar pits, and when the kings of Sodom and Gomorrah tried to run away from the battle, they fell into the pits; but the other three kings escaped to the mountains. 11 The four kings took everything in Sodom and Gomorrah, including the food, and went away. 12 Lot, Abram's nephew, was living in Sodom, so they took him and all his possessions.

13 But a man escaped and reported all this to Abram, the Hebrew, who was living near the sacred trees belonging to

f GARDEN OF THE LORD: *a reference to the Garden of Eden.*

GENESIS

Mamre the Amorite. Mamre and his brothers Eshcol and Aner were Abram's allies. 14 When Abram heard that his nephew had been captured, he called together all the fighting men in his camp, 318 in all, and pursued the four kings all the way to Dan. 15 There he divided his men into groups, attacked the enemy by night, and defeated them. He chased them as far as Hobah, north of Damascus, 16 and got back all the loot that had been taken. He also brought back his nephew Lot and his possessions, together with the women and the other prisoners.

Melchizedek Blesses Abram

17 When Abram came back from his victory over Chedorlaomer and the other kings, the king of Sodom went out to meet him in Shaveh Valley (also called King's Valley). 18 And Melchizedek, who was king of Salem and also a priest of the Most High God, brought bread and wine to Abram, 19 blessed him, and said, "May the Most High God, who made heaven and earth, bless Abram! 20 May the Most High God, who gave you victory over your enemies, be praised!" And Abram gave Melchizedek a tenth of all the loot he had recovered.

21 The king of Sodom said to Abram, "Keep the loot, but give me back all my people."

22 Abram answered, "I solemnly swear before the LORD, the Most High God, Maker of heaven and earth, 23 that I will not keep anything of yours, not even a thread or a sandal strap. Then you can never say, 'I am the one who made Abram rich.' 24 I will take nothing for myself. I will accept only what my men have used. But let my allies, Aner, Eshcol, and Mamre, take their share."

God's Covenant with Abram

15 After this, Abram had a vision and heard the LORD say to him, "Do not be afraid, Abram. I will shield you from danger and give you a great reward."

2 But Abram answered, "Sovereign LORD, what good will your reward do me, since I have no children? My only heir is Eliezer of Damascus.g 3 You have given me no children, and one of my slaves will inherit my property."

4 Then he heard the LORD speaking to him again: "This slave Eliezer will not inherit your property; your own son will be your heir." 5 The LORD took him outside and said, "Look at the sky and try to count the stars; you will have as many descendants as that."

6 Abram put his trust in the LORD, and because of this the LORD was pleased with him and accepted him.

7 Then the LORD said to him, "I am the LORD, who led you out of Ur in Babylonia, to give you this land as your own."

8 But Abram asked, "Sovereign LORD, how can I know that it will be mine?"

9 He answered, "Bring me a cow, a goat, and a ram, each of them three years old, and a dove and a pigeon." 10 Abram brought the animals to God, cut them in half, and placed the halves opposite each other in two rows; but he did not cut up the birds. 11 Vultures came down on the bodies, but Abram drove them off.

12 When the sun was going down, Abram fell into a deep sleep, and fear and terror came over him. 13 The LORD said to him, "Your descendants will be strangers in a foreign land; they will be slaves there and will be treated cruelly for four hundred years. 14 But I will punish the nation that enslaves them, and when they leave that foreign land, they will take great wealth with them. 15 You yourself will live to a ripe old age, die in peace, and be buried. 16 It will be four generations before your descendants come back here, because I will not drive out the Amorites until they become so wicked that they must be punished."

17 When the sun had set and it was dark, a smoking fire pot and a flaming torch suddenly appeared and passed between the pieces of the animals. 18 Then and there the LORD made a covenant with Abram. He said, "I promise to give your descendants all this land from the border of Egypt to the Euphrates River, 19 including the lands of the Kenites, the Kenizzites, the Kadmonites, 20 the Hittites, the Perizzites, the Rephaim, 21 the Amorites, the Canaanites, the Girgashites, and the Jebusites."

g My . . . Damascus; Hebrew unclear.

THE ANGEL OF THE LORD

The angel of the Lord in the Old Testament is a mysterious messenger of God. The Lord used this heavenly emissary to appear to human beings who otherwise would not be able to see him and live (Ex 33.20). The angel of the Lord performed actions associated with God, such as revelation, deliverance, and God's judgment. While similar in nature to other angels, the angel of the Lord occupies a higher station in heaven than angels in general.

The angel of the Lord appeared to the following Old Testament personalities and performed the following actions on God's behalf.

Personality(ies)	Action	Biblical Reference
Hagar	Instructed Hagar to return to Sarai (Sarah) and told her she would bear many descendants	Gn 16.7–10
Abraham	Prevented Abraham from sacrificing his son Isaac	Gn 22.11–13
Jacob	Wrestled with Jacob through the night and blessed him at daybreak	Gn 32.24–30
Moses	Spoke to Moses from the burning bush, promising to deliver the Israelites from enslavement	Ex 3.1–8
Israelites	Announced judgment against the Israelites for their sinful alliances with the Canaanites	Jg 2.1–3
Gideon	Commissioned Gideon to fight against the Midianites	Jg 6.11–24
Manoah and his wife	Announced the birth of their son and instructed them to dedicate the child to God as a Nazirite.	Jg 13.3–21

GENESIS

Hagar and Ishmael

16 Abram's wife Sarai had not borne him any children. But she had an Egyptian slave woman named Hagar, 2 and so she said to Abram, "The LORD has kept me from having children. Why don't you sleep with my slave? Perhaps she can have a child for me." Abram agreed with what Sarai said. 3 So she gave Hagar to him to be his concubine. (This happened after Abram had lived in Canaan for ten years.) 4 Abram had intercourse with Hagar, and she became pregnant. When she found out that she was pregnant, she became proud and despised Sarai.

5 Then Sarai said to Abram, "It's your fault that Hagar despises me.*h* I myself gave her to you, and ever since she found out that she was pregnant, she has despised me. May the LORD judge which of us is right, you or me!"

6 Abram answered, "Very well, she is your slave and under your control; do whatever you want with her." Then Sarai treated Hagar so cruelly that she ran away.

7 The angel of the LORD met Hagar at a spring in the desert on the road to Shur 8 and said, "Hagar, slave of Sarai, where have you come from and where are you going?"

She answered, "I am running away from my mistress."

9 He said, "Go back to her and be her slave." 10 Then he said, "I will give you so many descendants that no one will be able to count them. 11 You are going to have a son, and you will name him Ishmael,*i* because the LORD has heard your cry of distress. 12 But your son will live like a wild donkey; he will be against everyone, and everyone will be against him. He will live apart from all his relatives."

13 Hagar asked herself, "Have I really seen God and lived to tell about it?"*j* So she called the LORD, who had spoken to her, "A God Who Sees." 14 That is why people call the well between Kadesh and Bered "The Well of the Living One Who Sees Me."

15 Hagar bore Abram a son, and he named him Ishmael. 16 Abram was eighty-six years old at the time.

Circumcision, the Sign of the Covenant

17 When Abram was ninety-nine years old, the LORD appeared to him and said, "I am the Almighty God. Obey me and always do what is right. 2 I will make my covenant with you and give you many descendants." 3 Abram bowed down with his face touching the ground, and God said, 4 "I make this covenant with you: I promise that you will be the ancestor of many nations. 5 Your name will no longer be Abram, but Abraham,*k* because I am making you the ancestor of many nations. 6 I will give you many descendants, and some of them will be kings. You will have so many descendants that they will become nations.

7 "I will keep my promise to you and to your descendants in future generations as an everlasting covenant. I will be your God and the God of your descendants. 8 I will give to you and to your descendants this land in which you are now a foreigner. The whole land of Canaan will belong to your descendants forever, and I will be their God."

9 God said to Abraham, "You also must agree to keep the covenant with me, both you and your descendants in future generations. 10 You and your descendants must all agree to circumcise every male among you. 11-12 From now on you must circumcise every baby boy when he is eight days old, including slaves born in your homes and slaves bought from foreigners. This will show that there is a covenant between you and me. 13 Each one must be circumcised, and this will be a physical sign to show that my covenant with you is everlasting. 14 Any male who has not been circumcised will no longer be considered one of my people, because he has not kept the covenant with me."

15 God said to Abraham, "You must no longer call your wife Sarai; from now on her name is Sarah.*l* 16 I will bless her, and I will give you a son by her. I will bless her, and she will become the

---

h It's your fault . . . me; *or* May you suffer for this wrong done against me.　*i* ISHMAEL: *This name in Hebrew means "God hears."*　*j* Probable text lived to tell about it?; *Hebrew unclear.*　*k* ABRAHAM: *This name sounds like the Hebrew for "ancestor of many nations."*　*l* SARAH: *This name in Hebrew means "princess."*

GENESIS

mother of nations, and there will be kings among her descendants."

17 Abraham bowed down with his face touching the ground, but he began to laugh when he thought, "Can a man have a child when he is a hundred years old? Can Sarah have a child at ninety?" 18 He asked God, "Why not let Ishmael be my heir?"

19 But God said, "No. Your wife Sarah will bear you a son and you will name him Isaac.m I will keep my covenant with him and with his descendants forever. It is an everlasting covenant. 20 I have heard your request about Ishmael, so I will bless him and give him many children and many descendants. He will be the father of twelve princes, and I will make a great nation of his descendants. 21 But I will keep my covenant with your son Isaac, who will be born to Sarah about this time next year." 22 When God finished speaking to Abraham, he left him.

23 On that same day Abraham obeyed God and circumcised his son Ishmael and all the other males in his household, including the slaves born in his home and those he had bought. 24 Abraham was ninety-nine years old when he was circumcised, 25 and his son Ishmael was thirteen, 26 They were both circumcised on the same day, 27 together with all of Abraham's slaves.

A Son Is Promised to Abraham

18 The LORD appeared to Abraham at the sacred trees of Mamre. As Abraham was sitting at the entrance of his tent during the hottest part of the day, 2 he looked up and saw three men standing there. As soon as he saw them, he ran out to meet them. Bowing down with his face touching the ground, 3 he said, "Sirs, please do not pass by my home without stopping; I am here to serve you. 4 Let me bring some water for you to wash your feet; you can rest here beneath this tree. 5 I will also bring a bit of food; it will give you strength to continue your journey. You have honored me by coming to my home, so let me serve you."

They replied, "Thank you; we accept."

6 Abraham hurried into the tent and said to Sarah, "Quick, take a sack of your best flour, and bake some bread." 7 Then he ran to the herd and picked out a calf that was tender and fat, and gave it to a servant, who hurried to get it ready. 8 He took some cream, some milk, and the meat, and set the food before the men. There under the tree he served them himself, and they ate.

9 Then they asked him, "Where is your wife Sarah?"

"She is there in the tent," he answered.

10 One of them said, "Nine months from nown I will come back, and your wife Sarah will have a son."

Sarah was behind him, at the door of the tent, listening. 11 Abraham and Sarah were very old, and Sarah had stopped having her monthly periods. 12 So Sarah laughed to herself and said, "Now that I am old and worn out, can I still enjoy sex? And besides, my husband is old too."

13 Then the LORD asked Abraham, "Why did Sarah laugh and say, 'Can I really have a child when I am so old?' 14 Is anything too hard for the LORD? As I said, nine months from now I will return, and Sarah will have a son."

15 Because Sarah was afraid, she denied it. "I didn't laugh," she said.

"Yes, you did," he replied. "You laughed."

Abraham Pleads for Sodom

16 Then the men left and went to a place where they could look down at Sodom, and Abraham went with them to send them on their way. 17 And the LORD said to himself, "I will not hide from Abraham what I am going to do. 18 His descendants will become a great and mighty nation, and through him I will bless all the nations.o 19 I have chosen him in order that he may command his sons and his descendants to obey me and to do what is right and just. If they do, I will do everything for him that I have promised."

20 Then the LORD said to Abraham, "There are terrible accusations against Sodom and Gomorrah, and their sin is very great. 21 I must go down to find out whether or not the accusations which I have heard are true."

22 Then the two men left and went on

m ISAAC: This name in Hebrew means "he laughs." next year. o through . . . nations; or all the nations will ask me to bless them as I have blessed him. n Nine months from now; or This time

toward Sodom, but the LORD remained with Abraham. 23 Abraham approached the LORD and asked, "Are you really going to destroy the innocent with the guilty? 24 If there are fifty innocent people in the city, will you destroy the whole city? Won't you spare it in order to save the fifty? 25 Surely you won't kill the innocent with the guilty. That's impossible! You can't do that. If you did, the innocent would be punished along with the guilty. That is impossible. The judge of all the earth has to act justly."

26 The LORD answered, "If I find fifty innocent people in Sodom, I will spare the whole city for their sake."

27 Abraham spoke again: "Please forgive my boldness in continuing to speak to you, Lord. I am only a man and have no right to say anything. 28 But perhaps there will be only forty-five innocent people instead of fifty. Will you destroy the whole city because there are five too few?"

The LORD answered, "I will not destroy the city if I find forty-five innocent people."

29 Abraham spoke again: "Perhaps there will be only forty."

He replied, "I will not destroy it if there are forty."

30 Abraham said, "Please don't be angry, Lord, but I must speak again. What if there are only thirty?"

He said, "I will not do it if I find thirty."

31 Abraham said, "Please forgive my boldness in continuing to speak to you, Lord. Suppose that only twenty are found?"

He said, "I will not destroy the city if I find twenty."

32 Abraham said, "Please don't be angry, Lord, and I will speak only once more. What if only ten are found?"

He said, "I will not destroy it if there are ten." 33 After he had finished speaking with Abraham, the LORD went away, and Abraham returned home.

The Sinfulness of Sodom

19 When the two angels came to Sodom that evening, Lot was sitting at the city gate. As soon as he saw them, he got up and went to meet them. He bowed down before them 2 and said, "Sirs, I am here to serve you. Please come to my house. You can wash your feet and spend the night. In the morning you can get up early and go on your way."

But they answered, "No, we will spend the night here in the city square."

3 He kept on urging them, and finally they went with him to his house. Lot ordered his servants to bake some bread and prepare a fine meal for the guests. When it was ready, they ate it.

4 Before the guests went to bed, the men of Sodom surrounded the house. All the men of the city, both young and old, were there. 5 They called out to Lot and asked, "Where are the men who came to stay with you tonight? Bring them out to us!" The men of Sodom wanted to have sex with them.

6 Lot went outside and closed the door behind him. 7 He said to them, "Friends, I beg you, don't do such a wicked thing! 8 Look, I have two daughters who are still virgins. Let me bring them out to you, and you can do whatever you want with them. But don't do anything to these men; they are guests in my house, and I must protect them."

9 But they said, "Get out of our way, you foreigner! Who are you to tell us what to do? Out of our way, or we will treat you worse than them." They pushed Lot back and moved up to break down the door. 10 But the two men inside reached out, pulled Lot back into the house, and shut the door. 11 Then they struck all the men outside with blindness, so that they couldn't find the door.

Lot Leaves Sodom

12 The two men said to Lot, "If you have anyone else here — sons, daughters, sons-in-law, or any other relatives living in the city — get them out of here, 13 because we are going to destroy this place. The LORD has heard the terrible accusations against these people and has sent us to destroy Sodom."

14 Then Lot went to the men that his daughters were going to marry, and said, "Hurry up and get out of here; the LORD is going to destroy this place." But they thought he was joking.

15 At dawn the angels tried to make Lot hurry. "Quick!" they said. "Take your wife and your two daughters and get out, so that you will not lose your lives when the city is destroyed." 16 Lot hesitated. The LORD, however, had pity on him; so the men took him, his wife, and his two

daughters by the hand and led them out of the city. ¹⁷Then one of the angels said, "Run for your lives! Don't look back and don't stop in the valley. Run to the hills, so that you won't be killed."

¹⁸But Lot answered, "No, please don't make us do that, sir. ¹⁹You have done me a great favor and saved my life. But the hills are too far away; the disaster will overtake me, and I will die before I get there. ²⁰Do you see that little town? It is near enough. Let me go over there—you can see it is just a small place—and I will be safe."

²¹He answered, "All right, I agree. I won't destroy that town. ²²Hurry! Run! I can't do anything until you get there."

Because Lot called it small, the town was named Zoar.ᵖ

The Destruction of Sodom and Gomorrah

²³The sun was rising when Lot reached Zoar. ²⁴Suddenly the Lord rained burning sulfur on the cities of Sodom and Gomorrah ²⁵and destroyed them and the whole valley, along with all the people there and everything that grew on the land. ²⁶But Lot's wife looked back and was turned into a pillar of salt.

²⁷Early the next morning Abraham hurried to the place where he had stood in the presence of the Lord. ²⁸He looked down at Sodom and Gomorrah and the whole valley and saw smoke rising from the land, like smoke from a huge furnace. ²⁹But when God destroyed the cities of the valley where Lot was living, he kept Abraham in mind and allowed Lot to escape to safety.

The Origin of the Moabites and Ammonites

³⁰Because Lot was afraid to stay in Zoar, he and his two daughters moved up into the hills and lived in a cave. ³¹The older daughter said to her sister, "Our father is getting old, and there are no men in the whole worldᵠ to marry us so that we can have children. ³²Come on, let's get our father drunk, so that we can sleep with him and have children by him." ³³That night they gave him wine to drink, and the older daughter had inter-

course with him. But he was so drunk that he didn't know it.

³⁴The next day the older daughter said to her sister, "I slept with him last night; now let's get him drunk again tonight, and you sleep with him. Then each of us will have a child by our father." ³⁵So that night they got him drunk, and the younger daughter had intercourse with him. Again he was so drunk that he didn't know it. ³⁶In this way both of Lot's daughters became pregnant by their own father. ³⁷The older daughter had a son, whom she named Moab.ʳ He was the ancestor of the present-day Moabites. ³⁸The younger daughter also had a son, whom she named Benammi.ˢ He was the ancestor of the present-day Ammonites.

Abraham and Abimelech

20 Abraham moved from Mamre to the southern part of Canaan and lived between Kadesh and Shur. Later, while he was living in Gerar, ²he said that his wife Sarah was his sister. So King Abimelech of Gerar had Sarah brought to him. ³One night God appeared to him in a dream and said, "You are going to die, because you have taken this woman; she is already married."

⁴But Abimelech had not come near her, and he said, "Lord, I am innocent! Would you destroy me and my people? ⁵Abraham himself said that she was his sister, and she said the same thing. I did this with a clear conscience, and I have done no wrong."

⁶God replied in the dream, "Yes, I know that you did it with a clear conscience; so I kept you from sinning against me and did not let you touch her. ⁷But now, give the woman back to her husband. He is a prophet, and he will pray for you, so that you will not die. But if you do not give her back, I warn you that you are going to die, you and all your people."

⁸Early the next morning Abimelech called all his officials and told them what had happened, and they were terrified. ⁹Then Abimelech called Abraham and asked, "What have you done to us? What wrong have I done to you to make you

---

ᵖ ZOAR: *This name sounds like the Hebrew for "small."*   ᵠ the whole world; *or this land.*
ʳ MOAB: *This name sounds like the Hebrew for "from my father."*   ˢ BENAMMI: *This name in Hebrew means "son of my relative" and sounds like the Hebrew for "Ammonite."*

G
E
N
E
S
I
S

bring this disaster on me and my kingdom? No one should ever do what you have done to me. ¹⁰Why did you do it?"

¹¹Abraham answered, "I thought that there would be no one here who has reverence for God and that they would kill me to get my wife. ¹²She really is my sister. She is the daughter of my father, but not of my mother, and I married her. ¹³So when God sent me from my father's house into foreign lands, I said to her, 'You can show how loyal you are to me by telling everyone that I am your brother.'"

¹⁴Then Abimelech gave Sarah back to Abraham, and at the same time he gave him sheep, cattle, and slaves. ¹⁵He said to Abraham, "Here is my whole land; live anywhere you like." ¹⁶He said to Sarah, "I am giving your brother a thousand pieces of silver as proof to all who are with you that you are innocent; everyone will know that you have done no wrong."

¹⁷⁻¹⁸Because of what had happened to Sarah, Abraham's wife, the LORD had made it impossible for any woman in Abimelech's palace to have children. So Abraham prayed for Abimelech, and God healed him. He also healed his wife and his slave women, so that they could have children.

The Birth of Isaac

21 The LORD blessed Sarah, as he had promised, ²and she became pregnant and bore a son to Abraham when he was old. The boy was born at the time God had said he would be born. ³Abraham named him Isaac, ⁴and when Isaac was eight days old, Abraham circumcised him, as God had commanded. ⁵Abraham was a hundred years old when Isaac was born. ⁶Sarah said, "God has brought me joy and laughter.ᵗ Everyone who hears about it will laugh with me." ⁷Then she added, "Who would have said to Abraham that Sarah would nurse children? Yet I have borne him a son in his old age."

⁸The child grew, and on the day that he was weaned, Abraham gave a great feast.

Hagar and Ishmael Are Sent Away

⁹One day Ishmael, whom Hagar the Egyptian had borne to Abraham, was playing withᵘ Sarah's son Isaac.ᵛ ¹⁰Sarah saw them and said to Abraham, "Send this slave and her son away. The son of this woman must not get any part of your wealth, which my son Isaac should inherit." ¹¹This troubled Abraham very much, because Ishmael also was his son. ¹²But God said to Abraham, "Don't be worried about the boy and your slave Hagar. Do whatever Sarah tells you, because it is through Isaac that you will have the descendants I have promised. ¹³I will also give many children to the son of the slave woman, so that they will become a nation. He too is your son."

¹⁴Early the next morning Abraham gave Hagar some food and a leather bag full of water. He put the child on her back and sent her away. She left and wandered about in the wilderness of Beersheba. ¹⁵When the water was all gone, she left the child under a bush ¹⁶and sat down about a hundred yards away. She said to herself, "I can't bear to see my child die." While she was sitting there, sheʷ began to cry.

¹⁷God heard the boy crying, and from heaven the angel of God spoke to Hagar, "What are you troubled about, Hagar? Don't be afraid. God has heard the boy crying. ¹⁸Get up, go and pick him up, and comfort him. I will make a great nation out of his descendants." ¹⁹Then God opened her eyes, and she saw a well. She went and filled the leather bag with water and gave some to the boy. ²⁰God was with the boy as he grew up; he lived in the wilderness of Paran and became a skillful hunter. ²¹His mother got an Egyptian wife for him.

The Agreement between Abraham and Abimelech

²²At that time Abimelech went with Phicol, the commander of his army, and said to Abraham, "God is with you in everything you do. ²³So make a vow here in the presence of God that you will not deceive me, my children, or my descendants. I have been loyal to you, so promise that you will also be loyal to me and to

---

ᵗ LAUGHTER: *The name Isaac in Hebrew means "he laughs" (see also 17.17-19).*   ᵘ playing with; or making fun of.   ᵛ *Some ancient translations* with Sarah's son Isaac; *Hebrew does not have these words.*   ʷ she; *one ancient translation* the child.

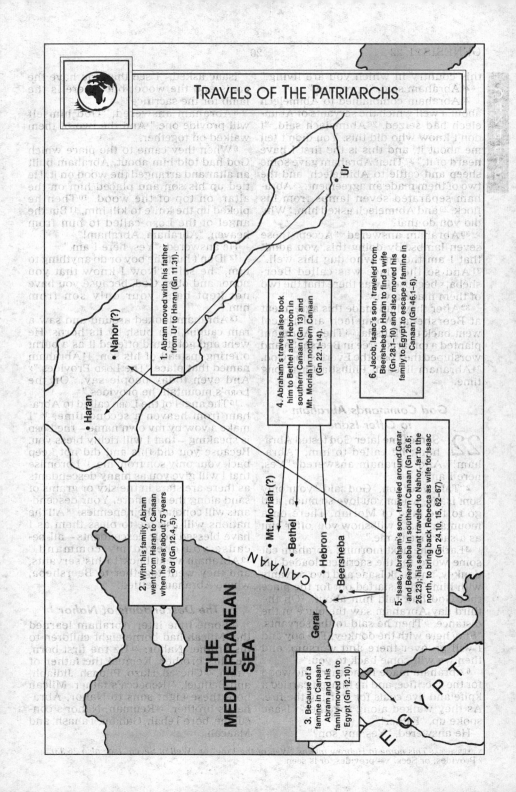

TRAVELS OF THE PATRIARCHS

Ur

Nahor (?)

Haran

1. Abram moved with his father from Ur to Haran (Gn 11.31).

2. With his family, Abram went from Haran to Canaan when he was about 75 years old (Gn 12.4, 5).

3. Because of a famine in Canaan, Abram and his family moved on to Egypt (Gn 12.10).

4. Abraham's travels also took him to Bethel and Hebron in southern Canaan (Gn 13) and Mt. Moriah in northern Canaan (Gn 22.1-14).

5. Isaac, Abraham's son, traveled around Gerar and Beersheba in southern Canaan (Gn 26.6; 26.23); his servant traveled to Nahor, far to the north, to bring back Rebeca as wife for Isaac (Gn 24.10, 15, 62-67).

6. Jacob, Isaac's son, traveled from Beersheba to Haran to find a wife (Gn 28.1-10) and also moved his family to Egypt to escape a famine in Canaan (Gn 46.1-6).

Mt. Moriah (?)

Bethel

Hebron

Beersheba

Gerar

CANAAN

THE MEDITERRANEAN SEA

EGYPT

this country in which you are living."
24 Abraham said, "I promise."
25 Abraham complained to Abimelech about a well which the servants of Abimelech had seized. 26 Abimelech said, "I don't know who did this. You didn't tell me about it, and this is the first I have heard of it." 27 Then Abraham gave some sheep and cattle to Abimelech, and the two of them made an agreement. 28 Abraham separated seven lambs from his flock, 29 and Abimelech asked him, "Why did you do that?"

30 Abraham answered, "Accept these seven lambs. By doing this, you admit that I am the one who dug this well." 31 And so the place was called Beersheba,ˣ because it was there that the two of them made a vow.

32 After they had made this agreement at Beersheba, Abimelech and Phicol went back to Philistia. 33 Then Abraham planted a tamarisk tree in Beersheba and worshiped the LORD, the Everlasting God. 34 Abraham lived in Philistia for a long time.

God Commands Abraham to Offer Isaac

22 Some time later God tested Abraham; he called to him, "Abraham!" And Abraham answered, "Yes, here I am!"

2 "Take your son," God said, "your only son, Isaac, whom you love so much, and go to the land of Moriah. There on a mountain that I will show you, offer him as a sacrifice to me."

3 Early the next morning Abraham cut some wood for the sacrifice, loaded his donkey, and took Isaac and two servants with him. They started out for the place that God had told him about. 4 On the third day Abraham saw the place in the distance. 5 Then he said to the servants, "Stay here with the donkey. The boy and I will go over there and worship, and then we will come back to you."

6 Abraham made Isaac carry the wood for the sacrifice, and he himself carried a knife and live coals for starting the fire. As they walked along together, 7 Isaac spoke up, "Father!"

He answered, "Yes, my son?"

Isaac asked, "I see that you have the coals and the wood, but where is the lamb for the sacrifice?"

8 Abraham answered, "God himself will provide one." And the two of them walked on together.

9 When they came to the place which God had told him about, Abraham built an altar and arranged the wood on it. He tied up his son and placed him on the altar, on top of the wood. 10 Then he picked up the knife to kill him. 11 But the angel of the LORD called to him from heaven, "Abraham, Abraham!"

He answered, "Yes, here I am."

12 "Don't hurt the boy or do anything to him," he said. "Now I know that you honor and obey God, because you have not kept back your only son from him."

13 Abraham looked around and saw a ram caught in a bush by its horns. He went and got it and offered it as a burnt offering instead of his son. 14 Abraham named that place "The LORD Provides."ʸ And even today people say, "On the LORD's mountain he provides."ᶻ

15 The angel of the LORD called to Abraham from heaven a second time, 16 "I make a vow by my own name—the LORD is speaking—that I will richly bless you. Because you did this and did not keep back your only son from me, 17 I promise that I will give you as many descendants as there are stars in the sky or grains of sand along the seashore. Your descendants will conquer their enemies. 18 All the nations will ask me to bless them as I have blessed your descendants—all because you obeyed my command." 19 Abraham went back to his servants, and they went together to Beersheba, where Abraham settled.

The Descendants of Nahor

20 Some time later Abraham learned that Milcah had borne eight children to his brother Nahor: 21 Uz the first-born, Buz his brother, Kemuel the father of Aram, 22 Chesed, Hazo, Pildash, Jidlaph, and Bethuel, 23 Rebecca's father. Milcah bore these eight sons to Nahor, Abraham's brother. 24 Reumah, Nahor's concubine, bore Tebah, Gaham, Tahash, and Maacah.

ˣ BEERSHEBA: *This name in Hebrew means "Well of the Vow" or "Well of Seven" (see also 26.33).*
ʸ Provides; *or* Sees.   ᶻ provides; *or* is seen.

Sarah Dies and Abraham Buys a Burial Ground

23 Sarah lived to be 127 years old. 2 She died in Hebron in the land of Canaan, and Abraham mourned her death.

3 He left the place where his wife's body was lying, went to the Hittites, and said, 4 "I am a foreigner living here among you; sell me some land, so that I can bury my wife."

5 They answered, 6 "Listen to us, sir. We look upon you as a mighty leader; bury your wife in the best grave that we have. Any of us would be glad to give you a grave, so that you can bury her."

7 Then Abraham bowed before them 8 and said, "If you are willing to let me bury my wife here, please ask Ephron son of Zohar 9 to sell me Machpelah Cave, which is near the edge of his field. Ask him to sell it to me for its full price, here in your presence, so that I can own it as a burial ground."

10 Ephron himself was sitting with the other Hittites at the meeting place at the city gate; he answered in the hearing of everyone there, 11 "Listen, sir; I will give you the whole field and the cave that is in it. Here in the presence of my own people, I will give it to you, so that you can bury your wife."

12 But Abraham bowed before the Hittites 13 and said to Ephron, so that everyone could hear, "May I ask you, please, to listen. I will buy the whole field. Accept my payment, and I will bury my wife there."

14 Ephron answered, 15 "Sir, land worth only four hundred pieces of silver — what is that between us? Bury your wife in it." 16 Abraham agreed and weighed out the amount that Ephron had mentioned in the hearing of the people — four hundred pieces of silver, according to the standard weights used by the merchants.

17 That is how the property which had belonged to Ephron at Machpelah east of Mamre, became Abraham's. It included the field, the cave which was in it, and all the trees in the field up to the edge of the property. 18 It was recognized as Abraham's property by all the Hittites who were there at the meeting.

19 Then Abraham buried his wife Sarah in that cave in the land of Canaan. 20 So the field which had belonged to the Hittites, and the cave in it, became the property of Abraham for a burial ground.

A Wife for Isaac

24 Abraham was now very old, and the LORD had blessed him in everything he did. 2 He said to his oldest servant, who was in charge of all that he had, "Place your hand between my thighs*a* and make a vow. 3 I want you to make a vow in the name of the LORD, the God of heaven and earth, that you will not choose a wife for my son from the people here in Canaan. 4 You must go back to the country where I was born and get a wife for my son Isaac from among my relatives."

5 But the servant asked, "What if the young woman will not leave home to come with me to this land? Shall I send your son back to the land you came from?"

6 Abraham answered, "Make sure that you don't send my son back there! 7 The LORD, the God of heaven, brought me from the home of my father and from the land of my relatives, and he solemnly promised me that he would give this land to my descendants. He will send his angel before you, so that you can get a wife there for my son. 8 If the young woman is not willing to come with you, you will be free from this promise. But you must not under any circumstances take my son back there." 9 So the servant put his hand between the thighs of Abraham, his master, and made a vow to do what Abraham had asked.

10 The servant, who was in charge of Abraham's property, took ten of his master's camels and went to the city where Nahor had lived in northern Mesopotamia. 11 When he arrived, he made the camels kneel down at the well outside the city. It was late afternoon, the time when women came out to get water. 12 He prayed, "LORD, God of my master Abraham, give me success today and keep your promise to my master. 13 Here I am at the well where the young women of the city will be coming to get water. 14 I will say to one of them, 'Please, lower your jar and let me have a drink.' If she says, 'Drink, and I will also bring water for your camels,' may she be the one that

---

a PLACE . . . THIGHS: *This was the way in which a vow was made absolutely unchangeable.*

you have chosen for your servant Isaac. If this happens, I will know that you have kept your promise to my master."

15 Before he had finished praying, Rebecca arrived with a water jar on her shoulder. She was the daughter of Bethuel, who was the son of Abraham's brother Nahor and his wife Milcah. 16 She was a very beautiful young woman and still a virgin. She went down to the well, filled her jar, and came back. 17 The servant ran to meet her and said, "Please give me a drink of water from your jar."

18 She said, "Drink, sir," and quickly lowered her jar from her shoulder and held it while he drank. 19 When he had finished, she said, "I will also bring water for your camels and let them have all they want." 20 She quickly emptied her jar into the animals' drinking trough and ran to the well to get more water, until she had watered all his camels. 21 The man kept watching her in silence, to see if the LORD had given him success.

22 When she had finished, the man took an expensive gold ring and put it in her nose and put two large gold bracelets on her arms. 23 He said, "Please tell me who your father is. Is there room in his house for my men and me to spend the night?"

24 "My father is Bethuel son of Nahor and Milcah," she answered. 25 "There is plenty of straw and fodder at our house, and there is a place for you to stay."

26 Then the man knelt down and worshiped the LORD. 27 He said, "Praise the LORD, the God of my master Abraham, who has faithfully kept his promise to my master. The LORD has led me straight to my master's relatives."

28 The young woman ran to her mother's house and told the whole story. 29 Now Rebecca had a brother named Laban, and he ran outside to go to the well where Abraham's servant was. 30 Laban had seen the nose ring and the bracelets on his sister's arms and had heard her say what the man had told her. He went to Abraham's servant, who was standing by his camels at the well, 31 and said, "Come home with me. You are a man whom the LORD has blessed. Why are you standing out here? I have a room ready for you in my house, and there is a place for your camels."

32 So the man went into the house, and Laban unloaded the camels and gave them straw and fodder. Then he brought water for Abraham's servant and his men to wash their feet. 33 When food was brought, the man said, "I will not eat until I have said what I have to say."

Laban said, "Go on and speak."

34 "I am the servant of Abraham," he began. 35 "The LORD has greatly blessed my master and made him a rich man. He has given him flocks of sheep and goats, cattle, silver, gold, male and female slaves, camels, and donkeys. 36 Sarah, my master's wife, bore him a son when she was old, and my master has given everything he owns to him. 37 My master made me promise with a vow to obey his command. He said, 'Do not choose a wife for my son from the young women in the land of Canaan. 38 Instead, go to my father's people, to my relatives, and choose a wife for him.' 39 And I asked my master, 'What if she will not come with me?' 40 He answered, 'The LORD, whom I have always obeyed, will send his angel with you and give you success. You will get for my son a wife from my own people, from my father's family. 41 There is only one way for you to be free from your vow: if you go to my relatives and they refuse you, then you will be free.'

42 "When I came to the well today, I prayed, 'LORD, God of my master Abraham, please give me success in what I am doing. 43 Here I am at the well. When a young woman comes out to get water, I will ask her to give me a drink of water from her jar. 44 If she agrees and also offers to bring water for my camels, may she be the one that you have chosen as the wife for my master's son.' 45 Before I had finished my silent prayer, Rebecca came with a water jar on her shoulder and went down to the well to get water. I said to her, 'Please give me a drink.' 46 She quickly lowered her jar from her shoulder and said, 'Drink, and I will also water your camels.' So I drank, and she watered the camels. 47 I asked her, 'Who is your father?' And she answered, 'My father is Bethuel son of Nahor and Milcah.' Then I put the ring in her nose and the bracelets on her arms. 48 I knelt down and worshiped the LORD. I praised the LORD, the God of my master Abraham, who had led me straight to my master's relative, where I found his daughter for my master's son. 49 Now, if you intend to fulfill your responsibility toward my master and treat him fairly, please tell

me; if not, say so, and I will decide what to do."

50 Laban and Bethuel answered, "Since this matter comes from the LORD, it is not for us to make a decision. 51 Here is Rebecca; take her and go. Let her become the wife of your master's son, as the LORD himself has said." 52 When the servant of Abraham heard this, he bowed down and worshiped the LORD. 53 Then he brought out clothing and silver and gold jewelry, and gave them to Rebecca. He also gave expensive gifts to her brother and to her mother.

54 Then Abraham's servant and the men with him ate and drank, and spent the night there. When they got up in the morning, he said, "Let me go back to my master."

55 But Rebecca's brother and her mother said, "Let her stay with us a week or ten days, and then she may go."

56 But he said, "Don't make us stay. The LORD has made my journey a success; let me go back to my master."

57 They answered, "Let's call her and find out what she has to say." 58 So they called Rebecca and asked, "Do you want to go with this man?"

"Yes," she answered.

59 So they let Rebecca and her old family servant go with Abraham's servant and his men. 60 And they gave Rebecca their blessing in these words:

"May you, sister, become the
mother of millions!
May your descendants conquer the
cities of their enemies!"

61 Then Rebecca and her young women got ready and mounted the camels to go with Abraham's servant, and they all started out.

62 Isaac had come into the wilderness of b "The Well of the Living One Who Sees Me" and was staying in the southern part of Canaan. 63 He went out in the early evening to take a walk in the fields and saw camels coming. 64 When Rebecca saw Isaac, she got down from her camel 65 and asked Abraham's servant, "Who is that man walking toward us in the field?"

"He is my master," the servant answered. So she took her scarf and covered her face.

66 The servant told Isaac everything he had done. 67 Then Isaac brought Rebecca into the tent that his mother Sarah had lived in, and she became his wife. Isaac loved Rebecca, and so he was comforted for the loss of his mother.

Other Descendants of Abraham
(1 Chronicles 1.32, 33)

25 Abraham married another woman, whose name was Keturah. 2 She bore him Zimran, Jokshan, Medan, Midian, Ishbak, and Shuah. 3 Jokshan was the father of Sheba and Dedan, and the descendants of Dedan were the Asshurim, the Letushim, and the Leummim. 4 The sons of Midian were Ephah, Epher, Hanoch, Abida, and Eldaah. All these were Keturah's descendants.

5 Abraham left everything he owned to Isaac; 6 but while he was still alive, he gave presents to the sons his other wives had borne him. Then he sent these sons to the land of the East, away from his son Isaac.

The Death and Burial of Abraham

7-8 Abraham died at the ripe old age of 175. 9 His sons Isaac and Ishmael buried him in Machpelah Cave, in the field east of Mamre that had belonged to Ephron son of Zohar the Hittite. 10 It was the field that Abraham had bought from the Hittites; both Abraham and his wife Sarah were buried there. 11 After the death of Abraham, God blessed his son Isaac, who lived near "The Well of the Living One Who Sees Me."

The Descendants of Ishmael
(1 Chronicles 1.28-31)

12 Ishmael, whom Hagar, the Egyptian slave of Sarah, bore to Abraham, 13 had the following sons, listed in the order of their birth: Nebaioth, Kedar, Adbeel, Mibsam, 14 Mishma, Dumah, Massa, 15 Hadad, Tema, Jetur, Naphish, and Kedemah. 16 They were the ancestors of twelve tribes, and their names were given to their villages and camping places. 17 Ishmael was 137 years old when he died. 18 The descendants of Ishmael lived in the territory between Havilah and Shur, to the east of Egypt on the way to Assyria. They lived apart from the other descendants of Abraham.

---

b Some ancient translations into the wilderness of; Hebrew from coming.

The Birth of Esau and Jacob

¹⁹This is the story of Abraham's son Isaac. ²⁰Isaac was forty years old when he married Rebecca, the daughter of Bethuel (an Aramean from Mesopotamia) and sister of Laban. ²¹Because Rebecca had no children, Isaac prayed to the LORD for her. The LORD answered his prayer, and Rebecca became pregnant. ²²She was going to have twins, and before they were born, they struggled against each other in her womb. She said, "Why should something like this happen to me?" So she went to ask the LORD for an answer.

²³The LORD said to her,

"Two nations are within you;
You will give birth to two rival
    peoples.
One will be stronger than the
    other;
The older will serve the younger."

²⁴The time came for her to give birth, and she had twin sons. ²⁵The first one was reddish, and his skin was like a hairy robe, so he was named Esau.^c ²⁶The second one was born holding on tightly to the heel of Esau, so he was named Jacob.^d Isaac was sixty years old when they were born.

Esau Sells His Rights as the First-Born Son

²⁷The boys grew up, and Esau became a skilled hunter, a man who loved the outdoors, but Jacob was a quiet man who stayed at home. ²⁸Isaac preferred Esau, because he enjoyed eating the animals Esau killed, but Rebecca preferred Jacob.

²⁹One day while Jacob was cooking some bean soup, Esau came in from hunting. He was hungry ³⁰and said to Jacob, "I'm starving; give me some of that red stuff." (That is why he was named Edom.^e)

³¹Jacob answered, "I will give it to you if you give me your rights as the first-born son."

³²Esau said, "All right! I am about to die; what good will my rights do me?"

³³Jacob answered, "First make a vow that you will give me your rights."

Esau made the vow and gave his rights to Jacob. ³⁴Then Jacob gave him some bread and some of the soup. He ate and drank and then got up and left. That was all Esau cared about his rights as the first-born son.

Isaac Lives at Gerar

26 There was another famine in the land besides the earlier one during the time of Abraham. Isaac went to Abimelech, king of the Philistines, at Gerar. ²The LORD had appeared to Isaac and had said, "Do not go to Egypt; stay in this land, where I tell you to stay. ³Live here, and I will be with you and bless you. I am going to give all this territory to you and to your descendants. I will keep the promise I made to your father Abraham. ⁴I will give you as many descendants as there are stars in the sky, and I will give them all this territory. All the nations will ask me to bless them as I have blessed your descendants. ⁵I will bless you, because Abraham obeyed me and kept all my laws and commands."

⁶So Isaac lived at Gerar. ⁷When the men there asked about his wife, he said that she was his sister. He would not admit that she was his wife, because he was afraid that the men there would kill him to get Rebecca, who was very beautiful. ⁸When Isaac had been there for some time, King Abimelech looked down from his window and saw Isaac and Rebecca making love. ⁹Abimelech sent for Isaac and said, "So she is your wife! Why did you say she was your sister?"

He answered, "I thought I would be killed if I said she was my wife."

¹⁰"What have you done to us?" Abimelech said. "One of my men might easily have slept with your wife, and you would have been responsible for our guilt." ¹¹Abimelech warned all the people: "Anyone who mistreats this man or his wife will be put to death."

¹²Isaac sowed crops in that land, and that year he harvested a hundred times as much as he had sown, because the LORD blessed him. ¹³He continued to prosper and became a very rich man. ¹⁴Because he had many herds of sheep and cattle and many servants, the Philistines were jealous of him. ¹⁵So they filled in all the wells which the servants of his

^c ESAU: *This name is taken to refer to Seir, the territory later inhabited by Esau's descendants; Seir sounds like the Hebrew for "hairy."* ^d JACOB: *This name sounds like the Hebrew for "heel."* ^e EDOM: *This name sounds like the Hebrew for "red."*

father Abraham had dug while Abraham was alive.

16 Then Abimelech said to Isaac, "Leave our country. You have become more powerful than we are." 17 So Isaac left and set up his camp in Gerar Valley, where he stayed for some time. 18 He dug once again the wells which had been dug during the time of Abraham and which the Philistines had stopped up after Abraham's death. Isaac gave the wells the same names that his father had given them.

19 Isaac's servants dug a well in the valley and found water. 20 The shepherds of Gerar quarreled with Isaac's shepherds and said, "This water belongs to us." So Isaac named the well "Quarrel."

21 Isaac's servants dug another well, and there was a quarrel about that one also, so he named it "Enmity." 22 He moved away from there and dug another well. There was no dispute about this one, so he named it "Freedom." He said, "Now the LORD has given us freedom to live in the land, and we will be prosperous here."

23 Isaac left and went to Beersheba. 24 That night the LORD appeared to him and said, "I am the God of your father Abraham. Do not be afraid; I am with you. I will bless you and give you many descendants because of my promise to my servant Abraham." 25 Isaac built an altar there and worshiped the LORD. Then he set up his camp there, and his servants dug another well.

The Agreement between Isaac and Abimelech

26 Abimelech came from Gerar with Ahuzzath his adviser and Phicol the commander of his army to see Isaac. 27 So Isaac asked, "Why have you now come to see me, when you were so unfriendly to me before and made me leave your country?"

28 They answered, "Now we know that the LORD is with you, and we think that there should be a solemn agreement between us. We want you to promise 29 that you will not harm us, just as we did not harm you. We were kind to you and let you go peacefully. Now it is clear that the LORD has blessed you." 30 Isaac prepared a feast for them, and they ate and drank.

31 Early next morning each man made his promise and sealed it with a vow. Isaac said good-bye to them, and they parted as friends.

32 On that day Isaac's servants came and told him about the well which they had dug. They said, "We have found water." 33 He named the well "Vow." That is how the city of Beersheba/ got its name.

Esau's Foreign Wives

34 When Esau was forty years old, he married two Hittites, Judith the daughter of Beeri, and Basemath the daughter of Elon. 35 They made life miserable for Isaac and Rebecca.

Isaac Blesses Jacob

27 Isaac was now old and had become blind. He sent for his older son Esau and said to him, "Son!"

"Yes," he answered.

2 Isaac said, "You see that I am old and may die soon. 3 Take your bow and arrows, go out into the country, and kill an animal for me. 4 Cook me some of that tasty food that I like, and bring it to me. After I have eaten it, I will give you my final blessing before I die."

5 While Isaac was talking to Esau, Rebecca was listening. So when Esau went out to hunt, 6 she said to Jacob, "I have just heard your father say to Esau, 7 'Bring me an animal and cook it for me. After I have eaten it, I will give you my blessing in the presence of the LORD before I die.' 8 Now, son," Rebecca continued, "listen to me and do what I say. 9 Go to the flock and pick out two fat young goats, so that I can cook them and make some of that food your father likes so much. 10 You can take it to him to eat, and he will give you his blessing before he dies."

11 But Jacob said to his mother, "You know that Esau is a hairy man, but I have smooth skin. 12 Perhaps my father will touch me and find out that I am deceiving him; in this way, I will bring a curse on myself instead of a blessing."

13 His mother answered, "Let any curse against you fall on me, my son; just do as I say, and go and get the goats for me." 14 So he went to get them and brought them to her, and she cooked the kind of food that his father liked. 15 Then she

/ BEERSHEBA: *This name in Hebrew means "Well of the Vow" or "Well of Seven" (see also 21.31).*

took Esau's best clothes, which she kept in the house, and put them on Jacob. 16She put the skins of the goats on his arms and on the hairless part of his neck. 17She handed him the tasty food, along with the bread she had baked.

18Then Jacob went to his father and said, "Father!"

"Yes," he answered. "Which of my sons are you?"

19Jacob answered, "I am your older son Esau; I have done as you told me. Please sit up and eat some of the meat that I have brought you, so that you can give me your blessing."

20Isaac said, "How did you find it so quickly, son?"

Jacob answered, "The LORD your God helped me find it."

21Isaac said to Jacob, "Please come closer so that I can touch you. Are you really Esau?" 22Jacob moved closer to his father, who felt him and said, "Your voice sounds like Jacob's voice, but your arms feel like Esau's arms." 23He did not recognize Jacob, because his arms were hairy like Esau's. He was about to give him his blessing, 24but asked again, "Are you really Esau?"

"I am," he answered.

25Isaac said, "Bring me some of the meat. After I eat it, I will give you my blessing." Jacob brought it to him, and he also brought him some wine to drink. 26Then his father said to him, "Come closer and kiss me, son." 27As he came up to kiss him, Isaac smelled his clothes — so he gave him his blessing. He said, "The pleasant smell of my son is like the smell of a field which the LORD has blessed. 28May God give you dew from heaven and make your fields fertile! May he give you plenty of grain and wine! 29May nations be your servants, and may peoples bow down before you. May you rule over all your relatives, and may your mother's descendants bow down before you. May those who curse you be cursed, and may those who bless you be blessed."

Esau Begs for Isaac's Blessing

30Isaac finished giving his blessing, and as soon as Jacob left, his brother Esau came in from hunting. 31He also cooked some tasty food and took it to his father. He said, "Please, father, sit up and eat some of the meat that I have brought you, so that you can give me your blessing."

32"Who are you?" Isaac asked.

"Your older son Esau," he answered.

33Isaac began to tremble and shake all over, and he asked, "Who was it, then, who killed an animal and brought it to me? I ate it just before you came. I gave him my final blessing, and so it is his forever."

34When Esau heard this, he cried out loudly and bitterly and said, "Give me your blessing also, father!"

35Isaac answered, "Your brother came and deceived me. He has taken away your blessing."

36Esau said, "This is the second time that he has cheated me. No wonder his name is Jacob.g He took my rights as the first-born son, and now he has taken away my blessing. Haven't you saved a blessing for me?"

37Isaac answered, "I have already made him master over you, and I have made all his relatives his slaves. I have given him grain and wine. Now there is nothing that I can do for you, son!"

38Esau continued to plead with his father: "Do you have only one blessing, father? Bless me too, father!" He began to cry.

39Then Isaac said to him,

"No dew from heaven for you,
No fertile fields for you.
40You will live by your sword,
But be your brother's slave.
Yet when you rebel,h
You will break away from his
control."

41Esau hated Jacob, because his father had given Jacob the blessing. He thought, "The time to mourn my father's death is near; then I will kill Jacob."

42But when Rebecca heard about Esau's plan, she sent for Jacob and said, "Listen, your brother Esau is planning to get even with you and kill you. 43Now, son, do what I say. Go at once to my brother Laban in Haran, 44and stay with him for a while, until your brother's anger cools down 45and he forgets what you have done to him. Then I will send someone to bring you back. Why should I lose both of my sons on the same day?"

---

g JACOB: *This name sounds like the Hebrew for "cheat."*   h rebel; or grow restless.

Isaac Sends Jacob to Laban

46 Rebecca said to Isaac, "I am sick and tired of Esau's foreign wives. If Jacob also marries one of these Hittites, I might as well die."

28 Isaac called Jacob, greeted him, and told him, "Don't marry a Canaanite. ²Go instead to Mesopotamia, to the home of your grandfather Bethuel, and marry one of the young women there, one of your uncle Laban's daughters. ³May Almighty God bless your marriage and give you many children, so that you will become the father of many nations! ⁴May he bless you and your descendants as he blessed Abraham, and may you take possession of this land, in which you have lived and which God gave to Abraham!" ⁵Isaac sent Jacob away to Mesopotamia, to Laban, who was the son of Bethuel the Aramean and the brother of Rebecca, the mother of Jacob and Esau.

Esau Takes Another Wife

6 Esau learned that Isaac had blessed Jacob and sent him away to Mesopotamia to find a wife. He also learned that when Isaac blessed him, he commanded him not to marry a Canaanite woman. ⁷He found out that Jacob had obeyed his father and mother and had gone to Mesopotamia. ⁸Esau then understood that his father Isaac did not approve of Canaanite women. ⁹So he went to Ishmael son of Abraham and married his daughter Mahalath, who was the sister of Nebaioth.

Jacob's Dream at Bethel

10 Jacob left Beersheba and started toward Haran. ¹¹At sunset he came to a holy place[i] and camped there. He lay down to sleep, resting his head on a stone. ¹²He dreamed that he saw a stairway reaching from earth to heaven, with angels going up and coming down on it. ¹³And there was the LORD standing beside him.[j] "I am the LORD, the God of Abraham and Isaac," he said. "I will give to you and to your descendants this land on which you are lying. ¹⁴They will be as numerous as the specks of dust on the earth. They will extend their territory in all directions, and through you and your descendants I will bless all the nations.[k]

15 Remember, I will be with you and protect you wherever you go, and I will bring you back to this land. I will not leave you until I have done all that I have promised you."

¹⁶Jacob woke up and said, "The LORD is here! He is in this place, and I didn't know it!" ¹⁷He was afraid and said, "What a terrifying place this is! It must be the house of God; it must be the gate that opens into heaven."

¹⁸Jacob got up early next morning, took the stone that was under his head, and set it up as a memorial. Then he poured olive oil on it to dedicate it to God. ¹⁹He named the place Bethel.[l] (The town there was once known as Luz.) ²⁰Then Jacob made a vow to the LORD: "If you will be with me and protect me on the journey I am making and give me food and clothing, ²¹and if I return safely to my father's home, then you will be my God. ²²This memorial stone which I have set up will be the place where you are worshiped, and I will give you a tenth of everything you give me."

Jacob Arrives at Laban's Home

29 Jacob continued on his way and went toward the land of the East. ²Suddenly he came upon a well out in the fields with three flocks of sheep lying around it. The flocks were watered from this well, which had a large stone over the opening. ³Whenever all the flocks came together there, the shepherds would roll the stone back and water them. Then they would put the stone back in place.

⁴Jacob asked the shepherds, "My friends, where are you from?"

"From Haran," they answered.

⁵He asked, "Do you know Laban, grandson of Nahor?"

"Yes, we do," they answered.

⁶"Is he well?" he asked.

"He is well," they answered. "Look, here comes his daughter Rachel with his flock."

⁷Jacob said, "Since it is still broad daylight and not yet time to bring the flocks in, why don't you water them and take them back to pasture?"

⁸They answered, "We can't do that until all the flocks are here and the stone

---

i a holy place; *or* a place.   *j* beside him; *or* on it.   *k* through you . . . nations; *or* all the nations will ask me to bless them as I have blessed you and your descendants.   *l* BETHEL: *This name in Hebrew means "house of God."*

has been rolled back; then we will water the flocks."

9 While Jacob was still talking with them, Rachel arrived with the flock. 10 When Jacob saw Rachel with his uncle Laban's flock, he went to the well, rolled the stone back, and watered the sheep. 11 Then he kissed her and began to cry for joy. 12 He told her, "I am your father's relative, the son of Rebecca."

She ran to tell her father; 13 and when he heard the news about his nephew Jacob, he ran to meet him, hugged him and kissed him, and brought him into the house. When Jacob told Laban everything that had happened, 14 Laban said, "Yes, indeed, you are my own flesh and blood." Jacob stayed there a whole month.

Jacob Serves Laban for Rachel and Leah

15 Laban said to Jacob, "You shouldn't work for me for nothing just because you are my relative. How much pay do you want?" 16 Laban had two daughters; the older was named Leah, and the younger Rachel. 17 Leah had lovely[m] eyes, but Rachel was shapely and beautiful.

18 Jacob was in love with Rachel, so he said, "I will work seven years for you, if you will let me marry Rachel."

19 Laban answered, "I would rather give her to you than to anyone else; stay here with me." 20 Jacob worked seven years so that he could have Rachel, and the time seemed like only a few days to him, because he loved her.

21 Then Jacob said to Laban, "The time is up; let me marry your daughter." 22 So Laban gave a wedding feast and invited everyone. 23 But that night, instead of Rachel, he took Leah to Jacob, and Jacob had intercourse with her. (24 Laban gave his slave woman Zilpah to his daughter Leah as her maid.) 25 Not until the next morning did Jacob discover that it was Leah. He went to Laban and said, "Why did you do this to me? I worked to get Rachel. Why have you tricked me?"

26 Laban answered, "It is not the custom here to give the younger daughter in marriage before the older. 27 Wait until the week's marriage celebrations are over, and I will give you Rachel, if you will work for me another seven years."

28 Jacob agreed, and when the week of marriage celebrations was over, Laban gave him his daughter Rachel as his wife. (29 Laban gave his slave woman Bilhah to his daughter Rachel as her maid.) 30 Jacob had intercourse with Rachel also, and he loved her more than Leah. Then he worked for Laban another seven years.

The Children Born to Jacob

31 When the LORD saw that Leah was loved less than Rachel, he made it possible for her to have children, but Rachel remained childless. 32 Leah became pregnant and gave birth to a son. She said, "The LORD has seen my trouble, and now my husband will love me"; so she named him Reuben.[n] 33 She became pregnant again and gave birth to another son. She said, "The LORD has given me this son also, because he heard that I was not loved"; so she named him Simeon.[o] 34 Once again she became pregnant and gave birth to another son. She said, "Now my husband will be bound more tightly to me, because I have borne him three sons"; so she named him Levi.[p] 35 Then she became pregnant again and gave birth to another son. She said, "This time I will praise the LORD"; so she named him Judah.[q] Then she stopped having children.

30 But Rachel had not borne Jacob any children, and so she became jealous of her sister and said to Jacob, "Give me children, or I will die."

2 Jacob became angry with Rachel and said, "I can't take the place of God. He is the one who keeps you from having children."

3 She said, "Here is my slave Bilhah; sleep with her, so that she can have a child for me. In this way I can become a mother through her." 4 So she gave Bilhah to her husband, and he had intercourse with her. 5 Bilhah became pregnant and bore Jacob a son. 6 Rachel said, "God has judged in my favor. He has heard my prayer and has given me a son"; so she named him Dan.[r] 7 Bilhah became pregnant again and bore Jacob a

---

m lovely; or weak.   n REUBEN: This name sounds like the Hebrew for "see, a son" and "has seen my trouble."   o SIMEON: This name sounds like the Hebrew for "hear."   p LEVI: This name sounds like the Hebrew for "bound."   q JUDAH: This name sounds like the Hebrew for "praise." r DAN: This name sounds like the Hebrew for "judge in favor."

second son. 8 Rachel said, "I have fought a hard fight with my sister, but I have won"; so she named him Naphtali.s

9 When Leah realized that she had stopped having children, she gave her slave Zilpah to Jacob as his wife. 10 Then Zilpah bore Jacob a son. 11 Leah said, "I have been lucky"; so she named him Gad.t 12 Zilpah bore Jacob another son, 13 and Leah said, "How happy I am! Now women will call me happy"; so she named him Asher.u

14 During the wheat harvest Reuben went into the fields and found mandrakes,v which he brought to his mother Leah. Rachel said to Leah, "Please give me some of your son's mandrakes."

15 Leah answered, "Isn't it enough that you have taken away my husband? Now you are even trying to take away my son's mandrakes."

Rachel said, "If you will give me your son's mandrakes, you can sleep with Jacob tonight."

16 When Jacob came in from the fields in the evening, Leah went out to meet him and said, "You are going to sleep with me tonight, because I have paid for you with my son's mandrakes." So he had intercourse with her that night.

17 God answered Leah's prayer, and she became pregnant and bore Jacob a fifth son. 18 Leah said, "God has given me my reward, because I gave my slave to my husband"; so she named her son Issachar.w 19 Leah became pregnant again and bore Jacob a sixth son. 20 She said, "God has given me a fine gift. Now my husband will accept me, because I have borne him six sons"; so she named him Zebulun.x 21 Later she bore a daughter, whom she named Dinah.

22 Then God remembered Rachel; he answered her prayer and made it possible for her to have children. 23 She became pregnant and gave birth to a son. She said, "God has taken away my disgrace by giving me a son. 24 May the LORD give me another son"; so she named him Joseph.y

Jacob's Bargain with Laban

25 After the birth of Joseph, Jacob said to Laban, "Let me go, so that I can return home. 26 Give me my wives and children that I have earned by working for you, and I will leave. You know how well I have served you."

27 Laban said to him, "Let me say this: I have learned by divination that the LORD has blessed me because of you. 28 Name your wages, and I will pay them."

29 Jacob answered, "You know how I have worked for you and how your flocks have prospered under my care. 30 The little you had before I came has grown enormously, and the LORD has blessed you wherever I went.z Now it is time for me to look out for my own interests."

31 "What shall I pay you?" Laban asked.

Jacob answered, "I don't want any wages. I will continue to take care of your flocks if you agree to this suggestion: 32 Let me go through all your flocks today and take every black lamba and every spotted or speckled young goat. That is all the wages I want. 33 In the future you can easily find out if I have been honest. When you come to check up on my wages, if I have any goat that isn't speckled or spotted or any sheep that isn't black, you will know that it has been stolen."

34 Laban answered, "Agreed. We will do as you suggest." 35 But that day Laban removed the male goats that had stripes or spots and all the females that were speckled and spotted or which had white on them; he also removed all the black sheep. He put his sons in charge of them, 36 and then went away from Jacob with this flock as far as he could travel in three days. Jacob took care of the rest of Laban's flocks.

37 Jacob got green branches of poplar, almond, and plane trees and stripped off some of the bark so that the branches had white stripes on them. 38 He placed these branches in front of the flocks at

---

s NAPHTALI: *This name sounds like the Hebrew for "fight."*   t GAD: *This name in Hebrew means* "luck."   u ASHER: *This name in Hebrew means "happy."*   v MANDRAKES: *Plants which were believed to produce fertility and were used as love charms.*   w ISSACHAR: *This name sounds like the Hebrew for "a man is hired" and "there is reward."*   x ZEBULUN: *This name sounds like the Hebrew for "accept" and "gift."*   y JOSEPH: *This name sounds like the Hebrew for "may he give another" and "he has taken away."*   z wherever I went; *or because of me.*   a *One ancient translation* every black lamb; *Hebrew* every spotted and speckled lamb, and every black lamb.

their drinking troughs. He put them there, because the animals mated when they came to drink. 39 So when the goats bred in front of the branches, they produced young that were streaked, speckled, and spotted.

40 Jacob kept the sheep separate from the goats and made them face in the direction of the streaked and black animals of Laban's flock. In this way he built up his own flock and kept it apart from Laban's.

41 When the healthy animals were mating, Jacob put the branches in front of them at the drinking troughs, so that they would breed among the branches. 42 But he did not put the branches in front of the weak animals. Soon Laban had all the weak animals, and Jacob all the healthy ones. 43 In this way Jacob became very wealthy. He had many flocks, slaves, camels, and donkeys.

Jacob Flees from Laban

31 Jacob heard that Laban's sons were saying, "Jacob has taken everything that belonged to our father. He got all his wealth from what our father owned." 2 He also saw that Laban was no longer as friendly as he had been earlier. 3 Then the LORD said to him, "Go back to the land of your fathers and to your relatives. I will be with you."

4 So Jacob sent word to Rachel and Leah to meet him in the field where his flocks were. 5 He said to them, "I have noticed that your father is not as friendly toward me as he has used to be; but my father's God has been with me. 6 You both know that I have worked for your father with all my strength. 7 Yet he has cheated me and changed my wages ten times. But God did not let him harm me. 8 Whenever Laban said, 'The speckled goats shall be your wages,' all the flocks produced speckled young. When he said, 'The striped goats shall be your wages,' all the flocks produced striped young. 9 God has taken flocks away from your father and given them to me.

10 "During the breeding season I had a dream, and I saw that the male goats that were mating were striped, spotted, and speckled. 11 The angel of God spoke to me in the dream and said, 'Jacob!' 'Yes,' I answered. 12 'Look,' he continued, 'all the male goats that are mating are striped, spotted, and speckled. I am mak-

ing this happen because I have seen all that Laban is doing to you. 13 I am the God who appeared to you at Bethel, where you dedicated a stone as a memorial by pouring olive oil on it and where you made a vow to me. Now get ready and go back to the land where you were born.'"

14 Rachel and Leah answered Jacob, "There is nothing left for us to inherit from our father. 15 He treats us like foreigners. He sold us, and now he has spent all the money he was paid for us. 16 All this wealth which God has taken from our father belongs to us and to our children. Do whatever God has told you."

17-18 So Jacob got ready to go back to his father in the land of Canaan. He put his children and his wives on the camels, and drove all his flocks ahead of him, with everything that he had gotten in Mesopotamia. 19 Laban had gone to shear his sheep, and during his absence Rachel stole the household gods that belonged to her father. 20 Jacob deceived Laban by not letting him know that he was leaving. 21 He took everything he owned and left in a hurry. He crossed the Euphrates River and started for the hill country of Gilead.

Laban Pursues Jacob

22 Three days later Laban was told that Jacob had fled. 23 He took his men with him and pursued Jacob for seven days until he caught up with him in the hill country of Gilead. 24 In a dream that night God came to Laban and said to him, "Be careful not to threaten Jacob in any way." 25 Jacob had set up his camp on a mountain, and Laban set up his camp with his relatives in the hill country of Gilead.

26 Laban said to Jacob, "Why did you deceive me and carry off my daughters like women captured in war? 27 Why did you deceive me and slip away without telling me? If you had told me, I would have sent you on your way with rejoicing and singing to the music of tambourines and harps. 28 You did not even let me kiss my grandchildren and my daughters good-bye. That was a foolish thing to do! 29 I have the power to do you harm, but last night the God of your father warned me not to threaten you in any way. 30 I know that you left because you were

so anxious to get back home, but why did you steal my household gods?"

31 Jacob answered, "I was afraid, because I thought that you might take your daughters away from me. 32 But if you find that anyone here has your gods, he will be put to death. Here, with our men as witnesses, look for anything that belongs to you and take what is yours." Jacob did not know that Rachel had stolen Laban's gods.

33 Laban went and searched Jacob's tent; then he went into Leah's tent, and the tent of the two slave women, but he did not find his gods. Then he went into Rachel's tent. 34 Rachel had taken the household gods and put them in a camel's saddlebag and was sitting on them. Laban searched through the whole tent, but did not find them. 35 Rachel said to her father, "Do not be angry with me, sir, but I am not able to stand up in your presence; I am having my monthly period." Laban searched but did not find his household gods.

36 Then Jacob lost his temper. "What crime have I committed?" he asked angrily. "What law have I broken that gives you the right to hunt me down? 37 Now that you have searched through all my belongings, what household article have you found that belongs to you? Put it out here where your men and mine can see it, and let them decide which one of us is right. 38 I have been with you now for twenty years; your sheep and your goats have not failed to reproduce, and I have not eaten any rams from your flocks. 39 Whenever a sheep was killed by wild animals, I always bore the loss myself. I didn't take it to you to show that it was not my fault. You demanded that I make good anything that was stolen during the day or during the night. 40 Many times I suffered from the heat during the day and from the cold at night. I was not able to sleep. 41 It was like that for the whole twenty years I was with you. For fourteen years I worked to win your two daughters—and six years for your flocks. And even then, you changed my wages ten times. 42 If the God of my fathers, the God of Abraham and Isaac,

had not been with me, you would have already sent me away empty-handed. But God has seen my trouble and the work I have done, and last night he gave his judgment."

The Agreement between Jacob and Laban

43 Laban answered Jacob, "These young women are my daughters; their children belong to me, and these flocks are mine. In fact, everything you see here belongs to me. But since I can do nothing to keep my daughters and their children, 44 I am ready to make an agreement with you. Let us make a pile of stones to remind us of our agreement."

45 So Jacob got a stone and set it up as a memorial. 46 He told his men to gather some rocks and pile them up. Then they ate a meal beside the pile of rocks. 47 Laban named it Jegar Sahadutha,[b] while Jacob named it Galeed.[c] 48 Laban said to Jacob, "This pile of rocks will be a reminder for both of us." That is why that place was named Galeed. 49 Laban also said, "May the LORD keep an eye on us while we are separated from each other." So the place was also named Mizpah.[d] 50 Laban went on, "If you mistreat my daughters or if you marry other women, even though I don't know about it, remember that God is watching us. 51 Here are the rocks that I have piled up between us, and here is the memorial stone. 52 Both this pile and this memorial stone are reminders. I will never go beyond this pile to attack you, and you must never go beyond it or beyond this memorial stone to attack me. 53 The God of Abraham and the God of Nahor[e] will judge between us." Then, in the name of the God whom his father Isaac worshiped, Jacob solemnly vowed to keep this promise. 54 He killed an animal, which he offered as a sacrifice on the mountain, and he invited his men to the meal. After they had eaten, they spent the night on the mountain. 55 Early the next morning Laban kissed his grandchildren and his daughters good-bye, and left to go back home.

---

b JEGAR SAHADUTHA: *This name in Aramaic means "a pile to remind us."*   c GALEED: *This name in Hebrew means "a pile to remind us."*   d MIZPAH: *This name sounds like the Hebrew for "place from which to watch."*   e ABRAHAM . . . NAHOR: *Abraham was Jacob's grandfather and Nahor was Laban's grandfather.*

Jacob Prepares to Meet Esau

32 As Jacob went on his way, some angels met him. 2 When he saw them, he said, "This is God's camp"; so he named the place Mahanaim.*f*

3 Jacob sent messengers ahead of him to his brother Esau in the country of Edom. 4 He instructed them to say: "I, Jacob, your obedient servant, report to my master Esau that I have been staying with Laban and that I have delayed my return until now. 5 I own cattle, donkeys, sheep, goats, and slaves. I am sending you word, sir, in the hope of gaining your favor."

6 When the messengers came back to Jacob, they said, "We went to your brother Esau, and he is already on his way to meet you. He has four hundred men with him." 7 Jacob was frightened and worried. He divided into two groups the people who were with him, and also his sheep, goats, cattle, and camels. 8 He thought, "If Esau comes and attacks the first group, the other may be able to escape."

9 Then Jacob prayed, "God of my grandfather Abraham and God of my father Isaac, hear me! You told me, LORD, to go back to my land and to my relatives, and you would make everything go well for me. 10 I am not worth all the kindness and faithfulness that you have shown me, your servant. I crossed the Jordan with nothing but a walking stick, and now I have come back with these two groups. 11 Save me, I pray, from my brother Esau. I am afraid—afraid that he is coming to attack us and destroy us all, even the women and children. 12 Remember that you promised to make everything go well for me and to give me more descendants than anyone could count, as many as the grains of sand along the seashore."

13-15 After spending the night there, Jacob chose from his livestock as a present for his brother Esau: 200 female goats and 20 males, 200 female sheep and 20 males, 30 milk camels with their young, 40 cows and 10 bulls, 20 female donkeys and 10 males. 16 He divided them into herds and put one of his servants in charge of each herd. He said to them, "Go ahead of me, and leave a space between each herd and the one behind it." 17 He ordered the first servant, "When my brother Esau meets you and asks, 'Who is your master? Where are you going? Who owns these animals in front of you?' 18 you must answer, 'They belong to your servant Jacob. He sends them as a present to his master Esau. Jacob himself is right behind us.' " 19 He gave the same order to the second, the third, and to all the others who were in charge of the herds: "This is what you must say to Esau when you meet him. 20 You must say, 'Yes, your servant Jacob is right behind us.' " Jacob was thinking, "I will win him over with the gifts, and when I meet him, perhaps he will forgive me." 21 He sent the gifts on ahead of him and spent that night in camp.

Jacob Wrestles at Peniel

22 That same night Jacob got up, took his two wives, his two concubines, and his eleven children, and crossed the Jabbok River. 23 After he had sent them across, he also sent across all that he owned, 24 but he stayed behind, alone.

Then a man came and wrestled with him until just before daybreak. 25 When the man saw that he was not winning the struggle, he hit Jacob on the hip, and it was thrown out of joint. 26 The man said, "Let me go; daylight is coming."

"I won't, unless you bless me," Jacob answered.

27 "What is your name?" the man asked.

"Jacob," he answered.

28 The man said, "Your name will no longer be Jacob. You have struggled with God and with men, and you have won; so your name will be Israel."*g*

29 Jacob said, "Now tell me your name."

But he answered, "Why do you want to know my name?" Then he blessed Jacob.

30 Jacob said, "I have seen God face-to-face, and I am still alive"; so he named the place Peniel.*h* 31 The sun rose as Jacob was leaving Peniel, and he was limping because of his hip. 32 Even today the descendants of Israel do not eat the muscle which is on the hip joint, because it was on this muscle that Jacob was hit.

f MAHANAIM: *This name in Hebrew means "two camps."* *g* ISRAEL: *This name sounds like the* Hebrew for *"he struggles with God" or "God struggles."* *h* PENIEL: *This name sounds like the* Hebrew for *"the face of God."*

THE CITY OF SHECHEM

Shechem was a fortified city on the edge of a fertile plain in central Palestine where main highways and trade routes converged. Associated particularly with Abraham, Jacob, and Joseph, Shechem was a place where many altars for worship of the one true God were erected.

When Abram (Abraham) entered Canaan about 1900 B.C., he stopped in Shechem. God appeared to him at Shechem and promised to give the land of Canaan to his descendants (Gn 12.6, 7). In response, Abram built an altar to the Lord.

Upon his return to Shechem many years later, Abraham's grandson Jacob also built an altar (Gn 33.18–20). John 4.12 says he dug a deep well there. Joseph visited his brothers when they were tending their father's herds at Shechem (Gn 37.12). Joseph's body was taken from Egypt during the Exodus and buried at Shechem (Js 24.32).

After Joshua led the Israelites to victory in Canaan, an altar was built at Shechem. Its construction was accompanied by a covenant-renewal ceremony in which offerings were given and the Law was read (Js 8.30–35). Shechem's location between barren Mount Ebal and fertile Mount Gerizim gave the ceremony symbolic meaning—the advantages of keeping the covenant were proclaimed from Gerizim, while the curses for breaking it were proclaimed from Ebal.

For a short time after the northern kingdom of Israel was founded, Shechem served as the capital city of this nation before Samaria was built and designated as the capital city (1 K 12.25).

Some scholars identify the New Testament town Sychar (Jn 4.5) with Shechem. If this is correct, then this is where Jesus spoke with the Samaritan woman at Jacob's well. He promised her living water that would become "a spring which will provide them with life-giving water and give them eternal life" (Jn 4.14).

Jacob Meets Esau

33 Jacob saw Esau coming with his four hundred men, so he divided the children among Leah, Rachel, and the two concubines. 2 He put the concubines and their children first, then Leah and her children, and finally Rachel and Joseph at the rear. 3 Jacob went ahead of them and bowed down to the ground seven times as he approached his brother. 4 But Esau ran to meet him, threw his arms around him, and kissed him. They were both crying. 5 When Esau looked around and saw the women and the children, he asked, "Who are these people with you?"

"These, sir, are the children whom God has been good enough to give me," Jacob answered. 6 Then the concubines came up with their children and bowed down; 7 then Leah and her children came, and last of all Joseph and Rachel came and bowed down.

8 Esau asked, "What about that other group I met? What did that mean?"

Jacob answered, "It was to gain your favor."

9 But Esau said, "I have enough, my brother; keep what you have."

10 Jacob said, "No, please, if I have gained your favor, accept my gift. To see your face is for me like seeing the face of God, now that you have been so friendly to me. 11 Please accept this gift which I have brought for you; God has been kind to me and given me everything I need." Jacob kept on urging him until he accepted.

12 Esau said, "Let's get ready and leave. I will go ahead of you."

13 Jacob answered, "You know that the children are weak, and I must think of the sheep and livestock with their young. If they are driven hard for even one day, the whole herd will die. 14 Please go on ahead of me, and I will follow slowly, going as fast as I can with the livestock and the children until I catch up with you in Edom."

15 Esau said, "Then let me leave some of my men with you."

But Jacob answered, "There is no need for that for I only want to gain your favor."*i* 16 So that day Esau started on his way back to Edom. 17 But Jacob went to Sukkoth, where he built a house for himself and shelters for his livestock. That is why the place was named Sukkoth.*j*

18 On his return from Mesopotamia Jacob arrived safely at the city of Shechem in the land of Canaan and set up his camp in a field near the city. 19 He bought that part of the field from the descendants of Hamor father of Shechem for a hundred pieces of silver. 20 He put up an altar there and named it for El, the God of Israel.

The Rape of Dinah

34 One day Dinah, the daughter of Jacob and Leah, went to visit some of the Canaanite women. 2 When Shechem son of Hamor the Hivite, who was chief of that region, saw her, he took her and raped her. 3 But he found the young woman so attractive that he fell in love with her and tried to win her affection.*k* 4 He told his father, "I want you to get Dinah for me as my wife."

5 Jacob learned that his daughter had been disgraced, but because his sons were out in the fields with his livestock, he did nothing until they came back. 6 Shechem's father Hamor went out to talk with Jacob, 7 just as Jacob's sons were coming in from the fields. When they heard about it, they were shocked and furious that Shechem had done such a thing and had insulted the people of Israel by raping Jacob's daughter. 8 Hamor said to him, "My son Shechem has fallen in love with your daughter; please let him marry her. 9 Let us make an agreement that there will be intermarriage between our people and yours. 10 Then you may stay here in our country with us; you may live anywhere you wish, trade freely, and own property."

11 Then Shechem said to Dinah's father and brothers, "Do me this favor, and I will give you whatever you want. 12 Tell me what presents you want, and set the payment for the bride as high as you wish; I will give you whatever you ask, if you will only let me marry her."

13 Because Shechem had disgraced their sister Dinah, Jacob's sons answered Shechem and his father Hamor in a deceitful way. 14 They said to him, "We cannot let our sister marry a man

---

i for I only want to gain your favor; *or* if it's all right with you.   *j* SUKKOTH: *This name in Hebrew means "shelters."*   *k* tried to win her affection; *or* comforted her.

who is not circumcised; that would be a disgrace for us. 15 We can agree only on the condition that you become like us by circumcising all your males. 16 Then we will agree to intermarriage. We will settle among you and become one people with you. 17 But if you will not accept our terms and be circumcised, we will take her and leave."

18 These terms seemed fair to Hamor and his son Shechem, 19 and the young man lost no time in doing what was suggested, because he was in love with Jacob's daughter. He was the most important member of his family.

20 Hamor and his son Shechem went to the meeting place at the city gate and spoke to the people of the town: 21 "These men are friendly; let them live in the land with us and travel freely. The land is large enough for them also. Let us marry their daughters and give them ours in marriage. 22 But these men will agree to live among us and be one people with us only on the condition that we circumcise all our males, as they are circumcised. 23 Won't all their livestock and everything else they own be ours? So let us agree that they can live among us." 24 All the citizens of the city agreed with what Hamor and Shechem proposed, and all the males were circumcised.

25 Three days later, when the men were still sore from their circumcision, two of Jacob's sons, Simeon and Levi, the brothers of Dinah, took their swords, went into the city without arousing suspicion, and killed all the men, 26 including Hamor and his son Shechem. Then they took Dinah from Shechem's house and left. 27 After the slaughter Jacob's other sons looted the town to take revenge for their sister's disgrace. 28 They took the flocks, the cattle, the donkeys, and everything else in the city and in the fields. 29 They took everything of value, captured all the women and children, and carried off everything in the houses.

30 Jacob said to Simeon and Levi, "You have gotten me into trouble; now the Canaanites, the Perizzites, and everybody else in the land will hate me. I do not have many men; if they all band together against me and attack me, our whole family will be destroyed."

31 But they answered, "We cannot let our sister be treated like a common whore."

God Blesses Jacob at Bethel

35 God said to Jacob, "Go to Bethel at once, and live there. Build an altar there to me, the God who appeared to you when you were running away from your brother Esau."

2 So Jacob said to his family and to all who were with him, "Get rid of the foreign gods that you have; purify yourselves and put on clean clothes. 3 We are going to leave here and go to Bethel, where I will build an altar to the God who helped me in the time of my trouble and who has been with me everywhere I have gone." 4 So they gave Jacob all the foreign gods that they had and also the earrings that they were wearing. He buried them beneath the oak tree near Shechem.

5 When Jacob and his sons started to leave, great fear fell on the people of the nearby towns, and they did not pursue them. 6 Jacob came with all his people to Luz, which is now known as Bethel, in the land of Canaan. 7 He built an altar there and named the place for the God of Bethel, because God had revealed himself to him there when he was running away from his brother. 8 Rebecca's nurse Deborah died and was buried beneath the oak south of Bethel. So it was named "Oak of Weeping."

9 When Jacob returned from Mesopotamia, God appeared to him again and blessed him. 10 God said to him, "Your name is Jacob, but from now on it will be Israel." So God named him Israel. 11 And God said to him, "I am Almighty God. Have many children. Nations will be descended from you, and you will be the ancestor of kings. 12 I will give you the land which I gave to Abraham and to Isaac, and I will also give it to your descendants after you." 13 Then God left him. 14 There, where God had spoken to him, Jacob set up a memorial stone and consecrated it by pouring wine and olive oil on it. 15 He named the place Bethel.

The Death of Rachel

16 Jacob and his family left Bethel, and when they were still some distance from Ephrath, the time came for Rachel to have her baby, and she was having difficult labor. 17 When her labor pains were at their worst, the midwife said to her, "Don't be afraid, Rachel; it's another

GENESIS

GENESIS

boy." 18 But she was dying, and as she breathed her last, she named her son Benoni,*l* but his father named him Benjamin.*m*

19 When Rachel died, she was buried beside the road to Ephrath, now known as Bethlehem. 20 Jacob set up a memorial stone there, and it still marks Rachel's grave to this day. 21 Jacob moved on and set up his camp on the other side of the tower of Eder.

The Sons of Jacob
(1 Chronicles 2.1, 2)

22 While Jacob was living in that land, Reuben had sexual intercourse with Bilhah, one of his father's concubines; Jacob heard about it and was furious.*n*

Jacob had twelve sons. 23 The sons of Leah were Reuben (Jacob's oldest son), Simeon, Levi, Judah, Issachar, and Zebulun. 24 The sons of Rachel were Joseph and Benjamin. 25 The sons of Rachel's slave Bilhah were Dan and Naphtali. 26 The sons of Leah's slave Zilpah were Gad and Asher. These sons were born in Mesopotamia.

The Death of Isaac

27 Jacob went to his father Isaac at Mamre, near Hebron, where Abraham and Isaac had lived. 28 Isaac lived to be a hundred and eighty years old 29 and died at a ripe old age; and his sons Esau and Jacob buried him.

The Descendants of Esau
(1 Chronicles 1.34-37)

36 These are the descendants of Esau, also called Edom. 2 Esau married Canaanite women: Adah, the daughter of Elon the Hittite; Oholibamah, the daughter of Anah son*o* of Zibeon the Hivite; 3 and Basemath, the daughter of Ishmael and sister of Nebaioth. 4 Adah bore Eliphaz; Basemath bore Reuel; 5 and Oholibamah bore Jeush, Jalam, and Korah. All these sons were born to Esau in the land of Canaan.

6 Then Esau took his wives, his sons, his daughters, and all the people of his house, along with all his livestock and all the possessions he had gotten in the land of Canaan, and went away from his brother Jacob to another land. 7 He left because the land where he and Jacob were living was not able to support them; they had too much livestock and could no longer stay together. 8 So Esau lived in the hill country of Edom.

9 These are the descendants of Esau, the ancestor of the Edomites. 10-13 Esau's wife Adah bore him one son, Eliphaz, and Eliphaz had five sons: Teman, Omar, Zepho, Gatam, and Kenaz. And by another wife, Timna, he had one more son, Amalek.

Esau's wife Basemath bore him one son, Reuel, and Reuel had four sons: Nahath, Zerah, Shammah, and Mizzah.

14 Esau's wife Oholibamah, the daughter of Anah son*o* of Zibeon, bore him three sons: Jeush, Jalam, and Korah.

15 These are the tribes descended from Esau. Esau's first son Eliphaz was the ancestor of the following tribes: Teman, Omar, Zepho, Kenaz, 16 Korah, Gatam, and Amalek. These were all descendants of Esau's wife Adah.

17 Esau's son Reuel was the ancestor of the following tribes: Nahath, Zerah, Shammah, and Mizzah. These were all descendants of Esau's wife Basemath.

18 The following tribes were descended from Esau by his wife Oholibamah, the daughter of Anah: Jeush, Jalam, and Korah. 19 All these tribes were descended from Esau.

The Descendants of Seir
(1 Chronicles 1.38-42)

20-21 The original inhabitants of the land of Edom were divided into tribes which traced their ancestry to the following descendants of Seir, a Horite: Lotan, Shobal, Zibeon, Anah, Dishon, Ezer, and Dishan.

22 Lotan was the ancestor of the clans of Hori and Heman. (Lotan had a sister named Timna.)

23 Shobal was the ancestor of the clans of Alvan, Manahath, Ebal, Shepho, and Onam.

24 Zibeon had two sons, Aiah and Anah. (This is the Anah who found the hot springs in the wilderness when he was taking care of his father's donkeys.) 25-26 Anah was the father of Dishon, who was the ancestor of the clans of Hemdan,

---

l BENONI: *This name in Hebrew means "son of my sorrow."*   *m* BENJAMIN: *This name in Hebrew means "son who will be fortunate."*   *n* *One ancient translation* and was furious; *Hebrew does not have these words.*   *o* *Some ancient translations* son; *Hebrew* daughter; *or* granddaughter.

Eshban, Ithran, and Cheran. Anah also had a daughter named Oholibamah.

27 Ezer was the ancestor of the clans of Bilhan, Zaavan, and Akan.

28 Dishan was the ancestor of the clans of Uz and Aran.

29-30 These are the Horite tribes in the land of Edom: Lotan, Shobal, Zibeon, Anah, Dishon, Ezer, and Dishan.

The Kings of Edom
(1 Chronicles 1.43-54)

31-39 Before there were any kings in Israel, the following kings ruled the land of Edom in succession:

Bela son of Beor from Dinhabah
Jobab son of Zerah from Bozrah
Husham from the region of Teman
Hadad son of Bedad from Avith
   (he defeated the Midianites in
   a battle in the country of
   Moab)
Samlah from Masrekah
Shaul from Rehoboth-on-the-River
Baal Hanan son of Achbor
Hadad from Pau (his wife was
   Mehetabel, the daughter of
   Matred and granddaughter of
   Mezahab)

40-43 Esau was the ancestor of the following Edomite tribes: Timna, Alvah, Jetheth, Oholibamah, Elah, Pinon, Kenaz, Teman, Mibzar, Magdiel, and Iram. The area where each of these tribes lived was known by the name of the tribe.

Joseph and His Brothers

37 Jacob continued to live in the land of Canaan, where his father had lived, 2 and this is the story of Jacob's family.

Joseph, a young man of seventeen, took care of the sheep and goats with his brothers, the sons of Bilhah and Zilpah, his father's concubines. He brought bad reports to his father about what his brothers were doing.

3 Jacob loved Joseph more than all his other sons, because he had been born to him when he was old. He made a long robe with full sleeves*p* for him. 4 When his brothers saw that their father loved Joseph more than he loved them, they hated their brother so much that they would not speak to him in a friendly manner.

5 One time Joseph had a dream, and when he told his brothers about it, they hated him even more. 6 He said, "Listen to the dream I had. 7 We were all in the field tying up sheaves of wheat, when my sheaf got up and stood up straight. Yours formed a circle around mine and bowed down to it."

8 "Do you think you are going to be a king and rule over us?" his brothers asked. So they hated him even more because of his dreams and because of what he said about them.

9 Then Joseph had another dream and told his brothers, "I had another dream, in which I saw the sun, the moon, and eleven stars bowing down to me."

10 He also told the dream to his father, and his father scolded him: "What kind of a dream is that? Do you think that your mother, your brothers, and I are going to come and bow down to you?" 11 Joseph's brothers were jealous of him, but his father kept thinking about the whole matter.

Joseph Is Sold and Taken to Egypt

12 One day when Joseph's brothers had gone to Shechem to take care of their father's flock, 13 Jacob said to Joseph, "I want you to go to Shechem, where your brothers are taking care of the flock."

Joseph answered, "I am ready."

14 His father told him, "Go and see if your brothers are safe and if the flock is all right; then come back and tell me." So his father sent him on his way from Hebron Valley.

Joseph arrived at Shechem 15 and was wandering around in the country when a man saw him and asked him, "What are you looking for?"

16 "I am looking for my brothers, who are taking care of their flock," he answered. "Can you tell me where they are?"

17 The man said, "They have already left. I heard them say that they were going to Dothan." So Joseph went after his brothers and found them at Dothan.

18 They saw him in the distance, and before he reached them, they plotted against him and decided to kill him. 19 They said to one another, "Here comes

---

p robe with full sleeves; *or* decorated robe.

GENESIS

that dreamer. 20Come on now, let's kill him and throw his body into one of the dry wells. We can say that a wild animal killed him. Then we will see what becomes of his dreams."

21Reuben heard them and tried to save Joseph. "Let's not kill him," he said. 22"Just throw him into this well in the wilderness, but don't hurt him." He said this, planning to save him from them and send him back to his father. 23When Joseph came up to his brothers, they ripped off his long robe with full sleeves.p 24Then they took him and threw him into the well, which was dry.

25While they were eating, they suddenly saw a group of Ishmaelites traveling from Gilead to Egypt. Their camels were loaded with spices and resins. 26Judah said to his brothers, "What will we gain by killing our brother and covering up the murder? 27Let's sell him to these Ishmaelites. Then we won't have to hurt him; after all, he is our brother, our own flesh and blood." His brothers agreed, 28and when some Midianite traders came by, the brothersq pulled Joseph out of the well and sold him for twenty pieces of silver to the Ishmaelites, who took him to Egypt.

29When Reuben came back to the well and found that Joseph was not there, he tore his clothes in sorrow. 30He returned to his brothers and said, "The boy is not there! What am I going to do?"

31Then they killed a goat and dipped Joseph's robe in its blood. 32They took the robe to their father and said, "We found this. Does it belong to your son?"

33He recognized it and said, "Yes, it is his! Some wild animal has killed him. My son Joseph has been torn to pieces!" 34Jacob tore his clothes in sorrow and put on sackcloth. He mourned for his son a long time. 35All his sons and daughters came to comfort him, but he refused to be comforted and said, "I will go down to the world of the dead still mourning for my son." So he continued to mourn for his son Joseph.

36Meanwhile, in Egypt the Midianites had sold Joseph to Potiphar, one of the king's officers, who was the captain of the palace guard.

Judah and Tamar

38 About that time Judah left his brothers and went to stay with a man named Hirah, who was from the town of Adullam. 2There Judah met a young Canaanite woman whose father was named Shua. He married her, 3and she bore him a son, whom he named Er. 4She became pregnant again and bore another son and named him Onan. 5Again she had a son and named him Shelah. Judah was at Achzib when the boy was born.

6For his first son Er, Judah got a wife whose name was Tamar. 7Er's conduct was evil, and it displeased the LORD, so the LORD killed him. 8Then Judah said to Er's brother Onan, "Go and sleep with your brother's widow. Fulfill your obligation to her as her husband's brother, so that your brother may have descendants." 9But Onan knew that the children would not belong to him, so when he had intercourse with his brother's widow, he let the semen spill on the ground, so that there would be no children for his brother. 10What he did displeased the LORD, and the LORD killed him also. 11Then Judah said to his daughter-in-law Tamar, "Return to your father's house and remain a widow until my son Shelah grows up." He said this because he was afraid that Shelah would be killed, as his brothers had been. So Tamar went back home.

12After some time Judah's wife died. When he had finished the time of mourning, he and his friend Hirah of Adullam went to Timnah, where his sheep were being sheared. 13Someone told Tamar that her father-in-law was going to Timnah to shear his sheep. 14So she changed from the widow's clothes she had been wearing, covered her face with a veil, and sat down at the entrance to Enaim, a town on the road to Timnah. As she well knew, Judah's youngest son Shelah was now grown up, and yet she had not been given to him in marriage.

15When Judah saw her, he thought that she was a prostitute, because she had her face covered. 16He went over to her at the side of the road and said, "All right, how much do you charge?" (He did not know that she was his daughter-in-law.)

p robe with full sleeves; or decorated robe.   q the brothers; Hebrew they.

She said, "What will you give me?"

17 He answered, "I will send you a young goat from my flock."

She said, "All right, if you will give me something to keep as a pledge until you send the goat."

18 "What shall I give you as a pledge?" he asked.

She answered, "Your seal with its cord and the walking stick you are carrying." He gave them to her. Then they had intercourse, and she became pregnant. 19 Tamar went home, took off her veil, and put her widow's clothes back on.

20 Judah sent his friend Hirah to take the goat and get back from the woman the articles he had pledged, but Hirah could not find her. 21 He asked some men at Enaim, "Where is the prostitute who was here by the road?"

"There has never been a prostitute here," they answered.

22 He returned to Judah and said, "I couldn't find her. The men of the place said that there had never been a prostitute there."

23 Judah said, "Let her keep the things. We don't want people to laugh at us. I did try to pay her, but you couldn't find her."

24 About three months later someone told Judah, "Your daughter-in-law Tamar has been acting like a whore, and now she is pregnant."

Judah ordered, "Take her out and burn her to death."

25 As she was being taken out, she sent word to her father-in-law: "I am pregnant by the man who owns these things. Look at them and see whose they are—this seal with its cord and this walking stick."

26 Judah recognized them and said, "She is in the right. I have failed in my obligation to her—I should have given her to my son Shelah in marriage." And Judah never had intercourse with her again.

27 When the time came for her to give birth, it was discovered that she was going to have twins. 28 While she was in labor, one of them put out an arm; the midwife caught it, tied a red thread around it, and said, "This one was born first." 29 But he pulled his arm back, and his brother was born first. Then the midwife said, "So this is how you break your way out!" So he was named Perez.r 30 Then his brother was born with the red thread on his arm, and he was named Zerah.s

Joseph and Potiphar's Wife

39 Now the Ishmaelites had taken Joseph to Egypt and sold him to Potiphar, one of the king's officers, who was the captain of the palace guard. 2 The LORD was with Joseph and made him successful. He lived in the house of his Egyptian master, 3 who saw that the LORD was with Joseph and had made him successful in everything he did. 4 Potiphar was pleased with him and made him his personal servant; so he put him in charge of his house and everything he owned. 5 From then on, because of Joseph the LORD blessed the household of the Egyptian and everything that he had in his house and in his fields. 6 Potiphar turned over everything he had to the care of Joseph and did not concern himself with anything except the food he ate.

Joseph was well-built and good-looking, 7 and after a while his master's wife began to desire Joseph and asked him to go to bed with her. 8 He refused and said to her, "Look, my master does not have to concern himself with anything in the house, because I am here. He has put me in charge of everything he has. 9 I have as much authority in this house as he has, and he has not kept back anything from me except you. How then could I do such an immoral thing and sin against God?" 10 Although she asked Joseph day after day, he would not go to bed with her.

11 But one day when Joseph went into the house to do his work, none of the house servants was there. 12 She caught him by his robe and said, "Come to bed with me." But he escaped and ran outside, leaving his robe in her hand. 13 When she saw that he had left his robe and had run out of the house, 14 she called to her house servants and said, "Look at this! This Hebrew that my husband brought to the house is insulting us. He came into my room and tried to rape me, but I screamed as loud as I could. 15 When

---

r PEREZ: This name in Hebrew means "breaking out." s ZERAH: This name sounds like a Hebrew word for the red brightness of dawn.

he heard me scream, he ran outside, leaving his robe beside me."

16 She kept his robe with her until Joseph's master came home. 17 Then she told him the same story: "That Hebrew slave that you brought here came into my room and insulted me. 18 But when I screamed, he ran outside, leaving his robe beside me."

19 Joseph's master was furious 20 and had Joseph arrested and put in the prison where the king's prisoners were kept, and there he stayed. 21 But the LORD was with Joseph and blessed him, so that the jailer was pleased with him. 22 He put Joseph in charge of all the other prisoners and made him responsible for everything that was done in the prison. 23 The jailer did not have to look after anything for which Joseph was responsible, because the LORD was with Joseph and made him succeed in everything he did.

Joseph Interprets the Prisoners' Dreams

40 Some time later the king of Egypt's wine steward and his chief baker offended the king. 2 He was angry with these two officials 3 and put them in prison in the house of the captain of the guard, in the same place where Joseph was being kept. 4 They spent a long time in prison, and the captain assigned Joseph as their servant.

5 One night there in prison the wine steward and the chief baker each had a dream, and the dreams had different meanings. 6 When Joseph came to them in the morning, he saw that they were upset. 7 He asked them, "Why do you look so worried today?"

8 They answered, "Each of us had a dream, and there is no one here to explain what the dreams mean."

"It is God who gives the ability to interpret dreams," Joseph said. "Tell me your dreams."

9 So the wine steward said, "In my dream there was a grapevine in front of me 10 with three branches on it. As soon as the leaves came out, the blossoms appeared, and the grapes ripened. 11 I was holding the king's cup; so I took the grapes and squeezed them into the cup and gave it to him."

12 Joseph said, "This is what it means: the three branches are three days. 13 In three days the king will release you, pardon you, and restore you to your position. You will give him his cup as you did before when you were his wine steward. 14 But please remember me when everything is going well for you, and please be kind enough to mention me to the king and help me get out of this prison. 15 After all, I was kidnapped from the land of the Hebrews, and even here in Egypt I didn't do anything to deserve being put in prison."

16 When the chief baker saw that the interpretation of the wine steward's dream was favorable, he said to Joseph, "I had a dream too; I was carrying three breadbaskets on my head. 17 In the top basket there were all kinds of baked goods for the king, and the birds were eating them."

18 Joseph answered, "This is what it means: the three baskets are three days. 19 In three days the king will release you—and have your head cut off! Then he will hang your body on a pole, and the birds will eat your flesh."

20 On his birthday three days later the king gave a banquet for all his officials; he released his wine steward and his chief baker and brought them before his officials. 21 He restored the wine steward to his former position, 22 but he executed the chief baker. It all happened just as Joseph had said. 23 But the wine steward never gave Joseph another thought—he forgot all about him.

Joseph Interprets the King's Dreams

41 After two years had passed, the king of Egypt dreamed that he was standing by the Nile River, 2 when seven cows, fat and sleek, came up out of the river and began to feed on the grass. 3 Then seven other cows came up; they were thin and bony. They came and stood by the other cows on the riverbank, 4 and the thin cows ate up the fat cows. Then the king woke up. 5 He fell asleep again and had another dream. Seven heads of grain, full and ripe, were growing on one stalk. 6 Then seven other heads of grain sprouted, thin and scorched by the desert wind, 7 and the thin heads of grain swallowed the full ones. The king woke up and realized that he had been dreaming. 8 In the morning he was worried, so he sent for all the magicians and wise men of Egypt. He told them his dreams, but no one could explain them to him.

9 Then the wine steward said to the king, "I must confess today that I have done wrong. 10 You were angry with the chief baker and me, and you put us in prison in the house of the captain of the guard. 11 One night each of us had a dream, and the dreams had different meanings. 12 A young Hebrew was there with us, a slave of the captain of the guard. We told him our dreams, and he interpreted them for us. 13 Things turned out just as he said: you restored me to my position, but you executed the baker."

14 The king sent for Joseph, and he was immediately brought from the prison. After he had shaved and changed his clothes, he came into the king's presence. 15 The king said to him, "I have had a dream, and no one can explain it. I have been told that you can interpret dreams."

16 Joseph answered, "I cannot, Your Majesty, but God will give a favorable interpretation."

17 The king said, "I dreamed that I was standing on the bank of the Nile, 18 when seven cows, fat and sleek, came up out of the river and began feeding on the grass. 19 Then seven other cows came up which were thin and bony. They were the poorest cows I have ever seen anywhere in Egypt. 20 The thin cows ate up the fat ones, 21 but no one would have known it, because they looked just as bad as before. Then I woke up. 22 I also dreamed that I saw seven heads of grain which were full and ripe, growing on one stalk. 23 Then seven heads of grain sprouted, thin and scorched by the desert wind, 24 and the thin heads of grain swallowed the full ones. I told the dreams to the magicians, but none of them could explain them to me."

25 Joseph said to the king, "The two dreams mean the same thing; God has told you what he is going to do. 26 The seven fat cows are seven years, and the seven full heads of grain are also seven years; they have the same meaning. 27 The seven thin cows which came up later and the seven thin heads of grain scorched by the desert wind are seven years of famine. 28 It is just as I told you—God has shown you what he is going to do. 29 There will be seven years of great plenty in all the land of Egypt. 30 After that, there will be seven years of famine, and all the good years will be forgotten, because the famine will ruin the country. 31 The time of plenty will be entirely forgotten, because the famine which follows will be so terrible. 32 The repetition of your dream means that the matter is fixed by God and that he will make it happen in the near future.

33 "Now you should choose some man with wisdom and insight and put him in charge of the country. 34 You must also appoint other officials and take a fifth of the crops during the seven years of plenty. 35 Order them to collect all the food during the good years that are coming, and give them authority to store up grain in the cities and guard it. 36 The food will be a reserve supply for the country during the seven years of famine which are going to come on Egypt. In this way the people will not starve."

Joseph Is Made Governor over Egypt

37 The king and his officials approved this plan, 38 and he said to them, "We will never find a better man than Joseph, a man who has God's spirit in him." 39 The king said to Joseph, "God has shown you all this, so it is obvious that you have greater wisdom and insight than anyone else. 40 I will put you in charge of my country, and all my people will obey your orders. Your authority will be second only to mine. 41 I now appoint you governor over all Egypt." 42 The king removed from his finger the ring engraved with the royal seal and put it on Joseph's finger. He put a fine linen robe on him, and placed a gold chain around his neck. 43 He gave him the second royal chariot to ride in, and his guard of honor went ahead of him and cried out, "Make way! Make way!" And so Joseph was appointed governor over all Egypt. 44 The king said to him, "I am the king—and no one in all Egypt shall so much as lift a hand or a foot without your permission." 45-46 He gave Joseph the Egyptian name Zaphenath Paneah, and he gave him a wife, Asenath, the daughter of Potiphera, a priest in the city of Heliopolis.

Joseph was thirty years old when he began to serve the king of Egypt. He left the king's court and traveled all over the land. 47 During the seven years of plenty the land produced abundant crops, 48 all

GENESIS

of which Joseph collected and stored in the cities. In each city he stored the food from the fields around it. [49] There was so much grain that Joseph stopped measuring it—it was like the sand of the sea.

[50] Before the years of famine came, Joseph had two sons by Asenath. [51] He said, "God has made me forget all my sufferings and all my father's family"; so he named his first son Manasseh.[t] [52] He also said, "God has given me children in the land of my trouble"; so he named his second son Ephraim.[u]

[53] The seven years of plenty that the land of Egypt had enjoyed came to an end, [54] and the seven years of famine began, just as Joseph had said. There was famine in every other country, but there was food throughout Egypt. [55] When the Egyptians began to be hungry, they cried out to the king for food. So he ordered them to go to Joseph and do what he told them. [56] The famine grew worse and spread over the whole country, so Joseph opened all the storehouses and sold grain to the Egyptians. [57] People came to Egypt from all over the world to buy grain from Joseph, because the famine was severe everywhere.

Joseph's Brothers Go to Egypt to Buy Grain

42 When Jacob learned that there was grain in Egypt, he said to his sons, "Why don't you do something? [2] I hear that there is grain in Egypt; go there and buy some to keep us from starving to death." [3] So Joseph's ten half brothers went to buy grain in Egypt, [4] but Jacob did not send Joseph's full brother Benjamin with them, because he was afraid that something might happen to him.

[5] The sons of Jacob came with others to buy grain, because there was famine in the land of Canaan. [6] Joseph, as governor of the land of Egypt, was selling grain to people from all over the world. So Joseph's brothers came and bowed down before him with their faces to the ground. [7] When Joseph saw his brothers, he recognized them, but he acted as if he did not know them. He asked them harshly, "Where do you come from?"

"We have come from Canaan to buy food," they answered.

[8] Although Joseph recognized his brothers, they did not recognize him. [9] He remembered the dreams he had dreamed about them and said, "You are spies; you have come to find out where our country is weak."

[10] "No, sir," they answered. "We have come as your slaves, to buy food. [11] We are all brothers. We are not spies, sir, we are honest men."

[12] Joseph said to them, "No! You have come to find out where our country is weak."

[13] They said, "We were twelve brothers in all, sir, sons of the same man in the land of Canaan. One brother is dead, and the youngest is now with our father."

[14] "It is just as I said," Joseph answered. "You are spies. [15] This is how you will be tested: I swear by the name of the king that you will never leave unless your youngest brother comes here. [16] One of you must go and get him. The rest of you will be kept under guard until the truth of what you say can be tested. Otherwise, as sure as the king lives, you are spies." [17] With that, he put them in prison for three days.

[18] On the third day Joseph said to them, "I am a God-fearing man, and I will spare your lives on one condition. [19] To prove that you are honest, one of you will stay in the prison where you have been kept; the rest of you may go and take back to your starving families the grain that you have bought. [20] Then you must bring your youngest brother to me. This will prove that you have been telling the truth, and I will not put you to death."

They agreed to this [21] and said to one another, "Yes, now we are suffering the consequences of what we did to our brother; we saw the great trouble he was in when he begged for help, but we would not listen. That is why we are in this trouble now."

[22] Reuben said, "I told you not to harm the boy, but you wouldn't listen. And now we are being paid back for his death." [23] Joseph understood what they said, but they did not know it, because they had been speaking to him through an interpreter. [24] Joseph left them and began to cry. When he was able to speak

[t] MANASSEH: This name sounds like the Hebrew for "cause to forget."   [u] EPHRAIM: This name sounds like the Hebrew for "give children."

again, he came back, picked out Simeon, and had him tied up in front of them.

Joseph's Brothers Return to Canaan

25 Joseph gave orders to fill his brothers' packs with grain, to put each man's money back in his sack, and to give them food for the trip. This was done. 26 The brothers loaded their donkeys with the grain they had bought, and then they left. 27 At the place where they spent the night, one of them opened his sack to feed his donkey and found his money at the top of the sack. 28 "My money has been returned to me," he called to his brothers. "Here it is in my sack!" Their hearts sank, and in fear they asked one another, "What has God done to us?"

29 When they came to their father Jacob in Canaan, they told him all that had happened to them: 30 "The governor of Egypt spoke harshly to us and accused us of spying against his country. 31 'We are not spies,' we answered, 'we are honest men. 32 We were twelve brothers in all, sons of the same father. One brother is dead, and the youngest is still in Canaan with our father.' 33 The man answered, 'This is how I will find out if you are honest men: One of you will stay with me; the rest will take grain for your starving families and leave. 34 Bring your youngest brother to me. Then I will know that you are not spies, but honest men; I will give your brother back to you, and you can stay here and trade.' "

35 Then when they emptied out their sacks, every one of them found his bag of money; and when they saw the money, they and their father Jacob were afraid. 36 Their father said to them, "Do you want to make me lose all my children? Joseph is gone; Simeon is gone; and now you want to take away Benjamin. I am the one who suffers!"

37 Reuben said to his father, "If I do not bring Benjamin back to you, you can kill my two sons. Put him in my care, and I will bring him back."

38 But Jacob said, "My son cannot go with you; his brother is dead, and he is the only one left. Something might happen to him on the way. I am an old man, and the sorrow you would cause me would kill me."

Joseph's Brothers Return to Egypt with Benjamin

43 The famine in Canaan got worse, 2 and when the family of Jacob had eaten all the grain which had been brought from Egypt, Jacob said to his sons, "Go back and buy a little food for us."

3 Judah said to him, "The man sternly warned us that we would not be admitted to his presence unless we had our brother with us. 4 If you are willing to send our brother with us, we will go and buy food for you. 5 If you are not willing, we will not go, because the man told us we would not be admitted to his presence unless our brother was with us."

6 Jacob said, "Why did you cause me so much trouble by telling the man that you had another brother?"

7 They answered, "The man kept asking about us and our family, 'Is your father still living? Do you have another brother?' We had to answer his questions. How could we know that he would tell us to bring our brother with us?"

8 Judah said to his father, "Send the boy with me, and we will leave at once. Then none of us will starve to death. 9 I will pledge my own life, and you can hold me responsible for him. If I do not bring him back to you safe and sound, I will always bear the blame. 10 If we had not waited so long, we could have been there and back twice by now."

11 Their father said to them, "If that is how it has to be, then take the best products of the land in your packs as a present for the governor: a little resin, a little honey, spices, pistachio nuts, and almonds. 12 Take with you also twice as much money, because you must take back the money that was returned in the top of your sacks. Maybe it was a mistake. 13 Take your brother and return at once. 14 May Almighty God cause the man to have pity on you, so that he will give Benjamin and your other brother back to you. As for me, if I must lose my children, I must lose them."

15 So the brothers took the gifts and twice as much money, and set out for Egypt with Benjamin. There they presented themselves to Joseph. 16 When Joseph saw Benjamin with them, he said to the servant in charge of his house, "Take these men to my house. They are going to

GENESIS

eat with me at noon, so kill an animal and prepare it." 17 The servant did as he was commanded and took the brothers to Joseph's house.

18 As they were being brought to the house, they were afraid and thought, "We are being brought here because of the money that was returned in our sacks the first time. They will suddenly attack us, take our donkeys, and make us his slaves." 19 So at the door of the house, they said to the servant in charge, 20 "If you please, sir, we came here once before to buy food. 21 When we set up camp on the way home, we opened our sacks, and each man found his money in the top of his sack — every bit of it. We have brought it back to you. 22 We have also brought some more money with us to buy more food. We do not know who put our money back in our sacks."

23 The servant said, "Don't worry. Don't be afraid. Your God, the God of your father, must have put the money in your sacks for you. I received your payment." Then he brought Simeon to them.

24 The servant took the brothers into the house. He gave them water so that they could wash their feet, and he fed their donkeys. 25 They got their gifts ready to present to Joseph when he arrived at noon, because they had been told that they were to eat with him. 26 When Joseph got home, they took the gifts into the house to him and bowed down to the ground before him. 27 He asked about their health and then said, "You told me about your old father — how is he? Is he still alive and well?"

28 They answered, "Your humble servant, our father, is still alive and well." And they knelt and bowed down before him.

29 When Joseph saw his brother Benjamin, he said, "So this is your youngest brother, the one you told me about. God bless you, my son." 30 Then Joseph left suddenly, because his heart was full of tender feelings for his brother. He was about to break down, so he went to his room and cried. 31 After he had washed his face, he came out, and controlling himself, he ordered the meal to be served. 32 Joseph was served at one table and his brothers at another. The Egyp-

tians who were eating there were served separately, because they considered it beneath their dignity to eat with Hebrews. 33 The brothers had been seated at the table, facing Joseph, in the order of their age from the oldest to the youngest. When they saw how they had been seated, they looked at one another in amazement. 34 Food was served to them from Joseph's table, and Benjamin was served five times as much as the rest of them. So they ate and drank with Joseph until they were drunk.

The Missing Cup

44 Joseph commanded the servant in charge of his house, "Fill the men's sacks with as much food as they can carry, and put each man's money in the top of his sack. 2 Put my silver cup in the top of the youngest brother's sack, together with the money for his grain." He did as he was told. 3 Early in the morning the brothers were sent on their way with their donkeys. 4 When they had gone only a short distance from the city, Joseph said to the servant in charge of his house, "Hurry after those men. When you catch up with them, ask them, 'Why have you paid back evil for good? 5 Why did you steal my master's silver cup?*v It is the one he drinks from, the one he uses for divination. You have committed a serious crime!' "

6 When the servant caught up with them, he repeated these words. 7 They answered him, "What do you mean, sir, by talking like this? We swear that we have done no such thing. 8 You know that we brought back to you from the land of Canaan the money we found in the top of our sacks. Why then should we steal silver or gold from your master's house? 9 Sir, if any one of us is found to have it, he will be put to death, and the rest of us will become your slaves."

10 He said, "I agree; but only the one who has taken the cup will become my slave, and the rest of you can go free." 11 So they quickly lowered their sacks to the ground, and each man opened his sack. 12 Joseph's servant searched carefully, beginning with the oldest and ending with the youngest, and the cup was found in Benjamin's sack. 13 The broth-

v *One ancient translation* Why did you steal my master's silver cup?; *Hebrew does not have these words.*

ers tore their clothes in sorrow, loaded their donkeys, and returned to the city.

14 When Judah and his brothers came to Joseph's house, he was still there. They bowed down before him, 15 and Joseph said, "What have you done? Didn't you know that a man in my position could find you out by practicing divination?"

16 "What can we say to you, sir?" Judah answered. "How can we argue? How can we clear ourselves? God has uncovered our guilt. All of us are now your slaves and not just the one with whom the cup was found."

17 Joseph said, "Oh, no! I would never do that! Only the one who had the cup will be my slave. The rest of you may go back safe and sound to your father."

Judah Pleads for Benjamin

18 Judah went up to Joseph and said, "Please, sir, allow me to speak with you freely. Don't be angry with me; you are like the king himself. 19 Sir, you asked us, 'Do you have a father or another brother?' 20 We answered, 'We have a father who is old and a younger brother, born to him in his old age. The boy's brother is dead, and he is the only one of his mother's children still alive; his father loves him very much.' 21 Sir, you told us to bring him here, so that you could see him, 22 and we answered that the boy could not leave his father; if he did, his father would die. 23 Then you said, 'You will not be admitted to my presence again unless your youngest brother comes with you.'

24 "When we went back to our father, we told him what you had said. 25 Then he told us to return and buy a little food. 26 We answered, 'We cannot go; we will not be admitted to the man's presence unless our youngest brother is with us. We can go only if our youngest brother goes also.' 27 Our father said to us, 'You know that my wife Rachel bore me only two sons. 28 One of them has already left me. He must have been torn to pieces by wild animals, because I have not seen him since he left. 29 If you take this one from me now and something happens to him, the sorrow you would cause me would kill me, as old as I am.'

30-31 "And now, sir," Judah continued, "if I go back to my father without the boy, as soon as he sees that the boy is not with me, he will die. His life is wrapped up with the life of the boy, and he is so old that the sorrow we would cause him would kill him. 32 What is more, I pledged my life to my father for the boy. I told him that if I did not bring the boy back to him, I would bear the blame all my life. 33 And now, sir, I will stay here as your slave in place of the boy; let him go back with his brothers. 34 How can I go back to my father if the boy is not with me? I cannot bear to see this disaster come upon my father."

Joseph Tells His Brothers Who He Is

45 Joseph was no longer able to control his feelings in front of his servants, so he ordered them all to leave the room. No one else was with him when Joseph told his brothers who he was. 2 He cried with such loud sobs that the Egyptians heard it, and the news was taken to the king's palace. 3 Joseph said to his brothers, "I am Joseph. Is my father still alive?" But when his brothers heard this, they were so terrified that they could not answer. 4 Then Joseph said to them, "Please come closer." They did, and he said, "I am your brother Joseph, whom you sold into Egypt. 5 Now do not be upset or blame yourselves because you sold me here. It was really God who sent me ahead of you to save people's lives. 6 This is only the second year of famine in the land; there will be five more years in which there will be neither plowing nor reaping. 7 God sent me ahead of you to rescue you in this amazing way and to make sure that you and your descendants survive. 8 So it was not really you who sent me here, but God. He has made me the king's highest official. I am in charge of his whole country; I am the ruler of all Egypt.

9 "Now hurry back to my father and tell him that this is what his son Joseph says: 'God has made me ruler of all Egypt; come to me without delay. 10 You can live in the region of Goshen, where you can be near me — you, your children, your grandchildren, your sheep, your goats, your cattle, and everything else that you have. 11 If you are in Goshen, I can take care of you. There will still be five years of famine; and I do not want you, your family, and your livestock to starve.' "

12 Joseph continued, "Now all of you, and you too, Benjamin, can see that I am

really Joseph. 13 Tell my father how powerful I am here in Egypt and tell him about everything that you have seen. Then hurry and bring him here."

14 He threw his arms around his brother Benjamin and began to cry; Benjamin also cried as he hugged him. 15 Then, still weeping, he embraced each of his brothers and kissed them. After that, his brothers began to talk with him.

16 When the news reached the palace that Joseph's brothers had come, the king and his officials were pleased. 17 He said to Joseph, "Tell your brothers to load their animals and to return to the land of Canaan. 18 Let them get their father and their families and come back here. I will give them the best land in Egypt, and they will have more than enough to live on. 19 Tell them also to take wagons with them from Egypt for their wives and small children and to bring their father with them. 20 They are not to worry about leaving their possessions behind; the best in the whole land of Egypt will be theirs."

21 Jacob's sons did as they were told. Joseph gave them wagons, as the king had ordered, and food for the trip. 22 He also gave each of them a change of clothes, but he gave Benjamin three hundred pieces of silver and five changes of clothes. 23 He sent his father ten donkeys loaded with the best Egyptian goods and ten donkeys loaded with grain, bread, and other food for the trip. 24 He sent his brothers off and as they left, he said to them, "Don't quarrel on the way."

25 They left Egypt and went back home to their father Jacob in Canaan. 26 "Joseph is still alive!" they told him. "He is the ruler of all Egypt!" Jacob was stunned and could not believe them.

27 But when they told him all that Joseph had said to them, and when he saw the wagons which Joseph had sent to take him to Egypt, he recovered from the shock. 28 "My son Joseph is still alive!" he said. "This is all I could ask for! I must go and see him before I die."

Jacob and His Family Go to Egypt

46 Jacob packed up all he had and went to Beersheba, where he offered sacrifices to the God of his father Isaac. 2 God spoke to him in a vision at night and called, "Jacob, Jacob!"

"Yes, here I am," he answered.

3 "I am God, the God of your father," he said. "Do not be afraid to go to Egypt; I will make your descendants a great nation there. 4 I will go with you to Egypt, and I will bring your descendants back to this land. Joseph will be with you when you die."

5 Jacob set out from Beersheba. His sons put him, their small children, and their wives in the wagons which the king of Egypt had sent. 6 They took their livestock and the possessions they had acquired in Canaan and went to Egypt. Jacob took all his descendants with him: 7 his sons, his grandsons, his daughters, and his granddaughters.

8 The members of Jacob's family who went to Egypt with him were his oldest son Reuben 9 and Reuben's sons: Hanoch, Pallu, Hezron, and Carmi. 10 Simeon and his sons: Jemuel, Jamin, Ohad, Jachin, Zohar, and Shaul, the son of a Canaanite woman. 11 Levi and his sons: Gershon, Kohath, and Merari. 12 Judah and his sons: Shelah, Perez, and Zerah. (Judah's other sons, Er and Onan, had died in Canaan.) Perez' sons were Hezron and Hamul. 13 Issachar and his sons: Tola, Puah, Jashub, and Shimron. 14 Zebulun and his sons: Sered, Elon, and Jahleel. 15 These are the sons that Leah had borne to Jacob in Mesopotamia, besides his daughter Dinah. In all, his descendants by Leah numbered thirty-three.

16 Gad and his sons: Zephon, Haggi, Shuni, Ezbon, Eri, Arod, and Areli. 17 Asher and his sons: Imnah, Ishvah, Ishvi, Beriah, and their sister Serah. Beriah's sons were Heber and Malchiel. 18 These sixteen are the descendants of Jacob by Zilpah, the slave woman whom Laban gave to his daughter Leah.

19 Jacob's wife Rachel bore him two sons: Joseph and Benjamin. 20 In Egypt Joseph had two sons, Manasseh and Ephraim, by Asenath, the daughter of Potiphera, a priest in Heliopolis. 21 Benjamin's sons were Bela, Becher, Ashbel, Gera, Naaman, Ehi, Rosh, Muppim, Huppim, and Ard. 22 These fourteen are the descendants of Jacob by Rachel.

23 Dan and his son Hushim. 24 Naphtali and his sons: Jahzeel, Guni, Jezer, and Shillem. 25 These seven are the descendants of Jacob by Bilhah, the slave woman whom Laban gave to his daughter Rachel.

26 The total number of the direct

descendants of Jacob who went to Egypt was sixty-six, not including his sons' wives. 27 Two sons were born to Joseph in Egypt, bringing to seventy the total number of Jacob's family who went there.

Jacob and His Family in Egypt

28 Jacob sent Judah ahead to ask Joseph to meet them in Goshen. When they arrived, 29 Joseph got in his chariot and went to Goshen to meet his father. When they met, Joseph threw his arms around his father's neck and cried for a long time. 30 Jacob said to Joseph, "I am ready to die, now that I have seen you and know that you are still alive."

31 Then Joseph said to his brothers and the rest of his father's family, "I must go and tell the king that my brothers and all my father's family, who were living in Canaan, have come to me. 32 I will tell him that you are shepherds and take care of livestock and that you have brought your flocks and herds and everything else that belongs to you. 33 When the king calls for you and asks what your occupation is, 34 be sure to tell him that you have taken care of livestock all your lives, just as your ancestors did. In this way he will let you live in the region of Goshen." Joseph said this because Egyptians will have nothing to do with shepherds.

47 So Joseph took five of his brothers and went to the king. He told him, "My father and my brothers have come from Canaan with their flocks, their herds, and all that they own. They are now in the region of Goshen." 2 He then presented his brothers to the king. 3 The king asked them, "What is your occupation?"

"We are shepherds, sir, just as our ancestors were," they answered. 4 "We have come to live in this country, because in the land of Canaan the famine is so severe that there is no pasture for our flocks. Please give us permission to live in the region of Goshen." 5 The king said to Joseph, "Now that your father and your brothers have arrived, 6 the land of Egypt is theirs. Let them settle in the region of Goshen, the best part of the land. And if there are any capable men among them, put them in charge of my own livestock."

7 Then Joseph brought his father Jacob and presented him to the king. Jacob gave the king his blessing, 8 and the king asked him, "How old are you?"

9 Jacob answered, "My life of wandering has lasted a hundred and thirty years. Those years have been few and difficult, unlike the long years of my ancestors in their wanderings." 10 Jacob gave the king a farewell blessing and left. 11 Then Joseph settled his father and his brothers in Egypt, giving them property in the best of the land near the city of Rameses, as the king had commanded. 12 Joseph provided food for his father, his brothers, and all the rest of his father's family, including the very youngest.

The Famine

13 The famine was so severe that there was no food anywhere, and the people of Egypt and Canaan became weak with hunger. 14 As they bought grain, Joseph collected all the money and took it to the palace. 15 When all the money in Egypt and Canaan was spent, the Egyptians came to Joseph and said, "Give us food! Don't let us die. Do something! Our money is all gone."

16 Joseph answered, "Bring your livestock; I will give you food in exchange for it if your money is all gone." 17 So they brought their livestock to Joseph, and he gave them food in exchange for their horses, sheep, goats, cattle, and donkeys. That year he supplied them with food in exchange for all their livestock.

18 The following year they came to him and said, "We will not hide the fact from you, sir, that our money is all gone and our livestock belongs to you. There is nothing left to give you except our bodies and our lands. 19 Don't let us die. Do something! Don't let our fields be deserted. Buy us and our land in exchange for food. We will be the king's slaves, and he will own our land. Give us grain to keep us alive and seed so that we can plant our fields."

20 Joseph bought all the land in Egypt for the king. Every Egyptian was forced to sell his land, because the famine was so severe; and all the land became the king's property. 21 Joseph made slaves of the people from one end of Egypt to the other. 22 The only land he did not buy was the land that belonged to the priests. They did not have to sell their lands, because the king gave them an allowance to live on. 23 Joseph said to the people,

GENESIS

"You see, I have now bought you and your lands for the king. Here is seed for you to sow in your fields. 24 At the time of harvest you must give one-fifth to the king. You can use the rest for seed and for food for yourselves and your families."

25 They answered, "You have saved our lives; you have been good to us, sir, and we will be the king's slaves." 26 So Joseph made it a law for the land of Egypt that one-fifth of the harvest should belong to the king. This law still remains in force today. Only the lands of the priests did not become the king's property.

Jacob's Last Request

27 The Israelites lived in Egypt in the region of Goshen, where they became rich and had many children. 28 Jacob lived in Egypt seventeen years, until he was a hundred and forty-seven years old. 29 When the time drew near for him to die, he called for his son Joseph and said to him, "Place your hand between my thighsʷ and make a solemn vow that you will not bury me in Egypt. 30 I want to be buried where my fathers are; carry me out of Egypt and bury me where they are buried."

Joseph answered, "I will do as you say."

31 Jacob said, "Make a vow that you will." Joseph made the vow, and Jacob gave thanks there on his bed.

Jacob Blesses Ephraim and Manasseh

48 Some time later Joseph was told that his father was ill. So he took his two sons, Manasseh and Ephraim, and went to see Jacob. 2 When Jacob was told that his son Joseph had come to see him, he gathered his strength and sat up in bed. 3 Jacob said to Joseph, "Almighty God appeared to me at Luz in the land of Canaan and blessed me. 4 He said to me, 'I will give you many children, so that your descendants will become many nations; I will give this land to your descendants as their possession forever.'"

5 Jacob continued, "Joseph, your two sons, who were born to you in Egypt before I came here, belong to me; Ephraim and Manasseh are just as much my sons as Reuben and Simeon. 6 If you have any more sons, they will not be considered mine; the inheritance they get will come through Ephraim and Manasseh. 7 I am doing this because of your mother Rachel. To my great sorrow she died in the land of Canaan, not far from Ephrath, as I was returning from Mesopotamia. I buried her there beside the road to Ephrath." (Ephrath is now known as Bethlehem.)

8 When Jacob saw Joseph's sons, he asked, "Who are these boys?"

9 Joseph answered, "These are my sons, whom God has given me here in Egypt."

Jacob said, "Bring them to me so that I may bless them." 10 Jacob's eyesight was failing because of his age, and he could not see very well. Joseph brought the boys to him, and he hugged them and kissed them. 11 Jacob said to Joseph, "I never expected to see you again, and now God has even let me see your children." 12 Then Joseph took them from Jacob's lap and bowed down before him with his face to the ground.

13 Joseph put Ephraim at Jacob's left and Manasseh at his right. 14 But Jacob crossed his hands, and put his right hand on the head of Ephraim, even though he was the younger, and his left hand on the head of Manasseh, who was the older. 15 Then he blessed Joseph:ˣ

"May God, whom my fathers
   Abraham and Isaac served,
   bless these boys!
May God, who has led me to this
   very day, bless them!
16 May the angel, who has rescued
   me from all harm, bless them!
May my name and the name of my
   fathers Abraham and Isaac
   live on through these boys!
May they have many children,
   many descendants!"

17 Joseph was upset when he saw that his father had put his right hand on Ephraim's head; so he took his father's hand to move it from Ephraim's head to the head of Manasseh. 18 He said to his father, "Not that way, father. This is the older boy; put your right hand on his head."

ʷ PLACE . . . THIGHS: *See 24.2.*   ˣ JOSEPH: *In blessing Ephraim and Manasseh, Jacob was in fact blessing Joseph.*

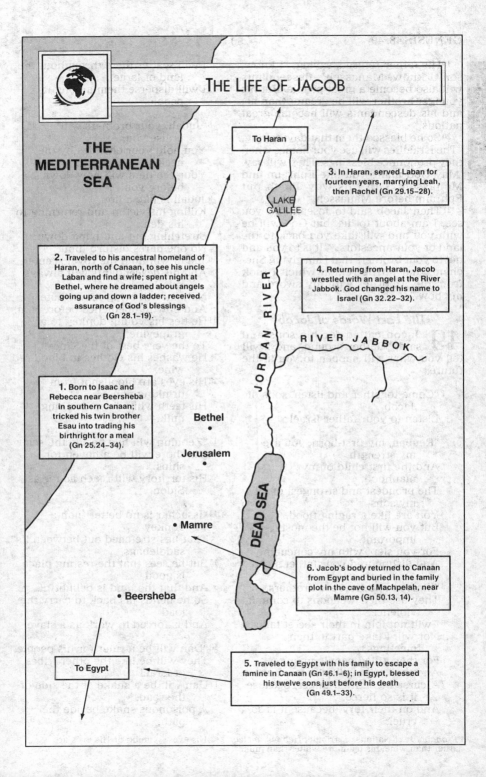

THE LIFE OF JACOB

THE MEDITERRANEAN SEA

To Haran

LAKE GALILEE

JORDAN RIVER

RIVER JABBOK

DEAD SEA

Bethel

Jerusalem

Mamre

Beersheba

To Egypt

3. In Haran, served Laban for fourteen years, marrying Leah, then Rachel (Gn 29.15–28).

4. Returning from Haran, Jacob wrestled with an angel at the River Jabbok. God changed his name to Israel (Gn 32.22–32).

2. Traveled to his ancestral homeland of Haran, north of Canaan, to see his uncle Laban and find a wife; spent night at Bethel, where he dreamed about angels going up and down a ladder; received assurance of God's blessings (Gn 28.1–19).

1. Born to Isaac and Rebecca near Beersheba in southern Canaan; tricked his twin brother Esau into trading his birthright for a meal (Gn 25.24–34).

6. Jacob's body returned to Canaan from Egypt and buried in the family plot in the cave of Machpelah, near Mamre (Gn 50.13, 14).

5. Traveled to Egypt with his family to escape a famine in Canaan (Gn 46.1–6); in Egypt, blessed his twelve sons just before his death (Gn 49.1–33).

19 His father refused, saying, "I know, son, I know. Manasseh's descendants will also become a great people. But his younger brother will be greater than he, and his descendants will become great nations."

20 So he blessed them that day, saying, "The Israelites will use your names when they pronounce blessings. They will say, 'May God make you like Ephraim and Manasseh.' " In this way Jacob put Ephraim before Manasseh.

21 Then Jacob said to Joseph, "As you see, I am about to die, but God will be with you and will take you back to the land of your ancestors. 22 It is to you and not to your brothers that I am giving Shechem, that fertile region which I took from the Amorites with my sword and my bow."

The Last Words of Jacob

49 Jacob called for his sons and said, "Gather around, and I will tell you what will happen to you in the future:

2 "Come together and listen, sons of Jacob.
Listen to your father Israel.

3 "Reuben, my first-born, you are my strength
And the first child of my manhood,
The proudest and strongest of all my sons.
4 You are like a raging flood,
But you will not be the most important,
For you slept with my concubine
And dishonored your father's bed.

5 "Simeon and Levi are brothers.
They use their weapons to commit violence.
6 I will not join in their secret talks,
Nor will I take part in their meetings,
For they killed people in anger
And they crippled bulls for sport.
7 A curse be on their anger, because it is so fierce,
And on their fury, because it is so cruel.

I will scatter them throughout the land of Israel.
I will disperse them among its people.

8 "Judah, your brothers will praise you.
You hold your enemies by the neck.
Your brothers will bow down before you.
9 Judah is like a lion,
Killing his victim and returning to his den,
Stretching out and lying down.
No one dares disturb him.
10 Judah will hold the royal scepter,
And his descendants will always rule.
Nations will bring him tribute y
And bow in obedience before him.
11 He ties his young donkey to a grapevine,
To the very best of the vines.
He washes his clothes in blood-red wine.
12 His eyes are bloodshot from drinking wine,
His teeth white from drinking milk. z

13 "Zebulun will live beside the sea.
His shore will be a haven for ships.
His territory will reach as far as Sidon.

14 "Issachar is no better than a donkey
That lies stretched out between its saddlebags.
15 But he sees that the resting place is good
And that the land is delightful.
So he bends his back to carry the load
And is forced to work as a slave.

16 "Dan will be a ruler for his people.
They will be like the other tribes of Israel.
17 Dan will be a snake at the side of the road,
A poisonous snake beside the path,

---

y Probable text Nations . . . tribute; Hebrew unclear.   z His eyes . . . milk; or His eyes are darker than wine, his teeth are whiter than milk.

That strikes at the horse's heel,
So that the rider is thrown off
backward.

18 "I wait for your deliverance, LORD.

19 "Gad will be attacked by a band of
robbers,
But he will turn and pursue them.

20 "Asher's land will produce rich
food.
He will provide food fit for a king.

21 "Naphtali is a deer that runs free,
Who bears lovely fawns.*a*

22 "Joseph is like a wild donkey by a
spring,
A wild colt on a hillside.*b*

23 His enemies attack him fiercely
And pursue him with their bows
and arrows.

24 But his bow remains steady,
And his arms are made strong*c*
By the power of the Mighty God of
Jacob,
By the Shepherd, the Protector of
Israel.

25 It is your father's God who
helps you,
The Almighty God who
blesses you
With blessings of rain from above
And of deep waters from beneath
the ground,
Blessings of many cattle and
children,

26 Blessings of grain and flowers,*d*
Blessings of ancient mountains,*e*
Delightful things from everlasting
hills.
May these blessings rest on the
head of Joseph,
On the brow of the one set apart
from his brothers.

27 "Benjamin is like a vicious wolf.
Morning and evening he kills and
devours."

28 These are the twelve tribes of Israel,
and this is what their father said as he
spoke a suitable word of farewell to
each son.

The Death and Burial of Jacob

29 Then Jacob commanded his sons,
"Now that I am going to join my people
in death, bury me with my fathers in the
cave that is in the field of Ephron the
Hittite, 30 at Machpelah east of Mamre in
the land of Canaan. Abraham bought
this cave and field from Ephron for a burial ground. 31 That is where they buried
Abraham and his wife Sarah; that is
where they buried Isaac and his wife Rebecca; and that is where I buried Leah.
32 The field and the cave in it were bought
from the Hittites. Bury me there."
33 When Jacob had finished giving instructions to his sons, he lay back down
and died

50 Joseph threw himself on his
father, crying and kissing his
face. 2 Then Joseph gave orders to em-
balm his father's body. 3 It took forty
days, the normal time for embalming.
The Egyptians mourned for him seventy
days.

4 When the time of mourning was over,
Joseph said to the king's officials,
"Please take this message to the king:
5 'When my father was about to die, he
made me promise him that I would bury
him in the tomb which he had prepared
in the land of Canaan. So please let me go
and bury my father, and then I will come
back.' "

6 The king answered, "Go and bury
your father, as you promised you would."

7 So Joseph went to bury his father. All
the king's officials, the senior men of his
court, and all the leading men of Egypt
went with Joseph. 8 His family, his brothers, and the rest of his father's family all
went with him. Only their small children
and their sheep, goats, and cattle stayed
in the region of Goshen. 9 Men in chariots
and men on horseback also went with
him; it was a huge group.

10 When they came to the threshing
place at Atad east of the Jordan, they
mourned loudly for a long time, and Joseph performed mourning ceremonies
for seven days. 11 When the citizens of

---

a Naphtali . . . fawns; *or* Naphtali is a spreading tree that puts out lovely branches.   *b* Joseph
. . . hillside; *or* Joseph is like a tree by a spring, a fruitful tree that spreads over a wall.   *c* But
. . . strong; *or* But their bows were broken and splintered, the muscles of their arms torn apart.
d *Probable text* grain and flowers; *Hebrew* your fathers are mightier than.   *e* *One ancient
translation* ancient mountains; *Hebrew* my ancestors to.

Canaan saw those people mourning at Atad, they said, "What a solemn ceremony of mourning the Egyptians are holding!" That is why the place was named Abel Mizraim.*f*

12 So Jacob's sons did as he had commanded them; 13 they carried his body to Canaan and buried it in the cave at Machpelah east of Mamre in the field which Abraham had bought from Ephron the Hittite for a burial ground. 14 After Joseph had buried his father, he returned to Egypt with his brothers and all who had gone with him for the funeral.

Joseph Reassures His Brothers

15 After the death of their father, Joseph's brothers said, "What if Joseph still hates us and plans to pay us back for all the harm we did to him?" 16 So they sent a message to Joseph: "Before our father died, 17 he told us to ask you, 'Please forgive the crime your brothers committed when they wronged you.' Now please forgive us the wrong that we, the servants of your father's God, have done." Joseph cried when he received this message.

18 Then his brothers themselves came and bowed down before him. "Here we are before you as your slaves," they said.

19 But Joseph said to them, "Don't be afraid; I can't put myself in the place of God. 20 You plotted evil against me, but God turned it into good, in order to preserve the lives of many people who are alive today because of what happened. 21 You have nothing to fear. I will take care of you and your children." So he reassured them with kind words that touched their hearts.

The Death of Joseph

22 Joseph continued to live in Egypt with his father's family; he was a hundred and ten years old when he died. 23 He lived to see Ephraim's children and grandchildren. He also lived to receive the children of Machir son of Manasseh into the family. 24 He said to his brothers, "I am about to die, but God will certainly take care of you and lead you out of this land to the land he solemnly promised to Abraham, Isaac, and Jacob." 25 Then Joseph asked his people to make a vow. "Promise me," he said, "that when God leads you to that land, you will take my body with you." 26 So Joseph died in Egypt at the age of a hundred and ten. They embalmed his body and put it in a coffin.

f ABEL MIZRAIM: *This name sounds like the Hebrew for "mourning of the Egyptians."*

EXODUS

Introduction

The name Exodus means "departure," and refers to the most important event in Israel's history, which is described in this book — the departure of the people of Israel from Egypt, where they had been slaves. The book has four main parts: 1) the freeing of the Hebrews from slavery; 2) their journey to Mount Sinai; 3) God's covenant with his people at Sinai, which gave them moral, civil, and religious laws to live by; and 4) the building and furnishing of a place of worship for Israel, and laws regarding the priests and the worship of God.

Above all, this book describes what God did, as he liberated his enslaved people and formed them into a nation with hope for the future.

The central human figure in the book is Moses, the man whom God chose to lead his people from Egypt. The most widely known part of the book is the list of the Ten Commandments in chapter 20.

Outline of Contents

The Israelites Are Treated Cruelly in Egypt

1 The sons of Jacob who went to Egypt with him, each with his family, were 2 Reuben, Simeon, Levi, Judah, 3 Issachar, Zebulun, Benjamin, 4 Dan, Naphtali, Gad, and Asher. 5 The total number of these people directly descended from Jacob was seventy.*a* His son Joseph was already in Egypt. 6 In the course of time Joseph, his brothers, and all the rest of that generation died, 7 but their descendants, the Israelites, had many children and became so numerous and strong that Egypt was filled with them.

8 Then, a new king, who knew nothing about Joseph, came to power in Egypt. 9 He said to his people, "These Israelites are so numerous and strong that they are a threat to us. 10 In case of war they might join our enemies in order to fight against us, and might escape from*b* the country. We must find some way to keep them from becoming even more numerous." 11 So the Egyptians put slave drivers over them to crush their spirits with hard la-bor. The Israelites built the cities of Pithom and Rameses to serve as supply centers for the king. 12 But the more the Egyptians oppressed the Israelites, the more they increased in number and the farther they spread through the land. The Egyptians came to fear the Israelites 13-14 and made their lives miserable by forcing them into cruel slavery. They made them work on their building projects and in their fields, and they had no pity on them.

15 Then the king of Egypt spoke to Shiphrah and Puah, the two midwives who helped the Hebrew women. 16 "When you help the Hebrew women give birth," he said to them, "kill the baby if it is a boy; but if it is a girl, let it live." 17 But the midwives were God-fearing and so did not obey the king; instead, they let the boys live. 18 So the king sent for the midwives and asked them, "Why are you doing this? Why are you letting the boys live?"

19 They answered, "The Hebrew women are not like Egyptian women; they give birth easily, and their babies

a One ancient translation seventy-five *(see Ac 7.14).*   *b* escape from; *or* take control of.

are born before either of us gets there."
20-21 Because the midwives were God-fearing, God was good to them and gave them families of their own. And the Israelites continued to increase and become strong. 22 Finally the king issued a command to all his people: "Take every newborn Hebrew boy and throw him into the Nile, but let all the girls live."

The Birth of Moses

2 During this time a man from the tribe of Levi married a woman of his own tribe, 2 and she bore him a son. When she saw what a fine baby he was, she hid him for three months. 3 But when she could not hide him any longer, she took a basket made of reeds and covered it with tar to make it watertight. She put the baby in it and then placed it in the tall grass at the edge of the river. 4 The baby's sister stood some distance away to see what would happen to him.

5 The king's daughter came down to the river to bathe, while her servants walked along the bank. Suddenly she noticed the basket in the tall grass and sent a slave woman to get it. 6 The princess opened it and saw a baby boy. He was crying, and she felt sorry for him. "This is one of the Hebrew babies," she said.

7 Then his sister asked her, "Shall I go and call a Hebrew woman to nurse the baby for you?"

8 "Please do," she answered. So the girl went and brought the baby's own mother. 9 The princess told the woman, "Take this baby and nurse him for me, and I will pay you." So she took the baby and nursed him. 10 Later, when the child was old enough, she took him to the king's daughter, who adopted him as her own son. She said to herself, "I pulled him out of the water, and so I name him Moses."c

Moses Escapes to Midian

11 When Moses had grown up, he went out to visit his people, the Hebrews, and he saw how they were forced to do hard labor. He even saw an Egyptian kill a Hebrew, one of Moses' own people. 12 Moses looked all around, and when he saw that no one was watching, he killed the Egyptian and hid his body in the sand. 13 The next day he went back and saw two Hebrew men fighting. He said to the one who was in the wrong, "Why are you beating up a fellow Hebrew?"

14 The man answered, "Who made you our ruler and judge? Are you going to kill me just as you killed that Egyptian?" Then Moses was afraid and said to himself, "People have found out what I have done." 15-16 When the king heard about what had happened, he tried to have Moses killed, but Moses fled and went to live in the land of Midian.

One day, when Moses was sitting by a well, seven daughters of Jethro, the priest of Midian, came to draw water and fill the troughs for their father's sheep and goats. 17 But some shepherds drove Jethro's daughters away. Then Moses went to their rescue and watered their animals for them. 18 When they returned to their father, he asked, "Why have you come back so early today?"

19 "An Egyptian rescued us from the shepherds," they answered, "and he even drew water for us and watered our animals."

20 "Where is he?" he asked his daughters. "Why did you leave the man out there? Go and invite him to eat with us."

21 So Moses decided to live there, and Jethro gave him his daughter Zipporah in marriage, 22 who bore him a son. Moses said to himself, "I am a foreigner in this land, and so I name him Gershom."d

23 Years later the king of Egypt died, but the Israelites were still groaning under their slavery and cried out for help. Their cry went up to God, 24 who heard their groaning and remembered his covenant with Abraham, Isaac, and Jacob. 25 He saw the slavery of the Israelites and was concerned for them.e

God Calls Moses

3 One day while Moses was taking care of the sheep and goats of his father-in-law Jethro, the priest of Midian, he led the flock across the desert and came to Sinai, the holy mountain. 2 There the angel of the LORD appeared to him as a flame coming from the middle of a

---

c MOSES: *This name sounds like the Hebrew for "pull out."* d GERSHOM: *This name sounds like the Hebrew for "foreigner."* e was concerned for them; *one ancient translation* revealed himself to them.

bush. Moses saw that the bush was on fire but that it was not burning up. 3 "This is strange," he thought. "Why isn't the bush burning up? I will go closer and see."

4 When the LORD saw that Moses was coming closer, he called to him from the middle of the bush and said, "Moses! Moses!"

He answered, "Yes, here I am."

5 God said, "Do not come any closer. Take off your sandals, because you are standing on holy ground. 6 I am the God of your ancestors, the God of Abraham, Isaac, and Jacob." So Moses covered his face, because he was afraid to look at God.

7 Then the LORD said, "I have seen how cruelly my people are being treated in Egypt; I have heard them cry out to be rescued from their slave drivers. I know all about their sufferings, 8 and so I have come down to rescue them from the Egyptians and to bring them out of Egypt to a spacious land, one which is rich and fertile and in which the Canaanites, the Hittites, the Amorites, the Perizzites, the Hivites, and the Jebusites now live. 9 I have indeed heard the cry of my people, and I see how the Egyptians are oppressing them. 10 Now I am sending you to the king of Egypt so that you can lead my people out of his country."

11 But Moses said to God, "I am nobody. How can I go to the king and bring the Israelites out of Egypt?"

12 God answered, "I will be with you, and when you bring the people out of Egypt, you will worship me on this mountain. That will be the proof that I have sent you."

13 But Moses replied, "When I go to the Israelites and say to them, 'The God of your ancestors sent me to you,' they will ask me, 'What is his name?' So what can I tell them?"

14 God said, "I am who I am. You must tell them: 'The one who is called I AM[f] has sent me to you.' 15 Tell the Israelites that I, the LORD, the God of their ancestors, the God of Abraham, Isaac, and Jacob, have sent you to them. This is my name forever; this is what all future generations are to call me. 16 Go and gather

the leaders of Israel together and tell them that I, the LORD, the God of their ancestors, the God of Abraham, Isaac, and Jacob, appeared to you. Tell them that I have come to them and have seen what the Egyptians are doing to them. 17 I have decided that I will bring them out of Egypt, where they are being treated cruelly, and will take them to a rich and fertile land—the land of the Canaanites, the Hittites, the Amorites, the Perizzites, the Hivites, and the Jebusites.

18 "My people will listen to what you say to them. Then you must go with the leaders of Israel to the king of Egypt and say to him, 'The LORD, the God of the Hebrews, has revealed himself to us. Now allow us to travel three days into the desert to offer sacrifices to the LORD, our God.' 19 I know that the king of Egypt will not let you go unless he is forced to do so. 20 But I will use my power and will punish Egypt by doing terrifying things there. After that he will let you go.

21 "I will make the Egyptians respect you so that when my people leave, they will not go empty-handed. 22 Every Israelite woman will go to her Egyptian neighbors and to any Egyptian woman living in her house and will ask for clothing and for gold and silver jewelry. The Israelites will put these things on their sons and daughters and carry away the wealth of the Egyptians."

God Gives Moses Miraculous Power

4 Then Moses answered the LORD, "But suppose the Israelites do not believe me and will not listen to what I say. What shall I do if they say that you did not appear to me?"

2 So the LORD asked him, "What are you holding?"

"A walking stick," he answered.

3 The LORD said, "Throw it on the ground." When Moses threw it down, it turned into a snake, and he ran away from it. 4 Then the LORD said to Moses, "Reach down and pick it up by the tail." So Moses reached down and caught it, and it became a walking stick again. 5 The LORD said, "Do this to prove to the Israelites that the LORD, the God of their

ancestors, the God of Abraham, Isaac, and Jacob, has appeared to you."

6 The LORD spoke to Moses again, "Put your hand inside your robe." Moses obeyed; and when he took his hand out, it was diseased, covered with white spots, like snow. 7 Then the LORD said, "Put your hand inside your robe again." He did so, and when he took it out this time, it was healthy, just like the rest of his body. 8 The LORD said, "If they will not believe you or be convinced by the first miracle, then this one will convince them. 9 If in spite of these two miracles they still will not believe you, and if they refuse to listen to what you say, take some water from the Nile and pour it on the ground. The water will turn into blood."

10 But Moses said, "No, LORD, don't send me. I have never been a good speaker, and I haven't become one since you began to speak to me. I am a poor speaker, slow and hesitant."

11 The LORD said to him, "Who gives man his mouth? Who makes him deaf or dumb? Who gives him sight or makes him blind? It is I, the LORD. 12 Now, go! I will help you to speak, and I will tell you what to say."

13 But Moses answered, "No, Lord, please send someone else."

14 At this the LORD became angry with Moses and said, "What about your brother Aaron, the Levite? I know that he can speak well. In fact, he is now coming to meet you and will be glad to see you. 15 You can speak to him and tell him what to say. I will help both of you to speak, and I will tell you both what to do. 16 He will be your spokesman and speak to the people for you. Then you will be like God, telling him what to say. 17 Take this walking stick with you; for with it you will perform miracles."

Moses Returns to Egypt

18 Then Moses went back to Jethro, his father-in-law, and said to him, "Please let me go back to my relatives in Egypt to see if they are still alive." Jethro agreed and told him good-bye.

19 While Moses was still in Midian, the LORD said to him, "Go back to Egypt, for all those who wanted to kill you are dead." 20 So Moses took his wife and his sons, put them on a donkey, and set out with them for Egypt, carrying the walking stick that God had told him to take.

21 Again the LORD said to Moses, "Now that you are going back to Egypt, be sure to perform before the king all the miracles which I have given you the power to do. But I will make the king stubborn, and he will not let the people go. 22 Then you must tell him that I, the LORD, say, 'Israel is my first-born son. 23 I told you to let my son go, so that he might worship me, but you refused. Now I am going to kill your first-born son.'"

24 At a camping place on the way to Egypt, the LORD met Moses and tried to kill him. 25-26 Then Zipporah, his wife, took a sharp stone, cut off the foreskin of her son, and touched Moses' feet[g] with it. Because of the rite of circumcision she said to Moses, "You are a husband of blood to me." And so the LORD spared Moses' life.

27 Meanwhile the LORD had said to Aaron, "Go into the desert to meet Moses." So he went to meet him at the holy mountain; and when he met him, he kissed him. 28 Then Moses told Aaron everything that the LORD had said when he told him to return to Egypt; he also told him about the miracles which the LORD had ordered him to perform. 29 So Moses and Aaron went to Egypt and gathered all the Israelite leaders together. 30 Aaron told them everything that the LORD had said to Moses, and then Moses performed all the miracles in front of the people. 31 They believed, and when they heard that the LORD had come to them and had seen how they were being treated cruelly, they bowed down and worshiped.

Moses and Aaron before the King of Egypt

5 Then Moses and Aaron went to the king of Egypt and said, "The LORD, the God of Israel, says, 'Let my people go, so that they can hold a festival in the desert to honor me.'"

2 "Who is the LORD?" the king demanded. "Why should I listen to him and let Israel go? I do not know the LORD; and I will not let Israel go."

3 Moses and Aaron replied, "The God of the Hebrews has revealed himself to

---

g FEET: This reference to "feet" is thought by some to be a euphemism for the genitals.

us. Allow us to travel three days into the desert to offer sacrifices to the LORD our God. If we don't do so, he will kill us with disease or by war."

4 The king said to Moses and Aaron, "What do you mean by making the people neglect their work? Get those slaves back to work! 5 You people have become more numerous than the Egyptians. And now you want to stop working!"

6 That same day the king commanded the Egyptian slave drivers and the Israelite foremen: 7 "Stop giving the people straw for making bricks. Make them go and find it for themselves. 8 But still require them to make the same number of bricks as before, not one brick less. They don't have enough work to do, and that is why they keep asking me to let them go and offer sacrifices to their God! 9 Make them work harder and keep them busy, so that they won't have time to listen to a pack of lies."

10 The slave drivers and the Israelite foremen went out and said to the Israelites, "The king has said that he will not supply you with any more straw. 11 He says that you must go and get it for yourselves wherever you can find it, but you must still make the same number of bricks." 12 So the people went all over Egypt looking for straw. 13 The slave drivers kept trying to force them to make the same number of bricks every day as they had made when they were given straw. 14 The Egyptian slave drivers beat the Israelite foremen, whom they had put in charge of the work. They demanded, "Why aren't you people making the same number of bricks that you made before?"

15 Then the foremen went to the king and complained, "Why do you do this to us, Your Majesty? 16 We are given no straw, but we are still ordered to make bricks! And now we are being beaten. It is your people that are at fault."

17 The king answered, "You are lazy and don't want to work, and that is why you ask me to let you go and offer sacrifices to the LORD. 18 Now get back to work! You will not be given any straw, but you must still make the same number of bricks." 19 The foremen realized that they were in trouble when they were told that they had to make the same number

of bricks every day as they had made before.

20 As they were leaving, they met Moses and Aaron, who were waiting for them. 21 They said to Moses and Aaron, "The LORD has seen what you have done and will punish you for making the king and his officers hate us. You have given them an excuse to kill us."

Moses Complains to the LORD

22 Then Moses turned to the LORD again and said, "Lord, why do you mistreat your people? Why did you send me here? 23 Ever since I went to the king to speak for you, he has treated them cruelly. And you have done nothing to help them!"

6 Then the LORD said to Moses, "Now you are going to see what I will do to the king. I will force him to let my people go. In fact, I will force him to drive them out of his land."

God Calls Moses

2 God spoke to Moses and said, "I am the LORD. 3 I appeared to Abraham, to Isaac, and to Jacob as Almighty God, but I did not make myself known to them by my holy name, the LORD. h 4 I also made my covenant with them, promising to give them the land of Canaan, the land in which they had lived as foreigners. 5 Now I have heard the groaning of the Israelites, whom the Egyptians have enslaved, and I have remembered my covenant. 6 So tell the Israelites that I say to them, 'I am the LORD; I will rescue you and set you free from your slavery to the Egyptians. I will raise my mighty arm to bring terrible punishment upon them, and I will save you. 7 I will make you my own people, and I will be your God. You will know that I am the LORD your God when I set you free from slavery in Egypt. 8 I will bring you to the land that I solemnly promised to give to Abraham, Isaac, and Jacob; and I will give it to you as your own possession. I am the LORD.' "

9 Moses told this to the Israelites, but they would not listen to him, because their spirit had been broken by their cruel slavery.

10 Then the LORD said to Moses, 11 "Go and tell the king of Egypt that he must let the Israelites leave his land."

12 But Moses replied, "Even the Israel-

h THE LORD: See 3.14.

ites will not listen to me, so why should the king? I am such a poor speaker."

13 The LORD commanded Moses and Aaron: "Tell the Israelites and the king of Egypt that I have ordered you to lead the Israelites out of Egypt."

The Family Record of Moses and Aaron

14 Reuben, Jacob's first-born, had four sons: Hanoch, Pallu, Hezron, and Carmi; they were the ancestors of the clans that bear their names. 15 Simeon had six sons: Jemuel, Jamin, Ohad, Jachin, Zohar, and Shaul, the son of a Canaanite woman; they were the ancestors of the clans that bear their names. 16 Levi had three sons: Gershon, Kohath, and Merari; they were the ancestors of the clans that bear their names. Levi lived 137 years. 17 Gershon had two sons: Libni and Shimei, and they had many descendants. 18 Kohath had four sons: Amram, Izhar, Hebron, and Uzziel. Kohath lived 133 years. 19 Merari had two sons: Mahli and Mushi. These are the clans of Levi with their descendants.

20 Amram married his father's sister Jochebed, who bore him Aaron and Moses. Amram lived 137 years. 21 Izhar had three sons: Korah, Nepheg, and Zichri. 22 Uzziel also had three sons: Mishael, Elzaphan, and Sithri.

23 Aaron married Elisheba, the daughter of Amminadab and sister of Nahshon; she bore him Nadab, Abihu, Eleazar, and Ithamar. 24 Korah had three sons: Assir, Elkanah, and Abiasaph; they were the ancestors of the divisions of the clan of Korah. 25 Eleazar, Aaron's son, married one of Putiel's daughters, who bore him Phinehas. These were the heads of the families and the clans of the tribe of Levi.

26 Aaron and Moses were the ones to whom the LORD said, "Lead the tribes of Israel out of Egypt." 27 They were the men who told the king of Egypt to free the Israelites.

The LORD's Command to Moses and Aaron

28 When the LORD spoke to Moses in the land of Egypt, 29 he said, "I am the LORD. Tell the king of Egypt everything I tell you."

30 But Moses answered, "You know that I am such a poor speaker; why should the king listen to me?"

7 The LORD said, "I am going to make you like God to the king, and your brother Aaron will speak to him as your prophet. 2 Tell Aaron everything I command you, and he will tell the king to let the Israelites leave his country. 3-4 But I will make the king stubborn, and he will not listen to you, no matter how many terrifying things I do in Egypt. Then I will bring severe punishment on Egypt and lead the tribes of my people out of the land. 5 The Egyptians will then know that I am the LORD, when I raise my hand against them and bring the Israelites out of their country." 6 Moses and Aaron did what the LORD commanded. 7 At the time when they spoke to the king, Moses was eighty years old, and Aaron was eighty-three.

Aaron's Walking Stick

8 The LORD said to Moses and Aaron, 9 "If the king demands that you prove yourselves by performing a miracle, tell Aaron to take his walking stick and throw it down in front of the king, and it will turn into a snake." 10 So Moses and Aaron went to the king and did as the LORD had commanded. Aaron threw his walking stick down in front of the king and his officers, and it turned into a snake. 11 Then the king called for his wise men and magicians, and by their magic they did the same thing. 12 They threw down their walking sticks, and the sticks turned into snakes. But Aaron's stick swallowed theirs. 13 The king, however, remained stubborn and, just as the LORD had said, the king would not listen to Moses and Aaron.

Disasters Strike Egypt

Blood

14 Then the LORD said to Moses, "The king is very stubborn and refuses to let the people go. 15 So go and meet him in the morning when he goes down to the Nile. Take with you the walking stick that was turned into a snake, and wait for him on the riverbank. 16 Then say to the king, 'The LORD, the God of the Hebrews, sent me to tell you to let his people go, so that they can worship him in the desert. But until now you have not listened. 17 Now, Your Majesty, the LORD says that

THE TEN PLAGUES OF EGYPT

The king of Egypt refused to release the Hebrew people from slavery and allow them to leave his country. So the Lord sent ten plagues upon the Egyptians to break the king's stubborn will and to demonstrate his power and superiority over the pagan gods of the Egyptians.

These plagues occurred within a period of about nine months, in the following order:

1. The water of the Nile River turned into blood (Ex 7.14–25).
2. Frogs covered the land of Egypt (Ex 8.1–15).
3. People and animals were covered with gnats (Ex 8.16–19).
4. Swarms of flies covered the land (Ex 8.20–32).
5. Disease killed the livestock of Egypt (Ex 9.1–7).
6. Boils and sores covered the Egyptians and their animals (Ex 9.8–12).
7. Hail destroyed plants and trees (Ex 9.13–35).
8. Swarms of locusts covered the land (Ex 10.1–20).
9. Total darkness covered Egypt for three days (Ex 10.21–29).
10. The Egyptian first-born, both of the people and of their animals, were destroyed by God's Angel of Death (Ex 11.1—12.30).

In all of these plagues, the Israelites were protected, while the Egyptians and their property were destroyed. The Israelites were delivered from the final plague when they marked their houses, at God's command, by putting the blood of a lamb on their doorposts. The Angel of Death "passed over" the Hebrew houses.

At this final demonstration of God's power, the King gave in and allowed Moses and the Israelites to leave Egypt. This deliverance became one of the most memorable occasions in the Israelites' history. The Passover is celebrated annually even today to commemorate God's deliverance of the Israelites from slavery.

E
X
O
D
U
S

you will find out who he is by what he is going to do. Look, I am going to strike the surface of the river with this stick, and the water will be turned into blood. 18 The fish will die, and the river will stink so much that the Egyptians will not be able to drink from it.' "

19 The LORD said to Moses, "Tell Aaron to take his stick and hold it out over all the rivers, canals, and pools in Egypt. The water will become blood, and all over the land there will be blood, even in the wooden tubs and stone jars."

20 Then Moses and Aaron did as the LORD commanded. In the presence of the king and his officers, Aaron raised his stick and struck the surface of the river, and all the water in it was turned into blood. 21 The fish in the river died, and it smelled so bad that the Egyptians could not drink from it. There was blood everywhere in Egypt. 22 Then the king's magicians did the same thing by means of their magic, and the king was as stubborn as ever. Just as the LORD had said, the king refused to listen to Moses and Aaron. 23 Instead, he turned and went back to his palace without paying any attention even to this. 24 All the Egyptians dug along the bank of the river for drinking water, because they were not able to drink water from the river.

25 Seven days passed after the LORD struck the river.

Frogs

8 Then the LORD said to Moses, "Go to the king and tell him that the LORD says, 'Let my people go, so that they can worship me. 2 If you refuse, I will punish your country by covering it with frogs. 3 The Nile will be so full of frogs that they will leave it and go into your palace, your bedroom, your bed, the houses of your officials and your people, and even into your ovens and baking pans. 4 They will jump up on you, your people, and all your officials.' "

5 The LORD said to Moses, "Tell Aaron to hold out his walking stick over the rivers, the canals, and the pools, and make frogs come up and cover the land of Egypt." 6 So Aaron held it out over all the water, and the frogs came out and covered the land. 7 But the magicians used magic, and they also made frogs come up on the land.

8 The king called for Moses and Aaron and said, "Pray to the LORD to take away these frogs, and I will let your people go, so that they can offer sacrifices to the LORD."

9 Moses replied, "I will be glad to pray for you. Just set the time when I am to pray for you, your officers, and your people. Then you will be rid of the frogs, and there will be none left except in the Nile."

10 The king answered, "Pray for me tomorrow."

Moses said, "I will do as you ask, and then you will know that there is no other god like the LORD, our God. 11 You, your officials, and your people will be rid of the frogs, and there will be none left except in the Nile." 12 Then Moses and Aaron left the king, and Moses prayed to the LORD to take away the frogs which he had brought on the king. 13 The LORD did as Moses asked, and the frogs in the houses, the courtyards, and the fields died. 14 The Egyptians piled them up in great heaps, until the land stank with them. 15 When the king saw that the frogs were dead, he became stubborn again and, just as the LORD had said, the king would not listen to Moses and Aaron.

Gnats

16 The LORD said to Moses, "Tell Aaron to strike the ground with his stick, and all over the land of Egypt the dust will change into gnats." 17 So Aaron struck the ground with his stick, and all the dust in Egypt was turned into gnats, which covered the people and the animals. 18 The magicians tried to use their magic to make gnats appear, but they failed. There were gnats everywhere, 19 and the magicians said to the king, "God has done this!" But the king was stubborn and, just as the LORD had said, the king would not listen to Moses and Aaron.

Flies

20 The LORD said to Moses, "Early tomorrow morning go and meet the king as he goes to the river, and tell him that the LORD says, 'Let my people go, so that they can worship me. 21 I warn you that if you refuse, I will punish you by sending flies on you, your officials, and your people. The houses of the Egyptians will be full of flies, and the ground will be covered with them. 22 But I will spare the region of Goshen, where my people live, so that there will be no flies there. I will do this

so that you will know that I, the Lord, am at work in this land. 23 I will make a distinction[i] between my people and your people. This miracle will take place tomorrow.' " 24 The Lord sent great swarms of flies into the king's palace and the houses of his officials. The whole land of Egypt was brought to ruin by the flies.

25 Then the king called for Moses and Aaron and said, "Go and offer sacrifices to your God here in this country."

26 "It would not be right to do that," Moses answered, "because the Egyptians would be offended by our sacrificing the animals that we offer to the Lord our God. If we use these animals and offend the Egyptians by sacrificing them where they can see us, they will stone us to death. 27 We must travel three days into the desert to offer sacrifices to the Lord our God, just as he commanded us."

28 The king said, "I will let you go to sacrifice to the Lord, your God, in the desert, if you do not go very far. Pray for me."

29 Moses answered, "As soon as I leave, I will pray to the Lord that tomorrow the flies will leave you, your officials, and your people. But you must not deceive us again and prevent the people from going to sacrifice to the Lord."

30 Moses left the king and prayed to the Lord, 31 and the Lord did as Moses asked. The flies left the king, his officials, and his people; not one fly remained. 32 But even this time the king became stubborn, and again he would not let the people go.

Death of the Animals

9 The Lord said to Moses, "Go to the king and tell him that the Lord, the God of the Hebrews, says, 'Let my people go, so that they may worship me. 2 If you again refuse to let them go, 3 I will punish you by sending a terrible disease on all your animals — your horses, donkeys, camels, cattle, sheep, and goats. 4 I will make a distinction between the animals of the Israelites and those of the Egyptians, and no animal that belongs to the Israelites will die. 5 I, the Lord, have set tomorrow as the time when I will do this.' "

6 The next day the Lord did as he had said, and all the animals of the Egyptians died, but not one of the animals of the Israelites died. 7 The king asked what had happened and was told that none of the animals of the Israelites had died. But he was stubborn and would not let the people go.

Boils

8 Then the Lord said to Moses and Aaron, "Take a few handfuls of ashes from a furnace; Moses is to throw them into the air in front of the king. 9 They will spread out like fine dust over all the land of Egypt, and everywhere they will produce boils that become open sores on the people and the animals." 10 So they got some ashes and stood before the king; Moses threw them into the air, and they produced boils that became open sores on the people and the animals. 11 The magicians were not able to appear before Moses, because they were covered with boils, like all the other Egyptians. 12 But the Lord made the king stubborn and, just as the Lord had said, the king would not listen to Moses and Aaron.

Hail

13 The Lord then said to Moses, "Early tomorrow morning meet with the king and tell him that the Lord, the God of the Hebrews, says, 'Let my people go, so that they may worship me. 14 This time I will punish not only your officials and your people, but I will punish you as well, so that you may know that there is no one like me in all the world. 15 If I had raised my hand to strike you and your people with disease, you would have been completely destroyed. 16 But to show you my power I have let you live so that my fame might spread over the whole world. 17 Yet you are still arrogant and refuse to let my people go. 18 This time tomorrow I will cause a heavy hailstorm, such as Egypt has never known in all its history. 19 Now give orders for your livestock and everything else you have in the open to be put under shelter. Hail will fall on the people and animals left outside unprotected, and they will all die.' " 20 Some of the king's officials were afraid because of what the Lord had said, and they brought their slaves and animals indoors for shelter. 21 Others, however, paid no attention to the Lord's warning and left

---

i Some ancient translations a distinction; *Hebrew* redemption.

EXODUS

their slaves and animals out in the open.

22 Then the LORD said to Moses, "Raise your hand toward the sky, and hail will fall over the whole land of Egypt—on the people, the animals, and all the plants in the fields." 23 So Moses raised his stick toward the sky, and the LORD sent thunder and hail, and lightning struck the ground. The LORD sent 24 a heavy hailstorm, with lightning flashing back and forth. It was the worst storm that Egypt had ever known in all its history. 25 All over Egypt the hail struck down everything in the open, including all the people and all the animals. It beat down all the plants in the fields and broke all the trees. 26 The region of Goshen, where the Israelites lived, was the only place where there was no hail.

27 The king sent for Moses and Aaron and said, "This time I have sinned; the LORD is in the right, and my people and I are in the wrong. 28 Pray to the LORD! We have had enough of this thunder and hail! I promise to let you go; you don't have to stay here any longer."

29 Moses said to him, "As soon as I go out of the city, I will lift up my hands in prayer to the LORD. The thunder will stop, and there will be no more hail, so that you may know that the earth belongs to the LORD. 30 But I know that you and your officials do not yet fear the LORD God."

31 The flax and the barley were ruined, because the barley was ripe, and the flax was budding. 32 But none of the wheat was ruined, because it ripens later.

33 Moses left the king, went out of the city, and lifted up his hands in prayer to the LORD. The thunder, the hail, and the rain all stopped. 34 When the king saw what had happened, he sinned again. He and his officials remained as stubborn as ever 35 and, just as the LORD had foretold through Moses, the king would not let the Israelites go.

Locusts

10 Then the LORD said to Moses, "Go and see the king. I have made him and his officials stubborn, in order that I may perform these miracles among them 2 and in order that you may be able to tell your children and grandchildren how I made fools of the Egyptians when I performed the miracles. All of you will know that I am the LORD."

3 So Moses and Aaron went to the king and said to him, "The LORD, the God of the Hebrews, says, 'How much longer will you refuse to submit to me? Let my people go, so that they may worship me. 4 If you keep on refusing, then I will bring locusts into your country tomorrow. 5 There will be so many that they will completely cover the ground. They will eat everything that the hail did not destroy, even the trees that are left. 6 They will fill your palaces and the houses of all your officials and all your people. They will be worse than anything your ancestors ever saw.'" Then Moses turned and left.

7 The king's officials said to him, "How long is this man going to give us trouble? Let the Israelite men go, so that they can worship the LORD their God. Don't you realize that Egypt is ruined?"

8 So Moses and Aaron were brought back to the king, and he said to them, "You may go and worship the LORD your God. But exactly who will go?"

9 Moses answered, "We will all go, including our children and our old people. We will take our sons and daughters, our sheep and goats, and our cattle, because we must hold a festival to honor the LORD."

10 The king said, "I swear by the LORD that I will never let you take your women and children! It is clear that you are plotting to revolt! 11 No! Only the men may go and worship the LORD if that is what you want." With that, Moses and Aaron were driven out of the king's presence.

12 Then the LORD said to Moses, "Raise your hand over the land of Egypt to bring the locusts. They will come and eat everything that grows, everything that has survived the hail." 13 So Moses raised his stick, and the LORD caused a wind from the east to blow on the land all that day and all that night. By morning it had brought the locusts. 14 They came in swarms and settled over the whole country. It was the largest swarm of locusts that had ever been seen or that ever would be seen again. 15 They covered the ground until it was black with them; they ate everything that the hail had left, including all the fruit on the trees. Not a green thing was left on any tree or plant in all the land of Egypt.

16 Then the king hurriedly called Moses and Aaron and said, "I have sinned against the LORD your God and

against you. 17 Now forgive my sin this one time and pray to the LORD your God to take away this fatal punishment from me." 18 Moses left the king and prayed to the LORD. 19 And the LORD changed the east wind into a very strong west wind, which picked up the locusts and blew them into the Gulf of Suez./ Not one locust was left in all of Egypt. 20 But the LORD made the king stubborn, and he did not let the Israelites go.

Darkness

21 The LORD then said to Moses, "Raise your hand toward the sky, and a darkness thick enough to be felt will cover the land of Egypt." 22 Moses raised his hand toward the sky, and there was total darkness throughout Egypt for three days. 23 The Egyptians could not see each other, and no one left his house during that time. But the Israelites had light where they were living.

24 The king called Moses and said, "You may go and worship the LORD; even your women and children may go with you. But your sheep, goats, and cattle must stay here."

25 Moses answered, "Then you would have to provide us with animals for sacrifices and burnt offerings to offer to the LORD our God. 26 No, we will take our animals with us; not one will be left behind. We ourselves must select the animals with which to worship the LORD our God. And until we get there, we will not know what animals to sacrifice to him."

27 The LORD made the king stubborn, and he would not let them go. 28 He said to Moses, "Get out of my sight! Don't let me ever see you again! On the day I do, you will die!"

29 "You are right," Moses answered, "You will never see me again."

Moses Announces the Death of the First-Born

11 Then the LORD said to Moses, "I will send only one more punishment on the king of Egypt and his people. After that he will let you leave. In fact, he will drive all of you out of here. 2 Now speak to the people of Israel and tell all of them to ask their neighbors for gold and silver jewelry." 3 The LORD made the Egyptians respect the Israelites. Indeed,

the officials and all the people considered Moses to be a very great man.

4 Moses then said to the king, "The LORD says, 'At about midnight I will go through Egypt, 5 and every first-born son in Egypt will die, from the king's son, who is heir to the throne, to the son of the slave woman who grinds grain. The first-born of all the cattle will die also. 6 There will be loud crying all over Egypt, such as there has never been before or ever will be again. 7 But not even a dog will bark at the Israelites or their animals. Then you will know that I, the LORD, make a distinction between the Egyptians and the Israelites.' " 8 Moses concluded by saying, "All your officials will come to me and bow down before me, and they will beg me to take all my people and go away. After that, I will leave." Then in great anger Moses left the king.

9 The LORD had said to Moses, "The king will continue to refuse to listen to you, in order that I may do more of my miracles in Egypt." 10 Moses and Aaron performed all these miracles before the king, but the LORD made him stubborn, and he would not let the Israelites leave his country.

The Passover

12 The LORD spoke to Moses and Aaron in Egypt: 2 "This month is to be the first month of the year for you. 3 Give these instructions to the whole community of Israel: On the tenth day of this month each man must choose either a lamb or a young goat for his household. 4 If his family is too small to eat a whole animal, he and his next-door neighbor may share an animal, in proportion to the number of people and the amount that each person can eat. 5 You may choose either a sheep or a goat, but it must be a one-year-old male without any defects. 6 Then, on the evening of the fourteenth day of the month, the whole community of Israel will kill the animals. 7 The people are to take some of the blood and put it on the doorposts and above the doors of the houses in which the animals are to be eaten. 8 That night the meat is to be roasted, and eaten with bitter herbs and with bread made without yeast. 9 Do not eat any of it raw or boiled, but eat it roasted whole, including the head, the

EXODUS

_____
/ GULF OF SUEZ: *See Red Sea in 13.18.*

legs, and the internal organs. 10 You must not leave any of it until morning; if any is left over, it must be burned. 11 You are to eat it quickly, for you are to be dressed for travel, with your sandals on your feet and your walking stick in your hand. It is the Passover Festival to honor me, the LORD.

12 "On that night I will go through the land of Egypt, killing every first-born male, both human and animal, and punishing all the gods of Egypt. I am the LORD. 13 The blood on the doorposts will be a sign to mark the houses in which you live. When I see the blood, I will pass over you and will not harm you when I punish the Egyptians. 14 You must celebrate this day as a religious festival to remind you of what I, the LORD, have done. Celebrate it for all time to come."

The Festival of Unleavened Bread

15 The LORD said, "For seven days you must not eat any bread made with yeast — eat only unleavened bread. On the first day you are to get rid of all the yeast in your houses, for if anyone during those seven days eats bread made with yeast, he shall no longer be considered one of my people. 16 On the first day and again on the seventh day you are to meet for worship. No work is to be done on those days, but you may prepare food. 17 Keep this festival, because it was on this day that I brought your tribes out of Egypt. For all time to come you must celebrate this day as a festival. 18 From the evening of the fourteenth day of the first month to the evening of the twenty-first day, you must not eat any bread made with yeast. 19-20 For seven days no yeast must be found in your houses, for if anyone, native-born or foreign, eats bread made with yeast, he shall no longer be considered one of my people."

The First Passover

21 Moses called for all the leaders of Israel and said to them, "Each of you is to choose a lamb or a young goat and kill it, so that your families can celebrate Passover. 22 Take a sprig of hyssop, dip it in the bowl containing[k] the animal's blood, and wipe the blood on the doorposts and the beam above the door of your house. Not one of you is to leave the

house until morning. 23 When the LORD goes through Egypt to kill the Egyptians, he will see the blood on the beams and the doorposts and will not let the Angel of Death enter your houses and kill you. 24 You and your children must obey these rules forever. 25 When you enter the land that the LORD has promised to give you, you must perform this ritual. 26 When your children ask you, 'What does this ritual mean?' 27 you will answer, 'It is the sacrifice of Passover to honor the LORD, because he passed over the houses of the Israelites in Egypt. He killed the Egyptians, but spared us.'"

The Israelites knelt down and worshiped. 28 Then they went and did what the LORD had commanded Moses and Aaron.

The Death of the First-Born

29 At midnight the LORD killed all the first-born sons in Egypt, from the king's son, who was heir to the throne, to the son of the prisoner in the dungeon; all the first-born of the animals were also killed. 30 That night, the king, his officials, and all the other Egyptians were awakened. There was loud crying throughout Egypt, because there was not one home in which there was not a dead son. 31 That same night the king sent for Moses and Aaron and said, "Get out, you and your Israelites! Leave my country; go and worship the LORD, as you asked. 32 Take your sheep, goats, and cattle, and leave. Also pray for a blessing on me."

33 The Egyptians urged the people to hurry and leave the country; they said, "We will all be dead if you don't leave." 34 So the people filled their baking pans with unleavened dough, wrapped them in clothing, and carried them on their shoulders. 35 The Israelites had done as Moses had said, and had asked the Egyptians for gold and silver jewelry and for clothes. 36 The LORD made the Egyptians respect the people and give them what they asked for. In this way the Israelites carried away the wealth of the Egyptians.

The Israelites Leave Egypt

37 The Israelites set out on foot from Rameses for Sukkoth. There were about 600,000 men, not counting women and

---

k dip it in the bowl containing; or put it on the threshold covered with.

ISRAEL AND THE EGYPTIANS

The history of Egypt stretches back to about 3000 B.C., at least a thousand years before the time of Abraham. During their formative years as a nation, the Israelites spent 430 years as slaves in Egypt (Ex 12.40) before they were released miraculously through God's power under the leadership of Moses.

According to the table of nations in the Book of Genesis, Egypt was founded by one of the sons of Ham (Gn 10.6, 13, 14).

Soon after arriving in the land of Canaan, Abraham migrated into Egypt for a time to escape a famine (Gn 12.10). Still later, Joseph was sold into Egyptian slavery by his brothers (Gn 37.12–36). Joseph rose to a position of prominence in the cabinet of the Egyptian king (Gn 41.37–46). This led Joseph's family to move to Egypt, and the Israelites were eventually enslaved when a new line of kings rose to power (Ex 1.6–14).

After the Israelites left Egypt, the once-powerful Egyptian Empire declined in strength and influence, becoming a second-rate political power. During the time of David and Solomon, Egypt's weakness and fragmentation contributed to the establishment of Israel as a strong nation. During Isaiah's time, the prophet warned the king of Judah about forming an alliance with Egypt against the Assyrians, predicting that "Egypt's protection will end in disaster" (Is 30.3).

The Egyptians worshiped many gods. Many of these were the personification of nature, including the earth, sun, and sky. Even the Nile River was thought to be divine because its periodic flooding enriched the soil of the Nile delta for a premium agricultural harvest. Several of the plagues God sent upon the Egyptians (Ex 7—12) affected the Nile, proving the weakness of the entire Egyptian religious system.

children. 38 A large number of other people and many sheep, goats, and cattle also went with them. 39 They baked unleavened bread from the dough that they had brought out of Egypt, for they had been driven out of Egypt so suddenly that they did not have time to get their food ready or to prepare leavened dough.

40 The Israelites had lived in Egypt for 430 years. 41 On the day the 430 years ended, all the tribes of the LORD's people left Egypt. 42 It was a night when the LORD kept watch to bring them out of Egypt; this same night is dedicated to the LORD for all time to come as a night when the Israelites must keep watch.

Regulations about Passover

43 The LORD said to Moses and Aaron, "These are the Passover regulations: No foreigner shall eat the Passover meal, 44 but any slave that you have bought may eat it if you circumcise him first. 45 No temporary resident or hired worker may eat it. 46 The whole meal must be eaten in the house in which it was prepared; it must not be taken outside. And do not break any of the animal's bones. 47 The whole community of Israel must celebrate this festival, 48 but no uncircumcised man may eat it. If a foreigner has settled among you and wants to celebrate Passover to honor the LORD, you must first circumcise all the males of his household. He is then to be treated like a native-born Israelite and may join in the festival. 49 The same regulations apply to native-born Israelites and to foreigners who settle among you." 50 All the Israelites obeyed and did what the LORD had commanded Moses and Aaron. 51 On that day the LORD brought the Israelite tribes out of Egypt.

Dedication of the First-Born

13 The LORD said to Moses, 2 "Dedicate all the first-born males to me, for every first-born male Israelite and every first-born male animal belongs to me."

The Festival of Unleavened Bread

3 Moses said to the people, "Remember this day — the day on which you left Egypt, the place where you were slaves.

This is the day the LORD brought you out by his great power. No leavened bread is to be eaten. 4 You are leaving Egypt on this day in the first month, the month of Abib. 5 The LORD solemnly promised your ancestors to give you the land of the Canaanites, the Hittites, the Amorites, the Hivites, and the Jebusites. When he brings you into that rich and fertile land, you must celebrate this festival in the first month of every year. 6 For seven days you must eat unleavened bread and on the seventh day there is to be a festival to honor the LORD. 7 For seven days you must not eat any bread made with yeast; there must be no yeast or leavened bread anywhere in your land. 8 When the festival begins, explain to your sons that you do all this because of what the LORD did for you when you left Egypt. 9 This observance will be a reminder, like something tied on your hand or on your forehead; it will remind you to continue to recite and study the Law of the LORD, because the LORD brought you out of Egypt by his great power. 10 Celebrate this festival at the appointed time each year.

The First-Born

11 "The LORD will bring you into the land of the Canaanites, which he solemnly promised to you and your ancestors. When he gives it to you, 12 you must offer every first-born male to the LORD. Every first-born male of your animals belongs to the LORD, 13 but you must buy back from him every first-born male donkey by offering a lamb in its place. If you do not want to buy back the donkey, break its neck. You must buy back every first-born male child of yours. 14 In the future, when your son asks what this observance means, you will answer him, 'By using great power the LORD brought us out of Egypt, the place where we were slaves. 15 When the king of Egypt was stubborn and refused to let us go, the LORD killed every first-born male in the land of Egypt, both human and animal. That is why we sacrifice every first-born male animal to the LORD, but buy back our first-born sons. 16 This observance will be a reminder, like something tied on our hands or on our foreheads; it will remind us that the LORD brought us out of Egypt by his great power.' "

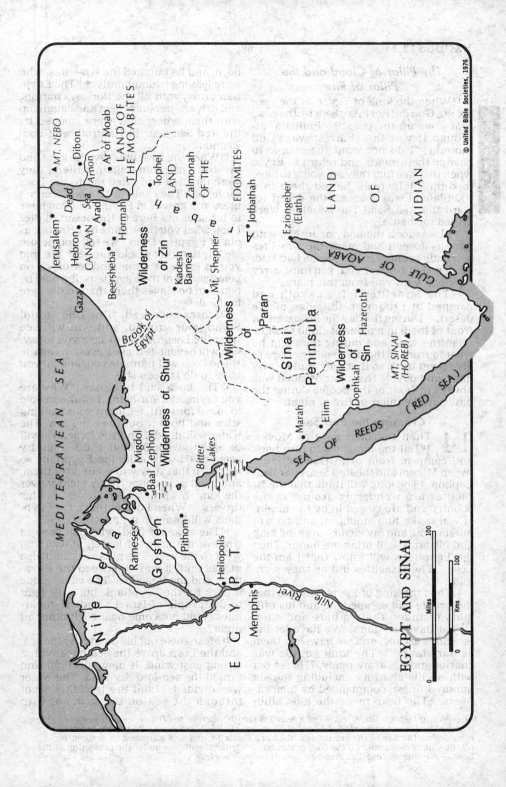

EGYPT AND SINAI

MEDITERRANEAN SEA

MT. NEBO
Dead
Sea
Dibon
Arnon
Ar of Moab
LAND OF THE MOABITES
Tophel
Jerusalem
Hebron
CANAAN
Arad
Hormah
Zalmonah
LAND OF THE EDOMITES
Beersheba
Gaza
Wilderness of Zin
Kadesh Barnea
Mt. Shepher
Jotbathah
LAND OF MIDIAN
Eziongeber (Elath)
Brook of Egypt
Wilderness of Paran
Mt. Shepher
Wilderness of Shur
Migdol
Baal Zephon
Wilderness of Shur
Bitter Lakes
Rameses
Goshen
Pithom
Nile Delta
Heliopolis
Marah
Elim
Hazeroth
Wilderness of Sin
Dophkah
MT. SINAI (HOREB)
Sinai Peninsula
SEA OF REEDS (RED SEA)
GULF OF AQABA
Memphis
Nile River
EGYPT

Miles
100
Kms
100
0

The Pillar of Cloud and the Pillar of Fire

17 When the king of Egypt let the people go, God did not take them by the road that goes up the coast to Philistia, although it was the shortest way. God thought, "I do not want the people to change their minds and return to Egypt when they see that they are going to have to fight." 18 Instead, he led them in a roundabout way through the desert toward the Red Sea.[l] The Israelites were armed for battle.

19 Moses took the body of Joseph with him, as Joseph had made the Israelites solemnly promise to do. Joseph had said, "When God rescues you, you must carry my body with you from this place."

20 The Israelites left Sukkoth and camped at Etham on the edge of the desert. 21 During the day the LORD went in front of them in a pillar of cloud to show them the way, and during the night he went in front of them in a pillar of fire to give them light, so that they could travel night and day. 22 The pillar of cloud was always in front of the people during the day, and the pillar of fire at night.

Crossing the Red Sea

14 Then the LORD said to Moses, 2 "Tell the Israelites to turn back and camp in front of Pi Hahiroth, between Migdol and the Red Sea, near Baal Zephon. 3 The king will think that the Israelites are wandering around in the country and are closed in by the desert. 4 I will make him stubborn, and he will pursue you, and my victory over the king and his army will bring me honor. Then the Egyptians will know that I am the LORD." The Israelites did as they were told.

5 When the king of Egypt was told that the people had escaped, he and his officials changed their minds and said, "What have we done? We have let the Israelites escape, and we have lost them as our slaves!" 6 The king got his war chariot and his army ready. 7 He set out with all his chariots, including the six hundred finest, commanded by their officers. 8 The LORD made the king stubborn, and he pursued the Israelites, who were leaving triumphantly.[m] 9 The Egyptian army, with all the horses, chariots, and drivers, pursued them and caught up with them where they were camped by the Red Sea near Pi Hahiroth and Baal Zephon.

10 When the Israelites saw the king and his army marching against them, they were terrified and cried out to the LORD for help. 11 They said to Moses, "Weren't there any graves in Egypt? Did you have to bring us out here in the desert to die? Look what you have done by bringing us out of Egypt! 12 Didn't we tell you before we left that this would happen? We told you to leave us alone and let us go on being slaves of the Egyptians. It would be better to be slaves there than to die here in the desert."

13 Moses answered, "Don't be afraid! Stand your ground, and you will see what the LORD will do to save you today; you will never see these Egyptians again. 14 The LORD will fight for you, and all you have to do is keep still."

15 The LORD said to Moses, "Why are you crying out for help? Tell the people to move forward. 16 Lift up your walking stick and hold it out over the sea. The water will divide, and the Israelites will be able to walk through the sea on dry ground. 17 I will make the Egyptians so stubborn that they will go in after them, and I will gain honor by my victory over the king, his army, his chariots, and his drivers. 18 When I defeat them, the Egyptians will know that I am the LORD."

19 The angel of God, who had been in front of the army of Israel, moved and went to the rear. The pillar of cloud also moved until it was 20 between the Egyptians and the Israelites. The cloud made it dark for the Egyptians, but gave light to the people of Israel,[n] and so the armies could not come near each other all night.

21 Moses held out his hand over the sea, and the LORD drove the sea back with a strong east wind. It blew all night and turned the sea into dry land. The water was divided, 22 and the Israelites went through the sea on dry ground, with

---

[l] RED SEA: (in Hebrew literally "Sea of Reeds") evidently referred to (1) a series of lakes and marshes between the head of the Gulf of Suez and the Mediterranean, the region generally regarded as the site of the events described in Exodus 13, and was also used to designate (2) the Gulf of Suez, and (3) the Gulf of Aqaba.   [m] triumphantly; or under the protection of the LORD.   [n] Probable text The cloud . . . Israel; Hebrew unclear.

walls of water on both sides. 23 The Egyptians pursued them and went after them into the sea with all their horses, chariots, and drivers. 24 Just before dawn the LORD looked down from the pillar of fire and cloud at the Egyptian army and threw them into a panic. 25 He made the wheels of their chariots get stuck, so that they moved with great difficulty. The Egyptians said, "The LORD is fighting for the Israelites against us. Let's get out of here!"

26 The LORD said to Moses, "Hold out your hand over the sea, and the water will come back over the Egyptians and their chariots and drivers." 27 So Moses held out his hand over the sea, and at daybreak the water returned to its normal level. The Egyptians tried to escape from the water, but the LORD threw them into the sea. 28 The water returned and covered the chariots, the drivers, and all the Egyptian army that had followed the Israelites into the sea; not one of them was left. 29 But the Israelites walked through the sea on dry ground, with walls of water on both sides.

30 On that day the LORD saved the people of Israel from the Egyptians, and the Israelites saw them lying dead on the seashore. 31 When the Israelites saw the great power with which the LORD had defeated the Egyptians, they stood in awe of the LORD; and they had faith in the LORD and in his servant Moses.

The Song of Moses

15 Then Moses and the Israelites sang this song to the LORD:

"I will sing to the LORD, because he
    has won a glorious victory;
he has thrown the horses and
    their riders into the sea.
2 The LORD is my strong defender;
    he is the one who has saved me.
He is my God, and I will
    praise him,
my father's God, and I will sing
    about his greatness.
3 The LORD is a warrior;
    the LORD is his name.

4 "He threw Egypt's army and its
    chariots into the sea;
the best of its officers were
    drowned in the Red Sea.
5 The deep sea covered them;

they sank to the bottom like a
    stone.

6 "Your right hand, LORD, is
    awesome in power;
it breaks the enemy in pieces.
7 In majestic triumph you overthrow
    your foes;
your anger blazes out and burns
    them up like straw.
8 You blew on the sea and the water
    piled up high;
it stood up straight like a wall;
the deepest part of the sea
    became solid.
9 The enemy said, 'I will pursue
    them and catch them;
I will divide their wealth and
    take all I want;
I will draw my sword and take
    all they have.'
10 But one breath from you, LORD,
    and the Egyptians were
    drowned;
they sank like lead in the
    terrible water.

11 "LORD, who among the gods is
    like you?
Who is like you, wonderful in
    holiness?
Who can work miracles and
    mighty acts like yours?
12 You stretched out your right hand,
    and the earth swallowed our
    enemies.
13 Faithful to your promise, you led
    the people you had rescued;
by your strength you guided
    them to your sacred land.
14 The nations have heard, and they
    tremble with fear;
the Philistines are seized with
    terror.
15 The leaders of Edom are terrified;
Moab's mighty men are
    trembling;
the people of Canaan lose their
    courage.
16 Terror and dread fall upon them.
They see your strength, O LORD,
    and stand helpless with fear
until your people have marched
    past —
the people you set free from
    slavery.
17 You bring them in and plant them
    on your mountain,

MANNA IN THE WILDERNESS

Manna was the food miraculously supplied by God to the Israelites during their years of wandering in the wilderness. The Lord told Moses, "Now I am going to cause food to rain down from the sky for all of you" (Ex 16.4). The spiritual purpose of the daily provision was that by sending hardships he could test the Israelites "so that in the end he could bless you with good things" (Dt 8.16).

The manna was to be gathered each day, except the Sabbath, by every household according to need (Ex 16.16–18). Manna gathered in excess of need melted in the sun or became infested with worms (Ex 16.20, 21). The miracle food, which fell like dew, is described as "something thin and flaky on the surface of the desert. It was as delicate as frost" (Ex 16.14). Although it was sticky when it appeared, the manna soon solidified so that it could be ground and baked into wafers or cakes. It tasted like "cakes made with honey" (Ex 16.31).

The exact nature of this miracle food remains a mystery, although it is compared to "a small white seed" (Ex 16.31). Some scholars believe it may have been a substance secreted by plant parasites as they fed on tamarisk trees in the wilderness. God supplied manna for forty years until the Israelites entered Canaan and the "food grown in Canaan" (Js 5.12) became available.

During the wilderness years, God provided water for the Israelites when Moses struck a rock with his stick (Ex 17.6). Quail were also miraculously supplied when the people complained they had no meat to eat with their manna (Ex 16.13).

Throughout the Bible, references are made to God's provision in the wilderness to show the Lord's continuing concern for his people. Jesus alluded to the "bread from heaven" given through Moses (Jn 6.32). But he described himself as the "bread of life," which permanently satisfies (Jn 6.35).

the place that you, LORD, have
  chosen for your home,
the Temple that you yourself
  have built.
18 You, LORD, will be king forever
  and ever."

The Song of Miriam

19 The Israelites walked through the
sea on dry ground. But when the Egyptian chariots with their horses and drivers went into the sea, the LORD brought
the water back, and it covered them.
20 The prophet Miriam, Aaron's sister,
took her tambourine, and all the women
followed her, playing tambourines and
dancing. 21 Miriam sang for them:
  "Sing to the LORD, because he has
    won a glorious victory;
  he has thrown the horses and
    their riders into the sea."

Bitter Water

22 Then Moses led the people of Israel
away from the Red Sea into the desert of
Shur. For three days they walked
through the desert, but found no water.
23 Then they came to a place called Marah, but the water there was so bitter that
they could not drink it. That is why it was
named Marah.º 24 The people complained to Moses and asked, "What are
we going to drink?" 25 Moses prayed earnestly to the LORD, and the LORD showed
him a piece of wood, which he threw into
the water; and the water became fit to
drink.
  There the LORD gave them laws to live
by, and there he also tested them. 26 He
said, "If you will obey me completely by
doing what I consider right and by keeping my commands, I will not punish you
with any of the diseases that I brought on
the Egyptians. I am the LORD, the one
who heals you."
27 Next they came to Elim, where there
were twelve springs and seventy palm
trees; there they camped by the water.

The Manna and the Quails

16 The whole Israelite community
set out from Elim, and on the fifteenth day of the second month after
they had left Egypt, they came to the
desert of Sin, which is between Elim and
Sinai. 2 There in the desert they all com-

plained to Moses and Aaron 3 and said to
them, "We wish that the LORD had killed
us in Egypt. There we could at least sit
down and eat meat and as much other
food as we wanted. But you have brought
us out into this desert to starve us all to
death."
4 The LORD said to Moses, "Now I am
going to cause food to rain down from
the sky for all of you. The people must go
out every day and gather enough for that
day. In this way I can test them to find out
if they will follow my instructions. 5 On
the sixth day they are to bring in twice as
much as usual and prepare it."
6 So Moses and Aaron said to all the
Israelites, "This evening you will know
that it was the LORD who brought you out
of Egypt. 7 In the morning you will see the
dazzling light of the LORD's presence. He
has heard your complaints against him—
yes, against him, because we are only
carrying out his instructions." 8 Then
Moses said, "It is the LORD who will give
you meat to eat in the evening and as
much bread as you want in the morning,
because he has heard how much you
have complained against him. When you
complain against us, you are really complaining against the LORD."
9 Moses said to Aaron, "Tell the whole
community to come and stand before the
LORD, because he has heard their complaints." 10 As Aaron spoke to the whole
community, they turned toward the
desert, and suddenly the dazzling light of
the LORD appeared in a cloud. 11 The LORD
said to Moses, 12 "I have heard the complaints of the Israelites. Tell them that at
twilight they will have meat to eat, and in
the morning they will have all the bread
they want. Then they will know that I,
the LORD, am their God."
13 In the evening a large flock of quails
flew in, enough to cover the camp, and in
the morning there was dew all around
the camp. 14 When the dew evaporated,
there was something thin and flaky on
the surface of the desert. It was as delicate as frost. 15 When the Israelites saw
it, they didn't know what it was and
asked each other, "What is it?"
  Moses said to them, "This is the food
that the LORD has given you to eat. 16 The
LORD has commanded that each of you
is to gather as much of it as he needs,

º MARAH: *This name in Hebrew means "bitter."*

two quarts for each member of his household."

17 The Israelites did this, some gathering more, others less. 18 When they measured it, those who gathered much did not have too much, and those who gathered less did not have too little. Each had gathered just what he needed. 19 Moses said to them, "No one is to keep any of it for tomorrow." 20 But some of them did not listen to Moses and saved part of it. The next morning it was full of worms and smelled rotten, and Moses was angry with them. 21 Every morning each one gathered as much as he needed; and when the sun grew hot, what was left on the ground melted.

22 On the sixth day they gathered twice as much food, four quarts for each person. All the leaders of the community came and told Moses about it, 23 and he said to them, "The LORD has commanded that tomorrow is a holy day of rest, dedicated to him. Bake today what you want to bake and boil what you want to boil. Whatever is left should be put aside and kept for tomorrow." 24 As Moses had commanded, they kept what was left until the next day; it did not spoil or get worms in it. 25 Moses said, "Eat this today, because today is the Sabbath, a day of rest dedicated to the LORD, and you will not find any food outside the camp. 26 You must gather food for six days, but on the seventh day, the day of rest, there will be none."

27 On the seventh day some of the people went out to gather food, but they did not find any. 28 Then the LORD said to Moses, "How much longer will you people refuse to obey my commands? 29 Remember that I, the LORD, have given you a day of rest, and that is why on the sixth day I will always give you enough food for two days. Everyone is to stay where he is on the seventh day and not leave his home." 30 So the people did no work on the seventh day.

31 The people of Israel called the food manna.p It was like a small white seed, and tasted like thin cakes made with honey. 32 Moses said, "The LORD has commanded us to save some manna, to be kept for our descendants, so that they can see the food which he gave us to eat

in the desert when he brought us out of Egypt." 33 Moses said to Aaron, "Take a jar, put two quarts of manna in it, and place it in the LORD's presence to be kept for our descendants." 34 As the LORD had commanded Moses, Aaron put it in front of the Covenant Box, so that it could be kept. 35 The Israelites ate manna for the next forty years, until they reached the land of Canaan, where they settled. (36 The standard dry measure then in use equaled twenty quarts.)

Water from the Rock
(Numbers 20.1-13)

17 The whole Israelite community left the desert of Sin, moving from one place to another at the command of the LORD. They camped at Rephidim, but there was no water there to drink. 2 They complained to Moses and said, "Give us water to drink."

Moses answered, "Why are you complaining? Why are you putting the LORD to the test?"

3 But the people were very thirsty and continued to complain to Moses. They said, "Why did you bring us out of Egypt? To kill us and our children and our livestock with thirst?"

4 Moses prayed earnestly to the LORD and said, "What can I do with these people? They are almost ready to stone me."

5 The LORD said to Moses, "Take some of the leaders of Israel with you, and go on ahead of the people. Take along the stick with which you struck the Nile. 6 I will stand before you on a rock at Mount Sinai. Strike the rock, and water will come out of it for the people to drink." Moses did so in the presence of the leaders of Israel.

7 The place was named Massah and Meribah,q because the Israelites complained and put the LORD to the test when they asked, "Is the LORD with us or not?"

War with the Amalekites

8 The Amalekites came and attacked the Israelites at Rephidim. 9 Moses said to Joshua, "Pick out some men to go and fight the Amalekites tomorrow. I will stand on top of the hill holding the stick that God told me to carry." 10 Joshua did as Moses commanded him and went out to fight the Amalekites, while Moses,

---

p MANNA: *This word sounds like the Hebrew for "what is it?" (see verse 15).*
q MASSAH . . . MERIBAH: *These names in Hebrew mean "testing" and "complaining."*

Aaron, and Hur went up to the top of the hill. 11 As long as Moses held up his arms, the Israelites won, but when he put his arms down, the Amalekites started winning. 12 When Moses' arms grew tired, Aaron and Hur brought a stone for him to sit on, while they stood beside him and held up his arms, holding them steady until the sun went down. 13 In this way Joshua totally defeated the Amalekites.

14 Then the LORD said to Moses, "Write an account of this victory, so that it will be remembered. Tell Joshua that I will completely destroy the Amalekites." 15 Moses built an altar and named it "The LORD is my Banner." 16 He said, "Hold high the banner of the LORD!r The LORD will continue to fight against the Amalekites forever!"

Jethro Visits Moses

18 Moses' father-in-law Jethro, the priest of Midian, heard about everything that God had done for Moses and the people of Israel when he led them out of Egypt. 2 So he came to Moses, bringing with him Moses' wife Zipporah, who had been left behind, 3 and Gershom and Eliezer, her two sons. (Moses had said, "I have been a foreigner in a strange land"; so he had named one son Gershom.s 4 He had also said, "The God of my father helped me and saved me from being killed by the king of Egypt"; so he had named the other son Eliezer.t) 5 Jethro came with Moses' wife and her two sons into the desert where Moses was camped at the holy mountain. 6 He had sent word to Moses that they were coming, 7 so Moses went out to meet him, bowed before him, and kissed him. They asked about each other's health and then went into Moses' tent. 8 Moses told Jethro everything that the LORD had done to the king and the people of Egypt in order to rescue the Israelites. He also told him about the hardships the people had faced on the way and how the LORD had saved them. 9 When Jethro heard all this, he was happy 10 and said, "Praise the LORD, who saved you from the king and the people of Egypt! Praise the LORD, who saved his people from slavery! 11 Now I know that the LORD is greater than all the gods, because he did this when the Egyp-

tians treated the Israelites with such contempt." 12 Then Jethro brought an offering to be burned whole and other sacrifices to be offered to God; and Aaron and all the leaders of Israel went with him to eat the sacred meal as an act of worship.

The Appointment of Judges
(Deuteronomy 1.9-18)

13 The next day Moses was settling disputes among the people, and he was kept busy from morning till night. 14 When Jethro saw everything that Moses had to do, he asked, "What is all this that you are doing for the people? Why are you doing this all alone, with people standing here from morning till night to consult you?"

15 Moses answered, "I must do this because the people come to me to learn God's will. 16 When two people have a dispute, they come to me, and I decide which one of them is right, and I tell them God's commands and laws."

17 Then Jethro said, "You are not doing this right. 18 You will wear yourself out and these people as well. This is too much for you to do alone. 19 Now let me give you some good advice, and God will be with you. It is right for you to represent the people before God and bring their disputes to him. 20 You should teach them God's commands and explain to them how they should live and what they should do. 21 But in addition, you should choose some capable men and appoint them as leaders of the people: leaders of thousands, hundreds, fifties, and tens. They must be God-fearing men who can be trusted and who cannot be bribed. 22 Let them serve as judges for the people on a permanent basis. They can bring all the difficult cases to you, but they themselves can decide all the smaller disputes. That will make it easier for you, as they share your burden. 23 If you do this, as God commands, you will not wear yourself out, and all these people can go home with their disputes settled."

24 Moses took Jethro's advice 25 and chose capable men from among all the Israelites. He appointed them as leaders of thousands, hundreds, fifties, and tens. 26 They served as judges for the people on

---

r *Probable text* Hold . . . LORD; *Hebrew unclear.*   s GERSHOM: *This name sounds like the Hebrew*
for "foreigner."   t ELIEZER: *This name sounds like the Hebrew for "God helps me."*

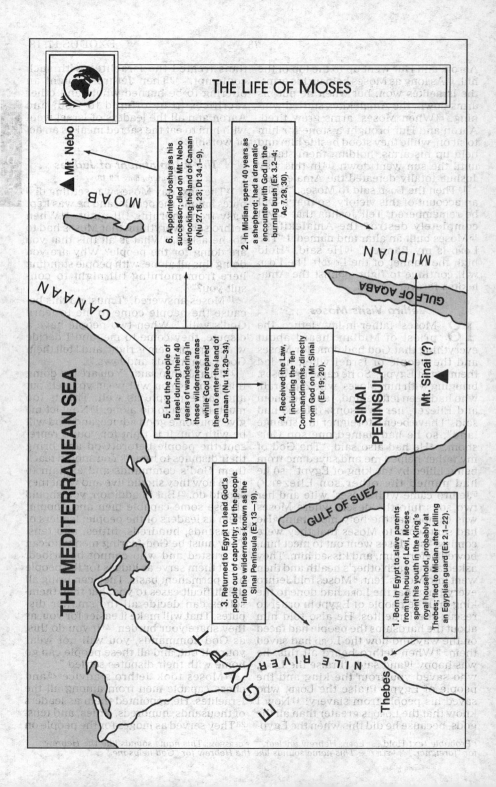

THE LIFE OF MOSES

MOAB

▲ Mt. Nebo

6. Appointed Joshua as his successor; died on Mt. Nebo overlooking the land of Canaan (Nu 27.18, 23; Dt 34.1–9).

2. In Midian, spent 40 years as a shepherd; had a dramatic encounter with God in the burning bush (Ex 3.2–4; Ac 7.29, 30).

CANAAN

MIDIAN

GULF OF AQABA

THE MEDITERRANEAN SEA

5. Led the people of Israel during their 40 years of wandering in these wilderness areas while God prepared them to enter the land of Canaan (Nu 14.20–34).

4. Received the Law, including the Ten Commandments, directly from God on Mt. Sinai. (Ex 19; 20).

SINAI PENINSULA

Mt. Sinai (?) ▲

GULF OF SUEZ

3. Returned to Egypt to lead God's people out of captivity; led the people into the wilderness known as the Sinai Peninsula (Ex 13–19).

1. Born in Egypt to slave parents from the house of Levi, Moses spent his youth in the King's royal household, probably at Thebes; fled to Midian after killing an Egyptian guard (Ex 2.1–22).

E G Y P T

NILE RIVER

Thebes ●

a permanent basis, bringing the difficult cases to Moses but deciding the smaller disputes themselves.

27 Then Moses said good-bye to Jethro, and Jethro went back home.

The Israelites at Mount Sinai

19 1-2 The people of Israel left Rephidim, and on the first day of the third month after they had left Egypt they came to the desert of Sinai. There they set up camp at the foot of Mount Sinai, 3 and Moses went up the mountain to meet with God.

The Lord called to him from the mountain and told him to say to the Israelites, Jacob's descendants: 4 "You saw what I, the Lord, did to the Egyptians and how I carried you as an eagle carries her young on her wings, and brought you here to me. 5 Now, if you will obey me and keep my covenant, you will be my own people. The whole earth is mine, but you will be my chosen people, 6 a people dedicated to me alone, and you will serve me as priests." 7 So Moses went down and called the leaders of the people together and told them everything that the Lord had commanded him. 8 Then all the people answered together, "We will do everything that the Lord has said," and Moses reported this to the Lord.

9 The Lord said to Moses, "I will come to you in a thick cloud, so that the people will hear me speaking with you and will believe you from now on."

Moses told the Lord what the people had answered, 10 and the Lord said to him, "Go to the people and tell them to spend today and tomorrow purifying themselves for worship. They must wash their clothes 11 and be ready the day after tomorrow. On that day I will come down on Mount Sinai, where all the people can see me. 12 Mark a boundary around the mountain that the people must not cross, and tell them not to go up the mountain or even get near it. If any of you set foot on it, you are to be put to death; 13 you must either be stoned or shot with arrows, without anyone touching you. This applies to both people and animals; they must be put to death. But when the trumpet is blown, then the people are to go up to the mountain."

14 Then Moses came down the mountain and told the people to get ready for worship. So they washed their clothes, 15 and Moses told them, "Be ready by the day after tomorrow and don't have sexual intercourse in the meantime."

16 On the morning of the third day there was thunder and lightning, a thick cloud appeared on the mountain, and a very loud trumpet blast was heard. All the people in the camp trembled with fear. 17 Moses led them out of the camp to meet God, and they stood at the foot of the mountain. 18 All of Mount Sinai was covered with smoke, because the Lord had come down on it in fire. The smoke went up like the smoke of a furnace, and all the people trembled violently. 19 The sound of the trumpet became louder and louder. Moses spoke, and God answered him with thunder. 20 The Lord came down on the top of Mount Sinai and called Moses to the top of the mountain. Moses went up 21 and the Lord said to him, "Go down and warn the people not to cross the boundary to come and look at me; if they do, many of them will die. 22 Even the priests who come near me must purify themselves, or I will punish them."

23 Moses said to the Lord, "The people cannot come up, because you commanded us to consider the mountain sacred and to mark a boundary around it."

24 The Lord replied, "Go down and bring Aaron back with you. But the priests and the people must not cross the boundary to come up to me, or I will punish them." 25 Moses then went down to the people and told them what the Lord had said.

The Ten Commandments
(Deuteronomy 5.1-21)

20 God spoke, and these were his words: 2 "I am the Lord your God who brought you out of Egypt, where you were slaves.

3 "Worship no god but me.

4 "Do not make for yourselves images of anything in heaven or on earth or in the water under the earth. 5 Do not bow down to any idol or worship it, because I am the Lord your God and I tolerate no rivals. I bring punishment on those who hate me and on their descendants down to the third and fourth generation. 6 But I show my love to thousands of

generations[u] of those who love me and obey my laws.

7 "Do not use my name for evil purposes, for I, the LORD your God, will punish anyone who misuses my name.

8 "Observe the Sabbath and keep it holy. 9 You have six days in which to do your work, 10 but the seventh day is a day of rest dedicated to me. On that day no one is to work—neither you, your children, your slaves, your animals, nor the foreigners who live in your country. 11 In six days I, the LORD, made the earth, the sky, the seas, and everything in them, but on the seventh day I rested. That is why I, the LORD, blessed the Sabbath and made it holy.

12 "Respect your father and your mother, so that you may live a long time in the land that I am giving you.

13 "Do not commit murder.

14 "Do not commit adultery.

15 "Do not steal.

16 "Do not accuse anyone falsely.

17 "Do not desire another man's house; do not desire his wife, his slaves, his cattle, his donkeys, or anything else that he owns."

The People's Fear
(Deuteronomy 5.22-33)

18 When the people heard the thunder and the trumpet blast and saw the lightning and the smoking mountain, they trembled with fear and stood a long way off. 19 They said to Moses, "If you speak to us, we will listen; but we are afraid that if God speaks to us, we will die."

20 Moses replied, "Don't be afraid; God has only come to test you and make you keep on obeying him, so that you will not sin." 21 But the people continued to stand a long way off, and only Moses went near the dark cloud where God was.

Laws about Altars

22 The LORD commanded Moses to tell the Israelites: "You have seen how I, the LORD, have spoken to you from heaven. 23 Do not make for yourselves gods of silver or gold to be worshiped in addition to me. 24 Make an altar of earth for me, and on it sacrifice your sheep and your cattle as offerings to be completely burned and as fellowship offerings. In every place that I set aside for you to worship me, I will come to you and bless you. 25 If you make an altar of stone for me, do not build it out of cut stones, because when you use a chisel on stones, you make them unfit for my use. 26 Do not build an altar for me with steps leading up to it; if you do, you will expose yourselves as you go up the steps.

The Treatment of Slaves
(Deuteronomy 15.12-18)

21 "Give the Israelites the following laws: 2 If you buy a Hebrew slave, he shall serve you for six years. In the seventh year he is to be set free without having to pay anything. 3 If he was unmarried when he became your slave, he is not to take a wife with him when he leaves; but if he was married when he became your slave, he may take his wife with him. 4 If his master gave him a wife and she bore him sons or daughters, the woman and her children belong to the master, and the man is to leave by himself. 5 But if the slave declares that he loves his master, his wife, and his children and does not want to be set free, 6 then his master shall take him to the place of worship. There he is to make him stand against the door or the doorpost and put a hole through his ear. Then he will be his slave for life.

7 "If a man sells his daughter as a slave, she is not to be set free, as male slaves are. 8 If she is sold to someone who intends to make her his wife, but he doesn't like her, then she is to be sold back to her father; her master cannot sell her to foreigners, because he has treated her unfairly. 9 If a man buys a female slave to give to his son, he is to treat her like a daughter. 10 If a man takes a second wife, he must continue to give his first wife the same amount of food and clothing and the same rights that she had before. 11 If he does not fulfill these duties to her, he must set her free and not receive any payment.

Laws about Violent Acts

12 "Whoever hits someone and kills him is to be put to death. 13 But if it was an accident and he did not mean to kill him, he can escape to a place which I will choose for you, and there he will be safe. 14 But when someone gets angry and

[u] thousands of generations; *or* thousands.

deliberately kills someone else, he is to be put to death, even if he has run to my altar for safety.

15 "Whoever hits his father or his mother is to be put to death.

16 "Whoever kidnaps someone, either to sell him or to keep him as a slave, is to be put to death.

17 "Whoever curses his father or his mother is to be put to death.

18-19 "If there is a fight and someone hits someone else with a stone or with his fist, but does not kill him, he is not to be punished. If the one who was hit has to stay in bed, but later is able to get up and walk outside with the help of a cane, the one who hit him is to pay for his lost time and take care of him until he gets well.

20 "If a slave owner takes a stick and beats his slave, whether male or female, and the slave dies on the spot, the owner is to be punished. 21 But if the slave does not die for a day or two, the master is not to be punished. The loss of his property is punishment enough.

22 "If some men are fighting and hurt a pregnant woman so that she loses her child, but she is not injured in any other way, the one who hurt her is to be fined whatever amount the woman's husband demands, subject to the approval of the judges. 23 But if the woman herself is injured, the punishment shall be life for life, 24 eye for eye, tooth for tooth, hand for hand, foot for foot, 25 burn for burn, wound for wound, bruise for bruise.

26 "If someone hits his male or female slave in the eye and puts it out, he is to free the slave as payment for the eye. 27 If he knocks out a tooth, he is to free the slave as payment for the tooth.

The Responsibility of Owners

28 "If a bull gores someone to death, it is to be stoned, and its flesh shall not be eaten; but its owner is not to be punished. 29 But if the bull had been in the habit of attacking people and its owner had been warned, but did not keep it penned up — then if it gores someone to death, it is to be stoned, and its owner is to be put to death also. 30 However, if the owner is allowed to pay a fine to save his life, he must pay the full amount required. 31 If the bull kills a boy or a girl, the same rule

applies. 32 If the bull kills a male or female slave, its owner shall pay the owner of the slave thirty pieces of silver, and the bull shall be stoned to death.

33 "If someone takes the cover off a pit or if he digs one and does not cover it, and a bull or a donkey falls into it, 34 he must pay for the animal. He is to pay the money to the owner and may keep the dead animal. 35 If someone's bull kills someone else's bull, the two of them shall sell the live bull and divide the money; they shall also divide up the meat from the dead animal. 36 But if it was known that the bull had been in the habit of attacking and its owner did not keep it penned up, he must make good the loss by giving the other man a live bull, but he may keep the dead animal.

Laws about Repayment

22 "If someone steals a cow or a sheep and kills it or sells it, he must pay five cows for one cow and four sheep for one sheep. 2-4 He must pay for what he stole. If he owns nothing, he shall be sold as a slave to pay for what he has stolen. If the stolen animal, whether a cow, a donkey, or a sheep, is found alive in his possession, he shall pay two for one.

"If a thief is caught breaking into a house at night and is killed, the one who killed him is not guilty of murder. But if it happens during the day, he is guilty of murder.

5 "If someone lets his animals graze in a field or a vineyard and they stray away and eat up the crops^v growing in someone else's field, he must make good the loss with the crops from his own fields or vineyards.

6 "If someone starts a fire in his own field and it spreads through the weeds to someone else's field and burns up grain that is growing or that has been cut and stacked, the one who started the fire is to pay for the damage.

7 "If anyone agrees to keep someone else's money or other valuables for him and they are stolen from his house, the thief, if found, shall repay double. 8 But if the thief is not found, the one who was keeping the valuables is to be brought to the place of worship and there he must

v If . . . crops; or If someone burns off a field or a vineyard, and lets the fire get out of control and burn up the crops.

take an oath that he has not stolen the other one's property.

9 "In every case of a dispute about property, whether it involves cattle, donkeys, sheep, clothing, or any other lost object, the two people claiming the property shall be taken to the place of worship. The one whom God declares to be guilty shall pay double to the other one.

10 "If anyone agrees to keep someone else's donkey, cow, sheep, or other animal for him, and the animal dies or is injured or is carried off in a raid, and if there was no witness, 11 the man must go to the place of worship and take an oath that he has not stolen the other man's animal. If the animal was not stolen, the owner shall accept the loss, and the other man need not repay him; 12 but if the animal was stolen, the man must repay the owner. 13 If it was killed by wild animals, the man is to bring the remains as evidence; he need not pay for what has been killed by wild animals.

14 "If anyone borrows an animal from someone else and it is injured or dies when its owner is not present, he must pay for it. 15 But if that happens when the owner is present, he need not repay. If it is a rented animal, the loss is covered by the rental price.

Moral and Religious Laws

16 "If a man seduces a virgin who is not engaged, he must pay the bride price for her and marry her. 17 But if her father refuses to let him marry her, he must pay the father a sum of money equal to the bride price for a virgin.

18 "Put to death any woman who practices magic.

19 "Put to death any man who has sexual relations with an animal.

20 "Condemn to death anyone who offers sacrifices to any god except to me, the LORD.

21 "Do not mistreat or oppress a foreigner; remember that you were foreigners in Egypt. 22 Do not mistreat any widow or orphan. 23 If you do, I, the LORD, will answer them when they cry out to me for help, 24 and I will become angry and kill you in war. Your wives will become widows, and your children will be fatherless.

25 "If you lend money to any of my people who are poor, do not act like a moneylender and require him to pay interest. 26 If you take someone's cloak as a pledge that he will pay you, you must give it back to him before the sun sets, 27 because it is the only covering he has to keep him warm. What else can he sleep in? When he cries out to me for help, I will answer him because I am merciful.

28 "Do not speak evil of God,w and do not curse a leader of your people.

29 "Give me the offerings from your grain, your wine, and your olive oil when they are due.

"Give me your first-born sons. 30 Give me the first-born of your cattle and your sheep. Let the first-born male stay with its mother for seven days, and on the eighth day offer it to me.

31 "You are my people, so you must not eat the meat of any animal that has been killed by wild animals; instead, give it to the dogs.

Justice and Fairness

23 "Do not spread false rumors, and do not help a guilty person by giving false testimony. 2 Do not follow the majority when they do wrong or when they give testimony that perverts justice. 3 Do not show partiality to a poor person at his trial.

4 "If you happen to see your enemy's cow or donkey running loose, take it back to him. 5 If his donkey has fallen under its load, help him get the donkey to its feet again; don't just walk off.

6 "Do not deny justice to a poor person when he appears in court. 7 Do not make false accusations, and do not put an innocent person to death, for I will condemn anyone who does such an evil thing. 8 Do not accept a bribe, for a bribe makes people blind to what is right and ruins the cause of those who are innocent.

9 "Do not mistreat a foreigner; you know how it feels to be a foreigner, because you were foreigners in Egypt.

The Seventh Year and the Seventh Day

10 "For six years plant your land and gather in what it produces. 11 But in the seventh year let it rest, and do not harvest anything that grows on it. The poor may eat what grows there, and the wild

w God; or the judges.

animals can have what is left. Do the same with your vineyards and your olive trees.

12 "Work six days a week, but do no work on the seventh day, so that your slaves and the foreigners who work for you and even your animals can rest.

13 "Listen to everything that I, the LORD, have said to you. Do not pray to other gods; do not even mention their names.

The Three Great Festivals
(Exodus 34.18-26; Deuteronomy 16.1-17)

14 "Celebrate three festivals a year to honor me. 15 In the month of Abib, the month in which you left Egypt, celebrate the Festival of Unleavened Bread in the way that I commanded you. Do not eat any bread made with yeast during the seven days of this festival. Never come to worship me without bringing an offering.

16 "Celebrate the Harvest Festival when you begin to harvest your crops.

"Celebrate the Festival of Shelters in the autumn, when you gather the fruit from your vineyards and orchards. 17 Every year at these three festivals all your men must come to worship me, the Lord your God.

18 "Do not offer bread made with yeast when you sacrifice an animal to me. The fat of animals sacrificed to me during these festivals is not to be left until the following morning.

19 "Each year bring to the house of the LORD your God the first grain that you harvest.

"Do not cook a young sheep or goat in its mother's milk.

Promises and Instructions

20 "I will send an angel ahead of you to protect you as you travel and to bring you to the place which I have prepared. 21 Pay attention to him and obey him. Do not rebel against him, for I have sent him, and he will not pardon such rebellion. 22 But if you obey him and do everything I command, I will fight against all your enemies. 23 My angel will go ahead of you and take you into the land of the Amorites, the Hittites, the Perizzites, the Canaanites, the Hivites, and the Jebusites, and I will destroy them. 24 Do not bow down to their gods or worship them, and

do not adopt their religious practices. Destroy their gods and break down their sacred stone pillars. 25 If you worship me, the LORD your God, I will bless you with food and water and take away all your sicknesses. 26 In your land no woman will have a miscarriage or be without children. I will give you long lives.

27 "I will make the people who oppose you afraid of me; I will bring confusion among the people against whom you fight, and I will make all your enemies turn and run from you. 28 I will throw your enemies into panic;*x* I will drive out the Hivites, the Canaanites, and the Hittites as you advance. 29 I will not drive them out within a year's time; if I did, the land would become deserted, and the wild animals would be too many for you. 30 Instead, I will drive them out little by little, until there are enough of you to take possession of the land. 31 I will make the borders of your land extend from the Gulf of Aqaba to the Mediterranean Sea and from the desert to the Euphrates River. I will give you power over the inhabitants of the land, and you will drive them out as you advance. 32 Do not make any agreement with them or with their gods. 33 Do not let those people live in your country; if you do, they will make you sin against me. If you worship their gods, it will be a fatal trap for you."

The Covenant Is Sealed

24 The LORD said to Moses, "Come up the mountain to me, you and Aaron, Nadab, Abihu, and seventy of the leaders of Israel; and while you are still some distance away, bow down in worship. 2 You alone, and none of the others, are to come near me. The people are not even to come up the mountain."

3 Moses went and told the people all the LORD's commands and all the ordinances, and all the people answered together, "We will do everything that the LORD has said." 4 Moses wrote down all the LORD's commands. Early the next morning he built an altar at the foot of the mountain and set up twelve stones, one for each of the twelve tribes of Israel. 5 Then he sent young men, and they burned sacrifices to the LORD and sacrificed some cattle as fellowship offerings. 6 Moses took half of the blood of the animals and put it in

---

x I will . . . panic; *or* I will send hornets among your enemies.

E
X
O
D
U
S

bowls; and the other half he threw against the altar. 7Then he took the book of the covenant, in which the Lord's commands were written, and read it aloud to the people. They said, "We will obey the Lord and do everything that he has commanded."

8Then Moses took the blood in the bowls and threw it on the people. He said, "This is the blood that seals the covenant which the Lord made with you when he gave all these commands."

9Moses, Aaron, Nadab, Abihu, and seventy of the leaders of Israel went up the mountain 10and they saw the God of Israel. Beneath his feet was what looked like a pavement of sapphire, as blue as the sky. 11God did not harm these leading men of Israel; they saw God, and then they ate and drank together.

Moses on Mount Sinai

12The Lord said to Moses, "Come up the mountain to me, and while you are here, I will give you two stone tablets which contain all the laws that I have written for the instruction of the people." 13Moses and his helper Joshua got ready, and Moses beganʸ to go up the holy mountain. 14Moses said to the leaders, "Wait here in the camp for us until we come back. Aaron and Hur are here with you; and so whoever has a dispute to settle can go to them."

15Moses went up Mount Sinai, and a cloud covered it. 16-17The dazzling light of the Lord's presence came down on the mountain. To the Israelites the light looked like a fire burning on top of the mountain. The cloud covered the mountain for six days, and on the seventh day the Lord called to Moses from the cloud. 18Moses went on up the mountain into the cloud. There he stayed for forty days and nights.

Offerings for the Sacred Tent
(Exodus 35.4-9)

25 The Lord said to Moses, 2"Tell the Israelites to make an offering to me. Receive whatever offerings anyone wishes to give. 3These offerings are to be: gold, silver, and bronze; 4fine linen; blue, purple, and red wool; cloth

made of goats' hair; 5rams' skin dyed red; fine leather; acacia wood; 6oil for the lamps; spices for the anointing oil and for the sweet-smelling incense; 7carnelians and other jewels to be set in the ephodᶻ of the High Priest and in his breastpiece. 8The people must make a sacred Tent for me, so that I may live among them. 9Make it and all its furnishings according to the plan that I will show you.

The Covenant Box
(Exodus 37.1-9)

10"Make a Box out of acacia wood, 45 inches long, 27 inches wide, and 27 inches high. 11Cover it with pure gold inside and out and put a gold border all around it. 12Make four carrying rings of gold for it and attach them to its four legs, with two rings on each side. 13Make carrying poles of acacia wood and cover them with gold 14and put them through the rings on each side of the Box. 15The poles are to be left in the rings and must not be taken out. 16Then put in the Box the two stone tablets that I will give you, on which the commandments are written.

17"Make a lid of pure gold, 45 inches long and 27 inches wide. 18Make two winged creaturesᵃ of hammered gold, 19one for each end of the lid. Make them so that they form one piece with the lid. 20The winged creatures are to face each other across the lid, and their outspread wings are to cover it. 21Put the two stone tablets inside the Box and put the lid on top of it. 22I will meet you there, and from above the lid between the two winged creatures I will give you all my laws for the people of Israel.

The Table for the Bread Offered to God
(Exodus 37.10-16)

23"Make a table out of acacia wood, 36 inches long, 18 inches wide, and 27 inches high. 24Cover it with pure gold and put a gold border around it. 25Make a rim 3 inches wide around it and a gold border around the rim. 26Make four carrying rings of gold for it and put them at the four corners, where the legs are.

ʸ Moses began; *one ancient translation* they began.　　ᶻ EPHOD: *In most contexts the term ephod refers to a type of shoulder garment, in certain respects resembling a vest. It was made of costly and colorful cloth and to it was attached a kind of pouch containing the Urim and Thummim, two objects used in determining God's will.*　　ᵃ WINGED CREATURES: *See Word List.*

27 The rings to hold the poles for carrying the table are to be placed near the rim. 28 Make the poles of acacia wood and cover them with gold. 29 Make plates, cups, jars, and bowls to be used for the wine offerings. All of these are to be made of pure gold. 30 The table is to be placed in front of the Covenant Box, and on the table there is always to be the sacred bread offered to me.

The Lampstand
(Exodus 37.17-24)

31 "Make a lampstand of pure gold. Make its base and its shaft of hammered gold; its decorative flowers, including buds and petals, are to form one piece with it. 32 Six branches shall extend from its sides, three from each side. 33 Each of the six branches is to have three decorative flowers shaped like almond blossoms with buds and petals. 34 The shaft of the lampstand is to have four decorative flowers shaped like almond blossoms with buds and petals. 35 There is to be one bud below each of the three pairs of branches. 36 The buds, the branches, and the lampstand are to be a single piece of pure hammered gold. 37 Make seven lamps for the lampstand and set them up so that they shine toward the front. 38 Make its tongs and trays of pure gold. 39 Use seventy-five pounds of pure gold to make the lampstand and all this equipment. 40 Take care to make them according to the plan that I showed you on the mountain.

The Tent of the LORD's Presence[b]
(Exodus 36.8-38)

26 "Make the interior of the sacred Tent, the Tent of my presence, out of ten pieces of fine linen woven with blue, purple, and red wool. Embroider them with figures of winged creatures. 2 Make each piece the same size, 14 yards long and 2 yards wide. 3 Sew five of them together in one set, and do the same with the other five. 4 Make loops of blue cloth on the edge of the outside piece in each set. 5 Put fifty loops on the first piece of the first set and fifty loops matching them on the last piece of the second set. 6 Make fifty gold hooks with which to join the two sets into one piece.

7 "Make a cover for the Tent out of eleven pieces of cloth made of goats' hair. 8 Make them all the same size, 15 yards long and 2 yards wide. 9 Sew five of them together in one set, and the other six in another set. Fold the sixth piece double over the front of the Tent. 10 Put fifty loops on the edge of the last piece of one set, and fifty loops on the edge of the other set. 11 Make fifty bronze hooks and put them in the loops to join the two sets so as to form one cover. 12 Hang the extra half piece over the back of the Tent. 13 The extra half yard on each side of the length is to hang over the sides of the Tent to cover it.

14 "Make two more coverings, one of rams' skin dyed red and the other of fine leather, to serve as the outer cover.

15 "Make upright frames for the Tent out of acacia wood. 16 Each frame is to be 15 feet long and 27 inches wide, 17 with two matching projections, so that the frames can be joined together. All the frames are to have these projections. 18 Make twenty frames for the south side 19 and forty silver bases to go under them, two bases under each frame to hold its two projections. 20 Make twenty frames for the north side of the Tent 21 and forty silver bases, two under each frame. 22 For the back of the Tent on the west, make six frames, 23 and two frames for the corners. 24 These corner frames are to be joined at the bottom and connected all the way to the top. The two frames that form the two corners are to be made in this way. 25 So there will be eight frames with their sixteen silver bases, two under each frame.

26 "Make fifteen crossbars of acacia wood, five for the frames on one side of the Tent, 27 five for the frames on the other side, and five for the frames on the west end, at the back. 28 The middle crossbar, set halfway up the frames, is to extend from one end of the Tent to the other. 29 Cover the frames with gold and fit them with gold rings to hold the crossbars, which are also to be covered with gold. 30 Set up the Tent according to the plan that I showed you on the mountain.

31 "Make a curtain of fine linen woven with blue, purple, and red wool. Embroider it with figures of winged creatures. 32 Hang it on four posts of acacia wood covered with gold, fitted with hooks, and

---

b TENT OF THE LORD'S PRESENCE: *See Word List.*

set in four silver bases. 33 Place the curtain under the row of hooks in the roof of the Tent, and put behind the curtain the Covenant Box containing the two stone tablets. The curtain will separate the Holy Place from the Most Holy Place. 34 Put the lid on the Covenant Box. 35 Outside the Most Holy Place put the table against the north side of the Tent and the lampstand against the south side.

36 "For the entrance of the Tent make a curtain of fine linen woven with blue, purple, and red wool and decorated with embroidery. 37 For this curtain make five posts of acacia wood covered with gold and fitted with gold hooks; make five bronze bases for these posts.

The Altar
(Exodus 38.1-7)

27 "Make an altar out of acacia wood. It is to be square, 7½ feet long and 7½ feet wide, and it is to be 4½ feet high. 2 Make projections at the top of the four corners. They are to form one piece with the altar, and the whole is to be covered with bronze. 3 Make pans for the greasy ashes, and make shovels, bowls, hooks, and fire pans. All this equipment is to be made of bronze. 4 Make a bronze grating and put four bronze carrying rings on its corners. 5 Put the grating under the rim of the altar, so that it reaches halfway up the altar. 6 Make carrying poles of acacia wood, cover them with bronze, 7 and put them in the rings on each side of the altar when it is carried. 8 Make the altar out of boards and leave it hollow, according to the plan that I showed you on the mountain.

The Enclosure for the Tent of the LORD's Presence
(Exodus 38.9-20)

9 "For the Tent of my presence make an enclosure out of fine linen curtains. On the south side the curtains are to be 50 yards long, 10 supported by twenty bronze posts in twenty bronze bases, with hooks and rods made of silver. 11 Do the same on the north side of the enclosure. 12 On the west side there are to be curtains 25 yards long, with ten posts and ten bases. 13 On the east side, where the entrance is, the enclosure is also to be 25 yards wide. 14-15 On each side of the entrance there are to be 7½ yards of curtains, with three posts and three bases. 16 For the entrance itself there is to be a curtain 10 yards long made of fine linen woven with blue, purple, and red wool, and decorated with embroidery. It is to be supported by four posts in four bases. 17 All the posts around the enclosure are to be connected with silver rods, and their hooks are to be made of silver and their bases of bronze. 18 The enclosure is to be 50 yards long, 25 yards wide, and 2½ yards high. The curtains are to be made of fine linen and the bases of bronze. 19 All the equipment that is used in the Tent and all the pegs for the Tent and for the enclosure are to be made of bronze.

Taking Care of the Lamp
(Leviticus 24.1-4)

20 "Command the people of Israel to bring you the best olive oil for the lamp, so that it can be lit each evening. 21 Aaron and his sons are to set up the lamp in the Tent of my presence outside the curtain which is in front of the Covenant Box. There in my presence it is to burn from evening until morning. This command is to be kept forever by the Israelites and their descendants.

Garments for the Priests
(Exodus 39.1-7)

28 "Summon your brother Aaron and his sons, Nadab, Abihu, Eleazar, and Ithamar. Separate them from the people of Israel, so that they may serve me as priests. 2 Make priestly garments for your brother Aaron, to provide him with dignity and beauty. 3 Call all the skilled workers to whom I have given ability, and tell them to make Aaron's clothes, so that he may be dedicated as a priest in my service. 4 Tell them to make a breastpiece, an ephod, a robe, an embroidered shirt, a turban, and a sash. They are to make these priestly garments for your brother Aaron and his sons, so that they can serve me as priests. 5 The skilled workers are to use blue, purple, and red wool, gold thread, and fine linen.

6 "They are to make the ephod of blue, purple, and red wool, gold thread, and fine linen, decorated with embroidery. 7 Two shoulder straps, by which it can be fastened, are to be attached to the sides. 8 A finely woven belt made of the same

materials is to be attached to the ephod so as to form one piece with it. ⁹Take two carnelian stones and engrave on them the names of the twelve sons of Jacob, ¹⁰in the order of their birth, with six on one stone and six on the other. ¹¹Have a skillful jeweler engrave on the two stones the names of the sons of Jacob, and mount the stones in gold settings. ¹²Put them on the shoulder straps of the ephod to represent the twelve tribes of Israel. In this way Aaron will carry their names on his shoulders, so that I, the LORD, will always remember my people. ¹³Make two gold settings ¹⁴and two chains of pure gold twisted like cords, and attach them to the settings.

The Breastpiece
(Exodus 39.8-21)

¹⁵"Make a breastpiece for the High Priest to use in determining God's will. It is to be made of the same materials as the ephod and with similar embroidery. ¹⁶It is to be square and folded double, 9 inches long and 9 inches wide. ¹⁷Mount four rows of precious stones on it; in the first row mount a ruby, a topaz, and a garnet; ¹⁸in the second row, an emerald, a sapphire, and a diamond; ¹⁹in the third row, a turquoise, an agate, and an amethyst; ²⁰and in the fourth row, a beryl, a carnelian, and a jasper. These are to be mounted in gold settings. ²¹Each of these twelve stones is to have engraved on it the name of one of the sons of Jacob, to represent the tribes of Israel. ²²For the breastpiece make chains of pure gold, twisted like cords. ²³Make two gold rings and attach them to the upper corners of the breastpiece, ²⁴and fasten the two gold cords to the two rings. ²⁵Fasten the other two ends of the cords to the two settings, and in this way attach them in front to the shoulder straps of the ephod. ²⁶Then make two rings of gold and attach them to the lower corners of the breastpiece on the inside edge next to the ephod. ²⁷Make two more gold rings and attach them to the lower part of the front of the two shoulder straps of the ephod, near the seam and above the finely woven belt. ²⁸Tie the rings of the breastpiece to the rings of the ephod with a blue cord, so that the breastpiece rests above the belt and does not come loose.

²⁹"When Aaron enters the Holy Place, he will wear this breastpiece engraved with the names of the tribes of Israel, so that I, the LORD, will always remember my people. ³⁰Put the Urim and Thummim[c] in the breastpiece, so that Aaron will carry them when he comes into my holy presence. At such times he must always wear this breastpiece, so that he can determine my will for the people of Israel.

The Other Priestly Garments
(Exodus 39.22-31)

³¹"The robe that goes under the ephod is to be made entirely of blue wool. ³²It is to have a hole for the head, and this hole is to be reinforced with a woven binding to keep it from tearing. ³³-³⁴All around its lower hem put pomegranates of blue, purple, and red wool, alternating with gold bells. ³⁵Aaron is to wear this robe when he serves as priest. When he comes into my presence in the Holy Place or when he leaves it, the sound of the bells will be heard, and he will not be killed.

³⁶"Make an ornament of pure gold and engrave on it 'Dedicated to the LORD.' ³⁷Tie it to the front of the turban with a blue cord. ³⁸Aaron is to wear it on his forehead, so that I, the LORD, will accept all the offerings that the Israelites dedicate to me, even if the people commit some error in offering them.

³⁹"Weave Aaron's shirt of fine linen and make a turban of fine linen and also a sash decorated with embroidery.

⁴⁰"Make shirts, sashes, and caps for Aaron's sons, to provide them with dignity and beauty. ⁴¹Put these clothes on your brother Aaron and his sons. Then ordain them and dedicate them by anointing them with olive oil, so that they may serve me as priests. ⁴²Make linen shorts for them, reaching from the waist to the thighs, so that they will not expose themselves. ⁴³Aaron and his sons must always wear them when they go into the Tent of my presence or approach the altar to serve as priests in the Holy Place, so that they will not be killed for exposing themselves. This is a permanent rule for Aaron and his descendants.

ᶜ URIM AND THUMMIM: *Two objects used by the priest to determine God's will; it is not known precisely how they were used.*

Instructions for Ordaining Aaron
and His Sons as Priests

(Leviticus 8.1-36)

29 "This is what you are to do to Aaron and his sons to dedicate them as priests in my service. Take one young bull and two rams without any defects. 2 Use the best wheat flour, but no yeast, and make some bread with olive oil, some without it, and some in the form of thin cakes brushed with oil. 3 Put them in a basket and offer them to me when you sacrifice the bull and the two rams.

4 "Bring Aaron and his sons to the entrance of the Tent of my presence, and have them take a ritual bath. 5 Then dress Aaron in the priestly garments — the shirt, the robe that goes under the ephod, the ephod, the breastpiece, and the belt. 6 Put the turban on him and tie on it the sacred sign of dedication engraved 'Dedicated to the LORD.' 7 Then take the anointing oil, pour it on his head, and anoint him.

8 "Bring his sons and put shirts on them; 9 put sashes around their waists and tie caps on their heads. That is how you are to ordain Aaron and his sons. They and their descendants are to serve me as priests forever.

10 "Bring the bull to the front of the Tent of my presence and tell Aaron and his sons to put their hands on its head. 11 Kill the bull there in my holy presence at the entrance of the Tent. 12 Take some of the bull's blood and with your finger put it on the projections of the altar. Then pour out the rest of the blood at the base of the altar. 13 Next, take all the fat which covers the internal organs, the best part of the liver, and the two kidneys with the fat on them, and burn them on the altar as an offering to me. 14 But burn the bull's flesh, its skin, and its intestines outside the camp. This is an offering to take away the sins of the priests.

15 "Take one of the rams and tell Aaron and his sons to put their hands on its head. 16 Kill it, and take its blood and throw it against all four sides of the altar. 17 Cut the ram in pieces; wash its internal organs and its hind legs, and put them on top of the head and the other pieces. 18 Burn the whole ram on the altar as a food offering. The odor of this offering pleases me.

19 "Take the other ram — the ram used for dedication — and tell Aaron and his sons to put their hands on its head. 20 Kill it, and take some of its blood and put it on the lobes of the right ears of Aaron and his sons, on the thumbs of their right hands and on the big toes of their right feet. Throw the rest of the blood against all four sides of the altar. 21 Take some of the blood that is on the altar and some of the anointing oil, and sprinkle it on Aaron and his clothes and on his sons and their clothes. He, his sons, and their clothes will then be dedicated to me.

22 "Cut away the ram's fat, the fat tail, the fat covering the internal organs, the best part of the liver, the two kidneys with the fat on them, and the right thigh. 23 From the basket of bread which has been offered to me, take one loaf of each kind: one loaf made with olive oil and one made without it and one thin cake. 24 Put all this food in the hands of Aaron and his sons and have them dedicate it to me as a special gift. 25 Then take it from them and burn it on the altar, on top of the burnt offering, as a food offering to me. The odor of this offering pleases me.

26 "Take the breast of this ram and dedicate it to me as a special gift. This part of the animal will be yours.

27 "When a priest is ordained, the breast and the thigh of the ram being used for the ordination are to be dedicated to me as a special gift and set aside for the priests. 28 It is my unchanging decision that when my people make their fellowship offerings, the breast and the thigh of the animal belong to the priests. This is the people's gift to me, the LORD.

29 "Aaron's priestly garments are to be handed on to his sons after his death, for them to wear when they are ordained. 30 The son of Aaron who succeeds him as priest and who goes into the Tent of my presence to serve in the Holy Place is to wear these garments for seven days.

31 "Take the meat of the ram used for the ordination of Aaron and his sons and boil it in a holy place. 32 At the entrance of the Tent of my presence they are to eat it along with the bread left in the basket. 33 They shall eat what was used in the ritual of forgiveness at their ordination. Only priests may eat this food, because it is sacred. 34 If some of the meat or some of the bread is not eaten by morning, it is to be burned; it is not to be eaten, for it is sacred.

35 "Perform the rites of ordination for Aaron and his sons for seven days exactly as I have commanded you. 36 Each day you must offer a bull as a sacrifice, so that sin may be forgiven. This will purify the altar. Then anoint it with olive oil to make it holy. 37 Do this every day for seven days. Then the altar will be completely holy, and anyone or anything that touches it will be harmed by the power of its holiness.d

The Daily Offerings
(Numbers 28.1-8)

38 "Every day for all time to come, sacrifice on the altar two one-year-old lambs. 39 Sacrifice one of the lambs in the morning and the other in the evening. 40 With the first lamb offer two pounds of fine wheat flour mixed with one quart of pure olive oil. Pour out one quart of wine as an offering. 41 Sacrifice the second lamb in the evening, and offer with it the same amounts of flour, olive oil, and wine as in the morning. This is a food offering to me, the LORD, and its odor pleases me. 42 For all time to come, this burnt offering is to be offered in my presence at the entrance of the Tent of my presence. That is where I will meet my people and speak to you. 43 There I will meet the people of Israel, and the dazzling light of my presence will make the place holy. 44 I will make the Tent and the altar holy, and I will set Aaron and his sons apart to serve me as priests. 45 I will live among the people of Israel, and I will be their God. 46 They will know that I am the LORD their God who brought them out of Egypt so that I could live among them. I am the LORD their God.

The Altar for Burning Incense
(Exodus 37.25-28)

30 "Make an altar out of acacia wood, for burning incense. 2 It is to be square, 18 inches long and 18 inches wide, and it is to be 36 inches high. Its projections at the four corners are to form one piece with it. 3 Cover its top, all four sides, and its projections with pure gold, and put a gold border around it. 4 Make two gold carrying rings for it and attach them below the border on two

sides to hold the poles with which it is to be carried. 5 Make these poles of acacia wood and cover them with gold. 6 Put this altar outside the curtain which hangs in front of the Covenant Box. That is the place where I will meet you. 7 Every morning when Aaron comes to take care of the lamps, he is to burn sweet-smelling incense on it. 8 He must do the same when he lights the lamps in the evening. This offering of incense is to continue without interruption for all time to come. 9 Do not offer on this altar any forbidden incense, any animal offering, or any grain offering, and do not pour out any wine offering on it. 10 Once a year Aaron is to perform the ritual for purifying the altar by putting on its four projections the blood of the animal sacrificed for sin. This is to be done every year for all time to come. This altar is to be completely holy, dedicated to me, the LORD."

The Tax for the Tent of the LORD's Presence

11 The LORD said to Moses, 12 "When you take a census of the people of Israel, each man is to pay me a price for his life, so that no disaster will come on him while the census is being taken. 13 Everyone included in the census must pay the required amount of money, weighed according to the official standard. Everyone must pay this as an offering to me. 14 Everyone being counted in the census, that is, every man twenty years old or older, is to pay me this amount. 15 The rich man is not to pay more, nor the poor man less, when they pay this amount for their lives. 16 Collect this money from the people of Israel and spend it for the upkeep of the Tent of my presence. This tax will be the payment for their lives, and I will remember to protect them."

The Bronze Basin

17 The LORD said to Moses, 18 "Make a bronze basin with a bronze base. Place it between the Tent and the altar, and put water in it. 19 Aaron and his sons are to use the water to wash their hands and feet 20 before they go into the Tent or approach the altar to offer the food

d BE HARMED BY THE POWER OF ITS HOLINESS: *It was believed that ordinary people or things would be harmed by touching something holy.*

EXODUS

offering. Then they will not be killed.
21 They must wash their hands and feet,
so that they will not die. This is a rule
which they and their descendants are to
observe forever."

The Anointing Oil

22 The LORD said to Moses, 23 "Take the
finest spices — 12 pounds of liquid myrrh,
6 pounds of sweet-smelling cinnamon, 6
pounds of sweet-smelling cane, 24 and 12
pounds of cassia (all weighed according
to the official standard). Add one gallon
of olive oil, 25 and make a sacred anointing oil, mixed like perfume. 26 Use it to
anoint the Tent of my presence, the Covenant Box, 27 the table and all its equipment, the lampstand and its equipment,
the altar for burning incense, 28 the altar
for burning offerings, together with all
its equipment, and the washbasin with
its base. 29 Dedicate these things in this
way, and they will be completely holy,
and anyone or anything that touches
them will be harmed by the power of its
holiness.e 30 Then anoint Aaron and his
sons, and ordain them as priests in my
service. 31 Say to the people of Israel,
'This holy anointing oil is to be used in
my service for all time to come. 32 It must
not be poured on ordinary men, and you
must not use the same formula to make
any mixture like it. It is holy, and you
must treat it as holy. 33 Whoever makes
any like it or uses any of it on anyone
who is not a priest will no longer be considered one of my people.' "

The Incense

34 The LORD said to Moses, "Take an
equal part of each of the following sweet
spices — stacte, onycha, galbanum, and
pure frankincense. 35 Use them to make
incense, mixed like perfume. Add salt to
keep it pure and holy. 36 Beat part of it
into a fine powder, take it into the Tent
of my presence, and sprinkle it in front of
the Covenant Box. Treat this incense as
completely holy. 37 Do not use the same
formula to make any incense like it for
yourselves. Treat it as a holy thing dedicated to me. 38 If anyone makes any like
it for use as perfume, he will no longer be
considered one of my people."

Craftsmen for the Tent of the LORD's Presence

(Exodus 35.30 – 36.1)

31 The LORD said to Moses, 2 "I have
chosen Bezalel, the son of Uri
and grandson of Hur, from the tribe of
Judah, 3 and I have filled him with my
power.f I have given him understanding, skill, and ability for every kind
of artistic work — 4 for planning skillful
designs and working them in gold, silver,
and bronze; 5 for cutting jewels to be set;
for carving wood; and for every other
kind of artistic work. 6 I have also selected Oholiab son of Ahisamach, from
the tribe of Dan, to work with him. I have
also given great ability to all the other
skilled workers, so that they can make
everything I have commanded to be
made: 7 the Tent of my presence, the Covenant Box and its lid, all the furnishings
of the Tent, 8 the table and its equipment,
the lampstand of pure gold and all its
equipment, the altar for burning incense,
9 the altar for burnt offerings and all its
equipment, the washbasin and its base,
10 the magnificent priestly garments for
Aaron and his sons to use when they
serve as priests, 11 the anointing oil, and
the sweet-smelling incense for the Holy
Place. In making all these things, they
are to do exactly as I have commanded you."

Sabbath, the Day of Rest

12 The LORD commanded Moses 13 to tell
the people of Israel, "Keep the Sabbath,
my day of rest, because it is a sign between you and me for all time to come, to
show that I, the LORD, have made you my
own people. 14 You must keep the day of
rest, because it is sacred. Whoever does
not keep it, but works on that day, is to
be put to death. 15 You have six days in
which to do your work, but the seventh
day is a solemn day of rest dedicated to
me. Whoever does any work on that day
is to be put to death. 16 The people of Israel are to keep this day as a sign of the
covenant. 17 It is a permanent sign between the people of Israel and me, because I, the LORD, made heaven and earth
in six days, and on the seventh day I
stopped working and rested."

18 When God had finished speaking to
Moses on Mount Sinai, he gave him the

---

e HARMED BY THE POWER OF ITS HOLINESS: *See 29.37.*   f *power;* or *spirit.*

two stone tablets on which God himself had written the commandments.

The Gold Bull-Calf

(Deuteronomy 9.6-29)

32 When the people saw that Moses had not come down from the mountain but was staying there a long time, they gathered around Aaron and said to him, "We do not know what has happened to this man Moses, who led us out of Egypt; so make us a god^g to lead us."

2 Aaron said to them, "Take off the gold earrings which your wives, your sons, and your daughters are wearing, and bring them to me." 3 So all the people took off their gold earrings and brought them to Aaron. 4 He took the earrings, melted them, poured the gold into a mold, and made a gold bull-calf. The people said, "Israel, this is our god, who led us out of Egypt!"

5 Then Aaron built an altar in front of the gold bull-calf and announced, "Tomorrow there will be a festival to honor the LORD." 6 Early the next morning they brought some animals to burn as sacrifices and others to eat as fellowship offerings. The people sat down to a feast, which turned into an orgy of drinking and sex.

7 The LORD said to Moses, "Hurry and go back down, because your people, whom you led out of Egypt, have sinned and rejected me. 8 They have already left the way that I commanded them to follow; they have made a bull-calf out of melted gold and have worshiped it and offered sacrifices to it. They are saying that this is their god, who led them out of Egypt. 9 I know how stubborn these people are. 10 Now, don't try to stop me. I am angry with them, and I am going to destroy them. Then I will make you and your descendants into a great nation."

11 But Moses pleaded with the LORD his God and said, "LORD, why should you be so angry with your people, whom you rescued from Egypt with great might and power? 12 Why should the Egyptians be able to say that you led your people out of Egypt, planning to kill them in the mountains and destroy them completely? Stop being angry; change your mind and do not bring this disaster on

your people. 13 Remember your servants Abraham, Isaac, and Jacob. Remember the solemn promise you made to them to give them as many descendants as there are stars in the sky and to give their descendants all that land you promised would be their possession forever." 14 So the LORD changed his mind and did not bring on his people the disaster he had threatened.

15 Moses went back down the mountain, carrying the two stone tablets with the commandments written on both sides. 16 God himself had made the tablets and had engraved the commandments on them.

17 Joshua heard the people shouting and said to Moses, "I hear the sound of battle in the camp."

18 Moses said, "That doesn't sound like a shout of victory or a cry of defeat; it's the sound of singing."

19 When Moses came close enough to the camp to see the bull-calf and to see the people dancing, he became furious. There at the foot of the mountain, he threw down the tablets he was carrying and broke them. 20 He took the bull-calf which they had made, melted it, ground it into fine powder, and mixed it with water. Then he made the people of Israel drink it. 21 He said to Aaron, "What did these people do to you, that you have made them commit such a terrible sin?"

22 Aaron answered, "Don't be angry with me; you know how determined these people are to do evil. 23 They said to me, 'We don't know what has happened to this man Moses, who brought us out of Egypt; so make us a god to lead us.' 24 I asked them to bring me their gold ornaments, and those who had any took them off and gave them to me. I threw the ornaments into the fire and out came this bull-calf!"

25 Moses saw that Aaron had let the people get out of control and make fools of themselves in front of their enemies. 26 So he stood at the gate of the camp and shouted, "Everyone who is on the LORD's side come over here!" So all the Levites gathered around him, 27 and he said to them, "The LORD God of Israel commands every one of you to put on your sword and go through the camp from this gate to the other and kill your brothers, your

^g a god; *or* some gods.

friends, and your neighbors." 28 The Levites obeyed, and killed about three thousand men that day. 29 Moses said to the Levites, "Today you have consecrated yourselves[h] as priests in the service of the LORD by killing your sons and brothers, so the LORD has given you his blessing."

30 The next day Moses said to the people, "You have committed a terrible sin. But now I will again go up the mountain to the LORD; perhaps I can obtain forgiveness for your sin." 31 Moses then returned to the LORD and said, "These people have committed a terrible sin. They have made a god out of gold and worshiped it. 32 Please forgive their sin; but if you won't, then remove my name from the book in which you have written the names of your people."

33 The LORD answered, "It is those who have sinned against me whose names I will remove from my book. 34 Now go, lead the people to the place I told you about. Remember that my angel will guide you, but the time is coming when I will punish these people for their sin."

35 So the LORD sent a disease on the people, because they had caused Aaron to make the gold bull-calf.

The LORD Orders Israel to Leave Mount Sinai

33 The LORD said to Moses, "Leave this place, you and the people you brought out of Egypt, and go to the land that I promised to give to Abraham, Isaac, and Jacob and to their descendants. 2 I will send an angel to guide you, and I will drive out the Canaanites, the Amorites, the Hittites, the Perizzites, the Hivites, and the Jebusites. 3 You are going to a rich and fertile land. But I will not go with you myself, because you are a stubborn people, and I might destroy you on the way."

4 When the people heard this, they began to mourn and did not wear jewelry any more. 5 For the LORD had commanded Moses to tell them, "You are a stubborn people. If I were to go with you even for a moment, I would completely destroy you. Now take off your jewelry, and I will decide what to do with you." 6 So after

they left Mount Sinai, the people of Israel no longer wore jewelry.

The Tent of the LORD's Presence

7 Whenever the people of Israel set up camp, Moses would take the sacred Tent and put it up some distance outside the camp. It was called the Tent of the LORD's presence, and anyone who wanted to consult the LORD would go out to it. 8 Whenever Moses went out there, the people would stand at the door of their tents and watch Moses until he entered it. 9 After Moses had gone in, the pillar of cloud would come down and stay at the door of the Tent, and the LORD would speak to Moses from the cloud. 10 As soon as the people saw the pillar of cloud at the door of the Tent, they would bow down. 11 The LORD would speak with Moses face-to-face, just as someone speaks with a friend. Then Moses would return to the camp. But the young man who was his helper, Joshua son of Nun, stayed in the Tent.

The LORD Promises to Be with His People

12 Moses said to the LORD, "It is true that you have told me to lead these people to that land, but you did not tell me whom you would send with me. You have said that you know me well and are pleased with me. 13 Now if you are, tell me your plans, so that I may serve you and continue to please you. Remember also that you have chosen this nation to be your own."

14 The LORD said, "I will go with you, and I will give you victory."

15 Moses replied, "If you do not go with us, don't make us leave this place. 16 How will anyone know that you are pleased with your people and with me if you do not go with us? Your presence with us will distinguish us from any other people on earth."

17 The LORD said to Moses, "I will do just as you have asked, because I know you very well and I am pleased with you."

18 Then Moses requested, "Please, let me see the dazzling light of your presence."

19 The LORD answered, "I will make all my splendor pass before you and in your

---

[h] *Some ancient translations* Today you have consecrated yourselves; *Hebrew* Consecrate yourselves today; *or* You have been consecrated today.

presence I will pronounce my sacred name. I am the LORD, and I show compassion and pity on those I choose. 20 I will not let you see my face, because no one can see me and stay alive, 21 but here is a place beside me where you can stand on a rock. 22 When the dazzling light of my presence passes by, I will put you in an opening in the rock and cover you with my hand until I have passed by. 23 Then I will take my hand away, and you will see my back but not my face."

The Second Set of Stone Tablets
(Deuteronomy 10.1-5)

34 The LORD said to Moses, "Cut two stone tablets like the first ones, and I will write on them the words that were on the first tablets, which you broke. 2 Get ready tomorrow morning, and come up Mount Sinai to meet me there at the top. 3 No one is to come up with you; no one is to be seen on any part of the mountain; and no sheep or cattle are to graze at the foot of the mountain." 4 So Moses cut two more stone tablets, and early the next morning he carried them up Mount Sinai, just as the LORD had commanded.

5 The LORD came down in a cloud, stood with him there, and pronounced his holy name, the LORD.[i] 6 The LORD then passed in front of him and called out, "I, the LORD, am a God who is full of compassion and pity, who is not easily angered and who shows great love and faithfulness. 7 I keep my promise for thousands of generations[j] and forgive evil and sin; but I will not fail to punish children and grandchildren to the third and fourth generation for the sins of their parents." 8 Moses quickly bowed down to the ground and worshiped. 9 He said, "Lord, if you really are pleased with me, I ask you to go with us. These people are stubborn, but forgive our evil and our sin, and accept us as your own people."

The Covenant Is Renewed
(Exodus 23.14-19; Deuteronomy 7.1-5; 16.1-17)

10 The LORD said to Moses, "I now make a covenant with the people of Israel. In their presence I will do great things such as have never been done anywhere on earth among any of the nations. All the people will see what great things I, the LORD, can do, because I am going to do an awesome thing for you. 11 Obey the laws that I am giving you today. I will drive out the Amorites, the Canaanites, the Hittites, the Perizzites, the Hivites, and the Jebusites, as you advance. 12 Do not make any treaties with the people of the country into which you are going, because this could be a fatal trap for you. 13 Instead, tear down their altars, destroy their sacred pillars, and cut down their symbols of the goddess Asherah.

14 "Do not worship any other god, because I, the LORD, tolerate no rivals. 15 Do not make any treaties with the people of the country, because when they worship their pagan gods and sacrifice to them, they will invite you to join them, and you will be tempted to eat the food they offer to their gods. 16 Your sons might marry those foreign women, who would lead them to be unfaithful to me and to worship their pagan gods.

17 "Do not make gods of metal and worship them.

18 "Keep the Festival of Unleavened Bread. As I have commanded you, eat unleavened bread for seven days in the month of Abib, because it was in that month that you left Egypt.

19 "Every first-born son and first-born male domestic animal belongs to me, 20 but you are to buy back every first-born donkey by offering a lamb in its place. If you do not buy it back, break its neck. Buy back every first-born son.

"No one is to appear before me without an offering.

21 "You have six days in which to do your work, but do not work on the seventh day, not even during plowing time or harvest.

22 "Keep the Harvest Festival when you begin to harvest the first crop of your wheat, and keep the Festival of Shelters in the autumn when you gather your fruit.

23 "Three times a year all of your men must come to worship me, the LORD, the God of Israel. 24 After I have driven out the nations before you and extended your territory, no one will try to conquer your country during the three festivals. 25 "Do not offer bread made with yeast

---

i THE LORD: *See 3.14, and Word List.*   *j* thousands of generations; *or thousands.*

E
X
O
D
U
S

EXODUS

when you sacrifice an animal to me. Do not keep until the following morning any part of the animal killed at the Passover Festival.

26 "Each year bring to the house of the Lord the first grain that you harvest.

"Do not cook a young sheep or goat in its mother's milk."

27 The Lord said to Moses, "Write these words down, because it is on the basis of these words that I am making a covenant with you and with Israel." 28 Moses stayed there with the Lord forty days and nights, eating and drinking nothing. He wrote on the tablets the words of the covenant — the Ten Commandments.

Moses Goes Down from Mount Sinai

29 When Moses went down from Mount Sinai carrying the Ten Commandments, his face was shining because he had been speaking with the Lord; but he did not know it. 30 Aaron and all the people looked at Moses and saw that his face was shining, and they were afraid to go near him. 31 But Moses called them, and Aaron and all the leaders of the community went to him, and Moses spoke with them. 32 After that, all the people of Israel gathered around him, and Moses gave them all the laws that the Lord had given him on Mount Sinai. 33 When Moses had finished speaking with them, he covered his face with a veil. 34 Whenever Moses went into the Tent of the Lord's presence to speak to the Lord, he would take the veil off. When he came out, he would tell the people of Israel everything that he had been commanded to say, 35 and they would see that his face was shining. Then he would put the veil back on until the next time he went to speak with the Lord.

Regulations for the Sabbath

35 Moses called together the whole community of the people of Israel and said to them, "This is what the Lord has commanded you to do: 2 You have six days in which to do your work, but the seventh day is to be sacred, a solemn day of rest dedicated to me, the Lord. Anyone who does any work on that day is to be put to death. 3 Do not even light a fire in your homes on the Sabbath."

Offerings for the Sacred Tent
(Exodus 25.1-9)

4 Moses said to all the people of Israel, "This is what the Lord has commanded: 5 Make an offering to the Lord. Everyone who wishes to do so is to bring an offering of gold, silver, or bronze; 6 fine linen; blue, purple, and red wool; cloth made of goats' hair; 7 rams' skin dyed red; fine leather; acacia wood; 8 oil for the lamps; spices for the anointing oil and for the sweet-smelling incense; 9 carnelians and other jewels to be set in the High Priest's ephod and in his breastpiece.

Articles for the Tent of the Lord's Presence
(Exodus 39.32-43)

10 "All the skilled workers among you are to come and make everything that the Lord commanded: 11 the Tent, its covering and its outer covering, its hooks and its frames, its crossbars, its posts, and its bases; 12 the Covenant Box, its poles, its lid, and the curtain to screen it off; 13 the table, its poles, and all its equipment; the bread offered to God; 14 the lampstand for the light and its equipment; the lamps with their oil; 15 the altar for burning incense and its poles; the anointing oil; the sweet-smelling incense; the curtain for the entrance of the Tent; 16 the altar on which to burn offerings, with its bronze grating attached, its poles, and all its equipment; the washbasin and its base; 17 the curtains for the enclosure, its posts and bases; the curtain for the entrance of the enclosure; 18 the Tent pegs and ropes for the Tent and the enclosure; 19 and the magnificent garments the priests are to wear when they serve in the Holy Place — the sacred clothes for Aaron the priest and for his sons."

The People Bring Their Offerings

20 All the people of Israel left, 21 and everyone who wished to do so brought an offering to the Lord for making the Tent of the Lord's presence. They brought everything needed for use in worship and for making the priestly garments. 22 All who wanted to, both men and women, brought decorative pins, earrings, rings, necklaces, and all kinds of gold jewelry and dedicated them to the Lord. 23 Everyone who had fine linen;

blue, purple, or red wool; cloth of goats' hair; rams' skin dyed red; or fine leather, brought it. 24 All who were able to contribute silver or bronze brought their offering for the LORD, and all who had acacia wood which could be used for any of the work brought it. 25 All the skilled women brought fine linen thread and thread of blue, purple, and red wool, which they had made. 26 They also made thread of goats' hair. 27 The leaders brought carnelians and other jewels to be set in the ephod and the breastpiece 28 and spices and oil for the lamps, for the anointing oil, and for the sweet-smelling incense. 29 All the people of Israel who wanted to brought their offering to the LORD for the work which he had commanded Moses to do.

Workers to Make the Tent of the LORD's Presence
(Exodus 31.1-11)

30 Moses said to the Israelites, "The LORD has chosen Bezalel, the son of Uri and grandson of Hur from the tribe of Judah. 31 God has filled him with his power[k] and given him skill, ability, and understanding for every kind of artistic work, 32 for planning skillful designs and working them in gold, silver, and bronze; 33 for cutting jewels to be set; for carving wood; and for every other kind of artistic work. 34 The LORD has given to him and to Oholiab son of Ahisamach, from the tribe of Dan, the ability to teach their crafts to others. 35 He has given them skill in all kinds of work done by engravers, designers, and weavers of fine linen; blue, purple, and red wool; and other cloth. They are able to do all kinds of work and are skillful designers.

36 "Bezalel, Oholiab, and all the other workers to whom the LORD has given skill and understanding, who know how to make everything needed to build the sacred Tent, are to make everything just as the LORD has commanded."

The People Bring Many Gifts

2 Moses called Bezalel, Oholiab, and all the other skilled men to whom the LORD had given ability and who were willing to help, and Moses told them to start working. 3 They received from him all the offerings which the Israelites had brought

for constructing the sacred Tent. But the people of Israel continued to bring Moses their offerings every morning. 4 Then the skilled men who were doing the work went 5 and told Moses, "The people are bringing more than is needed for the work which the LORD commanded to be done."

6 So Moses sent a command throughout the camp that no one was to make any further contribution for the sacred Tent; so the people did not bring any more. 7 What had already been brought was more than enough to finish all the work.

Making the Tent of the LORD's Presence
(Exodus 26.1-37)

8 The most skilled men among those doing the work made the Tent of the LORD's presence. They made it out of ten pieces of fine linen woven with blue, purple, and red wool and embroidered with figures of winged creatures. 9 Each piece was the same size, 14 yards long and 2 yards wide. 10 They sewed five of them together in one set and did the same with the other five. 11 They made loops of blue cloth on the edge of the outside piece in each set. 12 They put fifty loops on the first piece of the first set and fifty loops matching them on the last piece of the second set. 13 They made fifty gold hooks, with which to join the two sets into one piece.

14 Then they made a cover for the Tent out of eleven pieces of cloth made of goats' hair. 15 They made them all the same size, 15 yards long and 2 yards wide. 16 They sewed five of them together in one set and the other six in another set. 17 They put fifty loops on the edge of the last piece of one set and fifty loops on the edge of the other set. 18 They made fifty bronze hooks to join the two sets, so as to form one cover. 19 They made two more coverings, one of rams' skin dyed red and the other of fine leather, to serve as an outer cover.

20 They made upright frames of acacia wood for the Tent. 21 Each frame was 15 feet tall and 27 inches wide, 22 with two matching projections, so that the frames could be joined together. All the frames had these projections. 23 They made

k power; or spirit.

E
X
O
D
U
S

twenty frames for the south side [24] and forty silver bases to go under them, two bases under each frame to hold its two projections. [25] They made twenty frames for the north side of the Tent [26] and forty silver bases, two under each frame. [27] For the back of the Tent, on the west, they made six frames [28] and two frames for the corners. [29] These corner frames were joined at the bottom and connected all the way to the top. The two frames that formed the two corners were made in this way. [30] So there were eight frames and sixteen silver bases, two under each frame.

[31] They made fifteen crossbars of acacia wood, five for the frames on one side of the Tent, [32] five for the frames on the other side, and five for the frames on the west end, at the back. [33] The middle crossbar, set halfway up the frames, extended from one end of the Tent to the other. [34] They covered the frames with gold and fitted them with gold rings to hold the crossbars, which were also covered with gold.

[35] They made a curtain of fine linen, woven with blue, purple, and red wool and embroidered it with figures of winged creatures. [36] They made four posts of acacia wood to hold the curtain, covered them with gold, and fitted them with gold hooks. Then they made four silver bases to hold the posts. [37] For the entrance of the Tent they made a curtain of fine linen woven with blue, purple, and red wool and decorated with embroidery. [38] For this curtain they made five posts fitted with hooks, covered their tops and their rods with gold, and made five bronze bases for the posts.

Making the Covenant Box
(Exodus 25.10-22)

37 Bezalel made the Covenant Box out of acacia wood, 45 inches long, 27 inches wide, and 27 inches high. [2] He covered it with pure gold inside and out and put a gold border all around it. [3] He made four carrying rings of gold for it and attached them to its four feet, with two rings on each side. [4] He made carrying poles of acacia wood, covered them with gold, [5] and put them through the rings on each side of the Box. [6] He made a lid of pure gold, 45 inches long and 27 inches wide. [7] He made two winged creatures of hammered gold, [8] one for each

end of the lid. He made them so that they formed one piece with the lid. [9] The winged creatures faced each other across the lid, and their outspread wings covered it.

Making the Table for the Bread Offered to God
(Exodus 25.23-30)

[10] He made the table out of acacia wood, 36 inches long, 18 inches wide, and 27 inches high. [11] He covered it with pure gold and put a gold border around it. [12] He made a rim 3 inches wide around it and put a gold border around the rim. [13] He made four carrying rings of gold for it and put them at the four corners, where the legs were. [14] The rings to hold the poles for carrying the table were placed near the rim. [15] He made the poles of acacia wood and covered them with gold. [16] He made the dishes of pure gold for the table: the plates, the cups, the jars, and the bowls to be used for the wine offering.

Making the Lampstand
(Exodus 25.31-40)

[17] He made the lampstand of pure gold. He made its base and its shaft of hammered gold; its decorative flowers, including buds and petals, formed one piece with it. [18] Six branches extended from its sides, three from each side. [19] Each of the six branches had three decorative flowers shaped like almond blossoms with buds and petals. [20] The shaft of the lampstand had four decorative flowers shaped like almond blossoms with buds and petals. [21] There was one bud below each of the three pairs of branches. [22] The buds, the branches, and the lampstand were a single piece of pure hammered gold. [23] He made seven lamps for the lampstand, and he made its tongs and trays of pure gold. [24] He used seventy-five pounds of pure gold to make the lampstand and all its equipment.

Making the Altar for Burning Incense
(Exodus 30.1-5)

[25] He made an altar out of acacia wood, for burning incense. It was square, 18 inches long and 18 inches wide, and it was 36 inches high. Its projections at the four corners formed one piece with it.

26 He covered its top, all four sides, and its projections with pure gold and put a gold border around it. 27 He made two gold carrying rings for it and attached them below the border on the two sides, to hold the poles with which it was to be carried. 28 He made the poles of acacia wood and covered them with gold.

Making the Anointing Oil and the Incense
(Exodus 30.22-38)

29 He also made the sacred anointing oil and the pure sweet-smelling incense, mixed like perfume.

Making the Altar for Burning Offerings
(Exodus 27.1-8)

38 For burning offerings, he made an altar out of acacia wood. It was square, 7½ feet long and 7½ feet wide, and it was 4½ feet high. 2 He made the projections at the top of the four corners, so that they formed one piece with the altar. He covered it all with bronze. 3 He also made all the equipment for the altar: the pans, the shovels, the bowls, the hooks, and the fire pans. All this equipment was made of bronze. 4 He made a bronze grating and put it under the rim of the altar, so that it reached halfway up the altar. 5 He made four carrying rings and put them on the four corners. 6 He made carrying poles of acacia wood, covered them with bronze, 7 and put them in the rings on each side of the altar. The altar was made of boards and was hollow.

Making the Bronze Basin
(Exodus 30.18)

8 He made the bronze basin and its bronze base out of the mirrors belonging to the women who served at the entrance of the Tent of the LORD's presence.

The Enclosure for the Tent of the LORD's Presence
(Exodus 27.9-19)

9 For the Tent of the LORD's presence he made the enclosure out of fine linen curtains. On the south side the curtains were 50 yards long, 10 supported by twenty bronze posts in twenty bronze bases, with hooks and rods made of silver. 11 The enclosure was the same on the north side. 12 On the west side there were curtains 25 yards long, with ten posts and ten bases and with hooks and rods made of silver. 13 On the east side, where the entrance was, the enclosure was also 25 yards wide. 14-15 On each side of the entrance there were 7½ yards of curtains, with three posts and three bases. 16 All the curtains around the enclosure were made of fine linen. 17 The bases for the posts were made of bronze, and the hooks, the rods, and the covering of the tops of the posts were made of silver. All the posts around the enclosure were connected with silver rods. 18 The curtain for the entrance of the enclosure was made of fine linen woven with blue, purple, and red wool and decorated with embroidery. It was 10 yards long and 2½ yards high, like the curtains of the enclosure. 19 It was supported by four posts in four bronze bases. Their hooks, the covering of their tops, and their rods were made of silver. 20 All the pegs for the Tent and for the surrounding enclosure were made of bronze.

Metals Used in the Tent of the LORD's Presence

21 Here is a list of the amounts of the metals used in the Tent of the LORD's presence, where the two stone tablets were kept on which the Ten Commandments were written. The list was ordered by Moses and made by the Levites who worked under the direction of Ithamar son of Aaron the priest. 22 Bezalel, the son of Uri and grandson of Hur from the tribe of Judah, made everything that the LORD had commanded. 23 His helper, Oholiab son of Ahisamach, from the tribe of Dan, was an engraver, a designer, and a weaver of fine linen and of blue, purple, and red wool. 24 All the gold that had been dedicated to the LORD for the sacred Tent weighed 2,195 pounds, weighed according to the official standard. 25 The silver from the census of the community weighed 7,550 pounds, weighed according to the official standard. 26 This amount equaled the total paid by all persons enrolled in the census, each one paying the required amount, weighed according to the official standard. There were 603,550 men twenty years old or older enrolled in the

census. 27 Of the silver, 7,500 pounds were used to make the hundred bases for the sacred Tent and for the curtain, 75 pounds for each base. 28 With the remaining 50 pounds of silver Bezalel made the rods, the hooks for the posts, and the covering for their tops. 29 The bronze which was dedicated to the LORD amounted to 5,310 pounds. 30 With it he made the bases for the entrance of the Tent of the LORD's presence, the bronze altar with its bronze grating, all the equipment for the altar, 31 the bases for the surrounding enclosure and for the entrance of the enclosure, and all the pegs for the Tent and the surrounding enclosure.

Making the Garments for the Priests
(Exodus 28.1-14)

39 With the blue, purple, and red wool they made the magnificent garments which the priests were to wear when they served in the Holy Place. They made the priestly garments for Aaron, as the LORD had commanded Moses.

2 They made the ephod of fine linen; blue, purple, and red wool; and gold thread. 3 They hammered out sheets of gold and cut them into thin strips to be worked into the fine linen and into the blue, purple, and red wool. 4 They made two shoulder straps for the ephod and attached them to its sides, so that it could be fastened. 5 The finely woven belt, made of the same materials, was attached to the ephod so as to form one piece with it, as the LORD had commanded Moses. 6 They prepared the carnelians and mounted them in gold settings; they were skillfully engraved with the names of the twelve sons of Jacob. 7 They put them on the shoulder straps of the ephod to represent the twelve tribes of Israel, just as the LORD had commanded Moses.

Making the Breastpiece
(Exodus 28.15-30)

8 They made the breastpiece of the same materials as the ephod and with similar embroidery. 9 It was square and folded double, 9 inches long and 9 inches wide. 10 They mounted four rows of precious stones on it: in the first row they mounted a ruby, a topaz, and a garnet; 11 in the second row, an emerald, a sapphire, and a diamond; 12 in the third row,

a turquoise, an agate, and an amethyst; 13 and in the fourth row, a beryl, a carnelian, and a jasper. These were mounted in gold settings. 14 Each of the twelve stones had engraved on it the name of one of the sons of Jacob, in order to represent the twelve tribes of Israel. 15 For the breastpiece they made chains of pure gold, twisted like cords. 16 They made two gold settings and two gold rings and attached the two rings to the upper corners of the breastpiece. 17 They fastened the two gold cords to the two rings 18 and fastened the other two ends of the cords to the two settings and in this way attached them in front to the shoulder straps of the ephod. 19 They made two rings of gold and attached them to the lower corners of the breastpiece, on the inside edge next to the ephod. 20 They made two more gold rings and attached them to the lower part of the front of the two shoulder straps of the ephod, near the seam and above the finely woven belt. 21 Just as the LORD had commanded Moses, they tied the rings of the breastpiece to the rings of the ephod with a blue cord, so that the breastpiece rested above the belt and did not come loose.

Making the Other Priestly Garments
(Exodus 28.31-43)

22 The robe that goes under the ephod was made entirely of blue wool. 23 The hole for the head was reinforced with a woven binding to keep it from tearing. 24-26 All around its lower hem they put pomegranates of fine linen and of blue, purple, and red wool, alternating with bells of pure gold, just as the LORD had commanded Moses.

27 They made the shirts for Aaron and his sons, 28 and the turban, the caps, the linen shorts, 29 and the sash of fine linen and of blue, purple, and red wool, decorated with embroidery, as the LORD had commanded Moses. 30 They made the ornament, the sacred sign of dedication, out of pure gold, and they engraved on it "Dedicated to the LORD." 31 They tied it to the front of the turban with a blue cord, just as the LORD had commanded Moses.

The Completion of the Work
(Exodus 35.10-19)

32 All the work on the Tent of the LORD's presence was finally completed. The Is-

raelites made everything just as the LORD had commanded Moses. 33 They brought to Moses the Tent and all its equipment, its hooks, its frames, its crossbars, its posts, and its bases; 34 the covering of rams' skin dyed red; the covering of fine leather; the curtain; 35 the Covenant Box containing the stone tablets, its poles, and its lid; 36 the table and all its equipment, and the bread offered to God; 37 the lampstand of pure gold, its lamps, all its equipment, and the oil for the lamps; 38 the gold altar; the anointing oil; the sweet-smelling incense; the curtain for the entrance of the Tent; 39 the bronze altar with its bronze grating, its poles, and all its equipment; the washbasin and its base; 40 the curtains for the enclosure and its posts and bases; the curtain for the entrance of the enclosure and its ropes; the Tent pegs; all the equipment to be used in the Tent; 41 and the magnificent garments the priests were to wear in the Holy Place—the sacred clothes for Aaron the priest and for his sons. 42 The Israelites had done all the work just as the LORD had commanded Moses. 43 Moses examined everything and saw that they had made it all just as the LORD had commanded. So Moses blessed them.

Setting Up and Dedicating the Tent of the LORD's Presence

40 The LORD said to Moses, 2 "On the first day of the first month set up the Tent of the LORD's presence. 3 Place in it the Covenant Box containing the Ten Commandments and put the curtain in front of it. 4 Bring in the table and place the equipment on it. Also bring in the lampstand and set up the lamps on it. 5 Put the gold altar for burning incense in front of the Covenant Box and hang the curtain at the entrance of the Tent. 6 Put in front of the Tent the altar for burning offerings. 7 Put the washbasin between the Tent and the altar and fill it with water. 8 Put up the surrounding enclosure and hang the curtain at its entrance.

9 "Then dedicate the Tent and all its equipment by anointing it with the sacred oil, and it will be holy. 10 Next, dedicate the altar and all its equipment by anointing it, and it will be completely holy. 11 Also dedicate the washbasin and its base in the same way.

12 "Bring Aaron and his sons to the entrance of the Tent, and have them take a ritual bath. 13 Dress Aaron in the priestly garments, anoint him, and in this way consecrate him, so that he can serve me as priest. 14 Bring his sons and put the shirts on them. 15 Then anoint them, just as you anointed their father, so that they can serve me as priests. This anointing will make them priests for all time to come."

16 Moses did everything just as the LORD had commanded. 17 So on the first day of the first month of the second year after they left Egypt, the Tent of the LORD's presence was set up. 18 Moses put down its bases, set up its frames, attached its crossbars, and put up its posts. 19 He spread out the covering over the Tent and put the outer covering over it, just as the LORD had commanded. 20 Then he took the two stone tablets and put them in the Covenant Box. He put the poles in the rings of the Box and put the lid on it. 21 Then he put the Box in the Tent and hung up the curtain. In this way he screened off the Covenant Box, just as the LORD had commanded.

22 He put the table in the Tent, on the north side outside the curtain, 23 and placed on it the bread offered to the LORD, just as the LORD had commanded. 24 He put the lampstand in the Tent, on the south side, opposite the table, 25 and there in the LORD's presence he lit the lamps, just as the LORD had commanded. 26 He put the gold altar in the Tent, in front of the curtain, 27 and burned the sweet-smelling incense, just as the LORD had commanded. 28 He hung the curtain at the entrance of the Tent, 29 and there in front of the curtain he placed the altar for burning offerings. On it he sacrificed the burnt offering and the grain offering, just as the LORD had commanded. 30 He put the washbasin between the Tent and the altar and filled it with water. 31 Moses, Aaron, and his sons washed their hands and their feet there 32 whenever they went into the Tent or to the altar, just as the LORD had commanded. 33 Moses set up the enclosure around the Tent and the altar and hung the curtain at the entrance of the enclosure. So he finished all the work.

The Cloud over the Tent of the Lord's Presence

(Numbers 9.15-23)

34 Then the cloud covered the Tent and the dazzling light of the LORD's presence filled it. 35 Because of this, Moses could not go into the Tent. 36 The Israelites moved their camp to another place only when the cloud lifted from the Tent. 37 As long as the cloud stayed there, they did not move their camp. 38 During all their wanderings they could see the cloud of the LORD's presence over the Tent during the day and a fire burning above it during the night.

LEVITICUS

Introduction

Leviticus *contains regulations for worship and religious ceremonies in ancient Israel, and for the priests who were responsible for carrying out these instructions.*

The main theme of the book is the holiness of God and the ways in which his people were to worship and live so as to maintain their relationship with "the holy God of Israel."

The best known words from the book, found in 19.18, are those which Jesus called the second great commandment: "Love your neighbors as you love yourself."

Outline of Contents

Sacrifices Burned Whole

1 The LORD called to Moses from the Tent of the LORD's presence and gave him the following rules 2 for the Israelites to observe when they offer their sacrifices.

When you offer an animal sacrifice, it may be one of your cattle or one of your sheep or goats. 3 If you are offering one of your cattle as a burnt offering, you must bring a bull without any defects. You must present it at the entrance of the Tent of the LORD's presence so that the LORD will accept you. 4 You shall put your hand on its head, and it will be accepted as a sacrifice to take away your sins. 5 You shall kill the bull there, and the Aaronite priests shall present the blood to the LORD and then throw it against all four sides of the altar located at the entrance of the Tent. 6 Then you shall skin the animal and cut it up, 7 and the priests shall arrange firewood on the altar and light it. 8 They shall put on the fire the pieces of the animal, including the head and the fat. 9 You must wash the internal organs and the hind legs, and the officiating priest will burn the whole sacrifice on the altar. The odor of this food offering is pleasing to the LORD.

10 If you are offering one of your sheep or goats, it must be a male without any defects. 11 You shall kill it on the north side of the altar, and the priests shall throw its blood on all four sides of the altar. 12 After you cut it up, the officiating priest shall put on the fire all the parts, including the head and the fat. 13 You must wash the internal organs and the hind legs, and the priest will present the sacrifice to the LORD and burn all of it on the altar. The odor of this food offering is pleasing to the LORD.

14 If you are offering a bird as a burnt offering, it must be a dove or a pigeon. 15 The priest shall present it at the altar, wring its neck, and burn its head on the altar. Its blood shall be drained out against the side of the altar. 16 He shall remove the crop and its contents and throw them away on the east side of the altar where the ashes are put. 17 He shall take hold of its wings and tear its body open, without tearing the wings off, and then burn it whole on the altar. The odor of this food offering is pleasing to the LORD.

Grain Offerings

2 When any of you present an offering of grain to the LORD, you must first grind it into flour. You must put

olive oil and incense on it ²and bring it to the Aaronite priests. The officiating priest shall take a handful of the flour and oil and all of the incense and burn it on the altar as a token that it has all been offered to the Lord. The odor of this food offering is pleasing to the Lord. ³The rest of the grain offering belongs to the priests; it is very holy, since it is taken from the food offered to the Lord.

⁴If the offering is bread baked in an oven, it must be made without yeast. It may be thick loaves made of flour mixed with olive oil or thin cakes brushed with olive oil.

⁵If the offering is bread cooked on a griddle, it is to be made of flour mixed with olive oil but without yeast. ⁶Crumble it up and pour the oil on it when you present it as an offering.

⁷If the offering is bread cooked in a pan, it is to be made of flour and olive oil. ⁸Bring it as an offering to the Lord and present it to the priest, who will take it to the altar. ⁹The priest will take part of it as a token that it has all been offered to the Lord, and he will burn it on the altar. The odor of this food offering is pleasing to the Lord. ¹⁰The rest of the offering belongs to the priests; it is very holy, since it is taken from the food offered to the Lord.

¹¹None of the grain offerings which you present to the Lord may be made with yeast; you must never use yeast or honey in food offered to the Lord. ¹²An offering of the first grain that you harvest each year shall be brought to the Lord, but it is not to be burned on the altar. ¹³Put salt on every grain offering, because salt represents the covenant between you and God. (You must put salt on all your offerings.) ¹⁴When you bring to the Lord an offering of the first grain harvested, offer roasted grain or ground meal. ¹⁵Add olive oil and put incense on it. ¹⁶The priest will burn that part of the meal and oil that is to serve as a token, and also all the incense, as a food offering to the Lord.

Fellowship Offerings

3 When any of you offer one of your cattle as a fellowship offering, it is to be a bull or a cow without any defects.

²You shall put your hand on the head of the animal and kill it at the entrance of the Tent of the Lord's presence. The Aaronite priests shall throw the blood against all four sides of the altar ³and present the following parts of the animal as a food offering to the Lord: all the fat on the internal organs, ⁴the kidneys and the fat on them, and the best part of the liver. ⁵The priests shall burn all this on the altar along with the burnt offerings. The odor of this food offering is pleasing to the Lord.

⁶If a sheep or goat is used as a fellowship offering, it may be male or female, but it must be without any defects. ⁷If you offer a sheep, ⁸you shall put your hand on its head and kill it in front of the Tent. The priests shall throw its blood against all four sides of the altar ⁹and present the following parts of the animal as a food offering to the Lord: the fat, the entire fat tail cut off near the backbone, all the fat covering the internal organs, ¹⁰the kidneys and the fat on them, and the best part of the liver. ¹¹The officiating priest shall burn all this on the altar as a food offering to the Lord.

¹²If you offer a goat, ¹³you shall put your hand on its head and kill it in front of the Tent. The priests shall throw its blood against all four sides of the altar ¹⁴and present the following parts as a food offering to the Lord: all the fat on the internal organs, ¹⁵the kidneys and the fat on them, and the best part of the liver. ¹⁶The priest shall burn all this on the altar as a food offering pleasing to the Lord. All the fat belongs to the Lord. ¹⁷No Israelite may eat any fat or any blood; this is a rule to be kept forever by all Israelites wherever they live.

Offerings for Unintentional Sins

4 The Lord commanded Moses ²to tell the people of Israel that anyone who sinned and broke any of the Lord's commands without intending to, would have to observe the following rules.

³If it is the High Priest who sins and so brings guilt on the people, he shall present a young bull without any defects and sacrifice it to the Lord for his sin. ⁴He shall bring the bull to the entrance of the Tent, put his hand on its head, and kill it

there in the LORD's presence. 5Then the High Priest shall take some of the bull's blood and carry it into the Tent. 6He shall dip his finger in the blood and sprinkle it in front of the sacred curtain seven times. 7Then he shall put some of the blood on the projections at the corners of the incense altar in the Tent. He shall pour out the rest of the blood at the base of the altar used for burning sacrifices, which is at the entrance of the Tent. 8From this bull he shall take all the fat, the fat on the internal organs, 9the kidneys and the fat on them, and the best part of the liver. 10The priest shall take this fat and burn it on the altar used for the burnt offerings, just as he does with the fat from the animal killed for the fellowship offering. 11But he shall take its skin, all its flesh, its head, its legs, and its internal organs, including the intestines, 12carry it all outside the camp to the ritually clean place where the ashes are poured out, and there he shall burn it on a wood fire.

13If it is the whole community of Israel that sins and becomes guilty of breaking one of the LORD's commands without intending to, 14then as soon as the sin becomes known, the community shall bring a young bull as a sin offering. They shall bring it to the Tent of the LORD's presence; 15the leaders of the community shall put their hands on its head, and it shall be killed there. 16The High Priest shall take some of the bull's blood into the Tent, 17dip his finger in it, and sprinkle it in front of the curtain seven times. 18He shall put some of the blood on the projections at the corners of the incense altar inside the Tent and pour out the rest of it at the base of the altar used for burning sacrifices, which is at the entrance of the Tent. 19Then he shall take all its fat and burn it on the altar. 20He shall do the same thing with this bull as he does with the bull for the sin offering, and in this way he shall make the sacrifice for the people's sin, and they will be forgiven. 21Then he shall take the bull outside the camp and burn it, just as he burns the bull offered for his own sin. This is an offering to take away the sin of the community.

22If it is a ruler who sins and becomes guilty of breaking one of the LORD's commands without intending to, 23then as soon as the sin is called to his attention, he shall bring as his offering a male goat without any defects. 24He shall put his hand on its head and kill it on the north side of the altar, where the animals for the burnt offerings are killed. This is an offering to take away sin. 25The priest shall dip his finger in the blood of the animal, put it on the projections at the corners of the altar, and pour out the rest of it at the base of the altar. 26Then he shall burn all of its fat on the altar, just as he burns the fat of the animals killed for the fellowship offerings. In this way the priest shall offer the sacrifice for the sin of the ruler, and he will be forgiven.

27If any of you people sin and become guilty of breaking one of the LORD's commands without intending to, 28then as soon as the sin is called to your attention, you shall bring as your offering a female goat without any defects. 29You shall put your hand on its head and kill it on the north side of the altar, where the animals for the burnt offerings are killed. 30The priest shall dip his finger in the blood of the animal, put it on the projections at the corners of the altar, and pour out the rest of it at the base of the altar. 31Then he shall remove all its fat, just as the fat is removed from the animals killed for the fellowship offerings, and he shall burn it on the altar as an odor pleasing to the LORD. In this way the priest shall offer the sacrifice for the man's sin, and he will be forgiven.

32If you bring a sheep as a sin offering, it must be a female without any defects. 33You shall put your hand on its head and kill it on the north side of the altar, where the animals for the burnt offerings are killed. 34The priest shall dip his finger in the blood of the animal, put it on the projections at the corners of the altar, and pour out the rest of it at the base of the altar. 35Then he shall remove all its fat, just as the fat is removed from the sheep killed for the fellowship offerings, and he shall burn it on the altar along with the food offerings given to the LORD. In this way the priest shall offer the sacrifice for your sin, and you will be forgiven.

L
E
V
I
T
I
C
U
S

Cases Requiring Sin Offerings

5 Sin offerings are required in the following cases.

If you are officially summoned to give evidence in court and do not give information about something you have seen or heard, you must suffer the consequences. 2 If you unintentionally touch anything ritually unclean, such as a dead animal, you are unclean and guilty as soon as you realize what you have done. 3 If you unintentionally touch anything of human origin that is unclean, whatever it may be, you are guilty as soon as you realize what you have done. 4 If you make a careless vow, no matter what it is about, you are guilty as soon as you realize what you have done. 5 When you are guilty, you must confess the sin, 6 and as the penalty for your sin you must bring to the LORD a female sheep or goat as an offering. The priest shall offer the sacrifice for your sin.

7 If you cannot afford a sheep or a goat, you shall bring to the LORD as the payment for your sin two doves or two pigeons, one for a sin offering and the other for a burnt offering. 8 You shall bring them to the priest, who will first offer the bird for the sin offering. He will break its neck without pulling off its head 9 and sprinkle some of its blood against the side of the altar. The rest of the blood will be drained out at the base of the altar. This is an offering to take away sin. 10 Then he shall offer the second bird as a burnt offering, according to the regulations. In this way the priest shall offer the sacrifice for your sin, and you will be forgiven.

11 If you cannot afford two doves or two pigeons, you shall bring two pounds of flour as a sin offering. You shall not put any olive oil or any incense on it, because it is a sin offering, not a grain offering. 12 You shall bring it to the priest, who will take a handful of it as a token that it has all been offered to the LORD, and he will burn it on the altar as a food offering. It is an offering to take away sin. 13 In this way the priest shall offer the sacrifice for your sin, and you will be forgiven. The rest of the flour belongs to the priest, just as in the case of a grain offering.

Repayment Offerings

14 The LORD gave the following regulations to Moses. 15 If any of you sin unintentionally by failing to hand over the payments that are sacred to the LORD, you shall bring as your repayment offering to the LORD a male sheep or goat without any defects. Its value is to be determined according to the official standard. 16 You must make the payments you have failed to hand over and must pay an additional 20 percent. You shall give it to the priest, and the priest shall offer the animal as a sacrifice for your sin, and you will be forgiven.

17 If any of you sin unintentionally by breaking any of the LORD's commands, you are guilty and must pay the penalty. 18 You must bring to the priest as a repayment offering a male sheep or goat without any defects. Its value is to be determined according to the official standard. The priest shall offer the sacrifice for the sin which you committed unintentionally, and you will be forgiven. 19 It is a repayment offering for the sin you committed against the LORD.

6 The LORD gave the following regulations to Moses. 2 An offering is to be made if any of you sin against the LORD by refusing to return what another Israelite has left as a deposit or by stealing something from him or by cheating him 3 or by lying about something that has been lost and swearing that you did not find it. 4-5 When you sin in any of these ways, you must repay whatever you got by dishonest means. On the day you are found guilty, you must repay the owner in full, plus an additional 20 percent. 6 You shall bring to the priest as your repayment offering to the LORD a male sheep or goat without any defects. Its value is to be determined according to the official standard. 7 The priest shall offer the sacrifice for your sin, and you will be forgiven.

Sacrifices Burned Whole

8 The LORD commanded Moses 9 to give Aaron and his sons the following regulations for burnt offerings. A burnt offering is to be left on the altar all night long, and the fire is to be kept burning. 10 Then the priest, wearing his linen robe and linen shorts, shall remove the greasy ashes left on the altar and put them at the

side of the altar. 11 Then he shall change his clothes and take the ashes outside the camp to a ritually clean place. 12 The fire on the altar must be kept burning and never allowed to go out. Every morning the priest shall put firewood on it, arrange the burnt offering on it, and burn the fat of the fellowship offering. 13 The fire must always be kept burning on the altar and never allowed to go out.

Grain Offerings

14 The following are the regulations for grain offerings. An Aaronite priest shall present the grain offering to the LORD in front of the altar. 15 Then he shall take a handful of the flour and oil, and the incense on it, and burn it on the altar as a token that all of it has been offered to the LORD. The odor of this offering is pleasing to the LORD. 16-17 The priests shall eat the rest of it. It shall be made into bread baked without yeast and eaten in a holy place, the courtyard of the Tent of the LORD's presence. The LORD has given it to the priests as their part of the food offerings. It is very holy, like the sin offerings and the repayment offerings. 18 For all time to come any of the male descendants of Aaron may eat it as their continuing share of the food offered to the LORD. Anyone else who touches a food offering will be harmed by the power of its holiness.

19 The LORD gave Moses the following regulations 20 for the ordination of an Aaronite priest. On the day he is ordained, he shall present as an offering to the LORD two pounds of flour (the same amount as the daily grain offering), half in the morning and half in the evening. 21 It is to be mixed with oil and cooked on a griddle and then crumbled and presented as a grain offering, an odor pleasing to the LORD. 22 For all time to come this offering is to be made by every descendant of Aaron who is serving as High Priest. It shall be completely burned as a sacrifice to the LORD. 23 No part of a grain offering that a priest makes may be eaten; all of it must be burned.

Sin Offerings

24 The LORD commanded Moses 25 to give Aaron and his sons the following regulations for sin offerings. The animal for a sin offering shall be killed on the north side of the altar, where the animals for the burnt offerings are killed. This is a very holy offering. 26 The priest who sacrifices the animal shall eat it in a holy place, the courtyard of the Tent of the LORD's presence. 27 Anyone or anything that touches the flesh of the animal will be harmed by the power of its holiness. If any article of clothing is spattered with the animal's blood, it must be washed in a holy place. 28 Any clay pot in which the meat is boiled must be broken, and if a metal pot is used, it must be scrubbed and rinsed with water. 29 Any male of the priestly families may eat this offering; it is very holy. 30 But if any of the blood is brought into the Tent and used in the ritual to take away sin, the animal must not be eaten; it must be burned.

Repayment Offerings

7 The following are the regulations for repayment offerings, which are very holy. 2 The animal for this offering is to be killed on the north side of the altar, where the animals for the burnt offerings are killed, and its blood is to be thrown against all four sides of the altar. 3 All of its fat shall be removed and offered on the altar: the fat tail, the fat covering the internal organs, 4 the kidneys and the fat on them, and the best part of the liver. 5 The priest shall burn all the fat on the altar as a food offering to the LORD. It is a repayment offering. 6 Any male of the priestly families may eat it, but it must be eaten in a holy place, because it is very holy.

7 There is one regulation that applies to both the sin offering and the repayment offering: the meat belongs to the priest who offers the sacrifice. 8 The skin of an animal offered as a burnt offering belongs to the priest who offers the sacrifice. 9 Every grain offering that has been baked in an oven or prepared in a pan or on a griddle belongs to the priest who has offered it to God. 10 But all uncooked grain offerings, whether mixed with oil or dry, belong to all the Aaronite priests and must be shared equally among them.

Fellowship Offerings

11 The following are the regulations for the fellowship offerings presented to the LORD. 12 If you make this offering as a thanksgiving offering to God, you shall present, together with the animal to be sacrificed, an offering of bread made

without yeast: either thick loaves made of flour mixed with olive oil or thin cakes brushed with olive oil or cakes made of flour mixed with olive oil. 13 In addition, you shall offer loaves of bread baked with yeast. 14 You shall present one part of each kind of bread as a special contribution to the LORD; it belongs to the priest who takes the blood of the animal and throws it against the altar. 15 The flesh of the animal must be eaten on the day it is sacrificed; none of it may be left until the next morning.

16 If you bring a fellowship offering as fulfillment of a vow or as your own free-will offering, not all of it has to be eaten on the day it is offered, but any that is left over may be eaten on the following day. 17 Any meat that still remains on the third day must be burned. 18 If any of it is eaten on the third day, God will not accept your offering. The offering will not be counted to your credit but will be considered unclean, and whoever eats it will suffer the consequences. 19 If the meat comes into contact with anything ritually unclean, it must not be eaten, but must be burned.

Any of you that are ritually clean may eat the meat, 20 but if any of you who are not clean eat it, you shall no longer be considered one of God's people. 21 Also, if you eat the meat of this offering after you have touched anything ritually unclean, whether from a person or an animal, you shall no longer be considered one of God's people.

22 The LORD gave Moses the following regulations 23 for the people of Israel. No fat of cattle, sheep, or goats shall be eaten. 24 The fat of an animal that has died a natural death or has been killed by a wild animal must not be eaten, but it may be used for any other purpose. 25 Anyone who eats the fat of an animal that may be offered as a food offering to the LORD will no longer be considered one of God's people. 26 No matter where the Israelites live, they must never use the blood of birds or animals for food. 27 Anyone who breaks this law will no longer be considered one of God's people.

28 The LORD gave Moses the following regulations 29 for the people of Israel. When any of you offer a fellowship offering you must bring part of it as a special gift to the LORD, 30 bringing it with your own hands as a food offering. You shall bring the fat of the animal with its breast and present it as a special gift to the LORD. 31 The priest shall burn the fat on the altar, but the breast shall belong to the priests. 32 The right hind leg of the animal shall be given as a special contribution 33 to the priest who offers the blood and the fat of the fellowship offering. 34 The breast of the animal is a special gift, and the right hind leg is a special contribution that the LORD has taken from the people of Israel and given to the priests. This is what the people of Israel must give to the priests for all time to come. 35 This is the part of the food offered to the LORD that was given to Aaron and his sons on the day they were ordained as priests. 36 On that day the LORD commanded the people of Israel to give them this part of the offering. It is a regulation that the people of Israel must obey for all time to come.

37 These, then, are the regulations for the burnt offerings, the grain offerings, the sin offerings, the repayment offerings, the ordination offerings, and the fellowship offerings. 38 There on Mount Sinai in the desert, the LORD gave these commands to Moses on the day he told the people of Israel to make their offerings.

The Ordination of Aaron and His Sons
(Exodus 29.1-37)

8 The LORD said to Moses, 2 "Take Aaron and his sons to the entrance of the Tent of my presence and bring the priestly garments, the anointing oil, the young bull for the sin offering, the two rams, and the basket of unleavened bread. 3 Then call the whole community together there."

4 Moses did as the LORD had commanded, and when the community had assembled, 5 he said to them, "What I am now about to do is what the LORD has commanded."

6 Moses brought Aaron and his sons forward and had them take a ritual bath. 7 He put the shirt and the robe on Aaron and the sash around his waist. He put the ephod[a] on him and fastened it by put-

a EPHOD: *See Word List.*

ting its finely woven belt around his waist. 8 He put the breastpiece on him and put the Urim and Thummim*b* in it. 9 He placed the turban on his head, and on the front of it he put the gold ornament, the sacred sign of dedication, just as the LORD had commanded him.

10 Then Moses took the anointing oil and put it on the Tent of the LORD's presence and everything that was in it, and in this way he dedicated it all to the LORD. 11 He took some of the oil and sprinkled it seven times on the altar and its equipment and on the basin and its base, in order to dedicate them to the LORD. 12 He ordained Aaron by pouring some of the anointing oil on his head. 13 Next, Moses brought the sons of Aaron forward and put shirts on them, put sashes around their waists, and tied caps on their heads, just as the LORD had commanded.

14 Then Moses brought the young bull for the sin offering, and Aaron and his sons put their hands on its head. 15 Moses killed it and took some of the blood, and with his finger put it on the projections at the corners of the altar, in order to dedicate it. He then poured out the rest of the blood at the base of the altar. In this way he dedicated it and purified it. 16 Moses took all the fat on the internal organs, the best part of the liver, and the kidneys with the fat on them, and burned it all on the altar. 17 He took the rest of the bull, including its skin, flesh, and intestines, and burned it outside the camp, just as the LORD had commanded.

18 Next, Moses brought the ram for the burnt offering, and Aaron and his sons put their hands on its head. 19 Moses killed it and threw the blood on all four sides of the altar. 20-21 He cut the ram in pieces, washed the internal organs and the hind legs with water, and burned the head, the fat, and all the rest of the ram on the altar, just as the LORD had commanded. This burnt offering was a food offering, and its odor was pleasing to the LORD.

22 Then Moses brought the second ram, which was for the ordination of priests, and Aaron and his sons put their hands on its head. 23 Moses killed it and took some of the blood and put it on the lobe of Aaron's right ear, on the thumb of his right hand, and on the big toe of his right foot. 24 Then he brought Aaron's sons forward and put some of the blood on the lobes of their right ears, on the thumbs of their right hands, and on the big toes of their right feet. Moses then threw the rest of the blood on all four sides of the altar. 25 He took the fat, the fat tail, all the fat covering the internal organs, the best part of the liver, the kidneys with the fat on them, and the right hind leg. 26 Then he took one loaf of bread from the basket of unleavened bread dedicated to the LORD, one loaf made with oil, and one thin cake, and he put them on top of the fat and the right hind leg. 27 He put all of this food in the hands of Aaron and his sons, and they presented it as a special gift to the LORD. 28 Then Moses took the food from them and burned it on the altar, on top of the burnt offering, as an ordination offering. This was a food offering, and its odor was pleasing to the LORD. 29 Then Moses took the breast and presented it as a special gift to the LORD. It was Moses' part of the ordination ram. Moses did everything just as the LORD had commanded.

30 Moses took some of the anointing oil and some of the blood that was on the altar and sprinkled them on Aaron and his sons and on their clothes. In this way he consecrated them and their clothes to the LORD.

31 Moses said to Aaron and his sons, "Take the meat to the entrance of the Tent of the LORD's presence, boil it, and eat it there with the bread that is in the basket of ordination offerings, just as the LORD commanded. 32 Burn up any meat or bread that is left over. 33 You shall not leave the entrance of the Tent for seven days, until your ordination rites are completed. 34 The LORD commanded us to do what we have done today, in order to take away your sin. 35 You must stay at the entrance of the Tent day and night for seven days, doing what the LORD has commanded. If you don't, you will die. This is what the LORD has commanded me." 36 So Aaron and his sons did everything that the LORD had commanded through Moses.

---

b URIM AND THUMMIM: *Two objects used by the priest to determine God's will; it is not known precisely how they were used.*

Aaron Offers Sacrifices

9 The day after the ordination rites were completed, Moses called Aaron and his sons and the leaders of Israel. 2 He said to Aaron, "Take a young bull and a ram without any defects and offer them to the Lord, the bull for a sin offering and the ram for a burnt offering. 3 Then tell the people of Israel to take a male goat for a sin offering, a one-year-old calf, and a one-year-old lamb without any defects for a burnt offering, 4 and a bull and a ram for a fellowship offering. They are to sacrifice them to the Lord with the grain offering mixed with oil. They must do this because the Lord will appear to them today."

5 They brought to the front of the Tent everything that Moses had commanded, and the whole community assembled there to worship the Lord. 6 Moses said, "The Lord has commanded you to do all this, so that the dazzling light of his presence can appear to you." 7 Then he said to Aaron, "Go to the altar and offer the sin offering and the burnt offering to take away your sins and the sins of the people. Present this offering to take away the sins of the people, just as the Lord commanded."

8 Aaron went to the altar and killed the young bull which was for his own sin offering. 9 His sons brought him the blood, and he dipped his finger in it, put some of it on the projections at the corners of the altar, and poured out the rest of it at the base of the altar. 10 Then he burned on the altar the fat, the kidneys, and the best part of the liver, just as the Lord had commanded Moses. 11 But he burned the meat and the skin outside the camp.

12 He killed the animal which was for his own burnt offering. His sons brought him the blood, and he threw it on all four sides of the altar. 13 They handed him the head and the other pieces of the animal, and he burned them on the altar. 14 Then he washed the internal organs and the hind legs and burned them on the altar on top of the rest of the burnt offering.

15 After that, he presented the people's offerings. He took the goat that was to be offered for the people's sins, killed it, and offered it, as he had done with his own sin offering. 16 He also brought the animal for the burnt offering and offered it according to the regulations. 17 He presented the grain offering and took a handful of flour and burned it on the altar. (This was in addition to the daily burnt offering.) 18 He killed the bull and the ram as a fellowship offering for the people. His sons brought him the blood, and he threw it on all four sides of the altar. 19 Aaron put the fat parts of the bull and the ram 20 on top of the breasts of the animals and carried it all to the altar. He burned the fat on the altar 21 and presented the breasts and the right hind legs as the special gift to the Lord for the priests, as Moses had commanded.

22 When Aaron had finished all the sacrifices, he raised his hands over the people and blessed them, and then stepped down. 23 Moses and Aaron went into the Tent of the Lord's presence, and when they came out, they blessed the people, and the dazzling light of the Lord's presence appeared to all the people. 24 Suddenly the Lord sent a fire, and it consumed the burnt offering and the fat parts on the altar. When the people saw it, they all shouted and bowed down with their faces to the ground.

The Sin of Nadab and Abihu

10 Aaron's sons, Nadab and Abihu, each took his fire pan, put live coals in it, added incense, and presented it to the Lord. But this fire was not holy, because the Lord had not commanded them to present it. 2 Suddenly the Lord sent fire, and it burned them to death there in the presence of the Lord. 3 Then Moses said to Aaron, "This is what the Lord was speaking about when he said, 'All who serve me must respect my holiness; I will reveal my glory to my people.' "c But Aaron remained silent.

4 Moses called Mishael and Elzaphan, the sons of Uzziel, Aaron's uncle, and said to them, "Come here and carry your cousins' bodies away from the sacred Tent and put them outside the camp." 5 So they came and took hold of the clothing on the corpses and carried them outside the camp, just as Moses had commanded.

6 Then Moses said to Aaron and to his sons Eleazar and Ithamar, "Do not leave your hair uncombed or tear your clothes

---

c I will reveal my glory to my people; *or* my people must honor me.

to show that you are in mourning. If you do, you will die, and the LORD will be angry with the whole community. But all other Israelites are allowed to mourn this death caused by the fire which the LORD sent. 7 Do not leave the entrance of the Tent or you will die, because you have been consecrated by the anointing oil of the LORD." So they did as Moses said.

Rules for Priests

8 The LORD said to Aaron, 9 "You and your sons are not to enter the Tent of my presence after drinking wine or beer; if you do, you will die. This is a law to be kept by all your descendants. 10 You must distinguish between what belongs to God and what is for general use, between what is ritually clean and what is unclean. 11 You must teach the people of Israel all the laws which I have given to you through Moses."

12 Moses said to Aaron and his two remaining sons, Eleazar and Ithamar, "Take the grain offering that is left over from the food offered to the LORD, make unleavened bread with it and eat it beside the altar, because this offering is very holy. 13 Eat it in a holy place; it is the part that belongs to you and your sons from the food offered to the LORD. That is what the LORD commanded me. 14 But you and your families may eat the breast and the hind leg that are presented as the special gift and the special contribution to the LORD for the priests. You may eat them in any ritually clean place. These offerings have been given to you and your children as the part that belongs to you from the fellowship offerings of the people of Israel. 15 They shall bring the hind leg and the breast at the time the fat is presented as a food offering to the LORD. These parts belong to you and your children forever, just as the LORD commanded."

16 Moses asked about the goat for the sin offering and learned that it had already been burned. This made him angry at Eleazar and Ithamar, and he demanded, 17 "Why didn't you eat the sin offering in a sacred place? It is very holy, and the LORD has given it to you in order to take away the sin of the community. 18 Since its blood was not brought into the sacred Tent, you should have eaten the sacrifice there, as I commanded."

19 Aaron answered, "If I had eaten the sin offering today, would the LORD have approved? The people presented their sin offering to the LORD today, and they brought their burnt offering, but still these terrible things have happened to me." 20 When Moses heard this, he was satisfied.

Animals That May Be Eaten
(Deuteronomy 14.3-21)

11 The LORD gave Moses and Aaron the following regulations 2 for the people of Israel. You may eat any land animal 3 that has divided hoofs and that also chews the cud, 4-6 but you must not eat camels, rock badgers, or rabbits. These must be considered unclean; they chew the cud, but do not have divided hoofs. 7 Do not eat pigs. They must be considered unclean; they have divided hoofs, but do not chew the cud. 8 Do not eat these animals or even touch their dead bodies; they are unclean.

9 You may eat any kind of fish that has fins and scales, 10 but anything living in the water that does not have fins and scales must not be eaten. 11 Such creatures must be considered unclean. You must not eat them or even touch their dead bodies. 12 You must not eat anything that lives in the water and does not have fins and scales.

13-19 You must not eat any of the following birds: eagles, owls, hawks, falcons; buzzards, vultures, crows; ostriches; seagulls, storks, herons, pelicans, cormorants;d hoopoes; or bats.

20 All winged insects are unclean, 21 except those that hop. 22 You may eat locusts, crickets, or grasshoppers. 23 But all other small things that have wings and also crawl must be considered unclean.

24-28 If you touch the dead bodies of the following animals, you will be unclean until evening: all animals with hoofs, unless their hoofs are divided and they chew the cud, and all four-footed animals with paws. If you carry their dead bodies, you must wash your clothes, but you will still be unclean until evening. 29-30 Moles, rats, mice, and lizards must be considered unclean. 31 Whoever touches them or their dead bodies will be

d The identification of some of the birds in verses 13-19 is uncertain.

L
E
V
I
T
I
C
U
S

unclean until evening. 32 And if their dead bodies fall on anything, it will be unclean. This applies to any article of wood, cloth, leather, or sacking, no matter what it is used for. It shall be dipped in water, but it will remain unclean until evening. 33 And if their bodies fall into a clay pot, everything that is in it shall be unclean, and you must break the pot. 34 Any food which could normally be eaten, but on which water from such a pot has been poured, will be unclean, and anything drinkable in such a pot is unclean. 35 Anything on which the dead bodies fall is unclean; a clay stove or oven shall be broken, 36 but a spring or a cistern remains clean, although anything else that touches their dead bodies is unclean. 37 If one of them falls on seed that is going to be planted, the seed remains clean. 38 But if the seed is soaking in water and one of them falls on it, the seed is unclean.

39 If any animal that may be eaten dies, anyone who touches it will be unclean until evening. 40 And if any of you eat any part of the animal, you must wash your clothes, but you will still be unclean until evening; any of you who carry the dead body must wash your clothes, but you will still be unclean until evening.

41 You must not eat any of the small animals that move on the ground, 42 whether they crawl, or walk on four legs, or have many legs. 43 Do not make yourselves unclean by eating any of these. 44 I am the LORD your God, and you must keep yourselves holy, because I am holy. 45 I am the LORD who brought you out of Egypt so that I could be your God. You must be holy, because I am holy.

46 This, then, is the law about animals and birds, about everything that lives in the water, and everything that moves on the ground. 47 You must be careful to distinguish between what is ritually clean and unclean, between animals that may be eaten and those that may not.

The Purification of Women after Childbirth

12 The LORD gave Moses the following regulations 2 for the people of Israel. For seven days after a woman gives birth to a son, she is ritually unclean, as she is during her monthly period. 3 On the eighth day, the child shall

be circumcised. 4 Then it will be thirty-three more days until she is ritually clean from her loss of blood; she must not touch anything that is holy or enter the sacred Tent until the time of her purification is completed.

5 For fourteen days after a woman gives birth to a daughter, she is ritually unclean, as she is during her monthly period. Then it will be sixty-six more days until she is ritually clean from her loss of blood.

6 When the time of her purification is completed, whether for a son or daughter, she shall bring to the priest at the entrance of the Tent of the LORD's presence a one-year-old lamb for a burnt offering and a pigeon or a dove for a sin offering. 7 The priest shall present her offering to the LORD and perform the ritual to take away her impurity, and she will be ritually clean. This, then, is what a woman must do after giving birth.

8 If the woman cannot afford a lamb, she shall bring two doves or two pigeons, one for a burnt offering and the other for a sin offering, and the priest shall perform the ritual to take away her impurity, and she will be ritually clean.

Laws concerning Skin Diseases

13 The LORD gave Moses and Aaron these regulations. 2 If any of you have a sore on your skin or a boil or an inflammation which could develop into a dreaded skin disease, you shall be brought to the Aaronite priest. 3 The priest shall examine the sore, and if the hairs in it have turned white and the sore appears to be deeper than the surrounding skin, it is a dreaded skin disease, and the priest shall pronounce you unclean. 4 But if the sore is white and does not appear to be deeper than the skin around it and the hairs have not turned white, the priest shall isolate you for seven days. 5 The priest shall examine you again on the seventh day, and if in his opinion the sore looks the same and has not spread, he shall isolate you for another seven days. 6 The priest shall examine you again on the seventh day, and if the sore has faded and has not spread, he shall pronounce you ritually clean; it is only a sore. You shall wash your clothes and be ritually clean. 7 But if the sore spreads after the priest has examined you and pronounced you clean, you must appear before the priest again. 8 The priest will examine you again, and if it has spread, he shall pronounce you unclean; it is a dreaded skin disease.

9 If any of you have a dreaded skin disease, you shall be brought to the priest, 10 who will examine you. If there is a white sore on your skin which turns the hairs white and is full of pus, 11 it is a chronic skin disease. The priest shall pronounce you unclean; there is no need to isolate you, because you are obviously unclean. 12 If the skin disease spreads and covers you from head to foot, 13 the priest shall examine you again. If he finds that it actually has covered the whole body, he shall pronounce you ritually clean. If your whole skin has turned white, you are ritually clean. 14 But from the moment an open sore appears, you are unclean. 15 The priest shall examine you again, and if he sees an open sore, he shall pronounce you unclean. An open sore means a dreaded skin disease, and you are unclean. 16 But when the sore heals and becomes white again, you shall go to the priest, 17 who will examine you again. If the sore has turned white, you are ritually clean, and the priest shall pronounce you clean.

18 If any of you have a boil that has healed 19 and if afterward a white swelling or a reddish-white spot appears where the boil was, you shall go to the priest. 20 The priest shall examine you, and if the spot seems to be deeper than the surrounding skin and the hairs in it have turned white, he shall pronounce you unclean. It is a dreaded skin disease that has started in the boil. 21 But if the priest examines it and finds that the hairs in it have not turned white and that it is not deeper than the surrounding skin, but is light in color, the priest shall isolate you for seven days. 22 If the spot spreads, the priest shall pronounce you unclean; you are diseased. 23 But if it remains unchanged and does not spread, it is only the scar left from the boil, and the priest shall pronounce you ritually clean.

24 In case any of you have been burned, if the raw flesh becomes white or reddish-white, 25 the priest shall examine you. If the hairs in the spot have turned white and it appears deeper than the surrounding skin, it is a dreaded skin disease that has started in the burn, and the priest shall pronounce you unclean.

26 But if the hairs in it have not turned white and it is not deeper than the surrounding skin, but is light in color, the priest shall isolate you for seven days. 27 The priest shall examine you again on the seventh day, and if it is spreading, it is a dreaded skin disease, and the priest shall pronounce you unclean. 28 But if the spot remains unchanged and does not spread and is light in color, it is not a dreaded skin disease. The priest shall pronounce you ritually clean, because it is only a scar from the burn.

29 When any of you, male or female, have a sore on your head or chin, 30 the priest shall examine it. If it seems to be deeper than the surrounding skin and the hairs in it are yellowish and thin, it is a dreaded skin disease, and he shall pronounce you unclean. 31 If, when the priest examines you, the sore does not appear to be deeper than the surrounding skin, but there are still no healthy hairs in it, he shall isolate you for seven days. 32 The priest shall examine the sore again on the seventh day, and if it has not spread and there are no yellowish hairs in it and it does not seem to be deeper than the surrounding skin, 33 you shall shave the head except the area around the sore. The priest shall then isolate you for another seven days. 34 On the seventh day the priest shall again examine the sore, and if it has not spread and does not seem to be deeper than the surrounding skin, he shall pronounce you ritually clean. You shall wash your clothes, and you will be clean. 35 But if the sore spreads after you have been pronounced clean, 36 the priest shall examine you again. If the sore has spread, he need not look for yellowish hairs; you are obviously unclean. 37 But if in the priest's opinion the sore has not spread and healthy hairs are growing in it, the sore has healed, and the priest shall pronounce you ritually clean.

38 When any of you, male or female, have white spots on the skin, 39 the priest shall examine you. If the spots are dull white, it is only a blemish that has broken out on the skin; you are ritually clean.

40-41 If you lose your hair at the back or the front of your head, this does not make you unclean. 42 But if a reddish-white sore appears on the bald spot, it is a dreaded skin disease. 43 The priest shall

LEPERS AND LEPROSY

Leprosy, a disease mentioned often in the Bible, was a dreaded skin affliction in ancient times. Modern medicine has isolated several different types of leprosy, variously characterized by the formation of nodules, ulcers, deformities, and loss of feeling in the skin. In Old Testament times, a symptom used to diagnose the disease was the persistence of shiny white spots under the skin (Lv 13.3, 4).

Some medical experts believe the ancient disease was a severe type of psoriasis, or scaling of the skin, that is rarely seen today. It was probably more prevalent than Hansen's disease, the term generally used for leprosy today.

The leper, considered to be ceremonially unclean, was isolated and forced to live apart from others. Detailed instructions are given in the Book of Leviticus on how to recognize leprosy and how others were to be protected from those unfortunate enough to contract the dread disease. The leper was cast outside the camp (Lv 13.46), required to wear mourning clothes, and to cry out "Unclean, unclean!" to keep others at a safe distance (Lv 13.45, 46).

Several miraculous cures of leprosy are reported in the Bible. Both Moses (Ex 4.6, 7) and Miriam (Nu 12.10, 15) were afflicted with leprosy and cured by the Lord. God used the prophet Elisha to heal Naaman, a Syrian military officer, of his leprosy (2 K 5.1–14). In an expression of compassion, Jesus healed ten lepers, then told them to "let the priests examine you" (Lk 17.14) for specific instructions on how to reenter society. One of the lepers returned to express his thanks to Jesus (Lk 17.15–19).

This miraculous healing of the ten lepers was a clear sign of Jesus' messiahship, since leprosy was curable only by divine intervention.

examine you, and if there is a reddish-white sore, 44 the priest shall pronounce you unclean, because of the dreaded skin disease on your head.

45 If you have a dreaded skin disease, you must wear torn clothes, leave your hair uncombed, cover the lower part of your face, and call out, "Unclean, unclean!" 46 You remain unclean as long as you have the disease, and you must live outside the camp, away from others.

Laws concerning Mildew

47 When there is mildew*e* on clothing, whether wool or linen, 48 or on any piece of linen or wool cloth or on leather or anything made of leather, 49 if it is greenish or reddish, it is a spreading mildew and must be shown to the priest. 50 The priest shall examine it and put the object away for seven days. 51 He shall examine it again on the seventh day, and if the mildew has spread, the object is unclean. 52 The priest shall burn it, because it is a spreading mildew which must be destroyed by fire.

53 But if, when he examines it, the priest finds that the mildew has not spread on the object, 54 he shall order that it be washed and put away for another seven days. 55 Then he shall examine it, and if the mildew has not changed color, even though it has not spread, it is still unclean; you must burn the object, whether the rot is on the front or the back. 56 But if, when the priest examines it again, the mildew has faded, he shall tear it out of the clothing or leather. 57 Then, if the mildew reappears, it is spreading again, and the owner shall burn the object. 58 If he washes the object and the spot disappears, he shall wash it again, and it will be ritually clean.

59 This, then, is the law about mildew on clothing, whether it is wool or linen, or on linen or wool cloth or on anything made of leather; this is how the decision is made as to whether it is ritually clean or unclean.

Purification after Having Skin Diseases

14 The Lord gave Moses 2 the following regulations about the ritual purification of those of you cured of a dreaded skin disease. On the day you are to be pronounced clean, you shall be brought to the priest, 3 and the priest shall take you outside the camp and examine you. If the disease is healed, 4 the priest shall order that two ritually clean birds be brought, along with a piece of cedar wood, a red cord, and a sprig of hyssop. 5 Then the priest shall order that one of the birds be killed over a clay bowl containing fresh spring water. 6 He shall take the other bird and dip it, together with the cedar wood, the red cord, and the hyssop, in the blood of the bird that was killed. 7 He shall sprinkle the blood seven times on the one of you who is to be purified from your skin disease, and then he shall pronounce you clean. He shall let the live bird fly away over the open fields. 8 You shall wash your clothes, shave off all your hair, and take a bath; you will then be ritually clean. You may enter the camp, but you must live outside your tent for seven days. 9 On the seventh day you shall again shave your head, your beard, your eyebrows, and all the rest of the hair on your body; you shall wash your clothes and take a bath, and then you will be ritually clean.

10 On the eighth day you shall bring two male lambs and one female lamb a year old that are without any defects, five pounds of flour mixed with olive oil, and half a pint of olive oil. 11 The priest shall take you and these offerings to the entrance of the Tent of the Lord's presence. 12 Then the priest shall take one of the male lambs and together with the half pint of oil he shall offer it as a repayment offering. He shall present them as a special gift to the Lord for the priest. 13 He shall kill the lamb in the holy place where the animals for the sin offerings and the burnt offerings are killed. He must do this because the repayment offering, like the sin offering, belongs to the priest and is very holy. 14 The priest shall take some of the blood of the lamb and put it on the lobe of the right ear, on the thumb of the right hand, and on the big toe of the right foot of the one of you to be declared ritually clean. 15 The priest shall take some of the olive oil and pour it in the palm of his own left hand, 16 dip a finger of his right hand in it, and sprinkle some of it seven times there in the Lord's presence. 17 He shall take some of

e MILDEW: *The Hebrew word for "dreaded skin disease" and "mildew" is the same.*

LEVITICUS

the oil that is in the palm of his hand and some of the blood of the lamb and put them on the lobe of the right ear, on the thumb of the right hand, and on the big toe of the right foot of the one of you to be declared ritually clean. 18 He shall put the rest of the oil that is in the palm of his hand on your head. In this way he shall perform the ritual of purification.

19 Then the priest shall offer the sin offering and perform the ritual of purification. After that, he shall kill the animal for the burnt offering 20 and offer it with the grain offering on the altar. In this way the priest shall perform the ritual of purification, and you will be ritually clean.

21 If you are poor and cannot afford any more, you shall bring for your purification only one male lamb as your repayment offering, a special gift to the LORD for the priest. You shall bring only two pounds of flour mixed with olive oil for a grain offering and half a pint of olive oil. 22 You shall also bring two doves or two pigeons, one for the sin offering and one for the burnt offering. 23 On the eighth day of your purification you shall bring them to the priest at the entrance of the Tent. 24 The priest shall take the lamb and the olive oil and present them as a special gift to the LORD for the priest. 25 He shall kill the lamb and take some of the blood and put it on the lobe of your right ear, on the thumb of your right hand, and on the big toe of your right foot. 26 The priest shall pour some of the oil into the palm of his own left hand 27 and with a finger of his right hand sprinkle some of it seven times there in the LORD's presence. 28 He shall put some of the oil on the same places he put the blood: on the lobe of your right ear, on the thumb of your right hand, and on the big toe of your right foot. 29 The rest of the oil that is in his palm he shall put on your head and in this way perform the ritual of purification. 30 Then he shall offer one of the doves or pigeons 31 as the sin offering and the other as the burnt offering with the grain offering. In this way the priest shall perform the ritual of purification. 32 This is the law for those who have a dreaded skin disease but who cannot afford the normal offerings required for his purification.

Mildew in Houses

33 The LORD gave Moses and Aaron 34-35 the following regulations about houses affected by spreading mildew. (These were to apply after the people of Israel entered the land of Canaan, which the LORD was going to give them as their possession.) If any of you find that the LORD has sent mildew on your house, then you must go and tell the priest about it. 36 The priest shall order everything to be moved out of the house before he goes to examine the mildew; otherwise everything in the house will be declared unclean. Then he shall go to the house 37 and examine the mildew. If there are greenish or reddish spots that appear to be eating into the wall, 38 he shall leave the house and lock it up for seven days. 39 On the seventh day he shall return and examine it again. If the mildew has spread, 40 he shall order that the stones on which the mildew is found be removed and thrown into some unclean place outside the city. 41 After that he must have all the interior walls scraped and the plaster dumped in an unclean place outside the city. 42 Then other stones are to be used to replace the stones that were removed, and new plaster will be used to cover the walls.

43 If the mildew breaks out again in the house after the stones have been removed and the house has been scraped and plastered, 44 the priest shall go and look. If it has spread, the house is unclean. 45 It must be torn down, and its stones, its wood, and all its plaster must be carried out of the city to an unclean place. 46 Any who enter the house while it is locked up will be unclean until evening. 47 Any who lie down or eat in the house must wash their clothes.

48 If, when the priest comes to look, the mildew has not reappeared after the house has been replastered, he shall pronounce the house ritually clean, because the mildew has been completely removed. 49 To purify the house, he shall take two birds, some cedar wood, a red cord, and a sprig of hyssop. 50 He shall kill one of the birds over a clay bowl containing fresh spring water. 51 Then he shall take the cedar wood, the hyssop, the red cord, and the live bird and shall dip them in the blood of the bird that was killed and in the fresh water. And he

shall sprinkle the house seven times. [52] In this way he shall purify the house with the bird's blood, the fresh water, the live bird, the cedar wood, the hyssop, and the red cord. [53] Then he shall let the live bird fly away outside the city over the open fields. In this way he shall perform the ritual of purification for the house, and it will be ritually clean.

[54] These are the laws about dreaded skin diseases; [55-56] sores, boils, or inflammations; and about mildew in clothes or houses. [57] These laws determine when something is unclean and when it is clean.

Unclean Bodily Discharges

15 The LORD gave Moses and Aaron the following regulations [2] for the people of Israel. When any man has a discharge from his penis, the discharge is unclean, [3] whether the penis runs with it or is stopped up by it. [4] Any bed on which he sits or lies is unclean. [5] Anyone who touches his bed [6] or sits on anything the man has sat on must wash his clothes and take a bath, and he remains unclean until evening. [7] Anyone who touches the man with the discharge must wash his clothes and take a bath, and he remains unclean until evening. [8] If the man with the discharge spits on anyone who is ritually clean, that person must wash his clothes and take a bath, and he remains unclean until evening. [9] Any saddle or seat on which the man with the discharge sits is unclean. [10] Anyone who touches anything on which the man sat is unclean until evening. Anyone who carries anything on which the man sat must wash his clothes and take a bath, and he remains unclean until evening. [11] If a man who has a discharge touches one of you without first having washed his hands, you must wash your clothes and take a bath, and you remain unclean until evening. [12] Any clay pot that the man touches must be broken, and any wooden bowl that he touches must be washed.

[13] After the man is cured of his discharge, he must wait seven days and then wash his clothes and take a bath in fresh spring water, and he will be ritually clean. [14] On the eighth day he shall take two doves or two pigeons to the entrance of the Tent of the LORD's presence and give them to the priest. [15] The priest shall offer one of them as a sin offering and the other as a burnt offering. In this way he will perform the ritual of purification for the man.

[16] When a man has an emission of semen, he must bathe his whole body, and he remains unclean until evening. [17] Anything made of cloth or leather on which the semen falls must be washed, and it remains unclean until evening. [18] After sexual intercourse both the man and the woman must take a bath, and they remain unclean until evening.

[19] When a woman has her monthly period, she remains unclean for seven days. Anyone who touches her is unclean until evening. [20] Anything on which she sits or lies during her monthly period is unclean. [21-23] Any who touch her bed or anything on which she has sat must wash their clothes and take a bath, and they remain unclean until evening. [24] If a man has sexual intercourse with her during her period, he is contaminated by her impurity and remains unclean for seven days, and any bed on which he lies is unclean.

[25] If a woman has a flow of blood for several days outside her monthly period or if her flow continues beyond her regular period, she remains unclean as long as the flow continues, just as she is during her monthly period. [26] Any bed on which she lies and anything on which she sits during this time is unclean. [27] Any who touch them are unclean and must wash their clothes and take a bath; they remain unclean until evening. [28] After her flow stops, she must wait seven days, and then she will be ritually clean. [29] On the eighth day she shall take two doves or two pigeons to the priest at the entrance of the Tent of the LORD's presence. [30] The priest shall offer one of them as a sin offering and the other as a burnt offering, and in this way he will perform the ritual of purification for her.

[31] The LORD told Moses to warn the people of Israel about their uncleanness, so that they would not defile the Tent of his presence, which was in the middle of the camp. If they did, they would be killed.

[32] These are the regulations about a man who has a discharge or an emission of semen, [33] a woman during her monthly period, or a man who has sexual intercourse with a woman who is ritually unclean.

THE COVENANT BOX

The Covenant Box, also known as the ark of the covenant, was the object most sacred to the Israelites during their time in the wilderness.

Do we know what the Covenant Box looked like? We cannot be positive, but there is a clear and detailed description in the Old Testament (Ex 25.10–22). Archaeologists have discovered depictions of the Box (for example, a stone carving of the Box was found at the excavation of a synagogue in Capernaum).

From the biblical account, we can determine these facts about its physical appearance: It was a box about 45 inches long, 27 inches wide, and 27 inches high, made from acacia wood. Four poles were inserted into rings on the side of the Box so it could be carried by four men.

The lid on the Box, called the *mercy seat,* was made of gold. The Hebrew word traditionally translated mercy seat could be rendered *place of atonement,* because this was where the high priest sprinkled blood once each year on the Day of Atonement as the atonement for sin (Lv 16). Mounted on this lid were two winged creatures, which faced each other with outstretched wings. Inside the Box were the two stone tablets containing the Ten Commandments, which Moses had received from God at Mount Sinai (Ex 20). It also contained a golden jar of manna and Aaron's stick that sprouted leaves (He 9.4), reminders of God's provision for the needs of the Israelites in the wilderness.

The Israelites believed that God lived among them in the Tent between the wings of the cherubim above the lid. God spoke to Moses from this place (Nu 7.89) during their years of wandering in the wilderness as they were being prepared to enter the land promised by the Lord.

The Box was carried ahead of the Israelites when they left Mount Sinai (Nu 10.33); when they crossed the Jordan River to enter Canaan (Js 4.9–11); and when they circled the walls of Jericho before that city fell (Js 6.1–20). After many other travels, it was finally placed in Solomon's Temple in Jerusalem (1 K 8.1–9), only to disappear after the destruction of Jerusalem by the Babylonians between 587 B.C. and 586 B.C.

The Covenant Box served as a visible reminder of God's presence with the Israelites. The mercy seat, covered with gold, symbolized God's throne and his rule in the hearts of those who acknowledge him as their sovereign Lord.

The Day of Atonement

16 The LORD spoke to Moses after the death of the two sons of Aaron who were killed when they offered unholy fire to the LORD. 2 He said, "Tell your brother Aaron that only at the proper time is he to go behind the curtain into the Most Holy Place, because that is where I appear in a cloud above the lid on the Covenant Box. If he disobeys, he will be killed. 3 He may enter the Most Holy Place only after he has brought a young bull for a sin offering and a ram for a burnt offering."

4 Then the LORD gave the following instructions. Before Aaron goes into the Most Holy Place, he must take a bath and put on the priestly garments: the linen robe and shorts, the belt, and the turban. 5 The community of Israel shall give Aaron two male goats for a sin offering and a ram for a burnt offering. 6 He shall offer a bull as a sacrifice to take away his own sins and those of his family. 7 Then he shall take the two goats to the entrance of the Tent of the LORD's presence. 8 There he shall draw lots, using two stones, one marked "for the LORD" and the other "for Azazel."f 9 Aaron shall sacrifice the goat chosen by lot for the LORD and offer it as a sin offering. 10 The goat chosen for Azazel shall be presented alive to the LORD and sent off into the desert to Azazel, in order to take away the sins of the people.

11 When Aaron sacrifices the bull as the sin offering for himself and his family, 12 he shall take a fire pan full of burning coals from the altar and two handfuls of fine incense and bring them into the Most Holy Place. 13 There in the LORD's presence he shall put the incense on the fire, and the smoke of the incense will hide the lid of the Covenant Box so that he will not see it and die. 14 He shall take some of the bull's blood and with his finger sprinkle it on the front of the lid and then sprinkle some of it seven times in front of the Covenant Box.

15 After that, he shall kill the goat for the sin offering for the people, bring its blood into the Most Holy Place, and sprinkle it on the lid and then in front of the Covenant Box, as he did with the bull's blood. 16 In this way he will perform the ritual to purify the Most Holy Place from the uncleanness of the people of Israel and from all their sins. He must do this to the Tent, because it stands in the middle of the camp, which is ritually unclean. 17 From the time Aaron enters the Most Holy Place to perform the ritual of purification until he comes out, there must be no one in the Tent. When he has performed the ritual for himself, his family, and the whole community, 18 he must then go out to the altar for burnt offerings and purify it. He must take some of the bull's blood and some of the goat's blood and put it all over the projections at the corners of the altar. 19 With his finger he must sprinkle some of the blood on the altar seven times. In this way he is to purify it from the sins of the people of Israel and make it holy.

The Scapegoat

20 When Aaron has finished performing the ritual to purify the Most Holy Place, the rest of the Tent of the LORD's presence, and the altar, he shall present to the LORD the live goat chosen for Azazel.g 21 He shall put both of his hands on the goat's head and confess over it all the evils, sins, and rebellions of the people of Israel, and so transfer them to the goat's head. Then the goat is to be driven off into the desert by someone appointed to do it. 22 The goat will carry all their sins away with him into some uninhabited land.

23 Then Aaron shall go into the Tent, take off the priestly garments that he had put on before entering the Most Holy Place, and leave them there. 24 He must take a bath in a holy place and put on his own clothes. After that, he shall go out and offer the burnt offering to remove his own sins and those of the people. 25 He shall burn on the altar the fat of the animal for the sin offering. 26 The man who drove the goat into the desert to Azazel must wash his clothes and take a bath before he comes back into camp. 27 The bull and the goat used for the sin offering, whose blood was brought into the Most Holy Place to take away sin, shall be carried outside the camp and burned. Skin, meat, and intestines shall all be burned. 28 The one who burns them

---

f AZAZEL: The meaning of this Hebrew word is unknown; it may be the name of a desert demon.
g AZAZEL: See 16.8.

LEVITICUS

must wash his clothes and take a bath before he returns to camp.

Observing the Day of Atonement

29 The following regulations are to be observed for all time to come. On the tenth day of the seventh month the Israelites and the foreigners living among them must fast and must not do any work. 30 On that day the ritual is to be performed to purify them from all their sins, so that they will be ritually clean. 31 That day is to be a very holy day, one on which they fast and do no work at all. These regulations are to be observed for all time to come. 32 The High Priest, properly ordained and consecrated to succeed his father, is to perform the ritual of purification. He shall put on the priestly garments 33 and perform the ritual to purify the Most Holy Place, the rest of the Tent of the LORD's presence, the altar, the priests, and all the people of the community. 34 These regulations are to be observed for all time to come. This ritual must be performed once a year to purify the people of Israel from all their sins.

So Moses[h] did as the LORD had commanded.

The Sacredness of Blood

17 The LORD commanded Moses 2 to give Aaron and his sons and all the people of Israel the following regulations. 3-4 Any Israelites who kill a cow or a sheep or a goat as an offering to the LORD anywhere except at the entrance of the Tent of the LORD's presence have broken the Law. They have shed blood and shall no longer be considered God's people. 5 The meaning of this command is that the people of Israel shall now bring to the LORD the animals which they used to kill in the open country. They shall now bring them to the priest at the entrance of the Tent and kill them as fellowship offerings. 6 The priest shall throw the blood against the sides of the altar at the entrance of the Tent and burn the fat to produce an odor that is pleasing to the LORD. 7 The people of Israel must no longer be unfaithful to the LORD by killing their animals in the fields as sacrifices to the goat demons. The people of Israel must keep this regulation for all time to come.

8 Any Israelites or any foreigners living in the community who offer a burnt offering or any other sacrifice 9 as an offering to the LORD anywhere except at the entrance of the Tent shall no longer be considered God's people.

10 If any Israelites or any foreigners living in the community eat meat with blood still in it, the LORD will turn against them and no longer consider them his people. 11 The life of every living thing is in the blood, and that is why the LORD has commanded that all blood be poured out on the altar to take away the people's sins. Blood, which is life, takes away sins. 12 That is why the LORD has told the people of Israel that neither they nor any foreigner living among them shall eat any meat with blood still in it.

13 If any Israelites or any foreigners living in the community catch an animal or a bird which is ritually clean, they must pour its blood out on the ground and cover it with dirt. 14 The life of every living thing is in the blood, and that is why the LORD has told the people of Israel that they shall not eat any meat with blood still in it and that anyone who does so will no longer be considered one of his people.

15 Any people, Israelites or foreigners, who eat meat from an animal that has died a natural death or has been killed by wild animals must wash their clothes, take a bath, and wait until evening before they are ritually clean. 16 If they do not, they must suffer the consequences.

Forbidden Sexual Practices

18 The LORD told Moses 2 to say to the people of Israel, "I am the LORD your God. 3 Do not follow the practices of the people of Egypt, where you once lived, or of the people in the land of Canaan, where I am now taking you. 4 Obey my laws and do what I command. I am the LORD your God. 5 Follow the practices and the laws that I give you; you will save your life by doing so. I am the LORD."

6 The LORD gave the following regulations. Do not have sexual intercourse with any of your relatives. 7 Do not disgrace your father by having intercourse with your mother. You must not disgrace your own mother. 8 Do not disgrace your

h Moses; or Aaron.

father by having intercourse with any of his other wives. 9 Do not have intercourse with your sister or your stepsister, whether or not she was brought up in the same house with you. 10 Do not have intercourse with your granddaughter; that would be a disgrace to you. 11 Do not have intercourse with a half sister; she, too, is your sister. 12-13 Do not have intercourse with an aunt, whether she is your father's sister or your mother's sister. 14 Do not have intercourse with your uncle's wife; she, too, is your aunt. 15 Do not have intercourse with your daughter-in-law 16 or with your brother's wife. 17 Do not have intercourse with the daughter or granddaughter of a woman with whom you have had intercourse; they may be related to you, and that would be incest. 18 Do not take your wife's sister as one of your wives, as long as your wife is living.

19 Do not have intercourse with a woman during her monthly period, because she is ritually unclean. 20 Do not have intercourse with another man's wife; that would make you ritually unclean. 21 Do not hand over any of your children to be used in the worship of the god Molech, because that would bring disgrace on the name of God, the LORD. 22 No man is to have sexual relations with another man; God hates that. 23 No man or woman is to have sexual relations with an animal; that perversion makes you ritually unclean.

24 Do not make yourselves unclean by any of these acts, for that is how the pagans made themselves unclean, those pagans who lived in the land before you and whom the LORD is driving out so that you can go in. 25 Their actions made the land unclean, and so the LORD is punishing the land and making it reject the people who lived there. 26-27 They did all these disgusting things and made the land unclean, but you must not do them. All of you, whether Israelites or foreigners living with you, must keep the LORD's laws and commands, 28 and then the land will not reject you, as it rejected the pagans who lived there before you. 29 You know that whoever does any of these disgusting things will no longer be considered one of God's people.

30 And the LORD said, "Obey the commands I give and do not follow the practices of the people who lived in the land

before you, and do not make yourselves unclean by doing any of these things. I am the LORD your God."

Laws of Holiness and Justice

19 The LORD told Moses 2 to say to the community of Israel, "Be holy, because I, the LORD your God, am holy. 3 Each of you must respect your mother and your father, and must keep the Sabbath, as I have commanded. I am the LORD your God.

4 "Do not abandon me and worship idols; do not make gods of metal and worship them. I am the LORD your God.

5 "When you kill an animal for a fellowship offering, keep the regulations that I have given you, and I will accept the offering. 6 The meat must be eaten on the day the animal is killed or on the next day. Any meat left on the third day must be burned, 7 because it is ritually unclean, and if anyone eats it, I will not accept the offering. 8 Any who eat it will be guilty of treating as ordinary what is dedicated to me, and they will no longer be considered my people.

9 "When you harvest your fields, do not cut the grain at the edges of the fields, and do not go back to cut the heads of grain that were left. 10 Do not go back through your vineyard to gather the grapes that were missed or to pick up the grapes that have fallen; leave them for poor people and foreigners. I am the LORD your God.

11 "Do not steal or cheat or lie. 12 Do not make a promise in my name if you do not intend to keep it; that brings disgrace on my name. I am the LORD your God.

13 "Do not rob or take advantage of anyone. Do not hold back the wages of someone you have hired, not even for one night. 14 Do not curse the deaf or put something in front of the blind so as to make them stumble over it. Obey me; I am the LORD your God.

15 "Be honest and just when you make decisions in legal cases; do not show favoritism to the poor or fear the rich. 16 Do not spread lies about anyone, and when someone is on trial for his life, speak out if your testimony can help him. I am the LORD.

17 "Do not bear a grudge against others, but settle your differences with them, so that you will not commit a sin

because of them.i 18 Do not take revenge on others or continue to hate them, but love your neighbors as you love yourself. I am the LORD.

19 "Obey my commands. Do not cross-breed domestic animals. Do not plant two kinds of seed in the same field. Do not wear clothes made of two kinds of material.

20 "If a slave woman is the recognized concubine of a man and she has not been paid for and freed, then if another man has sexual relations with her, they will be punished, but noti put to death, since she is a slave. 21 The man shall bring a ram to the entrance of the Tent of my presence as his repayment offering, 22 and with it the priest shall perform the ritual of purification to remove the man's sin, and God will forgive him.

23 "When you come into the land of Canaan and plant any kind of fruit tree, consider the fruit ritually unclean for the first three years. During that time you must not eat it. 24 In the fourth year all the fruit shall be dedicated as an offering to show your gratitude to me,k the LORD. 25 But in the fifth year you may eat the fruit. If you do all this, your trees will bear more fruit. I am the LORD your God.

26 "Do not eat any meat with blood still in it. Do not practice any kind of magic. 27 Do not cut the hair on the sides of your head or trim your beard 28 or tattoo yourselves or cut gashes in your body to mourn for the dead. I am the LORD.

29 "Do not disgrace your daughters by making them temple prostitutes;l if you do, you will turn to other gods and the land will be full of immorality. 30 Keep the Sabbath, and honor the place where I am worshiped. I am the LORD.

31 "Do not go for advice to people who consult the spirits of the dead. If you do, you will be ritually unclean. I am the LORD your God.

32 "Show respect for old people and honor them. Reverently obey me; I am the LORD.

33 "Do not mistreat foreigners who are living in your land. 34 Treat them as you would an Israelite, and love them as you love yourselves. Remember that you were once foreigners in the land of Egypt. I am the LORD your God.

35 "Do not cheat anyone by using false measures of length, weight, or quantity. 36 Use honest scales, honest weights, and honest measures. I am the LORD your God, and I brought you out of Egypt. 37 Obey all my laws and commands. I am the LORD."

Penalties for Disobedience

20 The LORD told Moses 2 to say to the people of Israel, "Any of you or any foreigner living among you who gives any children to be used in the worship of the god Molech shall be stoned to death by the whole community. 3 If any of you give one of your children to Molech and make my sacred Tent unclean and disgrace my holy name, I will turn against you and will no longer consider you my people. 4 But if the community ignores what you have done and does not put you to death, 5 I myself will turn against you and your whole family and against all who join you in being unfaithful to me and worshiping Molech. I will no longer consider any of you my people.

6 "If any of you go for advice to people who consult the spirits of the dead, I will turn against you and will no longer consider you one of my people. 7 Keep yourselves holy, because I am the LORD your God. 8 Obey my laws, because I am the LORD and I make you holy."

9 The LORD gave the following regulations. Any of you that curse your father or mother shall be put to death; you are responsible for your own death.

10 If a man commits adultery with the wife of an Israelite, both he and the woman shall be put to death. 11 A man who has intercourse with one of his father's wives disgraces his father, and both he and the woman shall be put to death. They are responsible for their own death. 12 If a man has intercourse with his daughter-in-law, they shall both be put to death. They have committed incest and are responsible for their own death. 13 If a man has sexual relations with another man, they have done a disgusting thing, and both shall be put to death. They are

---

i so . . . them; or so that you do not commit this sin against them.   j they . . . not; or an investigation will be made but they will not be.   k to show your gratitude to me; or in praise of me.   l TEMPLE PROSTITUTES: These women were found in Canaanite temples, where fertility gods were worshiped. It was believed that intercourse with these prostitutes assured fertile fields and herds.

responsible for their own death. 14 If a man marries a woman and her mother, all three shall be burned to death because of the disgraceful thing they have done; such a thing must not be permitted among you. 15 If a man has sexual relations with an animal, he and the animal shall be put to death. 16 If a woman tries to have sexual relations with an animal, she and the animal shall be put to death. They are responsible for their own death.

17 If a man marries his sister or half sister, they shall be publicly disgraced and driven out of the community. He has had intercourse with his sister and must suffer the consequences. 18 If a man has intercourse with a woman during her monthly period, both of them are to be driven out of the community, because they have broken the regulations about ritual uncleanness.

19 If a man has intercourse with his aunt, both of them must suffer the consequences. 20 If a man has intercourse with his uncle's wife, he disgraces his uncle, and he and the woman will pay the penalty; neither one will have children. 21 If a man takes his brother's wife, they will die childless. He has done a ritually unclean thing and has disgraced his brother.

22 The LORD said, "Keep all my laws and commands, so that you will not be rejected by the land of Canaan, into which I am bringing you. 23 Do not adopt the customs of the people who live there; I am driving out those pagans so that you can enter the land. They have disgusted me with all their evil practices. 24 But I have promised you this rich and fertile land as your possession, and I will give it to you. I am the LORD your God, and I have set you apart from the other nations. 25 So then, you must make a clear distinction between animals and birds that are ritually clean and those that are not. Do not eat unclean animals or birds. I have declared them unclean, and eating them would make you unclean. 26 You shall be holy and belong only to me, because I am the LORD and I am holy. I have set you apart from the other nations so that you would belong to me alone.

27 "Any man or woman who consults the spirits of the dead shall be stoned to death; any of you that do this are responsible for your own death."

The Holiness of the Priests

21 The LORD commanded Moses to tell the Aaronite priests, "No priest is to make himself ritually unclean by taking part in the funeral ceremonies when a relative dies, 2 unless it is his mother, father, son, daughter, brother, 3 or unmarried sister living in his house. 4 He shall not make himself unclean at the death of those related to him by marriage. m

5 "No priest shall shave any part of his head or trim his beard or cut gashes on his body to show that he is in mourning. 6 He must be holy and must not disgrace my name. He offers food offerings to me, and he must be holy. 7 A priest shall not marry a woman who has been a prostitute or a woman who is not a virgin or who is divorced; he is holy. 8 The people must consider the priest holy, because he presents the food offerings to me. I am the LORD; I am holy and I make my people holy. 9 If a priest's daughter becomes a prostitute, she disgraces her father; she shall be burned to death.

10 "The High Priest has had the anointing oil poured on his head and has been consecrated to wear the priestly garments, so he must not leave his hair uncombed or tear his clothes to show that he is in mourning. 11-12 He has been dedicated to me and is not to make himself ritually unclean nor is he to defile my sacred Tent by leaving it and entering a house where there is a dead person, even if it is his own father or mother. 13 He shall marry a virgin, 14 not a widow or a divorced woman or a woman who has been a prostitute. He shall marry only a virgin from his own clan. 15 Otherwise, his children, who ought to be holy, will be ritually unclean. I am the LORD and I have set him apart as the High Priest."

16 The LORD commanded Moses 17 to tell Aaron, "None of your descendants who has any physical defects may present the food offering to me. This applies for all time to come. 18 No man with any physical defects may make the offering: no one who is blind, lame, disfigured, or deformed; 19 no one with a crippled hand or foot; 20 no one who is a hunchback or a

m Verse 4 in Hebrew is unclear.

dwarf; no one with any eye or skin disease; and no eunuch. 21 No descendant of Aaron the priest who has any physical defects may present the food offering to me. 22 Such a man may eat the food offered to me, both the holy food offering and the very holy food offering, 23 but because he has a physical defect, he shall not come near the sacred curtain or approach the altar. He must not profane these holy things, because I am the LORD and I make them holy."

24 This, then, is what Moses said to Aaron, the sons of Aaron, and to all the people of Israel.

The Holiness of the Offerings

22 The LORD commanded Moses 2 to tell Aaron and his sons, "You must not bring disgrace on my holy name, so treat with respect the sacred offerings that the people of Israel dedicate to me. I am the LORD. 3 If any of your descendants, while he is ritually unclean, comes near the sacred offerings which the people of Israel have dedicated to me, he can never again serve at the altar. This applies for all time to come. I am the LORD.

4 "None of the descendants of Aaron who has a dreaded skin disease or a discharge may eat any of the sacred offerings until he is ritually clean. Any priest is unclean if he touches anything which is unclean through contact with a corpse or if he has an emission of semen 5 or if he has touched an unclean animal or person. 6 Any priest who becomes unclean remains unclean until evening, and even then he may not eat any of the sacred offerings until he has taken a bath. 7 After the sun sets he is clean, and then he may eat the sacred offerings, which are his food. 8 He shall not eat the meat of any animal that has died a natural death or has been killed by wild animals; it will make him unclean. I am the LORD.

9 "All priests shall observe the regulations that I have given. Otherwise, they will become guilty and die, because they have disobeyed the sacred regulations. I am the LORD and I make them holy.

10 "Only a member of a priestly family may eat any of the sacred offerings; no one else may eat them — not even someone staying with a priest or hired by him. 11 But a priest's slaves, bought with his own money or born in his home, may eat the food the priest receives. 12 A priest's daughter who marries someone who is not a priest may not eat any of the sacred offerings. 13 But a widowed or divorced daughter who has no children and who has returned to live in her father's house as a dependent may eat the food her father receives as a priest. Only a member of a priestly family may eat any of it.

14 "If any people who are not members of a priestly family eat any of the sacred offerings without intending to, they must repay the priest its full value plus an additional 20 percent. 15 The priests shall not profane the sacred offerings 16 by letting any unauthorized people eat them; this would bring guilt and punishment on such people. I am the LORD and I make the offerings holy."

17 The LORD commanded Moses 18 to give Aaron and his sons and all the people of Israel the following regulations. When any Israelite or any foreigner living in Israel presents a burnt offering, whether as fulfillment of a vow or as a freewill offering, the animal must not have any defects. 19 To be accepted, it must be a male without any defects. 20 If you offer any animal that has any defects, the LORD will not accept it. 21 When anyone presents a fellowship offering to the LORD, whether as fulfillment of a vow or as a freewill offering, the animal must be without any defects if it is to be accepted. 22 Do not offer to the LORD any animal that is blind or crippled or mutilated, or that has a running sore or a skin eruption or scabs. Do not offer any such animals on the altar as a food offering. 23 As a freewill offering you may offer an animal that is stunted or not perfectly formed, but it is not acceptable in fulfillment of a vow. 24 Do not offer to the LORD any animal whose testicles have been crushed, cut, bruised, or torn off. This is not permitted in your land.

25 Do not offer as a food offering any animal obtained from a foreigner. Such animals are considered defective and are not acceptable.

26-27 When a calf or a lamb or a kid is born, it must not be taken from its mother for seven days, but after that it is acceptable as a food offering. 28 Do not sacrifice a cow and its calf or a sheep and its lamb or a goat and its kid on the same day. 29 When you offer a sacrifice of thanksgiving to the LORD, follow the rules so that you will be accepted; 30 eat it the same day and leave none of it until the next morning. 31 The LORD said, "Obey my commands; I am the LORD. 32 Do not bring disgrace on my holy name; all the people of Israel must acknowledge me to be holy. I am the LORD and I make you holy; 33 and I brought you out of Egypt to become your God. I am the LORD."

The Religious Festivals

23 The LORD gave Moses 2 the following regulations for the religious festivals, when the people of Israel are to gather for worship. 3 You have six days in which to do your work, but remember that the seventh day, the Sabbath, is a day of rest. On that day do not work, but gather for worship. The Sabbath belongs to the LORD, no matter where you live. 4 Proclaim the following festivals at the appointed times.

Passover and Unleavened Bread
(Numbers 28.16-25)

5 The Passover, celebrated to honor the LORD, begins at sunset on the fourteenth day of the first month. 6 On the fifteenth day the Festival of Unleavened Bread begins, and for seven days you must not eat any bread made with yeast. 7 On the first of these days you shall gather for worship and do none of your daily work. 8 Offer your food offerings to the LORD for seven days. On the seventh day you shall again gather for worship, but you shall do none of your daily work.

9-10 When you come into the land that the LORD is giving you and you harvest your grain, take the first sheaf to the priest. 11 He shall present it as a special offering to the LORD, so that you may be accepted. The priest shall present it the day after the Sabbath. 12 On the day you present the offering of grain, also sacrifice as a burnt offering a one-year-old male lamb that has no defects. 13 With it you shall present four pounds of flour mixed with olive oil as a food offering. The odor of this offering is pleasing to the LORD. You shall also present with it an offering of one quart of wine. 14 Do not eat any of the new grain, whether raw, roasted, or baked into bread, until you have brought this offering to God. This regulation is to be observed by all your descendants for all time to come.

The Harvest Festival
(Numbers 28.26-31)

15 Count seven full weeks from the day after the Sabbath on which you bring your sheaf of grain to present to the LORD. 16 On the fiftieth day, the day after the seventh Sabbath, present to the LORD another new offering of grain. 17 Each family is to bring two loaves of bread and present them to the LORD as a special gift. Each loaf shall be made of four pounds of flour baked with yeast and shall be presented to the LORD as an offering of the first grain to be harvested. 18 And with the bread the community is to present seven one-year-old lambs, one bull, and two rams, none of which may have any defects. They shall be offered as a burnt offering to the LORD, along with a grain offering and a wine offering. The odor of this offering is pleasing to the LORD. 19 Also offer one male goat as a sin offering and two one-year-old male lambs as a fellowship offering. 20 The priest shall present the bread with the two lambs as a special gift to the LORD for the priests. These offerings are holy. 21 On that day do none of your daily work, but gather for worship. Your descendants are to observe this regulation for all time to come, no matter where they live.

22 When you harvest your fields, do not cut the grain at the edges of the fields, and do not go back to cut the heads of grain that were left; leave them for poor people and foreigners. The LORD is your God.

The New Year Festival
(Numbers 29.1-6)

23-24 On the first day of the seventh month observe a special day of rest, and come together for worship when the trumpets sound. 25 Present a food offering to the LORD and do none of your daily work.

The Day of Atonement
(Numbers 29.7-11)

26-27 The tenth day of the seventh month is the day when the annual ritual is to be performed to take away the sins of the people. On that day do not eat anything at all; come together for worship, and present a food offering to the LORD. 28 Do no work on that day, because it is the day for performing the ritual to take away sin. 29 Any who eat anything on that day will no longer be considered God's people. 30 And if any do any work on that day, the LORD himself will put them to death. 31 This regulation applies to all your descendants, no matter where they live. 32 From sunset on the ninth day of the month to sunset on the tenth observe this day as a special day of rest, during which nothing may be eaten.

The Festival of Shelters
(Numbers 29.12-40)

33-34 The Festival of Shelters begins on the fifteenth day of the seventh month and continues for seven days. 35 On the first of these days come together for worship and do none of your daily work. 36 Each day for seven days you shall present a food offering. On the eighth day come together again for worship and present a food offering. It is a day for worship, and you shall do no work.

(37 These are the religious festivals on which you honor the LORD by gathering together for worship and presenting food offerings, burnt offerings, grain offerings, sacrifices, and wine offerings, as required day by day. 38 These festivals are in addition to the regular Sabbaths, and these offerings are in addition to your regular gifts, your offerings as fulfillment of vows, and your freewill offerings that you give to the LORD.)

39 When you have harvested your fields, celebrate this festival for seven days, beginning on the fifteenth day of the seventh month. The first day shall be a special day of rest. 40 On that day take some of the best fruit from your trees, take palm branches and limbs from leafy trees, and begin a religious festival to honor the LORD your God. 41 Celebrate it for seven days. This regulation is to be kept by your descendants for all time to come. 42 All the people of Israel shall live in shelters for seven days, 43 so that your descendants may know that the LORD made the people of Israel live in simple shelters when he led them out of Egypt. He is the LORD your God.

44 So in this way Moses gave the people of Israel the regulations for observing the religious festivals to honor the LORD.

Taking Care of the Lamps
(Exodus 27.20, 21)

24 The LORD told Moses 2 to give the following orders to the people of Israel: Bring pure olive oil of the finest quality for the lamps in the Tent, so that a light might be kept burning regularly. 3 Each evening Aaron shall light them and keep them burning until morning, there in the LORD's presence outside the curtain in front of the Covenant Box, which is in the Most Holy Place. This regulation is to be observed for all time to come. 4 Aaron shall take care of the lamps on the lampstand of pure gold and must see that they burn regularly in the LORD's presence.

The Bread Offered to God

5 Take twenty-four pounds of flour and bake twelve loaves of bread. 6 Put the loaves in two rows, six in each row, on the table covered with pure gold, which is in the LORD's presence. 7 Put some pure incense on each row, as a token food offering to the LORD to take the place of the bread. 8 Every Sabbath, for all time to come, the bread must be placed in the presence of the LORD. This is Israel's duty forever. 9 The bread belongs to Aaron and his descendants, and they shall eat it in a holy place, because this is a very holy part of the food offered to the LORD for the priests.

An Example of Just and Fair Punishment

10-11 There was a man whose father was an Egyptian and whose mother was an Israelite named Shelomith, the daughter of Dibri from the tribe of Dan. There in the camp this man quarreled with an Israelite. During the quarrel he cursed the LORD, so they took him to Moses, 12 put him under guard, and waited for the LORD to tell them what to do with him.

13 The LORD said to Moses, 14 "Take that man out of the camp. Everyone who heard him curse shall put his hands on the man's head to testify that he is guilty, and then the whole community shall stone him to death. 15 Then tell the people of Israel that anyone who curses God must suffer the consequences 16 and be put to death. Any Israelite or any foreigner living in Israel who curses the

THE JUBILEE YEAR

The Jubilee Year, also known as the Year of Restoration (Ez 46.17), was proclaimed on the fiftieth year after seven cycles of seven years. This fiftieth year was a time when specific instructions about property and slavery outlined in the Jewish law took effect (Lv 25.8–55).

The word *jubilee* comes from a Hebrew word meaning ram's horn or trumpet. The Jubilee Year was launched with a blast from a ram's horn on the Day of Atonement, signifying a call to celebration, liberation, and the beginning of a year for doing justice and loving mercy.

The fiftieth year was a special year in which to "proclaim freedom to all the inhabitants of the land" (Lv 25.10). Individuals who had sold themselves as slaves or indentured servants because of indebtedness were released from their debts and set free. If a family's land had been taken away because of indebtedness, this land was returned to the original owners in the Jubilee Year.

God apparently established the Jubilee Year to prevent the Israelites from oppressing and cheating one another (Lv 25.17). This law prevented a permanent system of classes from developing; it gave everyone the opportunity to start over, economically and socially.

LORD shall be stoned to death by the whole community.

17."Any who commit murder shall be put to death, 18 and any who kill an animal belonging to someone else must replace it. The principle is a life for a life. 19 "If any of you injure another person, whatever you have done shall be done to you. 20 If you break a bone, one of your bones shall be broken; if you put out an eye, one of your eyes shall be put out; if you knock out a tooth, one of your teeth shall be knocked out. Whatever injury you cause another person shall be done to you in return. 21 Whoever kills an animal shall replace it, but whoever kills a human being shall be put to death. 22 This law applies to all of you, to Israelites and to foreigners living among you, because I am the LORD your God."

23 When Moses had said this to the people of Israel, they took the man outside the camp and stoned him to death. In this way the people of Israel did what the LORD had commanded Moses.

The Seventh Year
(Deuteronomy 15.1-11)

25 The LORD spoke to Moses on Mount Sinai and commanded him 2 to give the following regulations to the people of Israel. When you enter the land that the LORD is giving you, you shall honor the LORD by not cultivating the land every seventh year. 3 You shall plant your fields, prune your vineyards, and gather your crops for six years. 4 But the seventh year is to be a year of complete rest for the land, a year dedicated to the LORD. Do not plant your fields or prune your vineyards. 5 Do not even harvest the grain that grows by itself without being planted, and do not gather the grapes from your unpruned vines; it is a year of complete rest for the land. 6 Although the land has not been cultivated during that year, it will provide food for you, your slaves, your hired men, the foreigners living with you, 7 your domestic animals, and the wild animals in your fields. Everything that it produces may be eaten.

The Year of Restoration

8 Count seven times seven years, a total of forty-nine years. 9 Then, on the tenth day of the seventh month, the Day of Atonement, send someone to blow a trumpet throughout the whole land. 10 In this way you shall set the fiftieth year apart and proclaim freedom to all the inhabitants of the land. During this year all property that has been sold shall be restored to the original owner or the descendants, and any who have been sold as slaves shall return to their families. 11 You shall not plant your fields or harvest the grain that grows by itself or gather the grapes in your unpruned vineyards. 12 The whole year shall be sacred for you; you shall eat only what the fields produce of themselves.

13 In this year all property that has been sold shall be restored to its original owner. 14 So when you sell land to an Israelite or buy land, do not deal unfairly. 15 The price is to be set according to the number of years the land can produce crops before the next Year of Restoration. 16 If there are many years, the price shall be higher, but if there are only a few years, the price shall be lower, because what is being sold is the number of crops the land can produce. 17 Do not cheat an Israelite, but obey the LORD your God.

The Problem of the Seventh Year

18 Obey all the LORD's laws and commands, so that you may live in safety in the land. 19 The land will produce its crops, and you will have all you want to eat and will live in safety.

20 But someone may ask what there will be to eat during the seventh year, when no fields are planted and no crops gathered. 21 The LORD will bless the land in the sixth year so that it will produce enough food for two years. 22 When you plant your fields in the eighth year, you will still be eating what you harvested during the sixth year, and you will have enough to eat until the crops you plant that year are harvested.

Restoration of Property

23 Your land must not be sold on a permanent basis, because you do not own it; it belongs to God, and you are like foreigners who are allowed to make use of it.

24 When land is sold, the right of the original owner to buy it back must be recognized. 25 If any of you Israelites become poor and are forced to sell your

land, your closest relative is to buy it back. 26 If you have no relative to buy it back, you may later become prosperous and have enough to buy it back yourself. 27 In that case you must pay to the one who bought it a sum that will make up for the years remaining until the next Year of Restoration, when you would in any event recover your land. 28 But if you do not have enough money to buy the land back, it remains under the control of the one who bought it until the next Year of Restoration. In that year it will be returned to its original owner.

29 If you sell a house in a walled city, you have the right to buy it back during the first full year from the date of sale. 30 But if you do not buy it back within the year, you lose the right of repurchase, and the house becomes the permanent property of the purchasers and their descendants; it will not be returned in the Year of Restoration. 31 But houses in unwalled villages are to be treated like fields; the original owner has the right to buy them back, and they are to be returned in the Year of Restoration. 32 However, Levites have the right to buy back at any time their property in the cities assigned to them. 33 If a house in one of these cities is sold by a Levite and is not bought back, it must be returned in the Year of Restoration,[n] because the houses which the Levites own in their cities are their permanent property among the people of Israel. 34 But the pasture land around the Levite cities shall never be sold; it is their property forever.

Loans to the Poor

35 If any Israelites living near you become poor and cannot support themselves, you must provide for them as you would for a hired worker, so that they can continue to live near you. 36 Do not charge Israelites any interest, but obey God and let them live near you. 37 Do not make them pay interest on the money you lend them, and do not make a profit on the food you sell them. 38 This is the command of the LORD your God, who brought you out of Egypt in order to give you the land of Canaan and to be your God.

Release of Slaves

39 If any Israelites living near you become so poor that they sell themselves to you as a slave, you shall not make them do the work of a slave. 40 They shall stay with you as hired workers and serve you until the next Year of Restoration. 41 At that time they and their children shall leave you and return to their family and to the property of their ancestors. 42 The people of Israel are the LORD's slaves, and he brought them out of Egypt; they must not be sold into slavery. 43 Do not treat them harshly, but obey your God. 44 If you need slaves, you may buy them from the nations around you. 45 You may also buy the children of the foreigners who are living among you. Such children born in your land may become your property, 46 and you may leave them as an inheritance to your children, whom they must serve as long as they live. But you must not treat any Israelites harshly.

47 Suppose a foreigner living with you becomes rich, while some Israelites become poor and sell themselves as slaves to that foreigner or to a member of that foreigner's family. 48 After they are sold, they still have the right to be bought back. A brother 49 or an uncle or a cousin or another close relative may buy them back; or if they themselves earn enough, they may buy their own freedom. 50 They must consult the one who bought them, and they must count the years from the time they sold themselves until the next Year of Restoration and must set the price for their release on the basis of the wages paid hired workers. 51-52 They must refund a part of the purchase price according to the number of years left, 53 as if they had been hired on an annual basis. Their master must not treat them harshly. 54 If they are not set free in any of these ways, they and their children must be set free in the next Year of Restoration. 55 Israelites cannot be permanent slaves, because the people of Israel are the LORD's slaves. He brought them out of Egypt; he is the LORD their God.

Blessings for Obedience

(Deuteronomy 7.12-24; 28.1-14)

26 The LORD said, "Do not make idols or set up statues, stone pillars, or carved stones to worship. I am

---

[n] *Probable text* If a house . . . Restoration; *Hebrew unclear.*

the LORD your God. 2 Keep the religious festivals and honor the place where I am worshiped. I am the LORD.

3 "If you live according to my laws and obey my commands, 4 I will send you rain at the right time, so that the land will produce crops and the trees will bear fruit. 5 Your crops will be so plentiful that you will still be harvesting grain when it is time to pick grapes, and you will still be picking grapes when it is time to plant grain. You will have all that you want to eat, and you can live in safety in your land.

6 "I will give you peace in your land, and you can sleep without being afraid of anyone. I will get rid of the dangerous animals in the land, and there will be no more war there. 7 You will be victorious over your enemies; 8 five of you will be able to defeat a hundred, and a hundred will be able to defeat ten thousand. 9 I will bless you and give you many children; I will keep my part of the covenant that I made with you. 10 Your harvests will be so plentiful that they will last for a year, and even then you will have to throw away what is left of the old harvest to make room for the new. 11 I will live among you in my sacred Tent, and I will never turn away from you. 12 I will be with you; I will be your God, and you will be my people. 13 I, the LORD your God, brought you out of Egypt so that you would no longer be slaves. I broke the power that held you down and I let you walk with your head held high."

Punishment for Disobedience
(Deuteronomy 28.15-68)

14 The LORD said, "If you will not obey my commands, you will be punished. 15 If you refuse to obey my laws and commands and break the covenant I have made with you, 16 I will punish you. I will bring disaster on you—incurable diseases and fevers that will make you blind and cause your life to waste away. You will plant your crops, but it will do you no good, because your enemies will conquer you and eat what you have grown. 17 I will turn against you, so that you will be defeated, and those who hate you will rule over you; you will be so terrified that you will run when no one is chasing you.

18 "If even after all of this you still do not obey me, I will increase your punishment seven times. 19 I will break your stubborn pride; there will be no rain, and your land will be dry and as hard as iron. 20 All your hard work will do you no good, because your land will not produce crops and the trees will not bear fruit.

21 "If you still continue to resist me and refuse to obey me, I will again increase your punishment seven times. 22 I will send dangerous animals among you, and they will kill your children, destroy your livestock, and leave so few of you that your roads will be deserted.

23 "If after all of this punishment you still do not listen to me, but continue to defy me, 24 then I will turn on you and punish you seven times harder than before. 25 I will bring war on you to punish you for breaking our covenant, and if you gather in your cities for safety, I will send incurable diseases among you, and you will be forced to surrender to your enemies. 26 I will cut off your food supply, so that ten women will need only one oven to bake all the bread they have. They will ration it out, and when you have eaten it all, you will still be hungry.

27 "If after all of this you still continue to defy me and refuse to obey me, 28 then in my anger I will turn on you and again make your punishment seven times worse than before. 29 Your hunger will be so great that you will eat your own children. 30 I will destroy your places of worship on the hills, tear down your incense altars, and throw your dead bodies on your fallen idols. In utter disgust 31 I will turn your cities into ruins, destroy your places of worship, and refuse to accept your sacrifices. 32 I will destroy your land so completely that the enemies who occupy it will be shocked at the destruction. 33 I will bring war on you and scatter you in foreign lands. Your land will be deserted, and your cities left in ruins. 34-35 Then the land will enjoy the years of complete rest that you would not give it; it will lie abandoned and get its rest while you are in exile in the land of your enemies.

36 "I will make those of you who are in exile so terrified that the sound of a leaf blowing in the wind will make you run. You will run as if you were being pursued in battle, and you will fall when there is no enemy near you. 37 You will stumble over one another when no one is chasing you, and you will be unable to fight against any enemy. 38 You will die

in exile, swallowed up by the land of your enemies. 39 The few of you who survive in the land of your enemies will waste away because of your own sin and the sin of your ancestors.

40 "But your descendants will confess their sins and the sins of their ancestors, who resisted me and rebelled against me, 41 and caused me to turn against them and send them into exile in the land of their enemies. At last, when your descendants are humbled and they have paid the penalty for their sin and rebellion, 42 I will remember my covenant with Jacob and with Isaac and with Abraham, and I will renew my promise to give my people the land. 43 First, however, the land must be rid of its people, so that it can enjoy its complete rest, and they must pay the full penalty for having rejected my laws and my commands. 44 But even then, when they are still in the land of their enemies, I will not completely abandon them or destroy them. That would put an end to my covenant with them, and I am the LORD their God. 45 I will renew the covenant that I made with their ancestors when I showed all the nations my power by bringing my people out of Egypt, in order that I, the LORD, might be their God."

46 All these are the laws and commands that the LORD gave to Moses on Mount Sinai for the people of Israel.

Laws concerning Gifts to the LORD

27 The LORD gave Moses 2 the following regulations for the people of Israel. When any of you have been given to the LORD in fulfillment of a special vow, you may be set free by the payment of the following sums of money, 3-7 according to the official standard:

—adult male, twenty to sixty years old: 50 pieces of silver
—adult female: 30 pieces of silver
—young male, five to twenty years old: 20 pieces of silver
—young female: 10 pieces of silver
—infant male under five: 5 pieces of silver
—infant female: 3 pieces of silver
—male above sixty years of age: 15 pieces of silver
—female above sixty: 10 pieces of silver

8 If any of you make a vow and are too poor to pay the standard price, you shall bring the person to the priest, and the priest will set a lower price, according to your ability to pay.

9 If your vow concerns an animal that is acceptable as an offering to the LORD, then every gift made to the LORD is sacred, 10 and you may not substitute another animal for it. If you do, both animals belong to the LORD. 11 But if your vow concerns a ritually unclean animal, which is not acceptable as an offering to the LORD, you shall take the animal to the priest. 12 The priest shall set a price for it, according to its good or bad qualities, and the price will be final. 13 If you wish to buy it back, you must pay the price plus an additional 20 percent.

14 When any of you dedicate your house to the LORD, the priest shall set the price according to its good or bad points, and the price will be final. 15 If you wish to buy your house back, you must pay the price plus an additional 20 percent.

16 If any of you dedicate part of your land to the LORD, the price shall be set according to the amount of seed it takes to sow it, at the rate of ten pieces of silver per bushel of barley. 17 If you dedicate the land immediately after a Year of Restoration, the full price applies. 18 If you dedicate it any time later, the priest shall estimate the cash value according to the number of years left until the next Year of Restoration, and set a reduced price. 19 If you wish to buy your field back, you must pay the price plus an additional 20 percent. 20 If you sell the field to someone else without first buying it back from the LORD, you lose the right to buy it back. 21 At the next Year of Restoration the field will become the LORD's permanent property; it shall belong to the priests.

22 If you dedicate to the LORD a field that you have bought, 23 the priest shall estimate its value according to the number of years until the next Year of Restoration, and you must pay the price that very day; the money belongs to the LORD. 24 At the Year of Restoration the field shall be returned to the original owner or to the descendants.

25 All prices shall be set according to the official standard.

26 The first-born of an animal already belongs to the LORD, so no one may dedicate it to him as a freewill offering. A calf, a lamb, or a kid belongs to the LORD,

27 but the first-born of an unclean animal may be bought back at the standard price plus an additional 20 percent. If it is not bought back, it may be sold to someone else at the standard price.

28 None of you may sell or buy back what you have unconditionally dedicated[o] to the LORD, whether it is a human being, an animal, or land. It belongs permanently to the LORD. 29 Not even human beings who have been unconditionally dedicated may be bought back; they must be put to death.

30 One tenth of all the produce of the land, whether grain or fruit, belongs to the LORD. 31 If you wish to buy any of it back, you must pay the standard price plus an additional 20 percent. 32 One of every ten domestic animals belongs to the LORD. When the animals are counted, every tenth one belongs to the LORD. 33 You may not arrange the animals so that the poor animals are chosen, and you may not make any substitutions. If you do substitute one animal for another, then both animals will belong to the LORD and may not be bought back.

34 These are the commands that the LORD gave Moses on Mount Sinai for the people of Israel.

[o] UNCONDITIONALLY DEDICATED: *Anything dedicated in this way belonged completely to the LORD and could not be used; it had to be destroyed.*

NUMBERS

Introduction

The book of Numbers tells the story of the Israelites during the nearly forty years from the time they left Mount Sinai until they reached the eastern border of the land that God had promised to give them. The name of the book refers to a prominent feature of the story, that is, the census which Moses took of the Israelites at Mount Sinai before their departure, and again in Moab, east of the Jordan, about a generation later. In the period between the two censuses the Israelites went to Kadesh Barnea on the southern border of Canaan, but failed to enter the promised land from there. After spending many years in that area, they went to the region east of the Jordan River, where part of the people settled and where the rest prepared to cross the river into Canaan.

The book of Numbers is an account of a people who were often discouraged and afraid in the face of hardship, and who rebelled against God and against Moses, the man God appointed to lead them. It is the story of God's faithful, persistent care for his people in spite of their weakness and disobedience, and of Moses' steadfast, if sometimes impatient, devotion both to God and to his people.

Outline of Contents

The First Census of Israel

1 On the first day of the second month in the second year after the people of Israel left Egypt, the LORD spoke to Moses there in the Tent of his presence in the Sinai Desert. He said, 2 "You and Aaron are to take a census of the people of Israel by clans and families. List the names of all the men 3 twenty years old or older who are fit for military service. 4 Ask one clan chief from each tribe to help you." 5-16 These are the men, leaders within their tribes, who were chosen from the community for this work:

Tribe	Clan chief
Reuben	Elizur son of Shedeur
Simeon	Shelumiel son of Zurishaddai
Judah	Nahshon son of Amminadab
Issachar	Nethanel son of Zuar
Zebulun	Eliab son of Helon
Ephraim	Elishama son of Ammihud
Manasseh	Gamaliel son of Pedahzur
Benjamin	Abidan son of Gideoni
Dan	Ahiezer son of Ammishaddai
Asher	Pagiel son of Ochran
Gad	Eliasaph son of Deuel
Naphtali	Ahira son of Enan

17 With the help of these twelve men Moses and Aaron 18 called together the whole community on the first day of the second month and registered all the people by clans and families. The names of all the men twenty years old or older were recorded and counted, 19 as the LORD had commanded. In the Sinai Desert, Moses registered the people. 20-46 The men twenty years old or older who were fit for military service were registered by name according to clan

N
U
M
B
E
R
S

and family, beginning with the tribe of Reuben, Jacob's oldest son. The totals were as follows:

Tribe	Number
Reuben	46,500
Simeon	59,300
Gad	45,650
Judah	74,600
Issachar	54,400
Zebulun	57,400
Ephraim	40,500
Manasseh	32,200
Benjamin	35,400
Dan	62,700
Asher	41,500
Naphtali	53,400
Total:	603,550

47 The Levites were not registered with the other tribes, 48 because the Lord had said to Moses, 49 "When you take a census of the men fit for military service, do not include the tribe of Levi. 50 Instead, put the Levites in charge of the Tent of my presence and all its equipment. They shall carry it and its equipment, serve in it, and set up their camp around it. 51 Whenever you move your camp, the Levites shall take the Tent down and set it up again at each new campsite. Anyone else who comes near the Tent shall be put to death. 52 The rest of the Israelites shall set up camp, company by company, each man with his own group and under his own banner. 53 But the Levites shall camp around the Tent to guard it, so that no one may come near and cause my anger to strike the community of Israel." 54 So the people of Israel did everything that the Lord had commanded Moses.

The Arrangement of the Tribes in Camp

2 The Lord gave Moses and Aaron the following instructions. 2 When the Israelites set up camp, each man will camp under the banner of his division and the flag of his own clan. The camp is to be set up all around the Tent.

3-9 On the east side, those under the banner of the division of Judah shall camp in their groups, under their leaders, as follows:

Tribe	Leader	Number
Judah	Nahshon son of Amminadab	74,600
Issachar	Nethanel son of Zuar	54,400
Zebulun	Eliab son of Helon	57,400
	Total:	186,400

The division of Judah shall march first.

10-16 On the south, those under the banner of the division of Reuben shall camp in their groups, under their leaders, as follows:

Tribe	Leader	Number
Reuben	Elizur son of Shedeur	46,500
Simeon	Shelumiel son of Zurishaddai	59,300
Gad	Eliasaph son of Deuel	45,650
	Total:	151,450

The division of Reuben shall march second.

17 Then, between the first two divisions and the last two the Levites are to march carrying the Tent. Each division shall march in the same order as they camp, each in position under its banner.

18-24 On the west, those under the banner of the division of Ephraim shall camp in their groups, under their leaders, as follows:

Tribe	Leader	Number
Ephraim	Elishama son of Ammihud	40,500
Manasseh	Gamaliel son of Pedahzur	32,200
Benjamin	Abidan son of Gideoni	35,400
	Total:	108,100

The division of Ephraim shall march third.

25-31 On the north, those under the banner of the division of Dan shall camp in their groups, under their leaders, as follows:

Tribe	Leader	Number
Dan	Ahiezer son of Ammishaddai	62,700
Asher	Pagiel son of Ochran	41,500
Naphtali	Ahira son of Enan	53,400
	Total:	157,600

The division of Dan shall march last. 32 The total number of the people of

Israel enrolled in the divisions, group by group, was 603,550. 33 As the LORD had commanded Moses, the Levites were not registered with the rest of the Israelites.

34 So the people of Israel did everything the LORD had commanded Moses. They camped, each under his own banner, and they marched, each with his own clan.

Aaron's Sons

3 This is the family of Aaron and Moses at the time the LORD spoke to Moses on Mount Sinai. 2 Aaron had four sons: Nadab, the oldest, Abihu, Eleazar, and Ithamar. 3 They were anointed and ordained as priests, 4 but Nadab and Abihu were killed when they offered unholy fire to the LORD in the Sinai Desert. They had no children, so Eleazar and Ithamar served as priests during Aaron's lifetime.

The Levites Are Appointed to Serve the Priests

5 The LORD said to Moses, 6 "Bring forward the tribe of Levi and appoint them as servants of Aaron the priest. 7 They shall do the work required for the Tent of my presence and perform duties for the priests and for the whole community. 8 They shall take charge of all the equipment of the Tent and perform the duties for the rest of the Israelites. 9 The only responsibility the Levites have is to serve Aaron and his sons. 10 You shall appoint Aaron and his sons to carry out the duties of the priesthood; anyone else who tries to do so shall be put to death."

11 The LORD said to Moses, 12-13 "The Levites are now to be mine. When I killed all the first-born of the Egyptians, I consecrated as my own the oldest son of each Israelite family and the first-born of every animal. Now, instead of having the first-born sons of Israel as my own, I have the Levites; they will belong to me. I am the LORD."

The Census of the Levites

14 In the Sinai Desert the LORD commanded Moses 15 to register the Levites by clans and families, enrolling every male a month old or older, 16 and Moses did so. 17-20 Levi had three sons: Gershon, Kohath, and Merari, who were the ancestors of the clans that bear their names. Gershon had two sons: Libni and Shimei; Kohath had four sons: Amram, Izhar, Hebron, and Uzziel; and Merari had two sons: Mahli and Mushi. They were the ancestors of the families that bear their names.

21 The clan of Gershon was composed of the families of Libni and Shimei. 22 The total number of males one month old or older that were enrolled was 7,500. 23 This clan was to camp on the west behind the Tent, 24 with Eliasaph son of Lael as chief of the clan. 25 They were responsible for the Tent, its inner cover, its outer cover, the curtain for the entrance, 26 the curtains for the court which is around the Tent and the altar, and the curtain for the entrance of the court. They were responsible for all the service connected with these items.

27 The clan of Kohath was composed of the families of Amram, Izhar, Hebron, and Uzziel. 28 The total number of males one month old or older that were enrolled was 8,600. 29 This clan was to camp on the south side of the Tent, 30 with Elizaphan son of Uzziel as chief of the clan. 31 They were responsible for the Covenant Box, the table, the lampstand, the altars, the utensils the priests use in the Holy Place, and the curtain at the entrance to the Most Holy Place. They were responsible for all the service connected with these items.

32 The chief of the Levites was Eleazar son of Aaron the priest. He was in charge of those who carried out the duties in the Holy Place.

33 The clan of Merari was composed of the families of Mahli and Mushi. 34 The total number of males one month old or older that were enrolled was 6,200. 35 This clan was to camp on the north side of the Tent, with Zuriel son of Abihail as chief of the clan. 36 They were assigned responsibility for the frames for the Tent, its bars, posts, bases, and all its fittings. They were responsible for all the service connected with these items. 37 They were also responsible for the posts, bases, pegs, and ropes for the outer court.

38 Moses and Aaron and his sons were to camp in front of the Tent on the east. They were responsible for carrying out the services performed in the Holy Place for the people of Israel. Anyone else who tried to do so was to be put to death. 39 The total number of all the Levite males one month old or older that Moses

enrolled by clans at the command of the LORD, was 22,000.

The Levites Take the Place of the First-Born Sons

40-41 The LORD said to Moses, "All of Israel's first-born sons belong to me. So register by name every first-born male Israelite, one month old or older. But in place of them I claim all the Levites as mine! I am the LORD! I also claim the livestock of the Levites in place of all the first-born of the livestock." **42** Moses obeyed, and registered all the first-born males **43** one month old or older; the total was 22,273.

44 The LORD said to Moses, **45** "Now dedicate the Levites as mine in place of all the first-born Israelite sons, and dedicate the livestock of the Levites in place of the first-born of the Israelites' livestock. **46** Since the first-born Israelite sons outnumber the Levites by 273, you must buy back the extra sons. **47** For each one pay five pieces of silver, according to the official standard, **48** and give this money to Aaron and his sons." **49** Moses obeyed and took **50** the 1,365 pieces of silver **51** and gave them to Aaron and his sons.

The Duties of the Levite Clan of Kohath

4 The LORD told Moses **2** to take a census of the Levite clan of Kohath by subclans and families, **3** and to register all the men between the ages of thirty and fifty who were qualified to work in the Tent of the LORD's presence. **4** Their service involves the most holy things.

5 The LORD gave Moses the following instructions. When it is time to break camp, Aaron and his sons shall enter the Tent, take down the curtain in front of the Covenant Box, and cover the Box with it. **6** They shall put a fine leather cover over it, spread a cloth of solid blue on top, and then insert the carrying poles.

7 They shall spread a blue cloth over the table for the bread offered to the LORD and put on it the dishes, the incense bowls, the offering bowls, and the jars for the wine offering. There shall always be bread on the table. **8** They shall spread a red cloth over all of this, put a fine leather cover over it, and then insert the carrying poles.

9 They shall take a blue cloth and cover the lampstand, with its lamps, tongs, trays, and all the olive oil containers. **10** They shall wrap it and all its equipment in a fine leather cover and place it on a carrying frame.

11 Next they shall spread a blue cloth over the gold altar, put a fine leather cover over it, and then insert the carrying poles. **12** They shall take all the utensils used in the Holy Place, wrap them in a blue cloth, put a fine leather cover over them, and place them on a carrying frame. **13** They shall remove the greasy ashes from the altar and spread a purple cloth over it. **14** They shall put on it all the equipment used in the service at the altar: fire pans, hooks, shovels, and basins. Then they shall put a fine leather cover over it and insert the carrying poles. **15** When it is time to break camp, the clan of Kohath shall come to carry the sacred objects only after Aaron and his sons have finished covering them and all their equipment. The Kohath clan must not touch the sacred objects, or they will die. These are the responsibilities of the Kohath clan whenever the Tent is moved.

16 Eleazar son of Aaron the priest shall be responsible for the whole Tent and for the oil for the lamps, the incense, the grain offerings, the anointing oil, and everything else in the Tent that has been consecrated to the LORD.

17 The LORD said to Moses and Aaron, **18** "Do not let the clan of Kohath **19** be killed by coming near these most sacred objects. To prevent this from happening, Aaron and his sons shall go in and assign each man his task and tell him what to carry. **20** But if the Kohathites enter the Tent and see the priests preparing the sacred objects for moving,[a] they will die."

The Duties of the Levite Clan of Gershon

21 The LORD told Moses **22** to take a census of the Levite clan of Gershon by subclans and families, **23** and to register all the men between the ages of thirty and fifty who were qualified to work in the Tent of the LORD's presence. **24** They shall

a see . . . moving; or see the sacred objects even for a moment.

be responsible for carrying the following objects: 25 the Tent, its inner cover, its outer cover, the fine leather cover on top of it, the curtain for the entrance, 26 the curtains and ropes for the court that is around the Tent and the altar, the curtains for the entrance of the court, and all the fittings used in setting up these objects. They shall perform all the tasks required for these things. 27 Moses and Aaron shall see to it that the Gershonites perform all the duties and carry everything that Aaron and his sons assign to them. 28 These are the responsibilities of the Gershon clan in the Tent; they shall carry them out under the direction of Ithamar son of Aaron the priest.

The Duties of the Levite Clan of Merari

29 The LORD told Moses to take a census of the Levite clan of Merari by subclans and families, 30 and to register all the men between the ages of thirty and fifty who were qualified to work in the Tent of the LORD's presence. 31 They shall be responsible for carrying the frames, bars, posts, and bases of the Tent, 32 and the posts, bases, pegs, and ropes of the court around the Tent, with all the fittings used in setting them up. Each man will be responsible for carrying specific items. 33 These are the responsibilities of the Merari clan in their service in the Tent; they shall carry them out under the direction of Ithamar son of Aaron the priest.

The Census of the Levites

34-48 Following the LORD's command, Moses, Aaron, and the leaders of the community took a census of the three Levite clans, Kohath, Gershon, and Merari. They did this by subclans and families and registered all the men between the ages of thirty and fifty who were qualified to work in the Tent of the LORD's presence, as follows:

Clan	Number
Kohath	2,750
Gershon	2,630
Merari	3,200
Total:	8,580

49 Each man was registered as the LORD had commanded Moses; and at the command of the LORD given through Moses,

each man was assigned responsibility for his task of serving or carrying.

Unclean People

5 The LORD said to Moses, 2 "Command the people of Israel to expel from the camp everyone with a dreaded skin disease or a bodily discharge and everyone who is unclean by contact with a corpse. 3 Send all these ritually unclean people out, so that they will not defile the camp, where I live among my people." 4 The Israelites obeyed and expelled them all from the camp.

Repayment for Wrongs Done

5 The LORD gave Moses 6 the following instructions for the people of Israel. When any of you are unfaithful to the LORD and commit a wrong against someone, 7 you must confess your sin and make full repayment, plus an additional 20 percent, to the person you have wronged. 8 But if that person has died and has no near relative to whom payment can be made, it shall be given to the LORD for the priest. This payment is in addition to the ram used to perform the ritual of purification for the guilty person. 9 Also every special contribution which the Israelites offer to the LORD belongs to the priest to whom they present it. 10 Each priest shall keep the offerings presented to him.

Cases of Wives with Suspicious Husbands

11 The LORD commanded Moses 12-14 to give the Israelites the following instructions. It may happen that a man becomes suspicious that his wife is unfaithful to him and has defiled herself by having intercourse with another man. But the husband may not be certain, for his wife may have kept it secret—there was no witness, and she was not caught in the act. Or it may happen that a husband becomes suspicious of his wife, even though she has not been unfaithful. 15 In either case the man shall take his wife to the priest. He shall also take the required offering of two pounds of barley flour, but he shall not pour any olive oil on it or put any incense on it, because it is an offering from a suspicious husband, made to bring the truth to light.

16 The priest shall bring the woman forward and have her stand in front of the

THE NAZIRITE VOW

The nazirite vow was an oath to abstain from certain worldly influences and to consecrate oneself to God. Among the Jews, the vow was an option for all persons, and it could be taken for a short period or for life. When the specified period was completed, the nazirite could appear before the priest for the ceremony of release. Nazirites who broke their vows could be restored only by observing specific restoration rites (Nu 6.9–20).

Nazirites expressed their dedication to God by (1) abstaining from all intoxicating drinks and grape products, (2) refusing to cut their hair, and (3) avoiding contact with the dead (Nu 6.3–7).

Persons associated with this nazirite vow in the Bible include Samson, Samuel, and John the Baptist. Samson's parents were told by the angel of the Lord that their son would be a nazirite until his death (Jg 13.7). Hannah dedicated Samuel to the nazirite way of life even before his birth (1 S 1.11, 28).

The self-denying life-style of John the Baptist indicates that he may have been a nazirite (Lk 1.15). John was so outspoken in his condemnation of sin in high places that he was executed by Herod, Roman governor of Palestine (Mk 6.17–28), at Herod's fortress palace in Machaerus.

The nazirite vow reminds us that God desires for all Christians to lead holy, separated lives. Such an exemplary witness requires God's grace and strong commitment on the believer's part to avoid corrupting influences.

altar. 17 He shall pour some holy water into a clay bowl and take some of the earth that is on the floor of the Tent of the LORD's presence and put it in the water to make it bitter. 18 Then he shall loosen the woman's hair and put the offering of flour in her hands. In his hands the priest shall hold the bowl containing the bitter water that brings a curse. 19 Then the priest shall make the woman agree to this oath spoken by the priest: "If you have not committed adultery, you will not be harmed by the curse that this water brings. 20 But if you have committed adultery, 21 may the LORD make your name a curse among your people. May he cause your genital organs to shrink and your stomach to swell up. 22 May this water enter your stomach and cause it to swell up and your genital organs to shrink."

The woman shall respond, "I agree; may the LORD do so."

23 Then the priest shall write this curse down and wash the writing off into the bowl of bitter water. 24 Before he makes the woman drink the water, which may then cause her bitter pain, 25 the priest shall take the offering of flour out of the woman's hands, hold it out in dedication to the LORD, and present it on the altar. 26 Then he shall take a handful of it as a token offering and burn it on the altar. Finally, he shall make the woman drink the water. 27 If she has committed adultery, the water will cause bitter pain; her stomach will swell up and her genital organs will shrink. Her name will become a curse among her people. 28 But if she is innocent, she will not be harmed and will be able to bear children.

29-30 This is the law in cases where a man is jealous and becomes suspicious that his wife has committed adultery. The woman shall be made to stand in front of the altar, and the priest shall perform this ritual. 31 The husband shall be free of guilt, but the woman, if guilty, must suffer the consequences.

Rules for Nazirites

6 The LORD commanded Moses 2 to give the following instructions to the people of Israel. Any of you, male or female, who make a special vow to become a nazirite and dedicate yourself to the LORD 3 shall abstain from wine and beer. You shall not drink any kind of drink made from grapes or eat any grapes or raisins. 4 As long as you are a nazirite, you shall not eat anything that comes from a grapevine, not even the seeds or skins of grapes.

5 As long as you are under the nazirite vow, you must not cut your hair or shave. You are bound by the vow for the full time that you are dedicated to the LORD, and you shall let your hair grow. 6-7 Your hair is the sign of your dedication to God, and so you must not defile yourself by going near a corpse, not even that of your father, mother, brother, or sister. 8 As long as you are a nazirite, you are consecrated to the LORD.

9 If your consecrated hair is defiled because you are right beside someone who suddenly dies, you must wait seven days and then shave your head; and so you become ritually clean. 10 On the eighth day you shall bring two doves or two pigeons to the priest at the entrance of the Tent of the LORD's presence. 11 The priest shall offer one as a sin offering and the other as a burnt offering, to perform the ritual of purification for you because of your contact with a corpse. On the same day you shall reconsecrate your hair 12 and rededicate to the LORD your time as a nazirite. The previous period of time doesn't count, because your consecrated hair was defiled. As a repayment offering you shall bring a one-year-old lamb.

13 When you complete your nazirite vow, you shall perform this ritual. You shall go to the entrance of the Tent 14 and present to the LORD three animals without any defects: a one-year-old male lamb for a burnt offering, a one-year-old ewe lamb for a sin offering, and a ram for a fellowship offering. 15 You shall also offer a basket of bread made without yeast: thick loaves made of flour mixed with olive oil and thin cakes brushed with olive oil, and in addition the required offerings of grain and wine.

16 The priest shall present all these to the LORD and offer the sin offering and the burnt offering. 17 He shall sacrifice the ram to the LORD as a fellowship offering, and offer it with the basket of bread; he shall also present the offerings of grain and wine. 18 At the entrance of the Tent you nazirites shall shave off your hair and put it on the fire on which the fellowship offering is being burned.

19 Then, when the shoulder of the ram

is boiled, the priest shall take it and put it, together with one thick loaf of bread and one thin cake from the basket, into the hands of the nazirite. 20 Next, the priest shall present them as a special gift to the LORD; they are a sacred offering for the priest, in addition to the breast and the leg of the ram which by law belong to the priest. After that, the nazirite may drink wine.

21 These are the regulations for you nazirites; but if you promise an offering beyond what your vow requires you to give, you must fulfill exactly the promise you made.

The Priestly Blessing

22 The LORD commanded Moses 23 to tell Aaron and his sons to use the following words in blessing the people of Israel:
24 May the LORD bless you and take
care of you;
25 May the LORD be kind and
gracious to you;
26 May the LORD look on you with
favor and give you peace.
27 And the LORD said, "If they pronounce my name as a blessing upon the people of Israel, I will bless them."

The Offerings of the Leaders

7 On the day Moses finished setting up the Tent of the LORD's presence, he anointed and dedicated the Tent and all its equipment, and the altar and all its equipment. 2 Then the clan chiefs who were leaders in the tribes of Israel, the same men who were in charge of the census, 3 brought their offerings to the LORD: six wagons and twelve oxen, a wagon for every two leaders and an ox for each leader. After they had presented them, 4 the LORD said to Moses, 5 "Accept these gifts for use in the work to be done for the Tent; give them to the Levites according to the work they have to do." 6 So Moses gave the wagons and the oxen to the Levites. 7 He gave two wagons and four oxen to the Gershonites, 8 and four wagons and eight oxen to the Merarites. All their work was to be done under the direction of Ithamar son of Aaron. 9 But Moses gave no wagons or oxen to the Kohathites, because the sacred objects they took care of had to be carried on their shoulders.

10 The leaders also brought offerings to celebrate the dedication of the altar.

When they were ready to present their gifts at the altar, 11 the LORD said to Moses, "Tell them that each day for a period of twelve days one of the leaders is to present his gifts for the dedication of the altar."

12-83 They presented their offerings in the following order:

Day	Tribe	Leader
1st	Judah	Nahshon son of Amminadab
2nd	Issachar	Nethanel son of Zuar
3rd	Zebulun	Eliab son of Helon
4th	Reuben	Elizur son of Shedeur
5th	Simeon	Shelumiel son of Zurishaddai
6th	Gad	Eliasaph son of Deuel
7th	Ephraim	Elishama son of Ammihud
8th	Manasseh	Gamaliel son of Pedahzur
9th	Benjamin	Abidan son of Gideoni
10th	Dan	Ahiezer son of Ammishaddai
11th	Asher	Pagiel son of Ochran
12th	Naphtali	Ahira son of Enan

The offerings each one brought were identical: one silver bowl weighing 50 ounces and one silver basin weighing 30 ounces, by the official standard, both of them full of flour mixed with oil for the grain offering; one gold dish weighing 4 ounces, full of incense; one young bull, one ram, and a one-year-old lamb, for the burnt offering; one goat for the sin offering; and two bulls, five rams, five goats, and five one-year-old lambs, for the fellowship offering.

84-88 The totals of the offerings brought by the twelve leaders for the dedication of the altar were as follows:
–twelve silver bowls and twelve
silver basins weighing a total
of 60 pounds
–twelve gold dishes weighing a
total of 48 ounces, filled with
incense
–twelve bulls, twelve rams, and
twelve one-year-old lambs,
plus the grain offerings that
go with them, for the burnt
offerings

—twelve goats for the sin offerings
—twenty-four bulls, sixty rams,
    sixty goats, sixty one-year-old
    lambs, for the fellowship
    offerings

89 When Moses went into the Tent to talk with the LORD, he heard the LORD speaking to him from above the lid on the Covenant Box, between the two winged creatures.b

Placing the Lamps

8 The LORD said to Moses, 2 "Tell Aaron that when he puts the seven lamps on the lampstand, he should place them so that the light shines toward the front." 3 Aaron obeyed and placed the lamps facing the front of the lampstand. 4 From top to bottom the lampstand was made of hammered gold, according to the pattern that the LORD had shown Moses.

The Purification and Dedication of the Levites

5 The LORD said to Moses, 6 "Separate the Levites from the rest of the people of Israel and purify them 7 in the following way: sprinkle them with the water of purification and have them shave their whole bodies and have them wash their clothes. Then they will be ritually clean. 8 Then they are to take a young bull and the required grain offering of flour mixed with olive oil; and you are to take another bull for the sin offering. 9 Then assemble the whole community of Israel and have the Levites stand in front of the Tent of my presence. 10 The people of Israel are to place their hands on the heads of the Levites, 11 and then Aaron shall dedicate the Levites to me as a special gift from the Israelites, so that they may do my work. 12 The Levites shall then put their hands on the heads of the two bulls; one is to be offered as a sin offering and the other as a burnt offering, in order to perform the ritual of purification for the Levites.

13 "Dedicate the Levites as a special gift to me, and put Aaron and his sons in charge of them. 14 Separate the Levites in this way from the rest of the Israelites, so that they will belong to me. 15 After you have purified and dedicated the Levites, they will be qualified to work in the Tent.

16 I have claimed them in the place of all the first-born sons of the Israelites, and they belong to me alone. 17 When I killed all the first-born in Egypt, I consecrated as my own the oldest son of each Israelite family and the first-born of every animal. 18 I am now taking the Levites instead of all the first-born of the Israelites, 19 and I assign the Levites to Aaron and his sons, as a gift from the Israelites, to work in the Tent for the people of Israel and to protect the Israelites from the disaster that would strike them if they came too near the Holy Place."

20 So Moses, Aaron, and all the people of Israel dedicated the Levites, as the LORD commanded Moses. 21 The Levites purified themselves and washed their clothes, and Aaron dedicated them as a special gift to the LORD. He also performed the ritual of purification for them. 22 The people did everything the LORD had commanded Moses concerning the Levites. And so the Levites were qualified to work in the Tent under Aaron and his sons.

23 The LORD said to Moses, 24 "From the age of twenty-five each Levite shall perform his duties in the Tent of my presence, 25 and at the age of fifty he shall retire. 26 After that, he may help his fellow Levites in performing their duties in the Tent, but he must not perform any service by himself. This is how you are to regulate the duties of the Levites."

The Second Passover

9 The LORD spoke to Moses in the Sinai Desert in the first month of the second year after the people of Israel had left Egypt. He said, 2-3 "On the fourteenth day of this month, beginning at sunset, the people of Israel are to observe the Passover according to all the rules and regulations for it." 4 So Moses told the people to observe the Passover, 5 and on the evening of the fourteenth day of the first month they did so in the Sinai Desert. The people did everything just as the LORD had commanded Moses.

6 But there were some people who were ritually unclean because they had touched a corpse, and they were not able to keep the Passover on that day. They went to Moses and Aaron 7 and said, "We are unclean because we have touched a

b WINGED CREATURES: See Word List.

corpse, but why should we be excluded from presenting the LORD's offering with the rest of the Israelites?"

⁸Moses answered, "Wait until I receive instructions from the LORD."

⁹The LORD told Moses ¹⁰to say to the people of Israel, "When any of you or your descendants are unclean from touching a corpse or are far away on a journey, but still want to keep the Passover, ¹¹you are permitted to observe it one month later instead, on the evening of the fourteenth day of the second month. Celebrate it with unleavened bread and bitter herbs. ¹²Do not leave any of the food until the following morning and do not break any of the animal's bones. Observe the Passover according to all the regulations. ¹³But if any of you are ritually clean and not away on a journey and do not observe the Passover, you shall no longer be considered my people, because you did not present the offering to me at the appointed time. You must suffer the consequences of your sin.

¹⁴"If foreigners living among you want to keep the Passover, they must observe it according to all the rules and regulations. The same law applies to everyone, whether native or foreigner."

The Fiery Cloud
(Exodus 40.34-38)

¹⁵⁻¹⁶On the day the Tent of the LORD's presence was set up, a cloud came and covered it. At night the cloud looked like fire. ¹⁷Whenever the cloud lifted, the people of Israel broke camp, and they set up camp again in the place where the cloud came down. ¹⁸The people broke camp at the command of the LORD, and at his command they set up camp. As long as the cloud stayed over the Tent, they stayed in the same camp. ¹⁹When the cloud stayed over the Tent for a long time, they obeyed the LORD and did not move on. ²⁰Sometimes the cloud remained over the Tent for only a few days; in any case, they remained in camp or moved, according to the command of the LORD. ²¹Sometimes the cloud remained only from evening until morning, and they moved on as soon as the cloud lifted. Whenever the cloud lifted, they moved on. ²²Whether it was two days, a month, a year, or longer, as long as the cloud remained over the Tent, they did not move on; but when it lifted, they moved.

²³They set up camp and broke camp in obedience to the commands which the LORD gave through Moses.

The Silver Trumpets

10 The LORD said to Moses, ²"Make two trumpets of hammered silver to use for calling the people together and for breaking camp. ³When long blasts are sounded on both trumpets, the whole community is to gather around you at the entrance to the Tent of my presence. ⁴But when only one trumpet is sounded, then only the leaders of the clans are to gather around you. ⁵When short blasts are sounded, the tribes camped on the east will move out. ⁶When short blasts are sounded a second time, the tribes on the south will move out. So short blasts are to be sounded to break camp, ⁷but in order to call the community together, long blasts are to be sounded. ⁸The trumpets are to be blown by Aaron's sons, the priests.

"The following rule is to be observed for all time to come. ⁹When you are at war in your land, defending yourselves against an enemy who has attacked you, sound the signal for battle on these trumpets. I, the LORD your God, will help you and save you from your enemies. ¹⁰Also on joyful occasions—at your New Moon Festivals and your other religious festivals—you are to blow the trumpets when you present your burnt offerings and your fellowship offerings. Then I will help you. I am the LORD your God."

The Israelites Break Camp

¹¹On the twentieth day of the second month in the second year after the people left Egypt, the cloud over the Tent of the LORD's presence lifted, ¹²and the Israelites started on their journey out of the Sinai Desert. The cloud came to rest in the wilderness of Paran.

¹³They began to march at the command of the LORD through Moses, ¹⁴and each time they moved, they were in the same order. Those under the banner of the division led by the tribe of Judah started out first, company by company, with Nahshon son of Amminadab in command. ¹⁵Nethanel son of Zuar was in command of the tribe of Issachar, ¹⁶and Eliab son of Helon was in command of the tribe of Zebulun.

¹⁷Then the Tent would be taken down,

and the clans of Gershon and Merari, who carried it, would start out.

18 Next, those under the banner of the division led by the tribe of Reuben would start out, company by company, with Elizur son of Shedeur in command. 19 Shelumiel son of Zurishaddai was in command of the tribe of Simeon, 20 and Eliasaph son of Deuel was in command of the tribe of Gad.

21 Then the Levite clan of Kohath would start out, carrying the sacred objects. By the time they arrived at the next camp, the Tent had been set up again. 22 Next, those under the banner of the division led by the tribe of Ephraim would start out, company by company, with Elishama son of Ammihud in command. 23 Gamaliel son of Pedahzur was in command of the tribe of Manasseh, 24 and Abidan son of Gideoni was in command of the tribe of Benjamin.

25 Finally, those under the banner of the division led by the tribe of Dan, serving as the rear guard of all the divisions, would start out, company by company, with Ahiezer son of Ammishaddai in command. 26 Pagiel son of Ochran was in command of the tribe of Asher, 27 and Ahira son of Enan was in command of the tribe of Naphtali. 28 This, then, was the order of march, company by company, whenever the Israelites broke camp and set out.

29 Moses said to his brother-in-law Hobab son of Jethro the Midianite, "We are about to start out for the place which the LORD said he would give us. He has promised to make Israel prosperous, so come with us, and we will share our prosperity with you."

30 Hobab answered, "No, I am going back to my native land."

31 "Please don't leave us," Moses said. "You know where we can camp in the wilderness, and you can be our guide. 32 If you come with us, we will share with you all the blessings that the LORD gives us."

The People Set Out

33 When the people left Sinai, the holy mountain, they traveled three days. The LORD's Covenant Box always went ahead of them to find a place for them to camp. 34 As they moved on from each camp, the cloud of the LORD was over them by day. 35 Whenever the Covenant Box started out, Moses would say, "Arise, LORD; scatter your enemies and put to flight those who hate you!" 36 And whenever it stopped, he would say, "Return, LORD, to the thousands of families of Israel."c

The Place Named Taberah

11 The people began to complain to the LORD about their troubles. When the LORD heard them, he became angry and sent fire on the people. It burned among them and destroyed one end of the camp. 2 The people cried out to Moses for help; he prayed to the LORD, and the fire died down. 3 So the place was named Taberah,d because there the fire of the LORD burned among them.

Moses Chooses Seventy Leaders

4 There were foreigners traveling with the Israelites. They had a strong craving for meat, and even the Israelites themselves began to complain: "If only we could have some meat! 5 In Egypt we used to eat all the fish we wanted, and it cost us nothing. Remember the cucumbers, the watermelons, the leeks, the onions, and the garlic we had? 6 But now our strength is gone. There is nothing at all to eat—nothing but this manna day after day!"

(7 Manna was like small seeds, whitish yellow in color. 8-9 It fell on the camp at night along with the dew. The next morning the people would go around and gather it, grind it or pound it into flour, and then boil it and make it into flat cakes. It tasted like bread baked with olive oil.)

10 Moses heard all the people complaining as they stood around in groups at the entrances of their tents. He was distressed because the LORD had become angry with them, 11 and he said to the LORD, "Why have you treated me so badly? Why are you displeased with me? Why have you given me the responsibility for all these people? 12 I didn't create them or bring them to birth! Why should you ask me to act like a nurse and carry them in my arms like babies all the way to the land you promised to their ancestors? 13 Where could I get enough meat

c Return . . . Israel; or Return, LORD, you who are like an army of millions for Israel.
d TABERAH: This name sounds like the Hebrew for "burning."

for all these people? They keep whining and asking for meat. 14I can't be responsible for all these people by myself; it's too much for me! 15If you are going to treat me like this, have pity on me and kill me, so that I won't have to endure your cruelty any longer."

16The LORD said to Moses, "Assemble seventy respected men who are recognized as leaders of the people, bring them to me at the Tent of my presence, and tell them to stand there beside you. 17I will come down and speak with you there, and I will take some of the spirit I have given you and give it to them. Then they can help you bear the responsibility for these people, and you will not have to bear it alone. 18Now tell the people, 'Purify yourselves for tomorrow; you will have meat to eat. The LORD has heard you whining and saying that you wished you had some meat and that you were better off in Egypt. Now the LORD will give you meat, and you will have to eat it. 19You will have to eat it not just for one or two days, or five, or ten, or even twenty days, 20but for a whole month, until it comes out of your ears, until you are sick of it. This will happen because you have rejected the LORD who is here among you and have complained to him that you should never have left Egypt.' "

21Moses said to the LORD, "Here I am leading 600,000 people, and you say that you will give them enough meat for a month? 22Could enough cattle and sheep be killed to satisfy them? Are all the fish in the sea enough for them?"

23"Is there a limit to my power?" the LORD answered. "You will soon see whether what I have said will happen or not!"

24So Moses went out and told the people what the LORD had said. He assembled seventy of the leaders and placed them around the Tent. 25Then the LORD came down in the cloud and spoke to him. He took some of the spirit he had given to Moses and gave it to the seventy leaders. When the spirit came on them, they began to shout like prophets, but not for long.

26Two of the seventy leaders, Eldad and Medad, had stayed in the camp and had not gone out to the Tent. There in the camp the spirit came on them, and they too began to shout like prophets. 27A young man ran out to tell Moses what Eldad and Medad were doing.

28Then Joshua son of Nun, who had been Moses' helper since he was a young man, spoke up and said to Moses, "Stop them, sir!"

29Moses answered, "Are you concerned about my interests? I wish that the LORD would give his spirit to all his people and make all of them shout like prophets!" 30Then Moses and the seventy leaders of Israel went back to camp.

The LORD Sends Quails

31Suddenly the LORD sent a wind that brought quails from the sea, flying three feet above the ground. They settled on the camp and all around it for miles and miles in every direction.e 32So all that day, all night, and all the next day, the people worked catching quails; no one gathered less than fifty bushels. They spread them out to dry all around the camp. 33While there was still plenty of meat for them to eat, the LORD became angry with the people and caused an epidemic to break out among them. 34That place was named Kibroth Hattaavah (which means "Graves of Craving"), because there they buried the people who had craved meat.

35From there the people moved to Hazeroth, where they made camp.

Miriam Is Punished

12 Moses had married a Cushitef woman, and Miriam and Aaron criticized him for it. 2They said, "Has the LORD spoken only throughg Moses? Hasn't he also spoken throughg us?" The LORD heard what they said. (3Moses was a humble man, more humble than anyone else on earth.)

4Suddenly the LORD said to Moses, Aaron, and Miriam, "I want the three of you to come out to the Tent of my presence." They went, 5and the LORD came down in a pillar of cloud, stood at the entrance of the Tent, and called out, "Aaron! Miriam!" The two of them stepped forward, 6and the LORD said, "Now hear what I have to say! When

---

e sea, flying . . . direction; or sea. They settled in the camp and all around it for miles and miles in every direction, until they were piled up three feet deep on the ground.   f Cushite (compare Hb 3.7); or Midianite; or Ethiopian.   g through; or to.

there are prophets among you,[h] I reveal myself to them in visions and speak to them in dreams. 7It is different when I speak with my servant Moses; I have put him in charge of all my people Israel.[i] 8So I speak to him face-to-face, clearly and not in riddles; he has even seen my form! How dare you speak against my servant Moses?"

9The LORD was angry with them; and so as he departed 10and the cloud left the Tent, Miriam's skin was suddenly covered with a dreaded disease and turned as white as snow. When Aaron looked at her and saw that she was covered with the disease, 11he said to Moses, "Please, sir, do not make us suffer this punishment for our foolish sin. 12Don't let her become like something born dead with half its flesh eaten away."

13So Moses cried out to the LORD, "O God, heal her!"

14The LORD answered, "If her father had spit in her face, she would have to bear her disgrace for seven days. So let her be shut out of the camp for a week, and after that she can be brought back in." 15Miriam was shut out of the camp for seven days, and the people did not move on until she was brought back in. 16Then they left Hazeroth and set up camp in the wilderness of Paran.

The Spies
(Deuteronomy 1.19-33)

13 The LORD said to Moses, 2"Choose one of the leaders from each of the twelve tribes and send them as spies to explore the land of Canaan, which I am giving to the Israelites." 3-15Moses obeyed and from the wilderness of Paran he sent out leaders, as follows:

Tribe	Leader
Reuben	Shammua son of Zaccur
Simeon	Shaphat son of Hori
Judah	Caleb son of Jephunneh
Issachar	Igal son of Joseph
Ephraim	Hoshea son of Nun
Benjamin	Palti son of Raphu
Zebulun	Gaddiel son of Sodi
Manasseh	Gaddi son of Susi
Dan	Ammiel son of Gemalli
Asher	Sethur son of Michael
Naphtali	Nahbi son of Vophsi
Gad	Geuel son of Machi

16These are the spies Moses sent to explore the land. He changed the name of Hoshea son of Nun to Joshua.

17When Moses sent them out, he said to them, "Go north from here into the southern part of the land of Canaan and then on into the hill country. 18Find out what kind of country it is, how many people live there, and how strong they are. 19Find out whether the land is good or bad and whether the people live in open towns or in fortified cities. 20Find out whether the soil is fertile and whether the land is wooded. And be sure to bring back some of the fruit that grows there." (It was the season when grapes were beginning to ripen.)

21So the men went north and explored the land from the wilderness of Zin in the south all the way to Rehob, near Hamath Pass in the north. 22They went first into the southern part of the land and came to Hebron, where the clans of Ahiman, Sheshai, and Talmai, the descendants of a race of giants called the Anakim, lived. (Hebron was founded seven years before Zoan in Egypt.) 23They came to Eshcol Valley, and there they cut off a branch which had one bunch of grapes on it so heavy that it took two men to carry it on a pole between them. They also brought back some pomegranates and figs. (24That place was named Eshcol[j] Valley because of the bunch of grapes the Israelites cut off there.)

25After exploring the land for forty days, the spies returned 26to Moses, Aaron, and the whole community of Israel at Kadesh in the wilderness of Paran. They reported what they had seen and showed them the fruit they had brought. 27They told Moses, "We explored the land and found it to be rich and fertile; and here is some of its fruit. 28But the people who live there are powerful, and their cities are very large and well fortified. Even worse, we saw the descendants of the giants there. 29Amalekites live in the southern part of the land; Hittites, Jebusites, and Amorites live in the hill country; and Canaanites

N
U
M
B
E
R
S

---

[h] *Some ancient translations* When . . . you; *Hebrew unclear.*   [i] I have put . . . Israel; *or he can* be trusted with all my affairs.   [j] ESHCOL: *This name in Hebrew means "bunch of grapes."*

live by the Mediterranean Sea and along the Jordan River."

30 Caleb silenced the people who were complaining against*k* Moses, and said, "We should attack now and take the land; we are strong enough to conquer it."

31 But the men who had gone with Caleb said, "No, we are not strong enough to attack them; the people there are more powerful than we are." 32 So they spread a false report among the Israelites about the land they had explored. They said, "That land doesn't even produce enough to feed the people who live there. Everyone we saw was very tall, 33 and we even saw giants there, the descendants of Anak. We felt as small as grasshoppers, and that is how we must have looked to them."

The People Complain

14 All night long the people cried out in distress. 2 They complained against Moses and Aaron, and said, "It would have been better to die in Egypt or even here in the wilderness! 3 Why is the LORD taking us into that land? We will be killed in battle, and our wives and children will be captured. Wouldn't it be better to go back to Egypt?" 4 So they said to one another, "Let's choose a leader and go back to Egypt!"

5 Then Moses and Aaron bowed to the ground in front of all the people. 6 And Joshua son of Nun and Caleb son of Jephunneh, two of the spies, tore their clothes in sorrow 7 and said to the people, "The land we explored is an excellent land. 8 If the LORD is pleased with us, he will take us there and give us that rich and fertile land. 9 Do not rebel against the LORD and don't be afraid of the people who live there. We will conquer them easily. The LORD is with us and has defeated the gods who protected them; so don't be afraid." 10 The whole community was threatening to stone them to death, but suddenly the people saw the dazzling light of the LORD's presence appear over the Tent.

Moses Prays for the People

11 The LORD said to Moses, "How much longer will these people reject me? How

much longer will they refuse to trust in me, even though I have performed so many miracles among them? 12 I will send an epidemic and destroy them, but I will make you the father of a nation that is larger and more powerful than they are!"

13 But Moses said to the LORD, "You brought these people out of Egypt by your power. When the Egyptians hear what you have done to your people, 14 they will tell it to the people who live in this land. These people have already heard that you, LORD, are with us, that you appear in plain sight when your cloud stops over us, and that you go before us in a pillar of cloud by day and a pillar of fire by night. 15 Now if you kill all your people, the nations who have heard of your fame will say 16 that you killed your people in the wilderness because you were not able to bring them into the land you promised to give them. 17 So now, LORD, I pray, show us your power and do what you promised when you said, 18 'I, the LORD, am not easily angered, and I show great love and faithfulness and forgive sin and rebellion. Yet I will not fail to punish children and grandchildren to the third and fourth generation for the sins of their parents.' 19 And now, LORD, according to the greatness of your unchanging love, forgive, I pray, the sin of these people, just as you have forgiven them ever since they left Egypt."

20 The LORD answered, "I will forgive them, as you have asked. 21 But I promise that as surely as I live and as surely as my presence fills the earth, 22 none of these people will live to enter that land. They have seen the dazzling light of my presence and the miracles that I performed in Egypt and in the wilderness, but they have tried my patience over and over again and have refused to obey me. 23 They will never enter the land which I promised to their ancestors. None of those who have rejected me will ever enter it. 24 But because my servant Caleb has a different attitude and has remained loyal to me, I will bring him into the land which he explored, and his descendants will possess the land 25 in whose valleys the Amalekites and the Canaanites now live. Turn back tomorrow and go into the

---

k complaining against; *or* gathered around.

wilderness in the direction of the Gulf of Aqaba."

The Lord Punishes the People for Complaining

26 The Lord said to Moses and Aaron, 27 "How much longer are these wicked people going to complain against me? I have heard enough of these complaints! 28 Now give them this answer: 'I swear that as surely as I live, I will do to you just what you have asked. I, the Lord, have spoken. 29 You will die and your corpses will be scattered across this wilderness. Because you have complained against me, none of you over twenty years of age will enter that land. 30 I promised to let you live there, but not one of you will, except Caleb and Joshua. 31 You said that your children would be captured, but I will bring them into the land that you rejected, and it will be their home. 32 You will die here in this wilderness. 33 Your children will wander in the wilderness for forty years, suffering for your unfaithfulness, until the last one of you dies. 34 You will suffer the consequences of your sin for forty years, one year for each of the forty days you spent exploring the land. You will know what it means to have me against you! 35 I swear that I will do this to you wicked people who have gathered together against me. Here in the wilderness every one of you will die. I, the Lord, have spoken.'"

36-37 The men Moses had sent to explore the land brought back a false report which caused the people to complain against the Lord. And so the Lord struck them with a disease, and they died. 38 Of the twelve spies only Joshua and Caleb survived.

The First Attempt to Invade the Land
(Deuteronomy 1.41-46)

39 When Moses told the Israelites what the Lord had said, they mourned bitterly. 40 Early the next morning they started out to invade the hill country, saying, "Now we are ready to go to the place which the Lord told us about. We admit that we have sinned."

41 But Moses said, "Then why are you disobeying the Lord now? You will not succeed! 42 Don't go. The Lord is not with

you, and your enemies will defeat you. 43 When you face the Amalekites and the Canaanites, you will die in battle; the Lord will not be with you, because you have refused to follow him."

44 Yet they still dared to go up into the hill country, even though neither the Lord's Covenant Box nor Moses left the camp. 45 Then the Amalekites and the Canaanites who lived there attacked and defeated them, and pursued them as far as Hormah.

Laws about Sacrifice

15 The Lord gave Moses 2 the following regulations for the people of Israel to observe in the land that he was going to give them. 3 A bull, a ram, a sheep, or a goat may be presented to the Lord as a burnt offering or as a sacrifice in fulfillment of a vow or as a freewill offering or as an offering at your regular religious festivals; the odor of these food offerings is pleasing to the Lord. 4-5 Whoever presents a sheep or a goat as a burnt offering to the Lord is to bring with each animal 2 pounds of flour mixed with 2 pints of olive oil as a grain offering, together with 2 pints of wine. 6 When a ram is offered, 4 pounds of flour mixed with 3 pints of olive oil are to be presented as a grain offering, 7 together with 3 pints of wine. The odor of these sacrifices is pleasing to the Lord. 8 When a bull is offered to the Lord as a burnt offering or as a sacrifice in fulfillment of a vow or as a fellowship offering, 9 a grain offering of 6 pounds of flour mixed with 4 pints of olive oil is to be presented, 10 together with 4 pints of wine. The odor of this sacrifice is pleasing to the Lord.

11 That is what shall be offered with each bull, ram, sheep, or goat. 12 When more than one animal is offered, the accompanying offering is to be increased proportionally. 13 All native Israelites are to do this when they present a food offering, an odor pleasing to the Lord. 14 And if at any time foreigners living among you, whether on a temporary or a permanent basis, make a food offering, an odor that pleases the Lord, they are to observe the same regulations. 15 For all time to come, the same[l] rules are

l Some ancient translations the same; Hebrew the congregation the same.

binding on you and on the foreigners who live among you. You and they are alike in the LORD's sight; 16the same laws and regulations apply to you and to them.

17The LORD gave Moses 18the following regulations for the people of Israel to observe in the land that he was going to give them. 19When any food produced there is eaten, some of it is to be set aside as a special contribution to the LORD. 20When you bake bread, the first loaf of the first bread made from the new grain is to be presented as a special contribution to the LORD. This is to be presented in the same way as the special contribution you make from the grain you thresh. 21For all time to come, this special gift is to be given to the LORD from the bread you bake.

22But suppose someone unintentionally fails to keep some of these regulations which the LORD has given Moses. 23And suppose that in the future the community fails to do everything that the LORD commanded through Moses. 24If the mistake was made because of the ignorance of the community, they are to offer a bull as a burnt offering, an odor that pleases the LORD, with the proper grain offering and wine offering. In addition, they are to offer a male goat as a sin offering. 25The priest shall perform the ritual of purification for the community, and they will be forgiven, because the mistake was unintentional and they brought their sin offering as a food offering to the LORD. 26The whole community of Israel and the foreigners living among them will be forgiven, because everyone was involved in the mistake.

27If any of you sin unintentionally, you are to offer a one-year-old female goat as a sin offering. 28At the altar the priest shall perform the ritual of purification to purify you from your sin, and you will be forgiven. 29The same regulation applies to all who unintentionally commit a sin, whether they are native Israelites or resident foreigners.

30But any who sin deliberately, whether they are natives or foreigners, are guilty of treating the LORD with contempt, and they shall be put to death, 31because they have rejected what the LORD said and have deliberately broken one of his commands. They are responsible for their own death.

The Man Who Broke the Sabbath

32Once, while the Israelites were still in the wilderness, a man was found gathering firewood on the Sabbath. 33He was taken to Moses, Aaron, and the whole community, 34and was put under guard, because it was not clear what should be done with him. 35Then the LORD said to Moses, "The man must be put to death; the whole community is to stone him to death outside the camp." 36So the whole community took him outside the camp and stoned him to death, as the LORD had commanded.

Rules about Tassels

37The LORD commanded Moses 38to say to the people of Israel: "Make tassels on the corners of your garments and put a blue cord on each tassel. You are to do this for all time to come. 39The tassels will serve as reminders, and each time you see them you will remember all my commands and obey them; then you will not turn away from me and follow your own wishes and desires. 40The tassels will remind you to keep all my commands, and you will belong completely to me. 41I am the LORD your God; I brought you out of Egypt to be your God. I am the LORD."

The Rebellion of Korah, Dathan, and Abiram

16 1-2Korah son of Izhar, from the Levite clan of Kohath, rebelled against the leadership of Moses. He was joined by three members of the tribe of Reuben—Dathan and Abiram, the sons of Eliab, and On son of Peleth—and by 250 other Israelites, well-known leaders chosen by the community. 3They assembled before Moses and Aaron and said to them, "You have gone too far! All the members of the community belong to the LORD, and the LORD is with all of us. Why, then, Moses, do you set yourself above the LORD's community?"

4When Moses heard this, he threw himself on the ground and prayed. 5Then he said to Korah and his followers, "Tomorrow morning the LORD will show us who belongs to him; he will let the one who belongs to him, that is, the one he has chosen, approach him at the altar. 6-7Tomorrow morning you and your followers take fire pans, put live coals and incense on them, and take them to the altar. Then we will see which of us the LORD has chosen. You Levites are the ones who have gone too far!"

8 Moses continued to speak to Korah. "Listen, you Levites! 9 Do you consider it a small matter that the God of Israel has set you apart from the rest of the community, so that you can approach him, perform your service in the LORD's Tent, and minister to the community and serve them? 10 He has let you and all the other Levites have this honor—and now you are trying to get the priesthood too! 11 When you complain against Aaron, it is really against the LORD that you and your followers are rebelling."

12 Then Moses sent for Dathan and Abiram, but they said, "We will not come! 13 Isn't it enough that you have brought us out of the fertile land of Egypt to kill us here in the wilderness? Do you also have to lord it over us? 14 You certainly have not brought us into a fertile land or given us fields and vineyards as our possession, and now you are trying to deceive us. We will not come!"

15 Moses became angry and said to the LORD, "Do not accept any offerings these men bring. I have not wronged any of them; I have not even taken one of their donkeys."

16 Moses said to Korah, "Tomorrow you and your 250 followers must come to the Tent of the LORD's presence; Aaron will also be there. 17 Each of you will take his fire pan, put incense on it, and then present it at the altar." 18 So they each took their fire pans, put live coals and incense on them, and stood at the entrance of the Tent with Moses and Aaron. 19 Then Korah gathered the whole community, and they stood facing Moses and Aaron at the entrance of the Tent. Suddenly the dazzling light of the LORD's presence appeared to the whole community, 20 and the LORD said to Moses and Aaron, 21 "Move back from these people, and I will destroy them immediately."

22 But Moses and Aaron bowed down with their faces to the ground and said, "O God, you are the source of all life. When one of us sins, do you become angry with the whole community?"

23 The LORD said to Moses, 24 "Tell the people to move away from the tents of Korah, Dathan, and Abiram."

25 Then Moses, accompanied by the leaders of Israel, went to Dathan and Abiram. 26 He said to the people, "Get away from the tents of these wicked men and don't touch anything that belongs to them. Otherwise, you will be wiped out with them for all their sins." 27 So they moved away from the tents of Korah, Dathan, and Abiram.

Dathan and Abiram had come out and were standing at the entrance of their tents, with their wives and children. 28 Moses said to the people, "This is how you will know that the LORD has sent me to do all these things and that it is not by my own choice that I have done them. 29 If these men die a natural death without some punishment from God, then the LORD did not send me. 30 But if the LORD does something unheard of, and the earth opens up and swallows them with all they own, so that they go down alive to the world of the dead, you will know that these men have rejected the LORD."

31 As soon as he had finished speaking, the ground under Dathan and Abiram split open 32 and swallowed them and their families, together with all of Korah's followers and their possessions. 33 So they went down alive to the world of the dead, with their possessions. The earth closed over them, and they vanished. 34 All the people of Israel who were there fled when they heard their cry. They shouted, "Run! The earth might swallow us too!"

35 Then the LORD sent a fire that blazed out and burned up the 250 men who had presented the incense.

The Fire Pans

36 Then the LORD said to Moses, 37 "Tell Eleazar son of Aaron the priest to remove the bronze fire pans from the remains of those who have been burned, and scatter the coals from the fire pans somewhere else, because the fire pans are holy. 38 They became holy when they were presented at the LORD's altar. So take the fire pans of these who were put to death for their sin, beat them into thin plates, and make a covering for the altar. It will be a warning to the people of Israel." 39 So Eleazar the priest took the fire pans and had them beaten into thin plates to make a covering for the altar. 40 This was a warning to the Israelites that no one who was not a descendant of Aaron should come to the altar to burn

incense for the LORD. Otherwise he would be destroyed like Korah and his men. All this was done as the LORD had commanded Eleazar through Moses.

Aaron Saves the People

41 The next day the whole community complained against Moses and Aaron and said, "You have killed some of the LORD's people." 42 After they had all gathered to protest to Moses and Aaron, they turned toward the Tent and saw that the cloud was covering it and that the dazzling light of the LORD's presence had appeared. 43 Moses and Aaron went and stood in front of the Tent, 44 and the LORD said to Moses, 45 "Move back from these people, and I will destroy them on the spot!"

The two of them bowed down with their faces to the ground, 46 and Moses said to Aaron, "Take your fire pan, put live coals from the altar in it, and put some incense on the coals. Then hurry with it to the people and perform the ritual of purification for them. Hurry! The LORD's anger has already broken out and an epidemic has already begun." 47 Aaron obeyed, took his fire pan and ran into the middle of the assembled people. When he saw that the plague had already begun, he put the incense on the coals and performed the ritual of purification for the people. 48 This stopped the plague, and he was left standing between the living and the dead. 49 The number of people who died was 14,700, not counting those who died in Korah's rebellion. 50 When the plague had stopped, Aaron returned to Moses at the entrance of the Tent.

Aaron's Walking Stick

17 The LORD said to Moses, 2 "Tell the people of Israel to give you twelve walking sticks, one from the leader of each tribe. Write each man's name on his stick 3 and then write Aaron's name on the stick representing Levi. There will be one stick for each tribal leader. 4 Take them to the Tent of my presence and put them in front of the Covenant Box, where I meet you. 5 Then the stick of the man I have chosen will sprout. In this way I will put a stop to the constant complaining of these Israelites against you."

6 So Moses spoke to the Israelites, and each of their leaders gave him a stick, one for each tribe, twelve in all, and Aaron's stick was put with them. 7 Moses then put all the sticks in the Tent in front of the LORD's Covenant Box.

8 The next day, when Moses went into the Tent, he saw that Aaron's stick, representing the tribe of Levi, had sprouted. It had budded, blossomed, and produced ripe almonds! 9 Moses took all the sticks and showed them to the Israelites. They saw what had happened, and each leader took his own stick back. 10 The LORD said to Moses, "Put Aaron's stick back in front of the Covenant Box. It is to be kept as a warning to the rebel Israelites that they will die unless their complaining stops." 11 Moses did as the LORD commanded.

12 The people of Israel said to Moses, "Then that's the end of us! 13 If anyone who even comes near the Tent must die, then we are all as good as dead!"

Duties of Priests and Levites

18 The LORD said to Aaron, "You, your sons, and the Levites must suffer the consequences of any guilt connected with serving in the Tent of my presence; but only you and your sons will suffer the consequences of service in the priesthood. 2 Bring in your relatives, the tribe of Levi, to work with you and help you while you and your sons are serving at the Tent. 3 They are to fulfill their duties to you and their responsibilities for the Tent, but they must not have any contact with sacred objects in the Holy Place or with the altar. If they do, both they and you will be put to death. 4 They are to work with you and fulfill their responsibilities for all the service in the Tent, but no unqualified person may work with you. 5 You and your sons alone must fulfill the responsibilities for the Holy Place and the altar, so that my anger will not again break out against the people of Israel. 6 I am the one who has chosen your relatives the Levites from among the Israelites as a gift to you. They are dedicated to me, so that they can carry out their duties in the Tent. 7 But you and your sons alone shall fulfill all the responsibilities of the priesthood that concern the altar and what is in the Most Holy Place. These things are your

responsibility, because I have given you the gift of the priesthood. Any unqualified person who comes near the sacred objects shall be put to death."

The Share of the Priests

8 The Lord said to Aaron, "Remember that I am giving you all the special contributions made to me that are not burned as sacrifices. I am giving them to you and to your descendants as the part assigned to you forever. 9 Of the most sacred offerings not burned on the altar, the following belong to you: the grain offerings, the sin offerings, and the repayment offerings. Everything that is presented to me as a sacred offering belongs to you and your sons. 10 You must eat these things in a holy place, and only males may eat them; consider them holy.

11 "In addition, any other special contributions that the Israelites present to me shall be yours. I am giving them to you, your sons, and your daughters for all time to come. Every member of your family who is ritually clean may eat them.

12 "I am giving you all the best of the first produce which the Israelites give me each year: olive oil, wine, and grain. 13 It all belongs to you. Every member of your family who is ritually clean may eat it.

14 "Everything in Israel that has been unconditionally dedicated to me belongs to you.

15 "Every first-born child or animal that the Israelites present to me belongs to you. But you must accept payment to buy back every first-born child, and must also accept payment for every first-born animal that is ritually unclean. 16 Children shall be bought back at the age of one month for the fixed price of five pieces of silver, according to the official standard. 17 But the first-born of cows, sheep, and goats are not to be bought back; they belong completely to me and are to be sacrificed. Throw their blood against the altar and burn their fat as a food offering, an odor pleasing to me. 18 The meat from them belongs to you, like the breast and the right hind leg of the special offering.

19 "I am giving to you, to your sons, and to your daughters, for all time to come, all the special contributions which the Israelites present to me. This is an un-

breakable covenant that I have made with you and your descendants."

20 The Lord said to Aaron, "You will not receive any property that can be inherited, and no part of the land of Israel will be assigned to you. I, the Lord, am all you need."

The Share of the Levites

21 The Lord said, "I have given to the Levites every tithe that the people of Israel present to me. This is in payment for their service in taking care of the Tent of my presence. 22 The other Israelites must no longer approach the Tent and in this way bring on themselves the penalty of death. 23 From now on only the Levites will take care of the Tent and bear the full responsibility for it. This is a permanent rule that applies also to your descendants. The Levites shall have no permanent property in Israel, 24 because I have given to them as their possession the tithe which the Israelites present to me as a special contribution. That is why I told them that they would have no permanent property in Israel."

The Levites' Tithe

25 The Lord commanded Moses 26 to say to the Levites: "When you receive from the Israelites the tithe that the Lord gives you as your possession, you must present a tenth of it as a special contribution to the Lord. 27 This special contribution will be considered as the equivalent of the offering which the farmer makes of new grain and new wine. 28 In this way you also will present the special contribution that belongs to the Lord from all the tithes which you receive from the Israelites. You are to give this special contribution for the Lord to Aaron the priest. 29 Give it from the best that you receive. 30 When you have presented the best part, you may keep the rest, just as the farmer keeps what is left after he makes his offering. 31 You and your families may eat the rest anywhere, because it is your wages for your service in the Tent. 32 You will not become guilty when you eat it, as long as you have presented the best of it to the Lord. But be sure not to profane the sacred gifts of the Israelites by eating any of the gifts before the best part is offered; if you do, you will be put to death."

NUMBERS

Ashes of the Red Cow

19 The LORD commanded Moses and Aaron [2] to give the Israelites the following regulations. Bring to Moses and Aaron a red cow which has no defects and which has never been worked, [3] and they will give it to Eleazar the priest. It is to be taken outside the camp and killed in his presence.[m] [4] Then Eleazar is to take some of its blood and with his finger sprinkle it seven times in the direction of the Tent. [5] The whole animal, including skin, meat, blood, and intestines, is to be burned in the presence of the priest. [6] Then he is to take some cedar wood, a sprig of hyssop, and a red cord and throw them into the fire. [7] After that, he is to wash his clothes and pour water over himself, and then he may enter the camp; but he remains ritually unclean until evening. [8] The one who burned the cow must also wash his clothes and pour water over himself, but he also remains unclean until evening. [9] Then someone who is ritually clean is to collect the ashes of the cow and put them in a ritually clean place outside the camp, where they are to be kept for the Israelite community to use in preparing the water for removing ritual uncleanness. This ritual is performed to remove sin. [10] The one who collected the ashes must wash his clothes, but he remains unclean until evening. This regulation is valid for all time to come, both for the Israelites and for the foreigners living among them.

Contact with a Corpse

[11] Those who touch a corpse are ritually unclean for seven days. [12] They must purify themselves with the water for purification on the third day and on the seventh day, and then they will be clean. But if they do not purify themselves on both the third and the seventh day, they will not be clean. [13] Those who touch a corpse and do not purify themselves remain unclean, because the water for purification has not been thrown over them. They defile the LORD's Tent, and they will no longer be considered God's people. [14] In the case of a person who dies in a tent, anyone who is in the tent at the time of death or who enters it becomes ritually unclean for seven days. [15] Every jar and pot in the tent that has no lid[n] on it also becomes unclean. [16] If any touch a person who has been killed or has died a natural death outdoors or if any touch a human bone or a grave, they become unclean for seven days.

[17] To remove the uncleanness, some ashes from the red cow which was burned to remove sin shall be taken and put in a pot, and fresh water added. [18] In the first case, someone who is ritually clean is to take a sprig of hyssop, dip it in the water, and sprinkle the tent, everything in it, and the people who were there. In the second case, someone who is ritually clean is to sprinkle the water on those who had touched the human bone or the dead body or the grave. [19] On the third day and on the seventh the person who is ritually clean is to sprinkle the water on the unclean persons. On the seventh day he is to purify those, who, after washing their clothes and pouring water over themselves, become ritually clean at sunset.

[20] Those who have become ritually unclean and do not purify themselves remain unclean, because the water for purification has not been thrown over them. They defile the LORD's Tent and will no longer be considered God's people. [21] You are to observe this rule for all time to come. The person who sprinkles the water for purification must also wash his clothes; anyone who touches the water remains ritually unclean until evening. [22] Whatever an unclean person touches is unclean, and anyone else who touches it remains unclean until evening.

Events at Kadesh
(Exodus 17.1-7)

20 In the first month the whole community of Israel came to the wilderness of Zin and camped at Kadesh. There Miriam died and was buried.

[2] There was no water where they camped, so the people gathered around Moses and Aaron [3] and complained: "It would have been better if we had died in front of the LORD's Tent along with the other Israelites. [4] Why have you brought us out into this wilderness? Just so that we can die here with our animals? [5] Why did you bring us out of Egypt into this

---

[m] It . . . presence; *or* He is to take it outside to the east of the camp and kill it.   [n] no lid; *or* no lid fastened.

miserable place where nothing will grow? There's no grain, no figs, no grapes, no pomegranates. There is not even any water to drink!" 6 Moses and Aaron moved away from the people and stood at the entrance of the Tent. They bowed down with their faces to the ground, and the dazzling light of the LORD's presence appeared to them.

7 The LORD said to Moses, 8 "Take the stick that is in front of the Covenant Box, and then you and Aaron assemble the whole community. There in front of them all speak to that rock over there, and water will gush out of it. In this way you will bring water out of the rock for the people, for them and their animals to drink." 9 Moses went and got the stick, as the LORD had commanded.

10 He and Aaron assembled the whole community in front of the rock, and Moses said, "Listen, you rebels! Do we have to get water out of this rock for you?" 11 Then Moses raised the stick and struck the rock twice with it, and a great stream of water gushed out, and all the people and animals drank.

12 But the LORD reprimanded Moses and Aaron. He said, "Because you did not have enough faith to acknowledge my holy power before the people of Israel, you will not lead them into the land that I promised to give them."

13 This happened at Meribah,o where the people of Israel complained against the LORD and where he showed them that he is holy.

The King of Edom Refuses to Let Israel Pass

14 Moses sent messengers from Kadesh to the king of Edom. They said, "This message is from your kinsmen, the tribes of Israel. You know the hardships we have suffered, 15 how our ancestors went to Egypt, where we lived many years. The Egyptians mistreated our ancestors and us, 16 and we cried to the LORD for help. He heard our cry and sent an angel, who led us out of Egypt. Now we are at Kadesh, a town at the border of your territory. 17 Please permit us to pass through your land. We and our cattle will not leave the road or go into your fields or

vineyards, and we will not drink from your wells. We will stay on the main roadp until we are out of your territory."

18 But the Edomites answered, "We refuse to let you pass through our country! If you try, we will march out and attack you."

19 The people of Israel said, "We will stay on the main road, and if we or our animals drink any of your water, we will pay for it — all we want is to pass through."

20 The Edomites repeated, "We refuse!" and they marched out with a powerful army to attack the people of Israel. 21 Because the Edomites would not let the Israelites pass through their territory, the Israelites turned and went another way.

The Death of Aaron

22 The whole community of Israel left Kadesh and arrived at Mount Hor, 23 on the border of Edom. There the LORD said to Moses and Aaron, 24 "Aaron is not going to enter the land which I promised to give to Israel; he is going to die, because the two of you rebelled against my command at Meribah. 25 Take Aaron and his son Eleazar up Mount Hor, 26 and there remove Aaron's priestly robes and put them on Eleazar. Aaron is going to die there." 27 Moses did what the LORD had commanded. They went up Mount Hor in the sight of the whole community, 28 and Moses removed Aaron's priestly robes and put them on Eleazar. There on the top of the mountain Aaron died, and Moses and Eleazar came back down. 29 The whole community learned that Aaron had died, and they all mourned for him for thirty days.

Victory over the Canaanites

21 When the Canaanite king of Arad in the southern part of Canaan heard that the Israelites were coming by way of Atharim, he attacked them and captured some of them. 2 Then the Israelites made a vow to the LORD: "If you will let us conquer these people, we will unconditionally dedicateq them and their cities to you and will destroy them." 3 The LORD heard them and helped them conquer the Canaanites. So the Israelites

---

o MERIBAH: This name in Hebrew means "complaining."   p main road; or King's Highway.
q UNCONDITIONALLY DEDICATE: Anything dedicated in this way belonged completely to the LORD and could not be used; it had to be destroyed.

completely destroyed them and their cities, and named the place Hormah.*r*

The Snake Made of Bronze

4 The Israelites left Mount Hor by the road that leads to the Gulf of Aqaba, in order to go around the territory of Edom. But on the way the people lost their patience 5 and spoke against God and Moses. They complained, "Why did you bring us out of Egypt to die in this desert, where there is no food or water? We can't stand any more of this miserable food!" 6 Then the LORD sent poisonous snakes among the people, and many Israelites were bitten and died. 7 The people came to Moses and said, "We sinned when we spoke against the LORD and against you. Now pray to the LORD to take these snakes away." So Moses prayed for the people. 8 Then the LORD told Moses to make a metal snake and put it on a pole, so that anyone who was bitten could look at it and be healed. 9 So Moses made a bronze snake and put it on a pole. Anyone who had been bitten would look at the bronze snake and be healed.

From Mount Hor to the Valley of the Moabites

10 The Israelites moved on and camped at Oboth. 11 After leaving that place, they camped at the ruins of Abarim in the wilderness east of Moabite territory. 12 Then they camped in Zered Valley. 13 From there they moved again and camped on the north side of the Arnon River, in the wilderness which extends into Amorite territory. (The Arnon was the border between the Moabites and the Amorites.) 14 That is why *The Book of the LORD's Battles* speaks of ". . . the town of Waheb in the area of Suphah, and the valleys; the Arnon River, 15 and the slope of the valleys that extend to the town of Ar and toward the border of Moab."

16 From there they went on to a place called Wells, where the LORD said to Moses, "Bring the people together, and I will give them water." 17 At that time the people of Israel sang this song:

"Wells, produce your water;
And we will greet it with a song —
18 The well dug by princes
And by leaders of the people,

Dug with a royal scepter
And with their walking sticks."

They moved from the wilderness to Mattanah, 19 and from there they went on to Nahaliel, and from Nahaliel to Bamoth, 20 and from Bamoth to the valley in the territory of the Moabites, below the top of Mount Pisgah, looking out over the desert.

Victory over King Sihon and King Og
(Deuteronomy 2.26 – 3.11)

21 Then the people of Israel sent messengers to the Amorite king Sihon to say: 22 "Let us pass through your land. We and our cattle will not leave the road and go into your fields or vineyards, and we will not drink water from your wells; we will stay on the main road*s* until we are out of your territory." 23 But Sihon would not permit the people of Israel to pass through his territory. He gathered his army and went out to Jahaz in the wilderness and attacked the Israelites. 24 But the Israelites killed many of the enemy in battle and occupied their land from the Arnon River north to the Jabbok, that is, to the Ammonites, because the Ammonite border was strongly defended.*t* 25 So the people of Israel captured all the Amorite cities, including Heshbon and all the surrounding towns, and settled in them. 26 Heshbon was the capital city of the Amorite king Sihon, who had fought against the former king of Moab and had captured all his land as far as the Arnon River. 27 That is why the poets sing,

"Come to Heshbon, to King
    Sihon's city!
We want to see it rebuilt and
    restored.
28 Once from this city of Heshbon
Sihon's army went forth like a
    fire;
It destroyed the city of Ar in Moab
And devoured*u* the hills of the
    upper Arnon.
29 How terrible for you, people of
    Moab!
You worshipers of Chemosh are
    brought to ruin!

r HORMAH: *This name in Hebrew means "destruction."*   *s* main road; *or* King's Highway.
t because . . . strongly defended; *some ancient translations* as far as Jazer on the Ammonite border.   *u* One ancient translation devoured; *Hebrew* the lords of.

Your god let the men become
   refugees,
And the women became captives
   of the Amorite king.
30 But now their descendants are
   destroyed,
All the way from Heshbon to
   Dibon,
From Nashim to Nophah, near
   Medeba."ᵛ

31 So the people of Israel settled in the territory of the Amorites, 32 and Moses sent men to find the best way to attack the city of Jazer. The Israelites captured it and its surrounding towns and drove out the Amorites living there.

33 Then the Israelites turned and took the road to Bashan, and King Og of Bashan marched out with his army to attack them at Edrei. 34 The LORD said to Moses, "Do not be afraid of him. I will give you victory over him, all his people, and his land. Do to him what you did to Sihon, the Amorite king who ruled at Heshbon." 35 So the Israelites killed Og, his sons, and all his people, leaving no survivors, and then they occupied his land.

The King of Moab Sends for Balaam

22 The Israelites moved on and set up camp in the plains of Moab east of the Jordan and opposite Jericho.

2 When the king of Moab, Balak son of Zippor, heard what the Israelites had done to the Amorites and how many Israelites there were, 3 he and all his people became terrified. 4 The Moabites said to the leaders of the Midianites, "This horde will soon destroy everything around us, like a bull eating the grass in a pasture." So King Balak 5 sent messengers to summon Balaam son of Beor, who was at Pethor near the Euphrates River in the land of Amaw. They brought him this message from Balak: "I want you to know that a whole nation has come from Egypt; its people are spreading out everywhere and threatening to take over our land. 6 They outnumber us, so please come and put a curse on them for me. Then perhaps we will be able to defeat them and drive them out of the land. I know that when you pronounce a blessing, people are blessed, and when you

pronounce a curse, they are placed under a curse."

7 So the Moabite and Midianite leaders took with them the payment for the curse, went to Balaam, and gave him Balak's message. 8 Balaam said to them, "Spend the night here, and tomorrow I will report to you whatever the LORD tells me." So the Moabite leaders stayed with Balaam.

9 God came to Balaam and asked, "Who are these people that are staying with you?"

10 He answered, "King Balak of Moab has sent them to tell me 11 that a people who came from Egypt has spread out over the whole land. He wants me to curse them for him, so that he can fight them and drive them out."

12 God said to Balaam, "Do not go with them, and do not put a curse on the people of Israel, because they have my blessing."

13 The next morning Balaam went to Balak's messengers and said, "Go back home; the LORD has refused to let me go with you." 14 So they returned to Balak and told him that Balaam had refused to come with them.

15 Then Balak sent a larger number of leaders, who were more important than the first. 16 They went to Balaam and gave him this message from Balak: "Please don't let anything prevent you from coming to me! 17 I will reward you richly and do anything you say. Please come and curse these people for me."

18 But Balaam answered, "Even if Balak gave me all the silver and gold in his palace, I could not disobey the command of the LORD my God in even the smallest matter. 19 But please spend the night, as the others did, so that I may learn whether or not the LORD has something else to tell me."

20 That night God came to Balaam and said, "If these men have come to ask you to go with them, get ready and go, but do only what I tell you." 21 So the next morning Balaam saddled his donkey and went with the Moabite leaders.

Balaam and His Donkey

22 God was angry that Balaam was going, and as Balaam was riding along on his donkey, accompanied by his two

servants, the angel of the LORD stood in the road to bar his way. 23 When the donkey saw the angel standing there holding a sword, it left the road and turned into the fields. Balaam beat the donkey and brought it back onto the road. 24 Then the angel stood where the road narrowed between two vineyards and had a stone wall on each side. 25 When the donkey saw the angel, it moved over against the wall and crushed Balaam's foot against it. Again Balaam beat the donkey. 26 Once more the angel moved ahead; he stood in a narrow place where there was no room at all to pass on either side. 27 This time, when the donkey saw the angel, it lay down. Balaam lost his temper and began to beat the donkey with his stick. 28 Then the LORD gave the donkey the power of speech, and it said to Balaam, "What have I done to you? Why have you beaten me these three times?"

29 Balaam answered, "Because you have made a fool of me! If I had a sword, I would kill you."

30 The donkey replied, "Am I not the same donkey on which you have ridden all your life? Have I ever treated you like this before?"

"No," he answered.

31 Then the LORD let Balaam see the angel standing there with his sword; and Balaam threw himself face downward on the ground. 32 The angel demanded, "Why have you beaten your donkey three times like this? I have come to bar your way, because you should not be making this journey.w 33 But your donkey saw me and turned aside three times. If it hadn't, I would have killed you and spared the donkey."

34 Balaam replied, "I have sinned. I did not know that you were standing in the road to oppose me; but now if you think it is wrong for me to go on, I will return home."

35 But the angel said, "Go on with these men, but say only what I tell you to say." So Balaam went on with them.

Balak Welcomes Balaam

36 When Balak heard that Balaam was coming, he went to meet him at Ar, a city on the Arnon River at the border of Moab. 37 Balak said to him, "Why didn't you come when I sent for you the first time? Did you think I wasn't able to reward you enough?"

38 Balaam answered, "I came, didn't I? But now, what power do I have? I can say only what God tells me to say." 39 So Balaam went with Balak to the town of Huzoth, 40 where Balak slaughtered cattle and sheep and gave some of the meat to Balaam and the leaders who were with him.

Balaam's First Prophecy

41 The next morning Balak took Balaam up to Bamoth Baal, from where Balaam could see a part of the people of

23 Israel. 1 He said to Balak, "Build seven altars here for me, and bring me seven bulls and seven rams."

2 Balak did as he was told, and he and Balaam offered a bull and a ram on each altar. 3 Then Balaam said to Balak, "Stand here by your burnt offering, while I go to see whether or not the LORD will meet me. I will tell you whatever he reveals to me." So he went alone to the top of a hill, 4 and God met him. Balaam said to him, "I have built the seven altars and offered a bull and a ram on each."

5 The LORD told Balaam what to say and sent him back to Balak to give him his message. 6 So he went back and found Balak still standing by his burnt offering with all the leaders of Moab.

7 Balaam uttered this prophecy:

"Balak king of Moab has
    brought me
From Syria, from the eastern
    mountains.
'Come speak for me,' he said.
'Put a curse on the people of
    Israel.'
8 How can I curse what God has
    not cursed,
Or speak of doom when the LORD
    has not?
9 From the high rocks I can see
    them;
I can watch them from the hills.
They are a nation that lives alone;
They know they are blessed more
    than other nations.
10 The descendants of Israel are like
    the dust —
There are too many of them to
    be counted.

---

w *Probable text* you should . . . journey; *Hebrew unclear.*

Let me end my days like one of
   God's people;
Let me die in peace like the
   righteous."

11 Then Balak said to Balaam, "What
have you done to me? I brought you here
to curse my enemies, but all you have
done is bless them."

12 He answered, "I can say only what
the LORD tells me to say."

Balaam's Second Prophecy

13 Then Balak said to Balaam, "Come
with me to another place from which you
can see only some of the Israelites. Curse
them for me from there." 14 He took him
to the field of Zophim on the top of
Mount Pisgah. There also he built seven
altars and offered a bull and a ram on
each of them.

15 Balaam said to Balak, "Stand here by
your burnt offering, and I will meet God
over there."

16 The LORD met Balaam, told him what
to say, and sent him back to Balak to give
him his message. 17 So he went back and
found Balak still standing by his burnt
offering, with the leaders of Moab. Balak
asked what the LORD had said, 18 and Balaam uttered this prophecy:

"Come, Balak son of Zippor,
   And listen to what I have to say.
19 God is not like people, who lie;
   He is not a human who changes
     his mind.
Whatever he promises, he does;
   He speaks, and it is done.
20 I have been instructed to bless,
   And when God blesses, I cannot
     call it back.
21 I foresee that Israel's future
   Will bring her no misfortune or
     trouble.
The LORD their God is with them;
   They proclaim that he is their
     king.
22 God has brought them out of
     Egypt;
   He fights for them like a wild ox.
23 There is no magic charm, no
     witchcraft,
   That can be used against the
     nation of Israel.x

Now people will say about Israel,
   'Look what God has done!'
24 The nation of Israel is like a
     mighty lion:
It doesn't rest until it has torn and
     devoured,
Until it has drunk the blood of
     those it has killed."

25 Then Balak said to Balaam, "You refuse to curse the people of Israel, but at
least don't bless them!"

26 Balaam answered, "Didn't I tell you
that I had to do everything that the LORD
told me?"

Balaam's Third Prophecy

27 Balak said, "Come with me, and I will
take you to another place. Perhaps God
will be willing to let you curse them for
me from there." 28 So he took Balaam to
the top of Mount Peor overlooking the
desert. 29 Balaam said to him, "Build
seven altars for me here and bring me
seven bulls and seven rams." 30 Balak did
as he was told, and offered a bull and a
ram on each altar.

24 By now Balaam knew that the
LORD wanted him to bless the
people of Israel, so he did not go to look
for omens, as he had done before. He
turned toward the desert 2 and saw the
people of Israel camped tribe by tribe.
The spirit of God took control of him,
3 and he uttered this prophecy:

"The message of Balaam son of
     Beor,
The words of the man who can
     see clearly,y
4 Who can hear what God is saying.
With staring eyes I see in a trance
   A vision from Almighty God.
5 The tents of Israel are beautiful,
6 Like long rows of palms
Or gardens beside a river,
Like aloes planted by the LORD
Or cedars beside the water.
7 They will have abundant rainfall
And plant their seed in
     well-watered fields.z
Their king shall be greater than
     Agag,
And his rule shall be extended
     far and wide.

---

x There ... Israel; *or* No magic charms are used in Israel, no witchcraft is practiced there.
y who can see clearly; *or* whose eyes are closed.   z *One ancient translation* They ... fields;
Hebrew unclear.

8 God brought them out of Egypt;
He fights for them like a wild ox.
They devour their enemies,
Crush their bones, smash their
arrows.
9 The nation is like a mighty lion;
When it is sleeping, no one dares
wake it.
Whoever blesses Israel will be
blessed,
And whoever curses Israel will
be cursed."

10 Balak clenched his fists in anger and said to Balaam, "I called you to curse my enemies, but three times now you have blessed them instead. 11 Now get on home! I promised to reward you, but the Lord has kept you from getting the reward."

12 Balaam answered, "I told the messengers you sent to me that 13 even if you gave me all the silver and gold in your palace, I could not disobey the command of the Lord by doing anything of myself. I will say only what the Lord tells me to say."

Balaam's Final Prophecies

14 Balaam said to Balak, "Now I am going back to my own people, but before I go, I am warning you what the people of Israel will do to your people in the future." 15 Then he uttered this prophecy:

"The message of Balaam son of
Beor,
The words of the man who can
see clearly,a
16 Who can hear what God is saying
And receive the knowledge that
comes from the Most High.
With staring eyes I see in a trance
A vision from Almighty God.
17 I look into the future,
And I see the nation of Israel.
A king, like a bright star, will
arise in that nation.
Like a comet he will come from
Israel.
He will strike the leaders of Moab
And beat down all the people of
Seth.b
18 He will conquer his enemies in
Edom

And make their land his property,
While Israel continues victorious.
19 The nation of Israel will trample
them down
And wipe out the last survivors."

20 Then in his vision Balaam saw the Amalekites and uttered this prophecy:
"Amalek was the most powerful
nation of all,
But at the end it will perish
forever."
21 In his vision he saw the Kenites, and uttered this prophecy:
"The place where you live is
secure,
Safe as a nest set high on a cliff,
22 But you Kenites will be destroyed
When Assyria takes you
captive."c
23 Balaam uttered this prophecy:
"Who are these people gathering
in the north?d
24 Invaders will sail from Cyprus;
They will conquer Assyria and
Eber,
But they, in turn, will perish
forever."
25 Then Balaam got ready and went back home, and Balak went on his way.

The People of Israel at Peor

25 When the Israelites were camped at Acacia Valley, the men began to have sexual intercourse with the Moabite women who were there. 2 These women invited them to sacrificial feasts, where the god of Moab was worshiped. The Israelites ate the food and worshiped the god 3 Baal of Peor. So the Lord was angry with them 4 and said to Moses, "Take all the leaders of Israel and, in obedience to me, execute them in broad daylight,e and then I will no longer be angry with the people." 5 Moses said to the officials, "Each of you is to kill every man in your tribe who has become a worshiper of Baal of Peor."

6 One of the Israelites took a Midianite woman into his tent in the sight of Moses and the whole community, while they were mourning at the entrance of the Tent of the Lord's presence. 7 When Phinehas, the son of Eleazar and grandson of Aaron the priest, saw this, he got up and left the assembly. He took a spear, 8 fol-

---

a who can see clearly; or whose eyes are closed.   b the people of Seth; or who are proud and violent.   c Verse 22 in Hebrew is unclear.   d Probable text Who . . . north; Hebrew unclear.
e in broad daylight; or publicly.

lowed the man and the woman into the tent, and drove the spear through both of them. In this way the epidemic that was destroying Israel was stopped, 9 but it had already killed twenty-four thousand people.

10 The LORD said to Moses, 11 "Because of what Phinehas has done, I am no longer angry with the people of Israel. He refused to tolerate the worship of any god but me, and that is why I did not destroy them in my anger. 12 So tell him that I am making a covenant with him that is valid for all time to come. 13 He and his descendants are permanently established as priests, because he did not tolerate any rivals to me and brought about forgiveness for the people's sin."

14 The name of the Israelite who was killed with the Midianite woman was Zimri son of Salu, the head of a family in the tribe of Simeon. 15 The woman's name was Cozbi. Zur, her father, was chief of a group of Midianite clans.

16 The LORD commanded Moses, 17 "Attack the Midianites and destroy them, 18 because of the evil they did to you when they deceived you at Peor, and because of Cozbi, who was killed at the time of the epidemic at Peor."

The Second Census

26 After the epidemic the LORD said to Moses and Eleazar son of Aaron, 2 "Take a census by families of the whole community of Israel, of all men twenty years old or older who are fit for military service." 3-4 Moses and Eleazar obeyed and called together all the men of that age group. They assembled in the plains of Moab across the Jordan River from Jericho.

These were the Israelites who came out of Egypt:

5 The tribe of Reuben (Reuben was the oldest son of Jacob): the clans of Hanoch, Pallu, 6 Hezron, and Carmi. 7 These clans numbered 43,730 men. 8 The descendants of Pallu were Eliab 9 and his sons Nemuel, Dathan, and Abiram. (These are the Dathan and Abiram who were chosen by the community. They defied Moses and Aaron and joined the followers of Korah when they rebelled against the LORD. 10 The ground opened and swallowed them, and they died with Korah and his followers when fire destroyed 250 men; they became a warning to the people.

11 But the sons of Korah were not killed.)

12 The tribe of Simeon: the clans of Nemuel, Jamin, Jachin, 13 Zerah, and Shaul. 14 These clans numbered 22,200 men.

15 The tribe of Gad: the clans of Zephon, Haggi, Shuni, 16 Ozni, Eri, 17 Arod, and Areli. 18 These clans numbered 40,500 men.

19-21 The tribe of Judah: the clans of Shelah, Perez, Zerah, Hezron, and Hamul. (Two of Judah's sons, Er and Onan, had died in the land of Canaan.) 22 These clans numbered 76,500 men.

23 The tribe of Issachar: the clans of Tola, Puah, 24 Jashub, and Shimron. 25 These clans numbered 64,300 men.

26 The tribe of Zebulun: the clans of Sered, Elon, and Jahleel. 27 These clans numbered 60,500 men.

28 The tribes of Joseph, who was the father of two sons, Manasseh and Ephraim.

29 The tribe of Manasseh. Machir son of Manasseh was the father of Gilead, and the following clans traced their ancestry to Gilead: 30 the clans of Iezer, Helek, 31 Asriel, Shechem, 32 Shemida, and Hepher. 33 Zelophehad son of Hepher had no sons, but only daughters; their names were Mahlah, Noah, Hoglah, Milcah, and Tirzah. 34 These clans numbered 52,700 men.

35 The tribe of Ephraim: the clans of Shuthelah, Becher, and Tahan. 36 The clan of Eran traced its descent from Shuthelah. 37 These clans numbered 32,500 men.

These are the clans descended from Joseph.

38 The tribe of Benjamin: the clans of Bela, Ashbel, Ahiram, 39 Shephupham, and Hupham. 40 The clans of Ard and Naaman traced their descent from Bela. 41 These clans numbered 45,600 men.

42 The tribe of Dan: the clan of Shuham, 43 which numbered 64,400 men.

44 The tribe of Asher: the clans of Imnah, Ishvi, and Beriah. 45 The clans of Heber and Malchiel traced their descent from Beriah. 46 Asher had a daughter named Serah. 47 These clans numbered 53,400 men.

48 The tribe of Naphtali: the clans of Jahzeel, Guni, 49 Jezer, and Shillem. 50 These clans numbered 45,400 men.

51 The total number of the Israelite men was 601,730.

52 The Lord said to Moses, 53 "Divide the land among the tribes, according to their size. 54-56 Divide the land by drawing lots, and give a large share to a large tribe and a small one to a small tribe."

57 The tribe of Levi consisted of the clans of Gershon, Kohath, and Merari. 58 Their descendants included the sub-clans of Libni, Hebron, Mahli, Mushi, and Korah. Kohath was the father of Amram, 59 who was married to Levi's daughter Jochebed, who was born in Egypt. She bore Amram two sons, Aaron and Moses, and a daughter, Miriam. 60 Aaron had four sons, Nadab, Abihu, Eleazar, and Ithamar. 61 Nadab and Abihu died when they offered unholy fire to the Lord. 62 The male Levites who were one month old or older numbered 23,000. They were listed separately from the rest of the Israelites, because they were not given any property in Israel.

63 All these clans were listed by Moses and Eleazar when they took a census of the Israelites in the plains of Moab across the Jordan River from Jericho. 64 There was not even one man left among those whom Moses and Aaron had listed in the first census in the Sinai Desert. 65 The Lord had said that all of them would die in the wilderness, and except for Caleb son of Jephunneh and Joshua son of Nun they all did.

The Daughters of Zelophehad

27 Mahlah, Noah, Hoglah, Milcah, and Tirzah were the daughters of Zelophehad son of Hepher, son of Gilead, son of Machir, son of Manasseh, son of Joseph. 2 They went and stood before Moses, Eleazar the priest, the leaders, and the whole community at the entrance of the Tent of the Lord's presence and said, 3 "Our father died in the wilderness without leaving any sons. He was not among the followers of Korah, who rebelled against the Lord; he died because of his own sin. 4 Just because he had no sons, why should our father's name disappear from Israel? Give us property among our father's relatives."

5 Moses presented their case to the Lord, 6 and the Lord said to him, 7 "What the daughters of Zelophehad request is right; give them property among their father's relatives. Let his inheritance pass on to them. 8 Tell the people of Israel that whenever a man dies without leaving a son, his daughter is to inherit his property. 9 If he has no daughter, his brothers are to inherit it. 10 If he has no brothers, his father's brothers are to inherit it. 11 If he has no brothers or uncles, then his nearest relative is to inherit it and hold it as his own property. The people of Israel are to observe this as a legal requirement, just as I, the Lord, have commanded you."

Joshua Is Chosen as Successor to Moses
(Deuteronomy 31.1-8)

12 The Lord said to Moses, "Go up the Abarim Mountains and look out over the land that I am giving to the Israelites. 13 After you have seen it, you will die, as your brother Aaron did, 14 because both of you rebelled against my command in the wilderness of Zin. When the whole community complained against me at Meribah, you refused to acknowledge my holy power before them." (Meribah is the spring at Kadesh in the wilderness of Zin.)

15 Moses prayed, 16 "Lord God, source of all life, appoint, I pray, a man who can lead the people 17 and can command them in battle, so that your community will not be like sheep without a shepherd."

18 The Lord said to Moses, "Take Joshua son of Nun, a capable man, and place your hands on his head. 19 Have him stand in front of Eleazar the priest and the whole community, and there before them all proclaim him as your successor. 20 Give him some of your own authority, so that the whole community of Israel will obey him. 21 He will depend on Eleazar the priest, who will learn my will by using the Urim and Thummim.*f* In this way Eleazar will direct Joshua and the whole community of Israel in all their affairs." 22 Moses did as the Lord had commanded him. He had Joshua stand before Eleazar the priest and the whole community. 23 As the Lord had commanded, Moses put his hands on Joshua's head and proclaimed him as his successor.

---

f URIM AND THUMMIM: *Two objects used by the priest to determine God's will; it is not known precisely how they were used.*

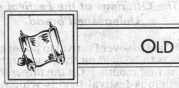

OLD TESTAMENT OFFERINGS

The patriarchs of the Old Testament—Abraham, Isaac, and Jacob—built altars and made sacrifices to God wherever they settled (Gn 12.8; 26.25; 28.18). Cain and Abel made the first offerings recorded in the Bible (Gn 4.3-5). Noah offered sacrifices of thanksgiving after the great flood (Gn 8.20). Most of these sacrifices involved the shedding of blood, a method God instituted to prepare his people for the Messiah's ultimate sacrifice for sins.

Several different types of offerings are specified by God throughout the Old Testament. These demonstrate human need and God's merciful provision.

The burnt offering involved a male animal that was wholly consumed by fire. The animal was killed and the priest collected the blood and sprinkled it about the altar (Nu 28.1-8). The burning symbolized the worshiper's desire to be purged of sinful acts. The grain offering described in Leviticus 2 was similar in purpose to the burnt offering. The grain was brought to the priest, who threw a portion on the fire, accompanied by the burning of incense.

The fellowship offering was a ritual meal shared with God, the priests, and often other worshipers (Lv 3). A voluntary animal offering was a sacrifice that expressed praise to God and fellowship with others. Jacob and Laban offered this sacrifice when they made a treaty (Gn 31.43-55). The sin offering was offered to make atonement for sins for which restitution was not possible (Lv 4.5-12). The repayment offering was made for lesser or unintentional offenses for which restitution was possible (Lv 5.14-19).

The Regular Offerings
(Exodus 29.38-46)

28 The LORD commanded Moses [2] to instruct the Israelites to present to God at the appointed times the required food offerings that are pleasing to him.

[3] These are the food offerings that are to be presented to the LORD: for the daily burnt offering, two one-year-old male lambs without any defects. [4] Offer the first lamb in the morning, and the second in the evening, [5] each with a grain offering of 2 pounds of flour, mixed with 2 pints of the best olive oil. [6] This is the daily offering that is completely burned, which was first offered at Mount Sinai as a food offering, an odor pleasing to the LORD. [7] As the wine offering with the first lamb, pour out at the altar 2 pints of wine. [8] In the evening offer the second lamb in the same way as the morning offering, together with its wine offering. It also is a food offering, an odor pleasing to the LORD.

The Sabbath Offering

[9] On the Sabbath day offer two one-year-old male lambs without any defects, 4 pounds of flour mixed with olive oil as a grain offering, and the wine offering. [10] This burnt offering is to be offered every Sabbath in addition to the daily offering with its wine offering.

The Offering on the First Day of the Month

[11] Present a burnt offering to the LORD at the beginning of each month: two young bulls, one ram, seven one-year-old male lambs, all without any defects. [12] As a grain offering, offer flour mixed with olive oil: with each bull, 6 pounds of flour; with the ram, 4 pounds; [13] and with each lamb, 2 pounds. These burnt offerings are food offerings, an odor pleasing to the LORD. [14] The proper wine offering is 4 pints of wine with each bull, 3 pints with the ram, and 2 pints with each lamb. This is the regulation for the burnt offering for the first day of each month throughout the year. [15] And in addition to the daily burnt offering with its wine offering, offer one male goat as a sin offering.

The Offerings at the Festival of Unleavened Bread
(Leviticus 23.5-14)

[16] The Passover Festival in honor of the LORD is to be held on the fourteenth day of the first month. [17] On the fifteenth day a religious festival begins which lasts seven days, during which only bread prepared without yeast is to be eaten. [18] On the first day of the festival you are to gather for worship, and no work is to be done. [19] Offer a burnt offering as a food offering to the LORD: two young bulls, one ram, and seven one-year-old male lambs, all without any defects. [20] Offer the proper grain offering of flour mixed with olive oil: 6 pounds with each bull, 4 pounds with the ram, [21] and 2 pounds with each lamb. [22] Also offer one male goat as a sin offering, and in this way perform the ritual of purification for the people. [23] Offer these in addition to the regular morning burnt offering. [24] In the same way, for seven days offer to the LORD a food offering, an odor pleasing to him. Offer this in addition to the daily burnt offering and wine offering. [25] Meet for worship on the seventh day and do no work.

The Offerings at the Harvest Festival
(Leviticus 23.15-22)

[26] On the first day of the Harvest Festival, when you present the offering of new grain to the LORD, you are to gather for worship, and no work is to be done. [27] Offer a burnt offering as an odor pleasing to the LORD: two young bulls, one ram, and seven one-year-old male lambs, all without any defects. [28] Offer the proper grain offering of flour mixed with olive oil: 6 pounds with each bull, 4 pounds with the ram, [29] and 2 pounds with each lamb. [30] Also offer one male goat as a sin offering, and in this way perform the ritual of purification for the people. [31] Offer these and the wine offering in addition to the daily burnt offering and grain offering.

The Offerings at the New Year Festival
(Leviticus 23.23-25)

29 On the first day of the seventh month you are to gather for worship, and no work is to be done. On that day trumpets are to be blown. 2 Present a burnt offering to the LORD, an odor pleasing to him: one young bull, one ram, and seven one-year-old male lambs, all without any defects. 3 Offer the proper grain offering of flour mixed with olive oil: 6 pounds of flour with the bull, 4 pounds with the ram, 4 and 2 pounds with each lamb. 5 Also offer one male goat as a sin offering, and in this way perform the ritual of purification for the people. 6 Offer these in addition to the regular burnt offering for the first day of the month with its grain offering, and the daily burnt offering with its grain offering and wine offering. These food offerings are an odor pleasing to the LORD.

The Offerings at the Day of Atonement
(Leviticus 23.26-32)

7 Gather for worship on the tenth day of the seventh month; eat no food and do no work. 8 Offer a burnt offering to the LORD, an odor pleasing to him: one young bull, one ram, and seven one-year-old male lambs, all without any defects. 9 Offer the proper grain offering of flour mixed with olive oil: 6 pounds of flour with the bull, 4 pounds with the ram, 10 and 2 pounds with each lamb. 11 Also offer one male goat as a sin offering, in addition to the goat offered in the ritual of purification for the people, and the daily burnt offering with its grain offering and wine offering.

The Offerings at the Festival of Shelters
(Leviticus 23.33-44)

12 Gather for worship on the fifteenth day of the seventh month. Celebrate this festival in honor of the LORD for seven days and do no work. 13 On this first day offer a food offering to the LORD, an odor pleasing to him: thirteen young bulls, two rams, and fourteen one-year-old male lambs, all without any defects. 14 Offer the proper grain offering of flour mixed with olive oil: 6 pounds of flour with each bull, 4 pounds with each ram, 15 and 2 pounds with each lamb, with the required wine offerings. 16 Also offer one male goat as a sin offering. Offer these in addition to the daily burnt offering with its grain offering and wine offering.
17 On the second day offer twelve young bulls, two rams, and fourteen one-year-old male lambs, all without any defects. 18-19 Offer with them all the other offerings required for the first day.
20 On the third day offer eleven young bulls, two rams, and fourteen one-year-old male lambs, all without any defects. 21-22 Offer with them all the other offerings required for the first day.
23 On the fourth day offer ten young bulls, two rams, and fourteen one-year-old male lambs, all without any defects. 24-25 Offer with them all the other offerings required for the first day.
26 On the fifth day offer nine young bulls, two rams, and fourteen one-year-old male lambs, all without any defects. 27-28 Offer with them all the other offerings required for the first day.
29 On the sixth day offer eight young bulls, two rams, and fourteen one-year-old male lambs, all without any defects. 30-31 Offer with them all the other offerings required for the first day.
32 On the seventh day offer seven young bulls, two rams, and fourteen one-year-old male lambs, all without any defects. 33-34 Offer with them all the other offerings required for the first day.
35 On the eighth day gather for worship and do no work. 36 Offer a burnt offering as a food offering to the LORD, an odor pleasing to him: one young bull, one ram, and seven one-year-old male lambs, all without any defects. 37-38 Offer with them all the other offerings required for the first day.
39 These are the regulations concerning the burnt offerings, grain offerings, wine offerings, and fellowship offerings that you are to make to the LORD at your appointed festivals. These are in addition to the offerings you give in fulfillment of a vow or as freewill offerings.
40 So Moses told the people of Israel everything that the LORD had commanded him.

Rules about Vows

30 Moses gave the following instructions to the leaders of the tribes of Israel. 2 When a man makes a vow to give something to the LORD or takes an oath to abstain from something, he must not break his promise, but must do everything that he said he would.
3 When a young woman still living in her father's house makes a vow to give

something to the LORD or promises to abstain from something, 4 she must do everything that she vowed or promised unless her father raises an objection when he hears about it. 5 But if her father forbids her to fulfill the vow when he hears about it, she is not required to keep it. The LORD will forgive her, because her father refused to let her keep it.

6 If an unmarried woman makes a vow, whether deliberately or carelessly, or promises to abstain from something, and then marries, 7 she must do everything that she vowed or promised unless her husband raises an objection when he hears about it. 8 But if her husband forbids her to fulfill the vow when he hears about it, she is not required to keep it. The LORD will forgive her.

9 A widow or a divorced woman must keep every vow she makes and every promise to abstain from something.

10 If a married woman makes a vow or promises to abstain from something, 11 she must do everything that she vowed or promised unless her husband raises an objection when he hears about it. 12 But if her husband forbids her to fulfill the vow when he hears about it, she is not required to keep it. The LORD will forgive her, because her husband prevented her from keeping her vow. 13 Her husband has the right to affirm or to annul any vow or promise that she has made. 14 But if, by the day after he hears of the vow, he has raised no objection, she must do everything that she has vowed or promised. He has affirmed the vow by not objecting on the day he heard of it. 15 But if he later annuls the vow, he must suffer the consequences for the failure to fulfill the vow.

16 These are the rules that the LORD gave Moses concerning vows made by an unmarried woman living in her father's house or by a married woman.

The Holy War against Midian

31 The LORD said to Moses, 2 "Punish the Midianites for what they did to the people of Israel. After you have done that, you will die."

3 So Moses said to the people, "Get ready for war, so that you can attack Midian and punish them for what they did to the LORD. 4 From each tribe of Israel send a thousand men to war."

5 So a thousand men were chosen from each tribe, a total of twelve thousand men ready for battle. 6 Moses sent them to war under the command of Phinehas son of Eleazar the priest, who took charge of the sacred objects and the trumpets for giving signals. 7 They attacked Midian, as the LORD had commanded Moses, and killed all the men, 8 including the five kings of Midian: Evi, Rekem, Zur, Hur, and Reba. They also killed Balaam son of Beor.

9 The people of Israel captured the Midianite women and children, took their cattle and their flocks, plundered all their wealth, 10 and burned all their cities and camps. 11 They took all the loot that they had captured, including the prisoners and the animals, 12 and brought them to Moses and Eleazar and to the community of the people of Israel, who were at the camp on the plains of Moab across the Jordan from Jericho.

The Army Returns

13 Moses, Eleazar, and all the other leaders of the community went out of the camp to meet the army. 14 Moses became angry with the officers, the commanders of battalions and companies, who had returned from the war. 15 He asked them, "Why have you kept all the women alive? 16 Remember that it was the women who followed Balaam's instructions and at Peor led the people to be unfaithful to the LORD. That was what brought the epidemic on the LORD's people. 17 So now kill every boy and kill every woman who has had sexual intercourse, 18 but keep alive for yourselves all the girls and all the women who are virgins. 19 Now all of you who have killed anyone or have touched a corpse must stay outside the camp for seven days. On the third day and on the seventh day purify yourselves and the women you have captured. 20 You must also purify every piece of clothing and everything made of leather, goats' hair, or wood."

21 Eleazar the priest said to the men who had returned from battle, "These are the regulations that the LORD has given to Moses. 22-23 Everything that will not burn, such as gold, silver, bronze, iron, tin, or lead, is to be purified by passing it through fire. Everything else is to be purified by the water for purification. 24 On the seventh day you must wash your

clothes; then you will be ritually clean and will be permitted to enter the camp."

Division of the Loot

25 The LORD said to Moses, 26 "You and Eleazar, together with the other leaders of the community, are to count everything that has been captured, including the prisoners and the animals. 27 Divide what was taken into two equal parts, one part for the soldiers and the other part for the rest of the community. 28 From the part that belongs to the soldiers, withhold as a tax for the LORD one out of every five hundred prisoners and the same proportion of the cattle, donkeys, sheep, and goats. 29 Give them to Eleazar the priest as a special contribution to the LORD. 30 From the part given to the rest of the people, take one out of every fifty prisoners and the same proportion of the cattle, donkeys, sheep, and goats. Give them to the Levites who are in charge of the LORD's Tent." 31 Moses and Eleazar did what the LORD commanded.

32-35 The following is a list of what was captured by the soldiers, in addition to what they kept for themselves: 675,000 sheep and goats, 72,000 cattle, 61,000 donkeys, and 32,000 virgins. 36-40 The half share of the soldiers was 337,500 sheep and goats, of which 675 were the tax for the LORD; 36,000 cattle for the soldiers, of which 72 were the tax for the LORD; 30,500 donkeys for the soldiers, of which 61 were the tax for the LORD; and 16,000 virgins for the soldiers, of which 32 were the tax for the LORD. 41 So Moses gave Eleazar the tax as a special contribution to the LORD, as the LORD had commanded.

42-46 The share of the community was the same as that for the soldiers: 337,500 sheep and goats, 36,000 cattle, 30,500 donkeys, and 16,000 virgins. 47 From this share Moses took one out of every fifty prisoners and animals, and as the LORD had commanded, gave them to the Levites who were in charge of the LORD's Tent.

48 Then the officers who had commanded the army went to Moses 49 and reported, "Sir, we have counted the soldiers under our command and not one of them is missing. 50 So we are bringing the gold ornaments, armlets, bracelets, rings, earrings, and necklaces that each of us has taken. We offer them to the

LORD as a payment for our lives, so that he will protect us." 51 Moses and Eleazar received the gold, all of which was in the form of ornaments. 52 The total contribution of the officers weighed over four hundred pounds. 53 Those who were not officers kept the loot they had taken. 54 So Moses and Eleazar took the gold to the Tent, so that the LORD would protect the people of Israel.

The Tribes East of the Jordan
(Deuteronomy 3.12-22)

32 The tribes of Reuben and Gad had a lot of livestock. When they saw how suitable the land of Jazer and Gilead was for cattle, 2 they went to Moses, Eleazar, and the other leaders of the community and said, 3-4 "This region which the LORD has helped the Israelites occupy — the towns of Ataroth, Dibon, Jazer, Nimrah, Heshbon, Elealeh, Sibmah, Nebo, and Beon — is good land for livestock, and we have so much livestock. 5 Please give us this land as our property, and do not make us cross the Jordan River and settle there."

6 Moses replied, "Do you want to stay here while the other Israelites go to war? 7 How dare you try to discourage the people of Israel from crossing the Jordan into the land which the LORD has given them? 8 That is what your fathers did when I sent them from Kadesh Barnea to explore the land. 9 They went as far as Eshcol Valley and saw the land, but when they returned, they discouraged the people from entering the land which the LORD had given them. 10 The LORD became angry that day and made a promise: 11 'I swear that because they did not remain loyal to me, none of the men twenty years old or older who came out of Egypt will enter the land that I promised to Abraham, Isaac, and Jacob.' 12 This included everyone, except Caleb son of Jephunneh the Kenizzite and Joshua son of Nun; they remained loyal to the LORD. 13 The LORD became angry with the people and made them wander in the wilderness forty years until that whole generation that had displeased him was dead. 14 And now you have taken your ancestors' place, a new generation of sinful people ready to bring down the fierce anger of the LORD on Israel again. 15 If you people of Reuben and Gad refuse to follow him now, he will

once again abandon all these people in the wilderness, and you will be responsible for their destruction."

16 They approached Moses and said, "First, allow us to build stone enclosures here for our sheep and fortified towns for our dependents. 17 Then we will be ready to go with the other Israelites into battle and lead the attack until we have settled them in the land that will be theirs. In the meantime, our dependents can live here in the fortified towns, safe from the people of this land. 18 We will not return to our homes until all the other Israelites have taken possession of the land assigned to them. 19 We will not take possession of any property among them on the other side of the Jordan, because we have received our share here east of the Jordan."

20 Moses answered, "If you really mean what you say, then here in the presence of the LORD get ready to go into battle. 21 All your fighting men are to cross the Jordan and under the command of the LORD they are to attack our enemies until the LORD defeats them 22 and takes possession of the land. After that, you may return, because you will have fulfilled your obligation to the LORD and to the other Israelites. Then the LORD will acknowledge that this land east of the Jordan is yours. 23 But if you do not keep your promise, I warn you that you will be sinning against the LORD. Make no mistake about it; you will be punished for your sin. 24 So build your towns and the enclosures for your sheep, but do what you have promised!"

25 The men of Gad and Reuben said, "Sir, we will do as you command. 26 Our wives and children and our cattle and sheep will remain here in the towns of Gilead. 27 But all of us are ready to go into battle under the LORD's command. We will cross the Jordan and fight, just as you have said."

28 So Moses gave these commands to Eleazar, Joshua, and the other leaders of Israel: 29 "If the men of Gad and Reuben cross the Jordan ready for battle at the LORD's command and if with their help you are able to conquer the land, then give them the land of Gilead as their property. 30 But if they do not cross the Jordan and go into battle with you, they are to receive their share of the property in the land of Canaan, as you do."

31 The men of Gad and Reuben answered, "Sir, we will do as the LORD has commanded. 32 Under his command we will cross into the land of Canaan and go into battle, so that we can retain our property here east of the Jordan."

33 So Moses assigned to the tribes of Gad and Reuben and to half the tribe of Manasseh all the territory of King Sihon of the Amorites and King Og of Bashan, including the towns and the country around them. 34 The tribe of Gad rebuilt the fortified towns of Dibon, Ataroth, Aroer, 35 Atroth Shophan, Jazer, Jogbehah, 36 Beth Nimrah, and Beth Haran. 37 The tribe of Reuben rebuilt Heshbon, Elealeh, Kiriathaim, 38 Nebo, Baal Meon (this name was changed), and Sibmah. They gave new names to the towns they rebuilt.

39 The clan of Machir son of Manasseh invaded the land of Gilead, occupied it, and drove out the Amorites who were there. 40 So Moses gave Gilead to the clan of Machir, and they lived there. 41 Jair, of the tribe of Manasseh, attacked and captured some villages and named them "Villages of Jair." 42 Nobah attacked and captured Kenath and its villages, and he renamed it Nobah, after himself.

The Journey from Egypt to Moab

33 The following account gives the names of the places where the Israelites set up camp after they left Egypt in their tribes under the leadership of Moses and Aaron. 2 At the command of the LORD, Moses wrote down the name of the place each time they set up camp.

3 The people of Israel left Egypt on the fifteenth day of the first month of the year, the day after the first Passover. Under the LORD's protection they left the city of Rameses in full view of the Egyptians, 4 who were burying the first-born sons that the LORD had killed. By doing this, the LORD showed that he was more powerful than the gods of Egypt.

5 The people of Israel left Rameses and set up camp at Sukkoth. 6 Their next camp was at Etham on the edge of the desert. 7 From there they turned back to Pi Hahiroth, east of Baal Zephon, and camped near Migdol. 8 They left Pi Hahiroth and passed through the Red

THE MEDITERRANEAN SEA

The Mediterranean Sea is a large body of water in the Middle East bordered by many important nations, including Israel, Greece, Lebanon, and Italy. Its southern coastline stretches 2,200 miles from the coast of Palestine to the Straits of Gibraltar off the coast of Spain. The sea is 80 miles wide at its narrowest point between Sicily and North Africa. Many ancient civilizations grew up around this sea, using it for transportation and commerce.

While the Israelites were wandering in the wilderness, they received instructions from God about the future boundaries of the land that God had promised to Abraham and his descendants. The Mediterranean Sea was established as the western boundary of their territory (Nu 34.6).

The Romans called it *Mare Nostrum,* or Our Sea, because of its importance to their empire in trade and commerce. In the time of Jesus and Paul, the Mediterranean was controlled by the Romans, who also used it to transport soldiers to the East to keep order in the provinces.

Perhaps the first people to exploit the trading advantages offered by the Mediterranean Sea were the Phoenicians. Through their fine port cities of Tyre and Sidon, they imported and exported goods from many nations of the ancient world. But the Israelites were never a seafaring people. Even Solomon, with all his wealth, formed an alliance with King Hiram of Tyre under which they conducted import and export services for the Israelites (1 K 9.27).

The Philistines also loved the sea. Some scholars believe they migrated to Palestine from their original home on the island of Crete, or Caphtor, in the Mediterranean.

The Mediterranean also played a key role in the early expansion of Christianity. Paul crossed the Mediterranean during his missionary journeys and set sail from many of its ports, including Caesarea (Ac 9.30), Seleucia (Ac 13.4), and Cenchreae (Ac 18.18). He was shipwrecked on the Mediterranean while sailing to Rome in late autumn (Ac 27).

Sea[g] into the desert of Shur; after a three days' march they camped at Marah. ⁹From there they went to Elim, where they camped, because there were twelve springs of water and seventy palm trees there.

¹⁰They left Elim and camped near the Gulf of Suez. ¹¹Their next camp was in the desert of Sin. ¹²Then they camped at Dophkah, ¹³and after that at Alush. ¹⁴Next was Rephidim, where there was no water for them to drink.

¹⁵⁻³⁷From Rephidim to Mount Hor they set up camp at the following places: the Sinai Desert, Kibroth Hattaavah (or "Graves of Craving"), Hazeroth, Rithmah, Rimmon Perez, Libnah, Rissah, Kehelathah, Mount Shepher, Haradah, Makheloth, Tahath, Terah, Mithkah, Hashmonah, Moseroth, Bene Jaakan, Hor Haggidgad, Jotbathah, Abronah, Eziongeber, the wilderness of Zin (that is, Kadesh), and Mount Hor, at the edge of the land of Edom.

³⁸⁻³⁹At the command of the LORD, Aaron the priest climbed Mount Hor. At the age of 123 he died there on the first day of the fifth month of the fortieth year after the Israelites had left Egypt.

⁴⁰The king of Arad in southern Canaan heard that the Israelites were coming.

⁴¹⁻⁴⁹From Mount Hor to the plains of Moab the Israelites set up camp at the following places: Zalmonah, Punon, Oboth, the ruins of Abarim in the territory of Moab, Dibon Gad, Almon Diblathaim, the Abarim Mountains near Mount Nebo, and in the plains of Moab across the Jordan River from Jericho, between Beth Jeshimoth and Acacia Valley.

Instructions before Crossing the Jordan

⁵⁰There in the plains of Moab across the Jordan from Jericho the LORD gave Moses ⁵¹the following instructions for Israel: "When you cross the Jordan into the land of Canaan, ⁵²you must drive out all the inhabitants of the land. Destroy all their stone and metal idols and all their places of worship. ⁵³Occupy the land and settle in it, because I am giving it to you. ⁵⁴Divide the land among the various tribes and clans by drawing lots, giving

a large piece of property to a large clan and a small one to a small clan. ⁵⁵But if you do not drive out the inhabitants of the land, those that are left will be as troublesome as splinters in your eyes and thorns in your sides, and they will fight against you. ⁵⁶If you do not drive them out, I will destroy you, as I planned to destroy them."

The Boundaries of the Land

34 The LORD gave Moses ²the following instructions for the people of Israel: "When you enter Canaan, the land which I am giving you, the borders of your territory will be as follows. ³The southern border will extend from the wilderness of Zin along the border of Edom. It will begin on the east at the southern end of the Dead Sea. ⁴Then it will turn southward toward Akrabbim Pass and continue on through Zin as far south as Kadesh Barnea. Then it will turn northwest to Hazar Addar and on to Azmon, ⁵where it will turn toward the valley at the border of Egypt and end at the Mediterranean.

⁶"The western border will be the Mediterranean Sea.

⁷"The northern border will follow a line from the Mediterranean to Mount Hor ⁸and from there to Hamath Pass. It will continue to Zedad ⁹and to Ziphron, and will end at Hazar Enan.

¹⁰"The eastern border will follow a line from Hazar Enan to Shepham. ¹¹It will then go south to Harbel, east of Ain, and on to the hills on the eastern shore of Lake Galilee, ¹²then south along the Jordan River to the Dead Sea.

"These will be the four borders of your land."

¹³So Moses said to the Israelites, "This is the land that you will receive by drawing lots, the land that the LORD has assigned to the nine and one-half tribes. ¹⁴The tribes of Reuben and Gad and the eastern half of Manasseh have received their property, divided according to their families, ¹⁵on the eastern side of the Jordan, opposite Jericho."

The Leaders Responsible for Dividing the Land

¹⁶The LORD said to Moses, ¹⁷"Eleazar the priest and Joshua son of Nun will

divide the land for the people. [18] Take also one leader from each tribe to help them divide it." [19-28] These are the men the LORD chose:

Tribe	Leader
Judah	Caleb son of Jephunneh
Simeon	Shelumiel son of Ammihud
Benjamin	Elidad son of Chislon
Dan	Bukki son of Jogli
Manasseh	Hanniel son of Ephod
Ephraim	Kemuel son of Shiphtan
Zebulun	Elizaphan son of Parnach
Issachar	Paltiel son of Azzan
Asher	Ahihud son of Shelomi
Naphtali	Pedahel son of Ammihud

[29] These are the men that the LORD assigned to divide the property for the people of Israel in the land of Canaan.

The Cities Assigned to the Levites

35 In the plains of Moab across the Jordan from Jericho the LORD said to Moses, [2] "Tell the Israelites that from the property they receive they must give the Levites some cities to live in and pasture land around the cities. [3] These cities will belong to the Levites, and they will live there. The pasture land will be for their cattle and all their other animals. [4] The pasture land is to extend outward from the city walls five hundred yards in each direction, [5] so that there is a square area measuring one thousand yards on each side, with the city in the middle. [6] You are to give the Levites six cities of refuge to which any of you can escape if you kill someone accidentally. In addition, give them forty-two other cities [7] with their pasture land, making a total of forty-eight. [8] The number of Levite cities in each tribe is to be determined according to the size of its territory."

The Cities of Refuge
(Deuteronomy 19.1-13; Joshua 20.1-9)

[9] The LORD told Moses [10] to say to the people of Israel: "When you cross the Jordan River and enter the land of Canaan, [11] you are to choose cities of refuge

to which any of you can escape if you kill someone accidentally. [12] There you will be safe from the dead person's relative who seeks revenge. No one accused of manslaughter is to be put to death without a public trial. [13] Choose six cities, [14] three east of the Jordan and three in the land of Canaan. [15] These will serve as cities of refuge for Israelites and for foreigners who are temporary or permanent residents. Anyone who kills someone accidentally can escape to one of them.

[16-18] "If, however, any of you use a weapon of iron or stone or wood to kill someone, you are guilty of murder and are to be put to death. [19] The dead person's nearest relative has the responsibility for putting the murderer to death. When he finds you, he is to kill you.

[20] "If you hate someone and kill him by pushing him down or by throwing something at him [21] or by striking him with your fist, you are guilty of murder and are to be put to death. The dead person's nearest relative has the responsibility for putting the murderer to death. When he finds you, he is to kill you.

[22] "But suppose you accidentally kill someone you do not hate, whether by pushing him down or by throwing something at him. [23] Or suppose that, without looking, you throw a stone that kills someone whom you did not intend to hurt and who was not your enemy. [24] In such cases the community shall judge in your favor and not in favor of the dead person's relative who is seeking revenge. [25] You are guilty only of manslaughter, and the community is to rescue you from the dead person's relative, and they are to return you to the city of refuge to which you had escaped. You must live there until the death of the man who is then High Priest. [26] If you leave the city of refuge to which you have escaped [27] and if the dead person's relative finds you and kills you, this act of revenge is not murder. [28] Any of you guilty of manslaughter must remain in the city of refuge until the death of the High Priest, but after that you may return home. [29] These rules apply to you and your descendants wherever you may live.

[30] "Those accused of murder may be found guilty and put to death only on the evidence of two or more witnesses; the evidence of one witness is not sufficient

to support an accusation of murder. 31 Murderers must be put to death. They cannot escape this penalty by the payment of money. 32 If they have fled to a city of refuge, do not allow them to make a payment in order to return home before the death of the High Priest. 33 If you did this, you would defile the land where you are living. Murder defiles the land, and except by the death of the murderer there is no way to perform the ritual of purification for the land where someone has been murdered. 34 Do not defile the land where you are living, because I am the LORD and I live among the people of Israel."

The Inheritance of Married Women

36 The heads of the families in the clan of Gilead, the son of Machir and grandson of Manasseh son of Joseph, went to Moses and the other leaders. 2 They said, "The LORD commanded you to distribute the land to the people of Israel by drawing lots. He also commanded you to give the property of our relative Zelophehad to his daughters. 3 But remember, if they marry men of another tribe, their property will then belong to that tribe, and the total allotted to us will be reduced. 4 In the Year of Restoration, when all property that has been

sold is restored to its original owners, the property of Zelophehad's daughters will be permanently added to the tribe into which they marry and will be lost to our tribe."

5 So Moses gave the people of Israel the following command from the LORD. He said, "What the tribe of Manasseh says is right, 6 and so the LORD says that the daughters of Zelophehad are free to marry anyone they wish but only within their own tribe. 7 The property of every Israelite will remain attached to his tribe. 8 Every woman who inherits property in an Israelite tribe must marry a man belonging to that tribe. In this way all Israelites will inherit the property of their ancestors, 9 and the property will not pass from one tribe to another. Each tribe will continue to possess its own property."

10-11 So Mahlah, Tirzah, Hoglah, Milcah, and Noah, the daughters of Zelophehad, did as the LORD had commanded Moses, and they married their cousins. 12 They married within the clans of the tribe of Manasseh son of Joseph, and their property remained in their father's tribe.

13 These are the rules and regulations that the LORD gave the Israelites through Moses in the plains of Moab across the Jordan River from Jericho.

DEUTERONOMY

Introduction

The book of Deuteronomy is organized as a series of addresses given by Moses to the people of Israel in the land of Moab, where they had stopped at the end of the long wilderness journey and were about to enter and occupy Canaan.

Some of the most important matters recorded in the book are as follows: 1) Moses recalls the great events of the past forty years. He appeals to the people to remember how God has led them through the wilderness and to be obedient and loyal to God. 2) Moses reviews the Ten Commandments and emphasizes the meaning of the First Commandment, calling the people to devotion to the Lord alone. Then he reviews the various laws that are to govern Israel's life in the promised land. 3) Moses reminds the people of the meaning of God's covenant with them, and calls for them to renew their commitment to its obligations. 4) Joshua is commissioned as the next leader of God's people. After singing a song celebrating God's faithfulness, and pronouncing a blessing on the tribes of Israel, Moses dies in Moab, east of the Jordan River.

The great theme of the book is that God has saved and blessed his chosen people, whom he loves; so his people are to remember this, and love and obey him, so that they may have life and continued blessing.

The key verses of the book are 6.4-6, and contain the words that Jesus called the greatest of all commandments: "Love the Lord your God with all your heart, with all your soul, and with all your strength."

Outline of Contents

Introduction

1 In this book are the words that Moses spoke to the people of Israel when they were in the wilderness east of the Jordan River. They were in the Jordan Valley near Suph, between the town of Paran on one side and the towns of Tophel, Laban, Hazeroth, and Dizahab on the other. (²It takes eleven days to travel from Mount Sinai to Kadesh Barnea by way of the hill country of Edom.) ³On the first day of the eleventh month of the fortieth year after they had left Egypt, Moses told the people everything the Lord had commanded him to tell them. ⁴This was after the Lord*a* had defeated King Sihon of the Amorites, who ruled in the town of Heshbon, and King Og of Bashan, who ruled in the towns of

Ashtaroth and Edrei. ⁵It was while the people were east of the Jordan in the territory of Moab that Moses began to explain God's laws and teachings.

He said, ⁶"When we were at Mount Sinai, the Lord our God said to us, 'You have stayed long enough at this mountain. ⁷Break camp and move on. Go to the hill country of the Amorites and to all the surrounding regions — to the Jordan Valley, to the hill country and the lowlands, to the southern region, and to the Mediterranean coast. Go to the land of Canaan and on beyond the Lebanon Mountains as far as the great Euphrates River. ⁸All of this is the land which I, the Lord, promised to give to your ancestors, Abraham, Isaac, and Jacob, and to their descendants. Go and occupy it.'"

---

a the Lord; or Moses.

Moses Appoints Judges
(Exodus 18.13-27)

9 Moses said to the people, "While we were still at Mount Sinai, I told you, 'The responsibility for leading you is too much for me. I can't do it alone. 10 The LORD your God has made you as numerous as the stars in the sky. 11 May the LORD, the God of your ancestors, make you increase a thousand times more and make you prosperous, as he promised! 12 But how can I alone bear the heavy responsibility for settling your disputes? 13 Choose some wise, understanding, and experienced men from each tribe, and I will put them in charge of you.' 14 And you agreed that this was a good thing to do. 15 So I took the wise and experienced leaders you chose from your tribes, and I placed them in charge of you. Some were responsible for a thousand people, some for a hundred, some for fifty, and some for ten. I also appointed other officials throughout the tribes.

16 "At that time I instructed them, 'Listen to the disputes that come up among your people. Judge every dispute fairly, whether it concerns only your own people or involves foreigners who live among you. 17 Show no partiality in your decisions; judge everyone on the same basis, no matter who they are. Do not be afraid of anyone, for the decisions you make come from God. If any case is too difficult for you, bring it to me, and I will decide it.' 18 At the same time I gave you instructions for everything else you were to do.

The Spies Are Sent Out from Kadesh Barnea
(Numbers 13.1-33)

19 "We did what the LORD our God commanded us. We left Mount Sinai and went through that vast and fearful desert on the way to the hill country of the Amorites. When we reached Kadesh Barnea, 20-21 I told you, 'You have now come to the hill country of the Amorites, which the LORD our God, the God of our ancestors, is giving us. Look, there it is. Go and occupy it as he commanded. Do not hesitate or be afraid.'

22 "But you came to me and said, 'Let's send men ahead of us to spy out the land, so that they can tell us the best route to take and what kind of cities are there.'

23 "That seemed like a good thing to do, so I selected twelve men, one from each tribe. 24 They went into the hill country as far as Eshcol Valley and explored it. 25 They brought us back some fruit they found there, and reported that the land which the LORD our God was giving us was very fertile.

26 "But you rebelled against the command of the LORD your God, and you would not enter the land. 27 You grumbled to one another: 'The LORD hates us. He brought us out of Egypt just to hand us over to these Amorites, so that they could kill us. 28 Why should we go there? We are afraid. The men we sent tell us that the people there are stronger and taller than we are, and that they live in cities with walls that reach the sky. They saw giants there!'

29 "But I told you, 'Don't be afraid of those people. 30 The LORD your God will lead you, and he will fight for you, just as you saw him do in Egypt 31 and in the desert. You saw how he brought you safely all the way to this place, just as a father would carry his son.' 32 But in spite of what I said, you still would not trust the LORD, 33 even though he always went ahead of you to find a place for you to camp. To show you the way, he went in front of you in a pillar of fire by night and in a pillar of cloud by day.

The LORD Punishes Israel
(Numbers 14.20-45)

34 "The LORD heard your complaints and became angry, and so he solemnly declared, 35 'Not one of you from this evil generation will enter the fertile land that I promised to give your ancestors. 36 Only Caleb son of Jephunneh will enter it. He has remained faithful to me, and I will give him and his descendants the land that he has explored.' 37 Because of you the LORD also became angry with me and said, 'Not even you, Moses, will enter the land. 38 But strengthen the determination of your helper, Joshua son of Nun. He will lead Israel to occupy the land.'

39 "Then the LORD said to all of us, 'Your children, who are still too young to know right from wrong, will enter the land — the children you said would be seized by your enemies. I will give the land to them, and they will occupy it. 40 But as for you people, turn around and go back into

the desert on the road to the Gulf of Aqaba.'

41 "You replied, 'Moses, we have sinned against the LORD. But now we will attack, just as the LORD our God commanded us.' Then each one of you got ready to fight, thinking it would be easy to invade the hill country.

42 "But the LORD said to me, 'Warn them not to attack, for I will not be with them, and their enemies will defeat them.' 43 I told you what the LORD had said, but you paid no attention. You rebelled against him, and in your pride you marched into the hill country. 44 Then the Amorites who lived in those hills came out against you like a swarm of bees. They chased you as far as Hormah and defeated you there in the hill country of Edom. 45 So you cried out to the LORD for help, but he would not listen to you or pay any attention to you.

The Years in the Desert

46 "So then, after we had stayed at Kadesh for a long time, 1 we finally turned and went into the desert, on the road to the Gulf of Aqaba, as the LORD had commanded, and we spent a long time wandering about in the hill country of Edom.

2 "Then the LORD told me 3 that we had spent enough time wandering about in those hills and that we should go north. 4 He told me to give you the following instructions: 'You are about to go through the hill country of Edom, the territory of your distant relatives, the descendants of Esau. They will be afraid of you, 5 but you must not start a war with them, because I am not going to give you so much as a square foot of their land. I have given Edom to Esau's descendants. 6 You may buy food and water from them.'

7 "Remember how the LORD your God has blessed you in everything that you have done. He has taken care of you as you wandered through this vast desert. He has been with you these forty years, and you have had everything you needed.

8 "So we moved on and left the road that goes from the towns of Elath and Eziongeber to the Dead Sea, and we turned northeast toward Moab. 9 The LORD said to me, 'Don't trouble the people of Moab, the descendants of Lot, or start

a war against them. I have given them the city of Ar, and I am not going to give you any of their land.' "

(10 A mighty race of giants called the Emim used to live in Ar. They were as tall as the Anakim, another race of giants. 11 Like the Anakim they were also known as Rephaim; but the Moabites called them Emim. 12 The Horites used to live in Edom, but the descendants of Esau chased them out, destroyed their nation, and settled there themselves, just as the Israelites later chased their enemies out of the land that the LORD gave them.)

13 "Then we crossed the Zered River as the LORD told us to do. 14 This was thirty-eight years after we had left Kadesh Barnea. All the fighting men of that generation had died, as the LORD had said they would. 15 The LORD kept on opposing them until he had destroyed them all.

16 "After they had all died, 17 the LORD said to us, 18 'Today you are to pass through the territory of Moab by way of Ar. 19 You will then be near the land of the Ammonites, the descendants of Lot. Don't trouble them or start a war against them, because I am not going to give you any of the land that I have given them.' "

(20 This territory is also known as the land of the Rephaim, the name of the people who used to live there; the Ammonites called them Zamzummim. 21 They were as tall as the Anakim. There were many of them, and they were a mighty race. But the LORD destroyed them, so that the Ammonites took over their land and settled there. 22 The LORD had done the same thing for the Edomites, the descendants of Esau, who live in the hill country of Edom. He destroyed the Horites, so that the Edomites took over their land and settled there, where they still live. 23 The land along the Mediterranean coast had been settled by people from the island of Crete. They had destroyed the Avvim, the original inhabitants, and had taken over all their land as far south as the city of Gaza.)

24 "After we had passed through Moab, the LORD told us, 'Now, start out and cross the Arnon River. I am placing in your power Sihon, the Amorite king of Heshbon, along with his land. Attack him, and begin occupying his land. 25 From today on I will make people everywhere afraid of you. Everyone will

tremble with fear at the mention of your name.'

Israel Defeats King Sihon
(Numbers 21.21-30)

26 "Then I sent messengers from the desert of Kedemoth to King Sihon of Heshbon with the following offer of peace: 27 'Let us pass through your country. We will go straight through and not leave the road. 28 We will pay for the food we eat and the water we drink. All we want to do is to pass through your country, 29 until we cross the Jordan River into the land that the LORD our God is giving us. The descendants of Esau, who live in Edom, and the Moabites, who live in Ar, allowed us to pass through their territory.'

30 "But King Sihon would not let us pass through his country. The LORD your God had made him stubborn and rebellious, so that we could defeat him and take his territory, which we still occupy. 31 "Then the LORD said to me, 'Look, I have made King Sihon and his land helpless before you; take his land and occupy it.' 32 Sihon came out with all his men to fight us near the town of Jahaz, 33 but the LORD our God put him in our power, and we killed him, his sons, and all his men. 34 At the same time we captured and destroyed every town, and put everyone to death, men, women, and children. We left no survivors. 35 We took the livestock and plundered the towns. 36 The LORD our God let us capture all the towns from Aroer, on the edge of the Arnon Valley, and the city in the middle of that valley, all the way to Gilead. No town had walls too strong for us. 37 But we did not go near the territory of the Ammonites or to the banks of the Jabbok River or to the towns of the hill country or to any other place where the LORD our God had commanded us not to go.

Israel Conquers King Og
(Numbers 21.31-35)

3 "Next, we moved north toward the region of Bashan, and King Og came out with all his men to fight us near the town of Edrei. 2 But the LORD said to me, 'Don't be afraid of him. I am going to give him, his men, and all his territory to you. Do the same thing to him that you did to Sihon the Amorite king who ruled in Heshbon.'

3 "So the LORD also placed King Og and his people in our power, and we slaughtered them all. 4 At the same time we captured all his towns—there was not one that we did not take. In all we captured sixty towns—the whole region of Argob, where King Og of Bashan ruled. 5 All these towns were fortified with high walls, gates, and bars to lock the gates, and there were also many villages without walls. 6 We destroyed all the towns and put to death all the men, women, and children, just as we did in the towns that belonged to King Sihon of Heshbon. 7 We took the livestock and plundered the towns.

8 "At that time we took from those two Amorite kings the land east of the Jordan River, from the Arnon River to Mount Hermon. (9 Mount Hermon is called Sirion by the Sidonians, and Senir by the Amorites.) 10 We took all the territory of King Og of Bashan: the cities on the plateau, the regions of Gilead and of Bashan, as far east as the towns of Salecah and Edrei."

(11 King Og was the last of the Rephaim. His coffin,[b] made of stone,[c] was six feet wide and almost fourteen feet long, according to standard measurements. It can still be seen in the Ammonite city of Rabbah.)

The Tribes That Settled East of the Jordan
(Numbers 32.1-42)

12 "When we took possession of the land, I assigned to the tribes of Reuben and Gad the territory north of the town of Aroer near the Arnon River and part of the hill country of Gilead, along with its towns. 13 To half the tribe of Manasseh I assigned the rest of Gilead and also all of Bashan, where Og had ruled, that is, the entire Argob region."

(Bashan was known as the land of the Rephaim. 14 Jair, from the tribe of Manasseh, took the entire region of Argob, that is, Bashan, as far as the border of Geshur and Maacah. He named the villages after himself, and they are still known as the villages of Jair.)

15 "I assigned Gilead to the clan of Machir of the tribe of Manasseh. 16 And to

---

b coffin; or bed.   c stone; or iron.

the tribes of Reuben and Gad I assigned the territory from Gilead to the Arnon River. The middle of the river was their southern boundary, and their northern boundary was the Jabbok River, part of which formed the Ammonite border. 17 On the west their territory extended to the Jordan River, from Lake Galilee in the north down to the Dead Sea in the south and to the foot of Mount Pisgah on the east.

18 "At the same time, I gave them the following instructions: 'The LORD our God has given you this land east of the Jordan to occupy. Now arm your fighting men and send them across the Jordan ahead of the other tribes of Israel, to help them occupy their land. 19 Only your wives, children, and livestock — I know you have a lot of livestock — will remain behind in the towns that I have assigned to you. 20 Help the other Israelites until they occupy the land that the LORD is giving them west of the Jordan and until the LORD lets them live there in peace, as he has already done here for you. After that, you may return to this land that I have assigned to you.'

21 "Then I instructed Joshua: 'You have seen all that the LORD your God did to those two kings, Sihon and Og; and he will do the same thing to everyone else whose land you invade. 22 Don't be afraid of them, for the LORD your God will fight for you.'

Moses Is Not Permitted to Enter Canaan

23 "At that time I earnestly prayed, 24 'Sovereign LORD, I know that you have shown me only the beginning of the great and wonderful things you are going to do. There is no god in heaven or on earth who can do the mighty things that you have done! 25 Let me cross the Jordan River, LORD, and see the fertile land on the other side, the beautiful hill country and the Lebanon Mountains.'

26 "But because of you people the LORD was angry with me and would not listen. Instead, he said, 'That's enough! Don't mention this again! 27 Go to the peak of Mount Pisgah and look to the north and to the south, to the east and to the west. Look carefully at what you see, because you will never go across the Jordan.

28 Give Joshua his instructions. Strengthen his determination, because he will lead the people across to occupy the land that you see.'

29 "So we remained in the valley opposite the town of Bethpeor."

Moses Urges Israel to Be Obedient

4 Then Moses said to the people, "Obey all the laws that I am teaching you, and you will live and occupy the land which the LORD, the God of your ancestors, is giving you. 2 Do not add anything to what I command you, and do not take anything away. Obey the commands of the LORD your God that I have given you. 3 You yourselves saw what the LORD did at Mount Peor. He destroyed everyone who worshiped Baal there, 4 but those of you who were faithful to the LORD your God are still alive today.

5 "I have taught you all the laws, as the LORD my God told me to do. Obey them in the land that you are about to invade and occupy. 6 Obey them faithfully, and this will show the people of other nations how wise you are. When they hear of all these laws, they will say, 'What wisdom and understanding this great nation has!'

7 "No other nation, no matter how great, has a god who is so near when they need him as the LORD our God is to us. He answers us whenever we call for help. 8 No other nation, no matter how great, has laws so just as those that I have taught you today. 9 Be on your guard! Make certain that you do not forget, as long as you live, what you have seen with your own eyes. Tell your children and your grandchildren 10 about the day you stood in the presence of the LORD your God at Mount Sinai,d when he said to me, 'Assemble the people. I want them to hear what I have to say, so that they will learn to obey me as long as they live and so that they will teach their children to do the same.'

11 "Tell your children how you went and stood at the foot of the mountain which was covered with thick clouds of dark smoke and fire blazing up to the sky. 12 Tell them how the LORD spoke to you from the fire, how you heard him speaking but did not see him in any form at all. 13 He told you what you must do to

---

d Sinai; or Horeb.

keep the covenant he made with you—you must obey the Ten Commandments, which he wrote on two stone tablets. [14] The LORD told me to teach you all the laws that you are to obey in the land that you are about to invade and occupy.

Warning against Idolatry

[15] "When the LORD spoke to you from the fire on Mount Sinai, you did not see any form. For your own good, then, make certain [16] that you do not sin by making for yourselves an idol in any form at all—whether man or woman, [17] animal or bird, [18] reptile or fish. [19] Do not be tempted to worship and serve what you see in the sky—the sun, the moon, and the stars. The LORD your God has given these to all other peoples for them to worship. [20] But you are the people he rescued from Egypt, that blazing furnace. He brought you out to make you his own people, as you are today. [21] Because of you the LORD your God was angry with me and solemnly declared that I would not cross the Jordan River to enter the fertile land which he is giving you. [22] I will die in this land and never cross the river, but you are about to go across and occupy that fertile land. [23] Be certain that you do not forget the covenant that the LORD your God made with you. Obey his command not to make yourselves any kind of idol, [24] because the LORD your God is like a flaming fire; he tolerates no rivals.

[25] "Even when you have been in the land a long time and have children and grandchildren, do not sin by making for yourselves an idol in any form at all. This is evil in the LORD's sight, and it will make him angry. [26] I call heaven and earth as witnesses against you today that, if you disobey me, you will soon disappear from the land. You will not live very long in the land across the Jordan that you are about to occupy. You will be completely destroyed. [27] The LORD will scatter you among other nations, where only a few of you will survive. [28] There you will serve gods made by human hands, gods of wood and stone, gods that cannot see or hear, eat or smell. [29] There you will look for the LORD your God, and if you search for him with all your heart, you will find him. [30] When you are in trouble and all those things happen to you, then you will finally turn to the LORD and obey

him. [31] He is a merciful God. He will not abandon you or destroy you, and he will not forget the covenant that he himself made with your ancestors.

[32] "Search the past, the time before you were born, all the way back to the time when God created human beings on the earth. Search the entire earth. Has anything as great as this ever happened before? Has anyone ever heard of anything like this? [33] Have any people ever lived after hearing a god speak to them from a fire, as you have? [34] Has any god ever dared to go and take a people from another nation and make them his own, as the LORD your God did for you in Egypt? Before your very eyes he used his great power and strength; he brought plagues and war, worked miracles and wonders, and caused terrifying things to happen. [35] The LORD has shown you this, to prove to you that he alone is God and that there is no other. [36] He let you hear his voice from heaven so that he could instruct you; and here on earth he let you see his holy fire, and he spoke to you from it. [37] Because he loved your ancestors, he chose you, and by his great power he himself brought you out of Egypt. [38] As you advanced, he drove out nations greater and more powerful than you, so that he might bring you in and give you their land, the land which still belongs to you. [39] So remember today and never forget: the LORD is God in heaven and on earth. There is no other god. [40] Obey all his laws that I have given you today, and all will go well with you and your descendants. You will continue to live in the land that the LORD your God is giving you to be yours forever."

The Cities of Refuge East of the Jordan

[41] Then Moses set aside three cities east of the Jordan River [42] to which a man could escape and be safe if he had accidentally killed someone who had not been his enemy. He could escape to one of these cities and not be put to death. [43] For the tribe of Reuben there was the city of Bezer, on the desert plateau; for the tribe of Gad there was Ramoth, in the territory of Gilead; and for the tribe of Manasseh there was Golan, in the territory of Bashan.

CITIES OF REFUGE

Six cities of refuge were designated throughout Israel in Old Testament times to provide a haven for people who killed other persons by accident. Protection like this was necessary because the relative of the person killed considered it his duty to slay the killer. Eligibility for refuge was determined by a judge. For convenience, three of the cities were located on either side of the Jordan River.

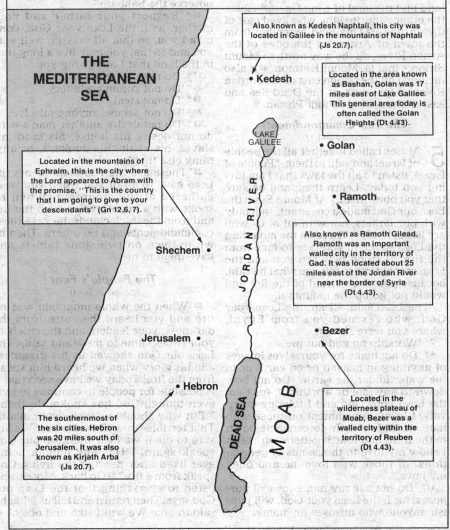

Also known as Kedesh Naphtali, this city was located in Galilee in the mountains of Naphtali (Js 20.7).

Located in the area known as Bashan, Golan was 17 miles east of Lake Galilee. This general area today is often called the Golan Heights (Dt 4.43).

THE MEDITERRANEAN SEA

Located in the mountains of Ephraim, this is the city where the Lord appeared to Abram with the promise, "This is the country that I am going to give to your descendants" (Gn 12.6, 7).

Also known as Ramoth Gilead, Ramoth was an important walled city in the territory of Gad. It was located about 25 miles east of the Jordan River near the border of Syria (Dt 4.43).

The southernmost of the six cities, Hebron was 20 miles south of Jerusalem. It was also known as Kirjath Arba (Js 20.7).

Located in the wilderness plateau of Moab, Bezer was a walled city within the territory of Reuben (Dt 4.43).

• Kedesh

LAKE GALILEE

• Golan

• Ramoth

JORDAN RIVER

Shechem •

Jerusalem •

• Bezer

• Hebron

DEAD SEA

MOAB

Introduction to the Giving of God's Law

44 Moses gave God's laws and teachings to the people of Israel. 45-46 It was after they had come out of Egypt and were in the valley east of the Jordan River, opposite the town of Bethpeor, that he gave them these laws. This was in the territory that had belonged to King Sihon of the Amorites, who had ruled in the town of Heshbon. Moses and the people of Israel defeated him when they came out of Egypt. 47 They occupied his land and the land of King Og of Bashan, the other Amorite king who lived east of the Jordan. 48 This land extended from the town of Aroer, on the edge of the Arnon River, all the way north to Mount Sirion,e that is, Mount Hermon. 49 It also included all the region east of the Jordan River as far south as the Dead Sea and east to the foot of Mount Pisgah.

The Ten Commandments
(Exodus 20.1-17)

5 Moses called together all the people of Israel and said to them, "People of Israel, listen to all the laws that I am giving you today. Learn them and be sure that you obey them. 2 At Mount Sinai the LORD our God made a covenant, 3 not only with our fathers, but with all of us who are living today. 4 There on the mountain the LORD spoke to you face-to-face from the fire. 5 I stood between you and the LORD at that time to tell you what he said, because you were afraid of the fire and would not go up the mountain.

"The LORD said, 6 'I am the LORD your God, who rescued you from Egypt, where you were slaves.

7 " 'Worship no god but me.

8 " 'Do not make for yourselves images of anything in heaven or on earth or in the water under the earth. 9 Do not bow down to any idol or worship it, for I am the LORD your God and I tolerate no rivals. I bring punishment on those who hate me and on their descendants down to the third and fourth generation. 10 But I show my love to thousands of generationsf of those who love me and obey my laws.

11 " 'Do not use my name for evil purposes, for I, the LORD your God, will punish anyone who misuses my name.

12 " 'Observe the Sabbath and keep it holy, as I, the LORD your God, have commanded you. 13 You have six days in which to do your work, 14 but the seventh day is a day of rest dedicated to me. On that day no one is to work — neither you, your children, your slaves, your animals, nor the foreigners who live in your country. Your slaves must rest just as you do. 15 Remember that you were slaves in Egypt, and that I, the LORD your God, rescued you by my great power and strength. That is why I command you to observe the Sabbath.

16 " 'Respect your father and your mother, as I, the LORD your God, command you, so that all may go well with you and so that you may live a long time in the land that I am giving you.

17 " 'Do not commit murder.

18 " 'Do not commit adultery.

19 " 'Do not steal.

20 " 'Do not accuse anyone falsely.

21 " 'Do not desire another man's wife; do not desire his house, his land, his slaves, his cattle, his donkeys, or anything else that he owns.'

22 "These are the commandments the LORD gave to all of you when you were gathered at the mountain. When he spoke with a mighty voice from the fire and from the thick clouds, he gave these commandments and no others. Then he wrote them on two stone tablets and gave them to me.

The People's Fear
(Exodus 20.18-21)

23 "When the whole mountain was on fire and you heard the voice from the darkness, your leaders and the chiefs of your tribes came to me 24 and said, 'The LORD our God showed us his greatness and his glory when we heard him speak from the fire! Today we have seen that it is possible for people to continue to live, even though God has spoken to them. 25 But why should we risk death again? That terrible fire will destroy us. We are sure to die if we hear the LORD our God speak again. 26 Has any human being ever lived after hearing the living God speak from a fire? 27 Go back, Moses, and listen to everything that the LORD our God says. Then return and tell us what he said to you. We will listen and obey.'

---

e One ancient translation Sirion; Hebrew Sion.   f thousands of generations; or thousands.

ISRAEL'S TRIBAL RIVALS

The twelve tribes of Israel encountered many tribal enemies, particularly during the Old Testament period before and after the conquest of Canaan. Important tribal rivals mentioned in the Bible are the Amalekites, Ammonites, Amorites, Edomites, Gibeonites, Horites, Hivites, Jebusites, Kenites, Midianites, and Moabites.

These tribal adversaries of Israel were nomadic people, although most of them lived in Canaan at one time or another. The Amorites, Hivites, and Jebusites were among the seven groups God commanded Israel to cast out of Canaan (Dt 7.1, 2). Several tribes, such as the Kenites, Midianites, and Moabites, were desert wanderers, migrating throughout the desert regions of the Dead Sea or Sinai with their flocks and herds.

Many of these tribal groups were distant relatives of the Israelites. The Midianites traced their ancestry to Midian, the son of Abraham (Gn 25.2). Three tribes—the Amorites, the Hivites, and the Jebusites— were descendants of Canaan, a son of Ham (Gn 10.6, 15–18). The Moabites and Ammonites were descendants of Lot (Gn 19.36–38).

Most of these tribes were warlike and often cruel and barbaric, constantly attacking Israel and other nations. Except those retained as slave laborers, they were eventually destroyed or expelled from Canaan. The Gibeonites became woodcutters and water carriers for Israel (Js 9.18–21). Solomon used the Hivites and other Canaanites who remained in the land as construction laborers (1 K 9.20, 21).

Israel's tribal rivals were generally idol worshipers. For this reason God commanded his people not to intermarry or make political alliances with these groups (Dt 7.1–4). The Moabites and Ammonites were especially rebuked by God because they refused to help the Israelites during their journey from Egypt to Canaan (Dt 23.3, 4).

28 "When the LORD heard this, he said to me, 'I have heard what these people said, and they are right. 29 If only they would always feel this way! If only they would always honor me and obey all my commands, so that everything would go well with them and their descendants forever. 30 Go and tell them to return to their tents. 31 But you, Moses, stay here with me, and I will give you all my laws and commands. Teach them to the people, so that they will obey them in the land that I am giving them.'

32 "People of Israel, be sure that you do everything that the LORD your God has commanded you. Do not disobey any of his laws. 33 Obey them all, so that everything will go well with you and so that you will continue to live in the land that you are going to occupy.

The Great Commandment

6 "These are all the laws that the LORD your God commanded me to teach you. Obey them in the land that you are about to enter and occupy. 2 As long as you live, you and your descendants are to honor the LORD your God and obey all his laws that I am giving you, so that you may live in that land a long time. 3 Listen to them, people of Israel, and obey them! Then all will go well with you, and you will become a mighty nation and live in that rich and fertile land, just as the LORD, the God of our ancestors, has promised.

4 "Israel, remember this! The LORD — and the LORD alone — is our God. g 5 Love the LORD your God with all your heart, with all your soul, and with all your strength. 6 Never forget these commands that I am giving you today. 7 Teach them to your children. Repeat them when you are at home and when you are away, when you are resting and when you are working. 8 Tie them on your arms and wear them on your foreheads as a reminder. 9 Write them on the doorposts of your houses and on your gates.

Warning against Disobedience

10 "Just as the LORD your God promised your ancestors, Abraham, Isaac, and Jacob, he will give you a land with large and prosperous cities which you did not build. 11 The houses will be full of good things which you did not put in them, and there will be wells that you did not dig, and vineyards and olive orchards that you did not plant. When the LORD brings you into this land and you have all you want to eat, 12 make certain that you do not forget the LORD who rescued you from Egypt, where you were slaves. 13 Honor the LORD your God, worship only him, and make your promises in his name alone. 14 Do not worship other gods, any of the gods of the peoples around you. 15 If you do worship other gods, the LORD's anger will come against you like fire and will destroy you completely, because the LORD your God, who is present with you, tolerates no rivals.

16 "Do not put the LORD your God to the test, as you did at Massah. 17 Be sure that you obey all the laws that he has given you. 18 Do what the LORD says is right and good, and all will go well with you. You will be able to take possession of the fertile land that the LORD promised your ancestors, 19 and you will drive out your enemies, as he promised.

20 "In times to come your children will ask you, 'Why did the LORD our God command us to obey all these laws?' 21 Then tell them, 'We were slaves of the king of Egypt, and the LORD rescued us by his great power. 22 With our own eyes we saw him work miracles and do terrifying things to the Egyptians and to their king and to all his officials. 23 He freed us from Egypt to bring us here and give us this land, as he had promised our ancestors he would. 24 Then the LORD our God commanded us to obey all these laws and to honor him. If we do, he will always watch over our nation and keep it prosperous. 25 If we faithfully obey everything that God has commanded us, he will be pleased with us.' h

The LORD's Own People
(Exodus 34.11-16)

7 "The LORD your God will bring you into the land that you are going to occupy, and he will drive many nations out of it. As you advance, he will drive out seven nations larger and more powerful than you: the Hittites, the Girgashites, the Amorites, the Canaanites, the Perizzites, the Hivites, and the Jebusites.

---

g The LORD . . . is our God; or The LORD, our God, is the only God; or The LORD our God is one.
h If we faithfully . . . with us; or The right thing for us to do is to obey faithfully everything that God has commanded us.

2 When the LORD your God places these people in your power and you defeat them, you must put them all to death. Do not make an alliance with them or show them any mercy. 3 Do not marry any of them, and do not let your children marry any of them, 4 because then they would lead your children away from the LORD to worship other gods. If that happens, the LORD will be angry with you and destroy you at once. 5 So then, tear down their altars, break their sacred stone pillars in pieces, cut down their symbols of the goddess Asherah, and burn their idols. 6 Do this because you belong to the LORD your God. From all the peoples on earth he chose you to be his own special people.

7 "The LORD did not love you and choose you because you outnumbered other peoples; you were the smallest nation on earth. 8 But the LORD loved you and wanted to keep the promise that he made to your ancestors. That is why he saved you by his great might and set you free from slavery to the king of Egypt. 9 Remember that the LORD your God is the only God and that he is faithful. He will keep his covenant and show his constant love to a thousand generations of those who love him and obey his commands, 10 but he will not hesitate to punish those who hate him. 11 Now then, obey what you have been taught; obey all the laws that I have given you today.

The Blessings of Obedience
(Deuteronomy 28.1-14)

12 "If you listen to these commands and obey them faithfully, then the LORD your God will continue to keep his covenant with you and will show you his constant love, as he promised your ancestors. 13 He will love you and bless you, so that you will increase in number and have many children; he will bless your fields, so that you will have grain, wine, and olive oil; and he will bless you by giving you many cattle and sheep. He will give you all these blessings in the land that he promised your ancestors he would give to you. 14 No people in the world will be as richly blessed as you. None of you nor any of your livestock will be sterile. 15 The LORD will protect you from all sickness, and he will not bring on you any of the dreadful diseases that you experienced in Egypt, but he will bring them on all your enemies. 16 Destroy every nation that the LORD your God places in your power, and do not show them any mercy. Do not worship their gods, for that would be fatal.

17 "Do not tell yourselves that these peoples outnumber you and that you cannot drive them out. 18 Do not be afraid of them; remember what the LORD your God did to the king of Egypt and to all his people. 19 Remember the terrible plagues that you saw with your own eyes, the miracles and wonders, and the great power and strength by which the LORD your God set you free. In the same way that he destroyed the Egyptians, he will destroy all these people that you now fear. 20 He will even cause panic[i] among them and will destroy those who escape and go into hiding. 21 So do not be afraid of these people. The LORD your God is with you; he is a great God and one to be feared. 22 Little by little he will drive out these nations as you advance. You will not be able to destroy them all at once, for, if you did, the number of wild animals would increase and be a threat to you. 23 The LORD will put your enemies in your power and make them panic until they are destroyed. 24 He will put their kings in your power. You will kill them, and they will be forgotten. No one will be able to stop you; you will destroy everyone. 25 Burn their idols. Do not desire the silver or gold that is on them, and do not take it for yourselves. If you do, that will be fatal, because the LORD hates idolatry. 26 Do not bring any of these idols into your homes, or the same curse will be on you that is on them. You must hate and despise these idols, because they are under the LORD's curse.

A Good Land to Be Possessed

8 "Obey faithfully all the laws that I have given you today, so that you may live, increase in number, and occupy the land that the LORD promised to your ancestors. 2 Remember how the LORD your God led you on this long journey through the desert these past forty years, sending hardships to test you, so that he might know what you intended to do and whether you would obey his

---

i cause panic; or send hornets, or send plagues.

commands. 3 He made you go hungry, and then he gave you manna to eat, food that you and your ancestors had never eaten before. He did this to teach you that you must not depend on bread alone to sustain you, but on everything that the LORD says. 4 During these forty years your clothes have not worn out, nor have your feet swollen up. 5 Remember that the LORD your God corrects and punishes you just as parents discipline their children. 6 So then, do as the LORD has commanded you: live according to his laws and obey him. 7 The LORD your God is bringing you into a fertile land — a land that has rivers and springs, and underground streams gushing out into the valleys and hills; 8 a land that produces wheat and barley, grapes, figs, pomegranates, olives, and honey. 9 There you will never go hungry or ever be in need. Its rocks have iron in them, and from its hills you can mine copper. 10 You will have all you want to eat, and you will give thanks to the LORD your God for the fertile land that he has given you.

Warnings against Forgetting the LORD

11 "Make certain that you do not forget the LORD your God; do not fail to obey any of his laws that I am giving you today. 12 When you have all you want to eat and have built good houses to live in 13 and when your cattle and sheep, your silver and gold, and all your other possessions have increased, 14 be sure that you do not become proud and forget the LORD your God who rescued you from Egypt, where you were slaves. 15 He led you through that vast and terrifying desert where there were poisonous snakes and scorpions. In that dry and waterless land he made water flow out of solid rock for you. 16 In the desert he gave you manna to eat, food that your ancestors had never eaten. He sent hardships on you to test you, so that in the end he could bless you with good things. 17 So then, you must never think that you have made yourselves wealthy by your own power and strength. 18 Remember that it is the LORD your God who gives you the power to become rich. He does this because he is still faithful today to the covenant that he made with your ancestors. 19 Never forget the LORD your God or turn

to other gods to worship and serve them. If you do, then I warn you today that you will certainly be destroyed. 20 If you do not obey the LORD, then you will be destroyed just like those nations that he is going to destroy as you advance.

The People's Disobedience

9 "Listen, people of Israel! Today you are about to cross the Jordan River and occupy the land belonging to nations greater and more powerful than you. Their cities are large, with walls that reach the sky. 2 The people themselves are tall and strong; they are giants, and you have heard it said that no one can stand against them. 3 But now you will see for yourselves that the LORD your God will go ahead of you like a raging fire. He will defeat them as you advance, so that you will drive them out and destroy them quickly, as he promised.

4 "After the LORD your God has driven them out for you, do not say to yourselves that he brought you in to possess this land because you deserved it. No, the LORD is going to drive these people out for you because they are wicked. 5 It is not because you are good and do what is right that the LORD is letting you take their land. He will drive them out because they are wicked and because he intends to keep the promise that he made to your ancestors, Abraham, Isaac, and Jacob. 6 You can be sure that the LORD is not giving you this fertile land because you deserve it. No, you are a stubborn people.

7 "Never forget how you made the LORD your God angry in the desert. From the day that you left Egypt until the day you arrived here, you have rebelled against him. 8 Even at Mount Sinai you made the LORD angry — angry enough to destroy you. 9 I went up the mountain to receive the stone tablets on which was written the covenant that the LORD had made with you. I stayed there forty days and nights and did not eat or drink anything. 10 Then the LORD gave me the two stone tablets on which he had written with his own hand what he had said to you from the fire on the day that you were gathered there at the mountain. 11 Yes, after those forty days and nights the LORD gave me the two stone tablets on which he had written the covenant.

12 "Then the LORD said to me, 'Go down

the mountain at once, because your people, whom you led out of Egypt, have become corrupt and have done evil. They have already turned away from what I commanded them to do, and they have made an idol for themselves.'

13 "The LORD also said to me, 'I know how stubborn these people are. 14 Don't try to stop me. I intend to destroy them so that no one will remember them any longer. Then I will make you the father of a nation larger and more powerful than they are.'

15 "So I turned and went down the mountain, carrying the two stone tablets on which the covenant was written. Flames of fire were coming from the mountain. 16 I saw that you had already disobeyed the command that the LORD your God had given you, and that you had sinned against him by making yourselves a metal idol in the form of a bull-calf. 17 So there in front of you I threw the stone tablets down and broke them to pieces. 18 Then once again I lay face downward in the LORD's presence for forty days and nights and did not eat or drink anything. I did this because you had sinned against the LORD and had made him angry. 19 I was afraid of the LORD's fierce anger, because he was furious enough to destroy you; but once again the LORD listened to me. 20 The LORD was also angry enough with Aaron to kill him, so I prayed for Aaron at the same time. 21 I took that sinful thing that you had made — that metal bull-calf — and threw it into the fire. Then I broke it in pieces, ground it to dust, and threw the dust into the stream that flowed down the mountain.

22 "You also made the LORD your God angry when you were at Taberah, Massah, and Kibroth Hattaavah. 23 And when he sent you from Kadesh Barnea with orders to go and take possession of the land that he was giving you, you rebelled against him; you did not trust him or obey him. 24 Ever since I have known you, you have rebelled against the LORD.

25 "So I lay face downward in the LORD's presence those forty days and nights, because I knew that he was determined to destroy you. 26 And I prayed, 'Sovereign LORD, don't destroy your own people, the people you rescued and

brought out of Egypt by your great strength and power. 27 Remember your servants, Abraham, Isaac, and Jacob, and do not pay any attention to the stubbornness, wickedness, and sin of this people. 28 Otherwise, the Egyptians will say that you were unable to take your people into the land that you had promised them. They will say that you took your people out into the desert to kill them, because you hated them. 29 After all, these are the people whom you chose to be your own and whom you brought out of Egypt by your great power and might.'

Moses Receives the Commandments Again
(Exodus 34.1-10)

10 "Then the LORD said to me, 'Cut two stone tablets like the first ones and make a wooden Box to put them in. Come up to me on the mountain, 2 and I will write on those tablets what I wrote on the tablets that you broke, and then you are to put them in the Box.'

3 "So I made a Box of acacia wood and cut two stone tablets like the first ones and took them up the mountain. 4 Then the LORD wrote on those tablets the same words that he had written the first time, the Ten Commandments that he gave you when he spoke from the fire on the day you were gathered at the mountain. The LORD gave me the tablets, 5 and I turned and went down the mountain. Then, just as the LORD had commanded, I put them in the Box that I had made — and they have been there ever since."

(6 The Israelites set out from the wells that belonged to the people of Jaakan, and went to Moserah. There Aaron died and was buried, and his son Eleazar succeeded him as priest. 7 From there they went to Gudgodah and then on to Jotbathah, a well-watered place. 8 At the mountain[j] the LORD appointed the men of the tribe of Levi to be in charge of the Covenant Box, to serve him as priests, and to pronounce blessings in his name. And these are still their duties. 9 That is why the tribe of Levi received no land as the other tribes did; what they received was the privilege of being the LORD's priests, as the LORD your God promised.)

10 "I stayed on the mountain forty days

j the mountain; or that time.

and nights, as I did the first time. The LORD listened to me once more and agreed not to destroy you. 11 Then he told me to go and lead you, so that you could take possession of the land that he had promised to give to your ancestors.

What God Demands

12 "Now, people of Israel, listen to what the LORD your God demands of you: Worship the LORD and do all that he commands. Love him, serve him with all your heart, 13 and obey all his laws. I am giving them to you today for your benefit. 14 To the LORD belong even the highest heavens; the earth is his also, and everything on it. 15 But the LORD's love for your ancestors was so strong that he chose you instead of any other people, and you are still his chosen people. 16 So then, from now on be obedient to the LORD and stop being stubborn. 17 The LORD your God is supreme over all gods and over all powers. He is great and mighty, and he is to be obeyed. He does not show partiality, and he does not accept bribes. 18 He makes sure that orphans and widows are treated fairly; he loves the foreigners who live with our people, and gives them food and clothes. 19 So then, show love for those foreigners, because you were once foreigners in Egypt. 20 Have reverence for the LORD your God and worship only him. Be faithful to him and make your promises in his name alone. 21 Praise him—he is your God, and you have seen with your own eyes the great and astounding things that he has done for you. 22 When your ancestors went to Egypt, there were only seventy of them. But now the LORD your God has made you as numerous as the stars in the sky.

The LORD's Greatness

11 "Love the LORD your God and always obey all his laws. 2 Remember today what you have learned about the LORD through your experiences with him. It was you, not your children, who had these experiences. You saw the LORD's greatness, his power, his might, 3 and his miracles. You saw what he did to the king of Egypt and to his entire country. 4 You saw how the LORD completely wiped out the Egyptian army, along with their horses and chariots, by

drowning them in the Red Sea[k] when they were pursuing you. 5 You know what the LORD did for you in the desert before you arrived here. 6 You recall what he did to Dathan and Abiram, the sons of Eliab of the tribe of Reuben. In the sight of everyone the earth opened up and swallowed them, along with their families, their tents, and all their servants and animals. 7 Yes, you are the ones who have seen all these great things that the LORD has done.

The Blessings of the Promised Land

8 "Obey everything that I have commanded you today. Then you will be able to cross the river and occupy the land that you are about to enter. 9 And you will live a long time in the rich and fertile land that the LORD promised to give your ancestors and their descendants. 10 The land that you are about to occupy is not like the land of Egypt, where you lived before. There, when you planted grain, you had to work hard to irrigate the fields; 11 but the land that you are about to enter is a land of mountains and valleys, a land watered by rain. 12 The LORD your God takes care of this land and watches over it throughout the year.

13 "So then, obey the commands that I have given you today; love the LORD your God and serve him with all your heart. 14 If you do, he will send rain on your land when it is needed, in the autumn and in the spring, so that there will be grain, wine, and olive oil for you, 15 and grass for your livestock. You will have all the food you want. 16 Do not let yourselves be led away from the LORD to worship and serve other gods. 17 If you do, the LORD will become angry with you. He will hold back the rain, and your ground will become too dry for crops to grow. Then you will soon die there, even though it is a good land that he is giving you.

18 "Remember these commands and cherish them. Tie them on your arms and wear them on your foreheads as a reminder. 19 Teach them to your children. Talk about them when you are at home and when you are away, when you are resting and when you are working. 20 Write them on the doorposts of your houses and on your gates. 21 Then you

[k] RED SEA: *See Word List.*

and your children will live a long time in the land that the LORD your God promised to give to your ancestors. You will live there as long as there is a sky above the earth.

22 "Obey faithfully everything that I have commanded you: Love the LORD your God, do everything he commands, and be faithful to him. 23 Then he will drive out all those nations as you advance, and you will occupy the land belonging to nations greater and more powerful than you. 24 All the ground that you march over will be yours. Your territory will extend from the desert in the south to the Lebanon Mountains in the north, and from the Euphrates River in the east to the Mediterranean Sea in the west. 25 Wherever you go in that land, the LORD your God will make the people fear you, as he has promised, and no one will be able to stop you.

26 "Today I am giving you the choice between a blessing and a curse — 27 a blessing, if you obey the commands of the LORD your God that I am giving you today; 28 but a curse, if you disobey these commands and turn away to worship other gods that you have never worshiped before. 29 When the LORD brings you into the land that you are going to occupy, you are to proclaim the blessing from Mount Gerizim and the curse from Mount Ebal. (30 These two mountains are west of the Jordan River in the territory of the Canaanites who live in the Jordan Valley. They are toward the west, not far from the sacred trees of Moreh near the town of Gilgal.) 31 You are about to cross the Jordan River and occupy the land that the LORD your God is giving you. When you take it and settle there, 32 be sure to obey all the laws that I am giving you today.

The One Place for Worship

12 "Here are the laws that you are to obey as long as you live in the land that the LORD, the God of your ancestors, is giving you. Listen to them! 2 In the land that you are taking, destroy all the places where the people worship their gods on high mountains, on hills, and under green trees. 3 Tear down their altars and smash their sacred stone pillars to pieces. Burn their symbols of the goddess Asherah and chop down their

idols, so that they will never again be worshiped at those places.

4 "Do not worship the LORD your God in the way that these people worship their gods. 5 Out of the territory of all your tribes the LORD will choose the one place where the people are to come into his presence and worship him. 6 There you are to offer your sacrifices that are to be burned and your other sacrifices, your tithes and your offerings, the gifts that you promise to the LORD, your freewill offerings, and the first-born of your cattle and sheep. 7 There, in the presence of the LORD your God, who has blessed you, you and your families will eat and enjoy the good things that you have worked for.

8 "When that time comes, you must not do as you have been doing. Until now you have all been worshiping as you please, 9 because you have not yet entered the land that the LORD your God is giving you, where you can live in peace. 10 When you cross the Jordan River, the LORD will let you occupy the land and live there. He will keep you safe from all your enemies, and you will live in peace. 11 The LORD will choose a single place where he is to be worshiped, and there you must bring to him everything that I have commanded: your sacrifices that are to be burned and your other sacrifices, your tithes and your offerings, and those special gifts that you have promised to the LORD. 12 Be joyful there in his presence, together with your children, your servants, and the Levites who live in your towns; remember that the Levites will have no land of their own. 13 You are not to offer your sacrifices wherever you choose; 14 you must offer them only in the one place that the LORD will choose in the territory of one of your tribes. Only there are you to offer your sacrifices that are to be burned and do all the other things that I have commanded you.

15 "But you are free to kill and eat your animals wherever you live. You may eat as many as the LORD gives you. All of you, whether ritually clean or unclean, may eat them, just as you would eat the meat of deer or antelope. 16 But you must not eat their blood; you must pour it out on the ground like water. 17 Nothing that you offer to the LORD is to be eaten in the places where you live: neither the tithes of your grain, your wine, or your olive

oil, nor the first-born of your cattle and sheep, the gifts that you promise to the LORD, your freewill offerings, or any other offerings. 18 You and your children, together with your servants and the Levites who live in your towns, are to eat these offerings only in the presence of the LORD your God, in the one place of worship chosen by the LORD your God. And you are to be happy there over everything that you have done. 19 Be sure, also, not to neglect the Levites, as long as you live in your land.

20 "When the LORD your God enlarges your territory, as he has promised, you may eat meat whenever you want to. 21 If the one place of worship is too far away, then, whenever you wish, you may kill any of the cattle or sheep that the LORD has given you, and you may eat the meat at home, as I have told you. 22 Anyone, ritually clean or unclean, may eat that meat, just as he would eat the meat of deer or antelope. 23 Only do not eat meat with blood still in it, for the life is in the blood, and you must not eat the life with the meat. 24 Do not use the blood for food; instead, pour it out on the ground like water. 25 If you obey this command, the LORD will be pleased, and all will go well for you and your descendants. 26 Take to the one place of worship your offerings and the gifts that you have promised the LORD. 27 Offer there the sacrifices which are to be completely burned on the LORD's altar. Also offer those sacrifices in which you eat the meat and pour the blood out on the altar. 28 Obey faithfully everything that I have commanded you, and all will go well for you and your descendants forever, because you will be doing what is right and what pleases the LORD your God.

Warning against Idolatry

29 "The LORD your God will destroy the nations as you invade their land, and you will occupy it and settle there. 30 After the LORD destroys those nations, make sure that you don't follow their religious practices, because that would be fatal. Don't try to find out how they worship their gods, so that you can worship in the same way. 31 Do not worship the LORD your God in the way they worship their gods, for in the worship of their gods they do all the disgusting things that the

LORD hates. They even sacrifice their children in the fires on their altars.

32 "Do everything that I have commanded you; do not add anything to it or take anything from it.

13 "Prophets or interpreters of dreams may promise a miracle or a wonder, 2 in order to lead you to worship and serve gods that you have not worshiped before. Even if what they promise comes true, 3 do not pay any attention to them. The LORD your God is using them to test you, to see if you love the LORD with all your heart. 4 Follow the LORD and honor him; obey him and keep his commands; worship him and be faithful to him. 5 But put to death any interpreters of dreams or prophets that tell you to rebel against the LORD, who rescued you from Egypt, where you were slaves. Such people are evil and are trying to lead you away from the life that the LORD has commanded you to live. They must be put to death, in order to rid yourselves of this evil.

6 "Even your brother or your son or your daughter or the wife you love or your closest friend may secretly encourage you to worship other gods, gods that you and your ancestors have never worshiped. 7 Some of them may encourage you to worship the gods of the people who live near you or the gods of those who live far away. 8 But do not let any of them persuade you; do not even listen to them. Show them no mercy or pity, and do not protect them. 9 Kill them! Be the first to stone them, and then let everyone else stone them too. 10 Stone them to death! They tried to lead you away from the LORD your God, who rescued you from Egypt, where you were slaves. 11 Then all the people of Israel will hear what happened; they will be afraid, and no one will ever again do such an evil thing.

12 "When you are living in the towns that the LORD your God gives you, you may hear 13 that some worthless people of your nation have misled the people of their town to worship gods that you have never worshiped before. 14 If you hear such a rumor, investigate it thoroughly; and if it is true that this evil thing did happen, 15 then kill all the people in that town and all their livestock too. Destroy that town completely. 16 Bring together all the possessions of the people who live

there and pile them up in the town square. Then burn the town and everything in it as an offering to the LORD your God. It must be left in ruins forever and never again be rebuilt. 17 Do not keep for yourselves anything that was condemned to destruction, and then the LORD will turn from his fierce anger and show you mercy. He will be merciful to you and make you a numerous people, as he promised your ancestors, 18 if you obey all his commands that I have given you today, and do what he requires.

A Forbidden Mourning Practice

14 "You are the people of the LORD your God. So when you mourn for the dead, don't gash yourselves or shave the front of your head, as other people do. 2 You belong to the LORD your God; he has chosen you to be his own people from among all the peoples who live on earth.

Clean and Unclean Animals
(Leviticus 11.1-47)

3 "Do not eat anything that the LORD has declared unclean. 4 You may eat these animals: cattle, sheep, goats, 5 deer, wild sheep, wild goats, or antelopes — 6 any animals that have divided hoofs and that also chew the cud. 7 But no animals may be eaten unless they have divided hoofs and also chew the cud. You may not eat camels, rabbits, or rock badgers. They must be considered unclean; they chew the cud but do not have divided hoofs. 8 Do not eat pigs. They must be considered unclean; they have divided hoofs but do not chew the cud. Do not eat any of these animals or even touch their dead bodies.

9 "You may eat any kind of fish that has fins and scales, 10 but anything living in the water that does not have fins and scales may not be eaten; it must be considered unclean.

11 "You may eat any clean bird. 12-18 But these are the kinds of birds you are not to eat: eagles, owls, hawks, falcons; buzzards, vultures, crows; ostriches; seagulls, storks, herons, pelicans, cormorants;[l] hoopoes; and bats.

19 "All winged insects are unclean; do not eat them. 20 You may eat any clean insect.

21 "Do not eat any animal that dies a natural death. You may let the foreigners who live among you eat it, or you may sell it to other foreigners. But you belong to the LORD your God; you are his people.

"Do not cook a young sheep or goat in its mother's milk.

The Law of the Tithe

22 "Set aside a tithe — a tenth of all that your fields produce each year. 23 Then go to the one place where the LORD your God has chosen to be worshiped; and there in his presence eat the tithes of your grain, wine, and olive oil, and the first-born of your cattle and sheep. Do this so that you may learn to honor the LORD your God always. 24 If the place of worship is too far from your home for you to carry there the tithe of the produce that the LORD has blessed you with, then do this: 25 Sell your produce and take the money with you to the one place of worship. 26 Spend it on whatever you want — beef, lamb, wine, beer — and there, in the presence of the LORD your God, you and your families are to eat and enjoy yourselves.

27 "Do not neglect the Levites who live in your towns; they have no property of their own. 28 At the end of every third year bring the tithe of all your crops and store it in your towns. 29 This food is for the Levites, since they own no property, and for the foreigners, orphans, and widows who live in your towns. They are to come and get all they need. Do this, and the LORD your God will bless you in everything you do.

The Seventh Year
(Leviticus 25.1-7)

15 "At the end of every seventh year you are to cancel the debts of those who owe you money. 2 This is how it is to be done. Each of you who has lent money to any Israelite is to cancel the debt; you must not try to collect the money; the LORD himself has declared the debt canceled. 3 You may collect what a foreigner owes you, but you must not collect what any of your own people owe you.

4 "The LORD your God will bless you in the land that he is giving you. Not one of your people will be poor 5 if you obey him and carefully observe everything that I

l The identification of some of these birds is uncertain.

command you today. 6The LORD will bless you, as he has promised. You will lend money to many nations, but you will not have to borrow from any; you will have control over many nations, but no nation will have control over you.

7"If in any of the towns in the land that the LORD your God is giving you there are Israelites in need, then do not be selfish and refuse to help them. 8Instead, be generous and lend them as much as they need. 9Do not refuse to lend them something, just because the year when debts are canceled is near. Do not let such an evil thought enter your mind. If you refuse to make the loan, they will cry out to the LORD against you, and you will be held guilty. 10Give to them freely and unselfishly, and the LORD will bless you in everything you do. 11There will always be some Israelites who are poor and in need, and so I command you to be generous to them.

The Treatment of Slaves
(Exodus 21.1-11)

12"If any Israelites, male or female, sell themselvesm to you as slaves, you are to release them after they have served you for six years. When the seventh year comes, you must let them go free. 13When you set them free, do not send them away empty-handed. 14Give to them generously from what the LORD has blessed you with—sheep, grain, and wine. 15Remember that you were slaves in Egypt and the LORD your God set you free; that is why I am now giving you this command.

16"But your slave may not want to leave; he may love you and your family and be content to stay. 17Then take him to the door of your house and there pierce his ear; he will then be your slave for life. Treat your female slave in the same way. 18Do not be resentful when you set slaves free; after all, they have served you for six years at half the cost of hired servants.n Do this, and the LORD your God will bless you in all that you do.

The First-Born Cattle and Sheep

19"Set aside for the LORD your God all the first-born males of your cattle and sheep; don't use any of these cattle for

work and don't shear any of these sheep. 20Each year you and your family are to eat them in the LORD's presence at the one place of worship. 21But if there is anything wrong with the animals, if they are crippled or blind or have any other serious defect, you must not sacrifice them to the LORD your God. 22You may eat such animals at home. All of you, whether ritually clean or unclean, may eat them, just as you eat deer or antelope. 23But do not use their blood for food; instead, you must pour it out on the ground like water.

The Passover
(Exodus 12.1-20)

16 "Honor the LORD your God by celebrating Passover in the month of Abib; it was on a night in that month that he rescued you from Egypt. 2Go to the one place of worship and slaughter there one of your sheep or cattle for the Passover meal to honor the LORD your God. 3When you eat this meal, do not eat bread prepared with yeast. For seven days you are to eat bread prepared without yeast, as you did when you had to leave Egypt in such a hurry. Eat this bread—it will be called the bread of suffering—so that as long as you live you will remember the day you came out of Egypt, that place of suffering. 4For seven days no one in your land is to have any yeast in the house; and the meat of the animal killed on the evening of the first day must be eaten that same night.

5-6"Slaughter the Passover animals at the one place of worship—and nowhere else in the land that the LORD your God will give you. Do it at sunset, the time of day when you left Egypt. 7Boil the meat and eat it at the one place of worship; and the next morning return home. 8For the next six days you are to eat bread prepared without yeast, and on the seventh day assemble to worship the LORD your God, and do no work on that day.

The Harvest Festival
(Exodus 34.22; Leviticus 23.15-21)

9"Count seven weeks from the time that you begin to harvest the grain, 10and then celebrate the Harvest Festival, to honor the LORD your God, by bringing him a freewill offering in proportion to the blessing he has given you. 11Be joyful

---

m sell themselves; *or* are sold.   n at half . . . servants; *or* and have worked twice as hard as hired servants.

in the LORD's presence, together with your children, your servants, and the Levites, foreigners, orphans, and widows who live in your towns. Do this at the one place of worship. 12 Be sure that you obey these commands; do not forget that you were slaves in Egypt.

The Festival of Shelters
(Leviticus 23.33-43)

13 "After you have threshed all your grain and pressed all your grapes, celebrate the Festival of Shelters for seven days. 14 Enjoy it with your children, your servants, and the Levites, foreigners, orphans, and widows who live in your towns. 15 Honor the LORD your God by celebrating this festival for seven days at the one place of worship. Be joyful, because the LORD has blessed your harvest and your work.

16 "All the men of your nation are to come to worship the LORD three times a year at the one place of worship: at Passover, Harvest Festival, and the Festival of Shelters. Each man is to bring a gift 17 as he is able, in proportion to the blessings that the LORD your God has given him.

The Administration of Justice

18 "Appoint judges and other officials in every town that the LORD your God gives you. These men are to judge the people impartially. 19 They are not to be unjust or show partiality in their judgments; and they are not to accept bribes, for gifts blind the eyes even of wise and honest men, and cause them to give wrong decisions. 20 Always be fair and just, so that you will occupy the land that the LORD your God is giving you and so that you will continue to live there.

21 "When you make an altar for the LORD your God, do not put beside it a wooden symbol of the goddess Asherah. 22 And do not set up any stone pillar for idol worship; the LORD hates them.

17 "Do not sacrifice to the LORD your God cattle or sheep that have any defects; the LORD hates this.

2 "Suppose you hear that in one of your towns some men or women have sinned against the LORD and broken his covenant 3 by worshiping and serving other gods or the sun or the moon or the stars,

contrary to the LORD's command. 4 If you hear such a report, then investigate it thoroughly. If it is true that this evil thing has happened in Israel, 5 then take them outside the town and stone them to death. 6 However, they may be put to death only if two or more witnesses testify against them; they are not to be put to death if there is only one witness. 7 The witnesses are to throw the first stones, and then the rest of the people are to stone them; in this way you will get rid of this evil.

8 "It may be that some cases will be too difficult for the local judges to decide, such as certain cases of property rights or of bodily injury or those cases that involve a distinction between murder and manslaughter. When this happens, go to the one place of worship chosen by the LORD your God, 9 and present your case to the levitical priests and to the judge who is in office at that time, and let them decide the case. 10 They will give their decision, and you are to do exactly as they tell you. 11 Accept their verdict and follow their instructions in every detail. 12 Anyone who dares to disobey either the judge or the priest on duty is to be put to death; in this way you will remove this evil from Israel. 13 Then everyone will hear of it and be afraid, and no one else will dare to act in such a way.

Instructions concerning a King

14 "After you have taken possession of the land that the LORD your God is going to give you and have settled there, then you will decide you need a king like all the nations around you. 15 Be sure that the man you choose to be king is the one whom the LORD has chosen. He must be one of your own people; do not make a foreigner your king. 16 The king is not to have a large number of horses for his army, and he is not to send people to Egypt to buy horses, o because the LORD has said that his people are never to return there. 17 The king is not to have many wives, because this would make him turn away from the LORD; and he is not to make himself rich with silver and gold. 18 When he becomes king, he is to have a copy of the book of God's laws and teachings made from the original copy kept by the levitical priests. 19 He is

o to buy horses; *or* in exchange for horses.

to keep this book near him and read from it all his life, so that he will learn to honor the LORD and to obey faithfully everything that is commanded in it. 20This will keep him from thinking that he is better than other Israelites and from disobeying the LORD's commands in any way. Then he will reign for many years, and his descendants will rule Israel for many generations.

The Share of the Priests

18 "The priestly tribe of Levi is not to receive any share of land in Israel; instead, they are to live on the offerings and other sacrifices given to the LORD. 2They are to own no land, as the other tribes do; their share is the privilege of being the LORD's priests, as the LORD has promised.

3"Whenever cattle or sheep are sacrificed, the priests are to be given the shoulder, the jaw, and the stomach. 4They are to receive the first share of the grain, wine, olive oil, and wool. 5The LORD chose from all your tribes the tribe of Levi to serve him as priests forever.

6"Any Levite who wants to may come from any town in Israel to the one place of worship 7and may serve there as a priest of the LORD his God, like the other Levites who are serving there. 8He is to receive the same amount of food as the other priests, and he may keep whatever his family sends him.p

Warning against Pagan Practices

9"When you come into the land that the LORD your God is giving you, don't follow the disgusting practices of the nations that are there. 10Don't sacrifice your children in the fires on your altars; and don't let your people practice divination or look for omens or use spells 11or charms, and don't let them consult the spirits of the dead. 12The LORD your God hates people who do these disgusting things, and that is why he is driving those nations out of the land as you advance. 13Be completely faithful to the LORD."

The Promise to Send a Prophet

14Then Moses said, "In the land you are about to occupy, people follow the advice of those who practice divination and look for omens, but the LORD your God does not allow you to do this. 15Instead, he will send you a prophet like me from among your own people, and you are to obey him.q

16"On the day that you were gathered at Mount Sinai, you begged not to hear the LORD speak again or to see his fiery presence any more, because you were afraid you would die. 17So the LORD said to me, 'They have made a wise request. 18I will send them a prophet like you from among their own people; I will tell him what to say, and her will tell the people everything I command. 19He will speak in my name, and Is will punish anyone who refuses to obey him. 20But if any prophet dares to speak a message in my name when I did not command him to do so, he must die for it, and so must any prophet who speaks in the name of other gods.'

21"You may wonder how you can tell when a prophet's message does not come from the LORD. 22If a prophet speaks in the name of the LORD and what he says does not come true, then it is not the LORD's message. That prophet has spoken on his own authority, and you are not to fear him.

The Cities of Refuge
(Numbers 35.9-34; Joshua 20.1-9)

19 "After the LORD your God has destroyed the people whose land he is giving you and after you have taken their cities and houses and settled there, 2-3divide the territory into three parts, each with a city that can be easily reached. Then any of you that kill will be able to escape to one of them for protection. 4If you accidentally kill someone who is not your enemy, you may escape to any of these cities and be safe. 5For example, if two of you go into the forest together to cut wood and if, as one of you is chopping down a tree, the ax head comes off the handle and kills the other, you can run to one of those three cities and be safe. 6If there were only one city, the distance to it might be too great, and the relative who is responsible for taking revenge for the killing might catch you and angrily kill an innocent person. After all, it was by accident that you killed

---

p Probable text and he may keep ... sends him; Hebrew unclear.   q a prophet ... him; or prophets ... them.   r a prophet ... him ... he; or prophets ... them ... they.   s He will speak ... and I; or When a prophet speaks in my name, I.

someone who was not your enemy. 7 This is why I order you to set aside three cities.

8 "When the LORD your God enlarges your territory, as he told your ancestors he would, and gives you all the land he has promised, 9 then you are to select three more cities. (He will give you this land if you do everything that I command you today and if you love the LORD your God and live according to his teachings.) 10 Do this, so that innocent people will not die and so that you will not be guilty of putting them to death in the land that the LORD is giving you.

11 "But suppose you deliberately murder your enemy in cold blood and then escape to one of those cities for protection. 12 In that case, the leaders of your own town are to send for you and hand you over to the relative responsible for taking revenge for the murder, so that you may be put to death. 13 No mercy will be shown to you. Israel must rid itself of murderers, so that all will go well.

Ancient Property Lines

14 "Do not move your neighbor's property line, established long ago in the land that the LORD your God is giving you.

Concerning Witnesses

15 "One witness is not enough to convict someone of a crime; at least two witnesses are necessary to prove that someone is guilty. 16 If any of you try to harm another by false accusations, 17 both of you are to go to the one place of worship and be judged by the priests and judges who are then in office. 18 The judges will investigate the case thoroughly; and if you have made a false accusation, 19 you are to receive the punishment the accused would have received. In this way your nation will get rid of this evil. 20 Then everyone else will hear what happened; they will be afraid, and no one will ever again do such an evil thing. 21 In such cases show no mercy; the punishment is to be a life for a life, an eye for an eye, a tooth for a tooth, a hand for a hand, and a foot for a foot.

Concerning War

20 "When you go out to fight against your enemies and you see chariots and horses and an army that outnum-

bers yours, do not be afraid of them. The LORD your God, who rescued you from Egypt, will be with you. 2 Before you start fighting, a priest is to come forward and say to the army, 3 'Men of Israel, listen! Today you are going into battle. Do not be afraid of your enemies or lose courage or panic. 4 The LORD your God is going with you, and he will give you victory.'

5 "Then the officers will address the men and say, 'Is there any man here who has just built a house, but has not yet dedicated it? If so, he is to go home. Otherwise, if he is killed in battle, someone else will dedicate his house. 6 Is there any man here who has just planted a vineyard, but has not yet had the chance to harvest its grapes? If so, he is to go home. Otherwise, if he is killed in battle, someone else will enjoy the wine. 7 Is there anyone here who is engaged to be married? If so, he is to go home. Otherwise, if he is killed in battle, someone else will marry the woman he is engaged to.'

8 "The officers will also say to the men, 'Is there any man here who has lost his nerve and is afraid? If so, he is to go home. Otherwise, he will destroy the morale of the others.' 9 When the officers have finished speaking to the army, leaders are to be chosen for each unit.

10 "When you go to attack a city, first give its people a chance to surrender. 11 If they open the gates and surrender, they are all to become your slaves and do forced labor for you. 12 But if the people of that city will not surrender, but choose to fight, surround it with your army. 13 Then, when the LORD your God lets you capture the city, kill every man in it. 14 You may, however, take for yourselves the women, the children, the livestock, and everything else in the city. You may use everything that belongs to your enemies. The LORD has given it to you. 15 That is how you are to deal with those cities that are far away from the land you will settle in.

16 "But when you capture cities in the land that the LORD your God is giving you, kill everyone. 17 Completely destroy all the people: the Hittites, the Amorites, the Canaanites, the Perizzites, the Hivites, and the Jebusites, as the LORD ordered you to do. 18 Kill them, so that they will not make you sin against the LORD by teaching you to do all the disgusting

things that they do in the worship of their gods.

19 "When you are trying to capture a city, do not cut down its fruit trees, even though the siege lasts a long time. Eat the fruit, but do not destroy the trees; the trees are not your enemies. 20 You may cut down the other trees and use them in the siege mounds until the city is captured.

Concerning Unsolved Murders

21 "Suppose someone is found murdered in a field in the land that the LORD your God is going to give you, and you do not know who killed him. 2 Your leaders and judges are to go out and measure the distance from the place where the body was found to each of the nearby towns. 3 Then the leaders of the town nearest to where the body was found are to select a young cow that has never been used for work. 4 They are to take it down to a spot near a stream that never runs dry and where the ground has never been plowed or planted, and there they are to break its neck. 5 The levitical priests are to go there also, because they are to decide every legal case involving violence. The LORD your God has chosen them to serve him and to pronounce blessings in his name. 6 Then all the leaders from the town nearest the place where the murdered person was found are to wash their hands over the cow 7 and say, 'We did not murder this one, and we do not know who did it. 8 LORD, forgive your people Israel, whom you rescued from Egypt. Forgive us and do not hold us responsible for the murder of an innocent person.' 9 And so, by doing what the LORD requires, you will not be held responsible for the murder.

Concerning Women Prisoners of War

10 "When the LORD your God gives you victory in battle and you take prisoners, 11 you may see among them a beautiful woman that you like and want to marry. 12 Take her to your home, where she will shave her head,^{t} cut her fingernails, 13 and change her clothes. She is to stay in your home and mourn for her parents for a month; after that, you may marry her. 14 Later, if you no longer want her,

^{t} shave her head; or trim her hair.

you are to let her go free. Since you forced her to have intercourse with you, you cannot treat her as a slave and sell her.

Concerning the First Son's Inheritance

15 "Suppose a man has two wives and they both bear him sons, but the first son is not the child of his favorite wife. 16 When the man decides how he is going to divide his property among his children, he is not to show partiality to the son of his favorite wife by giving him the share that belongs to the first-born son. 17 He is to give a double share of his possessions to his first son, even though he is not the son of his favorite wife. A man must acknowledge his first son and give him the share he is legally entitled to.

Concerning a Disobedient Son

18 "Suppose someone has a son who is stubborn and rebellious, a son who will not obey his parents, even though they punish him. 19 His parents are to take him before the leaders of the town where he lives and make him stand trial. 20 They are to say to them, 'Our son is stubborn and rebellious and refuses to obey us; he wastes money and is a drunkard.' 21 Then the men of the city are to stone him to death, and so you will get rid of this evil. Everyone in Israel will hear what has happened and be afraid.

Various Laws

22 "If someone has been put to death for a crime and the body is hung on a post, 23 it is not to remain there overnight. It must be buried the same day, because a dead body hanging on a post brings God's curse on the land. Bury the body, so that you will not defile the land that the LORD your God is giving you.

22 "If you see an Israelite's cow or sheep running loose, do not ignore it; take it back. 2 But if its owner lives a long way off or if you don't know who owns it, then take it home with you. When its owner comes looking for it, give it to him. 3 Do the same thing if you find a donkey, a piece of clothing, or anything else that an Israelite may have lost. 4 "If an Israelite's donkey or cow has

fallen down, don't ignore it; help him get the animal to its feet again.

5 "Women are not to wear men's clothing, and men are not to wear women's clothing; the LORD your God hates people who do such things.

6 "If you happen to find a bird's nest in a tree or on the ground with the mother bird sitting either on the eggs or with her young, you are not to take the mother bird. 7 You may take the young birds, but you must let the mother bird go, so that you will live a long and prosperous life.

8 "When you build a new house, be sure to put a railing around the edge of the roof. Then you will not be responsible if someone falls off and is killed.

9 "Do not plant any crop in the same field with your grapevines; if you do, you are forbidden to use either the grapes or the produce of the other crop.

10 "Do not hitch an ox and a donkey together for plowing.

11 "Do not wear cloth made by weaving wool and linen together.

12 "Sew tassels on the four corners of your clothes.

Laws concerning Sexual Purity

13 "Suppose a man marries a young woman and later he decides he doesn't want her. 14 So he makes up false charges against her, accusing her of not being a virgin when they got married.

15 "If this happens, the young woman's parents are to take the blood-stained wedding sheet that proves she was a virgin, and they are to show it in court to the town leaders. 16 Her father will say to them, 'I gave my daughter to this man in marriage, and now he doesn't want her. 17 He has made false charges against her, saying that she was not a virgin when he married her. But here is the proof that my daughter was a virgin; look at the blood-stains on the wedding sheet!' 18 Then the town leaders are to take the husband and beat him. 19 They are also to fine him a hundred pieces of silver and give the money to the young woman's father, because the man has brought disgrace on an Israelite woman. Moreover, she will continue to be his wife, and he can never divorce her as long as he lives.

20 "But if the charge is true and there is no proof that she was a virgin, 21 then they are to take her out to the entrance of her father's house, where the men of her city are to stone her to death. She has done a shameful thing among our people by having intercourse before she was married, while she was still living in her father's house. In this way you will get rid of this evil.

22 "If a man is caught having intercourse with another man's wife, both of them are to be put to death. In this way you will get rid of this evil.

23 "Suppose a man is caught in a town having intercourse with a young woman who is engaged to someone else. 24 You are to take them outside the town and stone them to death. She is to die because she did not cry out for help, although she was in a town, where she could have been heard. And the man is to die because he had intercourse with someone who was engaged. In this way you will get rid of this evil.

25 "Suppose a man out in the countryside rapes a young woman who is engaged to someone else. Then only the man is to be put to death; 26 nothing is to be done to the woman, because she has not committed a sin worthy of death. This case is the same as when one man attacks another man and murders him. 27 The man raped the engaged woman in the countryside, and although she cried for help, there was no one to help her.

28 "Suppose a man is caught raping a young woman who is not engaged. 29 He is to pay her father the bride price of fifty pieces of silver, and she is to become his wife, because he forced her to have intercourse with him. He can never divorce her as long as he lives.

30 "No man is to disgrace his father by having intercourse with any of his father's wives.

Exclusion from the LORD's People

23 "No man who has been castrated or whose penis has been cut off may be included among the LORD's people.

2 "No one born out of wedlock or any descendant of such a person, even in the tenth generation, may be included among the LORD's people.

3 "No Ammonite or Moabite — or any of their descendants, even in the tenth generation — may be included among the LORD's people. 4 They refused to provide you with food and water when you were on your way out of Egypt, and they hired

Balaam son of Beor, from the city of Pethor in Mesopotamia, to curse you. 5 But the LORD your God would not listen to Balaam; instead he turned the curse into a blessing, because he loved you. 6 As long as you are a nation, never do anything to help these nations or to make them prosperous.

7 "Do not despise the Edomites; they are your relatives. And do not despise the Egyptians; you once lived in their land. 8 From the third generation onward their descendants may be included among the LORD's people.

Keeping the Military Camp Clean

9 "When you are in camp in time of war, you are to avoid anything that would make you ritually unclean. 10 If a man becomes unclean because he has had a wet dream during the night, he is to go outside the camp and stay there. 11 Toward evening he is to wash himself, and at sunset he may come back into camp.

12 "You are to have a place outside the camp where you can go when you need to relieve yourselves. 13 Carry a stick as part of your equipment, so that when you have a bowel movement you can dig a hole and cover it up. 14 Keep your camp ritually clean, because the LORD your God is with you in your camp to protect you and to give you victory over your enemies. Do not do anything indecent that would cause the LORD to turn his back on you.

Various Laws

15 "If slaves run away from their owners and come to you for protection, do not send them back. 16 They may live in any of your towns that they choose, and you are not to treat them harshly.

17 "No Israelite, man or woman, is to become a temple prostitute. 18 Also, no money earned in this way may be brought into the house of the LORD your God in fulfillment of a vow. The LORD hates temple prostitutes.

19 "When you lend money or food or anything else to Israelites, do not charge them interest. 20 You may charge interest on what you lend to foreigners, but not on what you lend to Israelites. Obey this rule, and the LORD your God will bless

everything you do in the land that you are going to occupy.

21 "When you make a vow to the LORD your God, do not put off doing what you promised; the LORD will hold you to your vow, and it is a sin not to keep it. 22 It is no sin not to make a vow to the LORD, 23 but if you make one voluntarily, be sure that you keep it.

24 "When you walk along a path in someone else's vineyard, you may eat all the grapes you want, but you must not carry any away in a container. 25 When you walk along a path in someone else's grainfield, you may eat all the grain you can pull off with your hands, but you must not cut any grain with a sickle.

Divorce and Remarriage

24 "Suppose a man marries a woman and later decides that he doesn't want her, because he finds something about her that he doesn't like.u So he writes out divorce papers, gives them to her, and sends her away from his home. 2 Then suppose she marries another man, 3 and he also decides that he doesn't want her, so he also writes out divorce papers, gives them to her, and sends her away from his home. Or suppose her second husband dies. 4 In either case, her first husband is not to marry her again; he is to consider her defiled. If he married her again, it would be offensive to the LORD. You are not to commit such a terrible sin in the land that the LORD your God is giving you.

Various Laws

5 "When a man is newly married, he is not to be drafted into military service or any other public duty; he is to be excused from duty for one year, so that he can stay at home and make his wife happy.v

6 "When you lend someone something, you are not to take as security his millstones used for grinding his grain. This would take away the family's means of preparing food to stay alive.

7 "If any of you kidnap Israelites and make them your slaves or sell them into slavery, you are to be put to death. In this way your nation will get rid of this evil.

8 "When you are suffering from a dreaded skin disease, be sure to do exactly what the levitical priests tell you;

u something . . . like; or that she is guilty of some shameful conduct.   v make his wife happy; or be happy with his wife.

follow the instructions that I have given them. 9 Remember what the LORD your God did to Miriam as you were coming from Egypt.

10 "When you lend someone something, do not go into his house to get the garment he is going to give you as security; 11 wait outside and let him bring it to you himself. 12 If he is poor, do not keep it overnight; 13 return it to him each evening, so that he can have it to sleep in. Then he will be grateful, and the LORD your God will be pleased with you.

14 "Do not cheat poor and needy hired servants, whether they are Israelites or foreigners living in one of your towns. 15 Each day before sunset pay them for that day's work; they need the money and have counted on getting it. If you do not pay them, they will cry out against you to the LORD, and you will be guilty of sin.

16 "Parents are not to be put to death for crimes committed by their children, and children are not to be put to death for crimes committed by their parents; people are to be put to death only for a crime they themselves have committed.

17 "Do not deprive foreigners and orphans of their rights; and do not take a widow's garment as security for a loan. 18 Remember that you were slaves in Egypt and that the LORD your God set you free; that is why I have given you this command.

19 "When you gather your crops and fail to bring in some of the grain that you have cut, do not go back for it; it is to be left for the foreigners, orphans, and widows, so that the LORD your God will bless you in everything you do. 20 When you have picked your olives once, do not go back and get those that are left; they are for the foreigners, orphans, and widows. 21 When you have gathered your grapes once, do not go back over the vines a second time; the grapes that are left are for the foreigners, orphans, and widows. 22 Never forget that you were slaves in Egypt; that is why I have given you this command.

25 "Suppose two Israelites go to court to settle a dispute, and one is declared innocent and the other guilty. 2 If the guilty one is sentenced to be beaten, the judge is to make him lie face downward and have him whipped. The number of lashes will depend on the crime he has committed. 3 He may be given as many as forty lashes, but no more; more than that would humiliate him publicly.

4 "Do not muzzle an ox when you are using it to thresh grain.

Duty to a Dead Brother

5 "If two brothers live on the same property and one of them dies, leaving no son, then his widow is not to be married to someone outside the family; it is the duty of the dead man's brother to marry her. 6 The first son that they have will be considered the son of the dead man, so that his family line will continue in Israel. 7 But if the dead man's brother does not want to marry her, she is to go before the town leaders and say, 'My husband's brother will not do his duty; he refuses to give his brother a descendant among the people of Israel.' 8 Then the town leaders are to summon him and speak to him. If he still refuses to marry her, 9 his brother's widow is to go up to him in the presence of the town leaders, take off one of his sandals, spit in his face, and say, 'This is what happens to the man who refuses to give his brother a descendant.' 10 His family will be known in Israel as 'the family of the man who had his sandal pulled off.'

Other Laws

11 "If two men are having a fight and the wife of one tries to help her husband by grabbing hold of the other man's genitals, 12 show her no mercy; cut off her hand.

13-14 "Do not cheat when you use weights and measures. 15 Use true and honest weights and measures, so that you may live a long time in the land that the LORD your God is giving you. 16 The LORD hates people who cheat.

The Command to Kill the Amalekites

17 "Remember what the Amalekites did to you as you were coming from Egypt. 18 They had no fear of God, and so they attacked you from the rear when you were tired and exhausted, and killed all who were straggling behind. 19 So then, when the LORD your God has given you the land and made you safe from all your enemies who live around you, be sure to kill all the Amalekites, so that no one will

DEUTERONOMY

remember them any longer. Do not forget!

Harvest Offerings

26 "After you have occupied the land that the LORD your God is giving you and have settled there, ²each of you must place in a basket the first part of each crop that you harvest and you must take it with you to the one place of worship. ³Go to the priest in charge at that time and say to him, 'I now acknowledge to the LORD my God that I have entered the land that he promised our ancestors to give us.'

⁴"The priest will take the basket from you and place it before the altar of the LORD your God. ⁵Then, in the LORD's presence you will recite these words: 'My ancestor was a wandering Aramean, who took his family to Egypt to live. They were few in number when they went there, but they became a large and powerful nation. ⁶The Egyptians treated us harshly and forced us to work as slaves. ⁷Then we cried out for help to the LORD, the God of our ancestors. He heard us and saw our suffering, hardship, and misery. ⁸By his great power and strength he rescued us from Egypt. He worked miracles and wonders, and caused terrifying things to happen. ⁹He brought us here and gave us this rich and fertile land. ¹⁰So now I bring to the LORD the first part of the harvest that he has given me.'

"Then set the basket down in the LORD's presence and worship there. ¹¹Be grateful for the good things that the LORD your God has given you and your family; and let the Levites and the foreigners who live among you join in the celebration.

¹²"Every third year give the tithe—a tenth of your crops—to the Levites, the foreigners, the orphans, and the widows, so that in every community they will have all they need to eat. When you have done this, ¹³say to the LORD, 'None of the sacred tithe is left in my house; I have given it to the Levites, the foreigners, the orphans, and the widows, as you commanded me to do. I have not disobeyed or forgotten any of your commands concerning the tithe. ¹⁴I have not eaten any of it when I was mourning; I have not

taken any of it out of my house when I was ritually unclean; and I have not given any of it as an offering for the dead.ʷ I have obeyed you, O LORD; I have done everything you commanded concerning the tithe. ¹⁵Look down from your holy place in heaven and bless your people Israel; bless also the rich and fertile land that you have given us, as you promised our ancestors.'

The LORD's Own People

¹⁶"Today the LORD your God commands you to obey all his laws; so obey them faithfully with all your heart. ¹⁷Today you have acknowledged the LORD as your God; you have promised to obey him, to keep all his laws, and to do all that he commands. ¹⁸Today the LORD has accepted you as his own people, as he promised you; and he commands you to obey all his laws. ¹⁹He will make you greater than any other nation that he has created, and you will bring praise and honor to his name.ˣ You will be his own people, as he promised."

God's Laws Written on Stones

27 Then Moses, together with the leaders of Israel, said to the people, "Obey all the instructions that I am giving you today. ²On the day you cross the Jordan River and enter the land that the LORD your God is giving you, you are to set up some large stones, cover them with plaster, ³and write on them all these laws and teachings. When you have entered the rich and fertile land that the LORD, the God of your ancestors, promised you, ⁴and you are on the other side of the Jordan, set up these stones on Mount Ebal, as I am instructing you today, and cover them with plaster. ⁵Build an altar there made of stones that have had no iron tools used on them, ⁶because any altar you build for the LORD your God must be made of uncut stones. There you are to offer the sacrifices that are to be burned, ⁷and there you are to sacrifice and eat your fellowship offerings and be grateful in the presence of the LORD your God. ⁸On the stones covered with plaster write clearly every word of God's laws."

⁹Then Moses, together with the levitical priests, said to all the people of Israel, "Give me your attention, people of Israel,

---

ʷ *for the dead; or to the dead.*   ˣ *bring praise . . . name; or receive praise and honor.*

and listen to me. Today you have become the people of the LORD your God; 10so obey him and keep all his laws that I am giving you today."

The Curses on Disobedience

11Then Moses said to the people of Israel, 12"After you have crossed the Jordan, the following tribes are to stand on Mount Gerizim when the blessings are pronounced on the people: Simeon, Levi, Judah, Issachar, Joseph, and Benjamin. 13And the following tribes will stand on Mount Ebal when the curses are pronounced: Reuben, Gad, Asher, Zebulun, Dan, and Naphtali. 14The Levites will speak these words in a loud voice:

15" 'God's curse on anyone who makes an idol of stone, wood, or metal and secretly worships it; the LORD hates idolatry.'

"And all the people will answer, 'Amen!'

16" 'God's curse on anyone who dishonors his father or mother.'

"And all the people will answer, 'Amen!'

17" 'God's curse on anyone who moves a neighbor's property line.'

"And all the people will answer, 'Amen!'

18" 'God's curse on anyone who leads a blind person in the wrong direction.'

"And all the people will answer, 'Amen!'

19" 'God's curse on anyone who deprives foreigners, orphans, and widows of their rights.'

"And all the people will answer, 'Amen!'

20" 'God's curse on anyone who disgraces his father by having intercourse with any of his father's wives.'

"And all the people will answer, 'Amen!'

21" 'God's curse on anyone who has sexual relations with an animal.'

"And all the people will answer, 'Amen!'

22" 'God's curse on anyone who has intercourse with his sister or half sister.'

"And all the people will answer, 'Amen!'

23" 'God's curse on anyone who has intercourse with his mother-in-law.'

"And all the people will answer, 'Amen!'

24" 'God's curse on anyone who secretly commits murder.'

"And all the people will answer, 'Amen!'

25" 'God's curse on anyone who accepts money to murder an innocent person.'

"And all the people will answer, 'Amen!'

26" 'God's curse on anyone who does not obey all of God's laws and teachings.'

"And all the people will answer, 'Amen!'

The Blessings of Obedience
(Leviticus 26.3-13; Deuteronomy 7.12-24)

28 "If you obey the LORD your God and faithfully keep all his commands that I am giving you today, he will make you greater than any other nation on earth. 2Obey the LORD your God and all these blessings will be yours:

3"The LORD will bless your towns and your fields.

4"The LORD will bless you with many children, with abundant crops, and with many cattle and sheep.

5"The LORD will bless your grain crops and the food you prepare from them.

6"The LORD will bless everything you do.

7"The LORD will defeat your enemies when they attack you. They will attack from one direction, but they will run from you in all directions.

8"The LORD your God will bless your work and fill your barns with grain. He will bless you in the land that he is giving you.

9"If you obey the LORD your God and do everything he commands, he will make you his own people, as he has promised. 10Then all the peoples on earth will see that the LORD has chosen you to be his own people, and they will be afraid of you. 11The LORD will give you many children, many cattle, and abundant crops in the land that he promised your ancestors to give you. 12He will send rain in season from his rich storehouse in the sky and bless all your work, so that you will lend to many nations, but you will not have to borrow from any. 13The LORD your God will make you the leader among the nations and not a follower; you will always prosper and never fail if you obey faithfully all his commands that I am giving you today. 14But you must never disobey them in any way, or worship and serve other gods.

The Consequences of Disobedience
(Leviticus 26.14-46)

15 "But if you disobey the LORD your God and do not faithfully keep all his commands and laws that I am giving you today, all these evil things will happen to you: 16 "The LORD will curse your towns and your fields.

17 "The LORD will curse your grain crops and the food you prepare from them.

18 "The LORD will curse you by giving you only a few children, poor crops, and few cattle and sheep.

19 "The LORD will curse everything you do.

20 "If you do evil and reject the LORD, he will bring on you disaster, confusion, and trouble in everything you do, until you are quickly and completely destroyed. 21 He will send disease after disease on you until there is not one of you left in the land that you are about to occupy. 22 The LORD will strike you with infectious diseases, with swelling and fever; he will send drought and scorching winds to destroy your crops. These disasters will be with you until you die. 23 No rain will fall, and your ground will become as hard as iron. 24 Instead of rain, the LORD will send down duststorms and sandstorms until you are destroyed.

25 "The LORD will give your enemies victory over you. You will attack them from one direction, but you will run from them in all directions, and all the people on earth will be terrified when they see what happens to you. 26 When you die, birds and wild animals will come and eat your bodies, and there will be no one to scare them off. 27 The LORD will send boils on you, as he did on the Egyptians. He will make your bodies break out with sores. You will be covered with scabs, and you will itch, but there will be no cure. 28 The LORD will make you lose your mind; he will strike you with blindness and confusion. 29 You will grope about in broad daylight like someone blind, and you will not be able to find your way. You will not prosper in anything you do. You will be constantly oppressed and robbed, and there will be no one to help you.

30 "You will be engaged to a young woman — but someone else will marry her. You will build a house — but never live in it. You will plant a vineyard — but never eat its grapes. 31 Your cattle will be butchered before your very eyes, but you will not eat any of the meat. Your donkeys will be dragged away while you look on, and they will not be given back to you. Your sheep will be given to your enemies, and there will be no one to help you. 32 Your sons and daughters will be given as slaves to foreigners while you look on. Every day you will strain your eyes, looking in vain for your children to return. 33 A foreign nation will take all the crops that you have worked so hard to grow, while you receive nothing but constant oppression and harsh treatment. 34 Your sufferings will make you lose your mind. 35 The LORD will cover your legs with incurable, painful sores; boils will cover you from head to foot.

36 "The LORD will take you and your king away to a foreign land, where neither you nor your ancestors ever lived before; there you will serve gods made of wood and stone. 37 In the countries to which the LORD will scatter you, the people will be shocked at what has happened to you; they will make fun of you and ridicule you.

38 "You will plant plenty of seed, but reap only a small harvest, because the locusts will eat your crops. 39 You will plant vineyards and take care of them, but you will not gather their grapes or drink wine from them, because worms will eat the vines. 40 Olive trees will grow everywhere in your land, but you will not have any olive oil, because the olives will drop off. 41 You will have sons and daughters, but you will lose them, because they will be taken away as prisoners of war. 42 All your trees and crops will be devoured by insects.

43 "Foreigners who live in your land will gain more and more power, while you gradually lose yours. 44 They will have money to lend you, but you will have none to lend them. In the end they will be your rulers.

45 "All these disasters will come on you, and they will be with you until you are destroyed, because you did not obey the LORD your God and keep all the laws that he gave you. 46 They will be the evidence of God's judgment on you and your

descendants forever. 47 The LORD blessed you in every way, but you would not serve him with glad and joyful hearts. 48 So then, you will serve the enemies that the LORD is going to send against you. You will be hungry, thirsty, and naked — in need of everything. The LORDy will oppress you harshly until you are destroyed. 49 The LORD will bring against you a nation from the ends of the earth, a nation whose language you do not know. They will swoop down on you like an eagle. 50 They will be ruthless and show no mercy to anyone, young or old. 51 They will eat your livestock and your crops, and you will starve to death. They will not leave you any grain, wine, olive oil, cattle, or sheep; and you will die. 52 They will attack every town in the land that the LORD your God is giving you, and the high, fortified walls in which you trust will fall.

53 "When your enemies are besieging your towns, you will become so desperate for food that you will even eat the children that the LORD your God has given you. 54-55 Even the most refined man of noble birth will become so desperate during the siege that he will eat some of his own children because he has no other food. He will not even give any to his brother or to the wife he loves or to any of his children who are left. 56-57 Even the most refined woman of noble birth, so rich that she has never had to walk anywhere, will behave in the same way. When the enemy besieges her town, she will become so desperate for food that she will secretly eat her newborn child and the afterbirth as well. She will not share them with the husband she loves or with any of her children.

58 "If you do not obey faithfully all of God's teachings that are written in this book and if you do not honor the wonderful and awesome name of the LORD your God, 59 he will send on you and on your descendants incurable diseases and horrible epidemics that can never be stopped. 60 He will bring on you once again all the dreadful diseases you experienced in Egypt, and you will never recover. 61 He will also send all kinds of diseases and epidemics that are not mentioned in this book of God's laws and teachings, and you will be destroyed.

62 Although you become as numerous as the stars in the sky, only a few of you will survive, because you did not obey the LORD your God. 63 Just as the LORD took delight in making you prosper and in making you increase in number, so he will take delight in destroying you and in bringing ruin on you. You will be uprooted from the land that you are about to occupy.

64 "The LORD will scatter you among all the nations, from one end of the earth to the other, and there you will serve gods made of wood and stone, gods that neither you nor your ancestors have ever worshiped before. 65 You will find no peace anywhere, no place to call your own; the LORD will overwhelm you with anxiety, hopelessness, and despair. 66 Your life will always be in danger. Day and night you will be filled with terror, and you will live in constant fear of death. 67 Your hearts will pound with fear at everything you see. Every morning you will wish for evening; every evening you will wish for morning. 68 The LORD will send you back to Egypt in ships, even though hez said that you would never have to go there again. There you will try to sell yourselves to your enemies as slaves, but no one will want to buy you."

The LORD's Covenant with Israel in the Land of Moab

29 These are the terms of the covenant that the LORD commanded Moses to make with the people of Israel in the land of Moab; all this was in addition to the covenant which the LORD had made with them at Mount Sinai.

2 Moses called together all the people of Israel and said to them, "You saw for yourselves what the LORD did to the king of Egypt, to his officials, and to his entire country. 3 You saw the terrible plagues, the miracles, and the great wonders that the LORD performed. 4 But to this very day he has not let you understand what you have experienced. 5 For forty years the LORD led you through the desert, and your clothes and sandals never wore out. 6 You did not have bread to eat or wine or beer to drink, but the LORD provided for your needs in order to teach you that he is your God. 7 And when we came to this

y The LORD; or Your enemies.   z he; or I.

SODOM AND GOMORRAH

Located near the Dead Sea, Sodom and Gomorrah were two cities destroyed by God because of their wickedness and depravity. These cities, along with Admah, Zeboiim, and Zoar, were known as the "cities of the valley" (Gn 13.12; 19.25) in the rich, fertile flatlands south of the Dead Sea.

When Abraham gave his nephew Lot first choice of land in this area of Palestine, Lot chose the fertile, well-watered Jordan River Valley rather than the rocky hill country. Failing to consider the moral character of the inhabitants, Lot "camped near Sodom" (Gn 13.12).

Two angels were sent to warn Lot that God intended to destroy Sodom. A group of depraved citizens of Sodom wanted to abuse the two visitors sexually. The angels struck the Sodomites blind to save Lot (Gn 19.1–11), and Lot and his family fled the doomed city. Burning sulfur fell from heaven and consumed Sodom and Gomorrah, as well as Admah and Zeboiim (Dt 29.23). Only Zoar escaped destruction (Gn 19.30).

When Lot's wife looked back at the burning city of Sodom in disobedience of God's instructions, she was changed into a pillar of salt (Gn 19.26). A formation of salt, traditionally referred to as Lot's wife, may be seen today on the shores of the Dead Sea.

The destroyed cities of the plain were never rebuilt. Even Zoar eventually disappeared. Formations of salt, sulfur, and asphalt in the vicinity lead many scholars to believe that the cities of the plain are buried beneath the shallow waters of the southern end of the Dead Sea.

Before its destruction, this area was rich and productive. Today it is barren, with no plant life of any kind. Many of the Old Testament prophets, including Amos, reminded the Israelites of the destruction of Sodom and Gomorrah to call the people back to worship of the one true God (Am 4.11). In the New Testament, Paul quoted the prophet Isaiah's reference to the wickedness of the cities (Ro 9.29).

place, King Sihon of Heshbon and King Og of Bashan came out to fight against us. But we defeated them, [8] took their land, and divided it among the tribes of Reuben and Gad, and half the tribe of Manasseh. [9] Obey faithfully all the terms of this covenant, so that you will be successful in everything you do.

[10] "Today you are standing in the presence of the LORD your God, all of you— your leaders and officials, your men, [11] women, and children, and the foreigners who live among you and cut wood and carry water for you. [12] You are here today to enter into this covenant that the LORD your God is making with you and to accept its obligations, [13] so that the LORD may now confirm you as his people and be your God, as he promised you and your ancestors, Abraham, Isaac, and Jacob. [14] You are not the only ones with whom the LORD is making this covenant with its obligations. [15] He is making it with all of us who stand here in his presence today and also with our descendants who are not yet born.

[16] "You remember what life was like in Egypt and what it was like to travel through the territory of other nations. [17] You saw their disgusting idols made of wood, stone, silver, and gold. [18] Make sure that no man, woman, family, or tribe standing here today turns from the LORD our God to worship the gods of other nations. This would be like a root that grows to be a bitter and poisonous plant. [19] Make sure that there is no one here today who hears these solemn demands and yet convinces himself that all will be well with him, even if he stubbornly goes his own way. That would destroy all of you, good and evil alike. [20] The LORD will not forgive such a man. Instead, the LORD's burning anger will flame up against him, and all the disasters written in this book will fall on him until the LORD has destroyed him completely. [21] The LORD will make an example of him before all the tribes of Israel and will bring disaster on him in accordance with all the curses listed in the covenant that is written in this book of the LORD's teachings.

[22] "In future generations your descendants and foreigners from distant lands will see the disasters and sufferings that the LORD has brought on your land. [23] The fields will be a barren waste, covered with sulfur and salt; nothing will be planted, and not even weeds will grow there. Your land will be like the cities of Sodom and Gomorrah, of Admah and Zeboiim, which the LORD destroyed when he was furiously angry. [24] Then the whole world will ask, 'Why did the LORD do this to their land? What was the reason for his fierce anger?' [25] And the answer will be, 'It is because the LORD's people broke the covenant they had made with him, the God of their ancestors, when he brought them out of Egypt. [26] They served other gods that they had never worshiped before, gods that the LORD had forbidden them to worship. [27] And so the LORD became angry with his people and brought on their land all the disasters written in this book. [28] The LORD became furiously angry, and in his great anger he uprooted them from their land and threw them into a foreign land, and there they are today.'

[29] "There are some things that the LORD our God has kept secret; but he has revealed his Law, and we and our descendants are to obey it forever.

Conditions for Restoration and Blessing

30 "I have now given you a choice between a blessing and a curse. When all these things have happened to you, and you are living among the nations where the LORD your God has scattered you, you will remember the choice I gave you. [2] If you and your descendants will turn back to the LORD and with all your heart obey his commands that I am giving you today, [3] then the LORD your God will have mercy on you. He will bring you back from the nations where he has scattered you, and he will make you prosperous again. [4] Even if you are scattered to the farthest corners of the earth, the LORD your God will gather you together and bring you back, [5] so that you may again take possession of the land where your ancestors once lived. And he will make you more prosperous and more numerous than your ancestors ever were. [6] The LORD your God will give you and your descendants obedient hearts, so that you will love him with all your heart, and you will continue to live in that land. [7] He will turn all these curses against your enemies, who hated you

D
E
U
T
E
R
O
N
O
M
Y

and oppressed you, 8 and you will again obey him and keep all his commands that I am giving you today. 9 The LORD will make you prosperous in all that you do; you will have many children and a lot of livestock, and your fields will produce abundant crops. He will be as glad to make you prosperous as he was to make your ancestors prosperous, 10 but you will have to obey him and keep all his laws that are written in this book of his teachings. You will have to turn to him with all your heart.

11 "The command that I am giving you today is not too difficult or beyond your reach. 12 It is not up in the sky. You do not have to ask, 'Who will go up and bring it down for us, so that we can hear it and obey it?' 13 Nor is it on the other side of the ocean. You do not have to ask, 'Who will go across the ocean and bring it to us, so that we may hear it and obey it?' 14 No, it is here with you. You know it and can quote it, so now obey it.

15 "Today I am giving you a choice between good and evil, between life and death. 16 If you obey the commands of the LORD your God,a which I give you today, if you love him, obey him, and keep all his laws, then you will prosper and become a nation of many people. The LORD your God will bless you in the land that you are about to occupy. 17 But if you disobey and refuse to listen, and are led away to worship other gods, 18 you will be destroyed—I warn you here and now. You will not live long in that land across the Jordan that you are about to occupy. 19 I am now giving you the choice between life and death, between God's blessing and God's curse, and I call heaven and earth to witness the choice you make. Choose life. 20 Love the LORD your God, obey him and be faithful to him, and then you and your descendants will live long in the land that he promised to give your ancestors, Abraham, Isaac, and Jacob."

Joshua Becomes Moses' Successor

31 Moses continued speaking to the people of Israel, 2 and said, "I am now a hundred and twenty years old and am no longer able to be your leader. And besides this, the LORD has told me that I will not cross the Jordan. 3 The LORD your God himself will go before you and destroy the nations living there, so that you can occupy their land; and Joshua will be your leader, as the LORD has said. 4 The LORD will destroy those people, just as he defeated Sihon and Og, kings of the Amorites, and destroyed their country. 5 The LORD will give you victory over them, and you are to treat them exactly as I have told you. 6 Be determined and confident. Do not be afraid of them. Your God, the LORD himself, will be with you. He will not fail you or abandon you."

7 Then Moses called Joshua and said to him in the presence of all the people of Israel, "Be determined and confident; you are the one who will lead these people to occupy the land that the LORD promised to their ancestors. 8 The LORD himself will lead you and be with you. He will not fail you or abandon you, so do not lose courage or be afraid."

The Law Is to Be Read Every Seven Years

9 So Moses wrote down God's Law and gave it to the levitical priests, who were in charge of the LORD's Covenant Box, and to the leaders of Israel. 10 He commanded them, "At the end of every seven years, when the year that debts are canceled comes around, read this aloud at the Festival of Shelters. 11 Read it to the people of Israel when they come to worship the LORD your God at the one place of worship. 12 Call together all the men, women, and children, and the foreigners who live in your towns, so that everyone may hear it and learn to honor the LORD your God and to obey his teachings faithfully. 13 In this way your descendants who have never heard the Law of the LORD your God will hear it. And so they will learn to obey him as long as they live in the land that you are about to occupy across the Jordan."

The LORD's Last Instructions to Moses

14 Then the LORD said to Moses, "You do not have much longer to live. Call Joshua and bring him to the Tent, so that I may give him his instructions." Moses and Joshua went to the Tent, 15 and the LORD

a One ancient translation If you obey the commands of the LORD your God; Hebrew does not have these words.

appeared to them there in a pillar of cloud that stood by the door of the Tent.

16 The Lord said to Moses, "You will soon die, and after your death the people will become unfaithful to me and break the covenant that I made with them. They will abandon me and worship the pagan gods of the land they are about to enter. 17 When that happens, I will become angry with them; I will abandon them, and they will be destroyed. Many terrible disasters will come upon them, and then they will realize that these things are happening to them because I, their God, am no longer with them. 18 And I will refuse to help them then, because they have done evil and worshiped other gods.

19 "Now, write down this song. Teach it to the people of Israel, so that it will stand as evidence against them. 20 I will take them into this rich and fertile land, as I promised their ancestors. There they will have all the food they want, and they will live comfortably. But they will turn away and worship other gods. They will reject me and break my covenant, 21 and many terrible disasters will come on them. But this song will still be sung, and it will stand as evidence against them. Even now, before I take them into the land that I promised to give them, I know what they are thinking."

22 That same day Moses wrote down the song and taught it to the people of Israel.

23 Then the Lord spoke to Joshua son of Nun and told him, "Be confident and determined. You will lead the people of Israel into the land that I promised them, and I will be with you."

24 Moses wrote God's Law in a book, taking care not to leave out anything. 25 When he finished, he said to the levitical priests, who were in charge of the Lord's Covenant Box, 26 "Take this book of God's Law and place it beside the Covenant Box of the Lord your God, so that it will remain there as a witness against his people. 27 I know how stubborn and rebellious they are. They have rebelled against the Lord during my lifetime, and they will rebel even more after I am dead. 28 Assemble all your tribal leaders and officials before me, so that I can tell them these things; I will call heaven and earth

to be my witnesses against them. 29 I know that after my death the people will become wicked and reject what I have taught them. And in time to come they will meet with disaster, because they will have made the Lord angry by doing what he has forbidden."

The Song of Moses

30 Then Moses recited the entire song while all the people of Israel listened.

32 "Earth and sky, hear my words,
　　listen closely to what I say.
2 My teaching will fall like drops of rain
　　and form on the earth like dew.
My words will fall like showers on young plants,
　　like gentle rain on tender grass.
3 I will praise the name of the Lord,
　　and his people will tell of his greatness.

4 "The Lord is your mighty defender,
　　perfect and just in all his ways;
Your God is faithful and true;
　　he does what is right and fair.
5 But you are unfaithful, unworthy to be his people,[b]
　　a sinful and deceitful nation.
6 Is this the way you should treat the Lord,
　　you foolish, senseless people?
He is your father, your Creator,
　　he made you into a nation.

7 "Think of the past, of the time long ago;
　　ask your parents to tell you what happened,
　　ask the old people to tell of the past.
8 The Most High assigned nations their lands;
　　he determined where peoples should live.
He assigned to each nation a heavenly being,
9 　　but Jacob's descendants he chose for himself.

10 "He found them wandering through the desert,

---

b Probable text But you ... people; Hebrew unclear.

a desolate, wind-swept
  wilderness.
He protected them and cared for
  them,
  as he would protect himself.
11 Like an eagle teaching its young
    to fly,c
  catching them safely on its
    spreading wings,
  the LORD kept Israel from falling.
12 The LORD alone led his people
  without the help of a
    foreign god.

13 "He let them rule the highlands,
  and they ate what grew in the
    fields.
They found wild honey among the
    rocks;
  their olive trees flourished in
    stony ground.
14 Their cows and goats gave plenty
    of milk;
  they had the best sheep, goats,
    and cattle,
  the finest wheat, and the
    choicest wine.

15 "The LORD's people grew rich, but
    rebellious;
  they were fat and stuffed with
    food.
They abandoned God their Creator
  and rejected their mighty savior.
16 Their idolatry made the LORD
    jealous;
  the evil they did made him
    angry.
17 They sacrificed to gods that are
    not real,
  new gods their ancestors had
    never known,
  gods that Israel had never
    obeyed.
18 They forgot their God, their
    mighty savior,
  the one who had given them life.

19 "When the LORD saw this, he was
    angry
  and rejected his sons and
    daughters.
20 'I will no longer help them,' he
    said;

'then I will see what happens to
    them,
  those stubborn, unfaithful
    people.
21 With their idols they have made
    me angry,
  jealous with their so-called gods,
  gods that are really not gods.
So I will use a so-called nation to
  make them angry;
  I will make them jealous with a
    nation of fools.
22 My anger will flame up like fire
  and burn everything on earth.
It will reach to the world belowd
  and consume the roots of the
    mountains.

23 " 'I will bring on them endless
    disasters
  and use all my arrows against
    them.
24 They will die from hunger and
    fever;
  they will die from terrible
    diseases.
I will send wild animals to attack
    them,
  and poisonous snakes to bite
    them.
25 War will bring death in the streets;
  terrors will strike in the homes.
Young men and young women
    will die;
  neither babies nor old people
    will be spared.
26 I would have destroyed them
    completely,
  so that no one would remember
    them.
27 But I could not let their enemies
    boast
  that they had defeated my
    people,
  when it was I myself who had
    crushed them.'

28 "Israel is a nation without sense;
  they have no wisdom at all.
29 They fail to see why they were
    defeated;
  they cannot understand what
    happened.
30 Why were a thousand defeated
    by one,

---

c teaching its young to fly; or watching over its young.   d THE WORLD BELOW: This refers to the
world of the dead.

and ten thousand by only two?
The LORD, their God, had
    abandoned them;
    their mighty God had given
    them up.
31 Their enemies know that their
    own gods are weak,
    not mighty like Israel's God.
32 Their enemies, corrupt as Sodom
    and Gomorrah,
    are like vines that bear bitter
    and poisonous grapes,
33 like wine made from the venom
    of snakes.

34 "The LORD remembers what their
    enemies have done;
    he waits for the right time to
    punish them.
35 The LORD will take revenge and
    punish them;
    the time will come when they
    will fall;
    the day of their doom is near.
36 The LORD will rescue his people
    when he sees that their strength
    is gone.
He will have mercy on those who
    serve him,
    when he sees how helpless
    they are.
37 Then the LORD will ask his people,
    'Where are those mighty gods
    you trusted?
38 You fed them the fat of your
    sacrifices
    and offered them wine to drink.
Let them come and help you now;
    let them run to your rescue.

39 " 'I, and I alone, am God;
    no other god is real.
I kill and I give life, I wound and
    I heal,
    and no one can oppose what
    I do.
40 As surely as I am the living God,
    I raise my hand and I vow
41 that I will sharpen my flashing
    sword
    and see that justice is done.
I will take revenge on my enemies
    and punish those who hate me.
42 My arrows will drip with their
    blood,
    and my sword will kill all who
    oppose me.

I will spare no one who fights
    against me;
    even the wounded and prisoners
    will die.'

43 "Nations, you must praise the
    LORD's people —
    he punishes all who kill them.
He takes revenge on his enemies
    and forgives the sins of his
    people."

44 Moses and Joshua son of Nun recited
this song, so that the people of Israel
could hear it.

Moses' Final Instructions

45 When Moses had finished giving
God's teachings to the people, 46 he said,
"Be sure to obey all these commands that
I have given you today. Repeat them to
your children, so that they may faithfully
obey all of God's teachings. 47 These
teachings are not empty words; they are
your very life. Obey them and you will
live long in that land across the Jordan
that you are about to occupy."

48 That same day the LORD said to
Moses, 49 "Go to the Abarim Mountains
in the land of Moab opposite the city of
Jericho; climb Mount Nebo and look at
the land of Canaan that I am about to
give the people of Israel. 50 You will die
on that mountain as your brother Aaron
died on Mount Hor, 51 because both of
you were unfaithful to me in the presence
of the people of Israel. When you were at
the waters of Meribah, near the town of
Kadesh in the wilderness of Zin, you dishonored me in the presence of the people. 52 You will look at the land from a
distance, but you will not enter the land
that I am giving the people of Israel."

Moses Blesses the Tribes of Israel

33 These are the blessings that
Moses, the man of God, pronounced on the people of Israel before he
died.

2 The LORD came from Mount Sinai;
    he rose like the sun over Edom
    and shone on his people from
        Mount Paran.
Ten thousand angels were
    with him,

a flaming fire at his right
hand.*e*

³ The LORD loves his people *f*
and protects those who belong
to him.
So we bow at*g* his feet
and obey his commands.
⁴ We obey the Law that Moses
gave us,
our nation's most treasured
possession.
⁵ The LORD became king of his
people Israel
when their tribes and leaders
were gathered together.

⁶ Moses said about the tribe of Reuben:
"May Reuben never die out,
Although their people are few."

⁷ About the tribe of Judah he said:
"LORD, listen to their cry for help;
Unite them again with the other
tribes.
Fight for them, LORD,
And help them against their
enemies."*h*

⁸ About the tribe of Levi he said:
"You, LORD, reveal your will by the
Urim and Thummim*i*
Through your faithful servants, the
Levites;
You put them to the test at
Massah
And proved them true at the
waters of Meribah.
⁹ They showed greater loyalty
to you
Than to parents, brothers, or
children.
They obeyed your commands
And were faithful to your
covenant.
¹⁰ They will teach your people to
obey your Law;
They will offer sacrifices on your
altar.
¹¹ LORD, help their tribe to grow
strong;
Be pleased with what they do.
Crush all their enemies;

Let them never rise again."

¹² About the tribe of Benjamin he said:
"This is the tribe the LORD loves
and protects;
He guards them all the day long,
And he dwells in their midst."*i*

¹³ About the tribe of Joseph he said:
"May the LORD bless their land
with rain
And with water from under the
earth.
¹⁴ May their land be blessed with
sun-ripened fruit,
Rich with the best fruits of each
season.
¹⁵ May their ancient hills be covered
with choice fruit.
¹⁶ May their land be filled with all
that is good,
Blessed by the goodness of the
LORD,
Who spoke from the burning bush.
May these blessings come to the
tribe of Joseph,
Because he was the leader among
his brothers.
¹⁷ Joseph has the strength of a bull,
The horns of a wild ox.
His horns are Manasseh's
thousands
And Ephraim's ten thousands.
With them he gores the nations
And pushes them to the ends of
the earth."

¹⁸ About the tribes of Zebulun and Issachar he said:
"May Zebulun be prosperous in
their trade on the sea,
And may Issachar's wealth
increase at home.
¹⁹ They invite foreigners to their
mountain
And offer the right sacrifices
there.
They get their wealth from the sea
And from the sand along the
shore."

²⁰ About the tribe of Gad he said:

---

e Probable text Ten thousand . . . right hand; *Hebrew unclear.* *f One ancient translation* his
people; *Hebrew* the peoples. *g Probable text* bow at; *Hebrew unclear.* *h Probable text*
Fight for . . . enemies; *Hebrew* The tribe of Judah will fight for itself, and the LORD will help it
against its enemies. *i* URIM AND THUMMIM: *Two objects used by the priest to determine God's
will; it is not known precisely how they were used.* *j* And he . . . midst; *or* They live under his
protection.

"Praise God, who made their
    territory large.
Gad waits like a lion
To tear off an arm or a scalp.
21 They took the best of the land for
    themselves;
A leader's share was assigned to
    them.
They obeyed the LORD's commands
    and laws
When the leaders of Israel were
    gathered together."*k*

22 About the tribe of Dan he said:
"Dan is a young lion;
He leaps out from Bashan."

23 About the tribe of Naphtali he said:
"Naphtali is richly blessed by the
    LORD's good favor;
Their land reaches to the south
    from Lake Galilee."

24 About the tribe of Asher he said:
"Asher is blessed more than the
    other tribes.
May he be the favorite of his
    brothers,
And may his land be rich with
    olive trees.
25 May his towns be protected with
    iron gates,
And may he always live secure."

26 People of Israel, no god is like
    your God,
    riding in splendor across
        the sky,
    riding through the clouds to
        come to your aid.
27 God has always been your
    defense;
    his eternal arms are your
        support.
He drove out your enemies as you
    advanced,
    and told you to destroy them all.
28 So Jacob's descendants live in
    peace,
    secure in a land full of grain and
        wine,
    where dew from the sky waters
        the ground.
29 Israel, how happy you are!
There is no one like you,

a nation saved by the LORD.
The LORD himself is your shield
    and your sword,
    to defend you and give you
        victory.
Your enemies will come begging
    for mercy,
    and you will trample them
        down.

The Death of Moses

34 Moses went up from the plains of
Moab to Mount Nebo, to the top
of Mount Pisgah east of Jericho, and
there the LORD showed him the whole
land: the territory of Gilead as far north
as the town of Dan; 2 the entire territory
of Naphtali; the territories of Ephraim
and Manasseh; the territory of Judah as
far west as the Mediterranean Sea; 3 the
southern part of Judah; and the plain
that reaches from Zoar to Jericho, the
city of palm trees. 4 Then the LORD said to
Moses, "This is the land that I promised
Abraham, Isaac, and Jacob I would give
to their descendants. I have let you see it,
but I will not let you go there."

5 So Moses, the LORD's servant, died
there in the land of Moab, as the LORD
had said he would. 6 The LORD buried him
in a valley in Moab, opposite the town of
Bethpeor, but to this day no one knows
the exact place of his burial. 7 Moses was
a hundred and twenty years old when he
died; he was as strong as ever, and his
eyesight was still good. 8 The people of
Israel mourned for him for thirty days in
the plains of Moab.

9 Joshua son of Nun was filled with
wisdom, because Moses had appointed
him to be his successor. The people of
Israel obeyed Joshua and kept the commands that the LORD had given them
through Moses.

10 There has never been a prophet in
Israel like Moses; the LORD spoke with
him face-to-face. 11 No other prophet has
ever done miracles and wonders like
those that the LORD sent Moses to perform against the king of Egypt, his officials, and the entire country. 12 No other
prophet has been able to do the great and
terrifying things that Moses did in the
sight of all Israel.

k One ancient translation When the leaders . . . together; *Hebrew unclear.*

THE HISTORICAL BOOKS

The historical books include Joshua, Judges, Ruth, 1 and 2 Samuel, 1 and 2 Kings, 1 and 2 Chronicles, Ezra, Nehemiah, and Esther. In the Jewish canon, the books are split into two categories. (1) Joshua, Judges, 1 and 2 Samuel, and 1 and 2 Kings are called The Former Prophets. (2) All the rest are included in The Writings, the third major collection of the Hebrew Scripture.

The historical books do more than just present data about past events. They present the data in a form that tries to explain what the events mean and how God was working in them.

These books record the history of the period from the death of Moses to the time of the rebuilding of Jerusalem after the Exile of the Israelites.

Joshua marks the end of the Exodus period. Israel enters the land under a new generation of leaders, conquers the hill country, and enters into a great ceremony of covenant renewal at Shechem.

Judges is a collection of accounts of tribal heroes and heroines from the period between the time of Joshua and the time of Samuel. These are accounts of charismatic leaders who, in times of crisis, were called by God to save a part of the tribes from the oppression of an enemy. They teach an understanding of history in a pattern of faithfulness, unfaithfulness, judgment, and salvation in the political world.

Ruth emphasizes God working through a foreign woman to bring forth King David. It carries a strong warning against excluding anyone from a place among God's people.

1 and 2 Samuel record the end of the period of the judges and the rise of the kingship in Israel, with all the accompanying tensions between old ways and new ways. The narratives include the lives and rules of Samuel, Saul, and David.

1 and 2 Kings are the history of the monarchy from Solomon to the Exile. Solomon's glory, the building of the Temple, the division of the Kingdom, the destruction of the two kingdoms, and the rise of prophecy (Elijah and Elisha) are important themes in these books. Faithfulness to God is defined in social and political terms as well as religious terms.

1 and 2 Chronicles were written after the destruction of Jerusalem and try to answer the question "Why did God choose to punish his people in such a way?" The answer is found in history. God's people were unfaithful and what happened in social and political history is an expression of God's judgment on an unfaithful people.

Ezra picks up the themes of Chronicles and argues for national purity and exclusiveness.

Nehemiah is the account of the rebuilding of the walls of Jerusalem and the re-establishment of the covenant. It, too, argues for exclusiveness.

Esther is a delightful account of a Jewish heroine whose faithfulness saved her people from certain death.

The Book of
JOSHUA

Introduction

The Book of Joshua is the story of the Israelite invasion of Canaan under the leadership of Joshua, the successor of Moses. Notable events recorded in this book include the crossing of the Jordan, the fall of Jericho, the battle at Ai, and the renewal of the covenant between God and his people. One of the best-known passages in the book is, "Decide today whom you will serve . . . . As for my family and me, we will serve the LORD" (24.15).

Outline of Contents

God Commands Joshua to Conquer Canaan

1 After the death of the LORD's servant Moses, the LORD spoke to Moses' helper, Joshua son of Nun. 2 He said, "My servant Moses is dead. Get ready now, you and all the people of Israel, and cross the Jordan River into the land that I am giving them. 3 As I told Moses, I have given you and all my people the entire land that you will be marching over. 4 Your borders will reach from the desert in the south to the Lebanon Mountains in the north; from the great Euphrates River in the east, through the Hittite country, to the Mediterranean Sea in the west. 5 Joshua, no one will be able to defeat you as long as you live. I will be with you as I was with Moses. I will always be with you; I will never abandon you. 6 Be determined and confident, for you will be the leader of these people as they occupy this land which I promised their ancestors. 7 Just be determined, be confident; and make sure that you obey the whole Law that my servant Moses gave you. Do not neglect any part of it and you will succeed wherever you go. 8 Be sure that the book of the Law is always read in your worship. Study it day and night, and make sure that you obey everything written in it. Then you will be prosperous and successful. 9 Remember that I have commanded you to be determined and confident! Do not be afraid or discouraged, for I, the LORD your God, am with you wherever you go."

Joshua Gives Orders to the People

10 Then Joshua ordered the leaders to 11 go through the camp and say to the people, "Get some food ready, because in three days you are going to cross the Jordan River to occupy the land that the LORD your God is giving you."

12 Joshua said to the tribes of Reuben and Gad and to half the tribe of Manasseh, 13 "Remember how the LORD's servant Moses told you that the LORD your God would give you this land on the east side of the Jordan as your home. 14 Your wives, your children, and your livestock will stay here, but your soldiers, armed for battle, will cross over ahead of the other Israelites in order to help them 15 until they have occupied the land west of the Jordan that the LORD your God has given them. When he has given safety to all the tribes of Israel, then you may come back and settle here in your own land east of the Jordan, which Moses, the LORD's servant, gave to you."

16 They answered Joshua, "We will do everything you have told us and will go anywhere you send us. 17 We will obey

you, just as we always obeyed Moses, and may the LORD your God be with you as he was with Moses! 18 Whoever questions your authority or disobeys any of your orders will be put to death. Be determined and confident!"

Joshua Sends Spies into Jericho

2 Then Joshua sent two spies from the camp at Acacia with orders to go and secretly explore the land of Canaan, especially the city of Jericho. When they came to the city, they went to spend the night in the house of a prostitute named Rahab. 2 The king of Jericho heard that some Israelites had come that night to spy out the country, 3 so he sent word to Rahab: "The men in your house have come to spy out the whole country! Bring them out!"

4-6 "Some men did come to my house," she answered, "but I don't know where they were from. They left at sundown before the city gate was closed. I didn't find out where they were going, but if you start after them quickly, you can catch them." (Now Rahab had taken the two spies up on the roof and hidden them under some stalks of flax that she had put there.) 7 The king's men left the city, and then the gate was shut. They went looking for the Israelite spies as far as the place where the road crosses the Jordan.

8 Before the spies settled down for the night, Rahab went up on the roof 9 and said to them, "I know that the LORD has given you this land. Everyone in the country is terrified of you. 10 We have heard how the LORD dried up the Red Sea in front of you when you were leaving Egypt. We have also heard how you killed Sihon and Og, the two Amorite kings east of the Jordan. 11 We were afraid as soon as we heard about it; we have all lost our courage because of you. The LORD your God is God in heaven above and here on earth. 12 Now swear by him that you will treat my family as kindly as I have treated you, and give me some sign that I can trust you. 13 Promise me that you will save my father and mother, my brothers and sisters, and all their families! Don't let us be killed!"

14 The men said to her, "May God take our lives if we don't do as we say!ᵃ If you

do not tell anyone what we have been doing, we promise you that when the LORD gives us this land, we will treat you well."

15 Rahab lived in a house built into the city wall, so she let the men down from the window by a rope. 16 "Go into the hill country," she said, "or the king's men will find you. Hide there for three days until they come back. After that, you can go on your way."

17 The men said to her, "We will keep the promise that you have made us give. 18 This is what you must do. When we invade your land, tie this red cord to the window you let us down from. Get your father and mother, your brothers, and all your father's family together in your house. 19 If anyone goes out of the house, his death will be his own fault, and we will not be responsible; but if anyone in the house with you is harmed, then we will be responsible. 20 However, if you tell anyone what we have been doing, then we will not have to keep our promise which you have made us give you." 21 She agreed and sent them away. When they had gone, she tied the red cord to the window.

22 The spies went into the hills and hid. The king's men looked for them all over the countryside for three days, but they did not find them, so they returned to Jericho. 23 Then the two spies came down from the hills, crossed the river, and went back to Joshua. They told him everything that had happened, 24 and then said, "We are sure that the LORD has given us the whole country. All the people there are terrified of us."

The People of Israel Cross the Jordan

3 The next morning Joshua and all the people of Israel got up early, left the camp at Acacia, and went to the Jordan, where they camped while waiting to cross it. 2 Three days later the leaders went through the camp 3 and told the people, "When you see the priests carrying the Covenant Box of the LORD your God, break camp and follow them. 4 You have never been here before, so they will show you the way to go. But do not get near the Covenant Box; stay about half a mile behind it."

ᵃ May God . . . say; or We will protect you if you protect us.

5 Joshua told the people, "Purify yourselves, because tomorrow the LORD will perform miracles among you." 6 Then he told the priests to take the Covenant Box and go with it ahead of the people. They did as he said.

7 The LORD said to Joshua, "What I do today will make all the people of Israel begin to honor you as a great man, and they will realize that I am with you as I was with Moses. 8 Tell the priests carrying the Covenant Box that when they reach the river, they must wade in and stand near the bank."

9 Then Joshua said to the people, "Come here and listen to what the LORD your God has to say. 10 As you advance, he will surely drive out the Canaanites, the Hittites, the Hivites, the Perizzites, the Girgashites, the Amorites, and the Jebusites. You will know that the living God is among you 11 when the Covenant Box of the Lord of all the earth crosses the Jordan ahead of you. 12 Now choose twelve men, one from each of the tribes of Israel. 13 When the priests who carry the Covenant Box of the LORD of all the earth put their feet in the water, the Jordan will stop flowing, and the water coming downstream will pile up in one place."

14-15 It was harvest time, and the river was in flood.

When the people left the camp to cross the Jordan, the priests went ahead of them, carrying the Covenant Box. As soon as the priests stepped into the river, 16 the water stopped flowing and piled up, far upstream at Adam, the city beside Zarethan. The flow downstream to the Dead Sea was completely cut off, and the people were able to cross over near Jericho. 17 While the people walked across on dry ground, the priests carrying the LORD's Covenant Box stood on dry ground in the middle of the Jordan until all the people had crossed over.

Memorial Stones Are Set Up

4 When the whole nation had crossed the Jordan, the LORD said to Joshua, 2 "Choose twelve men, one from each tribe, 3 and command them to take twelve stones out of the middle of the Jordan, from the very place where the priests were standing. Tell them to carry these stones with them and to put them down where you camp tonight."

4 Then Joshua called the twelve men he had chosen, 5 and he told them, "Go into the Jordan ahead of the Covenant Box of the LORD your God. Each one of you take a stone on your shoulder, one for each of the tribes of Israel. 6 These stones will remind the people of what the LORD has done. In the future, when your children ask what these stones mean to you, 7 you will tell them that the water of the Jordan stopped flowing when the LORD's Covenant Box crossed the river. These stones will always remind the people of Israel of what happened here."

8 The men followed Joshua's orders. As the LORD had commanded Joshua, they took twelve stones from the middle of the Jordan, one for each of the tribes of Israel, carried them to the camping place, and put them down there. 9 Joshua also set up twelve stones in the middle of the Jordan, where the priests carrying the Covenant Box had stood. (Those stones are still there.) 10 The priests stood in the middle of the Jordan until everything had been done that the LORD ordered Joshua to tell the people to do. This is what Moses had commanded.

The people hurried across the river. 11 When they were all on the other side, the priests with the LORD's Covenant Box went on ahead of the people. 12 The men of the tribes of Reuben and Gad and of half the tribe of Manasseh, ready for battle, crossed ahead of the rest of the people, as Moses had told them to do. 13 In the presence of the LORD about forty thousand men ready for war crossed over to the plain near Jericho. 14 What the LORD did that day made the people of Israel consider Joshua a great man. They honored him all his life, just as they had honored Moses.

15 Then the LORD told Joshua 16 to command the priests carrying the Covenant Box to come up out of the Jordan. 17 Joshua did so, 18 and when the priests reached the riverbank, the river began flowing once more and flooded its banks again.

19 The people crossed the Jordan on the tenth day of the first month and camped at Gilgal, east of Jericho. 20 There Joshua set up the twelve stones taken from the Jordan. 21 And he said to the people of Israel, "In the future, when your children ask you what these stones mean, 22 you will tell them about the time when Israel

THE CITY OF JERICHO

Located near the Jordan River just north of the Dead Sea, Jericho is the site of one of the oldest continually inhabited cities in the world. Situated seventeen miles northeast of Jerusalem, Jericho has actually been positioned at three different sites within a few miles of one another. Throughout its long history the city has apparently changed location after sieges, earthquakes, and other catastrophes. Present-day Jericho is a small village (er-Riha) on the main highway from Jerusalem to Amman, Jordan.

Known as the "city of palm trees" (Jg 3.13) because of the trees that grow in its oasis location, Jericho at 800 feet below sea level sits lower than any other city on earth. Its position at the bottom of a deep gorge contributes to its hot, tropical climate.

Old Testament Jericho was the first city captured by Joshua in his invasion of Canaan. Under orders from the Lord, the Israelites marched around the massive walls of the fortified city for six days. On the seventh day the priests blew their trumpets and all the soldiers let out a loud shout. The walls came tumbling down, leaving the city exposed to the invaders (Js 6).

Excavations of Old Testament Jericho indicate that the site had been occupied for thousands of years before Joshua captured the city. Unfortunately, extensive archaeological excavations there have failed to uncover conclusive evidence of Joshua's conquest, because there are few remains from this period. This lack of evidence is most often attributed to centuries of erosion on the ruin.

New Testament Jericho, located about two miles south of the Old Testament site, is associated with the ministry of Jesus. The rough, hilly road from Jerusalem to Jericho was the setting for Jesus' famous parable of the Good Samaritan (Lk 10.30–37). On visits to Jericho, Jesus healed blind Bartimaeus (Mk 10.46–52) and brought salvation to Zacchaeus (Lk 19.1–10).

crossed the Jordan on dry ground. 23 Tell them that the LORD your God dried up the water of the Jordan for you until you had crossed, just as he dried up the Red Sea for us. 24 Because of this everyone on earth will know how great the LORD's power is, and you will honor the LORD your God forever."

5 All the Amorite kings west of the Jordan and all the Canaanite kings along the Mediterranean Sea heard that the LORD had dried up the Jordan until the people of Israel had crossed it. They became afraid and lost their courage because of the Israelites.

The Circumcision at Gilgal

2 Then the LORD told Joshua, "Make some knives out of flint and circumcise the Israelites." 3 So Joshua did as the LORD had commanded, and he circumcised the Israelites at a place called Circumcision Hill. 4-6 When the people of Israel left Egypt, all the males were already circumcised. However, during the forty years the people spent crossing the desert, none of the baby boys had been circumcised. Also, by the end of that time all the men who were of fighting age when they left Egypt had died because they had disobeyed the LORD. Just as he had sworn, they were not allowed to see the rich and fertile land that he had promised their ancestors. 7 The sons of these men had never been circumcised, and it was this new generation that Joshua circumcised.

8 After the circumcision was completed, the whole nation stayed in the camp until the wounds had healed. 9 The LORD said to Joshua, "Today I have removed from you the disgrace of being slaves in Egypt." That is why the place was named Gilgal,b the name it still has.

10 While the Israelites were camping at Gilgal on the plain near Jericho, they observed Passover on the evening of the fourteenth day of the month. 11 The next day was the first time they ate food grown in Canaan: roasted grain and bread made without yeast. 12 The manna stopped falling then, and the Israelites no longer had any. From that time on they ate food grown in Canaan.

b GILGAL: *This name sounds like the Hebrew for "removed."*

Joshua and the Man with a Sword

13 While Joshua was near Jericho, he suddenly saw a man standing in front of him, holding a sword. Joshua went up to him and asked, "Are you one of our soldiers, or an enemy?"

14 "Neither," the man answered. "I am here as the commander of the LORD's army."

Joshua threw himself on the ground in worship and said, "I am your servant, sir. What do you want me to do?" 15 And the commander of the LORD's army told him, "Take your sandals off; you are standing on holy ground." And Joshua did as he was told.

The Fall of Jericho

6 The gates of Jericho were kept shut and guarded to keep the Israelites out. No one could enter or leave the city. 2 The LORD said to Joshua, "I am putting into your hands Jericho, with its king and all its brave soldiers. 3 You and your soldiers are to march around the city once a day for six days. 4 Seven priests, each carrying a trumpet, are to go in front of the Covenant Box. On the seventh day you and your soldiers are to march around the city seven times while the priests blow the trumpets. 5 Then they are to sound one long note. As soon as you hear it, all the people are to give a loud shout, and the city walls will collapse. Then the whole army will go straight into the city."

6 Joshua called the priests and told them, "Take the Covenant Box, and seven of you go in front of it, carrying trumpets." 7 Then he ordered the people to start marching around the city, with an advance guard going on ahead of the LORD's Covenant Box.

8-9 So, just as Joshua had ordered, an advance guard started out ahead of the priests who were blowing trumpets; behind these came the priests who were carrying the Covenant Box, followed by a rear guard. All this time the trumpets were sounding. 10 But Joshua had ordered the people not to shout, not to say a word until he gave the order. 11 So he had this group of men take the LORD's Covenant Box around the city one time. Then they came back to camp and spent the night there.

JOSHUA

12-13 Joshua got up early the next morning, and for the second time the priests and soldiers marched around the city in the same order as the day before: first, the advance guard; next, the seven priests blowing the seven trumpets; then, the priests carrying the LORD's Covenant Box; and finally, the rear guard. All this time the trumpets were sounding. 14 On this second day they again marched around the city one time and then returned to camp. They did this for six days.

15 On the seventh day they got up at daybreak and marched seven times around the city in the same way—this was the only day that they marched around it seven times. 16 The seventh time around, when the priests were about to sound the trumpets, Joshua ordered the people to shout, and he said, "The LORD has given you the city! 17 The city and everything in it must be totally destroyed as an offering to the LORD. Only the prostitute Rahab and her household will be spared, because she hid our spies. 18 But you are not to take anything that is to be destroyed; if you do, you will bring trouble and destruction on the Israelite camp. 19 Everything made of silver, gold, bronze, or iron is set apart for the LORD. It is to be put in the LORD's treasury."

20 So the priests blew the trumpets. As soon as the people heard it, they gave a loud shout, and the walls collapsed. Then all the army went straight up the hill into the city and captured it. 21 With their swords they killed everyone in the city, men and women, young and old. They also killed the cattle, sheep, and donkeys.

22 Joshua then told the two men who had served as spies, "Go into the prostitute's house, and bring her and her family out, as you promised her." 23 So they went and brought Rahab out, along with her father and mother, her brothers, and the rest of her family. They took them all, family and slaves, to safety near the Israelite camp. 24 Then they set fire to the city and burned it to the ground, along with everything in it, except the things made of gold, silver, bronze, and iron, which they took and put in the LORD's treasury. 25 But Joshua spared the lives of the prostitute Rahab and all her relatives, because she had hidden the two spies that

he had sent to Jericho. (Her descendants have lived in Israel to this day.)

26 At this time Joshua issued a solemn warning: "Anyone who tries to rebuild the city of Jericho will be under the LORD's curse.

Whoever lays the foundation will lose his oldest son;
Whoever builds the gates will lose his youngest."

27 So the LORD was with Joshua, and his fame spread through the whole country.

Achan's Sin

7 The LORD's command to Israel not to take from Jericho anything that was to be destroyed was not obeyed. A man named Achan disobeyed that order, and so the LORD was furious with the Israelites. (Achan was the son of Carmi and grandson of Zabdi, and belonged to the clan of Zerah, a part of the tribe of Judah.)

2 Joshua sent some men from Jericho to Ai, a city east of Bethel, near Beth-aven, with orders to go and explore the land. When they had done so, 3 they reported back to Joshua: "There is no need for everyone to attack Ai. Send only about two or three thousand men. Don't send the whole army up there to fight; it is not a large city." 4 So about three thousand Israelites made the attack, but they were forced to retreat. 5 The men of Ai chased them from the city gate as far as some quarries and killed about thirty-six of them on the way down the hill. Then the Israelites lost their courage and were afraid.

6 Joshua and the leaders of Israel tore their clothes in grief, threw themselves to the ground before the LORD's Covenant Box, and lay there till evening, with dust on their heads to show their sorrow. 7 And Joshua said, "Sovereign LORD! Why did you bring us across the Jordan at all? To turn us over to the Amorites? To destroy us? Why didn't we just stay on the other side of the Jordan? 8 What can I say, O Lord, now that Israel has retreated from the enemy? 9 The Canaanites and everyone else in the country will hear about it. They will surround us and kill every one of us! And then what will you do to protect your honor?"

10 The LORD said to Joshua, "Get up! Why are you lying on the ground like this? 11 Israel has sinned! They have

JOSHUA'S VICTORIES

Under Joshua's leadership, the people of Israel entered Canaan to drive out the Canaanites and claim the land of promise. A careful study of the military campaigns described in the Book of Joshua shows that Joshua had a carefully planned strategy of conquest. His first campaign established the Israelites in the central part of Canaan, then conducted campaigns into the southern and northern parts of the land to complete the takeover. While these campaigns are described briefly in Joshua 1—11, they probably covered a period of about seven years. By the time Joshua died (Js 24.29), the Israelites had driven most of the Canaanites out of Palestine and divided the land among the twelve tribes of Israel.

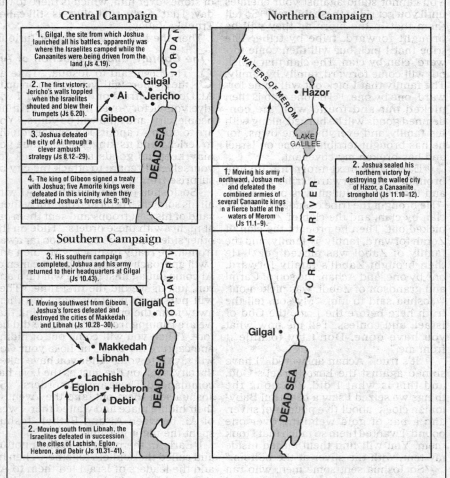

Central Campaign

1. Gilgal, the site from which Joshua launched all his battles, apparently was where the Israelites camped while the Canaanites were being driven from the land (Js 4.19).

2. The first victory; Jericho's walls toppled when the Israelites shouted and blew their trumpets (Js 6.20).

3. Joshua defeated the city of Ai through a clever ambush strategy (Js 8.12–29).

4. The king of Gibeon signed a treaty with Joshua; five Amorite kings were defeated in this vicinity when they attacked Joshua's forces (Js 9; 10).

Gilgal
Ai • Jericho
• Gibeon

JORDAN

DEAD SEA

Northern Campaign

WATERS OF MEROM

• Hazor

LAKE GALILEE

1. Moving his army northward, Joshua met and defeated the combined armies of several Canaanite kings in a fierce battle at the waters of Merom (Js 11.1–9).

2. Joshua sealed his northern victory by destroying the walled city of Hazor, a Canaanite stronghold (Js 11.10–12).

JORDAN RIVER

Gilgal •

DEAD SEA

Southern Campaign

3. His southern campaign completed, Joshua and his army returned to their headquarters at Gilgal (Js 10.43).

1. Moving southwest from Gibeon, Joshua's forces defeated and destroyed the cities of Makkedah and Libnah (Js 10.28–30).

Gilgal •

JORDAN RIV

• Makkedah
• Libnah
• Lachish
Eglon • • Hebron
• Debir

DEAD SEA

2. Moving south from Libnah, the Israelites defeated in succession the cities of Lachish, Eglon, Hebron, and Debir (Js 10.31–41).

broken the agreement with me that I ordered them to keep. They have taken some of the things condemned to destruction. They stole them, lied about it, and put them with their own things. 12 This is why the Israelites cannot stand against their enemies. They retreat from them because they themselves have now been condemned to destruction! I will not stay with you any longer unless you destroy the things you were ordered not to take! 13 Get up! Purify the people and get them ready to come before me. Tell them to be ready tomorrow, because I, the LORD God of Israel, have this to say: 'Israel, you have in your possession some things that I ordered you to destroy! You cannot stand against your enemies until you get rid of these things!' 14 So tell them that in the morning they will be brought forward, tribe by tribe. The tribe that I pick out will then come forward, clan by clan. The clan that I pick out will come forward, family by family. The family that I pick out will come forward, one by one. 15 The one who is then picked out and found with the condemned goods will be burned, along with his family and everything he owns, for he has brought terrible shame on Israel and has broken my covenant."

16 Early the next morning Joshua brought Israel forward, tribe by tribe, and the tribe of Judah was picked out. 17 He brought the tribe of Judah forward, clan by clan, and the clan of Zerah was picked out. Then he brought the clan of Zerah forward, family by family, and the family of Zabdi was picked out. 18 He then brought Zabdi's family forward, one by one, and Achan, the son of Carmi and grandson of Zabdi, was picked out. 19 Joshua said to him, "My son, tell the truth here before the LORD, the God of Israel, and confess. Tell me now what you have done. Don't try to hide it from me."

20 "It's true," Achan answered. "I have sinned against the LORD, Israel's God, and this is what I did. 21 Among the things we seized I saw a beautiful Babylonian cloak, about five pounds of silver, and a bar of gold weighing over one pound. I wanted them so much that I took them. You will find them buried inside my tent, with the silver at the bottom."

22 So Joshua sent some men, who ran to the tent and found that the condemned things really were buried there, with the silver at the bottom. 23 They brought them out of the tent, took them to Joshua and all the Israelites, and laid them down in the presence of the LORD. 24 Joshua, along with all the people of Israel, seized Achan, the silver, the cloak, the bar of gold, together with Achan's sons and daughters, his cattle, donkeys, and sheep, his tent, and everything else he owned; and they took them to Trouble Valley. 25 And Joshua said, "Why have you brought such trouble on us? The LORD will now bring trouble on you!" All the people then stoned Achan to death; they also stoned and burned his family and possessions. 26 They put a huge pile of stones over him, which is there to this day. That is why that place is still called Trouble Valley.

Then the LORD was no longer furious.

The Capture and Destruction of Ai

8 The LORD said to Joshua, "Take all the soldiers with you and go on up to Ai. Don't be afraid or discouraged. I will give you victory over the king of Ai; his people, city, and land will be yours. 2 You are to do to Ai and its king what you did to Jericho and its king, but this time you may keep its goods and livestock for yourselves. Prepare to attack the city by surprise from the rear."

3 So Joshua got ready to go to Ai with all his soldiers. He picked out thirty thousand of his best troops and sent them out at night 4 with these orders: "Hide on the other side of the city, but not too far away from it; be ready to attack. 5 My men and I will approach the city. When the men of Ai come out against us, we will turn and run, just as we did the first time. 6 They will pursue us until we have led them away from the city. They will think that we are running from them, as we did before. 7 Then you will come out of hiding and capture the city. The LORD your God will give it to you. 8 After you have taken the city, set it on fire, just as the LORD has commanded. These are your orders." 9 So Joshua sent them out, and they went to their hiding place and waited there, west of Ai, between Ai and Bethel. Joshua spent the night in camp.

10 Early in the morning Joshua got up and called the soldiers together. Then he and the leaders of Israel led them to Ai. 11 The soldiers with him went toward the

main entrance to the city and set up camp on the north side, with a valley between themselves and Ai. 12 He took about five thousand men and put them in hiding west of the city, between Ai and Bethel. 13 The soldiers were arranged for battle with the main camp north of the city and the rest of the men to the west. Joshua spent the night in the valley. 14 When the king of Ai saw Joshua's men, he acted quickly. He and all his men went out toward the Jordan Valley to fight the Israelites at the same place as before, not knowing that he was about to be attacked from the rear. 15 Joshua and his men pretended that they were retreating, and ran away toward the barren country. 16 All the men in the city had been called together to go after them, and as they pursued Joshua, they kept getting farther away from the city. 17 Every man in Ai*c* went after the Israelites, and the city was left wide open, with no one to defend it.

18 Then the LORD said to Joshua, "Point your spear at Ai; I am giving it to you." Joshua did as he was told, 19 and as soon as he lifted his hand, the men who had been hiding got up quickly, ran into the city and captured it. They immediately set the city on fire. 20 When the men of Ai looked back, they saw the smoke rising to the sky. There was no way for them to escape, because the Israelites who had run toward the barren country now turned around to attack them. 21 When Joshua and his men saw that the others had taken the city and that it was on fire, they turned around and began killing the men of Ai. 22 The Israelites in the city now came down to join the battle. So the men of Ai found themselves completely surrounded by Israelites, and they were all killed. No one got away, and no one lived through it 23 except the king of Ai. He was captured and taken to Joshua.

24 The Israelites killed every one of the enemy in the barren country where they had chased them. Then they went back to Ai and killed everyone there. 25-26 Joshua kept his spear pointed at Ai and did not put it down until every person there had been killed. The whole population of Ai was killed that day — twelve thousand men and women. 27 The Israelites kept for themselves the live-

stock and goods captured in the city, as the LORD had told Joshua. 28 Joshua burned Ai and left it in ruins. It is still like that today. 29 He hanged the king of Ai from a tree and left his body there until evening. At sundown Joshua gave orders for the body to be removed, and it was thrown down at the entrance to the city gate. They covered it with a huge pile of stones, which is still there today.

The Law Is Read at Mount Ebal

30 Then Joshua built on Mount Ebal an altar to the LORD, the God of Israel. 31 He made it according to the instructions that Moses, the LORD's servant, had given the Israelites, as it says in the Law of Moses: "an altar made of stones which have not been cut with iron tools." On it they offered burnt sacrifices to the LORD, and they also presented their fellowship offerings. 32 There, with the Israelites looking on, Joshua made on the stones*d* a copy of the Law which Moses had written. 33 The Israelites, with their leaders, officers, and judges, as well as the foreigners among them, stood on two sides of the LORD's Covenant Box, facing the levitical priests who carried it. Half of the people stood with their backs to Mount Gerizim and the other half with their backs to Mount Ebal. The LORD's servant Moses had commanded them to do this when the time came for them to receive the blessing. 34 Joshua then read aloud the whole Law, including the blessings and the curses, just as they are written in the book of the Law. 35 Every one of the commandments of Moses was read by Joshua to the whole gathering, which included women and children, as well as the foreigners living among them.

The Gibeonites Deceive Joshua

9 The victories of Israel became known to all the kings west of the Jordan — in the hills, in the foothills, and all along the coastal plain of the Mediterranean Sea as far north as Lebanon; these were the kings of the Hittites, the Amorites, the Canaanites, the Perizzites, the Hivites, and the Jebusites. 2 They all came together and joined forces to fight against Joshua and the Israelites.

3 But the people of Gibeon, who were Hivites, heard what Joshua had done to

c One ancient translation Ai; Hebrew Ai and Bethel.   d the stones; or stones.

Jericho and Ai, 4and they decided to deceive him. They went and got some food and loaded their donkeys with worn-out sacks and patched-up wineskins. 5They put on ragged clothes and worn-out sandals that had been mended. The bread they took with them was dry and moldy. 6Then they went to the camp at Gilgal and said to Joshua and the Israelites, "We have come from a distant land. We want you to make a treaty with us."

7But the Israelites said, "Why should we make a treaty with you? Maybe you live nearby."

8They said to Joshua, "We are at your service."

Joshua asked them, "Who are you? Where do you come from?"

9Then they told him this story: "We have come from a very distant land, sir, because we have heard of the LORD your God. We have heard about everything that he did in Egypt 10and what he did to the two Amorite kings east of the Jordan: King Sihon of Heshbon and King Og of Bashan, who lived in Ashtaroth. 11Our leaders and all the people that live in our land told us to get some food ready for a trip and to go and meet you. We were told to put ourselves at your service and ask you to make a treaty with us. 12Look at our bread. When we left home with it and started out to meet you, it was still warm. But look! Now it is dry and moldy. 13When we filled these wineskins, they were new, but look! They are torn. Our clothes and sandals are worn out from the long trip."

14The Israelites accepted some food from them, but did not consult the LORD about it. 15Joshua made a treaty of friendship with the people of Gibeon and allowed them to live. The leaders of the community of Israel gave their solemn promise to keep the treaty.

16Three days after the treaty had been made, the Israelites learned that these people did indeed live nearby. 17So the people of Israel started out and three days later arrived at the cities where these people lived: Gibeon, Chephirah, Beeroth, and Kiriath Jearim. 18But the Israelites could not kill them, because their leaders had made a solemn promise to them in the name of the LORD, Israel's God. All the people complained to the leaders about this, 19but they answered, "We have made our solemn promise to them in the name of the LORD God of Israel. Now we cannot harm them. 20We must let them live because of our promise; if we don't, God will punish us. 21Let them live, but they will have to cut wood and carry water for us." This was what the leaders suggested.

22Joshua ordered the people of Gibeon to be brought to him, and he asked them, "Why did you deceive us and tell us that you were from far away, when you live right here? 23Because you did this, God has condemned you. Your people will always be slaves, cutting wood and carrying water for the sanctuary of my God."

24They answered, "We did it, sir, because we learned that it was really true that the LORD your God had commanded his servant Moses to give you the whole land and to kill the people living in it as you advanced. We did it because we were terrified of you; we were in fear of our lives. 25Now we are in your power; do with us what you think is right." 26So this is what Joshua did: he protected them and did not allow the people of Israel to kill them. 27But at the same time he made them slaves, to cut wood and carry water for the people of Israel and for the LORD's altar. To this day they have continued to do this work in the place where the LORD has chosen to be worshiped.

The Amorites Are Defeated

10 Adonizedek, the king of Jerusalem,e heard that Joshua had captured and totally destroyed Ai and had killed its king, just as he had done to Jericho and its king. He also heard that the people of Gibeon had made peace with the Israelites and were living among them. 2The people of Jerusalem were greatly alarmed at this because Gibeon was as large as any of the cities that had a king; it was larger than Ai, and its men were good fighters. 3So Adonizedek sent the following message to King Hoham of Hebron, King Piram of Jarmuth, King Japhia of Lachish, and to King Debir of Eglon: 4"Come and help me attack Gibeon, because its people have made peace with Joshua and the Israelites." 5These five Amorite kings,

e JERUSALEM: *At that time it was a Jebusite city.*

the kings of Jerusalem, Hebron, Jarmuth, Lachish, and Eglon, joined forces, surrounded Gibeon, and attacked it.

6 The men of Gibeon sent word to Joshua at the camp in Gilgal: "Do not abandon us, sir! Come at once and help us! Save us! All the Amorite kings in the hill country have joined forces and have attacked us!"

7 So Joshua and his whole army, including the best troops, started out from Gilgal. 8 The LORD said to Joshua, "Do not be afraid of them. I have already given you the victory. Not one of them will be able to stand against you." 9 All night Joshua and his army marched from Gilgal to Gibeon, and they made a surprise attack on the Amorites. 10 The LORD made the Amorites panic at the sight of Israel's army. The Israelites slaughtered them at Gibeon and pursued them down the mountain pass at Beth Horon, keeping up the attack as far south as Azekah and Makkedah. 11 While the Amorites were running down the pass from the Israelite army, the LORD made large hailstones fall down on them all the way to Azekah. More were killed by the hailstones than by the Israelites.

12 On the day that the LORD gave the men of Israel victory over the Amorites, Joshua spoke to the LORD. In the presence of the Israelites he said,

"Sun, stand still over Gibeon;
Moon, stop over Aijalon Valley."

13 The sun stood still and the moon did not move until the nation had conquered its enemies. This is written in The Book of Jashar. The sun stood still in the middle of the sky and did not go down for a whole day. 14 Never before, and never since, has there been a day like it, when the LORD obeyed a human being. The LORD fought on Israel's side!

15 After this, Joshua and his army went back to the camp at Gilgal.

Joshua Captures the Five Amorite Kings

16 The five Amorite kings, however, had escaped and were hiding in the cave at Makkedah. 17 Someone found them, and Joshua was told where they were hiding. 18 He said, "Roll some big stones in front of the entrance to the cave. Place some guards there, 19 but don't stay there yourselves. Keep on after the enemy and

attack them from the rear; don't let them get to their cities! The LORD your God has given you victory over them." 20 Joshua and the men of Israel slaughtered them, although some managed to find safety inside their city walls and were not killed. 21 Then all of Joshua's men came back safe to him at the camp at Makkedah.

No one in the land dared even to speak against the Israelites.

22 Then Joshua said, "Open the entrance to the cave and bring those five kings out to me." 23 So the cave was opened, and the kings of Jerusalem, Hebron, Jarmuth, Lachish, and Eglon were brought out 24 and taken to Joshua. Joshua then called all the men of Israel to him and ordered the officers who had gone with him to come and put their feet on the necks of the kings. They did so. 25 Then Joshua said to his officers, "Don't be afraid or discouraged. Be determined and confident because this is what the LORD is going to do to all your enemies." 26 Then Joshua killed the kings and hanged them on five trees, where their bodies stayed until evening. 27 At sundown Joshua gave orders, and their bodies were taken down and thrown into the same cave where they had hidden earlier. Large stones were placed at the entrance to the cave, and they are still there.

Joshua Captures More Amorite Territory

28 Joshua attacked and captured Makkedah and its king that day. He put everyone in the city to death; no one was left alive. He did to the king of Makkedah what he had done to the king of Jericho.

29 After this, Joshua and his army went on from Makkedah to Libnah and attacked it. 30 The LORD also gave the Israelites victory over this city and its king. They spared no one, but killed every person in it. They did to the king what they had done to the king of Jericho.

31 After this, Joshua and his army went on from Libnah to Lachish, surrounded it and attacked it. 32 The LORD gave the Israelites victory over Lachish on the second day of the battle. Just as they had done at Libnah, they spared no one, but killed every person in the city. 33 King Horam of Gezer came to the aid of Lachish, but

Joshua defeated him and his army and left none of them alive.

34 Next, Joshua and his army went on from Lachish to Eglon, surrounded it and attacked it. 35 They captured it the same day and put everyone there to death, just as they had done at Lachish.

36 After this, Joshua and his army went from Eglon up into the hills to Hebron, attacked it 37 and captured it. They killed the king and everyone else in the city as well as in the nearby towns. Joshua condemned the city to total destruction, just as he had done to Eglon. No one in it was left alive.

38 Then Joshua and his army turned back to Debir and attacked it. 39 He captured it, with its king and all the nearby towns. They put everyone there to death. Joshua did to Debir and its king what he had done to Hebron and to Libnah and its king.

40 Joshua conquered the whole land. He defeated the kings of the hill country, the eastern slopes, and the western foothills, as well as those of the dry country in the south. He spared no one; everyone was put to death. This was what the LORD God of Israel had commanded. 41 Joshua's campaign took him from Kadesh Barnea in the south to Gaza near the coast, including all the area of Goshen, and as far north as Gibeon. 42 Joshua conquered all these kings and their territory in one campaign because the LORD, Israel's God, was fighting for Israel. 43 After this, Joshua and his army went back to the camp at Gilgal.

Joshua Defeats Jabin and His Allies

11 When the news of Israel's victories reached King Jabin of Hazor, he sent word to King Jobab of Madon, to the kings of Shimron and Achshaph, 2 and to the kings in the hill country in the north, in the Jordan Valley south of Lake Galilee, in the foothills, and on the coast near Dor. 3 He also sent word to the Canaanites on both sides of the Jordan, to the Amorites, the Hittites, the Perizzites, and the Jebusites in the hill country, as well as to the Hivites who lived at the foot of Mount Hermon in the land of Mizpah. 4 They came with all their soldiers — an army with as many men as there are grains of sand on the seashore. They also had many horses and chariots. 5 All of these kings joined forces and came together and set up camp at Merom Brook to fight against Israel.

6 The LORD said to Joshua, "Do not be afraid of them. By this time tomorrow I will have killed all of them for Israel. You are to cripple their horses and burn their chariots." 7 So Joshua and all his men attacked them by surprise at Merom Brook. 8 The LORD gave the Israelites victory over them; the Israelites attacked and pursued them as far north as Misrephoth Maim and Sidon, and as far east as the valley of Mizpah. The fight continued until none of the enemy was left alive. 9 Joshua did to them what the LORD had commanded: he crippled their horses and burned their chariots.

10 Joshua then turned back, captured Hazor and killed its king. (At that time Hazor was the most powerful of all those kingdoms.) 11 They put everyone there to death; no one was left alive, and the city was burned.

12 Joshua captured all these cities and their kings, putting everyone to death, just as Moses, the LORD's servant, had commanded. 13 However, the Israelites did not burn any of the cities built on mounds, except Hazor, which Joshua did burn. 14 The people of Israel took all the valuables and livestock from these cities and kept them for themselves. But they put every person to death; no one was left alive. 15 The LORD had given his commands to his servant Moses, Moses had given them to Joshua, and Joshua obeyed them. He did everything that the LORD had commanded Moses.

The Territory Taken by Joshua

16 Joshua captured all the land — the hill country and foothills, both north and south, all the area of Goshen and the dry country south of it, as well as the Jordan Valley. 17-18 The territory extended from Mount Halak in the south near Edom, as far as Baalgad in the north, in the valley of Lebanon south of Mount Hermon. Joshua was at war with the kings of this territory for a long time, but he captured them all and put them to death. 19 The only city that made peace with the people of Israel was Gibeon, where some of the Hivites lived. All the others were conquered in battle. 20 The LORD had made them determined to fight the Israelites, so that they would be condemned to total destruction and all be killed without

ISRAEL AND THE CANAANITES

The Canaanites, an ancient tribe highly developed in their culture, occupied Palestine long before the Israelites arrived to drive them out under the leadership of Joshua.

Archaeological evidence indicates the Canaanites must have settled the land of Canaan at least six hundred years before Joshua's time. They had a well-developed system of walled cities, including Jericho, Ai, Lachish, Hebron, and Hazor. Under God's leadership, Joshua was successful in taking these cities from the Canaanites (Js 6—12).

The Canaanites also had their own written language, based upon a unique alphabet, which they apparently developed. Discovery of a number of Canaanite documents at Ras Shamra in northern Palestine has given scholars many insights into Canaanite culture and daily life.

The religion of the Canaanite people posed a peculiar threat to the new inhabitants of Canaan. The Canaanites worshiped many pagan gods that appealed to their animal instincts. Baal, the god who controlled rain and fertility, was their main god.

Baal religion was basically a fertility cult. At temples scattered throughout their land, Canaanite worshipers participated in lewd, immoral acts with sacred prostitutes. Bestiality and child sacrifice were other evils associated with this depraved form of religion.

The threat of Baal worship explains why Moses issued a stern warning to the people of Israel about the Canaanites several years before they actually occupied the land promised by the Lord. "You must put them to death," Moses commanded. "Do not make an alliance with them or show them any mercy" (Dt 7.2).

Canaanite religion continued to exert its influence throughout the land for many years after Joshua's conquest. The Israelites had to be called back again and again to worship the one true God, who demanded holy and ethical living from his people.

mercy. This was what the LORD had commanded Moses.

21 At this time Joshua went and destroyed the race of giants called the Anakim who lived in the hill country—in Hebron, Debir, Anab, and in all the hill country of Judah and Israel. Joshua completely destroyed them and their cities. 22 None of the Anakim were left in the land of Israel; a few, however, were left in Gaza, Gath, and Ashdod. 23 Joshua captured the whole land, as the LORD had commanded Moses. Joshua gave it to the Israelites as their own and divided it into portions, one for each tribe.

So the people rested from war.

The Kings Defeated by Moses

12 The people of Israel had already conquered and occupied the land east of the Jordan, from the Arnon Valley up the Jordan Valley and as far north as Mount Hermon. They defeated two kings. 2 One was Sihon, the Amorite king who ruled at Heshbon. His kingdom included half of Gilead: from Aroer (on the edge of the Arnon Valley) and from the city in f the middle of that valley, as far as the Jabbok River, the border of Ammon; 3 it included the Jordan Valley from Lake Galilee south to Beth Jeshimoth (east of the Dead Sea) and on toward the foot of Mount Pisgah.

4 They also defeated King Og of Bashan, who was one of the last of the Rephaim; he ruled at Ashtaroth and Edrei. 5 His kingdom included Mount Hermon, Salecah, and all of Bashan as far as the boundaries of Geshur and Maacah, as well as half of Gilead, as far as the territory of King Sihon of Heshbon.

6 These two kings were defeated by Moses and the people of Israel. Moses, the LORD's servant, gave their land to the tribes of Reuben and Gad and to half the tribe of Manasseh, to be their possession.

The Kings Defeated by Joshua

7 Joshua and the people of Israel defeated all the kings in the territory west of the Jordan, from Baalgad in the valley of Lebanon to Mount Halak in the south near Edom. Joshua divided this land among the tribes and gave it to them as a permanent possession. 8 This portion included the hill country, the western foothills, the Jordan Valley and its foothills, the eastern slopes, and the dry country in the south. This land had been the home of the Hittites, the Amorites, the Canaanites, the Perizzites, the Hivites, and the Jebusites. 9 The people of Israel defeated the kings of the following cities: Jericho, Ai (near Bethel), 10 Jerusalem, Hebron, 11 Jarmuth, Lachish, 12 Eglon, Gezer, 13 Debir, Geder, 14 Hormah, Arad, 15 Libnah, Adullam, 16 Makkedah, Bethel, 17 Tappuah, Hepher, 18 Aphek, Lasharon, 19 Madon, Hazor, 20 Shimron Meron, Achshaph, 21 Taanach, Megiddo, 22 Kedesh, Jokneam (in Carmel), 23 Dor (on the coast), Goiim (in Galilee g), 24 and Tirzah—thirty-one kings in all.

The Land Still to Be Taken

13 Joshua was now very old. The LORD said to him, "You are very old, but there is still much land to be taken: 2 all the territory of Philistia and Geshur, 3 as well as all the territory of the Avvim to the south. (The land from the stream Shihor, at the Egyptian border, as far north as the border of Ekron was considered Canaanite; the kings of the Philistines lived at Gaza, Ashdod, Ashkelon, Gath, and Ekron.) 4 There is still all the Canaanite country, and Mearah (which belonged to the Sidonians), as far as Aphek, at the Amorite border; 5 the land of the Gebalites; all of Lebanon to the east, from Baalgad, which is south of Mount Hermon, to Hamath Pass. 6 This includes all the territory of the Sidonians, who live in the hill country between the Lebanon Mountains and Misrephoth Maim. I will drive all these peoples out as the people of Israel advance. You must divide the land among the Israelites, just as I have commanded you to do. 7 Now then, divide this land among the other nine tribes and half of the tribe of Manasseh, for them to possess as their own."

The Division of the Territory East of the Jordan

8 The tribes of Reuben and Gad and the other half of the tribe of Manasseh had already received the land that Moses, the LORD's servant, had given them; it was on the east side of the Jordan River. 9 Their

---

f Probable text (see 13.16; Dt 2.36) the city in; Hebrew does not have these words.   g One ancient translation Galilee; Hebrew Gilgal.

territory extended to Aroer (on the edge of the Arnon Valley) and the city in the middle of that valley and included all of the plateau from Medeba to Dibon. 10 It went as far as the border of Ammon and included all the cities that had been ruled by the Amorite king Sihon, who had ruled at Heshbon. 11 It included Gilead, the regions of Geshur and Maacah, all of Mount Hermon, and all of Bashan as far as Salecah. 12 It included the kingdom of Og, the last of the Rephaim, who had ruled at Ashtaroth and Edrei. Moses had defeated these people and driven them out. 13 However, the Israelites did not drive out the people of Geshur and Maacah; they still live in Israel.

14 Moses had given no land to the tribe of Levi. As the LORD had told Moses, they were to receive as their possession a share of the sacrifices burned on the altar to the LORD God of Israel.

The Territory Assigned to Reuben

15 Moses had given a part of the land to the families of the tribe of Reuben as their possession. 16 Their territory extended to Aroer (on the edge of the Arnon Valley) and the city in the middle of that valley and included all the plateau around Medeba. 17 It included Heshbon and all the cities on the plateau: Dibon, Bamoth Baal, Beth Baalmeon, 18 Jahaz, Kedemoth, Mephaath, 19 Kiriathaim, Sibmah, Zereth Shahar on the hill in the valley, 20 Bethpeor, the slopes of Mount Pisgah, and Beth Jeshimoth. 21 It included all the cities of the plateau and the whole kingdom of the Amorite king Sihon, who had ruled at Heshbon. Moses defeated him, as well as the rulers of Midian Evi, Rekem, Zur, Hur, and Reba. All of them had ruled the land for King Sihon. 22 Among those whom the people of Israel killed was the fortune teller Balaam son of Beor. 23 The Jordan was the western border of the tribe of Reuben. These were the cities and towns given to the families of the tribe of Reuben as their possession.

The Territory Assigned to Gad

24 Moses had also given a part of the land to the families of the tribe of Gad as their possession. 25 Their territory included Jazer and all the cities of Gilead,

half the land of Ammon as far as Aroer, which is east of Rabbah; 26 their land extended from Heshbon to Ramath Mizpeh and Betonim, from Mahanaim to the border of Lodebar. 27 In the Jordan Valley it included Beth Haram, Bethnimrah, Sukkoth, and Zaphon, the rest of the kingdom of King Sihon of Heshbon. Their western border was the Jordan River as far north as Lake Galilee. 28 These were the cities and towns given to the families of the tribe of Gad as their possession.

The Territory Assigned to East Manasseh

29 Moses had given a part of the land to the families of half the tribe of Manasseh as their possession. 30 Their territory extended to Mahanaim and included all of Bashan—the whole kingdom of Og, the king of Bashan, as well as all sixty of the villages of Jair in Bashan. 31 It included half of Gilead, as well as Ashtaroth and Edrei, the capital cities of Og's kingdom in Bashan. All this was given to half the families descended from Machir son of Manasseh.

32 This is how Moses divided the land east of Jericho and the Jordan when he was in the plains of Moab. 33 But Moses did not assign any land to the tribe of Levi. He told them that their possession was to be a share of the offerings to the LORD God of Israel.

The Division of the Territory West of the Jordan

14 What follows is an account of how the land of Canaan west of the Jordan was divided among the people of Israel. Eleazar the priest, Joshua son of Nun, and the leaders of the families of the Israelite tribes divided it among the population. 2 As the LORD had commanded Moses, the territories of the nine and one-half tribes west of the Jordan were determined by drawing lots.h 3-4 Moses had already assigned the land east of the Jordan to the other two and one-half tribes. (The descendants of Joseph were divided into two tribes: Manasseh and Ephraim.) However, Moses gave the Levites no portion of the territory. Instead, they received cities to live in, with fields for their cattle and flocks.

h DRAWING LOTS: *This was usually done by using specially marked stones to determine God's will.*

⁵The people of Israel divided the land as the LORD had commanded Moses.

Hebron Is Given to Caleb

⁶One day some people from the tribe of Judah came to Joshua at Gilgal. One of them, Caleb son of Jephunneh the Kenizzite, said to him, "You know what the LORD said in Kadesh Barnea about you and me to Moses, the man of God. ⁷I was forty years old when the LORD's servant Moses sent me from Kadesh Barnea to spy out this land. I brought an honest report back to him. ⁸The men who went with me, however, made our people afraid. But I faithfully obeyed the LORD my God. ⁹Because I did, Moses promised me that my children and I would certainly receive as our possession the land which I walked over. ¹⁰But now, look. It has been forty-five years since the LORD said that to Moses. That was when Israel was going through the desert, and the LORD, as he promised, has kept me alive ever since. Look at me! I am eighty-five years old ¹¹and am just as strong today as I was when Moses sent me out. I am still strong enough for war or for anything else. ¹²Now then, give me the hill country that the LORD promised me on that day when my men and I reported. We told you then that the race of giants called the Anakim were there in large walled cities. Maybe the LORD will be with me, and I will drive them out, just as the LORD said."

¹³Joshua blessed Caleb son of Jephunneh and gave him the city of Hebron as his possession. ¹⁴Hebron still belongs to the descendants of Caleb son of Jephunneh the Kenizzite, because he faithfully obeyed the LORD, the God of Israel. ¹⁵Before this, Hebron was called the city of Arba. (Arba had been the greatest of the Anakim.)

There was now peace in the land.

The Territory Assigned to Judah

15 The families of the tribe of Judah received a part of the land described as follows:

The land reached south to the southernmost point of the wilderness of Zin, at the border of Edom. ²This southern border ran from the south end of the Dead Sea, ³went southward from the Akrabbim Pass and on to Zin. It ran south of Kadesh Barnea, past Hezron and up to Addar, turned toward Karka, ⁴went on to Azmon, and followed the stream on the border of Egypt to the Mediterranean Sea, where the border ended. That was the southern border of Judah.

⁵The eastern border was the Dead Sea, all the way up to the inlet where the Jordan empties into it.

The northern border began there, ⁶extended up to Beth Hoglah, and went north of the ridge overlooking the Jordan Valley. Then it went up to the Stone of Bohan (Bohan was a son of Reuben), ⁷from Trouble Valley up to Debir, and then turned north toward Gilgal, which faces Adummim Pass on the south side of the valley. It then went on to the springs of Enshemesh, out to Enrogel, ⁸and up through Hinnom Valley on the south side of the hill where the Jebusite city of Jerusalem was located. The border then proceeded up to the top of the hill on the west side of Hinnom Valley, at the northern end of Rephaim Valley. ⁹From there it went to the Springs of Nephtoah and out to the cities near Mount Ephron. There it turned toward Baalah (or Kiriath Jearim), ¹⁰where it circled west of Baalah toward the hill country of Edom, went on the north side of Mount Jearim (or Chesalon), down to Beth Shemesh, and on past Timnah. ¹¹The border then went out to the hill north of Ekron, turned toward Shikkeron, past Mount Baalah, and on to Jamnia. It ended at the Mediterranean Sea, ¹²which formed the western border.

Within these borders lived the people of the families of Judah.

Caleb Conquers Hebron and Debir
(Judges 1.11-15)

¹³As the LORD commanded Joshua, part of the territory of Judah was given to Caleb son of Jephunneh, from the tribe of Judah. He received Hebron, the city belonging to Arba, father of Anak. ¹⁴Caleb drove the descendants of Anak out of the city—the clans of Sheshai, Ahiman, and Talmai. ¹⁵From there he went to attack the people living in Debir. (This city used to be called Kiriath Sepher.) ¹⁶Caleb said, "I will give my daughter Achsah in marriage to the man who succeeds in capturing Kiriath Sepher." ¹⁷Othniel, the son of Caleb's brother Kenaz, captured the city, so Caleb gave him his daughter Achsah in

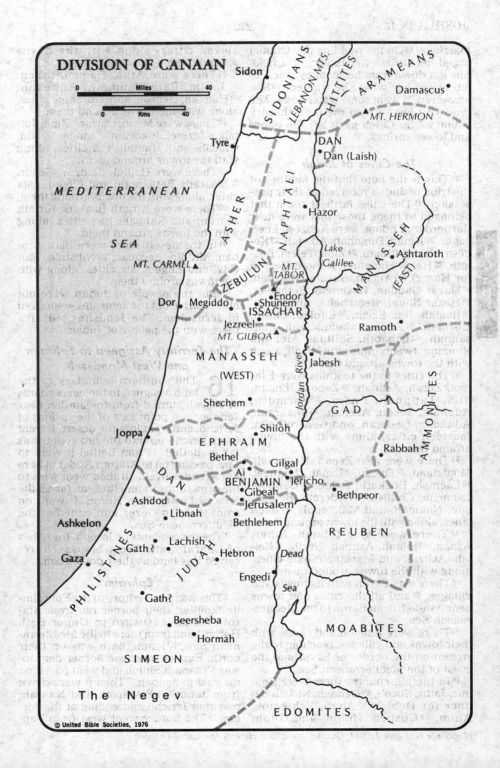

DIVISION OF CANAAN

Miles 0 — 40

Kms 0 — 40

MEDITERRANEAN

SEA

MT. CARMEL ▲

SIDONIANS

LEBANON MTS.

HITTITES

ARAMEANS

Sidon

Tyre

Damascus

▲ MT. HERMON

DAN

Dan (Laish)

ASHER

NAPHTALI

Hazor

MANASSEH (EAST)

Ashtaroth

Lake Galilee

ZEBULUN

MT. TABOR ▲

Endor

Shunem

Dor   Megiddo

ISSACHAR

Jezreel

MT. GILBOA ▲

Ramoth

MANASSEH

(WEST)

Jabesh

Shechem

GAD

Jordan River

Joppa

Shiloh

EPHRAIM

Bethel

DAN

Ai

BENJAMIN

Gilgal

Jericho

Rabbah

AMMONITES

Gibeah

Ashdod

Libnah

Jerusalem

Bethpeor

Bethlehem

REUBEN

Ashkelon

Lachish

Hebron

Gath?

Dead

Gaza

JUDAH

Engedi

Sea

PHILISTINES

Gath?

Beersheba

Hormah

MOABITES

SIMEON

The Negev

EDOMITES

© United Bible Societies, 1976

marriage. 18 On the wedding day Othniel urged her *i* to ask her father for a field. She got down from her donkey, and Caleb asked her what she wanted. 19 She answered, "I want some water holes. The land you have given me is in the dry country." So Caleb gave her the upper and lower springs.

The Cities of Judah

20 This is the land that the families of the tribe of Judah received as their possession. 21 The cities farthest south that belonged to them, those that were near the border of Edom, were Kabzeel, Eder, Jagur, 22 Kinah, Dimonah, Adadah, 23 Kedesh, Hazor, Ithnan, 24 Ziph, Telem, Bealoth, 25 Hazor Hadattah, Kerioth Hezron (or Hazor), 26 Amam, Shema, Moladah, 27 Hazar Gaddah, Heshmon, Bethpelet, 28 Hazar Shual, Beersheba, Biziothiah, 29 Baalah, Iim, Ezem, 30 Eltolad, Chesil, Hormah, 31 Ziklag, Madmannah, Sansannah, 32 Lebaoth, Shilhim, Ain, and Rimmon: twenty-nine cities in all, along with the towns around them.

33 The cities in the foothills were Eshtaol, Zorah, Ashnah, 34 Zanoah, Engannim, Tappuah, Enam, 35 Jarmuth, Adullam, Socoh, Azekah, 36 Shaaraim, Adithaim, Gederah, and Gederothaim: fourteen cities, along with the towns around them.

37 There were also Zenan, Hadashah, Migdalgad, 38 Dilean, Mizpah, Joktheel, 39 Lachish, Bozkath, Eglon, 40 Cabbon, Lahmam, Chitlish, 41 Gederoth, Bethdagon, Naamah, and Makkedah: sixteen cities, along with the towns around them.

42 There were also Libnah, Ether, Ashan, 43 Iphtah, Ashnah, Nezib, 44 Keilah, Achzib, and Mareshah: nine cities, along with the towns around them.

45 There was Ekron with its towns and villages, 46 and all the cities and towns near Ashdod, from Ekron to the Mediterranean Sea.

47 There were Ashdod and Gaza, with their towns and villages, reaching to the stream on the border of Egypt and the coast of the Mediterranean Sea.

48 In the hill country there were Shamir, Jattir, Socoh, 49 Dannah, Kiriath Sepher (or Debir), 50 Anab, Eshtemoa, Anim, 51 Goshen, Holon, and Giloh:

eleven cities, along with the towns around them.

52 There were Arab, Dumah, Eshan, 53 Janim, Beth Tappuah, Aphekah, 54 Humtah, Hebron, and Zior: nine cities, along with the towns around them.

55 There were Maon, Carmel, Ziph, Juttah, 56 Jezreel, Jokdeam, Zanoah, 57 Kain, Gibeah, and Timnah: ten cities, along with the towns around them.

58 There were Halhul, Bethzur, Gedor, 59 Maarath, Bethanoth, and Eltekon: six cities, along with the towns around them.

60 There were Kiriath Baal (or Kiriath Jearim) and Rabbah: two cities, along with the towns around them.

61 In the desert there were Beth Arabah, Middin, Secacah, 62 Nibshan, Salt City, and Engedi: six cities, along with the towns around them.

63 But the people of Judah were not able to drive out the Jebusites, who lived in Jerusalem. The Jebusites still live there with the people of Judah.

The Territory Assigned to Ephraim and West Manasseh

16 The southern boundary of the land assigned to the descendants of Joseph started from the Jordan near Jericho, at a point east of the springs of Jericho, and went into the desert. It went from Jericho up into the hill country as far as Bethel. 2 From Bethel it went to Luz, passing on to Ataroth Addar, where the Archites lived. 3 It then went west to the area of the Japhletites, as far as the area of Lower Beth Horon. It went on from there to Gezer and ended at the Mediterranean Sea.

4 The descendants of Joseph, the tribes of Ephraim and West Manasseh, received this land as their possession.

Ephraim

5 This was the territory of the Ephraimite families: their border ran from Ataroth Addar eastward to Upper Beth Horon, 6 and from there to the Mediterranean Sea. Michmethath was on their north. East of there the border bent toward Taanath Shiloh and went past it on the east to Janoah. 7 Then it went down from Janoah to Ataroth and Naarah, reaching Jericho and ending at the Jordan. 8 The border went west from Tap-

---

i Probable text (see Jg 1.14) Othniel urged her; Hebrew she urged Othniel.

puah to the stream Kanah and ended at the Mediterranean Sea. This was the land given to the families of the tribe of Ephraim as their possession, 9 along with some towns and villages that were within the borders of Manasseh, but given to the Ephraimites. 10 But they did not drive out the Canaanites who lived in Gezer, so the Canaanites have lived among the Ephraimites to this day, but they have been forced to work as slaves.

West Manasseh

17 A part of the land west of the Jordan was assigned to some of the families descended from Joseph's older son Manasseh. Machir, the father of Gilead, was Manasseh's oldest son and a military hero, so Gilead and Bashan, east of the Jordan, were assigned to him. 2 Land west of the Jordan was assigned to the rest of the families of Manasseh: Abiezer, Helek, Asriel, Shechem, Hepher, and Shemida. These were male descendants of Manasseh son of Joseph, and they were heads of families. 3 Zelophehad, son of Hepher, son of Gilead, son of Machir, son of Manasseh, did not have any sons, but only daughters. Their names were Mahlah, Noah, Hoglah, Milcah, and Tirzah. 4 They went to Eleazar the priest and to Joshua son of Nun and to the leaders, and said, "The LORD commanded Moses to give us, as well as our male relatives, a part of the land to possess." So, as the LORD had commanded, they were given land along with their male relatives. 5 This is why Manasseh received ten shares in addition to Gilead and Bashan on the east side of the Jordan, 6 since his female descendants as well as his male descendants were assigned land. The land of Gilead was assigned to the rest of the descendants of Manasseh.

7 The territory of Manasseh reached from Asher to Michmethath, east of Shechem. The border then went south to include the people of Entappuah. 8 The land around Tappuah belonged to Manasseh, but the town of Tappuah, on the border, belonged to the descendants of Ephraim. 9 The border then went down to the stream Kanah. The cities south of the stream belonged to Ephraim, even though they were in the territory of Ma-

nasseh. The border of Manasseh proceeded along the north side of the stream and ended at the Mediterranean Sea. 10 Ephraim was to the south, and Manasseh was to the north, with the Mediterranean Sea as their western border. Asher was to the northwest, and Issachar to the northeast. 11 Within the territories of Issachar and Asher, Manasseh possessed Beth Shan and Ibleam, along with their surrounding towns, as well as Dor (the one on the coast),j Endor, Taanach, Megiddo, and their surrounding towns. 12 The people of Manasseh, however, were not able to drive out the people living in those cities, so the Canaanites continued to live there. 13 Even when the Israelites became stronger, they did not drive out all the Canaanites, but they did force them to work for them.

Ephraim and West Manasseh Request More Land

14 The descendants of Joseph said to Joshua, "Why have you given us only one part of the land to possess as our own? There are very many of us because the LORD has blessed us."

15 Joshua answered, "If there are so many of you and the hill country of Ephraim is too small for you, then go into the forests and clear ground for yourselves in the land of the Perizzites and the Rephaim."

16 They replied, "The hill country is not big enough for us, but the Canaanites in the plains have iron chariots, both those who live in Beth Shan and its surrounding towns and those who live in Jezreel Valley."

17 Joshua said to the tribes of Ephraim and West Manasseh, "There are indeed many of you, and you are very powerful. You shall have more than one share. 18 The hill country will be yours. Even though it is a forest, you will clear it and take possession of it from one end to the other. As for the Canaanites, you will drive them out, even though they do have iron chariots and are a strong people."

The Division of the Rest of the Land

18 After they had conquered the land, the entire community of Israel assembled at Shiloh and set up the Tent of the LORD's presence. 2 There were

j Probable text Dor (the one on the coast); Hebrew unclear.

still seven tribes of the people of Israel who had not yet been assigned their share of the land. 3 So Joshua said to the people of Israel, "How long are you going to wait before you go in and take the land that the LORD, the God of your ancestors, has given you? 4 Let me have three men from each tribe. I will send them out over the whole country to map out the territory that they would like to have as their possession. Then they are to come back to me. 5 The land will be divided among them in seven parts; Judah will stay in its territory in the south, and Joseph in its territory in the north. 6 Write down a description of these seven divisions and bring it to me. Then I will draw lots*k* to consult the LORD our God for you. 7 The Levites, however, will not receive a share of the land with the rest of you, because their share is to serve as the LORD's priests. And of course, the tribes of Gad, Reuben, and East Manasseh have already received their land east of the Jordan, which Moses, the LORD's servant, gave to them."

8 The men went on their way to map out the land after Joshua had given them these instructions: "Go all over the land and map it out, and come back to me. And then here in Shiloh I will consult the LORD for you by drawing lots." 9 So the men went all over the land and set down in writing how they divided it into seven parts, making a list of the towns. Then they went back to Joshua in the camp at Shiloh. 10 Joshua drew lots to consult the LORD for them, and assigned each of the remaining tribes of Israel a certain part of the land.

The Territory Assigned to Benjamin

11 The territory belonging to the families of the tribe of Benjamin was the first to be assigned. Their land lay between the tribes of Judah and Joseph. 12 On the north their border began at the Jordan and then went up the slope north of Jericho and westward through the hill country as far as the desert of Bethaven. 13 The border then went to the slope on the south side of Luz (also called Bethel), then down to Ataroth Addar, on the mountain south of Lower Beth Horon. 14 The border then went in another direction, turning south from the western side

of this mountain and going to Kiriath Baal (or Kiriath Jearim), which belongs to the tribe of Judah. This was the western border. 15 The southern border started on the edge of Kiriath Jearim and went*l* to the Springs of Nephtoah. 16 It then went down to the foot of the mountain that overlooks Hinnom Valley, at the north end of Rephaim Valley. It then went south through Hinnom Valley, south of the Jebusite ridge, toward Enrogel. 17 It then turned north to Enshemesh and then on to Geliloth, opposite Adummim Pass. The border then went down to the Stone of Bohan (Bohan was a son of Reuben) 18 and passed north of the ridge overlooking the Jordan Valley. It then went down into the valley, 19 passing north of the ridge of Beth Hoglah, and ended at the northern inlet on the Dead Sea, where the Jordan River empties into it. This was the southern border. 20 The Jordan was the eastern border. These were the borders of the land which the families of the tribe of Benjamin received as their possession.

21 The cities belonging to the families of the tribe of Benjamin were Jericho, Beth Hoglah, Emek Keziz, 22 Beth Arabah, Zemaraim, Bethel, 23 Avvim, Parah, Ophrah, 24 Chepharammoni, Ophni, and Geba: twelve cities, along with the towns around them. 25 There were also Gibeon, Ramah, Beeroth, 26 Mizpah, Chephirah, Mozah, 27 Rekem, Irpeel, Taralah, 28 Zela, Haeleph, Jebus (or Jerusalem), Gibeah, and Kiriath Jearim: fourteen cities, along with the towns around them. This is the land which the families of the tribe of Benjamin received as their possession.

The Territory Assigned to Simeon

19 The second assignment made was for the families of the tribe of Simeon. Its territory extended into the land assigned to the tribe of Judah. 2 It included Beersheba, Sheba, Moladah, 3 Hazar Shual, Balah, Ezem, 4 Eltolad, Bethul, Hormah, 5 Ziklag, Beth Marcaboth, Hazar Susah, 6 Beth Lebaoth, and Sharuhen: thirteen cities, along with the towns around them.

7 There were also Ain, Rimmon, Ether, and Ashan: four cities, along with the towns around them. 8 This included all the towns around these cities as far as

---

k DRAW LOTS: *See 14.2.*   *l Probable text* and went; *Hebrew* and went westward.

Baalath Beer (or Ramah), in the south. This was the land which the families of the tribe of Simeon received as their possession. 9 Since Judah's assignment was larger than was needed, part of its territory was given to the tribe of Simeon.

The Territory Assigned to Zebulun

10 The third assignment made was for the families of the tribe of Zebulun. The land which they received reached as far as Sarid. 11 From there the border went west to Mareal, touching Dabbesheth and the stream east of Jokneam. 12 On the other side of Sarid it went east to the border of Chisloth Tabor, then to Daberath and up to Japhia. 13 It continued east from there to Gath Hepher and Ethkazin, turning in the direction of Neah on the way to Rimmon. 14 On the north the border turned toward Hannathon, ending at Iphtahel Valley. 15 It included Kattath, Nahalal, Shimron, Idalah, and Bethlehem: twelve cities, along with the towns around them. 16 These cities and their towns were in the land which the families of the tribe of Zebulun received as their possession.

The Territory Assigned to Issachar

17 The fourth assignment made was for the families of the tribe of Issachar. 18 Its area included Jezreel, Chesulloth, Shunem, 19 Hapharaim, Shion, Anaharath, 20 Rabbith, Kishion, Ebez, 21 Remeth, Engannim, Enhaddah, and Bethpazzez. 22 The border also touched Tabor, Shahazumah, and Beth Shemesh, ending at the Jordan. It included sixteen cities along with the towns around them. 23 These cities and their towns were in the land which the families of the tribe of Issachar received as their possession.

The Territory Assigned to Asher

24 The fifth assignment made was for the families of the tribe of Asher. 25 Its area included Helkath, Hali, Beten, Achshaph, 26 Allam Melech, Amad, and Mishal. On the west it touched Carmel and Shihor Libnath. 27 As it turned east, the border went to Bethdagon, touching Zebulun and Iphtahel Valley on the way north to Bethemek and Neiel. It continued north to Cabul, 28 Ebron, Rehob, Hammon, and Kanah, as far as Sidon.

29 The border then turned to Ramah, reaching the fortified city of Tyre; then it turned to Hosah and ended at the Mediterranean Sea. It included Mahalab, Achzib, 30 Ummah, Aphek, and Rehob: twenty-two cities, along with the towns around them. 31 These cities and their towns were in the land which the families of the tribe of Asher received as their possession.

The Territory Assigned to Naphtali

32 The sixth assignment made was for the families of the tribe of Naphtali. 33 Its border went from Heleph to the oak in Zaanannim, on to Adaminekeb and to Jamnia, as far as Lakkum, and ended at the Jordan. 34 There the border turned west to Aznoth Tabor, from there to Hukkok, touching Zebulun on the south, Asher on the west, and the Jordan[m] on the east. 35 The fortified cities were Ziddim, Zer, Hammath, Rakkath, Chinnereth, 36 Adamah, Ramah, Hazor, 37 Kedesh, Edrei, Enhazor, 38 Yiron, Migdalel, Horem, Bethanath, and Beth Shemesh: nineteen cities, along with the towns around them. 39 These cities and their towns were in the land which the families of the tribe of Naphtali received as their possession.

The Territory Assigned to Dan

40 The seventh assignment made was for the families of the tribe of Dan. 41 Its area included Zorah, Eshtaol, Irshemesh, 42 Shaalbim, Aijalon, Ithlah, 43 Elon, Timnah, Ekron, 44 Eltekeh, Gibbethon, Baalath, 45 Jehud, Beneberak, Gathrimmon, 46 Mejarkon, and Rakkon, as well as the territory around Joppa. 47 When the people of Dan lost their land, they went to Laish and attacked it. They captured it, killed its people, and claimed it for themselves. They settled there and changed the name of the city from Laish to Dan, naming it after their ancestor Dan. 48 These cities and their towns were in the land which the families of the tribe of Dan received as their possession.

The Final Assignment of the Land

49 When the people of Israel finished dividing up the land, they gave Joshua son of Nun a part of the land as his own. 50 As the LORD had commanded, they

m One ancient translation the Jordan; Hebrew Judah at the Jordan.

gave him the city he asked for: Timnath Serah, in the hill country of Ephraim. He rebuilt the city and settled there.

51 Eleazar the priest, Joshua son of Nun, and the leaders of the families of the tribes of Israel assigned these parts of the land by drawing lots[n] to consult the LORD at Shiloh, at the entrance of the Tent of the LORD's presence. In this way they finished dividing the land.

The Cities of Refuge

20 Then the LORD told Joshua 2 to say to the people of Israel, "Choose the cities of refuge that I had Moses tell you about. 3 If any of you accidentally kills someone, you can go there and escape the one who is looking for revenge. 4 You can run away to one of these cities, go to the place of judgment at the entrance to the city, and explain to the leaders what happened. Then they will let you into the city and give you a place to live in, so that you can stay there. 5 If the one looking for revenge follows you there, the people of the city must not hand you over to that one. They must protect you because you killed the person accidentally and not out of anger. 6 You may stay in the city until you have received a public trial and until the death of the man who is then the High Priest. Then you may go back home to your own town, from which you had run away."

7 So, on the west side of the Jordan they set aside Kedesh in Galilee, in the hill country of Naphtali; Shechem, in the hill country of Ephraim; and Hebron, in the hill country of Judah. 8 East of the Jordan, on the desert plateau east of Jericho, they chose Bezer in the territory of Reuben; Ramoth in Gilead, in the territory of Gad; and Golan in Bashan, in the territory of Manasseh. 9 These were the cities of refuge chosen for all the people of Israel and for any foreigner living among them. Any who killed a person accidentally could find protection there from the one looking for revenge; they could not be killed unless they had first received a public trial.

The Cities of the Levites

21 The leaders of the Levite families went to Eleazar the priest, Joshua son of Nun, and to the heads of the families of all the tribes of Israel. 2 There at Shiloh in the land of Canaan they said to them, "The LORD commanded through Moses that we were to be given cities to live in, as well as pasture land around them for our livestock." 3 So in accordance with the LORD's command the people of Israel gave the Levites certain cities and pasture lands out of their own territories.

4 The families of the Levite clan of Kohath were the first to be assigned cities. The families who were descended from Aaron the priest were assigned thirteen cities from the territories of Judah, Simeon, and Benjamin. 5 The rest of the clan of Kohath was assigned ten cities from the territories of Ephraim, Dan, and West Manasseh.

6 The clan of Gershon was assigned thirteen cities from the territories of Issachar, Asher, Naphtali, and East Manasseh.

7 The families of the clan of Merari were assigned twelve cities from the territories of Reuben, Gad, and Zebulun.

8 By drawing lots,[n] the people of Israel assigned these cities and their pasture lands to the Levites, as the LORD had commanded through Moses.

9 These are the names of the cities from the territories of Judah and Simeon which were given 10 to the descendants of Aaron who were of the clan of Kohath, which was descended from Levi. Their assignment was the first to be made. 11 They were given the city of Arba (Arba was Anak's father), now called Hebron, in the hill country of Judah, along with the pasture land surrounding it. 12 However, the fields of the city, as well as its towns, had already been given to Caleb son of Jephunneh as his possession.

13 In addition to Hebron (one of the cities of refuge), the following cities were assigned to the descendants of Aaron the priest: Libnah, 14 Jattir, Eshtemoa, 15 Holon, Debir, 16 Ain, Juttah, and Beth Shemesh, with their pasture lands: nine cities from the tribes of Judah and Simeon. 17 From the territory of Benjamin they were given four cities: Gibeon, Geba, 18 Anathoth, and Almon, with their pasture lands. 19 Thirteen cities in all, with their pasture lands, were given to the priests, the descendants of Aaron.

[n] DRAWING LOTS: See 14.2.

20 The other families of the Levite clan of Kohath were assigned some cities from the territory of Ephraim. 21 They were given four cities: Shechem and its pasture lands in the hill country of Ephraim (one of the cities of refuge), Gezer, 22 Kibzaim, and Beth Horon, with their pasture lands. 23 From the territory of Dan they were given four cities: Eltekeh, Gibbethon, 24 Aijalon, and Gathrimmon, with their pasture lands. 25 From the territory of West Manasseh they were given two cities: Taanach and Gathrimmon, with their pasture lands. 26 These families of the clan of Kohath received ten cities in all, with their pasture lands.

27 Another group of Levites, the clan of Gershon, received from the territory of East Manasseh two cities: Golan in Bashan (one of the cities of refuge) and Beeshterah, with their pasture lands. 28 From the territory of Issachar they received four cities: Kishion, Daberath, 29 Jarmuth, and Engannim, with their pasture lands. 30 From the territory of Asher they received four cities: Mishal, Abdon, 31 Helkath, and Rehob, with their pasture lands. 32 From the territory of Naphtali they received three cities: Kedesh in Galilee, with its pasture lands (one of the cities of refuge), Hammoth Dor, and Kartan, with their pasture lands. 33 The various families of the clan of Gershon received a total of thirteen cities with their pasture lands.

34 The rest of the Levites, the clan of Merari, received from the territory of Zebulun four cities: Jokneam, Kartah, 35 Dimnah, and Nahalal, with their pasture lands. 36 From the territory of Reuben they received four cities: Bezer, Jahaz, 37 Kedemoth, and Mephaath, with their pasture lands. 38 From the tribe of Gad they received four cities: Ramoth in Gilead, with its pasture lands (one of the cities of refuge), Mahanaim, 39 Heshbon, and Jazer, with their pasture lands. 40 So the clan of Merari was assigned a total of twelve cities.

41-42 From the land that the people of Israel possessed, a total of forty-eight cities, with the pasture lands around them, was given to the Levites.

Israel Takes Possession of the Land

43 So the LORD gave to Israel all the land that he had solemnly promised their ancestors he would give them. When they had taken possession of it, they settled down there. 44 The LORD gave them peace throughout the land, just as he had promised their ancestors. Not one of all their enemies had been able to stand against them, because the LORD gave the Israelites the victory over all their enemies. 45 The LORD kept every one of the promises that he had made to the people of Israel.

Joshua Sends the Eastern Tribes Home

22 Then Joshua called together the people of the tribes of Reuben, Gad, and East Manasseh. 2 He said to them, "You have done everything that Moses the LORD's servant ordered you to do, and you have obeyed all my commands. 3 All this time you have never once deserted the other Israelites. You have been careful to obey the commands of the LORD your God. 4 Now, as he promised, the LORD your God has given the other Israelites peace. So go back home to the land which you claimed for your own, the land on the east side of the Jordan, that Moses, the LORD's servant, gave you. 5 Make sure you obey the law that Moses commanded you: love the LORD your God, do his will, obey his commandments, be faithful to him, and serve him with all your heart and soul."

6-8 Joshua sent them home with his blessing and with these words: "You are going back home very rich, with a lot of livestock, silver, gold, bronze, iron, and many clothes. Share with your fellow tribesmen what you took from your enemies." Then they left for home.

Moses had given land east of the Jordan to one half of the tribe of Manasseh, but to the other half Joshua had given land west of the Jordan, along with the other tribes.

9 So the people of the tribes of Reuben, Gad, and East Manasseh went back home. They left the rest of the people of Israel at Shiloh in the land of Canaan and started out for their own land, the land of Gilead, which they had taken as the LORD had commanded them through Moses.

The Altar by the Jordan

10 When the tribes of Reuben, Gad, and East Manasseh arrived at Geliloth, still

on the west side° of the Jordan, they built a large, impressive altar there by the river. 11 The rest of the people of Israel were told, "Listen! The people of the tribes of Reuben, Gad, and East Manasseh have built an altar at Geliloth, on our side of the Jordan!" 12 When the people of Israel heard this, the whole community came together at Shiloh to go to war against the eastern tribes.

13 Then the people of Israel sent Phinehas, the son of Eleazar the priest, to the people of the tribes of Reuben, Gad, and East Manasseh in the land of Gilead. 14 Ten leading men went with Phinehas, one from each of the western tribes and each one the head of a family among the clans. 15 They came to the land of Gilead, to the people of Reuben, Gad, and East Manasseh, 16 and speaking for the whole community of the LORD, they said to them, "Why have you done this evil thing against the God of Israel? You have rebelled against the LORD by building this altar for yourselves! You are no longer following him! 17 Remember our sin at Peor, when the LORD punished his own people with an epidemic? We are still suffering because of that. Wasn't that sin enough? 18 Are you going to refuse to follow him now? If you rebel against the LORD today, he will be angry with everyone in Israel tomorrow. 19 Now then, if your land is not fit to worship in, come over into the LORD's land, where his Tent is. Claim some land among us. But don't rebel against the LORD or make rebels out of us by building an altar in addition to the altar of the LORD our God. 20 Remember how Achan son of Zerah refused to obey the command about the things condemned to destruction; the whole community of Israel was punished for that. Achan was not the only one who died because of his sin."

21 The people of the tribes of Reuben, Gad, and East Manasseh answered the heads of the families of the western tribes: 22 "The Mighty One is God! He is the LORD! The Mighty One is God! He is the LORD! He knows why we did this, and we want you to know too! If we rebelled and did not keep faith with the LORD, do not let us live any longer! 23 If we disobeyed the LORD and built our own altar to burn sacrifices on or to use for grain

offerings or fellowship offerings, let the LORD himself punish us. 24 No! We did it because we were afraid that in the future your descendants would say to ours, 'What do you have to do with the LORD, the God of Israel? 25 He made the Jordan a boundary between us and you people of Reuben and Gad. You have nothing to do with the LORD.' Then your descendants might make our descendants stop worshiping the LORD. 26 So we built an altar, not to burn sacrifices or make offerings, 27 but instead, as a sign for our people and yours, and for the generations after us, that we do indeed worship the LORD before his sacred Tent with our offerings to be burned and with sacrifices and fellowship offerings. This was to keep your descendants from saying that ours have nothing to do with the LORD. 28 It was our idea that, if this should ever happen, our descendants could say, 'Look! Our ancestors made an altar just like the LORD's altar. It was not for burning offerings or for sacrifice, but as a sign for our people and yours.' 29 We would certainly not rebel against the LORD or stop following him now by building an altar to burn offerings on or for grain offerings or sacrifices. We would not build any other altar than the altar of the LORD our God that stands in front of the Tent of his presence."

30 Phinehas the priest and the ten leading men of the community who were with him, the heads of families of the western tribes, heard what the people of the tribes of Reuben, Gad, and East Manasseh had to say, and they were satisfied. 31 Phinehas, the son of Eleazar the priest, said to them, "Now we know that the LORD is with us. You have not rebelled against him, and so you have saved the people of Israel from the LORD's punishment."

32 Then Phinehas and the leaders left the people of Reuben and Gad in the land of Gilead and went back to Canaan, to the people of Israel, and reported to them. 33 The Israelites were satisfied and praised God. They no longer talked about going to war to devastate the land where the people of Reuben and Gad had settled.

34 The people of Reuben and Gad said, "This altar is a witness to all of us that the

---

° still on the west side; or on the east side.

LORD is God." And so they named it "Witness."

Joshua's Farewell Address

23 Much later the LORD gave Israel security from their enemies around them. By that time Joshua was very old, 2 so he called all Israel, the elders, leaders, judges, and officers of the people, and said, "I am very old now. 3 You have seen everything that the LORD your God has done to all these nations because of you. The LORD your God has been fighting for you. 4 I have assigned as the possession of your tribes the land of the nations that are still left, as well as of all the nations that I have already conquered, from the Jordan River in the east to the Mediterranean Sea in the west. 5 The LORD your God will make them retreat from you, and he will drive them away as you advance. You shall have their land, as the LORD your God has promised you. 6 So be careful to obey and do everything that is written in the book of the Law of Moses. Do not neglect any part of it, 7 and then you will not associate with these peoples left among you or speak the names of their gods or use those names in taking vows or worship those gods or bow down to them. 8 Instead, be faithful to the LORD, as you have been till now. 9 The LORD has driven great and powerful nations out as you advanced, and no one has ever been able to stand against you. 10 Any one of you can make a thousand men run away, because the LORD your God is fighting for you, just as he promised. 11 Be careful, then, to love the LORD your God. 12 If you are disloyal and join with the nations that are still left among you and intermarry with them, 13 you may be sure that the LORD your God will no longer drive these nations out as you advance. Rather, they will be as dangerous for you as a trap or a pit and as painful as a whip on your back or thorns in your eyes. And this will last until none of you are left in this good land which the LORD your God has given you.

14 "Now my time has come to die. Every one of you knows in his heart and soul that the LORD your God has given you all the good things that he promised. Every promise he made has been kept; not one has failed. 15 But just as he kept every promise that he made to you, so he will carry out every threat. 16 If you do not keep the covenant which the LORD your God commanded you to keep and if you serve and worship other gods, then in his anger he will punish you, and soon none of you will be left in this good land that he has given you."

Joshua Speaks to the People at Shechem

24 Joshua gathered all the tribes of Israel together at Shechem. He called the elders, the leaders, the judges, and the officers of Israel, and they came into the presence of God. 2 Joshua said to all the people, "This is what the LORD, the God of Israel, has to say: 'Long ago your ancestors lived on the other side of the Euphrates River and worshiped other gods. One of those ancestors was Terah, the father of Abraham and Nahor. 3 Then I took Abraham, your ancestor, from the land across the Euphrates and led him through the whole land of Canaan. I gave him many descendants. I gave him Isaac, 4 and to Isaac I gave Jacob and Esau. I gave Esau the hill country of Edom as his possession, but your ancestor Jacob and his children went down to Egypt. 5 Later I sent Moses and Aaron, and I brought great trouble on Egypt. But I led you out; 6 I brought your ancestors out of Egypt, and the Egyptians pursued them with chariots and cavalry. But when your ancestors got to the Red Sea 7 they cried out to me for help, and I put darkness between them and the Egyptians. I made the sea come rolling over the Egyptians and drown them. You know what I did to Egypt.

" 'You lived in the desert a long time. 8 Then I brought you to the land of the Amorites, who lived on the east side of the Jordan. They fought you, but I gave you victory over them. You took their land, and I destroyed them as you advanced. 9 Then the king of Moab, Balak son of Zippor, fought against you. He sent word to Balaam son of Beor and asked him to put a curse on you. 10 But I would not listen to Balaam, so he blessed you, and in this way I rescued you from Balak. 11 You crossed the Jordan and came to Jericho. The men of Jericho fought you, as did the Amorites, the Perizzites, the Canaanites, the Hittites, the

Girgashites, the Hivites, and the Jebusites. But I gave you victory over them all. 12 As you advanced, I threw them into panic in order to drive out the two Amorite kings. Your swords and bows had nothing to do with it. 13 I gave you a land that you had never worked and cities that you had not built. Now you are living there and eating grapes from vines that you did not plant, and olives from trees that you did not plant.'

14 "Now then," Joshua continued, "honor the LORD and serve him sincerely and faithfully. Get rid of the gods which your ancestors used to worship in Mesopotamia and in Egypt, and serve only the LORD. 15 If you are not willing to serve him, decide today whom you will serve, the gods your ancestors worshiped in Mesopotamia or the gods of the Amorites, in whose land you are now living. As for my family and me, we will serve the LORD."

16 The people replied, "We would never leave the LORD to serve other gods! 17 The LORD our God brought our fathers and us out of slavery in Egypt, and we saw the miracles that he performed. He kept us safe wherever we went among all the nations through which we passed. 18 As we advanced into this land, the LORD drove out all the Amorites who lived here. So we also will serve the LORD; he is our God."

19 Joshua said to the people, "But you may not be able to serve the LORD. He is a holy God and will not forgive your sins. He will tolerate no rivals, 20 and if you leave him to serve foreign gods, he will turn against you and punish you. He will destroy you, even though he was good to you before."

21 The people said to Joshua, "No! We will serve the LORD."

22 Joshua told them, "You are your own witnesses to the fact that you have chosen to serve the LORD."

"Yes," they said, "we are witnesses."

p for; or with.

23 "Then get rid of those foreign gods that you have," he demanded, "and pledge your loyalty to the LORD, the God of Israel."

24 The people then said to Joshua, "We will serve the LORD our God. We will obey his commands."

25 So Joshua made a covenant for p the people that day, and there at Shechem he gave them laws and rules to follow. 26 Joshua wrote these commands in the book of the Law of God. Then he took a large stone and set it up under the oak tree in the LORD's sanctuary. 27 He said to all the people, "This stone will be our witness. It has heard all the words that the LORD has spoken to us. So it will be a witness against you, to keep you from rebelling against your God." 28 Then Joshua sent the people away, and everyone returned to their own part of the land.

Joshua and Eleazar Die

29 After that, the LORD's servant Joshua son of Nun died at the age of a hundred and ten. 30 They buried him on his own land at Timnath Serah in the hill country of Ephraim north of Mount Gaash.

31 As long as Joshua lived, the people of Israel served the LORD, and after his death they continued to do so as long as those leaders were alive who had seen for themselves everything that the LORD had done for Israel.

32 The body of Joseph, which the people of Israel had brought from Egypt, was buried at Shechem, in the piece of land that Jacob had bought from the sons of Hamor, the father of Shechem, for a hundred pieces of silver. This land was inherited by Joseph's descendants.

33 Eleazar son of Aaron died and was buried at Gibeah, the town in the hill country of Ephraim which had been given to his son Phinehas.

The Book of
JUDGES

Introduction

The Book of Judges is composed of stories from the lawless period of Israel's history between the invasion of Canaan and the establishment of the monarchy. These stories are about the exploits of national heroes called "judges," most of whom were military leaders rather than judges in the legal sense of the word. One of the better known of them is Samson, whose deeds are recorded in chapters 13—16.

The great lesson of the book is that Israel's survival depended on loyalty to God, while disloyalty always led to disaster. But there was more than this: even when the nation was disloyal to God and disaster came, God was always ready to save his people when they repented and turned to him again.

Outline of Contents

The Tribes of Judah and Simeon Capture Adonibezek

1 After Joshua's death the people of Israel asked the LORD, "Which of our tribes should be the first to go and attack the Canaanites?"

2 The LORD answered, "The tribe of Judah will go first. I am giving them control of the land."

3 The people of Judah said to the people of Simeon, "Go with us into the territory assigned to us, and we will fight the Canaanites together. Then we will go with you into the territory assigned to you." So the tribes of Simeon 4 and Judah went into battle together. The LORD gave them victory over the Canaanites and the Perizzites, and they defeated ten thousand men at Bezek. 5 They found Adonibezek there and fought him. 6 He ran away, but they chased him, caught him, and cut off his thumbs and big toes. 7 Adonibezek said, "Seventy kings with their thumbs and big toes cut off have picked up scraps under my table. God has now done to me what I did to them." He was taken to Jerusalem, where he died.

The Tribe of Judah Conquers Jerusalem and Hebron

8 The people of Judah attacked Jerusalem and captured it. They killed its people and set fire to the city. 9 After this they went on to fight the Canaanites who lived in the hill country, in the foothills, and in the dry country to the south. 10 They marched against the Canaanites living in the city of Hebron, which used to be called Kiriath Arba. There they defeated the clans of Sheshai, Ahiman, and Talmai.

Othniel Conquers the City of Debir

(Joshua 15.13-19)

11 From there the men of Judah marched against the city of Debir, at that time called Kiriath Sepher. 12 One of them, called Caleb, said, "I will give my daughter Achsah in marriage to the man who succeeds in capturing Kiriath Sepher." 13 Othniel, the son of Caleb's younger brother Kenaz, captured the city, so Caleb gave him his daughter Achsah in marriage. 14 On the wedding day Othniel urged her a to ask her father for a field. She got down from her donkey, and Caleb asked her what she wanted. 15 She answered, "I want some water holes. The land you have given me is in the dry country." So Caleb gave her the upper and lower springs.

The Victories of the Tribes of Judah and Benjamin

16 The descendants of Moses' father-in-law, the Kenite, went on with the people

a Some ancient translations Othniel urged her; Hebrew she urged Othniel.

of Judah from Jericho, the city of palm trees, into the barren country south of Arad in Judah. There they settled among the Amalekites.*b* 17 The people of Judah went with the people of Simeon, and together they defeated the Canaanites who lived in the city of Zephath. They put a curse on the city, destroyed it, and named it Hormah.*c* 18-19 The LORD helped the people of Judah, and they took possession of the hill country. But they did not capture *d* Gaza, Ashkelon, or Ekron, with their surrounding territories. These people living along the coast had iron chariots, and so the people of Judah were not able to drive them out. 20 As Moses had commanded, Hebron was given to Caleb, who drove out of the city the three clans descended from Anak. 21 But the people of the tribe of Benjamin did not drive out the Jebusites living in Jerusalem, and the Jebusites have continued to live there with the people of Benjamin ever since.

The Tribes of Ephraim and Manasseh Conquer Bethel

22-23 The tribes of Ephraim and Manasseh went to attack the city of Bethel, at that time called Luz. The LORD helped them. They sent spies to the city, 24 who saw a man leaving and said to him, "Show us how to get into the city, and we won't hurt you." 25 So he showed them, and the people of Ephraim and Manasseh killed everyone in the city, except this man and his family. 26 He later went to the land of the Hittites, built a city there, and named it Luz, which is still its name.

People Who Were Not Driven Out by the Israelites

27 The tribe of Manasseh did not drive out the people living in the cities of Beth Shan, Taanach, Dor, Ibleam, Megiddo, and the nearby towns; the Canaanites continued to live there. 28 When the Israelites became stronger, they forced the Canaanites to work for them, but still they did not drive them all out.

29 The tribe of Ephraim did not drive out the Canaanites living in the city of

Gezer, and so the Canaanites continued to live there with them.

30 The tribe of Zebulun did not drive out the people living in the cities of Kitron and Nahalal, and so the Canaanites continued to live there with them and were forced to work for them.

31 The tribe of Asher did not drive out the people living in the cities of Acco, Sidon, Ahlab, Achzib, Helbah, Aphek, and Rehob. 32 The people of Asher lived with the local Canaanites, since they had not been driven out.

33 The tribe of Naphtali did not drive out the people living in the cities of Beth Shemesh and Bethanath. The people of Naphtali lived with the local Canaanites, but forced them to work for them.

34 The Amorites forced the people of the tribe of Dan into the hill country and did not let them come down to the plain. 35 The Amorites continued to live at Aijalon, Shaalbim, and Mount Heres, but the tribes of Ephraim and Manasseh kept them under their rule and forced them to work for them.

36 North of Sela, the Edomite*e* border ran through Akrabbim Pass.

The Angel of the LORD at Bochim

2 The angel of the LORD went from Gilgal to Bochim and said to the Israelites, "I took you out of Egypt and brought you to the land that I promised to your ancestors. I said, 'I will never break my covenant with you. 2 You must not make any covenant with the people who live in this land. You must tear down their altars.' But you have not done what I told you. You have done just the opposite! 3 So I tell you now that I will not drive these people out as you advance. They will be your enemies,*f* and you will be trapped by the worship of their gods." 4 When the angel had said this, all the people of Israel began to cry, 5 and that is why the place is called Bochim.*g* There they offered sacrifices to the LORD.

The Death of Joshua

6 Joshua sent the people of Israel on their way, and each man went to take possession of his own share of the land. 7 As long as Joshua lived, the people of

b Some ancient translations Amalekites; Hebrew people.   c HORMAH: This name in Hebrew means "destruction."   d One ancient translation But they did not capture; Hebrew And they captured.   e One ancient translation Edomite; Hebrew Amorite.   f Some ancient translations enemies; Hebrew sides.   g BOCHIM: This name in Hebrew means "those who cry."

ISRAEL AND THE PHILISTINES

The Philistines were a fierce tribal people who lived in southwest Palestine. Also referred to as the sea people, the Philistines probably migrated to central Palestine from the island of Crete in the Mediterranean Sea (Gn 10.14; Am 9.7). Their presence in their new home was so prominent in Bible times that the entire land of Palestine was named for the coastal territory, Philistia, which they occupied along the Mediterranean.

The Philistines are mentioned prominently in the Bible during two distinct periods of biblical history—in Abraham's time and during the period of the judges and Kings Saul and David from about 1200 to 1000 B.C.

The Philistines of Abraham's time were peaceful, in contrast to those who are mentioned later. The earlier Philistines were governed in a single city-state by one king, Abimelech (Gn 26.1, 8). But the later Philistines were ruled by five lords, who united the Philistines into a confederation of five city-states—Ashkelon, Ashdod, Ekron, Gath, and Gaza (Js 13.3; Jg 3.3).

Archaeologists have discovered weapons of iron used by the Philistines against the Israelites. So strong was their threat that the tribe of Dan retreated to the north away from their territory. In Samuel's time, the Philistines destroyed the city of Shiloh, which served as the center of worship for the Israelites.

The threat of the Philistines was one factor that led the Israelites to ask for a king and a united kingdom. The first Israelite ruler, King Saul, and his sons were killed in a battle with the Philistines (1 S 31.1–4). But Saul's successor David was able to defeat the Philistines and break their power (1 Ch 18.1).

Israel served the LORD, and even after his death they continued to do so as long as the leaders were alive who had seen for themselves all the great things that the LORD had done for Israel. 8 The LORD's servant Joshua son of Nun died at the age of a hundred and ten. 9 He was buried in his own part of the land at Timnath Serah in the hill country of Ephraim north of Mount Gaash. 10 That whole generation also died, and the next generation forgot the LORD and what he had done for Israel.

Israel Stops Worshiping the LORD

11 Then the people of Israel sinned against the LORD and began to serve the Baals. 12 They stopped worshiping the LORD, the God of their ancestors, the God who had brought them out of Egypt, and they began to worship other gods, the gods of the peoples around them. They bowed down to them and made the LORD angry. 13 They stopped worshiping the LORD and served the Baals and the Astartes. 14 And so the LORD became furious with Israel and let raiders attack and rob them. He let the enemies all around overpower them, and the Israelites could no longer protect themselves. 15 Every time they would go into battle, the LORD was against them, just as he had said he would be. They were in great distress.

16 Then the LORD gave the Israelites leaders who saved them from the raiders. 17 But the Israelites paid no attention to their leaders. Israel was unfaithful to the LORD and worshiped other gods. Their fathers had obeyed the LORD's commands, but this new generation soon stopped doing so. 18 Whenever the LORD gave Israel a leader, the LORD would help that leader and would save the people from their enemies as long as that leader lived. The LORD would have mercy on them because they groaned under their suffering and oppression. 19 But when the leader died, the people would return to the old ways and behave worse than the previous generation. They would serve and worship other gods, and stubbornly continue their own evil ways. 20 Then the LORD would become furious with Israel and say, "This nation has broken the covenant that I commanded their ancestors to keep. Because they have not obeyed me, 21 I will no longer drive out any of the nations that were still in the land when Joshua died. 22 I will use them to find out whether or not these Israelites will follow my ways, as their ancestors did." 23 So the LORD allowed these nations to remain in the land; he did not give Joshua victory over them, nor did he drive them out soon after Joshua's death.

The Nations Remaining in the Land

3 So then, the LORD left some nations in the land to test the Israelites who had not been through the wars in Canaan. 2 He did this only in order to teach each generation of Israelites about war, especially those who had never been in battle before. 3 Those left in the land were the five Philistine cities, all the Canaanites, the Sidonians, and the Hivites who lived in the Lebanon Mountains from Mount Baal Hermon as far as Hamath Pass. 4 They were to be a test for Israel, to find out whether or not the Israelites would obey the commands that the LORD had given their ancestors through Moses. 5 And so the people of Israel settled down among the Canaanites, the Hittites, the Amorites, the Perizzites, the Hivites, and the Jebusites. 6 They intermarried with them and worshiped their gods.

Othniel

7 The people of Israel forgot the LORD their God; they sinned against him and worshiped the idols of Baal and Asherah. 8 So the LORD became angry with Israel and let King Cushan Rishathaim of Mesopotamia conquer them. They were subject to him for eight years. 9 Then the Israelites cried out to the LORD, and he sent someone to free them. This was Othniel, the son of Caleb's younger brother Kenaz. 10 The spirit of the LORD came upon him, and he became Israel's leader. Othniel went to war, and the LORD gave him the victory over the king of Mesopotamia. 11 There was peace in the land for forty years, and then Othniel died.

Ehud

12 The people of Israel sinned against the LORD again. Because of this the LORD made King Eglon of Moab stronger than Israel. 13 Eglon joined the Ammonites and the Amalekites; they defeated Israel and captured Jericho, the city of palm trees. 14 The Israelites were subject to Eglon for eighteen years.

15 Then the Israelites cried out to the LORD, and he sent someone to free them. This was Ehud, a left-handed man, who was the son of Gera, from the tribe of Benjamin. The people of Israel sent Ehud to King Eglon of Moab with gifts for him. 16 Ehud had made himself a double-edged sword about a foot and a half long. He had it fastened on his right side under his clothes. 17 Then he took the gifts to Eglon, who was a very fat man. 18 When Ehud had given him the gifts, he told the men who had carried them to go back home. 19 But Ehud himself turned back at the carved stones near Gilgal, went back to Eglon, and said, "Your Majesty, I have a secret message for you."

So the king ordered his servants, "Leave us alone!" And they all went out. 20 Then, as the king was sitting there alone in his cool room on the roof, Ehud went over to him and said, "I have a message from God for you." The king stood up. 21 With his left hand Ehud took the sword from his right side and plunged it into the king's belly. 22 The whole sword went in, handle and all, and the fat covered it up. Ehud did not pull it out of the king's belly, and it stuck out behind, between his legs. h 23 Then Ehud went outside, closed the doors behind him, locked them, 24 and left. The servants came and saw that the doors were locked, but they only thought that the king was inside, relieving himself. 25 They waited as long as they thought they should, but when he still did not open the door, they took the key and opened it. And there was their master, lying dead on the floor. 26 Ehud got away while they were waiting. He went past the carved stones and escaped to Seirah. 27 When he arrived there in the hill country of Ephraim, he blew a trumpet to call the people of Israel to battle; then he led them down from the hills. 28 He told them, "Follow me! The LORD has given you victory over your enemies, the Moabites." So they followed Ehud down and captured the place where the Moabites were to cross the Jordan; they did not allow anyone to cross. 29 That day they killed about ten thousand of the best Moabite soldiers; none of them escaped. 30 That day the Israelites defeated Moab, and there was peace in the land for eighty years.

Shamgar

31 The next leader was Shamgar son of Anath. He too rescued Israel, and did so by killing six hundred Philistines with an oxgoad.

Deborah and Barak

4 After Ehud died, the people of Israel sinned against the LORD again. 2 So the LORD let them be conquered by Jabin, a Canaanite king who ruled in the city of Hazor. The commander of his army was Sisera, who lived at Harosheth-of-the-Gentiles. 3 Jabin had nine hundred iron chariots, and he ruled the people of Israel with cruelty and violence for twenty years. Then the people of Israel cried out to the LORD for help.

4 Now Deborah, the wife of Lappidoth, was a prophet, and she was serving as a judge for the Israelites at that time. 5 She would sit under a certain palm tree between Ramah and Bethel in the hill country of Ephraim, and the people of Israel would go there for her decisions. 6 One day she sent for Barak son of Abinoam from the city of Kedesh in Naphtali and said to him, "The LORD, the God of Israel, has given you this command: 'Take ten thousand men from the tribes of Naphtali and Zebulun and lead them to Mount Tabor. 7 I will bring Sisera, the commander of Jabin's army, to fight you at the Kishon River. He will have his chariots and soldiers, but I will give you victory over him.' "

8 Then Barak replied, "I will go if you go with me, but if you don't go with me, I won't go either."

9 She answered, "All right, I will go with you, but you won't get any credit for the victory, because the LORD will hand Sisera over to a woman." So Deborah set off for Kedesh with Barak. 10 Barak called the tribes of Zebulun and Naphtali to Kedesh, and ten thousand men followed him. Deborah went with him.

11 In the meantime Heber the Kenite had set up his tent close to Kedesh near the oak tree at Zaanannim. He had moved away from the other Kenites, the descendants of Hobab, the brother-in-law of Moses.

12 When Sisera learned that Barak had gone up to Mount Tabor, 13 he called out his nine hundred iron chariots and all his

h Probable text it stuck . . . legs; Hebrew unclear.

men, and sent them from Harosheth-of-the-Gentiles to the Kishon River.

¹⁴Then Deborah said to Barak, "Go! The LORD is leading you! Today he has given you victory over Sisera." So Barak went down from Mount Tabor with his ten thousand men. ¹⁵When Barak attacked with his army, the LORD threw Sisera into confusion together with all his chariots and men. Sisera got down from his chariot and fled on foot. ¹⁶Barak pursued the chariots and the army to Harosheth-of-the-Gentiles, and Sisera's whole army was killed. Not a man was left.

¹⁷Sisera ran away to the tent of Jael, the wife of Heber the Kenite, because King Jabin of Hazor was at peace with Heber's family. ¹⁸Jael went out to meet Sisera and said to him, "Come in, sir; come into my tent. Don't be afraid." So he went in, and she hid him behind a curtain.ⁱ ¹⁹He said to her, "Please give me a drink of water; I'm thirsty." She opened a leather bag of milk, gave him a drink, and hid him again. ²⁰Then he told her, "Stand at the door of the tent, and if anyone comes and asks you if anyone is here, say no."

²¹Sisera was so tired that he fell sound asleep. Then Jael took a hammer and a tent peg, quietly went up to him, and killed him by driving the peg right through the side of his head and into the ground. ²²When Barak came looking for Sisera, Jael went out to meet him and said to him, "Come here! I'll show you the man you're looking for." So he went in with her, and there was Sisera on the ground, dead, with the tent peg through his head.

²³That day God gave the Israelites victory over Jabin, the Canaanite king. ²⁴They pressed harder and harder against him until they destroyed him.

The Song of Deborah and Barak

5 On that day Deborah and Barak son of Abinoam sang this song:

²Praise the LORD!
The Israelites were determined
to fight;
the people gladly volunteered.
³Listen, you kings!

Pay attention, you rulers!
I will sing and play music
to Israel's God, the LORD.
⁴LORD, when you left the mountains
of Seir,
when you came out of the region
of Edom,
the earth shook, and rain fell
from the sky.
Yes, water poured down from
the clouds.
⁵The mountains quaked before the
LORD of Sinai,
before the LORD, the God of
Israel.

⁶In the days of Shamgar son of
Anath,
in the days of Jael,
caravans no longer went through
the land,
and travelers used the back
roads.
⁷The towns of Israel stood
abandoned, Deborah;
they stood empty until you
came,ʲ
came like a mother for Israel.
⁸Then there was war in the land
when the Israelites chose new
gods.
Of the forty thousand men in
Israel,
did anyone carry shield or
spear?
⁹My heart is with the commanders
of Israel,
with the people who gladly
volunteered.
Praise the LORD!
¹⁰Tell ofᵏ it, you that ride on white
donkeys,
sitting on saddles,
and you that must walk
wherever you go.
¹¹Listen! The noisy crowds around
the wells
are telling of the LORD's
victories,
the victories of Israel's people!

Then the LORD's people marched
down from their cities.ˡ
¹²Lead on, Deborah, lead on!
Lead on! Sing a song! Lead on!

ⁱ hid him behind a curtain; *or* covered him with a rug.   ʲ abandoned, Deborah . . . you came;
or abandoned; they stood empty until I, Deborah, came.   ᵏ Tell of; *or* Think about.   ˡ from
their cities; *or* to their gates.

Forward, Barak son of Abinoam,
lead your captives away!
13 Then the faithful ones came down
to their leaders;
the LORD's people came to him[m]
ready to fight.
14 They came[n] from Ephraim into
the valley,[o]
behind the tribe of Benjamin
and its people.
The commanders came down from
Machir,
the officers down from Zebulun.
15 The leaders of Issachar came with
Deborah;
yes, Issachar came and
Barak too,
and they followed him into the
valley.
But the tribe of Reuben was
divided;
they could not decide to come.
16 Why did they stay behind with the
sheep?
To listen to shepherds calling
the flocks?
Yes, the tribe of Reuben was
divided;
they could not decide to come.
17 The tribe of Gad stayed east of the
Jordan,
and the tribe of Dan remained
by the ships.
The tribe of Asher stayed by the
seacoast;
they remained along the shore.
18 But the people of Zebulun and
Naphtali
risked their lives on the
battlefield.

19 At Taanach, by the stream of
Megiddo,
the kings came and fought;
the kings of Canaan fought,
but they took no silver away.
20 The stars fought from the sky;
as they moved across the sky,
they fought against Sisera.
21 A flood in the Kishon swept them
away—
the onrushing Kishon River.
I shall march, march on, with
strength!

22 Then the horses came
galloping on,
stamping the ground with their
hoofs.

23 "Put a curse on Meroz," says the
angel of the LORD,
"a curse, a curse on those who
live there.
They did not come to help the
LORD,
come as soldiers to fight
for him."

24 The most fortunate of women is
Jael,
the wife of Heber the Kenite—
the most fortunate of women
who live in tents.
25 Sisera asked for water, but she
gave him milk;
she brought him cream in a
beautiful bowl.
26 She took a tent peg in one hand,
a worker's hammer in the other;
she struck Sisera and crushed his
skull;
she pierced him through the
head.
27 He sank to his knees,
fell down and lay still at her
feet.
At her feet he sank to his knees
and fell;
he fell to the ground, dead.

28 Sisera's mother looked out of the
window;
she gazed[p] from behind the
lattice.
"Why is his chariot so late in
coming?" she asked.
"Why are his horses so slow to
return?"
29 Her wisest friends answered her,
and she told herself over and
over,
30 "They are only finding things to
capture and divide,
a woman or two for every
soldier,
rich cloth for Sisera,
embroidered pieces for the neck
of the queen."[q]

m One ancient translation him; Hebrew me.   n Probable text They came; Hebrew Their root.
o One ancient translation into the valley; Hebrew in Amalek.   p Some ancient translations
gazed; Hebrew cried out.   q Probable text queen; Hebrew plunder.

³¹So may all your enemies die like
that, O LORD,
but may your friends shine like
the rising sun!

And there was peace in the land for forty
years.

Gideon

6 Once again the people of Israel
sinned against the LORD, so he let the
people of Midian rule them for seven
years. ²The Midianites were stronger
than Israel, and the people of Israel hid
from them in caves and other safe places
in the hills. ³Whenever the Israelites
would plant their crops, the Midianites
would come with the Amalekites and the
desert tribes and attack them. ⁴They
would camp on the land and destroy the
crops as far south as the area around
Gaza. They would take all the sheep, cattle, and donkeys, and leave nothing for
the Israelites to live on. ⁵They would
come with their livestock and tents, as
thick as locusts. They and their camels
were too many to count. They came and
devastated the land, ⁶and Israel was
helpless against them.

⁷Then the people of Israel cried out to
the LORD for help against the Midianites,
⁸and he sent them a prophet who
brought them this message from the
LORD, the God of Israel: "I brought you
out of slavery in Egypt. ⁹I rescued you
from the Egyptians and from the people
who fought you here in this land. I drove
them out as you advanced, and I gave
you their land. ¹⁰I told you that I am the
LORD your God and that you should not
worship the gods of the Amorites, whose
land you are now living in. But you have
not listened to me."

¹¹Then the LORD's angel came to the
village of Ophrah and sat under the oak
tree that belonged to Joash, a man of the
clan of Abiezer. His son Gideon was
threshing some wheat secretly in a wine
press, so that the Midianites would not
see him. ¹²The LORD's angel appeared to
him there and said, "The LORD is with
you, brave and mighty man!"

¹³Gideon said to him, "If I may ask, sir,
why has all this happened to us if the
LORD is with us? What happened to all the
wonderful things that our fathers told us
the LORD used to do—how he brought
them out of Egypt? The LORD has abandoned us and left us to the mercy of the
Midianites."

¹⁴Then the LORD ordered him, "Go with
all your great strength and rescue Israel
from the Midianites. I myself am sending you."

¹⁵Gideon replied, "But Lord, how can I
rescue Israel? My clan is the weakest in
the tribe of Manasseh, and I am the least
important member of my family."

¹⁶The LORD answered, "You can do it
because I will help you. You will crush
the Midianites as easily as if they were
only one man."

¹⁷Gideon replied, "If you are pleased
with me, give me some proof that you are
really the LORD. ¹⁸Please do not leave until I bring you an offering of food."

He said, "I will stay until you come
back."

¹⁹So Gideon went into his house and
cooked a young goat and used a bushel
of flour to make bread without any yeast.
He put the meat in a basket and the broth
in a pot, brought them to the LORD's angel
under the oak tree, and gave them to him.
²⁰The angel told him, "Put the meat and
the bread on this rock, and pour the
broth over them." Gideon did so. ²¹Then
the LORD's angel reached out and touched
the meat and the bread with the end of
the stick he was holding. Fire came out
of the rock and burned up the meat and
the bread. Then the angel disappeared.

²²Gideon then realized that it was the
LORD's angel he had seen, and he said in
terror, "Sovereign LORD! I have seen your
angel face-to-face!"

²³But the LORD told him, "Peace. Don't
be afraid. You will not die." ²⁴Gideon
built an altar to the LORD there and
named it "The LORD is Peace." (It is still
standing at Ophrah, which belongs to the
clan of Abiezer.)

²⁵That night the LORD told Gideon,
"Take your father's bull and another bull
seven years old,ʳ tear down your
father's altar to Baal, and cut down the
symbol of the goddess Asherah, which is
beside it. ²⁶Build a well-constructed altar
to the LORD your God on top of this
mound. Then take the second bullˢ and

ʳ bull and another bull seven years old; *or* bull, the seven-year-old one.   ˢ the second bull; *or*
the bull.

burn it whole as an offering, using for firewood the symbol of Asherah you have cut down." 27 So Gideon took ten of his servants and did what the LORD had told him. He was too afraid of his family and the people in town to do it by day, so he did it at night.

28 When the people in town got up early the next morning, they found that the altar to Baal and the symbol of Asherah had been cut down, and that the second bull had been burned on the altar that had been built there. 29 They asked each other, "Who did this?" They investigated and found out that Gideon son of Joash had done it. 30 Then they said to Joash, "Bring your son out here, so that we can kill him! He tore down the altar to Baal and cut down the symbol of Asherah beside it."

31 But Joash said to all those who confronted him, "Are you arguing for Baal? Are you defending him? Anyone who argues for him will be killed before morning. If Baal is a god, let him defend himself. It is his altar that was torn down." 32 From then on Gideon was known as Jerubbaal,[t] because Joash said, "Let Baal defend himself; it is his altar that was torn down."

33 Then all the Midianites, the Amalekites, and the desert tribes assembled, crossed the Jordan River, and camped in Jezree Valley. 34 The spirit of the LORD took control of Gideon, and he blew a trumpet to call the men of the clan of Abiezer to follow him. 35 He sent messengers throughout the territory of both parts of Manasseh to call them to follow him. He sent messengers to the tribes of Asher, Zebulun, and Naphtali, and they also came to join him.

36 Then Gideon said to God, "You say that you have decided to use me to rescue Israel. 37 Well, I am putting some wool on the ground where we thresh the wheat. If in the morning there is dew only on the wool but not on the ground, then I will know that you are going to use me to rescue Israel." 38 That is exactly what happened. When Gideon got up early the next morning, he squeezed the wool and wrung enough dew out of it to fill a bowl with water. 39 Then Gideon said to God, "Don't be angry with me; let me speak just once more. Please let me make one

more test with the wool. This time let the wool be dry, and the ground be wet." 40 That night God did that very thing. The next morning the wool was dry, but the ground was wet with dew.

Gideon Defeats the Midianites

7 One day Gideon and all his men got up early and camped beside Harod Spring. The Midianite camp was in the valley to the north of them by Moreh Hill.

2 The LORD said to Gideon, "The men you have are too many for me to give them victory over the Midianites. They might think that they had won by themselves, and so give me no credit. 3 Announce to the people, 'Anyone who is afraid should go back home, and we will stay here at Mount Gilead.' " So twenty-two thousand went back, but ten thousand stayed.

4 Then the LORD said to Gideon, "You still have too many men. Take them down to the water, and I will separate them for you there. If I tell you a man should go with you, he will go. If I tell you a man should not go with you, he will not go." 5 Gideon took the men down to the water, and the LORD told him, "Separate everyone who laps up the water with his tongue like a dog, from everyone who gets down on his knees to drink." 6 There were three hundred men who scooped up water in their hands and lapped it; all the others got down on their knees to drink. 7 The LORD said to Gideon, "I will rescue you and give you victory over the Midianites with the three hundred men who lapped the water. Tell everyone else to go home." 8 So Gideon sent all the Israelites home, except the three hundred, who kept all the supplies and trumpets. The Midianite camp was below them in the valley.

9 That night the LORD commanded Gideon, "Get up and attack the camp; I am giving you victory over it. 10 But if you are afraid to attack, go down to the camp with your servant Purah. 11 You will hear what they are saying, and then you will have the courage to attack." So Gideon and his servant Purah went down to the edge of the enemy camp. 12 The Midianites, the Amalekites, and the desert tribesmen were spread out in the valley like a swarm of locusts, and they had as

---

[t] JERUBBAAL: *This name in Hebrew means "Let Baal defend himself."*

many camels as there are grains of sand on the seashore.

13 When Gideon arrived, he heard a man telling a friend about a dream. He was saying, "I dreamed that a loaf of barley bread rolled into our camp and hit a tent. The tent collapsed and lay flat on the ground."

14 His friend replied, "It's the sword of the Israelite, Gideon son of Joash! It can't mean anything else! God has given him victory over Midian and our whole army!"

15 When Gideon heard about the man's dream and what it meant, he fell to his knees and worshiped the Lord. Then he went back to the Israelite camp and said, "Get up! The Lord is giving you victory over the Midianite army!" 16 He divided his three hundred men into three groups and gave each man a trumpet and a jar with a torch inside it. 17 He told them, "When I get to the edge of the camp, watch me, and do what I do. 18 When my group and I blow our trumpets, then you blow yours all around the camp and shout, 'For the Lord and for Gideon!' "

19 Gideon and his one hundred men came to the edge of the camp a while before midnight, just after the guard had been changed. Then they blew the trumpets and broke the jars they were holding, 20 and the other two groups did the same. They all held the torches in their left hands, the trumpets in their right, and shouted, "A sword for the Lord and for Gideon!" 21 Every man stood in his place around the camp, and the whole enemy army ran away yelling. 22 While Gideon's men were blowing their trumpets, the Lord made the enemy troops attack each other with their swords. They ran toward Zarethan as far as Beth Shittah, as far as the town of Abel Meholah near Tabbath.

23 Then men from the tribes of Naphtali, Asher, and both parts of Manasseh were called out, and they pursued the Midianites. 24 Gideon sent messengers through all the hill country of Ephraim to say, "Come down and fight the Midianites. Hold the Jordan River and the streams as far as Bethbarah, to keep the Midianites from crossing them." The men of Ephraim were called together, and they held the Jordan River and the streams as far as Bethbarah. 25 They captured the two Midianite chiefs, Oreb and

Zeeb; they killed Oreb at Oreb Rock, and Zeeb at the Winepress of Zeeb. They continued to pursue the Midianites and brought the heads of Oreb and Zeeb to Gideon, who was now east of the Jordan.

The Final Defeat of the Midianites

8 Then the people of Ephraim said to Gideon, "Why didn't you call us when you went to fight the Midianites? Why did you treat us like this?" They complained bitterly about it.

2 But he told them, "What I was able to do is nothing compared with what you have done. Even the little that you people of Ephraim did is worth more than what my whole clan has done. 3 After all, through the power of God you killed the two Midianite chiefs, Oreb and Zeeb. What have I done to compare with that?" When he said this, they were no longer so angry.

4 By this time Gideon and his three hundred men had come to the Jordan River and had crossed it. They were exhausted, but were still pursuing the enemy. 5 When they arrived at Sukkoth, he said to the men of the town, "Please give my men some loaves of bread. They are exhausted, and I am chasing Zebah and Zalmunna, the Midianite kings."

6 But the leaders of Sukkoth said, "Why should we give your army any food? You haven't captured Zebah and Zalmunna yet."

7 So Gideon said, "All right! When the Lord has handed Zebah and Zalmunna over to me, I will beat you with thorns and briers from the desert!" 8 Gideon went on to Penuel and made the same request of the people there, but the men of Penuel gave the same answer as the men of Sukkoth. 9 So he said to them, "I am going to come back safe and sound, and when I do, I will tear this tower down!"

10 Zebah and Zalmunna were at Karkor with their army. Of the whole army of desert tribesmen, only about 15,000 were left; 120,000 soldiers had been killed. 11 Gideon went on the road along the edge of the desert, east of Nobah and Jogbehah, and attacked the army by surprise. 12 The two Midianite kings, Zebah and Zalmunna, ran away, but he pursued them and captured them, and caused their whole army to panic.

13 When Gideon was returning from

the battle by way of Heres Pass, 14he captured a young man from Sukkoth and questioned him. The young man wrote down for Gideon the names of the seventy-seven leading men of Sukkoth. 15Then Gideon went to the men of Sukkoth and said, "Remember when you refused to help me? You said that you couldn't give any food to my exhausted army because I hadn't captured Zebah and Zalmunna yet. Well, here they are!" 16He then took thorns and briers from the desert and used them to punish the leaders of Sukkoth. 17He also tore down the tower at Penuel and killed the men of that city.

18Then Gideon asked Zebah and Zalmunna, "What about the men you killed at Tabor?"

They answered, "They looked like you—every one of them like the son of a king."

19Gideon said, "They were my brothers, my own mother's sons. I solemnly swear that if you had not killed them, I would not kill you." 20Then he said to Jether, his oldest son, "Go ahead, kill them!" But the boy did not draw his sword. He hesitated, because he was still only a boy.

21Then Zebah and Zalmunna said to Gideon, "Come on, kill us yourself. It takes a man to do a man's job." So Gideon killed them and took the ornaments that were on the necks of their camels.

22After that, the Israelites said to Gideon, 'Be our ruler—you and your descendants after you. You have saved us from the Midianites."

23Gideon answered, "I will not be your ruler, nor will my son. The LORD will be your ruler." 24But he went on to say, "Let me ask one thing of you. Every one of you give me the earrings you took." (The Midianites, like other desert people, wore gold earrings.)

25The people answered, "We'll be glad to give them to you." They spread out a cloth, and everyone put on it the earrings that he had taken. 26The gold earrings that Gideon got weighed over forty pounds, and this did not include the ornaments, necklaces, and purple clothes that the kings of Midian wore, nor the collars that were around the necks of their camels. 27Gideon made an idol from the gold and put it in his hometown, Ophrah. All the Israelites abandoned God and went there to worship the idol. It was a trap for Gideon and his family.

28So Midian was defeated by the Israelites and was no longer a threat. The land was at peace for forty years, until Gideon died.

The Death of Gideon

29Gideon went back to his own home and lived there. 30He had seventy sons, because he had many wives. 31He also had a concubine in Shechem; she bore him a son, and he named him Abimelech. 32Gideon son of Joash died at a ripe old age and was buried in the tomb of his father Joash, at Ophrah, the town of the clan of Abiezer.

33After Gideon's death the people of Israel were unfaithful to God again and worshiped the Baals. They made Baal-of-the-Covenant their god, 34and no longer served the LORD their God, who had saved them from all their enemies around them. 35They were not grateful to the family of Gideon for all the good that he had done for Israel.

Abimelech

9 Gideon's son Abimelech went to the town of Shechem, where all his mother's relatives lived, and told them 2to ask the men of Shechem, "Which would you prefer? To have all seventy of Gideon's sons govern you or to have just one man? Remember that Abimelech is your own flesh and blood." 3His mother's relatives talked to the men of Shechem about this for him, and the men of Shechem decided to follow Abimelech because he was their relative. 4They gave him seventy pieces of silver from the temple of Baal-of-the-Covenant, and with this money he hired a bunch of worthless scoundrels to join him. 5He went to his father's house at Ophrah, and there on top of a single stone he killed his seventy brothers, Gideon's sons. But Jotham, Gideon's youngest son, hid and was not killed. 6Then all the men of Shechem and Bethmillo got together and went to the sacred oak tree at Shechem, where they made Abimelech king.

7When Jotham heard about this, he went and stood on top of Mount Gerizim and shouted out to them, "Listen to me, you men of Shechem, and God may listen to you! 8Once upon a time the trees went out to choose a king for themselves.

They said to the olive tree, 'Be our king.' 9 The olive tree answered, 'In order to govern you, I would have to stop producing my oil, which is used to honor gods and human beings.' 10 Then the trees said to the fig tree, 'You come and be our king.' 11 But the fig tree answered, 'In order to govern you, I would have to stop producing my good sweet fruit.' 12 So the trees then said to the grapevine, 'You come and be our king.' 13 But the vine answered, 'In order to govern you, I would have to stop producing my wine, that makes gods and human beings happy.' 14 So then all the trees said to the thorn bush, 'You come and be our king.' 15 The thorn bush answered, 'If you really want to make me your king, then come and take shelter in my shade. If you don't, fire will blaze out of my thorny branches and burn up the cedars of Lebanon.'

16 "Now then," Jotham continued, "were you really honest and sincere when you made Abimelech king? Did you respect Gideon's memory and treat his family properly, as his actions deserved? 17 Remember that my father fought for you. He risked his life to save you from the Midianites. 18 But today you turned against my father's family. You killed his sons — seventy men on a single stone — and just because Abimelech, his son by his servant woman, is your relative, you have made him king of Shechem. 19 Now then, if what you did today to Gideon and his family was sincere and honest, then be happy with Abimelech and let him be happy with you. 20 But if not, may fire blaze out from Abimelech and burn up the men of Shechem and Bethmillo. May fire blaze out from the men of Shechem and Bethmillo and burn Abimelech up." 21 Then because he was afraid of his brother Abimelech, Jotham ran away and went to live at Beer.

22 Abimelech ruled Israel for three years. 23 Then God made Abimelech and the men of Shechem hostile to each other, and they rebelled against Abimelech. 24 This happened so that Abimelech and the men of Shechem, who encouraged him to murder Gideon's seventy sons, would pay for their crime. 25 The men of Shechem put men in ambush against Abimelech on the mountaintops, and they robbed everyone who passed their way. Abimelech was told about this.

26 Then Gaal son of Ebed came to Shechem with his brothers, and the men of Shechem put their confidence in him. 27 They all went out into their vineyards and picked the grapes, made wine from them, and held a festival. They went into the temple of their god, where they ate and drank and made fun of Abimelech. 28 Gaal said, "What kind of men are we in Shechem? Why are we serving Abimelech? Who is he, anyway? The son of Gideon! And Zebul takes orders from him, but why should we serve him? Be loyal to your ancestor Hamor, who founded your clan! 29 I wish I were leading this people! I would get rid of Abimelech! I would tell[u] him, 'Reinforce your army, come on out and fight!' "

30 Zebul, the ruler of the city, became angry when he heard what Gaal had said. 31 He sent messengers to Abimelech at Arumah[v] to say, "Gaal son of Ebed and his brothers have come to Shechem, and they are not going to let you into the city. 32 Now then, you and your men should move by night and hide in the fields. 33 Get up tomorrow morning at sunrise and make a sudden attack on the city. Then when Gaal and his men come out against you, hit them with all you've got!"

34 So Abimelech and all his men made their move at night and hid outside Shechem in four groups. 35 When Abimelech and his men saw Gaal come out and stand at the city gate, they got up from their hiding places. 36 Gaal saw them and said to Zebul, "Look! There are men coming down from the mountaintops!"

"Those are not men," Zebul answered. "They are just shadows on the mountains."

37 Gaal said again, "Look! There are men coming down from the crest of the mountain and one group is coming along the road from the oak tree of the fortune-tellers!"

38 Then Zebul said to him, "Where is all your big talk now? You were the one who asked why we should serve this man Abimelech. These are the men you were

---

u One ancient translation I would tell; Hebrew He told.   v Probable text Arumah; Hebrew unclear.

making fun of. Go on out now and fight them." 39 Gaal led the men of Shechem out and fought Abimelech. 40 Abimelech started after Gaal, and Gaal ran. Many were wounded, even at the city gate. 41 Abimelech lived in Arumah, and Zebul drove Gaal and his brothers out of Shechem, so that they could no longer live there.

42 The next day Abimelech found out that the people of Shechem were planning to go out into the fields, 43 so he took his men, divided them into three groups, and hid in the fields, waiting. When he saw the people coming out of the city, he came out of hiding to kill them. 44 While Abimelech and his group hurried forward to guard the city gate, the other two companies attacked the people in the fields and killed them all. 45 The fighting continued all day long. Abimelech captured the city, killed its people, tore it down, and covered the ground with salt.

46 When all the leading men in the fort at Shechem heard about this, they sought safety in the stronghold of the temple of Baal-of-the-Covenant. 47 Abimelech was told that they had gathered there, 48 so he went up to Mount Zalmon with his men. There he took an ax, cut a limb off a tree, and put it on his shoulder. He told his men to hurry and do the same thing. 49 So everyone cut off a tree limb; then they followed Abimelech and piled the wood up against the stronghold. They set it on fire, with the people inside, and all the people of the fort died — about a thousand men and women.

50 Then Abimelech went to Thebez, surrounded that city, and captured it. 51 There was a strong tower there, and every man and woman in the city, including the leaders, ran to it. They locked themselves in and went up to the roof. 52 When Abimelech came to attack the tower, he went up to the door to set the tower on fire. 53 But a woman threw a millstone down on his head and fractured his skull. 54 Then he quickly called the young man who was carrying his weapons and told him, "Draw your sword and kill me. I don't want it said that a woman killed me." So the young man ran him through, and he died. 55 When the Israelites saw that Abimelech was dead, they all went home.

56 And so it was that God paid Abimelech back for the crime that he committed against his father in killing his seventy brothers. 57 God also made the men of Shechem suffer for their wickedness, just as Jotham, Gideon's son, said they would when he cursed them.

Tola

10 After Abimelech's death Tola, the son of Puah and grandson of Dodo, came to free Israel. He was from the tribe of Issachar and lived at Shamir in the hill country of Ephraim. 2 He was Israel's leader for twenty-three years. Then he died and was buried at Shamir.

Jair

3 After Tola came Jair from Gilead. He led Israel for twenty-two years. 4 He had thirty sons who rode thirty donkeys. They had thirty cities in the land of Gilead, which are still called the villages of Jair. 5 Jair died and was buried at Kamon.

Jephthah

6 Once again the Israelites sinned against the LORD by worshiping the Baals and the Astartes, as well as the gods of Syria, of Sidon, of Moab, of Ammon, and of Philistia. They abandoned the LORD and stopped worshiping him. 7 So the LORD became angry with the Israelites, and let the Philistines and the Ammonites conquer them. 8 For eighteen years they oppressed and persecuted all the Israelites who lived in Amorite country east of the Jordan River in Gilead. 9 The Ammonites even crossed the Jordan to fight the tribes of Judah, Benjamin, and Ephraim. Israel was in great distress.

10 Then the Israelites cried out to the LORD and said, "We have sinned against you, for we left you, our God, and worshiped the Baals."

11 The LORD gave them this answer: "The Egyptians, the Amorites, the Ammonites, the Philistines, 12 the Sidonians, the Amalekites, and the Maonites oppressed you in the past, and you cried out to me. Did I not save you from them? 13 But you still left me and worshiped other gods, so I am not going to rescue you again. 14 Go and cry out to the gods you have chosen. Let them rescue you when you get in trouble."

15 But the people of Israel said to the LORD, "We have sinned. Do whatever you like, but please, save us today." 16 So they

ISRAEL'S JUDGES

After the death of Joshua, the nation of Israel was ruled by judges, or heroic figures, until the united monarchy was established under King Saul. The era of the judges was a time of instability and moral depravity, a dark period when "everyone did whatever they wanted" (Jg 17.6). The judges tried to rally the people against their enemies, but many of the judges were morally weak and the people often turned to idolatry. The well-known judges are portrayed on this map.

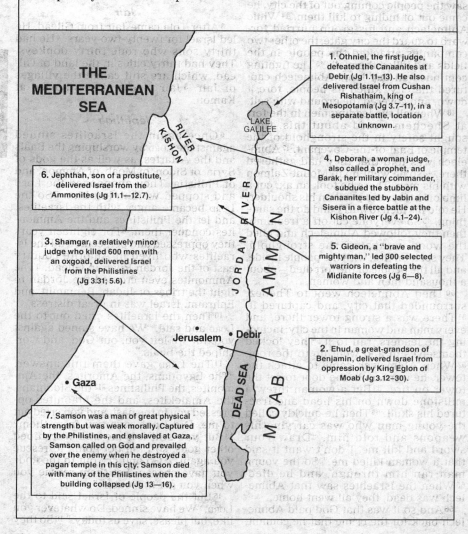

THE MEDITERRANEAN SEA

LAKE GALILEE

RIVER KISHON

JORDAN RIVER

AMMON

MOAB

DEAD SEA

Jerusalem • Debir

• Gaza

1. Othniel, the first judge, defeated the Canaanites at Debir (Jg 1.11–13). He also delivered Israel from Cushan Rishathaim, king of Mesopotamia (Jg 3.7–11), in a separate battle, location unknown.

4. Deborah, a woman judge, also called a prophet, and Barak, her military commander, subdued the stubborn Canaanites led by Jabin and Sisera in a fierce battle at the Kishon River (Jg 4.1–24).

6. Jephthah, son of a prostitute, delivered Israel from the Ammonites (Jg 11.1—12.7).

5. Gideon, a "brave and mighty man," led 300 selected warriors in defeating the Midianite forces (Jg 6—8).

3. Shamgar, a relatively minor judge who killed 600 men with an oxgoad, delivered Israel from the Philistines (Jg 3.31; 5.6).

2. Ehud, a great-grandson of Benjamin, delivered Israel from oppression by King Eglon of Moab (Jg 3.12–30).

7. Samson was a man of great physical strength but was weak morally. Captured by the Philistines, and enslaved at Gaza, Samson called on God and prevailed over the enemy when he destroyed a pagan temple in this city. Samson died with many of the Philistines when the building collapsed (Jg 13—16).

got rid of their foreign gods and worshiped the LORD; and he became troubled over Israel's distress.

17 Then the Ammonite army prepared for battle and camped in Gilead. The people of Israel came together and camped at Mizpah in Gilead. 18 There the people and the leaders of the Israelite tribes asked one another, "Who will lead the fight against the Ammonites? Whoever does will be the leader of everyone in Gilead."

11 Jephthah, a brave soldier from Gilead, was the son of a prostitute. His father Gilead 2 had other sons by his wife, and when they grew up, they forced Jephthah to leave home. They told him, "You will not inherit anything from our father; you are the son of another woman." 3 Jephthah fled from his brothers and lived in the land of Tob. There he attracted a group of worthless men, and they went around with him.

4 It was some time later that the Ammonites went to war against Israel. 5 When this happened, the leaders of Gilead went to bring Jephthah back from the land of Tob. 6 They told him, "Come and lead us, so that we can fight the Ammonites."

7 But Jephthah answered, "You hated me so much that you forced me to leave my father's house. Why come to me now that you're in trouble?"

8 They said to Jephthah, "We are turning to you now because we want you to go with us and fight the Ammonites and lead all the people of Gilead."

9 Jephthah said to them, "If you take me back home to fight the Ammonites and the LORD gives me victory, I will be your ruler."

10 They replied, "We agree. The LORD is our witness." 11 So Jephthah went with the leaders of Gilead, and the people made him their ruler and leader. Jephthah stated his terms at Mizpah in the presence of the LORD.

12 Then Jephthah sent messengers to the king of Ammon to say, "What is your quarrel with us? Why have you invaded our country?"

13 The king of Ammon answered Jephthah's messengers, "When the Israelites came out of Egypt, they took away my land from the Arnon River to the Jabbok River and the Jordan River. Now you must give it back peacefully."

14 Jephthah sent messengers back to the king of Ammon 15 with this answer: "It is not true that Israel took away the land of Moab or the land of Ammon. 16 This is what happened: when the Israelites left Egypt, they went through the desert to the Gulf of Aqaba and came to Kadesh. 17 Then they sent messengers to the king of Edom to ask permission to go through his land. But the king of Edom would not let them. They also asked the king of Moab, but neither would he let them go through his land. So the Israelites stayed at Kadesh. 18 Then they went on through the desert, going around the land of Edom and the land of Moab until they came to the east side of Moab, on the other side of the Arnon River. They camped there, but they did not cross the Arnon because it was the boundary of Moab. 19 Then the Israelites sent messengers to Sihon, the Amorite king of Heshbon, and asked him for permission to go through his country to their own land. 20 But Sihon would not let Israel do it. He brought his whole army together, camped at Jahaz, and attacked Israel. 21 But the LORD, the God of Israel, gave the Israelites victory over Sihon and his army. So the Israelites took possession of all the territory of the Amorites who lived in that country. 22 They occupied all the Amorite territory from the Arnon in the south to the Jabbok in the north and from the desert on the east to the Jordan on the west. 23 So it was the LORD, the God of Israel, who drove out the Amorites for his people, the Israelites. 24 Are you going to try to take it back? You can keep whatever your god Chemosh has given you. But we are going to keep everything that the LORD, our God, has taken for us. 25 Do you think you are any better than Balak son of Zippor, king of Moab? He never challenged Israel, did he? Did he ever go to war against us? 26 For three hundred years Israel has occupied Heshbon and Aroer, and the towns around them, and all the cities on the banks of the Arnon River. Why haven't you taken them back in all this time? 27 No, I have not done you any wrong. You are doing wrong by making war on me. The LORD is the judge. He will decide today between the Israelites and the Ammonites." 28 But the king of Ammon paid no attention to this message from Jephthah.

29 Then the spirit of the LORD came

upon Jephthah. He went through Gilead and Manasseh and returned to Mizpah in Gilead and went on to Ammon. 30 Jephthah promised the LORD: "If you will give me victory over the Ammonites, 31 I will burn as an offering the first person that comes out of my house to meet me, when I come back from the victory. I will offer that person to you as a sacrifice."

32 So Jephthah crossed the river to fight the Ammonites, and the LORD gave him victory. 33 He struck at them from Aroer to the area around Minnith, twenty cities in all, and as far as Abel Keramim. There was a great slaughter, and the Ammonites were defeated by Israel.

Jephthah's Daughter

34 When Jephthah went back home to Mizpah, there was his daughter coming out to meet him, dancing and playing the tambourine. She was his only child. 35 When he saw her, he tore his clothes in sorrow and said, "Oh, my daughter! You are breaking my heart! Why must it be you that causes me pain? I have made a solemn promise to the LORD, and I cannot take it back!"

36 She told him, "If you have made a promise to the LORD, do what you said you would do to me, since the LORD has given you revenge on your enemies, the Ammonites." 37 But she asked her father, "Do this one thing for me. Leave me alone for two months, so that I can go with my friends to wander in the mountains and grieve that I must die a virgin." 38 He told her to go and sent her away for two months. She and her friends went up into the mountains and grieved because she was going to die unmarried and childless. 39 After two months she came back to her father. He did what he had promised the LORD, and she died still a virgin.

This was the origin of the custom in Israel 40 that the Israelite women would go out for four days every year to grieve for the daughter of Jephthah of Gilead.

Jephthah and the Ephraimites

12 The men of Ephraim prepared for battle; they crossed the Jordan River to Zaphon and said to Jephthah, "Why did you cross the border to fight the Ammonites without calling us to go with you? We'll burn the house down over your head!"

2 But Jephthah told them, "My people and I had a serious quarrel with the Ammonites. I did call you, but you would not rescue me from them. 3 When I saw that you were not going to, I risked my life and crossed the border to fight them, and the LORD gave me victory over them. So why are you coming up to fight me now?" 4 Then Jephthah brought all the men of Gilead together, fought the men of Ephraim and defeated them. (The Ephraimites had said, "You Gileadites in Ephraim and Manasseh, you are deserters from Ephraim!") 5 In order to keep the Ephraimites from escaping, the Gileadites captured the places where the Jordan could be crossed. When any Ephraimite who was trying to escape would ask permission to cross, the men of Gilead would ask, "Are you an Ephraimite?" If he said, "No," 6 they would tell him to say "Shibboleth." But he would say "Sibboleth," because he could not pronounce it correctly. Then they would grab him and kill him there at one of the Jordan River crossings. At that time forty-two thousand of the Ephraimites were killed.

7 Jephthah led Israel for six years. Then he died and was buried in his hometown[w] in Gilead.

Ibzan, Elon, and Abdon

8 After Jephthah, Ibzan from Bethlehem led Israel. 9 He had thirty sons and thirty daughters. He gave his daughters in marriage outside the clan and brought thirty young women from outside the clan for his sons to marry. Ibzan led Israel for seven years, 10 then he died and was buried at Bethlehem.

11 After Ibzan, Elon from Zebulun led Israel for ten years. 12 Then he died and was buried at Aijalon in the territory of Zebulun.

13 After Elon, Abdon son of Hillel from Pirathon led Israel. 14 He had forty sons and thirty grandsons, who rode on seventy donkeys. Abdon led Israel for eight years, 15 then he died and was buried at Pirathon in the territory of Ephraim in the hill country of the Amalekites.

w One ancient translation his hometown; Hebrew the towns.

The Birth of Samson

13 The Israelites sinned against the LORD again, and he let the Philistines rule them for forty years.

2 At that time there was a man named Manoah from the town of Zorah. He was a member of the tribe of Dan. His wife had never been able to have children. 3 The LORD's angel appeared to her and said, "You have never been able to have children, but you will soon be pregnant and have a son. 4 Be sure not to drink any wine or beer, or eat any forbidden food; 5 and after your son is born, you must never cut his hair, because from the day of his birth he will be dedicated to God as a nazirite.x He will begin the work of rescuing Israel from the Philistines."

6 Then the woman went and told her husband, "A man of God has come to me, and he looked as frightening as the angely of God. I didn't ask him where he came from, and he didn't tell me his name. 7 But he did tell me that I would become pregnant and have a son. He told me not to drink any wine or beer, or eat any forbidden food, because the boy is to be dedicated to God as a nazirite as long as he lives."

8 Then Manoah prayed to the LORD, "Please, LORD, let the man of God that you sent come back to us and tell us what we must do with the boy when he is born." 9 God did what Manoah asked, and his angel came back to the woman while she was sitting in the field. Her husband Manoah was not with her, 10 so she ran at once and told him, "Look! The man who came to me the other day has appeared to me again."

11 Manoah got up and followed his wife. He went to the man and asked, "Are you the man who talked to my wife?"

"Yes," he answered.

12 Then Manoah said, "Now then, when your words come true, what must the boy do? What kind of a life must he lead?"

13 The LORD's angel answered, "Your wife must be sure to do everything that I have told her. 14 She must not eat anything that comes from the grapevine; she must not drink any wine or beer, or eat any forbidden food. She must do everything that I have told her."

15-16 Not knowing that it was the LORD's angel, Manoah said to him, "Please do not go yet. Let us cook a young goat for you."

But the angel said, "If I do stay, I will not eat your food. But if you want to prepare it, burn it as an offering to the LORD."

17 Manoah replied, "Tell us your name, so that we can honor you when your words come true."

18 The angel asked, "Why do you want to know my name? It is a name of wonder."z

19 So Manoah took a young goat and some grain, and offered them on the rock altar to the LORD who works wonders.a 20-21 While the flames were going up from the altar, Manoah and his wife saw the LORD's angel go up toward heaven in the flames. Manoah realized then that the man had been the LORD's angel, and he and his wife threw themselves face downward on the ground. They never saw the angel again.

22 Manoah said to his wife, "We are sure to die, because we have seen God!"

23 But his wife answered, "If the LORD had wanted to kill us, he would not have accepted our offerings; he would not have shown us all this or told us such things at this time."

24 The woman gave birth to a son and named him Samson. The child grew and the LORD blessed him. 25 And the LORD's power began to strengthen him while he was between Zorah and Eshtaol in the Camp of Dan.

Samson and the Woman from Timnah

14 One day Samson went down to Timnah, where he noticed a certain young Philistine woman. 2 He went back home and told his father and mother, "There is a Philistine woman down at Timnah who caught my attention. Get her for me; I want to marry her."

3 But his father and mother asked him, "Why do you have to go to those heathen Philistines to get a wife? Can't you find someone in our own clan, among all our people?"

But Samson told his father, "She is the

x NAZIRITE *A person who showed devotion to God by taking vows not to drink wine or beer or allow any hair to be cut or touch corpses (see Nu 6.1-8).* y the angel; *or* an angel. z name of wonder; *or* mysterious name. a *Some ancient translations* who works wonders; *Hebrew* and working wonders while Manoah and his wife watched.

one I want you to get for me. I like her."

4 His parents did not know that it was the LORD who was leading Samson to do this, for the LORD was looking for a chance to fight the Philistines. At this time the Philistines were ruling Israel.

5 So Samson went down to Timnah with his father and mother. As they were going through the vineyards there, he heard a young lion roaring. 6 Suddenly the power of the LORD made Samson strong, and he tore the lion apart with his bare hands, as if it were a young goat. But he did not tell his parents what he had done.

7 Then he went and talked to the young woman, and he liked her. 8 A few days later Samson went back to marry her. On the way he left the road to look at the lion he had killed, and he was surprised to find a swarm of bees and some honey inside the dead body. 9 He scraped the honey out into his hands and ate it as he walked along. Then he went to his father and mother and gave them some. They ate it, but Samson did not tell them that he had taken the honey from the dead body of a lion.

10 His father went to the woman's house, and Samson gave a banquet there. This was a custom among the young men. 11 When the Philistines saw him, they sent thirty young men to stay with him. 12-13 Samson said to them, "Let me tell you a riddle. I'll bet each one of you a piece of fine linen and a change of fine clothes that you can't tell me its meaning before the seven days of the wedding feast are over."

"Tell us your riddle," they said. "Let's hear it."

14 He said,

"Out of the eater came something
    to eat;
Out of the strong came something
    sweet."

Three days later they had still not figured out what the riddle meant.

15 On the fourth[b] day they said to Samson's wife, "Trick your husband into telling us what the riddle means. If you don't, we'll set fire to your father's house and burn you with it.[c] You two invited us so that you could rob us, didn't you?"

16 So Samson's wife went to him in

tears and said, "You don't love me! You just hate me! You told my friends a riddle and didn't tell me what it means!"

He said, "Look, I haven't even told my father and mother. Why should I tell you?" 17 She cried about it for the whole seven days of the feast. But on the seventh day he told her what the riddle meant, for she nagged him so about it. Then she told the Philistines. 18 So on the seventh day, before Samson went into the bedroom,[d] the men of the city said to him,

"What could be sweeter than
    honey?
What could be stronger than a
    lion?"

Samson replied,

"If you hadn't been plowing with
    my cow,
You wouldn't know the
    answer now."

19 Suddenly the power of the LORD made him strong, and he went down to Ashkelon, where he killed thirty men, stripped them, and gave their fine clothes to the men who had solved the riddle. After that, he went back home, furious about what had happened, 20 and his wife was given to the man that had been his best man at the wedding.

15 Some time later Samson went to visit his wife during the wheat harvest and took her a young goat. He told her father, "I want to go to my wife's room."

But he wouldn't let him go in. 2 He told Samson, "I really thought that you hated her, so I gave her to your friend. But her younger sister is prettier, anyway. You can have her, instead."

3 Samson said, "This time I'm not going to be responsible for what I do to the Philistines!" 4 So he went and caught three hundred foxes. Two at a time, he tied their tails together and put torches in the knots. 5 Then he set fire to the torches and turned the foxes loose in the Philistine wheat fields. In this way he burned up not only the wheat that had been harvested but also the wheat that was still in the fields. The olive orchards were also burned. 6 When the Philistines asked who had done this, they learned that Samson had done it because his father-

---

b *Some ancient translations* fourth; *Hebrew* seventh.   c set fire . . . you with it; *or* burn you and your family.   d *Probable text* bedroom; *Hebrew* sun.

in-law, a man from Timnah, had given
Samson's wife to a friend of Samson's.
So the Philistines went and burned the
woman to death and burned down her
father's house.e

7 Samson told them, "So this is how
you act! I swear that I won't stop until I
pay you back!" 8 He attacked them
fiercely and killed many of them. Then
he went and stayed in the cave in the cliff
at Etam.

Samson Defeats the Philistines

9 The Philistines came and camped in
Judah, and attacked the town of Lehi.
10 The men of Judah asked them, "Why
are you attacking us?"

They answered, "We came to take
Samson prisoner and to treat him as he
treated us." 11 So these three thousand
men of Judah went to the cave in the cliff
at Etam and said to Samson, "Don't you
know that the Philistines are our rulers?
What have you done to us?"

He answered, "I did to them just what
they did to me."

12 They told him, "We have come here
to tie you up, so we can hand you over to
them."

Samson said, "Give me your word that
you won't kill me yourselves."

13 "All right," they said, "we are only
going to tie you up and hand you over to
them. We won't kill you." So they tied
him up with two new ropes and brought
him back from the cliff.

14 When he got to Lehi, the Philistines
came running toward him, shouting at
him. Suddenly the power of the LORD
made him strong, and he broke the ropes
around his arms and hands as if they
were burnt thread. 15 Then he found a
jawbone of a donkey that had recently
died. He reached down and picked it up,
and killed a thousand men with it. 16 So
Samson sang,

"With the jawbone of a donkey I
  killed a thousand men;
With the jawbone of a donkey I
  piled them up in piles."f

17 After that, he threw the jawbone away.
The place where this happened was
named Ramath Lehi.g

18 Then Samson became very thirsty,
so he called to the LORD and said, "You

gave me this great victory; am I now going to die of thirst and be captured by
these heathen Philistines?" 19 Then God
opened a hollow place in the ground
there at Lehi, and water came out of it.
Samson drank it and began to feel much
better. So the spring was named Hakkore;h it is still there at Lehi.

20 Samson led Israel for twenty years
while the Philistines ruled the land.

Samson at Gaza

16 One day Samson went to the Philistine city of Gaza, where he met
a prostitute and went to bed with her.
2 The people of Gaza found out that Samson was there, so they surrounded the
place and waited for him all night long at
the city gate. They were quiet all night,
thinking to themselves, "We'll wait until
daybreak, and then we'll kill him." 3 But
Samson stayed in bed only until midnight. Then he got up and took hold of
the city gate and pulled it up—doors,
posts, lock, and all. He put them on his
shoulders and carried them far off to the
top of the hill overlooking Hebron.

Samson and Delilah

4 After this, Samson fell in love with a
woman named Delilah, who lived in So-
rek Valley. 5 The five Philistine kings
went to her and said, "Trick Samson into
telling you why he is so strong and how
we can overpower him, tie him up, and
make him helpless. Each one of us will
give you eleven hundred pieces of
silver."

6 So Delilah said to Samson, "Please
tell me what makes you so strong. If
someone wanted to tie you up and make
you helpless, how could he do it?"

7 Samson answered, "If they tie me up
with seven new bowstrings that are not
dried out, I'll be as weak as anybody
else."

8 So the Philistine kings brought Delilah seven new bowstrings that were not
dried out, and she tied Samson up. 9 She
had some men waiting in another room,
so she shouted, "Samson! The Philistines
are coming!" But he snapped the bowstrings just as thread breaks when fire
touches it. So they still did not know the
secret of his strength.

e burned the woman ... house; or burned the woman and her family to death. f PILES: This
word sounds like the Hebrew for "donkey." g RAMATH LEHI: This name in Hebrew means
"Jawbone Hill." h HAKKORE: This name in Hebrew means "caller."

10 Delilah told Samson, "Look, you've been making a fool of me and not telling me the truth. Please tell me how someone could tie you up."

11 He told her, "If they tie me with new ropes that have never been used, I'll be as weak as anybody else."

12 So Delilah got some new ropes and tied him up. Then she shouted, "Samson! The Philistines are coming!" The men were waiting in another room. But he snapped the ropes off his arms like thread.

13 Delilah said to Samson, "You're still making a fool of me and not telling me the truth. Tell me how someone could tie you up."

He told her, "If you weave my seven locks of hair into a loom, and make it tight with a peg, I'll be as weak as anybody else."

14 Delilah then lulled him to sleep, took his seven locks of hair, and wove them into the loom.[i] She made it tight with a peg and shouted, "Samson! The Philistines are coming!" But he woke up and pulled his hair loose from the loom.

15 So she said to him, "How can you say you love me, when you don't mean it? You've made a fool of me three times, and you still haven't told me what makes you so strong." 16 She kept on asking him, day after day. He got so sick and tired of her bothering him about it 17 that he finally told her the truth. "My hair has never been cut," he said. "I have been dedicated to God as a nazirite[j] from the time I was born. If my hair were cut, I would lose my strength and be as weak as anybody else."

18 When Delilah realized that he had told her the truth, she sent a message to the Philistine kings and said, "Come back one more time. He has told me the truth." Then they came and brought the money with them. 19 Delilah lulled Samson to sleep in her lap and then called a man, who cut off[k] Samson's seven locks of hair. Then she began to torment him, for he had lost his strength. 20 Then she shouted, "Samson! The Philistines are coming!" He woke up and thought, "I'll get loose and go free, as always." He did not know that the LORD had left him.

21 The Philistines captured him and put his eyes out. They took him to Gaza, chained him with bronze chains, and put him to work grinding at the mill in the prison. 22 But his hair started growing back.

The Death of Samson

23 The Philistine kings met together to celebrate and offer a great sacrifice to their god Dagon. They sang, "Our god has given us victory over our enemy Samson!" 24-25 They were enjoying themselves, and so they said, "Call Samson, and let's make him entertain us!"[l] When they brought Samson out of the prison, they made him entertain them[m] and made him stand between the columns. When the people saw him, they sang praise to their god: "Our god has given us victory over our enemy, who devastated our land and killed so many of us!" 26 Samson said to the boy who was leading him by the hand, "Let me touch the columns that hold up the building. I want to lean on them." 27 The building was crowded with men and women. All five Philistine kings were there, and there were about three thousand men and women on the roof, watching Samson entertain them.[n]

28 Then Samson prayed, "Sovereign LORD, please remember me; please, God, give me my strength just this one time more, so that with this one blow I can get even with the Philistines for putting out my two eyes." 29 So Samson took hold of the two middle columns holding up the building. Putting one hand on each column, he pushed against them 30 and shouted, "Let me die with the Philistines!" He pushed with all his might, and the building fell down on the five kings and everyone else. Samson killed more people at his death than he had killed during his life.

31 His brothers and the rest of his family came down to get his body. They took him and buried him between Zorah and Eshtaol in the tomb of his father Manoah. He had been Israel's leader for twenty years.

i One ancient translation and make it tight (in verse 13) . . . into the loom (in verse 14); Hebrew does not have these words.   j NAZIRITE: See 13.5.   k Probable text who cut off; Hebrew and she cut off.   l make him entertain us; or make fun of him.   m made him entertain them; or made fun of him.   n entertain them; or and making fun of him.

Micah's Idols

17 There was once a man named Micah, who lived in the hill country of Ephraim. 2 He told his mother, "When someone stole those eleven hundred pieces of silver from you, you put a curse on the robber. I heard you do it. Look, I have the money. I am the one who took it."

His mother said, "May the LORD bless you, my son!" 3 He gave the money back to his mother, and she said, "To keep the curse from falling on my son, I myself am solemnly dedicating the silver to the LORD. It will be used to make a wooden idol covered with silver. So now I will give the pieces of silver back to you." 4 Then he gave them back to his mother. She took two hundred of the pieces of silver and gave them to a metalworker, who made an idol, carving it from wood and covering it with the silver. It was placed in Micah's house.

5 This man Micah had his own place of worship. He made some idols and an ephod,[o] and appointed one of his sons as his priest. 6 There was no king in Israel at that time; everyone did whatever they wanted.

7 At that same time there was a young Levite who had been living in the town of Bethlehem in Judah. 8 He left Bethlehem to find another place to live. While he was traveling, he came to Micah's house in the hill country of Ephraim. 9 Micah asked him, "Where do you come from?"

He answered, "I am a Levite from Bethlehem in Judah. I am looking for a place to live."

10 Micah said, "Stay with me. Be my adviser and priest, and I will give you ten pieces of silver a year, some clothes, and your food."[p] 11 The young Levite agreed to stay with Micah and became like a son to him. 12 Micah appointed him as his priest, and he lived in Micah's home. 13 Micah said, "Now that I have a Levite as my priest, I know that the LORD will make things go well for me."

Micah and the Tribe of Dan

18 There was no king in Israel at that time. In those days the tribe of Dan was looking for territory to claim and settle in because they had not yet received any land of their own among the tribes of Israel. 2 So the people of Dan chose five qualified[q] men out of all the families in the tribe and sent them from the towns of Zorah and Eshtaol with instructions to explore the land and spy on it. When they arrived in the hill country of Ephraim, they stayed at Micah's house. 3 While they were there, they recognized the accent of the young Levite, so they went up to him and asked, "What are you doing here? Who brought you here?"

4 He answered, "I have an arrangement with Micah, who pays me to serve as his priest."

5 They said to him, "Please ask God if we are going to be successful on our trip."

6 The priest answered, "You have nothing to worry about. The LORD is taking care of you on this trip."

7 So the five men left and went to the town of Laish. They saw how the people there lived in security like the Sidonians. They were a peaceful, quiet people, with no argument with anyone; they had all they needed.[r] They lived far away from the Sidonians and had no dealings with any other people. 8 When the five men returned to Zorah and Eshtaol, the people asked them what they had found out. 9 "Come on," they replied. "Let's attack Laish. We saw the land, and it's very good. Don't stay here doing nothing; hurry! Go on in and take it over! 10 When you get there, you will find that the people don't suspect a thing. It is a big country; it has everything a person could want, and God has given it to you."

11 So six hundred men from the tribe of Dan left Zorah and Eshtaol, ready for battle. 12 They went up and camped west of Kiriath Jearim in Judah. That is why the place is still called Camp of Dan. 13 They went on from there and came to Micah's house in the hill country of Ephraim.

14 Then the five men who had gone to spy on the country around Laish said to their companions, "Did you know that here in one of these houses there is a wooden idol covered with silver? There are also other idols and an ephod. What do you think we should do?" 15 So they

[o] EPHOD: *See Word List.* [p] *Probable text* your food; *Hebrew* your food. So the Levite went.
[q] qualified; *or* brave. [r] *Probable text* They were . . . needed; *Hebrew unclear.*

went into Micah's house, where the young Levite lived, and asked the Levite how he was getting along. 16 Meanwhile the six hundred Danite soldiers, ready for battle, were standing at the gate. 17 The five spies went straight on into the house and took the wooden idol covered with silver, the other idols, and the ephod, while the priest stayed at the gate with the six hundred armed men.

18 When the men went into Micah's house and took the sacred objects, the priest asked them, "What are you doing?"

19 They told him, "Keep quiet. Don't say a word. Come with us and be our priest and adviser. Wouldn't you rather be a priest for a whole Israelite tribe than for the family of one man?" 20 This made the priest very happy, so he took the sacred objects and went along with them. 21 They turned around and started off, with their children, their livestock, and their belongings going ahead. 22 They had traveled a good distance from the house when Micah called his neighbors out for battle. They caught up with the Danites 23 and shouted at them. The Danites turned around and asked Micah, "What's the matter? Why all this mob?"

24 Micah answered, "What do you mean, 'What's the matter?' You take my priest and the gods that I made, and walk off! What have I got left?"

25 The Danites told him, "You had better not say anything else unless you want these men to get angry and attack you. You and your whole family would die." 26 Then the Danites went on. Micah saw that they were too strong for him, so he turned and went back home.

27-28 After the Danites had taken the priest and the things that Micah had made, they went and attacked Laish, that town of peaceful, quiet people which was in the same valley as Bethrehob. They killed the inhabitants and burned the town. There was no one to save them, because Laish was a long way from Sidon, and they had no dealings with any other people. The Danites rebuilt the town and settled down there. 29 They changed its name from Laish to Dan, after their ancestor Dan, the son of Jacob. 30 The Danites set up the idol to be worshiped, and Jonathan, the son of Gershom and grandson of Moses, served as a priest for the Danites, and his descend-

ants served as their priests until the people were taken away into exile. 31 Micah's idol remained there as long as the Tent where God was worshiped remained at Shiloh.

The Levite and His Concubine

19 In those days before Israel had a king, there was a Levite living far back in the hill country of Ephraim. He took a young woman from Bethlehem in Judah to be his concubine. 2 But she became angry with him, went back to her father's house in Bethlehem, and stayed there four months. 3 Then the man decided to go after her and try to persuade her to return to him. He took his servant and two donkeys with him. The woman showed the Levite into the house, and when her father saw him, he gave him a hearty greeting. 4 The father insisted that he stay, and so he stayed for three days. The couple had their meals and spent the nights there. 5 On the morning of the fourth day they woke up early and got ready to go. But the woman's father said to the Levite, "Have something to eat first. You'll feel better. You can go later."

6 So the two men sat down and ate and drank together. Then the woman's father told him, "Please spend the night and enjoy yourself."

7 The Levite got up to go, but the father urged him to stay, so he spent another night there. 8 Early in the morning of the fifth day he started to leave, but the woman's father said, "Eat something, please. Wait until later in the day." So the two men ate together.

9 When the man, his concubine, and the servant once more started to leave, the father said, "Look, it's almost evening now; you might as well stay all night. It will be dark soon; stay here and have a good time. Tomorrow you can get up early for the trip and go home."

10-11 But the man did not want to spend another night there, so he and his concubine started on their way, with their servant and two donkeys with pack saddles. It was late in the day when they came near Jebus (that is, Jerusalem), so the servant said to his master, "Why don't we stop and spend the night here in this Jebusite city?"

12-13 But his master said, "We're not going to stop in a city where the people are not Israelites. We'll pass on by and go a little farther and spend the night at Gibeah or Ramah." 14 So they passed by Jebus and continued on their way. It was sunset when they came to Gibeah in the territory of the tribe of Benjamin. 15 They turned off the road to go and spend the night there. They went into town and sat down in the city square, but no one offered to take them home for the night.

16 While they were there, an old man came by at the end of a day's work on the farm. He was originally from the hill country of Ephraim, but he was now living in Gibeah. (The other people there were from the tribe of Benjamin.) 17 The old man noticed the traveler in the city square and asked him, "Where do you come from? Where are you going?"

18 The Levite answered, "We have been in Bethlehem in Judah, and now we are on our way home s deep in the hill country of Ephraim. No one will put us up for the night, 19 even though we have fodder and straw for our donkeys, as well as bread and wine for my concubine and me and for my servant. We have everything we need."

20 The old man said, "You are welcome in my home! I'll take care of you; you don't have to spend the night in the square." 21 So he took them home with him and fed their donkeys. His guests washed their feet and had a meal.

22 They were enjoying themselves when all of a sudden some sexual perverts from the town surrounded the house and started beating on the door. They said to the old man, "Bring out that man that came home with you! We want to have sex with him!"

23 But the old man went outside and said to them, "No, my friends! Please! Don't do such an evil, immoral thing! This man is my guest. 24 Look! Here is his concubine and my own virgin daughter, I'll bring them out now, and you can have them. Do whatever you want to with them. But don't do such an awful thing to this man!" 25 But the men would not listen to him. So the Levite took his concubine and put her outside with them. They raped her and abused her all night long and didn't stop until morning.

26 At dawn the woman came and fell down at the door of the old man's house, where her husband was. She was still there when daylight came. 27 Her husband got up that morning, and when he opened the door to go on his way, he found his concubine lying in front of the house with her hands reaching for the door. 28 He said, "Get up. Let's go." But there was no answer. So he put her body across the donkey and started on his way home. 29 When he arrived, he went in the house and got a knife. He took his concubine's body, cut it into twelve pieces, and sent one piece to each of the twelve tribes of Israel. 30 Everyone who saw it said, "We have never heard of such a thing! Nothing like this has ever happened since the Israelites left Egypt! We have to do something about this! What will it be?"

Israel Prepares for War

20 All the people of Israel from Dan in the north to Beersheba in the south, as well as from the land of Gilead in the east, answered the call. They gathered in one body in the Lord's presence at Mizpah. 2 The leaders of all the tribes of Israel were present at this gathering of God's people, and there were 400,000 foot soldiers. 3 Meanwhile the people of Benjamin heard that all the other Israelites had gathered at Mizpah.

The Israelites asked, "Tell us, how was this crime committed?" 4 The Levite whose concubine had been murdered answered, "My concubine and I went to Gibeah in the territory of Benjamin to spend the night. 5 The men of Gibeah came to get me and surrounded the house at night. They intended to kill me; instead they raped my concubine, and she died. 6 I took her body, cut it in pieces, and sent one piece to each of the twelve tribes of Israel. These people have committed an evil and immoral act among us. 7 All of you here are Israelites. What are we going to do about this?"

8 All the people stood up together and said, "None of us, whether he lives in a tent or in a house, will go home. 9 This is what we will do: we will draw lots and choose some men to attack Gibeah. t 10 One tenth of the men in Israel will provide food for the army, and the others will go and punish Gibeah u for this

---

s One ancient translation home; Hebrew to the house of the Lord.   t One ancient translation to attack Gibeah; Hebrew to Gibeah.   u One ancient translation Gibeah; Hebrew Geba.

immoral act that they have committed in Israel." [11] So all the men in Israel assembled with one purpose — to attack the town.

[12] The Israelite tribes sent messengers all through the territory of the tribe of Benjamin to say, "What is this crime that you have committed? [13] Now hand over those perverts in Gibeah, so that we can kill them and remove this evil from Israel." But the people of Benjamin paid no attention to the other Israelites. [14] From all the cities of Benjamin they came to Gibeah to fight the other people of Israel. [15-16] They called out twenty-six thousand soldiers from their cities that day. Besides these, the citizens of Gibeah gathered seven hundred specially chosen men[v] who were left-handed. Every one of them could sling a stone at a strand of hair and never miss. [17] Not counting the tribe of Benjamin, the Israelites gathered 400,000 trained soldiers.

The War against the Benjaminites

[18] The Israelites went to the place of worship at Bethel, and there they asked God, "Which tribe should attack the Benjaminites first?"

The LORD answered, "The tribe of Judah."

[19] So the Israelites started out the next morning and camped near the city of Gibeah. [20] They went to attack the army of Benjamin, and placed the soldiers in position facing the city. [21] The army of Benjamin came out of the city, and before the day was over they had killed twenty-two thousand Israelite soldiers. [22-23] Then the Israelites went to the place of worship and mourned in the presence of the LORD until evening. They asked him, "Should we go again into battle against our brothers the Benjaminites?"

The LORD answered, "Yes."

So the Israelite army was encouraged, and they placed their soldiers in position again, where they had been the day before. [24] They marched against the army of Benjamin a second time. [25] And for the second time the Benjaminites came out of Gibeah, and this time they killed eighteen thousand trained Israelite soldiers.

[26] Then all the people of Israel went up to Bethel and mourned. They sat there in the LORD's presence and did not eat until evening. They offered fellowship sacrifices and burned some sacrifices whole — all in the presence of the LORD. [27-28] God's Covenant Box was there at Bethel in those days, and Phinehas, the son of Eleazar and grandson of Aaron, was in charge of it. The people asked the LORD, "Should we go out to fight our brothers the Benjaminites again, or should we give up?"

The LORD answered, "Fight. Tomorrow I will give you victory over them."

[29] So the Israelites put some soldiers in hiding around Gibeah. [30] Then for the third straight day they marched against the army of Benjamin and placed their soldiers in battle position facing Gibeah, as they had done before. [31] The Benjaminites came out to fight and were led away from the city. As they had before, they began killing some Israelites in the open country, on the road to Bethel and on the road to Gibeah. They killed about thirty Israelites. [32] The Benjaminites said, "We've beaten them just as before."

But the Israelites had planned to retreat and lead them away from the city onto the roads. [33] So when the main army of the Israelites pulled back and regrouped at Baaltamar, the men surrounding Gibeah suddenly rushed out of their hiding places in the rocky country around the city.[w] [34] Ten thousand men, specially chosen out of all Israel, attacked Gibeah, and the fighting was hard. The Benjaminites had not realized that they were about to be destroyed. [35] The LORD gave Israel victory over the army of Benjamin. The Israelites killed 25,100 of the enemy that day, [36] and the Benjaminites realized they were defeated.

How the Israelites Won

The main body of the Israelite army had retreated from the Benjaminites because they were relying on the men that they had put in hiding around Gibeah. [37] These men ran quickly toward Gibeah; they spread out in the city and killed everyone there. [38] The main Israelite

v *Some ancient translations* men; *Hebrew* men. In all this number there were seven hundred specially chosen men.   w *One ancient translation* the city (that is, Gibeah); *Hebrew* Geba.

army and the men in hiding had arranged a signal. When they saw a big cloud of smoke going up from the town, [39] the Israelites out on the battlefield were to turn around. By this time the Benjaminites had already killed the thirty Israelites. They told themselves, "Yes, we've beaten them just as before." [40] Then the signal appeared; a cloud of smoke began to go up from the town. The Benjaminites looked behind them and were amazed to see the whole city going up in flames. [41] Then the Israelites turned around, and the Benjaminites were thrown into panic because they realized that they were about to be destroyed. [42] They retreated from the Israelites and ran toward the open country, but they could not escape. They were caught between the main army and the men who were now coming out of the city,[x] and they were destroyed. [43] The Israelites had the enemy trapped, and without stopping they pursued them as far as a point east of Gibeah, killing them as they went.[y] [44] Eighteen thousand of the best Benjaminite soldiers were killed. [45] The others turned and ran toward the open country to Rimmon Rock. Five thousand of them were killed on the roads. The Israelites continued to pursue the rest to Gidom, killing two thousand. [46] In all, twenty-five thousand Benjaminites were killed that day — all of them brave soldiers.

[47] But six hundred men were able to escape to the open country to Rimmon Rock, and they stayed there four months. [48] The Israelites turned back against the rest of the Benjaminites and killed them all — men, women, and children, and animals as well. They burned every town in the area.

Wives for the Tribe of Benjamin

21 When the Israelites had gathered at Mizpah, they had made a solemn promise to the LORD: "None of us will allow a Benjaminite to marry a daughter of ours." [2] So now the people of Israel went to Bethel and sat there in the presence of God until evening. Loudly and bitterly they mourned: [3] "LORD God of Israel, why has this happened? Why is

the tribe of Benjamin about to disappear from Israel?"

[4] Early the next morning the people got up and built an altar there. They offered fellowship sacrifices and burned some sacrifices whole. [5] They asked, "Is there any group out of all the tribes of Israel that did not go to the gathering in the LORD's presence at Mizpah?" (They had taken a solemn oath that anyone who had not gone to Mizpah would be put to death.) [6] The people of Israel felt sorry for their brothers the Benjaminites and said, "Today Israel has lost one of its tribes. [7] What shall we do to provide wives for the men of Benjamin who are left? We have made a solemn promise to the LORD that we will not give them any of our daughters."

[8] When they asked if there was some group out of the tribes of Israel that had not gone to the gathering at Mizpah, they found out that no one from Jabesh in Gilead had been there; [9] at the roll call of the army no one from Jabesh had responded. [10] So the assembly sent twelve thousand of their bravest men with the orders, "Go and kill everyone in Jabesh, including women and children. [11] Kill all the males, and also every woman who is not a virgin." [12] They found four hundred young virgins among the people in Jabesh, so they brought them to the camp at Shiloh, which is in the land of Canaan.

[13] Then the whole assembly sent word to the Benjaminites who were at Rimmon Rock and offered to end the war. [14] The Benjaminites came back, and the other Israelites gave them the young women from Jabesh whom they had not killed. But there were not enough of them.

[15] The people felt sorry for the Benjaminites because the LORD had broken the unity of the tribes of Israel. [16] So the leaders of the gathering said, "There are no more women in the tribe of Benjamin. What shall we do to provide wives for the men who are left? [17] Israel must not lose one of its twelve tribes. We must find a way for the tribe of Benjamin to survive, [18] but we cannot allow them to marry our daughters, because we have put a curse on anyone who allows a Benjaminite to marry one of our daughters."

---

[x] *Probable text* city; *Hebrew* cities.   [y] *Verse 43 in Hebrew is unclear.*

19 Then they thought, "The yearly festival of the LORD at Shiloh is coming soon." (Shiloh is north of Bethel, south of Lebonah, and east of the road between Bethel and Shechem.) **20** They told the Benjaminites, "Go and hide in the vineyards **21** and watch. When the young women of Shiloh come out to dance during the festival, you come out of the vineyards. Each of you take a wife by force from among them and take her back to the territory of Benjamin with you. **22** If their fathers or brothers come to youᶻ and protest, youᵃ can tell them, 'Please let us keep them, because we did not take them from you in battle to be our wives. And since you did not give them to us, you are not guilty of breaking your promise.'"

23 The Benjaminites did this; each of them chose a wife from the young women who were dancing at Shiloh and carried her away. Then they went back to their own territory, rebuilt their towns, and lived there. **24** At the same time the rest of the Israelites left, and every man went back to his own tribe and family and to his own property.

25 There was no king in Israel at that time. Everyone did whatever they pleased.

ᶻ *One ancient translation* you; *Hebrew* us.　　ᵃ *Probable text* you; *Hebrew* we.

The Book of
RUTH

Introduction

The peaceful story of Ruth is set in the violent times of The Book of Judges. Ruth, a Moabite woman, is married to an Israelite. When he dies, Ruth shows uncommon loyalty to her Israelite mother-in-law and deep devotion to the God of Israel. In the end she finds a new husband among her former husband's relatives, and through this marriage becomes the great-grandmother of David, Israel's greatest king.

The stories of Judges show the disaster that came when God's people turned away from him. Ruth shows the blessing that came to a foreigner who turned to Israel's God and so became part of his faithful people.

Outline of Contents

Elimelech and His Family Move to Moab

1 1-2 Long ago, in the days before Israel had a king, there was a famine in the land. So a man named Elimelech, who belonged to the clan of Ephrath and who lived in Bethlehem in Judah, went with his wife Naomi and their two sons Mahlon and Chilion to live for a while in the country of Moab. While they were living there, 3 Elimelech died, and Naomi was left alone with her two sons, 4 who married Moabite women, Orpah and Ruth. About ten years later 5 Mahlon and Chilion also died, and Naomi was left all alone, without husband or sons.

Naomi and Ruth Return to Bethlehem

6 Some time later Naomi heard that the LORD had blessed his people by giving them good crops; so she got ready to leave Moab with her daughters-in-law. 7 They started out together to go back to Judah, but on the way 8 she said to them, "Go back home and stay with your mothers. May the LORD be as good to you as you have been to me and to those who have died. 9 And may the LORD make it possible for each of you to marry again and have a home."

So Naomi kissed them good-bye. But they started crying 10 and said to her,

"No! We will go with you to your people."

11 "You must go back, my daughters," Naomi answered. "Why do you want to come with me? Do you think I could have sons again for you to marry? 12 Go back home, for I am too old to get married again. Even if I thought there was still hope, and so got married tonight and had sons, 13 would you wait until they had grown up? Would this keep you from marrying someone else? No, my daughters, you know that's impossible. The LORD has turned against me, and I feel very sorry for you."[a]

14 Again they started crying. Then Orpah kissed her mother-in-law good-bye and went back home,[b] but Ruth held on to her. 15 So Naomi said to her, "Ruth, your sister-in-law has gone back to her people and to her god.[c] Go back home with her."

16 But Ruth answered, "Don't ask me to leave you! Let me go with you. Wherever you go, I will go; wherever you live, I will live. Your people will be my people, and your God will be my God. 17 Wherever you die, I will die, and that is where I will be buried. May the LORD's worst punishment come upon me if I let anything but death[d] separate me from you!"

18 When Naomi saw that Ruth was determined to go with her, she said nothing more.

---

a sorry for you; *or* bitter about what has happened to you.   b *One ancient translation* and went back home; *Hebrew does not have these words.*   c god; *or* gods.   d anything but death; *or* even death.

OLD TESTAMENT WOMEN

One of the outstanding women of the Old Testament was Hannah, who prayed for a son and then dedicated him to the Lord even before he was born. Hannah's faithfulness was rewarded in the person of Samuel, who served his nation as prophet, priest, and judge during a crucial time in its history (1 S 1—7).

Other outstanding women of the Old Testament are listed below.

Name	Description	Biblical Reference
Bathsheba	Wife of David; mother of Solomon	2 S 11.3, 27
Deborah	A judge who defeated the Canaanites under Sisera	Jg 4.4
Delilah	Philistine woman who tricked Samson	Jg 16.4, 5
Dinah	Only daughter of Jacob	Gn 30.21
Esther	Jewish captive in Persia; saved her people from destruction by Haman	Es 2.16, 17
Eve	First woman	Gn 3.20
Gomer	The prophet Hosea's unfaithful wife	Ho 1.2, 3
Hagar	Sarai's (Sarah's) maid; mother of Ishmael	Gn 16.3–16
Jezebel	Wicked wife of King Ahab of Israel	1 K 16.30, 31
Jochebed	Mother of Moses	Ex 6.20
Miriam	Sister of Aaron; a prophet	Ex 15.20
Naomi	Ruth's mother-in-law	Ru 1.2, 4
Orpah	Ruth's sister-in-law	Ru 1.4
Rachel	Wife of Jacob	Gn 29.28
Rahab	Prostitute who harbored Israel's spies; ancestor of Jesus	Js 2.1–3; Mt 1.5
Ruth	Wife of Boaz and mother of Obed; ancestor of Jesus	Ru 4.13, 17; Mt 1.5
Sarah	Wife of Abram; mother of Isaac	Gn 11.29; 21.2, 3
Tamar	A daughter of David	2 S 13.1
Zipporah	Wife of Moses	Ex 2.21

19They went on until they came to Bethlehem. When they arrived, the whole town became excited, and the women there exclaimed, "Is this really Naomi?"

20"Don't call me Naomi," she answered; "call me Marah,e because Almighty God has made my life bitter. 21When I left here, I had plenty, but the LORD has brought me back without a thing. Why call me Naomi when the LORD Almighty has condemned me and sent me trouble?"

22This, then, was how Naomi came back from Moab with Ruth, her Moabite daughter-in-law. When they arrived in Bethlehem, the barley harvest was just beginning.

Ruth Works in the Field of Boaz

2 Naomi had a relative named Boaz, a rich and influential man who belonged to the family of her husband Elimelech. 2One day Ruth said to Naomi, "Let me go to the fields to gather the grain that the harvest workers leave. I am sure to find someone who will let me work with him."

Naomi answered, "Go ahead, daughter."

3So Ruth went out to the fields and walked behind the workers, picking up the heads of grain which they left. It so happened that she was in a field that belonged to Boaz.

4Some time later Boaz himself arrived from Bethlehem and greeted the workers. "The LORD be with you!" he said.

"The LORD bless you!" they answered.

5Boaz asked the man in charge, "Who is that young woman?"

6The man answered, "She is the foreigner who came back from Moab with Naomi. 7She asked me to let her follow the workers and gather grain. She has been working since early morning and has just now stopped to rest for a while under the shelter."

8Then Boaz said to Ruth, "Let me give you some advice. Don't gather grain anywhere except in this field. Work with the women here; 9watch them to see where they are reaping and stay with them. I have ordered my men not to molest you. And whenever you are thirsty, go and drink from the water jars that they have filled."

10Ruth bowed down with her face touching the ground, and said to Boaz, "Why should you be so concerned about me? Why should you be so kind to a foreigner?"

11Boaz answered, "I have heard about everything that you have done for your mother-in-law since your husband died. I know how you left your father and mother and your own country and how you came to live among a people you had never known before. 12May the LORD reward you for what you have done. May you have a full reward from the LORD God of Israel, to whom you have come for protection!"

13Ruth answered, "You are very kindf to me, sir. You have made me feel better by speaking gently to me, even though I am not the equal of one of your servants."

14At mealtime Boaz said to Ruth, "Come and have a piece of bread, and dip it in the sauce." So she sat with the workers, and Boaz passed some roasted grain to her. She ate until she was satisfied, and she still had some food left over.

15-16After she had left to go and gather grain, Boaz ordered the workers, "Let her gather grain even where the bundles are lying, and don't say anything to stop her. Besides that, pull out some heads of grain from the bundles and leave them for her to pick up."

17So Ruth gathered grain in the field until evening, and when she had beaten it out, she found she had nearly twenty-five pounds. 18She took the grain back into town and showed her mother-in-law how much she had gathered. She also gave her the food left over from the meal. 19Naomi asked her, "Where did you gather all this grain today? Whose field have you been working in? May God bless the man who took an interest in you!"

So Ruth told Naomi that she had been working in a field belonging to a man named Boaz.

20"May the LORD bless Boaz!" Naomi exclaimed. "The LORD always keeps his promises to the living and the dead." And she went on, "That man is a close relative

R
U
T
H

---

e NAOMI . . . MARAH: In Hebrew Naomi means "pleasant" and Marah means "bitter."   f You are very kind; or Please be kind.

of ours, one of those responsible for taking care of us."

21 Then Ruth said, "Best of all, he told me to keep gathering grain with his workers until they finish the harvest."

22 Naomi said to Ruth, "Yes, daughter, it will be better for you to work with the women in Boaz' field. You might be molested if you went to someone else's field." 23 So Ruth worked with them and gathered grain until all the barley and wheat had been harvested. And she continued to live with her mother-in-law.

Ruth Finds a Husband

3 Some time later Naomi said to Ruth, "I must find a husband for you, so that you will have a home of your own. 2 Remember that this man Boaz, whose women you have been working with, is our relative. Now listen. This evening he will be threshing the barley. 3 So wash yourself, put on some perfume, and get dressed in your best clothes. Then go where he is threshing, but don't let him know you are there until he has finished eating and drinking. 4 Be sure to notice where he lies down, and after he falls asleep, go and lift the covers and lie down at his feet. He will tell you what to do."

5 Ruth answered, "I will do everything you say."

6 So Ruth went to the threshing place and did just what her mother-in-law had told her. 7 When Boaz had finished eating and drinking, he was in a good mood. He went to the pile of barley and lay down to sleep. Ruth slipped over quietly, lifted the covers and lay down at his feet. 8 During the night he woke up suddenly, turned over, and was surprised to find a woman lying at his feet. 9 "Who are you?" he asked.

"It's Ruth, sir," she answered. "Because you are a close relative, you are responsible for taking care of me. So please marry me."

10 "The LORD bless you," he said. "You are showing even greater family loyalty in what you are doing now than in what you did for your mother-in-law. You might have gone looking for a young man, either rich or poor, but you haven't. 11 Now don't worry, Ruth. I will do everything you ask; as everyone in town knows, you are a fine woman. 12 It is true that I am a close relative and am responsible for you, but there is a man who is a closer relative than I am. 13 Stay here the rest of the night, and in the morning we will find out whether or not he will take responsibility for you. If so, well and good; if not, then I swear by the living LORD that I will take the responsibility. Now lie down and stay here till morning."

14 So she lay there at his feet, but she got up before it was light enough for her to be seen, because Boaz did not want anyone to know that she had been there. 15 Boaz said to her, "Take off your cloak and spread it out here." She did, and he poured out almost fifty pounds of barley and helped her lift it to her shoulder. Then she returned to town with it. 16 When she arrived home, her mother-in-law asked her, "How did you get along, daughter?"

Ruth told her everything that Boaz had done for her. 17 She added, "He told me I must not come back to you empty-handed, so he gave me all this barley."

18 Naomi said to her, "Now be patient, Ruth, until you see how this all turns out. Boaz will not rest today until he settles the matter."

Boaz Marries Ruth

4 Boaz went to the meeting place at the town gate and sat down there. Then Elimelech's nearest relative, the man whom Boaz had mentioned, came by, and Boaz called to him, "Come over here, my friend, and sit down." So he went over and sat down. 2 Then Boaz got ten of the leaders of the town and asked them to sit down there too. When they were seated, 3 he said to his relative, "Now that Naomi has come back from Moab, she wants to sell the field that belonged to our relative Elimelech, 4 and I think you ought to know about it. Now then, if you want it, buy it in the presence of these men sitting here. But if you don't want it, say so, because the right to buy it belongs first to you and then to me."

The man said, "I will buy it."

5 Boaz said, "Very well, if you buy the field from Naomi, then you are also buying Ruth,g the Moabite widow, so that

g *Some ancient translations* Naomi . . . Ruth; *Hebrew* Naomi and from Ruth.

the field will stay in the dead man's family."

6 The man answered, "In that case I will give up my right to buy the field, because it would mean that my own children would not inherit it. You buy it; I would rather not."

7 Now in those days, to settle a sale or an exchange of property, it was the custom for the seller to take off his sandal and give it to the buyer. In this way the Israelites showed that the matter was settled.

8 So when the man said to Boaz, "You buy it," he took off his sandal and gave it to Boaz.[h] 9 Then Boaz said to the leaders and all the others there, "You are all witnesses today that I have bought from Naomi everything that belonged to Elimelech and to his sons Chilion and Mahlon. 10 In addition, Ruth the Moabite, Mahlon's widow, becomes my wife. This will keep the property in the dead man's family, and his family line will continue among his people and in his hometown. You are witnesses to this today."

11 The leaders and the others said, "Yes, we are witnesses. May the LORD make your wife become like Rachel and Leah, who bore many children to Jacob.

May you become rich in the clan of Ephrath and famous in Bethlehem. 12 May the children that the LORD will give you by this young woman make your family like the family of Perez, the son of Judah and Tamar."

Boaz and His Descendants

13 So Boaz took Ruth home as his wife. The LORD blessed her, and she became pregnant and had a son. 14 The women said to Naomi, "Praise the LORD! He has given you a grandson today to take care of you. May the boy become famous in Israel! 15 Your daughter-in-law loves you, and has done more for you than seven sons. And now she has given you a grandson, who will bring new life to you and give you security in your old age." 16 Naomi took the child, held him close,[i] and took care of him.

17 The women of the neighborhood named the boy Obed. They told everyone, "A son has been born to Naomi!"

Obed became the father of Jesse, who was the father of David.

18-22 This is the family line from Perez to David: Perez, Hezron, Ram, Amminadab, Nahshon, Salmon, Boaz, Obed, Jesse, David.

h One ancient translation and gave it to Boaz; Hebrew does not have these words.   i held him close; or adopted him.

The First Book of

SAMUEL

Introduction

The book of First Samuel *records the transition in Israel from the period of the judges to the monarchy. This change in Israel's national life revolved mainly around three men: Samuel, the last of the great judges; Saul, Israel's first king; and David, whose early adventures before coming to power are interwoven with the accounts of Samuel and Saul.*

The theme of this book, like that of other historical writings in the Old Testament, is that faithfulness to God brings success, while disobedience brings disaster. This is stated clearly in the Lord's message to the priest Eli in 2.30: "I will honor those who honor me, and I will treat with contempt those who despise me."

The book records mixed feelings about the establishment of the monarchy. The Lord himself was regarded as the real king of Israel, but in response to the people's request the Lord chose a king for them. The important fact was that both the king and the people of Israel lived under the sovereignty and judgment of God (2.7-10). Under God's laws the rights of all people, rich and poor alike, were to be maintained.

Outline of Contents

1
S
A
M
U
E
L

Elkanah and His Family at Shiloh

1 There was a man named Elkanah, from the tribe of Ephraim, who lived in the town of Ramah in the hill country of Ephraim. He was the son of Jeroham and grandson of Elihu, and belonged to the family of Tohu, a part of the clan of Zuph. ²Elkanah had two wives, Hannah and Peninnah. Peninnah had children, but Hannah did not. ³Every year Elkanah went from Ramah to worship and offer sacrifices to the Lord Almighty at Shiloh, where Hophni and Phinehas, the two sons of Eli, were priests of the Lord. ⁴Each time Elkanah offered his sacrifice, he would give one share of the meat to Peninnah and one share to each of her children. ⁵And even though he loved Hannah very much he would give her only one share, because *a* the Lord had kept her from having children. ⁶Peninnah, her rival, would torment and humiliate her, because the Lord had kept her childless. ⁷This went on year after year; whenever they went to the house of the Lord, Peninnah would upset Hannah so much that she would cry and refuse to eat anything. ⁸Her husband Elkanah would ask her, "Hannah, why are you crying? Why won't you eat? Why are you always so sad? Don't I mean more to you than ten sons?"

Hannah and Eli

9-10 One time, after they had finished their meal in the house of the Lord at Shiloh, Hannah got up. She was deeply distressed, and she cried bitterly as she prayed to the Lord. Meanwhile, Eli the priest was sitting in his place by the door. ¹¹Hannah made a solemn promise: "Lord Almighty, look at me, your servant! See my trouble and remember me! Don't forget me! If you give me a son, I promise that I will dedicate him to you for his whole life and that he will never have his hair cut."*b*

¹²Hannah continued to pray to the Lord for a long time, and Eli watched her lips. ¹³She was praying silently; her lips

---

a And even ... because; *or* To Hannah, however, he would give a special share, because he loved her very much, even though. *b* NEVER HAVE HIS HAIR CUT: *A sign of dedication to the Lord* (see Nu 6.5).

were moving, but she made no sound. So Eli thought that she was drunk, 14and he said to her, "Stop making a drunken show of yourself! Stop your drinking and sober up!"

15"No, I'm not drunk, sir," she answered. "I haven't been drinking! I am desperate, and I have been praying, pouring out my troubles to the LORD. 16Don't think I am a worthless woman. I have been praying like this because I'm so miserable."

17"Go in peace," Eli said, "and may the God of Israel give you what you have asked him for."

18"May you always think kindly of me," she replied. Then she went away, ate some food, and was no longer sad.

Samuel's Birth and Dedication

19The next morning Elkanah and his family got up early, and after worshiping the LORD, they went back home to Ramah. Elkanah had intercourse with his wife Hannah, and the LORD answered her prayer. 20So it was that she became pregnant and gave birth to a son. She named him Samuel,c and explained, "I asked the LORD for him."

21The time came again for Elkanah and his family to go to Shiloh and offer to the LORD the yearly sacrifice and the special sacrifice he had promised. 22But this time Hannah did not go. She told her husband, "As soon as the child is weaned, I will take him to the house of the LORD, where he will stay all his life."

23Elkanah answered, "All right, do whatever you think best; stay at home until you have weaned him. And may the LORD make yourd promise come true." So Hannah stayed at home and nursed her child.

24After she had weaned him, she took him to Shiloh, taking along a three-year-old bull,e a bushel of flour, and a leather bag full of wine. She took Samuel, young as he was, to the house of the LORD at Shiloh. 25After they had killed the bull, they took the child to Eli. 26Hannah said to him, "Excuse me, sir. Do you remember me? I am the woman you saw standing here, praying to the LORD. 27I asked him for this child, and he gave me what I asked for. 28So I am ded-

icating him to the LORD. As long as he lives, he will belong to the LORD."

Then theyf worshiped the LORD there.

Hannah's Prayer

2 Hannah prayed:

"The LORD has filled my heart
    with joy;
how happy I am because of
    what he has done!
I laugh at my enemies;
    how joyful I am because God
    has helped me!

2 "No one is holy like the LORD;
    there is none like him,
    no protector like our God.
3 Stop your loud boasting;
    silence your proud words.
For the LORD is a God who knows,
    and he judges all that people do.
4 The bows of strong soldiers are
    broken,
    but the weak grow strong.
5 The people who once were
    well fed
now hire themselves out to get
    food,
    but the hungry are hungry no
    more.
The childless wife has borne seven
    children,
    but the mother of many is left
    with none.
6 The LORD kills and restores to life;
    he sends people to the world of
    the dead
    and brings them back again.
7 He makes some people poor and
    others rich;
    he humbles some and makes
    others great.
8 He lifts the poor from the dust
    and raises the needy from their
    misery.
He makes them companions of
    princes
    and puts them in places of
    honor.
The foundations of the earth
    belong to the LORD;
    on them he has built the world.

1 SAMUEL

---

c SAMUEL: *This name, which in Hebrew means "name of God," is here related to the Hebrew verb for "ask."*   d *Some ancient translations* your; *Hebrew* his.   e *Some ancient translations* a three-year-old bull; *Hebrew* three bulls.   f *Some ancient translations* they; *Hebrew* he.

9"He protects the lives of his
faithful people,
but the wicked disappear in
darkness;
a man does not triumph by his
own strength.
10The Lord's enemies will be
destroyed;
he will thunder against them
from heaven.
The Lord will judge the whole
world;
he will give power to his king,
he will make his chosen king
victorious."

11Then Elkanah went back home to
Ramah, but the boy Samuel stayed in
Shiloh and served the Lord under the
priest Eli.

The Sons of Eli

12The sons of Eli were scoundrels.
They paid no attention to the Lord 13or
to the regulations concerning what the
priests could demand from the people.
Instead, when someone was offering a
sacrifice, the priest's servant would
come with a three-pronged fork. While
the meat was still cooking, 14he would
stick the fork into the cooking pot, and
whatever the fork brought out belonged
to the priest. All the Israelites who came
to Shiloh to offer sacrifices were treated
like this. 15In addition, even before the
fat was taken off and burned, the priest's
servant would come and say to the one
offering the sacrifice, "Give me some
meat for the priest to roast; he won't accept boiled meat from you, only raw
meat."
16If the person answered, "Let us do
what is right and burn the fat first; then
take what you want," the priest's servant
would say, "No! Give it to me now! If you
don't, I will have to take it by force!"
17This sin of the sons of Eli was extremely serious in the Lord's sight, because they treated the offerings to the
Lord with such disrespect.

Samuel at Shiloh

18In the meantime the boy Samuel
continued to serve the Lord, wearing a
sacred linen apron. 19Each year his
mother would make a little robe and
take it to him when she accompanied
her husband to offer the yearly sacrifice.
20Then Eli would bless Elkanah and his
wife, and say to Elkanah, "May the Lord
give you other children by this woman
to take the place of the one you dedicated to him."
After that they would go back home.
21The Lord did bless Hannah, and she
had three more sons and two daughters.
The boy Samuel grew up in the service
of the Lord.

Eli and His Sons

22Eli was now very old. He kept hearing about everything his sons were doing to the Israelites and that they were
even sleeping with the women who
worked at the entrance to the Tent of the
Lord's presence. 23So he said to them,
"Why are you doing these things? Everybody tells me about the evil you are doing. 24Stop it, my sons! This is an awful
thing the people of the Lord are talking
about! 25If anyone sins against someone
else, God can defend the one who is
wrong; but who can defend someone
who sins against the Lord?"
But they would not listen to their
father, for the Lord had decided to kill
them.
26The boy Samuel continued to grow
and to gain favor both with the Lord and
with people.

The Prophecy against Eli's Family

27A prophet came to Eli with this message from the Lord: "When your ancestor Aaron and his family were slaves of
the king of Egypt, I revealed myself to
Aaron. 28From all the tribes of Israel I
chose his family to be my priests, to
serve at the altar, to burn the incense,
and to wear the ephodᵍ to consult me.
And I gave them the right to keep a
share of the sacrifices burned on the altar. 29Why, then, do you look with
greedʰ at the sacrifices and offerings
which I require from my people? Why,
Eli, do you honor your sons more than
me by letting them fatten themselves on
the best parts of all the sacrifices my
people offer to me? 30I, the Lord God of
Israel, promised in the past that your

ᵍ EPHOD: See Word List.   ʰ One ancient translation look with greed; Hebrew unclear.

THE CITY OF SHILOH

Shiloh was a small Old Testament village about twenty miles north of Jerusalem. It was important because it served as the religious center for the Israelites during the period of the judges before the kingdom was united under the leadership of David.

Numerous references are made to Shiloh during this period as the city where the "Tent where God was worshiped" was located (Jg 18.31). These references are probably to the Tent with its Covenant Box—or perhaps a permanent building that housed the Tent—because the Temple was not constructed until Solomon was king.

Hannah prayed for a son at Shiloh. God granted this request by sending Samuel. During his boyhood, Samuel worked with the high priest Eli at Shiloh. One of the most beautiful stories of the Old Testament is about Samuel's response to the voice of the Lord. Thinking his master Eli was calling him, he awakened the high priest to find out what the high priest wanted. Finally, it dawned on both that God was calling Samuel in a unique revelation of his will for the boy. Samuel's response to God's next call was, "Speak; your servant is listening" (1 S 3.1–10).

Samuel eventually succeeded Eli. The Tent was located in Shiloh during Samuel's early years as priest (1 S 1.9; 4.3, 4). However, during a battle with the Philistines, the Covenant Box was captured by Israel's enemies because God had forsaken Shiloh as the center of worship (Ps 78.60). When the Box was returned to Israel by the Philistines, it was not placed at Shiloh (2 S 6.2–17). It was lodged instead at Kiriath Jearim (1 Ch 13.3–14).

After the Box was moved to another city, Shiloh gradually lost its importance. This loss was made complete when Jerusalem was established as capital of the kingdom in David's time. In the days of the prophet Jeremiah, Shiloh was in ruin (Jr 7.12, 14). It became an inhabited town again in the days of the Greeks and Romans several centuries later.

family and your clan would serve me as priests for all time. But now I say that I won't have it any longer! Instead, I will honor those who honor me, and I will treat with contempt those who despise me. 31 Listen, the time is coming when I will kill all the young men in your family and your clan, so that no man in your family will live to be old. 32 You will be troubled and look with envy*i* on all the blessings I will give to the other people of Israel, but no one in your family will ever again live to old age. 33 Yet I will keep one of your descendants alive, and he will serve me as priest. But he*j* will become blind and lose all hope, and all your other descendants will die a violent death. 34 When your two sons Hophni and Phinehas both die on the same day, this will show you that everything I have said will come true. 35 I will choose a priest who will be faithful to me and do everything I want him to. I will give him descendants, who will always serve in the presence of my chosen king. 36 Any of your descendants who survive will have to go to that priest and ask him for money and food, and beg to be allowed to help the priests, in order to have something to eat."

The LORD Appears to Samuel

3 In those days, when the boy Samuel was serving the LORD under the direction of Eli, there were very few messages from the LORD, and visions from him were quite rare. 2 One night Eli, who was now almost blind, was sleeping in his own room; 3 Samuel was sleeping in the sanctuary, where the sacred Covenant Box was. Before dawn, while the lamp was still burning, 4 the LORD called Samuel. He answered, "Yes, sir!" 5 and ran to Eli and said, "You called me, and here I am."

But Eli answered, "I didn't call you; go back to bed." So Samuel went back to bed.

6-7 The LORD called Samuel again. The boy did not know that it was the LORD, because the LORD had never spoken to him before. So he got up, went to Eli, and said, "You called me, and here I am."

But Eli answered, "My son, I didn't call you; go back to bed."

8 The LORD called Samuel a third time; he got up, went to Eli, and said, "You called me, and here I am."

Then Eli realized that it was the LORD who was calling the boy, 9 so he said to him, "Go back to bed; and if he calls you again, say, 'Speak, LORD, your servant is listening.'" So Samuel went back to bed.

10 The LORD came and stood there, and called as he had before, "Samuel! Samuel!"

Samuel answered, "Speak; your servant is listening."

11 The LORD said to him, "Some day I am going to do something to the people of Israel that is so terrible that everyone who hears about it will be stunned. 12 On that day I will carry out all my threats against Eli's family, from beginning to end. 13 I have already told him*k* that I am going to punish his family forever because his sons have spoken evil things against me. Eli knew they were doing this, but he did not stop them. 14 So I solemnly declare to the family of Eli that no sacrifice or offering will ever be able to remove the consequences of this terrible sin."

15 Samuel stayed in bed until morning; then he got up and opened the doors of the house of the LORD. He was afraid to tell Eli about the vision. 16 Eli called him, "Samuel, my boy!"

"Yes, sir," answered Samuel.

17 "What did the LORD tell you?" Eli asked. "Don't keep anything from me. God will punish you severely if you don't tell me everything he said." 18 So Samuel told him everything; he did not keep anything back. Eli said, "He is the LORD; he will do whatever seems best to him."

19 As Samuel grew up, the LORD was with him and made come true everything that Samuel said. 20 So all the people of Israel, from one end of the country to the other, knew that Samuel was indeed a prophet of the LORD. 21 The LORD continued to reveal himself at Shiloh, where he had appeared to Samuel and had spoken to him. And when Samuel spoke, all Israel listened.

i Probable text look with envy; *Hebrew unclear.*
k One ancient translation I have already told him;

j One ancient translation he; *Hebrew* you.
Hebrew I will tell him.

The Capture of the Covenant Box

4 At that time the Philistines gathered to go to war against Israel, so[l] the Israelites set out to fight them. The Israelites set up their camp at Ebenezer and the Philistines at Aphek. 2 The Philistines attacked, and after fierce fighting they defeated the Israelites and killed about four thousand men on the battlefield. 3 When the survivors came back to camp, the leaders of Israel said, "Why did the LORD let the Philistines defeat us today? Let's go and bring the LORD's Covenant Box from Shiloh, so that he[m] will go with us and save us from our enemies." 4 So they sent messengers to Shiloh and got the Covenant Box of the LORD Almighty, who is enthroned above the winged creatures.[n] And Eli's two sons, Hophni and Phinehas, came along with the Covenant Box.

5 When the Covenant Box arrived, the Israelites gave such a loud shout of joy that the earth shook. 6 The Philistines heard the shouting and said, "Listen to all that shouting in the Hebrew camp! What does it mean?" When they found out that the LORD's Covenant Box had arrived in the Hebrew camp, 7 they were afraid, and said, "A god has come into their camp! We're lost! Nothing like this has ever happened to us before! 8 Who can save us from those powerful gods? They are the gods who slaughtered the Egyptians in the desert! 9 Be brave, Philistines! Fight like men, or we will become slaves to the Hebrews, just as they were our slaves. So fight like men!"

10 The Philistines fought hard and defeated the Israelites, who went running to their homes. There was a great slaughter: thirty thousand Israelite soldiers were killed. 11 God's Covenant Box was captured, and Eli's sons, Hophni and Phinehas, were both killed.

The Death of Eli

12 A man from the tribe of Benjamin ran all the way from the battlefield to Shiloh and arrived there the same day. To show his grief, he had torn his clothes and put dirt on his head. 13 Eli, who was very worried about the Covenant Box, was sitting in his seat beside the road, staring. The man spread the news throughout the town, and everyone cried out in fear. 14 Eli heard the noise and asked, "What is all this noise about?" The man hurried to Eli to tell him the news. (15 Eli was now ninety-eight years old and almost completely blind.) 16 The man said, "I have escaped from the battle and have run all the way here today."

Eli asked him, "What happened, my son?"

17 The messenger answered, "Israel ran away from the Philistines; it was a terrible defeat for us! Besides that, your sons Hophni and Phinehas were killed, and God's Covenant Box was captured!"

18 When the man mentioned the Covenant Box, Eli fell backward from his seat beside the gate. He was so old and fat that the fall broke his neck, and he died. He had been a leader in Israel for forty years.

The Death of the Widow of Phinehas

19 Eli's daughter-in-law, the wife of Phinehas, was pregnant, and it was almost time for her baby to be born. When she heard that God's Covenant Box had been captured and that her father-in-law and her husband were dead, she suddenly went into labor and gave birth. 20 As she was dying, the women helping her said to her, "Be brave! You have a son!" But she paid no attention and did not answer. 21 She named the boy Ichabod,[o] explaining, "God's glory has left Israel"—referring to the capture of the Covenant Box and the death of her father-in-law and her husband. 22 "God's glory has left Israel," she said, "because God's Covenant Box has been captured."

The Covenant Box among the Philistines

5 After the Philistines captured the Covenant Box, they carried it from Ebenezer to their city of Ashdod, 2 took it into the temple of their god Dagon, and set it up beside his statue. 3 Early the next morning the people of Ashdod saw that the statue of Dagon had fallen face downward on the ground in front of the LORD's Covenant Box. So they lifted it up and put it back in its place. 4 Early the

CAPTURE OF THE COVENANT BOX

The Covenant Box, a sacred portable chest, was the most sacred object in the Tent and the Temple. It symbolized God's presence and his covenant with Israel. Believing the Box would protect them in battle, the army of Israel carried the sacred chest into conflict with the Philistines. The Philistines captured the Box but were eager to return it when they were visited by a series of plagues.

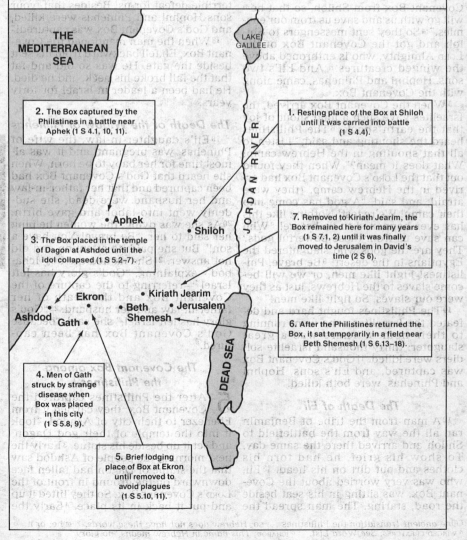

THE MEDITERRANEAN SEA

LAKE GALILEE

JORDAN RIVER

DEAD SEA

2. The Box captured by the Philistines in a battle near Aphek (1 S 4.1, 10, 11).

1. Resting place of the Box at Shiloh until it was carried into battle (1 S 4.4).

• Aphek

• Shiloh

3. The Box placed in the temple of Dagon at Ashdod until the idol collapsed (1 S 5.2–7).

7. Removed to Kiriath Jearim, the Box remained here for many years (1 S 7.1, 2) until it was finally moved to Jerusalem in David's time (2 S 6).

Ekron
• Kiriath Jearim
• Beth • Jerusalem
Ashdod • Gath • Shemesh

6. After the Philistines returned the Box, it sat temporarily in a field near Beth Shemesh (1 S 6.13–18).

4. Men of Gath struck by strange disease when Box was placed in this city (1 S 5.8, 9).

5. Brief lodging place of Box at Ekron until removed to avoid plagues (1 S 5.10, 11).

following morning they saw that the statue had again fallen down in front of the Covenant Box. This time its head and both its arms were broken off and were lying in the doorway; only the body was left. (5 That is why even today the priests of Dagon and all his worshipers in Ashdod step over that place and do not walk on it.)

6 The Lord punished the people of Ashdod severely and terrified them. He punished them and the people in the surrounding territory by causing them to have tumors.ᴾ 7 When they saw what was happening, they said, "The God of Israel is punishing us and our god Dagon. We can't let the Covenant Box stay here any longer." 8 So they sent messengers and called together all five of the Philistine kings and asked them, "What shall we do with the Covenant Box of the God of Israel?"

"Take it over to Gath," they answered; so they took it to Gath, another Philistine city. 9 But after it arrived there, the Lord punished that city too and caused a great panic. He punished them with tumors which developed in all the people of the city, young and old alike. 10 So they sent the Covenant Box to Ekron, another Philistine city; but when it arrived there, the people cried out, "They have brought the Covenant Box of the God of Israel here, in order to kill us all!" 11 So again they sent for all the Philistine kings and said, "Send the Covenant Box of Israel back to its own place, so that it won't kill us and our families." There was panic throughout the city because God was punishing them so severely. 12 Even those who did not die developed tumors and the people cried out to their gods for help.

The Return of the Covenant Box

6 After the Lord's Covenant Box had been in Philistia for seven months, 2 the people called the priests and the magicians and asked, "What shall we do with the Covenant Box of the Lord? If we send it back where it belongs, what shall we send with it?"

3 They answered, "If you return the Covenant Box of the God of Israel, you must, of course, send with it a gift to him

to pay for your sin. The Covenant Box must not go back without a gift. In this way you will be healed, and you will find out why he has kept on punishing you."

4 "What gift shall we send him?" the people asked.

They answered, "Five gold models of tumors and five gold mice, one of each for each Philistine king. The same plague was sent on all of you and on the five kings. 5 You must make these models of the tumors and of the mice that are ravaging your country, and you must give honor to the God of Israel. Perhaps he will stop punishing you, your gods, and your land. 6 Why should you be stubborn, as the king of Egypt and the Egyptians were? Don't forget how God made fools of them until they let the Israelites leave Egypt. 7 So prepare a new wagon and two cows that have never been yoked; hitch them to the wagon and drive their calves back to the barn. 8 Take the Lord's Covenant Box, put it on the wagon, and place in a box beside it the gold models that you are sending to him as a gift to pay for your sins. Start the wagon on its way and let it go by itself. 9 Then watch it go; if it goes toward the town of Beth Shemesh, this means that it is the God of the Israelites who has sent this terrible disaster on us. But if it doesn't, then we will know that he did not send the plague; it was only a matter of chance."

10 They did what they were told: they took two cows and hitched them to the wagon, and shut the calves in the barn. 11 They put the Covenant Box in the wagon, together with the box containing the gold models of the mice and of the tumors. 12 The cows started off on the road to Beth Shemesh and headed straight toward it, without turning off the road. They were mooing as they went. The five Philistine kings followed them as far as the border of Beth Shemesh.

13 The people of Beth Shemesh were reaping wheat in the valley, when suddenly they looked up and saw the Covenant Box. They were overjoyed at the sight. 14 The wagon came to a field belonging to a man named Joshua, who lived in Beth Shemesh, and it stopped

---

ᴾ TUMORS: *The association of tumors with an abundance of mice suggests that this was a case of bubonic plague (see 6.5).*

there near a large rock. The people chopped up the wooden wagon and killed the cows and burned them as a burnt sacrifice to the LORD. 15 The Levites lifted off the Covenant Box of the LORD and the box with the gold models in it, and placed them on the large rock. Then the people of Beth Shemesh offered burnt sacrifices and other sacrifices to the LORD. 16 The five Philistine kings watched them do this and then went back to Ekron that same day.

17 The Philistines sent the five gold tumors to the LORD as a gift to pay for their sins, one each for the cities of Ashdod, Gaza, Ashkelon, Gath, and Ekron. 18 They also sent gold mice, one for each of the cities ruled by the five Philistine kings, both the fortified towns and the villages without walls. The large rock in the field of Joshua of Beth Shemesh, on which they placed the LORD's Covenant Box, is still there as a witness to what happened.

19 The LORD killed seventy of the men of Beth Shemesh because they looked inside the Covenant Box. And the people mourned because the LORD had caused such a great slaughter among them.

The Covenant Box at Kiriath Jearim

20 So the men of Beth Shemesh said, "Who can stand before the LORD, this holy God? Where can we send him to get him away from us?" 21 They sent messengers to the people of Kiriath Jearim to say, "The Philistines have returned the LORD's Covenant Box. Come down and get it."

7 So the people of Kiriath Jearim got the LORD's Covenant Box and took it to the house of a man named Abinadab, who lived on a hill. They consecrated his son Eleazar to be in charge of it.

Samuel Rules Israel

2 The Covenant Box of the LORD stayed in Kiriath Jearim a long time, some twenty years. During this time all the Israelites cried to the LORD for help.

3 Samuel said to the people of Israel, "If you are going to turn to the LORD with all your hearts, you must get rid of all the foreign gods and the images of the goddess Astarte. Dedicate yourselves completely to the LORD and worship only him, and he will rescue you from the power of the Philistines." 4 So the Israel-

ites got rid of their idols of Baal and Astarte, and worshiped only the LORD.

5 Then Samuel called for all the Israelites to meet at Mizpah, telling them, "I will pray to the LORD for you there." 6 So they all gathered at Mizpah. They drew some water and poured it out as an offering to the LORD and fasted that whole day. They said, "We have sinned against the LORD." (It was at Mizpah where Samuel settled disputes among the Israelites.)

7 When the Philistines heard that the Israelites had gathered at Mizpah, the five Philistine kings started out with their men to attack them. The Israelites heard about it and were afraid, 8 and said to Samuel, "Keep praying to the LORD our God to save us from the Philistines." 9 Samuel killed a young lamb and burned it whole as a sacrifice to the LORD. Then he prayed to the LORD to help Israel, and the LORD answered his prayer. 10 While Samuel was offering the sacrifice, the Philistines moved forward to attack; but just then the LORD thundered from heaven against them. They became completely confused and fled in panic. 11 The Israelites marched out from Mizpah and pursued the Philistines almost as far as Bethcar, killing them along the way.

12 Then Samuel took a stone, set it up between Mizpah and Shen, and said, "The LORD has helped us all the way" — and he named it "Stone of Help." 13 So the Philistines were defeated, and the LORD prevented them from invading Israel's territory as long as Samuel lived. 14 All the cities which the Philistines had captured between Ekron and Gath were returned to Israel, and so Israel got back all its territory. And there was peace also between the Israelites and the Canaanites.

15 Samuel ruled Israel as long as he lived. 16 Every year he would go around to Bethel, Gilgal, and Mizpah, and in these places he would settle disputes. 17 Then he would go back to his home in Ramah, where also he would serve as judge. In Ramah he built an altar to the LORD.

The People Ask for a King

8 When Samuel grew old, he made his sons judges in Israel. 2 The older son was named Joel and the younger

one Abijah; they were judges in Beersheba. ³But they did not follow their father's example; they were interested only in making money, so they accepted bribes and did not decide cases honestly.

⁴Then all the leaders of Israel met together, went to Samuel in Ramah, ⁵and said to him, "Look, you are getting old and your sons don't follow your example. So then, appoint a king to rule over us, so that we will have a king, as other countries have." ⁶Samuel was displeased with their request for a king; so he prayed to the Lord, ⁷and the Lord said, "Listen to everything the people say to you. You are not the one they have rejected; I am the one they have rejected as their king. ⁸Ever since I brought them out of Egypt, they have turned away from me and worshiped other gods; and now they are doing to you what they have always done to me. ⁹So then, listen to them, but give them strict warnings and explain how their kings will treat them."

¹⁰Samuel told the people who were asking him for a king everything that the Lord had said to him. ¹¹"This is how your king will treat you," Samuel explained. "He will make soldiers of your sons; some of them will serve in his war chariots, others in his cavalry, and others will run before his chariots. ¹²He will make some of them officers in charge of a thousand men, and others in charge of fifty men. Your sons will have to plow his fields, harvest his crops, and make his weapons and the equipment for his chariots. ¹³Your daughters will have to make perfumes for him and work as his cooks and his bakers. ¹⁴He will take your best fields, vineyards, and olive groves, and give them to his officials. ¹⁵He will take a tenth of your grain and of your grapes for his court officers and other officials. ¹⁶He will take your servants *q* and your best cattle *q* and donkeys, and make them work for him. ¹⁷He will take a tenth of your flocks. And you yourselves will become his slaves. ¹⁸When that time comes, you will complain bitterly because of your king, whom you yourselves chose, but the Lord will not listen to your complaints."

¹⁹The people paid no attention to Samuel, but said, "No! We want a king, ²⁰so that we will be like other nations, with our own king to rule us and to lead us out to war and to fight our battles." ²¹Samuel listened to everything they said and then went and told it to the Lord. ²²The Lord answered, "Do what they want and give them a king." Then Samuel told all the men of Israel to go back home.

Saul Meets Samuel

9 There was a wealthy and influential man named Kish, from the tribe of Benjamin; he was the son of Abiel and grandson of Zeror, and belonged to the family of Becorath, a part of the clan of Aphiah. ²He had a son named Saul, a handsome man in the prime of life. Saul was a foot taller than anyone else in Israel and more handsome as well.

³Some donkeys belonging to Kish had wandered off, so he said to Saul, "Take one of the servants with you and go and look for the donkeys." ⁴They went through the hill country of Ephraim and the region of Shalishah, but did not find them; so they went on through the region of Shaalim, but the donkeys were not there. Then they went through the territory of Benjamin, but still did not find them. ⁵When they came into the region of Zuph, Saul said to his servant, "Let's go back home, or my father might stop thinking about the donkeys and start worrying about us."

⁶The servant answered, "Wait! In this town there is a holy man who is highly respected because everything he says comes true. Let's go to him, and maybe he can tell us where we can find the donkeys."

⁷"If we go to him, what can we give him?" Saul asked. "There is no food left in our packs, and we don't have a thing to give him, do we?"

⁸The servant answered, "I have a small silver coin. I can give him that, and then he will tell us where we can find them."

⁹⁻¹¹Saul replied, "A good idea! Let's go." So they went to the town where the holy man lived. As they were going up the hill to the town, they met some young women who were coming out to draw water. They asked these women, "Is the seer in town?"

---

q One ancient translation cattle; *Hebrew* young men.

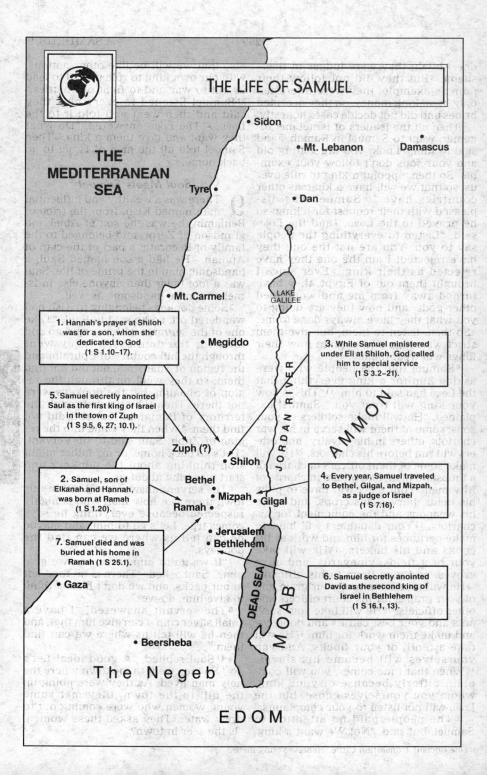

THE LIFE OF SAMUEL

THE
MEDITERRANEAN
SEA

• Sidon

• Mt. Lebanon   Damascus

• Tyre •

• Dan

LAKE
GALILEE

• Mt. Carmel

1. Hannah's prayer at Shiloh was for a son, whom she dedicated to God (1 S 1.10–17).

• Megiddo

3. While Samuel ministered under Eli at Shiloh, God called him to special service (1 S 3.2–21).

AMMON

5. Samuel secretly anointed Saul as the first king of Israel in the town of Zuph (1 S 9.5, 6, 27; 10.1).

Zuph (?)

• Shiloh

JORDAN RIVER

2. Samuel, son of Elkanah and Hannah, was born at Ramah (1 S 1.20).

Bethel
• Mizpah • Gilgal
Ramah •

4. Every year, Samuel traveled to Bethel, Gilgal, and Mizpah, as a judge of Israel (1 S 7.16).

7. Samuel died and was buried at his home in Ramah (1 S 25.1).

• Jerusalem
• Bethlehem

DEAD SEA

MOAB

• Gaza

6. Samuel secretly anointed David as the second king of Israel in Bethlehem (1 S 16.1, 13).

• Beersheba

The Negeb

EDOM

(At that time a prophet was called a seer, and so whenever someone wanted to ask God a question, he would say, "Let's go to the seer.")

12-13 "Yes, he is," the young women answered. "In fact, he is just ahead of you. If you hurry, you will catch up with him. As soon as you go into town, you will find him. He arrived in town today because the people are going to offer a sacrifice on the altar on the hill. The people who are invited won't start eating until he gets there, because he has to bless the sacrifice first. If you go now, you will find him before he goes up the hill to eat." 14 So Saul and his servant went on to the town, and as they were going in, they saw Samuel coming out toward them on his way to the place of worship.

15 Now on the previous day the LORD had told Samuel, 16 "Tomorrow about this time I will send you a man from the tribe of Benjamin; anoint him as ruler of my people Israel, and he will rescue them from the Philistines. I have seen the suffering of my people and have heard their cries for help."

17 When Samuel caught sight of Saul, the LORD said to him, "This is the man I told you about. He will rule my people." 18 Then Saul went over to Samuel, who was near the gate, and asked, "Tell me, where does the seer live?"

19 Samuel answered, "I am the seer. Go on ahead of me to the place of worship. Both of you are to eat with me today. Tomorrow morning I will answer all your questions and send you on your way. 20 As for the donkeys that were lost three days ago, don't worry about them; they have already been found. But who is it that the people of Israel want so much?r It is you — you and your father's family."

21 Saul answered, "I belong to the tribe of Benjamin, the smallest tribe in Israel, and my family is the least important one in the tribe. Why, then, do you talk like this to me?"

22 Then Samuel led Saul and his servant into the large room and gave them a place at the head of the table where the guests, about thirty in all, were seated. 23 Samuel said to the cook, "Bring the piece of meat I gave you, which I told you to set aside." 24 So the cook brought the choice piece of the leg and placed it before Saul. Samuels said, "Look, here is the piece that was kept for you. Eat it. I saved it for you to eat at this time with the people I invited."t

So Saul ate with Samuel that day. 25 When they went down from the place of worship to the town, they fixed up a bed for Saulu on the roof,v 26 and he slept there.w

Samuel Anoints Saul as Ruler

At dawn Samuel called to Saul on the roof, "Get up, and I will send you on your way." Saul got up, and he and Samuel went out to the street together. 27 When they arrived at the edge of town, Samuel said to Saul, "Tell the servant to go on ahead of us." The servant left, and Samuel continued, "Stay here a minute, and I will tell you what God has said."

10 Then Samuel took a jar of olive oil and poured it on Saul's head, kissed him, and said, "The LORD anoints you as ruler of his people Israel. You will rule his people and protect them from all their enemies. And this is the proof to you that the LORD has chosen youx to be the ruler of his people: 2 When you leave me today, you will meet two men near Rachel's tomb at Zelzah in the territory of Benjamin. They will tell you that the donkeys you were looking for have been found, so that your father isn't worried any more about them but about you, and he keeps asking, 'What shall I do about my son?' 3 You will go on from there until you come to the sacred tree at Tabor, where you will meet three men on their way to offer a sacrifice to God at Bethel. One of them will be leading three young goats, another one will be carrying three loaves of bread, and the third one will have a leather bag full of wine. 4 They will greet you and offer you two of the loaves, which you are to accept. 5 Then you will go to the Hill of God in Gibeah,

---

r who is it . . . much?; or who is to have the most desirable thing in Israel?   s Some ancient translations Samuel; Hebrew He (that is, the cook).   t Probable text I saved it . . . invited; Hebrew unclear.   u One ancient translation they fixed up a bed for Saul; Hebrew he spoke with Saul.   v ON THE ROOF: At that time houses had flat roofs, and it was common for people to sleep on them.   w Some ancient translations and he slept there; Hebrew they got up early.   x Some ancient translations as ruler of his people . . . the LORD has chosen you; Hebrew does not have these words.

where there is a Philistine camp. At the entrance to the town you will meet a group of prophets coming down from the altar on the hill, playing harps, drums, flutes, and lyres. They will be dancing and shouting. 6 Suddenly the spirit of the LORD will take control of you, and you will join in their religious dancing and shouting and will become a different person. 7 When these things happen, do whatever God leads you to do. 8 You will go ahead of me to Gilgal, where I will meet you and offer burnt sacrifices and fellowship sacrifices. Wait there seven days until I come and tell you what to do."

9 When Saul turned to leave Samuel, God gave Saul a new nature. And everything Samuel had told him happened that day. 10 When Saul and his servant arrived at Gibeah, a group of prophets met him. Suddenly the spirit of God took control of him, and he joined in their ecstatic dancing and shouting. 11 People who had known him before saw him doing this and asked one another, "What has happened to the son of Kish? Has Saul become a prophet?" 12 A man who lived there asked, "How about these other prophets—who do you think their fathers are?" This is how the saying originated, "Has even Saul become a prophet?" 13 When Saul finished his ecstatic dancing and shouting, he went to the altar on the hill.

14 Saul's uncle saw him and the servant, and he asked them, "Where have you been?"

"Looking for the donkeys," Saul answered. "When we couldn't find them, we went to see Samuel."

15 "And what did he tell you?" Saul's uncle asked.

16 "He told us that the animals had been found," Saul answered—but he did not tell his uncle what Samuel had said about his becoming king.

Saul Is Acclaimed as King

17 Samuel called the people together for a religious gathering at Mizpah 18 and said to them, "The LORD, the God of Israel, says, 'I brought you out of Egypt and rescued you from the Egyptians and all the other peoples who were oppressing you. 19 I am your God, the one who rescues you from all your troubles and difficulties, but today you have rejected me and have asked me to give you a king. Very well, then, gather yourselves before the LORD by tribes and by clans.'"

20 Then Samuel had each tribe come forward, and the LORD picked the tribe of Benjamin. 21 Then Samuel had the families of the tribe of Benjamin come forward, and the family of Matri was picked out. Then the men of the family of Matri came forward,y and Saul son of Kish was picked out. They looked for him, but when they could not find him, 22 they asked the LORD, "Is there still someone else?"

The LORD answered, "Saul is over there, hiding behind the supplies."

23 So they ran and brought Saul out to the people, and they could see that he was a foot taller than anyone else. 24 Samuel said to the people, "Here is the man the LORD has chosen! There is no one else among us like him."

All the people shouted, "Long live the king!"

25 Samuel explained to the people the rights and duties of a king, and then wrote them in a book, which he deposited in a holy place. Then he sent everyone home. 26 Saul also went back home to Gibeah. Some powerful men,z whose hearts God had touched, went with him. 27 But some worthless people said, "How can this fellow do us any good?" They despised Saul and did not bring him any gifts.

Saul Defeats the Ammonites

11 About a month later King Nahash of Ammon led his army against the town of Jabesh in the territory of Gilead and besieged it. The men of Jabesh said to Nahash, "Make a treaty with us, and we will accept you as our ruler."

2 Nahash answered, "I will make a treaty with you on one condition: I will put out everyone's right eye and so bring disgrace on all Israel."

3 The leaders of Jabesh said, "Give us

y One ancient translation Then the men of the family of Matri came forward; Hebrew does not have these words.   z One ancient translation Some powerful men; Hebrew The army.

seven days to send messengers throughout the land of Israel. If no one will help us, then we will surrender to you."

4 The messengers arrived at Gibeah, where Saul lived, and when they told the news, the people started crying in despair. 5 Saul was just then coming in from the field with his oxen, and he asked, "What's wrong? Why is everyone crying?" They told him what the messengers from Jabesh had reported. 6 When Saul heard this, the spirit of God took control of him, and he became furious. 7 He took two oxen, cut them in pieces, and had messengers carry the pieces throughout the land of Israel with this warning: "Whoever does not follow Saul and Samuel into battle will have this done to his oxen!"

The people of Israel were afraid of what the LORD might do, and all of them, without exception, came out together. 8 Saul gathered them at Bezek: there were 300,000 from Israel and 30,000 from Judah. 9 They said to the messengers from Jabesh, "Tell your people that before noon tomorrow they will be rescued." When the people of Jabesh received the message, they were overjoyed 10 and said to Nahash, "Tomorrow we will surrender to you, and you can do with us whatever you wish."

11 That night Saul divided his men into three groups, and at dawn the next day they rushed into the enemy camp and attacked the Ammonites. By noon they had slaughtered them. The survivors scattered, each man running off by himself.

12 Then the people of Israel said to Samuel, "Where are the people who said that Saul should not be our king? Hand them over to us, and we will kill them!"

13 But Saul said, "No one will be put to death today, for this is the day the LORD rescued Israel." 14 And Samuel said to them, "Let us all go to Gilgal and once more proclaim Saul as our king." 15 So they all went to Gilgal, and there at the holy place they proclaimed Saul king. They offered fellowship sacrifices, and Saul and all the people of Israel celebrated the event.

Samuel Addresses the People

12 Then Samuel said to the people of Israel, "I have done what you asked me to do. I have given you a king to rule you, 2 and now you have him to lead you. As for me, I am old and gray, and my sons are with you. I have been your leader from my youth until now. 3 Here I am. If I have done anything wrong, accuse me now in the presence of the LORD and the king he has chosen. Have I taken anybody's cow or anybody's donkey? Have I cheated or oppressed anyone? Have I accepted a bribe from anyone? If I have done any of these things, I will pay back what I have taken."

4 The people answered, "No, you have not cheated us or oppressed us; you have not taken anything from anyone."

5 Samuel replied, "The LORD and the king he has chosen are witnesses today that you have found me to be completely innocent."

"Yes, the LORD is our witness," they answered.

6 Samuel continued, "The LORD is the one who chose Moses and Aaron and who brought your ancestors out of Egypt. 7 Now stand where you are, and I will accuse you before the LORD by reminding youᶜ of all the mighty actions the LORD did to save you and your ancestors. 8 When Jacob and his family went to Egypt and the Egyptians oppressed them,ᵇ your ancestors cried to the LORD for help, and he sent Moses and Aaron, who brought them out of Egypt and settled them in this land. 9 But the people forgot the LORD their God, and so he let the Philistines and the king of Moab and Sisera, commander of the army of the city of Hazor, fight against your ancestors and conquer them. 10 Then they cried to the LORD for help and said, 'We have sinned, because we turned away from you, LORD, and worshiped the idols of Baal and Astarte. Rescue us from our enemies, and we will worship you!' 11 And the LORD sent Gideon, Barak,ᶜ Jephthah, and finally me. Each of us rescued you from your enemies, and you lived in safety. 12 But when you saw that King Nahash of Ammon was about to

---

ᵃ *One ancient translation* by reminding you; *Hebrew does not have these words.*
ᵇ *One ancient translation* and the Egyptians oppressed them; *Hebrew does not have these words.*
ᶜ *Some ancient translations* Barak; *Hebrew* Bedan.

attack you, you rejected the Lord as your king and said to me, 'We want a king to rule us.'

13 "Now here is the king you chose; you asked for him, and now the Lord has given him to you. 14 All will go well with you if you honor the Lord your God, serve him, listen to him, and obey his commands, and if you and your king follow him. 15 But if you do not listen to the Lord but disobey his commands, he will be against you and your king.d 16 So then, stand where you are, and you will see the great thing which the Lord is going to do. 17 It's the dry season, isn't it? But I will pray, and the Lord will send thunder and rain. When this happens, you will realize that you committed a great sin against the Lord when you asked him for a king."

18 So Samuel prayed, and on that same day the Lord sent thunder and rain. Then all the people became afraid of the Lord and of Samuel, 19 and they said to Samuel, "Please, sir, pray to the Lord your God for us, so that we won't die. We now realize that, besides all our other sins, we have sinned by asking for a king."

20 "Don't be afraid," Samuel answered. "Even though you have done such an evil thing, do not turn away from the Lord, but serve him with all your heart. 21 Don't go after e false gods; they cannot help you or save you, for they are not real. 22 The Lord has made a solemn promise, and he will not abandon you, for he has decided to make you his own people. 23 As for me, the Lord forbid that I should sin against him by no longer praying for you. Instead, I will teach you what is good and right for you to do. 24 Obey the Lord and serve him faithfully with all your heart. Remember the great things he has done for you. 25 But if you continue to sin, you and your king will be destroyed."

War against the Philistines

13 f 2 Saul picked three thousand men, keeping two thousand of them with him in Michmash and in the hill country of Bethel and sending one thousand with his son Jonathan to Gibeah, in the territory of the tribe of Benjamin. The rest of the men Saul sent home.

3 Jonathan killed the Philistine commanderg in Geba, and all the Philistines heard about it. Then Saul sent messengers to call the Hebrews to war by blowing a trumpet throughout the whole country. 4 All the Israelites were told that Saul had killed the Philistine commander and that the Philistines hated them. So the people answered the call to join Saul at Gilgal.

5 The Philistines assembled to fight the Israelites; they had thirty thousand war chariots, six thousand cavalry troops, and as many soldiers as there are grains of sand on the seashore. They went to Michmash, east of Bethaven, and camped there. 6 Then they launched a strong attack against the Israelites, putting them in a desperate situation. Some of the Israelites hid in caves and holes or among the rocks or in pits and wells; 7 others crossed the Jordan River into the territories of Gad and Gilead.

Saul was still at Gilgal, and the people with him were trembling with fear. 8 He waited seven days for Samuel, as Samuel had instructed him to do, but Samuel still had not come to Gilgal. The people began to desert Saul, 9 so he said to them, "Bring me the burnt sacrifices and the fellowship sacrifices." He offered a burnt sacrifice, 10 and just as he was finishing, Samuel arrived. Saul went out to meet him and welcome him, 11 but Samuel said, "What have you done?"

Saul answered, "The people were deserting me, and you had not come when you said you would; besides that, the Philistines are gathering at Michmash. 12 So I thought, 'The Philistines are going to attack me here in Gilgal, and I have not tried to win the Lord's favor.' So I felt I had to offer a sacrifice."

13 "That was a foolish thing to do," Samuel answered. "You have not obeyed the command the Lord your God gave you. If you had obeyed, he would have let you and your descendants rule over Israel forever. 14 But now your rule will not continue. Because you have dis-

d One ancient translation your king; Hebrew your ancestors.   e Some ancient translations after; Hebrew because after.   f One ancient translation does not have verse 1; Hebrew has as verse 1 Saul was . . . years old when he became king, and he was king of Israel for two years. The Hebrew text is defective at two points in this verse.   g killed the Philistine commander; or defeated the Philistines camping.

obeyed him, the Lord will find the kind of man he wants and make him ruler of his people."

15 Samuel left Gilgal and went on his way. The rest of the people followed Saul as he went to join his soldiers. They went from Gilgal*h* to Gibeah in the territory of Benjamin. Saul inspected his troops, about six hundred men. 16 Saul, his son Jonathan, and their men camped in Geba in the territory of Benjamin; the Philistine camp was at Michmash. 17 The Philistine soldiers went out on raids from their camp in three groups: one group went toward Ophrah in the territory of Shual, 18 another went toward Beth Horon, and the other one went to the border overlooking Zeboim Valley and the wilderness.

19 There were no blacksmiths in Israel because the Philistines were determined to keep the Hebrews from making swords and spears. (20 The Israelites had to go to the Philistines to get their plows, hoes, axes, and sickles*i* sharpened; 21 the charge was one small coin for sharpening axes and for fixing goads,*j* and two coins for sharpening plows or hoes.) 22 And so on the day of battle none of the Israelite soldiers except Saul and his son Jonathan had swords or spears. 23 The Philistines sent a group of soldiers to defend Michmash Pass.

Jonathan's Daring Deed

14 One day Jonathan said to the young man who carried his weapons, "Let's go across to the Philistine camp." But Jonathan did not tell his father Saul, 2 who was camping under a pomegranate tree in Migron, not far from Gibeah; he had about six hundred men with him. 3 (The priest carrying the ephod was Ahijah, the son of Ichabod's brother Ahitub, who was the son of Phinehas and grandson of Eli, the priest of the Lord in Shiloh.) The men did not know that Jonathan had left.

4 In Michmash Pass, which Jonathan had to go through to get over to the Philistine camp, there were two large jagged rocks, one on each side of the pass: one was called Bozez and the other Se-

neh. 5 One was on the north side of the pass, facing Michmash, and the other was on the south side, facing Geba.

6 Jonathan said to the young man, "Let's cross over to the camp of those heathen Philistines. Maybe the Lord will help us; if he does, nothing can keep him from giving us the victory, no matter how few of us there are."

7 The young man answered, "Whatever you want to do,*k* I'm with you."

8 "All right," Jonathan said. "We will go across and let the Philistines see us. 9 If they tell us to wait for them to come to us, then we will stay where we are. 10 But if they tell us to go to them, then we will, because that will be the sign that the Lord has given us victory over them."

11 So they let the Philistines see them, and the Philistines said, "Look! Some Hebrews are coming out of the holes they have been hiding in!" 12 Then they called out to Jonathan and the young man, "Come on up here! We have something to tell*l* you!"

Jonathan said to the young man, "Follow me. The Lord has given Israel victory over them." 13 Jonathan climbed up out of the pass on his hands and knees, and the young man followed him. Jonathan attacked the Philistines and knocked them down, and the young man killed them. 14 In that first slaughter Jonathan and the young man killed about twenty men in an area of about half an acre.*m* 15 All the Philistines in the countryside were terrified; the raiders and the soldiers in the camp trembled with fear; the earth shook, and there was great panic.

The Defeat of the Philistines

16 Saul's men on watch at Gibeah in the territory of Benjamin saw the Philistines running in confusion. 17 So Saul said to his men, "Count the soldiers and find out who is missing." They did so and found that Jonathan and the young man who carried his weapons were missing. 18 "Bring the ephod*n* here," Saul said to Ahijah the priest. (On that day Ahijah was carrying it in front of the

---

h Some ancient translations on his way . . . went from Gilgal; *Hebrew does not have these words.* *i One ancient translation* sickles; *Hebrew* plows. *j Probable text* the charge . . . fixing goads; *Hebrew unclear.* *k One ancient translation* you want to do; *Hebrew* you want to do. Turn. *l* tell; *or* show. *m Probable text* in an area of about half an acre; *Hebrew unclear.* *n One ancient translation* ephod (see 2.28); *Hebrew* Covenant Box.

people of Israel.)ᵒ ¹⁹As Saul was speaking to the priest, the confusion in the Philistine camp kept getting worse, so Saul said to him, "There's no time to consult the LORD!" ²⁰Then he and his men marched into battle against the Philistines, who were fighting each other in complete confusion. ²¹Some Hebrews, who had been on the Philistine side and had gone with them to the camp, changed sidesᵖ and joined Saul and Jonathan. ²²Others, who had been hiding in the hills of Ephraim, heard that the Philistines were running away, so they also joined in and attacked the Philistines, ²³fighting all the way beyond Bethaven. The LORD saved Israel that day.

Events after the Battle

²⁴The Israelites were weak with hunger that day, because Saul, with a solemn oath, had given the order: "A curse be on anyone who eats any food today before I take revenge on my enemies." So nobody had eaten anything all day. ²⁵They allᵠ came into a wooded area and found honey everywhere. ²⁶The woods were full of honey, but no one ate any of it because they were all afraid of Saul's curse. ²⁷But Jonathan had not heard his father threaten the people with a curse; so he reached out with the stick he was carrying, dipped it in a honeycomb, and ate some honey. At once he felt much better. ²⁸But one of the men told him, "We are all weak from hunger, but your father threatened us and said, 'A curse be on anyone who eats any food today.'"

²⁹Jonathan answered, "What a terrible thing my father has done to our people! See how much better I feel because I ate some honey! ³⁰How much better it would have been today if our people had eaten the food they took when they defeated the enemy. Just think how many more Philistines they would have killed!"

³¹That day the Israelites defeated the Philistines, fighting all the way from Michmash to Aijalon. By this time the Israelites were very weak from hunger, ³²and so they rushed over to what they had captured from the enemy, took sheep and cattle, slaughtered them on the spot, and ate the meat with the blood still in it. ³³Saul was told, "Look, the people are sinning against the LORD by eating meat with the blood in it."

"You are traitors!" Saul cried out. "Roll a big stone over hereʳ to me." ³⁴Then he gave another order: "Go among the people and tell them all to bring their cattle and sheep here. They are to slaughter them and eat them here; they must not sin against the LORD by eating meat with blood in it." So that night they all brought their cattle and slaughtered them there. ³⁵Saul built an altar to the LORD, the first one that he built.

³⁶Saul said to his men, "Let's go down and attack the Philistines in the night, plunder them until dawn, and kill them all."

"Do whatever you think best," they answered.

But the priest said, "Let's consult God first."

³⁷So Saul asked God, "Shall I attack the Philistines? Will you give us victory?" But God did not answer that day. ³⁸Then Saul said to the leaders of the people, "Come here and find out what sin was committed today. ³⁹I promise by the living LORD, who gives Israel victory, that the guilty one will be put to death, even if he is my son Jonathan." But no one said anything. ⁴⁰Then Saul said to them, "All of you stand over there, and Jonathan and I will stand over here."

"Do whatever you think best," they answered.

⁴¹Saul said to the LORD, the God of Israel, "LORD, why have you not answered me today? LORD, God of Israel, answer me by the sacred stones. If the guilt is Jonathan's or mine, answer by the Urim; but if it belongs to your people Israel,ˢ answer by the Thummim."ᵗ The answer indicated Jonathan and Saul; and the people were cleared. ⁴²Then Saul said, "Decide between my son Jonathan and

---

ᵒ *One ancient translation* On that day ... Israel; *Hebrew* Because on that day God's Covenant Box and the people of Israel.   ᵖ *Some ancient translations* changed sides again; *Hebrew* around also.   ᵠ *Probable text* They all; *Hebrew* All the land.   ʳ *One ancient translation* here; *Hebrew* today.   ˢ *Some ancient translations* answer me by the sacred stones ... your people Israel; *Hebrew does not have these words.*   ᵗ URIM ... THUMMIM: *Two stones used by the priest to determine God's will; it is not known precisely how they were used.*

SAUL'S MILITARY CAMPAIGNS

As the first king of the united kingdom of Israel, Saul's major task was to subdue the nation's enemies. At first, he won several decisive battles. But his campaigns bogged down when he turned his attention to David, attempting to wipe out what he perceived as a threat to his power. Saul and his sons were eventually killed by the Philistines.

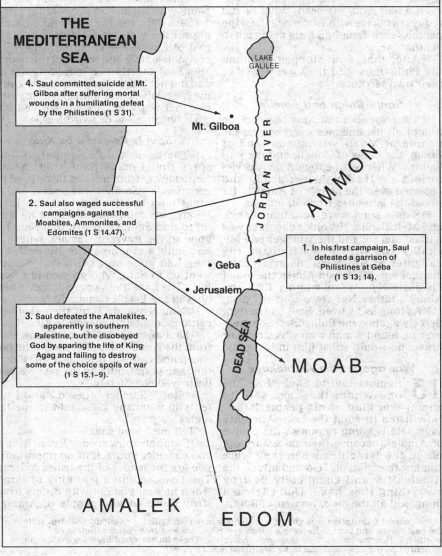

THE MEDITERRANEAN SEA

LAKE GALILEE

4. Saul committed suicide at Mt. Gilboa after suffering mortal wounds in a humiliating defeat by the Philistines (1 S 31).

• Mt. Gilboa

JORDAN RIVER

AMMON

2. Saul also waged successful campaigns against the Moabites, Ammonites, and Edomites (1 S 14.47).

1. In his first campaign, Saul defeated a garrison of Philistines at Geba (1 S 13; 14).

• Geba

• Jerusalem

3. Saul defeated the Amalekites, apparently in southern Palestine, but he disobeyed God by sparing the life of King Agag and failing to destroy some of the choice spoils of war (1 S 15.1–9).

DEAD SEA

MOAB

AMALEK

EDOM

me." And Jonathan was indicated.
43 Then Saul asked Jonathan, "What
have you done?"

Jonathan answered, "I ate a little
honey with the stick I was holding. Here
I am—I am ready to die."

44 Saul said to him, "May God strike
me dead if you are not put to death!"

45 But the people said to Saul, "Will
Jonathan, who won this great victory for
Israel, be put to death? No! We promise
by the living LORD that he will not lose
even a hair from his head. What he did
today was done with God's help." So the
people saved Jonathan from being put to
death.

46 After that, Saul stopped pursuing
the Philistines, and they went back to
their own territory.

Saul's Reign and Family

47 After Saul became king of Israel, he
fought all his enemies everywhere: the
people of Moab, of Ammon, and of
Edom, the kings of Zobah, and the Philistines. Wherever he fought he was vic-
torious.u 48 He fought heroically and
defeated even the people of Amalek. He
saved the Israelites from all attacks.

49 Saul's sons were Jonathan, Ishvi,
and Malchishua. His older daughter was
named Merab, and the younger one Michal. 50 His wife was Ahinoam, the
daughter of Ahimaaz; his army commander was his cousin Abner, the son of
his uncle Ner. 51 Saul's father Kish and
Abner's father Ner were sons of Abiel.

52 As long as he lived, Saul had to fight
fiercely against the Philistines. So whenever he found a man who was strong or
brave, he would enlist him in his army.

War against the Amalekites

15 Samuel said to Saul, "I am the
one whom the LORD sent to
anoint you king of his people Israel.
Now listen to what the LORD Almighty
says. 2 He is going to punish the people
of Amalek because their ancestors opposed the Israelites when they were
coming from Egypt. 3 Go and attack the
Amalekites and completely destroy
everything they have. Don't leave a
thing; kill all the men, women, children,

and babies; the cattle, sheep, camels,
and donkeys."

4 Saul called his forces together and inspected them at Telem: there were
200,000 soldiers from Israel and 10,000
from Judah. 5 Then he and his men went
to the city of Amalek and waited in ambush
in a dry riverbed. 6 He sent a warning to the
Kenites, a people whose ancestors had
been kind to the Israelites when they
came from Egypt: "Go away and leave
the Amalekites, so that I won't kill you
along with them." So the Kenites left.

7 Saul defeated the Amalekites, fighting all the way from Havilah to Shur,
east of Egypt; 8 he captured King Agag
of Amalek alive and killed all the people.
9 But Saul and his men spared Agag's life
and did not kill the best sheep and cattle,
the best calves and lambs,v or anything
else that was good; they destroyed only
what was useless or worthless.w

Saul Is Rejected as King

10 The LORD said to Samuel, 11 "I am
sorry that I made Saul king; he has
turned away from me and disobeyed my
commands." Samuel was angry, and all
night long he pleaded with the LORD.
12 Early the following morning he went
off to find Saul. He heard that Saul had
gone to the town of Carmel, where he
had built a monument to himself, and
then had gone on to Gilgal. 13 Samuel
went up to Saul, who greeted him, saying, "The LORD bless you, Samuel! I have
obeyed the LORD's command."

14 Samuel asked, "Why, then, do I hear
cattle mooing and sheep bleating?"

15 Saul answered, "My men took them
from the Amalekites. They kept the best
sheep and cattle to offer as a sacrifice to
the LORD your God, and the rest we have
destroyed completely."x

16 "Stop," Samuel ordered, "and I will
tell you what the LORD said to me last
night."

"Tell me," Saul said.

17 Samuel answered, "Even though
you consider yourself of no importance,
you are the leader of the tribes of Israel.
The LORD anointed you king of Israel,
18 and he sent you out with orders to destroy those wicked people of Amalek.

---

u One ancient translation was victorious; Hebrew acted wickedly.   v One ancient translation
the best calves and lambs; Hebrew unclear.   w Some ancient translations useless or
worthless; Hebrew unclear.   x DESTROYED COMPLETELY: These animals had been unconditionally
dedicated to the LORD and had to be destroyed (see Lv 27.28).

He told you to fight until you had killed them all. 19 Why, then, did you not obey him? Why did you rush to grab the loot, and so do what displeases the LORD?"

20 "I did obey the LORD," Saul replied. "I went out as he told me to, brought back King Agag, and killed all the Amalekites. 21 But my men did not kill the best sheep and cattle that they captured; instead, they brought them here to Gilgal to offer as a sacrifice to the LORD your God."

22 Samuel said, "Which does the LORD prefer: obedience or offerings and sacrifices? It is better to obey him than to sacrifice the best sheep to him. 23 Rebellion against him is as bad as witchcraft, and arrogance is as sinful as idolatry. Because you rejected the LORD's command, he has rejected you as king."

24 "Yes, I have sinned," Saul replied. "I disobeyed the LORD's command and your instructions. I was afraid of my men and did what they wanted. 25 But now I beg you, forgive my sin and go back with me, so that I can worship the LORD."

26 "I will not go back with you," Samuel answered. "You rejected the LORD's command, and he has rejected you as king of Israel."

27 Then Samuel turned to leave, but Saul caught hold of his cloak, and it tore. 28 Samuel said to him, "The LORD has torn the kingdom of Israel away from you today and given it to someone who is a better man than you. 29 Israel's majestic God does not lie or change his mind. He is not a human being—he does not change his mind."

30 "I have sinned," Saul replied. "But at least show me respect in front of the leaders of my people and all of Israel. Go back with me so that I can worship the LORD your God." 31 So Samuel went back with him, and Saul worshiped the LORD.

32 "Bring King Agag here to me," Samuel ordered. Agag came to him, trembling with fear, thinking to himself, "What a bitter thing it is to die!"y 33 Samuel said, "As your sword has made many mothers childless, so now your mother will become childless." And he cut Agag to pieces in front of the altar in Gilgal.

34 Then Samuel went to Ramah, and King Saul went home to Gibeah. 35 As long as Samuel lived, he never again saw the king; but he grieved over him. The LORD was sorry that he had made Saul king of Israel.

David Is Anointed King

16 The LORD said to Samuel, "How long will you go on grieving over Saul? I have rejected him as king of Israel. But now get some olive oil and go to Bethlehem, to a man named Jesse, because I have chosen one of his sons to be king."

2 "How can I do that?" Samuel asked. "If Saul hears about it, he will kill me!"

The LORD answered, "Take a calf with you and say that you are there to offer a sacrifice to the LORD. 3 Invite Jesse to the sacrifice, and I will tell you what to do. You will anoint as king the man I tell you to."

4 Samuel did what the LORD told him to do and went to Bethlehem, where the city leaders came trembling to meet him and asked, "Is this a peaceful visit, seer?"

5 "Yes," he answered. "I have come to offer a sacrifice to the LORD. Purify yourselves and come with me." He also told Jesse and his sons to purify themselves, and he invited them to the sacrifice.

6 When they arrived, Samuel saw Jesse's son Eliab and said to himself, "This man standing here in the LORD's presence is surely the one he has chosen." 7 But the LORD said to him, "Pay no attention to how tall and handsome he is. I have rejected him, because I do not judge as people judge. They look at the outward appearance, but I look at the heart."

8 Then Jesse called his son Abinadab and brought him to Samuel. But Samuel said, "No, the LORD hasn't chosen him either." 9 Jesse then brought Shammah. "No, the LORD hasn't chosen him either," Samuel said. 10 In this way Jesse brought seven of his sons to Samuel. And Samuel said to him, "No, the LORD hasn't chosen any of these." 11 Then he asked him, "Do you have any more sons?"

Jesse answered, "There is still the youngest, but he is out taking care of the sheep."

y trembling with fear . . . die; or confidently, thinking to himself, "Surely the bitter danger of death is past!"

"Tell him to come here," Samuel said. "We won't offer the sacrifice until he comes." 12So Jesse sent for him. He was a handsome, healthy young man, and his eyes sparkled. The LORD said to Samuel, "This is the one—anoint him!" 13Samuel took the olive oil and anointed David in front of his brothers. Immediately the spirit of the LORD took control of David and was with him from that day on. Then Samuel returned to Ramah.

David in Saul's Court

14The LORD's spirit left Saul, and an evil spirit sent by the LORD tormented him. 15His servants said to him, "We know that an evil spirit sent by God is tormenting you. 16So give us the order, sir, and we will look for a man who knows how to play the harp. Then when the evil spirit comes on you, the man can play his harp, and you will be all right again."

17Saul ordered them, "Find me a man who plays well and bring him to me." 18One of his attendants said, "Jesse of the town of Bethlehem has a son who is a good musician. He is also a brave and handsome man, a good soldier, and an able speaker. The LORD is with him."

19So Saul sent messengers to Jesse to say, "Send me your son David, the one who takes care of the sheep." 20Jesse sent David to Saul with a young goat, a donkey loaded with bread, and a leather bag full of wine. 21David came to Saul and entered his service. Saul liked him very much and chose him as the man to carry his weapons. 22Then Saul sent a message to Jesse: "I like David. Let him stay here in my service." 23From then on, whenever the evil spirit sent by God came on Saul, David would get his harp and play it. The evil spirit would leave, and Saul would feel better and be all right again.

Goliath Challenges the Israelites

17 The Philistines gathered for battle in Socoh, a town in Judah; they camped at a place called Ephes Dammim, between Socoh and Azekah. 2Saul and the Israelites assembled and camped in Elah Valley, where they got ready to fight the Philistines. 3The Philistines lined up on one hill and the Israelites on another, with a valley between them.

4A man named Goliath, from the city of Gath, came out from the Philistine camp to challenge the Israelites. He was over nine feet z tall 5and wore bronze armor that weighed about 125 pounds and a bronze helmet. 6His legs were also protected by bronze armor, and he carried a bronze javelin slung over his shoulder. 7His spear was as thick as the bar on a weaver's loom, and its iron head weighed about fifteen pounds. A soldier walked in front of him carrying his shield. 8Goliath stood and shouted at the Israelites, "What are you doing there, lined up for battle? I am a Philistine, you slaves of Saul! Choose one of your men to fight me. 9If he wins and kills me, we will be your slaves; but if I win and kill him, you will be our slaves. 10Here and now I challenge the Israelite army. I dare you to pick someone to fight me!" 11When Saul and his men heard this, they were terrified.

David in Saul's Camp

12David was the son of Jesse, who was an Ephrathite from Bethlehem in Judah. Jesse had eight sons, and at the time Saul was king, he was already a very old man.a 13His three oldest sons had gone with Saul to war. The oldest was Eliab, the next was Abinadab, and the third was Shammah. 14David was the youngest son, and while the three oldest brothers stayed with Saul, 15David would go back to Bethlehem from time to time, to take care of his father's sheep.

16Goliath challenged the Israelites every morning and evening for forty days.

17One day Jesse said to David, "Take a half-bushel of this roasted grain and these ten loaves of bread, and hurry with them to your brothers in the camp. 18And take these ten cheeses to the commanding officer. Find out how your brothers are getting along and bring back something to show that you saw them and that they are well. 19King Saul, your brothers, and all the other Israelites are in Elah Valley fighting the Philistines."

20David got up early the next morn-

---

z Hebrew nine feet; one ancient Hebrew manuscript and one ancient translation seven feet.
a Some ancient translations a very old man; Hebrew unclear.

ing, left someone else in charge of the sheep, took the food, and went as Jesse had told him to. He arrived at the camp just as the Israelites were going out to their battle line, shouting the war cry. 21 The Philistine and the Israelite armies took positions for battle, facing each other. 22 David left the food with the officer in charge of the supplies, ran to the battle line, went to his brothers, and asked how they were getting along. 23 As he was talking with them, Goliath came forward and challenged the Israelites as he had done before. And David heard him. 24 When the Israelites saw Goliath, they ran away in terror. 25 "Look at him!" they said to each other. "Listen to his challenge! King Saul has promised to give a big reward to the man who kills him; the king will also give him his daughter to marry and will not require his father's family to pay taxes."*b*

26 David asked the men who were near him, "What will the man get who kills this Philistine and frees Israel from this disgrace? After all, who is this heathen Philistine to defy the army of the living God?" 27 They told him what would be done for the man who killed Goliath.

28 Eliab, David's oldest brother, heard David talking to the men. He became angry with David and said, "What are you doing here? Who is taking care of those sheep of yours out there in the wilderness? You smart aleck, you! You just came to watch the fighting!"

29 "Now what have I done?" David asked. "Can't I even ask a question?" 30 He turned to another man and asked him the same question, and every time he asked, he got the same answer.

31 Some men heard what David had said, and they told Saul, who sent for him. 32 David said to Saul, "Your Majesty, no one should be afraid of this Philistine! I will go and fight him."

33 "No," answered Saul. "How could you fight him? You're just a boy, and he has been a soldier all his life!"

34 "Your Majesty," David said, "I take care of my father's sheep. Any time a lion or a bear carries off a lamb, 35 I go after it, attack it, and rescue the lamb. And if the lion or bear turns on me, I grab it by the throat and beat it to death. 36 I have killed lions and bears, and I will

do the same to this heathen Philistine, who has defied the army of the living God. 37 The LORD has saved me from lions and bears; he will save me from this Philistine."

"All right," Saul answered. "Go, and the LORD be with you." 38 He gave his own armor to David for him to wear: a bronze helmet, which he put on David's head, and a coat of armor. 39 David strapped Saul's sword over the armor and tried to walk, but he couldn't, because he wasn't used to wearing them. "I can't fight with all this," he said to Saul. "I'm not used to it." So he took it all off. 40 He took his shepherd's stick and then picked up five smooth stones from the stream and put them in his bag. With his sling ready, he went out to meet Goliath.

David Defeats Goliath

41 The Philistine started walking toward David, with his shield bearer walking in front of him. He kept coming closer, 42 and when he got a good look at David, he was filled with scorn for him because he was just a nice, good-looking boy. 43 He said to David, "What's that stick for? Do you think I'm a dog?" And he called down curses from his god on David. 44 "Come on," he challenged David, "and I will give your body to the birds and animals to eat."

45 David answered, "You are coming against me with sword, spear, and javelin, but I come against you in the name of the LORD Almighty, the God of the Israelite armies, which you have defied. 46 This very day the LORD will put you in my power; I will defeat you and cut off your head. And I will give the bodies of the Philistine soldiers to the birds and animals to eat. Then the whole world will know that Israel has a God, 47 and everyone here will see that the LORD does not need swords or spears to save his people. He is victorious in battle, and he will put all of you in our power."

48 Goliath started walking toward David again, and David ran quickly toward the Philistine battle line to fight him. 49 He reached into his bag and took out a stone, which he slung at Goliath. It hit him on the forehead and broke his skull, and Goliath fell face downward on the ground. 50 And so, without a sword, Da-

---

b to pay taxes; or either to pay taxes or serve him.

vid defeated and killed Goliath with a sling and a stone! 51 He ran to him, stood over him, took Goliath's sword out of its sheath, and cut off his head and killed him.

When the Philistines saw that their hero was dead, they ran away. 52 The men of Israel and Judah shouted and ran after them, pursuing them all the way to Gath c and to the gates of Ekron. The Philistines fell wounded all along the road that leads to Shaaraim, as far as Gath and Ekron. 53 When the Israelites came back from pursuing the Philistines, they looted their camp. 54 David got Goliath's head and took it to Jerusalem, but he kept Goliath's weapons in his own tent.

David Is Presented to Saul

55 When Saul saw David going out to fight Goliath, he asked Abner, the commander of his army, "Abner, whose son is he?"

"I have no idea, Your Majesty," Abner answered.

56 "Then go and find out," Saul ordered.

57 So when David returned to camp after killing Goliath, Abner took him to Saul. David was still carrying Goliath's head. 58 Saul asked him, "Young man, whose son are you?"

"I am the son of your servant Jesse from Bethlehem," David answered.

18 Saul and David finished their conversation. After that, Saul's son Jonathan was deeply attracted to David and came to love him as much as he loved himself. 2 Saul kept David with him from that day on and did not let him go back home. 3 Jonathan swore eternal friendship with David because of his deep affection for him. 4 He took off the robe he was wearing and gave it to David, together with his armor and also his sword, bow, and belt. 5 David was successful in all the missions on which Saul sent him, and so Saul made him an officer in his army. This pleased all of Saul's officers and men.

Saul Becomes Jealous of David

6 As David was returning after killing Goliath and as the soldiers were coming back home, women from every town in Israel came out to meet King Saul. They were singing joyful songs, dancing, and playing tambourines and lyres. 7 In their celebration the women sang, "Saul has killed thousands, but David tens of thousands." 8 Saul did not like this, and he became very angry. He said, "For David they claim tens of thousands, but only thousands for me. They will be making him king next!" 9 And so he was jealous and suspicious of David from that day on.

10 The next day an evil spirit from God suddenly took control of Saul, and he raved in his house like a madman. David was playing the harp, as he did every day, and Saul was holding a spear. 11 "I'll pin him to the wall," Saul said to himself, and he threw the spear at him twice; but David dodged each time.

12 Saul was afraid of David because the LORD was with David but had abandoned him. 13 So Saul sent him away and put him in command of a thousand men. David led his men in battle 14 and was successful in all he did, because the LORD was with him. 15 Saul noticed David's success and became even more afraid of him. 16 But everyone in Israel and Judah loved David because he was such a successful leader.

David Marries Saul's Daughter

17 Then Saul said to David, "Here is my older daughter Merab. I will give her to you as your wife on condition that you serve me as a brave and loyal soldier, and fight the LORD's battles." (Saul was thinking that in this way the Philistines would kill David, and he would not have to do it himself.)

18 David answered, "Who am I and what is my family that I should become the king's son-in-law?" 19 But when the time came for Merab to be given to David, she was given instead to a man named Adriel from Meholah.

20 Saul's daughter Michal, however, fell in love with David, and when Saul heard of this, he was pleased. 21 He said to himself, "I'll give Michal to David; I will use her to trap him, and he will be killed by the Philistines." So for the second time Saul said to David, "You will be my son-in-law." 22 He ordered his officials to speak privately with David and

c *One ancient translation* Gath; *Hebrew* a valley.

tell him, "The king is pleased with you and all his officials like you; now is a good time for you to marry his daughter."

23 So they told this to David, and he answered, "It's a great honor to become the king's son-in-law, too great for someone poor and insignificant like me."

24 The officials told Saul what David had said, 25 and Saul ordered them to tell David: "All the king wants from you as payment for the bride are the foreskins of a hundred dead Philistines, as revenge on his enemies." (This was how Saul planned to have David killed by the Philistines.) 26 Saul's officials reported to David what Saul had said, and David was delighted with the thought of becoming the king's son-in-law. Before the day set for the wedding, 27 David and his men went and killed two hundred Philistines. He took their foreskins to the king and counted them all out to him, so that he might become his son-in-law. So Saul had to give his daughter Michal in marriage to David.

28 Saul realized clearly that the LORD was with David and also that his daughter Michal loved him. 29 So he became even more afraid of David and was his enemy as long as he lived.

30 The Philistine armies would come and fight, but in every battle David was more successful than any of Saul's other officers. As a result David became very famous.

David Is Persecuted by Saul

19 Saul told his son Jonathan and all his officials that he planned to kill[d] David. But Jonathan was very fond of David, 2 and so he told him, "My father is trying to kill you. Please be careful tomorrow morning; hide in some secret place and stay there. 3 I will go and stand by my father in the field where you are hiding, and I will speak to him about you. If I find out anything, I will let you know."

4 Jonathan praised David to Saul and said, "Sir, don't do wrong to your servant David. He has never done you any wrong; on the contrary, everything he has done has been a great help to you. 5 He risked his life when he killed Goli-

ath, and the LORD won a great victory for Israel. When you saw it, you were glad. Why, then, do you now want to do wrong to an innocent man and kill David for no reason at all?"

6 Saul was convinced by what Jonathan said and made a vow in the LORD's name that he would not kill David. 7 So Jonathan called David and told him everything; then he took him to Saul, and David served the king as he had before.

8 War with the Philistines broke out again. David attacked them and defeated them so thoroughly that they fled.

9 One day an evil spirit from the LORD took control of Saul. He was sitting in his house with his spear in his hand, and David was there, playing his harp. 10 Saul tried to pin David to the wall with his spear, but David dodged, and the spear stuck in the wall. David ran away and escaped.

11 That same night Saul sent some men to watch David's house and kill him the next morning. Michal, David's wife, warned him, "If you don't get away tonight, tomorrow you will be dead." 12 She let him down from a window, and he ran away and escaped. 13 Then she took the household idol, laid it on the bed, put a pillow made of goats' hair at its head, and put a cover over it. 14 When Saul's men came to get David, Michal told them that he was sick. 15 But Saul sent them back to see David for themselves. He ordered them, "Carry him here in his bed, and I will kill him." 16 They went inside and found the household idol in the bed and the goats' hair pillow at its head. 17 Saul asked Michal, "Why have you tricked me like this and let my enemy escape?"

She answered, "He said he would kill me if I didn't help him escape."

18 David escaped and went to Samuel in Ramah and told him everything that Saul had done to him. Then he and Samuel went to Naioth and stayed there. 19 Saul was told that David was in Naioth in Ramah, 20 so he sent some men to arrest him. They saw[e] the group of prophets dancing and shouting, with Samuel as their leader. Then the spirit of God took control of Saul's men, and they also began to dance and shout. 21 When Saul

d that he planned to kill; or to kill.   _e Some ancient translations They saw; Hebrew He saw._

heard of this, he sent more messengers, and they also began to dance and shout. He sent messengers the third time, and the same thing happened to them. 22 Then he himself started out to Ramah. When he came to the large well in Secu, he asked where Samuel and David were and was told that they were at Naioth. 23 As he was going there, the spirit of God took control of him also, and he danced and shouted all the way to Naioth. 24 He took off his clothes and danced and shouted in Samuel's presence, and lay naked all that day and all that night. (This is how the saying originated, "Has even Saul become a prophet?")

Jonathan Helps David

20 Then David fled from Naioth in Ramah and went to Jonathan. "What have I done?" he asked. "What crime have I committed? What wrong have I done to your father to make him want to kill me?"

2 Jonathan answered, "God forbid that you should die! My father tells me everything he does, important or not, and he would not hide this from me. It just isn't so!"

3 But David answered,f "Your father knows very well how much you like me, and he has decided not to let you know what he plans to do, because you would be deeply hurt. I swear to you by the living LORD that I am only a step away from death!"

4 Jonathan said, "I'll do anything you want."

5 "Tomorrow is the New Moon Festival," David replied, "and I am supposed to eat with the king. But if it's all right with you, I will go and hide in the fields until the evening of the day after tomorrow. 6 If your father notices that I am not at the table, tell him that I begged your permission to hurry home to Bethlehem, since it's the time for the annual sacrifice there for my whole family. 7 If he says, 'All right,' I will be safe; but if he becomes angry, you will know that he is determined to harm me. 8 Please do me this favor, and keep the sacred promise you made to me. But if I'm guilty, kill me

yourself! Why take me to your father to be killed?"

9 "Don't even think such a thing!" Jonathan answered. "If I knew for sure that my father was determined to harm you, wouldn't I tell you?"

10 David then asked, "Who will let me know if your father answers you angrily?"

11 "Let's go out to the fields," Jonathan answered. So they went, 12 and Jonathan said to David, "May the LORD God of Israel be our witness!g At this time tomorrow and on the following day I will question my father. If his attitude toward you is good, I will send you word. 13 If he intends to harm you, may the LORD strike me dead if I don't let you know about it and get you safely away. May the LORD be with you as he was with my father! 14 And if I remain alive, please keep your sacred promise and be loyal to me; but if I die,h 15 show the same kind of loyalty to my family forever. And when the LORD has completely destroyed all your enemies, 16 may our promise to each other still be unbroken. If it is broken, the LORD will punish you."i

17 Once again Jonathan made David promise to love him, for Jonathan loved David as much as he loved himself. 18 Then Jonathan said to him, "Since tomorrow is the New Moon Festival, your absence will be noticed if you aren't at the meal. 19 The day after tomorrow your absence will be noticedj even more; so go to the place where you hid yourself the other time, and hide behind the pile of stones there.k 20 I will then shoot three arrows at it, as though it were a target. 21 Then I will tell my servant to go and find them. And if I tell him, 'Look, the arrows are on this side of you; get them,' that means that you are safe and can come out. I swear by the living LORD that you will be in no danger. 22 But if I tell him, 'The arrows are on the other side of you,' then leave, because the LORD is sending you away. 23 As for the promise we have made to each other, the LORD will make sure that we will keep it forever."

---

f One ancient translation answered; Hebrew made a vow again.   g One ancient translation be our witness; Hebrew does not have these words.   h Some ancient translations if I die; Hebrew that I may not die.   i Verses 15-16 in Hebrew are unclear.   j Some ancient translations your absence will be noticed; Hebrew go down.   k Probable text the pile of stones there; Hebrew the Ezel Stone.

24 So David hid in the fields. At the New Moon Festival, King Saul came to the meal 25 and sat in his usual place by the wall. Abner sat next to him, and Jonathan sat across the table from him.*l* David's place was empty, 26 but Saul said nothing that day, because he thought, "Something has happened to him, and he is not ritually pure." 27 On the following day, the day after the New Moon Festival, David's place was still empty, and Saul asked Jonathan, "Why didn't David come to the meal either yesterday or today?"

28 Jonathan answered, "He begged me to let him go to Bethlehem. 29 'Please let me go,' he said, 'because our family is celebrating the sacrificial feast in town, and my brother ordered me to be there. So then, if you are my friend, let me go and see my relatives.' That is why he isn't in his place at your table."

30 Saul became furious with Jonathan and said to him, "How rebellious and faithless your mother was! Now I know you are taking sides with David and are disgracing yourself and that mother of yours! 31 Don't you realize that as long as David is alive, you will never be king of this country? Now go and bring him here—he must die!"

32 "Why should he die?" Jonathan replied. "What has he done?"

33 At that, Saul threw his spear at Jonathan to kill him, and Jonathan realized that his father was really determined to kill David. 34 Jonathan got up from the table in a rage and ate nothing that day—the second day of the New Moon Festival. He was deeply distressed about David, because Saul had insulted him. 35 The following morning Jonathan went to the fields to meet David, as they had agreed. He took a young boy with him 36 and said to him, "Run and find the arrows I'm going to shoot." The boy ran, and Jonathan shot an arrow beyond him. 37 When the boy reached the place where the arrow had fallen, Jonathan shouted to him, "The arrow is farther on! 38 Don't just stand there! Hurry up!" The boy picked up the arrow and returned to his master, 39 not knowing what it all meant; only Jonathan and David knew. 40 Jonathan gave his weapons to the boy and told him to take them back to town. 41 After the boy had left, David got up from behind the pile of stones,*m* fell on his knees and bowed with his face to the ground three times. Both he and Jonathan were crying as they kissed each other; David's grief was even greater than Jonathan's.*n* 42 Then Jonathan said to David, "God be with you. The LORD will make sure that you and I, and your descendants and mine, will forever keep the sacred promise we have made to each other." Then David left, and Jonathan went back to the town.

David Flees from Saul

21 David went to the priest Ahimelech in Nob. Ahimelech came out trembling to meet him and asked, "Why did you come here all by yourself?"

2 "I am here on the king's business," David answered. "He told me not to let anyone know what he sent me to do. As for my men, I have told them to meet me at a certain place. 3 Now, then, what supplies do you have? Give me five loaves of bread or anything else you have."

4 The priest said, "I don't have any ordinary bread, only sacred bread; you can have it if your men haven't had sexual relations recently."

5 "Of course they haven't," answered David. "My men always keep themselves ritually pure even when we go out on an ordinary mission; how much more this time when we are on a special mission!"

6 So the priest gave David the sacred bread, because the only bread he had was the loaves offered to God, which had been removed from the sacred table and replaced by fresh bread.

(7 Saul's chief herdsman, Doeg, who was from Edom, happened to be there that day, because he had to fulfill a religious obligation.)

8 David said to Ahimelech, "Do you have a spear or a sword you can give me? The king's orders made me leave in such a hurry that I didn't have time to get my sword or any other weapon."

9 Ahimelech answered, "I have the sword of Goliath the Philistine, whom you killed in Elah Valley; it is behind the

l One ancient translation sat across the table from him; *Hebrew* stood up.   *m Probable text* the pile of stones; *Hebrew* the south.   *n Probable text* David's grief was even greater than Jonathan's; *Hebrew unclear.*

ephod, wrapped in a cloth. If you want it, take it — it's the only weapon here."

"Give it to me," David said. "There is not a better sword anywhere!"

10 So David left, fleeing from Saul, and went to King Achish of Gath. 11 The king's officials said to Achish, "Isn't this David, the king of his country? This is the man about whom the women sang, as they danced, 'Saul has killed thousands, but David has killed tens of thousands.'"

12 Their words made a deep impression on David, and he became very much afraid of King Achish. 13 So whenever David was around them, he pretended to be insane and acted like a madman when they tried to restrain him; he would scribble on the city[o] gates and let spit drool down his beard. 14 So Achish said to his officials, "Look! The man is crazy! Why did you bring him to me? 15 Don't I have enough madmen already? Why bring another one to bother me with his crazy actions right here in my own house?"

The Slaughter of the Priests

22 David fled from the city of Gath and went to a cave near the town of Adullam. When his brothers and the rest of the family heard that he was there, they joined him. 2 People who were oppressed or in debt or dissatisfied went to him, about four hundred men in all, and he became their leader.

3 David went on from there to Mizpah in Moab and said to the king of Moab, "Please let my father and mother come and stay with you until I find out what God is going to do for me." 4 So David left his parents with the king of Moab, and they stayed there as long as David was hiding out in the cave.

5 Then the prophet Gad came to David and said, "Don't stay here; go at once to the land of Judah." So David left and went to the forest of Hereth.

6 One day Saul was in Gibeah, sitting under a tamarisk tree on a hill, with his spear in his hand, and all his officers were standing around him. He was told that David and his men had been located, 7 and he said to his officers, "Listen, men of Benjamin! Do you think that

David will give fields and vineyards to all of you, and make you officers in his army? 8 Is that why you are plotting against me? Not one of you told me that my own son had made an alliance with David. No one is concerned about me or tells me that David, one of my own men, is right now looking for a chance to kill me, and that my son has encouraged him!"

9 Doeg was standing there with Saul's officers, and he said, "I saw David when he went to Ahimelech son of Ahitub in Nob. 10 Ahimelech asked the LORD what David should do, and then he gave David some food and the sword of Goliath the Philistine."

11 So King Saul sent for the priest Ahimelech and all his relatives, who were also priests in Nob, and they came to him. 12 Saul said to Ahimelech, "Listen, Ahimelech!"

"At your service, sir," he answered.

13 Saul asked him, "Why are you and David plotting against me? Why did you give him some food and a sword, and consult God for him? Now he has turned against me and is waiting for a chance to kill me!"

14 Ahimelech answered, "David is the most faithful officer you have! He is your own son-in-law, captain of[p] your bodyguard, and highly respected by everyone in the royal court. 15 Yes, I consulted God for him, and it wasn't the first time.[q] As for plotting against you, Your Majesty must not accuse me or anyone else in my family. I don't know anything about this matter!"

16 The king said, "Ahimelech, you and all your relatives must die." 17 Then he said to the guards standing near him, "Kill the LORD's priests! They conspired with David and did not tell me that he had run away, even though they knew it all along." But the guards refused to lift a hand to kill the LORD's priests. 18 So Saul said to Doeg, "You kill them!" — and Doeg killed them all. On that day he killed eighty-five priests who were qualified to carry the ephod. 19 Saul also had all the other inhabitants of Nob, the city of priests, put to death: men and women, children and babies, cattle, donkeys, and sheep — they were all killed.

o city; or palace.   p Some ancient translations captain of; Hebrew he turned to.   q Yes, I consulted . . . time; or Now, have I done something wrong today by consulting God for him? Not at all!

20 But Abiathar, one of Ahimelech's sons, escaped, and went and joined David. 21 He told him how Saul had slaughtered the priests of the LORD. 22 David said to him, "When I saw Doeg there that day, I knew that he would be sure to tell Saul. So I am responsible *r* for the death of all your relatives. 23 Stay with me and don't be afraid. Saul wants to kill both you and me, but you will be safe with me."

David Saves the Town of Keilah

23 David heard that the Philistines were attacking the town of Keilah and were stealing the newly harvested grain. 2 So he asked the LORD, "Shall I go and attack the Philistines?"

"Yes," the LORD answered. "Attack them and save Keilah."

3 But David's men said to him, "We have enough to be afraid of here in Judah; it will be much worse if we go to Keilah and attack the Philistine forces!" 4 So David consulted the LORD again, and the LORD said to him, "Go and attack Keilah, because I will give you victory over the Philistines." 5 So David and his men went to Keilah and attacked the Philistines; they killed many of them and took their livestock. And so it was that David saved the town.

6 When Abiathar son of Ahimelech escaped and joined David in Keilah, he took the ephod with him.

7 Saul was told that David had gone to Keilah, and he said, "God has put him in my power. David has trapped himself by going into a walled town with fortified gates." 8 So Saul called his troops to war, to march against Keilah and besiege David and his men.

9 When David heard that Saul was planning to attack him, he said to the priest Abiathar, "Bring the ephod here." 10 Then David said, "LORD, God of Israel, I have heard that Saul is planning to come to Keilah and destroy it on account of me, your servant. 11 Will the citizens of Keilah hand me over to Saul? Will Saul really come, as I have heard? LORD, God of Israel, I beg you to answer me!"

The LORD answered, "Saul will come."

12 "And will the citizens of Keilah hand my men and me over to Saul?" David asked again.

"They will," the LORD answered.

13 So David and his men — about six hundred in all — left Keilah at once and kept on the move. When Saul heard that David had escaped from Keilah, he gave up his plan.

David in the Hill Country

14 David stayed in hiding in the hill country, in the wilderness near Ziph. Saul was always trying to find him, but God did not turn David over to him. 15 David saw that Saul was out to kill him.

David was at Horesh, in the wilderness near Ziph. 16 Jonathan went to him there and encouraged him with assurances of God's protection, 17 saying to him, "Don't be afraid. My father Saul won't be able to harm you. He knows very well that you are the one who will be the king of Israel and that I will be next in rank to you." 18 The two of them made a sacred promise of friendship to each other. David stayed at Horesh, and Jonathan went home.

19 Some people from Ziph went to Saul at Gibeah and said, "David is hiding out in our territory at Horesh on Mount Hachilah, in the southern part of the Judean wilderness. 20 We know, Your Majesty, how much you want to capture him; so come to our territory, and we will make sure that you catch him."

21 Saul answered, "May the LORD bless you for being so kind to me! 22 Go and make sure once more; find out for certain where he is and who has seen him there. I hear that he is very cunning. 23 Find out exactly the places where he hides, and be sure to bring back a report to me right away. Then I will go with you, and if he is still in the region, I will hunt him down, even if I have to search the whole land of Judah."

24 So they left and returned to Ziph ahead of Saul. David and his men were in the wilderness of Maon, in a desolate valley in the southern part of the Judean wilderness. 25 Saul and his men set out to look for David, but he heard about it and went to a rocky hill in the wilderness of Maon and stayed there. When Saul heard about this, he went after David. 26 Saul and his men were on one side of the hill, separated from David and his

r Some ancient translations I am responsible; *Hebrew* I have turned.

men, who were on the other side. They were hurrying to get away from Saul and his men, who were closing in on them and were about to capture them. 27 Just then a messenger arrived and said to Saul, "Come back at once! The Philistines are invading the country!" 28 So Saul stopped pursuing David and went to fight the Philistines. That is why that place is called Separation Hill. 29 David left and went to the region of Engedi, where he stayed in hiding.

David Spares Saul's Life

24 When Saul came back from fighting the Philistines, he was told that David was in the wilderness near Engedi. 2 Saul took three thousand of the best soldiers in Israel and went looking for David and his men east of Wild Goat Rocks. 3 He came to a cave close to some sheep pens by the road and went in to relieve himself. It happened to be the very cave in which David and his men were hiding far back in the cave. 4 They said to him, "This is your chance! The LORD has told you that he would put your enemy in your power and you could do to him whatever you wanted to." David crept over and cut off a piece of Saul's robe without Saul's knowing it. 5 But then David's conscience began to hurt, 6 and he said to his men, "May the LORD keep me from doing any harm to my master, whom the LORD chose as king! I must not harm him in the least, because he is the king chosen by the LORD!" 7 So David convinced his men that they should not attack Saul.

Saul got up, left the cave, and started away. 8 Then David went out after him and called to him, "Your Majesty!" Saul turned around, and David bowed down to the ground in respect 9 and said, "Why do you listen to people who say that I am trying to harm you? 10 You can see for yourself that just now in the cave the LORD put you in my power. Some of my men told me to kill you, but I felt sorry for you and said that I would not harm you in the least, because you are the one whom the LORD chose to be king. 11 Look, my father, look at the piece of your robe I am holding! I could have killed you, but instead I only cut this off. This should convince you that I have no thought of rebelling against you or of harming you. You are hunting me down to kill me,

even though I have not done you any wrong. 12 May the LORD judge which one of us is wrong! May he punish you for your action against me, for I will not harm you in the least. 13 You know the old saying, 'Evil is done only by evil people.' And so I will not harm you. 14 Look at what the king of Israel is trying to kill! Look at what he is chasing! A dead dog, a flea! 15 The LORD will judge, and he will decide which one of us is wrong. May he look into the matter, defend me, and save me from you."

16 When David had finished speaking, Saul said, "Is that really you, David my son?" And he started crying. 17 Then he said to David, "You are right, and I am wrong. You have been so good to me, while I have done such wrong to you! 18 Today you have shown how good you are to me, because you did not kill me, even though the LORD put me in your power. 19 How often does someone catch an enemy and then let him get away unharmed? The LORD bless you for what you have done to me today! 20 Now I am sure that you will be king of Israel and that the kingdom will continue under your rule. 21 But promise me in the LORD's name that you will spare my descendants, so that my name and my family's name will not be completely forgotten." 22 David promised that he would.

Then Saul went back home, and David and his men went back to their hiding place.

The Death of Samuel

25 Samuel died, and all the Israelites came together and mourned for him. Then they buried him at his home in Ramah.

David and Abigail

After this, David went to the wilderness of Paran. 2-3 There was a man of the clan of Caleb named Nabal, who was from the town of Maon, and who owned land near the town of Carmel. He was a very rich man, the owner of three thousand sheep and one thousand goats. His wife Abigail was beautiful and intelligent, but he was a mean, bad-tempered man.

Nabal was shearing his sheep in Carmel, 4 and David, who was in the wilderness, heard about it, 5 so he sent ten young men with orders to go to Carmel, find Nabal, and give him his greetings. 6 He instructed them to say to Nabal: "David sends you greetings, my friend, with his best wishes for you, your family, and all that is yours. 7 He heard that you were shearing your sheep, and he wants you to know that your shepherds have been with us and we did not harm them. Nothing that belonged to them was stolen all the time they were at Carmel. 8 Just ask them, and they will tell you. We have come on a feast day, and David asks you to receive us kindly. Please give what you can to us your servants and to your dear friend David."

9 David's men delivered this message to Nabal in David's name. Then they waited there, 10 and Nabal finally answered, "David? Who is he? I've never heard of him! The country is full of runaway slaves nowadays! 11 I'm not going to take my bread and water, and the animals I have butchered for my sheepshearers, and give them to people who come from I don't know where!"

12 David's men went back to him and told him what Nabal had said. 13 "Buckle on your swords!" he ordered, and they all did. David also buckled on his sword and left with about four hundred of his men, leaving two hundred behind with the supplies.

14 One of Nabal's servants said to Nabal's wife Abigail, "Have you heard? David sent some messengers from the wilderness with greetings for our master, but he insulted them. 15 Yet they were very good to us; they never bothered us, and all the time we were with them in the fields, nothing that belonged to us was stolen. 16 They protected us day and night the whole time we were with them looking after our flocks. 17 Please think this over and decide what to do. This could be disastrous for our master and all his family. He is so mean that he won't listen to anybody!"

18 Abigail quickly gathered two hundred loaves of bread, two leather bags full of wine, five roasted sheep, two bushels of roasted grain, a hundred bunches of raisins, and two hundred cakes of dried figs, and loaded them on donkeys. 19 Then she said to the serv-

ants, "You go on ahead and I will follow you." But she said nothing to her husband.

20 She was riding her donkey around a bend on a hillside when suddenly she met David and his men coming toward her. 21 David had been thinking, "Why did I ever protect that fellow's property out here in the wilderness? Not a thing that belonged to him was stolen, and this is how he pays me back for the help I gave him! 22 May God strike me*s* dead if I don't kill every last one of those men before morning!"

23 When Abigail saw David, she quickly dismounted and threw herself on the ground 24 at David's feet, and said to him, "Please, sir, listen to me! Let me take the blame. 25 Please, don't pay any attention to Nabal, that good-for-nothing! He is exactly what his name means—a fool!*t* I wasn't there when your servants arrived, sir. 26 It is the Lord who has kept you from taking revenge and killing your enemies. And now I swear to you by the living Lord that your enemies and all who want to harm you will be punished like Nabal. 27 Please, sir, accept this present I have brought you, and give it to your men. 28 Please forgive me, sir, for any wrong I have done. The Lord will make you king, and your descendants also, because you are fighting his battles; and you will not do anything evil*u* as long as you live. 29 If anyone should attack you and try to kill you, the Lord your God will keep you safe, as someone guards a precious treasure. As for your enemies, however, he will throw them away, as someone hurls stones with a sling. 30 And when the Lord has done all the good things he has promised you and has made you king of Israel, 31 then you will not have to feel regret or remorse, sir, for having killed without cause or for having taken your own revenge. And when the Lord has blessed you, sir, please do not forget me."

32 David said to her, "Praise the Lord, the God of Israel, who sent you today to meet me! 33 Thank God for your good sense and for what you have done today in keeping me from the crime of murder and from taking my own revenge. 34 The

---

s One ancient translation me; Hebrew my enemies.   *t* A FOOL: This is the meaning of the Hebrew name Nabal.   *u* you will not do anything evil; or no evil will happen to you.

LORD has kept me from harming you. But I swear by the living God of Israel that if you had not hurried to meet me, all of Nabal's men would have been dead by morning!" 35 Then David accepted what she had brought him and said to her, "Go back home and don't worry. I will do what you want."

36 Abigail went back to Nabal, who was at home having a feast fit for a king. He was drunk and in a good mood, so she did not tell him anything until the next morning. 37 Then, after he had sobered up, she told him everything. He suffered a stroke and was completely paralyzed. 38 Some ten days later the LORD struck Nabal and he died.

39 When David heard that Nabal had died, he said, "Praise the LORD! He has taken revenge on Nabal for insulting me and has kept me his servant from doing wrong. The LORD has punished Nabal for his evil."

Then David sent a proposal of marriage to Abigail. 40 His servants went to her at Carmel and said to her, "David sent us to take you to him to be his wife."

41 Abigail bowed down to the ground and said, "I am his servant, ready to wash the feet of his servants." 42 She rose quickly and mounted her donkey. Accompanied by her five maids, she went with David's servants and became his wife.

43 David had married Ahinoam from Jezreel, and now Abigail also became his wife. 44 Meanwhile, Saul had given his daughter Michal, who had been David's wife, to Palti son of Laish, who was from the town of Gallim.

David Spares Saul's Life Again

26 Some men from Ziph came to Saul at Gibeah and told him that David was hiding on Mount Hachilah at the edge of the Judean wilderness. 2 Saul went at once with three thousand of the best soldiers in Israel to the wilderness of Ziph to look for David, 3 and camped by the road on Mount Hachilah. David was still in the wilderness, and when he learned that Saul had come to look for him, 4 he sent spies and found out that Saul was indeed there. 5 He went at once and located the exact place where Saul and Abner son of Ner, commander of Saul's army, slept. Saul slept inside the camp, and his men camped around him.

6 Then David asked Ahimelech the Hittite, and Abishai the brother of Joab (their mother was Zeruiah), "Which of you two will go to Saul's camp with me?"

"I will," Abishai answered.

7 So that night David and Abishai entered Saul's camp and found Saul sleeping in the center of the camp with his spear stuck in the ground near his head. Abner and the troops were sleeping around him. 8 Abishai said to David, "God has put your enemy in your power tonight. Now let me plunge his own spear through him and pin him to the ground with just one blow—I won't have to strike twice!"

9 But David said, "You must not harm him! The LORD will certainly punish whoever harms his chosen king. 10 By the living LORD," David continued, "I know that the LORD himself will kill Saul, either when his time comes to die a natural death or when he dies in battle. 11 The LORD forbid that I should try to harm the one whom the LORD has made king! Let's take his spear and his water jar, and go." 12 So David took the spear and the water jar from right beside Saul's head, and he and Abishai left. No one saw it or knew what had happened or even woke up—they were all sound asleep, because the LORD had sent a heavy sleep on them all.

13 Then David crossed over to the other side of the valley to the top of the hill, a safe distance away, 14 and shouted to Saul's troops and to Abner, "Abner! Can you hear me?"

"Who is that shouting and waking up the king?" Abner asked.

15 David answered, "Abner, aren't you the greatest man in Israel? So why aren't you protecting your master, the king? Just now someone entered the camp to kill your master. 16 You failed in your duty, Abner! I swear by the living LORD that all of you deserve to die, because you have not protected your master, whom the LORD made king. Look! Where is the king's spear? Where is the water jar that was right by his head?"

17 Saul recognized David's voice and asked, "David, is that you, my son?"

"Yes, Your Majesty," David answered. 18 And he added, "Why, sir, are you still pursuing me, your servant? What have I done? What crime have I committed? 19 Your Majesty, listen to what I have to say. If it is the LORD who has turned you against me, an offering to him will make him change his mind; but if some people have done it, may the LORD's curse fall on them. For they have driven me out from the LORD's land to a country where I can only worship foreign gods. 20 Don't let me be killed on foreign soil, away from the LORD. Why should the king of Israel come to kill a flea like me? Why should he hunt me down like a wild bird?"

21 Saul answered, "I have done wrong. Come back, David, my son! I will never harm you again, because you have spared my life tonight. I have been a fool! I have done a terrible thing!"

22 David replied, "Here is your spear, Your Majesty. Let one of your men come over and get it. 23 The LORD rewards those who are faithful and righteous. Today he put you in my power, but I did not harm you, whom the LORD made king. 24 Just as I have spared your life today, may the LORD do the same to me and free me from all troubles!"

25 Saul said to David, "God bless you, my son! You will succeed in everything you do!"

So David went on his way, and Saul returned home.

David among the Philistines

27 David said to himself, "One of these days Saul will kill me. The best thing for me to do is to escape to Philistia. Then Saul will give up looking for me in Israel, and I will be safe." 2 So David and his six hundred men went over at once to Achish son of Maoch, king of Gath. 3 David and his men settled there in Gath with their families. David had his two wives with him, Ahinoam from Jezreel, and Abigail, Nabal's widow, from Carmel. 4 When Saul heard that David had fled to Gath, he gave up trying to find him.

5 David said to Achish, "If you are my friend, let me have a small town to live in. There is no need, sir, for me to live with you in the capital city." 6 So Achish gave him the town of Ziklag, and for this reason Ziklag has belonged to the kings of Judah ever since. 7 David lived in Philistia for sixteen months.

8 During that time David and his men would attack the people of Geshur, Girzi, and Amalek, who had been living in the region a very long time. He would raid their land as far as Shur, all the way down to Egypt, 9 killing all the men and women and taking the sheep, cattle, donkeys, camels, and even the clothes. Then he would come back to Achish, 10 who would ask him, "Where did you go on a raid this time?" and David would tell him that he had gone to the southern part of Judah or to the territory of the clan of Jerahmeel or to the territory where the Kenites lived. 11 David would kill everyone, men and women, so that no one could go back to Gath and report what he and his men had really done. This is what David did the whole time he lived in Philistia. 12 But Achish trusted David and said to himself, "He is hated so much by his own people the Israelites that he will have to serve me all his life."

28 Some time later the Philistines gathered their troops to fight Israel, and Achish said to David, "Of course you understand that you and your men are to fight on my side."

2 "Of course," David answered. "I am your servant, and you will see for yourself what I can do."

Achish said, "Good! I will make you my permanent bodyguard."

Saul Consults a Medium

3 Now Samuel had died, and all the Israelites had mourned for him and had buried him in his hometown of Ramah. Saul had forced all the fortunetellers and mediums to leave Israel.

4 The Philistine troops assembled and camped near the town of Shunem; Saul gathered the Israelites and camped at Mount Gilboa. 5 When Saul saw the Philistine army, he was terrified, 6 and so he asked the LORD what to do. But the LORD did not answer him at all, either by dreams or by the use of Urim and Thummim or by prophets. 7 Then Saul ordered his officials, "Find me a woman who is a medium, and I will go and consult her."

"There is one in Endor," they answered.

8 So Saul disguised himself; he put on different clothes, and after dark he went with two of his men to see the woman. "Consult the spirits for me and tell me what is going to happen," he said to her. "Call up the spirit of the man I name."

9 The woman answered, "Surely you know what King Saul has done, how he

forced the fortunetellers and mediums to leave Israel.ᵛ Why, then, are you trying to trap me and get me killed?"

10 Then Saul made a sacred vow. "By the living LORD I promise that you will not be punished for doing this," he told her.

11 "Whom shall I call up for you?" the woman asked.

"Samuel," he answered.

12 When the woman saw Samuel, she screamed and said to Saul, "Why have you tricked me? You are King Saul!"

13 "Don't be afraid!" the king said to her. "What do you see?"

"I see a spirit coming up from the earth," she answered.

14 "What does it look like?" he asked.

"It's an old man coming up," she answered. "He is wearing a cloak."

Then Saul knew that it was Samuel, and he bowed to the ground in respect.

15 Samuel said to Saul, "Why have you disturbed me? Why did you make me come back?"

Saul answered, "I am in great trouble! The Philistines are at war with me, and God has abandoned me. He doesn't answer me any more, either by prophets or by dreams. And so I have called you, for you to tell me what I must do."

16 Samuel said, "Why do you call me when the LORD has abandoned you and become your enemy? 17 The LORD has done to you what he told you through me: he has taken the kingdom away from you and given it to David instead. 18 You disobeyed the LORD's command and did not completely destroy the Amalekites and all they had. That is why the LORD is doing this to you now. 19 He will give you and Israel over to the Philistines. Tomorrow you and your sons will join me, and the LORD will also give the army of Israel over to the Philistines."

20 At once Saul fell down and lay stretched out on the ground, terrified by what Samuel had said. He was weak, because he had not eaten anything all day and all night. 21 The woman went over to him and saw that he was terrified, so she said to him, "Please, sir, I risked my life by doing what you asked. 22 Now please do what I ask. Let me fix you some food. You must eat so that you will be strong enough to travel."

23 Saul refused and said he would not eat anything. But his officers also urged him to eat. He finally gave in, got up from the ground, and sat on the bed. 24 The woman quickly killed a calf which she had been fattening. Then she took some flour, prepared it, and baked some bread without yeast. 25 She set the food before Saul and his officers, and they ate it. And they left that same night.

David Is Rejected by the Philistines

29 The Philistines brought all their troops together at Aphek, while the Israelites camped at the spring in Jezreel Valley. 2 The five Philistine kings marched out with their units of a hundred and of a thousand men; David and his men marched in the rear with King Achish. 3 The Philistine commanders saw them and asked, "What are these Hebrews doing here?"

Achish answered, "This is David, an official of King Saul of Israel. He has been with me for quite some time now. He has done nothing I can find fault with since the day he came over to me."

4 But the Philistine commanders were angry with Achish and said to him, "Send that fellow back to the town you gave him. Don't let him go into battle with us; he might turn against us during the fighting. What better way is there for him to win back his master's favor than by the death of our men? 5 After all, this is David, the one about whom the women sang, as they danced, 'Saul has killed thousands, but David has killed tens of thousands.'"

6 Achish called David and said to him, "I swear by the living God of Israel that you have been loyal to me; and I would be pleased to have you go with me and fight in this battle. I have not found any fault in you from the day you came over to me. But the other kings don't approve of you. 7 So go back home in peace, and don't do anything that would displease them."

8 David answered, "What have I done wrong, sir? If, as you say, you haven't found any fault in me since the day I started serving you, why shouldn't I go with you, my master and king, and fight your enemies?"

9 "I agree," Achish replied. "I consider

ᵛ he forced . . . Israel; or he put to death the fortunetellers and mediums in Israel.

you as loyal as an angel of God. But the other kings have said that you can't go with us into battle. 10So then, David, tomorrow morning all of you who left Saul and came over to me will have to get up early and leave as soon as it's light."

11So David and his men started out early the following morning to go back to Philistia, and the Philistines went on to Jezreel.

The War against the Amalekites

30 Two days later David and his men arrived back at Ziklag. The Amalekites had raided southern Judah and attacked Ziklag. They had burned down the town 2and captured all the women; they had not killed anyone, but had taken everyone with them when they left. 3When David and his men arrived, they found that the town had been burned down and that their wives, sons, and daughters had been carried away. 4David and his men started crying and did not stop until they were completely exhausted. 5Even David's two wives, Ahinoam and Abigail, had been taken away.

6David was now in great trouble, because his men were all very bitter about losing their children, and they were threatening to stone him; but the LORD his God gave him courage. 7David said to the priest Abiathar son of Ahimelech, "Bring me the ephod," and Abiathar brought it to him. 8David asked the LORD, "Shall I go after those raiders? And will I catch them?"

He answered, "Go after them; you will catch them and rescue the captives."

9So David and his six hundred men started out, and when they arrived at Besor Brook, some of them stayed there. 10David continued on his way with four hundred men; the other two hundred men were too tired to cross the brook and so stayed behind. 11The men with David found a young Egyptian out in the country and brought him to David. They gave him some food and water, 12some dried figs, and two bunches of raisins. After he had eaten, his strength returned; he had not had anything to eat or drink for three full days. 13David asked him, "Who is your master, and where are you from?"

"I am an Egyptian, the slave of an Amalekite," he answered. "My master left me behind three days ago because I got sick. 14We had raided the territory of the Cherethites in the southern part of Judah and the territory of the clan of Caleb, and we burned down Ziklag."

15"Will you lead me to those raiders?" David asked him.

He answered, "I will if you promise me in God's name that you will not kill me or hand me over to my master." 16And he led David to them.

The raiders were scattered all over the place, eating, drinking, and celebrating because of the enormous amount of loot they had captured from Philistia and Judah. 17At dawn the next day David attacked them and fought until evening. Except for four hundred young men who mounted camels and got away, none of them escaped. 18David rescued everyone and everything the Amalekites had taken, including his two wives; 19nothing at all was missing. David got back all his men's sons and daughters, and all the loot the Amalekites had taken. 20He also recovered all the flocks and herds; his men drove all the livestock in front of themw and said, "This belongs to David!"

21Then David went back to the two hundred men who had been too weak to go with him and had stayed behind at Besor Brook. They came forward to meet David and his men, and David went up to them and greeted them warmly. 22But some mean and worthless men who had gone with David said, "They didn't go with us, and so we won't give them any of the loot. They can take their wives and children and go away."

23But David answered, "My brothers, you can't do this with what the LORD has given us! He kept us safe and gave us victory over the raiders. 24No one can agree with what you say! All must share alike: whoever stays behind with the supplies gets the same share as the one who goes into battle." 25David made this a rule, and it has been followed in Israel ever since.

26When David returned to Ziklag, he sent part of the loot to his friends, the leaders of Judah, with the message, "Here is a present for you from the loot

w *Probable text* his men .... front of them; *Hebrew unclear.*

we took from the LORD's enemies." 27 He sent it to the people in Bethel, to the people in Ramah in the southern part of Judah, and to the people in the towns of Jattir, 28 Aroer, Siphmoth, Eshtemoa, 29 and Racal; to the clan of Jerahmeel, to the Kenites, 30 and to the people in the towns of Hormah, Borashan, Athach, 31 and Hebron. He sent it to all the places where he and his men had roamed.

The Death of Saul and His Sons
(1 Chronicles 10.1-12)

31 The Philistines fought a battle against the Israelites on Mount Gilboa. Many Israelites were killed there, and the rest of them, including King Saul and his sons, fled. 2 But the Philistines caught up with them and killed three of Saul's sons, Jonathan, Abinadab, and Malchishua. 3 The fighting was heavy around Saul, and he himself was hit by enemy arrows and badly wounded. 4 He said to the young man carrying his weapons, "Draw your sword and kill me, so that these godless Philistines won't gloat over me and kill me." But the young man was too terrified to do it. So Saul took his own sword and threw himself on it. 5 The young man saw that Saul was dead, so he too threw himself on his own sword and

died with Saul. 6 And that is how Saul, his three sons, and the young man died; all of Saul's men died that day. 7 When the Israelites on the other side of Jezreel Valley and east of the Jordan River heard that the Israelite army had fled and that Saul and his sons had been killed, they abandoned their towns and fled. Then the Philistines came and occupied the towns.

8 The day after the battle the Philistines went to plunder the corpses, and they found the bodies of Saul and his three sons lying on Mount Gilboa. 9 They cut off Saul's head, stripped off his armor, and sent messengers with them throughout Philistia to tell the good news to their idols and to their people. 10 Then they put his weapons in the temple of the goddess Astarte, and they nailed his body to the wall of the city of Beth Shan.

11 When the people of Jabesh in Gilead heard what the Philistines had done to Saul, 12 the bravest men started out and marched all night to Beth Shan. They took down the bodies of Saul and his sons from the wall, brought them back to Jabesh, and burned them there. 13 Then they took the bones and buried them under the tamarisk tree in town, and fasted for seven days.

The Second Book of
SAMUEL

Introduction

Second Samuel, *the sequel to* First Samuel, *is the history of David's reign as king, first over Judah in the south (chapters 1–4) and then over the whole nation, including Israel in the north (chapters 5–24). It is a vivid account of how David, in order to extend his kingdom and consolidate his position, had to struggle with enemies within the nation as well as with foreign powers. David is shown to be a man of deep faith and devotion to God, and one who was able to win the loyalty of his people. Yet he is also shown as being sometimes ruthless and willing to commit terrible sins to serve his own desires and ambitions. But when he is confronted with his sins by the Lord's prophet Nathan, he confesses them and accepts the punishment that God sends.*

The life and achievements of David impressed the people of Israel so much that in later times of national distress, when they longed for another king, it was for one who would be "a son of David," that is, a descendant of David who would be like him.

Outline of Contents

David Learns of Saul's Death

1 After Saul's death David came back from his victory over the Amalekites and stayed in Ziklag for two days. 2 The next day a young man arrived from Saul's camp. To show his grief, he had torn his clothes and put dirt on his head. He went to David and bowed to the ground in respect. 3 David asked him, "Where have you come from?"

"I have escaped from the Israelite camp," he answered.

4 "Tell me what happened," David said.

"Our army ran away from the battle," he replied, "and many of our men were killed. Saul and his son Jonathan were also killed."

5 "How do you know that Saul and Jonathan are dead?" David asked him.

6 He answered, "I happened to be on Mount Gilboa, and I saw that Saul was leaning on his spear and that the chariots and cavalry of the enemy were closing in on him. 7 Then he turned around, saw me, and called to me. I answered, 'Yes, sir!' 8 He asked who I was, and I told him that I was an Amalekite. 9 Then he said, 'Come here and kill me! I have been badly wounded, and I'm about to die.' 10 So I went up to him and killed him, because I knew that he would die anyway as soon as he fell. Then I took the crown from his head and the bracelet from his arm, and I have brought them to you, sir."

11 David tore his clothes in sorrow, and all his men did the same. 12 They grieved and mourned and fasted until evening for Saul and Jonathan and for Israel, the people of the LORD, because so many had been killed in battle.

13 David asked the young man who had brought him the news, "Where are you from?"

He answered, "I'm an Amalekite, but I live in your country."

14 David asked him, "How is it that you dared kill the LORD's chosen king?" 15 Then David called one of his men and said, "Kill him!" The man struck the Amalekite and mortally wounded him, 16 and David said to the Amalekite, "You brought this on yourself. You condemned yourself when you confessed that you killed the one whom the LORD chose to be king."

David's Lament for Saul and Jonathan

17 David sang this lament for Saul and his son Jonathan, 18 and ordered it*a* to be taught to the people of Judah. (It is recorded in *The Book of Jashar.*)

19 "On the hills of Israel our leaders
   are dead!
The bravest of our soldiers have
   fallen!
20 Do not announce it in Gath
   or in the streets of Ashkelon.
Do not make the women of
   Philistia glad;
   do not let the daughters of
   pagans rejoice.

21 "May no rain or dew fall on
   Gilboa's hills;
   may its fields be always barren!
For the shields of the brave lie
   there in disgrace;
   the shield of Saul is no longer
   polished with oil.
22 Jonathan's bow was deadly,
   the sword of Saul was merciless,
striking down the mighty, killing
   the enemy.

23 "Saul and Jonathan, so wonderful
   and dear;
together in life, together in
   death;
swifter than eagles, stronger
   than lions.

2 SAMUEL

a One ancient translation it; *Hebrew* the bow.

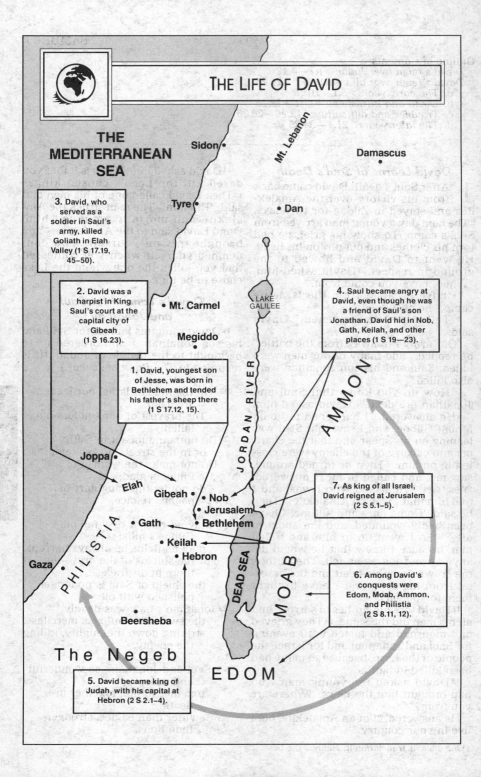

THE LIFE OF DAVID

THE MEDITERRANEAN SEA

Sidon

Mt. Lebanon

Damascus

Tyre

Dan

3. David, who served as a soldier in Saul's army, killed Goliath in Elah Valley (1 S 17.19, 45–50).

2. David was a harpist in King Saul's court at the capital city of Gibeah (1 S 16.23).

Mt. Carmel

LAKE GALILEE

Megiddo

4. Saul became angry at David, even though he was a friend of Saul's son Jonathan. David hid in Nob, Gath, Keilah, and other places (1 S 19–23).

1. David, youngest son of Jesse, was born in Bethlehem and tended his father's sheep there (1 S 17.12, 15).

JORDAN RIVER

AMMON

Joppa

Elah

Gibeah • Nob

Jerusalem

Gath • Bethlehem

7. As king of all Israel, David reigned at Jerusalem (2 S 5.1–5).

Keilah

Hebron

Gaza

PHILISTIA

DEAD SEA

MOAB

6. Among David's conquests were Edom, Moab, Ammon, and Philistia (2 S 8.11, 12).

Beersheba

The Negeb

EDOM

5. David became king of Judah, with his capital at Hebron (2 S 2.1–4).

24 "Women of Israel, mourn for Saul!
   He clothed you in rich scarlet
      dresses
   and adorned you with jewels
      and gold.

25 "The brave soldiers have fallen,
   they were killed in battle.
   Jonathan lies dead in the hills.

26 "I grieve for you, my brother
      Jonathan;
   how dear you were to me!
   How wonderful was your love
      for me,
   better even than the love of
      women.

27 "The brave soldiers have fallen,
   their weapons abandoned and
      useless."

David Is Made King of Judah

2 After this, David asked the LORD, "Shall I go and take control of one of the towns of Judah?"

"Yes," the LORD answered.

"Which one?" David asked.

"Hebron," the LORD said. 2 So David went to Hebron, taking with him his two wives: Ahinoam, who was from Jezreel, and Abigail, Nabal's widow, who was from Carmel. 3 He also took his men and their families, and they settled in the towns around Hebron. 4 Then the men of Judah came to Hebron and anointed David as king of Judah.

When David heard that the people of Jabesh in Gilead had buried Saul, 5 he sent some men there with the message: "May the LORD bless you for showing your loyalty to your king by burying him. 6 And now may the LORD be kind and faithful to you. I too will treat you well because of what you have done. 7 Be strong and brave! Saul your king is dead, and the people of Judah have anointed me as their king."

Ishbosheth Is Made King of Israel

8 The commander of Saul's army, Abner son of Ner, had fled with Saul's son Ishbosheth across the Jordan to Mahanaim. 9 There Abner made Ishbosheth king of the territories of Gilead, Asher,[b] Jezreel, Ephraim, and Benjamin, and in-

deed over all Israel. 10 He was forty years old when he was made king of Israel, and he ruled for two years.

But the tribe of Judah was loyal to David, 11 and he ruled in Hebron over Judah for seven and a half years.

War between Israel and Judah

12 Abner and the officials of Ishbosheth went from Mahanaim to the city of Gibeon. 13 Joab, whose mother was Zeruiah, and David's other officials met them at the pool, where they all sat down, one group on one side of the pool and the other group on the opposite side. 14 Abner said to Joab, "Let's have some of the young men from each side fight an armed contest."

"All right," Joab answered.

15 So twelve men, representing Ishbosheth and the tribe of Benjamin, fought twelve of David's men. 16 Each man caught his opponent by the head and plunged his sword into his opponent's side, so that all twenty-four of them fell down dead together. And so that place in Gibeon is called "Field of Swords."

17 Then a furious battle broke out, and Abner and the Israelites were defeated by David's men. 18 The three sons of Zeruiah were there: Joab, Abishai, and Asahel. Asahel, who could run as fast as a wild deer, 19 started chasing Abner, running straight for him. 20 Abner looked back and said, "Is that you, Asahel?"

"Yes," he answered.

21 "Stop chasing me!" Abner said. "Run after one of the soldiers and take what he has." But Asahel kept on chasing him. 22 Once more Abner said to him, "Stop chasing me! Why force me to kill you? How could I face your brother Joab?" 23 But Asahel would not quit; so Abner, with a backward thrust[c] of his spear, struck him through the stomach so that the spear came out at his back. Asahel dropped to the ground dead, and everyone who came to the place where he was lying stopped and stood there.

24 But Joab and Abishai started out after Abner, and at sunset they came to the hill of Ammah, which is to the east of Giah on the road to the wilderness of Gibeon. 25 The men from the tribe of Benjamin gathered around Abner again

---

b One ancient translation Asher; Hebrew Assyria. Hebrew unclear.

c Probable text with a backward thrust;

and took their stand on the top of a hill.
26 Abner called out to Joab, "Do we have
to go on fighting forever? Can't you see
that in the end there will be nothing but
bitterness? We are your relatives. How
long will it be before you order your men
to stop chasing us?"

27 "I swear by the living God," Joab answered, "that if you had not spoken, my
men would have kept on chasing you
until tomorrow morning." 28 Then Joab
blew the trumpet as a signal for his men
to stop pursuing the Israelites; and so
the fighting stopped.

29 Abner and his men marched
through the Jordan Valley all that night;
they crossed the Jordan River, and after
marching all the next morning, they arrived back at Mahanaim.

30 When Joab gave up the chase, he
gathered all his men and found that
nineteen of them were missing, in addition to Asahel. 31 David's men had killed
360 of Abner's men from the tribe of
Benjamin. 32 Joab and his men took Asahel's body and buried it in the family
tomb at Bethlehem. Then they marched
all night and at dawn arrived back at
Hebron.

3 The fighting between the forces
supporting Saul's family and those
supporting David went on for a long
time. As David became stronger and
stronger, his opponents became weaker
and weaker.

David's Sons

2 The following six sons, in order of
their birth, were born to David at Hebron: Amnon, whose mother was Ahinoam, from Jezreel; 3 Chileab, whose
mother was Abigail, Nabal's widow,
from Carmel; Absalom, whose mother
was Maacah, the daughter of King Talmai of Geshur; 4 Adonijah, whose
mother was Haggith; Shephatiah, whose
mother was Abital; 5 Ithream, whose
mother was Eglah. All of these sons
were born in Hebron.

Abner Joins David

6 As the fighting continued between
David's forces and the forces loyal to
Saul's family, Abner became more and
more powerful among Saul's followers.
7 One day Ishbosheth son of Saul ac-

cused Abner of sleeping with Saul's concubine Rizpah, the daughter of Aiah.
8 This made Abner furious. "Do you
think that I would betray Saul? Do you
really think I'm serving Judah?" he exclaimed. "From the very first I have been
loyal to the cause of your father Saul, his
brothers, and his friends, and I have
kept you from being defeated by David;
yet today you find fault with me about a
woman! 9-10 The LORD promised David
that he would take the kingdom away
from Saul and his descendants and
would make David king of both Israel
and Judah, from one end of the country
to the other. Now may God strike me
dead if I don't make this come true!"
11 Ishbosheth was so afraid of Abner that
he could not say a word.

12 Abner sent messengers to David,
who at that time was at Hebron,d to say,
"Who is going to rule this land? Make an
agreement with me, and I will help you
win all Israel over to your side."

13 "Good!" David answered. "I will
make an agreement with you on one
condition: you must bring Saul's daughter Michal to me when you come to see
me." 14 And David also sent messengers
to Ishbosheth to say, "Give me back my
wife Michal. I paid a hundred Philistine
foreskins in order to marry her." 15 So
Ishbosheth had her taken from her husband Paltiel son of Laish. 16 Paltiel followed her all the way to the town of
Bahurim, crying as he went. But when
Abner said, "Go back home," he did.

17 Abner went to the leaders of Israel
and said to them, "For a long time you
have wanted David to be your king.
18 Now here is your chance. Remember
that the LORD has said, 'I will use my
servant David to rescue my people Israel
from the Philistines and from all their
other enemies.'" 19 Abner spoke also to
the people of the tribe of Benjamin and
then went to Hebron to tell David what
the people of Benjamin and of Israel had
agreed to do.

20 When Abner came to David at Hebron with twenty men, David gave a
feast for them. 21 Abner told David, "I
will go now and win all Israel over to
Your Majesty. They will accept you
as king, and then you will get what you
have wanted and will rule over the

d One ancient translation at Hebron; Hebrew where he (Abner) was.

whole land." David gave Abner a guarantee of safety and sent him on his way.

Abner Is Murdered

22 Later on Joab and David's other officials returned from a raid, bringing a large amount of loot with them. Abner, however, was no longer there at Hebron with David, because David had sent him away with a guarantee of safety. 23 When Joab and his men arrived, he was told that Abner had come to King David and had been sent away with a guarantee of safety. 24 So Joab went to the king and said to him, "What have you done? Abner came to you — why did you let him go like that? 25 He came here to deceive you and to find out everything you do and everywhere you go. Surely you know that!"

26 After leaving David, Joab sent messengers to get Abner, and they brought him back from Sirah Well; but David knew nothing about it. 27 When Abner arrived in Hebron, Joab took him aside at the gate, as though he wanted to speak privately with him, and there he stabbed him in the stomach. And so Abner was murdered because he had killed Joab's brother Asahel. 28 When David heard the news, he said, "The LORD knows that my subjects and I are completely innocent of the murder of Abner. 29 May the punishment for it fall on Joab and all his family! In every generation may there be some man in his family who has gonorrhea or a dreaded skin disease or is fit only to do a woman's work or is killed in battle or doesn't have enough to eat!" 30 So Joab and his brother Abishai took revenge on Abner for killing their brother Asahel in the battle at Gibeon.

Abner Is Buried

31 Then David ordered Joab and his men to tear their clothes, wear sackcloth, and mourn for Abner. And at the funeral King David himself walked behind the coffin. 32 Abner was buried at Hebron, and the king wept aloud at the grave, and so did all the people. 33 David sang this lament for Abner:

"Why did Abner have to die like a
    fool?
34 His hands were not tied,

And his feet were not bound;
    He died like someone killed by
        criminals!"
And the people wept for him again.
35 All day long the people tried to get David to eat something, but he made a solemn promise, "May God strike me dead if I eat anything before the day is over!" 36 They took note of this and were pleased. Indeed, everything the king did pleased the people. 37 All of David's people and all the people in Israel understood that the king had no part in the murder of Abner. 38 The king said to his officials, "Don't you realize that this day a great leader in Israel has died? 39 Even though I am the king chosen by God, I feel weak today. These sons of Zeruiah are too violent for me. May the LORD punish these criminals as they deserve!"

Ishbosheth Is Murdered

4 When Saul's son Ishbosheth heard that Abner had been killed in Hebron, he was afraid, and all the people of Israel were alarmed. 2 Ishbosheth had two officers who were leaders of raiding parties, Baanah and Rechab, sons of Rimmon, from Beeroth in the tribe of Benjamin. (Beeroth is counted as part of Benjamin. 3 Its original inhabitants had fled to Gittaim, where they have lived ever since.)

4 Another descendant of Saul was Jonathan's son Mephibosheth, who was five years old when Saul and Jonathan were killed. When the news about their death came from the city of Jezreel, his nurse picked him up and fled; but she was in such a hurry that she dropped him, and he became crippled.

5 Rechab and Baanah set out for Ishbosheth's house and arrived there about noon, while he was taking his midday rest. 6 The woman at the door had become drowsy while she was sifting wheat and had fallen asleep, so Rechab and Baanah slipped in.e 7 Once inside, they went to Ishbosheth's bedroom, where he was sound asleep, and killed him. Then they cut off his head, took it with them, and walked all night through the Jordan Valley. 8 They presented the head to King David at Hebron and said to him, "Here is the head of Ishbosheth,

---

e Verse 6 follows one ancient translation; Hebrew They went on into the house carrying wheat, and struck him in the belly. Then Rechab and his brother Baanah escaped.

the son of your enemy Saul, who tried to kill you. Today the LORD has allowed Your Majesty to take revenge on Saul and his descendants."

9 David answered them, "I take a vow by the living LORD, who has saved me from all dangers! 10 The messenger who came to me at Ziklag and told me of Saul's death thought he was bringing good news. I seized him and had him put to death. That was the reward I gave him for his good news! 11 How much worse it will be for evil men who murder an innocent man asleep in his own house! I will now take revenge on you for murdering him and will wipe you off the face of the earth!" 12 David gave the order, and his soldiers killed Rechab and Baanah and cut off their hands and feet, which they hung up near the pool in Hebron. They took Ishbosheth's head and buried it in Abner's tomb there at Hebron.

David Becomes King of Israel and Judah
(1 Chronicles 11.1-9; 14.1-7)

5 Then all the tribes of Israel went to David at Hebron and said to him, "We are your own flesh and blood. 2 In the past, even when Saul was still our king, you led the people of Israel in battle, and the LORD promised you that you would lead his people and be their ruler." 3 So all the leaders of Israel came to King David at Hebron. He made a sacred alliance with them, they anointed him, and he became king of Israel. 4 David was thirty years old when he became king, and he ruled for forty years. 5 He ruled in Hebron over Judah for seven and a half years, and in Jerusalem over all Israel and Judah for thirty-three years.

6 The time came when King David and his men set out to attack Jerusalem. The Jebusites, who lived there, thought that David would not be able to conquer the city, and so they said to him, "You will never get in here; even the blind and the crippled could keep you out." (7 But David did capture their fortress of Zion, and it became known as "David's City.")

8 That day David said to his men, "Does anybody here hate the Jebusites as much as I do? Enough to kill them?

Then go up through the water tunnel and attack those poor blind cripples." (That is why it is said, "The blind and the crippled cannot enter the LORD's house.")*f*

9 After capturing the fortress, David lived in it and named it "David's City." He built the city around it, starting at the place where land was filled in on the east side of the hill. 10 He grew stronger all the time, because the LORD God Almighty was with him.

11 King Hiram of Tyre sent a trade mission to David; he provided him with cedar logs and with carpenters and stone masons to build a palace. 12 And so David realized that the LORD had established him as king of Israel and was making his kingdom prosperous for the sake of his people.

13 After moving from Hebron to Jerusalem, David took more concubines and wives, and had more sons and daughters. 14 The following children were born to him in Jerusalem: Shammua, Shobab, Nathan, Solomon, 15 Ibhar, Elishua, Nepheg, Japhia, 16 Elishama, Eliada, and Eliphelet.

Victory over the Philistines
(1 Chronicles 14.8-17)

17 The Philistines were told that David had been made king of Israel, so their army set out to capture him. When David heard of it, he went down to a fortified place. 18 The Philistines arrived at Rephaim Valley and occupied it. 19 David asked the LORD, "Shall I attack the Philistines? Will you give me the victory?"

"Yes, attack!" the LORD answered. "I will give you the victory!"

20 So David went to Baal Perazim and there he defeated the Philistines. He said, "The LORD has broken through my enemies like a flood." And so that place is called Baal Perazim.*g* 21 When the Philistines fled, they left their idols behind, and David and his men carried them away.

22 Then the Philistines went back to Rephaim Valley and occupied it again. 23 Once more David consulted the LORD, who answered, "Don't attack them from here, but go around and get ready to at-

---

f Verse 8 in Hebrew is unclear.   g BAAL PERAZIM: This name in Hebrew means "Lord of the Breakthrough."

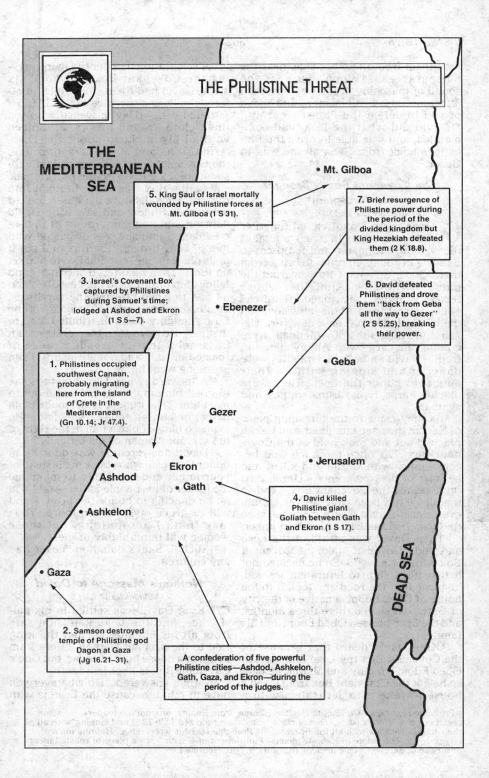

THE PHILISTINE THREAT

THE MEDITERRANEAN SEA

• Mt. Gilboa

5. King Saul of Israel mortally wounded by Philistine forces at Mt. Gilboa (1 S 31).

7. Brief resurgence of Philistine power during the period of the divided kingdom but King Hezekiah defeated them (2 K 18.8).

3. Israel's Covenant Box captured by Philistines during Samuel's time; lodged at Ashdod and Ekron (1 S 5—7).

• Ebenezer

6. David defeated Philistines and drove them ''back from Geba all the way to Gezer'' (2 S 5.25), breaking their power.

1. Philistines occupied southwest Canaan, probably migrating here from the island of Crete in the Mediterranean (Gn 10.14; Jr 47.4).

• Geba

• Gezer

• Ekron

• Jerusalem

Ashdod

• Gath

4. David killed Philistine giant Goliath between Gath and Ekron (1 S 17).

• Ashkelon

• Gaza

DEAD SEA

2. Samson destroyed temple of Philistine god Dagon at Gaza (Jg 16.21–31).

A confederation of five powerful Philistine cities—Ashdod, Ashkelon, Gath, Gaza, and Ekron—during the period of the judges.

tack them from the other side, near the balsam trees. [24] When you hear the sound of marching in the treetops, then attack because I will be marching ahead of you to defeat the Philistine army." [25] David did what the LORD had commanded, and was able to drive the Philistines back from Geba all the way to Gezer.

The Covenant Box Is Brought to Jerusalem
(1 Chronicles 13.1-14; 15.25 — 16.6, 43)

6 Once more David called together the best soldiers in Israel, a total of thirty thousand men, [2] and led them to Baalah[h] in Judah, in order to bring from there God's Covenant Box, bearing the name of the LORD Almighty, whose throne is above the winged creatures.[i] [3] They took it from Abinadab's home on the hill and placed it on a new cart. Uzzah and Ahio, sons of Abinadab, were guiding the cart, [4] with Ahio walking in front. [5] David and all the Israelites were dancing and singing with all their might[j] to honor the LORD. They were playing harps, lyres, drums, rattles, and cymbals.

[6] As they came to the threshing place of Nacon, the oxen stumbled, and Uzzah reached out and took hold of the Covenant Box. [7] At once the LORD God became angry with Uzzah and killed him because of his irreverence.[k] Uzzah died there beside the Covenant Box, [8] and so that place has been called Perez Uzzah[l] ever since. David was furious because the LORD had punished Uzzah in anger.

[9] Then David was afraid of the LORD and said, "How can I take the Covenant Box with me now?" [10] So he decided not to take it with him to Jerusalem; instead, he turned off the road and took it to the house of Obed Edom, a native of the city of Gath. [11] It stayed there three months, and the LORD blessed Obed Edom and his family.

[12] King David heard that because of the Covenant Box the LORD had blessed Obed Edom's family and all that he had; so he got the Covenant Box from Obed's house to take it to Jerusalem with a great celebration. [13] After the men carrying the Covenant Box had gone six steps, David had them stop while he offered the LORD a sacrifice of a bull and a fattened calf. [14] David, wearing only a linen cloth around his waist, danced with all his might to honor the LORD. [15] And so he and all the Israelites took the Covenant Box up to Jerusalem with shouts of joy and the sound of trumpets.

[16] As the Box was being brought into the city, Michal, Saul's daughter, looked out of the window and saw King David dancing and jumping around in the sacred dance, and she was disgusted with him. [17] They brought the Box and put it in its place in the Tent that David had set up for it. Then he offered sacrifices and fellowship offerings to the LORD. [18] When he had finished offering the sacrifices, he blessed the people in the name of the LORD Almighty [19] and distributed food to them all. He gave each man and woman in Israel a loaf of bread, a piece of roasted meat,[m] and some raisins. Then everyone went home.

[20] Afterward, when David went home to greet his family, Michal came out to meet him. "The king of Israel made a big name for himself today!" she said. "He exposed himself like a fool in the sight of the servant women of his officials!"

[21] David answered, "I was dancing to honor the LORD, who chose me instead of your father and his family to make me the leader of his people Israel. And I will go on dancing to honor the LORD, [22] and will disgrace myself even more. You[n] may think I am nothing, but those women will think highly of me!"

[23] Michal, Saul's daughter, never had any children.

Nathan's Message to David
(1 Chronicles 17.1-15)

7 King David was settled in his palace, and the LORD kept him safe from all his enemies. [2] Then the king said to the prophet Nathan, "Here I am living in a house built of cedar, but God's Covenant Box is kept in a tent!"

[3] Nathan answered, "Do whatever you have in mind, because the LORD is with

---

[h] *Probable text (see 1 Ch 13.6)* to Baalah; *Hebrew* from Baaley, *or* from the leaders.   [i] WINGED CREATURES: *See Word List.*   [j] *One ancient translation (and see 1 Ch 13.8)* and singing with all their might; *Hebrew* with all the fir trees.   [k] *Probable text* his irreverence; *Hebrew unclear.*
[l] PEREZ UZZAH: *This name in Hebrew means "Punishment of Uzzah."*   [m] a piece of roasted meat; *or* a cake of dates.   [n] *One ancient translation* You; *Hebrew* I.

you." 4But that night the LORD said to Nathan, 5"Go and tell my servant David that I say to him, 'You are not the one to build a temple for me to live in. 6From the time I rescued the people of Israel from Egypt until now, I have never lived in a temple; I have traveled around living in a tent. 7In all my traveling with the people of Israel I never asked any of the leaders[o] that I appointed why they had not built me a temple made of cedar.'

8"So tell my servant David that I, the LORD Almighty, say to him, 'I took you from looking after sheep in the fields and made you the ruler of my people Israel. 9I have been with you wherever you have gone, and I have defeated all your enemies as you advanced. I will make you as famous as the greatest leaders in the world. 10-11I have chosen a place for my people Israel and have settled them there, where they will live without being oppressed any more. Ever since they entered this land, they have been attacked by violent people, but this will not happen again. I promise to keep you safe from all your enemies and to give you descendants. 12When you die and are buried with your ancestors, I will make one of your sons king and will keep his kingdom strong. 13He will be the one to build a temple for me, and I will make sure that his dynasty continues forever. 14I will be his father, and he will be my son. When he does wrong, I will punish him as a father punishes his son. 15But I will not withdraw my support from him as I did from Saul, whom I removed so that you could be king. 16You will always have descendants, and I will make your kingdom last forever. Your dynasty will never end.'"

17Nathan told David everything that God had revealed to him.

David's Prayer of Thanksgiving
(1 Chronicles 17.16-27)

18Then King David went into the Tent of the LORD's presence, sat down and prayed, "Sovereign LORD, I am not worthy of what you have already done for me, nor is my family. 19Yet now you are doing even more, Sovereign LORD; you have made promises about my descendants in the years to come. And you let a man see this.[p] Sovereign LORD! 20What more can I say to you! You know me, your servant. 21It was your will and purpose to do this; you have done all these great things in order to instruct me. 22How great you are, Sovereign LORD! There is none like you; we have always known that you alone are God. 23There is no other nation on earth like Israel, whom you rescued from slavery to make them your own people. The great and wonderful things you did for them[q] have spread your fame throughout the world. You drove out[r] other nations and their gods as your people advanced, the people whom you set free from Egypt to be your own. 24You have made Israel your own people forever, and you, LORD, have become their God.

25"And now, LORD God, fulfill for all time the promise you made about me and my descendants, and do what you said you would. 26Your fame will be great, and people will forever say, 'The LORD Almighty is God over Israel.' And you will preserve my dynasty for all time. 27LORD Almighty, God of Israel! I have the courage to pray this prayer to you, because you have revealed all this to me, your servant, and have told me that you will make my descendants kings.

28"And now, Sovereign LORD, you are God; you always keep your promises, and you have made this wonderful promise to me. 29I ask you to bless my descendants so that they will continue to enjoy your favor. You, Sovereign LORD, have promised this, and your blessing will rest on my descendants forever."

David's Military Victories
(1 Chronicles 18.1-17)

8 Some time later King David attacked the Philistines again, defeated them, and ended their control over the land.[s]

2Then he defeated the Moabites. He made the prisoners lie down on the ground and put two out of every three of

---

[o] *Probable text (see 1 Ch 17.6)* leaders; *Hebrew* tribes.   [p] *Probable text* you let a man see this; *Hebrew* this is a law for human beings.   [q] *Probable text* them; *Hebrew* you (plural).   [r] *One ancient translation (and see 1 Ch 17.21)* You drove out; *Hebrew* for your land.   [s] *Probable text* over the land; *Hebrew unclear.*

them to death. So the Moabites became his subjects and paid taxes to him.

3 Then he defeated the king of the Syrian state of Zobah, Hadadezer son of Rehob, as Hadadezer was on his way to restore his control over the territory by the upper Euphrates River. 4 David captured seventeen hundred of his cavalry and twenty thousand of his foot soldiers. He kept enough horses for a hundred chariots and crippled all the rest.

5 When the Syrians of Damascus sent an army to help King Hadadezer, David attacked it and killed twenty-two thousand men. 6 Then he set up military camps in*t* their territory, and they became his subjects and paid taxes to him. The LORD made David victorious everywhere. 7 David captured the gold shields carried by Hadadezer's officials and took them to Jerusalem. 8 He also took a great quantity of bronze from Betah and Berothai, cities ruled by Hadadezer.

9 King Toi of Hamath heard that David had defeated all of Hadadezer's army. 10 So he sent his son Joram to greet King David and congratulate him for his victory over Hadadezer, against whom Toi had fought many times. Joram took David presents made of gold, silver, and bronze. 11 King David dedicated them for use in worship, along with the silver and gold he took from the nations he had conquered — 12 Edom, Moab, Ammon, Philistia, and Amalek — as well as part of the loot he had taken from Hadadezer.

13 David became even more famous when he returned from killing eighteen thousand Edomites in Salt Valley. 14 He set up military camps*u* throughout Edom, and the people there became his subjects. The LORD made David victorious everywhere.

15 David ruled over all of Israel and made sure that his people were always treated fairly and justly. 16 Joab, whose mother was Zeruiah, was the commander of the army; Jehoshaphat son of Ahilud was in charge of the records; 17 Zadok son of Ahitub and Ahimelech son of Abiathar were priests; Seraiah was the court secretary; 18 Benaiah son of Jehoiada was in charge of*v* David's bodyguards; and David's sons were priests.

David and Mephibosheth

9 One day David asked, "Is there anyone left of Saul's family? If there is, I would like to show him kindness for Jonathan's sake."

2 There was a servant of Saul's family named Ziba, and he was told to go to David. "Are you Ziba?" the king asked.

"At your service, sir," he answered.

3 The king asked him, "Is there anyone left of Saul's family to whom I can show loyalty and kindness, as I promised God I would?"

Ziba answered, "There is still one of Jonathan's sons. He is crippled."

4 "Where is he?" the king asked.

"At the home of Machir son of Ammiel in Lodebar," Ziba answered. 5 So King David sent for him.

6 When Mephibosheth, the son of Jonathan and grandson of Saul, arrived, he bowed down before David in respect. David said, "Mephibosheth," and he answered, "At your service, sir."

7 "Don't be afraid," David replied. "I will be kind to you for the sake of your father Jonathan. I will give you back all the land that belonged to your grandfather Saul, and you will always be welcome at my table."

8 Mephibosheth bowed again and said, "I am no better than a dead dog, sir! Why should you be so good to me?"

9 Then the king called Ziba, Saul's servant, and said, "I am giving Mephibosheth, your master's grandson, everything that belonged to Saul and his family. 10 You, your sons, and your servants will farm the land for your master Saul's family and bring in the harvest, to provide food for them. But Mephibosheth himself will always be a guest at my table." (Ziba had fifteen sons and twenty servants.)

11 Ziba answered, "I will do everything Your Majesty commands."

So Mephibosheth ate at the king's*w* table, just like one of the king's sons. 12 Mephibosheth had a young son named Mica. All the members of Ziba's family became servants of Mephibosheth. 13 So Mephibosheth, who was crippled in both feet, lived in Jerusalem, eating all his meals at the king's table.

---

t set up military camps in; *or* placed military commanders over.   *u* set up military camps; *or* placed military commanders.   *v* *Some ancient translations* was in charge of; *Hebrew does not have these words.*   *w* *One ancient translation* the king's; *Hebrew* my.

David Defeats the Ammonites and the Syrians

(1 Chronicles 19.1-19)

10 Some time later King Nahash of Ammon died, and his son Hanun became king. 2 King David said, "I must show loyal friendship to Hanun, as his father Nahash did to me." So David sent messengers to express his sympathy.

When they arrived in Ammon, 3 the Ammonite leaders said to the king, "Do you think that it is in your father's honor that David has sent these men to express sympathy to you? Of course not! He has sent them here as spies to explore the city, so that he can conquer us!"

4 Hanun seized David's messengers, shaved off one side of their beards, cut off their clothes at the hips, and sent them away. 5 They were too ashamed to return home. When David heard about what had happened, he sent word for them to stay in Jericho and not return until their beards had grown again.

6 The Ammonites realized that they had made David their enemy, so they hired twenty thousand Syrian soldiers from Bethrehob and Zobah, twelve thousand men from Tob, and the king of Maacah with a thousand men. 7 David heard of it and sent Joab against them with the whole army. 8 The Ammonites marched out and took up their position at the entrance to Rabbah, their capital city, while the others, both the Syrians and the men from Tob and Maacah, took up their position in the open countryside.

9 Joab saw that the enemy troops would attack him in front and from the rear, so he chose the best of Israel's soldiers and put them in position facing the Syrians. 10 He placed the rest of his troops under the command of his brother Abishai, who put them in position facing the Ammonites. 11 Joab said to him, "If you see that the Syrians are defeating me, come and help me, and if the Ammonites are defeating you, I will go and help you. 12 Be strong and courageous! Let's fight hard for our people and for the cities of our God. And may the LORD's will be done!"

13 Joab and his men advanced to attack, and the Syrians fled. 14 When the Ammonites saw the Syrians running away, they fled from Abishai and retreated into the city. Then Joab turned back from fighting the Ammonites and went back to Jerusalem.

15 The Syrians realized that they had been defeated by the Israelites, and so they called all their troops together. 16 King Hadadezer sent for the Syrians who were on the east side of the Euphrates River, and they came to Helam under the command of Shobach, commander of the army of King Hadadezer of Zobah. 17 When David heard of it, he gathered the Israelite troops, crossed the Jordan River, and marched to Helam, where the Syrians took up their position facing him. The fighting began, 18 and the Israelites drove the Syrian army back. David and his men killed seven hundred Syrian chariot drivers and forty thousand cavalry, and they wounded Shobach, the enemy commander, who died on the battlefield. 19 When the kings who were subject to Hadadezer realized that they had been defeated by the Israelites, they made peace with them and became their subjects. And the Syrians were afraid to help the Ammonites any more.

David and Bathsheba

11 The following spring, at the time of the year when kings usually go to war, David sent out Joab with his officers and the Israelite army; they defeated the Ammonites and besieged the city of Rabbah. But David himself stayed in Jerusalem.

2 One day, late in the afternoon, David got up from his nap and went to the palace roof. As he walked around up there, he saw a woman taking a bath in her house. She was very beautiful. 3 So he sent a messenger to find out who she was, and learned that she was Bathsheba, the daughter of Eliam and the wife of Uriah the Hittite. 4 David sent messengers to get her; they brought her to him and he made love to her. (She had just finished her monthly ritual of purification.) Then she went back home. 5 Afterward she discovered that she was pregnant and sent a message to David to tell him.

6 David then sent a message to Joab: "Send me Uriah the Hittite." So Joab sent him to David. 7 When Uriah arrived, David asked him if Joab and the troops were well, and how the fighting was go-

ISRAEL AND THE HITTITES

The Hittites were a people of the ancient world who flourished in Asia Minor and surrounding regions between about 1900 B.C. and 1200 B.C. While the Hittites are mentioned prominently in the Bible, some scholars questioned the existence of these people for many years because there was little physical evidence of their empire. But recent discoveries of Hittite culture by archaeologists have confirmed the accuracy of the biblical accounts.

The Hittite nation, with Hattusa as capital, eventually spread into northern Syria, then into the land of Canaan. Hittites are mentioned in the Bible during the earliest time of Israel's history.

When Sarah died, Abraham bought a burial cave from Ephron the Hittite (Gn 23.10–20). Isaac's son Esau took two Hittite women as wives (Gn 26.34). Several centuries later, the Hittites were included among the groups that would have to be driven out of Canaan before Israel could possess the land (Ex 3.8; Dt 7.1).

In David's time, Abimelech the Hittite was a trusted companion of David during his flight from Saul (1 S 26.6). Uriah the Hittite, Bathsheba's husband, was sent to his death by David to cover up his adultery with Bathsheba (2 S 11.14, 15). Since Uriah was a brave soldier in David's army, this shows that at least some of the Hittites had been assimilated into Israelite culture by this time in their history.

In Solomon's time, Solomon disobeyed God's instructions and married a Hittite woman to seal an alliance with these ancient people (1 K 11.1, 2). The prohibition against such a marriage shows how objectionable the Hittite religious system was in God's eyes. The Hittites worshiped many different pagan gods, including several adopted from the Egyptians and the Babylonians. Solomon's marriage became a corrupting influence that pulled the nation of Israel away from worship of the one true God (1 K 11.9–13).

ing. 8Then he said to Uriah, "Go on home and rest a while." Uriah left, and David had a present sent to his home. 9But Uriah did not go home; instead he slept at the palace gate with the king's guards. 10When David heard that Uriah had not gone home, he asked him, "You have just returned after a long absence; why didn't you go home?"

11Uriah answered, "The men of Israel and Judah are away in battle, and the Covenant Box is with them; my commander Joab and his officers are camping out in the open. How could I go home, eat and drink, and sleep with my wife? By all that's sacred, I swear that I could never do such a thing!"

12So David said, "Then stay here the rest of the day, and tomorrow I'll send you back." So Uriah stayed in Jerusalem that day and the next. 13David invited him to supper and got him drunk. But again that night Uriah did not go home; instead he slept on his blanketx in the palace guardroom.

14The next morning David wrote a letter to Joab and sent it by Uriah. 15He wrote: "Put Uriah in the front line, where the fighting is heaviest, then retreat and let him be killed." 16So while Joab was besieging the city, he sent Uriah to a place where he knew the enemy was strong. 17The enemy troops came out of the city and fought Joab's forces; some of David's officers were killed, and so was Uriah.

18Then Joab sent a report to David telling him about the battle, 19and he instructed the messenger, "After you have told the king all about the battle, 20he may get angry and ask you, 'Why did you go so near the city to fight them? Didn't you realize that they would shoot arrows from the walls? 21Don't you remember how Abimelech son of Gideon was killed? It was at Thebez, where a woman threw a millstone down from the wall and killed him. Why, then, did you go so near the wall?' If the king asks you this, tell him, 'Your officer Uriah was also killed.' "

22So the messenger went to David and told him what Joab had commanded him to say. 23He said, "Our enemies were stronger than we and came out of the city to fight us in the open, but we drove them back to the city gate. 24Then they shot arrows at us from the wall, and some of Your Majesty's officers were killed; your officer Uriah was also killed."

25David said to the messenger, "Encourage Joab and tell him not to be upset, since you never can tell who will die in battle. Tell him to launch a stronger attack on the city and capture it."

26When Bathsheba heard that her husband had been killed, she mourned for him. 27When the time of mourning was over, David had her brought to the palace; she became his wife and bore him a son. But the LORD was not pleased with what David had done.

Nathan's Message and David's Repentance

12 The LORD sent the prophet Nathan to David. Nathan went to him and said, "There were two men who lived in the same town; one was rich and the other poor. 2The rich man had many cattle and sheep, 3while the poor man had only one lamb, which he had bought. He took care of it, and it grew up in his home with his children. He would feed it some of his own food, let it drink from his cup, and hold it in his lap. The lamb was like a daughter to him. 4One day a visitor arrived at the rich man's home. The rich man didn't want to kill one of his own animals to fix a meal for him; instead, he took the poor man's lamb and prepared a meal for his guest."

5David became very angry at the rich man and said, "I swear by the living LORD that the man who did this ought to die! 6For having done such a cruel thing, he must pay back four times as much as he took."

7"You are that man," Nathan said to David. "And this is what the LORD God of Israel says: 'I made you king of Israel and rescued you from Saul. 8I gave you his kingdom and his wives; I made you king over Israel and Judah. If this had not been enough, I would have given you twice as much. 9Why, then, have you disobeyed my commands? Why did you do this evil thing? You had Uriah killed in battle; you let the Ammonites kill him, and then you took his wife! 10Now, in every generation some of your

x blanket; or cot.

descendants will die a violent death because you have disobeyed me and have taken Uriah's wife. [11] I swear to you that I will cause someone from your own family to bring trouble on you. You will see it when I take your wives from you and give them to another man; and he will have intercourse with them in broad daylight. [12] You sinned in secret, but I will make this happen in broad daylight for all Israel to see.' "

[13] "I have sinned against the LORD," David said.

Nathan replied, "The LORD forgives you; you will not die. [14] But because you have shown such contempt for the LORD in doing this, your child will die." [15] Then Nathan went home.

David's Son Dies

The LORD caused the child that Uriah's wife had borne to David to become very sick. [16] David prayed to God that the child would get well. He refused to eat anything, and every night he went into his room and spent the night lying on the floor. [17] His court officials went to him and tried to make him get up, but he refused and would not eat anything with them. [18] A week later the child died, and David's officials were afraid to tell him the news. They said, "While the child was living, David wouldn't answer us when we spoke to him. How can we tell him that his child is dead? He might do himself some harm!"

[19] When David noticed them whispering to each other, he realized that the child had died. So he asked them, "Is the child dead?"

"Yes, he is," they answered.

[20] David got up from the floor, took a bath, combed his hair, and changed his clothes. Then he went and worshiped in the house of the LORD. When he returned to the palace, he asked for food and ate it as soon as it was served. [21] "We don't understand this," his officials said to him. "While the child was alive, you wept for him and would not eat; but as soon as he died, you got up and ate!"

[22] "Yes," David answered, "I did fast and weep while he was still alive. I thought that the LORD might be merciful to me and not let the child die. [23] But now

that he is dead, why should I fast? Could I bring the child back to life? I will some day go to where he is, but he can never come back to me."

Solomon Is Born

[24] Then David comforted his wife Bathsheba. He had intercourse with her, and she bore a son, whom David named Solomon. The LORD loved the boy [25] and commanded the prophet Nathan to name the boy Jedidiah,[y] because the LORD loved him.

David Captures Rabbah

(1 Chronicles 20.1-3)

[26] Meanwhile Joab continued his campaign against Rabbah, the capital city of Ammon, and was about to capture it. [27] He sent messengers to David to report: "I have attacked Rabbah and have captured its water supply. [28] Now gather the rest of your forces, attack the city and take it yourself. I don't want to get the credit for capturing it." [29] So David gathered his forces, went to Rabbah, attacked it, and conquered it. [30] From the head of the idol of the Ammonite god Molech[z] David took a gold crown which weighed about seventy-five pounds and had a jewel in it. David took the jewel and put it in his own crown.[a] He also took a large amount of loot from the city [31] and put its people to work with saws, iron hoes, and iron axes, and forced them to work at[b] making bricks. He did the same to the people of all the other towns of Ammon. Then he and his men returned to Jerusalem.

Amnon and Tamar

13 David's son Absalom had a beautiful unmarried sister named Tamar. Amnon, another of David's sons, fell in love with her. [2] He was so much in love with her that he became sick, because it seemed impossible for him to have her; as a virgin, she was kept from meeting men. [3] But he had a friend, a very shrewd man named Jonadab, son of David's brother Shammah. [4] Jonadab said to Amnon, "You are the king's son, yet day after day I see you looking sad. What's the matter?"

"I'm in love with Tamar, the sister of

---

[y] JEDIDIAH: *This name in Hebrew means "Beloved of the LORD."* [z] idol of the Ammonite god Molech; *or* Ammonite king. [a] jewel . . . crown; *or* crown and put it on his own head. [b] *Probable text (see 1 Ch 20.3)* work at; *Hebrew* pass through.

my half brother Absalom," he answered.

⁵Jonadab said to him, "Pretend that you are sick and go to bed. When your father comes to see you, say to him, 'Please ask my sister Tamar to come and feed me. I want her to fix the food here where I can see her, and then serve it to me herself.' " ⁶So Amnon pretended that he was sick and went to bed.

King David went to see him, and Amnon said to him, "Please let Tamar come and make a few cakes here where I can see her, and then serve them to me herself."

⁷So David sent word to Tamar in the palace: "Go to Amnon's house and fix him some food." ⁸She went there and found him in bed. She took some dough, prepared it, and made some cakes there where he could see her. Then she baked the cakes ⁹and emptied them out of the pan for him to eat, but he wouldn't. He said, "Send everyone away"—and they all left. ¹⁰Then he said to her, "Bring the cakes here to my bed and serve them to me yourself." She took the cakes and went over to him. ¹¹As she offered them to him, he grabbed her and said, "Come to bed with me!"

¹²"No," she said. "Don't force me to do such a degrading thing! That's awful! ¹³How could I ever hold up my head in public again? And you—you would be completely disgraced in Israel. Please, speak to the king, and I'm sure that he will give me to you." ¹⁴But he would not listen to her; and since he was stronger than she was, he overpowered her and raped her.

¹⁵Then Amnon was filled with a deep hatred for her; he hated her now even more than he had loved her before. He said to her, "Get out!"

¹⁶"No," she answered. "To send me away like this is a greater crime*c* than what you just did!"

But Amnon would not listen to her; ¹⁷he called in his personal servant and said, "Get this woman out of my sight! Throw her out and lock the door!" ¹⁸The servant put her out and locked the door.

Tamar was wearing a long robe with full sleeves,*d* the usual clothing for an unmarried princess in those days.*e*

¹⁹She sprinkled ashes on her head, tore her robe, and with her face buried in her hands went away crying. ²⁰When her brother Absalom saw her, he asked, "Has Amnon molested you? Please, sister, don't let it upset you so much. He is your half brother, so don't tell anyone about it." So Tamar lived in Absalom's house, sad and lonely.

²¹When King David heard what had happened, he was furious. ²²And Absalom hated Amnon so much for having raped his sister Tamar that he would no longer even speak to him.

Absalom's Revenge

²³Two years later Absalom was having his sheep sheared at Baal Hazor, near the town of Ephraim, and he invited all the king's sons to be there. ²⁴He went to King David and said, "Your Majesty, I am having my sheep sheared. Will you and your officials come and take part in the festivities?"

²⁵"No, my son," the king answered. "It would be too much trouble for you if we all went." Absalom insisted, but the king would not give in, and he asked Absalom to leave.

²⁶But Absalom said, "Well, then, will you at least let my brother Amnon come?"

"Why should he?" the king asked. ²⁷But Absalom kept on insisting until David finally let Amnon and all his other sons go with Absalom.

Absalom prepared a banquet fit for a king*f* ²⁸and instructed his servants: "Notice when Amnon has had too much to drink, and then when I give the order, kill him. Don't be afraid. I will take the responsibility myself. Be brave and don't hesitate!" ²⁹So the servants followed Absalom's instructions and killed Amnon. All the rest of David's sons mounted their mules and fled.

³⁰While they were on their way home, David was told: "Absalom has killed all your sons—not one of them is left!" ³¹The king stood up, tore his clothes in sorrow, and threw himself to the ground. The servants who were there with him tore their clothes also. ³²But Jonadab, the son of David's brother

---

c Probable text To send me ... crime; *Hebrew unclear.*   *d* long robe with full sleeves; *or* decorated robe *(see Gn 37.3).*   *e Probable text* in those days; *Hebrew garments.*   *f Some ancient translations* Absalom prepared a banquet fit for a king; *Hebrew does not have these words.*

Shammah, said, "Your Majesty, they haven't killed all your sons. Only Amnon is dead. You could tell by looking at Absalom that he had made up his mind to do this from the time that Amnon raped his sister Tamar. 33 So don't believe the news that all your sons are dead; only Amnon was killed."

34 In the meantime Absalom had fled.

Just then the soldier on sentry duty saw a large crowd coming down the hill on the road from Horonaim.g He went to the king and reported what he had seen.h 35 Jonadab said to David, "Those are your sons coming, just as I said they would." 36 As soon as he finished saying this, David's sons came in; they started crying, and David and his officials also cried bitterly.

37-38 Absalom fled and went to the king of Geshur, Talmai son of Ammihud, and stayed there three years. David mourned a long time for his son Amnon; 39 but when he got over Amnon's death, he was filled with longing for his son Absalom.

Joab Arranges for Absalom's Return

14 Joab knew that King David missed Absalom very much, 2 so he sent for a clever woman who lived in Tekoa. When she arrived, he said to her, "Pretend that you are in mourning; put on your mourning clothes, and don't comb your hair. Act like a woman who has been in mourning for a long time. 3 Then go to the king and say to him what I tell you to say." Then Joab told her what to say.

4 The woman went to the king, bowed down to the ground in respect, and said, "Help me, Your Majesty!"

5 "What do you want?" he asked her.

"I am a poor widow, sir," she answered. "My husband is dead. 6 Sir, I had two sons, and one day they got into a quarrel out in the fields, where there was no one to separate them, and one of them killed the other. 7 And now, sir, all my relatives have turned against me and are demanding that I hand my son over to them, so that they can kill him for murdering his brother. If they do this, I will be left without a son. They will destroy my last hope and leave my hus-

band without a son to keep his name alive."

8 "Go back home," the king answered, "and I will take care of the matter."

9 "Your Majesty," she said, "whatever you do, my family and I will take the blame; you and the royal family are innocent."

10 The king replied, "If anyone threatens you, bring him to me, and he will never bother you again."

11 She said, "Your Majesty, please pray to the LORD your God, so that my relative who is responsible for avenging the death of my son will not commit a greater crime by killing my other son."

"I promise by the living LORD," David replied, "that your son will not be harmed in the least."

12 "Please, Your Majesty, let me say just one more thing," the woman said.

"All right," he answered.

13 She said to him, "Why have you done such a wrong to God's people? You have not allowed your own son to return from exile, and so you have condemned yourself by what you have just said. 14 We will all die; we are like water spilled on the ground, which can't be gathered again. Even God does not bring the dead back to life, but the king can at least find a way to bring a man back from exile.i 15 Now, Your Majesty, the reason I have come to speak to you is that the people threatened me, and so I said to myself that I would speak to you in the hope that you would do what I ask. 16 I thought you would listen to me and save me from the one who is trying to kill my son and me and so remove us from the land God gave his people. 17 I said to myself that your promise, sir, would make me safe, because the king is like God's angel and can distinguish good from evil.j May the LORD your God be with you!"

18 The king answered, "I'm going to ask you a question, and you must tell me the whole truth."

"Ask me anything, Your Majesty," she answered.

19 "Did Joab put you up to this?" he asked her.

She answered, "I swear by all that is sacred, Your Majesty, that there is no

---

g *Probable text* from Horonaim; *Hebrew* behind him.   h *One ancient translation* He went . . . had seen; *Hebrew does not have these words.*   i *Probable text* Even God . . . from exile; *Hebrew unclear.*   j can distinguish good from evil; *or* knows everything.

way to avoid answering your question.*
It was indeed your officer Joab who told
me what to do and what to say. 20 But he
did it in order to straighten out this
whole matter. Your Majesty is as wise as
the angel of God and knows everything
that happens."

21 Later on the king said to Joab, "I
have decided to do what you want. Go
and get the young man Absalom and
bring him back here."

22 Joab threw himself to the ground in
front of David in respect, and said, "God
bless you, Your Majesty! Now I know
that you are pleased with me, because
you have granted my request." 23 Then
he got up and went to Geshur and
brought Absalom back to Jerusalem.
24 The king, however, gave orders that
Absalom should not live in the palace. "I
don't want to see him," the king said. So
Absalom lived in his own house and did
not appear before the king.

Absalom Is Reconciled to David

25 There was no one in Israel as famous for his good looks as Absalom; he
had no defect from head to toe. 26 His
hair was very thick, and he had to cut it
once a year, when it grew too long and
heavy. It would weigh about five pounds
according to the royal standard of
weights. 27 Absalom had three sons and
one daughter named Tamar, a very
beautiful woman.

28 Absalom lived two years in Jerusalem without seeing the king. 29 Then he
sent for Joab, to ask him to go to the
king for him; but Joab would not come.
Again Absalom sent for him, and again
Joab refused to come. 30 So Absalom
said to his servants, "Look, Joab's field
is next to mine, and it has barley growing in it. Go and set fire to it." So they
went and set the field on fire.

31 Joab went to Absalom's house and
demanded, "Why did your servants set
fire to my field?"

32 Absalom answered, "Because you
wouldn't come when I sent for you. I
wanted you to go to the king and ask for
me: 'Why did I leave Geshur and come
here? It would have been better for me to
have stayed there.' " And Absalom went
on, "I want you to arrange for me to see

the king, and if I'm guilty, then let him
put me to death."

33 So Joab went to King David and told
him what Absalom had said. The king
sent for Absalom, who went to him and
bowed down to the ground in front of
him. The king welcomed him with a kiss.

Absalom Plans Rebellion

15 After this, Absalom provided a
chariot and horses for himself,
and an escort of fifty men. 2 He would get
up early and go and stand by the road at
the city gate. Whenever someone came
there with a dispute that he wanted the
king to settle, Absalom would call him
over and ask him where he was from.
And after the man had told him what
tribe he was from, 3 Absalom would say,
"Look, the law is on your side, but there
is no representative of the king to hear
your case." 4 And he would add, "How I
wish I were a judge! Then anyone who
had a dispute or a claim could come to
me, and I would give him justice."
5 When the man would approach Absalom to bow down before him, Absalom
would reach out, take hold of him, and
kiss him. 6 Absalom did this with every
Israelite who came to the king for judgment, and so he won their loyalty.

7 After four *l* years Absalom said to
King David, "Sir, let me go to Hebron
and keep a promise I made to the LORD.
8 While I was living in Geshur in Syria, I
promised the LORD that if he would take
me back to Jerusalem, I would worship
him in Hebron."*m*

9 "Go in peace," the king said. So Absalom went to Hebron. 10 But he sent messengers to all the tribes of Israel to say,
"When you hear the sound of trumpets,
shout, 'Absalom has become king at Hebron!' " 11 There were two hundred men
who at Absalom's invitation had gone
from Jerusalem with him; they knew
nothing of the plot and went in all good
faith. 12 And while he was offering sacrifices, Absalom also sent to the town of
Gilo for Ahithophel, who was one of
King David's advisers. The plot against
the king gained strength, and Absalom's
followers grew in number.

---

k there is . . . . question; *or* you are absolutely right.   *l* *Some ancient translations* four; *Hebrew*
forty.   *m* *One ancient translation* in Hebron; *Hebrew does not have these words.*

David Flees from Jerusalem

13 A messenger reported to David, "The Israelites are pledging their loyalty to Absalom."

14 So David said to all his officials who were with him in Jerusalem, "We must get away at once if we want to escape from Absalom! Hurry! Or else he will soon be here and defeat us and kill everyone in the city!"

15 "Yes, Your Majesty," they answered. "We are ready to do whatever you say."

16 So the king left, accompanied by all his family and officials, except for ten concubines, whom he left behind to take care of the palace.

17 As the king and all his men were leaving the city, they stopped at the last house. 18 All his officials stood^n next to him as the royal bodyguards passed by in front of him. The six hundred soldiers who had followed him from Gath also passed by, 19 and the king said to Ittai, their leader, "Why are you going with us? Go back and stay with the new king. You are a foreigner, a refugee away from your own country. 20 You have lived here only a short time, so why should I make you wander around with me? I don't even know where I'm going. Go back and take all your people with you—and may the LORD be kind and faithful to you."^{o}

21 But Ittai answered, "Your Majesty, I swear to you in the LORD's name that I will always go with you wherever you go, even if it means death."

22 "Fine!" David answered. "March on!" So Ittai went on with all his men and their dependents. 23 The people cried loudly as David's followers left. The king crossed Kidron Brook, followed by his men, and together they went out toward the wilderness.

24 Zadok the priest was there, and with him were the Levites, carrying the sacred Covenant Box. They set it down^p and didn't pick it up again until all the people had left the city. The priest Abiathar was there too.^{q} 25 Then the king said to Zadok, "Take the Covenant Box back to the city. If the LORD is pleased with me, some day he will let me come back to see it and the place where it

stays. 26 But if he isn't pleased with me—well, then, let him do to me what he wishes." 27 And he went on to say to Zadok, "Look,^{r} take your son Ahimaaz and Abiathar's son Jonathan and go back to the city in peace. 28 Meanwhile, I will wait at the river crossings in the wilderness until I receive news from you." 29 So Zadok and Abiathar took the Covenant Box back into Jerusalem and stayed there.

30 David went on up the Mount of Olives crying; he was barefoot and had his head covered as a sign of grief. All who followed him covered their heads and cried also. 31 When David was told^s that Ahithophel had joined Absalom's rebellion, he prayed, "Please, LORD, turn Ahithophel's advice into nonsense!"

32 When David reached the top of the hill, where there was a place of worship, his trusted friend Hushai the Archite met him with his clothes torn and with dirt on his head. 33 David said to him, "You will be of no help to me if you come with me, 34 but you can help me by returning to the city and telling Absalom that you will now serve him as faithfully as you served his father. And do all you can to oppose any advice that Ahithophel gives. 35 The priests Zadok and Abiathar will be there; tell them everything you hear in the king's palace. 36 They have their sons Ahimaaz and Jonathan with them, and you can send them to me with all the information you gather."

37 So Hushai, David's friend, returned to the city just as Absalom was arriving.

David and Ziba

16 When David had gone a little beyond the top of the hill, he was suddenly met by Ziba, the servant of Mephibosheth, who had with him a couple of donkeys loaded with two hundred loaves of bread, a hundred bunches of raisins, a hundred bunches of fresh fruit, and a leather bag full of wine. 2 King David asked him, "What are you going to do with all that?"

Ziba answered, "The donkeys are for Your Majesty's family to ride, the bread and the fruit are for the men to eat, and

---

^{n} *Probable text* stood; *Hebrew* passed. ^{o} *One ancient translation* and may the LORD be kind and faithful to you; *Hebrew* kindness and faithfulness. ^{p} *Probable text* set it down; *Hebrew* poured it out. ^{q} *Probable text* was there too; *Hebrew* went up. ^{r} *Some ancient translations* Look; *Hebrew* Are you the seer? ^{s} *One ancient translation* was told; *Hebrew* told.

the wine is for them to drink when they get tired in the wilderness."

3 "Where is Mephibosheth, the grandson of your master Saul?" the king asked him.

"He is staying in Jerusalem," Ziba answered, "because he is convinced that the Israelites will now restore to him the kingdom of his grandfather Saul."

4 The king said to Ziba, "Everything that belonged to Mephibosheth is yours."

"I am your servant," Ziba replied. "May I always please Your Majesty!"

David and Shimei

5 When King David arrived at Bahurim, one of Saul's relatives, Shimei son of Gera, came out to meet him, cursing him as he came. **6** Shimei started throwing stones at David and his officials, even though David was surrounded by his men and his bodyguards. **7** Shimei cursed him and said, "Get out! Get out! Murderer! Criminal! **8** You took Saul's kingdom, and now the LORD is punishing you for murdering so many of Saul's family. The LORD has given the kingdom to your son Absalom, and you are ruined, you murderer!"

9 Abishai, whose mother was Zeruiah, said to the king, "Your Majesty, why do you let this dog curse you? Let me go over there and cut off his head!"

10 "This is none of your business," the king said to Abishai and his brother Joab. "If he curses me because the LORD told him to, who has the right to ask why he does it?" **11** And David said to Abishai and to all his officials, "My own son is trying to kill me; so why should you be surprised at this Benjaminite? The LORD told him to curse; so leave him alone and let him do it. **12** Perhaps the LORD will notice my misery[t] and give me some blessings to take the place of his curse." **13** So David and his men continued along the road. Shimei kept up with them, walking on the hillside; he was cursing and throwing stones and dirt at them as he went. **14** The king and all his men were worn out when they reached the Jordan,[u] and there they rested.

Absalom in Jerusalem

15 Absalom and all the Israelites with him entered Jerusalem, and Ahithophel was with them. **16** When Hushai, David's trusted friend, met Absalom, he shouted, "Long live the king! Long live the king!"

17 "What has happened to your loyalty to your friend David?" Absalom asked him. "Why didn't you go with him?"

18 Hushai answered, "How could I? I am for the one chosen by the LORD, by these people, and by all the Israelites. I will stay with you. **19** After all, whom should I serve, if not my master's son? As I served your father, so now I will serve you."

20 Then Absalom turned to Ahithophel and said, "Now that we are here, what do you advise us to do?"

21 Ahithophel answered, "Go and have intercourse with your father's concubines whom he left behind to take care of the palace. Then everyone in Israel will know that your father regards you as his enemy, and your followers will be greatly encouraged." **22** So they set up a tent for Absalom on the palace roof, and in the sight of everyone Absalom went in and had intercourse with his father's concubines.

23 Any advice that Ahithophel gave in those days was accepted as though it were the very word of God; both David and Absalom followed it.

Hushai Misleads Absalom

17 Not long after that, Ahithophel said to Absalom, "Let me choose twelve thousand men, and tonight I will set out after David. **2** I will attack him while he is tired and discouraged. He will be frightened, and all his men will run away. I will kill only the king **3** and then bring back all his men to you, like a bride returning to her husband. You want to kill only one man;[v] the rest of the people will be safe." **4** This seemed like good advice to Absalom and all the Israelite leaders.

5 Absalom said, "Now call Hushai, and let us hear what he has to say." **6** When Hushai arrived, Absalom said to him, "This is the advice that Ahithophel has

---

t Some ancient translations misery; *Hebrew* wickedness.   *u One ancient translation* the Jordan; *Hebrew does not have these words.   v One ancient translation* like a bride . . . only one man; *Hebrew* like the return of the whole, so is the man you seek.

given us; shall we follow it? If not, you tell us what to do."

7 Hushai answered, "The advice Ahithophel gave you this time is no good. 8 You know that your father David and his men are hard fighters and that they are as fierce as a mother bear robbed of her cubs. Your father is an experienced soldier and does not stay with his men at night. 9 Right now he is probably hiding in a cave or some other place. As soon as David attacks your men, whoever hears about it will say that your men have been defeated. 10 Then even the bravest men, as fearless as lions, will be afraid because everyone in Israel knows that your father is a great soldier and that his men are hard fighters. 11 My advice is that you bring all the Israelites together from one end of the country to the other, as many as the grains of sand on the seashore, and that you lead them personally in battle. 12 We will find David wherever he is, and attack him before he knows what's happening. Neither he nor any of his men will survive. 13 If he retreats into a city, our people will all bring ropes and just pull the city*w* into the valley below. Not a single stone will be left there on top of the hill."

14 Absalom and all the Israelites said, "Hushai's advice is better than Ahithophel's." The LORD had decided that Ahithophel's good advice would not be followed, so that disaster would come on Absalom.

David Is Warned and Escapes

15 Then Hushai told the priests Zadok and Abiathar what advice he had given to Absalom and the Israelite leaders and what advice Ahithophel had given. 16 Hushai added, "Quick, now! Send a message to David not to spend the night at the river crossings in the wilderness, but to cross the Jordan at once, so that he and his men won't all be caught and killed."

17 Abiathar's son Jonathan and Zadok's son Ahimaaz were waiting at the spring of Enrogel, on the outskirts of Jerusalem, because they did not dare be seen entering the city. A servant woman would regularly go and tell them what was happening, and then they would go and tell King David. 18 But one day a boy happened to see them, and he told Absalom; so they hurried off to hide in the house of a certain man in Bahurim. He had a well near his house, and they got down in it. 19 The man's wife took a covering, spread it over the opening of the well and scattered grain over it, so that no one would notice anything. 20 Absalom's officials came to the house and asked the woman, "Where are Ahimaaz and Jonathan?"

"They crossed the river," she answered.

The men looked for them but could not find them, and so they returned to Jerusalem. 21 After they left, Ahimaaz and Jonathan came up out of the well and went and reported to King David. They told him what Ahithophel had planned against him and said, "Hurry up and cross the river." 22 So David and his men started crossing the Jordan, and by daybreak they had all gone across.

23 When Ahithophel saw that his advice had not been followed, he saddled his donkey and went back to his hometown. After putting his affairs in order, he hanged himself. He was buried in the family grave.

24 David had reached the town of Mahanaim by the time Absalom and the Israelites had crossed the Jordan. (25 Absalom had put Amasa in command of the army in the place of Joab. Amasa was the son of Jether the Ishmaelite;*x* his mother was Abigail, the daughter of Nahash and the sister of Joab's mother Zeruiah.) 26 Absalom and his men camped in the land of Gilead.

27 When David arrived at Mahanaim, he was met by Shobi son of Nahash, from the city of Rabbah in Ammon, and by Machir son of Ammiel, from Lodebar, and by Barzillai, from Rogelim in Gilead. 28-29 They brought bowls, clay pots, and bedding, and also food for David and his men: wheat, barley, meal, roasted grain, beans, peas,*y* honey, cheese, cream, and some sheep. They knew that David and his men would get hungry, thirsty, and tired in the wilderness.

---

w Some ancient translations the city; *Hebrew* him.   *x One ancient translation (and see 1 Ch 2.17)* Ishmaelite; *Hebrew* Israelite.   *y Some ancient translations* peas; *Hebrew* peas and roasted grain.

the Jordan River by the men of Judah, who had come to Gilgal to escort him across the river. 16 At the same time the Benjaminite Shimei son of Gera from Bahurim hurried to the Jordan to meet King David. 17 He had with him a thousand men from the tribe of Benjamin. And Ziba, the servant of Saul's family, also came with his fifteen sons and twenty servants, and they arrived at the Jordan before the king. 18 They crossed[b] the river to escort the royal party across and to do whatever the king wanted.

David Shows Kindness to Shimei

As the king was getting ready to cross, Shimei threw himself down in front of him 19 and said, "Your Majesty, please forget the wrong I did that day you left Jerusalem. Don't hold it against me or think about it any more. 20 I know, sir, that I have sinned, and this is why I am the first one from the northern tribes to come and meet Your Majesty today."

21 Abishai son of Zeruiah spoke up: "Shimei should be put to death because he cursed the one whom the LORD chose as king."

22 But David said to Abishai and his brother Joab, "Who asked your opinion? Are you going to give me trouble? I am the one who is king of Israel now, and no Israelite will be put to death today." 23 And he said to Shimei, "I give you my word that you will not be put to death."

David Shows Kindness to Mephibosheth

24 Then Mephibosheth, Saul's grandson, came down to meet the king. He had not washed his feet, trimmed his beard, or washed his clothes from the time the king left Jerusalem until he returned victorious. 25 When Mephibosheth arrived from[c] Jerusalem to meet the king, the king said to him, "Mephibosheth, you didn't go with me. Why not?"

26 He answered, "As you know, Your Majesty, I am crippled. I told my servant to saddle my donkey so that I could ride along with you, but he betrayed me. 27 He lied about me to Your Majesty, but you are like God's angel, so do what seems right to you. 28 All of my father's family deserved to be put to death by

Your Majesty, but you gave me the right to eat at your table. I have no right to ask for any more favors from Your Majesty."

29 The king answered, "You don't have to say anything more. I have decided that you and Ziba will share Saul's property."

30 "Let Ziba have it all," Mephibosheth answered. "It's enough for me that Your Majesty has come home safely."

David Shows Kindness to Barzillai

31 Barzillai, from Gilead, had also come down from Rogelim to escort the king across the Jordan. 32 Barzillai was a very old man, eighty years old. He was very rich and had supplied the king with food while he was staying at Mahanaim. 33 The king said to him, "Come with me to Jerusalem, and I will take care of you."

34 But Barzillai answered, "I don't have long to live; why should I go with Your Majesty to Jerusalem? 35 I am already eighty years old, and nothing gives me pleasure any more. I can't taste what I eat and drink, and I can't hear the voices of singers. I would only be a burden to Your Majesty. 36 I don't deserve such a great reward. So I will go just a little way with you beyond the Jordan. 37 Then let me go back home and die near my parents' grave. Here is my son Chimham, who will serve you; take him with you, Your Majesty, and do for him as you think best."

38 The king answered, "I will take him with me and do for him whatever you want. And I will do for you anything you ask." 39 Then David and all of his men crossed the Jordan. He kissed Barzillai and gave him his blessing, and Barzillai went back home.

Judah and Israel Argue over the King

40 When the king had crossed, escorted by all the people of Judah and half the people of Israel, he went on to Gilgal, and Chimham went with him. 41 Then all the Israelites went to the king and said to him, "Your Majesty, why did our brothers, the men of Judah, think they had the right to take you away and

2 SAMUEL

b Probable text They crossed; Hebrew The crossing crossed.   c One ancient translation from; Hebrew at.

escort you, your family, and your men across the Jordan?"

42 The men of Judah answered, "We did it because the king is one of us. So why should this make you angry? He hasn't paid for our food nor has he given us anything."

43 The Israelites replied, "We have ten times as many claims on King David as you have, even if he is one of you. Why do you look down on us? Don't forget that we were the first to talk about bringing the king back!"

But the men of Judah were more violent in making their claims than the men of Israel.

Sheba's Rebellion

20 There happened to be in Gilgal a worthless character named Sheba son of Bikri, of the tribe of Benjamin. He blew the trumpet and called out, "Down with David! We won't follow him! Men of Israel, let's go home!" 2 So the Israelites deserted David and went with Sheba, but the men of Judah remained loyal and followed David from the Jordan to Jerusalem.

3 When David arrived at his palace in Jerusalem, he took the ten concubines he had left to take care of the palace, and put them under guard. He provided for their needs, but did not have intercourse with them. They were kept confined for the rest of their lives, living like widows.

4 The king said to Amasa, "Call the men of Judah together and be back here with them by the day after tomorrow." 5 Amasa went to call them, but he did not get back by the time the king had told him to. 6 So the king said to Abishai, "Sheba will give us more trouble than Absalom. Take my men and go after him, or else he may occupy some fortified towns and escape from us." 7 So Joab's men, the royal bodyguards, and all the other soldiers left Jerusalem with Abishai to go after Sheba. 8 When they reached the large rock at Gibeon, Amasa met them. Joab was dressed for battle, with a sword in its sheath fastened to his belt. As he came forward, the sword fell out. 9 Joab said to Amasa, "How are you, my friend?" and took hold of his beard with his right hand in order to kiss him. 10 Amasa was not on guard against the sword that Joab was holding in his other hand, and Joab stabbed him in the belly, and his insides spilled out on the ground. He died immediately, and Joab did not have to strike again.

Then Joab and his brother Abishai went on after Sheba. 11 One of Joab's men stood by Amasa's body and called out, "Everyone who is for Joab and David follow Joab!" 12 Amasa's body, covered with blood, was lying in the middle of the road. Joab's man saw that everybody was stopping, so he dragged the body from the road out into the field and threw a blanket over it. 13 After the body had been removed from the road, everyone followed Joab in pursuit of Sheba.

14 Sheba passed through the territory of all the tribes of Israel and came to the city of Abel Beth Maacah, and all the members of the clan of Bikri[d] assembled and followed him into the city. 15 Joab's men heard that Sheba was there, and so they went and besieged the city. They built ramps of earth against the outer wall and also began to dig under the wall to make it fall down. 16 There was a wise woman in the city who shouted from the wall, "Listen! Listen! Tell Joab to come here; I want to speak with him." 17 Joab went, and she asked, "Are you Joab?"

"Yes, I am," he answered.

"Listen to me, sir," she said.

"I'm listening," he answered.

18 She said, "Long ago they used to say, 'Go and get your answer in the city of Abel'—and that's just what they did. 19 Ours is a great city, one of the most peaceful and loyal in Israel. Why are you trying to destroy it? Do you want to ruin what belongs to the LORD?"

20 "Never!" Joab answered. "I will never ruin or destroy your city! 21 That is not our plan. A man named Sheba son of Bikri, who is from the hill country of Ephraim, started a rebellion against King David. Hand over this one man, and I will withdraw from the city."

"We will throw his head over the wall to you," she said. 22 Then she went to the people of the city with her plan, and they cut off Sheba's head and threw it over the wall to Joab. He blew the trumpet as a signal for his men to leave the city, and

d *Probable text* Bikri; *Hebrew* Beri.

they went back home. And Joab returned to Jerusalem to the king.

David's Officials

23 Joab was in command of the army of Israel; Benaiah son of Jehoiada was in charge of David's bodyguards; 24 Adoniram was in charge of the forced labor; Jehoshaphat son of Ahilud was in charge of the records; 25 Sheva was the court secretary; Zadok and Abiathar were the priests, 26 and Ira from the town of Jair was also one of David's priests.

Saul's Descendants Are Put to Death

21 During David's reign there was a severe famine which lasted for three full years. So David consulted the LORD about it, and the LORD said, "Saul and his family are guilty of murder; he put the people of Gibeon to death." (2 The people of Gibeon were not Israelites; they were a small group of Amorites whom the Israelites had promised to protect, but Saul had tried to destroy them because of his zeal for the people of Israel and Judah.) 3 So David summoned the people of Gibeon and said to them, "What can I do for you? I want to make up for the wrong that was done to you, so that you will bless the LORD's people."

4 They answered, "Our quarrel with Saul and his family can't be settled with silver or gold, nor do we want to kill any Israelite."

"What, then, do you think I should do for you?" David asked.

5 They answered, "Saul wanted to destroy us and leave none of us alive anywhere in Israel. 6 So hand over seven of his male descendants, and we will hang them before the LORD at Gibeah, the hometown of Saul, the LORD's chosen king."

"I will hand them over," the king answered.

7 But because of the sacred promise that he and Jonathan had made to each other, David spared Jonathan's son Mephibosheth, the grandson of Saul. 8 However, he took Armoni and Mephibosheth, the two sons that Rizpah the daughter of Aiah had borne to Saul; he also took the five sons of Saul's daughter Merab, whom she had borne to Adriel son of Barzillai, who was from Meholah. 9 David handed them over to the people of Gibeon, who hanged them on the mountain before the LORD — and all seven of them died together. It was late in the spring, at the beginning of the barley harvest, when they were put to death.

10 Then Saul's concubine Rizpah, the daughter of Aiah, used sackcloth to make a shelter for herself on the rock where the corpses were, and she stayed there from the beginning of harvest until the autumn rains came. During the day she would keep the birds away from the corpses, and at night she would protect them from wild animals.

11 When David heard what Rizpah had done, 12 he went and got the bones of Saul and of his son Jonathan from the people of Jabesh in Gilead. (They had stolen them from the public square in Beth Shan, where the Philistines had hanged the bodies on the day they killed Saul on Mount Gilboa.) 13 David took the bones of Saul and Jonathan and also gathered up the bones of the seven men who had been hanged. 14 Then they buried the bones of Saul and Jonathan in the grave of Saul's father Kish, in Zela in the territory of Benjamin, doing all that the king had commanded. And after that, God answered their prayers for the country.

Battles against Philistine Giants
(1 Chronicles 20.4-8)

15 There was another war between the Philistines and Israel, and David and his men went and fought the Philistines. During one of the battles David grew tired. 16 A giant named Ishbibenob, who was carrying a bronze spear that weighed about seven and a half pounds and who was wearing a new sword, thought he could kill David. 17 But Abishai son of Zeruiah came to David's help, attacked the giant, and killed him. Then David's men made David promise that he would never again go out with them to battle. "You are the hope of Israel, and we don't want to lose you," they said.

18 After this there was a battle with the Philistines at Gob, during which Sibbecai from Hushah killed a giant named Saph.

19 There was another battle with the Philistines at Gob, and Elhanan son of

Jair *e* from Bethlehem killed Goliath
from Gath, whose spear had a shaft as
thick as the bar on a weaver's loom.
20 Then there was another battle at
Gath, where there was a giant who loved
to fight. He had six fingers on each hand
and six toes on each foot. **21** He defied the
Israelites, and Jonathan, the son of David's brother Shammah, killed him.
22 These four were descendants of the
giants of Gath, and they were killed by
David and his men.

David's Song of Victory

(Psalm 18)

22 When the LORD saved David
from Saul and his other enemies,
David sang this song to the LORD:

2 The LORD is my protector;
he is my strong fortress.
3 My God is my protection,
and with him I am safe.
He protects me like a shield;
he defends me and keeps me
safe.
He is my savior;
he protects me and saves me
from violence.
4 I call to the LORD,
and he saves me from my
enemies.
Praise the LORD!

5 The waves of death were all
around me;
the waves of destruction rolled
over me.
6 The danger of death was
around me,
and the grave set its trap for me.
7 In my trouble I called to the LORD;
I called to my God for help.
In his temple he heard my voice;
he listened to my cry for help.

8 Then the earth trembled and
shook;
the foundations of the sky
rocked and quivered
because God was angry!
9 Smoke poured out of his nostrils,
a consuming flame and burning
coals from his mouth.

10 He tore the sky open and came
down,
with a dark cloud under his feet.
11 He flew swiftly on his winged
creature;*f*
he traveled on the wings of the
wind.
12 He covered himself with darkness;
thick clouds, full of *g* water,
surrounded him;
13 burning coals flamed up from
the lightning before him.

14 Then the LORD thundered from
the sky,
and the voice of Almighty God
was heard.
15 He shot his arrows and scattered
his enemies;
with flashes of lightning he sent
them running.
16 The floor of the ocean was laid
bare,
and the foundations of the earth
were uncovered
when the LORD rebuked his
enemies
and roared at them in anger.

17 The LORD reached down from
above and took hold of me;
he pulled me out of the deep
waters.
18 He rescued me from my powerful
enemies
and from all those who
hate me—
they were too strong for me.
19 When I was in trouble, they
attacked me,
but the LORD protected me.
20 He helped me out of danger;
he saved me because he was
pleased with me.

21 The LORD rewards me because I do
what is right;
he blesses me because I am
innocent.
22 I have obeyed the law of the LORD;
I have not turned away from
my God.
23 I have observed all his laws;
I have not disobeyed his
commands.

---

*e Probable text (see 1 Ch 20.5) Jair; Hebrew Jaareoregim.   f WINGED CREATURE: See Word List.
g Some ancient translations (and see Ps 18.11) full of; Hebrew unclear.*

24 He knows that I am faultless,
   that I have kept myself from
     doing wrong.
25 And so he rewards me because I
     do what is right,
   because he knows that I am
     innocent.

26 O Lord, you are faithful to those
     who are faithful to you,
   and completely good to those [h]
     who are perfect.
27 You are pure to those who are
     pure,
   but hostile to those who are
     wicked.
28 You save those who are humble,
   but you humble those who are
     proud.

29 You, Lord, are my light;
   you dispel my darkness.
30 You give me strength to attack
     my enemies
   and power to overcome their
     defenses.

31 This God — how perfect are his
     deeds,
   how dependable his words!
   He is like a shield
     for all who seek his protection.
32 The Lord alone is God;
   God alone is our defense.
33 This God is my strong refuge;
   he makes [i] my pathway safe.
34 He makes me sure-footed as a
     deer;
   he keeps me safe on the
     mountains.
35 He trains me for battle,
   so that I can use the
     strongest bow.

36 O Lord, you protect me and
     save me;
   your help has made me great.
37 You have kept me from being
     captured,
   and I have never fallen.
38 I pursue my enemies and defeat
     them;

I do not stop until I destroy
     them.
39 I strike them down, and they
     cannot rise;
   they lie defeated before me.
40 You give me strength for the battle
   and victory over my enemies.
41 You make my enemies run
     from me;
   I destroy those who hate me.
42 They look for help, but no one
     saves them;
   they call to the Lord, but he does
     not answer.
43 I crush them, and they become
     like dust;
   I trample on them like mud in
     the streets.

44 You saved me from my rebellious
     people
   and maintained my rule over
     the nations;
   people I did not know have now
     become my subjects.
45 Foreigners bow before me;
   when they hear me, they obey.
46 They lose their courage
   and come trembling [j] from their
     fortresses.

47 The Lord lives! Praise my
     defender!
   Proclaim the greatness of the
     strong God who saves me!
48 He gives me victory over my
     enemies;
   he subdues the nations under me
49   and saves me from my foes.

   O Lord, you give me victory over
     my enemies
   and protect me from
     violent men.
50 And so I praise you among the
     nations;
   I sing praises to you.
51 God gives great victories to his
     king;
   he shows constant love to the
     one he has chosen,
   to David and his descendants
     forever.

---

[h] *Probable text (see Ps 18.25)* those; *Hebrew the strong.*   [i] *Probable text (see Ps 18.32)* he
makes; *Hebrew unclear.*   [j] *Probable text (see Ps 18.45)* come trembling; *Hebrew* come ready
to fight.

David's Last Words

23 David son of Jesse was the man whom God made great, whom the God of Jacob chose to be king, and who was the composer of beautiful songs for Israel. These are David's last words:

2 The spirit of the LORD speaks
    through me;
  his message is on my lips.
3 The God of Israel has spoken;
    the protector of Israel said
      to me:
  "The king who rules with justice,
    who rules in obedience to God,
4 is like the sun shining on a
    cloudless dawn,
  the sun that makes the grass
    sparkle after rain."

5 And that is how God will bless my
    descendants,
  because he has made an eternal
    covenant with me,
  an agreement that will not be
    broken,
  a promise that will not be
    changed.
  That is all I desire;
    that will be my victory,
    and God will surely bring it
      about.
6 But godless people are like thorns
    that are thrown away;
  no one can touch them
    barehanded.
7 You must use an iron tool or a
    spear;
  they will be burned
    completely.[k]

David's Famous Soldiers

(1 Chronicles 11.10-41)

8 These are the names of David's famous soldiers: the first was Josheb Basshebeth from Tachemon, who was the leader of "The Three";[l] he fought with his spear[m] against eight hundred men and killed them all in one battle.

9 The second of the famous three was Eleazar son of Dodo, of the clan of Ahoh. One day he and David challenged the Philistines who had gathered for battle. The Israelites fell back, 10 but he stood his ground and fought the Philistines until his hand was so cramped that he could not let go of his sword. The LORD won a great victory that day. After it was over, the Israelites returned to where Eleazar was and stripped the armor from the dead.

11 The third of the famous three was Shammah son of Agee from Harar. The Philistines had gathered at Lehi, where there was a field of peas. The Israelites fled from the Philistines, 12 but Shammah stood his ground in the field, defended it, and killed the Philistines. The LORD won a great victory that day.

13 Near the beginning of harvest time[n] three of "The Thirty" went down to Adullam Cave, where David was, while a band of Philistines was camping in Rephaim Valley. 14 At that time David was on a fortified hill, and a group of Philistines had occupied Bethlehem. 15 David grew homesick and said, "How I wish someone would bring me a drink of water from the well by the gate at Bethlehem!" 16 The three famous soldiers forced their way through the Philistine camp, drew some water from the well, and brought it back to David. But he would not drink it; instead he poured it out as an offering to the LORD 17 and said, "LORD, I could never drink this! It would be like drinking the blood of these men who risked their lives!" So he refused to drink it.

Those were the brave deeds of the three famous soldiers.

18 Joab's brother Abishai (their mother was Zeruiah) was the leader of "The Famous Thirty." He fought with his spear against three hundred men and killed them, and became famous among "The Thirty."[o] 19 He was the most famous of "The Thirty"[p] and became their leader, but he was not as famous as "The Three."

20 Benaiah son of Jehoiada from Kabzeel was another famous soldier; he did many brave deeds, including killing two great Moabite warriors. He once went down into a pit on a snowy day and killed a lion. 21 He also killed an Egyptian, a huge man who was armed with a

---

k Verses 6-7 in Hebrew are unclear.   *l One ancient translation "The Three"; Hebrew the third.* *m Probable text (see 1 Ch 11.11) he fought with his spear; Hebrew unclear.*   *n Probable text Near the beginning of harvest time; Hebrew unclear.*   *o One ancient translation "The Thirty"; Hebrew "The Three."*   *p Probable text "The Thirty"; Hebrew "The Three."*

spear. Benaiah attacked him with his club, snatched the spear from the Egyptian's hand, and killed him with it. [22] Those were the brave deeds of Benaiah, who was one of "The Thirty."[p] [23] He was outstanding among them, but was not as famous as "The Three." David put him in charge of his bodyguard.

[24-39] Other members of "The Thirty" included:

Asahel, Joab's brother
Elhanan son of Dodo from Bethlehem
Shammah and Elika from Harod
Helez from Pelet
Ira son of Ikkesh from Tekoa
Abiezer from Anathoth
Mebunnai from Hushah
Zalmon from Ahoh
Maharai from Netophah
Heleb son of Baanah from Netophah
Ittai son of Ribai from Gibeah in Benjamin
Benaiah from Pirathon
Hiddai from the valleys near Gaash
Abialbon from Arabah
Azmaveth from Bahurim
Eliahba from Shaalbon
The sons of Jashen
Jonathan
Shammah from Harar
Ahiam son of Sharar from Harar
Eliphelet son of Ahasbai from Maacah
Eliam son of Ahithophel from Gilo
Hezro from Carmel
Paarai from Arab
Igal son of Nathan from Zobah
Bani from Gad
Zelek from Ammon
Naharai from Beeroth, Joab's armorbearer
Ira and Gareb from Jattir
Uriah the Hittite.

There were thirty-seven famous soldiers in all.

David Takes a Census
(1 Chronicles 21.1-27)

24 On another occasion the LORD was angry with Israel, and he made David bring trouble on them. The LORD said to him, "Go and count the peo-ple of Israel and Judah." [2] So David gave orders to Joab, the commander of his army: "Go with your officers through all the tribes of Israel from one end of the country to the other, and count the people. I want to know how many there are."

[3] But Joab answered the king, "Your Majesty, may the LORD your God make the people of Israel a hundred times more numerous than they are now, and may you live to see him do it. But why does Your Majesty want to do this?" [4] But the king made Joab and his officers obey his order; they left his presence and went out to count the people of Israel.

[5] They crossed the Jordan and camped south of Aroer, the city in the middle of the valley, in the territory of Gad.[q] From there they went north to Jazer, [6] and on to Gilead and to Kadesh, in Hittite territory.[r] Then they went to Dan, and from Dan they went[s] west to Sidon. [7] Then they went south to the fortified city of Tyre, on to all the cities of the Hivites and the Canaanites, and finally to Beersheba, in the southern part of Judah. [8] So after nine months and twenty days they returned to Jerusalem, having traveled through the whole country. [9] They reported to the king the total number of men capable of military service: 800,000 in Israel and 500,000 in Judah.

[10] But after David had taken the census, his conscience began to hurt, and he said to the LORD, "I have committed a terrible sin in doing this! Please forgive me. I have acted foolishly."

[11-12] The LORD said to Gad, David's prophet, "Go and tell David that I am giving him three choices. I will do whichever he chooses." The next morning, after David had gotten up, [13] Gad went to him, told him what the LORD said, and asked, "Which is it to be? Three[t] years of famine in your land or three months of running away from your enemies or three days of an epidemic in your land? Now think it over, and tell me what answer to take back to the LORD."

2 SAMUEL

14 David answered, "I am in a desperate situation! But I don't want to be punished by people. Let the LORD himself be the one to punish us, for he is merciful." 15 So the LORD sent an epidemic on Israel, which lasted from that morning until the time that he had chosen. From one end of the country to the other seventy thousand Israelites died. 16 When the LORD's angel was about to destroy Jerusalem, the LORD changed his mind about punishing the people and said to the angel who was killing them, "Stop! That's enough!" The angel was by the threshing place of Araunah, a Jebusite.

17 David saw the angel who was killing the people, and said to the LORD, "I am the guilty one. I am the one who did wrong. What have these poor people done? You should punish me and my family."

18 That same day Gad went to David and said to him, "Go up to Araunah's threshing place and build an altar to the LORD." 19 David obeyed the LORD's command and went as Gad had told him to.

20 Araunah looked down and saw the king and his officials coming up to him. He threw himself on the ground in front of David 21 and asked, "Your Majesty, why are you here?"

David answered, "To buy your threshing place and build an altar for the LORD, in order to stop the epidemic."

22 "Take it, Your Majesty," Araunah said, "and offer to the LORD whatever you wish. Here are these oxen to burn as an offering on the altar; here are their yokes and the threshing boards to use as fuel." 23 Araunah gave it all to the king u and said to him, "May the LORD your God accept your offering."

24 But the king answered, "No, I will pay you for it. I will not offer to the LORD my God sacrifices that have cost me nothing." And he bought the threshing place and the oxen for fifty pieces of silver. 25 Then he built an altar to the LORD and offered burnt offerings and fellowship offerings. The LORD answered his prayer, and the epidemic in Israel was stopped.

u *Probable text* to the king; *Hebrew* to the king the king.

2
S
A
M
U
E
L

The First Book of
KINGS

Introduction

First Kings continues the history of the Israelite monarchy begun in the books of Samuel. It may be divided into three parts: 1) The succession of Solomon as king of Israel and Judah, and the death of his father David. 2) The reign and achievements of Solomon. Especially noteworthy is the building of the Temple in Jerusalem. 3) The division of the nation into the northern and southern kingdoms, and the stories of the kings who ruled them down to the middle of the ninth century B.C.

In the two books of Kings each ruler is judged according to his loyalty to God, and national success is seen as depending on this loyalty, while idolatry and disobedience lead to disaster. The kings of the northern kingdom all fail the test, while the record of Judah's kings is mixed.

Prominent in the book of First Kings are the prophets of the Lord, those courageous spokesmen for God who warned the people not to worship idols and not to disobey God. Especially notable is Elijah and the story of his contest with the priests of Baal (chapter 18).

Outline of Contents

King David in His Old Age

1 King David was now a very old man, and although his servants covered him with blankets, he could not keep warm. 2 So his officials said to him, "Your Majesty, let us find a young woman to stay with you and take care of you. She will lie close to you and keep you warm." 3 A search was made all over Israel for a beautiful young woman, and in Shunem they found such a woman named Abishag, and brought her to the king. 4 She was very beautiful, and waited on the king and took care of him, but he did not have intercourse with her.

Adonijah Claims the Throne

5-6 Now that Absalom was dead, Adonijah, the son of David and Haggith, was the oldest surviving son. He was a very handsome man. David had never repri-manded him about anything, and he was ambitious to be king. He provided for himself chariots, horses, and an escort of fifty men. 7 He talked with Joab (whose mother was Zeruiah) and with Abiathar the priest, and they agreed to support his cause. 8 But Zadok the priest, Benaiah son of Jehoiada, Nathan the prophet, Shimei, Rei, and David's bodyguards were not on Adonijah's side.

9 One day Adonijah offered a sacrifice of sheep, bulls, and fattened calves at Snake Rock, near the spring of Enrogel. He invited the other sons of King David and the king's officials who were from Judah to come to this sacrificial feast, 10 but he did not invite his half brother Solomon or Nathan the prophet or Benaiah or the king's bodyguards.

Solomon Is Made King

11 Then Nathan went to Bathsheba, Solomon's mother, and asked her,

"Haven't you heard that Haggith's son Adonijah has made himself king? And King David doesn't know anything about it! 12If you want to save your life and the life of your son Solomon, I would advise you to 13go at once to King David and ask him, 'Your Majesty, didn't you solemnly promise me that my son Solomon would succeed you as king? How is it, then, that Adonijah has become king?' " 14And Nathan added, "Then, while you are still talking with King David, I will come in and confirm your story."

15So Bathsheba went to see the king in his bedroom. He was very old, and Abishag, the young woman from Shunem, was taking care of him. 16Bathsheba bowed low before the king, and he asked, "What do you want?"

17She answered, "Your Majesty, you made me a solemn promise in the name of the LORD your God that my son Solomon would be king after you. 18But Adonijah has already become king, and you don't know anything about it. 19He has offered a sacrifice of many bulls, sheep, and fattened calves, and he invited your sons, and Abiathar the priest, and Joab the commander of your army to the feast, but he did not invite your son Solomon. 20Your Majesty, all the people of Israel are looking to you to tell them who is to succeed you as king. 21If you don't, as soon as you are dead, my son Solomon and I will be treated as traitors."

22She was still speaking, when Nathan arrived at the palace. 23The king was told that the prophet was there, and Nathan went in and bowed low before the king. 24Then he said, "Your Majesty, have you announced that Adonijah would succeed you as king? 25This very day he has gone and offered a sacrifice of many bulls, sheep, and fattened calves. He invited all your sons, Joab the commander of your army,a and Abiathar the priest, and right now they are feasting with him and shouting, 'Long live King Adonijah!' 26But he did not invite me, sir, or Zadok the priest or Benaiah or Solomon. 27Did Your Majesty approve all this and not even tell your officials who is to succeed you as king?"

28King David said, "Ask Bathsheba to come back in"—and she came and stood before him. 29Then he said to her, "I promise you by the living LORD, who has rescued me from all my troubles, 30that today I will keep the promise I made to you in the name of the LORD, the God of Israel, that your son Solomon would succeed me as king."

31Bathsheba bowed low and said, "May my lord the king live forever!"

32Then King David sent for Zadok, Nathan, and Benaiah. When they came in, 33he said to them, "Take my court officials with you; have my son Solomon ride my own mule, and escort him down to Gihon Spring, 34where Zadok and Nathan are to anoint him as king of Israel. Then blow the trumpet and shout, 'Long live King Solomon!' 35Follow him back here when he comes to sit on my throne. He will succeed me as king, because he is the one I have chosen to be the ruler of Israel and Judah."

36"It shall be done," answered Benaiah, "and may the LORD your God confirm it! 37As the LORD has been with Your Majesty, may he also be with Solomon and make his reign even more prosperous than yours."

38So Zadok, Nathan, Benaiah, and the royal bodyguards put Solomon on King David's mule and escorted him to Gihon Spring. 39Zadok took the container of olive oil which he had brought from the Tent of the LORD's presence, and anointed Solomon. They blew the trumpet, and all the people shouted, "Long live King Solomon!" 40Then they all followed him back, shouting for joy and playing flutes, making enough noise to shake the ground.

41As Adonijah and all his guests were finishing the feast, they heard the noise. And when Joab heard the trumpet, he asked, "What's the meaning of all that noise in the city?" 42Before he finished speaking, Jonathan, the son of the priest Abiathar, arrived. "Come on in," Adonijah said. "You're a good man—you must be bringing good news."

43"I'm afraid not," Jonathan answered. "His Majesty King David has made Solomon king. 44He sent Zadok, Nathan, Benaiah, and the royal bodyguards to escort him. They had him ride on the king's mule, 45and Zadok and Na-

---

a One ancient translation Joab the commander of your army; Hebrew your army commanders.

than anointed him as king at Gihon Spring. Then they went into the city, shouting for joy, and the people are now in an uproar. That's the noise you just heard. 46 Solomon is now the king. 47 What is more, the court officials went in to pay their respects to His Majesty King David and said, 'May your God make Solomon even more famous than you, and may Solomon's reign be even more prosperous than yours.' Then King David bowed in worship on his bed 48 and prayed, 'Let us praise the LORD, the God of Israel, who has today made one of my descendants succeed me as king, and has let me live to see it!'"

49 Then Adonijah's guests were afraid, and they all got up and left, each going his own way. 50 Adonijah, in great fear of Solomon, went to the Tent of the LORD's presence and took hold of the corners of the altar.b 51 King Solomon was told that Adonijah was afraid of him and that he was holding on to the corners of the altar and had said, "First, I want King Solomon to swear to me that he will not have me put to death."

52 Solomon replied, "If he is loyal, not even a hair on his head will be touched; but if he is not, he will die." 53 King Solomon then sent for Adonijah and had him brought down from the altar. Adonijah went to the king and bowed low before him, and the king said to him, "You may go home."

David's Last Instructions to Solomon

2 When David was about to die, he called his son Solomon and gave him his last instructions: 2 "My time to die has come. Be confident and determined, 3 and do what the LORD your God orders you to do. Obey all his laws and commands, as written in the Law of Moses, so that wherever you go you may prosper in everything you do. 4 If you obey him, the LORD will keep the promise he made when he told me that my descendants would rule Israel as long as they were careful to obey his commands faithfully with all their heart and soul.

5 "There is something else. You remember what Joab did to me by killing the two commanders of Israel's armies,

Abner son of Ner and Amasa son of Jether. You remember how he murdered them in time of peace as revenge for deaths they had caused in time of war. He killed innocent men,c and now I bear the responsibility for what he did, and I sufferd the consequences. 6 You know what to do; you must not let him die a natural death.

7 "But show kindness to the sons of Barzillai from Gilead and take care of them, because they were kind to me when I was fleeing from your brother Absalom.

8 "There is also Shimei son of Gera, from the town of Bahurim in Benjamin. He cursed me bitterly the day I went to Mahanaim, but when he met me at the Jordan River, I gave him my solemn promise in the name of the LORD that I would not have him killed. 9 But you must not let him go unpunished. You know what to do, and you must see to it that he is put to death."

The Death of David

10 David died and was buried in David's City. 11 He had been king of Israel for forty years, ruling seven years in Hebron and thirty-three years in Jerusalem. 12 Solomon succeeded his father David as king, and his royal power was firmly established.

The Death of Adonijah

13 Then Adonijah, whose mother was Haggith, went to Bathsheba, who was Solomon's mother. "Is this a friendly visit?" she asked.

"It is," he answered, 14 and then he added, "I have something to ask of you."

"What is it?" she asked.

15 He answered, "You know that I should have become king and that everyone in Israel expected it. But it happened differently, and my brother became king because it was the LORD's will. 16 And now I have one request to make; please do not refuse me."

"What is it?" Bathsheba asked.

17 He answered, "Please ask King Solomon—I know he won't refuse you— to let me have Abishag, the young woman from Shunem, as my wife."

---

b CORNERS OF THE ALTAR: Small projections at the four corners of the altar that looked like horns. Anyone holding on to them was safe from being killed.   c Some ancient translations innocent men; Hebrew men in battle.   d Some ancient translations I bear ... and I suffer; Hebrew he bears ... and he suffers.

18 "Very well," she answered. "I will speak to the king for you."

19 So Bathsheba went to the king to speak to him on behalf of Adonijah. The king stood up to greet his mother and bowed to her. Then he sat on his throne and had another one brought in on which she sat at his right. 20 She said, "I have a small favor to ask of you; please do not refuse me."

"What is it, mother?" he asked. "I will not refuse you."

21 She answered, "Let your brother Adonijah have Abishag as his wife."

22 "Why do you ask me to give Abishag to him?" the king asked. "You might as well ask me to give him the throne too. After all, he is my older brother, and Abiathar the priest and Joab are on his side!"e 23 Then Solomon made a solemn promise in the LORD's name, "May God strike me dead if I don't make Adonijah pay with his life for asking this! 24 The LORD has firmly established me on the throne of my father David; he has kept his promise and given the kingdom to me and my descendants. I swear by the living LORD that Adonijah will die this very day!"

25 So King Solomon gave orders to Benaiah, who went out and killed Adonijah.

Abiathar's Banishment and Joab's Death

26 Then King Solomon said to Abiathar the priest, "Go to your country home in Anathoth. You deserve to die, but I will not have you put to death now, for you were in charge of the LORD's Covenant Box while you were with my father David, and you shared in all his troubles."

27 Then Solomon dismissed Abiathar from serving as a priest of the LORD, and so made come true what the LORD had said in Shiloh about the priest Eli and his descendants.

28 Joab heard what had happened. (He had supported Adonijah, but not Absalom.) So he fled to the Tent of the LORD's presence and took hold of the corners of the altar.f 29 When the news reached King Solomon that Joab had fled to the Tent and was by the altar, Solomon sent a messenger to Joab to ask him why he had fled to the altar. Joab answered that he had fled to the LORD because he was afraid of Solomon. So King Solomon sent Benaiahg to kill Joab. 30 He went to the Tent of the LORD's presence and said to Joab, "The king orders you to come out."

"No," Joab answered. "I will die here." Benaiah went back to the king and told him what Joab had said.

31 "Do what Joab says," Solomon answered. "Kill him and bury him. Then neither I nor any other of David's descendants will any longer be held responsible for what Joab did when he killed innocent men. 32 The LORD will punish Joab for those murders, which he committedh without my father David's knowledge. Joab killed two innocent men who were better men than he: Abner, commander of the army of Israel, and Amasa, commander of the army of Judah. 33 The punishment for their murders will fall on Joab and on his descendants forever. But the LORD will always give success to David's descendants who sit on his throne."

34 So Benaiah went to the Tent of the LORD's presence and killed Joab, and he was buried at his home in the open country. 35 The king made Benaiah commander of the army in Joab's place and put Zadok the priest in Abiathar's place.

The Death of Shimei

36 Then the king sent for Shimei and said to him, "Build a house for yourself here in Jerusalem. Live in it and don't leave the city. 37 If you ever leave and go beyond Kidron Brook, you will certainly die — and you yourself will be to blame."

38 "Very well, Your Majesty," Shimei answered. "I will do what you say." So he lived in Jerusalem a long time.

39 Three years later, however, two of Shimei's slaves ran away to the king of Gath, Achish son of Maacah. When Shimei heard that they were in Gath, 40 he saddled his donkey and went to King Achish in Gath, to find his slaves. He found them and brought them back home. 41 When Solomon heard what Shimei had done, 42 he sent for him and

---

e Some ancient translations and Abiathar the priest . . . on his side; Hebrew unclear.   f CORNERS OF THE ALTAR: See 1.50.   g One ancient translation Solomon sent a messenger . . . sent Benaiah; Hebrew Solomon sent Benaiah.   h will punish . . . committed; or will kill Joab, because he committed those murders.

said, "I made you promise in the LORD's name not to leave Jerusalem. And I warned you that if you ever did, you would certainly die. Did you not agree to it and say that you would obey me? 43 Why, then, have you broken your promise and disobeyed my command? 44 You know very well all the wrong that you did to my father David. The LORD will punish you for it. 45 But he will bless me, and he will make David's kingdom secure forever."

46 Then the king gave orders to Benaiah, who went out and killed Shimei. Solomon was now in complete control.

Solomon Prays for Wisdom
(2 Chronicles 1.3-12)

3 Solomon made an alliance with the king of Egypt by marrying his daughter. He brought her to live in David's City until he had finished building his palace, the Temple, and the wall around Jerusalem. 2 A temple had not yet been built for the LORD, and so the people were still offering sacrifices at many different altars. 3 Solomon loved the LORD and followed the instructions of his father David, but he also slaughtered animals and offered them as sacrifices on various altars.

4 On one occasion he went to Gibeon to offer sacrifices because that was where the most famous altar was. He had offered hundreds of burnt offerings there in the past. 5 That night the LORD appeared to him in a dream and asked him, "What would you like me to give you?"

6 Solomon answered, "You always showed great love for my father David, your servant, and he was good, loyal, and honest in his relation with you. And you have continued to show him your great and constant love by giving him a son who today rules in his place. 7 O LORD God, you have let me succeed my father as king, even though I am very young and don't know how to rule. 8 Here I am among the people you have chosen to be your own, a people who are so many that they cannot be counted. 9 So give me the wisdom I need to rule your people with justice and to know the difference between good and evil. Otherwise, how would I ever be able to rule this great people of yours?"

10 The Lord was pleased that Solomon

had asked for this, 11 and so he said to him, "Because you have asked for the wisdom to rule justly, instead of long life for yourself or riches or the death of your enemies, 12 I will do what you have asked. I will give you more wisdom and understanding than anyone has ever had before or will ever have again. 13 I will also give you what you have not asked for: all your life you will have wealth and honor, more than that of any other king. 14 And if you obey me and keep my laws and commands, as your father David did, I will give you a long life."

15 Solomon woke up and realized that God had spoken to him in the dream. Then he went to Jerusalem and stood in front of the LORD's Covenant Box and offered burnt offerings and fellowship offerings to the LORD. After that he gave a feast for all his officials.

Solomon Judges a Difficult Case

16 One day two prostitutes came and presented themselves before King Solomon. 17 One of them said, "Your Majesty, this woman and I live in the same house, and I gave birth to a baby boy at home while she was there. 18 Two days after my child was born, she also gave birth to a baby boy. Only the two of us were there in the house — no one else was present. 19 Then one night she accidentally rolled over on her baby and smothered it. 20 She got up during the night, took my son from my side while I was asleep, and carried him to her bed; then she put the dead child in my bed. 21 The next morning, when I woke up and was going to nurse my baby, I saw that it was dead. I looked at it more closely and saw that it was not my child."

22 But the other woman said, "No! The living child is mine, and the dead one is yours!"

The first woman answered back, "No! The dead child is yours, and the living one is mine!"

And so they argued before the king.

23 Then King Solomon said, "Each of you claims that the living child is hers and that the dead child belongs to the other one." 24 He sent for a sword, and when it was brought, 25 he said, "Cut the living child in two and give each woman half of it."

26 The real mother, her heart full of

love for her son, said to the king, "Please, Your Majesty, don't kill the child! Give it to her!"

But the other woman said, "Don't give it to either of us; go on and cut it in two."

27 Then Solomon said, "Don't kill the child! Give it to the first woman—she is its real mother."

28 When the people of Israel heard of Solomon's decision, they were all filled with deep respect for him, because they knew then that God had given him the wisdom to settle disputes fairly.

Solomon's Officials

4 Solomon was king of all Israel, 2 and these were his high officials:
The priest: Azariah son of Zadok
3 The court secretaries: Elihoreph and Ahijah, sons of Shisha
In charge of the records: Jehoshaphat son of Ahilud
4 Commander of the army: Benaiah son of Jehoiada
Priests: Zadok and Abiathar
5 Chief of the district governors: Azariah son of Nathan
Royal Adviser: the priest Zabud son of Nathan
6 In charge of the palace servants: Ahishar
In charge of the forced labor: Adoniram son of Abda
7 Solomon appointed twelve men as district governors in Israel. They were to provide food from their districts for the king and his household, each man being responsible for one month out of the year. 8 The following are the names of these twelve officers and the districts they were in charge of:
Benhur: the hill country of Ephraim
9 Bendeker: the cities of Makaz, Shaalbim, Beth Shemesh, Elon, and Beth Hanan
10 Benhesed: the cities of Arubboth and Socoh and all the territory of Hepher
11 Benabinadab, who was married to Solomon's daughter Taphath: the whole region of Dor
12 Baana son of Ahilud: the cities of Taanach, Megiddo, and all the region near Beth Shan, near

the town of Zarethan, south of the town of Jezreel, as far as the city of Abel Meholah and the city of Jokmeam
13 Bengeber: the city of Ramoth in Gilead, and the villages in Gilead belonging to the clan of Jair, a descendant of Manasseh, and the region of Argob in Bashan, sixty large towns in all, fortified with walls and with bronze bars on the gates
14 Ahinadab son of Iddo: the district of Mahanaim
15 Ahimaaz, who was married to Basemath, another of Solomon's daughters: the territory of Naphtali
16 Baana son of Hushai: the region of Asher and the town of Bealoth
17 Jehoshaphat son of Paruah: the territory of Issachar
18 Shimei son of Ela: the territory of Benjamin
19 Geber son of Uri: the region of Gilead, which had been ruled by King Sihon of the Amorites and King Og of Bashan
Besides these twelve, there was one governor over the whole land.

Solomon's Prosperous Reign

20 The people of Judah and Israel were as numerous as the grains of sand on the seashore; they ate and drank, and were happy. 21 Solomon's kingdom included all the nations from the Euphrates River to Philistia and the Egyptian border. They paid him taxes and were subject to him all his life.

22 The supplies Solomon needed each day were 150 bushels of fine flour and 300 bushels of meal; 23 10 stall-fed cattle, 20 pasture-fed cattle, and 100 sheep, besides deer, gazelles, roebucks, and poultry.

24 Solomon ruled over all the land west of the Euphrates River, from Tiphsah on the Euphrates as far west as the city of Gaza. All the kings west of the Euphrates were subject to him, and he was at peace with all the neighboring countries. 25 As long as he lived, the people throughout Judah and Israel lived in safety, each family with its own grapevines and fig trees.

1 KINGS

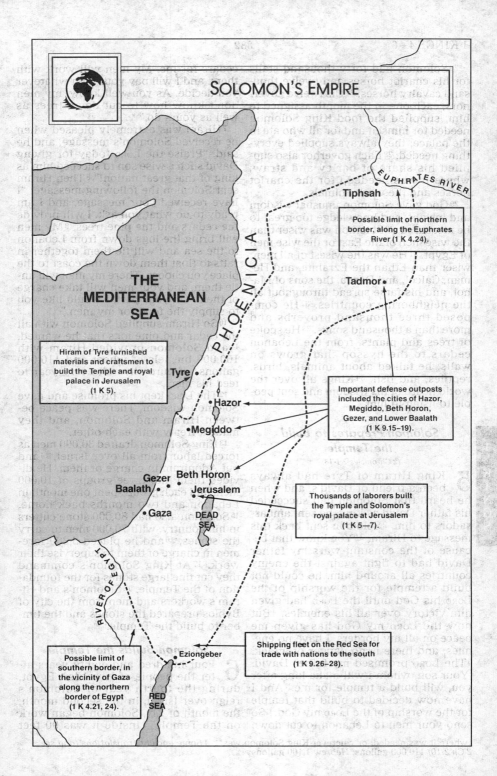

SOLOMON'S EMPIRE

EUPHRATES RIVER

Tiphsah

Possible limit of northern
border, along the Euphrates
River (1 K 4.24).

Tadmor

PHOENICIA

THE
MEDITERRANEAN
SEA

Hiram of Tyre furnished
materials and craftsmen to
build the Temple and royal
palace in Jerusalem
(1 K 5).

Tyre

Hazor

Important defense outposts
included the cities of Hazor,
Megiddo, Beth Horon,
Gezer, and Lower Baalath
(1 K 9.15–19).

Megiddo

Gezer   Beth Horon
Baalath   Jerusalem

Thousands of laborers built
the Temple and Solomon's
royal palace at Jerusalem
(1 K 5–7).

Gaza   DEAD
            SEA

Possible limit of
southern border, in
the vicinity of Gaza
along the northern
border of Egypt
(1 K 4.21, 24).

RIVER OF EGYPT

Eziongeber

Shipping fleet on the Red Sea for
trade with nations to the south
(1 K 9.26–28).

RED
SEA

26 Solomon had forty thousand stalls for his chariot horses and twelve thousand cavalry horses. 27 His twelve governors, each one in the month assigned to him, supplied the food King Solomon needed for himself and for all who ate in the palace; they always supplied everything needed. 28 Each governor also supplied his share of barley and straw, where it was needed,[i] for the chariot horses and the work animals.

29 God gave Solomon unusual wisdom and insight, and knowledge too great to be measured. 30 Solomon was wiser than the wise men of the East or the wise men of Egypt. 31 He was the wisest of all men: wiser than Ethan the Ezrahite, and Heman, Calcol, and Darda, the sons of Mahol, and his fame spread throughout all the neighboring countries. 32 He composed three thousand proverbs and more than a thousand songs. 33 He spoke of trees and plants, from the Lebanon cedars to the hyssop that grows on walls; he talked about animals, birds, reptiles, and fish. 34 Kings all over the world heard of his wisdom and sent people to listen to him.

Solomon Prepares to Build the Temple
(2 Chronicles 2.1-18)

5 King Hiram of Tyre had always been a friend of David's, and when he heard that Solomon had succeeded his father David as king, he sent ambassadors to him. 2 Solomon sent back this message to Hiram: 3 "You know that because of the constant wars my father David had to fight against the enemy countries all around him, he could not build a temple for the worship of the LORD his God until the LORD had given him victory over all his enemies. 4 But now the LORD my God has given me peace on all my borders. I have no enemies, and there is no danger of attack. 5 The LORD promised my father David, 'Your son, whom I will make king after you, will build a temple for me.' And I have now decided to build that temple for the worship of the LORD my God. 6 So send your men to Lebanon to cut down

cedars for me. My men will work with them, and I will pay your men whatever you decide. As you well know, my men don't know how to cut down trees as well as yours do."

7 Hiram was extremely pleased when he received Solomon's message, and he said, "Praise the LORD today for giving David such a wise son to succeed him as king of that great nation!" 8 Then Hiram sent Solomon the following message: "I have received your message, and I am ready to do what you ask. I will provide the cedars and the pine trees. 9 My men will bring the logs down from Lebanon to the sea and will tie them together in rafts to float them down the coast to the place you choose. There my men will untie them, and your men will take charge of them. On your part, I would like you to supply the food for my men."

10 So Hiram supplied Solomon with all the cedar and pine logs that he wanted, 11 and Solomon provided Hiram with 100,000 bushels of wheat and 110,000 gallons[j] of pure olive oil every year to feed his men.

12 The LORD kept his promise and gave Solomon wisdom. There was peace between Hiram and Solomon, and they made a treaty with each other.

13 King Solomon drafted 30,000 men as forced labor from all over Israel, 14 and put Adoniram in charge of them. He divided them into three groups of 10,000 men, and each group spent one month in Lebanon and two months back home. 15 Solomon also had 80,000 stone cutters in hill country, with 70,000 men to carry the stones, 16 and he placed 3,300 foremen in charge of them to supervise their work. 17 At King Solomon's command they cut fine large stones for the foundation of the Temple. 18 Solomon's and Hiram's workers and men from the city of Byblos prepared the stones and the timber to build the Temple.

Solomon Builds the Temple

6 Four hundred and eighty years after the people of Israel left Egypt, during the fourth year of Solomon's reign over Israel, in the second month, the month of Ziv, Solomon began work on the Temple. 2 Inside it was 90 feet

---

i where it was needed; or wherever King Solomon was.   j Some ancient translations (and see
2 Ch 2.10) 110,000 gallons; Hebrew 1,100 gallons.

long, 30 feet wide, and 45 feet high. ³The entrance room was 15 feet deep and 30 feet wide, as wide as the sanctuary itself. ⁴The walls of the Temple had openings in them, narrower on the outside than on the inside. ⁵Against the outside walls, on the sides and the back of the Temple, a three-storied annex was built, each story 7½ feet high. ⁶Each room in the lowest story was 7½ feet wide, in the middle story 9 feet wide, and in the top story 10½ feet wide. The Temple wall on each floor was thinner than on the floor below, so that the rooms could rest on the wall without having their beams built into it.

⁷The stones with which the Temple was built had been prepared at the quarry, so that there was no noise made by hammers, axes, or any other iron tools as the Temple was being built.

⁸The entrance to the lowest*k* story of the annex was on the south side of the Temple, with stairs leading up to the second and third stories. ⁹So King Solomon finished building the Temple. He put in a ceiling made of beams and boards of cedar. ¹⁰The three-storied annex, each story*l* 7½ feet high, was built against the outside walls of the Temple, and was joined to them by cedar beams.

¹¹The LORD said to Solomon, ¹²"If you obey all my laws and commands, I will do for you what I promised your father David. ¹³I will live among my people Israel in this Temple that you are building, and I will never abandon them."

¹⁴So Solomon finished building the Temple.

The Interior Furnishings
of the Temple
(2 Chronicles 3.8-14)

¹⁵The inside walls were covered with cedar panels from the floor to the ceiling, and the floor was made of pine. ¹⁶An inner room, called the Most Holy Place, was built in the rear of the Temple. It was 30 feet long and was partitioned off by cedar boards reaching from the floor to the ceiling.*m* ¹⁷The room in front of the Most Holy Place was 60 feet long. ¹⁸The cedar panels were decorated with carvings of gourds and flowers; the whole interior was covered with cedar, so that the stones of the walls could not be seen.

¹⁹In the rear of the Temple an inner room was built, where the LORD's Covenant Box was to be placed. ²⁰This inner room was 30 feet long, 30 feet wide, and 30 feet high, all covered with pure gold. The altar was covered with cedar panels.*n* ²¹The inside of the Temple was covered with gold, and gold chains were placed across the entrance of the inner room, which was also covered with gold. ²²The whole interior of the Temple was covered with gold, as well as the altar in the Most Holy Place.

²³Two winged creatures were made of olive wood and placed in the Most Holy Place, each one 15 feet tall. ²⁴⁻²⁶Both were of the same size and shape. Each had two wings, each wing 7½ feet long, so that the distance from one wing tip to the other was 15 feet. ²⁷They were placed side by side in the Most Holy Place, so that two of their outstretched wings touched each other in the middle of the room, and the other two wings touched the walls. ²⁸The two winged creatures were covered with gold.

²⁹The walls of the main room and of the inner room were all decorated with carved figures of winged creatures, palm trees, and flowers. ³⁰Even the floor was covered with gold.

³¹A double door made of olive wood was set in place at the entrance of the Most Holy Place; the top of the doorway was a pointed arch. ³²The doors were decorated with carved figures of winged creatures, palm trees, and flowers. The doors, the winged creatures, and the palm trees were covered with gold. ³³For the entrance to the main room a rectangular doorframe of olive wood was made. ³⁴There were two folding doors made of pine ³⁵and decorated with carved figures of winged creatures, palm trees, and flowers, which were evenly covered with gold.

³⁶An inner court was built in front of the Temple, enclosed with walls which had one layer of cedar beams for every three layers of stone.

³⁷The foundation of the Temple was laid in the second month, the month of

---

k Some ancient translations lowest; *Hebrew* middle.   *l Probable text* three-storied annex, each story; *Hebrew* three-storied annex.   *m One ancient translation* ceiling; *Hebrew* walls.
n Verse 20 in Hebrew is unclear.

Ziv, in the fourth year of Solomon's reign. [38] In the eighth month, the month of Bul, in the eleventh year of Solomon's reign, the Temple was completely finished exactly as it had been planned. It had taken Solomon seven years to build it.

Solomon's Palace

7 Solomon also built a palace for himself, and it took him thirteen years. [2-3] The Hall of the Forest of Lebanon[o] was 150 feet long, 75 feet wide, and 45 feet high. It had three[p] rows of cedar pillars, 15 in each row, with cedar beams resting on them. The ceiling was of cedar, extending over storerooms, which were supported by the pillars. [4] On each of the two side walls there were three rows of windows. [5] The doorways and the windows[q] had rectangular frames, and the three rows of windows in each wall faced the opposite rows.

[6] The Hall of Columns was 75 feet long and 45 feet wide. It had a covered porch, supported by columns.

[7] The Throne Room, also called the Hall of Judgment, where Solomon decided cases, had cedar panels from the floor to the rafters.[r]

[8] Solomon's own quarters, in another court behind the Hall of Judgment, were made like the other buildings. He also built the same kind of house for his wife, the daughter of the king of Egypt.

[9] All these buildings and the great court were made of fine stones from the foundations to the eaves. The stones were prepared at the quarry and cut to measure, with their inner and outer sides trimmed with saws. [10] The foundations were made of large stones prepared at the quarry, some of them twelve feet long and others fifteen feet long. [11] On top of them were other stones, cut to measure, and cedar beams. [12] The palace court, the inner court of the Temple, and the entrance room of the Temple had walls with one layer of cedar beams for every three layers of cut stones.

Huram's Task

[13] King Solomon sent for a man named Huram, a craftsman living in the city of Tyre, who was skilled in bronze work. [14] His father, who was no longer living, was from Tyre, and had also been a skilled bronze craftsman; his mother was from the tribe of Naphtali. Huram was an intelligent and experienced craftsman. He accepted King Solomon's invitation to be in charge of all the bronze work.

The Two Bronze Columns
(2 Chronicles 3.15-17)

[15] Huram cast two bronze columns, each one 27 feet tall and 18 feet in circumference,[s] and placed them at the entrance of the Temple. [16] He also made two bronze capitals, each one 7½ feet tall, to be placed on top of the columns. [17] The top of each column was decorated with a design of interwoven chains[t] [18] and two rows of bronze pomegranates. [19] The capitals were shaped like lilies, 6 feet tall, [20] and were placed on a rounded section which was above the chain design. There were 200 pomegranates in two rows around each[u] capital.

[21] Huram placed these two bronze columns in front of the entrance of the Temple: the one on the south side was named Jachin[v] and the one on the north was named Boaz.[w] [22] The lily-shaped bronze capitals were on top of the columns.

And so the work on the columns was completed.

The Bronze Tank
(2 Chronicles 4.2-5)

[23] Huram made a round tank of bronze, 7½ feet deep, 15 feet in diameter, and 45 feet in circumference. [24] All around the outer edge of the rim of the tank[x] were two rows of bronze gourds, which had been cast all in one piece with the rest of the tank. [25] The tank rested on the backs of twelve bronze bulls that faced outward, three facing in each

---

[o] HALL OF THE FOREST OF LEBANON: *A large ceremonial hall in the palace, probably so called because it was paneled in cedar.*   [p] *One ancient translation* three; *Hebrew* four.   [q] *One ancient translation* windows; *Hebrew* doorposts.   [r] *Some ancient translations* rafters; *Hebrew* floor.   [s] *Some ancient translations* each one . . . circumference; *Hebrew* the first column was 27 feet tall and the second column was 18 feet in circumference.   [t] *Verse 17 in Hebrew is unclear.*   [u] *One ancient translation* each; *Hebrew* the second.   [v] JACHIN: *This name sounds like the Hebrew for "he (God) establishes."*   [w] BOAZ: *This name sounds like the Hebrew for "by his (God's) strength."*   [x] *Probable text* All around . . . tank; *Hebrew unclear.*

direction. 26The sides of the tank were 3 inches thick. Its rim was like the rim of a cup, curving outward like the petals of a lily. The tank held about 10,000 gallons.

The Bronze Carts

27Huram also made ten bronze carts; each was 6 feet long, 6 feet wide, and 4½ feet high. 28They were made of square panels which were set in frames, 29with the figures of lions, bulls, and winged creatures on the panels; and on the frames, above and underneath the lions and bulls, there were spiral figures in relief. 30Each cart had four bronze wheels with bronze axles. At the four corners were bronze supports for a basin; the supports were decorated with spiral figures in relief. 31There was a circular frame on top for the basin. It projected upward 18 inches from the top of the cart and 7 inches down into it. It had carvings around it. 32The wheels were 25 inches high; they were under the panels, and the axles were of one piece with the carts. 33The wheels were like chariot wheels; their axles, rims, spokes, and hubs were all of bronze. 34There were four supports at the bottom corners of each cart, which were of one piece with the cart. 35There was a 9-inch band around the top of each cart; its supports and the panels were of one piece with the cart. 36The supports and panels were decorated with figures of winged creatures, lions, and palm trees, wherever there was space for them, with spiral figures all around. 37This, then, is how the carts were made; they were all alike, having the same size and shape.

38Huram also made ten basins, one for each cart. Each basin was 6 feet in diameter and held 200 gallons. 39He placed five of the carts on the south side of the Temple, and the other five on the north side; the tank he placed at the southeast corner.

Summary List of Temple Furnishings

(2 Chronicles 4.11 – 5.1)

40-45Huram also made pots, shovels, and bowls. He completed all his work for King Solomon for the LORD's Temple. This is what he made:
The two columns
The two bowl-shaped capitals on
top of the columns

The design of interwoven chains
on each capital
The 400 bronze pomegranates, in
two rows of 100 each around
the design on each capital
The ten carts
The ten basins
The tank
The twelve bulls supporting the
tank
The pots, shovels, and bowls
All this equipment for the Temple, which Huram made for King Solomon, was of polished bronze. 46The king had it all made in the foundry between Sukkoth and Zarethan, in the Jordan Valley. 47Solomon did not have these bronze objects weighed, because there were too many of them, and so their weight was never determined.

48Solomon also had gold furnishings made for the Temple: the altar, the table for the bread offered to God, 49the ten lampstands that stood in front of the Most Holy Place, five on the south side and five on the north; the flowers, lamps, and tongs; 50the cups, lamp snuffers, bowls, dishes for incense, and the pans used for carrying live coals; and the hinges for the doors of the Most Holy Place and of the outer doors of the Temple. All these furnishings were made of gold.

51When King Solomon finished all the work on the Temple, he placed in the Temple storerooms all the things that his father David had dedicated to the LORD—the silver, gold, and other articles.

The Covenant Box Is Brought to the Temple

(2 Chronicles 5.2 – 6.2)

8 Then King Solomon summoned all the leaders of the tribes and clans of Israel to come to him in Jerusalem in order to take the LORD's Covenant Box from Zion, David's City, to the Temple. 2They all assembled during the Festival of Shelters in the seventh month, in the month of Ethanim. 3When all the leaders had gathered, the priests lifted the Covenant Box 4and carried it to the Temple. The Levites and the priests also moved the Tent of the LORD's presence and all its equipment to the Temple. 5King Solomon and all the people of Is-

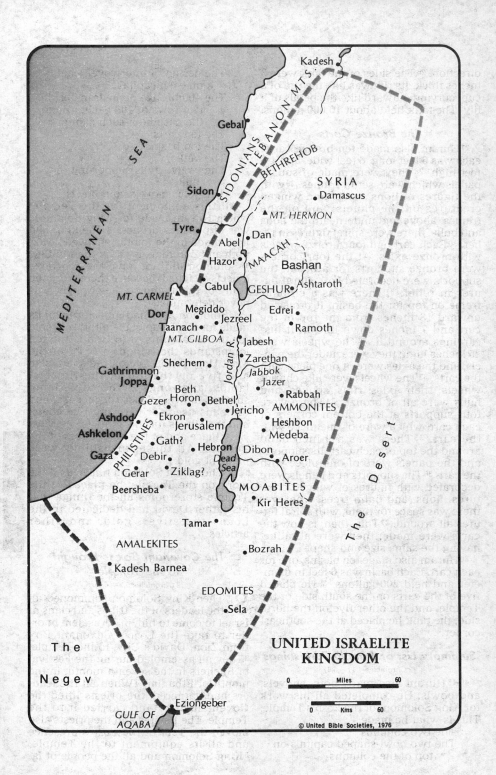

MEDITERRANEAN SEA

Kadesh

Gebal

LEBANON MTS.

SIDONIANS

BETHREHOB

SYRIA

Damascus

Sidon

MT. HERMON

Tyre

Abel   Dan

Hazor   MAACAH

Bashan

Cabul   GESHUR   Ashtaroth

MT. CARMEL

Dor   Megiddo   Edrei

Taanach   Jezreel

MT. GILBOA   Ramoth

Jabesh

Zarethan

Shechem   Jabbok

Gathrimmon   Jazer

Joppa

Beth   Rabbah

Horon   Bethel   AMMONITES

Gezer   Jericho   Heshbon

Ashdod   Ekron   Medeba

Ashkelon   Jerusalem

PHILISTINES   Gath?   Hebron   Dibon

Gaza   Debir   Dead   Aroer

Gerar   Ziklag?   Sea

Beersheba   MOABITES

Kir Heres

Tamar

AMALEKITES   Bozrah

Kadesh Barnea

EDOMITES

Sela

The   Jordan R.

Negev   The   Desert

Eziongeber

UNITED ISRAELITE KINGDOM

GULF OF
AQABA

0   Miles   60

0   Kms   60

© United Bible Societies, 1976

rael assembled in fo[r] of the Covenant Box and sacrificed...o many to count. sheep and cattle...ried the Covenant 6Then the priests...e and put it in the Box into the Te[mple]...neath the winged Most Holy Pla[ce]...utstretched wings creatures. 7Th...he poles it was car- covered the bo...a the poles could be ried by. 8The...nding directly in seen by any...o[n]ly Place, but from front of the M...oles are still there nowhere else...nothing inside the today.) 9The...the two stone tab- Covenant B[ox] ad placed there at lets which...e LORD made a cov- Mount Sin...le of Israel as they enant wi...gypt.

were co...ere leaving the Tem-
10 As...filled with a cloud
ple, it...dazzling light of the
11 shi...nd they could not go
their duties. 12 Then
LOR[D]
ba...ve placed the sun in
S[?]
...ve chosen to live in
...nd darkness.
...built a majestic temple
...or you to live in
...

[?]Address to the People
Chronicles 6.3-11)

...As th...ple stood there, King Sol- ...on tur...face them, and he asked od's bl...ng on them. 15 He said, Praise th...rd God of Israel! He has kept the...ise he made to my father David, wh...he told him, 16 'From the time I brou...my people out of Egypt, I have not c...en any city in all the land of Israel i...hich a temple should be built where...would be worshiped. But I chose you...avid, to rule my people.'"

17 And So...mon continued, "My father David plan...ed to build a temple for the worship of...he LORD God of Israel, 18 but the LORD sa...d to him, 'You were right in wanting to...uild a temple for me, 19 but you will nev...er build it. It is your son, your own son, who will build my temple.'

20 "And now the LORD has kept his promise. I have succeeded my father as

king of Israel, and I have built the Temple for the worship of the LORD God of Israel. 21 I have also provided a place in the Temple for the Covenant Box containing the stone tablets of the covenant which the LORD made with our ancestors when he brought them out of Egypt."

Solomon's Prayer
(2 Chronicles 6.12-42)

22 Then in the presence of the people Solomon went and stood in front of the altar, where he raised his arms 23 and prayed, "LORD God of Israel, there is no god like you in heaven above or on earth below! You keep your covenant with your people and show them your love when they live in wholehearted obedience to you. 24 You have kept the promise you made to my father David; today every word has been fulfilled. 25 And now, LORD God of Israel, I pray that you will also keep the other promise you made to my father when you told him that there would always be one of his descendants ruling as king of Israel, provided they obeyed you as carefully as he did. 26 So now, O God of Israel, let everything come true that you promised to my father David, your servant.

27 "But can you, O God, really live on earth? Not even all of heaven is large enough to hold you, so how can this Temple that I have built be large enough? 28 LORD my God, I am your servant. Listen to my prayer, and grant the requests I make to you today. 29 Watch over this Temple day and night, this place where you have chosen to be worshiped. Hear me when I face this Temple and pray. 30 Hear my prayers and the prayers of your people when they face this place and pray. In your home in heaven hear us and forgive us.

31 "When a person is accused of wronging another and is brought to your altar in this Temple to take an oath that he is innocent, 32 O LORD, listen in heaven and judge your servants. Punish the guilty one as he deserves, and acquit the one who is innocent.

33 "When your people Israel are defeated by their enemies because they have sinned against you, and then when they turn to you and come to this Temple, humbly praying to you for

y One ancient translation You ... sky; Hebrew does not have these words.

1 KINGS

forgiveness, 34listen to them in heaven. Forgive the sins of your people and bring them back to the land which you gave to their ancestors.

35 "When you hold back the rain because your people have sinned against you, and then when they repent and face this Temple, humbly praying to you, 36listen to them in heaven. Forgive the sins of the king and of the people of Israel, and teach them to do what is right. Then, O LORD, send rain on this land of yours, which you gave to your people as a permanent possession.

37 "When there is famine in the land or an epidemic or the crops are destroyed by scorching winds or swarms of locusts, or when your people are attacked by their enemies, or when there is disease or sickness among them, 38listen to their prayers. If any of your people Israel, out of heartfelt sorrow, stretch out their hands in prayer toward this Temple, 39hear their prayer. Listen to them in your home in heaven, forgive them, and help them. You alone know the thoughts of the human heart. Deal with each person as he deserves, 40so that your people may obey you all the time they live in the land which you gave to our ancestors.

41-42 "When a foreigner who lives in a distant land hears of your fame and of the great things you have done for your people and comes to worship you and to pray at this Temple, 43listen to his prayer. In heaven, where you live, hear him and do what he asks you to do, so that all the peoples of the world may know you and obey you, as your people Israel do. Then they will know that this Temple I have built is the place where you are to be worshiped.

44 "When you command your people to go into battle against their enemies and they pray to you, wherever they are, facing this city which you have chosen and this Temple which I have built for you, 45listen to their prayers. Hear them in heaven and give them victory.

46 "When your people sin against you—and there is no one who does not sin—and in your anger you let their enemies defeat them and take them as prisoners to some other land, even if that land is far away, 47listen to your people's prayers. If there in that land they repent and pray to you, confessing how

sinful and wicke_____ their prayers, O _____ hey have been, hear they truly and sinc___D. 48If in that land to you as they fa_ly repent and pray which you gave to_oward this land city which you hav_ ancestors, this Temple which I __osen, and this 49then listen to the_built for you, home in heaven hea_yers. In your ful to them. 50Forgiv_and be merci- their rebellion agair_eir sins and their enemies treat th_and make 51They are your own ___kindness. brought out of Egyr_____ furnace. _hom you

52 "Sovereign LORD, _lazing look with favor on you and their king, and hea_ays whenever they call to ___el 53You chose them from all _____ be your own people, as y_____ through your servant Mos_ brought our ancestors out o

The Final Praye_

54After Solomon had finis_ to the LORD, he stood up in_ altar, where he had been k___ uplifted hands. 55In a lo___ asked God's blessings on a___ assembled there. He said ____ LORD who has given his _eo__ he promised he would. He ____ the generous promises he m____ his servant Moses. 57May t___ God be with us as he was ___ cestors; may he never leave_ don us; 58may he make us___ him, so that we will alwa__ wants us to live, keeping all_____ commands he gave our anc_s. 59May the LORD our God remembe_ all times this prayer and these pet_ns I have made to him. May he alwa_e merciful to the people of Israel and their king, according to their daily nee_ 60And so all the nations of the wor_will know that the LORD alone is God_here is no other. 61May you, his peopl_always be faithful to the LORD our God_obeying all his laws and commands_as you do today."

The Dedication of the Temple
(2 Chronicles 7.4-10)

62Then King Solomon and all the people there offered sacrifices to the LORD. 63He sacrificed 22,000 head of cattle and

120,000 sheep as fellowship offerings. And so the king and all the people dedicated the Temple. 64 That same day he also consecrated the central part of the courtyard, the area in front of the Temple, and then he offered there the sacrifices burned whole, the grain offerings, and the fat of the animals for the fellowship offerings. He did this because the bronze altar was too small for all these offerings.

65 There at the Temple, Solomon and all the people of Israel celebrated the Festival of Shelters for seven[z] days. There was a huge crowd of people from as far away as Hamath Pass in the north and the Egyptian border in the south. 66 On the eighth day Solomon sent the people home. They all praised him and went home happy because of all the blessings that the LORD had given his servant David and his people Israel.

God Appears to Solomon Again
(2 Chronicles 7.11-22)

9 After King Solomon had finished building the Temple and the palace and everything else he wanted to build, 2 the LORD appeared to him again, as he had in Gibeon. 3 The LORD said to him, "I have heard your prayer. I consecrate this Temple which you have built as the place where I shall be worshiped forever. I will watch over it and protect it for all time. 4 If you will serve me in honesty and integrity, as your father David did, and if you obey my laws and do everything I have commanded you, 5 I will keep the promise I made to your father David when I told him that Israel would always be ruled by his descendants. 6 But if you or your descendants stop following me, disobey the laws and commands I have given you, and worship other gods, 7 then I will remove my people Israel from the land that I have given them. I will also abandon this Temple which I have consecrated as the place where I am to be worshiped. People everywhere will ridicule Israel and treat her with contempt. 8 This Temple will become a pile of ruins,[a] and everyone who passes by will be shocked and amazed. 'Why did the LORD do this to this land and this Temple?' they will ask.

9 People will answer, 'It is because they abandoned the LORD their God, who brought their ancestors out of Egypt. They gave their allegiance to other gods and worshiped them. That is why the LORD has brought this disaster on them.' "

Solomon's Agreement with Hiram
(2 Chronicles 8.1, 2)

10 It took Solomon twenty years to build the Temple and his palace. 11 King Hiram of Tyre had provided him with all the cedar and pine and with all the gold he wanted for this work. After it was finished, King Solomon gave Hiram twenty towns in the region of Galilee. 12 Hiram went to see them, and he did not like them. 13 So he said to Solomon, "So these, my brother, are the towns you have given me!" For this reason the area is still called Cabul.[b] 14 Hiram had sent Solomon almost five tons of gold.

Further Achievements of Solomon
(2 Chronicles 8.3-18)

15 King Solomon used forced labor to build the Temple and the palace, to fill in land on the east side of the city, and to build the city wall. He also used it to rebuild the cities of Hazor, Megiddo, and Gezer. (16 The king of Egypt had attacked Gezer and captured it, killing its inhabitants and setting fire to the city. Then he gave it as a wedding present to his daughter when she married Solomon, 17 and Solomon rebuilt it.) Using his forced labor, Solomon also rebuilt Lower Beth Horon, 18 Baalath, Tamar in the wilderness of Judah, 19 the cities where his supplies were kept, the cities for his horses and chariots, and everything else he wanted to build in Jerusalem, in Lebanon, and elsewhere in his kingdom. 20-21 For his forced labor Solomon used the descendants of the people of Canaan whom the Israelites had not killed when they took possession of their land. These included Amorites, Hittites, Perizzites, Hivites, and Jebusites, whose descendants continue to be slaves down to the present time. 22 Solomon did not make slaves of Israelites; they served as his soldiers, officers, commanders, chariot captains, and cavalry. 23 There were 550 officials in charge of

---

[z] *One ancient translation* seven; *Hebrew* fourteen.   [a] *Some ancient translations* a pile of ruins; *Hebrew* high.   [b] CABUL: *This name sounds like "ke-bal," the Hebrew for "worthless."*

the forced labor working on Solomon's various building projects.

24 Solomon filled in the land on the east side of the city, after his wife, the daughter of the king of Egypt, had moved from David's City to the palace Solomon built for her.

25 Three times a year Solomon offered burnt offerings and fellowship offerings on the altar he had built to the LORD. He also burned incense[c] to the LORD. And so he finished building the Temple.

26 King Solomon also built a fleet of ships at Eziongeber, which is near Elath on the shore of the Gulf of Aqaba, in the land of Edom. 27 King Hiram sent some experienced sailors from his fleet to serve with Solomon's men. 28 They sailed to the land of Ophir and brought back to Solomon about sixteen tons of gold.

The Visit of the Queen of Sheba
(2 Chronicles 9.1-12)

10 The queen of Sheba heard of Solomon's fame,[d] and she traveled to Jerusalem to test him with difficult questions. 2 She brought with her a large group of attendants, as well as camels loaded with spices, jewels, and a large amount of gold. When she and Solomon met, she asked him all the questions that she could think of. 3 He answered them all; there was nothing too difficult for him to explain. 4 The queen of Sheba heard Solomon's wisdom and saw the palace he had built. 5 She saw the food that was served at his table, the living quarters for his officials, the organization of his palace staff and the uniforms they wore, the servants who waited on him at feasts, and the sacrifices he offered in the Temple. It left her breathless and amazed. 6 She said to King Solomon, "What I heard in my own country about you[e] and your wisdom is true! 7 But I couldn't believe it until I had come and seen it all for myself. But I didn't hear even half of it; your wisdom and wealth are much greater than what I was told. 8 How fortunate are your wives![f] And how fortunate your servants, who are always in your presence and are privileged to hear your wise sayings! 9 Praise

the LORD your God! He has shown how pleased he is with you by making you king of Israel. Because his love for Israel is eternal, he has made you their king so that you can maintain law and justice."

10 She presented to King Solomon the gifts she had brought: almost five tons of gold and a very large amount of spices and jewels. The amount of spices she gave him was by far the greatest that he ever received at any time.

(11 Hiram's fleet, which had brought gold from Ophir, also brought from there a large amount of juniper wood and jewels. 12 Solomon used the wood to build railings in the Temple and the palace, and also to make harps and lyres for the musicians. It was the finest juniper wood ever imported into Israel; none like it has ever been seen again.)

13 King Solomon gave the queen of Sheba everything she asked for, besides all the other customary gifts that he had generously given her. Then she and her attendants returned to the land of Sheba.

King Solomon's Wealth
(2 Chronicles 9.13-29)

14 Every year King Solomon received over twenty-five tons of gold, 15 in addition to the taxes[g] paid by merchants, the profits from trade, and tribute paid by the Arabian kings and the governors of the Israelite districts.

16 Solomon made two hundred large shields and had each one overlaid with almost fifteen pounds of gold. 17 He also made three hundred smaller shields, overlaying each one of them with nearly four pounds of gold. He had all these shields placed in the Hall of the Forest of Lebanon.[h]

18 He also had a large throne made. Part of it was covered with ivory and the rest of it was covered with the finest gold. 19-20 The throne had six steps leading up to it, with the figure of a lion at each end of every step, a total of twelve lions. At the back of the throne was the figure of a bull's head, and beside each of the two armrests was the figure of a lion. No throne like this had ever existed in any other kingdom.

---

c Hebrew has two additional words, the meaning of which is unclear.   d Probable text (see 2 Ch 9.1) Solomon's fame; Hebrew Solomon's fame concerning the name of the LORD.   e you; or your deeds.   f Some ancient translations wives; Hebrew men.   g Some ancient translations taxes; Hebrew men.   h HALL OF THE FOREST OF LEBANON: See 7.2-3.

21 All of Solomon's drinking cups were made of gold, and all the utensils in the Hall of the Forest of Lebanon were of pure gold. No silver was used, since it was not considered valuable in Solomon's day. 22 He had a fleet of ocean-going ships sailing with Hiram's fleet. Every three years his fleet would return, bringing gold, silver, ivory, apes, and monkeys.

23 King Solomon was richer and wiser than any other king, 24 and the whole world wanted to come and listen to the wisdom that God had given him. 25 Everyone who came brought him a gift — articles of silver and gold, robes, weapons, spices, horses, and mules. This continued year after year.

26 Solomon built up a force of fourteen hundred chariots and twelve thousand cavalry horses. Some of them he kept in Jerusalem and the rest he stationed in various other cities. 27 During his reign silver was as common in Jerusalem as stone, and cedar was as plentiful as ordinary sycamore in the foothills of Judah. 28 The king's agents controlled the export of horses from Musri*i* and Cilicia,*j* 29 and the export of chariots from Egypt. They supplied the Hittite and Syrian kings with horses and chariots, selling chariots for 600 pieces of silver each and horses for 150 each.

Solomon Turns Away from God

11 Solomon loved many foreign women. Besides the daughter of the king of Egypt he married Hittite women and women from Moab, Ammon, Edom, and Sidon. 2 He married them even though the LORD had commanded the Israelites not to intermarry with these people, because they would cause the Israelites to give their loyalty to other gods. 3 Solomon married seven hundred princesses and also had three hundred concubines. They made him turn away from God, 4 and by the time he was old they had led him into the worship of foreign gods. He was not faithful to the LORD his God, as his father David had been. 5 He worshiped Astarte, the goddess of Sidon, and Molech, the disgusting god of Ammon. 6 He sinned against the LORD and was not true to him

as his father David had been. 7 On the mountain east of Jerusalem he built a place to worship Chemosh, the disgusting god of Moab, and a place to worship Molech, the disgusting god of Ammon. 8 He also built places of worship where all his foreign wives could burn incense and offer sacrifices to their own gods.

9-10 Even though the LORD, the God of Israel, had appeared to Solomon twice and had commanded him not to worship foreign gods, Solomon did not obey the LORD but turned away from him. So the LORD was angry with Solomon 11 and said to him, "Because you have deliberately broken your covenant with me and disobeyed my commands, I promise that I will take the kingdom away from you and give it to one of your officials. 12 However, for the sake of your father David I will not do this in your lifetime, but during the reign of your son. 13 And I will not take the whole kingdom away from him; instead, I will leave him one tribe for the sake of my servant David and for the sake of Jerusalem, the city I have made my own."

Solomon's Enemies

14 So the LORD caused Hadad, of the royal family of Edom, to turn against Solomon. 15-16 Long before this, when David had conquered Edom, Joab the commander of his army had gone there to bury the dead. He and his men remained in Edom six months, and during that time they killed every male in Edom 17 except Hadad and some of his father's Edomite servants, who escaped to Egypt. (At that time Hadad was just a child.) 18 They left Midian and went to Paran, where some other men joined them. Then they traveled to Egypt and went to the king, who gave Hadad some land and a house and provided him with food. 19 Hadad won the friendship of the king, and the king gave his sister-in-law, the sister of Queen Tahpenes, to Hadad in marriage. 20 She bore him a son, Genubath, who was raised by the queen in the palace, where he lived with the king's sons.

21 When the news reached Hadad in Egypt that David had died and that Joab the commander of the army was dead,

1 KINGS

i Probable text Musri; Hebrew Egypt.   j MUSRI AND CILICIA: Two ancient countries in what is now southeast Turkey which were centers of horse breeding in Solomon's time.

Hadad said to the king, "Let me go back to my own country."

22 "Why?" the king asked. "Have I failed to give you something? Is that why you want to go back home?"

"Just let me go," Hadad answered the king. And he went back to his country.[k] As king of Edom, Hadad was an evil, bitter enemy of Israel.[l]

23 God also caused Rezon son of Eliada to turn against Solomon. Rezon had fled from his master, King Hadadezer of Zobah, 24 and had become the leader of a gang of outlaws. (This happened after David had defeated Hadadezer and had slaughtered his Syrian allies.) Rezon and his gang went and lived in Damascus, where his followers made him king of Syria. 25 He was an enemy of Israel during the lifetime of Solomon.

God's Promise to Jeroboam

26 Another man who turned against King Solomon was one of his officials, Jeroboam son of Nebat, from Zeredah in Ephraim. His mother was a widow named Zeruah. 27 This is the story of the revolt.

Solomon was filling in the land on the east side of Jerusalem and repairing the city walls. 28 Jeroboam was an able young man, and when Solomon noticed how hard he worked, he put him in charge of all the forced labor in the territory of the tribes of Manasseh and Ephraim. 29 One day, as Jeroboam was traveling from Jerusalem, the prophet Ahijah from Shiloh met him alone on the road in the open country. 30 Ahijah took off the new robe he was wearing, tore it into twelve pieces, 31 and said to Jeroboam, "Take ten pieces for yourself, because the LORD, the God of Israel, says to you, 'I am going to take the kingdom away from Solomon, and I will give you ten tribes. 32 Solomon will keep one tribe for the sake of my servant David and for the sake of Jerusalem, the city I have chosen to be my own from the whole land of Israel. 33 I am going to do this because Solomon has rejected me and has[m] worshiped foreign gods: Astarte, the goddess of Sidon; Chemosh, the god

of Moab; and Molech, the god of Ammon. Solomon has[n] disobeyed me; he has done wrong and has not kept my laws and commands as his father David did. 34 But I will not take the whole kingdom away from Solomon, and I will keep him in power as long as he lives. This I will do for the sake of my servant David, whom I chose and who obeyed my laws and commands. 35 I will take the kingdom away from Solomon's son and will give you ten tribes, 36 but I will let Solomon's son keep one tribe, so that I will always have a descendant of my servant David ruling in Jerusalem, the city I have chosen as the place where I am worshiped. 37 Jeroboam, I will make you king of Israel, and you will rule over all the territory that you want. 38 If you obey me completely, live by my laws, and win my approval by doing what I command, as my servant David did, I will always be with you. I will make you king of Israel and will make sure that your descendants rule after you, just as I have done for David. 39 Because of Solomon's sin I will punish the descendants of David, but not for all time.' "

40 And so Solomon tried to kill Jeroboam, but he escaped to King Shishak of Egypt and stayed there until Solomon's death.

The Death of Solomon
(2 Chronicles 9.29-31)

41 Everything else that Solomon did, his career, and his wisdom, are all recorded in *The History of Solomon*. 42 He was king in Jerusalem over all Israel for forty years. 43 He died and was buried in David's City, and his son Rehoboam succeeded him as king.

The Northern Tribes Revolt
(2 Chronicles 10.1-19)

12 Rehoboam went to Shechem, where all the people of northern Israel had gathered to make him king. 2 When Jeroboam son of Nebat, who had gone to Egypt to escape from King Solomon, heard this news, he returned

---

[k] *One ancient translation* And he went back to his country; *Hebrew does not have these words.* [l] *One ancient translation* As king . . . Israel; *in Hebrew this sentence, with some differences, comes at the end of verse 25.* [m] *Some ancient translations* Solomon has . . . and has; *Hebrew they have . . . and have.* [n] *Some ancient translations* Solomon has; *Hebrew They have.*

from⁰ Egypt. ³The people of the northern tribes sent for him, and then they all went together to Rehoboam and said to him, ⁴"Your father Solomon treated us harshly and placed heavy burdens on us. If you make these burdens lighter and make life easier for us, we will be your loyal subjects."

⁵"Come back in three days and I will give you my answer," he replied. So they left.

⁶King Rehoboam consulted the older men who had served as his father Solomon's advisers. "What answer do you advise me to give these people?" he asked.

⁷They replied, "If you want to serve this people well, give a favorable answer to their request, and they will always serve you loyally."

⁸But he ignored the advice of the older men and went instead to the young men who had grown up with him and who were now his advisers. ⁹"What do you advise me to do?" he asked. "What shall I say to the people who are asking me to make their burdens lighter?"

¹⁰They replied, "This is what you should tell them: 'My little finger is thicker than my father's waist!' ¹¹Tell them, 'My father placed heavy burdens on you; I will make them even heavier. He beat you with whips; I'll flog you with bullwhips!'"

¹²Three days later Jeroboam and all the people returned to King Rehoboam, as he had instructed them. ¹³The king ignored the advice of the older men and spoke harshly to the people, ¹⁴as the younger men had advised. He said, "My father placed heavy burdens on you; I will make them even heavier. He beat you with whips; I'll flog you with bullwhips!" ¹⁵It was the will of the LORD to bring about what he had spoken to Jeroboam son of Nebat through the prophet Ahijah from Shiloh. This is why the king did not pay any attention to the people.

¹⁶When the people saw that the king would not listen to them, they shouted, "Down with David and his family! What have they ever done for us? People of Israel, let's go home! Let Rehoboam look out for himself!"

So the people of Israel rebelled,

¹⁷leaving Rehoboam as king only of the people who lived in the territory of Judah.

¹⁸Then King Rehoboam sent Adoniram, who was in charge of the forced labor, to go to the Israelites, but they stoned him to death. At this, Rehoboam hurriedly got in his chariot and escaped to Jerusalem. ¹⁹Ever since that time the people of the northern kingdom of Israel have been in rebellion against the dynasty of David.

²⁰When the people of Israel heard that Jeroboam had returned from Egypt, they invited him to a meeting of the people and made him king of Israel. Only the tribe of Judah remained loyal to David's descendants.

Shemaiah's Prophecy
(2 Chronicles 11.1-4)

²¹When Rehoboam arrived in Jerusalem, he called together 180,000 of the best soldiers from the tribes of Judah and Benjamin. He intended to go to war and restore his control over the northern tribes of Israel. ²²But God told the prophet Shemaiah ²³to give this message to Rehoboam and to all the people of the tribes of Judah and Benjamin: ²⁴"Do not attack your own relatives, the people of Israel. Go home, all of you. What has happened is my will." They all obeyed the LORD's command and went back home.

Jeroboam Turns Away from God

²⁵King Jeroboam of Israel fortified the town of Shechem in the hill country of Ephraim and lived there for a while. Then he left and fortified the town of Penuel. ²⁶⁻²⁷He said to himself, "As things are now, if my people go to Jerusalem and offer sacrifices to the LORD in the Temple there, they will transfer their allegiance to King Rehoboam of Judah and will kill me."

²⁸After thinking it over, he made two bull-calves of gold and said to his people, "You have been going long enough to Jerusalem to worship. People of Israel, here are your gods who brought you out of Egypt!" ²⁹He placed one of the gold bull-calves in Bethel and the other in Dan. ³⁰And so the people sinned, going to worship in Bethel and in Dan.ᵖ

⁰ *Some ancient translations (and see 2 Ch 10.2)* returned from; *Hebrew* remained in.
ᵖ *One ancient translation* in Bethel and in Dan; *Hebrew* in Dan.

1 KINGS

31 Jeroboam also built places of worship on hilltops, and he chose priests from families who were not of the tribe of Levi.

Worship at Bethel Is Condemned

32 Jeroboam also instituted a religious festival on the fifteenth day of the eighth month, like the festival in Judah. On the altar in Bethel he offered sacrifices to the gold bull-calves he had made, and he placed there in Bethel the priests serving at the places of worship he had built. 33 And on the fifteenth day of the eighth month, the day that he himself had set, he went to Bethel and offered a sacrifice on the altar in celebration of the festival he had instituted for the people of Israel.

13 At the LORD's command a prophet from Judah went to Bethel and arrived there as Jeroboam stood at the altar to offer the sacrifice. 2 Following the LORD's command, the prophet denounced the altar: "O altar, altar, this is what the LORD says: A child, whose name will be Josiah, will be born to the family of David. He will slaughter on you the priests serving at the pagan altars who offer sacrifices on you, and he will burn human bones on you." 3 And the prophet went on to say, "This altar will fall apart, and the ashes on it will be scattered. Then you will know that the LORD has spoken through me."

4 When King Jeroboam heard this, he pointed at him and ordered, "Seize that man!" At once the king's arm became paralyzed so that he couldn't pull it back. 5 The altar suddenly fell apart and the ashes spilled to the ground, as the prophet had predicted in the name of the LORD. 6 King Jeroboam said to the prophet, "Please pray for me to the LORD your God, and ask him to heal my arm!"

The prophet prayed to the LORD, and the king's arm was healed. 7 Then the king said to the prophet, "Come home with me and have something to eat. I will reward you for what you have done."

8 The prophet answered, "Even if you gave me half of your wealth, I would not go with you or eat or drink anything with you. 9 The LORD has commanded me not to eat or drink a thing, and not to return home the same way I came." 10 So he did not go back the same way he had come, but by another road.

The Old Prophet of Bethel

11 At that time there was an old prophet living in Bethel. His sons*q* came and told him what the prophet from Judah had done in Bethel that day and what he had said to King Jeroboam. 12 "Which way did he go when he left?" the old prophet asked them. They showed him*r* the road 13 and he told them to saddle his donkey for him. They did so, and he rode off 14 down the road after the prophet from Judah and found him sitting under an oak tree. "Are you the prophet from Judah?" he asked.

"I am," the man answered.

15 "Come home and have a meal with me," he said.

16 But the prophet from Judah answered, "I can't go home with you or accept your hospitality. And I won't eat or drink anything with you here, 17 because the LORD has commanded me not to eat or drink a thing, and not to return home the same way I came."

18 Then the old prophet from Bethel said to him, "I, too, am a prophet just like you, and at the LORD's command an angel told me to take you home with me and offer you my hospitality." But the old prophet was lying.

19 So the prophet from Judah went home with the old prophet and had a meal with him. 20 As they were sitting at the table, the word of the LORD came to the old prophet, 21 and he cried out to the prophet from Judah, "The LORD says that you disobeyed him and did not do what he commanded. 22 Instead, you returned and ate a meal in a place he had ordered you not to eat in. Because of this you will be killed, and your body will not be buried in your family grave."

23 After they had finished eating, the old prophet saddled the donkey for the prophet from Judah, 24 who rode off. On the way a lion met him and killed him. His body lay on the road, and the donkey and the lion stood beside it. 25 Some

---

q Some ancient translations sons; Hebrew son. Hebrew saw.   *r Some ancient translations showed him;*

men passed by and saw the body on the road, with the lion standing near by. They went on into Bethel and reported what they had seen.

26 When the old prophet heard about it, he said, "That is the prophet who disobeyed the LORD's command! And so the LORD sent the lion to attack and kill him, just as the LORD said he would." 27 Then he said to his sons, "Saddle my donkey for me." They did so, 28 and he rode off and found the prophet's body lying on the road, with the donkey and the lion still standing by it. The lion had not eaten the body or attacked the donkey. 29 The old prophet picked up the body, put it on the donkey, and brought it back to Bethel to mourn over it and bury it. 30 He buried it in his own family grave, and he and his sons mourned over it, saying, "Oh my brother, my brother!" 31 After the burial the prophet said to his sons, "When I die, bury me in this grave and lay my body next to his. 32 The words that he spoke at the LORD's command against the altar in Bethel and against all the places of worship in the towns of Samaria will surely come true."

Jeroboam's Fatal Sin

33 King Jeroboam of Israel still did not turn from his evil ways but continued to choose priests from ordinary families to serve at the altars he had built. He ordained as priest anyone who wanted to be one. 34 This sin on his part brought about the ruin and total destruction of his dynasty.

The Death of Jeroboam's Son

14 At that time King Jeroboam's son Abijah got sick. 2 Jeroboam said to his wife, "Disguise yourself so that no one will recognize you, and go to Shiloh, where the prophet Ahijah lives, the one who said I would be king of Israel. 3 Take him ten loaves of bread, some cakes, and a jar of honey. Ask him what is going to happen to our son, and he will tell you."

4 So she went to Ahijah's home in Shiloh. Old age had made Ahijah blind. 5 The LORD had told him that Jeroboam's wife was coming to ask him about her son, who was sick. And the LORD told Ahijah what to say.

When Jeroboam's wife arrived, she pretended to be someone else. 6 But when Ahijah heard her coming in the door, he said, "Come in. I know you are Jeroboam's wife. Why are you pretending to be someone else? I have bad news for you. 7 Go and tell Jeroboam that this is what the LORD, the God of Israel, says to him: 'I chose you from among the people and made you the ruler of my people Israel. 8 I took the kingdom away from David's descendants and gave it to you. But you have not been like my servant David, who was completely loyal to me, obeyed my commands, and did only what I approve of. 9 You have committed far greater sins than those who ruled before you. You have rejected me and have aroused my anger by making idols and metal images to worship. 10 Because of this I will bring disaster on your dynasty and will kill all your male descendants, young and old alike. I will get rid of your family; they will be swept away like dung. 11 Any members of your family who die in the city will be eaten by dogs, and any who die in the open country will be eaten by vultures. I, the LORD, have spoken.'"

12 And Ahijah went on to say to Jeroboam's wife, "Now go back home. As soon as you enter the town, your son will die. 13 All the people of Israel will mourn for him and bury him. He will be the only member of Jeroboam's family who will be properly buried, because he is the only one with whom the LORD, the God of Israel, is pleased. 14 The LORD is going to place a king over Israel who will put an end to Jeroboam's dynasty.s 15 The LORD will punish Israel, and she will shake like a reed shaking in a stream. He will uproot the people of Israel from this good land which he gave to their ancestors, and he will scatter them beyond the Euphrates River, because they have aroused his anger by making idols of the goddess Asherah. 16 The LORD will abandon Israel because Jeroboam sinned and led the people of Israel into sin."

17 Jeroboam's wife went back to Tirzah. Just as she entered her home, the child died. 18 The people of Israel mourned for him and buried him, as the

s Hebrew has five additional words, the meaning of which is unclear.

LORD had said through his servant, the prophet Ahijah.

The Death of Jeroboam

19 Everything else that King Jeroboam did, the wars he fought and how he ruled, are all recorded in *The History of the Kings of Israel.* 20 Jeroboam ruled as king for twenty-two years. He died and was buried, and his son Nadab succeeded him as king.

King Rehoboam of Judah
(2 Chronicles 11.5 – 12.15)

21 Solomon's son Rehoboam was forty-one years old when he became king of Judah, and he ruled seventeen years in Jerusalem, the city which the LORD had chosen from all the territory of Israel as the place where he was to be worshiped. Rehoboam's mother was Naamah from Ammon.

22 The people of Judah sinned against the LORD and did more to arouse his anger against them than all their ancestors had done. 23 They built places of worship for false gods and put up stone pillars and symbols of Asherah to worship on the hills and under shady trees. 24 Worst of all, there were men and women who served as prostitutes at those pagan places of worship. The people of Judah practiced all the shameful things done by the people whom the LORD had driven out of the land as the Israelites advanced into the country.

25 In the fifth year of Rehoboam's reign King Shishak of Egypt attacked Jerusalem. 26 He took away all the treasures in the Temple and in the palace, including the gold shields Solomon had made. 27 To replace them, King Rehoboam made bronze shields and entrusted them to the officers responsible for guarding the palace gates. 28 Every time the king went to the Temple, the guards carried the shields and then returned them to the guardroom.

29 Everything else that King Rehoboam did is recorded in *The History of the Kings of Judah.* 30 During all this time Rehoboam and Jeroboam were constantly at war with each other. 31 Rehoboam died and was buried in the royal tombs in David's City and his son Abijah succeeded him as king.

King Abijah of Judah
(2 Chronicles 13.1 – 14.1)

15 In the eighteenth year of the reign of King Jeroboam of Israel, Abijah became king of Judah, 2 and he ruled three years in Jerusalem. His mother was Maacah, the daughter of Absalom. 3 He committed the same sins as his father and was not completely loyal to the LORD his God, as his great-grandfather David had been. 4 But for David's sake the LORD his God gave Abijah a son to rule after him in Jerusalem and to keep Jerusalem secure. 5 The LORD did this because David had done what pleased him and had never disobeyed any of his commands, except in the case of Uriah the Hittite. 6 The war which had begun between Rehoboam and Jeroboam continued throughout Abijah's lifetime. 7 And everything else that Abijah did is recorded in *The History of the Kings of Judah.*

8 Abijah died and was buried in David's City, and his son Asa succeeded him as king.

King Asa of Judah
(2 Chronicles 15.16 – 16.6)

9 In the twentieth year of the reign of King Jeroboam of Israel, Asa became king of Judah, 10 and he ruled forty-one years in Jerusalem. His grandmother was Maacah, the daughter of Absalom. 11 Asa did what pleased the LORD, as his ancestor David had done. 12 He expelled from the country all the male and female prostitutes serving at the pagan places of worship, and he removed all the idols his predecessors had made. 13 He removed his grandmother Maacah from her position as queen mother, because she had made an obscene idol of the fertility goddess Asherah. Asa cut down the idol and burned it in Kidron Valley. 14 Even though Asa did not destroy all the pagan places of worship, he remained faithful to the LORD all his life. 15 He placed in the Temple all the objects his father had dedicated to God, as well as the gold and silver objects that he himself dedicated.

16 King Asa of Judah and King Baasha of Israel were constantly at war with each other as long as they were in power. 17 Baasha invaded Judah and started to fortify Ramah in order to cut

off all traffic in and out of Judah. ¹⁸So King Asa took all the silver and gold that was left in the Temple and the palace, and sent it by some of his officials to Damascus, to King Benhadad of Syria, the son of Tabrimmon and grandson of Hezion, with this message: ¹⁹"Let us be allies, as our fathers were. This silver and gold is a present for you. Now break your alliance with King Baasha of Israel, so that he will have to pull his troops out of my territory."

²⁰King Benhadad agreed to Asa's proposal and sent his commanding officers and their armies to attack the cities of Israel. They captured Ijon, Dan, Abel Beth Maacah, the area near Lake Galilee, and the whole territory of Naphtali. ²¹When King Baasha heard what had happened, he stopped fortifying Ramah and went to Tirzah.

²²Then King Asa sent out an order throughout all of Judah requiring everyone, without exception, to help carry away from Ramah the stones and timber that Baasha had been using to fortify it. With this material Asa fortified Mizpah and Geba, a city in the territory of Benjamin.

²³Everything else that King Asa did, his brave deeds and the towns he fortified, are all recorded in *The History of the Kings of Judah.* But in his old age he was crippled by a foot disease. ²⁴Asa died and was buried in the royal tombs in David's City, and his son Jehoshaphat succeeded him as king.

King Nadab of Israel

²⁵In the second year of the reign of King Asa of Judah, King Jeroboam's son Nadab became king of Israel, and he ruled for two years. ²⁶Like his father before him, he sinned against the LORD and led Israel into sin.

²⁷Baasha son of Ahijah, of the tribe of Issachar, plotted against Nadab and killed him as Nadab and his army were besieging the city of Gibbethon in Philistia. ²⁸This happened during the third year of the reign of King Asa of Judah. And so Baasha succeeded Nadab as king of Israel. ²⁹At once he began killing all the members of Jeroboam's family. In accordance with what the LORD had said through his servant, the prophet Ahijah from Shiloh, all of Jeroboam's family were killed; not one survived. ³⁰This

happened because Jeroboam aroused the anger of the LORD, the God of Israel, by the sins that he committed and that he caused Israel to commit.

³¹Everything else that Nadab did is recorded in *The History of the Kings of Israel.* ³²King Asa of Judah and King Baasha of Israel were constantly at war with each other as long as they were in power.

King Baasha of Israel

³³In the third year of the reign of King Asa of Judah, Baasha son of Ahijah became king of all Israel, and he ruled in Tirzah for twenty-four years. ³⁴Like King Jeroboam before him, he sinned against the LORD and led Israel into sin.

16 The LORD spoke to the prophet Jehu son of Hanani and gave him this message for Baasha: ²"You were a nobody, but I made you the leader of my people Israel. And now you have sinned like Jeroboam and have led my people into sin. Their sins have aroused my anger, ³and so I will do away with you and your family, just as I did with Jeroboam. ⁴Any members of your family who die in the city will be eaten by dogs, and any who die in the open country will be eaten by vultures."

⁵Everything else that Baasha did and all his brave deeds are recorded in *The History of the Kings of Israel.* ⁶Baasha died and was buried in Tirzah, and his son Elah succeeded him as king.

⁷That message from the LORD against Baasha and his family was given by the prophet Jehu because of the sins that Baasha committed against the LORD. He aroused the LORD's anger not only because of the evil he did, just as King Jeroboam had done before him, but also because he killed all of Jeroboam's family.

King Elah of Israel

⁸In the twenty-sixth year of the reign of King Asa of Judah, Elah son of Baasha became king of Israel, and he ruled in Tirzah for two years. ⁹Zimri, one of his officers who was in charge of half of the king's chariots, plotted against him. One day in Tirzah, Elah was getting drunk in the home of Arza, who was in charge of the palace. ¹⁰Zimri entered the house, assassinated Elah, and succeeded him as king. This happened in the

1 KINGS

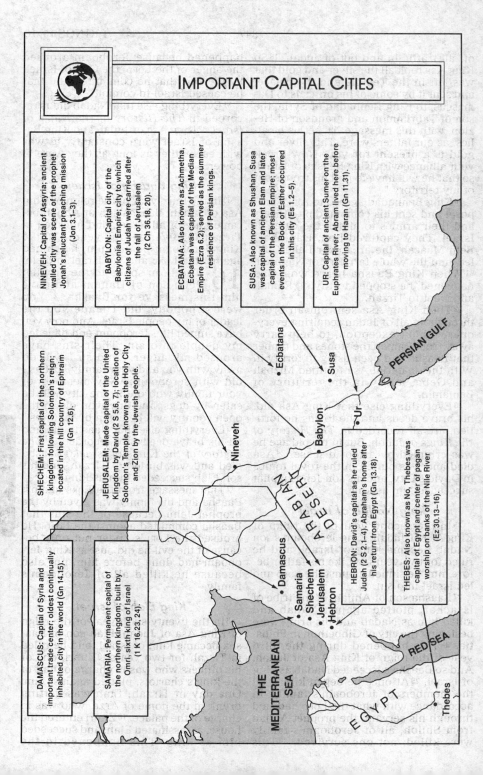

IMPORTANT CAPITAL CITIES

NINEVEH: Capital of Assyria; ancient walled city was scene of the prophet Jonah's reluctant preaching mission (Jon 3.1-3).

BABYLON: Capital city of the Babylonian Empire; city to which citizens of Judah were carried after the fall of Jerusalem (2 Ch 36.18, 20).

ECBATANA: Also known as Achmetha, Ecbatana was capital of the Median Empire (Ezra 6.2); served as the summer residence of Persian kings.

SUSA: Also known as Shushan, Susa was capital of ancient Elam and later capital of the Persian Empire; most events in the Book of Esther occurred in this city (Es 1.2–5).

UR: Capital of ancient Sumer on the Euphrates River; Abram lived here before moving to Haran (Gn 11.31).

SHECHEM: First capital of the northern kingdom following Solomon's reign; located in the hill country of Ephraim (Gn 12.6).

JERUSALEM: Made capital of the United Kingdom by David (2 S 5.6, 7); location of Solomon's Temple, known as the Holy City and Zion by the Jewish people.

DAMASCUS: Capital of Syria and important trade center; oldest continually inhabited city in the world (Gn 14.15).

SAMARIA: Permanent capital of the northern kingdom; built by Omri, sixth king of Israel (1 K 16.23, 24).

HEBRON: David's capital as he ruled Judah (2 S 2.1–4). Abraham's home after his return from Egypt (Gn 13.18).

THEBES: Also known as No, Thebes was capital of Egypt and center of pagan worship on banks of the Nile River (Ez 30.13–16).

PERSIAN GULF

• Ecbatana

• Susa

• Nineveh

• Babylon

• Ur

ARABIAN DESERT

• Damascus

• Samaria
• Shechem
• Jerusalem
• Hebron

THE MEDITERRANEAN SEA

RED SEA

EGYPT

• Thebes

twenty-seventh year of the reign of King Asa of Judah.

11 As soon as Zimri became king he killed off all the members of Baasha's family. Every male relative and friend was put to death. 12 And so, in accordance with what the LORD had said against Baasha through the prophet Jehu, Zimri killed all the family of Baasha. 13 Because of their idolatry and because they led Israel into sin, Baasha and his son Elah had aroused the anger of the LORD, the God of Israel. 14 Everything else that Elah did is recorded in *The History of the Kings of Israel*.

King Zimri of Israel

15 In the twenty-seventh year of the reign of King Asa of Judah, Zimri ruled in Tirzah over Israel for seven days. The Israelite troops were besieging the city of Gibbethon in Philistia, 16 and when they heard that Zimri had plotted against the king and assassinated him, then and there they all proclaimed their commander Omri king of Israel. 17 Omri and his troops left Gibbethon and went and besieged Tirzah. 18 When Zimri saw that the city had fallen, he went into the palace's inner fortress, set the palace on fire, and died in the flames. 19 This happened because of his sins against the LORD. Like his predecessor Jeroboam, he displeased the LORD by his own sins and by leading Israel into sin. 20 Everything else that Zimri did, including the account of his conspiracy, is recorded in *The History of the Kings of Israel*.

King Omri of Israel

21 The people of Israel were divided; some of them wanted to make Tibni son of Ginath king, and the others were in favor of Omri. 22 In the end, those in favor of Omri won out; Tibni died and Omri became king. 23 So in the thirty-first year of the reign of King Asa of Judah, Omri became king of Israel, and he ruled for twelve years. The first six years he ruled in Tirzah, 24 and then he bought the hill of Samaria for six thousand pieces of silver from a man named Shemer. Omri fortified the hill, built a town there, and named it Samaria, after Shemer, the former owner of the hill.

25 Omri sinned against the LORD more than any of his predecessors. 26 Like Jeroboam before him, he aroused the anger of the LORD, the God of Israel, by his sins and by leading the people into sin and idolatry. 27 Everything else that Omri did and all his accomplishments are recorded in *The History of the Kings of Israel*. 28 Omri died and was buried in Samaria, and his son Ahab succeeded him as king.

King Ahab of Israel

29 In the thirty-eighth year of the reign of King Asa of Judah, Ahab son of Omri became king of Israel, and he ruled in Samaria for twenty-two years. 30 He sinned against the LORD more than any of his predecessors. 31 It was not enough for him to sin like King Jeroboam; he went further and married Jezebel, the daughter of King Ethbaal of Sidon, and worshiped Baal. 32 He built a temple to Baal in Samaria, made an altar for him, and put it in the temple. 33 He also put up an image of the goddess Asherah. He did more to arouse the anger of the LORD, the God of Israel, than all the kings of Israel before him. 34 During his reign Hiel from Bethel rebuilt Jericho. As the LORD had foretold through Joshua son of Nun, Hiel lost his oldest son Abiram when he laid the foundation of Jericho, and his youngest son Segub when he built the gates.

Elijah and the Drought

17 A prophet named Elijah, from Tishbe in Gilead, said to King Ahab, "In the name of the LORD, the living God of Israel, whom I serve, I tell you that there will be no dew or rain for the next two or three years until I say so."

2 Then the LORD said to Elijah, 3 "Leave this place and go east and hide yourself near Cherith Brook, east of the Jordan. 4 The brook will supply you with water to drink, and I have commanded ravens to bring you food there."

5 Elijah obeyed the LORD's command, and went and stayed by Cherith Brook. 6 He drank water from the brook, and ravens brought him bread and meat every morning and every evening. 7 After a while the brook dried up because of the lack of rain.

Elijah and the Widow in Zarephath

8 Then the LORD said to Elijah, 9 "Now go to the town of Zarephath, near Sidon,

and stay there. I have commanded a widow who lives there to feed you." 10 So Elijah went to Zarephath, and as he came to the town gate, he saw a widow gathering firewood. "Please bring me a drink of water," he said to her. 11 And as she was going to get it, he called out, "And please bring me some bread, too."

12 She answered, "By the living Lord your God I swear that I don't have any bread. All I have is a handful of flour in a bowl and a bit of olive oil in a jar. I came here to gather some firewood to take back home and prepare what little I have for my son and me. That will be our last meal, and then we will starve to death."

13 "Don't worry," Elijah said to her. "Go on and prepare your meal. But first make a small loaf from what you have and bring it to me, and then prepare the rest for you and your son. 14 For this is what the Lord, the God of Israel, says: 'The bowl will not run out of flour or the jar run out of oil before the day that I, the Lord, send rain.'"

15 The widow went and did as Elijah had told her, and all of them had enough food for many days. 16 As the Lord had promised through Elijah, the bowl did not run out of flour nor did the jar run out of oil.

17 Some time later the widow's son got sick; he got worse and worse, and finally he died. 18 She said to Elijah, "Man of God, why did you do this to me? Did you come here to remind God of my sins and so cause my son's death?"

19 "Give the boy to me," Elijah said. He took the boy from her arms, carried him upstairs to the room where he was staying, and laid him on the bed. 20 Then he prayed aloud, "O Lord my God, why have you done such a terrible thing to this widow? She has been kind enough to take care of me, and now you kill her son!" 21 Then Elijah stretched himself out on the boy three times and prayed, "O Lord my God, restore this child to life!" 22 The Lord answered Elijah's prayer; the child started breathing again and revived.

23 Elijah took the boy back downstairs to his mother and said to her, "Look, your son is alive!"

24 She answered, "Now I know that you are a man of God and that the Lord really speaks through you!"

Elijah and the Prophets of Baal

18 After some time, in the third year of the drought, the Lord said to Elijah, "Go and present yourself to King Ahab, and I will send rain." 2 So Elijah started out.

The famine in Samaria was at its worst, 3 so Ahab called in Obadiah, who was in charge of the palace. (Obadiah was a devout worshiper of the Lord, 4 and when Jezebel was killing the Lord's prophets, Obadiah took a hundred of them, hid them in caves in two groups of fifty, and provided them with food and water.) 5 Ahab said to Obadiah, "Let us go and lookᵗ at every spring and every stream bed in the land to see if we can find enough grass to keep the horses and mules alive. Maybe we won't have to kill any of our animals." 6 They agreed on which part of the land each one would explore, and set off in different directions.

7 As Obadiah was on his way, he suddenly met Elijah. He recognized him, bowed low before him, and asked, "Is it really you, sir?"

8 "Yes, I'm Elijah," he answered. "Go and tell your master the king that I am here."

9 Obadiah answered, "What have I done that you want to put me in danger of being killed by King Ahab? 10 By the living Lord, your God, I swear that the king has made a search for you in every country in the world. Whenever the ruler of a country reported that you were not in his country, Ahab would require that ruler to swear that you could not be found. 11 And now you want me to go and tell him that you are here? 12 What if the spirit of the Lord carries you off to some unknown place as soon as I leave? Then, when I tell Ahab that you are here and he can't find you, he will put me to death. Remember that I have been a devout worshiper of the Lord ever since I was a boy. 13 Haven't you heard that when Jezebel was killing the prophets of the Lord I hid a hundred of them in caves, in two groups of fifty, and supplied them with food and water? 14 So how can you order me to go and tell the

---

ᵗ One ancient translation Let us go and look; Hebrew You go and look.

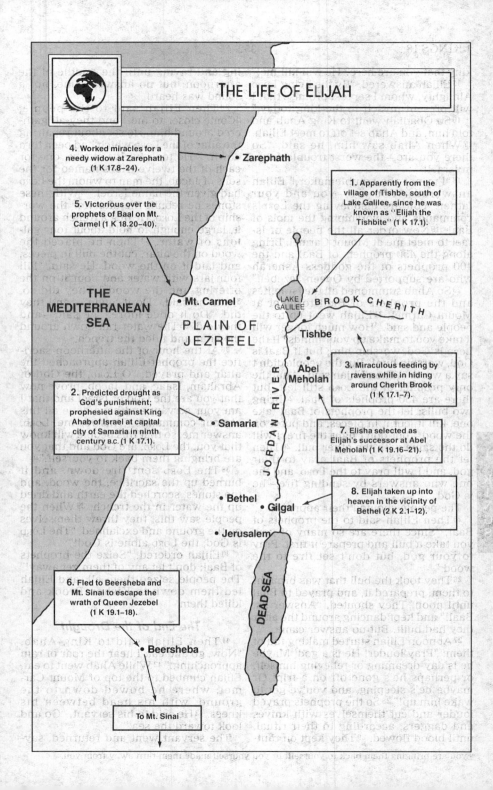

THE LIFE OF ELIJAH

4. Worked miracles for a needy widow at Zarephath (1 K 17.8–24).

• Zarephath

1. Apparently from the village of Tishbe, south of Lake Galilee, since he was known as "Elijah the Tishbite" (1 K 17.1).

5. Victorious over the prophets of Baal on Mt. Carmel (1 K 18.20–40).

THE MEDITERRANEAN SEA

• Mt. Carmel

LAKE GALILEE

BROOK CHERITH

PLAIN OF JEZREEL

Tishbe

Abel Meholah

3. Miraculous feeding by ravens while in hiding around Cherith Brook (1 K 17.1–7).

2. Predicted drought as God's punishment; prophesied against King Ahab of Israel at capital city of Samaria in ninth century B.C. (1 K 17.1).

• Samaria

JORDAN RIVER

7. Elisha selected as Elijah's successor at Abel Meholah (1 K 19.16–21).

• Bethel

• Gilgal

8. Elijah taken up into heaven in the vicinity of Bethel (2 K 2.1–12).

• Jerusalem

DEAD SEA

6. Fled to Beersheba and Mt. Sinai to escape the wrath of Queen Jezebel (1 K 19.1–18).

• Beersheba

To Mt. Sinai

king that you are here? He will kill me!"

15 Elijah answered, "By the living Lord Almighty, whom I serve, I promise that I will present myself to the king today."

16 So Obadiah went to King Ahab and told him, and Ahab set off to meet Elijah. 17 When Ahab saw him, he said, "So there you are—the worst troublemaker in Israel!"

18 "I'm not the troublemaker," Elijah answered. "You are—you and your father. You are disobeying the Lord's commands and worshiping the idols of Baal. 19 Now order all the people of Israel to meet me at Mount Carmel. Bring along the 450 prophets of Baal and the 400 prophets of the goddess Asherah who are supported by Queen Jezebel."

20 So Ahab summoned all the Israelites and the prophets of Baal to meet at Mount Carmel. 21 Elijah went up to the people and said, "How much longer will it take you to make up your minds? If the Lord is God, worship him; but if Baal is God, worship him!" But the people didn't say a word. 22 Then Elijah said, "I am the only prophet of the Lord still left, but there are 450 prophets of Baal. 23 Bring two bulls; let the prophets of Baal take one, kill it, cut it in pieces, and put it on the wood—but don't light the fire. I will do the same with the other bull. 24 Then let the prophets of Baal pray to their god, and I will pray to the Lord, and the one who answers by sending fire—he is God."

The people shouted their approval.

25 Then Elijah said to the prophets of Baal, "Since there are so many of you, you take a bull and prepare it first. Pray to your god, but don't set fire to the wood."

26 They took the bull that was brought to them, prepared it, and prayed to Baal until noon. They shouted, "Answer us, Baal!" and kept dancing around the altar they had built. But no answer came.

27 At noon Elijah started making fun of them: "Pray louder! He is a god! Maybe he is day-dreaming or relieving himself, or perhaps he's gone off on a trip! Or maybe he's sleeping, and you've got to wake him up!" 28 So the prophets prayed louder and cut themselves with knives and daggers, according to their ritual, until blood flowed. 29 They kept on rant-

ing and raving until the middle of the afternoon; but no answer came, not a sound was heard.

30 Then Elijah said to the people, "Come closer to me," and they all gathered around him. He set about repairing the altar of the Lord which had been torn down. 31 He took twelve stones, one for each of the twelve tribes named for the sons of Jacob, the man to whom the Lord had given the name Israel. 32 With these stones he rebuilt the altar for the worship of the Lord. He dug a trench around it, large enough to hold about four gallons of water. 33 Then he placed the wood on the altar, cut the bull in pieces, and laid it on the wood. He said, "Fill four jars with water and pour it on the offering and the wood." They did so, 34 and he said, "Do it again"—and they did. "Do it once more," he said—and they did. 35 The water ran down around the altar and filled the trench.

36 At the hour of the afternoon sacrifice the prophet Elijah approached the altar and prayed, "O Lord, the God of Abraham, Isaac, and Jacob, prove now that you are the God of Israel and that I am your servant and have done all this at your command. 37 Answer me, Lord, answer me, so that this people will know that you, the Lord, are God and that you are bringing them back to yourself."u

38 The Lord sent fire down, and it burned up the sacrifice, the wood, and the stones, scorched the earth and dried up the water in the trench. 39 When the people saw this, they threw themselves on the ground and exclaimed, "The Lord is God; the Lord alone is God!"

40 Elijah ordered, "Seize the prophets of Baal; don't let any of them get away!" The people seized them all, and Elijah led them down to Kishon Brook and killed them.

The End of the Drought

41 Then Elijah said to King Ahab, "Now, go and eat. I hear the roar of rain approaching." 42 While Ahab went to eat, Elijah climbed to the top of Mount Carmel, where he bowed down to the ground, with his head between his knees. 43 He said to his servant, "Go and look toward the sea."

The servant went and returned, say-

u you are bringing them back to yourself; or you yourself made them turn away from you.

ing, "I didn't see a thing." Seven times in all Elijah told him to go and look. 44 The seventh time he returned and said, "I saw a little cloud no bigger than a man's hand, coming up from the sea."

Elijah ordered his servant, "Go to King Ahab and tell him to get in his chariot and go back home before the rain stops him."

45 In a little while the sky was covered with dark clouds, the wind began to blow, and a heavy rain began to fall. Ahab got in his chariot and started back to Jezreel. 46 The power of the LORD came on Elijah; he fastened his clothes tight around his waist and ran ahead of Ahab all the way to Jezreel.

Elijah on Mount Sinai

19 King Ahab told his wife Jezebel everything that Elijah had done and how he had put all the prophets of Baal to death. 2 She sent a message to Elijah: "May the gods strike me dead if by this time tomorrow I don't do the same thing to you that you did to the prophets." 3 Elijah was afraid and fled for his life; he took his servant and went to Beersheba in Judah.

Leaving the servant there, 4 Elijah walked a whole day into the wilderness. He stopped and sat down in the shade of a tree and wished he would die. "It's too much, LORD," he prayed. "Take away my life; I might as well be dead!"

5 He lay down under the tree and fell asleep. Suddenly an angel touched him and said, "Wake up and eat." 6 He looked around and saw a loaf of bread and a jar of water near his head. He ate and drank, and lay down again. 7 The LORD's angel returned and woke him up a second time, saying, "Get up and eat, or the trip will be too much for you." 8 Elijah got up, ate and drank, and the food gave him enough strength to walk forty days to Sinai, the holy mountain. 9 There he went into a cave to spend the night.

Suddenly the LORD spoke to him, "Elijah, what are you doing here?"

10 He answered, "LORD God Almighty, I have always served you — you alone. But the people of Israel have broken their covenant with you, torn down your altars, and killed all your prophets. I am

the only one left — and they are trying to kill me!"

11 "Go out and stand before me on top of the mountain," the LORD said to him. Then the LORD passed by and sent a furious wind that split the hills and shattered the rocks — but the LORD was not in the wind. The wind stopped blowing, and then there was an earthquake — but the LORD was not in the earthquake. 12 After the earthquake there was a fire — but the LORD was not in the fire. And after the fire there was the soft whisper of a voice.

13 When Elijah heard it, he covered his face with his cloak and went out and stood at the entrance of the cave. A voice said to him, "Elijah, what are you doing here?"

14 He answered, "LORD God Almighty, I have always served you — you alone. But the people of Israel have broken their covenant with you, torn down your altars, and killed all your prophets. I am the only one left — and they are trying to kill me."

15 The LORD said, "Return to the wilderness near Damascus, then enter the city and anoint Hazael as king of Syria; 16 anoint Jehu son of Nimshi as king of Israel, and anoint Elisha son of Shaphat from Abel Meholah to succeed you as prophet. 17 Anyone who escapes being put to death by Hazael will be killed by Jehu, and anyone who escapes Jehu will be killed by Elisha. 18 Yet I will leave seven thousand people alive in Israel — all those who are loyal to me and have not bowed to Baal or kissed his idol."

The Call of Elisha

19 Elijah left and found Elisha plowing with a team of oxen; there were eleven teams ahead of him, and he was plowing with the last one. Elijah took off his cloak and put it on Elisha. 20 Elisha then left his oxen, ran after Elijah, and said, "Let me kiss my father and mother goodbye, and then I will go with you."

Elijah answered, "All right, go back. I'm not stopping you!"v

21 Then Elisha went to his team of oxen, killed them, and cooked the meat, using the yoke as fuel for the fire. He gave the meat to the people, and they ate

v All right . . . you; or Go on, but come back, because what I have just done to you is important.

it. Then he went and followed Elijah as his helper.

War with Syria

20 King Benhadad of Syria gathered all his troops, and supported by thirty-two other rulers with their horses and chariots, he marched up, laid siege to Samaria, and launched attacks against it. ²He sent messengers into the city to King Ahab of Israel to say, "King Benhadad demands that ³you surrender to him your silver and gold, your women and the strongest of your children."

⁴"Tell my lord, King Benhadad, that I agree; he can have me and everything I own," Ahab answered.

⁵Later the messengers came back to Ahab with another demand from Benhadad: "I sent you word that you were to hand over to me your silver and gold, your women and your children. ⁶Now, however, I will send my officers to search your palace and the homes of your officials, and to take everything theyʷ consider valuable. They will be there about this time tomorrow."

⁷King Ahab called in all the leaders of the country and said, "You see that this man wants to ruin us. He sent me a message demanding my wives and children, my silver and gold, and I agreed."

⁸The leaders and the people answered, "Don't pay any attention to him; don't give in."

⁹So Ahab replied to Benhadad's messengers, "Tell my lord the king that I agreed to his first demand, but I cannot agree to the second."

The messengers left and then returned with another message ¹⁰from Benhadad: "I will bring enough men to destroy this city of yours and carry off the rubble in their hands. May the gods strike me dead if I don't!"

¹¹King Ahab answered, "Tell King Benhadad that a real soldier does his bragging *after* a battle, not before it."

¹²Benhadad received Ahab's answer as he and his allies, the other rulers, were drinking in their tents. He ordered his men to get ready to attack the city, and so they moved into position.

¹³Meanwhile, a prophet went to King Ahab and said, "The Lord says, 'Don't be afraid of that huge army! I will give you victory over it today, and you will know that I am the Lord.'"

¹⁴"Who will lead the attack?" Ahab asked.

The prophet answered, "The Lord says that the young soldiers under the command of the district governors are to do it."

"Who will command the main force?" the king asked.

"You," the prophet answered.

¹⁵So the king called out the young soldiers who were under the district commanders, 232 in all. Then he called out the Israelite army, a total of seven thousand men.

¹⁶The attack began at noon, as Benhadad and his thirty-two allies were getting drunk in their tents. ¹⁷The young soldiers advanced first. Scouts sent out by Benhadad reported to him that a group of soldiers was coming out of Samaria. ¹⁸He ordered, "Take them alive, no matter whether they are coming to fight or to ask for peace."

¹⁹The young soldiers led the attack, followed by the Israelite army, ²⁰and each one killed the man he fought. The Syrians fled, with the Israelites in hot pursuit, but Benhadad escaped on horseback, accompanied by some of the cavalry. ²¹King Ahab took to the field, capturedˣ the horses and chariots, and inflicted a severe defeat on the Syrians.

²²Then the prophet went to King Ahab and said, "Go back and build up your forces and make careful plans, because the king of Syria will attack again next spring."

The Second Syrian Attack

²³King Benhadad's officials said to him, "The gods of Israel are mountain gods, and that is why the Israelites defeated us. But we will certainly defeat them if we fight them in the plains. ²⁴Now, remove the thirty-two rulers from their commands and replace them with field commanders. ²⁵Then call up an army as large as the one that deserted you, with the same number of horses and chariots. We will fight the Israelites

---

ʷ *Some ancient translations* they; *Hebrew* you.
destroyed.

ˣ *One ancient translation* captured; *Hebrew*

in the plains, and this time we will defeat them."

King Benhadad agreed and followed their advice. 26 The following spring he called up his men and marched with them to the city of Aphek to attack the Israelites. 27 The Israelites were called up and equipped; they marched out and camped in two groups facing the Syrians. The Israelites looked like two small flocks of goats compared to the Syrians, who spread out over the countryside.

28 A prophet went to King Ahab and said, "This is what the LORD says: 'Because the Syrians say that I am a god of the hills and not of the plains, I will give you victory over their huge army, and you and your people will know that I am the LORD.' "

29 For seven days the Syrians and the Israelites stayed in their camps, facing each other. On the seventh day they started fighting, and the Israelites killed a hundred thousand Syrians. 30 The survivors fled into the city of Aphek, where the city walls fell on twenty-seven thousand of them.

Benhadad also escaped into the city and took refuge in the back room of a house. 31 His officials went to him and said, "We have heard that the Israelite kings are merciful. Give us permission to go to the king of Israel with sackcloth around our waists and ropes around our necks, and maybe he will spare your life." 32 So they wrapped sackcloth around their waists and ropes around their necks, went to Ahab and said, "Your servant Benhadad pleads with you for his life."

Ahab answered, "Is he still alive? Good! He's like a brother to me!"

33 Benhadad's officials were watching for a good sign, and when Ahab said "brother," they took it up at once, and said, "As you say, Benhadad is your brother!"

"Bring him to me," Ahab ordered. When Benhadad arrived, Ahab invited him to get in the chariot with him. 34 Benhadad said to him, "I will restore to you the towns my father took from your father, and you may set up a commercial center for yourself in Damascus, just as my father did in Samaria."

Ahab replied, "On these terms, then, I will set you free." He made a treaty with him and let him go.

A Prophet Condemns Ahab

35 At the LORD's command a member of a group of prophets ordered a fellow prophet to hit him. But he refused, 36 so he said to him, "Because you have disobeyed the LORD's command, a lion will kill you as soon as you leave me." And as soon as he left, a lion came along and killed him.

37 Then this same prophet went to another man and said, "Hit me!" This man did so; he hit him a hard blow and hurt him. 38 The prophet bandaged his face with a cloth, to disguise himself, and went and stood by the road, waiting for the king of Israel to pass. 39 As the king was passing by, the prophet called out to him and said, "Your Majesty, I was fighting in the battle when a soldier brought a captured enemy to me and said, 'Guard this man; if he escapes, you will pay for it with your life or else pay a fine of three thousand pieces of silver.' 40 But I got busy with other things, and the man escaped."

The king answered, "You have pronounced your own sentence, and you will have to pay the penalty."

41 The prophet tore the cloth from his face, and at once the king recognized him as one of the prophets. 42 The prophet then said to the king, "This is the word of the LORD: 'Because you allowed the man to escape whom I had ordered to be killed, you will pay for it with your life, and your army will be destroyed for letting his army escape.' "

43 The king went back home to Samaria, worried and depressed.

Naboth's Vineyard

21 Near King Ahab's palace in Jezreel there was a vineyard owned by a man named Naboth. 2 One day Ahab said to Naboth, "Let me have your vineyard; it is close to my palace, and I want to use the land for a vegetable garden. I will give you a better vineyard for it or, if you prefer, I will pay you a fair price."

3 "I inherited this vineyard from my ancestors," Naboth replied. "The LORD forbid that I should let you have it!"

4 Ahab went home, depressed and angry over what Naboth had said to him. He lay down on his bed, facing the wall, and would not eat. 5 His wife Jezebel

went to him and asked, "Why are you so depressed? Why won't you eat?"

6 He answered, "Because of what Naboth said to me. I offered to buy his vineyard or, if he preferred, to give him another one for it, but he told me that I couldn't have it!"

7 "Well, are you the king or aren't you?" Jezebel replied. "Get out of bed, cheer up, and eat. I will get you Naboth's vineyard!"

8 Then she wrote some letters, signed Ahab's name to them, sealed them with his seal, and sent them to the officials and leading citizens of Jezreel. 9 The letters said: "Proclaim a day of fasting, call the people together, and give Naboth the place of honor. 10 Get a couple of scoundrels to accuse him to his face of cursing God and the king. Then take him out of the city and stone him to death."

11 The officials and leading citizens of Jezreel did what Jezebel had commanded. 12 They proclaimed a day of fasting, called the people together, and gave Naboth the place of honor. 13 The two scoundrels publicly accused him of cursing God and the king, and so he was taken outside the city and stoned to death. 14 The message was sent to Jezebel: "Naboth has been put to death."

15 As soon as Jezebel received the message, she said to Ahab, "Naboth is dead. Now go and take possession of the vineyard which he refused to sell to you." 16 At once Ahab went to the vineyard to take possession of it.

17 Then the LORD said to Elijah, the prophet from Tishbe, 18 "Go to King Ahab of Samaria. You will find him in Naboth's vineyard, about to take possession of it. 19 Tell him that I, the LORD, say to him, 'After murdering the man, are you taking over his property as well?' Tell him that this is what I say: 'In the very place that the dogs licked up Naboth's blood they will lick up your blood!'"

20 When Ahab saw Elijah, he said, "Have you caught up with me, my enemy?"

"Yes, I have," Elijah answered. "You have devoted yourself completely to doing what is wrong in the LORD's sight. 21 So the LORD says to you, 'I will bring disaster on you. I will do away with you and get rid of every male in your family, young and old alike. 22 Your family will become like the family of King Jeroboam son of Nebat and like the family of King Baasha son of Ahijah, because you have stirred up my anger by leading Israel into sin.' 23 And concerning Jezebel, the LORD says that dogs will eat her body in the city of Jezreel. 24 Any of your relatives who die in the city will be eaten by dogs, and any who die in the open country will be eaten by vultures."

(25 There was no one else who had devoted himself so completely to doing wrong in the LORD's sight as Ahab—all at the urging of his wife Jezebel. 26 He committed the most shameful sins by worshiping idols, as the Amorites had done, whom the LORD had driven out of the land as the people of Israel advanced.)

27 When Elijah finished speaking, Ahab tore his clothes, took them off, and put on sackcloth. He refused food, slept in the sackcloth, and went about gloomy and depressed.

28 The LORD said to the prophet Elijah, 29 "Have you noticed how Ahab has humbled himself before me? Since he has done this, I will not bring disaster on him during his lifetime; it will be during his son's lifetime that I will bring disaster on Ahab's family."

The Prophet Micaiah Warns Ahab
(2 Chronicles 18.2-27)

22 There was peace between Israel and Syria for the next two years, 2 but in the third year King Jehoshaphat of Judah went to see King Ahab of Israel.

3 Ahab asked his officials, "Why is it that we have not done anything to get back Ramoth in Gilead from the king of Syria? It belongs to us!" 4 And Ahab asked Jehoshaphat, "Will you go with me to attack Ramoth?"

"I am ready when you are," Jehoshaphat answered, "and so are my soldiers and my cavalry. 5 But first let's consult the LORD."

6 So Ahab called in the prophets, about four hundred of them, and asked them, "Should I go and attack Ramoth, or not?"

"Attack it," they answered. "The Lord will give you victory."

7 But Jehoshaphat asked, "Isn't there another prophet through whom we can consult the LORD?"

8 Ahab answered, "There is one more, Micaiah son of Imlah. But I hate him because he never prophesies anything good for me; it's always something bad."

"You shouldn't say that!" Jehoshaphat replied.

9 Then Ahab called in a court official and told him to go and get Micaiah at once.

10 The two kings, dressed in their royal robes, were sitting on their thrones at the threshing place just outside the gate of Samaria, and all the prophets were prophesying in front of them. 11 One of them, Zedekiah son of Chenaanah, made iron horns and said to Ahab, "This is what the LORD says: 'With these you will fight the Syrians and totally defeat them.' " 12 All the other prophets said the same thing. "March against Ramoth and you will win," they said. "The LORD will give you victory."

13 Meanwhile, the official who had gone to get Micaiah said to him, "All the other prophets have prophesied success for the king, and you had better do the same."

14 But Micaiah answered, "By the living LORD I promise that I will say what he tells me to!"

15 When he appeared before King Ahab, the king asked him, "Micaiah, should King Jehoshaphat and I go and attack Ramoth, or not?"

"Attack!" Micaiah answered. "Of course you'll win. The LORD will give you victory."

16 But Ahab replied, "When you speak to me in the name of the LORD, tell the truth! How many times do I have to tell you that?"

17 Micaiah answered, "I can see the army of Israel scattered over the hills like sheep without a shepherd. And the LORD said, 'These men have no leader; let them go home in peace.' "

18 Ahab said to Jehoshaphat, "Didn't I tell you that he never prophesies anything good for me? It's always something bad!"

19 Micaiah went on: "Now listen to what the LORD says! I saw the LORD sitting on his throne in heaven, with all his angels standing beside him. 20 The LORD asked, 'Who will deceive Ahab so that he will go and be killed at Ramoth?' Some of the angels said one thing, and others said something else, 21 until a spirit stepped forward, approached the LORD, and said, 'I will deceive him.' 22 'How?' the LORD asked. The spirit replied, 'I will go and make all of Ahab's prophets tell lies.' The LORD said, 'Go and deceive him. You will succeed.' "

23 And Micaiah concluded: "This is what has happened. The LORD has made these prophets of yours lie to you. But he himself has decreed that you will meet with disaster!"

24 Then the prophet Zedekiah went up to Micaiah, slapped his face, and asked, "Since when did the LORD's spirit leave me and speak to you?"

25 "You will find out when you go into some back room to hide," Micaiah replied.

26 Then King Ahab ordered one of his officers, "Arrest Micaiah and take him to Amon, the governor of the city, and to Prince Joash. 27 Tell them to throw him in prison and to put him on bread and water until I return safely."

28 "If you return safely," Micaiah exclaimed, "then the LORD has not spoken through me!" And he added, "Listen, everyone, to what I have said!"

The Death of Ahab
(2 Chronicles 18.28-34)

29 Then King Ahab of Israel and King Jehoshaphat of Judah went to attack the city of Ramoth in Gilead. 30 Ahab said to Jehoshaphat, "As we go into battle, I will disguise myself, but you wear your royal garments." So the king of Israel went into battle in disguise.

31 The king of Syria had ordered his thirty-two chariot commanders to attack no one else except the king of Israel. 32 So when they saw King Jehoshaphat, they all thought that he was the king of Israel, and they turned to attack him. But when he cried out, 33 they realized that he was not the king of Israel, and they stopped their attack. 34 By chance, however, a Syrian soldier shot an arrow which struck King Ahab between the joints of his armor. "I'm wounded!" he cried out to his chariot driver. "Turn around and pull out of the battle!"

35 While the battle raged on, King Ahab remained propped up in his chariot, facing the Syrians. The blood from his wound ran down and covered the bottom of the chariot, and at evening he

1
K
I
N
G
S

died. 36 Near sunset the order went out through the Israelite ranks: "Each of you go back to your own country and city!"

37 So died King Ahab. His body was taken to Samaria and buried. 38 His chariot was cleaned up at the pool of Samaria, where dogs licked up his blood and prostitutes washed themselves, as the LORD had said would happen.

39 Everything else that King Ahab did, including an account of his palace decorated with ivory and of all the cities he built, is recorded in The History of the Kings of Israel. 40 At his death his son Ahaziah succeeded him as king.

King Jehoshaphat of Judah

(2 Chronicles 20.31 — 21.1)

41 In the fourth year of the reign of King Ahab of Israel, Jehoshaphat son of Asa became king of Judah 42 at the age of thirty-five, and he ruled in Jerusalem for twenty-five years. His mother was Azubah, the daughter of Shilhi. 43 Like his father Asa before him, he did what was right in the sight of the LORD; but the places of worship were not destroyed, and the people continued to offer sacrifices and burn incense there. 44 Jehoshaphat made peace with the king of Israel.

45 Everything else that Jehoshaphat did, all his bravery and his battles, are recorded in The History of the Kings of Judah. 46 He got rid of all the male and female prostitutes serving at the pagan altars who were still left from the days of his father Asa.

47 The land of Edom had no king; it was ruled by a deputy appointed by the king of Judah.

48 King Jehoshaphat had ocean-going ships built to sail to the land of Ophir for gold; but they were wrecked at Eziongeber and never sailed. 49 Then King Ahaziah of Israel offered to let his men sail with Jehoshaphat's men, but Jehoshaphat refused the offer.

50 Jehoshaphat died and was buried in the royal tombs in David's City, and his son Jehoram succeeded him as king.

King Ahaziah of Israel

51 In the seventeenth year of the reign of King Jehoshaphat of Judah, Ahaziah son of Ahab became king of Israel, and he ruled in Samaria for two years. 52 He sinned against the LORD, following the wicked example of his father Ahab, his mother Jezebel, and King Jeroboam, who had led Israel into sin. 53 He worshiped and served Baal, and like his father before him, he aroused the anger of the LORD, the God of Israel.

The Second Book of

KINGS

Introduction

Second Kings *continues the history of the two Israelite kingdoms where* First Kings *leaves off. The book may be divided into two parts: 1) The story of the two kingdoms from the middle of the ninth century B.C. down to the fall of Samaria and the end of the northern kingdom in 722 B.C. 2) The story of the kingdom of Judah from the fall of the kingdom of Israel down to the capture and destruction of Jerusalem by King Nebuchadnezzar of Babylonia in 586 B.C. The book ends with an account of Gedaliah as governor of Judah under the Babylonians and a report of the release of King Jehoiachin of Judah from prison in Babylon.*

These national disasters took place because of the unfaithfulness of the kings and people of Israel and Judah. The destruction of Jerusalem and the exile of many of the people of Judah was one of the great turning points of Israelite history.

The prophet who stands out in Second Kings is Elijah's successor Elisha.

Outline of Contents

Elijah and King Ahaziah

1 After the death of King Ahab of Israel the country of Moab rebelled against Israel.

2 King Ahaziah of Israel fell off the balcony on the roof of his palace in Samaria and was seriously injured. So he sent some messengers to consult Baalzebub, the god of the Philistine city of Ekron, in order to find out whether or not he would recover. 3 But an angel of the LORD commanded Elijah, the prophet from Tishbe, to go and meet the messengers of King Ahaziah and ask them, "Why are you going to consult Baalzebub, the god of Ekron? Is it because you think there is no god in Israel? 4 Tell the king that the LORD says, 'You will not recover from your injuries; you will die!' "

Elijah did as the LORD commanded, 5 and the messengers returned to the king. "Why have you come back?" he asked.

6 They answered, "We were met by a man who told us to come back and tell you that the LORD says to you, 'Why are you sending messengers to consult Baalzebub, the god of Ekron? Is it because you think there is no god in Israel? You will not recover from your injuries; you will die!' "

7 "What did the man look like?" the king asked.

8 "He was wearing a cloak made of animal skins, tied with[a] a leather belt," they answered.

"It's Elijah!" the king exclaimed.

9 Then he sent an officer with fifty men to get Elijah. The officer found him sitting on a hill and said to him, "Man of God, the king orders you to come down."

10 "If I am a man of God," Elijah answered, "may fire come down from heaven and kill you and your men!" At once fire came down and killed the officer and his men.

11 The king sent another officer with fifty men, who went up[b] and said to Elijah, "Man of God, the king orders you to come down at once!"

12 "If I am a man of God," Elijah answered, "may fire come down from heaven and kill you and your men!" At once the fire of God came down and killed the officer and his men.

13 Once more the king sent an officer with fifty men. He went up the hill, fell on his knees in front of Elijah, and pleaded, "Man of God, be merciful to me and my men. Spare our lives! 14 The two other officers and their men were killed by fire from heaven; but please be merciful to me!"

15 The angel of the LORD said to Elijah, "Go down with him, and don't be afraid." So Elijah went with the officer to the king 16 and said to him, "This is what the LORD says: 'Because you sent messengers to consult Baalzebub, the god of Ekron — as if there were no god in Israel to consult — you will not get well; you will die!' "

17 Ahaziah died, as the LORD had said through Elijah. Ahaziah had no sons, so his brother[c] Joram succeeded him as king in the second year of the reign of Jehoram son of Jehoshaphat, king of Judah.

18 Everything else that King Ahaziah did is recorded in *The History of the Kings of Israel.*

Elijah Is Taken Up to Heaven

2 The time came for the LORD to take Elijah up to heaven in a whirlwind. Elijah and Elisha set out from Gilgal,

---

a was wearing . . . with; or was a hairy man and wore.   b One ancient translation went up; Hebrew answered.   c Some ancient translations his brother; Hebrew does not have these words.

THE JORDAN RIVER

The Jordan River has such an important role in biblical history that many visitors to the Holy Land ask to be baptized in its waters near Jericho, where Jesus was baptized by John (Mt 3.13).

This famous river begins as a small stream in the foothills of Mount Hermon near Caesarea Philippi (now called Banias), then passes through the Sea of Galilee, and finally ends in the Dead Sea in southern Palestine. Popularly, the name *Jordan* is thought to mean descender or the river that rushes down, which it does at the rate of 25 feet per mile along its twisting 100-mile journey. Its descent ranges from about 1,200 feet above sea level to about 1,286 feet below sea level. The place where it enters the Dead Sea is the lowest point on earth.

Through the centuries, the Jordan has served as a natural boundary between Palestine and other nations. In the period between the Old Testament and the New Testament, the Jordan River formed the main eastern boundary of the Persian and Greek province of Judea. The Decapolis, a federation of ten Greek cities, was formed on the eastern side of the Jordan in the Greek period.

The Old Testament speaks of the Jordan as the site of the land favored by Lot (Gn 13.10, 11); the place where Israel would cross into the land of Canaan in Joshua's time (Dt 3.20, 25, 27); and the scene of events in Elijah's and Elisha's lives (1 K 17.2-5; 2 K 2.13-15).

Because the Jordan is a short and rather shallow river, it was compared unfavorably by Naaman the leper to the two larger rivers in his homeland of Syria. When the prophet Elisha directed him to dip in the Jordan to be healed of his leprosy, he replied, "Aren't the rivers Abana and Pharpar, back in Damascus, better than Israel? I could have washed in them and been cured" (2 K 5.12).

But his servants persuaded him to do as Elisha asked, and Naaman was healed.

2 and on the way Elijah said to Elisha, "Now stay here; the LORD has ordered me to go to Bethel."

But Elisha answered, "I swear by my loyalty to the living LORD and to you that I will not leave you." So they went on to Bethel.

3 A group of prophets who lived there went to Elisha and asked him, "Do you know that the LORD is going to take your master away from you today?"

"Yes, I know," Elisha answered. "But let's not talk about it."

4 Then Elijah said to Elisha, "Now stay here; the LORD has ordered me to go to Jericho."

But Elisha answered, "I swear by my loyalty to the living LORD and to you that I will not leave you." So they went on to Jericho.

5 A group of prophets who lived there went to Elisha and asked him, "Do you know that the LORD is going to take your master away from you today?"

"Yes, I know," Elisha answered. "But let's not talk about it."

6 Then Elijah said to Elisha, "Now stay here; the LORD has ordered me to go to the Jordan River."

But Elisha answered, "I swear by my loyalty to the living LORD and to you that I will not leave you." So they went on, 7 and fifty of the prophets followed them to the Jordan. Elijah and Elisha stopped by the river, and the fifty prophets stood a short distance away. 8 Then Elijah took off his cloak, rolled it up, and struck the water with it; the water divided, and he and Elisha crossed to the other side on dry ground. 9 There, Elijah said to Elisha, "Tell me what you want me to do for you before I am taken away."

"Let me receive the share of your power that will make me your successor,"d Elisha answered.

10 "That is a difficult request to grant," Elijah replied. "But you will receive it if you see me as I am being taken away from you; if you don't see me, you won't receive it."

11 They kept talking as they walked on; then suddenly a chariot of fire pulled by horses of fire came between them, and Elijah was taken up to heaven by a whirlwind. 12 Elisha saw it and cried out

to Elijah, "My father, my father! Mighty defender of Israel! You are gone!" And he never saw Elijah again.

In grief Elisha tore his cloak in two. 13 Then he picked up Elijah's cloak that had fallen from him, and went back and stood on the bank of the Jordan. 14 He struck the water with Elijah's cloak and said, "Where is the LORD, the God of Elijah?" Then he struck the water again, and it divided, and he walked over to the other side. 15 The fifty prophets from Jericho saw him and said, "The power of Elijah is on Elisha!" They went to meet him, bowed down before him, 16 and said, "There are fifty of us here, all strong men. Let us go and look for your master. Maybe the spirit of the LORD has carried him away and left him on some mountain or in some valley."

"No, you must not go," Elisha answered.

17 But they insisted until he gave in and let them go. The fifty of them went and looked high and low for Elijah for three days, but didn't find him. 18 Then they returned to Elisha, who had waited at Jericho, and he said to them, "Didn't I tell you not to go?"

Miracles of Elisha

19 Some men from Jericho went to Elisha and said, "As you know, sir, this is a fine city, but the water is bad and causes miscarriages."

20 "Put some salt in a new bowl and bring it to me," he ordered. They brought it to him, 21 and he went to the spring, threw the salt in the water, and said, "This is what the LORD says: 'I make this water pure, and it will not cause any more deaths or miscarriages.' " 22 And that water has been pure ever since, just as Elisha said it would be.

23 Elisha left Jericho to go to Bethel, and on the way some boys came out of a town and made fun of him. "Get out of here, baldy!" they shouted.

24 Elisha turned around, glared at them, and cursed them in the name of the LORD. Then two she-bears came out of the woods and tore forty-two of the boys to pieces.

25 Elisha went on to Mount Carmel and later returned to Samaria.

d THE SHARE . . . SUCCESSOR: Elisha asked for the share that the first-born son inherited by law from his father (see Dt 21.17).

War between Israel and Moab

3 In the eighteenth year of the reign of King Jehoshaphat of Judah, Joram son of Ahab became king of Israel, and he ruled in Samaria for twelve years. 2 He sinned against the Lord, but he was not as bad as his father or his mother Jezebel; he pulled down the image his father had made for the worship of Baal. 3 Yet, like King Jeroboam son of Nebat before him, he led Israel into sin and would not stop.

4 King Mesha of Moab raised sheep, and every year he gave as tribute to the king of Israel 100,000 lambs and the wool from 100,000 sheep. 5 But when King Ahab of Israel died, Mesha rebelled against Israel. 6 At once King Joram left Samaria and gathered all his troops. 7 He sent word to King Jehoshaphat of Judah: "The king of Moab has rebelled against me; will you join me in war against him?"

"I will," King Jehoshaphat replied. "I am at your disposal, and so are my men and my horses. 8 What route shall we take for the attack?"

"We will go the long way through the wilderness of Edom," Joram answered.

9 So King Joram and the kings of Judah and Edom set out. After marching seven days, they ran out of water, and there was none left for the men or the pack animals. 10 "We're done for!" King Joram exclaimed. "The Lord has put the three of us at the mercy of the king of Moab!"

11 King Jehoshaphat asked, "Is there a prophet here through whom we can consult the Lord?"

An officer of King Joram's forces answered, "Elisha son of Shaphat is here. He was Elijah's assistant."

12 "He is a true prophet," King Jehoshaphat said. So the three kings went to Elisha.

13 "Why should I help you?" Elisha said to the king of Israel. "Go and consult those prophets that your father and mother consulted."

"No!" Joram replied. "It is the Lord who has put us three kings at the mercy of the king of Moab."

14 Elisha answered, "By the living Lord, whom I serve, I swear that I would

have nothing to do with you if I didn't respect your ally, King Jehoshaphat of Judah. 15 Now get me a musician."

As the musician played his harp, the power of the Lord came on Elisha, 16 and he said, "This is what the Lord says: 'Dig ditches all over this dry stream bed. 17 Even though you will not see any rain or wind, this stream bed will be filled with water, and you, your livestock, and your pack animals will have plenty to drink.' " 18 And Elisha continued, "But this is an easy thing for the Lord to do; he will also give you victory over the Moabites. 19 You will conquer all their beautiful fortified cities; you will cut down all their fruit trees, stop all their springs, and ruin all their fertile fields by covering them with stones."

20 The next morning, at the time of the regular morning sacrifice, water came flowing from the direction of Edom and covered the ground.

21 When the Moabites heard that the three kings had come to attack them, all the men who could bear arms, from the oldest to the youngest, were called out and stationed at the border. 22 When they got up the following morning, the sun was shining on the water, making it look as red as blood. 23 "It's blood!" they exclaimed. "The three enemy armies must have fought and killed each other! Let's go and loot their camp!"

24 But when they reached the camp, the Israelites attacked them and drove them back. The Israelites kept up the pursuit,e slaughtering the Moabites 25 and destroying their cities. As they passed by a fertile field, every Israelite would throw a stone on it until finally all the fields were covered; they also stopped up the springs and cut down the fruit trees. At last only the capital city of Kir Heresf was left, and the slingers surrounded it and attacked it.

26 When the king of Moab realized that he was losing the battle, he took seven hundred swordsmen with him and tried to force his way through the enemy lines and escape to the king of Syria,g but he failed. 27 So he took his oldest son, who was to succeed him as king, and offered him on the city wall as a sacrifice to the god of Moab. The Israelites were terri-

---

e *One ancient translation* kept up the pursuit; *Hebrew unclear.* f *Probable text only the* capital city of Kir Heres; *Hebrew unclear.* g *One ancient translation* Syria; *Hebrew* Edom.

fied[h] and so they drew back from the city and returned to their own country.

Elisha Helps a Poor Widow

4 The widow of a member of a group of prophets went to Elisha and said, "Sir, my husband has died! As you know, he was a God-fearing man, but now a man he owed money to has come to take away my two sons as slaves in payment for my husband's debt."

2 "What shall I do for you?" he asked. "Tell me, what do you have at home?"

"Nothing at all, except a small jar of olive oil," she answered.

3 "Go to your neighbors and borrow as many empty jars as you can," Elisha told her. 4 "Then you and your sons go into the house, close the door, and start pouring oil into the jars. Set each one aside as soon as it is full."

5 So the woman went into her house with her sons, closed the door, took the small jar of olive oil, and poured oil into the jars as her sons brought them to her. 6 When they had filled all the jars, she asked if there were any more. "That was the last one," one of her sons answered. And the olive oil stopped flowing. 7 She went back to Elisha, the prophet, who said to her, "Sell the olive oil and pay all your debts, and there will be enough money left over for you and your sons to live on."

Elisha and the Rich Woman from Shunem

8 One day Elisha went to Shunem, where a rich woman lived. She invited him to a meal, and from then on every time he went to Shunem he would have his meals at her house. 9 She said to her husband, "I am sure that this man who comes here so often is a holy man. 10 Let's build a small room on the roof, put a bed, a table, a chair, and a lamp in it, and he can stay there whenever he visits us."

11 One day Elisha returned to Shunem and went up to his room to rest. 12 He told his servant Gehazi to go and call the woman. When she came, 13 he said to Gehazi, "Ask her what I can do for her in return for all the trouble she has had in providing for our needs. Maybe she would like me to go to the king or the army commander and put in a good word for her."

"I have all I need here among my own people," she answered.

14 Elisha asked Gehazi, "What can I do for her then?"

He answered, "Well, she has no son, and her husband is an old man."

15 "Tell her to come here," Elisha ordered. She came and stood in the doorway, 16 and Elisha said to her, "By this time next year you will be holding a son in your arms."

"Oh!" she exclaimed. "Please, sir, don't lie to me. You are a man of God!"

17 But, as Elisha had said, at about that time the following year she gave birth to a son.

18 Some years later, at harvest time, the boy went out one morning to join his father, who was in the field with the harvest workers. 19 Suddenly he cried out to his father, "My head hurts! My head hurts!"

"Carry the boy to his mother," the father said to a servant. 20 The servant carried the boy back to his mother, who held him in her lap until noon, at which time he died. 21 She carried him up to Elisha's room, put him on the bed and left, closing the door behind her. 22 Then she called her husband and said to him, "Send a servant here with a donkey. I need to go to the prophet Elisha. I'll be back as soon as I can."

23 "Why do you have to go today?" her husband asked. "It's neither a Sabbath nor a New Moon Festival."[i]

"Never mind," she answered. 24 Then she had the donkey saddled, and ordered the servant, "Make the donkey go as fast as it can, and don't slow down unless I tell you to." 25 So she set out and went to Mount Carmel, where Elisha was.

Elisha saw her coming while she was still some distance away, and he said to his servant Gehazi, "Look, there comes the woman from Shunem! 26 Hurry to her and find out if everything is all right with her, her husband, and her son."

She told Gehazi that everything was all right, 27 but when she came to Elisha, she bowed down before him and took

---

[h] TERRIFIED, *either because of what Chemosh, the god of the Moabites, might do, or because of what the* LORD, *the God of the Israelites, might do.*   [i] SABBATH ... NEW MOON FESTIVAL: *Such holy days were thought to be the best time to consult a prophet.*

hold of his feet. Gehazi was about to push her away, but Elisha said, "Leave her alone. Can't you see she's deeply distressed? And the LORD has not told me a thing about it."

28 The woman said to him, "Sir, did I ask you for a son? Didn't I tell you not to get my hopes up?"

29 Elisha turned to Gehazi and said, "Hurry! Take my walking stick and go. Don't stop to greet anyone you meet, and if anyone greets you, don't take time to answer. Go straight to the house and hold my stick over the boy."

30 The woman said to Elisha, "I swear by my loyalty to the living LORD and to you that I will not leave you!" So the two of them started back together. 31 Gehazi went on ahead and held Elisha's stick over the child, but there was no sound or any other sign of life. So he went back to meet Elisha and said, "The boy didn't wake up."

32 When Elisha arrived, he went alone into the room and saw the boy lying dead on the bed. 33 He closed the door and prayed to the LORD. 34 Then he lay down on the boy, placing his mouth, eyes, and hands on the boy's mouth, eyes, and hands. As he lay stretched out over the boy, the boy's body started to get warm. 35 Elisha got up, walked around the room, and then went back and again stretched himself over the boy. The boy sneezed seven times and then opened his eyes. 36 Elisha called Gehazi and told him to call the boy's mother. When she came in, he said to her, "Here's your son." 37 She fell at Elisha's feet, with her face touching the ground; then she took her son and left.

Two More Miracles

38 Once, when there was a famine throughout the land, Elisha returned to Gilgal. While he was teaching a group of prophets, he told his servant to put a big pot on the fire and make some stew for them. 39 One of them went out in the fields to get some herbs. He found a wild vine and picked as many gourds as he could carry. He brought them back and sliced them up into the stew, not knowing what they were. 40 The stew was poured out for the men to eat, but as soon as they tasted it they exclaimed to Elisha, "It's poisoned!"—and wouldn't eat it. 41 Elisha asked for some meal, threw it into the pot, and said, "Pour out some more stew for them." And then there was nothing wrong with it.

42 Another time, a man came from Baal Shalishah, bringing Elisha twenty loaves of bread made from the first barley harvested that year, and some freshly-cut heads of grain. Elisha told his servant to feed the group of prophets with this, 43 but he answered, "Do you think this is enough for a hundred men?"

Elisha replied, "Give it to them to eat, because the LORD says that they will eat and still have some left over." 44 So the servant set the food before them, and as the LORD had said, they all ate, and there was still some left over.

Naaman Is Cured

5 Naaman, the commander of the Syrian army, was highly respected and esteemed by the king of Syria, because through Naaman the LORD had given victory to the Syrian forces. He was a great soldier, but he suffered from a dreaded skin disease. 2 In one of their raids against Israel, the Syrians had carried off a little Israelite girl, who became a servant of Naaman's wife. 3 One day she said to her mistress, "I wish that my master could go to the prophet who lives in Samaria! He would cure him of his disease." 4 When Naaman heard of this, he went to the king and told him what the girl had said. 5 The king said, "Go to the king of Israel and take this letter to him."

So Naaman set out, taking thirty thousand pieces of silver, six thousand pieces of gold, and ten changes of fine clothes. 6 The letter that he took read: "This letter will introduce my officer Naaman. I want you to cure him of his disease."

7 When the king of Israel read the letter, he tore his clothes in dismay and exclaimed, "How can the king of Syria expect me to cure this man? Does he think that I am God,*j* with the power of life and death? It's plain that he is trying to start a quarrel with me!"

8 When the prophet Elisha heard what had happened, he sent word to the king:

---

j God; or a god.

"Why are you so upset? Send the man to me, and I'll show him that there is a prophet in Israel!"

9 So Naaman went with his horses and chariot and stopped at the entrance to Elisha's house. 10 Elisha sent a servant out to tell him to go and wash himself seven times in the Jordan River, and he would be completely cured of his disease. 11 But Naaman left in a rage, saying, "I thought that he would at least come out to me, pray to the Lord his God, wave his hand over the diseased spot,*k* and cure me! 12 Besides, aren't the rivers Abana and Pharpar, back in Damascus, better than any river in Israel? I could have washed in them and been cured!"

13 His servants went up to him and said, "Sir, if the prophet had told you to do something difficult, you would have done it. Now why can't you just wash yourself, as he said, and be cured?" 14 So Naaman went down to the Jordan, dipped himself in it seven times, as Elisha had instructed, and he was completely cured. His flesh became firm and healthy like that of a child. 15 He returned to Elisha with all his men and said, "Now I know that there is no god but the God of Israel; so please, sir, accept a gift from me."

16 Elisha answered, "By the living Lord, whom I serve, I swear that I will not accept a gift."

Naaman insisted that he accept it, but he would not. 17 So Naaman said, "If you won't accept my gift, then let me have two mule-loads of earth to take home with me,*l* because from now on I will not offer sacrifices or burnt offerings to any god except the Lord. 18 So I hope that the Lord will forgive me when I accompany my king to the temple of Rimmon, the god of Syria, and worship him. Surely the Lord will forgive me!"

19 "Go in peace," Elisha said. And Naaman left.

He had gone only a short distance, 20 when Elisha's servant Gehazi said to himself, "My master has let Naaman get away without paying a thing! He should have accepted what that Syrian offered him. By the living Lord I will run after him and get something from him." 21 So he set off after Naaman. When Naaman saw a man running after him, he got down from his chariot to meet him, and asked, "Is something wrong?"

22 "No," Gehazi answered. "But my master sent me to tell you that just now two members of the group of prophets in the hill country of Ephraim arrived, and he would like you to give them three thousand pieces of silver and two changes of fine clothes."

23 "Please take six thousand pieces of silver," Naaman replied. He insisted on it, tied up the silver in two bags, gave them and two changes of fine clothes to two of his servants, and sent them on ahead of Gehazi. 24 When they reached the hill where Elisha lived, Gehazi took the two bags and carried them into the house. Then he sent Naaman's servants back. 25 He went back into the house, and Elisha asked him, "Where have you been?"

"Oh, nowhere, sir," he answered.

26 But Elisha said, "Wasn't I there in spirit when the man got out of his chariot to meet you? This is no time to accept money and clothes, olive groves and vineyards, sheep and cattle, or servants! 27 And now Naaman's disease will come upon you, and you and your descendants will have it forever!"

When Gehazi left, he had the disease — his skin was as white as snow.

The Recovery of the Ax Head

6 One day the group of prophets that Elisha was in charge of complained to him, "The place where we live is too small! 2 Give us permission to go to the Jordan and cut down some trees, so that we can build a place to live."

"All right," Elisha answered.

3 One of them urged him to go with them; he agreed, 4 and they set out together. When they arrived at the Jordan, they began to work. 5 As one of them was cutting down a tree, suddenly his iron ax head fell in the water. "What shall I do, sir?" he exclaimed to Elisha. "It was a borrowed ax!"

6 "Where did it fall?" Elisha asked.

The man showed him the place, and Elisha cut off a stick, threw it in the water, and made the ax head float. 7 "Take

k the diseased spot; or this place. *l* EARTH TO TAKE HOME WITH ME: *It was then believed that a god could be worshiped only on his own land.*

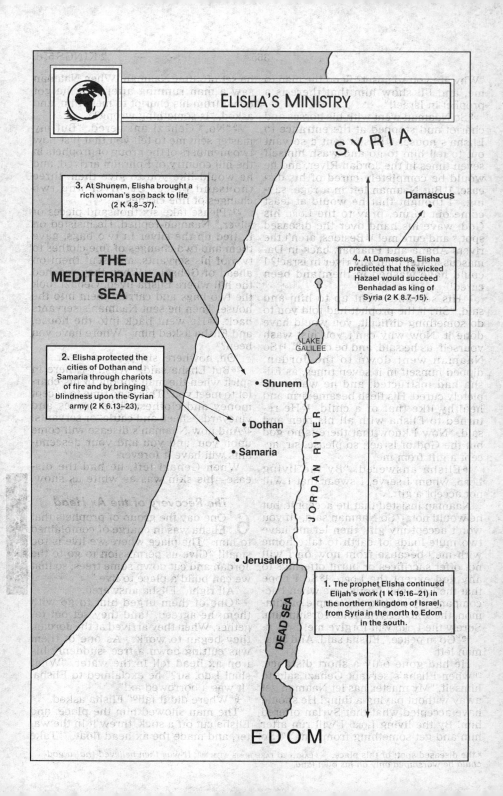

ELISHA'S MINISTRY

SYRIA

Damascus

THE MEDITERRANEAN SEA

LAKE GALILEE

JORDAN RIVER

• Shunem

• Dothan

• Samaria

• Jerusalem

DEAD SEA

EDOM

3. At Shunem, Elisha brought a rich woman's son back to life (2 K 4.8–37).

4. At Damascus, Elisha predicted that the wicked Hazael would succeed Benhadad as king of Syria (2 K 8.7–15).

2. Elisha protected the cities of Dothan and Samaria through chariots of fire and by bringing blindness upon the Syrian army (2 K 6.13–23).

1. The prophet Elisha continued Elijah's work (1 K 19.16–21) in the northern kingdom of Israel, from Syria in the north to Edom in the south.

it out," he ordered, and the man reached down and picked it up.

The Syrian Army Is Defeated

8 The king of Syria was at war with Israel. He consulted his officers and chose a place to set up his camp. 9 But Elisha sent word to the king of Israel, warning him not to go near that place, because the Syrians were waiting in ambush there. 10 So the king of Israel warned the people who lived in that place, and they were on guard. This happened several times.

11 The Syrian king became greatly upset over this; he called in his officers and asked them, "Which one of you is on the side of the king of Israel?"

12 One of them answered, "No one is, Your Majesty. The prophet Elisha tells the king of Israel what you say even in the privacy of your own room."

13 "Find out where he is," the king ordered, "and I will capture him."

When he was told that Elisha was in Dothan, 14 he sent a large force there with horses and chariots. They reached the town at night and surrounded it. 15 Early the next morning Elisha's servant got up, went out of the house, and saw the Syrian troops with their horses and chariots surrounding the town. He went back to Elisha and exclaimed, "We are doomed, sir! What shall we do?"

16 "Don't be afraid," Elisha answered. "We have more on our side than they have on theirs." 17 Then he prayed, "O LORD, open his eyes and let him see!" The LORD answered his prayer, and Elisha's servant looked up and saw the hillside covered with horses and chariots of fire all around Elisha.

18 When the Syrians attacked, Elisha prayed, "O LORD, strike these men blind!" The LORD answered his prayer and struck them blind. 19 Then Elisha went to them and said, "You are on the wrong road; this is not the town you are looking for. Follow me, and I will lead you to the man you are after." And he led them to Samaria.

20 As soon as they had entered the city, Elisha prayed, "Open their eyes, LORD, and let them see." The LORD answered his prayer; he restored their sight, and they saw that they were inside Samaria.

21 When the king of Israel saw the Syrians, he asked Elisha, "Shall I kill them, sir? Shall I kill them?"

22 "No," he answered. "Not even soldiers you had captured in combat would you put to death. Give them something to eat and drink, and let them return to their king." 23 So the king of Israel provided a great feast for them; and after they had eaten and drunk, he sent them back to the king of Syria. From then on the Syrians stopped raiding the land of Israel.

The Siege of Samaria

24 Some time later King Benhadad of Syria led his entire army against Israel and laid siege to the city of Samaria. 25 As a result of the siege the food shortage in the city was so severe that a donkey's head cost eighty pieces of silver, and half a pound of dove's dung *m* cost five pieces of silver.

26 The king of Israel was walking by on the city wall when a woman cried out, "Help me, Your Majesty!"

27 He replied, "If the LORD won't help you, what help can I provide? Do I have any wheat or wine? 28 What's your trouble?"

She answered, "The other day this woman here suggested that we eat my child, and then eat her child the next day. 29 So we cooked my son and ate him. The next day I told her that we would eat her son, but she had hidden him!"

30 Hearing this, the king tore his clothes in dismay, and the people who were close to the wall could see that he was wearing sackcloth under his clothes. 31 He exclaimed, "May God strike me dead if Elisha is not beheaded before the day is over!" 32 And he sent a messenger to get Elisha.

Meanwhile Elisha was at home with some elders who were visiting him. Before the king's messenger arrived, Elisha said to the elders, "That murderer is sending someone to kill me! Now, when he gets here, shut the door and don't let him come in. The king himself will be right behind him." 33 He had hardly finished saying this, when the king *n*

m DOVE'S DUNG: *This may be a popular term for a vegetable such as wild onions.* *n* Probable text king; Hebrew messenger.

arrived and said, "It's the LORD who has brought this trouble on us! Why should I wait any longer for him to do something?"

7 Elisha answered, "Listen to what the LORD says! By this time tomorrow you will be able to buy in Samaria ten pounds of the best wheat or twenty pounds of barley for one piece of silver."

2 The personal attendant of the king said to Elisha, "That can't happen — not even if the LORD himself were to send grain[o] at once!"

"You will see it happen, but you won't get to eat any of the food," Elisha replied.

The Syrian Army Leaves

3 Four men who were suffering from a dreaded skin disease were outside the gates of Samaria, and they said to each other, "Why should we wait here until we die? 4 It's no use going into the city, because we would starve to death in there; but if we stay here, we'll die also. So let's go to the Syrian camp; the worst they can do is kill us, but maybe they will spare our lives." 5 So, as it began to get dark, they went to the Syrian camp, but when they reached it, no one was there. 6 The Lord had made the Syrians hear what sounded like the advance of a large army with horses and chariots, and the Syrians thought that the king of Israel had hired Hittite and Egyptian kings and their armies to attack them. 7 So that evening the Syrians had fled for their lives, abandoning their tents, horses, and donkeys, and leaving the camp just as it was.

8 When the four men reached the edge of the camp, they went into a tent, ate and drank what was there, grabbed the silver, gold, and clothing they found, and went off and hid them; then they returned, entered another tent, and did the same thing. 9 But then they said to each other, "We shouldn't be doing this! We have good news, and we shouldn't keep it to ourselves. If we wait until morning to tell it, we are sure to be punished. Let's go right now and tell the king's officers!" 10 So they left the Syrian camp, went back to Samaria, and called out to the guards at the gates: "We went to the Syrian camp and didn't see or hear anybody; the horses and donkeys have not been untied, and the tents are just as the Syrians left them."

11 The guards announced the news, and it was reported in the palace. 12 It was still night, but the king got out of bed and said to his officials, "I'll tell you what the Syrians are planning! They know about the famine here, so they have left their camp to go and hide in the countryside. They think that we will leave the city to find food, and then they will take us alive and capture the city."

13 One of his officials said, "The people here in the city are doomed anyway, like those that have already died. So let's send some men with five of the horses that are left, so that we can find out what has happened."[p] 14 They chose some men, and the king sent them in two chariots with instructions to go and find out what had happened to the Syrian army. 15 The men went as far as the Jordan, and all along the road they saw the clothes and equipment that the Syrians had abandoned as they fled. Then they returned and reported to the king. 16 The people of Samaria rushed out and looted the Syrian camp. And as the LORD had said, ten pounds of the best wheat or twenty pounds of barley were sold for one piece of silver.

17 It so happened that the king of Israel had put the city gate under the command of the officer who was his personal attendant. The officer was trampled to death there by the people and died, as Elisha had predicted when the king went to see him. 18 Elisha had told the king that by that time the following day ten pounds of the best wheat or twenty pounds of barley would be sold in Samaria for one piece of silver, 19 to which the officer had answered, "That can't happen — not even if the LORD himself were to send grain[q] at once!" And Elisha had replied, "You will see it happen, but you won't get to eat any of the food." 20 And that is just what happened to him — he died, trampled to death by the people at the city gate.

The Woman from Shunem Returns

8 Now Elisha had told the woman who lived in Shunem, whose son he had brought back to life, that the LORD

---

[o] grain; or rain.   [p] Verse 13 in Hebrew is unclear.   [q] grain; or rain.

was sending a famine on the land, which would last for seven years, and that she should leave with her family and go and live somewhere else. 2 She had followed his instructions and had gone with her family to live in Philistia for the seven years.

3 At the end of the seven years she returned to Israel and went to the king to ask that her house and her land be restored to her. 4 She found the king talking with Gehazi, Elisha's servant; the king wanted to know about Elisha's miracles. 5 While Gehazi was telling the king how Elisha had brought a dead person back to life, the woman made her appeal to the king. Gehazi said to him, "Your Majesty, here is the woman and here is her son whom Elisha brought back to life!" 6 In answer to the king's question, she confirmed Gehazi's story, and so the king called an official and told him to give back to her everything that was hers, including the value of all the crops that her fields had produced during the seven years she had been away.

Elisha and King Benhadad of Syria

7 Elisha went to Damascus at a time when King Benhadad of Syria was sick. When the king was told that Elisha was there, 8 he said to Hazael, one of his officials, "Take a gift to the prophet and ask him to consult the LORD to find out whether or not I am going to get well." 9 So Hazael loaded forty camels with all kinds of the finest products of Damascus and went to Elisha. When Hazael met him, he said, "Your servant King Benhadad has sent me to ask you whether or not he will recover from his sickness."

10 Elisha answered, "The LORD has revealed to me that he will die; but go to him and tell him that he will recover." 11 Then Elisha stared at him with a horrified look on his face until Hazael became ill at ease. Suddenly Elisha burst into tears. 12 "Why are you crying, sir?" Hazael asked.

"Because I know the horrible things you will do against the people of Israel," Elisha answered. "You will set their fortresses on fire, slaughter their finest young men, batter their children to

death, and rip open their pregnant women."

13 "How could I ever be that powerful?" Hazael asked. "I'm a nobody!"

"The LORD has shown me that you will be king of Syria," Elisha replied.

14 Hazael went back to Benhadad, who asked him, "What did Elisha say?"

"He told me that you would certainly get well," Hazael answered. 15 But on the following day Hazael took a blanket, soaked it in water, and smothered the king.

And Hazael succeeded Benhadad as king of Syria.

King Jehoram of Judah
(2 Chronicles 21.1-20)

16 In the fifth year of the reign of Joram son of Ahab as king of Israel,[r] Jehoram son of Jehoshaphat became king of Judah 17 at the age of thirty-two, and he ruled in Jerusalem for eight years. 18 His wife was Ahab's daughter, and like the family of Ahab he followed the evil ways of the kings of Israel. He sinned against the LORD, 19 but the LORD was not willing to destroy Judah, because he had promised his servant David that his descendants would always continue to rule.

20 During Jehoram's reign Edom revolted against Judah and became an independent kingdom. 21 So Jehoram set out with all his chariots to Zair, where the Edomite army surrounded them. During the night he and his chariot commanders managed to break out and escape, and his soldiers scattered to their homes. 22 Edom has been independent of[s] Judah ever since. During this same period the city of Libnah also revolted.

23 Everything else that Jehoram did is recorded in The History of the Kings of Judah. 24 Jehoram died and was buried in the royal tombs in David's City, and his son Ahaziah succeeded him as king.

King Ahaziah of Judah
(2 Chronicles 22.1-6)

25 In the twelfth year of the reign of Joram son of Ahab as king of Israel, Ahaziah son of Jehoram became king of Judah 26 at the age of twenty-two, and he ruled in Jerusalem for one year. His mother was Athaliah, the daughter of King Ahab and granddaughter of King

---

r Some ancient translations Israel; Hebrew Israel, Jehoshaphat being king of Judah.
s independent of; or in revolt against.

KING JEHU'S BLACK OBELISK

During the period of Old Testament history from about 900 to 700 B.C., the Assyrians were the dominant world power. One of the powerful Assyrian kings, Shalmaneser III (reigned 859–824 B.C.), erected a large stone monument on which he recorded his military victories. This impressive archaeological find, known as the Black Obelisk, contains a relief sculpture depicting the visit of King Jehu of Israel (reigned 841–814 B.C.) to pay tribute to Shalmaneser.

Placed outside the royal palace at Nimrud in Assyria, the monument is more than six feet high. Chiseled carefully in stone is a series of detailed drawings, with accompanying inscriptions that commemorate Shalmaneser's numerous military campaigns. The obelisk shows an event not mentioned in the Bible—Jehu bowing before Shalmaneser, with numerous Israelite servants and aids standing by with gifts for the Assyrian king.

Tribute, or compulsory payments to protect a weaker nation against a more powerful foe, was often levied by aggressor nations such as the Assyrians during Old Testament times.

After being anointed king of Israel by the prophet Elisha, Jehu eliminated all threats to his rule by killing all members of the family of Ahab, whom he succeeded (2 K 9; 10). As a ruler, Jehu was a weak king who failed to eliminate Baal worship from the land.

The Black Obelisk is a valuable archaeological find, because it helps establish a date for Jehu's rule, as well as an overall chronology for this period of Israel's history. It also shows us what an Israelite king from this period must have looked like. This is the only image or drawing of an Israelite king that has been discovered by archaeologists.

Omri of Israel. 27 Since Ahaziah was related to King Ahab by marriage, he sinned against the Lord, just as Ahab's family did.

28 King Ahaziah joined King Joram of Israel in a war against King Hazael of Syria. The armies clashed at Ramoth in Gilead, and Joram was wounded in battle. 29 He returned to the city of Jezreel to recover from his wounds, and Ahaziah went there to visit him.

Jehu Is Anointed King of Israel

9 Meanwhile the prophet Elisha called one of the young prophets and said to him, "Get ready and go to Ramoth in Gilead. Take this jar of olive oil with you, 2 and when you get there look for Jehu, the son of Jehoshaphat and grandson of Nimshi. Take him to a private room away from his companions, 3 pour this olive oil on his head, and say, 'The Lord proclaims that he anoints you king of Israel.' Then leave there as fast as you can."

4 So the young prophet went to Ramoth, 5 where he found the army officers in a conference. He said, "Sir, I have a message for you."

Jehu asked, "Which one of us are you speaking to?"

"To you, sir," he replied. 6 Then the two of them went indoors, and the young prophet poured the olive oil on Jehu's head and said to him, "The Lord, the God of Israel, proclaims: 'I anoint you king of my people Israel. 7 You are to kill your master the king, that son of Ahab, so that I may punish Jezebel for murdering my prophets and my other servants. 8 All of Ahab's family and descendants are to die; I will get rid of every male in his family, young and old alike. 9 I will treat his family as I did the families of King Jeroboam of Israel and of King Baasha of Israel. 10 Jezebel will not be buried; her body will be eaten by dogs in the territory of Jezreel.' " After saying this, the young prophet left the room and fled.

11 Jehu went back to his fellow officers, who asked him, "Is everything all right? What did that crazy fellow want with you?"

"You know what he wanted," Jehu answered.

12 "No we don't!" they replied. "Tell us what he said!"

"He told me that the Lord proclaims: 'I anoint you king of Israel.' "

13 At once Jehu's fellow officers spread their cloaks at the top of the steps for Jehu to stand on, blew trumpets, and shouted, "Jehu is king!"

King Joram of Israel Is Killed

14-15 Then Jehu plotted against King Joram, who was in Jezreel, where he had gone to recover from the wounds which he had received in the battle at Ramoth against King Hazael of Syria. So Jehu said to his fellow officers, "If you are with me, make sure that no one slips out of Ramoth to go and warn the people in Jezreel." 16 Then he got into his chariot and set off for Jezreel. Joram had still not recovered, and King Ahaziah of Judah was there, visiting him.

17 A guard on duty in the watchtower at Jezreel saw Jehu and his men approaching. "I see some men riding up!" he called out.

Joram replied, "Send a rider to find out if they are friends or enemies."

18 The messenger rode out to Jehu and said to him, "The king wants to know if you come as a friend."

"That's none of your business!" Jehu answered. "Fall in behind me."

The guard on the watchtower reported that the messenger had reached the group but was not returning. 19 Another messenger was sent out, who asked Jehu the same question. Again Jehu answered, "That's none of your business! Fall in behind me."

20 Once more the guard reported that the messenger had reached the group but was not returning. And he added, "The leader of the group is driving his chariot like a madman, just like Jehu!"

21 "Get my chariot ready," King Joram ordered. It was done, and he and King Ahaziah rode out, each in his own chariot, to meet Jehu. They met him at the field which had belonged to Naboth. 22 "Are you coming in peace?" Joram asked him.

"How can there be peace," Jehu answered, "when we still have all the witchcraft and idolatry that your mother Jezebel started?"

23 "It's treason, Ahaziah!" Joram cried out, as he turned his chariot around and fled. 24 Jehu drew his bow, and with all his strength shot an arrow that struck

Joram in the back and pierced his heart. Joram fell dead in his chariot, 25 and Jehu said to his aide Bidkar, "Get his body and throw it in the field that belonged to Naboth. Remember that when you and I were riding together behind King Joram's father Ahab, the LORD spoke these words against Ahab: 26 'I saw the murder of Naboth and his sons yesterday. And I promise that I will punish you here in this same field.' So take Joram's body," Jehu ordered his aide, "and throw it in the field that belonged to Naboth, so as to fulfill the LORD's promise."

King Ahaziah of Judah Is Killed

27 King Ahaziah saw what happened, so he fled in his chariot toward the town of Beth Haggan, pursued by Jehu. "Kill him too!" Jehu ordered his men, and they wounded him t as he drove his chariot on the road up to Gur, near the town of Ibleam. But he managed to keep on going until he reached the city of Megiddo, where he died. 28 His officials took his body back to Jerusalem in a chariot and buried him in the royal tombs in David's City.

29 Ahaziah had become king of Judah in the eleventh year that Joram son of Ahab was king of Israel.

Queen Jezebel Is Killed

30 Jehu arrived in Jezreel. Jezebel, having heard what had happened, put on eye shadow, arranged her hair, and stood looking down at the street from a window in the palace. 31 As Jehu came through the gate, she called out, "You Zimri! u You assassin! Why are you here?"

32 Jehu looked up and shouted, "Who is on my side?" Two or three palace officials looked down at him from a window, 33 and Jehu said to them, "Throw her down!" They threw her down, and her blood spattered on the wall and on the horses. Jehu drove his horses and chariot over her body, 34 entered the palace, and had a meal. Only then did he say, "Take that cursed woman and bury her; after all, she is a king's daughter." 35 But the men who went out to bury her found nothing except her skull and the bones of her hands and feet. 36 When they reported this to Jehu, he said, "This is what the LORD said would happen, when he spoke through his servant Elijah: 'Dogs will eat Jezebel's body in the territory of Jezreel. 37 Her remains will be scattered there like dung, so that no one will be able to identify them.' "

The Descendants of Ahab Are Killed

10 There were seventy descendants of King Ahab living in the city of Samaria. Jehu wrote a letter and sent copies to the rulers of the city, v to the leading citizens, and to the guardians of Ahab's descendants. The letter read: 2 "You are in charge of the king's descendants, and you have at your disposal chariots, horses, weapons, and fortified cities. So then, as soon as you receive this letter, 3 you are to choose the best qualified of the king's descendants, make him king, and fight to defend him."

4 The rulers of Samaria were terrified. "How can we oppose Jehu," they said, "when neither King Joram nor King Ahaziah could?" 5 So the officer in charge of the palace and the official in charge of the city, together with the leading citizens and the guardians, sent this message to Jehu: "We are your servants, and we are ready to do anything you say. But we will not make anyone king; do whatever you think best."

6 Jehu wrote them another letter: "If you are with me and are ready to follow my orders, bring the heads of King Ahab's descendants to me at Jezreel by this time tomorrow."

The seventy descendants of King Ahab were under the care of the leading citizens of Samaria, who were bringing them up. 7 When Jehu's letter was received, the leaders of Samaria killed all seventy of Ahab's descendants, put their heads in baskets, and sent them to Jehu at Jezreel.

8 When Jehu was told that the heads of Ahab's descendants had been brought, he ordered them to be piled up in two heaps at the city gate and to be left there until the following morning. 9 In the morning he went out to the gate and said to the people who were there, "I was the

---

t *Some ancient translations* and they wounded him; *Hebrew does not have these words.*
u ZIMRI: *An Israelite army officer who assassinated the king of Israel (see 1 K 16.8-12).*
v *Some ancient translations* the city; *Hebrew* Jezreel.

one who plotted against King Joram and killed him; you are not responsible for that. But who killed all these? 10 This proves that everything that the LORD said about the descendants of Ahab will come true. The LORD has done what he promised through his prophet Elijah." 11 Then Jehu put to death all the other relatives of Ahab living in Jezreel, and all his officers, close friends, and priests; not one of them was left alive.

The Relatives of King Ahaziah Are Killed

12 Jehu left Jezreel to go to Samaria. On the way, at a place called "Shepherds' Camp," 13 he met some relatives of the late King Ahaziah of Judah and asked them, "Who are you?"

"Ahaziah's relatives," they answered. "We are going to Jezreel to pay our respects to the children of Queen Jezebel and to the rest of the royal family." 14 Jehu ordered his men, "Take them alive!" They seized them, and he put them to death near a pit there. There were forty-two people in all, and not one of them was left alive.

All Remaining Relatives of Ahab Are Killed

15 Jehu started out again, and on his way he was met by Jonadab son of Rechab. Jehu greeted him and said, "You and I think alike. Will you support me?"

"I will," Jonadab answered.

"Give me your hand, then," Jehu replied. They clasped hands, and Jehu helped him up into the chariot, 16 saying, "Come with me and see for yourself how devoted I am to the LORD." And they rode on together to Samaria. 17 When they arrived there, Jehu killed all of Ahab's relatives, not sparing even one. This is what the LORD had told Elijah would happen.

The Worshipers of Baal Are Killed

18 Jehu called the people of Samaria together and said, "King Ahab served the god Baal a little, but I will serve him much more. 19 Call together all the prophets of Baal, all his worshipers, and all his priests. No one is excused; I am going to offer a great sacrifice to Baal, and whoever is not present will be put to death." (This was a trick on the part of

Jehu by which he meant to kill all the worshipers of Baal.) 20 Then Jehu ordered, "Proclaim a day of worship in honor of Baal!" The proclamation was made, 21 and Jehu sent word throughout all the land of Israel. All who worshiped Baal came; not one of them failed to come. They all went into the temple of Baal, filling it from one end to the other. 22 Then Jehu ordered the priest in charge of the sacred robes to bring the robes out and give them to the worshipers. 23 After that, Jehu himself went into the temple with Jonadab son of Rechab and said to the people there, "Make sure that only worshipers of Baal are present and that no worshiper of the LORD has come in." 24 Then he and Jonadab went in to offer sacrifices and burnt offerings to Baal. He had stationed eighty men outside the temple and had instructed them: "You are to kill all these people; anyone who lets one of them escape will pay for it with his life!"

25 As soon as Jehu had presented the offerings, he said to the guards and officers, "Go in and kill them all; don't let anyone escape!" They went in with drawn swords, killed them all, and dragged the bodies outside. Then they went on into the inner sanctuary of the temple, 26 brought out the sacred pillar that was there, and burned it. 27 So they destroyed the sacred pillar and the temple, and turned the temple into a latrine—which it still is today.

28 That was how Jehu wiped out the worship of Baal in Israel. 29 But he imitated the sin of King Jeroboam, who led Israel into the sin of worshiping the gold bull-calves he set up in Bethel and in Dan. 30 The LORD said to Jehu, "You have done to Ahab's descendants everything I wanted you to do. So I promise you that your descendants, down to the fourth generation, will be kings of Israel." 31 But Jehu did not obey with all his heart the Law of the LORD, the God of Israel; instead, he followed the example of Jeroboam, who led Israel into sin.

The Death of Jehu

32 At that time the LORD began to reduce the size of Israel's territory. King Hazael of Syria conquered all the Israelite territory 33 east of the Jordan, as far south as the town of Aroer on the Arnon River—this included the territories of

Gilead and Bashan, where the tribes of Gad, Reuben, and East Manasseh lived.

34 Everything else that Jehu did, including his brave deeds, is recorded in *The History of the Kings of Israel.* 35 He died and was buried in Samaria, and his son Jehoahaz succeeded him as king. 36 Jehu had ruled in Samaria as king of Israel for twenty-eight years.

Queen Athaliah of Judah
(2 Chronicles 22.10 – 23.15)

11 As soon as King Ahaziah's mother Athaliah learned of her son's murder, she gave orders for all the members of the royal family to be killed. 2 Only Ahaziah's son Joash escaped. He was about to be killed with the others, but was rescued by his aunt Jehosheba, who was King Jehoram's daughter and Ahaziah's half sister. She took him and his nurse into a bedroom in the Temple and hid him from Athaliah, so that he was not killed. 3 For six years Jehosheba took care of the boy and kept him hidden in the Temple, while Athaliah ruled as queen.

4 But in the seventh year Jehoiada the priest sent for the officers in charge of the royal bodyguard and of the palace guards, and told them to come to the Temple, where he made them agree under oath to what he planned to do. He showed them King Ahaziah's son Joash 5 and gave them the following orders: "When you come on duty on the Sabbath, one third of you are to guard the palace; 6 another third are to stand guard at the Sur Gate, and the other third are to stand guard at the gate behind the other guards.w 7 The two groups that go off duty on the Sabbath are to stand guard at the Temple to protect the king. 8 You are to guard King Joash with drawn swords and stay with him wherever he goes. Anyone who comes near you is to be killed."

9 The officers obeyed Jehoiada's instructions and brought their men to him — those going off duty on the Sabbath and those going on duty. 10 He gave the officers the spearsx and shields that had belonged to King David and had

been kept in the Temple, 11 and he stationed the men with drawn swords all around the front of the Temple, to protect the king. 12 Then Jehoiada led Joash out, placed the crown on his head, and gave him a copy of the laws governing kingship. Then Joash was anointed and proclaimed king. The people clapped their hands and shouted, "Long live the king!"

13 Queen Athaliah heard the noise being made by the guards and the people, so she hurried to the Temple, where the crowd had gathered. 14 There she saw the new king standing by the column at the entrance of the Temple, as was the custom. He was surrounded by the officers and the trumpeters, and the people were all shouting joyfully and blowing trumpets. Athaliah tore her clothes in distress and shouted, "Treason! Treason!"

15 Jehoiada did not want Athaliah killed in the Temple area, so he ordered the army officers: "Take her out between the rows of guards, and kill anyone who tries to rescue her." 16 They seized her, took her to the palace, and there at the Horse Gate they killed her.

Jehoiada's Reforms
(2 Chronicles 23.16-21)

17 The priest Jehoiada had King Joash and the people make a covenant with the LORD that they would be the LORD's people; he also made a covenant between the king and the people. 18 Then the people went to the temple of Baal and tore it down; they smashed the altars and the idols, and killed Mattan, the priest of Baal, in front of the altars.

Jehoiada put guards on duty at the Temple, 19 and then he, the officers, the royal bodyguard, and the palace guards escorted the king from the Temple to the palace, followed by all the people. Joash entered by the Guard Gate and took his place on the throne. 20 All the people were filled with happiness, and the city was quiet, now that Athaliah had been killed in the palace.

21 Joash became king of Judah at the age of seven.

w *Hebrew has an additional word, the meaning of which is unclear.*   x *Some ancient translations (and see 2 Ch 23.9) spears; Hebrew spear.*

King Joash of Judah
(2 Chronicles 24.1-16)

12 In the seventh year of the reign of King Jehu of Israel, Joash became king of Judah, and he ruled in Jerusalem for forty years. His mother was Zibiah from the city of Beersheba. ²Throughout his life he did what pleased the LORD, because Jehoiada the priest instructed him. ³However, the pagan places of worship were not destroyed, and the people continued to offer sacrifices and burn incense there.

⁴Joash called the priests and ordered them to save up the money paid in connection with the sacrifices in the Temple, both the dues paid for the regular sacrifices and the money given as freewill gifts. ⁵Each priest was to be responsible for the money brought by those he served, and the money was to be used to repair the Temple, as needed.

⁶But by the twenty-third year of Joash's reign the priests still had not made any repairs in the Temple. ⁷So he called in Jehoiada and the other priests and asked them, "Why aren't you repairing the Temple? From now on you are not to keep the money you receive; you must hand it over, so that the repairs can be made." ⁸The priests agreed to this and also agreed not to make the repairs in the Temple.

⁹Then Jehoiada took a box, made a hole in the lid, and placed the box by the altar, on the right side as one enters the Temple. The priests on duty at the entrance put in the box all the money given by the worshipers. ¹⁰Whenever there was a large amount of money in the box, the royal secretary and the High Priest would come, melt down the silver, and weigh it.ʸ ¹¹After recording the exact amount, they would hand the silver over to the men in charge of the work in the Temple, and these would pay the carpenters, the builders, ¹²the masons, and the stone cutters, buy the timber and the stones used in the repairs, and pay all other necessary expenses. ¹³None of the money, however, was used to pay for making silver cups, bowls, trumpets, or tools for tending the lamps, or any other article of silver or of gold. ¹⁴It was all used to pay the workers and to buy the

materials used in the repairs. ¹⁵The men in charge of the work were thoroughly honest, so there was no need to require them to account for the funds. ¹⁶The money given for the repayment offerings and for the offerings for sin was not deposited in the box; it belonged to the priests.

¹⁷At that time King Hazael of Syria attacked the city of Gath and conquered it; then he decided to attack Jerusalem. ¹⁸King Joash of Judah took all the offerings that his predecessors Jehoshaphat, Jehoram, and Ahaziah had dedicated to the LORD, added to them his own offerings and all the gold in the treasuries of the Temple and the palace, and sent them all as a gift to King Hazael, who then led his army away from Jerusalem.

¹⁹Everything else that King Joash did is recorded in *The History of the Kings of Judah.*

²⁰⁻²¹King Joash's officials plotted against him, and two of them, Jozacar son of Shimeath and Jehozabad son of Shomer, killed him at the house built on the land that was filled in on the east side of Jerusalem, on the road that goes down to Silla. Joash was buried in the royal tombs in David's City, and his son Amaziah succeeded him as king.

King Jehoahaz of Israel

13 In the twenty-third year of the reign of Joash son of Ahaziah as king of Judah, Jehoahaz son of Jehu became king of Israel, and he ruled in Samaria for seventeen years. ²Like King Jeroboam before him, he sinned against the LORD and led Israel into sin; he never gave up his evil ways. ³So the LORD was angry with Israel, and he allowed King Hazael of Syria and his son Benhadad to defeat Israel time after time. ⁴Then Jehoahaz prayed to the LORD, and the LORD, seeing how harshly the king of Syria was oppressing the Israelites, answered his prayer. ⁵The LORD sent Israel a leader, who freed them from the Syrians, and so the Israelites lived in peace, as before. ⁶But they still did not give up the sins into which King Jeroboam had led Israel, but kept onᶻ committing them; and the image of the goddess Asherah remained in Samaria.

ʸ melt down the silver, and weigh it; *or* count the money, and tie it up in bags.
ᶻ *Some ancient translations* kept on; *Hebrew* he kept on.

7 Jehoahaz had no armed forces left except fifty cavalry troops, ten chariots, and ten thousand foot soldiers, because the king of Syria had destroyed the rest, trampling them down like dust.

8 Everything else that Jehoahaz did and all his brave deeds are recorded in *The History of the Kings of Israel.* 9 He died and was buried in Samaria, and his son Jehoash succeeded him as king.

King Jehoash of Israel

10 In the thirty-seventh year of the reign of King Joash of Judah, Jehoash son of Jehoahaz became king of Israel, and he ruled in Samaria for sixteen years. 11 He too sinned against the LORD and followed the evil example of King Jeroboam, who had led Israel into sin. 12 Everything else that Jehoash did, including his bravery in the war against King Amaziah of Judah, is recorded in *The History of the Kings of Israel.* 13 Jehoash died and was buried in the royal tombs in Samaria, and his son Jeroboam II succeeded him as king.

The Death of Elisha

14 The prophet Elisha was sick with a fatal disease, and as he lay dying, King Jehoash of Israel went to visit him. "My father, my father!" he exclaimed as he wept. "You have been the mighty defender of Israel!"

15 "Get a bow and some arrows," Elisha ordered him. Jehoash got them, 16 and Elisha told him to get ready to shoot. The king did so, and Elisha placed his hands on the king's hands. 17 Then, following the prophet's instructions, the king opened the window that faced toward Syria. "Shoot the arrow!" Elisha ordered. As soon as the king shot the arrow, the prophet exclaimed, "You are the LORD's arrow, with which he will win victory over Syria. You will fight the Syrians in Aphek until you defeat them."

18 Then Elisha told the king to take the other arrows and strike the ground with them. The king struck the ground three times, and then stopped. 19 This made Elisha angry, and he said to the king, "You should have struck five or six times, and then you would have won complete victory over the Syrians; but now you will defeat them only three times."

20 Elisha died and was buried.

Every year bands of Moabites used to invade the land of Israel. 21 One time during a funeral, one of those bands was seen, and the people threw the corpse into Elisha's tomb and ran off,[a] As soon as the body came into contact with Elisha's bones, the man came back to life and stood up.

War between Israel and Syria

22 King Hazael of Syria oppressed the Israelites during all of Jehoahaz' reign, 23 but the LORD was kind and merciful to them. He would not let them be destroyed, but helped them because of his covenant with Abraham, Isaac, and Jacob. He has never forgotten his people. 24 At the death of King Hazael of Syria his son Benhadad became king. 25 Then King Jehoash of Israel defeated Benhadad three times and recaptured the cities that had been taken by Benhadad during the reign of Jehoahaz, the father of Jehoash.

King Amaziah of Judah

(2 Chronicles 25.1-24)

14 In the second year of the reign of Jehoash son of Jehoahaz as king of Israel, Amaziah son of Joash became king of Judah 2 at the age of twenty-five, and he ruled in Jerusalem for twenty-nine years. His mother was Jehoaddin from Jerusalem. 3 He did what was pleasing to the LORD, but he was not like his ancestor King David; instead, he did what his father Joash had done. 4 He did not tear down the pagan places of worship, and the people continued to offer sacrifices and burn incense there.

5 As soon as Amaziah was firmly in power, he executed the officials who had killed his father, the king. 6 However, he did not kill their children but followed what the LORD had commanded in the Law of Moses: "Parents are not to be put to death for crimes committed by their children, and children are not to be put to death for crimes committed by their parents; people are to be put to death only for a crime they themselves have committed."

---

a One ancient translation and ran off; *Hebrew* and he ran off.

7 Amaziah killed ten thousand Edomite soldiers in Salt Valley; he captured the city of Sela in battle and called it Joktheel, the name it still has.

8 Then Amaziah sent messengers to King Jehoash of Israel, challenging him to fight.b 9 But King Jehoash sent back the following reply: "Once a thorn bush on the Lebanon Mountains sent a message to a cedar: 'Give your daughter in marriage to my son.' A wild animal passed by and trampled the bush down. 10 Now Amaziah, you have defeated the Edomites, and you are filled with pride. Be satisfied with your fame and stay at home. Why stir up trouble that will only bring disaster on you and your people?"

11 But Amaziah refused to listen, so King Jehoash marched out with his men and fought against him at Beth Shemesh in Judah. 12 Amaziah's army was defeated, and all his soldiers fled to their homes. 13 Jehoash took Amaziah prisoner, advanced on Jerusalem, and tore down the city wall from Ephraim Gate to the Corner Gate, a distance of two hundred yards. 14 He took all the silver and gold he could find, all the Temple equipment and all the palace treasures, and carried them back to Samaria. He also took hostages with him.

15 Everything else that Jehoash did, including his bravery in the war against King Amaziah of Judah, is recorded in *The History of the Kings of Israel.* 16 Jehoash died and was buried in the royal tombs in Samaria, and his son Jeroboam II succeeded him as king.

The Death of King Amaziah of Judah
(2 Chronicles 25.25-28)

17 King Amaziah of Judah lived fifteen years after the death of King Jehoash of Israel. 18 Everything else that Amaziah did is recorded in *The History of the Kings of Judah.*

19 There was a plot in Jerusalem to assassinate Amaziah, so he fled to the city of Lachish, but his enemies followed him there and killed him. 20 His body was carried back to Jerusalem on a horse and was buried in the royal tombs in David's City. 21 The people of Judah then crowned his sixteen-year-old son

Uzziah as king. 22 Uzziah reconquered and rebuilt Elath after his father's death.

King Jeroboam II of Israel

23 In the fifteenth year of the reign of Amaziah son of Joash as king of Judah, Jeroboam son of Jehoash became king of Israel, and he ruled in Samaria for forty-one years. 24 He sinned against the LORD, following the wicked example of his predecessor King Jeroboam son of Nebat, who led Israel into sin. 25 He reconquered all the territory that had belonged to Israel, from Hamath Pass in the north to the Dead Sea in the south. This was what the LORD, the God of Israel, had promised through his servant the prophet Jonah son of Amittai from Gath Hepher.

26 The LORD saw the terriblec suffering of the Israelites; there was no one at all to help them. 27 But it was not the LORD's purpose to destroy Israel completely and forever, so he rescued them through King Jeroboam II.

28 Everything else that Jeroboam II did, his brave battles, and how he restored Damascus and Hamath to Israel,d are all recorded in *The History of the Kings of Israel.* 29 Jeroboam died and was buried in the royal tombs, and his son Zechariah succeeded him as king.

King Uzziah of Judah
(2 Chronicles 26.1-23)

15 In the twenty-seventh year of the reign of King Jeroboam II of Israel, Uzziah son of Amaziah became king of Judah 2 at the age of sixteen, and he ruled in Jerusalem for fifty-two years. His mother was Jecoliah from Jerusalem. 3 Following the example of his father, he did what was pleasing to the LORD. 4 But the pagan places of worship were not destroyed, and the people continued to offer sacrifices and burn incense there. 5 The LORD struck Uzziah with a dreaded skin disease that stayed with him the rest of his life. He lived in a separate house, relieved of all duties, while his son Jotham governed the country.

6 Everything else that Uzziah did is recorded in *The History of the Kings of Judah.* 7 Uzziah died and was buried in the royal burial ground in David's City,

and his son Jotham succeeded him as king.

King Zechariah of Israel

8 In the thirty-eighth year of the reign of King Uzziah of Judah, Zechariah son of Jeroboam II became king of Israel, and he ruled in Samaria for six months. 9 He, like his predecessors, sinned against the LORD. He followed the wicked example of King Jeroboam son of Nebat, who led Israel into sin. 10 Shallum son of Jabesh conspired against King Zechariah, assassinated him at Ibleam,e and succeeded him as king.

11 Everything else that Zechariah did is recorded in The History of the Kings of Israel.

12 So the promise was fulfilled which the LORD had made to King Jehu: "Your descendants down to the fourth generationf will be kings of Israel."

King Shallum of Israel

13 In the thirty-ninth year of the reign of King Uzziah of Judah, Shallum son of Jabesh became king of Israel, and he ruled in Samaria for one month.

14 Menahem son of Gadi went from Tirzah to Samaria, assassinated Shallum, and succeeded him as king. 15 Everything else that Shallum did, including an account of his conspiracy, is recorded in The History of the Kings of Israel. 16 As Menahem was on his way from Tirzah, he completely destroyed the city of Tappuah,g its inhabitants, and the surrounding territory, because the city did not surrender to him. He even ripped open the bellies of all the pregnant women.

King Menahem of Israel

17 In the thirty-ninth year of the reign of King Uzziah of Judah, Menahem son of Gadi became king of Israel, and he ruled in Samaria for ten years. 18 He sinned against the LORD, for until the day of his death he followed the wicked example of King Jeroboam son of Nebat, who led Israel into sin. 19 Tiglath Pileser, the emperor of Assyria, invaded Israel, and Menahem gave him thirty-eight tons of silver to gain his support in strengthening Menahem's power over the coun-

try. 20 Menahem got the money from the rich men of Israel by forcing each one to contribute fifty pieces of silver. So Tiglath Pileser went back to his own country.

21 Everything else that Menahem did is recorded in The History of the Kings of Israel. 22 He died and was buried, and his son Pekahiah succeeded him as king.

King Pekahiah of Israel

23 In the fiftieth year of the reign of King Uzziah of Judah, Pekahiah son of Menahem became king of Israel, and he ruled in Samaria for two years. 24 He sinned against the LORD, following the wicked example of King Jeroboam son of Nebat, who led Israel into sin. 25 An officer of Pekahiah's forces, Pekah son of Remaliah, plotted with fifty men from Gilead, assassinated Pekahiah in the palace's inner fortressh in Samaria, and succeeded him as king.

26 Everything else that Pekahiah did is recorded in The History of the Kings of Israel.

King Pekah of Israel

27 In the fifty-second year of the reign of King Uzziah of Judah, Pekah son of Remaliah became king of Israel, and he ruled in Samaria for twenty years. 28 He sinned against the LORD, following the wicked example of King Jeroboam son of Nebat, who led Israel into sin.

29 It was while Pekah was king that Tiglath Pileser, the emperor of Assyria, captured the cities of Ijon, Abel Beth Maacah, Janoah, Kedesh, and Hazor, and the territories of Gilead, Galilee, and Naphtali, and took the people to Assyria as prisoners.

30 In the twentieth year of the reign of Jotham son of Uzziah as king of Judah, Hoshea son of Elah plotted against King Pekah, assassinated him, and succeeded him as king. 31 Everything else that Pekah did is recorded in The History of the Kings of Israel.

King Jotham of Judah
(2 Chronicles 27.1-9)

32 In the second year of the reign of Pekah son of Remaliah as king of Israel, Jotham son of Uzziah became king of

e One ancient translation at Ibleam; Hebrew before people.   f FOURTH GENERATION: Zechariah was Jehu's great-great-grandson.   g One ancient translation Tappuah; Hebrew Tiphsah.
h Hebrew has two additional words, the meaning of which is unclear.

Judah [33] at the age of twenty-five, and he ruled in Jerusalem for sixteen years. His mother was Jerusha, the daughter of Zadok. [34] Following the example of his father Uzziah, Jotham did what was pleasing to the Lord. [35] But the pagan places of worship were not destroyed, and the people continued to offer sacrifices and burn incense there. It was Jotham who built the North Gate of the Temple.

[36] Everything else that Jotham did is recorded in *The History of the Kings of Judah*. [37] It was while he was king that the Lord first sent King Rezin of Syria and King Pekah of Israel to attack Judah. [38] Jotham died and was buried in the royal tombs in David's City, and his son Ahaz succeeded him as king.

King Ahaz of Judah
(2 Chronicles 28.1-27)

16 In the seventeenth year of the reign of Pekah son of Remaliah as king of Israel, Ahaz son of Jotham became king of Judah [2] at the age of twenty, and he ruled in Jerusalem for sixteen years. He did not follow the good example of his ancestor King David; instead, he did what was not pleasing to the Lord his God [3] and followed the example of the kings of Israel. He even sacrificed his own son as a burnt offering to idols, imitating the disgusting practice of the people whom the Lord had driven out of the land as the Israelites advanced. [4] At the pagan places of worship, on the hills, and under every shady tree, Ahaz offered sacrifices and burned incense.

[5] King Rezin of Syria and King Pekah of Israel attacked Jerusalem and besieged it, but could not defeat Ahaz. ([6] At the same time the king of Edom[i] regained control of the city of Elath and drove out the Judeans who lived there. The Edomites settled in Elath and still live there.) [7] Ahaz sent men to Tiglath Pileser, the emperor of Assyria, with this message: "I am your devoted servant. Come and rescue me from the kings of Syria and of Israel, who are attacking me." [8] Ahaz took the silver and gold from the Temple and the palace treasury, and sent it as a present to the em-

peror. [9] Tiglath Pileser, in answer to Ahaz' plea, marched out with his army against Damascus, captured it, killed King Rezin, and took the people to Kir as prisoners.

[10] When King Ahaz went to Damascus to meet Emperor Tiglath Pileser, he saw the altar there and sent back to Uriah the priest an exact model of it, down to the smallest details. [11] So Uriah built an altar just like it and finished it before Ahaz returned. [12] On his return from Damascus, Ahaz saw that the altar was finished, [13] so he burned animal sacrifices and grain offerings on it and poured a wine offering and the blood of a fellowship offering on it. [14] The bronze altar dedicated to the Lord was between the new altar and the Temple, so Ahaz moved it to the north side of his new altar. [15] Then he ordered Uriah: "Use this large altar of mine for the morning burnt offerings and the evening grain offerings, for the burnt offerings and grain offerings of the king and the people, and for the people's wine offerings. Pour on it the blood of all the animals that are sacrificed. But keep the bronze altar for me to use for divination." [16] Uriah did as the king commanded.

[17] King Ahaz took apart the bronze carts used in the Temple and removed the basins that were on them. He also took the bronze tank from the backs of the twelve bronze bulls and placed it on a stone foundation. [18] And in order to please the Assyrian emperor, Ahaz also removed from the Temple the platform for the royal throne and closed up the king's private entrance to the Temple.[j]

[19] Everything else that King Ahaz did is recorded in *The History of the Kings of Judah*. [20] Ahaz died and was buried in the royal tombs in David's City, and his son Hezekiah succeeded him as king.

King Hoshea of Israel

17 In the twelfth year of the reign of King Ahaz of Judah, Hoshea son of Elah became king of Israel, and he ruled in Samaria for nine years. [2] He sinned against the Lord, but not as much as the kings who had ruled Israel before him. [3] Emperor Shalmaneser of Assyria made war against him; Hoshea surren-

---

i *Probable text* the king of Edom; *Hebrew* King Rezin of Syria.   j *Verse 18 in Hebrew is unclear.*

dered to Shalmaneser and paid him tribute every year. 4 But one year Hoshea sent messengers to So, king of Egypt,*k* asking for his help, and stopped paying the annual tribute to Assyria. When Shalmaneser learned of this, he had Hoshea arrested and put in prison.

The Fall of Samaria

5 Then Shalmaneser invaded Israel and besieged Samaria. In the third year of the siege, 6 which was the ninth year of the reign of Hoshea, the Assyrian emperor*l* captured Samaria, took the Israelites to Assyria as prisoners, and settled some of them in the city of Halah, some near the Habor River in the district of Gozan and some in the cities of Media. 7 Samaria fell because the Israelites sinned against the LORD their God, who had rescued them from the king of Egypt and had led them out of Egypt. They worshiped other gods, 8 followed the customs of the people whom the LORD had driven out as his people advanced, and adopted customs introduced by the kings of Israel.*m* 9 The Israelites did*n* things that the LORD their God disapproved of. They built pagan places of worship in all their towns, from the smallest village to the largest city. 10 On all the hills and under every shady tree they put up stone pillars and images of the goddess Asherah, 11 and they burned incense on all the pagan altars, following the practice of the people whom the LORD had driven out of the land. They aroused the LORD's anger with all their wicked deeds 12 and disobeyed the LORD's command not to worship idols.

13 The LORD had sent his messengers and prophets to warn Israel and Judah: "Abandon your evil ways and obey my commands, which are contained in the Law I gave to your ancestors and which I handed on to you through my servants the prophets." 14 But they would not obey; they were stubborn like their ancestors, who had not trusted in the LORD their God. 15 They refused to obey his instructions, they did not keep the covenant he had made with their ancestors, and they disregarded his warnings. They worshiped worthless idols and became worthless themselves, and they followed the customs of the surrounding nations, disobeying the LORD's command not to imitate them. 16 They broke all the laws of the LORD their God and made two metal bull-calves to worship; they also made an image of the goddess Asherah, worshiped the stars, and served the god Baal. 17 They sacrificed their sons and daughters as burnt offerings to pagan gods; they consulted mediums and fortunetellers, and they devoted themselves completely to doing what is wrong in the LORD's sight, and so aroused his anger. 18 The LORD was angry with the Israelites and banished them from his sight, leaving only the kingdom of Judah.

19 But even the people of Judah did not obey the laws of the LORD their God; they imitated the customs adopted by the people of Israel. 20 The LORD rejected all the Israelites, punishing them and handing them over to cruel enemies until at last he had banished them from his sight.

21 After the LORD had separated Israel from Judah, the Israelites made Jeroboam son of Nebat their king. Jeroboam caused them to abandon the LORD and led them into terrible sins. 22 They followed Jeroboam and continued to practice all the sins he had committed, 23 until at last the LORD banished them from his sight, as he had warned through his servants the prophets that he would do. So the people of Israel were taken into exile to Assyria, where they still live.

The Assyrians Settle in Israel

24 The emperor of Assyria took people from the cities of Babylon, Cuth, Ivvah, Hamath, and Sepharvaim, and settled them in the cities of Samaria*o* in place of the exiled Israelites. They took possession of these cities and lived there. 25 When they first settled there, they did not worship the LORD, and so he sent lions, which killed some of them. 26 The emperor of Assyria was told that the people he had settled in the cities of Samaria did not know the law of the god of that land, and so the god had sent lions, which were killing them. 27 So the

---

k So, king of Egypt; *or* the king of Egypt at Sais, *l* ASSYRIAN EMPEROR: *Probably Sargon II, the successor of Shalmaneser.   m Probable text* and adopted . . . Israel; *Hebrew unclear.*   *n* did; *or said.   o* SAMARIA: *The name of the capital city was applied to the territory of the former kingdom of Israel.*

emperor commanded: "Send back one of the priests we brought as prisoners; have him[p] go back and live there, in order to teach the people the law of the god of that land." 28 So an Israelite priest who had been deported from Samaria went and lived in Bethel, where he taught the people how to worship the LORD.

29 But the people who settled in Samaria continued to make their own idols, and they placed them in the shrines that the Israelites had built. Each different group made idols in the cities they were living in: 30 the people of Babylon made idols of the god Succoth Benoth; the people of Cuth, idols of Nergal; the people of Hamath, idols of Ashima; 31 the people of Ivvah, idols of Nibhaz and Tartak; and the people of Sepharvaim sacrificed their children as burnt offerings to their gods Adrammelech and Anammelech. 32 These people also worshiped the LORD and chose from among their own number all sorts of people to serve as priests at the pagan places of worship and to offer sacrifices for them there. 33 So they worshiped the LORD, but they also worshiped their own gods according to the customs of the countries from which they had come.

34 They still carry on their old customs to this day. They do not worship the LORD nor do they obey the laws and commands which he gave to the descendants of Jacob, whom he named Israel. 35 The LORD had made a covenant with them and had ordered them: "Do not worship other gods; do not bow down to them or serve them or offer sacrifices to them. 36 You shall obey me, the LORD, who brought you out of Egypt with great power and strength; you are to bow down to me and offer sacrifices to me. 37 You shall always obey the laws and commands that I wrote for you. You shall not obey other gods, 38 and you shall not forget the covenant I made with you. 39 You shall obey me, the LORD your God, and I will rescue you from your enemies." 40 But those people would not listen, and they continued to follow their old customs.

41 So those people worshiped the LORD, but they also worshiped their idols; and

to this day their descendants continue to do the same.

King Hezekiah of Judah
(2 Chronicles 29.1, 2; 31.1)

18 In the third year of the reign of Hoshea son of Elah as king of Israel, Hezekiah son of Ahaz became king of Judah 2 at the age of twenty-five, and he ruled in Jerusalem for twenty-nine years. His mother was Abijah, the daughter of Zechariah. 3 Following the example of his ancestor King David, he did what was pleasing to the LORD. 4 He destroyed the pagan places of worship, broke the stone pillars, and cut down the images of the goddess Asherah. He also broke in pieces the bronze snake that Moses had made, which was called Nehushtan. Up to that time the people of Israel had burned incense in its honor. 5 Hezekiah trusted in the LORD, the God of Israel; Judah never had another king like him, either before or after his time. 6 He was faithful to the LORD and never disobeyed him, but carefully kept all the commands that the LORD had given Moses. 7 So the LORD was with him, and he was successful in everything he did. He rebelled against the emperor of Assyria and refused to submit to him. 8 He defeated the Philistines and raided their settlements, from the smallest village to the largest city, including Gaza and its surrounding territory.

9 In the fourth year of Hezekiah's reign—which was the seventh year of King Hoshea's reign over Israel— Emperor Shalmaneser of Assyria invaded Israel and besieged Samaria. 10 In the third year of the siege Samaria fell; this was the sixth year of Hezekiah's reign and the ninth year of Hoshea's reign. 11 The Assyrian emperor[q] took the Israelites to Assyria as prisoners and settled some of them in the city of Halah, some near the Habor River in the district of Gozan, and some in the cities of Media.

12 Samaria fell because the Israelites did not obey the LORD their God, but broke the covenant he had made with them and disobeyed all the laws given by Moses, the servant of the LORD. They would not listen and they would not obey.

---

p Some ancient translations him; Hebrew them.　　q ASSYRIAN EMPEROR: See 17.6.

2 KINGS

The Assyrians Threaten Jerusalem
(2 Chronicles 32.1-19; Isaiah 36.1-22)

13 In the fourteenth year of the reign of King Hezekiah, Sennacherib, the emperor of Assyria, attacked the fortified cities of Judah and conquered them. 14 Hezekiah sent a message to Sennacherib, who was in Lachish: "I have done wrong; please stop your attack, and I will pay whatever you demand." The emperor's answer was that Hezekiah should send him ten tons of silver and one ton of gold. 15 Hezekiah sent him all the silver in the Temple and in the palace treasury; 16 he also stripped the gold from the temple doors and the gold with which he himself had covered the doorposts, and he sent it all to Sennacherib. 17 The Assyrian emperor sent a large army from Lachish to attack Hezekiah at Jerusalem; it was commanded by his three highest officials. When they arrived at Jerusalem, they occupied the road where the cloth makers work by the ditch that brings water from the upper pool. 18 Then they sent for King Hezekiah, and three of his officials went out to meet them: Eliakim son of Hilkiah, who was in charge of the palace; Shebna, the court secretary; and Joah son of Asaph, who was in charge of the records. 19 One of the Assyrian officials told them that the emperor wanted to know what made King Hezekiah so confident. 20 He demanded, "Do you think that words can take the place of military skill and might? Who do you think will help you rebel against Assyria? 21 You are expecting Egypt to help you, but that would be like using a reed as a walking stick—it would break and jab your hand. That is what the king of Egypt is like when anyone relies on him."

22 The Assyrian official went on, "Or will you tell me that you are relying on the LORD your God? It was the LORD's shrines and altars that Hezekiah destroyed, when he told the people of Judah and Jerusalem to worship only at the altar in Jerusalem. 23 I will make a bargain with you in the name of the emperor. I will give you two thousand horses if you can find that many men to ride them! 24 You are no match for even the lowest ranking Assyrian official, and yet you expect the Egyptians to send you chariots and cavalry! 25 Do you think I have attacked your country and destroyed it without the LORD's help? The LORD himself told me to attack it and destroy it."

26 Then Eliakim, Shebna, and Joah told the official, "Speak Aramaic to us, sir. We understand it. Don't speak Hebrew; all the people on the wall are listening."

27 He replied, "Do you think you and the king are the only ones the emperor sent me to say all these things to? No, I am also talking to the people who are sitting on the wall, who will have to eat their excrement and drink their urine, just as you will."

28 Then the official stood up and shouted in Hebrew, "Listen to what the emperor of Assyria is telling you! 29 He warns you not to let Hezekiah deceive you. Hezekiah can't save you. 30 And don't let him persuade you to rely on the LORD. Don't think that the LORD will save you and that he will stop our Assyrian army from capturing your city. 31 Don't listen to Hezekiah. The emperor of Assyria commands you to come out of the city and surrender. You will all be allowed to eat grapes from your own vines and figs from your own trees, and to drink water from your own wells— 32 until the emperor resettles you in a country much like your own, where there are vineyards to give wine and there is grain for making bread; it is a land of olives, olive oil, and honey. If you do what he commands, you will not die, but live. Don't let Hezekiah fool you into thinking that the LORD will rescue you. 33 Did the gods of any other nations save their countries from the emperor of Assyria? 34 Where are they now, the gods of Hamath and Arpad? Where are the gods of Sepharvaim, Hena, and Ivvah? Did anyone save Samaria? 35 When did any of the gods of all these countries ever save their country from our emperor? Then what makes you think the LORD can save Jerusalem?"

36 The people kept quiet, just as King Hezekiah had told them to; they did not say a word. 37 Then Eliakim, Shebna, and Joah tore their clothes in grief, and went and reported to the king what the Assyrian official had said.

The King Asks Isaiah's Advice
(Isaiah 37.1-7)

19 As soon as King Hezekiah heard their report, he tore his clothes in grief, put on sackcloth, and went to the Temple of the LORD. 2 He sent Eliakim, the official in charge of the palace, Shebna, the court secretary, and the senior priests to the prophet Isaiah son of Amoz. They also were wearing sackcloth. 3 This is the message which he told them to give Isaiah: "Today is a day of suffering; we are being punished and are in disgrace. We are like a woman who is ready to give birth, but is too weak to do it. 4 The Assyrian emperor has sent his chief official to insult the living God. May the LORD your God hear these insults and punish those who spoke them. So pray to God for those of our people who survive."

5 When Isaiah received King Hezekiah's message, 6 he sent back this answer: "The LORD tells you not to let the Assyrians frighten you with their claims that he cannot save you. 7 The LORD will cause the emperor to hear a rumor that will make him go back to his own country, and the LORD will have him killed there."

The Assyrians Send Another Threat
(Isaiah 37.8-20)

8 The Assyrian official learned that the emperor had left Lachish and was fighting against the nearby city of Libnah; so he went there to consult him. 9 Word reached the Assyrians that the Egyptian army, led by King Tirhakah of Ethiopia,*r* was coming to attack them. When the emperor heard this, he sent a letter to King Hezekiah of Judah 10 to tell him, "The god you are trusting in has told you that you will not fall into my hands, but don't let that deceive you. 11 You have heard what an Assyrian emperor does to any country he decides to destroy. Do you think that you can escape? 12 My ancestors destroyed the cities of Gozan, Haran, and Rezeph, and killed the people of Betheden who lived in Telassar, and none of their gods could save them. 13 Where are the kings of the cities of Hamath, Arpad, Sepharvaim, Hena, and Ivvah?"

14 King Hezekiah took the letter from the messengers and read it. Then he went to the Temple, placed the letter there in the presence of the LORD, 15 and prayed, "O LORD, the God of Israel, seated on your throne above the winged creatures, you alone are God, ruling all the kingdoms of the world. You created the earth and the sky. 16 Now, LORD, look at what is happening to us. Listen to all the things that Sennacherib is saying to insult you, the living God. 17 We all know, LORD, that the emperors of Assyria have destroyed many nations, made their lands desolate, 18 and burned up their gods—which were no gods at all, only images of wood and stone made by human hands. 19 Now, LORD our God, rescue us from the Assyrians, so that all the nations of the world will know that only you, O LORD, are God."

Isaiah's Message to the King
(Isaiah 37.21-38)

20 Then Isaiah sent a message telling King Hezekiah that in answer to the king's prayer 21 the LORD had said, "The city of Jerusalem laughs at you, Sennacherib, and makes fun of you. 22 Whom do you think you have been insulting and ridiculing? You have been disrespectful to me, the holy God of Israel. 23 You sent your messengers to boast to me that with all your chariots you had conquered the highest mountains of Lebanon. You boasted that there you cut down the tallest cedars and the finest cypress trees and that you reached the deepest parts of the forests. 24 You boasted that you dug wells and drank water in foreign lands and that the feet of your soldiers tramped the Nile River dry.

25 "Have you never heard that I planned all this long ago? And now I have carried it out. I gave you the power to turn fortified cities into piles of rubble. 26 The people who lived there were powerless; they were frightened and stunned. They were like grass in a field or weeds growing on a roof when the hot east wind blasts them.*s*

---

r Hebrew Cush: Cush is the ancient name of the extensive territory south of the First Cataract of the Nile River. This region was called Ethiopia in Graeco-Roman times, and included within its borders most of modern Sudan and some of present-day Ethiopia (Abyssinia).   s Probable text when the hot east wind blasts them; Hebrew blasted before they are grown.

27 "But I know everything about you, what you do and where you go. I know how you rage against me. 28 I have received the report of that rage and that pride of yours, and now I will put a hook through your nose and a bit in your mouth, and take you back by the same road you came."

29 Then Isaiah said to King Hezekiah, "Here is a sign of what will happen. This year and next you will have only wild grain to eat, but the following year you will be able to plant your grain and harvest it, and plant vines and eat grapes. 30 Those in Judah who survive will flourish like plants that send roots deep into the ground and produce fruit. 31 There will be people in Jerusalem and on Mount Zion who will survive, because the Lord is determined to make this happen.

32 "And this is what the Lord has said about the Assyrian emperor: 'He will not enter this city or shoot a single arrow against it. No soldiers with shields will come near the city, and no siege mounds will be built around it. 33 He will go back by the same road he came, without entering this city. I, the Lord, have spoken. 34 I will defend this city and protect it, for the sake of my own honor and because of the promise I made to my servant David.'"

35 That night an angel of the Lord went to the Assyrian camp and killed 185,000 soldiers. At dawn the next day there they lay, all dead! 36 Then the Assyrian emperor Sennacherib withdrew and returned to Nineveh. 37 One day, when he was worshiping in the temple of his god Nisroch, two of his sons, Adrammelech and Sharezer, killed him with their swords and then escaped to the land of Ararat. Another of his sons, Esarhaddon, succeeded him as emperor.

King Hezekiah's Illness and Recovery

(Isaiah 38.1-8, 21, 22; 2 Chronicles 32.24-26)

20 About this time King Hezekiah became sick and almost died. The prophet Isaiah son of Amoz went to see him and said to him, "The Lord tells you that you are to put everything in or-

der, because you will not recover. Get ready to die."

2 Hezekiah turned his face to the wall and prayed: 3 "Remember, Lord, that I have served you faithfully and loyally and that I have always tried to do what you wanted me to." And he began to cry bitterly.

4 Isaiah left the king, but before he had passed through the central courtyard of the palace the Lord told him to go back to Hezekiah, ruler of the Lord's people, and say to him, "I, the Lord, the God of your ancestor David, have heard your prayer and seen your tears. I will heal you, and in three days you will go to the Temple. 6 I will let you live fifteen years longer. I will rescue you and this city Jerusalem from the emperor of Assyria. I will defend this city, for the sake of my own honor and because of the promise I made to my servant David."

7 Then Isaiah told the king's attendants to put on his boil a paste made of figs, and he would get well.ᵗ 8 King Hezekiah asked, "What is the sign to prove that the Lord will heal me and that three days later I will be able to go to the Temple?"

9 Isaiah replied, "The Lord will give you a sign to prove that he will keep his promise. Now, would you prefer to have the shadow on the stairway go forward ten steps or go back ten steps?"ᵘ

10 Hezekiah answered, "It's easy to have the shadow go forward ten steps!ᵛ Have it go back ten steps."ᵛ

11 Isaiah prayed to the Lord, and the Lord made the shadow go back ten stepsᵛ on the stairwayʷ set up by King Ahaz.

Messengers from Babylonia

(Isaiah 39.1-8)

12 About that same time the king of Babylonia, Merodach Baladan, the son of Baladan, heard that King Hezekiah had been sick, so he sent him a letter and a present. 13 Hezekiah welcomed the messengers and showed them his wealth—his silver and gold, his spices and perfumes, and all his military equipment. There was nothing in his storerooms or anywhere in his kingdom that

---

ᵗ *One ancient translation (and see Is 38.21)* figs, and he would get well; *Hebrew* figs. They did so, and he got well. ᵘ stairway . . . steps . . . steps . . . ; *or* sundial . . . degrees . . . degrees. ᵛ steps; *or* degrees. ʷ stairway; *or* sundial. *Archaeological evidence suggests that the stairway referred to in this passage was one specially constructed to tell time.*

he did not show them. 14 Then the prophet Isaiah went to King Hezekiah and asked, "Where did these men come from and what did they say to you?"

Hezekiah answered, "They came from a very distant country, from Babylonia."

15 "What did they see in the palace?"

"They saw everything. There is nothing in the storerooms that I didn't show them."

16 Isaiah then told the king, "The Lord Almighty says that 17 a time is coming when everything in your palace, everything that your ancestors have stored up to this day, will be carried off to Babylonia. Nothing will be left. 18 Some of your own direct descendants will be taken away and made eunuchs to serve in the palace of the king of Babylonia."

19 King Hezekiah understood this to mean that there would be peace and security during his lifetime, so he replied, "The message you have given me from the Lord is good."

The End of Hezekiah's Reign
(2 Chronicles 32.32, 33)

20 Everything else that King Hezekiah did, his brave deeds, and an account of how he built a reservoir and dug a tunnel to bring water into the city, are all recorded in *The History of the Kings of Judah.* 21 Hezekiah died, and his son Manasseh succeeded him as king.

King Manasseh of Judah
(2 Chronicles 33.1-20)

21 Manasseh was twelve years old when he became king of Judah, and he ruled in Jerusalem for fifty-five years. His mother was Hephzibah. 2 Following the disgusting practices of the nations whom the Lord had driven out of the land as his people advanced, Manasseh sinned against the Lord. 3 He rebuilt the pagan places of worship that his father Hezekiah had destroyed; he built altars for the worship of Baal and made an image of the goddess Asherah, as King Ahab of Israel had done. Manasseh also worshiped the stars. 4 He built pagan altars in the Temple, the place that the Lord had said was where he should be worshiped. 5 In the two courtyards of the Temple he built altars for the worship of the stars. 6 He sacrificed his son

as a burnt offering. He practiced divination and magic and consulted[x] fortune-tellers and mediums. He sinned greatly against the Lord and stirred up his anger. 7 He placed the symbol of the goddess Asherah in the Temple, the place about which the Lord had said to David and his son Solomon: "Here in Jerusalem, in this Temple, is the place that I have chosen out of all the territory of the twelve tribes of Israel as the place where I am to be worshiped. 8 And if the people of Israel will obey all my commands and keep the whole Law that my servant Moses gave them, then I will not allow them to be driven out of the land that I gave to their ancestors." 9 But the people of Judah did not obey the Lord, and Manasseh led them to commit even greater sins than those committed by the nations whom the Lord had driven out of the land as his people advanced.

10 Through his servants the prophets the Lord said, 11 "King Manasseh has done these disgusting things, things far worse than what the Canaanites did; and with his idols he has led the people of Judah into sin. 12 So I, the Lord God of Israel, will bring such a disaster on Jerusalem and Judah that everyone who hears about it will be stunned. 13 I will punish Jerusalem as I did Samaria, as I did King Ahab of Israel and his descendants. I will wipe Jerusalem clean of its people, as clean as a plate that has been wiped and turned upside down. 14 I will abandon the people who survive, and will hand them over to their enemies, who will conquer them and plunder their land. 15 I will do this to my people because they have sinned against me and have stirred up my anger from the time their ancestors came out of Egypt to this day."

16 Manasseh killed so many innocent people that the streets of Jerusalem were flowing with blood; he did this in addition to leading the people of Judah into idolatry, causing them to sin against the Lord.

17 Everything else that Manasseh did, including the sins he committed, is recorded in *The History of the Kings of Judah.* 18 Manasseh died and was buried in the palace garden, the garden of

---

x consulted; *or* brought back.

Uzza, and his son Amon succeeded him as king.

King Amon of Judah
(2 Chronicles 33.21-25)

19 Amon was twenty-two years old when he became king of Judah, and he ruled in Jerusalem for two years. His mother was Meshullemeth, the daughter of Haruz from the town of Jotbah. 20 Like his father Manasseh, he sinned against the LORD; 21 he imitated his father's actions, and he worshiped the idols that his father had worshiped. 22 He rejected the LORD, the God of his ancestors, and disobeyed the LORD's commands.

23 Amon's officials plotted against him and assassinated him in the palace. 24 The people of Judah killed Amon's assassins and made his son Josiah king.

25 Everything else that Amon did is recorded in *The History of the Kings of Judah.* 26 Amon was buried in the tomb in the garden of Uzza, and his son Josiah succeeded him as king.

King Josiah of Judah
(2 Chronicles 34.1, 2)

22 Josiah was eight years old when he became king of Judah, and he ruled in Jerusalem for thirty-one years. His mother was Jedidah, the daughter of Adaiah from the town of Bozkath. 2 Josiah did what was pleasing to the LORD; he followed the example of his ancestor King David, strictly obeying all the laws of God.

The Book of the Law Is Discovered
(2 Chronicles 34.8-28)

3 In the eighteenth year of his reign, King Josiah sent the court secretary Shaphan, the son of Azaliah and grandson of Meshullam, to the Temple with the order: 4 "Go to the High Priest Hilkiah and get a report on the amount of money that the priests on duty at the entrance to the Temple have collected from the people. 5 Tell him to give the money to the men who are in charge of the repairs in the Temple. They are to pay 6 the carpenters, the builders, and the masons, and buy the timber and the stones used in the repairs. 7 The men in charge of the work are thoroughly honest, so there is no need to require them to account for the funds."

8 Shaphan delivered the king's order to Hilkiah, and Hilkiah told him that he had found the book of the Law in the Temple. Hilkiah gave him the book, and Shaphan read it. 9 Then he went back to the king and reported: "Your servants have taken the money that was in the Temple and have handed it over to the men in charge of the repairs." 10 And then he said, "I have here a book that Hilkiah gave me." And he read it aloud to the king.

11 When the king heard the book being read, he tore his clothes in dismay, 12 and gave the following order to Hilkiah the priest, to Ahikam son of Shaphan, to Achbor son of Micaiah, to Shaphan, the court secretary, and to Asaiah, the king's attendant: 13 "Go and consult the LORD for me and for all the people of Judah about the teachings of this book. The LORD is angry with us because our ancestors have not done what this book says must be done."

14 Hilkiah, Ahikam, Achbor, Shaphan, and Asaiah went to consult a woman named Huldah, a prophet who lived in the newer part of Jerusalem. (Her husband Shallum, the son of Tikvah and grandson of Harhas, was in charge of the Temple robes.) They described to her what had happened, 15 and she told them to go back to the king and give him 16 the following message from the LORD: "I am going to punish Jerusalem and all its people, as written in the book that the king has read. 17 They have rejected me and have offered sacrifices to other gods, and so have stirred up my anger by all they have done. My anger is aroused against Jerusalem, and it will not die down. 18 As for the king himself, this is what I, the LORD God of Israel, say: You listened to what is written in the book, 19 and you repented and humbled yourself before me, tearing your clothes and weeping, when you heard how I threatened to punish Jerusalem and its people. I will make it a terrifying sight, a place whose name people will use as a curse. But I have heard your prayer, 20 and the punishment which I am going to bring on Jerusalem will not come until after your death. I will let you die in peace."

The men returned to King Josiah with this message.

Josiah Does Away with Pagan Worship

(2 Chronicles 34.3-7, 29-33)

23 King Josiah summoned all the leaders of Judah and Jerusalem, [2] and together they went to the Temple, accompanied by the priests and the prophets and all the rest of the people, rich and poor alike. Before them all the king read aloud the whole book of the covenant which had been found in the Temple. [3] He stood by the royal column and made a covenant with the LORD to obey him, to keep his laws and commands with all his heart and soul, and to put into practice the demands attached to the covenant, as written in the book. And all the people promised to keep the covenant.

[4] Then Josiah ordered the High Priest Hilkiah, his assistant priests, and the guards on duty at the entrance to the Temple to bring out of the Temple all the objects used in the worship of Baal, of the goddess Asherah, and of the stars. The king burned all these objects outside the city near Kidron Valley and then had the ashes taken to Bethel. [5] He removed from office the priests that the kings of Judah had ordained to offer sacrifices[y] on the pagan altars in the cities of Judah and in places near Jerusalem—all the priests who offered sacrifices to Baal, to the sun, the moon, the planets, and the stars. [6] He removed from the Temple the symbol of the goddess Asherah, took it out of the city to Kidron Valley, burned it, pounded its ashes to dust, and scattered it over the public burying ground. [7] He destroyed the living quarters in the Temple occupied by the temple prostitutes.[z] (It was there that women wove robes used in the worship of Asherah.) [8] He brought to Jerusalem the priests who were in the cities of Judah, and throughout the whole country he desecrated the altars where they had offered sacrifices. He also tore down the altars dedicated to the goat demons near the gate built by Joshua, the city governor, which was to the left of the main gate as one enters the city. [9] Those priests were not allowed to serve in the Temple, but they could eat the unleavened bread provided for their fellow priests.

[10] King Josiah also desecrated Topheth, the pagan place of worship in Hinnom Valley, so that no one could sacrifice his son or daughter as a burnt offering to the god Molech. [11] He also removed the horses that the kings of Judah had dedicated to the worship of the sun, and he burned the chariots used in this worship. (These were kept in the temple courtyard, near the gate and not far from the living quarters of Nathan Melech, a high official.) [12] The altars which the kings of Judah had built on the palace roof above King Ahaz' quarters, King Josiah tore down, along with the altars put up by King Manasseh in the two courtyards of the Temple; he smashed the altars to bits[a] and threw them into Kidron Valley. [13] Josiah desecrated the altars that King Solomon had built east of Jerusalem, south of the Mount of Olives,[b] for the worship of disgusting idols—Astarte the goddess of Sidon, Chemosh the god of Moab, and Molech the god of Ammon. [14] King Josiah broke the stone pillars to pieces, cut down the symbols of the goddess Asherah, and the ground where they had stood he covered with human bones.

[15] Josiah also tore down the place of worship in Bethel, which had been built by King Jeroboam son of Nebat, who led Israel into sin. Josiah pulled down the altar, broke its stones into pieces,[c] and pounded them to dust; he also burned the image of Asherah. [16] Then Josiah looked around and saw some tombs there on the hill; he had the bones taken out of them and burned on the altar. In this way he desecrated the altar, doing what the prophet had predicted long before during the festival as King Jeroboam was standing by the altar. King Josiah looked around and saw the tomb of the prophet[d] who had made this pre-

---

[y] *Some ancient translations* to offer sacrifices; *Hebrew* and he offered sacrifices.
[z] TEMPLE PROSTITUTES: *Men and women who practiced prostitution in the worship of fertility gods.*
[a] *Probable text* smashed ... to bits; *Hebrew unclear.*   [b] MOUNT OF OLIVES: *Hebrew here refers to it as "Mount of Destruction" or "Mount of Sin."*   [c] *One ancient translation* broke its stones into pieces; *Hebrew* burned the altar.   [d] *One ancient translation* during the festival ... the prophet; *Hebrew does not have these words.*

diction. 17 "Whose tomb is that?" he asked.

The people of Bethel answered, "It is the tomb of the prophet who came from Judah and predicted these things that you have done to this altar."

18 "Leave it as it is," Josiah ordered. "His bones are not to be moved."

So his bones were not moved, neither were those of the prophet who had come from Samaria.

19 In every city of Israel King Josiah tore down all the pagan places of worship which had been built by the kings of Israel, who thereby aroused the LORD's anger. He did to all those altars what he had done in Bethel. 20 He killed all the pagan priests on the altars where they served, and he burned human bones on every altar. Then he returned to Jerusalem.

Josiah Celebrates the Passover
(2 Chronicles 35.1-19)

21 King Josiah ordered the people to celebrate the Passover in honor of the LORD their God, as written in the book of the covenant. 22 No Passover like this one had ever been celebrated by any of the kings of Israel or of Judah, since the time when judges ruled the nation. 23 Now at last, in the eighteenth year of the reign of Josiah, the Passover was celebrated in Jerusalem.

Other Changes Made by Josiah

24 In order to enforce the laws written in the book that the High Priest Hilkiah had found in the Temple, King Josiah removed from Jerusalem and the rest of Judah all the mediums and fortunetellers, and all the household gods, idols, and all other pagan objects of worship. 25 There had never been a king like him before, who served the LORD with all his heart, mind, and strength, obeying all the Law of Moses; nor has there been a king like him since.

26 But the LORD's fierce anger had been aroused against Judah by what King Manasseh had done, and even now it did not die down. 27 The LORD said, "I will do to Judah what I have done to Israel: I will banish the people of Judah from my sight, and I will reject Jerusalem, the city I chose, and the Temple, the place I said was where I should be worshiped."

The End of Josiah's Reign
(2 Chronicles 35.20 — 36.1)

28 Everything else that King Josiah did is recorded in *The History of the Kings of Judah*. 29 While Josiah was king, King Neco of Egypt led an army to the Euphrates River to help the emperor of Assyria. King Josiah tried to stop the Egyptian army at Megiddo and was killed in battle. 30 His officials placed his body in a chariot and took it back to Jerusalem, where he was buried in the royal tombs.

The people of Judah chose Josiah's son Joahaz and anointed him king.

King Joahaz of Judah
(2 Chronicles 36.2-4)

31 Joahaz was twenty-three years old when he became king of Judah, and he ruled in Jerusalem for three months. His mother was Hamutal, the daughter of Jeremiah from the city of Libnah. 32 Following the example of his ancestors, he sinned against the LORD. 33 His reign ended when King Neco of Egypt took him prisoner in Riblah, in the land of Hamath, and made Judah pay 7,500 pounds of silver and 75 pounds of gold as tribute. 34 King Neco made Josiah's son Eliakim king of Judah as successor to Josiah, and changed his name to Jehoiakim. Joahaz was taken to Egypt by King Neco, and there he died.

King Jehoiakim of Judah
(2 Chronicles 36.5-8)

35 King Jehoiakim collected a tax from the people in proportion to their wealth, in order to raise the amount needed to pay the tribute demanded by the king of Egypt.

36 Jehoiakim was twenty-five years old when he became king of Judah, and he ruled in Jerusalem for eleven years. His mother was Zebidah, the daughter of Pedaiah from the town of Rumah. 37 Following the example of his ancestors, Jehoiakim sinned against the LORD.

24 While Jehoiakim was king, King Nebuchadnezzar of Babylonia invaded Judah, and for three years Jehoiakim was forced to submit to his rule; then he rebelled. 2 The LORD sent armed bands of Babylonians, Syrians, Moabites, and Ammonites against Jehoiakim to destroy Judah, as the LORD had said through his servants the prophets that

he would do. ³This happened at the
LORD's command, in order to banish the
people of Judah from his sight because
of all the sins that King Manasseh had
committed, ⁴and especially because of
all the innocent people he had killed.
The LORD could not forgive Manasseh for
that.

⁵Everything that Jehoiakim did is recorded in *The History of the Kings of
Judah.* ⁶Jehoiakim died, and his son Je-
hoiakin succeeded him as king.

⁷The king of Egypt and his army never
marched out of Egypt again, because the
king of Babylonia now controlled all the
territory that had belonged to Egypt,
from the Euphrates River to the northern border of Egypt.

King Jehoiachin of Judah
(2 Chronicles 36.9, 10)

⁸Jehoiachin was eighteen years old
when he became king of Judah, and he
ruled in Jerusalem for three months. His
mother was Nehushta, the daughter of
Elnathan from Jerusalem. ⁹Following
the example of his father, Jehoiachin
sinned against the LORD.

¹⁰It was during his reign that the
Babylonian army, commanded by King
Nebuchadnezzar's officers, marched
against Jerusalem and besieged it.
¹¹During the siege Nebuchadnezzar
himself came to Jerusalem, ¹²and King
Jehoiachin, along with his mother, his
sons, his officers, and the palace officials, surrendered to the Babylonians. In
the eighth year of Nebuchadnezzar's
reign he took Jehoiachin prisoner ¹³and
carried off to Babylon all the treasures
in the Temple and the palace. As the
LORD had foretold, Nebuchadnezzar
broke up all the gold utensils which
King Solomon had made for use in the
Temple. ¹⁴Nebuchadnezzar carried
away as prisoners the people of Jerusalem, all the royal princes, and all the
leading men, ten thousand in all. He also
deported all the skilled workers, including the blacksmiths, leaving only the
poorest of the people behind in Judah.

¹⁵Nebuchadnezzar took Jehoiachin to
Babylon as a prisoner, together with Jehoiachin's mother, his wives, his officials, and the leading men of Judah.
¹⁶Nebuchadnezzar deported all the important men to Babylonia, seven thousand in all, and one thousand skilled
workers, including the blacksmiths, all
of them able-bodied men fit for military
duty.

¹⁷Nebuchadnezzar made Jehoiachin's
uncle Mattaniah king of Judah and
changed his name to Zedekiah.

King Zedekiah of Judah
(2 Chronicles 36.11, 12; Jeremiah 52.1-3a)

¹⁸Zedekiah was twenty-one years old
when he became king of Judah, and he
ruled in Jerusalem for eleven years. His
mother was Hamutal, the daughter of
Jeremiah from the city of Libnah. ¹⁹King
Zedekiah sinned against the LORD, just
as King Jehoiakim had done. ²⁰The LORD
became so angry with the people of Jerusalem and Judah that he banished
them from his sight.

The Fall of Jerusalem
(2 Chronicles 36.13-21; Jeremiah 52.3b-11)

25 Zedekiah rebelled against King
Nebuchadnezzar of Babylonia,
and so Nebuchadnezzar came with all
his army and attacked Jerusalem on the
tenth day of the tenth month of the ninth
year of Zedekiah's reign. They set up
camp outside the city, built siege walls
around it, ²and kept it under siege until
Zedekiah's eleventh year. ³On the ninth
day of the fourth month*e* of that same
year, when the famine was so bad that
the people had nothing left to eat, ⁴the
city walls were broken through. Although the Babylonians were surrounding the city, all the soldiers escaped
during the night. They left by way of the
royal garden, went through the gateway
connecting the two walls, and fled in the
direction of the Jordan Valley. ⁵But the
Babylonian army pursued King Zedekiah, captured him in the plains near
Jericho, and all his soldiers deserted
him. ⁶Zedekiah was taken to King Nebuchadnezzar, who was in the city of Riblah, and there Nebuchadnezzar passed
sentence on him. ⁷While Zedekiah was
looking on, his sons were put to death;
then Nebuchadnezzar had Zedekiah's
eyes put out, placed him in chains, and
took him to Babylon.

e Probable text (see Jr 52.6) the fourth month; Hebrew the month.

The Destruction of the Temple
(Jeremiah 52.12-33)

8 On the seventh day of the fifth month of the nineteenth year of King Nebuchadnezzar of Babylonia, Nebuzaradan, adviser to the king and commander of his army, entered Jerusalem. 9 He burned down the Temple, the palace, and the houses of all the important people in Jerusalem, 10 and his soldiers tore down the city walls. 11 Then Nebuzaradan took away to Babylonia the people who were left in the city, the remaining skilled workers,*f* and those who had deserted to the Babylonians. 12 But he left in Judah some of the poorest people, who owned no property, and put them to work in the vineyards and fields.

13 The Babylonians broke in pieces the bronze columns and the carts that were in the Temple, together with the large bronze tank, and they took all the bronze to Babylon. 14 They also took away the shovels and the ash containers used in cleaning the altar, the tools used in tending the lamps, the bowls used for catching the blood from the sacrifices, the bowls used for burning incense, and all the other bronze articles used in the Temple service. 15 They took away everything that was made of gold or silver, including the small bowls and the pans used for carrying live coals. 16 The bronze objects that King Solomon had made for the Temple — the two columns, the carts, and the large tank — were too heavy to weigh. 17 The two columns were identical: each one was 27 feet high, with a bronze capital on top, 4½ feet high. All around each capital was a bronze grillwork decorated with pomegranates made of bronze.

The People of Judah Are Taken to Babylonia
(Jeremiah 52.24-27)

18 In addition, Nebuzaradan, the commanding officer, took away as prisoners Seraiah the High Priest, Zephaniah the priest next in rank, and the three other important Temple officials. 19 From the city he took the officer who had been in command of the troops, five of the king's personal advisers who were still in the city, the commander's assistant, who was in charge of military records, and sixty other important men. 20 Nebuzaradan took them to the king of Babylonia, who was in the city of Riblah 21 in the territory of Hamath. There the king had them beaten and put to death.

So the people of Judah were carried away from their land into exile.

Gedaliah, Governor of Judah
(Jeremiah 40.7-9; 41.1-3)

22 King Nebuchadnezzar of Babylonia made Gedaliah, the son of Ahikam and grandson of Shaphan, governor of Judah, and placed him in charge of all those who had not been taken away to Babylonia. 23 When the Judean officers and soldiers who had not surrendered heard about this, they joined Gedaliah at Mizpah. These officers were Ishmael son of Nethaniah, Johanan son of Kareah, Seraiah son of Tanhumeth from the town of Netophah, and Jezaniah from Maacah. 24 Gedaliah said to them, "I give you my word that there is no need for you to be afraid of the Babylonian officials. Settle in this land, serve the king of Babylonia, and all will go well with you."

25 But in the seventh month of that year, Ishmael, the son of Nethaniah and grandson of Elishama, a member of the royal family, went to Mizpah with ten men, attacked Gedaliah, and killed him. He also killed the Israelites and Babylonians who were there with him. 26 Then all the Israelites, rich and poor alike, together with the army officers, left and went to Egypt, because they were afraid of the Babylonians.

Jehoiachin Is Released from Prison
(Jeremiah 52.31-34)

27 In the year that Evilmerodach became king of Babylonia, he showed kindness to King Jehoiachin of Judah by releasing him from prison. This happened on the twenty-seventh day of the twelfth month of the thirty-seventh year after Jehoiachin had been taken away as prisoner. 28 Evilmerodach treated him kindly and gave him a position of

---

f Probable text (see Jr 52.15) skilled workers; *Hebrew* crowd.

greater honor than he gave the other kings who were exiles with him in Babylonia. 29 So Jehoiachin was permitted to change from his prison clothes and to dine at the king's table for the rest of his life. 30 Each day, for as long as he lived, he was given a regular allowance for his needs.

The First Book of
CHRONICLES

Introduction

First and Second Chronicles are largely a retelling of events recorded in the books of Samuel and Kings, but from a different point of view. Two main purposes govern the account of the history of the Israelite monarchy in the books of Chronicles:

1) To show that in spite of the disasters that had fallen upon the kingdoms of Israel and Judah, God was still keeping his promises to the nation and was working out his plan for his people through those who were living in Judah. As a basis for this assurance, the writer looked to the great achievements of David and Solomon, to the reforms of Jehoshaphat, Hezekiah, and Josiah, and to the people who remained faithful to God.

2) To describe the origin of the worship of God in the Temple at Jerusalem and especially the organization of the priests and Levites, by which the worship was carried out. David is presented as the real founder of the Temple and its ritual, even though it is Solomon who builds the Temple.

Outline of Contents

From Adam to Abraham
(Genesis 5.1-32; 10.1-32; 11.10-26)

1 Adam was the father of Seth, Seth was the father of Enosh, Enosh the father of Kenan, 2 Kenan the father of Mahalalel, Mahalalel the father of Jared. 3 Jared was the father of Enoch, who was the father of Methuselah; Methuselah was the father of Lamech, 4 who was the father of Noah. Noah had three sons: Shem, Ham, and Japheth.

5 The sons of Japheth — Gomer, Magog, Madai, Javan, Tubal, Meshech, and Tiras — were the ancestors of the peoples who bear their names. 6 The descendants of Gomer were the people of Ashkenaz, Riphath, and Togarmah. 7 The descendants of Javan were the people of Elishah, Spain, Cyprus, and Rhodes.

8 The sons of Ham — Cush, Egypt, Libya, and Canaan — were the ancestors of the peoples who bear their names. 9 The descendants of Cush were the people of Seba, Havilah, Sabtah, Raamah, and Sabteca. The descendants of Raamah were the people of Sheba and Dedan. (10 Cush had a son named Nimrod, who became the world's first great conqueror.) 11 The descendants of Egypt were the people of Lydia, Anam, Lehab, Naphtuh, 12 Pathrus, Casluh, and of Crete (from whom the Philistines were descended). 13 Canaan's sons — Sidon, the oldest, and Heth — were the ancestors of the peoples who bear their names. 14 Canaan was also the ancestor of the Jebusites, the Amorites, Girgashites, 15 Hivites, Arkites, Sinites, 16 Arvadites, Zemarites, and Hamathites.

17 Shem's sons — Elam, Asshur, Arpachshad, Lud, Aram, Uz, Hul, Gether, and Meshek — were the ancestors of the peoples who bear their names. 18 Arpachshad was the father of Shelah, who was the father of Eber. 19 Eber had two sons; one was named Peleg,a because during his time the people of the world were divided, and the other was named Joktan. 20 The descendants of Joktan were the people of Almodad, Sheleph, Hazarmaveth, Jerah, 21 Hadoram, Uzal, Diklah, 22 Ebal, Abimael, Sheba, 23 Ophir, Havilah, and Jobab.

24 The family line from Shem to Abram is as follows: Shem, Arpachshad, Shelah, 25 Eber, Peleg, Reu, 26 Serug, Nahor, Terah, 27 and Abram (also known as Abraham).

a PELEG: This name sounds like the Hebrew for "divide."

The Descendants of Ishmael
(Genesis 25.12-16)

28 Abraham had two sons, Isaac and Ishmael. 29 The sons of Ishmael became the heads of twelve tribes: Nebaioth (from the name of Ishmael's oldest son), Kedar, Adbeel, Mibsam, 30 Mishma, Dumah, Massa, Hadad, Tema, 31 Jetur, Naphish, and Kedemah.

32 Abraham had a concubine named Keturah, who bore him six sons: Zimran, Jokshan, Medan, Midian, Ishbak, and Shuah. Jokshan had two sons: Sheba and Dedan. 33 Midian had five sons: Ephah, Epher, Hanoch, Abida, and Eldaah.

The Descendants of Esau
(Genesis 36.1-19)

34 Abraham's son Isaac had two sons, Esau and Jacob. 35 Esau's sons were Eliphaz, Reuel, Jeush, Jalam, and Korah. 36 Eliphaz became the ancestor of the following tribes: Teman, Omar, Zephi, Gatam, Kenaz, Timna, and Amalek. 37 And Reuel became the ancestor of the tribes of Nahath, Zerah, Shammah, and Mizzah.

The Original Inhabitants of Edom
(Genesis 36.20-30)

38-42 The original inhabitants of Edom were descended from the following sons of Seir:

Lotan, who was the ancestor of the clans of Hori and Homam. (Lotan had a sister named Timna.)

Shobal, who was the ancestor of the clans of Alvan, Manahath, Ebal, Shephi, and Onam.

Zibeon, who had two sons, Aiah and Anah. Anah was the father of Dishon, and Dishon was the ancestor of the clans of Hamran, Eshban, Ithran, and Cheran.

Ezer, who was the ancestor of the clans of Bilhan, Zaavan, and Jaakan.

Dishan, who was the ancestor of the clans of Uz and Aran.

The Kings of Edom
(Genesis 36.31-43)

43-50 The following kings ruled the land of Edom one after the other, in the time before there were any kings in Israel:

Bela son of Beor from Dinhabah

Jobab son of Zerah from Bozrah

Husham from the region of Teman

Hadad son of Bedad from Avith (he defeated the Midianites in a battle in the country of Moab)

Samlah from Masrekah

Shaul from Rehoboth-on-the-River

Baal Hanan son of Achbor

Hadad from Pau (his wife was Mehetabel, the daughter of Matred and granddaughter of Mezahab)

51 The people of Edom were divided into the following tribes: Timna, Alvah, Jetheth, 52 Oholibamah, Elah, Pinon, 53 Kenaz, Teman, Mibzar, 54 Magdiel, and Iram.

The Descendants of Judah

2 Jacob had twelve sons: Reuben, Simeon, Levi, Judah, Issachar, Zebulun, 2 Dan, Joseph, Benjamin, Naphtali, Gad, and Asher.

3 Judah had five sons in all. By his wife Bathshua, a Canaanite, he had three sons: Er, Onan, and Shelah. His oldest son, Er, was so evil that the Lord killed him. 4 By his daughter-in-law Tamar, Judah had two more sons, Perez and Zerah.

5 Perez had two sons, Hezron and Hamul. 6 His brother Zerah had five sons: Zimri, Ethan, Heman, Calcol, and Darda. 7 Achan[b] son of Carmi, one of Zerah's descendants, brought disaster on the people of Israel by keeping loot that had been devoted to God.

8 Ethan had one son, Azariah.

The Family Tree of King David

9 Hezron had three sons: Jerahmeel, Ram, and Caleb. 10 The family line from Ram to Jesse is as follows: Ram, Amminadab, Nahshon (a prominent man of the tribe of Judah), 11 Salmon, Boaz, 12 Obed, and Jesse. 13 Jesse had seven sons. In order of age they were: Eliab, Abinadab, Shammah, 14 Nethanel, Raddai, 15 Ozem, and David. 16 He also had two daughters, Zeruiah and Abigail.

Jesse's daughter Zeruiah had three sons: Abishai, Joab, and Asahel. 17 His

---

[b] ACHAN: *This is his name in Js 7.1. The Hebrew text here calls him "Achar," which means "disaster."*

other daughter Abigail married Jether, a descendant of Ishmael, and they had a son named Amasa.

The Descendants of Hezron

18 Hezron's son Caleb married Azubah and had a daughter named Jerioth. She had[c] three sons: Jesher, Shobab, and Ardon. 19 After the death of Azubah, Caleb married Ephrath, and they had a son named Hur. 20 Hur's son was Uri, and his grandson was Bezalel.

21 When Hezron was sixty years old, he married Machir's daughter, the sister of Gilead. They had a son named Segub, 22 and Segub had a son named Jair. Jair ruled[d] twenty-three cities in the territory of Gilead. 23 But the kingdoms of Geshur and Aram conquered sixty towns there, including the villages of Jair and Kenath, and the towns nearby. All the people who lived there were descendants of Machir, the father of Gilead. 24 After Hezron died, his son Caleb married Ephrath, his father's widow.[e] They had a son named Ashhur, who founded the town of Tekoa.

The Descendants of Jerahmeel

25 Jerahmeel, the oldest son of Hezron, had five sons: Ram, the oldest, Bunah, Oren, Ozem, and Ahijah. 26-27 Ram had three sons: Maaz, Jamin, and Eker. Jerahmeel had another wife, a woman named Atarah, and they had a son, Onam. 28 Onam had two sons, Shammai and Jada, and Shammai also had two sons, Nadab and Abishur.

29 Abishur married a woman named Abihail, and they had two sons, Ahban and Molid. 30 Abishur's brother Nadab had two sons, Seled and Appaim, but Seled died without having any sons. 31 Appaim was the father of Ishi, Ishi was the father of Sheshan, and Sheshan the father of Ahlai.

32 Jada, the brother of Shammai, had two sons, Jether and Jonathan, but Jether died without having any sons. 33 Jonathan had two sons, Peleth and Zaza. All these were descendants of Jerahmeel.

34 Sheshan had no sons, only daughters. He had an Egyptian servant named Jarha, 35 to whom he gave one of his daughters in marriage. They had a son named Attai. 36 The family line from Attai to Elishama is as follows: Attai, Nathan, Zabad, 37 Ephlal, Obed, 38 Jehu, Azariah, 39 Helez, Eleasah, 40 Sismai, Shallum, 41 Jekamiah, and Elishama.

Other Descendants of Caleb

42 The oldest son of Caleb, Jerahmeel's brother, was named Mesha. Mesha was the father of Ziph, who was the father of Mareshah, who was the father of Hebron.[f] 43 Hebron had four sons: Korah, Tappuah, Rekem, and Shema. 44 Shema was the father of Raham and the grandfather of Jorkeam. Rekem, Shema's brother, was the father of Shammai, 45 who was the father of Maon, who was the father of Bethzur.

46 Caleb had a concubine named Ephah, and by her he had three more sons: Haran, Moza, and Gazez. Haran also had a son named Gazez.

(47 A man named Jahdai had six sons: Regem, Jotham, Geshan, Pelet, Ephah, and Shaaph.)

48 Caleb had another concubine, Maacah, who bore him two sons, Sheber and Tirhanah. 49 Later she had two more sons: Shaaph, who founded the town of Madmannah; and Shevah, who founded the towns of Machbenah and Gibea.

In addition, Caleb had a daughter named Achsah.

50 The following are also descendants of Caleb.

Hur was the oldest son of Caleb and his wife Ephrath. Hur's son Shobal founded Kiriath Jearim, 51 his second son Salma founded Bethlehem, and his third son Hareph founded Bethgader.

52 Shobal, the founder of Kiriath Jearim, was the ancestor of the people of Haroeh, of half the inhabitants of Menuhoth, 53 and of the following clans that lived in Kiriath Jearim: the Ithrites, Puthites, Shumathites, and Mishraites. (The people of the cities of Zorah and Eshtaol were members of these clans.)

54 Salma, the founder of Bethlehem, was the ancestor of the people of Netophath, of Atroth Beth Joab, and of the Zorites, who were one of the two clans in Manahath.

(55 The following clans of experts in

---

c *Some ancient translations* had a daughter.... She had; *Hebrew unclear.*   d *ruled; or owned.*
e *Some ancient translations* his son ... widow; *Hebrew unclear.*   f *Probable text* father of
Mareshah ... Hebron; *Hebrew unclear.*

writing and copying documents lived in the town of Jabez: the Tirathites, Shimeathites, and Sucathites. They were Kenites who had intermarried with the Rechabites.)

King David's Children

3 1-3 The following, in order of age, are David's sons who were born while he was in Hebron:

Amnon, whose mother was
　Ahinoam from Jezreel
Daniel, whose mother was
　Abigail from Carmel
Absalom, whose mother was
　Maacah, daughter of King
　Talmai of Geshur
Adonijah, whose mother was
　Haggith
Shephatiah, whose mother was
　Abital
Ithream, whose mother was
　Eglah

4 All six were born in Hebron during the seven and a half years that David ruled there.

In Jerusalem he ruled as king for thirty-three years, 5 and many sons were born to him there.

His wife Bathsheba, daughter of Ammiel, bore him four sons: Shimea, Shobab, Nathan, and Solomon.

6 He had nine other sons: Ibhar, Elishua, Elpelet, 7 Nogah, Nepheg, Japhia, 8 Elishama, Eliada, and Eliphelet. 9 In addition to all these sons, David had sons by his concubines. He also had a daughter, Tamar.

The Descendants of King Solomon

10 This is the line of King Solomon's descendants from father to son: Solomon, Rehoboam, Abijah, Asa, Jehoshaphat, 11 Jehoram, Ahaziah, Joash, 12 Amaziah, Uzziah, Jotham, 13 Ahaz, Hezekiah, Manasseh, 14 Amon, and Josiah. 15 Josiah had four sons: Johanan, Jehoiakim, Zedekiah, and Joahaz. 16 Jehoiakim had two sons: Jehoiachin and Zedekiah.

The Descendants of King Jehoiachin

17 These are the descendants of King Jehoiachin, who was taken prisoner by the Babylonians. Jehoiachin had seven sons: Shealtiel, 18 Malchiram, Pedaiah,

Shenazzar, Jekamiah, Hoshama, and Nedabiah. 19 Pedaiah had two sons, Zerubbabel and Shimei. Zerubbabel was the father of two sons, Meshullam and Hananiah, and one daughter, Shelomith. 20 He had five other sons: Hashubah, Ohel, Berechiah, Hasadiah, and Jushab Hesed.

21 Hananiah had two sons, Pelatiah and Jeshaiah. Jeshaiah was the father of Rephaiah, who was the father of Arnan, the father of Obadiah, the father of Shecaniah.g 22 Shecaniah had one son, Shemaiah, and five grandsons: Hattush, Igal, Bariah, Neariah, and Shaphat. 23 Neariah had three sons: Elioenai, Hizkiah, and Azrikam. 24 Elioenai had seven sons: Hodaviah, Eliashib, Pelaiah, Akkub, Johanan, Delaiah, and Anani.

The Descendants of Judah

4 These are some of the descendants of Judah: Perez, Hezron, Carmi, Hur, and Shobal. 2 Shobal was the father of Reaiah, who was the father of Jahath, the father of Ahumai and Lahad, the ancestors of the people who lived in Zorah.

3-4 Hur was the oldest son of his father Caleb's wife Ephrath, and his descendants founded the city of Bethlehem. Hur had three sons: Etam, Penuel, and Ezer. Etam had three sons:h Jezreel, Ishma, and Idbash, and one daughter, Hazzelelponi. Penuel founded the city of Gedor, and Ezer founded Hushah.

5 Ashhur, who founded the town of Tekoa, had two wives, Helah and Naarah. 6 He and Naarah had four sons: Ahuzzam, Hepher, Temeni, and Haahashtari. 7 Ashhur and Helah had three sons: Zereth, Izhar, and Ethnan.

8 Koz was the father of Anub and Zobebah, and the ancestor of the clans descended from Aharhel son of Harum.

9 There was a man named Jabez, who was the most respected member of his family. His mother had given him the name Jabez,i because his birth had been very painful. 10 But Jabez prayed to the God of Israel, "Bless me, God, and give me much land. Be with me and keep me from anything evil that might cause me pain." And God gave him what he prayed for.

---

g *Verse 21 in Hebrew is unclear.* h *Some ancient translations* sons; *Hebrew* fathers.
i JABEZ: *This name sounds like the Hebrew for "pain."*

Other Family Lists

11 Caleb, the brother of Shuhah, had a son, Mehir. Mehir was the father of Eshton, 12 who had three sons: Bethrapha, Paseah, and Tehinnah. Tehinnah was the founder of the city of Nahash. The descendants of these men lived in Recah.

13 Kenaz had two sons, Othniel and Seraiah. Othniel also had two sons, Hathath and Meonothai.ⁱ 14 Meonothai was the father of Ophrah.

Seraiah was the father of Joab, the founder of Handcraft Valley, where all the people were skilled workers.

15 Caleb son of Jephunneh had three sons: Iru, Elah, and Naam. And Elah was the father of Kenaz.

16 Jehallelel had four sons: Ziph, Ziphah, Tiria, and Asarel.

17-18 Ezrah had four sons: Jether, Mered, Epher, and Jalon. Mered married Bithiah, a daughter of the king of Egypt, and they had a daughter, Miriam, and two sons, Shammai and Ishbah. Ishbah founded the town of Eshtemoa. Mered also married a woman from the tribe of Judah, and they had three sons: Jered, who founded the town of Gedor; Heber, founder of the town of Soco; and Jekuthiel, founder of the town of Zanoah.

19 Hodiah married the sister of Naham. Their descendants founded the clan of Garm, which lived in the town of Keilah, and the clan of Maacath, which lived in the town of Eshtemoa.ᵏ

20 Shimon had four sons: Amnon, Rinnah, Benhanan, and Tilon.

Ishi had two sons: Zoheth and Benzoheth.

The Descendants of Shelah

21 Shelah was one of Judah's sons. His descendants included Er, who founded the town of Lecah; Laadah, founder of the town of Mareshah; the clan of linen weavers, who lived in the town of Beth Ashbea; 22 Jokim and the people who lived in the town of Cozeba; and Joash and Saraph, who married Moabite women and then settled in Bethlehem.ⁱ (These traditions are very old.) 23 They were potters in the service of the king and lived in the towns of Netaim and Gederah.

The Descendants of Simeon

24 Simeon had five sons: Nemuel, Jamin, Jarib, Zerah, and Shaul. 25 Shaul's son was Shallum, his grandson was Mibsam, and his great-grandson was Mishma. 26 Then from Mishma the line descended through Hammuel, Zaccur, and Shimei. 27 Shimei had sixteen sons and six daughters, but his relatives had fewer children, and the tribe of Simeon did not grow as much as the tribe of Judah did.

28 Down to the time of King David the descendants of Simeon lived in the following towns: Beersheba, Moladah, Hazarshual, 29 Bilhah, Ezem, Tolad, 30 Bethuel, Hormah, Ziklag, 31 Beth Marcaboth, Hazarsusim, Bethbiri, and Shaaraim. 32 They also lived in five other places: Etam, Ain, Rimmon, Tochen, and Ashan, 33 and the surrounding villages, as far southwest as the town of Baalath. These are the records which they kept of their families and of the places where they lived.

34-38 The following men were the heads of their clans:

Meshobab, Jamlech, Joshah son of Amaziah, Joel,
Jehu (the son of Joshibiah, the son of Seraiah, the son of Asiel),
Elioenai, Jaakobah, Jeshohaiah, Asaiah, Adiel, Jesimiel, Benaiah,
Ziza (the son of Shiphi, the son of Allon, a descendant of Jedaiah, Shimri, and Shemaiah).

Because their families continued to grow, 39 they spread out westward almost to Gerarᵐ and pastured their sheep on the eastern side of the valley in which that city is located. 40 They found plenty of fertile pasture lands there in a stretch of open country that was quiet and peaceful. The people who had lived there before were Hamites.

41 In the time of King Hezekiah of Judah, the men named above went to Gerar and destroyed the tents and huts of the people who lived there.ⁿ They drove

---

ⁱ Some ancient translations Meonothai; Hebrew does not have this name.   ᵏ Verse 19 in Hebrew is unclear.   ⁱ Probable text settled in Bethlehem; Hebrew unclear.   ᵐ Some ancient translations Gerar; Hebrew Gedor.   ⁿ the tents and huts . . . there; or the tents of the people who lived there, and the Meunites also.

the people out and settled there permanently because there was plenty of pasture for their sheep. 42 Five hundred other members of the tribe of Simeon went east to Edom. They were led by the sons of Ishi: Pelatiah, Neariah, Rephaiah, and Uzziel. 43 There they killed the surviving Amalekites, and they have lived there ever since.

The Descendants of Reuben

5 These are the descendants of Reuben, the oldest of Jacob's sons. (Because he had sex with one of his father's concubines, he lost the rights belonging to the first-born son, and those rights were given to Joseph. 2 It was the tribe of Judah, however, that became the strongest and provided a ruler for all the tribes.) 3 Reuben, the oldest of Jacob's sons, had four sons: Hanoch, Pallu, Hezron, and Carmi.

4-6 These are the descendants of Joel from generation to generation: Shemaiah, Gog, Shimei, Micah, Reaiah, Baal, and Beerah. The Assyrian emperor, Tiglath Pileser, captured Beerah, a leader of the tribe, and deported him.

7 The family records list the following clan leaders in the tribe of Reuben: Jeiel, Zechariah, 8 and Bela, the son of Azaz and grandson of Shema, of the clan of Joel. This clan lived in Aroer and in the territory from there north to Nebo and Baal Meon. 9 They had large herds in the land of Gilead, and so they occupied the land as far east as the desert that stretches all the way to the Euphrates River.

10 In the time of King Saul the tribe of Reuben attacked the Hagrites, killed them in battle, and occupied their land in the eastern part of Gilead.

The Descendants of Gad

11 The tribe of Gad lived to the north of Reuben in the land of Bashan as far east as Salecah. 12 Joel was the founder of the leading clan, and Shapham of the second most important clan. Janai and Shaphat were founders of other clans in Bashan. 13 The other members of the tribe belonged to the following seven clans: Michael, Meshullam, Sheba, Jorai, Jacan, Zia, and Eber. 14 They were

descendants of Abihail son of Huri, whose ancestors were traced back as follows: Abihail, Huri, Jaroah, Gilead, Michael, Jeshishai, Jahdo, Buz. 15 Ahi, the son of Abdiel and grandson of Guni, was head of these clans. 16 They lived in the territory of Bashan and Gilead, in the towns there and all over the pasture lands of Sharon. (17 These records were compiled in the days of King Jotham of Judah and King Jeroboam II of Israel.)

The Armies of the Eastern Tribes

18 In the tribes of Reuben, Gad, and East Manasseh there were 44,760 soldiers, well-trained in the use of shields, swords, and bows. 19 They went to war against the Hagrite tribes of Jetur, Naphish, and Nodab. 20 They put their trust in God and prayed to him for help, and God answered their prayers and made them victorious over the Hagrites and their allies. 21 They captured from the enemy 50,000 camels, 250,000 sheep, and 2,000 donkeys, and took 100,000 prisoners of war. 22 They killed many of the enemy, because the war was God's will. And they went on living in that territory until the exile.o

The People of East Manasseh

23 The people of East Manasseh settled in the territory of Bashan as far north as Baal Hermon, Senir, and Mount Hermon, and their population increased greatly. 24 The following were the heads of their clans: Epher, Ishi, Eliel, Azriel, Jeremiah, Hodaviah, and Jahdiel. They were all outstanding soldiers, well-known leaders of their clans.

The Eastern Tribes Are Deported

25 But the people were unfaithful to the God of their ancestors and deserted him to worship the gods of the nations whom God had driven out of the land. 26 So God caused Emperor Pul of Assyria (also known as Tiglath Pileser) to invade their country. He deported the tribes of Reuben, Gad, and East Manasseh and settled them permanently in Halah, Habor, and Hara, and by the Gozan River.

o THE EXILE: About 733 B.C. the Assyrians conquered northern Israel and the Israelite territory east of the Jordan River and deported the people (see 2 K 15.29).

The Family Line of the High Priests

6 Levi had three sons: Gershon, Kohath, and Merari. 2 Kohath had four sons: Amram, Izhar, Hebron, and Uzziel.

3 Amram had two sons, Aaron and Moses, and one daughter, Miriam. Aaron had four sons: Nadab, Abihu, Eleazar, and Ithamar.

4 The descendants of Eleazar from generation to generation are as follows: Phinehas, Abishua, 5 Bukki, Uzzi, 6 Zerahiah, Meraioth, 7 Amariah, Ahitub, 8 Zadok, Ahimaaz, 9 Azariah, Johanan, 10 Azariah (the one who served in the Temple which King Solomon built in Jerusalem), 11 Amariah, Ahitub, 12 Zadok, Shallum, 13 Hilkiah, Azariah, 14 Seraiah, Jehozadak. 15 King Nebuchadnezzar deported Jehozadak along with the other people of Judah and Jerusalem whom the LORD sent into exile.

Other Descendants of Levi

16 Levi had three sons: Gershon, Kohath, and Merari. 17 Each of them also had sons. Gershon was the father of Libni and Shimei; 18 Kohath was the father of Amram, Izhar, Hebron, and Uzziel; 19 and Merari was the father of Mahli and Mushi.

20 These are the descendants of Gershon from generation to generation: Libni, Jahath, Zimmah, 21 Joah, Iddo, Zerah, Jeatherai.

22 These are the descendants of Kohath from generation to generation: Amminadab, Korah, Assir, 23 Elkanah, Ebiasaph, Assir, 24 Tahath, Uriel, Uzziah, Shaul.

25 Elkanah had two sons, Amasai and Ahimoth. 26 These are Ahimoth's descendants from generation to generation: Elkanah, Zophai, Nahath, 27 Eliab, Jeroham, Elkanah.

28 Samuel had two sons: Joel,p the older, and Abijah, the younger.

29 These are the descendants of Merari from generation to generation: Mahli, Libni, Shimei, Uzzah, 30 Shimea, Haggiah, Asaiah.

The Temple Musicians

31 These are the men whom King David put in charge of the music at the place of worship in Jerusalem after the Covenant Box was moved there. 32 They took regular turns of duty at the Tent of the LORD's presence during the time before King Solomon built the Temple. 33 The family lines of those who held this office are as follows:

The clan of Kohath: Heman, the leader of the first choir, was the son of Joel. His family line went back to Jacob as follows: Heman, Joel, Samuel, 34 Elkanah, Jeroham, Eliel, Toah, 35 Zuph, Elkanah, Mahath, Amasai, 36 Elkanah, Joel, Azariah, Zephaniah, 37 Tahath, Assir, Ebiasaph, Korah, 38 Izhar, Kohath, Levi, Jacob.

39 Asaph was leader of the second choir. His family line went back to Levi as follows: Asaph, Berechiah, Shimea, 40 Michael, Baaseiah, Malchijah, 41 Ethni, Zerah, Adaiah, 42 Ethan, Zimmah, Shimei, 43 Jahath, Gershon, Levi.

44 Ethan of the clan of Merari was the leader of the third choir. His family line went back to Levi as follows: Ethan, Kishi, Abdi, Malluch, 45 Hashabiah, Amaziah, Hilkiah, 46 Amzi, Bani, Shemer, 47 Mahli, Mushi, Merari, Levi.

48 The other Levites were assigned all the other duties at the place of worship.

The Descendants of Aaron

49 Aaron and his descendants presented the offerings of incense and offered the sacrifices that were burnt on the altar. They were responsible for all the worship in the Most Holy Place and for the sacrifices by which God forgives Israel's sins. They did all this in accordance with the instructions given by Moses, God's servant. 50 This is the line of Aaron's descendants: Eleazar, Phinehas, Abishua, 51 Bukki, Uzzi, Zerahiah, 52 Meraioth, Amariah, Ahitub, 53 Zadok, Ahimaaz.

Where the Levites Lived

54 This is the territory assigned to the descendants of Aaron of the clan of Kohath. They received the first share of the land assigned to the Levites. 55 This included Hebron in the territory of Judah and the pasture lands around it. 56 The fields and villages, however, that belonged to the city were assigned to Caleb son of Jephunneh. 57-59 The following towns were assigned to Aaron's

p *Some ancient translations (see also 1 S 8.2)* Joel; *Hebrew does not have this name.*

descendants: Hebron, a city of refuge,q Jattir, and the towns of Libnah, Eshtemoa, Hilen, Debir, Ashan, and Beth Shemesh, with their pasture lands. 60 In the territory of Benjamin they were assigned the following towns with their pasture lands: Geba, Alemeth, and Anathoth. This made a total of thirteen towns for all their families to live in. 61 Ten towns in the territory of West Manasseh were assigned by lot to the rest of the clan of Kohath, family by family.

62 To the clan of Gershon, family by family, were assigned thirteen towns in the territories of Issachar, Asher, Naphtali, and East Manasseh in Bashan. 63 In the same way, twelve towns in the territories of Reuben, Gad, and Zebulun were assigned to the clan of Merari, family by family. 64 In this way the people of Israel assigned towns for the Levites to live in, together with the pasture lands around the towns. (65 The towns in the territories of Judah, Simeon, and Benjamin, mentioned above, were also assigned by drawing lots.)

66 Some of the families of the clan of Kohath were assigned towns and pasture lands in the territory of Ephraim: 67 Shechem, the city of refuge in the hills of Ephraim, Gezer, 68 Jokmeam, Beth Horon, 69 Aijalon, and Gath Rimmon. 70 In the territory of West Manasseh they were assigned the towns of Aner and Bileam with the surrounding pasture lands.

71 The families of the clan of Gershon were assigned the following towns, with the surrounding pasture lands:

In the territory of East Manasseh: Golan in Bashan, and Ashtaroth.

72 In the territory of Issachar: Kedesh, Daberath, 73 Ramoth, and Anem.

74 In the territory of Asher: Mashal, Abdon, 75 Hukok, and Rehob.

76 In the territory of Naphtali: Kedesh in Galilee, Hammon, and Kiriathaim.

77 The remaining families of the clan of Merari were assigned the following towns with the surrounding pasture lands:

In the territory of Zebulun: Rimmono and Tabor.

78 In the territory of Reuben, east of the Jordan River beyond Jericho: Bezer on the plateau, Jahzah, 79 Kedemoth, and Mephaath.

80 In the territory of Gad: Ramoth in Gilead, Mahanaim, 81 Heshbon, and Jazer.

The Descendants of Issachar

7 Issachar had four sons: Tola, Puah, Jashub, and Shimron.

2 Tola had six sons: Uzzi, Rephaiah, Jeriel, Jahmai, Ibsam, and Shemuel. They were heads of families of the clan of Tola and were famous soldiers. At the time of King David their descendants numbered 22,600.

3 Uzzi had one son, Izrahiah. Izrahiah and his four sons, Michael, Obadiah, Joel, and Isshiah, were all heads of families. 4 They had so many wives and children that their descendants were able to provide 36,000 men for military duty.

5 The official records of all the families of the tribe of Issachar listed 87,000 men eligible for military duty.

The Descendants of Benjamin and Dan

6 Benjamin had three sons: Bela, Becher, and Jediael.

7 Bela had five sons: Ezbon, Uzzi, Uzziel, Jerimoth, and Iri. They were heads of families in the clan and were all famous soldiers. Their descendants included 22,034 men eligible for military duty.

8 Becher had nine sons: Zemirah, Joash, Eliezer, Elioenai, Omri, Jeremoth, Abijah, Anathoth, and Alemeth. 9 The official record of their descendants by families listed 20,200 men eligible for military duty.

10 Jediael had one son, Bilhan, and Bilhan had seven sons: Jeush, Benjamin, Ehud, Chenaanah, Zethan, Tarshish, and Ahishahar. 11 They were heads of families in the clan and were all famous soldiers. Their descendants included 17,200 men eligible for military duty. 12 Shuppim and Huppim also belonged to this tribe.

Dan had one son, Hushim.r

q CITY OF REFUGE: *If anyone accidentally killed someone, he could escape to one of these cities and be safe from revenge (see Js 20.1-9).*   r Probable text Shuppim . . . Hushim (see Gn 46.23; Nu 26.39, 42); Hebrew And Shuppim and Huppim, sons of Ir; Hushim son of Aher.

The Descendants of Naphtali

13 Naphtali had four sons: Jahziel, Guni, Jezer, and Shallum. (They were descendants of Bilhah.s)

The Descendants of Manasseh

14 By his Aramean concubine, Manasseh had two sons, Asriel and Machir. Machir was the father of Gilead. 15 Machir found a wife for Huppim and one for Shuppim. His sister's name was Maacah. Machir's second son was Zelophehad, and he had only daughters.

16 Maacah, Machir's wife, gave birth to two sons, whom they named Peresh and Sheresh. Peresh had two sons, Ulam and Rakem, 17 and Ulam had a son named Bedan. These are all descendants of Gilead, the son of Machir and grandson of Manasseh.

18 Gilead's sister Hammolecheth had three sons: Ishod, Abiezer, and Mahlah. (19 Shemida had four sons: Ahian, Shechem, Likhi, and Aniam.)

The Descendants of Ephraim

20 These are the descendants of Ephraim from generation to generation: Shuthelah, Bered, Tahath, Eleadah, Tahath, 21 Zabad, Shuthelah. Ephraim had two other sons besides Shuthelah: Ezer and Elead, who were killed when they tried to steal the livestock belonging to the native inhabitants of Gath. 22 Their father Ephraim mourned for them for many days, and his relatives came to comfort him. 23 Then he had intercourse with his wife again, and she became pregnant and had a son. They named him Beriah,t because of the trouble that had come to their family.

24 Ephraim had a daughter named Sheerah. She built the towns of Upper and Lower Beth Horon, and Uzzen Sheerah.

25 Ephraim also had a son named Rephah, whose descendants were as follows: Resheph, Telah, Tahan, 26 Ladan, Ammihud, Elishama, 27 Nun, Joshua. 28 The territory which they took and settled included Bethel and the towns around it, as far east as Naaran and as far west as Gezer and the towns around it. It also included the cities of Shechem and Ayyah, and the towns around them.

29 The descendants of Manasseh controlled the cities of Beth Shan, Taanach, Megiddo, and Dor, and the towns around them.

All these are the places where the descendants of Joseph son of Jacob lived.

The Descendants of Asher

30 These are the descendants of Asher. He had four sons: Imnah, Ishvah, Ishvi, and Beriah; and one daughter, Serah.

31 Beriah had two sons, Heber and Malchiel. (Malchiel founded the city of Birzaith.)

32 Heber had three sons: Japhlet, Shomer, and Hotham; and one daughter, Shua.

33 Japhlet also had three sons: Pasach, Bimhal, and Ashvath.

34 His brother Shomer had three sons: Rohgah, Jehubbah, and Aram.

35 His brother Hothamu had four sons: Zophah, Imna, Shelesh, and Amal.

36 The descendants of Zophah were Suah, Harnepher, Shual, Beri, Imrah, 37 Bezer, Hod, Shamma, Shilshah, Ithran, and Beera.

38 The descendants of Jether were Jephunneh, Pispa, and Ara, 39 and the descendants of Ulla were Arah, Hanniel, and Rizia.

40 All of these were descendants of Asher. They were heads of families, famous fighting men, outstanding leaders. Asher's descendants included 26,000 men eligible for military duty.

The Descendants of Benjamin

8 Benjamin had five sons. In order of age they were Bela, Ashbel, Aharah, 2 Nohah, and Rapha.

3 The descendants of Bela were Addar, Gera, Abihud, 4 Abishua, Naaman, Ahoah, 5 Gera, Shephuphan, and Huram.

6-7 The descendants of Ehud were Naaman, Ahijah, and Gera. They were heads of families that lived in Geba, but which were forced out and went to live in Manahath. Gera, the father of Uzza and Ahihud, led them in this move.

8-9 Shaharaim divorced two wives, Hushim and Baara. Later, when he lived in the country of Moab, he married Hodesh

---

s BILHAH: *A concubine of Jacob and the mother of his two sons Dan and Naphtali.*   t BERIAH: *This name sounds like the Hebrew for "in trouble."*   u *Probable text (see verse 32)* Hotham; *Hebrew* Helem.

and had seven sons: Jobab, Zibia, Mesha, Malcam, 10 Jeuz, Sachia, and Mirmah. His sons all became heads of families.

11 He also had two sons by Hushim: Abitub and Elpaal.

12 Elpaal had three sons: Eber, Misham, and Shemed. It was Shemed who built the cities of Ono and Lod and the surrounding villages.

The Benjaminites in Gath and Aijalon

13 Beriah and Shema were heads of families that settled in the city of Aijalon and drove out the people who lived in the city of Gath. 14 Beriah's descendants included Ahio, Shashak, Jeremoth, 15 Zebadiah, Arad, Eder, 16 Michael, Ishpah, and Joha.

The Benjaminites in Jerusalem

17 Elpaal's descendants included Zebadiah, Meshullam, Hizki, Heber, 18 Ishmerai, Izliah, and Jobab.

19 Shimei's descendants included Jakim, Zichri, Zabdi, 20 Elienai, Zillethai, Eliel, 21 Adaiah, Beraiah, and Shimrath.

22 Shashak's descendants included Ishpan, Eber, Eliel, 23 Abdon, Zichri, Hanan, 24 Hananiah, Elam, Anthothijah, 25 Iphdeiah, and Penuel.

26 Jeroham's descendants included Shamsherai, Shehariah, Athaliah, 27 Jaareshiah, Elijah, and Zichri.

28 These were the ancestral heads of families and their principal descendants who lived in Jerusalem.

The Benjaminites in Gibeon and Jerusalem

29 Jeiel v founded the city of Gibeon and settled there. His wife was named Maacah, 30 and his oldest son, Abdon. His other sons were Zur, Kish, Baal, Ner, w Nadab, 31 Gedor, Ahio, Zechariah, 32 and Mikloth, the father of Shimeah. Their descendants lived in Jerusalem near other families of their clan.

The Family of King Saul

33 Ner was the father of Kish, and Kish was the father of King Saul. Saul had four sons: Jonathan, Malchishua, Abinadab, and Eshbaal. x 34 Jonathan was the father of Meribbaal, y who was the father of Micah.

35 Micah had four sons: Pithon, Melech, Tarea, and Ahaz. 36 Ahaz was the father of Jehoaddah, who was the father of three sons: Alemeth, Azmaveth, and Zimri. Zimri was the father of Moza, 37 Moza the father of Binea, Binea of Raphah, Raphah of Eleasah, and Eleasah of Azel.

38 Azel had six sons: Azrikam, Bocheru, Ishmael, Sheariah, Obadiah, and Hanan. 39 Azel's brother Eshek had three sons: Ulam, Jeush, and Eliphelet.

40 Ulam's sons were outstanding soldiers and archers. He had a hundred and fifty sons and grandsons in all. All those named above were members of the tribe of Benjamin.

The People Who Returned from Captivity

9 All the people of Israel were listed according to their families, and this information was recorded in *The Book of the Kings of Israel.*

The people of Judah had been deported to Babylon as punishment for their sins. 2 The first to return to their property in the cities included Israelite citizens, priests, Levites, and Temple workers. 3 People from the tribes of Judah, Benjamin, Ephraim, and Manasseh went to live in Jerusalem.

4-6 There were 690 families of the tribe of Judah who lived in Jerusalem.

The descendants of Judah's son Perez had as their leader Uthai, the son of Ammihud and grandson of Omri. His other ancestors included Imri and Bani.

The descendants of Judah's son Shelah had as their leader Asaiah, who was the head of his family.

The descendants of Judah's son Zerah had Jeuel as their leader.

7-8 The following members of the tribe of Benjamin lived in Jerusalem:
  Sallu son of Meshullam, who was the son of Hodaviah, the son of Hassenuah
  Ibneiah son of Jeroham
  Elah, the son of Uzzi and grandson of Michri

---

v *Probable text (and see 9.35)* Jeiel; *Hebrew does not have this name.*   w *One ancient translation (and see 9.36)* Ner; *Hebrew does not have this name.*   x ESHBAAL: *Called Ishbosheth in 2 S 2.8 and elsewhere in 2 Samuel.*   y MERIBBAAL: *Called Mephibosheth in 2 S 4.4 and elsewhere in 2 Samuel.*

Meshullam son of Shephatiah, who was the son of Reuel, the son of Ibnijah

9 There were 956 families of this tribe living there. All the men named above were heads of families.

The Priests Who Lived in Jerusalem

10-12 The following priests lived in Jerusalem:

Jedaiah, Jehoiarib, and Jachin

Azariah son of Hilkiah (the chief official in the Temple), whose ancestors included Meshullam, Zadok, Meraioth, and Ahitub

Adaiah son of Jeroham, whose ancestors included Pashhur and Malchijah

Maasai son of Adiel, whose ancestors included Jahzerah, Meshullam, Meshillemith, and Immer

13 The priests who were heads of families totaled 1,760. They were experts in all the work carried on in the Temple.

The Levites Who Lived in Jerusalem

14-16 The following Levites lived in Jerusalem:

Shemaiah son of Hasshub, whose ancestors included Azrikam and Hashabiah, of the clan of Merari

Bakbakkar, Heresh, and Galal

Mattaniah son of Mica, whose ancestors included Zichri and Asaph

Obadiah son of Shemaiah, whose ancestors included Galal and Jeduthun

Berechiah, the son of Asa and grandson of Elkanah, who lived in the territory that belonged to the town of Netophah

The Temple Guards Who Lived in Jerusalem

17 The following Temple guards lived in Jerusalem: Shallum, Akkub, Talmon, and Ahiman. Shallum was their leader. 18 Down to that time members of their clans had been stationed at the eastern entrance to the King's Gate.[z] Formerly they had stood guard at the gates to the camps of the Levites.

19 Shallum, the son of Kore and grandson of Ebiasaph, together with his fellow members of the clan of Korah, was responsible for guarding the entrance to the Tent of the LORD's presence, just as their ancestors had been when they were in charge of the LORD's camp. 20 Phinehas son of Eleazar—may the LORD be with him!—had supervised them at one time.

21 Zechariah son of Meshelemiah was also a guard at the entrance to the Tent of the LORD's presence.

22 In all, 212 men were chosen as guards for the entrances and gates. They were registered according to the villages where they lived. It was King David and the prophet Samuel who had put their ancestors in these responsible positions. 23 They and their descendants continued to guard the gates to the Temple. 24 There was a gate facing in each direction, north, south, east, and west, and each had a chief guard. 25 These guards were assisted by their relatives, who lived in the villages and who had to take turns at guard duty for seven days at a time. 26 The four chief guards were Levites and had the final responsibility. They were also responsible for the rooms in the Temple and for the supplies kept there. 27 They lived near the Temple, because it was their duty to guard it and to open the gates every morning.

The Other Levites

28 Other Levites were responsible for the utensils used in worship. They checked them out and checked them back in every time they were used. 29 Others were in charge of the other sacred equipment, and of the flour, wine, olive oil, incense, and spices. 30 But the responsibility for mixing the spices belonged to the priests.

31 A Levite named Mattithiah, oldest son of Shallum, of the clan of Korah, was responsible for preparing the baked offerings.[a] 32 Members of the clan of Kohath were responsible for preparing the sacred bread[b] for the Temple every Sabbath.

---

z KING'S GATE: The east gate of the Temple, through which the king usually entered. a BAKED OFFERINGS: Thin cakes of flour and olive oil which were baked and then presented as offerings to God (see Lv 2.4-6). b SACRED BREAD: Twelve loaves of bread which were placed on a table in the Temple each Sabbath as an offering to God (see Lv 24.5-9).

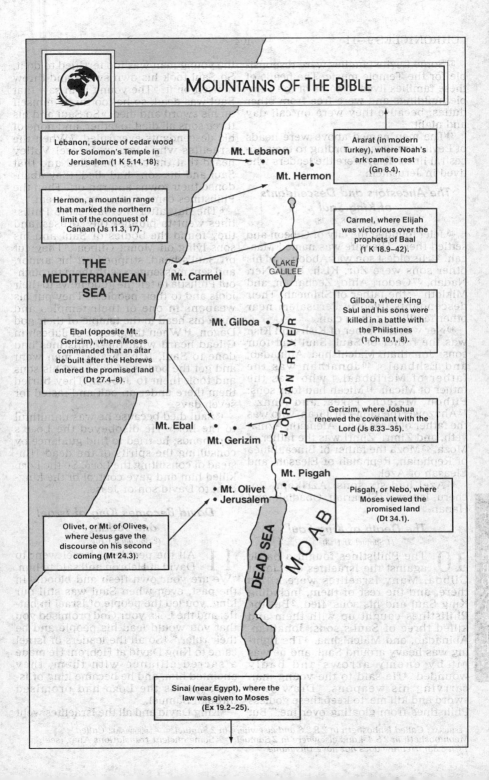

MOUNTAINS OF THE BIBLE

Lebanon, source of cedar wood for Solomon's Temple in Jerusalem (1 K 5.14, 18).

Ararat (in modern Turkey), where Noah's ark came to rest (Gn 8.4).

Hermon, a mountain range that marked the northern limit of the conquest of Canaan (Js 11.3, 17).

Carmel, where Elijah was victorious over the prophets of Baal (1 K 18.9–42).

THE MEDITERRANEAN SEA

Gilboa, where King Saul and his sons were killed in a battle with the Philistines (1 Ch 10.1, 8).

Ebal (opposite Mt. Gerizim), where Moses commanded that an altar be built after the Hebrews entered the promised land (Dt 27.4–8).

Gerizim, where Joshua renewed the covenant with the Lord (Js 8.33–35).

Pisgah, or Nebo, where Moses viewed the promised land (Dt 34.1).

Olivet, or Mt. of Olives, where Jesus gave the discourse on his second coming (Mt 24.3).

Sinai (near Egypt), where the law was given to Moses (Ex 19.2–25).

Mt. Lebanon

Mt. Hermon

LAKE GALILEE

Mt. Carmel

Mt. Gilboa

JORDAN RIVER

Mt. Ebal

Mt. Gerizim

Mt. Pisgah

Mt. Olivet
Jerusalem

MOAB

DEAD SEA

33 Some Levite families were responsible for the Temple music. The heads of these families lived in some of the Temple buildings and were free from other duties, because they were on call day and night.

34 The men named above were heads of Levite families, according to their ancestral lines. They were the leaders who lived in Jerusalem.

The Ancestors and Descendants of King Saul
(1 Chronicles 8.29-38)

35 Jeiel founded the city of Gibeon and settled there. His wife was named Maacah. 36 His oldest son was Abdon, and his other sons were Zur, Kish, Baal, Ner, Nadab, 37 Gedor, Ahio, Zechariah, and Mikloth, 38 the father of Shimeah. Their descendants lived in Jerusalem near other families of their clan.

39 Ner was the father of Kish, and Kish was the father of Saul. Saul had four sons: Jonathan, Malchishua, Abinadab, and Eshbaal.c 40 Jonathan was the father of Meribbaal,d who was the father of Micah. 41 Micah had four sons: Pithon, Melech, Tarea, and Ahaz.e 42 Ahaz was the father of Jarah, who was the father of three sons: Alemeth, Azmaveth, and Zimri. Zimri was the father of Moza, 43 Moza the father of Binea, Binea of Rephaiah, Rephaiah of Eleasah, and Eleasah of Azel.

44 Azel had six sons: Azrikam, Bocheru, Ishmael, Sheariah, Obadiah, and Hanan.

The Death of King Saul
(1 Samuel 31.1-13)

10 The Philistines fought a battle against the Israelites on Mount Gilboa. Many Israelites were killed there, and the rest of them, including King Saul and his sons, fled. 2 But the Philistines caught up with them and killed three of Saul's sons, Jonathan, Abinadab, and Malchishua. 3 The fighting was heavy around Saul, and he was hit by enemy arrows and badly wounded. 4 He said to the young man carrying his weapons, "Draw your sword and kill me, to keep these godless Philistines from gloating over me." But the young man was too terrified to do it. So Saul took his own sword and threw himself on it. 5 The young man saw that Saul was dead, so he too threw himself on his sword and died. 6 So Saul and his three sons all died together, and none of his descendants ever ruled. 7 When the Israelites who lived in Jezreel Valley heard that the army had fled and that Saul and his sons had died, they abandoned their towns and ran off. Then the Philistines came and occupied them.

8 The day after the battle the Philistines went to plunder the corpses, and they found the bodies of Saul and his sons lying on Mount Gilboa. 9 They cut off Saul's head, stripped off his armor, and sent messengers with them throughout Philistia to tell the good news to their idols and to their people. 10 They put his weapons in one of their temples and hung his head in the temple of their god Dagon. 11 When the people of Jabesh in Gilead heard what the Philistines had done to Saul, 12 the bravest men went and got the bodies of Saul and his sons and took them to Jabesh. They buried them there under an oak and fasted for seven days.

13 Saul died because he was unfaithful to the LORD. He disobeyed the LORD's commands; he tried to find guidance by consulting the spirits of the dead 14 instead of consulting the LORD. So the LORD killed him and gave control of the kingdom to David son of Jesse.

David Becomes King of Israel and Judah
(2 Samuel 5.1-10)

11 All the people of Israel went to David at Hebron and said to him, "We are your own flesh and blood. 2 In the past, even when Saul was still our king, you led the people of Israel in battle, and the LORD your God promised you that you would lead his people and be their ruler." 3 So all the leaders of Israel came to King David at Hebron. He made a sacred alliance with them, they anointed him, and he became king of Israel, just as the LORD had promised through Samuel.

4 King David and all the Israelites went

c ESHBAAL: *Called Ishbosheth in 2 S 2.8 and elsewhere in 2 Samuel.*   d MERIBBAAL: *Called Mephibosheth in 2 S 4.4 and elsewhere in 2 Samuel.*   e *Some ancient translations Ahaz (see 1 Ch 8.35); Hebrew does not have this name.*

THE CITY OF JERUSALEM

When David became king of Judah, one of his first acts was to capture Jerusalem from the Jebusites and make the city the capital of his kingdom (2 S 5.6–10; 1 Ch 11.4–9). The city served from that point on as the religious and political capital of the Jewish nation.

Jerusalem was a good choice as a capital city site. Easy to defend because of its hilltop location, it was also centrally located between the northern and southern tribes of the nation. David's first task as king was to unite these tribes under his leadership. This is probably why he selected Jerusalem as his capital.

Jerusalem grew into a magnificent city under Solomon, David's son and successor. Solomon built the Temple as the place of worship for the Israelites (1 K 6; 7; 2 Ch 3; 4). He also planted many vineyards, orchards, and gardens to beautify the city.

Several centuries after Solomon's time, the Babylonians destroyed Jerusalem and carried its inhabitants into captivity. Although the Temple and the city and its surrounding walls were rebuilt by the returning Jewish exiles some time later, Jerusalem was not restored to its previous splendor. This task, ironically, fell to Herod the Great, Roman ruler of Palestine about the time of Jesus. He restored the Temple to its previous state in an attempt to appease the Jewish people and also built several other beautiful buildings in Jerusalem. This building program continued throughout the period of Jesus' public ministry.

The Holy City played a significant role in the life and ministry of Jesus. At the age of twelve, he went to Jerusalem, where he amazed the temple leaders with his wisdom and knowledge (Lk 2.47). At the close of his public ministry, he was crucified, buried, and resurrected at Jerusalem.

As Jesus had predicted (Mt 23.37–39), the city of Jerusalem was destroyed in A.D. 70 when the Jewish people rebelled against Roman authority.

and attacked the city of Jerusalem. It was then known as Jebus, and the Jebusites, the original inhabitants of the land, were still living there. 5 The Jebusites told David he would never get inside the city, but David captured their fortress of Zion, and it became known as "David's City." 6 David said, "The first man to kill a Jebusite will be commander of the army!" Joab, whose mother was Zeruiah, led the attack and became commander. 7 Because David went to live in the fortress, it came to be called "David's City." 8 He rebuilt the city, starting at the place where land was filled in on the east side of the hill, and Joab restored the rest of the city. 9 David grew stronger and stronger, because the LORD Almighty was with him.

David's Famous Soldiers
(2 Samuel 23.8-39)

10 This is the list of David's famous soldiers. Together with the rest of the people of Israel, they helped him become king, as the LORD had promised, and they kept his kingdom strong.

11 First was Jashobeam of the clan of Hachmon, the leader of "The Three."ᶠ He fought with his spear against three hundred men and killed them all in one battle. 12 Next among the famous "Three" was Eleazar son of Dodo, of the clan of Ahoh. 13 He fought on David's side against the Philistines at the battle of Pas Dammim. He was in a barley field when the Israelites started to run away, 14 so he and his men took a stand in the middle of the field and fought the Philistines. The LORD gave him a great victory.

15 One day three of the thirty leading soldiers went to a rock where David was staying near Adullam Cave, while a band of Philistines was camping in Rephaim Valley. 16 At that time David was on a fortified hill, and a group of Philistines had occupied Bethlehem. 17 David got homesick and said, "How I wish someone would bring me a drink of water from the well by the gate in Bethlehem!" 18 The three famous soldiers forced their way through the Philistine camp, drew some water from the well, and brought it back to David. But he would not drink it; instead he poured it out as an offering to the LORD 19 and said, "I could never drink this! It would be like drinking the blood of these men who risked their lives!" So he refused to drink it. These were the brave deeds of the three famous soldiers.

20 Joab's brother Abishai was the leader of "The Famous Thirty."ᵍ He fought with his spear against three hundred men and killed them, and became famous among "The Thirty."ʰ 21 He was the most famous of "The Thirty"ⁱ and became their leader, but he was not as famous as "The Three."

22 Benaiah son of Jehoiada from Kabzeel was a famous soldier; he did many brave deeds, including killing two great Moabite warriors. He once went down into a pit on a snowy day and killed a lion. 23 He also killed an Egyptian, a huge man seven and a half feet tall, who was armed with a gigantic spear. Benaiah attacked him with a club, snatched the spear from the Egyptian's hand, and killed him with it. 24 Those were the brave deeds of Benaiah, who was one of "The Thirty."ʲ 25 He was outstanding among "The Thirty," but not as famous as "The Three." David put him in charge of his bodyguard.

26-47 These are the other outstanding soldiers:

Asahel, Joab's brother
Elhanan son of Dodo from
  Bethlehem
Shammoth from Harod
Helez from Pelet
Ira son of Ikkesh from Tekoa
Abiezer from Anathoth
Sibbecai from Hushah
Ilai from Ahoh
Maharai from Netophah
Heled son of Baanah from
  Netophah
Ithai son of Ribai from Gibeah
  in Benjamin
Benaiah from Pirathon
Hurai from the valleys near
  Gaash
Abiel from Arbah
Azmaveth from Bahurum
Eliahba from Shaalbon

ᶠ One ancient translation (see also 2 S 23.8) "The Three"; Hebrew "The Thirty."   ᵍ One ancient translation Thirty; Hebrew Three.   ʰ One ancient translation (see also 2 S 23.18) "The Thirty"; Hebrew "The Three."   ⁱ Probable text (see 2 S 23.19) most famous of "The Thirty"; Hebrew unclear.   ʲ Probable text "The Thirty"; Hebrew "The Three."

Hashem[k] from Gizon
Jonathan son of Shagee from
  Harar
Ahiam son of Sachar from
  Harar
Eliphal son of Ur
Hepher from Mecherah
Ahijah from Pelon
Hezro from Carmel
Naarai son of Ezbai
Joel brother of Nathan
Mibhar son of Hagri
Zelek from Ammon
Naharai, Joab's armorbearer,
  from Beeroth
Ira and Gareb from Jattir
Uriah the Hittite
Zabad son of Ahlai
Adina son of Shiza (a leading
  member of the tribe of
  Reuben, with his own group
  of thirty soldiers)
Hanan son of Maacah
Joshaphat from Mithan
Uzzia from Ashterah
Shamma and Jeiel, sons of
  Hotham, from Aroer
Jediael and Joha, sons of
  Shimri, from Tiz
Eliel from Mahavah
Jeribai and Joshaviah, sons of
  Elnaam
Ithmah from Moab
Eliel, Obed, and Jaasiel from
  Zobah[l]

David's Early Followers from the Tribe of Benjamin

12 David was living in Ziklag, where he had gone to escape from King Saul. There he was joined by many experienced, reliable soldiers, 2members of the tribe of Benjamin, to which Saul belonged. They could shoot arrows and sling stones either right-handed or left-handed. 3-7They were under the command of Ahiezer and Joash, sons of Shemaah, from Gibeah.

These were the soldiers:
Jeziel and Pelet, sons of
  Azmaveth
Beracah and Jehu from
  Anathoth

Ishmaiah from Gibeon, a famous
  soldier and one of the leaders
  of "The Thirty"
Jeremiah, Jahaziel, Johannan,
  and Jozabad, from Gederah
Eluzai, Jerimoth, Bealiah,
  Shemariah, and Shephatiah,
  from Hariph
Elkanah, Isshiah, Azarel, Joezer,
  and Jashobeam, of the clan of
  Korah
Joelah and Zebadiah, sons of
  Jeroham, from Gedor

David's Followers from the Tribe of Gad

8These are the names of the famous, experienced soldiers from the tribe of Gad who joined David's troops when he was at the desert fort. They were experts with shields and spears, as fierce looking as lions and as quick as mountain deer. 9-13They were ranked in the following order: Ezer, Obadiah, Eliab, Mishmannah, Jeremiah, Attai, Eliel, Johanan, Elzabad, Jeremiah, and Machbannai.

14Some of these men from the tribe of Gad were senior officers in command of a thousand men, and others were junior officers in command of a hundred. 15In the first month of one year, the time when the Jordan River overflowed its banks, they crossed the river, scattering the people who lived in the valleys both east and west of the river.

Followers from Benjamin and Judah

16Once a group of men from the tribes of Benjamin and Judah went out to the fort where David was. 17David went to meet them and said, "If you are coming as friends to help me, you are welcome here. Join us! But if you intend to betray me to my enemies, even though I have not tried to hurt you, the God of our ancestors will know it and punish you."

18God's spirit took control of one of them, Amasai, who later became the commander of "The Thirty," and he called out,

"David son of Jesse, we are yours!
Success to you and those who
  help you!
God is on your side."

---

[k] *Probable text* Hashem; *Hebrew* the sons of Hashem. unclear.   [l] *Probable text* from Zobah; *Hebrew*

David welcomed them and made them officers in his army.

Followers from Manasseh

19 Some soldiers from the tribe of Manasseh went over to David's side when he was marching out with the Philistines to fight King Saul. Actually he did not help the Philistines, for their kings were afraid that he would betray them to his former master Saul, so they sent him back to Ziklag. 20 These are the soldiers from Manasseh who went over to David's side when he was returning: Adnah, Jozabad, Jediael, Michael, Jozabad, Elihu, and Zillethai. In Manasseh they had all commanded units of a thousand men. 21 They served David as officers over his troops, m because they were all outstanding soldiers. Later they were officers in the Israelite army. 22 Almost every day new men joined David's forces, so that his army was soon enormous.

List of David's Forces

23-37 When David was at Hebron, many trained soldiers joined his army to help make him king in place of Saul, as the LORD had promised. Their numbers were as follows:
Judah: 6,800 well-equipped men, armed with shields and spears;
Simeon: 7,100 well-trained men;
Levi: 4,600 men;
Followers of Jehoiada, descendant of Aaron: 3,700 men;
Relatives of Zadok, an able young fighter: 22 leading men;
Benjamin (Saul's own tribe): 3,000 men (most of the people of Benjamin had remained loyal to Saul);
Ephraim: 20,800 men famous in their own clans;
West Manasseh: 18,000 men chosen to go and make David king;
Issachar: 200 leaders, together with the men under their command (these leaders knew what Israel should do and the best time to do it);
Zebulun: 50,000 loyal and reliable men ready to fight, trained to use all kinds of weapons;
Naphtali: 1,000 leaders, together with

37,000 men armed with shields and spears;
Dan: 28,600 trained men;
Asher: 40,000 men ready for battle;
Tribes east of the Jordan—Reuben, Gad, and East Manasseh: 120,000 men trained to use all kinds of weapons.
38 All these soldiers, ready for battle, went to Hebron, determined to make David king over all Israel. All the rest of the people of Israel were united in the same purpose. 39 They spent three days there with David, feasting on the food and drink which their relatives had prepared for them. 40 From as far away as the northern tribes of Issachar, Zebulun, and Naphtali, people came bringing donkeys, camels, mules, and oxen loaded with food—flour, figs, raisins, wine, and olive oil. They also brought cattle and sheep to kill and eat. All this was an expression of the joy that was felt throughout the whole country.

The Covenant Box Is Moved from Kiriath Jearim
(2 Samuel 6.1-11)

13 King David consulted with all the officers in command of units of a thousand men and units of a hundred men. 2 Then he announced to all the people of Israel, "If you give your approval and if it is the will of the LORD our God, let us send messengers to the rest of our people and to the priests and Levites in their towns, and tell them to assemble here with us. 3 Then we will go and get God's Covenant Box, which was ignored while Saul was king." 4 The people were pleased with the suggestion and agreed to it.

5 So David assembled the people of Israel from all over the country, from the Egyptian border in the south to Hamath Pass in the north, in order to bring the Covenant Box from Kiriath Jearim to Jerusalem. 6 David and the people went to the city of Baalah, that is, to Kiriath Jearim, in the territory of Judah, to get the Covenant Box of God, which bears the name of the LORD enthroned above the winged creatures. 7 At Abinadab's house they brought out the Covenant Box and put it on a new cart. Uzzah and Ahio guided the cart, 8 while David and all the people danced with all their might to

---

m They served David . . . troops; or They helped David fight against the bands of raiders.

honor God. They sang and played musical instruments — harps, drums, cymbals, and trumpets.

9 As they came to the threshing place of Chidon, the oxen stumbled, and Uzzah reached out and took hold of the Covenant Box. 10 At once the LORD became angry with Uzzah and killed him for touching the Box. He died there in God's presence, 11 and so that place has been called Perez Uzzah[n] ever since. David was furious because the LORD had punished Uzzah in anger.

12 Then David was afraid of God and said, "How can I take the Covenant Box with me now?" 13 So David did not take it with him to Jerusalem. Instead, he left it at the house of a man named Obed Edom, a native of the city of Gath. 14 It stayed there three months, and the LORD blessed Obed Edom's family and everything that belonged to him.

David's Activities in Jerusalem
(2 Samuel 5.11-16)

14 King Hiram of Tyre sent a trade mission to David; he provided him with cedar logs and with stonemasons and carpenters to build a palace. 2 And so David realized that the LORD had established him as king of Israel and was making his kingdom prosperous for the sake of his people.

3 There in Jerusalem, David married more wives and had more sons and daughters. 4 The following children were born to him in Jerusalem: Shammua, Shobab, Nathan, Solomon, 5 Ibhar, Elishua, Elpelet, 6 Nogah, Nepheg, Japhia, 7 Elishama, Beeliada,[o] and Eliphelet.

Victory over the Philistines
(2 Samuel 5.17-25)

8 When the Philistines heard that David had now been made king over the whole country of Israel, their army went out to capture him. So David marched out to meet them. 9 The Philistines arrived at Rephaim Valley and began plundering. 10 David asked God, "Shall I attack the Philistines? Will you give me the victory?"

The LORD answered, "Yes, attack! I will give you the victory!"

11 So David attacked them at Baal Perazim and defeated them. He said, "God has used me to break through the enemy army like a flood." So that place is called Baal Perazim.[p] 12 When the Philistines fled, they left their idols behind, and David gave orders for them to be burned.

13 Soon the Philistines returned to the valley and started plundering it again. 14 Once more David consulted God, who answered, "Don't attack them from here, but go around and get ready to attack them from the other side, near the balsam trees. 15 When you hear the sound of marching in the treetops, then attack, because I will be marching ahead of you to defeat the Philistine army." 16 David did what God had commanded, and so he drove the Philistines back from Gibeon all the way to Gezer. 17 David's fame spread everywhere, and the LORD made every nation afraid of him.

Getting Ready to Move the Covenant Box

15 For his own use, David built houses in David's City.[q] He also prepared a place for God's Covenant Box and put up a tent for it. 2 Then he said, "Only Levites should carry the Covenant Box, because they are the ones the LORD chose to carry it and to serve him forever." 3 So David summoned all the people of Israel to Jerusalem in order to bring the Covenant Box to the place he had prepared for it. 4 Next he sent for the descendants of Aaron and for the Levites. 5 From the Levite clan of Kohath came Uriel, in charge of 120 members of his clan; 6 from the clan of Merari came Asaiah, in charge of 220; 7 from the clan of Gershon, Joel, in charge of 130; 8 from the clan of Elizaphan, Shemaiah, in charge of 200; 9 from the clan of Hebron, Eliel, in charge of 80; 10 and from the clan of Uzziel, Amminadab, in charge of 112.

11 David called in the priests Zadok and Abiathar and the six Levites, Uriel, Asaiah, Joel, Shemaiah, Eliel, and Amminadab. 12 He said to the Levites, "You are the leaders of the Levite clans. Purify yourselves and your fellow Levites, so that you can bring the Covenant Box of

---

[n] PEREZ UZZAH: This name in Hebrew means "Punishment of Uzzah." [o] BEELIADA: Called Eliada in 3.8. [p] BAAL PERAZIM: This name in Hebrew means "Lord of the Breakthrough." [q] DAVID'S CITY: That part of Jerusalem which David had captured from the original inhabitants, the Jebusites (see 2 S 5.6-10).

the LORD God of Israel to the place I have prepared for it. 13 Because you were not there to carry it the first time, the LORD our God punished us for not worshiping him as we should have done."

14 Then the priests and the Levites purified themselves in order to move the Covenant Box of the LORD God of Israel. 15 The Levites carried it on poles on their shoulders, as the LORD had commanded through Moses.

16 David commanded the leaders of the Levites to assign various Levites to sing and to play joyful music on harps and cymbals. 17-21 From the clans of singers they chose the following men to play the brass cymbals: Heman son of Joel, his relative Asaph son of Berechiah, and Ethan son of Kushaiah, of the clan of Merari. To assist them they chose the following Levites to play the high-pitched harps: Zechariah, Jaaziel, Shemiramoth, Jehiel, Unni, Eliab, Maaseiah, and Benaiah.

To play the low-pitched harps they chose the following Levites: Mattithiah, Eliphelehu, Mikneiah, Azaziah, and the Temple guards, Obed Edom and Jeiel. 22 Because of his skill in music Chenaniah was chosen to be in charge of the levitical musicians. 23-24 Berechiah and Elkanah, along with Obed Edom and Jehiah, were chosen as guards for the Covenant Box. The priests Shebaniah, Joshaphat, Nethanel, Amasai, Zechariah, Benaiah, and Eliezer were chosen to blow trumpets in front of the Covenant Box.

Moving the Covenant Box to Jerusalem
(2 Samuel 6.12-22)

25 So King David, the leaders of Israel, and the military commanders went to the house of Obed Edom to get the Covenant Box, and they had a great celebration. 26 They sacrificed seven bulls and seven sheep, to make sure that God would help the Levites who were carrying the Covenant Box. 27 David was wearing a robe made of the finest linen, and so were the musicians, Chenaniah their leader, and the Levites who carried the Box. David also wore a linen ephod. 28 So all the Israelites accompanied the Covenant Box up to Jerusalem with

shouts of joy, the sound of trumpets, horns, and cymbals, and the music of harps.

29 As the Box was being brought into the city, Michal, Saul's daughter, looked out of the window and saw King David dancing and leaping for joy, and she was disgusted with him.

16 They took the Covenant Box to the tent which David had prepared for it and put it inside. Then they offered sacrifices and fellowship offerings to God. 2 After David had finished offering the sacrifices, he blessed the people in the name of the LORD 3 and distributed food to them all. He gave each man and woman in Israel a loaf of bread, a piece of roasted meat,[r] and some raisins.

4 David appointed some of the Levites to lead the worship of the LORD, the God of Israel, in front of the Covenant Box, by singing and praising him. 5 Asaph was appointed leader, with Zechariah as his assistant. Jeiel, Shemiramoth, Jehiel, Mattithiah, Eliab, Benaiah, Obed Edom, and Jeiel were to play harps. Asaph was to sound the cymbals, 6 and two priests, Benaiah and Jahaziel, were to blow trumpets regularly in front of the Covenant Box. 7 It was then that David first gave Asaph and the other Levites the responsibility for singing praises to the LORD.

A Song of Praise
(Psalms 105.1-15; 96.1-13; 106.1, 47, 48)

8 Give thanks to the LORD, proclaim his greatness;
   tell the nations what he has done.
9 Sing praise to the LORD;
   tell the wonderful things he has done.
10 Be glad that we belong to him;
   let all who worship him rejoice!
11 Go to the LORD for help,
   and worship him continually.
12-13 You descendants of Jacob, God's servant,
   descendants of Israel, whom God chose,
   remember the miracles that God performed
   and the judgments that he gave.
14 The LORD is our God;

---

[r] *a piece of roasted meat; or a cake of dates.*

his commands are for all the
world.
15 Never forget God's covenant,
which he made to last forever,
16   the covenant he made with
Abraham,
the promise he made to Isaac.
17 The LORD made a covenant with
Jacob,
one that will last forever.
18 "I will give you the land of
Canaan," he said.
"It will be your own possession."

19 God's people were few in number,
strangers in the land of Canaan.
20 They wandered from country to
country,
from one kingdom to another.
21 But God let no one oppress them;
to protect them, he warned the
kings:
22 "Don't harm my chosen servants;
do not touch my prophets."

23 Sing to the LORD, all the world!
Proclaim every day the good
news that he has saved us.
24 Proclaim his glory to the nations,
his mighty deeds to all peoples.

25 The LORD is great and is to be
highly praised;
he is to be honored more than
all the gods.
26 The gods of all other nations are
only idols,
but the LORD created the
heavens.
27 Glory and majesty surround him,
power and joy fill his Temple.

28 Praise the LORD, all people on
earth,
praise his glory and might.
29 Praise the LORD's glorious name;
bring an offering and come into
his Temple.
Bow down before the Holy One
when he appears;s
30   tremble before him, all the
earth!
The earth is set firmly in place
and cannot be moved.
31 Be glad, earth and sky!

Tell the nations that the LORD
is king.
32 Roar, sea, and every creature
in you;
be glad, fields, and everything
in you!
33 The trees in the woods will shout
for joy
when the LORD comes to rule the
earth.

34 Give thanks to the LORD, because
he is good;
his love is eternal.
35 Say to him, "Save us, O God our
Savior;
gather us together; rescue us
from the nations,
so that we may be thankful
and praise your holy name."
36 Praise the LORD, the God of Israel!
Praise him now and forever!

Then all the people said, "Amen," and
praised the LORD.

Worship at Jerusalem and Gibeon

37 King David put Asaph and the other
Levites in permanent charge of the worship that was held at the place where the
Covenant Box was kept. They were to
perform their duties there day by day.
38 Obed Edom son of Jeduthun and sixty-
eight men of his clan were to assist
them. Hosah and Obed Edom were in
charge of guarding the gates.

39 Zadok the priest and his fellow
priests, however, were in charge of the
worship of the LORD at the place of worship in Gibeon. 40 Every morning and
evening they were to burn sacrifices
whole on the altar in accordance with
what was written in the Law which the
LORD gave to Israel. 41 There with them
were Heman and Jeduthun and the others who were specifically chosen to sing
praises to the LORD for his eternal love.
42 Heman and Jeduthun also had charge
of the trumpets and cymbals and the
other instruments which were played
when the songs of praise were sung. The
members of Jeduthun's clan were in
charge of guarding the gates.

43 Then everyone went home, and David went home to spend some time with
his family.

s when he appears; or in garments of worship.

Nathan's Message to David
(2 Samuel 7.1-17)

17 King David was now living in his palace. One day he sent for the prophet Nathan and said to him, "Here I am living in a house built of cedar, but the LORD's Covenant Box is kept in a tent!"

2 Nathan answered, "Do whatever you have in mind, because God is with you."

3 But that night God said to Nathan, 4 "Go and tell my servant David that I say to him, 'You are not the one to build a temple for me to live in. 5 From the time I rescued the people of Israel from Egypt until now I have never lived in a temple; I have always lived in tents and moved from place to place. 6 In all my traveling with the people of Israel I never asked any of the leaders that I appointed why they had not built me a temple made of cedar.'

7 "So tell my servant David that I, the LORD Almighty, say to him, 'I took you from looking after sheep in the fields and made you the ruler of my people Israel. 8 I have been with you wherever you have gone, and I have defeated all your enemies as you advanced. I will make you as famous as the greatest leaders in the world. 9-10 I have chosen a place for my people Israel and have settled them there, where they will live without being oppressed any more. Ever since they entered this land they have been attacked by violent people, but this will not happen again. I promise to defeat all your enemies and to give you descendants. 11 When you die and are buried with your ancestors, I will make one of your sons king and will keep his kingdom strong. 12 He will be the one to build a temple for me, and I will make sure that his dynasty continues forever. 13 I will be his father, and he will be my son. I will not withdraw my support from him as I did from Saul, whom I removed so that you could be king. 14 I will put him in charge of my people and my kingdom forever. His dynasty will never end.'"

15 Nathan told David everything that God had revealed to him.

David's Prayer of Thanksgiving
(2 Samuel 7.18-29)

16 Then King David went into the Tent of the LORD's presence, sat down, and prayed, "I am not worthy of what you have already done for me, LORD God, nor is my family. 17 Yet now you are doing even more; you have made promises about my descendants in the years to come, and you, LORD God, are already treating me like someone great.[t] 18 What more can I say to you! You know me well, and yet you honor me, your servant. 19 It was your will and purpose to do this for me and to show me my future greatness. 20 LORD, there is none like you; we have always known that you alone are God. 21 There is no other nation on earth like Israel, whom you rescued from slavery to make them your own people. The great and wonderful things you did for them spread your fame throughout the world. You rescued your people from Egypt and drove out other nations as your people advanced. 22 You have made Israel your own people forever, and you, LORD, have become their God.

23 "And now, O LORD, fulfill for all time the promise you made about me and my descendants, and do what you said you would. 24 Your fame will be great, and people will forever say, 'The LORD Almighty is God over Israel.' And you will preserve my dynasty for all time. 25 I have the courage to pray this prayer to you, my God, because you have revealed all this to me, your servant, and have told me that you will make my descendants kings. 26 You, LORD, are God, and you have made this wonderful promise to me. 27 I ask you to bless my descendants so that they will continue to enjoy your favor. You, LORD, have blessed them, and your blessing will rest on them forever."

David's Military Victories
(2 Samuel 8.1-18)

18 Some time later King David attacked the Philistines again and defeated them. He took out of their control the city of Gath and its surrounding villages. 2 He also defeated the Moabites, who became his subjects and paid taxes to him.

---

[t] *Probable text* and you, LORD God ... great; *Hebrew unclear.*

THE DEAD SEA

The Dead Sea is a lake about 50 miles long and 10 miles wide in southern Palestine. The Jordan River and other smaller streams flow into it, but, because it lies at the lowest point on the earth, no water flows out of it. Because of its rapid water loss through evaporation, salts and other minerals have become highly concentrated in it. This has made the lake unfit for marine life; thus its name, "The Dead Sea."

In Abraham's time five cities known as the "cities of the plain" were situated at the south end of the Dead Sea (Gn 14.2, 3, 8). Because of their great wickedness, four of these cities—Sodom, Gomorrah, Admah, and Zeboiim—were destroyed by earthquake and fire (Gn 19.28, 29; Dt 29.23). Many scholars believe the remains of these cities were covered in later years by the Dead Sea as the waters shifted when other earthquakes struck the area.

In addition to the destruction of Sodom and Gomorrah, many other biblical events occurred along the shores of the Dead Sea. The springs of Engedi provided a refuge for David in his flight from King Saul (1 S 24.1). In the Salt Valley south of the Dead Sea, David was victorious over the Edomites (2 S 8.13; 1 Ch 18.12, 13).

The Dead Sea is also famous because of the discovery of ancient biblical manuscripts in the caves on its northwest coast. Known as the Dead Sea Scrolls, these manuscripts include a complete copy of the Book of Isaiah and portions of several other books of the Bible, as well as many non-biblical manuscripts. They are dated to the period between 250 B.C. and A.D. 135.

These manuscripts, some of the earliest copies of biblical texts yet discovered, helped scholars establish dates for several important biblical events and gave helpful information on the development of the Hebrew language.

Other names for the Dead Sea used in the Bible are the Salt Sea, the Sea of Arabah, and the eastern sea.

3 Next, David attacked King Hadadezer of the Syrian state of Zobah, near the territory of Hamath, because Hadadezer was trying to gain control of the territory by the upper Euphrates River. 4 David captured a thousand of his chariots, seven thousand cavalry troops, and twenty thousand foot soldiers. He kept enough horses for a hundred chariots and crippled all the rest.

5 When the Syrians of Damascus sent an army to help King Hadadezer, David attacked it and killed twenty-two thousand men. 6 Then he set up military camps in their territory, and they became his subjects and paid taxes to him. The LORD made David victorious everywhere. 7 David captured the gold shields carried by Hadadezer's officials and took them to Jerusalem. 8 He also took a great quantity of bronze from Tibhath and Kun, cities ruled by Hadadezer. (Solomon later used this bronze to make the tank, the columns, and the bronze utensils for the Temple.)

9 King Toi of Hamath heard that David had defeated Hadadezer's entire army. 10 So he sent his son Joram to greet King David and congratulate him for his victory over Hadadezer, against whom Toi had fought many times. Joram brought David presents made of gold, silver, and bronze. 11 King David dedicated them for use in worship, along with the silver and gold he took from the nations he conquered—Edom, Moab, Ammon, Philistia, and Amalek.

12 Abishai, whose mother was Zeruiah, defeated the Edomites in Salt Valley and killed eighteen thousand of them. 13 He set up military camps throughout Edom, and the people there became King David's subjects. The LORD made David victorious everywhere.

14 David ruled over all Israel and made sure that his people were always treated fairly and justly. 15 Abishai's brother Joab was commander of the army; Jehoshaphat son of Ahilud was in charge of the records; 16 Zadok son of Ahitub and Ahimelech son of Abiathar were priests; Seraiah[u] was court secretary; 17 Benaiah son of Jehoiada was in charge of David's bodyguards; and King David's sons held high positions in his service.

David Defeats the Ammonites and the Syrians

(2 Samuel 10.1-19)

19 Some time later King Nahash of Ammon died, and his son Hanun became king. 2 King David said, "I must show loyal friendship to Hanun, as his father Nahash did to me." So David sent messengers to express his sympathy.

When they arrived in Ammon and called on King Hanun, 3 the Ammonite leaders said to the king, "Do you think that it is in your father's honor that David has sent these men to express sympathy to you? Of course not! He has sent them here as spies to explore the land, so that he can conquer it!"

4 Hanun seized David's messengers, shaved off their beards, cut off their clothes at the hips, and sent them away. 5 They were too ashamed to return home. When David heard what had happened, he sent word for them to stay in Jericho and not return until their beards had grown again.

6 King Hanun and the Ammonites realized that they had made David their enemy, so they paid nearly forty tons of silver to hire chariots and charioteers from Upper Mesopotamia and from the Syrian states of Maacah and Zobah. 7 The thirty-two thousand chariots they hired and the army of the king of Maacah came and camped near Medeba. The Ammonites too came out from all their cities and got ready to fight.

8 When David heard what was happening, he sent out Joab and the whole army. 9 The Ammonites marched out and took up their position at the entrance to Rabbah, their capital city, and the kings who had come to help took up their position in the open countryside.

10 Joab saw that the enemy troops would attack him in front and from the rear, so he chose the best of Israel's soldiers and put them in position facing the Syrians. 11 He placed the rest of his troops under the command of his brother Abishai, who put them in position facing the Ammonites. 12 Joab said to him, "If you see that the Syrians are defeating me, come and help me, and if the Ammonites are defeating you, I will go and help you. 13 Be strong and courageous! Let's fight hard for our people

---

u *Probable text (see 2 S 8.17)* Seraiah; *Hebrew* Shavsha.

and for the cities of our God. And may the LORD's will be done."

14 Joab and his men advanced to attack, and the Syrians fled. 15 When the Ammonites saw the Syrians running away, they fled from Abishai and retreated into the city. Then Joab went back to Jerusalem.

16 The Syrians realized that they had been defeated by the Israelites, so they brought troops from the Syrian states on the east side of the Euphrates River and placed them under the command of Shobach, commander of the army of King Hadadezer of Zobah. 17 When David heard of it, he gathered the Israelite troops, crossed the Jordan River, and put them in position facing the Syrians. The fighting began, 18 and the Israelites drove the Syrian army back. David and his men killed seven thousand Syrian chariot drivers and forty thousand foot soldiers. They also killed the Syrian commander, Shobach. 19 When the kings who were subject to Hadadezer realized that they had been defeated by Israel, they made peace with David and became his subjects. 20 The Syrians were never again willing to help the Ammonites.

David Captures Rabbah
(2 Samuel 12.26-31)

20 The following spring, at the time of the year when kings usually go to war, Joab led out the army and invaded the land of Ammon; King David, however, stayed in Jerusalem. They besieged the city of Rabbah, attacked it, and destroyed it. 2 The Ammonite idol Molech[v] had a gold crown which weighed about seventy-five pounds. In it there was a jewel, which David took and put in his own crown. He also took a large amount of loot from the city. 3 He took the people of the city and put them to work with saws, iron hoes, and axes. He did the same to the people of all the other towns of Ammon. Then he and his men returned to Jerusalem.

Battles against Philistine Giants
(2 Samuel 21.15-22)

4 Later on, war broke out again with the Philistines at Gezer. This was when Sibbecai from Hushah killed a giant

named Sippai, and the Philistines were defeated.

5 There was another battle with the Philistines, and Elhanan son of Jair killed Lahmi, the brother of Goliath from Gath, whose spear had a shaft as thick as the bar on a weaver's loom.

6 Another battle took place at Gath, where there was a giant with six fingers on each hand and six toes on each foot. He was a descendant of the ancient giants. 7 He defied the Israelites, and Jonathan, the son of David's brother Shammah, killed him.

8 These three, who were killed by David and his men, were descendants of the giants at Gath.

David Takes a Census
(2 Samuel 24.1-25)

21 Satan wanted to bring trouble on the people of Israel, so he made David decide to take a census. 2 David gave orders to Joab and the other officers, "Go through Israel, from one end of the country to the other, and count the people. I want to know how many there are."

3 Joab answered, "May the LORD make the people of Israel a hundred times more numerous than they are now! Your Majesty, they are all your servants. Why do you want to do this and make the whole nation guilty?" 4 But the king made Joab obey the order. Joab went out, traveled through the whole country of Israel, and then returned to Jerusalem. 5 He reported to King David the total number of men capable of military service: 1,100,000 in Israel and 470,000 in Judah. 6 Because Joab disapproved of the king's command, he did not take any census of the tribes of Levi and Benjamin.

7 God was displeased with what had been done, so he punished Israel. 8 David said to God, "I have committed a terrible sin in doing this! Please forgive me. I have acted foolishly."

9 Then the LORD said to Gad, David's prophet, 10 "Go and tell David that I am giving him three choices. I will do whichever he chooses."

11 Gad went to David, told him what the LORD had said, and asked, "Which is it to be? 12 Three years of famine? Or

v *Ammonite idol Molech; or Ammonite king.*

three months of running away from the armies of your enemies? Or three days during which the LORD attacks you with his sword and sends an epidemic on your land, using his angel to bring death throughout Israel? What answer shall I give the LORD?"

13 David replied to Gad, "I am in a desperate situation! But I don't want to be punished by people. Let the LORD himself be the one to punish me, because he is merciful."

14 So the LORD sent an epidemic on the people of Israel, and seventy thousand of them died. 15 Then he sent an angel to destroy Jerusalem, but he changed his mind and said to the angel, "Stop! That's enough!" The angel was standing by the threshing place of Araunah, a Jebusite.

16 David saw the angel standing in midair, holding his sword in his hand, ready to destroy Jerusalem. Then David and the leaders of the people—all of whom were wearing sackcloth—bowed low, with their faces touching the ground. 17 David prayed, "O God, I am the one who did wrong. I am the one who ordered the census. What have these poor people done? LORD, my God, punish me and my family, and spare your people."

18 The angel of the LORD told Gad to command David to go and build an altar to the LORD at Araunah's threshing place. 19 David obeyed the LORD's command and went, as Gad had told him to. 20 There at the threshing place Araunah and his four sons were threshing wheat, and when they saw the angel, the sons ran and hid. 21 As soon as Araunah saw King David approaching, he left the threshing place and bowed low, with his face touching the ground. 22 David said to him, "Sell me your threshing place, so that I can build an altar to the LORD, to stop the epidemic. I'll give you the full price."

23 "Take it, Your Majesty," Araunah said, "and do whatever you wish. Here are these oxen to burn as an offering on the altar, and here are the threshing boards to use as fuel, and wheat to give as an offering. I give it all to you."

24 But the king answered, "No, I will pay you the full price. I will not give as an offering to the LORD something that belongs to you, something that costs me

nothing." 25 And he paid Araunah six hundred gold coins for the threshing place. 26 He built an altar to the LORD there and offered burnt offerings and fellowship offerings. He prayed, and the LORD answered him by sending fire from heaven to burn the sacrifices on the altar.

27 The LORD told the angel to put his sword away, and the angel obeyed. 28 David saw by this that the LORD had answered his prayer, so he offered sacrifices on the altar at Araunah's threshing place. 29 The Tent of the LORD's presence which Moses had made in the wilderness, and the altar on which sacrifices were burned were still at the place of worship at Gibeon at this time; 30 but David was not able to go there to worship God, because he was afraid of the sword of the LORD's angel.

22 So David said, "This is where the Temple of the LORD God will be. Here is the altar where the people of Israel are to offer burnt offerings."

Preparations for Building the Temple

2 King David gave orders for all the foreigners living in the land of Israel to assemble, and he put them to work. Some of them prepared stone blocks for building the Temple. 3 He supplied a large amount of iron for making nails and clamps for the wooden gates, and so much bronze that no one could weigh it. 4 He had the people of Tyre and Sidon bring him a large number of cedar logs. 5 David thought, "The Temple that my son Solomon is to build must be splendid and world-famous. But he is young and inexperienced, so I must make preparations for it." So David got large amounts of the materials ready before he died.

6 He sent for his son Solomon and commanded him to build a temple for the LORD, the God of Israel. 7 David said to him, "Son, I wanted to build a temple to honor the LORD my God. 8 But the LORD told me that I had killed too many people and fought too many wars. And so, because of all the bloodshed I have caused, he would not let me build a temple for him. 9 He did, however, make me a promise. He said, 'You will have a son who will rule in peace, because I will give him peace from all his enemies. His

name will be Solomon,ᵂ because during his reign I will give Israel peace and security. ¹⁰He will build a temple for me. He will be my son, and I will be his father. His dynasty will rule Israel forever.' "

¹¹David continued, "Now, son, may the LORD your God be with you, and may he keep his promise to make you successful in building a temple for him. ¹²And may the LORD your God give you insight and wisdom so that you may govern Israel according to his Law. ¹³If you obey all the laws which the LORD gave to Moses for Israel, you will be successful. Be determined and confident, and don't let anything make you afraid. ¹⁴As for the Temple, by my efforts I have accumulated almost four thousand tons of gold and nearly forty thousand tons of silver to be used in building it. Besides that, there is an unlimited supply of bronze and iron. I also have wood and stone ready, but you must get more. ¹⁵You have many workers. There are stonecutters to work in the quarries, and there are masons and carpenters, as well as a large number of skilled workers of every sort who can work ¹⁶with gold, silver, bronze, and iron. Now begin the work, and may the LORD be with you."

¹⁷David commanded all the leaders of Israel to help Solomon. ¹⁸He said, "The LORD your God has been with you and given you peace on all sides. He let me conquer all the people who used to live in this land, and they are now subject to you and to the LORD. ¹⁹Now serve the LORD your God with all your heart and soul. Start building the Temple, so that you can place in it the Covenant Box of the LORD and all the other sacred objects used in worshiping him."

23 When David was very old, he made his son Solomon king of Israel.

The Work of the Levites

²King David brought together all the Israelite leaders and all the priests and Levites. ³He took a census of all the male Levites aged thirty or older. The total was thirty-eight thousand. ⁴The king assigned twenty-four thousand to administer the work of the Temple, six

thousand to keep records and decide disputes, ⁵four thousand to do guard duty, and four thousand to praise the LORD, using the musical instruments provided by the king for this purpose.

⁶David divided the Levites into three groups, according to their clans: Gershon, Kohath, and Merari.

⁷Gershon had two sons: Ladan and Shimei. ⁸Ladan had three sons: Jehiel, Zetham, and Joel, ⁹who were the heads of the clans descended from Ladan. (Shimei had three sons: Shelomoth, Haziel, and Haran.)ˣ ¹⁰⁻¹¹Shimei had four sons: Jahath, Zina, Jeush, and Beriah, in order of age. Jeush and Beriah did not have many descendants, so they were counted as one clan.

¹²Kohath had four sons: Amram, Izhar, Hebron, and Uzziel. ¹³His oldest son, Amram, was the father of Aaron and Moses. (Aaron and his descendants were set apart to be in charge of the sacred objects forever, to burn incense in the worship of the LORD, to serve him, and to bless the people in his name. ¹⁴But the sons of Moses, the man of God, were included among the Levites.) ¹⁵Moses had two sons, Gershom and Eliezer. ¹⁶The leader among Gershom's sons was Shebuel. ¹⁷Eliezer had only one son, Rehabiah, but Rehabiah had many descendants.

¹⁸Kohath's second son, Izhar, had a son, Shelomith, the head of the clan. ¹⁹Kohath's third son, Hebron, had four sons: Jeriah, Amariah, Jahaziel, and Jekameam. ²⁰Kohath's fourth son, Uzziel, had two sons, Micah and Isshiah.

²¹Merari had two sons, Mahli and Mushi. Mahli also had two sons, Eleazar and Kish, ²²but Eleazar died without having any sons, only daughters. His daughters married their cousins, the sons of Kish. ²³Merari's second son, Mushi, had three sons: Mahli, Eder, and Jeremoth.

²⁴These were the descendants of Levi, by clans and families, every one of them registered by name. Each of his descendants, twenty years of age or older, had a share in the work of the LORD's Temple.

²⁵David said, "The LORD God of Israel has given peace to his people, and he

---

ᵂ SOLOMON: *This name is formed from the Hebrew word "shalom," which means "peace and security."* ˣ SHIMEI ... HARAN: *The relation of this list to the list of Shimei's sons in verse 10 is not clear.*

himself will live in Jerusalem forever. 26 So there is no longer any need for the Levites to carry the Tent of the LORD's presence and all the equipment used in worship." 27 On the basis of David's final instructions all Levites were registered for service when they reached the age of twenty, 28 and were assigned the following duties: to help the priests descended from Aaron with the Temple worship, to take care of its courtyards and its rooms, and to keep undefiled everything that is sacred; 29 to be responsible for the bread offered to God, the flour used in offerings, the wafers made without yeast, the baked offerings, and the flour mixed with olive oil; to weigh and measure the Temple offerings; 30 and to praise and glorify the LORD every morning and every evening 31 and whenever offerings to the LORD are burned on the Sabbath, the New Moon Festival, and other festivals. Rules were made specifying the number of Levites assigned to do this work each time. The Levites were assigned the duty of worshiping the LORD for all time. 32 They were given the responsibility of taking care of the Tent of the LORD's presence and the Temple, and of assisting their relatives, the priests descended from Aaron, in the Temple worship.

The Work Assigned to the Priests

24 These are the groups to which the descendants of Aaron belong. Aaron had four sons: Nadab, Abihu, Eleazar, and Ithamar. 2 Nadab and Abihu died before their father did, and left no descendants, so their brothers Eleazar and Ithamar became priests. 3 King David organized the descendants of Aaron into groups according to their duties. He was assisted in this by Zadok, a descendant of Eleazar, and by Ahimelech, a descendant of Ithamar. 4 The descendants of Eleazar were organized into sixteen groups, while the descendants of Ithamar were organized into eight; this was done because there were more male heads of families among the descendants of Eleazar. 5 Since there were Temple officials and spiritual leaders among the descendants of both Eleazar and Ithamar, assignments were made by drawing lots. 6 The descendants of Eleazar and of Ithamar took turns drawing lots. Then they were registered

by Shemaiah son of Nethanel, a Levite secretary. The king, his officials, the priest Zadok, Ahimelech son of Abiathar, and the heads of the priestly families and of the Levite families, were all witnesses.

7-18 This is the order in which the twenty-four family groups were given their assignments: 1) Jehoiarib; 2) Jedaiah; 3) Harim; 4) Seorim; 5) Malchijah; 6) Mijamin; 7) Hakkoz; 8) Abijah; 9) Jeshua; 10) Shecaniah; 11) Eliashib; 12) Jakim; 13) Huppah; 14) Jeshebeab; 15) Bilgah; 16) Immer; 17) Hezir; 18) Happizzez; 19) Pethahiah; 20) Jehezkel; 21) Jachin; 22) Gamul; 23) Delaiah; 24) Maaziah.

19 These men were registered according to their assignments for going to the Temple and performing the duties established by their ancestor Aaron in obedience to the commands of the LORD God of Israel.

The List of the Levites

20 These are other heads of families descended from Levi:

Jehdeiah, a descendant of Amram through Shebuel;

21 Isshiah, a descendant of Rehabiah;

22 Jahath, a descendant of Izhar through Shelomith;

23 Jeriah, Amariah, Jehaziel, and Jekameam, sons of Hebron, in order of age;

24 Shamir, a descendant of Uzziel through Micah;

25 Zechariah, a descendant of Uzziel through Isshiah, Micah's brother;

26 Mahli, Mushi, and Jaaziah, descendants of Merari. 27 Jaaziah had three sons: Shoham, Zaccur, and Ibri. 28-29 Mahli had two sons, Eleazar and Kish. Eleazar had no sons, but Kish had one son, Jerahmeel. 30 Mushi had three sons: Mahli, Eder, and Jeremoth.

These are the families of the Levites.

31 The head of each family and one of his younger brothers drew lots for their assignments, just as their relatives, the priests descended from Aaron, had done. King David, Zadok, Ahimelech, and the heads of families of the priests and of the Levites were witnesses.

The Temple Musicians

25 King David and the leaders of the Levites chose the following Levite clans to lead the worship services: Asaph, Heman, and Jeduthun. They were to proclaim God's messages, accompanied by the music of harps and cymbals. This is the list of persons chosen to lead the worship, with the type of service that each group performed:

2 The four sons of Asaph: Zaccur, Joseph, Nethaniah, and Asharelah. They were under the direction of Asaph, who proclaimed God's messages whenever the king commanded.

3 The six sons of Jeduthun: Gedaliah, Zeri, Jeshaiah, Shimei, Hashabiah, and Mattithiah. Under the direction of their father they proclaimed God's message, accompanied by the music of harps, and sang praise and thanks to the LORD.

4 The fourteen sons of Heman: Bukkiah, Mattaniah, Uzziel, Shebuel, Jerimoth, Hananiah, Hanani, Eliathah, Giddalti, Romamti Ezer, Joshbekashah, Mallothi, Hothir, and Mahazioth. 5 God gave to Heman, the king's prophet, these fourteen sons and also three daughters, as he had promised, in order to give power to Heman. 6 All of his sons played cymbals and harps under their father's direction, to accompany the Temple worship. And Asaph, Jeduthun, and Heman were under orders from the king.

7 All these twenty-four men were experts; and their fellow Levites were trained musicians. There were 288 men in all.

8 To determine the assignment of duties they all drew lots, whether they were young or old, experts or beginners.

9-31 These 288 men were divided according to families into twenty-four groups of twelve, with a leader in charge of each group. This is the order in which they were on duty: 1) Joseph of the family of Asaph; 2) Gedaliah; 3) Zaccur; 4) Zeri; 5) Nethaniah; 6) Bukkiah; 7) Asharelah; 8) Jeshaiah; 9) Mattaniah; 10) Shimei; 11) Uzziel; 12) Hashabiah; 13) Shebuel; 14) Mattithiah; 15) Jerimoth; 16) Hananiah; 17) Joshbekashah; 18) Hanani; 19) Mallothi; 20) Eliathah; 21) Hothir; 22) Giddalti; 23) Mahazioth; 24) Romamti Ezer.

The Temple Guards

26 These are the assignments of work for the Levites who served as Temple guards. From the clan of Ko-

rah there was Meshelemiah son of Kore, of the family of Asaph. 2 He had seven sons, listed in order of age: Zechariah, Jediael, Zebadiah, Jathniel, 3 Elam, Jehohanan, and Eliehoenai.

4 There was also Obed Edom, whom God blessed by giving him eight sons, listed in order of age: Shemaiah, Jehozabad, Joah, Sachar, Nethanel, 5 Ammiel, Issachar, and Peullethai.

6-7 Obed Edom's oldest son, Shemaiah, had six sons: Othni, Rephael, Obed, Elzabad, Elihu, and Semachiah. They were important men in their clan because of their great ability; the last two were especially talented.

8 Obed Edom's family furnished a total of sixty-two highly qualified men for this work.

9 Meshelemiah's family furnished eighteen qualified men.

10 From the clan of Merari there was Hosah, who had four sons: Shimri (his father made him the leader, even though he was not the oldest son), 11 Hilkiah, Tebaliah, and Zechariah. In all there were thirteen members of Hosah's family who were Temple guards.

12 The Temple guards were divided into groups, according to families, and they were assigned duties in the Temple, just as the other Levites were. 13 Each family, regardless of size, drew lots to see which gate it would be responsible for. 14 Shelemiah drew the east gate, and his son Zechariah, a man who always gave good advice, drew the north gate. 15 Obed Edom was allotted the south gate, and his sons were allotted to guard the storerooms. 16 Shuppim and Hosah were allotted the west gate and the Shallecheth Gate on the upper road. Guard duty was divided into assigned periods, one after another. 17 On the east, six guards were on duty each day, on the north, four, and on the south, four. Four guards were stationed at the storerooms daily, two at each storeroom. 18 Near the western pavilion there were four guards by the road and two at the pavilion itself. 19 This is the assignment of guard duty to the clan of Korah and the clan of Merari.

Other Temple Duties

20 Others of their fellow Levites[y] were in charge of the Temple treasury and the

storerooms for gifts dedicated to God. 21 Ladan, one of the sons of Gershon, was the ancestor of several family groups, including the family of his son Jehiel. 22 Ladan's two other sons, Zetham and Joel, had charge of the Temple treasury and storerooms.

23 Duties were also assigned to the descendants of Amram, Izhar, Hebron, and Uzziel.

24 Shebuel, of the clan of Moses' son Gershom, was the chief official responsible for the Temple treasury. 25 Through Gershom's brother Eliezer he was related to Shelomith. Eliezer was the father of Rehabiah, who was the father of Jeshaiah, the father of Joram, the father of Zichri, the father of Shelomith. 26 Shelomith and the members of his family were in charge of all the gifts dedicated to God by King David, the heads of families, leaders of clan groups, and army officers. 27 They took some of the loot they captured in battle and dedicated it for use in the Temple. 28 Shelomith and his family were in charge of everything that had been dedicated for use in the Temple, including the gifts brought by the prophet Samuel, by King Saul, by Abner son of Ner, and by Joab son of Zeruiah.

Duties of Other Levites

29 Among the descendants of Izhar, Chenaniah and his sons were assigned administrative duties: keeping records and settling disputes for the people of Israel.

30 Among the descendants of Hebron, Hashabiah and seventeen hundred of his relatives, all outstanding men, were put in charge of the administration of all religious and civil matters in Israel west of the Jordan River. 31 Jeriah was the leader of the descendants of Hebron. In the fortieth year that David was king, an investigation was made of the family line of Hebron's descendants, and outstanding soldiers belonging to this family were found living at Jazer in the territory of Gilead. 32 King David chose twenty-seven hundred outstanding heads of families from Jeriah's relatives and put them in charge of administering all religious and civil matters in Israel

east of the Jordan River—the territories of Reuben, Gad, and East Manasseh.

Military and Civil Organization

27 This is the list of the Israelite heads of families and clan leaders and their officials who administered the work of the kingdom. Each month of the year a different group of twenty-four thousand men was on duty under the commander for that month.

2-15 The following were the commanders for each month:

> First month: Jashobeam son of Zabdiel (he was a member of the clan of Perez, a part of the tribe of Judah)
> Second month: Dodai, a descendant of Ahohi (Mikloth was his second in command)z
> Third month: Benaiah son of Jehoiada the priest; he was the leader of "The Thirty" (his son Ammizabad succeeded him as commander of this group)
> Fourth month: Asahel, brother of Joab (his son Zebadiah succeeded him)
> Fifth month: Shamhuth, a descendant of Izhar
> Sixth month: Ira son of Ikkesh from Tekoa
> Seventh month: Helez, an Ephraimite from Pelon
> Eighth month: Sibbecai from Hushah (he was a member of the clan of Zerah, a part of the tribe of Judah)
> Ninth month: Abiezer from Anathoth in the territory of the tribe of Benjamin
> Tenth month: Maharai from Netophah (he was a member of the clan of Zerah)
> Eleventh month: Benaiah from Pirathon in the territory of the tribe of Ephraim
> Twelfth month: Heldai from Netophah (he was a descendant of Othniel)

Administration of the Tribes of Israel

16-22 This is the list of the administrators of the tribes of Israel:

z Probable text Mikloth . . . command; Hebrew unclear.

Tribe	Administrator
Reuben	Eliezer son of Zichri
Simeon	Shephatiah son of Maacah
Levi	Hashabiah son of Kemuel
Aaron	Zadok
Judah	Elihu, one of King David's brothers
Issachar	Omri son of Michael
Zebulun	Ishmaiah son of Obadiah
Naphtali	Jeremoth son of Azriel
Ephraim	Hoshea son of Azaziah
West Manasseh	Joel son of Pedaiah
East Manasseh	Iddo son of Zechariah
Benjamin	Jaasiel son of Abner
Dan	Azarel son of Jeroham

23 King David did not take a census of the people who were under the age of twenty, because of the LORD's promise to make the people of Israel as numerous as the stars in the sky. 24 Joab, whose mother was Zeruiah, began to take a census, but he did not complete it. God punished Israel because of this census, so the final figures were never recorded in King David's official records.

Administrators of the Royal Property

25-31 This is the list of those who administered the royal property:

Royal storerooms: Azmaveth son of Adiel
Local storerooms: Jonathan son of Uzziah
Farm labor: Ezri son of Chelub
Vineyards: Shimei from Ramah
Wine cellars: Zabdi from Shepham
Olive and sycamore trees (in the western foothills): Baal Hanan from Geder
Olive oil storage: Joash
Cattle in the Plain of Sharon: Shitrai from Sharon
Cattle in the valleys: Shaphat son of Adlai
Camels: Obil, an Ishmaelite
Donkeys: Jehdeiah from Meronoth

Sheep and goats: Jaziz, a Hagrite

David's Personal Advisers

32 Jonathan, King David's uncle, was a skillful adviser and a scholar. He and Jehiel son of Hachmoni were in charge of the education of the king's sons. 33 Ahithophel was adviser to the king, and Hushai the Archite was the king's friend and counselor. 34 After Ahithophel died, Abiathar and Jehoiada son of Benaiah became advisers. Joab was commander of the royal army.

David's Instructions for the Temple

28 King David commanded all the officials of Israel to assemble in Jerusalem. So all the officials of the tribes, the officials who administered the work of the kingdom, the leaders of the clans, the supervisors of the property and livestock that belonged to the king and his sons—indeed all the palace officials, leading soldiers, and important men—gathered in Jerusalem.

2 David stood before them and addressed them: "My friends, listen to me. I wanted to build a permanent home for the Covenant Box, the footstool of the LORD our God. I have made preparations for building a temple to honor him, 3 but he has forbidden me to do it, because I am a soldier and have shed too much blood. 4 The LORD, the God of Israel, chose me and my descendants to rule Israel forever. He chose the tribe of Judah to provide leadership, and out of Judah he chose my father's family. From all that family it was his pleasure to take me and make me king over all Israel. 5 He gave me many sons, and out of them all he chose Solomon to rule over Israel, the LORD's kingdom.

6 "The LORD said to me, 'Your son Solomon is the one who will build my Temple. I have chosen him to be my son, and I will be his father. 7 I will make his kingdom last forever if he continues to obey carefully all my laws and commands as he does now.'

8 "So now, my people, in the presence of our God and of this assembly of all Israel, the LORD's people, I charge you to obey carefully everything that the LORD our God has commanded us, so that you may continue to possess this good land

and so that you may hand it on to succeeding generations forever."

⁹And to Solomon he said, "My son, I charge you to acknowledge your father's God and to serve him with an undivided heart and a willing mind. He knows all our thoughts and desires. If you go to him, he will accept you; but if you turn away from him, he will abandon you forever. ¹⁰You must realize that the Lord has chosen you to build his holy Temple. Now do it — and do it with determination."

¹¹David gave Solomon the plans for all the Temple buildings, for the storerooms and all the other rooms, and for the Most Holy Place, where sins are forgiven. ¹²He also gave him the plans for all he had in mind for the courtyards and the rooms around them, and for the storerooms for the Temple equipment and the gifts dedicated to the Lord. ¹³David also gave him the plans for organizing the priests and Levites to perform their duties, to do the work of the Temple, and to take care of all the Temple utensils. ¹⁴He gave instructions as to how much silver and gold was to be used for making the utensils, ¹⁵for each lamp and lampstand, ¹⁶for the silver tables, and for each gold table on which were placed the loaves of bread offered to God. ¹⁷He also gave instructions as to how much pure gold was to be used in making forks, bowls, and jars, how much silver and gold in making dishes, ¹⁸and how much pure gold in making the altar on which incense was burned and in making the chariot for the winged creatures that spread their wings over the Lord's Covenant Box. ¹⁹King David said, "All this is contained in the plan written according to the instructions which the Lord himself gave me to carry out."

²⁰King David said to his son Solomon, "Be confident and determined. Start the work and don't let anything stop you. The Lord God, whom I serve, will be with you. He will not abandon you, but he will stay with you until you finish the work to be done on his Temple. ²¹The priests and the Levites have been assigned duties to perform in the Temple. Workers with every kind of skill are eager to help you, and all the people and their leaders are at your command."

Gifts for Building the Temple

29 King David announced to the whole assembly: "My son Solomon is the one whom God has chosen, but he is still young and lacks experience. The work to be done is tremendous, because this is not a palace for people but a temple for the Lord God. ²I have made every effort to prepare materials for the Temple — gold, silver, bronze, iron, timber, precious stones and gems, stones for mosaics, and quantities of marble. ³Over and above all this that I have provided, I have given silver and gold from my personal property because of my love for God's Temple. ⁴I have given 115 tons of the finest gold and 265 tons of pure silver for decorating the walls of the Temple ⁵and for all the objects which the skilled workers are to make. Now who else is willing to give a generous offering to the Lord?"

⁶Then the heads of the clans, the officials of the tribes, the commanders of the army, and the administrators of the royal property volunteered to give ⁷the following for the work on the Temple: 190 tons of gold, 380 tons of silver, 675 tons of bronze, and 3,750 tons of iron. ⁸Those who had precious stones gave them to the Temple treasury, which was administered by Jehiel of the Levite clan of Gershon. ⁹The people had given willingly to the Lord, and they were happy that so much had been given. King David also was extremely happy.

David Praises God

¹⁰There in front of the whole assembly King David praised the Lord. He said, "Lord God of our ancestor Jacob, may you be praised forever and ever! ¹¹You are great and powerful, glorious, splendid, and majestic. Everything in heaven and earth is yours, and you are king, supreme ruler over all. ¹²All riches and wealth come from you; you rule everything by your strength and power; and you are able to make anyone great and strong. ¹³Now, our God, we give you thanks, and we praise your glorious name.

¹⁴"Yet my people and I cannot really give you anything, because everything is a gift from you, and we have only given back what is yours already. ¹⁵You know, O Lord, that we pass through life like ex-

iles and strangers, as our ancestors did. Our days are like a passing shadow, and we cannot escape death. 16O LORD, our God, we have brought together all this wealth to build a temple to honor your holy name, but it all came from you and all belongs to you. 17I know that you test everyone's heart and are pleased with people of integrity. In honesty and sincerity I have willingly given all this to you, and I have seen how your people who are gathered here have been happy to bring offerings to you. 18LORD God of our ancestors Abraham, Isaac, and Jacob, keep such devotion forever strong in your people's hearts and keep them always faithful to you. 19Give my son Solomon a wholehearted desire to obey everything that you command and to build the Temple for which I have made these preparations."

20Then David commanded the people, "Praise the LORD your God!" And the whole assembly praised the LORD, the God of their ancestors, and they bowed low and gave honor to the LORD and also to the king.

21The following day they killed animals as sacrifices, dedicating them to the LORD, and then gave them to the people to eat. In addition, they sacrificed a thousand bulls, a thousand rams, and a thousand lambs, which they burned whole on the altar. They also brought the offerings of wine. 22So that day they were very happy as they ate and drank in the presence of the LORD.

For a second time they proclaimed Solomon king. In the name of the LORD they anointed him as their ruler and Zadok as priest. 23So Solomon succeeded his father David on the throne which the LORD had established. He was a successful king, and the whole nation of Israel obeyed him. 24All the officials and soldiers, and even all of David's other sons, promised to be loyal to Solomon as king. 25The LORD made the whole nation stand in awe of Solomon, and he made him more glorious than any other king that had ruled Israel.

Summary of David's Reign

26David son of Jesse ruled over all Israel 27for forty years. He ruled in Hebron for seven years and in Jerusalem for thirty-three. 28He died at a ripe old age, wealthy and respected, and his son Solomon succeeded him as king. 29The history of King David from beginning to end is recorded in the records of the three prophets, Samuel, Nathan, and Gad. 30The records tell how he ruled, how powerful he was, and all the things that happened to him, to Israel, and to the surrounding kingdoms.

The Second Book of
CHRONICLES

Introduction

Second Chronicles *begins where* First Chronicles *ends. It describes the rule of King Solomon, records the revolt of the northern tribes led by Jeroboam against Rehoboam, King Solomon's son and successor, and continues an account of the history of the kingdom of Judah until the fall of Jerusalem in 586 B.C.*

Outline of Contents

2 CHRONICLES

King Solomon Prays for Wisdom
(1 Kings 3.1-15)

1 Solomon, the son of King David, took firm control of the kingdom of Israel, and the LORD his God blessed him and made him very powerful.

2 King Solomon gave an order to all the officers in charge of units of a thousand men and of a hundred men, all the government officials, all the heads of families, and all the rest of the people, 3 commanding them to go with him to the place of worship at Gibeon. They went there because that was where the Tent of the LORD's presence was located, which Moses, the LORD's servant, had made in the wilderness. (4 The Covenant Box, however, was in Jerusalem, kept in a tent which King David had set up when he brought the Box from Kiriath Jearim.) 5 The bronze altar which had been made by Bezalel, the son of Uri and grandson of Hur, was also in Gibeon in front of the Tent of the LORD's presence. King Solomon and all the people worshiped the LORD there. 6 In front of the Tent the king worshiped the LORD by offering sacrifices on the bronze altar; he had a thousand animals killed and burned whole on it.

7 That night God appeared to Solomon and asked, "What would you like me to give you?"

8 Solomon answered, "You always showed great love for my father David, and now you have let me succeed him as king. 9 O LORD God, fulfill the promise you made to my father. You have made me king over a people who are so many that they cannot be counted, 10 so give me the wisdom and knowledge I need to rule over them. Otherwise, how would I ever be able to rule this great people of yours?"

11 God replied to Solomon, "You have made the right choice. Instead of asking for wealth or treasure or fame or the death of your enemies or even for long life for yourself, you have asked for wisdom and knowledge so that you can rule my people, over whom I have made you king. 12 I will give you wisdom and knowledge. And in addition, I will give you more wealth, treasure, and fame than any king has ever had before or will ever have again."

King Solomon's Power and Wealth
(1 Kings 10.26-29)

13 So Solomon left[a] the place of worship at Gibeon, where the Tent of the LORD's presence was, and returned to Jerusalem. There he ruled over Israel. 14 He built up a force of fourteen hundred chariots and twelve thousand cavalry horses. Some of them he kept in Jerusalem, and the rest he stationed in various other cities. 15 During his reign silver and gold became as common in Jerusalem as stone, and cedar was as plentiful as ordinary sycamore in the foothills of Judah. 16 The king's agents controlled the export of horses from Musri[b] and Cilicia,[c] 17 and the export of chariots from Egypt. They supplied the Hittite and Syrian kings with horses and chariots, selling chariots for 600 pieces of silver each and horses for 150 each.[d]

Preparations for Building the Temple
(1 Kings 5.1-18)

2 King Solomon decided to build a temple where the LORD would be worshiped, and also to build a palace for himself. 2 He put 70,000 men to work transporting materials, and 80,000 to work cutting stone in the hill country. There were 3,600 others responsible for supervising the work.

3 Solomon sent a message to King Hiram of Tyre: "Do business with me as you did with my father, King David, when you sold him cedar logs for building his palace. 4 I am building a temple to honor the LORD my God. It will be a holy place where my people and I will worship him by burning incense of fragrant spices, where we will present offerings of sacred bread to him continuously, and where we will offer burnt offerings every morning and evening, as well as on Sabbaths, New Moon Festivals, and other holy days honoring the LORD our God. He has commanded Israel to do this forever. 5 I intend to build a great temple, because our God is greater than any other god. 6 Yet no one can really build a temple for God, because even all the vastness of heaven

---

a Some ancient translations left; Hebrew came to.   b Probable text Musri; Hebrew Egypt.
c MUSRI AND CILICIA: Two ancient countries in what is now southeast Turkey which were centers of horse breeding in Solomon's time.   d Verses 16-17 in Hebrew are unclear.

THE CITY OF JOPPA

The modern city of Jaffa, a suburb of Tel Aviv, Israel, is located on the coast of the Mediterranean Sea, about midway between the northern and southern borders of the country. In biblical times, the city was called Joppa, a name that means beautiful.

This city is first mentioned in the Bible as a portion of the land allotted to the tribe of Dan (Js 19.46). In later years, the prophet Jonah tried to escape his call to preach to the city of Nineveh by going to Joppa to catch a ship bound for Spain (Jon 1.3).

Joppa was the only natural harbor on the Mediterranean Sea between Egypt and Accho (or Ptolemais), north of Mount Carmel. It served as a maritime shipping center for the inland city of Jerusalem in both Old and New Testament times. Solomon's Temple at Jerusalem was built in part with cedar logs from Phoenicia. These were floated on rafts from the forests of Lebanon to Joppa, where they were hauled by land to the temple site (2 Ch 2.16).

Two New Testament personalities are connected with Joppa. The city was the home of Tabitha, or Dorcas (Ac 9.36–43). After Tabitha was restored to life by Simon Peter, many people believed in the Lord.

Simon the tanner also lived at Joppa (Ac 10.32). While praying on the roof of Simon's house, Simon Peter received his famous vision of a sheet descending from heaven (Ac 10.9–22). This vision led Peter to the conviction that "God treats everyone on the same basis. Those who fear him and do what is right are acceptable to him" (Ac 10.34, 35). From that point on, Peter preached the gospel of Christ to Gentiles, as well as to his own Jewish countrymen.

cannot contain him. How then can I build a temple that would be anything more than a place to burn incense to God? 7Now send me a man with skill in engraving, in working gold, silver, bronze, and iron, and in making blue, purple, and red cloth. He will work with the craftsmen of Judah and Jerusalem whom my father David selected. 8I know how skillful your lumbermen are, so send me cedar, cypress, and juniper logs from Lebanon. I am ready to send my men to assist yours 9in preparing large quantities of timber, because this temple I intend to build will be large and magnificent. 10As provisions for your lumbermen, I will send you 100,000 bushels of wheat, 100,000 bushels of barley, 110,000 gallons of wine, and 110,000 gallons of olive oil."

11King Hiram sent Solomon a letter in reply. He wrote, "Because the LORD loves his people, he has made you their king. 12Praise the LORD God of Israel, Creator of heaven and earth! He has given King David a wise son, full of understanding and skill, who now plans to build a temple for the LORD and a palace for himself. 13I am sending you a wise and skillful master metalworker named Huram. 14His mother was a member of the tribe of Dan and his father was a native of Tyre. He knows how to make things out of gold, silver, bronze, iron, stone, and wood. He can work with blue, purple, and red cloth, and with linen. He can do all sorts of engraving and can follow any design suggested to him. Let him work with your skilled workers and with those who worked for your father, King David. 15So now send us the wheat, barley, wine, and olive oil that you promised. 16In the mountains of Lebanon we will cut down all the cedars you need, tie them together in rafts, and float them by sea as far as Joppa. From there you can take them to Jerusalem."

Construction of the Temple Begins
(1 Kings 6.1-38)

17King Solomon took a census of all the foreigners living in the land of Israel, similar to the census his father David had taken. There were 153,600 resident foreigners. 18He assigned 70,000 of them to transport materials and 80,000 to cut

stones in the mountains, and appointed 3,600 supervisors to make sure the work was done.

3 King David, Solomon's father, had already prepared a place for the Temple. It was in Jerusalem, on Mount Moriah, where the LORD appeared to David, at the place which Araunah the Jebusite had used as a threshing place. King Solomon began the construction 2in the second month of the fourth year that he was king. 3The Temple which King Solomon built was 90 feet long and 30 feet wide. 4The entrance room was the full width of the Temple, 30 feet, and was 180 feet high. The inside of the room was overlaid with pure gold. 5The main room was paneled with cedar and overlaid with fine gold, in which were worked designs of palm trees and chain patterns. 6The king decorated the Temple with beautiful precious stones and with gold imported from the land of Parvaim. 7He used the gold to overlay the Temple walls, the rafters, the entryways, and the doors. On the walls the workers carved designs of winged creatures.*e* 8The inner room, called the Most Holy Place, was 30 feet long and 30 feet wide, which was the full width of the Temple. Twenty-five tons of gold were used to cover the walls of the Most Holy Place; 9twenty ounces of gold were used for making nails, and the walls of the upper rooms were also covered with gold.

10The king also had his workers make two winged creatures out of metal, cover them with gold, and place them in the Most Holy Place, 11-13where they stood side by side facing the entrance. Each had two wings, each wing 7½ feet long, which were spread out so that they touched each other in the center of the room and reached to the wall on either side of the room, stretching across the full width of 30 feet. 14A curtain for the Most Holy Place was made of linen and of other material, which was dyed blue, purple, and red, with designs of the winged creatures worked into it.

The Two Bronze Columns
(1 Kings 7.15-22)

15The king had two columns made, each one 52 feet tall, and placed them in front of the Temple. Each one had a

e WINGED CREATURES: *See Word List.*

THE TEMPLE

The Temple, located in Jerusalem, was the center of the religious life of the Jewish people. In this sanctuary devoted to worship of the one true God, priests offered sacrifices to God to atone for the sins of the nation of Israel. Through temple services, the Jewish people pledged their lives to follow the laws and teachings of their creator.

Before the Temple was built, the Tent was used as a place of worship by the Israelites. During much of their history, the Tent was moved from place to place to accompany the nation of Israel in their wanderings (Ex 40). But after they settled in their permanent home in Canaan, God commanded through his servant David that the Temple be constructed. This more ornate structure, devoted to worship, would be a permanent fixture in their capital city (1 Ch 28).

Three separate temples were actually built in Jerusalem across a period of about a thousand years in Jewish history. All three were built on the same site—on a hill known as Mount Moriah in the eastern section of the Holy City (2 Ch 3.1).

The first temple, built by King Solomon, stood on a platform about ten feet high with ten steps leading to an entrance flanked by two stone pillars. Thousands of common laborers and skilled craftsmen were involved in its construction (1 K 6; 7; 2 Ch 3; 4). This building was destroyed by the Babylonians when they captured Jerusalem. But Cyrus, king of Persia, authorized reconstruction of this building on the same site when he allowed the Jewish people to return to Jerusalem (Ezra 1).

Several centuries later, Herod the Great, Roman ruler of Palestine, ordered construction of the third temple to appease the Jewish people. This temple was the structure to which Jesus referred in speaking of his resurrection (Jn 2.19, 20). As he predicted, this temple was destroyed by the Romans about 40 years after his resurrection and ascension.

The accounts of Solomon's Temple in the Old Testament suggest it had an inner courtyard, as well as an outer courtyard. The three main objects in the inner courtyard were (1) the bronze altar used for burnt offerings (1 K 8.22, 64; 9.25); (2) the bronze tank, which held water for ritual washings by the priests (1 K 7.23–26); and (3) twelve bulls, apparently also cast bronze, which held the bronze tank on their backs (1 K 7.25).

In the inner courtyard was an area known as the holy place, which contained the golden incense altar, the table with showbread, ten lampstands, and utensils used for offering sacrifices (1 K 7.48–50). Beyond this area was a room known as the Most Holy Place, a restricted place which only the high priest could enter. Even he could go into this area only once a year—on the Day of Atonement when he went inside to make atonement for his own sins and then for the sins of the people (Lv 16). In this room was the Covenant Box, containing the stone tablets on which the Ten Commandments were written. God's presence was manifested in the Most Holy Place as a cloud (1 K 8.5–11).

capital 7½ feet tall. 16The tops of the columns were decorated with a design of interwoven chains and one hundred bronze pomegranates.*f* 17The columns were set at the sides of the Temple entrance: the one on the south side was named Jachin*g* and the one on the north side was named Boaz.*h*

Equipment for the Temple
(1 Kings 7.23-51)

4 King Solomon had a bronze altar made, which was 30 feet square and 15 feet high. 2He also made a round tank of bronze, 7½ feet deep, 15 feet in diameter, and 45 feet in circumference. 3All around the outer edge of the rim of the tank*i* were two rows of decorations, one above the other. The decorations were in the shape of bulls, which had been cast all in one piece with the rest of the tank. 4The tank rested on the backs of twelve bronze bulls that faced outward, three facing in each direction. 5The sides of the tank were 3 inches thick. Its rim was like the rim of a cup, curving outward like the petals of a flower. The tank held about 15,000 gallons. 6They also made ten basins, five to be placed on the south side of the Temple and five on the north side. They were to be used to rinse the parts of the animals that were burned as sacrifices. The water in the large tank was for the priests to use for washing.

7-8They made ten gold lampstands according to the usual pattern, and ten tables, and placed them in the main room of the Temple, five lampstands and five tables on each side. They also made a hundred gold bowls.

9They made an inner courtyard for the priests, and also an outer courtyard. The doors in the gates between the courtyards were covered with bronze. 10The tank was placed near the southeast corner of the Temple.

11-16Huram also made pots, shovels, and bowls. He completed all the objects that he had promised King Solomon he would make for the Temple:
The two columns

The two bowl-shaped capitals on top of the columns
The design of interwoven chains on each capital
The 400 bronze pomegranates arranged in two rows around the design of each capital
The ten*j* carts
The ten basins
The tank
The twelve bulls supporting the tank
The pots, shovels, and forks
Huram the master metalworker made all these objects*k* out of polished bronze, as King Solomon had commanded, for use in the Temple of the LORD.

17The king had them all made in the foundry between Sukkoth and Zeredah*l* in the Jordan Valley. 18So many objects were made that no one determined the total weight of the bronze used.

19King Solomon also had gold furnishings made for the Temple: the altar and the tables for the bread offered to God; 20the lampstands and the lamps of fine gold that were to burn in front of the Most Holy Place, according to plan; 21the flower decorations, the lamps, and the tongs; 22the lamp snuffers, the bowls, the dishes for incense, and the pans used for carrying live coals. All these objects were made of pure gold. The outer doors of the Temple and the doors to the Most Holy Place were overlaid with gold.

5 When King Solomon finished all the work on the Temple, he placed in the Temple storerooms all the things that his father David had dedicated to the LORD—the silver, gold, and other articles.

The Covenant Box Is Brought to the Temple
(1 Kings 8.1-9)

2Then King Solomon summoned all the leaders of the tribes and clans of Israel to assemble in Jerusalem, in order to take the LORD's Covenant Box from Zion, David's City,*m* to the Temple. 3They all assembled at the time of the

---

f Verse 16 in Hebrew is unclear.   *g JACHIN: This name sounds like the Hebrew for "he (God) establishes."*   *h BOAZ: This name sounds like the Hebrew for "by his (God's) strength."*
i Probable text All around . . . tank; Hebrew unclear.   *j Probable text (see 1 K 7.40-45) ten; Hebrew he made.*   *k One ancient translation all these objects; Hebrew all their objects.*
l ZEREDAH (see Zarethan, 1 K 7.46).   *m DAVID'S CITY: See Word List.*

Festival of Shelters. 4When all the leaders had gathered, then the Levites lifted the Covenant Box 5and carried it to the Temple. The priests and the Levites also moved the Tent of the LORD's presence and all its equipment to the Temple. 6King Solomon and all the people of Israel assembled in front of the Covenant Box and sacrificed a large number of sheep and cattle—too many to count. 7Then the priests carried the Covenant Box of the LORD into the Temple and put it in the Most Holy Place, beneath the winged creatures. 8Their outstretched wings covered the Box and the poles it was carried by. 9The ends of the poles could be seen by anyone standing directly in front of the Most Holy Place, but from nowhere else. (The poles are still there today.) 10There was nothing inside the Covenant Box except the two stone tablets which Moses had placed there at Mount Sinai, when the LORD made a covenant with the people of Israel as they were coming from Egypt.

The Glory of the LORD

11-14All the priests present, regardless of the group to which they belonged, had consecrated themselves. And all the Levite musicians—Asaph, Heman, and Jeduthun, and the members of their clans—were wearing linen clothing. The Levites stood near the east side of the altar with cymbals and harps, and with them were 120 priests playing trumpets. The singers were accompanied in perfect harmony by trumpets, cymbals, and other instruments, as they praised the LORD singing:

"Praise the LORD, because he is
    good,
And his love is eternal."

As the priests were leaving the Temple, it was suddenly filled with a cloud shining with the dazzling light of the LORD's presence, and they could not continue the service of worship.

Solomon's Address to the People
(1 Kings 8.12-21)

6 Then King Solomon prayed,
"LORD, you have chosen to live
    in clouds and darkness.
2Now I have built a majestic temple
    for you,
    a place for you to live in
      forever."

3All the people of Israel were standing there. The king turned to face them and asked God's blessing on them. 4He said, "Praise the LORD God of Israel! He has kept the promise he made to my father David when he said to him, 5'From the time I brought my people out of Egypt until now, I did not choose any city in the land of Israel as the place to build a temple where I would be worshiped, and I did not choose anyone to lead my people Israel. 6But now I have chosen Jerusalem as the place where I will be worshiped, and you, David, to rule my people.'"

7And Solomon continued, "My father David planned to build a temple for the worship of the LORD God of Israel, 8but the LORD said to him, 'You were right in wanting to build a temple for me, 9but you will never build it. It is your son, your own son, who will build my temple.'

10"Now the LORD has kept his promise: I have succeeded my father as king of Israel, and I have built a temple for the worship of the LORD God of Israel. 11I have placed in the Temple the Covenant Box, which contains the stone tablets of the covenant which the LORD made with the people of Israel."

Solomon's Prayer
(1 Kings 8.22-53)

12Then in the presence of the people Solomon went and stood in front of the altar and raised his arms in prayer. (13Solomon had made a bronze platform and put it in the middle of the courtyard. It was eight feet square and five feet high. He mounted this platform, knelt down where everyone could see him, and raised his hands toward heaven.) 14He prayed, "LORD God of Israel, in all heaven and earth there is no god like you. You keep your covenant with your people and show them your love when they live in wholehearted obedience to you. 15You have kept the promise you made to my father David; today every word has been fulfilled. 16Now, LORD God of Israel, keep the other promise you made to my father when you told him that there would always be one of his descendants ruling as king of Israel, provided that they carefully obeyed your Law just as he did. 17So now, LORD God of Israel, let everything come true

2
C
H
R
O
N
I
C
L
E
S

that you promised to your servant David.

18 "But can you, O God, really live on earth among men and women? Not even all of heaven is large enough to hold you, so how can this Temple that I have built be large enough? 19 LORD my God, I am your servant. Listen to my prayer and grant the requests I make to you. 20 Watch over this Temple day and night. You have promised that this is where you will be worshiped, so hear me when I face this Temple and pray. 21 Hear my prayers and the prayers of your people Israel when they face this place and pray. In your home in heaven hear us and forgive us.

22 "When people are accused of wronging others and are brought to your altar in this Temple to take an oath that they are innocent, 23 O LORD, listen in heaven and judge your servants. Punish the guilty ones as they deserve and acquit the innocent.

24 "When your people Israel are defeated by their enemies because they have sinned against you and then when they turn to you and come to this Temple, humbly praying to you for forgiveness, 25 listen to them in heaven. Forgive the sins of your people and bring them back to the land which you gave to them and to their ancestors.

26 "When you hold back the rain because your people have sinned against you and then when they repent and face this Temple, humbly praying to you, 27 O LORD, listen to them in heaven and forgive the sins of your servants, the people of Israel, and teach them to do what is right. Then, O LORD, send rain on this land of yours, which you gave to your people as a permanent possession.

28 "When there is famine in the land or an epidemic or the crops are destroyed by scorching winds or swarms of locusts, or when your people are attacked by their enemies, or when there is disease or sickness among them, 29 listen to their prayers. If any of your people Israel, out of heartfelt sorrow, stretch out their hands in prayer toward this Temple, 30 hear their prayer. Listen to them in your home in heaven and forgive

them. You alone know the thoughts of the human heart. Deal with each of us as we deserve, 31 so that your people may honor you and obey you all the time they live in the land which you gave to our ancestors.

32 "When foreigners who live in a distant land hear how great and powerful you are and how you are always ready to act, and then they come to pray at this Temple, 33 listen to their prayers. In heaven, where you live, hear them and do what they ask you to do, so that all the peoples of the world may know you and obey you, as your people Israel do. Then they will know that this Temple I have built is where you are to be worshiped.

34 "When you command your people to go into battle against their enemies and they pray to you, wherever they are, facing this city which you have chosen and this Temple which I have built for you, 35 listen to their prayers. Hear them in heaven and give them victory.

36 "When your people sin against you—and there is no one who does not sin—and in your anger you let their enemies defeat them and take them as prisoners to some other land, even if that land is far away, 37 listen to your people's prayers. If there in that land they repent and pray to you, confessing how sinful and wicked they have been, hear their prayers, O LORD. 38 If in that land they truly and sincerely repent and pray to you as they face toward this land which you gave to our ancestors, this city which you have chosen, and this Temple which I have built for you, 39 then listen to their prayers. In your home in heaven hear them and be merciful to them and forgive all the sins of your people.

40 "Now, O my God, look on us and listen to the prayers offered in this place. 41 Rise up now, LORD God, and with the Covenant Box, the symbol of your power, enter the Temple and stay here forever. Bless your priests in all they do, and may all your people be happy because of your goodness to them. 42 LORD God, do not reject the king you have chosen. Remember the love you had for your servant David."n

n the love you ... David; or your servant David's loyal service.

The Dedication of the Temple
(1 Kings 8.62-66)

7 When King Solomon finished his prayer, fire came down from heaven and burned up the sacrifices that had been offered, and the dazzling light of the LORD's presence filled the Temple. 2 Because the Temple was full of the dazzling light, the priests could not enter it. 3 When the people of Israel saw the fire fall from heaven and the light fill the Temple, they fell face downward on the pavement, worshiping God and praising him for his goodness and his eternal love. 4 Then Solomon and all the people offered sacrifices to the LORD. 5 He sacrificed 22,000 head of cattle and 120,000 sheep as fellowship offerings. And so he and all the people dedicated the Temple. 6 The priests stood in the places that were assigned to them, and facing them stood the Levites, praising the LORD with the musical instruments that King David had provided and singing the hymn, "His Love Is Eternal!" as they had been commissioned by David. The priests blew trumpets while all the people stood.

7 Solomon consecrated the central part of the courtyard, the area in front of the Temple, and then offered there the sacrifices burned whole, the grain offerings, and the fat from the fellowship offerings. He did this because the bronze altar which he had made was too small for all these offerings.

8 Solomon and all the people of Israel celebrated the Festival of Shelters for seven days. There was a huge crowd of people from as far away as Hamath Pass in the north and the Egyptian border in the south. 9 They had spent seven days for the dedication of the altar and then seven more days for the festival. On the last day they had a closing celebration, 10 and on the following day, the twenty-third day of the seventh month, Solomon sent the people home. They were happy about all the blessings that the LORD had given to his people Israel, to David, and to Solomon.

God Appears to Solomon Again
(1 Kings 9.1-9)

11 After King Solomon had finished the Temple and the palace, successfully completing all his plans for them, 12 the LORD appeared to him at night. He said to him, "I have heard your prayer, and I accept this Temple as the place where sacrifices are to be offered to me. 13 Whenever I hold back the rain or send locusts to eat up the crops or send an epidemic on my people, 14 if they pray to me and repent and turn away from the evil they have been doing, then I will hear them in heaven, forgive their sins, and make their land prosperous again. 15 I will watch over this Temple and be ready to hear all the prayers that are offered here, 16 because I have chosen it and consecrated it as the place where I will be worshiped forever. I will watch over it and protect it for all time. 17 If you serve me faithfully as your father David did, obeying my laws and doing everything I have commanded you, 18 I will keep the promise I made to your father David when I told him that Israel would always be ruled by his descendants. 19 But if you and your people ever disobey the laws and commands I have given you and worship other gods, 20 then I will remove you from the land that I gave you, and I will abandon this Temple that I have consecrated as the place where I am to be worshiped. People everywhere will ridicule it and treat it with contempt. 21 "The Temple is now greatly honored, but then everyone who passes by it will be amazed and will ask, 'Why did the LORD do this to this land and this Temple?' 22 People will answer, 'It is because they abandoned the LORD their God, who brought their ancestors out of Egypt. They gave their allegiance to other gods and worshiped them. That is why the LORD has brought this disaster on them.'"

Solomon's Achievements
(1 Kings 9.10-28)

8 It took Solomon twenty years to build the Temple and his palace. 2 He also rebuilt the cities that King Hiram had given him, and sent Israelites to settle in them. 3 He captured the territory of Hamath and Zobah 4 and fortified the city of Palmyra in the desert. He rebuilt all the cities in Hamath that were centers for storing supplies. 5 Solomon also rebuilt the following cities: Upper Beth Horon and Lower Beth Horon (fortified cities with gates that could be barred),

6the city of Baalath, all the cities where he stored supplies, and the cities where his horses and chariots were stationed. He carried out all his plans for building in Jerusalem, in Lebanon, and throughout the territory that he ruled over. 7-8 Solomon employed at forced labor all the descendants of the people of Canaan whom the Israelites had not killed when they took possession of the land. These included Hittites, Amorites, Perizzites, Hivites, and Jebusites, whose descendants continue to be slaves down to the present time. 9 Israelites were not used at forced labor, but served as soldiers, officers, chariot commanders, and cavalry troops. 10 There were 250 officials in charge of the forced labor working on the various building projects.

11 Solomon moved his wife, the daughter of the king of Egypt, from David's City to a house he built for her. He said, "She must not live in the palace of King David of Israel, because any place where the Covenant Box has been is holy."

12 Solomon offered sacrifices to the LORD on the altar which he had built in front of the Temple. 13 He offered burnt offerings according to the requirements of the Law of Moses for each holy day: Sabbaths, New Moon Festivals, and the three annual festivals—the Festival of Unleavened Bread, the Harvest Festival, and the Festival of Shelters. 14 Following the rules laid down by his father David, he organized the daily work of the priests and of the Levites who assisted the priests in singing hymns and in doing their work. He also organized the Temple guards in sections for performing their daily duties at each gate, in accordance with the commands of David, the man of God. 15 The instructions which David had given the priests and the Levites concerning the storehouses and other matters were carried out in detail.

16 By this time all of Solomon's projects had been completed. From the laying of the foundation of the LORD's Temple to its completion, all the work had been successful.

17 Then Solomon went to Eziongeber and Elath, ports on the shore of the Gulf of Aqaba, in the land of Edom. 18 King Hiram sent him ships under the command of his own officers and with experienced sailors. They sailed with Solomon's officers to the land of Ophir and brought back to Solomon about sixteen tons of gold.

The Visit of the Queen of Sheba
(1 Kings 10.1-13)

9 The queen of Sheba heard of King Solomon's fame, and she traveled to Jerusalem to test him with difficult questions. She brought with her a large group of attendants, as well as camels loaded with spices, jewels, and a large amount of gold. When she and Solomon met, she asked him all the questions that she could think of. 2 He answered them all; there was nothing too difficult for him to explain. 3 The queen of Sheba heard Solomon's wisdom and saw the palace he had built. 4 She saw the food that was served at his table, the living quarters for his officials, the organization of his palace staff and the uniforms they wore, the clothing of the servants who waited on him at feasts, and the sacrifices he offeredᵒ in the Temple. It left her breathless and amazed.

5 She said to the king, "What I heard in my own country about youᵖ and your wisdom is true! 6 I did not believe what they told me until I came and saw for myself. I had not heard of even half your wisdom. You are even wiser than people say. 7 How fortunate are those who serve you, who are always in your presence and are privileged to hear your wise sayings! 8 Praise the LORD your God! He has shown how pleased he is with you by making you king, to rule in his name. Because he loves his people Israel and wants to preserve them forever, he has made you their king so that you can maintain law and justice."

9 She presented to King Solomon the gifts she had brought: almost five tons of gold and a very large amount of spices and jewels. There have never been any other spices as fine as those that the queen of Sheba gave to King Solomon.

(10 The sailors of King Hiram and of King Solomon who brought gold from Ophir also brought juniper wood and

---

ᵒ *Probable text (see 1 K 10.5)* sacrifices he offered; *Hebrew* his upper rooms.   ᵖ you; *or your* deeds.

jewels. [11]Solomon used the wood to make stairs for the Temple and for his palace, and to make harps and lyres for the musicians. Nothing like that had ever been seen before in the land of Judah.)

[12]King Solomon gave the queen of Sheba everything she asked for. This was in addition to what he gave her in exchange for the gifts[q] she brought to him. Then she and her attendants returned to the land of Sheba.

King Solomon's Wealth
(1 Kings 10.14-25)

[13]Every year King Solomon received over twenty-five tons of gold, [14]in addition to the taxes paid by the traders and merchants. The kings of Arabia and the governors of the Israelite districts also brought him silver and gold. [15]Solomon made two hundred large shields, each of which was covered with about fifteen pounds of beaten gold, [16]and three hundred smaller shields, each covered with about eight pounds of beaten gold. He had them all placed in the Hall of the Forest of Lebanon.[r]

[17]The king also had a large throne made. Part of it was covered with ivory and the rest of it was covered with pure gold. [18]Six steps led up to the throne, and there was a footstool attached to it, covered with gold. There were arms on each side of the throne, and the figure of a lion stood at each side. [19]Twelve figures of lions were on the steps, one at either end of each step. No throne like this had ever existed in any other kingdom.

[20]All of King Solomon's drinking cups were made of gold, and all the utensils in the Hall of the Forest of Lebanon were of pure gold. Silver was not considered valuable in Solomon's day. [21]He had a fleet of ocean-going ships sailing with King Hiram's fleet. Every three years his fleet would return, bringing gold, silver, ivory, apes, and monkeys.

[22]King Solomon was richer and wiser than any other king in the world. [23]They all consulted him, to hear the wisdom that God had given him. [24]Each of them brought Solomon gifts—articles of silver and gold, robes, weapons, spices,

horses, and mules. This continued year after year.

[25]King Solomon also had four thousand stalls for his chariots and horses, and had twelve thousand cavalry horses. Some of them he kept in Jerusalem and the rest he stationed in various other cities. [26]He was supreme ruler of all the kings in the territory from the Euphrates River to Philistia and the Egyptian border. [27]During his reign silver was as common in Jerusalem as stone, and cedar was as plentiful as ordinary sycamore in the foothills of Judah. [28]Solomon imported horses from Musri[s] and from every other country.

Summary of Solomon's Reign
(1 Kings 11.41-43)

[29]The rest of the history of Solomon from beginning to end is recorded in *The History of Nathan the Prophet,* in *The Prophecy of Ahijah of Shiloh,* and in *The Visions of Iddo the Prophet,* which also deal with the reign of King Jeroboam of Israel. [30]Solomon ruled in Jerusalem over all Israel for forty years. [31]He died and was buried in David's City, and his son Rehoboam succeeded him as king.

The Northern Tribes Revolt
(1 Kings 12.1-20)

10 Rehoboam went to Shechem, where all the people of northern Israel had gathered to make him king. [2]When Jeroboam son of Nebat, who had gone to Egypt to escape from King Solomon, heard this news, he returned home. [3]The people of the northern tribes sent for him, and they all went together to Rehoboam and said to him, [4]"Your father placed heavy burdens on us. If you make these burdens lighter and make life easier for us, we will be your loyal subjects."

[5]Rehoboam replied, "Give me three days to consider the matter. Then come back." So the people left.

[6]King Rehoboam consulted the older men who had served as his father Solomon's advisers. "What answer do you advise me to give these people?" he asked.

[7]They replied, "If you are kind to these people and try to please them by giving

---

[q] *Probable text* he gave her in exchange for the gifts; *Hebrew unclear.*   [r] HALL OF THE FOREST OF LEBANON: *A large ceremonial hall in the palace, probably so called because it was paneled in cedar.*   [s] *Probable text (see 1.16)* Musri; *Hebrew* Egypt.

a considerate answer, they will always serve you loyally."

8 But he ignored the advice of the older men and went instead to the young men who had grown up with him and who were now his advisers. 9 "What do you advise me to do?" he asked. "What shall I say to the people who are asking me to make their burdens lighter?"

10 They replied, "This is what you should tell them: 'My little finger is thicker than my father's waist.' 11 Tell them, 'My father placed heavy burdens on you; I will make them even heavier. He beat you with whips; I'll flog you with bullwhips!'"

12 Three days later Jeroboam and all the people returned to King Rehoboam, as he had instructed them. 13 The king ignored the advice of the older men and spoke harshly to the people, 14 as the younger men had advised. He said, "My father placed heavy burdens on you; I will make them even heavier. He beat you with whips; I'll flog you with bullwhips!" 15 It was the will of the LORD God to bring about what he had spoken to Jeroboam son of Nebat through the prophet Ahijah from Shiloh. This is why the king did not pay any attention to the people.

16 When the people saw that the king would not listen to them, they shouted, "Down with David and his family! What have they ever done for us? People of Israel, let's go home! Let Rehoboam look out for himself!"

So the people of Israel rebelled, 17 leaving Rehoboam as king only of the people who lived in the territory of Judah.

18 Then King Rehoboam sent Adoniram, who was in charge of the forced labor, to go to the Israelites, but they stoned him to death. At this, Rehoboam hurriedly got in his chariot and escaped to Jerusalem. 19 Ever since that time the people of the northern kingdom of Israel have been in rebellion against the dynasty of David.

Shemaiah's Prophecy
(1 Kings 12.21-24)

11 When King Rehoboam arrived in Jerusalem, he called together 180,000 of the best soldiers from the tribes of Benjamin and Judah. He intended to go to war and restore his con-

trol over the northern tribes of Israel. 2 But the LORD told the prophet Shemaiah 3 to give this message to King Rehoboam and to all the people of the tribes of Judah and Benjamin: 4 "Do not attack your own relatives. Go home, all of you. What has happened is my will." They obeyed the LORD's command and did not go to fight Jeroboam.

Rehoboam Fortifies the Cities

5 Rehoboam remained in Jerusalem and had fortifications built for the following cities of Judah and Benjamin: 6 Bethlehem, Etam, Tekoa, 7 Bethzur, Soco, Adullam, 8 Gath, Mareshah, Ziph, 9 Adoraim, Lachish, Azekah, 10 Zorah, Aijalon, and Hebron. 11 He had them strongly fortified and appointed a commander for each of them, and in each one he placed supplies of food, olive oil, and wine, 12 and also shields and spears. In this way he kept Judah and Benjamin under his control.

Priests and Levites Come to Judah

13 From all the territory of Israel priests and Levites came south to Judah. 14 The Levites abandoned their pastures and other land and moved to Judah and Jerusalem, because King Jeroboam of Israel and his successors would not let them serve as priests of the LORD. 15 Jeroboam appointed priests of his own to serve at the pagan places of worship and to worship demons and the idols he made in the form of bull-calves. 16 From all the tribes of Israel people who sincerely wanted to worship the LORD, the God of Israel, followed the Levites to Jerusalem, so that they could offer sacrifices to the LORD, the God of their ancestors. 17 This strengthened the kingdom of Judah, and for three years they supported Rehoboam son of Solomon and lived as they had under the rule of King David and King Solomon.

Rehoboam's Family

18 Rehoboam married Mahalath, whose father was Jerimoth son of David and whose mother was Abihail, the daughter of Eliab and granddaughter of Jesse. 19 They had three sons, Jeush, Shemariah, and Zaham. 20 Later he married Maacah, the daughter of Absalom, and they had four sons: Abijah, Attai, Ziza, and Shelomith. 21 In all, Rehoboam

had eighteen wives and sixty concubines, and he fathered twenty-eight sons and sixty daughters. Of all his wives and concubines he loved Maacah best, 22 and he favored her son Abijah over all his other children, choosing him as the one to succeed him as king. 23 Rehoboam wisely assigned responsibilities to his sons and stationed them throughout Judah and Benjamin in the fortified cities. He provided generously for them and also secured many wives for them.

An Egyptian Invasion of Judah
(1 Kings 14.25-28)

12 As soon as Rehoboam had established his authority as king, he and all his people abandoned the Law of the LORD. 2 In the fifth year of Rehoboam's reign their disloyalty to the LORD was punished. King Shishak of Egypt attacked Jerusalem 3 with an army of twelve hundred chariots, sixty thousand cavalry, and more soldiers than could be counted, including Libyan, Sukkite, and Ethiopian[t] troops. 4 He captured the fortified cities of Judah and advanced as far as Jerusalem.

5 Shemaiah the prophet went to King Rehoboam and the Judean leaders who had gathered in Jerusalem to escape Shishak. He said to them, "This is the LORD's message to you: 'You have abandoned me, so now I have abandoned you to Shishak.'"

6 The king and the leaders admitted that they had sinned, and they said, "What the LORD is doing is just."

7 When the LORD saw this, he spoke again to Shemaiah and said to him, "Because they admit their sin, I will not destroy them. But when Shishak attacks, they will barely survive. Jerusalem will not feel the full force of my anger, 8 but Shishak will conquer them, and they will learn the difference between serving me and serving earthly rulers."

9 King Shishak came to Jerusalem and took the treasures from the Temple and from the palace. He took everything, including the gold shields that King Solomon had made. 10 To replace them, Rehoboam made bronze shields and entrusted them to the officers responsible for guarding the palace gates. 11 Every time the king went to the Temple, the guards carried the shields and then returned them to the guardroom. 12 Because he submitted to the LORD, the LORD's anger did not completely destroy him, and things went well for Judah.

Summary of Rehoboam's Reign

13 Rehoboam ruled in Jerusalem and increased his power as king. He was forty-one years old when he became king, and he ruled for seventeen years in Jerusalem, the city which the LORD had chosen from all the territory of Israel as the place where he was to be worshiped. Rehoboam's mother was Naamah, from the land of Ammon. 14 He did what was evil, because he did not try to find the LORD's will.

15 Rehoboam's acts from beginning to end and his family records are found in *The History of Shemaiah the Prophet* and *The History of Iddo the Prophet.* Rehoboam and Jeroboam were constantly at war with each other. 16 Rehoboam died and was buried in the royal tombs in David's City and his son Abijah succeeded him as king.

Abijah's War with Jeroboam
(1 Kings 15.1-8)

13 In the eighteenth year of the reign of King Jeroboam of Israel, Abijah became king of Judah, 2 and he ruled three years in Jerusalem. His mother was Micaiah daughter of Uriel, from the city of Gibeah.

War broke out between Abijah and Jeroboam. 3 Abijah raised an army of 400,000 soldiers, and Jeroboam opposed him with an army of 800,000.

4 The armies met in the hill country of Ephraim. King Abijah went up Mount Zemaraim and called out to Jeroboam and the Israelites: "Listen to me!" he said. 5 "Don't you know that the LORD, the God of Israel, made an unbreakable covenant with David, giving him and his descendants kingship over Israel forever? 6 Jeroboam son of Nebat rebelled against Solomon, his king. 7 Later he gathered together a group of worthless scoundrels, and they forced their will on

t *Hebrew* Cushite(s): *Cush is the ancient name of the extensive territory south of the First Cataract of the Nile River. This region was called Ethiopia in Graeco-Roman times, and included within its borders most of modern Sudan and some of present-day Ethiopia (Abyssinia).*

2 CHRONICLES

Rehoboam son of Solomon, who was too young and inexperienced to resist them. [8] Now you propose to fight against the royal authority that the LORD gave to David's descendants. You have a huge army and have with you the gold bull-calves that Jeroboam made to be your gods. [9] You drove out the LORD's priests, the descendants of Aaron, and you drove out the Levites. In their place you appointed priests in the same way that other nations do. Anybody who comes along with a bull or seven sheep can get himself consecrated as a priest of those so-called gods of yours.

[10] "But we still serve the LORD our God and have not abandoned him. Priests descended from Aaron perform their duties, and Levites assist them. [11] Every morning and every evening they offer him incense and animal sacrifices burned whole. They present the offerings of bread on a table that is ritually clean, and every evening they light the lamps on the gold lampstand. We do what the LORD has commanded, but you have abandoned him. [12] God himself is our leader and his priests are here with trumpets, ready to blow them and call us to battle against you. People of Israel, don't fight against the LORD, the God of your ancestors! You can't win!"

[13] Meanwhile Jeroboam had sent some of his troops to ambush the Judean army from the rear, while the rest faced them from the front. [14] The Judeans looked around and saw that they were surrounded. They cried to the LORD for help, and the priests blew the trumpets. [15] The Judeans gave a loud shout, and led by Abijah, they attacked; God defeated Jeroboam and the Israelite army. [16] The Israelites fled from the Judeans, and God let the Judeans overpower them. [17] Abijah and his army dealt the Israelites a crushing defeat—half a million of Israel's best soldiers were killed. [18] And so the people of Judah were victorious over Israel, because they relied on the LORD, the God of their ancestors.

[19] Abijah pursued Jeroboam's army and occupied some of his cities: Bethel, Jeshanah, and Ephron, and the villages near each of these cities. [20] Jeroboam never regained his power during Abijah's reign. Finally the LORD struck him down, and he died.

[21] Abijah, however, grew more powerful. He had fourteen wives and fathered twenty-two sons and sixteen daughters. [22] The rest of the history of Abijah, what he said and what he did, is written in *The History of Iddo the Prophet.*

King Asa Defeats the Ethiopians

14 King Abijah died and was buried in the royal tombs in David's City. His son Asa succeeded him as king, and under Asa the land enjoyed peace for ten years. [2] Asa pleased the LORD, his God, by doing what was right and good. [3] He removed the foreign altars and the pagan places of worship, broke down the sacred stone columns, and cut down the symbols of the goddess Asherah. [4] He commanded the people of Judah to do the will of the LORD, the God of their ancestors, and to obey his teachings and commands. [5] Because he abolished the pagan places of worship and the incense altars from all the cities of Judah, the kingdom was at peace under his rule. [6] He built fortifications for the cities of Judah during this time, and for several years there was no war, because the LORD gave him peace. [7] He told the people of Judah, "Let us fortify the cities by building walls and towers, and gates that can be shut and barred. We have control of the land because we have done the will of the LORD our God. He has protected us and given us security on every side." And so they built and prospered. [8] King Asa had an army of 300,000 men from Judah, armed with shields and spears, and 280,000 men from Benjamin, armed with shields and bows. All of them were brave, well-trained men.

[9] An Ethiopian[t] named Zerah invaded Judah with an army of a million men and three hundred chariots and advanced as far as Mareshah. [10] Asa went out to fight him, and both sides took up their positions at Zephathah Valley near Mareshah. [11] Asa prayed to the LORD his God, "O LORD, you can help a weak army as easily as a powerful one. Help us now,

[t] Hebrew Cushite(s): *Cush is the ancient name of the extensive territory south of the First Cataract of the Nile River. This region was called Ethiopia in Graeco-Roman times, and included within its borders most of modern Sudan and some of present-day Ethiopia (Abyssinia).*

O LORD our God, because we are relying on you, and in your name we have come out to fight against this huge army. LORD, you are our God; no one can hope to defeat you."

12 The LORD defeated the Ethiopian[t] army when Asa and the Judean army attacked them. They fled, 13 and Asa and his troops pursued them as far as Gerar. So many of the Ethiopians[t] were killed that the army was unable to rally and fight.[u] They were overpowered by the LORD and his army, and the army took large amounts of loot. 14 Then they were able to destroy the cities in the area around Gerar, because the people there were terrified of the LORD. The army plundered all those cities and captured large amounts of loot. 15 They also attacked the camps of some shepherds, capturing large numbers of sheep and camels. Then they returned to Jerusalem.

Asa's Reforms

15 The spirit of God came upon Azariah son of Oded, 2 and he went to meet King Asa. He called out, "Listen to me, King Asa, and all you people of Judah and Benjamin! The LORD is with you as long as you are with him. If you look for him, he will let you find him, but if you turn away, he will abandon you. 3 For a long time Israel lived without the true God, without priests to teach them, and without a law. 4 But when trouble came, they turned to the LORD, the God of Israel. They searched for him and found him. 5 In those days no one could come and go in safety, because there was trouble and disorder in every land. 6 One nation oppressed another nation, and one city oppressed another city, because God was bringing trouble and distress on them. 7 But you must be strong and not be discouraged. The work that you do will be rewarded."

8 When Asa heard the prophecy that Azariah son of[v] Oded had spoken, he was encouraged. He did away with all the idols in the land of Judah and Benjamin and all the idols in the cities he had captured in the hill country of Ephraim. He also repaired the altar of the LORD that stood in the Temple courtyard.

9 Many people had come over to Asa's side from Ephraim, Manasseh, and Simeon, and were living in his kingdom, because they had seen that the LORD was with him. Asa summoned all of them and the people of Judah and Benjamin. 10 They assembled in Jerusalem in the third month of the fifteenth year that Asa was king. 11 On that day they offered sacrifices to the LORD from the loot they had brought back: seven hundred head of cattle and seven thousand sheep. 12 They made a covenant in which they agreed to worship the LORD, the God of their ancestors, with all their heart and soul. 13 Anyone, young or old, male or female, who did not worship him was to be put to death. 14 In a loud voice they took an oath in the LORD's name that they would keep the covenant, and then they shouted and blew trumpets. 15 All the people of Judah were happy because they had made this covenant with all their heart. They took delight in worshiping the LORD, and he accepted them and gave them peace on every side.

16 King Asa removed his grandmother Maacah from her position as queen mother, because she had made an obscene idol of the fertility goddess Asherah. Asa cut down the idol, chopped it up, and burned the pieces in Kidron Valley. 17 Even though Asa did not destroy all the pagan places of worship in the land, he remained faithful to the LORD all his life. 18 He placed in the Temple all the objects his father Abijah had dedicated to God, as well as the gold and silver objects that he himself dedicated. 19 There was no more war until the thirty-fifth year of his reign.

Troubles with Israel
(1 Kings 15.17-22)

16 In the thirty-sixth year of the reign of King Asa of Judah, King Baasha of Israel invaded Judah and started to fortify Ramah in order to cut off all traffic in and out of Judah. 2 So

---

[t] Hebrew Cushite(s): *Cush is the ancient name of the extensive territory south of the First Cataract of the Nile River. This region was called Ethiopia in Graeco-Roman times, and included within its borders most of modern Sudan and some of present-day Ethiopia (Abyssinia).*   [u] So many of the Ethiopians ... fight; *or* The Ethiopians were completely defeated; not one of them was left alive.   [v] Some ancient translations Azariah son of; Hebrew does not have these words.

Asa took silver and gold from the treasuries of the Temple and the palace and sent it to Damascus, to King Benhadad of Syria, with this message: 3 "Let us be allies, as our fathers were. This silver and gold is a present for you. Now break your alliance with King Baasha of Israel so that he will have to pull his troops out of my territory."

4 Benhadad agreed to Asa's proposal and sent his commanding officers and their armies to attack the cities of Israel. They captured Ijon, Dan, Abel Beth Maacah, and all the cities of Naphtali where supplies were stored. 5 When King Baasha heard what was happening, he stopped fortifying Ramah and abandoned the work. 6 Then King Asa gathered men from throughout Judah and had them carry off the stones and timbers that Baasha had been using at Ramah, and they used them to fortify the cities of Geba and Mizpah.

The Prophet Hanani

7 At that time the prophet Hanani went to King Asa and said, "Because you relied on the king of Syria instead of relying on the Lord your God, the army of the king of Israel[w] has escaped from you. 8 Didn't the Ethiopians[x] and the Libyans have large armies with many chariots and cavalry troops? But because you relied on the Lord, he gave you victory over them. 9 The Lord keeps close watch over the whole world, to give strength to those whose hearts are loyal to him. You have acted foolishly, and so from now on you will always be at war." 10 This made Asa so angry with the prophet that he had him put in chains. It was at this same time that Asa began treating some of the people cruelly.

The End of Asa's Reign
(1 Kings 15.23, 24)

11 All the events of Asa's reign from beginning to end are recorded in The History of the Kings of Judah and Israel. 12 In the thirty-ninth year that Asa was king, he was crippled by a severe foot disease; but even then he did not turn to the Lord for help, but to doctors. 13 Two years later he died 14 and was buried in the rock tomb which he had carved out for himself in David's City. They used spices and perfumed oils to prepare his body for burial, and they built a huge bonfire to mourn his death.

Jehoshaphat Becomes King

17 Jehoshaphat succeeded his father Asa as king and strengthened his position against Israel. 2 He stationed troops in the fortified cities of Judah, in the Judean countryside, and in the cities which Asa had captured in the territory of Ephraim. 3 The Lord blessed Jehoshaphat because he followed the example of his father's early life and did not worship Baal. 4 He served his father's God, obeyed God's commands, and did not act the way the kings of Israel did. 5 The Lord gave Jehoshaphat firm control over the kingdom of Judah, and all the people brought him gifts, so that he became wealthy and highly honored. 6 He took pride in serving the Lord and destroyed all the pagan places of worship and the symbols of the goddess Asherah in Judah.

7 In the third year of his reign he sent out the following officials to teach in the cities of Judah: Benhail, Obadiah, Zechariah, Nethanel, and Micaiah. 8 They were accompanied by nine Levites and two priests. The Levites were Shemaiah, Nethaniah, Zebadiah, Asahel, Shemiramoth, Jehonathan, Adonijah, Tobijah, and Tobadonijah; and the priests were Elishama and Jehoram. 9 They took the book of the Law of the Lord and went through all the towns of Judah, teaching it to the people.

Jehoshaphat's Greatness

10 The Lord made all the surrounding kingdoms afraid to go to war against King Jehoshaphat. 11 Some of the Philistines brought Jehoshaphat a large amount of silver and other gifts, and some Arabs brought him 7,700 sheep and 7,700 goats. 12 So Jehoshaphat continued to grow more and more powerful. Throughout Judah he built fortifications and cities, 13 where supplies were stored in huge amounts.

w One ancient translation Israel; Hebrew Syria. x Hebrew Cushites: Cush is the ancient name of the extensive territory south of the First Cataract of the Nile River. This region was called Ethiopia in Graeco-Roman times, and included within its borders most of modern Sudan and some of present-day Ethiopia (Abyssinia).

In Jerusalem he stationed outstanding officers, 14 according to their clans. Adnah was the commander of the troops from the clans of Judah, and he had 300,000 soldiers under him. 15 Second in rank was Jehohanan, with 280,000 soldiers, 16 and third was Amasiah son of Zichri, with 200,000. (Amasiah had volunteered to serve the LORD.) 17 The commander of the troops from the clans of Benjamin was Eliada, an outstanding soldier, in command of 200,000 men armed with shields and bows. 18 His second in command was Jehozabad with 180,000 men, well-equipped for battle. 19 These soldiers served the king in Jerusalem, and in addition he stationed others in the other fortified cities of Judah.

The Prophet Micaiah Warns Ahab
(1 Kings 22.1-28)

18 When King Jehoshaphat of Judah became rich and famous, he arranged a marriage between a member of his family and the family of King Ahab of Israel. 2 A number of years later Jehoshaphat went to the city of Samaria to visit Ahab. To honor Jehoshaphat and those with him, Ahab had a large number of sheep and cattle slaughtered for a feast. He tried to persuade Jehoshaphat to join him in attacking the city of Ramoth in Gilead. 3 He asked, "Will you go with me to attack Ramoth?"

Jehoshaphat replied, "I am ready when you are, and so is my army. We will join you." 4 Then he added, "But first let's consult the LORD."

5 So Ahab called in the prophets, about four hundred of them, and asked them, "Should I go and attack Ramoth, or not?"

"Attack it," they answered. "God will give you victory."

6 But Jehoshaphat asked, "Isn't there another prophet through whom we can consult the LORD?"

7 Ahab answered, "There is one more, Micaiah son of Imlah. But I hate him because he never prophesies anything good for me; it's always something bad."

"You shouldn't say that!" Jehoshaphat replied.

8 So King Ahab called in a court official and told him to go and get Micaiah at once.

9 The two kings, dressed in their royal robes, were sitting on their thrones at the threshing place just outside the gate of Samaria, and all the prophets were prophesying in front of them. 10 One of them, Zedekiah son of Chenaanah, made iron horns and said to Ahab, "This is what the LORD says, 'With these you will fight the Syrians and totally defeat them.' " 11 All the other prophets said the same thing. "March against Ramoth and you will win," they said. "The LORD will give you victory."

12 Meanwhile, the official who had gone to get Micaiah said to him, "All the other prophets have prophesied success for the king, and you had better do the same."

13 But Micaiah answered, "By the living LORD I will say what my God tells me to!"

14 When he appeared before King Ahab, the king asked him, "Micaiah, should King Jehoshaphat and I go and attack Ramoth, or not?"

"Attack!" Micaiah answered. "Of course you'll win. The LORD will give you victory."

15 But Ahab replied, "When you speak to me in the name of the LORD, tell the truth! How many times do I have to tell you that?"

16 Micaiah answered, "I can see the army of Israel scattered over the hills like sheep without a shepherd. And the LORD said, 'These men have no leader; let them go home in peace.' "

17 Ahab said to Jehoshaphat, "I told you that he never prophesies anything good for me; it's always something bad!"

18 Micaiah went on: "Now listen to what the LORD says! I saw the LORD sitting on his throne in heaven, with all his angels standing beside him. 19 The LORD asked, 'Who will deceive Ahab so that he will go and get killed at Ramoth?' Some of the angels said one thing, and others said something else, 20 until a spirit stepped forward, approached the LORD, and said, 'I will deceive him.' 'How?' the LORD asked. 21 The spirit replied, 'I will go and make all of Ahab's prophets tell lies.' The LORD said, 'Go and deceive him. You will succeed.' "

22 And Micaiah concluded: "This is what has happened. The LORD has made these prophets of yours lie to you. But he

himself has decreed that you will meet with disaster!"

23 Then the prophet Zedekiah went up to Micaiah, slapped his face, and asked, "Since when did the LORD's spirit leave me and speak to you?"

24 "You will find out when you go into some back room to hide," Micaiah replied.

25 Then King Ahab ordered one of his officers, "Arrest Micaiah and take him to Amon, the governor of the city, and to Prince Joash. 26 Tell them to throw him in prison and to put him on bread and water until I return safely."

27 "If you return safely," Micaiah exclaimed, "then the LORD has not spoken through me!" And he added, "Listen, everyone, to what I have said!"

The Death of Ahab
(1 Kings 22.29-35)

28 Then King Ahab of Israel and King Jehoshaphat of Judah went to attack the city of Ramoth in Gilead. 29 Ahab said to Jehoshaphat, "As we go into battle, I will disguise myself, but you wear your royal garments." So the king of Israel went into battle in disguise.

30 The king of Syria had ordered his chariot commanders to attack no one else except the king of Israel. 31 So when they saw King Jehoshaphat, they all thought that he was the king of Israel, and they turned to attack him. But Jehoshaphat gave a shout, and the LORD God rescued him and turned the attack away from him. 32 The chariot commanders saw that he was not the king of Israel, so they stopped pursuing him. 33 By chance, however, a Syrian soldier shot an arrow which struck King Ahab between the joints of his armor. "I'm wounded!" he cried out to his chariot driver. "Turn around and pull out of the battle!" 34 While the battle raged on, King Ahab remained propped up in his chariot, facing the Syrians. At sunset he died.

A Prophet Reprimands Jehoshaphat

19 King Jehoshaphat of Judah returned safely to his palace in Jerusalem. 2 A prophet, Jehu son of Hanani, went to meet the king and said to him, "Do you think it is right to help those who are wicked and to take the side of those who hate the LORD? What you have done has brought the LORD's anger on you. 3 But even so, there is some good in you. You have removed all the symbols of the goddess Asherah which people worshiped, and you have tried to follow God's will."

Jehoshaphat's Reforms

4 Even though King Jehoshaphat lived in Jerusalem, he traveled regularly among the people, from Beersheba in the south to the edge of the hill country of Ephraim in the north, in order to call the people back to the LORD, the God of their ancestors. 5 He appointed judges in each of the fortified cities of Judah 6 and instructed them: "Be careful in pronouncing judgment; you are not acting on human authority, but on the authority of the LORD, and he is with you when you pass sentence. 7 Honor the LORD and act carefully, because the LORD our God does not tolerate fraud or partiality or the taking of bribes."

8 In Jerusalem Jehoshaphat appointed Levites, priests, and some of the leading citizens as judges in cases involving a violation of the Law of the LORD or legal disputes between inhabitants of the city.y 9 He gave them the following instructions: "You must perform your duties in reverence for the LORD, faithfully obeying him in everything you do. 10 Whenever your fellow citizens from any of the cities bring before you a case of homicide or any other violation of a law or commandment, you must instruct them carefully how to conduct themselves during the trial, so that they do not become guilty of sinning against the LORD. Unless you do, you and your fellow citizens will feel the force of the LORD's anger. But if you do your duty, you will not be guilty. 11 Amariah the High Priest will have final authority in all religious cases, and Zebadiah son of Ishmael, governor of Judah, will have final authority in all civil cases. The Levites have the responsibility of seeing that the decisions of the courts are carried out. Be courageous and carry out these instructions, and may the LORD be on the side of the right!"

---

y Some ancient translations between . . . city; Hebrew unclear.

War against Edom

20 Some time later the armies of Moab and Ammon, together with their allies, the Meunites,*z* invaded Judah. 2 Some messengers came and announced to King Jehoshaphat: "A large army from Edom has come from the other side of the Dead Sea to attack you. They have already captured Hazazon Tamar." (This is another name for Engedi.) 3 Jehoshaphat was frightened and prayed to the LORD for guidance. Then he gave orders for a fast to be observed throughout the country. 4 From every city of Judah people hurried to Jerusalem to ask the LORD for guidance, 5 and they and the people of Jerusalem gathered in the new courtyard of the Temple. King Jehoshaphat went and stood before them 6 and prayed aloud, "O LORD God of our ancestors, you rule in heaven over all the nations of the world. You are powerful and mighty, and no one can oppose you. 7 You are our God. When your people Israel moved into this land, you drove out the people who were living here and gave the land to the descendants of Abraham, your friend, to be theirs forever. 8 They have lived here and have built a temple to honor you, knowing 9 that if any disaster struck them to punish them—a war,*a* an epidemic, or a famine—then they could come and stand in front of this Temple where you are worshiped. They could pray to you in their trouble, and you would hear them and rescue them.

10 "Now the people of Ammon, Moab, and Edom have attacked us. When our ancestors came out of Egypt, you did not allow them to enter those lands, so our ancestors went around them and did not destroy them. 11 This is how they repay us—they come to drive us out of the land that you gave us. 12 You are our God! Punish them, for we are helpless in the face of this large army that is attacking us. We do not know what to do, but we look to you for help."

13 All the men of Judah, with their wives and children, were standing there at the Temple. 14 The spirit of the LORD came upon a Levite who was present in the crowd. His name was Jahaziel son of Zechariah; he was a member of the clan of Asaph and was descended from Asaph through Mattaniah, Jeiel, and Benaiah. 15 Jahaziel said, "Your Majesty and all you people of Judah and Jerusalem, the LORD says that you must not be discouraged or be afraid to face this large army. The battle depends on God, not on you. 16 Attack them tomorrow as they come up the pass at Ziz. You will meet them at the end of the valley that leads to the wild country near Jeruel. 17 You will not have to fight this battle. Just take up your positions and wait; you will see the LORD give you victory. People of Judah and Jerusalem, do not hesitate or be afraid. Go out to battle, and the LORD will be with you!"

18 Then King Jehoshaphat bowed low, with his face touching the ground, and all the people bowed with him and worshiped the LORD. 19 The members of the Levite clans of Kohath and Korah stood up and with a loud shout praised the LORD, the God of Israel.

20 Early the next morning the people went out to the wild country near Tekoa. As they were starting out, Jehoshaphat addressed them with these words: "People of Judah and Jerusalem! Put your trust in the LORD your God, and you will stand your ground. Believe what his prophets tell you, and you will succeed." 21 After consulting with the people, the king ordered some musicians to put on the robes they wore on sacred occasions and to march ahead of the army, singing: "Praise the LORD! His love is eternal!"

22 When they began to sing, the LORD threw the invading armies into a panic. 23 The Ammonites and the Moabites attacked the Edomite army and completely destroyed it, and then they turned on each other in savage fighting. 24 When the Judean army reached a tower that was in the desert, they looked toward the enemy and saw that they were all lying on the ground dead. Not one had escaped.

25 Jehoshaphat and his troops moved in to take the loot, and they found many cattle,*b* supplies, clothing, and other valuable objects. They spent three days gathering the loot, but there was so much that they could not take

---

z One ancient translation Meunites; *Hebrew* Ammonites.   *a* struck . . . war; *or* struck them—a devastating war.   *b One ancient translation* cattle; *Hebrew* among them.

everything. 26On the fourth day they assembled in Beracah Valley and praised the Lord for all he had done. That is why the valley is called "Beracah."c 27Jehoshaphat led his troops back to Jerusalem in triumph, because the Lord had defeated their enemies. 28When they reached the city, they marched to the Temple to the music of harps and trumpets. 29Every nation that heard how the Lord had defeated Israel's enemies was terrified, 30so Jehoshaphat ruled in peace, and God gave him security on every side.

The End of Jehoshaphat's Reign
(1 Kings 22.41-50)

31Jehoshaphat had become king of Judah at the age of thirty-five and had ruled in Jerusalem for twenty-five years. His mother was Azubah, the daughter of Shilhi. 32Like his father Asa before him, he did what was right in the sight of the Lord; 33but the pagan places of worship were not destroyed. The people still did not turn wholeheartedly to the worship of the God of their ancestors.

34Everything else that Jehoshaphat did, from the beginning of his reign to its end, is recorded in *The History of Jehu Son of Hanani*, which is a part of *The History of the Kings of Israel*.

35At one time King Jehoshaphat of Judah made an alliance with King Ahaziah of Israel, who did many wicked things. 36At the port of Eziongeber they built ocean-going ships. 37But Eliezer son of Dodavahu, from the town of Mareshah, warned Jehoshaphat, "Because you have made an alliance with Ahaziah, the Lord will destroy what you have built." And the ships were wrecked and never sailed.

21 Jehoshaphat died and was buried in the royal tombs in David's City and his son Jehoram succeeded him as king.

King Jehoram of Judah
(2 Kings 8.17-24)

2Jehoram son of King Jehoshaphat of Judah had six brothers: Azariah, Jehiel, Zechariah, Azariahu, Michael, and Shephatiah. 3Their father gave them large amounts of gold, silver, and other valuable possessions, and placed each one in charge of one of the fortified cities of Judah. But because Jehoram was the oldest, Jehoshaphat made him his successor. 4When Jehoram was in firm control of the kingdom, he had all his brothers killed, and also some Israelite officials.

5Jehoram became king at the age of thirty-two, and he ruled in Jerusalem for eight years. 6He followed the wicked example of King Ahab and the other kings of Israel, because he had married one of Ahab's daughters. He sinned against the Lord, 7but the Lord was not willing to destroy the dynasty of David, because he had made a covenant with David and promised that his descendants would always continue to rule.

8During Jehoram's reign Edom revolted against Judah and became an independent kingdom. 9So Jehoram and his officers set out with chariots and invaded Edom. There the Edomite army surrounded them, but during the night they managed to break out and escape. 10Edom has been independent ofd Judah ever since. During this same period the city of Libnah also revolted, because Jehoram had abandoned the Lord, the God of his ancestors. 11He even built pagan places of worship in the Judean highlands and led the people of Judah and Jerusalem to sin against the Lord.

12The prophet Elijah sent Jehoram a letter, which read as follows: "The Lord, the God of your ancestor David, condemns you, because you did not follow the example of your father, King Jehoshaphat, or that of your grandfather, King Asa. 13Instead, you have followed the example of the kings of Israel and have led the people of Judah and Jerusalem into being unfaithful to God, just as Ahab and his successors led Israel into unfaithfulness. You even murdered your brothers, who were better men than you are. 14As a result, the Lord will severely punish your people, your children, and your wives, and will destroy your possessions. 15You yourself will suffer a painful intestinal disease that will grow worse day by day."

16Some Philistines and Arabs lived

c BERACAH: *This name in Hebrew means "praise."*   d independent of; *or in revolt against.*

near where some Ethiopians[e] had settled along the coast. The LORD caused them to go to war against Jehoram. [17]They invaded Judah, looted the royal palace, and carried off as prisoners all the king's wives and sons except Ahaziah, his youngest son.

[18]Then after all this, the LORD brought on the king a painful disease of the intestines. [19]For almost two years it grew steadily worse until finally the king died in agony. His subjects did not light a bonfire in mourning for him as had been done for his ancestors.

[20]Jehoram had become king at the age of thirty-two and had ruled in Jerusalem for eight years. Nobody was sorry when he died. They buried him in David's City, but not in the royal tombs.

King Ahaziah of Judah
(2 Kings 8.25-29; 9.21-28)

22 Some Arabs had led a raid and killed all of King Jehoram's sons except Ahaziah, the youngest. So now the people of Jerusalem made Ahaziah king as his father's successor. [2-3]Ahaziah became king at the age of twenty-two,[f] and he ruled in Jerusalem for one year. Ahaziah also followed the example of King Ahab's family, since his mother Athaliah—the daughter of King Ahab and granddaughter of King Omri of Israel—gave him advice that led him into evil. [4]He sinned against the LORD, because after his father's death other members of King Ahab's family became his advisers, and they led to his downfall. [5]Following their advice, he joined King Joram of Israel in a war against King Hazael of Syria. The armies clashed at Ramoth in Gilead, and Joram was wounded in battle. [6]He returned to the city of Jezreel to recover from his wounds, and Ahaziah went there to visit him. [7]God used this visit to Joram to bring about Ahaziah's downfall. While Ahaziah was there, he and Joram were confronted by a man named Jehu son of Nimshi, whom the LORD had chosen to destroy the dynasty of Ahab. [8]As Jehu was carrying out God's sentence on the

dynasty, he came across a group made up of Judean leaders and of Ahaziah's nephews that had accompanied Ahaziah on his visit. Jehu killed them all. [9]A search was made for Ahaziah, and he was found hiding in Samaria. They took him to Jehu and put him to death. But they did bury his body out of respect for his grandfather King Jehoshaphat, who had done all he could to serve the LORD.

No member of Ahaziah's family was left who could rule the kingdom.

Queen Athaliah of Judah
(2 Kings 11.1-3)

[10]As soon as King Ahaziah's mother Athaliah learned of her son's murder, she gave orders for all the members of the royal family of Judah to be killed. [11]Ahaziah had a half sister, Jehosheba, who was married to a priest named Jehoiada. She secretly rescued one of Ahaziah's sons, Joash, took him away from the other princes who were about to be murdered and hid him and a nurse in a bedroom at the Temple. By keeping him hidden, she saved him from death at the hands of Athaliah. [12]For six years he remained there in hiding, while Athaliah ruled as queen.

The Revolt against Athaliah
(2 Kings 11.4-16)

23 After waiting six years Jehoiada the priest decided that it was time to take action. He made a pact with five army officers: Azariah son of Jeroham, Ishmael son of Jehohanan, Azariah son of Obed, Maaseiah son of Adaiah, and Elishaphat son of Zichri. [2]They traveled to all the cities of Judah and brought back with them to Jerusalem the Levites and all the heads of the clans. [3]They all gathered in the Temple, and there they made a covenant with Joash, the king's son. Jehoiada said to them, "Here is the son of the late king. He is now to be king, as the LORD promised that King David's descendants would be. [4]This is what we will do. When the priests and Levites come on duty on the

Sabbath, one third of them will guard the Temple gates, 5 another third will guard the royal palace, and the rest will be stationed at the Foundation Gate. All the people will assemble in the Temple courtyard. 6 No one is to enter the Temple buildings except the priests and the Levites who are on duty. They may enter, because they are consecrated, but the rest of the people must obey the LORD's instructions and stay outside. 7 The Levites are to stand guard around the king, with their swords drawn, and are to stay with the king wherever he goes. Anyone who tries to enter the Temple is to be killed."

8 The Levites and the people of Judah carried out Jehoiada's instructions. The men were not dismissed when they went off duty on the Sabbath, so the commanders had available both those coming on duty and those going off. 9 Jehoiada gave the officers the spears and shields that had belonged to King David and had been kept in the Temple. 10 He stationed the men with drawn swords all around the front of the Temple, to protect the king. 11 Then Jehoiada led Joash out, placed the crown on his head, and gave him a copy of the laws governing kingship. And so he was made king. Jehoiada the priest and his sons anointed Joash, and everyone shouted, "Long live the king!"

12 Athaliah heard the people cheering for the king, so she hurried to the Temple, where the crowd had gathered. 13 There she saw the new king at the Temple entrance, standing by the column reserved for kings and surrounded by the army officers and the trumpeters. All the people were shouting joyfully and blowing trumpets, and the Temple musicians with their instruments were leading the celebration. She tore her clothes in distress and shouted, "Treason! Treason!"

14 Jehoiada did not want Athaliah killed in the Temple area, so he called out the army officers and said, "Take her out between the rows of guards, and kill anyone who tries to rescue her." 15 They seized her, took her to the palace, and there at the Horse Gate they killed her.

Jehoiada's Reforms
(2 Kings 11.17-20)

16 The priest Jehoiada had King Joash and the people join him in making a covenant that they would be the LORD's people. 17 Then they all went to the temple of Baal and tore it down. They smashed the altars and idols there and killed Mattan, the priest of Baal, in front of the altars. 18 Jehoiada put the priests and Levites in charge of the work of the Temple. They were to carry out the duties assigned to them by King David and to burn the sacrifices offered to the LORD in accordance with the Law of Moses. They were also in charge of the music and the celebrations. 19 Jehoiada also put guards on duty at the Temple gates to keep out anyone who was ritually unclean.

20 The army officers, the leading citizens, the officials, and all the rest of the people joined Jehoiada in a procession that brought the king from the Temple to the palace. They entered by the main gate, and the king took his place on the throne. 21 All the people were filled with happiness, and the city was quiet, now that Athaliah had been killed.

King Joash of Judah
(2 Kings 12.1-16)

24 Joash became king of Judah at the age of seven, and he ruled in Jerusalem for forty years. His mother was Zibiah from the city of Beersheba. 2 He did what was pleasing to the LORD as long as Jehoiada the priest was alive. 3 Jehoiada chose two wives for King Joash, and they bore him sons and daughters.

4 After he had been king for a while, Joash decided to have the Temple repaired. 5 He ordered the priests and the Levites to go to the cities of Judah and collect from all the people enough money to make the annual repairs on the Temple. He told them to act promptly, but the Levites delayed, 6 so he called in Jehoiada, their leader, and demanded, "Why haven't you seen to it that the Levites collect from Judah and Jerusalem the tax which Moses, the servant of the LORD, required the people g to pay for support of the Tent of the LORD's presence?"

(7 The followers of Athaliah, that cor-

g Probable text required the people; Hebrew unclear.

rupt woman,[h] had damaged the Temple and had used many of the sacred objects in the worship of Baal.) 8 The king ordered the Levites to make a box for contributions and to place it at the Temple gate. 9 They sent word throughout Jerusalem and Judah for everyone to bring to the LORD the tax which Moses, God's servant, had first collected in the wilderness. 10 This pleased the people and their leaders, and they brought their tax money and filled the box with it. 11 Every day the Levites would take the box to the royal official who was in charge of it. Whenever it was full, the royal secretary and the High Priest's representative would take the money out and return the box to its place. And so they collected a large sum of money.

12 The king and Jehoiada would give the money to those who were in charge of repairing the Temple, and they hired stonemasons, carpenters, and metalworkers to make the repairs. 13 All of them worked hard, and they restored the Temple to its original condition, as solid as ever. 14 When the repairs were finished, the remaining gold and silver was given to the king and Jehoiada, who used it to have bowls and other utensils made for the Temple.

Jehoiada's Policies Are Reversed

As long as Jehoiada was alive, sacrifices were offered regularly at the Temple. 15 After reaching the very old age of a hundred and thirty, he died. 16 They buried him in the royal tombs in David's City in recognition of the service he had done for the people of Israel, for God, and for the Temple.

17 But once Jehoiada was dead, the leaders of Judah persuaded King Joash to listen to them instead. 18 And so the people stopped worshiping in the Temple of the LORD, the God of their ancestors, and began to worship idols and the images of the goddess Asherah. Their guilt for these sins brought the LORD's anger on Judah and Jerusalem. 19 The LORD sent prophets to warn them to return to him, but the people refused to listen. 20 Then the spirit of God took control of Zechariah son of Jehoiada the

priest. He stood where the people could see him and called out, "The LORD God asks why you have disobeyed his commands and are bringing disaster on yourselves! You abandoned him, so he has abandoned you!" 21 King Joash joined in a conspiracy against Zechariah, and on the king's orders the people stoned Zechariah in the Temple courtyard. 22 The king forgot about the loyal service that Zechariah's father Jehoiada had given him, and he had Zechariah killed. As Zechariah was dying, he called out, "May the LORD see what you are doing and punish you!"

The End of Joash's Reign

23 When autumn came that year, the Syrian army attacked Judah and Jerusalem, killed all the leaders, and took large amounts of loot back to Damascus. 24 The Syrian army was small, but the LORD let them defeat a much larger Judean army because the people had abandoned him, the LORD God of their ancestors. In this way King Joash was punished. 25 He was severely wounded, and when the enemy withdrew, two of his officials plotted against him and killed him in his bed to avenge the murder of the son[i] of Jehoiada the priest. He was buried in David's City, but not in the royal tombs. (26 Those who plotted against him were Zabad, the son of an Ammonite woman named Shimeath, and Jehozabad, the son of a Moabite woman named Shimrith.) 27 The *Commentary on the Book of Kings* contains the stories of the sons of Joash, the prophecies spoken against him, and the record of how he rebuilt the Temple. His son Amaziah succeeded him as king.

King Amaziah of Judah
(2 Kings 14.2-6)

25 Amaziah became king at the age of twenty-five, and he ruled in Jerusalem for twenty-nine years. His mother was Jehoaddin from Jerusalem. 2 He did what was pleasing to the LORD, but did it reluctantly. 3 As soon as he was firmly in power, he executed the officials who had murdered his father. 4 He did not, however, execute their children, but followed what the LORD had commanded in the Law of Moses: "Parents are not to

---

[h] *that corrupt woman; or whom she corrupted.* sons.

[i] *Some ancient translations* son; *Hebrew* sons.

be put to death for crimes committed by their children, and children are not to be put to death for crimes committed by their parents; people are to be put to death only for crimes they themselves have committed."

War against Edom
(2 Kings 14.7)

5 King Amaziah organized all the men of the tribes of Judah and Benjamin into army units, according to the clans they belonged to, and placed officers in command of units of a thousand and units of a hundred. This included all men twenty years of age or older, 300,000 in all. They were picked troops, ready for battle, skilled in using spears and shields. 6 In addition, he hired 100,000 soldiers from Israel at a cost of about four tons of silver. 7 But a prophet went to the king and said to him, "Don't take these Israelite soldiers with you. The LORD is not with these people from the Northern Kingdom. 8 You may think that they will make you stronger *j* in battle, but it is God who has the power to give victory or defeat, and he will let your enemies defeat you."

9 Amaziah asked the prophet, "But what about all that silver I have already paid for them?"

The prophet replied, "The LORD can give you back more than that!" 10 So Amaziah sent the hired troops away and told them to go home. At this they went home, bitterly angry with the people of Judah.

11 Amaziah summoned up his courage and led his army to Salt Valley. There they fought and killed ten thousand Edomite soldiers 12 and captured another ten thousand. They took the prisoners to the top of the cliff at the city of Sela and threw them off, so that they were killed on the rocks below.

13 Meanwhile the Israelite soldiers that Amaziah had not allowed to go into battle with him attacked the Judean cities between Samaria and Beth Horon, killed three thousand men, and captured quantities of loot.

14 When Amaziah returned from defeating the Edomites, he brought their idols back with him, set them up, worshiped them, and burned incense to them. 15 This made the LORD angry, so he sent a prophet to Amaziah. The prophet demanded, "Why have you worshiped foreign gods that could not even save their own people from your power?"

16 "Since when," Amaziah interrupted, "have we made you adviser to the king? Stop talking, or I'll have you killed!"

The prophet stopped, but not before saying, "Now I know that God has decided to destroy you because you have done all this and have ignored my advice."

War against Israel
(2 Kings 14.8-20)

17 King Amaziah of Judah and his advisers plotted against Israel. He then sent a message to King Jehoash of Israel, who was the son of Jehoahaz and grandson of Jehu, challenging him to fight. *k* 18 Jehoash sent this answer to Amaziah: "Once a thorn bush in the Lebanon Mountains sent a message to a cedar: 'Give your daughter in marriage to my son.' A wild animal passed by and trampled the bush down. 19 Now Amaziah, you boast that you have defeated the Edomites, but I advise you to stay at home. Why stir up trouble that will only bring disaster on you and your people?"

20 But Amaziah refused to listen. It was God's will for Amaziah to be defeated, because he had worshiped the Edomite idols. 21 So King Jehoash of Israel went into battle against King Amaziah of Judah. They met at Beth Shemesh in Judah, 22 the Judean army was defeated, and the soldiers fled to their homes. 23 Jehoash captured Amaziah and took him to Jerusalem. There he tore down the city wall from Ephraim Gate to the Corner Gate, a distance of two hundred yards. 24 He took back to Samaria as loot all the gold and silver in the Temple, the Temple equipment guarded by the descendants of Obed Edom, and the palace treasures. He also took hostages with him.

25 King Amaziah of Judah outlived King Jehoash of Israel by fifteen years. 26 All the other things that Amaziah did from the beginning to the end of his reign are recorded in *The History of the*

---

j Some ancient translations You may . . . stronger; *Hebrew unclear.* *k challenging him to fight; or inviting him to a conference.*

Kings of Judah and Israel. 27Ever since the time when he rebelled against the LORD, there had been a plot against him in Jerusalem. Finally he fled to the city of Lachish, but his enemies followed him there and killed him. 28His body was carried to Jerusalem on a horse, and he was buried in the royal tombs in David's City.

King Uzziah of Judah
(2 Kings 14.21, 22; 15.1-7)

26 All the people of Judah chose Amaziah's sixteen-year-old son Uzziah to succeed his father as king. (2It was after the death of Amaziah that Uzziah recaptured Elath and rebuilt the city.)

3Uzziah became king at the age of sixteen, and he ruled in Jerusalem for fifty-two years. His mother was Jecoliah from Jerusalem. 4Following the example of his father, he did what was pleasing to the LORD. 5As long as Zechariah, his religious adviser, was living, he served the LORD faithfully, and God blessed him.

6Uzziah went to war against the Philistines. He tore down the walls of the cities of Gath, Jamnia, and Ashdod, and built fortified cities near Ashdod and in the rest of Philistia. 7God helped him defeat the Philistines, the Arabs living at Gurbaal, and the Meunites. 8The Ammonites paid tribute to Uzziah, and he became so powerful that his fame spread even to Egypt.

9Uzziah strengthened the fortifications of Jerusalem by building towers at the Corner Gate, at the Valley Gate, and where the wall turned. 10He also built fortified towers in the open country and dug many cisterns, because he had large herds of livestock in the western foothills and plains. Because he loved farming, he encouraged the people to plant vineyards in the hill country and to farm the fertile land.

11He had a large army ready for battle. Its records were kept by his secretaries Jeiel and Maaseiah under the supervision of Hananiah, a member of the king's staff. 12The army was commanded by 2,600 officers. 13Under them were 307,500 soldiers able to fight effectively for the king against his enemies. 14Uzziah supplied the army with shields, spears, helmets, coats of armor, bows and arrows, and stones for slinging. 15In Jerusalem his inventors made equipment for shooting arrows and for throwing large stones from the towers and corners of the city wall. His fame spread everywhere, and he became very powerful because of the help he received from God.

Uzziah Is Punished for His Pride

16But when King Uzziah became strong, he grew arrogant, and that led to his downfall. He defied the LORD his God by going into the Temple to burn incense on the altar of incense. 17Azariah the priest, accompanied by eighty strong and courageous priests, followed the king 18to resist him. They said, "Uzziah! You have no right to burn incense to the LORD. Only the priests who are descended from Aaron have been consecrated to do this. Leave this holy place. You have offended the LORD God, and you no longer have his blessing."

19Uzziah was standing there in the Temple beside the incense altar and was holding an incense burner. He became angry with the priests, and immediately a dreaded skin disease broke out on his forehead. 20Azariah and the other priests stared at the king's forehead in horror and then forced him to leave the Temple. He hurried to get out, because the LORD had punished him.

21For the rest of his life King Uzziah was ritually unclean because of his disease. Unable to enter the Temple again, he lived in his own house, relieved of all duties, while his son Jotham governed the country.

22The prophet Isaiah son of Amoz recorded all the other things that King Uzziah did during his reign. 23Uzziah died and was buried in the royal burial ground, but because of his disease he was not buried in the royal tombs. His son Jotham succeeded him as king.

King Jotham of Judah
(2 Kings 15.32-38)

27 Jotham became king at the age of twenty-five, and he ruled in Jerusalem for sixteen years. His mother was Jerushah, the daughter of Zadok. 2He did what was pleasing to the LORD, just as his father had done; but unlike his father he did not sin by burning incense[l] in the Temple. The people, however, went on sinning.

3 It was Jotham who built the North Gate of the Temple and did extensive work on the city wall in the area of Jerusalem called Ophel. 4 In the mountains of Judah he built cities, and in the forests he built forts and towers. 5 He fought against the king of Ammon and his army and defeated them. Then he forced the Ammonites to pay him the following tribute each year for three years: four tons of silver, fifty thousand bushels of wheat, and fifty thousand bushels of barley. 6 Jotham grew powerful because he faithfully obeyed the LORD his God. 7 The other events of Jotham's reign, his wars, and his policies, are all recorded in *The History of the Kings of Israel and Judah.* 8 Jotham was twenty-five years old when he became king, and he ruled in Jerusalem for sixteen years. 9 He died and was buried in David's City and his son Ahaz succeeded him as king.

King Ahaz of Judah
(2 Kings 16.1-4)

28 Ahaz became king at the age of twenty, and he ruled in Jerusalem for sixteen years. He did not follow the good example of his ancestor King David; instead, he did what was not pleasing to the LORD 2 and followed the example of the kings of Israel. He had metal images of Baal made, 3 burned incense in Hinnom Valley, and even sacrificed his own sons as burnt offerings to idols, imitating the disgusting practice of the people whom the LORD had driven out of the land as the Israelites advanced. 4 At the pagan places of worship, on the hills, and under every shady tree Ahaz offered sacrifices and burned incense.

War with Syria and Israel
(2 Kings 16.5)

5-6 Because King Ahaz sinned, the LORD his God let the king of Syria defeat him and take a large number of Judeans back to Damascus as prisoners. The LORD also let the king of Israel, Pekah son of Remaliah, defeat Ahaz and kill 120,000 of the bravest Judean soldiers

in one day. The LORD, the God of their ancestors, permitted this to happen, because the people of Judah had abandoned him. 7 An Israelite soldier named Zichri killed King Ahaz' son Maaseiah, the palace administrator Azrikam, and Elkanah, who was second in command to the king. 8 Even though the Judeans were their own relatives, the Israelite army captured 200,000 women and children as prisoners and took them back to Samaria, along with large amounts of loot.

The Prophet Oded

9 A man named Oded, a prophet of the LORD, lived in the city of Samaria. He met the returning Israelite army with its Judean prisoners as it was about to enter the city, and he said, "The LORD God of your ancestors was angry with Judah and let you defeat them, but now he has heard of the vicious way you slaughtered them. 10 And now you intend to make the men and women of Jerusalem and Judah your slaves. Don't you know that you also have committed sins against the LORD your God? 11 Listen to me! These prisoners are your brothers and sisters. Let them go, or the LORD will punish you in his anger."

12 Four of the leading men of the Northern Kingdom, Azariah son of Jehohanan, Berechiah son of Meshillemoth, Jehizkiah son of Shallum, and Amasa son of Hadlai also opposed the actions of the army. 13 They said, "Don't bring those prisoners here! We have already sinned against the LORD and made him angry enough to punish us. Now you want to do something that will increase our guilt." 14 So then the army handed the prisoners and the loot over to the people and their leaders, 15 and the four men were appointed to provide the prisoners with clothing from the captured loot. They gave them clothes and sandals to wear, gave them enough to eat and drink, and put olive oil on their wounds. Those who were too weak to walk were put on donkeys, and all the prisoners were taken back to Judean territory at Jericho, the city of palm trees. Then the Israelites returned home to Samaria.

---

l he did not sin by burning incense; *or* he did not take part in the worship.

Ahaz Asks Assyria for Help
(2 Kings 16.7-9)

16-17 The Edomites began to raid Judah again and captured many prisoners, so King Ahaz asked Tiglath Pileser, the emperor of Assyria, to send help. 18 At this same time the Philistines were raiding the towns in the western foothills and in southern Judah. They captured the cities of Beth Shemesh, Aijalon, and Gederoth, and the cities of Soco, Timnah, and Gimzo with their villages, and settled there permanently. 19 Because King Ahaz of Judah had violated the rights of his people and had defied the LORD, the LORD brought troubles on Judah. 20 The Assyrian emperor, instead of helping Ahaz, opposed him and caused him trouble. 21 So Ahaz took the gold from the Temple, the palace, and the homes of the leaders of the people, and gave it to the emperor, but even this did not help.

The Sins of Ahaz

22 When his troubles were at their worst, that man Ahaz sinned against the LORD more than ever. 23 He offered sacrifices to the gods of the Syrians, who had defeated him. He said, "The Syrian gods helped the kings of Syria, so if I sacrifice to them, they may help me too." This brought disaster on him and on his nation. 24 In addition, he took all the Temple equipment and broke it in pieces. He closed the Temple and set up altars in every part of Jerusalem. 25 In every city and town in Judah he built pagan places of worship, where incense was to be burned to foreign gods. In this way he brought on himself the anger of the LORD, the God of his ancestors. 26 All the other events of his reign, from beginning to end, are recorded in *The History of the Kings of Judah and Israel.* 27 King Ahaz died and was buried in Jerusalem, but not in the royal tombs. His son Hezekiah succeeded him as king.

King Hezekiah of Judah
(2 Kings 18.1-3)

29 Hezekiah became king of Judah at the age of twenty-five, and he ruled in Jerusalem for twenty-nine years. His mother was Abijah, the daughter of Zechariah. 2 Following the example of his ancestor King David, he did what was pleasing to the LORD.

The Purification of the Temple

3 In the first month of the year after Hezekiah became king, he reopened the gates of the Temple and had them repaired. 4 He assembled a group of priests and Levites in the east courtyard of the Temple 5 and spoke to them there. He said, "You Levites are to consecrate yourselves and purify the Temple of the LORD, the God of your ancestors. Remove from the Temple everything that defiles it. 6 Our ancestors were unfaithful to the LORD our God and did what was displeasing to him. They abandoned him and turned their backs on the place where he dwells. 7 They closed the doors of the Temple, let the lamps go out, and failed to burn incense or offer burnt offerings in the Temple of the God of Israel. 8 Because of this the LORD has been angry with Judah and Jerusalem, and what he has done to them has shocked and frightened everyone. You know this very well. 9 Our fathers were killed in battle, and our wives and children have been taken away as prisoners.

10 "I have now decided to make a covenant with the LORD, the God of Israel, so that he will no longer be angry with us. 11 My sons, do not lose any time. You are the ones that the LORD has chosen to burn incense to him and to lead the people in worshiping him."

12-14 The following Levites were there:
From the clan of Kohath, Mahath son of Amasai and Joel son of Azariah
From the clan of Merari, Kish son of Abdi and Azariah son of Jehallelel
From the clan of Gershon, Joah son of Zimmah and Eden son of Joah
From the clan of Elizaphan, Shimri and Jeuel
From the clan of Asaph, Zechariah and Mattaniah
From the clan of Heman, Jehuel and Shimei
From the clan of Jeduthun, Shemaiah and Uzziel

15 These men assembled their fellow Levites, and they all made themselves ritually clean. Then, as the king had commanded them to do, they began to

make the Temple ritually clean, according to the Law of the Lord. *m* 16 The priests went inside the Temple to purify it, and they carried out into the Temple courtyard everything that was ritually unclean. From there the Levites took it all outside the city to Kidron Valley.

17 The work was begun on the first day of the first month, and by the eighth day they had finished it all, including the entrance room to the Temple. Then they worked for the next eight days, until the sixteenth of the month, preparing the Temple for worship.

The Temple Is Rededicated

18 The Levites made the following report to King Hezekiah: "We have completed the ritual purification of the whole Temple, including the altar for burnt offerings, the table for the sacred bread, and all their equipment. 19 We have also brought back all the equipment which King Ahaz took away during those years he was unfaithful to God, and we have rededicated it. It is all in front of the Lord's altar."

20 Without delay King Hezekiah assembled the leading men of the city, and together they went to the Temple. 21 As an offering to take away the sins of the royal family and of the people of Judah and to purify the Temple, they took seven bulls, seven sheep, seven lambs, and seven goats. The king told the priests, who were descendants of Aaron, to offer the animals as sacrifices on the altar. 22 The priests killed the bulls first, then the sheep, and then the lambs, and sprinkled the blood of each sacrifice on the altar. 23 Finally they took the goats to the king and to the other worshipers, who laid their hands on them. 24 Then the priests killed the goats and poured their blood on the altar as a sacrifice to take away the sin of all the people, for the king had commanded that burnt offerings and sin offerings be made for all Israel.

25 The king followed the instructions that the Lord had given to King David through Gad, the king's prophet, and through the prophet Nathan; he stationed Levites in the Temple, with harps and cymbals, 26 instruments like those that King David had used. The priests also stood there with trumpets. 27 Hezekiah gave the order for the burnt offering to be presented; and as the offering began, the people sang praise to the Lord, and the musicians began to play the trumpets and all the other instruments. 28 Everyone who was there joined in worship, and the singing and the rest of the music continued until all the sacrifices had been burned. 29 Then King Hezekiah and all the people knelt down and worshiped God. 30 The king and the leaders of the nation told the Levites to sing to the Lord the songs of praise that were written by David and by Asaph the prophet. So everyone sang with great joy as they knelt and worshiped God.

31 Hezekiah said to the people, "Now that you are ritually clean, bring sacrifices as offerings of thanksgiving to the Lord." They obeyed, and some of them also voluntarily brought animals to be sacrificed as burnt offerings. 32 They brought 70 bulls, 100 sheep, and 200 lambs as burnt offerings for the Lord; 33 they also brought 600 bulls and 3,000 sheep as sacrifices for the people to eat. 34 Since there were not enough priests to kill all these animals, the Levites helped them until the work was finished. By then more priests had made themselves ritually clean. (The Levites were more faithful in keeping ritually clean than the priests were.) 35 In addition to offering the sacrifices that were burned whole, the priests were responsible for burning the fat that was offered from the sacrifices which the people ate, and for pouring out the wine that was presented with the burnt offerings.

And so worship in the Temple was begun again. 36 King Hezekiah and the people were happy, because God had helped them to do all this so quickly.

Preparations for Passover

30 1-3 The people had not been able to celebrate the Passover Festival at the proper time in the first month, because not enough priests were ritually clean and not many people had assembled in Jerusalem. So King Hezekiah, his officials, and the people of Jerusalem agreed to celebrate it in the second

---

m Then, as the king ... Lord; *or* Then they began to make the Temple ritually clean, as the king, who was acting at the Lord's command, had ordered them to do.

month, and the king sent word to all the people of Israel and Judah. He took special care to send letters to the tribes of Ephraim and Manasseh, inviting them to come to the Temple in Jerusalem to celebrate the Passover in honor of the Lord, the God of Israel. 4 The king and the people were pleased with their plan, 5 so they invited all the Israelites, from Dan in the north to Beersheba in the south, to come together in Jerusalem and celebrate the Passover according to the Law, in larger numbers than ever before. 6 Messengers went out at the command of the king and his officials through all Judah and Israel with the following invitation:

"People of Israel, you have survived the Assyrian conquest of the land. Now return to the Lord, the God of Abraham, Isaac, and Jacob, and he will return to you. 7 Do not be like your ancestors and your Israelite relatives who were unfaithful to the Lord their God. As you can see, he punished them severely. 8 Do not be stubborn as they were, but obey the Lord. Come to the Temple in Jerusalem, which the Lord your God has made holy forever, and worship him so that he will no longer be angry with you. 9 If you return to the Lord, then those who have taken your relatives away as prisoners will take pity on them and let them come back home. The Lord your God is kind and merciful, and if you return to him, he will accept you."

10 The messengers went to every city in the territory of the tribes of Ephraim and Manasseh, and as far north as the tribe of Zebulun, but people laughed at them and made fun of them. 11 Still, there were some from the tribes of Asher, Manasseh, and Zebulun who were willing to come to Jerusalem. 12 God was also at work in Judah and united the people in their determination to obey his will by following the commands of the king and his officials.

Passover Is Celebrated

13 A great number of people gathered in Jerusalem in the second month to celebrate the Festival of Unleavened Bread. 14 They took all the altars that had been used in Jerusalem for offering sacrifices and burning incense and threw them into Kidron Valley. 15 And on the fourteenth day of the month they killed the lambs for the Passover sacrifice. The priests and Levites who were not ritually clean became so ashamed that they dedicated themselves to the Lord, and now they could sacrifice burnt offerings in the Temple. 16 They took their places in the Temple according to the instructions in the Law of Moses, the man of God. The Levites gave the blood of the sacrifices to the priests, who sprinkled it on the altar. 17 Because many of the people were not ritually clean, they could not kill the Passover lambs, so the Levites did it for them and dedicated the lambs to the Lord. 18 In addition, many of those who had come from the tribes of Ephraim, Manasseh, Issachar, and Zebulun had not performed the ritual of purification, and so they were observing Passover improperly. King Hezekiah offered this prayer for them: 19 "O Lord, the God of our ancestors, in your goodness forgive those who are worshiping you with all their heart, even though they are not ritually clean." 20 The Lord answered Hezekiah's prayer; he forgave the people and did not harm them. 21 For seven days the people who had gathered in Jerusalem celebrated the Festival of Unleavened Bread with great joy, and day after day the Levites and the priests praised the Lord with all their strength. n 22 Hezekiah praised the Levites for their skill in conducting the worship of the Lord.

A Second Celebration

After the seven days during which they offered sacrifices in praise of the Lord, the God of their ancestors, 23 they all decided to celebrate for another seven days. So they celebrated with joy. 24 King Hezekiah contributed 1,000 bulls and 7,000 sheep for the people to kill and eat, and the officials gave them another 1,000 bulls and 10,000 sheep. A large number of priests went through the ritual of purification. 25 So everyone was happy—the people of Judah, the priests, the Levites, the people who had come from the north, and the foreigners who had settled permanently in Israel and Judah. 26 The city of Jerusalem was filled with joy, because nothing like this had

n *Probable text* with all their strength; *Hebrew* with mighty instruments.

happened since the days of King Solomon, the son of David. 27 The priests and the Levites asked the LORD's blessing on the people. In his home in heaven God heard their prayers and accepted them.

Hezekiah Reforms Religious Life

31 After the festival ended, all the people of Israel went to every city in Judah and broke the stone pillars, cut down the symbols of the goddess Asherah, and destroyed the altars and the pagan places of worship. They did the same thing throughout the rest of Judah, and the territories of Benjamin, Ephraim, and Manasseh; then they all returned home.

2 King Hezekiah reestablished the organization of the priests and Levites, under which they each had specific duties. These included offering the burnt offerings and the fellowship offerings, taking part in the Temple worship, and giving praise and thanks in the various parts of the Temple. 3 From his own flocks and herds he provided animals for the burnt offerings each morning and evening, and for those offered on the Sabbath, at the New Moon Festival, and at the other festivals which are required by the Law of the LORD.

4 In addition, the king told the people of Jerusalem to bring the offerings to which the priests and the Levites were entitled, so that they could give all their time to the requirements of the Law of the LORD. 5 As soon as the order was given, the people of Israel brought gifts of their finest grain, wine, olive oil, honey, and other farm produce, and they also brought the tithes° of everything they had. 6 All the people who lived in the cities of Judah brought tithes of their cattle and sheep, and they also brought large quantities of gifts which they dedicated to the LORD their God. 7 The gifts started arriving in the third month and continued to pile up for the next four months. 8 When King Hezekiah and his officials saw how much had been given, they praised the LORD and praised his people Israel. 9 The king spoke to the priests and the Levites about these gifts,

10 and Azariah the High Priest, a descendant of Zadok, said to him, "Since the people started bringing their gifts to the Temple, there has been enough to eat and a large surplus besides. We have all this because the LORD has blessed his people."

11 On the king's orders they prepared storerooms in the Temple area 12 and put all the gifts and tithes in them for safekeeping. They placed a Levite named Conaniah in charge and made his brother Shimei his assistant. 13 Ten Levites were assigned to work under them: Jehiel, Azaziah, Nahath, Asahel, Jerimoth, Jozabad, Eliel, Ismachiah, Mahath, and Benaiah. All this was done under the authority of King Hezekiah and Azariah the High Priest. 14 Kore son of Imnah, a Levite who was chief guard at the East Gate of the Temple, was in charge of receiving the gifts offered to the LORD and of distributing them. 15 In the other cities where priests lived, he was faithfully assisted in this by other Levites: Eden, Miniamin, Jeshua, Shemaiah, Amariah, and Shecaniah. They distributed the food equally to their fellow Levites according to what their duties were, 16 and not by clans. They gave a share to all males thirtyp years of age or older who had daily responsibilities in the Temple in accordance with their positions. 17 The priests were assigned their duties by clans, and the Levites twenty years of age or older were assigned theirs by work groups. 18 They were all registered together with their wives, children, and other dependents, because they were required to be ready to perform their sacred duties at any time. 19 Among the priests who lived in the cities assigned to Aaron's descendants or in the pasture lands belonging to these cities, there were responsible men who distributed the food to all the males in the priestly families and to everyone who was on the rolls of the Levite clans.

20 Throughout all Judah, King Hezekiah did what was right and what was pleasing to the LORD his God. 21 He was successful, because everything he did for the Temple or in observance of the Law, he did in a spirit of complete loyalty and devotion to his God.

° GIFTS . . . TITHES: *The gifts were for the priests, and the tithes for the Levites (see Nu 18).*
p *Probable text* thirty; *Hebrew* three.

The Assyrians Threaten Jerusalem
(2 Kings 18.13-37; 19.14-19, 35-37; Isaiah 36.1-22; 37.8-38)

32 After these events, in which King Hezekiah served the LORD faithfully, Sennacherib, the emperor of Assyria, invaded Judah. He besieged the fortified cities and gave orders for his army to break their way through the walls. 2 When Hezekiah saw that Sennacherib intended to attack Jerusalem also, 3-4 he and his officials decided to cut off the supply of water outside the city in order to keep the Assyrians from having any water when they got near Jerusalem. The officials led a large number of people out and stopped up all the springs, so that no more water flowed out of them. 5 The king strengthened the city's defenses by repairing the wall, building towers on it,*a* and building an outer wall. In addition, he repaired the defenses built on the land that was filled in on the east side of the old part of Jerusalem. He also had a large number of spears and shields made. 6 He placed all the men in the city under the command of army officers and had them assemble in the open square at the city gate. He said to them, 7 "Be determined and confident, and don't be afraid of the Assyrian emperor or of the army he is leading. We have more power on our side than he has on his. 8 He has human power, but we have the LORD our God to help us and to fight our battles." The people were encouraged by these words of their king.

9 Some time later, while Sennacherib and his army were still at Lachish, he sent the following message to Hezekiah and the people of Judah who were with him in Jerusalem: 10 "I, Sennacherib, Emperor of Assyria, ask what gives you people the confidence to remain in Jerusalem under siege. 11 Hezekiah tells you that the LORD your God will save you from our power, but Hezekiah is deceiving you and will let you die of hunger and thirst. 12 He is the one who destroyed the LORD's shrines and altars and then told the people of Judah and Jerusalem to worship and burn incense at one altar only. 13 Don't you know what my ancestors and I have done to the people of other nations? Did the gods of any other

nation save their people from the emperor of Assyria? 14 When did any of the gods of all those countries ever save their country from us? Then what makes you think that your god can save you? 15 Now don't let Hezekiah deceive you or mislead you like that. Don't believe him! No god of any nation has ever been able to save his people from any Assyrian emperor. So certainly this god of yours can't save you!"

16 The Assyrian officials said even worse things about the LORD God and Hezekiah, the LORD's servant. 17 The letter that the emperor wrote defied the LORD, the God of Israel. It said, "The gods of the nations have not saved their people from my power, and neither will Hezekiah's god save his people from me." 18 The officials shouted this in Hebrew in order to frighten and discourage the people of Jerusalem who were on the city wall, so that it would be easier to capture the city. 19 They talked about the God of Jerusalem in the same way that they talked about the gods of the other peoples, idols made by human hands.

20 Then King Hezekiah and the prophet Isaiah son of Amoz prayed to God and cried out to him for help. 21 The LORD sent an angel that killed the soldiers and officers of the Assyrian army. So the emperor went back to Assyria disgraced. One day when he was in the temple of his god, some of his sons killed him with their swords.

22 In this way the LORD rescued King Hezekiah and the people of Jerusalem from the power of Sennacherib, the emperor of Assyria, and also from their other enemies. He let the people live in peace*r* with all the neighboring countries. 23 Many people came to Jerusalem, bringing offerings to the LORD and gifts to Hezekiah, so that from then on all the nations held Hezekiah in honor.

Hezekiah's Illness and Pride
(2 Kings 20.1-3, 12-19; Isaiah 38.1-3; 39.1-8)

24 About this time King Hezekiah became sick and almost died. He prayed, and the LORD gave him a sign that he would recover. 25 But Hezekiah was too proud to show gratitude for what the LORD had done for him, and Judah and

---

a Some ancient translations building towers on it; *Hebrew* building on the towers.
r Some ancient translations He let the people live in peace; *Hebrew* He led the people.

Jerusalem suffered for it. 26 Finally, however, Hezekiah and the people of Jerusalem humbled themselves, and so the LORD did not punish the people until after Hezekiah's death.

Hezekiah's Wealth and Splendor

27 King Hezekiah became very wealthy, and everyone held him in honor. He had storerooms built for his gold, silver, precious stones, spices, shields, and other valuable objects. 28 In addition, he had storehouses built for his grain, wine, and olive oil; barns for his cattle; and pens for his sheep. 29 Besides all this, God gave him sheep and cattle and so much other wealth that he built many cities. 30 It was King Hezekiah who blocked the outlet for Gihon Spring and channeled the water to flow through a tunnel to a point inside the walls of Jerusalem. Hezekiah succeeded in everything he did, 31 and even when the Babylonian ambassadors came to inquire about the unusual event that had happened in the land, God let Hezekiah go his own way only in order to test his character.

The End of Hezekiah's Reign
(2 Kings 20.20, 21)

32 Everything else that King Hezekiah did and his devotion to the LORD are recorded in *The Vision of the Prophet Isaiah Son of Amoz* and in *The History of the Kings of Judah and Israel.* 33 Hezekiah died and was buried in the upper section of the royal tombs. All the people of Judah and Jerusalem paid him great honor at his death. His son Manasseh succeeded him as king.

King Manasseh of Judah
(2 Kings 21.1-9)

33 Manasseh was twelve years old when he became king of Judah, and he ruled in Jerusalem for fifty-five years. 2 Following the disgusting practices of the nations whom the LORD had driven out of the land as his people advanced, Manasseh sinned against the LORD. 3 He rebuilt the pagan places of worship that his father Hezekiah had destroyed. He built altars for the worship of Baal, made images of the goddess Asherah, and worshiped the stars. 4 He built pagan altars in the Temple, the place that the LORD had said was where

he should be worshiped forever. 5 In the two courtyards of the Temple he built altars for the worship of the stars. 6 He sacrificed his sons in Hinnom Valley as burnt offerings. He practiced divination and magic and consulted fortunetellers and mediums. He sinned greatly against the LORD and stirred up his anger. 7 He placed an image in the Temple, the place about which God had said to David and his son Solomon: "Here in Jerusalem, in this Temple, is the place that I have chosen out of all the territory of the twelve tribes of Israel as the place where I am to be worshiped. 8 And if the people of Israel will obey all my commands and keep the whole Law that my servant Moses gave them, then I will not allow them to be driven out of the land that I gave to their ancestors." 9 Manasseh led the people of Judah to commit even greater sins than those committed by the nations whom the LORD had driven out of the land as his people advanced.

Manasseh Repents

10 Although the LORD warned Manasseh and his people, they refused to listen. 11 So the LORD let the commanders of the Assyrian army invade Judah. They captured Manasseh, stuck hooks in him, put him in chains, and took him to Babylon. 12 In his suffering he became humble, turned to the LORD his God, and begged him for help. 13 God accepted Manasseh's prayer and answered it by letting him go back to Jerusalem and rule again. This convinced Manasseh that the LORD was God.

14 After this, Manasseh increased the height of the outer wall on the east side of David's City, from a point in the valley near Gihon Spring north to the Fish Gate and the area of the city called Ophel. He also stationed an army officer in command of a unit of troops in each of the fortified cities of Judah. 15 He removed from the Temple the foreign gods and the image that he had placed there, and the pagan altars that were on the hill where the Temple stood and in other places in Jerusalem; he took all these things outside the city and threw them away. 16 He also repaired the altar where the LORD was worshiped, and he sacrificed fellowship offerings and thanksgiving offerings on it. He commanded all the people of Judah to worship the LORD,

the God of Israel. [17] Although the people continued to offer sacrifices at other places of worship, they offered them only to the LORD.

The End of Manasseh's Reign
(2 Kings 21.17, 18)

[18] Everything else that Manasseh did, the prayer he made to his God, and the messages of the prophets who spoke to him in the name of the LORD, the God of Israel, are all recorded in *The History of the Kings of Israel*. [19] The king's prayer and God's answer to it, and an account of the sins he committed before he repented—the evil he did, the pagan places of worship and the symbols of the goddess Asherah that he made and the idols that he worshiped—are all recorded in *The History of the Prophets*. [20] Manasseh died and was buried at the palace, and his son Amon succeeded him as king.

King Amon of Judah
(2 Kings 21.19-26)

[21] Amon was twenty-two years old when he became king of Judah, and he ruled in Jerusalem for two years. [22] Like his father Manasseh, he sinned against the LORD, and he worshiped the idols that his father had worshiped. [23] But unlike his father, he did not become humble and turn to the LORD; he was even more sinful than his father had been.

[24] Amon's officials plotted against him and assassinated him in the palace. [25] The people of Judah killed Amon's assassins and made his son Josiah king.

King Josiah of Judah
(2 Kings 22.1, 2)

34 Josiah was eight years old when he became king of Judah, and he ruled in Jerusalem for thirty-one years. [2] He did what was pleasing to the LORD; he followed the example of his ancestor King David, strictly obeying all the laws of God.

Josiah Attacks Pagan Worship

[3] In the eighth year that Josiah was king, while he was still very young, he began to worship the God of his ancestor King David. Four years later he began to destroy the pagan places of worship, the symbols of the goddess Asherah, and all the other idols. [4] Under

his direction the altars where Baal was worshiped were smashed, and the incense altars near them were torn down. They ground to dust the images of Asherah and all the other idols and then scattered the dust on the graves of the people who had sacrificed to them. [5] He burned the bones of the pagan priests on the altars where they had worshiped. By doing all this, he made Judah and Jerusalem ritually clean again. [6] He did the same thing in the cities and the devastated areas of Manasseh, Ephraim, and Simeon, and as far north as Naphtali. [7] Throughout the territory of the Northern Kingdom he smashed the altars and the symbols of Asherah, ground the idols to dust, and broke into bits all the incense altars. Then he returned to Jerusalem.

The Book of the Law Is Discovered
(2 Kings 22.3-20)

[8] In the eighteenth year of his reign, after he had purified the land and the Temple by ending pagan worship, King Josiah sent three men to repair the Temple of the LORD God: Shaphan son of Azaliah, Maaseiah, the governor of Jerusalem, and Joah son of Joahaz, a high official. [9] The money that the Levite guards had collected in the Temple was turned over to Hilkiah the High Priest. (It had been collected from the people of Ephraim and Manasseh and the rest of the Northern Kingdom, and from the people of Judah, Benjamin, and Jerusalem.) [10] This money was then handed over to the three men in charge of the Temple repairs, and they gave it to [11] the carpenters and the builders to buy the stones and the timber used to repair the buildings that the kings of Judah had allowed to decay. [12] The men who did the work were thoroughly honest. They were supervised by four Levites: Jahath and Obadiah of the clan of Merari, and Zechariah and Meshullam of the clan of Kohath. (The Levites were all skillful musicians.) [13] Other Levites were in charge of transporting materials and supervising the workers on various jobs, and others kept records or served as guards.

[14] While the money was being taken out of the storeroom, Hilkiah found the book of the Law of the LORD, the Law that God had given to Moses. [15] He said

to Shaphan, "I have found the book of the Law here in the Temple." He gave Shaphan the book, 16 and Shaphan took it to the king. He reported, "We have done everything that you commanded. 17 We have taken the money that was kept in the Temple and handed it over to the workers and their supervisors." 18 Then he added, "I have here a book that Hilkiah gave me." And he read it aloud to the king.

19 When the king heard the book being read, he tore his clothes in dismay 20 and gave the following order to Hilkiah, to Ahikam son of Shaphan, to Abdon[s] son of Micaiah, to Shaphan, the court secretary, and to Asaiah, the king's attendant: 21 "Go and consult the LORD for me and for the people who still remain in Israel and Judah. Find out about the teachings of this book. The LORD is angry with us because our ancestors have not obeyed the word of the LORD and have not done what this book says must be done."

22 At the king's command, Hilkiah and the others went to consult a woman named Huldah, a prophet who lived in the newer part of Jerusalem. (Her husband Shallum, the son of Tikvah and grandson of Harhas, was in charge of the Temple robes.) They described to her what had happened, 23 and she told them to go back to the king and give him 24 the following message from the LORD: "I am going to punish Jerusalem and all its people with the curses written in the book that was read to the king. 25 They have rejected me and have offered sacrifices to other gods, and so have stirred up my anger by all they have done. My anger is aroused against Jerusalem, and it will not die down. 26 As for the king himself, this is what I, the LORD God of Israel, say: You listened to what is written in the book, 27 and you repented and humbled yourself before me, tearing your clothes and weeping, when you heard how I threatened to punish Jerusalem and its people. I have heard your prayer, 28 and the punishment which I am going to bring on Jerusalem will not come until after your death. I will let you die in peace."

The men returned to King Josiah with this message.

Josiah Makes a Covenant to Obey the LORD
(2 Kings 23.1-20)

29 King Josiah summoned all the leaders of Judah and Jerusalem, 30 and together they went to the Temple, accompanied by the priests and the Levites and all the rest of the people, rich and poor alike. Before them all the king read aloud the whole book of the covenant, which had been found in the Temple. 31 He stood by the royal column[t] and made a covenant with the LORD to obey him, to keep his laws and commands with all his heart and soul, and to put into practice the demands attached to the covenant, as written in the book. 32 He made the people of Benjamin and everyone else present in Jerusalem promise to keep the covenant. And so the people of Jerusalem obeyed the requirements of the covenant they had made with the God of their ancestors. 33 King Josiah destroyed all the disgusting idols that were in the territory belonging to the people of Israel, and as long as he lived, he required the people to serve the LORD, the God of their ancestors.

Josiah Celebrates the Passover
(2 Kings 23.21-23)

35 King Josiah celebrated the Passover at Jerusalem in honor of the LORD; on the fourteenth day of the first month they killed the animals for the festival. 2 He assigned to the priests the duties they were to perform in the Temple and encouraged them to do them well. 3 He also gave these instructions to the Levites, the teachers of Israel, who were dedicated to the LORD: "Put the sacred Covenant Box in the Temple that King Solomon, the son of David, built. You are no longer to carry it from place to place, but you are to serve the LORD your God and his people Israel. 4 Take your places in the Temple by clans, according to the responsibilities assigned to you by King David and his son King Solomon, 5 and arrange yourselves so that some of you will be available to help each family of the people of Israel. 6 You are to kill the Passover lambs and goats. Now make yourselves ritually clean and

---

s ABDON: *Achbor in 2 K 22.12.*   t *Probable text (see 2 K 23.3)* by the royal column; *Hebrew in his place.*

prepare the sacrifices in order that your fellow Israelites may follow the instructions which the LORD gave through Moses."

7 For the use of the people at the Passover, King Josiah contributed from his own herds and flocks 30,000 sheep, lambs, and young goats, and 3,000 bulls. 8 His officials also made contributions for the people, the priests, and the Levites to use. And the officials in charge of the Temple — Hilkiah, the High Priest, Zechariah, and Jehiel — gave the priests 2,600 lambs and young goats and 300 bulls for sacrifices during the festival. 9 The leaders of the Levites — Conaniah, Shemaiah and his brother Nethanel, Hashabiah, Jeiel, and Jozabad — contributed 5,000 lambs and young goats and 500 bulls for the Levites to offer as sacrifices.

10 When everything was arranged for the Passover, the priests and the Levites took their posts, as commanded by the king. 11 After the lambs and goats had been killed, the Levites skinned them, and the priests sprinkled the blood on the altar. 12 Then they divided among the people, by family groups, the animals for burnt offerings, so that they could offer them according to the instructions in the Law of Moses. 13 The Levites roasted the Passover sacrifices over the fire, according to the regulations, and boiled the sacred offerings in pots, kettles, and pans, and quickly distributed the meat to the people. 14 After this was done, the Levites provided meat for themselves and for the priests descended from Aaron, for the priests were kept busy until night, burning the animals that were burned whole and the fat of the sacrifices. 15 The following musicians of the Levite clan of Asaph were in the places assigned to them by King David's instructions: Asaph, Heman, and Jeduthun, the king's prophet. The guards at the Temple gates did not need to leave their posts, because the other Levites prepared the Passover for them. 16 So, as King Josiah had commanded, everything was done that day for the worship of the LORD, the keeping of the Passover Festival, and the offering of burnt offerings on the altar. 17 For seven days all the people of Israel who were present celebrated the Passover and the Festival of Unleavened Bread. 18 Since the days of

the prophet Samuel, the Passover had never been celebrated like this. None of the former kings had ever celebrated a Passover like this one celebrated by King Josiah, the priests, the Levites, and the people of Judah, Israel, and Jerusalem 19 in the eighteenth year of Josiah's reign.

The End of Josiah's Reign
(2 Kings 23.28-30)

20 After King Josiah had done all this for the Temple, King Neco of Egypt led an army to fight at Carchemish on the Euphrates River. Josiah tried to stop him, 21 but Neco sent Josiah this message: "This war I am fighting does not concern you, King of Judah. I have not come to fight you, but to fight my enemies, and God has told me to hurry. God is on my side, so don't oppose me, or he will destroy you." 22 But Josiah was determined to fight. He refused to listen to what God was saying through King Neco, so he disguised himself and went into battle on the plain of Megiddo.

23 During the battle King Josiah was struck by Egyptian arrows. He ordered his servants, "Take me away; I'm badly hurt!" 24 They lifted him out of his chariot, placed him in a second chariot which he had there, and took him to Jerusalem. There he died and was buried in the royal tombs. All the people of Judah and Jerusalem mourned his death.

25 The prophet Jeremiah composed a lament for King Josiah. It has become a custom in Israel for the singers, both men and women, to use this song when they mourn for him. The song is found in the collection of laments.

26 Everything that Josiah did — his devotion to the LORD, his obedience to the Law, 27 and his history from beginning to end — is all recorded in *The History of the Kings of Israel and Judah*.

King Joahaz of Judah
(2 Kings 23.30-35)

36 The people of Judah chose Josiah's son Joahaz and anointed him king in Jerusalem. 2 Joahaz was twenty-three years old when he became king of Judah, and he ruled in Jerusalem for three months. 3 King Neco of Egypt took him prisoner and made Judah pay 7,500 pounds of silver and 75 pounds of gold as tribute. 4 Neco made Joahaz' brother Eliakim king of Judah and changed his name to Jehoiakim. Joahaz was taken to Egypt by Neco.

King Jehoiakim of Judah
(2 Kings 23.36 – 24.7)

5 Jehoiakim was twenty-five years old when he became king of Judah, and he ruled in Jerusalem for eleven years. He sinned against the LORD his God. 6 King Nebuchadnezzar of Babylonia invaded Judah, captured Jehoiakim, and took him to Babylonia in chains. 7 Nebuchadnezzar carried off some of the treasures of the Temple and put them in his palace in Babylon. 8 Everything that Jehoiakim did, including his disgusting practices and the evil he committed, is recorded in *The History of the Kings of Israel and Judah*. His son Jehoiachin succeeded him as king.

King Jehoiachin of Judah
(2 Kings 24.8-17)

9 Jehoiachin was eighteenu years old when he became king of Judah, and he ruled in Jerusalem for three months and ten days. He too sinned against the LORD. 10 When spring came, King Nebuchadnezzar took Jehoiachin to Babylonia as a prisoner and carried off the treasures of the Temple. Then Nebuchadnezzar made Jehoiachin's unclev Zedekiah king of Judah and Jerusalem.

King Zedekiah of Judah
(2 Kings 24.18-20; Jeremiah 52.1-3a)

11 Zedekiah was twenty-one years old when he became king of Judah, and he ruled in Jerusalem for eleven years. 12 He sinned against the LORD and did not listen humbly to the prophet Jeremiah, who spoke the word of the LORD.

The Fall of Jerusalem
(2 Kings 25.1-21; Jeremiah 52.3b-11)

13 Zedekiah rebelled against King Nebuchadnezzar, who had forced him to swear in God's name that he would be loyal. He stubbornly refused to repent and return to the LORD, the God of Israel. 14 In addition, the leaders of Judah, the priests, and the people followed the sin-ful example of the nations around them in worshiping idols, and so they defiled the Temple, which the LORD himself had made holy. 15 The LORD, the God of their ancestors, had continued to send prophets to warn his people, because he wanted to spare them and the Temple. 16 But they made fun of God's messengers, ignoring his words and laughing at his prophets, until at last the LORD's anger against his people was so great that there was no escape.

17 So the LORD brought the king of Babylonia to attack them. The king killed the young men of Judah even in the Temple. He had no mercy on anyone, young or old, man or woman, sick or healthy. God handed them all over to him. 18 The king of Babylonia looted the Temple, the Temple treasury, and the wealth of the king and his officials, and took everything back to Babylon. 19 He burned down the Temple and the city, with all its palaces and its wealth, and broke down the city wall. 20 He took all the survivors to Babylonia, where they served him and his descendants as slaves until the rise of the Persian Empire. 21 And so what the LORD had foretold through the prophet Jeremiah was fulfilled: "The land will lie desolate for seventy years, to make up for the Sabbath restw that has not been observed."

Cyrus Commands the Jews to Return
(Ezra 1.1-4)

22 In the first year that Cyrus of Persia was emperor,x the LORD made what he had said through the prophet Jeremiah come true. He prompted Cyrus to issue the following command and send it out in writing to be read aloud everywhere in his empire:

23 "This is the command of Cyrus, Emperor of Persia. The LORD, the God of Heaven, has made me ruler over the whole world and has given me the responsibility of building a temple for him in Jerusalem in Judah. Now, all of you who are God's people, go there, and may the LORD your God be with you."

---

u *Some ancient translations (and see 2 K 24.8)* eighteen; *Hebrew* eight.   v *Some ancient translations (and see 2 K 24.17)* uncle; *Hebrew* brother.   w SABBATH REST: *A reference to the requirement of the Law that every seventh year the land was not to be farmed (see Lv 25.1-7).*   x EMPEROR: *King Cyrus of Persia occupied the city of Babylon in 539 B.C. and began to reign as the emperor of Babylonia.*

The Book of
EZRA

Introduction

The Book of Ezra, *as a sequel to* Chronicles, *describes the return of some of the Jewish exiles from Babylon and the restoration of life and worship in Jerusalem. These events are presented in the following stages: 1) The first group of Jewish exiles returns from Babylonia at the order of Cyrus, the Persian emperor. 2) The Temple is rebuilt and dedicated, and the worship of God restored in Jerusalem. 3) Years later another group of Jews returns to Jerusalem under the leadership of Ezra, an expert in the Law of God, who helps the people reorganize their religious and social life in order to safeguard the spiritual heritage of Israel.*

Outline of Contents

Cyrus Commands the Jews to Return

1 In the first year that Cyrus of Persia was emperor,[a] the LORD made what he had said come true through the prophet Jeremiah come true. He prompted Cyrus to issue the following command and send it out in writing to be read aloud everywhere in his empire:

2 "This is the command of Cyrus, Emperor of Persia. The LORD, the God of Heaven, has made me ruler over the whole world and has given me the responsibility of building a temple for him in Jerusalem in Judah. 3 May God be with all of you who are his people. You are to go to Jerusalem and rebuild the Temple of the LORD, the God of Israel, the God who is worshiped in Jerusalem. 4 If any of his people in exile need help to return, their neighbors are to give them this help. They are to provide them with silver and gold, supplies and pack animals, as well as offerings to present in the Temple of God in Jerusalem."

5 Then the heads of the clans of the tribes of Judah and Benjamin, the priests and Levites, and everyone else whose heart God had moved got ready to go and rebuild the LORD's Temple in Jerusalem. 6 All their neighbors helped them by giving them many things: silver utensils, gold, supplies, pack animals, other valuables, and offerings for the Temple.

7 Emperor Cyrus gave them back the bowls and cups that King Nebuchadnezzar had taken from the Temple in Jerusalem and had put in the temple of his gods. 8 He handed them over to Mithredath, chief of the royal treasury, who made an inventory of them for Sheshbazzar, the governor of Judah, 9-10 as follows:

gold bowls for offerings	30
silver bowls for offerings	1,000
other bowls	29
small gold bowls	30
small silver bowls	410
other utensils	1,000

11 In all there were 5,400 gold and silver bowls and other articles which Sheshbazzar took with him when he and the other exiles went from Babylon to Jerusalem.

The List of Those Who Returned from Exile

(Nehemiah 7.4-73)

2 Many of the exiles left the province of Babylon and returned to Jerusalem and Judah, all to their own hometowns. Their families had been living in exile in Babylonia ever since King Nebuchadnezzar had taken them there as

---

a EMPEROR: *King Cyrus of Persia occupied the city of Babylon in 539 B.C. and began to reign as the emperor of Babylonia.*

prisoners. 2 Their leaders were Zerubbabel, Joshua, Nehemiah, Seraiah, Reelaiah, Mordecai, Bilshan, Mispar, Bigvai, Rehum, and Baanah.

This is the list of the clans of Israel, with the number of those from each clan who returned from exile:

3-20 Parosh - 2,172
Shephatiah - 372
Arah - 775
Pahath Moab (descendants of Jeshua and Joab) - 2,812
Elam - 1,254
Zattu - 945
Zaccai - 760
Bani - 642
Bebai - 623
Azgad - 1,222
Adonikam - 666
Bigvai - 2,056
Adin - 454
Ater (also called Hezekiah) - 98
Bezai - 323
Jorah - 112
Hashum - 223
Gibbar - 95

21-35 People whose ancestors had lived in the following towns also returned:

Bethlehem - 123
Netophah - 56
Anathoth - 128
Azmaveth - 42
Kiriath Jearim, Chephirah, and Beeroth - 743
Ramah and Geba - 621
Michmash - 122
Bethel and Ai - 223
Nebo - 52
Magbish - 156
The other Elam - 1,254
Harim - 320
Lod, Hadid, and Ono - 725
Jericho - 345
Senaah - 3,630

36-39 This is the list of the priestly clans that returned from exile:

Jedaiah (descendants of Jeshua) - 973
Immer - 1,052
Pashhur - 1,247
Harim - 1,017

40-42 Clans of Levites who returned from exile:

Jeshua and Kadmiel (descendants of Hodaviah) - 74

Temple musicians (descendants of Asaph) - 128
Temple guards (descendants of Shallum, Ater, Talmon, Akkub, Hatita, and Shobai) - 139

43-54 Clans of Temple workers who returned from exile:

Ziha, Hasupha, Tabbaoth,
Keros, Siaha, Padon,
Lebanah, Hagabah, Akkub,
Hagab, Shamlai, Hanan,
Giddel, Gahar, Reaiah,
Rezin, Nekoda, Gazzam,
Uzza, Paseah, Besai,
Asnah, Meunim, Nephisim,
Bakbuk, Hakupha, Harhur,
Bazluth, Mehida, Harsha,
Barkos, Sisera, Temah,
Neziah, and Hatipha

55-57 Clans of Solomon's servants who returned from exile:

Sotai, Hassophereth, Peruda,
Jaalah, Darkon, Giddel,
Shephatiah, Hattil, Pochereth
Hazzebaim, and Ami

58 The total number of descendants of the Temple workers and of Solomon's servants who returned from exile was 392.

59-60 There were 652 belonging to the clans of Delaiah, Tobiah, and Nekoda who returned from the towns of Tel Melah, Tel Harsha, Cherub, Addan, and Immer; but they could not prove that they were descendants of Israelites.

61-62 The following priestly clans could find no record to prove their ancestry: Habaiah, Hakkoz, and Barzillai. (The ancestor of the priestly clan of Barzillai had married a woman from the clan of Barzillai of Gilead and had taken the name of his father-in-law's clan.) Since they were unable to prove who their ancestors were, they were not accepted as priests. 63 The Jewish governor told them that they could not eat the food offered to God until there was a priest who could use the Urim and Thummim.b

64-67 Total number of exiles who returned - 42,360
Their male and female servants - 7,337
Male and female musicians - 200
Horses - 736
Mules - 245

b URIM AND THUMMIM: *Two objects used by the priest to determine God's will; it is not known precisely how they were used.*

to Jerusalem and forced the Jews to stop rebuilding the city.

Work on the Temple Begins Again

24 Work on the Temple had been stopped and had remained at a standstill until the second year of the reign of Emperor Darius of Persia. 5 1 At that time two prophets, Haggai and Zechariah son of Iddo, began to speak in the name of the God of Israel to the Jews who lived in Judah and Jerusalem. 2 When Zerubbabel son of Shealtiel and Joshua son of Jehozadak heard their messages, they began to rebuild the Temple in Jerusalem, and the two prophets helped them.

3 Almost at once Governor Tattenai of West-of-Euphrates, Shethar Bozenai, and their fellow officials came to Jerusalem and demanded: "Who gave you orders to build this Temple and equip it?" 4 They*j* also asked for the names of all the men who were helping build the Temple. 5 But God was watching over the Jewish leaders, and the Persian officials decided to take no action until they could write to Emperor Darius and receive a reply. 6 This is the report that they sent to the emperor:

7 "To Emperor Darius, may you rule in peace.

8 "Your Majesty should know that we went to the province of Judah and found that the Temple of the great God is being rebuilt with large stone blocks and with wooden beams set in the wall. The work is being done with great care and is moving ahead steadily.

9 "We then asked the leaders of the people to tell us who had given them authority to rebuild the Temple and to equip it. 10 We also asked them their names so that we could inform you who the leaders of this work are.

11 "They answered, 'We are servants of the God of heaven and earth, and we are rebuilding the Temple which was originally built and equipped many years ago by a powerful king of Israel. 12 But because our ancestors made the God of Heaven angry, he let them be conquered by King Nebuchadnezzar of Babylonia, a king of the Chaldean dynasty. The Temple was destroyed, and the people were taken into exile in Babylonia. 13 Then in the first year of the reign of King Cyrus as emperor of Babylonia, Cyrus issued orders for the Temple to be rebuilt. 14 He restored the gold and silver Temple utensils which Nebuchadnezzar had taken from the Temple in Jerusalem and had placed in the temple in Babylon. Emperor Cyrus turned these utensils over to a man named Sheshbazzar, whom he appointed governor of Judah. 15 The emperor told him to take them and return them to the Temple in Jerusalem, and to rebuild the Temple where it had stood before. 16 So Sheshbazzar came and laid its foundation; construction has continued from then until the present, but it is still not finished.'

17 "Now, if it please Your Majesty, have a search made in the royal records in Babylon to find whether or not Emperor Cyrus gave orders for this Temple in Jerusalem to be rebuilt, and then inform us what your will is in this matter."

Emperor Cyrus' Order Is Rediscovered

6 So Emperor Darius issued orders for a search to be made in the royal records that were kept in Babylon. 2 But it was in the city of Ecbatana in the province of Media that a scroll was found, containing the following record:

3 "In the first year of his reign Emperor Cyrus commanded that the Temple in Jerusalem be rebuilt as a place where sacrifices are made and offerings are burned. The Temple is to be ninety feet high and ninety feet wide. 4 The walls are to be built with one layer of wood on top of each three layers of stone. All expenses are to be paid by the royal treasury. 5 Also the gold and silver utensils which King Nebuchadnezzar brought to Babylon from the Temple in Jerusalem are to be returned to their proper place in the Jerusalem Temple."

j Some ancient translations They; *Aramaic* We.

OLD TESTAMENT JOURNEYS

One of the most famous travelers of the Old Testament was Abraham. He accompanied his family as they moved from Ur in Babylonia to the city of Haran in upper Mesopotamia (Gn 11.31, 32). Later he moved his family from Haran to Canaan in response to God's call (Gn 12.1–5). Still later he moved his flocks and herds into Egypt to escape a severe famine throughout Canaan (Gn 12.10). He eventually returned to southern Canaan, where he spent the rest of his life as a wandering herdsman in the region around Hebron and the central hill country of Shechem. A Moslem mosque in modern Hebron supposedly marks the site of Abraham's tomb in southern Palestine.

Following is a list of some of the journeys made by other Old Testament personalities:

Personality(ies)	Description of Journey	Biblical Reference
Jacob	From Hebron to ancestral Haran to find a wife	Gn 28; 29
Joseph	From Canaan to Egypt, sold into slavery by his brothers	Gn 37
Jacob and his family	To Egypt to escape a famine in Canaan	Gn 42—46
Moses	From Egypt to Midian after killing an Egyptian; back to Egypt to lead his people out of slavery	Ex 2.14, 15; Ex 3; 4
Israelites	From Egypt to the Promised Land	Ex 12 and following
Ruth	From Moab to mother-in-law Naomi's ancestral home in Bethlehem	Ru 1
Saul	From Gibeah to Ramah to be anointed first king of Israel	1 S 1.1; 1 S 9.1—10.1
Samuel	From Ramah to Bethlehem to anoint David as king	1 S 16
David	From Philistia to Hebron to become king of Judah; from Hebron to Jerusalem to capture the city and become king over all Israel	2 S 2.1–4; 2 S 5.7–12
Solomon	From Jerusalem to Gibeon to offer sacrifices and ask for wisdom	1 K 3.4–9
Queen of Sheba	From Arabia to Jerusalem to pay a royal visit to Solomon	1 K 10
Elijah	From Jezreel to escape Jezebel's wrath	1 K 18.46; 19
Naaman	From Syria to Samaria to be healed by Elisha	2 K 5
Captives of Judah	From Jerusalem to captivity in Babylon; from captivity in Babylon to freedom in Jerusalem	2 Ch 36.20; Ezra 1
Ezra	From Babylonia to Jerusalem "teaching all its laws and regulations to the people of Israel"	Ezra 7.1–10
Nehemiah	From Babylonia to Jerusalem to rebuild the city wall	Ne 1; 2

Emperor Darius Orders the Work to Continue

6 Then Emperor Darius sent the following reply:

"To Tattenai, governor of West-of-Euphrates, Shethar Bozenai, and your fellow officials in West-of-Euphrates.

"Stay away from the Temple 7 and do not interfere with its construction. Let the governor of Judah and the Jewish leaders rebuild the Temple of God where it stood before. 8 I hereby command you to help them rebuild it. Their expenses are to be paid promptly out of the royal funds received from taxes in West-of-Euphrates, so that the work is not interrupted. 9 Day by day, without fail, you are to give the priests in Jerusalem whatever they tell you they need: young bulls, sheep, or lambs to be burned as offerings to the God of Heaven, or wheat, salt, wine, or olive oil. 10 This is to be done so that they can offer sacrifices that are acceptable to the God of Heaven and pray for his blessing on me and my sons. 11 I further command that if any disobey this order, a wooden beam is to be torn out of their houses, sharpened on one end, and then driven through their bodies. And their houses are to be made a rubbish heap. 12 May the God who chose Jerusalem as the place where he is to be worshiped overthrow any king or nation that defies this command and tries to destroy the Temple there. I, Darius, have commanded. My command is to be fully obeyed."

The Temple Is Dedicated

13 Then Governor Tattenai, Shethar Bozenai, and their fellow officials did exactly as the emperor had commanded. 14 The Jewish leaders made good progress with the building of the Temple, encouraged by the prophets Haggai and Zechariah. They completed the Temple as they had been commanded by the God of Israel and by Cyrus, Darius, and Artaxerxes, emperors of Persia. 15 They finished the Temple on the third day of the month Adar in the sixth year of the reign of Emperor Darius. 16 Then the people of Israel—the priests, the Levites, and all the others who had returned from exile—joyfully dedicated the Temple. 17 For the dedication they offered 100 bulls, 200 sheep, and 400 lambs as sacrifices, and 12 goats as offerings for sin, one for each tribe of Israel. 18 They also organized the priests and the Levites for the Temple services in Jerusalem, according to the instructions contained in the book of Moses.

The Passover

19 The people who had returned from exile celebrated Passover on the fourteenth day of the first month of the following year. 20 All the priests and the Levites had purified themselves and were ritually clean. The Levites killed the animals for the Passover sacrifices for all the people who had returned, for the priests, and for themselves. 21 The sacrifices were eaten by all the Israelites who had returned from exile and by all those who had given up the pagan ways of the other people who were living in the land and who had come to worship the Lord God of Israel. 22 For seven days they joyfully celebrated the Festival of Unleavened Bread. They were full of joy because the Lord had made the emperor of Assyria[k] favorable to them, so that he supported them in their work of rebuilding the Temple of the God of Israel.

Ezra Arrives in Jerusalem

7 Many years later, when Artaxerxes was emperor of Persia, there was a man named Ezra. He traced his ancestors back to Aaron, the High Priest, as follows: Ezra was the son of Seraiah, son of Azariah, son of Hilkiah, 2 son of Shallum, son of Zadok, son of Ahitub, 3 son of Amariah, son of Azariah, son of Meraioth, 4 son of Zerahiah, son of Uzzi, son of Bukki, 5 son of Abishua, son of Phinehas, son of Eleazar, son of Aaron.

6-7 Ezra was a scholar with a thorough knowledge of the Law which the Lord, the God of Israel, had given to Moses. Because Ezra had the blessing of the Lord his God, the emperor gave him everything he asked for. In the seventh year of the reign of Artaxerxes, Ezra set

E Z R A

---

k EMPEROR OF ASSYRIA: *Apparently a reference to the Persian emperor who then also ruled the territory once occupied by Assyria, Israel's ancient enemy.*

out from Babylonia for Jerusalem with a group of Israelites which included priests, Levites, Temple musicians, Temple guards, and workers. 8-9They left Babylonia on the first day of the first month, and with God's help they arrived in Jerusalem on the first day of the fifth month. 10Ezra had devoted his life to studying the Law of the LORD, to practicing it, and to teaching all its laws and regulations to the people of Israel.

The Document Which Emperor Artaxerxes Gave to Ezra

11Emperor Artaxerxes gave the following document to Ezra, the priest and scholar, who had a thorough knowledge of the laws and commands which the LORD had given to Israel:

12"From Emperor Artaxerxes[l] to the priest Ezra, scholar in the Law of the God of Heaven.[m]

13"I command that throughout my empire all the Israelite people, priests, and Levites that so desire be permitted to go with you to Jerusalem. 14I, together with my seven counselors, send you to investigate the conditions in Jerusalem and Judah in order to see how well the Law of your God, which has been entrusted to you, is being obeyed. 15You are to take with you the gold and silver offerings which I and my counselors desire to give to the God of Israel, whose Temple is in Jerusalem. 16You are also to take all the silver and gold which you collect throughout the province of Babylon and the offerings which the Israelite people and their priests give for the Temple of their God in Jerusalem. 17"You are to spend this money carefully and buy bulls, rams, lambs, grain, and wine and offer them on the altar of the Temple in Jerusalem. 18You may use the silver and gold that is left over for whatever you and your people desire, in accordance with the will of your God. 19You are to present to God in Jerusalem all the utensils that have been given to you for use in the Temple services. 20And anything else which you need for the Temple,

you may get from the royal treasury.

21"I command all the treasury officials in West-of-Euphrates Province to provide promptly for Ezra, the priest and scholar in the Law of the God of Heaven, everything he asks you for, 22up to a limit of 7,500 pounds of silver, 500 bushels of wheat, 550 gallons of wine, 550 gallons of olive oil, and as much salt as needed. 23You must be careful to provide everything which the God of Heaven requires for his Temple, and so make sure that he is never angry with me or with those who reign after me. 24You are forbidden to collect any taxes from the priests, Levites, musicians, guards, workers, or anyone else connected with this Temple.

25"You, Ezra, using the wisdom which your God has given you, are to appoint administrators and judges to govern all the people in West-of-Euphrates who live by the Law of your God. You must teach that Law to anyone who does not know it. 26If any disobey the laws of your God or the laws of the empire, they are to be punished promptly: by death or by exile or by confiscation of their property or by imprisonment."

Ezra Praises God

27Ezra said, "Praise the LORD, the God of our ancestors! He has made the emperor willing to honor in this way the Temple of the LORD in Jerusalem. 28By God's grace I have won the favor of the emperor, of his counselors, and of all his powerful officials; the LORD my God has given me courage, and I have been able to persuade many of the heads of the clans of Israel to return with me."

The People Who Returned from Exile

8 This is the list of the heads of the clans who had been in exile in Babylonia and who returned with Ezra to Jerusalem when Artaxerxes was emperor:

2-14Gershom, of the clan of Phinehas
Daniel, of the clan of Ithamar

---

l Verses 12-26 are in Aramaic (see also 4.7).   m Aramaic has an additional word, the meaning of which is unclear.

Hattush son of Shecaniah, of the clan of David

Zechariah, of the clan of Parosh, with 150 men of his clan (there were records of their family lines)

Eliehoenai son of Zerahiah, of the clan of Pahath Moab, with 200 men

Shecaniah son of Jahaziel, of the clan of Zattu,[n] with 300 men

Ebed son of Jonathan, of the clan of Adin, with 50 men

Jeshaiah son of Athaliah, of the clan of Elam, with 70 men

Zebadiah son of Michael, of the clan of Shephatiah, with 80 men

Obadiah son of Jehiel, of the clan of Joab, with 218 men

Shelomith son of Josiphiah, of the clan of Bani,[o] with 160 men

Zechariah son of Bebai, of the clan of Bebai, with 28 men

Johanan son of Hakkatan, of the clan of Azgad, with 110 men

Eliphelet, Jeuel, and Shemaiah, of the clan of Adonikam, with 60 men (they returned at a later date)

Uthai and Zaccur, of the clan of Bigvai, with 70 men

Ezra Finds Levites for the Temple

15 I assembled the entire group by the canal that runs to the town of Ahava, and we camped there three days. I found that there were priests in the group, but no Levites. 16 I sent for nine of the leaders: Eliezer, Ariel, Shemaiah, Elnathan, Jarib, Elnathan, Nathan, Zechariah, and Meshullam, and for two teachers, Joiarib and Elnathan. 17 I sent them to Iddo, head of the community at Casiphia, to ask him and his associates, the Temple workers, to send us people to serve God in the Temple. 18 Through God's grace they sent us Sherebiah, an able man, a Levite from the clan of Mahli; and eighteen of his sons and brothers came with him. 19 They also sent Hashabiah and Jeshaiah of the clan of Merari, with twenty of their relatives. 20 In addition there were 220 Temple workers whose ancestors had been designated by King David and his officials to assist the Levites. They were all listed by name.

Ezra Leads the People in Fasting and Prayer

21 There by the Ahava Canal I gave orders for us all to fast and humble ourselves before our God and to ask him to lead us on our journey and protect us and our children and all our possessions. 22 I would have been ashamed to ask the emperor for a troop of cavalry to guard us from any enemies during our journey, because I had told him that our God blesses everyone who trusts him, but that he is displeased with and punishes anyone who turns away from him. 23 So we fasted and prayed for God to protect us, and he answered our prayers.

The Gifts for the Temple

24 From among the leading priests I chose Sherebiah, Hashabiah, and ten others. 25 Then I weighed out the silver, the gold, and the utensils which the emperor, his advisers and officials, and the people of Israel had given to be used in the Temple, and I gave it to the priests. 26-27 This is what I gave them:

silver - 25 tons
100 silver utensils - 150 pounds
gold - 7,500 pounds
20 gold bowls - 270 ounces
2 fine bronze bowls, equal in value to gold bowls

28 I said to them, "You are sacred to the LORD, the God of your ancestors, and so are all the silver and gold utensils brought to him as freewill offerings. 29 Guard them carefully until you reach the Temple. There in the priests' rooms weigh them and turn them over to the leaders of the priests and of the Levites, and to the leaders of the people of Israel in Jerusalem." 30 So the priests and the Levites took charge of the silver, the gold, and the utensils, to take them to the Temple in Jerusalem.

The Return to Jerusalem

31 It was on the twelfth day of the first month that we left the Ahava Canal to go to Jerusalem. Our God was with us and protected us from enemy attacks and from ambush as we traveled. 32 When we reached Jerusalem, we rested three days. 33 Then on the fourth day we went to the Temple, weighed the

---

n One ancient translation (see also 2.8) Zattu; Hebrew does not have this name.
o One ancient translation (see also 2.10) Bani; Hebrew does not have this name.

silver, the gold, and the utensils, and turned them over to Meremoth the priest, son of Uriah. With him were Eleazar son of Phinehas and two Levites, Jozabad son of Jeshua and Noadiah son of Binnui. 34 Everything was counted and weighed, and a complete record was made at the same time.

35 All those who had returned from exile then brought offerings to be burned as sacrifices to the God of Israel. They offered 12 bulls for all Israel, 96 rams, and 77 lambs; they also offered 12 goats to purify themselves from sin. All these animals were burned as sacrifices to the LORD. 36 They also took the document the emperor had given them and gave it to the governors and officials of West-of-Euphrates Province, who then gave their support to the people and the Temple worship.

Ezra Learns of Intermarriages with Non-Jews

9 After all this had been done, some of the leaders of the people of Israel came and told me that the people, the priests, and the Levites had not kept themselves separate from the people in the neighboring countries of Ammon, Moab, and Egypt or from the Canaanites, Hittites, Perizzites, Jebusites, and Amorites. They were doing the same disgusting things which these people did. 2 Jewish men were marrying foreign women, and so God's holy people had become contaminated. The leaders and officials were the chief offenders. 3 When I heard this, I tore my clothes in despair, tore my hair and my beard, and sat down crushed with grief. 4 I sat there grieving until the time for the evening sacrifice to be offered, and people began to gather around me—all those who were frightened because of what the God of Israel had said about the sins of those who had returned from exile.

5 When the time came for the evening sacrifice, I got up from where I had been grieving, and still wearing my torn clothes, I knelt in prayer and stretched out my hands to the LORD my God. 6 I said, "O God, I am too ashamed to raise my head in your presence. Our sins pile up higher than our heads; they reach as high as the heavens. 7 From the days of our ancestors until now, we,

your people, have sinned greatly. Because of our sins we, our kings, and our priests have fallen into the hands of foreign kings, and we have been slaughtered, robbed, and carried away as prisoners. We have been totally disgraced, as we still are today. 8 Now for a short time, O LORD our God, you have been gracious to us and have let some of us escape from slavery and live in safety in this holy place. You have let us escape from slavery and have given us new life. 9 We were slaves, but you did not leave us in slavery. You made the emperors of Persia favor us and permit us to go on living and to rebuild your Temple, which was in ruins, and to find safety here in Judah and Jerusalem.

10 "But now, O God, what can we say after all that has happened? We have again disobeyed the commands 11 that you gave us through your servants, the prophets. They told us that the land we were going to occupy was an impure land because the people who lived in it filled it from one end to the other with disgusting, filthy actions. 12 They told us that we were never to intermarry with those people and never to help them prosper or succeed if we wanted to enjoy the land and pass it on to our descendants forever. 13 Even after everything that has happened to us in punishment for our sins and wrongs, we know that you, our God, have punished us less than we deserve and have allowed us to survive. 14 Then how can we ignore your commandments again and intermarry with these wicked people? If we do, you will be so angry that you will destroy us completely and let no one survive. 15 LORD God of Israel, you are just, but you have let us survive. We confess our guilt to you; we have no right to come into your presence."

The Plan for Ending Mixed Marriages

10 While Ezra was bowing in prayer in front of the Temple, weeping and confessing these sins, a large group of Israelites—men, women, and children—gathered around him, weeping bitterly. 2 Then Shecaniah son of Jehiel, of the clan of Elam, said to Ezra, "We have broken faith with God by marrying foreign women, but even so

there is still hope for Israel. ³Now we must make a solemn promise to our God that we will send these women and their children away. We will do what you and the others who honor God's commands advise us to do. We will do what God's Law demands. ⁴It is your responsibility to act. We are behind you, so go ahead and get it done."

⁵So Ezra began by making the leaders of the priests, of the Levites, and of the rest of the people take an oath that they would do what Shecaniah had proposed. ⁶Then he went from in front of the Temple into the living quarters of Jehohanan son of Eliashib, and spent the night *p* there grieving over the unfaithfulness of the exiles. He did not eat or drink anything.

⁷A message was sent throughout Jerusalem and Judah that all those who had returned from exile were to meet in Jerusalem ⁸by order of the leaders of the people. If any failed to come within three days, all their property would be confiscated, and they would lose their right to be members of the community. ⁹Within the three days, on the twentieth day of the ninth month, all the men living in the territory of Judah and Benjamin came to Jerusalem and assembled in the Temple square. It was raining hard, and because of the weather and the importance of the meeting everyone was trembling.

¹⁰Ezra the priest stood up and spoke to them. He said, "You have been faithless and have brought guilt on Israel by marrying foreign women. ¹¹Now then, confess your sins to the LORD, the God of your ancestors, and do what pleases him. Separate yourselves from the foreigners living in our land and get rid of your foreign wives."

¹²The people shouted in answer, "We will do whatever you say." ¹³But they added, "The crowd is too big, and it's raining hard. We can't stand here in the open like this. This isn't something that can be done in one or two days, because so many of us are involved in this sin. ¹⁴Let our officials stay in Jerusalem and take charge of the matter. Then let anyone who has a foreign wife come at a set time, together with the leaders and the judges of his city. In this way God's anger over this situation will be turned away." ¹⁵No one was opposed to the plan except Jonathan son of Asahel and Jahzeiah son of Tikvah, who had the support of Meshullam and of Shabbethai, a Levite.

¹⁶The returned exiles accepted the plan, so Ezra the priest appointed *q* men from among the heads of the clans and recorded their names. On the first day of the tenth month they began their investigation, ¹⁷and within the next three months they investigated all the cases of men with foreign wives.

The Men Who Had Foreign Wives

¹⁸This is the list of the men who had foreign wives:

Priests, listed by clans:

Clan of Joshua and his brothers, sons of Jehozadak: Maaseiah, Eliezer, Jarib, and Gedaliah. ¹⁹They promised to divorce their wives, and they offered a ram as a sacrifice for their sins.

²⁰Clan of Immer: Hanani and Zebadiah

²¹Clan of Harim: Maaseiah, Elijah, Shemaiah, Jehiel, and Uzziah

²²Clan of Pashhur: Elioenai, Maaseiah, Ishmael, Nethanel, Jozabad, and Elasah

²³*Levites:*

Jozabad, Shimei, Kelaiah (also called Kelita), Pethahiah, Judah, and Eliezer

²⁴*Musicians:*

Eliashib

Temple guards:

Shallum, Telem, and Uri

²⁵*Others:*

Clan of Parosh: Ramiah, Izziah, Malchijah, Mijamin, Eleazar, Malchijah, and Benaiah

²⁶Clan of Elam: Mattaniah, Zechariah, Jehiel, Abdi, Jeremoth, and Elijah

²⁷Clan of Zattu: Elioenai, Eliashib, Mattaniah, Jeremoth, Zabad, and Aziza

²⁸Clan of Bebai: Jehohanan, Hananiah, Zabbai, and Athlai

²⁹Clan of Bani: Meshullam, Malluch,

p One ancient translation spent the night; *Hebrew* went.   *q Some ancient translations* appointed; *Hebrew unclear.*

Adaiah, Jashub, Sheal, and Jeremoth
30 Clan of Pahath Moab: Adna, Chelal, Benaiah, Maaseiah, Mattaniah, Bezalel, Binnui, and Manasseh
31-32 Clan of Harim: Eliezer, Isshijah, Malchijah, Shemaiah, Shimeon, Benjamin, Malluch, and Shemariah
33 Clan of Hashum: Mattenai, Mattattah, Zabad, Eliphelet, Jeremai, Manasseh, and Shimei
34-37 Clan of Bani: Maadai, Amram, Uel, Benaiah, Bedeiah, Cheluhi, Vaniah,

Meremoth, Eliashib, Mattaniah, Mattenai, and Jaasu
38-42 Clan of Binnui: Shimei, Shelemiah, Nathan, Adaiah, Machnadebai, Shashai, Sharai, Azarel, Shelemiah, Shemariah, Shallum, Amariah, and Joseph
43 Clan of Nebo: Jeiel, Mattithiah, Zabad, Zebina, Jaddai, Joel, and Benaiah
44 All these men had foreign wives. They divorced them and sent them and their children away.r

r *Verse 44 in Hebrew is unclear.*

The Book of
NEHEMIAH

Introduction
The Book of Nehemiah *may be divided into four parts: 1) The return of Nehemiah to Jerusalem, where he has been sent by the Persian emperor to govern Judah. 2) The rebuilding of the walls of Jerusalem. 3) The solemn reading of the Law of God by Ezra and the people's confession of sin. 4) Further activities of Nehemiah as governor of Judah.*

A notable feature of the book is the record of Nehemiah's deep dependence on God and his frequent prayers to him.

Outline of Contents

1 This is the account of what Nehemiah son of Hacaliah accomplished.

Nehemiah's Concern for Jerusalem
In the month of Kislev in the twentieth year that Artaxerxes was emperor of Persia, I, Nehemiah, was in Susa, the capital city. 2 Hanani, one of my brothers, arrived from Judah with another group, and I asked them about Jerusalem and about the other Jews who had returned from exile in*a* Babylonia. 3 They told me that those who had survived and were back in the homeland*b* were in great difficulty and that the for-

eigners who lived nearby looked down on them. They also told me that the walls of Jerusalem were still broken down and that the gates had not been restored since the time they were burned. 4 When I heard all this, I sat down and wept.

For several days I mourned and did not eat. I prayed to God, 5 "LORD God of Heaven! You are great, and we stand in fear of you. You faithfully keep your covenant with those who love you and do what you command. 6 Look at me, LORD, and hear my prayer, as I pray day and night for your servants, the people of Israel. I confess that we, the people of

a had returned from exile in; or had not been exiled to.   b had survived and . . . homeland; or had remained in the homeland and had not gone into exile.

Israel, have sinned. My ancestors and I have sinned. [7] We have acted wickedly against you and have not done what you commanded. We have not kept the laws which you gave us through Moses, your servant. [8] Remember now what you told Moses: 'If you people of Israel are unfaithful to me, I will scatter you among the other nations. [9] But then if you turn back to me and do what I have commanded you, I will bring you back to the place where I have chosen to be worshiped, even though you are scattered to the ends of the earth.'

[10] "Lord, these are your servants, your own people. You rescued them by your great power and strength. [11] Listen now to my prayer and to the prayers of all your other servants who want to honor you. Give me success today and make the emperor merciful to me."

In those days I was the emperor's wine steward.

Nehemiah Goes to Jerusalem

2 One day four months later, when Emperor Artaxerxes was dining, I took the wine to him. He had never seen me look sad before, [2] so he asked, "Why are you looking so sad? You aren't sick, so it must be that you're unhappy."

I was startled [3] and answered, "May Your Majesty live forever! How can I keep from looking sad when the city where my ancestors are buried is in ruins and its gates have been destroyed by fire?"

[4] The emperor asked, "What is it that you want?"

I prayed to the God of Heaven, [5] and then I said to the emperor, "If Your Majesty is pleased with me and is willing to grant my request, let me go to the land of Judah, to the city where my ancestors are buried, so that I can rebuild the city."

[6] The emperor, with the empress sitting at his side, approved my request. He asked me how long I would be gone and when I would return, and I told him.

[7] Then I asked him to grant me the favor of giving me letters to the governors of West-of-Euphrates Province, [c] instructing them to let me travel to Judah. [8] I asked also for a letter to Asaph, keeper of the royal forests, instructing

him to supply me with timber for the gates of the fort that guards the Temple, for the city walls, and for the house I was to live in. The emperor gave me all I asked for, because God was with me.

[9] The emperor sent some army officers and a troop of cavalry with me, and I made the journey to West-of-Euphrates. There I gave the emperor's letters to the governors. [10] But Sanballat, from the town of Beth Horon, and Tobiah, an official in the province of Ammon, heard that someone had come to work for the good of the people of Israel, and they were highly indignant.

[11] I went on to Jerusalem, and for three days [12] I did not tell anyone what God had inspired me to do for Jerusalem. Then in the middle of the night I got up and went out, taking a few of my companions with me. The only animal we took was the donkey that I rode on. [13] It was still night as I left the city through the Valley Gate on the west and went south past Dragon's Fountain to the Rubbish Gate. As I went, I inspected the broken walls of the city and the gates that had been destroyed by fire. [14] Then on the east side of the city I went north to the Fountain Gate and the King's Pool. The donkey I was riding could not find any path through the rubble, [15] so I went down into Kidron Valley and rode along, looking at the wall. Then I returned the way I had come and went back into the city through the Valley Gate.

[16] None of the local officials knew where I had gone or what I had been doing. So far I had not said anything to any of the other Jews—the priests, the leaders, the officials, or anyone else who would be taking part in the work. [17] But now I said to them, "See what trouble we are in because Jerusalem is in ruins and its gates are destroyed! Let's rebuild the city walls and put an end to our disgrace." [18] And I told them how God had been with me and helped me, and what the emperor had said to me.

They responded, "Let's start rebuilding!" And they got ready to start the work.

[19] When Sanballat, Tobiah, and an Arab named Geshem heard what we

---

[c] WEST-OF-EUPHRATES PROVINCE: *Under Persian rule the land of Israel was part of this large Persian province west of the Euphrates River.*

were planning to do, they laughed at us and said, "What do you think you're doing? Are you going to rebel against the emperor?"

20 I answered, "The God of Heaven will give us success. We are his servants, and we are going to start building. But you have no right to any property in Jerusalem, and you have no share in its traditions."

Rebuilding the Wall of Jerusalem

3 This is how the city wall was rebuilt.d The High Priest Eliashib and his fellow priests rebuilt the Sheep Gate, dedicated it, and put the gates in place. They dedicated the wall as far as the Tower of the Hundred and the Tower of Hananel.

2 The men of Jericho built the next section.

Zaccur son of Imri built the next section.

3 The clan of Hassenaah built the Fish Gate. They put the beams and the gates in place, and put in the bolts and bars for locking the gate.

4 Meremoth, the son of Uriah and grandson of Hakkoz, built the next section.

Meshullam, the son of Berechiah and grandson of Meshezabel, built the next section.

Zadok son of Baana built the next section.

5 The men of Tekoa built the next section, but the leading men of the town refused to do the manual labor assigned them by the supervisors.

6 Joiada son of Paseah and Meshullam son of Besodeiah rebuilt Jeshanah Gate.e They put the beams and the gates in place, and put in the bolts and bars for locking the gate.

7 Melatiah from Gibeon, Jadon from Meronoth, and the men of Gibeon and Mizpah built the next section, as far as the residence of the governor of West-of-Euphrates.

8 Uzziel son of Harhaiah, a goldsmith, built the next section.

Hananiah, a maker of perfumes, built the next section, as far as Broad Wall.

9 Rephaiah son of Hur, ruler of half of the Jerusalem District, built the next section.

10 Jedaiah son of Harumaph built the next section, which was near his own house.

Hattush son of Hashabneiah built the next section.

11 Malchijah son of Harim and Hasshub son of Pahath Moab built both the next section and the Tower of the Ovens.

12 Shallum son of Hallohesh, ruler of the other half of the Jerusalem District, built the next section. (His daughters helped with the work.)

13 Hanun and the inhabitants of the city of Zanoah rebuilt the Valley Gate. They put the gates in place, put in the bolts and the bars for locking the gate, and repaired the wall for fifteen hundred feet, as far as the Rubbish Gate.

14 Malchijah son of Rechab, ruler of the Beth Haccherem District, rebuilt the Rubbish Gate. He put the gates in place, and put in the bolts and the bars for locking the gate.

15 Shallum son of Colhozeh, ruler of the Mizpah District, rebuilt the Fountain Gate. He covered the gateway, put the gates in place, and put in the bolts and the bars. At the Pool of Shelah he built the wall next to the royal garden, as far as the stairs leading down from David's City.

16 Nehemiah son of Azbuk, ruler of half of the Bethzur District, built the next section, as far as David's tomb, the pool, and the barracks.

Levites Who Worked on the Wall

17 The following Levites rebuilt the next several sections of the wall:

Rehum son of Bani built the next section;

Hashabiah, ruler of half of the Keilah District, built the next section on behalf of his district;

18 Bavvai son of Henadad, ruler of the other half of the Keilah District, built the next section;

19 Ezer son of Jeshua, ruler of Mizpah, built the next section in front of the armory, as far as the place where the wall turns;

20 Baruch son of Zabbai built the next

---

d CITY WALL WAS REBUILT: According to the following report, the rebuilding of the wall started at the middle of the north side and proceeded counterclockwise around the city. Many of the places mentioned cannot be identified.   e Jeshanah Gate; or the Old Gate.

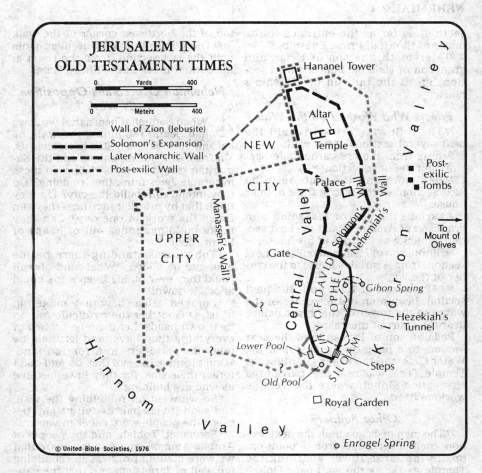

JERUSALEM IN OLD TESTAMENT TIMES

```
0        Yards        400
0        Meters       400
```

—————— Wall of Zion (Jebusite)
– – – – Solomon's Expansion
— — — Later Monarchic Wall
· · · · · · Post-exilic Wall

Hananel Tower

Altar

Temple

NEW CITY

Palace

Post-exilic Tombs

To Mount of Olives

UPPER CITY

Manasseh's Wall?

Central Valley

Solomon's Wall

Nehemiah's Wall

Gate

CITY OF DAVID

OPHEL

Gihon Spring

Hezekiah's Tunnel

Lower Pool

Old Pool

SILOAM

Steps

Kidron Valley

Royal Garden

Hinnom Valley

Enrogel Spring

© United Bible Societies, 1976

section, as far as the entrance to the house of the High Priest Eliashib;

21 Meremoth, the son of Uriah and grandson of Hakkoz, built the next section, up to the far end of Eliashib's house.

Priests Who Worked on the Wall

22 The following priests rebuilt the next several sections of the wall:

Priests from the area around Jerusalem built the next section;

23 Benjamin and Hasshub built the next section, which was in front of their houses;

Azariah, the son of Maaseiah and grandson of Ananiah, built the next section, which was in front of his house;

24 Binnui son of Henadad built the next section, from Azariah's house to the corner of the wall;

25-26 Palal son of Uzai built the next section, beginning at the corner of the wall and the tower of the upper palace near the court of the guard;

Pedaiah son of Parosh built the next section, to a point on the east near the Water Gate and the tower guarding the Temple. (This was near that part of the city called Ophel, where the Temple workers lived.)

Other Builders

27 The men of Tekoa built the next section, their second one, from a point opposite the large tower guarding the Temple as far as the wall near Ophel.

28 A group of priests built the next section, going north from the Horse Gate, each one building in front of his own house.

29 Zadok son of Immer built the next section, which was in front of his house.

Shemaiah son of Shecaniah, keeper of the East Gate, built the next section.

30 Hananiah son of Shelemiah and Hanun, the sixth son of Zalaph, built the next section, their second one.

Meshullam son of Berechiah built the next section, which was in front of his house.

31 Malchijah, a goldsmith, built the next section, as far as the building used by the Temple workers and the merchants, which was by the Miphkad*f* Gate to the Temple, near the room on top of the northeast corner of the wall.

32 The goldsmiths and the merchants built the last section, from the room at the corner as far as the Sheep Gate.

Nehemiah Overcomes Opposition to His Work

4 When Sanballat heard that we Jews had begun rebuilding the wall, he became furious and began to ridicule us. 2 In front of his companions and the Samaritan troops he said, "What do these miserable Jews think they're doing? Do they intend to rebuild the city? Do they think that by offering sacrifices they can finish the work in one day? Can they make building stones out of heaps of burnt rubble?"

3 Tobiah was standing there beside him, and he added, "What kind of wall could they ever build? Even a fox could knock it down!"

4 I prayed, "Hear how they make fun of us, O God! Let their ridicule fall on their own heads. Let them be robbed of everything they have, and let them be taken as prisoners to a foreign land. 5 Don't forgive the evil they do and don't forget their sins, for they have insulted us who are building."

6 So we went on rebuilding the wall, and soon it was half its full height, because the people were eager to work.

7 Sanballat, Tobiah, and the people of Arabia, Ammon, and Ashdod heard that we were making progress in rebuilding the wall of Jerusalem and that the gaps in the wall were being closed, and they became very angry. 8 So they all plotted together to come and attack Jerusalem and create confusion, 9 but we prayed to our God and kept men on guard against them day and night.

10 The people of Judah had a song they sang:

"We grow weak carrying burdens;
There's so much rubble to take
     away.
How can we build the wall today?"

11 Our enemies thought we would not see them or know what was happening until they were already upon us, killing us and putting an end to our work. 12 But time after time Jews who were living among our enemies came to warn us of the plans our enemies were making

f Miphkad; or Mustering, or Watch.

against us.[g] 13 So I armed the people with swords, spears, and bows, and stationed them by clans behind the wall, wherever it was still unfinished.

14 I saw that the people were worried, so I said to them and to their leaders and officials, "Don't be afraid of our enemies. Remember how great and terrifying the Lord is, and fight for your relatives, your children, your wives, and your homes." 15 Our enemies heard that we had found out what they were plotting, and they realized that God had defeated their plans. Then all of us went back to rebuilding the wall.

16 From then on half of my men worked and half stood guard, wearing coats of armor and armed with spears, shields, and bows. And our leaders gave their full support to the people 17 who were rebuilding the wall. Even those who carried building materials worked with one hand and kept a weapon in the other, 18 and everyone who was building kept a sword strapped to their waist. The man who was to sound the alarm on the bugle stayed with me. 19 I told the people and their officials and leaders, "The work is spread out over such a distance that we are widely separated from one another on the wall. 20 If you hear the bugle, gather around me. Our God will fight for us." 21 So every day, from dawn until the stars came out at night, half of us worked on the wall, while the other half stood guard with spears.

22 During this time I told the men in charge that they and all their helpers had to stay in Jerusalem at night, so that we could guard the city at night as well as work in the daytime. 23 I didn't take off my clothes even at night, neither did any of my companions nor my servants nor my bodyguards. And we all kept our weapons at hand.[h]

Oppression of the Poor

5 Some time later many of the people, both men and women, began to complain against the other Jews. 2 Some said, "We have large families, we need grain to keep us alive."

3 Others said, "We have had to mortgage our fields and vineyards and houses to get enough grain to keep us from starving."

4 Still others said, "We had to borrow money to pay the royal tax on our fields and vineyards. 5 We are of the same race as the other Jews. Aren't our children just as good as theirs? But we have to make slaves of our children. Some of our daughters have already been sold as slaves. We are helpless because our fields and vineyards have been taken away from us."

6 When I heard their complaints, I grew angry 7 and decided to act. I denounced the leaders and officials of the people and told them, "You are oppressing your own relatives!"

I called a public assembly to deal with the problem 8 and said, "As far as we have been able, we have been buying back our Jewish relatives who had to sell themselves to foreigners. Now you are forcing your own relatives to sell themselves to you, their own people!" The leaders were silent and could find nothing to say.

9 Then I said, "What you are doing is wrong! You ought to obey God and do what's right. Then you would not give our enemies, the Gentiles, any reason to ridicule us. 10 I have let the people borrow money and grain from me, and so have my companions and those who work for me. Now let's give up all our claims to repayment. 11 Cancel all the debts[i] they owe you—money or grain or wine or olive oil. And give them back their fields, vineyards, olive groves, and houses right now!"

12 The leaders replied, "We'll do as you say. We'll give the property back and not try to collect the debts."

I called in the priests and made the leaders swear in front of them to keep the promise they had just made. 13 Then I took off the sash[j] I was wearing around my waist and shook it out. "This is how God will shake any of you who don't keep your promise," I said. "God will take away your houses and everything you own, and will leave you with nothing."

g Probable text the plans our enemies were making against us; Hebrew unclear.
h Probable text weapons at hand; Hebrew unclear.   i One ancient translation debts; Hebrew
unclear.   j SASH: Clothing in those days had no pockets, so small items were tucked into the
sash that was worn like a belt around the waist. Shaking it out was a symbol of losing
everything.

Everyone who was present said, "Amen!" and praised the LORD. And the leaders kept their promise.

Nehemiah's Unselfishness

14 During all the twelve years that I was governor of the land of Judah, from the twentieth year that Artaxerxes was emperor until his thirty-second year, neither my relatives nor I ate the food I was entitled to have as governor. 15 Every governor who had been in office before me had been a burden to the people and had demanded forty silver coins a day *k* for food and wine. Even their servants had oppressed the people. But I acted differently, because I honored God. 16 I put all my energy into rebuilding the wall and did not acquire any property. Everyone who worked for me joined in the rebuilding. 17 I regularly fed at my table a hundred and fifty of the Jewish people and their leaders, besides all the people who came to me from the surrounding nations. 18 Every day I served one beef, six of the best sheep, and many chickens, and every ten days I provided a fresh supply of wine. But I knew what heavy burdens the people had to bear, and so I did not claim the allowance that the governor is entitled to.

19 I pray you, O God, remember to my credit everything that I have done for this people.

Plots against Nehemiah

6 Sanballat, Tobiah, Geshem, and the rest of our enemies heard that we had finished building the wall and that there were no gaps left in it, although we still had not set up the gates in the gateways. 2 So Sanballat and Geshem sent me a message, suggesting that I meet with them in one of the villages in the Plain of Ono. This was a trick of theirs to try to harm me. 3 I sent messengers to say to them, "I am doing important work and can't go down there. I am not going to let the work stop just to go and see you."

4 They sent me the same message four times, and each time I sent them the same reply.

5 Then Sanballat sent one of his servants to me with a fifth message, this one in the form of an unsealed letter.*l* 6 It read:

"Geshem tells me that a rumor is going around among the neighboring peoples that you and the Jewish people intend to revolt and that this is why you are rebuilding the wall. He also says you plan to make yourself king 7 and that you have arranged for some prophets to proclaim in Jerusalem that you are the king of Judah. His Majesty is certain to hear about this, so I suggest that you and I meet to talk the situation over."

8 I sent a reply to him: "Nothing of what you are saying is true. You have made it all up yourself."

9 They were trying to frighten us into stopping work. I prayed, "But now, God, make me strong!"

10 About this time I went to visit Shemaiah, the son of Delaiah and grandson of Mehetabel, who was unable to leave his house. He said to me, "You and I must go and hide together in the Holy Place of the Temple and lock the doors, because they are coming to kill you. Any night now they will come to kill you."

11 I answered, "I'm not the kind of person that runs and hides. Do you think I would try to save my life by hiding in the Temple? I won't do it."

12 When I thought it over, I realized that God had not spoken to Shemaiah, but that Tobiah and Sanballat had bribed him to give me this warning. 13 They hired him to frighten me into sinning, so that they could ruin my reputation and humiliate me.

14 I prayed, "God, remember what Tobiah and Sanballat have done and punish them. Remember that woman Noadiah and all the other prophets who tried to frighten me."

The Conclusion of the Work

15 After fifty-two days of work the entire wall was finished on the twenty-fifth day of the month of Elul. 16 When our enemies in the surrounding nations heard this, they realized that they had lost face, since everyone knew that the work had been done with God's help. 17 During all this time the Jewish lead-

---

k One ancient translation a day; *Hebrew unclear.*   *l* UNSEALED LETTER: *Leaving a letter unsealed was a deliberate way of making certain that its contents would become widely known.*

ers had been in correspondence with Tobiah. 18 Many people in Judah were on his side because of his Jewish father-in-law, Shecaniah son of Arah. In addition, his son Jehohanan had married the daughter of Meshullam son of Berechiah. 19 People would talk in front of me about all the good deeds Tobiah had done and would tell him everything I said. And he kept sending me letters to try to frighten me.

7 And now the wall had been rebuilt, the gates had all been put in place, and the Temple guards, the members of the sacred choir, and the other Levites had been assigned their work. 2 I put two men in charge of governing the city of Jerusalem: my brother Hanani and Hananiah, commanding officer of the fortress. Hananiah was a reliable and God-fearing man without equal. 3 I told them not to have the gates of Jerusalem opened in the morning until well after sunrise and to have them closed and barred before the guards went off duty at sunset. I also told them to appoint guards from among the people who lived in Jerusalem and to assign some of them to specific posts and others to patrol the area around their own houses.

The List of Those Who Returned from Exile

(Ezra 2.1-70)

4 Jerusalem was a large city, but not many people were living in it, and not many houses had been built yet. 5 God inspired me to assemble the people and their leaders and officials and to check their family records. I located the records of those who had first returned from captivity, and this is the information I found:

6 Many of the exiles left the province of Babylon and returned to Jerusalem and Judah, each to his own hometown. Their families had been living in exile in Babylonia ever since King Nebuchadnezzar had taken them there as prisoners. 7 Their leaders were Zerubbabel, Joshua, Nehemiah, Azariah, Raamiah, Nahamani, Mordecai, Bilshan, Mispereth, Bigvai, Nehum, and Baanah.

8-25 This is the list of the clans of Israel, with the number of those from each clan who returned from exile:

Parosh - 2,172

Shephatiah - 372
Arah - 652
Pahath Moab (descendants of Jeshua and Joab) - 2,818
Elam - 1,254
Zattu - 845
Zaccai - 760
Binnui - 648
Bebai - 628
Azgad - 2,322
Adonikam - 667
Bigvai - 2,067
Adin - 655
Ater (also called Hezekiah) - 98
Hashum - 328
Bezai - 324
Hariph - 112
Gibeon - 95

26-38 People whose ancestors had lived in the following towns also returned:

Bethlehem and Netophah - 188
Anathoth - 128
Beth Azmaveth - 42
Kiriath Jearim, Chephirah, and Beeroth - 743
Ramah and Geba - 621
Michmash - 122
Bethel and Ai - 123
The other Nebo - 52
The other Elam - 1,254
Harim - 320
Jericho - 345
Lod, Hadid, and Ono - 721
Senaah - 3,930

39-42 This is the list of the priestly clans that returned from exile:

Jedaiah (descendants of Jeshua) - 973
Immer - 1,052
Pashhur - 1,247
Harim - 1,017

43-45 Clans of Levites who returned from exile:

Jeshua and Kadmiel (descendants of Hodaviah) - 74
Temple musicians (descendants of Asaph) - 148
Temple guards (descendants of Shallum, Ater, Talmon, Akkub, Hatita, and Shobai) - 138

46-56 Clans of Temple workers who returned from exile:

Ziha, Hasupha, Tabbaoth,
Keros, Sia, Padon,
Lebana, Hagaba, Shalmai,
Hanan, Giddel, Gahar,
Reaiah, Rezin, Nekoda,
Gazzam, Uzza, Paseah,

NEHEMIAH

Besai, Meunim, Nephushesim,
Bakbuk, Hakupha, Harhur,
Bazlith, Mehida, Harsha,
Barkos, Sisera, Temah,
Neziah, and Hatipha.

57-59 Clans of Solomon's servants who returned from exile:

Sotai, Sophereth, Perida,
Jaalah, Darkon, Giddel,
Shephatiah, Hattil, Pochereth
Hazzebaim, and Amon.

60 The total number of descendants of the Temple workers and of Solomon's servants who returned from exile was 392.

61-62 There were 642 belonging to the clans of Delaiah, Tobiah, and Nekoda who returned from the towns of Tel Melah, Tel Harsha, Cherub, Addon, and Immer; but they could not prove that they were descendants of Israelites.

63-64 The following priestly clans could find no record to prove their ancestry: Hobaiah, Hakkoz, and Barzillai. (The ancestor of the priestly clan of Barzillai had married a woman from the clan of Barzillai of Gilead and taken the name of his father-in-law's clan.) Since they were unable to prove who their ancestors were, they were not accepted as priests. **65** The Jewish governor told them that they could not eat the food offered to God until there was a priest who could use the Urim and Thummim.*m*

66-69 Total number of exiles who returned - 42,360.

Their male and female
    servants - 7,337
Male and female musicians - 245
Horses - 736
Mules - 245
Camels - 435
Donkeys - 6,720

70-72 Many of the people contributed to help pay the cost of restoring the Temple:

The governor	270	ounces of gold
	50	ceremonial bowls
	530	robes for priests
Heads of clans	337	pounds of gold

	3,215	pounds of silver
The rest of the people	337	pounds of gold
	2,923	pounds of silver
	67	robes for priests

73 The priests, the Levites, the Temple guards, the musicians, many of the ordinary people, the Temple workers — all the people of Israel — settled in the towns and cities of Judah.

Ezra Reads the Law to the People

8 By the seventh month the people of Israel were all settled in their towns. On the first day of that month they all assembled in Jerusalem, in the square just inside the Water Gate. They asked Ezra, the priest and scholar of the Law which the LORD had given Israel through Moses, to get the book of the Law. **2** So Ezra brought it to the place where the people had gathered — men, women, and the children who were old enough to understand. **3** There in the square by the gate he read the Law to them from dawn until noon, and they all listened attentively.

4 Ezra was standing on a wooden platform that had been built for the occasion. The following men stood at his right: Mattithiah, Shema, Anaiah, Uriah, Hilkiah, and Maaseiah; and the following stood at his left: Pedaiah, Mishael, Malchijah, Hashum, Hashbaddanah, Zechariah, and Meshullam.

5 As Ezra stood there on the platform high above the people, they all kept their eyes fixed on him. As soon as he opened the book, they all stood up. **6** Ezra said, "Praise the LORD, the great God!"

All the people raised their arms in the air and answered, "Amen! Amen!" They knelt in worship, with their faces to the ground.

7 Then they rose and stood in their places, and the following Levites explained the Law to them: Jeshua, Bani, Sherebiah, Jamin, Akkub, Shabbethai, Hodiah, Maaseiah, Kelita, Azariah, Jozabad, Hanan, and Pelaiah. **8** They gave an oral translation*n* of God's Law and

m URIM AND THUMMIM: *Two objects used by the priest to determine God's will; it is not known precisely how they were used.* *n* TRANSLATION: *The Law was written in Hebrew, but in Babylonia the Jews had adopted Aramaic as the language for daily life. Because of this a translation was necessary.*

explained⁰ it so that the people could understand it.

9 When the people heard what the Law required, they were so moved that they began to cry. So Nehemiah, who was the governor, Ezra, the priest and scholar of the Law, and the Levites who were explaining the Law told all the people, "This day is holy to the LORD your God, so you are not to mourn or cry. 10 Now go home and have a feast. Share your food and wine with those who don't have enough. Today is holy to our Lord, so don't be sad. The joy that the LORD gives you will make you strong."

11 The Levites went around calming the people and telling them not to be sad on such a holy day. 12 So all the people went home and ate and drank joyfully and shared what they had with others, because they understood what had been read to them.

The Festival of Shelters

13 The next day the heads of the clans, together with the priests and the Levites, went to Ezra to study the teachings of the Law. 14 They discovered that the Law, which the LORD gave through Moses, ordered the people of Israel to live in temporary shelters during the Festival of Shelters. 15 So they gave the following instructions and sent themᵖ all through Jerusalem and the other cities and towns: "Go out to the hills and get branches from pines, olives, myrtles, palms, and other trees to make shelters according to the instructions written in the Law."

16 So the people got branches and built shelters on the flat roofs of their houses, in their yards, in the Temple courtyard, and in the public squares by the Water Gate and by the Ephraim Gate. 17 All the people who had come back from captivity built shelters and lived in them. This was the first time it had been done since the days of Joshua son of Nun, and everybody was excited and happy. 18 From the first day of the festival to the last they read a part of God's Law every day. They celebrated for seven days, and on the eighth day there was a closing ceremony, as required in the Law.

The People Confess Their Sins

9 1-2 On the twenty-fourth day of the same month the people of Israel gathered to fast in order to show sorrow for their sins. They had already separated themselves from all foreigners. They wore sackcloth and put dust on their heads as signs of grief. Then they stood and began to confess the sins that they and their ancestors had committed. 3 For about three hours the Law of the LORD their God was read to them, and for the next three hours they confessed their sins and worshiped the LORD their God.

4 There was a platform for the Levites, and on it stood Jeshua, Bani, Kadmiel, Shebaniah, Bunni, Sherebiah, Bani, and Chenani. They prayed aloud to the LORD their God.

5 The following Levites gave a call to worship: Jeshua, Kadmiel, Bani, Hashabneiah, Sherebiah, Hodiah, Shebaniah, and Pethahiah. They said:
"Stand up and praise the LORD
      your God;
   praise him forever and ever!
Let everyone praise his glorious
      name,
   although no human praise is
      great enough."

The Prayer of Confession

6 And then the people of Israel prayed this prayer:
"You, LORD, you alone are LORD;
   you made the heavens and the
      stars of the sky.
You made land and sea and
      everything in them;
   you gave life to all.
The heavenly powers bow down
      and worship you.
7 You, LORD God, chose Abram
   and led him out of Ur in
      Babylonia;
   you changed his name to
      Abraham.
8 You found that he was faithful
      to you,
   and you made a covenant
      with him.
You promised to give him the land
      of the Canaanites,

⁰ They gave . . . explained; or They read God's Law and then translated it, explaining.
ᵖ Probable text So they . . . sent them; Hebrew It also ordered that the following instructions be sent.

the land of the Hittites and the
Amorites,
the land of the Perizzites, the
Jebusites, the Girgashites,
to be a land where his
descendants would live.
You kept your promise, because
you are faithful.

9 "You saw how our ancestors
suffered in Egypt;
you heard their call for help at
the Red Sea.
10 You worked amazing miracles
against the king,
against his officials and the
people of his land,
because you knew how they
oppressed your people.
You won then the fame you still
have today.
11 Through the sea you made a path
for your people
and led them through on dry
ground.
Those who pursued them drowned
in deep water,
as a stone sinks in the
raging sea.
12 With a cloud you led them in
daytime,
and at night you lighted their
way with fire.
13 At Mount Sinai you came down
from heaven;
you spoke to your people
and gave them good laws and
sound teachings.
14 You taught them to keep your
Sabbaths holy,
and through your servant Moses
you gave them your laws.

15 "When they were hungry, you
gave them bread from heaven,
and water from a rock when
they were thirsty.
You told them to take control of
the land
which you had promised to give
them.
16 But our ancestors grew proud and
stubborn
and refused to obey your
commands.
17 They refused to obey; they forgot
all you did;

they forgot the miracles you had
performed.
In their pride they chose a leader
to take them back to slavery in
Egypt.
But you are a God who forgives;
you are gracious and loving,
slow to be angry.
Your mercy is great; you did not
forsake them.
18 They made an idol in the shape of
a bull-calf
and said it was the god who led
them from Egypt!
How much they insulted you,
LORD!
19 But you did not abandon them
there in the desert,
for your mercy is great.
You did not take away the cloud
or the fire
that showed them the path by
day and night.
20 In your goodness you told them
what they should do;
you fed them manna and gave
them water to drink.
21 Through forty years in the desert
you provided all that they
needed;
their clothing never wore out,
and their feet were not swollen
with pain.

22 "You let them conquer nations and
kingdoms,
lands that bordered their own.
They conquered the land of
Heshbon, where Sihon ruled,
and the land of Bashan, where
Og was king.
23 You gave them as many children
as there are stars in the sky,
and let them conquer and live in
the land
that you had promised their
ancestors to give them.
24 They conquered the land of
Canaan;
you overcame the people living
there.
You gave your people the power
to do as they pleased
with the people and kings of
Canaan.
25 Your people captured fortified
cities,

fertile land, houses full of
wealth,
cisterns already dug,
olive trees, fruit trees, and
vineyards.
They ate all they wanted and
grew fat;
they enjoyed all the good things
you gave them.

26 "But your people rebelled and
disobeyed you;
they turned their backs on
your Law.
They killed the prophets who
warned them,
who told them to turn back
to you.
They insulted you time after time,
27 so you let their enemies conquer
and rule them.
In their trouble they called to you
for help,
and you answered them from
heaven.
In your great mercy you sent them
leaders
who rescued them from their
foes.
28 When peace returned, they sinned
again,
and again you let their enemies
conquer them.
Yet when they repented and asked
you to save them,
in heaven you heard, and time
after time
you rescued them in your great
mercy.
29 You warned them to obey your
teachings,
but in pride they rejected your
laws,
although keeping your Law is
the way to life.
Hard-headed and stubborn, they
refused to obey.
30 Year after year you patiently
warned them.
You inspired your prophets to
speak,
but your people were deaf,
so you let them be conquered
by other nations.
31 And yet, because your mercy is
great,
you did not forsake or destroy
them.

You are a gracious and
merciful God!

32 "O God, our God, how great
you are!
How terrifying, how powerful!
You faithfully keep your covenant
promises.
From the time when Assyrian
kings oppressed us,
even till now, how much we
have suffered!
Our kings, our leaders, our priests
and prophets,
our ancestors, and all our people
have suffered.
Remember how much we have
suffered!
33 You have done right to punish us;
you have been faithful, even
though we have sinned.
34 Our ancestors, our kings, leaders,
and priests
have not kept your Law.
They did not listen to your
commands and warnings.
35 With your blessing, kings ruled
your people
when they lived in the broad,
fertile land you gave them;
but they failed to turn from sin
and serve you.
36 And now we are slaves in the land
that you gave us,
this fertile land which gives us
food.
37 What the land produces goes to
the kings
that you put over us because we
sinned.
They do as they please with us
and our livestock,
and we are in deep distress!"

The People Sign an Agreement

38 Because of all that has happened,
we, the people of Israel, hereby make a
solemn written agreement, and our leaders, our Levites, and our priests put their
seals to it.

10 The first to sign was the governor, Nehemiah son of Hacaliah,
and then Zedekiah signed. The following also signed:

2-8 *Priests:*
Seraiah, Azariah, Jeremiah,
Pashhur, Amariah, Malchijah,

Hattush, Shebaniah, Malluch,
Harim, Meremoth, Obadiah,
Daniel, Ginnethon, Baruch,
Meshullam, Abijah, Mijamin,
Maaziah, Bilgai, and Shemaiah.

9-13 *Levites:*
Jeshua son of Azaniah,
Binnui of the clan of Henadad,
Kadmiel, Shebaniah, Hodiah,
Kelita, Pelaiah, Hanan,
Mica, Rehob, Hashabiah,
Zaccur, Sherebiah, Shebaniah,
Hodiah, Bani, and Beninu.

14-27 *Leaders of the people:*
Parosh, Pahath Moab,
Elam, Zattu, Bani,
Bunni, Azgad, Bebai,
Adonijah, Bigvai, Adin,
Ater, Hezekiah, Azzur,
Hodiah, Hashum, Bezai,
Hariph, Anathoth, Nebai,
Magpiash, Meshullam, Hezir,
Meshezabel, Zadok, Jaddua,
Pelatiah, Hanan, Anaiah,
Hoshea, Hananiah, Hasshub,
Hallohesh, Pilha, Shobek,
Rehum, Hashabnah, Maaseiah,
Ahiah, Hanan, Anan,
Malluch, Harim, and Baanah.

The Agreement

28 We, the people of Israel, the priests, the Levites, the Temple guards, the Temple musicians, the Temple workers, and all others who in obedience to God's Law have separated themselves from the foreigners living in our land, we, together with our wives and all our children old enough to understand, 29 do hereby join with our leaders in an oath, under penalty of a curse if we break it, that we will live according to God's Law, which God gave through his servant Moses; that we will obey all that the LORD, our Lord, commands us; and that we will keep all his laws and requirements.

30 We will not intermarry with the foreigners living in our land.

31 If foreigners bring grain or anything else to sell to us on the Sabbath or on any other holy day, we will not buy from them.

Every seventh year we will not farm the land, and we will cancel all debts. 32 Every year we will each contribute one-eighth of an ounce of silver to help pay the expenses of the Temple.

33 We will provide for the Temple worship the following: the sacred bread, the daily grain offering, the animals to be burned each day as sacrifices, the sacred offerings for Sabbaths, New Moon Festivals, and other festivals, the other sacred offerings, the offerings to take away the sins of Israel, and anything else needed for the Temple.

34 We, the people, priests, and Levites, will draw lots each year to determine which clans are to provide wood to burn the sacrifices offered to the LORD our God, according to the requirements of the Law.

35 We will take to the Temple each year an offering of the first grain we harvest and of the first fruit that ripens on our trees.

36 The first son born to each of us we will take to the priests in the Temple and there, as required by the Law, dedicate him to God. We will also dedicate the first calf born to each of our cows, and the first lamb or kid born to each of our sheep or goats.

37 We will take to the priests in the Temple the dough made from the first grain harvested each year and our other offerings of wine, olive oil, and all kinds of fruit.

We will take to the Levites, who collect tithes in our farming villages, the tithes from the crops that grow on our land. 38 Priests who are descended from Aaron are to be with the Levites when tithes are collected, and for use in the Temple the Levites are to take to the Temple storerooms one-tenth of all the tithes they collect. 39 The people of Israel and the Levites are to take the contributions of grain, wine, and olive oil to the storerooms where the utensils for the Temple are kept and where the priests who are on duty, the Temple guards, and the members of the Temple choir have their quarters.

We will not neglect the house of our God.

The People Who Lived in Jerusalem

11 The leaders settled in Jerusalem, and the rest of the people drew lots to choose one family out of every ten to go and live in the holy city of Jerusalem, while the rest were to live in the

other cities and towns. 2 The people
praised anyone else who volunteered to
live in Jerusalem. 3 In the other towns
and cities the people of Israel, the
priests, the Levites, the Temple workers,
and the descendants of Solomon's servants lived on their own property in their
own towns.

The following is the list of the leading citizens of the province of Judah who lived in Jerusalem:

4 *Members of the tribe of Judah:*

Athaiah, the son of Uzziah and grandson of Zechariah. His other ancestors included Amariah, Shephatiah, and Mahalalel, descendants of Judah's son Perez.

5 Maaseiah, the son of Baruch and grandson of Colhozeh. His other ancestors included Hazaiah, Adaiah, Joiarib, and Zechariah, descendants of Judah's son Shelah.

6 Of the descendants of Perez, 468 outstanding soldiers lived in Jerusalem.

7 *Members of the tribe of Benjamin:*

Sallu, the son of Meshullam and grandson of Joed. His other ancestors included Pedaiah, Kolaiah, Maaseiah, Ithiel, and Jeshaiah.

8 Gabbai and Sallai, close relatives[q] of Sallu.

In all, 928 Benjaminites lived in Jerusalem. 9 Joel son of Zichri was their
leader, and Judah son of Hassenuah was
the second ranking official in the city.

10 *Priests:*

Jedaiah son of Joiarib, and Jachin.

11 Seraiah, the son of Hilkiah and
grandson of Meshullam. His ancestors
included Zadok, Meraioth, and Ahitub,
who was the High Priest. 12 In all, 822
members of this clan served in the
Temple.

Adaiah, the son of Jeroham and
grandson of Pelaliah. His ancestors included Amzi, Zechariah, Pashhur, and
Malchijah. 13 In all, 242 members of this
clan were heads of families.

Amashsai, the son of Azarel and
grandson of Ahzai. His ancestors included Meshillemoth and Immer.
14 There were 128 members of this clan
who were outstanding soldiers. Their
leader was Zabdiel, a member of a leading family.[r]

15 *Levites:*

Shemaiah, the son of Hasshub and grandson of Azrikam. His ancestors included Hashabiah and Bunni.

16 Shabbethai and Jozabad, prominent Levites in charge of the work outside the Temple.

17 Mattaniah, the son of Mica and grandson of Zabdi, a descendant of Asaph. He led the Temple choir in singing the prayer of thanksgiving.

Bakbukiah, who was Mattaniah's assistant.

Abda, the son of Shammua and grandson of Galal, a descendant of Jeduthun.

18 In all, 284 Levites lived in the holy city of Jerusalem.

19 *Temple guards:*

Akkub, Talmon, and their relatives, 172 in all.

20 The rest of the people of Israel and
the remaining priests and Levites lived
on their own property in the other cities
and towns of Judah. 21 The Temple
workers lived in the part of Jerusalem
called Ophel and worked under the supervision of Ziha and Gishpa.

22 The supervisor of the Levites who
lived in Jerusalem was Uzzi, the son of
Bani and grandson of Hashabiah. His
ancestors included Mattaniah and Mica,
and he belonged to the clan of Asaph,
the clan that was responsible for the music in the Temple services. 23 There were
royal regulations stating how the clans
should take turns in leading the Temple
music each day.

24 Pethahiah son of Meshezabel, of the
clan of Zerah and the tribe of Judah, represented the people of Israel at the Persian court.

The People in Other Towns and Cities

25 Many of the people lived in towns
near their farms. Those who were of the
tribe of Judah lived in Kiriath Arba, Dibon, and Jekabzeel, and in the villages
near these cities. 26 They also lived in the
cities of Jeshua, Moladah, Bethpelet,

[q] *One ancient translation* close relatives; *Hebrew* after him. [r] a member of a leading family; *or* son of Haggedolim.

27and Hazarshual, and in Beersheba and the villages around it. 28They lived in the city of Ziklag, in Meconah and its villages, 29in Enrimmon, in Zorah, in Jarmuth, 30in Zanoah, in Adullam, and in the villages near these towns. They lived in Lachish and on the farms nearby, and in Azekah and its villages. That is to say, the people of Judah lived in the territory between Beersheba in the south and Hinnom Valley in the north.

31The people of the tribe of Benjamin lived in Geba, Michmash, Ai, Bethel and the nearby villages, 32Anathoth, Nob, Ananiah, 33Hazor, Ramah, Gittaim, 34Hadid, Zeboim, Neballat, 35Lod, and Ono, and in Craftsmen's Valley. 36Some groups of Levites that had lived in the territory of Judah were assigned to live with the people of Benjamin.

List of Priests and Levites

12 The following is a list of the priests and Levites who returned from exile with Zerubbabel son of Shealtiel and with the High Priest Joshua:

2-7Priests:

Seraiah, Jeremiah, Ezra,
Amariah, Malluch, Hattush,
Shecaniah, Rehum, Meremoth,
Iddo, Ginnethoi, Abijah,
Mijamin, Maadiah, Bilgah,
Shemaiah, Joiarib, Jedaiah,
Sallu, Amok, Hilkiah, and Jedaiah.
These men were leaders among all their fellow priests in the days of Joshua.

8Levites:

The following were in charge of the singing of hymns of thanksgiving: Jeshua, Binnui, Kadmiel, Sherebiah, Judah, and Mattaniah.
9The following formed the choir that sang the responses: Bakbukiah, Unno, and their fellow Levites.

Descendants of the High Priest Joshua

10Joshua was the father of Joiakim; Joiakim was the father of Eliashib; Eliashib was the father of Joiada; 11Joiada was the father of Jonathan; and Jonathan was the father of Jaddua.

Heads of the Priestly Clans

12-21When Joiakim was High Priest, the following priests were the heads of the priestly clans:

Priest	Clan
Meraiah	Seraiah
Hananiah	Jeremiah
Meshullam	Ezra
Jehohanan	Amariah
Jonathan	Malluchi
Joseph	Shebaniah
Adna	Harim
Helkai	Meraioth
Zechariah	Iddo
Meshullam	Ginnethon
Zichri	Abijah
...s	Miniamin
Piltai	Moadiah
Shammua	Bilgah
Jehonathan	Shemaiah
Mattenai	Joiarib
Uzzi	Jedaiah
Kallai	Sallai
Eber	Amok
Hashabiah	Hilkiah
Nethanel	Jedaiah

Record of the Priestly and Levite Families

22A record was kept of the heads of the Levite families and of the priestly families during the lifetimes of the following High Priests: Eliashib, Joiada, Jonathan, and Jaddua. This record was finished when Darius was emperor of Persia.
23The heads of the Levite families, however, were recorded in the official records only until the time of Jonathan, the grandson of Eliashib.

Assignment of Duties in the Temple

24Under the direction of Hashabiah, Sherebiah, Jeshua, Binnui,t and Kadmiel, the Levites were organized into groups. Two groups at a time praised God responsively and gave thanks to him, in accordance with the instructions given by King David, the man of God.
25The following Temple guards were in charge of guarding the storerooms by the gates to the Temple: Mattaniah, Bakbukiah, Obadiah, Meshullam, Talmon, and Akkub.

s In Hebrew a name is missing from the list.   t Probable text (see 10.9 and 12.8) Binnui; Hebrew son of.

26 These people lived during the time of Joiakim, the son of Joshua and grandson of Jehozadak, and the time of Nehemiah the governor, and the time of Ezra, the priest who was a scholar of the Law.

Nehemiah Dedicates the City Wall

27 When the city wall of Jerusalem was dedicated, the Levites were brought in from wherever they were living, so that they could join in celebrating the dedication with songs of thanksgiving and with the music of cymbals and harps. 28 The Levite families of singers gathered from the area where they had settled around Jerusalem and from the towns around Netophah, 29 and from Bethgilgal, Geba, and Azmaveth. 30 The priests and the Levites performed ritual purification for themselves, the people, the gates, and the city wall.

31 I assembled the leaders of Judah on top of the wall and put them in charge of two large groups to march around the city, giving thanks to God.

The first group went to the right on top of the wall toward the Rubbish Gate.ᵘ 32 Hoshaiah marched behind the singers, followed by half the leaders of Judah. 33-35 The following priests, blowing trumpets, marched next: Azariah, Ezra, Meshullam, Judah, Benjamin, Shemaiah, and Jeremiah. Next came Zechariah, the son of Jonathan and grandson of Shemaiah. (His ancestors also included Mattaniah, Micaiah, and Zaccur, of the clan of Asaph.) 36 He was followed by other members of his clan — Shemaiah, Azarel, Milalai, Gilalai, Maai, Nethanel, Judah, and Hanani — all of whom carried musical instruments of the kind played by King David, the man of God. Ezra the scholar led this group in the procession. 37 At the Fountain Gate they went up the steps that led to David's City, past David's palace, and back to the wall at the Water Gate, on the east side of the city.

38 The other group of those who gave thanks went to the left along the top of the wall, and I followed with half of the people. We marched past the Tower of the Ovens to the Broad Wall, 39 and from there we went past Ephraim Gate, Jeshanah Gate,ᵛ the Fish Gate, the Tower of Hananel, and the Tower of the Hundred, to the Sheep Gate. We ended our march near the gate to the Temple.

40 So both the groups that were giving thanks to God reached the Temple area. In addition to the leaders who were with me, 41 my group included the following priests, blowing trumpets: Eliakim, Maaseiah, Miniamin, Micaiah, Elioenai, Zechariah, and Hananiah; 42 and they were followed by Maaseiah, Shemaiah, Eleazar, Uzzi, Jehohanan, Malchijah, Elam, and Ezer. The singers, led by Jezrahiah, sang at the top of their voices.

43 That day many sacrifices were offered, and the people were full of joy because God had made them very happy. The women and the children joined in the celebration, and the noise they all made could be heard for miles.

Providing for Worship in the Temple

44 At that time men were put in charge of the storerooms where contributions for the Temple were kept, including the tithes and the first grain and fruit that ripened each year. These men were responsible for collecting from the farms near the various cities the contributions for the priests and the Levites which the Law required. All the people of Judah were pleased with the priests and the Levites, 45 because they performed the ceremonies of purification and the other rituals that God had commanded. The Temple musicians and the Temple guards also performed their duties in accordance with the regulations made by King David and his son Solomon. 46 From the time of King David and the musician Asaph long ago, the musicians have led songs of praise and thanksgiving to God. 47 In the time of Zerubbabel and also in the time of Nehemiah, all the people of Israel gave daily gifts for the support of the Temple musicians and the Temple guards. The people gave a sacred offering to the Levites, and the Levites gave the required portion to the priests.

Separation from Foreigners

13 When the Law of Moses was being read aloud to the people, they came to the passage that said that

---

ᵘ RUBBISH GATE: *The two groups started somewhere on the southwestern part of the city wall and went in opposite directions until they met in front of the Temple in the northeastern part of the city.*   ᵛ Ephraim Gate, Jeshanah Gate; *or* Ephraim Gate (also called the Old Gate).

no Ammonite or Moabite was ever to be permitted to join God's people. 2 This was because the people of Ammon and Moab did not give food and water to the Israelites on their way out of Egypt. Instead, they paid money to Balaam to curse Israel, but our God turned the curse into a blessing. 3 When the people of Israel heard this law read, they excluded all foreigners from the community.

Nehemiah's Reforms

4 The priest Eliashib, who was in charge of the Temple storerooms, had for a long time been on good terms with Tobiah. 5 He allowed Tobiah to use a large room that was intended only for storing offerings of grain and incense, the equipment used in the Temple, the offerings for the priests, and the tithes of grain, wine, and olive oil given to the Levites, to the Temple musicians, and to the Temple guards. 6 While this was going on, I was not in Jerusalem, because in the thirty-second year that Artaxerxes[w] was king of Babylon I had gone back to report to him. After some time I received his permission 7 and returned to Jerusalem. There I was shocked to find that Eliashib had allowed Tobiah to use a room in the Temple. 8 I was furious and threw out all of Tobiah's belongings. 9 I gave orders for the rooms to be ritually purified and for the Temple equipment, grain offerings, and incense to be put back.

10 I also learned that the Temple musicians and other Levites had left Jerusalem and gone back to their farms, because the people had not been giving them enough to live on. 11 I reprimanded the officials for letting the Temple be neglected. And I brought the Levites and musicians back to the Temple and put them to work again. 12 Then all the people of Israel again started bringing to the Temple storerooms their tithes of grain, wine, and olive oil. 13 I put the following men in charge of the storerooms: Shelemiah, a priest; Zadok, a scholar of the Law; and Pedaiah, a Levite. Hanan, the son of Zaccur and grandson of Mattaniah, was to be their assistant. I knew I could trust these men to be honest in distributing the supplies to the other workers.

14 Remember, my God, all these things that I have done for your Temple and its worship.

15 At that time I saw people in Judah pressing juice from grapes on the Sabbath. Others were loading grain, wine, grapes, figs, and other things on their donkeys and taking them into Jerusalem; I warned them not to sell anything on the Sabbath. 16 Some people from the city of Tyre were living in Jerusalem, and they brought fish and all kinds of goods into the city to sell to our people on the Sabbath. 17 I reprimanded the Jewish leaders and told them, "Look at the evil you're doing! You're making the Sabbath unholy. 18 This is exactly why God punished your ancestors when he brought destruction on this city. And yet you insist on bringing more of God's anger down on Israel by profaning the Sabbath."

19 So I gave orders for the city gates to be shut at the beginning of every Sabbath, as soon as evening[x] began to fall, and not to be opened again until the Sabbath was over. I stationed some of my men at the gates to make sure that nothing was brought into the city on the Sabbath. 20 Once or twice merchants who sold all kinds of goods spent Friday night outside the city walls. 21 I warned them, "It's no use waiting out there for morning to come. If you try this again, I'll use force on you." From then on they did not come back on the Sabbath. 22 I ordered the Levites to purify themselves and to go and guard the gates to make sure that the Sabbath was kept holy.

Remember me, O God, for this also, and spare me because of your great love.

23 At that time I also discovered that many of the Jewish men had married women from Ashdod, Ammon, and Moab. 24 Half of their children spoke the language of Ashdod or some other language and didn't know how to speak our language. 25 I reprimanded the men, called down curses on them, beat them, and pulled out their hair. Then I made them take an oath in God's name that

---

w ARTAXERXES: *As emperor of Persia, Artaxerxes also had the title "King of Babylon."*
x EVENING: *The Jewish day begins at sunset.*

never again would they or their children intermarry with foreigners. 26 I told them, "It was foreign women that made King Solomon sin. Here was a man who was greater than any of the kings of other nations. God loved him and made him king over all of Israel, and yet he fell into this sin. 27 Are we then to follow your example and disobey our God by marrying foreign women?"

28 Joiada was the son of Eliashib the High Priest, but one of Joiada's sons married the daughter of Sanballat, from the town of Beth Horon, so I made Joiada leave Jerusalem.

29 Remember, God, how those people defiled both the office of priest and the covenant you made with the priests and the Levites.

30 I purified the people from everything foreign; I prepared regulations for the priests and the Levites so that all of them would know their duties; 31 I arranged for the wood used for burning the offerings to be brought at the proper times, and for the people to bring their offerings of the first grain and first fruits that ripened.

Remember all this, O God, and give me credit for it.

The Book of
ESTHER

Introduction

The events of The Book of Esther, which take place at the winter residence of the Persian emperor, center around a Jewish heroine named Esther, who by her great courage and devotion to her people saved them from being exterminated by their enemies. The book explains the background and meaning of the Jewish festival of Purim.

Outline of Contents

Queen Vashti Defies King Xerxes

1 1-2 From his royal throne in Persia's capital city of Susa, King Xerxes ruled 127 provinces, all the way from India to Ethiopia.a 3 In the third year of his reign he gave a banquet for all his officials and administrators. The armies of Persia and Media were present, as well as the governors and noblemen of the provinces. 4 For six whole months he made a show of the riches of the imperial court with all its splendor and majesty.

5 After that, the king gave a banquet for all the people in the capital city of Susa, rich and poor alike. It lasted a whole week and was held in the gardens of the royal palace. 6 The courtyard there was decorated with blue and white cotton curtains, tied by cords of fine purple linen to silver rings on marble columns. Couches made of gold and silver had been placed in the courtyard, which was paved with white marble, red feldspar, shining mother-of-pearl, and blue turquoise. 7 Drinks were served in gold cups, no two of them alike, and the king was generous with the royal wine. 8 There were no limits on the drinks; the king had given orders to the palace

a *Hebrew Cush: Cush is the ancient name of the extensive territory south of the First Cataract of the Nile River. This region was called Ethiopia in Graeco-Roman times, and included within its borders most of modern Sudan and some of present-day Ethiopia (Abyssinia).*

ESTHER

servants that everyone could have as much as they wanted.[b]

9 Meanwhile, inside the royal palace Queen Vashti was giving a banquet for the women.

10 On the seventh day of his banquet the king was drinking and feeling happy, so he called in the seven eunuchs who were his personal servants, Mehuman, Biztha, Harbona, Bigtha, Abagtha, Zethar, and Carkas. 11 He ordered them to bring in Queen Vashti, wearing her royal crown. The queen was a beautiful woman, and the king wanted to show off her beauty to the officials and all his guests. 12 But when the servants told Queen Vashti of the king's command, she refused to come. This made the king furious.

13 Now it was the king's custom to ask for expert opinion on questions of law and order, so he called for his advisers, who would know what should be done. 14 Those he most often turned to for advice were Carshena, Shethar, Admatha, Tarshish, Meres, Marsena, and Memucan — seven officials of Persia and Media who held the highest offices in the kingdom. 15 He said to these men, "I, King Xerxes, sent my servants to Queen Vashti with a command, and she refused to obey it! What does the law say that we should do with her?"

16 Then Memucan declared to the king and his officials: "Queen Vashti has insulted not only the king but also his officials — in fact, every man in the empire! 17 Every woman in the empire will start looking down on her husband as soon as she hears what the queen has done. They'll say, 'King Xerxes commanded Queen Vashti to come to him, and she refused.' 18 When the wives of the royal officials of Persia and Media hear about the queen's behavior, they will be telling their husbands about it before the day is out. Wives everywhere will have no respect for their husbands, and husbands will be angry with their wives. 19 If it please Your Majesty, issue a royal proclamation that Vashti may never again appear before the king. Have it written into the laws of Persia and Media, so that it can never be changed. Then give her place as queen to some better woman. 20 When your proclamation is made known all over this huge empire, every woman will treat her husband with proper respect, whether he's rich or poor."

21 The king and his officials liked this idea, and the king did what Memucan suggested. 22 To each of the royal provinces he sent a message in the language and the system of writing of that province, saying[c] that every husband should be the master of his home and speak with final authority.

Esther Becomes Queen

2 Later, even after the king's anger had cooled down, he kept thinking about what Vashti had done and about his proclamation against her. 2 So some of the king's advisers who were close to him suggested, "Why don't you make a search to find some beautiful young virgins? 3 You can appoint officials in every province of the empire and have them bring all these beautiful young women to your harem here in Susa, the capital city. Put them in the care of Hegai, the eunuch who is in charge of your women, and let them be given a beauty treatment. 4 Then take the young woman you like best and make her queen in Vashti's place."

The king thought this was good advice, so he followed it.

5 There in Susa lived a Jew named Mordecai son of Jair; he was from the tribe of Benjamin and was a descendant of Kish and Shimei. 6 When King Nebuchadnezzar of Babylon took King Jehoiachin of Judah into exile from Jerusalem, along with a group of captives, Mordecai was among them. 7 He had a cousin, Esther, whose Hebrew name was Hadassah; she was a beautiful young woman, and had a good figure. At the death of her parents, Mordecai had adopted her and brought her up as his own daughter.

8 When the king had issued his new proclamation and many young women were being brought to Susa, Esther was among them. She too was put in the royal palace in the care of Hegai, who had charge of the harem. 9 Hegai liked Esther, and she won his favor. He lost no

---

[b] There were no limits ... wanted; or But no one was forced to drink; the king had given orders to the palace servants that everyone could have as much or as little as they wanted.
[c] saying; or in order.

time in beginning her beauty treatment of massage and special diet. He gave her the best place in the harem and assigned seven young women specially chosen from the royal palace to serve her.

10 Now, on the advice of Mordecai, Esther had kept it secret that she was Jewish. 11 Every day Mordecai would walk back and forth in front of the courtyard of the harem, in order to find out how she was getting along and what was going to happen to her.

12 The regular beauty treatment for the women lasted a year — massages with oil of myrrh for six months and with oil of balsam for six more. After that, each woman would be taken in turn to King Xerxes. 13 When she went from the harem to the palace, she could wear whatever she wanted. 14 She would go there in the evening, and the next morning she would be taken to another harem and put in the care of Shaashgaz, the eunuch in charge of the king's concubines. She would not go to the king again unless he liked her enough to ask for her by name.

15 The time came for Esther to go to the king. Esther — the daughter of Abihail and the cousin of Mordecai, who had adopted her as his daughter; Esther — admired by everyone who saw her. When her turn came, she wore just what Hegai, the eunuch in charge of the harem, advised her to wear. 16 So in Xerxes' seventh year as king, in the tenth month, the month of Tebeth, Esther was brought to King Xerxes in the royal palace. 17 The king liked her more than any of the other women, and more than any of the others she won his favor and affection. He placed the royal crown on her head and made her queen in place of Vashti. 18 Then the king gave a great banquet in Esther's honor and invited all his officials and administrators. He proclaimed a holiday[d] for the whole empire and distributed gifts worthy of a king.

Mordecai Saves the King's Life

19 Meanwhile Mordecai had been appointed by the king to an administrative position. 20 As for Esther, she had still not let it be known that she was Jewish. Mordecai had told her not to tell anyone,

and she obeyed him in this, just as she had obeyed him when she was a little girl under his care.

21 During the time that Mordecai held office in the palace, Bigthana and Teresh, two of the palace eunuchs who guarded the entrance to the king's rooms, became hostile to King Xerxes and plotted to assassinate him. 22 Mordecai learned about it and told Queen Esther, who then told the king what Mordecai had found out. 23 There was an investigation, and it was discovered that the report was true, so both men were hanged on the gallows. The king ordered an account of this to be written down in the official records of the empire.

Haman Plots to Destroy the Jews

3 Some time later King Xerxes promoted a man named Haman to the position of prime minister. Haman was the son of Hammedatha, a descendant of Agag.[e] 2 The king ordered all the officials in his service to show their respect for Haman by kneeling and bowing to him. They all did so, except for Mordecai, who refused to do it. 3 The other officials in the royal service asked him why he was disobeying the king's command; 4 day after day they urged him to give in, but he would not listen to them. "I am a Jew," he explained, "and I cannot bow to Haman." So they told Haman about this, wondering if he would tolerate Mordecai's conduct. 5 Haman was furious when he realized that Mordecai was not going to kneel and bow to him, 6 and when he learned that Mordecai was a Jew, he decided to do more than punish Mordecai alone. He made plans to kill every Jew in the whole Persian Empire.

7 In the twelfth year of King Xerxes' rule, in the first month, the month of Nisan, Haman ordered the lots to be cast ("purim," they were called) to find out the right day and month to carry out his plot. The thirteenth day of the twelfth month, the month of Adar, was decided on.

8 So Haman told the king, "There is a certain race of people scattered all over your empire and found in every province. They observe customs that are not

---

d holiday; or remission of taxes.   e AGAG: An Amalekite king; his people were traditional enemies of the people of Israel.

THE JEWISH CALENDAR

The Jewish people used two kinds of calendars:
Civil Calendar—official calendar of kings, childbirth, and contracts.
Sacred Calendar—from which festivals were computed.

NAMES OF MONTHS	CORRESPONDS WITH	NUMBER OF DAYS	MONTH OF CIVIL YEAR	MONTH OF SACRED YEAR
ETHANIM	Sept.–Oct.	30	1st	7th
BUL	Oct.–Nov.	29 or 30	2nd	8th
KISLEV	Nov.–Dec.	29 or 30	3rd	9th
TEBETH	Dec.–Jan.	29	4th	10th
SHEBAT	Jan.–Feb.	30	5th	11th
***ADAR**	Feb.–Mar.	29 or 30	6th	12th
NISAN	Mar.–Apr.	30	7th	1st
ZIV	Apr.–May	29	8th	2nd
SIVAN	May–June	30	9th	3rd
TAMMUZ	June–July	29	10th	4th
AB	July–Aug.	30	11th	5th
ELUL	Aug.–Sept.	29	12th	6th

*Hebrew months were alternately 30 and 29 days long. Their year, shorter than ours, had 354 days. Therefore, about every 3 years (7 times in 19 years) an extra 29-day month, VEADAR, was added between ADAR and NISAN.

like those of any other people. Moreover, they do not obey the laws of the empire, so it is not in your best interests to tolerate them. 9 If it please Your Majesty, issue a decree that they are to be put to death. If you do, I guarantee that I will be able to put 375 tons of silver into the royal treasury for the administration of the empire."

10 The king took off his ring, which was used to stamp proclamations and make them official, and gave it to the enemy of the Jewish people, Haman son of Hammedatha, the descendant of Agag. 11 The king told him, "The people and their money are yours; do as you like with them."

12 So on the thirteenth day of the first month Haman called the king's secretaries and dictated a proclamation to be translated into every language and system of writing used in the empire and to be sent to all the rulers, governors, and officials. It was issued in the name of King Xerxes and stamped with his ring. 13 Runners took this proclamation to every province of the empire. It contained the instructions that on a single day, the thirteenth day of Adar, all Jews — young and old, women and children — were to be killed. They were to be slaughtered without mercy and their belongings were to be taken. 14 The contents of the proclamation were to be made public in every province, so that everyone would be prepared when that day came.

15 At the king's command the decree was made public in the capital city of Susa, and runners carried the news to the provinces. The king and Haman sat down and had a drink while the city of Susa was being thrown into confusion.

Mordecai Asks for Esther's Help

4 When Mordecai learned of all that had been done, he tore his clothes in anguish. Then he dressed in sackcloth, covered his head with ashes, and walked through the city, wailing loudly and bitterly, 2 until he came to the entrance of the palace. He did not go in because no one wearing sackcloth was allowed inside. 3 Throughout all the provinces, wherever the king's proclamation was made known, there was loud mourning among the Jews. They fasted, wept, wailed, and most of them put on sackcloth and lay in ashes.

4 When Esther's servant women and eunuchs told her what Mordecai was doing, she was deeply disturbed. She sent Mordecai some clothes to put on instead of the sackcloth, but he would not accept them. 5 Then she called Hathach, one of the palace eunuchs appointed as her servant by the king, and told him to go to Mordecai and find out what was happening and why. 6 Hathach went to Mordecai in the city square at the entrance of the palace. 7 Mordecai told him everything that had happened to him and just how much money Haman had promised to put into the royal treasury if all the Jews were killed. 8 He gave Hathach a copy of the proclamation that had been issued in Susa, ordering the destruction of the Jews. Mordecai asked him to take it to Esther, explain the situation to her, and have her go and plead with the king and beg him to have mercy on her people. 9 Hathach did this, 10 and Esther gave him this message to take back to Mordecai: 11 "If anyone, man or woman, goes to the inner courtyard and sees the king without being summoned, that person must die. That is the law; everyone, from the king's advisers to the people in the provinces, knows that. There is only one way to get around this law: if the king holds out his gold scepter to someone, then that person's life is spared. But it has been a month since the king sent for me."

12 When Mordecai received Esther's message, 13 he sent her this warning: "Don't imagine that you are safer than any other Jew just because you are in the royal palace. 14 If you keep quiet at a time like this, help will come from heaven to the Jews, and they will be saved, but you will die and your father's family will come to an end. Yet who knows — maybe it was for a time like this that you were made queen!"

15 Esther sent Mordecai this reply: 16 "Go and get all the Jews in Susa together; hold a fast and pray for me. Don't eat or drink anything for three days and nights. My servant women and I will be doing the same. After that, I will go to the king, even though it is against the law. If I must die for doing it, I will die."

ESTHER

17 Mordecai then left and did everything that Esther had told him to do.

Esther Invites the King and Haman to a Banquet

5 On the third day of her fast Esther put on her royal robes and went and stood in the inner courtyard of the palace, facing the throne room. The king was inside, seated on the royal throne, facing the entrance. 2 When the king saw Queen Esther standing outside, she won his favor, and he held out to her the gold scepter. She then came up and touched the tip of it. 3 "What is it, Queen Esther?" the king asked. "Tell me what you want, and you shall have it—even if it is half my empire."

4 Esther replied, "If it please Your Majesty, I would like you and Haman to be my guests tonight at a banquet I am preparing for you."

5 The king then ordered Haman to come quickly, so that they could be Esther's guests. So the king and Haman went to Esther's banquet. 6 Over the wine the king asked her, "Tell me what you want, and you shall have it. I will grant your request, even if you ask for half my empire."

7 Esther replied, 8 "If Your Majesty is kind enough to grant my request, I would like you and Haman to be my guests tomorrow at another banquet that I will prepare for you. At that time I will tell you what I want."

Haman Plots to Kill Mordecai

9 When Haman left the banquet he was happy and in a good mood. But then he saw Mordecai at the entrance of the palace, and when Mordecai did not rise or show any sign of respect as he passed, Haman was furious with him. 10 But he controlled himself and went on home. Then he invited his friends to his house and asked his wife Zeresh to join them. 11 He boasted to them about how rich he was, how many sons he had, how the king had promoted him to high office, and how much more important he was than any of the king's other officials. 12 "What is more," Haman went on, "Queen Esther gave a banquet for no one but the king and me, and we are invited back tomorrow. 13 But none of this

means a thing to me as long as I see that Jew Mordecai sitting at the entrance of the palace."

14 So his wife and all his friends suggested, "Why don't you have a gallows built, seventy-five feet tall? Tomorrow morning you can ask the king to have Mordecai hanged on it, and then you can go to the banquet happy."

Haman thought this was a good idea, so he had the gallows built.

The King Honors Mordecai

6 That same night the king could not get to sleep, so he had the official records of the empire brought and read to him. 2 The part they read included the account of how Mordecai had uncovered a plot to assassinate the king—the plot made by Bigthana and Teresh, the two palace eunuchs who had guarded the king's rooms. 3 The king asked, "How have we honored and rewarded Mordecai for this?"

His servants answered, "Nothing has been done for him."

4 "Are any of my officials in the palace?" the king asked.

Now Haman had just entered the courtyard; he had come to ask the king to have Mordecai hanged on the gallows that was now ready. 5 So the servants answered, "Haman is here, waiting to see you."

"Show him in," said the king.

6 So Haman came in, and the king said to him, "There is someone I wish very much to honor. What should I do for this man?"

Haman thought to himself, "Now who could the king want to honor so much? Me, of course."

7-8 So he answered the king, "Have royal robes brought for this man—robes that you yourself wear. Have a royal ornament[f] put on your own horse. 9 Then have one of your highest noblemen dress the man in these robes and lead him, mounted on the horse, through the city square. Have the nobleman announce as they go: 'See how the king rewards someone he wishes to honor!' "

10 Then the king said to Haman, "Hurry and get the robes and the horse, and provide these honors for Mordecai the Jew. Do everything for him that you

---

[f] ORNAMENT: *Probably a type of crown.*

PERSIAN CUSTOMS IN THE BOOK OF ESTHER

The Book of Esther records events during the reign of King Xerxes in the fifth century B.C. at Susa (Shushan), administrative capital of the Persian Empire. After the death of Darius I (the Persian king who had allowed any Jews who desired to return to their homeland to do so), his son Xerxes became king. Xerxes was the king who became dissatisfied with his queen Vashti and banished her, marrying Esther.

Royal Persian feasts were noted for their splendor and opulence. Esther describes the Persian custom of eating while reclining on beds or couches. "Drinks were served in gold cups, no two of them alike" (Es 1.7).

Special laws protected the Persian king. Esther 1.14 refers to the seven officials who "held the highest offices in the kingdom." These were the chief nobles who were his advisors. Only a person summoned by the king could visit him, a custom which signified his royalty, as well as protected him from would-be assassins. Esther feared going to Xerxes without being called because the punishment for such a visit was death (Es 4.11).

The Persian Empire boasted about a well-organized postal system (Es 3.13). The king's ring (Es 8.8) was the signet ring, or the royal seal, with which official documents were signed. In ancient Persia documents were sealed in two ways: with a signet ring if they were written on papyrus, or with a cylinder seal if written on clay tablets. Among the objects excavated at the royal city of Persepolis was a cylinder seal, which belonged to King Xerxes.

The Book of Esther also refers to "the laws of Persia and Media" (1.19). This phrase describes the ironclad nature of the laws that governed the Persian Empire. Once a law was issued, it could not be changed or revoked—not even by the king himself.

have suggested. You will find him sitting at the entrance of the palace."

11 So Haman got the robes and the horse, and he put the robes on Mordecai. Mordecai got on the horse, and Haman led him through the city square, announcing to the people as they went: "See how the king rewards a man he wishes to honor!"

12 Mordecai then went back to the palace entrance while Haman hurried home, covering his face in embarrassment. 13 He told his wife and all his friends everything that had happened to him. Then she and those wise friends of his told him, "You are beginning to lose power to Mordecai. He is a Jew, and you cannot overcome him. He will certainly defeat you."

Haman Is Put to Death

14 While they are still talking, the palace eunuchs arrived in a hurry to

7 take Haman to Esther's banquet. ¹And so the king and Haman went to eat with Esther ²for a second time. Over the wine the king asked her again, "Now, Queen Esther, what do you want? Tell me and you shall have it. I'll even give you half the empire."

3 Queen Esther answered, "If it please Your Majesty to grant my humble request, my wish is that I may live and that my people may live. 4 My people and I have been sold for slaughter. If it were nothing more serious than being sold into slavery, I would have kept quiet and not bothered you about it;g but we are about to be destroyed — exterminated!"

5 Then King Xerxes asked Queen Esther, "Who dares to do such a thing? Where is this man?"

6 Esther answered, "Our enemy, our persecutor, is this evil man Haman!"

Haman faced the king and queen with terror. 7 The king got up in a fury, left the room, and went outside to the palace gardens. Haman could see that the king was determined to punish him for this, so he stayed behind to beg Queen Esther for his life. 8 He had just thrown himself down on Esther's couch to beg for mercy, when the king came back into the room from the gardens. Seeing this, the king cried out, "Is this man going to

rape the queen right here in front of me, in my own palace?"

The king had no sooner said this than the eunuchs covered Haman's head. 9 Then one of them, who was named Harbonah, said, "Haman even went so far as to build a gallows at his house so that he could hang Mordecai, who saved Your Majesty's life. And it's seventy-five feet tall!"

"Hang Haman on it!" the king commanded.

10 So Haman was hanged on the gallows that he had built for Mordecai. Then the king's anger cooled down.

The Jews Are Told to Fight Back

8 That same day King Xerxes gave Queen Esther all the property of Haman, the enemy of the Jews. Esther told the king that Mordecai was related to her, and from then on Mordecai was allowed to enter the king's presence. 2 The king took off his ring with his seal on it (which he had taken back from Haman) and gave it to Mordecai. Esther put Mordecai in charge of Haman's property.

3 Then Esther spoke to the king again, throwing herself at his feet and crying. She begged him to do something to stop the evil plot that Haman, the descendant of Agag,h had made against the Jews. 4 The king held out the gold scepter to her, so she stood up and said, 5 "If it please Your Majesty, and if you care about me and if it seems right to you, please issue a proclamation to keep Haman's orders from being carried out — those orders that the son of Hammedatha the descendant of Agag gave for the destruction of all the Jews in the empire. 6 How can I endure it if this disaster comes on my people, and my own relatives are killed?"

7 King Xerxes then said to Queen Esther and Mordecai, the Jew, "Look, I have hanged Haman for his plot against the Jews, and I have given Esther his property. 8 But a proclamation issued in the king's name and stamped with the royal seal cannot be revoked. You may, however, write to the Jews whatever you like; and you may write it in my name and stamp it with the royal seal."

9 This happened on the twenty-third

---

g *Probable text* and not . . . it; *Hebrew unclear.*   h AGAG: *See 3.1.*

day of the third month, the month of Sivan. Mordecai called the king's secretaries and dictated letters to the Jews and to the governors, administrators, and officials of all the 127 provinces from India to Ethiopia.[i] The letters were written to each province in its own language and system of writing and to the Jews in their language and system of writing. 10 Mordecai had the letters written in the name of King Xerxes, and he stamped them with the royal seal. They were delivered by riders mounted on fast horses from the royal stables.

11 These letters explained that the king would allow the Jews in every city to organize for self-defense. If armed men of any nationality in any province attacked the Jewish men, their children, or their women, the Jews could fight back and destroy the attackers; they could slaughter them to the last man and take their possessions. 12 This decree was to take effect throughout the Persian Empire on the day set for the slaughter of the Jews, the thirteenth of Adar, the twelfth month. 13 It was to be proclaimed as law and made known to everyone in every province, so that the Jews would be ready to take revenge on their enemies when that day came. 14 At the king's command the riders mounted royal horses and rode off at top speed. The decree was also made public in Susa, the capital city.

15 Mordecai left the palace, wearing royal robes of blue and white, a cloak of fine purple linen, and a magnificent gold crown. Then the streets of Susa rang with cheers and joyful shouts. 16 For the Jews there was joy and relief, happiness and a sense of victory. 17 In every city and province, wherever the king's proclamation was read, the Jews held a joyful holiday with feasting and happiness. In fact, many other people became Jews, because they were afraid of them now.

The Jews Destroy Their Enemies

9 The thirteenth day of Adar came, the day on which the royal proclamation was to take effect, the day when the enemies of the Jews were hoping to get them in their power. But instead, the Jews triumphed over them. 2 In the Jewish quarter of every city[j] in the empire the Jews organized to attack anyone who tried to harm them. People everywhere were afraid of them, and no one could stand against them. 3 In fact, all the provincial officials — governors, administrators, and royal representatives — helped the Jews because they were all afraid of Mordecai. 4 It was well-known throughout the empire that Mordecai was now a powerful man in the palace and was growing more powerful. 5 So the Jews could do what they wanted with their enemies. They attacked them with swords and slaughtered them.

6 In Susa, the capital city itself, the Jews killed five hundred people. 7-10 Among them were the ten sons of Haman son of Hammedatha, the enemy of the Jews: Parshandatha, Dalphon, Aspatha, Poratha, Adalia, Aridatha, Parmashta, Arisai, Aridai, and Vaizatha. However, there was no looting.

11 That same day the number of people killed in Susa was reported to the king. 12 He then said to Queen Esther, "In Susa alone the Jews have killed five hundred people, including Haman's ten sons. What must they have done out in the provinces! What do you want now? You shall have it. Tell me what else you want, and you shall have it."

13 Esther answered, "If it please Your Majesty, let the Jews in Susa do again tomorrow what they were allowed to do today. And have the bodies of Haman's ten sons hung from the gallows." 14 The king ordered this to be done, and the proclamation was issued in Susa. The bodies of Haman's ten sons were publicly displayed. 15 On the fourteenth day of Adar the Jews of Susa got together again and killed three hundred more people in the city. But again, they did no looting.

16 The Jews in the provinces also organized and defended themselves. They rid themselves of their enemies by killing seventy-five thousand people who hated them. But they did no looting. 17 This was on the thirteenth day of Adar. On the next day, the fourteenth,

[i] Hebrew Cush: Cush is the ancient name of the extensive territory south of the First Cataract of the Nile River. This region was called Ethiopia in Graeco-Roman times, and included within its borders most of modern Sudan and some of present-day Ethiopia (Abyssinia).
[j] In the Jewish quarter of every city; or In every Jewish city.

there was no more killing, and they made it a joyful day of feasting. 18 The Jews of Susa, however, made the fifteenth a holiday, since they had slaughtered their enemies on the thirteenth and fourteenth and then stopped on the fifteenth. 19 This is why Jews who live in small towns observe the fourteenth day of the month of Adar as a joyous holiday, a time for feasting and giving gifts of food to one another.

The Festival of Purim

20 Mordecai had these events written down and sent letters to all the Jews, near and far, throughout the Persian Empire, 21 telling them to observe the fourteenth and fifteenth days of Adar as holidays every year. 22 These were the days on which the Jews had rid themselves of their enemies; this was a month that had been turned from a time of grief and despair into a time of joy and happiness. They were told to observe these days with feasts and parties, giving gifts of food to one another and to the poor. 23 So the Jews followed Mordecai's instructions, and the celebration became an annual custom.

24 Haman son of Hammedatha—the descendant of Agag and the enemy of the Jewish people—had cast lots ("purim," they were called) to determine the day for destroying the Jews; he had planned to wipe them out. 25 But Esther went to the king, and the king issued written orders with the result that Haman suffered the fate he had planned for the Jews—he and his sons were hanged from the gallows. 26 That is why the holidays are called Purim. Because of Mordecai's letter and because of all that had happened to them, 27 the Jews made it a rule for themselves, their descendants,

and anyone who might become a Jew, that at the proper time each year these two days would be regularly observed according to Mordecai's instructions. 28 It was resolved that every Jewish family of every future generation in every province and every city should remember and observe the days of Purim for all time to come.

29 Then Queen Esther, the daughter of Abihail, along with Mordecai, also wrote a letter, putting her full authority behind the letter about Purim, which Mordecai had written earlier. 30 The letter was addressed to all the Jews, and copies were sent to all the 127 provinces of the Persian Empire. It wished the Jews peace and security 31 and directed them and their descendants to observe the days of Purim at the proper time, just as they had adopted rules for the observance of fasts and times of mourning. This was commanded by both Mordecai and Queen Esther. 32 Esther's command, confirming the rules for Purim, was written down on a scroll.

The Greatness of Xerxes and Mordecai

10 King Xerxes imposed forced labor on the people of the coastal regions of his empire as well as on those of the interior. 2 All the great and wonderful things he did, as well as the whole story of how he promoted Mordecai to high office, are recorded in the official records of the kings of Persia and Media. 3 Mordecai the Jew was second in rank only to King Xerxes himself. He was honored and well-liked by his fellow Jews. He worked for the good of his people and for the security of all their descendants.

POETICAL AND WISDOM BOOKS

In the Hebrew canon, these books are included in The Writings. The books of poetry include the Psalms, Song of Songs, and Lamentations. The wisdom books are Job, Proverbs, and Ecclesiastes. This does not mean all poetry in the Bible is found in Psalms and Song of Songs, nor that all wisdom is found in only three books. Poetry abounds in the Torah and the Prophets. Much of the wisdom literature is written in poetic form. On the other hand, wisdom is also found throughout the Bible.

The Psalms were the hymn book and prayer book of the second temple, and continue to be used in the same way by the Jewish community today. Traditionally, the Psalms were ascribed to David, but a reading of the subheads shows there are several collections of Psalms, including many by David, but also collections credited to the sons of Korah, to Asaph, to Solomon, even to Moses. There are also many kinds of Psalms, just as there are many types of hymns in a modern hymnal. There are songs of praise and thanksgiving, songs of ascent which were sung going up to the temple, royal psalms, prayers, laments, and so on. The Psalms are one of the favorite books for Christians and many of the biblical passages that are most meaningful come from the Psalms.

Song of Songs is a collection of love poems, which are beautiful expressions of human love at its best. They remind us that God is present in all of life.

Lamentations is a collection of poems of deep bitterness and grief over the destruction of Jerusalem and the Temple by the Babylonians in 586 B.C.

Wisdom literature also takes several different forms. Sometimes it is short sayings on how to cope with life. The theme is usually how virture can triumph over wrong. Sometimes wisdom takes the form of riddles. Or wisdom can be reflections on the meaning of life or on the life of faith (what we might call philosophy).

The heart of wisdom literature is a theology of creation and life. God has made the world and everything in it. We can learn something about God and life by observing nature. Because God is in all of life, we are called to live joyfully as well as responsibly. A great deal of wisdom literature deals with how to live the good life, that is, the life God approves.

Job begins with the undeserved suffering of the patriarch Job and reflects on the meaning of suffering and God's relationship to one who suffers unjustly. Job suffers most because he refuses to deny his own integrity or the integrity of God.

Proverbs is a collection of sayings about how to live the good life. It also contains the great passage on the personification of wisdom as God's hand-maid, delighting in the works of creation.

Ecclesiastes reads almost like a diary of a spiritual journey. The author deals with ultimate questions of life and death, while talking about the routines of daily life. He reflects on what his life has meant from youth to old age, and how God has played a part in that life.

The Book of

JOB

Introduction

The Book of Job *is the story of a good man who suffers total disaster—he loses all his children and property and is afflicted with a repulsive disease. Then in three series of poetic dialogues the author shows how Job's friends and Job himself react to these calamities. In the end, God himself, whose dealings with the human race have been a prominent part of the discussion, appears to Job.*

The friends of Job explain his suffering in traditional religious terms. Since God, so they assume, always rewards good and punishes evil, the sufferings of Job can only mean that he has sinned. But for Job this is too simple; he does not deserve such cruel punishment, because he has been an unusually good and righteous man. He cannot understand how God can let so much evil happen to one like himself, and he boldly challenges God. Job does not lose his faith, but he does long to be justified before God and to regain his honor as a good man.

God does not give an answer to Job's questions, but he does respond to Job's faith by overwhelming him with a poetic picture of his divine power and wisdom. Job then humbly acknowledges God as wise and great, and repents of the wild and angry words he had used.

The prose conclusion records how Job is restored to his former condition, with even greater prosperity than before. God reprimands Job's friends for failing to understand the meaning of Job's suffering. Only Job had really sensed that God is greater than traditional religion had depicted him.

Outline of Contents

Satan Tests Job

1 There was a man named Job, living in the land of Uz,*a* who worshiped God and was faithful to him. He was a good man, careful not to do anything evil. ²He had seven sons and three daughters, ³and owned seven thousand sheep, three thousand camels, one thousand head of cattle, and five hundred donkeys. He also had a large number of servants and was the richest man in the East.

⁴Job's sons used to take turns giving a feast, to which all the others would come, and they always invited their three sisters to join them. ⁵The morning after each feast, Job would get up early and offer sacrifices for each of his children in order to purify them. He always did this because he thought that one of them might have sinned by insulting God unintentionally.

⁶When the day came for the heavenly beings*b* to appear before the LORD, Satan*c* was there among them. ⁷The LORD asked him, "What have you been doing?"

Satan answered, "I have been walking here and there, roaming around the earth."

⁸"Did you notice my servant Job?" the

---

a UZ: *An area whose exact location is unknown.*   *b* HEAVENLY BEINGS: *Supernatural beings who serve God in heaven.*   *c* SATAN: *A supernatural being whose name indicates he was regarded as the opponent of human beings.*

LORD asked. "There is no one on earth as faithful and good as he is. He worships me and is careful not to do anything evil."

9 Satan replied, "Would Job worship you if he got nothing out of it? 10 You have always protected him and his family and everything he owns. You bless everything he does, and you have given him enough cattle to fill the whole country. 11 But now suppose you take away everything he has—he will curse you to your face!"

12 "All right," the LORD said to Satan, "everything he has is in your power, but you must not hurt Job himself." So Satan left.

Job's Children and Wealth Are Destroyed

13 One day when Job's children were having a feast at the home of their oldest brother, 14 a messenger came running to Job. "We were plowing the fields with the oxen," he said, "and the donkeys were in a nearby pasture. 15 Suddenly the Sabeans d attacked and stole them all. They killed every one of your servants except me. I am the only one who escaped to tell you."

16 Before he had finished speaking, another servant came and said, "Lightning struck the sheep and the shepherds and killed them all. I am the only one who escaped to tell you."

17 Before he had finished speaking, another servant came and said, "Three bands of Chaldean e raiders attacked us, took away the camels, and killed all your servants except me. I am the only one who escaped to tell you."

18 Before he had finished speaking, another servant came and said, "Your children were having a feast at the home of your oldest son, 19 when a storm swept in from the desert. It blew the house down and killed them all. I am the only one who escaped to tell you."

20 Then Job got up and tore his clothes in grief. He shaved his head and threw himself face downward on the ground. 21 He said, "I was born with nothing, and I will die with nothing. The LORD gave, and now he has taken away. May his name be praised!"

22 In spite of everything that had happened, Job did not sin by blaming God.

Satan Tests Job Again

2 When the day came for the heavenly beings to appear before the LORD again, Satan was there among them. 2 The LORD asked him, "Where have you been?"

Satan answered, "I have been walking here and there, roaming around the earth."

3 "Did you notice my servant Job?" the LORD asked. "There is no one on earth as faithful and good as he is. He worships me and is careful not to do anything evil. You persuaded me to let you attack him for no reason at all, but Job is still as faithful as ever."

4 Satan replied, "A person will give up everything in order to stay alive. 5 But now suppose you hurt his body—he will curse you to your face!"

6 So the LORD said to Satan, "All right, he is in your power, but you are not to kill him."

7 Then Satan left the LORD's presence and made sores break out all over Job's body. 8 Job went and sat by the garbage dump and took a piece of broken pottery to scrape his sores. 9 His wife said to him, "You are still as faithful as ever, aren't you? Why don't you curse God and die?"

10 Job answered, "You are talking nonsense! When God sends us something good, we welcome it. How can we complain when he sends us trouble?" Even in all this suffering Job said nothing against God.

Job's Friends Come

11 Three of Job's friends were Eliphaz, from the city of Teman, Bildad, from the land of Shuah, and Zophar, from the land of Naamah. When they heard how much Job had been suffering, they decided to go and comfort him. 12 While they were still a long way off they saw Job, but did not recognize him. When they did, they began to weep and wail, tearing their clothes in grief and throwing dust into the air and on their heads. 13 Then they sat there on the ground with him for seven days and nights without

---

d SABEANS: A tribe of wandering raiders from the south.   e CHALDEANS: A tribe of wandering raiders from the north.

saying a word, because they saw how much he was suffering.

Job's Complaint to God

3 Finally Job broke the silence and cursed the day on which he had been born.

Job

2-3 O God, put a curse on the day I
   was born;
   put a curse on the night when I
      was conceived!
4 Turn that day into darkness, God.
   Never again remember that day;
   never again let light shine on it.
5 Make it a day of gloom and thick
      darkness;
   cover it with clouds, and blot out
      the sun.
6 Blot that night out of the year,
   and never let it be counted
      again;
7   make it a barren, joyless night.
8 Tell the sorcerers to curse
      that day,
   those who know how to control
      Leviathan.*f*
9 Keep the morning star from
      shining;
   give that night no hope of dawn.
10 Curse that night for letting me be
      born,
   for exposing me to trouble and
      grief.

11 I wish I had died in my mother's
      womb
   or died the moment I was born.
12 Why did my mother hold me on
      her knees?
   Why did she feed me at her
      breast?
13 If I had died then, I would be at
      rest now,
14   sleeping like the kings and
      rulers
   who rebuilt ancient palaces.
15 Then I would be sleeping like
      princes
   who filled their houses with gold
      and silver,
16   or sleeping like a stillborn child.
17 In the grave wicked people stop
      their evil,

and tired workers find rest at
   last.
18 Even prisoners enjoy peace,
   free from shouts and harsh
      commands.
19 Everyone is there, the famous and
   the unknown,
   and slaves at last are free.

20 Why let people go on living in
      misery?
   Why give light to those in grief?
21 They wait for death, but it never
      comes;
   they prefer a grave to any
      treasure.
22 They are not happy till they are
   dead and buried;
23   God keeps their future hidden
   and hems them in on every side.
24 Instead of eating, I mourn,
   and I can never stop groaning.
25 Everything I fear and dread comes
      true.
26 I have no peace, no rest,
   and my troubles never end.

The First Dialogue
(4.1 — 14.22)

4

Eliphaz

1-2 Job, will you be annoyed if I
      speak?
   I can't keep quiet any longer.
3 You have taught many people
   and given strength to feeble
      hands.
4 When someone stumbled, weak
      and tired,
   your words encouraged him to
      stand.
5 Now it's your turn to be in trouble,
   and you are too stunned to
      face it.
6 You worshiped God, and your life
      was blameless;
   and so you should have
      confidence and hope.
7 Think back now. Name a single
      case
   where someone righteous met
      with disaster.
8 I have seen people plow fields of
      evil

f LEVIATHAN: Some take this to be the crocodile, others a legendary monster. Magicians were thought to be able to make him cause eclipses of the sun.

and plant wickedness like seed;
now they harvest wickedness
and evil.
9 Like a storm, God destroys them
in his anger.
10 The wicked roar and growl like
lions,
but God silences them and
breaks their teeth.
11 Like lions with nothing to kill
and eat,
they die, and all their children
are scattered.

12 Once a message came quietly,
so quietly I could hardly hear it.
13 Like a nightmare it disturbed my
sleep.
14   I trembled and shuddered;
my whole body shook with fear.
15 A light breeze touched my face,
and my skin crawled with fright.
16 I could see something standing
there;
I stared, but couldn't tell what
it was.
Then I heard a voice out of the
silence:
17 "Can anyone be righteous in the
sight of*g* God
or be before*h* his Creator?
18 God does not trust his heavenly
servants;
he finds fault even with his
angels.
19 Do you think he will trust a
creature of clay,
a thing of dust that can be
crushed like a moth?
20 We may be alive in the morning,
but die unnoticed before evening
comes.
21 All that we have is taken away;
we die, still lacking wisdom."

5 Call out, Job. See if anyone
answers.
Is there any angel to whom you
can turn?
2 To worry yourself to death with
resentment
would be a foolish, senseless
thing to do.
3 I have seen fools who looked
secure,

but I called down a sudden curse
on their homes.
4 Their children can never find
safety;
no one stands up to defend them
in court.
5 Hungry people will eat the fool's
crops—
even the grain growing among
thorns*i*—
and thirsty people will envy his
wealth.
6 Evil does not grow in the soil,
nor does trouble grow out of the
ground.
7 No indeed! We bring trouble on
ourselves,
as surely as sparks fly up from
a fire.*j*

8 If I were you, I would turn to God
and present my case to him.
9 We cannot understand the great
things he does,
and to his miracles there is
no end.
10 He sends rain on the land
and he waters the fields.
11 Yes, it is God who raises the
humble
and gives joy to all who mourn.
12-13 He upsets the plans of cunning
people,
and traps the wise in their own
schemes,
so that nothing they do
succeeds;
14   even at noon they grope in
darkness.
15 But God saves the poor*k* from
death;
he saves the needy from
oppression.
16 He gives hope to the poor and
silences the wicked.

17 Happy is the person whom God
corrects!
Do not resent it when he
rebukes you.
18 God bandages the wounds he
makes;
his hand hurts you, and his
hand heals.

---

g righteous in the sight of; *or more righteous than.*
i *Probable text even . . . thorns; Hebrew unclear.*
the sky.   *k* *Probable text poor; Hebrew unclear.*
h be pure before; *or be more pure than.*
j sparks fly up from a fire; *or birds fly up to*

JOB

19 Time after time he will save you
    from harm;
20 when famine comes, he will
    keep you alive,
    and in war protect you from
    death.
21 God will rescue you from slander;
    he will save you when
    destruction comes.
22 You will laugh at violence and
    hunger
    and not be afraid of wild
    animals.
23 The fields you plow will be free
    of rocks;
    wild animals will never
    attack you.
24 Then you will live at peace in your
    tent;
    when you look at your sheep,
    you will find them safe.
25 You will have as many children
    as there are blades of grass in a
    pasture.
26 Like wheat that ripens till harvest
    time,
    you will live to a ripe old age.
27 Job, we have learned this by long
    study.
    It is true, so now accept it.

6

Job

1-2 If my troubles and griefs were
    weighed on scales,
3   they would weigh more than the
    sands of the sea,
    so my wild words should not
    surprise you.
4 Almighty God has shot me with
    arrows,
    and their poison spreads
    through my body.
    God has lined up his terrors
    against me.

5 A donkey is content when eating
    grass,
    and a cow is quiet when
    eating hay.
6 But who can eat flat, unsalted
    food?

What taste is there in the white
    of an egg?
7 I have no appetite for food like
    that,
    and everything I eat makes me
    sick.*l*

8 Why won't God give me what
    I ask?
    Why won't he answer my
    prayer?
9 If only he would go ahead and
    kill me!
10 If I knew he would, I would leap
    for joy,
    no matter how great my pain.
    I know that God is holy;
    I have never opposed what he
    commands.
11 What strength do I have to keep
    on living?
    Why go on living when I have
    no hope?
12 Am I made of stone? Is my body
    bronze?
13 I have no strength left to save
    myself;
    there is nowhere I can turn for
    help.

14 In trouble*m* like this I need loyal
    friends —
    whether I've forsaken God
    or not.
15 But you, my friends, you deceive
    me like streams
    that go dry when no rain comes.
16 The streams are choked with snow
    and ice,
17 but in the heat they disappear,
    and the stream beds lie bare
    and dry.
18 Caravans get lost looking for
    water;
    they wander and die in the
    desert.
19 Caravans from Sheba and Tema
    search,
20 but their hope dies beside dry
    streams.
21 You are like*n* those streams
    to me,*o*
    you see my fate and draw back
    in fear.

l Probable text sick; *Hebrew unclear.*   *m Probable text* trouble; *Hebrew unclear.*
n Probable text like; *Hebrew* because.   *o Some ancient translations* and one; *Hebrew
manuscript* to me; *most Hebrew manuscripts have two different expressions:* nothing *in the
text and* to him *in the margin.*

22 Have I asked you to give me a gift
    or to bribe someone on my
    behalf
23   or to save me from some enemy
    or tyrant?

24 All right, teach me; tell me my
    faults.
    I will be quiet and listen to you.
25 Honest words are convincing,
    but you are talking nonsense.
26 You think I am talking nothing but
    wind;
    then why do you answer my
    words of despair?
27 You would even roll dice for
    orphan slaves
    and make yourselves rich off
    your closest friends!
28 Look me in the face. I won't lie.
29 You have gone far enough. Stop
    being unjust.
    Don't condemn me. I'm in the
    right.
30 But you think I am lying —
    you think I can't tell right from
    wrong.

7 Human life is like forced army
    service,
    like a life of hard manual labor,
2   like a slave longing for cool
    shade;
    like a worker waiting to be paid.
3 Month after month I have nothing
    to live for;
    night after night brings me grief.
4 When I lie down to sleep, the
    hours drag;
    I toss all night and long for
    dawn.
5 My body is full of worms;
    it is covered with scabs;
    pus runs out of my sores.
6 My days pass by without hope,
    pass faster than a weaver's
    shuttle.p

7 Remember, O God, my life is only
    a breath;
    my happiness has already
    ended.
8 You see me now, but never again.
    If you look for me, I'll be gone.

9-10 Like a cloud that fades and is
    gone,
    we humans die and never
    return;
    we are forgotten by all who
    knew us.
11 No! I can't be quiet!
    I am angry and bitter.
    I have to speak.

12 Why do you keep me under
    guard?
    Do you think I am a sea
    monster?q
13 I lie down and try to rest;
    I look for relief from my pain.
14 But you — you terrify me with
    dreams;
    you send me visions and
    nightmares
15   until I would rather be strangled
    than live in this miserable body.
16 I give up; I am tired of living.
    Leave me alone. My life makes no
    sense.

17 Why are people so important
    to you?
    Why pay attention to what
    they do?
18 You inspect them every morning
    and test them every minute.
19 Won't you look away long enough
    for me to swallow my spit?
20 Are you harmed by my sin, you
    jailer?
    Why use me for your target
    practice?
    Am I so great a burden to you?
21 Can't you ever forgive my sin?
    Can't you pardon the wrong
    I do?
    Soon I will be in my grave,
    and I'll be gone when you look
    for me.

8

Bildad
1-2 Are you finally through with your
    windy speech?
3 God never twists justice;
    he never fails to do what is
    right.

---

p WEAVER'S SHUTTLE: *A small device in the loom which carries threads back and forth rapidly in
weaving cloth.*   q SEA MONSTER: *A reference to ancient stories in which sea monsters had to be
guarded so that they would not escape and do damage.*

4 Your children must have sinned
   against God,
   and so he punished them as they
   deserved.
5 But turn now and plead with
   Almighty God;
6   if you are so honest and pure,
   then God will come and
   help you
   and restore your household as
   your reward.
7 All the wealth you lost will be
   nothing
   compared with what God will
   give you then.

8 Look for a moment at ancient
   wisdom;
   consider the truths our ancestors
   learned.
9 Our life is short, we know nothing
   at all;
   we pass like shadows across the
   earth.
10 But let the ancient wise people
   teach you;
   listen to what they had to say:

11 "Reeds can't grow where there is
   no water;
   they are never found outside a
   swamp.
12 If the water dries up, they are the
   first to wither,
   while still too small to be cut
   and used.
13 Godless people are like those
   reeds;
   their hope is gone, once God is
   forgotten.
14 They trust a thread—a
   spider's web.
15   If they lean on a web, will it
   hold them up?
   If they grab for a thread, will it
   help them stand?"

16 Evil people sprout like weeds in
   the sun,
   like weeds that spread all
   through the garden.
17 Their roots wrap around the
   stones
   and hold fast to[r] every rock.
18 But then pull them up—

no one will ever know they were
   there.
19 Yes, that's all the joy evil people
   have;
   others now come and take their
   places.

20 But God will never abandon the
   faithful
   or ever give help to evil people.
21 He will let you laugh and shout
   again,
22   but he will bring disgrace on
   those who hate you,
   and the homes of the wicked
   will vanish.

9
Job

1-2 Yes, I've heard all that before.
   But how can a human being win
   a case against God?
3 How can anyone argue with him?
   He can ask a thousand questions
   that no one could ever answer.[s]
4 God is so wise and powerful;
   no one can stand up
   against him.
5 Without warning he moves
   mountains
   and in anger he destroys them.
6 God sends earthquakes and
   shakes the ground;
   he rocks the pillars that support
   the earth.
7 He can keep the sun from rising,
   and the stars from shining at
   night.
8 No one helped God spread out the
   heavens
   or trample the sea monster's
   back.[t]
9 God hung the stars in the sky—the
   Dipper,
   Orion, the Pleiades, and the
   stars of the south.
10 We cannot understand the great
   things he does,
   and to his miracles there is
   no end.

11 God passes by, but I cannot
   see him.

---

r *Probable text* hold fast to; *Hebrew* see.   s He can ask . . . answer; *or* Someone could ask him
a thousand questions, and he would not answer.   t TRAMPLE THE SEA MONSTER'S BACK: *A reference
to ancient stories in which a sea monster was killed and then trampled (see also 26.13).*

12 He takes what he wants, and no
    one can stop him;
    no one dares ask him, "What are
    you doing?"
13 God's anger is constant. He
    crushed his enemies
    who helped Rahab,ᵘ the sea
    monster, oppose him.
14 So how can I find words to
    answer God?
15 Though I am innocent, all I can do
    is beg for mercy from God my
    judge.
16 Yet even then, if he lets me speak,
    I can't believe he would listen
    to me.
17 He sends storms to batter and
    bruise me
    without any reason at all.
18 He won't let me catch my breath;
    he has filled my life with
    bitterness.
19 Should I try force? Try force
    on God?
    Should I take him to court? Could
    anyone make him go?ᵛ
20 I am innocent and faithful, but my
    words sound guilty,
    and everything I say seems to
    condemn me.
21-22 I am innocent, but I no longer
    care.
    I am sick of living. Nothing
    matters;
    innocent or guilty, God will
    destroy us.
23 When an innocent person
    suddenly dies,
    God laughs.
24 God gave the world to the wicked.
    He made all the judges blind.
    And if God didn't do it, who did?

25 My days race by, not one of them
    good.
26 My life passes like the swiftest
    boat,
    as fast as an eagle swooping
    down on a rabbit.
27-28 If I smile and try to forget my
    pain,
    all my suffering comes back to
    haunt me;
    I know that God does hold me
    guilty.

29 Since I am held guilty, why should
    I bother?
30 No soap can wash away my
    sins.
31 God throws me into a pit with
    filth,
    and even my clothes are
    ashamed of me.
32 If God were human, I could
    answer him;
    we could go to court to decide
    our quarrel.
33 But there is no one to step
    between us —
    no one to judge both God
    and me.
34 Stop punishing me, God!
    Keep your terrors away!
35 I am not afraid. I am going to talk
    because I know my own heart.

10 I am tired of living.
       Listen to my bitter complaint.
2 Don't condemn me, God.
    Tell me! What is the charge
    against me?
3 Is it right for you to be so cruel?
    To despise what you yourself
    have made?
    And then to smile on the
    schemes of wicked people?
4 Do you see things as we do?
5 Is your life as short as ours?
6 Then why do you track down all
    my sins
    and hunt down every fault I
    have?
7 You know that I am not guilty,
    that no one can save me
    from you.

8 Your hands formed and
    shaped me,
    and nowʷ those same hands
    destroy me.
9 Remember that you made me from
    clay;ˣ
    are you going to crush me back
    to dust?
10 You gave my father strength to
    beget me;
    you made me grow in my
    mother's womb.
11 You formed my body with bones
    and sinews

ᵘ RAHAB: *A legendary sea monster which represented the forces of chaos and evil.*
ᵛ *Probable text* make him go; *Hebrew* make me go.   ʷ *Some ancient translations* and now;
Hebrew together.   ˣ *One ancient translation* from clay; *Hebrew* like clay.

and covered the bones with
muscles and skin.

12 You have given me life and
constant love,
and your care has kept me alive.
13 But now I know that all that time
you were secretly planning to
harm me.
14 You were watching to see if I
would sin,
so that you could refuse to
forgive me.
15 As soon as I sin, I'm in trouble
with you,
but when I do right, I get no
credit.
I am miserable and covered with
shame.y
16 If I have any success at all,
you hunt me down like a lion;
to hurt me you even work
miracles.
17 You always have some witness
against me;
your anger toward me grows
and grows;
you always plan some new
attack.

18 Why, God, did you let me be born?
I should have died before
anyone saw me.
19 To go from the womb straight to
the grave
would have been as good as
never existing.
20 Isn't my life almost over? Leave
me alone!
Let me enjoy the time I have
left.
21 I am going soon and will never
come back—
going to a land that is dark and
gloomy,
22 a land of darkness, shadows,
and confusion,
where the light itself is
darkness.

11
Zophar

1-2 Will no one answer all this
nonsense?
Does talking so much put you in
the right?

3 Job, do you think we can't
answer you?
That your mocking words will
leave us speechless?
4 You claim that what you say is
true;
you claim you are pure in the
sight of God.
5 How I wish God would
answer you!
6 He would tell you there are many
sides to wisdom;
there are things too deep for
human knowledge.
God is punishing you less than
you deserve.

7 Can you discover the limits and
bounds
of the greatness and power
of God?
8 The sky is no limit for God,
but it lies beyond your reach.
God knows the world of the dead,
but you do not know it.
9 God's greatness is broader than
the earth,
wider than the sea.
10 If God arrests you and brings you
to trial,
who is there to stop him?
11 God knows which people are
worthless;
he sees all their evil deeds.
12 Stupid people will start being wise
when wild donkeys are born
tame.

13 Put your heart right, Job. Reach
out to God.
14 Put away evil and wrong from
your home.
15 Then face the world again, firm
and courageous.
16 Then all your troubles will fade
from your memory,
like floods that are past and
remembered no more.
17 Your life will be brighter than
sunshine at noon,
and life's darkest hours will
shine like the dawn.
18 You will live secure and full of
hope;
God will protect you and give
you rest.

y *Probable text* covered with shame; *Hebrew* see my shame.

19 You won't be afraid of your
      enemies;
   many people will ask you for
      help.
20 But the wicked will look around in
      despair
   and find that there is no way to
      escape.
   Their one hope is that death will
      come.

12
Job

1-2 Yes, you are the voice of the
      people.
   When you die, wisdom will die
      with you.
3 But I have as much sense as you
      have;
   I am in no way inferior to you;
   everyone knows all that you
      have said.
4 Even my friends laugh at me now;
   they laugh, although I am
      righteous and blameless;
   but there was a time when God
      answered my prayers.
5 You have no troubles, and yet you
      make fun of me;
   you hit someone who is about to
      fall.
6 But thieves and godless people live
      in peace,
   though their only god is their
      own strength.

7 Even birds and animals have
      much they could teach you;
8   ask the creatures of earth and
      sea for their wisdom.
9 All of them know that the LORD's
      hand made them.
10 It is God who directs the lives of
      his creatures;
   everyone's life is in his power.
11 But just as your tongue enjoys
      tasting food,
   your ears enjoy hearing words.

12-13 Old people have wisdom,
   but God has wisdom and power.
   Old people have insight;
   God has insight and power
      to act.
14 When God tears down, who can
      rebuild,

and who can free those God
      imprisons?
15 Drought comes when God
      withholds rain;
   floods come when he turns
      water loose.
16 God is strong and always
      victorious;
   both deceived and deceiver are
      in his power.
17 He takes away the wisdom of
      rulers
   and makes leaders act like fools.
18 He dethrones kings and makes
      them prisoners;
19   he humbles priests and men of
      power.
20 He silences those who are trusted,
   and takes the wisdom of old
      people away.
21 He disgraces those in power
   and puts an end to the strength
      of rulers.
22 He sends light to places dark as
      death.
23 He makes nations strong and
      great,
   but then he defeats and destroys
      them.
24 He makes their leaders foolish
   and lets them wander confused
      and lost;
25   they grope in the dark and
      stagger like drunkards.

13

1-2 Everything you say, I have
      heard before.
   I understand it all; I know as
      much as you do.
   I'm not your inferior.
3 But my dispute is with God,
      not you;
   I want to argue my case
      with him.
4 You cover up your ignorance with
      lies;
   you are like doctors who can't
      heal anyone.
5 Say nothing, and someone may
      think you are wise!

6 Listen while I state my case.
7   Why are you lying?
   Do you think your lies will
      benefit God?
8 Are you trying to defend him?

Are you going to argue his case
in court?
9 If God looks at you closely, will he
find anything good?
Do you think you can fool God
the way you fool others?
10 Even though your prejudice is
hidden,
he will reprimand you,
11 and his power will fill you with
terror.
12 Your proverbs are as useless as
ashes;
your arguments are as weak as
clay.
13 Be quiet and give me a chance to
speak,
and let the results be what they
will.

14 I am[z] ready to risk my life.
15 I've lost all hope, so what if God
kills me?
I am going to state my case
to him.
16 It may even be that my boldness
will save me,
since no wicked person would
dare to face God.
17 Now listen to my words of
explanation.
18 I am ready to state my case,
because I know I am in the
right.

19 Are you coming to accuse
me, God?
If you do, I am ready to be silent
and die.
20 Let me ask for two things; agree
to them,
and I will not try to hide
from you:
21 stop punishing me, and don't
crush me with terror.

22 Speak first, O God, and I will
answer.
Or let me speak, and you
answer me.
23 What are my sins? What wrongs
have I done?
What crimes am I charged with?

24 Why do you avoid me?

Why do you treat me like an
enemy?
25 Are you trying to frighten me? I'm
nothing but a leaf;
you are attacking a piece of dry
straw.

26 You bring bitter charges
against me,
even for what I did when I was
young.
27 You bind chains on my feet;
you watch every step I take,
and even examine my footprints.
28 As a result, I crumble like rotten
wood,
like a moth-eaten coat.

14

We are all born weak and
helpless.
All lead the same short, troubled
life.
2 We grow and wither as quickly as
flowers;
we disappear like shadows.
3 Will you even look at me, God,
or put me on trial and judge me?
4 Nothing clean can ever come
from anything as unclean as
human beings.
5 The length of our lives is decided
beforehand—
the number of months we will
live.
You have settled it, and it can't be
changed.
6 Look away from us and leave us
alone;[a]
let us enjoy our hard life—if
we can.[b]

7 There is hope for a tree that has
been cut down;
it can come back to life and
sprout.
8 Even though its roots grow old,
and its stump dies in the ground,
9 with water it will sprout like a
young plant.
10 But we die, and that is the end
of us;
we die, and where are we then?

11 Like rivers that stop running,
and lakes that go dry,

z One ancient translation I am; Hebrew Why am I.   a One Hebrew manuscript and leave us
alone; most Hebrew manuscripts so that we may rest.   b let us . . . can; or until we finish our
day of hard work.

12 people die, never to rise.
   They will never wake up while the
      sky endures;
   they will never stir from their
      sleep.

13 I wish you would hide me in the
      world of the dead;
   let me be hidden until your
      anger is over,
   and then set a time to
      remember me.
14 If a man dies, can he come back to
      life?
   But I will wait for better times,
      wait till this time of trouble is
      ended.
15 Then you will call, and I will
      answer,
   and you will be pleased with me,
      your creature.
16 Then you will watch every step I
      take,
   but you will not keep track of
      my sins.
17 You will forgive them and put
      them away;
   you will wipe out all the wrongs
      I have done.

18 There comes a time when
      mountains fall
   and solid cliffs are moved away.
19 Water will wear down rocks,
   and heavy rain will wash away
      the soil;
   so you destroy our hope for life.
20 You overpower us and send us
      away forever;
   our faces are twisted in death.
21 Our children win honor, but we
      never know it,
   nor are we told when they are
      disgraced.
22 We feel only the pain of our own
      bodies
   and the grief of our own minds.

The Second Dialogue
(15.1 — 21.34)

15
Eliphaz

1-2 Empty words, Job! Empty words!
   3 No one who is wise would talk the
      way you do

or defend himself with such
   meaningless words.
4 If you had your way, no one
      would fear God;
   no one would pray to him.
5 Your wickedness is evident by
      what you say;
   you are trying to hide behind
      clever words.
6 There is no need for me to
      condemn you;
   you are condemned by every
      word you speak.

7 Do you think you were the first
      person born?
   Were you there when God made
      the mountains?
8 Did you overhear the plans God
      made?
   Does human wisdom belong to
      you alone?
9 There is nothing you know that we
      don't know.
10 We learned our wisdom from
      gray-haired people —
   those born before your father.

11 God offers you comfort; why still
      reject it?
   We have spoken for him with
      calm, even words.
12 But you are excited and glare at us
      in anger.
13 You are angry with God and
      denounce him.

14 Can any human being be really
      pure?
   Can anyone be right with God?
15 Why, God does not trust even his
      angels;
   even they are not pure in his
      sight.
16 And we drink evil as if it were
      water;
   yes, we are corrupt; we are
      worthless.

17 Now listen, Job, to what I know.
18 Those who are wise have taught
      me truths
   which they learned from their
      ancestors,
   and they kept no secrets hidden.
19 Their land was free from
      foreigners;

there was no one to lead them
away from God.

20 The wicked who oppress others
will be in torment as long as
they live.
21 Voices of terror will scream in
their ears,
and robbers attack when they
think they are safe.
22 They have no hope of escaping
from darkness,
for somewhere a sword is
waiting to kill them,
23   and vultures*c* are waiting*d* to
eat their corpses.
They know their future is dark;
24   disaster, like a powerful king,
is waiting to attack them.

25 That is the fate of those
who shake their fists at God
and defy the Almighty.
26-27 They are proud and rebellious;
they stubbornly hold up their
shields
and rush to fight against God.

28 They are the ones who captured
cities
and seized houses whose owners
had fled,
but war will destroy those cities
and houses.
29 They will not remain rich for long;
nothing they own will last.
Even their shadows*e* will vanish,
30   and they will not escape from
darkness.
They will be like trees
whose branches are burned by
fire,
whose blossoms*f* are blown
away by the wind.
31 If they are foolish enough to trust
in evil,
then evil will be their reward.
32 Before their time is up they will
wither,*g*
wither like a branch and never
be green again.
33 They will be like vines that lose
their unripe grapes;

like olive trees that drop their
blossoms.
34 There will be no descendants for
godless people,
and fire will destroy the homes
built by bribery.
35 These are the ones who plan
trouble and do evil;
their hearts are always full of
deceit.

16
Job

1-2 I have heard words like that
before;
the comfort you give is only
torment.
3 Are you going to keep on talking
forever?
Do you always have to have the
last word?
4 If you were in my place and I in
yours,
I could say everything you are
saying.
I could shake my head wisely
and drown you with a flood of
words.
5 I could strengthen you with advice
and keep talking to comfort you.

6 But nothing I say helps,
and being silent does not calm
my pain.
7 You have worn me out, God;
you have let my family be killed.
8   You have seized me; you are my
enemy.
I am skin and bones,
and people take that as proof of
my guilt.*h*

9 In anger God tears me limb from
limb;
he glares at me with hate.
10 People sneer at me;
they crowd around me and slap
my face.
11 God has handed me over to evil
people.

---

c One ancient translation vultures; *Hebrew* where is he?   *d One ancient translation* are
waiting; *Hebrew* he wanders.   *e One ancient translation* shadows; *Hebrew unclear.*
f One ancient translation blossoms; *Hebrew* mouth.   *g Some ancient translations* wither;
Hebrew be filled.   *h Verses 7-8 in Hebrew are unclear.*

12 I was living in peace,
  but God took me by the throat
  and battered me and
  crushed me.
God uses me for target practice
13   and shoots arrows at me from
  every side—
  arrows that pierce and
  wound me;
  and even then he shows no pity.
14 He wounds me again and again;
  he attacks like a soldier gone
  mad with hate.

15 I mourn and wear clothes made of
  sackcloth,
  and I sit here in the dust
  defeated.
16 I have cried until my face is red,
  and my eyes are swollen and
  circled with shadows,
17   but I am not guilty of any
  violence,
  and my prayer to God is sincere.

18 O Earth, don't hide the wrongs
  done to me!
  Don't let my call for justice be
  silenced!
19 There is someone in heaven
  to stand up for me and take my
  side.
20 My friends scorn me;
  my eyes pour out tears to God.
21 I want someone to plead with God
  for me,
  as one pleads for a friend.
22 My years are passing now,
  and I walk the road of no return.

17 ¹ The end of my life is near. I
  can hardly breathe;
  there is nothing left for me but
  the grave.
² I watch how bitterly everyone
  mocks me.
³ I am being honest, God. Accept
  my word.
  There is no one else to support
  what I say.
⁴ You have closed their minds to
  reason;
  don't let them triumph over
  me now.

5 In the old proverb someone
  betrays his friends for money,
  and his children suffer for it.ⁱ
6 And now people use this proverb
  against me;
  they come and spit in my face.
7 My grief has almost made me
  blind;
  my arms and legs are as thin as
  shadows.
8 Those who claim to be honest are
  shocked,
  and they all condemn me as
  godless.
9 Those who claim to be respectable
  are more and more convinced
  they are right.
10 But if all of them came and stood
  before me,
  I would not find even one of
  them wise.

11 My days have passed; my plans
  have failed;
  my hope is gone.
12 But my friends say night is
  daylight;
  they say that light is near,
  but I know I remain in darkness.
13 My only hope is the world of the
  dead,
  where I will lie down to sleep in
  the dark.
14 I will call the grave my father,
  and the worms that eat me
  I will call my mother and my
  sisters.
15 Where is there any hope for me?
  Who sees any?
16 Hope will not go with meʲ
  when I go down to the world of
  the dead.

18

Bildad

1-2 Job, can't people like you ever be
  quiet?
  If you stopped to listen, we
  could talk to you.
³ What makes you think we are as
  stupid as cattle?
⁴ You are only hurting yourself with
  your anger.

ⁱ someone . . . suffer for it; or someone entertains his friends while his children go hungry.
ʲ One ancient translation with me; Hebrew unclear.

Will the earth be deserted
  because you are angry?
Will God move mountains to
  satisfy you?

5 The light of the wicked will still be
  put out;
  its flame will never burn again.
6 The lamp in their tents will be
  darkened.
7 Their steps were firm, but now
  they stumble;
  they fall — victims of their own
  advice.
8 They walk into a net, and their
  feet are caught;
9   a trap catches their heels and
  holds them.
10 On the ground a snare is hidden;
  a trap has been set in their path.

11 All around them terror is waiting;
  it follows them at every step.
12 They used to be rich, but now they
  go hungry;
  disaster stands and waits at their
  side.
13 A deadly disease spreads over
  their bodies
  and causes their arms and legs
  to rot.
14 They are torn from the tents
  where they lived secure,
  and are dragged off to face King
  Death.
15 Now anyone may live in their
  tents — k
  after sulfur is sprinkled to
  disinfect them!l
16 Their roots and branches are
  withered and dry.
17 Their fame is ended at home and
  abroad;
  no one remembers them any
  more.
18 They will be driven out of the land
  of the living,
  driven from light into darkness.
19 They have no descendants, no
  survivors.
20 From east to west, all who hear of
  their fate
  shudder and tremble with fear.
21 That is the fate of evil people,
  the fate of those who care
  nothing for God.

19

Job

1-2 Why do you keep tormenting me
  with words?
3 Time after time you insult me
  and show no shame for the way
  you abuse me.
4 Even if I have done wrong,
  how does that hurt you?
5 You think you are better than
  I am,
  and regard my troubles as proof
  of my guilt.
6 Can't you see it is God who has
  done this?
  He has set a trap to catch me.
7 I protest his violence,
  but no one is listening;
  no one hears my cry for justice.
8 God has blocked the way, and I
  can't get through;
  he has hidden my path in
  darkness.
9 He has taken away all my wealth
  and destroyed my reputation.
10 He batters me from every side.
  He uproots my hope
  and leaves me to wither and die.
11 God is angry and rages
  against me;
  he treats me like his worst
  enemy.
12 He sends his army to attack me;
  they dig trenches and lay siege
  to my tent.

13 God has made my own family
  forsake me;
  I am a stranger to those who
  knew me;
14   my relatives and friends are
  gone.
15 Those who were guests in my
  house have forgotten me;
  my servant women treat me like
  a stranger and a foreigner.
16 When I call a servant, he doesn't
  answer —
  even when I beg him to help me.
17 My wife can't stand the smell of
  my breath,
  and my own brothers won't
  come near me.

---

k Now anyone may live in their tents; *Hebrew unclear.*   l TO DISINFECT THEM: *Sulfur was used in the ancient world as a disinfectant and to clean rooms that had contained corpses.*

18 Children despise me and laugh
  when they see me.
19 My closest friends look at me with
  disgust;
  those I loved most have turned
  against me.
20 My skin hangs loose on my bones;
  I have barely escaped with my
  life.m
21 You are my friends! Take pity
  on me!
  The hand of God has struck me
  down.
22 Why must you persecute me the
  way God does?
  Haven't you tormented me
  enough?

23 How I wish that someone would
  remember my words
  and record them in a book!
24 Or with a chisel carve my words
  in stone
  and write them so that they
  would last forever.n
25 But I know there is someone in
  heaven
  who will come at last to my
  defense.
26 Even after my skin is eaten by
  disease,
  while still in this bodyo I will
  see God.p
27 I will see him with my own eyes,
  and he will not be a stranger.

My courage failed because you
  said,
28 "How can we torment him?"
  You looked for some excuse to
  attack me.
29 But now, be afraid of the sword—
  the sword that brings God's
  wrath on sin,
  so that you will know there is
  one who judges.q

20

Zophar

1-2 Job, you upset me. Now I'm
  impatient to answer.
3 What you have said is an insult,

but I know how to reply to you.

4 Surely you know that from ancient
  times,
  when we humans were first
  placed on earth,
5 no wicked people have been
  happy for long.
6 They may grow great, towering to
  the sky,
  so great that their heads reach
  the clouds,
7 but they will be blown away like
  dust.
  Those who used to know them
  will wonder where they have
  gone.
8 They will vanish like a dream, like
  a vision at night,
  and never be seen again.
9 The wicked will disappear from
  the place where they used to
  live;
10 and their children will make
  good what they stole from the
  poor.
11 Their bodies used to be young and
  vigorous,
  but soon they will turn to dust.

12-13 Evil tastes so good to them
  that they keep some in their
  mouths to enjoy its flavor.
14 But in their stomachs the food
  turns bitter,
  as bitter as any poison could be.
15 The wicked vomit up the wealth
  they stole;
  God takes it back, even out of
  their stomachs.
16 What the evil people swallow is
  like poison;
  it kills them like the bite of a
  deadly snake.
17 They will not live to see rivers of
  olive oilr
  or streams that flow with milk
  and honey.
18 They will have to give up all they
  have worked for;
  they will have no chance to
  enjoy their wealth,
19 because they oppressed and
  neglected the poor

---

m Verse 20 in Hebrew is unclear.   n last forever; or be on record.   o while still in this body; or although not in this body.   p Verse 26 in Hebrew is unclear.   q one who judges; or a judgment.   r Probable text They will . . . oil; Hebrew unclear.

and seized houses someone else
had built.
20 Their greed is never satisfied.
21 When they eat, there is nothing
left over,
but now their prosperity comes
to an end.
22 At the height of their success
all the weight of misery will
crush them.
23 Let them eat all they want!
God will punish them in fury
and anger.
24 When they try to escape from an
iron sword,
a bronze bow will shoot them
down.
25 Arrows stick through their bodies;
the shiny points drip with their
blood,
and terror grips their hearts.
26 Everything they have saved is
destroyed;
a fire not lit by human hands
burns them and all their family.
27 Heaven reveals their sin,
and the earth gives testimony
against them.
28 All their wealth will be destroyed
in the flood of God's anger.

29 This is the fate of wicked people,
the fate that God assigns to
them.

21
Job

1-2 Listen to what I am saying;
that is all the comfort I ask
from you.
3 Give me a chance to speak and
then,
when I am through, sneer if you
like.

4 My quarrel is not with mortals;
I have good reason to be
impatient.
5 Look at me. Isn't that enough
to make you stare in shocked
silence?
6 When I think of what has
happened to me,
I am stunned, and I tremble and
shake.

7 Why does God let evil people live,
let them grow old and prosper?
8 They have children and
grandchildren,
and live to watch them all
grow up.
9 God does not bring disaster on
their homes;
they never have to live in terror.
10 Yes, all their cattle breed
and give birth without trouble.
11 Their children run and play like
lambs
12 and dance to the music of harps
and flutes.
13 They live out their lives in peace
and quietly die without
suffering.

14 The wicked tell God to leave them
alone;
they don't want to know his will
for their lives.
15 They think there is no need to
serve God
nor any advantage in praying
to him.
16 They claim they succeed by their
own strength,
but their way of thinking I can't
accept.

17 Was a wicked person's light ever
put out?
Did one of them ever meet with
disaster?
Did God ever punish the wicked in
anger
18 and blow them away like straw
in the wind,
or like dust carried away in a
storm?

19 You claim God punishes a child
for the sins of his father.
No! Let God punish the sinners
themselves;
let him show that he does it
because of *their* sins.
20 Let sinners bear their own
punishment;
let them feel the wrath of
Almighty God.
21 When our lives are over,
do we really care whether our
children are happy?
22 Can anyone teach God,

who judges even those in high
places?

23-24 Some people stay healthy till the
day they die;
they die happy and at ease,
their bodies well-nourished.
25 Others have no happiness at all;
they live and die with bitter
hearts.
26 But all alike die and are buried;
they all are covered with worms.

27 I know what spiteful thoughts you
have.
28 You ask, "Where are the homes of
great people now,
those who practiced evil?"

29 Haven't you talked with people
who travel?
Don't you know the reports they
bring back?
30 On the day God is angry and
punishes,
it is the wicked who are always
spared.
31 There is no one to accuse the
wicked
or pay them back for all they
have done.
32 When they are carried to the
graveyard,
to their well-guarded tombs,
33   thousands join the funeral
procession,
and even the earth lies gently on
their bodies.

34 And you! You try to comfort me
with nonsense!
Every answer you give is a lie!

The Third Dialogue
(22.1 – 27.23)

22
Eliphaz
1-2 Is there anyone, even the wisest,
who could ever be of use
to God?
3 Does your doing right benefit God,
or does your being good help
him at all?
4 It is not because you stand in awe
of God

that he reprimands you and
brings you to trial.
5 No, it's because you have sinned
so much;
it's because of all the evil
you do.
6 To make a brother repay you the
money he owed,
you took away his clothes and
left him nothing to wear.
7 You refused water to those who
were tired,
and refused to feed those who
were hungry.
8 You used your power and your
position
to take over the whole land.
9 You not only refused to help
widows,
but you also robbed and
mistreated orphans.
10 So now there are pitfalls all
around you,
and suddenly you are full of
fear.
11 It has grown so dark that you
cannot see,
and a flood overwhelms you.

12 Doesn't God live in the highest
heavens
and look down on the stars,
even though they are high?
13 And yet you ask, "What does God
know?
He is hidden by clouds — how
can he judge us?"
14 You think the thick clouds keep
him from seeing,
as he walks on the dome of
the sky.

15 Are you determined to walk in the
paths
that evil people have always
followed?
16 Even before their time had come,
they were washed away by a
flood.
17 These are the ones who
rejected God
and believed that he could do
nothing to them.
18 And yet it was God who made
them prosperous —
I can't understand the thoughts
of the wicked.

JOB

19 Good people are glad and the
   innocent laugh
   when they see the wicked
   punished.
20 All that the wicked own is
   destroyed,
   and fire burns up anything that
   is left.

21 Now, Job, make peace with God
   and stop treating him like an
   enemy;
   if you do, then he will bless you.
22 Accept the teaching he gives;
   keep his words in your heart.
23 Yes, you must humbly*s* return
   to God
   and put an end to all the evil
   that is done in your house.
24 Throw away your gold;
   dump your finest gold in the dry
   stream bed.
25 Let Almighty God be your gold,
   and let him be silver, piled high
   for you.
26 Then you will always trust in God
   and find that he is the source of
   your joy.
27 When you pray, he will
   answer you,
   and you will keep the vows you
   made.
28 You will succeed in all you do,
   and light will shine on your
   path.
29 God brings down the proud*t*
   and saves the humble.
30 He will rescue you if you are
   innocent,*u*
   if what you do is right.*v*

23

Job

1-2 I still rebel and complain
   against God;
   I cannot keep from groaning.
3 How I wish I knew where to
   find him,
   and knew how to go where
   he is.
4 I would state my case before him
   and present all the arguments in
   my favor.

5 I want to know what he would say
   and how he would answer me.
6 Would God use all his strength
   against me?
   No, he would listen as I spoke.
7 I am honest; I could reason
   with God;
   he would declare me innocent*w*
   once and for all.

8 I have searched in the East, but
   God is not there;
   I have not found him when I
   searched in the West.
9 God has been at work in the North
   and the South,
   but still I have not seen him.
10 Yet God knows every step I take;
   if he tests me, he will find me
   pure.
11 I follow faithfully the road he
   chooses,
   and never wander to either side.
12 I always do what God commands;
   I follow his will, not my own
   desires.

13 He never changes. No one can
   oppose him
   or stop him from doing what he
   wants to do.
14 He will fulfill what he has planned
   for me;
   that plan is just one of the many
   he has;
15   I tremble with fear before him.
16-17 Almighty God has destroyed my
   courage.
   It is God, not the dark, that makes
   me afraid—
   even though the darkness has
   made me blind.

24

Why doesn't God set a time for
   judging,
   a day of justice for those who
   serve him?

2 People move property lines to get
   more land;
   they steal sheep and put them
   with their own flocks.
3 They take donkeys that belong to
   orphans,

---

s One ancient translation humbly; *Hebrew* be built up.   *t Probable text* proud; *Hebrew
unclear.   u Some ancient translations* innocent; *Hebrew* not innocent.   *v Verse 30 in Hebrew
is unclear.   w* he would declare me innocent; *or* then my rights would be safe.

and keep a widow's ox till she
  pays her debts.
4 They prevent the poor from
    getting their rights
  and force the needy to run and
    hide.

5 So the poor, like wild donkeys,
    search for food in the dry
    wilderness;
  nowhere else can they find food
    for their children.
6 They have to harvest fields they
    don't own,ˣ
  and gather grapes in vineyards
    of the wicked.
7 At night they sleep with nothing to
    cover them,
  nothing to keep them from the
    cold.
8 They are drenched by the rain that
    falls on the mountains,
  and they huddle beside the rocks
    for shelter.

9 Evil people make slaves of
    fatherless infants
  and take the children of the poor
    in payment for debts.
10 But the poor must go out with no
    clothes to protect them;
  they must go hungry while
    harvesting wheat.
11 They press olives for oil, and
    grapes for wine,
  but they themselves are thirsty.
12 In the cities the wounded and
    dying cry out,
  but God ignores their prayers.

13 There are those who reject the
    light;
  they don't understand it or go
    where it leads.
14 At dawn the murderer gets up
  and goes out to kill the poor,
  and at night he steals.
15 The adulterer waits for twilight to
    come;
  he covers his face so that no one
    can see him.
16 At night thieves break into houses,
  but by day they hide and avoid
    the light.
17 They fear the light of day,

but darkness holds no terror for
  them.

[Zophar]ʸ
18 The wicked are swept away by
    floods,
  and the land they own is under
    God's curse;
  they no longer go to work in
    their vineyards.
19 As snow vanishes in heat and
    drought,
  so sinners vanish from the land
    of the living.
20 Not even their mothers remember
    them now;
  they are eaten by worms and
    destroyed like fallen trees.
21 That happens because they
    mistreated widows
  and showed no kindness to
    childless women.
22 God, in his strength, destroys the
    mighty;
  God acts—and the wicked die.
23 God may let them live secure,
  but keeps an eye on them all the
    time.
24 For a while the wicked prosper,
  but then they wither like weeds,
  like stalks of grain that have
    been cut down.
25 Can anyone deny that this is so?
  Can anyone prove that my words
    are not true?

25
Bildad
1-2 God is powerful; all must stand in
      awe of him;
  he keeps his heavenly kingdom
    in peace.
3 Can anyone count the angels who
    serve him?
  Is there any place where God's
    light does not shine?
4 Can anyone be righteous or pure
    in God's sight?
5 In his eyes even the moon is not
    bright,
  or the stars pure.
6 Then what about a human being,
    that worm, that insect?

ˣ FIELDS THEY DON'T OWN: *Having been cheated out of their own land, the poor are forced to work
for others for very small pay.*   ʸ Zophar is not named in the text, but this speech is usually
assigned to him.

What is a human life worth in
God's eyes?

26
Job

1-2 What a big help you are to me —
poor, weak man that I am!
3 You give such good advice
and share your knowledge with
a fool like me!
4 Who do you think will hear all
your words?
Who inspired you to speak like
this?

[Bildad] z

5 The spirits of the dead tremble
in the waters under the earth.
6 The world of the dead lies open
to God;
no covering shields it from his
sight.
7 God stretched out the northern sky
and hung the earth in empty
space.
8 It is God who fills the clouds with
water
and keeps them from bursting
with the weight.
9 He hides the full moon behind a
cloud.
10 He divided light from darkness
by a circle drawn on the face of
the sea.
11 When he threatens the pillars that
hold up the sky,
they shake and tremble with
fear.
12 It is his strength that conquered
the sea;a
by his skill he destroyed the
monster Rahab.b
13 It is his breath that made the sky
clear,
and his hand that killed the
escaping monster.c
14 But these are only hints of his
power,
only the whispers that we have
heard.
Who can know how truly great
God is?

27
Job

1-2 I swear by the living
Almighty God,
who refuses me justice and
makes my life bitter —
3 as long as God gives me breath,
4 my lips will never say anything
evil,
my tongue will never tell a lie.
5 I will never say that you men are
right;
I will insist on my innocence to
my dying day.
6 I will never give up my claim to be
right;
my conscience is clear.

7 May all who oppose me and fight
against me
be punished like the wicked and
the unrighteous.
8 What hope is there for the godless
in the hour when God demands
their life?
9 When trouble comes, will God
hear their cries?
10 They should have desired the joy
he gives;
they should have constantly
prayed to him.

11 Let me teach you how great is
God's power,
and explain what Almighty God
has planned.
12 But no, after all, you have seen for
yourselves;
so why do you talk such
nonsense?

[Zophar]d

13 This is how Almighty God
punishes wicked, violent people.
14 They may have many sons,
but all will be killed in war;
their children never have
enough to eat.
15 Those who survive will die from
disease,
and even their widows will not
mourn their death.

---

z Bildad is not named in the text, but this speech is usually assigned to him.
a CONQUERED THE SEA: A reference to an ancient story in which the sea fought against God.
b RAHAB: See 9.13.   c ESCAPING MONSTER: See 9.8.   d Zophar is not named in the text, but this
speech is usually assigned to him.

16 The wicked may have too much
     silver to count
   and more clothes than anyone
     needs;
17 but some good person will wear
     the clothes,
   and someone honest will get the
     silver.
18 The wicked build houses like a
     spider's web[e]
   or like the hut of a slave
     guarding the fields.
19 One last time[f] they will lie down
     rich,
   and when they wake up, they
     will find their wealth gone.
20 Terror will strike like a sudden
     flood;
   a wind in the night will blow
     them away;
21   the east wind will sweep them
     from their homes;
22   it will blow down on them
     without pity
   while they try their best to
     escape.
23 The wind howls at them as
     they run,
   frightening them with
     destructive power.

In Praise of Wisdom[g]

28 There are mines where silver
          is dug;
   There are places where gold is
     refined.
2 We dig iron out of the ground
   And melt copper out of the stones.
3 Miners explore the deepest
     darkness.
   They search the depths of the
     earth
   And dig for rocks in the darkness.
4 Far from where anyone lives
   Or human feet ever travel,
   They dig the shafts of mines.
   There they work in loneliness,
   Clinging to ropes in the pits.
5 Food grows out of the earth,
   But underneath the same earth
   All is torn up and crushed.
6 The stones of the earth contain
     sapphires,
   And its dust contains gold.

7 No hawk sees the roads to the
     mines,
   And no vulture ever flies over
     them.
8 No lion or other fierce beast
   Ever travels those lonely roads.
9 Miners dig the hardest rocks,
   Dig mountains away at their base.
10 As they tunnel through the rocks,
   They discover precious stones.
11 They dig to the sources of[h] rivers
   And bring to light what is hidden.
12 But where can wisdom be found?
   Where can we learn to
     understand?
13 Wisdom is not to be found among
     mortals;
   No one knows its true value.
14 The depths of the oceans and seas
   Say that wisdom is not found
     there.
15 It cannot be bought with silver or
     gold.
16 The finest gold and jewels
   Cannot equal its value.
17 It is worth more than gold,
   Than a gold vase or finest glass.
18 The value of wisdom is more
   Than coral or crystal or rubies.
19 The finest topaz and the purest
     gold
   Cannot compare with the value of
     wisdom.

20 Where, then, is the source of
     wisdom?
   Where can we learn to
     understand?
21 No living creature can see it,
   Not even a bird in flight.
22 Even death and destruction
   Admit they have heard only
     rumors.

23 God alone knows the way,
   Knows the place where wisdom is
     found,
24 Because he sees the ends of the
     earth,
   Sees everything under the sky.
25 When God gave the wind its
     power

---

e *Some ancient translations* spider's web; *Hebrew* moth *or* bird's nest.
f *Some ancient translations* One last time; *Hebrew* They will not be gathered.
g *The Hebrew text does not indicate who is speaking in this chapter.*
h *Some ancient translations* dig to the sources of; *Hebrew* bind from trickling.

And determined the size of
  the sea;
26 When God decided where the rain
    would fall,
  And the path that the
    thunderclouds travel;
27 It was then he saw wisdom and
    tested its worth —
  He gave it his approval.

28 God said to us humans,
  "To be wise, you must have
    reverence for the Lord.
  To understand, you must turn
    from evil."

Job's Final Statement of His Case

29 Job began speaking again.

Job

2 If only my life could once again
    be as it was when God watched
    over me.
3 God was always with me then
    and gave me light as I walked
    through the darkness.
4 Those were the days when I was
    prosperous,
  and the friendship of God
    protected my home.
5 Almighty God was with me then,
    and I was surrounded by all my
    children.
6 My cows and goats gave plenty of
    milk,
  and my olive trees grew in the
    rockiest soil.
7 Whenever the city elders met
    and I took my place among
    them,
8   young men stepped aside as
      soon as they saw me,
    and old men stood up to show
      me respect.
9 The leaders of the people would
    stop talking;
10   even the most important men
      kept silent.

11 Everyone who saw me or heard
    of me
  had good things to say about
    what I had done.
12 When the poor cried out, I helped
    them;
  I gave help to orphans who had
    nowhere to turn.

13 People who were in deepest
    misery praised me,
  and I helped widows find
    security.
14 I have always acted justly and
    fairly.
15 I was eyes for the blind,
    and feet for the lame.
16 I was like a father to the poor
    and took the side of strangers in
    trouble.
17 I destroyed the power of cruel men
    and rescued their victims.

18 I always expected to live a long
    life
  and to die at home in comfort.
19 I was like a tree whose roots
    always have water
  and whose branches are wet
    with dew.
20 Everyone was always praising me,
    and my strength never
    failed me.
21 When I gave advice, people were
    silent
  and listened carefully to what I
    said;
22   they had nothing to add when I
      had finished.
  My words sank in like drops of
    rain;
23   everyone welcomed them
    just as farmers welcome rain in
      spring.
24 I smiled on them when they had
    lost confidence;
  my cheerful face encouraged
    them.
25 I took charge and made the
    decisions;
  I led them as a king leads his
    troops,
  and gave them comfort in their
    despair.

30 But men younger than I am
    make fun of me now!
  Their fathers have always been so
    worthless
  that I wouldn't let them help my
    dogs guard sheep.
2 They were a bunch of
    worn-out men,
  too weak to do any work for me.
3 They were so poor and hungry
    that they would gnaw dry
    roots —

at night, in wild, desolate places.
4 They pulled up the plants of the
    desert and ate them,
    even the tasteless roots of the
    broom tree!
5 Everyone drove them away with
    shouts,
    as if they were shouting at
    thieves.
6 They had to live in caves,
    in holes dug in the sides of cliffs.
7 Out in the wilds they howled like
    animals
    and huddled together under the
    bushes.
8 A worthless bunch of nameless
    nobodies!
    They were driven out of the
    land.

9 Now they come and laugh at me;
    I am nothing but a joke to them.
10 They treat me with disgust;
    they think they are too good
    for me,
    and even come and spit in my
    face.
11 Because God has made me weak
    and helpless,
    they turn against me with all
    their fury.
12 This mob attacks me head-on;
    they send me running; they
    prepare their final assault.
13 They cut off my escape and try to
    destroy me;
    and there is no one to stop[i]
    them.
14 They pour through the holes in my
    defenses
    and come crashing down on top
    of me;
15 I am overcome with terror;
    my dignity is gone like a puff of
    wind,
    and my prosperity like a cloud.

16 Now I am about to die;
    there is no relief for my
    suffering.
17 At night my bones all ache;
    the pain that gnaws me never
    stops.
18 God seizes me by my collar
    and twists my clothes out of
    shape.

19 He throws me down in the mud;
    I am no better than dirt.

20 I call to you, O God, but you never
    answer;
    and when I pray, you pay no
    attention.
21 You are treating me cruelly;
    you persecute me with all your
    power.
22 You let the wind blow me away;
    you toss me about in a raging
    storm.
23 I know you are taking me off to
    my death,
    to the fate in store for everyone.
24 Why do you attack a ruined man,
    one who can do nothing but beg
    for pity?[i]
25 Didn't I weep with people in
    trouble
    and feel sorry for those in need?
26 I hoped for happiness and light,
    but trouble and darkness came
    instead.
27 I am torn apart by worry and
    pain;
    I have had day after day of
    suffering.
28 I go about in gloom, without any
    sunshine;
    I stand up in public and plead
    for help.
29 My voice is as sad and lonely
    as the cries of a jackal or an
    ostrich.
30 My skin has turned dark; I am
    burning with fever.
31 Where once I heard joyful music,
    now I hear only mourning and
    weeping.

31

I have made a solemn promise
    never to look with lust at a
    woman.

2 What does Almighty God do to us?
    How does he repay human
    deeds?
3 He sends disaster and ruin
    to those who do wrong.
4 God knows everything I do;
    he sees every step I take.

5 I swear I have never acted
    wickedly

---

[i] Probable text stop; Hebrew help.   [i] Verse 24 in Hebrew is unclear.

and never tried to deceive
  others.
6 Let God weigh me on honest
  scales,
  and he will see how innocent
  I am.
7 If I have turned from the right
  path
  or let myself be attracted to evil,
  if my hands are stained with sin,
8 then let my crops be destroyed,
  or let others eat the food I grow.

9 If I have been attracted to my
  neighbor's wife,
  and waited, hidden, outside her
  door,
10 then let my wife cook another
  man's food
  and sleep in another man's bed.
11 Such wickedness should be
  punished by death.
12 It would be like a destructive,
  hellish fire,
  consuming everything I have.

13 When any of my servants
  complained against me,
  I would listen and treat them
  fairly.
14 If I did not, how could I then
  face God?
  What could I say when God
  came to judge me?
15 The same God who created me
  created my servants also.

16 I have never refused to help the
  poor;
  never have I let widows live in
  despair
17 or let orphans go hungry while
  I ate.
18 All my life I have taken care of
  them.^{k}

19 When I found someone in need,
  too poor to buy clothes,
20 I would give him clothing made
  of wool
  that had come from my own
  flock of sheep.
  Then he would praise me with all
  his heart.

21 If I have ever cheated an orphan,

knowing I could win in court,
22 then may my arms be broken;
  may they be torn from my
  shoulders.
23 Because I fear God's punishment,
  I could never do such a thing.

24 I have never trusted in riches
25 or taken pride in my wealth.
26 I have never worshiped the sun in
  its brightness
  or the moon in all its beauty.
27 I have not been led astray to
  honor them
  by kissing my hand in reverence
  to them.
28 Such a sin should be punished by
  death;
  it denies Almighty God.

29 I have never been glad when my
  enemies suffered,
  or pleased when they met with
  disaster;
30 I never sinned by praying for
  their death.
31 All those who work for me know
  that I have always welcomed
  strangers.
32 I invited travelers into my home
  and never let them sleep in the
  streets.

33 Others try to hide their sins,
  but I have never concealed mine.
34 I have never feared what people
  would say;
  I have never kept quiet or stayed
  indoors
  because I feared their scorn.

35 Will no one listen to what I am
  saying?
  I swear that every word is true.
  Let Almighty God answer me.

  If the charges my opponent brings
  against me
  were written down so that I
  could see them,
36 I would wear them proudly on my
  shoulder
  and place them on my head like
  a crown.
37 I would tell God everything I have
  done,

^{k} All my life . . . them; Hebrew unclear.

and hold my head high in his
presence.

38 If I have stolen the land I farm
and taken it from its rightful
owners —
39 if I have eaten the food that
grew there
but let the farmers that grew
it starve —
40 then instead of wheat and
barley,
may weeds and thistles grow.

The words of Job are ended.

The Speeches of Elihu
(32.1 — 37.24)

32 Because Job was convinced of
his own innocence, the three
men gave up trying to answer him. 2 But
a bystander named Elihu could not control his anger any longer, because Job
was justifying himself and blaming God.
(Elihu was the son of Barakel, a
descendant of Buz, and belonged to the
clan of Ram.) 3 He was also angry with
Job's three friends. They could not find
any way to answer Job, and this made it
appear that God was in the wrong. 4 Because Elihu was the youngest one there,
he had waited until everyone finished
speaking. 5 When he saw that the three
men could not answer Job, he was angry
6 and began to speak.

Elihu

I am young, and you are old,
so I was afraid to tell you what I
think.
7 I told myself that you ought to
speak,
that you older men should share
your wisdom.
8 But it is the spirit of Almighty God
that comes to us and gives us
wisdom.
9 It is not growing old that makes us
wise
or helps us to know what is
right.
10 So now I want you to listen to me;
let me tell you what I think.

11 I listened patiently while you were
speaking

and waited while you searched
for wise phrases.
12 I paid close attention and heard
you fail;
you have not disproved what
Job has said.
13 How can you claim you have
discovered wisdom?
God must answer Job, for you
have failed.
14 Job was speaking to you, not
to me,
but I would never answer the
way you did.

15 Words have failed them, Job;
they have no answer for you.
16 Shall I go on waiting when they
are silent?
They stand there with nothing
more to say.
17 No, I will give my own
answer now
and tell you what I think.
18 I can hardly wait to speak.
I can't hold back the words.
19 If I don't get a chance to speak,
I will burst like a wineskin full
of new wine.
20 I can't stand it; I have to speak.
21 I will not take sides in this debate;
I am not going to flatter anyone.
22 I don't know how to flatter,
and God would quickly punish
me if I did.

33 And now, Job, listen carefully
to all that I have to say.
2 I am ready to say what's on my
mind.
3 All my words are sincere,
and I am speaking the truth.
4 God's spirit made me and gave
me life.

5 Answer me if you can. Prepare
your arguments.
6 You and I are the same in God's
sight,
both of us were formed from
clay.
7 So you have no reason to fear me;
I will not overpower you.

8 Now this is what I heard you say:
9 "I am not guilty; I have done
nothing wrong.
I am innocent and free from sin.

JOB

10 But God finds excuses for
   attacking me
   and treats me like an enemy.
11 He binds chains on my feet;
   he watches every move I make."

12 But I tell you, Job, you are wrong.
   God is greater than any human
   being.
13 Why do you accuse God
   of never answering our
   complaints?
14 Although God speaks again and
   again,
   no one pays attention to what he
   says.
15 At night when people are asleep,
   God speaks in dreams and
   visions.
16 He makes them listen to what he
   says,
   and they are frightened at his
   warnings.
17 God speaks to make them stop
   their sinning
   and to save them from becoming
   proud.
18 He will not let them be destroyed;
   he saves them from death itself.
19 God corrects us by sending
   sickness
   and filling our bodies with pain.
20 Those who are sick lose their
   appetites,
   and even the finest food looks
   revolting.
21 Their bodies waste away to
   nothing;
   you can see all their bones;
22 they are about to go to the world
   of the dead.

23 Perhaps an angel may come to
   their aid —
   one of God's thousands of
   angels,
   who remind us of our duty.
24 In mercy the angel will say,
   "Release them!
   They are not to go down to the
   world of the dead.
   Here is the ransom to set them
   free."
25 Their bodies will grow young and
   strong again;
26 when they pray, God will
   answer;
   they will worship God with joy;

God will set things right for
   them again.
27 Each one will say in public, "I
   have sinned.
   I have not done right, but God
   spared me.
28 He kept me from going to the
   world of the dead,
   and I am still alive."

29 God does all this again and again;
30 each one saves a person's life,
   and gives him the joy of living.

31 Now, Job, listen to what I am
   saying;
   be quiet and let me speak.
32 But if you have something to say,
   let me hear it;
   I would gladly admit you are in
   the right.
33 But if not, be quiet and listen
   to me,
   and I will teach you how to be
   wise.

34

1-2 You men are so wise, so
   clever;
   listen now to what I am saying.
3 You know good food when you
   taste it,
   but not wise words when you
   hear them.
4 It is up to us to decide the case.
5 Job claims that he is innocent,
   that God refuses to give him
   justice.
6 He asks, "How could I lie and say
   I am wrong?
   I am fatally wounded, but I am
   sinless."

7 Have you ever seen anyone like
   this man Job?
   He never shows respect for God.
8 He likes the company of evil
   people
   and goes around with sinners.
9 He says that it never does any
   good
   to try to follow God's will.

10 Listen to me, you men who
   understand!
   Will Almighty God do what is
   wrong?
11 He rewards people for what
   they do

and treats them as they deserve.
12 Almighty God does not do evil;
he is never unjust to anyone.
13 Did God get his power from
someone else?
Did someone put him in charge
of the world?
14 If God took back the breath of life,
15 then everyone living would die
and turn into dust again.

16 Now listen to me, if you are wise.
17 Are you condemning the
righteous God?
Do you think that *he* hates
justice?
18 God condemns kings and rulers
when they are worthless or
wicked.
19 He does not take the side of rulers
nor favor the rich over the poor,
for he created everyone.
20 We may suddenly die at night.
God strikes us down and we
perish;
he kills the mighty with no
effort at all.
21 He watches every step we take.
22 There is no darkness dark enough
to hide a sinner from God.
23 God does not need to set a time*l*
for us to go and be judged
by him.
24 He does not need an investigation
to remove leaders and replace
them with others.
25 Because he knows what they do;
he overthrows them and crushes
them by night.
26 He punishes sinners where all can
see it,
27 because they have stopped
following him
and ignored all his commands.
28 They forced the poor to cry out
to God,
and he heard their calls for help.

29 If God decided to do nothing at all,
no one could criticize him.
If he hid his face, we would be
helpless.
30 There would be nothing that
nations could do
to keep godless oppressors from
ruling them.

31 Job, have you confessed your sins
to God
and promised not to sin again?
32 Have you asked God to show you
your faults,
and have you agreed to stop
doing evil?
33 Since you object to what God
does,
can you expect him to do what
you want?
The decision is yours, not mine;
tell us now what you think.

34 Any sensible person will surely
agree;
and the wise who hear me
will say
35 that Job is speaking from
ignorance
and that nothing he says makes
sense.
36 Think through everything that Job
says;
you will see that he talks like an
evil man.
37 To his sins he adds rebellion;
in front of us all he mocks God.

35

1-2 It is not right, Job, for you
to say
that you are innocent in God's
sight,
3 or to ask God, "How does my sin
affect you?
What have I gained by not
sinning?"
4 I am going to answer you and
your friends too.

5 Look at the sky! See how high the
clouds are!
6 If you sin, that does no harm
to God.
If you do wrong many times,
does that affect him?
7 Do you help God by being so
righteous?
There is nothing God needs
from you.
8 Others suffer from your sins,
and the good you do helps them.

9 When people are oppressed, they
groan;

---

l Probable text a time; *Hebrew* yet.

they cry for someone to save
them.
10 But they don't turn to God, their
Creator,
who gives them hope in their
darkest hours.
11 They don't turn to God, who
makes us wise,
wiser than any animal or bird.
12 They cry for help, but God doesn't
answer,
for they are proud and evil.
13 It is useless for them to cry out;
Almighty God does not see or
hear them.

14 Job, you say you can't see God;
but wait patiently—your case is
before him.
15 You think that God does not
punish,
that he pays little attention
to sin.
16 It is useless for you to go on
talking;
it is clear you don't know what
you are saying.

36

1-2 Be patient and listen a little
longer
to what I am saying on God's
behalf.
3 My knowledge is wide; I will use
what I know
to show that God, my Creator, is
just.
4 Nothing I say to you is false;
you see before you a truly
wise man.

5 How strong God is! He despises
no one;
there is nothing he doesn't
understand.
6 He does not let sinners live on,
and he always treats the poor
with justice.
7 He protects those who are
righteous;
he allows them to rule like kings
and lets them be honored
forever.
8 But if people are bound in chains,
suffering for what they have
done,
9 God shows them their sins and
their pride.

10 He makes them listen to his
warning
to turn away from evil.
11 If they obey God and serve him,
they live out their lives in peace
and prosperity.
12 But if not, they will die in
ignorance
and cross the stream into the
world of the dead.

13 Those who are godless keep on
being angry,
and even when punished, they
don't pray for help.
14 They die while they are still
young,
worn out by a life of disgrace.
15 But God teaches people through
suffering
and uses distress to open their
eyes.

16 God brought you out of trouble,
and let you enjoy security;
your table was piled high with
food.
17 But now you are being punished
as you deserve.
18 Be careful not to let bribes
deceive you,
or riches lead you astray.
19 It will do you no good to cry out
for help;
all your strength can't help
you now.
20 Don't wish for night to come,
the time when nations will
perish.
21 Be careful not to turn to evil;
your suffering was sent to keep
you from it.

22 Remember how great is God's
power;
he is the greatest teacher of all.
23 No one can tell God what to do
or accuse him of doing evil.
24 He has always been praised for
what he does;
you also must praise him.
25 Everyone has seen what he has
done;
but we can only watch from a
distance.m

m but we can only watch from a distance; or no one understands it all.

J
O
B

26 We cannot fully know his
greatness
or count the number of his
years.
27 It is God who takes water from the
earth
and turns it into drops of rain.
28 He lets the rain pour from the
clouds
in showers for all human beings.
29 No one knows how the clouds
move
or how the thunder roars
through the sky, where God
dwells.
30 He sends lightning through all
the sky,
but the depths of the sea remain
dark.
31 This is how he feeds[n] the people
and provides an abundance of
food.
32 He seizes the lightning with his
hands
and commands it to hit the
mark.
33 Thunder announces the
approaching storm,
and the cattle know it is coming.

37

1 The storm makes my heart
beat wildly.
2 Listen, all of you, to the voice
of God,
to the thunder that comes from
his mouth.
3 He sends the lightning across
the sky,
from one end of the earth to the
other.
4 Then the roar of his voice is
heard,
the majestic sound of thunder,
and all the while the lightning
flashes.
5 At God's command amazing things
happen,
wonderful things that we can't
understand.
6 He commands snow to fall on the
earth,
and sends torrents of drenching
rain.
7 He brings our work to a stop;
he shows us what he can do.[o]

8 The wild animals go to their dens.
9 The storm winds come from the
south,
and the biting cold from the
north.
10 The breath of God freezes the
waters,
and turns them to solid ice.
11 Lightning flashes from the
clouds,[p]
12 as they move at God's will.
They do all that God commands,
everywhere throughout the
world.
13 God sends rain to water the earth;
he may send it to punish us,
or to show us his favor.

14 Pause a moment, Job, and listen;
consider the wonderful things
God does.
15 Do you know how God gives the
command
and makes lightning flash from
the clouds?
16 Do you know how clouds float in
the sky,
the work of God's amazing skill?
17 No, you can only suffer in the heat
when the south wind oppresses
the land.
18 Can you help God stretch out
the sky
and make it as hard as polished
metal?
19 Teach us what to say to God;
our minds are blank; we have
nothing to say.
20 I won't ask to speak with God;
why should I give him a chance
to destroy me?

21 And now the light in the sky is
dazzling,
too bright for us to look at it;
and the sky has been swept
clean by the wind.
22 A golden glow is seen in the north,
and the glory of God fills us
with awe.
23 God's power is so great that we
cannot come near him;
he is righteous and just in his
dealings with us.

n *Probable text* feeds; *Hebrew* judges.   o *One ancient translation* us what he can do; *Hebrew*
this to those whom he has made.   p *Verse 11 in Hebrew is unclear.*

24 No wonder, then, that everyone is
    awed by him,
  and that he ignores those who
    claim to be wise.

The LORD Answers Job

38 Then out of the storm the LORD
     spoke to Job.

The LORD

2 Who are you to question my
    wisdom
  with your ignorant, empty
    words?
3 Now stand up straight
  and answer the questions I
    ask you.
4 Were you there when I made the
    world?
  If you know so much, tell me
    about it.
5 Who decided how large it
    would be?
  Who stretched the measuring
    line over it?
  Do you know all the answers?
6 What holds up the pillars that
    support the earth?
  Who laid the cornerstone of the
    world?
7 In the dawn of that day the stars
    sang together,
  and the heavenly beings*q*
    shouted for joy.

8 Who closed the gates to hold back
    the sea*r*
  when it burst from the womb of
    the earth?
9 It was I who covered the sea with
    clouds
  and wrapped it in darkness.
10 I marked a boundary for the sea
  and kept it behind bolted gates.
11 I told it, "So far and no farther!
  Here your powerful waves must
    stop."
12 Job, have you ever in all your life
  commanded a day to dawn?
13 Have you ordered the dawn to
    seize the earth
  and shake the wicked from their
    hiding places?
14 Daylight makes the hills and
    valleys stand out
  like the folds of a garment,

clear as the imprint of a seal on
    clay.
15 The light of day is too bright for
    the wicked
  and restrains them from doing
    violence.

16 Have you been to the springs in
    the depths of the sea?
  Have you walked on the floor of
    the ocean?
17 Has anyone ever shown you the
    gates
  that guard the dark world of the
    dead?
18 Have you any idea how big the
    world is?
  Answer me if you know.

19 Do you know where the light
    comes from
  or what the source of
    darkness is?
20 Can you show them how far to go,
  or send them back again?
21 I am sure you can, because you're
    so old
  and were there when the world
    was made!

22 Have you ever visited the
    storerooms,
  where I keep the snow and the
    hail?
23 I keep them ready for times of
    trouble,
  for days of battle and war.
24 Have you been to the place where
    the sun comes up,
  or the place from which the east
    wind blows?

25 Who dug a channel for the
    pouring rain
  and cleared the way for the
    thunderstorm?
26 Who makes rain fall where no one
    lives?
27 Who waters the dry and thirsty
    land,
  so that grass springs up?
28 Does either the rain or the dew
    have a father?
29 Who is the mother of the ice and
    the frost,
30   which turn the waters to stone

---

q HEAVENLY BEINGS: *See 1.6.*   *r* TO HOLD BACK THE SEA: *See 26.12.*

and freeze the face of the sea?

31 Can you tie the Pleiades together
or loosen the bonds that hold
Orion?
32 Can you guide the stars season by
season
and direct the Big and the Little
Dipper?
33 Do you know the laws that govern
the skies,
and can you make them apply to
the earth?

34 Can you shout orders to the clouds
and make them drench you with
rain?
35 And if you command the lightning
to flash,
will it come to you and say, "At
your service"?
36 Who tells the ibis[s] when the Nile
will flood,
or who tells the rooster that rain
will fall?[t]
37 Who is wise enough to count the
clouds
and tilt them over to pour out
the rain,
38 rain that hardens the dust into
lumps?

39 Do you find food for lions to eat,
and satisfy hungry young lions
40 when they hide in their caves,
or lie in wait in their dens?
41 Who is it that feeds the ravens
when they wander about
hungry,
when their young cry to me for
food?

39

1 Do you know when mountain
goats are born?
Have you watched wild deer
give birth?
2 Do you know how long they carry
their young?
Do you know the time for their
birth?
3 Do you know when they will
crouch down
and bring their young into the
world?
4 In the wilds their young grow
strong;

they go away and don't come
back.

5 Who gave the wild donkeys their
freedom?
Who turned them loose and let
them roam?
6 I gave them the desert to be their
home,
and let them live on the salt
plains.
7 They keep far away from the
noisy cities,
and no one can tame them and
make them work.
8 The mountains are the pastures
where they feed,
where they search for anything
green to eat.

9 Will a wild ox work for you?
Is he willing to spend the night
in your stable?
10 Can you hold one with a rope and
make him plow?
Or make him pull a harrow in
your fields?
11 Can you rely on his great strength
and expect him to do your heavy
work?
12 Do you expect him to bring in
your harvest
and gather the grain from your
threshing place?

13 How fast the wings of an ostrich
beat!
But no ostrich can fly like a
stork.[u]
14 The ostrich leaves her eggs on the
ground
for the heat in the soil to warm
them.
15 She is unaware that a foot may
crush them
or a wild animal break them.
16 She acts as if the eggs were not
hers,
and is unconcerned that her
efforts were wasted.
17 It was I who made her foolish
and did not give her wisdom.
18 But when she begins to run,[v]
she can laugh at any horse and
rider.

---

s IBIS: *A bird in ancient Egypt that was believed to announce the flooding of the Nile River.*
t *Verse 36 in Hebrew is unclear.*　u *Verse 13 in Hebrew is unclear.*　v *Probable text* run;
Hebrew unclear.

19 Was it you, Job, who made horses
    so strong
    and gave them their flowing
    manes?
20 Did you make them leap like
    locusts
    and frighten people with their
    snorting?
21 They eagerly paw the ground in
    the valley;
    they rush into battle with all
    their strength.
22 They do not know the meaning of
    fear,
    and no sword can turn them
    back.
23 The weapons which their riders
    carry
    rattle and flash in the
    sun.
24 Trembling with excitement, the
    horses race ahead;
    when the trumpet blows, they
    can't stand still.
25 At each blast of the trumpet they
    snort;
    they can smell a battle before
    they get near,
    and they hear the officers
    shouting commands.

26 Does a hawk learn from you how
    to fly
    when it spreads its wings toward
    the south?
27 Does an eagle wait for your
    command
    to build its nest high in the
    mountains?
28 It makes its home on the highest
    rocks
    and makes the sharp peaks its
    fortress.
29 From there it watches near and
    far
    for something to kill and
    eat.
30 Around dead bodies the eagles
    gather,
    and the young eagles drink the
    blood.

40

1-2 Job, you challenged
    Almighty God;
    will you give up now, or will you
    answer?

Job

3-4 I spoke foolishly, LORD. What can I
    answer?
    I will not try to say anything
    else.
5 I have already said more than I
    should.

6 Then out of the storm the LORD spoke
to Job once again.

The LORD

7 Now stand up straight,
    and answer my questions.
8 Are you trying to prove that I am
    unjust —
    to put me in the wrong and
    yourself in the right?
9 Are you as strong as I am?
    Can your voice thunder as loud
    as mine?
10 If so, stand up in your honor and
    pride;
    clothe yourself with majesty and
    glory.
11 Look at those who are proud;
    pour out your anger and humble
    them.
12 Yes, look at them and bring them
    down;
    crush the wicked where they
    stand.
13 Bury them all in the ground;
    bind them in the world of the
    dead.
14 Then I will be the first to
    praise you
    and admit that you won the
    victory yourself.

15 Look at the monster Behemoth;w
    I created him and I created you.
    He eats grass like a cow,
16   but what strength there is in his
     body,
     and what power there is in his
     muscles!
17 His tail stands up like a cedar,
    and the muscles in his legs are
    strong.
18 His bones are as strong as bronze,
    and his legs are like iron bars.

19 The most amazing of all my
    creatures!
    Only his Creator can defeat him.

w BEHEMOTH: *Some identify this with the hippopotamus, others with a legendary creature.*

20 Grass to feed him grows
    on the hills where wild beasts
    play.*x*

21 He lies down under the thorn
    bushes,
    and hides among the reeds in
    the swamp.

22 The thorn bushes and the willows
    by the stream
    give him shelter in their shade.

23 He is not afraid of a rushing river;
    he is calm when the Jordan
    dashes in his face.

24 Who can blind his eyes and
    capture him?
    Or who can catch his snout in a
    trap?

41

Can you catch Leviathan*y* with
    a fishhook
or tie his tongue down with a
    rope?

2 Can you put a rope through his
    snout
    or put a hook through his jaws?

3 Will he beg you to let him go?
    Will he plead with you for
    mercy?

4 Will he make an agreement
    with you
    and promise to serve you
    forever?

5 Will you tie him like a pet bird,
    like something to amuse your
    servant women?

6 Will fishermen bargain over him?
    Will merchants cut him up to
    sell?

7 Can you fill his hide with fishing
    spears
    or pierce his head with a
    harpoon?

8 Touch him once and you'll never
    try it again;
    you'll never forget the fight!

9 Anyone who sees Leviathan
    loses courage and falls to the
    ground.

10 When he is aroused, he is fierce;
    no one would dare to stand
    before him.

11 Who can attack him and still be
    safe?

No one in all the world can
    do it.*z*

12 Let me tell you about Leviathan's
    legs
    and describe how great and
    strong he is.

13 No one can tear off his outer coat
    or pierce the armor*a* he wears.

14 Who can make him open his jaws,
    ringed with those terrifying
    teeth?

15 His back*b* is made of rows of
    shields,
    fastened together and hard as
    stone.

16 Each one is joined so tight to the
    next,
    not even a breath can come
    between.

17 They all are fastened so firmly
    together
    that nothing can ever pull them
    apart.

18 Light flashes when he sneezes,
    and his eyes glow like the
    rising sun.

19 Flames blaze from his mouth,
    and streams of sparks fly out.

20 Smoke comes pouring out of his
    nose,
    like smoke from weeds burning
    under a pot.

21 His breath starts fires burning;
    flames leap out of his mouth.

22 His neck is so powerful
    that all who meet him are
    terrified.

23 There is not a weak spot in his
    skin;
    it is as hard and unyielding as
    iron.

24 His stony heart is without fear,
    as unyielding and hard as a
    millstone.

25 When he rises up, even the
    strongest*c* are frightened;
    they are helpless with fear.

26 There is no sword that can
    wound him;
    no spear or arrow or lance that
    can harm him.

27 For him iron is as flimsy as straw,
    and bronze as soft as rotten
    wood.

---

x Verse 20 in Hebrew is unclear.   *y* LEVIATHAN: *See 3.8.*   *z Verse 11 in Hebrew is unclear.*
a One ancient translation armor; *Hebrew* bridle.   *b Some ancient translations* back; *Hebrew*
pride.   *c* strongest; *or* gods.

28 There is no arrow that can make
      him run;
    rocks thrown at him are like bits
      of straw.
29 To him a club is a piece of straw,
    and he laughs when men throw
      spears.
30 The scales on his belly are like
      jagged pieces of pottery;
    they tear up the muddy ground
      like a threshing sledge.d
31 He churns up the sea like boiling
      water
    and makes it bubble like a pot
      of oil.
32 He leaves a shining path
      behind him
    and turns the sea to white foam.
33 There is nothing on earth to
      compare with him;
    he is a creature that has no fear.
34 He looks down on even the
      proudest animals;
    he is king of all wild beasts.

42   Then Job answered the LORD.

Job

2 I know, LORD, that you are
      all-powerful;
    that you can do everything you
      want.
3 You ask how I dare question your
      wisdom
    when I am so very ignorant.
    I talked about things I did not
      understand,
    about marvels too great for me
      to know.
4 You told me to listen while you
      spoke
    and to try to answer your
      questions.
5 In the past I knew only what
      others had told me,
    but now I have seen you with
      my own eyes.

6 So I am ashamed of all I have said
    and repent in dust and ashes.

Conclusion

7 After the LORD had finished speaking
to Job, he said to Eliphaz, "I am angry
with you and your two friends, because
you did not speak the truth about me,
the way my servant Job did. 8 Now take
seven bulls and seven rams to Job and
offer them as a sacrifice for yourselves.
Job will pray for you, and I will answer
his prayer and not disgrace you the way
you deserve. You did not speak the truth
about me as he did."

9 Eliphaz, Bildad, and Zophar did what
the LORD had told them to do, and the
LORD answered Job's prayer.

10 Then, after Job had prayed for his
three friends, the LORD made him prosperous again and gave him twice as
much as he had had before. 11 All Job's
brothers and sisters and former friends
came to visit him and feasted with him
in his house. They expressed their sympathy and comforted him for all the
troubles the LORD had brought on him.
Each of them gave him some money and
a gold ring.

12 The LORD blessed the last part of
Job's life even more than he had blessed
the first. Job owned fourteen thousand
sheep, six thousand camels, two thousand head of cattle, and one thousand
donkeys. 13 He was the father of seven
sons and three daughters. 14 He called
the oldest daughter Jemimah, the second Keziah, and the youngest Keren
Happuch.e 15 There were no other
women in the whole world as beautiful
as Job's daughters. Their father gave
them a share of the inheritance along
with their brothers.

16 Job lived a hundred and forty years
after this, long enough to see his grandchildren and great-grandchildren.
17 And then he died at a very great age.

d THRESHING SLEDGES: *These had sharp pieces of iron or stone fastened beneath them.*
e *In Hebrew the names of Job's daughters suggest beauty both by their sound and by their
meaning.* JEMIMAH *means "dove";* KEZIAH *means "cassia," a variety of cinnamon used as a
perfume; and* KEREN HAPPUCH *means a small box used for eye make-up.*

HEBREW POETRY

When applied to the Bible, the word *poetry* has a meaning different from the typical English language structure to which we are accustomed. The main characteristic of Hebrew poetry is parallelism. This is a construction in which the content of one line is repeated, contrasted, or advanced by the content of the next—a type of sense rhythm characterized by thought arrangement rather than by word arrangement or rhyme.

There are three main types of parallelism in the Old Testament. Each is found in abundance in the Book of Psalms.

In **synonymous parallelism**, the second line of a poetic construction expresses essentially the same idea as the first: "The LORD Almighty is with us;/the God of Jacob is our refuge" (Ps 46.11).

In **antithetic parallelism**, the second line introduces a thought that is the direct opposite of the first idea: "The righteous are guided and protected by the LORD,/but the evil are on the way to their doom" (Ps 1.6).

In **progressive parallelism**, part of the first line of the poetic expression is repeated in the second line, but something more is added: "The ocean depths raise their voice, O LORD;/they raise their voice and roar" (Ps 93.3).

Another literary device the biblical writers used to give their psalms a peculiar style was the **alphabetic acrostic**. The best example of this technique is Psalm 119, which contains twenty-two different sections of eight verses each. In the original language, each verse in the major divisions of the psalm begins with the Hebrew letter that appears as the heading for that section.

PSALMS

Introduction

The book of Psalms is the hymnbook and prayer book of the Bible. Composed by different authors over a long period of time, these hymns and prayers were collected and used by the people of Israel in their worship, and eventually this collection was included in their Scriptures.

These religious poems are of many kinds: there are hymns of praise and worship of God; prayers for help, protection, and salvation; pleas for forgiveness; songs of thanksgiving for God's blessings; and petitions for the punishment of enemies. These prayers are both personal and national; some portray the most intimate feelings of one person, while others represent the needs and feelings of all the people of God.

The psalms were used by Jesus, quoted by the writers of the New Testament, and became the treasured book of worship of the Christian Church from its beginning.

Outline of Contents

The 150 psalms are grouped into five collections, or books, as follows:

BOOK ONE

(Psalms 1–41)

True Happiness

1 Happy are those
  who reject the advice of evil
    people,
  who do not follow the example
    of sinners
  or join those who have no use
    for God.
2 Instead, they find joy in obeying
    the Law of the LORD,
  and they study it day and night.
3 They are like trees that grow
    beside a stream,
  that bear fruit at the right time,
  and whose leaves do not dry up.
  They succeed in everything
    they do.

4 But evil people are not like this
    at all;
  they are like straw that the wind
    blows away.
5 Sinners will be condemned by God

and kept apart from God's own
    people.
6 The righteous are guided and
    protected by the LORD,
  but the evil are on the way to
    their doom.

God's Chosen King

2 Why do the nations plan
    rebellion?
  Why do people make their
    useless plots?
2 Their kings revolt,
    their rulers plot together against
      the LORD
  and against the king he chose.
3 "Let us free ourselves from their
    rule," they say;
  "let us throw off their control."

4 From his throne in heaven the
    Lord laughs
  and mocks their feeble plans.
5 Then he warns them in anger
  and terrifies them with his fury.
6 "On Zion,ᵃ my sacred hill," he
    says,
  "I have installed my king."

ᵃ ZION: The term "Zion" (originally a designation for "David's City," the Jebusite stronghold captured by King David's forces) was later extended in meaning to refer to the hill on which the Temple stood.

7 "I will announce," says the king,
   "what the LORD has declared.
   He said to me: 'You are my son;
   today I have become your
   father.
8 Ask, and I will give you all the
   nations;
   the whole earth will be yours.
9 You will break them with an
   iron rod;
   you will shatter them in pieces
   like a clay pot.' "

10 Now listen to this warning, you
   kings;
   learn this lesson, you rulers of
   the world:
11 Serve the LORD with fear;
   tremble 12 and bow down
   to him; b
   or else his anger will be quickly
   aroused,
   and you will suddenly die.
   Happy are all who go to him for
   protection.

Morning Prayer for Help c

3 I have so many enemies, LORD,
   so many who turn against me!
2 They talk about me and say,
   "God will not help him."

3 But you, O LORD, are always my
   shield from danger;
   you give me victory
   and restore my courage.
4 I call to the LORD for help,
   and from his sacred hill d he
   answers me.

5 I lie down and sleep,
   and all night long the LORD
   protects me.
6 I am not afraid of the thousands of
   enemies
   who surround me on every side.

7 Come, LORD! Save me, my God!
   You punish all my enemies
   and leave them powerless to
   harm me.
8 Victory comes from the LORD —
   may he bless his people.

Evening Prayer for Help e

4 Answer me when I pray,
   O God, my defender!
   When I was in trouble, you
   helped me.
   Be kind to me now and hear my
   prayer.

2 How long will you people
   insult me?
   How long will you love what is
   worthless
   and go after what is false?

3 Remember that the LORD has
   chosen the righteous for
   his own,
   and he hears me when I call
   to him.

4 Tremble with fear and stop
   sinning;
   think deeply about this,
   when you lie in silence on your
   beds.
5 Offer the right sacrifices to the
   LORD,
   and put your trust in him.

6 There are many who pray:
   "Give us more blessings, O LORD.
   Look on us with kindness!"
7 But the joy that you have
   given me
   is more than they will ever have
   with all their grain and wine.

8 When I lie down, I go to sleep in
   peace;
   you alone, O LORD, keep me
   perfectly safe.

A Prayer for Protection e

5 Listen to my words, O LORD,
   and hear my sighs.
2 Listen to my cry for help,
   my God and king!

   I pray to you, O LORD;
3 you hear my voice in the
   morning;
   at sunrise I offer my prayer f
   and wait for your answer.

---

b Probable text tremble . . . him; some other possible texts with trembling kiss his feet and
with trembling kiss the Son and tremble and kiss the mighty one; Hebrew unclear.
c HEBREW TITLE: A psalm by David, after he ran away from his son Absalom.   d SACRED HILL: See 2.6.
e HEBREW TITLE: A psalm by David.   f prayer; or sacrifice.

4 You are not a God who is pleased
  with wrongdoing;
   you allow no evil in your
   presence.
5 You cannot stand the sight of the
  proud;
   you hate all wicked people.
6 You destroy all liars
   and despise violent, deceitful
   people.

7 But because of your great love
   I can come into your house;
   I can worship in your holy Temple
   and bow down to you in
   reverence.
8 LORD, I have so many enemies!
   Lead me to do your will;
   make your way plain for me to
   follow.

9 What my enemies say can never
  be trusted;
   they only want to destroy.
  Their words are flattering and
  smooth,
   but full of deadly deceit.
10 Condemn and punish them,
  O God;
   may their own plots cause their
   ruin.
  Drive them out of your presence
   because of their many sins
   and their rebellion against you.

11 But all who find safety in you will
   rejoice;
   they can always sing for joy.
  Protect those who love you;
   because of you they are truly
   happy.
12 You bless those who obey you,
   LORD;
   your love protects them like a
   shield.

A Prayer for Help in Time
of Trouble g

6 LORD, don't be angry and
   rebuke me!
   Don't punish me in your anger!
2 I am worn out, O LORD; have pity
   on me!

Give me strength; I am
  completely exhausted
3   and my whole being is deeply
   troubled.
  How long, O LORD, will you wait
   to help me?

4 Come and save me, LORD;
   in your mercy rescue me from
   death.
5 In the world of the dead you are
   not remembered;
   no one can praise you there.

6 I am worn out with grief;
   every night my bed is damp
   from my weeping;
   my pillow is soaked with tears.
7 I can hardly see;
   my eyes are so swollen
   from the weeping caused by my
   enemies.

8 Keep away from me, you evil
  people!
  The LORD hears my weeping;
9   he listens to my cry for help
   and will answer my prayer.
10 My enemies will know the bitter
   shame of defeat;
   in sudden confusion they will be
   driven away.

A Prayer for Justice h

7 O LORD, my God, I come to you for
   protection;
   rescue me and save me from all
   who pursue me,
2 or else like a lion they will carry
   me off
   where no one can save me,
   and there they will tear me to
   pieces.

3-4 O LORD, my God, if I have wronged
  anyone,
   if I have betrayed a friend
   or without cause done violence
   to my enemy i —
   if I have done any of these
   things —
5 then let my enemies pursue me
   and catch me,
   let them cut me down and
   kill me

---

g HEBREW TITLE: *A psalm by David.*   h HEBREW TITLE: *A song which David sang to the LORD because
of Cush the Benjaminite.*   i without cause done violence to my enemy; or shown mercy to
someone who wronged me unjustly.

and leave me lifeless on the
ground!

6 Rise in your anger, O LORD!
Stand up against the fury of my
enemies;
rouse yourself and help me!
Justice is what you demand,
7 so bring together all the peoples
around you,
and rule over them from
above.ʲ
8 You are the judge of all people.
Judge in my favor, O LORD;
you know that I am innocent.
9 You are a righteous God
and judge our thoughts and
desires.
Stop the wickedness of evildoers
and reward those who are good.

10 God is my protector;
he saves those who obey him.
11 God is a righteous judge
and always condemns the
wicked.
12 If they do not change their ways,
God will sharpen his sword.
He bends his bow and makes it
ready;
13 he takes up his deadly weapons
and aims his burning arrows.

14 See how wicked people think up
evil;
they plan trouble and practice
deception.
15 But in the traps they set for others,
they themselves get caught.
16 So they are punished by their own
evil
and are hurt by their own
violence.

17 I thank the LORD for his justice;
I sing praises to the LORD, the
Most High.

God's Glory and Human Dignity ᵏ

8 O LORD, our Lord,
your greatness is seen in all the
world!
Your praise reaches up to the
heavens;

2 it is sung by children and
babies.
You are safe and secure from all
your enemies;
you stop anyone who
opposes you.

3 When I look at the sky, which you
have made,
at the moon and the stars, which
you set in their places—
4 what are human beings, that you
think of them;
mere mortals, that you care for
them?

5 Yet you made them inferior only
to yourself; ˡ
you crowned them with glory
and honor.
6 You appointed them rulers over
everything you made;
you placed them over all
creation:
7 sheep and cattle, and the wild
animals too;
8 the birds and the fish
and the creatures in the seas.

9 O LORD, our Lord,
your greatness is seen in all the
world!

Thanksgiving to God for His Justice ᵐ

9 I will praise you, LORD, with all my
heart;
I will tell of all the wonderful
things you have done.
2 I will sing with joy because of you.
I will sing praise to you,
Almighty God.

3 My enemies turn back when you
appear;
they fall down and die.
4 You are fair and honest in your
judgments,
and you have judged in my
favor.

5 You have condemned the heathen
and destroyed the wicked;

ʲ Probable text rule over them from above; Hebrew return above over them.
ᵏ HEBREW TITLE: A psalm by David.   ˡ yourself; or the gods, or the angels.
ᵐ HEBREW TITLE: A psalm by David.

they will be remembered no
    more.
6 Our enemies are finished forever;
    you have destroyed their cities,
    and they are completely
    forgotten.

7 But the LORD is king forever;
    he has set up his throne for
    judgment.
8 He rules the world with
    righteousness;
    he judges the nations with
    justice.

9 The LORD is a refuge for the
    oppressed,
    a place of safety in times of
    trouble.
10 Those who know you, LORD, will
    trust you;
    you do not abandon anyone who
    comes to you.

11 Sing praise to the LORD, who rules
    in Zion!
    Tell every nation what he has
    done!
12 God remembers those who suffer;
    he does not forget their cry,
    and he punishes those who
    wrong them.

13 Be merciful to me, O LORD!
    See the sufferings my enemies
    cause me!
    Rescue me from death, O LORD,
14   that I may stand before the
    people of Jerusalem
    and tell them all the things for
    which I praise you.
    I will rejoice because you
    saved me.

15 The heathen have dug a pit and
    fallen in;
    they have been caught in their
    own trap.
16 The LORD has revealed himself by
    his righteous judgments,
    and the wicked are trapped by
    their own deeds.

17 Death is the destiny of all the
    wicked,
    of all those who reject God.
18 The needy will not always be
    neglected;

the hope of the poor will not be
    crushed forever.

19 Come, LORD! Do not let anyone
    defy you!
    Bring the heathen before you
    and pronounce judgment on
    them.
20 Make them afraid, O LORD;
    make them know that they are
    only mortal beings.

A Prayer for Justice

10 Why are you so far away,
        O LORD?
    Why do you hide yourself when
    we are in trouble?
2 The wicked are proud and
    persecute the poor;
    catch them in the traps they
    have made.

3 The wicked are proud of their evil
    desires;
    the greedy curse and reject the
    LORD.
4 The wicked do not care about the
    LORD;
    in their pride they think that
    God doesn't matter.

5 The wicked succeed in everything.
    They cannot understand God's
    judgments;
    they sneer at their enemies.
6 They say to themselves, "We will
    never fail;
    we will never be in trouble."
7 Their speech is filled with curses,
    lies, and threats;
    they are quick to speak hateful,
    evil words.

8 They hide themselves in the
    villages,
    waiting to murder innocent
    people.
    They spy on their helpless victims;
9   they wait in their hiding place
    like lions.
    They lie in wait for the poor;
    they catch them in their traps
    and drag them away.

10 The helpless victims lie crushed;
    brute strength has defeated
    them.

11 The wicked say to themselves,
   "God doesn't care!
   He has closed his eyes and will
      never see me!"

12 O LORD, punish those wicked
      people!
   Remember those who are
      suffering!
13 How can the wicked despise God
   and say to themselves, "He will
      not punish me"?

14 But you do see; you take notice of
      trouble and suffering
   and are always ready to help.
   The helpless commit themselves
      to you;
   you have always helped the
      needy.

15 Break the power of wicked and
      evil people;
   punish them for the wrong they
      have done
   until they do it no more.

16 The LORD is king forever and ever.
   Those who worship other gods
      will vanish from his land.

17 You will listen, O LORD, to the
      prayers of the lowly;
   you will give them courage.
18 You will hear the cries of the
      oppressed and the orphans;
   you will judge in their favor,
   so that mortal men may cause
      terror no more.

Confidence in the LORD[n]

11 I trust in the LORD for safety.
      How foolish of you to say
         to me,
   "Fly away like a bird to the
      mountains,[o]
2   because the wicked have drawn
      their bows and aimed their
         arrows
   to shoot from the shadows at
      good people.
3 There is nothing a good person
      can do
   when everything falls apart."

4 The LORD is in his holy temple;
   he has his throne in heaven.
   He watches people everywhere
   and knows what they are doing.
5 He examines the good and the
      wicked alike;
   the lawless he hates with all his
      heart.

6 He sends down flaming coals[p]
   and burning sulfur on the
      wicked;
   he punishes them with scorching
      winds.
7 The LORD is righteous and loves
      good deeds;
   those who do them will live in
      his presence.

A Prayer for Help[q]

12 Help us, LORD!
      There is not a good person
         left;
   honest people can no longer be
      found.
2 All of them lie to one another;
   they deceive each other with
      flattery.

3 Silence those flattering tongues,
      O LORD!
   Close those boastful mouths
      that say,
4 "With our words we get what we
      want.
   We will say what we wish,
   and no one can stop us."

5 "But now I will come," says the
      LORD,
   "because the needy are
      oppressed
   and the persecuted groan in
      pain.
   I will give them the security they
      long for."

6 The promises of the LORD can be
      trusted;
   they are as genuine as silver
   refined seven times in the
      furnace.

7-8 The wicked are everywhere,

and everyone praises what is
evil.
Keep us always safe, O LORD,
and preserve us from such
people.

A Prayer for Help *q*

13 How much longer will you
forget me, LORD? Forever?
How much longer will you hide
yourself from me?
2 How long must I endure trouble?
How long will sorrow fill my
heart day and night?
How long will my enemies
triumph over me?

3 Look at me, O LORD my God, and
answer me.
Restore my strength; don't let
me die.
4 Don't let my enemies say, "We
have defeated him."
Don't let them gloat over my
downfall.

5 I rely on your constant love;
I will be glad, because you will
rescue me.
6 I will sing to you, O LORD,
because you have been good
to me.

Human Wickedness *r*

(Psalm 53)

14 Fools say to themselves,
"There is no God!"
They are all corrupt,
and they have done terrible
things;
there is no one who does what is
right.

2 The LORD looks down from heaven
at us humans
to see if there are any who are
wise,
any who worship him.
3 But they have all gone wrong;
they are all equally bad.
Not one of them does what is
right,
not a single one.

4 "Don't they know?" asks the LORD.

"Are all these evildoers
ignorant?
They live by robbing my people,
and they never pray to me."

5 But then they will be terrified,
for God is with those who
obey him.
6 Evildoers frustrate the plans of the
humble,
but the LORD is their protection.

7 How I pray that victory
will come to Israel from Zion.
How happy the people of Israel
will be
when the LORD makes them
prosperous again!

What God Requires *s*

15 LORD, who may enter your
Temple?
Who may worship on Zion, your
sacred hill? *t*

2 Those who obey God in everything
and always do what is right,
whose words are true and sincere,
3   and who do not slander others.
They do no wrong to their friends
nor spread rumors about their
neighbors.
4 They despise those whom God
rejects,
but honor those who obey the
LORD.
They always do what they
promise,
no matter how much it may cost.
5 They make loans without charging
interest
and cannot be bribed to testify
against the innocent.

Whoever does these things will
always be secure.

A Prayer of Confidence *u*

16 Protect me, O God; I trust in
you for safety.
2 I say to the LORD, "You are my
Lord;
all the good things I have come
from you."

---

q HEBREW TITLE: *A psalm by David.*   *r* HEBREW TITLE: *By David.*   *s* HEBREW TITLE: *A psalm by David.*
t SACRED HILL: *See 2.6.*   *u* HEBREW TITLE: *A psalm by David.*

³How excellent are the LORD's
  faithful people!
  My greatest pleasure is to be
    with them.

⁴Those who rush to other gods
  bring many troubles on
    themselves.ᵛ
  I will not take part in their
    sacrifices;
  I will not worship their gods.

⁵You, LORD, are all I have,
  and you give me all I need;
  my future is in your hands.
⁶How wonderful are your gifts
    to me;
  how good they are!

⁷I praise the LORD, because he
    guides me,
  and in the night my conscience
    warns me.
⁸I am always aware of the LORD's
    presence;
  he is near, and nothing can
    shake me.

⁹And so I am thankful and glad,
  and I feel completely secure,
¹⁰because you protect me from the
    power of death.
  I have served you faithfully,
  and you will not abandon me to
    the world of the dead.

¹¹You will show me the path that
    leads to life;
  your presence fills me with joy
  and brings me pleasure
    forever.

The Prayer of an Innocent Personʷ

17 Listen, O LORD, to my plea for
    justice;
  pay attention to my cry
    for help!
  Listen to my honest prayer.
²You will judge in my favor,
  because you know what is right.

³You know my heart.
  You have come to me at night;
  you have examined me
    completely

and found no evil desire
  in me.
I speak no evil, ⁴as others do;
  I have obeyed your command
  and have not followed paths of
    violence.
⁵I have always walked in
    your way
  and have never strayed from it.

⁶I pray to you, O God, because you
    answer me;
  so turn to me and listen to my
    words.
⁷Reveal your wonderful love and
    save me;
  at your side I am safe from my
    enemies.

⁸Protect me as you would your very
    eyes;
  hide me in the shadow of your
    wings
⁹ from the attacks of the wicked.

Deadly enemies surround me;
¹⁰ they have no pity and speak
    proudly.
¹¹They are around me now,
    wherever I turn,
  watching for a chance to pull me
    down.
¹²They are like lions, waiting
    for me,
  wanting to tear me to pieces.

¹³Come, LORD! Oppose my enemies
  and defeat them!
Save me from the wicked by your
    sword;
¹⁴ save me from those who in this
    life have all they want.
Punish them with the sufferings
  you have stored up
    for them;
  may there be enough for their
    children
  and some left over for their
    children's children!

¹⁵But I will see you, because I have
    done no wrong;
  and when I awake, your
    presence will fill me
    with joy.

ᵛ *Probable text* Those . . . themselves; *Hebrew unclear.*   ʷ HEBREW TITLE: *A prayer by David.*

David's Song of Victory[x]
(2 Samuel 22.1-51)

18 How I love you, LORD!
  You are my defender.

2 The LORD is my protector;
  he is my strong fortress.
My God is my protection,
  and with him I am safe.
He protects me like a shield;
  he defends me and keeps me
    safe.
3 I call to the LORD,
  and he saves me from my
    enemies.
Praise the LORD!

4 The danger of death was all
    around me;
  the waves of destruction rolled
    over me.
5 The danger of death was
    around me,
  and the grave set its trap for me.
6 In my trouble I called to the LORD;
  I called to my God for help.
In his temple he heard my voice;
  he listened to my cry for help.

7 Then the earth trembled and
    shook;
  the foundations of the mountains
    rocked and quivered,
  because God was angry.
8 Smoke poured out of his nostrils,
  a consuming flame and burning
    coals from his mouth.
9 He tore the sky open and came
    down
  with a dark cloud under his feet.
10 He flew swiftly on his winged
    creature;[y]
  he traveled on the wings of the
    wind.
11 He covered himself with darkness;
  thick clouds, full of water,
    surrounded him.
12 Hailstones and flashes of fire
  came from the lightning
    before him
  and broke through the dark
    clouds.

13 Then the LORD thundered from
    the sky;
  and the voice of the Most High
    was heard.[z]
14 He shot his arrows and scattered
    his enemies;
  with flashes of lightning he sent
    them running.
15 The floor of the ocean was laid
    bare,
  and the foundations of the earth
    were uncovered,
when you rebuked your enemies,
  LORD,
  and roared at them in anger.

16 The LORD reached down from
    above and took hold of me;
  he pulled me out of the deep
    waters.
17 He rescued me from my powerful
    enemies
  and from all those who
    hate me—
  they were too strong for me.
18 When I was in trouble, they
    attacked me,
  but the LORD protected me.
19 He helped me out of danger;
  he saved me because he was
    pleased with me.

20 The LORD rewards me because I do
    what is right;
  he blesses me because I am
    innocent.
21 I have obeyed the law of the LORD;
  I have not turned away from
    my God.
22 I have observed all his laws;
  I have not disobeyed his
    commands.
23 He knows that I am faultless,
  that I have kept myself from
    doing wrong.
24 And so he rewards me because I
    do what is right,
  because he knows that I am
    innocent.

25 O LORD, you are faithful to those
  who are faithful to you;
  completely good to those who
    are perfect.

---

x HEBREW TITLE: *The words that David, the LORD's servant, sang to the LORD on the day the LORD saved him from Saul and all his other enemies.*   y WINGED CREATURE: *See Word List.*
z *One ancient translation (and see 2 S 22.14) was heard; Hebrew was heard hailstones and flashes of fire.*

26 You are pure to those who are
     pure,
     but hostile to those who are
     wicked.
27 You save those who are humble,
     but you humble those who are
     proud.

28 O Lord, you give me light;
     you dispel my darkness.
29 You give me strength to attack
     my enemies
     and power to overcome their
     defenses.

30 This God—how perfect are his
     deeds!
     How dependable his words!
   He is like a shield
     for all who seek his protection.
31 The Lord alone is God;
     God alone is our defense.
32 He is the God who makes me
     strong,
     who makes my pathway safe.
33 He makes me sure-footed as a
     deer;
     he keeps me safe on the
     mountains.
34 He trains me for battle,
     so that I can use the
     strongest bow.

35 O Lord, you protect me and
     save me;
     your care has made me great,
     and your power has kept me
     safe.
36 You have kept me from being
     captured,
     and I have never fallen.
37 I pursue my enemies and catch
     them;
     I do not stop until I destroy
     them.
38 I strike them down, and they
     cannot rise;
     they lie defeated before me.
39 You give me strength for the battle
     and victory over my enemies.
40 You make my enemies run
     from me;
     I destroy those who hate me.
41 They cry for help, but no one
     saves them;

they call to the Lord, but he does
     not answer.
42 I crush them, so that they become
     like dust
     which the wind blows away.
   I trample on them like mud in the
     streets.

43 You saved me from a rebellious
     people
     and made me ruler over the
     nations;
     people I did not know have now
     become my subjects.
44 Foreigners bow before me;
     when they hear me, they obey.
45 They lose their courage
     and come trembling from their
     fortresses.

46 The Lord lives! Praise my
     defender!
   Proclaim the greatness of the
     God who saves me.
47 He gives me victory over my
     enemies;
     he subdues the nations under me
48   and saves me from my foes.

   O Lord, you give me victory over
     my enemies
     and protect me from violent
     people.
49 And so I praise you among the
     nations;
     I sing praises to you.

50 God gives great victories to his
     king;
     he shows constant love to the
     one he has chosen,
     to David and his descendants
     forever.

God's Glory in Creation [a]

19 How clearly the sky reveals
          God's glory!
     How plainly it shows what he
     has done!
2 Each day announces it to the
     following day;
     each night repeats it to the next.
3 No speech or words are used,
     no sound is heard;
4 yet their message [b] goes out to all
     the world

---

a HEBREW TITLE: *A psalm by David.*   b *Some ancient translations* message; *Hebrew* line.

and is heard to the ends of the
 earth.
God made a home in the sky for
 the sun;
5 it comes out in the morning like
 a happy bridegroom,
 like an athlete eager to run a
  race.
6 It starts at one end of the sky
 and goes across to the other.
 Nothing can hide from its heat.

The Law of the LORD

7 The law of the LORD is perfect;
 it gives new strength.
The commands of the LORD are
 trustworthy,
 giving wisdom to those who
  lack it.
8 The laws of the LORD are right,
 and those who obey them are
  happy.
The commands of the LORD are
 just
 and give understanding to the
  mind.
9 Reverence for the LORD is good;
 it will continue forever.
The judgments of the LORD are
 just;
 they are always fair.
10 They are more desirable than the
 finest gold;
 they are sweeter than the purest
  honey.
11 They give knowledge to me, your
 servant;
 I am rewarded for obeying them.

12 None of us can see our own
 errors;
 deliver me, LORD, from hidden
  faults!
13 Keep me safe, also, from willful
 sins;
 don't let them rule over me.
Then I shall be perfect
 and free from the evil of sin.

14 May my words and my thoughts
 be acceptable to you,
 O LORD, my refuge and my
  redeemer!

A Prayer for Victory[c]

20 May the LORD answer you when
 you are in trouble!
May the God of Jacob
 protect you!
2 May he send you help from his
 Temple
 and give you aid from Mount
  Zion.
3 May he accept all your offerings
 and be pleased with all your
  sacrifices.
4 May he give you what you desire
 and make all your plans
  succeed.
5 Then we will shout for joy over
 your victory
 and celebrate your triumph by
  praising our God.
May the LORD answer all your
 requests.

6 Now I know that the LORD gives
 victory to his chosen king;
 he answers him from his holy
  heaven
 and by his power gives him
  great victories.
7 Some trust in their war chariots
 and others in their horses,
 but we trust in the power of the
  LORD our God.
8 Such people will stumble and fall,
 but we will rise and stand firm.

9 Give victory to the king, O LORD;
 answer[d] us when we call.

Praise for Victory[e]

21 The king is glad, O LORD,
 because you gave him
  strength;
 he rejoices because you made
  him victorious.
2 You have given him his heart's
 desire;
 you have answered his request.

3 You came to him with great
 blessings
 and set a crown of gold on his
  head.
4 He asked for life, and you gave it,
 a long and lasting life.

---

c HEBREW TITLE: *A psalm by David.*   d *Some ancient translations* answer; *Hebrew* he will answer.
e HEBREW TITLE: *A psalm by David.*

5His glory is great because of your
   help;
   you have given him fame and
     majesty.
6Your blessings are with him
   forever,
   and your presence fills him
     with joy.

7The king trusts in the LORD
   Almighty;
   and because of the LORD's
     constant love
   he will always be secure.
8The king will capture all his
   enemies;
   he will capture everyone who
     hates him.
9He will destroy them like a blazing
   fire
   when he appears.

   The LORD will devour them in his
     anger,
   and fire will consume them.
10None of their descendants will
   survive;
   the king will kill them all.

11They make their plans, and plot
   against him,
   but they will not succeed.
12He will shoot his arrows at them
   and make them turn and run.

13We praise you, LORD, for your
   great strength!
   We will sing and praise your
     power.

A Cry of Anguish and a Song of Praise e

22 My God, my God, why have
      you abandoned me?
I have cried desperately for help,
   but still it does not come.
2During the day I call to you,
   my God,
   but you do not answer;
I call at night,
   but get no rest.
3But you are enthroned as the
   Holy One,
   the one whom Israel
     praises.

4Our ancestors put their trust
   in you;
   they trusted you, and you saved
     them.
5They called to you and escaped
   from danger;
   they trusted you and were not
     disappointed.

6But I am no longer a human
   being; I am a worm,
   despised and scorned by
     everyone!
7All who see me make fun of me;
   they stick out their tongues and
     shake their heads.
8"You relied on the LORD,"
   they say.
   "Why doesn't he save you?
If the LORD likes you,
   why doesn't he help you?"

9It was you who brought me safely
   through birth,
   and when I was a baby, you
     kept me safe.
10I have relied on you since the day
   I was born,
   and you have always been
     my God.
11Do not stay away from me!
   Trouble is near,
   and there is no one to help.

12Many enemies surround me like
   bulls;
   they are all around me,
   like fierce bulls from the land of
     Bashan.
13They open their mouths like lions,
   roaring and tearing at me.

14My strength is gone,
   gone like water spilled on the
     ground.
   All my bones are out of joint;
   my heart is like melted wax.
15My throat f is as dry as dust,
   and my tongue sticks to the roof
     of my mouth.
   You have left me for dead in the
     dust.

16An evil gang is around me;
   like a pack of dogs they close in
     on me;

---

e HEBREW TITLE: *A psalm by David.*   f *Probable text* throat; *Hebrew* strength.

they tear at^g my hands and feet.
17 All my bones can be seen.
My enemies look at me and
stare.
18 They gamble for my clothes
and divide them among
themselves.

19 O Lord, don't stay away from me!
Come quickly to my rescue!
20 Save me from the sword;
save my life from these dogs.
21 Rescue me from these lions;
I am helpless^h before these wild
bulls.

22 I will tell my people what you
have done;
I will praise you in their
assembly:
23 "Praise him, you servants of the
Lord!
Honor him, you descendants of
Jacob!
Worship him, you people of
Israel!
24 He does not neglect the poor or
ignore their suffering;
he does not turn away from
them,
but answers when they call for
help."

25 In the full assembly I will praise
you for what you have done;
in the presence of those who
worship you
I will offer the sacrifices I
promised.
26 The poor will eat as much as they
want;
those who come to the Lord will
praise him.
May they prosper forever!

27 All nations will remember the
Lord.
From every part of the world
they will turn to him;
all races will worship him.
28 The Lord is king,
and he rules the nations.

29 All proud people will bow down
to him; ⁱ
all mortals will bow down
before him.
30 Future generations will serve him;
they will speak of the Lord to
the coming generation.
31 People not yet born will be told:
"The Lord saved his people."

The Lord Our Shepherd^j

23 The Lord is my shepherd;
I have everything I need.
2 He lets me rest in fields of green
grass
and leads me to quiet pools of
fresh water.
3 He gives me new strength.
He guides me in the right paths,
as he has promised.
4 Even if I go through the deepest
darkness,
I will not be afraid, Lord,
for you are with me.
Your shepherd's rod and staff
protect me.

5 You prepare a banquet for me,
where all my enemies can
see me;
you welcome me as an honored
guest
and fill my cup to the brim.
6 I know that your goodness and
love will be with me all my
life;
and your house will be my home
as long as I live.

The Great King^j

24 The world and all that is in it
belong to the Lord;
the earth and all who live on it
are his.
2 He built it on the deep waters
beneath the earth
and laid its foundations in the
ocean depths.

3 Who has the right to go up the
Lord's hill?^k
Who may enter his holy
Temple?

---

^g Some ancient translations they tear at; others they tie; Hebrew like a lion.
^h Some ancient translations I am helpless; Hebrew you answered me.   ⁱ Probable text will
bow down to him; Hebrew will eat and bow down.   ^j HEBREW TITLE: A psalm by David.
^k THE LORD'S HILL: The hill in Jerusalem on which the Temple was built.

4Those who are pure in act and in
thought,
who do not worship idols
or make false promises.
5The LORD will bless them and save
them;
God will declare them innocent.
6Such are the people who come
to God,
who come into the presence of
the God of Jacob.

7Fling wide the gates,
open the ancient doors,
and the great king will come in.
8Who is this great king?
He is the LORD, strong and mighty,
the LORD, victorious in battle.

9Fling wide the gates,
open the ancient doors,
and the great king will come in.
10Who is this great king?
The triumphant LORD—he is the
great king!

A Prayer for Guidance and Protection[l]

25 To you, O LORD, I offer my
prayer;
2 in you, my God, I trust.
Save me from the shame of defeat;
don't let my enemies gloat
over me!
3Defeat does not come to those
who trust in you,
but to those who are quick to
rebel against you.

4Teach me your ways, O LORD;
make them known to me.
5Teach me to live according to your
truth,
for you are my God, who
saves me.
I always trust in you.

6Remember, O LORD, your kindness
and constant love
which you have shown from
long ago.
7Forgive the sins and errors of my
youth.
In your constant love and
goodness,
remember me, LORD!

8Because the LORD is righteous and
good,
he teaches sinners the path they
should follow.
9He leads the humble in the
right way
and teaches them his will.
10With faithfulness and love he
leads
all who keep his covenant and
obey his commands.

11Keep your promise, LORD, and
forgive my sins,
for they are many.
12Those who have reverence for the
LORD
will learn from him the path
they should follow.
13They will always be prosperous,
and their children will possess
the land.
14The LORD is the friend of those
who obey him
and he affirms his covenant with
them.

15I look to the LORD for help at all
times,
and he rescues me from danger.
16Turn to me, LORD, and be merciful
to me,
because I am lonely and weak.
17Relieve me of my worries
and save me from all my
troubles.
18Consider my distress and suffering
and forgive all my sins.

19See how many enemies I have;
see how much they hate me.
20Protect me and save me;
keep me from defeat.
I come to you for safety.
21May my goodness and honesty
preserve me,
because I trust in you.

22From all their troubles, O God,
save your people Israel!

The Prayer of a Good Person[l]

26 Declare me innocent, O LORD,
because I do what is right
and trust you completely.
2Examine me and test me, LORD;

----

l HEBREW TITLE: By David.

judge my desires and thoughts.
3 Your constant love is my guide;
   your faithfulness always
     leads me.*m*

4 I do not keep company with
   worthless people;
   I have nothing to do with
     hypocrites.
5 I hate the company of the evil
   and avoid the wicked.

6 Lord, I wash my hands to show
   that I am innocent
   and march in worship around
     your altar.
7 I sing a hymn of thanksgiving
   and tell of all your wonderful
     deeds.

8 I love the house where you live,
   O Lord,
   the place where your glory
     dwells.
9 Do not destroy me with the
     sinners;
   spare me from the fate of
     murderers —
10   those who do evil all the time
   and are always ready to take
     bribes.

11 As for me, I do what is right;
   be merciful to me and
     save me!

12 I am safe from all dangers;
   in the assembly of his people I
     praise the Lord.

A Prayer of Praise[n]

27 The Lord is my light and my
     salvation;
   I will fear no one.
The Lord protects me from all
     danger;
   I will never be afraid.

2 When evil people attack me and
   try to kill me,
   they stumble and fall.
3 Even if a whole army
   surrounds me,
   I will not be afraid;

even if enemies attack me,
   I will still trust God.*o*

4 I have asked the Lord for one
     thing;
   one thing only do I want:
to live in the Lord's house all my
     life,
   to marvel there at his goodness,
   and to ask for his guidance.
5 In times of trouble he will
     shelter me;
   he will keep me safe in his
     Temple
   and make me secure on a high
     rock.
6 So I will triumph over my enemies
   around me.
   With shouts of joy I will offer
     sacrifices in his Temple;
   I will sing, I will praise the Lord.

7 Hear me, Lord, when I call to you!
   Be merciful and answer me!
8 When you said, "Come
     worship me,"
   I answered, "I will come, Lord."
9   Don't hide yourself from me!

Don't be angry with me;
   don't turn your servant away.
You have been my help;
   don't leave me, don't
     abandon me,
   O God, my savior.
10 My father and mother may
     abandon me,
   but the Lord will take care
     of me.

11 Teach me, Lord, what you want
     me to do,
   and lead me along a safe path,
   because I have many
     enemies.
12 Don't abandon me to my enemies,
   who attack me with lies and
     threats.

13 I know that I will live to see
   the Lord's goodness in this
     present life.
14 Trust in the Lord.
   Have faith, do not despair.
   Trust in the Lord.

---

m your faithfulness always leads me; *or* I live in loyalty to you.   *n* HEBREW TITLE: *By David.*
o still trust God; *or* not lose courage.

A Prayer for Help[p]

28 O LORD, my defender, I call
to you.
Listen to my cry!
If you do not answer me,
  I will be among those who go
    down to the world of the dead.
2 Hear me when I cry to you for
    help,
  when I lift my hands toward
    your holy Temple.
3 Do not condemn me with the
    wicked,
  with those who do evil —
  those whose words are friendly,
  but who have hatred in their
    hearts.

4 Punish them for what they have
    done,
  for the evil they have committed.
  Punish them for all their deeds;
  give them what they deserve!
5 They take no notice of what the
    LORD has done
  or of what he has made;
  so he will punish them
    and destroy them forever.

6 Give praise to the LORD;
  he has heard my cry for help.
7 The LORD protects and defends me;
  I trust in him.
  He gives me help and makes me
    glad;
  I praise him with joyful songs.

8 The LORD protects his people;
  he defends and saves his chosen
    king.
9 Save your people, LORD,
  and bless those who are yours.
  Be their shepherd,
  and take care of them forever.

The Voice of the LORD in the Storm[q]

29 Praise the LORD, you heavenly
    beings;
  praise his glory and power.
2 Praise the LORD's glorious name;
  bow down before the Holy One
    when he appears.[r]

3 The voice of the LORD is heard on
    the seas;
  the glorious God thunders,
  and his voice echoes over the
    ocean.
4 The voice of the LORD is heard
  in all its might and majesty.

5 The voice of the LORD breaks the
    cedars,
  even the cedars of Lebanon.
6 He makes the mountains of
    Lebanon jump like calves
  and makes Mount Hermon leap
    like a young bull.

7 The voice of the LORD makes the
    lightning flash.
8 His voice makes the desert shake;
  he shakes the desert of Kadesh.
9 The LORD's voice shakes the oaks[s]
  and strips the leaves from the
    trees
  while everyone in his Temple
    shouts, "Glory to God!"

10 The LORD rules over the deep
    waters;
  he rules as king forever.
11 The LORD gives strength to his
    people
  and blesses them with peace.

A Prayer of Thanksgiving[t]

30 I praise you, LORD, because you
    have saved me
  and kept my enemies from
    gloating over me.
2 I cried to you for help, O LORD
    my God,
  and you healed me;
3   you kept me from the grave.
  I was on my way to the depths
    below,[u]
  but you restored my life.

4 Sing praise to the LORD,
  all his faithful people!
  Remember what the Holy One has
    done,
  and give him thanks!
5 His anger lasts only a moment,
  his goodness for a lifetime.
  Tears may flow in the night,

---

p HEBREW TITLE: *By David.*   q HEBREW TITLE: *A psalm by David.*   r *when he appears; or in garments
of worship; or in his beautiful Temple.*   s *Probable text* shakes the oaks; *Hebrew* makes the
deer give birth.   t HEBREW TITLE: *A song for the dedication of the Temple; a psalm by David.*
u THE DEPTHS BELOW: *The world of the dead (see 6.5).*

but joy comes in the morning.

6 I felt secure and said to myself,
  "I will never be defeated."
7 You were good to me, LORD;
  you protected me like a
    mountain fortress.
  But then you hid yourself
    from me,
  and I was afraid.

8 I called to you, LORD;
  I begged for your help:
9 "What will you gain from my
    death?
  What profit from my going to
    the grave?
  Are dead people able to
    praise you?
  Can they proclaim your
    unfailing goodness?
10 Hear me, LORD, and be merciful!
  Help me, LORD!"

11 You have changed my sadness
    into a joyful dance;
  you have taken away my sorrow
  and surrounded me with joy.
12 So I will not be silent;
  I will sing praise to you.
  LORD, you are my God;
  I will give you thanks forever.

A Prayer of Trust in God v

31 I come to you, LORD, for
      protection;
  never let me be defeated.
  You are a righteous God;
  save me, I pray!
2 Hear me! Save me now!
  Be my refuge to protect me;
  my defense to save me.

3 You are my refuge and defense;
  guide me and lead me as you
    have promised.
4 Keep me safe from the trap that
    has been set for me;
  shelter me from danger.
5 I place myself in your care.
  You will save me, LORD;
  you are a faithful God.

6 You hate those who worship false
    gods,
  but I trust in you.

7 I will be glad and rejoice
  because of your constant love.
  You see my suffering;
  you know my trouble.
8 You have not let my enemies
    capture me;
  you have given me freedom to
    go where I wish.

9 Be merciful to me, LORD,
  for I am in trouble;
  my eyes are tired from so much
    crying;
  I am completely worn out.
10 I am exhausted by sorrow,
  and weeping has shortened my
    life.
  I am weak from all my troubles; w
  even my bones are wasting
    away.
11 All my enemies, and especially my
    neighbors,
  treat me with contempt.
  Those who know me are afraid
    of me;
  when they see me in the street,
    they run away.
12 Everyone has forgotten me, as
    though I were dead;
  I am like something thrown
    away.
13 I hear many enemies whispering;
  terror is all around me.
  They are making plans
    against me,
  plotting to kill me.

14 But my trust is in you, O LORD;
  you are my God.
15 I am always in your care;
  save me from my enemies,
  from those who persecute me.
16 Look on your servant with
    kindness;
  save me in your constant love.
17 I call to you, LORD;
  don't let me be disgraced.
  May the wicked be disgraced;
  may they go silently down to the
    world of the dead.
18 Silence those liars —
  all the proud and arrogant
  who speak with contempt about
    the righteous.

---

v HEBREW TITLE: A psalm by David.   w Some ancient translations troubles; Hebrew iniquity.

19 How wonderful are the good
    things
  you keep for those who
    honor you!
Everyone knows how good
    you are,
  how securely you protect those
    who trust you.
20 You hide them in the safety of
    your presence
  from the plots of others;
in a safe shelter you hide them
    from the insults of their enemies.

21 Praise the LORD!
How wonderfully he showed his
    love for me
  when I was surrounded and
    attacked!
22 I was afraid and thought
    that he had driven me out of his
    presence.
But he heard my cry,
  when I called to him for help.

23 Love the LORD, all his faithful
    people.
The LORD protects the faithful,
  but punishes the proud as they
    deserve.
24 Be strong, be courageous,
  all you that hope in the LORD.

*Confession and Forgiveness*x

32 Happy are those whose sins are
    forgiven,
  whose wrongs are pardoned.
2 Happy is the one whom the LORD
    does not accuse of doing
    wrong
and who is free from all deceit.

3 When I did not confess my sins,
  I was worn out from crying all
    day long.
4 Day and night you punished me,
    LORD;
  my strength was completely
    drained,
  as moisture is dried up by the
    summer heat.

5 Then I confessed my sins to you;
  I did not conceal my
    wrongdoings.
I decided to confess them to you,

and you forgave all my sins.

6 So all your loyal people should
    pray to you in times of need;y
  when a great flood of trouble
    comes rushing in,
  it will not reach them.
7 You are my hiding place;
  you will save me from trouble.
I sing aloud of your salvation,
  because you protect me.

8 The LORD says, "I will teach you
    the way you should go;
  I will instruct you and
    advise you.
9 Don't be stupid like a horse or a
    mule,
  which must be controlled with a
    bit and bridle
to make it submit."

10 The wicked will have to suffer,
  but those who trust in the LORD
  are protected by his constant
    love.
11 You that are righteous, be glad
    and rejoice
because of what the LORD has
    done.
You that obey him, shout for joy!

A Song of Praise

33 All you that are righteous,
    shout for joy for what the
    LORD has done;
praise him, all you that
    obey him.
2 Give thanks to the LORD with
    harps,
  sing to him with stringed
    instruments.
3 Sing a new song to him,
  play the harp with skill, and
    shout for joy!

4 The words of the LORD are true,
  and all his works are
    dependable.
5 The LORD loves what is righteous
    and just;
  his constant love fills the earth.

6 The LORD created the heavens by
    his command,

---

x HEBREW TITLE: *A poem by David.*   y *Some ancient translations* need; *Hebrew* finding only.

the sun, moon, and stars by his
spoken word.
7 He gathered all the seas into one
place;
he shut up the ocean depths in
storerooms.

8 Worship the LORD, all the earth!
Honor him, all peoples of the
world!
9 When he spoke, the world was
created;
at his command everything
appeared.

10 The LORD frustrates the purposes
of the nations;
he keeps them from carrying out
their plans.
11 But his plans endure forever;
his purposes last eternally.
12 Happy is the nation whose God is
the LORD;
happy are the people he has
chosen for his own!

13 The LORD looks down from
heaven
and sees all of us humans.
14 From where he rules, he looks
down
on all who live on earth.
15 He forms all their thoughts
and knows everything they do.

16 A king does not win because of
his powerful army;
a soldier does not triumph
because of his strength.
17 War horses are useless for
victory;
their great strength cannot save.

18 The LORD watches over those who
obey him,
those who trust in his constant
love.
19 He saves them from death;
he keeps them alive in times of
famine.

20 We put our hope in the LORD;
he is our protector and our help.
21 We are glad because of him;
we trust in his holy name.

22 May your constant love be with
us, LORD,
as we put our hope in you.

In Praise of God's Goodness z

34 I will always thank the LORD;
I will never stop praising him.
2 I will praise him for what he has
done;
may all who are oppressed listen
and be glad!
3 Proclaim with me the LORD's
greatness;
let us praise his name together!

4 I prayed to the LORD, and he
answered me;
he freed me from all my fears.
5 The oppressed look to him and are
glad;
they will never be disappointed.
6 The helpless call to him, and he
answers;
he saves them from all their
troubles.
7 His angel guards those who honor
the LORD
and rescues them from danger.

8 Find out for yourself how good the
LORD is.
Happy are those who find safety
with him.
9 Honor the LORD, all his people;
those who obey him have all
they need.
10 Even lions go hungry for lack of
food,
but those who obey the LORD
lack nothing good.

11 Come, my young friends, and
listen to me,
and I will teach you to honor the
LORD.
12 Would you like to enjoy life?
Do you want long life and
happiness?
13 Then keep from speaking evil
and from telling lies.
14 Turn away from evil and do good;
strive for peace with all your
heart.

z HEBREW TITLE: *By David, who left the presence of Abimelech after pretending to be crazy
and being sent away by him.*

15 The LORD watches over the
   righteous
   and listens to their cries;
16 but he opposes those who do evil,
   so that when they die, they are
   soon forgotten.
17 The righteous call to the LORD, and
   he listens;
   he rescues them from all their
   troubles.
18 The LORD is near to those who are
   discouraged;
   he saves those who have lost all
   hope.

19 Good people suffer many troubles,
   but the LORD saves them from
   them all;
20 the LORD preserves them
   completely;
   not one of their bones is broken.
21 Evil will kill the wicked;
   those who hate the righteous
   will be punished.

22 The LORD will save his people;
   those who go to him for
   protection will be spared.

A Prayer for Help a

35 Oppose those who oppose me,
   LORD,
   and fight those who fight
   against me!
2 Take your shield and armor
   and come to my rescue.
3 Lift up your spear and war ax
   against those who pursue me.
   Promise that you will save me.

4 May those who try to kill me
   be defeated and disgraced!
   May those who plot against me
   be turned back and confused!
5 May they be like straw blown by
   the wind
   as the angel of the LORD pursues
   them!
6 May their path be dark and
   slippery
   while the angel of the LORD
   strikes them down!

7 Without any reason they laid a
   trap for me

and dug a deep hole to
   catch me.
8 But destruction will catch them
   before they know it;
   they will be caught in their own
   trap
   and fall to their destruction!

9 Then I will be glad because of the
   LORD;
   I will be happy because he
   saved me.
10 With all my heart I will say to the
   LORD,
   "There is no one like you.
   You protect the weak from the
   strong,
   the poor from the oppressor."

11 Evil people testify against me
   and accuse me of crimes I know
   nothing about.
12 They pay me back evil for good,
   and I sink in despair.
13 But when they were sick, I dressed
   in mourning;
   I deprived myself of food;
   I prayed with my head bowed low,
14   as I would pray for a friend or a
   brother.
   I went around bent over in
   mourning,
   as one who mourns for his
   mother.

15 But when I was in trouble, they
   were all glad
   and gathered around to make
   fun of me;
   strangers beat me
   and kept striking me.
16 Like those who would mock a
   cripple, b
   they glared at me with hate.

17 How much longer, Lord, will you
   just look on?
   Rescue me from their attacks;
   save my life from these lions!
18 Then I will thank you in the
   assembly of your people;
   I will praise you before them all.

19 Don't let my enemies, those liars,
   gloat over my defeat.

---

a HEBREW TITLE: *By David.*   b *Probable text* Like those . . . cripple; *Hebrew unclear.*

Don't let those who hate me for no
reason
smirk with delight over my
sorrow.

20 They do not speak in a
friendly way;
instead they invent all kinds of
lies about peace-loving people.
21 They accuse me, shouting,
"We saw what you did!"
22 But you, O Lord, have seen this.
So don't be silent, Lord;
don't keep yourself far away!
23 Rouse yourself, O Lord, and
defend me;
rise up, my God, and plead my
cause.
24 You are righteous, O Lord, so
declare me innocent;
don't let my enemies gloat
over me.
25 Don't let them say to themselves,
"We are rid of him!
That's just what we wanted!"

26 May those who gloat over my
suffering
be completely defeated and
confused;
may those who claim to be better
than I am
be covered with shame and
disgrace.

27 May those who want to see me
acquitted
shout for joy and say again and
again,
"How great is the Lord!
He is pleased with the success of
his servant."
28 Then I will proclaim your
righteousness,
and I will praise you all day
long.

Human Wickedness c

36 Sin speaks to the wicked deep
in their hearts;
they reject God and do not have
reverence for him.
2 Because they think so highly of
themselves,

they think that God will not
discover their sin and
condemn it.
3 Their speech is wicked and full of
lies;
they no longer do what is wise
and good.
4 They make evil plans as they lie
in bed;
nothing they do is good,
and they never reject anything
evil.

The Goodness of God

5 Lord, your constant love reaches
the heavens;
your faithfulness extends to the
skies.
6 Your righteousness is towering
like the mountains;
your justice is like the depths of
the sea.
People and animals are in your
care.

7 How precious, O God, is your
constant love!
We find d protection under the
shadow of your wings.
8 We feast on the abundant food
you provide;
you let us drink from the river
of your goodness.
9 You are the source of all life,
and because of your light we see
the light.

10 Continue to love those who
know you
and to do good to those who are
righteous.
11 Do not let proud people attack me
or the wicked make me run
away.

12 See where evil people have fallen.
There they lie, unable to rise.

The Destiny of the Wicked and of the Good e

37 Don't be worried on account of
the wicked;
don't be jealous of those who do
wrong.

c HEBREW TITLE: By David, the Lord's servant.   d precious, O God, is . . . find; or precious is your
constant love! Gods and people find.   e HEBREW TITLE: By David.

2 They will soon disappear like
   grass that dries up;
   they will die like plants that
   wither.

3 Trust in the LORD and do good;
   live in the land and be safe.
4 Seek your happiness in the LORD,
   and he will give you your heart's
   desire.

5 Give yourself to the LORD;
   trust in him, and he will
   help you;
6 he will make your righteousness
   shine like the noonday sun.

7 Be patient and wait for the LORD
   to act;
   don't be worried about those
   who prosper,
   or those who succeed in their
   evil plans.

8 Don't give in to worry or anger;
   it only leads to trouble.
9 Those who trust in the LORD will
   possess the land,
   but the wicked will be
   driven out.

10 Soon the wicked will disappear;
   you may look for them, but you
   won't find them;
11 but the humble will possess the
   land
   and enjoy prosperity and peace.

12 The wicked plot against good
   people
   and glare at them with hate.
13 But the Lord laughs at wicked
   people,
   because he knows they will soon
   be destroyed.

14 The wicked draw their swords and
   bend their bows
   to kill the poor and needy,
   to slaughter those who do what
   is right;
15 but they will be killed by their
   own swords,
   and their bows will be smashed.

16 The little that a good person owns
   is worth more than the wealth of
   all the wicked,

17 because the LORD will take away
   the strength of the wicked,
   but protect those who are good.

18 The LORD takes care of those who
   obey him,
   and the land will be theirs
   forever.
19 They will not suffer when times
   are bad;
   they will have enough in time of
   famine.
20 But the wicked will die;
   the enemies of the LORD will
   vanish like wild flowers;
   they will disappear like smoke.

21 The wicked borrow and never pay
   back,
   but good people are generous
   with their gifts.
22 Those who are blessed by the LORD
   will possess the land,
   but those who are cursed by him
   will be driven out.

23 The LORD guides us in the way we
   should go
   and protects those who
   please him.
24 If they fall, they will not stay
   down,
   because the LORD will help
   them up.

25 I am old now; I have lived a long
   time,
   but I have never seen good
   people abandoned by the LORD
   or their children begging for
   food.
26 At all times they give freely and
   lend to others,
   and their children are a blessing.

27 Turn away from evil and do good,
   and your descendants will
   always live in the land;
28 for the LORD loves what is right
   and does not abandon his
   faithful people.
   He protects them forever,
   but the descendants of the
   wicked will be driven out.
29 The righteous will possess the land
   and live in it forever.

30 The words of good people are
    wise,
    and they are always fair.
31 They keep the law of their God in
    their hearts
    and never depart from it.

32 Wicked people watch good people
    and try to kill them;
33 but the LORD will not abandon
    them to their enemy's power
    or let them be condemned when
    they are on trial.

34 Put your hope in the LORD and
    obey his commands;
    he will honor you by giving you
    the land,
    and you will see the wicked
    driven out.

35 I once knew someone wicked who
    was a tyrant;
    he towered over everyone like a
    cedar of Lebanon; f
36 but later I g passed by, and he
    wasn't there;
    I looked for him, but couldn't
    find him.

37 Notice good people, observe the
    righteous;
    peaceful people have
    descendants,
38 but sinners are completely
    destroyed,
    and their descendants are
    wiped out.

39 The LORD saves the righteous
    and protects them in times of
    trouble.
40 He helps them and rescues them;
    he saves them from the wicked,
    because they go to him for
    protection.

The Prayer of a Sufferer h

38 O LORD, don't punish me in
    your anger!
2 You have wounded me with your
    arrows;
    you have struck me down.

3 Because of your anger, I am in
    great pain;
    my whole body is diseased
    because of my sins.
4 I am drowning in the flood of my
    sins;
    they are a burden too heavy to
    bear.

5 Because I have been foolish,
    my sores stink and rot.
6 I am bent over, I am crushed;
    I mourn all day long.
7 I am burning with fever
    and I am near death.
8 I am worn out and utterly crushed;
    my heart is troubled, and I
    groan with pain.

9 O Lord, you know what I long for;
    you hear all my groans.
10 My heart is pounding, my strength
    is gone,
    and my eyes have lost their
    brightness.
11 My friends and neighbors will not
    come near me,
    because of my sores;
    even my family keeps away
    from me.
12 Those who want to kill me lay
    traps for me,
    and those who want to hurt me
    threaten to ruin me;
    they never stop plotting
    against me.

13 I am like the deaf and cannot
    hear,
    like the dumb and cannot speak.
14 I am like those who do not
    answer,
    because they cannot hear.

15 But I trust in you, O LORD;
    and you, O Lord my God, will
    answer me.
16 Don't let my enemies gloat over
    my distress;
    don't let them boast about my
    downfall!
17 I am about to fall
    and am in constant pain.

18 I confess my sins;

---

f One ancient translation like a cedar of Lebanon; Hebrew unclear.
g Some ancient translations I; Hebrew he.   h HEBREW TITLE: A psalm by David; a lament.

they fill me with anxiety.
19 My enemies are healthy and
    strong;
    there are many who hate me for
    no reason.
20 Those who pay back evil for good
    are against me because I try to
    do right.

21 Do not abandon me, O LORD;
    do not stay away, my God!
22 Help me now, O Lord my savior!

The Confession of a Sufferer[i]

39 I said, "I will be careful about
       what I do
    and will not let my tongue make
    me sin;
    I will not say anything
    while evil people are near."
2 I kept quiet, not saying a word,
    not even about anything good!
    But my suffering only grew worse,
3   and I was overcome with
    anxiety.
    The more I thought, the more
    troubled I became;
    I could not keep from asking:
4 "LORD, how long will I live?
    When will I die?
    Tell me how soon my life
    will end."

5 How short you have made my life!
    In your sight my lifetime seems
    nothing.
    Indeed every living being is no
    more than a puff of wind,
6   no more than a shadow.
    All we do is for nothing;
    we gather wealth, but don't
    know who will get it.

7 What, then, can I hope for, Lord?
    I put my hope in you.
8 Save me from all my sins,
    and don't let fools make fun
    of me.
9 I will keep quiet, I will not say a
    word,
    for you are the one who made
    me suffer like this.
10 Don't punish me any more!
    I am about to die from your
    blows.

11 You punish our sins by your
    rebukes,
    and like a moth you destroy
    what we love.
    Indeed we are no more than a puff
    of wind!

12 Hear my prayer, LORD,
    and listen to my cry;
    come to my aid when I weep.
    Like all my ancestors
    I am only your guest for a little
    while.
13 Leave me alone so that I may have
    some happiness
    before I go away and am no
    more.

A Song of Praise[i]

40 I waited patiently for the LORD's
       help;
    then he listened to me and heard
    my cry.
2 He pulled me out of a
    dangerous pit,
    out of the deadly quicksand.
    He set me safely on a rock
    and made me secure.
3 He taught me to sing a new song,
    a song of praise to our God.
    Many who see this will take
    warning
    and will put their trust in the
    LORD.

4 Happy are those who trust the
    LORD,
    who do not turn to idols
    or join those who worship false
    gods.
5 You have done many things for
    us, O LORD our God;
    there is no one like you!
    You have made many wonderful
    plans for us.
    I could never speak of them all —
    their number is so great!

6 You do not want sacrifices and
    offerings;
    you do not ask for animals
    burned whole on the altar
    or for sacrifices to take away
    sins.
    Instead, you have given me ears to
    hear you,

---

i HEBREW TITLE: *A psalm by David.*

7 and so I answered, "Here I am;
   your instructions for me are in
      the book of the Law.*ʲ*
8 How I love to do your will,
      my God!
   I keep your teaching in my
      heart."

9 In the assembly of all your people,
      LORD,
   I told the good news that you
      save us.
   You know that I will never stop
      telling it.
10 I have not kept the news of
      salvation to myself;
   I have always spoken of your
      faithfulness and help.
   In the assembly of all your people
      I have not been silent
   about your loyalty and constant
      love.

11 LORD, I know you will never stop
      being merciful to me.
   Your love and loyalty will
      always keep me safe.

A Prayer for Help
(Psalm 70)

12 I am surrounded by many
      troubles —
   too many to count!
   My sins have caught up with me,
      and I can no longer see;
   they are more than the hairs of
      my head,
   and I have lost my courage.
13 Save me, LORD! Help me now!
14 May those who try to kill me
      be completely defeated and
      confused.
   May those who are happy because
      of my troubles
   be turned back and disgraced.
15 May those who make fun of me
      be dismayed by their defeat.

16 May all who come to you
      be glad and joyful.
   May all who are thankful for your
      salvation
   always say, "How great is the
      LORD!"

17 I am weak and poor, O Lord,
   but you have not forgotten me.
   You are my savior and my God —
   hurry to my aid!

A Prayer in Sickness*ᵏ*

41 Happy are those who are
   concerned for the poor;
   the LORD will help them when
      they are in trouble.
2 The LORD will protect them and
      preserve their lives;
   he will make them happy in the
      land;
   he will not abandon them to the
      power of their enemies.
3 The LORD will help them when
      they are sick
   and will restore them to health.

4 I said, "I have sinned against you,
      LORD;
   be merciful to me and heal me."
5 My enemies say cruel things
      about me.
   They want me to die and be
      forgotten.
6 Those who come to see me are not
      sincere;
   they gather bad news about me
   and then go out and tell it
      everywhere.
7 All who hate me whisper to each
      other about me,
   they imagine the worst
      about*ˡ* me.
8 They say, "He is fatally ill;
   he will never leave his bed
      again."
9 Even my best friend, the one I
      trusted most,
   the one who shared my food,
   has turned against me.

10 Be merciful to me, LORD, and
      restore my health,
   and I will pay my enemies back.
11 They will not triumph over me,
   and I will know that you are
      pleased with me.
12 You will help me, because I do
      what is right;
   you will keep me in your
      presence forever.

ʲ your instructions . . . Law; *or* my devotion to you is recorded in your book.
ᵏ HEBREW TITLE: *A psalm by David.*   *ˡ* imagine the worst about; *or* make evil plans to harm.

13 Praise the LORD, the God of Israel!
Praise him now and forever!

Amen! Amen!

BOOK TWO

(Psalms 42–72)

The Prayer of Someone in Exile [m]

42 As a deer longs for a stream of
cool water,
so I long for you, O God.
2 I thirst for you, the living God.
When can I go and worship in
your presence?
3 Day and night I cry,
and tears are my only food;
all the time my enemies ask me,
"Where is your God?"

4 My heart breaks when I remember
the past,
when I went with the crowds to
the house of God
and led them as they walked
along,
a happy crowd, singing and
shouting praise to God.
5 Why am I so sad?
Why am I so troubled?
I will put my hope in God,
and once again I will praise him,
my savior and my God.

6-7 Here in exile my heart is breaking,
and so I turn my thoughts
to him.
He has sent waves of sorrow over
my soul;
chaos roars at me like a flood,
like waterfalls thundering down
to the Jordan
from Mount Hermon and Mount
Mizar.
8 May the LORD show his constant
love during the day,
so that I may have a song at
night,
a prayer to the God of my life.

9 To God, my defender, I say,
"Why have you forgotten me?
Why must I go on suffering
from the cruelty of my
enemies?"

10 I am crushed by their insults,
as they keep on asking me,
"Where is your God?"

11 Why am I so sad?
Why am I so troubled?
I will put my hope in God,
and once again I will praise him,
my savior and my God.

The Prayer of Someone in Exile
(Continuation of Psalm 42)

43 O God, declare me innocent,
and defend my cause against
the ungodly;
deliver me from lying and evil
people!
2 You are my protector;
why have you abandoned me?
Why must I go on suffering
from the cruelty of my enemies?

3 Send your light and your truth;
may they lead me
and bring me back to Zion, your
sacred hill, [n]
and to your Temple, where you
live.
4 Then I will go to your altar,
O God;
you are the source of my
happiness.
I will play my harp and sing
praise to you,
O God, my God.

5 Why am I so sad?
Why am I so troubled?
I will put my hope in God,
and once again I will praise him,
my savior and my God.

A Prayer for Protection [o]

44 With our own ears we have
heard it, O God—
our ancestors have told us
about it,
about the great things you did in
their time,
in the days of long ago:
2 how you yourself drove out the
heathen
and established your people in
their land;
how you punished the other
nations

---

m HEBREW TITLE: *A poem by the clan of Korah.*   n SACRED HILL: *See 2.6.*   o HEBREW TITLE: *A poem by
the clan of Korah.*

and caused your own to prosper.
3 Your people did not conquer the
  land with their swords;
  they did not win it by their own
    power;
  it was by your power and your
    strength,
  by the assurance of your
    presence,
  which showed that you loved
    them.

4 You are my king and my God;
  you give *p* victory to your
    people,
5 and by your power we defeat
    our enemies.
6 I do not trust in my bow
  or in my sword to save me;
7 but you have saved us from our
    enemies
  and defeated those who hate us.
8 We will always praise you
  and give thanks to you forever.

9 But now you have rejected us and
    let us be defeated;
  you no longer march out with
    our armies.
10 You made us run from our
    enemies,
  and they took for themselves
    what was ours.
11 You allowed us to be slaughtered
    like sheep;
  you scattered us in foreign
    countries.
12 You sold your own people for a
    small price
  as though they had little value. *q*

13 Our neighbors see what you did
    to us,
  and they mock us and laugh
    at us.
14 You have made us a joke among
    the nations;
  they shake their heads at us in
    scorn.
15 I am always in disgrace;
  I am covered with shame
16 from hearing the sneers and
    insults
  of my enemies and those who
    hate me.

17 All this has happened to us,
  even though we have not
    forgotten you
  or broken the covenant you
    made with us.
18 We have not been disloyal to you;
  we have not disobeyed your
    commands.
19 Yet you left us helpless among
    wild animals;
  you abandoned us in deepest
    darkness.

20 If we had stopped worshiping
    our God
  and prayed to a foreign god,
21 you would surely have
    discovered it,
  because you know our secret
    thoughts.
22 But it is on your account that we
    are being killed all the time,
  that we are treated like sheep to
    be slaughtered.

23 Wake up, Lord! Why are you
    asleep?
  Rouse yourself! Don't reject us
    forever!
24 Why are you hiding from us?
  Don't forget our suffering and
    trouble!

25 We fall crushed to the ground;
  we lie defeated in the dust.
26 Come to our aid!
  Because of your constant love
    save us!

A Royal Wedding Song *r*

 Beautiful words fill my mind,
  as I compose this song for the
    king.
  Like the pen of a good writer
  my tongue is ready with a poem.

2 You are the most handsome
    of men;
  you are an eloquent speaker.
  God has always blessed you.
3 Buckle on your sword, mighty
    king;
  you are glorious and majestic.

4 Ride on in majesty to victory

---

p Some ancient translations and my God; you give; *Hebrew* O God; give.   *q as . . . value; or*
and made no profit from the sale.   *r* HEBREW TITLE: *A poem by the clan of Korah; a love song.*

for the defense of truth and
  justice!ˢ
Your strength will win you great
  victories!
⁵Your arrows are sharp,
  they pierce the hearts of your
    enemies;
  nations fall down at your feet.

⁶The kingdom that God has given
    youᵗ
  will last forever and ever.
You rule over your people with
    justice;
⁷ you love what is right and hate
    what is evil.
  That is why God, your God, has
    chosen you
  and has poured out more
    happiness on you
  than on any other king.
⁸The perfume of myrrh and aloes is
    on your clothes;
  musicians entertain you in
    palaces decorated with ivory.
⁹Among the women of your court
    are daughters of kings,
  and at the right of your throne
    stands the queen,
  wearing ornaments of finest
    gold.

¹⁰Bride of the king, listen to what
    I say—
  forget your people and your
    relatives.
¹¹Your beauty will make the king
    desire you;
  he is your master, so you must
    obey him.
¹²The people of Tyre will bring you
    gifts;
  rich people will try to win your
    favor.

¹³The princess is in the palace—how
    beautiful she is!
  Her gown is made of gold
    thread.
¹⁴In her colorful gown she is led to
    the king,
  followed by her bridesmaids,
  and they also are brought
    to him.
¹⁵With joy and gladness they come

and enter the king's palace.

¹⁶You, my king, will have many
    sons
  to succeed your ancestors as
    kings,
  and you will make them rulers
    over the whole earth.
¹⁷My song will keep your fame alive
    forever,
  and everyone will praise you for
    all time to come.

God Is with Usᵘ

46 God is our shelter and strength,
      always ready to help in times
        of trouble.
²So we will not be afraid, even if
    the earth is shaken
  and mountains fall into the
    ocean depths;
³even if the seas roar and rage,
  and the hills are shaken by the
    violence.

⁴There is a river that brings joy to
    the city of God,
  to the sacred house of the Most
    High.
⁵God is in that city, and it will
    never be destroyed;
  at early dawn he will come to
    its aid.
⁶Nations are terrified, kingdoms are
    shaken;
  God thunders, and the earth
    dissolves.

⁷The Lord Almighty is with us;
  the God of Jacob is our refuge.

⁸Come and see what the Lord has
    done.
  See what amazing things he has
    done on earth.
⁹He stops wars all over the world;
  he breaks bows, destroys spears,
  and sets shields on fire.
¹⁰"Stop fighting," he says, "and
    know that I am God,
  supreme among the nations,
  supreme over the world."

¹¹The Lord Almighty is with us;
  the God of Jacob is our refuge.

ˢ *Probable text* and justice; *Hebrew* and meekness of justice.   ᵗ The kingdom that God has
given you; *or* Your kingdom, O God; *or* Your divine kingdom.   ᵘ HEBREW TITLE: *A song by
the clan of Korah.*

The Supreme Ruler[v]

47 Clap your hands for joy, all
peoples!
Praise God with loud songs!
2 The LORD, the Most High, is to be
feared;
he is a great king, ruling over all
the world.
3 He gave us victory over the
peoples;
he made us rule over the
nations.
4 He chose for us the land where we
live,
the proud possession of his
people, whom he loves.

5 God goes up to his throne.
There are shouts of joy and the
blast of trumpets,
as the LORD goes up.
6 Sing praise to God;
sing praise to our king!
7 God is king over all the world;
praise him with songs!

8 God sits on his sacred throne;
he rules over the nations.
9 The rulers of the nations assemble
with the people[w] of the God of
Abraham.
More powerful than all armies
is he;
he rules supreme.

Zion, the City of God[x]

48 The LORD is great and is to be
highly praised
in the city of our God, on his
sacred hill.[y]
2 Zion, the mountain of God, is high
and beautiful;
the city of the great king brings
joy to all the world.
3 God has shown that there is safety
with him
inside the fortresses of the city.

4 The kings gathered together
and came to attack Mount Zion.
5 But when they saw it, they were
amazed;
they were afraid and ran away.

6 There they were seized with fear
and anguish,
like a woman about to bear a
child,
7 like ships tossing in a furious
storm.

8 We have heard what God has
done,
and now we have seen it
in the city of our God, the LORD
Almighty;
he will keep the city safe forever.

9 Inside your Temple, O God,
we think of your constant love.
10 You are praised by people
everywhere,
and your fame extends over all
the earth.
You rule with justice;
11 let the people of Zion be glad!
You give right judgments;
let there be joy in the cities of
Judah!

12 People of God, walk around Zion
and count the towers;
13 take notice of the walls and
examine the fortresses,
so that you may tell the next
generation:
14 "This God is our God forever
and ever;
he will lead us for all time to
come."

The Foolishness of Trusting
in Riches[z]

49 Hear this, everyone!
Listen, all people everywhere,
2 great and small alike,
rich and poor together.
3 My thoughts will be clear;
I will speak words of wisdom.
4 I will turn my attention to
proverbs
and explain their meaning as I
play the harp.

5 I am not afraid in times of danger
when I am surrounded by
enemies,

---

v HEBREW TITLE: *A psalm by the clan of Korah.*   w *Probable text* with the people; *Hebrew* the people.
x HEBREW TITLE: *A psalm by the clan of Korah; a song.*   y SACRED HILL: *See 2.6.*
z HEBREW TITLE: *A psalm by the clan of Korah.*

6 by evil people who trust in their
   riches
   and boast of their great wealth.
7 We can never redeem ourselves;
   we cannot pay God the price for
      our lives,
8   because the payment for a
      human life is too great.
   What we could pay would never
      be enough
9   to keep us from the grave,
      to let us live forever.

10 Anyone can see that even the
      wise die,
   as well as the foolish and stupid.
   They all leave their riches to
      their descendants.
11 Their graves *a* are their homes
      forever;
   there they stay for all time,
   though they once had lands of
      their own.
12 Our greatness cannot keep us
      from death;
   we will still die like the animals.

13 See what happens to those who
      trust in themselves,
   the fate of those *b* who are
      satisfied with their wealth—
14 they are doomed to die like sheep,
   and Death will be their
      shepherd.
   The righteous will triumph over
      them,
   as their bodies quickly decay
   in the world of the dead far from
      their homes. *c*
15 But God will rescue me;
   he will save me from the power
      of death.

16 Don't be upset when someone
      becomes rich,
   when his wealth grows even
      greater;
17 he cannot take it with him when
      he dies;
   his wealth will not go with him
      to the grave.
18 Even if someone is satisfied with
      this life
   and is praised because he is
      successful,

19 he will join all his ancestors in
      death,
   where the darkness lasts
      forever.
20 Our greatness cannot keep us
      from death;
   we will still die like the animals.

True Worship *d*

50 The Almighty God, the LORD,
      speaks;
   he calls to the whole earth from
      east to west.
2 God shines from Zion,
   the city perfect in its beauty.

3 Our God is coming, but not in
      silence;
   a raging fire is in front of him,
   a furious storm around him.
4 He calls heaven and earth as
      witnesses
   to see him judge his people.
5 He says, "Gather my faithful
      people to me,
   those who made a covenant with
      me by offering a sacrifice."
6 The heavens proclaim that God is
      righteous,
   that he himself is judge.

7 "Listen, my people, and I will
      speak;
   I will testify against you, Israel.
   I am God, your God.
8 I do not reprimand you because of
      your sacrifices
   and the burnt offerings you
      always bring me.
9 And yet I do not need bulls from
      your farms
   or goats from your flocks;
10 all the animals in the forest are
      mine
   and the cattle on thousands of
      hills.
11 All the wild birds are mine
   and all living things in the fields.

12 "If I were hungry, I would not ask
      you for food,
   for the world and everything in
      it is mine.
13 Do I eat the flesh of bulls
   or drink the blood of goats?

---

a Some ancient translations graves; *Hebrew* inner thoughts.   *b One ancient translation* the
fate of those; *Hebrew* after them.   *c* in . . . homes.; *Hebrew unclear.*   *d* HEBREW TITLE: *A psalm
by Asaph.*

14 Let the giving of thanks be your
    sacrifice to God,*e*
  and give the Almighty all that
    you promised.
15 Call to me when trouble comes;
  I will save you,
  and you will praise me."

16 But God says to the wicked,
  "Why should you recite my
    commandments?
  Why should you talk about my
    covenant?
17 You refuse to let me correct you;
  you reject my commands.
18 You become the friend of every
    thief you see,
  and you associate with
    adulterers.

19 "You are always ready to speak
    evil;
  you never hesitate to tell lies.
20 You are ready to accuse your own
    relatives
  and to find fault with them.
21 You have done all this, and I have
    said nothing,
  so you thought that I am
    like you.
  But now I reprimand you
  and make the matter plain
    to you.

22 "Listen to this, you that ignore me,
  or I will destroy you,
  and there will be no one to
    save you.
23 Giving thanks is the sacrifice that
    honors me,
  and I will surely save all who
    obey me."

A Prayer for Forgiveness*f*

51
Be merciful to me, O God,
    because of your constant
    love.
  Because of your great mercy
  wipe away my sins!
2 Wash away all my evil
  and make me clean from my sin!

3 I recognize my faults;
  I am always conscious of my
    sins.

4 I have sinned against you — only
    against you —
  and done what you consider
    evil.
  So you are right in judging me;
  you are justified in
    condemning me.
5 I have been evil from the day I
    was born;
  from the time I was conceived, I
    have been sinful.

6 Sincerity and truth are what you
    require;
  fill my mind with your wisdom.
7 Remove my sin, and I will be
    clean;
  wash me, and I will be whiter
    than snow.
8 Let me hear the sounds of joy and
    gladness;
  and though you have crushed
    me and broken me,
  I will be happy once again.
9 Close your eyes to my sins
  and wipe out all my evil.

10 Create a pure heart in me, O God,
  and put a new and loyal spirit
    in me.
11 Do not banish me from your
    presence;
  do not take your holy spirit
    away from me.
12 Give me again the joy that comes
    from your salvation,
  and make me willing to
    obey you.
13 Then I will teach sinners your
    commands,
  and they will turn back to you.

14 Spare my life, O God, and
    save me,*g*
  and I will gladly proclaim your
    righteousness.
15 Help me to speak, Lord,
  and I will praise you.

16 You do not want sacrifices,
  or I would offer them;
  you are not pleased with burnt
    offerings.
17 My sacrifice is a humble spirit,
    O God;

---

e Let the giving . . . to God; *or* Offer your thanksgiving sacrifice to God.   *f* HEBREW TITLE: *A psalm by David, after the prophet Nathan had spoken to him about his adultery with Bathsheba.* *g* Spare my life . . . me; *or* O God my savior, keep me from the crime of murder.

you will not reject a humble
and repentant heart.

18 O God, be kind to Zion and
help her;
rebuild the walls of
Jerusalem.
19 Then you will be pleased with
proper sacrifices
and with our burnt
offerings;
and bulls will be sacrificed on
your altar.

God's Judgment and Grace[h]

52 Why do you boast, great one,
of your evil?
God's faithfulness is eternal.
2 You make plans to ruin others;
your tongue is like a sharp
razor.
You are always inventing lies.
3 You love evil more than good
and falsehood more than truth.
4 You love to hurt people with your
words, you liar!

5 So God will ruin you forever;
he will take hold of you and
snatch you from your home;
he will remove you from the
world of the living.
6 Righteous people will see this and
be afraid;
then they will laugh at you
and say,
7 "Look, here is someone who did
not depend on God for safety,
but trusted instead in great
wealth
and looked for security in being
wicked."

8 But I am like an olive tree growing
in the house of God;
I trust in his constant love
forever and ever.
9 I will always thank you, God, for
what you have done;
in the presence of your
people
I will proclaim that you are
good.

Human Wickedness[i]

(Psalm 14)

53 Fools say to themselves,
"There is no God."
They are all corrupt,
and they have done terrible
things;
there is no one who does what
is right.

2 God looks down from heaven at
people
to see if there are any who are
wise,
any who worship him.
3 But they have all turned away;
they are all equally bad.
Not one of them does what is
right,
not a single one.

4 "Don't they know?" God asks.
"Are these evildoers ignorant?
They live by robbing my people,
and they never pray to me."

5 But then they will become
terrified,
as they have never been before,
for God will scatter the bones of
the enemies of his people.
God has rejected them,
and so Israel will totally defeat
them.

6 How I pray that victory
will come to Israel from Zion.
How happy the people of Israel
will be
when God makes them
prosperous again!

A Prayer for Protection from Enemies[j]

54 Save me by your power,
O God;
set me free by your might!
2 Hear my prayer, O God;
listen to my words!
3 Proud people are coming to
attack me;
cruel people are trying to
kill me—

---

[h] HEBREW TITLE: *A poem by David, after Doeg the Edomite went to Saul and told him that David had gone to the house of Ahimelech.*   [i] HEBREW TITLE: *A poem by David.*   [j] HEBREW TITLE: *A poem by David, after the men from Ziph went to Saul and told him that David was hiding in their territory.*

P
S
A
L
M
S

those who do not care
  about God.

4 But God is my helper.
  The Lord is my defender.
5 May God use their own evil to
  punish my enemies.
  He will destroy them because he
    is faithful.

6 I will gladly offer you a sacrifice,
  O Lord;
  I will give you thanks
  because you are good.
7 You have rescued me from all my
    troubles,
  and I have seen my enemies
    defeated.

The Prayer of Someone Betrayed by a Friend k

55 Hear my prayer, O God;
    don't turn away from my
      plea!
2 Listen to me and answer me;
  I am worn out by my worries.
3 I am terrified by the threats of my
    enemies,
  crushed by the oppression of the
    wicked.
  They bring trouble on me;
  they are angry with me and
    hate me.

4 I am terrified,
  and the terrors of death
    crush me.
5 I am gripped by fear and
    trembling;
  I am overcome with horror.
6 I wish I had wings like a dove.
  I would fly away and find rest.
7 I would fly far away
  and make my home in the
    desert.
8 I would hurry and find myself a
    shelter
  from the raging wind and the
    storm.
9 Confuse the speech of my
    enemies, O Lord!

I see violence and riots in the city,
10   surrounding it day and night,
  filling it with crime and trouble.
11 There is destruction everywhere;

the streets are full of oppression
  and fraud.

12 If it were an enemy making fun
    of me,
  I could endure it;
  if it were an opponent boasting
    over me,
  I could hide myself from him.
13 But it is you, my companion,
  my colleague and close friend.
14 We had intimate talks with each
    other
  and worshiped together in the
    Temple.
15 May my enemies die before their
    time;
  may they go down alive into the
    world of the dead!
Evil is in their homes and in their
  hearts.

16 But I call to the Lord God for help,
  and he will save me.
17 Morning, noon, and night
  my complaints and groans go up
    to him,
  and he will hear my voice.
18 He will bring me safely back
  from the battles that I fight
  against so many enemies.
19 God, who has ruled from eternity,
  will hear me and defeat them;
  for they refuse to change,
  and they do not fear him.

20 My former companion attacked his
    friends;
  he broke his promises.
21 His words were smoother than
    cream,
  but there was hatred in his
    heart;
  his words were as soothing as oil,
  but they cut like sharp swords.

22 Leave your troubles with the Lord,
  and he will defend you;
  he never lets honest people be
    defeated.

23 But you, O God, will bring those
    murderers and liars to their
    graves
  before half their life is over.
As for me, I will trust in you.

---

k HEBREW TITLE: *A poem by David.*

A Prayer of Trust in God[l]

56

Be merciful to me, O God,
　　because I am under attack;
my enemies persecute me all the
　　time.
2 All day long my opponents
　　attack me.
There are so many who fight
　　against me.
3 When I am afraid, O LORD
　　Almighty,
　I put my trust in you.
4 I trust in God and am not afraid;
　I praise him for what he has
　　promised.
What can a mere human being
　　do to me?

5 My enemies make trouble for me
　　all day long;
　they are always thinking up
　　some way to hurt me!
6 They gather in hiding places
　and watch everything I do,
　hoping to kill me.
7 Punish[m] them, O God, for their
　　evil;
　defeat those people in your
　　anger!

8 You know how troubled I am;
　you have kept a record of my
　　tears.
　Aren't they listed in your book?
9 The day I call to you,
　my enemies will be turned back.
I know this: God[n] is on my side—
10 　the LORD, whose promises I
　　praise.
11 In him I trust, and I will not be
　　afraid.
What can a mere human being
　　do to me?

12 O God, I will offer you what I
　　have promised;
　I will give you my offering of
　　thanksgiving,
13 because you have rescued me from
　　death
　and kept me from defeat.
And so I walk in the presence
　　of God,

in the light that shines on the
　　living.

A Prayer for Help[o]

57

Be merciful to me, O God, be
　　merciful,
because I come to you for safety.
In the shadow of your wings I find
　　protection
until the raging storms are over.

2 I call to God, the Most High,
　to God, who supplies my every
　　need.
3 He will answer from heaven and
　　save me;
　he will defeat my oppressors.
God will show me his constant
　　love and faithfulness.

4 I am surrounded by enemies,
　who are like lions hungry for
　　human flesh.
Their teeth are like spears and
　　arrows;
　their tongues are like sharp
　　swords.

5 Show your greatness in the sky,
　　O God,
　and your glory over all the
　　earth.

6 My enemies have spread a net to
　　catch me;
　I am overcome with distress.
They dug a pit in my path,
　but fell into it themselves.

7 I have complete confidence,
　　O God;
　I will sing and praise you!
8 Wake up, my soul!
　Wake up, my harp and lyre!
　I will wake up the sun.
9 I will thank you, O Lord, among
　　the nations.
　I will praise you among the
　　peoples.
10 Your constant love reaches the
　　heavens;
　your faithfulness touches the
　　skies.
11 Show your greatness in the sky,
　　O God,

[l] HEBREW TITLE: *A psalm by David, after the Philistines captured him in Gath.*
[m] *Probable text* Punish; *Hebrew* Save.　　[n] I know this: God; *or* Because I know that God.
[o] HEBREW TITLE: *A psalm by David, after he fled from Saul in the cave.*

and your glory over all the earth.

A Prayer for God to Punish the Wicked[D]

58 Do you rulers[q] ever give a just decision?
Do you judge everyone fairly?
2 No! You think only of the evil you can do,
and commit crimes of violence in the land.

3 Evildoers go wrong all their lives;
they tell lies from the day they are born.
4 They are full of poison like snakes;
they stop up their ears like a deaf cobra,
5 which does not hear the voice of the snake charmer,
or the chant of the clever magician.

6 Break the teeth of these fierce lions, O God.
7 May they disappear like water draining away;
may they be crushed like weeds on a path.[r]
8 May they be like snails that dissolve into slime;
may they be like a baby born dead that never sees the light.
9 Before they know it, they are cut down like weeds;
in his fierce anger God will blow them away
while they are still living.[s]

10 The righteous will be glad when they see sinners punished;
they will wade through the blood of the wicked.
11 People will say, "The righteous are indeed rewarded;
there is indeed a God who judges the world."

A Prayer for Safety[t]

59 Save me from my enemies, my God;
protect me from those who attack me!
2 Save me from those evil people;
rescue me from those murderers!

3 Look! They are waiting to kill me;
cruel people are gathering against me.
It is not because of any sin or wrong I have done,
4 nor because of any fault of mine, O LORD,
that they hurry to their places.

5 Rise, LORD God Almighty, and come to my aid;
see for yourself, God of Israel!
Wake up and punish the heathen;
show no mercy to evil traitors!

6 They come back in the evening,
snarling like dogs as they go about the city.
7 Listen to their insults and threats.
Their tongues are like swords in their mouths,
yet they think that no one hears them.

8 But you laugh at them, LORD;
you mock all the heathen.
9 I have confidence in your strength;
you are my refuge, O God.
10 My God loves me and will come to me;
he will let me see my enemies defeated.

11 Do not kill them, O God, or my people may forget.
Scatter them by your strength and defeat them,
O Lord, our protector.
12 Sin is on their lips; all their words are sinful;
may they be caught in their pride!
Because they curse and lie,
13 destroy them in your anger;
destroy them completely.
Then everyone will know that God rules in Israel,
that his rule extends over all the earth.

[D] HEBREW TITLE: *A psalm by David.* [q] *rulers; or gods.* [r] *Probable text may . . . path; Hebrew unclear.* [s] *Verse 9 in Hebrew is unclear.* [t] HEBREW TITLE: *A psalm by David, after Saul sent men to watch his house in order to kill him.*

14 My enemies come back in the
evening,
snarling like dogs as they go
about the city,
15 like dogs roaming about for food
and growling if they do not find
enough.

16 But I will sing about your
strength;
every morning I will sing aloud
of your constant love.
You have been a refuge for me,
a shelter in my time of trouble.
17 I will praise you, my defender.
My refuge is God,
the God who loves me.

A Prayer for Deliverance u

60 You have rejected us, God, and
defeated us;
you have been angry with us—
but now turn back to us. v
2 You have made the land tremble,
and you have cut it open;
now heal its wounds, because it
is falling apart.
3 You have made your people suffer
greatly;
we stagger around as though we
were drunk.
4 You have warned those who have
reverence for you,
so that they might escape
destruction.
5 Save us by your might; answer
our prayer,
so that the people you love may
be rescued.

6 From his sanctuary w God has
said,
"In triumph I will divide
Shechem
and distribute Sukkoth Valley to
my people.
7 Gilead is mine, and Manasseh too;
Ephraim is my helmet
and Judah my royal scepter.
8 But I will use Moab as my
washbowl,
and I will throw my sandals on
Edom,
as a sign that I own it.

Did the Philistines think they
would shout in triumph
over me?"

9 Who, O God, will take me into the
fortified city?
Who will lead me to Edom?
10 Have you really rejected us?
Aren't you going to march out
with our armies?
11 Help us against the enemy;
human help is worthless.
12 With God on our side we will win;
he will defeat our enemies.

A Prayer for Protection x

61 Hear my cry, O God;
listen to my prayer!
2 In despair and far from home
I call to you!

Take me to a safe refuge,
3 for you are my protector,
my strong defense against my
enemies.

4 Let me live in your sanctuary all
my life;
let me find safety under your
wings.
5 You have heard my promises,
O God,
and you have given me what
belongs to those who
honor you.

6 Add many years to the king's life;
let him live on and on!
7 May he rule forever in your
presence, O God;
protect him with your constant
love and faithfulness.

8 So I will always sing praises
to you,
as I offer you daily what I have
promised.

Confidence in God's Protection y

62 I wait patiently for God to
save me;
I depend on him alone.
2 He alone protects and saves me;
he is my defender,

u HEBREW TITLE: A psalm by David, for teaching, when he fought against the Arameans from
Naharaim and from Zobah, and Joab turned back and killed 12,000 Edomites in Salt Valley.
v angry with us ... us; or angry with us and turned your back on us.   w From his sanctuary; or
In his holiness.   x HEBREW TITLE: By David.   y HEBREW TITLE: A psalm by David.

and I shall never be defeated.

3 How much longer will all of you
    attack someone
  who is no stronger than a
    broken-down fence?
4 You only want to bring him down
    from his place of honor;
  you take pleasure in lies.
  You speak words of blessing,
    but in your heart you curse him.

5 I depend on God alone;
  I put my hope in him.
6 He alone protects and saves me;
    he is my defender,
    and I shall never be defeated.
7 My salvation and honor depend
    on God;
  he is my strong protector;
  he is my shelter.

8 Trust in God at all times, my
    people.
  Tell him all your troubles,
    for he is our refuge.

9 Human beings are all like a puff
    of breath;
  great and small alike are
    worthless.
  Put them on the scales, and they
    weigh nothing;
  they are lighter than a mere
    breath.
10 Don't put your trust in violence;
  don't hope to gain anything by
    robbery;
  even if your riches increase,
    don't depend on them.

11 More than once I have heard
    God say
  that power belongs to him
12   and that his love is constant.
  You yourself, O Lord, reward
    everyone according to their
    deeds.

Longing for God z

63 O God, you are my God,
    and I long for you.
  My whole being desires you;
  like a dry, worn-out, and
    waterless land,

my soul is thirsty for you.
2 Let me see you in the sanctuary;
  let me see how mighty and
    glorious you are.
3 Your constant love is better than
    life itself,
  and so I will praise you.
4 I will give you thanks as long as I
    live;
  I will raise my hands to you in
    prayer.
5 My soul will feast and be satisfied,
  and I will sing glad songs of
    praise to you.

6 As I lie in bed, I remember you;
  all night long I think of you,
7   because you have always been
    my help.
  In the shadow of your wings I sing
    for joy.
8 I cling to you,
  and your hand keeps me safe.

9 Those who are trying to kill me
  will go down into the world of
    the dead.
10 They will be killed in battle,
  and their bodies eaten by
    wolves.
11 Because God gives him victory,
  the king will rejoice.
  Those who make promises in
    God's name will praise him,
  but the mouths of liars will be
    shut.

A Prayer for Protection a

64 I am in trouble, God—listen to
    my prayer!
  I am afraid of my enemies—save
    my life!
2 Protect me from the plots of the
    wicked,
  from mobs of evil people.
3 They sharpen their tongues like
    swords
  and aim cruel words like arrows.
4 They are quick to spread their
    shameless lies;
  they destroy good people with
    cowardly slander.
5 They encourage each other in their
    evil plots;

z HEBREW TITLE: *A psalm by David, when he was in the desert of Judea.*   a HEBREW TITLE: *A psalm by David.*

they talk about where they will
place their traps.
"No one can see them," they say.
6 They make evil plans and say,
"We have planned a perfect
crime."
The human heart and mind are a
mystery.

7 But God shoots his arrows at
them,
and suddenly they are wounded.
8 He will destroy them because of
those words; b
all who see them will shake
their heads.
9 They will all be afraid;
they will think about what God
has done
and tell about his deeds.
10 All righteous people will rejoice
because of what the LORD has
done.
They will find safety in him;
all good people will praise him.

Praise and Thanksgiving c

65 O God, it is right for us to
praise you in Zion
and keep our promises to you,
2   because you answer prayers.
People everywhere will come
to you
3   on account of their sins.
Our faults defeat us, d
but you forgive them.
4 Happy are those whom you
choose,
whom you bring to live in your
sanctuary.
We shall be satisfied with the
good things of your house,
the blessings of your sacred
Temple.

5 You answer us by giving us
victory,
and you do wonderful things to
save us.
People all over the world
and across the distant seas trust
in you.
6 You set the mountains in place by
your strength,
showing your mighty power.

7 You calm the roar of the seas
and the noise of the waves;
you calm the uproar of the
peoples.
8 The whole world stands in awe
of the great things that you have
done.
Your deeds bring shouts of joy
from one end of the earth to the
other.

9 You show your care for the land
by sending rain;
you make it rich and fertile.
You fill the streams with water;
you provide the earth with
crops.
This is how you do it:
10   you send abundant rain on the
plowed fields
and soak them with water;
you soften the soil with showers
and cause the young plants to
grow.
11 What a rich harvest your goodness
provides!
Wherever you go there is plenty.
12 The pastures are filled with flocks;
the hillsides are full of joy.
13 The fields are covered with sheep;
the valleys are full of wheat.
Everything shouts and sings
for joy.

A Song of Praise and Thanksgiving e

66 Praise God with shouts of joy,
all people!
2 Sing to the glory of his name;
offer him glorious praise!
3 Say to God, "How wonderful are
the things you do!
Your power is so great
that your enemies bow down in
fear before you.
4 Everyone on earth worships you;
they sing praises to you,
they sing praises to your
name."

5 Come and see what God has done,
his wonderful acts among
people.
6 He changed the sea into dry
land;

b Probable text He will destroy them because of those words; Hebrew They will destroy him,
those words are against them.   c HEBREW TITLE: A psalm by David; a song.
d One ancient translation us; Hebrew me.   e HEBREW TITLE: A song.

our ancestors crossed the river
  on foot.
There we rejoiced because of what
  he did.
7 He rules forever by his might
    and keeps his eyes on the
      nations.
    Let no rebels rise against
      him.
8 Praise our God, all nations;
    let your praise be heard.
9 He has kept us alive
    and has not allowed us to fall.

10 You have put us to the test,
    God;
    as silver is purified by fire,
    so you have tested us.
11 You let us fall into a trap
    and placed heavy burdens on
      our backs.
12 You let our enemies trample us;
    we went through fire and
      flood,
    but now you have brought us to
      a place of safety. *f*

13 I will bring burnt offerings to your
    house;
    I will offer you what I promised.
14 I will give you what I said I would
    when I was in trouble.
15 I will offer sheep to be burned on
    the altar;
    I will sacrifice bulls and goats,
    and the smoke will go up to
      the sky.

16 Come and listen, all who
    honor God,
    and I will tell you what he has
      done for me.
17 I cried to him for help;
    I praised him with songs.
18 If I had ignored my sins,
    the Lord would not have listened
      to me.
19 But God has indeed heard me;
    he has listened to my prayer.

20 I praise God,
    because he did not reject my
      prayer
    or keep back his constant love
      from me.

A Song of Thanksgiving *g*

67 God, be merciful to us and
    bless us;
    look on us with kindness,
2 so that the whole world may know
    your will;
    so that all nations may know
    your salvation.

3 May the peoples praise you,
    O God;
    may all the peoples praise you!

4 May the nations be glad and sing
    for joy,
    because you judge the peoples
    with justice
    and guide every nation on earth.

5 May the peoples praise you,
    O God;
    may all the peoples praise you!

6 The land has produced its harvest;
    God, our God, has blessed us.
7 God has blessed us;
    may all people everywhere
    honor him.

A National Song of Triumph *h*

68 God rises up and scatters his
    enemies.
    Those who hate him run away
    in defeat.
2 As smoke is blown away, so he
    drives them off;
    as wax melts in front of the fire,
    so do the wicked perish in God's
    presence.
3 But the righteous are glad and
    rejoice in his presence;
    they are happy and shout
    for joy.

4 Sing to God, sing praises to his
    name;
    prepare a way for him who rides
    on the clouds. *i*
    His name is the LORD — be glad
    in his presence!

5 God, who lives in his sacred
    Temple,
    cares for orphans and protects
    widows.

f Some ancient translations safety; *Hebrew* overflowing.   *g* HEBREW TITLE: *A psalm; a song.*
h HEBREW TITLE: *A psalm by David; a song.*   *i* on the clouds; *or* across the desert.

6 He gives the lonely a home to
live in
and leads prisoners out into
happy freedom,
but rebels will have to live in a
desolate land.

7 O God, when you led your people,
when you marched across the
desert,
8 the earth shook, and the sky
poured down rain,
because of the coming of the
God of Sinai,[j]
the coming of the God of Israel.
9 You caused abundant rain to fall
and restored your worn-out
land;
10 your people made their home
there;
in your goodness you provided
for the poor.

11 The Lord gave the command,
and many women carried the
news:
12 "Kings and their armies are
running away!"
The women at home divided
what was captured:
13   figures of doves covered with
silver,
whose wings glittered with fine
gold.
(Why did some of you stay among
the sheep pens on the day of
battle?)
14 When Almighty God scattered the
kings on Mount Zalmon,
he caused snow to fall there.

15 What a mighty mountain is
Bashan,
a mountain of many peaks!
16 Why from your mighty peaks do
you look with scorn
on the mountain[k] on which God
chose to live?
The LORD will live there forever!

17 With his many thousands of
mighty chariots
the Lord comes from Sinai[l]
into the holy place.
18 He goes up to the heights,

taking many captives with him;
he receives gifts from rebellious
people.
The LORD God will live there.

19 Praise the Lord,
who carries our burdens day
after day;
he is the God who saves us.
20 Our God is a God who saves;
he is the LORD, our Lord,
who rescues us from death.

21 God will surely break the heads of
his enemies,
of those who persist in their
sinful ways.
22 The Lord has said, "I will bring
your enemies back from
Bashan;
I will bring them back from the
depths of the ocean,
23 so that you may wade in their
blood,
and your dogs may lap up as
much as they want."

24 O God, your march of triumph is
seen by all,
the procession of God, my king,
into his sanctuary.
25 The singers are in front, the
musicians are behind,
in between are the young
women beating the
tambourines.
26 "Praise God in the meeting of his
people;
praise the LORD, all you
descendants of Jacob!"
27 First comes Benjamin, the smallest
tribe,
then the leaders of Judah with
their group,
followed by the leaders of
Zebulun and Naphtali.

28 Show your power, O God,
the power you have used on our
behalf
29   from your Temple in Jerusalem,
where kings bring gifts to you.
30 Rebuke Egypt, that wild animal in
the reeds;

---

[j] GOD OF SINAI: *As the people of Israel went from Egypt to Canaan, God revealed himself to them at Mount Sinai (see Ex 19.16-25).*   [k] MOUNTAIN: *See 2.6.*   [l] *Probable text* comes from Sinai; *Hebrew* in them, Sinai.

P
S
A
L
M
S

rebuke the nations, that herd of
bulls with their calves,
until they all bow down and
offer you their silver.
Scatter those people who love to
make war!*m*

31 Ambassadors*n* will come from
Egypt;
the Ethiopians*o* will raise their
hands in prayer to God.

32 Sing to God, kingdoms of the
world,
sing praise to the Lord,
33 to him who rides in the sky,
the ancient sky.
Listen to him shout with a mighty
roar.
34 Proclaim God's power;
his majesty is over Israel,
his might is in the skies.
35 How awesome is God as he comes
from his sanctuary —
the God of Israel!
He gives strength and power to his
people.

Praise God!

A Cry for Help*p*

69 Save me, O God!
The water is up to my neck;
2 I am sinking in deep mud,
and there is no solid ground;
I am out in deep water,
and the waves are about to
drown me.
3 I am worn out from calling for
help,
and my throat is aching.
I have strained my eyes,
looking for your help.

4 Those who hate me for no reason
are more numerous than the
hairs of my head.
My enemies tell lies against me;
they are strong and want to
kill me.
They made me give back things I
did not steal.

5 My sins, O God, are not hidden
from you;
you know how foolish I have
been.
6 Don't let me bring shame on those
who trust in you,
Sovereign LORD Almighty!
Don't let me bring disgrace to
those who worship you,
O God of Israel!
7 It is for your sake that I have been
insulted
and that I am covered with
shame.
8 I am like a stranger to my
relatives,
like a foreigner to my family.

9 My devotion to your Temple burns
in me like a fire;
the insults which are hurled at
you fall on me.
10 I humble myself*q* by fasting,
and people insult me;
11 I dress myself in clothes of
mourning,
and they laugh at me.
12 They talk about me in the streets,
and drunkards make up songs
about me.

13 But as for me, I will pray to you,
LORD;
answer me, God, at a time you
choose.
Answer me because of your great
love,
because you keep your promise
to save.
14 Save me from sinking in the mud;
keep me safe from my enemies,
safe from the deep water.
15 Don't let the flood come over me;
don't let me drown in the depths
or sink into the grave.

16 Answer me, LORD, in the goodness
of your constant love;
in your great compassion turn
to me!
17 Don't hide yourself from your
servant;

---

*m Verse 30 in Hebrew is unclear.   n Some ancient translations Ambassadors; Hebrew unclear.
o Hebrew Cushites: Cush is the ancient name of the extensive territory south of the First
Cataract of the Nile River. This region was called Ethiopia in Graeco-Roman time, and
included within its borders most of modern Sudan and some of present-day Ethiopia
(Abyssinia).   p HEBREW TITLE: By David.   q Some ancient translations humble myself;
Hebrew cry.*

I am in great trouble — answer
me now!
18 Come to me and save me;
rescue me from my enemies.

19 You know how I am insulted,
how I am disgraced and
dishonored;
you see all my enemies.
20 Insults have broken my heart,
and I am in despair.
I had hoped for sympathy, but
there was none;
for comfort, but I found none.
21 When I was hungry, they gave me
poison;
when I was thirsty, they offered
me vinegar.

22 May their banquets cause their
ruin;
may their sacred feasts cause
their downfall.
23 Strike them with blindness!
Make their backs always weak!
24 Pour out your anger on them;
let your indignation overtake
them.
25 May their camps be left deserted;
may no one be left alive in their
tents.
26 They persecute those whom you
have punished;
they talk about the sufferings of
those you have wounded.
27 Keep a record of all their sins;
don't let them have any part in
your salvation.
28 May their names be erased from
the book of the living;
may they not be included in the
list of your people.

29 But I am in pain and despair;
lift me up, O God, and save me!

30 I will praise God with a song;
I will proclaim his greatness by
giving him thanks.
31 This will please the LORD more
than offering him cattle,
more than sacrificing a
full-grown bull.
32 When the oppressed see this, they
will be glad;

those who worship God will be
encouraged.
33 The LORD listens to those in need
and does not forget his people in
prison.

34 Praise God, O heaven and earth,
seas and all creatures in them.
35 He will save Jerusalem
and rebuild the towns of Judah.
His people will live there and
possess the land;
36   the descendants of his servants
will inherit it,
and those who love him will live
there.

A Prayer for Help [r]
(Psalm 40.13-17)

70 Save me, O God!
LORD, help me now!
2 May those who try to kill me
be defeated and confused.
May those who are happy because
of my troubles
be turned back and disgraced.
3 May those who make fun of me
be dismayed by their defeat.

4 May all who come to you
be glad and joyful.
May all who are thankful for your
salvation
always say, "How great is God!"

5 I am weak and poor;
come to me quickly, O God.
You are my savior and my LORD —
hurry to my aid!

The Prayer of an Elderly Person

71 LORD, I have come to you for
protection;
never let me be defeated!
2 Because you are righteous, help
me and rescue me.
Listen to me and save me!
3 Be my secure shelter
and a strong fortress [s] to
protect me;
you are my refuge and defense.

4 My God, rescue me from wicked
people,
from the power of cruel and evil
people.

---

[r] HEBREW TITLE: *A psalm by David; a lament.*   [s] *One ancient translation* a strong fortress; *Hebrew*
to go always you commanded.

P
S
A
L
M
S

5 Sovereign Lord, I put my hope
      in you;
   I have trusted in you since I was
      young.
6 I have relied on you all my
      life;
   you have protected[t] me since
      the day I was born.
   I will always praise you.

7 My life has been an example to
      many,
   because you have been my
      strong defender.
8 All day long I praise you
   and proclaim your glory.
9 Do not reject me now that I
      am old;
   do not abandon me now that I
      am feeble.
10 My enemies want to kill me;
   they talk and plot against me.
11 They say, "God has abandoned
      him;
   let's go after him and catch
      him;
   there is no one to rescue him."

12 Don't stay so far away, O God;
   my God, hurry to my aid!
13 May those who attack me
   be defeated and destroyed.
   May those who try to hurt me
   be shamed and disgraced.
14 I will always put my hope in you;
   I will praise you more and more.
15 I will tell of your goodness;
   all day long I will speak of your
      salvation,
   though it is more than I can
      understand.
16 I will go in the strength of the
      Lord God;
   I will proclaim your goodness,
      yours alone.

17 You have taught me ever since I
      was young,
   and I still tell of your wonderful
      acts.
18 Now that I am old and my hair is
      gray,
   do not abandon me, O God!
   Be with me while I proclaim your
      power and might
   to all generations to come.

19 Your righteousness, God, reaches
      the skies.
   You have done great things;
   there is no one like you.
20 You have sent troubles and
      suffering on me,
   but you will restore my strength;
   you will keep me from the
      grave.
21 You will make me greater than
      ever;
   you will comfort me again.

22 I will indeed praise you with the
      harp;
   I will praise your faithfulness,
      my God.
   On my harp I will play hymns
      to you,
   the Holy One of Israel.
23 I will shout for joy as I play
      for you;
   with my whole being I will sing
   because you have saved me.
24 I will speak of your righteousness
      all day long,
   because those who tried to
      harm me
   have been defeated and
      disgraced.

A Prayer for the King[u]

72 Teach the king to judge with
      your righteousness, O God;
   share with him your own justice,
2 so that he will rule over your
      people with justice
   and govern the oppressed with
      righteousness.
3 May the land enjoy prosperity;
   may it experience righteousness.
4 May the king judge the poor
      fairly;
   may he help the needy
   and defeat their oppressors.
5 May your people worship you as
      long as the sun shines,
   as long as the moon gives light,
      for ages to come.

6 May the king be like rain on the
      fields,
   like showers falling on the land.
7 May righteousness flourish in his
      lifetime,

---

t Some ancient translations protected; Hebrew unclear.   u HEBREW TITLE: By Solomon.

and may prosperity last as long
as the moon gives light.

8 His kingdom will reach from sea
to sea,
from the Euphrates to the ends
of the earth.
9 The peoples of the desert will bow
down before him;
his enemies will throw
themselves to the ground.
10 The kings of Spain and of the
islands will offer him gifts;
the kings of Sheba and Seba[v]
will bring him offerings.
11 All kings will bow down
before him;
all nations will serve him.

12 He rescues the poor who call
to him,
and those who are needy and
neglected.
13 He has pity on the weak and poor;
he saves the lives of those in
need.
14 He rescues them from oppression
and violence;
their lives are precious to him.

15 Long live the king!
May he be given gold from
Sheba;[w]
may prayers be said for him at
all times;
may God's blessings be on him
always!
16 May there be plenty of grain in the
land;
may the hills be covered with
crops,
as fruitful as those of Lebanon.
May the cities be filled with
people,
like fields full of grass.
17 May the king's name never be
forgotten;
may his fame last as long as
the sun.
May all nations ask God to bless
them
as he has blessed the king.[x]

18 Praise the LORD, the God of Israel!

He alone does these wonderful
things.
19 Praise his glorious name forever!
May his glory fill the whole world.

Amen! Amen!

20 This is the end of the prayers of
David son of Jesse.

BOOK THREE

(Psalms 73–89)

The Justice of God[y]

73 God is indeed good to Israel,
to those who have pure
hearts.
2 But I had nearly lost confidence;
my faith was almost gone
3 because I was jealous of the proud
when I saw that things go well
for the wicked.

4 They do not suffer pain;
they are strong and healthy.
5 They do not suffer as other
people do;
they do not have the troubles
that others have.
6 And so they wear pride like a
necklace
and violence like a robe;
7 their hearts pour out evil,[z]
and their minds are busy with
wicked schemes.
8 They laugh at other people and
speak of evil things;
they are proud and make plans
to oppress others.
9 They speak evil of God in heaven
and give arrogant orders to
everyone on earth,
10 so that even God's people turn to
them
and eagerly believe whatever
they say.[a]
11 They say, "God will not know;
the Most High will not find out."
12 That is what the wicked are like.
They have plenty and are
always getting more.

[v] SHEBA AND SEBA: *Sheba was toward the south in Arabia and Seba was on the opposite side of
the Red Sea.*   [w] SHEBA: *See 72.10.*   [x] *as he has blessed the king; or and may they wish
happiness for the king.*   [y] HEBREW TITLE: *By Asaph.*   [z] *Some ancient translations their hearts
pour out evil; Hebrew unclear.*   [a] *Verse 10 in Hebrew is unclear.*

13 Is it for nothing, then, that I have
    kept myself pure
    and have not committed sin?
14 O God, you have made me suffer
    all day long;
    every morning you have
    punished me.

15 If I had said such things,
    I would not be acting as one of
    your people.
16 I tried to think this problem
    through,
    but it was too difficult for me
17   until I went into your Temple.
    Then I understood what will
    happen to the wicked.

18 You will put them in slippery
    places
    and make them fall to
    destruction!
19 They are instantly destroyed;
    they go down to a horrible end.
20 They are like a dream that goes
    away in the morning;
    when you rouse yourself,
    O Lord, they disappear.

21 When my thoughts were bitter
    and my feelings were hurt,
22 I was as stupid as an animal;
    I did not understand you.
23 Yet I always stay close to you,
    and you hold me by the hand.
24 You guide me with your
    instruction
    and at the end you will receive
    me with honor.
25 What else do I have in heaven
    but you?
    Since I have you, what else
    could I want on earth?
26 My mind and my body may grow
    weak,
    but God is my strength;
    he is all I ever need.

27 Those who abandon you will
    certainly perish;
    you will destroy those who are
    unfaithful to you.
28 But as for me, how wonderful to
    be near God,

to find protection with the
    Sovereign LORD
and to proclaim all that he has
    done!

A Prayer for National Deliverance [b]

74

Why have you abandoned us
    like this, O God?
Will you be angry with your
    own people forever?
2 Remember your people, whom you
    chose for yourself long ago,
    whom you brought out of
    slavery to be your own tribe.
    Remember Mount Zion, where
    once you lived.
3 Walk over these total ruins;
    our enemies have destroyed
    everything in the Temple.

4 Your enemies have shouted in
    triumph in your Temple;
    they have placed their flags
    there as signs of victory.
5 They looked like woodsmen
    cutting down trees with their
    axes. [c]
6 They smashed all the wooden
    panels
    with their axes and sledge
    hammers.
7 They wrecked your Temple and
    set it on fire;
    they desecrated the place where
    you are worshiped.
8 They wanted to crush us
    completely;
    they burned down every holy
    place in the land.

9 All our sacred symbols are gone;
    there are no prophets left,
    and no one knows how long this
    will last.
10 How long, O God, will our
    enemies laugh at you?
    Will they insult your name
    forever?
11 Why have you refused to help us?
    Why do you keep your hands
    behind you? [d]

12 But you have been our king from
    the beginning, O God;
    you have saved us many times.

b HEBREW TITLE: *A poem by Asaph.*   c *Verse 5 in Hebrew is unclear.*   d *Probable text* Why do
you keep your hands behind you; *Hebrew unclear.*

13 With your mighty strength you
    divided the sea
and smashed the heads of the
    sea monsters;
14 you crushed the heads of the
    monster Leviathan e
and fed his body to desert
    animals. f
15 You made springs and fountains
    flow;
you dried up large rivers.
16 You created the day and the night;
    you set the sun and the moon in
    their places;
17 you set the limits of the earth;
    you made summer and winter.

18 But remember, O LORD, that your
    enemies laugh at you,
that they are godless and
    despise you.
19 Don't abandon your helpless
    people to their cruel enemies;
don't forget your persecuted
    people!

20 Remember the covenant you made
    with us.
There is violence in every dark
    corner of the land.
21 Don't let the oppressed be put to
    shame;
let those poor and needy people
    praise you.

22 Rouse yourself, God, and defend
    your cause!
Remember that godless people
    laugh at you all day long.
23 Don't forget the angry shouts of
    your enemies,
the continuous noise made by
    your foes.

God the Judge g

75 We give thanks to you, O God,
    we give thanks to you!
We proclaim how great you are
and tell of h the wonderful
    things you have done.

2 "I have set a time for judgment,"
    says God,

"and I will judge with fairness.
3 Though every living creature
    tremble
and the earth itself be shaken,
I will keep its foundations firm.
4 I tell the wicked not to be
    arrogant;
5   I tell them to stop their
    boasting."

6 Judgment does not come from the
    east or from the west,
from the north or from the
    south; i
7 it is God who is the judge,
    condemning some and acquitting
    others.
8 The LORD holds a cup in his hand,
    filled with the strong wine of his
    anger.
He pours it out, and all the wicked
    drink it;
they drink it down to the last
    drop.

9 But I will never stop speaking of
    the God of Jacob
or singing praises to him.
10 He will break the power of the
    wicked,
but the power of the righteous
    will be increased.

God the Victor j

76 God is known in Judah;
    his name is honored in Israel.
2 He has his home in Jerusalem;
    he lives on Mount Zion.
3 There he broke the arrows of the
    enemy,
their shields and swords, yes, all
    their weapons.

4 How glorious you are, O God!
How majestic, as you return
    from the mountains
where you defeated your foes.
5 Their brave soldiers have been
    stripped of all they had
and now are sleeping the sleep
    of death;
all their strength and skill was
    useless.

e LEVIATHAN: *A legendary monster which was a symbol of the forces of chaos and evil.*
f *animals; or* people.   g HEBREW TITLE: *A psalm by Asaph; a song.*   h *Some ancient translations*
We proclaim how great you are and tell of; *Hebrew* Your name is near and they tell of.
i *Probable text* from the north or from the south; *Hebrew* from the wilderness of the mountains.
j HEBREW TITLE: *A psalm by Asaph; a song.*

6 When you threatened them, O God
    of Jacob,
  the horses and their riders fell
    dead.

7 But you, LORD, are feared by all.
  No one can stand in your
    presence
  when you are angry.
8 You made your judgment known
    from heaven;
  the world was afraid and kept
    silent,
9 when you rose up to pronounce
    judgment,
  to save all the oppressed on
    earth.

10 Human anger only results in more
    praise for you;
  those who survive the wars will
    keep your festivals.*k*

11 Give the LORD your God what you
    promised him;
  bring gifts to him, all you
    nearby nations.
  God makes everyone fear him;
12   he humbles proud princes
    and terrifies great kings.

Comfort in Time of Distress *l*

77
I cry aloud to God;
  I cry aloud, and he hears me.
2 In times of trouble I pray to the
    Lord;
  all night long I lift my hands in
    prayer,
  but I cannot find comfort.
3 When I think of God, I sigh;
  when I meditate, I feel
    discouraged.

4 He keeps me awake all night;
  I am so worried that I cannot
    speak.
5 I think of days gone by
  and remember years of
    long ago.
6 I spend the night in deep
    thought; *m*
  I meditate, and this is what I ask
    myself:
7 "Will the Lord always reject us?

Will he never again be pleased
    with us?
8 Has he stopped loving us?
  Does his promise no longer
    stand?
9 Has God forgotten to be merciful?
  Has anger taken the place of his
    compassion?"
10 Then I said, "What hurts me most
    is this—
  that God is no longer
    powerful."*n*

11 I will remember your great deeds,
    LORD;
  I will recall the wonders you did
    in the past.
12 I will think about all that you have
    done;
  I will meditate on all your
    mighty acts.

13 Everything you do, O God, is holy.
  No god is as great as you.
14 You are the God who works
    miracles;
  you showed your might among
    the nations.
15 By your power you saved your
    people,
  the descendants of Jacob and of
    Joseph.

16 When the waters saw you, O God,
    they were afraid,
  and the depths of the sea
    trembled.
17 The clouds poured down rain;
  thunder crashed from the sky,
  and lightning flashed in all
    directions.
18 The crash of your thunder
    rolled out,
  and flashes of lightning lit up
    the world;
  the earth trembled and shook.
19 You walked through the waves;
  you crossed the deep sea,
  but your footprints could not be
    seen.
20 You led your people like a
    shepherd,
  with Moses and Aaron in
    charge.

---

k One ancient translation will keep your festivals; *verse 10 in Hebrew is unclear.*
l HEBREW TITLE: *A psalm by Asaph.*   *m Some ancient translations* deep thought; *Hebrew* song.
n Verse 10 in Hebrew is unclear.

God and His People o

78 Listen, my people, to my
teaching,
and pay attention to what I say.
2 I am going to use wise sayings
and explain mysteries from the
past,
3   things we have heard and
known,
things that our ancestors told us.
4 We will not keep them from our
children;
we will tell the next generation
about the LORD's power and his
great deeds
and the wonderful things he has
done.

5 He gave laws to the people of
Israel
and commandments to the
descendants of Jacob.
He instructed our ancestors
to teach his laws to their
children,
6 so that the next generation might
learn them
and in turn should tell their
children.
7 In this way they also will put their
trust in God
and not forget what he has
done,
but always obey his
commandments.
8 They will not be like their
ancestors,
a rebellious and disobedient
people,
whose trust in God was never firm
and who did not remain faithful
to him.

9 The Ephraimites, armed with bows
and arrows,
ran away on the day of battle.
10 They did not keep their covenant
with God;
they refused to obey his law.
11 They forgot what he had done,
the miracles they had seen him
perform.
12 While their ancestors watched,
God performed miracles
in the plain of Zoan in the land
of Egypt.

13 He divided the sea and took them
through it;
he made the waters stand like
walls.
14 By day he led them with a cloud
and all night long with the light
of a fire.
15 He split rocks open in the desert
and gave them water from the
depths.
16 He caused a stream to come out of
the rock
and made water flow like a
river.

17 But they continued to sin
against God,
and in the desert they rebelled
against the Most High.
18 They deliberately put God to the
test
by demanding the food they
wanted.
19 They spoke against God and said,
"Can God supply food in the
desert?
20 It is true that he struck the rock,
and water flowed out in a
torrent;
but can he also provide us with
bread
and give his people meat?"

21 And so the LORD was angry when
he heard them;
he attacked his people with fire,
and his anger against them
grew,
22 because they had no faith in him
and did not believe that he
would save them.
23 But he spoke to the sky above
and commanded its doors to
open;
24 he gave them grain from heaven,
by sending down manna for
them to eat.
25 So they ate the food of angels,
and God gave them all they
wanted.
26 He also caused the east wind to
blow,
and by his power he stirred up
the south wind;
27 and to his people he sent down
birds,

o HEBREW TITLE: *A poem by Asaph.*

P
S
A
L
M
S

as many as the grains of sand
    on the shore;
28 they fell in the middle of the camp
    all around the tents.
29 So the people ate and were
    satisfied;
    God gave them what they
    wanted.
30 But they had not yet satisfied their
    craving
    and were still eating,
31 when God became angry with
    them
    and killed their strongest men,
    the best young men of Israel.

32 In spite of all this the people kept
    sinning;
    in spite of his miracles they did
    not trust him.
33 So he ended their days like a
    breath
    and their lives with sudden
    disaster.
34 Whenever he killed some of them,
    the rest would turn to him;
    they would repent and pray
    earnestly to him.
35 They remembered that God was
    their protector,
    that the Almighty came to
    their aid.
36 But their words were all lies;
    nothing they said was sincere.
37 They were not loyal to him;
    they were not faithful to their
    covenant with him.

38 But God was merciful to his
    people.
    He forgave their sin
    and did not destroy them.
    Many times he held back his
    anger
    and restrained his fury.
39 He remembered that they were
    only mortal beings,
    like a wind that blows by and is
    gone.

40 How often they rebelled against
    him in the desert;
    how many times they made
    him sad!
41 Again and again they put God to
    the test

and brought pain to the Holy
    God of Israel.
42 They forgot his great power
    and the day when he saved them
    from their enemies
43   and performed his mighty acts
    and miracles
    in the plain of Zoan in the land
    of Egypt.
44 He turned the rivers into blood,
    and the Egyptians had no water
    to drink.
45 He sent flies among them, that
    tormented them,
    and frogs that ruined their land.
46 He sent locusts to eat their crops
    and to destroy their fields.
47 He killed their grapevines with
    hail
    and their fig trees with frost.
48 He killed their cattle with hail
    and their flocks with lightning.ᵖ
49 He caused them great distress
    by pouring out his anger and
    fierce rage,
    which came as messengers of
    death.
50 He did not restrain his anger
    or spare their lives,
    but killed them with a plague.
51 He killed the first-born sons
    of all the families of Egypt.

52 Then he led his people out like a
    shepherd
    and guided them through the
    desert.
53 He led them safely, and they were
    not afraid;
    but the sea came rolling over
    their enemies.
54 He brought them to his holy land,
    to the mountains which he
    himself conquered.
55 He drove out the inhabitants as his
    people advanced;
    he divided their land among the
    tribes of Israel
    and gave their homes to his
    people.

56 But they rebelled against
    Almighty God
    and put him to the test.
    They did not obey his
    commandments,

ᵖ hail ... lightning; or terrible disease ... deadly plague.

57 but were rebellious and disloyal
   like their ancestors,
   unreliable as a crooked arrow.
58 They angered him with their
   heathen places of worship,
   and with their idols they made
   him furious.
59 God was angry when he saw it,
   so he rejected his people
   completely.
60 He abandoned his tent in Shiloh,q
   the home where he had lived
   among us.
61 He allowed our enemies to capture
   the Covenant Box,
   the symbol of his power and
   glory.
62 He was angry with his own people
   and let them be killed by their
   enemies.
63 Young men were killed in war,
   and young women had no one to
   marry.
64 Priests died by violence,
   and their widows were not
   allowed to mourn.

65 At last the Lord woke up as
   though from sleep;
   he was like a strong man excited
   by wine.
66 He drove his enemies back
   in lasting and shameful defeat.
67 But he rejected the descendants of
   Joseph;
   he did not select the tribe of
   Ephraim.
68 Instead he chose the tribe of Judah
   and Mount Zion, which he
   dearly loves.
69 There he built his Temple
   like his home in heaven;
   he made it firm like the earth
   itself,
   secure for all time.

70 He chose his servant David;
   he took him from the pastures,
71 where he looked after his flocks,
   and he made him king of Israel,
   the shepherd of the people
   of God.
72 David took care of them with
   unselfish devotion
   and led them with skill.

A Prayer for the Nation's Deliverancer

79 O God, the heathen have
   invaded your land.
   They have desecrated your holy
   Temple
   and left Jerusalem in ruins.
2 They left the bodies of your people
   for the vultures,
   the bodies of your servants for
   wild animals to eat.
3 They shed your people's blood like
   water;
   blood flowed like water all
   through Jerusalem,
   and no one was left to bury the
   dead.
4 The surrounding nations insult us;
   they laugh at us and mock us.

5 LORD, will you be angry with us
   forever?
   Will your anger continue to burn
   like fire?
6 Turn your anger on the nations
   that do not worship you,
   on the people who do not pray
   to you.
7 For they have killed your people;
   they have ruined your country.

8 Do not punish us for the sins of
   our ancestors.
   Have mercy on us now;
   we have lost all hope.
9 Help us, O God, and save us;
   rescue us and forgive our sins
   for the sake of your own honor.
10 Why should the nations ask us,
   "Where is your God?"
   Let us see you punish the nations
   for shedding the blood of your
   servants.

11 Listen to the groans of the
   prisoners,
   and by your great power free
   those who are condemned
   to die.
12 Lord, pay the other nations back
   seven times
   for all the insults they have
   hurled at you.
13 Then we, your people, the sheep of
   your flock,

q SHILOH: *The central place of worship for the people of Israel before the time of King David.*
r HEBREW TITLE: *A psalm by Asaph.*

will thank you forever
and praise you for all time to
come.

A Prayer for the Nation's Restoration[s]

80 Listen to us, O Shepherd of
Israel;
hear us, leader of your flock.
Seated on your throne above the
winged creatures,
2 reveal yourself to the tribes of
Ephraim, Benjamin, and
Manasseh.
Show us your strength;
come and save us!

3 Bring us back, O God!
Show us your mercy, and we
will be saved!

4 How much longer, LORD God
Almighty,
will you be angry with your
people's prayers?
5 You have given us sorrow to eat,
a large cup of tears to drink.
6 You let the surrounding nations
fight over our land;
our enemies insult us.

7 Bring us back, Almighty God!
Show us your mercy, and we
will be saved!

8 You brought a grapevine out of
Egypt;
you drove out other nations and
planted it in their land.
9 You cleared a place for it to grow;
its roots went deep, and it
spread out over the whole
land.
10 It covered the hills with its shade;
its branches overshadowed the
giant cedars.
11 It extended its branches to the
Mediterranean Sea
and as far as the Euphrates
River.
12 Why did you break down the
fences around it?
Now anyone passing by can
steal its grapes;
13 wild hogs trample it down,
and wild animals feed on it.

14 Turn to us, Almighty God!
Look down from heaven at us;
come and save your people!
15 Come and save this grapevine that
you planted,
this young vine you made grow
so strong!

16 Our enemies have set it on fire
and cut it down;
look at them in anger and
destroy them!
17 Preserve and protect the people
you have chosen,
the nation you made so strong.
18 We will never turn away from you
again;
keep us alive, and we will
praise you.

19 Bring us back, LORD God Almighty.
Show us your mercy, and we
will be saved.

A Song for a Festival[t]

81 Shout for joy to God our
defender;
sing praise to the God of Jacob!
2 Start the music and beat the
tambourines;
play pleasant music on the harps
and the lyres.
3 Blow the trumpet for the festival,
when the moon is new and
when the moon is full.
4 This is the law in Israel,
an order from the God of Jacob.
5 He gave it to the people of Israel
when he attacked the land of
Egypt.

I hear an unknown voice saying,
6 "I took the burdens off your backs;
I let you put down your loads of
bricks.
7 When you were in trouble, you
called to me, and I saved you.
From my hiding place in the
storm, I answered you.
I put you to the test at the
springs of Meribah.
8 Listen, my people, to my warning;
Israel, how I wish you would
listen to me!
9 You must never worship
another god.

s HEBREW TITLE: *A psalm by Asaph; a testimony.*   t HEBREW TITLE: *By Asaph.*

10 I am the LORD your God,
who brought you out of Egypt.
Open your mouth, and I will
feed you.

11 "But my people would not listen
to me;
Israel would not obey me.
12 So I let them go their stubborn
ways
and do whatever they wanted.
13 How I wish my people would
listen to me;
how I wish they would obey me!
14 I would quickly defeat their
enemies
and conquer all their foes.
15 Those who hate me would bow in
fear before me;
their punishment would last
forever.
16 But I would feed you with the
finest wheat
and satisfy you with wild
honey."

God the Supreme Ruler u

82 God presides in the heavenly
council;
in the assembly of the gods he
gives his decision:
2 "You must stop judging unjustly;
you must no longer be partial to
the wicked!
3 Defend the rights of the poor and
the orphans;
be fair to the needy and the
helpless.
4 Rescue them from the power of
evil people.

5 "How ignorant you are! How
stupid!
You are completely corrupt,
and justice has disappeared from
the world.
6 'You are gods,' I said,
'all of you are children of the
Most High.'
7 But you will die like mortals;
your life will end like that of any
prince."

8 Come, O God, and rule the world;
all the nations are yours.

A Prayer for the Defeat of Israel's Enemies v

83 O God, do not keep silent;
do not be still, do not be
quiet!
2 Look! Your enemies are in revolt,
and those who hate you are
rebelling.
3 They are making secret plans
against your people;
they are plotting against those
you protect.
4 "Come," they say, "let us destroy
their nation,
so that Israel will be forgotten
forever."

5 They agree on their plan
and form an alliance
against you:
6 the people of Edom and the
Ishmaelites;
the people of Moab and the
Hagrites;
7 the people of Gebal, Ammon, and
Amalek,
and of Philistia and Tyre.
8 Assyria has also joined them
as a strong ally of the
Ammonites and Moabites, the
descendants of Lot.

9 Do to them what you did to the
Midianites,
and to Sisera and Jabin at the
Kishon River.
10 You defeated them at Endor,
and their bodies rotted on the
ground.
11 Do to their leaders what you did
to Oreb and Zeeb;
defeat all their rulers as you did
Zebah and Zalmunna,
12 who said, "We will take for
our own
the land that belongs to God."

13 Scatter them like dust, O God,
like straw blown away by the
wind.
14 As fire burns the forest,
as flames set the hills on fire,
15 chase them away with your storm
and terrify them with your fierce
winds.

---

u HEBREW TITLE: *A psalm by Asaph.*　　v HEBREW TITLE: *A psalm by Asaph; a song.*

16 Cover their faces with shame,
O Lord,
and make them acknowledge
your power.
17 May they be defeated and terrified
forever;
may they die in complete
disgrace.
18 May they know that you alone are
the Lord,
supreme ruler over all the earth.

Longing for God's House w

84 How I love your Temple, Lord
Almighty!
2 How I want to be there!
I long to be in the Lord's
Temple.
With my whole being I sing for joy
to the living God.
3 Even the sparrows have built a
nest,
and the swallows have their own
home;
they keep their young near your
altars,
Lord Almighty, my king and
my God.
4 How happy are those who live in
your Temple,
always singing praise to you.

5 How happy are those whose
strength comes from you,
who are eager to make the
pilgrimage to Mount Zion.
6 As they pass through the dry
valley of Baca,
it becomes a place of springs;
the autumn rain fills it with
pools.
7 They grow stronger as they go;
they will see the God of gods on
Zion.

8 Hear my prayer, Lord God
Almighty.
Listen, O God of Jacob!
9 Bless our king, O God,
the king you have chosen.

10 One day spent in your Temple
is better than a thousand
anywhere else;
I would rather stand at the gate of
the house of my God

than live in the homes of the
wicked.
11 The Lord is our protector and
glorious king,
blessing us with kindness and
honor.
He does not refuse any good thing
to those who do what is right.
12 Lord Almighty, how happy are
those who trust in you!

A Prayer for the Nation's Welfare w

85 Lord, you have been merciful to
your land;
you have made Israel
prosperous again.
2 You have forgiven your people's
sins
and pardoned all their wrongs.
3 You stopped being angry with
them
and held back your furious rage.

4 Bring us back, O God our savior,
and stop being displeased
with us!
5 Will you be angry with us forever?
Will your anger never cease?
6 Make us strong again,
and we, your people, will
praise you.
7 Show us your constant love,
O Lord,
and give us your saving help.

8 I am listening to what the Lord
God is saying;
he promises peace to us, his own
people,
if we do not go back to our
foolish ways.
9 Surely he is ready to save those
who honor him,
and his saving presence will
remain in our land.

10 Love and faithfulness will meet;
righteousness and peace will
embrace.
11 Human loyalty will reach up from
the earth,
and God's righteousness will
look down from heaven.
12 The Lord will make us prosperous,
and our land will produce rich
harvests.

w HEBREW TITLE: *A psalm by the clan of Korah.*

13 Righteousness will go before the
LORD
and prepare the path for him.

A Prayer for Help x

86 Listen to me, LORD, and
answer me,
for I am helpless and weak.
2 Save me from death, because I am
loyal to you;
save me, for I am your servant
and I trust in you.

3 You are my God, so be merciful
to me;
I pray to you all day long.
4 Make your servant glad, O Lord,
because my prayers go up
to you.
5 You are good to us and forgiving,
full of constant love for all who
pray to you.

6 Listen, LORD, to my prayer;
hear my cries for help.
7 I call to you in times of trouble,
because you answer my prayers.

8 There is no god like you, O Lord,
not one has done what you have
done.
9 All the nations that you have
created
will come and bow down to you;
they will praise your greatness.
10 You are mighty and do wonderful
things;
you alone are God.

11 Teach me, LORD, what you want
me to do,
and I will obey you faithfully;
teach me to serve you with
complete devotion.
12 I will praise you with all my heart,
O Lord my God;
I will proclaim your greatness
forever.
13 How great is your constant love
for me!
You have saved me from the
grave itself.

14 Proud people are coming against
me, O God;
a cruel gang is trying to
kill me—
people who pay no attention
to you.
15 But you, O Lord, are a merciful
and loving God,
always patient, always kind and
faithful.
16 Turn to me and have mercy
on me;
strengthen me and save me,
because I serve you just as my
mother did.
17 Show me proof of your goodness,
LORD;
those who hate me will be
ashamed
when they see that you have
given me comfort and help.

In Praise of Jerusalem y

87 The LORD built his city on the
sacred hill; z
2   more than any other place in
Israel
he loves the city of Jerusalem.
3 Listen, city of God,
to the wonderful things he says
about you:

4 "I will include Egypt and
Babylonia
when I list the nations that
obey me;
the people of Philistia, Tyre, and
Ethiopia a
I will number among the
inhabitants of Jerusalem."

5 Of Zion it will be said
that all nations belong there
and that the Almighty will make
her strong.
6 The LORD will write a list of the
peoples
and include them all as citizens
of Jerusalem.
7 They dance and sing,
"In Zion is the source of all our
blessings."

x HEBREW TITLE: *A prayer by David*   y HEBREW TITLE: *A psalm by the clan of Korah; a song.*
z SACRED HILL: *See 2.6.*   a Hebrew Cush: *Cush is the ancient name of the extensive territory
south of the First Cataract of the Nile River. This region was called Ethiopia in Graeco-Roman
time, and included within its borders most of modern Sudan and some of present-day Ethiopia
(Abyssinia).*

P
S
A
L
M
S

A Cry for Help[b]

88 LORD God, my savior, I cry out
all day,
and at night I come before you.
2 Hear my prayer;
listen to my cry for help!

3 So many troubles have fallen
on me
that I am close to death.
4 I am like all others who are about
to die;
all my strength is gone.[c]
5 I am abandoned among the dead;
I am like the slain lying in their
graves,
those you have forgotten
completely,
who are beyond your help.
6 You have thrown me into the
depths of the tomb,
into the darkest and deepest pit.
7 Your anger lies heavy on me,
and I am crushed beneath its
waves.

8 You have caused my friends to
abandon me;
you have made me repulsive to
them.
I am closed in and cannot escape;
9   my eyes are weak from
suffering.
LORD, every day I call to you
and lift my hands to you in
prayer.

10 Do you perform miracles for the
dead?
Do they rise up and praise you?
11 Is your constant love spoken of in
the grave
or your faithfulness in the place
of destruction?
12 Are your miracles seen in that
place of darkness
or your goodness in the land of
the forgotten?

13 LORD, I call to you for help;
every morning I pray to you.
14 Why do you reject me, LORD?
Why do you turn away
from me?

15 Ever since I was young, I have
suffered and been near death;
I am worn out[d] from the burden
of your punishments.
16 Your furious anger crushes me;
your terrible attacks destroy me.
17 All day long they surround me like
a flood;
they close in on me from every
side.
18 You have made even my closest
friends abandon me,
and darkness is my only
companion.

A Hymn in Time of National Trouble[e]

89 O LORD, I will always sing of
your constant love;
I will proclaim your faithfulness
forever.
2 I know that your love will last for
all time,
that your faithfulness is as
permanent as the sky.
3 You said, "I have made a covenant
with the man I chose;
I have promised my servant
David,
4 'A descendant of yours will always
be king;
I will preserve your dynasty
forever.' "

5 The heavens sing of the wonderful
things you do;
the holy ones sing of your
faithfulness, LORD.
6 No one in heaven is like you,
LORD;
none of the heavenly beings is
your equal.
7 You are feared in the council of
the holy ones;
they all stand in awe of you.

8 LORD God Almighty, none is as
mighty as you;
in all things you are faithful,
O LORD.
9 You rule over the powerful sea;
you calm its angry waves.
10 You crushed the monster Rahab[f]
and killed it;

---

b HEBREW TITLE: *A psalm by the clan of Korah; a song. A poem by Heman the Ezrahite.*
c all my strength is gone; *or there is no help for me.*   d *Probable text* I am worn out; *Hebrew
unclear.*   e HEBREW TITLE: *A poem by Ethan the Ezrahite.*   f RAHAB: *A legendary sea monster
which represented the forces of chaos and evil.*

with your mighty strength you
 defeated your enemies.
11 Heaven is yours, the earth also;
 you made the world and
 everything in it.
12 You created the north and the
 south;
 Mount Tabor and Mount
 Hermon sing to you for joy.
13 How powerful you are!
 How great is your strength!
14 Your kingdom is founded on
 righteousness and justice;
 love and faithfulness are shown
 in all you do.

15 How happy are the people who
 worship you with songs,
 who live in the light of your
 kindness!
16 Because of you they rejoice all day
 long,
 and they praise you for your
 goodness.
17 You give us great victories;
 in your love you make us
 triumphant.
18 You, O LORD, chose our protector;
 you, the Holy God of Israel,
 gave us our king.

God's Promise to David

19 In a vision long ago you said to
 your faithful servants,
 "I have given help to a famous
 soldier;
 I have given the throne to one I
 chose from the people.
20 I have made my servant David
 king
 by anointing him with holy oil.
21 My strength will always be
 with him,
 my power will make him strong.
22 His enemies will never succeed
 against him;
 the wicked will not defeat him.
23 I will crush his foes
 and kill everyone who
 hates him.
24 I will love him and be loyal
 to him;
 I will make him always
 victorious.
25 I will extend his kingdom
 from the Mediterranean to the
 Euphrates River.
26 He will say to me,

'You are my father and my God;
 you are my protector and
 savior.'
27 I will make him my first-born son,
 the greatest of all kings.
28 I will always keep my promise
 to him,
 and my covenant with him will
 last forever.
29 His dynasty will be as permanent
 as the sky;
 a descendant of his will always
 be king.

30 "But if his descendants disobey
 my law
 and do not live according to my
 commands,
31 if they disregard my instructions
 and do not keep my
 commandments,
32 then I will punish them for their
 sins;
 I will make them suffer for their
 wrongs.
33 But I will not stop loving David
 or fail to keep my promise
 to him.
34 I will not break my covenant
 with him
 or take back even one promise I
 made him.

35 "Once and for all I have promised
 by my holy name:
 I will never lie to David.
36 He will always have descendants,
 and I will watch over his
 kingdom as long as the sun
 shines.
37 It will be as permanent as the
 moon,
 that faithful witness in the sky."

Lament over the Defeat of the King

38 But you are angry with your
 chosen king;
 you have deserted and
 rejected him.
39 You have broken your covenant
 with your servant
 and thrown his crown in the
 dirt.
40 You have torn down the walls of
 his city
 and left his forts in ruins.
41 All who pass by steal his
 belongings;

P S A L M S

all his neighbors laugh at him.
42 You have given the victory to his
    enemies;
  you have made them all happy.
43 You have made his weapons
    useless
  and let him be defeated in battle.
44 You have taken away his royal
    scepter g
  and knocked his throne to the
    ground.
45 You have made him old before his
    time
  and covered him with disgrace.

A Prayer for Deliverance

46 LORD, will you hide yourself
    forever?
  How long will your anger burn
    like fire?
47 Remember how short my life is;
  remember that you created all of
    us mortal!
48 Who can live and never die?
  How can we humans keep
    ourselves from the grave?

49 Lord, where are the former proofs
    of your love?
  Where are the promises you
    made to David?
50 Don't forget how I, your servant,
    am insulted,
  how I endure all the curses h of
    the heathen.
51 Your enemies insult your chosen
    king, O LORD!
  They insult him wherever he
    goes.

52 Praise the LORD forever!

Amen! Amen!

BOOK FOUR

(Psalms 90–106)

Of God and Human Beings i

90 O Lord, you have always been
      our home.
  2 Before you created the hills
    or brought the world into being,
    you were eternally God,
    and will be God forever.

3 You tell us to return to what we
    were;
  you change us back to dust.
4 A thousand years to you are like
    one day;
  they are like yesterday, already
    gone,
  like a short hour in the
    night.
5 You carry us away like a flood;
  we last no longer than a
    dream.
  We are like weeds that sprout in
    the morning,
6 that grow and burst into bloom,
    then dry up and die in the
    evening.

7 We are destroyed by your anger;
  we are terrified by your fury.
8 You place our sins before you,
  our secret sins where you can
    see them.

9 Our life is cut short by your
    anger;
  it fades away like a whisper.
10 Seventy years is all we have—
  eighty years, if we are strong;
  yet all they bring us is trouble and
    sorrow;
  life is soon over, and we are
    gone.

11 Who has felt the full power of
    your anger?
  Who knows what fear your fury
    can bring?
12 Teach us how short our life is,
  so that we may become wise.

13 How much longer will your anger
    last?
  Have pity, O LORD, on your
    servants!
14 Fill us each morning with your
    constant love,
  so that we may sing and be glad
    all our life.
15 Give us now as much happiness as
    the sadness you gave us
  during all our years of misery.
16 Let us, your servants, see your
    mighty deeds;
  let our descendants see your
    glorious might.

g Probable text royal scepter; Hebrew purity. h Probable text curses; Hebrew crowds.
i HEBREW TITLE: A prayer by Moses, the man of God.

17 Lord our God, may your blessings
   be with us.
   Give us success in all we do!

God Our Protector

91 Whoever goes to the LORD for
   safety,
   whoever remains under the
   protection of the Almighty,
2 can say to him,
   "You are my defender and
   protector.
   You are my God; in you I trust."
3 He will keep you safe from all
   hidden dangers
   and from all deadly diseases.
4 He will cover you with his wings;
   you will be safe in his care;
   his faithfulness will protect and
   defend you.
5 You need not fear any dangers at
   night
   or sudden attacks during the day
6   or the plagues that strike in the
   dark
   or the evils that kill in daylight.

7 A thousand may fall dead
   beside you,
   ten thousand all around you,
   but you will not be harmed.
8 You will look and see
   how the wicked are punished.

9 You have made the LORD your ʲ
   defender,
   the Most High your protector,
10 and so no disaster will strike you,
   no violence will come near your
   home.
11 God will put his angels in charge
   of you
   to protect you wherever you go.
12 They will hold you up with their
   hands
   to keep you from hurting your
   feet on the stones.
13 You will trample down lions and
   snakes,
   fierce lions and poisonous
   snakes.

14 God says, "I will save those who
   love me
   and will protect those who
   acknowledge me as LORD.
15 When they call to me, I will
   answer them;
   when they are in trouble, I will
   be with them.
   I will rescue them and honor
   them.
16 I will reward them with long life;
   I will save them."

A Song of Praise ᵏ

92 How good it is to give thanks
   to you, O LORD,
   to sing in your honor, O Most
   High God,
2 to proclaim your constant love
   every morning
   and your faithfulness every
   night,
3 with the music of stringed
   instruments
   and with melody on the harp.
4 Your mighty deeds, O LORD, make
   me glad;
   because of what you have done,
   I sing for joy.

5 How great are your actions, LORD!
   How deep are your thoughts!
6 This is something a fool cannot
   know;
   someone who is stupid cannot
   understand:
7 the wicked may grow like weeds,
   those who do wrong may
   prosper;
   yet they will be totally destroyed,
8   because you, LORD, are supreme
   forever.

9 We know that your enemies
   will die,
   and all the wicked will be
   defeated.
10 You have made me as strong as a
   wild ox;
   you have blessed me with
   happiness.
11 I have seen the defeat of my
   enemies
   and heard the cries of the
   wicked.

12 The righteous will flourish like
   palm trees;
   they will grow like the cedars of
   Lebanon.

ʲ *Probable text your; Hebrew my.*   ᵏ HEBREW TITLE: *A psalm; a song for the Sabbath.*

¹³They are like trees planted in the
  house of the LORD,
  that flourish in the Temple of
  our God,
¹⁴ that still bear fruit in old age
  and are always green and
  strong.
¹⁵This shows that the LORD is just,
  that there is no wrong in my
  protector.

God the King

93 The LORD is king.
  He is clothed with majesty
  and strength.
The earth is set firmly in place
  and cannot be moved.
²Your throne, O LORD, has been
  firm from the beginning,
  and you existed before time
  began.

³The ocean depths raise their voice,
  O LORD;
  they raise their voice and roar.
⁴The LORD rules supreme in heaven,
  greater than the roar of the
  ocean,
  more powerful than the waves of
  the sea.

⁵Your laws are eternal, LORD,
  and your Temple is holy indeed,
  forever and ever.

God the Judge of All

94 LORD, you are a God who
  punishes;
  reveal your anger!
²You are the judge of us all;
  rise and give the proud what
  they deserve!
³How much longer will the wicked
  be glad?
  How much longer, LORD?
⁴How much longer will criminals
  be proud
  and boast about their crimes?

⁵They crush your people, LORD;
  they oppress those who belong
  to you.
⁶They kill widows and orphans,
  and murder the strangers who
  live in our land.

⁷They say, "The LORD does not
  see us;
  the God of Israel does not
  notice."

⁸My people, how can you be such
  stupid fools?
  When will you ever learn?
⁹God made our ears — can't he
  hear?
  He made our eyes — can't he see?
¹⁰He scolds the nations — won't he
  punish them?[l]
  He is the teacher of us all —
  hasn't he any knowledge?
¹¹The LORD knows what we think;
  he knows how senseless our
  reasoning is.

¹²LORD, how happy are those you
  instruct,
  the ones to whom you teach
  your law!
¹³You give them rest from days of
  trouble
  until a pit is dug to trap the
  wicked.
¹⁴The LORD will not abandon his
  people;
  he will not desert those who
  belong to him.
¹⁵Justice will again be found in the
  courts,
  and all righteous people will
  support it.

¹⁶Who stood up for me against the
  wicked?
  Who took my side against the
  evildoers?
¹⁷If the LORD had not helped me,
  I would have gone quickly to the
  land of silence.[m]
¹⁸I said, "I am falling";
  but your constant love, O LORD,
  held me up.
¹⁹Whenever I am anxious and
  worried,
  you comfort me and make me
  glad.

²⁰You have nothing to do with
  corrupt judges,
  who make injustice legal,
²¹ who plot against good people

---

[l] them?; *or* our wicked leaders?   [m] LAND OF SILENCE: *The world of the dead (see 6.5).*

and sentence the innocent to
death.
22 But the LORD defends me;
my God protects me.
23 He will punish them for their
wickedness
and destroy them for their sins;
the LORD our God will destroy
them.

A Song of Praise

95 Come, let us praise the LORD!
Let us sing for joy to God,
who protects us!
2 Let us come before him with
thanksgiving
and sing joyful songs of praise.
3 For the LORD is a mighty God,
a mighty king over all the gods.
4 He rules over the whole earth,
from the deepest caves to the
highest hills.
5 He rules over the sea, which he
made;
the land also, which he himself
formed.

6 Come, let us bow down and
worship him;
let us kneel before the LORD, our
Maker!
7 He is our God;
we are the people he cares for,
the flock for which he provides.

Listen today to what he says:
8 "Don't be stubborn, as your
ancestors were at Meribah,
as they were that day in the
desert at Massah.
9 There they put me to the test and
tried me,
although they had seen what I
did for them.
10 For forty years I was disgusted
with those people.
I said, 'How disloyal they are!
They refuse to obey my
commands.'
11 I was angry and made a solemn
promise:
'You will never enter the land
where I would have given you
rest.' "

God the Supreme King
(1 Chronicles 16.23-33)

96 Sing a new song to the LORD!
Sing to the LORD, all the
world!
2 Sing to the LORD, and praise
him!
Proclaim every day the good
news that he has saved us.
3 Proclaim his glory to the
nations,
his mighty deeds to all peoples.

4 The LORD is great and is to be
highly praised;
he is to be honored more than
all the gods.
5 The gods of all other nations are
only idols,
but the LORD created the
heavens.
6 Glory and majesty surround
him;
power and beauty fill his
Temple.

7 Praise the LORD, all people on
earth;
praise his glory and might.
8 Praise the LORD's glorious
name;
bring an offering and come into
his Temple.
9 Bow down before the Holy One
when he appears; [n]
tremble before him, all the
earth!

10 Say to all the nations, "The LORD
is king!
The earth is set firmly in place
and cannot be moved;
he will judge the peoples with
justice."
11 Be glad, earth and sky!
Roar, sea, and every creature
in you;
12 be glad, fields, and everything
in you!
The trees in the woods will shout
for joy
13 when the LORD comes to rule the
earth.
He will rule the peoples of the
world
with justice and fairness.

[n] *when he appears; or in garments of worship.*

God the Supreme Ruler

97 The LORD is king! Earth, be
glad!
Rejoice, you islands of the seas!
2 Clouds and darkness
surround him;
he rules with righteousness and
justice.
3 Fire goes in front of him
and burns up his enemies
around him.
4 His lightning lights up the world;
the earth sees it and trembles.
5 The hills melt like wax before the
LORD,
before the Lord of all the earth.
6 The heavens proclaim his
righteousness,
and all the nations see his glory.

7 Everyone who worships idols is
put to shame;
all the gods bow down[o] before
the LORD.
8 The people of Zion are glad,
and the cities of Judah rejoice
because of your judgments,
O LORD.
9 LORD Almighty, you are ruler of all
the earth;
you are much greater than all
the gods.

10 The LORD loves those who hate
evil;[p]
he protects the lives of his
people;
he rescues them from the power
of the wicked.
11 Light shines on the righteous,
and gladness on the good.
12 All you that are righteous be glad
because of what the LORD has
done!
Remember what the holy God has
done,
and give thanks to him.

God the Ruler of the World[q]

98 Sing a new song to the LORD;
he has done wonderful
things!
By his own power and holy
strength

he has won the victory.
2 The LORD announced his victory;
he made his saving power
known to the nations.
3 He kept his promise to the people
of Israel
with loyalty and constant love
for them.
All people everywhere have seen
the victory of our God.

4 Sing for joy to the LORD, all the
earth;
praise him with songs and
shouts of joy!
5 Sing praises to the LORD!
Play music on the harps!
6 Blow trumpets and horns,
and shout for joy to the LORD,
our king.

7 Roar, sea, and every creature
in you;
sing, earth, and all who live
on you!
8 Clap your hands, you rivers;
you hills, sing together with joy
before the LORD,
9 because he comes to rule the
earth.
He will rule the peoples of the
world
with justice and fairness.

God the Supreme King

99 The LORD is king,
and the people tremble.
He sits on his throne above the
winged creatures,
and the earth shakes.
2 The LORD is mighty in Zion;
he is supreme over all the
nations.
3 Everyone will praise his great and
majestic name.
Holy is he!

4 Mighty king,[r] you love what is
right;
you have established justice in
Israel;
you have brought righteousness
and fairness.
5 Praise the LORD our God;

o all the gods bow down; or bow down, all gods.   p Probable text The LORD loves those who
hate evil; Hebrew Hate evil, you who love the LORD.   q HEBREW TITLE: A psalm.
r Probable text Mighty king; Hebrew The might of the king.

worship before his throne!
Holy is he!

6 Moses and Aaron were his priests,
and Samuel was one who
prayed to him;
they called to the LORD, and he
answered them.
7 He spoke to them from the pillar
of cloud;
they obeyed the laws and
commands that he gave them.

8 O LORD, our God, you answered
your people;
you showed them that you are a
God who forgives,
even though you punished them
for their sins.
9 Praise the LORD our God,
and worship at his sacred hill! s
The LORD our God is holy.

A Hymn of Praise t

100 Sing to the LORD, all the
world!
2 Worship the LORD with joy;
come before him with happy
songs!

3 Acknowledge that the LORD is God.
He made us, and we belong
to him;
we are his people, we are his
flock.

4 Enter the Temple gates with
thanksgiving;
go into its courts with praise.
Give thanks to him and
praise him.

5 The LORD is good;
his love is eternal
and his faithfulness lasts
forever.

A King's Promise u

101 My song is about loyalty and
justice,
and I sing it to you, O LORD.
2 My conduct will be faultless.
When will you come to me?

I will live a pure life in my house
3 and will never tolerate evil.

I hate the actions of those who
turn away from God;
I will have nothing to do with
them.
4 I will not be dishonest v
and will have no dealings with
evil. w
5 I will get rid of anyone
who whispers evil things about
someone else;
I will not tolerate anyone
who is proud and arrogant.

6 I will approve of those who are
faithful to God
and will let them live in my
palace.
Those who are completely honest
will be allowed to serve me.

7 No liar will live in my palace;
no hypocrite will remain in my
presence.
8 Day after day I will destroy
the wicked in our land;
I will expel all who are evil
from the city of the LORD.

The Prayer of a Troubled Youth x

102 Listen to my prayer, O LORD,
and hear my cry for help!
2 When I am in trouble,
don't turn away from me!
Listen to me,
and answer me quickly when I
call!

3 My life is disappearing like smoke;
my body is burning like fire.
4 I am beaten down like dry grass;
I have lost my desire for food.
5 I groan aloud;
I am nothing but skin and
bones.
6 I am like a wild bird in the desert,
like an owl in abandoned ruins.
7 I lie awake;
I am like a lonely bird on a
housetop.
8 All day long my enemies
insult me;
those who mock me use my
name in cursing.

9-10 Because of your anger and fury,

---

s SACRED HILL: *See 2.6.*   t HEBREW TITLE: *A psalm of thanksgiving.*   u HEBREW TITLE: *A psalm by David.*   v not be dishonest; *or stay away from dishonest people.*   w evil; *or evil people.*
x HEBREW TITLE: *A prayer by a weary sufferer who pours out his complaints to the LORD.*

ashes are my food,
and my tears are mixed with my
drink.
You picked me up and threw me
away.
11 My life is like the evening
shadows;
I am like dry grass.

12 But you, O Lord, are king forever;
all generations will
remember you.
13 You will rise and take pity on
Zion;
the time has come to have
mercy on her;
this is the right time.
14 Your servants love her,
even though she is destroyed;
they have pity on her,
even though she is in ruins.

15 The nations will fear the Lord;
all the kings of the earth will
fear his power.
16 When the Lord rebuilds Zion,
he will reveal his greatness.
17 He will hear his forsaken people
and listen to their prayer.

18 Write down for the coming
generation what the Lord has
done,
so that people not yet born will
praise him.
19 The Lord looked down from his
holy place on high,
he looked down from heaven to
earth.
20 He heard the groans of prisoners
and set free those who were
condemned to die.
21 And so his name will be
proclaimed in Zion,
and he will be praised in
Jerusalem
22 when nations and kingdoms
come together
and worship the Lord.

23 The Lord has made me weak while
I am still young;
he has shortened my life.
24 O God, do not take me away now
before I grow old.

O Lord, you live forever;
25 long ago you created the earth,
and with your own hands you
made the heavens.
26 They will disappear, but you will
remain;
they will all wear out like
clothes.
You will discard them like clothes,
and they will vanish.
27 But you are always the same,
and your life never ends.
28 Our children will live in safety,
and under your protection
their descendants will be secure.

The Love of God y

103
Praise the Lord, my soul!
All my being, praise his
holy name!
2 Praise the Lord, my soul,
and do not forget how kind
he is.
3 He forgives all my sins
and heals all my diseases.
4 He keeps me from the grave
and blesses me with love and
mercy.
5 He fills my life z with good things,
so that I stay young and strong
like an eagle.

6 The Lord judges in favor of the
oppressed
and gives them their rights.
7 He revealed his plans to Moses
and let the people of Israel see
his mighty deeds.
8 The Lord is merciful and loving,
slow to become angry and full of
constant love.
9 He does not keep on rebuking;
he is not angry forever.
10 He does not punish us as we
deserve
or repay us according to our
sins and wrongs.
11 As high as the sky is above the
earth,
so great is his love for those
who honor him.
12 As far as the east is from the west,
so far does he remove our sins
from us.
13 As a father is kind to his children,

y HEBREW TITLE: By David.   z Probable text my life; Hebrew unclear.

so the LORD is kind to those who
  honor him.
14 He knows what we are made of;
  he remembers that we are dust.

15 As for us, our life is like grass.
  We grow and flourish like a wild
    flower;
16   then the wind blows on it, and it
    is gone—
  no one sees it again.
17 But for those who honor the LORD,
  his love lasts forever,
  and his goodness endures for all
    generations
18 of those who are true to his
    covenant
  and who faithfully obey his
    commands.

19 The LORD placed his throne in
    heaven;
  he is king over all.
20 Praise the LORD, you strong and
    mighty angels,
  who obey his commands,
  who listen to what he says.
21 Praise the LORD, all you heavenly
    powers,
  you servants of his, who do his
    will!
22 Praise the LORD, all his creatures
  in all the places he rules.
  Praise the LORD, my soul!

In Praise of the Creator

104 Praise the LORD, my soul!
  O LORD, my God, how
    great you are!
  You are clothed with majesty and
    glory;
2   you cover yourself with light.
  You have spread out the heavens
    like a tent
3   and built your home on the
    waters above.a
  You use the clouds as your chariot
  and ride on the wings of the
    wind.
4 You use the winds as your
    messengers
  and flashes of lightning as your
    servants.

5 You have set the earth firmly on
  its foundations,

and it will never be moved.
6 You placed the ocean over it like a
    robe,
  and the water covered the
    mountains.
7 When you rebuked the waters,
    they fled;
  they rushed away when they
    heard your shout of command.
8 They flowed over the mountains
  and into the valleys,
  to the place you had made for
    them.
9 You set a boundary they can never
    pass,
  to keep them from covering the
    earth again.

10 You make springs flow in the
    valleys,
  and rivers run between the hills.
11 They provide water for the wild
    animals;
  there the wild donkeys quench
    their thirst.
12 In the trees near by,
  the birds make their nests and
    sing.

13 From the sky you send rain on the
    hills,
  and the earth is filled with your
    blessings.
14 You make grass grow for the
    cattle
  and plants for us to use,
  so that we can grow our crops
15   and produce wine to make us
    happy,
  olive oil to make us cheerful,
  and bread to give us strength.

16 The cedars of Lebanon get plenty
    of rain—
  the LORD's own trees, which he
    planted.
17 There the birds build their nests;
  the storks nest in the fir trees.
18 The wild goats live in the high
    mountains,
  and the rock badgers hide in the
    cliffs.

19 You created the moon to mark the
    months;
  the sun knows the time to set.

---

a THE WATERS ABOVE: *A reference to the waters above the celestial dome (Gn 1.6, 7).*

20 You made the night, and in the
   darkness
   all the wild animals come out.
21 The young lions roar while they
   hunt,
   looking for the food that God
   provides.
22 When the sun rises, they go back
   and lie down in their dens.
23 Then people go out to do their
   work
   and keep working until evening.

24 LORD, you have made so many
   things!
   How wisely you made them all!
   The earth is filled with your
   creatures.
25 There is the ocean, large and wide,
   where countless creatures live,
   large and small alike.
26 The ships sail on it, and in it plays
   Leviathan,
   that sea monster which you
   made.b

27 All of them depend on you
   to give them food when they
   need it.
28 You give it to them, and they
   eat it;
   you provide food, and they are
   satisfied.
29 When you turn away, they are
   afraid;
   when you take away your
   breath, they die
   and go back to the dust from
   which they came.
30 But when you give them breath,c
   they are created;
   you give new life to the earth.

31 May the glory of the LORD last
   forever!
   May the LORD be happy with
   what he has made!
32 He looks at the earth, and it
   trembles;
   he touches the mountains, and
   they pour out smoke.

33 I will sing to the LORD all my life;
   as long as I live I will sing
   praises to my God.

34 May he be pleased with my song,
   for my gladness comes
   from him.
35 May sinners be destroyed from the
   earth;
   may the wicked be no more.

Praise the LORD, my soul!
Praise the LORD!

God and His People

(*1 Chronicles 16.8-22*)

105 Give thanks to the LORD,
     proclaim his greatness;
   tell the nations what he has
   done.
2 Sing praise to the LORD;
   tell the wonderful things he has
   done.
3 Be glad that we belong to him;
   let all who worship him rejoice.
4 Go to the LORD for help;
   and worship him continually.
5-6 You descendants of Abraham, his
   servant;
   you descendants of Jacob, the
   man he chose:
   remember the miracles that God
   performed
   and the judgments that he gave.

7 The LORD is our God;
   his commands are for all the
   world.
8 He will keep his covenant forever,
   his promises for a thousand
   generations.
9 He will keep the agreement he
   made with Abraham
   and his promise to Isaac.
10 The LORD made a covenant with
   Jacob,
   one that will last forever.
11 "I will give you the land of
   Canaan," he said.
   "It will be your own possession."

12 God's people were few in number,
   strangers in the land of Canaan.
13 They wandered from country to
   country,
   from one kingdom to another.
14 But God let no one oppress them;
   to protect them, he warned the
   kings:

---

b in it plays . . . made; *or* Leviathan is there, that sea monster you made to amuse you.
c give them breath; *or* send out your spirit.

15 "Don't harm my chosen servants;
    do not touch my prophets."

16 The LORD sent famine to their
      country
    and took away all their food.
17 But he sent a man ahead of
      them,
    Joseph, who had been sold as a
      slave.
18 His feet were kept in chains,
    and an iron collar was around
      his neck,
19   until what he had predicted
        came true.
    The word of the LORD proved him
      right.
20 Then the king of Egypt had him
      released;
    the ruler of nations set him
      free.
21 He put him in charge of his
      government
    and made him ruler over all the
      land,
22   with power over the king's
        officials
    and authority to instruct his
      advisers.

23 Then Jacob went to Egypt
    and settled in that country.
24 The LORD gave many children to
      his people
    and made them stronger than
      their enemies.
25 He made the Egyptians hate his
      people
    and treat his servants with
      deceit.

26 Then he sent his servant Moses,
    and Aaron, whom he had
      chosen.
27 They did God's mighty acts
    and performed miracles in
      Egypt.
28 God sent darkness on the country,
    but the Egyptians did not obey d
      his command.
29 He turned their rivers into blood
    and killed all their fish.
30 Their country was overrun with
    frogs;

even the palace was filled with
  them.
31 God commanded, and flies and
      gnats
    swarmed throughout the whole
      country.
32 He sent hail and lightning on their
      land
    instead of rain;
33 he destroyed their grapevines and
      fig trees
    and broke down all the
      trees.
34 He commanded, and the locusts
      came,
    countless millions of them;
35 they ate all the plants in the
      land;
    they ate all the crops.
36 He killed the first-born sons
    of all the families of Egypt.

37 Then he led the Israelites out;
    they carried silver and
      gold,
    and all of them were healthy
      and strong.
38 The Egyptians were afraid of
      them
    and were glad when they left.
39 God put a cloud over his people
    and a fire at night to give them
      light.
40 They e asked, and he sent quails;
    he gave them food from heaven
      to satisfy them.
41 He opened a rock, and water
      gushed out,
    flowing through the desert like a
      river.
42 He remembered his sacred
      promise
    to Abraham his servant.

43 So he led his chosen people out,
    and they sang and shouted
      for joy.
44 He gave them the lands of other
      peoples
    and let them take over their
      fields,
45 so that his people would obey his
      laws
    and keep all his commands.

Praise the LORD!

d Some ancient translations did not obey; Hebrew obeyed.   e Some ancient translations
They; Hebrew He.

The Lord's Goodness to His People

106 Praise the Lord!

Give thanks to the Lord,
    because he is good;
    his love is eternal.
2 Who can tell all the great things
    he has done?
    Who can praise him enough?
3 Happy are those who obey his
    commands,
    who always do what is right.

4 Remember me, Lord, when you
    help your people;
    include me when you save them.
5 Let me see the prosperity of your
    people
    and share in the happiness of
    your nation,
    in the glad pride of those who
    belong to you.

6 We have sinned as our
    ancestors did;
    we have been wicked and evil.
7 Our ancestors in Egypt did not
    understand God's wonderful
    acts;
    they forgot the many times he
    showed them his love,
    and they rebelled against the
    Almighty *f* at the Red Sea.
8 But he saved them, as he had
    promised,
    in order to show his great
    power.
9 He gave a command to the
    Red Sea,
    and it dried up;
    he led his people across on dry
    land.
10 He saved them from those who
    hated them;
    he rescued them from their
    enemies.
11 But the water drowned their
    enemies;
    not one of them was left.
12 Then his people believed his
    promises
    and sang praises to him.

13 But they quickly forgot what he
    had done

and acted without waiting for
    his advice.
14 They were filled with craving in
    the desert
    and put God to the test;
15 so he gave them what they
    asked for,
    but also sent a terrible disease
    among them.

16 There in the desert they were
    jealous of Moses
    and of Aaron, the Lord's holy
    servant.
17 Then the earth opened up and
    swallowed Dathan
    and buried Abiram and his
    family;
18 fire came down on their followers
    and burned up those wicked
    people.

19 They made a gold bull-calf at
    Sinai
    and worshiped that idol;
20 they exchanged the glory of God
    for the image of an animal that
    eats grass.
21 They forgot the God who had
    saved them
    by his mighty acts in Egypt.
22 What wonderful things he did
    there!
    What amazing things at the
    Red Sea!
23 When God said that he would
    destroy his people,
    his chosen servant, Moses, stood
    up against God
    and kept his anger from
    destroying them.

24 Then they rejected the pleasant
    land,
    because they did not believe
    God's promise.
25 They stayed in their tents and
    grumbled
    and would not listen to the Lord.
26 So he gave them a solemn
    warning
    that he would make them die in
    the desert
27   and scatter their descendants
    among the heathen,

---

f Probable text the Almighty; *Hebrew* the sea.

letting them die in foreign
countries.

28 Then at Peor, God's people joined
in the worship of Baal
and ate sacrifices offered to
dead gods.
29 They stirred up the LORD's anger
by their actions,
and a terrible disease broke out
among them.
30 But Phinehas stood up and
punished the guilty,
and the plague was stopped.
31 This has been remembered in his
favor ever since
and will be for all time to come.

32 At the springs of Meribah the
people made the LORD angry,
and Moses was in trouble on
their account.
33 They made him so bitter
that he spoke without stopping
to think.

34 They did not kill the heathen,
as the LORD had commanded
them to do,
35 but they intermarried with them
and adopted their pagan ways.
36 God's people worshiped idols,
and this caused their
destruction.
37 They offered their own sons and
daughters
as sacrifices to the idols of
Canaan.
38 They killed those innocent
children,
and the land was defiled by
those murders.
39 They made themselves impure by
their actions
and were unfaithful to God.

40 So the LORD was angry with his
people;
he was disgusted with them.
41 He abandoned them to the power
of the heathen,
and their enemies ruled over
them.
42 They were oppressed by their
enemies

and were in complete subjection
to them.
43 Many times the LORD rescued his
people,
but they chose to rebel
against him
and sank deeper into sin.
44 Yet the LORD heard them when
they cried out,
and he took notice of their
distress.
45 For their sake he remembered his
covenant,
and because of his great love he
relented.
46 He made all their oppressors
feel sorry for them.

47 Save us, O LORD our God,
and bring us back from among
the nations,
so that we may be thankful
and praise your holy name.

48 Praise the LORD, the God of Israel;
praise him now and forever!
Let everyone say, "Amen!"

Praise the LORD!

BOOK FIVE

(Psalms 107–150)

In Praise of God's Goodness

107 "Give thanks to the LORD,
because he is good;
his love is eternal!"
2 Repeat these words in praise to
the LORD,
all you whom he has saved.
He has rescued you from your
enemies
3   and has brought you back from
foreign countries,
from east and west, from north
and south. g

4 Some wandered in the trackless
desert
and could not find their way to a
city to live in.
5 They were hungry and thirsty
and had given up all hope.
6 Then in their trouble they called to
the LORD,

---

g *Probable text* south; *Hebrew* the Mediterranean Sea *(meaning "west").*

and he saved them from their
distress.
7 He led them by a straight road
to a city where they could live.
8 They must thank the Lord for his
constant love,
for the wonderful things he did
for them.
9 He satisfies those who are thirsty
and fills the hungry with good
things.

10 Some were living in gloom and
darkness,
prisoners suffering in chains,
11 because they had rebelled against
the commands of
Almighty God
and had rejected his
instructions.
12 They were worn out from hard
work;
they would fall down, and no
one would help.
13 Then in their trouble they called to
the Lord,
and he saved them from their
distress.
14 He brought them out of their
gloom and darkness
and broke their chains in pieces.
15 They must thank the Lord for his
constant love,
for the wonderful things he did
for them.
16 He breaks down doors of bronze
and smashes iron bars.

17 Some were fools, suffering
because of their sins
and because of their evil;
18 they couldn't stand the sight of
food
and were close to death.
19 Then in their trouble they called to
the Lord,
and he saved them from their
distress.
20 He healed them with his command
and saved them from the grave.
21 They must thank the Lord for his
constant love,
for the wonderful things he did
for them.
22 They must thank him with
sacrifices,
and with songs of joy must tell
all that he has done.

23 Some sailed over the ocean in
ships,
earning their living on the seas.
24 They saw what the Lord can do,
his wonderful acts on the seas.
25 He commanded, and a mighty
wind began to blow
and stirred up the waves.
26 The ships were lifted high in
the air
and plunged down into the
depths.
In such danger the sailors lost
their courage;
27 they stumbled and staggered
like drunks —
all their skill was useless.
28 Then in their trouble they called to
the Lord,
and he saved them from their
distress.
29 He calmed the raging storm,
and the waves became quiet.
30 They were glad because of the
calm,
and he brought them safe to the
port they wanted.
31 They must thank the Lord for his
constant love,
for the wonderful things he did
for them.
32 They must proclaim his greatness
in the assembly of the people
and praise him before the
council of the leaders.

33 The Lord made rivers dry up
completely
and stopped springs from
flowing.
34 He made rich soil become a salty
wasteland
because of the wickedness of
those who lived there.
35 He changed deserts into pools of
water
and dry land into flowing
springs.
36 He let hungry people settle there,
and they built a city to live in.
37 They sowed the fields and planted
grapevines
and reaped an abundant harvest.
38 He blessed his people, and they
had many children;
he kept their herds of cattle
from decreasing.

39 When God's people were defeated
and humiliated
by cruel oppression and
suffering,
40 he showed contempt for their
oppressors
and made them wander in
trackless deserts.
41 But he rescued the needy from
their misery
and made their families increase
like flocks.
42 The righteous see this and are
glad,
but all the wicked are put to
silence.

43 May those who are wise think
about these things;
may they consider the LORD's
constant love.

A Prayer for Help against Enemies [h]

(Psalm 57.7-11; 60.5-12)

108

I have complete confidence,
O God!
I will sing and praise you!
Wake up, my soul!
2 Wake up, my harp and lyre!
I will wake up the sun.
3 I will thank you, O LORD, among
the nations.
I will praise you among the
peoples.
4 Your constant love reaches above
the heavens;
your faithfulness touches the
skies.

5 Show your greatness in the sky,
O God,
and your glory over all the
earth.
6 Save us by your might; answer my
prayer,
so that the people you love may
be rescued.

7 From his sanctuary [i] God has
said,
"In triumph I will divide
Shechem
and distribute Sukkoth Valley to
my people.
8 Gilead is mine, and Manasseh too;

Ephraim is my helmet
and Judah my royal scepter.
9 But I will use Moab as my
washbowl,
and I will throw my sandals on
Edom,
as a sign that I own it.
I will shout in triumph over the
Philistines."

10 Who, O God, will take me into the
fortified city?
Who will lead me to Edom?
11 Have you really rejected us?
Aren't you going to march out
with our armies?
12 Help us against the enemy;
human help is worthless.
13 With God on our side we will win;
he will defeat our enemies.

The Complaint of Someone in Trouble [j]

109

I praise you, God; don't
remain silent!
2 Wicked people and liars have
attacked me.
They tell lies about me,
3 and they say evil things
about me,
attacking me for no reason.
4 They oppose me, even though I
love them
and have prayed for them. [k]
5 They pay me back evil for good
and hatred for love.

6 Choose some corrupt judge to try
my enemy,
and let one of his own enemies
accuse him.
7 May he be tried and found guilty;
may even his prayer be
considered a crime!
8 May his life soon be ended;
may someone else take his job!
9 May his children become orphans,
and his wife a widow!
10 May his children be homeless
beggars;
may they be driven from [l] the
ruins they live in!
11 May his creditors take away all
his property,

h HEBREW TITLE: A psalm by David; a song.   i From his sanctuary; or In his holiness.
j HEBREW TITLE: A psalm by David.   k Probable text have prayed for them; Hebrew unclear.
l One ancient translation be driven from; Hebrew seek.

and may strangers get
everything he worked for.
12 May no one ever be kind to him
or care for the orphans he
leaves behind.
13 May all his descendants die,
and may his name be forgotten
in the next generation.
14 May the LORD remember the evil of
his ancestors
and never forgive his mother's
sins.
15 May the LORD always remember
their sins,
but may they themselves be
completely forgotten!

16 That man never thought of being
kind;
he persecuted and killed
the poor, the needy, and the
helpless.
17 He loved to curse—may he be
cursed!
He hated to give blessings—may
no one bless him!
18 He cursed as naturally as he
dressed himself;
may his own curses soak into
his body like water
and into his bones like oil!
19 May they cover him like clothes
and always be around him like
a belt!

20 LORD, punish my enemies in
that way—
those who say such evil things
against me!
21 But my Sovereign LORD, help me
as you have promised,
and rescue me because of the
goodness of your love.
22 I am poor and needy;
I am hurt to the depths of my
heart.
23 Like an evening shadow I am
about to vanish;
I am blown away like an insect.
24 My knees are weak from lack of
food;
I am nothing but skin and
bones.

25 When people see me, they laugh
at me;
they shake their heads in scorn.

26 Help me, O LORD my God;
because of your constant love,
save me!
27 Make my enemies know
that you are the one who
saves me.
28 They may curse me, but you will
bless me.
May my persecutors be
defeated,m
and may I, your servant, be
glad.
29 May my enemies be covered with
disgrace;
may they wear their shame like
a robe.

30 I will give loud thanks to the LORD;
I will praise him in the assembly
of the people,
31 because he defends the poor
and saves them from those who
condemn them to death.

The LORD and His Chosen King n

110
The LORD said to my lord,
"Sit here at my right side
until I put your enemies under
your feet."
2 From Zion the LORD will extend
your royal power.
"Rule over your enemies," he
says.
3 On the day you fight your
enemies,
your people will volunteer.
Like the dew of early morning
your young men will come to
you on the sacred hills.o

4 The LORD made a solemn promise
and will not take it back:
"You will be a priest forever
in the priestly order of
Melchizedek."p

5 The Lord is at your right side;
when he becomes angry, he will
defeat kings.

---

m One ancient translation May my persecutors be defeated; Hebrew They persecuted me and
were defeated.   n HEBREW TITLE: A psalm by David.   o Verse 3 in Hebrew is unclear.
p in the priestly order of Melchizedek; or like Melchizedek; or in the line of succession to
Melchizedek.

6 He will pass judgment on the
nations
and fill the battlefield with
corpses;
he will defeat kings all over the
earth.
7 The king will drink from the
stream by the road,
and strengthened, he will stand
victorious.

In Praise of the LORD

111
Praise the LORD!

With all my heart I will thank the
LORD
in the assembly of his
people.
2 How wonderful are the things the
LORD does!
All who are delighted with them
want to understand them.
3 All he does is full of honor and
majesty;
his righteousness is eternal.

4 The LORD does not let us forget his
wonderful actions;
he is kind and merciful.
5 He provides food for those who
honor him;
he never forgets his
covenant.
6 He has shown his power to his
people
by giving them the lands of
foreigners.

7 In all he does he is faithful and
just;
all his commands are
dependable.
8 They last for all time;
they were given in truth and
righteousness.
9 He set his people free
and made an eternal covenant
with them.
Holy and mighty is he!
10 The way to become wise is to
honor the LORD; q
he gives sound judgment
to all who obey his commands.
He is to be praised forever.

The Happiness of a Good Person

112
Praise the LORD!

Happy is the person who honors
the LORD,
who takes pleasure in obeying
his commands.
2 The good man's children will be
powerful in the land;
his descendants will be blessed.
3 His family will be wealthy and
rich,
and he will be prosperous
forever.

4 Light shines in the darkness for
good people,
for those who are merciful, kind,
and just.
5 Happy is the person who is
generous with his loans,
who runs his business honestly.
6 A good person will never fail;
he will always be remembered.

7 He is not afraid of receiving bad
news;
his faith is strong, and he trusts
in the LORD.
8 He is not worried or afraid;
he is certain to see his enemies
defeated.
9 He gives generously to the needy,
and his kindness never fails;
he will be powerful and
respected.
10 The wicked see this and are angry;
they glare in hate and disappear;
their hopes are gone forever.

In Praise of the LORD's Goodness

113
Praise the LORD!

You servants of the LORD,
praise his name!
2 May his name be praised,
now and forever.
3 From the east to the west
praise the name of the LORD!
4 The LORD rules over all nations;
his glory is above the heavens.

5 There is no one like the LORD
our God.
He lives in the heights above,
6   but he bends down

---

q The way . . . the LORD; or The most important part of wisdom is honoring the LORD.

to see the heavens and the earth.
7 He raises the poor from the dust;
  he lifts the needy from their
    misery
8 and makes them companions of
    princes,
  the princes of his people.
9 He honors the childless wife in her
    home;
  he makes her happy by giving
    her children.

Praise the LORD!

A Passover Song

114 When the people of Israel
      left Egypt,
  when Jacob's descendants left
    that foreign land,
2 Judah became the Lord's holy
    people,
  Israel became his own
    possession.

3 The Red Sea looked and ran
    away;
  the Jordan River stopped
    flowing.
4 The mountains skipped like goats;
  the hills jumped around like
    lambs.

5 What happened, Sea, to make you
    run away?
  And you, O Jordan, why did you
    stop flowing?
6 You mountains, why did you skip
    like goats?
  You hills, why did you jump
    around like lambs?

7 Tremble, earth, at the Lord's
    coming,
  at the presence of the God of
    Jacob,
8 who changes rocks into pools of
    water
  and solid cliffs into flowing
    springs.

The One True God

115 To you alone, O LORD, to you
      alone,
  and not to us, must glory be
    given

because of your constant love
  and faithfulness.

2 Why should the nations ask us,
  "Where is your God?"
3 Our God is in heaven;
  he does whatever he wishes.
4 Their gods are made of silver and
    gold,
  formed by human hands.
5 They have mouths, but cannot
    speak,
  and eyes, but cannot see.
6 They have ears, but cannot hear,
  and noses, but cannot smell.
7 They have hands, but cannot feel,
  and feet, but cannot walk;
  they cannot make a sound.
8 May all who made them and who
    trust in them
  become r like the idols they
    have made.

9 Trust in the LORD, you people of
    Israel.
  He helps you and protects you.
10 Trust in the LORD, you priests
    of God.
  He helps you and protects you.
11 Trust in the LORD, all you that
    worship him.
  He helps you and protects you.

12 The LORD remembers us and will
    bless us;
  he will bless the people of Israel
  and all the priests of God.
13 He will bless everyone who
    honors him,
  the great and the small alike.

14 May the LORD give you children—
  you and your descendants!
15 May you be blessed by the LORD,
  who made heaven and earth!

16 Heaven belongs to the LORD alone,
  but he gave the earth to us
    humans.
17 The LORD is not praised by the
    dead,
  by any who go down to the land
    of silence. s

---

r May all . . . become; or All who made them and who trust in them will become.
s LAND OF SILENCE: The world of the dead (see 6.5).

18 But we, the living, will give thanks
to him
now and forever.

Praise the LORD!

Someone Saved from Death Praises God

116 I love the LORD, because he
hears me;
he listens to my prayers.
2 He listens to me
every time I call to him.
3 The danger of death was all
around me;
the horrors of the grave closed
in on me;
I was filled with fear and
anxiety.
4 Then I called to the LORD,
"I beg you, LORD, save me!"

5 The LORD is merciful and good;
our God is compassionate.
6 The LORD protects the helpless;
when I was in danger, he
saved me.
7 Be confident, my heart,
because the LORD has been good
to me.

8 The LORD saved me from death;
he stopped my tears
and kept me from defeat.
9 And so I walk in the presence of
the LORD
in the world of the living.
10 I kept on believing, even when I
said,
"I am completely crushed,"
11 even when I was afraid and said,
"No one can be trusted."

12 What can I offer the LORD
for all his goodness to me?
13 I will bring a wine offering to the
LORD,
to thank him for saving me.
14 In the assembly of all his people
I will give him what I have
promised.

15 How painful it is to the LORD
when one of his people dies!
16 I am your servant, LORD;
I serve you just as my
mother did.

You have saved me from death.
17 I will give you a sacrifice of
thanksgiving
and offer my prayer to you.
18-19 In the assembly of all your people,
in the sanctuary of your Temple
in Jerusalem,
I will give you what I have
promised.

Praise the LORD!

In Praise of the LORD

117 Praise the LORD, all nations!
Praise him, all peoples!
2 His love for us is strong,
and his faithfulness is eternal.

Praise the LORD!

A Prayer of Thanks for Victory

118 Give thanks to the LORD,
because he is good,
and his love is eternal.
2 Let the people of Israel say,
"His love is eternal."
3 Let the priests of God say,
"His love is eternal."
4 Let all who worship him say,
"His love is eternal."

5 In my distress I called to the LORD;
he answered me and set me free.
6 The LORD is with me, I will not be
afraid;
what can anyone do to me?
7 It is the LORD who helps me,
and I will see my enemies
defeated.
8 It is better to trust in the LORD
than to depend on people.
9 It is better to trust in the LORD
than to depend on human
leaders.

10 Many enemies were around me;
but I destroyed them by the
power of the LORD!
11 They were around me on every
side;
but I destroyed them by the
power of the LORD!
12 They swarmed around me like
bees,
but they burned out as quickly
as a brush fire;
by the power of the LORD I
destroyed them.

13 I was fiercely attacked and was
     being defeated,
     but the LORD helped me.
14 The LORD makes me powerful and
     strong;
     he has saved me.

15 Listen to the glad shouts of victory
     in the tents of God's people:
     "The LORD's mighty power has
     done it!
16   His power has brought us
     victory—
     his mighty power in battle!"

17 I will not die; instead, I will live
     and proclaim what the LORD has
     done.
18 He has punished me severely,
     but he has not let me die.

19 Open to me the gates of the
     Temple;
     I will go in and give thanks to
     the LORD!

20 This is the gate of the LORD;
     only the righteous can come in.

21 I praise you, LORD, because you
     heard me,
     because you have given me
     victory.

22 The stone which the builders
     rejected as worthless
     turned out to be the most
     important of all.
23 This was done by the LORD;
     what a wonderful sight it is!
24 This is the day of the LORD's
     victory;
     let us be happy, let us celebrate!
25 Save us, LORD, save us!
     Give us success, O LORD!

26 May God bless the one who comes
     in the name of the LORD!
     From the Temple of the LORD we
     bless you.
27 The LORD is God; he has been good
     to us.
     With branches in your hands, start
     the festival
     and march around the altar.

28 You are my God, and I give you
     thanks;

     I will proclaim your greatness.

29 Give thanks to the LORD, because
     he is good,
     and his love is eternal.

The Law of the LORD

119 Happy are those whose lives
     are faultless,
     who live according to the law of
     the LORD.
2 Happy are those who follow his
     commands,
     who obey him with all their
     heart.
3 They never do wrong;
     they walk in the LORD's ways.
4 LORD, you have given us your laws
     and told us to obey them
     faithfully.
5 How I hope that I shall be faithful
     in keeping your instructions!
6 If I pay attention to all your
     commands,
     then I will not be put to shame.
7 As I learn your righteous
     judgments,
     I will praise you with a pure
     heart.
8 I will obey your laws;
     never abandon me!

Obedience to the Law of the LORD

9 How can young people keep their
     lives pure?
     By obeying your commands.
10 With all my heart I try to
     serve you;
     keep me from disobeying your
     commandments.
11 I keep your law in my heart,
     so that I will not sin against you.
12 I praise you, O LORD;
     teach me your ways.
13 I will repeat aloud
     all the laws you have given.
14 I delight in following your
     commands
     more than in having great
     wealth.
15 I study your instructions;
     I examine your teachings.
16 I take pleasure in your laws;
     your commands I will not forget.

Happiness in the Law of the LORD

17 Be good to me, your servant,
    so that I may live and obey your
    teachings.
18 Open my eyes, so that I may see
    the wonderful truths in
    your law.
19 I am here on earth for just a little
    while;
    do not hide your commands
    from me.
20 My heart aches with longing;
    I want to know your judgments
    at all times.
21 You reprimand the proud;
    cursed are those who disobey
    your commands.
22 Free me from their insults and
    scorn,
    because I have kept your laws.
23 The rulers meet and plot
    against me,
    but I will study your teachings.
24 Your instructions give me
    pleasure;
    they are my advisers.

Determination to Obey the Law of the LORD

25 I lie defeated in the dust;
    revive me, as you have
    promised.
26 I confessed all I have done, and
    you answered me;
    teach me your ways.
27 Help me to understand your laws,
    and I will meditate on your
    wonderful teachings.ᵗ
28 I am overcome by sorrow;
    strengthen me, as you have
    promised.
29 Keep me from going the
    wrong way,
    and in your goodness teach me
    your law.
30 I have chosen to be obedient;
    I have paid attention to your
    judgments.
31 I have followed your instructions,
    LORD;
    don't let me be put to shame.
32 I will eagerly obey your
    commands,
    because you will give me more
    understanding.

A Prayer for Understanding

33 Teach me, LORD, the meaning of
    your laws,
    and I will obey them at all times.
34 Explain your law to me, and I will
    obey it;
    I will keep it with all my heart.
35 Keep me obedient to your
    commandments,
    because in them I find
    happiness.
36 Give me the desire to obey your
    laws
    rather than to get rich.
37 Keep me from paying attention to
    what is worthless;
    be good to me, as you have
    promised.
38 Keep your promise to me, your
    servant —
    the promise you make to those
    who obey you.
39 Save me from the insults I fear;
    how wonderful are your
    judgments!
40 I want to obey your commands;
    give me new life, for you are
    righteous.

Trusting the Law of the LORD

41 Show me how much you love me,
    LORD,
    and save me according to your
    promise.
42 Then I can answer those who
    insult me
    because I trust in your word.
43 Enable me to speak the truth at
    all times,
    because my hope is in your
    judgments.
44 I will always obey your law,
    forever and ever.
45 I will live in perfect freedom,
    because I try to obey your
    teachings.
46 I will announce your commands
    to kings
    and I will not be ashamed.
47 I find pleasure in obeying your
    commands,
    because I love them.
48 I respect and love your
    commandments;
    I will meditate on your
    instructions.

ᵗ teachings; or deeds.

PSALMS

Confidence in the Law of the Lord

49 Remember your promise to me,
     your servant;
     it has given me hope.
50 Even in my suffering I was
     comforted
     because your promise gave me
     life.
51 The proud are always scornful
     of me,
     but I have not departed from
     your law.
52 I remember your judgments of
     long ago,
     and they bring me comfort,
     O Lord.
53 When I see the wicked breaking
     your law,
     I am filled with anger.
54 During my brief earthly life
     I compose songs about your
     commands.
55 In the night I remember you, Lord,
     and I think about your law.
56 I find my happiness
     in obeying your commands.

Devotion to the Law of the Lord

57 You are all I want, O Lord;
     I promise to obey your laws.
58 I ask you with all my heart
     to have mercy on me, as you
     have promised!
59 I have considered my conduct,
     and I promise to follow your
     instructions.
60 Without delay I hurry
     to obey your commands.
61 The wicked have laid a trap
     for me,
     but I do not forget your law.
62 In the middle of the night I
     wake up
     to praise you for your righteous
     judgments.
63 I am a friend of all who serve you,
     of all who obey your laws.
64 Lord, the earth is full of your
     constant love;
     teach me your commandments.

The Value of the Law of the Lord

65 You have kept your promise, Lord,
     and you are good to me, your
     servant.
66 Give me wisdom and knowledge,
     because I trust in your
     commands.

67 Before you punished me, I used to
     go wrong,
     but now I obey your word.
68 How good you are—how kind!
     Teach me your commands.
69 The proud have told lies about me,
     but with all my heart I obey
     your instructions.
70 They have no understanding,
     but I find pleasure in your law.
71 My punishment was good for me,
     because it made me learn your
     commands.
72 The law that you gave means
     more to me
     than all the money in the world.

The Justice of the Law of the Lord

73 You created me, and you keep me
     safe;
     give me understanding, so that I
     may learn your laws.
74 Those who honor you will be glad
     when they see me,
     because I trust in your promise.
75 I know that your judgments are
     righteous, Lord,
     and that you punished me
     because you are faithful.
76 Let your constant love comfort me,
     as you have promised me, your
     servant.
77 Have mercy on me, and I will live
     because I take pleasure in
     your law.
78 May the proud be ashamed for
     falsely accusing me;
     as for me, I will meditate on
     your instructions.
79 May those who honor you come
     to me—
     all those who know your
     commands.
80 May I perfectly obey your
     commandments
     and be spared the shame of
     defeat.

A Prayer for Deliverance

81 I am worn out, Lord, waiting for
     you to save me;
     I place my trust in your word.
82 My eyes are tired from watching
     for what you promised,
     while I ask, "When will you
     help me?"
83 I am as useless as a discarded
     wineskin;

yet I have not forgotten your
  commands.
84 How much longer must I wait?
  When will you punish those who
  persecute me?
85 The proud, who do not obey
  your law,
  have dug pits to trap me.
86 Your commandments are all
  trustworthy;
  people persecute me with lies—
  help me!
87 They have almost succeeded in
  killing me,
  but I have not neglected your
  commands.
88 Because of your constant love be
  good to me,
  so that I may obey your laws.

Faith in the Law of the LORD

89 Your word, O LORD, will last
  forever;
  it is eternal in heaven.
90 Your faithfulness endures through
  all the ages;
  you have set the earth in place,
  and it remains.
91 All things remain to this day
  because of your command,
  because they are all your
  servants.
92 If your law had not been the
  source of my joy,
  I would have died from my
  sufferings.
93 I will never neglect your
  instructions,
  because by them you have kept
  me alive.
94 I am yours—save me!
  I have tried to obey your
  commands.
95 The wicked are waiting to kill me,
  but I will meditate on your laws.
96 I have learned that everything has
  limits;
  but your commandment is
  perfect.

Love for the Law of the LORD

97 How I love your law!
  I think about it all day long.
98 Your commandment is with me all
  the time

and makes me wiser than my
  enemies.
99 I understand more than all my
  teachers,
  because I meditate on your
  instructions.
100 I have greater wisdom than those
  who are old,
  because I obey your commands.
101 I have avoided all evil conduct,
  because I want to obey your
  word.
102 I have not neglected your
  instructions,
  because you yourself are my
  teacher.
103 How sweet is the taste of your
  instructions—
  sweeter even than honey!
104 I gain wisdom from your laws,
  and so I hate all bad conduct.

Light from the Law of the LORD

105 Your word is a lamp to guide me
  and a light for my path.
106 I will keep my solemn promise
  to obey your just instructions.
107 My sufferings, LORD, are terrible
  indeed;
  keep me alive, as you have
  promised.
108 Accept my prayer of thanks,
  O LORD,
  and teach me your commands.
109 I am always ready to risk my life;
  I[u] have not forgotten your law.
110 The wicked lay a trap for me,
  but I have not disobeyed your
  commands.
111 Your commandments are my
  eternal possession;
  they are the joy of my heart.
112 I have decided to obey your laws
  until the day I die.

Safety in the Law of the LORD

113 I hate those who are not
  completely loyal to you,
  but I love your law.
114 You are my defender and
  protector;
  I put my hope in your promise.
115 Go away from me, you sinful
  people.
  I will obey the commands of
  my God.

u I am always ready to risk my life; I; or My life is in constant danger, but I.

116 Give me strength, as you
    promised, and I shall live;
    don't let me be disappointed in
    my hope!
117 Hold me, and I will be safe,
    and I will always pay attention
    to your commands.
118 You reject everyone who disobeys
    your laws;
    their deceitful schemes are
    useless.
119 You treat all the wicked like
    rubbish,
    and so I love your instructions.
120 Because of you I am afraid;
    I am filled with fear because of
    your judgments.

Obedience to the Law of the LORD

121 I have done what is right and
    good;
    don't abandon me to my
    enemies!
122 Promise that you will help your
    servant;
    don't let the arrogant
    oppress me!
123 My eyes are tired from watching
    for your saving help,
    for the deliverance you
    promised.
124 Treat me according to your
    constant love,
    and teach me your commands.
125 I am your servant; give me
    understanding,
    so that I may know your
    teachings.
126 LORD, it is time for you to act,
    because people are disobeying
    your law.
127 I love your commands more than
    gold,
    more than the finest gold.
128 And so I follow all your
    instructions; v
    I hate all wrong ways.

Desire to Obey the Law of the LORD

129 Your teachings are wonderful;
    I obey them with all my heart.
130 The explanation of your teachings
    gives light
    and brings wisdom to the
    ignorant.
131 In my desire for your commands
    I pant with open mouth.
132 Turn to me and have mercy on me
    as you do on all those who
    love you.
133 As you have promised, keep me
    from falling;
    don't let me be overcome by
    evil.
134 Save me from those who
    oppress me,
    so that I may obey your
    commands.
135 Bless me with your presence
    and teach me your laws.
136 My tears pour down like a river,
    because people do not obey
    your law.

The Justice of the Law of the LORD

137 You are righteous, LORD,
    and your laws are just.
138 The rules that you have given
    are completely fair and right.
139 My anger burns in me like a fire,
    because my enemies disregard
    your commands.
140 How certain your promise is!
    How I love it!
141 I am unimportant and despised,
    but I do not neglect your
    teachings.
142 Your righteousness will last
    forever,
    and your law is always true.
143 I am filled with trouble and
    anxiety,
    but your commandments bring
    me joy.
144 Your instructions are always just;
    give me understanding, and I
    shall live.

A Prayer for Deliverance

145 With all my heart I call to you;
    answer me, LORD, and I will obey
    your commands!
146 I call to you;
    save me, and I will keep your
    laws.
147 Before sunrise I call to you for
    help;
    I place my hope in your
    promise.
148 All night long I lie awake,
    to meditate on your instructions.

v *Some ancient translations* all your instructions; *Hebrew unclear.*

149 Because your love is constant,
      hear me, O LORD;
    show your mercy, and preserve
      my life!
150 My cruel persecutors are coming
      closer,
    people who never keep
      your law.
151 But you are near to me, LORD,
    and all your commands are
      permanent.
152 Long ago I learned about your
      instructions;
    you made them to last forever.

A Plea for Help

153 Look at my suffering, and
      save me,
    because I have not neglected
      your law.
154 Defend my cause, and set me free;
    save me, as you have promised.
155 The wicked will not be saved,
    for they do not obey your laws.
156 But your compassion, LORD, is
      great;
    show your mercy and save me!
157 I have many enemies and
      oppressors,
    but I do not fail to obey your
      laws.
158 When I look at those traitors, I am
      filled with disgust,
    because they do not keep your
      commands.
159 See how I love your instructions,
      LORD.
    Your love never changes, so
      save me!
160 The heart of your law is truth,
    and all your righteous judgments
      are eternal.

Dedication to the Law of the LORD

161 Powerful people attack me
      unjustly,
    but I respect your law.
162 How happy I am because of your
      promises—
    as happy as someone who finds
      rich treasure.
163 I hate and detest all lies,
    but I love your law.
164 Seven times each day I thank you
    for your righteous judgments.

165 Those who love your law have
      perfect security,
    and there is nothing that can
      make them fall.
166 I wait for you to save me, LORD,
    and I do what you command.
167 I obey your teachings;
    I love them with all my heart.
168 I obey your commands and your
      instructions;
    you see everything I do.

A Prayer for Help

169 Let my cry for help reach you,
      LORD!
    Give me understanding, as you
      have promised.
170 Listen to my prayer,
    and save me according to your
      promise!
171 I will always praise you,
    because you teach me your laws.
172 I will sing about your law,
    because your commands are
      just.
173 Always be ready to help me,
    because I follow your
      commands.
174 How I long for your saving help,
      O LORD!
    I find happiness in your law.
175 Give me life, so that I may
      praise you;
    may your instructions help me.
176 I wander about like a lost sheep;
    so come and look for me, your
      servant,
    because I have not neglected
      your laws.

A Prayer for Help

120 When I was in trouble, I
        called to the LORD,
    and he answered me.
2 Save me, LORD,
    from liars and deceivers.

3 You liars, what will God do
    to you?
    How will he punish you?
4 With a soldier's sharp arrows,
    with red-hot coals!

5 Living among you is as bad as
      living in Meshech
    or among the people of Kedar. w

w MESHECH . . . KEDAR: *Two distant regions, whose people were regarded as savages.*

6 I have lived too long
  with people who hate peace!
7 When I speak of peace,
  they are for war.

The LORD Our Protector

121 I look to the mountains;
  where will my help come
  from?
2 My help will come from the LORD,
  who made heaven and earth.

3 He will not let you fall;
  your protector is always awake.

4 The protector of Israel
  never dozes or sleeps.
5 The LORD will guard you;
  he is by your side to protect you.
6 The sun will not hurt you during
  the day,
  nor the moon during the night.

7 The LORD will protect you from all
  danger;
  he will keep you safe.
8 He will protect you as you come
  and go
  now and forever.

In Praise of Jerusalem x

122 I was glad when they said
  to me,
  "Let us go to the LORD's house."
2 And now we are here,
  standing inside the gates of
  Jerusalem!

3 Jerusalem is a city restored
  in beautiful order and harmony.
4 This is where the tribes come,
  the tribes of Israel,
  to give thanks to the LORD
  according to his command.
5 Here the kings of Israel
  sat to judge their people.

6 Pray for the peace of Jerusalem:
  "May those who love you
  prosper.
7   May there be peace inside your
  walls
  and safety in your palaces."
8 For the sake of my relatives and
  friends

I say to Jerusalem, "Peace be
  with you!"
9 For the sake of the house of the
  LORD our God
I pray for your prosperity.

A Prayer for Mercy

123 LORD, I look up to you,
  up to heaven, where you
  rule.
2 As a servant depends on his
  master,
  as a maid depends on her
  mistress,
  so we will keep looking to you,
  O LORD our God,
  until you have mercy on us.

3 Be merciful to us, LORD, be
  merciful;
  we have been treated with so
  much contempt.
4 We have been mocked too long by
  the rich
  and scorned by proud
  oppressors.

God the Protector of His People x

124 What if the LORD had not
  been on our side?
Answer, O Israel!

2 "If the LORD had not been on our
  side
  when our enemies attacked us,
3 then they would have swallowed
  us alive
  in their furious anger against us;
4 then the flood would have carried
  us away,
  the water would have
  covered us,
5   the raging torrent would have
  drowned us."

6 Let us thank the LORD,
  who has not let our enemies
  destroy us.
7 We have escaped like a bird from
  a hunter's trap;
  the trap is broken, and we are
  free!
8 Our help comes from the LORD,
  who made heaven and earth.

x HEBREW TITLE: By David.

The Security of God's People

125 Those who trust in the LORD
are like Mount Zion,
which can never be shaken,
never be moved.
2 As the mountains surround
Jerusalem,
so the LORD surrounds his
people,
now and forever.

3 The wicked will not always rule
over the land of the righteous;
if they did, the righteous
themselves might do evil.
4 LORD, do good to those who are
good,
to those who obey your
commands.
5 But when you punish the wicked,
punish also those who abandon
your ways.

Peace be with Israel!

A Prayer for Deliverance

126 When the LORD brought us
back to Jerusalem,[y]
it was like a dream!
2 How we laughed, how we sang
for joy!
Then the other nations said
about us,
"The LORD did great things for
them."
3 Indeed he did great things for us;
how happy we were!

4 LORD, make us prosperous again,[z]
just as the rain brings water
back to dry riverbeds.
5 Let those who wept as they
planted their crops,
gather the harvest with joy!

6 Those who wept as they went out
carrying the seed
will come back singing for joy,
as they bring in the harvest.

In Praise of God's Goodness[a]

127 If the LORD does not build
the house,
the work of the builders is
useless;

if the LORD does not protect the
city,
it does no good for the sentries
to stand guard.
2 It is useless to work so hard for a
living,
getting up early and going to
bed late.
For the LORD provides for those he
loves,
while they are asleep.

3 Children are a gift from the LORD;
they are a real blessing.
4 The sons a man has when he is
young
are like arrows in a soldier's
hand.
5 Happy is the man who has many
such arrows.
He will never be defeated
when he meets his enemies in
the place of judgment.

The Reward of Obedience to the LORD

128 Happy are those who obey
the LORD,
who live by his commands.

2 Your work will provide for your
needs;
you will be happy and
prosperous.
3 Your wife will be like a fruitful
vine in your home,
and your children will be like
young olive trees around
your table.
4 A man who obeys the LORD
will surely be blessed like this.

5 May the LORD bless you from Zion!
May you see Jerusalem prosper
all the days of your life!
6 May you live to see your
grandchildren!

Peace be with Israel!

A Prayer against Israel's Enemies

129 Israel, tell us how your
enemies have
persecuted you
ever since you were young.

[y] brought us back to Jerusalem; *or* made Jerusalem prosperous again.   [z] make us prosperous again; *or* take us back to our land.   [a] HEBREW TITLE: *By Solomon.*

2 "Ever since I was young,
  my enemies have persecuted me
    cruelly,
  but they have not overcome me.
3 They cut deep wounds in my back
  and made it like a plowed field.
4 But the LORD, the righteous one,
  has freed me from slavery."

5 May everyone who hates Zion
  be defeated and driven back.
6 May they all be like grass growing
    on the housetops,
  which dries up before it can
    grow;
7   no one gathers it up
  or carries it away in bundles.
8 No one who passes by will say,
  "May the LORD bless you!
  We bless you in the name of the
    LORD."

A Prayer for Help

130 From the depths of my
        despair I call to you,
        LORD.
2 Hear my cry, O Lord;
  listen to my call for help!
3 If you kept a record of our sins,
  who could escape being
    condemned?
4 But you forgive us,
  so that we should stand in awe
    of you.

5 I wait eagerly for the LORD's help,
  and in his word I trust.
6 I wait for the Lord
  more eagerly than sentries wait
    for the dawn—
  than sentries wait for the dawn.

7 Israel, trust in the LORD,
  because his love is constant
  and he is always willing to save.
8 He will save his people Israel
  from all their sins.

A Prayer of Humble Trust b

131 LORD, I have given up my
        pride
  and turned away from my
    arrogance.
  I am not concerned with great
    matters

b HEBREW TITLE: By David.

or with subjects too difficult
    for me.
2 Instead, I am content and at
    peace.
  As a child lies quietly in its
    mother's arms,
  so my heart is quiet within me.
3 Israel, trust in the LORD
  now and forever!

In Praise of the Temple

132 LORD, do not forget David
        and all the hardships he
        endured.
2 Remember, LORD, what he
    promised,
  the vow he made to you, the
    Mighty God of Jacob:
3 "I will not go home or go to
    bed;
4   I will not rest or sleep,
5   until I provide a place for the
    LORD,
  a home for the Mighty God of
    Jacob."

6 In Bethlehem we heard about the
    Covenant Box,
  and we found it in the fields of
    Jearim.
7 We said, "Let us go to the LORD's
    house;
  let us worship before his
    throne."

8 Come to the Temple, LORD, with
    the Covenant Box,
  the symbol of your power,
  and stay here forever.
9 May your priests do always what
    is right;
  may your people shout for joy!

10 You made a promise to your
    servant David;
  do not reject your chosen king,
    LORD.
11 You made a solemn promise to
    David—
  a promise you will not take
    back:
  "I will make one of your sons
    king,
  and he will rule after you.
12 If your sons are true to my
    covenant

and to the commands I give
them,
their sons, also, will succeed you
for all time as kings."

13 The LORD has chosen Zion;
he wants to make it his
home:
14 "This is where I will live forever;
this is where I want to rule.
15 I will richly provide Zion with all
she needs;
I will satisfy her poor with
food.
16 I will bless her priests in all
they do,
and her people will sing and
shout for joy.
17 Here I will make one of David's
descendants a great king;
here I will preserve the rule of
my chosen king.
18 I will cover his enemies with
shame,
but his kingdom will prosper
and flourish."

In Praise of Living in Peace [b]

133 How wonderful it is, how
pleasant,
for God's people to live together
in harmony!
2 It is like the precious anointing oil
running down from Aaron's
head and beard,
down to the collar of his
robes.
3 It is like the dew on Mount
Hermon,
falling on the hills of Zion.
That is where the LORD has
promised his blessing —
life that never ends.

A Call to Praise God

134 Come, praise the LORD,
all his servants,
all who serve in his Temple at
night.
2 Raise your hands in prayer in the
Temple,
and praise the LORD!

3 May the LORD, who made heaven
and earth,
bless you from Zion!

A Hymn of Praise

135 Praise the LORD!
Praise his name, you servants of
the LORD,
2 who stand in the LORD's house,
in the Temple of our God.
3 Praise the LORD, because he is
good;
sing praises to his name,
because he is kind. [c]
4 He chose Jacob for himself,
the people of Israel for his own.

5 I know that our LORD is great,
greater than all the gods.
6 He does whatever he wishes
in heaven and on earth,
in the seas and in the depths
below.
7 He brings storm clouds from the
ends of the earth;
he makes lightning for the
storms,
and he brings out the wind from
his storeroom.

8 In Egypt he killed all the first-born
of people and animals alike.
9 There he performed miracles and
wonders
to punish the king and all his
officials.
10 He destroyed many nations
and killed powerful kings:
11 Sihon, king of the Amorites,
Og, king of Bashan,
and all the kings in Canaan.
12 He gave their lands to his people;
he gave them to Israel.

13 LORD, you will always be
proclaimed as God;
all generations will
remember you.
14 The LORD will defend his people;
he will take pity on his servants.

15 The gods of the nations are made
of silver and gold;
they are formed by human
hands.
16 They have mouths, but cannot
speak,
and eyes, but cannot see.
17 They have ears, but cannot hear;

P
S
A
L
M
S

---

[b] HEBREW TITLE: *By David.*   [c] he is kind; *or* it is pleasant to do so.

they are not even able to
   breathe.
18 May all who made them and who
      trust in them
   become *d* like the idols they
      have made!

19 Praise the LORD, people of Israel;
   praise him, you priests of God!
20 Praise the LORD, you Levites;
   praise him, all you that
      worship him!
21 Praise the LORD in Zion,
   in Jerusalem, his home.

Praise the LORD!

A Hymn of Thanksgiving

136 Give thanks to the LORD,
        because he is good;
   his love is eternal.
2 Give thanks to the greatest of all
      gods;
   his love is eternal.
3 Give thanks to the mightiest of all
      lords;
   his love is eternal.

4 He alone performs great miracles;
   his love is eternal.
5 By his wisdom he made the
      heavens;
   his love is eternal;
6 he built the earth on the deep
      waters;
   his love is eternal.
7 He made the sun and the moon;
   his love is eternal;
8 the sun to rule over the day;
   his love is eternal;
9 the moon and the stars to rule
      over the night;
   his love is eternal.

10 He killed the first-born sons of the
      Egyptians;
   his love is eternal.
11 He led the people of Israel out of
      Egypt;
   his love is eternal;
12 with his strong hand, his
      powerful arm;
   his love is eternal.
13 He divided the Red Sea;
   his love is eternal;
14 he led his people through it;

his love is eternal;
15 but he drowned the king of Egypt
      and his army;
   his love is eternal.

16 He led his people through the
      desert;
   his love is eternal.
17 He killed powerful kings;
   his love is eternal;
18 he killed famous kings;
   his love is eternal;
19 Sihon, king of the Amorites;
   his love is eternal;
20 and Og, king of Bashan;
   his love is eternal.
21 He gave their lands to his people;
   his love is eternal;
22 he gave them to Israel, his servant;
   his love is eternal.

23 He did not forget us when we
      were defeated;
   his love is eternal;
24 he freed us from our enemies;
   his love is eternal.
25 He gives food to every living
      creature;
   his love is eternal.

26 Give thanks to the God of heaven;
   his love is eternal.

A Lament of Israelites in Exile

137 By the rivers of Babylon we
        sat down;
   there we wept when we
      remembered Zion.
2 On the willows near by
   we hung up our harps.
3 Those who captured us told us to
      sing;
   they told us to entertain them:
   "Sing us a song about Zion."

4 How can we sing a song to the
   LORD
   in a foreign land?
5 May I never be able to play the
      harp again
   if I forget you, Jerusalem!
6 May I never be able to sing again
   if I do not remember you,
   if I do not think of you as my
      greatest joy!

d May all . . . become; *or* All who made them and who trust in them will become.

7Remember, LORD, what the
	Edomites did
	the day Jerusalem was captured.
Remember how they kept saying,
	"Tear it down to the ground!"

8Babylon, you will be destroyed.
Happy are those who pay you
	back
	for what you have done to us—
9	who take your babies
	and smash them against a rock.

A Prayer of Thanksgiving e

138 I thank you, LORD, with all
	my heart;
	I sing praise to you before the
	gods.
2I face your holy Temple,
	bow down, and praise your
	name
because of your constant love and
	faithfulness,
	because you have shown that
	your name and your
	commands are supreme.f
3You answered me when I called
	to you;
	with your strength you
	strengthened me.

4All the kings in the world will
	praise you, LORD,
	because they have heard your
	promises.
5They will sing about what you
	have done
	and about your great glory.
6Even though you are so high
	above,
	you care for the lowly,
	and the proud cannot hide
	from you.

7When I am surrounded by
	troubles,
	you keep me safe.
You oppose my angry enemies
	and save me by your power.
8You will do everything you have
	promised;
	LORD, your love is eternal.
	Complete the work that you
	have begun.

God's Complete Knowledge and Care g

139 LORD, you have examined me
	and you know me.
2You know everything I do;
	from far away you understand
	all my thoughts.
3You see me, whether I am
	working or resting;
	you know all my actions.
4Even before I speak,
	you already know what I
	will say.
5You are all around me on every
	side;
	you protect me with your power.
6Your knowledge of me is too deep;
	it is beyond my understanding.

7Where could I go to escape
	from you?
	Where could I get away from
	your presence?
8If I went up to heaven, you would
	be there;
	if I lay down in the world of the
	dead, you would be there.
9If I flew away beyond the east
	or lived in the farthest place in
	the west,
10you would be there to lead me,
	you would be there to help me.
11I could ask the darkness to
	hide me
	or the light around me to turn
	into night,
12but even darkness is not dark
	for you,
	and the night is as bright as
	the day.
	Darkness and light are the same
	to you.

13You created every part of me;
	you put me together in my
	mother's womb.
14I praise you because you are to be
	feared;
	all you do is strange and
	wonderful.
	I know it with all my heart.
15When my bones were being
	formed,
	carefully put together in my
	mother's womb,

e HEBREW TITLE: *By David.* f *Probable text* your name and your commands are supreme; *Hebrew* your command is greater than all your name. g HEBREW TITLE: *A psalm by David.*

when I was growing there in
        secret,
    you knew that I was there—
16   you saw me before I was born.
    The days allotted to me
    had all been recorded in your
        book,
    before any of them ever began.
17 O God, how difficult I find your
        thoughts; *h*
    how many of them there are!
18 If I counted them, they would be
        more than the grains of sand.
    When I awake, I am still
        with you.

19 O God, how I wish you would kill
        the wicked!
    How I wish violent people would
        leave me alone!
20 They say wicked things about you;
    they speak evil things against
        your name. *i*
21 O LORD, how I hate those who
        hate you!
    How I despise those who rebel
        against you!
22 I hate them with a total hatred;
    I regard them as my enemies.

23 Examine me, O God, and know
        my mind;
    test me, and discover my
        thoughts.
24 Find out if there is any evil in me
    and guide me in the
        everlasting way. *j*

A Prayer for Protection *k*

140   Save me, LORD, from
        evildoers;
    keep me safe from violent
        people.
2 They are always plotting evil,
    always stirring up quarrels.
3 Their tongues are like deadly
        snakes;
    their words are like a cobra's
        poison.

4 Protect me, LORD, from the power
        of the wicked;
    keep me safe from violent
        people

who plot my downfall.
5 The proud have set a trap for me;
    they have laid their snares,
    and along the path they have set
        traps to catch me.

6 I say to the LORD, "You are
        my God."
    Hear my cry for help, LORD!
7 My Sovereign LORD, my strong
        defender,
    you have protected me in battle.
8 LORD, don't give the wicked what
        they want;
    don't let their plots succeed.

9 Don't let my enemies be
        victorious; *l*
    make their threats against me
        fall back on them.
10 May red-hot coals fall on them;
    may they be thrown into a pit
        and never get out.
11 May those who accuse others
        falsely not succeed;
    may evil overtake violent people
        and destroy them.

12 LORD, I know that you defend the
        cause of the poor
    and the rights of the needy.
13 The righteous will praise you
        indeed;
    they will live in your presence.

An Evening Prayer *m*

141   I call to you, LORD; help
        me now!
    Listen to me when I call to you.
2 Receive my prayer as incense,
    my uplifted hands as an evening
        sacrifice.

3 LORD, place a guard at my mouth,
    a sentry at the door of my lips.
4 Keep me from wanting to do
        wrong
    and from joining evil people in
        their wickedness.
    May I never take part in their
        feasts.

5 Good people may punish me and
    rebuke me in kindness,

---

h how difficult I find your thoughts; *or* how precious are your thoughts to me.
i *Probable text* they speak . . . name; *Hebrew unclear.*   *j* the everlasting way; *or* the ways of
my ancestors.   *k* HEBREW TITLE: *A psalm by David.*   *l* *Probable text* Don't let my enemies be
victorious; *Hebrew unclear.*   *m* HEBREW TITLE: *A psalm by David.*

but I will never accept honor
from evil people,
because I am always praying
against their evil deeds.
6 When their rulers are thrown
down from rocky cliffs,
the people will admit that my
words were true.
7 Like wood that is split and
chopped into bits,
so their bones are scattered at
the edge of the grave.n

8 But I keep trusting in you, my
Sovereign LORD.
I seek your protection;
don't let me die!
9 Protect me from the traps they
have set for me,
from the snares of those
evildoers.
10 May the wicked fall into their own
traps
while I go by unharmed.

A Prayer for Helpo

142 I call to the LORD for help;
I plead with him.
2 I bring him all my complaints;
I tell him all my troubles.
3 When I am ready to give up,
he knows what I should do.
In the path where I walk,
my enemies have hidden a trap
for me.
4 When I look beside me,
I see that there is no one to
help me,
no one to protect me.
No one cares for me.

5 LORD, I cry to you for help;
you, LORD, are my protector;
you are all I want in this
life.
6 Listen to my cry for help,
for I am sunk in despair.
Save me from my enemies;
they are too strong for me.
7 Set me free from my distress; p
then in the assembly of your
people I will praise you
because of your goodness to me.

A Prayer for Helpq

143 LORD, hear my prayer!
In your righteousness listen
to my plea;
answer me in your faithfulness!
2 Don't put me, your servant, on
trial;
no one is innocent in your sight.

3 My enemies have hunted me down
and completely defeated me.
They have put me in a dark
prison,
and I am like those who died
long ago.
4 So I am ready to give up;
I am in deep despair.

5 I remember the days gone by;
I think about all that you have
done,
I bring to mind all your deeds.
6 I lift up my hands to you in
prayer;
like dry ground my soul is
thirsty for you.

7 Answer me now, LORD!
I have lost all hope.
Don't hide yourself from me,
or I will be among those who go
down to the world of the dead.
8 Remind me each morning of your
constant love,
for I put my trust in you.
My prayers go up to you;
show me the way I should go.

9 I go to you for protection, LORD;
rescue me from my enemies.
10 You are my God;
teach me to do your will.
Be good to me, and guide me on a
safe path.

11 Rescue me, LORD, as you have
promised;
in your goodness save me from
my troubles!
12 Because of your love for me, kill
my enemies
and destroy all my oppressors,
for I am your servant.

---

n Verses 5-7 in Hebrew are unclear.   o HEBREW TITLE: A poem by David, when he was in the cave;
a prayer.   p distress; or prison.   q HEBREW TITLE: A psalm by David.

A King Thanks God for Victory[r]

144 Praise the LORD, my
protector!
He trains me for battle
and prepares me for war.
2 He is my protector and defender,
my shelter and savior,
in whom I trust for safety.
He subdues the nations under me.

3 LORD, what are mortals, that you
notice them;
mere mortals, that you pay
attention to us?
4 We are like a puff of wind;
our days are like a passing
shadow.

5 O LORD, tear the sky open and
come down;
touch the mountains, and they
will pour out smoke.
6 Send flashes of lightning and
scatter your enemies;
shoot your arrows and send
them running.
7 Reach down from above,
pull me out of the deep water,
and rescue me;
save me from the power of
foreigners,
8 who never tell the truth
and lie even under oath.

9 I will sing you a new song, O God;
I will play the harp and sing
to you.
10 You give victory to kings
and rescue your servant David.
11 Save me from my cruel enemies;
rescue me from the power of
foreigners,
who never tell the truth
and lie even under oath.

12 May our sons in their youth
be like plants that grow up
strong.
May our daughters be like stately
columns
which adorn the corners of a
palace.
13 May our barns be filled
with crops of every kind.
May the sheep in our fields

bear young by the tens of
thousands.
14 May our cattle reproduce
plentifully
without miscarriage or loss.
May there be no cries of distress
in our streets.

15 Happy is the nation of whom this
is true;
happy are the people whose God
is the LORD!

A Hymn of Praise[s]

145 I will proclaim your
greatness, my God and
king;
I will thank you forever and
ever.
2 Every day I will thank you;
I will praise you forever and
ever.
3 The LORD is great and is to be
highly praised;
his greatness is beyond
understanding.

4 What you have done will be
praised from one generation to
the next;
they will proclaim your mighty
acts.
5 They will speak of your glory and
majesty,
and I will meditate on your
wonderful deeds.
6 People will speak of your mighty
deeds,
and I will proclaim your
greatness.
7 They will tell about all your
goodness
and sing about your kindness.
8 The LORD is loving and merciful,
slow to become angry and full of
constant love.
9 He is good to everyone
and has compassion on all he
made.
10 All your creatures, LORD, will
praise you,
and all your people will give you
thanks.
11 They will speak of the glory of
your royal power

r HEBREW TITLE: *By David.*   s HEBREW TITLE: *A song of praise by David.*

and tell of your might,
12 so that everyone will know your
     mighty deeds
  and the glorious majesty of your
     kingdom.
13 Your rule is eternal,
  and you are king forever.

The Lord is faithful to his
     promises;
  he is merciful in all his acts.
14 He helps those who are in trouble;
  he lifts those who have fallen.

15 All living things look hopefully
     to you,
  and you give them food when
     they need it.
16 You give them enough
  and satisfy the needs of all.

17 The Lord is righteous in all he
     does,
  merciful in all his acts.
18 He is near to those who call
     to him,
  who call to him with sincerity.
19 He supplies the needs of those
     who honor him;
  he hears their cries and saves
     them.
20 He protects everyone who
     loves him,
  but he will destroy the wicked.

21 I will always praise the Lord;
  let all his creatures praise his
     holy name forever.

In Praise of God the Savior

146
Praise the Lord!
  Praise the Lord, my soul!
2 I will praise him as long as I live;
  I will sing to my God all my life.

3 Don't put your trust in human
     leaders;
  no human being can save you.
4 When they die, they return to the
     dust;
  on that day all their plans come
     to an end.

5 Happy are those who have the
     God of Jacob to help them
  and who depend on the Lord
     their God,

6   the Creator of heaven, earth,
       and sea,
    and all that is in them.
  He always keeps his promises;
7   he judges in favor of the
       oppressed
    and gives food to the hungry.

  The Lord sets prisoners free
8   and gives sight to the blind.
  He lifts those who have fallen;
    he loves his righteous people.
9 He protects the strangers who live
     in our land;
  he helps widows and orphans,
  but takes the wicked to their
     ruin.

10 The Lord is king forever.
  Your God, O Zion, will reign for
     all time.

Praise the Lord!

In Praise of God the Almighty

147
Praise the Lord!
  It is good to sing praise to
     our God;
  it is pleasant and right to
     praise him.
2 The Lord is restoring Jerusalem;
  he is bringing back the exiles.
3 He heals the broken-hearted
  and bandages their wounds.

4 He has decided the number of the
     stars
  and calls each one by name.
5 Great and mighty is our Lord;
  his wisdom cannot be measured.
6 He raises the humble,
  but crushes the wicked to the
     ground.

7 Sing hymns of praise to the Lord;
  play music on the harp to
     our God.
8 He spreads clouds over the sky;
  he provides rain for the earth
  and makes grass grow on the
     hills.
9 He gives animals their food
  and feeds the young ravens
     when they call.

10 His pleasure is not in strong
     horses,

nor his delight in brave soldiers;
11 but he takes pleasure in those who
  honor him,
  in those who trust in his
  constant love.

12 Praise the LORD, O Jerusalem!
  Praise your God, O Zion!
13 He keeps your gates strong;
  he blesses your people.
14 He keeps your borders safe
  and satisfies you with the finest
  wheat.

15 He gives a command to the
  earth,
  and what he says is quickly
  done.
16 He spreads snow like a blanket
  and scatters frost like dust.
17 He sends hail like gravel;
  no one can endure the cold he
  sends!
18 Then he gives a command, and the
  ice melts;
  he sends the wind, and the
  water flows.

19 He gives his message to his
  people,
  his instructions and laws to
  Israel.
20 He has not done this for other
  nations;
  they do not know his laws.

  Praise the LORD!

A Call for the Universe to Praise God

148
Praise the LORD!

Praise the LORD from
  heaven,
  you that live in the heights
  above.
2 Praise him, all his angels,
  all his heavenly armies.

3 Praise him, sun and moon;
  praise him, shining stars.
4 Praise him, highest heavens,
  and the waters above the sky.t

5 Let them all praise the name of
  the LORD!
  He commanded, and they were
  created;
6   by his command they were fixed
  in their places forever,
  and they cannot disobey.u

7 Praise the LORD from the earth,
  sea monsters and all ocean
  depths;
8 lightning and hail, snow and
  clouds,
  strong winds that obey his
  command.

9 Praise him, hills and mountains,
  fruit trees and forests;
10 all animals, tame and wild,
  reptiles and birds.

11 Praise him, kings and all
  peoples,
  princes and all other rulers;
12 young women and young men,
  old people and children too.

13 Let them all praise the name of
  the LORD!
  His name is greater than all
  others;
  his glory is above earth and
  heaven.
14 He made his nation strong,
  so that all his people
  praise him—
  the people of Israel, so dear
  to him.

  Praise the LORD!

A Hymn of Praise

149
Praise the LORD!

Sing a new song to the LORD;
  praise him in the assembly of
  his faithful people!
2 Be glad, Israel, because of your
  Creator;
  rejoice, people of Zion, because
  of your king!
3 Praise his name with
  dancing;
  play drums and harps in praise
  of him.

t WATERS ABOVE THE SKY: See Gn 1.6, 7.   u by his command . . . disobey; or he has fixed them in
their places for all time, by a command that lasts forever.

⁴The Lord takes pleasure in his
　　people;
　　he honors the humble with
　　　victory.
⁵Let God's people rejoice in their
　　triumph
　　and sing joyfully all night
　　　long.
⁶Let them shout aloud as they
　　praise God,
　　with their sharp swords in their
　　　hands
⁷　to defeat the nations
　　and to punish the peoples;
⁸　to bind their kings in chains,
　　their leaders in chains of iron;
⁹　to punish the nations as God has
　　commanded.
　This is the victory of God's people.

Praise the Lord!

Praise the Lord!

150
Praise the Lord!

Praise God in his Temple!
　Praise his strength in heaven!
²Praise him for the mighty things
　he has done.
　Praise his supreme greatness.

³Praise him with trumpets.
　Praise him with harps and lyres.
⁴Praise him with drums and
　dancing.
　Praise him with harps and
　flutes.
⁵Praise him with cymbals.
　Praise him with loud cymbals.
⁶Praise the Lord, all living
　creatures!

Praise the Lord!

PSALMS

PROVERBS

Introduction

The book of Proverbs is a collection of moral and religious teachings in the form of sayings and proverbs. Much of it has to do with practical, everyday concerns. It begins with the reminder that "To have knowledge, you must first have reverence for the LORD," and then goes on to deal with matters not only of religious morality, but also of common sense and good manners. Its many short sayings reveal the insights of ancient Israelite teachers about what a wise person will do in certain situations. Some of these concern family relations, others, business dealings. Some deal with matters of etiquette in social relationships, and others with the need of self-control. Much is said about such qualities as humility, patience, respect for the poor, and loyalty to friends.

Outline of Contents

The Value of Proverbs

1 The proverbs of Solomon, son of David and king of Israel.

2 Here are proverbs that will help you recognize wisdom and good advice, and understand sayings with deep meaning. 3 They can teach you how to live intelligently and how to be honest, just, and fair. 4 They can make an inexperienced person clever and teach young people how to be resourceful. 5 These proverbs can even add to the knowledge of the wise and give guidance to the educated, 6 so that they can understand the hidden meanings of proverbs and the problems that the wise raise.

Advice to the Young

7 To have knowledge, you must first have reverence for the LORD.a Stupid people have no respect for wisdom and refuse to learn.

8 My child, pay attention to what your father and mother tell you. 9 Their teaching will improve your character as a handsome turban or a necklace improves your appearance.

10 My child, when sinners tempt you, don't give in. 11 Suppose they say, "Come on; let's find someone to kill! Let's attack some innocent people for the fun of it! 12 They may be alive and well when we find them, but they'll be dead when we're through with them! 13 We'll find all kinds of riches and fill our houses with loot! 14 Come and join us, and we'll all share what we steal."

15 My child, don't go with people like that. Stay away from them. 16 They can't wait to do something bad. They're always ready to kill. 17 It does no good to spread a net when the bird you want to catch is watching, 18 but people like that are setting a trap for themselves, a trap in which they will die. 19 Robbery always claims the life of the robber — this is what happens tob anyone who lives by violence.

Wisdom Calls

20 Listen! Wisdom is calling out in the streets and marketplaces, 21 calling loudly at the city gates and wherever people come together:

22 "Foolish people! How long do you want to be foolish? How long will you enjoy making fun of knowledge? Will you never learn? 23 Listen when I reprimand you; I will give you good advice and share my knowledge with you. 24 I have been calling you, inviting you to come, but you would not listen. You paid

---

a To ... LORD; or The most important part of knowledge is having reverence for the LORD.
b One ancient translation what happens to; Hebrew the path of.

no attention to me. 25 You have ignored all my advice and have not been willing to let me correct you. 26 So when you get into trouble, I will laugh at you. I will make fun of you when terror strikes— 27 when it comes on you like a storm, bringing fierce winds of trouble, and you are in pain and misery. 28 Then you will call for wisdom, but I will not answer. You may look for me everywhere, but you will not find me. 29 You have never had any use for knowledge and have always refused to obey the LORD. 30 You have never wanted my advice or paid any attention when I corrected you. 31 So then, you will get what you deserve, and your own actions will make you sick. 32 Inexperienced people die because they reject wisdom. Stupid people are destroyed by their own lack of concern. 33 But whoever listens to me will have security. He will be safe, with no reason to be afraid."

The Rewards of Wisdom

2 My child, learn what I teach you and never forget what I tell you to do. 2 Listen to what is wise and try to understand it. 3 Yes, beg for knowledge; plead for insight. 4 Look for it as hard as you would for silver or some hidden treasure. 5 If you do, you will know what it means to fear the LORD and you will succeed in learning about God. 6 It is the LORD who gives wisdom; from him come knowledge and understanding. 7 He provides help and protection for those who are righteous and honest. 8 He protects those who treat others fairly, and guards those who are devoted to him.

9 If you listen to me, you will know what is right, just, and fair. You will know what you should do. 10 You will become wise, and your knowledge will give you pleasure. 11 Your insight and understanding will protect you 12 and prevent you from doing the wrong thing. They will keep you away from people who stir up trouble by what they say— 13 those who have abandoned a righteous life to live in the darkness of sin, 14 those who find pleasure in doing wrong and who enjoy senseless evil, 15 unreliable people who cannot be trusted.

16 You will be able to resist any immoral woman who tries to seduce you with her smooth talk, 17 who is faithless to her own husband and forgets her sacred vows. 18 If you go to her house, you are traveling the road to death. To go there is to approach the world of the dead. 19 No one who visits her ever comes back. He never returns to the road to life. 20 So you must follow the example of good people and live a righteous life. 21 Righteous people—people of integrity—will live in this land of ours. 22 But God will snatch the wicked from the land and pull sinners out of it like plants from the ground.

Advice to the Young

3 My child, don't forget what I teach you. Always remember what I tell you to do. 2 My teaching will give you a long and prosperous life. 3 Never let go of loyalty and faithfulness. Tie them around your neck; write them on your heart. 4 If you do this, both God and people will be pleased with you.

5 Trust in the LORD with all your heart. Never rely on what you think you know. 6 Remember the LORD in everything you do, and he will show you the right way. 7 Never let yourself think that you are wiser than you are; simply obey the LORD and refuse to do wrong. 8 If you do, it will be like good medicine, healing your wounds and easing your pains. 9 Honor the LORD by making him an offering from the best of all that your land produces. 10 If you do, your barns will be filled with grain, and you will have too much wine to store it all.

11 My child, when the LORD corrects you, pay close attention and take it as a warning. 12 The LORD corrects those he loves, as parents correct a child of whom they are proud. 13 Happy is anyone who becomes wise—who comes to have understanding. 14 There is more profit in it than there is in silver; it is worth more to you than gold. 15 Wisdom is more valuable than jewels; nothing you could want can compare with it. 16 Wisdom offers you long life, as well as wealth and honor. 17 Wisdom can make your life pleasant and lead you safely through it. 18 Those who become wise are happy; wisdom will give them life.

19 The LORD created the earth by his wisdom;
　　by his knowledge he set the sky
　　　in place.

PROVERBS

20 His wisdom caused the rivers to flow
and the clouds to give rain to the earth.

21 My child, hold on to your wisdom and insight. Never let them get away from you. 22 They will provide you with life — a pleasant and happy life. 23 You can go safely on your way and never even stumble. 24 You will not be afraid when you go to bed, and you will sleep soundly through the night. 25 You will not have to worry about sudden disasters, such as come on the wicked like a storm. 26 The LORD will keep you safe. He will not let you fall into a trap.

27 Whenever you possibly can, do good to those who need it. 28 Never tell your neighbors to wait until tomorrow if you can help them now. 29 Don't plan anything that will hurt your neighbors; they live beside you, trusting you. 30 Don't argue with others for no reason when they have never done you any harm. 31 Don't be jealous of violent people or decide to act as they do, 32 because the LORD hates people who do evil, but he takes righteous people into his confidence. 33 The LORD puts a curse on the homes of the wicked, but blesses the homes of the righteous. 34 He has no use for conceited people, but shows favor to those who are humble. 35 Wise people will gain an honorable reputation, but stupid people will only add to their own disgrace.

The Benefits of Wisdom

4 My children, listen to what your father teaches you. Pay attention, and you will have understanding. 2 What I am teaching you is good, so remember it all. 3 When I was only a little boy, my parents' only son, 4 my father would teach me. He would say, "Remember what I say and never forget it. Do as I tell you, and you will live. 5 Get wisdom and insight! Do not forget or ignore what I say. 6 Do not abandon wisdom, and she will protect you; love her, and she will keep you safe. 7 Getting wisdom is the most important thing you can do. Whatever else you get, get insight. 8 Love wisdom, and she will make you great. Embrace her,c and she will bring you honor. 9 She will be your crowning glory."

10 Listen to me, my child. Take seriously what I am telling you, and you will live a long life. 11 I have taught you wisdom and the right way to live. 12 Nothing will stand in your way if you walk wisely, and you will not stumble when you run. 13 Always remember what you have learned. Your education is your life — guard it well. 14 Do not go where evil people go. Do not follow the example of the wicked. 15 Don't do it! Keep away from evil! Refuse it and go on your way. 16 Wicked people cannot sleep unless they have done something wrong. They lie awake unless they have hurt someone. 17 Wickedness and violence are like food and drink to them.

18 The road the righteous travel is like the sunrise, getting brighter and brighter until daylight has come. 19 The road of the wicked, however, is dark as night. They fall, but cannot see what they have stumbled over.

20 My child, pay attention to what I say. Listen to my words. 21 Never let them get away from you. Remember them and keep them in your heart. 22 They will give life and health to anyone who understands them. 23 Be careful how you think; your life is shaped by your thoughts. 24 Never say anything that isn't true. Have nothing to do with lies and misleading words. 25 Look straight ahead with honest confidence; don't hang your head in shame. 26 Plan carefully what you do, and whatever you do will turn out right. 27 Avoid evil and walk straight ahead. Don't go one step off the right way.

Warning against Adultery

5 My child, pay attention and listen to my wisdom and insight. 2 Then you will know how to behave properly, and your words will show that you have knowledge. 3 The lips of another man's wife may be as sweet as honey and her kisses as smooth as olive oil, 4 but when it is all over, she leaves you nothing but bitterness and pain. 5 She will take you down to the world of the dead; the road she walks is the road to death. 6 She does not stay on the road to life; but wanders off, and does not realize what is happening.

7 Now listen to me, sons, and never

---

c Embrace her; or Prize her highly.

forget what I am saying. 8Keep away from such a woman! Don't even go near her door! 9If you do, others will gain the respect that you once had, and you will die young at the hands of merciless people. 10Yes, strangers will take all your wealth, and what you have worked for will belong to someone else. 11You will lie groaning on your deathbed, your flesh and muscles being eaten away, 12and you will say, "Why would I never learn? Why would I never let anyone correct me? 13I wouldn't listen to my teachers. I paid no attention to them. 14And suddenly I found myself*d* publicly disgraced."

15Be faithful to your own wife and give your love to her alone. 16Children that you have by other women will do you no good. 17Your children should grow up to help you, not strangers. 18So be happy with your wife and find your joy with the woman you married— 19pretty and graceful as a deer. Let her charms keep you happy; let her surround you with her love. 20Son, why should you give your love to another woman? Why should you prefer the charms of another man's wife? 21The LORD sees everything you do. Wherever you go, he is watching. 22The sins of the wicked are a trap. They get caught in the net of their own sin. 23They die because they have no self-control. Their utter stupidity will send them to their graves.

More Warnings

6 My child, have you promised to be responsible for someone else's debts? 2Have you been caught by your own words, trapped by your own promises? 3Well then, my child, you are in that person's power, but this is how to get out of it: hurry to him, and beg him to release you. 4Don't let yourself go to sleep or even stop to rest. 5Get out of the trap like a bird or a deer escaping from a hunter.

6Lazy people should learn a lesson from the way ants live. 7They have no leader, chief, or ruler, 8but they store up their food during the summer, getting ready for winter. 9How long is the lazy man going to lie around? When is he ever going to get up? 10"I'll just take a short nap," he says; "I'll fold my hands and rest a while." 11But while he sleeps, poverty will attack him like an armed robber.

12Worthless, wicked people go around telling lies. 13They wink and make gestures to deceive you, 14all the while planning evil in their perverted minds, stirring up trouble everywhere. 15Because of this, disaster will strike them without warning, and they will be fatally wounded.

16-19There are seven things that the LORD hates and cannot tolerate:
A proud look,
  a lying tongue,
  hands that kill innocent people,
  a mind that thinks up wicked plans,
  feet that hurry off to do evil,
  a witness who tells one lie after
    another,
and someone who stirs up trouble
    among friends.

Warning against Adultery

20Son, do what your father tells you and never forget what your mother taught you. 21Keep their words with you always, locked in your heart. 22Their teaching will lead you when you travel, protect you at night, and advise you during the day. 23Their instructions are a shining light; their correction can teach you how to live. 24It can keep you away from bad women, from the seductive words of other men's wives. 25Don't be tempted by their beauty; don't be trapped by their flirting eyes. 26A man can hire a prostitute for the price of a loaf of bread, but adultery will cost him all he has.

27Can you carry fire against your chest without burning your clothes? 28Can you walk on hot coals without burning your feet? 29It is just as dangerous to sleep with another man's wife. Whoever does it will suffer. 30People don't despise a thief if he steals food when he is hungry;*e* 31yet if he is caught, he must pay back seven times more—he must give up everything he has. 32But a man who commits adultery doesn't have any sense. He is just destroying himself. 33He will be dishonored and beaten up; he will be

---

d And suddenly ... myself; or I was about to be. people despise ... hungry?

e People don't despise ... hungry; or Don't

permanently disgraced. 34 A husband is never angrier than when he is jealous; his revenge knows no limits. 35 He will not accept any payment; no amount of gifts will satisfy his anger.

7 My child, remember what I say and never forget what I tell you to do. 2 Do what I say, and you will live. Be as careful to follow my teaching as you are to protect your eyes. 3 Keep my teaching with you all the time; write it on your heart. 4 Treat wisdom as your sister, and insight as your closest friend. 5 They will keep you away from other men's wives, from women with seductive words.

The Immoral Woman

6 Once I was looking out the window of my house, 7 and I saw many inexperienced young men, but noticed one foolish fellow in particular. 8 He was walking along the street near the corner where a certain woman lived. He was passing near her house 9 in the evening after it was dark. 10 And then she met him; she was dressed like a prostitute and was making plans. 11 She was a bold and shameless woman who always walked the streets 12 or stood waiting at a corner, sometimes in the streets, sometimes in the marketplace. 13 She threw her arms around the young man, kissed him, looked him straight in the eye, and said, 14 "I made my offerings today and have the meat from the sacrifices. 15 So I came out looking for you. I wanted to find you, and here you are! 16 I've covered my bed with sheets of colored linen from Egypt. 17 I've perfumed it with myrrh, aloes, and cinnamon. 18 Come on! Let's make love all night long. We'll be happy in each other's arms. 19 My husband isn't at home. He's on a long trip. 20 He took plenty of money with him and won't be back for two weeks." 21 So she tempted him with her charms, and he gave in to her smooth talk. 22 Suddenly he was going with her like an ox on the way to be slaughtered, like a deer prancing into a trap/ 23 where an arrow would pierce its heart. He was like a bird going into a net — he did not know that his life was in danger.

24 Now then, sons, listen to me. Pay attention to what I say. 25 Do not let such a woman win your heart; don't go wan-dering after her. 26 She has been the ruin of many men and caused the death of too many to count. 27 If you go to her house, you are on the way to the world of the dead. It is a shortcut to death.

In Praise of Wisdom

8 Listen! Wisdom is calling out. Reason is making herself heard. 2 On the hilltops near the road and at the crossroads she stands. 3 At the entrance to the city, beside the gates, she calls: 4 "I appeal to all of you; I call to everyone on earth. 5 Are you immature? Learn to be mature. Are you foolish? Learn to have sense. 6 Listen to my excellent words; all I tell you is right. 7 What I say is the truth; lies are hateful to me. 8 Everything I say is true; nothing is false or misleading. 9 To those with insight, it is all clear; to the well-informed, it is all plain. 10 Choose my instruction instead of silver; choose knowledge rather than the finest gold.

11 "I am Wisdom, I am better than jewels; nothing you want can compare with me. 12 I am Wisdom, and I have insight; I have knowledge and sound judgment. 13 To honor the LORD is to hate evil; I hate pride and arrogance, evil ways and false words. 14 I make plans and carry them out. I have understanding, and I am strong. 15 I help kings to govern and rulers to make good laws. 16 Every ruler on earth governs with my help, officials and nobles alike. 17 I love those who love me; whoever looks for me can find me.

f Probable text like a deer prancing into a trap; Hebrew unclear.

18 I have riches and honor to give,
    prosperity and success.
19 What you get from me is better
    than the finest gold,
    better than the purest silver.
20 I walk the way of righteousness;
    I follow the paths of justice,
21 giving wealth to those who
    love me,
    filling their houses with
    treasures.

22 "The LORD created me first of all,
    the first of his works, long ago.
23 I was made in the very beginning,
    at the first, before the world
    began.
24 I was born before the oceans,
    when there were no springs of
    water.
25 I was born before the mountains,
    before the hills were set in
    place,
26 before God made the earth and its
    fields
    or even the first handful of soil.
27 I was there when he set the sky in
    place,
    when he stretched the horizon
    across the ocean,
28 when he placed the clouds in
    the sky,
    when he opened the springs of
    the ocean
29 and ordered the waters of the sea
    to rise no further than he said,
    I was there when he laid the
    earth's foundations.
30 I was beside him like an
    architect,g
    I was his daily source of joy,
    always happy in his presence—
31 happy with the world
    and pleased with the human
    race.

32 "Now, young people, listen to me.
    Do as I say, and you will be
    happy.
33 Listen to what you are taught.
    Be wise; do not neglect it.
34 Those who listen to me will be
    happy—
    those who stay at my door
    every day,

waiting at the entrance to my
    home.
35 Those who find me find life,
    and the LORD will be pleased
    with them.
36 Those who do not find me hurt
    themselves;
    anyone who hates me loves
    death."

Wisdom and Stupidity

9 Wisdom has built her house and made seven columns for it. 2 She has had an animal killed for a feast, mixed spices in the wine, and set the table. 3 She has sent her servant women to call out from the highest place in town: 4 "Come in, ignorant people!" And to the foolish she says, 5 "Come, eat my food and drink the wine that I have mixed. 6 Leave the company of ignorant people, and live. Follow the way of knowledge."

7 If you correct conceited people, you will only be insulted. If you reprimand evil people, you will only get hurt. 8 Never correct conceited people; they will hate you for it. But if you correct the wise, they will respect you. 9 Anything you say to the wise will make them wiser. Whatever you tell the righteous will add to their knowledge.

10 To be wise you must first have reverence for the LORD. If you know the Holy One, you have understanding. 11 Wisdom will add years to your life. 12 You are the one who will profit if you have wisdom, and if you reject it, you are the one who will suffer.

13 Stupidity is like a loud, ignorant, shameless woman.h 14 She sits at the door of her house or on a seat in the highest part of town, 15 and calls out to people passing by, who are minding their own business: 16 "Come in, ignorant people!" To the foolish she says, 17 "Stolen water is sweeter. Stolen bread tastes better." 18 Her victims do not know that the people die who go to her house, that those who have already entered are now deep in the world of the dead.

Solomon's Proverbs

10 These are Solomon's proverbs: Wise children make their fathers proud of them; foolish ones bring their mothers grief.

---

g an architect; or a little child.   h Verse 13 in Hebrew is unclear.

2 Wealth you get by dishonesty will do you no good, but honesty can save your life.

3 The Lord will not let good people go hungry, but he will keep the wicked from getting what they want.

4 Being lazy will make you poor, but hard work will make you rich.

5 A sensible person gathers the crops when they are ready; it is a disgrace to sleep through the time of harvest.

6 Good people will receive blessings. The words of the wicked hide a violent nature.

7 Good people will be remembered as a blessing, but the wicked will soon be forgotten.

8 Sensible people accept good advice. People who talk foolishly will come to ruin.

9 Honest people are safe and secure, but the dishonest will be caught.

10 Someone who holds back the truth causes trouble, but one who openly criticizes works for peace. *i*

11 A good person's words are a fountain of life, but a wicked person's words hide a violent nature.

12 Hate stirs up trouble, but love forgives all offenses.

13 Intelligent people talk sense, but stupid people need to be punished.

14 The wise get all the knowledge they can, but when fools speak, trouble is not far off.

15 Wealth protects the rich; poverty destroys the poor.

16 The reward for doing good is life, but sin leads only to more sin.

17 People who listen when they are corrected will live, but those who will not admit that they are wrong are in danger.

18 Anyone who hides hatred is a liar. Anyone who spreads gossip is a fool.

19 The more you talk, the more likely you are to sin. If you are wise, you will keep quiet.

20 A good person's words are like pure silver; a wicked person's ideas are worthless.

21 A good person's words will benefit many people, but you can kill yourself with stupidity.

22 It is the Lord's blessing that makes you wealthy. Hard work can make you no richer. *j*

23 It is foolish to enjoy doing wrong. Intelligent people take pleasure in wisdom.

24 The righteous get what they want, but the wicked will get what they fear most.

25 Storms come, and the wicked are blown away, but honest people are always safe.

26 Never get a lazy person to do something for you; he will be as irritating as vinegar on your teeth or smoke in your eyes.

27 Obey the Lord, and you will live longer. The wicked die before their time.

28 The hopes of good people lead to joy, but wicked people can look forward to nothing.

29 The Lord protects honest people, but destroys those who do wrong.

30 Righteous people will always have security, but the wicked will not survive in the land.

31 Righteous people speak wisdom, but the tongue that speaks evil will be stopped.

32 Righteous people know the kind thing to say, but the wicked are always saying things that hurt.

11

The Lord hates people who use dishonest scales. He is happy with honest weights.

2 People who are proud will soon be disgraced. It is wiser to be modest.

3 If you are good, you are guided by honesty. People who can't be trusted are destroyed by their own dishonesty.

4 Riches will do you no good on the day you face death, but honesty can save your life.

5 Honesty makes a good person's life easier, but the wicked will cause their own downfall.

6 Righteousness rescues those who are honest, but those who can't be trusted are trapped by their own greed.

7 When the wicked die, their hope dies with them. Confidence placed in riches comes to nothing.

8 The righteous are protected from trouble; it comes to the wicked instead.

9 You can be ruined by the talk of god-

---

i One ancient translation but one . . . peace; *Hebrew repeats verse 8b.* *j* Hard work . . . richer; or And the Lord does not add sorrow to your wealth.

less people, but the wisdom of the righteous can save you.

10 A city is happy when honest people have good fortune, and there are joyful shouts when the wicked die.

11 A city becomes great when the righteous give it their blessing; but a city is brought to ruin by the words of the wicked.

12 It is foolish to speak scornfully of others. If you are smart, you will keep quiet.

13 No one who gossips can be trusted with a secret, but you can put confidence in someone who is trustworthy.

14 A nation will fall if it has no guidance. Many advisers mean security.

15 If you promise to pay a stranger's debt, you will regret it. You are better off if you don't get involved.

16 A gracious woman is respected, but a woman without virtue is a disgrace.

Lazy people will never have money,*k* but aggressive people will get rich.

17 You do yourself a favor when you are kind. If you are cruel, you only hurt yourself.

18 Wicked people do not really gain anything, but if you do what is right, you are certain to be rewarded.

19 Anyone who is determined to do right will live, but anyone who insists on doing wrong will die.

20 The LORD hates evil-minded people, but loves those who do right.

21 You can be sure that evil people will be punished, but the righteous will escape.

22 Beauty in a woman without good judgment is like a gold ring in a pig's snout.

23 What good people want always results in good; when the wicked get what they want, everyone is angry.*l*

24 Some people spend their money freely and still grow richer. Others are cautious, and yet grow poorer.

25 Be generous, and you will be prosperous. Help others, and you will be helped.

26 People curse someone who hoards grain, waiting for a higher price, but they praise the one who puts it up for sale.

27 If your goals are good, you will be respected, but if you are looking for trouble, that is what you will get.

28 Those who depend on their wealth will fall like the leaves of autumn, but the righteous will prosper like the leaves of summer.

29 Those who bring trouble on their families will have nothing at the end. Foolish people will always be servants to the wise.

30 Righteousness*m* gives life, but violence*n* takes it away.

31 Those who are good are rewarded here on earth, so you can be sure that wicked and sinful people will be punished.

12 Any who love knowledge want to be told when they are wrong. It is stupid to hate being corrected.

2 The LORD is pleased with good people, but condemns those who plan evil.

3 Wickedness does not give security, but righteous people stand firm.

4 A good wife is her husband's pride and joy; but a wife who brings shame on her husband is like a cancer in his bones.

5 Honest people will treat you fairly; the wicked only want to deceive you.

6 The words of the wicked are murderous, but the words of the righteous rescue those who are threatened.

7 The wicked meet their downfall and leave no descendants, but the families of the righteous live on.

8 If you are intelligent, you will be praised; if you are stupid, people will look down on you.

9 It is better to be an ordinary person working for a living than to play the part of someone great but go hungry.

10 Good people take care of their animals, but wicked people are cruel to theirs.

11 A hard-working farmer has plenty to eat, but it is stupid to waste time on useless projects.

12 All that wicked people want is to find evil things to do, but the righteous stand firm.*o*

13 The wicked are trapped by their own words, but honest people get themselves out of trouble.

k One ancient translation but a woman ... money; Hebrew does not have these words.
l everyone is angry; or God punishes them. m One ancient translation Righteousness; Hebrew A righteous person. n Probable text violence; Hebrew a wise person. o Verse 12 in Hebrew is unclear.

¹⁴Your reward depends on what you say and what you do; you will get what you deserve.

¹⁵Stupid people always think they are right. Wise people listen to advice.

¹⁶When a fool is annoyed, he quickly lets it be known. Smart people will ignore an insult.

¹⁷When you tell the truth, justice is done, but lies lead to injustice.

¹⁸Thoughtless words can wound as deeply as any sword, but wisely spoken words can heal.

¹⁹A lie has a short life, but truth lives on forever.

²⁰Those who plan evil are in for a rude surprise, but those who work for good will find happiness.

²¹Nothing bad happens to righteous people, but the wicked have nothing but trouble.

²²The LORD hates liars, but is pleased with those who keep their word.

²³Smart people keep quiet about what they know, but stupid people advertise their ignorance.

²⁴Hard work will give you power; being lazy will make you a slave.

²⁵Worry can rob you of happiness, but kind words will cheer you up.

²⁶The righteous person is a guide to his friend, but the path of the wicked leads them astray.

²⁷If you are lazy, you will never get what you are after, but if you work hard, you will get a fortune.^p

²⁸Righteousness is the road to life; wickedness ^q is the road to death.

13 Wise children pay attention when their parents correct them, but arrogant people never admit they are wrong.

²Good people will be rewarded for what they say, but those who are deceitful are hungry for violence.

³Be careful what you say and protect your life. A careless talker destroys himself.

⁴No matter how much a lazy person may want something, he will never get it. A hard worker will get everything he wants.

⁵Honest people hate lies, but the words of wicked people are shameful and disgraceful.

⁶Righteousness protects the innocent; wickedness is the downfall of sinners.

⁷Some people pretend to be rich, but have nothing. Others pretend to be poor, but own a fortune.

⁸The rich have to use their money to save their lives, but no one threatens the poor.

⁹The righteous are like a light shining brightly; the wicked are like a lamp flickering out.

¹⁰Arrogance causes nothing but trouble. It is wiser to ask for advice.

¹¹The more easily you get your wealth, the sooner you will lose it. The harder it is to earn, the more you will have.

¹²When hope is crushed, the heart is crushed, but a wish come true fills you with joy.

¹³If you refuse good advice, you are asking for trouble; follow it and you are safe.

¹⁴The teachings of the wise are a fountain of life; they will help you escape when your life is in danger.

¹⁵Intelligence wins respect, but those who can't be trusted are on the road to ruin.^r

¹⁶Sensible people always think before they act, but stupid people advertise their ignorance.

¹⁷Unreliable messengers cause trouble, but those who can be trusted bring peace.

¹⁸Someone who will not learn will be poor and disgraced. Anyone who listens to correction is respected.

¹⁹How good it is to get what you want! Stupid people refuse to turn away from evil.

²⁰Keep company with the wise and you will become wise. If you make friends with stupid people, you will be ruined.

²¹Trouble follows sinners everywhere, but righteous people will be rewarded with good things.

²²Good people will have wealth to leave to their grandchildren, but the wealth of sinners will go to the righteous.

²³Unused fields could yield plenty of food for the poor, but unjust people keep them from being farmed.^s

---

p Verse 27 in Hebrew is unclear.   q One ancient translation wickedness; Hebrew path.
r One ancient translation road to ruin; Hebrew permanent road.   s Verse 23 in Hebrew is unclear.

24 If you don't punish your children, you don't love them. If you do love them, you will correct them.

25 The righteous have enough to eat, but the wicked are always hungry.

14 Homes are made by the wisdom of women, but are destroyed by foolishness.

2 Be honest and you show that you have reverence for the LORD; be dishonest and you show that you do not.

3 Proud fools talk too much; the words of the wise protect them.

4 Without any oxen to pull the plow your barn will be empty, but with them it will be full of grain. *t*

5 A reliable witness always tells the truth, but an unreliable one tells nothing but lies.

6 Conceited people can never become wise, but intelligent people learn easily.

7 Stay away from foolish people; they have nothing to teach you.

8 Why is a clever person wise? Because he knows what to do. Why is a stupid person foolish? Because he only thinks he knows.

9 Foolish people don't care if they sin, but good people want to be forgiven. *u*

10 Your joy is your own; your bitterness is your own. No one can share them with you.

11 A good person's house will still be standing after an evildoer's house has been destroyed.

12 What you think is the right road may lead to death.

13 Laughter may hide sadness. When happiness is gone, sorrow is always there.

14 Bad people will get what they deserve. Good people will be rewarded for their deeds. *v*

15 A fool will believe anything; smart people watch their step.

16 Sensible people are careful to stay out of trouble, but stupid people are careless and act too quickly.

17 People with a hot temper do foolish things; wiser people remain calm. *w*

18 Ignorant people get what their foolishness deserves, but the clever are rewarded with knowledge.

19 Evil people will have to bow down to the righteous and humbly beg their favor.

20 No one likes the poor, not even their neighbors, but the rich have many friends.

21 If you want to be happy, be kind to the poor; it is a sin to despise anyone.

22 You will earn the trust and respect of others if you work for good; if you work for evil, you are making a mistake.

23 Work and you will earn a living; if you sit around talking you will be poor.

24 Wise people are rewarded with wealth, but fools are known by *x* their foolishness.

25 A witness saves lives when he tells the truth; when he tells lies, he betrays people.

26 Reverence for the LORD gives confidence and security to a man and his family.

27 Do you want to avoid death? Reverence for the LORD is a fountain of life.

28 A king's greatness depends on how many people he rules; without them he is nothing.

29 If you stay calm, you are wise, but if you have a hot temper, you only show how stupid you are.

30 Peace of mind makes the body healthy, but jealousy is like a cancer.

31 If you oppress poor people, you insult the God who made them; but kindness shown to the poor is an act of worship.

32 Wicked people bring about their own downfall by their evil deeds, but good people are protected by their integrity. *y*

33 Wisdom is in every thought of intelligent people; fools know nothing *z* about wisdom.

34 Righteousness makes a nation great; sin is a disgrace to any nation.

35 Kings are pleased with competent officials, but they punish those who fail them.

15 A gentle answer quiets anger, but a harsh one stirs it up.

2 When wise people speak, they make knowledge attractive, but stupid people spout nonsense.

---

t your barn will be . . . grain; or you may grow a little grain, but with them you can grow much more.   u Verse 9 in Hebrew is unclear.   v Probable text for their deeds; Hebrew from upon them.   w One ancient translation remain calm; Hebrew are hated.   x Probable text are known by; Hebrew unclear.   y Some ancient translations integrity; Hebrew death. z One ancient translation nothing; Hebrew does not have this word.

³The LORD sees what happens everywhere; he is watching us, whether we do good or evil.

⁴Kind words bring life, but cruel words crush your spirit.

⁵It is foolish to ignore what your parents taught you; it is wise to accept their correction.

⁶Righteous people keep their wealth, but the wicked lose theirs when hard times come.

⁷Knowledge is spread by people who are wise, not by fools.

⁸The LORD is pleased when good people pray, but hates the sacrifices that the wicked bring him.

⁹The LORD hates the ways of evil people, but loves those who do what is right.

¹⁰If you do what is wrong, you will be severely punished; you will die if you do not let yourself be corrected.

¹¹Not even the world of the dead can keep the LORD from knowing what is there; how then can we hide our thoughts from God?

¹²Conceited people do not like to be corrected; they never ask for advice from those who are wiser.

¹³When people are happy, they smile, but when they are sad, they look depressed.

¹⁴Intelligent people want to learn, but stupid people are satisfied with ignorance.

¹⁵The life of the poor is a constant struggle, but happy people always enjoy life.

¹⁶Better to be poor and fear the LORD than to be rich and in trouble.

¹⁷Better to eat vegetables with people you love than to eat the finest meat where there is hate.

¹⁸Hot tempers cause arguments, but patience brings peace.

¹⁹If you are lazy, you will meet difficulty everywhere, but if you are honest, you will have no trouble.

²⁰Wise children make their fathers happy. Only fools despise their mothers.

²¹Stupid people are happy with their foolishness, but the wise will do what is right.

²²Get all the advice you can, and you will succeed; without it you will fail.

²³What a joy it is to find just the right word for the right occasion!

²⁴Wise people walk the road that leads upward to life, not the road that leads downward to death.

²⁵The LORD will destroy the homes of arrogant men, but he will protect a widow's property.

²⁶The LORD hates evil thoughts, but he is pleased with friendly words.

²⁷Try to make a profit dishonestly, and you get your family in trouble. Don't take bribes and you will live longer.

²⁸Good people think before they answer. Evil people have a quick reply, but it causes trouble.

²⁹When good people pray, the LORD listens, but he ignores those who are evil.

³⁰Smiling faces make you happy, and good news makes you feel better.

³¹If you pay attention when you are corrected, you are wise.

³²If you refuse to learn, you are hurting yourself. If you accept correction, you will become wiser.

³³Reverence for the LORD is an education in itself. You must be humble before you can ever receive honors.

16

We may make our plans, but God has the last word.ᵃ

²You may think everything you do is right, but the LORD judges your motives.

³Ask the LORD to bless your plans, and you will be successful in carrying them out.

⁴Everything the LORD has made has its destiny; and the destiny of the wicked is destruction.

⁵The LORD hates everyone who is arrogant; he will never let them escape punishment.

⁶Be loyal and faithful, and God will forgive your sin. Obey the LORD and nothing evil will happen to you.

⁷When you please the LORD, you can makeᵇ your enemies into friends.

⁸It is better to have a little, honestly earned, than to have a large income, dishonestly gained.

⁹You may make your plans, but God directs your actions.

¹⁰The king speaks with divine authority; his decisions are always right.

¹¹The LORD wants weights and measures to be honest and every sale to be fair.

ᵃ God . . . word; *or* God inspires our words.　　ᵇ you can make; *or* he will make.

12 Kings cannot tolerate evil,c because justice is what makes a government strong.

13 A king wants to hear the truth and will favor those who speak it.

14 A wise person will try to keep the king happy; if the king becomes angry, someone may die.

15 The king's favor is like the clouds that bring rain in the springtime—life is there.

16 It is better—much better—to have wisdom and knowledge than gold and silver.

17 Those who are good travel a road that avoids evil; so watch where you are going—it may save your life.

18 Pride leads to destruction, and arrogance to downfall.

19 It is better to be humble and stay poor than to be one of the arrogant and get a share of their loot.

20 Pay attention to what you are taught, and you will be successful; trust in the LORD and you will be happy.

21 A wise, mature person is known for his understanding. The more pleasant his words, the more persuasive he is.

22 Wisdom is a fountain of life to the wise, but trying to educate stupid people is a waste of time.

23 Intelligent people think before they speak; what they say is then more persuasive.

24 Kind words are like honey—sweet to the taste and good for your health.

25 What you think is the right road may lead to death.

26 A laborer's appetite makes him work harder, because he wants to satisfy his hunger.

27 Evil people look for ways to harm others; even their words burn with evil.

28 Gossip is spread by wicked people; they stir up trouble and break up friendships.

29 Violent people deceive their friends and lead them to disaster.

30 Watch out for people who grin and wink at you; they have thought of something evil.

31 Long life is the reward of the righteous; gray hair is a glorious crown.

32 It is better to be patient than powerful. It is better to win control over yourself than over whole cities.

33 People cast lots to learn God's will, but God himself determines the answer.

17 Better to eat a dry crust of bread with peace of mind than have a banquet in a house full of trouble.

2 A shrewd servant will gain authority over a master's worthless son and receive a part of the inheritance.

3 Gold and silver are tested by fire, and a person's heart is tested by the LORD.

4 Evil people listen to evil ideas, and liars listen to lies.

5 If you make fun of poor people, you insult the God who made them. You will be punished if you take pleasure in someone's misfortune.

6 Grandparents are proud of their grandchildren, just as children are proud of their parents.

7 Respected people do not tell lies, and fools have nothing worthwhile to say.

8 Some people think a bribe works like magic; they believe it can do anything.

9 If you want people to like you, forgive them when they wrong you. Remembering wrongs can break up a friendship.

10 An intelligent person learns more from one rebuke than a fool learns from being beaten a hundred times.

11 Death will come like a cruel messenger to wicked people who are always stirring up trouble.

12 It is better to meet a mother bear robbed of her cubs than to meet some fool busy with a stupid project.

13 If you repay good with evil, you will never get evil out of your house.

14 The start of an argument is like the first break in a dam; stop it before it goes any further.

15 Condemning the innocent or letting the wicked go—both are hateful to the LORD.

16 It does a fool no good to spend money on an education, because he has no common sense.

17 Friends always show their love. What are relatives for if not to share trouble?

18 Only someone with no sense would promise to be responsible for someone else's debts.

19 To like sin is to like making trouble.

c Kings . . . evil; or It is intolerable for kings to do evil.

If you brag all the time,*d* you are asking for trouble.

20 Anyone who thinks and speaks evil can expect to find nothing good—only disaster.

21 There is nothing but sadness and sorrow for parents whose children do foolish things.

22 Being cheerful keeps you healthy. It is slow death to be gloomy all the time.

23 Corrupt judges accept secret bribes, and then justice is not done.

24 An intelligent person aims at wise action, but a fool starts off in many directions.

25 Foolish children bring grief to their fathers and bitter regrets to their mothers.

26 It is not right to make an innocent person pay a fine; justice is perverted when good people are punished.

27 Those who are sure of themselves do not talk all the time. People who stay calm have real insight. 28 After all, even fools may be thought wise and intelligent if they stay quiet and keep their mouths shut.

18 People who do not get along with others are interested only in themselves; they will disagree with what everyone else knows is right.

2 A fool does not care whether he understands a thing or not; all he wants to do is show how smart he is.

3 Sin and shame go together. Lose your honor, and you will get scorn in its place.

4 A person's words can be a source of wisdom, deep as the ocean, fresh as a flowing stream.

5 It is not right to favor the guilty and keep the innocent from receiving justice.

6 When some fool starts an argument, he is asking for a beating.

7 When a fool speaks, he is ruining himself; he gets caught in the trap of his own words.

8 Gossip is so tasty—how we love to swallow it!

9 A lazy person is as bad as someone who is destructive.

10 The LORD is like a strong tower, where the righteous can go and be safe.

11 Rich people, however, imagine that their wealth protects them like high, strong walls around a city.

12 No one is respected unless he is humble; arrogant people are on the way to ruin.

13 Listen before you answer. If you don't, you are being stupid and insulting.

14 Your will to live can sustain you when you are sick, but if you lose it, your last hope is gone.

15 Intelligent people are always eager and ready to learn.

16 Do you want to meet an important person? Take a gift and it will be easy.

17 The first person to speak in court always seems right until his opponent begins to question him.

18 If two powerful people are opposing each other in court, casting lots can settle the issue.

19 Help your relatives and they will protect you like a strong city wall,*e* but if you quarrel with them, they will close their doors to you.

20 You will have to live with the consequences of everything you say. 21 What you say can preserve life or destroy it; so you must accept the consequences of your words.

22 Find a wife and you find a good thing; it shows that the LORD is good to you.

23 When the poor speak, they have to be polite, but when the rich answer, they are rude.

24 Some friendships do*f* not last, but some friends are more loyal than brothers.

19 It is better to be poor but honest than to be a lying fool.

2 Enthusiasm without knowledge is not good; impatience will get you into trouble.

3 Some people ruin themselves by their own stupid actions and then blame the LORD.

4 Rich people are always finding new friends, but the poor cannot keep the few they have.

5 If you tell lies in court, you will be punished—there will be no escape.

6 Everyone tries to gain the favor of important people; everyone claims the friendship of those who give out favors.

---

d brag . . . time; or make a show of your wealth. Hebrew unclear. f Some ancient translations Some friendships do; Hebrew Someone with friends does. *e Some ancient translations Help . . . wall;*

7 Even the relatives of a poor person have no use for him; no wonder he has no friends. No matter how hard he tries, he cannot win any.g

8 Do yourself a favor and learn all you can; then remember what you learn and you will prosper.

9 No one who tells lies in court can escape punishment; he is doomed.

10 Fools should not live in luxury, and slaves should not rule over noblemen.

11 If you are sensible, you will control your temper. When someone wrongs you, it is a great virtue to ignore it.

12 The king's anger is like the roar of a lion, but his favor is like welcome rain.

13 Stupid children can bring their parents to ruin. A nagging wife is like water going drip-drip-drip.

14 A man can inherit a house and money from his parents, but only the LORD can give him a sensible wife.

15 Go ahead and be lazy; sleep on, but you will go hungry.

16 Keep God's laws and you will live longer; if you ignore them, you will die.

17 When you give to the poor, it is like lending to the LORD, and the LORD will pay you back.

18 Discipline your children while they are young enough to learn. If you don't, you are helping them destroy themselves.h

19 If someone has a hot temper, let him take the consequences. If you get him out of trouble once, you will have to do it again.

20 If you listen to advice and are willing to learn, one day you will be wise.

21 People may plan all kinds of things, but the LORD's will is going to be done.

22 It is a disgrace to be greedy;i poor people are better off than liars.

23 Obey the LORD and you will live a long life, content and safe from harm.

24 Some people are too lazy to put food in their own mouths.

25 Arrogance should be punished, so that people who don't know any better can learn a lesson. If you are wise, you will learn when you are corrected.

26 Only a shameful, disgraceful person would mistreat his father or turn his mother away from his home.

27 My child, when you stop learning, you will soon neglect what you already know.

28 There is no justice where a witness is determined to hurt someone. Wicked people love the taste of evil.

29 A conceited fool is sure to get a beating.

20 Drinking too much makes you loud and foolish. It's stupid to get drunk.

2 Fear an angry king as you would a growling lion; making him angry is suicide.

3 Any fool can start arguments; the honorable thing is to stay out of them.

4 A farmer too lazy to plow his fields at the right time will have nothing to harvest.

5 A person's thoughts are like water in a deep well, but someone with insight can draw them out.

6 Everyone talks about how loyal and faithful he is, but just try to find someone who really is!

7 Children are fortunate if they have a father who is honest and does what is right.

8 The king sits in judgment and knows evil when he sees it.

9 Can anyone really say that his conscience is clear, that he has gotten rid of his sin?

10 The LORD hates people who use dishonest weights and measures.

11 Even children show what they are by what they do; you can tell if they are honest and good.

12 The LORD has given us eyes to see with and ears to listen with.

13 If you spend your time sleeping, you will be poor. Keep busy and you will have plenty to eat.

14 The customer always complains that the price is too high, but then he goes off and brags about the bargain he got.

15 If you know what you are talking about, you have something more valuable than gold or jewels.

16 Anyone stupid enough to promise to be responsible for a stranger's debts ought to have their own property held to guarantee payment.

17 What you get by dishonesty you

PROVERBS

---

g *Probable text* No matter . . . any; *Hebrew unclear.*   h *If you . . . themselves; or But don't punish them so hard that you kill them.*   i *get him out . . . again; or try to get him out of trouble, you only make things worse.*   j *It . . . greedy; or Loyalty is what is desired in a person.*

may enjoy like the finest food, but sooner or later it will be like a mouthful of sand.

18 Get good advice and you will succeed; don't go charging into battle without a plan.

19 A gossip can never keep a secret. Stay away from people who talk too much.

20 If you curse your parents, your life will end like a lamp that goes out in the dark.

21 The more easily you get your wealth, the less good it will do you.

22 Don't take it on yourself to repay a wrong. Trust the LORD and he will make it right.

23 The LORD hates people who use dishonest scales and weights.

24 The LORD has determined our path; how then can anyone understand the direction his own life is taking?

25 Think carefully before you promise an offering to God. You might regret it later.

26 A wise king will find out who is doing wrong, and will punish him without pity.

27 The LORD gave us mind and conscience; we cannot hide from ourselves.

28 A king will remain in power as long as his rule is honest, just, and fair.

29 We admire the strength of youth and respect the gray hair of age.

30 Sometimes it takes a painful experience to make us change our ways.

21 The LORD controls the mind of a king as easily as he directs the course of a stream.

2 You may think that everything you do is right, but remember that the LORD judges your motives.

3 Do what is right and fair; that pleases the LORD more than bringing him sacrifices.

4 Wicked people are controlled by their conceit and arrogance, and this is sinful.

5 Plan carefully and you will have plenty; if you act too quickly, you will never have enough.

6 The riches you get by dishonesty soon disappear, but not before they lead you into the jaws of death.

7 The wicked are doomed by their own violence; they refuse to do what is right.

8 Guilty people walk a crooked path; the innocent do what is right.

9 Better to live on the roof than share the house with a nagging wife.

10 Wicked people are always hungry for evil; they have no mercy on anyone.

11 When someone who is conceited gets his punishment, even an unthinking person learns a lesson. One who is wise will learn from what he is taught.

12 God, the righteous one, knows what goes on in the homes of the wicked, and he will bring the wicked down to ruin.

13 If you refuse to listen to the cry of the poor, your own cry for help will not be heard.

14 If someone is angry with you, a gift given secretly will calm him down.

15 When justice is done, good people are happy, but evil people are brought to despair.

16 Death is waiting for anyone who wanders away from good sense.

17 Indulging in luxuries, wine, and rich food will never make you wealthy.

18 The wicked bring on themselves the suffering they try to cause good people.

19 Better to live out in the desert than with a nagging, complaining wife.

20 Wise people live in wealth and luxury, but stupid people spend their money as fast as they get it.

21 Be kind and honest and you will live a long life; others will respect you and treat you fairly.

22 A shrewd general can take a city defended by strong men, and destroy the walls they relied on.

23 If you want to stay out of trouble, be careful what you say.

24 Show me a conceited person and I will show you someone who is arrogant, proud, and inconsiderate.

25 Lazy people who refuse to work are only killing themselves; 26 all they do is think about what they would like to have. The righteous, however, can give, and give generously.

27 The LORD hates it when wicked people offer him sacrifices, especially if they do it from evil motives.

28 The testimony of a liar is not believed, but the word of someone who thinks matters through is accepted.

29 Righteous people are sure of themselves; the wicked have to pretend as best they can.

30 Human wisdom, brilliance, insight—they are of no help if the LORD is against you.

31 You can get horses ready for battle, but it is the LORD who gives victory.

22 If you have to choose between a good reputation and great wealth, choose a good reputation.

2 The rich and the poor have this in common: the LORD made them both.

3 Sensible people will see trouble coming and avoid it, but an unthinking person will walk right into it and regret it later.

4 Obey the LORD, be humble, and you will get riches, honor, and a long life.

5 If you love your life, stay away from the traps that catch the wicked along the way.

6 Teach children how they should live, and they will remember it all their life.

7 Poor people are slaves of the rich. Borrow money and you are the lender's slave.

8 If you plant the seeds of injustice, disaster will spring up, and your oppression of others will end.

9 Be generous and share your food with the poor. You will be blessed for it.

10 Get rid of a conceited person, and then there will be no more arguments, quarreling, or name-calling.

11 If you love purity of heart and graciousness of speech, the king will be your friend.

12 The LORD sees to it that truth is kept safe by disproving the words of liars.

13 Lazy people stay at home; they say a lion might get them if they go outside.

14 Adultery is a trap—it catches those with whom the LORD is angry.

15 Children just naturally do silly, careless things, but a good spanking will teach them how to behave.

16 If you make gifts to rich people or oppress the poor to get rich, you will become poor yourself.

The Thirty Wise Sayings

17 Listen, and I will teach you what the wise have said. Study their teachings, 18 and you will be glad if you remember them and can quote them. 19 I want you to put your trust in the LORD; that is why I am going to tell them to you now. 20 I have written down thirty sayings for you. They contain knowledge and good advice, 21 and will teach you what the truth really is. Then when you are sent to find it out, you will bring back the right answer.

-1-

22 Don't take advantage of the poor just because you can; don't take advantage of those who stand helpless in court. 23 The LORD will argue their case for them and threaten the life of anyone who threatens theirs.

-2-

24 Don't make friends with people who have hot, violent tempers. 25 You might learn their habits and not be able to change.

-3-

26 Don't promise to be responsible for someone else's debts. 27 If you should be unable to pay, they will take away even your bed.

-4-

28 Never move an old property line that your ancestors established.

-5-

29 Show me someone who does a good job, and I will show you someone who is better than most and worthy of the company of kings.

-6-

23 When you sit down to eat with someone important, keep in mind who he is.[k] 2 If you have a big appetite, restrain yourself. 3 Don't be greedy for the fine food he serves; he may be trying to trick you.

-7-

4 Be wise enough not to wear yourself out trying to get rich. 5 Your money can be gone in a flash, as if it had grown wings and flown away like an eagle.

-8-

6 Don't eat at the table of a stingy person or be greedy for the fine food he serves. 7 "Come on and have some more," he says, but he doesn't mean it. What he thinks is what he really is. 8 You will vomit up what you have eaten, and all your flattery will be wasted.

k keep . . . is; *or notice carefully what is before you.*

-9-

⁹Don't try to talk sense to a fool; he can't appreciate it.

-10-

¹⁰Never move an old property line or take over land owned by orphans. ¹¹The LORD is their powerful defender, and he will argue their case against you.

-11-

¹²Pay attention to your teacher and learn all you can.

-12-

¹³Don't hesitate to discipline children. A good spanking won't kill them. ¹⁴As a matter of fact, it may save their lives.

-13-

¹⁵My child, if you become wise, I will be very happy. ¹⁶I will be proud when I hear you speaking words of wisdom.

-14-

¹⁷Don't be envious of sinful people; let reverence for the LORD be the concern of your life. ¹⁸If it is, you have a bright future.

-15-

¹⁹Listen, my child, be wise and give serious thought to the way you live. ²⁰Don't associate with people who drink too much wine or stuff themselves with food. ²¹Drunkards and gluttons will be reduced to poverty. If all you do is eat and sleep, you will soon be wearing rags.

-16-

²²Listen to your father; without him you would not exist. When your mother is old, show her your appreciation. ²³Truth, wisdom, learning, and good sense—these are worth paying for, but too valuable for you to sell. ²⁴A righteous person's parents have good reason to be happy. You can take pride in a wise child. ²⁵Let your father and mother be proud of you; give your mother that happiness.

-17-

²⁶Pay close attention, son, and let my

life be your example. ²⁷Prostitutes and immoral women are a deadly trap. ²⁸They wait for you like robbers and cause many men to be unfaithful.

-18-

²⁹⁻³⁰Show me people who drink too much, who have to try out fancy drinks, and I will show you people who are miserable and sorry for themselves, always causing trouble and always complaining. Their eyes are bloodshot, and they have bruises that could have been avoided. ³¹Don't let wine tempt you, even though it is rich red, and it sparkles in the cup, and it goes down smoothly. ³²The next morning you will feel as if you had been bitten by a poisonous snake. ³³Weird sights will appear before your eyes, and you will not be able to think or speak clearly. ³⁴You will feel as if you were out on the ocean, seasick, swinging high up in the rigging of a tossing ship. ³⁵"I must have been hit," you will say; "I must have been beaten up, but I don't remember it. Why can't I wake up? I need another drink."

-19-

24 Don't be envious of evil people, and don't try to make friends with them. ²Causing trouble is all they ever think about; every time they open their mouth someone is going to be hurt.

-20-

³Homes are built on the foundation of wisdom and understanding.ˡ ⁴Where there is knowledge, the rooms are furnished with valuable, beautiful things.

-21-

⁵Being wise is better than being strong;ᵐ yes, knowledge is more important than strength. ⁶After all, you must make careful plans before you fight a battle, and the more good advice you get, the more likely you are to win.

-22-

⁷Wise sayings are too deep for stupid people to understand. They have nothing to say when important matters are being discussed.

ˡ *Homes . . . understanding; or* It takes care to lay the foundations of a house, and skill to build it.
ᵐ *Some ancient translations* Being wise is better than being strong; *Hebrew* A person is wise in strength.

-23-

8 If you are always planning evil, you will earn a reputation as a troublemaker. 9 Any scheme a fool thinks up is sinful. People hate a person who has nothing but scorn for others.

-24-

10 If you are weak in a crisis, you are weak indeed.

-25-

11 Don't hesitate to rescue someone who is about to be executed unjustly. 12 You may say that it is none of your business, but God knows and judges your motives. He keeps watch on you; he knows. And he will reward you according to what you do.

-26-

13 My child, eat honey; it is good. And just as honey from the comb is sweet on your tongue, 14 you may be sure that wisdom is good for the soul. Get wisdom and you have a bright future.

-27-

15 Don't be like the wicked who scheme to rob honest people or to take away their homes. 16 No matter how often honest people fall, they always get up again; but disaster destroys the wicked.

-28-

17 Don't be glad when your enemies meet disaster, and don't rejoice when they stumble. 18 The LORD will know if you are gloating, and he will not like it; and then maybe he won't punish them.

-29-

19 Don't let evil people worry you; don't be envious of them. 20 A wicked person has no future—nothing to look forward to.

-30-

21 Have reverence for the LORD, my child, and honor the king. Have nothing to do with people who rebel against them; 22 such people could be ruined in a moment. Do you realize the disaster that God or the king can cause?

More Wise Sayings

23 The wise have also said these things: It is wrong for judges to be prejudiced. 24 If they pronounce a guilty person innocent, they will be cursed and hated by everyone. 25 Judges who punish the guilty, however, will be prosperous and enjoy a good reputation.

26 An honest answer is a sign of true friendship.

27 Don't build your house and establish a home until your fields are ready, and you are sure that you can earn a living.

28 Don't give evidence against others without good reason, or say misleading things about them. 29 Don't say, "I'll do to them just what they did to me! I'll get even with them!"

30 I walked through the fields and vineyards of a lazy, stupid person. 31 They were full of thorn bushes and overgrown with weeds. The stone wall around them had fallen down. 32 I looked at this, thought about it, and learned a lesson from it: 33 Go ahead and take your nap; go ahead and sleep. Fold your hands and rest awhile, 34 but while you are asleep, poverty will attack you like an armed robber.

More of Solomon's Proverbs

25 Here are more of Solomon's proverbs, copied by scribes at the court of King Hezekiah of Judah.

2 We honor God for what he conceals; we honor kings for what they explain.

3 You never know what a king is thinking; his thoughts are beyond us, like the heights of the sky or the depths of the ocean.

4 Take the impurities out of silver and the artist can produce a thing of beauty. 5 Keep evil advisers away from the king and his government will be known for its justice.

6 When you stand before the king, don't try to impress him and pretend to be important. 7 It is better to be asked to take a higher position than to be told to give your place to someone more important.

8 Don't be too quick to go to court about something you have seen. If another witness later proves you wrong, what will you do then?

9 If you and your neighbor have a difference of opinion, settle it between

yourselves and do not reveal any secrets. [10]Otherwise everyone will learn that you can't keep a secret, and you will never live down the shame.

[11]An idea well-expressed is like a design of gold, set in silver.

[12]A warning given by an experienced person to someone willing to listen is more valuable than gold rings or jewelry made of the finest gold.

[13]A reliable messenger is refreshing to the one who sends him, like cold water in the heat of harvest time.

[14]People who promise things that they never give are like clouds and wind that bring no rain.

[15]Patient persuasion can break down the strongest resistance and can even convince rulers.

[16]Never eat more honey than you need; too much may make you vomit. [17]Don't visit your neighbors too often; they may get tired of you and come to hate you.

[18]A false accusation is as deadly as a sword, a club, or a sharp arrow.

[19]Depending on an unreliable person in a crisis is like trying to chew with a loose tooth or walk with a crippled foot.

[20]Singing to a person who is depressed is like taking off a person's clothes on a cold day or like rubbing salt in a wound.

[21]If your enemies are hungry, feed them; if they are thirsty, give them a drink. [22]You will make them burn with shame, and the Lord will reward you.

[23]Gossip brings anger just as surely as the north wind brings rain.

[24]Better to live on the roof than share the house with a nagging wife.

[25]Finally hearing good news from a distant land is like a drink of cold water when you are dry and thirsty.

[26]A good person who gives in to someone who is evil reminds you of a polluted spring or a poisoned well.

[27]Too much honey is bad for you, and so is trying to win too much praise.[n]

[28]If you cannot control your anger, you are as helpless as a city without walls, open to attack.

26 Praise for a fool is out of place, like snow in summer or rain at harvest time.

[2]Curses cannot hurt you unless you deserve them. They are like birds that fly by and never light.

[3]You have to whip a horse, you have to bridle a donkey, and you have to beat a fool.

[4]If you answer a silly question, you are just as silly as the person who asked it.

[5]Give a silly answer to a silly question, and the one who asked it will realize that he's not as smart as he thinks.

[6]If you let a fool deliver a message, you might as well cut off your own feet; you are asking for trouble.

[7]A fool can use a proverb about as well as crippled people can use their legs.

[8]Praising someone who is stupid makes as much sense as tying a stone in a sling.

[9]A fool quoting a wise saying reminds you of a drunk trying to pick a thorn out of his hand.

[10]An employer who hires any fool that comes along is only hurting everybody concerned.[o]

[11]A fool doing some stupid thing a second time is like a dog going back to its vomit.

[12]The most stupid fool is better off than those who think they are wise when they are not.

[13]Why don't lazy people ever get out of the house? What are they afraid of? Lions?

[14]Lazy people turn over in bed. They get no farther than a door swinging on its hinges.

[15]Some people are too lazy to put food in their own mouths.

[16]A lazy person will think he is smarter than seven men who can give good reasons for their opinions.

[17]Getting involved in an argument that is none of your business is like going down the street and grabbing a dog by the ears.

[18-19]Someone who tricks someone else and then claims that he was only joking is like a crazy person playing with a deadly weapon.

[20]Without wood, a fire goes out; without gossip, quarreling stops.

[21]Charcoal keeps the embers glowing, wood keeps the fire burning, and troublemakers keep arguments alive.

---

[n] Probable text and so . . . praise; Hebrew unclear.   [o] Verse 10 in Hebrew is unclear.

22Gossip is so tasty! How we love to swallow it!

23Insincere p talk that hides what you are really thinking is like a fine glaze q on a cheap clay pot.

24A hypocrite hides hate behind flattering words. 25They may sound fine, but don't believe him, because his heart is filled to the brim with hate. 26He may disguise his hatred, but everyone will see the evil things he does.

27People who set traps for others get caught themselves. People who start landslides get crushed.

28You have to hate someone to want to hurt him with lies. Insincere talk brings nothing but ruin.

27 Never boast about tomorrow. You don't know what will happen between now and then.

2Let other people praise you—even strangers; never do it yourself.

3The weight of stone and sand is nothing compared to the trouble that stupidity can cause.

4Anger is cruel and destructive, but it is nothing compared to jealousy.

5Better to correct someone openly than to let him think you don't care for him at all.

6Friends mean well, even when they hurt you. But when an enemy puts his arm around your shoulder—watch out!

7When you are full, you will refuse honey, but when you are hungry, even bitter food tastes sweet.

8Anyone away from home is like a bird away from its nest.

9Perfume and fragrant oils make you feel happier, but trouble shatters your peace of mind.r

10Do not forget your friends or your father's friends. If you are in trouble, don't ask a relative for help; a nearby neighbor can help you more than relatives who are far away.

11Be wise, my child, and I will be happy; I will have an answer for anyone who criticizes me.

12Sensible people will see trouble coming and avoid it, but an unthinking person will walk right into it and regret it later.

13Any people stupid enough to prom-ise to be responsible for a stranger's debtss deserve to have their own property held to guarantee payment.

14You might as well curse your friends as wake them up early in the morning with a loud greeting.

15A nagging wife is like water going drip-drip-drip on a rainy day. 16How can you keep her quiet? Have you ever tried to stop the wind or ever tried to hold a handful of oil?t

17People learn from one another, just as iron sharpens iron.

18Take care of a fig tree and you will have figs to eat. Servants who take care of their master will be honored.

19It is your own face that you see reflected in the water and it is your own self that you see in your heart.

20Human desires are like the world of the dead—there is always room for more.

21Fire tests gold and silver; a person's reputation can also be tested.

22Even if you beat fools half to death, you still can't beat their foolishness out of them.

23Look after your sheep and cattle as carefully as you can, 24because wealth is not permanent. Not even nations last forever. 25You cut the hay and then cut the grass on the hillsides while the next crop of hay is growing. 26You can make clothes from the wool of your sheep and buy land with the money you get from selling some of your goats. 27The rest of the goats will provide milk for you and your family, and for your servant women as well.

28 The wicked run when no one is chasing them, but an honest person is as brave as a lion.

2When a nation sins, it will have one ruler after another. But a nation will be strong and endure when it has intelligent, sensible leaders.

3Someone in authority who oppresses poor people is like a driving rain that destroys the crops.

4If you have no regard for the law, you are on the side of the wicked; but if you obey it, you are against them.

5Evil people do not know what justice

p One ancient translation Insincere; Hebrew Burning.   q Probable text fine glaze; Hebrew unrefined silver.   r One ancient translation but trouble . . . mind; Hebrew unclear.
s One ancient translation stranger's debts; Hebrew stranger's debts or those of an immoral woman.   t Probable text or ever . . . oil; Hebrew unclear.

is, but those who worship the LORD understand it well.

6 Better to be poor and honest than rich and dishonest.

7 Young people who obey the law are intelligent. Those who make friends with good-for-nothings are a disgrace to their parents.

8 If you get rich by charging interest and taking advantage of people, your wealth will go to someone who is kind to the poor.

9 If you do not obey the law, God will find your prayers too hateful to hear.

10 If you trick an honest person into doing evil, you will fall into your own trap.

The innocent will be well rewarded.

11 Rich people always think they are wise, but a poor person who has insight into character knows better.

12 When good people come to power, everybody celebrates, but when bad people rule, people stay in hiding.

13 You will never succeed in life if you try to hide your sins. Confess them and give them up; then God will show mercy to you.

14 Always obey the LORD and you will be happy. If you are stubborn, you will be ruined.

15 Poor people are helpless against a wicked ruler; he is as dangerous as a growling lion or a prowling bear.

16 A ruler without good sense will be a cruel tyrant. One who hates dishonesty will rule a long time.

17 Someone guilty of murder is digging his own grave as fast as he can. Don't try to stop him.

18 Be honest and you will be safe. If you are dishonest, you will suddenly fall.

19 A hard-working farmer has plenty to eat. People who waste time will always be poor.

20 Honest people will lead a full, happy life. But if you are in a hurry to get rich, you are going to be punished.

21 Prejudice is wrong. But some judges will do wrong to get even the smallest bribe.

22 Selfish people are in such a hurry to get rich that they do not know when poverty is about to strike.

23 Correct someone, and afterward he will appreciate it more than flattery.

24 Anyone who thinks it isn't wrong to steal from his parents is no better than a common thief.

25 Selfishness only causes trouble. You are much better off to trust the LORD.

26 It is foolish to follow your own opinions. Be safe, and follow the teachings of wiser people.

27 Give to the poor and you will never be in need. If you close your eyes to the poor, many people will curse you.

28 People stay in hiding when the wicked come to power. But when they fall from power, the righteous will rule again.

29 If you get more stubborn every time you are corrected, one day you will be crushed and never recover.

2 Show me a righteous ruler and I will show you a happy people. Show me a wicked ruler and I will show you a miserable people.

3 If you appreciate wisdom, your parents will be proud of you.

It is a foolish waste to spend money on prostitutes.

4 When the king is concerned with justice, the nation will be strong, but when he is only concerned with money, he will ruin his country.

5 If you flatter your friends, you set a trap for yourself.u

6 Evil people are trapped in their own sins, while honest people are happy and free.

7 A good person knows the rights of the poor, but wicked people cannot understand such things.

8 People with no regard for others can throw whole cities into turmoil. Those who are wise keep things calm.

9 When an intelligent person brings a lawsuit against a fool, the fool only laughs and becomes loud and abusive.

10 Bloodthirsty people hate anyone who's honest, but righteous people will protectv the life of such a person.

11 Stupid people express their anger openly, but sensible people are patient and hold it back.

12 If a ruler pays attention to false information, all his officials will be liars.

13 A poor person and his oppressor

u yourself; or them.   v Probable text protect; Hebrew seek.

have this in common — the LORD gave eyes to both of them.

14 If a king defends the rights of the poor, he will rule for a long time.

15 Correction and discipline are good for children. If they have their own way, they will make their mothers ashamed of them.

16 When evil people are in power, crime increases. But the righteous will live to see the downfall of such people.

17 Discipline your children and you can always be proud of them. They will never give you reason to be ashamed.

18 A nation without God's guidance is a nation without order. Happy are those who keep God's law!

19 You cannot correct servants just by talking to them. They may understand you, but they will pay no attention.

20 There is more hope for a stupid fool than for someone who speaks without thinking.

21 If you give your servants everything they want from childhood on, some day they will take over everything you own.*w*

22 People with quick tempers cause a lot of quarreling and trouble.

23 Arrogance will bring your downfall, but if you are humble, you will be respected.

24 A thief's partner is his own worst enemy. He will be punished if he tells the truth in court, and God will curse him if he doesn't.

25 It is dangerous to be concerned with what others think of you, but if you trust the LORD, you are safe.

26 Everybody wants the good will of the ruler, but only from the LORD can you get justice.

27 The righteous hate the wicked, and the wicked hate the righteous.

The Words of Agur

30 These are the solemn words of Agur son of Jakeh:

"God is not with me, God is not with me,
    and I am helpless.*x*
2 I am more like an animal than a
    human being;
I do not have the sense we
    humans should have.

3 I have never learned any wisdom,
    and I know nothing at all
    about God.
4 Have any ever mastered heavenly
    knowledge?
Have any ever caught the wind
    in their hands?
Or wrapped up water in a piece
    of cloth?
Or fixed the boundaries of the
    earth?
Who are they, if you know? Who
    are their children?
5 "God keeps every promise he makes. He is like a shield for all who seek his protection. 6 If you claim that he said something that he never said, he will reprimand you and show that you are a liar."

More Proverbs

7 I ask you, God, to let me have two things before I die: 8 keep me from lying, and let me be neither rich nor poor. So give me only as much food as I need. 9 If I have more, I might say that I do not need you. But if I am poor, I might steal and bring disgrace on my God.

10 Never criticize servants to their master. You will be cursed and suffer for it.

11 There are people who curse their fathers and do not show their appreciation for their mothers.

12 There are people who think they are pure when they are as filthy as they can be.

13 There are people who think they are so good — oh, how good they think they are!

14 There are people who take cruel advantage of the poor and needy; that is the way they make their living.

15 A leech has two daughters, and both are named "Give me!"

There are four things that are never satisfied:
16 the world of the dead,
    a woman without children,
    dry ground that needs rain,
    and a fire burning out of control.
17 If you make fun of your father or despise your mother in her old age,*y* you ought to be eaten by vultures or have your eyes picked out by wild ravens.

---

w they . . . own; *or* you will not be able to control them.   *x* *Probable text* "God . . . helpless; *Hebrew unclear.*   *y* *One ancient translation* mother in her old age; *Hebrew* mother's obedience.

¹⁸There are four things that are too mysterious for me to understand:
¹⁹an eagle flying in the sky,
a snake moving on a rock,
a ship finding its way over the sea,
and a man and a woman falling in love.

²⁰This is how an unfaithful wife acts: she commits adultery, takes a bath, and says, "But I haven't done anything wrong!"

²¹There are four things that the earth itself cannot tolerate:
²²a slave who becomes a king,
a fool who has all he wants to eat,
²³a hateful woman who gets married,
and a servant woman who takes the place of her mistress.

²⁴There are four animals in the world that are small, but very, very clever:
²⁵Ants: they are weak, but they store up their food in the summer.
²⁶Rock badgers: they are not strong either, but they make their homes among the rocks.
²⁷Locusts: they have no king, but they move in formation.
²⁸Lizards: you can hold one in your hand, but you can find them in palaces.

²⁹There are four things that are impressive to watch as they walk:
³⁰lions, strongest of all animals and afraid of none;
³¹goats, strutting roosters,
and kings in front of their people.[z]

³²If you have been foolish enough to be arrogant and plan evil, stop and think! ³³If you churn milk, you get butter. If you hit someone's nose, it bleeds. If you stir up anger, you get into trouble.

Advice to a King

31 These are the solemn words which King Lemuel's mother said to him:

²"You are my own dear son, the answer to my prayers. What shall I tell you? ³Don't spend all your energy on sex and all your money on women; they have destroyed kings. ⁴Listen, Lemuel. Kings should not drink wine or have a craving for alcohol. ⁵When they drink, they forget the laws and ignore the rights of people in need. ⁶Alcohol is for people who are dying, for those who are in misery. ⁷Let them drink and forget their poverty and unhappiness.

⁸"Speak up for people who cannot speak for themselves. Protect the rights of all who are helpless. ⁹Speak for them and be a righteous judge. Protect the rights of the poor and needy."

The Capable Wife

¹⁰How hard it is to find a capable wife! She is worth far more than jewels!

¹¹Her husband puts his confidence in her, and he will never be poor.

¹²As long as she lives, she does him good and never harm.

¹³She keeps herself busy making wool and linen cloth.

¹⁴She brings home food from out-of-the-way places, as merchant ships do.

¹⁵She gets up before daylight to prepare food for her family and to tell her servant women what to do.

¹⁶She looks at land and buys it, and with money she has earned she plants a vineyard.

¹⁷She is a hard worker, strong and industrious.

¹⁸She knows the value of everything she makes, and works late into the night.

¹⁹She spins her own thread and weaves her own cloth.

²⁰She is generous to the poor and needy.

²¹She doesn't worry when it snows, because her family has warm clothing.

²²She makes bedspreads and wears clothes of fine purple linen.

²³Her husband is well known, one of the leading citizens.

²⁴She makes clothes and belts, and sells them to merchants.

²⁵She is strong and respected and not afraid of the future.

²⁶She speaks with a gentle wisdom.

²⁷She is always busy and looks after her family's needs.

²⁸Her children show their appreciation, and her husband praises her.

z *Verse 31 in Hebrew is unclear.*

29 He says, "Many women are good wives, but you are the best of them all."

30 Charm is deceptive and beauty disappears, but a woman who honors the Lord should be praised.

31 Give her credit for all she does. She deserves the respect of everyone.

ECCLESIASTES

Introduction

The book of Ecclesiastes *contains the thoughts of "the Philosopher," a man who reflected deeply on how short and contradictory human life is, with its mysterious injustices and frustrations, and concluded that "life is useless." He could not understand the ways of God, who controls human destiny. Yet, in spite of this, he advised people to work hard, and to enjoy the gifts of God as much and as long as they could.*

Many of the Philosopher's thoughts appear negative and even depressing. But the fact that this book is in the Bible shows that biblical faith is broad enough to take into account such pessimism and doubt. Many have taken comfort in seeing themselves in the mirror of Ecclesiastes, and have discovered that the same Bible which reflects these thoughts also offers the hope in God that gives life its greater meaning.

Outline of Contents

Life Is Useless

1 These are the words of the Philosopher, David's son, who was king in Jerusalem.

2 It is useless, useless, said the Philosopher. Life is useless, all useless. 3 You spend your life working, laboring, and what do you have to show for it? 4 Generations come and generations go, but the world stays just the same. 5 The sun still rises, and it still goes down, going wearily back to where it must start all over again. 6 The wind blows south, the wind blows north — round and round and back again. 7 Every river flows into the sea, but the sea is not yet full. The water returns to where the rivers began, and starts all over again. 8 Everything leads to weariness — a weariness too great for words. Our eyes can never see enough to be satisfied; our ears can never hear enough. 9 What has happened before will happen again. What has been done before will be done again. There is nothing new in the whole world. 10 "Look," they say, "here is something new!" But no, it has all happened before, long before we were born. 11 No one remembers what has happened in the past, and no one in days to come will remember what happens between now and then.

The Philosopher's Experience

12 I, the Philosopher, have been king over Israel in Jerusalem. 13 I determined that I would examine and study all the things that are done in this world.

God has laid a miserable fate upon us. 14 I have seen everything done in this world, and I tell you, it is all useless. It is like chasing the wind. 15 You can't straighten out what is crooked; you can't count things that aren't there.

16 I told myself, "I have become a great man, far wiser than anyone who ruled Jerusalem before me. I know what wisdom and knowledge really are." 17 I was determined to learn the difference between knowledge and foolishness, wisdom and madness. But I found out that I might as well be chasing the wind. 18 The wiser you are, the more worries you have; the more you know, the more it hurts.

2 I decided to enjoy myself and find out what happiness is. But I found that this is useless, too. 2 I discovered that laughter is foolish, that pleasure does you no good. 3 Driven on by my desire for wisdom, I decided to cheer myself up with wine and have a good time. I thought that this might be the best way people can spend their short lives on earth.

⁴I accomplished great things. I built myself houses and planted vineyards. ⁵I planted gardens and orchards, with all kinds of fruit trees in them; ⁶I dug ponds to irrigate them. ⁷I bought many slaves, and there were slaves born in my household. I owned more livestock than anyone else who had ever lived in Jerusalem. ⁸I also piled up silver and gold from the royal treasuries of the lands I ruled. Men and women sang to entertain me, and I had all the women a man could want.

⁹Yes, I was great, greater than anyone else who had ever lived in Jerusalem, and my wisdom never failed me. ¹⁰Anything I wanted, I got. I did not deny myself any pleasure. I was proud of everything I had worked for, and all this was my reward. ¹¹Then I thought about all that I had done and how hard I had worked doing it, and I realized that it didn't mean a thing. It was like chasing the wind—of no use at all. ¹²After all, a king can only do what previous kings have done.

So I started thinking about what it meant to be wise or reckless or foolish. ¹³Oh, I know, "Wisdom is better than foolishness, just as light is better than darkness. ¹⁴The wise can see where they are going, and fools cannot." But I also know that the same fate is waiting for us all. ¹⁵I thought to myself, "What happens to fools is going to happen to me, too. So what have I gained from being so wise?" "Nothing," I answered, "not a thing." ¹⁶No one remembers the wise, and no one remembers fools. In days to come, we will all be forgotten. We must all die—wise and foolish alike. ¹⁷So life came to mean nothing to me, because everything in it had brought me nothing but trouble. It had all been useless; I had been chasing the wind.

¹⁸Nothing that I had worked for and earned meant a thing to me, because I knew that I would have to leave it to my successor, ¹⁹and he might be wise, or he might be foolish—who knows? Yet he will own everything I have worked for, everything my wisdom has earned for me in this world. It is all useless. ²⁰So I came to regret that I had worked so hard. ²¹You work for something with all your wisdom, knowledge, and skill, and then you have to leave it all to someone who hasn't had to work for it. It is use-

less, and it isn't right! ²²You work and worry your way through life, and what do you have to show for it? ²³As long as you live, everything you do brings nothing but worry and heartache. Even at night your mind can't rest. It is all useless.

²⁴The best thing we can do is eat and drink and enjoy what we have earned. And yet, I realized that even this comes from God. ²⁵How else could you have anything to eat or enjoy yourself at all? ²⁶God gives wisdom, knowledge, and happiness to those who please him, but he makes sinners work, earning and saving, so that what they get can be given to those who please him. It is all useless. It is like chasing the wind.

A Time for Everything

3 Everything that happens in this world happens at the time God chooses.

²He sets the time for birth and the
    time for death,
the time for planting and the time
    for pulling up,
³the time for killing and the time
    for healing,
the time for tearing down and the
    time for building.
⁴He sets the time for sorrow and
    the time for joy,
the time for mourning and the
    time for dancing,
⁵the time for making love and the
    time for not making love,
the time for kissing and the time
    for not kissing,
⁶He sets the time for finding and
    the time for losing,
the time for saving and the time
    for throwing away,
⁷the time for tearing and the time
    for mending,
the time for silence and the time
    for talk.
⁸He sets the time for love and the
    time for hate,
the time for war and the time for
    peace.

⁹What do we gain from all our work? ¹⁰I know the heavy burdens that God has laid on us. ¹¹He has set the right time for everything. He has given us a desire to know the future, but never gives us the satisfaction of fully understanding what he does. ¹²So I realized that all we

can do is be happy and do the best we can while we are still alive. 13 All of us should eat and drink and enjoy what we have worked for. It is God's gift.

14 I know that everything God does will last forever. You can't add anything to it or take anything away from it. And one thing God does is to make us stand in awe of him. 15 Whatever happens or can happen has already happened before. God makes the same thing happen again and again.

Injustice in the World

16 In addition, I have also noticed that in this world you find wickedness where justice and right ought to be. 17 I told myself, "God is going to judge the righteous and the evil alike, because every thing, every action, will happen at its own set time."a 18 I decided that God is testing us, to show us that we are no better than animals. 19 After all, the same fate awaits human beings and animals alike. One dies just like the other. They are the same kind of creature. A human being is no better off than an animal, because life has no meaning for either. 20 They are both going to the same place—the dust. They both came from it; they will both go back to it. 21 How can anyone be sure that the human spirit goes upward while an animal's spirit goes down into the ground? 22 So I realized then that the best thing we can do is enjoy what we have worked for. There is nothing else we can do.b There is no way for us to know what will happen after we die.

4 Then I looked again at all the injustice that goes on in this world. The oppressed were crying, and no one would help them. No one would help them, because their oppressors had power on their side. 2 I envy those who are dead and gone; they are better off than those who are still alive. 3 But better off than either are those who have never been born, who have never seen the injustice that goes on in this world.

4 I have also learned why people work so hard to succeed: it is because they envy the things their neighbors have. But it is useless. It is like chasing the wind. 5 They say that we would be fools to fold our hands and let ourselves starve to death. 6 Maybe so, but it is better to have only a little, with peace of mind, than be busy all the time with both hands, trying to catch the wind.

7 I have noticed something else in life that is useless. 8 Here is someone who lives alone. He has no son, no brother, yet he is always working, never satisfied with the wealth he has. For whom is he working so hard and denying himself any pleasure? This is useless, too—and a miserable way to live.

9 Two are better off than one, because together they can work more effectively. 10 If one of them falls down, the other can help him up. But if someone is alone and falls, it's just too bad, because there is no one to help him. 11 If it is cold, two can sleep together and stay warm, but how can you keep warm by yourself? 12 Two people can resist an attack that would defeat one person alone. A rope made of three cords is hard to break.

13-14 Someone may rise from poverty to become king of his country, or go from prison to the throne, but if in his old age he is too foolish to take advice, he is not as well off as a young man who is poor but intelligent. 15 I thought about all the people who live in this world, and I realized that somewhere among them there is a young man who will take the king's place. 16 There may be no limit to the number of people a king rules; when he is gone, no one will be grateful for what he has done. It is useless. It is like chasing the wind.

Don't Make Rash Promises

5 Be careful about going to the Temple. It is better to go there to learn than to offer sacrifices like foolish people who don't know right from wrong. 2 Think before you speak, and don't make any rash promises to God. He is in heaven and you are on earth, so don't say any more than you have to. 3 The more you worry, the more likely you are to have bad dreams, and the more you talk, the more likely you are to say something foolish. 4 So when you make a promise to God, keep it as quickly as possible. He has no use for a fool. Do what you promise to do. 5 Better not to promise at all than to make a promise

---

a *Probable text* its own set time; *Hebrew* its own set time there.   b what we have . . . do; *or* our work, because we are going to have to do it anyway.

and not keep it. 6 Don't let your own words lead you into sin, so that you have to tell God's priest that you didn't mean it. Why make God angry with you? Why let him destroy what you have worked for? 7 No matter how much you dream, how much useless work you do, or how much you talk, you must still stand in awe of God.

Life Is Useless

8 Don't be surprised when you see that the government oppresses the poor and denies them justice and their rights. Every official is protected by someone higher, and both are protected by still higher officials. 9 Even a king depends on the harvest.c

10 If you love money, you will never be satisfied; if you long to be rich, you will never get all you want. It is useless. 11 The richer you are, the more mouths you have to feed. All you gain is the knowledge that you are rich. 12 Workers may or may not have enough to eat, but at least they can get a good night's sleep. The rich, however, have so much that they stay awake worrying.

13 Here is a terrible thing that I have seen in this world: people save up their money for a time when they may need it,d 14 and then lose it all in some bad deal and end up with nothing left to pass on to their children. 15 We leave this world just as we entered it — with nothing. In spite of all our work there is nothing we can take with us. 16 It isn't right! We go just as we came. We labor, trying to catch the wind, and what do we get? 17 We get to live our lives in darkness and grief,e worried, angry, and sick.

18 Here is what I have found out: the best thing we can do is eat and drink and enjoy what we have worked for during the short life that God has given us; this is our fate. 19 If God gives us wealth and property and lets us enjoy them, we should be grateful and enjoy what we have worked for. It is a gift from God. 20 Since God has allowed us to be happy, we will not worry too much about how short life is.

6 I have noticed that in this world a serious injustice is done. 2 God will give us wealth, honor, and property, yes, everything we want, but then will not let us enjoy it. Some stranger will enjoy it instead. It is useless, and it just isn't right. 3 We may have a hundred children and live a long time, but no matter how long we live, if we do not get our share of happiness and do not receive a decent burial, then I say that a baby born dead is better off. 4 It does that baby no good to be born; it disappears into darkness, where it is forgotten. 5 It never sees the light of day or knows what life is like, but at least it has found rest — 6 more so than the man who never enjoys life, though he may live two thousand years. After all, both of them are going to the same place.

7 We do all our work just to get something to eat, but we never have enough. 8 How are the wise better off than fools? What good does it do the poor to know how to face life? 9 It is useless; it is like chasing the wind. It is better to be satisfied with what you have than to be always wanting something else.

10 Everything that happens was already determined long ago, and we all know that youf cannot argue with someone who is stronger than you. 11 The longer you argue, the more useless it is, and you are no better off. 12 How can anyone know what is best for us in this short, useless life of ours — a life that passes like a shadow? How can we know what will happen in the world after we die?

Thoughts about Life

7 A good reputation is better than expensive perfume; and the day you die is better than the day you are born.

2 It is better to go to a home where there is mourning than to one where there is a party, because the living should always remind themselves that death is waiting for us all.

3 Sorrow is better than laughter; it may sadden your face, but it sharpens your understanding.

4 Someone who is always thinking about happiness is a fool. A wise person thinks about death.

5It is better to have wise people reprimand you than to have stupid people sing your praises.

6When a fool laughs, it is like thorns crackling in a fire. It doesn't mean a thing.

7You may be wise, but if you cheat someone, you are acting like a fool. If you take a bribe, you ruin your character.

8The end of something is better than its beginning.

Patience is better than pride.

9Keep your temper under control; it is foolish to harbor a grudge.

10Never ask, "Oh, why were things so much better in the old days?" It's not an intelligent question.

11Everyone who lives ought to be wise; it is as good as receiving an inheritance 12and will give you as much security as money can. Wisdom keeps you safe—this is the advantage of knowledge.

13Think about what God has done. How can anyone straighten out what God has made crooked? 14When things are going well for you, be glad, and when trouble comes, just remember: God sends both happiness and trouble; you never know what is going to happen next.g

15My life has been useless, but in it I have seen everything. Some good people may die while others live on, even though they are evil. 16So don't be too good or too wise—why kill yourself? 17But don't be too wicked or too foolish, either—why die before you have to? 18Avoid both extremes. If you have reverence for God, you will be successful anyway.

19Wisdom does more for a person than ten rulers can do for a city.

20There is no one on earth who does what is right all the time and never makes a mistake.

21Don't pay attention to everything people say—you may hear your servant insulting you, 22and you know yourself that you have insulted other people many times.

23I used my wisdom to test all of this. I was determined to be wise, but it was beyond me. 24How can anyone discover what life means? It is too deep for us, too hard to understand. 25But I devoted myself to knowledge and study; I was determined to find wisdom and the answers to my questions, and to learn how wicked and foolish stupidity is.

26I found something more bitter than death—the woman who is like a trap. The love she offers you will catch you like a net, and her arms around you will hold you like a chain. A man who pleases God can get away, but she will catch the sinner. 27Yes, said the Philosopher, I found this out little by little while I was looking for answers. 28I have looked for other answers but have found none. I found one man in a thousand that I could respect, but not one woman. 29This is all that I have learned: God made us plain and simple, but we have made ourselves very complicated.

8 Only the wise know what things really mean. Wisdom makes them smile and makes their frowns disappear.

Obey the King

2Do what the king says,h and don't make any rash promises to God. 3The king can do anything he likes, so depart from his presence; don't stay in such a dangerous place. 4The king acts with authority, and no one can challenge what he does. 5As long as you obey his commands, you are safe, and a wise person knows how and when to do it. 6There is a right time and a right way to do everything, but we know so little! 7None of us knows what is going to happen, and there is no one to tell us. 8No one can keep from dying or put off the day of death. That is a battle we cannot escape; we cannot cheat our way out.

The Wicked and the Righteous

9I saw all this when I thought about the things that are done in this world, a world where some people have power and others have to suffer under them. 10Yes, I have seen the wicked buried and in their graves, but on the way back from the cemetery people praise them in the very city where they did their evil.i It is useless.

11Why do people commit crimes so readily? Because crime is not punished quickly enough. 12A sinner may commit

g you . . . next; or you cannot find fault with him.   h Some ancient translations Do what the king says; Hebrew unclear.   i Verse 10 in Hebrew is unclear.

a hundred crimes and still live. Oh yes, I know what they say: "If you obey God, everything will be all right, 13but it will not go well for the wicked. Their life is like a shadow and they will die young, because they do not obey God." 14But this is nonsense. Look at what happens in the world: sometimes the righteous get the punishment of the wicked, and the wicked get the reward of the righteous. I say it is useless.

15So I am convinced that we should enjoy ourselves, because the only pleasure we have in this life is eating and drinking and enjoying ourselves. We can at least do this as we labor during the life that God has given us in this world.

16Whenever I tried to become wise and learn what goes on in the world, I realized that you could stay awake night and day 17and never be able to understand what God is doing. However hard you try, you will never find out. The wise may claim to know, but they don't.

9 I thought long and hard about all this and saw that God controls the actions of wise and righteous people, even their love and their hate. No one knows anything about what lies ahead. 2It makes no difference.j The same fate comes to the righteous and the wicked, to the good and the bad,k to those who are religious and those who are not, to those who offer sacrifices and those who do not. A good person is no better off than a sinner; one who takes an oath is no better off than one who does not. 3One fate comes to all alike, and this is as wrong as anything that happens in this world. As long as people live, their minds are full of evil and madness, and suddenly they die. 4But anyone who is alive in the world of the living has some hope; a live dog is better off than a dead lion. 5Yes, the living know they are going to die, but the dead know nothing. They have no further reward; they are completely forgotten. 6Their loves, their hates, their passions, all died with them. They will never again take part in anything that happens in this world.

7Go ahead—eat your food and be happy; drink your wine and be cheerful.

It's all right with God. 8Always look happy and cheerful. 9Enjoy life with the one you love, as long as you live the useless life that God has given you in this world. Enjoy every useless day of it, because that is all you will get for all your trouble. 10Work hard at whatever you do, because there will be no action, no thought, no knowledge, no wisdom in the world of the dead—and that is where you are going.

11I realized another thing, that in this world fast runners do not always win the races, and the brave do not always win the battles. The wise do not always earn a living, intelligent people do not always get rich, and capable people do not always rise to high positions. Bad luck happens to everyone. 12You never know when your time is coming. Like birds suddenly caught in a trap, like fish caught in a net, we are trapped at some evil moment when we least expect it.

Thoughts on Wisdom and Foolishness

13There is something else I saw, a good example of how wisdom is regarded in this world. 14There was a little town without many people in it. A powerful king attacked it. He surrounded it and prepared to break through the walls. 15Someone lived there who was poor, but so clever that he could have saved the town. But no one thought about him.l 16I have always said that wisdom is better than strength, but no one thinks of the poor as wise or pays any attention to what they say. 17It is better to listen to the quiet words of someone wise than to the shouts of a ruler at a council of fools. 18Wisdom does more good than weapons, but one sinner can undo a lot of good.

10 Dead flies can make a whole bottle of perfume stink, and a little stupidity can cancel out the greatest wisdom.

2It is natural for the wise to do the right thing and for fools to do the wrong thing. 3Their stupidity will be evident even to strangers they meet along the way; they let everyone know that they are fools.

---

j hate. No one ... difference; or hate, but no one knows whether it is out of love or hate. 2It makes no difference what lies ahead of us.   k Some ancient translations and the bad; Hebrew does not have these words.   l he could have ... him; or he saved the town. But later on no one remembered him.

ECCLESIASTES

4 If your ruler becomes angry with you, do not hand in your resignation; serious wrongs may be pardoned if you keep calm.*m*

5 Here is an injustice I have seen in the world—an injustice caused by rulers. 6 Stupid people are given positions of authority while the rich are ignored. 7 I have seen slaves on horseback while noblemen go on foot like slaves.

8 If you dig a pit, you fall in it; if you break through a wall, a snake bites you. 9 If you work in a stone quarry, you get hurt by stones. If you split wood, you get hurt doing it. 10 If your ax is dull and you don't sharpen it, you have to work harder to use it. It is smarter to plan ahead. 11 Knowing how to charm a snake is of no use if you let the snake bite first. 12 What the wise say brings them honor, but fools are destroyed by their own words. 13 They start out with silly talk and end up with pure madness. 14 A fool talks on and on.

No one knows what is going to happen next, and no one can tell us what will happen after we die.

15 Only someone too stupid to find his way home would wear himself out with work.

16 A country is in trouble when its king is a youth and its leaders feast all night long. 17 But a country is fortunate to have a king who makes his own decisions and leaders who eat at the proper time, who control themselves and don't get drunk.

18 When you are too lazy to repair your roof, it will leak, and the house will fall in.

19 Feasting makes you happy and wine cheers you up, but you can't have either without money.

20 Don't criticize the king, even silently, and don't criticize the rich, even in the privacy of your bedroom. A bird might carry the message and tell them what you said.

What a Wise Person Does

11 Invest your money in foreign trade, and one of these days you will make a profit. 2 Put your investments in several places—many places even—because you never know what kind of bad luck you are going to have in this world.

3 No matter which direction a tree falls, it will lie where it fell. When the clouds are full, it rains. 4 If you wait until the wind and the weather are just right, you will never plant anything and never harvest anything. 5 God made everything, and you can no more understand what he does than you understand how new life begins in the womb of a pregnant woman. 6 Do your planting in the morning and in the evening, too. You never know whether it will all grow well or whether one planting will do better than the other.

7 It is good to be able to enjoy the pleasant light of day. 8 Be grateful for every year you live. No matter how long you live, remember that you will be dead much longer. There is nothing at all to look forward to.

Advice to Young People

9 Young people, enjoy your youth. Be happy while you are still young. Do what you want to do, and follow your heart's desire. But remember that God is going to judge you for whatever you do. 10 Don't let anything worry you or cause you pain. You aren't going to be young very long.

12 So remember your Creator*n* while you are still young, before those dismal days and years come when you will say, "I don't enjoy life." 2 That is when the light of the sun, the moon, and the stars will grow dim for you, and the rain clouds will never pass away. 3 Then your arms, that have protected you, will tremble, and your legs, now strong, will grow weak. Your teeth will be too few to chew your food, and your eyes too dim to see clearly. 4 Your ears will be deaf to the noise of the street. You will barely be able to hear the mill as it grinds or music as it plays, but even the song of a bird will wake you from sleep. 5 You will be afraid of high places, and walking will be dangerous. Your hair will turn white; you will hardly be able to drag yourself along, and all desire will be gone.

We are going to our final resting place, and then there will be mourning in the streets. 6 The silver chain will

m keep calm; or submit to him.   n The Hebrew expression for your Creator sounds like the Hebrew for your grave.

snap, and the golden lamp will fall and break; the rope at the well will break, and the water jar will be shattered. [7]Our bodies will return to the dust of the earth, and the breath of life will go back to God, who gave it to us.

[8]Useless, useless, said the Philosopher. It is all useless.

The Summing Up

[9]But because the Philosopher was wise, he kept on teaching the people what he knew. He studied proverbs and honestly tested their truth. [10]The Philosopher tried to find comforting words, but the words he wrote were honest.

[11]The sayings of the wise are like the sharp sticks that shepherds use to guide sheep, and collected proverbs are as lasting as firmly driven nails. They have been given by God, the one Shepherd of us all.

[12]My child, there is something else to watch out for. There is no end to the writing of books, and too much study will wear you out.

[13]After all this, there is only one thing to say: Have reverence for God, and obey his commands, because this is all that we were created for. [14]God is going to judge everything we do, whether good or bad, even things done in secret.

SONG OF SONGS

Introduction

The Song of Songs *is a series of love poems, for the most part in the form of songs addressed by a man to a woman, and by the woman to the man. In some translations, the book is called* The Song of Solomon, *because it is attributed to Solomon in the Hebrew title.*

These songs have often been interpreted by Jews as a picture of the relationship between God and his people, and by Christians as a picture of the relationship between Christ and the Church.

Outline of Contents

1 The most beautiful of songs, by Solomon.[a]

The First Song

The Woman

[2]Your lips cover me with kisses;
    your love is better than wine.
[3]There is a fragrance about you;
    the sound of your name
    recalls it.
No woman could keep from
    loving you.

[4]Take me with you, and we'll run
    away;
    be my king and take me to your
    room.
We will be happy together,
    drink deep, and lose ourselves in
    love.
No wonder all women love
    you!
[5]Women of Jerusalem, I am dark
    but[b] beautiful,
    dark as the desert tents of
    Kedar,

---

a by Solomon; *or* dedicated to Solomon, *or* about Solomon.   *b* but; *or* and.

but beautiful as the draperies in
Solomon's palace.
6 Don't look down on me because of
my color,
because the sun has tanned me.
My brothers were angry with me
and made me work in the
vineyard.
I had no time to care for myself.
7 Tell me, my love,
Where will you lead your flock
to graze?
Where will they rest from the
noonday sun?
Why should I need to look for you
among the flocks of the other
shepherds?c

The Man

8 Don't you know the place,
loveliest of women?
Go and follow the flock;
find pasture for your goats
near the tents of the shepherds.

9 You, my love, excite men
as a mare excites the stallions of
Pharaoh's chariots.
10 Your hair is beautiful upon your
cheeks
and falls along your neck like
jewels.
11 But we will make for you a chain
of gold
with ornaments of silver.

The Woman

12 My king was lying on his couch,
and my perfume filled the air
with fragrance.
13 My lover has the scent of myrrh
as he lies upon my breasts.
14 My lover is like the wild flowers
that bloom in the vineyards at
Engedi.

The Man

15 How beautiful you are, my love;
how your eyes shine with love!

The Woman

16 How handsome you are, my
dearest;
how you delight me!
The green grass will be our bed;

17   the cedars will be the beams of
our house,
and the cypress trees the ceiling.

2 I am only a wild flower in Sharon,
a lily in a mountain valley.

The Man

2 Like a lily among thorns
is my darling among women.

The Woman

3 Like an apple tree among the trees
of the forest,
so is my dearest compared to
other men.
I love to sit in its shadow,
and its fruit is sweet to my taste.
4 He brought me to his banquet hall
and raised the banner of love
over me.
5 Restore my strength with raisins
and refresh me with apples!
I am weak from passion.
6 His left hand is under my head,
and his right hand caresses me.
7 Promise me, women of Jerusalem;
swear by the swift deer and the
gazelles
that you will not interrupt our
love.

The Second Song

The Woman

8 I hear my lover's voice.
He comes running over the
mountains,
racing across the hills to me.
9 My lover is like a gazelle,
like a young stag.
There he stands beside the wall.
He looks in through the window
and glances through the lattice.
10 My lover speaks to me.

The Man

Come then, my love;
my darling, come with me.
11 The winter is over; the rains have
stopped;
12   in the countryside the flowers
are in bloom.
This is the time for singing;
the song of doves is heard in the
fields.
13 Figs are beginning to ripen;

c *Probable text* Why should I . . . shepherds; *Hebrew unclear.*

the air is fragrant with
  blossoming vines.
Come then, my love;
  my darling, come with me.
14 You are like a dove that hides
  in the crevice of a rock.
Let me see your lovely face
  and hear your enchanting voice.

15 Catch the foxes, the little foxes,
  before they ruin our vineyard in
  bloom.

The Woman

16 My lover is mine, and I am his.
He feeds his flock among the lilies
17   until the morning breezes blow
  and the darkness disappears.
Return, my darling, like a gazelle,
  like a stag on the mountains of
  Bether.*d*

3 Asleep on my bed, night after
  night
  I dreamed of the one I love;
  I was looking for him, but
  couldn't find him.
2 I went wandering through the city,
  through its streets and alleys.
I looked for the one I love.
  I looked, but couldn't find him.
3 The sentries patrolling the city
  saw me.
I asked them, "Have you found
  my lover?"
4 As soon as I left them, I
  found him.
I held him and wouldn't let him go
  until I took him to my mother's
  house,
  to the room where I was born.

5 Promise me, women of Jerusalem;
  swear by the swift deer and the
  gazelles
  that you will not interrupt our
  love.

The Third Song

The Woman

6 What is this coming from the
  desert like a column of smoke,
  fragrant with incense and
  myrrh,
  the incense sold by the traders?
7 Solomon is coming, carried on his
  throne;

sixty soldiers form the
  bodyguard,
  the finest soldiers in Israel.
8 All of them are skillful with the
  sword;
  they are battle-hardened
  veterans.
Each of them is armed with a
  sword,
  on guard against a night attack.
9 King Solomon is carried on a
  throne
  made of the finest wood.
10 Its posts are covered with silver;
  over it is cloth embroidered with
  gold.
Its cushions are covered with
  purple cloth,
  lovingly woven by the women of
  Jerusalem.
11 Women of Zion, come and see
  King Solomon.
He is wearing the crown that his
  mother placed on his head
  on his wedding day,
  on the day of his gladness
  and joy.

The Man

4 How beautiful you are, my love!
  How your eyes shine with
  love behind your veil.
Your hair dances like a flock of
  goats
  bounding down the hills of
  Gilead.
2 Your teeth are as white as sheep
  that have just been shorn and
  washed.
Not one of them is missing;
  they are all perfectly matched.
3 Your lips are like a scarlet ribbon;
  how lovely they are when you
  speak.
Your cheeks glow behind your
  veil.
4 Your neck is like the tower of
  David,
  round and smooth,*e*
  with a necklace like a thousand
  shields hung around it.
5 Your breasts are like gazelles,
  twin deer feeding among lilies.
6 I will stay on the hill of myrrh,
  the hill of incense,
  until the morning breezes blow

d mountains of Bether; *or* rugged mountains.   *e* round and smooth; *Hebrew unclear.*

and the darkness disappears.
⁷How beautiful you are, my love;
how perfect you are!

⁸Come with me from the Lebanon
Mountains, my bride;
come with me from Lebanon.
Come down from the top of Mount
Amana,
from Mount Senir and Mount
Hermon,
where the lions and leopards
live.
⁹The look in your eyes, my
sweetheart and bride,
and the necklace you are
wearing
have stolen my heart.
¹⁰Your love delights me,
my sweetheart and bride.
Your love is better than wine;
your perfume more fragrant
than any spice.
¹¹The taste of honey is on your lips,
my darling;
your tongue is milk and honey
for me.
Your clothing has all the fragrance
of Lebanon.

¹²My sweetheart, my bride, is a
secret garden,
a walled garden, a private
spring;
¹³ there the plants flourish.
They grow like an orchard of
pomegranate trees
and bear the finest fruits.
There is no lack of henna and
nard,
¹⁴ of saffron, calamus, and
cinnamon,
or incense of every kind.
Myrrh and aloes grow there
with all the most fragrant
perfumes.
¹⁵Fountains water the garden,
streams of flowing water,
brooks gushing down from the
Lebanon Mountains.

The Woman
¹⁶Wake up, North Wind.
South Wind, blow on my garden;
fill the air with fragrance.
Let my lover come to his garden
and eat the best of its fruits.

The Man

5 I have entered my garden,
my sweetheart, my bride.
I am gathering my spices and
myrrh;
I am eating my honey and
honeycomb;
I am drinking my wine and milk.

The Women
Eat, lovers, and drink
until you are drunk with love!

The Fourth Song

The Woman
²While I slept, my heart was
awake.
I dreamed my lover knocked at
the door.

The Man
Let me come in, my darling,
my sweetheart, my dove.
My head is wet with dew,
and my hair is damp from the
mist.

The Woman
³I have already undressed;
why should I get dressed again?
I have washed my feet;
why should I get them dirty
again?

⁴My lover put his hand to the door,
and I was thrilled that he was
near.
⁵ I was ready to let him come in.
My hands were covered with
myrrh,
my fingers with liquid myrrh,
as I grasped the handle of the
door.
⁶I opened the door for my lover,
but he had already gone.
How I wanted to hear his
voice!
I looked for him, but couldn't
find him;
I called to him, but heard no
answer.

⁷The sentries patrolling the city
found me;
they struck me and bruised me;
the guards at the city wall tore
off my cape.

8 Promise me, women of Jerusalem,
  that if you find my lover,
  you will tell him I am weak from
    passion.

The Women

9 Most beautiful of women,
  is your lover different from
    everyone else?
  What is there so wonderful
    about him
  that we should give you our
    promise?

The Woman

10 My lover is handsome and
    strong;
   he is one in ten thousand.
11 His face is bronzed and smooth;
   his hair is wavy,
     black as a raven.
12 His eyes are as beautiful as doves
     by a flowing brook,
   doves washed in milk and
     standing by the stream.*f*
13 His cheeks are as lovely as a
     garden
   that is full of herbs and
     spices.
   His lips are like lilies,
     wet with liquid myrrh.
14 His hands are well-formed,
     and he wears rings set with
       gems.
   His body is like smooth ivory,*g*
     with sapphires set in it.
15 His thighs are columns of
     alabaster
   set in sockets of gold.
   He is majestic, like the Lebanon
     Mountains
   with their towering cedars.
16 His mouth is sweet to kiss;
   everything about him
     enchants me.
   This is what my lover is like,
     women of Jerusalem.

The Women

6 Most beautiful of women,
    where has your lover gone?
  Tell us which way your lover
    went,
  so that we can help you
    find him.

The Woman

2 My lover has gone to his garden,
  where the balsam trees grow.
  He is feeding his flock in the
    garden
  and gathering lilies.
3 My lover is mine, and I am his;
  he feeds his flock among the
    lilies.

The Fifth Song

The Man

4 My love, you are as beautiful as
    Jerusalem,
  as lovely as the city of Tirzah,
  as breathtaking as these great
    cities.*h*
5 Turn your eyes away from me;
  they are holding me captive.
  Your hair dances like a flock of
    goats
  bounding down the hills of
    Gilead.
6 Your teeth are as white as a flock
    of sheep
  that have just been washed.
  Not one of them is missing;
  they are all perfectly matched.
7 Your cheeks glow behind your
    veil.
8 Let the king have sixty queens,
    eighty concubines,
  young women without number!
9 But I love only one,
  and she is as lovely as a dove.
  She is her mother's only daughter,
    her mother's favorite child.
  All women look at her and
    praise her;
  queens and concubines sing her
    praises.

10 Who is this whose glance is like
     the dawn?
   She is beautiful and bright,
     as dazzling as the sun or the
       moon.*i*
11 I have come down among the
     almond trees
   to see the young plants in the
     valley,
   to see the new leaves on the
     vines
   and the blossoms on the
     pomegranate trees.

---

f and standing by the stream; *Hebrew unclear.*
h as breathtaking as . . . cities; *Hebrew unclear.*
g like smooth ivory; *Hebrew unclear.*
i as dazzling as . . . moon; *Hebrew unclear.*

12 I am trembling; you have made me
    as eager for love
    as a chariot driver is for battle.[j]

The Women

13 Dance, dance,[k] girl of Shulam.
    Let us watch you as you dance.

The Woman

    Why do you want to watch me
    as I dance between the rows of
    onlookers?

The Man

7 What a magnificent young woman
    you are!
    How beautiful are your feet in
    sandals.
    The curve of your thighs
    is like the work of an artist.
2 A bowl is there,
    that never runs out of spiced
    wine.
    A sheaf of wheat is there,
    surrounded by lilies.
3 Your breasts are like twin deer,
    like two gazelles.
4 Your neck is like a tower of ivory.
    Your eyes are like the pools in the
    city of Heshbon,
    near the gate of that great city.
    Your nose is as lovely as the tower
    of Lebanon
    that stands guard at Damascus.
5 Your head is held high like Mount
    Carmel.
    Your braided hair shines like the
    finest satin;
    its beauty[l] could hold a king
    captive.

6 How pretty you are, how beautiful;
    how complete the delights of
    your love.
7 You are as graceful as a palm tree,
    and your breasts are clusters of
    dates.
8 I will climb the palm tree
    and pick its fruit.
    To me your breasts are like
    bunches of grapes,
    your breath like the fragrance of
    apples,

9   and your mouth like the finest
    wine.

The Woman

    Then let the wine flow straight to
    my lover,
    flowing over his lips and teeth.[m]
10 I belong to my lover, and he
    desires me.
11 Come, darling, let's go out to the
    countryside
    and spend the night in the
    villages.[n]
12 We will get up early and look at
    the vines
    to see whether they've started to
    grow,
    whether the blossoms are
    opening
    and the pomegranate trees are
    in bloom.
    There I will give you my love.
13 You can smell the scent of
    mandrakes,
    and all the pleasant fruits are
    near our door.
    Darling, I have kept for you
    the old delights and the new.

8 I wish that you were my brother,
    that my mother had nursed you
    at her breast.
    Then, if I met you in the street,
    I could kiss you and no one
    would mind.
2 I would take you to my mother's
    house,
    where you could teach me love.
    I would give you spiced wine,
    my pomegranate wine to drink.

3 Your left hand is under my head,
    and your right hand
    caresses me.

4 Promise me, women of Jerusalem,
    that you will not interrupt our
    love.

The Sixth Song

The Women

5 Who is this coming from the
    desert,
    arm in arm with her lover?

---

[j] *Verse 12 in Hebrew is unclear.*   [k] *Dance, dance; or* Come back, come back.
[l] beauty; *Hebrew unclear.*   [m] *Some ancient translations* lips and teeth; *Hebrew* lips of those
who sleep.   [n] villages; *or* fields.

The Woman

Under the apple tree I woke you,
in the place where you were
born.
6 Close your heart to every love but
mine;
hold no one in your arms
but me.
Love is as powerful as death;
passion is as strong as death
itself.
It bursts into flame
and burns like a raging fire.
7 Water cannot put it out;
no flood can drown it.
But if any tried to buy love with
their wealth,
contempt is all they would get.

The Woman's Brothers

8 We have a young sister,
and her breasts are still small.
What will we do for her
when a young man comes
courting?
9 If she is a wall,
we will build her a silver tower.
But if she is a gate,
we will protect her with panels
of cedar.

The Woman

10 I am a wall,
and my breasts are its towers.
My lover knows that with him
I find contentment and peace.

The Man

11 Solomon has a vineyard
in a place called Baal
Hamon.
There are farmers who rent it
from him;
each one pays a thousand silver
coins.
12 Solomon is welcome to his
thousand coins,
and the farmers to two hundred
as their share;
I have a vineyard of my own!

13 Let me hear your voice from the
garden, my love;
my companions are waiting to
hear you speak.

The Woman

14 Come to me, my lover, like a
gazelle,
like a young stag on the
mountains where spices grow.

SONG OF SONGS

THE PROPHETS

Prophets in Israel were persons who interpreted the actions of God in the events of history. They tried to keep alive the memory of the Exodus and re-interpret the meaning of the ancient faith for new times. The writings are called the major and minor prophets. The terms *major* and *minor* have to do with the size of the books, not the importance of the message.

In roughly chronological order, the prophets are listed below.

Amos preached in the northern kingdom of Israel. His message included an emphasis on social justice as an expression of the covenant.

Hosea described the relationship between God and Israel as a marriage.

Isaiah of Jerusalem was a counselor to kings. During this time there were two major crises—the war with Syria and the Assyrian threats. Isaiah saw those events as expressions of God's rule over the nations. The latter part of the book of Isaiah is a collection of great hymns and poems about the hope of restoration at the end of the Exile.

Micah preached in Jerusalem the same time as Isaiah. He cried out against the injustice practiced in both Samaria and Jerusalem but also lifted up the vision of a great day of peace and salvation, with Jerusalem as the center of God's Kingdom.

Zephaniah condemned the idolatry and injustice practiced by the kings of Judah.

Jeremiah had the longest career of any of the prophets. Over this long career, his message changed as world events changed and called forth new understandings of the work of God.

Joel lived in a time of a great locust plague, which he saw as the beginning of the judgment of God. His message is primarily a call to national repentance.

Habakkuk preached near the end of the seventh century B.C., a time when the Babylonians were on the march and overrunning all the little kingdoms of the Middle East.

Nahum was written at the time of the fall of Ninevah. His work includes a hymn about a God who is slow to anger but who will punish those who defy him.

Ezekiel was a priest taken to Babylon. Before 586, he preached a message of judgment and doom. After 586 he focused on hope and salvation.

Haggai and Zechariah preached in Jerusalem during the reign of Darius of Persia. Their message was that the Temple was to be rebuilt and the people were to come together into a purified and faithful community.

Malachi told of the coming day of the Lord, and accused the people and priests of indifference, doubt, and immorality.

Opinion is divided as to the chronological placement of the following prophets:

Obadiah is the shortest book in the Old Testament. It is a song of anger toward the Edomites for their part in the destruction of Jerusalem.

Jonah is the story of a prophet driven by God to proclaim salvation and mercy even to Israel's enemies.

Daniel was written to offer hope and consolation to Jews who were suffering persecution.

The Book of
ISAIAH

Introduction

The Book of Isaiah is named for a great prophet who lived in Jerusalem in the latter half of the eighth century B.C. This book may be divided into three principal parts:

1) Chapters 1–39 come from a time when Judah, the southern kingdom, was threatened by a powerful neighbor, Assyria. Isaiah saw that the real threat to the life of Judah was not simply the might of Assyria, but the nation's own sin and disobedience toward God, and their lack of trust in him. In vivid words and actions the prophet called the people and their leaders to a life of righteousness and justice, and warned that failure to listen to God would bring doom and destruction. Isaiah also foretold a time of world-wide peace and the coming of a descendant of David who would be the ideal king.

2) Chapters 40–55 speak to a time when many of the people of Judah were in exile in Babylon, crushed and without hope. The prophet proclaimed that God would set his people free and take them home to Jerusalem to begin a new life. A notable theme of these chapters is that God is the Lord of history, and his plan for his people includes their mission to all nations, who will be blessed through Israel. The passages about "the Servant of the Lord" are among the best known of the Old Testament.

3) Chapters 56–66 for the most part speak to a time when people were back in Jerusalem and needed reassurance that God was going to fulfill his promises to the nation. Concern is expressed for righteousness and justice, and also for Sabbath observance, sacrifice, and prayer. A notable passage is 61.1-2, words used by Jesus at the beginning of his ministry to express his calling.

Outline of Contents

---

1 This book contains the messages about Judah and Jerusalem which God revealed to Isaiah son of Amoz during the time when Uzziah, Jotham, Ahaz, and Hezekiah were kings of Judah.

God Reprimands His People

2 The LORD said, "Earth and sky, listen to what I am saying! The children I brought up have rebelled against me. 3 Cattle know who owns them, and donkeys know where their master feeds them. But that is more than my people Israel know. They don't understand at all."

4 You are doomed, you sinful nation, you corrupt and evil people! Your sins drag you down! You have rejected the LORD, the holy God of Israel, and have turned your backs on him. 5 Why do you keep on rebelling? Do you want to be punished even more? Israel, your head is already covered with wounds, and your heart and mind are sick. 6 From head to foot there is not a healthy spot on your body. You are covered with bruises and sores and open wounds. Your wounds have not been cleaned or bandaged. No medicine has been put on them.

7 Your country has been devastated, and your cities have been burned to the ground. While you look on, foreigners take over your land and bring everything to ruin. 8 Jerusalem alone is left, a city under siege — as defenseless as a guard's hut in a vineyard or a shed in a cucumber field. 9 If the LORD Almighty had not let some of the people survive, Jerusalem would have been totally destroyed, just as Sodom and Gomorrah were.

10 Jerusalem, your rulers and your people are like those of Sodom and Go-

morrah. Listen to what the Lord is saying to you. Pay attention to what our God is teaching you. [11]He says, "Do you think I want all these sacrifices you keep offering to me? I have had more than enough of the sheep you burn as sacrifices and of the fat of your fine animals. I am tired of the blood of bulls and sheep and goats. [12]Who asked you to bring me all this when you come to worship me? Who asked you to do all this tramping around in my Temple? [13]It's useless to bring your offerings. I am disgusted with the smell of the incense you burn. I cannot stand your New Moon Festivals, your Sabbaths, and your religious gatherings; they are all corrupted by your sins. [14]I hate your New Moon Festivals and holy days; they are a burden that I am tired of bearing.

[15]"When you lift your hands in prayer, I will not look at you. No matter how much you pray, I will not listen, for your hands are covered with blood. [16]Wash yourselves clean. Stop all this evil that I see you doing. Yes, stop doing evil [17]and learn to do right. See that justice is done—help those who are oppressed, give orphans their rights, and defend widows."

[18]The Lord says, "Now, let's settle the matter. You are stained red with sin, but I will wash you as clean as snow.[a] Although your stains are deep red, you will be as white as wool.[b] [19]If you will only obey me, you will eat the good things the land produces. [20]But if you defy me, you are doomed to die. I, the Lord, have spoken."

The Sinful City

[21]The city that once was faithful is behaving like a whore! At one time it was filled with righteous people, but now only murderers remain. [22]Jerusalem, you were once like silver, but now you are worthless; you were like good wine, but now you are only water. [23]Your leaders are rebels and friends of thieves; they are always accepting gifts and bribes. They never defend orphans in court or listen when widows present their case.

[24]So now, listen to what the Lord Almighty, Israel's powerful God, is saying: "I will take revenge on you, my enemies, and you will cause me no more trouble. [25]I will take action against you. I will purify you the way metal is refined, and will remove all your impurity. [26]I will give you rulers and advisers like those you had long ago. Then Jerusalem will be called the righteous, faithful city."

[27]Because the Lord is righteous, he will save Jerusalem and everyone there who repents. [28]But he will crush everyone who sins and rebels against him; he will kill everyone who forsakes him.

[29]You will be sorry that you worshiped trees and planted sacred gardens.[c] [30]You will wither like a dying oak, like a garden that no one waters. [31]Just as straw is set on fire by a spark, so powerful people will be destroyed by their own evil deeds, and no one will be able to stop the destruction.

Everlasting Peace
(Micah 4.1-3)

2 Here is the message which God gave to Isaiah son of Amoz about Judah and Jerusalem:

[2]In days to come
  the mountain where the Temple
    stands
  will be the highest one of all,
  towering above all the hills.
Many nations will come streaming
    to it,
[3] and their people will say,
"Let us go up the hill of the Lord,[d]
  to the Temple of Israel's God.
He will teach us what he wants us
    to do;
  we will walk in the paths he has
    chosen.
For the Lord's teaching comes
    from Jerusalem;
  from Zion he speaks to his
    people."

[4]He will settle disputes among
    great nations.
They will hammer their swords
    into plows

---

[a] sin, but . . . snow; *or* sin; do you think I will wash you as clean as snow?   [b] Although your . . . wool; *or* Your stains are deep red; do you think you will be as white as wool?
[c] SACRED GARDENS: *People believed that dedicating a garden to a fertility god would cause him to bless their crops.*   [d] HILL OF THE LORD: *Mount Zion, the hill in Jerusalem which formed part of the area on which the Temple was built.*

and their spears into pruning
knives.
Nations will never again go
to war,
never prepare for battle again.
5 Now, descendants of Jacob, let us
walk in the light which the LORD
gives us!

Arrogance Will Be Destroyed

6 O God, you have forsaken your people, the descendants of Jacob! The land
is full of magic practices from the East
and from Philistia.e The people follow
foreign customs. 7 Their land is full of silver and gold, and there is no end to their
treasures. Their land is full of horses,
and there is no end to their chariots.
8 Their land is full of idols, and they worship objects that they have made with
their own hands.

9 Everyone will be humiliated and disgraced. Do not forgive them, LORD!

10 They will hide in caves in the rocky
hills or dig holes in the ground to try to
escape from the LORD's anger and to hide
from his power and glory! 11 A day is
coming when human pride will be ended
and human arrogance destroyed. Then
the LORD alone will be exalted. 12 On that
day the LORD Almighty will humble
everyone who is powerful, everyone
who is proud and conceited. 13 He will
destroy the tall cedars of Lebanon and
all the oaks in the land of Bashan. 14 He
will level the high mountains and hills,
15 every high tower, and the walls of
every fortress. 16 He will sink even the
largest and most beautiful ships.
17-18 Human pride will be ended, and human arrogance will be destroyed. Idols
will completely disappear, and the LORD
alone will be exalted on that day.

19 People will hide in caves in the
rocky hills or dig holes in the ground to
try to escape from the LORD's anger and
to hide from his power and glory, when
he comes to shake the earth. 20 When
that day comes, they will throw away
the gold and silver idols they have made,
and abandon them to the moles and the
bats. 21 When the LORD comes to shake
the earth, people will hide in holes and
caves in the rocky hills to try to escape

from his anger and to hide from his
power and glory.

22 Put no more confidence in mortals.
What are they worth?

Chaos in Jerusalem

3 Now the Lord, the Almighty LORD, is
about to take away from Jerusalem
and Judah everything and everyone that
the people depend on. He is going to
take away their food and their water,
2 their heroes and their soldiers, their
judges and their prophets, their fortunetellers and their statesmen, 3 their
military and civilian leaders, their
politicians and everyone who uses
magic to control events. 4 The LORD will
let the people be governed by immature
boys. 5 Everyone will take advantage of
everyone else. Young people will not respect their elders, and worthless people
will not respect their superiors.

6 A time will come when the members
of a clan will choose one of their number
and say to him, "You at least have something to wear, so be our leader in this
time of trouble."

7 But he will answer, "Not me! I can't
help you. I don't have any food or
clothes either. Don't make me your
leader!"

8 Yes, Jerusalem is doomed! Judah is
collapsing! Everything they say and do
is against the LORD; they openly insult
God himself. 9 Their prejudices will be
held against them. They sin as openly as
the people of Sodom did. They are
doomed, and they have brought it on
themselves.

10 The righteous will be happy,f and
things will go well for them. They will
get to enjoy what they have worked for.
11 But evil people are doomed; what they
have done to others will now be done to
them.

12 Moneylenders oppress my people,
and their creditors cheat them.

My people, your leaders are misleading you, so that you do not know which
way to turn.

The LORD Judges His People

13 The LORD is ready to state his case;
he is ready to judge his people.g 14 The
LORD is bringing the elders and leaders

---

e Probable text The land ... Philistia; Hebrew unclear.   f Probable text The righteous will be
happy; Hebrew Say to the righteous.   g Some ancient translations his people; Hebrew the
peoples.

of his people to judgment. He makes this accusation: "You have plundered vineyards, and your houses are full of what you have taken from the poor. 15 You have no right to crush my people and take advantage of the poor. I, the Sovereign LORD Almighty, have spoken."

A Warning to the Women of Jerusalem

16 The LORD said, "Look how proud the women of Jerusalem are! They walk along with their noses in the air. They are always flirting. They take dainty little steps, and the bracelets on their ankles jingle. 17 But I will punish them—I will shave their heads and leave them bald."

18 A day is coming when the Lord will take away from the women of Jerusalem everything they are so proud of—the ornaments they wear on their ankles, on their heads, on their necks, 19 and on their wrists. He will take away their veils 20 and their hats; the magic charms they wear on their arms and at their waists; 21 the rings they wear on their fingers and in their noses; 22 all their fine robes, gowns, cloaks, and purses; 23 their revealing garments, their linen handkerchiefs, and the scarves and long veils they wear on their heads.

24 Instead of using perfumes, they will stink; instead of fine belts, they will wear coarse ropes; instead of having beautiful hair, they will be bald; instead of fine clothes, they will be dressed in rags; their beauty will be turned to shame!

25 The men of the city, yes, even the strongest men, will be killed in war. 26 The city gates will mourn and cry, and the city itself will be like a woman sitting on the ground, stripped naked.

4 When that time comes, seven women will grab hold of one man and say, "We can feed and clothe ourselves, but please let us say you are our husband, so that we won't have to endure the shame of being unmarried."

Jerusalem Will Be Restored

2 The time is coming when the LORD will make every plant and tree in the land grow large and beautiful. All the people of Israel who survive will take delight and pride in the crops that the land produces. 3 Everyone who is left in Jerusalem, whom God has chosen for survival, will be called holy. 4 By his power the Lord will judge and purify the nation and wash away the guilt of Jerusalem and the blood that has been shed there. 5 Then over Mount Zion and over all who are gathered there, the LORD will send a cloud in the daytime and smoke and a bright flame at night. God's glory will cover and protect the whole city. 6 His glory will shade the city from the heat of the day and make it a place of safety, sheltered from the rain and storm.

The Song of the Vineyard

5 Listen while I sing you this song,
   a song of my friend and his
      vineyard:
My friend had a vineyard
   on a very fertile hill.
2 He dug the soil and cleared it of
      stones;
   he planted the finest vines.
He built a tower to guard them,
   dug a pit for treading the grapes.
He waited for the grapes to ripen,
   but every grape was sour.

3 So now my friend says, "You people who live in Jerusalem and Judah, judge between my vineyard and me. 4 Is there anything I failed to do for it? Then why did it produce sour grapes and not the good grapes I expected?

5 "Here is what I am going to do to my vineyard: I will take away the hedge around it, break down the wall that protects it, and let wild animals eat it and trample it down. 6 I will let it be overgrown with weeds. I will not trim the vines or hoe the ground; instead, I will let briers and thorns cover it. I will even forbid the clouds to let rain fall on it."

7 Israel is the vineyard of the LORD
      Almighty;
   the people of Judah are the
      vines he planted.
He expected them to do what was
      good,
   but instead they committed
      murder.
He expected them to do what was
      right,
   but their victims cried out for
      justice.

The Evil That People Do

8 You are doomed! You buy more houses and fields to add to those you already have. Soon there will be no place for anyone else to live, and you alone will live in the land. 9 I have heard the LORD Almighty say, "All these big, fine houses will be empty ruins. 10 The grapevines growing on five acres of land will yield only five gallons of wine. Ten bushels of seed will produce only one bushel of grain."

11 You are doomed! You get up early in the morning to start drinking, and you spend long evenings getting drunk. 12 At your feasts you have harps and tambourines and flutes — and wine. But you don't understand what the LORD is doing, 13 and so you will be carried away as prisoners. Your leaders will starve to death, and the common people will die of thirst, 14 The world of the dead is hungry for them, and it opens its mouth wide. It gulps down the nobles of Jerusalem along with the noisy crowd of common people.

15 Everyone will be disgraced, and all who are proud will be humbled. 16 But the LORD Almighty shows his greatness by doing what is right, and he reveals his holiness by judging his people. 17 In the ruins of the cities lambs will eat grass and young goats will find pasture.h

18 You are doomed! You are unable to break free from your sins. 19 You say, "Let the LORD hurry up and do what he says he will, so that we can see it. Let Israel's holy God carry out his plans; let's see what he has in mind."

20 You are doomed! You call evil good and call good evil. You turn darkness into light and light into darkness. You make what is bitter sweet, and what is sweet you make bitter.

21 You are doomed! You think you are wise, so very clever.

22 You are doomed! Heroes of the wine bottle! Brave and fearless when it comes to mixing drinks! 23 But for just a bribe you let the guilty go free, and you keep the innocent from getting justice. 24 So now, just as straw and dry grass shrivel and burn in the fire, your roots will rot and your blossoms will dry up and blow away, because you have rejected what the LORD Almighty, Israel's holy God,

has taught us. 25 The LORD is angry with his people and has stretched out his hand to punish them. The mountains will shake, and the bodies of those who die will be left in the streets like rubbish. Yet even then the LORD's anger will not be ended, but his hand will still be stretched out to punish.

26 The LORD gives a signal to call for a distant nation.i He whistles for them to come from the ends of the earth. And here they come, swiftly, quickly! 27 None of them grow tired; none of them stumble. They never doze or sleep. Not a belt is loose; not a sandal strap is broken. 28 Their arrows are sharp, and their bows are ready to shoot. Their horses' hoofs are as hard as flint, and their chariot wheels turn like a whirlwind. 29 The soldiers roar like lions that have killed an animal and are carrying it off where no one can take it away from them.

30 When that day comes, they will roar over Israel as loudly as the sea. Look at this country! Darkness and distress! The light is swallowed by darkness.

God Calls Isaiah to Be a Prophet

6 In the year that King Uzziah died, I saw the Lord. He was sitting on his throne, high and exalted, and his robe filled the whole Temple. 2 Around him flaming creatures were standing, each of which had six wings. Each creature covered its face with two wings, and its body with two, and used the other two for flying. 3 They were calling out to each other:

"Holy, holy, holy!
The LORD Almighty is holy!
His glory fills the world."

4 The sound of their voices made the foundation of the Temple shake, and the Temple itself became filled with smoke.

5 I said, "There is no hope for me! I am doomed because every word that passes my lips is sinful, and I live among a people whose every word is sinful. And yet, with my own eyes I have seen the King, the LORD Almighty."

6 Then one of the creatures flew down to me, carrying a burning coal that he had taken from the altar with a pair of tongs. 7 He touched my lips with the burning coal and said, "This has touched

---

h Verse 17 in Hebrew is unclear.   i Probable text a distant nation; Hebrew distant nations.

your lips, and now your guilt is gone, and your sins are forgiven."

8 Then I heard the Lord say, "Whom shall I send? Who will be our messenger?"

I answered, "I will go! Send me!"

9 So he told me to go and give the people this message: "No matter how much you listen, you will not understand. No matter how much you look, you will not know what is happening." 10 Then he said to me, "Make the minds of these people dull, their ears deaf, and their eyes blind, so that they cannot see or hear or understand. If they did, they might turn to me and be healed."

11 I asked, "How long will it be like this, Lord?"

He answered, "Until the cities are ruined and empty—until the houses are uninhabited—until the land itself is a desolate wasteland. 12 I will send the people far away and make the whole land desolate. 13 Even if one person out of ten remains in the land, he too will be destroyed; he will be like the stump of an oak tree that has been cut down."

(The stump represents a new beginning for God's people.)

A Message for King Ahaz

7 When King Ahaz, the son of Jotham and grandson of Uzziah, ruled Judah, war broke out. Rezin, king of Syria, and Pekah son of Remaliah, king of Israel, attacked Jerusalem, but were unable to capture it.

2 When word reached the king of Judah that the armies of Syria were already in the territory of Israel, he and all his people were so terrified that they trembled like trees shaking in the wind.

3 The Lord said to Isaiah, "Take your son Shear Jashub,[j] and go to meet King Ahaz. You will find him on the road where the cloth makers work, at the end of the ditch that brings water from the upper pool. 4 Tell him to keep alert, to stay calm, and not to be frightened or disturbed. The anger of King Rezin and his Syrians and of King Pekah is no more dangerous than the smoke from

two smoldering sticks of wood. 5 Syria, together with Israel and its king, has made a plot. 6 They intend to invade Judah, terrify the people into joining their side, and then put Tabeel's son on the throne.

7 "But I, the Lord, declare that this will never happen. 8 Why? Because Syria is no stronger than Damascus, its capital city, and Damascus is no stronger than King Rezin. As for Israel, within sixty-five years it will be too shattered to survive as a nation. 9 Israel is no stronger than Samaria, its capital city, and Samaria is no stronger than King Pekah.

"If your faith is not enduring, you will not endure."

The Sign of Immanuel

10 The Lord sent another message to Ahaz: 11 "Ask the Lord your God to give you a sign. It can be from deep in the world of the dead or from high up in heaven."

12 Ahaz answered, "I will not ask for a sign. I refuse to put the Lord to the test."

13 To that Isaiah replied, "Listen, now, descendants of King David. It's bad enough for you to wear out the patience of people—do you have to wear out God's patience too? 14 Well then, the Lord himself will give you a sign: a young woman[k] who is pregnant will have a son and will name him 'Immanuel.'[l] 15 By the time he is old enough to make his own decisions, people will be drinking milk and eating honey.[m] 16 Even before that time comes, the lands of those two kings who terrify you will be deserted.

17 "The Lord is going to bring on you, on your people, and on the whole royal family, days of trouble worse than any that have come since the kingdom of Israel separated from Judah—he is going to bring the king of Assyria.

18 "When that time comes, the Lord will whistle as a signal for the Egyptians to come like flies from the farthest branches of the Nile, and for the Assyrians to come from their land like bees. 19 They will swarm in the rugged valleys

---

[j] SHEAR JASHUB: This name in Hebrew means "A few will come back" (see 10.20-22).
[k] YOUNG WOMAN: The Hebrew word here translated "young woman" is not the specific term for "virgin," but refers to any young woman of marriageable age. The use of "virgin" in Mt 1.23 reflects a Greek translation of the Old Testament, made some 500 years after Isaiah.
[l] IMMANUEL: This name in Hebrew means "God is with us."   [m] MILK AND HONEY: These foods were associated with the earlier days of Israel's history.

and in the caves in the rocks, and they will cover every thorn bush and every pasture.

20 "When that time comes, the Lord will hire a barber from across the Euphrates — the emperor of Assyria! — and he will shave off your beards and the hair on your heads and your bodies.

21 "When that time comes, even if a farmer has been able to save only one young cow and two goats, 22 they will give so much milk that he will have all he needs. Yes, the few survivors left in the land will have milk and honey to eat.

23 "When that time comes, the fine vineyards, each with a thousand vines and each worth a thousand pieces of silver, will be overgrown with thorn bushes and briers. 24 People will go hunting there with bows and arrows. Yes, the whole country will be full of briers and thorn bushes. 25 All the hills where crops were once planted will be so overgrown with thorns that no one will go there. It will be a place where cattle and sheep graze."

Isaiah's Son as a Sign to the People

8 The Lord said to me, "Take a large piece of writing material and write on it in large letters:n 'Quick Loot, Fast Plunder.' 2 Get two reliable men, the priest Uriah and Zechariah son of Jeberechiah, to serve as witnesses."

3 Some time later my wife became pregnant. When our son was born, the Lord said to me, "Name him 'Quick-Loot-Fast-Plunder.' 4 Before the boy is old enough to say 'Mamma' and 'Daddy,' all the wealth of Damascus and all the loot of Samaria will be carried off by the king of Assyria."

The Emperor of Assyria Is Coming

5 The Lord spoke to me again. 6 He said, "Because these people have rejected the quiet waters of Shiloah Brooko and tremblep before King Rezin and King Pekah, 7 I, the Lord, will bring the emperor of Assyria and all his forces to attack Judah. They will advance like the flood waters of the Euphrates River, overflowing all its banks. 8 They will sweep through Judah in a flood, rising shoulder high and covering everything."

God is with us! His outspread wings protect the land.q

9 Gather together in fear, you nations! Listen, you distant parts of the earth. Get ready to fight, but be afraid! Yes, get ready, but be afraid! 10 Make your plans! But they will never succeed. Talk all you want to! But it is all useless, because God is with us.

The Lord Warns the Prophet

11 With his great power the Lord warned me not to follow the road which the people were following. He said, 12 "Do not join in the schemes of the people and do not be afraid of the things that they fear. 13 Remember that I, the Lord Almighty, am holy; I am the one you must fear. 14 Because of my awesome holiness I am like a stone that people stumble over; I am like a trap that will catch the people of the kingdoms of Judah and Israel and the people of Jerusalem. 15 Many will stumble; they will fall and be crushed. They will be caught in a trap."

Warning against Consulting the Dead

16 You, my disciples, are to guard and preserve the messages that God has given me. 17 The Lord has hidden himself from his people, but I trust him and place my hope in him.

18 Here I am with the children the Lord has given me. The Lord Almighty, whose throne is on Mount Zion, has sent us as living messages to the people of Israel.

19 But people will tell you to ask for messages from fortunetellers and mediums, who chirp and mutter. They will say, "After all, people should ask for messages from the spirits and consult the dead on behalf of the living."

20 You are to answer them, "Listen to what the Lord is teaching you! Don't listen to mediums — what they tell you cannot keep trouble away."r

ISAIAH

---

n large letters; or letters that everyone can read.
the large spring on the eastern side of Jerusalem.
q everything." God . . . land; or everything. They will spread out over the land. God be with us!"
r Verse 20 in Hebrew is unclear.
o SHILOAH BROOK: A stream which flowed from
p Probable text tremble; Hebrew rejoice.

A Time of Trouble

21 The people will wander through the land, discouraged and hungry. In their hunger and their anger they will curse their king and their God. They may look up to the sky 22 or stare at the ground, but they will see nothing but trouble and darkness, terrifying darkness into which 9 they are being driven. 1 There will be no way for them to escape from this time of trouble.

The Future King

The land of the tribes of Zebulun and Naphtali was once disgraced, but the future will bring honor to this region, from the Mediterranean eastward to the land on the other side of the Jordan, and even to Galilee itself, where the foreigners live.

2 The people who walked in darkness
  have seen a great light.
They lived in a land of shadows,
  but now light is shining on them.
3 You have given them great joy,s
  Lord;
  you have made them happy.
They rejoice in what you have done,
  as people rejoice when they harvest grain
  or when they divide captured wealth.
4 For you have broken the yoke that burdened them
  and the rod that beat their shoulders.
You have defeated the nation
  that oppressed and exploited your people,
  just as you defeated the army of Midian long ago.
5 The boots of the invading army
  and all their bloodstained clothing
  will be destroyed by fire.
6 A child is born to us!
  A son is given to us!
  And he will be our ruler.
He will be called, "Wonderfult Counselor,"
  "Mighty God," "Eternal Father,"
"Prince of Peace."
7 His royal power will continue to grow;
  his kingdom will always be at peace.
He will rule as King David's successor,
  basing his power on right and justice,
  from now until the end of time.
The Lord Almighty is determined to do all this.

The Lord Will Punish Israel

8 The Lord has pronounced judgment on the kingdom of Israel, on the descendants of Jacob. 9 All the people of Israel, everyone who lives in the city of Samaria, will know that he has done this. Now they are proud and arrogant. They say, 10 "The brick buildings have fallen down, but we will replace them with stone buildings. The beams of sycamore wood have been cut down, but we will replace them with the finest cedar." 11 The Lord has stirred up their enemiesu to attack them. 12 Syria on the east and Philistia on the west have opened their mouths to devour Israel. Yet even so the Lord's anger is not ended; his hand is still stretched out to punish.

13 The people of Israel have not repented; even though the Lord Almighty has punished them, they have not returned to him. 14 In a single day the Lord will punish Israel's leaders and its people; he will cut them off, head and tail. 15 The old and honorable men are the head — and the tail is the prophets whose teachings are lies! 16 Those who lead these people have misled them and totally confused them. 17 And so the Lord will not let any of the young men escape, and he will not show pity on any of the widows and orphans, because all the people are godless and wicked and everything they say is evil. Yet even so the Lord's anger will not be ended, but his hand will still be stretched out to punish.

18 The wickedness of the people burns like a fire that destroys thorn bushes and thistles. It burns like a forest fire that sends up columns of smoke. 19 Because

s Probable text You have given them great joy; Hebrew You have increased the nation.
t Wonderful; or Wise.   u Probable text their enemies; Hebrew the enemies of Rezin.

the LORD Almighty is angry, his punishment burns like a fire throughout the land and destroys the people, and it is each of us for ourselves. 20 Everywhere in the country people snatch and eat any bit of food they can find, but their hunger is never satisfied. They even eat their own children! 21 The people of Manasseh and the people of Ephraim attack each other, and together they attack Judah. Yet even so the LORD's anger is not ended; his hand is still stretched out to punish.

10 You are doomed! You make unjust laws that oppress my people. 2 That is how you keep the poor from having their rights and from getting justice. That is how you take the property that belongs to widows and orphans. 3 What will you do when God punishes you? What will you do when he brings disaster on you from a distant country? Where will you run to find help? Where will you hide your wealth? 4 You will be killed in battle or dragged off as prisoners. Yet even so the LORD's anger will not be ended; his hand will still be stretched out to punish.

The Emperor of Assyria as the Instrument of God

5 The LORD said, "Assyria! I use Assyria like a club to punish those with whom I am angry. 6 I sent Assyria to attack a godless nation, people who have made me angry. I sent them to loot and steal and trample the people like dirt in the streets."

7 But the Assyrian emperor has his own violent plans in mind. He is determined to destroy many nations. 8 He boasts, "Every one of my commanders is a king! 9 I conquered the cities of Calno and Carchemish, the cities of Hamath and Arpad. I conquered Samaria and Damascus. 10 I reached out to punish those kingdoms that worship idols, idols more numerous than those of Jerusalem and Samaria. 11 I have destroyed Samaria and all its idols, and I will do the same to Jerusalem and the images that are worshiped there."

12 But the Lord says, "When I finish what I am doing on Mount Zion and in Jerusalem, I will punish the emperor of Assyria for all his boasting and all his pride."

13 The emperor of Assyria boasts, "I have done it all myself. I am strong and wise and clever. I wiped out the boundaries between nations and took the supplies they had stored. Like a bull I have trampled the people who live there. 14 The nations of the world were like a bird's nest, and I gathered their wealth as easily as gathering eggs. Not a wing fluttered to scare me off; no beak opened to scream at me!"

15 But the LORD says, "Can an ax claim to be greater than the one who uses it? Is a saw more important than the one who saws with it? A club doesn't lift up a person; a person lifts up a club."

16 The LORD Almighty is going to send disease to punish those who are now well-fed. In their bodies there will be a fire that burns and burns. 17 God, the light of Israel, will become a fire. Israel's holy God will become a flame, which in a single day will burn up everything, even the thorns and thistles. 18 The rich forests and farmlands will be totally destroyed, in the same way that a fatal sickness destroys someone. 19 There will be so few trees left that even a child will be able to count them.

A Few Will Come Back

20 A time is coming when the people of Israel who have survived will not rely any more on the nation that almost destroyed them. They will truly put their trust in the LORD, Israel's holy God. 21 A few of the people of Israel will come back to their mighty God. 22 Even though now there are as many people of Israel as there are grains of sand by the sea, only a few will come back. Destruction is in store for the people, and it is fully deserved. 23 Yes, throughout the whole country the Sovereign LORD Almighty will bring destruction, as he said he would.

The LORD Will Punish Assyria

24 The Sovereign LORD Almighty says to his people who live in Zion, "Do not be afraid of the Assyrians, even though they oppress you as the Egyptians used to do. 25 In only a little while I will finish punishing you, and then I will destroy them. 26 I, the LORD Almighty, will beat them with my whip as I did the people of Midian at Oreb Rock. I will punish Assyria as I punished Egypt. 27 When that

ISAIAH

time comes, I will free you from the power of Assyria, and their yoke will no longer be a burden on your shoulders."v

The Invader Attacks

28 The enemy army has captured the city of Ai!w They have passed through Migron! They left their supplies at Michmash! 29 They have crossed the pass and are spending the night at Geba! The people in the town of Ramah are terrified, and the people in King Saul's hometown of Gibeah have run away. 30 Shout, people of Gallim! Listen, people of Laishah! Answer, people of Anathoth! 31 The people of Madmenah and Gebim are running for their lives. 32 Today the enemy are in the town of Nob, and there they are shaking their fists at Mount Zion, at the city of Jerusalem.

33 The LORD Almighty will bring them crashing down like branches cut off a tree. The proudest and highest of them will be cut down and humiliated. 34 The LORD will cut them down as trees in the heart of the forest are cut down with an ax, as even the finest trees of Lebanon fall!

The Peaceful Kingdom

11 The royal line of David is like a tree that has been cut down; but just as new branches sprout from a stump, so a new king will arise from among David's descendants.

2 The spirit of the LORD will give him
   wisdom
and the knowledge and skill to
   rule his people.
He will know the LORD's will and
   honor him,
3 and find pleasure in
   obeying him.
He will not judge by appearance
   or hearsay;
4 he will judge the poor fairly
   and defend the rights of the
   helpless.
At his command the people will be
   punished,
   and evil persons will die.

5 He will rule his people with justice
   and integrity.

6 Wolves and sheep will live
   together in peace,
and leopards will lie down with
   young goats.
Calves and lion cubs will feedx
   together,
and little children will take care
   of them.
7 Cows and bears will eat together,
   and their calves and cubs will lie
   down in peace.
Lions will eat straw as cattle do.
8 Even a baby will not be harmed
   if it plays near a poisonous
   snake.
9 On Zion, God's sacred hill,
   there will be nothing harmful or
   evil.
The land will be as full of
   knowledge of the LORD
as the seas are full of water.

The Exiled People Will Return

10 A day is coming when the new king from the royal line of David will be a symbol to the nations. They will gather in his royal city and give him honor. 11 When that day comes, the Lord will once again use his power and bring back home those of his people who are left in Assyria and Egypt, in the lands of Pathros, Ethiopia,y Elam, Babylonia, and Hamath, and in the coastlands and on the islands of the sea. 12 The Lord will raise a signal flag to show the nations that he is gathering together again the scattered people of Israel and Judah and bringing them back from the four corners of the earth. 13 The kingdom of Israel will not be jealous of Judah any more, and Judah will not be the enemy of Israel. 14 Together they will attack the Philistines on the west and plunder the people who live to the east. They will conquer the people of Edom and Moab, and the people of Ammon will obey them. 15 The LORD will dry up the Gulf of Suez, and he will bring a hot wind to dry up the Euphrates, leaving only seven

---

v Hebrew has three additional words, the meaning of which is unclear.   w Ai: This and the other places mentioned in verses 28-32 were located near Jerusalem, along the way by which an invader would come to attack from the north.   x Some ancient translations will feed; Hebrew and well-fed cattle.   y Hebrew Cush: Cush is the ancient name of the extensive territory south of the First Cataract of the Nile River. This region was called Ethiopia in Graeco-Roman times, and included within its borders most of modern Sudan and some of present-day Ethiopia (Abyssinia).

tiny streams, so that anyone can walk across. 16 There will be a highway out of Assyria for those of his people Israel who have survived there, just as there was for their ancestors when they left Egypt.

Hymn of Thanksgiving

12 A day is coming when people will sing,
"I praise you, LORD! You were
angry with me,
but now you comfort me and
are angry no longer.
2 God is my savior;
I will trust him and not be
afraid.
The LORD gives me power and
strength;
he is my savior.
3 As fresh water brings joy to the
thirsty,
so God's people rejoice when
he saves them."

4 A day is coming when people will
sing,
"Give thanks to the LORD! Call for
him to help you!
Tell all the nations what he has
done!
Tell them how great he is!
5 Sing to the LORD because of the
great things he has done.
Let the whole world hear the
news.
6 Let everyone who lives in Zion
shout and sing!
Israel's holy God is great,
and he lives among his people."

God Will Punish Babylon

13 This is a message about Babylon, which Isaiah son of Amoz received from God.
2 On the top of a barren hill raise the battle flag! Shout to the soldiers and raise your arm as the signal for them to attack the gates of the proud city. 3 The LORD has called out his proud and confident soldiers to fight a holy war and punish those he is angry with.

4 Listen to the noise on the mountains — the sound of a great crowd of people, the sound of nations and kingdoms gathering. The LORD of Armies is preparing his troops for battle. 5 They are coming from far-off countries at the ends of the earth. In his anger the LORD is coming to devastate the whole country.

6 Howl in pain! The day of the LORD is near, the day when the Almighty brings destruction. 7 Everyone's hands will hang limp, and everyone's courage will fail. 8 They will all be terrified and overcome with pain, like the pain of a woman in labor. They will look at each other in fear, and their faces will burn with shame. 9 The day of the LORD is coming — that cruel day of his fierce anger and fury. The earth will be made a wilderness, and every sinner will be destroyed. 10 Every star and every constellation will stop shining, the sun will be dark when it rises, and the moon will give no light.

11 The LORD says, "I will bring disaster on the earth and punish all wicked people for their sins. I will humble everyone who is proud and punish everyone who is arrogant and cruel. 12 Those who survive will be scarcer than gold. 13 I will make the heavens tremble, and the earth will be shaken out of its place on that day when I, the LORD Almighty, show my anger.

14 "The foreigners living in Babylon will run away to their homelands, scattering like deer escaping from hunters, like sheep without a shepherd. 15 Anyone who is caught will be stabbed to death. 16 While they look on helplessly, their babies will be battered to death, their houses will be looted, and their wives will be raped."

17 The LORD says, "I am stirring up the Medes z to attack Babylon. They care nothing for silver and are not tempted by gold. 18 With their bows and arrows they will kill the young men. They will show no mercy to babies and take no pity on children. 19 Babylonia is the most beautiful kingdom of all; it is the pride of its people. But I, the LORD, will overthrow Babylon as I did Sodom and Gomorrah! 20 No one will ever live there again. No wandering Arab will ever pitch a tent there, and no shepherd will ever pasture a flock there. 21 It will be a place where desert animals live and where owls build their nests. Ostriches will live there, and wild goats will prance through the ruins.

z MEDES: *People of a nation northeast of Babylonia, which became part of the Persian Empire.*

22 The towers and palaces will echo with the cries of hyenas and jackals. Babylon's time has come! Her days are almost over."

The Return from Exile

14 The LORD will once again be merciful to his people Israel and choose them as his own. He will let them live in their own land again, and foreigners will come and live there with them. 2 Many nations will help the people of Israel return to the land which the LORD gave them, and there the nations will serve Israel as slaves. Those who once captured Israel will now be captured by Israel, and the people of Israel will rule over those who once oppressed them.

The King of Babylon in the World of the Dead

3 The LORD will give the people of Israel relief from their pain and suffering and from the hard work they were forced to do. 4 When he does this, they are to mock the king of Babylon and say:

"The cruel king has fallen! He will never oppress anyone again! 5 The LORD has ended the power of the evil rulers 6 who angrily oppressed the peoples and never stopped persecuting the nations they had conquered. 7 Now at last the whole world enjoys rest and peace, and everyone sings for joy. 8 The cypress trees and the cedars of Lebanon rejoice over the fallen king, because there is no one to cut them down, now that he is gone!

9 "The world of the dead is getting ready to welcome the king of Babylon. The ghosts of those who were powerful on earth are stirring about. The ghosts of kings are rising from their thrones. 10 They all call out to him, 'Now you are as weak as we are! You are one of us! 11 You used to be honored with the music of harps, but now here you are in the world of the dead. You lie on a bed of maggots and are covered with a blanket of worms.' "

12 King of Babylon, bright morning star, you have fallen from heaven! In the past you conquered nations, but now you have been thrown to the ground. 13 You were determined to climb up to heaven and to place your throne above the highest stars. You thought you would sit like a king on that mountain in the north where the gods assemble. 14 You said you would climb to the tops of the clouds and be like the Almighty. 15 But instead, you have been brought down to the deepest part of the world of the dead.

16 The dead will stare and gape at you. They will ask, "Is this the man who shook the earth and made kingdoms tremble? 17 Is this the man who destroyed cities and turned the world into a desert? Is this the man who never freed his prisoners or let them go home?"

18 All the kings of the earth lie in their magnificent tombs, 19 but you have no tomb, and your corpse is thrown out to rot. It is covered by the bodies of soldiers killed in battle, thrown with them into a rocky pit, and trampled down. 20 Because you ruined your country and killed your own people, you will not be buried like other kings. None of your evil family will survive. 21 Let the slaughter begin! The sons of this king will die because of their ancestors' sins. None of them will ever rule the earth or cover it with cities.

God Will Destroy Babylon

22 The LORD Almighty says, "I will attack Babylon and bring it to ruin. I will leave nothing — no children, no survivors at all. I, the LORD, have spoken. 23 I will turn Babylon into a marsh, and owls will live there. I will sweep Babylon with a broom that will sweep everything away. I, the LORD Almighty, have spoken."

God Will Destroy the Assyrians

24 The LORD Almighty has sworn an oath: "What I have planned will happen. What I have determined to do will be done. 25 I will destroy the Assyrians in my land of Israel and trample them on my mountains. I will free my people from the Assyrian yoke and from the burdens they have had to bear. 26 This is my plan for the world, and my arm is stretched out to punish the nations." 27 The LORD Almighty is determined to do this; he has stretched out his arm to punish, and no one can stop him.

God Will Destroy the Philistines

28 This is a message that was proclaimed in the year that King Ahaz died.

29 People of Philistia, the rod that beat you is broken, but you have no reason to be glad. When one snake dies, a worse one comes in its place. A snake's egg hatches a flying dragon. 30 The LORD will be a shepherd to the poor of his people and will let them live in safety. But he will send a terrible famine on you Philistines, and it will not leave any of you alive.

31 Howl and cry for help, all you Philistine cities! Be terrified, all of you! A cloud of dust is coming from the north — it is an army with no cowards in its ranks.

32 How shall we answer the messengers that come to us from Philistia? We will tell them that the LORD has established Zion and that his suffering people will find safety there.

God Will Destroy Moab

15 This is a message about Moab. The cities of Ar and Kir are destroyed in a single night, and silence covers the land of Moab. 2 The people of Dibon*a* climb the hill to weep at the shrine. The people of Moab wail in grief over the cities of Nebo and Medeba; they have shaved their heads and their beards in grief. 3 The people in the streets are dressed in sackcloth; in the city squares and on the rooftops people mourn and cry. 4 The people of Heshbon and Elealeh cry out, and their cry can be heard as far away as Jahaz. Even the soldiers tremble; their courage is gone. 5 My heart cries out for Moab! The people have fled to the town of Zoar, and to Eglath Shelishiyah. Some climb the road to Luhith, weeping as they go; some escape to Horonaim, grieving loudly. 6 Nimrim Brook is dry, the grass beside it has withered, and nothing green is left. 7 The people go across the Valley of Willows, trying to escape with all their possessions. 8 Everywhere at Moab's borders the sound of crying is heard. It is heard at the towns of Eglaim and Beerelim 9 At the town of Dibon the river is red with blood, and God has something even worse in store for the people there. Yes, there will be a bloody slaughter of everyone left in Moab.

Moab's Hopeless Situation

16 From the city of Sela in the desert the people of Moab send a lamb as a present to the one who rules in Jerusalem. 2 They wait on the banks of the Arnon River and move aimlessly back and forth, like birds driven from their nest.

3 They say to the people of Judah, "Tell us what to do. Protect us like a tree that casts a cool shadow in the heat of noon, and let us rest in your shade. We are refugees; hide us where no one can find us. 4 Let us stay in your land. Protect us from those who want to destroy us."

(Oppression and destruction will end, and those who are devastating the country will be gone. 5 Then one of David's descendants will be king, and he will rule the people with faithfulness and love. He will be quick to do what is right, and he will see that justice is done.)

6 The people of Judah say, "We have heard how proud the people of Moab are. We know that they are arrogant and conceited, but their boasts are empty."

7 The people of Moab will weep because of the troubles they suffer. They will all weep when they remember the fine food they used to eat in the city of Kir Heres. They will be driven to despair. 8 The farms near Heshbon and the vineyards of Sibmah are destroyed — those vineyards whose wine used to make the rulers of the nations drunk. At one time the vines spread as far as the city of Jazer, and eastward into the desert, and westward to the other side of the Dead Sea. 9 Now I weep for Sibmah's vines as I weep for Jazer. My tears fall for Heshbon and Elealeh, because there is no harvest to make the people glad. 10 No one is happy now in the fertile fields. No one shouts or sings in the vineyards. No one tramples grapes to make wine; the shouts of joy are ended.*b* 11 I groan with sadness for Moab, with grief for Kir Heres. 12 The people of Moab wear themselves out going to their mountain shrines and to their temples to pray, but it will do them no good.

13 That is the message the LORD gave earlier about Moab. 14 And now the LORD

---

a Probable text people of Dibon; *Hebrew* people and Dibon.   *b One ancient translation* the shouts of joy are ended; *Hebrew* I have ended the shouts of joy.

says, "In exactly three years Moab's great wealth will disappear. Of its many people, only a few will survive, and they will be weak."

God Will Punish Syria and Israel

17 The LORD said, "Damascus will not be a city any longer; it will be only a pile of ruins. 2 The cities of Syria will be deserted forever.c They will be a pasture for sheep and cattle, and no one will drive them away. 3 Israel will be defenseless, and Damascus will lose its independence. Those Syrians who survive will be in disgrace like the people of Israel. I, the LORD Almighty, have spoken."

4 The LORD said, "A day is coming when Israel's greatness will come to an end, and its wealth will be replaced by poverty. 5 Israel will be like a field where the grain has been cut and harvested, as desolate as a field in Rephaim Valley when it has been picked bare. 6 Only a few people will survive, and Israel will be like an olive tree from which all the olives have been picked except two or three at the very top, or a few that are left on the lower branches. I, the LORD God of Israel, have spoken."

7 When that day comes, people will turn for help to their Creator, the holy God of Israel. 8 They will no longer rely on the altars they made with their own hands, or trust in their own handiwork—symbols of the goddess Asherah and altars for burning incense.

9 When that day comes, well-defended cities will be deserted and left in ruins like the cities that the Hivites and the Amoritesd abandoned as they fled from the people of Israel.

10 Israel, you have forgotten the God who rescues you and protects you like a mighty rock. Instead, you plant sacred gardense in order to worship a foreign god. 11 But even if they sprouted and blossomed the very morning you planted them, there would still be no harvest. There would be only trouble and incurable pain.

Enemy Nations Are Defeated

12 Powerful nations are in commotion with a sound like the roar of the sea, like the crashing of huge waves. 13 The nations advance like rushing waves, but God reprimands them and they retreat, driven away like dust on a mountainside, like straw in a whirlwind. 14 At evening they cause terror, but by morning they are gone. That is the fate of everyone who plunders our land.

God Will Punish Ethiopia

18 Beyond the rivers of Ethiopiaf there is a land where the sound of wings is heard. 2 From that land ambassadors come down the Nile in boats made of reeds. Go back home, swift messengers! Take a message back to your land divided by rivers, to your strong and powerful nation, to your tall and smooth-skinned people, who are feared all over the world.

3 Listen, everyone who lives on earth! Look for a signal flag to be raised on the mountaintops! Listen for the blowing of the bugle! 4 The LORD said to me, "I will look down from heaven as quietly as the dew forms in the warm nights of harvest time, as serenely as the sun shines in the heat of the day. 5 Before the grapes are gathered, when the blossoms have all fallen and the grapes are ripening, the enemy will destroy the Ethiopiansf as easily as a knife cuts branches from a vine. 6 The corpses of their soldiers will be left exposed to the birds and the wild animals. In summer the birds will feed on them, and in winter, the animals."

7 A time is coming when the LORD Almighty will receive offerings from this land divided by rivers, this strong and powerful nation, this tall and smooth-skinned people, who are feared all over the world. They will come to Mount Zion, where the LORD Almighty is worshiped.

God Will Punish Egypt

19 This is a message about Egypt. The LORD is coming to Egypt, riding swiftly on a cloud. The Egyptian

---

c One ancient translation The cities . . . forever; Hebrew The cities of Aroer are deserted.
d One ancient translation the Hivites and the Amorites; Hebrew woodland and hill country.
e SACRED GARDENS: See 1.29.   f Hebrew Cush(ites): Cush is the ancient name of the extensive territory south of the First Cataract of the Nile River. This region was called Ethiopia in Graeco-Roman times, and included within its borders most of modern Sudan and some of present-day Ethiopia (Abyssinia).

idols tremble before him, and the people of Egypt lose their courage. 2 The LORD says, "I will stir up civil war in Egypt and turn brother against brother and neighbor against neighbor. Rival cities will fight each other, and rival kings will struggle for power. 3 I am going to frustrate the plans of the Egyptians and destroy their morale. They will ask their idols to help them, and they will go and consult mediums and ask the spirits of the dead for advice. 4 I will hand the Egyptians over to a tyrant, to a cruel king who will rule them. I, the LORD Almighty, have spoken."

5 The water will be low in the Nile, and the river will gradually dry up. 6 The channels of the river will stink as they slowly go dry. Reeds and rushes will wither, 7 and all the crops planted along the banks of the Nile will dry up and be blown away. 8 Everyone who earns a living by fishing in the Nile will groan and cry; their hooks and their nets will be useless. 9 Those who make linen cloth will be in despair; 10 weavers and skilled workers will be broken and depressed.

11 The leaders of the city of Zoan are fools! Egypt's wisest people give stupid advice! How do they dare to tell the king that they are successors to the ancient scholars and kings? 12 King of Egypt, where are those clever advisers of yours? Perhaps they can tell you what plans the LORD Almighty has for Egypt. 13 The leaders of Zoan and Memphis are fools. They were supposed to lead the nation, but they have misled it. 14 The LORD has made them give confusing advice. As a result, Egypt does everything wrong and staggers like a drunk slipping on his own vomit. 15 No one in Egypt, rich or poor, important or unknown, can offer help.

Egypt Will Worship the LORD

16 A time is coming when the people of Egypt will be as timid as women. They will tremble in terror when they see that the LORD Almighty has stretched out his hand to punish them. 17 The people of Egypt will be terrified of Judah every time they are reminded of the fate that the LORD Almighty has prepared for them.

18 When that time comes, the Hebrew language will be spoken in five Egyptian cities. The people there will take their oaths in the name of the LORD Almighty. One of the cities will be called, "City of the Sun."

19 When that time comes, there will be an altar to the LORD in the land of Egypt and a stone pillar dedicated to him at the Egyptian border. 20 They will be symbols of the LORD Almighty's presence in Egypt. When the people there are oppressed and call out to the LORD for help, he will send someone to rescue them. 21 The LORD will reveal himself to the Egyptian people, and then they will acknowledge and worship him, and bring him sacrifices and offerings. They will make solemn promises to him and do what they promise. 22 The LORD will punish the Egyptians, but then he will heal them. They will turn to him, and he will hear their prayers and heal them.

23 When that time comes, there will be a highway between Egypt and Assyria. The people of these two countries will travel back and forth between them, and the two nations will worship together. 24 When that time comes, Israel will rank with Egypt and Assyria, and these three nations will be a blessing to all the world. 25 The LORD Almighty will bless them and say, "I will bless you, Egypt, my people; you, Assyria, whom I created; and you, Israel, my chosen people."

The Sign of the Naked Prophet

20 Under the orders of Emperor Sargon of Assyria, the commander-in-chief of the Assyrian army attacked the Philistine city of Ashdod. 2 Three years earlier the LORD had told Isaiah son of Amoz to take off his sandals and the sackcloth he was wearing. He obeyed and went around naked and barefoot. 3 When Ashdod was captured, the LORD said, "My servant Isaiah has been going around naked and barefoot for three years. This is a sign of what will happen to Egypt and Ethiopia.f 4 The emperor of Assyria will lead

---

f Hebrew Cush(ites): Cush is the ancient name of the extensive territory south of the First Cataract of the Nile River. This region was called Ethiopia in Graeco-Roman times, and included within its borders most of modern Sudan and some of present-day Ethiopia (Abyssinia).

away naked the prisoners he captures from those two countries. Young and old, they will walk barefoot and naked, with their buttocks exposed, bringing shame on Egypt. 5 Those who have put their trust in Ethiopia*f* and have boasted about Egypt will be disillusioned, their hopes shattered. 6 When that time comes, the people who live along the coast of Philistia will say, 'Look at what has happened to the people we relied on to protect us from the emperor of Assyria! How will we ever survive?' "

A Vision of the Fall of Babylon

21 This is a message about Babylonia.

Like a whirlwind sweeping across the desert, disaster will come from a terrifying land. 2 I have seen a vision of cruel events, a vision of betrayal and destruction.

Army of Elam, attack! Army of Media, lay siege to the cities! God will put an end to the suffering which Babylon has caused.

3 What I saw and heard in the vision has filled me with terror and pain, pain like that of a woman in labor. 4 My head is spinning, and I am trembling with fear. I had been longing for evening to come, but it has brought me nothing but terror.

5 In the vision a banquet is ready; rugs are spread for the guests to sit on. They are eating and drinking. Suddenly the command rings out: "Officers! Prepare your shields!"

6 Then the Lord said to me, "Go and post a sentry, and tell him to report what he sees. 7 If he sees riders coming on horseback, two by two, and riders on donkeys and camels, he is to observe them carefully."

8 The sentry calls out, "Sir, I have been standing guard at my post day and night."

9 Suddenly, here they come! Riders on horseback, two by two. The sentry gives the news, "Babylon has fallen! All the idols they worshiped lie shattered on the ground."

10 My people Israel, you have been threshed like wheat, but now I have announced to you the good news that I have heard from the Lord Almighty, the God of Israel.

A Message about Edom

11 This is a message about Edom.

Someone calls to me from Edom, "Sentry, how soon will the night be over? Tell me how soon it will end."

12 I answer, "Morning is coming, but night will come again. If you want to ask again, come back and ask."

A Message about Arabia

13 This is a message about Arabia.

People of Dedan, you whose caravans camp in the barren country of Arabia, 14 give water to the thirsty people who come to you. You people of the land of Tema, give food to the refugees. 15 People are fleeing to escape from swords that are ready to kill them, from bows that are ready to shoot, from all the dangers of war.

16 Then the Lord said to me, "In exactly one year the greatness of the tribes of Kedar will be at an end. 17 The archers are the bravest warriors of Kedar, but few of them will be left. I, the Lord God of Israel, have spoken."

A Message about Jerusalem

22 This is a message about the Valley of Vision.

What is happening? Why are all the people of the city celebrating on the roofs of the houses? 2 The whole city is in an uproar, filled with noise and excitement.

Your people who died in this war did not die fighting. 3 All your leaders ran away and were captured before they shot a single arrow. 4 Now leave me alone to weep bitterly over all those of my people who have died. Don't try to comfort me. 5 This is a time of panic, defeat, and confusion in the Valley of Vision, and the Sovereign Lord Almighty has sent it on us. The walls of our city have been battered down, and cries for help have echoed among the hills.

6 The soldiers from the land of Elam came riding on horseback, armed with

f Hebrew Cush(ites): Cush is the ancient name of the extensive territory south of the First Cataract of the Nile River. This region was called Ethiopia in Graeco-Roman times, and included within its borders most of modern Sudan and some of present-day Ethiopia (Abyssinia).

bows and arrows. Soldiers from the land of Kir had their shields ready. 7 The fertile valleys of Judah were filled with chariots; soldiers on horseback stood in front of Jerusalem's gates. 8 All of Judah's defenses crumbled.

When that happened, you brought weapons out of the arsenal. 9-10 You found the places where the walls of Jerusalem needed repair. You inspected all the houses in Jerusalem and tore some of them down to get stones to repair the city walls. In order to store water, 11 you built a reservoir inside the city to hold the water flowing down from the old pool. But you paid no attention to God, who planned all this long ago and who caused it to happen.

12 The Sovereign Lord Almighty was calling you then to weep and mourn, to shave your heads and wear sackcloth. 13 Instead, you laughed and celebrated. You killed sheep and cattle to eat, and you drank wine. You said, "We might as well eat and drink! Tomorrow we'll be dead."

14 The Sovereign Lord Almighty himself spoke to me and said, "This evil will never be forgiven them as long as they live. I, the Sovereign Lord Almighty, have spoken."

A Warning to Shebna

15 The Sovereign Lord Almighty told me to go to Shebna, the manager of the royal household, and say to him, 16 "Who do you think you are? What right do you have to carve a tomb for yourself out of the rocky hillside? 17 You may be important, but the Lord will pick you up and throw you away. 18 He will pick you up like a ball and throw you into a much larger country. You will die there beside the chariots you were so proud of. You are a disgrace to your master's household. 19 The Lord will remove you from office and bring you down from your high position."

20 The Lord said to Shebna, "When that happens, I will send for my servant Eliakim son of Hilkiah. 21 I will put your official robe and belt on him and give him all the authority you have had. He will be like a father to the people of Jerusalem and Judah. 22 I will give him complete authority under the king, the descendant of David. He will have the keys of office; what he opens, no one will shut, and what he shuts, no one will open. 23 I will fasten him firmly in place like a peg, and he will be a source of honor to his whole family.

24 "But all his relatives and dependents will become a burden to him. They will hang on him like pots and bowls hanging from a peg! 25 When that happens, the peg that was firmly fastened will pull loose and fall. And that will be the end of everything that was hanging on it." The Lord has spoken.

A Message about Phoenicia

23 This is a message about Tyre.

Howl with grief, you sailors out on the ocean! Your home port of Tyre has been destroyed; its houses and its harbor are in ruins. As your ships return from Cyprus, you learn the news. 2 Wail, you merchants of Sidon! You sent agents 3 across the sea to buy and sell the grain that grew in Egypt and to do business with all the nations.

4 City of Sidon, you are disgraced! The sea and the great ocean depths disown you and say, "I never had any children. I never raised sons or daughters."

5 Even the Egyptians will be shocked and dismayed when they learn that Tyre has been destroyed.

6 Howl with grief, you people of Phoenicia! Try to escape to Spain! 7 Can this be the joyful city of Tyre, founded so long ago? Is this the city that sent settlers across the sea to establish colonies? 8 Who was it that planned to bring all this on Tyre, that imperial city, whose merchant princes were the most honored men on earth? 9 The Lord Almighty planned it. He planned it in order to put an end to their pride in what they had done and to humiliate their honored ones.

10 Go and farm the land, you people in the colonies in Spain! There is no one to protect you any more. g 11 The Lord has stretched out his hand over the sea and overthrown kingdoms. He has commanded that the Phoenician centers of commerce be destroyed. 12 City of Sidon, your happiness has ended, and your people are oppressed. Even if they escape to Cyprus, they will still not be safe.

g Verse 10 in Hebrew is unclear.

(13 It was the Babylonians, not the Assyrians, who let the wild animals overrun Tyre. It was the Babylonians who put up siege towers, tore down the fortifications of Tyre, and left the city in ruins.h)

14 Howl with grief, you sailors out on the ocean! The city you relied on has been destroyed.

15 A time is coming when Tyre will be forgotten for seventy years, the lifetime of a king. When those years are over, Tyre will be like the prostitute in the song:

16 Take your harp, go round the
       town,
   you poor forgotten whore!
   Play and sing your songs again
       to bring men back once more.

17 When the seventy years are over, the LORD will let Tyre go back to her old trade, and she will hire herself out to all the kingdoms of the world. 18 The money she earns by commerce will be dedicated to the LORD. She will not store it away, but those who worship the LORD will use her money to buy the food and the clothing they need.

The LORD Will Punish the Earth

24 The LORD is going to devastate the earth and leave it desolate. He will twist the earth's surface and scatter its people. 2 Everyone will meet the same fate—the priests and the people, slaves and masters, buyers and sellers, lenders and borrowers, rich and poor. 3 The earth will lie shattered and ruined. The LORD has spoken and it will be done.

4 The earth dries up and withers; the whole world grows weak; both earth and sky decay. 5 The people have defiled the earth by breaking God's laws and by violating the covenant he made to last forever. 6 So God has pronounced a curse on the earth. Its people are paying for what they have done. Fewer and fewer remain alive. 7 The grapevines wither, and wine is becoming scarce. Everyone who was once happy is now sad, 8 and the joyful music of their harps and drums has ceased. 9 There is no more happy singing over wine; no one enjoys its taste any more. 10 In the city everything is in chaos, and people lock

themselves in their houses for safety. 11 People shout in the streets because there is no more wine. Happiness is gone forever; it has been banished from the land. 12 The city is in ruins, and its gates have been broken down. 13 This is what will happen in every nation all over the world. It will be like the end of harvest, when the olives have been beaten off every tree and the last grapes picked from the vines.

14 Those who survive will sing for joy. Those in the West will tell how great the LORD is, 15 and those in the East will praise him. The people who live along the sea will praise the LORD, the God of Israel. 16 From the most distant parts of the world we will hear songs in praise of Israel, the righteous nation.

But there is no hope for me! I am wasting away! Traitors continue to betray, and their treachery grows worse and worse. 17 Listen to me, everyone! There are terrors, pits, and traps waiting for you. 18 Anyone who tries to escape from the terror will fall in a pit, and anyone who escapes from the pit will be caught in a trap. Torrents of rain will pour from the sky, and earth's foundations will shake. 19 The earth will crack and shatter and split open. 20 The earth itself will stagger like a drunk, sway like a hut in a storm. The world is weighed down by its sins; it will collapse and never rise again.

21 A time is coming when the LORD will punish the powers above and the rulers of the earth. 22 God will crowd kings together like prisoners in a pit. He will shut them in prison until the time of their punishment comes. 23 The moon will grow dark, and the sun will no longer shine, for the LORD Almighty will be king. He will rule in Jerusalem on Mount Zion, and the leaders of the people will see his glory.

A Hymn of Praise

25 LORD, you are my God;
       I will honor you and praise
       your name.
   You have done amazing things;
       you have faithfully carried out
       the plans you made long ago.
   2 You have turned cities into ruins

---

h Verse 13 in Hebrew is unclear.

and destroyed their
fortifications.
The palaces which our enemies
built
are gone forever.
3 The people of powerful nations
will praise you;
you will be feared in the cities of
cruel nations.
4 The poor and the helpless have
fled to you
and have been safe in times of
trouble.
You give them shelter from storms
and shade from the burning
heat.
Cruel enemies attack like a winter
storm,*
5 like drought in a dry land.
But you, LORD, have silenced our
enemies;
you silence the shouts of cruel
people,
as a cloud cools a hot day.

God Prepares a Banquet

6 Here on Mount Zion the LORD
Almighty will prepare a banquet for all
the nations of the world—a banquet of
the richest food and the finest wine.
7 Here he will suddenly remove the cloud
of sorrow that has been hanging over all
the nations. 8 The Sovereign LORD will
destroy death forever! He will wipe
away the tears from everyone's eyes and
take away the disgrace his people have
suffered throughout the world. The LORD
himself has spoken.
9 When it happens, everyone will say,
"He is our God! We have put our trust in
him, and he has rescued us. He is the
LORD! We have put our trust in him, and
now we are happy and joyful because he
has saved us."

God Will Punish Moab

10 The LORD will protect Mount Zion,
but the people of Moab will be trampled
down the way straw is trampled in manure. 11 They will reach out their hands
as if they were trying to swim, but God
will humiliate them, and their hands will
sink helplessly. 12 He will destroy the
fortresses of Moab with their high walls
and bring them tumbling down into the
dust.

God Will Give His People Victory

26 A day is coming when the people will sing this song in the land
of Judah:
Our city is strong!
God himself defends its walls!
2 Open the city gates
and let the faithful nation enter,
the nation whose people do what
is right.
3 You, LORD, give perfect peace
to those who keep their purpose
firm
and put their trust in you.
4 Trust in the LORD forever;
he will always protect us.
5 He has humbled those who were
proud;
he destroyed the strong city they
lived in,
and sent its walls crashing into
the dust.
6 Those who were oppressed walk
over it now
and trample it under their feet.

7 LORD, you make the path smooth
for good people;
the road they travel is level.
8 We follow your will and put our
hope in you;
you are all that we desire.
9 At night I long for you with all my
heart;
when you judge the earth and its
people,
they will all learn what
justice is.
10 Even though you are kind to the
wicked,
they never learn to do what is
right.
Even here in a land of righteous
people
they still do wrong;
they refuse to recognize your
greatness.
11 Your enemies do not know that
you will punish them.
LORD, put them to shame and let
them suffer;
let them suffer the punishment
you have prepared.
Show them how much you love
your people.

Probable text winter storm; *Hebrew* storm against a wall.

12 You will give us prosperity, LORD;
everything that we achieve
is the result of what you do.*j*
13 LORD our God, we have been ruled
by others,
but you alone are our LORD.
14 Now they are dead and will not
live again;
their ghosts will not rise,
for you have punished them and
destroyed them.
No one remembers them any
more.
15 LORD, you have made our nation
grow,
enlarging its territory on every
side;
and this has brought you honor.
16 You punished your people, LORD,
and in anguish they prayed
to you.*k*
17 You, LORD, have made us cry out,
as a woman in labor cries out in
pain.
18 We were in pain and agony,
but we gave birth to nothing.
We have won no victory for our
land;
we have accomplished nothing.*l*

19 Those of our people who have
died will live again!
Their bodies will come back to
life.
All those sleeping in their graves
will wake up and sing for joy.
As the sparkling dew refreshes the
earth,
so the LORD will revive those
who have long been dead.

Judgment and Restoration

20 Go into your houses, my people, and shut the door behind you. Hide yourselves for a little while until God's anger is over. 21 The LORD is coming from his heavenly dwelling place to punish the people of the earth for their sins. The murders that were secretly committed on the earth will be revealed, and the ground will no longer hide those who have been killed.

27 On that day the LORD will use his powerful and deadly sword to punish Leviathan, that wriggling, twisting dragon, and to kill the monster *m* that lives in the sea.

2 On that day the LORD will say of his pleasant vineyard, 3 "I watch over it and water it continually. I guard it night and day so that no one will harm it. 4 I am no longer angry with the vineyard. If there were thorns and briers to fight against, I would burn them up completely. 5 But if the enemies of my people want my protection, let them make peace with me. Yes, let them make peace with me."

6 In the days to come the people of Israel, the descendants of Jacob, will take root like a tree, and they will blossom and bud. The earth will be covered with the fruit they produce.

7 Israel has not been punished by the LORD as severely as its enemies nor lost as many people. 8 The LORD punished his people by sending them into exile. He took them away with a cruel wind from the east.*n* 9 But Israel's sins will be forgiven only when the stones of pagan altars are ground up like chalk, and no more incense altars or symbols of the goddess Asherah are left.

10 The fortified city lies in ruins. It is deserted like an empty wilderness. It has become a pasture for cattle, where they can rest and graze. 11 The branches of the trees are withered and broken, and women gather them for firewood. Because the people have understood nothing, God their Creator will not pity them or show them any mercy.

12 On that day, from the Euphrates to the Egyptian border, the LORD will gather his people one by one, as threshing separates the wheat from the chaff. 13 When that day comes, a trumpet will be blown to call back from Assyria and Egypt all the Israelites who are in exile there. They will come and worship the LORD in Jerusalem, on his sacred hill.*o*

A Warning to the Northern Kingdom

28 The kingdom of Israel is doomed! Its glory is fading like the crowns of flowers on the heads of its drunken leaders. Their proud heads are

---

j everything that . . . do; or you treat us according to what we do.   k Verse 16 in Hebrew is unclear.   l We have won . . . nothing; Hebrew unclear.   m LEVIATHAN . . . MONSTER: Legendary monsters which were symbols of the nations oppressing Israel.   n Verse 8 in Hebrew is unclear.   o SACRED HILL: See 2.3.

well perfumed, but there they lie, dead drunk. 2 The Lord has someone strong and powerful ready to attack them, someone who will come like a hailstorm, like a torrent of rain, like a rushing, overpowering flood, and will overwhelm the land. 3 The pride of those drunken leaders will be trampled underfoot. 4 The fading glory of those proud leaders will disappear like the first figs of the season, picked and eaten as soon as they are ripe.

5 A day is coming when the LORD Almighty will be like a glorious crown of flowers for his people who survive. 6 He will give a sense of justice to those who serve as judges, and courage to those who defend the city gates from attack.

Isaiah and the Drunken Prophets of Judah

7 Even the prophets and the priests are so drunk that they stagger. They have drunk so much wine and liquor that they stumble in confusion. The prophets are too drunk to understand the visions that God sends, and the priests are too drunk to decide the cases that are brought to them. 8 The tables where they sit are all covered with vomit, and not a clean spot is left.

9 They complain about me. They say, "Who does that man think he's teaching? Who needs his message? It's only good for babies that have just stopped nursing! 10 He is trying to teach us letter by letter, line by line, lesson by lesson."

11 If you won't listen to me, then God will use foreigners speaking some strange-sounding language to teach you a lesson. 12 He offered rest and comfort to all of you, but you refused to listen to him. 13 That is why the LORD is going to teach you letter by letter, line by line, lesson by lesson. Then you will stumble with every step you take. You will be wounded, trapped, and taken prisoner.

A Cornerstone for Zion

14 Now you arrogant leaders who rule here in Jerusalem over this people, listen to what the LORD is saying. 15 You boast that you have made a treaty with death and reached an agreement with the world of the dead. You are certain that disaster will spare you when it comes,

because you depend on lies and deceit to keep you safe. 16 This, now, is what the Sovereign LORD says: "I am placing in Zion a foundation that is firm and strong. In it I am putting a solid cornerstone on which are written the words, 'Faith that is firm is also patient.' 17 Justice will be the measuring line for the foundation, and honesty will be its plumb line."

Hailstorms will sweep away all the lies you depend on, and floods will destroy your security. 18 The treaty you have made with death will be abolished, and your agreement with the world of the dead will be canceled. When disaster sweeps down, you will be overcome. 19 It will strike you again and again, morning after morning. You will have to bear it day and night. Each new message from God will bring new terror! 20 You will be like the person in the proverb, who tries to sleep in a bed too short to stretch out on, with a blanket too narrow to wrap himself in. 21 The LORD will fight as he did at Mount Perazim and in the valley of Gibeon, in order to do what he intends to do — strange as his actions may seem. He will complete his work, his mysterious work.

22 Don't laugh at the warning I am giving you! If you do, it will be even harder for you to escape. I have heard the LORD Almighty's decision to destroy the whole country.

God's Wisdom

23 Listen to what I am saying; pay attention to what I am telling you. 24 Farmers don't constantly plow their fields and keep getting them ready for planting. 25 Once they have prepared the soil, they plant the seeds of herbs such as dill and cumin. They plant rows of wheat and barley,p and at the edges of their fields they plant other grain. 26 They know how to do their work, because God has taught them. 27 They never use a heavy club to beat out dill seeds or cumin seeds; instead they use light sticks of the proper size. 28 They do not ruin the wheat by threshing it endlessly, and they know how to thresh it by driving a cart over it without bruising the grains. 29 All this wisdom comes from the LORD

---

p Hebrew has an additional word, the meaning of which is unclear.

Almighty. The plans God makes are wise, and they always succeed.

The Fate of Jerusalem

29 God's altar, Jerusalem itself, is doomed! The city where David camped is doomed! Let another year or two come and go, with its feasts and festivals, 2 and then God will bring disaster on the city that is called "God's altar." There will be weeping and wailing, and the whole city will be like an altar covered with blood. 3 God will attack the city, surround it, and besiege it. 4 Jerusalem will be like a ghost struggling to speak from under the ground, a muffled voice coming from the dust.

5 Jerusalem, all the foreigners who attack you will be blown away like dust, and their terrifying armies will fly away like straw. Suddenly and unexpectedly 6 the LORD Almighty will rescue you with violent thunderstorms and earthquakes. He will send windstorms and raging fire; 7 then all the armies of the nations attacking the city of God's altar, all their weapons and equipment — everything — will vanish like a dream, like something imagined in the night. 8 All the nations that assemble to attack Jerusalem will be like a starving person who dreams he is eating and wakes up hungry, or like someone dying of thirst who dreams he is drinking and wakes with a dry throat.

Disregarded Warnings

9 Go ahead and be stupid! Go ahead and be blind! Get drunk without any wine! Stagger without drinking a drop! 10 The LORD has made you drowsy, ready to fall into a deep sleep. The prophets should be the eyes of the people, but God has blindfolded them. 11 The meaning of every prophetic vision will be hidden from you; it will be like a sealed scroll. If you take it to someone who knows how to read and ask him to read it to you, he will say he can't because it is sealed. 12 If you give it to someone who can't read and ask him to read it to you, he will answer that he doesn't know how.

13 The Lord said, "These people claim to worship me, but their words are meaningless, and their hearts are somewhere else. Their religion is nothing but human rules and traditions, which they have simply memorized. 14 So I will startle them with one unexpected blow after another. Those who are wise will turn out to be fools, and all their cleverness will be useless."

Hope for the Future

15 Those who try to hide their plans from the LORD are doomed! They carry out their schemes in secret and think no one will see them or know what they are doing. 16 They turn everything upside down. Which is more important, the potter or the clay? Can something you have made say, "You didn't make me"? Or can it say, "You don't know what you are doing"?

17 As the saying goes, before long the dense forest will become farmland, and the farmland will go back to forest.

18 When that day comes, the deaf will be able to hear a book being read aloud, and the blind, who have been living in darkness, will open their eyes and see. 19 Poor and humble people will once again find the happiness which the LORD, the holy God of Israel, gives. 20 It will be the end of those who oppress others and show contempt for God. Every sinner will be destroyed. 21 God will destroy those who slander others, those who prevent the punishment of criminals, and those who tell lies to keep honest people from getting justice.

22 So now the LORD, the God of Israel, who rescued Abraham from trouble, says, "My people, you will not be disgraced any longer, and your faces will no longer be pale with shame. 23 When you see the children that I will give you, then you will acknowledge that I am the holy God of Israel. You will honor me and stand in awe of me. 24 Foolish people will learn to understand, and those who are always grumbling will be glad to be taught."

A Useless Treaty with Egypt

30 The LORD has spoken: "Those who rule Judah are doomed because they rebel against me. They follow plans that I did not make, and sign treaties against my will, piling one sin on another. 2 They go to Egypt for help without asking for my advice. They want Egypt to protect them, so they put their trust in Egypt's king. 3 But the king will be powerless to help them, and Egypt's protection will end in disaster. 4 Although their ambassadors have

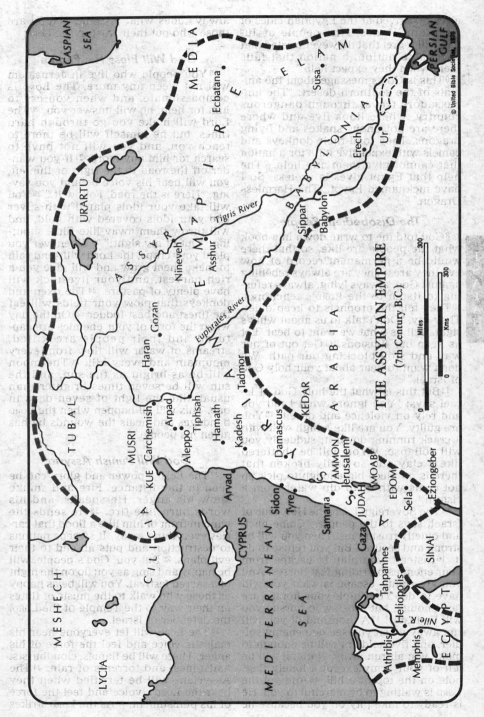

THE ASSYRIAN EMPIRE
(7th Century B.C.)

© United Bible Societies, 1976

CASPIAN SEA

PERSIAN GULF

MEDIA

Ecbatana

URARTU

ELAM

Susa

ASSYRIAN EMPIRE

BABYLONIA

Erech

Ur

Nineveh

Asshur

Gozan

Haran

Tigris River

Sippar

Babylon

TUBAL

MUSRI

Carchemish

Arpad

Euphrates River

Tiphsah

Aleppo

Hamath

KEDAR

Kadesh

Tadmor

MESHECH

KUE

ARABIA

Damascus

LYCIA

CILICIA

Arvad

AMMON

Sidon

Tyre

Jerusalem

MOAB

Samaria

JUDAH

EDOM

Gaza

Sela

Eziongeber

CYPRUS

MEDITERRANEAN SEA

SINAI

Tahpanhes

EGYPT

Heliopolis

Nile R.

Athribis

Memphis

Miles
300

Kms
300

already arrived at the Egyptian cities of Zoan and Hanes, 5 the people of Judah will regret that they ever trusted that unreliable nation, a nation that fails them when they expect help."

6 This is God's message about the animals of the southern desert: "The ambassadors travel through dangerous country, where lions live and where there are poisonous snakes and flying dragons. They load their donkeys and camels with expensive gifts for a nation that cannot give them any help. 7 The help that Egypt gives is useless. So I have nicknamed Egypt, 'The Harmless Dragon.' "

The Disobedient People

8 God told me to write down in a book what the people are like, so that there would be a permanent record of how evil they are. 9 They are always rebelling against God, always lying, always refusing to listen to the LORD's teachings. 10 They tell the prophets to keep quiet. They say, "Don't talk to us about what's right. Tell us what we want to hear. Let us keep our illusions. 11 Get out of our way and stop blocking our path. We don't want to hear about your holy God of Israel."

12 But this is what the holy God of Israel says: "You ignore what I tell you and rely on violence and deceit. 13 You are guilty. You are like a high wall with a crack running down it; suddenly you will collapse. 14 You will be shattered like a clay pot, so badly broken that there is no piece big enough to pick up hot coals with or to dip water from a cistern."

15 The Sovereign LORD, the Holy One of Israel, says to the people, "Come back and quietly trust in me. Then you will be strong and secure." But you refuse to do it. 16 Instead, you plan to escape from your enemies by riding fast horses. And you are right — escape is what you will have to do! You think your horses are fast enough, but those who pursue you will be faster! 17 A thousand of you will run away when you see one enemy soldier, and five soldiers will be enough to make you all run away. Nothing will be left of your army except a lonely flagpole on the top of a hill. 18 And yet the LORD is waiting to be merciful to you. He is ready to take pity on you because he always does what is right. Happy are those who put their trust in the LORD.

God Will Bless His People

19 You people who live in Jerusalem will not weep any more. The LORD is compassionate, and when you cry to him for help, he will answer you. 20 The Lord will make you go through hard times, but he himself will be there to teach you, and you will not have to search for him any more. 21 If you wander off the road to the right or the left, you will hear his voice behind you saying, "Here is the road. Follow it." 22 You will take your idols plated with silver and your idols covered with gold, and will throw them away like filth, shouting, "Out of my sight!" 23 Whenever you plant your crops, the Lord will send rain to make them grow and will give you a rich harvest, and your livestock will have plenty of pasture. 24 The oxen and donkeys that plow your fields will eat the finest and best fodder. 25 On the day when the forts of your enemies are captured and their people are killed, streams of water will flow from every mountain and every hill. 26 The moon will be as bright as the sun, and the sun will be seven times brighter than usual, like the light of seven days in one. This will all happen when the LORD bandages and heals the wounds he has given his people.

God Will Punish Assyria

27 The LORD's power and glory can be seen in the distance. Fire and smoke show his anger. He speaks, and his words burn like fire. 28 He sends the wind in front of him like a flood that carries everything away. It sweeps nations to destruction and puts an end to their evil plans. 29 But you, God's people, will be happy and sing as you do on the night of a sacred festival. You will be as happy as those who walk to the music of flutes on their way to the Temple of the LORD, the defender of Israel.

30 The LORD will let everyone hear his majestic voice and feel the force of his anger. There will be flames, cloudbursts, hailstones, and torrents of rain. 31 The Assyrians will be terrified when they hear the LORD's voice and feel the force of his punishment. 32 As the LORD strikes

them again and again, his people will keep time with the music of drums and harps. God himself will fight against the Assyrians. 33 Long ago a place was prepared where a huge fire will burn the emperor of Assyria. It is deep and wide, and piled high with wood. The LORD will breathe out a stream of flame to set it on fire.

God Will Protect Jerusalem

31 Those who go to Egypt for help are doomed! They are relying on Egypt's vast military strength—horses, chariots, and soldiers. But they do not rely on the LORD, the holy God of Israel, or ask him for help. 2 He knows what he is doing! He sends disaster. He carries out his threats to punish evil people and those who protect them. 3 The Egyptians are not gods—they are only human. Their horses are not supernatural. When the LORD acts, the strong nation will crumble, and the weak nation it helped will fall. Both of them will be destroyed.

4 The LORD said to me, "No matter how shepherds yell and shout, they can't scare away a lion from an animal that it has killed; in the same way, there is nothing that can keep me, the LORD Almighty, from protecting Mount Zion. 5 Just as a bird hovers over its nest to protect its young, so I, the LORD Almighty, will protect Jerusalem and defend it."

6 God said, "People of Israel, you have sinned against me and opposed me. But now, come back to me! 7 A time is coming when all of you will throw away the sinful idols you made out of silver and gold. 8 Assyria will be destroyed in war, but not by human power. The Assyrians will run from battle, and their young men will be made slaves. 9 Their emperor will run away in terror, and the officers will be so frightened that they will abandon their battle flags." The LORD has spoken—the LORD who is worshiped in Jerusalem and whose fire burns there for sacrifices.

A King with Integrity

32 Some day there will be a king who rules with integrity, and national leaders who govern with justice. 2 Each of them will be like a shelter from the wind and a place to hide from storms. They will be like streams flowing in a desert, like the shadow of a giant rock in a barren land. 3 Their eyes and ears will be open to the needs of the people. 4 They will not be impatient any longer, but they will act with understanding and will say what they mean. 5 No one will think that a fool is honorable or say that a scoundrel is honest. 6 A fool speaks foolishly and thinks up evil things to do. What he does and what he says are an insult to the LORD, and he never feeds the hungry or gives thirsty people anything to drink. 7 A stupid person is evil and does evil things; he plots to ruin the poor with lies and to keep them from getting their rights. 8 But an honorable person acts honestly and stands firm for what is right.

Judgment and Restoration

9 You women who live an easy life, free from worries, listen to what I am saying. 10 You may be satisfied now, but this time next year you will be in despair because there will be no grapes for you to gather. 11 You have been living an easy life, free from worries; but now, tremble with fear! Strip off your clothes and tie rags around your waist. 12 Beat your breasts in grief because the fertile fields and the vineyards have been destroyed, 13 and thorn bushes and briers are growing on my people's land. Weep for all the houses where people were happy and for the city that was full of life. 14 Even the palace will be abandoned and the capital city totally deserted. Homes and the forts that guarded them will be in ruins forever. Wild donkeys will roam there, and sheep will find pasture there.

15 But once more God will send us his spirit. The wasteland will become fertile, and fields will produce rich crops. 16 Everywhere in the land righteousness and justice will be done. 17 Because everyone will do what is right, there will be peace and security forever. 18 God's people will be free from worries, and their homes peaceful and safe. (19 But hail will fall on the forests, and the city will be torn down.) 20 How happy everyone will be with plenty of water for the crops and safe pasture everywhere for the donkeys and cattle.

ISAIAH

A Prayer for Help

33 Our enemies are doomed! They have robbed and betrayed, although no one has robbed them or betrayed them. But their time to rob and betray will end, and they themselves will become victims of robbery and treachery.

2 LORD, have mercy on us. We have put our hope in you. Protect us day by day and save us in times of trouble. 3 When you fight for us, nations run away from the noise of battle. 4 Their belongings are pounced upon and taken as loot.

5 How great the LORD is! He rules over everything. He will fill Jerusalem with justice and integrity 6 and give stability to the nation. He always protects his people and gives them wisdom and knowledge. Their greatest treasure is their reverence for the LORD.

7 The brave are calling for help. The ambassadors who tried to bring about peace are crying bitterly. 8 The highways are so dangerous that no one travels on them. Treaties are broken and agreements are violated. No one is respected any more. 9 The land lies idle and deserted. The forests of Lebanon have withered, the fertile valley of Sharon is like a desert, and in Bashan and on Mount Carmel the leaves are falling from the trees.

The LORD Warns His Enemies

10 The LORD says to the nations, "Now I will act. I will show how powerful I am. 11 You make worthless plans and everything you do is useless. My spirit is like a fire that will destroy you.q 12 You will crumble like rocks burned to make lime, like thorns burned to ashes. 13 Let everyone near and far hear what I have done and acknowledge my power."

14 The sinful people of Zion are trembling with fright. They say, "God's judgment is like a fire that burns forever. Can any of us survive a fire like that?" 15 You can survive if you say and do what is right. Don't use your power to cheat the poor and don't accept bribes. Don't join with those who plan to commit murder or to do other evil things. 16 Then you will be safe; you will be as secure as if in a strong fortress. You will have food to eat and water to drink.

The Glorious Future

17 Once again you will see a king ruling in splendor over a land that stretches in all directions. 18 Your old fears of foreign tax collectors and spies will be only a memory. 19 You will no longer see any arrogant foreigners who speak a language that you can't understand. 20 Look at Zion, the city where we celebrate our religious festivals. Look at Jerusalem! What a safe place it will be to live in! It will be like a tent that is never moved, whose pegs are never pulled up and whose ropes never break. 21 The LORD will show us his glory. We will live beside broad rivers and streams, but hostile ships will not sail on them.r 22-23 All the rigging on those ships is useless; the sails cannot be spread! We will seize all the wealth of enemy armies, and there will be so much that even the lame can get a share. The LORD himself will be our king; he will rule over us and protect us. 24 No one who lives in our land will ever again complain of being sick, and all sins will be forgiven.

God Will Punish His Enemies

34 Come, people of all nations! Gather around and listen. Let the whole earth and everyone living on it come here and listen. 2 The LORD is angry with all the nations and all their armies. He has condemned them to destruction. 3 Their corpses will not be buried, but will lie there rotting and stinking; and the mountains will be red with blood. 4 The sun, moon, and stars will crumble to dust. The sky will disappear like a scroll being rolled up, and the stars will fall like leaves dropping from a vine or a fig tree.

5 The LORD has prepared his sword in heaven, and now it will strike Edom, those people whom he has condemned to destruction. 6 His sword will be covered with their blood and fat, like the blood and fat of lambs and goats that are sacrificed. The LORD will offer this sacrifice in the city of Bozrah; he will make this a great slaughter in the land of Edom. 7 The people will fall like wild oxen and young bulls, and the earth will

---

q *One ancient translation* My spirit . . . you; *Hebrew* You are destroying yourselves.
r *Verse 21 in Hebrew is unclear.*

SENNACHERIB'S PRISM

The monument known as Sennacherib's Prism is a fascinating artifact from Assyria's past. It gives a different account than the Bible about an important event in Israel's history—a siege against Jerusalem conducted by King Sennacherib of Assyria (ruled 705–681 B.C.) about 690 B.C. (Is 36; 37).

The fifteen-inch high clay prism contains a well-preserved Assyrian script that verifies the attack on Jerusalem and King Hezekiah of Judah by Assyrian forces. "As to Hezekiah, the Jew, he did not submit to my yoke," the prism reads. "I laid siege to 46 of his strong cities, walled forts and to countless small cities in their vicinity, and conquered them . . . . [Hezekiah] I made a prisoner in Jerusalem, his royal residence, like a bird in a cage."

While Sennacherib's siege against Jerusalem is a verified historical fact, it is interesting that Sennacherib's account does not mention how the siege ended. This leads to suspicion among historians that the siege failed, since the Assyrians never mentioned their defeats in their official records—only their victories.

The biblical account indicates that Sennacherib suffered a crushing defeat in his siege of Jerusalem because of divine intervention. During the night, thousands of soldiers in the Assyrian army died through the action of the angel of the Lord (2 K 19.35). Some scholars believe God used a deadly plague as an instrument of judgment against the enemies of his people.

Rulers of the ancient world used monuments such as this prism on which to record their exploits. These documents of stone and clay have survived for centuries in the rubble and ruin of ancient cities. They provide valuable insight into life in Bible times, confirming and, in many cases, adding valuable information about biblical events.

be red with blood and covered with fat.
⁸This is the time when the LORD will rescue Zion and take vengeance on her
enemies.

⁹The rivers of Edom will turn into tar,
and the soil will turn into sulfur. The
whole country will burn like tar. ¹⁰It will
burn day and night, and smoke will rise
from it forever. The land will lie waste
age after age, and no one will ever travel
through it again. ¹¹Owls and ravens will
take over the land. The LORD will make it
a barren waste again, as it was before
the creation. ¹²There will be no king to
rule the country, and the leaders will all
be gone.ˢ ¹³Thorns and thistles will
grow up in all the palaces and walled
towns, and jackals and owls will live in
them. ¹⁴Wild animals will roam there,
and demons will call to each other. The
night monsterᵗ will come there looking
for a place to rest. ¹⁵Owls will build their
nests, lay eggs, hatch their young, and
care for them there. Vultures will gather
there, one after another.

¹⁶Search in the LORD's book of living
creatures and read what it says. Not one
of these creatures will be missing, and
not one will be without its mate. The
LORD has commanded it to be so; he himself will bring them together. ¹⁷It is the
LORD who will divide the land among
them and give each of them a share.
They will live in the land age after age,
and it will belong to them forever.

The Road of Holiness

35 The desert will rejoice,
　　and flowers will bloom in
　　　the wastelands.
²The desert will sing and shout
　　for joy;
　it will be as beautiful as the
　　Lebanon Mountains
　and as fertile as the fields of
　　Carmel and Sharon.
Everyone will see the LORD's
　splendor,
　see his greatness and power.

³Give strength to hands that are
　tired
　and to knees that tremble with
　weakness.
⁴Tell everyone who is discouraged,

"Be strong and don't be afraid!
　God is coming to your rescue,
　coming to punish your enemies."

⁵The blind will be able to see,
　and the deaf will hear.
⁶The lame will leap and dance,
　and those who cannot speak will
　　shout for joy.
　Streams of water will flow through
　　the desert;
⁷　the burning sand will become a
　　lake,
　and dry land will be filled with
　　springs.
　Where jackals used to live,
　marsh grass and reeds will
　　grow.

⁸There will be a highway there,
　called "The Road of Holiness."
No sinner will ever travel that
　road;
　no fools will mislead those who
　　follow it.ᵘ
⁹No lions will be there;
　no fierce animals will pass
　　that way.
Those whom the LORD has
　rescued
　will travel home by that road.
¹⁰They will reach Jerusalem with
　gladness,
　singing and shouting for joy.
They will be happy forever,
　forever free from sorrow and
　　grief.

The Assyrians Threaten Jerusalem
(2 Kings 18.13-27; 2 Chronicles 32.1-19)

36 In the fourteenth year that Hezekiah was king of Judah, Sennacherib, the emperor of Assyria,
attacked the fortified cities of Judah and
captured them. ²Then he ordered his
chief official to go from Lachish to Jerusalem with a large military force to demand that King Hezekiah surrender.
The official occupied the road where the
cloth makers work, by the ditch that
brings water from the upper pool. ³Three Judeans came out to meet him:
the official in charge of the palace, Elia-
kim son of Hilkiah; the court secretary,
Shebna; and the official in charge of the

ˢ Verse 12 in Hebrew begins with a word, the meaning of which is unclear.　ᵗ NIGHT MONSTER: A
female demon, believed to live in desolate places.　ᵘ Probable text no fools . . . follow it;
Hebrew unclear.

records, Joah son of Asaph. 4The Assyrian official told them that the emperor wanted to know what made King Hezekiah so confident. 5He demanded, "Do you think that words can take the place of military skill and might? Who do you think will help you rebel against Assyria? 6You are expecting Egypt to help you, but that would be like using a reed as a walking stick — it would break and would jab your hand. That is what the king of Egypt is like when anyone relies on him."

7The Assyrian official went on, "Or will you tell me that you are relying on the LORD your God? It was the LORD's shrines and altars that Hezekiah destroyed when he told the people of Judah and Jerusalem to worship at one altar only. 8I will make a bargain with you in the name of the emperor. I will give you two thousand horses if you can find that many riders. 9You are no match for even the lowest ranking Assyrian official, and yet you expect the Egyptians to send you chariots and horsemen. 10Do you think I have attacked your country and destroyed it without the LORD's help? The LORD himself told me to attack it and destroy it."

11Then Eliakim, Shebna, and Joah told the official, "Speak Aramaic to us. We understand it. Don't speak Hebrew; all the people on the wall are listening."

12He replied, "Do you think you and the king are the only ones the emperor sent me to say all these things to? No, I am also talking to the people who are sitting on the wall, who will have to eat their excrement and drink their urine, just as you will."

13Then the official stood up and shouted in Hebrew, "Listen to what the emperor of Assyria is telling you. 14He warns you not to let Hezekiah deceive you. Hezekiah can't save you. 15And don't let him persuade you to rely on the LORD. Don't think that the LORD will save you and that he will stop our Assyrian army from capturing your city. 16Don't listen to Hezekiah! The emperor of Assyria commands you to come out of the city and surrender. You will all be allowed to eat grapes from your own vines and figs from your own trees, and to drink water from your own wells — 17until the emperor resettles you in a country much like your own, where there are vineyards to give wine and there is grain for making bread. 18Don't let Hezekiah fool you into thinking that the LORD will rescue you. Did the gods of any other nations save their countries from the emperor of Assyria? 19Where are they now, the gods of Hamath and Arpad? Where are the gods of Sepharvaim? Did anyone save Samaria? 20When did any of the gods of all these countries ever save their country from our emperor? Then what makes you think the LORD can save Jerusalem?"

21The people kept quiet, just as King Hezekiah had told them to; they did not say a word. 22Then Eliakim, Shebna, and Joah tore their clothes in grief and went and reported to the king what the Assyrian official had said.

The King Asks Isaiah's Advice
(2 Kings 19.1-7)

37 As soon as King Hezekiah heard their report, he tore his clothes in grief, put on sackcloth, and went to the Temple of the LORD. 2He sent Eliakim, the official in charge of the palace, Shebna, the court secretary, and the senior priests to the prophet Isaiah son of Amoz. They also were wearing sackcloth. 3This is the message which he told them to give to Isaiah: "Today is a day of suffering; we are being punished and are in disgrace. We are like a woman who is ready to give birth, but is too weak to do it. 4The Assyrian emperor has sent his chief official to insult the living God. May the LORD your God hear these insults and punish those who spoke them. So pray to God for those of our people who survive."

5When Isaiah received King Hezekiah's message, 6he sent back this answer: "The LORD tells you not to let the Assyrians frighten you by their claims that he cannot save you. 7The LORD will cause the emperor to hear a rumor that will make him go back to his own country, and the LORD will have him killed there."

The Assyrians Send Another Threat
(2 Kings 19.8-19)

8The Assyrian official learned that the emperor had left Lachish and was fighting against the nearby city of Libnah; so he went there to consult him. 9Word reached the Assyrians that the Egyptian army, led by King Tirhakah of Ethiopia,[v] was coming to attack them. When the emperor heard this, he sent a letter to King Hezekiah [10] of Judah to tell him: "The god you are trusting in has told you that you will not fall into my hands, but don't let that deceive you. [11] You have heard what an Assyrian emperor does to any country he decides to destroy. Do you think that you can escape? [12] My ancestors destroyed the cities of Gozan, Haran, and Rezeph, and killed the people of Betheden who lived in Telassar, and none of their gods could save them. [13] Where are the kings of the cities of Hamath, Arpad, Sepharvaim, Hena, and Ivvah?"

[14] King Hezekiah took the letter from the messengers and read it. Then he went to the Temple, placed the letter there in the presence of the LORD, [15] and prayed, [16] "Almighty LORD, God of Israel, seated above the winged creatures, you alone are God, ruling all the kingdoms of the world. You created the earth and the sky. [17] Now, LORD, hear us and look at what is happening to us. Listen to all the things that Sennacherib is saying to insult you, the living God. [18] We all know, LORD, that the emperors of Assyria have destroyed many nations, made their lands desolate, [19] and burned up their gods—which were no gods at all, only images of wood and stone made by human hands. [20] Now, LORD our God, rescue us from the Assyrians, so that all the nations of the world will know that you alone are God."

Isaiah's Message to the King
(2 Kings 19.20-37)

[21] Then Isaiah sent a message telling King Hezekiah that in answer to the king's prayer [22] the LORD had said, "The city of Jerusalem laughs at you, Sennacherib, and makes fun of you. [23] Whom do you think you have been insulting and ridiculing? You have been disrespectful to me, the holy God of Israel. [24] You sent your servants to boast to me that with all your chariots you had conquered the highest mountains of Lebanon. You boasted that there you cut down the tallest cedars and the finest cy-

press trees, and that you reached the deepest parts of the forests. [25] You boasted that you dug wells and drank water in foreign lands, and that the feet of your soldiers tramped the Nile River dry.

[26] "Have you never heard that I planned all this long ago? And now I have carried it out. I gave you the power to turn fortified cities into piles of rubble. [27] The people who lived there were powerless; they were frightened and stunned. They were like grass in a field or weeds growing on a roof when the hot east wind blasts them.[w]

[28] "But I know everything about you, what you do and where you go. I know how you rage against me. [29] I have received the report of that rage and that pride of yours, and now I will put a hook through your nose and a bit in your mouth and will take you back by the same road you came."

[30] Then Isaiah said to King Hezekiah, "Here is a sign of what will happen. This year and next you will have only wild grain to eat, but the following year you will be able to plant grain and harvest it, and plant vines and eat grapes. [31] Those in Judah who survive will flourish like plants that send roots deep into the ground and produce fruit. [32] There will be people in Jerusalem and on Mount Zion who will survive, because the LORD Almighty is determined to make this happen.

[33] "And this is what the LORD has said about the Assyrian emperor: 'He will not enter this city or shoot a single arrow against it. No soldiers with shields will come near the city, and no siege mounds will be built around it. [34] He will go back by the same road he came, without entering this city. I, the LORD, have spoken. [35] I will defend this city and protect it, for the sake of my own honor and because of the promise I made to my servant David.' "

[36] An angel of the LORD went to the Assyrian camp and killed 185,000 soldiers. At dawn the next day there they lay, all dead! [37] Then the Assyrian emperor Sennacherib withdrew and returned to Nineveh. [38] One day when he was

---

[v] Hebrew Cush: Cush is the ancient name of the extensive territory south of the First Cataract of the Nile River. This region was called Ethiopia in Graeco-Roman times, and included within its borders most of modern Sudan and some of present-day Ethiopia (Abyssinia).
[w] Probable text when the hot east wind blasts them; Hebrew blasted before they are grown.

HEZEKIAH'S WATER TUNNEL

The long underground shaft known as Hezekiah's water tunnel, or the Siloam tunnel, was dug through solid rock under the city wall of Jerusalem by King Hezekiah of Judah in the eighth century B.C. (2 K 20.20). The tunnel linking the Gihon Spring outside the city walls to the water reservoir known as the Pool of Siloam inside the city walls was dug to provide water to the city in case of a prolonged siege by Assyrian forces.

Built about 700 B.C., the crooked shaft is 1,750 feet long, often running 60 feet below the surface of the earth. It was discovered in 1838, but little scientific exploration and excavation work was done on the channel until 1866. Not until 1910 was it cleared of debris left by the destruction of Jerusalem in 586 B.C. A walk through Hezekiah's tunnel is a popular activity for modern tourists while visiting Jerusalem.

An inscription in Hebrew found in the tunnel near the Pool of Siloam describes the construction project. Two separate crews worked from opposite ends and eventually met in the middle of the shaft. Digging far below the earth's surface in bedrock, they labored for months in semidarkness with crude hand tools under difficult breathing conditions. But their hard work was rewarded when the Pool of Siloam began to fill with precious water that would spell the difference between life and death for Jerusalem if the Assyrians should attack the city.

A tactic used by besieging armies against walled cities was to cut off food and water supplies to the people inside (2 K 6.25–29). Hezekiah's tunnel and pool was more than a marvel of ancient engineering; it was a brilliant survival strategy.

Hezekiah's tunnel may not have been the first water shaft dug at Jerusalem. Some scholars believe David captured the city from the Jebusites about three hundred years before Hezekiah's time by gaining entrance to the walled city through a water shaft (2 S 5.6–8).

worshiping in the temple of his god Nisroch, two of his sons, Adrammelech and
Sharezer, killed him with their swords
and then escaped to the land of Ararat.
Another of his sons, Esarhaddon, succeeded him as emperor.

King Hezekiah's Illness and Recovery

(2 Kings 20.1-11; 2 Chronicles 32.24-26)

38 About this time King Hezekiah
became sick and almost died.
The prophet Isaiah son of Amoz went to
see him and said to him, "The LORD tells
you that you are to put everything in order because you will not recover. Get
ready to die."

2 Hezekiah turned his face to the wall
and prayed: 3 "Remember, LORD, that I
have served you faithfully and loyally,
and that I have always tried to do what
you wanted me to." And he began to cry
bitterly.

4 Then the LORD commanded Isaiah 5 to
go back to Hezekiah and say to him, "I,
the LORD, the God of your ancestor David, have heard your prayer and seen
your tears; I will let you live fifteen years
longer. 6 I will rescue you and this city of
Jerusalem from the emperor of Assyria,
and I will continue to protect the city."

21 Isaiah told the king to put a paste
made of figs on his boil, and he would
get well. 22 Then King Hezekiah asked,
"What is the sign to prove that I will be
able to go to the Temple?"x

7 Isaiah replied, "The LORD will give
you a sign to prove that he will keep his
promise. 8 On the stairway built by King
Ahaz, the LORD will make the shadow go
back ten steps." And the shadow moved
back ten steps.y

9 After Hezekiah recovered from his
illness, he wrote this song of praise:

10 I thought that in the prime of life
    I was going to the world of the
        dead,
    Never to live out my life.
11 I thought that in this world of the
        living
    I would never again see the LORD
    Or any living person.
12 My life was cut off and ended,

Like a tent that is taken down,
Like cloth that is cut from a loom.
I thought that God was ending my
    life.z
13 All night I cried out with pain,
    As if a lion were breaking my
        bones.
I thought that God was ending my
    life.a
14 My voice was thin and weak,
    And I moaned like a dove.
My eyes grew tired from looking
    to heaven.
LORD, rescue me from all this
    trouble.
15 What can I say? The LORD has
    done this.
My heart is bitter, and I cannot
    sleep.b

16 Lord, I will live for you, for you
    alone;
Heal me and let me live.c
17 My bitterness will turn into peace.
You save d my life from all
    danger;
You forgive all my sins.
18 No one in the world of the dead
    can praise you;
The dead cannot trust in your
    faithfulness.
19 It is the living who praise you,
    As I praise you now.
Parents tell their children how
    faithful you are.
20 LORD, you have healed me.
We will play harps and sing your
    praise,
Sing praise in your Temple as long
    as we live.e

Messengers from Babylonia

(2 Kings 20.12-19)

39 About that same time the king of
Babylonia, Merodach Baladan,
son of Baladan, heard that King Hezekiah had been sick, so he sent him a letter and a present. 2 Hezekiah welcomed
the messengers and showed them his
wealth—his silver and gold, his spices
and perfumes, and all his military equipment. There was nothing in his storerooms or anywhere in his kingdom that

---

x *Verses 21-22 are moved here from the end of the chapter (see 2 K 20.6-9).*   y *stairway . . . ten
steps . . . steps; or sundial . . . ten degrees . . . degrees (see 2 K 20.9-11).*   z *I thought . . . my life;
Hebrew unclear.*   a *Verse 13 in Hebrew is unclear.*   b *One ancient translation suggests I
cannot sleep; Hebrew unclear.*   c *Verses 15 and 16 in Hebrew are unclear.*
d *Some ancient translations save; Hebrew love.*   e *Verses 21-22 are placed after verse 6.*

he did not show them. ³ Then the prophet Isaiah went to King Hezekiah and asked, "Where did these messengers come from and what did they say to you?"

Hezekiah answered, "They came from a very distant country, from Babylonia."

⁴ "What did they see in the palace?"

"They saw everything. There is nothing in the storerooms that I didn't show them."

⁵ Isaiah then told the king, "The LORD Almighty says that ⁶ a time is coming when everything in your palace, everything that your ancestors have stored up to this day, will be carried off to Babylonia. Nothing will be left. ⁷ Some of your own direct descendants will be taken away and made eunuchs to serve in the palace of the king of Babylonia."

⁸ King Hezekiah understood this to mean that there would be peace and security during his lifetime, so he replied, "The message you have given me from the LORD is good."

Words of Hope

40 "Comfort my people," says our God. "Comfort them!
² Encourage the people of
　Jerusalem.
Tell them they have suffered long
　enough
　and their sins are now
　　forgiven.ᶠ
I have punished them in full for all
　their sins."

³ A voice cries out,
"Prepare in the wilderness a road
　for the LORD!
　Clear the way in the desert for
　our God!
⁴ Fill every valley;
　level every mountain.
The hills will become a plain,
　and the rough country will be
　made smooth.
⁵ Then the glory of the LORD will be
　revealed,
　and all people will see it.

The LORD himself has promised
　this."

⁶ A voice cries out, "Proclaim a
　message!"
"What message shall I proclaim?"
　I ask.
"Proclaim that all human beings
　are like grass;
　they last no longer than wild
　flowers.
⁷ Grass withers and flowers fade
　when the LORD sends the wind
　blowing over them.
People are no more enduring
　than grass.
⁸ Yes, grass withers and flowers
　fade,
　but the word of our God endures
　forever."

⁹ Jerusalem, go up on a high
　mountain
　and proclaim the good news!
Call out with a loud voice, Zion;
　announce the good news!ᵍ
Speak out and do not be afraid.
Tell the towns of Judah
　that their God is coming!

¹⁰ The Sovereign LORD is coming to
　rule with power,
　bringing with him the people he
　has rescued.ʰ
¹¹ He will take care of his flock like
　a shepherd;
he will gather the lambs
　together
and carry them in his arms;
he will gently lead their
　mothers.

Israel's Incomparable God

¹² Can anyone measure the ocean by
　handfuls
　or measure the sky with his
　hands?
Can anyone hold the soil of the
　earth in a cup
　or weigh the mountains and hills
　on scales?
¹³ Can anyone tell the LORD what
　to do?
Who can teach him or give him
　advice?

ᶠ and their sins are now forgiven; or they have paid for what they did.　ᵍ Jerusalem, go up . . .
news!; or Go up on a high mountain and proclaim the good news to Jerusalem! Call out with a
loud voice and announce the good news to Zion!　ʰ the people he has rescued; or the rewards
he has for his people.

¹⁴With whom does God consult
    in order to know and understand
    and to learn how things should
    be done?

¹⁵To the LORD the nations are
    nothing,
    no more than a drop of water;
    the distant islands are as light as
    dust.
¹⁶All the animals in the forests of
    Lebanon
    are not enough for a sacrifice to
    our God,
    and its trees are too few to
    kindle the fire.
¹⁷The nations are nothing at all
    to him.

¹⁸To whom can God be compared?
    How can you describe what he
    is like?
¹⁹He is not like an idol that workers
    make,
    that metalworkers cover with
    gold
    and set in a base of silver.
²⁰Anyone who cannot afford silver
    or gold *i*
    chooses wood that will not rot.
    He finds a skillful worker
    to make an image that won't fall
    down.

²¹Do you not know?
    Were you not told long ago?
    Have you not heard how the
    world began?
²²It was made by the one who sits
    on his throne
    above the earth and beyond
    the sky;
    the people below look as tiny as
    ants.
    He stretched out the sky like a
    curtain,
    like a tent in which to live.

²³He brings down powerful rulers
    and reduces them to nothing.
²⁴They are like young plants,
    just set out and barely rooted.
    When the LORD sends a wind,
    they dry up and blow away like
    straw.

²⁵To whom can the holy God be
    compared?
    Is there anyone else like him?
²⁶Look up at the sky!
    Who created the stars you see?
    The one who leads them out like
    an army,
    he knows how many there are
    and calls each one by name!
    His power is so great —
    not one of them is ever missing!

²⁷Israel, why then do you complain
    that the LORD doesn't know your
    troubles
    or care if you suffer injustice?
²⁸Don't you know? Haven't you
    heard?
    The LORD is the everlasting God;
    he created all the world.
    He never grows tired or weary.
    No one understands his
    thoughts.
²⁹He strengthens those who are
    weak and tired.
³⁰Even those who are young grow
    weak;
    young people can fall exhausted.
³¹But those who trust in the LORD for
    help
    will find their strength renewed.
    They will rise on wings like
    eagles;
    they will run and not get weary;
    they will walk and not grow
    weak.

God's Assurance to Israel

41 God says,
    "Be silent and listen to me,
    you distant lands!
    Get ready to present your case
    in court;
    you will have your chance to
    speak.
    Let us come together to decide
    who is right.

²"Who was it that brought the
    conqueror from the east *j*
    and makes him triumphant
    wherever he goes?
    Who gives him victory over kings
    and nations?

i Verses 19-20a in Hebrew are unclear.   *j* THE CONQUEROR FROM THE EAST: *Cyrus, the emperor of
Persia (see 45.1).*

His sword strikes them down as
  if they were dust.
His arrows scatter them like
  straw before the wind.
3 He follows in pursuit and marches
    safely on,
  so fast that he hardly touches
    the ground!
4 Who was it that made this
    happen?
  Who has determined the course
    of history?
I, the LORD, was there at the
    beginning,
  and I, the LORD, will be there at
    the end.

5 "The people of distant lands have
    seen what I have done;
  they are frightened and tremble
    with fear.
  So they all assemble and come.
6 The skilled workers help and
    encourage each other.
7 The carpenter says to the
    goldsmith, 'Well done!'
  The one who beats the idol
    smooth
  encourages the one who nails it
    together.
  They say, 'The soldering is
    good' —
  and they fasten the idol in place
    with nails.

8 "But you, Israel my servant,
  you are the people that I have
    chosen,
  the descendants of Abraham, my
    friend.
9 I brought you from the ends of the
    earth;
  I called you from its farthest
    corners
  and said to you, 'You are my
    servant.'
I did not reject you, but chose you.
10 Do not be afraid — I am with you!
  I am your God — let nothing
    terrify you!
  I will make you strong and
    help you;
  I will protect you and save you.

11 "Those who are angry with you
  will know the shame of defeat.
  Those who fight against you
    will die

12   and will disappear from the
      earth.
13 I am the LORD your God;
  I strengthen you and tell you,
  'Do not be afraid; I will
    help you.' "

14 The LORD says,
  "Small and weak as you are,
    Israel,
  don't be afraid; I will help you.
I, the holy God of Israel, am the
    one who saves you.
15 I will make you like a threshing
    board,
  with spikes that are new and
    sharp.
  You will thresh mountains and
    destroy them;
  hills will crumble into dust.
16 You will toss them in the air,
  the wind will carry them off,
  and they will be scattered by the
    storm.
  Then you will be happy because I
    am your God;
  you will praise me, the holy God
    of Israel.

17 "When my people in their need
    look for water,
  when their throats are dry with
    thirst,
  then I, the LORD, will answer their
    prayer;
  I, the God of Israel, will never
    abandon them.
18 I will make rivers flow among
    barren hills
  and springs of water run in the
    valleys.
  I will turn the desert into pools of
    water
  and the dry land into flowing
    springs.
19 I will make cedars grow in the
    desert,
  and acacias and myrtles and
    olive trees.
  Forests will grow in barren land,
    forests of pine and juniper and
    cypress.
20 People will see this and know
    that I, the LORD, have done it.
  They will come to understand
    that Israel's holy God has made
    it happen."

The Lord's Challenge to False Gods

21 The Lord, the king of Israel, has this
to say:

"You gods of the nations, present
your case.
Bring the best arguments you
have!
22 Come here and predict what will
happen,
so that we will know it when it
takes place.
Explain to the court the events of
the past,
and tell us what they
mean.
23 Tell us what the future holds—
then we will know that you are
gods!
Do something good or bring some
disaster;
fill us with fear and awe!
24 You and all you do are
nothing;
those who worship you are
disgusting!

25 "I have chosen a man who lives in
the east;*k*
I will bring him to attack from
the north.
He tramples on rulers as if they
were mud,
like a potter trampling
clay.
26 Which of you predicted that this
would happen,
so that we could say that you
were right?
None of you said a word about it;
no one heard you say a
thing!
27 I, the Lord, was the first to tell
Zion the news;
I sent a messenger to Jerusalem
to say,
'Your people are coming! They
are coming home!'*l*
28 When I looked among the gods,
none of them had a thing to
say;
not one could answer the
questions I asked.
29 All these gods are useless;
they can do nothing at all—
these idols are weak and
powerless."

The Lord's Servant

42 The Lord says,
"Here is my servant, whom I
strengthen—
the one I have chosen, with
whom I am pleased.
I have filled him with my Spirit,
and he will bring justice to every
nation.
2 He will not shout or raise his voice
or make loud speeches in the
streets.
3 He will not break off a bent reed
nor put out a flickering lamp.
He will bring lasting justice to all.
4 He will not lose hope or courage;
he will establish justice on the
earth.
Distant lands eagerly wait for
his teaching."

5 God created the heavens and
stretched them out;
he fashioned the earth and all
that lives there;
he gave life and breath to all its
people.
And now the Lord God says to his
servant,
6 "I, the Lord, have called you and
given you power
to see that justice is done on
earth.
Through you I will make a
covenant with all peoples;
through you I will bring light to
the nations.
7 You will open the eyes of the blind
and set free those who sit in
dark prisons.

8 "I alone am the Lord your God.
No other god may share my
glory;
I will not let idols share my
praise.
9 The things I predicted have now
come true.
Now I will tell you of new things
even before they begin to
happen."

A Song of Praise

10 Sing a new song to the Lord;
sing his praise, all the world!
Praise him, you that sail the sea;

---

k A MAN WHO LIVES IN THE EAST: See 41.2.   *l* Verse 27 in Hebrew is unclear.

praise him, all creatures of
the sea!
Sing, distant lands and all who
live there!
11 Let the desert and its towns
praise God;
let the people of Kedar
praise him!
Let those who live in the city of
Sela
shout for joy from the tops of
the mountains!
12 Let those who live in distant lands
give praise and glory to the
LORD!
13 The LORD goes out to fight like a
warrior;
he is ready and eager for battle.
He gives a war cry, a battle
shout;
he shows his power against his
enemies.

God Promises to Help His People

14 God says,
"For a long time I kept silent;
I did not answer my people.
But now the time to act has come;
I cry out like a woman in labor.
15 I will destroy the hills and
mountains
and dry up the grass and trees.
I will turn the river valleys into
deserts *m*
and dry up the pools of water.

16 "I will lead my blind people
by roads they have never
traveled.
I will turn their darkness into light
and make rough country smooth
before them.
These are my promises,
and I will keep them without
fail.
17 All who trust in idols,
who call images their gods,
will be humiliated and
disgraced."

Israel's Failure to Learn

18 The LORD says,
"Listen, you deaf people!
Look closely, you that are blind!
19 Is anyone more blind than my
servant,

more deaf than the messenger I
send?
20 Israel, you have seen so much,
but what has it meant to you?
You have ears to hear with,
but what have you really
heard?"

21 The LORD is a God who is eager to
save,
so he exalted his laws and
teachings,
and he wanted his people to
honor them.
22 But now his people have been
plundered;
they are locked up in dungeons
and hidden away in prisons.
They were robbed and plundered,
with no one to come to their
rescue.

23 Will any of you listen to this?
From now on will you listen
with care?
24 Who gave Israel up to the looters?
It was the LORD himself, against
whom we sinned!
We would not live as he wanted us
to live
or obey the teachings he
gave us.
25 So he made us feel the force of his
anger
and suffer the violence of war.
Like fire his anger burned
throughout Israel,
but we never knew what was
happening;
we learned nothing at all
from it.

God Promises to Rescue His People

43 Israel, the LORD who created you
says,
"Do not be afraid—I will
save you.
I have called you by name—you
are mine.
2 When you pass through deep
waters, I will be with you;
your troubles will not
overwhelm you.
When you pass through fire, you
will not be burned;

---

m Probable text deserts; Hebrew coastlands.

the hard trials that come will not
hurt you.
3 For I am the LORD your God,
the holy God of Israel, who
saves you.
I will give up Egypt to set you
free;
I will give up Ethiopia[n] and
Seba.
4 I will give up whole nations to
save your life,
because you are precious to me
and because I love you and give
you honor.
5 Do not be afraid—I am with you!

"From the distant east and the
farthest west
I will bring your people home.
6 I will tell the north to let them go
and the south not to hold them
back.
Let my people return from distant
lands,
from every part of the world.
7 They are my own people,
and I created them to bring me
glory."

Israel Is the LORD's Witness

8 God says,
"Summon my people to court.
They have eyes, but they are
blind;
they have ears, but they are
deaf!
9 Summon the nations to come to
the trial.
Which of their gods can predict
the future?
Which of them foretold what is
happening now?
Let these gods bring in their
witnesses
to prove that they are right,
to testify to the truth of their
words.

10 "People of Israel, you are my
witnesses;
I chose you to be my servant,
so that you would know me and
believe in me
and understand that I am the
only God.

Besides me there is no other god;
there never was and never
will be.
11 "I alone am the LORD,
the only one who can save you.
12 I predicted what would happen,
and then I came to your aid.
No foreign god has ever done this;
you are my witnesses.
13 I am God and always will be.
No one can escape from my
power;
no one can change what I do."

Escape from Babylon

14 Israel's holy God, the LORD who
saves you, says,
"To save you, I will send an army
against Babylon;
I will break down the city gates,
and the shouts of her people will
turn into crying.
15 I am the LORD, your holy God.
I created you, Israel, and I am
your king."

16 Long ago the LORD made a road
through the sea,
a path through the swirling
waters.
17 He led a mighty army to
destruction,
an army of chariots and horses.
Down they fell, never to rise,
snuffed out like the flame of a
lamp!

18 But the LORD says,
"Do not cling to events of the past
or dwell on what happened
long ago.
19 Watch for the new thing I am
going to do.
It is happening already—you
can see it now!
I will make a road through the
wilderness
and give you streams of water
there.
20 Even the wild animals will
honor me;
jackals and ostriches will
praise me

---

[n] *Hebrew* Cush: *Cush is the ancient name of the extensive territory south of the First Cataract
of the Nile River. This region was called Ethiopia in Graeco-Roman times, and included within
its borders most of modern Sudan and some of present-day Ethiopia (Abyssinia).*

when I make rivers flow in the
desert
to give water to my chosen
people.
21 They are the people I made for
myself,
and they will sing my praises!"

Israel's Sin

22 The LORD says,
"But you were tired of me, Israel;
you did not worship me.
23 You did not bring me your burnt
offerings of sheep;
you did not honor me with your
sacrifices.
I did not burden you by
demanding offerings
or wear you out by asking for
incense.
24 You didn't buy incense for me
or satisfy me with the fat of
your animals.
Instead you burdened me with
your sins;
you wore me out with the
wrongs you have committed.
25 And yet, I am the God who
forgives your sins,
and I do this because of who
I am.
I will not hold your sins
against you.

26 "Let us go to court; bring your
accusation!
Present your case to prove you
are in the right!
27 Your earliest ancestor[o] sinned;
your leaders sinned against me,
28 and your rulers profaned[p] my
sanctuary.
So I brought destruction on Israel;
I let my own people be insulted."

The LORD Is the Only God

44 The LORD says,
"Listen now, Israel, my
servant,
my chosen people, the
descendants of Jacob.
2 I am the LORD who created you;
from the time you were born, I
have helped you.
Do not be afraid; you are my
servant,
my chosen people whom I love.

3 "I will give water to the thirsty
land
and make streams flow on the
dry ground.
I will pour out my spirit on your
children
and my blessing on your
descendants.
4 They will thrive like well-watered
grass,
like willows by streams of
running water.

5 "One by one, people will say, 'I am
the LORD's.'
They will come to join the
people of Israel.
They each will mark the name of
the LORD on their arms
and call themselves one of God's
people."

6 The LORD, who rules and protects
Israel,
the LORD Almighty, has this
to say:
"I am the first, the last, the
only God;
there is no other god but me.
7 Could anyone else have done what
I did?
Who could have predicted all
that would happen
from the very beginning to the
end of time?[q]
8 Do not be afraid, my people!
You know that from ancient times
until now
I have predicted all that would
happen,
and you are my witnesses.
Is there any other god?
Is there some powerful god I never
heard of?"

Idolatry Is Ridiculed

9 All those who make idols are worthless, and the gods they prize so highly
are useless. Those who worship these
gods are blind and ignorant—and they
will be disgraced. 10 It does no good to

[o] YOUR EARLIEST ANCESTOR: *A reference to Jacob or to Abraham, or possibly to Adam.*
[p] *One ancient translation* your rulers profaned; *Hebrew* I profaned the rulers of.
[q] *Verse 7 in Hebrew is unclear.*

make a metal image to worship as a god!
[11] Everyone who worships it will be humiliated. The people who make idols are human beings and nothing more. Let them come and stand trial—they will be terrified and will suffer disgrace.

[12] The metalworker takes a piece of metal and works with it over a fire. His strong arm swings a hammer to pound the metal into shape. As he works, he gets hungry, thirsty, and tired.

[13] The carpenter measures the wood. He outlines a figure with chalk, carves it out with his tools, and makes it in the form of a man, a handsome human figure, to be placed in his house. [14] He might cut down cedars to use, or choose oak or cypress wood from the forest. Or he might plant a laurel tree and wait for the rain to make it grow. [15] A person uses part of a tree for fuel and part of it for making an idol. With one part he builds a fire to warm himself and bake bread; with the other part he makes a god and worships it. [16] With some of the wood he makes a fire; he roasts meat, eats it, and is satisfied. He warms himself and says, "How nice and warm! What a beautiful fire!" [17] The rest of the wood he makes into an idol, and then he bows down and worships it. He prays to it and says, "You are my god— save me!"

[18] Such people are too stupid to know what they are doing. They close their eyes and their minds to the truth. [19] The maker of idols hasn't the wit or the sense to say, "Some of the wood I burned up. I baked some bread on the coals, and I roasted meat and ate it. And the rest of the wood I made into an idol. Here I am bowing down to a block of wood!"

[20] It makes as much sense[r] as eating ashes. His foolish ideas have so misled him that he is beyond help. He won't admit to himself that the idol he holds in his hand is not a god at all.

The LORD, the Creator and Savior

[21] The LORD says,
"Israel, remember this;
    remember that you are my
        servant.
I created you to be my servant,
    and I will never forget you.

[22] I have swept your sins away like a
        cloud.
    Come back to me; I am the one
        who saves you."

[23] Shout for joy, you heavens!
    Shout, deep places of the earth!
Shout for joy, mountains, and
        every tree of the forest!
The LORD has shown his greatness
    by saving his people Israel.

[24] "I am the LORD, your savior;
    I am the one who created you.
I am the LORD, the Creator of all
        things.
    I alone stretched out the
        heavens;
    when I made the earth, no one
        helped me.
[25] I make fools of fortunetellers
    and frustrate the predictions of
        astrologers.
The words of the wise I refute
    and show that their wisdom is
        foolishness.
[26] But when my servant makes a
        prediction,
    when I send a messenger to
        reveal my plans,
    I make those plans and
        predictions come true.
I tell Jerusalem that people will
        live there again,
    and the cities of Judah that they
        will be rebuilt.
    Those cities will rise from the
        ruins.
[27] With a word of command I dry up
        the ocean.
[28] I say to Cyrus, 'You are the one
        who will rule for me;
    you will do what I want you
        to do:
    you will order that Jerusalem be
        rebuilt
    and that the foundations of the
        Temple be laid.' "

The LORD Appoints Cyrus

45 The LORD has chosen Cyrus to
        be king.
He has appointed him to conquer
        nations;
    he sends him to strip kings of
        their power;

---

[r] It makes as much sense; *or* It will do him as much good.

the LORD will open the gates of
cities for him.
To Cyrus the LORD says,
2 "I myself will prepare your way,
leveling mountains and hills.
I will break down bronze gates
and smash their iron bars.
3 I will give you treasures from
dark, secret places;
then you will know that I am the
LORD
and that the God of Israel has
called you by name.
4 I appoint you to help my servant
Israel,
the people that I have chosen.
I have given you great honor,
although you do not know me.

5 "I am the LORD; there is no
other god.
I will give you the strength you
need,
although you do not know me.
6 I do this so that everyone
from one end of the world to the
other
may know that I am the LORD
and that there is no other god.
7 I create both light and darkness;
I bring both blessing and
disaster.
I, the LORD, do all these things.
8 I will send victory from the sky
like rain;
the earth will open to receive it
and will blossom with freedom
and justice.
I, the LORD, will make this
happen."

The LORD of Creation and History

9 Does a clay pot dare argue with its
maker,
a pot that is like all the others?
Does the clay ask the potter what
he is doing?
Does the pot complain that its
maker has no skill?
10 Do we dare say to our parents,
"Why did you make me like
this?"
11 The LORD, the holy God of Israel,
the one who shapes the future,
says:

"You have no right to question me
about my children
or to tell me what I ought to do!
12 I am the one who made the earth
and created human beings to
live there.
By my power I stretched out the
heavens;
I control the sun, the moon, and
the stars.
13 I myself have stirred Cyrus to
action
to fulfill my purpose and put
things right.
I will straighten out every road
that he travels.
He will rebuild my city,
Jerusalem,
and set my captive people free.
No one has hired him or bribed
him to do this."
The LORD Almighty has spoken.

14 The LORD says to Israel,
"The wealth of Egypt and
Ethiopia[s] will be yours,
and the tall men of Seba will be
your slaves;
they will follow you in chains.
They will bow down to you and
confess,
'God is with you—he alone
is God.
15 The God of Israel, who saves his
people,
is a God who conceals himself.
16 Those who make idols will all be
ashamed;
all of them will be disgraced.
17 But Israel is saved by the LORD,
and her victory lasts forever;
her people will never be
disgraced.' "

18 The LORD created the heavens—
he is the one who is God!
He formed and made the earth—
he made it firm and lasting.
He did not make it a desolate
waste,
but a place for people to live.
It is he who says, "I am the LORD,
and there is no other god.
19 I have not spoken in secret
or kept my purpose hidden.

[s] *Hebrew* Cush: *Cush is the ancient name of the extensive territory south of the First Cataract of the Nile River. This region was called Ethiopia in Graeco-Roman times, and included within its borders most of modern Sudan and some of present-day Ethiopia (Abyssinia).*

I did not require the people of
    Israel
  to look for me in a desolate
    waste.
  I am the LORD, and I speak the
    truth;
  I make known what is right."

The LORD of the World and the Idols of Babylon

20 The LORD says,
  "Come together, people of the
    nations,
  all who survive the fall of the
    empire;
  present yourselves for the trial!
  The people who parade with their
    idols of wood
  and pray to gods that cannot
    save them—
    those people know nothing
    at all!
21 Come and present your case in
    court;
  let the defendants consult one
    another.
  Who predicted long ago what
    would happen?
  Was it not I, the LORD, the God
    who saves his people?
  There is no other god.

22 "Turn to me now and be saved,
    people all over the world!
  I am the only God there is.
23 My promise is true,
    and it will not be changed.
  I solemnly promise by all that
    I am:
    Everyone will come and kneel
    before me
    and vow to be loyal to me.

24 "They will say that only
    through me
  are victory and strength to be
    found;
  but all who hate me will suffer
    disgrace.
25 I, the LORD, will rescue all the
    descendants of Jacob,
  and they will give me praise.

46 "This is the end for Babylon's
    gods!
  Bel and Nebo once were
    worshiped,

  but now they are loaded on
    donkeys,
  a burden for the backs of tired
    animals.
2 The idols cannot save
    themselves;
  they are captured and carried
    away.
This is the end for Babylon's gods!

3 "Listen to me, descendants of
    Jacob,
  all who are left of my people.
  I have cared for you from the time
    you were born.
4 I am your God and will take care
    of you
  until you are old and your hair
    is gray.
  I made you and will care for you;
    I will give you help and
    rescue you.

5 "To whom will you compare me?"
    says the LORD.
  "Is there anyone else like me?
6 People open their purses and pour
    out gold;
  they weigh out silver on the
    scales.
  They hire a goldsmith to make
    a god;
  then they bow down and
    worship it.
7 They lift it to their shoulders and
    carry it;
  they put it in place, and there it
    stands,
  unable to move from where it is.
  If any pray to it, it cannot answer
    or save them from disaster.

8 "Remember this, you sinners;
    consider what I have done.
9 Remember what happened
    long ago;
  acknowledge that I alone
    am God
  and that there is no one else
    like me.
10 From the beginning I predicted the
    outcome;
  long ago I foretold what would
    happen.
  I said that my plans would never
    fail,
  that I would do everything I
    intended to do.

11 I am calling a man to come from
       the east;[t]
     he will swoop down like a hawk
     and accomplish what I have
        planned.
     I have spoken, and it will be done.

12 "Listen to me, you stubborn people
     who think that victory is far
        away.
13 I am bringing the day of victory
     near—
     it is not far away at all,
     My triumph will not be delayed.
     I will save Jerusalem
     and bring honor to Israel there."

Judgment on Babylon

47 The LORD says,
       "Babylon, come down from
          your throne,
     and sit in the dust on the
        ground.
     You were once like a virgin, a city
        unconquered,
       but you are soft and delicate no
          longer!
     You are now a slave!
2 Turn the millstone! Grind the
        flour!
     Off with your veil! Strip off your
        fine clothes!
     Lift up your skirts to cross the
        streams![u]
3 People will see you naked;
     they will see you humbled and
        shamed.
     I will take vengeance, and no one
        will stop me."

4 The holy God of Israel sets us
       free—
     his name is the LORD Almighty.

5 The LORD says to Babylon,
     "Sit in silence and darkness;
       no more will they call you the
          queen of nations!
6 I was angry with my people;
     I treated them as no longer
        mine:
     I put them in your power,
       and you showed them no mercy;
     even the aged you treated
        harshly.

7 You thought you would always be
       a queen,
     and did not take these things to
        heart
     or think how it all would end.

8 "Listen to this, you lover of
       pleasure,
     you that think you are safe and
        secure.
     You claim you are as great
        as God—
       that there is no one else
          like you.
     You thought that you would never
       be a widow
     or suffer the loss of your
        children.
9 But in a moment, in a single day,
       both of these things will happen.
     In spite of all the magic you use,
       you will lose your husband and
          children.

10 "You felt sure of yourself in your
       evil;
     you thought that no one could
        see you.
     Your wisdom and knowledge led
       you astray,
     and you said to yourself, 'I
        am God—
       there is no one else like me.'
11 Disaster will come upon you,
     and none of your magic can
        stop it.
     Ruin will come on you suddenly—
       ruin you never dreamed of!
12 Keep all your magic spells and
       charms;
     you have used them since you
        were young.
     Perhaps they will be of some help
        to you;
       perhaps you can frighten your
          enemies.
13 You are powerless in spite of the
       advice you get.
     Let your astrologers come forward
       and save you—
     those people who study the
        stars,
     who map out the zones of the
        heavens

---

[t] A MAN TO COME FROM THE EAST: See 41.2.   [u] CROSS THE STREAMS: This probably refers to going
into exile.

and tell you from month to
month
what[v] is going to happen
to you.

14 "They will be like bits of straw,
and a fire will burn them up!
They will not even be able to save
themselves —
the flames will be too hot for
them,
not a cozy fire to warm
themselves by.
15 That is all the good they will
do you —
those astrologers you've
consulted all your life.
They all will leave you and go
their own way,
and none will be left to
save you."

God Is Lord of the Future

48 Listen to this, people of Israel,
you that are descended from
Judah:
You swear by the name of the
Lord
and claim to worship the God of
Israel —
but you don't mean a word
you say.
2 And yet you are proud to say
that you are citizens of the holy
city
and that you depend on
Israel's God,
whose name is the Lord
Almighty.

3 The Lord says to Israel,
"Long ago I predicted what would
take place;
then suddenly I made it happen.
4 I knew that you would prove to be
stubborn,
as rigid as iron and unyielding
as bronze.
5 And so I predicted your future
long ago,
announcing events before they
took place,
to keep you from claiming
that your idols and images made
them happen.

6 "All I foretold has now taken
place;
you have to admit my
predictions were right.
Now I will tell you of new things
to come,
events that I did not reveal
before.
7 Only now am I making them
happen;
nothing like this took place in
the past.
If it had, you would claim that you
knew all about it.
8 I knew that you couldn't be
trusted,
that you have always been
known as a rebel.
That is why you never heard of
this at all,
why no word of it ever came to
your ears.

9 "In order that people will praise
my name,
I am holding my anger in check;
I am keeping it back and will
not destroy you.
10 I have tested you in the fire of
suffering,
as silver is refined in a furnace.
But I have found that you are
worthless.
11 What I do is done for my own
sake —
I will not let my name be
dishonored
or let anyone else share the
glory
that should be mine and mine
alone."

Cyrus, the Lord's Chosen Leader

12 The Lord says,
"Listen to me, Israel, the people I
have called!
I am God, the first, the last, the
only God!
13 My hands made the earth's
foundations
and spread the heavens out.
When I summon earth and sky,
they come at once and present
themselves.

14 "Assemble and listen, all of you!

v Some ancient translations what; Hebrew from what.

None of the gods could predict
that the man I have chosen
would attack Babylon;
he will do what I want him
to do.
15 I am the one who spoke and
called him;
I led him out and gave him
success.

16 "Now come close to me and hear
what I say.
From the beginning I have
spoken openly
and have always made my
words come true."
(Now the Sovereign Lord has given me
his power and sent me.)

The Lord's Plan for His People

17 The holy God of Israel,
the Lord who saves you, says:
"I am the Lord your God,
the one who wants to teach you
for your own good
and direct you in the way you
should go.

18 "If only you had listened to my
commands!
Then blessings would have flowed
for you
like a stream that never
goes dry.
Victory would have come to you
like the waves that roll on the
shore.
19 Your descendants would be as
numerous as grains of sand,
and I would have made sure
they were never destroyed."

20 Go out from Babylon, go free!
Shout the news gladly; make it
known everywhere:
"The Lord has saved his servant
Israel!"
21 When the Lord led his people
through a hot, dry desert,
they did not suffer from thirst.
He made water come from a rock
for them;
he split the rock open, and water
flowed out.

22 "There is no safety for sinners,"
says the Lord.

Israel, A Light to the Nations

49 Listen to me, distant nations,
you people who live far
away!
Before I was born, the Lord
chose me
and appointed me to be his
servant.
2 He made my words as sharp as a
sword.
With his own hand he
protected me.w
He made me like an arrow,
sharp and ready for use.
3 He said to me, "Israel, you are my
servant;
because of you, people will
praise me."

4 I said, "I have worked, but how
hopeless it is!
I have used up my strength, but
have accomplished nothing."
Yet I can trust the Lord to defend
my cause;
he will reward me for what I do.

5 Before I was born, the Lord
appointed me;
he made me his servant to bring
back his people,
to bring back the scattered
people of Israel.
The Lord gives me honor;
he is the source of my strength.

6 The Lord said to me,
"I have a greater task for you, my
servant.
Not only will you restore to
greatness
the people of Israel who have
survived,
but I will also make you a light to
the nations—
so that all the world may be
saved."

7 Israel's holy God and savior says
to the one who is deeply
despised,
who is hated by the nations
and is the servant of rulers:

w With his own hand . . . me; or He kept me hidden in his hand.

"Kings will see you released
  and will rise to show their
    respect;
princes also will see it,
  and they will bow low to
    honor you."

This will happen because the LORD
    has chosen his servant;
the holy God of Israel keeps his
    promises.

The Restoration of Jerusalem

8 The LORD says to his people,
  "When the time comes to save
      you, I will show you favor
    and answer your cries for help.
  I will guard and protect you
    and through you make a
        covenant with all peoples.
  I will let you settle once again
    in your land that is now laid
        waste.
9 I will say to the prisoners, 'Go
      free!'
    and to those who are in
        darkness,
    'Come out to the light!'
  They will be like sheep that graze
      on the hills;
10   they will never be hungry or
        thirsty.
    Sun and desert heat will not hurt
        them,
    for they will be led by one who
        loves them.
    He will lead them to springs of
        water.

11 "I will make a highway across the
        mountains
    and prepare a road for my
        people to travel.
12 My people will come from far
        away,
    from the north and the west,
    and from Aswan^x in the south."

13 Sing, heavens! Shout for joy,
      earth!
    Let the mountains burst into
        song!
  The LORD will comfort his people;
    he will have pity on his suffering
        people.

14 But the people of Jerusalem said,
  "The LORD has abandoned us!
    He has forgotten us."
15 So the LORD answers,
  "Can a woman forget her own
        baby
    and not love the child she bore?
  Even if a mother should forget her
        child,
    I will never forget you.
16 Jerusalem, I can never forget you!
    I have written your name on the
        palms of my hands.

17 "Those who will rebuild you are
        coming soon,
    and those who destroyed you
        will leave.
18 Look around and see what is
        happening!
    Your people are assembling—
        they are coming home!
  As surely as I am the living God,
    you will be proud of your
        people,
    as proud as a bride is of her
        jewels.

19 "Your country was ruined and
        desolate—
    but now it will be too small
    for those who are coming to live
        there.
  And those who left you in ruins
    will be far removed from you.
20 Your people who were born in
        exile
    will one day say to you,
  'This land is too small—
    we need more room to live in!'
21 Then you will say to yourself,
  'Who bore all these children
        for me?
  I lost my children and could have
        no more.
  I was exiled and driven away—
    who brought these children up?
  I was left all alone—
    where did these children come
        from?' "

22 The Sovereign LORD says to his
people:
  "I will signal to the nations,
    and they will bring your
        children home.

---

x ASWAN: *A city in southern Egypt, where a large Jewish community had settled.*

23 Kings will be like fathers to you;
   queens will be like mothers.
They will bow low before you and
   honor you;
   they will humbly show their
   respect for you.
Then you will know that I am the
   LORD;
   no one who waits for my help
   will be disappointed."

24 Can you take away a soldier's
   loot?
   Can you rescue the prisoners of
   a tyrant?

25 The LORD replies,
   "That is just what is going to
   happen.
The soldier's prisoners will be
   taken away,
   and the tyrant's loot will be
   seized.
I will fight against whoever
   fights you,
   and I will rescue your children.
26 I will make your oppressors kill
   each other;
   they will be drunk with murder
   and rage.
Then all people will know that I
   am the LORD,
   the one who saves you and sets
   you free.
They will know that I am Israel's
   powerful God."

50 The LORD says,
   "Do you think I sent my
      people away
   like a man who divorces his
      wife?
   Where, then, are the papers of
      divorce?
Do you think I sold you into
   captivity
   like a man who sells his children
   as slaves?
No, you went away captive
   because of your sins;
   you were sent away because of
   your crimes.

2 "Why did my people fail to
   respond
   when I went to them to save
   them?

Why did they not answer when I
   called?
Am I too weak to save them?
I can dry up the sea with a
   command
   and turn rivers into a desert,
   so that the fish in them die for
   lack of water.
3 I can make the sky turn dark,
   as if it were in mourning for the
   dead."

The Obedience of the LORD's Servant

4 The Sovereign LORD has taught me
      what to say,
   so that I can strengthen the
   weary.
Every morning he makes me eager
   to hear what he is going to
   teach me.
5 The LORD has given me
   understanding,
   and I have not rebelled
   or turned away from him.
6 I bared my back to those who
      beat me.
   I did not stop them when they
   insulted me,
   when they pulled out the hairs
   of my beard
   and spit in my face.

7 But their insults cannot hurt me
   because the Sovereign LORD
   gives me help.
I brace myself to endure them.
   I know that I will not be
   disgraced,
8   for God is near,
   and he will prove me innocent.
Does anyone dare bring charges
   against me?
   Let us go to court together!
   Let him bring his accusation!
9 The Sovereign LORD himself
   defends me —
   who, then, can prove me guilty?
All my accusers will disappear;
   they will vanish like moth-eaten
   cloth.

10 All of you that honor the LORD
   and obey the words of his
   servant,
   the path you walk may be dark
   indeed,
   but trust in the LORD, rely on
   your God.

11 All of you that plot to destroy
others
will be destroyed by your own
plots.
The LORD himself will make this
happen;
you will suffer a miserable fate.

Words of Comfort to Jerusalem

51 The LORD says,
"Listen to me, you that want
to be saved,
you that come to me for help.
Think of the rock from which you
came,
the quarry from which you
were cut.
2 Think of your ancestor, Abraham,
and of Sarah, from whom you
are descended.
When I called Abraham, he was
childless,
but I blessed him and gave him
children;
I made his descendants
numerous.

3 "I will show compassion to
Jerusalem,
to all who live in her ruins.
Though her land is a desert, I will
make it a garden,
like the garden I planted in
Eden.
Joy and gladness will be there,
and songs of praise and thanks
to me.

4 "Listen to me, my people,
listen to what I say:
I give my teaching to the nations;
my laws will bring them light.
5 I will come quickly and save them;
the time of my victory is near.
I myself will rule over the nations.
Distant lands wait for me to
come;
they wait with hope for me to
save them.
6 Look up at the heavens; look at
the earth!
The heavens will disappear like
smoke;
the earth will wear out like old
clothing,

and all its people will die like
flies.
But the deliverance I bring will
last forever;
my victory will be final.

7 "Listen to me, you that know what
is right,
who have my teaching fixed in
your hearts.
Do not be afraid when people
taunt and insult you;
8 they will vanish like moth-eaten
clothing!
But the deliverance I bring will
last forever;
my victory will endure for all
time."

9 Wake up, LORD, and help us!
Use your power and save us;
use it as you did in ancient
times.
It was you that cut the sea
monster Rahab[y] to pieces.
10 It was you also who dried up
the sea
and made a path through the
water,
so that those you were saving
could cross.
11 Those whom you have rescued
will reach Jerusalem with
gladness,
singing and shouting for joy.
They will be happy forever,
forever free from sorrow and
grief.

12 The LORD says,
"I am the one who
strengthens you.
Why should you fear mortals,
who are no more enduring than
grass?
13 Have you forgotten the LORD who
made you,
who stretched out the heavens
and laid the earth's foundations?
Why should you live in constant
fear
of the fury of those who
oppress you,
of those who are ready to
destroy you?

y RAHAB: *A legendary sea monster, which represented the forces of chaos and evil, was
sometimes a symbol of Egypt.*

Their fury can no longer
   touch you.
14 Those who are prisoners will soon
   be set free;
   they will live a long life
   and have all the food they need.

15 "I am the LORD your God;
   I stir up the sea
   and make its waves roar.
My name is the LORD Almighty!
16 I stretched out^z the heavens
   and laid the earth's foundations;
I say to Jerusalem, 'You are my
   people!
I have given you my teaching,
and I protect you with my
   hand.' "

The End of Jerusalem's Suffering

17 Jerusalem, wake up!
   Rouse yourself and get up!
You have drunk the cup of
   punishment
   that the LORD in his anger gave
   you to drink;
you drank it down, and it made
   you stagger.
18 There is no one to lead you,
   no one among your people
   to take you by the hand.

19 A double disaster has fallen
   on you:
   your land has been devastated
   by war,
   and your people have starved.
There is no one to show you
   sympathy.
20 At the corner of every street
   your people collapse from
   weakness;
   they are like deer caught in a
   hunter's net.
They have felt the force of God's
   anger.

21 You suffering people of Jerusalem,
   you that stagger as though you
   were drunk,
22 the LORD your God defends you
   and says,
"I am taking away the cup
   that I gave you in my anger.
You will no longer have to drink

the wine that makes you
   stagger.
23 I will give it to those who
   oppressed you,
to those who made you lie down
   in the streets
and trampled on you as if you
   were dirt."

God Will Rescue Jerusalem

52 Jerusalem, be strong and great
   again!
Holy city of God, clothe yourself
   with splendor!
The heathen will never enter your
   gates again.
2 Shake yourself free, Jerusalem!
Rise from the dust and sit on
   your throne!
Undo the chains that bind you,
   captive people of Zion!

3 The Sovereign LORD says to his people, "When you became slaves, no
money was paid for you; in the same
way nothing will be paid to set you free.
4 When you went to live in Egypt as foreigners, you did so of your own free will;
Assyria, however, took you away by
force and paid nothing for you. 5 And
now in Babylonia the same thing has
happened: you are captives, and nothing
was paid for you. Those who rule over
you boast and brag and constantly show
contempt for me. 6 In time to come you
will acknowledge that I am God and that
I have spoken to you."

7 How wonderful it is to see
   a messenger coming across the
   mountains,
   bringing good news, the news of
   peace!
He announces victory and says to
   Zion,
"Your God is king!"
8 Those who guard the city are
   shouting,
   shouting together for joy.
They can see with their own eyes
   the return of the LORD to Zion.

9 Break into shouts of joy,
   you ruins of Jerusalem!
The LORD will rescue his city
   and comfort his people.

I
S
A
I
A
H

---

^z *One ancient translation* stretched out; *Hebrew* planted.

10 The LORD will use his holy power;
    he will save his people,
    and all the world will see it.
11 Be sure to leave Babylonia,
    all you that carry the Temple
      equipment.
    Touch no forbidden thing;*a*
    keep yourselves holy and leave.
12 This time you will not have to
      leave in a hurry;
    you will not be trying to escape.
    The LORD your God will lead you
      and protect you on every side.

The Suffering Servant

13 The LORD says,
    "My servant will succeed in his
      task;
    he will be highly honored.*b*
14 Many people were shocked when
      they saw him;
    he was so disfigured that he
      hardly looked human.
15 But now many nations will marvel
      at him,
    and kings will be speechless
      with amazement.
    They will see and understand
      something they had never
      known."

53 The people reply,
    "Who would have believed
      what we now report?
    Who could have seen the LORD's
      hand in this?
2 It was the will of the LORD that his
      servant
    grow like a plant taking root in
      dry ground.
    He had no dignity or beauty
      to make us take notice of him.
    There was nothing attractive
      about him,
    nothing that would draw us
      to him.
3 We despised him and
      rejected him;
    he endured suffering and pain.
    No one would even look at him —
    we ignored him as if he were
      nothing.

4 "But he endured the suffering that
      should have been ours,

    the pain that we should have
      borne.
    All the while we thought that his
      suffering
    was punishment sent by God.
5 But because of our sins he was
      wounded,
    beaten because of the evil
      we did.
    We are healed by the punishment
      he suffered,
    made whole by the blows he
      received.
6 All of us were like sheep that were
      lost,
    each of us going his own way.
    But the LORD made the punishment
      fall on him,
    the punishment all of us
      deserved.

7 "He was treated harshly, but
      endured it humbly;
    he never said a word.
    Like a lamb about to be
      slaughtered,
    like a sheep about to be sheared,
    he never said a word.
8 He was arrested and sentenced
      and led off to die,
    and no one cared about his fate.
    He was put to death for the sins of
      our people.
9 He was placed in a grave with
      those who are evil,
    he was buried with the rich,
    even though he had never
      committed a crime
    or ever told a lie."

10 The LORD says,
    "It was my will that he should
      suffer;
    his death was a sacrifice to
      bring forgiveness.
    And so he will see his
      descendants;
    he will live a long life,
    and through him my purpose
      will succeed.
11 After a life of suffering, he will
      again have joy;
    he will know that he did not
      suffer in vain.

---

a FORBIDDEN THING: *Any object that was considered ritually unclean.*   *b* he will be highly
honored; *or* he will be restored to greatness and honor.

My devoted servant, with whom I
  am pleased,
will bear the punishment of
  many
and for his sake I will forgive
  them.
12 And so I will give him a place of
  honor,
a place among the great and
  powerful.
He willingly gave his life
and shared the fate of evil men.
He took the place of many sinners
and prayed that they might be
  forgiven."c

The Lord's Love for Israel

54 Jerusalem, you have been like a
  childless woman,
but now you can sing and shout
  for joy.
Now you will have more children
than a woman whose husband
  never left her.
2 Make the tent you live in larger;
lengthen its ropes and
  strengthen the pegs!
3 You will extend your boundaries
  on all sides;
your people will get back the
  land
that the other nations now
  occupy.
Cities now deserted will be filled
  with people.

4 Do not be afraid—you will not be
  disgraced again;
you will not be humiliated.
You will forget your unfaithfulness
  as a young wife,
and your desperate loneliness as
  a widow.
5 Your Creator will be like a
  husband to you—
the Lord Almighty is his name.
The holy God of Israel will
  save you—
he is the ruler of all the world.

6 Israel, you are like a young wife,
  deserted by her husband and
  deeply distressed.
But the Lord calls you back to him
  and says:
7 "For one brief moment I left you;

with deep love I will take you
  back.
8 I turned away angry for only a
  moment,
but I will show you my love
  forever."
So says the Lord who saves you.

9 "In the time of Noah I promised
never again to flood the earth.
Now I promise not to be angry
  with you again;
I will not reprimand or
  punish you.
10 The mountains and hills may
  crumble,
but my love for you will
  never end;
I will keep forever my promise
  of peace."
So says the Lord who loves you.

The Future Jerusalem

11 The Lord says,
"O Jerusalem, you suffering,
  helpless city,
with no one to comfort you,
I will rebuild your foundations
  with precious stones.
12 I will build your towers with
  rubies,
your gates with stones that glow
  like fire,
and the wall around you with
  jewels.

13 "I myself will teach your people
and give them prosperity and
  peace.
14 Justice and right will make you
  strong.
You will be safe from
  oppression and terror.
15 Whoever attacks you,
does it without my consent;
whoever fights against you will
  fall.

16 "I create the blacksmith,
who builds a fire and forges
  weapons.
I also create the soldier,
who uses the weapons to kill.
17 But no weapon will be able to
  hurt you;

c prayed that they might be forgiven; or suffered the punishment they deserved.

you will have an answer for all
who accuse you.
I will defend my servants
and give them victory."

The Lord has spoken.

God's Offer of Mercy

55 The Lord says,
"Come, everyone who is
thirsty—
here is water!
Come, you that have no money—
buy grain and eat!
Come! Buy wine and milk—
it will cost you nothing!
2 Why spend money on what does
not satisfy?
Why spend your wages and still
be hungry?
Listen to me and do what I say,
and you will enjoy the best food
of all.

3 "Listen now, my people, and come
to me;
come to me, and you will have
life!
I will make a lasting covenant
with you
and give you the blessings I
promised to David.
4 I made him a leader and
commander of nations,
and through him I showed them
my power.
5 Now you will summon foreign
nations;
at one time they did not
know you,
but now they will come running
to join you!
I, the Lord your God, the holy God
of Israel,
will make all this happen;
I will give you honor and glory."

6 Turn to the Lord and pray to him,
now that he is near.
7 Let the wicked leave their way of
life
and change their way of
thinking.
Let them turn to the Lord,
our God;
he is merciful and quick to
forgive.

8 "My thoughts," says the Lord, "are
not like yours,
and my ways are different from
yours.
9 As high as the heavens are above
the earth,
so high are my ways and
thoughts above yours.

10 "My word is like the snow and the
rain
that come down from the sky to
water the earth.
They make the crops grow
and provide seed for planting
and food to eat.
11 So also will be the word that I
speak—
it will not fail to do what I plan
for it;
it will do everything I send it
to do.

12 "You will leave Babylon with
joy;
you will be led out of the city in
peace.
The mountains and hills will burst
into singing,
and the trees will shout for
joy.
13 Cypress trees will grow where
now there are briers;
myrtle trees will come up in
place of thorns.
This will be a sign that will last
forever,
a reminder of what I, the Lord,
have done."

God's People Will Include
All Nations

56 The Lord says to his people, "Do
what is just and right, for soon I
will save you. 2 I will bless those who always observe the Sabbath and do not
misuse it. I will bless those who do nothing evil."

3 A foreigner who has joined the
Lord's people should not say, "The Lord
will not let me worship with his people."
A man who has been castrated should
never think that because he cannot have
children, he can never be part of God's
people. 4 The Lord says to such a man, "If
you honor me by observing the Sabbath
and if you do what pleases me and faith-

fully keep my covenant, [5] then your name will be remembered in my Temple and among my people longer than if you had sons and daughters. You will never be forgotten."

[6] And the LORD says to those foreigners who become part of his people, who love him and serve him, who observe the Sabbath and faithfully keep his covenant: [7] "I will bring you to Zion, my sacred hill,[d] give you joy in my house of prayer, and accept the sacrifices you offer on my altar. My Temple will be called a house of prayer for the people of all nations."

[8] The Sovereign LORD, who has brought his people Israel home from exile, has promised that he will bring still other people to join them.

Israel's Leaders Are Condemned

[9] The LORD has told the foreign nations to come like wild animals and devour his people. [10] He says, "All the leaders, who are supposed to warn my people, are blind! They know nothing. They are like watch dogs that don't bark—they only lie around and dream. How they love to sleep! [11] They are like greedy dogs that never get enough. These leaders have no understanding. They each do as they please and seek their own advantage. [12] 'Let's get some wine,' these drunkards say, 'and drink all we can hold! Tomorrow will be even better than today!' "

Israel's Idolatry Is Condemned

57 Good people die, and no one understands or even cares. But when they die, no calamity can hurt them. [2] Those who live good lives find peace and rest in death.

[3] Come here to be judged, you sinners! You are no better than sorcerers, adulterers, and prostitutes. [4] Who are you making fun of? Who are you liars jeering at? [5] You worship the fertility gods by having sex under those sacred trees of yours. You offer your children as sacrifices in the rocky caves near stream beds. [6] You take smooth stones from there and worship them as gods. You pour out wine as offerings to them and bring them grain offerings. Do you think I am pleased with all this? [7] You go to the high mountains to offer sacrifices and

have sex. [8] You set up your obscene idols just inside your front doors. You forsake me; you take off your clothes and climb in your large beds with your lovers, whom you pay to sleep with you. And there you satisfy your lust. [9] You put on your perfumes and ointments and go to worship the god Molech. To find gods to worship, you send messengers far and wide, even to the world of the dead. [10] You wear yourselves out looking for other gods, but you never give up. You think your obscene idols give you strength, and so you never grow weak.

[11] The LORD says, "Who are these gods that make you afraid, so that you tell me lies and forget me completely? Have you stopped honoring me because I have kept silent for so long? [12] You think that what you do is right, but I will expose your conduct, and your idols will not be able to help you. [13] When you cry for help, let those idols of yours save you! A puff of wind will carry them off! But those who trust in me will live in the land and will worship me in my Temple."

God's Promise of Help and Healing

[14] The LORD says, "Let my people return to me. Remove every obstacle from their path! Build the road and make it ready!

[15] "I am the high and holy God, who lives forever. I live in a high and holy place, but I also live with people who are humble and repentant, so that I can restore their confidence and hope. [16] I gave my people life, and I will not continue to accuse them or be angry with them forever.[e] [17] I was angry with them because of their sin and greed, and so I punished them and abandoned them. But they were stubborn and kept on going their own way.

[18] "I have seen how they acted, but I will heal them. I will lead them and help them, and I will comfort those who mourn. [19] I offer peace to all, both near and far! I will heal my people. [20] But evil people are like the restless sea, whose waves never stop rolling in, bringing filth and muck. [21] There is no safety for sinners," says the LORD.

---

[d] SACRED HILL: See 2.3.   [e] I gave my people ... forever; or I will not continue to accuse them or be angry with them forever, for then they would die—the very people to whom I gave life.

True Fasting

58 The LORD says, "Shout as loud as you can! Tell my people Israel about their sins! [2] They worship me every day, claiming that they are eager to know my ways and obey my laws. They say they want me to give them just laws and that they take pleasure in worshiping me."

[3] The people ask, "Why should we fast if the LORD never notices? Why should we go without food if he pays no attention?"

The LORD says to them, "The truth is that at the same time you fast, you pursue your own interests and oppress your workers. [4] Your fasting makes you violent, and you quarrel and fight. Do you think this kind of fasting will make me listen to your prayers? [5] When you fast, you make yourselves suffer; you bow your heads low like a blade of grass and spread out sackcloth and ashes to lie on. Is that what you call fasting? Do you think I will be pleased with that?

[6] "The kind of fasting I want is this: Remove the chains of oppression and the yoke of injustice, and let the oppressed go free. [7] Share your food with the hungry and open your homes to the homeless poor. Give clothes to those who have nothing to wear, and do not refuse to help your own relatives.

[8] "Then my favor will shine on you like the morning sun, and your wounds will be quickly healed. I will always be with you to save you; my presence will protect you on every side. [9] When you pray, I will answer you. When you call to me, I will respond.

"If you put an end to oppression, to every gesture of contempt, and to every evil word; [10] if you give food to the hungry and satisfy those who are in need, then the darkness around you will turn to the brightness of noon. [11] And I will always guide you and satisfy you with good things. I will keep you strong and well. You will be like a garden that has plenty of water, like a spring of water that never goes dry. [12] Your people will rebuild what has long been in ruins, building again on the old foundations. You will be known as the people who rebuilt the walls, who restored the ruined houses."

The Reward for Keeping the Sabbath

[13] The LORD says, "If you treat the Sabbath as sacred and do not pursue your own interests on that day; if you value my holy day and honor it by not traveling, working, or talking idly on that day, [14] then you will find the joy that comes from serving me. I will make you honored all over the world, and you will enjoy the land I gave to your ancestor, Jacob. I, the LORD, have spoken."

The Prophet Condemns the People's Sins

59 Don't think that the LORD is too weak to save you or too deaf to hear your call for help! [2] It is because of your sins that he doesn't hear you. It is your sins that separate you from God when you try to worship him. [3] You are guilty of lying, violence, and murder.

[4] You go to court, but you do not have justice on your side. You depend on lies to win your case. You carry out your plans to hurt others. [5-6] The evil plots you make are as deadly as the eggs of a poisonous snake. Crush an egg, out comes a snake! But your plots will do you no good—they are as useless as clothing made of cobwebs! [7] You are always planning something evil, and you can hardly wait to do it. You never hesitate to murder innocent people. You leave ruin and destruction wherever you go, [8] and no one is safe when you are around. Everything you do is unjust. You follow a crooked path, and no one who walks that path will ever be safe.

The People Confess Their Sin

[9] The people say, "Now we know why God does not save us from those who oppress us. We hope for light to walk by, but there is only darkness, [10] and we grope about like blind people. We stumble at noon, as if it were night, as if we were in the dark world of the dead. [11] We are frightened and distressed. We long for God to save us from oppression and wrong, but nothing happens.

[12] "LORD, our crimes against you are many. Our sins accuse us. We are well aware of them all. [13] We have rebelled against you, rejected you, and refused to follow you. We have oppressed others and turned away from you. Our

thoughts are false; our words are lies. 14 Justice is driven away, and right cannot come near. Truth stumbles in the public square, and honesty finds no place there. 15 There is so little honesty that those who stop doing evil find themselves the victims of crime."

The LORD Prepares to Rescue His People

The LORD has seen this, and he is displeased that there is no justice. 16 He is astonished to see that there is no one to help the oppressed. So he will use his own power to rescue them and to win the victory. 17 He will wear justice like a coat of armor and saving power like a helmet. He will clothe himself with the strong desire to set things right and to punish and avenge the wrongs that people suffer. 18 He will punish his enemies according to what they have done, even those who live in distant lands. 19 From east to west everyone will fear him and his great power. He will come like a rushing river, like a strong wind.

20 The LORD says to his people, "I will come to Jerusalem to defend you and to save all of you that turn from your sins. 21 And I make a covenant with you: I have given you my power and my teachings to be yours forever, and from now on you are to obey me and teach your children and your descendants to obey me for all time to come."

The Future Glory of Jerusalem

60 Arise, Jerusalem, and shine like the sun;
The glory of the LORD is shining on you!
2 Other nations will be covered by darkness,
But on you the light of the LORD will shine;
The brightness of his presence will be with you.
3 Nations will be drawn to your light,
And kings to the dawning of your new day.

4 Look around you and see what is happening:
Your people are gathering to come home!
Your sons will come from far away;

Your daughters will be carried like children.
5 You will see this and be filled with joy;
You will tremble with excitement.
The wealth of the nations will be brought to you;
From across the sea their riches will come.

6 Great caravans of camels will come, from Midian and Ephah.
They will come from Sheba, bringing gold and incense.
People will tell the good news of what the LORD has done!
7 All the sheep of Kedar and Nebaioth
Will be brought to you as sacrifices
And offered on the altar to please the LORD.
The LORD will make his Temple more glorious than ever.

8 What are these ships that skim along like clouds,
Like doves returning home?
9 They are ships coming from distant lands,
Bringing God's people home.
They bring with them silver and gold
To honor the name of the LORD,
The holy God of Israel,
Who has made all nations honor his people.

10 The LORD says to Jerusalem,
"Foreigners will rebuild your walls,
And their kings will serve you.
In my anger I punished you,
But now I will show you my favor and mercy.
11 Day and night your gates will be open,
So that the kings of the nations
May bring you their wealth.
12 But nations that do not serve you
Will be completely destroyed.

13 "The wood of the pine, the juniper, and the cypress,
The finest wood from the forests of Lebanon,
Will be brought to rebuild you, Jerusalem,

To make my Temple beautiful,
To make my city glorious.
14 The descendants of those who
    oppressed you will come
And bow low to show their
    respect.
All who once despised you will
    worship at your feet.
They will call you 'The City of the
    LORD,'
'Zion, the City of Israel's
    Holy God.'

15 "You will no longer be forsaken
    and hated,
A city deserted and desolate.
I will make you great and
    beautiful,
A place of joy forever and ever.
16 Nations and kings will care
    for you
As a mother nurses her child.
You will know that I, the LORD,
    have saved you,
That the mighty God of Israel sets
    you free.

17 "I will bring you gold instead of
    bronze,
Silver and bronze instead of iron
    and wood,
And iron instead of stone.
Your rulers will no longer
    oppress you;
I will make them rule with justice
    and peace.
18 The sounds of violence will be
    heard no more;
Destruction will not shatter your
    country again.
I will protect and defend you like
    a wall;
You will praise me because I have
    saved you.

19 "No longer will the sun be your
    light by day
Or the moon be your light by
    night;
I, the LORD, will be your eternal
    light;
The light of my glory will shine
    on you.
20 Your days of grief will come to
    an end.
I, the LORD, will be your eternal
    light,

More lasting than the sun and
    moon.
21 Your people will all do what is
    right,
And will possess the land forever.
I planted them, I made them,
To reveal my greatness to all.
22 Even your smallest and humblest
    family
Will become as great as a
    powerful nation.
When the right time comes,
I will make this happen quickly.
I am the LORD!"

The Good News of Deliverance

61 The Sovereign LORD has filled
    me with his Spirit.
He has chosen me and sent me
To bring good news to the poor,
To heal the broken-hearted,
To announce release to captives
And freedom to those in prison.
2 He has sent me to proclaim
That the time has come
When the LORD will save his
    people
And defeat their enemies.
He has sent me to comfort all who
    mourn,
3 To give to those who mourn in
    Zion
Joy and gladness instead of grief,
A song of praise instead of
    sorrow.
They will be like trees
That the LORD himself has planted.
They will all do what is right,
And God will be praised for what
    he has done.
4 They will rebuild cities that have
    long been in ruins.

5 My people, foreigners will
    serve you.
They will take care of your flocks
And farm your land and tend your
    vineyards.
6 And you will be known as the
    priests of the LORD,
The servants of our God.
You will enjoy the wealth of the
    nations
And be proud that it is yours.
7 Your shame and disgrace are
    ended.
You will live in your own land,
And your wealth will be doubled;

Your joy will last forever.

8 The LORD says,
"I love justice and I hate
    oppression and crime.
I will faithfully reward my
    people
And make an eternal covenant
    with them.
9 They will be famous among the
    nations;
Everyone who sees them will
    know
That they are a people whom I
    have blessed."

10 Jerusalem rejoices because of
    what the LORD has done.
She is like a bride dressed for her
    wedding.
God has clothed her with salvation
    and victory.
11 As surely as seeds sprout and
    grow,
The Sovereign LORD will save his
    people,
And all the nations will
    praise him.

62

I will speak out to encourage
    Jerusalem;
I will not be silent until she is
    saved,
And her victory shines like a torch
    in the night.
2 Jerusalem, the nations will see you
    victorious!
All their kings will see your glory.
You will be called by a new name,
A name given by the LORD
    himself.
3 You will be like a beautiful crown
    for the LORD.
4 No longer will you be called
    "Forsaken,"
Or your land be called "The
    Deserted Wife."
Your new name will be "God Is
    Pleased with Her."
Your land will be called "Happily
    Married,"
Because the LORD is pleased
    with you
And will be like a husband to your
    land.
5 Like a young man taking a virgin
    as his bride,

He who formed you will
    marry you.
As a groom is delighted with his
    bride,
So your God will delight in you.

6 On your walls, Jerusalem, I have
    placed sentries;
They must never be silent day or
    night.
They must remind the LORD of his
    promises
And never let him forget
    them.
7 They must give him no rest until
    he restores Jerusalem
And makes it a city the whole
    world praises.

8 The LORD has made a solemn
    promise,
And by his power he will carry
    it out:
"Your grain will no longer be food
    for your enemies,
And foreigners will no longer
    drink your wine.
9 But you that planted and
    harvested the grain
Will eat the bread and praise the
    LORD.
You that tended and gathered the
    grapes
Will drink the wine in the courts
    of my Temple."

10 People of Jerusalem, go out of the
    city
And build a road for your
    returning people!
Prepare a highway; clear it of
    stones!
Put up a signal so that the nations
    can know
11 That the LORD is announcing to all
    the earth:
"Tell the people of Jerusalem
That the LORD is coming to
    save you,
Bringing with him the people he
    has rescued."
12 You will be called "God's Holy
    People,"
"The People the LORD Has Saved."
Jerusalem will be called "The City
    That God Loves,"
"The City That God Did Not
    Forsake."

The Lord's Victory over the Nations

63 "Who is this coming from the city of Bozrah in Edom? Who is this so splendidly dressed in red, marching along[f] in power and strength?"

It is the Lord, powerful to save, coming to announce his victory.

2 "Why is his clothing so red, like that of someone who tramples grapes to make wine?"

3 The Lord answers, "I have trampled the nations like grapes, and no one came to help me. I trampled them in my anger, and their blood has stained all my clothing. 4 I decided that the time to save my people had come; it was time to punish their enemies. 5 I was amazed when I looked and saw that there was no one to help me. But my anger made me strong, and I won the victory myself. 6 In my anger I trampled whole nations and shattered them. I poured out their lifeblood on the ground."

The Lord's Goodness to Israel

7 I will tell of the Lord's unfailing
    love;
  I praise him for all he has done
    for us.
  He has richly blessed the people of
    Israel
    because of his mercy and
      constant love.

8 The Lord said, "They are my people; they will not deceive me." And so he saved them 9 from all their suffering. It was not an angel, but the Lord himself who saved them. In his love and compassion he rescued them. He had always taken care of them in the past, 10 but they rebelled against him and made his holy spirit sad. So the Lord became their enemy and fought against them.

11 But then they[g] remembered the past, the days of Moses, the servant of the Lord, and they asked, "Where now is the Lord, who saved the leaders of his people from the sea? Where is the Lord, who gave his spirit to Moses? 12-13 Where is the Lord, who by his power did great things through Moses, dividing the waters of the sea and leading his people through the deep water, to win everlasting fame for himself?"

Led by the Lord, they were as surefooted as wild horses, and never stumbled. 14 As cattle are led into a fertile valley, so the Lord gave his people rest. He led his people and brought honor to his name.

A Prayer for Mercy and Help

15 Lord, look upon us from heaven, where you live in your holiness and glory. Where is your great concern for us? Where is your power? Where are your love and compassion? Do not ignore us. 16 You are our father. Our ancestors Abraham and Jacob do not acknowledge us, but you, Lord, are our father, the one who has always rescued us. 17 Why do you let us stray from your ways? Why do you make us so stubborn that we turn away from you? Come back, for the sake of those who serve you, for the sake of the people who have always been yours.

18 We, your holy people, were driven out by our enemies for a little while; they trampled down your sanctuary.[h] 19 You treat us as though you had never been our ruler, as though we had never been your people.

64 Why don't you tear the sky open and come down? The mountains would see you and shake with fear. 2 They would tremble like water boiling over a hot fire. Come and reveal your power to your enemies, and make the nations tremble at your presence! 3 There was a time when you came and did terrifying things that we did not expect; the mountains saw you and shook with fear. 4 No one has ever seen or heard of a God like you, who does such deeds for those who put their hope in him. 5 You welcome those who find joy in doing what is right, those who remember how you want them to live. You were angry with us, but we went on sinning; in spite of your great anger we have continued to do wrong since ancient times.[i] 6 All of us have been sinful; even our best actions are filthy through and through. Because of our sins we are like leaves that wither and are blown away by the wind. 7 No one turns to you in prayer; no one goes to you for help. You have hidden yourself from us and

---

f *Some ancient translations* marching along; *Hebrew* bowed down.   g *Probable text* they; *Hebrew* he.   h *Verse 18 in Hebrew is unclear.*   i *Probable text* in spite of . . . ancient times; *Hebrew unclear.*

have abandoned⟍ us because of our sins.

8 But you are our father, LORD. We are like clay, and you are like the potter. You created us, 9 so do not be too angry with us or hold our sins against us forever. We are your people; be merciful to us. 10 Your sacred cities are like a desert; Jerusalem is a deserted ruin, 11 and our Temple, the sacred and beautiful place where our ancestors praised you, has been destroyed by fire. All the places we loved are in ruins. 12 LORD, are you unmoved by all this? Are you going to do nothing and make us suffer more than we can endure?

God's Punishment of the Rebellious

65 The LORD said, "I was ready to answer my people's prayers, but they did not pray. I was ready for them to find me, but they did not even try. The nation did not pray to me, even though I was always ready to answer, 'Here I am; I will help you.' 2 I have always been ready to welcome my people, who stubbornly do what is wrong and go their own way. 3 They shamelessly keep on making me angry. They offer pagan sacrifices at sacred gardens k and burn incense on pagan altars. 4 At night they go to caves and tombs to consult the spirits of the dead. They eat pork and drink broth made from meat offered in pagan sacrifices. 5 And then they say to others, 'Keep away from us; we are too holy for you to touch!' I cannot stand people like that—my anger against them is like a fire that never goes out.

6 "I have already decided on their punishment, and their sentence is written down. I will not overlook what they have done, but will repay them 7 for their sins and the sins of their ancestors. They have burned incense at pagan hill shrines and spoken evil of me. So I will punish them as their past deeds deserve."

8 The LORD says, "No one destroys good grapes; instead, they make wine with them. Neither will I destroy all my people—I will save those who serve me. 9 I will bless the Israelites who belong to the tribe of Judah, and their descendants will possess my land of mountains. My chosen people, who serve me, will live there. 10 They will worship me and will lead their sheep and cattle to pasture in the Plain of Sharon in the west and in Trouble Valley in the east.

11 "But it will be different for you that forsake me, who ignore Zion, my sacred hill,ˡ and worship Gad and Meni, the gods of luck and fate. 12 It will be your fate to die a violent death, because you did not answer when I called you or listen when I spoke. You chose to disobey me and do evil. 13 And so I tell you that those who worship and obey me will have plenty to eat and drink, but you will be hungry and thirsty. They will be happy, but you will be disgraced. 14 They will sing for joy, but you will cry with a broken heart. 15 My chosen people will use your name as a curse. I, the Sovereign LORD, will put you to death. But I will give a new name to those who obey me. 16 Anyone in the land who asks for a blessing will ask to be blessed by the faithful God. Whoever takes an oath will swear by the name of the faithful God. The troubles of the past will be gone and forgotten."

The New Creation

17 The LORD says, "I am making a new earth and new heavens. The events of the past will be completely forgotten. 18 Be glad and rejoice forever in what I create. The new Jerusalem I make will be full of joy, and her people will be happy. 19 I myself will be filled with joy because of Jerusalem and her people. There will be no weeping there, no calling for help. 20 Babies will no longer die in infancy, and all people will live out their life span. Those who live to be a hundred will be considered young. To die before that would be a sign that I had punished them. 21-22 People will build houses and get to live in them—they will not be used by someone else. They will plant vineyards and enjoy the wine—it will not be drunk by others. Like trees, my people will live long lives. They will fully enjoy the things that they have worked for. 23 The work they do will be successful, and their children will not meet with disaster. I will bless them and their descendants for all time to come.

⟍ Some ancient translations abandoned; Hebrew melted.   k SACRED GARDENS: See 1.29.
ˡ SACRED HILL: See 2.3.

24 Even before they finish praying to me,
I will answer their prayers. 25 Wolves
and lambs will eat together; lions will
eat straw, as cattle do, and snakes will
no longer be dangerous. On Zion, my sacred hill,[l] there will be nothing harmful
or evil."

The Lord Judges the Nations

66 The Lord says, "Heaven is my
throne, and the earth is my footstool. What kind of house, then, could
you build for me, what kind of place for
me to live in? 2 I myself created the
whole universe! I am pleased with those
who are humble and repentant, who fear
me and obey me.

3 "The people do as they please. It's all
the same to them whether they kill a bull
as a sacrifice or sacrifice a human being;
whether they sacrifice a lamb or break a
dog's neck; whether they present a grain
offering or offer pigs' blood; whether
they offer incense or pray to an idol.
They take pleasure in disgusting ways of
worship. 4 So I will bring disaster upon
them — the very things they are afraid
of — because no one answered when I
called or listened when I spoke. They
chose to disobey me and do evil."

5 Listen to what the Lord says, you that
fear him and obey him: "Because you
are faithful to me, some of your own
people hate you and will have nothing to
do with you. They mock you and say,
'Let the Lord show his greatness and
save you, so that we may see you rejoice.' But they themselves will be disgraced! 6 Listen! That loud noise in the
city, that sound in the Temple, is the
sound of the Lord punishing his
enemies!

7 "My holy city is like a woman who
suddenly gives birth to a child without
ever going into labor. 8 Has anyone ever
seen or heard of such a thing? Has a
nation ever been born in a day? Zion
will not have to suffer long, before the nation is born. 9 Do not think that I will
bring my people to the point of birth
and not let them be born." The Lord has
spoken.

10 Rejoice with Jerusalem; be glad
    for her,
  all you that love this city!

Rejoice with her now,
    all you that have mourned
    for her!
11 You will enjoy her prosperity,
    like a child at its mother's
    breast.

12 The Lord says, "I will bring you lasting prosperity; the wealth of the nations
will flow to you like a river that never
goes dry. You will be like a child that is
nursed by its mother, carried in her
arms, and treated with love. 13 I will
comfort you in Jerusalem, as a mother
comforts her child. 14 When you see this
happen, you will be glad; it will make
you strong and healthy. Then you will
know that I, the Lord, help those who
obey me, and I show my anger against
my enemies."

15 The Lord will come with fire. He will
ride on the wings of a storm to punish
those he is angry with. 16 By fire and
sword he will punish all the people of the
world whom he finds guilty — and many
will be put to death.

17 The Lord says, "The end is near for
those who purify themselves for pagan
worship, who go in procession to sacred
gardens,[m] and who eat pork and mice
and other disgusting foods. 18 I know[n]
their thoughts and their deeds. I am
coming[o] to gather the people of all the
nations. When they come together, they
will see what my power can do 19 and
will know that I am the one who punishes them.

"But I will spare some of them and
send them to the nations and the distant
lands that have not heard of my fame or
seen my greatness and power: to Spain,
Libya,[p] and Lydia, with its skilled archers, and to Tubal and Greece. Among
these nations they will proclaim my
greatness. 20 They will bring back all
your people from the nations as a gift to
me. They will bring them to my sacred
hill[q] in Jerusalem on horses, mules, and
camels, and in chariots and wagons, just
as Israelites bring grain offerings to the
Temple in ritually clean containers.
21 I will make some of them priests and
Levites.

22 "Just as the new earth and the new
heavens will endure by my power, so
your descendants and your name will

---

[l] SACRED HILL: *See 2.3.*   [m] SACRED GARDENS: *See 1.29.*   [n] *Some ancient translations* I know;
Hebrew I.   [o] *Some ancient translations* I am coming; *Hebrew* He is coming.
[p] *One ancient translation* Libya; *Hebrew* Pul.   [q] SACRED HILL: *See 2.3.*

endure. 23 On every New Moon Festival and every Sabbath people of every nation will come to worship me here in Jerusalem," says the Lord. 24 "As they leave, they will see the dead bodies of those who have rebelled against me. The worms that eat them will never die, and the fire that burns them will never be put out. The sight of them will be disgusting to all people."

The Book of
JEREMIAH

Introduction

The prophet Jeremiah lived during the latter part of the seventh century and the first part of the sixth century B.C. During his long ministry he warned God's people of the catastrophe that was to fall upon the nation because of their idolatry and sin. He lived to see this prediction come true with the fall of Jerusalem to the Babylonian king, Nebuchadnezzar, the destruction of the city and the Temple, and the exile to Babylonia of Judah's king and many of the people. He also foretold the eventual return of the people from exile and the restoration of the nation.

The Book of Jeremiah may be divided into the following parts: 1) The call of Jeremiah. 2) Messages from God to the nation of Judah and its rulers during the reigns of Josiah, Jehoiakim, Jehoiachin, and Zedekiah. 3) Material from the memoirs of Baruch, Jeremiah's secretary, including various prophecies and important events from the life of Jeremiah. 4) Messages from the Lord about various foreign nations. 5) A historical appendix, giving an account of the fall of Jerusalem, and the exile to Babylonia.

Jeremiah was a sensitive man who deeply loved his people, and who hated to have to pronounce judgment upon them. In many passages he spoke with deep emotion about the things he suffered because God had called him to be a prophet. The word of the Lord was like fire in his heart — he could not keep it back.

Some of the greatest words in the book point beyond Jeremiah's own troubled time to the day when there would be a new covenant, one that God's people would keep without a teacher to remind them, because it would be written on their hearts (31.31-34).

Outline of Contents

1 This book is the account of what was said by Jeremiah son of Hilkiah, one of the priests of the town of Anathoth in the territory of Benjamin. ²The LORD spoke to Jeremiah in the thirteenth year that Josiah son of Amon was king of Judah, ³ and he spoke to him again when Josiah's son Jehoiakim was king. After that, the LORD spoke to him many times, until the eleventh year of the reign of Zedekiah son of Josiah. In the fifth month of that year the people of Jerusalem were taken into exile.

The Call of Jeremiah

⁴The LORD said to me, ⁵ "I chose you before I gave you life, and before you were born I selected you to be a prophet to the nations."

⁶I answered, "Sovereign LORD, I don't know how to speak; I am too young."

⁷But the LORD said to me, "Do not say that you are too young, but go to the people I send you to, and tell them everything I command you to say. ⁸Do not be afraid of them, for I will be with you to protect you. I, the LORD, have spoken!"

⁹Then the LORD reached out, touched my lips, and said to me, "Listen, I am giving you the words you must speak. ¹⁰Today I give you authority over nations and kingdoms to uproot and to pull down, to destroy and to overthrow, to build and to plant."

Two Visions

¹¹The LORD asked me, "Jeremiah, what do you see?"

I answered, "A branch of an almond tree."

¹² "You are right," the LORD said, "and I

am watching[a] to see that my words come true."

13 Then the LORD spoke to me again. "What else do you see?" he asked.

I answered, "I see a pot boiling in the north, and it is about to tip over this way."

14 He said to me, "Destruction will boil over from the north on all who live in this land, 15 because I am calling all the nations in the north to come. Their kings will set up their thrones at the gates of Jerusalem and around its walls and also around the other cities of Judah. 16 I will punish my people because they have sinned; they have abandoned me, have offered sacrifices to other gods, and have made idols and worshiped them. 17 Get ready, Jeremiah; go and tell them everything I command you to say. Do not be afraid of them now, or I will make you even more afraid when you are with them. 18-19 Listen, Jeremiah! Everyone in this land—the kings of Judah, the officials, the priests, and the people—will be against you. But today I am giving you the strength to resist them; you will be like a fortified city, an iron pillar, and a bronze wall. They will not defeat you, for I will be with you to protect you. I, the LORD, have spoken."

God's Care for Israel

2 The LORD told me 2 to proclaim this message to everyone in Jerusalem.
"I remember how faithful you
    were when you were young,
  how you loved me when we
    were first married;
you followed me through the
    desert,
  through a land that had not been
    planted.
3 Israel, you belonged to me alone;
  you were my sacred possession.
I sent suffering and disaster
  on everyone who hurt you.
I, the LORD, have spoken."

The Sin of Israel's Ancestors

4 Listen to the LORD's message, you descendants of Jacob, you tribes of Israel. 5 The LORD says:
"What accusation did your
    ancestors bring against me?

What made them turn away
    from me?
They worshiped worthless idols
  and became worthless
    themselves.
6 They did not care about me,
  even though I rescued them
    from Egypt
and led them through the
    wilderness:
  a land of deserts and sand pits,
  a dry and dangerous land
  where no one lives
  and no one will even travel.
7 I brought them into a fertile land,
  to enjoy its harvests and its
    other good things.
But instead they ruined my land;
  they defiled the country I had
    given them.
8 The priests did not ask, 'Where is
    the LORD?'
  My own priests did not
    know me.
The rulers rebelled against me;
  the prophets spoke in the name
    of Baal
  and worshiped useless idols.

The LORD's Case against His People

9 "And so I, the LORD, will state my
    case against my people again.
I will bring charges against their
    descendants.
10 Go west to the island of Cyprus,
  and send someone eastward to
    the land of Kedar.
You will see that nothing like
  this has ever happened before.
11 No other nation has ever changed
    its gods,
  even though they were not real.
But my people have
    exchanged me,
  the God who has brought them
    honor,
  for gods that can do nothing for
    them.
12 And so I command the sky to
    shake with horror,
  to be amazed and astonished,
13   for my people have committed
    two sins:
they have turned away from me,
  the spring of fresh water,
  and they have dug cisterns,

---

[a] WATCHING: *This word in Hebrew sounds like the Hebrew for "almond."*

cracked cisterns that can hold
no water at all.

The Results of Israel's Unfaithfulness

14 "Israel is not a slave;
he was not born into slavery.
Why then do his enemies hunt
him down?
15 They have roared at him like
lions;
they have made his land a
desert,
and his towns lie in ruins,
completely abandoned.
16 Yes, the people of Memphis and
Tahpanhes
have cracked his skull.
17 Israel, you brought this on
yourself!
You deserted me, the LORD
your God,
while I was leading you along
the way.
18 What do you think you will gain
by going to Egypt
to drink water from the Nile?
What do you think you will gain
by going to Assyria
to drink water from the
Euphrates?
19 Your own evil will punish you,
and your turning from me will
condemn you.
You will learn how bitter and
wrong it is
to abandon me, the LORD
your God,
and no longer to remain faithful
to me.
I, the Sovereign LORD Almighty,
have spoken."

Israel Refuses to Worship the LORD

20 The Sovereign LORD says,
"Israel, long ago you rejected my
authority;
you refused to obey me and
worship me.
On every high hill
and under every green tree
you worshiped fertility gods.
21 I planted you like a choice vine
from the very best seed.
But look what you have become!
You are like a rotten, worthless
vine.

22 Even if you washed with the
strongest soap,
I would still see the stain of your
guilt.
23 How can you say you have not
defiled yourself,
that you have never worshiped
Baal?
Look how you sinned in the
valley;
see what you have done.
You are like a wild camel in heat,
running around loose,
24   rushing into the desert.b
When she is in heat, who can
control her?
No male that wants her has to
trouble himself;
she is always available in
mating season.
25 Israel, don't wear your feet out,
or let your throat become dry
from chasing after other gods.
But you say, 'No! I can't turn back.
I have loved foreign gods
and will go after them.' "

Israel Deserves to Be Punished

26 The LORD says, "Just as a thief is disgraced when caught, so all you people of
Israel will be disgraced—your kings and
officials, your priests and prophets.
27 You will all be disgraced—you that
say that a tree is your father and that a
rock is your mother. This will happen
because you turned away from me instead of turning to me. But when you are
in trouble, you ask me to come and
save you.
28 "Where are the gods that you made
for yourselves? When you are in trouble,
let them save you—if they can! Judah,
you have as many gods as you have cities. 29 What is your complaint? Why
have you rebelled against me? 30 I
punished you, but it did no good; you
would not let me correct you. Like a raging lion, you have murdered your prophets. 31 People of Israel, listen to what I am
saying. Have I been like a desert to you,
like a dark and dangerous land? Why,
then, do you say that you will do as you
please, that you will never come back to
me? 32 Does a young woman forget her
jewelry, or a bride her wedding dress?
But my people have forgotten me for

b Probable text rushing into the desert; Hebrew a wild donkey used to the desert.

more days than can be counted. 33 You certainly know how to chase after lovers. Even the worst of women can learn from you. 34 Your clothes are stained with the blood of the poor and innocent, not with the blood of burglars.

"But in spite of all this, 35 you say, 'I am innocent; surely the LORD is no longer angry with me.' But I, the LORD, will punish you because you deny that you have sinned. 36 You have cheapened yourself by turning to the gods of other nations. You will be disappointed by Egypt, just as you were by Assyria. 37 You will turn away from Egypt, hanging your head in shame. I, the LORD, have rejected those you trust; you will not gain anything from them."

Unfaithful Israel

3 The LORD says, "If a man divorces his wife, and she leaves him and becomes another man's wife, he cannot take her back again. This would completely defile the land. But, Israel, you have had many lovers, and now you want to return to me! 2 Look up at the hilltops. Is there any place where you have not acted like a prostitute? You waited for lovers along the roadside, as an Arab waits for victims in the desert. You have defiled the land with your prostitution. 3 That is why the rains were held back, and the spring showers did not come. You even look like a prostitute; you have no shame. 4 "And now you say to me, 'You are my father, and you have loved me ever since I was a child. 5 You won't always be angry; you won't be mad at me forever.' Israel, that is what you said, but you did all the evil you could."

Israel and Judah Must Repent

6 When Josiah was king, the LORD said to me, "Have you seen what Israel, that unfaithful woman, has done? She has turned away from me, and on every high hill and under every green tree she has acted like a prostitute. 7 I thought that after she had done all this, she would surely return to me. But she did not return, and her unfaithful sister Judah saw it all. 8 Judah also saw that I divorced Israel and sent her away because she had turned from me and had become a prostitute. But Judah, Israel's unfaithful sister, was not afraid. She too became a

prostitute 9 and was not at all ashamed. She defiled the land, and she committed adultery by worshiping stones and trees. 10 And after all this, Judah, Israel's unfaithful sister, only pretended to return to me; she was not sincere. I, the LORD, have spoken."

11 Then the LORD told me that, even though Israel had turned away from him, she had proved to be better than unfaithful Judah. 12 He told me to go and say to Israel, "Unfaithful Israel, come back to me. I am merciful and will not be angry; I will not be angry with you forever. 13 Only admit that you are guilty and that you have rebelled against the LORD, your God. Confess that under every green tree you have given your love to foreign gods and that you have not obeyed my commands. I, the LORD, have spoken.

14 "Unfaithful people, come back; you belong to me. I will take one of you from each town and two from each clan, and I will bring you back to Mount Zion. 15 I will give you rulers who obey me, and they will rule you with wisdom and understanding. 16 Then when you have become numerous in that land, people will no longer talk about my Covenant Box. They will no longer think about it or remember it; they will not even need it, nor will they make another one. 17 When that time comes, Jerusalem will be called 'The Throne of the LORD,' and all nations will gather there to worship me. They will no longer do what their stubborn and evil hearts tell them. 18 Israel will join with Judah, and together they will come from exile in the country in the north and will return to the land that I gave your ancestors as a permanent possession."

The Idolatry of God's People

19 The LORD says,
"Israel, I wanted to accept you as
my child
and give you a delightful land,
the most beautiful land in all the
world.
I wanted you to call me father
and never again turn away
from me.
20 But like an unfaithful wife,
you have not been faithful
to me.
I, the LORD, have spoken."

21 A noise is heard on the hilltops:
    it is the people of Israel crying
        and pleading
    because they have lived sinful
        lives
    and have forgotten the LORD
        their God.
22 Return, all of you who have turned
        away from the LORD;
    he will heal you and make you
        faithful.

You say, "Yes, we are coming to the LORD because he is our God. 23 We were not helped at all by our pagan worship on the hilltops. Help for Israel comes only from the LORD our God. 24 But the worship of Baal, the god of shame, has made us lose flocks and herds, sons and daughters — everything that our ancestors have worked for since ancient times. 25 We should lie down in shame and let our disgrace cover us. We and our ancestors have always sinned against the LORD our God; we have never obeyed his commands."

A Call to Repentance

4 The LORD says, "People of Israel, if you want to turn, then turn back to me. If you are faithful to me and remove the idols I hate, 2 it will be right for you to swear by my name. Then c all the nations will ask me to bless them, and they will praise me."

3 The LORD says to the people of Judah and Jerusalem, "Plow up your unplowed fields; do not plant your seeds among thorns. 4 Keep your covenant with me, your LORD, and dedicate yourselves to me, you people of Judah and Jerusalem. If you don't, my anger will burn like fire because of the evil things you have done. It will burn, and there will be no one to put it out."

Judah Is Threatened with Invasion

5 Blow the trumpet throughout the
        land!
    Shout loud and clear!
    Tell the people of Judah and
        Jerusalem
        to run to the fortified cities.
6 Point the way to Zion!
    Run for safety! Don't delay!
    The LORD is bringing disaster

and great destruction from the
        north.
7 Like a lion coming from its hiding
        place,
    a destroyer of nations has
        set out.
He is coming to destroy Judah.
The cities of Judah will be left in
        ruins,
    and no one will live in them.
8 So put on sackcloth, and weep and
        wail
    because the fierce anger of the
        LORD
    has not turned away from
        Judah.

9 The LORD said, "On that day kings and officials will lose their courage; priests will be shocked and prophets will be astonished."

10 Then I said, "Sovereign LORD, you have completely deceived the people of Jerusalem! You have said there would be peace, but a sword is at their throats."

11 The time is coming when the people of Jerusalem will be told that a scorching wind is blowing in from the desert toward them. It will not be a gentle wind that only blows away the chaff — 12 the wind that comes at the LORD'S command will be much stronger than that! It is the LORD himself who is pronouncing judgment on his people.

Judah Is Surrounded by Enemies

13 Look, the enemy is coming like clouds. Their war chariots are like a whirlwind, and their horses are faster than eagles. We are lost! We are doomed!

14 Jerusalem, wash the evil from your heart, so that you may be saved. How long will you go on thinking sinful thoughts?

15 Messengers from the city of Dan and from the hills of Ephraim announce the bad news. 16 They have come to warn the nations and to tell Jerusalem that enemies are coming from a country far away. These enemies will shout against the cities of Judah 17 and will surround Jerusalem like men guarding a field, because her people have rebelled against the LORD. The LORD has spoken.

---

c it will be right . . . name. Then; or and if you swear by my name and are truthful, just, and righteous, then.

18 Judah, you have brought this on yourself by the way you have lived and by the things you have done. Your sin has caused this suffering; it has stabbed you through the heart.

Jeremiah's Sorrow for His People

19 The pain! I can't bear the pain!
My heart! My heart is beating
    wildly!
I can't keep quiet;
I hear the trumpets
    and the shouts of battle.
20 One disaster follows another;
    the whole country is left in
    ruins.
Suddenly our tents are destroyed;
    their curtains are torn to pieces.
21 How long must I see the battle
    raging
    and hear the blasts of trumpets?
22 The LORD says, "My people are
    stupid;
    they don't know me.
They are like foolish children;
    they have no understanding.
They are experts at doing what is
    evil,
    but failures at doing what is
    good."

Jeremiah's Vision of the Coming Destruction

23 I looked at the earth—it was a
    barren waste;
    at the sky—there was no light.
24 I looked at the mountains—they
    were shaking,
    and the hills were rocking back
    and forth.
25 I saw that there were no people;
    even the birds had flown away.
26 The fertile land had become a
    desert;
    its cities were in ruins
    because of the LORD's fierce
    anger.
(27 The LORD has said that the whole earth will become a wasteland, but that he will not completely destroy it.)
28 The earth will mourn;
    the sky will grow dark.
The LORD has spoken
    and will not change his mind.
He has made his decision
    and will not turn back.
29 At the noise of the cavalry and
    archers

everyone will run away.
Some will run to the forest;
    others will climb up among the
    rocks.
Every town will be left empty,
    and no one will live in them
    again.
30 Jerusalem, you are doomed!
Why do you dress in scarlet?
Why do you put on jewelry and
    paint your eyes?
You are making yourself beautiful
    for nothing!
Your lovers have rejected you
    and want to kill you.
31 I heard a cry, like a woman in
    labor,
    a scream like a woman bearing
    her first child.
It was the cry of Jerusalem
    gasping for breath,
    stretching out her hand and
    saying,
"I am doomed!
    They are coming to kill me!"

The Sin of Jerusalem

5 People of Jerusalem, run through
    your streets!
Look around! See for
    yourselves!
Search the marketplaces!
Can you find one person
    who does what is right
    and tries to be faithful to God?
If you can, the LORD will forgive
    Jerusalem.
2 Even though you claim to worship
    the LORD,
    you do not mean what you say.
3 Surely the LORD looks for
    faithfulness.
He struck you, but you paid no
    attention;
    he crushed you, but you refused
    to learn.
You were stubborn and would not
    turn from your sins.
4 Then I thought, "These are only
    the poor and ignorant.
They behave foolishly;
    they don't know what their God
    requires,
    what the LORD wants them to do.
5 I will go to the people in power
    and talk with them.
Surely they know what their God
    requires,

what the LORD wants them
to do."
But all of them have rejected the
LORD's authority
and refuse to obey him.
⁶That is why lions from the forest
will kill them;
wolves from the desert will tear
them to pieces,
and leopards will prowl through
their towns.
If those people go out, they will be
torn apart
because their sins are numerous
and time after time they have
turned from God.
⁷The LORD asked, "Why should I
forgive the sins of my people?
They have abandoned me
and have worshiped gods that
are not real.
I fed my people until they were
full,
but they committed adultery
and spent their time with
prostitutes.
⁸They were like well-fed stallions
wild with desire,
each lusting for his neighbor's
wife.
⁹Shouldn't I punish them for these
things
and take revenge on a nation
such as this?
¹⁰I will send enemies to cut down
my people's vineyards,
but not to destroy them
completely.
I will tell them to strip away the
branches,
because those branches are not
mine.
¹¹The people of Israel and Judah
have betrayed me completely.
I, the LORD, have spoken."

The LORD Rejects Israel

¹²The LORD's people have denied him
and have said, "He won't really do any-
thing.ᵈ We won't have hard times; we
won't have war or famine." ¹³⁻¹⁴They
have said that the prophets are nothing
but windbags and that they have no
message from the LORD. The LORD God
Almighty said to me, "Jeremiah, because

these people have said such things, I will
make my words like a fire in your
mouth. The people will be like wood,
and the fire will burn them up."

¹⁵People of Israel, the LORD is bringing
a nation from far away to attack you. It
is a strong and ancient nation, a nation
whose language you do not know.
¹⁶Their archers are mighty soldiers who
kill without mercy. ¹⁷They will devour
your crops and your food; they will kill
your sons and your daughters. They will
slaughter your flocks and your herds
and destroy your vines and fig trees. The
fortified cities in which you trust will be
destroyed by their army.

¹⁸The LORD says, "Yet even in those
days I will not completely destroy my
people. ¹⁹When they ask why I did all
these things, tell them, Jeremiah, that
just as they turned away from me and
served foreign gods in their own land, so
they will serve strangers in a land that is
not theirs."

God Warns His People

²⁰The LORD says, "Tell the descendants
of Jacob, tell the people of Judah: ²¹Pay
attention, you foolish and stupid people,
who have eyes, but cannot see, and have
ears, but cannot hear. ²²I am the LORD;
why don't you fear me? Why don't you
tremble before me? I placed the sand as
the boundary of the sea, a permanent
boundary that it cannot cross. The sea
may toss, but it cannot go beyond it; the
waves may roar, but they cannot break
through. ²³But you people! You are stubborn and rebellious; you have turned
aside and left me. ²⁴You never thought
to honor me, even though I send the autumn rains and the spring rains and give
you the harvest season each year. ²⁵In-
stead, your sins have kept these good
things from you.

²⁶"Evildoers live among my people;
they lie in wait like those who lay nets to
catch birds,ᵉ but they have set their
traps to catch people. ²⁷Just as a hunter
fills a cage with birds, they have filled
their houses with loot. That is why they
are powerful and rich, ²⁸why they are fat
and well fed. There is no limit to their
evil deeds. They do not give orphans

ᵈ He won't . . . anything; or We don't want anything to do with him.　　ᵉ Probable text they . . .
birds; Hebrew unclear.

their rights or show justice to the oppressed. 29 "But I, the LORD, will punish them for these things; I will take revenge on this nation. 30 A terrible and shocking thing has happened in the land: 31 prophets speak nothing but lies; priests rule as the prophets command, and my people offer no objections. But what will they do when it all comes to an end?"

Jerusalem Is Surrounded by Enemies

6 People of Benjamin, run for safety! Escape from Jerusalem! Sound the trumpet in Tekoa and build a signal fire in Beth Haccherem. Disaster and destruction are about to come from the north. 2 The city of Zion is beautiful, but it will be destroyed; 3 kings will camp there with their armies. They will pitch their tents around the city, and each of them will camp wherever they want. 4 They will say, "Prepare to attack Jerusalem! Get ready! We'll attack at noon!" But then they will say, "It's too late, the day is almost over, and the evening shadows are growing long. 5 We'll attack by night; we'll destroy the city's fortresses."

6 The LORD Almighty has ordered these kings to cut down trees and build mounds in order to besiege Jerusalem. He has said, "I will punish this city because it is full of oppression. 7 As a well keeps its water fresh, so Jerusalem keeps its evil fresh. I hear violence and destruction in the city; sickness and wounds are all I see. 8 People of Jerusalem, let these troubles be a warning to you, or else I will abandon you; I will turn your city into a desert, a place where no one lives."

Rebellious Israel

9 The LORD Almighty said to me, "Israel will be stripped clean like a vineyard from which every grape has been picked. So you must rescue everyone you can while there is still time."

10 I answered, "Who would listen to me if I spoke to them and warned them? They are stubborn and refuse to listen to your message; they laugh at what you tell me to say. 11 Your anger against them burns in me too, LORD, and I can't hold it in any longer."

Then the LORD said to me, "Pour out my anger on the children in the streets and on the gatherings of the young people. Husbands and wives will be taken away, and even the very old will not be spared. 12 Their houses will be given to others, and so will their fields and their wives. I am going to punish the people of this land. 13 Everyone, great and small, tries to make money dishonestly; even prophets and priests cheat the people. 14 They act as if my people's wounds were only scratches. 'All is well,' they say, when all is not well. 15 Were they ashamed because they did these disgusting things? No, they were not at all ashamed; they don't even know how to blush. And so they will fall as others have fallen; when I punish them, that will be the end of them. I, the LORD, have spoken."

Israel Rejects God's Way

16 The LORD said to his people, "Stand at the crossroads and look. Ask for the ancient paths and where the best road is. Walk in it, and you will live in peace." But they said, "No, we will not!" 17 Then the LORD appointed sentries to listen for the trumpet's warning. But they said, "We will not listen."

18 So the LORD said, "Listen, you nations, and learn what is going to happen to my people. 19 Listen, earth! As punishment for all their schemes I am bringing ruin on these people, because they have rejected my teaching and have not obeyed my words. 20 What do I care about the incense they bring me from Sheba, or the spices from a distant land? I will not accept their offerings or be pleased with their sacrifices. 21 And so I will make these people stumble and fall. Parents and children will die, and so will friends and neighbors."

Invasion from the North

22 The LORD says, "People are coming from a country in the north; a mighty nation far away is preparing for war. 23 They have taken up their bows and swords; they are cruel and merciless. They sound like the roaring sea, as they ride their horses. They are ready for battle against Jerusalem."

24 "We have heard the news," say the people of Jerusalem, "and our hands hang limp; we are seized by anguish and pain like a woman in labor. 25 We don't dare go to the countryside or walk on

JEREMIAH

the roads, because our enemies are armed and terror is all around us."

26 The LORD says to his people, "Put on sackcloth and roll in ashes. Mourn with bitter tears as you would for an only child, because the one who comes to destroy you will suddenly attack. 27 Jeremiah, test my people, as you would test metal, and find out what they are like. 28 They are all stubborn rebels, hard as bronze and iron. They are all corrupt, going around and spreading gossip. 29 The furnace burns fiercely, but the waste metals do not melt and run off. It is useless to go on refining my people, because those who are evil are not taken away. 30 They will be called worthless dross, because I, the LORD, have rejected them."

Jeremiah Preaches in the Temple

7 1-3 The LORD sent me to the gate of the Temple where the people of Judah went in to worship. He told me to stand there and announce what the LORD Almighty, the God of Israel, had to say to them: "Change the way you are living and the things you are doing, and I will let you go on living here. 4 Stop believing those deceitful words, 'We are safe! This is the LORD's Temple, this is the LORD's Temple, this is the LORD's Temple!'

5 "Change the way you are living and stop doing the things you are doing. Be fair in your treatment of one another. 6 Stop taking advantage of aliens, orphans, and widows. Stop killing innocent people in this land. Stop worshiping other gods, for that will destroy you. 7 If you change, I will let you go on living here in the land which I gave your ancestors as a permanent possession.

8 "Look, you put your trust in deceitful words. 9 You steal, murder, commit adultery, tell lies under oath, offer sacrifices to Baal, and worship gods that you had not known before. 10 You do these things I hate, and then you come and stand in my presence, in my own Temple, and say, 'We are safe!' Do you think that my Temple is a hiding place for robbers? I have seen what you are doing. 12 Go to Shiloh,f the first place where I chose to be worshiped, and see what I did to it because of the sins of my people Israel.

13 You have committed all these sins, and even though I spoke to you over and over again, you refused to listen. You would not answer when I called you. 14 And so, what I did to Shiloh I will do to this Temple of mine, in which you trust. Here in this place that I gave to your ancestors and you, I will do the same thing that I did to Shiloh. 15 I will drive you out of my sight as I drove out your relatives, the people of Israel. I, the LORD, have spoken."

The People's Disobedience

16 The LORD said, "Jeremiah, do not pray for these people. Do not cry or pray on their behalf; do not plead with me, for I will not listen to you. 17 Don't you see what they are doing in the cities of Judah and in the streets of Jerusalem? 18 The children gather firewood, the men build fires, and the women mix dough to bake cakes for the goddess they call the Queen of Heaven. They also pour out offerings of wine to other gods, in order to hurt me. 19 But am I really the one they are hurting? No, they are hurting themselves and bringing shame on themselves. 20 And so I, the Sovereign LORD, will pour out my fierce anger on this Temple. I will pour it out on people and animals alike, and even on the trees and the crops. My anger will be like a fire that no one can put out.

21 "My people, some sacrifices you burn completely on the altar, and some you are permitted to eat. But what I, the LORD, say is that you might as well eat them all. 22 I gave your ancestors no commands about burnt offerings or any other kinds of sacrifices when I brought them out of Egypt. 23 But I did command them to obey me, so that I would be their God and they would be my people. And I told them to live the way I had commanded them, so that things would go well for them. 24 But they did not obey or pay any attention. Instead, they did whatever their stubborn and evil hearts told them to do, and they became worse instead of better. 25 From the day that your ancestors came out of Egypt until this very day I have kept on sending to you my servants, the prophets. 26 Yet no one listened or paid any attention. In-

---

f SHILOH: *The city where the Covenant Box was kept in the time of Eli (see 1 S 1.3). The city was destroyed, probably by the Philistines.*

stead, you became more stubborn and rebellious than your ancestors.

27 "So, Jeremiah, you will speak all these words to my people, but they will not listen to you; you will call them, but they will not answer. 28 You will tell them that their nation does not obey me, the LORD their God, or learn from their punishment. Faithfulness is dead. No longer is it even talked about.

Sinful Deeds in Hinnom Valley

29 "Mourn, people of Jerusalem;
    cut off your hair and throw it
    away.
Sing a funeral song on the
    hilltops,
    because I, the LORD, am angry
    and have rejected my people.
30 "The people of Judah have done an evil thing. They have placed their idols, which I hate, in my Temple and have defiled it. 31 In Hinnom Valley they have built an altar called Topheth, so that they can sacrifice their sons and daughters in the fire. I did not command them to do this — it did not even enter my mind. 32 And so, the time will come when it will no longer be called Topheth or Hinnom Valley, but Slaughter Valley. They will bury people there because there will be nowhere else to bury them. 33 The corpses will be food for the birds and wild animals, and there will be no one to scare them off. 34 The land will become a desert. In the cities of Judah and in the streets of Jerusalem I will put an end to the sounds of joy and gladness and to the happy sounds of wedding feasts.

8 "At that time the bones of the kings and of the officials of Judah, as well as the bones of the priests, of the prophets, and of the other people who lived in Jerusalem, will be taken out of their graves. 2 Instead of being gathered and buried, their bones will be like manure lying on the ground. They will be spread out before the sun, the moon, and the stars, which these people have loved and served, and which they have consulted and worshiped. 3 And the people of this evil nation who survive, who live in the places where I have scattered them, will prefer to die rather than to go on living. I, the LORD Almighty, have spoken."

Sin and Punishment

4 The LORD told me to say to his people, "When someone falls down, doesn't he get back up? If someone misses the road, doesn't he turn back? 5 Why then, my people, do you turn away from me without ever turning back? You cling to your idols and refuse to return to me. 6 I listened carefully, but you did not speak the truth. Not one of you has been sorry for your wickedness; not one of you has asked, 'What have I done wrong?' Each of you keep on going your own way, like a horse rushing into battle. 7 Even storks know when it is time to return; doves, swallows, and thrushes know when it is time to migrate. But, my people, you do not know the laws by which I rule you. 8 How can you say that you are wise and that you know my laws? Look, the laws have been changed by dishonest scribes. 9 Your wise men are put to shame; they are confused and trapped. They have rejected my words; what wisdom do they have now? 10 So I will give their fields to new owners and their wives to other men. Everyone, great and small, tries to make money dishonestly. Even prophets and priests cheat the people. 11 They act as if my people's wounds were only scratches. 'All is well,' they say, when all is not well. 12 My people, were you ashamed because you did these disgusting things? No, you were not ashamed at all; you don't even know how to blush! And so you will fall as others have fallen; when I punish you, that will be the end of you. I, the LORD, have spoken.

13 "I wanted to gather my people, as a farmer gathers a harvest; but they are like a vine with no grapes; like a fig tree with no figs; even the leaves have withered. Therefore, I have allowed outsiders to take over the land."g

14 "Why are we sitting still?" God's people ask. "Come on, we will run to the fortified cities and die there. The LORD our God has condemned us to die; he has given us poison to drink, because we have sinned against him. 15 We hoped for peace and a time of healing, but it was no use; terror came instead. 16 Our enemies are already in the city of Dan; we hear the snorting of their horses. The whole land trembles when their horses

g Therefore . . . land; Hebrew unclear.

JEREMIAH

neigh. Our enemies have come to destroy our land and everything in it, our city and all its people."

17 "Watch out!" the LORD says, "I am sending snakes among you, poisonous snakes that cannot be charmed, and they will bite you."

Jeremiah's Sorrow for His People

18 My sorrow cannot be healed; *h*
I am sick at heart.
19 Listen! Throughout the land
I hear my people crying out,
"Is the LORD no longer in Zion?
Is Zion's king no longer there?"
The LORD, their king, replies,
"Why have you made me angry by
worshiping your idols
and by bowing down to your
useless foreign gods?"
20 The people cry out,
"The summer is gone, the harvest
is over,
but we have not been saved."

21 My heart has been crushed
because my people are crushed;
I mourn; I am completely
dismayed.
22 Is there no medicine in Gilead? *i*
Are there no doctors there?
Why, then, have my people not
been healed?

9 I wish my head were a well of
water,
and my eyes a fountain of tears,
so that I could cry day and night
for my people who have been
killed.
2 I wish I had a place to stay in the
desert
where I could get away from my
people.
They are all unfaithful,
a mob of traitors.
3 They are always ready to tell lies;
dishonesty instead of truth rules
the land.

The LORD says,
"My people do one evil thing after
another
and do not acknowledge me as
their God."

4 Everyone must be on guard
against their friends,
and no one can trust their
relatives;
for all relatives are as deceitful as
Jacob,
and everyone slanders their
friends.
5-6 They all mislead their friends,
and no one tells the truth;
they have taught their tongues
to lie
and will not give up their
sinning.
They do one violent thing after
another,
and one deceitful act follows
another.

The LORD says that his people
reject him.
7 Because of this the LORD Almighty
says,
"I will refine my people like metal
and put them to the test.
My people have done evil—
what else can I do with them?
8 Their tongues are like deadly
arrows;
they always tell lies.
Everyone speaks friendly words to
their neighbors,
but they are really setting a trap
for them.
9 Will I not punish them for these
things?
Will I not take revenge on a
nation like this?
I, the LORD, have spoken."

10 I said, "I will mourn for the
mountains
and weep for the pastures,
because they have dried up,
and no one travels through
them.
The sound of livestock is no
longer heard;
birds and wild animals have fled
and gone."

11 The LORD says, "I will make
Jerusalem a pile of ruins,
a place where jackals live;

---

h Probable text My sorrow . . . healed; Hebrew unclear. i GILEAD: A region east of the Jordan, famous for plants that were used for medicinal purposes.

the cities of Judah will become a
desert,
a place where no one lives."

12 I asked, "LORD, why is the land devastated and dry as a desert, so that no one travels through it? Who is wise enough to understand this? To whom have you explained it so that they can tell others?"

13 The LORD answered, "This has happened because my people have abandoned the teaching that I gave them. They have not obeyed me or done what I told them. 14 Instead, they have been stubborn and have worshiped the idols of Baal as their ancestors taught them to do. 15 So then, listen to what I, the LORD Almighty, the God of Israel, will do: I will give my people bitter plants to eat and poison to drink. 16 I will scatter them among nations that neither they nor their ancestors have heard about, and I will send armies against them until I have completely destroyed them."

The People of Jerusalem Cry Out for Help

17 The LORD Almighty said,
"Think about what is happening!
Call for the mourners to come,
for the women who sing funeral
songs."

18 The people said,
"Tell them to hurry and sing a
funeral song for us,
until our eyes fill with tears,
and our eyelids are wet from
crying."

19 Listen to the sound of crying in
Zion:
"We are ruined!
We are completely disgraced!
We must leave our land;
our homes have been torn
down."

20 I said,
"Listen to the LORD, you women,
and pay attention to his words.
Teach your daughters how to
mourn,

and your friends how to sing a
funeral song.
21 Death has come in through our
windows
and entered our palaces;
it has cut down the children in the
streets
and the young men in the
marketplaces.
22 Dead bodies are scattered
everywhere,
like piles of manure on the
fields,
like grain cut and left behind by
the reapers,
grain that no one gathers.
This is what the LORD has told me
to say."

23 The LORD says,
"The wise should not boast of their
wisdom,
nor the strong of their strength,
nor the rich of their wealth.
24 If any want to boast,
they should boast that they
know and understand me,
because my love is constant,
and I do what is just and right.
These are the things that
please me.
I, the LORD, have spoken."

25-26 The LORD says, "The time is coming when I will punish the people of Egypt, Judah, Edom, Ammon, Moab, and the desert people, who have their hair cut short. All these people are circumcised, but have not kept the covenant it symbolizes. None of these people and none of the people of Israel have kept my covenant."

Idolatry and True Worship

10 People of Israel, listen to the message that the LORD has for you. 2 He says,
"Do not follow the ways of other
nations;
do not be disturbed by unusual
sights in the sky,
even though other nations are
terrified.
3 The religion of these people is
worthless.

---

j HAIR CUT SHORT: The desert people cut their hair short in honor of their god, a pagan practice forbidden to the Israelites (see Lv 19.27).

A tree is cut down in the forest;
   it is carved by the tools of the
     woodworker
4 and decorated with silver and
     gold.
It is fastened down with nails
   to keep it from falling over.
5 Such idols are like scarecrows in
   a field of melons;
  they cannot speak;
they have to be carried
  because they cannot walk.
Do not be afraid of them:
  they can cause you no harm,
  and they can do you no good."

6 Lord, there is no one like you;
  you are mighty,
  and your name is great and
    powerful.
7 Who would not honor you, the
   king of all nations?
  You deserve to be honored.
There is no one like you
  among all the wise men of the
   nations
  or among any of their kings.
8 All of them are stupid and foolish.
  What can they learn from
   wooden idols?k
9 Their idols are covered with silver
   from Spain
  and with gold from Uphaz,
  all the work of artists;
  they are dressed in violet and
    purple cloth
  woven by skilled weavers.
10 But you, Lord, are the true God;
  you are the living God
  and the eternal king.
When you are angry, the world
   trembles;
  the nations cannot endure your
   anger.

(11 You people must tell them that the
gods who did not make the earth and the
sky will be destroyed. They will no
longer exist anywhere on earth.)

A Hymn of Praise to God

12 The Lord made the earth by his
   power;
  by his wisdom he created the
   world

and stretched out the heavens.
13 At his command the waters above
   the skyl roar;
  he brings clouds from the ends
   of the earth.
He makes lightning flash in the
   rain
  and sends the wind from his
   storeroom.
14 At the sight of this, people feel
   stupid and senseless;
  those who make idols are
   disillusioned,
  because the gods they make are
   false and lifeless.
15 They are worthless and should be
   despised;
  they will be destroyed when the
   Lord comes to deal with them.
16 The God of Jacob is not like them;
  he is the one who made
   everything,
  and he has chosen Israel to be
   his very own people.
The Lord Almighty is his name.

The Coming Exile

17 People of Jerusalem, you are under
siege! Gather up your belongings. 18 The
Lord is going to throw you out of this
land; he is going to crush you until not
one of you is left. The Lord has spoken.
19 The people of Jerusalem cried out,
  "How badly we are hurt!
   Our wounds will not heal.
And we thought this was
   something we could endure!
20 Our tents are ruined;
  the ropes that held them have
   broken.
Our children have all gone away;
  there is no one left to put up our
   tents again;
  there is no one to hang their
   curtains."

21 I answered, "Our leaders are
   stupid;
  they do not ask the Lord for
   guidance.
This is why they have failed,
  and our people have been
   scattered.
22 Listen! News has come!

k What can ... idols?; or What their idols teach is worthless. l WATERS ABOVE THE SKY: See
Gn 1.6-8.

There is a great commotion in a
  nation to the north;
its army will turn the cities of
  Judah into a desert,
a place where jackals live."

23 LORD, I know that none of us are
  in charge of our own destiny;
none of us have control over our
  own life.
24 Correct your people, LORD,
  but do not be too hard on us
or punish us when you are
  angry;
that would be the end of us.
25 Turn your anger on the nations
  that do not worship you
and on the people who
  reject you.
They have killed your people;
  they have destroyed us
  completely
and left our country in ruins.

Jeremiah and the Covenant

11 The LORD said to me, 2 "Listen to
the terms of the covenant. Tell
the people of Judah and of Jerusalem
3 that I, the LORD God of Israel, have
placed a curse on everyone who does
not obey the terms of this covenant. 4 It is
the covenant I made with their ancestors
when I brought them out of Egypt, the
land that was like a blazing furnace to
them. I told them to obey me and to do
everything that I had commanded. I told
them that if they obeyed, they would be
my people and I would be their God.
5 Then I would keep the promise I made
to their ancestors that I would give them
the rich and fertile land which they now
have."

I said, "Yes, LORD."

6 Then the LORD said to me, "Go to the
cities of Judah and to the streets of Jerusalem. Proclaim my message there and
tell the people to listen to the terms of
the covenant and to obey them. 7 When I
brought their ancestors out of Egypt, I
solemnly warned them to obey me, and
I have kept on warning the people until
this day. 8 But they did not listen or obey.
Instead, everyone continued to be as
stubborn and evil as ever. I had commanded them to keep the covenant, but

they refused. So I brought on them all
the punishments described in it."

9 Then the LORD said to me, "The people of Judah and of Jerusalem are plotting against me. 10 They have gone back
to the sins of their ancestors, who refused to do what I said; they have worshiped other gods. Both Israel and Judah
have broken the covenant that I made
with their ancestors. 11 So now I, the
LORD, warn them that I am going to bring
destruction on them, and they will not
escape. And when they cry out to me for
help, I will not listen to them. 12 Then the
people of Judah and of Jerusalem will go
to the gods to whom they offer sacrifices
and will cry out to them for help. But
those gods will not be able to save them
when this destruction comes. 13 The people of Judah have as many gods as they
have cities, and the inhabitants of Jerusalem have set up as many altars for sacrifices to that disgusting god Baal as
there are streets in the city. 14 Jeremiah,
don't pray to me or plead with me on
behalf of these people. When they are in
trouble and call to me for help, I will not
listen to them."

15 The LORD says, "The people I love
are doing evil things. What right do they
have to be in my Temple? Do they think
they can prevent disaster by making
promisesm and by offering animal sacrifices? Will they then rejoice? 16 I once
called them a leafy olive tree, full of
beautiful fruit; but now, with a roar like
thunder I will set its leaves on fire and
break its branches.

17 "I, the LORD Almighty, planted Israel
and Judah; but now I threaten them with
disaster. They have brought this on
themselves because they have done
wrong; they have made me angry by offering sacrifices to Baal."

A Plot against Jeremiah's Life

18 The LORD informed me of the plots
that my enemies were making against
me. 19 I was like a trusting lamb taken
out to be killed, and I did not know that
it was against me that they were planning evil things. They were saying,
"Let's chop down the tree while it is still
healthy;n let's kill him so that no one
will remember him any more."

m One ancient translation promises; Hebrew many.   n Probable text while it is still healthy;
Hebrew with its bread.

20 Then I prayed, "Almighty LORD, you are a just judge; you test people's thoughts and feelings. I have placed my cause in your hands; so let me watch you take revenge on these people."

21 The people of Anathoth wanted me killed, and they told me that they would kill me if I kept on proclaiming the LORD's message. **22** So the LORD Almighty said, "I will punish them! Their young men will be killed in war; their children will die of starvation. **23** I have set a time for bringing disaster on the people of Anathoth, and when that time comes, none of them will survive."

Jeremiah Questions the LORD

12 "LORD, if I argued my case
    with you,
  you would prove to be right.
Yet I must question you about
    matters of justice.
Why are the wicked so
    prosperous?
  Why do dishonest people
    succeed?
2 You plant them, and they take
    root;
  they grow and bear fruit.
They always speak well of you,
  yet they do not really care
    about you.
3 But, LORD, you know me;
  you see what I do
  and how I love you.
Drag these evil people away like
    sheep to be butchered;
  guard them until it is time for
    them to be slaughtered.
4 How long will our land be dry,
  and the grass in every field be
    withered?
Animals and birds are dying
  because of the wickedness of
    our people,
  people who say, 'God doesn't
    see what we are doing.' "*o*

5 The LORD said,
"Jeremiah, if you get tired racing
    against people,
  how can you race against
    horses?
If you can't even stand up in open
    country,

how will you manage in the
    jungle by the Jordan?
6 Even your relatives, members of
    your own family, have
    betrayed you;
  they join in the attacks
    against you.
Do not trust them, even though
  they speak friendly words."

The LORD's Sorrow because of His People

7 The LORD says,
"I have abandoned Israel;
  I have rejected my chosen
    nation.
I have given the people I love
  into the power of their enemies.
8 My chosen people have turned
    against me;
  like a lion in the forest
  they have roared at me,
  and so I hate them.
9 My chosen people are like a bird
    attacked from all sides by
    hawks.
Call the wild animals
  to come and join in the feast!
10 Many foreign rulers have
    destroyed my vineyard;
  they have trampled down my
    fields;
  they have turned my lovely land
    into a desert.
11 They have made it a wasteland;
  it lies desolate before me.
The whole land has become a
    desert,
  and no one cares.
12 Across all the desert highlands
    people have come to plunder.
I have sent war to destroy the
    entire land;
  no one can live in peace.
13 My people planted wheat, but
    gathered weeds;
  they have worked hard, but got
    nothing for it.
Because of my fierce anger
  their crops have failed."

The LORD's Promise to Israel's Neighbors

14 The LORD says, "I have something to say about Israel's neighbors who have ruined the land I gave to my people Is-

---

o Some ancient translations what we are doing; *Hebrew* our latter end.

rael. I will take those wicked people away from their countries like an uprooted plant, and I will rescue Judah from them. 15But after I have taken them away, I will have mercy on them; I will bring each nation back to its own land and to its own country. 16If with all their hearts they will accept the religion of my people and will swear, 'As the LORD lives — as they once taught my people to swear by Baal — then they will also be a part of my people and will prosper. 17But if any nation will not obey, then I will completely uproot it and destroy it. I, the LORD, have spoken."

The Linen Shorts

13 The LORD told me to go and buy myself some linen shorts and to put them on; but he told me not to put them in water. 2So I bought them and put them on. 3Then the LORD spoke to me again and said, 4"Go to the Euphrates River and hide the shorts in a hole in the rocks." 5So I went and hid them near the Euphrates.

6Some time later the LORD told me to go back to the Euphrates and get the shorts. 7So I went back, and when I found the place where I had hidden them, I saw that they were ruined and were no longer any good.

8Then the LORD spoke to me again. He said, 9"This is how I will destroy the pride of Judah and the great pride of Jerusalem. 10These evil people have refused to obey me. They have been as stubborn and wicked as ever, and have worshiped and served other gods. So then, they will become like these shorts that are no longer any good. 11Just as shorts fit tightly around the waist, so I intended all the people of Israel and Judah to hold tightly to me. I did this so that they would be my people and would bring praise and honor to my name; but they would not obey me."

The Wine Jar

12The LORD God said to me, "Jeremiah, tell the people of Israel that every wine jar should be filled with wine. They will answer that they know every wine jar should be filled with wine. 13Then tell them that I, the LORD, am going to fill the people in this land with wine until they

are drunk: the kings, who are David's descendants, the priests, the prophets, and all the people of Jerusalem. 14Then I will smash them like jars against one another, old and young alike. No pity, compassion, or mercy will stop me from killing them."

Jeremiah Warns against Pride

15People of Israel, the LORD has
    spoken!
Be humble and listen to him.
16Honor the LORD, your God,
    before he brings darkness,
    and you stumble on the
      mountains;
before he turns into deep darkness
    the light you hoped for.
17If you will not listen,
    I will cry in secret because of
      your pride;
I will cry bitterly, and my tears
    will flow
because the LORD's people have
    been taken away as captives.

18The LORD said to me, "Tell the king and his mother to come down from their thrones, because their beautiful crowns have fallen from their heads.p 19The towns of southern Judah are under siege; no one can get through to them. All the people of Judah have been taken away into exile."

20Jerusalem, look! Your enemies are coming down from the north! Where are the people entrusted to your care, your people you were so proud of? 21What will you say when people you thought were your friends conquer you and rule over you?q You will be in pain like a woman giving birth. 22If you ask why all this has happened to you — why your clothes have been torn off and you have been raped — it is because your sin is so terrible. 23Can people change the color of their skin, or a leopard remove its spots? If they could, then you that do nothing but evil could learn to do what is right. 24The LORD will scatter you like straw that is blown away by the desert wind. 25He has said that this will be your fate. This is what he has decided to do with you, because you have forgotten him and have trusted in false gods.

p Some ancient translations from their heads; Hebrew unclear.   q Probable text What ... over you; Hebrew unclear.

26 The LORD himself will strip off your clothes and expose you to shame. 27 He has seen you do the things he hates. He has seen you go after pagan gods on the hills and in the fields, like a man lusting after his neighbor's wife or like a stallion after a mare. People of Jerusalem, you are doomed! When will you ever be pure?

The Terrible Drought

14 The LORD said to me concerning the drought,

2 "Judah is in mourning;
  its cities are dying,
its people lie on the ground in
  sorrow,
and Jerusalem cries out for help.
3 The rich people send their
    servants for water;
  they go to the cisterns,
  but find no water;
  they come back with their jars
    empty.
Discouraged and confused,
  they hide their faces.
4 Because there is no rain
  and the ground is dried up,
  the farmers are sick at heart;
  they hide their faces.
5 In the field the mother deer
  abandons her newborn fawn
  because there is no grass.
6 The wild donkeys stand on the
    hilltops
  and pant for breath like
    jackals;
  their eyesight fails them
  because they have no food.
7 My people cry out to me,
  'Even though our sins accuse us,
  help us, LORD, as you have
    promised.
We have turned away from you
    many times;
  we have sinned against you.
8 You are Israel's only hope;
  you are the one who saves us
    from disaster.
Why are you like a stranger in our
    land,
  like a traveler who stays for
    only one night?
9 Why are you like someone taken
    by surprise,
  like a soldier powerless to help?
Surely, LORD, you are with us!

We are your people;
  do not abandon us.' "

10 The LORD says about these people, "They love to run away from me, and they will not control themselves. So I am not pleased with them. I will remember the wrongs they have done and punish them because of their sins."

11 The LORD said to me, "Do not ask me to help these people. 12 Even if they fast, I will not listen to their cry for help; and even if they offer me burnt offerings and grain offerings, I will not be pleased with them. Instead, I will kill them in war and by starvation and disease."

13 Then I said, "Sovereign LORD, you know that the prophets are telling the people that there will be no war or starvation, because you have promised, they say, that there will be only peace in our land."

14 But the LORD replied, "The prophets are telling lies in my name; I did not send them, nor did I give them any orders or speak one word to them. The visions they talk about have not come from me; their predictions are worthless things that they have imagined. 15 I, the LORD, tell you what I am going to do to those prophets whom I did not send but who speak in my name and say war and starvation will not strike this land—I will kill them in war and by starvation. 16 The people to whom they have said these things will be killed in the same way. Their bodies will be thrown out into the streets of Jerusalem, and there will be no one to bury them. This will happen to all of them—including their wives, their sons, and their daughters. I will make them pay for their wickedness."

17 The LORD commanded me to tell the people about my sorrow and to say:
  "May my eyes flow with tears day
    and night,
  may I never stop weeping,
  for my people are deeply wounded
    and are badly hurt.
18 When I go out in the fields,
  I see the bodies of men killed
    in war;
  when I go into the towns,
  I see people starving to death.
Prophets and priests carry on their
    work,

but they don't know what they are doing."[r]

The People Plead with the LORD

19 LORD, have you completely rejected
    Judah?
Do you hate the people of Zion?
Why have you hurt us so badly
    that we cannot be healed?
We looked for peace, but nothing
    good happened;
we hoped for healing, but terror
    came instead.
20 We have sinned against you, LORD;
we confess our own sins
    and the sins of our ancestors.
21 Remember your promises and do
    not despise us;
do not bring disgrace on
    Jerusalem,
the place of your glorious
    throne.
Do not break the covenant you
    made with us.
22 None of the idols of the nations
    can send rain;
the sky by itself cannot make
    showers fall.
We have put our hope in you,
    O LORD our God,
because you are the one who
    does these things.

Doom for the People of Judah

15 Then the LORD said to me, "Even
if Moses and Samuel were standing here pleading with me, I would not
show these people any mercy. Make
them go away; make them get out of my
sight. 2 When they ask you where they
should go, tell them that I have said:
Some are doomed to die by
    disease—
    that's where they will go!
Others are doomed to die in war—
    that's where they will go!
Some are doomed to die of
    starvation—
    that's where they will go!
Others are doomed to be taken
    away as prisoners—
    that's where they will go!
3 I, the LORD, have decided that four terrible things will happen to them: they will
be killed in war; their bodies will be

dragged off by dogs; birds will eat them,
and wild animals will devour what is left
over. 4 I will make all the people of the
world horrified at them because of what
Hezekiah's son Manasseh did in Jerusalem when he was king of Judah."
5 The LORD says,
"Who will pity you, people of
    Jerusalem,
    and who will grieve over you?
Who will stop long enough
    to ask how you are?
6 You people have rejected me;
    you have turned your backs
        on me.
So I reached out and crushed you
    because I was tired of
        controlling my anger.[s]
7 In every town in the land
    I threw you to the wind like
        straw.
I destroyed you, my people,
    I killed your children
    because you did not stop your
        evil ways.
8 There are more widows in your
        land
    than grains of sand by the sea.
I killed your young men in their
        prime
    and made their mothers suffer.
I suddenly struck them
    with anguish and terror.
9 The mother who lost her seven
        children has fainted,
    gasping for breath.
Her daylight has turned to
        darkness;
    she is disgraced and sick at
        heart.
I will let your enemies kill
    those of you who are still alive.
I, the LORD, have spoken."

Jeremiah Complains to the LORD

10 What an unhappy man I am! Why
did my mother bring me into the world?
I have to quarrel and argue with everyone in the land. I have not lent any
money or borrowed any; yet everyone
curses me. 11 LORD, may all their curses
come true if I have not served[t] you well,
if I have not pleaded with you on behalf
of my enemies when they were in trouble and distress. (12 No one can break

[r] Prophets ... doing; or Prophets and priests have been dragged away to a land they know
nothing about.   [s] you because ... anger; or you; I was tired of feeling sorry for you.
[t] Probable text LORD, ... served; Hebrew unclear.

JEREMIAH

iron, especially the iron from the north that is mixed with bronze.)

13 The Lord said to me, "I will send enemies to carry away the wealth and treasures of my people, in order to punish them for the sins they have committed throughout the land. 14 I will make them serve their enemies in a land they know nothing about, because my anger is like fire, and it will burn forever."

15 Then I said, "Lord, you understand. Remember me and help me. Let me have revenge on those who persecute me. Do not be so patient with them that they succeed in killing me. Remember that it is for your sake that I am insulted. 16 You spoke to me, and I listened to every word. I belong to you, Lord God Almighty, and so your words filled my heart with joy and happiness. 17 I did not spend my time with other people, laughing and having a good time. In obedience to your orders I stayed by myself and was filled with anger. 18 Why do I keep on suffering? Why are my wounds incurable? Why won't they heal? Do you intend to disappoint me like a stream that goes dry in the summer?"

19 To this the Lord replied, "If you return, I will take you back, and you will be my servant again. If instead of talking nonsense you proclaim a worthwhile message, you will be my prophet again. The people will come back to you, and you will not need to go to them. 20 I will make you like a solid bronze wall as far as they are concerned. They will fight against you, but they will not defeat you. I will be with you to protect you and keep you safe. 21 I will rescue you from the power of wicked and violent people. I, the Lord, have spoken."

The Lord's Will for Jeremiah's Life

16 Again the Lord spoke to me and said, 2 "Do not marry or have children in a place like this. 3 I will tell you what is going to happen to the children who are born here and to their parents. 4 They will die of terrible diseases, and no one will mourn for them or bury them. Their bodies will lie like piles of manure on the ground. They will be killed in war or die of starvation, and their bodies will be food for the birds and the wild animals.

5 "You must not enter a house where there is mourning. Do not grieve for anyone. I will no longer bless my people with peace or show them love and mercy. 6 The rich and the poor will die in this land, but no one will bury them or mourn for them. Not one of you will gash yourself or shave your head to show your grief. 7 No one will eat or drink with anyone to offer comfort when a loved one dies. No one will show sympathy, not even for someone who has lost a father or mother.

8 "Do not enter a house where people are feasting. Do not sit down with them to eat and drink. 9 Listen to what I, the Lord Almighty, the God of Israel, have to say. I will silence the sounds of joy and gladness and the happy sounds of wedding feasts. The people here will live to see this happen.

10 "When you tell them all this, they will ask you why I have decided to punish them so harshly. They will ask what crime they are guilty of and what sin they have committed against the Lord their God. 11 Then tell them that the Lord has said, 'Your ancestors turned away from me and worshiped and served other gods. They abandoned me and did not obey my teachings. 12 But you have done even worse than your ancestors. All of you are stubborn and evil, and you do not obey me. 13 So then, I will throw you out of this land into a land that neither you nor your ancestors have ever known. And there you will serve other gods day and night, and I will show you no mercy.' "

The Return from Exile

14 The Lord says, "The time is coming when people will no longer swear by me as the living God who brought the people of Israel out of the land of Egypt. 15 Instead, they will swear by me as the living God who brought the people of Israel out of a northern land and out of all the other countries where I had scattered them. I will bring them back to their own country, to the land that I gave their ancestors. I, the Lord, have spoken."

The Coming Punishment

16 The Lord says, "I am sending for many fishermen to come and catch these people. Then I will send for many hunters to hunt them down on every mountain and hill and in the caves among the

rocks. 17I see everything they do. Nothing is hidden from me; their sins do not escape my sight. 18I will make them pay double for their sin and wickedness, because they have defiled my land with idols that are as lifeless as corpses, and have filled it with their false gods."

Jeremiah's Prayer of Confidence in the LORD

19LORD, you are the one who protects me and gives me strength; you help me in times of trouble. Nations will come to you from the ends of the earth and say, "Our ancestors had nothing but false gods, nothing but useless idols. 20Can people make their own gods? No, if they did, those would not really be gods."

21"So then," says the LORD, "once and for all I will make the nations know my power and my might; they will know that I am the LORD."

The Sin and Punishment of Judah

17 The LORD says, "People of Judah, your sin is written with an iron pen; it is engraved on your hearts with a diamond point and carved on the corners of your altars. 2Your people worship at the altars and the symbols that have been set up for the goddess Asherah by every green tree and on the hilltops 3and on the mountains in the open country. I will have your enemies take away your wealth and your treasures because of all the sins you have committed[u] throughout your land. 4You will have to give up[v] the land I gave you, and I will make you serve your enemies in a land you know nothing about, because my anger is like a fire, and it will burn forever."

Various Sayings

5The LORD says,
"I will condemn those
who turn away from me
and put their trust in human beings,
in the strength of mortals.
6He is like a bush in the desert,
which grows in the dry wasteland,
on salty ground where nothing else grows.

Nothing good ever happens to him.

7"But I will bless the person
who puts his trust in me.
8He is like a tree growing near a stream
and sending out roots to the water.
It is not afraid when hot weather comes,
because its leaves stay green;
it has no worries when there is no rain;
it keeps on bearing fruit.

9"Who can understand the human heart?
There is nothing else so deceitful;
it is too sick to be healed.
10I, the LORD, search the minds
and test the hearts of people.
I treat each of them according to the way they live,
according to what they do."

11The person who gets money dishonestly
is like a bird that hatches eggs it didn't lay.
In the prime of life he will lose his riches,
and in the end he is nothing but a fool.

12Our Temple is like a glorious throne,
standing on a high mountain from the beginning.

13LORD, you are Israel's hope;
all who abandon you will be put to shame.
They will disappear like names written in the dust,[w]
because they have abandoned you, the LORD,
the spring of fresh water.

Jeremiah Asks the LORD for Help

14LORD, heal me and I will be completely well; rescue me and I will be perfectly safe. You are the one I praise!
15The people say to me, "Where are

---

u *Probable text* because of all the sins you have committed; *Hebrew* your high places for sins.
v *Probable text* You . . . give up; *Hebrew unclear.*   w *disappear . . . dust; or* go to the world of the dead.

those threats the LORD made against us? Let him carry them out now!"

16 But, LORD, I never urged you to bring disaster on them;*x I did not wish a time of trouble for them. LORD, you know this; you know what I have said. 17 Do not be a terror to me; you are my place of safety when trouble comes. 18 Bring disgrace on those who persecute me, but spare me, LORD. Fill them with terror, but do not terrify me. Bring disaster on them and break them to pieces.

On Observing the Sabbath

19 The LORD said to me, "Jeremiah, go and announce my message at the People's Gate, through which the kings of Judah enter and leave the city; then go to all the other gates of Jerusalem. 20 Tell the kings and all the people of Judah and everyone who lives in Jerusalem and enters these gates, to listen to what I say. 21 Tell them that if they love their lives, they must not carry any load on the Sabbath; they must not carry anything in through the gates of Jerusalem 22 or carry anything out of their houses on the Sabbath. They must not work on the Sabbath; they must observe it as a sacred day, as I commanded their ancestors. 23 Their ancestors did not listen to me or pay any attention. Instead, they became stubborn; they would not obey me or learn from me.

24 "Tell these people that they must obey all my commands. They must not carry any load in through the gates of this city on the Sabbath. They must observe the Sabbath as a sacred day and must not do any work at all. 25 Then their kings and princes will enter the gates of Jerusalem and have the same royal power that David had. Together with the people of Judah and of Jerusalem, they will ride in chariots and on horses, and the city of Jerusalem will always be filled with people. 26 People will come from the towns of Judah and from the villages around Jerusalem; they will come from the territory of Benjamin, from the foothills, from the mountains, and from southern Judah. They will bring to my Temple burnt offerings and sacrifices, grain offerings and incense, as well as thank offerings. 27 But they must obey me and observe the Sabbath

as a sacred day. They must not carry any load through the gates of Jerusalem on that day, for if they do, I will set the gates of Jerusalem on fire. Fire will burn down the palaces of Jerusalem, and no one will be able to put it out."

Jeremiah at the Potter's House

18 The LORD said to me, 2 "Go down to the potter's house, where I will give you my message." 3 So I went there and saw the potter working at his wheel. 4 Whenever a piece of pottery turned out imperfect, he would take the clay and make it into something else.

5 Then the LORD said to me, 6 "Don't I have the right to do with you people of Israel what the potter did with the clay? You are in my hands just like clay in the potter's hands. 7 If at any time I say that I am going to uproot, break down, or destroy any nation or kingdom, 8 but then that nation turns from its evil, I will not do what I said I would. 9 On the other hand, if I say that I am going to plant or build up any nation or kingdom, 10 but then that nation disobeys me and does evil, I will not do what I said I would. 11 Now then, tell the people of Judah and of Jerusalem that I am making plans against them and getting ready to punish them. Tell them to stop living sinful lives — to change their ways and the things they are doing. 12 They will answer, 'No, why should we? We will all be just as stubborn and evil as we want to be.'"

The People Reject the LORD

13 The LORD says,
"Ask every nation if such a thing
    has ever happened before.
The people of Israel have done a
    terrible thing!
14 Are Lebanon's rocky heights ever
    without snow?
Do its cool mountain streams
    ever run dry?
15 Yet my people have forgotten me;
    they burn incense to idols.
They have stumbled in the way
    they should go;
they no longer follow the old
    ways;
they walk on unmarked paths.

x *Probable text* bring disaster on them; *Hebrew* from being a shepherd after you.

16 They have made this land a thing
of horror,
    to be despised forever.
All who pass by will be shocked at
what they see;
    they will shake their heads in
amazement.
17 I will scatter my people before
their enemies,
    like dust blown by the east
wind.
I will turn my back on them;
    I will not help them when the
disaster comes."

A Plot against Jeremiah

18 Then the people said, "Let's do
something about Jeremiah! There will
always be priests to instruct us, the wise
to give us counsel, and prophets to proclaim God's message. Let's bring
charges against him and stop listening
to what he says."

19 So I prayed, "LORD, hear what I am
saying and listen to what my enemies
are saying about me. 20 Is evil the payment for good? Yet they have dug a pit
for me to fall in. Remember how I came
to you and spoke on their behalf, so that
you would not deal with them in anger.
21 But now, LORD, let their children starve
to death; let them be killed in war. Let
the women lose their husbands and children; let the men die of disease and the
young men be killed in battle. 22 Send a
mob to plunder their homes without
warning; make them cry out in terror.
They have dug a pit for me to fall in and
have set traps to catch me. 23 But, LORD,
you know all their plots to kill me. Do
not forgive their evil or pardon their sin.
Throw them down in defeat and deal
with them while you are angry."

The Broken Jar

19 The LORD told me to go and buy a
clay jar. He also told me to take
some of the elders of the people and
some of the older priests, 2 and to go
through Potsherd Gate out to Hinnom
Valley. There I was to proclaim the message that he would give me. 3 The LORD
told me to say, "Kings of Judah and people of Jerusalem, listen to what I, the
LORD Almighty, the God of Israel, have to
say. I am going to bring such a disaster
on this place that everyone who hears
about it will be stunned. 4 I am going to

do this because the people have abandoned me and defiled this place by offering sacrifices here to other gods — gods
that neither they nor their ancestors nor
the kings of Judah have known anything
about. They have filled this place with
the blood of innocent people, 5 and they
have built altars for Baal in order to
burn their children in the fire as sacrifices. I never commanded them to do
this; it never even entered my mind. 6 So
then, the time will come when this place
will no longer be called Topheth or Hinnom Valley. Instead, it will be known as
Slaughter Valley. 7 In this place I will
frustrate all the plans of the people of
Judah and Jerusalem. I will let their enemies triumph over them and kill them in
battle. I will give their corpses to the
birds and the wild animals as food.
8 I will bring such terrible destruction on
this city that everyone who passes by
will be shocked and amazed. 9 The enemy will surround the city and try to kill
its people. The siege will be so terrible
that the people inside the city will eat
one another and even their own
children."

10 Then the LORD told me to break the
jar in front of those who had gone with
me 11 and to tell them that the LORD
Almighty had said, "I will break this
people and this city, and it will be like
this broken clay jar that cannot be put
together again. People will bury their
dead even in Topheth because there
will be nowhere else to bury them.
12 I promise that I will make this city and
its inhabitants like Topheth. 13 The
houses of Jerusalem, the houses of the
kings of Judah, and indeed all the
houses on whose roofs incense has been
burned to the stars and where wine has
been poured out as an offering to other
gods — they will all be as unclean as
Topheth."

14 Then I left Topheth, where the LORD
had sent me to proclaim his message. I
went and stood in the court of the Temple and told all the people 15 that the
LORD Almighty, the God of Israel, had
said, "I am going to bring on this city
and on every nearby town all the punishment that I said I would, because you
are stubborn and will not listen to what
I say."

JEREMIAH

Jeremiah's Conflict with Pashhur the Priest

20 When the priest Pashhur son of Immer, who was the chief officer of the Temple, heard me proclaim these things, ²he had me beaten and placed in chains near the upper Benjamin Gate in the Temple. ³The next morning, after Pashhur had released me from the chains, I said to him, "The LORD did not name you Pashhur. The name he has given you is 'Terror Everywhere.' ⁴The LORD himself has said, 'I am going to make you a terror to yourself and to your friends, and you will see them all killed by the swords of their enemies. I am going to put all the people of Judah under the power of the king of Babylonia; he will take some away as prisoners to his country and put others to death. ⁵I will also let their enemies plunder all the wealth of this city and seize all its possessions and property, even the treasures of the kings of Judah, and carry everything off to Babylonia. ⁶As for you, Pashhur, you and all your family will also be captured and taken off to Babylonia. There you will die and be buried, along with all your friends to whom you have told so many lies.' "

Jeremiah Complains to the LORD

⁷LORD, you have deceived me,
    and I was deceived.
You are stronger than I am,
    and you have overpowered me.
Everyone makes fun of me;
    they laugh at me all day long.

⁸Whenever I speak, I have to
        cry out
    and shout, "Violence!
        Destruction!"
LORD, I am ridiculed and scorned
        all the time
    because I proclaim your
        message.
⁹But when I say, "I will forget the
        LORD
    and no longer speak in his
        name,"
then your message is like a fire
    burning deep within me.
I try my best to hold it in,
    but can no longer keep it back.
¹⁰I hear everybody whispering,
    "Terror is everywhere!

So let's report him to the
        authorities!"
Even my close friends wait for my
        downfall.
"Perhaps he can be tricked,"
        they say;
    "then we can catch him and get
        revenge."
¹¹But you, LORD, are on my side,
        strong and mighty,
    and those who persecute me will
        fail.
They will be disgraced forever,
    because they cannot succeed.
Their disgrace will never be
    forgotten.
¹²But, Almighty LORD, you test
        people justly;
    you know what is in their hearts
        and minds.
So let me see you take revenge on
        my enemies,
    for I have placed my cause in
        your hands.
¹³Sing to the LORD!
    Praise the LORD!
He rescues the oppressed from the
    power of evil people.

¹⁴Curse the day I was born!
Forget the day my mother gave me
        birth!
¹⁵Curse the one who made my
        father glad
    by bringing him the news,
    "It's a boy! You have a son!"
¹⁶May he be like those cities
    that the LORD destroyed without
        mercy.
May he hear cries of pain in the
        morning
    and the battle alarm at noon,
17   for not killing me before I was
        born.
Then my mother's womb would
    have been my grave.
¹⁸Why was I born?
    Was it only to have trouble and
        sorrow,
    to end my life in disgrace?

Jerusalem's Defeat Is Predicted

21 King Zedekiah of Judah sent to me Pashhur son of Malchiah and the priest Zephaniah son of Maaseiah with this request: ²"Please speak to the LORD for us, because King Nebuchadnezzar of Babylonia and his army are besieging the city. Maybe the LORD will perform one of his miracles for us and force Nebuchadnezzar to retreat."

3 Then the LORD spoke to me, and I told those who had been sent to me 4to tell Zedekiah that the LORD, the God of Israel, had said, "Zedekiah, I am going to defeat your army that is fighting against the king of Babylonia and his army. I will pile up your soldiers' weapons in the center of the city. 5 I will fight against you with all my might, my anger, my wrath, and my fury. 6 I will kill everyone living in this city; people and animals alike will die of a terrible disease. 7 But as for you, your officials, and the people who survive the war, the famine, and the disease—I will let all of you be captured by King Nebuchadnezzar and by your enemies, who want to kill you. Nebuchadnezzar will put you to death. He will not spare any of you or show mercy or pity to any of you. I, the LORD, have spoken."

8 Then the LORD told me to say to the people, "Listen! I, the LORD, am giving you a choice between the way that leads to life and the way that leads to death. 9 Anyone who stays in the city will be killed in war or by starvation or disease. But those who go out and surrender to the Babylonians, who are now attacking the city, will not be killed; they will at least escape with their life. 10 I have made up my mind not to spare this city, but to destroy it. It will be given over to the king of Babylonia, and he will burn it to the ground. I, the LORD, have spoken."

Judgment on the Royal House of Judah

11-12 The LORD told me to give this message to the royal house of Judah, the descendants of David: "Listen to what I, the LORD, am saying. See that justice is done every day. Protect the person who is being cheated from the one who is cheating him. If you don't, the evil you are doing will make my anger burn like a fire that cannot be put out. 13 You, Jerusalem, are sittingʸ high above the valleys, like a rock rising above the plain. But I will fight against you. You say that no one can attack you or break through your defenses. 14 But I will punish you for what you have done. I will set your

palace on fire, and the fire will burn down everything around it. I, the LORD, have spoken."

Jeremiah's Message to the Royal House of Judah

22 1-2 The LORD told me to go to the palace of the king of Judah, the descendant of David, and there tell the king, his officials, and the people of Jerusalem to listen to what the LORD had said: 3 "I, the LORD, command you to do what is just and right. Protect the person who is being cheated from the one who is cheating him. Do not mistreat or oppress aliens, orphans, or widows; and do not kill innocent people in this holy place. 4 If you really do as I have commanded, then David's descendants will continue to be kings. And they, together with their officials and their people, will continue to pass through the gates of this palace in chariots and on horses. 5 But if you do not obey my commands, then I swear to you that this palace will fall into ruins. I, the LORD, have spoken.

6 "To me, Judah's royal palace is as beautiful as the land of Gilead and as the Lebanon Mountains; but I will make it a desolate place where no one lives. 7 I am sending men to destroy it. They will all bring their axes, cut down its beautiful cedar pillars, and throw them into the fire.

8 "Afterward many foreigners will pass by and ask one another why I, the LORD, have done such a thing to this great city. 9 Then they will answer that it is because you have abandoned your covenant with me, your God, and have worshiped and served other gods."

Jeremiah's Message concerning Joahaz

10 People of Judah, do not weep for
   King Josiah;
  do not mourn his death.
But weep bitterly for Joahaz,
  his son;
  they are taking him away, never
   to return,
  never again to see the land
   where he was born.

11 The LORD says concerning Josiah's son Joahaz, who succeeded his father as king of Judah, "He has gone away from

ʸ You, Jerusalem, are sitting; or You are enthroned.

here, never to return. 12 He will die in the country where they have taken him, and he will never again see this land."

Jeremiah's Message concerning Jehoiakim

13 Doomed is the one who builds his house by injustice
and enlarges it by dishonesty;
who makes his people work for nothing
and does not pay their wages.
14 Doomed is the one who says,
"I will build myself a mansion
with spacious rooms upstairs."
So he puts windows in his house,
panels it with cedar,
and paints it red.
15 Does it make you a better king
if you build houses of cedar,
finer than those of others?
Your father enjoyed a full life.
He was always just and fair,
and he prospered in everything
he did.
16 He gave the poor a fair trial,
and all went well with him.
That is what it means to know the
LORD.
17 But you can only see your selfish
interests;
you kill the innocent
and violently oppress your
people.
The LORD has spoken.

18 So then, the LORD says about Josiah's son Jehoiakim, king of Judah,
"No one will mourn his death
or say,
'How terrible, my friend, how
terrible!'
No one will weep for him or cry,
'My lord! My king!'
19 With the funeral honors of a
donkey,
he will be dragged away
and thrown outside Jerusalem's
gates."

Jeremiah's Message about the Fate of Jerusalem

20 People of Jerusalem, go to
Lebanon and shout,
go to the land of Bashan
and cry;

call out from the mountains of
Moab,
because all your allies have been
defeated.
21 The LORD spoke to you when you
were prosperous,
but you refused to listen.
That is what you've done all your
life;
you never would obey the LORD.
22 Your leaders will be blown away
by the wind,
your allies taken as prisoners
of war,
your city disgraced and put to
shame
because of all the evil you have
done.
23 You rest secure among the cedars
brought from Lebanon;
but how pitiful you'll be when
pains strike you,
pains like those of a woman in
labor.

God's Judgment on Jehoiachin

24 The LORD said to King Jehoiachin, son of King Jehoiakim of Judah, "As surely as I am the living God, even if you were the signet ring on my right hand, I would pull you off 25 and give you to people you are afraid of, people who want to kill you. I will give you to King Nebuchadnezzar of Babylonia and his soldiers. 26 I am going to force you and your mother into exile. You will go to a country where neither of you was born, and both of you will die there. 27 You will long to see this country again, but you will never return."
28 I said, "Has King Jehoiachin become like a broken jar that is thrown away and that no one wants? Is that why he and his children have been taken into exile to a land they know nothing about?"
29 O land, land, land!
Listen to what the LORD has said:
30 "This man is condemned to lose
his children,
to be a man who will never
succeed.
He will have no descendants
who will rule in Judah
as David's successors.
I, the LORD, have spoken."

Hope for the Future

23 How terrible will be the LORD's judgment on those rulers who destroy and scatter his people! ²This is what the LORD, the God of Israel, says about the rulers who were supposed to take care of his people: "You have not taken care of my people; you have scattered them and driven them away. Now I am going to punish you for the evil you have done. ³I will gather the rest of my people from the countries where I have scattered them, and I will bring them back to their homeland. They will have many children and increase in number. ⁴I will appoint rulers to take care of them. My people will no longer be afraid or terrified, and I will not punish them again.ᶻ I, the LORD, have spoken."

⁵The LORD says, "The time is coming when I will choose as king a righteous descendant of David. That king will rule wisely and do what is right and just throughout the land. ⁶When he is king, the people of Judah will be safe, and the people of Israel will live in peace. He will be called 'The LORD Our Salvation.'

⁷"The time is coming," says the LORD, "when people will no longer swear by me as the living God who brought the people of Israel out of the land of Egypt. ⁸Instead, they will swear by me as the living God who brought the people of Israel out of a northern land and out of all the other countries where I had scattered them. Then they will live in their own land."

Jeremiah's Message about the Prophets

⁹My heart is crushed,
    and I am trembling.
Because of the LORD,
    because of his holy words,
I am like a man who is drunk,
    someone who has had too much
        wine.
¹⁰The land is full of people
    unfaithful to the LORD;
they live wicked lives and
    misuse their power.
Because of the LORD's curse the
    land mourns
    and the pastures are dry.

¹¹The LORD says,

"The prophets and the priests are
    godless;
I have caught them doing evil in
    the Temple itself.
¹²The paths they follow will be
    slippery and dark;
I will make them stumble and
    fall.
I am going to bring disaster on
    them;
    the time of their punishment is
        coming.
I, the LORD, have spoken.
¹³I have seen the sin of Samaria's
    prophets:
    they have spoken in the name of
        Baal
    and have led my people astray.
¹⁴But I have seen the prophets in
    Jerusalem do even worse:
    they commit adultery and tell
        lies;
    they help people to do wrong,
        so that no one stops doing what
            is evil.
To me they are all as bad
    as the people of Sodom and
        Gomorrah.

¹⁵"So then, this is what I, the LORD Almighty, say about the prophets of Jerusalem:

I will give them bitter plants to eat
    and poison to drink,
because they have spread
    ungodliness throughout the
        land."

¹⁶The LORD Almighty said to the people of Jerusalem, "Do not listen to what the prophets say; they are filling you with false hopes. They tell you what they have imagined and not what I have said. ¹⁷To the people who refuse to listen to what I have said, they keep saying that all will go well with them. And they tell everyone who is stubborn that disaster will never touch them."

¹⁸I said, "None of these prophets has ever known the LORD's secret thoughts. None of them has ever heard or understood his message, or ever listened or paid attention to what he said. ¹⁹His anger is a storm, a furious wind that will rage over the heads of the wicked, ²⁰and it will not end until he has done everything he intends to do. In days to come

---

ᶻ I will not punish them again; *or* not one of them will be missing.

his people will understand this clearly."

21 The LORD said, "I did not send these prophets, but even so they went. I did not give them any message, but still they spoke in my name. 22 If they had known my secret thoughts, then they could have proclaimed my message to my people and could have made them give up the evil lives they live and the wicked things they do.

23 "I am a God who is everywhere and not in one place only. 24 No one can hide where I cannot see them. Do you not know that I am everywhere in heaven and on earth? 25 I know what those prophets have said who speak lies in my name and claim that I have given them my messages in their dreams. 26 How much longer will those prophets mislead my people with the lies they have invented? 27 They think that the dreams they tell will make my people forget me, just as their ancestors forgot me and turned to Baal. 28 The prophet who has had a dream should say it is only a dream, but the prophet who has heard my message should proclaim that message faithfully. What good is straw compared with wheat? 29 My message is like a fire and like a hammer that breaks rocks in pieces. 30 I am against those prophets who take each other's words and proclaim them as my message. 31 I am also against those prophets who speak their own words and claim they came from me. 32 Listen to what I, the LORD, say! I am against the prophets who tell their dreams that are full of lies. They tell these dreams and lead my people astray with their lies and their boasting. I did not send them or order them to go, and they are of no help at all to the people. I, the LORD, have spoken."

The LORD's Burden

33 The LORD said to me, "Jeremiah, when one of my people or a prophet or a priest asks you, 'What is the LORD's message?' you are to say, 'You are a burden*a* to the LORD, and he is going to get rid of you.' 34 If any of my people or a prophet or a priest even uses the words 'the LORD's burden,' I will punish them and their families. 35 Instead, each one of them should ask their friends and their

relatives, 'What answer has the LORD given? What has the LORD said?' 36 So they must no longer use the words 'the LORD's burden,' because if any of them do, I will make my message a real burden to them. The people have perverted the words of their God, the living God, the LORD Almighty. 37 Jeremiah, ask the prophets, 'What answer did the LORD give you? What did the LORD say?' 38 And if they disobey my command and use the words 'the LORD's burden,' then tell them that 39 I will certainly pick them up*b* and throw them far away from me, both them and the city that I gave to them and their ancestors. 40 I will bring on them everlasting shame and disgrace that will never be forgotten."

Two Baskets of Figs

24 The LORD showed me two baskets of figs placed in front of the Temple. (This was after King Nebuchadnezzar of Babylonia had taken away Jehoiakim's son, King Jehoiachin of Judah, as a prisoner from Jerusalem to Babylonia, together with the leaders of Judah, the craftworkers, and the skilled workers.) 2 The first basket contained good figs, those that ripen early; the other one contained bad figs, too bad to eat. 3 Then the LORD said to me, "Jeremiah, what do you see?"

I answered, "Figs. The good ones are very good, and the bad ones are very bad, too bad to eat."

4 So the LORD said to me, 5 "I, the LORD, the God of Israel, consider that the people who were taken away to Babylonia are like these good figs, and I will treat them with kindness. 6 I will watch over them and bring them back to this land. I will build them up and not tear them down; I will plant them and not pull them up. 7 I will give them the desire to know that I am the LORD. Then they will be my people, and I will be their God, because they will return to me with all their heart.

8 "As for King Zedekiah of Judah, the politicians around him, and the rest of the people of Jerusalem who have stayed in this land or moved to Egypt—I, the LORD, will treat them all like these figs that are too bad to be eaten. 9 I will

---

a The Hebrew word for message *and* burden *is the same.*   *b The Hebrew verb for* pick up *comes from the same root as the Hebrew word for* message *and* burden.

bring such a disaster on them that all the nations of the world will be terrified. People will make fun of them, ridicule them, and use their name as a curse everywhere I scatter them. 10I will bring war, starvation, and disease on them until there is not one of them left in the land that I gave to them and their ancestors."

The Enemy from the North

25 In the fourth year that Jehoiakim son of Josiah was king of Judah, I received a message from the LORD concerning all the people of Judah. (This was the first year that Nebuchadnezzar was king of Babylonia.) 2I said to all the people of Judah and of Jerusalem, 3"For twenty-three years, from the thirteenth year that Josiah son of Amon was king of Judah until this very day, the LORD has spoken to me, and I have never failed to tell you what he said. But you have paid no attention. 4You would not listen or pay attention, even though the LORD has continued to send you his servants the prophets. 5They told you to turn from your wicked way of life and from the evil things you are doing, so that you could go on living in the land that the LORD gave you and your ancestors as a permanent possession. 6They told you not to worship and serve other gods and not to make the LORD angry by worshiping the idols you had made. If you had obeyed the LORD, then he would not have punished you. 7But the LORD himself says that you refused to listen to him. Instead, you made him angry with your idols and have brought his punishment on yourselves.

8"So then, because you would not listen to him, the LORD Almighty says, 9'I am going to send for all the peoples from the north and for my servant, King Nebuchadnezzar of Babylonia. I am going to bring them to fight against Judah and its inhabitants and against all the neighboring nations. I am going to destroy this nation and its neighbors and leave them in ruins forever, a terrible and shocking sight. I, the LORD, have spoken. 10I will silence their shouts of joy and gladness and the happy sounds of wedding feasts. They will have no oil for their lamps, and there will be no more grain. 11This whole land will be left in ruins and will be a shocking sight, and the neighboring

nations will serve the king of Babylonia for seventy years. 12After that I will punish Babylonia and its king for their sin. I will destroy that country and leave it in ruins forever. 13I will punish Babylonia with all the disasters that I threatened to bring on the nations when I spoke through Jeremiah—all the disasters recorded in this book. 14I will pay the Babylonians back for what they have done, and many nations and great kings will make slaves of them.'"

God's Judgment on the Nations

15The LORD, the God of Israel, said to me, "Here is a wine cup filled with my anger. Take it to all the nations to whom I send you, and make them drink from it. 16When they drink from it, they will stagger and go out of their minds because of the war I am sending against them."

17So I took the cup from the LORD's hand, gave it to all the nations to whom the LORD had sent me, and made them drink from it. 18Jerusalem and all the towns of Judah, together with its kings and leaders, were made to drink from it, so that they would become a desert, a terrible and shocking sight, and so that people would use their name as a curse—as they still do.

19-26Here is the list of all the others who had to drink from the cup:

the king of Egypt, his officials and
    leaders;
all the Egyptians and all the
    foreigners in Egypt;
all the kings of the land of Uz;
all the kings of the Philistine cities
    of Ashkelon, Gaza, Ekron, and
    what remains of Ashdod;
all the people of Edom, Moab, and
    Ammon;
all the kings of Tyre and Sidon;
all the kings of the Mediterranean
    lands;
the cities of Dedan, Tema,
    and Buz;
all the people who cut their hair
    short;
all the kings of Arabia;
all the kings of the desert tribes;
all the kings of Zimri, Elam, and
    Media;
all the kings of the north, far and
    near, one after another.
Every nation on the face of the earth

had to drink from it. Last of all, the king of Babylonia will drink from it.

27 Then the Lord said to me, "Tell the people that I, the Lord Almighty, the God of Israel, am commanding them to drink until they are drunk and vomit, until they fall down and cannot get up, because of the war that I am sending against them. 28 And if they refuse to take the cup from your hand and drink from it, then tell them that the Lord Almighty has said that they will still have to drink from it. 29 I will begin my work of destruction in my own city. Do they think they will go unpunished? No, they will be punished, for I am going to send war on all the people on earth. I, the Lord Almighty, have spoken.

30 "You, Jeremiah, must proclaim everything I have said. You must tell these people,

'The Lord will roar from heaven
    and thunder from the heights of
        heaven.
He will roar against his people;
    he will shout like a man
        treading grapes.
Everyone on earth will hear him,
31   and the sound will echo to the
        ends of the earth.
The Lord has a case against the
        nations.
He will bring all people to trial
    and put the wicked to death.
The Lord has spoken.' "

32 The Lord Almighty says that disaster is coming on one nation after another, and a great storm is gathering at the far ends of the earth. 33 On that day the bodies of those whom the Lord has killed will lie scattered from one end of the earth to the other. No one will mourn for them, and they will not be taken away and buried. They will lie on the ground like piles of manure.

34 Cry, you leaders, you shepherds of my people, cry out loud! Mourn and roll in the dust. The time has come for you to be slaughtered,c and you will be butchered like rams.d 35 There will be no way for you to escape. 36-37 You moan and cry out in distress because the Lord in his anger has destroyed your nation and left your peaceful country in ruins. 38 The

Lord has abandoned his people e like a lion that leaves its cave. The horrors of war and the Lord's fierce anger have turned the country into a desert.

Jeremiah Is Brought to Trial

26 Soon after Jehoiakim son of Josiah became king of Judah, 2 the Lord said to me, "Stand in the court of the Temple and proclaim all I have commanded you to say to the people who come from the towns of Judah to worship there. Do not leave out anything. 3 Perhaps the people will listen and give up their evil ways. If they do, then I will change my mind about the destruction I plan to bring on them for all their wicked deeds."

4 The Lord told me to say to the people, "I, the Lord, have said that you must obey me by following the teaching that I gave you, 5 and by paying attention to the words of my servants, the prophets, whom I have kept on sending to you. You have never obeyed what they said. 6 If you continue to disobey, then I will do to this Temple what I did to Shiloh,f and all the nations of the world will use the name of this city as a curse."

7 The priests, the prophets, and all the people heard me saying these things in the Temple, 8 and as soon as I had finished all that the Lord had commanded me to speak, they grabbed me and shouted, "You ought to be killed for this! 9 Why have you said in the Lord's name that this Temple will become like Shiloh and that this city will be destroyed and no one will live in it?" Then the people crowded around me.

10 When the leaders of Judah heard what had happened, they hurried from the royal palace to the Temple and took their places at the New Gate. 11 Then the priests and the prophets said to the leaders and to the people, "This man deserves to be sentenced to death because he has spoken against our city. You heard him with your own ears."

12 Then I said, "The Lord sent me to proclaim everything that you heard me say against this Temple and against this city. 13 You must change the way you are living and the things you are doing, and must obey the Lord your God. If you do,

---

c Hebrew has an additional word, the meaning of which is unclear.   d One ancient translation rams; Hebrew vessels.   e The Lord . . . people; or The Lord's people run away.
f shiloh: See 7.12.

ISRAEL AND THE BABYLONIANS

Babylonia was an ancient pagan empire between the Tigris and Euphrates rivers in southern Mesopotamia. A long, narrow country, it was about forty miles wide at its widest point, covering an area of about eight thousand square miles. It was bordered on the north by Assyria, on the south and west by the Arabian desert, and on the southeast by the Persian Gulf.

The fortunes of the Babylonians rose and fell during the long sweep of Old Testament history. In its early history Hammurabi emerged as the ruler of the nation. He expanded the borders of the empire and organized its laws into a written system. This was about the time that Abraham's family left Ur, one of the ancient cities of lower Babylonia (Gn 11.27–32).

During its long history, Babylonia was constantly at war with Assyria, its neighbor to the north. About 1270 B.C. the Assyrians overpowered Babylonia, reducing its power and influence so effectively that it remained a second-rate nation for the next six or seven centuries. But this began to change dramatically when Nebuchadnezzar became ruler of Babylonia about 605 B.C. During his reign of forty-four years, the Babylonians built an empire, which stretched from north of the Mediterranean Sea to the south through Israel along the Red Sea to the Persian Gulf in the east.

Because of his long reign and many military conquests, Nebuchadnezzar is mentioned several times in the Old Testament (2 K 24.10–17; Dn 1.1–3). Between July 587 and 586 B.C. the Babylonian army under Nebuchadnezzar's leadership destroyed Jerusalem and carried Israel's leading citizens to Babylon as captives (2 Ch 36.6–13). This was a fulfillment of the warning of the prophets Jeremiah and Ezekiel that God would punish his people unless they turned from their idolatry to worship of the one true God (Jr 27; Ez 23.17–21).

The Babylonians had a system of gods, each with a main temple in a particular city. The system included gods of heaven, air, ocean, sun, moon, storms, love, and war. Their worship included elaborate festivals and many different types of priests, especially the exorcist and the diviner, whose function was to drive away evil spirits.

Babylonian dominance of the ancient world came to an end with the fall of their capital city, Babylon, to the Persians about 539 B.C. This was a clear fulfillment of the prophecies of Isaiah and Jeremiah. They predicted God would punish the Babylonians because of their destruction of Jerusalem and their deportation of the citizens of Judah into captivity (Is 14.22; 21.9; 43.14; Jr 50.9; 51.37).

he will change his mind about the destruction that he said he would bring on you. 14 As for me, I am in your power! Do with me whatever you think is fair and right. 15 But be sure of this: if you kill me, you and the people of this city will be guilty of killing an innocent man, because it is the LORD who sent me to give you this warning."

16 Then the leaders and the people said to the priests and the prophets, "This man spoke to us in the name of the LORD our God; he should not be put to death."

17 After that, some of the elders stood up and said to the people who had gathered, 18 "When Hezekiah was king of Judah, the prophet Micah of Moresheth told all the people that the LORD Almighty had said,

'Zion will be plowed like a field;
Jerusalem will become a pile of ruins,
and the Temple hill will become a forest.'

19 King Hezekiah and the people of Judah did not put Micah to death. Instead, Hezekiah honored the LORD and tried to win his favor. And the LORD changed his mind about the disaster that he said he would bring on them. Now we are about to bring a terrible disaster on ourselves."

(20 There was another man, Uriah son of Shemaiah from Kiriath Jearim, who spoke in the name of the LORD against this city and nation just as Jeremiah did. 21 When King Jehoiakim and his soldiers and officials heard what Uriah had said, the king tried to have him killed. But Uriah heard about it; so he fled in terror and escaped to Egypt. 22 King Jehoiakim, however, sent Elnathan son of Achbor and some other men to Egypt to get Uriah. 23 They brought him back to King Jehoiakim, who had him killed and his body thrown into the public burial ground.)

24 But because I had the support of Ahikam son of Shaphan, I was not handed over to the people and killed.

Jeremiah Wears an Ox Yoke

27 Soon after Josiah's son Zedekiah became king of Judah, the LORD told me 2 to make myself a yoke out of leather straps and wooden crossbars and to put it on my neck. 3 Then the LORD told me to send a message[g] to the kings of Edom, Moab, Ammon, Tyre, and Sidon through their ambassadors who had come to Jerusalem to see King Zedekiah. 4 The LORD Almighty, the God of Israel, told me to command them to tell their kings that the LORD had said: 5 "By my great power and strength I created the world, human beings, and all the animals that live on the earth; and I give it to anyone I choose. 6 I am the one who has placed all these nations under the power of my servant, King Nebuchadnezzar of Babylonia, and I have made even the wild animals serve him. 7 All nations will serve him, and they will serve his son and his grandson until the time comes for his own nation to fall. Then his nation will serve powerful nations and great kings.

8 "But if any nation or kingdom will not submit to his rule, then I will punish that nation by war, starvation, and disease until I have let Nebuchadnezzar destroy it completely. 9 Do not listen to your prophets or to those who claim they can predict the future, either by dreams or by calling up the spirits of the dead or by magic. They all tell you not to submit to the king of Babylonia. 10 They are deceiving you and will cause you to be taken far away from your country. I will drive you out, and you will be destroyed. 11 But if any nation submits to the king of Babylonia and serves him, then I will let it stay on in its own land, to farm it and live there. I, the LORD, have spoken."

12 I said the same thing to King Zedekiah of Judah, "Submit to the king of Babylonia. Serve him and his people, and you will live. 13 Why should you and your people die in war or of starvation or disease? That is what the LORD has said will happen to any nation that does not submit to the king of Babylonia. 14 Do not listen to the prophets who tell you not to surrender to him. They are deceiving you. 15 The LORD himself has said that he did not send them and that they are lying to you in his name. And so he will drive you out, and you will be killed, you and the prophets who are telling you these lies."

16 Then I told the priests and the people that the LORD had said: "Do not listen

g Probable text a message; Hebrew them.

to the prophets who say that the Temple treasures will soon be brought back from Babylonia. They are lying to you. 17 Don't listen to them! Submit to the king of Babylonia and you will live! Why should this city become a pile of ruins? 18 If they are really prophets and if they have my message, let them ask me, the LORD Almighty, not to allow the treasures that remain in the Temple and in the royal palace to be taken to Babylonia."

(19-20) When King Nebuchadnezzar took away to Babylonia the king of Judah, Jehoiachin son of Jehoiakim, and the leading men of Judah and Jerusalem, he left the columns, the bronze tank, the carts, and some of the other Temple treasures.)

21 "Listen to what I, the LORD Almighty, the God of Israel, say about the treasures that are left in the Temple and in the royal palace in Jerusalem: 22 They will be taken to Babylonia and will remain there until I turn my attention to them. Then I will bring them back and restore them to this place. I, the LORD, have spoken."

Jeremiah and the Prophet Hananiah

28 That same year,h in the fifth month of the fourth year that Zedekiah was king, Hananiah son of Azzur, a prophet from the town of Gibeon, spoke to me in the Temple. In the presence of the priests and of the people he told me 2 that the LORD Almighty, the God of Israel, had said: "I have broken the power of the king of Babylonia. 3 Within two years I will bring back to this place all the Temple treasures that King Nebuchadnezzar took to Babylonia. 4 I will also bring back the king of Judah, Jehoiachin son of Jehoiakim, along with all of the people of Judah who went into exile in Babylonia. Yes, I will break the power of the king of Babylonia. I, the LORD, have spoken."

5 Then in the presence of the priests and of all the people who were standing in the Temple, I said to Hananiah, 6 "Wonderful! I hope the LORD will do this! I certainly hope he will make your prophecy come true and will bring back from Babylonia all the Temple treasures

and all the people who were taken away as prisoners. 7 But listen to what I say to you and to the people. 8 The prophets who spoke long ago, before my time and yours, predicted that war, starvation, and disease would come to many nations and powerful kingdoms. 9 But a prophet who predicts peace can only be recognized as a prophet whom the LORD has truly sent when that prophet's predictions come true."

10 Then Hananiah took the yoke off my neck, broke it in pieces, 11 and said in the presence of all the people, "The LORD has said that this is how he will break the yoke that King Nebuchadnezzar has put on the neck of all the nations; and he will do this within two years." Then I left.

12 Some time after this the LORD told me 13 to go and tell Hananiah: "The LORD has said that you may be able to break a wooden yoke, but hei will replace it with an iron yoke. 14 The LORD Almighty, the God of Israel, has said that he will put an iron yoke on all these nations and that they will serve King Nebuchadnezzar of Babylonia. The LORD has said that he will make even the wild animals serve Nebuchadnezzar."

15 Then I told Hananiah this, and added, "Listen, Hananiah! The LORD did not send you, and you are making these people believe a lie. 16 And so the LORD himself says that he is going to get rid of you. Before this year is over you will die because you have told the people to rebel against the LORD."

17 And Hananiah died in the seventh month of that same year.

Jeremiah's Letter to the Jews in Babylonia

29 I wrote a letter to the priests, the prophets, the leaders of the people, and to all the others whom Nebuchadnezzar had taken away as prisoners from Jerusalem to Babylonia. 2 I wrote it after King Jehoiachin, his mother, the palace officials, the leaders of Judah and of Jerusalem, the engravers, and the skilled workers had been taken into exile. 3 I gave the letter to Elasah son of Shaphan and to Gemariah son of Hilkiah, whom King Zedekiah of

h One ancient translation That same year; Hebrew That same year at the beginning of his reign.
i One ancient translation he; Hebrew you.

Judah was sending to King Nebuchadnezzar of Babylonia. It said:

4 "The LORD Almighty, the God of Israel, says to all those people whom he allowed Nebuchadnezzar to take away as prisoners from Jerusalem to Babylonia: 5 'Build houses and settle down. Plant gardens and eat what you grow in them. 6 Marry and have children. Then let your children get married, so that they also may have children. You must increase in numbers and not decrease. 7 Work for the good of the cities where I have made you go as prisoners. Pray to me on their behalf, because if they are prosperous, you will be prosperous too. 8 I, the LORD, the God of Israel, warn you not to let yourselves be deceived by the prophets who live among you or by any others who claim they can predict the future. Do not pay any attention to their *i* dreams. 9 They are telling you lies in my name. I did not send them. I, the LORD Almighty, have spoken.'

10 "The LORD says, 'When Babylonia's seventy years are over, I will show my concern for you and keep my promise to bring you back home. 11 I alone know the plans I have for you, plans to bring you prosperity and not disaster, plans to bring about the future you hope for. *k* 12 Then you will call to me. You will come and pray to me, and I will answer you. 13 You will seek me, and you will find me because you will seek me with all your heart. 14 Yes, I say, you will find me, and I will restore you to your land. I will gather you from every country and from every place to which I have scattered you, and I will bring you back to the land from which I had sent you away into exile. I, the LORD, have spoken.'

15 "You say that the LORD has given you prophets in Babylonia. 16 Listen to what the LORD says about the king who rules the kingdom that David ruled and about the people of this city, that is, your relatives who were not taken away as prisoners with you. 17 The LORD Almighty says, 'I am bringing war, starvation, and disease on them, and I will make them like figs that are too rotten to be eaten. 18 I will pursue them with war, starvation, and disease, and all the nations of the world will be horrified at what they see. Everywhere I scatter them, people will be shocked and terrified at what has happened to them. People will make fun of them and use their name as a curse. 19 This will happen to them because they did not obey the message that I kept on sending to them through my servants the prophets. They refused to listen. 20 All of you whom I sent into exile in Babylonia, listen to what I, the LORD, say.'

21 "The LORD Almighty, the God of Israel, has spoken about Ahab son of Kolaiah and Zedekiah son of Maaseiah, who are telling you lies in his name. He has said that he will hand them over to the power of King Nebuchadnezzar of Babylonia, who will put them to death before your eyes. 22 When the people who were taken away as prisoners from Jerusalem to Babylonia want to bring a curse on someone, they will say, 'May the LORD treat you like Zedekiah and Ahab, whom the king of Babylonia roasted alive!' 23 This will be their fate because they are guilty of terrible sins—they have committed adultery and have told lies in the LORD's name. This was against the LORD's will; he knows what they have done, and he is a witness against them. *l* The LORD has spoken."

The Letter of Shemaiah

24-25 The LORD Almighty, the God of Israel, gave me a message for Shemaiah of Nehelam, who had sent a letter in his own name to all the people of Jerusalem and to the priest Zephaniah son of Maaseiah and to all the other priests. In this letter Shemaiah wrote to Zephaniah:

26 "The LORD made you a priest in place of Jehoiada, and you are now the chief officer *m* in the Temple. It is your duty to see that every crazy

---

i Probable text their; *Hebrew* your.   *k* the future you hope for; *or* a future full of hope.
l done, and he . . . them; *or* done; he saw them do it.   *m Some ancient translations* officer;
Hebrew officers.

person who pretends to be a prophet is placed in chains with an iron collar around the neck. 27 Why haven't you done this to Jeremiah of Anathoth, who has been speaking as a prophet to the people? 28 He must be stopped because he told the people in Babylonia that they would be prisoners there a long time and should build houses, settle down, plant gardens, and eat what they grow."

29 Zephaniah read the letter to me, 30 and then the LORD told me 31-32 to send to all the prisoners in Babylon this message about Shemaiah: "I, the LORD, will punish Shemaiah and all of his descendants. I did not send him, but he spoke to you as if he were a prophet, and he made you believe lies. He will have no descendants among you. He will not live to see the good things that I am going to do for my people, because he told them to rebel against me. I, the LORD, have spoken."

The LORD's Promises to His People

30 The LORD, the God of Israel, 2 said to me, "Write down in a book everything that I have told you, 3 because the time is coming when I will restore my people, Israel and Judah. I will bring them back to the land that I gave their ancestors, and they will take possession of it again. I, the LORD, have spoken."

4 The LORD says to the people of Israel and Judah,

5 "I heard a cry of terror,
     a cry of fear and not of peace.
6 Now stop and think!
     Can a man give birth to a child?
Why then do I see every man with
     his hands on his stomach
     like a woman in labor?
     Why is everyone so pale?
7 A terrible day is coming;
     no other day can compare
       with it —
     a time of distress for my people,
     but they will survive."

8 The LORD Almighty says, "When that day comes, I will break the yoke that is around their neck and remove their chains, and they will no longer be the slaves of foreigners. 9 Instead, they will serve me, the LORD their God, and a descendant of David, whom I will enthrone as king.

10 "My people, do not be afraid;
     people of Israel, do not be
       terrified.
I will rescue you from that
     faraway land,
     from the land where you are
       prisoners.
You will come back home and live
     in peace;
     you will be secure, and no one
       will make you afraid.
11 I will come to you and save you.
I will destroy all the nations
     where I have scattered you,
     but I will not destroy you.
I will not let you go unpunished;
     but when I punish you, I will be
       fair.
I, the LORD, have spoken."

12 The LORD says to his people,
     "Your wounds are incurable,
     your injuries cannot be healed.
13 There is no one to take care
       of you,
     no remedy for your sores,
     no hope of healing for you.
14 All your lovers have forgotten you;
     they no longer care about you.
I have attacked you like an enemy;
     your punishment has been harsh
     because your sins are many
     and your wickedness is great.
15 Complain no more about your
       injuries;
     there is no cure for you.
I punished you like this
     because your sins are many
     and your wickedness is great.
16 But now, all who devour you will
       be devoured,
     and all your enemies will be
       taken away as prisoners.
All who oppress you will be
       oppressed,
     and all who plunder you will be
       plundered.
17 I will make you well again;
     I will heal your wounds,
     though your enemies say,
     'Zion is an outcast;
     no one cares about her.'
I, the LORD, have spoken."

18 The LORD says,

"I will restore my people to their
    land
  and have mercy on every family;
  Jerusalem will be rebuilt,
    and its palace restored.
19 The people who live there will
    sing praise;
  they will shout for joy.
By my blessing they will increase
    in numbers;
  my blessing will bring them
    honor.
20 I will restore the nation's ancient
    power
  and establish it firmly again;
  I will punish all who oppress
    them.
21-22 Their ruler will come from their
    own nation,
  their prince from their own
    people.
He will approach me when I
    invite him,
  for who would dare come
    uninvited?
They will be my people,
  and I will be their God.
  I, the LORD, have spoken."

23-24 The LORD's anger is a storm, a furious wind that will rage over the heads of the wicked. It will not end until he has done all that he intends to do. In days to come his people will understand this clearly.

Israel's Return Home

31 The LORD says, "The time is coming when I will be the God of all the tribes of Israel, and they will be my people. 2 In the desert I showed mercy to those people who had escaped death. When the people of Israel longed for rest, 3 I appeared to them[n] from far away. People of Israel, I have always loved you, so I continue to show you my constant love. 4 Once again I will rebuild you. Once again you will take up your tambourines and dance joyfully. 5 Once again you will plant vineyards on the hills of Samaria, and those who plant them will eat what the vineyards produce. 6 Yes, the time is coming when sentries will call out on the hills of Ephraim,

'Let's go up to Zion, to the LORD our
God.' "
7 The LORD says,
  "Sing with joy for Israel,
    the greatest of the nations.
Sing your song of praise,
  'The LORD has saved his[o]
    people;
  he has rescued all who are left.'
8 I will bring them from the north
  and gather them from the ends
    of the earth.
The blind and the lame will come
    with them,
  pregnant women and those
    about to give birth.
They will come back a great
    nation.
9 My people will return weeping,
  praying as I lead them back.
I will guide them to streams of
    water,
  on a smooth road where they
    will not stumble.
I am like a father to Israel,
  and Ephraim is my oldest son."

10 The LORD says,
  "Nations, listen to me
  and proclaim my words on the
    far-off shores.
I scattered my people, but I will
    gather them
  and guard them as a shepherd
    guards his flock.
11 I have set Israel's people free
  and have saved them from a
    mighty nation.
12 They will come and sing for joy on
    Mount Zion
  and be delighted with my gifts—
  gifts of grain and wine and
    olive oil,
  gifts of sheep and cattle.
They will be like a well-watered
    garden;
  they will have everything they
    need.
13 Then the young women will dance
    and be happy,
  and men, young and old, will
    rejoice.
I will comfort them and turn their
    mourning into joy,
  their sorrow into gladness.

---

n One ancient translation them; Hebrew me.   o Some ancient translations The LORD has saved his; Hebrew LORD, save your.

14 I will fill the priests with the
  richest food
and satisfy all the needs of my
  people.
I, the LORD, have spoken."

The LORD's Mercy on Israel

15 The LORD says,
"A sound is heard in Ramah,
  the sound of bitter weeping.
Rachel is crying for her children;
  they are gone,
and she refuses to be comforted.
16 Stop your crying
  and wipe away your tears.
All that you have done for your
  children
will not go unrewarded;
  they will return from the
  enemy's land.
17 There is hope for your future;
  your children will come back
  home.
I, the LORD, have spoken.

18 "I hear the people of Israel say in
  grief,
'LORD, we were like an untamed
  animal,
  but you taught us to obey.
Bring us back;
  we are ready to return to you,
  the LORD our God.
19 We turned away from you,
  but soon we wanted to return.
After you had punished us,
  we hung our heads in grief.
We were ashamed and disgraced
  because we sinned when we
  were young.'

20 "Israel, you are my dearest child,
  the one I love best.
Whenever I mention your name,
  I think[p] of you with love.
My heart goes out to you;
  I will be merciful.
21 Set up signs and mark the road;
  find again the way by which you
  left.
Come back, people of Israel,
  come home to the towns you
  left.
22 How long will you hesitate,
  faithless people?

I have created something new and
  different,
as different as a woman
  protecting a man."[q]

The Future Prosperity
of God's People

23 The LORD Almighty, the God of Israel, says, "When I restore the people to
their land, they will once again say in
the land of Judah and in its towns,
'May the LORD bless the sacred
  hill[r] of Jerusalem,
  the holy place where he lives.'
24 People will live in Judah and in all its
towns, and there will be farmers, and
shepherds with their flocks. 25 I will refresh those who are weary and will satisfy with food everyone who is weak
from hunger. 26 So then, people will say,
'I went to sleep and woke up refreshed.'
27 "I, the LORD, say that the time is coming when I will fill the land of Israel and
Judah with people and animals. 28 And
just as I took care to uproot, to pull
down, to overthrow, to destroy, and to
demolish them, so I will take care to
plant them and to build them up.
29 When that time comes, people will no
longer say,
'The parents ate the sour grapes,
But the children got the sour
  taste.'
30 Instead, those who eat sour grapes will
have their own teeth set on edge; and
everyone will die because of their
own sin."
31 The LORD says, "The time is coming
when I will make a new covenant with
the people of Israel and with the people
of Judah. 32 It will not be like the old covenant that I made with their ancestors
when I took them by the hand and led
them out of Egypt. Although I was like a
husband to them, they did not keep that
covenant. 33 The new covenant that I will
make with the people of Israel will be
this: I will put my law within them and
write it on their hearts. I will be their
God, and they will be my people. 34 None
of them will have to teach a neighbor to
know the LORD, because all will know
me, from the least to the greatest. I will
forgive their sins and I will no longer

J
E
R
E
M
I
A
H

---

p I mention . . . I think; or I threaten to punish, I still think.   q as different . . . man; Hebrew
unclear   r SACRED HILL: Mount Zion, the hill in Jerusalem which formed part of the Temple and
palace area.

remember their wrongs. I, the LORD, have spoken."

35 The LORD provides the sun for light by day,
the moon and the stars to shine at night.
He stirs up the sea and makes it roar;
his name is the LORD Almighty.
36 He promises that as long as the natural order lasts,
so long will Israel be a nation.
37 If one day the sky could be measured
and the foundations of the earth explored,
only then would he reject the people of Israel
because of all they have done.
The LORD has spoken.

38 "The time is coming," says the LORD, "when all of Jerusalem will be rebuilt as my city, from Hananel Tower west to the Corner Gate. 39 And the boundary line will continue from there on the west to the hill of Gareb and then around to Goah. 40 The entire valley, where the dead are buried and garbage is dumped, and all the fields above Kidron Brook as far as the Horse Gate to the east, will be sacred to me. The city will never again be torn down or destroyed."

Jeremiah Buys a Field

32 The LORD spoke to me in the tenth year that Zedekiah was king of Judah, which was also the eighteenth year of King Nebuchadnezzar of Babylonia. 2 At that time the army of the king of Babylonia was attacking Jerusalem, and I was locked up in the courtyard of the royal palace. 3 King Zedekiah had imprisoned me there and had accused me of announcing that the LORD had said, "I am going to let the king of Babylonia capture this city, 4 and King Zedekiah will not escape. He will be handed over to the king of Babylonia; he will see him face-to-face and will speak to him in person. 5 Zedekiah will be taken to Babylonia, and he will remain there until I deal with him. Even if he fights the Babylonians, he will not be successful. I, the LORD, have spoken."

6 The LORD told me 7 that Hanamel, my uncle Shallum's son, would come to me with the request to buy his field at Ana-

thoth in the territory of Benjamin, because I was his nearest relative and had the right to buy it for myself. 8 Then, just as the LORD had said, Hanamel came to me there in the courtyard and asked me to buy the field. So I knew that the LORD had really spoken to me. 9 I bought the field from Hanamel and weighed out the money to him; the price came to seventeen pieces of silver. 10 I signed and sealed the deed, had it witnessed, and weighed out the money on scales. 11 Then I took both copies of the deed of purchase—the sealed copy containing the contract and its conditions, and the open copy— 12 and gave them to Baruch, the son of Neriah and grandson of Mahseiah. I gave them to him in the presence of Hanamel and of the witnesses who had signed the deed of purchase and of the people who were sitting in the courtyard. 13 Before them all I said to Baruch, 14 "The LORD Almighty, the God of Israel, has ordered you to take these deeds, both the sealed deed of purchase and the open copy, and to place them in a clay jar, so that they may be preserved for years to come. 15 The LORD Almighty, the God of Israel, has said that houses, fields, and vineyards will again be bought in this land."

Jeremiah's Prayer

16 After I had given the deed of purchase to Baruch, I prayed, 17 "Sovereign LORD, you made the earth and the sky by your great power and might; nothing is too difficult for you. 18 You have shown constant love to thousands, but you also punish people for the sins of their parents. You are a great and powerful God; you are the LORD Almighty. 19 You make wise plans and do mighty things; you see everything that people do, and you reward them according to their actions. 20 Long ago you performed miracles and wonders in Egypt, and you have continued to perform them to this day, both in Israel and among all the other nations, so that you are now known everywhere. 21 By means of miracles and wonders that terrified our enemies, you used your power and might to bring your people Israel out of Egypt. 22 You gave them this rich and fertile land, as you had promised their ancestors. 23 But when they came into this land and took possession of it, they did not obey your commands

or live according to your teaching; they did nothing that you had ordered them to do. And so you brought all this destruction on them. 24 "The Babylonians have built siege mounds around the city to capture it, and they are attacking. War, starvation, and disease will make the city fall into their hands. You can see that all you have said has come true. 25 Yet, Sovereign Lord, you are the one who ordered me to buy the field in the presence of witnesses, even though the city is about to be captured by the Babylonians."

26 Then the Lord said to me, 27 "I am the Lord, the God of all people. Nothing is too difficult for me. 28 I am going to give this city over to King Nebuchadnezzar of Babylonia and his army; they will capture it 29 and set it on fire. They will burn it down, together with the houses where people have made me angry by burning incense to Baal on the rooftops and by pouring out wine offerings to other gods. 30 From the very beginning of their history the people of Israel and the people of Judah have displeased me and made me angry by what they have done. 31 The people of this city have made me angry and furious from the day it was built. I have decided to destroy it 32 because of all the evil that has been done by the people of Judah and Jerusalem, together with their kings and leaders, their priests and prophets. 33 They turned their backs on me; and though I kept on teaching them, they would not listen and learn. 34 They even placed their disgusting idols in the Temple built for my worship, and they have defiled it. 35 They have built altars to Baal in Hinnom Valley, to sacrifice their sons and daughters to the god Molech. I did not command them to do this, and it did not even enter my mind that they would do such a thing and make the people of Judah sin."

A Promise of Hope

36 The Lord, the God of Israel, said to me, "Jeremiah, the people are saying that war, starvation, and disease will make this city fall into the hands of the king of Babylonia. Now listen to what else I have to say. 37 I am going to gather the people from all the countries where I have scattered them in my anger and fury, and I am going to bring them back to this place and let them live here in safety. 38 Then they will be my people, and I will be their God. 39 I will give them a single purpose in life: to honor me for all time, for their own good and the good of their descendants. 40 I will make an eternal covenant with them. I will never stop doing good things for them, and I will make them fear me with all their heart, so that they will never turn away from me. 41 I will take pleasure in doing good things for them, and I will establish them permanently in this land.

42 "Just as I have brought this disaster on these people, so I am going to give them all the good things that I have promised. 43 The people are saying that this land will be like a desert where neither people nor animals live, and that it will be given over to the Babylonians. But fields will once again be bought in this land. 44 People will buy them, and the deeds will be signed, sealed, and witnessed. This will take place in the territory of Benjamin, in the villages around Jerusalem, in the towns of Judah, and in the towns in the hill country, in the foothills, and in southern Judah. I will restore the people to their land. I, the Lord, have spoken."

Another Promise of Hope

33 While I was still in prison in the courtyard, the Lord's message came to me again. 2 The Lord, who made the earth, who formed it and set it in place, spoke to me. He whose name is the Lord said, 3 "Call to me, and I will answer you; I will tell you wonderful and marvelous things that you know nothing about. 4 I, the Lord, the God of Israel, say that the houses of Jerusalem and the royal palace of Judah will be torn down as a result of the siege and the attack. 5 Some will fight against the Babylonians, who will fill the houses s with the corpses of those whom I am going to strike down in my anger and fury. I have turned away from this city because of the evil things that its people have done. 6 But I will heal this city and its people and restore them to health. I will show them abundant peace and se-

s In verses 4 and 5 as a result . . . houses; Hebrew unclear.

curity. 7I will make Judah and Israel prosperous, and I will rebuild them as they were before. 8I will purify them from the sins that they have committed against me, and I will forgive their sins and their rebellion. 9Jerusalem will be a source of joy, honor, and pride to me; and every nation in the world will fear and tremble when they hear about the good things that I do for the people of Jerusalem and about the prosperity that I bring to the city."

10The LORD said, "People are saying that this place is like a desert, that it has no people or animals living in it. And they are right; the towns of Judah and the streets of Jerusalem are empty; no people or animals live there. But in these places you will hear again 11the shouts of gladness and joy and the happy sounds of wedding feasts. You will hear people sing as they bring thank offerings to my Temple; they will say,

'Give thanks to the LORD Almighty,
    because he is good
    and his love is eternal.'

I will make this land as prosperous as it was before. I, the LORD, have spoken."

12The LORD Almighty said, "In this land that is like a desert and where no people or animals live, there will once again be pastures where shepherds can take their sheep. 13In the towns in the hill country, in the foothills, and in southern Judah, in the territory of Benjamin, in the villages around Jerusalem, and in the towns of Judah, shepherds will once again count their sheep. I, the LORD, have spoken."

14The LORD said, "The time is coming when I will fulfill the promise that I made to the people of Israel and Judah. 15At that time I will choose as king a righteous descendant of David. That king will do what is right and just throughout the land. 16The people of Judah and of Jerusalem will be rescued and will live in safety. The city will be called 'The LORD Our Salvation.' 17I, the LORD, promise that there will always be a descendant of David to be king of Israel 18and that there will always be priests from the tribe of Levi to serve me and to offer burnt offerings, grain offerings, and sacrifices."

19The LORD said to me, 20"I have made a covenant with the day and with the night, so that they always come at their proper times; and that covenant can never be broken. 21In the same way I have made a covenant with my servant David that he would always have a descendant to be king, and I have made a covenant with the priests from the tribe of Levi that they would always serve me; and those covenants can never be broken. 22I will increase the number of descendants of my servant David and the number of priests from the tribe of Levi, so that it will be as impossible to count them as it is to count the stars in the sky or the grains of sand on the seashore."

23The LORD said to me, 24"Have you noticed how people are saying that I have rejected Israel and Judah, the two families that I chose? And so they look with contempt on my people and no longer consider them a nation. 25But I, the LORD, have a covenant with day and night, and I have made the laws that control earth and sky. 26And just as surely as I have done this, so I will maintain my covenant with Jacob's descendants and with my servant David. I will choose one of David's descendants to rule over the descendants of Abraham, Isaac, and Jacob. I will be merciful to my people and make them prosperous again."

A Message for Zedekiah

34 The LORD spoke to me when King Nebuchadnezzar of Babylonia and his army, supported by troops from all the nations and races that were subject to him, were attacking Jerusalem and its nearby towns. 2The LORD, the God of Israel, told me to go and say to King Zedekiah of Judah, "I, the LORD, will hand this city over to the king of Babylonia, and he will burn it down. 3You will not escape; you will be captured and handed over to him. You will see him face-to-face and talk to him in person; then you will go to Babylonia. 4Zedekiah, listen to what I say about you. You will not be killed in battle. 5You will die in peace, and as people burned incense when they buried your ancestors, who were kings before you, in the same way they will burn incense for you. They will mourn over you and say, 'Our king is dead!' I, the LORD, have spoken."

6Then I gave this message to King

Zedekiah in Jerusalem 7while the army of the king of Babylonia was attacking the city. The army was also attacking Lachish and Azekah, the only other fortified cities left in Judah.

Deceitful Treatment of Slaves

8King Zedekiah and the people of Jerusalem had made an agreement to set free 9their Hebrew slaves, both male and female, so that no one would have an Israelite as a slave. 10All the people and their leaders agreed to free their slaves and never to enslave them again. They did set them free, 11but later they changed their minds, took them back, and forced them to become slaves again. 12Then the LORD, 13the God of Israel, told me to say to the people: "I made a covenant with your ancestors when I rescued them from Egypt and set them free from slavery. I told them that 14every seven years they were to set free any Hebrew slave who had served them for six years. But your ancestors would not pay any attention to me or listen to what I said. 15Just a few days ago you changed your minds and did what pleased me. All of you agreed to set all Israelites free, and you made a covenant in my presence, in the Temple where I am worshiped. 16But then you changed your minds again and dishonored me. All of you took back the slaves whom you had set free as they desired, and you forced them into slavery again. 17So now, I, the LORD, say that you have disobeyed me; you have not given all Israelites their freedom. Very well, then, I will give you freedom: the freedom to die by war, disease, and starvation. I will make every nation in the world horrified at what I do to you. 18-19The officials of Judah and of Jerusalem, together with the palace officials, the priests, and all the leaders, made a covenant with me by walking between the two halves of a bull that they had cut in two. But they broke the covenant and did not keep its terms. So I will do to these people what they did to the bull. 20I will hand them over to their enemies, who want to kill them, and their corpses will be eaten by birds and wild animals. 21I will also hand over King Zedekiah of Judah and his officials to those who want to kill them. I will hand them over to the Babylonian army, which has stopped its attack against

you. 22I will give the order, and they will return to this city. They will attack it, capture it, and burn it down. I will make the towns of Judah like a desert where no one lives. I, the LORD, have spoken."

Jeremiah and the Rechabites

35 When Jehoiakim son of Josiah was king of Judah, the LORD said to me, 2"Go to the members of the Rechabite clan and talk to them. Then bring them into one of the rooms in the Temple and offer them some wine." 3So I took the entire Rechabite clan—Jaazaniah (the son of another Jeremiah, who was Habazziniah's son) and all his brothers and sons—4and brought them to the Temple. I took them into the room of the disciples of the prophet Hanan son of Igdaliah. This room was above the room of Maaseiah son of Shallum, an important official in the Temple, and near the rooms of the other officials. 5Then I placed cups and bowls full of wine before the Rechabites, and I said to them, "Have some wine."

6But they answered, "We do not drink wine. Our ancestor Jonadab son of Rechab told us that neither we nor our descendants were ever to drink any wine. 7He also told us not to build houses or farm the land and not to plant vineyards or buy them. He commanded us always to live in tents, so that we might remain in this land where we live like strangers. 8We have obeyed all the instructions that Jonadab gave us. We ourselves never drink wine, and neither do our wives, our sons, or our daughters. 9-10We do not build houses for homes— we live in tents—and we own no vineyards, fields, or grain. We have fully obeyed everything that our ancestor Jonadab commanded us. 11But when King Nebuchadnezzar invaded the country, we decided to come to Jerusalem to get away from the Babylonian and Syrian armies. That is why we are living in Jerusalem."

12-13Then the LORD Almighty, the God of Israel, told me to go and say to the people of Judah and Jerusalem, "I, the LORD, ask you why you refuse to listen to me and to obey my instructions. 14Jonadab's descendants have obeyed his command not to drink wine, and to this very day none of them drink any. But I have kept on speaking to you, and you have not obeyed me. 15 I have continued to send you all my servants the prophets, and they have told you to give up your evil ways and to do what is right. They warned you not to worship and serve other gods, so that you could go on living in the land that I gave you and your ancestors. But you would not listen to me or pay any attention to me. 16 Jonadab's descendants have obeyed the command that their ancestor gave them, but you people have not obeyed me. 17 So now, I, the LORD Almighty, the God of Israel, will bring on you people of Judah and of Jerusalem all the destruction that I promised. I will do this because you would not listen when I spoke to you, and you would not answer when I called you."

18 Then I told the Rechabite clan that the LORD Almighty, the God of Israel, had said, "You have obeyed the command that your ancestor Jonadab gave you; you have followed all his instructions, and you have done everything he commanded you. 19 So I, the LORD Almighty, the God of Israel, promise that Jonadab son of Rechab will always have a male descendant to serve me."

Baruch Reads the Scroll in the Temple

36 In the fourth year that Jehoiakim son of Josiah was king of Judah, the LORD said to me, 2 "Get a scroll and write on it everything that I have told you about Israel and Judah and all the nations. Write everything that I have told you from the time I first spoke to you, when Josiah was king, up to the present. 3 Perhaps when the people of Judah hear about all the destruction that I intend to bring on them, they will turn from their evil ways. Then I will forgive their wickedness and their sins."

4 So I called Baruch son of Neriah and dictated to him everything that the LORD had said to me. And Baruch wrote it all down on a scroll. 5 Then I gave Baruch the following instructions: "I am no longer allowed to go into the Temple. 6 But I want you to go there the next time the people are fasting. You are to read the scroll aloud, so that they will hear everything that the LORD has said to me

and that I have dictated to you. Do this where everyone can hear you, including the people of Judah who have come in from their towns. 7 Perhaps they will pray to the LORD and turn from their evil ways, because the LORD has threatened this people with his terrible anger and fury." 8 So Baruch read the LORD's words in the Temple exactly as I had told him to do.

9 In the ninth month of the fifth year that Jehoiakim was king of Judah, the people fasted to gain the LORD's favor. The fast was kept by all who lived in Jerusalem and by all who came there from the towns of Judah. 10 Then, while all the people were listening, Baruch read from the scroll everything that I had said. He did this in the Temple, from the room of Gemariah son of Shaphan, the court secretary. His room was in the upper court near the entrance of the New Gate of the Temple.

The Scroll Is Read to the Officials

11 Micaiah, the son of Gemariah and grandson of Shaphan, heard Baruch read from the scroll what the LORD had said. 12 Then he went to the royal palace, to the room of the court secretary, where all the officials were in session. Elishama, the court secretary, Delaiah son of Shemaiah, Elnathan son of Achbor, Gemariah son of Shaphan, Zedekiah son of Hananiah, and all the other officials were there. 13 Micaiah told them everything that he had heard Baruch read to the people. 14 Then the officials sent Jehudi (the son of Nethaniah, grandson of Shelemiah, and great-grandson of Cushi) to tell Baruch to bring the scroll that he had read to the people. Baruch brought them the scroll. 15 "Sit down," they said, "and read the scroll to us." So Baruch did. 16 After he had read it, they turned to one another in alarm and said to Baruch, "We must report this to the king." 17 Then they asked him, "Tell us, now, how did you come to write all this? Did Jeremiah dictate it to you?"

18 Baruch answered, "Jeremiah dictated every word of it to me, and I wrote it down in ink on this scroll."

19 Then they told him, "You and Jeremiah must go and hide. Don't let anyone know where you are."

The King Burns the Scroll

20 The officials put the scroll in the room of Elishama, the court secretary, and went to the king's court, where they reported everything to the king. 21 Then the king sent Jehudi to get the scroll. He took it from the room of Elishama and read it to the king and all the officials who were standing around him. 22 It was winter and the king was sitting in his winter palace in front of the fire. 23 As soon as Jehudi finished reading three or four columns, the king cut them off with a small knife and threw them into the fire. He kept doing this until the entire scroll was burned up. 24 But neither the king nor any of his officials who heard all this was afraid or showed any sign of sorrow. 25 Although Elnathan, Delaiah, and Gemariah begged the king not to burn the scroll, he paid no attention to them. 26 Then he ordered Prince Jerahmeel, together with Seraiah son of Azriel and Shelemiah son of Abdeel, to arrest me and my secretary Baruch. But the LORD had hidden us.

Jeremiah Writes Another Scroll

27 After King Jehoiakim had burned the scroll that I had dictated to Baruch, the LORD told me 28 to take another scroll and write on it everything that had been on the first one. 29 The LORD told me to say to the king, "You have burned the scroll, and you have asked Jeremiah why he wrote that the king of Babylonia would come and destroy this land and kill its people and its animals. 30 So now, I, the LORD, say to you, King Jehoiakim, that no descendant of yours will ever rule over David's kingdom. Your corpse will be thrown out where it will be exposed to the sun during the day and to the frost at night. 31 I will punish you, your descendants, and your officials because of the sins all of you commit. Neither you nor the people of Jerusalem and of Judah have paid any attention to my warnings, and so I will bring on all of you the disaster that I have threatened."

32 Then I took another scroll and gave it to my secretary Baruch, and he wrote down everything that I dictated. He wrote everything that had been on the first scroll and similar messages that I dictated to him.

Zedekiah's Request to Jeremiah

37 King Nebuchadnezzar of Babylonia made Zedekiah son of Josiah king of Judah in the place of Jehoiachin son of Jehoiakim. 2 But neither Zedekiah nor his officials nor the people obeyed the message which the LORD had given me.

3 King Zedekiah sent Jehucal son of Shelemiah and the priest Zephaniah son of Maaseiah to ask me to pray to the LORD our God on behalf of our nation. 4 I had not yet been put in prison and was still moving about freely among the people. 5 The Babylonian army had been besieging Jerusalem, but when they heard that the Egyptian army had crossed the Egyptian border, they retreated.

6 Then the LORD, the God of Israel, told me 7 to say to Zedekiah, "The Egyptian army is on its way to help you, but it will return home. 8 Then the Babylonians will come back, attack the city, capture it, and burn it down. 9 I, the LORD, warn you not to deceive yourselves into thinking that the Babylonians will not come back, because they will. 10 Even if you defeat the whole Babylonian army, so that only wounded men are left, lying in their tents, they would still get up and burn this city to the ground."

Jeremiah Is Arrested and Imprisoned

11 The Babylonian army retreated from Jerusalem because the Egyptian army was approaching. 12 So I started to leave Jerusalem and go to the territory of Benjamin to take possession of my share of the family property. 13 But when I reached the Benjamin Gate, the officer in charge of the soldiers on duty there, a man by the name of Irijah, the son of Shelemiah and grandson of Hananiah, stopped me and said, "You are deserting to the Babylonians!"

14 I answered, "That's not so! I'm not deserting." But Irijah would not listen to me. Instead, he arrested me and took me to the officials. 15 They were furious with me and had me beaten and locked up in the house of Jonathan, the court secretary, whose house had been made into a prison. 16 I was put in an underground cell and kept there a long time.

17 Later on King Zedekiah sent for me,

and there in the palace he asked me privately, "Is there any message from the LORD?"

"There is," I answered, and added, "You will be handed over to the king of Babylonia." 18 Then I asked, "What crime have I committed against you or your officials or this people, to make you put me in prison? 19 What happened to your prophets who told you that the king of Babylonia would not attack you or the country? 20 And now, Your Majesty, I beg you to listen to me and do what I ask. Please do not send me back to the prison in Jonathan's house. If you do, I will surely die there."

21 So King Zedekiah ordered me to be locked up in the palace courtyard. I stayed there, and each day I was given a loaf of bread from the bakeries until all the bread in the city was gone.

Jeremiah in a Dry Well

38 Shephatiah son of Mattan, Gedaliah son of Pashhur, Jehucal son of Shelemiah, and Pashhur son of Malchiah heard that I was telling the people that 2 the LORD had said, "Whoever stays on in the city will die in war or of starvation or disease. But those who go out and surrender to the Babylonians will not be killed; they will at least escape with their life." 3 I was also telling them that the LORD had said, "I am going to give the city to the Babylonian army, and they will capture it."

4 Then the officials went to the king and said, "This man must be put to death. By talking like this he is making the soldiers in the city lose their courage, and he is doing the same thing to everyone else left in the city. He is not trying to help the people; he only wants to hurt them."

5 King Zedekiah answered, "Very well, then, do what you want to with him; I can't stop you." 6 So they took me and let me down by ropes into Prince Malchiah's well, which was in the palace courtyard. There was no water in the well, only mud, and I sank down in it.

7 However, Ebedmelech the Ethiopian,t a eunuch who worked in the royal palace, heard that they had put me

in the well. At that time the king was holding court at the Benjamin Gate. 8 So Ebedmelech went there and said to the king, 9 "Your Majesty, what these men have done is wrong. They have put Jeremiah in the well, where he is sure to die of starvation, since there is no more food in the city." 10 Then the king ordered Ebedmelech to take with him three men and to pull me out of the well before I died. 11 So Ebedmelech went with the men to the palace storeroom and got some worn-out clothing which he let down to me by ropes. 12 He told me to put the rags under my arms, so that the ropes wouldn't hurt me. I did this, 13 and they pulled me up out of the well. After that I was kept in the courtyard.

Zedekiah Asks Jeremiah's Advice

14 On another occasion King Zedekiah had me brought to him at the third entrance to the Temple, and he said, "I am going to ask you a question, and I want you to tell me the whole truth."

15 I answered, "If I tell you the truth, you will put me to death, and if I give you advice, you won't pay any attention."

16 So King Zedekiah promised me in secret, "I swear by the living God, the God who gave us life, that I will not put you to death or hand you over to the men who want to kill you."

17 Then I told Zedekiah that the LORD Almighty, the God of Israel, had said, "If you surrender to the king of Babylonia's officers, your life will be spared, and this city will not be burned down. Both you and your family will be spared. 18 But if you do not surrender, then this city will be handed over to the Babylonians, who will burn it down, and you will not escape from them."

19 But the king answered, "I am afraid of our own people who have deserted to the Babylonians. I may be handed over to them and tortured."

20 I said, "You will not be handed over to them. I beg you to obey the LORD's message; then all will go well with you, and your life will be spared. 21 But the LORD has shown me in a vision what will happen if you refuse to surrender. 22 In it

t *Hebrew* Cushite: *Cush is the ancient name of the extensive territory south of the First Cataract of the Nile River. This region was called Ethiopia in Graeco-Roman times, and included within its borders most of modern Sudan and some of present-day Ethiopia (Abyssinia).*

I saw all the women left in Judah's royal palace being led out to the king of Babylonia's officers. Listen to what they were saying as they went:

'The king's best friends
    misled him,
they overruled him.
And now that his feet have sunk
    in the mud,
    his friends have left him.' "

23 Then I added, "All your women and children will be taken out to the Babylonians, and you yourself will not escape from them. You will be taken prisoner by the king of Babylonia, and this city will be burned to the ground."

24 Zedekiah replied, "Don't let anyone know about this conversation, and your life will not be in danger. 25 If the officials hear that I have talked with you, they will come and ask you what we said. They will promise not to put you to death if you tell them everything. 26 Just tell them you were begging me not to send you back to prison to die there."

27 Then all the officials came and questioned me, and I told them exactly what the king had told me to say. There was nothing else they could do, because no one had overheard the conversation. 28 And I was kept in the palace courtyard until the day Jerusalem was captured.

The Fall of Jerusalem

39 In the tenth month of the ninth year that Zedekiah was king of Judah, King Nebuchadnezzar of Babylonia came with his whole army and attacked Jerusalem. 2 On the ninth day of the fourth month of Zedekiah's eleventh year as king, the city walls were broken through.

(3 When Jerusalem was captured,u all the high officials of the king of Babylonia came and took their places at the Middle Gate, including Nergal Sharezer, Samgar Nebo, Sarsechim, and another Nergal Sharezer.v)

4 When King Zedekiah and all his soldiers saw what was happening, they tried to escape from the city during the night. They left by way of the royal garden, went through the gateway connect-

ing the two walls, and escaped in the direction of the Jordan Valley. 5 But the Babylonian army pursued them and captured Zedekiah in the plains near Jericho. Then they took him to King Nebuchadnezzar, who was in the city of Riblah in the territory of Hamath, and there Nebuchadnezzar passed sentence on him. 6 At Riblah he put Zedekiah's sons to death while Zedekiah was looking on, and he also had the officials of Judah executed. 7 After that, he had Zedekiah's eyes put out and had him placed in chains to be taken to Babylonia. 8 Meanwhile, the Babylonians burned down the royal palace and the houses of the people and tore down the walls of Jerusalem. 9 Finally Nebuzaradan, the commanding officer, took away as prisoners to Babylonia the people who were left in the city, together with those who had deserted to him. 10 He left in the land of Judah some of the poorest people, who owned no property, and he gave them vineyards and fields.

Jeremiah's Release

11 But King Nebuchadnezzar commanded Nebuzaradan, the commanding officer, to give the following order: 12 "Go and find Jeremiah and take good care of him. Do not harm him, but do for him whatever he wants." 13 So Nebuzaradan, together with the high officials Nebushazban and Nergal Sharezer and all the other officers of the king of Babylonia, 14 had me brought from the palace courtyard. They put me under the care of Gedaliah, the son of Ahikam and grandson of Shaphan, who was to see that I got home safely. And so I stayed there among the people.

Hope for Ebedmelech

15 While I was still imprisoned in the palace courtyard, the LORD told me 16 to tell Ebedmelech the Ethiopianw that the LORD Almighty, the God of Israel, had said, "Just as I said I would, I am going to bring upon this city destruction and not prosperity. And when this happens, you will be there to see it. 17 But I, the LORD, will protect you, and you will not

u When Jerusalem was captured; these words are moved here from the end of chapter 38.
v The names and titles of these men are unclear.   w Hebrew Cushite: Cush is the ancient name of the extensive territory south of the First Cataract of the Nile River. This region was called Ethiopic in Graeco-Roman times, and included within its borders most of modern Sudan and some of present-day Ethiopia (Abyssinia).

be handed over to the people you are afraid of. 18 I will keep you safe, and you will not be put to death. You will escape with your life because you have put your trust in me. I, the LORD, have spoken."

Jeremiah Stays with Gedaliah

40 The LORD spoke to me after Nebuzaradan, the commanding officer, had set me free at Ramah. I had been taken there in chains, along with all the other people from Jerusalem and Judah who were being taken away as prisoners to Babylonia.

2 The commanding officer took me aside and said, "The LORD your God threatened this land with destruction, 3 and now he has done what he said he would. All this happened because your people sinned against the LORD and disobeyed him. 4 Now, I am taking the chains off your wrists and setting you free. If you want to go to Babylonia with me, you may do so, and I will take care of you. But if you don't want to go, you don't have to. You have the whole country to choose from, and you may go wherever you wish."

5 When I did not answer,x Nebuzaradan said, "Go back to Gedaliah, the son of Ahikam and grandson of Shaphan, whom the king of Babylonia has made governor of the towns of Judah. You may stay with him and live among the people, or you may go anywhere you think you should." Then he gave me a present and some food to take with me, and let me go on my way. 6 I went to stay with Gedaliah in Mizpah and lived among the people who were left in the land.

Gedaliah, Governor of Judah
(2 Kings 25.22-24)

7 Some of the Judean officers and soldiers had not surrendered. They heard that the king of Babylonia had made Gedaliah governor of the land and had placed him in charge of all those who had not been taken away to Babylonia — the poorest people in the land. 8 So Ishmael son of Nethaniah, Johanan son of Kareah, Seraiah son of Tanhumeth, the sons of Ephai from Netophah, and Jeza-

niah from Maacah went with their men to Gedaliah at Mizpah. 9 Gedaliah said to them, "I give you my word that there is no need for you to be afraid to surrender to the Babylonians. Settle in this land, serve the king of Babylonia, and all will go well with you. 10 I myself will stay in Mizpah and be your representative when the Babylonians come here. But you can gather and store up wine, fruit, and olive oil, and live in the villages you occupy." 11 Meanwhile, all the Israelites who were in Moab, Ammon, Edom, and other countries, heard that the king of Babylonia had allowed some Israelites to stay on in Judah and that he had made Gedaliah their governor. 12 So they left the places where they had been scattered, and returned to Judah. They came to Gedaliah at Mizpah, and there they gathered in large amounts of wine and fruit.

Gedaliah Is Murdered
(2 Kings 25.25, 26)

13 After this, Johanan and the leaders of the soldiers who had not surrendered came to Gedaliah at Mizpah 14 and said to him, "Don't you know that King Baalis of Ammon has sent Ishmael to murder you?" But Gedaliah did not believe it. 15 Then Johanan said privately to him, "Let me go and kill Ishmael, and no one will know who did it. Why should he be allowed to murder you? That would cause all the Jews who have gathered around you to be scattered, and it would bring disaster on all the people who are left in Judah."

16 But Gedaliah answered, "Don't do it! What you are saying about Ishmael is not true!"

41 In the seventh month of that year, Ishmael, the son of Nethaniah and grandson of Elishama, a member of the royal family and one of the king's chief officers, went to Mizpah with ten men to see Governor Gedaliah. While they were all eating a meal together, 2 Ishmael and the ten men with him pulled out their swords and killed Gedaliah. 3 Ishmael also killed all the Israelites who were with Gedaliah at Mizpah and the Babylonian soldiers who happened to be there.

x When I did not answer; or Then, before he left.

4 The next day, before anyone knew about Gedaliah's murder, 5 eighty men arrived from Shechem, Shiloh, and Samaria. They had shaved off their beards, torn their clothes, and gashed themselves. They were taking grain and incense to offer in the Temple. 6 So Ishmael went out from Mizpah to meet them weeping as he went. When he came to them, he said, "Please come in to see Gedaliah." 7 As soon as they were inside the city, Ishmael and his men killed them and threw their bodies in a well.

8 But there were ten men in the group who said to Ishmael, "Please don't kill us! We have wheat, barley, olive oil, and honey hidden in the fields." So he spared them. 9 The well into which Ishmael threw the bodies of the men he had killed was the large one[y] that King Asa had dug when he was being attacked by King Baasha of Israel. Ishmael filled the well with the bodies. 10 Then he made prisoners of the king's daughters and all the rest of the people in Mizpah, whom Nebuzaradan the commanding officer had placed under the care of Gedaliah. Ishmael took them prisoner and started off in the direction of the territory of Ammon.

11 Johanan and all the army leaders with him heard of the crime that Ishmael had committed. 12 So they went after him with their men and overtook him near the large pool at Gibeon. 13 When Ishmael's prisoners saw Johanan and the leaders of the forces with him, they were glad, 14 and turned and ran to them. 15 But Ishmael and eight of his men got away from Johanan and escaped to the land of Ammon.

16 Then Johanan and the leaders of the forces with him took charge of the people whom Ishmael had taken away as prisoners from Mizpah after murdering Gedaliah—soldiers, women, children, and eunuchs. 17-18 They were afraid of the Babylonians because Ishmael had murdered Gedaliah, whom the king of Babylonia had made governor of the land. So they set out for Egypt, in order to get away from the Babylonians. On the way they stopped at Chimham near Bethlehem.

The People Ask Jeremiah to Pray for Them

42 Then all the army leaders, including Johanan son of Kareah and Azariah[z] son of Hoshaiah, came with people of every class 2 and said to me, "Please do what we ask you! Pray to the LORD our God for us. Pray for all of us who have survived. Once there were many of us; but now only a few of us are left, as you can see. 3 Pray that the LORD our God will show us the way we should go and what we should do."

4 I answered, "Very well, then. I will pray to the LORD our God, just as you have asked, and whatever he says, I will tell you. I will not keep back anything from you."

5 Then they said to me, "May the LORD be a true and faithful witness against us if we do not obey all the commands that the LORD our God gives you for us. 6 Whether it pleases us or not, we will obey the LORD our God, to whom we are asking you to pray. All will go well with us if we obey him."

The LORD's Answer to Jeremiah's Prayer

7 Ten days later the LORD spoke to me; 8 so I called together Johanan, all the army leaders who were with him, and all the other people. 9 I said to them, "The LORD, the God of Israel, to whom you sent me with your request has said, 10 'If you are willing to go on living in this land, then I will build you up and not tear you down; I will plant you and not pull you up. The destruction I brought on you has caused me great sorrow. 11 Stop being afraid of the king of Babylonia. I am with you, and I will rescue you from his power. 12 Because I am merciful, I will make him have mercy on you and let you go back home. I, the LORD, have spoken.'

13-15 "But you people who are left in Judah must not disobey the LORD your God and refuse to live in this land. You must not say, 'No, we will go and live in Egypt, where we won't face war any more or hear the call to battle or go hungry.' If you say this, then the LORD Almighty, the God of Israel, says, 'If you are determined to go and live in Egypt,

y One ancient translation was the large one; Hebrew by means of Gedaliah.
z One ancient translation (see also 43.2) Azariah; Hebrew Jezaniah.

16then the war that you fear will overtake you, and the hunger you dread will follow you, and you will die there in Egypt. 17All the people who are determined to go and live in Egypt will die either in war or of starvation or disease. Not one of them will survive, not one will escape the disaster that I am going to bring on them.'

18"The Lord, the God of Israel, says, 'Just as my anger and fury were poured out on the people of Jerusalem, so my fury will be poured out on you if you go to Egypt. You will be a horrifying sight; people will make fun of you and use your name as a curse. You will never see this place again.'"

19Then I continued, "The Lord has told you people who are left in Judah not to go to Egypt. And so I warn you now 20that you are making a fatal mistake. You asked me to pray to the Lord our God for you, and you promised that you would do everything that he commands. 21And now I have told you, but you are disobeying everything that the Lord our God sent me to tell you. 22So then, remember this: you will die in war or of starvation or disease in the land where you want to go and live."

Jeremiah Is Taken to Egypt

43 I finished telling the people everything that the Lord their God had sent me to tell them. 2Then Azariah son of Hoshaiah and Johanan son of Kareah and all the other arrogant men said to me, "You are lying. The Lord our God did not send you to tell us not to go and live in Egypt. 3Baruch son of Neriah has stirred you up against us, so that the Babylonians will gain power over us and can either kill us or take us away to Babylonia." 4So neither Johanan nor any of the army officers nor any of the people would obey the Lord's command to remain in the land of Judah. 5Then Johanan and all the army officers took everybody left in Judah away to Egypt, together with all the people who had returned from the nations where they had been scattered: 6the men, the women, the children, and the king's daughters. They took everyone whom Nebuzaradan the commanding officer had left under the care of Gedaliah, including Baruch and me. 7They disobeyed the Lord's command and went into Egypt as far as the city of Tahpanhes.

8There the Lord said to me, 9"Get some large stones and bury them in the mortar of the pavementa in front of the entrance to the government building here in the city, and let some of the Israelites see you do it. 10Then tell them that I, the Lord Almighty, the God of Israel, am going to bring my servant King Nebuchadnezzar of Babylonia to this place, and heb will put his throne over these stones that youc buried, and will spread the royal tent over them. 11Nebuchadnezzar will come and defeat Egypt. Those people who are doomed to die of disease will die of disease, those doomed to be taken away as prisoners will be taken away as prisoners, and those doomed to be killed in war will be killed in war. 12I will set fire to the temples of Egypt's gods, and the king of Babylonia will either burn their gods or carry them off. As shepherds pick their clothes clean of lice, so the king of Babylonia will pick the land of Egypt clean and then leave victorious. 13He will destroy the sacred stone monuments at Heliopolis in Egypt and will burn down the temples of the Egyptian gods."

The Lord's Message to the Israelites in Egypt

44 The Lord spoke to me concerning all the Israelites living in Egypt, in the cities of Migdol, Tahpanhes, and Memphis, and in the southern part of the country. 2The Lord Almighty, the God of Israel, said, "You yourselves have seen the destruction I brought on Jerusalem and all the other cities of Judah. Even now they are still in ruins, and no one lives in them 3because their people had done evil and had made me angry. They offered sacrifices to other gods and served gods that neither they nor you nor your ancestors ever worshiped. 4I kept sending you my servants the prophets, who told you not to do this terrible thing that I hate. 5But you would not listen or pay any attention. You would not give up your evil practice of

---

a Probable text bury them . . . pavement; Hebrew unclear.   b Some ancient translations he; Hebrew I.   c Some ancient translations you; Hebrew I.

sacrificing to other gods. 6 So I poured out my anger and fury on the towns of Judah and on the streets of Jerusalem, and I set them on fire. They were left in ruins and became a horrifying sight, as they are today.

7 "And so I, the LORD Almighty, the God of Israel, now ask why you are doing such an evil thing to yourselves. Do you want to bring destruction on men and women, children and babies, so that none of your people will be left? 8 Why do you make me angry by worshiping idols and by sacrificing to other gods here in Egypt, where you have come to live? Are you doing this just to destroy yourselves, so that every nation on earth will make fun of you and use your name as a curse? 9 Have you forgotten all the wicked things that have been done in the towns of Judah and in the streets of Jerusalem by your ancestors, by the kings of Judah and their wives, and by you and your wives? 10 But to this day you have not humbled yourselves. You have not honored me or lived according to all the laws that I gave you and your ancestors.

11 "So then, I, the LORD Almighty, the God of Israel, will turn against you and destroy all Judah. 12 As for the people of Judah who are left and are determined to go and live in Egypt, I will see to it that all of them are destroyed. All of them, great and small, will die in Egypt, either in war or of starvation. They will be a horrifying sight; people will make fun of them and use their name as a curse. 13 I will punish those who live in Egypt just as I punished Jerusalem — with war, starvation, and disease. 14 None of the people of Judah who are left and have come to Egypt to live will escape or survive. Not one of them will return to Judah, where they long to live once again. No one will return except a few refugees."

15 Then all the men who knew that their wives offered sacrifices to other gods, and all the women who were standing there, including the Israelites who lived in southern Egypt — a large crowd in all — said to me, 16 "We refuse to listen to what you have told us in the name of the LORD. 17 We will do everything that we said we would. We will offer sacrifices to our goddess, the Queen of Heaven, and we will pour out wine offerings to her, just as we and our ancestors, our king and our leaders, used to do in the towns of Judah and in the streets of Jerusalem. Then we had plenty of food, we were prosperous, and had no troubles. 18 But ever since we stopped sacrificing to the Queen of Heaven and stopped pouring out wine offerings to her, we have had nothing, and our people have died in war and of starvation."

19 And the women added, "When we baked cakes shaped like the Queen of Heaven, offered sacrifices to her, and poured out wine offerings to her, our husbands approved of what we were doing."

20 Then I said to all the men and the women who had answered me in this way, 21 "As for the sacrifices which you and your ancestors, your kings and your leaders, and the people of the land offered in the towns of Judah and in the streets of Jerusalem — do you think that the LORD did not know about them or that he forgot them? 22 This very day your land lies in ruins and no one lives in it. It has become a horrifying sight, and people use its name as a curse because the LORD could no longer endure your wicked and evil practices. 23 This present disaster has come on you because you offered sacrifices to other gods and sinned against the LORD by not obeying all his commands."

24-25 I told all the people, especially the women, what the LORD Almighty, the God of Israel, was saying to the people of Judah living in Egypt: "Both you and your wives have made solemn promises to the Queen of Heaven. You promised that you would offer sacrifices to her and pour out wine offerings to her, and you have kept your promises. Very well, then! Keep your promises! Carry out your vows! 26 But now listen to the vow that I, the LORD, have made in my mighty name to all you Israelites in Egypt: Never again will I let any of you use my name to make a vow by saying, 'I swear by the living Sovereign LORD!' 27 I will see to it that you will not prosper, but will be destroyed. All of you will die, either in war or of disease, until not one of you is left. 28 But a few of you will escape death and return from Egypt to Judah. Then the survivors will know whose words have come true, mine or theirs.

J
E
R
E
M
I
A
H

29I, the LORD, will give you proof that I will punish you in this place and that my promise to bring destruction on you will come true. 30I will hand over King Hophra of Egypt to his enemies who want to kill him, just as I handed over King Zedekiah of Judah to King Nebuchadnezzar of Babylonia, who was his enemy and wanted to kill him."

God's Promise to Baruch

45 In the fourth year that Jehoiakim son of Josiah was king of Judah, Baruch wrote down what I had dictated to him. Then I told him 2that the LORD, the God of Israel, had said, "Baruch, 3you are saying, 'I give up! The LORD has added sorrow to my troubles. I am worn out from groaning, and I can't find any rest!'

4"But I, the LORD, am tearing down what I have built and pulling up what I have planted. I will do this to the entire earth. 5Are you looking for special treatment for yourself? Don't do it. I am bringing disaster on all people, but you will at least escape with your life, wherever you go. I, the LORD, have spoken."

Egypt's Defeat at Carchemish

46 The LORD spoke to me about the nations, 2beginning with Egypt. This is what he said about the army of King Neco of Egypt, which King Nebuchadnezzar of Babylonia defeated at Carchemish near the Euphrates River in the fourth year that Jehoiakim was king of Judah:

3"The Egyptian officers shout,
'Get your shields ready
    and march into battle!
4Harness your horses and mount
        them!
Fall in line and put on your
        helmets!
    Sharpen your spears!
    Put on your armor!'

5"But what do I see?" asks the
        LORD.
"They are turning back in terror.
    Their soldiers are beaten back;
    overcome with fear, they run as
        fast as they can

and do not look back.
6Those who run fast cannot get
        away;
    the soldiers cannot escape.
In the north, by the Euphrates,
    they stumble and fall.
7Who is this that rises like the Nile,
    like a river flooding its banks?
8It is Egypt, rising like the Nile,
    like a river flooding its banks.
Egypt said, 'I will rise and cover
        the world;
    I will destroy cities and the
        people who live there.
9Command the horses to go
    and the chariots to roll!
Send out the soldiers:
    men from Ethiopiad and Libya,
        carrying shields,
    and skilled archers from
        Lydia.' "

10This is the day of the Sovereign
    LORD Almighty:
today he will take revenge;
today he will punish his
        enemies.
His sword will eat them until it is
        full,
    and drink their blood until it is
        satisfied.
Today the Almighty sacrifices his
        victims
    in the north, by the Euphrates.
11People of Egypt, go to Gileade
    and look for medicine!
All your medicine has proved
        useless;
    nothing can heal you.
12Nations have heard of your
        shame;
    everyone has heard you cry.
One soldier trips over another,
    and both of them fall to the
        ground.

The Coming of Nebuchadnezzar

13When King Nebuchadnezzar of Babylonia came to attack Egypt, the LORD spoke to me. He said, 14"Proclaim it in the towns of Egypt, in Migdol, Memphis, and Tahpanhes:
    'Get ready to defend yourselves;

d Hebrew Cush: Cush is the ancient name of the extensive territory south of the First Cataract of the Nile River. This region was called Ethiopia in Graeco-Roman times, and included within its borders most of modern Sudan and some of present-day Ethiopia (Abyssinia).
e GILEAD: See 8.22.

all you have will be destroyed
   in war!
15 Why has your mighty god Apis
   fallen?
   The LORD has struck him down!'
16 Your soldiers have stumbled and
   fallen;*f*
   each one says to the other,
   'Hurry! Let's go home to our
      people
   and escape the enemy's sword!'

17 "Give the king of Egypt a new
      name—
   'Noisy Braggart Who Missed His
      Chance.'
18 I, the LORD Almighty, am king.
   I am the living God.
   As Mount Tabor towers above the
      mountains
   and Mount Carmel stands high
      above the sea,
   so will be the strength of the one
      who attacks you.
19 Get ready to be taken prisoner,
   you people of Egypt!
   Memphis will be made a desert,
   a ruin where no one lives.
20 Egypt is like a splendid cow,
   attacked by a stinging fly from
      the north.
21 Even her hired soldiers
   are helpless as calves.
   They did not stand and fight;
   all of them turned and ran.
   The day of their doom had
      arrived,
   the time of their destruction.
22 Egypt runs away, hissing like a
      snake,
   as the enemy's army
      approaches.
   They attack her with axes,
   like people cutting down trees
23   and destroying a thick forest.
   Their soldiers are too many to
      count;
   they outnumber the locusts.
24 The people of Egypt are put to
      shame;
   they are conquered by the
      people of the north.
   I, the LORD, have spoken."

25 The LORD Almighty, the God of Israel, says, "I am going to punish Amon,
the god of Thebes, together with Egypt
and its gods and kings. I am going to
take the king of Egypt and all who put
their trust in him, 26 and hand them over
to those who want to kill them, to King
Nebuchadnezzar of Babylonia and his
army. But later on, people will live in
Egypt again, as they did in times past. I,
the LORD, have spoken.

The LORD Will Save His People

27 "My people, do not be afraid,
   people of Israel, do not be
      terrified.
   I will rescue you from that
      faraway land,
   from the land where you are
      prisoners.
   You will come back home and live
      in peace;
   you will be secure, and no one
      will make you afraid.
28 I will come to you and save you.
   I will destroy all the nations
      where I have scattered you,
   but I will not destroy you.
   I will not let you go unpunished;
   but when I punish you, I will be
      fair.
   I, the LORD, have spoken."

The LORD's Message about Philistia

47   Before the king of Egypt attacked Gaza, the LORD spoke to
me about Philistia. 2 He said:
   "Look! Waters are rising in the
      north
   and will rush like a river in
      flood.
   They will cover the land and
      everything on it,
   cities and the people who live
      there.
   People will call out for help;
   everyone on earth will cry
      bitterly.
3 They will hear the hoofbeats of
      horses,
   the clatter of chariots,
   the rumble of wheels.
   Parents will not turn back for their
      children;
   their hands will hang limp at
      their sides.
4 The time has come to destroy
   Philistia,

f Probable text Your soldiers . . . fallen; *Hebrew unclear.*

JEREMIAH

to cut off from Tyre and Sidon
all the help that remains.
I, the Lord, will destroy the
Philistines,
all who came from the shores of
Crete.
5 Great sorrow has come to the
people of Gaza,
and Ashkelon's people are silent.
How long will the rest of
Philistia mourn?
6 You cry out, 'Sword of the Lord!
How long will you go on
slashing?
Go back to your scabbard,
stay there and rest!'
7 But how can it rest,
when I have given it work to do?
I have commanded it to attack
Ashkelon
and the people who live on the
coast."

The Destruction of Moab

48 This is what the Lord Almighty
said about Moab:
"Pity the people of Nebo—
their town is destroyed!
Kiriathaim is captured,
its mighty fortress torn down,
and its people put to shame;
2   the splendor of Moab is gone.
The enemy have captured
Heshbon
and plot to destroy the nation of
Moab.
The town of Madmen will be
silenced;
armies will march against it.
3 The people of Horonaim cry out,
'Violence! Destruction!'

4 "Moab has been destroyed;
listen to the children crying.
5 Hear the sound of their sobs
along the road up to Luhith,
the cries of distress
on the way down to Horonaim.
6 'Quick, run for your lives!'
they say.
'Run like a wild desert donkey!'

7 "Moab, you trusted in your
strength and your wealth,
but now even you will be
conquered;
your god Chemosh will go into
exile,

along with his princes and
priests.
8 Not a town will escape the
destruction;
both valley and plain will be
ruined.
I, the Lord, have spoken.
9 Set up a tombstone for Moab;
it will soon be destroyed.
Its towns will be left in ruins,
and no one will live there
again."

(10 Curse those who do not do the
Lord's work with all their heart! Curse
those who do not slash and kill!)

The Cities of Moab Are Destroyed

11 The Lord said, "Moab has always
lived secure and has never been taken
into exile. Moab is like wine left to settle
undisturbed and never poured from jar
to jar. Its flavor has never been ruined,
and it tastes as good as ever.
12 "So now, the time is coming when I
will send people to pour Moab out like
wine. They will empty its wine jars and
break them in pieces. 13 Then the Moabites will be disillusioned with their god
Chemosh, just as the Israelites were disillusioned with Bethel, a god in whom
they trusted.
14 "Men of Moab, why do you claim
to be heroes,
brave soldiers tested in war?
15 Moab and its cities are destroyed;
its finest young men have been
slaughtered.
I am the king, the Lord Almighty,
and I have spoken.
16 Moab's doom approaches;
its ruin is coming soon.

17 "Mourn for that nation, you that
live nearby,
all of you that know its fame.
Say, 'Its powerful rule has been
broken;
its glory and might are no more.'
18 You that live in Dibon,
come down from your place of
honor
and sit on the ground in the
dust;
Moab's destroyer is here
and has left its forts in ruins.
19 You that live in Aroer,
stand by the road and wait;

ask those who are running
away,
find out from them what has
happened.
20 'Moab has fallen,' they will
answer,
'weep for it; it is disgraced.
Announce along the Arnon River
that Moab is destroyed!'

21 "Judgment has come on the cities of
the plateau: on Holon, Jahzah, Mephaath, 22 Dibon, Nebo, Beth Diblathaim,
23 Kiriathaim, Bethgamul, Bethmeon,
24 Kerioth, and Bozrah. Judgment has
come on all the cities of Moab, far and
near. 25 Moab's might has been crushed;
its power has been destroyed. I, the
LORD, have spoken."

Moab Will Be Humbled

26 The LORD said, "Make Moab drunk,
because it has rebelled against me.
Moab will roll in its own vomit, and
people will laugh. 27 Moab, remember
how you made fun of the people of
Israel? You treated them as though
they had been caught with a gang of
robbers.
28 "You people who live in Moab, leave
your towns! Go and live on the cliffs! Be
like the dove that makes its nest in the
sides of a ravine. 29 Moab is very proud!
I have heard how proud, arrogant, and
conceited the people are, how much they
think of themselves. 30 I, the LORD, know
of their arrogance. Their boasts amount
to nothing, and the things they do will
not last. 31 And so I will weep for everyone in Moab and for the people of Kir
Heres. 32 I will cry for the people of Sibmah, even more than for the people of
Jazer. City of Sibmah, you are like a
vine whose branches reach across the
Dead Sea and go as far as Jazer. But
now your summer fruits and your
grapes have been destroyed. 33 Happiness and joy have been taken away from
the fertile land of Moab. I have made the
wine stop flowing from the wine
presses; there is no one to make the wine
and shout for joy.
34 "The people of Heshbon and Elealeh
cry out,g and their cry can be heard as

far as Jahaz; it can be heard by the people in Zoar, and it is heard as far as Horonaim and Eglath Shelishiyah. Even
Nimrim Brook has dried up. 35 I will stop
the people of Moab from making burnt
offerings at their places of worship and
from offering sacrifices to their gods. I,
the LORD, have spoken.
36 "So my heart mourns for Moab and
for the people of Kir Heres, like someone
playing a funeral song on a flute, because everything they owned is gone.
37 All of them have shaved their heads
and cut off their beards. They have all
made gashes on their hands, and everyone is wearing sackcloth. 38 On all the
housetops of Moab and in all its public
squares there is nothing but mourning,
because I have broken Moab like a jar
that no one wants. 39 Moab has been
shattered! Cry out! Moab has been disgraced. It is in ruins, and all the surrounding nations make fun of it. I, the
LORD, have spoken."

No Escape for Moab

40 The LORD has promised that a nation
will swoop down on Moab like an eagle
with its outspread wings, 41 and the
towns and fortresses will be captured.
On that day Moab's soldiers will be as
frightened as a woman in labor. 42 Moab
will be destroyed and will no longer be a
nation, because it rebelled against me.
43 Terror, pits, and traps are waiting for
the people of Moab. The LORD has spoken. 44 Whoever tries to escape the terror
will fall into the pits, and whoever
climbs out of the pits will be caught in
the traps, because the LORD has set the
time for Moab's destruction. 45 Helpless
refugees try to find protection in Heshbon, the city that King Sihon once ruled,
but it is in flames.h Fire has burned
up the frontiers and the mountain
heights of the war-loving people of
Moab. 46 Pity the people of Moab! The
people who worshiped Chemosh have
been destroyed, and their sons and
daughters have been taken away as
prisoners.
47 But in days to come the LORD will
make Moab prosperous again. All of this
is what the LORD has said will happen to
Moab.

J
E
R
E
M
I
A
H

---

g Probable text Heshbon . . . cry out; Hebrew unclear.   h Heshbon, the city . . . flames; or the
city of Heshbon, but it is in flames and the palace of King Sihon is burning.

The LORD's Judgment on Ammon

49 This is what the LORD said about Ammon: "Where are the men of Israel? Is there no one to defend their land? Why have they let the people who worship Molech take the territory of the tribe of Gad and settle there? 2 But the time is coming when I will make the people of the capital city of Rabbah hear the noise of battle, and it will be left in ruins and its villages burned to the ground. Then Israel will take its land back from those who took it from them. 3 People of Heshbon, cry out! Ai is destroyed! Women of Rabbah, go into mourning! Put on sackcloth and mourn. Run about in confusion. Your god Molech will be taken into exile, together with his priests and princes. 4 Why do you unfaithful people boast? Your strength is failing. Why do you trust in your power and say that no one would dare attack you? 5 I will bring terror on you from every side. You will all run away. Each one will run for his life, and there will be no one to bring your troops together again.

6 "But later on I will make Ammon prosperous again. I, the LORD, have spoken."

The LORD's Judgment on Edom

7 This is what the LORD Almighty said about Edom: "Have the people of Edom lost their good judgment? Can their advisers no longer tell them what to do? Has all their wisdom disappeared? 8 People of Dedan, turn and run! Hide! I am going to destroy Esau's descendants because the time has come for me to punish them. 9 When people pick grapes, they leave a few on the vines, and when robbers come at night, they take only what they want. 10 But I* have stripped Esau's descendants completely and uncovered their hiding places, so that they can no longer hide. All the people of Edom are destroyed. Not one of them is left. 11 Leave your orphans with me, and I will take care of them. Your widows can depend on me.

12 "If even those who did not deserve to be punished had to drink from the cup of punishment, do you think that you will go unpunished? No, you must drink from the cup! 13 I myself have sworn that the city of Bozrah will become a horrifying sight and a desert; people will make fun of it and use its name as a curse. All the nearby villages will be in ruins forever. I, the LORD, have spoken."

14 I said, "Edom, I have received a message from the LORD. He has sent a messenger to tell the nations to assemble their armies and to get ready to attack you. 15 The LORD is going to make you weak, and no one will respect you. 16 Your pride has deceived you. No one fears you as much as you think they do. You live on the rocky cliffs, high on top of the mountain; but even though you live as high up as an eagle, the LORD will bring you down. The LORD has spoken."

17 The LORD said, "The destruction that will come on Edom will be so terrible that everyone who passes by will be shocked and terrified. 18 The same thing will happen to Edom that happened to Sodom and Gomorrah, when they and the nearby towns were destroyed. No one will ever live there again. I, the LORD, have spoken. 19 Like a lion coming out of the thick woods along the Jordan River up to the green pasture land, I will come and make the Edomites run away suddenly from their country. Then the leader I choose will rule the nation. Who can be compared to me? Who would dare challenge me? What ruler could oppose me? 20 So listen to the plan that I have made against the people of Edom, and to what I intend to do to the people of the city of Teman. Even their children will be dragged off, and everyone will be horrified. 21 When Edom falls, there will be such a noise that the entire earth will shake, and the cries of alarm will be heard as far away as the Gulf of Aqaba. 22 The enemy will attack Bozrah like an eagle swooping down with outspread wings. On that day Edom's soldiers will be as frightened as a woman in labor."

The LORD's Judgment on Damascus

23 This is what the LORD said about Damascus: "The people in the cities of Hamath and Arpad are worried and troubled because they have heard bad news. Anxiety rolls over them like a sea, and they cannot rest. 24 The people of Damascus are weak and have fled in

*they leave a few ... they take only what they want. 10 But I; or they leave nothing ... they take everything. 10 And so I.

terror. They are in pain and misery like a woman in labor. 25 The famous city that used to be happy[j] is completely deserted. 26 On that day her young men will be killed in the city streets, and all her soldiers destroyed. 27 I will set the walls of Damascus on fire and will burn down King Benhadad's palaces. I, the LORD Almighty, have spoken."

Judgment on the Tribe of Kedar and the City of Hazor

28 This is what the LORD said about the tribe of Kedar and the districts controlled by Hazor, which were conquered by King Nebuchadnezzar of Babylonia: "Attack the people of Kedar and destroy that tribe of eastern people! 29 Seize their tents and their flocks, their tent curtains and everything in their tents. Take their camels and tell the people, 'Terror is all around you!'

30 "People of Hazor, I, the LORD, warn you to run far away and hide. King Nebuchadnezzar of Babylonia has plotted against you, and this is what he says, 31 'Come on! We'll attack those people that feel safe and secure! Their city has no gates or locks and is completely unprotected.'

32 "Take their camels and all their livestock! I will scatter in every direction those people who cut their hair short, and I will bring disaster on them from every side. 33 Hazor will be made a desert forever, a place where only jackals live. No one will ever live there again. I, the LORD, have spoken."

The LORD's Judgment on Elam

34 Soon after Zedekiah became king of Judah, the LORD Almighty spoke to me about the country of Elam. 35 He said, "I will kill all the archers who have made Elam so powerful. 36 I will make winds blow against Elam from all directions, and I will scatter her people everywhere, until there is no country where her refugees have not gone. 37 I will make the people of Elam afraid of their enemies, who want to kill them. In my great anger I will destroy the people of Elam and send armies against them until I have wiped them out. 38 I will destroy their kings and leaders, and set up my throne there. 39 But later on I will make the people of Elam prosperous again. I, the LORD, have spoken."

Babylon's Capture

50 This is the message that the LORD gave me about the city of Babylon and its people:

2 "Tell the news to the nations!
   Proclaim it!
   Give the signal and announce
      the news!
   Do not keep it a secret!
Babylon has fallen!
   Her god Marduk has been
      shattered!
   Babylon's idols are put to shame;
      her disgusting images are
         crushed!

3 "A nation from the north has come to attack Babylonia and will make it a desert. People and animals will run away, and no one will live there."

Israel's Return

4 The LORD says, "When that time comes, the people of both Israel and Judah will come weeping, looking for me, their God. 5 They will ask the way to Zion and then go in that direction. They will make an eternal covenant with me and never break it.

6 "My people are like sheep whose shepherds have let them get lost in the mountains. They have wandered like sheep from one mountain to another, and they have forgotten where their home is. 7 They are attacked by all who find them. Their enemies say, 'They sinned against the LORD, and so what we have done is not wrong. Their ancestors trusted in the LORD, and they themselves should have remained faithful to him.'

8 "People of Israel, run away from Babylon! Leave the country! Be the first to leave! 9 I am going to stir up a group of strong nations in the north and make them attack Babylonia. They will line up in battle against the country and conquer it. They are skillful hunters, shooting arrows that never miss the mark. 10 Babylonia will be looted, and those who loot it will take everything they want. I, the LORD, have spoken."

---

j *Some ancient translations* happy; *Hebrew* my happiness.

Babylon's Fall

11 The LORD says, "People of Babylonia, you plundered my nation. You are happy and glad, going about like a cow threshing grain or like a neighing horse, 12 but your own great city will be humiliated and disgraced. Babylonia will be the least important nation of all; it will become a dry and waterless desert. 13 Because of my anger no one will live in Babylon; it will be left in ruins, and all who pass by will be shocked and amazed.

14 "Archers, line up for battle against Babylon and surround it. Shoot all your arrows at Babylon, because it has sinned against me, the LORD. 15 Raise the war cry all around the city! Now Babylon has surrendered. Its walls have been broken through and torn down.k I am taking my revenge on the Babylonians. So take your revenge on them, and treat them as they have treated others. 16 Do not let seeds be planted in that country nor let a harvest be gathered. Every foreigner living there will be afraid of the attacking army and will go back home."

Israel's Return

17 The LORD says, "The people of Israel are like sheep, chased and scattered by lions. First, they were attacked by the emperor of Assyria, and then King Nebuchadnezzar of Babylonia gnawed on their bones. 18 Because of this, I, the LORD Almighty, the God of Israel, will punish King Nebuchadnezzar and his country, just as I punished the emperor of Assyria. 19 I will restore the people of Israel to their land. They will eat the food that grows on Mount Carmel and in the region of Bashan, and they will eat all they want of the crops that grow in the territories of Ephraim and Gilead. 20 When that time comes, no sin will be found in Israel and no wickedness in Judah, because I will forgive those people whose lives I have spared. I, the LORD, have spoken."

God's Judgment on Babylonia

21 The LORD says, "Attack the people of Merathaim and of Pekod. Kill and destroy them.l Do everything I command you. I, the LORD, have spoken. 22 The noise of battle is heard in the land, and there is great destruction. 23 Babylonia hammered the whole world to pieces, and now that hammer is shattered! All the nations are shocked at what has happened to that country. 24 Babylonia, you fought against me, and you have been caught in the trap I set for you, even though you did not know it. 25 I have opened the place where my weapons are stored, and in my anger I have taken them out, because I, the Sovereign LORD Almighty, have work to do in Babylonia. 26 Attack it from every side and break open the places where its grain is stored! Pile up the loot like piles of grain! Destroy the country! Leave nothing at all! 27 Kill all their soldiers! Slaughter them! The people of Babylonia are doomed! The time has come for them to be punished!"

(28 Refugees escape from Babylonia and come to Jerusalem, and they tell how the LORD our God took revenge for what the Babylonians had done to his Temple.)

29 "Tell the archers to attack Babylon. Send out everyone who knows how to use the bow and arrow. Surround the city and don't let anyone escape. Pay it back for all it has done, and treat it as it has treated others, because it acted with pride against me, the Holy One of Israel. 30 So its young men will be killed in the city streets, and all its soldiers will be destroyed on that day. I, the LORD, have spoken.

31 "Babylonia, you are filled with pride, so I, the Sovereign LORD Almighty, am against you! The time has come for me to punish you. 32 Your proud nation will stumble and fall, and no one will help you up. I will set your cities on fire, and everything around will be destroyed."

33 The LORD Almighty says, "The people of Israel and of Judah are oppressed. All who captured them are guarding them closely and will not let them go. 34 But the one who will rescue them is strong—his name is the LORD Almighty. He himself will take up their cause and will bring peace to the earth, but trouble to the people of Babylonia."

35 The LORD says,

---

k Hebrew has an additional word, the meaning of which is unclear.   l One ancient translation them; Hebrew after them.

"Death to Babylonia!
　Death to its people,
　　to its rulers, to its people of
　　　wisdom.
36 Death to its lying prophets—
　　what fools they are!
　Death to its soldiers—
　　how terrified they are!
37 Destroy its horses and chariots!
　Death to its hired soldiers—
　　how weak they are!
　Destroy its treasures;
　　plunder and loot.
38 Bring a drought on its land
　　and dry up its rivers.
　Babylonia is a land of terrifying
　　idols
　　that have made fools of the
　　　people.

39 "And so Babylon will be haunted by demons and evil spirits, *m* and by unclean birds. Never again will people live there, not for all time to come. 40 The same thing will happen to Babylon that happened to Sodom and Gomorrah, when I destroyed them and the nearby towns. No one will ever live there again. I, the LORD, have spoken.

41 "People are coming from a country
　　in the north,
　a mighty nation far away;
　　many kings are preparing
　　　for war.
42 They have taken their bows and
　　swords;
　　they are cruel and merciless.
　They sound like the roaring sea,
　　as they ride their horses.
　They are ready for battle against
　　Babylonia.
43 The king of Babylonia hears the
　　news,
　　and his hands hang limp.
　He is seized by anguish,
　　by pain like a woman in labor.

44 "Like a lion coming out of the thick woods along the Jordan up to the green pasture land, I, the LORD, will come and make the Babylonians run away suddenly from their city. Then the leader I choose will rule the nation. Who can be compared to me? Who would dare challenge me? What ruler could oppose me? 45 So listen to the plan that I have made against the city of Babylon and to what I intend to do to its people. Even their

children will be dragged off, and everyone will be horrified. 46 When Babylon falls, there will be such a noise that the entire earth will shake, and the cries of alarm will be heard by the other nations."

Further Judgment on Babylonia

51 The LORD says, "I am bringing a destructive wind *n* against Babylonia and its people. 2 I will send foreigners to destroy Babylonia like a wind that blows straw away. When that day of destruction comes, they will attack from every side and leave the land bare. 3 Don't give its soldiers time to shoot their arrows or to put on their armor. Do not spare the young men! Destroy the whole army! 4 They will be wounded and die in the streets of their cities. 5 I, the LORD God Almighty, have not abandoned Israel and Judah, even though they have sinned against me, the Holy One of Israel. 6 Run away from Babylonia! Run for your lives! Do not be killed because of Babylonia's sin. I am now taking my revenge and punishing it as it deserves. 7 Babylonia was like a gold cup in my hand, making the whole world drunk. The nations drank its wine and went out of their minds. 8 Babylonia has suddenly fallen and is destroyed! Mourn over it! Get medicine for its wounds, and maybe it can be healed. 9 Foreigners living there said, 'We tried to help Babylonia, but it was too late. Let's leave now and go back home. God has punished Babylonia with all his might and has destroyed it completely.' "

10 The LORD says, "My people shout, 'The LORD has shown that we are in the right. Let's go and tell the people in Jerusalem what the LORD our God has done.' "

11 The LORD has stirred up the kings of Media, because he intends to destroy Babylonia. That is how he will take revenge for the destruction of his Temple.

The attacking officers command, "Sharpen your arrows! Get your shields ready! 12 Give the signal to attack Babylon's walls. Strengthen the guard! Post the sentries! Place troops in ambush!"

The LORD has done what he said he would do to the people of Babylonia. 13 That country has many rivers and rich

---

m demons and evil spirits; *or* wildcats and jackals.　　*n* destructive wind; *or* destroying spirit.

treasures, but its time is up, and its thread of life is cut. 14 The LORD Almighty has sworn by his own life that he will bring many men to attack Babylonia like a swarm of locusts, and they will shout with victory.

A Hymn of Praise to God

15 The LORD made the earth by his power;
by his wisdom he created the world
and stretched out the heavens.
16 At his command the waters above the sky[o] roar;
he brings clouds from the ends of the earth.
He makes lightning flash in the rain
and sends the wind from his storeroom.
17 At the sight of this, people feel stupid and senseless;
those who make idols are disillusioned
because the gods they make are false and lifeless.
18 They are worthless and should be despised;
they will be destroyed when the LORD comes to deal with them.
19 The God of Jacob is not like them;
he is the one who made everything,
and he has chosen Israel to be his very own people.
The LORD Almighty is his name.

The LORD's Hammer

20 The LORD says,
"Babylonia, you are my hammer, my weapon of war.
I used you to crush nations and kingdoms,
21 to shatter horses and riders,
to shatter chariots and their drivers,
22 to kill men and women,
to slay old and young,
to kill boys and girls,
23 to slaughter shepherds and their flocks,
to slaughter farmers and their plow horses,
to crush rulers and high officials."

Babylonia's Punishment

24 The LORD says, "You will see me repay Babylonia and its people for all the evil they did to Jerusalem. 25 Babylonia, you are like a mountain that destroys the whole world, but I, the LORD, am your enemy. I will take hold of you, level you to the ground, and leave you in ashes. 26 None of the stones from your ruins will ever be used again for building. You will be like a desert forever. I, the LORD, have spoken.

27 "Give the signal to attack! Blow the trumpet so that the nations can hear! Prepare the nations for war against Babylonia! Tell the kingdoms of Ararat, Minni, and Ashkenaz to attack. Appoint an officer to lead the attack. Bring up the horses like a swarm of locusts. 28 Prepare the nations for war against Babylonia. Send for the kings of Media, their leaders and officials, and the armies of all the countries they control. 29 The earth trembles and shakes because the LORD is carrying out his plan to make Babylonia a desert, where no one lives. 30 The Babylonian soldiers have stopped fighting and remain in their forts. They have lost their courage and have become helpless. The city gates are broken down, and the houses are on fire. 31 Messenger after messenger runs to tell the king of Babylonia that his city has been broken into from every side. 32 The enemy have captured the river crossing and have set the fortresses on fire. The Babylonian soldiers have panicked. 33 Soon the enemy will cut them down and trample them like grain on a threshing place. I, the LORD Almighty, the God of Israel, have spoken."

34 The king of Babylonia cut
Jerusalem up
and ate it.
He emptied the city like a jar;
like a monster he swallowed it.
He took what he wanted
and threw the rest away.
35 Let the people of Zion say,
"May Babylonia be held responsible
for the violence done to us!"
Let the people of Jerusalem say,
"May Babylonia be held responsible
for what we have suffered!"

---

o WATERS ABOVE THE SKY: See Gn 1.6-8.

The LORD Will Help Israel

36 And so the LORD said to the people of Jerusalem, "I will take up your cause and will make your enemies pay for what they did to you. I will dry up the source of Babylonia's water and make its rivers go dry. 37 That country will become a pile of ruins where wild animals live. It will be a horrible sight; no one will live there, and all who see it will be terrified. 38 The Babylonians all roar like lions and growl like lion cubs. 39 Are they greedy? I will prepare them a feast and make them drunk and happy. They will go to sleep and never wake up. 40 I will take them to be slaughtered, like lambs, goats, and rams. I, the LORD, have spoken."

Babylon's Fate

41 The LORD says about Babylon: "The city that the whole world praised has been captured! What a horrifying sight Babylon has become to the nations! 42 The sea has rolled over Babylon and covered it with roaring waves. 43 The towns have become a horrifying sight and are like a waterless desert, where no one lives or even travels. 44 I will punish Bel, the god of Babylonia, and make him give up his stolen goods; the nations will not worship him any more.

"Babylon's walls have fallen. 45 People of Israel, run away from there! Run for your life from my fierce anger. 46 Do not lose courage or be afraid because of the rumors you hear. Every year a different rumor spreads — rumors of violence in the land and of one king fighting another. 47 And so the time is coming when I will deal with Babylonia's idols. The whole country will be put to shame, and all its people will be killed. 48 Everything on earth and in the sky will shout for joy when Babylonia falls to the people who come from the north to destroy it. 49 Babylonia caused the death of people all over the world, and now Babylonia will fall because it caused the death of so many Israelites. I, the LORD, have spoken."

God's Message to the Israelites in Babylonia

50 The LORD says to his people in Babylonia: "You have escaped death! Now go! Don't wait! Though you are far from home, think about me, your LORD, and remember Jerusalem. 51 You say, 'We've been disgraced and made ashamed; we feel completely helpless because foreigners have taken over the holy places in the Temple.' 52 So then, I say that the time is coming when I will deal with Babylon's idols, and the wounded will groan throughout the country. 53 Even if Babylon could climb to the sky and build a strong fortress there, I would still send people to destroy it. I, the LORD, have spoken."

Further Destruction on Babylon

54 The LORD says,
"Listen to the sound of crying in
    Babylon,
  of mourning for the destruction
    in the land.
55 I am destroying Babylon
  and putting it to silence.
The armies rush in like roaring
    waves
  and attack with noisy shouts.
56 They have come to destroy
    Babylon;
  its soldiers are captured,
  and their bows are broken.
I am a God who punishes evil,
  and I will treat Babylon as it
    deserves.
57 I will make its rulers drunk —
  men of wisdom, leaders, and
    soldiers.
They will go to sleep and never
    wake up.
  I, the king, have spoken;
  I am the LORD Almighty.
58 The walls of mighty Babylon will
    be thrown to the ground,
  and its towering gates burned
    down.
The work of the nations is all for
    nothing;
  their efforts go up in flames.
I, the LORD Almighty, have
    spoken."

Jeremiah's Message Is Sent to Babylonia

59 King Zedekiah's personal attendant was Seraiah, the son of Neriah and grandson of Mahseiah. In the fourth year that Zedekiah was king of Judah, Seraiah was going to Babylonia with him, and I gave him some instructions. 60 I wrote in a book an account of all the

destruction that would come on Babylonia, as well as all these other things about Babylonia. 61 I told Seraiah, "When you get to Babylon, be sure to read aloud to the people everything that is written here. 62 Then pray, 'LORD, you have said that you would destroy this place, so that there would be no living creatures in it, neither people nor animals, and it would be like a desert forever.' 63 Seraiah, when you finish reading this book to the people, then tie it to a rock and throw it into the Euphrates River 64 and say, 'This is what will happen to Babylonia — it will sink and never rise again because of the destruction that the LORD is going to bring on it.' "p

The words of Jeremiah end here.

The Fall of Jerusalem
(2 Kings 24.18 — 25.7)

52 Zedekiah was twenty-one years old when he became king of Judah, and he ruled in Jerusalem for eleven years. His mother's name was Hamutal, the daughter of the Jeremiah who lived in the city of Libnah. 2 King Zedekiah sinned against the LORD, just as King Jehoiakim had done. 3 The LORD became so angry with the people of Jerusalem and Judah that he banished them from his sight.

Zedekiah rebelled against King Nebuchadnezzar of Babylonia, 4 and so Nebuchadnezzar came with all his army and attacked Jerusalem on the tenth day of the tenth month of the ninth year of Zedekiah's reign. They set up camp outside the city, built siege walls around it, 5 and kept it under siege until Zedekiah's eleventh year. 6 On the ninth day of the fourth month of that same year, when the famine was so bad that the people had nothing left to eat, 7 the city walls were broken through. Although the Babylonians were surrounding the city, all the soldiers escaped during the night. They left by way of the royal garden, went through the gateway connecting the two walls, and fled in the direction of the Jordan Valley. 8 But the Babylonian army pursued King Zedekiah, captured him in the plains near Jericho, and all his soldiers deserted him. 9 Zedekiah

was taken to King Nebuchadnezzar, who was in the city of Riblah in the territory of Hamath, and there Nebuchadnezzar passed sentence on him. 10 At Riblah he put Zedekiah's sons to death while Zedekiah was looking on and he also had the officials of Judah executed. 11 After that, he had Zedekiah's eyes put out and had him placed in chains and taken to Babylon. Zedekiah remained in prison in Babylon until the day he died.

The Destruction of the Temple
(2 Kings 25.8-17)

12 On the tenth day of the fifth month of the nineteenth year of King Nebuchadnezzar of Babylonia, Nebuzaradan, adviser to the king and commander of his army, entered Jerusalem. 13 He burned down the Temple, the palace, and the houses of all the important people in Jerusalem; 14 and his soldiers tore down the city walls. 15 Then Nebuzaradan took away to Babyloniaq the people who were left in the city, the remaining skilled workers, and those who had deserted to the Babylonians. 16 But he left in Judah some of the poorest people, who owned no property, and he put them to work in the vineyards and fields.

17 The Babylonians broke in pieces the bronze columns and the carts that were in the Temple, together with the large bronze tank, and they took all the bronze to Babylon. 18 They also took away the shovels and the ash containers used in cleaning the altar, the tools used in tending the lamps, the bowls used for catching the blood from the sacrifices, the bowls used for burning incense, and all the other bronze articles used in the Temple service. 19 They took away everything that was made of gold or silver: the small bowls, the pans used for carrying live coals, the bowls for holding the blood from the sacrifices, the ash containers, the lampstands, the bowls used for incense, and the bowls used for pouring out wine offerings. 20 The bronze objects that King Solomon had made for the Temple — the two columns, the carts, the large tank, and the twelve bulls that supported it — were too heavy to weigh. 21-22 The two columns were identical: each one was 27 feet high and

p One ancient translation on it; Hebrew on it and they will become tired out.
q Probable text Babylonia; Hebrew Babylonia some of the poorest of the people.

18 feet around. They were hollow, and the metal was 3 inches thick. On top of each column was a bronze capital 7½ feet high, and all around it was a grill-work decorated with pomegranates, all of which was also made of bronze. 23 On the grillwork of each column there were a hundred pomegranates in all, and ninety-six of these were visible from the ground.

The People of Judah Are Taken to Babylonia

(2 Kings 25.18-21, 27-30)

24 In addition, Nebuzaradan, the commanding officer, took away as prisoners Seraiah the High Priest, Zephaniah the priest next in rank, and the three other important Temple officials. 25 From the city he took the officer who had been in command of the troops, seven of the king's personal advisers who were still in the city, the commander's assistant, who was in charge of military records, and sixty other important men. 26 Nebuzaradan took them to the king of Babylonia, who was in the city of Riblah 27 in the territory of Hamath. There the king had them beaten and put to death.

So the people of Judah were carried away from their land into exile. 28 This is the record of the people that Nebuchadnezzar took away as prisoners: in his seventh year as king he carried away 3,023; 29 in his eighteenth year, 832 from Jerusalem; 30 and in his twenty-third year, 745 — taken away by Nebuzaradan. In all, 4,600 people were taken away.

31 In the year that Evil-merodach became king of Babylonia, he showed kindness to King Jehoiachin of Judah by releasing him from prison. This happened on the twenty-fifth day of the twelfth month of the thirty-seventh year after Jehoiachin had been taken away as a prisoner. 32 Evilmerodach treated him kindly and gave him a position of greater honor than he gave the other kings who were exiles with him in Babylonia. 33 So Jehoiachin was permitted to change from his prison clothes and to dine at the king's table for the rest of his life. 34 Each day for as long as he lived, he was given a regular allowance for his needs.

LAMENTATIONS

Introduction

The book of Lamentations is a collection of five poems lamenting the destruction of Jerusalem in 586 B.C., and its aftermath of ruin and exile. In spite of the mournful nature of most of the book, there is also the note of trust in God and hope for the future. These poems are used by the Jews in worship on the annual days of fasting and mourning which commemorate the national disaster of 586 B.C.

Outline of Contents

The Sorrows of Jerusalem

1 How lonely lies Jerusalem, once
    so full of people!
Once honored by the world, she
    is now like a widow;
The noblest of cities has fallen
    into slavery.

2 All night long she cries; tears run
    down her cheeks.
Of all her former friends, not
    one is left to comfort her.
Her allies have betrayed her and
    are all against her now.

3 Judah's people are helpless slaves,
    forced away from home.*a*
They live in other lands, with no
    place to call their own —
Surrounded by enemies, with no
    way to escape.

4 No one comes to the Temple now
    to worship on the holy days.
The young women who sang
    there suffer, and the priests
    can only groan.
The city gates stand empty, and
    Zion is in agony.

5 Her enemies succeeded; they hold
    her in their power.
The LORD has made her suffer
    for all her many sins;
Her children have been captured
    and taken away.

6 The splendor of Jerusalem is a
    thing of the past.
Her leaders are like deer that
    are weak from hunger,
Whose strength is almost gone
    as they flee from the
    hunters.

7 A lonely ruin now, Jerusalem
    recalls her ancient splendor.
When she fell to the enemy,
    there was no one to help her;
Her conquerors laughed at her
    downfall.

8 Her honor is gone; she is naked
    and held in contempt.
She groans and hides her face in
    shame.
Jerusalem made herself filthy
    with terrible sin.

9 Her uncleanness was easily seen,
    but she showed no concern for
    her fate.
Her downfall was terrible; no
    one can comfort her.
Her enemies have won, and she
    cries to the LORD for mercy.

10 The enemies robbed her of all her
    treasures.
She saw them enter the Temple
    itself,
Where the LORD had forbidden
    Gentiles to go.

11 Her people groan as they look for
    something to eat;
They exchange their treasures
    for food to keep themselves
    alive.
"Look at me, LORD," the city
    cries; "see me in my
    misery."

12 "Look at me!" she cries to
    everyone who passes by.*b*
"No one has ever had pain like
    mine,
Pain that the LORD brought on
    me in the time of his anger.

13 "He sent fire from above, a fire
    that burned inside me.
He set a trap for me and brought
    me to the ground.
Then he abandoned me and left
    me in constant pain.

14 "He took note of all my sins and
    tied them all together;
He hung them around my neck,
    and I grew weak beneath the
    weight.
The Lord gave me to my foes,
    and I was helpless against
    them.

15 "The Lord laughed at all my
    strongest soldiers;

---

*a are helpless ... home; or fled from home, from the misery of slavery.   b Look ... by; or May
this not happen to you that pass by; or Does this mean nothing to you that pass by?*

He sent an army to destroy my
young men.
He crushed my people like
grapes in a wine press.

16 "That is why my eyes are
overflowing with tears.
No one can comfort me; no one
can give me courage.
The enemy has conquered me;
my people have nothing left.

17 "I stretch out my hands, but no
one will help me.
The LORD has called enemies
against me from every side;
They treat me like some filthy
thing.

18 "But the LORD is just, for I have
disobeyed him.
Listen to me, people
everywhere; look at me in my
pain.
My young men and women have
been taken away captive.

19 "I called to my allies, but they
refused to help me.
The priests and the leaders died
in the city streets,
Looking for food to keep
themselves alive.

20 "Look, O LORD, at my agony, at the
anguish of my soul!
My heart is broken in sorrow for
my sins.
There is murder in the streets;
even indoors there is death.

21 "Listen c to my groans; there is no
one to comfort me.
My enemies are glad that you
brought disaster on me.
Bring d the day you promised;
make my enemies suffer as
I do.

22 "Condemn them for all their
wickedness;
Punish them as you punished me
for my sins.
I groan in misery, and I am sick
at heart."

The Lord's Punishment of Jerusalem

2 The Lord in his anger has covered
Zion with darkness.
Its heavenly splendor he has
turned into ruins.
On the day of his anger he
abandoned even his Temple.

2 The Lord destroyed without mercy
every village in Judah
And tore down the forts that
defended the land.
He brought disgrace on the
kingdom and its rulers.

3 In his fury he shattered the
strength of Israel;
He refused to help us when the
enemy came.
He raged against us like fire,
destroying everything.

4 He aimed his arrows at us like an
enemy;
He killed all those who were our
joy and delight.
Here in Jerusalem we felt his
burning anger.

5 Like an enemy, the Lord has
destroyed Israel;
He has left her forts and palaces
in ruins.
He has brought on the people of
Judah unending sorrow.

6 He smashed to pieces the Temple
where we worshiped him;
He has put an end to holy days
and Sabbaths.
King and priest alike have felt
the force of his anger.

7 The Lord rejected his altar and
deserted his holy Temple;
He allowed the enemy to tear
down its walls.
They shouted in victory where
once we had worshiped in joy.

8 The LORD was determined that the
walls of Zion should fall;
He measured them off to make
sure of total destruction.

c One ancient translation Listen; Hebrew They listened.   d One ancient translation Bring;
Hebrew You brought.

The towers and walls now lie in
ruins together.

9 The gates lie buried in rubble,
their bars smashed to pieces.
The king and the noblemen now
are in exile.
The Law is no longer taught,
and the prophets have no
visions from the LORD.

10 Jerusalem's old men sit on the
ground in silence,
With dust on their heads and
sackcloth on their bodies.
Young women bow their heads
to the ground.

11 My eyes are worn out with
weeping; my soul is in
anguish.
I am exhausted with grief at the
destruction of my people.
Children and babies are fainting
in the streets of the city.

12 Hungry and thirsty, they cry to
their mothers;
They fall in the streets as though
they were wounded,
And slowly die in their mothers'
arms.

13 O Jerusalem, beloved Jerusalem,
what can I say?
How can I comfort you? No one
has ever suffered like this.
Your disaster is boundless as the
ocean; there is no possible
hope.

14 Your prophets had nothing to tell
you but lies;
Their preaching deceived you by
never exposing your sin.
They made you think you did
not need to repent.

15 People passing by the city look at
you in scorn.
They shake their heads and
laugh at Jerusalem's ruins:
"Is this that lovely city? Is this
the pride of the world?"

16 All your enemies mock you and
glare at you with hate.
They curl their lips and sneer,
"We have destroyed it!
This is the day we have
waited for!"

17 The LORD has finally done what he
threatened to do:
He has destroyed us without
mercy, as he warned us
long ago.
He gave our enemies victory,
gave them joy at our
downfall.

18 O Jerusalem, let your very walls
cry out to the Lord!e
Let your tears flow like rivers
night and day;
Wear yourself out with weeping
and grief!

19 All through the night get up again
and again to cry out to the
Lord;
Pour out your heart and beg him
for mercy on your children —
Children starving to death on
every street corner!

20 Look, O LORD! Why are you
punishing us like this?
Women are eating the bodies of
the children they loved!
Priests and prophets are being
killed in the Temple itself!

21 Young and old alike lie dead in
the streets,
Young men and women, killed
by enemy swords.
You slaughtered them without
mercy on the day of your
anger.

22 You invited my enemies to hold a
carnival of terror all
around me,
And no one could escape on that
day of your anger.
They murdered my children,
whom I had raised and
loved.

e Probable text O Jerusalem . . . Lord; Hebrew Their hearts cried out to the Lord, O wall of
Jerusalem.

Punishment, Repentance, and Hope

3 I am one who knows what it is to be punished by God.
2 He drove me deeper and deeper into darkness
3 And beat me again and again with merciless blows.

4 He has left my flesh open and raw, and has broken my bones.
5 He has shut me in a prison of misery and anguish.
6 He has forced me to live in the stagnant darkness of death.

7 He has bound me in chains; I am a prisoner with no hope of escape.
8 I cry aloud for help, but God refuses to listen;
9 I stagger as I walk; stone walls block me wherever I turn.

10 He waited for me like a bear; he pounced on me like a lion.
11 He chased me off the road, tore me to pieces, and left me.
12 He drew his bow and made me the target for his arrows.

13 He shot his arrows deep into my body.
14 People laugh at me all day long; I am a joke to them all.
15 Bitter suffering is all he has given me for food and drink.

16 He rubbed my face in the ground and broke my teeth on rocks.
17 I have forgotten what health and peace and happiness are.
18 I do not have much longer to live; my hope in the LORD is gone.

19 The thought of my pain, my homelessness, is bitter poison.
20 I think of it constantly, and my spirit is depressed.
21 Yet hope returns when I remember this one thing:

22 The LORD's unfailing love and mercy still continue,
23 Fresh as the morning, as sure as the sunrise.
24 The LORD is all I have, and so in him I put my hope.

25 The LORD is good to everyone who trusts in him,
26 So it is best for us to wait in patience—to wait for him to save us—
27 And it is best to learn this patience in our youth.

28 When we suffer, we should sit alone in silent patience;
29 We should bow in submission, for there may still be hope.
30 Though beaten and insulted, we should accept it all.

31 The Lord is merciful and will not reject us forever.
32 He may bring us sorrow, but his love for us is sure and strong.
33 He takes no pleasure in causing us grief or pain.

34 The Lord knows when our spirits are crushed in prison;
35 He knows when we are denied the rights he gave us;
36 When justice is perverted in court, he knows.

37 The will of the Lord alone is always carried out.*f*
38 Good and evil alike take place at his command.
39 Why should we ever complain when we are punished for our sin?*g*

40 Let us examine our ways and turn back to the LORD.
41 Let us open our hearts to God in heaven and pray,
42 "We have sinned and rebelled, and you, O LORD, have not forgiven us.

43 "You pursued us and killed us; your mercy was hidden by your anger,
44 By a cloud of fury too thick for our prayers to get through.

f The will . . . out; *or* No one can make anything happen unless the Lord is willing.
g Why should . . . sin?; *or* Why should we complain about being punished for sin, as long as we are still alive?

45 You have made us the garbage
    dump of the world.

46 "We are insulted and mocked by
    all our enemies.
47 We have been through disaster
    and ruin; we live in danger
    and fear.
48 My eyes flow with rivers of tears
    at the destruction of my
    people.

49 "My tears will pour out in a
    ceaseless stream
50 Until the LORD looks down from
    heaven and sees us.
51 My heart is grieved when I see
    what has happened to the
    women of the city.

52 "I was trapped like a bird by
    enemies who had no cause to
    hate me.
53 They threw me alive into a pit
    and closed the opening with a
    stone.
54 Water began to close over me,
    and I thought death was near.

55 "From the bottom of the pit,
    O LORD, I cried out to you,
56 And when I begged you to listen
    to my cry, you heard.
57 You answered me and told me
    not to be afraid.

58 "You came to my rescue, Lord,
    and saved my life.
59 Judge in my favor; you know
    the wrongs done against me.
60 You know how my enemies hate
    me and how they plot
    against me.

61 "You have heard them insult me,
    O LORD; you know all their
    plots.
62 All day long they talk about me
    and make their plans.
63 From morning till night they
    make fun of me.

64 "Punish them for what they have
    done, O LORD;
65 Curse them and fill them with
    despair!

66 Hunt them down and wipe them
    off the earth!"

Jerusalem after Its Fall

4 Our glittering gold has grown dull;
    the stones of the Temple lie
    scattered in the streets.

2 Zion's young people were as
    precious to us as gold,
    but now they are treated like
    common clay pots.

3 Even a mother wolf will nurse her
    cubs,
    but my people are like ostriches,
    cruel to their young.

4 They let their babies die of hunger
    and thirst;
    children are begging for food
    that no one will give them.

5 People who once ate the finest
    foods die starving in the
    streets;
    those raised in luxury are
    pawing through garbage for
    food.

6 My people have been punished
    even more than the
    inhabitants of Sodom,
    which met a sudden downfall at
    the hands of God.

7 Our princes[h] were undefiled and
    pure as snow,
    vigorous and strong, glowing
    with health.

8 Now they lie unknown in the
    streets, their faces blackened
    in death;
    their skin, dry as wood, has
    shriveled on their bones.

9 Those who died in the war were
    better off than those who died
    later,
    who starved slowly to death,
    with no food to keep them
    alive.

10 The disaster that came to my
    people brought horror;

h princes; or Nazirites.

loving mothers boiled their own children for food.

11 The LORD turned loose the full force of his fury;
he lit a fire in Zion that burned it to the ground.

12 No one anywhere, not even rulers of foreign nations,
believed that any invader could enter Jerusalem's gates.

13 But it happened, because her prophets sinned and her priests were guilty
of causing the death of innocent people.

14 Her leaders wandered through the streets as though blind,
so stained with blood that no one would touch them.

15 "Get away!" people shouted. "You're defiled! Don't touch me!"
So they wandered from nation to nation, welcomed by no one.

16 The LORD had no more concern for them; he scattered them himself.
He showed no regard for our priests and leaders.

17 For help that never came, we looked until we could look no longer.
We kept waiting for help from a nation that had none to give.

18 The enemy was watching for us; we could not even walk in the streets.
Our days were over; the end had come.

19 Swifter than eagles swooping from the sky, they chased us down.
They tracked us down in the hills; they took us by surprise in the desert.

20 They captured the source of our life, the king the LORD had chosen,
the one we had trusted to protect us from every invader.

21 Laugh on, people of Edom and Uz; be glad while you can.
Your disaster is coming too; you too will stagger naked in shame.

22 Zion has paid for her sin; the LORD will not keep us in exile any longer.
But Edom, the LORD will punish you; he will expose your guilty acts.

A Prayer for Mercy

5 Remember, O LORD, what has happened to us.
Look at us, and see our disgrace.

2 Our property is in the hands of strangers;
foreigners are living in our homes.

3 Our fathers have been killed by the enemy,
and now our mothers are widows.

4 We must pay for the water we drink;
we must buy the wood we need for fuel.

5 Driven hard like donkeys or camels,
we are tired, but are allowed no rest.

6 To get food enough to stay alive, we went begging to Egypt and Assyria.

7 Our ancestors sinned, but now they are gone,
and we are suffering for their sins.

8 Our rulers are no better than slaves,
and no one can save us from their power.

9 Murderers roam through the countryside;

we risk our lives when we look for food.

10 Hunger has made us burn with fever
until our skin is as hot as an oven.

11 Our wives have been raped on Mount Zion itself;
in every Judean village our daughters have been forced to submit.

12 Our leaders have been taken and hanged;
our elders are shown no respect.

13 Our young men are forced to grind grain like slaves;
boys go staggering under heavy loads of wood.

14 The old people no longer sit at the city gate,
and the young people no longer make music.

15 Happiness has gone out of our lives;

grief has taken the place of our dances.

16 Nothing is left of all we were proud of.
We sinned, and now we are doomed.

17 We are sick at our very hearts
and can hardly see through our tears,

18 because Mount Zion lies lonely and deserted,
and wild jackals prowl through its ruins.

19 But you, O Lord, are king forever
and will rule to the end of time.

20 Why have you abandoned us so long?
Will you ever remember us again?

21 Bring us back to you, Lord! Bring us back!
Restore our ancient glory.

22 Or have you rejected us forever?
Is there no limit to your anger?

The Book of
EZEKIEL

Introduction

The prophet Ezekiel lived in exile in Babylon during the period before and after the fall of Jerusalem in 586 B.C. His message was addressed both to the exiles in Babylonia and to the people of Jerusalem. The Book of Ezekiel has six principal parts: 1) God's call to Ezekiel to be a prophet. 2) Warnings to the people about God's judgment on them and about the coming fall and destruction of Jerusalem. 3) Messages from the Lord regarding his judgment upon the various nations that oppressed and misled his people. 4) Comfort for Israel after the fall of Jerusalem and the promise of a brighter future. 5) The prophecy against Gog. 6) Ezekiel's picture of a restored Temple and nation.

Ezekiel was a man of deep faith and great imagination. Many of his insights came in the form of visions, and many of his messages were expressed in vivid symbolic actions. Ezekiel emphasized the need for inner renewal of the heart and spirit, and the responsibility of each individual for his own sins. He also proclaimed his hope for the renewal of the life of the nation. As a priest, as well as prophet, he had special interest in the Temple and in the need for holiness.

Outline of Contents

EZEKIEL'S FIRST VISION OF GOD
(1.1 – 7.27)

God's Throne

1 On the fifth day of the fourth month of the thirtieth year,ᵃ I, Ezekiel the priest, son of Buzi, was living with the Jewish exiles by the Chebar River in Babylonia. The sky opened, and I saw a vision of God. (2 It was the fifth year since King Jehoiachin had been taken into exile.) 3 There in Babylonia beside the Chebar River, I heard the LORD speak to me, and I felt his power.

4 I looked up and saw a windstorm coming from the north. Lightning was flashing from a huge cloud, and the sky around it was glowing. Where the lightning was flashing, something shone like bronze. 5 At the center of the storm I saw what looked like four living creatures in human form, 6 but each of them had four faces and four wings. 7 Their legs were straight, and they had hoofs like those of a bull. They shone like polished bronze. 8 In addition to their four faces and four wings, they each had four human hands, one under each wing. 9 Two wings of each creature were spread out so that the creatures formed a square, with their wing tips touching. When they moved, they moved as a group without turning their bodies.

10 Each living creature had four different faces: a human face in front, a lion's face at the right, a bull's face at the left, and an eagle's face at the back. 11 Two wingsᵇ of each creature were raised so that they touched the tips of the wings of the creatures next to it, and their other two wings were folded against their bodies. 12 Each creature faced all four directions, and so the group could go wherever they wished, without having to turn.

13 Amongᶜ the creatures there was something that looked like a blazing torch, constantly moving. The fire would blaze up and shoot out flashes of light-

---

ᵃ THIRTIETH YEAR: *It is not known to what year this refers.*   ᵇ *Some ancient translations* Two wings; *Hebrew* Their faces, their wings.   ᶜ *Some ancient translations* Among; *Hebrew* And the likeness of.

ning. 14The creatures themselves darted back and forth with the speed of lightning.

15As I was looking at the four creatures I saw four wheels touching the ground, one beside each of them.*d* 16All four wheels were alike; each one shone like a precious stone, and each had another wheel intersecting it at right angles, 17so that the wheels could move in any of the four directions. 18The rims of the wheels were covered with eyes.*e* 19Whenever the creatures moved, the wheels moved with them, and if the creatures rose up from the earth, so did the wheels. 20The creatures went wherever they wished, and the wheels did exactly what the creatures did, because the creatures controlled them. 21So every time the creatures moved or stopped or rose in the air, the wheels did exactly the same.

22Above the heads of the creatures there was something that looked like a dome made of dazzling crystal. 23There under the dome stood the creatures, each stretching out two wings toward the ones next to it and covering its body with the other two wings. 24I heard the noise their wings made in flight; it sounded like the roar of the sea, like the noise of a huge army, like the voice of Almighty God. When they stopped flying, they folded their wings, 25but there was still a sound coming from above the dome over their heads.

26Above the dome there was something that looked like a throne made of sapphire, and sitting on the throne was a figure that looked like a human being. 27The figure seemed to be shining like bronze in the middle of a fire. It shone all over with a bright light 28that had in it all the colors of the rainbow. This was the dazzling light which shows the presence of the LORD.

God Calls Ezekiel to Be a Prophet

When I saw this, I fell face downward on the ground. Then I heard a voice

2 1saying, "Mortal man, stand up. I want to talk to you." 2While the voice was speaking, God's spirit entered me and raised me to my feet, and I heard the voice continue, 3"Mortal man, I am sending you to the people of Israel. They have rebelled and turned against me and are still rebels, just as their ancestors were. 4They are stubborn and do not respect me, so I am sending you to tell them what I, the Sovereign LORD, am saying to them. 5Whether those rebels listen to you or not, they will know that a prophet has been among them.

6"But you, mortal man, must not be afraid of them or of anything they say. They will defy and despise you; it will be like living among scorpions. Still, don't be afraid of those rebels or of anything they say. 7You will tell them whatever I tell you to say, whether they listen or not. Remember what rebels they are.

8"Mortal man, listen to what I tell you. Don't be rebellious like them. Open your mouth and eat what I am going to give you." 9I saw a hand reaching out toward me, and it was holding a scroll. 10The hand unrolled the scroll, and I saw that there was writing on both sides—cries of grief were written there, and wails and groans.

3 God said, "Mortal man, eat this scroll; then go and speak to the people of Israel."

2So I opened my mouth, and he gave me the scroll to eat. 3He said, "Mortal man, eat this scroll that I give you; fill your stomach with it." I ate it, and it tasted as sweet as honey.

4Then God said, "Mortal man, go to the people of Israel and say to them whatever I tell you to say. 5I am not sending you to a nation that speaks a difficult foreign language, but to the Israelites. 6If I sent you to great nations that spoke difficult languages you didn't understand, they would listen to you. 7But none of the people of Israel will be willing to listen; they will not even listen to me. All of them are stubborn and defiant. 8Now I will make you as stubborn and as tough as they are. 9I will make you as firm as a rock, as hard as a diamond; don't be afraid of those rebels."

10God continued, "Mortal man, pay close attention and remember everything I tell you. 11Then go to the people of your nation who are in exile and tell them what I, the Sovereign LORD, am saying to you, whether they pay attention to you or not."

12Then God's spirit lifted me up, and I

---

d Some ancient translations them; Hebrew their faces.   *e Verse 18 in Hebrew is unclear.*

heard behind me the loud roar of a voice that said, "Praise the glory of the LORD in heaven above!" 13 I heard the wings of the creatures beating together in the air, and the noise of the wheels, as loud as an earthquake. 14 The power of the LORD came on me with great force, and as his spirit carried me off, I felt bitter and angry. 15 So I came to Tel Abib beside the Chebar River, where the exiles were living, and for seven days I stayed there, overcome by what I had seen and heard.

The LORD Appoints Ezekiel as a Lookout
(Ezekiel 33.1-9)

16 After the seven days had passed, the LORD spoke to me. 17 "Mortal man," he said, "I am making you a lookout for the nation of Israel. You will pass on to them the warnings I give you. 18 If I announce that someone evil is going to die but you do not warn him to change his ways so that he can save his life, he will die, still a sinner, but I will hold you responsible for his death. 19 If you do warn an evil man and he doesn't stop sinning, he will die, still a sinner, but your life will be spared.

20 "If someone truly good starts doing evil and I put him in a dangerous situation, he will die if you do not warn him. He will die because of his sins — I will not remember the good he did — and I will hold you responsible for his death. 21 If you do warn a good man not to sin and he listens to you and doesn't sin, he will stay alive, and your life will also be spared."

Ezekiel Will Be Unable to Talk

22 I felt the powerful presence of the LORD and heard him say to me, "Get up and go out into the valley. I will talk to you there."

23 So I went out into the valley, and there I saw the glory of the LORD, just as I had seen it beside the Chebar River. I fell face downward on the ground, 24 but God's spirit entered me and raised me to my feet. The LORD said to me, "Go home and shut yourself up in the house. 25 You will be tied with ropes, mortal man, and you will not be able to go out in public. 26 I will paralyze your tongue so that you

won't be able to warn these rebellious people. 27 Then, when I speak to you again and give you back the power of speech, you will tell them what I, the Sovereign LORD, am saying. Some of them will listen, but some will ignore you, for they are a nation of rebels."

Ezekiel Acts Out the Siege of Jerusalem

4 God said, "Mortal man, get a brick, put it in front of you, and scratch lines on it to represent the city of Jerusalem. 2 Then, to represent a siege, put trenches, earthworks, camps, and battering rams all around it. 3 Take an iron pan and set it up like a wall between you and the city. Face the city. It is under siege, and you are the one besieging it. This will be a sign to the nation of Israel.

4-5 "Then lie down on your left side, and I*f* will place on you the guilt of the nation of Israel. For 390 days you will stay there and suffer because of their guilt. I have sentenced you to one day for each year their punishment will last. 6 When you finish that, turn over on your right side and suffer for the guilt of Judah for forty days — one day for each year of their punishment.

7 "Fix your eyes on the siege of Jerusalem. Shake your fist at the city and prophesy against it. 8 I will tie you up so that you cannot turn from one side to the other until the siege is over.

9 "Now take some wheat, barley, beans, peas, millet, and spelt. Mix them all together and make bread. That is what you are to eat during the 390 days you are lying on your left side. 10 You will be allowed eight ounces of bread a day, and it will have to last until the next day. 11 You will also have a limited amount of water to drink, two cups a day. 12 You are to build a fire out of dried human excrement, bake bread on the fire, and eat it where everyone can see you."

13 The LORD said, "This represents the way the Israelites will have to eat food which the Law forbids,*g* when I scatter them to foreign countries."

14 But I replied, "No, Sovereign LORD! I have never defiled myself. From childhood on I have never eaten meat from

---

f Probable text I; *Hebrew* you.   *g* FOOD WHICH THE LAW FORBIDS: *The Law of Moses prohibited the eating of certain foods as being ritually unclean (see Lv 11).*

any animal that died a natural death or was killed by wild animals. I have never eaten any food considered unclean."

15 So God said, "Very well. I will let you use cow dung instead, and you can bake your bread on that."

16 And he added, "Mortal man, I am going to cut off the supply of bread for Jerusalem. The people there will be distressed and anxious as they measure out the food they eat and the water they drink. 17 They will run out of bread and water; they will be in despair, and they will waste away because of their sins."

Ezekiel Cuts His Hair

5 The LORD said, "Mortal man, take a sharp sword and use it to shave off your beard and all your hair. Then weigh the hair on scales and divide it into three parts. 2 Burn up a third of it in the city when the siege is over. Take another third and chop it up with your sword as you move around outside the city. Scatter the remaining third to the winds, and I will pursue it with my sword. 3 Keep back a few hairs and wrap them in the hem of your clothes. 4 Then take a few of them out again, throw them in the fire, and let them burn up. From them fire will spread to the whole nation of Israel."

5 The Sovereign LORD said, "Look at Jerusalem. I put her at the center of the world, with other countries all around her. 6 But Jerusalem rebelled against my commands and showed that she was more wicked than the other nations, more disobedient than the countries around her. Jerusalem rejected my commands and refused to keep my laws. 7 Now listen, Jerusalem, to what I, the Sovereign LORD, am saying. By not obeying my laws or keeping my commands, you have caused more trouble than the nations around you. You have followed the customs of other nations. 8 And so I, the Sovereign LORD, am telling you that I am your enemy. I will pass judgment on you where all the nations can see it. 9 Because of all the things you do that I hate, I will punish Jerusalem as I have never done before and will never do again. 10 As a result, parents in Jerusalem will eat their children, and children will eat their parents. I will punish you and scatter in every direction any who are left alive.

11 "Therefore, as I am the living God— this is the word of the Sovereign LORD— because you defiled my Temple with all the evil, disgusting things you did, I will cut you down without mercy. 12 A third of your people will die from sickness and hunger in the city; a third will be cut down by swords outside the city; and I will scatter the last third to the winds and pursue them with a sword.

13 "You will feel all the force of my anger and rage until I am satisfied. When all this happens, you will be convinced that I, the LORD, have spoken to you because I am outraged at your unfaithfulness. 14 Everyone from the nations around you who passes by will sneer at you and keep their distance.

15 "When I am angry and furious with you and punish you, all the nations around you will be terrified. They will look at you with disgust and make fun of you. 16 I will cut off your supply of food and let you starve. You[h] will feel the pains of hunger like sharp arrows sent to destroy you. 17 I will send hunger and wild animals to kill your children, and will send sickness, violence, and war to kill you. I, the LORD, have spoken."

The LORD Condemns Idolatry

6 The LORD spoke to me. 2 "Mortal man," he said, "look toward the mountains of Israel and give them my message. 3 Tell the mountains of Israel to hear the Sovereign LORD's word—to hear what I, the Sovereign LORD, am telling the mountains, the hills, the gorges, and the valleys: I will send a sword to destroy the places where people worship idols. 4 The altars will be torn down and the incense altars broken. All the people there will be killed in front of their idols. 5 I will scatter the corpses of the people of Israel; I will scatter their bones all around the altars. 6 All the cities of Israel will be destroyed, so that all their altars and their idols will be smashed to pieces, their incense altars will be shattered, and everything they made will disappear. 7 People will be killed everywhere, and those who survive will acknowledge that I am the LORD.

8 "I will let some escape the slaughter

h Probable text You; Hebrew They.

and be scattered among the nations, [9] where they will live in exile. There they will remember me and know that I have punished them and disgraced them,[i] because their faithless hearts deserted me and they preferred idols to me. And they will be disgusted with themselves because of the evil and degrading things they have done. [10] They will know that I am the LORD and that my warnings were not empty threats."

[11] The Sovereign LORD said, "Wring your hands! Stamp your feet! Cry in sorrow because of all the evil, disgusting things the Israelites have done. They are going to die in war or of starvation or disease. [12] Those far away will get sick and die; those nearby will be killed in war; those who survive will starve to death. They will feel all the force of my anger. [13] Corpses will be scattered among the idols and around the altars, scattered on every high hill, on the top of every mountain, under every green tree and every large oak, in every place where they burned sacrifices to their idols. Then everyone will know that I am the LORD. [14] Yes, I will reach out and destroy their country. I will make it a wasteland from the southern desert to the city of Riblah in the north, not sparing any place where the Israelites live. Then everyone will know that I am the LORD."

The End Is Near for Israel

7 The LORD spoke to me. [2] "Mortal man," he said, "this is what I, the Sovereign LORD, am saying to the land of Israel: This is the end for the whole land! [3] "Israel, the end has come. You will feel my anger, because I am judging you for what you have done. I will pay you back for all your disgusting conduct. [4] I will not spare you or show you any mercy. I am going to punish you for the disgusting things you have done, so that you will know that I am the LORD."

[5] This is what the Sovereign LORD is saying: "One disaster after another is coming on you. [6] It's all over. This is the end. You are finished. [7] The end is coming for you people who live in the land. The time is near when there will be no more celebrations at the mountain shrines, only confusion.[j]

[8] "Very soon now you will feel all the force of my anger. I am judging you for what you have done, and I will pay you back for all your disgusting conduct. [9] I will not spare you or show you any mercy. I am going to punish you for the disgusting things you have done, so that you will know that I am the LORD and that I am the one who punishes you."

[10] The day of disaster is coming. Violence is flourishing. Pride is at its height.[k] [11] Violence produces more wickedness. Nothing of theirs will remain, nothing of their wealth, their splendor, or their glory.

[12] The time is coming. The day is near when buying and selling will have no more meaning, because God's punishment will fall on everyone alike. [13] No merchants will live long enough to get back what they have lost, because God's anger is on everyone. Those who are evil cannot survive.[l] [14] The trumpet blows, and everyone gets ready. But no one goes off to war, for God's anger will fall on everyone alike.

Punishment for Israel's Sins

[15] There is fighting in the streets, and sickness and hunger in the houses. Anyone who is out in the country will die in the fighting, and anyone in the city will be a victim of sickness and hunger. [16] Some will escape to the mountains like doves frightened from the valleys. All of them will moan over their sins.[m] [17] Everyone's hands will be weak, and their knees will shake. [18] They will put on sackcloth and they will tremble all over. Their heads will be shaved, and they will all be disgraced. [19] They will throw their gold and silver away in the streets like garbage, because neither silver nor gold can save them when the LORD pours out his fury. They cannot use it to satisfy their desires or fill their stomachs. Gold and silver led them into sin. [20] Once they were proud of their beautiful jewels, but they used them to make disgusting idols. That is why the LORD has made their wealth repulsive to them.

[21] "I will let foreigners rob them," says

---

[i] *Some ancient translations* disgraced them; *Hebrew* I am disgraced.
[j] *Probable text* celebrations . . . confusion; *Hebrew unclear.* [k] *Probable text* Pride is at its height; *Hebrew unclear.* [l] *Verse 13 in Hebrew is unclear.* [m] *Verse 16 in Hebrew is unclear.*

the Lord, "and lawbreakers will take all their wealth and defile it. 22 I will not interfere when my treasured Temple is profaned, when robbers break into it and defile it.

23 "Everything is in confusion[n] — the land is full of murders and the cities are full of violence. 24 I will bring the most evil nations here and let them have your homes. Your strongest men will lose their confidence when I let the nations profane the places where you worship. 25 Despair is coming. You will look for peace and never find it. 26 One disaster will follow another, and a steady stream of bad news will pour in. You will beg the prophets to reveal what they foresee. The priests will have nothing to teach the people, and the elders will have no advice to give. 27 The king will mourn, the prince will give up hope, and the people will shake with fear. I will punish you for all you have done, and will judge you in the same way as you have judged others. This will show you that I am the Lord."

EZEKIEL'S SECOND VISION OF GOD (8.1 – 10.22)

Idolatry in Jerusalem

8 On the fifth day of the sixth month of the sixth year of our exile, the leaders of the exiles from Judah were sitting in my house with me. Suddenly the power of the Sovereign Lord came on me. 2 I looked up and saw a vision of a fiery human form. From the waist down his body looked like fire, and from the waist up he was shining like polished bronze. 3 He reached out what seemed to be a hand and grabbed me by the hair. Then in this vision God's spirit lifted me high in the air and took me to Jerusalem. He took me to the inner entrance of the north gate of the Temple, where there was an idol that was an outrage to God.

4 There I saw the dazzling light that shows the presence of Israel's God, just as I had seen it when I was by the Chebar River. 5 God said to me, "Mortal man, look toward the north." I looked, and there near the altar by the entrance of

the gateway I saw the idol that was an outrage to God.

6 God said to me, "Mortal man, do you see what is happening? Look at the disgusting things the people of Israel are doing here, driving me farther and farther away from my holy place. You will see even more disgraceful things than this."

7 He took me to the entrance of the outer courtyard and showed me a hole in the wall. 8 He said, "Mortal man, break through the wall here." I broke through it and found a door. 9 He told me, "Go in and look at the evil, disgusting things they are doing there." 10 So I went in and looked. The walls were covered with drawings of snakes and other unclean animals,[o] and of the other things which the Israelites were worshiping. 11 Seventy Israelite leaders were there, including Jaazaniah son of Shaphan. Each one was holding an incense burner, and smoke was rising from the incense. 12 God asked me, "Mortal man, do you see what the Israelite leaders are doing in secret? They are all worshiping in a room full of images. Their excuse is: 'The Lord doesn't see us! He has abandoned the country.'"

13 Then the Lord said to me, "You are going to see them do even more disgusting things than that." 14 So he took me to the north gate of the Temple and showed me women weeping over the death of the god Tammuz.[p]

15 He asked, "Mortal man, do you see that? You will see even more disgusting things." 16 So he took me to the inner courtyard of the Temple. There near the entrance of the sanctuary, between the altar and the porch, were about twenty-five men. They had turned their backs to the sanctuary and were bowing low toward the east, worshiping the rising sun.

17 The Lord said to me, "Mortal man, do you see that? These people of Judah are not satisfied with merely doing all the disgusting things you have seen here and with spreading violence throughout the country. No, they must come and do them right here in the Temple and make me even more angry. Look how they

---

[n] One ancient translation Everything is in confusion; *Hebrew unclear.*   [o] UNCLEAN ANIMALS: *The Law of Moses prohibited the eating of certain animals as being ritually unclean (see 4.13; Lv 11).*   [p] TAMMUZ: *A god who was thought to die when vegetation died and to come to life the next year. Women would mourn his ritual death.*

insult me in the most offensive way possible!*q* 18They will feel all the force of my anger. I will not spare them or show them any mercy. They will shout prayers to me as loud as they can, but I will not listen to them."

Jerusalem Is Punished

9 Then I heard God shout, "Come here, you men who are going to punish the city. Bring your weapons with you." 2At once six men came from the outer north gate of the Temple, each one carrying a weapon. With them was a man dressed in linen clothes, carrying something to write with. They all came and stood by the bronze altar.

3Then the dazzling light of the presence of the God of Israel rose up from the winged creatures*r* where it had been, and moved to the entrance of the Temple. The LORD called to the man dressed in linen, 4"Go through the whole city of Jerusalem and put a mark on the forehead of everyone who is distressed and troubled because of all the disgusting things being done in the city."

5And I heard God say to the other men, "Follow him through the city and kill. Spare no one; have mercy on no one. 6Kill the old men, young men, young women, mothers, and children. But don't touch anyone who has the mark on his forehead. Start here at my Temple." So they began with the leaders who were standing there at the Temple.

7God said to them, "Defile the Temple. Fill its courtyards with corpses. Get to work!" So they began to kill the people in the city.*s*

8While the killing was going on, I was there alone. I threw myself face downward on the ground and shouted, "Sovereign LORD, are you so angry with Jerusalem that you are going to kill everyone left in Israel?"

9God answered, "The people of Israel and Judah are guilty of terrible sins. They have committed murder all over the land and have filled Jerusalem with crime. They say that I, the LORD, have abandoned their country and that I don't see them. 10But I will not have pity on them; I will do to them what they have done to others."

11Then the man wearing linen clothes returned and reported to the LORD, "I have carried out your orders."

The Glory of the LORD Leaves the Temple

10 I looked at the dome over the heads of the living creatures*t* and above them was something that seemed to be a throne made of sapphire. 2God said to the man wearing linen clothes, "Go between the wheels under the creatures and fill your hands with burning coals. Then scatter the coals over the city."

I watched him go. 3The creatures were standing to the south of the Temple when he went in, and a cloud filled the inner courtyard. 4The dazzling light of the LORD's presence rose up from the creatures and moved to the entrance of the Temple. Then the cloud filled the Temple, and the courtyard was blazing with the light. 5The noise made by the creatures' wings was heard even in the outer courtyard. It sounded like the voice of Almighty God.

6When the LORD commanded the man wearing linen clothes to take some fire from between the wheels that were under the creatures, the man went in and stood by one of the wheels. 7One of the creatures reached his hand into the fire that was there among them, picked up some coals, and put them in the hands of the man in linen. The man took the coals and left.

8I saw that each creature had what looked like a human hand under each of its wings. 9-10I also saw that there were four wheels, all alike, one beside each creature. The wheels shone like precious stones, and each one had another wheel which intersected it at right angles. 11When the creatures moved, they could go in any direction without turning. They all moved together in the direction they wanted to go, without having to turn around. 12Their bodies, backs, hands, wings, and wheels were covered with eyes. 13I heard a voice calling out, "Whirling wheels."

14Each creature had four faces. The first was the face of a bull, the second a

q IN THE MOST OFFENSIVE WAY POSSIBLE: *A reference to a pagan rite of putting a branch to the nose.* r WINGED CREATURES: *See 1.5-12.* s work!" So they ... city.; *or* work! Go on and start killing the people in the city!" t LIVING CREATURES: *See 1.5-12.*

human face, the third the face of a lion, and the fourth the face of an eagle. 15 (They were the same creatures that I had seen by the Chebar River.) When the creatures rose in the air 16 and moved, the wheels went with them. Whenever they spread their wings to fly, the wheels still went with them. 17 When the creatures stopped, the wheels stopped; and when the creatures flew, the wheels went with them, because the creatures controlled them.

18 Then the dazzling light of the Lord's presence left the entrance of the Temple and moved to a place above the creatures. 19 They spread their wings and flew up from the earth while I was watching, and the wheels went with them. They paused at the east gate of the Temple, and the dazzling light was over them. 20 I recognized them as the same creatures which I had seen beneath the God of Israel at the Chebar River.

21 Each of them had four faces, four wings, and what looked like a human hand under each wing. 22 Their faces looked exactly like the faces u I had seen by the Chebar River. Each creature moved straight ahead.

Jerusalem Is Condemned

11 God's spirit lifted me up and took me to the east gate of the Temple. There near the gate I saw twenty-five men, including Jaazaniah son of Azzur and Pelatiah son of Benaiah, two leaders of the nation.

2 God said to me, "Mortal man, these men make evil plans and give bad advice in this city. 3 They say, 'We will soon be building houses again. v The city is like a cooking pot, and we are like the meat in it, but at least it protects us from the fire.' 4 Now then, denounce them, mortal man."

5 The spirit of the Lord took control of me, and the Lord told me to give the people this message: "People of Israel, I know what you are saying and what you are planning. 6 You have murdered so many people here in the city that the streets are full of corpses.

7 "So this is what I, the Sovereign Lord, am saying to you. This city is a cooking pot all right, but what is the meat? The corpses of those you have killed! You will not be here—I will throw you out of the city! 8 Are you afraid of swords? I will bring soldiers with swords to attack you. 9 I will take you out of the city and hand you over to foreigners. I have sentenced you to death, 10 and you will be killed in battle in your own country. Then everyone will know that I am the Lord. 11 This city will not protect you the way a pot protects the meat in it. I will punish you wherever you may be in the land of Israel. 12 You will know that I am the Lord and that while you were keeping the laws of the neighboring nations, you were breaking my laws and disobeying my commands."

13 While I was prophesying, Pelatiah dropped dead. I threw myself face downward on the ground and shouted, "No, Sovereign Lord! Are you going to kill everyone left in Israel?"

God's Promise to the Exiles

14 The Lord spoke to me. 15 "Mortal man," he said, "the people who live in Jerusalem are talking about you and those of your nation who are in exile. They say, 'The exiles are too far away to worship the Lord. He has given us possession of the land.'

16 "Now tell your fellow exiles what I am saying. I am the one who sent them to live in far-off nations and scattered them in other countries. Yet, for the time being I will be present with them in the lands where they have gone.

17 "So tell them what I, the Sovereign Lord, am saying. I will gather them out of the countries where I scattered them, and will give the land of Israel back to them. 18 When they return, they are to get rid of all the filthy, disgusting idols they find. 19 I will give them a new heart and a new mind. I will take away their stubborn heart of stone and will give them an obedient heart. 20 Then they will keep my laws and faithfully obey all my commands. They will be my people, and I will be their God. 21 But I will punish the people who love to worship filthy, disgusting idols. I will punish them for what they have done." The Sovereign Lord has spoken.

---

u *Probable text* the faces; *Hebrew* the faces and them.   v We will . . . again; *or* We won't be building houses any time soon.

God's Glory Leaves Jerusalem

22 The living creatures began to fly, and the wheels went with them. The dazzling light of the presence of the God of Israel was over them. 23 Then the dazzling light left the city and moved to the mountain east of it. 24 In the vision the spirit of God lifted me up and brought me back to the exiles in Babylonia. Then the vision faded, 25 and I told the exiles everything that the LORD had shown me.

The Prophet as a Refugee

12 The LORD spoke to me. 2 "Mortal man," he said, "you are living among rebellious people. They have eyes, but they see nothing; they have ears, but they hear nothing, because they are rebellious.

3 "Now, mortal man, pack a bundle just as a refugee would and start out before nightfall. Let everyone see you leaving and going to another place. Maybe those rebels will notice you.w 4 While it is still daylight, pack your bundle for exile, so that they can see you, and then let them watch you leave in the evening as if you were going into exile. 5 While they are watching, break a hole through the wall of your house and take your pack out through it. 6 Let them watch you putting your pack on your shoulder and going out into the dark with your eyes covered, so that you can't see where you are going. What you do will be a warning to the Israelites."

7 I did what the LORD told me to do. That day I packed a bundle as a refugee would, and that evening as it was getting dark I dug a hole in the wall with my hands and went out. While everyone watched, I put the pack on my shoulder and left.

8 The next morning the LORD spoke to me. 9 "Mortal man," he said, "now that those Israelite rebels are asking you what you're doing, 10 tell them what I, the Sovereign LORD, am saying to them. This message is for the prince ruling in Jerusalem and for all the people who live there. 11 Tell them that what you have done is a sign of what will happen to them—they will be refugees and captives. 12 The prince who is ruling them will shoulder his pack in the dark and escape through a hole that they dig for him in the wall. He will cover his eyes and not see where he is going. 13 But I will spread out my net and trap him in it. Then I will take him to the city of Babylon, where he will die without having seen it. 14 I will scatter in every direction all the members of his court and his advisers and bodyguards, and people will search for them to kill them.

15 "When I scatter them among the other nations and in foreign countries, they will know that I am the LORD. 16 I will let a few of them survive the war, the famine, and the diseases, so that there among the nations they will realize how disgusting their actions have been and will acknowledge that I am the LORD."

The Sign of the Trembling Prophet

17 The LORD spoke to me. 18 "Mortal man," he said, "tremble when you eat, and shake with fear when you drink. 19 Tell the whole nation that this is the message of the Sovereign LORD to the people of Jerusalem who are still living in their land: They will tremble when they eat and shake with fear when they drink. Their land will be stripped bare, because everyone who lives there is lawless. 20 Cities that are now full of people will be destroyed, and the country will be made a wilderness. Then they will know that I am the LORD."

A Popular Proverb and an Unpopular Message

21 The LORD spoke to me. 22 "Mortal man," he said, "why do the people of Israel repeat this proverb: 'Time goes by, and predictions come to nothing'? 23 Now tell them what I, the Sovereign LORD, have to say about that. I will put an end to that proverb. It won't be repeated in Israel any more. Tell them instead: The time has come, and the predictions are coming true!

24 "Among the people of Israel there will be no more false visions or misleading prophecies. 25 I, the LORD, will speak to them, and what I say will be done. There will be no more delay. In your own lifetime, you rebels, I will do what I have warned you I would do. I have spoken," says the Sovereign LORD.

26 The LORD said to me, 27 "Mortal man,

w Maybe those . . . you; or Maybe they will then realize that they are rebels.

the Israelites think that your visions and prophecies are about the distant future. 28 So tell them that I, the Sovereign LORD, am saying: There will be no more delay. What I have said will be done. I, the Sovereign LORD, have spoken!"

Prophecy against False Male Prophets

13 The LORD spoke to me. 2 "Mortal man," he said, "denounce the prophets of Israel who make up their own prophecies. Tell them to listen to the word of the LORD."

3 This is what the Sovereign LORD says: "These foolish prophets are doomed! They provide their own inspiration and invent their own visions. 4 People of Israel, your prophets are as useless as foxes living among the ruins of a city. 5 They don't guard the places where the walls have crumbled, nor do they rebuild the walls, and so Israel cannot be defended when war comes on the day of the LORD. 6 Their visions are false, and their predictions are lies. They claim that they are speaking my message, but I have not sent them. Yet they expect their words to come true! 7 I tell them: Those visions you see are false, and the predictions you make are lies. You say that they are my words, but I haven't spoken to you!"

8 So the Sovereign LORD says to them, "Your words are false, and your visions are lies. I am against you. 9 I am about to punish you prophets who have false visions and make misleading predictions. You will not be there when my people gather to make decisions; your names will not be included in the list of the citizens of Israel; you will never return to your land. Then you will know that I am the Sovereign LORD.

10 "The prophets mislead my people by saying that all is well. All is certainly not well! My people have put up a wall of loose stones, and then the prophets have come and covered it with whitewash. 11 Tell the prophets that their wall is going to fall down. I will send a pouring rain. Hailstones will fall on it, and a strong wind will blow against it. 12 The wall will collapse, and everyone will ask you what good the whitewash did."

13 Now this is what the Sovereign LORD says: "In my anger I will send a strong wind, pouring rain, and hailstones to destroy the wall. 14 I intend to break down the wall they whitewashed, to shatter it, and to leave the foundation stones bare. It will collapse and kill you all. Then everyone will know that I am the LORD.

15 "The wall and those who covered it with whitewash will feel the force of my anger. Then I will tell you that the wall is gone and so are those who whitewashed it — 16 those prophets who assured Jerusalem that all was well, when all was not well!" The Sovereign LORD has spoken.

Prophecy against False Female Prophets

17 The LORD said, "Now, mortal man, look at the women among your people who make up predictions. Denounce them 18 and tell them what the Sovereign LORD is saying to them:

"You women are doomed! You sew magic wristbands for everyone and make magic scarves for everyone to wear on their heads, so that they can have power over other people's lives. You want to possess the power of life and death over my people and to use it for your own benefit. 19 You dishonor me in front of my people in order to get a few handfuls of barley and a few pieces of bread. You kill people who don't deserve to die, and you keep people alive who don't deserve to live. So you tell lies to my people, and they believe you."

20 Now this is what the Sovereign LORD says: "I hate the wristbands that you use in your attempt to control life and death. I will rip them off your arms and set free the people that you were controlling. x 21 I will rip off your scarves and let my people escape from your power once and for all. Then you will know that I am the LORD.

22 "By your lies you discourage good people, whom I do not wish to hurt. You prevent evil people from giving up evil and saving their lives. 23 So now your false visions and misleading predictions are over. I am rescuing my people from your power, so that you will know that I am the LORD."

x In verse 20 in Hebrew a word occurs twice, the meaning of which is unclear.

God Condemns Idolatry

14 Some of the leaders of the Israelites came to consult me about the Lord's will. 2 Then the Lord spoke to me. 3 "Mortal man," he said, "these men have given their hearts to idols and are letting idols lead them into sin. Do they think I will give them an answer?

4 "Now speak to them and tell them what I, the Sovereign Lord, am saying to them: Each of you Israelites who have given your heart to idols and let them lead you into sin and who then come to consult a prophet, will get an answer from me — the answer that your many idols deserve! 5 All those idols have turned the Israelites away from me, but by my answer I hope to win back their loyalty.

6 "Now then, tell the Israelites what I, the Sovereign Lord, am saying: Turn back and leave your disgusting idols.

7 "Whenever one of you Israelites or one of you foreigners who live in the Israelite community turn away from me and worship idols, and then go to consult a prophet, I, the Lord, will give you your answer! 8 I will oppose you. I will make an example of you. I will remove you from the community of my people, so that all of you will know that I am the Lord.

9 "If any prophets are deceived into giving a false answer, it is because I, the Lord, have deceived them. I will remove them from the people of Israel. 10 Both prophets and anyone who consults them will get the same punishment. 11 I will do this to keep the Israelites from deserting me and defiling themselves by their sins. They are to be my people, and I will be their God." The Sovereign Lord has spoken.

Noah, Danel, and Job

12 The Lord spoke to me. 13 "Mortal man," he said, "if a country sins and is unfaithful to me, I will reach out and destroy its supply of food. I will send a famine and kill people and animals alike. 14 Even if those three men, Noah, Danel,y and Job, were living there, their goodness would save only their own lives." The Sovereign Lord has spoken.

15 "Or I might send wild animals to kill the people, making the land so dangerous that no one could travel through it, 16 and even if those three men lived there — as surely as I, the Sovereign Lord, am the living God — they would not be able to save even their own children. They would save only their own lives, and the land would become a wilderness.

17 "Or I might bring war on that country and send destructive weapons to wipe out people and animals alike, 18 and even if those three men lived there — as surely as I, the Sovereign Lord, am the living God — they would not be able to save even their children, but only their own lives.

19 "If I send an epidemic on that country and in my anger take many lives, killing people and animals, 20 even if Noah, Danel, and Job lived there — as surely as I, the Sovereign Lord, am the living God — they would not be able to save even their own children. Their goodness would save only their own lives."

21 This is what the Sovereign Lord is saying: "I will send my four worst punishments on Jerusalem — war, famine, wild animals, and disease — to destroy people and animals alike. 22 If some survive and save their children, look at them when they come to you. See how evil they are, and be convinced that the punishment I am bringing on Jerusalem is justified; 23 then you will know that there was good reason for everything I did." The Sovereign Lord has spoken.

A Parable about a Vine

15 The Lord spoke to me. 2 "Mortal man," he said, "how does a vine compare with a tree? What good is a branch of a grapevine compared with the trees of the forest? 3 Can you use it to make anything? Can you even make a peg out of it to hang things on? 4 It is only good for building a fire. And when the ends are burned up and the middle is charred, can you make anything out of it? 5 It was useless even before it was burned. Now that the fire has burned it and charred it, it is even more useless."

6 Now this is what the Sovereign Lord is saying: "Just as a vine is taken from the forest and burned, so I will take the people who live in Jerusalem 7 and will

y Danel; or Daniel (see 28.3), an ancient hero, known for his righteous life.

punish them. They have escaped one fire, but now fire will burn them up. When I punish them, you will know that I am the LORD. ⁸They have been unfaithful to me, and so I will make the country a wilderness." The Sovereign LORD has spoken.

Jerusalem the Unfaithful

16 The LORD spoke to me again. ²"Mortal man," he said, "point out to Jerusalem what disgusting things she has done. ³Tell Jerusalem what the Sovereign LORD is saying to her:

"You were born in the land of Canaan. Your father was an Amorite, and your mother was a Hittite.ᶻ ⁴When you were born, no one cut your umbilical cord or washed youᵃ or rubbed you with salt or wrapped you in cloths. ⁵No one took enough pity on you to do any of these things for you. When you were born, no one loved you. You were thrown out in an open field.

⁶"Then I passed by and saw you squirming in your own blood. You were covered with blood, but I wouldn't let you die. ⁷I made you grow like a healthy plant. You grew strong and tall and became a young woman.ᵇ Your breasts were well-formed, and your hair had grown, but you were naked.

⁸"As I passed by again, I saw that the time had come for you to fall in love. I covered your naked body with my coat and promised to love you. Yes, I made a marriage covenant with you, and you became mine." This is what the Sovereign LORD says.

⁹"Then I took water and washed the blood off you. I rubbed olive oil on your skin. ¹⁰I dressed you in embroidered gowns and gave you shoes of the best leather, a linen headband, and a silk cloak. ¹¹I put jewels on you—bracelets and necklaces. ¹²I gave you a nose ring and earrings and a beautiful crown to wear. ¹³You had ornaments of gold and silver, and you always wore clothes of embroidered linen and silk. You ate bread made from the best flour, and had honey and olive oil to eat. Your beauty was dazzling, and you became a queen. ¹⁴You became famous in every nation for your perfect beauty, because I was the one who made you so lovely." This is what the Sovereign LORD says.

¹⁵"But you took advantage of your beauty and fame to sleep with everyone who came along.ᶜ ¹⁶You used some of your clothes to decorate your places of worship, and just like a prostitute,ᵈ you gave yourself to everyone. ¹⁷You took the silver and gold jewelry that I had given you, used it to make male images, and committed adultery with them. ¹⁸You took the embroidered clothes I gave you and put them on the images, and you offered to the images the olive oil and incense I had given you. ¹⁹I gave you food—the best flour, olive oil, and honey—but you offered it as a sacrifice to win the favor of idols." This is what the Sovereign LORD says.

²⁰"Then you took the sons and the daughters you had borne me and offered them as sacrifices to idols. Wasn't it bad enough to be unfaithful to me, ²¹without taking my children and sacrificing them to idols? ²²During your disgusting life as a prostitute you never once remembered your childhood—when you were naked, squirming in your own blood."

Jerusalem's Life as a Prostitute

²³The Sovereign LORD said, "You are doomed! Doomed! You did all that evil, and then ²⁴by the side of every road you built places to worship idols and practice prostitution. ²⁵You dragged your beauty through the mud. You offered yourself to everyone who came by, and you were more of a prostitute every day. ²⁶You let your lustful neighbors, the Egyptians, go to bed with you, and used your prostitution to make me angry.

²⁷"Now I have raised my hand to punish you and to take away your share of my blessing. I have handed you over to the Philistines, who hate you and are disgusted with your immoral actions.

²⁸"Because you were not satisfied by the others, you went running after the Assyrians. You were their prostitute, but they didn't satisfy you either. ²⁹You were also a prostitute for the

---

ᶻ AMORITE . . . HITTITE: *The Israelites regarded these people as immoral and idolatrous.*
ᵃ *Hebrew has an additional word, the meaning of which is unclear.*   ᵇ *Probable text* young woman; *Hebrew unclear.*   ᶜ *Hebrew has two additional words, the meaning of which is unclear.*   ᵈ *Hebrew has four additional words, the meaning of which is unclear.*

Babylonians, that nation of merchants, but they didn't satisfy you either."

30 This *e* is what the Sovereign LORD is saying: "You have done all this like a shameless prostitute. 31 On every street you built places to worship idols and practice prostitution. But you are not out for money like a common prostitute. 32 You are like a woman who commits adultery with strangers instead of loving her husband. 33 A prostitute is paid, but you gave presents to all your lovers and bribed them to come from everywhere to sleep with you. 34 You are a special kind of prostitute. No one forced you to become one. You didn't get paid; you paid them! Yes, you are different."

God's Judgment on Jerusalem

35 Now then, Jerusalem, you whore! Hear what the LORD is saying.

36 This is what the Sovereign LORD says: "You stripped off your clothes, and like a prostitute, you gave yourself to your lovers and to all your disgusting idols, and you killed your children as sacrifices to idols. 37 Because of this I will bring all your former lovers together—the ones you liked and the ones you hated. I will bring them around you in a circle, and then I will strip off your clothes and let them see you naked. 38 I will condemn you for adultery and murder, and in my anger and fury I will punish you with death. 39 I will put you in their power, and they will tear down the places where you engage in prostitution and worship idols. They will take away your clothes and jewels and leave you completely naked.

40 "They will stir up a crowd to stone you, and they will cut you to pieces with their swords. 41 They will burn your houses down and let crowds of women see your punishment. I will make you stop being a prostitute and make you stop giving gifts to your lovers. 42 Then my anger will be over, and I will be calm. I will not be angry or jealous any more. 43 You have forgotten how I treated you when you were young, and you have made me angry by all the things you did. That is why I have made you pay for them all. Why did you add sexual immorality to all the other disgusting things

you did?" The Sovereign LORD has spoken.

Like Mother, Like Daughter

44 The LORD said, "People will use this proverb about you, Jerusalem: 'Like mother, like daughter.' 45 You really are your mother's daughter. She detested her husband and her children. You are like your sisters, who hated their husbands and their children. You and your sister cities had a Hittite mother and an Amorite *f* father.

46 "Your older sister, with her villages, is Samaria, in the north. Your younger sister, with her villages, is Sodom, in the south. 47 Were you satisfied to follow in their footsteps and copy their disgusting actions? No, in only a little while you were acting worse than they were in everything you did.

48 "As surely as I am the living God," the Sovereign LORD says, "your sister Sodom and her villages never did the evil that you and your villages have done. 49 She and her daughters were proud because they had plenty to eat and lived in peace and quiet, but they did not take care of the poor and the underprivileged. 50 They were proud and stubborn and did the things that I hate, so I destroyed them, as you well know.

51 "Samaria did not sin half as much as you have. You have acted more disgustingly than she ever did. Your corruption makes your sisters look innocent by comparison. 52 And now you will have to endure your disgrace. Your sins are so much worse than those of your sisters that they look innocent beside you. Now blush and bear your shame, because you make your sisters look pure."

Sodom and Samaria Will Be Restored

53 The LORD said to Jerusalem, "I will make them prosperous again—Sodom and her villages and Samaria and her villages. Yes, I will make you prosperous too. 54 You will be ashamed of yourself, and your disgrace will show your sisters how well-off they are. 55 They will become prosperous again, and you and your villages will also be restored. 56 Didn't you joke about Sodom in those

---

e Verse 30 in Hebrew begins with three words, the meaning of which is unclear. f HITTITE ...
AMORITE: See 16.3.

days when you were proud [57] and before the evil you did had been exposed? Now you are just like her — a joke to the Edomites, the Philistines, and your other neighbors who hate you. [58] You must suffer for the obscene, disgusting things you have done." The LORD has spoken.

A Covenant That Lasts Forever

[59] The Sovereign LORD says, "I will treat you the way you deserve, because you ignored your promises and broke the covenant. [60] But I will honor the covenant I made with you when you were young, and I will make a covenant with you that will last forever. [61] You will remember how you have acted, and be ashamed of it when you get your older sister and your younger sister back. I will let them be like daughters to you, even though this was not part of my covenant with you. [62] I will renew my covenant with you, and you will know that I am the LORD. [63] I will forgive all the wrongs you have done, but you will remember them and be too ashamed to open your mouth." The Sovereign LORD has spoken.

The Parable of the Eagles and the Vine

17 The LORD spoke to me. [2] "Mortal man," he said, "tell the Israelites a parable [3] to let them know what I, the Sovereign LORD, am saying to them: There was a giant eagle with beautiful feathers and huge wings, spread wide. He flew to the Lebanon Mountains and broke off the top of a cedar tree, [4] which he carried to a land of commerce and placed in a city of merchants. [5] Then he took a young plant from the land of Israel and planted it in a fertile field, [g] where there was always water to make it grow. [6] The plant sprouted and became a low, wide-spreading grapevine. The branches grew upward toward the eagle, and the roots grew deep. The vine was covered with branches and leaves.

[7] "There was another giant eagle with huge wings and thick plumage. And now the vine sent its roots toward him and turned its leaves toward him, in the hope that he would give it more water than there was in the garden where it was growing. [h] [8] But the vine had already been planted in a fertile, well-watered field so that it could grow leaves and bear grapes and be a magnificent vine.

[9] "So I, the Sovereign LORD, ask: Will this vine live and grow? Won't the first eagle pull it up by its roots, pull off the grapes, and break off the branches and let them wither? It will not take much strength or a mighty nation to pull it up. [10] Yes, it is planted, but will it live and grow? Won't it wither when the east wind strikes it? Won't it wither there where it is growing?"

The Parable Is Explained

[11] The LORD said to me, [12] "Ask these rebels if they know what the parable means. Tell them that the king of Babylonia came to Jerusalem and took the king and his officials back with him to Babylonia. [13] He took one of the king's family, made a treaty with him, and made him swear to be loyal. He took important men as hostages [14] to keep the nation from rising again and to make sure that the treaty would be kept. [15] But the king of Judah rebelled and sent agents to Egypt to get horses and a large army. Will he succeed? Can he get away with that? He cannot break the treaty and go unpunished!

[16] "As surely as I am the living God," says the Sovereign LORD, "this king will die in Babylonia because he broke his oath and the treaty he had made with the king of Babylonia, who put him on the throne. [17] Even the powerful army of the king of Egypt will not be able to help him fight when the Babylonians build earthworks and dig trenches in order to kill many people. [18] He broke his oath and the treaty he had made. He did all these things, and now he will not escape."

[19] The Sovereign LORD says, "As surely as I am the living God, I will punish him for breaking the treaty which he swore in my name to keep. [20] I will spread out a hunter's net and catch him in it. I will take him to Babylonia and punish him there, because he was unfaithful to me. [21] His best soldiers will be killed in battle, and the survivors will be scattered in

---

g *Hebrew has an additional word, the meaning of which is unclear.*   h *And now the vine . . . growing; or And now the vine turned away from the garden where it was growing and sent its roots toward him and turned its leaves toward him, in the hope that he would give it water.*

every direction. Then you will know that
I, the Lord, have spoken."

God's Promise of Hope

22 This is what the Sovereign Lord
says:
"I will take the top of a tall cedar
    and break off a tender sprout;
I will plant it on a high mountain,
23   on Israel's highest mountain.
It will grow branches and bear
        seed
    and become a magnificent cedar.
Birds of every kind will live there
    and find shelter in its shade.
24 All the trees in the land will know
    that I am the Lord.
I cut down the tall trees
    and make small trees grow tall.
I wither up the green trees
    and make the dry trees become
        green.
I, the Lord, have spoken. I will do what I
have said I would do."

Individual Responsibility

18 The Lord spoke to me 2 and said,
    "What is this proverb people
keep repeating in the land of Israel?
    'The parents ate the sour grapes,
    But the children got the sour
        taste.'
3 "As surely as I am the living God,"
says the Sovereign Lord, "you will not
repeat this proverb in Israel any more.
4 The life of every person belongs to me,
the life of the parent as well as that of
the child. The person who sins is the one
who will die.
5 "Suppose there is a truly good man,
righteous and honest. 6 He doesn't worship the idols of the Israelites or eat the
sacrifices offered at forbidden shrines.
He doesn't seduce another man's wife or
have intercourse with a woman during
her period. 7 He doesn't cheat or rob anyone. He returns what a borrower gives
him as security; he feeds the hungry and
gives clothing to the naked. 8 He doesn't
lend money for profit. He refuses to do
evil and gives an honest decision in any
dispute. 9 Such a man obeys my commands and carefully keeps my laws. He
is righteous, and he will live," says the
Sovereign Lord.

10 "Then suppose this man has a son
who robs and kills, who does any i of
these things 11 that the father never did.
He eats sacrifices offered at forbidden
shrines and seduces other men's wives.
12 He cheats the poor, he robs, he keeps
what a borrower gives him as security.
He goes to pagan shrines, worships disgusting idols, 13 and lends money for
profit. Will he live? No, he will not. He
has done all these disgusting things, and
so he will die. He will be to blame for his
own death.
14 "Now suppose this second man has
a son. He sees all the sins his father
practiced, but does not follow his example. 15 He doesn't worship the idols of the
Israelites or eat the sacrifices offered at
forbidden shrines. He doesn't seduce another man's wife 16 or oppress anyone or
rob anyone. He returns what a borrower
gives him as security. He feeds the hungry and gives clothing to the naked.
17 He refuses to do evil j and doesn't
lend money for profit. He keeps my laws
and obeys my commands. He will not
die because of his father's sins, but he
will certainly live. 18 His father, on the
other hand, cheated and robbed k and
always did evil to everyone. And so he
died because of the sins he himself had
committed.
19 "But you ask, 'Why shouldn't the
son suffer because of his father's sins?'
The answer is that the son did what was
right and good. He kept my laws and followed them carefully, and so he will certainly live. 20 It is the one who sins who
will die. A son is not to suffer because of
his father's sins, nor a father because of
the sins of his son. Good people will be
rewarded for doing good, and evil people will suffer for the evil they do.
21 "If someone evil stops sinning and
keeps my laws, if he does what is right
and good, he will not die; he will certainly live. 22 All his sins will be forgiven,
and he will live, because he did what is
right. 23 Do you think I enjoy seeing evil
people die?" asks the Sovereign Lord.
"No, I would rather see them repent and
live.
24 "But if a righteous person stops doing good and starts doing all the evil,
disgusting things that evil people do,

---

i *Some ancient translations* who does any; *Hebrew unclear.*   j *Some ancient translations (see*
also verse 8) to do evil; *Hebrew* from the poor.   k *Some ancient translations* robbed; *Hebrew*
unclear.

will he go on living? No! None of the good he did will be remembered. He will die because of his unfaithfulness and his sins.

25 "But you say, 'What the Lord does isn't right.' Listen to me, you Israelites. Do you think my way of doing things isn't right? It is your way that isn't right. 26 When a righteous person stops doing good and starts doing evil and then dies, he dies because of the evil he has done. 27 When someone evil stops sinning and does what is right and good, he saves his life. 28 He realizes what he is doing and stops sinning, so he will certainly not die, but go on living. 29 And you Israelites say, 'What the Lord does isn't right.' You think my way isn't right, do you? It is your way that isn't right.

30 "Now I, the Sovereign Lord, am telling you Israelites that I will judge each of you by what you have done. Turn away from all the evil you are doing, and don't let your sin destroy you. 31 Give up all the evil you have been doing, and get yourselves new minds and hearts. Why do you Israelites want to die? 32 I do not want anyone to die," says the Sovereign Lord. "Turn away from your sins and live."

A Song of Sorrow

19 The Lord told me to sing this song of sorrow for two princes of Israel:

2 What a lioness your mother was!
She raised her cubs among the
    fierce male lions.
3 She raised a cub and taught him
    to hunt;
    he learned to eat people.
4 The nations heard about him
    and trapped him in a pit.
With hooks they dragged him off
    to Egypt.
5 She waited until she saw all hope
    was gone.
Then she raised another of her
    cubs,
    and he grew into a fierce lion.
6 When he was full-grown,
    he prowled with the other lions.
He too learned to hunt and eat
    people.

7 He wrecked forts,[l] he ruined
    towns.
The people of the land were
    terrified
    every time he roared.
8 The nations gathered to fight him;
    people came from everywhere.
They spread their hunting nets
    and caught him in their trap.
9 They put him in a cage
    and took him to the king of
        Babylonia.
They kept him under guard,
    so that his roar would never be
        heard again
    on the hills of Israel.

10 Your mother was like a
    grapevine[m]
    planted near a stream.
Because there was plenty of water,
    the vine was covered with leaves
        and fruit.
11 Its branches were strong
    and grew to be royal scepters.
The vine grew tall enough to reach
    the clouds;
    everyone saw how leafy and tall
        it was.
12 But angry hands pulled it up by
    the roots
    and threw it to the ground.
The east wind dried up its fruit.
Its branches were broken off;
    they dried up and were burned.
13 Now it is planted in the desert,
    in a dry and waterless land.
14 The stem of the vine caught fire;
    fire burned up its branches and
        fruit.
The branches will never again be
    strong,
    will never be royal scepters.
This is a song of sorrow; it has been sung again and again.

The Lord's Will and Human Defiance

20 It was the tenth day of the fifth month of the seventh year of our exile. Some of the leaders of the Israelite community came to consult me about the Lord's will, and they sat down in front of me. 2 Then the Lord spoke to me. 3 "Mortal man," he said, "speak to these leaders and tell them that the Sovereign

---

l One ancient translation wrecked forts; Hebrew unclear, the meaning of which is unclear.   m Hebrew has an additional word,

Lord is saying: You have come to ask my will, have you? As surely as I am the living God, I will not let you ask me anything. I, the Sovereign Lord, have spoken.

4 "Are you ready to pass sentence on them, mortal man? Then do so. Remind them of the disgusting things their ancestors did. 5 Tell them what I am saying. When I chose Israel, I made them a promise. I revealed myself to them in Egypt and told them: I am the Lord your God. 6 It was then that I promised to take them out of Egypt and lead them to a land I had chosen for them, a rich and fertile land, the finest land of all. 7 I told them to throw away the disgusting idols they loved and not to make themselves unclean with the false gods of Egypt, because I am the Lord their God. 8 But they defied me and refused to listen. They did not throw away their disgusting idols or give up the Egyptian gods. I was ready to let them feel the full force of my anger there in Egypt. 9 But I did not, since that would have brought dishonor to my name, for in the presence of the people among whom they were living I had announced to Israel that I was going to lead them out of Egypt.

10 "And so I led them out of Egypt into the desert. 11 I gave them my commands and taught them my laws, which bring life to anyone who obeys them. 12 I made the keeping of the Sabbath a sign of the agreement between us, to remind them that I, the Lord, make them holy. 13 But even in the desert they defied me. They broke my laws and rejected my commands, which bring life to anyone who obeys them. They completely profaned the Sabbath. I was ready to let them feel the force of my anger there in the desert and to destroy them. 14 But I did not, since that would have brought dishonor to my name among the nations which had seen me lead Israel out of Egypt. 15 So I made a vow in the desert that I would not take them to the land I had given them, a rich and fertile land, the finest land of all. 16 I made the vow because they had rejected my commands, broken my laws, and profaned the Sabbath — they preferred to worship their idols.

17 "But then I took pity on them. I decided not to kill them there in the desert. 18 Instead, I warned the young people among them: Do not keep the laws your ancestors made; do not follow their customs or defile yourselves with their idols. 19 I am the Lord your God. Obey my laws and my commands. 20 Make the Sabbath a holy day, so that it will be a sign of the covenant we made, and will remind you that I am the Lord your God.

21 "But that generation also defied me. They broke my laws and did not keep my commands, which bring life to anyone who obeys them. They profaned the Sabbath. I was ready to let them feel the force of my anger there in the desert and to kill them all. 22 But I did not, since that would have brought dishonor to my name among the nations which had seen me bring Israel out of Egypt. 23 So I made another vow in the desert. I vowed that I would scatter them all over the world. 24 I did this because they had rejected my commands, broken my laws, profaned the Sabbath, and worshiped the same idols their ancestors had served.

25 "Then I gave them laws that are not good and commands that do not bring life. 26 I let them defile themselves with their own offerings, and I let them sacrifice their first-born sons. This was to punish them and show them that I am the Lord.

27 "Now then, mortal man, tell the Israelites what I, the Sovereign Lord, am saying to them. This is another way their ancestors insulted me by their unfaithfulness. 28 I brought them to the land I had promised to give them. When they saw the high hills and green trees, they offered sacrifices at all of them. They made me angry by the sacrifices they burned and by the wine they brought as offerings. 29 I asked them: What are these high places where you go? So they have been called 'High Places'[n] ever since. 30 Now tell the Israelites what I am saying: Why must you commit the same sins your ancestors did and go running after their idols? 31 Even today you offer the same gifts and defile yourselves with the same idols by sacrificing your children to them in the fire. And then you Israelites still come to ask what my will

---

[n] HIGH PLACES: *Pagan places of worship which the Hebrews were forbidden to use. The Hebrew word translated "High Places" sounds like the Hebrew for "where you go."*

is! As surely as I, the Sovereign LORD, am the living God, I will not let you ask me anything. 32 You have made up your minds that you want to be like the other nations, like the people who live in other countries and worship trees and rocks. But that will never be.

God Punishes and Forgives

33 "As surely as I, the Sovereign LORD, am the living God, I warn you that in my anger I will rule over you with a strong hand, with all my power. 34 I will show you my power and my anger when I gather you together and bring you back from all the countries where you have been scattered. 35 I will bring you into the 'Desert of the Nations,' and there I will condemn you to your face. 36 I will now condemn you just as I condemned your ancestors in the Sinai Desert," says the Sovereign LORD.

37 "I will take firm control of you and make you obey my covenant. 38 I will take away from among you those who are rebellious and sinful. I will take them out of the lands where they are living now, but I will not let them return to the land of Israel. Then you will know that I am the LORD."

39 The Sovereign LORD says, "And now, all you Israelites, suit yourselves! Go on and serve your idols! But I warn you that after this you will have to obey me and stop dishonoring my holy name by offering gifts to your idols. 40 There in the land, on my holy mountain,o the high mountain of Israel, all you people of Israel will worship me. I will be pleased with you and will expect you to bring me your sacrifices, your best offerings, and your holy gifts. 41 After I bring you out of the countries where you have been scattered and gather you together, I will accept the sacrifices that you burn, and the nations will see that I am holy. 42 When I bring you back to Israel, the land that I promised I would give to your ancestors, then you will know that I am the LORD. 43 Then you will remember all the disgraceful things you did and how you defiled yourselves. You will be disgusted with yourselves because of all the evil things you did. 44 When I act to protect my honor, you Israelites will know that I

am the LORD, because I do not deal with you as your wicked, evil actions deserve." The Sovereign LORD has spoken.

Fire in the South

45 The LORD spoke to me. 46 "Mortal man," he said, "look toward the south. Speak against the south and prophesy against the forest of the south. 47 Tell the southern forest to hear what the Sovereign LORD is saying: Look! I am starting a fire, and it will burn up every tree in you, whether green or dry. Nothing will be able to put it out. It will spread from south to north, and everyone will feel the heat of the flames. 48 They will all see that I, the LORD, set it on fire and that no one can put it out."

49 But I protested, "Sovereign LORD, don't make me do it! Everyone is already complaining that I always speak in riddles."

The LORD's Sword

21 The LORD spoke to me. 2 "Mortal man," he said, "denounce Jerusalem. Denounce the places where people worship. Warn the land of Israel 3 that I, the LORD, am saying: I am your enemy. I will draw my sword and kill all of you, good and evil alike. 4 I will use my sword against everyone from south to north. 5 Everyone will know that I, the LORD, have drawn my sword and that I will not put it away.

6 "Mortal man, groan as if your heart is breaking with despair. Groan in sorrow where everyone can watch you. 7 When they ask you why you are groaning, tell them it is because of the news that is coming. When it comes, their hearts will be filled with fear, their hands will hang limp, their courage will fail, and their knees will tremble. The time has come; it is here." The Sovereign LORD has spoken.

8 The LORD said to me, 9 "Mortal man, prophesy. Tell the people what I, the Lord, am saying:

A sword, a sword is sharpened
    and polished.
10 It is sharpened to kill,
    polished to flash like lightning.
There can be no rejoicing,

---

o HOLY MOUNTAIN: *Mount Zion, the hill in Jerusalem which formed part of the Temple and palace area.*

WARFARE IN BIBLE TIMES

In Old Testament times, the nation of Israel often waged war against its enemies. One notable example is the war of conquest led by Joshua to drive the Canaanites from the land the Lord promised Israel. To the Israelites, this was a holy war undertaken at God's command and carried out under his guidance and protection. Just before they attacked the city of Jericho, for example, Joshua issued this order to the priests and soldiers who were marching around the city walls: "The LORD has given you the city" (Js 6.16).

The weapons used by Joshua and his warriors were the simple arms of the time: the bow and arrow, the sling, the sword, the spear or lance, the battle ax, and various pieces of protective armor. His warfare techniques included threats, intimidation, ambush and surprise attack, siege warfare against walled cities, and hand-to-hand combat.

But there is a noticeable progression throughout Old Testament history in the types of weapons used and how warfare was carried out. By the time of Solomon, mounted warriors with more sophisticated weapons were a part of Israel's armed forces. Solomon also had a fleet of chariots at his command for swift attacks against enemy forces (1 K 10.26).

As the nation of Israel increased its weaponry, it came to rely more on military might and less on God's guidance and protection as the key to victory in battle. Many of the prophets of the Old Testament condemned the kings of Israel and Judah for leading the people to place their trust in the sword rather than in the word of God.

Some of the most striking warfare imagery in the Old Testament is found in the Book of Ezekiel. In a vision, the prophet saw the attack of Jerusalem by the Babylonians. He described how a besieging army gained entrance to a walled city. The king of Babylon gave orders for his army "to place battering rams against the gates, to throw up earthworks, and to dig trenches" (Ez 21.22).

for my people have disregarded
every warning and
punishment.*p*

11 The sword is being polished,
to make it ready for use.
It is sharpened and polished,
to be put in the hands of a killer.

12 Howl in grief, mortal man;
this sword is meant for my
people
and for all the leaders of Israel.
They are going to be killed
with all the rest of my people.
Beat your breast in despair!

13 I am testing my people,
and if they refuse to repent,
all these things will happen to
them.*q*

14 "Now, mortal man, prophesy. Clap
your hands, and the sword will strike
again and again. It is a sword that kills,
a sword that terrifies*r* and slaughters.
15 It makes my people lose courage and
stumble. I am threatening their city with
a sword*s* that flashes like lightning and
is ready to kill. 16 Cut to the right and the
left, you sharp sword! Cut wherever you
turn.*t* 17 I also will clap my hands, and
my anger will be over. I, the LORD, have
spoken."

The Sword of the King of Babylonia

18 The LORD spoke to me. 19 "Mortal
man," he said, "mark out two roads by
which the king of Babylonia can come
with his sword. Both of them are to start
in the same country. Put up a signpost
where the roads fork.*u* 20 One will show
the king the way to the Ammonite city of
Rabbah, and the other the way to Judah,
to the fortified city, Jerusalem. 21 The
king of Babylonia stands by the signpost
at the fork of the road. To discover
which way to go, he shakes the arrows;*v* he consults his idols; he examines the liver of a sacrificed animal.
22 Now! His right hand holds the arrow
marked 'Jerusalem'! It tells him to go
and set up battering rams, to shout the
battle cry, to place battering rams
against the gates, to throw up earthworks, and to dig trenches. 23 The people

of Jerusalem won't believe this because
of the treaties they have made. But this
prediction is to remind them of their
sins and to warn them that they will be
captured. 24 This then is what I, the
Sovereign LORD, am saying: Your sins
are exposed. Everyone knows how
guilty you are. You show your sins in
your every action. You stand condemned, and I will hand you over to
your enemies.

25 "You wicked, unholy ruler of Israel,
your day, the day of your final punishment, is coming. 26 I, the Sovereign LORD,
have spoken. Take off your crown and
your turban. Nothing will be the same
again. Raise the poor to power! Bring
down those who are ruling! 27 Ruin, ruin!
Yes, I will make the city a ruin. But this
will not happen until the one comes
whom I have chosen to punish the city.
To him I will give it.

A Sword and the Ammonites

28 "Mortal man, prophesy. Announce
what I, the Sovereign LORD, am saying to
the Ammonites, who are insulting Israel.
Say to them:
'A sword is ready to destroy;
It is polished to kill, to flash like
lightning.
29 The visions that you see are false, and
the predictions you make are lies. You
are wicked and evil, and your day is
coming, the day of your final punishment. The sword is going to fall on your
necks.

30 " 'Put up the sword! I will judge you
in the place where you were created, in
the land where you were born. 31 You
will feel my anger when I turn it loose on
you like a blazing fire. And I will hand
you over to brutal men, experts at destruction. 32 You will be destroyed by
fire. Your blood will be shed in your own
country, and no one will remember you
any more.' " The LORD has spoken.

The Crimes of Jerusalem

22 The LORD spoke to me. 2 "Mortal
man," he said, "are you ready to
judge the city that is full of murderers?

---

p Probable text There ... punishment; *Hebrew unclear.*   *q Verse 13 in Hebrew is unclear.*
r Some ancient translations terrifies; *Hebrew unclear.*   *s Probable text* threatening ... sword;
Hebrew unclear.   *t Verse 16 in Hebrew is unclear.*   *u Probable text* Put ... fork; *Hebrew*
unclear.   *v* SHAKES THE ARROWS: *When faced with a decision, people in ancient times would*
sometimes take a handful of arrows, throw them down, and study the pattern in which they
fell, in order to learn what to do.

Make clear to her all the disgusting things she has done. ³Tell the city what I, the Sovereign LORD, am saying: Because you have murdered so many of your own people and have defiled yourself by worshiping idols, your time is coming. ⁴You are guilty of those murders and are defiled by the idols you made, and so your day is coming, your time is up! That is why I have let the nations make fun of you and all the countries sneer at you. ⁵Countries nearby and countries far away sneer at you because of your lawlessness. ⁶All Israel's leaders trust in their own strength and commit murder. ⁷None of you in the city honor your parents. You cheat foreigners and take advantage of widows and orphans. ⁸You have no respect for the holy places, and you don't keep the Sabbath. ⁹Some of your people tell lies about others in order to have them put to death. Some of them eat sacrifices offered to idols. Some are always satisfying their lusts. ¹⁰Some of them sleep with their father's wife. Some force women to have intercourse with them during their period. ¹¹Some commit adultery, and others seduce their daughters-in-law or their half sisters. ¹²Some of your people murder for pay. Some charge interest on the loans they make to other Israelites and get rich by taking advantage of them. They have forgotten me." The Sovereign LORD has spoken.

¹³"I will bring my fist down on your robberies and murders. ¹⁴Do you think you will have any courage left or have strength enough to lift your hand when I am finished with you? I, the LORD, have spoken, and I keep my word. ¹⁵I will scatter your people to every country and nation and will put an end to your evil actions. ¹⁶And so the other nations will dishonor you, but you will know that I am the LORD."

God's Refining Furnace

¹⁷The LORD said to me, ¹⁸"Mortal man, the Israelites are of no use to me. They are like waste metal—copper, tin, iron, and lead—left over after silver has been refined in a furnace. ¹⁹So now I, the Sovereign LORD, am telling them that they are just as useless as that. I will

bring them all together in Jerusalem ²⁰in the same way that the ore of silver, copper, iron, lead, and tin is put in a refining furnace. My anger and rage will melt them the way fire melts ore. ²¹Yes, I will gather them in Jerusalem, build a fire under them, and melt them with my anger. ²²They will be melted in Jerusalem the way silver is melted in a furnace, and then they will know that they are feeling the anger of the LORD."

The Sins of Israel's Leaders

²³The LORD spoke to me again. ²⁴"Mortal man," he said, "tell the Israelites that their land is unholy, and so I am punishing it in my anger. ²⁵The leadersʷ are like lions roaring over the animals they have killed. They kill the people, take all the money and property they can get, and by their murders leave many widows. ²⁶The priests break my law and have no respect for what is holy. They make no distinction between what is holy and what is not. They do not teach the difference between clean and unclean things, and they ignore the Sabbath. As a result the people of Israel do not respect me. ²⁷The government officials are like wolves tearing apart the animals they have killed. They commit murder in order to get rich. ²⁸The prophets have hidden these sins like workers covering a wall with whitewash. They see false visions and make false predictions. They claim to speak the word of the Sovereign LORD, but I, the LORD, have not spoken to them. ²⁹The wealthy cheat and rob. They mistreat the poor and take advantage of foreigners. ³⁰I looked for someone who could build a wall, who could stand in the places where the walls have crumbled and defend the land when my anger is about to destroy it, but I could find no one. ³¹So I will turn my anger loose on them, and like a fire I will destroy them for what they have done." The Sovereign LORD has spoken.

The Sinful Sisters

23 The LORD spoke to me. ²"Mortal man," he said, "there were once two sisters. ³When they were young, living in Egypt, they lost their virginity and became prostitutes. ⁴The older one was

ʷ One ancient translation The leaders; Hebrew A conspiracy of her prophets.

named Oholah[x] (she represents Samaria), and the younger one was named Oholibah[y] (she represents Jerusalem). I married both of them, and they bore me children. 5 Although she was mine, Oholah continued to be a prostitute and was full of lust for her lovers from Assyria. 6 They were soldiers in uniforms of purple, noblemen and high-ranking officers; all of them were handsome young cavalry officers. 7 She was the whore for all the Assyrian officers, and her lust led her to defile herself by worshiping Assyrian idols. 8 She continued what she had begun as a prostitute in Egypt, where she lost her virginity. From the time she was a young woman, men slept with her and treated her like a prostitute. 9 So I handed her over to her Assyrian lovers whom she wanted so much. 10 They stripped her naked, seized her sons and daughters, and then killed her with a sword. Women everywhere gossiped about her fate.

11 "Even though her sister Oholibah saw this, she was wilder and more of a prostitute than Oholah had ever been. 12 She too was full of lust for the Assyrian noblemen and officers — soldiers in bright uniforms — and for the cavalry officers, all of those handsome young men. 13 I saw that she was completely immoral, that the second sister was as bad as the first.

14-15 "She sank deeper and deeper in her immorality. She was attracted by the images of high Babylonian officials carved into the wall and painted bright red, with sashes around their waists and fancy turbans on their heads. 16 As soon as she saw them, she was filled with lust and sent messengers to them in Babylonia. 17 The Babylonians came to have sex with her. They used her and defiled her so much that finally she became disgusted with them. 18 She exposed herself publicly and let everyone know she was a whore. I was as disgusted with her as I had been with her sister. 19 She became more of a prostitute than ever, acting the way she did as a young woman, when she was a prostitute in Egypt. 20 She was filled with lust for oversexed men who had all the lustfulness of donkeys or stallions." (21 Oholibah, you wanted to repeat the immorality you were guilty of as a young woman in Egypt, where men played with your breasts and you lost your virginity.)

God's Judgment on the Younger Sister

22 "Now then, Oholibah, this is what I, the Sovereign LORD, am saying to you. You are tired of those lovers, but I will make them angry with you and bring them to surround you. 23 I will bring all the Babylonians and Chaldeans, men from Pekod, Shoa, and Koa, and all the Assyrians. I will gather all those handsome young noblemen and officers, all those important officials and high-ranking cavalry officers. 24 They will attack you from the north,[z] bringing a large army with chariots and supply wagons. Protected by shields and helmets, they will surround you. I will hand you over to them, and they will judge you by their own laws. 25 Because I am angry with you, I will let them deal with you in their anger. They will cut off your nose and your ears and kill your children. Yes, they will take your sons and daughters from you and burn them alive. 26 They will tear off your clothes and take your jewels. 27 I will put a stop to your lust and to the obscenities you have committed ever since you were in Egypt. You won't look at any more idols or think about Egypt any more."

28 This is what the Sovereign LORD says: "I will hand you over to people you hate and are disgusted with. 29 And because they hate you, they will take away everything you have worked for and leave you stripped naked, exposed like a prostitute. Your lust and your prostitution 30 have brought this on you. You were a prostitute for the nations and defiled yourself with their idols. 31 You followed in your sister's footsteps, and so I will give you the same cup of punishment to drink."

32 The Sovereign LORD says,
"You will drink from your
    sister's cup;
it is large and deep.
Everyone will scorn and
    mock you;
the cup is full.

---

x OHOLAH: *This name in Hebrew means "her sanctuary."* y OHOLIBAH: *This name in Hebrew means "my sanctuary is in her."* z *One ancient translation* north; *Hebrew unclear.*

33 It will make you miserable and
drunk,
that cup of fear and ruin,
your sister Samaria's cup.
34 You will drink and drain it dry,
and with its broken pieces
tear your breast.
I, the Sovereign LORD, have spoken."

35 Now this is what the Sovereign LORD
is saying: "Because you forgot me and
turned your back on me, you will suffer
for your lust and your prostitution."

God's Judgment on Both Sisters

36 The LORD said to me, "Mortal man,
are you ready to judge Oholah and Oholibah? Accuse them of the disgusting
things they have done. 37 They have
committed adultery and murder —
adultery with idols and murder of the
children they bore me. They sacrificed
my children to their idols. 38 And that is
not all they did. They profaned my Temple and broke the Sabbath, which I had
established. 39 The very day that they
killed my children as sacrifices to idols,
they came to my Temple and profaned it!

40 "Again and again they sent messengers to invite men to come from a great
distance, and the men came. The two sisters would bathe and put on eye shadow
and jewelry. 41 They would sit on a beautiful couch, and in front of them they
would have a table covered with good
things, including the incense and the olive oil that I had given them. 42 The
sound of a carefree crowd could be
heard, a group of men brought in from
the desert. They put bracelets on the
women's arms and beautiful crowns on
their heads. 43 And I said to myself that
they were using as a prostitute a woman
worn out by adultery.ᵃ 44 They went
back to these prostitutes again and
again. They went back to Oholah and
Oholibah, those immoral women.
45 Righteous men will condemn them on
the charge of adultery and murder, because they practice adultery and their
hands are stained with blood."

46 This is what the Sovereign LORD
says: "Bring a mob to terrorize them and
rob them. 47 Let the mob stone them and
attack them with swords, kill their children, and burn down their houses.
48 Throughout the land I will put a stop to
immorality, as a warning to every
woman not to commit adultery as they
did. 49 And you two sisters — I will punish
you for your immorality and your sin of
worshiping idols. Then you will know
that I am the Sovereign LORD."

The Corroded Cooking Pot

24 On the tenth day of the tenth
month of the ninth year of our
exile, the LORD spoke to me. 2 "Mortal
man," he said, "write down today's date,
because this is the day that the king of
Babylonia is beginning the siege of Jerusalem. 3 Tell my rebellious people this
parable that I, the Sovereign LORD, have
for them:

Set the pot on the fire
and fill it up with water.
4 Put in the best pieces of meat —
the shoulders and the legs —
fill it with choice bony
pieces too.
5 Use the meat of the finest
sheep;
pile the woodᵇ under the pot.
Let the water boil;
boil the bones and the meat."

6 This is what the Sovereign LORD is
saying: "The city of murderers is
doomed! It is like a corroded pot that is
never cleaned. Piece after piece of meat
is taken out, and not one is left. 7 There
was murder in the city, but the blood
was not spilled on the ground where the
dust could hide it; it was spilled on a
bare rock. 8 I have left the blood there,
where it cannot be hidden, where it demands angry revenge."

9 This is what the Sovereign LORD is
saying: "The city of murderers is
doomed! I myself will pile up the firewood. 10 Bring more wood! Fan the
flames! Cook the meat! Boil away the
broth!ᶜ Burn up the bones! 11 Now set
the empty bronze pot on the coals and
let it get red-hot. Then the pot will be
ritually pure again after the corrosion is
burned off, 12 although all that corrosion
will not disappear in the flames.ᵈ 13 Jerusalem, your immoral actions have defiled you. Although I tried to purify you,
you remained defiled. You will not be

ᵃ *Verses 42-43 in Hebrew are unclear.*   ᵇ *Probable text* wood; *Hebrew* bones.
ᶜ *Some ancient translations* Boil away the broth!; *Hebrew unclear.*   ᵈ *Verse 12 in Hebrew
begins with two words, the meaning of which is unclear.*

pure again until you have felt the full force of my anger. [14]I, the LORD, have spoken. The time has come for me to act. I will not ignore your sins or show pity or be merciful. You will be punished for what you have done." The Sovereign LORD has spoken.

The Death of the Prophet's Wife

[15]The LORD spoke to me. [16]"Mortal man," he said, "with one blow I am going to take away the person you love most. You are not to complain or cry or shed any tears. [17]Don't let your sobbing be heard. Do not go bareheaded or barefoot as a sign of mourning. Don't cover your face or eat the food that mourners eat."

[18]Early in the day I was talking with the people. That evening my wife died, and the next day I did as I had been told. [19]The people asked me, "Why are you acting like this?"

[20]So I said to them, "The LORD spoke to me and told me [21]to give you Israelites this message: You are proud of the strength of the Temple. You like to look at it and to visit it, but the LORD is going to profane it. And the younger members of your families who are left in Jerusalem will be killed in war. [22]Then you will do what I have done. You will not cover your faces or eat the food that mourners eat. [23]You will not go bareheaded or barefoot or mourn or cry. You will waste away because of your sins, and you will groan to one another. [24]Then I will be a sign to you; you will do everything I have done. The LORD says that when this happens, you will know that he is the Sovereign LORD."

[25]The LORD said, "Now, mortal man, I will take away from them the strong Temple that was their pride and joy, which they liked to look at and to visit. And I will take away their sons and daughters. [26]On the day that I do this, some who escape the destruction will come and tell you about it. [27]That same day you will get back the power of speech which you had lost, and you will talk with them. In this way you will be a sign to the people, and they will know that I am the LORD."

Prophecy against Ammon

25 The LORD spoke to me. [2]"Mortal man," he said, "denounce the country of Ammon. [3]Tell them to listen to what I, the Sovereign LORD, am saying: You were delighted to see my Temple profaned, to see the land of Israel devastated, to see the people of Judah go into exile. [4]Because you were glad, I will let the tribes from the eastern desert conquer you. They will set up their camps in your country and settle there. They will eat the fruit and drink the milk that should have been yours. [5]I will turn the city of Rabbah into a place to keep camels, and the whole country of Ammon will become a place to keep sheep, so that you will know I am the LORD.

[6]"This is what the Sovereign LORD is saying: You clapped your hands and jumped for joy. You despised the land of Israel. [7]Because you did, I will hand you over to other nations who will rob you and plunder you. I will destroy you so completely that you will not be a nation any more or have a country of your own. Then you will know that I am the LORD."

Prophecy against Moab

[8]The Sovereign LORD said, "Because Moab[e] has said that Judah is like all the other nations, [9]I will let the cities that defend the border of Moab be attacked, including even the finest cities—Beth Jeshimoth, Baal Meon, and Kiriathaim. [10]I will let the tribes of the eastern desert conquer Moab, together with Ammon, so that Moab[f] will no longer be a nation. [11]I will punish Moab, and they will know that I am the LORD."

Prophecy against Edom

[12]The Sovereign LORD said, "The people of Edom took cruel revenge on Judah, and that revenge has brought lasting guilt on Edom. [13]Now I announce that I will punish Edom and kill every person and animal there. I will make it a wasteland, from the city of Teman to the city of Dedan, and the people will be killed in battle. [14]My people Israel will take revenge on Edom for me, and they will make Edom feel my furious anger. Edom will know what it means to be the

---

e *Some ancient translations* Moab; *Hebrew* Moab and Seir.   f *Probable text* Moab; *Hebrew* Ammon.

TYRE AND SIDON

Tyre and Sidon were two Phoenician seaport cities about twenty-five miles apart on the coast of the Mediterranean Sea. For the most part, Israel had a good relationship with these cities. The Phoenician king, Hiram, was a trading partner of both David and Solomon. He provided building materials, as well as skilled tradesmen to help build the Temple and Solomon's palace complex in the city of Jerusalem.

Why, then, did the prophet Ezekiel utter such bitter words against Tyre (Ez 26)? It was probably because of the taunting attitude Tyre demonstrated when the nation of Judah was overrun by the Babylonians (Ez 26.2). Judah's collapse meant that Phoenicia was a region with little competition in central Palestine. Their trade monopoly complete, Tyre and Sidon rejoiced. Their insatiable greed and prideful attitude led Ezekiel to issue his bitter condemnation.

When Ezekiel spoke these words, the cities of Tyre and Sidon had no peers on the Mediterranean shores. As early as 1000 B.C. the two cities had emerged as important population centers. As the leader of a group of small city-states, Sidon first grew to prominence in trade. After a time, it was eclipsed by Tyre, which established an empire based on maritime trade. The ships of Tyre sailed as far away as Great Britain and North Africa on trading ventures.

As predicted by Ezekiel, the cities of Tyre and Sidon were eventually judged by God. Tyre was thought to be invincible because part of the city was located off-shore, completely surrounded by the sea. But the Greek conqueror Alexander the Great built a causeway to the city and destroyed it in 332 B.C. After the Romans became the dominant world power, they rebuilt Tyre. The ruins of this city are visible today.

Both Tyre and Sidon are mentioned in the New Testament. Jesus visited both cities during his ministry (Mt 15.21-28). Paul also visited a Christian community in Tyre, staying with believers there for a week during his third missionary journey (Ac 21.1-6).

object of my revenge." The Sovereign LORD has spoken.

Prophecy against Philistia

15 The Sovereign LORD said, "The Philistines have taken cruel revenge on their agelong enemies and destroyed them in their hate. 16 And so I am announcing that I will attack the Philistines and wipe them out. I will destroy everyone left living there on the Philistine Plain. 17 I will punish them severely and take full revenge on them. They will feel my anger. Then they will know that I am the LORD."

Prophecy against Tyre

26 On the first day of the ... month[g] of the eleventh year of our exile, the LORD spoke to me. 2 "Mortal man," he said, "this is what the people in the city of Tyre are cheering about. They shout, 'Jerusalem is shattered! Her commercial power is gone! She won't be our rival any more!'

3 "Now then, this is what I, the Sovereign LORD, am saying: I am your enemy, city of Tyre. I will bring many nations to attack you, and they will come like the waves of the sea. 4 They will destroy your city walls and tear down your towers. Then I will sweep away all the dust and leave only a bare rock. 5 Fishermen will dry their nets on it, there where it stands in the sea. I, the Sovereign LORD, have spoken. The nations will plunder Tyre, 6 and with their swords they will kill those who live in her towns on the mainland. Then Tyre will know that I am the LORD."

7 The Sovereign LORD says, "I am going to bring the greatest king of all — King Nebuchadnezzar of Babylonia — to attack Tyre. He will come from the north with a huge army, with horses and chariots and with cavalry. 8 Those who live in the towns on the mainland will be killed in the fighting. The enemy will dig trenches, build earthworks, and make a solid wall of shields against you. 9 They will pound in your walls with battering rams and tear down your towers with iron bars. 10 The clouds of dust raised by their horses will cover you. The noise of their horses pulling wagons and chariots will shake your walls as they pass

through the gates of the ruined city. 11 Their cavalry will storm through your streets, killing your people with their swords. Your mighty pillars will be thrown to the ground. 12 Your enemies will help themselves to your wealth and merchandise. They will pull down your walls and shatter your luxurious houses. They will take the stones and wood and all the rubble, and dump them into the sea. 13 I will put an end to all your songs, and I will silence the music of your harps. 14 I will leave only a bare rock where fishermen can dry their nets. The city will never be rebuilt. I, the Sovereign LORD, have spoken."

15 The Sovereign LORD has this to say to the city of Tyre: "When you are being conquered, the people who live along the coast will be terrified at the screams of those who are slaughtered. 16 All the kings of the seafaring nations will come down from their thrones. They will take off their robes and their embroidered clothes and sit trembling on the ground. They will be so terrified at your fate that they will not be able to stop trembling. 17 They will sing this funeral song for you:

> The famous city is destroyed!
> Her ships have been swept[h] from
> the seas.
> The people of this city ruled the
> seas
> And terrified all who lived on the
> coast.
> 18 Now, on the day it has fallen,
> The islands are trembling,
> And their people are shocked at
> such destruction."

19 The Sovereign LORD says: "I will make you as desolate as ruined cities where no one lives. I will cover you with the water of the ocean depths. 20 I will send you down to the world of the dead to join the people who lived in ancient times. I will make you stay in that underground world among eternal ruins, keeping company with the dead. As a result you will never again be inhabited and take your place[i] in the land of the living. 21 I will make you a terrifying example, and that will be the end of you. People may look for you, but you will

---

g month; *the Hebrew text does not specify the month.*   h *Some ancient translations* swept; Hebrew inhabited.   i *One ancient translation* and take your place; *Hebrew unclear.*

ISRAEL AND THE PHOENICIANS

The Phoenicians lived on a narrow strip of land northwest of Palestine on the eastern shore of the Mediterranean Sea in the area now known as Lebanon and coastal Syria. A people who once occupied the land of Canaan, the Phoenicians were driven out by Israel and crowded onto this narrow strip of coastline.

Hemmed in by the ocean and the Lebanon mountains, the Phoenicians took to the sea to expand their empire. This led them to become distinguished seafaring merchants who founded many colonies along the Mediterranean. The nation was at the pinnacle of its power and prosperity from 1050 to 850 B.C.

With excellent ports such as Tyre and Sidon and a good supply of timber (cypress, pine, and cedar), the Phoenicians became noted shipbuilders and sea merchants (Ez 27.8, 9). Since the Israelites disliked the sea, the Phoenicians generally enjoyed good working relations with Israel. Hiram of Tyre, a friend of David and Solomon, helped Israel equip its merchant fleet (1 K 9.26–28).

Phoenician religion was largely a carryover from the Canaanite worship system, which included child sacrifice. The gods were mainly male and female nature deities with Baal as the primary god. The marriage of King Ahab to Jezebel, a Phoenician woman, was a corrupting influence on Israel. Ahab allowed Jezebel to place the prophets of Baal in influential positions (1 K 18.19). King Solomon lapsed into idolatry by worshiping Astarte, the supreme goddess of the Sidonians (1 K 11.5).

The Phoenician cities of Tyre and Sidon are mentioned often in the New Testament. Jesus healed a demon-possessed girl in this area (Mt 15.21–28). Early Christian believers witnessed in Phoenicia after leaving Jerusalem (Ac 11.19). Paul often traveled through the area (Ac 15.3).

never be found." The Sovereign LORD has spoken.

A Funeral Song for Tyre

27 The LORD said to me, 2 "Mortal man, sing a funeral song for Tyre, 3 that city which stands at the edge of the sea and does business with the people living on every seacoast. Tell her what the Sovereign LORD is saying:

"Tyre, you boasted of your perfect
beauty.
4 Your home is the sea.
Your builders made you like a
beautiful ship;
5 They used fir trees from Mount
Hermon for timber
And a cedar from Lebanon for
your mast.
6 They took oak trees from Bashan
to make oars;
They made your deck out of pine
from Cyprus
And inlaid it with ivory.
7 Your sails were made of linen,
Embroidered linen from Egypt,
Easily recognized from afar.
Your awnings were made of finest
cloth,
Of purple from the island of
Cyprus.
8 Your oarsmen were from the cities
of Sidon and Arvad.
Your own skillful men were the
sailors.
9 The ship's carpenters
Were well-trained men from
Byblos.
Sailors from every seagoing ship
Did business in your shops.

10 "Soldiers from Persia, Lydia, and Libya served in your army. They hung their shields and their helmets in your barracks. They are the men who won glory for you. 11 Soldiers from Arvad guarded your walls, and troops from Gamad guarded your towers. They hung their shields on your walls. They are the ones who made you beautiful.

12 "You did business in Spain and took silver, iron, tin, and lead in payment for your abundant goods. 13 You did business in Greece, Tubal, and Meshech and traded your goods for slaves and for articles of bronze. 14 You sold your goods for workhorses, war-horses, and mules from Beth Togarmah. 15 The people of Rhodes[i] traded with you; people of many coastal lands gave you ivory and ebony in exchange for your goods. 16 The people of Syria bought your merchandise and your many products. They gave emeralds, purple cloth, embroidery, fine linen, coral, and rubies in payment for your wares. 17 Judah and Israel paid for your goods with wheat,[k] honey, olive oil, and spices. 18-19 The people of Damascus bought your merchandise and your products, paying for them with wine from Helbon and wool from Sahar.[l] They traded wrought iron and spices for your goods. 20 The people of Dedan traded saddle blankets for your goods. 21 The Arabians and the rulers of the land of Kedar paid for your merchandise with lambs, sheep, and goats. 22 For your goods the merchants of Sheba and Raamah traded jewels, gold, and the finest spices. 23 The cities of Haran, Canneh, and Eden, the merchants of Sheba, the cities of Asshur and Chilmad—they all traded with you. 24 They sold you luxurious clothing, purple cloth, and embroidery, brightly colored carpets, and well-made cords and ropes. 25 Your merchandise was carried in fleets of the largest cargo ships.

"You were like a ship at sea
Loaded with heavy cargo.
26 When your oarsmen brought you
out to sea,
An east wind wrecked you far
from land.
27 All your wealth of merchandise,
All the sailors in your crew,
Your ship's carpenters and your
merchants,
Every soldier on board the ship—
All, all were lost at sea
When your ship was wrecked.
28 The shouts of the drowning sailors
Echoed on the shore.

29 "Every ship is now deserted,
And every sailor has gone ashore.
30 They all mourn bitterly for you,
Throwing dust on their heads and
rolling in ashes.
31 They shave their heads for you
And dress themselves in sackcloth.

Their hearts are bitter as they
    weep.
32 They chant a funeral song for you:
    'Who can be compared to Tyre,
    To Tyre now silent in the sea?
33 When your merchandise went
      overseas,
    You filled the needs of every
      nation.
    Kings were made rich
    By the wealth of your goods.
34 Now you are wrecked in the sea;
    You have sunk to the ocean
      depths.
    Your goods and all who worked
      for you
    Have vanished with you in
      the sea.'

35 "Everyone who lives along the coast is shocked at your fate. Even their kings are terrified, and fear is written on their faces. 36 You are gone, gone forever, and merchants all over the world are terrified, afraid that they will share your fate."

Prophecy against the King of Tyre

28 The LORD spoke to me. 2 "Mortal man," he said, "tell the ruler of Tyre what I, the Sovereign LORD, am saying to him: Puffed up with pride, you claim to be a god. You say that like a god you sit on a throne, surrounded by the seas. You may pretend to be a god, but, no, you are mortal, not divine. 3 You think you are wiser than Danel,*m* that no secret can be kept from you. 4 Your wisdom and skill made you rich with treasures of gold and silver. 5 You made clever business deals and kept on making profits. How proud you are of your wealth!

6 "Now then, this is what I, the Sovereign LORD, am saying: Because you think you are as wise as a god, 7 I will bring ruthless enemies to attack you. They will destroy all the beautiful things you have acquired by skill and wisdom. 8 They will kill you and send you to a watery grave. 9 When they come to kill you, will you still claim that you are a god? When you face your murderers, you will be mortal and not at all divine. 10 You will die like a dog at the hand of godless foreigners. I, the Sovereign LORD, have given the command."

The Fall of the King of Tyre

11 The LORD spoke to me again. 12 "Mortal man," he said, "grieve for the fate that is waiting for the king of Tyre. Tell him what I, the Sovereign LORD, am saying: You were once an example of perfection. How wise and handsome you were! 13 You lived in Eden, the garden of God, and wore gems of every kind: rubies and diamonds; topaz, beryl, carnelian, and jasper; sapphires, emeralds, and garnets. You had ornaments of gold. They were made for you*n* on the day you were created. 14 I put a terrifying angel there to guard you.*o* You lived on my holy mountain and walked among sparkling gems. 15 Your conduct was perfect from the day you were created until you began to do evil. 16 You were busy buying and selling, and this led you to violence and sin. So I forced you to leave my holy mountain, and the angel who guarded you drove you away from the sparkling gems. 17 You were proud of being handsome, and your fame made you act like a fool. Because of this I hurled you to the ground and left you as a warning to other kings. 18 You did such evil in buying and selling that your places of worship were corrupted. So I set fire to the city and burned it to the ground. All who look at you now see you reduced to ashes. 19 You are gone, gone forever, and all the nations that had come to know you are terrified, afraid that they will share your fate."

Prophecy against Sidon

20 The LORD said to me, 21 "Mortal man, denounce the city of Sidon. 22 Tell the people there what I, the Sovereign LORD, say about them: I am your enemy, Sidon; people will praise me because of what I do to you. They will know that I am the LORD, when I show how holy I am by punishing those who live in you. 23 I will send diseases on you and make blood flow in your streets. You will be attacked from every side, and your people will be killed. Then you will know that I am the LORD."

---

m Danel; or Daniel (see 14.14).   *n Probable text They were made for you; Hebrew unclear.*
o One ancient translation I put . . . you; Hebrew unclear.

EZEKIEL

Israel Will Be Blessed

24 The LORD said, "None of the surrounding nations that treated Israel with scorn will ever again be like thorns and briers to hurt Israel. And they will know that I am the Sovereign LORD."

25 The Sovereign LORD said, "I will bring back the people of Israel from the nations where I scattered them, and all the nations will know that I am holy. The people of Israel will live in their own land, the land that I gave to my servant Jacob. 26 They will live there in safety. They will build houses and plant vineyards. I will punish all their neighbors who treated them with scorn, and Israel will be secure. Then they will know that I am the LORD their God."

Prophecy against Egypt

29 On the twelfth day of the tenth month of the tenth year of our exile, the LORD spoke to me. 2 "Mortal man," he said, "denounce the king of Egypt. Tell him how he and all the land of Egypt will be punished. 3 Say that this is what the Sovereign LORD is telling the king of Egypt: I am your enemy, you monster crocodile, lying in the river. You say that the Nile is yours and that you made it.p 4 I am going to put a hook through your jaw and make the fish in your river stick fast to you. Then I will pull you up out of the Nile, with all the fish sticking to you. 5 I will throw you and all those fish into the desert. Your body will fall on the ground and be left unburied. I will give it to the birds and animals for food. 6 Then all the people of Egypt will know that I am the LORD."

The LORD says, "The Israelites relied on you Egyptians for support, but you were no better than a weak stick. 7 When they leaned on you, you broke, pierced their armpits, and made them wrench their backs.q 8 Now then, I, the Sovereign LORD, am telling you that I will have troops attack you with swords, and they will kill your people and your animals. 9 Egypt will become an empty wasteland. Then you will know that I am the LORD.

"Because you said that the Nile is yours and you made it, 10 I am your enemy and the enemy of your Nile. I will make all of Egypt an empty wasteland, from the city of Migdol in the north to the city of Aswan in the south, all the way to the Ethiopianr border. 11 No human being or animal will walk through it. For forty years nothing will live there. 12 I will make Egypt the most desolate country in the world. For forty years the cities of Egypt will lie in ruins, ruins worse than those of any other city. I will make the Egyptians refugees. They will flee to every country and live among other peoples."

13 The Sovereign LORD says, "After forty years I will bring the Egyptians back from the nations where I have scattered them, 14 and I will let them live in southern Egypt, their original home. There they will be a weak kingdom, 15 the weakest kingdom of all, and they will never again rule other nations. I will make them so unimportant that they will not be able to bend any other nation to their will. 16 Israel will never again depend on them for help. Egypt's fate will remind Israel how wrong it was to rely on them. Then Israel will know that I am the Sovereign LORD."

King Nebuchadnezzar Will Conquer Egypt

17 On the first day of the first month of the twenty-seventh year of our exile, the LORD spoke to me. 18 "Mortal man," he said, "King Nebuchadnezzar of Babylonia launched an attack on Tyre. He made his soldiers carry such heavy loads that their heads were rubbed bald and their shoulders were worn raw, but neither the king nor his army got anything for all their trouble. 19 So now this is what I, the Sovereign LORD, am saying: I am giving the land of Egypt to King Nebuchadnezzar. He will loot and plunder it and carry off all the wealth of Egypt as his army's pay. 20 I am giving him Egypt in payment for his services, because his army was working for me. I, the Sovereign LORD, have spoken.

p Some ancient translations you made it; Hebrew you made yourself.
q One ancient translation wrench their backs; Hebrew make their backs stand.
r Hebrew Cushite (Cush): Cush is the ancient name of the extensive territory south of the First Cataract of the Nile River. This region was called Ethiopia in Graeco-Roman times, and included within its borders most of modern Sudan and some of present-day Ethiopia (Abyssinia).

21 "When that happens, I will make the people of Israel strong and let you, Ezekiel, speak out where everyone can hear you, so that they will know that I am the LORD."

The LORD Will Punish Egypt

30 The LORD spoke to me again. 2 "Mortal man," he said, "prophesy and announce what I, the Sovereign LORD, am saying. You are to shout these words:

A day of terror is coming!
3 The day is near, the day when the
  LORD will act,
A day of clouds and trouble for
  the nations.
4 There will be war in Egypt
And great distress in Ethiopia.r
Many in Egypt will be killed;
The country will be plundered
And left in ruins.
5 "That war will also kill the soldiers hired from Ethiopia,r Libya, Lydia, Arabia, Kub, and even from among my own people."

6 The LORD says, "From Migdol in the north to Aswan in the south, all Egypt's defenders will be killed in battle. Egypt's proud army will be destroyed. I, the Sovereign LORD, have spoken. 7 The land will be the most desolate in the world, and its cities will be left totally in ruins. 8 When I set fire to Egypt and all her defenders are killed, then they will know that I am the LORD.

9 "When that day comes and Egypt is destroyed, I will send messengers in ships to arouse the unsuspecting people of Ethiopia,r and they will be terrified. That day is coming!"

10 The Sovereign LORD says, "I will use King Nebuchadnezzar of Babylonia to put an end to Egypt's wealth. 11 He and his ruthless army will come to devastate the land. They will attack Egypt with swords, and the land will be full of corpses. 12 I will dry up the Nile and put Egypt under the power of evil people. Foreigners will devastate the whole country. I, the LORD, have spoken."

13 The Sovereign LORD says, "I will destroy the idols and the false gods in Memphis. There will be no one to rule

Egypt, and I will terrify all the people. 14 I will make southern Egypt desolate and set fire to the city of Zoan in the north. I will punish the capital city of Thebes. 15 I will let the city of Pelusium, Egypt's great fortress, feel my fury. I will destroy the wealth of Thebes. 16 I will set fire to Egypt, and Pelusium will be in agony. The walls of Thebes will be broken down, and the city will be flooded.s 17 The young men of the cities of Heliopolis and Bubastis will die in the war, and the other people will be taken prisoner. 18 Darkness will fall on Tahpanhes when I break the power of Egypt and put an end to the strength they were so proud of. A cloud will cover Egypt, and the people of all her cities will be taken prisoner. 19 When I punish Egypt in this way, they will know that I am the LORD."

The Broken Power of the King of Egypt

20 On the seventh day of the first month of the eleventh year of our exile, the LORD spoke to me. 21 "Mortal man," he said, "I have broken the arm of the king of Egypt. No one has bandaged it or put it in a sling so that it could heal and be strong enough to hold a sword again. 22 Now then, this is what I, the Sovereign LORD, say: I am the enemy of the king of Egypt. I am going to break both his arms—the good one and the one already broken—and the sword will fall from his hand. 23 I am going to scatter the Egyptians throughout the world. 24 Then I will make the arms of the king of Babylonia strong and put my sword in his hands. But I will break the arms of the king of Egypt, and he will groan and die in front of his enemy. 25 Yes, I will weaken him and strengthen the king of Babylonia. When I give him my sword and he points it toward Egypt, everyone will know that I am the LORD. 26 I will scatter the Egyptians throughout the world. Then they will know that I am the LORD."

Egypt Is Compared to a Cedar Tree

31 On the first day of the third month of the eleventh year of our exile, the LORD spoke to me. 2 "Mortal

---

r *Hebrew* Cushite (Cush): *Cush is the ancient name of the extensive territory south of the First Cataract of the Nile River. This region was called Ethiopia in Graeco-Roman times, and included within its borders most of modern Sudan and some of present-day Ethiopia (Abyssinia).*   s *One ancient translation* flooded; *Hebrew unclear.*

man," he said, "say to the king of Egypt
and all his people:

How powerful you are!
What can I compare you to?
[3] You are like *t* a cedar in Lebanon,
With beautiful, shady branches,
A tree so tall it reaches the
clouds. *u*
[4] There was water to make it grow,
And underground rivers to feed it.
They watered the place where the
tree was growing
And sent streams to all the trees
of the forest.
[5] Because it was well-watered,
It grew taller than other trees.
Its branches grew thick and long.
[6] Every kind of bird built nests in its
branches;
The wild animals bore their young
in its shelter;
The nations of the world rested in
its shade.
[7] How beautiful the tree was —
So tall, with such long branches.
Its roots reached down to the
deep-flowing streams.
[8] No cedar in God's garden could
compare with it.
No fir tree ever had such
branches,
And no plane tree such limbs.
No tree in God's own garden was
so beautiful.
[9] I made it beautiful, with spreading
branches.
It was the envy of every tree in
Eden, the garden of God.

[10] "Now then, I, the Sovereign LORD,
will tell you what is going to happen to
that tree that grew until it reached the
clouds. *u* As it grew taller it grew proud;
[11] so I have rejected it and will let a foreign ruler have it. He will give that tree
what it deserves for its wickedness.
[12] Ruthless foreigners will cut it down
and leave it. Its branches and broken
limbs will fall on every mountain and
valley in the country. All the nations that
have been living in its shade will go
away. [13] The birds will come and perch
on the fallen tree, and the wild animals
will walk over its branches. [14] And so
from now on, no tree, no matter how

well-watered it is, will grow that tall
again or push its top through the
clouds *u* and reach such a height. All of
them are doomed to die like mortals,
doomed to join those who go down to
the world of the dead."

[15] This is what the Sovereign LORD
says: "On the day when the tree goes to
the world of the dead, I will make the
underground waters cover it as a sign of
mourning. I will hold back the rivers and
not let the many streams flow out. Because the tree has died, I will bring darkness over the Lebanon Mountains and
make all the trees of the forest wither.
[16] When I send it down to the world of
the dead, the noise of its downfall will
shake the nations. All the trees of Eden
and all the choice, well-watered trees of
Lebanon who have gone to the world below will be pleased at its downfall.
[17] They will go with it to the world of the
dead to join those that have already
fallen. And all who live under its shadow
will be scattered among the nations. *v*

[18] "The tree is the king of Egypt and all
his people. Not even the trees in Eden
were so tall and impressive. But now,
like the trees of Eden, it will go down to
the world of the dead and join the ungodly and those killed in battle. I have
spoken," says the Sovereign LORD.

The King of Egypt Is Compared to a Crocodile

32 On the first day of the twelfth
month of the twelfth year of our
exile, the LORD spoke to me. [2] "Mortal
man," he said, "give a solemn warning to
the king of Egypt. Give him this message
from me: You act like a lion among the
nations, but you are more like a crocodile splashing through a river. You
muddy the water with your feet and pol-
lute the rivers. [3] When many nations
gather, I will catch you in my net and let
them drag the net ashore. [4] I will throw
you out on the ground and bring all the
birds and animals of the world to feed on
you. [5] I will cover mountains and valleys
with your rotting corpse. [6] I will pour out
your blood until it spreads over the
mountains and fills the streams. [7] When
I destroy you, I will cover the sky and
blot out the stars. The sun will hide be-

---

t Probable text You are like; *Hebrew* Assyria is.
thick branches.   *v Probable text* And all . . . nations; *Hebrew unclear.*
u One ancient translation clouds; *Hebrew*

hind the clouds, and the moon will give no light. 8 I will put out all the lights of heaven and plunge your world into darkness. I, the Sovereign LORD, have spoken.

9 "Many nations will be troubled when I spread the news of your destruction through countries you never heard of. 10 What I do to you will shock many nations. When I swing my sword, kings will shudder with fright. On the day you fall, all of them will tremble in fear for their own lives."

11 The Sovereign LORD says to the king of Egypt, "You will face the sword of the king of Babylonia. 12 I will let soldiers from cruel nations draw their swords and kill all your people. All your people and everything else that you are proud of will be destroyed. 13 I will slaughter your cattle at every water hole. There will be no people or cattle to muddy the water any more. 14 I will let your waters settle and become clear and let your rivers run calm. I, the Sovereign LORD, have spoken. 15 When I make Egypt a desolate wasteland and destroy all who live there, they will know that I am the LORD. 16 This solemn warning will become a funeral song. The women of the nations will sing it to mourn for Egypt and all its people. I, the Sovereign LORD, have spoken."

The World of the Dead

17 On the fifteenth day of the first month[w] of the twelfth year of our exile, the LORD spoke to me. 18 "Mortal man," he said, "mourn for all the many people of Egypt. Send them down with the other powerful nations to the world of the dead. 19 Say to them:

"Do you think you are more
    beautiful than anyone else?
You will go down to the world of
    the dead
    and lie there among the
    ungodly.

20 "The people of Egypt will fall with those who are killed in battle. A sword is ready to kill them all.[x] 21 The greatest heroes and those who fought on the Egyptian side welcome the Egyptians to the world of the dead. They shout: 'The ungodly who were killed in battle have come down here, and here they lie!'

22 "Assyria is there, with the graves of her soldiers all around. They were all killed in battle, 23 and their graves are in the deepest parts of the world of the dead. All her soldiers fell in battle, and their graves surround her tomb. Yet once they terrified the land of the living.

24 "Elam is there, with the graves of her soldiers all around. They were all killed in battle, and they went down, uncircumcised, to the world of the dead. In life they spread terror, but now they lie dead and disgraced. 25 Elam lies down among those killed in battle, and the graves of her soldiers are all around her. They are all uncircumcised, all killed in battle. In life they spread terror, but now they lie dead and disgraced, sharing the fate of those killed in battle.

26 "Meshech and Tubal are there, with the graves of their soldiers all around. They are all uncircumcised, all killed in battle. Yet once they terrified the living. 27 They were not given honorable burial like the heroes of ancient times,[y] who went fully armed to the world of the dead, their swords placed under their heads and their shields[z] over their bodies. These heroes were once powerful enough to terrify the living.

28 "That is how the Egyptians will lie crushed among the uncircumcised who were killed in battle.

29 "Edom is there with her kings and rulers. They were powerful soldiers, but now they lie in the world of the dead with the uncircumcised who were killed in battle.

30 "All the princes of the north are there, and so are the Sidonians. Their power once spread terror, but now they go down in disgrace with those killed in battle and are laid to rest, uncircumcised. They share the disgrace of those who go down to the world of the dead.

31 "The sight of all these who were killed in battle will be a comfort to the king of Egypt and his army," says the Sovereign LORD. 32 "I caused the king of Egypt to terrorize the living, but he and all his army will be killed and laid to rest with all the

---

w One ancient translation of the first month; Hebrew does not have these words.
x Probable text A sword . . . all; Hebrew unclear.   y Some ancient translations of ancient times; Hebrew of the uncircumcised.   z Probable text shields; Hebrew iniquities.

uncircumcised who die in battle." The Sovereign LORD has spoken.

God Appoints Ezekiel as a Lookout
(Ezekiel 3.16-21)

33 The LORD spoke to me. ²"Mortal man," he said, "tell your people what happens when I bring war to a land. The people of that country choose one of their number to be a lookout. ³When he sees the enemy approaching, he sounds the alarm to warn everyone. ⁴If someone hears it but pays no attention and the enemy comes and kills him, then he is to blame for his own death. ⁵His death is his own fault, because he paid no attention to the warning. If he had paid attention, he could have escaped. ⁶If, however, the lookout sees the enemy coming and does not sound the alarm, the enemy will come and kill those sinners, but I will hold the lookout responsible for their death.

⁷"Now, mortal man, I am making you a lookout for the nation of Israel. You must pass on to them the warnings I give you. ⁸If I announce that an evil person is going to die but you do not warn him to change his ways so that he can save his life, then he will die, still a sinner, and I will hold you responsible for his death. ⁹If you do warn an evil person and he doesn't stop sinning, he will die, still a sinner, but your life will be spared."

Individual Responsibility

¹⁰The LORD spoke to me. "Mortal man," he said, "repeat to the Israelites what they are saying: 'We are burdened with our sins and the wrongs we have done. We are wasting away. How can we live?' ¹¹Tell them that as surely as I, the Sovereign LORD, am the living God, I do not enjoy seeing sinners die. I would rather see them stop sinning and live. Israel, stop the evil you are doing. Why do you want to die?

¹²"Now, mortal man, tell the Israelites that when someone good sins, the good he has done will not save him. If an evil person stops doing evil, he won't be punished, and if a good man starts sinning, his life will not be spared. ¹³I may promise life to someone good, but if he starts thinking that his past goodness is enough and begins to sin, I will not remember any of the good he did. He will die because of his sins. ¹⁴I may warn

someone evil that he is going to die, but if he stops sinning and does what is right and good — ¹⁵for example, if he returns the security he took for a loan or gives back what he stole — if he stops sinning and follows the laws that give life, he will not die, but live. ¹⁶I will forgive the sins he has committed, and he will live because he has done what is right and good.

¹⁷"And your people say that what I do isn't right! No, it's their way that isn't right. ¹⁸When someone righteous stops doing good and starts doing evil, he will die for it. ¹⁹When someone evil quits sinning and does what is right and good, he has saved his life. ²⁰But Israel, you say that what I do isn't right. I am going to judge you by what you do."

The News of Jerusalem's Fall

²¹On the fifth day of the tenth month of the twelfth year of our exile, someone who had escaped from Jerusalem came and told me that the city had fallen. ²²The evening before he came, I had felt the powerful presence of the LORD. When the man arrived the next morning, the LORD gave me back the power of speech.

The Sins of the People

²³The LORD spoke to me. ²⁴"Mortal man," he said, "the people who are living in the ruined cities of the land of Israel are saying: 'Abraham was only one man, and he was given the whole land. There are many of us, so now the land is ours.'

²⁵"Tell them what I, the Sovereign LORD, am saying: You eat meat with the blood still in it. You worship idols. You commit murder. What makes you think that the land belongs to you? ²⁶You rely on your swords. Your actions are disgusting. Everyone commits adultery. What makes you think that the land is yours?

²⁷"Tell them that I, the Sovereign LORD, warn them that as surely as I am the living God, the people who live in the ruined cities will be killed. Those living in the country will be eaten by wild animals. Those hiding in the mountains and in caves will die of disease. ²⁸I will make the country a desolate wasteland, and the power they were so proud of will come to an end. The mountains of Israel will be so wild that no one will be able to

travel through them. 29 When I punish the people for their sins and make the country a wasteland, then they will know that I am the LORD."

The Results of the Prophet's Message

30 The LORD said, "Mortal man, your people are talking about you when they meet by the city walls or in the doorways of their houses. They say to one another, 'Let's go and hear what word has come from the LORD now.' 31 So my people crowd in to hear what you have to say, but they don't do what you tell them to do. Loving words are on their lips, but they continue their greedy ways. 32 To them you are nothing more than an entertainer singing love songs or playing a harp. They listen to all your words and don't obey a single one of them. 33 But when all your words come true — and they will come true — then they will know that a prophet has been among them."

The Shepherds of Israel

34 The LORD spoke to me. 2 "Mortal man," he said, "denounce the rulers of Israel. Prophesy to them, and tell them what I, the Sovereign LORD, say to them: You are doomed, you shepherds of Israel! You take care of yourselves, but never tend the sheep. 3 You drink the milk, wear clothes made from the wool, and kill and eat the finest sheep. But you never tend the sheep. 4 You have not taken care of the weak ones, healed the ones that are sick, bandaged the ones that are hurt, brought back the ones that wandered off, or looked for the ones that were lost. Instead, you treated them cruelly. 5 Because the sheep had no shepherd, they were scattered, and wild animals killed and ate them. 6 So my sheep wandered over the high hills and the mountains. They were scattered over the face of the earth, and no one looked for them or tried to find them.

7 "Now, you shepherds, listen to what I, the LORD, am telling you. 8 As surely as I am the living God, you had better listen to me. My sheep have been attacked by wild animals that killed and ate them because there was no shepherd. My shepherds did not try to find the sheep. They were taking care of themselves and not the sheep. 9 So listen to me, you shep-

herds. 10 I, the Sovereign LORD, declare that I am your enemy. I will take my sheep away from you and never again let you be their shepherds; never again will I let you take care only of yourselves. I will rescue my sheep from you and not let you eat them.

The Good Shepherd

11 "I, the Sovereign LORD, tell you that I myself will look for my sheep and take care of them 12 in the same way as shepherds take care of their sheep that were scattered and are brought together again. I will bring them back from all the places where they were scattered on that dark, disastrous day. 13 I will take them out of foreign countries, gather them together, and bring them back to their own land. I will lead them back to the mountains and the streams of Israel and will feed them in pleasant pastures. 14 I will let them graze in safety in the mountain meadows and the valleys and in all the green pastures of the land of Israel. 15 I myself will be the shepherd of my sheep, and I will find them a place to rest. I, the Sovereign LORD, have spoken.

16 "I will look for those that are lost, bring back those that wander off, bandage those that are hurt, and heal those that are sick; but those that are fat and strong I will destroy, because I am a shepherd who does what is right.

17 "Now then, my flock, I, the Sovereign LORD, tell you that I will judge each of you and separate the good from the bad, the sheep from the goats. 18 Some of you are not satisfied with eating the best grass; you even trample down what you don't eat! You drink the clear water and muddy what you don't drink! 19 My other sheep have to eat the grass you trample down and drink the water you muddy.

20 "So now, I, the Sovereign LORD, tell you that I will judge between you strong sheep and the weak sheep. 21 You pushed the sick ones aside and butted them away from the flock. 22 But I will rescue my sheep and not let them be mistreated any more. I will judge each of my sheep and separate the good from the bad. 23 I will give them a king like my servant David to be their one shepherd, and he will take care of them. 24 I, the LORD, will be their God, and a king like my servant David will be their ruler. I

have spoken. 25 I will make a covenant with them that guarantees their security. I will get rid of all the dangerous animals in the land, so that my sheep can live safely in the fields and sleep in the forests.

26 "I will bless them and let them live around my sacred hill.ª There I will bless them with showers of rain when they need it. 27 The trees will bear fruit, the fields will produce crops, and everyone will live in safety on his own land. When I break my people's chains and set them free from those who made them slaves, then they will know that I am the LORD. 28 The heathen nations will not plunder them any more, and the wild animals will not kill and eat them. They will live in safety, and no one will terrify them. 29 I will give them fertile fields and put an end to hunger in the land. The other nations will not sneer at them any more. 30 Everyone will know that I protect Israel and that they are my people. I, the Sovereign LORD, have spoken.

31 "You, my sheep, the flock that I feed, are my people, and I am your God," says the Sovereign LORD.

God's Punishment of Edom

35 The LORD spoke to me. 2 "Mortal man," he said, "denounce the country of Edom. 3 Tell the people what I, the Sovereign LORD, am saying:
"I am your enemy, mountains of Edom!
I will make you a desolate wasteland.
4 I will leave your cities in ruins And your land desolate;
Then you will know that I am the LORD.

5 "You were Israel's constant enemy and let her people be slaughtered in the time of her disaster, the time of final punishment for her sins. 6 So then—as surely as I, the Sovereign LORD, am the living God—death is your fate, and you cannot escape it. You are guilty ofᵇ murder, and murder will follow you. 7 I will make the hill country of Edom a wasteland and kill everyone who travels through it. 8 I will cover the mountains with corpses, and the bodies of those who are killed in battle will cover the hills and valleys. 9 I will make you deso-

late forever, and no one will live in your cities again. Then you will know that I am the LORD.

10 "You said that the two nations, Judah and Israel, together with their lands, belonged to you and that you would possess them, even though I, the LORD, was their God. 11 So then, as surely as I, the Sovereign LORD, am the living God, I will pay you back for your anger, your jealousy, and your hate toward my people. They will know that I am punishing you for what you did to them. 12 Then you will know that I, the LORD, heard you say with contempt that the mountains of Israel were desolate and that they were yours to devour. 13 I have heard the wild, boastful way you have talked against me."

14 The Sovereign LORD says, "I will make you so desolate that the whole world will rejoice at your downfall, 15 just as you rejoiced at the devastation of Israel, my own possession. The mountains of Seir, yes, all the land of Edom, will be desolate. Then everyone will know that I am the LORD."

God's Blessing on Israel

36 The LORD said, "Mortal man, speak to the mountains of Israel and tell them to listen to the message which I, 2 the Sovereign LORD, have for them: Israel's enemies gloated and said, 'Now those ancient hills are ours!'

3 "Prophesy, then, and announce what I, the Sovereign LORD, am saying. When the neighboring nations captured and plundered the mountains of Israel, everyone made fun of Israel. 4 So now listen to what I, the Sovereign LORD, say to you mountains and hills, to you brooks and valleys, to you places that were left in ruins, and to you deserted cities which were plundered and mocked by all the surrounding nations.

5 "I, the Sovereign LORD, have spoken out in the heat of my anger against the surrounding nations, and especially against Edom. With glee and contempt they captured my land and took possession of its pastures.

6 "So prophesy to the land of Israel; tell the mountains, hills, brooks, and valleys what I, the Sovereign LORD, am saying in jealous anger because of the way the na-

---

ª SACRED HILL: See 20.40.   ᵇ One ancient translation are guilty of; Hebrew hate.

tions have insulted and humiliated them. 7I, the Sovereign LORD, solemnly promise that the surrounding nations will be humiliated. 8But on the mountains of Israel the trees will again grow leaves and bear fruit for you, my people Israel. You are going to come home soon. 9I am on your side, and I will make sure that your land is plowed again and crops are planted on it. 10I will make your population grow. You will live in the cities and rebuild everything that was left in ruins. 11I will make people and cattle increase in number. There will be more of you than ever before, and you will have many children. I will let you live there as you used to live, and I will make you more prosperous than ever. Then you will know that I am the LORD. 12I will bring you, my people Israel, back to live again in the land. It will be your own land, and it will never again let your children starve.

13"I, the Sovereign LORD, say: It is true that people say that the land eats people and that it robs the nation of its children. 14But from now on it will no longer eat people and rob you of your children. I, the Sovereign LORD, have spoken. 15The land will no longer have to listen to the nations making fun of it or see the peoples sneer at it. The land will no longer rob the nation of its children. I, the Sovereign LORD, have spoken."

Israel's New Life

16The LORD spoke to me. 17"Mortal man," he said, "when the Israelites were living in their land, they defiled it by the way they lived and acted. I regarded their behavior as being as ritually unclean as a woman is during her monthly period.c 18I let them feel the force of my anger because of the murders they had committed in the land and because of the idols by which they had defiled it. 19I condemned them for the way they lived and acted, and I scattered them through foreign countries. 20Wherever they went, they brought disgrace on my holy name, because people would say, 'These are the people of the LORD, but they had to leave his land.' 21That made me concerned for my holy name, since

the Israelites brought disgrace on it everywhere they went.

22"Now then, give the Israelites the message that I, the Sovereign LORD, have for them: What I am going to do is not for the sake of you Israelites, but for the sake of my holy name, which you have disgraced in every country where you have gone. 23When I demonstrate to the nations the holiness of my great name— the name you disgraced among them— then they will know that I am the LORD. I, the Sovereign LORD, have spoken. I will use you to show the nations that I am holy. 24I will take you from every nation and country and bring you back to your own land. 25I will sprinkle clean water on you and make you clean from all your idols and everything else that has defiled you. 26I will give you a new heart and a new mind. I will take away your stubborn heart of stone and give you an obedient heart. 27I will put my spirit in you and will see to it that you follow my laws and keep all the commands I have given you. 28Then you will live in the land I gave your ancestors. You will be my people, and I will be your God. 29I will save you from everything that defiles you. I will command the grain to be plentiful, so that you will not have any more famines. 30I will increase the yield of your fruit trees and your fields, so that there will be no more famines to disgrace you among the nations. 31You will remember your evil conduct and the wrongs that you committed, and you will be disgusted with yourselves because of your sins and your iniquities. 32Israel, I want you to know that I am not doing all this for your sake. I want you to feel the shame and disgrace of what you are doing. I, the Sovereign LORD, have spoken."

33The Sovereign LORD says, "When I make you clean from all your sins, I will let you live in your cities again and let you rebuild the ruins. 34Everyone who used to walk by your fields saw how overgrown and wild they were, but I will let you farm them again. 35Everyone will talk about how this land, which was once a wilderness, has become like the Garden of Eden, and how the cities which were torn down, looted, and left

---

c RITUALLY UNCLEAN ... PERIOD: *This is based on the view of ritual uncleanness described in the Law of Moses (see Lv 15.19).*

in ruins, are now inhabited and fortified. 36 Then the neighboring nations that have survived will know that I, the LORD, rebuild ruined cities and replant waste fields. I, the LORD, have promised that I would do this — and I will."

37 The Sovereign LORD says, "I will once again let the Israelites ask me for help, and I will let them increase in numbers like a flock of sheep. 38 The cities that are now in ruins will then be as full of people as Jerusalem was once full of the sheep which were offered as sacrifices at a festival. Then they will know that I am the LORD."

The Valley of Dry Bones

37 I felt the powerful presence of the LORD, and his spirit took me and set me down in a valley where the ground was covered with bones. 2 He led me all around the valley, and I could see that there were very many bones and that they were very dry. 3 He said to me, "Mortal man, can these bones come back to life?"

I replied, "Sovereign LORD, only you can answer that!"

4 He said, "Prophesy to the bones. Tell these dry bones to listen to the word of the LORD. 5 Tell them that I, the Sovereign LORD, am saying to them: I am going to put breath into you and bring you back to life. 6 I will give you sinews and muscles, and cover you with skin. I will put breath into you and bring you back to life. Then you will know that I am the LORD."

7 So I prophesied as I had been told. While I was speaking, I heard a rattling noise, and the bones began to join together. 8 While I watched, the bones were covered with sinews and muscles, and then with skin. But there was no breath in the bodies.

9 God said to me, "Mortal man, prophesy to the wind. d Tell the wind that the Sovereign LORD commands it to come from every direction, to breathe into these dead bodies, and to bring them back to life."

10 So I prophesied as I had been told. Breath entered the bodies, and they came to life and stood up. There were enough of them to form an army.

11 God said to me, "Mortal man, the people of Israel are like these bones. They say that they are dried up, without any hope and with no future. 12 So prophesy to my people Israel and tell them that I, the Sovereign LORD, am going to open their graves. I am going to take them out and bring them back to the land of Israel. 13 When I open the graves where my people are buried and bring them out, they will know that I am the LORD. 14 I will put my breath in them, bring them back to life, and let them live in their own land. Then they will know that I am the LORD. I have promised that I would do this — and I will. I, the LORD, have spoken."

Judah and Israel in One Kingdom

15 The LORD spoke to me again. 16 "Mortal man," he said, "take a wooden stick and write on it the words, 'The kingdom of Judah.' Then take another stick and write on it the words, 'The kingdom of Israel.' 17 Then hold the two sticks end to end in your hand so that they look like one stick. 18 When your people ask you to tell them what this means, 19 tell them that I, the Sovereign LORD, am going to take the stick representing Israel and put it with the one that represents Judah. Out of the two I will make one stick and hold it in my hand.

20 "Hold in your hand the two sticks and let the people see them. 21 Then tell them that I, the Sovereign LORD, am going to take all my people out of the nations where they have gone, gather them together, and bring them back to their own land. 22 I will unite them into one nation in the land, on the mountains of Israel. They will have one king to rule over them, and they will no longer be divided into two nations or split into two kingdoms. 23 They will not defile themselves with disgusting idols any more or corrupt themselves with sin. I will free them from all the ways in which they sin and betray me. I will purify them; they will be my people, and I will be their God. 24 A king like my servant David will be their king. They will all be united under one ruler and will obey my laws faithfully. 25 They will live on the land I gave to my servant Jacob, the land where their ancestors lived. They will live there forever, and so will their chil-

---

d wind; or spirit. *The same Hebrew word may mean* wind, or spirit, or breath.

dren and all their descendants. A king like my servant David will rule them forever. 26 I will make a covenant with them that guarantees their security forever. I will establish them and increase their population, and will see to it that my Temple stands forever in their land. 27 I will live there with them; I will be their God, and they will be my people. 28 When I place my Temple there to be among them forever, then the nations will know that I, the LORD, have chosen Israel to be my own people."

Gog as the Instrument of God

38 The LORD spoke to me. 2 "Mortal man," he said, "denounce Gog, chief ruler of the nations of Meshech and Tubal in the land of Magog. Denounce him 3 and tell him that I, the Sovereign LORD, am his enemy. 4 I will turn him around, put hooks in his jaws, and drag him and all his troops away. His army, with its horses and uniformed riders, is enormous, and every soldier carries a shield and is armed with a sword. 5 Troops from Persia, Ethiopia,e and Libya are with him, and all have shields and helmets. 6 All the fighting men of the lands of Gomer and Beth Togarmah in the north are with him, and so are men from many other nations. 7 Tell him to get ready and have all his troops ready at his command. 8 After many years I will order him to invade a country where the people were brought back together from many nations and have lived without fear of war. He will invade the mountains of Israel, which were desolate and deserted so long, but where all the people now live in safety. 9 He and his army and the many nations with him will attack like a storm and cover the land like a cloud."

10 This is what the Sovereign LORD says to Gog: "When that time comes, you will start thinking up an evil plan. 11 You will decide to invade a helpless country where the people live in peace and security in unwalled towns that have no defenses. 12 You will plunder and loot the people who live in cities that were once in ruins. They have been gathered from the nations, and now they have livestock and property and live at the crossroads of the world. 13 The people of Sheba and Dedan and the merchants from the towns of Spain will ask you, 'Have you assembled your army and attacked in order to loot and plunder? Do you intend to get silver and gold, livestock and property, and march off with all those spoils?' "

14 So the Sovereign LORD sent me to tell Gog what he was saying to him: "Now while my people Israel live in security, you will set outf 15 to come from your place in the far north, leading a large, powerful army of soldiers from many nations, all of them on horseback. 16 You will attack my people Israel like a storm moving across the land. When the time comes, I will send you to invade my land in order to show the nations who I am, to show my holiness by what I do through you. 17 You are the one I was talking about long ago, when I announced through my servants, the prophets of Israel, that in days to come I would bring someone to attack Israel." The Sovereign LORD has spoken.

God's Punishment of Gog

18 The Sovereign LORD says, "On the day when Gog invades Israel, I will become furious. 19 I declare in the heat of my anger that on that day there will be a severe earthquake in the land of Israel. 20 Every fish and bird, every animal large and small, and every human being on the face of the earth will tremble for fear of me. Mountains will fall, cliffs will crumble, and every wall will collapse. 21 I will terrify Gog with all sorts of calamities.g I, the Sovereign LORD, have spoken. His men will turn their swords against one another. 22 I will punish him with disease and bloodshed. Torrents of rain and hail, together with fire and sulfur, will pour down on him and his army and on the many nations that are on his side. 23 In this way I will show all the nations that I am great and that I am holy. They will know then that I am the LORD."

E
Z
E
K
I
E
L

e Hebrew Cush: Cush is the ancient name of the extensive territory south of the First Cataract of the Nile River. This region was called Ethiopia in Graeco-Roman times, and included within its borders most of modern Sudan and some of present-day Ethiopia (Abyssinia). f One ancient translation set out; Hebrew know.   g One ancient translation terrify . . . calamities; Hebrew unclear.

The Defeat of Gog

39 The Sovereign LORD said, "Mortal man, denounce Gog, the chief ruler of the nations of Meshech and Tubal, and tell him that I am his enemy. 2 I will turn him in a new direction and lead him out of the far north until he comes to the mountains of Israel. 3 Then I will knock his bow out of his left hand and his arrows out of his right hand. 4 Gog and his army and his allies will fall dead on the mountains of Israel, and I will let their bodies be food for all the birds and wild animals. 5 They will fall dead in the open field. I, the Sovereign LORD, have spoken. 6 I will start a fire in the land of Magog and along all the seacoasts where people live undisturbed, and everyone will know that I am the LORD. 7 I will make sure that my people Israel know my holy name, and I will not let my name be disgraced any more. Then the nations will know that I, the LORD, am the holy God of Israel."

8 The Sovereign LORD said, "The day I spoke about is certain to come. 9 The people who live in the cities of Israel will go out and collect the abandoned weapons for firewood. They will build fires with the shields, bows, arrows, spears, and clubs, and have enough to last for seven years. 10 They will not have to gather firewood in the fields or cut down trees in the forest, because they will have the abandoned weapons to burn. They will loot and plunder those who looted and plundered them." The Sovereign LORD has spoken.

The Burial of Gog

11 The LORD said, "When all this happens, I will give Gog a burial ground there in Israel, in Travelers' Valley, east of the Dead Sea.ʰ Gog and all his army will be buried there, and the valley will be called 'The Valley of Gog's Army.' 12 It will take the Israelites seven months to bury all the corpses and make the land clean again. 13 Everyone in the land will help bury them, and they will be honored for this on the day of my victory. I, the Sovereign LORD, have spoken. 14 After the seven months are over, men will be chosen to travel through the land in order to find and bury those bodiesⁱ

remaining on the ground, so that they can make the land clean. 15 As they go up and down the country, every time they find a human bone, they will put a marker beside it so that the gravediggers can come and bury it in the Valley of Gog's Army. 16 (There will be a town nearby named after the army.) And so the land will be made clean again."

17 The Sovereign LORD said to me, "Mortal man, call all the birds and animals to come from all around to eat the sacrifice I am preparing for them. It will be a huge feast on the mountains of Israel, where they can eat meat and drink blood. 18 They are to eat the bodies of soldiers and drink the blood of the rulers of the earth, all of whom will be killed like rams or lambs or goats or fat bulls. 19 When I kill these people like sacrifices, the birds and animals are to eat all the fat they can hold and to drink blood until they are drunk. 20 At my table they will eat all they can hold of horses and their riders and of soldiers and fighting men. I, the Sovereign LORD, have spoken."

The Restoration of Israel

21 The LORD said, "I will let the nations see my glory and show them how I use my power to carry out my just decisions. 22 The Israelites will know from then on that I am the LORD their God. 23 And the nations will know that the Israelites went into exile because of the sins which they committed against me. I turned away from them and let their enemies defeat them and kill them in battle. 24 I gave them what they deserved for their uncleanness and their wickedness, and I turned away from them."

25 The Sovereign LORD said, "But now I will be merciful to Jacob's descendants, the people of Israel, and make them prosperous again. I will protect my holy name. 26 When they are once more living in safety in their own land, with no one to threaten them, they will be able to forget how they were disgraced for having betrayed me. 27 In order to show to the many nations that I am holy, I will bring my people back from all the countries where their enemies live. 28 Then my

---

ʰ *Hebrew has four additional words, the meaning of which is unclear.*
ⁱ *Some ancient translations* those bodies; *Hebrew* the travelers.

people will know that I am the LORD their God. They will know this, because I sent them into captivity and now gather them and bring them back into their own land, not leaving even one of them behind. [29] I will pour out my spirit on the people of Israel and never again turn away from them. I, the Sovereign LORD, have spoken."

A VISION OF THE FUTURE TEMPLE (40.1 — 48.35)

Ezekiel Is Taken to Jerusalem

40 It was the tenth day of the new year, which was the twenty-fifth year after we had been taken into exile and the fourteenth year after Jerusalem was captured. On that day I felt the powerful presence of the LORD, and he carried me away. [2] In a vision God took me to the land of Israel and put me on a high mountain. I saw in front of me[j] a group of buildings that looked like a city. [3] He took me closer, and I saw a man who shone like bronze. He was holding a linen tape measure and a measuring rod and was standing by a gateway.

[4] He said to me, "Watch, mortal man. Listen carefully and pay close attention to everything I show you, because this is why you were brought here. You are to tell the people of Israel everything you see."

The East Gate

[5] What I saw was the Temple, and there was a wall around it. The man took his measuring rod, which was 10 feet long, and measured the wall. It was 10 feet high and 10 feet thick. [6] Then he went to the gateway that faced east. He went up the steps, and at the top he measured the entrance; it was 10 feet deep.[k] [7] Beyond it there was a passageway, which had three guardrooms on each side. Each of the rooms was square, 10 feet on each side, and the walls between them were 8 feet thick. Beyond the guardrooms there was a passageway 10 feet long that led to an entrance room which faced the Temple. [8-9] He measured this room and found it was 14 feet deep. It formed that end of

the gateway which was nearest the Temple, and at its far end the walls were 4 feet thick. ([10] These guardrooms on each side of the passageway were all the same size, and the walls between them were all of the same thickness.)

[11] Next, the man measured the width of the passageway in the gateway. It was 22 feet altogether, and the space between the open gates was 16 feet. [12] In front of each of the guardrooms there was a low wall 20 inches high and 20 inches thick. (The rooms were 10 feet square.) [13] Then he measured the distance from the back wall[l] of one room to the back wall[l] of the room across the passageway from it, and it was 42 feet. [14] The room at the far end led out to a courtyard. He measured that room and found it was 34 feet wide.[m] [15] The total length of the gateway from the outside wall of the gate to the far side of the last room was 84 feet. [16] There were small openings in the outside walls of all the rooms and also in the inner walls between the rooms. There were palm trees carved on the inner walls that faced the passageway.

The Outer Courtyard

[17] The man took me through the gateway into the courtyard. There were thirty rooms built against the outer wall, and in front of them there was an area paved with stones, [18] which extended around the courtyard. This outer courtyard was at a lower level than the inner courtyard. [19] There was a gateway at a higher level that led to the inner courtyard. The man measured the distance between the two gateways, and it was 168 feet.[n]

The North Gate

[20] Then the man measured the gateway on the north side that led into the outer courtyard. [21] The three guardrooms on each side of the passageway, the walls between them, and the entrance room all had the same measurements as those in the east gateway. The total length of the gateway was 84 feet and the width 42 feet. [22] The entrance room, the windows, and the carved palm

---

[j] One ancient translation in front of me; Hebrew in the south.   [k] One ancient translation deep; Hebrew deep, one entrance 10 feet deep.   [l] Probable text back wall; Hebrew roof. [m] Verse 14 in Hebrew is unclear.   [n] Hebrew has two additional words, the meaning of which is unclear.

trees were like those in the east gate. Here seven steps led up to the gate, and the entrance room was at the end facing the courtyard. 23 Across the courtyard from this north gateway was another gateway leading to the inner courtyard, just as there was on the east side. The man measured the distance between these two gateways, and it was 168 feet.

The South Gate

24 Next, the man took me to the south side, and there we saw another gateway. He measured its inner walls and its entrance room, and they were the same as the others. 25 There were windows in the rooms of this gateway just as in the others. The total length of the gateway was 84 feet and the width 42 feet. 26 Seven steps led up to it, and its entrance room was also at the end facing the courtyard. There were palm trees carved on the inner walls that faced the passageway. 27 Here, too, there was a gateway leading to the inner courtyard. The man measured the distance to this second gateway, and it was 168 feet.

The Inner Courtyard: The South Gate

28 The man took me through the south gateway into the inner courtyard. He measured the gateway, and it was the same size as the gateways in the outer wall. 29-30 Its guardrooms, its entrance room, and its inner walls were the same size as those in the other gateways. There were also windows in the rooms of this gateway. The total length was 84 feet and the width 42 feet. 31 Its entrance room faced the other courtyard, and palm trees were carved on the walls along the passageway. Eight steps led up to this gate.

The Inner Courtyard: The East Gate

32 The man took me through the east gateway into the inner courtyard. He measured the gateway, and it was the same size as the others. 33 Its guardrooms, its entrance room, and its inner walls measured the same as those in the other gateways. There were windows all around, and in the entrance room also. The total length was 84 feet and the

width 42 feet. 34 The entrance room faced the outer courtyard. Palm trees were carved on the walls along the passageway. Eight steps led up to this gate.

The Inner Courtyard: The North Gate

35 Then the man took me to the north gateway. He measured it, and it was the same size as the others. 36 Like them, it also had guardrooms, decorated inner walls, an entrance room, and windows all around. Its total length was 84 feet and its width 42 feet. 37 The entrance roomo faced the outer courtyard. Palm trees were carved on the walls along the passageway. Eight steps led up to this gate.

Buildings Near the North Gate

38 In the outer courtyard there was an annex attached to the inner gateway on the north side. It opened into the entrance room that faced the courtyard, and there they washed the carcasses of the animals to be burned whole as sacrifices. 39 In this entrance room there were four tables, two on each side of the room. It was on these tables that they killed the animals to be offered as sacrifices, either to be burned whole or to be sacrifices for sin or as repayment offerings. 40 Outside the room there were four similar tables, two on either side of the entrance of the north gate. 41 Altogether there were eight tables on which the animals to be sacrificed were killed: four inside the room and four out in the courtyard. 42 The four tables in the annex, used to prepare the offerings to be burned whole, were of cut stone. They were 20 inches high, and their tops were 30 inches square. All the equipment used in killing the sacrificial animals was kept on these tables. 43 Ledges 3 inches wide ran around the edge of the tables. All the meat to be offered in sacrifice was placed on the tables.p

44 Then he brought me into the inner court. There were two rooms opening on the inner court, one facing south beside the north gateway and the other facing north beside the south gateway.q 45 The man told me that the room which faced

o Some ancient translations entrance room; Hebrew inner wall.   p Verse 43 in Hebrew is unclear.   q One ancient translation Then . . . south gateway; verse 44 in Hebrew is unclear.

south was for the priests who served in the Temple, 46and the room which faced north was for the priests who served at the altar. All the priests are descended from Zadok; they are the only members of the tribe of Levi who are permitted to go into the LORD's presence to serve him.

The Inner Courtyard and the Temple Building

47The man measured the inner courtyard, and it was 168 feet square. The Temple was on the west side, and in front of it was an altar. 48Then he took me into the entrance room of the Temple. He measured the entranceway: it was 9 feet deep and 24 feet wide,r with walls 5 feet thick on either side. 49Steps led up to the entrance room, which was 34 feet wide and 20 feet deep.s There were two columns, one on each side of the entrance.

41 Next, the man took me into the central room, the Holy Place. He measured the passageway into it: it was 10 feet deept 2and 18 feet wide, with walls 8 feet thick on either side. He measured the room itself: it was 68 feet long and 34 feet wide.

3Then he went to the innermost room. He measured the passageway into it: it was 3 feet deep and 10 feet wide, with walls on either side 12 feet thick.u 4He measured the room itself, and it was 34 feet square. This room was beyond the central room. Then he said to me, "This is the Most Holy Place."

The Rooms Built against the Temple Walls

5The man measured the thickness of the inner wall of the Temple building, and it was 10 feet. Against this wall, all around the Temple, was a series of small rooms 7 feet wide. 6These rooms were in three stories, with thirty rooms on each floor. The Temple's outer wall on each floor was thinner than on the floor below, so that the rooms could rest on the wall without being anchored into it. 7And so the Temple walls, when seen from the outside, seemed to have the same thickness all the way to the top.

Against the Temple's outer wall, on the outside of the rooms, two wide stairways were built, so that it was possible to go from the lower story to the middle and the upper stories.v 8-11The outside wall of these rooms was 8 feet thick; there was one door into the rooms on the north side of the Temple, and one into those on the south side. I saw that there was a terrace 8 feet wide around the Temple; it was 10 feet above the ground and it was level with the foundation of the rooms by the Temple walls. Between the terrace and the buildings used by the priests there was an open space 34 feet across, along the sides of the Temple.

The Building on the West

12At the far end of the open space on the west side of the Temple there was a building 150 feet long and 116 feet wide; its walls were 9 feet thick all around.

The Total Measurements of the Temple Building

13The man measured the outside of the Temple, and it was 168 feet long. And from the back of the Temple, across the open space to the far side of the building to the west, the distance was also 168 feet. 14The distance across the front of the Temple, including the open space on either side, was also 168 feet. 15He measured the length of the building to the west, including its galleries on both sides, and it was also 168 feet.

Details of the Temple Building

The entrance room of the Temple, the Holy Place, and the Most Holy Place 16were all paneled with wood from the floor to the windows. These windows could be covered.w 17The inside walls of the Temple, up as high as above the doors, were completely covered with carvingsx 18of palm trees and winged creatures. Palm trees alternated with creatures, one following the other, all the way around the room. Each creature had two faces: 19a human face that was turned toward the palm tree on one side, and a lion's face that was turned toward the tree on the other side. It was like this

r One ancient translation and 24 feet wide; Hebrew does not have these words.
s One ancient translation 20 feet deep; Hebrew 18 feet deep. t Hebrew has two additional words, the meaning of which is unclear. u One ancient translation with walls on either side 12 feet thick; Hebrew and 12 feet thick. v Verse 7 in Hebrew is unclear. w Verse 16 in Hebrew is unclear. x Verse 17 in Hebrew is unclear.

all around the wall, [20]from the floor to above the doors. [21]The doorposts of the Holy Place were square.

The Wooden Altar

In front of the entrance of the Most Holy Place there was something that looked like [22]a wooden altar. It was 5 feet high and 4 feet wide. Its corner posts, its base,[y] and its sides were all made of wood. The man said to me, "This is the table which stands in the presence of the LORD."

The Doors

[23]There was a door at the end of the passageway to the Holy Place and one also at the end of the passageway to the Most Holy Place. [24]They were double doors that swung open in the middle. [25]There were palm trees and winged creatures carved on the doors of the Holy Place, just as there were on the walls. And there was a wooden covering over the outside of the doorway of the entrance room. [26]At the sides of this room there were windows, and the walls were decorated with palm trees.[z]

Two Buildings Near the Temple

42 Then the man took me into the outer courtyard and led me to a building on the north side of the Temple, not far from the building at the west end of the Temple. [2]This building was 168 feet long and 84 feet wide. [3]On one side it faced the space 34 feet wide which was alongside the Temple, and on the other side it faced the pavement of the outer courtyard. It was built on three levels, each one set further back than the one below it. [4]Along the north side of this building was a passageway 16 feet wide and 168 feet long,[a] with entrances on that side. [5]The rooms at the upper level of the building were narrower than those at the middle and lower levels because they were set further back. [6]The rooms at all three levels were on terraces and were not supported by columns like the other buildings in the courtyard. [7-8]At the lower level the outer wall of the building was solid for 84 feet,

half its length; and there were rooms in the remaining 84 feet. At the top level there were rooms in the entire length of the building. [9-10]Below these rooms at the east end of the building, where the wall of the courtyard began,[b] there was an entrance into the outer courtyard.

At the south[c] side of the Temple there was an identical building not far from the building at the west end of the Temple. [11]In front of the rooms there was a passageway just like the one on the north side. It had the same measurements, the same design, and the same kind of entrances. [12]There was a door under the rooms on the south side of the building, at the east end where the wall began.

[13]The man said to me, "Both these buildings are holy. In them the priests who enter the LORD's presence eat the holiest offerings. Because the rooms are holy, the priests will place the holiest offerings there: the offerings of grain and the sacrifices offered for sin or as repayment offerings. [14]When priests have been in the Temple and want to go to the outer courtyard, they must leave in these rooms the holy clothing they wore while serving the LORD. They must put on other clothes before going out to the area where the people gather."

The Measurements of the Temple Area

[15]When the man had finished measuring inside the Temple area, he took me out through the east gate and then measured the outside of the area. [16]He took the measuring rod and measured the east side, and it was 840 feet. [17-19]Then he measured the north side, the south side, and the west side; each side had the same length, 840 feet,[d] [20]so that the wall enclosed a square 840 feet on each side. The wall served to separate what was holy from what was not.

The LORD Returns to the Temple

43 The man took me to the gate that faces east, [2]and there I saw coming from the east the dazzling light of the presence of the God of Israel. God's

[y] Some ancient translations base; Hebrew length.   [z] Hebrew has three additional words, the meaning of which is unclear.   [a] Some ancient translations 168 feet long; Hebrew a way of 20 inches.   [b] One ancient translation where the wall of the courtyard began; Hebrew in the breadth of the wall of the courtyard.   [c] One ancient translation south; Hebrew east.
[d] Verses 16-19 in Hebrew are unclear.

voice sounded like the roar of the sea, and the earth shone with the dazzling light. ³This vision was like the one I had seen when God came to destroy Jerusalem, and the one I saw by the Chebar River. Then I threw myself face downward on the ground. ⁴The dazzling light passed through the east gate and went into the Temple.

⁵The LORD's spirit lifted me up and took me into the inner courtyard, where I saw that the Temple was filled with the glory of the LORD. ⁶The man stood beside me there, and I heard the LORD speak to me out of the Temple: ⁷"Mortal man, here is my throne. I will live here among the people of Israel and rule them forever. Neither the people of Israel nor their kings will ever again disgrace my holy name by worshiping other gods or by burying the corpses ofᵉ their dead kings. ⁸The kings built the doorsills and doorposts of their palace right against the doorsills and doorposts of my Temple, so that there was only a wall between us. They disgraced my holy name by all the disgusting things they did, and so in my anger I destroyed them. ⁹Now they must stop worshiping other gods and remove the corpses ofᶠ their kings. If they do, I will live among them forever."

¹⁰And the LORD continued, "Mortal man, tell the people of Israel about the Temple, and let them study its plan. Make them ashamed of their sinful actions. ¹¹Then if they are ashamed of what they have done, explain the plan of the Temple to them: its design, its entrances and exits, its shape, the arrangement of everything, and all its rules and regulations. Write all this down for them so that they can see how everything is arranged and can carry out all the rules. ¹²This is the law of the Temple: All the area surrounding it on the top of the mountain is sacred and holy."

The Altar

¹³These are the measurements of the altar, using the same unit of measure as in measuring the Temple. All around the base of the altar there was a gutter 20 inches deep and 20 inches wide, with a rim at the outside edge 10 inches high. ¹⁴The lowest section of the altar, from the top of the base, was 4 feet high. The next section was set back from the edge 20 inches all around, and was 7 feet high. The section after that was also set back from the edge 20 inches all around. ¹⁵This top section, on which the sacrifices were burned, was also 7 feet high. The projections on the four corners were higher than the rest of the top. ¹⁶The top of the altar was a square, 20 feet on each side. ¹⁷The middle section was also a square, 24 feet on each side, with a rim at the outside edge 10 inches high. (The gutter was 20 inches wide.) The steps going up the altar were on the east side.

The Consecration of the Altar

¹⁸The Sovereign LORD said to me, "Mortal man, listen to what I tell you. When the altar is built, you are to dedicate it by burning sacrifices on it and by sprinkling on it the blood of the animals that were sacrificed. ¹⁹Those priests belonging to the tribe of Levi who are descended from Zadok are the only ones who are to come into my presence to serve me. I, the Sovereign LORD, command this. You will give them a young bull to offer as a sacrifice for sin. ²⁰You are to take some of its blood and put it on the projections on the top corners of the altar, on the corners of the middle section of the altar, and all around its edges. In this way you will purify the altar and consecrate it. ²¹You are to take the bull that is offered as a sacrifice for sin and burn it at the specified place outside the Temple area. ²²The next day you are to take a male goat without any defects and offer it as a sacrifice for sin. Purify the altar with its blood the same way you did with the bull. ²³When you have finished doing that, take a young bull and a young ram, both of them without any defects, ²⁴and bring them to me. The priests will sprinkle salt on them and burn them as an offering to me. ²⁵Each day for seven days you are to offer a goat, a bull, and a ram as sacrifices for sin. All of them must be without any defects. ²⁶For seven days the priests are

E
Z
E
K
I
E
L

ᵉ by burying the corpses of; or by putting up monuments to.   ᶠ remove the corpses of; or remove the monuments to.

to consecrate the altar and make it ready for use. 27When the week is over, the priests are to begin offering on the altar the burnt offerings and the fellowship offerings of the people. Then I will be pleased with all of you. I, the Sovereign Lord, have spoken."

The Use of the East Gate

44 The man led me to the outer gate at the east side of the Temple area. The gate was closed, 2and the Lord said to me, "This gate will stay closed and will never be opened. No human being is allowed to use it, because I, the Lord God of Israel, have entered through it. It is to remain closed. 3The ruling prince, however, may go there to eat a holy meal in my presence. He is to enter and leave the gateway through the entrance room at the inner end."

Rules for Admission to the Temple

4Then the man took me through the north gate to the front of the Temple. As I looked, I saw that the Temple of the Lord was filled with the dazzling light of his presence. I threw myself face downward on the ground, 5and the Lord said to me, "Mortal man, pay attention to everything you see and hear. I am going to tell you the rules and regulations for the Temple. Note carefully which persons are allowed to go in and out of the Temple, and which persons are not allowed.

6"Tell those rebellious people of Israel that I, the Sovereign Lord, will no longer tolerate the disgusting things that they have been doing. 7They have profaned my Temple by letting uncircumcised foreigners, people who do not obey me, enter the Temple when the fat and the blood of the sacrifices are being offered to me. So my people have broken my covenant by all the disgusting things they have done. 8They have not taken charge of the sacred rituals in my Temple, but instead have put foreigners in charge.

9"I, the Sovereign Lord, declare that no uncircumcised foreigner, no one who disobeys me, will enter my Temple, not even a foreigner who lives among the people of Israel."

The Levites Are Excluded from the Priesthood

10The Lord said to me, "I am punishing those Levites who, together with the rest of the people of Israel, deserted me and worshiped idols. 11They may serve me in the Temple by taking charge of the gates and by performing the work of the Temple. They may kill the animals which the people offer for burnt offerings and for sacrifices, and they are to be on duty to serve the people. 12But because they conducted the worship of idols for the people of Israel and in this way led the people into sin, I, the Sovereign Lord, solemnly swear that they must be punished. 13They are not to serve me as priests or to go near anything that is holy to me or to enter the Most Holy Place. This is the punishment for the disgusting things they have done. 14I am assigning to them the menial work that is to be done in the Temple."

The Priests

15The Sovereign Lord said, "Those priests belonging to the tribe of Levi who are descended from Zadok, however, continued to serve me faithfully in the Temple when the rest of the people of Israel turned away from me. So now they are the ones who are to serve me and come into my presence to offer me the fat and the blood of the sacrifices. 16They alone will enter my Temple, serve at my altar, and conduct the Temple worship. 17When they enter the gateway to the inner courtyard of the Temple, they are to put on linen clothing. They must not wear anything made of wool when they are on duty in the inner courtyard or in the Temple. 18So that they won't perspire, they are to wear linen turbans and linen trousers, but no belt. 19Before they go to the outer courtyard where the people are, they must first take off the clothes they wore on duty in the Temple and leave them in the holy rooms. They are to put on other clothing in order to keep their sacred clothing from harming the people.g

20"Priests must neither shave their heads nor let their hair grow long. They are to keep it a proper length. 21Priests must not drink any wine before going

g HARMING THE PEOPLE: *It was believed that ordinary people would be harmed by touching something holy.*

into the inner courtyard. 22 No priest may marry a divorced woman; he is to marry only an Israelite virgin or the widow of another priest.

23 "The priests are to teach my people the difference between what is holy and what is not, and between what is ritually clean and what is not. 24 When a legal dispute arises, the priests are to decide the case according to my laws. They are to keep the religious festivals according to my rules and regulations, and they are to keep the Sabbaths holy.

25 "A priest is not to become ritually unclean by touching a corpse, unless it is one of his parents, one of his children or a brother or an unmarried sister. 26 After he has become clean again, he must wait seven days 27 and then go into the inner courtyard of the Temple and offer a sacrifice for his purification, so that he can serve in the Temple again. I, the Sovereign LORD, have spoken.

28 "The priests have the priesthood as their share of what I have given Israel to be handed down from one generation to another. They are not to hold property in Israel; I am all they need. 29 The grain offerings, the sin offerings, and the repayment offerings will be the priests' food, and they are to receive everything in Israel that is set apart for me. 30 The priests are to have the best of all the first harvest and of everything else that is offered to me. Each time the people bake bread, they are to give the priests the first loaf as an offering, and my blessing will rest on their homes. 31 The priests must not eat any bird or animal that dies a natural death or is killed by another animal."

The LORD's Portion of the Country

45 When the land is divided to give each tribe a share, one part is to be dedicated to the LORD. It is to be 10 miles long by 8 miles[h] wide. The entire area will be holy. 2 In this area there is to be a square plot of land for the Temple, 840 feet on each side, entirely surrounded by an open space 84 feet wide. 3 Half of this area, a section 10 miles by 4 miles, is to be measured off; it will contain the Temple, the holiest place of all.

4 It will be a holy part of the country, set aside for the priests who serve the LORD in his Temple. It will contain their houses and the section of land for the Temple. 5 The other half of the area is to be set aside as the possession of the Levites, who do the work in the Temple. There will be towns there for them to live in.[i]

6 Next to the holy area, another section, 10 miles long and 2 miles wide, is to be set aside for a city where any of the people of Israel may live.

Land for the Prince

7 Land is also to be set aside for the ruling prince. From the west boundary of the holy area it will extend west to the Mediterranean Sea; and from the east boundary it will extend to the eastern border of the country, so that its length will be the same as the length of one of the areas allotted to the tribes of Israel. 8 This area will be the share the ruling prince will have in the land of Israel, so that he will no longer oppress the people, but will let the rest of the country belong to the tribes of Israel.

Rules for the Prince

9 The Sovereign LORD said, "You have sinned too long, you rulers of Israel! Stop your violence and oppression. Do what is right and just. You must never again drive my people off their land. I, the Sovereign LORD, am telling you this.

10 "Everyone must use honest weights and measures:

11 "The ephah for dry measure is to be equal to the bath for liquid measure. The standard is the homer.[j] The resulting measures are as follows:

> 1 homer = 10 ephahs = 10 baths

12 "Your weights are to be as follows:

> 20 gerahs = 1 shekel[k]
> 60 shekels = 1 mina

13-15 "This is the basis on which you are to make your offerings:

> Wheat: 1/60th of your harvest
> Barley: 1/60th of your harvest
> Olive oil: 1/100th of the yield of your trees

(Measure it by the bath: 10 baths = 1 homer = 1 kor.)

---

h One ancient translation 8 miles; Hebrew 4 miles. i One ancient translation towns there for them to live in; Hebrew twenty rooms. j HOMER: A unit of dry or liquid measure, about 5 bushels or 175 quarts; so an ephah or a bath would be about 1/2 bushel or 17.5 quarts. k SHEKEL: In Ezekiel's time this unit of weight was about 0.4 ounce or 11.4 grams.

Sheep: 1 sheep out of every 200 from the meadows of Israel

"You are to bring grain offerings, animals to be burned whole, and animals for fellowship offerings, so that your sins will be forgiven. I, the Sovereign LORD, command it.

16 "All the people of the land must take[l] these offerings to the ruling prince of Israel. 17 It will be his duty to provide the animals to be burned whole, the grain offerings, and the wine offerings for the whole nation of Israel at the New Moon Festivals, the Sabbaths, and the other festivals. He is to provide the sin offerings, the grain offerings, the offerings to be burned whole, and the fellowship offerings, to take away the sins of the people of Israel."

The Festivals

(Exodus 12.1-20; Leviticus 23.33-43)

18 The Sovereign LORD said, "On the first day of the first month you are to sacrifice a bull without any defects and purify the Temple. 19 The priest will take some of the blood of this sin offering and put it on the doorposts of the Temple, on the four corners of the altar, and on the posts of the gateways to the inner courtyard. 20 On the seventh day of the month you are to do the same thing on behalf of anyone who sins unintentionally or through ignorance. In this way you will keep the Temple holy.

21 "On the fourteenth day of the first month you will begin the celebration of the Passover Festival. For seven days everyone will eat bread made without yeast. 22 On the first day of the festival the ruling prince must offer a bull as a sacrifice for his sins and for those of all the people. 23 On each of the seven days of the festival he is to sacrifice to the LORD seven bulls and seven rams without any defects and burn them whole. He is also to sacrifice a male goat each day as a sin offering. 24 For each bull and each ram that is sacrificed, there is to be an offering of half a bushel of grain and three quarts of olive oil.

25 "For the Festival of Shelters, which begins on the fifteenth day of the seventh month, the prince will offer on each of the seven days the same sacrifice for sin, the same offerings to be burned whole, and the same offerings of grain and olive oil."

The Prince and the Festivals

46 The Sovereign LORD says, "The east gateway to the inner courtyard must be kept closed during the six working days, but it is to be opened on the Sabbath and at the New Moon Festival. 2 The ruling prince will go from the outer courtyard into the entrance room of the gateway and stand beside the posts of the gate while the priests burn his sacrifices whole and offer his fellowship offerings. There at the gate he must worship and then go back out. The gate must not be shut until evening. 3 Each Sabbath and each New Moon Festival all the people are also to bow down and worship the LORD in front of the gate. 4 On the Sabbath the prince is to bring to the LORD, as sacrifices to be burned whole, six lambs and one ram, all without any defects. 5 With each ram he is to bring an offering of half a bushel of grain, and with each lamb he is to bring whatever he wants to give. For each half-bushel of grain offering he is to bring three quarts of olive oil. 6 At the New Moon Festival he will offer a young bull, six lambs, and a ram, all without any defects. 7 With each bull and each ram the offering is to be half a bushel of grain, and with each lamb the offering is to be whatever the prince wants to give. Three quarts of olive oil are to be offered with each half-bushel of grain. 8 The prince must leave the entrance room of the gateway and go out by the same way he went in.

9 "When the people come to worship the LORD at any festival, those who enter by the north gate are to leave by the south gate after they have worshiped, and those who enter by the south gate are to leave by the north gate. No one may go out by the same way he entered, but must leave by the opposite gate. 10 The prince is to come in when the people come, and leave when they leave. 11 On the feast days and at the festivals the grain offering will be half a bushel with each bull or ram, and whatever the worshiper wants to give with each lamb. Three quarts of olive oil are to be offered with each half-bushel of grain.

---

l Probable text must take; *Hebrew unclear.*

12 "When the ruling prince wants to make a voluntary offering to the Lord, either an offering to be burned whole or a fellowship offering, the east gate to the inner courtyard will be opened for him. He is to make the offering in the same way he does on the Sabbath, and the gate is to be closed after he goes back out."

The Daily Offering

13 The Lord says, "Every morning a one-year-old lamb without any defects is to be burned whole as an offering to the Lord. This offering must be made every day. 14 Also an offering of five pounds of flour is to be made every morning, along with one quart of olive oil for mixing with the flour. The rules for this offering to the Lord are to be in force forever. 15 The lamb, the flour, and the olive oil are to be offered to the Lord every morning forever."

The Prince and the Land

16 The Sovereign Lord commands: "If the ruling prince gives any of the land he owns to one of his sons as a present, it will belong to that son as a part of his family property. 17 But if the ruling prince gives any of his land to anyone who is in his service, it will become the prince's property again when the Year of Restoration m comes. It belongs to him, and only he and his sons can own it permanently. 18 The ruling prince must not take any of the people's property away from them. Any land he gives to his sons must be from the land that is assigned to him, so that he will not oppress any of my people by taking their land."

The Temple Kitchens

19 Then the man took me to the entrance of the rooms facing north near the gate on the south side of the inner courtyard. These are holy rooms for the priests. He pointed out a place on the west side of the rooms 20 and said, "This is the place where the priests are to boil the meat offered as sacrifices for sin or as repayment offerings, and to bake the offerings of flour, so that nothing holy is carried to the outer courtyard, where it might harm the people." n

21-22 Then he led me to the outer courtyard and showed me that in each of its four corners there was a smaller o courtyard, 68 feet long and 48 feet wide. 23 Each one had a stone wall around it, with fireplaces built against the wall. 24 The man told me, "These are the kitchens where the Temple servants are to boil the sacrifices the people offer."

The Stream Flowing from the Temple

47 The man led me back to the entrance of the Temple. Water was coming out from under the entrance and flowing east, the direction the Temple faced. It was flowing down from under the south part of the Temple past the south side of the altar. 2 The man then took me out of the Temple area by way of the north gate and led me around to the gate that faces east. A small stream of water was flowing out at the south side of the gate. 3 With his measuring rod the man measured 560 yards downstream to the east and told me to wade through the stream there. The water came only to my ankles. 4 Then he measured another 560 yards, and the water came up to my knees. Another 560 yards farther down, the water was up to my waist. 5 He measured 560 yards more, and there the stream was so deep I could not wade through it. It was too deep to cross except by swimming. 6 He said to me, "Mortal man, note all this carefully."

Then the man took me back to the riverbank, 7 and when I got there, I saw that there were very many trees on each bank. 8 He said to me, "This water flows through the land to the east and down into the Jordan Valley and to the Dead Sea. When it flows into the Dead Sea, it replaces the salt water of that sea with fresh water. 9 Wherever the stream flows, there will be all kinds of animals and fish. The stream will make the water of the Dead Sea fresh, and wherever it flows, it will bring life. 10 From the Springs of Engedi all the way to the Springs of Eneglaim, there will be fishermen on the shore of the sea, and they

m YEAR OF RESTORATION: Every fifty years, all Israelites were required to give freedom to any Israelites who had become slaves because of debts; they were also to give back to the original owner, or his heirs, any ancestral land that had been sold for debt (see Lv 25.8-55).
n HARM THE PEOPLE: See 44.19.   o One ancient translation smaller; Hebrew enclosed.

will spread out their nets there to dry. There will be as many different kinds of fish there as there are in the Mediterranean Sea. [11] But the water in the marshes and ponds along the shore will not be made fresh. They will remain there as a source of salt. [12] On each bank of the stream all kinds of trees will grow to provide food. Their leaves will never wither, and they will never stop bearing fruit. They will have fresh fruit every month, because they are watered by the stream that flows from the Temple. The trees will provide food, and their leaves will be used for healing people."

The Boundaries of the Land

[13] The Sovereign LORD said, "These are the boundaries of the land that is to be divided among the twelve tribes, with the tribe of Joseph receiving two sections.[p] [14] I solemnly promised your ancestors that I would give them possession of this land; now divide it equally among you.

[15] "The northern boundary runs eastward from the Mediterranean Sea to the city of Hethlon, to Hamath Pass, to city of Zedad,[q] [16] to the cities of Berothah and Sibraim (they are located between the territory of the kingdom of Damascus and that of the kingdom of Hamath), and to the city of Ticon (located by the border of the district of Hauran). [17] So the northern boundary runs from the Mediterranean eastward to Enon City, with the border regions of Damascus and Hamath to the north of it.

[18] "The eastern boundary runs south from a point between the territory of Damascus and that of Hauran, with the Jordan River forming the boundary between the land of Israel on the west and Gilead on the east, as far as Tamar[r] on the Dead Sea.

[19] "The southern boundary runs southwest from Tamar to the oasis of Kadesh Meribah and then northwest along the Egyptian border to the Mediterranean Sea.

[20] "The western boundary is formed by the Mediterranean and runs north to a point west of Hamath Pass.

[21] "Divide this land among your tribes; [22] it is to be your permanent possession. The foreigners who are living among you and who have had children born here are also to receive their share of the land when you divide it. They are to be treated like full Israelite citizens and are to draw lots for shares of the land along with the tribes of Israel. [23] All foreign residents will receive their share with the people of the tribe among whom they are living. I, the Sovereign LORD, have spoken."

The Division of the Land among the Tribes

48 [1-7] The northern boundary of the land runs eastward from the Mediterranean Sea to the city of Hethlon, to Hamath Pass, to Enon City, to the boundary between the kingdoms of Damascus and Hamath. Each tribe is to receive one section of land extending from the eastern boundary west to the Mediterranean Sea,[s] in the following order from north to south:

    Dan
    Asher
    Naphtali
    Manasseh
    Ephraim
    Reuben
    Judah

The Special Section in the Center of the Land

[8] The next section of the land is to be set apart for special use. It is to be 10 miles wide from north to south, and the same length from east to west as the sections given to the tribes. The Temple will be located within this section.

[9] In the center of this section, a special area 10 miles by 8 miles[t] is to be dedicated to the LORD. [10] The priests are to have a portion of this holy area. From east to west their portion is to measure 10 miles, and from north to south, 4 miles. The Temple of the LORD is to be located in the middle of this area. [11] This holy area is to be for the priests who are descendants of Zadok. They served me faithfully and did not join the rest of the

[p] TWO SECTIONS: *The tribes of Manasseh and Ephraim, the sons of Joseph, were each given one section.* [q] *One ancient translation* Hamath Pass, to the city of Zedad; *Hebrew* Zedad Pass to the city of Hamath. [r] *Some ancient translations* Tamar; *Hebrew unclear.*
[s] *One ancient translation* extending . . . Sea; *Hebrew* having an eastern boundary and a western boundary. [t] *Probable text (see 45.1)* 8 miles; *Hebrew* 4 miles.

Israelites in doing wrong, as the other members of the tribe of Levi did. 12 So they are to have a special area next to the area belonging to the Levites, and it will be the holiest of all. 13 The Levites also are to have a special area, south of that of the priests. It too is to be 10 miles from east to west, by 4 miles from north to south. 14 The area dedicated to the Lord is the best part of all the land, and none of it may be sold or exchanged or transferred to anyone else. It is holy and belongs to the Lord.

15 The part of the special area that is left, 10 miles by 2 miles, is not holy, but is for the general use of the people. They may live there and use the land. The city is to be in the center of it, 16 and it will be a square, 2,520 yards on each side. 17 All around the city on each side there will be an open space 140 yards across. 18 The land that is left after the city has been built in the area immediately to the south of the holy area — 4 miles by 2 miles on the east and 4 miles by 2 miles on the west — is to be used as farmland by the people who live in the city. 19 Anyone who lives in the city, no matter which tribe he comes from, may farm that land.

20 And so the total area in the center of the section which was set apart will be a square measuring 10 miles on each side, and it will include the area occupied by the city.

21-22 To the east and to the west of this area which contains the Temple, the priests' land, the Levites' land, and the city, the remaining land belongs to the ruling prince. It reaches east to the eastern boundary and west to the Mediterranean Sea, and is bounded on the north by the section belonging to Judah and on the south by the one belonging to Benjamin.

Land for the Other Tribes

23-27 South of this special section, each of the remaining tribes is to receive one section of land running from the eastern boundary west to the Mediterranean Sea, in the following order from north to south:

Benjamin
Simeon
Issachar
Zebulun
Gad

28 On the south side of the portion given to the tribe of Gad, the boundary runs southwest from Tamar to the oasis of Kadesh, and then northwest along the Egyptian border to the Mediterranean Sea.

29 The Sovereign Lord said, "That is the way the land is to be divided into sections for the tribes of Israel to possess."

The Gates of Jerusalem

30-34 There are twelve entrances to the city of Jerusalem. Each of the four walls measures 2,520 yards and has three gates in it, each named for one of the tribes. The gates in the north wall are named for Reuben, Judah, and Levi; those in the east wall, for Joseph, Benjamin, and Dan; those in the south wall, for Simeon, Issachar, and Zebulun; and those in the west wall are named for Gad, Asher, and Naphtali. 35 The total length of the wall on all four sides of the city is 10,080 yards. The name of the city from now on will be "The-Lord-Is-Here!"

The Book of
DANIEL

Introduction

The Book of Daniel *was written during a time when the Jews were suffering greatly under the persecution and oppression of a pagan king. Using stories and accounts of visions, the writer encourages the people of his time with the hope that God will bring the tyrant down and restore sovereignty to God's people.*

The book has two main parts: 1) Stories about Daniel and some of his fellow exiles, who through their faith in God and obedience to him triumph over their enemies. These stories are set in the time of the Babylonian and Persian Empires. 2) A series of visions seen by Daniel, which in the form of symbols present the successive rise and fall of several empires, beginning with Babylonia, and predict the downfall of the pagan oppressor and the victory of God's people.

Outline of Contents

THE STORY OF DANIEL AND HIS FRIENDS (1.1 — 6.28)

The Young Men at Nebuchadnezzar's Court

1 In the third year that Jehoiakim was king of Judah, King Nebuchadnezzar of Babylonia attacked Jerusalem and surrounded the city. 2 The Lord let him capture King Jehoiakim and seize some of the Temple treasures. He took some prisoners back with him to the temple of his gods in Babylon, and put the captured treasures in the temple storerooms.

3 The king ordered Ashpenaz, his chief official, to select from among the Israelite exiles some young men of the royal family and of the noble families. 4 They had to be handsome, intelligent, well-trained, quick to learn, and free from physical defects, so that they would be qualified to serve in the royal court. Ashpenaz was to teach them to read and write the Babylonian language. 5 The king also gave orders that every day they were to be given the same food and wine as the members of the royal court. After three years of this training they were to appear before the king. 6 Among those chosen were Daniel, Hananiah,

Mishael, and Azariah, all of whom were from the tribe of Judah. 7 The chief official gave them new names: Belteshazzar, Shadrach, Meshach, and Abednego.

8 Daniel made up his mind not to let himself become ritually unclean by eating the food and drinking the wine of the royal court, so he asked Ashpenaz to help him, 9 and God made Ashpenaz sympathetic to Daniel. 10 Ashpenaz, however, was afraid of the king, so he said to Daniel, "The king has decided what you are to eat and drink, and if you don't look as fit as the other young men, he may kill me."

11 So Daniel went to the guard whom Ashpenaz had placed in charge of him and his three friends. 12 "Test us for ten days," he said. "Give us vegetables to eat and water to drink. 13 Then compare us with the young men who are eating the food of the royal court, and base your decision on how we look."

14 He agreed to let them try it for ten days. 15 When the time was up, they looked healthier and stronger than all those who had been eating the royal food. 16 So from then on the guard let them continue to eat vegetables instead of what the king provided.

17 God gave the four young men knowledge and skill in literature and

philosophy. In addition, he gave Daniel skill in interpreting visions and dreams.

18 At the end of the three years set by the king, Ashpenaz took all the young men to Nebuchadnezzar. 19 The king talked with them all, and Daniel, Hananiah, Mishael, and Azariah impressed him more than any of the others. So they became members of the king's court. 20 No matter what question the king asked or what problem he raised, these four knew ten times more than any fortuneteller or magician in his whole kingdom. 21 Daniel remained at the royal court until Cyrus, the emperor of Persia, conquered Babylonia.

Nebuchadnezzar's Dream

2 In the second year that Nebuchadnezzar was king, he had a dream. It worried him so much that he couldn't sleep, 2 so he sent for his fortunetellers, magicians, sorcerers, and wizards to come and explain the dream to him. When they came and stood before the king, 3 he said to them, "I'm worried about a dream I've had. I want to know what it means."

4 They answered the king in Aramaic,a "May Your Majesty live forever! Tell us your dream, and we will explain it to you."

5 The king said to them, "I have made up my mind that you must tell me the dream and then tell me what it means. If you can't, I'll have you torn limb from limb and make your houses a pile of ruins. 6 But if you can tell me both the dream and its meaning, I will reward you with gifts and great honor. Now then, tell me what the dream was and what it means."

7 They answered the king again, "If Your Majesty will only tell us what the dream was, we will explain it."

8 At that, the king exclaimed, "Just as I thought! You are trying to gain time, because you see that I have made up my mind 9 to give all of you the same punishment if you don't tell me the dream. You have agreed among yourselves to go on telling me lies because you hope that in time things will change. Tell me what the dream was, and then I will know that you can also tell me what it means."

10 The advisers replied, "There is no one on the face of the earth who can tell Your Majesty what you want to know. No king, not even the greatest and most powerful, has ever made such a demand of his fortunetellers, magicians, and wizards. 11 What Your Majesty is asking for is so difficult that no one can do it for you except the gods, and they do not live among human beings."

12 At that, the king flew into a rage and ordered the execution of all the royal advisers in Babylon. 13 So the order was issued for all of them to be killed, including Daniel and his friends.

God Shows Daniel What the Dream Means

14 Then Daniel went to Arioch, commander of the king's bodyguard, who had been ordered to carry out the execution. Choosing his words carefully, 15 he asked Arioch why the king had issued such a harsh order. So Arioch told Daniel what had happened.

16 Daniel went at once and obtained royal permission for more time, so that he could tell the king what the dream meant. 17 Then Daniel went home and told his friends Hananiah, Mishael, and Azariah what had happened. 18 He told them to pray to the God of heaven for mercy and to ask him to explain the mystery to them so that they would not be killed along with the other advisers in Babylon. 19 Then that same night the mystery was revealed to Daniel in a vision, and he praised the God of heaven:

20 "God is wise and powerful!
  Praise him forever and ever.
21 He controls the times and the
    seasons;
  he makes and unmakes kings;
  it is he who gives wisdom and
    understanding.
22 He reveals things that are deep
    and secret;
  he knows what is hidden in
    darkness,
  and he himself is surrounded by
    light.
23 I praise you and honor you, God
    of my ancestors.
  You have given me wisdom and
    strength;
  you have answered my prayer

a From here to the end of chapter 7, the language used is Aramaic, not Hebrew.

and shown us what to tell the king."

Daniel Tells the King the Dream and Explains It

24 So Daniel went to Arioch, whom the king had commanded to execute the royal advisers. He said to him, "Don't put them to death. Take me to the king, and I will tell him what his dream means."

25 At once Arioch took Daniel into King Nebuchadnezzar's presence and told the king, "I have found one of the Jewish exiles who can tell Your Majesty the meaning of your dream."

26 The king said to Daniel (who was also called Belteshazzar), "Can you tell me what I dreamed and what it means?"

27 Daniel replied, "Your Majesty, there is no wizard, magician, fortuneteller, or astrologer who can tell you that. 28 But there is a God in heaven, who reveals mysteries. He has informed Your Majesty what will happen in the future. Now I will tell you the dream, the vision you had while you were asleep.

29 "While Your Majesty was sleeping, you dreamed about the future; and God, who reveals mysteries, showed you what is going to happen. 30 Now, this mystery was revealed to me, not because I am wiser than anyone else, but so that Your Majesty may learn the meaning of your dream and understand the thoughts that have come to you.

31 "Your Majesty, in your vision you saw standing before you a giant statue, bright and shining, and terrifying to look at. 32 Its head was made of the finest gold; its chest and arms were made of silver; its waist and hips of bronze, 33 its legs of iron, and its feet partly of iron and partly of clay. 34 While you were looking at it, a great stone broke loose from a cliff without anyone touching it, struck the iron and clay feet of the statue, and shattered them. 35 At once the iron, clay, bronze, silver, and gold crumbled and became like the dust on a threshing place in summer. The wind carried it all away, leaving not a trace. But the stone grew to be a mountain that covered the whole earth.

36 "This was the dream. Now I will tell Your Majesty what it means. 37 Your Majesty, you are the greatest of all kings. The God of heaven has made you emperor and given you power, might, and honor. 38 He has made you ruler of all the inhabited earth and ruler over all the animals and birds. You are the head of gold. 39 After you there will be another empire, not as great as yours, and after that a third, an empire of bronze, which will rule the whole earth. 40 And then there will be a fourth empire, as strong as iron, which shatters and breaks everything. And just as iron shatters everything, it will shatter and crush all the earlier empires. 41 You also saw that the feet and the toes were partly clay and partly iron. This means that it will be a divided empire. It will have something of the strength of iron, because there was iron mixed with the clay. 42 The toes — partly iron and partly clay — mean that part of the empire will be strong and part of it weak. 43 You also saw that the iron was mixed with the clay. This means that the rulers of that empire will try to unite their families by intermarriage, but they will not be able to, any more than iron can mix with clay. 44 At the time of those rulers the God of heaven will establish a kingdom that will never end. It will never be conquered, but will completely destroy all those empires and then last forever. 45 You saw how a stone broke loose from a cliff without anyone touching it and how it struck the statue made of iron, bronze, clay, silver, and gold. The great God is telling Your Majesty what will happen in the future. I have told you exactly what you dreamed, and have given you its true meaning."

The King Rewards Daniel

46 Then King Nebuchadnezzar bowed to the ground and gave orders for sacrifices and offerings to be made to Daniel. 47 The king said, "Your God is the greatest of all gods, the Lord over kings, and the one who reveals mysteries. I know this because you have been able to explain this mystery." 48 Then he gave Daniel a high position, presented him with many splendid gifts, put him in charge of the province of Babylon, and made him the head of all the royal advisers. 49 At Daniel's request the king put Shadrach, Meshach, and Abednego in charge of the affairs of the province of

Babylon; Daniel, however, remained at the royal court.

Nebuchadnezzar Commands Everyone to Worship a Gold Statue

3 King Nebuchadnezzar had a gold statue made, ninety feet high and nine feet wide, and he had it set up in the plain of Dura in the province of Babylon. [2] Then the king gave orders for all his officials to come together—the princes, governors, lieutenant governors, commissioners, treasurers, judges, magistrates, and all the other officials of the provinces. They were to attend the dedication of the statue which King Nebuchadnezzar had set up. [3] When all these officials gathered for the dedication and stood in front of the statue, [4] a herald announced in a loud voice, "People of all nations, races, and languages! [5] You will hear the sound of the trumpets, followed by the playing of oboes, lyres, zithers, and harps; and then all the other instruments will join in. As soon as the music starts, you are to bow down and worship the gold statue that King Nebuchadnezzar has set up. [6] Anyone who does not bow down and worship will immediately be thrown into a blazing furnace." [7] And so, as soon as they heard the sound of the instruments, the people of all the nations, races, and languages bowed down and worshiped the gold statue which King Nebuchadnezzar had set up.

Daniel's Three Friends Are Accused of Disobedience

[8] It was then that some Babylonians took the opportunity to denounce the Jews. [9] They said to King Nebuchadnezzar, "May Your Majesty live forever! [10] Your Majesty has issued an order that as soon as the music starts, everyone is to bow down and worship the gold statue, [11] and that anyone who does not bow down and worship it is to be thrown into a blazing furnace. [12] There are some Jews whom you put in charge of the province of Babylon—Shadrach, Meshach, and Abednego—who are disobeying Your Majesty's orders. They do not worship your god or bow down to the statue you set up."

[13] At that, the king flew into a rage and ordered the three men to be brought before him. [14] He said to them, "Shadrach, Meshach, and Abednego, is it true that you refuse to worship my god and to bow down to the gold statue I have set up? [15] Now then, as soon as you hear the sound of the trumpets, oboes, lyres, zithers, harps, and all the other instruments, bow down and worship the statue. If you do not, you will immediately be thrown into a blazing furnace. Do you think there is any god who can save you?"

[16] Shadrach, Meshach, and Abednego answered, "Your Majesty, we will not try to defend ourselves. [17] If the God whom we serve is able to save us from the blazing furnace and from your power, then he will.[b] [18] But even if he doesn't, Your Majesty may be sure that we will not worship your god, and we will not bow down to the gold statue that you have set up."

Daniel's Three Friends Are Sentenced to Death

[19] Then Nebuchadnezzar lost his temper, and his face turned red with anger at Shadrach, Meshach, and Abednego. So he ordered the furnace to be heated seven times hotter than usual. [20] And he commanded the strongest men in his army to tie the three men up and throw them into the blazing furnace. [21] So they tied them up, fully dressed—shirts, robes, caps, and all—and threw them into the blazing furnace. [22] Now because the king had given strict orders for the furnace to be made extremely hot, the flames burned up the guards who took the men to the furnace. [23] Then Shadrach, Meshach, and Abednego, still tied up, fell into the heart of the blazing fire.

[24] Suddenly Nebuchadnezzar leaped to his feet in amazement. He asked his officials, "Didn't we tie up three men and throw them into the blazing furnace?"

They answered, "Yes, we did, Your Majesty."

[25] "Then why do I see four men walking around in the fire?" he asked. "They are not tied up, and they show no sign of being hurt—and the fourth one looks like an angel."[c]

D
A
N
I
E
L

---

b If the God ... will; or If it is true that we refuse to worship your god or bow down to the gold statue you set up, the God whom we serve is able to save us from the blazing furnace and from your power—and he will.   c angel; or a son of the gods; or a son of God.

The Three Men Are Released and Promoted

26 So Nebuchadnezzar went up to the door of the blazing furnace and called out, "Shadrach! Meshach! Abednego! Servants of the Supreme God! Come out!" And they came out at once. 27 All the princes, governors, lieutenant governors, and other officials of the king gathered to look at the three men, who had not been harmed by the fire. Their hair was not singed, their clothes were not burned, and there was no smell of smoke on them.

28 The king said, "Praise the God of Shadrach, Meshach, and Abednego! He sent his angel and rescued these men who serve and trust him. They disobeyed my orders and risked their lives rather than bow down and worship any god except their own.

29 "And now I command that if anyone of any nation, race, or language speaks disrespectfully of the God of Shadrach, Meshach, and Abednego, he is to be torn limb from limb, and his house is to be made a pile of ruins. There is no other god who can rescue like this."

30 And the king promoted Shadrach, Meshach, and Abednego to higher positions in the province of Babylon.

Nebuchadnezzar's Second Dream

4 King Nebuchadnezzar sent the following message to the people of all nations, races, and languages in the world:

"Greetings! 2 Listen to my account of the wonders and miracles which the Supreme God has shown me.

3 "How great are the wonders God
   shows us!
How powerful are the miracles he
   performs!
God is king forever; he will rule
   for all time.

4 "I was living comfortably in my palace, enjoying great prosperity. 5 But I had a frightening dream and saw terrifying visions while I was asleep. 6 I ordered all the royal advisers in Babylon to be brought to me so that they could tell me what the dream meant. 7 Then all the fortunetellers, magicians, wizards, and astrologers were brought in, and I told them my dream, but they could not explain it to me. 8 Then Daniel came in. (He is also called Belteshazzar, after the name of my god.) The spirit of the holy gods[d] is in him, so I told him what I had dreamed. I said to him: 9 Belteshazzar, chief of the fortunetellers, I know that the spirit of the holy gods[d] is in you and that you understand all mysteries. This is[e] my dream. Tell me what it means.

10 "While I was asleep, I had a vision of a huge tree in the middle of the earth. 11 It grew bigger and bigger until it reached the sky and could be seen by everyone in the world. 12 Its leaves were beautiful, and it was loaded down with fruit—enough for the whole world to eat. Wild animals rested in its shade, birds built nests in its branches, and every kind of living being ate its fruit.

13 "While I was thinking about the vision, I saw coming down from heaven an angel, alert and watchful. 14 He proclaimed in a loud voice, 'Cut the tree down and chop off its branches; strip off its leaves and scatter its fruit. Drive the animals from under it and the birds out of its branches. 15 But leave the stump in the ground with a band of iron and bronze around it. Leave it there in the field with the grass.

" 'Now let the dew fall on this man, and let him live with the animals and the plants. 16 For seven years he will not have a human mind, but the mind of an animal. 17 This is the decision of the alert and watchful angels. So then, let all people everywhere know that the Supreme God has power over human kingdoms and that he can give them to anyone he chooses—even to those who are least important.'

18 "This is the dream I had," said King Nebuchadnezzar. "Now, Belteshazzar, tell me what it means. None of my royal advisers could tell me, but you can, because the spirit of the holy gods[f] is in you."

Daniel Explains the Dream

19 At this, Daniel, who is also called Belteshazzar, was so alarmed that he could not say anything. The king said to him, "Belteshazzar, don't let the dream and its message alarm you."

Belteshazzar replied, "Your Majesty, I

---

d gods; *or* God.   e *Probable text* This is; *Aramaic* Visions of.   f gods; *or* God.

wish that the dream and its explanation applied to your enemies and not to you. [20] The tree, so tall that it reached the sky, could be seen by everyone in the world. [21] Its leaves were beautiful, and it had enough fruit on it to feed the whole world. Wild animals rested under it, and birds made their nests in its branches.

[22] "Your Majesty, you are the tree, tall and strong. You have grown so great that you reach the sky, and your power extends over the whole world. [23] While Your Majesty was watching, an angel came down from heaven and said, 'Cut the tree down and destroy it, but leave the stump in the ground. Wrap a band of iron and bronze around it, and leave it there in the field with the grass. Let the dew fall on this man, and let him live there with the animals for seven years.'

[24] "This, then, is what it means, Your Majesty, and this is what the Supreme God has declared will happen to you. [25] You will be driven away from human society and will live with wild animals. For seven years you will eat grass like an ox and sleep in the open air, where the dew will fall on you. Then you will admit that the Supreme God controls all human kingdoms and that he can give them to anyone he chooses. [26] The angel ordered the stump to be left in the ground. This means that you will become king again when you acknowledge that God rules all the world. [27] So then, Your Majesty, follow my advice. Stop sinning, do what is right, and be merciful to the poor.[g] Then you will continue to be prosperous."

[28] All this did happen to King Nebuchadnezzar. [29] Only twelve months later, while he was walking around on the roof of his royal palace in Babylon, [30] he said, "Look how great Babylon is! I built it as my capital city to display my power and might, my glory and majesty."

[31] Before the words were out of his mouth, a voice spoke from heaven, "King Nebuchadnezzar, listen to what I say! Your royal power is now taken away from you. [32] You will be driven away from human society, live with wild animals, and eat grass like an ox for seven years. Then you will acknowledge

that the Supreme God has power over human kingdoms and that he can give them to anyone he chooses."

[33] The words came true immediately. Nebuchadnezzar was driven out of human society and ate grass like an ox. The dew fell on his body, and his hair grew as long as eagle feathers and his nails as long as bird claws.

Nebuchadnezzar Praises God

[34] "When the seven years had passed," said the king, "I looked up at the sky, and my sanity returned. I praised the Supreme God and gave honor and glory to the one who lives forever.

"He will rule forever,
   and his kingdom will last for
     all time.
[35] He looks on the people of the
   earth as nothing;
   angels in heaven and people
   on earth
   are under his control.
No one can oppose his will
   or question what he does.

[36] "When my sanity returned, my honor, my majesty, and the glory of my kingdom were given back to me. My officials and my noblemen welcomed me, and I was given back my royal power with even greater honor than before.

[37] "And now, I, Nebuchadnezzar, praise, honor, and glorify the King of Heaven. Everything he does is right and just, and he can humble anyone who acts proudly."

Belshazzar's Banquet

5 One night King Belshazzar invited a thousand noblemen to a great banquet, and they drank wine together. [2] While they were drinking, Belshazzar gave orders to bring in the gold and silver cups and bowls which his father[h] Nebuchadnezzar had carried off from the Temple in Jerusalem. The king sent for them so that he, his noblemen, his wives, and his concubines could drink out of them. [3] At once the gold cups and bowls were brought in, and they all drank wine out of them [4] and praised gods made of gold, silver, bronze, iron, wood, and stone.

---

[g] Stop sinning . . . to the poor; *cr* Make up for your sins by doing what is right and by being merciful to the poor.   [h] *There were several kings of Babylonia between Nebuchadnezzar and Belshazzar. Father may mean predecessor, or the name Nebuchadnezzar may be used for Nabonidus.*

DANIEL

5 Suddenly a human hand appeared and began writing on the plaster wall of the palace, where the light from the lamps was shining most brightly. And the king saw the hand as it was writing. 6 He turned pale and was so frightened that his knees began to shake. 7 He shouted for someone to bring in the magicians, wizards, and astrologers. When they came in, the king said to them, "Anyone who can read this writing and tell me what it means will be dressed in robes of royal purple, wear a gold chain of honor around his neck, and be the third in power in the kingdom." 8 The royal advisers came forward, but none of them could read the writing or tell the king what it meant. 9 In his distress King Belshazzar grew even paler, and his noblemen had no idea what to do.

10 The queen mother heard the noise made by the king and his noblemen and entered the banquet hall. She said, "May Your Majesty live forever! Please do not be so disturbed and look so pale. 11 There is a man in your kingdom who has the spirit of the holy gods*i* in him. When your father was king, this man showed good sense, knowledge, and wisdom like the wisdom of the gods. And King Nebuchadnezzar, your father,*j* made him chief of the fortune-tellers, magicians, wizards, and astrologers. 12 He has unusual ability and is wise and skillful in interpreting dreams, solving riddles, and explaining mysteries; so send for this man Daniel, whom the king named Belteshazzar, and he will tell you what all this means."

Daniel Explains the Writing

13 Daniel was brought at once into the king's presence, and the king said to him, "Are you Daniel, that Jewish exile whom my father the king brought here from Judah? 14 I have heard that the spirit of the holy gods*k* is in you and that you are skillful and have knowledge and wisdom. 15 The advisers and magicians were brought in to read this writing and tell me what it means, but they could not discover the meaning. 16 Now I have heard that you can find hidden meanings and explain mysteries. If you can read this writing and tell me what it

means, you will be dressed in robes of royal purple, wear a gold chain of honor around your neck, and be the third in power in the kingdom."

17 Daniel replied, "Keep your gifts for yourself or give them to someone else. I will read for Your Majesty what has been written and tell you what it means. 18 "The Supreme God made your father Nebuchadnezzar a great king and gave him dignity and majesty. 19 He was so great that people of all nations, races, and languages were afraid of him and trembled. If he wanted to kill someone, he did; if he wanted to keep someone alive, he did. He honored or disgraced anyone he wanted to. 20 But because he became proud, stubborn, and cruel, he was removed from his royal throne and lost his place of honor. 21 He was driven away from human society, and his mind became like that of an animal. He lived with wild donkeys, ate grass like an ox, and slept in the open air with nothing to protect him from the dew. Finally he admitted that the Supreme God controls all human kingdoms and can give them to anyone he chooses.

22 "But you, his son, have not humbled yourself, even though you knew all this. 23 You acted against the Lord of heaven and brought in the cups and bowls taken from his Temple. You, your noblemen, your wives, and your concubines drank wine out of them and praised gods made of gold, silver, bronze, iron, wood, and stone — gods that cannot see or hear and that do not know anything. But you did not honor the God who determines whether you live or die and who controls everything you do. 24 That is why God has sent the hand to write these words.

25 "This is what was written: 'Number, number, weight, divisions.' 26 And this is what it means: *number*, God has numbered the days of your kingdom and brought it to an end; 27 *weight*, you have been weighed on the scales and found to be too light; 28 *divisions*, your kingdom is divided up and given to the Medes and Persians."*l*

29 Immediately Belshazzar ordered his servants to dress Daniel in a robe of royal purple and to hang a gold chain of honor around his neck. And he made

---

i gods; *or* God.   *j* your father (*see 5.2*).   *k* gods; *or* God.   *l* PERSIANS: *In Aramaic the word for "Persians" sounds like the word for "division."*

him the third in power in the kingdom. ³⁰That same night Belshazzar, the king of Babylonia, was killed; ³¹and Darius the Mede, who was then sixty-two years old, seized the royal power.

Daniel in the Pit of Lions

6 Darius decided to appoint a hundred and twenty governors to hold office throughout his empire. ²In addition, he chose Daniel and two others to supervise the governors and to look after the king's interests. ³Daniel soon showed that he could do better work than the other supervisors or the governors. Because he was so outstanding, the king considered putting him in charge of the whole empire. ⁴Then the other supervisors and the governors tried to find something wrong with the way Daniel administered the empire, but they couldn't, because Daniel was reliable and did not do anything wrong or dishonest. ⁵They said to each other, "We are not going to find anything of which to accuse Daniel unless it is something in connection with his religion."

⁶So they went to see the king and said, "King Darius, may Your Majesty live forever! ⁷All of us who administer your empire—the supervisors, the governors, the lieutenant governors, and the other officials—have agreed that Your Majesty should issue an order and enforce it strictly. Give orders that for thirty days no one be permitted to request anything from any god or from any human being except from Your Majesty. Anyone who violates this order is to be thrown into a pit filled with lions. ⁸So let Your Majesty issue this order and sign it, and it will be in force, a law of the Medes and Persians, which cannot be changed." ⁹And so King Darius signed the order. ¹⁰When Daniel learned that the order had been signed, he went home. In an upstairs room of his house there were windows that faced toward Jerusalem. There, just as he had always done, he knelt down at the open windows and prayed to God three times a day.

¹¹When Daniel's enemies observed him praying to God, ¹²all of them went together to the king to accuse Daniel. They said, "Your Majesty, you signed an order that for the next thirty days anyone who requested anything from any god or from any human being except

you, would be thrown into a pit filled with lions."

The king replied, "Yes, that is a strict order, a law of the Medes and Persians, which cannot be changed."

¹³Then they said to the king, "Daniel, one of the exiles from Judah, does not respect Your Majesty or obey the order you issued. He prays regularly three times a day."

¹⁴When the king heard this, he was upset and did his best to find some way to rescue Daniel. He kept trying until sunset. ¹⁵Then Daniel's enemies came back to the king and said to him, "Your Majesty knows that according to the laws of the Medes and Persians no order which the king issues can be changed."

¹⁶So the king gave orders for Daniel to be taken and thrown into the pit filled with lions. He said to Daniel, "May your God, whom you serve so loyally, rescue you." ¹⁷A stone was put over the mouth of the pit, and the king placed his own royal seal and the seal of his noblemen on the stone, so that no one could rescue Daniel. ¹⁸Then the king returned to the palace and spent a sleepless night, without food or any form of entertainment.

¹⁹At dawn the king got up and hurried to the pit. ²⁰When he got there, he called out anxiously, "Daniel, servant of the living God! Was the God you serve so loyally able to save you from the lions?"

²¹Daniel answered, "May Your Majesty live forever! ²²God sent his angel to shut the mouths of the lions so that they would not hurt me. He did this because he knew that I was innocent and because I have not wronged you, Your Majesty."

²³The king was overjoyed and gave orders for Daniel to be pulled up out of the pit. So they pulled him up and saw that he had not been hurt at all, for he trusted God. ²⁴Then the king gave orders to arrest all those who had accused Daniel, and he had them thrown, together with their wives and children, into the pit filled with lions. Before they even reached the bottom of the pit, the lions pounced on them and broke all their bones.

²⁵Then King Darius wrote to the people of all nations, races, and languages on earth:

"Greetings! ²⁶I command that

throughout my empire everyone should fear and respect Daniel's God.

"He is a living God,
and he will rule forever.
His kingdom will never be destroyed,
and his power will never come to an end.
27 He saves and rescues;
he performs wonders and miracles
in heaven and on earth.
He saved Daniel from being killed by the lions."

28 Daniel prospered during the reign of Darius and the reign of Cyrus the Persian.

DANIEL DESCRIBES HIS VISIONS (7.1 – 12.13)

Daniel's Vision of the Four Beasts

7 In the first year that Belshazzar was king of Babylonia, I had a dream and saw a vision in the night. I wrote the dream down, and this is the record 2 of what I saw that night:

Winds were blowing from all directions and lashing the surface of the ocean. 3 Four huge beasts came up out of the ocean, each one different from the others. 4 The first one looked like a lion, but had wings like an eagle. While I was watching, the wings were torn off. The beast was lifted up and made to stand up straight. And then a human mind was given to it.

5 The second beast looked like a bear standing on its hind legs. It was holding three ribs between its teeth, and a voice said to it, "Go on, eat as much meat as you can!"

6 While I was watching, another beast appeared. It looked like a leopard, but on its back there were four wings, like the wings of a bird, and it had four heads. It had a look of authority about it.

7 As I was watching, a fourth beast appeared. It was powerful, horrible, terrifying. With its huge iron teeth it crushed its victims, and then it trampled on them. Unlike the other beasts, it had ten horns. 8 While I was staring at the horns, I saw a little horn coming up among the others. It tore out three of the horns that were already there. This horn had hu-

man eyes and a mouth that was boasting proudly.

The Vision of the One Who Has Been Living Forever

9 While I was looking, thrones were put in place. One who had been living forever sat down on one of the thrones. His clothes were white as snow, and his hair was like pure wool. His throne, mounted on fiery wheels, was blazing with fire, 10 and a stream of fire was pouring out from it. There were many thousands of people there to serve him, and millions of people stood before him. The court began its session, and the books were opened.

11 While I was looking, I could still hear the little horn bragging and boasting. As I watched, the fourth beast was killed, and its body was thrown into the flames and destroyed. 12 The other beasts had their power taken away, but they were permitted to go on living for a limited time.

13 During this vision in the night, I saw what looked like a human being. He was approaching me, surrounded by clouds, and he went to the one who had been living forever and was presented to him. 14 He was given authority, honor, and royal power, so that the people of all nations, races, and languages would serve him. His authority would last forever, and his kingdom would never end.

The Visions Are Explained

15 The visions I saw alarmed me, and I was deeply disturbed.[m] 16 I went up to one of those standing there and asked him to explain it all. So he told me the meaning. 17 He said, "These four huge beasts are four empires which will arise on earth. 18 And the people of the Supreme God will receive royal power and keep it forever and ever."

19 Then I wanted to know more about the fourth beast, which was not like any of the others — the terrifying beast which crushed its victims with its bronze claws and iron teeth and then trampled on them. 20 And I wanted to know about the ten horns on its head and the horn that had come up afterward and had made three of the horns fall. It had eyes and a mouth and was boasting proudly. It was

m Aramaic has two additional words, the meaning of which is unclear.

more terrifying than any of the others. 21 While I was looking, that horn made war on God's people and conquered them. 22 Then the one who had been living forever came and pronounced judgment in favor of[n] the people of the Supreme God. The time had arrived for God's people to receive royal power.

23 This is the explanation I was given: "The fourth beast is a fourth empire that will be on the earth and will be different from all other empires. It will crush the whole earth and trample it down. 24 The ten horns are ten kings who will rule that empire. Then another king will appear; he will be very different from the earlier ones and will overthrow three kings. 25 He will speak against the Supreme God and oppress God's people. He will try to change their religious laws and festivals, and God's people will be under his power for three and a half years. 26 Then the heavenly court will sit in judgment, take away his power, and destroy him completely. 27 The power and greatness of all the kingdoms on earth will be given to the people of the Supreme God. Their royal power will never end, and all rulers on earth will serve and obey them."

28 This is the end of the account. I was so frightened that I turned pale, and I kept everything to myself.

Daniel's Vision of a Ram and a Goat

8 In the third year that Belshazzar was king, I saw a second vision.[o] 2 In the vision I suddenly found myself in the walled city of Susa in the province of Elam. I was standing by the Ulai River, 3 and there beside the river I saw a ram that had two long horns, one of which was longer and newer than the other. 4 I watched the ram butting with his horns to the west, the north, and the south. No animal could stop him or escape his power. He did as he pleased and grew arrogant.

5 While I was wondering what this meant, a goat came rushing out of the west, moving so fast that his feet didn't touch the ground. He had one prominent horn between his eyes. 6 He came toward the ram, which I had seen standing be-

side the river, and rushed at him with all his force. 7 I watched him attack the ram. He was so angry that he smashed into him and broke the two horns. The ram had no strength to resist. He was thrown to the ground and trampled on, and there was no one who could save him.

8 The goat grew more and more arrogant, but at the height of his power his horn was broken. In its place four prominent horns came up, each pointing in a different direction. 9 Out of one of these four horns grew a little horn, whose power extended toward the south and the east and toward the Promised Land. 10 It grew strong enough to attack the army of heaven, the stars themselves, and it threw some of them to the ground and trampled on them. 11 It even defied the Prince of the heavenly army, stopped the daily sacrifices offered to him, and ruined the Temple. 12 People sinned there instead of offering the proper daily sacrifices,[p] and true religion was thrown to the ground. The horn was successful in everything it did.

13 Then I heard one angel ask another, "How long will these things that were seen in the vision continue? How long will an awful sin replace the daily sacrifices? How long will the army of heaven and the Temple be trampled on?"

14 I heard the other angel answer, "It will continue for 2,300 evenings and mornings, during which sacrifices will not be offered. Then the Temple will be restored."

The Angel Gabriel Explains the Vision

15 I was trying to understand what the vision meant, when suddenly someone was standing in front of me. 16 I heard a voice call out over the Ulai River, "Gabriel, explain to him the meaning of what he saw." 17 Gabriel came and stood beside me, and I was so terrified that I fell to the ground.

He said to me, "Mortal man, understand the meaning. The vision has to do with the end of the world." 18 While he was talking, I fell to the ground unconscious. But he took hold of me, raised me to my feet, 19 and said, "I am showing

---

[n] pronounced judgment in favor of; *or* gave the right to judge to   [o] *Beginning at 8.1, the rest of this book is in Hebrew (see 2.4).*   [p] People . . . sacrifices; *Hebrew unclear.*

you what the result of God's anger will be. The vision refers to the time of the end.

20 "The ram you saw that had two horns represents the kingdoms of Media and Persia. 21 The goat represents the kingdom of Greece, and the prominent horn between his eyes is the first king. 22 The four horns that came up when the first horn was broken represent the four kingdoms into which that nation will be divided and which will not be as strong as the first kingdom.

23 "When the end of those kingdoms is near and they have become so wicked that they must be punished, there will be a stubborn, vicious, and deceitful king. 24 He will grow strong—but not by his own power. He will cause terrible destruction and be successful in everything he does. He will bring destruction on powerful men and on God's own people. 25 Because he is cunning, he will succeed in his deceitful ways. He will be proud of himself and destroy many people without warning. He will even defy the greatest King of all, but he will be destroyed without the use of any human power. 26 This vision about the evening and morning sacrifices which has been explained to you will come true. But keep it secret now, because it will be a long time before it does come true."

27 I was depressed and ill for several days. Then I got up and went back to the work that the king had assigned to me, but I was puzzled by the vision and could not understand it.

Daniel Prays for His People

9 Darius the Mede, who was the son of Xerxes, ruled over the kingdom of Babylonia. 2 In the first year of his reign I was studying the sacred books and thinking about the seventy years that Jerusalem would be in ruins, according to what the LORD had told the prophet Jeremiah. 3 And I prayed earnestly to the Lord God, pleading with him, fasting, wearing sackcloth, and sitting in ashes. 4 I prayed to the LORD my God and confessed the sins of my people.

I said, "Lord God, you are great, and we honor you. You are faithful to your covenant and show constant love to those who love you and do what you command.

5 "We have sinned, we have been evil, we have done wrong. We have rejected what you commanded us to do and have turned away from what you showed us was right. 6 We have not listened to your servants the prophets, who spoke in your name to our kings, our rulers, our ancestors, and our whole nation. 7 You, Lord, always do what is right, but we have always brought disgrace on ourselves. This is true of all of us who live in Judea and in Jerusalem and of all the Israelites whom you scattered in countries near and far because they were unfaithful to you. 8 Our kings, our rulers, and our ancestors have acted shamefully and sinned against you, Lord. 9 You are merciful and forgiving, although we have rebelled against you. 10 We did not listen to you, O LORD our God, when you told us to live according to the laws which you gave us through your servants the prophets. 11 All Israel broke your laws and refused to listen to what you said. We sinned against you, and so you brought on us the curses that are written in the Law of Moses, your servant. 12 You did what you said you would do to us and our rulers. You punished Jerusalem more severely than any other city on earth, 13 giving us all the punishment described in the Law of Moses. But even now, O LORD our God, we have not tried to please you by turning from our sins or by following your truth. 14 You, O LORD our God, were prepared to punish us, and you did, because you always do what is right, and we did not listen to you.

15 "O Lord our God, you showed your power by bringing your people out of Egypt, and your power is still remembered. We have sinned; we have done wrong. 16 You have defended us in the past, so do not be angry with Jerusalem any longer. It is your city, your sacred hill.q All the people in the neighboring countries look down on Jerusalem and on your people because of our sins and the evil our ancestors did. 17 O God, hear my prayer and pleading. Restore your Temple, which has been destroyed; restore it so that everyone will know that you are God. 18 Listen to us, O God; look

q SACRED HILL: Mount Zion (see Zion in Word List).

at us and see the trouble we are in and the suffering of the city that bears your name. We are praying to you because you are merciful, not because we have done right. [19]Lord, hear us. Lord, forgive us. Lord, listen to us, and act! In order that everyone will know that you are God, do not delay! This city and these people are yours."

Gabriel Explains the Prophecy

[20]I went on praying, confessing my sins and the sins of my people Israel and pleading with the LORD my God to restore his holy Temple. [21]While I was praying, Gabriel, whom I had seen in the earlier vision, came flying down to where I was. It was the time for the evening sacrifice to be offered. [22]He explained, "Daniel, I have come here to help you understand the prophecy. [23]When you began to plead with God, he answered you. He loves you, and so I have come to tell you the answer. Now pay attention while I explain the vision. [24]"Seven times seventy years is the length of time God has set for freeing your people and your holy city from sin and evil. Sin will be forgiven and eternal justice established, so that the vision and the prophecy will come true, and the holy Temple[r] will be rededicated. [25]Note this and understand it: From the time the command is given to rebuild Jerusalem until God's chosen leader comes, seven times seven years will pass. Jerusalem will be rebuilt with streets and strong defenses, and will stand for seven times sixty-two years, but this will be a time of troubles. [26]And at the end of that time God's chosen leader will be killed unjustly.[s] The city and the Temple will be destroyed by the invading army of a powerful ruler. The end will come like a flood, bringing the war and destruction which God has prepared. [27]That ruler will have a firm agreement with many people for seven years, and when half this time is past, he will put an end to sacrifices and offerings. The Awful Horror[t] will be placed on the highest point of the Temple and will remain there until the one who put it there meets the end which God has prepared for him."

Daniel's Vision by the Tigris River

10 In the third year that Cyrus was emperor of Persia, a message was revealed to Daniel, who is also called Belteshazzar. The message was true but extremely hard to understand.[u] It was explained to him in a vision.

[2]At that time I was mourning for three weeks. [3]I did not eat any rich food or any meat, drink any wine, or comb my hair until the three weeks were past.

[4]On the twenty-fourth day of the first month of the year I was standing on the bank of the mighty Tigris River. [5]I looked up and saw someone who was wearing linen clothes and a belt of fine gold. [6]His body shone like a jewel. His face was as bright as a flash of lightning, and his eyes blazed like fire. His arms and legs shone like polished bronze, and his voice sounded like the roar of a great crowd.

[7]I was the only one who saw the vision. Those who were with me did not see anything, but they were terrified and ran and hid. [8]I was left there alone, watching this amazing vision. I had no strength left, and my face was so changed that no one could have recognized me. [9]When I heard his voice, I fell to the ground unconscious and lay there face downward. [10]Then a hand took hold of me and raised me to my hands and knees; I was still trembling.

[11]The angel said to me, "Daniel, God loves you. Stand up and listen carefully to what I am going to say. I have been sent to you." When he had said this, I stood up, still trembling.

[12]Then he said, "Daniel, don't be afraid. God has heard your prayers ever since the first day you decided to humble yourself in order to gain understanding. I have come in answer to your prayer. [13]The angel prince of the kingdom of Persia opposed me for twenty-one days. Then Michael, one of the chief angels, came to help me, because I had been left there alone in Persia. [14]I have come to make you understand what will happen to your people in the future. This is a vision about the future."

[15]When he said this, I stared at the ground, speechless. [16]Then the angel,

DANIEL

---

[r] Temple; or altar.   [s] One ancient translation unjustly; Hebrew unclear.   [t] THE AWFUL HORROR: A pagan image set up in the Jerusalem Temple by foreign conquerors (see 1 Macc 1.54-61).
[u] but extremely hard to understand; or and it was about a great war.

who looked like a human being, reached out and touched my lips. I said to him, "Sir, this vision makes me so weak that I can't stop trembling. 17 I am like a slave standing before his master. How can I talk to you? I have no strength or breath left in me."

18 Once more he took hold of me, and I felt stronger. 19 He said, "God loves you, so don't let anything worry you or frighten you."

When he had said this, I felt even stronger and said, "Sir, tell me what you have to say. You have made me feel better."

20-21 He said, "Do you know why I came to you? It is to reveal to you what is written in the Book of Truth. Now I have to go back and fight the guardian angel of Persia. After that the guardian angel of Greece will appear. There is no one to help me except Michael, Israel's guardian angel. v

11 1 He is w responsible for helping and defending me. 2 And what I am now going to tell you is true."

The Kingdoms of Egypt and Syria

The angel said, "Three more kings will rule over Persia, followed by a fourth, who will be richer than all the others. At the height of his power and wealth he will challenge the kingdom of Greece.

3 "Then a heroic king will appear. He will rule over a huge empire and do whatever he wants. 4 But at the height of his power his empire will break up and be divided into four parts. Kings not descended from him will rule in his place, but they will not have the power that he had.

5 "The king of Egypt will be strong. One of his generals, however, will be even stronger and rule a greater kingdom. 6 After a number of years the king of Egypt will make an alliance with the king of Syria and give him his daughter in marriage. But the alliance will not last, and she, her husband, her child, x and the servants who went with her will all be killed. 7 Soon afterward one of her relatives will become king. He will attack the army of the king of Syria, enter their fortress, and defeat them. 8 He will

carry back to Egypt the images of their gods and the articles of gold and silver dedicated to those gods. After several years of peace 9 the king of Syria will invade Egypt, but he will be forced to retreat.

10 "The sons of the king of Syria will prepare for war and gather a large army. One of them will sweep on like a flood and attack an enemy fortress. 11 In his anger the king of Egypt will go to war against the king of Syria and capture his huge army. 12 He will be proud of his victory and of the many soldiers he has killed, but he will not continue to be victorious.

13 "The king of Syria will go back and gather a larger army than he had before. When the proper time comes, he will return with a large, well-equipped army. 14 Then many people will rebel against the king of Egypt. And some violent people from your nation, Daniel, will rebel because of a vision they have seen, but they will be defeated. 15 So the king of Syria will lay siege to a fortified city and capture it. The soldiers of Egypt will not continue to fight; even the best of them will not have enough strength. 16 The Syrian invader will do with them as he pleases, without opposition. He will stand in the Promised Land and have it completely in his power.

17 "The king of Syria will plan an expedition, using his whole army. Then, in order to destroy his enemy's kingdom, he will make an alliance with him and offer him his daughter y in marriage; but his plan will not succeed. 18 After that he will attack the nations by the sea and conquer many of them. But a foreign leader will defeat him and put an end to his arrogance; indeed he will turn the arrogance of Syria's king back on him. z 19 The king will return to the fortresses of his own land, but he will be defeated, and that will be the end of him.

20 "He will be followed by another king, who will send an officer to oppress the people with taxes in order to increase the wealth of his kingdom. In a short time that king will be killed, but not publicly and not in battle."

---

v *Probable text* guardian angel; *Hebrew* guardian angel. And I, in the first year of Darius the Mede.
w *One ancient translation* He is; *Hebrew* I am.   x *Some ancient translations* her child;
Hebrew her father.   y his daughter; *or* a young woman.   z *Probable text* his arrogance . . . on him; *Hebrew unclear.*

The Evil King of Syria

21 The angel went on to explain: "The next king of Syria will be an evil man who has no right to be king, but he will come unexpectedly and seize power by trickery. 22 Anyone who opposes him, even God's High Priest, will be swept away and wiped out. 23 By making treaties, he will deceive other nations, and he will grow stronger and stronger, even though he rules only a small nation. 24 He will invade a wealthy province without warning and will do things that none of his ancestors ever did. Then he will divide among his followers the goods and property he has captured in war. He will make plans to attack fortresses, but his time will soon run out.

25 "He will boldly raise a large army to attack the king of Egypt, who will prepare to fight back with a huge and powerful army. But the king of Egypt will be deceived and will not be successful. 26 His closest advisers will ruin him. Many of his soldiers will be killed, and his army will be wiped out. 27 Then the two kings will sit down to eat at the same table, but their motives will be evil, and they will lie to each other. They will not get what they want, because the time for it has not yet come. 28 The king of Syria will return home with all the loot he has captured, determined to destroy the religion of God's people. He will do as he pleases and then return to his own land.

29 "Later on he will invade Egypt again, but this time things will turn out differently. 30 The Romans will come in ships and oppose him, and he will be frightened.

"Then he will turn back in a rage and try to destroy the religion of God's people. He will follow the advice of those who have abandoned that religion. 31 Some of his soldiers will make the Temple ritually unclean. They will stop the daily sacrifices and set up The Awful Horror.a 32 By deceit the king will win the support of those who have already abandoned their religion, but those who follow God will fight back. 33 Wise leaders of the people will share their wisdom with many others. But for a while some of them will be killed in battle or be burned to death, and some will be robbed and made prisoners. 34 While the killing is going on, God's people will receive a little help, even though many who join them will do so for selfish reasons. 35 Some of those wise leaders will be killed, but as a result of this the people will be purified. This will continue until the end comes, the time that God has set.

36 "The king of Syria will do as he pleases. He will boast that he is greater than any god, superior even to the Supreme God. He will be able to do this until the time when God punishes him. God will do exactly what he has planned. 37 The king will ignore the god his ancestors served, and also the god that women love. In fact, he will ignore every god, because he will think he is greater than any of them. 38 Instead, he will honor the god who protects fortresses. He will offer gold, silver, jewels, and other rich gifts to a god his ancestors never worshiped. 39 To defend his fortresses he will use people who worship a foreign god. He will give great honor to those who accept him as ruler, put them into high offices, and give them land as a reward.

40 "When the king of Syria's final hour has almost come, the king of Egypt will attack him, and the king of Syria will fight back with all his power, using chariots, horses, and many ships. He will invade many countries, like the waters of a flood. 41 He will even invade the Promised Land and kill tens of thousands, but the countries of Edom, Moab, and what is left of Ammon will escape. 42 When he invades all those countries, even Egypt will not be spared. 43 He will take away Egypt's hidden treasures of gold and silver and its other prized possessions. He will conquer Libya and Ethiopia.b 44 Then news that comes from the east and the north will frighten him, and he will fight furiously, killing many people. 45 He will even set up his huge royal tents between the sea and the mountain on which the Temple stands. But he will die, with no one there to help him."

---

a THE AWFUL HORROR: See 9.27.　b Hebrew Cush: Cush is the ancient name of the extensive territory south of the First Cataract of the Nile River. This region was called Ethiopia in Graeco-Roman times, and included within its borders most of modern Sudan and some of present-day Ethiopia (Abyssinia).

The Time of the End

12 The angel wearing linen clothes said, "At that time the great angel Michael, who guards your people, will appear. Then there will be a time of troubles, the worst since nations first came into existence. When that time comes, all the people of your nation whose names are written in God's book will be saved. ² Many of those who have already died will live again: some will enjoy eternal life, and some will suffer eternal disgrace. ³ The wise leaders will shine with all the brightness of the sky. And those who have taught many people to do what is right will shine like the stars forever."

⁴ He said to me, "And now, Daniel, close the book and put a seal on it until the end of the world. Meanwhile, many people will waste their efforts trying to understand what is happening."

⁵ Then I saw two men standing by a river, one on each bank. ⁶ One of them asked the angel who was standing further upstream, "How long will it be until these amazing events come to an end?"

⁷ The angel raised both hands toward the sky and made a solemn promise in the name of the Eternal God. I heard him say, "It will be three and a half years. When the persecution of God's people ends, all these things will have happened."

⁸ I heard what he said, but I did not understand it. So I asked, "But, sir, how will it all end?"

⁹ He answered, "You must go now, Daniel, because these words are to be kept secret and hidden until the end comes. ¹⁰ Many people will be purified. Those who are wicked will not understand but will go on being wicked; only those who are wise will understand.

¹¹ "From the time the daily sacrifices are stopped, that is, from the time of The Awful Horror,ᶜ 1,290 days will pass. ¹² Happy are those who remain faithful until 1,335 days are over!

¹³ "And you, Daniel, be faithful to the end. Then you will die, but you will rise to receive your reward at the end of time."

ᶜ THE AWFUL HORROR: *See 9.27.*

The Book of
HOSEA

Introduction
The prophet Hosea preached in the northern kingdom of Israel, after the prophet Amos, during the troubled times before the fall of Samaria in 721 B.C. He was especially concerned about the idolatry of the people and their faithlessness toward God. Hosea boldly pictured this faithlessness in terms of his own disastrous marriage to an unfaithful woman. Just as his wife Gomer turned out to be unfaithful to him, so God's people had deserted the Lord. For this, judgment would fall on Israel. Yet in the end God's constant love for his people would prevail, and he would win the nation back to himself and restore the relationship. This love is expressed in the moving words: "How can I give you up, Israel? How can I abandon you? . . . My heart will not let me do it! My love for you is too strong" (11.8).

Outline of Contents

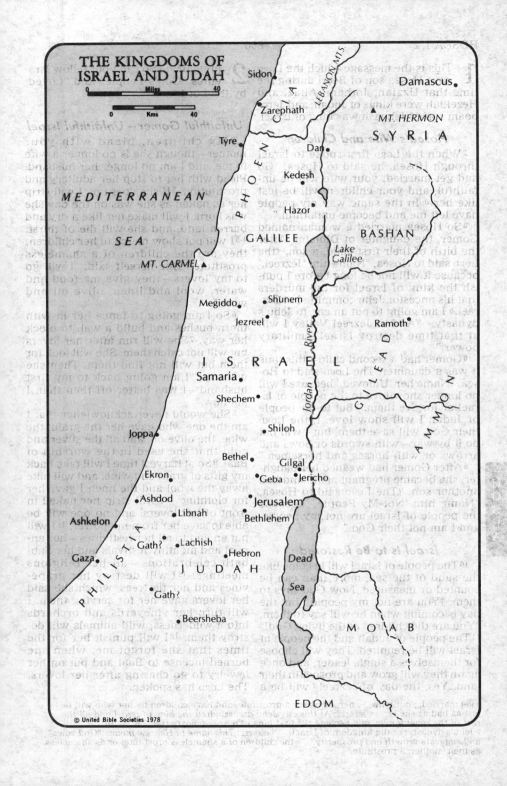

THE KINGDOMS OF
ISRAEL AND JUDAH

Miles
0   40

Kms
0   40

MEDITERRANEAN

SEA

Sidon
Zarephath
Tyre
Kedesh
Hazor

Damascus

MT. HERMON

SYRIA

Dan

PHOENICIA

LEBANON MTS.

GALILEE
MT. CARMEL

Lake
Galilee

BASHAN

Megiddo   Shunem
        Jezreel
                Ramoth

ISRAEL

Samaria

Shechem

Joppa

GILEAD

AMMON

Shiloh
Bethel
Gilgal
Ekron   Geba   Jericho
Ashdod
Ashkelon   Libnah   Jerusalem
Gath?   Bethlehem
Gaza   Lachish
        Hebron

PHILISTIA

JUDAH

Dead
Sea

MOAB

Gath?

Beersheba

EDOM

© United Bible Societies 1978

1 This is the message which the LORD gave Hosea son of Beeri during the time that Uzziah, Jotham, Ahaz, and Hezekiah were kings of Judah, and Jeroboam son of Jehoash was king of Israel.

Hosea's Wife and Children

2 When the LORD first spoke to Israel through Hosea, he said to Hosea, "Go and get married; your wife will be unfaithful, and your children will be just like her.[a] In the same way my people have left me and become unfaithful."

3 So Hosea married a woman named Gomer, the daughter of Diblaim. After the birth of their first child, a son, 4 the LORD said to Hosea, "Name him 'Jezreel,' because it will not be long before I punish the king of Israel for the murders that his ancestor Jehu committed at Jezreel.[b] I am going to put an end to Jehu's dynasty.[c] 5 And in Jezreel Valley I will at that time destroy Israel's military power."

6 Gomer had a second child—this time it was a daughter. The LORD said to Hosea, "Name her 'Unloved,' because I will no longer show love to the people of Israel or forgive them. 7 But to the people of Judah I will show love. I, the LORD their God, will save them, but I will not do it by war—with swords or bows and arrows or with horses and horsemen."

8 After Gomer had weaned her daughter, she became pregnant again and had another son. 9 The LORD said to Hosea, "Name him 'Not-My-People,' because the people of Israel are not my people, and I am not their God."

Israel Is to Be Restored

10 The people of Israel will become like the sand of the sea, more than can be counted or measured. Now God says to them, "You are not my people," but the day is coming when he will say to them, "You are the children of the living God!" 11 The people of Judah and the people of Israel will be reunited. They will choose for themselves a single leader, and once again they will grow and prosper in their land. Yes, the day of Jezreel[d] will be a

2 great day! 1 So call your fellow Israelites "God's People" and "Loved-by-the-Lord."

Unfaithful Gomer — Unfaithful Israel

2 My children, plead with your mother—though she is no longer a wife to me, and I am no longer her husband. Plead with her to stop her adultery and prostitution. 3 If she does not, I will strip her as naked as she was on the day she was born. I will make her like a dry and barren land, and she will die of thirst. 4-5 I will not show mercy to her children; they are the children of a shameless prostitute.[e] She herself said, "I will go to my lovers—they give me food and water, wool and linen, olive oil and wine."

6 So I am going to fence her in with thorn bushes and build a wall to block her way. 7 She will run after her lovers but will not catch them. She will look for them but will not find them. Then she will say, "I am going back to my first husband—I was better off then than I am now."

8 She would never acknowledge that I am the one who gave her the grain, the wine, the olive oil, and all the silver and gold that she used in the worship of Baal. 9 So at harvest time I will take back my gifts of grain and wine, and will take away the wool and the linen I gave her for clothing. 10 I will strip her naked in front of her lovers, and no one will be able to save her from my power. 11 I will put an end to all her festivities—her annual and monthly festivals and her Sabbath celebrations—all her religious meetings. 12 I will destroy her grapevines and her fig trees, which she said her lovers gave her for serving them. I will turn her vineyards and orchards into a wilderness; wild animals will destroy them. 13 I will punish her for the times that she forgot me, when she burned incense to Baal and put on her jewelry to go chasing after her lovers. The LORD has spoken.

---

a get married; your wife . . . her; or marry a prostitute, and have children by her who will be just as bad as she is. b JEZREEL: At this city Jehu assassinated the king of Israel and all the rest of the royal family, and became the first king of a new dynasty (see 2 K 9–10). c Jehu's dynasty; or the kingdom of Israel. d JEZREEL: This name in Hebrew means "God sows" and suggests growth and prosperity. e the children of a shameless prostitute; or as shameless as their mother, a prostitute.

The LORD's Love for His People

14 So I am going to take her into the desert again; there I will win her back with words of love. 15 I will give back to her the vineyards she had and make Trouble Valley a door of hope. She will respond to me there as she did when she was young, when she came from Egypt. 16 Then once again she will call me her husband—she will no longer call me her Baal.[f] 17 I will never let her speak the name of Baal again.

18 At that time I will make a covenant with all the wild animals and birds, so that they will not harm my people. I will also remove all weapons of war from the land, all swords and bows, and will let my people live in peace and safety.

19 Israel, I will make you my wife;
   I will be true and faithful;
   I will show you constant love
      and mercy
   and make you mine forever.
20 I will keep my promise and make
      you mine,
   and you will acknowledge me as
      LORD.
21-22 At that time I will answer the
      prayers of my people Israel.[g]
   I will make rain fall on the
      earth,
   and the earth will produce grain
      and grapes and olives.
23 I will establish my people in the
      land and make them prosper.
   I will show love to those who were
      called "Unloved,"
   and to those who were called
      "Not-My-People,"
   I will say, "You are my people,"
      and they will answer "You are
      our God."

Hosea and the Unfaithful Woman

3 The LORD said to me, "Go again[h] and show your love for a woman who is committing adultery with a lover. You must love her just as I still love the people of Israel, even though they turn to other gods and like to take offerings of raisins to idols."[i]

2 So I paid fifteen pieces of silver and seven bushels of barley to buy her. 3 I told her that for a long time she would have to wait for me without being a prostitute or committing adultery; and during this time I would wait for her. 4 In just this way the people of Israel will have to live for a long time without kings or leaders, without sacrifices or sacred stone pillars, without idols or images to use for divination. 5 But the time will come when the people of Israel will once again turn to the LORD their God and to a descendant of David their king. Then they will fear the LORD and will receive his good gifts.

The LORD's Accusation against Israel

4 The LORD has an accusation to bring against the people who live in this land. Listen, Israel, to what he says: "There is no faithfulness or love in the land, and the people do not acknowledge me as God. 2 They make promises and break them; they lie, murder, steal, and commit adultery. Crimes increase, and there is one murder after another. 3 And so the land will dry up, and everything that lives on it will die. All the animals and birds, and even the fish, will die."

The LORD Accuses the Priests

4 The LORD says, "Let no one accuse the people or reprimand them—my complaint is against you priests.[j] 5 Night and day you blunder on, and the prophets do no better than you. I am going to destroy Israel, your mother. 6 My people are doomed because they do not acknowledge me. You priests have refused to acknowledge me and have rejected my teaching, and so I reject you and will not acknowledge your sons as my priests.

7 "The more of you priests there are, the more you sin against me, and so I will turn your honor into disgrace. 8 You grow rich from the sins of my people, and so you want them to sin more and more. 9 You will suffer the same punishment as the people! I will punish you and

---

f BAAL: This title of the Canaanite god means "Lord"; another meaning of the word is "husband."   g ISRAEL: The Hebrew text here refers to Israel as Jezreel (see 1.4, 11).
h The LORD . . . again; or The LORD spoke to me again. He said, "Go . . ."   i OFFERINGS OF RAISINS TO IDOLS: Dried grapes were used in the worship of fertility gods, who were believed to give abundant harvests to their worshipers.   j Probable text my complaint is against you priests; Hebrew your people are like those with a complaint against the priests.

make you pay for the evil you do. 10 You
will eat your share of the sacrifices, but
still be hungry. You will worship the fertility gods, but still have no children, because you have turned away from me to
follow other gods."

The LORD Condemns Pagan Worship

11 The LORD says, "Wine, both old and
new, is robbing my people of their
senses! 12 They ask for revelations from
a piece of wood! A stick tells them what
they want to know! They have left me.
Like a woman who becomes a prostitute, they have given themselves to other
gods. 13 At sacred places on the mountaintops they offer sacrifices, and on the
hills they burn incense under tall,
spreading trees, because the shade is so
pleasant!

"As a result, your daughters serve as
prostitutes, and your daughters-in-law
commit adultery. 14 Yet I will not punish
them for this, because you yourselves go
off with temple prostitutes,[k] and together with them you offer pagan sacrifices. As the proverb says, 'A people
without sense will be ruined.'

15 "Even though you people of Israel
are unfaithful to me, may Judah not be
guilty of the same thing. Don't worship
at Gilgal or Bethaven,[l] or make promises there in the name of the living LORD.
16 The people of Israel are as stubborn as
mules. How can I feed them like lambs
in a meadow? 17 The people of Israel are
under the spell of idols. Let them go
their own way. 18 After drinking much
wine, they delight in their prostitution,
preferring disgrace to honor. 19 They will
be carried away as by the wind, and they
will be ashamed of their pagan sacrifices.[m,n]

5 "Listen to this, you priests! Pay attention, people of Israel! Listen, you
that belong to the royal family! You are
supposed to judge with justice—so judgment will fall on you! You have become
a trap at Mizpah, a net spread on Mount
Tabor, 2 a deep pit at Acacia City,[o] and
I will punish all of you. 3 I know what
Israel is like—she cannot hide from me.
She has been unfaithful, and her people
are unfit to worship me."

Hosea Warns against Idolatry

4 The evil that the people have done
keeps them from returning to their God.
Idolatry has a powerful hold on them,
and they do not acknowledge the LORD.
5 The arrogance of the people of Israel
cries out against them. Their sins make
them stumble and fall, and the people of
Judah fall with them. 6 They take their
sheep and cattle to offer as sacrifices to
the LORD, but it does them no good. They
cannot find him, for he has left them.
7 They have been unfaithful to the LORD;
their children do not belong to him. So
now they and their lands will soon be
destroyed.

War between Judah and Israel

8 Blow the war trumpets in Gibeah!
Sound the alarm in Ramah! Raise the
war cry at Bethaven![p] Into battle, men
of Benjamin! 9 The day of punishment is
coming, and Israel will be ruined. People
of Israel, this will surely happen!

10 The LORD says, "I am angry because
the leaders of Judah have invaded Israel
and stolen land from her. So I will pour
out punishment on them like a flood.
11 Israel is suffering oppression; she has
lost land that was rightfully hers, because she insisted on going for help to
those who had none to give.[q] 12 I will
bring destruction on Israel and ruin on
the people of Judah.

13 "When Israel saw how sick she was
and when Judah saw her own wounds,
then Israel went to Assyria to ask the
great emperor for help, but he could not
cure them or heal their wounds. 14 I will
attack the people of Israel and Judah
like a lion. I myself will tear them to
pieces and then leave them. When I drag
them off, no one will be able to save
them.

15 "I will abandon my people until they

[k] TEMPLE PROSTITUTES: *These women were found in Canaanite temples, where fertility gods were worshiped. It was believed that intercourse with these prostitutes assured fertile fields and herds.* [l] BETHAVEN: *This name means "house of evil" or "house of idolatry" and in this passage refers to the city of Bethel, a name which means "house of God." See also 10.8.*
[m] sacrifices; *some ancient translations* altars. [n] *Verses 17-19 in Hebrew are unclear.*
[o] *Probable text* a deep pit at Acacia City; *Hebrew unclear.* [p] BETHAVEN: *This name means "house of evil" or "house of idolatry" and in this passage refers to the city of Bethel, a name which means "house of God." See also 10.8.* [q] *Probable text* those who had none to give; *Hebrew* command.

have suffered enough for their sins and come looking for me. Perhaps in their suffering they will try to find me."

The People's Insincere Repentance

6 The people say, "Let's return to the Lord! He has hurt us, but he will be sure to heal us; he has wounded us, but he will bandage our wounds, won't he? 2 In two or three days he will revive us, and we will live in his presence. 3 Let us try to know the Lord. He will come to us as surely as the day dawns, as surely as the spring rains fall upon the earth."

4 But the Lord says, "Israel and Judah, what am I going to do with you? Your love for me disappears as quickly as morning mist; it is like dew, that vanishes early in the day. 5 That is why I have sent my prophets to you with my message of judgment and destruction. What I want from you is plain and clear: 6 I want your constant love, not your animal sacrifices. I would rather have my people know me than burn offerings to me.

7 "But as soon as they entered the land at Adam,ʳ they broke the covenant I had made with them. 8 Gilead is a city full of evil people and murderers. 9 The priests are like a gang of robbers who wait in ambush for someone. Even on the road to the holy place at Shechem they commit murder. And they do all this evil deliberately! 10 I have seen a horrible thing in Israel: my people have defiled themselves by worshiping idols. 11 "And as for you, people of Judah, I have set a time to punish you also for what you are doing.

7 "Whenever I want to heal my people Israel and make them prosperous again, all I can see is their wickedness and the evil they do. They cheat one another; they break into houses and steal; they rob people in the streets. 2 It never enters their heads that I will remember all this evil; but their sins surround them, and I cannot avoid seeing them."

Conspiracy in the Palace

3 The Lord says, "People deceive the king and his officers by their evil plots. 4 They are all treacherous and disloyal.

Their hatred smolders like the fire in an oven, which is not stirred by the baker until the dough is ready to bake. 5 On the day of the king's celebration they made the king and his officials drunk and foolish with wine. 6 Yes, they burnedˢ like an oven with their plotting. All night their anger smoldered, and in the morning it burst into flames. 7 "In the heat of their anger they murdered their rulers. Their kings have been assassinated one after another, but no one prays to me for help."

Israel and the Nations

8 The Lord says, "The people of Israel are like a half-baked loaf of bread. They rely on the nations around them 9 and do not realize that this reliance on foreigners has robbed them of their strength. Their days are numbered, but they don't even know it. 10 The arrogance of the people of Israel cries out against them. In spite of everything that has happened, they have not returned to me, the Lord their God. 11 Israel flits around like a silly pigeon; first her people call on Egypt for help, and then they run to Assyria! 12 But I will spread out a net and catch them like birds as they go by. I will punish them for the evil they have done.ᵗ

13 "They are doomed! They have left me and rebelled against me. They will be destroyed. I wanted to save them, but their worship of me was false. 14 They have not prayed to me sincerely, but instead they throw themselves down and wail as the heathen do. When they pray for grain and wine, they gash themselves like pagans. What rebels they are! 15 Even though I was the one who brought them up and made them strong, they plotted against me. 16 They keep on turning away from me to a god that is powerless.ᵘ They are as unreliable as a crooked bow. Because their leaders talk arrogantly, they will die a violent death, and the Egyptians will laugh."

The Lord Condemns Israel for Idol Worship

8 The Lord says, "Sound the alarm! Enemies are swooping down on my land like eagles! My people have broken

---

ʳ *Probable text* But . . . at Adam; *Hebrew* But like Adam.   ˢ *One ancient translation* burned; *Hebrew* drew near.   ᵗ *Probable text* the evil they have done; *Hebrew* the report to their congregation.   ᵘ *Probable text* a god that is powerless; *Hebrew unclear.*

the covenant I made with them and have rebelled against my teaching. 2 Even though they call me their God and claim that they are my people and that they know me, 3 they have rejected what is good. Because of this their enemies will pursue them.

4 "My people chose kings, but they did it on their own. They appointed leaders, but without my approval. They took their silver and gold and made idols — for their own destruction. 5 I hate the gold bull worshiped by the people of the city of Samaria. I am furious with them. How long will it be before they give up their idolatry? 6 An Israelite craftsman made the idol, and it is not a god at all! The gold bull worshiped in Samaria will be smashed to pieces! 7 When they sow the wind, they will reap a storm! A field of grain that doesn't ripen can never produce any bread. But even if it did, foreigners would eat it up. 8 Israel has become like any other nation and is as useless as a broken pot. 9 Stubborn as wild donkeys, the people of Israel go their own way. They have gone off to seek help from Assyria and have paid other nations to protect them. 10 But now I am going to gather them together and punish them. Soon they will writhe in pain when the emperor of Assyria oppresses them.

11 "The more altars the people of Israel build for removing sin, the more places they have for sinning! 12 I write down countless teachings for the people, but they reject them as strange and foreign. 13 They offer sacrifices to me and eat the meat of the sacrifices.v But I, the LORD, am not pleased with them, and now I will remember their sin and punish them for it; I will send them back to Egypt!

14 "The people of Israel have built palaces, but they have forgotten their own Maker. The people of Judah have built fortified cities. But I will send fire that will burn down their palaces and their cities."

Hosea Announces Punishment for Israel

9 People of Israel, stop celebrating your festivals like pagans. You have turned away from your God and have been unfaithful to him. All over the land you have sold yourselves like prostitutes to the god Baal and have loved the grain you thought he paid you with! 2 But soon you will not have enough grain and olive oil, and there will be no wine. 3 The people of Israel will not remain in the LORD's land, but will have to go back to Egypt and will have to eat forbidden foodw in Assyria. 4 In those foreign lands they will not be able to make wine offerings to the LORD or bring their sacrifices to him. Their food will defile everyone who eats it, like food eaten at funerals. It will be used only to satisfy their hunger; none of it will be taken as an offering to the LORD's Temple. 5 And when the time comes for the appointed festivals in honor of the LORD, what will they do then? 6 When the disaster comes and the people are scattered, the Egyptians will gather them up — gather them for burial there at Memphis! Their treasures of silver and the places where their homes once stood will be overgrown with weeds and thorn bushes.

7 The time for punishment has come, the time when people will get what they deserve. When that happens, Israel will know it! "This prophet," you say, "is a fool. This inspired man is insane." You people hate me so much because your sin is so great. 8 God has sent me as a prophet to warn his people Israel. Yet wherever I go, you try to trap me like a bird. Even in God's Temple the people are the prophet's enemies. 9 They are hopelessly evil in what they do, just as they were at Gibeah.x God will remember their sin and punish them for it.

Israel's Sin and Its Consequences

10 The LORD says, "When I first found Israel, it was like finding grapes growing in the desert. When I first saw your ancestors, it was like seeing the first ripe figs of the season. But when they came

v They offer . . . the sacrifices; Hebrew unclear.   w FORBIDDEN FOOD: The Law of Moses prohibited the eating of certain foods as being ritually unclean (see Lv 11).   x GIBEAH: At this city some Israelites of the tribe of Benjamin raped a Levite's concubine; this caused a civil war that almost wiped out the Benjaminites (see Jg 19–21).

to Mount Peor, they began to worship Baal and soon became as disgusting as the gods they loved. 11 Israel's greatness will fly away like a bird, and there will be no more children born to them, no more women pregnant, no more children conceived. 12 But even if they did bring up children, I would take them away and not leave one alive. When I abandon these people, terrible things will happen to them."

13 LORD, I can see their children being hunted downy and killed. 14 What shall I ask you to do to these people? Make their women barren! Make them unable to nurse their babies!

The LORD's Judgment on Israel

15 The LORD says, "All their evildoing began in Gilgal. It was there that I began to hate them. And because of the evil they have done, I will drive them out of my land. I will not love them any more; all their leaders have rebelled against me. 16 The people of Israel are like a plant whose roots have dried up and which bears no fruit. They will have no children, but even if they did, I would kill the children so dear to them."

The Prophet Speaks about Israel

17 The God I serve will reject his people, because they have not listened to him. They will become wanderers among the nations. 1 The people of Israel were like a grapevine that was full of grapes. The more prosperous they were, the more altars they built. The more productive their land was, the more beautiful they made the sacred stone pillars they worship. 2 The people whose hearts are deceitful must now suffer for their sins. God will break down their altars and destroy their sacred pillars.

3 These people will soon be saying, "We have no king because we did not fear the LORD. But what could a king do for us anyway?" 4 They utter empty words and make false promises and useless treaties. Justice has become injustice, growing like poisonous weeds in a plowed field.

5 The people who live in the city of Samaria will be afraid and will mourn the loss of the gold bullz at Bethaven. a They and the priests who serve the idol will weep over it. They will wail when it is stripped of its golden splendor. 6 The idol will be carried off to Assyria as tribute to the great emperor. The people of Israel will be disgraced and put to shame because of the advice they followed. 7 Their king will be carried off, like a chip of wood on water. 8 The hilltop shrines of Aven,a where the people of Israel worship idols, will be destroyed. Thorns and weeds will grow up over their altars. The people will call out to the mountains, "Hide us!" and to the hills, "Cover us!"

The LORD Pronounces Judgment on Israel

9 The LORD says, "The people of Israel have not stopped sinning against me since the time of their sin at Gibeah.b So at Gibeah war will catch up with them. 10 I will attackc this sinful people and punish them. Nations will join together against them, and they will be punished for their many sins.

11 "Israel was once like a well-trained young cow, ready and willing to thresh grain. But I decided to put a yoked on her beautiful neck and to harness her for harder work. I made Judah pull the plow and Israel pull the harrow. 12 I said, 'Plow new ground for yourselves, plant righteousness, and reap the blessings that your devotion to me will produce. It is time for you to turn to me, your LORD, and I will come and pour out blessings upon you.' 13 But instead you planted evil and reaped its harvest. You have eaten the fruit produced by your lies.

"Because you trusted in your chariotse and in the large number of your soldiers, 14 war will come to your people, and all your fortresses will be destroyed. It will be like the day when King Shalman destroyed the city of Betharbel in battle, and mothers and their children

H
O
S
E
A

---

y Probable text being hunted down; Hebrew unclear.   z Some ancient translations bull;
Hebrew cows.   a BETHAVEN: This name means "house of evil" or "house of idolatry" and in this
passage refers to the city of Bethel, a name which means "house of God." In verse 8, Bethaven
is called Aven. See also 4.15 and 5.8.   b GIBEAH: See 9.9.   c One ancient translation I will
attack; Hebrew In my desire.   d Probable text put a yoke; Hebrew spare.
e One ancient translation chariots; Hebrew way.

were crushed to death. 15 That is what will happen to you, people of Bethel, because of the terrible evil that you have done. As soon as the battle begins, the king of Israel will die."

God's Love for His Rebellious People

11 The LORD says,
"When Israel was a child, I loved him
and called him out of Egypt as my son.*f*
2 But the more I*g* called to him,
the more he turned away from me.*h*
My people sacrificed to Baal;
they burned incense to idols.
3 Yet I was the one who taught Israel to walk.

I took my people up in my arms,*i*
but they did not acknowledge that I took care of them.
4 I drew them to me with affection and love.

I picked them up and held them to my cheek;
I bent down to them and fed them.*j*

5 "They refuse to return to me, and so they must return to Egypt, and Assyria will rule them. 6 War will sweep through their cities and break down the city gates. It will destroy my people because they do what they themselves think best. 7 They insist on turning away from me. They will cry out because of the yoke that is on them, but no one will lift it from them.*k*

8 "How can I give you up, Israel?
How can I abandon you?
Could I ever destroy you as I did Admah,
or treat you as I did Zeboiim?
My heart will not let me do it!
My love for you is too strong.
9 I will not punish you in my anger;
I will not destroy Israel again.
For I am God and not a mere human being.
I, the Holy One, am with you.
I will not come to you in anger.

10 "My people will follow me when I roar like a lion at their enemies. They will hurry to me from the west. 11 They will come from Egypt, as swiftly as birds, and from Assyria, like doves. I will bring them to their homes again. I, the LORD, have spoken."

Israel and Judah Are Condemned

12 The LORD says, "The people of Israel have surrounded me with lies and deceit, and the people of Judah are still rebelling against me, the faithful and holy

12 God. 1 Everything that the people of Israel do from morning to night is useless and destructive. Treachery and acts of violence increase among them. They make treaties with Assyria and do business with Egypt."

2 The LORD has an accusation to bring against the people of Judah; he is also going to punish Israel for the way her people act. He will pay them back for what they have done. 3 Their ancestor Jacob struggled with his twin brother Esau while the two of them were still in their mother's womb; when Jacob grew up, he fought against God—4 he fought against an angel and won. He wept and asked for a blessing. And at Bethel God came to our ancestor Jacob and spoke with him.*l* 5 This was the LORD God Almighty—the LORD is the name by which he is to be worshiped. 6 So now, descendants of Jacob, trust in your God and return to him. Be loyal and just, and wait patiently for your God to act.

Further Words of Judgment

7 The LORD says, "The people of Israel are as dishonest as the Canaanites; they love to cheat their customers with false scales. 8 'We are rich,' they say. 'We've made a fortune. And no one can accuse us of getting rich dishonestly.' 9 But I, the LORD your God who led you out of Egypt, I will make you live in tents again, as you did when I came to you in the desert.

10 "I spoke to the prophets and gave them many visions, and through the prophets I gave my people warnings. 11 Yet idols are worshiped in Gilead, and those who worship them will die. Bulls are sacrificed in Gilgal, and the altars

---

f him, and called him . . . son; *or* him; from the time he left Egypt I have called him my son.
g One ancient translation I; Hebrew they. *h* One ancient translation me; Hebrew them.
i One ancient translation I . . . my arms; Hebrew He . . . his arms. *j* Verse 4 in Hebrew is unclear. *k* Verse 7 in Hebrew is unclear. *l* Some ancient translations him; Hebrew us.

there will become piles of stone in the open fields."

12 Our ancestor Jacob had to flee to Mesopotamia, where, in order to get a wife, he worked for another man and took care of his sheep. 13 The LORD sent a prophet to rescue the people of Israel from slavery in Egypt and to take care of them. 14 The people of Israel have made the LORD bitterly angry; they deserve death for their crimes. Their Lord will punish them for the disgrace they have brought on him.

Final Judgment on Israel

13 In the past, when the tribe of Ephraim spoke, the other tribes of Israel were afraid; they looked up to Ephraim. But the people sinned by worshiping Baal, and for this they will die. 2 They still keep on sinning by making metal images to worship—idols of silver, designed by human minds, made by human hands. And then they say, "Offer sacrifices to them!" How can anyone kiss those idols—idols in the shape of bulls!m 3 And so these people will disappear like morning mist, like the dew that vanishes early in the day. They will be like chaff which the wind blows from the threshing place, like smoke from a chimney.

4 The LORD says, "I am the LORD your God, who led you out of Egypt. You have no God but me. I alone am your savior. 5 I took care of you in a dry, desert land. 6 But when you entered the good land, you became full and satisfied, and then you grew proud and forgot me. 7 So I will attack you like a lion. Like a leopard I will lie in wait along your path. 8 I will attack you like a bear that has lost her cubs, and I will tear you open. Like a lion I will devour you on the spot, and will tear you to pieces like a wild animal.

9 "I will destroy you, people of Israel! Then who can help you?n 10 You asked for a king and for leaders, but how can they save the nation?o 11 In my anger I have given you kings, and in my fury I have taken them away.

12 "Israel's sin and guilt are on record, and the records are safely stored away. 13 Israel has a chance to live, but is too foolish to take it—like a child about to be born, who refuses to come out of the womb. 14 I will not save this people from the world of the dead or rescue them from the power of death. Bring onp your plagues, death! Bring onp your destruction, world of the dead! I will no longer have pity for this people. 15 Even though Israel flourishes like weeds,q I will send a hot east wind from the desert, and it will dry up their springs and wells. It will take away everything of value. 16 Samaria must be punished for rebelling against me. Her people will die in war; babies will be dashed to the ground, and pregnant women will be ripped open."

Hosea's Plea to Israel

14 Return to the LORD your God, people of Israel. Your sin has made you stumble and fall. 2 Return to the LORD and let this prayer be your offering to him: "Forgive all our sins and accept our prayer, and we will praise you as we have promised. 3 Assyria can never save us, and war horses cannot protect us. We will never again say to our idols that they are our God. O LORD, you show mercy to those who have no one else to turn to."

The LORD Promises New Life for Israel

4 The LORD says,
"I will bring my people back
    to me.
I will love them with all my heart;
    no longer am I angry with them.
5 I will be to the people of Israel
    like rain in a dry land.
They will blossom like flowers;
    they will be firmly rooted
    like the trees of Lebanon.
6 They will be alive with new
        growth,
    and beautiful like olive trees.
They will be fragrant
    like the cedars of Lebanon.
7 Once again they will live under
    my protection.
They will grow crops of grain
    and be fruitful like a vineyard.
They will be as famous as the
    wine of Lebanon.

---

m *Probable text* And then they ... bulls!; *Hebrew unclear.*   n *One ancient translation* who can help you?; *Hebrew* in me is your help.   o *Verse 10 in Hebrew is unclear.*   p *Some ancient translations* Bring on; *Hebrew* I will be.   q *Probable text* like weeds; *Hebrew* among brothers.

8 The people of Israel[r] will have
    nothing more to do with idols;
  I will answer their prayers and
    take care of them.
  Like an evergreen tree I will
    shelter them;
  I am the source of all their
    blessings."

Conclusion

9 May those who are wise understand
what is written here, and may they take
it to heart. The LORD's ways are right,
and righteous people live by following
them, but sinners stumble and fall because they ignore them.

[r] *One ancient translation* The people of Israel; *Hebrew* Israel, I.

The Book of
JOEL

Introduction

*Little is known about the prophet Joel, and it is not clear just when he lived. But it
seems likely that the book comes from the fifth or fourth century B.C., during the time
of the Persian Empire. Joel describes a terrible invasion of locusts and a devastating
drought in Palestine. In these events he sees a sign of the coming day of the Lord, a time
when the Lord will punish those who oppose his righteous will. The prophet conveys the
Lord's call to the people to repent, and his promise of restoration and blessing for his
people. Noteworthy is the promise that God will send his Spirit upon all the people, men
and women, young and old alike.*

Outline of Contents

H O S E A

1

This is the LORD's message to Joel
son of Pethuel,

The People Mourn the Destruction
of the Crops

2 Pay attention, you older people;
    everyone in Judah, listen.
  Has anything like this ever
    happened
    in your time or the time of your
    ancestors?
3 Tell your children about it;
    they will tell their children,
    who in turn will tell the next
    generation.

4 Swarm after swarm of locusts
    settled on the crops;
  what one swarm left, the next
    swarm devoured.
5 Wake up and weep, you
    drunkards;

  cry, you wine-drinkers;
    the grapes for making new wine
    have been destroyed.

6 An army of locusts has attacked
    our land;
  they are powerful and too many
    to count;
  their teeth are as sharp as those
    of a lion.
7 They have destroyed our
    grapevines
    and chewed up our fig trees.
  They have stripped off the bark,
    till the branches are white.

8 Cry, you people, like a young
    woman who mourns the death
    of the man she was going to
    marry.
9 There is no grain or wine to offer
    in the Temple;

the priests mourn because they
have no offerings for the Lord.

10 The fields are bare;
the ground mourns
because the grain is destroyed,
the grapes are dried up,
and the olive trees are withered.

11 Grieve, you farmers;
cry, you that take care of the
vineyards,
because the wheat, the barley,
yes all the crops are destroyed.

12 The grapevines and fig trees have
withered;
all the fruit trees have wilted
and died.
The joy of the people is gone.

13 Put on sackcloth and weep,
you priests who serve at the
altar!
Go into the Temple and mourn all
night!
There is no grain or wine to offer
your God.

14 Give orders for a fast;
call an assembly!
Gather the leaders
and all the people of Judah
into the Temple of the Lord
your God
and cry out to him!

15 The day of the Lord is near,
the day when the Almighty
brings destruction.
What terror that day will bring!

16 We look on helpless as our crops
are destroyed.
There is no joy in the Temple of
our God.

17 The seeds die in the dry earth.
There is no grain to be stored,
and so the empty granaries are
in ruins.

18 The cattle are bellowing in distress
because there is no pasture for
them;
the flocks of sheep also suffer.

19 I cry out to you, Lord,
because the pastures and trees
are dried up,
as though a fire had burned
them.

20 Even the wild animals cry out
to you

because the streams have
become dry.

The Locusts as a Warning of the Day of the Lord

2 Blow the trumpet; sound the
alarm
on Zion, God's sacred hill.[a]
Tremble, people of Judah!
The day of the Lord is coming
soon.

2 It will be a dark and gloomy day,
a black and cloudy day.
The great army of locusts
advances
like darkness spreading over the
mountains.
There has never been anything
like it,
and there never will be again.

3 Like fire they eat up the plants.
In front of them the land is like
the Garden of Eden,
but behind them it is a barren
desert.
Nothing escapes them.

4 They look like horses;
they run like war-horses.

5 As they leap on the tops of the
mountains,
they rattle like chariots;
they crackle like dry grass on
fire.
They are lined up like a great
army ready for battle.

6 As they approach, everyone is
terrified;
every face turns pale.

7 They attack like warriors;
they climb the walls like
soldiers.
They all keep marching straight
ahead
and do not change direction

8 or get in each other's way.
They swarm through defenses,
and nothing can stop them.

9 They rush against the city;
they run over the walls;
they climb up the houses
and go in through the windows
like thieves.

10 The earth shakes as they advance;
the sky trembles.

a SACRED HILL: *Mount Zion (see Zion in Word List).*

The sun and the moon grow dark,
and the stars no longer shine.
11 The LORD thunders commands to
his army.
The troops that obey him
are many and mighty.
How terrible is the day of the
LORD!
Who will survive it?

A Call to Repentance

12 "But even now," says the LORD,
"repent sincerely and return
to me
with fasting and weeping and
mourning.
13 Let your broken heart show your
sorrow;
tearing your clothes is not
enough."

Come back to the LORD your God.
He is kind and full of mercy;
he is patient and keeps his
promise;
he is always ready to forgive
and not punish.
14 Perhaps the LORD your God will
change his mind
and bless you with abundant
crops.
Then you can offer him grain and
wine.

15 Blow the trumpet on Mount Zion;
give orders for a fast and call an
assembly!
16 Gather the people together;
prepare them for a sacred
meeting;
bring the old people;
gather the children
and the babies too.
Even newly married couples
must leave their homes and
come.
17 The priests, serving the LORD
between the altar and the
entrance of the Temple,
must weep and pray:
"Have pity on your people, LORD.
Do not let other nations despise
us and mock us
by saying, 'Where is
your God?' "

God Restores Fertility to the Land

18 Then the LORD showed concern for
his land;
he had mercy on his people.
19 He answered them:
"Now I am going to give you
grain and wine and olive oil,
and you will be satisfied.
Other nations will no longer
despise you.
20 I will remove the locust army that
came from the north
and will drive some of them into
the desert.
Their front ranks will be driven
into the Dead Sea,
their rear ranks into the
Mediterranean.
Their dead bodies will stink.
I will destroy them because of all
they have done to you.

21 "Fields, don't be afraid,
but be joyful and glad
because of all the LORD has done
for you.
22 Animals, don't be afraid.
The pastures are green;
the trees bear their fruit,
and there are plenty of figs and
grapes.

23 "Be glad, people of Zion,
rejoice at what the LORD your
God has done for you.
He has given you the right
amount of autumn rain;b
he has poured down the winter
rain for you
and the spring rain as before.
24 The threshing places will be full of
grain;
the pits beside the presses will
overflow with wine and
olive oil.
25 I will give you back what you lost
in the years when swarms of
locusts ate your crops.
It was I who sent this army
against you.
26 Now you will have plenty to eat,
and be satisfied.
You will praise the LORD
your God,
who has done wonderful things
for you.

---

b right amount of autumn rain; or autumn rain because he is just.

My people will never be
despised again.
27 Then, Israel, you will know that
I am among you
and that I, the LORD, am
your God
and there is no other.
My people will never be
despised again.

The Day of the LORD

28 "Afterward I will pour out my
Spirit on everyone:
your sons and daughters will
proclaim my message;
your old people will have
dreams,
and your young people will see
visions.
29 At that time I will pour out my
Spirit
even on servants, both men and
women.

30 "I will give warnings of that day
in the sky and on the earth;
there will be bloodshed, fire, and
clouds of smoke.
31 The sun will be darkened,
and the moon will turn red as
blood
before the great and terrible day
of the LORD comes.
32 But all who ask the LORD for help
will be saved.
As the LORD has said,
'Some in Jerusalem will escape;
those whom I choose will
survive.' "

God Will Judge the Nations

3 The LORD says,
"At that time I will restore
the prosperity of Judah and
Jerusalem.
2 I will gather all the nations
and bring them to the Valley of
Judgment.
There I will judge them
for all they have done to my
people.
They have scattered the Israelites
in foreign countries
and divided Israel, my land.
3 They threw dice to decide
who would get the captives.

They sold boys and girls into
slavery
to pay for prostitutes and wine.

4 "What are you trying to do to me,
Tyre, Sidon, and all of Philistia? Are you
trying to pay me back for something? If
you are, I will quickly pay you back!
5 You have taken my silver and gold and
carried my rich treasures into your temples. 6 You have taken the people of Judah and Jerusalem far from their own
country and sold them to the Greeks.
7 Now I am going to bring them out of the
places to which you have sold them. I
will do to you what you have done to
them. 8 I will let your sons and daughters
be sold to the people of Judah; they will
sell them to the far-off Sabeans. I, the
LORD, have spoken.

9 "Make this announcement among
the nations:
'Prepare for war;
call your warriors;
gather all your soldiers and
march!
10 Hammer the points of your plows
into swords
and your pruning knives into
spears.
Even the weak must fight.
11 Hurryᶜ and come,
all you surrounding nations,
and gather in the valley.' "

Send down, O LORD, your army to
attack them!

12 "The nations must get ready
and come to the Valley of
Judgment.
There I, the LORD, will sit to judge
all the surrounding nations.
13 They are very wicked;
cut them down like grain
at harvest time;
crush them as grapes are crushed
in a full wine press
until the wine runs over."

14 Thousands and thousands
are in the Valley of Judgment.
It is there that the day of the LORD
will soon come.

ᶜ Probable text Hurry; Hebrew Help.

15 The sun and the moon grow dark,
   and the stars no longer shine.

God Will Bless His People

16 The LORD roars from Mount Zion;
   his voice thunders from
      Jerusalem;
   earth and sky tremble.
   But he will defend his people.
17 "Then, Israel, you will know that I
      am the LORD your God.
   I live on Zion, my sacred hill.
   Jerusalem will be a sacred city;
      foreigners will never conquer it
      again.
18 At that time the mountains will be
      covered with vineyards,
   and cattle will be found on every
      hill;

there will be plenty of water for
   all of Judah.
A stream will flow from the
      Temple of the LORD,
   and it will water Acacia Valley.

19 "Egypt will become a desert,
   and Edom a ruined waste,
   because they attacked the land of
      Judah
   and killed its innocent
      people.
20-21 I will avenge^d those who were
      killed;
   I will not spare the guilty.
But Judah and Jerusalem will be
      inhabited forever,
   and I, the LORD, will live on
      Mount Zion."

d *Some ancient translations* avenge; *Hebrew* declare innocent.

The Book of
AMOS

Introduction

Amos was the first prophet in the Bible whose message was recorded at length. Although he came from a town in Judah, he preached to the people of the northern kingdom of Israel, about the middle of the eighth century B.C. It was a time of great prosperity, notable religious piety, and apparent security. But Amos saw that prosperity was limited to the wealthy, and that it fed on injustice and on oppression of the poor. Religious observance was insincere, and security more apparent than real. With passion and courage he preached that God would punish the nation. He called for justice to "flow like a stream," and said, "Perhaps the Lord will be merciful to the people of this nation who are still left alive" (5.15).

Outline of Contents

1 These are the words of Amos, a shepherd from the town of Tekoa. Two years before the earthquake, when Uzziah was king of Judah and Jeroboam son of Jehoash was king of Israel, God revealed to Amos all these things about Israel.

2 Amos said,

"The LORD roars from Mount
      Zion;
   his voice thunders from
      Jerusalem.
The pastures dry up,
   and the grass on Mount Carmel
      turns brown."

J
O
E
L

God's Judgment on Israel's Neighbors

Syria

3 The LORD says, "The people of Damascus have sinned again and again, and for this I will certainly punish them. They treated the people of Gilead with savage cruelty. 4 So I will send fire upon the palace built by King Hazael and I will burn down the fortresses of King Benhadad. 5 I will smash the city gates of Damascus and remove the inhabitants of Aven Valley and the ruler of Betheden. The people of Syria will be taken away as prisoners to the land of Kir."

Philistia

6 The LORD says, "The people of Gaza have sinned again and again, and for this I will certainly punish them. They carried off a whole nation and sold them as slaves to the people of Edom. 7 So I will send fire upon the city walls of Gaza and burn down its fortresses. 8 I will remove the rulers of the cities of Ashdod and Ashkelon. I will punish the city of Ekron, and all the Philistines who are left will die."

Tyre

9 The LORD says, "The people of Tyre have sinned again and again, and for this I will certainly punish them. They carried off a whole nation into exile in the land of Edom, and did not keep the treaty of friendship they had made. 10 So I will send fire upon the city walls of Tyre and burn down its fortresses."

Edom

11 The LORD says, "The people of Edom have sinned again and again, and for this I will certainly punish them. They hunted down their relatives,*a* the Israelites, and showed them no mercy. Their anger had no limits, and they never let it die. 12 So I will send fire upon the city of Teman and burn down the fortresses of Bozrah."

Ammon

13 The LORD says, "The people of Ammon have sinned again and again, and for this I will certainly punish them. In their wars for more territory they even ripped open pregnant women in Gilead. 14 So I will send fire upon the city walls of Rabbah and burn down its fortresses. Then there will be shouts on the day of battle, and the fighting will rage like a storm. 15 Their king and his officers will go into exile."

Moab

2 The LORD says, "The people of Moab have sinned again and again, and for this I will certainly punish them. They dishonored the bones of the king of Edom by burning them to ashes. 2 I will send fire upon the land of Moab and burn down the fortresses of Kerioth. The people of Moab will die in the noise of battle while soldiers are shouting and trumpets are sounding. 3 I will kill the ruler of Moab and all the leaders of the land."

Judah

4 The LORD says, "The people of Judah have sinned again and again, and for this I will certainly punish them. They have despised my teachings and have not kept my commands. They have been led astray by the same false gods that their ancestors served. 5 So I will send fire upon Judah and burn down the fortresses of Jerusalem."

God's Judgment on Israel

6 The LORD says, "The people of Israel have sinned again and again, and for this I will certainly punish them. They sell into slavery honest people who cannot pay their debts, the poor who cannot repay even the price of a pair of sandals. 7 They trample*b* down the weak and helpless and push the poor out of the way. A man and his father have intercourse with the same slave woman, and so profane my holy name. 8 At every place of worship people sleep on clothing that they have taken from the poor as security for debts. In the temple of their God they drink wine which they have taken from those who owe them money.

9 "And yet, my people, it was for your sake that I totally destroyed the Amorites, who were as tall as cedar trees and as strong as oaks. 10 I brought you out of

A
M
O
S

---

a THEIR RELATIVES: *The Israelites were descended from Jacob, who was the brother of Esau, the ancestor of the Edomites.*   *b* trample; *Hebrew unclear.*

THE CITY OF SAMARIA

Samaria is probably best known as the setting for Jesus' visit with the woman at the well (Jn 4.5–42). But Samaria's importance as both a city and a region was well established long before the time of Jesus. This ancient city is second only to Jerusalem and Babylon in the number of times it is mentioned in the Bible.

One of the most striking features of Samaria was its hilltop location. Built by King Omri as the capital of the northern kingdom of Israel, it contributed significantly to the history and culture of ancient Israel.

Samaria was one of the few major Jewish cities actually founded and built from the ground up by the Israelites. They took most of their cities from other nations and then either rebuilt or renovated them into distinctively Jewish population centers.

After succeeding Omri as king, Ahab (reigned 874–853 B.C.) remodeled and expanded Omri's beautiful palace in the city of Samaria. Some of Ahab's decorations, especially the expensive ivory with which he adorned his furniture and palace walls, have been discovered by archaeologists. But in spite of its wealth and splendor, the city fell to the Assyrians in 722 B.C., fulfilling Amos' prophecy of its destruction (Am 3.11–15). The citizens of Samaria were carried away to Assyria as captives.

After its fall to the Assyrians, Samaria continued to be inhabited by several different groups under the successive authority of Assyria, Babylonia, Persia, Greece, and Rome. Herod the Great, Roman governor of Palestine (ruled 37–4 B.C.), made many improvements to the city and renamed it Sebaste—the Greek term for Augustus—in honor of the emperor of Rome.

Egypt, led you through the desert for forty years, and gave you the land of the Amorites to be your own. ¹¹I chose some of your sons to be prophets and some of your young men to be nazirites.ᶜ Isn't this true, people of Israel? I, the LORD, have spoken. ¹²But you made the nazirites drink wine, and ordered the prophets not to speak my message. ¹³And now I will crush you to the ground, and you will groan like a cart loaded with grain. ¹⁴Not even fast runners will escape; strong men will lose their strength, and soldiers will not be able to save their own lives. ¹⁵Archers will not stand their ground, fast runners will not get away, and men on horses will not escape with their lives. ¹⁶On that day even the bravest soldiers will drop their weapons and run." The LORD has spoken.

3 People of Israel, listen to this message which the LORD has spoken about you, the entire nation that he brought out of Egypt: ²"Of all the nations on earth, you are the only one I have known and cared for. That is what makes your sins so terrible, and that is why I must punish you for them."

The Prophet's Task

³Do two people start traveling together without arranging to meet?

⁴Does a lion roar in the forest unless he has found a victim?

Does a young lion growl in his den unless he has caught something?

⁵Does a bird get caught in a trap if the trap has not been baited?

Does a trap spring unless something sets it off?

⁶Does the war trumpet sound in a city without making the people afraid?

Does disaster strike a city unless the LORD sends it?

⁷The Sovereign LORD never does anything without revealing his plan to his servants, the prophets.

⁸When a lion roars, who can keep from being afraid?

When the Sovereign LORD speaks, who can keep from proclaiming his message?

The Doom of Samaria

⁹Announce to those who live in the palaces of Egypt and Ashdod: "Gather together in the hills around Samaria and see the great disorder and the crimes being committed there."

¹⁰The LORD says, "These people fill their mansions with things taken by crime and violence. They don't even know how to be honest. ¹¹And so an enemy will surround their land, destroy their defenses, and plunder their mansions."

¹²The LORD says, "As a shepherd recovers only two legs or an ear of a sheep that a lion has eaten, so only a few will survive of Samaria's people, who now recline on luxurious couches.ᵈ ¹³Listen now, and warn the descendants of Jacob," says the Sovereign LORD Almighty. ¹⁴"On the day when I punish the people of Israel for their sins, I will destroy the altars of Bethel. The corners of every altar will be broken off and will fall to the ground. ¹⁵I will destroy winter houses and summer houses. The houses decorated with ivory will fall in ruins; every large house will be destroyed."

4 Listen to this, you women of Samaria, who grow fat like the well-fed cows of Bashan, who mistreat the weak, oppress the poor, and demand that your husbands keep you supplied with liquor! ²As the Sovereign LORD is holy, he has promised, "The days will come when they will drag you away with hooks; every one of you will be like a fish on a hook. ³You will be dragged to the nearest break in the wall and thrown out."ᵉ

Israel's Failure to Learn

⁴The Sovereign LORD says, "People of Israel, go to the holy place in Bethel and sin, if you must! Go to Gilgal and sin with all your might! Go ahead and bring animals to be sacrificed morning after morning, and bring your tithes every third day. ⁵Go on and offer your bread in thanksgiving to God, and brag about the extra offerings you bring! This is the kind of thing you love to do.

⁶"I was the one who brought famine to all your cities, yet you did not come back to me. ⁷I kept it from raining when your crops needed it most. I sent rain on one city, but not on another. Rain fell on one field, but another field dried up. ⁸Weak

---

ᶜ NAZIRITES: *Israelites who showed their devotion to God by taking vows not to drink wine or beer or cut their hair or touch corpses (see Nu 6.1-8).*   ᵈ *luxurious couches; Hebrew unclear.*
ᵉ *Hebrew has an additional word, the meaning of which is unclear.*

with thirst, the people of several cities went to a city where they hoped to find water, but there was not enough to drink. Still you did not come back to me.

9 "I sent a scorching wind to dry up your crops. The locusts ate up all your gardens and vineyards, your fig trees and olive trees. Still you did not come back to me.

10 "I sent a plague on you like the one I sent on Egypt. I killed your young men in battle and took your horses away. I filled your nostrils with the stink of dead bodies in your camps. Still you did not come back to me.

11 "I destroyed some of you as I destroyed Sodom and Gomorrah. Those of you who survived were like a burning stick saved from a fire. Still you did not come back to me," says the LORD. 12 "So then, people of Israel, I am going to punish you. And because I am going to do this, get ready to face my judgment!"

13 God is the one who made the
    mountains
  and created the winds.
He makes his thoughts known to
    people;
  he changes day into night.
He walks on the heights of the
    earth.
This is his name: the LORD God
    Almighty!

A Call to Repentance

5 Listen, people of Israel, to this funeral song which I sing over you:

2 Virgin Israel has fallen,
  Never to rise again!
She lies abandoned on the ground,
  And no one helps her up.

3 The Sovereign LORD says, "A city in Israel sends out a thousand soldiers, but only a hundred return; another city sends out a hundred, but only ten come back."

4 The LORD says to the people of Israel, "Come to me, and you will live. 5 Do not go to Beersheba to worship. Do not try to find me at Bethel — Bethel will come to nothing. Do not go to Gilgal — her people are doomed to exile."

6 Go to the LORD, and you will live. If you do not go, he will sweep down like fire on the people of Israel. The fire will burn up the people of Bethel, and no one will be able to put it out. 7 You are doomed, you that twist justice and cheat people out of their rights!

8 The LORD made the stars,
  the Pleiades and Orion.
He turns darkness into daylight
  and day into night.
He calls for the waters of the sea
  and pours them out on the earth.
His name is the LORD.
9 He brings destruction on the
  mighty and their strongholds.

10 You people hate anyone who challenges injustice and speaks the whole truth in court. 11 You have oppressed the poor and robbed them of their grain. And so you will not live in the fine stone houses you build or drink wine from the beautiful vineyards you plant. 12 I know how terrible your sins are and how many crimes you have committed. You persecute good people, take bribes, and prevent the poor from getting justice in the courts. 13 And so, keeping quiet in such evil times is the smart thing to do!

14 Make it your aim to do what is right, not what is evil, so that you may live. Then the LORD God Almighty really will be with you, as you claim he is. 15 Hate what is evil, love what is right, and see that justice prevails in the courts. Perhaps the LORD will be merciful to the people of this nation who are still left alive.

16 And so the Sovereign LORD Almighty says, "There will be wailing and cries of sorrow in the city streets. Even farmers will be called to mourn the dead along with those who are paid to mourn. 17 There will be wailing in all the vineyards. All this will take place because I am coming to punish you." The LORD has spoken.

18 How terrible it will be for you who long for the day of the LORD! What good will that day do you? For you it will be a day of darkness and not of light. 19 It will be like someone who runs from a lion and meets a bear! Or like someone who comes home and puts his hand on the wall — only to be bitten by a snake! 20 The day of the LORD will bring darkness and not light; it will be a day of gloom, without any brightness.

21 The LORD says, "I hate your religious festivals; I cannot stand them! 22 When

AHAB'S IVORY HOUSE AT SAMARIA

During Old Testament times, ivory was a rare and expensive item found only in the palaces of kings and the homes of the very wealthy. Ornate ivory carvings were inlaid in furniture and the wooden paneling used in elegant homes. A mark of the wealth of King Solomon was his royal throne made of ivory (2 Ch 9.17).

After Solomon's reign and the division of his kingdom into two separate nations, the upper classes of the northern kingdom continued the lavish display of their wealth by using ivory in their homes and palaces. The prophet Amos condemned these people for these excesses and for exploiting the poor, predicting that those who rested upon "luxurious couches" would be judged by God (Am 6.4).

King Ahab of Israel was an avid builder who loved to display his wealth with ornate buildings and elegant furnishings. He completed and adorned the capital city of Samaria, which his father Omri had begun several years before. Excavations of the royal palace in Samaria have yielded evidence of the extravagant practices Amos condemned. The outside of Ahab's house was faced with white stone, which gave it the appearance of ivory (1 K 22.39; Amos 3.15). It was also decorated throughout with numerous ivory carvings and inlaid ivory panels.

The two-story palace was constructed on a high hill, surrounded by numerous courtyards. One of these courtyards featured a large pool. Excavators believe this may have been the pool where the blood of Ahab was washed from his chariot after he was killed in battle (1 K 22.38). Discovered nearby was a large storeroom, which contained five hundred pieces of ivory, ready to be inlaid in walls and furniture throughout the royal palace.

you bring me burnt offerings and grain offerings, I will not accept them; I will not accept the animals you have fattened to bring me as offerings. 23 Stop your noisy songs; I do not want to listen to your harps. 24 Instead, let justice flow like a stream, and righteousness like a river that never goes dry.

25 "People of Israel, I did not demand sacrifices and offerings during those forty years that I led you through the desert. 26 But now, because you have worshiped images of Sakkuth, your king god, and of Kaiwan, your star god, you will have to carry those images 27 when I take you into exile in a land beyond Damascus," says the LORD, whose name is Almighty God.

The Destruction of Israel

6 How terrible it will be for you that have such an easy life in Zion and for you that feel safe in Samaria—you great leaders of this great nation Israel, you to whom the people go for help! 2 Go and look at the city of Calneh. Then go on to the great city of Hamath and on down to the Philistine city of Gath. Were they any better than the kingdoms of Judah and Israel? Was their territory larger than yours? 3 You refuse to admit that a day of disaster is coming, but what you do only brings that day closer. 4 How terrible it will be for you that stretch out on your luxurious couches, feasting on veal and lamb! 5 You like to compose songs, as David did, and play them on harps. 6 You drink wine by the bowlful and use the finest perfumes, but you do not mourn over the ruin of Israel. 7 So you will be the first to go into exile. Your feasts and banquets will come to an end.

8 The Sovereign LORD Almighty has given this solemn warning: "I hate the pride of the people of Israel; I despise their luxurious mansions. I will give their capital city and everything in it to the enemy."

9 If there are ten men left in a family, they will die. 10 The dead man's relative, the one in charge of the funeral, will take the body out of the house. The relative will call to whoever is still left in the house, "Is anyone else there with you?"

The person will answer, "No!"

Then the relative will say, "Be quiet! We must be careful not even to mention the LORD's name."ᶠ

11 When the LORD gives the command, houses large and small will be smashed to pieces. 12 Do horses gallop on rocks? Does anyone plow the sea with oxen? Yet you have turned justice into poison, and right into wrong.

13 You brag about capturing the town of Lodebar.ᵍ You boast, "We were strong enough to take Karnaim."ʰ

14 The LORD God Almighty himself says, "People of Israel, I am going to send a foreign army to occupy your country. It will oppress you from Hamath Pass in the north to the Brook of the Arabah in the south."

A Vision of Locusts

7 I had a vision from the Sovereign LORD. In it I saw him create a swarm of locusts just after the king's share of the hay had been cut and the grass was starting to grow again. 2 In my vision I saw the locusts eat up every green thing in the land, and then I said, "Sovereign LORD, forgive your people! How can they survive? They are so small and weak!"

3 The LORD changed his mind and said, "What you saw will not take place."

A Vision of Fire

4 I had another vision from the Sovereign LORD. In it I saw him preparing to punish his people with fire. The fire burned up the great ocean under the earth and started to burn up the land. 5 Then I said, "Stop, O Sovereign LORD! How can your people survive? They are so small and weak!"

6 The LORD changed his mind again and said, "This will not take place either."

A Vision of a Plumb Line

7 I had another vision from the LORD. In it I saw him standing beside a wall that had been built with the use of a plumb line, and there was a plumb line in his hand. 8 He asked me, "Amos, what do you see?"

"A plumb line," I answered.

Then he said, "I am using it to show that my people are like a wall that is out

---

ᶠ Verse 10 in Hebrew is unclear.   ᵍ LODEBAR: This name sounds like the Hebrew for "nothing."
ʰ KARNAIM: The name of this small town means "horns," a symbol of strength.

of line. I will not change my mind again about punishing them. 9 The places where Isaac's descendants worship will be destroyed. The holy places of Israel will be left in ruins. I will bring the dynasty of King Jeroboam to an end."

Amos and Amaziah

10 Amaziah, the priest of Bethel, then sent a report to King Jeroboam of Israel: "Amos is plotting against you among the people. His speeches will destroy the country. 11 This is what he says: 'Jeroboam will die in battle, and the people of Israel will be taken away from their land into exile.' "

12 Amaziah then said to Amos, "That's enough, prophet! Go on back to Judah and do your preaching there. Let *them* pay you for it. 13 Don't prophesy here at Bethel any more. This is the king's place of worship, the national temple."

14 Amos answered, "I am not the kind of prophet who prophesies for pay. I am a herdsman, and I take care of fig trees. 15 But the LORD took me from my work as a shepherd and ordered me to come and prophesy to his people Israel. 16 So now listen to what the LORD says. You tell me to stop prophesying, to stop raving against the people of Israel. 17 And so, Amaziah, the LORD says to you, 'Your wife will become a prostitute in the city, and your children will be killed in war. Your land will be divided up and given to others, and you yourself will die in a heathen country. And the people of Israel will certainly be taken away from their own land into exile.' "

A Vision of a Basket of Fruit

8 I had another vision from the Sovereign LORD. In it I saw a basket of fruit. 2 The LORD asked, "Amos, what do you see?"

"A basket of fruit," I answered.

The LORD said to me, "The end*i* has come for my people Israel. I will not change my mind again about punishing them. 3 On that day the songs in the palace will become cries of mourning. There will be dead bodies everywhere. They will be cast out in silence."*j*

Israel's Doom

4 Listen to this, you that trample on the needy and try to destroy the poor of the country. 5 You say to yourselves, "We can hardly wait for the holy days to be over so that we can sell our grain. When will the Sabbath end, so that we can start selling again? Then we can overcharge, use false measures, and fix the scales to cheat our customers. 6 We can sell worthless wheat at a high price. We'll find someone poor who can't pay his debts, not even the price of a pair of sandals, and we'll buy him as a slave."

7 The LORD, the God of Israel, has sworn, "I will never forget their evil deeds. 8 And so the earth will quake, and everyone in the land will be in distress. The whole country will be shaken; it will rise and fall like the Nile River. 9 The time is coming when I will make the sun go down at noon and the earth grow dark in daytime. I, the Sovereign LORD, have spoken. 10 I will turn your festivals into funerals and change your glad songs into cries of grief. I will make you shave your heads and wear sackcloth, and you will be like parents mourning for their only child. That day will be bitter to the end.

11 "The time is coming when I will send famine on the land. People will be hungry, but not for bread; they will be thirsty, but not for water. They will hunger and thirst for a message from the LORD. I, the Sovereign LORD, have spoken. 12 People will wander from the Dead Sea to the Mediterranean and then on around from the north to the east. They will look everywhere for a message from the LORD, but they will not find it. 13 On that day even healthy young men and women will collapse from thirst. 14 Those who swear by the idols of Samaria, who say, 'By the god of Dan' or 'By the god of Beersheba' — those people will fall and not rise again."

The LORD's Judgments

9 I saw the Lord standing by the altar. He gave the command: "Strike the tops of the Temple columns so hard that the foundation will shake. Break them off and let them fall on the heads of the people. I will kill the rest of the people in war. No one will get away; not one

i END: *The Hebrew words for "end" and "fruit" sound alike.*   *j* out in silence; *or* out. Silence!

will escape. ²Even if they dig their way down to the world of the dead, I will catch them. Even if they climb up to heaven, I will bring them down. ³If they hide on the top of Mount Carmel, I will search for them and catch them. If they hide from me at the bottom of the sea, I will command the sea monster[k] to bite them. ⁴If they are taken away into captivity by their enemies, I will order them to be put to death. I am determined to destroy them, not to help them."

⁵The Sovereign Lord Almighty
    touches the earth,
      and it quakes;
      all who live there mourn.
The whole world rises and falls
    like the Nile River.
⁶The Lord builds his home in the
    heavens,
      and over the earth he puts the
      dome of the sky.
He calls for the waters of the sea
    and pours them out on the earth.
His name is the Lord!

⁷The Lord says, "People of Israel, I think as much of the people of Ethiopia[l] as I do of you. I brought the Philistines from Crete and the Syrians from Kir, just as I brought you from Egypt. ⁸I, the Sovereign Lord, am watching this sinful kingdom of Israel, and I will destroy it from the face of the earth. But I will not destroy all the descendants of Jacob.

⁹"I will give the command and shake the people of Israel like grain in a sieve. I will shake them among the nations to remove all who are worthless. ¹⁰The sinners among my people will be killed in war—all those who say, 'God will not let any harm come near us.'"

The Future Restoration of Israel

¹¹The Lord says, "A day is coming when I will restore the kingdom of David, which is like a house fallen into ruins. I will repair its walls and restore it. I will rebuild it and make it as it was long ago. ¹²And so the people of Israel will conquer what is left of the land of Edom and all the nations that were once mine," says the Lord, who will cause this to happen.

¹³"The days are coming," says the
    Lord,
    "when grain will grow faster
      than it can be harvested,
    and grapes will grow faster than
      the wine can be made.
The mountains will drip with
    sweet wine,
    and the hills will flow with it.
¹⁴I will bring my people back to
    their land.
They will rebuild their ruined
    cities and live there;
they will plant vineyards and
    drink the wine;
they will plant gardens and eat
    what they grow.
¹⁵I will plant my people on the land
    I gave them,
    and they will not be pulled up
    again."
The Lord your God has spoken.

AMOS

[k] SEA MONSTER: *It was believed that the sea was inhabited by a great monster. This creature, like all others, was regarded as under God's control.* [l] Hebrew Cush: *Cush is the ancient name of the extensive territory south of the First Cataract of the Nile River. This region was called Ethiopia in Graeco-Roman times, and included within its borders most of modern Sudan and some of present-day Ethiopia (Abyssinia).*

The Book of
OBADIAH

Introduction

This short book comes from some undetermined time after the fall of Jerusalem in 586 B.C., when Edom, Judah's age-old enemy to the southeast, not only rejoiced over the fall of Jerusalem but took advantage of Judah's plight to loot the city and help the invader. Obadiah prophesied that Edom would be punished and defeated, along with other nations that were the enemies of Israel.

Outline of Contents

---

¹This is the prophecy of Obadiah — what the Sovereign Lord said about the nation of Edom.

The Lord Will Punish Edom

The Lord has sent his messenger
　　to the nations,
　　and we have heard his message:
　　"Get ready! Let us go to war
　　　　against Edom!"
²The Lord says to Edom,
　　"I will make you weak;
　　everyone will despise you.
³Your pride has deceived you.
　　Your capital is a fortress of solid
　　　　rock;
　　your home is high in the
　　　　mountains,
　　and so you say to yourself,
　　'Who can ever pull me down?'
⁴Even though you make your home
　　as high as an eagle's nest,
　　so that it seems to be among the
　　　　stars,
　　yet I will pull you down.

⁵"When thieves come at night,
　　they take only what they want.
　　When people gather grapes,
　　they always leave a few.
　　But your enemies have wiped you
　　　　out completely.
⁶Descendants of Esau, your
　　　　treasures have been looted.
⁷Your allies have deceived you;
　　they have driven you from your
　　　　country.

People who were at peace with
　　you have now conquered you.
　　Those friends who ate with you
　　　　have laid a trap for you;
　　they say of you, 'Where is all
　　　　that cleverness he had?'

⁸"On the day I punish Edom,
　　I will destroy their clever men
　　and wipe out all their wisdom.
⁹The fighting men of Teman will be
　　　　terrified,
　　and every soldier in Edom will
　　　　be killed.

Reasons for Edom's Punishment

¹⁰"Because you robbed and killed
　　your relatives,ᵃ the descendants
　　　　of Jacob,
　　you will be destroyed and
　　　　dishonored forever.
¹¹You stood aside on that day
　　when enemies broke down their
　　　　gates.
　　You were as bad as those
　　　　strangers
　　who carried off Jerusalem's
　　　　wealth
　　and divided it among
　　　　themselves.
¹²You should not have gloated
　　over the misfortune of your
　　　　relatives in Judah.
　　You should not have been glad
　　　　on the day of their ruin.
　　You should not have laughed at
　　　　them
　　in their distress.

ᵃ YOUR RELATIVES: The Israelites were descended from Jacob, who was the brother of Esau, the ancestor of the Edomites.

¹³You should not have entered the
city of my people
to gloat over their suffering
and to seize their riches
on the day of their disaster.
¹⁴You should not have stood at the
crossroads
to catch those trying to escape.
You should not have handed them
over to the enemy
on the day of their distress.

God Will Judge the Nations

¹⁵"The day is near when I, the LORD,
will judge all nations.
Edom, what you have done
will be done to you.
You will get back what you have
given.
¹⁶My people have drunk a bitter cup
of punishment
on my sacred hill.^b
But all the surrounding nations
will drink
a still more bitter cup of
punishment;
they will drink it all and vanish
away.

The Victory of Israel

¹⁷"But on Mount Zion some will
escape,
and it will be a sacred place.
The people of Jacob will possess

^b SACRED HILL: *Mount Zion (see Zion in Word List).*

the land that is theirs by right.
¹⁸The people of Jacob and of Joseph
will be like fire;
they will destroy the people of
Esau
as fire burns stubble.
No descendant of Esau will
survive.
I, the LORD, have spoken.

¹⁹"People from southern Judah will
occupy Edom;
those from the western foothills
will capture Philistia.
Israelites will possess the territory
of Ephraim and Samaria;
the people of Benjamin will take
Gilead.
²⁰The army of exiles from northern
Israel
will return and conquer
Phoenicia as far north as
Zarephath.
The exiles from Jerusalem who
are in Sardis
will capture the towns of
southern Judah.
²¹The victorious men
of Jerusalem
will attack Edom and rule
over it.
And the LORD himself will be
king."

The Book of
JONAH

Introduction

The Book of Jonah *is unlike other prophetic books of the Bible in that it is a narrative, describing the adventures of a prophet who tried to disobey God's command. God told him to go to Nineveh, the capital of the great empire of Assyria, Israel's deadly enemy. But Jonah did not want to go there with God's message, because he was convinced that God would not carry out his threat to destroy the city. After a series of dramatic events, he reluctantly obeyed, and finally sulked when his message of doom did not come true.*

The book portrays God's absolute sovereignty over his creation. But above all it portrays God as a God of love and mercy, who would rather forgive and save even the enemies of his people, than punish and destroy them.

Outline of Contents

Jonah Disobeys the LORD

One day the LORD spoke to Jonah son of Amittai. ² He said, "Go to Nineveh, that great city, and speak out against it; I am aware of how wicked its people are." ³ Jonah, however, set out in the opposite direction in order to get away from the LORD. He went to Joppa, where he found a ship about to go to Spain. He paid his fare and went aboard with the crew to sail to Spain, where he would be away from the LORD.

⁴ But the LORD sent a strong wind on the sea, and the storm was so violent that the ship was in danger of breaking up. ⁵ The sailors were terrified and cried out for help, each one to his own god. Then, in order to lessen the danger,ᵃ they threw the cargoᵇ overboard. Meanwhile, Jonah had gone below and was lying in the ship's hold, sound asleep.

⁶ The captain found him there and said to him, "What are you doing asleep? Get up and pray to your god for help. Maybe he will feel sorry for us and spare our lives."

⁷ The sailors said to each other, "Let's draw lots and find out who is to blame for getting us into this danger." They did so, and Jonah's name was drawn. ⁸ So they said to him, "Now, then, tell us! Who is to blame for this? What are you doing here? What country do you come from? What is your nationality?"

⁹ "I am a Hebrew," Jonah answered. "I worship the LORD, the God of heaven, who made land and sea." ¹⁰ Jonah went on to tell them that he was running away from the LORD.

The sailors were terrified, and said to him, "That was an awful thing to do!"ᶜ ¹¹ The storm was getting worse all the time, so the sailors asked him, "What should we do to you to stop the storm?"

¹² Jonah answered, "Throw me into the sea, and it will calm down. I know it is my fault that you are caught in this violent storm."

¹³ Instead, the sailors tried to get the ship to shore, rowing with all their might. But the storm was becoming worse and worse, and they got nowhere. ¹⁴ So they cried out to the LORD, "O LORD, we pray, don't punish us with death for taking this man's life! You, O LORD, are responsible for all this; it is your doing." ¹⁵ Then they picked Jonah up and threw him into the sea, and it calmed down at once. ¹⁶ This made the sailors so afraid of the LORD that they offered a sacrifice and promised to serve him.

¹⁷ At the LORD's command a large fish swallowed Jonah, and he was inside the fish for three days and three nights.

Jonah's Prayer

From deep inside the fish Jonah prayed to the LORD his God:

² "In my distress, O LORD, I called
    to you,
  and you answered me.
From deep in the world of the
    dead
  I cried for help, and you
    heard me.
³ You threw me down into the
    depths,
  to the very bottom of the sea,
  where the waters were all
    around me,
  and all your mighty waves rolled
    over me.
⁴ I thought I had been banished
    from your presence
  and would never see your holy
    Temple again.
⁵ The water came over me and
    choked me;
  the sea covered me completely,
  and seaweed wrapped around
    my head.
⁶ I went down to the very roots of
    the mountains,

ᵃ lessen the danger; *or* lighten the ship. ᵇ cargo; *or* equipment. ᶜ and said . . . to do!; *or* and asked him, "Why did you have to run away like that?"

THE CITY OF NINEVEH

Founded by Nimrod, great-grandson of Noah (Gn 10.6–12), Nineveh was for many years the capital city of the mighty Assyrian Empire.

At the height of its prosperity, Nineveh was a "great city" (Jon 1.2; 3.2) with a population of 120,000 (Jon 4.11). It would have taken a traveler three days to go around greater Nineveh, with its numerous outlying suburbs, and a day's journey to reach the center of the city (Jon 3.4).

The most famous biblical personality connected with ancient Nineveh was the prophet Jonah. Assyrian kings were cruel and ruthless. This pagan nation had invaded and pillaged the homeland of the Israelites on numerous occasions when Jonah visited Nineveh. The prophet wanted the city destroyed—not saved—because of its wickedness. But the people repented and were spared by a compassionate God (Jon 3.10). God's love for a pagan people was deeper than his messenger could understand or accept.

Nineveh was eventually destroyed about 150 years after Jonah's visit. It fell after a long siege by an alliance of Medes, Babylonians, and Scythians. The attackers entered the city through walls made weak by a flooding of the Khosr and Tigris rivers. The sun-dried bricks of its buildings were also dissolved. This was a remarkable fulfillment of the prophecy of Nahum: "The gates of the river burst open; the palace is filled with terror" (Nh 2.6).

Significant archaeological discoveries at Nineveh include the temples of Nabu and Ishtar, Assyrian gods, and the palaces of three Assyrian kings—Ashurbanipal, Ashurnasirpal, and Sennacherib. One of the most important discoveries was the royal library of Ashurbanipal, which contained over sixteen thousand cuneiform tablets. These include Mesopotamian stories of creation and the flood, as well as many other religious and historical texts.

Nineveh was one of the oldest cities of the ancient Near East. Excavations down to the virgin soil indicate the site was first occupied about 4500 B.C.

into the land whose gates lock
shut forever.*d*
But you, O L<small>ORD</small> my God,
brought me back from the
depths alive.
7 When I felt my life slipping away,
then, O L<small>ORD</small>, I prayed to you,
and in your holy Temple you
heard me.
8 Those who worship worthless
idols
have abandoned their loyalty
to you.
9 But I will sing praises to you;
I will offer you a sacrifice
and do what I have promised.
Salvation comes from the L<small>ORD</small>!"
10 Then the L<small>ORD</small> ordered the fish to
spit Jonah up on the beach, and it did.

Jonah Obeys the L<small>ORD</small>

3 Once again the L<small>ORD</small> spoke to Jonah. 2 He said, "Go to Nineveh, that
great city, and proclaim to the people the
message I have given you." 3 So Jonah
obeyed the L<small>ORD</small> and went to Nineveh, a
city so large that it took three days to
walk through it. 4 Jonah started through
the city, and after walking a whole day,
he proclaimed, "In forty days Nineveh
will be destroyed!"

5 The people of Nineveh believed
God's message. So they decided that
everyone should fast, and all the people,
from the greatest to the least, put on
sackcloth to show that they had
repented.

6 When the king of Nineveh heard
about it, he got up from his throne, took
off his robe, put on sackcloth, and sat
down in ashes. 7 He sent out a proclamation to the people of Nineveh: "This is an
order from the king and his officials: No
one is to eat anything; all persons, cattle,
and sheep are forbidden to eat or drink.
8 All persons and animals must wear
sackcloth. Everyone must pray earnestly to God and must give up their
wicked behavior and their evil actions.
9 Perhaps God will change his mind; per-

haps he will stop being angry, and we
will not die!"

10 God saw what they did; he saw that
they had given up their wicked behavior. So he changed his mind and did not
punish them as he had said he would.

Jonah's Anger and God's Mercy

4 Jonah was very unhappy about this
and became angry. 2 So he prayed,
"L<small>ORD</small>, didn't I say before I left home that
this is just what you would do? That's
why I did my best to run away to Spain!
I knew that you are a loving and merciful God, always patient, always kind,
and always ready to change your mind
and not punish. 3 Now then, L<small>ORD</small>, let me
die. I am better off dead than alive."

4 The L<small>ORD</small> answered, "What right do
you have to be angry?"

5 Jonah went out east of the city and
sat down. He made a shelter for himself
and sat in its shade, waiting to see what
would happen to Nineveh. 6 Then the
L<small>ORD</small> God made a plant grow up over Jonah to give him some shade, so that he
would be more comfortable. Jonah was
extremely pleased with the plant. 7 But at
dawn the next day, at God's command, a
worm attacked the plant, and it died.
8 After the sun had risen, God sent a hot
east wind, and Jonah was about to faint
from the heat of the sun beating down
on his head. So he wished he were
dead.*e* "I am better off dead than alive,"
he said.

9 But God said to him, "What right do
you have to be angry about the plant?"

Jonah replied, "I have every right to be
angry—angry enough to die!"

10 The L<small>ORD</small> said to him, "This plant
grew up in one night and disappeared
the next; you didn't do anything for it
and you didn't make it grow—yet you
feel sorry for it! 11 How much more, then,
should I have pity on Nineveh, that great
city. After all, it has more than 120,000
innocent children in it, as well as many
animals!"

---

d THE LAND WHOSE GATES LOCK SHUT FOREVER: *A reference to the world of the dead (see 2.2).*
e wished he were dead; *or* prayed that he would die.

The Book of

MICAH

M
I
C
A
H

Introduction

The prophet Micah, a contemporary of Isaiah, was from a country town in Judah, the southern kingdom. He was convinced that Judah was about to face the same kind of national catastrophe that Amos had predicted for the northern kingdom, and for the same reason God would punish the hateful injustice of the people. Micah's message, however, contains more clear and notable signs of hope for the future.

Passages especially worth noting are the picture of universal peace under God (4.1-4); the prediction of a great king who would come from the family line of David and bring peace to the nation (5.2-5a); and, in a single verse (6.8), the summary of much that the prophets of Israel had to say: "What he requires of us is this: to do what is just, to show constant love, and to live in humble fellowship with our God."

Outline of Contents

1 During the time that Jotham, Ahaz, and Hezekiah were kings of Judah, the LORD gave this message to Micah, who was from the town of Moresheth. The LORD revealed to Micah all these things about Samaria and Jerusalem.

A Lament for Samaria and Jerusalem

2 Hear this, all you nations;
   listen to this, all who live on
      earth!
   The Sovereign LORD will testify
      against you.
   Listen! He speaks from his
      heavenly temple.
3 The LORD is coming from his holy
      place;
   he will come down and walk on
      the tops of the mountains.
4 Then the mountains will melt
      under him
   like wax in a fire;
   they will pour down into the
      valleys
   like water pouring down a hill.

5 All this will happen because the people of Israel have sinned and rebelled against God. Who is to blame for Israel's rebellion? Samaria, the capital city itself! Who is guilty of idolatry in Judah?

Jerusalem itself! 6 So the LORD says, "I will make Samaria a pile of ruins in the open country, a place for planting grapevines. I will pour the rubble of the city down into the valley, and will lay bare the city's foundations. 7 All its precious idols will be smashed to pieces, everything given to its temple prostitutes will be destroyed by fire, and all its images will become a desolate heap. Samaria acquired these things for its fertility rites, and now her enemies will carry them off for temple prostitutes elsewhere."

8 Then Micah said, "Because of this I will mourn and lament. To show my sorrow, I will walk around barefoot and naked. I will howl like a jackal and wail like an ostrich. 9 Samaria's wounds cannot be healed, and Judah is about to suffer in the same way; destruction has reached the gates of Jerusalem itself, where my people live."

The Enemy Approaches Jerusalem

10 Don't tell our enemies in Gath about our defeat; don't let them see you weeping. People of Beth Leaphrah,ᵃ show your despair by rolling in the dust! 11 You people of Shaphir, go into exile, naked and ashamed. Those who live in Zaanan do not dare to come out of their

ᵃ BETH LEAPHRAH: *The prophet speaks of outlying towns (verses 10-14) which an enemy army approaching Jerusalem would attack.*

city. When you hear the people of Bethezel mourn, you will know that there is no refuge there. 12 The people of Maroth anxiously wait for relief, because the Lord has brought disaster close to Jerusalem. 13 You that live in Lachish, hitch the horses to the chariots. You imitated the sins of Israel and so caused Jerusalem to sin. 14 And now, people of Judah, say good-bye to the town of Moresheth Gath. The kings of Israel will get no help from the town of Achzib.

15 People of Mareshah, the Lord will hand you over to an enemy, who is going to capture your town. The leaders of Israel will go and hide in the cave at Adullam. 16 People of Judah, cut off your hair in mourning for the children you love. Make yourselves as bald as vultures, because your children will be taken away from you into exile.

The Fate of Those Who Oppress the Poor

2 How terrible it will be for those who lie awake and plan evil! When morning comes, as soon as they have the chance, they do the evil they planned. 2 When they want fields, they seize them; when they want houses, they take them. No one's family or property is safe.

3 And so the Lord says, "I am planning to bring disaster on you, and you are going not be able to escape it. You are going to find yourselves in trouble, and then you will not walk so proudly any more. 4 When that time comes, people will use the story about you as an example of disaster, and they will sing this song of despair about your experience:

We are completely ruined!
The Lord has taken our land away
And given it to those who took us captive."b

5 So then, when the time comes for the land to be given back to the Lord's people, there will be no share for any of you.

6 The people preach at me and say, "Don't preach at us. Don't preach about all that. God is not going to disgrace us.

7 Do you think the people of Israel are under a curse?c Has the Lord lost his patience? Would he really do such things? Doesn't hed speak kindly to those who do right?"

8 The Lord replies, "You attack my peoplee like enemies. Men return from battle, thinking they are safe at home, but there you are, waiting to steal the coats off their backs. 9 You drive the women of my people out of the homes they love, and you have robbed their children of my blessings forever. 10 Get up and go; there is no safety here any more. Your sins have doomed this place to destruction.

11 "These people want the kind of prophet who goes around full of lies and deceit and says, 'I prophesy that wine and liquor will flow for you.'

12 "But I will gather you together, all you people of Israel that are left. I will bring you together like sheep returning to the fold. Like a pasture full of sheep, your land will once again be filled with many people."

13 God will open the way for them and lead them out of exile. They will break out of the city gates and go free. Their king, the Lord himself, will lead them out.

Micah Denounces Israel's Leaders

3 Listen, you rulers of Israel! You are supposed to be concerned about justice, 2 yet you hate what is good and you love what is evil. You skin my people alive and tear the flesh off their bones. 3 You eat my people up. You strip off their skin, break their bones, and chop them up like meat for the pot. 4 The time is coming when you will cry out to the Lord, but he will not answer you. He will not listen to your prayers, for you have done evil.

5 My people are deceived by prophets who promise peace to those who pay them, but threaten war for those who don't. To these prophets the Lord says, 6 "Prophets, your day is almost over; the sun is going down on you. Because you mislead my people, you will have no more prophetic visions, and you will not be able to predict anything." 7 Those who

b Probable text those who took us captive; Hebrew rebels.   c Probable text under a curse; Hebrew unclear.   d One ancient translation Doesn't he; Hebrew Don't I.   e Probable text You attack my people; Hebrew Recently my people have attacked.

predict the future will be disgraced by their failure. They will all be humiliated because God does not answer them.

⁸But as for me, the LORD fills me with his spirit and power, and gives me a sense of justice and the courage to tell the people of Israel what their sins are. ⁹Listen to me, you rulers of Israel, you that hate justice and turn right into wrong. ¹⁰You are building God's city, Jerusalem, on a foundation of murder and injustice. ¹¹The city's rulers govern for bribes, the priests interpret the Law for pay, the prophets give their revelations for money — and they all claim that the LORD is with them. "No harm will come to us," they say. "The LORD is with us."

¹²And so, because of you, Zion will be plowed like a field, Jerusalem will become a pile of ruins, and the Temple hill will become a forest.

The LORD's Universal Reign of Peace
(Isaiah 2.2-4)

4 In days to come
　　the mountain where the
　　　　Temple stands
　　will be the highest one of all,
　　　　towering above all the
　　　　　　hills.
　Many nations will come streaming
　　　　to it,
　² 　and their people will say,
　　"Let us go up the hill of the
　　　　LORD,ᶠ
　　to the Temple of Israel's
　　　　God.
　He will teach us what he wants us
　　　　to do;
　　we will walk in the paths he has
　　　　chosen.
　For the LORD's teaching comes
　　　　from Jerusalem;
　　from Zion he speaks to his
　　　　people."

³He will settle disputes among the
　　　　nations,
　　among the great powers near
　　　　and far.
　They will hammer their swords
　　　　into plows
　　and their spears into pruning
　　　　knives.

Nations will never again go
　　　　to war,
　　never prepare for battle
　　　　again.
⁴Everyone will live in peace
　　among their own vineyards and
　　　　fig trees,
　　and no one will make them
　　　　afraid.
　The LORD Almighty has promised
　　　　this.

⁵Each nation worships and obeys its own god, but we will worship and obey the LORD our God forever and ever.

Israel Will Return from Exile

⁶"The time is coming," says the LORD, "when I will gather together the people I punished, those who have suffered in exile. ⁷They are crippled and far from home, but I will make a new beginning with those who are left, and they will become a great nation. I will rule over them on Mount Zion from that time on and forever."

⁸And you, Jerusalem, where God, like a shepherd from his lookout tower, watches over his people, will once again be the capital of the kingdom that was yours. ⁹Why do you cry out so loudly? Why are you suffering like a woman in labor? Is it because you have no king, and your counselors are dead? ¹⁰Twist and groan,ᵍ people of Jerusalem, like a woman giving birth, for now you will have to leave the city and live in the open country. You will have to go to Babylon, but there the LORD will save you from your enemies. ¹¹Many nations have gathered to attack you. They say, "Jerusalem must be destroyed! We will see this city in ruins!" ¹²But these nations do not know what is in the LORD's mind. They do not realize that they have been gathered together to be punished in the same way that grain is brought in to be threshed.

¹³The LORD says, "People of Jerusalem, go and punish your enemies! I will make you as strong as a bull with iron horns and bronze hoofs. You will crush many nations, and the wealth they got by violence you will present to me, the Lord of the whole world."

ᶠ HILL OF THE LORD: *Mount Zion (see Zion in Word List).* 　 ᵍ *Probable text groan; Hebrew bring forth.*

THE CITY OF BETHLEHEM

Located in the hill country of Judah in southern Palestine, the humble village of Bethlehem is famous as the home of David and the birthplace of Jesus Christ. Bethlehem is situated five miles south of Jerusalem.

The region around Bethlehem today is known for its fertile hills and valleys. Its busy marketplaces and religious shrines continue to attract tourists. Bethlehem's main attraction is the Church of Nativity, which is supposedly built over the birthplace of Jesus. Most scholars agree this is one of the best authenticated sites in the Holy Land. The present building, erected over the cave area, which served as a stable for the crowded inn, was built by the Roman emperor Justinian I in the sixth century A.D. The city and the church are especially popular as destinations for pilgrims during Christmas celebrations.

Bethlehem is also closely associated with King David, Israel's favorite king. Known as the city of David, Bethlehem is his ancestral home and the site where Samuel anointed David as Saul's successor. The prophet Micah foresaw the coming of a Ruler in the line of David who would be born in Bethlehem (Mic 5.2). The city was the original home of Naomi, and it served as the setting for much of the Book of Ruth.

Other popular attractions at Bethlehem for Holy Land tourists are the fields of Boaz, where Ruth gleaned grain after the fields had been harvested, and Shepherds' Field, where the angel of the Lord announced the birth of Jesus to the shepherds (Lk 2.8–18).

The name *Bethlehem* means house of bread, probably commemorating the reputation of the entire region as a grain-producing center in Old Testament times. How appropriate that Jesus Christ, who is the bread of life, was born in a town with such a name.

5 People of Jerusalem, gather your forces![h] We are besieged! They are attacking the leader of Israel!

God Promises a Ruler from Bethlehem

2 The LORD says, "Bethlehem Ephrathah, you are one of the smallest towns in Judah, but out of you I will bring a ruler for Israel, whose family line goes back to ancient times."

3 So the LORD will abandon his people to their enemies until the woman who is to give birth has her son. Then those Israelites who are in exile will be reunited with their own people. 4 When he comes, he will rule his people with the strength that comes from the LORD and with the majesty of the LORD God himself. His people will live in safety because people all over the earth will acknowledge his greatness, 5 and he will bring peace.

Deliverance and Punishment

When the Assyrians invade our country and break through our defenses, we will send our strongest leaders to fight them. 6 By force of arms they will conquer Assyria, the land of Nimrod, and they[i] will save us from the Assyrians when they invade our territory.

7 The people of Israel who survive will be like refreshing dew sent by the LORD for many nations, like showers on growing plants. They will depend on God, not people. 8 Those who are left among the nations will be like a lion hunting for food in a forest or a pasture: it gets in among the sheep, pounces on them, and tears them to pieces—and there is no hope of rescue. 9 Israel will conquer her enemies and destroy them all.

10 The LORD says, "At that time I will take away your horses and destroy your chariots. 11 I will destroy the cities in your land and tear down all your defenses. 12 I will destroy the magic charms you use and leave you without any fortunetellers. 13 I will destroy your idols and sacred stone pillars; no longer will you worship the things that you yourselves have made. 14 I will pull down the images of the goddess Asherah in your land and destroy your cities. 15 And in my great anger I will take revenge on all nations that have not obeyed me."

The LORD's Case against Israel

6 Listen to the LORD's case against Israel.

Arise, O LORD, and present your case; let the mountains and the hills hear what you say. 2 You mountains, you everlasting foundations of the earth, listen to the LORD's case! The LORD has a case against his people. He is going to bring an accusation against Israel.

3 The LORD says, "My people, what have I done to you? How have I been a burden to you? Answer me. 4 I brought you out of Egypt; I rescued you from slavery; I sent Moses, Aaron, and Miriam to lead you. 5 My people, remember what King Balak of Moab planned to do to you and how Balaam son of Beor answered him. Remember the things that happened on the way from the camp at Acacia to Gilgal. Remember these things and you will realize what I did in order to save you."

What the LORD Requires

6 What shall I bring to the LORD, the God of heaven, when I come to worship him? Shall I bring the best calves to burn as offerings to him? 7 Will the LORD be pleased if I bring him thousands of sheep or endless streams of olive oil? Shall I offer him my first-born child to pay for my sins? 8 No, the LORD has told us what is good. What he requires of us is this: to do what is just, to show constant love, and to live in humble fellowship with our God.

9 It is wise to fear the LORD. He calls to the city, "Listen, you people who assemble in the city![j] 10 In the houses of evil people are treasures which they got dishonestly. They use false measures, a thing that I hate.[k] 11 How can I forgive those who use false scales and weights? 12 Your rich people exploit the poor, and all of you are liars. 13 So I have already begun[l] your ruin and destruction because of your sins. 14 You will eat, but not be satisfied—in fact you will still be hungry. You will carry things off, but you will not be able to save them;

---

[h] Probable text People . . . forces!; Hebrew unclear.   [i] Probable text they; Hebrew he.
[j] Probable text who assemble in the city; Hebrew and who appointed it. Yet.   [k] Verse 10 in Hebrew is unclear.   [l] Some ancient translations begun; Hebrew made sick.

anything you do save I will destroy in war. [15] You will sow grain, but not harvest the crop. You will press oil from olives, but never get to use it. You will make wine, but never drink it. [16] This will happen because you have followed the evil practices of King Omri and of his son, King Ahab. You have continued their policies, and so I will bring you to ruin, and everyone will despise you. People[m] everywhere will treat you with contempt."[n]

Israel's Moral Corruption

7 It's hopeless! I am like a hungry person who finds no fruit left on the trees and no grapes on the vines. All the grapes and all the tasty figs have been picked. [2] There is not an honest person left in the land, no one loyal to God. Everyone is waiting for a chance to commit murder. Everyone hunts down their own people. [3] They are all experts at doing evil. Officials and judges ask for bribes. The influential people tell them what they want, and so they scheme together.[o] [4] Even the best and most honest of them are as worthless as weeds.

The day has come when God will punish the people, as he warned them through their watchmen, the prophets. Now they are in confusion. [5] Don't believe your neighbor or trust your friend. Be careful what you say even to your husband or wife. [6] In these times sons treat their fathers like fools, daughters oppose their mothers, and young women quarrel with their mothers-in-law; your enemies are the members of your own family.

[7] But I will watch for the LORD; I will wait confidently for God, who will save me. My God will hear me.

The LORD Brings Salvation

[8] Our enemies have no reason to gloat over us. We have fallen, but we will rise again. We are in darkness now, but the LORD will give us light. [9] We have sinned against the LORD, so now we must endure his anger for a while. But in the end

he will defend us and right the wrongs that have been done to us. He will bring us out to the light; we will live to see him save us. [10] Then our enemies will see this and be disgraced — the same enemies who taunted us by asking, "Where is the LORD your God?" We will see them defeated, trampled[p] down like mud in the streets.

[11] People of Jerusalem, the time to rebuild the city walls is coming. At that time your territory will be enlarged. [12] Your people will return to you from everywhere — from Assyria in the east, from Egypt in the south, from the region of the Euphrates River, from distant seas and far-off mountains. [13] But the earth will become a desert because of the wickedness of those who live on it.

The LORD's Compassion on Israel

[14] Be a shepherd to your people, LORD, the people you have chosen. Although they live apart in the wilderness, there is fertile land around them. Let them go and feed in the rich pastures of Bashan and Gilead, as they did long ago.

[15] Work miracles for us,[q] LORD, as you did in the days when you brought us out of Egypt. [16] The nations will see this and be frustrated in spite of all their strength. In dismay they will close their mouths and cover their ears. [17] They will crawl in the dust like snakes; they will come from their fortresses, trembling and afraid. They will turn in fear to the LORD our God.

[18] There is no other god like you, O LORD; you forgive the sins of your people who have survived. You do not stay angry forever, but you take pleasure in showing us your constant love. [19] You will be merciful to us once again. You will trample our sins underfoot and send them to the bottom of the sea! [20] You will show your faithfulness and constant love to your people, the descendants of Abraham and of Jacob, as you promised our ancestors long ago.

---

[m] One ancient translation People; Hebrew My people.   [n] People . . . contempt; or As my people you will everywhere be treated with contempt.   [o] and so they scheme together; Hebrew unclear.   [p] We will see . . . trampled; or We will gloat over them as they lie trampled. [q] Probable text Work miracles for us; Hebrew I will work miracles for him.

The Book of
NAHUM

Introduction

The Book of Nahum *is a poem celebrating the fall of Nineveh, the capital city of Israel's ancient and oppressive enemy, the Assyrians. The fall of Nineveh, near the end of the seventh century B.C., is seen as the judgment of God upon a cruel and arrogant nation.*

Outline of Contents

1 This is a message about Nineveh, the account of a vision seen by Nahum, who was from Elkosh.

The LORD's Anger against Nineveh

2 The LORD God tolerates no rivals;
he punishes those who
oppose him.
In his anger he pays them back.
3 The LORD does not easily become
angry,
but he is powerful
and never lets the guilty go
unpunished.

Where the LORD walks, storms
arise;
the clouds are the dust raised
by his feet!
4 He commands the sea, and it
dries up!
He makes the rivers go dry.
The fields of Bashan wither,
Mount Carmel turns brown,
and the flowers of Lebanon fade.
5 Mountains quake in the presence
of the LORD;
hills melt before him.
The earth shakes when the LORD
appears;
the world and all its people
tremble.
6 When he is angry, who can
survive?
Who can survive his terrible
fury?
He pours out his flaming anger;
rocks crumble to dust
before him.

7 The LORD is good;
he protects his people in times
of trouble;
he takes care of those who turn
to him.
8 Like a great rushing flood he
completely destroys his
enemies;*a*
he sends to their death those
who oppose him.
9 What are you plotting against the
LORD?
He will destroy you.
No one opposes him more than
once.
10 Like tangled thorns and dry straw
you drunkards will be
burned up!

11 From you, Nineveh, there came someone full of wicked schemes, who plotted against the LORD. 12 This is what the LORD says to his people Israel: "Even though the Assyrians are strong and numerous, they will be destroyed and disappear. My people, I made you suffer, but I will not do it again. 13 I will now end Assyria's power over you and break the chains that bind you."

14 This is what the LORD has decreed about the Assyrians: "They will have no descendants to carry on their name. I will destroy the idols that are in the temples of their gods. I am preparing a grave for the Assyrians — they don't deserve to live!"

15 Look, a messenger is coming over the mountains with good news! He is on his way to announce the victory! People

---

a Some ancient translations his enemies; *Hebrew* its place.

of Judah, celebrate your festivals and give God what you solemnly promised him. The wicked will never invade your land again. They have been totally destroyed!

The Fall of Nineveh

2 Nineveh, you are under attack!
The power that will shatter
  you has come.
Prepare the defenses!
Guard the road!
Prepare for battle!
(2 The LORD is about to restore the glory of Israel, as it was before her enemies plundered her.)
3 The enemy soldiers carry red
    shields
  and wear uniforms of red.
They are preparing to attack!
  Their chariots flash like fire!
  Their horses*b* prance!

4 Chariots dash wildly through the
    streets,
  rushing back and forth in the
    city squares.
They flash like torches
  and dart about like lightning.
5 The officers are summoned;
  they stumble as they press
    forward.

The attackers rush to the wall
  and set up the shield for the
    battering ram.
6 The gates by the river burst open;
  the palace is filled with terror.
7 The queen is taken captive;
  her servants moan like doves
  and beat their breasts in sorrow.
8 Like water from a broken dam
  the people rush from Nineveh!*c*
"Stop! Stop!" the cry rings out—
  but no one turns back.

9 Plunder the silver!
  Plunder the gold!
The city is full of treasure!

10 Nineveh is destroyed, deserted,
    desolate!
  Hearts melt with fear;
  knees tremble, strength is gone;
  faces grow pale.

11 Where now is the city
  that was like a den of lions,
  the place where young lions
    were fed,
  where the lion and the lioness
    would go
  and their cubs would be safe?
12 The lion killed his prey
  and tore it to pieces for his mate
    and her cubs;
  he filled his den with torn flesh.

13 "I am your enemy!" says the LORD Almighty. "I will burn up your chariots. Your soldiers will be killed in war, and I will take away everything that you took from others. The demands of your envoys will no longer be heard."

3 Doomed is the lying, murderous
    city,
  full of wealth to be looted and
    plundered!
2 Listen! The crack of the whip,
  the rattle of wheels,
  the gallop of horses,
  the jolting of chariots!
3 Cavalry troops charge,
  swords flash, spears gleam!
Corpses are piled high,
  dead bodies without number—
  men stumble over them!
4 Nineveh the whore is being
    punished.
Attractive and full of deadly
    charms,
  she enchanted nations and
    enslaved*d* them.

5 The LORD Almighty says,
"I will punish you, Nineveh!
  I will strip you naked
  and let the nations see you,
  see you in all your shame.
6 I will treat you with contempt
  and cover you with filth.
People will stare at you in
    horror.
7 All who see you will shrink back.
  They will say, 'Nineveh lies in
    ruins!
  Who has any sympathy for her?
  Who will want to comfort her?' "

8 Nineveh, are you any better than

---

b Some ancient translations horses; *Hebrew* cypresses. Nineveh; *Hebrew unclear.*   *d* enslaved; *or* seduced.   *c Probable text* Like water . . .

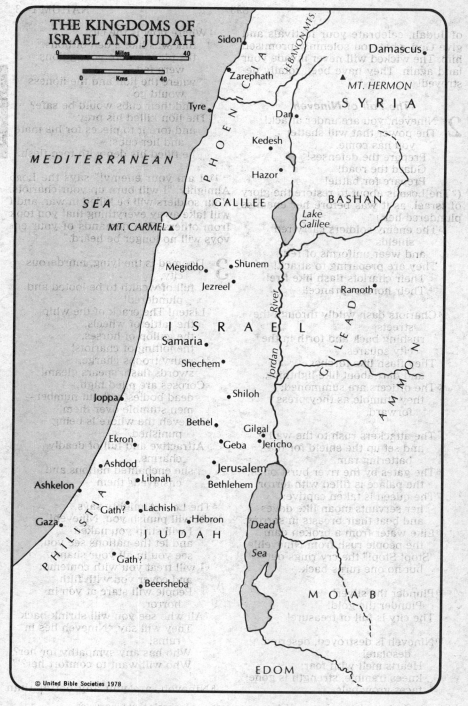

THE KINGDOMS OF ISRAEL AND JUDAH

0 — Miles — 40

0 — Kms — 40

MEDITERRANEAN

SEA

Sidon

Zarephath

Tyre

PHOENICIA

LEBANON MTS.

Damascus

MT. HERMON

SYRIA

Dan

Kedesh

Hazor

GALILEE

Lake
Galilee

BASHAN

MT. CARMEL

Megiddo

Shunem

Jezreel

Ramoth

ISRAEL

Samaria

Shechem

GILEAD

Jordan River

Shiloh

Joppa

Bethel

AMMON

Ekron

Geba

Gilgal

Jericho

Ashdod

Libnah

Jerusalem

Bethlehem

Ashkelon

Gath?

Lachish

Gaza

PHILISTIA

Hebron

JUDAH

Dead

Sea

Gath?

Beersheba

MOAB

EDOM

© United Bible Societies 1978

Thebes, the capital of Egypt? She too had a river to protect her like a wall — the Nile was her defense. 9 She ruled Ethiopia*e* and Egypt, there was no limit to her power; Libya was her ally. 10 Yet the people of Thebes were carried off into exile. At every street corner their children were beaten to death. Their leading men were carried off in chains and divided among their captors.

11 Nineveh, you too will fall into a drunken stupor! You too will try to escape from your enemies. 12 All your fortresses will be like fig trees with ripe figs: shake the trees, and the fruit falls right into your mouth! 13 Your soldiers are helpless, and your country stands defenseless before your enemies. Fire will destroy the bars across your gates. 14 Draw water to prepare for a siege, and strengthen your fortresses! Trample the clay to make bricks, and get the brick molds ready! 15 No matter what you do,

you will still be burned to death or killed in battle. You will be wiped out like crops eaten up by locusts.

You multiplied like locusts! 16 You produced more merchants than there are stars in the sky! But now they are gone, like locusts that spread their wings and fly away. 17 Your officials are like a swarm of locusts that stay in the walls on a cold day. But when the sun comes out, they fly away, and no one knows where they have gone!

18 Emperor of Assyria, your governors are dead, and your noblemen are asleep forever! Your people are scattered on the mountains, and there is no one to bring them home again. 19 There is no remedy for your injuries, and your wounds cannot be healed. All those who hear the news of your destruction clap their hands for joy. Did anyone escape your endless cruelty?

---

e Hebrew Cush: Cush is the ancient name of the extensive territory south of the First Cataract of the Nile River. This region was called Ethiopia in Graeco-Roman times, and included within its borders most of modern Sudan and some of present-day Ethiopia (Abyssinia).

The Book of
HABAKKUK

Introduction

The words of the prophet Habakkuk come from near the end of the seventh century B.C., at a time when the Babylonians were in power. He was deeply disturbed by the violence of these cruel people, and asked the Lord, "So why are you silent while they destroy people who are more righteous than they are?" (1.13). The Lord's answer was that he would take action in his own good time, and meanwhile "those who are righteous will live because they are faithful to God" (2.4).

The rest of the book is a prophecy of doom on the unrighteous, with a concluding psalm celebrating the greatness of God and expressing the undying faith of the poet.

Outline of Contents

1 This is the message that the LORD revealed to the prophet Habakkuk.

Habakkuk Complains of Injustice

2 O LORD, how long must I call for help before you listen, before you save us from violence? 3 Why do you make me see such trouble? How can you stand to look on such wrongdoing? Destruction and violence are all around me, and there is fighting and quarreling everywhere. 4 The law is weak and useless,

and justice is never done. Evil people get the better of the righteous, and so justice is perverted.

The Lord's Reply

5 Then the Lord said to his people, "Keep watching the nations around you, and you will be astonished at what you see. I am going to do something that you will not believe when you hear about it. 6 I am bringing the Babylonians to power, those fierce, restless people. They are marching out across the world to conquer other lands. 7 They spread fear and terror, and in their pride they are a law to themselves.

8 "Their horses are faster than leopards, fiercer than hungry wolves. Their cavalry troops come riding from distant lands; their horses paw the ground. They come swooping down like eagles attacking their prey.

9 "Their armies advance in violent conquest, and everyone is terrified as they approach.a Their captives are as numerous as grains of sand. 10 They treat kings with contempt and laugh at high officials. No fortress can stop them — they pile up earth against it and capture it. 11 Then they sweep on like the wind and are gone, these men whose power is their god."

Habakkuk Complains to the Lord Again

12 Lord, from the very beginning you are God. You are my God, holy and eternal. Lord, my God and protector, you have chosen the Babylonians and made them strong so that they can punish us. 13 But how can you stand these treacherous, evil men? Your eyes are too holy to look at evil, and you cannot stand the sight of people doing wrong. So why are you silent while they destroy people who are more righteous than they are? 14 How can you treat people like fish or like a swarm of insects that have no ruler to direct them? 15 The Babylonians catch people with hooks, as though they were fish. They drag them off in nets and shout for joy over their catch! 16 They even worship their nets and offer sacrifices to them, because their nets

provide them with the best of everything.

17 Are they going to use their swords forever and keep on destroying nations without mercy?

The Lord's Answer to Habakkuk

2 I will climb my watchtower and wait to see what the Lord will tell me to say and what answer heb will give to my complaint.

2 The Lord gave me this answer: "Write down clearly on tablets what I reveal to you, so that it can be read at a glance. 3 Put it in writing, because it is not yet time for it to come true. But the time is coming quickly, and what I show you will come true. It may seem slow in coming, but wait for it; it will certainly take place, and it will not be delayed. 4 And this is the message: 'Those who are evil will not survive,c but those who are righteous will live because they are faithful to God.' "

Doom on the Unrighteous

5 Wealth is deceitful. Greedy people are proud and restless — like death itself they are never satisfied. That is why they conquer nation after nation for themselves. 6 The conquered people will taunt their conquerors and show their scorn for them. They will say, "You take what isn't yours, but you are doomed! How long will you go on getting rich by forcing your debtors to pay up?"

7 But before you know it, you that have conquered others will be in debt yourselves and be forced to pay interest. Enemies will come and make you tremble. They will plunder you! 8 You have plundered the people of many nations, but now those who have survived will plunder you because of the murders you have committed and because of your violence against the people of the world and its cities.d

9 You are doomed! You have made your family rich with what you took by violence, and have tried to make your own home safe from harm and danger! 10 But your schemes have brought shame on your family; by destroying many nations you have only brought ruin on yourself. 11 Even the stones of the walls

---

a Probable text and everyone . . . approach; Hebrew unclear.   b One ancient translation he; Hebrew I.   c Probable text will not survive; Hebrew unclear.   d the people . . . cities; or the land, the city, and those who live in it.

cry out against you, and the rafters echo the cry. 12 You are doomed! You founded a city on crime and built it up by murder. 13 The nations you conquered wore themselves out in useless labor, and all they have built goes up in flames. The LORD Almighty has done this. 14 But the earth will be as full of the knowledge of the LORD's glory as the seas are full of water.

15 You are doomed! In your fury you humiliated and disgraced your neighbors; you made them stagger as though they were drunk. 16 You in turn will be covered with shame instead of honor. You yourself will drink and stagger. The LORD will make you drink your own cup of punishment, and your honor will be turned to disgrace. 17 You have cut down the forests of Lebanon; now you will be cut down. You killed its animals; now animals will terrify you. This will happen because of the murders you have committed and because of your violence against the people of the world and its cities.*d*

18 What's the use of an idol? It is only something that a human being has made, and it tells you nothing but lies. What good does it do for its maker to trust it — a god that can't even talk! 19 You are doomed! You say to a piece of wood, "Wake up!" or to a block of stone, "Get up!" Can an idol reveal anything to you? It may be covered with silver and gold, but there is no life in it.

20 The LORD is in his holy Temple; let everyone on earth be silent in his presence.

A Prayer of Habakkuk

3 This is a prayer of the prophet Habakkuk:*e*

2 O LORD, I have heard of what you have done,
and I am filled with awe.
Now do again in our times
the great deeds you used to do.
Be merciful, even when you are angry.

3 God is coming again from Edom;
the holy God is coming from the hills of Paran.
His splendor covers the heavens,
and the earth is full of his praise.
4 He comes with the brightness of lightning;
light flashes from his hand,
there where his power is hidden.
5 He sends disease before him
and commands death to follow him.
6 When he stops, the earth shakes;
at his glance the nations tremble.
The eternal mountains are shattered;
the everlasting hills sink down,
the hills where he walked in ancient times.

7 I saw the people of Cushan afraid
and the people of Midian tremble.
8 Was it the rivers that made you angry, LORD?
Was it the sea that made you furious?
You rode upon the clouds;
the storm cloud was your chariot,
as you brought victory to your people.
9 You got ready to use your bow,
ready to shoot your arrows.*f*
Your lightning split open the earth.
10 When the mountains saw you, they trembled;
water poured down from the skies.
The waters under the earth roared,
and their waves rose high.
11 At the flash of your speeding arrows
and the gleam of your shining spear,
the sun and the moon stood still.
12 You marched across the earth in anger;
in fury you trampled the nations.
13 You went out to save your people,
to save your chosen king.
You struck down the leader of the wicked

---

d the people . . . cities; or the land, the city, and those who live in it.   e Hebrew has an additional phrase, the meaning of which is unclear.   f Probable text ready to shoot your arrows; Hebrew unclear.

and completely destroyed his
    followers.g
14 Your arrows pierced the
    commander of his army
    when it came like a storm to
    scatter us,
    gloating like those who secretly
    oppress the poor.h
15 You trampled the sea with your
    horses,
    and the mighty waters foamed.

16 I hear all this, and I tremble;
    my lips quiver with fear.
    My body goes limp,
    and my feet stumblei
    beneath me.

    I will quietly wait for the time to
    come

when God will punish those who
    attack us.

17 Even though the fig trees have no
    fruit
    and no grapes grow on the
    vines,
    even though the olive crop fails
    and the fields produce no grain,
    even though the sheep all die
    and the cattle stalls are empty,
18 I will still be joyful and glad,
    because the LORD God is my
    savior.
19 The Sovereign LORD gives me
    strength.
    He makes me sure-footed as a
    deer
    and keeps me safe on the
    mountains.

g *Probable text* completely . . . followers; *Hebrew unclear.*   h *Verse 14 in Hebrew is unclear.*
i *Probable text* my feet stumble; *Hebrew* I am excited, because.

The Book of
ZEPHANIAH

Introduction

The prophet Zephaniah preached in the latter part of the seventh century B.C.,
probably in the decade before King Josiah's religious reforms of 621 B.C. The book
contains the familiar prophetic themes: A day of doom and destruction is threatened,
when Judah will be punished for her worship of other gods. The Lord will punish other
nations also. Although Jerusalem is doomed, in time the city will be restored, with a
humble and righteous people living there.

Outline of Contents

1 This is the message that the LORD
    gave to Zephaniah during the time
that Josiah son of Amon was king of Judah. (Zephaniah was descended from
King Hezekiah through Amariah, Gedaliah, and Cushi.)

The Day of the LORD's Judgment

2 The LORD said, "I am going to destroy
everything on earth, 3 all human beings

and animals, birds and fish. I will bring
about the downfall ofa the wicked. I will
destroy everyone, and no survivors will
be left. I, the LORD, have spoken.

4 "I will punish the people of Jerusalem
and of all Judah. I will destroy the last
trace of the worship of Baal there, and
no one will even remember the pagan
priests who serve him. 5 I will destroy
anyone who goes up on the roof and

a *Probable text* I will bring about the downfall of; *Hebrew* the stumbling blocks.

worships the sun, the moon, and the stars. I will also destroy those who worship me and swear loyalty to me, but then take oaths in the name of the god Molech. 6 I will destroy those who have turned back and no longer follow me, those who do not come to me or ask me to guide them."

7 The day is near when the LORD will sit in judgment; so be silent in his presence. The LORD is preparing to sacrifice his people and has invited enemies to plunder Judah. 8 "On that day of slaughter," says the LORD, "I will punish the officials, the king's sons, and all who practice foreign customs. 9 I will punish all who worship like pagans and who steal and kill in order to fill their master's house[b] with loot.

10 "On that day," says the LORD, "you will hear the sound of crying at the Fish Gate in Jerusalem. You will hear wailing in the newer part of the city and a great crashing sound in the hills. 11 Wail and cry when you hear this, you that live in the lower part of the city, because all the merchants will be dead!

12 "At that time I will take a lamp and search Jerusalem. I will punish the people who are self-satisfied and confident, who say to themselves, 'The LORD never does anything, one way or the other.' 13 Their wealth will be looted and their houses destroyed. They will never live in the houses they are building or drink wine from the vineyards they are planting."

14 The great day of the LORD is near—very near and coming fast! That day will be bitter, for even[c] the bravest soldiers will cry out in despair! 15 It will be a day of fury, a day of trouble and distress, a day of ruin and destruction, a day of darkness and gloom, a black and cloudy day, 16 a day filled with the sound of war trumpets and the battle cry of soldiers attacking fortified cities and high towers.

17 The LORD says, "I will bring such disasters on the human race that everyone will grope about like someone blind. They have sinned against me, and now their blood will be poured out like water, and their dead bodies will lie rotting on the ground."

18 On the day when the LORD shows his fury, not even all their silver and gold will save them. The whole earth will be destroyed by the fire of his anger. He will put an end—a sudden end—to everyone who lives on earth.

A Plea for Repentance

2 Shameless nation, come to your senses 2 before you are driven away like chaff blown by the wind, before the burning anger of the LORD comes upon you, before the day when he shows his fury. 3 Turn to the LORD, all you humble people of the land, who obey his commands. Do what is right, and humble yourselves before the LORD. Perhaps you will escape punishment on the day when the LORD shows his anger.

The Doom of the Nations around Israel

4 No one will be left in the city of Gaza. Ashkelon will be deserted. The people of Ashdod will be driven out in half a day,[d] and the people of Ekron will be driven from their city. 5 You Philistines are doomed, you people who live along the coast. The LORD has passed sentence on you. He will destroy you, and not one of you will be left. 6 Your land by the sea will become open fields with shepherd's huts and sheep pens. 7 The people of Judah who survive will occupy your land. They will pasture their flocks there and sleep in the houses of Ashkelon. The LORD their God will be with them and make them prosper again.

8 The LORD Almighty says, "I have heard the people of Moab and Ammon insulting and taunting my people, and boasting that they would seize their land. 9 As surely as I am the living LORD, the God of Israel, I swear that Moab and Ammon are going to be destroyed like Sodom and Gomorrah. They will become a place of salt pits and everlasting ruin, overgrown with weeds. Those of my people who survive will plunder them and take their land."

10 That is how the people of Moab and Ammon will be punished for their pride and arrogance and for insulting the people of the LORD Almighty. 11 The LORD will terrify them. He will reduce the gods

---

b their master's house; or the temple of their god.   c That day . . . even; or Listen! That terrible
day is coming when even.   d in half a day; or by a surprise attack at noontime.

ZECHARIAH

of the earth to nothing, and then every nation will worship him, each in its own land.

12 The LORD will also put the people of Ethiopia*e* to death.

13 The LORD will use his power to destroy Assyria. He will make the city of Nineveh a deserted ruin, a waterless desert. 14 It will be a place where flocks, herds, and animals of every kind will lie down. Owls will live among its ruins and hoot from the windows. Crows*f* will caw on the doorsteps. The cedar wood of her buildings will be stripped away. 15 That is what will happen to the city that is so proud of its own power and thinks it is safe. Its people think that their city is the greatest in the world. What a desolate place it will become, a place where wild animals will rest! Everyone who passes by will shrink back in horror.

Jerusalem's Sin and Redemption

3 Jerusalem is doomed, that corrupt, rebellious city that oppresses its own people. 2 It has not listened to the LORD or accepted his discipline. It has not put its trust in the LORD or asked for his help. 3 Its officials are like roaring lions; its judges are like hungry wolves, too greedy to leave a bone until morning. 4 The prophets are irresponsible and treacherous; the priests defile what is sacred, and twist the law of God to their own advantage. 5 But the LORD is still in the city; he does what is right and never what is wrong. Every morning without fail, he brings justice to his people. And yet the unrighteous people there keep on doing wrong and are not ashamed.

6 The LORD says, "I have wiped out whole nations; I have destroyed their cities and left their walls and towers in ruins. The cities are deserted; the streets are empty — no one is left. 7 I thought that then my people would have reverence for me and accept my discipline, that they would never forget*g* the lesson

I taught them. But soon they were behaving as badly as ever.

8 "Just wait," the LORD says. "Wait for the day when I rise to accuse the nations. I have made up my mind to gather nations and kingdoms in order to let them feel the force of my anger. The whole earth will be destroyed by the fire of my fury.

9 "Then I will change the people of the nations, and they will pray to me alone and not to other gods. They will all obey me. 10 Even from distant Ethiopia*h* my scattered people will bring offerings to me. 11 At that time you, my people, will no longer need to be ashamed that you rebelled against me. I will remove everyone who is proud and arrogant, and you will never again rebel against me on my sacred hill.*i* 12 I will leave there a humble and lowly people, who will come to me for help. 13 The people of Israel who survive will do no wrong to anyone, tell no lies, nor try to deceive. They will be prosperous and secure, afraid of no one."

A Song of Joy

14 Sing and shout for joy, people of Israel!
Rejoice with all your heart, Jerusalem!
15 The LORD has stopped your punishment;
he has removed all your enemies.
The LORD, the king of Israel, is with you;
there is no reason now to be afraid.
16 The time is coming when they will say to Jerusalem,
"Do not be afraid, city of Zion!
Do not let your hands hang limp!
17 The LORD your God is with you;
his power gives you victory.
The LORD will take delight in you,
and in his love he will give you new life.*j*

---

e Hebrew Cush: *Cush is the ancient name of the extensive territory south of the First Cataract of the Nile River. This region was called Ethiopia in Graeco-Roman times, and included within its borders most of modern Sudan and some of present-day Ethiopia (Abyssinia).*
f Some ancient translations Crows; *Hebrew* Desolation.   *g Some ancient translations* they would never forget; *Hebrew* their dwelling would not be cut off.   *h Hebrew* Cush: *Cush is the ancient name of the extensive territory south of the First Cataract of the Nile River. This region was called Ethiopia in Graeco-Roman times, and included within its borders most of modern Sudan and some of present-day Ethiopia (Abyssinia).*   *i* SACRED HILL: *Mount Zion (see* Zion *in Word List).*   *j Some ancient translations* give you new life; *Hebrew* be silent.

He will sing and be joyful
   over you,
18 as joyful as people at a festival."
The LORD says,
"I have ended the threat of doom
   and taken away your
   disgrace.k
19 The time is coming!
I will punish your oppressors;
I will rescue all the lame
   and bring the exiles home.

I will turn their shame to honor,
   and all the world will praise
   them.
20 The time is coming!
I will bring your scattered people
   home;
I will make you famous
   throughout the world
and make you prosperous once
   again."
The LORD has spoken.

k Verse 18 in Hebrew is unclear.

The Book of
HAGGAI

Introduction

The Book of Haggai *is a collection of brief messages that came from the Lord through the prophet Haggai in 520 B.C. The people had returned from exile and had lived in Jerusalem for some years, but the Temple still lay in ruins. The messages urge the leaders of the people to rebuild the Temple, and the Lord promises prosperity and peace in the future for a renewed and purified people.*

Outline of Contents

The LORD's Command to Rebuild the Temple

1 During the second year that Darius was emperor of Persia, on the first day of the sixth month, the LORD spoke through the prophet Haggai. The message was for the governor of Judah, Zerubbabel son of Shealtiel, and for the High Priest, Joshua son of Jehozadak.
2 The LORD Almighty said to Haggai, "These people say that this is not the right time to rebuild the Temple." 3 The LORD then gave this message to the people through the prophet Haggai: 4 "My people, why should you be living in well-built houses while my Temple lies in ruins? 5 Don't you see what is happening to you? 6 You have planted much grain, but have harvested very little. You have food to eat, but not enough to make you full. You have wine to drink, but not

enough to get drunk on! You have clothing, but not enough to keep you warm. And workers cannot earn enough to live on. 7 Can't you see why this has happened? 8 Now go up into the hills, get lumber, and rebuild the Temple; then I will be pleased and will be worshiped as I should be.

9 "You hoped for large harvests, but they turned out to be small. And when you brought the harvest home, I blew it away.a Why did I do that? Because my Temple lies in ruins while every one of you is busy working on your own house. 10 That is why there is no rain and nothing can grow. 11 I have brought drought on the land—on its hills, grainfields, vineyards, and olive orchards—on every crop the ground produces, on people and animals, on everything you try to grow."

a I blew it away; or I spoiled it.

The People Obey the Lord's Command

12 Then Zerubbabel and Joshua and all the people who had returned from the exile[b] in Babylonia, did what the Lord their God told them to do. They were afraid and obeyed the prophet Haggai, the Lord's messenger. 13 Then Haggai gave the Lord's message to the people: "I will be with you—that is my promise." 14 The Lord inspired everyone to work on the Temple: Zerubbabel, the governor of Judah; Joshua, the High Priest, and all the people who had returned from the exile.[b] They began working on the Temple of the Lord Almighty, their God, 15 on the twenty-fourth day of the sixth month of the second year that Darius was emperor.

The Splendor of the New Temple

2 On the twenty-first day of the seventh month of that same year, the Lord spoke again through the prophet Haggai. 2 He told Haggai to speak to Zerubbabel, the governor of Judah, to Joshua, the High Priest, and to the people, and to say to them, 3 "Is there anyone among you who can still remember how splendid the Temple used to be? How does it look to you now? It must seem like nothing at all. 4 But now don't be discouraged, any of you. Do the work, for I am with you. 5 When you came out of Egypt, I promised that I would always be with you. I am still with you, so do not be afraid.

6 "Before long I will shake heaven and earth, land and sea. 7 I will overthrow all the nations, and their treasures will be brought here, and the Temple will be filled with wealth. 8 All the silver and gold of the world is mine. 9 The new Temple will be more splendid than the old one, and there I will give my people prosperity and peace." The Lord Almighty has spoken.

The Prophet Consults the Priests

10 On the twenty-fourth day of the ninth month of the second year that Darius was emperor, the Lord Almighty spoke again to the prophet Haggai. 11 He said, "Ask the priests for a ruling on this question: 12 Suppose someone takes a piece of consecrated meat from a sacrifice and carries it in a fold of his robe. If he then lets his robe touch any bread, cooked food, wine, olive oil, or any kind of food at all, will it make that food consecrated also?"

When the question was asked, the priests answered, "No."

13 Then Haggai asked, "Suppose someone is defiled because he has touched a dead body. If he then touches any of these foods, will that make them defiled too?"

The priests answered, "Yes."

14 Then Haggai said, "The Lord says that the same thing applies to the people of this nation and to everything they produce; and so everything they offer on the altar is defiled."

The Lord Promises His Blessing

15 The Lord says, "Can't you see what has happened to you? Before you started to rebuild the Temple, 16 you would go to a pile of grain expecting to find twenty bushels, but there would be only ten. You would go to draw fifty gallons of wine from a vat, but find only twenty. 17 I sent scorching winds and hail to ruin everything you tried to grow, but still you did not repent. 18 Today is the twenty-fourth day of the ninth month, the day that the foundation of the Temple has been completed. See what is going to happen from now on. 19 Although there is no grain left, and the grapevines, fig trees, pomegranates, and olive trees have not yet produced, yet from now on I will bless you."

The Lord's Promise to Zerubbabel

20 On that same day, the twenty-fourth of the month, the Lord gave Haggai a second message 21 for Zerubbabel, the governor of Judah: "I am about to shake heaven and earth 22 and overthrow kingdoms and end their power. I will overturn chariots and their drivers; the horses will die, and their riders will kill one another. 23 On that day I will take you, Zerubbabel my servant, and I will appoint you to rule in my name. You are the one I have chosen." The Lord Almighty has spoken.

---

b who had returned from the exile; *or* who had not gone into exile.

The Book of
ZECHARIAH

Introduction

The Book of Zechariah *has two distinct parts: 1) Chapters 1–8 Prophecies from the prophet Zechariah, dated at various times in the years from 520 to 518 B.C. These are largely in the form of visions, and deal with the restoration of Jerusalem, the rebuilding of the Temple, the purification of God's people, and the messianic age to come. 2) Chapters 9–14 A collection of messages about the expected Messiah and the final judgment.*

Outline of Contents

The Lord Calls His People to Return to Him

1 In the eighth month of the second year that Darius was emperor of Persia, the Lord gave this message to the prophet Zechariah, the son of Berechiah and grandson of Iddo. 2 The Lord Almighty told Zechariah to say to the people, "I, the Lord, was very angry with your ancestors, 3 but now I say to you, 'Return to me, and I will return to you. 4 Do not be like your ancestors. Long ago the prophets gave them my message, telling them not to live evil, sinful lives any longer. But they would not listen to me or obey me. 5 Your ancestors and those prophets are no longer alive. 6 Through my servants the prophets I gave your ancestors commands and warnings, but they disregarded them and suffered the consequences. Then they repented and acknowledged that I, the Lord Almighty, had punished them as they deserved and as I had determined to do.' "

The Prophet's Vision of the Horses

7 In the second year that Darius was emperor, on the twenty-fourth day of the eleventh month (the month of Shebat), the Lord gave me a message in a vision at night. 8 I saw someone riding a red horse. He had stopped among some myrtle trees in a valley, and behind him were other horses — red, dappled, and white. 9 I asked him, "Sir, what do these horses mean?"

He answered, "I will show you what

they mean. 10 The Lord sent them to go and inspect the earth."

11 They reported to the angel: "We have been all over the world and have found that the whole world lies helpless and subdued."

12 Then the angel said, "Almighty Lord, you have been angry with Jerusalem and the cities of Judah for seventy years now. How much longer will it be before you show them mercy?"

13 The Lord answered the angel with comforting words, 14 and the angel told me to proclaim what the Lord Almighty had said: "I have a deep love and concern for Jerusalem, my holy city, 15 and I am very angry with the nations that enjoy quiet and peace. For while I was holding back my anger against my people, those nations made the sufferings of my people worse. 16 So I have come back to Jerusalem to show mercy to the city. My Temple will be restored, and the city will be rebuilt."

17 The angel also told me to proclaim: "The Lord Almighty says that his cities will be prosperous again and that he will once again help Jerusalem and claim the city as his own."

The Vision of the Horns

18 In another vision I saw four ox horns. 19 I asked the angel that had been speaking to me, "What do these horns mean?"

He answered, "They stand for the world powers that have scattered the people of Judah, Israel, and Jerusalem."

20 Then the Lord showed me four

workers with hammers. 21 I asked, "What have they come to do?"

He answered, "They have come to terrify and overthrow the nations that completely crushed the land of Judah and scattered its people."

The Vision of the Measuring Line

2 In another vision I saw a man with a measuring line in his hand. 2 "Where are you going?" I asked.

"To measure Jerusalem," he answered, "to see how long and how wide it is."

3 Then I saw the angel who had been speaking to me step forward, and another angel came to meet him. 4 The first one said to the other, "Run and tell that young man with the measuring line that there are going to be so many people and so much livestock in Jerusalem that it will be too big to have walls. 5 The LORD has promised that he himself will be a wall of fire around the city to protect it and that he will live there in all his glory."

The Exiles Are Called to Come Home

6-7 The LORD said to his people, "I scattered you in all directions. But now, you exiles, escape from Babylonia and return to Jerusalem. 8 Anyone who strikes you strikes what is most precious to me."

So the LORD Almighty[a] sent me with this message for the nations that had plundered his people: 9 "The LORD himself will fight against you, and you will be plundered by the people who were once your servants."

When this happens, everyone will know that the LORD Almighty sent me.

10 The LORD said, "Sing for joy, people of Jerusalem! I am coming to live among you!"

11 At that time many nations will come to the LORD and become his people. He will live among you, and you will know

that he has sent me to you. 12 Once again Judah will be the special possession of the LORD in his sacred land, and Jerusalem will be the city he loves most of all.

13 Be silent, everyone, in the presence of the LORD, for he is coming from his holy dwelling place.

The Prophet's Vision of the High Priest

3 In another vision the LORD showed me the High Priest Joshua standing before the angel of the LORD. And there beside Joshua stood Satan,[b] ready to bring an accusation against him. 2 The angel of the LORD[c] said to Satan, "May the LORD condemn you, Satan! May the LORD, who loves Jerusalem, condemn you. This man is like a stick snatched from the fire."

3 Joshua was standing there, wearing filthy clothes. 4 The angel said to his heavenly attendants, "Take away the filthy clothes this man is wearing." Then he said to Joshua, "I have taken away your sin and will give you new clothes to wear."

5 He commanded the attendants to put[d] a clean turban on Joshua's head. They did so, and then they put the new clothes on him while the angel of the LORD stood there.

6 Then the angel told Joshua that 7 the LORD Almighty had said: "If you obey my laws and perform the duties I have assigned you, then you will continue to be in charge of my Temple and its courts, and I will hear your prayers, just as I hear the prayers of the angels who are in my presence. 8 Listen then, Joshua, you who are the High Priest; and listen, you fellow priests of his, you that are the sign of a good future: I will reveal my servant, who is called The Branch! 9 I am placing in front of Joshua a single stone with seven facets. I will engrave an inscription on it, and in a single day I will take away the sin of this land. 10 When that day comes, each of you will invite your neighbor to come and enjoy peace

and security, surrounded by your vineyards and fig trees."

The Vision of the Lampstand

4 The angel who had been speaking to me came again and roused me as if I had been sleeping. 2 "What do you see?" he asked.

"A lampstand made of gold," I answered. "At the top is a bowl for the oil. On the lampstand are seven lamps, each one with places for seven wicks. 3 There are two olive trees beside the lampstand, one on each side of it." 4 Then I asked the angel, "What do these things stand for, sir?"

5 "Don't you know?" he asked me.

"No, I don't, sir," I replied.

10b The angel said to me, "The seven lamps are the seven eyes of the LORD, which see all over the earth."e 11 Then I asked him, "What do the two olive trees on either side of the lampstand mean? 12 And what is the meaning of the two olive branches beside the two gold pipes from which the olive oil pours?"

13 He asked me, "Don't you know?"

"No, I don't, sir," I answered.

14 Then he said, "These are the two men whom God has chosen and anointed to serve him, the Lord of the whole earth."

God's Promise to Zerubbabel

6 The angel told me to give Zerubbabel this message from the LORD: "You will succeed, not by military might or by your own strength, but by my spirit. 7 Obstacles as great as mountains will disappear before you. You will rebuild the Temple, and as you put the last stone in place, the people will shout, 'Beautiful, beautiful!' "

8 Another message came to me from the LORD. 9 He said, "Zerubbabel has laid the foundation of the Temple, and he will finish the building. When this happens, my people will know that it is I who sent you to them. 10a They are disappointed because so little progress is being made. But they will see Zerubbabel continuing to build the Temple, and they will be glad."

The Vision of the Flying Scroll

5 I looked again, and this time I saw a scroll flying through the air. 2 The angel asked me what I saw. I answered, "A scroll flying through the air; it is thirty feet long and fifteen feet wide."

3 Then he said to me, "On it is written the curse that is to go out over the whole land. On one side of the scroll it says that every thief will be removed from the land; and on the other side it says that everyone who tells lies under oath will also be taken away. 4 The LORD Almighty says that he will send this curse out, and it will enter the house of every thief and the house of everyone who tells lies under oath. It will remain in their houses and leave them in ruins."

The Vision of the Woman in the Basket

5 The angel appeared again and said, "Look! Something else is coming!"

6 "What is it?" I asked.

He replied, "It is a basket, and it stands for the sinf of the whole land."

7 The basket had a lid made of lead. As I watched, the lid was raised, and there in the basket sat a woman! 8 The angel said, "This represents wickedness." Then he pushed her down into the basket and put the lid back down. 9 I looked up and saw two women flying toward me with powerful wings like those of a stork. They picked up the basket and flew off with it.

10 I asked the angel, "Where are they taking it?"

11 He answered, "To Babylonia, where they will build a temple for it. When the temple is finished, the basket will be placed there to be worshiped."

The Vision of the Four Chariots

6 I had another vision. This time I saw four chariots coming out from between two bronze mountains. 2 The first chariot was pulled by red horses, the second by black horses, 3 the third by white horses, and the fourth by dappled horses. 4 Then I asked the angel, "Sir, what do these chariots mean?"

5 He answered, "These are the four winds; they have just come from the presence of the Lord of all the earth."

e Verses 10b-14 are moved here from the end of the chapter in order to retain the natural sequence of the narrative.   f Some ancient translations sin; Hebrew eye.

6 The chariot pulled by the black horses was going north to Babylonia, the white horses were going to the west, and the dappled horses were going to the country in the south. 7 As the dappled horses came out, they were impatient to go and inspect the earth. The angel said, "Go and inspect the earth!" — and they did. 8 Then the angel cried out to me, "The horses that went north to Babylonia have quieted the LORD's anger."

The Command to Crown Joshua

9 The LORD gave me this message. 10 He said, "Take the gifts given by the exiles Heldai, Tobijah, and Jedaiah, and go at once to the home of Josiah son of Zephaniah. All of them have returned from exile in Babylonia. 11 Make a crown out of the silver and gold they have given, and put it on the head of the High Priest, Joshua son of Jehozadak. 12 Tell him that the LORD Almighty says, 'The man who is called The Branch will flourish where he is and rebuild the LORD's Temple. 13 He is the one who will build it and receive the honor due a king, and he will rule his people. A priest will stand by his throne, and they will work together in peace and harmony.' 14 The crown will be a memorial in the LORD's Temple in honor of Heldai,g Tobijah, Jedaiah, and Josiah."h

15 Men who live far away will come and help to rebuild the Temple of the LORD. And when it is rebuilt, you will know that the LORD Almighty sent me to you. This will all happen if you fully obey the commands of the LORD your God.

The LORD Condemns Insincere Fasting

7 In the fourth year that Darius was emperor, on the fourth day of the ninth month (the month of Kislev), the LORD gave me a message. 2 The people of Bethel had sent Sharezer and Regemmelech and their men to the Temple of the LORD Almighty to pray for the LORD's blessing 3 and to ask the priests and the prophets this question: "Should we continue to mourn because of the destruction of the Temple, by fasting in the fifth month as we have done for so many years now?"

4 This is the message of the LORD that came to me. 5 He said, "Tell the people of the land and the priests that when they fasted and mourned in the fifth and seventh months during these seventy years, it was not in honor of me. 6 And when they ate and drank, it was for their own satisfaction."

7 This is what the LORD said through the earlier prophets at the time when Jerusalem was prosperous and filled with people and when there were many people living not only in the towns around the city but also in the southern region and in the western foothills.

Disobedience, the Cause of Exile

8 The LORD gave this message to Zechariah: 9 "Long ago I gave these commands to my people: 'You must see that justice is done, and must show kindness and mercy to one another. 10 Do not oppress widows, orphans, foreigners who live among you, or anyone else in need. And do not plan ways of harming one another.'

11 "But my people stubbornly refused to listen. They closed their minds 12 and made their hearts as hard as rock. Because they would not listen to the teaching which I sent through the prophets who lived long ago, I became very angry. 13 Because they did not listen when I spoke, I did not answer when they prayed. 14 Like a storm I swept them away to live in foreign countries. This good land was left a desolate place, with no one living in it."

The LORD Promises to Restore Jerusalem

8 The LORD Almighty gave this message to Zechariah: 2 "I have longed to help Jerusalem because of my deep love for her people, a love which has made me angry with her enemies. 3 I will return to Jerusalem, my holy city, and live there. It will be known as the faithful city, and the hill of the LORD Almightyi will be called the sacred hill. 4 Once again old men and women, so old that they use canes when they walk, will be sitting in the city squares. 5 And the

---

g One ancient translation Heldai; Hebrew Helem.   h One ancient translation Josiah; Hebrew Hen.   i HILL OF THE LORD ALMIGHTY: Mount Zion (see Zion in Word List).

streets will again be full of boys and girls playing.

6 "This may seem impossible to those of the nation who are now left, but it's not impossible for me. 7 I will rescue my people from the lands where they have been taken, 8 and will bring them back from east and west to live in Jerusalem. They will be my people, and I will be their God, ruling over them faithfully and justly.

9 "Have courage! You are now hearing the same words the prophets spoke at the time the foundation was being laid for rebuilding my Temple. 10 Before that time no one could afford to hire either men or animals, and no one was safe from enemies. I turned people against one another. 11 But now I am treating the survivors of this nation differently. 12 They will plant their crops in peace. Their vines will bear grapes, the earth will produce crops, and there will be plenty of rain. I will give all these blessings to the people of my nation who survive. 13 People of Judah and Israel! In the past foreigners have cursed one another by saying, 'May the same disasters fall on you that fell on Judah and Israel!' But I will save you, and then those foreigners will say to one another, 'May you receive the same blessings that came to Judah and Israel!' So have courage and don't be afraid."

14 The LORD Almighty says, "When your ancestors made me angry, I planned disaster for them and did not change my mind, but carried out my plans. 15 But now I am planning to bless the people of Jerusalem and Judah. So don't be afraid. 16 These are the things you should do: Speak the truth to one another. In the courts give real justice — the kind that brings peace. 17 Do not plan ways of harming one another. Do not give false testimony under oath. I hate lying, injustice, and violence."

18 The LORD Almighty gave this message to Zechariah: 19 "The fasts held in the fourth, fifth, seventh, and tenth months will become festivals of joy and gladness for the people of Judah. You must love truth and peace."

20 The LORD Almighty says, "The time is coming when people from many *i* cit-

ies will come to Jerusalem. 21 Those from one city will say to those from another, 'We are going to worship the LORD Almighty and pray for his blessing. Come with us!' 22 Many *i* peoples and powerful nations will come to Jerusalem to worship the LORD Almighty and to pray for his blessing. 23 In those days ten foreigners will come to one Jew and say, 'We want to share in your destiny, because we have heard that God is with you.' "

Judgment on Neighboring Nations

9 This is the LORD's message:
He has decreed punishment for the land of Hadrach and for the city of Damascus. Not only the tribes of Israel but also the capital of Syria belong to the LORD. 2 Hamath, which borders on Hadrach, also belongs to him, and so do the cities of Tyre and Sidon, with all their skill. 3 Tyre has built fortifications for herself and has piled up so much silver and gold that it is as common as dirt! 4 But the Lord will take away everything she has. He will throw her wealth into the sea, and the city will be burned to the ground.

5 The city of Ashkelon will see this and be afraid. The city of Gaza will see it and suffer great pain. So will Ekron, and her hopes will be shattered. Gaza will lose her king, and Ashkelon will be left deserted. 6 People of mixed race will live in Ashdod. The LORD says, "I will humble all these proud Philistines. 7 They will no longer eat meat with blood in it, or other forbidden food. All the survivors will become part of my people and be like a clan in the tribe of Judah. Ekron will become part of my people, as the Jebusites *k* did. 8 I will guard my land and keep armies from passing through it. I will not allow tyrants to oppress my people any more. I have seen how my people have suffered."

The Future King

9 Rejoice, rejoice, people of Zion!
    Shout for joy, you people of
        Jerusalem!
    Look, your king is coming
        to you!
He comes triumphant and
    victorious,

---

i many; or great.   *k* JEBUSITES: *The original inhabitants of Jerusalem, who became David's subjects after he captured the city.*

but humble and riding on a
  donkey —
on a colt, the foal of a donkey.
10 The LORD says,
"I will remove the war chariots
    from Israel
  and take the horses from
    Jerusalem;
  the bows used in battle will be
    destroyed.
Your king will make peace among
    the nations;
  he will rule from sea to sea,
  from the Euphrates River to the
    ends of the earth."

The Restoration of God's People

11 The LORD says,
  "Because of my covenant with you
    that was sealed by the blood of
    sacrifices,
  I will set your people free —
    free from the waterless pit of
    exile.
12 Return, you exiles who now have
    hope;
  return to your place of safety.
Now I tell you that I will repay
    you twice over
  with blessing for all you have
    suffered.
13 I will use Judah like a
    soldier's bow
  and Israel like the arrows.
I will use the men of Zion like a
    sword,
  to fight the men of Greece."

14 The LORD will appear above his
    people;
  he will shoot his arrows like
    lightning.
The Sovereign LORD will sound
    the trumpet;
  he will march in the storms
    from the south.
15 The LORD Almighty will protect
    his people,
  and they will destroy their
    enemies.
They will shout in battle like
    drunk men
  and will shed the blood of their
    enemies;

it will flow like the blood of a
    sacrifice
  poured on the altar from a
    bowl.*l*

16 When that day comes, the LORD
    will save his people,
  as a shepherd saves his flock
    from danger.
They will shine in his land
  like the jewels of a crown.
17 How good and beautiful the land
    will be!
The young people will grow
    strong on its grain and wine.

The LORD Promises Deliverance

10 Ask the LORD for rain in the
spring of the year. It is the LORD
who sends rain clouds and showers,
making the fields green for everyone.
2 People consult idols and fortunetellers,
but the answers they get are lies and
nonsense. Some interpret dreams, but
only mislead you; the comfort they give
is useless. So the people wander about
like lost sheep. They are in trouble because
they have no leader.

3 The LORD says, "I am angry with
those foreigners who rule my people,
and I am going to punish them. The people
of Judah are mine, and I, the LORD
Almighty, will take care of them. They
will be my powerful war-horses. 4 From
among them will come rulers, leaders,
and commanders to govern my people.*m*
5 The people of Judah will be victorious
like soldiers who trample their enemies
in the mud of the streets. They will fight
because the LORD is with them, and they
will defeat even the enemy cavalry.

6 "I will make the people of Judah
    strong;
  I will rescue the people of Israel.
I will have compassion on them
  and bring them all back home.
They will be as though I had never
    rejected them.
I am the LORD their God; I will
  answer their prayers.
7 The people of Israel will be strong
    like soldiers,
  happy like those who have been
    drinking wine.

l Verse 15 in Hebrew is unclear.   *m* From among ... people; or All oppressors — rulers, leaders,
and commanders — will depart together from Judah.

Their descendants will remember
this victory
and be glad because of what the
LORD has done.

8"I will call my people
and gather them together.
I will rescue them
and make them as numerous as
they used to be.
9Though I have scattered them
among the nations,
yet in far-off places they will
remember me.
They and their children will
survive
and return home together.
10From Egypt and Assyria I will
bring them home
and settle them in their own
country.
I will settle them in Gilead and
Lebanon also;
the whole land will be filled
with people.
11When they pass through their sea
of trouble,
I, the LORD, will strike the waves,
and the depths of the Nile will
go dry.
Proud Assyria will be humbled,
and mighty Egypt will lose her
power.
12I will make my people strong;
they will worship and obey me."
The LORD has spoken.

The Fall of the Tyrants

11 Open your doors, Lebanon,
so that fire can burn down
your cedar trees!n
2Weep and wail, cypress trees—
the cedars have fallen;
those glorious trees have been
destroyed!
Weep and wail, oaks of Bashan—
the dense forest has been cut
down!
3The rulers cry out in grief;
their glory is gone!
Listen to the roaring of the lions;
their forest home along the
Jordan is destroyed!

The Two Shepherds

4The LORD my God said to me, "Act the part of the shepherdo of a flock of sheep that are going to be butchered. 5Their owners kill them and go unpunished. They sell the meat and say, 'Praise the LORD! We are rich!' Even their own shepherds have no pity on them."

(6 The LORD said, "I will no longer pity anyone on earth. I myself will put all the people in the power of their rulers. These rulers will devastate the earth, and I will not save it from their power.")

7Those who bought and sold the sheep hired me, and I became the shepherd of the sheep that were going to be butchered. I took two sticks: one I called "Favor" and the other "Unity." And I took care of the flock. 8I lost patience with three other shepherds, who hated me, and I got rid of them all in a single month. 9Then I said to the flock, "I will not be your shepherd any longer. Let those die who are to die. Let those be destroyed who are to be destroyed. Those who are left will destroy one another." 10Then I took the stick called "Favor" and broke it, to cancel the covenant which the LORD had made with all the nations. 11So the covenant was canceled on that day. Those who bought and sold the sheep were watching me, and they knew that the LORD was speaking through what I did. 12I said to them, "If you are willing, give me my wages. But if not, keep them." So they paid me thirty pieces of silver as my wages.

13The LORD said to me, "Put them in the Temple treasury."p So I took the thirty pieces of silver—the magnificent sum they thought I was worth—and put them in the Temple treasury. 14Then I broke the second stick, the one called "Unity," and the unity of Judah and Israel was shattered.

15Then the LORD said to me, "Once again act the part of a shepherd, this time a worthless one. 16I have put a shepherd in charge of my flock, but he does not help the sheep that are threatened by destruction; nor does he look for the lost, or heal those that are hurt, or feed the healthy. Instead, he eats the meat of the fattest sheep and tears off

n CEDAR TREES: *Trees are used here as symbols of powerful nations or their kings.*
o SHEPHERD: *Shepherd is used here as a symbol of a king or leader, and sheep as symbols of his people or followers.*   p *Some ancient translations* Put them in the Temple treasury; *Hebrew* Give them to the potter.

their hoofs. 17That worthless shepherd is doomed! He has abandoned his flock. War will totally destroy his power. His arm will wither, and his right eye will go blind."

The Future Deliverance of Jerusalem

12 This is a message about Israel from the LORD, the LORD who spread out the skies, created the earth, and gave life to man. He says, 2"I will make Jerusalem like a cup of wine; the nations around her will drink and stagger like drunks. And when they besiege Jerusalem, the cities of the rest of Judah will also be besieged. 3But when that time comes, I will make Jerusalem like a heavy stone—any nation that tries to lift it will be hurt. All the nations of the world will join forces to attack her. 4At that time I will terrify all their horses and make all their riders go crazy. I will watch over the people of Judah, but I will make the horses of their enemies blind. 5Then the clans of Judah will say to themselves, 'The LORD God Almighty gives strength to his people who live in Jerusalem.'

6"At that time I will make the clans of Judah like a fire in a forest or in a field of ripe grain—they will destroy all the surrounding nations. The people of Jerusalem will remain safe in the city.

7"I, the LORD, will give victory to the armies of Judah first, so that the honor which the descendants of David and the people of Jerusalem will receive will be no greater than that of the rest of Judah. 8At that time the LORD will protect those who live in Jerusalem, and even the weakest among them will become as strong as David was. The descendants of David will lead them like the angel of the LORD, like God himself. 9At that time I will destroy every nation that tries to attack Jerusalem.

10"I will fill the descendants of David and the other people of Jerusalem with the spirit of mercy and the spirit of prayer. They will look at the one whom they stabbed to death, and they will mourn for him like those who mourn for an only child. They will mourn bitterly, like those who have lost their first-born son. 11At that time the mourning in Jeru-

salem will be as great as the mourning for Hadad Rimmon*q* in the plain of Megiddo. 12-14Each family in the land will mourn by itself: the family descended from David, the family descended from Nathan, the family descended from Levi, the family descended from Shimei, and all the other families. Each family will mourn by itself, and the men of each family will mourn separately from the women.

13 "When that time comes," says the LORD Almighty, "a fountain will be opened to purify the descendants of David and the people of Jerusalem from their sin and idolatry. 2At that time I will remove the names of the idols from the land, and no one will remember them any more. I will get rid of anyone who claims to be a prophet and will take away the desire to worship idols. 3Then if anyone still insists on prophesying, his own father and mother will tell him that he must be put to death, because he claimed to speak the LORD's word, but spoke lies instead. When he prophesies, his own father and mother will stab him to death. 4When that time comes, no prophet will be proud of his visions or act like a prophet or wear a prophet's coarse garment in order to deceive people. 5Instead, he will say, 'I am not a prophet. I am a farmer—I have farmed the land all my life.' 6Then if someone asks him, 'What are those wounds on your chest?' he will answer, 'I got them at a friend's house.' "

The Command to Kill God's Shepherd

7The LORD Almighty says, "Wake up, sword, and attack the shepherd*r* who works for me! Kill him, and the sheep will be scattered. I will attack my people 8and throughout the land two-thirds of the people will die. 9And I will test the third that survives and will purify them as silver is purified by fire. I will test them as gold is tested. Then they will pray to me, and I will answer them. I will tell them that they are my people, and they will confess that I am their God."

q HADAD RIMMON: *Probably a name for Baal, the god of vegetation in Canaan and Syria. When the vegetation died each year, the worshipers thought that the god had died, and they mourned his death.*   *r* SHEPHERD: *See 11.4.*

Jerusalem and the Nations

14 The day when the LORD will sit in judgment is near. Then Jerusalem will be looted, and the loot will be divided up before your eyes. ²The LORD will bring all the nations together to make war on Jerusalem. The city will be taken, the houses looted, and the women raped. Half of the people will go into exile, but the rest of them will not be taken away from the city. ³Then the LORD will go out and fight against those nations, as he has fought in times past. ⁴At that time he will stand on the Mount of Olives, to the east of Jerusalem. Then the Mount of Olives will be split in two from east to west by a large valley. Half of the mountain will move northward, and half of it southward. ⁵You will escape through this valley that divides the mountain in two.ˢ You will flee as your ancestors did when the earthquake struck in the time of King Uzziah of Judah. The LORD my God will come, bringing all the angels with him.

⁶When that time comes, there will no longer be cold or frost,ᵗ ⁷nor any darkness. There will always be daylight, even at nighttime. When this will happen is known only to the LORD.

⁸When that day comes, fresh water will flow from Jerusalem, half of it to the Dead Sea and the other half to the Mediterranean. It will flow all year long, in the dry season as well as the wet. ⁹Then the LORD will be king over all the earth; everyone will worship him as God and know him by the same name.

¹⁰The whole region, from Geba in the north to Rimmon in the south, will be made level. Jerusalem will tower above the land around it; the city will reach from the Benjamin Gate to the Corner Gate, where there had been an earlier gate, and from the Tower of Hananel to the royal wine presses. ¹¹The people will live there in safety, no longer threatened by destruction.

¹²The LORD will bring a terrible disease on all the nations that make war on Jerusalem. Their flesh will rot away while they are still alive; their eyes and their tongues will rot away.

¹³At that time the LORD will make them so confused and afraid that everyone will seize the man next to him and attack him. ¹⁴The men of Judah will fight to defend Jerusalem. They will take as loot the wealth of all the nations—gold, silver, and clothing in great abundance.

¹⁵A terrible disease will also fall on the horses, the mules, the camels, and the donkeys—on all the animals in the camps of the enemy.

¹⁶Then all of the survivors from the nations that have attacked Jerusalem will go there each year to worship the LORD Almighty as king and to celebrate the Festival of Shelters. ¹⁷If any nation refuses to go and worship the LORD Almighty as king, then rain will not fall on their land. ¹⁸If the Egyptians refuse to celebrate the Festival of Shelters, then they will be struck by the same disease that the LORD will send on every nation that refuses to go. ¹⁹This will be the punishment that will fall on Egypt and on all the other nations if they do not celebrate the Festival of Shelters.

²⁰At that time even the harness bells of the horses will be inscribed with the words "Dedicated to the LORD." The cooking pots in the Temple will be as sacred as the bowls before the altar. ²¹Every cooking pot in Jerusalem and in all Judah will be set apart for use in the worship of the LORD Almighty. The people who offer sacrifices will use them for boiling the meat of the sacrifices. When that time comes, there will no longer be any merchant in the Temple of the LORD Almighty.

ˢ *Probable text* You will escape ... in two; *Hebrew unclear.*   ᵗ *Probable text* cold or frost; *Hebrew unclear.*

The Book of
MALACHI

Introduction

The Book of Malachi *comes from some time in the fifth century B.C. after the Temple in Jerusalem was rebuilt. The prophet's main concern is to call priests and people to renew their faithfulness to their covenant with God. It is clear that there is laxity and corruption in the life and worship of God's people. Priests and people are cheating God by not giving him the offerings that are rightly due him, and by not living according to his teaching. But the Lord will come to judge and purify his people, sending ahead of him his messenger to prepare the way and to proclaim his covenant.*

Outline of Contents

---

1 This is the message that the LORD gave Malachi to tell the people of Israel.

The LORD's Love for Israel

2 The LORD says to his people, "I have always loved you."

But they reply, "How have you shown your love for us?"

The LORD answers, "Esau and Jacob were brothers, but I have loved Jacob and his descendants, 3 and have hated Esau and his descendants. I have devastated Esau's hill country and abandoned the land to jackals."

4 If Esau's descendants, the Edomites, say, "Our towns have been destroyed, but we will rebuild them," then the LORD will reply, "Let them rebuild — I will tear them down again. People will call them 'The evil country' and 'The nation with whom the LORD is angry forever.'"

5 The people of Israel are going to see this with their own eyes, and they will say, "The LORD is mighty even outside the land of Israel!"

The LORD Reprimands the Priests

6 The LORD Almighty says to the priests, "Children honor their parents, and servants honor their masters. I am your father — why don't you honor me? I am your master — why don't you respect me? You despise me, and yet you ask, 'How have we despised you?' 7 This is how — by offering worthless food on my altar. Then you ask, 'How have we failed to respect you?' I will tell you — by showing contempt for my altar. 8 When you bring a blind or sick or lame animal to sacrifice to me, do you think there's nothing wrong with that? Try giving an animal like that to the governor! Would he be pleased with you or grant you any favors?"

9 Now, you priests, try asking God to be good to us. He will not answer your prayer, and it will be your fault. 10 The LORD Almighty says, "I wish one of you would close the Temple doors so as to prevent you from lighting useless fires on my altar. I am not pleased with you; I will not accept the offerings you bring me. 11 People from one end of the world to the other honor me. Everywhere they burn incense to me and offer acceptable sacrifices. All of them honor me! 12 But you dishonor me when you say that my altar is worthless and when you offer on it food that you despise. 13 You say, 'How tired we are of all this!' and you turn up your nose at me. As your offering to me you bring a stolen animal or one that is lame or sick. Do you think I will accept that from you? 14 A curse on the cheater who sacrifices a worthless animal to me, when he has in his flock a good animal that he promised to give me! For I am a great king, and people of all nations fear me."

2 The LORD Almighty says to the priests, "This command is for you: 2 You must honor me by what you do. If you will not listen to what I say, then I will bring a curse on you. I will put a curse on the things you receive for your

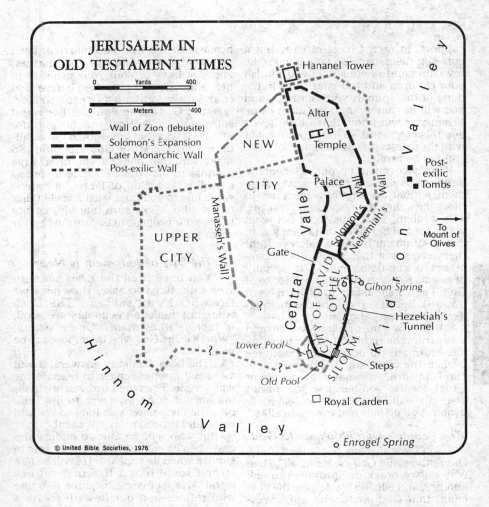

JERUSALEM IN
OLD TEMPLE STATES

(Map: Jerusalem in Old Testament Times)

Wall of Zion (Jebusite)
Solomon's Expansion
Later Monarchic Wall
Post-exilic Wall

Hananel Tower

NEW

CITY

Altar
Temple

Palace

Manasseh's Wall?

UPPER

CITY

Gate

Central Valley

Solomon's Wall

Nehemiah's Wall

CITY OF DAVID

OPHEL

Gihon Spring

Hezekiah's Tunnel

Lower Pool

SILOAM

Steps

Old Pool

Royal Garden

Hinnom

Valley

Enrogel Spring

Kidron Valley

Post-exilic Tombs

To Mount of Olives

© United Bible Societies, 1976

support. In fact, I have already put a curse on them, because you do not take my command seriously. ³I will punish your children and rub your faces in the dung of the animals you sacrifice—and you will be taken out to the dung heap. ⁴Then you will know that I have given you this command, so that my covenant with the priests, the descendants of Levi, will not be broken.

⁵"In my covenant I promised them life and well-being, and this is what I gave them, so that they might respect me. In those days they did respect and fear me. ⁶They taught what was right, not what was wrong. They lived in harmony with me; they not only did what was right themselves, but they also helped many others to stop doing evil. ⁷It is the duty of priests to teach the true knowledge of God. People should go to them to learn my will, because they are the messengers of the LORD Almighty.

⁸"But now you priests have turned away from the right path. Your teaching has led many to do wrong. You have broken the covenant I made with you. ⁹So I, in turn, will make the people of Israel despise you because you do not obey my will, and when you teach my people, you do not treat everyone alike."

The People's Unfaithfulness to God

¹⁰Don't we all have the same father? Didn't the same God create us all? Then why do we break our promises to one another, and why do we despise the covenant that God made with our ancestors? ¹¹The people of Judah have broken their promise to God and done a horrible thing in Jerusalem and all over the country. They have defiled the Temple which the LORD loves. Men have married women who worship foreign gods. ¹²May the LORD remove from the community of Israel those who did this, and never again let them participate in the offerings our nation brings to the LORD Almighty.ᵃ

¹³This is another thing you do. You drown the LORD's altar with tears, weeping and wailing because he no longer accepts the offerings you bring him. ¹⁴You ask why he no longer accepts them. It is because he knows you have broken your

promise to the wife you married when you were young. She was your partner, and you have broken your promise to her, although you promised before God that you would be faithful to her. ¹⁵Didn't God make you one body and spirit with her?ᵇ What was his purpose in this? It was that you should have children who are truly God's people. So make sure that none of you breaks his promise to his wife. ¹⁶"I hate divorce," says the LORD God of Israel. "I hate it when one of you does such a cruel thing to his wife. Make sure that you do not break your promise to be faithful to your wife."

The Day of Judgment Is Near

¹⁷You have tired the LORD out with your talk. But you ask, "How have we tired him?" By saying, "The LORD Almighty thinks all evildoers are good; in fact he likes them." Or by asking, "Where is the God who is supposed to be just?"

3 The LORD Almighty answers, "I will send my messenger to prepare the way for me. Then the Lord you are looking for will suddenly come to his Temple. The messenger you long to see will come and proclaim my covenant."

²But who will be able to endure the day when he comes? Who will be able to survive when he appears? He will be like strong soap, like a fire that refines metal. ³He will come to judge like one who refines and purifies silver. As a metalworker refines silver and gold, so the LORD's messenger will purify the priests, so that they will bring to the LORD the right kind of offerings. ⁴Then the offerings which the people of Judah and Jerusalem bring to the LORD will be pleasing to him, as they used to be in the past.

⁵The LORD Almighty says, "I will appear among you to judge, and I will testify at once against those who practice magic, against adulterers, against those who give false testimony, those who cheat employees out of their wages, and those who take advantage of widows, orphans, and foreigners—against all who do not respect me.

ᵃ One ancient translation May ... Almighty; Hebrew unclear.   ᵇ Probable text Didn't God ... her; Hebrew unclear.

The Payment of Tithes

6 "I am the LORD, and I do not change. And so you, the descendants of Jacob, are not yet completely lost. 7 You, like your ancestors before you, have turned away from my laws and have not kept them. Turn back to me, and I will turn to you. But you ask, 'What must we do to turn back to you?' 8 I ask you, is it right for a person to cheat God? Of course not, yet you are cheating me. 'How?' you ask. In the matter of tithes and offerings. 9 A curse is on all of you because the whole nation is cheating me. 10 Bring the full amount of your tithes to the Temple, so that there will be plenty of food there. Put me to the test and you will see that I will open the windows of heaven and pour out on you in abundance all kinds of good things. 11 I will not let insects destroy your crops, and your grapevines will be loaded with grapes. 12 Then the people of all nations will call you happy, because your land will be a good place to live.

God's Promise of Mercy

13 "You have said terrible things about me," says the LORD. "But you ask, 'What have we said about you?' 14 You have said, 'It's useless to serve God. What's the use of doing what he says or of trying to show the LORD Almighty that we are sorry for what we have done? 15 As we see it, proud people are the ones who are happy. Evil people not only prosper, but they test God's patience with their evil deeds and get away with it.' "

16 Then the people who feared the LORD spoke to one another, and the LORD listened and heard what they said. In his presence, there was written down in a book a record of those who feared the LORD and respected him. 17 "They will be my people," says the LORD Almighty. "On the day when I act, they will be my very own. I will be merciful to them as parents are merciful to the children who serve them. 18 Once again my people will see the difference between what happens to the righteous and to the wicked, to the person who serves me and the one who does not."

The Day of the LORD Is Coming

4 The LORD Almighty says, "The day is coming when all proud and evil people will burn like straw. On that day they will burn up, and there will be nothing left of them. 2 But for you who obey me, my saving power will rise on you like the sun and bring healing like the sun's rays. You will be as free and happy as calves let out of a stall. 3 On the day when I act, you will overcome the wicked, and they will be like dust under your feet.

4 "Remember the teachings of my servant Moses, the laws and commands which I gave him at Mount Sinai for all the people of Israel to obey.

5 "But before the great and terrible day of the LORD comes, I will send you the prophet Elijah. 6 He will bring fathers and children together again; otherwise I would have to come and destroy your country."

MALACHI

NEW TESTAMENT

THE GOSPELS

The word *gospel* is from the Anglo-Saxon *godspell*, meaning good news. Ultimately the word comes from the Greek *euangelion*, also meaning good news. Gospel can mean the good news preached by Jesus, or the good news preached about Jesus. These two meanings are the ones found in the Bible. Gospel can also mean the books that contain the memories of Jesus, the gospels we find in our New Testaments.

Gospels are not biographies. They are accounts of the life and teaching of Jesus, but they are also reflections on who Jesus is and what he means for the world. Each of the gospel writers wanted to say something specific about the meaning of Jesus and carefully selected materials and arranged them to carry his own particular emphasis. The gospels contain a great deal of historical information, but that information is always interpreted by the writers to show Jesus as Son of God and Savior of the world.

There are four gospels. Matthew, Mark, and Luke are called Synoptic Gospels, because they follow a common synopsis, or outline. These three gospels can be studied in a parallel manner because they follow the same basic outline, use many of the same words, and are in the same order. The Gospel of John is entirely different from the other three. It does not follow the same outline, has a three-year ministry for Jesus instead of one year, and contains long reflections about the meaning of Jesus instead of short sayings and parables.

Matthew begins by placing Jesus within the whole story of salvation. Jesus is son of Abraham and son of David, the fulfillment of all the promises to God's people. The teaching material in Matthew is organized into five great sections, the best-known of which is the Sermon on the Mount. Many have said Matthew saw Jesus as a second Moses, giving a new Torah to God's people.

Mark is probably the oldest of the gospels. Tradition says it was written in Rome by John Mark and contains the memories of Peter. The crucifixion and resurrection are the key to understanding who Jesus is—nearly one-half of the gospel deals with these events. Mark does not have any birth narratives, but begins with the preaching of John the Baptist.

Luke's special interest is in the oppressed and outcasts of society, especially women and the poor. His gospel begins with the births of John the Baptist and of Jesus. It has the only story of Jesus between his birth and ministry, the episode in the temple at the age of twelve. Some of the best-loved parables—the Good Samaritan, the Lost Son, and the Rich Man and Lazarus—are found only in Luke's gospel.

John has less narrative and no parables, but a series of long reflections on Jesus as divine Son of God. The gospel begins with a great hymn on the Word who was always God and became flesh for the salvation of the world. That Word is Jesus. John also contains a series of miracles as signs pointing to Jesus, and the "I AM" sayings, which express what Jesus means in a series of striking metaphors.

The Gospel according to
MATTHEW

Introduction

The Gospel according to Matthew *tells the good news that Jesus is the promised Savior, the one through whom God fulfilled the promises he made to his people in the Old Testament. This good news is not only for the Jewish people, among whom Jesus was born and lived, but for the whole world.*

Matthew is carefully arranged. It begins with the birth of Jesus, describes his baptism and temptation, and then takes up his ministry of preaching, teaching, and healing in Galilee. After this the Gospel records Jesus' journey from Galilee to Jerusalem and the events of Jesus' last week, culminating in his crucifixion and resurrection.

This Gospel presents Jesus as the great Teacher, who has the authority to interpret the Law of God, and who teaches about the Kingdom of God. Much of his teaching is gathered by subject matter into five collections: (1) the Sermon on the Mount, which concerns the character, duties, privileges, and destiny of the citizens of the Kingdom of heaven (chapters 5–7); (2) instructions to the twelve disciples for their mission (chapter 10); (3) parables about the Kingdom of heaven (chapter 13); (4) teaching on the meaning of discipleship (chapter 18); and (5) teaching about the end of the present age and the coming of the Kingdom of God (chapters 24–25).

Outline of Contents

The Ancestors of Jesus Christ
(Luke 3.23-38)

1 This is the list of the ancestors of Jesus Christ, a descendant of David, who was a descendant of Abraham.

2-6a From Abraham to King David, the following ancestors are listed: Abraham, Isaac, Jacob, Judah and his brothers; then Perez and Zerah (their mother was Tamar), Hezron, Ram, Amminadab, Nahshon, Salmon, Boaz (his mother was Rahab), Obed (his mother was Ruth), Jesse, and King David.

6b-11 From David to the time when the people of Israel were taken into exile in Babylon, the following ancestors are listed: David, Solomon (his mother was the woman who had been Uriah's wife), Rehoboam, Abijah, Asa, Jehoshaphat, Jehoram, Uzziah, Jotham, Ahaz, Hezekiah, Manasseh, Amon, Josiah, and Jehoiachin and his brothers.

12-16 From the time after the exile in Babylon to the birth of Jesus, the following ancestors are listed: Jehoiachin, Shealtiel, Zerubbabel, Abiud, Eliakim, Azor, Zadok, Achim, Eliud, Eleazar, Matthan, Jacob, and Joseph, who married Mary, the mother of Jesus, who was called the Messiah.

17 So then, there were fourteen generations from Abraham to David, and fourteen from David to the exile in Babylon, and fourteen from then to the birth of the Messiah.

The Birth of Jesus Christ
(Luke 2.1-7)

18 This was how the birth of Jesus Christ took place. His mother Mary was engaged to Joseph, but before they were married, she found out that she was going to have a baby by the Holy Spirit. 19 Joseph was a man who always did what was right, but he did not want to disgrace Mary publicly; so he made plans to break the engagement privately. 20 While he was thinking about this, an angel of the Lord appeared to him in a dream and said, "Joseph, descendant of David, do not be afraid to

take Mary to be your wife. For it is by the Holy Spirit that she has conceived. 21 She will have a son, and you will name him Jesus — because he will save his people from their sins."

22 Now all this happened in order to make come true what the Lord had said through the prophet, 23 "A virgin will become pregnant and have a son, and he will be called Immanuel" (which means, "God is with us").

24 So when Joseph woke up, he married Mary, as the angel of the Lord had told him to. 25 But he had no sexual relations with her before she gave birth to her son. And Joseph named him Jesus.

Visitors from the East

2 Jesus was born in the town of Bethlehem in Judea, during the time when Herod was king. Soon afterward, some men who studied the stars came from the East to Jerusalem 2 and asked, "Where is the baby born to be the king of the Jews? We saw his star when it came up in the east, and we have come to worship him."

3 When King Herod heard about this, he was very upset, and so was everyone else in Jerusalem. 4 He called together all the chief priests and the teachers of the Law and asked them, "Where will the Messiah be born?"

5 "In the town of Bethlehem in Judea," they answered. "For this is what the prophet wrote:
6 'Bethlehem in the land of Judah,
    you are by no means the least of
      the leading cities of Judah;
for from you will come a leader
    who will guide my people
      Israel.' "

7 So Herod called the visitors from the East to a secret meeting and found out from them the exact time the star had appeared. 8 Then he sent them to Bethlehem with these instructions: "Go and make a careful search for the child; and when you find him, let me know, so that I too may go and worship him."

9-10 And so they left, and on their way they saw the same star they had seen in the East. When they saw it, how happy they were, what joy was theirs! It went ahead of them until it stopped over the place where the child was. 11 They went into the house, and when they saw the child with his mother Mary, they knelt down and worshiped him. They brought out their gifts of gold, frankincense, and myrrh, and presented them to him.

12 Then they returned to their country by another road, since God had warned them in a dream not to go back to Herod.

The Escape to Egypt

13 After they had left, an angel of the Lord appeared in a dream to Joseph and said, "Herod will be looking for the child in order to kill him. So get up, take the child and his mother and escape to Egypt, and stay there until I tell you to leave."

14 Joseph got up, took the child and his mother, and left during the night for Egypt, 15 where he stayed until Herod died. This was done to make come true what the Lord had said through the prophet, "I called my Son out of Egypt."

The Killing of the Children

16 When Herod realized that the visitors from the East had tricked him, he was furious. He gave orders to kill all the boys in Bethlehem and its neighborhood who were two years old and younger — this was done in accordance with what he had learned from the visitors about the time when the star had appeared.

17 In this way what the prophet Jeremiah had said came true:
18 "A sound is heard in Ramah,
    the sound of bitter weeping.
Rachel is crying for her children;
    she refuses to be comforted,
    for they are dead."

The Return from Egypt

19 After Herod died, an angel of the Lord appeared in a dream to Joseph in Egypt 20 and said, "Get up, take the child and his mother, and go back to the land of Israel, because those who tried to kill the child are dead." 21 So Joseph got up, took the child and his mother, and went back to Israel.

22 But when Joseph heard that Archelaus had succeeded his father Herod as king of Judea, he was afraid to go there. He was given more instructions in a dream, so he went to the province of Galilee 23 and made his home in a town named Nazareth. And so what the prophets had said came true: "He will be called a Nazarene."

THE CITY OF NAZARETH

A town of lower Galilee where Jesus spent his boyhood years (Mt 2.23), Nazareth is located about thirty miles from the Mediterranean Sea. Its mild climate and sheltered location in the hills of Galilee made Nazareth an ideal place to live.

Nazareth is not mentioned in the Old Testament, although artifacts discovered on the site indicate that Nazareth was a settled community at least 1,500 years before the New Testament era. In Jesus' time, the town apparently had a bad reputation in morals and religion. This may have prompted Nathanael, when he first learned of Jesus of Nazareth, to ask, "Can anything good come from Nazareth?" (Jn 1.46).

The angel appeared to Mary at Nazareth and informed her of the coming birth of Jesus (Lk 1.26-38). After their sojourn in Egypt (Mt 2.19-22), Joseph and Mary brought Jesus back to Nazareth where they had lived before his birth (Mt 2.23). Here Jesus spent the greater part of his life (Lk 3.23). Apparently he was well received as a young man (Lk 2.42; 4.16), but his townspeople later rejected him (Mk 6.1-6).

Because of his close association with the city, he became known as Jesus of Nazareth (Jn 1.45). There was also prophetic significance to his being known as a Nazarene—"what the prophets had said came true: 'He will be called a Nazarene' " (Mt 2.23).

Modern Nazareth, known as En-Nasira, is a city of about 30,000 people. Its location on the site of old Nazareth makes it impossible to conduct extensive archaeological excavations. The Church of the Annunciation, the major tourist attraction, has a special significance for all Bible students. This church contains a cave where, according to legend, the angel Gabriel appeared to Mary (Lk 1.26-31). Rebuilding and excavation work on this site has turned up evidence that a Christian church existed at this location as early as the fourth century A.D.

The Preaching of John the Baptist
(Mark 1.1-8; Luke 3.1-18; John 1.19-28)

3 At that time John the Baptist came to the desert of Judea and started preaching. 2 "Turn away from your sins," he said, "because the Kingdom of heaven is near!" 3 John was the man the prophet Isaiah was talking about when he said,

"Someone is shouting in the
　　desert,
'Prepare a road for the Lord;
make a straight path for him to
　　travel!' "

4 John's clothes were made of camel's hair; he wore a leather belt around his waist, and his food was locusts and wild honey. 5 People came to him from Jerusalem, from the whole province of Judea, and from all over the country near the Jordan River. 6 They confessed their sins, and he baptized them in the Jordan.

7 When John saw many Pharisees and Sadducees coming to him to be baptized, he said to them, "You snakes — who told you that you could escape from the punishment God is about to send? 8 Do those things that will show that you have turned from your sins. 9 And don't think you can escape punishment by saying that Abraham is your ancestor. I tell you that God can take these rocks and make descendants for Abraham! 10 The ax is ready to cut down the trees at the roots; every tree that does not bear good fruit will be cut down and thrown in the fire. 11 I baptize you with water to show that you have repented, but the one who will come after me will baptize you with the Holy Spirit and fire. He is much greater than I am; and I am not good enough even to carry his sandals. 12 He has his winnowing shovel with him to thresh out all the grain. He will gather his wheat into his barn, but he will burn the chaff in a fire that never goes out."

The Baptism of Jesus
(Mark 1.9-11; Luke 3.21, 22)

13 At that time Jesus arrived from Galilee and came to John at the Jordan to be baptized by him. 14 But John tried to make him change his mind. "I ought to be baptized by you," John said, "and yet you have come to me!"

15 But Jesus answered him, "Let it be so for now. For in this way we shall do all that God requires." So John agreed.

16 As soon as Jesus was baptized, he came up out of the water. Then heaven was opened to him, and he saw the Spirit of God coming down like a dove and lighting on him. 17 Then a voice said from heaven, "This is my own dear Son, with whom I am pleased."

The Temptation of Jesus
(Mark 1.12, 13; Luke 4.1-13)

4 Then the Spirit led Jesus into the desert to be tempted by the Devil. 2 After spending forty days and nights without food, Jesus was hungry. 3 Then the Devil came to him and said, "If you are God's Son, order these stones to turn into bread."

4 But Jesus answered, "The scripture says, 'Human beings cannot live on bread alone, but need every word that God speaks.' "

5 Then the Devil took Jesus to Jerusalem, the Holy City, set him on the highest point of the Temple, 6 and said to him, "If you are God's Son, throw yourself down, for the scripture says,

'God will give orders to his angels
　　about you;
they will hold you up with their
　　hands,
so that not even your feet will be
　　hurt on the stones.' "

7 Jesus answered, "But the scripture also says, 'Do not put the Lord your God to the test.' "

8 Then the Devil took Jesus to a very high mountain and showed him all the kingdoms of the world in all their greatness. 9 "All this I will give you," the Devil said, "if you kneel down and worship me."

10 Then Jesus answered, "Go away, Satan! The scripture says, 'Worship the Lord your God and serve only him!' "

11 Then the Devil left Jesus; and angels came and helped him.

Jesus Begins His Work in Galilee
(Mark 1.14, 15; Luke 4.14, 15)

12 When Jesus heard that John had been put in prison, he went away to Galilee. 13 He did not stay in Nazareth, but went to live in Capernaum, a town by Lake Galilee, in the territory of Zebulun and Naphtali. 14 This was done to make

come true what the prophet Isaiah had said,

15 "Land of Zebulun and land of Naphtali,
  on the road to the sea, on the other side of the Jordan,
  Galilee, land of the Gentiles!
16 The people who live in darkness will see a great light.
  On those who live in the dark land of death
  the light will shine."

17 From that time Jesus began to preach his message: "Turn away from your sins, because the Kingdom of heaven is near!"

Jesus Calls Four Fishermen
(Mark 1.16-20; Luke 5.1-11)

18 As Jesus walked along the shore of Lake Galilee, he saw two brothers who were fishermen, Simon (called Peter) and his brother Andrew, catching fish in the lake with a net. 19 Jesus said to them, "Come with me, and I will teach you to catch people." 20 At once they left their nets and went with him.

21 He went on and saw two other brothers, James and John, the sons of Zebedee. They were in their boat with their father Zebedee, getting their nets ready. Jesus called them, 22 and at once they left the boat and their father, and went with him.

Jesus Teaches, Preaches, and Heals
(Luke 6.17-19)

23 Jesus went all over Galilee, teaching in the synagogues, preaching the Good News about the Kingdom, and healing people who had all kinds of disease and sickness. 24 The news about him spread through the whole country of Syria, so that people brought to him all those who were sick, suffering from all kinds of diseases and disorders: people with demons, and epileptics, and paralytics — and Jesus healed them all. 25 Large crowds followed him from Galilee and the Ten Towns, from Jerusalem, Judea, and the land on the other side of the Jordan.

The Sermon on the Mount

5 Jesus saw the crowds and went up a hill, where he sat down. His disciples gathered around him, 2 and he began to teach them:

True Happiness
(Luke 6.20-23)

3 "Happy are those who know they are spiritually poor;
  the Kingdom of heaven belongs to them!
4 "Happy are those who mourn;
  God will comfort them!
5 "Happy are those who are humble;
  they will receive what God has promised!
6 "Happy are those whose greatest desire is to do what God requires;
  God will satisfy them fully!
7 "Happy are those who are merciful to others;
  God will be merciful to them!
8 "Happy are the pure in heart;
  they will see God!
9 "Happy are those who work for peace;
  God will call them his children!
10 "Happy are those who are persecuted because they do what God requires;
  the Kingdom of heaven belongs to them!

11 "Happy are you when people insult you and persecute you and tell all kinds of evil lies against you because you are my followers. 12 Be happy and glad, for a great reward is kept for you in heaven. This is how the prophets who lived before you were persecuted.

Salt and Light
(Mark 9.50; Luke 14.34, 35)

13 "You are like salt for the whole human race. But if salt loses its saltiness, there is no way to make it salty again. It has become worthless, so it is thrown out and people trample on it.

14 "You are like light for the whole world. A city built on a hill cannot be hid. 15 No one lights a lamp and puts it under a bowl; instead it is put on the lampstand, where it gives light for everyone in the house. 16 In the same way your light must shine before people, so that they will see the good things you do and praise your Father in heaven.

Teaching about the Law

17 "Do not think that I have come to do away with the Law of Moses and the teachings of the prophets. I have not come to do away with them, but to make

THE SERMON ON THE MOUNT

Jesus' long discourse known as the Sermon on the Mount (Mt 5—7) is so named because he taught his disciples and the crowds that followed him from a mountainside at the beginning of his public ministry (Mt 5.1). The traditional site of the Sermon is marked today by a beautiful little church, the Chapel on the Mount of Beatitudes, one of the major stopping points for tourists who visit the Holy Land.

The ten major sections of the Sermon on the Mount are as follows:

1. True happiness (5.3–12): The blessed rewards of living as citizens of Christ's kingdom.

2. The lessons of salt and light (5.13–16): The effects of Christian living on the world.

3. True righteousness (5.17–48): The deeper meaning of the law of God.

4. Practice without hypocrisy (6.1–18): The right motives for giving, praying, and fasting.

5. The Christian's concerns (6.19–34): Serving God with singleness of purpose and putting the concerns of his kingdom first are actions that free us from anxiety over lesser things.

6. Warning against judgment (7.1–6): The dangers of judging others harshly and carelessly.

7. Invitation to prayer (7.7–12): The blessings and privileges of prayer.

8. The two ways (7.13, 14): Choose the narrow way, not the broad way that leads to destruction.

9. A tree and its fruit (7.15–20): "Be on your guard for false prophets."

10. The importance of deeds (7.21–29): To obey God is far better than talking about your obedience.

their teachings come true. 18 Remember that as long as heaven and earth last, not the least point nor the smallest detail of the Law will be done away with—not until the end of all things.[a] 19 So then, whoever disobeys even the least important of the commandments and teaches others to do the same, will be least in the Kingdom of heaven. On the other hand, whoever obeys the Law and teaches others to do the same, will be great in the Kingdom of heaven. 20 I tell you, then, that you will be able to enter the Kingdom of heaven only if you are more faithful than the teachers of the Law and the Pharisees in doing what God requires.

Teaching about Anger

21 "You have heard that people were told in the past, 'Do not commit murder; anyone who does will be brought to trial.' 22 But now I tell you: if you are angry[b] with your brother you will be brought to trial, if you call your brother 'You good-for-nothing!' you will be brought before the Council, and if you call your brother a worthless fool you will be in danger of going to the fire of hell. 23 So if you are about to offer your gift to God at the altar and there you remember that your brother has something against you, 24 leave your gift there in front of the altar, go at once and make peace with your brother, and then come back and offer your gift to God.

25 "If someone brings a lawsuit against you and takes you to court, settle the dispute while there is time, before you get to court. Once you are there, you will be turned over to the judge, who will hand you over to the police, and you will be put in jail. 26 There you will stay, I tell you, until you pay the last penny of your fine.

Teaching about Adultery

27 "You have heard that it was said, 'Do not commit adultery.' 28 But now I tell you: anyone who looks at a woman and wants to possess her is guilty of committing adultery with her in his heart. 29 So if your right eye causes you to sin, take it out and throw it away! It is much better for you to lose a part of your body than to have your whole body

thrown into hell. 30 If your right hand causes you to sin, cut it off and throw it away! It is much better for you to lose one of your limbs than to have your whole body go off to hell.

Teaching about Divorce
(Matthew 19.9; Mark 10.11, 12; Luke 16.18)

31 "It was also said, 'Anyone who divorces his wife must give her a written notice of divorce.' 32 But now I tell you: if a man divorces his wife for any cause other than her unfaithfulness, then he is guilty of making her commit adultery if she marries again; and the man who marries her commits adultery also.

Teaching about Vows

33 "You have also heard that people were told in the past, 'Do not break your promise, but do what you have vowed to the Lord to do.' 34 But now I tell you: do not use any vow when you make a promise. Do not swear by heaven, for it is God's throne; 35 nor by earth, for it is the resting place for his feet; nor by Jerusalem, for it is the city of the great King. 36 Do not even swear by your head, because you cannot make a single hair white or black. 37 Just say 'Yes' or 'No'— anything else you say comes from the Evil One.

Teaching about Revenge
(Luke 6.29, 30)

38 "You have heard that it was said, 'An eye for an eye, and a tooth for a tooth.' 39 But now I tell you: do not take revenge on someone who wrongs you. If anyone slaps you on the right cheek, let him slap your left cheek too. 40 And if someone takes you to court to sue you for your shirt, let him have your coat as well. 41 And if one of the occupation troops forces you to carry his pack one mile, carry it two miles. 42 When someone asks you for something, give it to him; when someone wants to borrow something, lend it to him.

Love for Enemies
(Luke 6.27, 28, 32-36)

43 "You have heard that it was said, 'Love your friends, hate your enemies.' 44 But now I tell you: love your enemies and pray for those who persecute you,

---

[a] the end of all things; or all its teachings come true.   [b] if you are angry; some manuscripts have if without cause you are angry.

MATTHEW

⁴⁵so that you may become the children of your Father in heaven. For he makes his sun to shine on bad and good people alike, and gives rain to those who do good and to those who do evil. ⁴⁶Why should God reward you if you love only the people who love you? Even the tax collectors do that! ⁴⁷And if you speak only to your friends, have you done anything out of the ordinary? Even the pagans do that! ⁴⁸You must be perfect—just as your Father in heaven is perfect.

Teaching about Charity

6 "Make certain you do not perform your religious duties in public so that people will see what you do. If you do these things publicly, you will not have any reward from your Father in heaven.

²"So when you give something to a needy person, do not make a big show of it, as the hypocrites do in the houses of worship and on the streets. They do it so that people will praise them. I assure you, they have already been paid in full. ³But when you help a needy person, do it in such a way that even your closest friend will not know about it. ⁴Then it will be a private matter. And your Father, who sees what you do in private, will reward you.

Teaching about Prayer
(Luke 11.2-4)

⁵"When you pray, do not be like the hypocrites! They love to stand up and pray in the houses of worship and on the street corners, so that everyone will see them. I assure you, they have already been paid in full. ⁶But when you pray, go to your room, close the door, and pray to your Father, who is unseen. And your Father, who sees what you do in private, will reward you.

⁷"When you pray, do not use a lot of meaningless words, as the pagans do, who think that their gods will hear them because their prayers are long. ⁸Do not be like them. Your Father already knows what you need before you ask him. ⁹This, then, is how you should pray:

'Our Father in heaven:
    May your holy name be
        honored;
10   may your Kingdom come;
    may your will be done on earth
        as it is in heaven.
11   Give us today the food we
        need.c
12   Forgive us the wrongs we have
        done,
    as we forgive the wrongs that
        others have done to us.
13   Do not bring us to hard testing,
        but keep us safe from the
        Evil One.'d

¹⁴"If you forgive others the wrongs they have done to you, your Father in heaven will also forgive you. ¹⁵But if you do not forgive others, then your Father will not forgive the wrongs you have done.

Teaching about Fasting

¹⁶"And when you fast, do not put on a sad face as the hypocrites do. They neglect their appearance so that everyone will see that they are fasting. I assure you, they have already been paid in full. ¹⁷When you go without food, wash your face and comb your hair, ¹⁸so that others cannot know that you are fasting—only your Father, who is unseen, will know. And your Father, who sees what you do in private, will reward you.

Riches in Heaven
(Luke 12.33, 34)

¹⁹"Do not store up riches for yourselves here on earth, where moths and rust destroy, and robbers break in and steal. ²⁰Instead, store up riches for yourselves in heaven, where moths and rust cannot destroy, and robbers cannot break in and steal. ²¹For your heart will always be where your riches are.

The Light of the Body
(Luke 11.34-36)

²²"The eyes are like a lamp for the body. If your eyes are sound, your whole body will be full of light; ²³but if your eyes are no good, your body will be in darkness. So if the light in you is darkness, how terribly dark it will be!

c we need; *or* for today, *or* for tomorrow.   d *Some manuscripts add* For yours is the kingdom, and the power, and the glory forever. Amen.

God and Possessions
(Luke 16.13; 12.22-31)

24 "You cannot be a slave of two masters; you will hate one and love the other; you will be loyal to one and despise the other. You cannot serve both God and money.

25 "This is why I tell you: do not be worried about the food and drink you need in order to stay alive, or about clothes for your body. After all, isn't life worth more than food? And isn't the body worth more than clothes? 26 Look at the birds: they do not plant seeds, gather a harvest and put it in barns; yet your Father in heaven takes care of them! Aren't you worth much more than birds? 27 Can any of you live a bit longer[e] by worrying about it?

28 "And why worry about clothes? Look how the wild flowers grow: they do not work or make clothes for themselves. 29 But I tell you that not even King Solomon with all his wealth had clothes as beautiful as one of these flowers. 30 It is God who clothes the wild grass — grass that is here today and gone tomorrow, burned up in the oven. Won't he be all the more sure to clothe you? What little faith you have!

31 "So do not start worrying: 'Where will my food come from? or my drink? or my clothes?' 32 (These are the things the pagans are always concerned about.) Your Father in heaven knows that you need all these things. 33 Instead, be concerned above everything else with the Kingdom of God and with what he requires of you, and he will provide you with all these other things. 34 So do not worry about tomorrow; it will have enough worries of its own. There is no need to add to the troubles each day brings.

Judging Others
(Luke 6.37, 38, 41, 42)

7 "Do not judge others, so that God will not judge you, 2 for God will judge you in the same way you judge others, and he will apply to you the same rules you apply to others. 3 Why, then, do you look at the speck in your brother's eye and pay no attention to the log in your own eye? 4 How dare you say to your brother, 'Please, let me take

that speck out of your eye,' when you have a log in your own eye? 5 You hypocrite! First take the log out of your own eye, and then you will be able to see clearly to take the speck out of your brother's eye.

6 "Do not give what is holy to dogs — they will only turn and attack you. Do not throw your pearls in front of pigs — they will only trample them underfoot.

Ask, Seek, Knock
(Luke 11.9-13)

7 "Ask, and you will receive; seek, and you will find; knock, and the door will be opened to you. 8 For everyone who asks will receive, and anyone who seeks will find, and the door will be opened to those who knock. 9 Would any of you who are fathers give your son a stone when he asks for bread? 10 Or would you give him a snake when he asks for a fish? 11 As bad as you are, you know how to give good things to your children. How much more, then, will your Father in heaven give good things to those who ask him!

12 "Do for others what you want them to do for you: this is the meaning of the Law of Moses and of the teachings of the prophets.

The Narrow Gate
(Luke 13.24)

13 "Go in through the narrow gate, because the gate to hell is wide and the road that leads to it is easy, and there are many who travel it. 14 But the gate to life is narrow and the way that leads to it is hard, and there are few people who find it.

A Tree and Its Fruit
(Luke 6.43, 44)

15 "Be on your guard against false prophets; they come to you looking like sheep on the outside, but on the inside they are really like wild wolves. 16 You will know them by what they do. Thorn bushes do not bear grapes, and briers do not bear figs. 17 A healthy tree bears good fruit, but a poor tree bears bad fruit. 18 A healthy tree cannot bear bad fruit, and a poor tree cannot bear good fruit. 19 And any tree that does not bear good fruit is cut down and thrown in the

---

[e] live a bit longer; *or* grow a bit taller.

fire. 20 So then, you will know the false prophets by what they do.

I Never Knew You
(Luke 13.25-27)

21 "Not everyone who calls me 'Lord, Lord' will enter the Kingdom of heaven, but only those who do what my Father in heaven wants them to do. 22 When the Judgment Day comes, many will say to me, 'Lord, Lord! In your name we spoke God's message, by your name we drove out many demons and performed many miracles!' 23 Then I will say to them, 'I never knew you. Get away from me, you wicked people!'

The Two House Builders
(Luke 6.47-49)

24 "So then, anyone who hears these words of mine and obeys them is like a wise man who built his house on rock. 25 The rain poured down, the rivers flooded over, and the wind blew hard against that house. But it did not fall, because it was built on rock.

26 "But anyone who hears these words of mine and does not obey them is like a foolish man who built his house on sand. 27 The rain poured down, the rivers flooded over, the wind blew hard against that house, and it fell. And what a terrible fall that was!"

The Authority of Jesus

28 When Jesus finished saying these things, the crowd was amazed at the way he taught. 29 He wasn't like the teachers of the Law; instead, he taught with authority.

Jesus Heals a Man
(Mark 1.40-45; Luke 5.12-16)

8 When Jesus came down from the hill, large crowds followed him. 2 Then a man suffering from a dreaded skin disease came to him, knelt down before him, and said, "Sir, if you want to, you can make me clean."*f*

3 Jesus reached out and touched him. "I do want to," he answered. "Be clean!" At once the man was healed of his disease. 4 Then Jesus said to him, "Listen! Don't tell anyone, but go straight to the priest and let him examine you; then in order to prove to everyone that you are

cured, offer the sacrifice that Moses ordered."

Jesus Heals a Roman Officer's Servant
(Luke 7.1-10)

5 When Jesus entered Capernaum, a Roman officer met him and begged for help: 6 "Sir, my servant is sick in bed at home, unable to move and suffering terribly."

7 "I will go and make him well," Jesus said.

8 "Oh no, sir," answered the officer. "I do not deserve to have you come into my house. Just give the order, and my servant will get well. 9 I, too, am a man under the authority of superior officers, and I have soldiers under me. I order this one, 'Go!' and he goes; and I order that one, 'Come!' and he comes; and I order my slave, 'Do this!' and he does it."

10 When Jesus heard this, he was surprised and said to the people following him, "I tell you, I have never found anyone in Israel with faith like this. 11 I assure you that many will come from the east and the west and sit down with Abraham, Isaac, and Jacob at the feast in the Kingdom of heaven. 12 But those who should be in the Kingdom will be thrown out into the darkness, where they will cry and gnash their teeth." 13 Then Jesus said to the officer, "Go home, and what you believe will be done for you."

And the officer's servant was healed that very moment.

Jesus Heals Many People
(Mark 1.29-34; Luke 4.38-41)

14 Jesus went to Peter's home, and there he saw Peter's mother-in-law sick in bed with a fever. 15 He touched her hand; the fever left her, and she got up and began to wait on him.

16 When evening came, people brought to Jesus many who had demons in them. Jesus drove out the evil spirits with a word and healed all who were sick. 17 He did this to make come true what the prophet Isaiah had said, "He himself took our sickness and carried away our diseases."

---

f MAKE ME CLEAN: *This disease was considered to make a person ritually unclean.*

LAKE GALILEE

The beautiful Lake Galilee, also referred to in the Bible as Lake Tiberias (Jn 6.1) and Lake Gennesaret (Lk 5.1), was the geographical center of much of the ministry of Jesus. Almost thirteen miles long and about eight miles wide, the freshwater lake is surrounded by high mountains. Interestingly, Lake Galilee is one of the lowest points on earth, standing 690 feet below sea level.

The region around Lake Galilee in the upper Jordan River valley in northern Palestine is a lush garden, with an abundance of fertile soil, water, fish, and a hot climate. About 200,000 people, mostly Gentiles, were scattered in the many towns along the shores of the lake and throughout the upper Jordan valley when Jesus taught and healed in Palestine.

Because of their openness to new ideas, Jesus appealed to the common people of Galilee. Jesus recruited eleven of his disciples from this area. Many of them, including brothers Peter and Andrew and brothers James and John, were fishermen who earned their livelihood from the waters of this lake. Settlements along the shores of Lake Galilee in the time of Jesus included Tiberias, Magdala, Capernaum, and Bethsaida. In this region Jesus taught the multitudes and healed the sick (Mt 15.29–31).

Powerful winds sometimes sweep down from the mountains along the shores of the lake, clashing with heat waves rising from the water's surface. The resulting turbulence creates sudden, violent storms. This is probably the type of storm that Jesus calmed on the lake in response to the pleas of his disciples. "What kind of man is this?" they said. "Even the winds and the waves obey him" (Mt 8.27).

The Would-Be Followers of Jesus
(Luke 9.57-62)

18 When Jesus noticed the crowd around him, he ordered his disciples to go to the other side of the lake. 19 A teacher of the Law came to him. "Teacher," he said, "I am ready to go with you wherever you go."

20 Jesus answered him, "Foxes have holes, and birds have nests, but the Son of Man has no place to lie down and rest."

21 Another man, who was a disciple, said, "Sir, first let me go back and bury my father."

22 "Follow me," Jesus answered, "and let the dead bury their own dead."

Jesus Calms a Storm
(Mark 4.35-41; Luke 8.22-25)

23 Jesus got into a boat, and his disciples went with him. 24 Suddenly a fierce storm hit the lake, and the boat was in danger of sinking. But Jesus was asleep. 25 The disciples went to him and woke him up. "Save us, Lord!" they said. "We are about to die!"

26 "Why are you so frightened?" Jesus answered. "What little faith you have!" Then he got up and ordered the winds and the waves to stop, and there was a great calm.

27 Everyone was amazed. "What kind of man is this?" they said. "Even the winds and the waves obey him!"

Jesus Heals Two Men with Demons
(Mark 5.1-20; Luke 8.26-39)

28 When Jesus came to the territory of Gadara on the other side of the lake, he was met by two men who came out of the burial caves there. These men had demons in them and were so fierce that no one dared travel on that road. 29 At once they screamed, "What do you want with us, you Son of God? Have you come to punish us before the right time?"

30 Not far away there was a large herd of pigs feeding. 31 So the demons begged Jesus, "If you are going to drive us out, send us into that herd of pigs."

32 "Go," Jesus told them; so they left and went off into the pigs. The whole herd rushed down the side of the cliff into the lake and was drowned.

33 The men who had been taking care of the pigs ran away and went into the town, where they told the whole story and what had happened to the men with the demons. 34 So everyone from the town went out to meet Jesus; and when they saw him, they begged him to leave their territory.

Jesus Heals a Paralyzed Man
(Mark 2.1-12; Luke 5.17-26)

9 Jesus got into the boat and went back across the lake to his own town,g 2 where some people brought to him a paralyzed man, lying on a bed. When Jesus saw how much faith they had, he said to the paralyzed man, "Courage, my son! Your sins are forgiven."

3 Then some teachers of the Law said to themselves, "This man is speaking blasphemy!"

4 Jesus perceived what they were thinking, and so he said, "Why are you thinking such evil things? 5 Is it easier to say, 'Your sins are forgiven,' or to say, 'Get up and walk'? 6 I will prove to you, then, that the Son of Man has authority on earth to forgive sins." So he said to the paralyzed man, "Get up, pick up your bed, and go home!"

7 The man got up and went home. 8 When the people saw it, they were afraid, and praised God for giving such authority to people.

Jesus Calls Matthew
(Mark 2.13-17; Luke 5.27-32)

9 Jesus left that place, and as he walked along, he saw a tax collector, named Matthew, sitting in his office. He said to him, "Follow me."

Matthew got up and followed him.

10 While Jesus was having a meal in Matthew's house,h many tax collectors and other outcasts came and joined Jesus and his disciples at the table. 11 Some Pharisees saw this and asked his disciples, "Why does your teacher eat with such people?"

12 Jesus heard them and answered, "People who are well do not need a doctor, but only those who are sick. 13 Go and find out what is meant by the scripture that says: 'It is kindness that I want, not animal sacrifices.' I have not come to call respectable people, but outcasts."

---

g HIS OWN TOWN: *Capernaum (see 4.13).*   h in Matthew's house; *or* in his (*that is,* Jesus') house.

The Question about Fasting
(Mark 2.18-22; Luke 5.33-39)

14 Then the followers of John the Baptist came to Jesus, asking, "Why is it that we and the Pharisees fast often, but your disciples don't fast at all?"

15 Jesus answered, "Do you expect the guests at a wedding party to be sad as long as the bridegroom is with them? Of course not! But the day will come when the bridegroom will be taken away from them, and then they will fast.

16 "No one patches up an old coat with a piece of new cloth, for the new patch will shrink and make an even bigger hole in the coat. 17 Nor does anyone pour new wine into used wineskins, for the skins will burst, the wine will pour out, and the skins will be ruined. Instead, new wine is poured into fresh wineskins, and both will keep in good condition."

The Official's Daughter and the Woman Who Touched Jesus' Cloak
(Mark 5.21-43; Luke 8.40-56)

18 While Jesus was saying this, a Jewish official came to him, knelt down before him, and said, "My daughter has just died; but come and place your hands on her, and she will live."

19 So Jesus got up and followed him, and his disciples went along with him.

20 A woman who had suffered from severe bleeding for twelve years came up behind Jesus and touched the edge of his cloak. 21 She said to herself, "If only I touch his cloak, I will get well."

22 Jesus turned around and saw her, and said, "Courage, my daughter! Your faith has made you well." At that very moment the woman became well.

23 Then Jesus went into the official's house. When he saw the musicians for the funeral and the people all stirred up, 24 he said, "Get out, everybody! The little girl is not dead—she is only sleeping!" Then they all started making fun of him. 25 But as soon as the people had been put out, Jesus went into the girl's room and took hold of her hand, and she got up. 26 The news about this spread all over that part of the country.

Jesus Heals Two Blind Men

27 Jesus left that place, and as he walked along, two blind men started following him. "Have mercy on us, Son of David!" they shouted.

28 When Jesus had gone indoors, the two blind men came to him, and he asked them, "Do you believe that I can heal you?"

"Yes, sir!" they answered.

29 Then Jesus touched their eyes and said, "Let it happen, then, just as you believe!"—30 and their sight was restored. Jesus spoke sternly to them, "Don't tell this to anyone!"

31 But they left and spread the news about Jesus all over that part of the country.

Jesus Heals a Man Who Could Not Speak

32 As the men were leaving, some people brought to Jesus a man who could not talk because he had a demon. 33 But as soon as the demon was driven out, the man started talking, and everyone was amazed. "We have never seen anything like this in Israel!" they exclaimed.

34 But the Pharisees said, "It is the chief of the demons who gives Jesus the power to drive out demons."

Jesus Has Pity for the People

35 Jesus went around visiting all the towns and villages. He taught in the synagogues, preached the Good News about the Kingdom, and healed people with every kind of disease and sickness. 36 As he saw the crowds, his heart was filled with pity for them, because they were worried and helpless, like sheep without a shepherd. 37 So he said to his disciples, "The harvest is large, but there are few workers to gather it in. 38 Pray to the owner of the harvest that he will send out workers to gather in his harvest."

The Twelve Apostles
(Mark 3.13-19; Luke 6.12-16)

10 Jesus called his twelve disciples together and gave them authority to drive out evil spirits and to heal every disease and every sickness. 2 These are the names of the twelve apostles: first, Simon (called Peter) and his brother Andrew; James and his brother John, the sons of Zebedee; 3 Philip and Bartholomew; Thomas and Matthew, the tax collector; James son of Alphaeus, and Thaddaeus; 4 Simon the

Patriot, and Judas Iscariot, who betrayed Jesus.

The Mission of the Twelve
(Mark 6.7-13; Luke 9.1-6)

5 These twelve men were sent out by Jesus with the following instructions: "Do not go to any Gentile territory or any Samaritan towns. 6 Instead, you are to go to the lost sheep of the people of Israel. 7 Go and preach, 'The Kingdom of heaven is near!' 8 Heal the sick, bring the dead back to life, heal those who suffer from dreaded skin diseases, and drive out demons. You have received without paying, so give without being paid. 9 Do not carry any gold, silver, or copper money in your pockets; 10 do not carry a beggar's bag for the trip or an extra shirt or shoes or a walking stick. Workers should be given what they need.

11 "When you come to a town or village, go in and look for someone who is willing to welcome you, and stay with him until you leave that place. 12 When you go into a house, say, 'Peace be with you.' 13 If the people in that house welcome you, let your greeting of peace remain; but if they do not welcome you, then take back your greeting. 14 And if some home or town will not welcome you or listen to you, then leave that place and shake the dust off your feet. 15 I assure you that on the Judgment Day God will show more mercy to the people of Sodom and Gomorrah than to the people of that town!

Coming Persecutions
(Mark 13.9-13; Luke 21.12-17)

16 "Listen! I am sending you out just like sheep to a pack of wolves. You must be as cautious as snakes and as gentle as doves. 17 Watch out, for there will be those who will arrest you and take you to court, and they will whip you in the synagogues. 18 For my sake you will be brought to trial before rulers and kings, to tell the Good News to them and to the Gentiles. 19 When they bring you to trial, do not worry about what you are going to say or how you will say it; when the time comes, you will be given what you will say. 20 For the words you will speak will not be yours; they will come from the Spirit of your Father speaking through you.

21 "People will hand over their own brothers to be put to death, and fathers will do the same to their children; children will turn against their parents and have them put to death. 22 Everyone will hate you because of me. But whoever holds out to the end will be saved. 23 When they persecute you in one town, run away to another one. I assure you that you will not finish your work in all the towns of Israel before the Son of Man comes.

24 "No pupil is greater than his teacher; no slave is greater than his master. 25 So a pupil should be satisfied to become like his teacher, and a slave like his master. If the head of the family is called Beelzebul, the members of the family will be called even worse names!

Whom to Fear
(Luke 12.2-7)

26 "So do not be afraid of people. Whatever is now covered up will be uncovered, and every secret will be made known. 27 What I am telling you in the dark you must repeat in broad daylight, and what you have heard in private you must announce from the housetops. 28 Do not be afraid of those who kill the body but cannot kill the soul; rather be afraid of God, who can destroy both body and soul in hell. 29 For only a penny you can buy two sparrows, yet not one sparrow falls to the ground without your Father's consent. 30 As for you, even the hairs of your head have all been counted. 31 So do not be afraid; you are worth much more than many sparrows!

Confessing and Rejecting Christ
(Luke 12.8, 9)

32 "Those who declare publicly that they belong to me, I will do the same for them before my Father in heaven. 33 But those who reject me publicly, I will reject before my Father in heaven.

Not Peace, but a Sword
(Luke 12.51-53; 14.26, 27)

34 "Do not think that I have come to bring peace to the world. No, I did not come to bring peace, but a sword. 35 I came to set sons against their fathers, daughters against their mothers, daughters-in-law against their mothers-in-law; 36 your worst enemies will be the members of your own family.

37 "Those who love their father or

mother more than me are not fit to be my disciples; those who love their son or daughter more than me are not fit to be my disciples. 38 Those who do not take up their cross and follow in my steps are not fit to be my disciples. 39 Those who try to gain their own life will lose it; but those who lose their life for my sake will gain it.

Rewards
(Mark 9.41)

40 "Whoever welcomes you welcomes me; and whoever welcomes me welcomes the one who sent me. 41 Whoever welcomes God's messenger because he is God's messenger, will share in his reward. And whoever welcomes a good man because he is good, will share in his reward. 42 You can be sure that whoever gives even a drink of cold water to one of the least of these my followers because he is my follower, will certainly receive a reward."

The Messengers from John the Baptist
(Luke 7.18-35)

11 When Jesus finished giving these instructions to his twelve disciples, he left that place and went off to teach and preach in the towns near there.

2 When John the Baptist heard in prison about the things that Christ was doing, he sent some of his disciples to him. 3 "Tell us," they asked Jesus, "are you the one John said was going to come, or should we expect someone else?"

4 Jesus answered, "Go back and tell John what you are hearing and seeing: 5 the blind can see, the lame can walk, those who suffer from dreaded skin diseases are made clean, i the deaf hear, the dead are brought back to life, and the Good News is preached to the poor. 6 How happy are those who have no doubts about me!"

7 While John's disciples were leaving, Jesus spoke about him to the crowds: "When you went out to John in the desert, what did you expect to see? A blade of grass bending in the wind? 8 What did you go out to see? A man dressed up in fancy clothes? People who

dress like that live in palaces! 9 Tell me, what did you go out to see? A prophet? Yes indeed, but you saw much more than a prophet. 10 For John is the one of whom the scripture says: 'God said, I will send my messenger ahead of you to open the way for you.' 11 I assure you that John the Baptist is greater than anyone who has ever lived. But the one who is least in the Kingdom of heaven is greater than John. 12 From the time John preached his message until this very day the Kingdom of heaven has suffered violent attacks, j and violent men try to seize it. 13 Until the time of John all the prophets and the Law of Moses spoke about the Kingdom; 14 and if you are willing to believe their message, John is Elijah, whose coming was predicted. 15 Listen, then, if you have ears!

16 "Now, to what can I compare the people of this day? They are like children sitting in the marketplace. One group shouts to the other, 17 'We played wedding music for you, but you wouldn't dance! We sang funeral songs, but you wouldn't cry!' 18 When John came, he fasted and drank no wine, and everyone said, 'He has a demon in him!' 19 When the Son of Man came, he ate and drank, and everyone said, 'Look at this man! He is a glutton and wine drinker, a friend of tax collectors and other outcasts!' God's wisdom, however, is shown to be true by its results."

The Unbelieving Towns
(Luke 10.13-15)

20 The people in the towns where Jesus had performed most of his miracles did not turn from their sins, so he reproached those towns. 21 "How terrible it will be for you, Chorazin! How terrible for you too, Bethsaida! If the miracles which were performed in you had been performed in Tyre and Sidon, the people there would have long ago put on sackcloth and sprinkled ashes on themselves, to show that they had turned from their sins! 22 I assure you that on the Judgment Day God will show more mercy to the people of Tyre and Sidon than to you! 23 And as for you, Capernaum! Did you want to lift yourself up to heaven? You will be thrown down to hell! If the miracles which were per-

i MADE CLEAN: See 8.2.　j has suffered violent attacks; or has been coming violently.

M
A
T
T
H
E
W

formed in you had been performed in Sodom, it would still be in existence today! 24 You can be sure that on the Judgment Day God will show more mercy to Sodom than to you!"

Come to Me and Rest
(Luke 10.21, 22)

25 At that time Jesus said, "Father, Lord of heaven and earth! I thank you because you have shown to the unlearned what you have hidden from the wise and learned. 26 Yes, Father, this was how you were pleased to have it happen.

27 "My Father has given me all things. No one knows the Son except the Father, and no one knows the Father except the Son and those to whom the Son chooses to reveal him.

28 "Come to me, all of you who are tired from carrying heavy loads, and I will give you rest. 29 Take my yoke and put it on you, and learn from me, because I am gentle and humble in spirit; and you will find rest. 30 For the yoke I will give you is easy, and the load I will put on you is light."

The Question about the Sabbath
(Mark 2.23-28; Luke 6.1-5)

12 Not long afterward Jesus was walking through some wheat fields on a Sabbath. His disciples were hungry, so they began to pick heads of wheat and eat the grain. 2 When the Pharisees saw this, they said to Jesus, "Look, it is against our Law for your disciples to do this on the Sabbath!"

3 Jesus answered, "Have you never read what David did that time when he and his men were hungry? 4 He went into the house of God, and he and his men ate the bread offered to God, even though it was against the Law for them to eat it — only the priests were allowed to eat that bread. 5 Or have you not read in the Law of Moses that every Sabbath the priests in the Temple actually break the Sabbath law, yet they are not guilty? 6 I tell you that there is something here greater than the Temple. 7 The scripture says, 'It is kindness that I want, not animal sacrifices.' If you really knew what this means, you would not condemn people who are not guilty; 8 for the Son of Man is Lord of the Sabbath."

The Man with a Paralyzed Hand
(Mark 3.1-6; Luke 6.6-11)

9 Jesus left that place and went to a synagogue, 10 where there was a man who had a paralyzed hand. Some people were there who wanted to accuse Jesus of doing wrong, so they asked him, "Is it against our Law to heal on the Sabbath?"

11 Jesus answered, "What if one of you has a sheep and it falls into a deep hole on the Sabbath? Will you not take hold of it and lift it out? 12 And a human being is worth much more than a sheep! So then, our Law does allow us to help someone on the Sabbath." 13 Then he said to the man with the paralyzed hand, "Stretch out your hand."

He stretched it out, and it became well again, just like the other one. 14 Then the Pharisees left and made plans to kill Jesus.

God's Chosen Servant

15 When Jesus heard about the plot against him, he went away from that place; and large crowds followed him. He healed all the sick 16 and gave them orders not to tell others about him. 17 He did this so as to make come true what God had said through the prophet Isaiah:
18 "Here is my servant, whom I have
    chosen,
    the one I love, and with whom I
    am pleased.
    I will send my Spirit upon him,
    and he will announce my
    judgment to the nations.
19 He will not argue or shout,
    or make loud speeches in the
    streets.
20 He will not break off a bent reed,
    nor put out a flickering lamp.
    He will persist until he causes
    justice to triumph,
21 and on him all peoples will put
    their hope."

Jesus and Beelzebul
(Mark 3.20-30; Luke 11.14-23)

22 Then some people brought to Jesus a man who was blind and could not talk because he had a demon. Jesus healed the man, so that he was able to talk and see. 23 The crowds were all amazed at what Jesus had done. "Could he be the Son of David?" they asked.

24 When the Pharisees heard this, they replied, "He drives out demons only because their ruler Beelzebul gives him power to do so."

25 Jesus knew what they were thinking, and so he said to them, "Any country that divides itself into groups which fight each other will not last very long. And any town or family that divides itself into groups which fight each other will fall apart. 26 So if one group is fighting another in Satan's kingdom, this means that it is already divided into groups and will soon fall apart! 27 You say that I drive out demons because Beelzebul gives me the power to do so. Well, then, who gives your followers the power to drive them out? What your own followers do proves that you are wrong! 28 No, it is not Beelzebul, but God's Spirit, who gives me the power to drive out demons, which proves that the Kingdom of God has already come upon you.

29 "No one can break into a strong man's house and take away his belongings unless he first ties up the strong man; then he can plunder his house.

30 "Anyone who is not for me is really against me; anyone who does not help me gather is really scattering. 31 For this reason I tell you: people can be forgiven any sin and any evil thing they say; k but whoever says evil things against the Holy Spirit will not be forgiven. 32 Anyone who says something against the Son of Man can be forgiven; but whoever says something against the Holy Spirit will not be forgiven — now or ever.

A Tree and Its Fruit
(Luke 6.43-45)

33 "To have good fruit you must have a healthy tree; if you have a poor tree, you will have bad fruit. A tree is known by the kind of fruit it bears. 34 You snakes — how can you say good things when you are evil? For the mouth speaks what the heart is full of. 35 A good person brings good things out of a treasure of good things; a bad person brings bad things out of a treasure of bad things.

36 "You can be sure that on the Judgment Day you will have to give account of every useless word you have ever spoken. 37 Your words will be used to judge you — to declare you either innocent or guilty."

The Demand for a Miracle
(Mark 8.11, 12; Luke 11.29-32)

38 Then some teachers of the Law and some Pharisees spoke up. "Teacher," they said, "we want to see you perform a miracle."

39 "How evil and godless are the people of this day!" Jesus exclaimed. "You ask me for a miracle? No! The only miracle you will be given is the miracle of the prophet Jonah. 40 In the same way that Jonah spent three days and nights in the big fish, so will the Son of Man spend three days and nights in the depths of the earth. 41 On the Judgment Day the people of Nineveh will stand up and accuse you, because they turned from their sins when they heard Jonah preach; and I tell you that there is something here greater than Jonah! 42 On the Judgment Day the Queen of Sheba will stand up and accuse you, because she traveled all the way from her country to listen to King Solomon's wise teaching; and I assure you that there is something here greater than Solomon!

The Return of the Evil Spirit
(Luke 11.24-26)

43 "When an evil spirit goes out of a person, it travels over dry country looking for a place to rest. If it can't find one, 44 it says to itself, 'I will go back to my house.' So it goes back and finds the house empty, clean, and all fixed up. 45 Then it goes out and brings along seven other spirits even worse than itself, and they come and live there. So when it is all over, that person is in worse shape than at the beginning. This is what will happen to the evil people of this day."

Jesus' Mother and Brothers
(Mark 3.31-35; Luke 8.19-21)

46 Jesus was still talking to the people when his mother and brothers arrived. They stood outside, asking to speak with him. 47 So one of the people there said to him, "Look, your mother and brothers are standing outside, and they want to speak with you." l

k *evil thing they say; or evil thing they say against God.*   l *Some manuscripts do not have verse 47.*

48 Jesus answered, "Who is my mother? Who are my brothers?" 49 Then he pointed to his disciples and said, "Look! Here are my mother and my brothers! 50 Whoever does what my Father in heaven wants is my brother, my sister, and my mother."

The Parable of the Sower
(Mark 4.1-9; Luke 8.4-8)

13 That same day Jesus left the house and went to the lakeside, where he sat down to teach. 2 The crowd that gathered around him was so large that he got into a boat and sat in it, while the crowd stood on the shore. 3 He used parables to tell them many things.

"Once there was a man who went out to sow grain. 4 As he scattered the seed in the field, some of it fell along the path, and the birds came and ate it up. 5 Some of it fell on rocky ground, where there was little soil. The seeds soon sprouted, because the soil wasn't deep. 6 But when the sun came up, it burned the young plants; and because the roots had not grown deep enough, the plants soon dried up. 7 Some of the seed fell among thorn bushes, which grew up and choked the plants. 8 But some seeds fell in good soil, and the plants bore grain: some had one hundred grains, others sixty, and others thirty."

9 And Jesus concluded, "Listen, then, if you have ears!"

The Purpose of the Parables
(Mark 4.10-12; Luke 8.9, 10)

10 Then the disciples came to Jesus and asked him, "Why do you use parables when you talk to the people?"

11 Jesus answered, "The knowledge about the secrets of the Kingdom of heaven has been given to you, but not to them. 12 For the person who has something will be given more, so that he will have more than enough; but the person who has nothing will have taken away from him even the little he has. 13 The reason I use parables in talking to them is that they look, but do not see, and they listen, but do not hear or understand. 14 So the prophecy of Isaiah applies to them:

"This people will listen and listen,
    but not understand;
they will look and look, but
    not see,

15 because their minds are dull,
    and they have stopped up their
      ears
    and have closed their eyes.
Otherwise, their eyes would see,
    their ears would hear,
    their minds would understand,
and they would turn to me,
      says God,
    and I would heal them.'

16 "As for you, how fortunate you are! Your eyes see and your ears hear. 17 I assure you that many prophets and many of God's people wanted very much to see what you see, but they could not, and to hear what you hear, but they did not.

Jesus Explains the Parable of the Sower
(Mark 4.13-20; Luke 8.11-15)

18 "Listen, then, and learn what the parable of the sower means. 19 Those who hear the message about the Kingdom but do not understand it are like the seeds that fell along the path. The Evil One comes and snatches away what was sown in them. 20 The seeds that fell on rocky ground stand for those who receive the message gladly as soon as they hear it. 21 But it does not sink deep into them, and they don't last long. So when trouble or persecution comes because of the message, they give up at once. 22 The seeds that fell among thorn bushes stand for those who hear the message; but the worries about this life and the love for riches choke the message, and they don't bear fruit. 23 And the seeds sown in the good soil stand for those who hear the message and understand it: they bear fruit, some as much as one hundred, others sixty, and others thirty."

The Parable of the Weeds

24 Jesus told them another parable: "The Kingdom of heaven is like this. A man sowed good seed in his field. 25 One night, when everyone was asleep, an enemy came and sowed weeds among the wheat and went away. 26 When the plants grew and the heads of grain began to form, then the weeds showed up. 27 The man's servants came to him and said, 'Sir, it was good seed you sowed in your field; where did the weeds come from?' 28 'It was some enemy who did this,' he answered. 'Do you want us to go

and pull up the weeds?' they asked him. 29 'No,' he answered, 'because as you gather the weeds you might pull up some of the wheat along with them. 30 Let the wheat and the weeds both grow together until harvest. Then I will tell the harvest workers to pull up the weeds first, tie them in bundles and burn them, and then to gather in the wheat and put it in my barn.' "

The Parable of the Mustard Seed
(Mark 4.30-32; Luke 13.18, 19)

31 Jesus told them another parable: "The Kingdom of heaven is like this. A man takes a mustard seed and sows it in his field. 32 It is the smallest of all seeds, but when it grows up, it is the biggest of all plants. It becomes a tree, so that birds come and make their nests in its branches."

The Parable of the Yeast
(Luke 13.20, 21)

33 Jesus told them still another parable: "The Kingdom of heaven is like this. A woman takes some yeast and mixes it with a bushel of flour until the whole batch of dough rises."

Jesus' Use of Parables
(Mark 4.33, 34)

34 Jesus used parables to tell all these things to the crowds; he would not say a thing to them without using a parable. 35 He did this to make come true what the prophet had said,

"I will use parables when I speak to them;
I will tell them things unknown since the creation of the world."

Jesus Explains the Parable of the Weeds

36 When Jesus had left the crowd and gone indoors, his disciples came to him and said, "Tell us what the parable about the weeds in the field means."

37 Jesus answered, "The man who sowed the good seed is the Son of Man; 38 the field is the world; the good seed is the people who belong to the Kingdom; the weeds are the people who belong to the Evil One; 39 and the enemy who sowed the weeds is the Devil. The harvest is the end of the age, and the harvest workers are angels. 40 Just as the weeds are gathered up and burned in the fire, so the same thing will happen at the end of the age: 41 the Son of Man will send out his angels to gather up out of his Kingdom all those who cause people to sin and all others who do evil things, 42 and they will throw them into the fiery furnace, where they will cry and gnash their teeth. 43 Then God's people will shine like the sun in their Father's Kingdom. Listen, then, if you have ears!

The Parable of the Hidden Treasure

44 "The Kingdom of heaven is like this. A man happens to find a treasure hidden in a field. He covers it up again, and is so happy that he goes and sells everything he has, and then goes back and buys that field.

The Parable of the Pearl

45 "Also, the Kingdom of heaven is like this. A man is looking for fine pearls, 46 and when he finds one that is unusually fine, he goes and sells everything he has, and buys that pearl.

The Parable of the Net

47 "Also, the Kingdom of heaven is like this. Some fishermen throw their net out in the lake and catch all kinds of fish. 48 When the net is full, they pull it to shore and sit down to divide the fish: the good ones go into the buckets, the worthless ones are thrown away. 49 It will be like this at the end of the age: the angels will go out and gather up the evil people from among the good 50 and will throw them into the fiery furnace, where they will cry and gnash their teeth.

New Truths and Old

51 "Do you understand these things?" Jesus asked them.

"Yes," they answered.

52 So he replied, "This means, then, that every teacher of the Law who becomes a disciple in the Kingdom of heaven is like a homeowner who takes new and old things out of his storage room."

Jesus Is Rejected at Nazareth
(Mark 6.1-6; Luke 4.16-30)

53 When Jesus finished telling these parables, he left that place 54 and went back to his hometown. He taught in the synagogue, and those who heard him

M
A
T
T
H
E
W

were amazed. "Where did he get such wisdom?" they asked. "And what about his miracles? [55] Isn't he the carpenter's son? Isn't Mary his mother, and aren't James, Joseph, Simon, and Judas his brothers? [56] Aren't all his sisters living here? Where did he get all this?" [57] And so they rejected him.

Jesus said to them, "A prophet is respected everywhere except in his hometown and by his own family." [58] Because they did not have faith, he did not perform many miracles there.

The Death of John the Baptist
(Mark 6.14-29; Luke 9.7-9)

14 At that time Herod, the ruler of Galilee, heard about Jesus. [2] "He is really John the Baptist, who has come back to life," he told his officials. "That is why he has this power to perform miracles."

[3] For Herod had earlier ordered John's arrest, and he had him tied up and put in prison. He had done this because of Herodias, his brother Philip's wife. [4] For some time John the Baptist had told Herod, "It isn't right for you to be married to Herodias!" [5] Herod wanted to kill him, but he was afraid of the Jewish people, because they considered John to be a prophet.

[6] On Herod's birthday the daughter of Herodias danced in front of the whole group. Herod was so pleased [7] that he promised her, "I swear that I will give you anything you ask for!"

[8] At her mother's suggestion she asked him, "Give me here and now the head of John the Baptist on a plate!"

[9] The king was sad, but because of the promise he had made in front of all his guests he gave orders that her wish be granted. [10] So he had John beheaded in prison. [11] The head was brought in on a plate and given to the girl, who took it to her mother. [12] John's disciples came, carried away his body, and buried it; then they went and told Jesus.

Jesus Feeds Five Thousand
(Mark 6.30-44; Luke 9.10-17; John 6.1-14)

[13] When Jesus heard the news about John, he left there in a boat and went to a lonely place by himself. The people heard about it, and so they left their towns and followed him by land. [14] Jesus got out of the boat, and when he saw the large crowd, his heart was filled with pity for them, and he healed their sick.

[15] That evening his disciples came to him and said, "It is already very late, and this is a lonely place. Send the people away and let them go to the villages to buy food for themselves."

[16] "They don't have to leave," answered Jesus. "You yourselves give them something to eat!"

[17] "All we have here are five loaves and two fish," they replied.

[18] "Then bring them here to me," Jesus said. [19] He ordered the people to sit down on the grass; then he took the five loaves and the two fish, looked up to heaven, and gave thanks to God. He broke the loaves and gave them to the disciples, and the disciples gave them to the people. [20] Everyone ate and had enough. Then the disciples took up twelve baskets full of what was left over. [21] The number of men who ate was about five thousand, not counting the women and children.

Jesus Walks on the Water
(Mark 6.45-52; John 6.15-21)

[22] Then Jesus made the disciples get into the boat and go on ahead to the other side of the lake, while he sent the people away. [23] After sending the people away, he went up a hill by himself to pray. When evening came, Jesus was there alone; [24] and by this time the boat was far out in the lake, tossed about by the waves, because the wind was blowing against it.

[25] Between three and six o'clock in the morning Jesus came to the disciples, walking on the water. [26] When they saw him walking on the water, they were terrified. "It's a ghost!" they said, and screamed with fear.

[27] Jesus spoke to them at once. "Courage!" he said. "It is I. Don't be afraid!"

[28] Then Peter spoke up. "Lord, if it is really you, order me to come out on the water to you."

[29] "Come!" answered Jesus. So Peter got out of the boat and started walking on the water to Jesus. [30] But when he noticed the strong wind, he was afraid and started to sink down in the water. "Save me, Lord!" he cried.

[31] At once Jesus reached out and grabbed hold of him and said, "What little faith you have! Why did you doubt?"

32 They both got into the boat, and the wind died down. 33 Then the disciples in the boat worshiped Jesus. "Truly you are the Son of God!" they exclaimed.

Jesus Heals the Sick in Gennesaret
(Mark 6.53-56)

34 They crossed the lake and came to land at Gennesaret, 35 where the people recognized Jesus. So they sent for the sick people in all the surrounding country and brought them to Jesus. 36 They begged him to let the sick at least touch the edge of his cloak; and all who touched it were made well.

The Teaching of the Ancestors
(Mark 7.1-13)

15 Then some Pharisees and teachers of the Law came from Jerusalem to Jesus and asked him, 2 "Why is it that your disciples disobey the teaching handed down by our ancestors? They don't wash their hands in the proper way before they eat!"

3 Jesus answered, "And why do you disobey God's command and follow your own teaching? 4 For God said, 'Respect your father and your mother,' and 'If you curse your father or your mother, you are to be put to death.' 5 But you teach that if people have something they could use to help their father or mother, but say, 'This belongs to God,' 6 they do not need to honor their father.m In this way you disregard God's command, in order to follow your own teaching. 7 You hypocrites! How right Isaiah was when he prophesied about you!

8 'These people, says God, honor me
   with their words,
   but their heart is really far away
   from me.
9 It is no use for them to
   worship me,
   because they teach human rules
   as though they were my
   laws!' "

The Things That Make a Person Unclean
(Mark 7.14-23)

10 Then Jesus called the crowd to him and said to them, "Listen and understand! 11 It is not what goes into your mouth that makes you ritually unclean;

rather, what comes out of it makes you unclean."

12 Then the disciples came to him and said, "Do you know that the Pharisees had their feelings hurt by what you said?"

13 "Every plant which my Father in heaven did not plant will be pulled up," answered Jesus. 14 "Don't worry about them! They are blind leaders of the blind; and when one blind man leads another, both fall into a ditch."

15 Peter spoke up, "Explain this saying to us."

16 Jesus said to them, "You are still no more intelligent than the others. 17 Don't you understand? Anything that goes into your mouth goes into your stomach and then on out of your body. 18 But the things that come out of the mouth come from the heart, and these are the things that make you ritually unclean. 19 For from your heart come the evil ideas which lead you to kill, commit adultery, and do other immoral things; to rob, lie, and slander others. 20 These are the things that make you unclean. But to eat without washing your hands as they say you should — this doesn't make you unclean."

A Woman's Faith
(Mark 7.24-30)

21 Jesus left that place and went off to the territory near the cities of Tyre and Sidon. 22 A Canaanite woman who lived in that region came to him. "Son of David!" she cried out. "Have mercy on me, sir! My daughter has a demon and is in a terrible condition."

23 But Jesus did not say a word to her. His disciples came to him and begged him, "Send her away! She is following us and making all this noise!"

24 Then Jesus replied, "I have been sent only to the lost sheep of the people of Israel."

25 At this the woman came and fell at his feet. "Help me, sir!" she said.

26 Jesus answered, "It isn't right to take the children's food and throw it to the dogs."

27 "That's true, sir," she answered, "but even the dogs eat the leftovers that fall from their masters' table."

28 So Jesus answered her, "You are a

---

m *their father; some manuscripts have* their father or mother.

woman of great faith! What you want will be done for you." And at that very moment her daughter was healed.

Jesus Heals Many People

29 Jesus left there and went along by Lake Galilee. He climbed a hill and sat down. 30 Large crowds came to him, bringing with them the lame, the blind, the crippled, the dumb, and many other sick people, whom they placed at Jesus' feet; and he healed them. 31 The people were amazed as they saw the dumb speaking, the crippled made whole, the lame walking, and the blind seeing; and they praised the God of Israel.

Jesus Feeds Four Thousand
(Mark 8.1-10)

32 Jesus called his disciples to him and said, "I feel sorry for these people, because they have been with me for three days and now have nothing to eat. I don't want to send them away without feeding them, for they might faint on their way home."

33 The disciples asked him, "Where will we find enough food in this desert to feed this crowd?"

34 "How much bread do you have?" Jesus asked.

"Seven loaves," they answered, "and a few small fish."

35 So Jesus ordered the crowd to sit down on the ground. 36 Then he took the seven loaves and the fish, gave thanks to God, broke them, and gave them to the disciples; and the disciples gave them to the people. 37 They all ate and had enough. Then the disciples took up seven baskets full of pieces left over. 38 The number of men who ate was four thousand, not counting the women and children.

39 Then Jesus sent the people away, got into a boat, and went to the territory of Magadan.

The Demand for a Miracle
(Mark 8.11-13; Luke 12.54-56)

16 Some Pharisees and Sadducees who came to Jesus wanted to trap him, so they asked him to perform a miracle for them, to show that God approved of him. 2 But Jesus answered, "When the sun is setting, you say,

'We are going to have fine weather, because the sky is red.' 3 And early in the morning you say, 'It is going to rain, because the sky is red and dark.' You can predict the weather by looking at the sky, but you cannot interpret the signs concerning these times![n] 4 How evil and godless are the people of this day! You ask me for a miracle? No! The only miracle you will be given is the miracle of Jonah."

So he left them and went away.

The Yeast of the Pharisees and Sadducees
(Mark 8.14-21)

5 When the disciples crossed over to the other side of the lake, they forgot to take any bread. 6 Jesus said to them, "Take care; be on your guard against the yeast of the Pharisees and Sadducees."

7 They started discussing among themselves, "He says this because we didn't bring any bread."

8 Jesus knew what they were saying, so he asked them, "Why are you discussing among yourselves about not having any bread? What little faith you have! 9 Don't you understand yet? Don't you remember when I broke the five loaves for the five thousand men? How many baskets did you fill? 10 And what about the seven loaves for the four thousand men? How many baskets did you fill? 11 How is it that you don't understand that I was not talking to you about bread? Guard yourselves from the yeast of the Pharisees and Sadducees!"

12 Then the disciples understood that he was not warning them to guard themselves from the yeast used in bread but from the teaching of the Pharisees and Sadducees.

Peter's Declaration about Jesus
(Mark 8.27-30; Luke 9.18-21)

13 Jesus went to the territory near the town of Caesarea Philippi, where he asked his disciples, "Who do people say the Son of Man is?"

14 "Some say John the Baptist," they answered. "Others say Elijah, while others say Jeremiah or some other prophet."

15 "What about you?" he asked them. "Who do you say I am?"

---

[n] Some manuscripts do not have the words of Jesus in verses 2-3.

16 Simon Peter answered, "You are the Messiah, the Son of the living God."

17 "Good for you, Simon son of John!" answered Jesus. "For this truth did not come to you from any human being, but it was given to you directly by my Father in heaven. 18 And so I tell you, Peter: you are a rock, and on this rock foundation I will build my church, and not even death will ever be able to overcome it. 19 I will give you the keys of the Kingdom of heaven; what you prohibit on earth will be prohibited in heaven, and what you permit on earth will be permitted in heaven."

20 Then Jesus ordered his disciples not to tell anyone that he was the Messiah.

Jesus Speaks about His Suffering and Death
(Mark 8.31 — 9.1; Luke 9.22-27)

21 From that time on Jesus began to say plainly to his disciples, "I must go to Jerusalem and suffer much from the elders, the chief priests, and the teachers of the Law. I will be put to death, but three days later I will be raised to life."

22 Peter took him aside and began to rebuke him. "God forbid it, Lord!" he said. "That must never happen to you!"

23 Jesus turned around and said to Peter, "Get away from me, Satan! You are an obstacle in my way, because these thoughts of yours don't come from God, but from human nature."

24 Then Jesus said to his disciples, "If any of you want to come with me, you must forget yourself, carry your cross, and follow me. 25 For if you want to save your own life, you will lose it; but if you lose your life for my sake, you will find it. 26 Will you gain anything if you win the whole world but lose your life? Of course not! There is nothing you can give to regain your life. 27 For the Son of Man is about to come in the glory of his Father with his angels, and then he will reward each one according to his deeds. 28 I assure you that there are some here who will not die until they have seen the Son of Man come as King."

The Transfiguration
(Mark 9.2-13; Luke 9.28-36)

17 Six days later Jesus took with him Peter and the brothers James and John and led them up a high mountain where they were alone. 2 As they looked on, a change came over Jesus: his face was shining like the sun, and his clothes were dazzling white. 3 Then the three disciples saw Moses and Elijah talking with Jesus. 4 So Peter spoke up and said to Jesus, "Lord, how good it is that we are here! If you wish, I will make three tents here, one for you, one for Moses, and one for Elijah."

5 While he was talking, a shining cloud came over them, and a voice from the cloud said, "This is my own dear Son, with whom I am pleased — listen to him!"

6 When the disciples heard the voice, they were so terrified that they threw themselves face downward on the ground. 7 Jesus came to them and touched them. "Get up," he said. "Don't be afraid!" 8 So they looked up and saw no one there but Jesus.

9 As they came down the mountain, Jesus ordered them, "Don't tell anyone about this vision you have seen until the Son of Man has been raised from death."

10 Then the disciples asked Jesus, "Why do the teachers of the Law say that Elijah has to come first?"

11 "Elijah is indeed coming first," answered Jesus, "and he will get everything ready. 12 But I tell you that Elijah has already come and people did not recognize him, but treated him just as they pleased. In the same way they will also mistreat the Son of Man."

13 Then the disciples understood that he was talking to them about John the Baptist.

Jesus Heals a Boy with a Demon
(Mark 9.14-29; Luke 9.37-43a)

14 When they returned to the crowd, a man came to Jesus, knelt before him, 15 and said, "Sir, have mercy on my son! He is an epileptic and has such terrible attacks that he often falls in the fire or into water. 16 I brought him to your disciples, but they could not heal him."

17 Jesus answered, "How unbelieving and wrong you people are! How long must I stay with you? How long do I have to put up with you? Bring the boy here to me!" 18 Jesus gave a command to the demon, and it went out of the boy, and at that very moment he was healed.

19 Then the disciples came to Jesus in private and asked him, "Why couldn't we drive the demon out?"

MATTHEW

20 "It was because you do not have enough faith," answered Jesus. "I assure you that if you have faith as big as a mustard seed, you can say to this hill, 'Go from here to there!' and it will go. You could do anything!"o

Jesus Speaks Again about His Death
(Mark 9.30-32; Luke 9.43b-45)

22 When the disciples all came together in Galilee, Jesus said to them, "The Son of Man is about to be handed over to those 23 who will kill him; but three days later he will be raised to life."

The disciples became very sad.

Payment of the Temple Tax

24 When Jesus and his disciples came to Capernaum, the collectors of the Temple tax came to Peter and asked, "Does your teacher pay the Temple tax?"

25 "Of course," Peter answered.

When Peter went into the house, Jesus spoke up first, "Simon, what is your opinion? Who pays duties or taxes to the kings of this world? The citizens of the country or the foreigners?"

26 "The foreigners," answered Peter.

"Well, then," replied Jesus, "that means that the citizens don't have to pay. 27 But we don't want to offend these people. So go to the lake and drop in a line. Pull up the first fish you hook, and in its mouth you will find a coin worth enough for my Temple tax and yours. Take it and pay them our taxes."

Who Is the Greatest?
(Mark 9.33-37; Luke 9.46-48)

18 At that time the disciples came to Jesus, asking, "Who is the greatest in the Kingdom of heaven?"

2 So Jesus called a child to come and stand in front of them, 3 and said, "I assure you that unless you change and become like children, you will never enter the Kingdom of heaven. 4 The greatest in the Kingdom of heaven is the one who humbles himself and becomes like this child. 5 And whoever welcomes in my name one such child as this, welcomes me.

Temptations to Sin
(Mark 9.42-48; Luke 17.1, 2)

6 "If anyone should cause one of these little ones to lose his faith in me, it would be better for that person to have a large millstone tied around his neck and be drowned in the deep sea. 7 How terrible for the world that there are things that make people lose their faith! Such things will always happen — but how terrible for the one who causes them!

8 "If your hand or your foot makes you lose your faith, cut it off and throw it away! It is better for you to enter life without a hand or a foot than to keep both hands and both feet and be thrown into the eternal fire. 9 And if your eye makes you lose your faith, take it out and throw it away! It is better for you to enter life with only one eye than to keep both eyes and be thrown into the fire of hell.

The Parable of the Lost Sheep
(Luke 15.3-7)

10 "See that you don't despise any of these little ones. Their angels in heaven, I tell you, are always in the presence of my Father in heaven.p

12 "What do you think a man does who has one hundred sheep and one of them gets lost? He will leave the other ninety-nine grazing on the hillside and go and look for the lost sheep. 13 When he finds it, I tell you, he feels far happier over this one sheep than over the ninety-nine that did not get lost. 14 In just the same way your q Father in heaven does not want any of these little ones to be lost.

When Someone Sins

15 "If your brother sins against you,r go to him and show him his fault. But do it privately, just between yourselves. If he listens to you, you have won your brother back. 16 But if he will not listen to you, take one or two other persons with you, so that 'every accusation may be upheld by the testimony of two or more witnesses,' as the scripture says. 17 And if he will not listen to them, then tell the whole thing to the church. Finally, if he will not listen to the church, treat him

---

o *Some manuscripts add verse 21:* But only prayer and fasting can drive this kind out; nothing else can *(see Mk 9.29).* p *Some manuscripts add verse 11:* For the Son of Man came to save the lost *(see Lk 19.10).* q *your; some manuscripts have* my. r *Some manuscripts do not have* against you.

as though he were a pagan or a tax collector.

Prohibiting and Permitting

18 "And so I tell all of you: what you prohibit on earth will be prohibited in heaven, and what you permit on earth will be permitted in heaven. 19 "And I tell you more: whenever two of you on earth agree about anything you pray for, it will be done for you by my Father in heaven. 20 For where two or three come together in my name, I am there with them."

The Parable of the Unforgiving Servant

21 Then Peter came to Jesus and asked, "Lord, if my brother keeps on sinning against me, how many times do I have to forgive him? Seven times?"

22 "No, not seven times," answered Jesus, "but seventy times seven,s 23 because the Kingdom of heaven is like this. Once there was a king who decided to check on his servants' accounts. 24 He had just begun to do so when one of them was brought in who owed him millions of dollars. 25 The servant did not have enough to pay his debt, so the king ordered him to be sold as a slave, with his wife and his children and all that he had, in order to pay the debt. 26 The servant fell on his knees before the king. 'Be patient with me,' he begged, 'and I will pay you everything!' 27 The king felt sorry for him, so he forgave him the debt and let him go.

28 "Then the man went out and met one of his fellow servants who owed him a few dollars. He grabbed him and started choking him. 'Pay back what you owe me!' he said. 29 His fellow servant fell down and begged him, 'Be patient with me, and I will pay you back!' 30 But he refused; instead, he had him thrown into jail until he should pay the debt. 31 When the other servants saw what had happened, they were very upset and went to the king and told him everything. 32 So he called the servant in. 'You worthless slave!' he said. 'I forgave you the whole amount you owed me, just because you asked me to. 33 You should have had mercy on your fellow servant, just as I had mercy on you.' 34 The king was very

---

s seventy times seven; or seventy-seven times.

angry, and he sent the servant to jail to be punished until he should pay back the whole amount."

35 And Jesus concluded, "That is how my Father in heaven will treat every one of you unless you forgive your brother from your heart."

Jesus Teaches about Divorce
(Mark 10.1-12)

19 When Jesus finished saying these things, he left Galilee and went to the territory of Judea on the other side of the Jordan River. 2 Large crowds followed him, and he healed them there.

3 Some Pharisees came to him and tried to trap him by asking, "Does our Law allow a man to divorce his wife for whatever reason he wishes?"

4 Jesus answered, "Haven't you read the scripture that says that in the beginning the Creator made people male and female? 5 And God said, 'For this reason a man will leave his father and mother and unite with his wife, and the two will become one.' 6 So they are no longer two, but one. No human being must separate, then, what God has joined together."

7 The Pharisees asked him, "Why, then, did Moses give the law for a man to hand his wife a divorce notice and send her away?"

8 Jesus answered, "Moses gave you permission to divorce your wives because you are so hard to teach. But it was not like that at the time of creation. 9 I tell you, then, that any man who divorces his wife for any cause other than her unfaithfulness, commits adultery if he marries some other woman."

10 His disciples said to him, "If this is how it is between a man and his wife, it is better not to marry."

11 Jesus answered, "This teaching does not apply to everyone, but only to those to whom God has given it. 12 For there are different reasons why men cannot marry: some, because they were born that way; others, because men made them that way; and others do not marry for the sake of the Kingdom of heaven. Let him who can accept this teaching do so."

Jesus Blesses Little Children
(Mark 10.13-16; Luke 18.15-17)

13 Some people brought children to Jesus for him to place his hands on them and to pray for them, but the disciples scolded the people. 14 Jesus said, "Let the children come to me and do not stop them, because the Kingdom of heaven belongs to such as these."

15 He placed his hands on them and then went away.

The Rich Young Man
(Mark 10.17-31; Luke 18.18-30)

16 Once a man came to Jesus. "Teacher," he asked, "what good thing must I do to receive eternal life?"

17 "Why do you ask me concerning what is good?" answered Jesus. "There is only One who is good. Keep the commandments if you want to enter life."

18 "What commandments?" he asked.

Jesus answered, "Do not commit murder; do not commit adultery; do not steal; do not accuse anyone falsely; 19 respect your father and your mother; and love your neighbor as you love yourself."

20 "I have obeyed all these commandments," the young man replied. "What else do I need to do?"

21 Jesus said to him, "If you want to be perfect, go and sell all you have and give the money to the poor, and you will have riches in heaven; then come and follow me."

22 When the young man heard this, he went away sad, because he was very rich.

23 Jesus then said to his disciples, "I assure you: it will be very hard for rich people to enter the Kingdom of heaven. 24 I repeat: it is much harder for a rich person to enter the Kingdom of God than for a camel to go through the eye of a needle."

25 When the disciples heard this, they were completely amazed. "Who, then, can be saved?" they asked.

26 Jesus looked straight at them and answered, "This is impossible for human beings, but for God everything is possible."

27 Then Peter spoke up. "Look," he said, "we have left everything and followed you. What will we have?"

28 Jesus said to them, "You can be sure that when the Son of Man sits on his glorious throne in the New Age, then you twelve followers of mine will also sit on thrones, to rule the twelve tribes of Israel. 29 And everyone who has left houses or brothers or sisters or father or mother or children or fields for my sake, will receive a hundred times more and will be given eternal life. 30 But many who now are first will be last, and many who now are last will be first.

The Workers in the Vineyard

20 "The Kingdom of heaven is like this. Once there was a man who went out early in the morning to hire some men to work in his vineyard. 2 He agreed to pay them the regular wage, a silver coin a day, and sent them to work in his vineyard. 3 He went out again to the marketplace at nine o'clock and saw some men standing there doing nothing, 4 so he told them, 'You also go and work in the vineyard, and I will pay you a fair wage.' 5 So they went. Then at twelve o'clock and again at three o'clock he did the same thing. 6 It was nearly five o'clock when he went to the marketplace and saw some other men still standing there, 'Why are you wasting the whole day here doing nothing?' he asked them. 7 'No one hired us,' they answered. 'Well, then, you go and work in the vineyard,' he told them.

8 "When evening came, the owner told his foreman, 'Call the workers and pay them their wages, starting with those who were hired last and ending with those who were hired first.' 9 The men who had begun to work at five o'clock were paid a silver coin each. 10 So when the men who were the first to be hired came to be paid, they thought they would get more; but they too were given a silver coin each. 11 They took their money and started grumbling against the employer. 12 'These men who were hired last worked only one hour,' they said, 'while we put up with a whole day's work in the hot sun—yet you paid them the same as you paid us!' 13 'Listen, friend,' the owner answered one of them, 'I have not cheated you. After all, you agreed to do a day's work for one silver coin. 14 Now take your pay and go home. I want to give this man who was hired last as much as I gave you. 15 Don't I have the right to do as I wish with my

own money? Or are you jealous because I am generous?' "

16 And Jesus concluded, "So those who are last will be first, and those who are first will be last."

Jesus Speaks a Third Time about His Death

(Mark 10.32-34; Luke 18.31-34)

17 As Jesus was going up to Jerusalem, he took the twelve disciples aside and spoke to them privately, as they walked along. 18 "Listen," he told them, "we are going up to Jerusalem, where the Son of Man will be handed over to the chief priests and the teachers of the Law. They will condemn him to death 19 and then hand him over to the Gentiles, who will make fun of him, whip him, and crucify him; but three days later he will be raised to life."

A Mother's Request

(Mark 10.35-45)

20 Then the wife of Zebedee came to Jesus with her two sons, bowed before him, and asked him for a favor.

21 "What do you want?" Jesus asked her.

She answered, "Promise me that these two sons of mine will sit at your right and your left when you are King."

22 "You don't know what you are asking for," Jesus answered the sons. "Can you drink the cup of suffering that I am about to drink?"

"We can," they answered.

23 "You will indeed drink from my cup," Jesus told them, "but I do not have the right to choose who will sit at my right and my left. These places belong to those for whom my Father has prepared them."

24 When the other ten disciples heard about this, they became angry with the two brothers. 25 So Jesus called them all together and said, "You know that the rulers of the heathen have power over them, and the leaders have complete authority. 26 This, however, is not the way it shall be among you. If one of you wants to be great, you must be the servant of the rest; 27 and if one of you wants to be first, you must be the slave of the others—28 like the Son of Man, who did

not come to be served, but to serve and to give his life to redeem many people."

Jesus Heals Two Blind Men

(Mark 10.46-52; Luke 18.35-43)

29 As Jesus and his disciples were leaving Jericho, a large crowd was following. 30 Two blind men who were sitting by the road heard that Jesus was passing by, so they began to shout, "Son of David! Have mercy on us, sir!"

31 The crowd scolded them and told them to be quiet. But they shouted even more loudly, "Son of David! Have mercy on us, sir!"

32 Jesus stopped and called them. "What do you want me to do for you?" he asked them.

33 "Sir," they answered, "we want you to give us our sight!"

34 Jesus had pity on them and touched their eyes; at once they were able to see, and they followed him.

The Triumphant Entry into Jerusalem

(Mark 11.1-11; Luke 19.28-40; John 12.12-19)

21 As Jesus and his disciples approached Jerusalem, they came to Bethphage at the Mount of Olives. There Jesus sent two of the disciples on ahead 2 with these instructions: "Go to the village there ahead of you, and at once you will find a donkey tied up with her colt beside her. Untie them and bring them to me. 3 And if anyone says anything, tell him, 'The Master[t] needs them'; and then he will let them go at once."

4 This happened in order to make come true what the prophet had said:

5 "Tell the city of Zion,
  Look, your king is coming
    to you!
  He is humble and rides on a
    donkey
  and on a colt, the foal of a
    donkey."

6 So the disciples went and did what Jesus had told them to do: 7 they brought the donkey and the colt, threw their cloaks over them, and Jesus got on. 8 A large crowd of people spread their cloaks on the road while others cut branches from the trees and spread them on the road. 9 The crowds walking in front of Jesus and those walking be-

---

[t] The Master; or Their owner.

M
A
T
T
H
E
W

hind began to shout, "Praise to David's Son! God bless him who comes in the name of the Lord! Praise be to God!"

10 When Jesus entered Jerusalem, the whole city was thrown into an uproar. "Who is he?" the people asked.

11 "This is the prophet Jesus, from Nazareth in Galilee," the crowds answered.

Jesus Goes to the Temple
(Mark 11.15-19; Luke 19.45-48; John 2.13-22)

12 Jesus went into the Temple and drove out all those who were buying and selling there. He overturned the tables of the moneychangers and the stools of those who sold pigeons, 13 and said to them, "It is written in the Scriptures that God said, 'My Temple will be called a house of prayer.' But you are making it a hideout for thieves!"

14 The blind and the crippled came to him in the Temple, and he healed them. 15 The chief priests and the teachers of the Law became angry when they saw the wonderful things he was doing and the children shouting in the Temple, "Praise to David's Son!" 16 So they asked Jesus, "Do you hear what they are saying?"

"Indeed I do," answered Jesus. "Haven't you ever read this scripture? 'You have trained children and babies to offer perfect praise.'"

17 Jesus left them and went out of the city to Bethany, where he spent the night.

Jesus Curses the Fig Tree
(Mark 11.12-14, 20-24)

18 On his way back to the city early next morning, Jesus was hungry. 19 He saw a fig tree by the side of the road and went to it, but found nothing on it except leaves. So he said to the tree, "You will never again bear fruit!" At once the fig tree dried up.

20 The disciples saw this and were astounded. "How did the fig tree dry up so quickly?" they asked.

21 Jesus answered, "I assure you that if you believe and do not doubt, you will be able to do what I have done to this fig tree. And not only this, but you will even be able to say to this hill, 'Get up and throw yourself in the sea,' and it will. 22 If you believe, you will receive whatever you ask for in prayer."

The Question about Jesus' Authority
(Mark 11.27-33; Luke 20.1-8)

23 Jesus came back to the Temple; and as he taught, the chief priests and the elders came to him and asked, "What right do you have to do these things? Who gave you such right?"

24 Jesus answered them, "I will ask you just one question, and if you give me an answer, I will tell you what right I have to do these things. 25 Where did John's right to baptize come from: was it from God or from human beings?"

They started to argue among themselves, "What shall we say? If we answer, 'From God,' he will say to us, 'Why, then, did you not believe John?' 26 But if we say, 'From human beings,' we are afraid of what the people might do, because they are all convinced that John was a prophet." 27 So they answered Jesus, "We don't know."

And he said to them, "Neither will I tell you, then, by what right I do these things.

The Parable of the Two Sons

28 "Now, what do you think? There was once a man who had two sons. He went to the older one and said, 'Son, go and work in the vineyard today.' 29 'I don't want to,' he answered, but later he changed his mind and went. 30 Then the father went to the other son and said the same thing. 'Yes, sir,' he answered, but he did not go. 31 Which one of the two did what his father wanted?"

"The older one," they answered.

So Jesus said to them, "I tell you: the tax collectors and the prostitutes are going into the Kingdom of God ahead of you. 32 For John the Baptist came to you showing you the right path to take, and you would not believe him; but the tax collectors and the prostitutes believed him. Even when you saw this, you did not later change your minds and believe him.

The Parable of the Tenants in the Vineyard
(Mark 12.1-12; Luke 20.9-19)

33 "Listen to another parable," Jesus said. "There was once a landowner who planted a vineyard, put a fence around it, dug a hole for the wine press, and built a watchtower. Then he rented the

vineyard to tenants and left home on a trip. 34 When the time came to gather the grapes, he sent his slaves to the tenants to receive his share of the harvest. 35 The tenants grabbed his slaves, beat one, killed another, and stoned another. 36 Again the man sent other slaves, more than the first time, and the tenants treated them the same way. 37 Last of all he sent his son to them. 'Surely they will respect my son,' he said. 38 But when the tenants saw the son, they said to themselves, 'This is the owner's son. Come on, let's kill him, and we will get his property!' 39 So they grabbed him, threw him out of the vineyard, and killed him.

40 "Now, when the owner of the vineyard comes, what will he do to those tenants?" Jesus asked.

41 "He will certainly kill those evil men," they answered, "and rent the vineyard out to other tenants, who will give him his share of the harvest at the right time."

42 Jesus said to them, "Haven't you ever read what the Scriptures say?
'The stone which the builders
     rejected as worthless
     turned out to be the most
     important of all.
This was done by the Lord;
     what a wonderful sight it is!'

43 "And so I tell you," added Jesus, "the Kingdom of God will be taken away from you and given to a people who will produce the proper fruits."u

45 The chief priests and the Pharisees heard Jesus' parables and knew that he was talking about them, 46 so they tried to arrest him. But they were afraid of the crowds, who considered Jesus to be a prophet.

The Parable of the Wedding Feast
(Luke 14.15-24)

22 Jesus again used parables in talking to the people. 2 "The Kingdom of heaven is like this. Once there was a king who prepared a wedding feast for his son. 3 He sent his servants to tell the invited guests to come to the feast, but they did not want to come. 4 So he sent other servants with this message for the guests: 'My feast is ready now; my steers and prize calves have

been butchered, and everything is ready. Come to the wedding feast!' 5 But the invited guests paid no attention and went about their business: one went to his farm, another to his store, 6 while others grabbed the servants, beat them, and killed them. 7 The king was very angry; so he sent his soldiers, who killed those murderers and burned down their city. 8 Then he called his servants and said to them, 'My wedding feast is ready, but the people I invited did not deserve it. 9 Now go to the main streets and invite to the feast as many people as you find.' 10 So the servants went out into the streets and gathered all the people they could find, good and bad alike; and the wedding hall was filled with people.

11 "The king went in to look at the guests and saw a man who was not wearing wedding clothes. 12 'Friend, how did you get in here without wedding clothes?' the king asked him. But the man said nothing. 13 Then the king told the servants, 'Tie him up hand and foot, and throw him outside in the dark. There he will cry and gnash his teeth.' "

14 And Jesus concluded, "Many are invited, but few are chosen."

The Question about Paying Taxes
(Mark 12.13-17; Luke 20.20-26)

15 The Pharisees went off and made a plan to trap Jesus with questions. 16 Then they sent to him some of their disciples and some members of Herod's party. "Teacher," they said, "we know that you tell the truth. You teach the truth about God's will for people, without worrying about what others think, because you pay no attention to anyone's status. 17 Tell us, then, what do you think? Is it against our Law to pay taxes to the Roman Emperor, or not?"

18 Jesus, however, was aware of their evil plan, and so he said, "You hypocrites! Why are you trying to trap me? 19 Show me the coin for paying the tax!" They brought him the coin, 20 and he asked them, "Whose face and name are these?"

21 "The Emperor's," they answered.

So Jesus said to them, "Well, then, pay to the Emperor what belongs to the

---

u *Some manuscripts add verse 44:* Whoever falls on this stone will be cut to pieces; and if the stone falls on someone, it will crush him to dust *(see Lk 20.18).*

Emperor, and pay to God what belongs to God."

22 When they heard this, they were amazed; and they left him and went away.

The Question about Rising from Death

(Mark 12.18-27; Luke 20.27-40)

23 That same day some Sadducees came to Jesus and claimed that people will not rise from death. 24 "Teacher," they said, "Moses said that if a man who has no children dies, his brother must marry the widow so that they can have children who will be considered the dead man's children. 25 Now, there were seven brothers who used to live here. The oldest got married and died without having children, so he left his widow to his brother. 26 The same thing happened to the second brother, to the third, and finally to all seven. 27 Last of all, the woman died. 28 Now, on the day when the dead rise to life, whose wife will she be? All of them had married her."

29 Jesus answered them, "How wrong you are! It is because you don't know the Scriptures or God's power. 30 For when the dead rise to life, they will be like the angels in heaven and will not marry. 31 Now, as for the dead rising to life: haven't you ever read what God has told you? He said, 32 'I am the God of Abraham, the God of Isaac, and the God of Jacob.' He is the God of the living, not of the dead."

33 When the crowds heard this, they were amazed at his teaching.

The Great Commandment

(Mark 12.28-34; Luke 10.25-28)

34 When the Pharisees heard that Jesus had silenced the Sadducees, they came together, 35 and one of them, a teacher of the Law, tried to trap him with a question. 36 "Teacher," he asked, "which is the greatest commandment in the Law?"

37 Jesus answered, " 'Love the Lord your God with all your heart, with all your soul, and with all your mind.' 38 This is the greatest and the most important commandment. 39 The second most important commandment is like it:

'Love your neighbor as you love yourself.' 40 The whole Law of Moses and the teachings of the prophets depend on these two commandments."

The Question about the Messiah

(Mark 12.35-37; Luke 20.41-44)

41 When some Pharisees gathered together, Jesus asked them, 42 "What do you think about the Messiah? Whose descendant is he?"

"He is David's descendant," they answered.

43 "Why, then," Jesus asked, "did the Spirit inspire David to call him 'Lord'? David said,

44 'The Lord said to my Lord:
    Sit here at my right side
    until I put your enemies under
       your feet.'

45 If, then, David called him 'Lord,' how can the Messiah be David's descendant?"

46 No one was able to give Jesus any answer, and from that day on no one dared to ask him any more questions.

Jesus Warns against the Teachers of the Law and the Pharisees

(Mark 12.38, 39; Luke 11.43, 46; 20.45, 46)

23 Then Jesus spoke to the crowds and to his disciples. 2 "The teachers of the Law and the Pharisees are the authorized interpreters of Moses' Law. 3 So you must obey and follow everything they tell you to do; do not, however, imitate their actions, because they don't practice what they preach. 4 They tie onto people's backs loads that are heavy and hard to carry, yet they aren't willing even to lift a finger to help them carry those loads. 5 They do everything so that people will see them. Look at the straps with scripture verses on them which they wear on their foreheads and arms, and notice how large they are! Notice also how long are the tassels on their cloaks!*v* 6 They love the best places at feasts and the reserved seats in the synagogues; 7 they love to be greeted with respect in the marketplaces and to have people call them 'Teacher.' 8 You must not be called 'Teacher,' because you are all equal and have only one Teacher. 9 And you must not call anyone

---

v TASSELS ON THEIR CLOAKS: These tassels were worn as a sign of devotion to God (see Nu 15.37-41).

here on earth 'Father,' because you have only the one Father in heaven. 10 Nor should you be called 'Leader,' because your one and only leader is the Messiah. 11 The greatest one among you must be your servant. 12 Whoever makes himself great will be humbled, and whoever humbles himself will be made great.

Jesus Condemns Their Hypocrisy
(Mark 12.40; Luke 11.39-42, 44, 52; 20.47)

13 "How terrible for you, teachers of the Law and Pharisees! You hypocrites! You lock the door to the Kingdom of heaven in people's faces, but you yourselves don't go in, nor do you allow in those who are trying to enter!w

15 "How terrible for you, teachers of the Law and Pharisees! You hypocrites! You sail the seas and cross whole countries to win one convert; and when you succeed, you make him twice as deserving of going to hell as you yourselves are!

16 "How terrible for you, blind guides! You teach, 'If someone swears by the Temple, he isn't bound by his vow; but if he swears by the gold in the Temple, he is bound.' 17 Blind fools! Which is more important, the gold or the Temple which makes the gold holy? 18 You also teach, 'If someone swears by the altar, he isn't bound by his vow; but if he swears by the gift on the altar, he is bound.' 19 How blind you are! Which is the more important, the gift or the altar which makes the gift holy? 20 So then, when a person swears by the altar, he is swearing by it and by all the gifts on it; 21 and when he swears by the Temple, he is swearing by it and by God, who lives there; 22 and when someone swears by heaven, he is swearing by God's throne and by him who sits on it.

23 "How terrible for you, teachers of the Law and Pharisees! You hypocrites! You give to God one tenth even of the seasoning herbs, such as mint, dill, and cumin, but you neglect to obey the really important teachings of the Law, such as justice and mercy and honesty. These you should practice, without neglecting the others. 24 Blind guides! You strain a fly out of your drink, but swallow a camel!

25 "How terrible for you, teachers of the Law and Pharisees! You hypocrites! You clean the outside of your cup and plate, while the inside is full of what you have gotten by violence and selfishness. 26 Blind Pharisee! Clean what is inside the cup first, and then the outside will be clean too!

27 "How terrible for you, teachers of the Law and Pharisees! You hypocrites! You are like whitewashed tombs, which look fine on the outside but are full of bones and decaying corpses on the inside. 28 In the same way, on the outside you appear good to everybody, but inside you are full of hypocrisy and sins.

Jesus Predicts Their Punishment
(Luke 11.47-51)

29 "How terrible for you, teachers of the Law and Pharisees! You hypocrites! You make fine tombs for the prophets and decorate the monuments of those who lived good lives; 30 and you claim that if you had lived during the time of your ancestors, you would not have done what they did and killed the prophets. 31 So you actually admit that you are the descendants of those who murdered the prophets! 32 Go on, then, and finish up what your ancestors started! 33 You snakes and children of snakes! How do you expect to escape from being condemned to hell? 34 And so I tell you that I will send you prophets and wise men and teachers; you will kill some of them, crucify others, and whip others in the synagogues and chase them from town to town. 35 As a result, the punishment for the murder of all innocent people will fall on you, from the murder of innocent Abel to the murder of Zechariah son of Berechiah, whom you murdered between the Temple and the altar. 36 I tell you indeed: the punishment for all these murders will fall on the people of this day!

Jesus' Love for Jerusalem
(Luke 13.34, 35)

37 "Jerusalem, Jerusalem! You kill the prophets and stone the messengers God

---

w *Some manuscripts add verse 14:* How terrible for you, teachers of the Law and Pharisees! You hypocrites! You take advantage of widows and rob them of their homes, and then make a show of saying long prayers! Because of this your punishment will be all the worse! *(see Mk 12.40).*

M
A
T
T
H
E
W

has sent you! How many times I wanted to put my arms around all your people, just as a hen gathers her chicks under her wings, but you would not let me! 38 And so your Temple will be abandoned and empty. 39 From now on, I tell you, you will never see me again until you say, 'God bless him who comes in the name of the Lord.' "

Jesus Speaks of the Destruction of the Temple

(Mark 13.1, 2; Luke 21.5, 6)

24 Jesus left and was going away from the Temple when his disciples came to him to call his attention to its buildings. 2 "Yes," he said, "you may well look at all these. I tell you this: not a single stone here will be left in its place; every one of them will be thrown down."

Troubles and Persecutions

(Mark 13.3-13; Luke 21.7-19)

3 As Jesus sat on the Mount of Olives, the disciples came to him in private. "Tell us when all this will be," they asked, "and what will happen to show that it is the time for your coming and the end of the age."

4 Jesus answered, "Watch out, and do not let anyone fool you. 5 Many men, claiming to speak for me, will come and say, 'I am the Messiah!' and they will fool many people. 6 You are going to hear the noise of battles close by and the news of battles far away; but do not be troubled. Such things must happen, but they do not mean that the end has come. 7 Countries will fight each other; kingdoms will attack one another. There will be famines and earthquakes everywhere. 8 All these things are like the first pains of childbirth.

9 "Then you will be arrested and handed over to be punished and be put to death. Everyone will hate you because of me. 10 Many will give up their faith at that time; they will betray one another and hate one another. 11 Then many false prophets will appear and fool many people. 12 Such will be the spread of evil that many people's love will grow cold. 13 But whoever holds out to the end will be saved. 14 And this Good News about the Kingdom will be preached through all the world for a witness to all people; and then the end will come.

The Awful Horror

(Mark 13.14-23; Luke 21.20-24)

15 "You will see 'The Awful Horror' of which the prophet Daniel spoke. It will be standing in the holy place." (Note to the reader: understand what this means!) 16 "Then those who are in Judea must run away to the hills. 17 Someone who is on the roof of a house must not take the time to go down and get any belongings from the house. 18 Someone who is in the field must not go back to get a cloak. 19 How terrible it will be in those days for women who are pregnant and for mothers with little babies! 20 Pray to God that you will not have to run away during the winter or on a Sabbath! 21 For the trouble at that time will be far more terrible than any there has ever been, from the beginning of the world to this very day. Nor will there ever be anything like it again. 22 But God has already reduced the number of days; had he not done so, nobody would survive. For the sake of his chosen people, however, God will reduce the days.

23 "Then, if anyone says to you, 'Look, here is the Messiah!' or 'There he is!' — do not believe it. 24 For false Messiahs and false prophets will appear; they will perform great miracles and wonders in order to deceive even God's chosen people, if possible. 25 Listen! I have told you this ahead of time.

26 "Or, if people should tell you, 'Look, he is out in the desert!' — don't go there; or if they say, 'Look, he is hiding here!' — don't believe it. 27 For the Son of Man will come like the lightning which flashes across the whole sky from the east to the west.

28 "Wherever there is a dead body, the vultures will gather.

The Coming of the Son of Man

(Mark 13.24-27; Luke 21.25-28)

29 "Soon after the trouble of those days, the sun will grow dark, the moon will no longer shine, the stars will fall from heaven, and the powers in space will be driven from their courses. 30 Then the sign of the Son of Man will appear in the sky; and all the peoples of earth will weep as they see the Son of Man coming on the clouds of heaven with power and

great glory. 31 The great trumpet will sound, and he will send out his angels to the four corners of the earth, and they will gather his chosen people from one end of the world to the other.

The Lesson of the Fig Tree
(Mark 13.28-31; Luke 21.29-33)

32 "Let the fig tree teach you a lesson. When its branches become green and tender and it starts putting out leaves, you know that summer is near. 33 In the same way, when you see all these things, you will know that the time is near, ready to begin.x 34 Remember that all these things will happen before the people now living have all died. 35 Heaven and earth will pass away, but my words will never pass away.

No One Knows the Day and Hour
(Mark 13.32-37; Luke 17.26-30, 34-36)

36 "No one knows, however, when that day and hour will come—neither the angels in heaven nor the Son;y the Father alone knows. 37 The coming of the Son of Man will be like what happened in the time of Noah. 38 In the days before the flood people ate and drank, men and women married, up to the very day Noah went into the boat; 39 yet they did not realize what was happening until the flood came and swept them all away. That is how it will be when the Son of Man comes. 40 At that time two men will be working in a field: one will be taken away, the other will be left behind. 41 Two women will be at a mill grinding meal: one will be taken away, the other will be left behind. 42 Watch out, then, because you do not know what day your Lord will come. 43 If the owner of a house knew the time when the thief would come, you can be sure that he would stay awake and not let the thief break into his house. 44 So then, you also must always be ready, because the Son of Man will come at an hour when you are not expecting him.

The Faithful or the Unfaithful Servant
(Luke 12.41-48)

45 "Who, then, is a faithful and wise servant? It is the one that his master has placed in charge of the other servants to give them their food at the proper time. 46 How happy that servant is if his master finds him doing this when he comes home! 47 Indeed, I tell you, the master will put that servant in charge of all his property. 48 But if he is a bad servant, he will tell himself that his master will not come back for a long time, 49 and he will begin to beat his fellow servants and to eat and drink with drunkards. 50 Then that servant's master will come back one day when the servant does not expect him and at a time he does not know. 51 The master will cut him in piecesz and make him share the fate of the hypocrites. There he will cry and gnash his teeth.

The Parable of the Ten Young Women

25 "At that time the Kingdom of heaven will be like this. Once there were ten young women who took their oil lamps and went out to meet the bridegroom. 2 Five of them were foolish, and the other five were wise. 3 The foolish ones took their lamps but did not take any extra oil with them, 4 while the wise ones took containers full of oil for their lamps. 5 The bridegroom was late in coming, so they began to nod and fall asleep.

6 "It was already midnight when the cry rang out, 'Here is the bridegroom! Come and meet him!' 7 The ten young women woke up and trimmed their lamps. 8 Then the foolish ones said to the wise ones, 'Let us have some of your oil, because our lamps are going out.' 9 'No, indeed,' the wise ones answered, 'there is not enough for you and for us. Go to the store and buy some for yourselves.' 10 So the foolish ones went off to buy some oil; and while they were gone, the bridegroom arrived. The five who were ready went in with him to the wedding feast, and the door was closed.

11 "Later the others arrived. 'Sir, sir! Let us in!' they cried out. 12 'Certainly not! I don't know you,' the bridegroom answered."

13 And Jesus concluded, "Watch out, then, because you do not know the day or the hour.

x the time is near, ready to begin; *or* he is near, ready to come.   y *Some manuscripts do not* have nor the Son.   z cut him in pieces; *or* throw him out.

The Parable of the Three Servants

(Luke 19.11-27)

14 "At that time the Kingdom of heaven will be like this. Once there was a man who was about to leave home on a trip; he called his servants and put them in charge of his property. 15 He gave to each one according to his ability: to one he gave five thousand gold coins, to another he gave two thousand, and to another he gave one thousand. Then he left on his trip. 16 The servant who had received five thousand coins went at once and invested his money and earned another five thousand. 17 In the same way the servant who had received two thousand coins earned another two thousand. 18 But the servant who had received one thousand coins went off, dug a hole in the ground, and hid his master's money.

19 "After a long time the master of those servants came back and settled accounts with them. 20 The servant who had received five thousand coins came in and handed over the other five thousand. 'You gave me five thousand coins, sir,' he said. 'Look! Here are another five thousand that I have earned.' 21 'Well done, you good and faithful servant!' said his master. 'You have been faithful in managing small amounts, so I will put you in charge of large amounts. Come on in and share my happiness!' 22 Then the servant who had been given two thousand coins came in and said, 'You gave me two thousand coins, sir. Look! Here are another two thousand that I have earned.' 23 'Well done, you good and faithful servant!' said his master. 'You have been faithful in managing small amounts, so I will put you in charge of large amounts. Come on in and share my happiness!' 24 Then the servant who had received one thousand coins came in and said, 'Sir, I know you are a hard man; you reap harvests where you did not plant, and you gather crops where you did not scatter seed. 25 I was afraid, so I went off and hid your money in the ground. Look! Here is what belongs to you.' 26 'You bad and lazy servant!' his master said. 'You knew, did you, that I reap harvests where I did not plant, and gather crops where I did not scatter seed? 27 Well, then, you should have deposited my money in the bank, and I would have received it all back with interest when I returned. 28 Now, take the money away from him and give it to the one who has ten thousand coins. 29 For to every person who has something, even more will be given, and he will have more than enough; but the person who has nothing, even the little that he has will be taken away from him. 30 As for this useless servant—throw him outside in the darkness; there he will cry and gnash his teeth.'

The Final Judgment

31 "When the Son of Man comes as King and all the angels with him, he will sit on his royal throne, 32 and the people of all the nations will be gathered before him. Then he will divide them into two groups, just as a shepherd separates the sheep from the goats. 33 He will put the righteous people at his right and the others at his left. 34 Then the King will say to the people on his right, 'Come, you that are blessed by my Father! Come and possess the kingdom which has been prepared for you ever since the creation of the world. 35 I was hungry and you fed me, thirsty and you gave me a drink; I was a stranger and you received me in your homes, 36 naked and you clothed me; I was sick and you took care of me, in prison and you visited me.' 37 The righteous will then answer him, 'When, Lord, did we ever see you hungry and feed you, or thirsty and give you a drink? 38 When did we ever see you a stranger and welcome you in our homes, or naked and clothe you? 39 When did we ever see you sick or in prison, and visit you?' 40 The King will reply, 'I tell you, whenever you did this for one of the least important of these followers of mine, you did it for me!'

41 "Then he will say to those on his left, 'Away from me, you that are under God's curse! Away to the eternal fire which has been prepared for the Devil and his angels! 42 I was hungry but you would not feed me, thirsty but you would not give me a drink; 43 I was a stranger but you would not welcome me in your homes, naked but you would not clothe me; I was sick and in prison but you would not take care of me.' 44 Then they will answer him, 'When, Lord, did we ever see you hungry or thirsty or a

stranger or naked or sick or in prison, and we would not help you?' 45 The King will reply, 'I tell you, whenever you refused to help one of these least important ones, you refused to help me.' 46 These, then, will be sent off to eternal punishment, but the righteous will go to eternal life."

The Plot against Jesus
(Mark 14.1, 2; Luke 22.1, 2; John 11.45-53)

26 When Jesus had finished teaching all these things, he said to his disciples, 2 "In two days, as you know, it will be the Passover Festival, and the Son of Man will be handed over to be crucified."

3 Then the chief priests and the elders met together in the palace of Caiaphas, the High Priest, 4 and made plans to arrest Jesus secretly and put him to death. 5 "We must not do it during the festival," they said, "or the people will riot."

Jesus Is Anointed at Bethany
(Mark 14.3-9; John 12.1-8)

6 Jesus was in Bethany at the house of Simon, a man who had suffered from a dreaded skin disease. 7 While Jesus was eating, a woman came to him with an alabaster jar filled with an expensive perfume, which she poured on his head. 8 The disciples saw this and became angry. "Why all this waste?" they asked. 9 "This perfume could have been sold for a large amount and the money given to the poor!"

10 Jesus knew what they were saying, and so he said to them, "Why are you bothering this woman? It is a fine and beautiful thing that she has done for me. 11 You will always have poor people with you, but you will not always have me. 12 What she did was to pour this perfume on my body to get me ready for burial. 13 Now, I assure you that wherever this gospel is preached all over the world, what she has done will be told in memory of her."

Judas Agrees to Betray Jesus
(Mark 14.10, 11; Luke 22.3-6)

14 Then one of the twelve disciples — the one named Judas Iscariot — went to the chief priests 15 and asked, "What will you give me if I betray Jesus to you?" They counted out thirty silver coins and gave them to him. 16 From then on Judas was looking for a good chance to hand Jesus over to them.

Jesus Eats the Passover Meal with His Disciples
(Mark 14.12-21; Luke 22.7-13, 21-23; John 13.21-30)

17 On the first day of the Festival of Unleavened Bread the disciples came to Jesus and asked him, "Where do you want us to get the Passover meal ready for you?"

18 "Go to a certain man in the city," he said to them, "and tell him: 'The Teacher says, My hour has come; my disciples and I will celebrate the Passover at your house.' "

19 The disciples did as Jesus had told them and prepared the Passover meal.

20 When it was evening, Jesus and the twelve disciples sat down to eat. 21 During the meal Jesus said, "I tell you, one of you will betray me."

22 The disciples were very upset and began to ask him, one after the other, "Surely, Lord, you don't mean me?"

23 Jesus answered, "One who dips his bread in the dish with me will betray me. 24 The Son of Man will die as the Scriptures say he will, but how terrible for that man who will betray the Son of Man! It would have been better for that man if he had never been born!"

25 Judas, the traitor, spoke up. "Surely, Teacher, you don't mean me?" he asked.

Jesus answered, "So you say."

The Lord's Supper
(Mark 14.22-26; Luke 22.14-20; 1 Corinthians 11.23-25)

26 While they were eating, Jesus took a piece of bread, gave a prayer of thanks, broke it, and gave it to his disciples. "Take and eat it," he said; "this is my body."

27 Then he took a cup, gave thanks to God, and gave it to them. "Drink it, all of you," he said; 28 "this is my blood, which seals God's covenant, my blood poured out for many for the forgiveness of sins. 29 I tell you, I will never again drink this wine until the day I drink the new wine with you in my Father's Kingdom."

30 Then they sang a hymn and went out to the Mount of Olives.

Jesus Predicts Peter's Denial
(Mark 14.27-31; Luke 22.31-34; John 13.36-38)

31 Then Jesus said to them, "This very night all of you will run away and leave me, for the scripture says, 'God will kill the shepherd, and the sheep of the flock will be scattered.' 32 But after I am raised to life, I will go to Galilee ahead of you."

33 Peter spoke up and said to Jesus, "I will never leave you, even though all the rest do!"

34 Jesus said to Peter, "I tell you that before the rooster crows tonight, you will say three times that you do not know me."

35 Peter answered, "I will never say that, even if I have to die with you!"

And all the other disciples said the same thing.

Jesus Prays in Gethsemane
(Mark 14.32-42; Luke 22.39-46)

36 Then Jesus went with his disciples to a place called Gethsemane, and he said to them, "Sit here while I go over there and pray." 37 He took with him Peter and the two sons of Zebedee. Grief and anguish came over him, 38 and he said to them, "The sorrow in my heart is so great that it almost crushes me. Stay here and keep watch with me."

39 He went a little farther on, threw himself face downward on the ground, and prayed, "My Father, if it is possible, take this cup of suffering from me! Yet not what I want, but what you want." 40 Then he returned to the three disciples and found them asleep; and he said to Peter, "How is it that you three were not able to keep watch with me for even one hour? 41 Keep watch and pray that you will not fall into temptation. The spirit is willing, but the flesh is weak."

42 Once more Jesus went away and prayed, "My Father, if this cup of suffering cannot be taken away unless I drink it, your will be done." 43 He returned once more and found the disciples asleep; they could not keep their eyes open.

44 Again Jesus left them, went away, and prayed the third time, saying the same words. 45 Then he returned to the disciples and said, "Are you still sleeping and resting? Look! The hour has come for the Son of Man to be handed over to the power of sinners. 46 Get up, let us go. Look, here is the man who is betraying me!"

The Arrest of Jesus
(Mark 14.43-50; Luke 22.47-53; John 18.3-12)

47 Jesus was still speaking when Judas, one of the twelve disciples, arrived. With him was a large crowd armed with swords and clubs and sent by the chief priests and the elders. 48 The traitor had given the crowd a signal: "The man I kiss is the one you want. Arrest him!"

49 Judas went straight to Jesus and said, "Peace be with you, Teacher," and kissed him.

50 Jesus answered, "Be quick about it, friend!"[a]

Then they came up, arrested Jesus, and held him tight. 51 One of those who were with Jesus drew his sword and struck at the High Priest's slave, cutting off his ear. 52 "Put your sword back in its place," Jesus said to him. "All who take the sword will die by the sword. 53 Don't you know that I could call on my Father for help, and at once he would send me more than twelve armies of angels? 54 But in that case, how could the Scriptures come true which say that this is what must happen?"

55 Then Jesus spoke to the crowd, "Did you have to come with swords and clubs to capture me, as though I were an outlaw? Every day I sat down and taught in the Temple, and you did not arrest me. 56 But all this has happened in order to make come true what the prophets wrote in the Scriptures."

Then all the disciples left him and ran away.

Jesus before the Council
(Mark 14.53-65; Luke 22.54, 55, 63-71; John 18.13, 14, 19-24)

57 Those who had arrested Jesus took him to the house of Caiaphas, the High Priest, where the teachers of the Law and the elders had gathered together. 58 Peter followed from a distance, as far as the courtyard of the High Priest's house. He went into the courtyard and sat down with the guards to see how it would all come out. 59 The chief priests and the whole Council tried to find some

---

[a] Be quick about it, friend!; *or* Why are you here, friend?

false evidence against Jesus to put him to death; 60 but they could not find any, even though many people came forward and told lies about him. Finally two men stepped up 61 and said, "This man said, 'I am able to tear down God's Temple and three days later build it back up.' "

62 The High Priest stood up and said to Jesus, "Have you no answer to give to this accusation against you?" 63 But Jesus kept quiet. Again the High Priest spoke to him, "In the name of the living God I now put you under oath: tell us if you are the Messiah, the Son of God."

64 Jesus answered him, "So you say. But I tell all of you: from this time on you will see the Son of Man sitting at the right side of the Almighty and coming on the clouds of heaven!"

65 At this the High Priest tore his clothes and said, "Blasphemy! We don't need any more witnesses! You have just heard his blasphemy! 66 What do you think?"

They answered, "He is guilty and must die."

67 Then they spat in his face and beat him; and those who slapped him 68 said, "Prophesy for us, Messiah! Guess who hit you!"

Peter Denies Jesus
(Mark 14.66-72; Luke 22.56-62; John 18.15-18, 25-27)

69 Peter was sitting outside in the courtyard when one of the High Priest's servant women came to him and said, "You, too, were with Jesus of Galilee."

70 But he denied it in front of them all. "I don't know what you are talking about," he answered, 71 and went on out to the entrance of the courtyard. Another servant woman saw him and said to the men there, "He was with Jesus of Nazareth."

72 Again Peter denied it and answered, "I swear that I don't know that man!"

73 After a little while the men standing there came to Peter. "Of course you are one of them," they said. "After all, the way you speak gives you away!"

74 Then Peter said, "I swear that I am telling the truth! May God punish me if I am not! I do not know that man!"

Just then a rooster crowed, 75 and Peter remembered what Jesus had told him: "Before the rooster crows, you will say three times that you do not know me." He went out and wept bitterly.

Jesus Is Taken to Pilate
(Mark 15.1; Luke 23.1, 2; John 18.28-32)

27 Early in the morning all the chief priests and the elders made their plans against Jesus to put him to death. 2 They put him in chains, led him off, and handed him over to Pilate, the Roman governor.

The Death of Judas
(Acts 1.18, 19)

3 When Judas, the traitor, learned that Jesus had been condemned, he repented and took back the thirty silver coins to the chief priests and the elders. 4 "I have sinned by betraying an innocent man to death!" he said.

"What do we care about that?" they answered. "That is your business!"

5 Judas threw the coins down in the Temple and left; then he went off and hanged himself.

6 The chief priests picked up the coins and said, "This is blood money, and it is against our Law to put it in the Temple treasury." 7 After reaching an agreement about it, they used the money to buy Potter's Field, as a cemetery for foreigners. 8 That is why that field is called "Field of Blood" to this very day.

9 Then what the prophet Jeremiah had said came true: "They took the thirty silver coins, the amount the people of Israel had agreed to pay for him, 10 and used the money to buy the potter's field, as the Lord had commanded me."

Pilate Questions Jesus
(Mark 15.2-5; Luke 23.3-5; John 18.33-38)

11 Jesus stood before the Roman governor, who questioned him. "Are you the king of the Jews?" he asked.

"So you say," answered Jesus. 12 But he said nothing in response to the accusations of the chief priests and elders. 13 So Pilate said to him, "Don't you hear all these things they accuse you of?"

14 But Jesus refused to answer a single word, with the result that the Governor was greatly surprised.

Jesus Is Sentenced to Death
(Mark 15.6-15; Luke 23.13-25; John 18.39–19.16)

15 At every Passover Festival the Roman governor was in the habit of setting free any one prisoner the crowd asked for. 16 At that time there was a well-

known prisoner named Jesus Barabbas. 17 So when the crowd gathered, Pilate asked them, "Which one do you want me to set free for you? Jesus Barabbas or Jesus called the Messiah?" 18 He knew very well that the Jewish authorities had handed Jesus over to him because they were jealous.

19 While Pilate was sitting in the judgment hall, his wife sent him a message: "Have nothing to do with that innocent man, because in a dream last night I suffered much on account of him."

20 The chief priests and the elders persuaded the crowd to ask Pilate to set Barabbas free and have Jesus put to death. 21 But Pilate asked the crowd, "Which one of these two do you want me to set free for you?"

"Barabbas!" they answered.

22 "What, then, shall I do with Jesus called the Messiah?" Pilate asked them.

"Crucify him!" they all answered.

23 But Pilate asked, "What crime has he committed?"

Then they started shouting at the top of their voices: "Crucify him!"

24 When Pilate saw that it was no use to go on, but that a riot might break out, he took some water, washed his hands in front of the crowd, and said, "I am not responsible for the death of this man! This is your doing!"

25 The whole crowd answered, "Let the responsibility for his death fall on us and on our children!"

26 Then Pilate set Barabbas free for them; and after he had Jesus whipped, he handed him over to be crucified.

The Soldiers Make Fun of Jesus
(Mark 15.16-20; John 19.2, 3)

27 Then Pilate's soldiers took Jesus into the governor's palace, and the whole company gathered around him. 28 They stripped off his clothes and put a scarlet robe on him. 29 Then they made a crown out of thorny branches and placed it on his head, and put a stick in his right hand; then they knelt before him and made fun of him. "Long live the King of the Jews!" they said. 30 They spat on him, and took the stick and hit him over the head. 31 When they had finished making fun of him, they took the robe off and put his own clothes back on him. Then they led him out to crucify him.

Jesus Is Crucified
(Mark 15.21-32; Luke 23.26-43; John 19.17-27)

32 As they were going out, they met a man from Cyrene named Simon, and the soldiers forced him to carry Jesus' cross. 33 They came to a place called Golgotha, which means, "The Place of the Skull." 34 There they offered Jesus wine mixed with a bitter substance; but after tasting it, he would not drink it.

35 They crucified him and then divided his clothes among them by throwing dice. 36 After that they sat there and watched him. 37 Above his head they put the written notice of the accusation against him: "This is Jesus, the King of the Jews." 38 Then they crucified two bandits with Jesus, one on his right and the other on his left.

39 People passing by shook their heads and hurled insults at Jesus: 40 "You were going to tear down the Temple and build it back up in three days! Save yourself if you are God's Son! Come on down from the cross!"

41 In the same way the chief priests and the teachers of the Law and the elders made fun of him: 42 "He saved others, but he cannot save himself! Isn't he the king of Israel? If he will come down off the cross now, we will believe in him! 43 He trusts in God and claims to be God's Son. Well, then, let us see if God wants to save him now!"

44 Even the bandits who had been crucified with him insulted him in the same way.

The Death of Jesus
(Mark 15.33-41; Luke 23.44-49; John 19.28-30)

45 At noon the whole country was covered with darkness, which lasted for three hours. 46 At about three o'clock Jesus cried out with a loud shout, *"Eli, Eli, lema sabachthani?"* which means, "My God, my God, why did you abandon me?"

47 Some of the people standing there heard him and said, "He is calling for Elijah!" 48 One of them ran up at once, took a sponge, soaked it in cheap wine, put it on the end of a stick, and tried to make him drink it.

49 But the others said, "Wait, let us see if Elijah is coming to save him!"

50 Jesus again gave a loud cry and breathed his last.

51 Then the curtain hanging in the Temple was torn in two from top to bottom. The earth shook, the rocks split apart, 52 the graves broke open, and many of God's people who had died were raised to life. 53 They left the graves, and after Jesus rose from death, they went into the Holy City, where many people saw them.

54 When the army officer and the soldiers with him who were watching Jesus saw the earthquake and everything else that happened, they were terrified and said, "He really was the Son of God!"

55 There were many women there, looking on from a distance, who had followed Jesus from Galilee and helped him. 56 Among them were Mary Magdalene, Mary the mother of James and Joseph, and the wife of Zebedee.

The Burial of Jesus
(Mark 15.42-47; Luke 23.50-56; John 19.38-42)

57 When it was evening, a rich man from Arimathea arrived; his name was Joseph, and he also was a disciple of Jesus. 58 He went into the presence of Pilate and asked for the body of Jesus. Pilate gave orders for the body to be given to Joseph. 59 So Joseph took it, wrapped it in a new linen sheet, 60 and placed it in his own tomb, which he had just recently dug out of solid rock. Then he rolled a large stone across the entrance to the tomb and went away. 61 Mary Magdalene and the other Mary were sitting there, facing the tomb.

The Guard at the Tomb

62 The next day, which was a Sabbath, the chief priests and the Pharisees met with Pilate 63 and said, "Sir, we remember that while that liar was still alive he said, 'I will be raised to life three days later.' 64 Give orders, then, for his tomb to be carefully guarded until the third day, so that his disciples will not be able to go and steal the body, and then tell the people that he was raised from death. This last lie would be even worse than the first one."

65 "Take a guard," Pilate told them; "go and make the tomb as secure as you can."

66 So they left and made the tomb secure by putting a seal on the stone and leaving the guard on watch.

The Resurrection
(Mark 16.1-10; Luke 24.1-12; John 20.1-10)

28 After the Sabbath, as Sunday morning was dawning, Mary Magdalene and the other Mary went to look at the tomb. 2 Suddenly there was a violent earthquake; an angel of the Lord came down from heaven, rolled the stone away, and sat on it. 3 His appearance was like lightning, and his clothes were white as snow. 4 The guards were so afraid that they trembled and became like dead men.

5 The angel spoke to the women. "You must not be afraid," he said. "I know you are looking for Jesus, who was crucified. 6 He is not here; he has been raised, just as he said. Come here and see the place where he was lying. 7 Go quickly now, and tell his disciples, 'He has been raised from death, and now he is going to Galilee ahead of you; there you will see him!' Remember what I have told you."

8 So they left the tomb in a hurry, afraid and yet filled with joy, and ran to tell his disciples.

9 Suddenly Jesus met them and said, "Peace be with you." They came up to him, took hold of his feet, and worshiped him. 10 "Do not be afraid," Jesus said to them. "Go and tell my brothers to go to Galilee, and there they will see me."

The Report of the Guard

11 While the women went on their way, some of the soldiers guarding the tomb went back to the city and told the chief priests everything that had happened. 12 The chief priests met with the elders and made their plan; they gave a large sum of money to the soldiers 13 and said, "You are to say that his disciples came during the night and stole his body while you were asleep. 14 And if the Governor should hear of this, we will convince him that you are innocent, and you will have nothing to worry about."

15 The guards took the money and did what they were told to do. And so that is the report spread around by the Jews to this very day.

Jesus Appears to His Disciples
(Mark 16.14-18; Luke 24.36-49; John 20.19-23; Acts 1.6-8)

16 The eleven disciples went to the hill in Galilee where Jesus had told them to go. 17 When they saw him, they wor-

MATTHEW

shiped him, even though some of them doubted. [18] Jesus drew near and said to them, "I have been given all authority in heaven and on earth. [19] Go, then, to all peoples everywhere and make them my disciples: baptize them in the name of the Father, the Son, and the Holy Spirit, [20] and teach them to obey everything I have commanded you. And I will be with you always, to the end of the age."

The Gospel according to

MARK

Introduction

The Gospel according to Mark *begins with the statement that it is "the Good News about Jesus Christ, the Son of God." Jesus is pictured as a man of action and authority. His authority is seen in his teaching, in his power over demons, and in forgiving people's sins. Jesus speaks of himself as the Son of Man, who came to give his life to set people free from sin.*

Mark presents the story of Jesus in a straightforward, vigorous way, with emphasis on what Jesus did, rather than on his words and teachings. After a brief prologue about John the Baptist and the baptism and temptation of Jesus, the writer immediately takes up Jesus' ministry of healing and teaching. As time goes on, the followers of Jesus come to understand him better, but Jesus' opponents become more hostile. The closing chapters report the events of Jesus' last week of earthly life, especially his crucifixion and resurrection.

The two endings to the Gospel, which are enclosed in brackets, are generally regarded as written by someone other than the author of Mark.

Outline of Contents

The Preaching of John the Baptist

(Matthew 3.1-12; Luke 3.1-18; John 1.19-28)

1 This is the Good News about Jesus Christ, the Son of God.*a* 2 It began as the prophet Isaiah had written:

"God said, 'I will send my
    messenger ahead of you
to open the way for you.'
3 Someone is shouting in the desert,
    'Get the road ready for the
        Lord;
    make a straight path for him to
        travel!'"

4 So John appeared in the desert, baptizing and preaching.*b* "Turn away from your sins and be baptized," he told the people, "and God will forgive your sins." 5 Many people from the province of Judea and the city of Jerusalem went out to hear John. They confessed their sins, and he baptized them in the Jordan River.

6 John wore clothes made of camel's hair, with a leather belt around his waist, and his food was locusts and wild honey. 7 He announced to the people, "The man who will come after me is much greater than I am. I am not good enough even to bend down and untie his sandals. 8 I baptize you with water, but he will baptize you with the Holy Spirit."

The Baptism and Temptation of Jesus

(Matthew 3.13—4.11; Luke 3.21, 22; 4.1-13)

9 Not long afterward Jesus came from Nazareth in the province of Galilee, and was baptized by John in the Jordan. 10 As soon as Jesus came up out of the water, he saw heaven opening and the Spirit coming down on him like a dove. 11 And a voice came from heaven, "You are my own dear Son. I am pleased with you."

12 At once the Spirit made him go into the desert, 13 where he stayed forty days, being tempted by Satan. Wild animals were there also, but angels came and helped him.

---

a Some manuscripts do not have the Son of God. *b* John appeared in the desert, baptizing and preaching; some manuscripts have John the Baptist appeared in the desert, preaching.

Jesus Calls Four Fishermen
(Matthew 4.12-22; Luke 4.14, 15; 5.1-11)

14 After John had been put in prison, Jesus went to Galilee and preached the Good News from God. 15 "The right time has come," he said, "and the Kingdom of God is near! Turn away from your sins and believe the Good News!"

16 As Jesus walked along the shore of Lake Galilee, he saw two fishermen, Simon and his brother Andrew, catching fish with a net. 17 Jesus said to them, "Come with me, and I will teach you to catch people." 18 At once they left their nets and went with him.

19 He went a little farther on and saw two other brothers, James and John, the sons of Zebedee. They were in their boat getting their nets ready. 20 As soon as Jesus saw them, he called them; they left their father Zebedee in the boat with the hired men and went with Jesus.

A Man with an Evil Spirit
(Luke 4.31-37)

21 Jesus and his disciples came to the town of Capernaum, and on the next Sabbath Jesus went to the synagogue and began to teach. 22 The people who heard him were amazed at the way he taught, for he wasn't like the teachers of the Law; instead, he taught with authority.

23 Just then a man with an evil spirit came into the synagogue and screamed, 24 "What do you want with us, Jesus of Nazareth? Are you here to destroy us? I know who you are — you are God's holy messenger!"

25 Jesus ordered the spirit, "Be quiet, and come out of the man!"

26 The evil spirit shook the man hard, gave a loud scream, and came out of him. 27 The people were all so amazed that they started saying to one another, "What is this? Is it some kind of new teaching? This man has authority to give orders to the evil spirits, and they obey him!"

28 And so the news about Jesus spread quickly everywhere in the province of Galilee.

Jesus Heals Many People
(Matthew 8.14-17; Luke 4.38-41)

29 Jesus and his disciples, including James and John, left the synagogue and went straight to the home of Simon and Andrew. 30 Simon's mother-in-law was sick in bed with a fever, and as soon as Jesus arrived, he was told about her. 31 He went to her, took her by the hand, and helped her up. The fever left her, and she began to wait on them.

32 After the sun had set and evening had come, people brought to Jesus all the sick and those who had demons. 33 All the people of the town gathered in front of the house. 34 Jesus healed many who were sick with all kinds of diseases and drove out many demons. He would not let the demons say anything, because they knew who he was.

Jesus Preaches in Galilee
(Luke 4.42-44)

35 Very early the next morning, long before daylight, Jesus got up and left the house. He went out of town to a lonely place, where he prayed. 36 But Simon and his companions went out searching for him, 37 and when they found him, they said, "Everyone is looking for you."

38 But Jesus answered, "We must go on to the other villages around here. I have to preach in them also, because that is why I came."

39 So he traveled all over Galilee, preaching in the synagogues and driving out demons.

Jesus Heals a Man
(Matthew 8.1-4; Luke 5.12-16)

40 A man suffering from a dreaded skin disease came to Jesus, knelt down, and begged him for help. "If you want to," he said, "you can make me clean."c

41 Jesus was filled with pity,d and reached out and touched him. "I do want to," he answered. "Be clean!" 42 At once the disease left the man, and he was clean. 43 Then Jesus spoke sternly to him and sent him away at once, 44 after saying to him, "Listen, don't tell anyone about this. But go straight to the priest and let him examine you; then in order to prove to everyone that you are cured, offer the sacrifice that Moses ordered."

---

c MAKE ME CLEAN: *This disease was considered to make a person ritually unclean.*
d pity; *some manuscripts have* anger.

THE CITY OF CAPERNAUM

One of the sites in modern Israel that stirs the soul of the Christian is the ruins of the synagogue that has been uncovered at Capernaum. Here, walking through the ruins, one can imagine Jesus healing the sick and teaching the people about the kingdom of God. This fishing town on the shores of Lake Galilee was the center of his activities soon after he began his public ministry.

Although the synagogue visited by tourists at Capernaum does not date to the time of Jesus, it was probably built in the second or third century A.D., and we may imagine Jesus ministering in just such a place (Mk 1.21). In Capernaum Jesus healed many people, including a Roman soldier's paralyzed servant (Mt 8.5–13), a paralyzed man carried by his friends (Mk 2.1–12), Simon's mother-in-law (Mk 1.29–31), and a nobleman's son (Jn 4.46–54).

While walking by Lake Galilee near Capernaum, Jesus called Peter, Andrew, James, and John to become his disciples (Mk 1.16–21). It was also at Capernaum that he called the tax collector Matthew (Mk 2.1, 13, 14). After the feeding of the five thousand, he delivered his discourse on the bread of life near this city (Jn 6.32–59).

Jesus was deeply concerned about the lack of belief demonstrated by the citizens of Capernaum. He pronounced a curse upon the city (Mt 11.23, 24) and predicted its ruin (Lk 10.15). So strikingly did his prophecy come true that only recently has the site of Capernaum been positively identified.

The name *Capernaum* means village of Nahum. It was probably named for the man who owned the land where the village first grew up—an unknown person not to be confused with the prophet Nahum of the Old Testament.

M
A
R
K

45 But the man went away and began to spread the news everywhere. Indeed, he talked so much that Jesus could not go into a town publicly. Instead, he stayed out in lonely places, and people came to him from everywhere.

Jesus Heals a Paralyzed Man
(Matthew 9.1-8; Luke 5.17-26)

2 A few days later Jesus went back to Capernaum, and the news spread that he was at home. 2 So many people came together that there was no room left, not even out in front of the door. Jesus was preaching the message to them 3 when four men arrived, carrying a paralyzed man to Jesus. 4 Because of the crowd, however, they could not get the man to him. So they made a hole in the roof right above the place where Jesus was. When they had made an opening, they let the man down, lying on his mat. 5 Seeing how much faith they had, Jesus said to the paralyzed man, "My son, your sins are forgiven."

6 Some teachers of the Law who were sitting there thought to themselves, 7 "How does he dare talk like this? This is blasphemy! God is the only one who can forgive sins!"

8 At once Jesus knew what they were thinking, so he said to them, "Why do you think such things? 9 Is it easier to say to this paralyzed man, 'Your sins are forgiven,' or to say, 'Get up, pick up your mat, and walk'? 10 I will prove to you, then, that the Son of Man has authority on earth to forgive sins." So he said to the paralyzed man, 11 "I tell you, get up, pick up your mat, and go home!"

12 While they all watched, the man got up, picked up his mat, and hurried away. They were all completely amazed and praised God, saying, "We have never seen anything like this!"

Jesus Calls Levi
(Matthew 9.9-13; Luke 5.27-32)

13 Jesus went back again to the shore of Lake Galilee. A crowd came to him, and he started teaching them. 14 As he walked along, he saw a tax collector, Levi son of Alphaeus, sitting in his office. Jesus said to him, "Follow me." Levi got up and followed him.

15 Later on Jesus was having a meal in Levi's house.e A large number of tax collectors and other outcasts was following Jesus, and many of them joined him and his disciples at the table. 16 Some teachers of the Law, who were Pharisees, saw that Jesus was eating with these outcasts and tax collectors, so they asked his disciples, "Why does he eat with such people?"

17 Jesus heard them and answered, "People who are well do not need a doctor, but only those who are sick. I have not come to call respectable people, but outcasts."

The Question about Fasting
(Matthew 9.14-17; Luke 5.33-39)

18 On one occasion the followers of John the Baptist and the Pharisees were fasting. Some people came to Jesus and asked him, "Why is it that the disciples of John the Baptist and the disciples of the Pharisees fast, but yours do not?"

19 Jesus answered, "Do you expect the guests at a wedding party to go without food? Of course not! As long as the bridegroom is with them, they will not do that. 20 But the day will come when the bridegroom will be taken away from them, and then they will fast.

21 "No one uses a piece of new cloth to patch up an old coat, because the new patch will shrink and tear off some of the old cloth, making an even bigger hole. 22 Nor does anyone pour new wine into used wineskins, because the wine will burst the skins, and both the wine and the skins will be ruined. Instead, new wine must be poured into fresh wineskins."

The Question about the Sabbath
(Matthew 12.1-8; Luke 6.1-5)

23 Jesus was walking through some wheat fields on a Sabbath. As his disciples walked along with him, they began to pick the heads of wheat. 24 So the Pharisees said to Jesus, "Look, it is against our Law for your disciples to do that on the Sabbath!"

25 Jesus answered, "Have you never read what David did that time when he needed something to eat? He and his men were hungry, 26 so he went into the house of God and ate the bread offered to God. This happened when Abiathar

e in Levi's house; or in his (that is, Jesus') house.

was the High Priest. According to our Law only the priests may eat this bread—but David ate it and even gave it to his men."

27 And Jesus concluded, "The Sabbath was made for the good of human beings; they were not made for the Sabbath. 28 So the Son of Man is Lord even of the Sabbath."

The Man with a Paralyzed Hand
(Matthew 12.9-14; Luke 6.6-11)

3 Then Jesus went back to the synagogue, where there was a man who had a paralyzed hand. 2 Some people were there who wanted to accuse Jesus of doing wrong; so they watched him closely to see whether he would cure the man on the Sabbath. 3 Jesus said to the man, "Come up here to the front." 4 Then he asked the people, "What does our Law allow us to do on the Sabbath? To help or to harm? To save someone's life or to destroy it?"

But they did not say a thing. 5 Jesus was angry as he looked around at them, but at the same time he felt sorry for them, because they were so stubborn and wrong. Then he said to the man, "Stretch out your hand." He stretched it out, and it became well again. 6 So the Pharisees left the synagogue and met at once with some members of Herod's party, and they made plans to kill Jesus.

A Crowd by the Lake

7 Jesus and his disciples went away to Lake Galilee, and a large crowd followed him. They had come from Galilee, from Judea, 8 from Jerusalem, from the territory of Idumea, from the territory on the east side of the Jordan, and from the region around the cities of Tyre and Sidon. All these people came to Jesus because they had heard of the things he was doing. 9 The crowd was so large that Jesus told his disciples to get a boat ready for him, so that the people would not crush him. 10 He had healed many people, and all the sick kept pushing their way to him in order to touch him. 11 And whenever the people who had evil spirits in them saw him, they would fall down before him and scream, "You are the Son of God!"

12 Jesus sternly ordered the evil spirits not to tell anyone who he was.

Jesus Chooses the Twelve Apostles
(Matthew 10.1-4; Luke 6.12-16)

13 Then Jesus went up a hill and called to himself the men he wanted. They came to him, 14 and he chose twelve, whom he named apostles. "I have chosen you to be with me," he told them. "I will also send you out to preach, 15 and you will have authority to drive out demons."

16 These are the twelve he chose: Simon (Jesus gave him the name Peter); 17 James and his brother John, the sons of Zebedee (Jesus gave them the name Boanerges, which means "Men of Thunder"); 18 Andrew, Philip, Bartholomew, Matthew, Thomas, James son of Alphaeus, Thaddaeus, Simon the Patriot, 19 and Judas Iscariot, who betrayed Jesus.

Jesus and Beelzebul
(Matthew 12.22-32; Luke 11.14-23; 12.10)

20 Then Jesus went home. Again such a large crowd gathered that Jesus and his disciples had no time to eat. 21 When his family heard about it, they set out to take charge of him, because people were saying, "He's gone mad!"

22 Some teachers of the Law who had come from Jerusalem were saying, "He has Beelzebul in him! It is the chief of the demons who gives him the power to drive them out."

23 So Jesus called them to him and spoke to them in parables: "How can Satan drive out Satan? 24 If a country divides itself into groups which fight each other, that country will fall apart. 25 If a family divides itself into groups which fight each other, that family will fall apart. 26 So if Satan's kingdom divides into groups, it cannot last, but will fall apart and come to an end.

27 "No one can break into a strong man's house and take away his belongings unless he first ties up the strong man; then he can plunder his house.

28 "I assure you that people can be forgiven all their sins and all the evil things they may say. *f* 29 But whoever says evil things against the Holy Spirit will never be forgiven, because he has committed

f evil things they may say; or evil things they may say against God.

an eternal sin." (30 Jesus said this because some people were saying, "He has an evil spirit in him.")

Jesus' Mother and Brothers
(Matthew 12.46-50; Luke 8.19-21)

31 Then Jesus' mother and brothers arrived. They stood outside the house and sent in a message, asking for him. 32 A crowd was sitting around Jesus, and they said to him, "Look, your mother and your brothers and sisters are outside, and they want you."

33 Jesus answered, "Who is my mother? Who are my brothers?" 34 He looked at the people sitting around him and said, "Look! Here are my mother and my brothers! 35 Whoever does what God wants is my brother, my sister, my mother."

The Parable of the Sower
(Matthew 13.1-9; Luke 8.4-8)

4 Again Jesus began to teach beside Lake Galilee. The crowd that gathered around him was so large that he got into a boat and sat in it. The boat was out in the water, and the crowd stood on the shore at the water's edge. 2 He used parables to teach them many things, saying to them:

3 "Listen! Once there was a man who went out to sow grain. 4 As he scattered the seed in the field, some of it fell along the path, and the birds came and ate it up. 5 Some of it fell on rocky ground, where there was little soil. The seeds soon sprouted, because the soil wasn't deep. 6 Then, when the sun came up, it burned the young plants; and because the roots had not grown deep enough, the plants soon dried up. 7 Some of the seed fell among thorn bushes, which grew up and choked the plants, and they didn't bear grain. 8 But some seeds fell in good soil, and the plants sprouted, grew, and bore grain: some had thirty grains, others sixty, and others one hundred."

9 And Jesus concluded, "Listen, then, if you have ears!"

The Purpose of the Parables
(Matthew 13.10-17; Luke 8.9, 10)

10 When Jesus was alone, some of those who had heard him came to him with the twelve disciples and asked him to explain the parables. 11 "You have been given the secret of the Kingdom of God," Jesus answered. "But the others, who are on the outside, hear all things by means of parables, 12 so that,

'They may look and look,
    yet not see;
they may listen and listen,
    yet not understand.
For if they did, they would turn
    to God,
    and he would forgive them.' "

Jesus Explains the Parable of the Sower
(Matthew 13.18-23; Luke 8.11-15)

13 Then Jesus asked them, "Don't you understand this parable? How, then, will you ever understand any parable? 14 The sower sows God's message. 15 Some people are like the seeds that fall along the path; as soon as they hear the message, Satan comes and takes it away. 16 Other people are like the seeds that fall on rocky ground. As soon as they hear the message, they receive it gladly. 17 But it does not sink deep into them, and they don't last long. So when trouble or persecution comes because of the message, they give up at once. 18 Other people are like the seeds sown among the thorn bushes. These are the ones who hear the message, 19 but the worries about this life, the love for riches, and all other kinds of desires crowd in and choke the message, and they don't bear fruit. 20 But other people are like seeds sown in good soil. They hear the message, accept it, and bear fruit: some thirty, some sixty, and some one hundred."

A Lamp under a Bowl
(Luke 8.16-18)

21 Jesus continued, "Does anyone ever bring in a lamp and put it under a bowl or under the bed? Isn't it put on the lampstand? 22 Whatever is hidden away will be brought out into the open, and whatever is covered up will be uncovered. 23 Listen, then, if you have ears!"

24 He also said to them, "Pay attention to what you hear! The same rules you use to judge others will be used by God to judge you—but with even greater severity. 25 Those who have something will be given more, and those who have nothing will have taken away from them even the little they have."

The Parable of the Growing Seed

26 Jesus went on to say, "The Kingdom of God is like this. A man scatters seed in his field. 27 He sleeps at night, is up and about during the day, and all the while the seeds are sprouting and growing. Yet he does not know how it happens. 28 The soil itself makes the plants grow and bear fruit; first the tender stalk appears, then the head, and finally the head full of grain. 29 When the grain is ripe, the man starts cutting it with his sickle, because harvest time has come.

The Parable of the Mustard Seed
(Matthew 13.31, 32, 34; Luke 13.18, 19)

30 "What shall we say the Kingdom of God is like?" asked Jesus. "What parable shall we use to explain it? 31 It is like this. A man takes a mustard seed, the smallest seed in the world, and plants it in the ground. 32 After a while it grows up and becomes the biggest of all plants. It puts out such large branches that the birds come and make their nests in its shade."

33 Jesus preached his message to the people, using many other parables like these; he told them as much as they could understand. 34 He would not speak to them without using parables, but when he was alone with his disciples, he would explain everything to them.

Jesus Calms a Storm
(Matthew 8.23-27; Luke 8.22-25)

35 On the evening of that same day Jesus said to his disciples, "Let us go across to the other side of the lake." 36 So they left the crowd; the disciples got into the boat in which Jesus was already sitting, and they took him with them. Other boats were there too. 37 Suddenly a strong wind blew up, and the waves began to spill over into the boat, so that it was about to fill with water. 38 Jesus was in the back of the boat, sleeping with his head on a pillow. The disciples woke him up and said, "Teacher, don't you care that we are about to die?"

39 Jesus stood up and commanded the wind, "Be quiet!" and he said to the waves, "Be still!" The wind died down, and there was a great calm. 40 Then Jesus said to his disciples, "Why are you frightened? Do you still have no faith?"

41 But they were terribly afraid and began to say to one another, "Who is this man? Even the wind and the waves obey him!"

Jesus Heals a Man with Evil Spirits
(Matthew 8.28-34; Luke 8.26-39)

5 Jesus and his disciples arrived on the other side of Lake Galilee, in the territory of Gerasa. 2 As soon as Jesus got out of the boat, he was met by a man who came out of the burial caves there. This man had an evil spirit in him 3 and lived among the tombs. Nobody could keep him tied with chains any more; 4 many times his feet and his hands had been tied, but every time he broke the chains and smashed the irons on his feet. He was too strong for anyone to control him. 5 Day and night he wandered among the tombs and through the hills, screaming and cutting himself with stones.

6 He was some distance away when he saw Jesus; so he ran, fell on his knees before him, 7 and screamed in a loud voice, "Jesus, Son of the Most High God! What do you want with me? For God's sake, I beg you, don't punish me!" (8 He said this because Jesus was saying, "Evil spirit, come out of this man!")

9 So Jesus asked him, "What is your name!"

The man answered, "My name is 'Mob'—there are so many of us!" 10 And he kept begging Jesus not to send the evil spirits out of that region.

11 There was a large herd of pigs nearby, feeding on a hillside. 12 So the spirits begged Jesus, "Send us to the pigs, and let us go into them." 13 He let them go, and the evil spirits went out of the man and entered the pigs. The whole herd— about two thousand pigs in all—rushed down the side of the cliff into the lake and was drowned.

14 The men who had been taking care of the pigs ran away and spread the news in the town and among the farms. People went out to see what had happened, 15 and when they came to Jesus, they saw the man who used to have the mob of demons in him. He was sitting there, clothed and in his right mind; and they were all afraid. 16 Those who had seen it told the people what had happened to the man with the demons, and about the pigs.

17 So they asked Jesus to leave their territory.

18 As Jesus was getting into the boat, the man who had had the demons begged him, "Let me go with you!"

19 But Jesus would not let him. Instead, he told him, "Go back home to your family and tell them how much the Lord has done for you and how kind he has been to you."

20 So the man left and went all through the Ten Towns, telling what Jesus had done for him. And all who heard it were amazed.

Jairus' Daughter and the Woman Who Touched Jesus' Cloak
(Matthew 9.18-26; Luke 8.40-56)

21 Jesus went back across to the other side of the lake. There at the lakeside a large crowd gathered around him. 22 Jairus, an official of the local synagogue, arrived, and when he saw Jesus, he threw himself down at his feet 23 and begged him earnestly, "My little daughter is very sick. Please come and place your hands on her, so that she will get well and live!"

24 Then Jesus started off with him. So many people were going along with Jesus that they were crowding him from every side.

25 There was a woman who had suffered terribly from severe bleeding for twelve years, 26 even though she had been treated by many doctors. She had spent all her money, but instead of getting better she got worse all the time. 27 She had heard about Jesus, so she came in the crowd behind him, 28 saying to herself, "If I just touch his clothes, I will get well."

29 She touched his cloak, and her bleeding stopped at once; and she had the feeling inside herself that she was healed of her trouble. 30 At once Jesus knew that power had gone out of him, so he turned around in the crowd and asked, "Who touched my clothes?"

31 His disciples answered, "You see how the people are crowding you; why do you ask who touched you?"

32 But Jesus kept looking around to see who had done it. 33 The woman realized what had happened to her, so she came, trembling with fear, knelt at his feet, and told him the whole truth. 34 Jesus said to her, "My daughter, your faith has made

you well. Go in peace, and be healed of your trouble."

35 While Jesus was saying this, some messengers came from Jairus' house and told him, "Your daughter has died. Why bother the Teacher any longer?"

36 Jesus paid no attention to g what they said, but told him, "Don't be afraid, only believe." 37 Then he did not let anyone else go on with him except Peter and James and his brother John. 38 They arrived at Jairus' house, where Jesus saw the confusion and heard all the loud crying and wailing. 39 He went in and said to them, "Why all this confusion? Why are you crying? The child is not dead—she is only sleeping!"

40 They started making fun of him, so he put them all out, took the child's father and mother and his three disciples, and went into the room where the child was lying. 41 He took her by the hand and said to her, *"Talitha, koum,"* which means, "Little girl, I tell you to get up!"

42 She got up at once and started walking around. (She was twelve years old.) When this happened, they were completely amazed. 43 But Jesus gave them strict orders not to tell anyone, and he said, "Give her something to eat."

Jesus Is Rejected at Nazareth
(Matthew 13.53-58; Luke 4.16-30)

6 Jesus left that place and went back to his hometown, followed by his disciples. 2 On the Sabbath he began to teach in the synagogue. Many people were there; and when they heard him, they were all amazed. "Where did he get all this?" they asked. "What wisdom is this that has been given him? How does he perform miracles? 3 Isn't he the carpenter, the son of Mary, and the brother of James, Joseph, Judas, and Simon? Aren't his sisters living here?" And so they rejected him.

4 Jesus said to them, "Prophets are respected everywhere except in their own hometown and by their relatives and their family."

5 He was not able to perform any miracles there, except that he placed his hands on a few sick people and healed them. 6 He was greatly surprised, because the people did not have faith.

---

g paid no attention to; *or* overheard.

Jesus Sends Out the Twelve Disciples
(Matthew 10.5-15; Luke 9.1-6)

Then Jesus went to the villages around there, teaching the people. 7 He called the twelve disciples together and sent them out two by two. He gave them authority over the evil spirits 8 and ordered them, "Don't take anything with you on the trip except a walking stick— no bread, no beggar's bag, no money in your pockets. 9 Wear sandals, but don't carry an extra shirt." 10 He also told them, "Wherever you are welcomed, stay in the same house until you leave that place. 11 If you come to a town where people do not welcome you or will not listen to you, leave it and shake the dust off your feet. That will be a warning to them!"

12 So they went out and preached that people should turn away from their sins. 13 They drove out many demons, and rubbed olive oil on many sick people and healed them.

The Death of John the Baptist
(Matthew 14.1-12; Luke 9.7-9)

14 Now King Herod[h] heard about all this, because Jesus' reputation had spread everywhere. Some people were saying, "John the Baptist has come back to life! That is why he has this power to perform miracles."

15 Others, however, said, "He is Elijah."

Others said, "He is a prophet, like one of the prophets of long ago."

16 When Herod heard it, he said, "He is John the Baptist! I had his head cut off, but he has come back to life!" 17 Herod himself had ordered John's arrest, and he had him tied up and put in prison. Herod did this because of Herodias, whom he had married, even though she was the wife of his brother Philip. 18 John the Baptist kept telling Herod, "It isn't right for you to marry your brother's wife!"

19 So Herodias held a grudge against John and wanted to kill him, but she could not because of Herod. 20 Herod was afraid of John because he knew that John was a good and holy man, and so he kept him safe. He liked to listen to him, even though he became greatly disturbed every time he heard him.

21 Finally Herodias got her chance. It was on Herod's birthday, when he gave a feast for all the top government officials, the military chiefs, and the leading citizens of Galilee. 22 The daughter of Herodias[i] came in and danced, and pleased Herod and his guests. So the king said to the girl, "What would you like to have? I will give you anything you want." 23 With many vows he said to her, "I swear that I will give you anything you ask for, even as much as half my kingdom!"

24 So the girl went out and asked her mother, "What shall I ask for?"

"The head of John the Baptist," she answered.

25 The girl hurried back at once to the king and demanded, "I want you to give me here and now the head of John the Baptist on a plate!"

26 This made the king very sad, but he could not refuse her because of the vows he had made in front of all his guests. 27 So he sent off a guard at once with orders to bring John's head. The guard left, went to the prison, and cut John's head off; 28 then he brought it on a plate and gave it to the girl, who gave it to her mother. 29 When John's disciples heard about this, they came and got his body, and buried it.

Jesus Feeds Five Thousand
(Matthew 14.13-21; Luke 9.10-17; John 6.1-14)

30 The apostles returned and met with Jesus, and told him all they had done and taught. 31 There were so many people coming and going that Jesus and his disciples didn't even have time to eat. So he said to them, "Let us go off by ourselves to some place where we will be alone and you can rest a while." 32 So they started out in a boat by themselves to a lonely place.

33 Many people, however, saw them leave and knew at once who they were; so they went from all the towns and ran ahead by land and arrived at the place ahead of Jesus and his disciples. 34 When Jesus got out of the boat, he saw this large crowd, and his heart was filled with pity for them, because they were

---

h KING HEROD: *Herod Antipas, ruler of Galilee.* i The daughter of Herodias; *some manuscripts have His daughter Herodias.*

M
A
R
K

like sheep without a shepherd. So he began to teach them many things. 35 When it was getting late, his disciples came to him and said, "It is already very late, and this is a lonely place. 36 Send the people away, and let them go to the nearby farms and villages in order to buy themselves something to eat."

37 "You yourselves give them something to eat," Jesus answered.

They asked, "Do you want us to go and spend two hundred silver coins*j* on bread in order to feed them?"

38 So Jesus asked them, "How much bread do you have? Go and see."

When they found out, they told him, "Five loaves and also two fish."

39 Jesus then told his disciples to make all the people divide into groups and sit down on the green grass. 40 So the people sat down in rows, in groups of a hundred and groups of fifty. 41 Then Jesus took the five loaves and the two fish, looked up to heaven, and gave thanks to God. He broke the loaves and gave them to his disciples to distribute to the people. He also divided the two fish among them all. 42 Everyone ate and had enough. 43 Then the disciples took up twelve baskets full of what was left of the bread and the fish. 44 The number of men who were fed was five thousand.

Jesus Walks on the Water
(Matthew 14.22-33; John 6.15-21)

45 At once Jesus made his disciples get into the boat and go ahead of him to Bethsaida, on the other side of the lake, while he sent the crowd away. 46 After saying good-bye to the people, he went away to a hill to pray. 47 When evening came, the boat was in the middle of the lake, while Jesus was alone on land. 48 He saw that his disciples were straining at the oars, because they were rowing against the wind; so sometime between three and six o'clock in the morning, he came to them, walking on the water. He was going to pass them by,*k* 49 but they saw him walking on the water. "It's a ghost!" they thought, and screamed. 50 They were all terrified when they saw him.

Jesus spoke to them at once, "Cour-

age!" he said. "It is I. Don't be afraid!" 51 Then he got into the boat with them, and the wind died down. The disciples were completely amazed, 52 because they had not understood the real meaning of the feeding of the five thousand; their minds could not grasp it.

Jesus Heals the Sick in Gennesaret
(Matthew 14.34-36)

53 They crossed the lake and came to land at Gennesaret, where they tied up the boat. 54 As they left the boat, people recognized Jesus at once. 55 So they ran throughout the whole region; and wherever they heard he was, they brought to him the sick lying on their mats. 56 And everywhere Jesus went, to villages, towns, or farms, people would take their sick to the marketplaces and beg him to let the sick at least touch the edge of his cloak. And all who touched it were made well.

The Teaching of the Ancestors
(Matthew 15.1-9)

7 Some Pharisees and teachers of the Law who had come from Jerusalem gathered around Jesus. 2 They noticed that some of his disciples were eating their food with hands that were ritually unclean—that is, they had not washed them in the way the Pharisees said people should.

(3 For the Pharisees, as well as the rest of the Jews, follow the teaching they received from their ancestors: they do not eat unless they wash their hands in the proper way; 4 nor do they eat anything that comes from the market unless they wash it first.*l* And they follow many other rules which they have received, such as the proper way to wash cups, pots, copper bowls, and beds.*m*)

5 So the Pharisees and the teachers of the Law asked Jesus, "Why is it that your disciples do not follow the teaching handed down by our ancestors, but instead eat with ritually unclean hands?"

6 Jesus answered them, "How right Isaiah was when he prophesied about you! You are hypocrites, just as he wrote:

---

j SILVER COINS: *A silver coin was the daily wage of a rural worker (see Mt 20.2).*   *k* pass them by; *or* join them.   *l* anything that comes from the market unless they wash it first; *or anything after they come from the market unless they wash themselves first.*   *m* *Some manuscripts do not have* and beds.

'These people, says God, honor me with their words,

but their heart is really far away from me.

7 It is no use for them to worship me,

because they teach human rules as though they were my laws!'

8 "You put aside God's command and obey human teachings."

9 And Jesus continued, "You have a clever way of rejecting God's law in order to uphold your own teaching. 10 For Moses commanded, 'Respect your father and your mother,' and, 'If you curse your father or your mother, you are to be put to death.' 11 But you teach that if people have something they could use to help their father or mother, but say, 'This is Corban' (which means, it belongs to God), 12 they are excused from helping their father or mother. 13 In this way the teaching you pass on to others cancels out the word of God. And there are many other things like this that you do."

The Things That Make a Person Unclean
(Matthew 15.10-20)

14 Then Jesus called the crowd to him once more and said to them, "Listen to me, all of you, and understand. 15 There is nothing that goes into you from the outside which can make you ritually unclean. Rather, it is what comes out of you that makes you unclean."[n]

17 When he left the crowd and went into the house, his disciples asked him to explain this saying. 18 "You are no more intelligent than the others," Jesus said to them. "Don't you understand? Nothing that goes into you from the outside can really make you unclean, 19 because it does not go into your heart but into your stomach and then goes on out of the body." (In saying this, Jesus declared that all foods are fit to be eaten.)

20 And he went on to say, "It is what comes out of you that makes you unclean. 21 For from the inside, from your heart, come the evil ideas which lead you to do immoral things, to rob, kill, 22 commit adultery, be greedy, and do all sorts of evil things; deceit, indecency, jealousy, slander, pride, and folly — 23 all

these evil things come from inside you and make you unclean."

A Woman's Faith
(Matthew 15.21-28)

24 Then Jesus left and went away to the territory near the city of Tyre. He went into a house and did not want anyone to know he was there, but he could not stay hidden. 25 A woman, whose daughter had an evil spirit in her, heard about Jesus and came to him at once and fell at his feet. 26 The woman was a Gentile, born in the region of Phoenicia in Syria. She begged Jesus to drive the demon out of her daughter. 27 But Jesus answered, "Let us first feed the children. It isn't right to take the children's food and throw it to the dogs."

28 "Sir," she answered, "even the dogs under the table eat the children's leftovers!"

29 So Jesus said to her, "Because of that answer, go back home, where you will find that the demon has gone out of your daughter!"

30 She went home and found her child lying on the bed; the demon had indeed gone out of her.

Jesus Heals a Deaf-Mute

31 Jesus then left the neighborhood of Tyre and went on through Sidon to Lake Galilee, going by way of the territory of the Ten Towns. 32 Some people brought him a man who was deaf and could hardly speak, and they begged Jesus to place his hands on him. 33 So Jesus took him off alone, away from the crowd, put his fingers in the man's ears, spat, and touched the man's tongue. 34 Then Jesus looked up to heaven, gave a deep groan, and said to the man, "Ephphatha," which means, "Open up!"

35 At once the man was able to hear, his speech impediment was removed, and he began to talk without any trouble. 36 Then Jesus ordered the people not to speak of it to anyone; but the more he ordered them not to, the more they told it. 37 And all who heard were completely amazed. "How well he does everything!" they exclaimed. "He even causes the deaf to hear and the dumb to speak!"

[n] Some manuscripts add verse 16: Listen, then, if you have ears! (see 4.23).

Jesus Feeds Four Thousand People
(Matthew 15.32-39)

8 Not long afterward another large crowd came together. When the people had nothing left to eat, Jesus called the disciples to him and said, 2 "I feel sorry for these people, because they have been with me for three days and now have nothing to eat. 3 If I send them home without feeding them, they will faint as they go, because some of them have come a long way."

4 His disciples asked him, "Where in this desert can anyone find enough food to feed all these people?"

5 "How much bread do you have?" Jesus asked.

"Seven loaves," they answered.

6 He ordered the crowd to sit down on the ground. Then he took the seven loaves, gave thanks to God, broke them, and gave them to his disciples to distribute to the crowd; and the disciples did so. 7 They also had a few small fish. Jesus gave thanks for these and told the disciples to distribute them too. 8-9 Everybody ate and had enough— there were about four thousand people. Then the disciples took up seven baskets full of pieces left over. Jesus sent the people away 10 and at once got into a boat with his disciples and went to the district of Dalmanutha.

The Pharisees Ask for a Miracle
(Matthew 16.1-4)

11 Some Pharisees came to Jesus and started to argue with him. They wanted to trap him, so they asked him to perform a miracle to show that God approved of him. 12 But Jesus gave a deep groan and said, "Why do the people of this day ask for a miracle? No, I tell you! No such proof will be given to these people!"

13 He left them, got back into the boat, and started across to the other side of the lake.

The Yeast of the Pharisees and of Herod
(Matthew 16.5-12)

14 The disciples had forgotten to bring enough bread and had only one loaf with them in the boat. 15 "Take care," Jesus warned them, "and be on your guard against the yeast of the Pharisees and the yeast of Herod."

16 They started discussing among themselves: "He says this because we don't have any bread."

17 Jesus knew what they were saying, so he asked them, "Why are you discussing about not having any bread? Don't you know or understand yet? Are your minds so dull? 18 You have eyes—can't you see? You have ears—can't you hear? Don't you remember 19 when I broke the five loaves for the five thousand people? How many baskets full of leftover pieces did you take up?"

"Twelve," they answered.

20 "And when I broke the seven loaves for the four thousand people," asked Jesus, "how many baskets full of leftover pieces did you take up?"

"Seven," they answered.

21 "And you still don't understand?" he asked them.

Jesus Heals a Blind Man at Bethsaida

22 They came to Bethsaida, where some people brought a blind man to Jesus and begged him to touch him. 23 Jesus took the blind man by the hand and led him out of the village. After spitting on the man's eyes, Jesus placed his hands on him and asked him, "Can you see anything?"

24 The man looked up and said, "Yes, I can see people, but they look like trees walking around."

25 Jesus again placed his hands on the man's eyes. This time the man looked intently, his eyesight returned, and he saw everything clearly. 26 Jesus then sent him home with the order, "Don't go back into the village."

Peter's Declaration about Jesus
(Matthew 16.13-20; Luke 9.18-21)

27 Then Jesus and his disciples went away to the villages near Caesarea Philippi. On the way he asked them, "Tell me, who do people say I am?"

28 "Some say that you are John the Baptist," they answered; "others say that you are Elijah, while others say that you are one of the prophets."

29 "What about you?" he asked them. "Who do you say I am?"

Peter answered, "You are the Messiah."

30 Then Jesus ordered them, "Do not tell anyone about me."

Jesus Speaks about His Suffering and Death
(Matthew 16.21-28; Luke 9.22-27)

31 Then Jesus began to teach his disciples: "The Son of Man must suffer much and be rejected by the elders, the chief priests, and the teachers of the Law. He will be put to death, but three days later he will rise to life." **32** He made this very clear to them. So Peter took him aside and began to rebuke him. **33** But Jesus turned around, looked at his disciples, and rebuked Peter. "Get away from me, Satan," he said. "Your thoughts don't come from God but from human nature!"

34 Then Jesus called the crowd and his disciples to him. "If any of you want to come with me," he told them, "you must forget yourself, carry your cross, and follow me. **35** For if you want to save your own life, you will lose it; but if you lose your life for me and for the gospel, you will save it. **36** Do you gain anything if you win the whole world but lose your life? Of course not! **37** There is nothing you can give to regain your life. **38** If you are ashamed of me and of my teaching in this godless and wicked day, then the Son of Man will be ashamed of you when he comes in the glory of his Father with the holy angels."

9 And he went on to say, "I tell you, there are some here who will not die until they have seen the Kingdom of God come with power."

The Transfiguration
(Matthew 17.1-13; Luke 9.28-36)

2 Six days later Jesus took with him Peter, James, and John, and led them up a high mountain, where they were alone. As they looked on, a change came over Jesus, **3** and his clothes became shining white—whiter than anyone in the world could wash them. **4** Then the three disciples saw Elijah and Moses talking with Jesus. **5** Peter spoke up and said to Jesus, "Teacher, how good it is that we are here! We will make three tents, one for you, one for Moses, and one for Elijah." **6** He and the others were so frightened that he did not know what to say.

7 Then a cloud appeared and covered them with its shadow, and a voice came from the cloud, "This is my own dear Son—listen to him!" **8** They took a quick look around but did not see anyone else; only Jesus was with them.

9 As they came down the mountain, Jesus ordered them, "Don't tell anyone what you have seen, until the Son of Man has risen from death."

10 They obeyed his order, but among themselves they started discussing the matter, "What does this 'rising from death' mean?" **11** And they asked Jesus, "Why do the teachers of the Law say that Elijah has to come first?"

12 His answer was, "Elijah is indeed coming first in order to get everything ready. Yet why do the Scriptures say that the Son of Man will suffer much and be rejected? **13** I tell you, however, that Elijah has already come and that people treated him just as they pleased, as the Scriptures say about him."

Jesus Heals a Boy with an Evil Spirit
(Matthew 17.14-21; Luke 9.37-43a)

14 When they joined the rest of the disciples, they saw a large crowd around them and some teachers of the Law arguing with them. **15** When the people saw Jesus, they were greatly surprised, and ran to him and greeted him. **16** Jesus asked his disciples, "What are you arguing with them about?"

17 A man in the crowd answered, "Teacher, I brought my son to you, because he has an evil spirit in him and cannot talk. **18** Whenever the spirit attacks him, it throws him to the ground, and he foams at the mouth, grits his teeth, and becomes stiff all over. I asked your disciples to drive the spirit out, but they could not."

19 Jesus said to them, "How unbelieving you people are! How long must I stay with you? How long do I have to put up with you? Bring the boy to me!" **20** They brought him to Jesus.

As soon as the spirit saw Jesus, it threw the boy into a fit, so that he fell on the ground and rolled around, foaming at the mouth. **21** "How long has he been like this?" Jesus asked the father.

"Ever since he was a child," he replied. **22** "Many times the evil spirit has tried to kill him by throwing him in the fire and into water. Have pity on us and help us, if you possibly can!"

23 "Yes," said Jesus, "if you yourself

MARK

can! Everything is possible for the person who has faith."

24 The father at once cried out, "I do have faith, but not enough. Help me have more!"

25 Jesus noticed that the crowd was closing in on them, so he gave a command to the evil spirit. "Deaf and dumb spirit," he said, "I order you to come out of the boy and never go into him again!"

26 The spirit screamed, threw the boy into a bad fit, and came out. The boy looked like a corpse, and everyone said, "He is dead!" 27 But Jesus took the boy by the hand and helped him rise, and he stood up.

28 After Jesus had gone indoors, his disciples asked him privately, "Why couldn't we drive the spirit out?"

29 "Only prayer can drive this kind out," answered Jesus; "nothing else can."

Jesus Speaks Again about His Death
(Matthew 17.22, 23; Luke 9.43b-45)

30 Jesus and his disciples left that place and went on through Galilee. Jesus did not want anyone to know where he was, 31 because he was teaching his disciples: "The Son of Man will be handed over to those who will kill him. Three days later, however, he will rise to life."

32 But they did not understand what this teaching meant, and they were afraid to ask him.

Who Is the Greatest?
(Matthew 18.1-5; Luke 9.46-48)

33 They came to Capernaum, and after going indoors Jesus asked his disciples, "What were you arguing about on the road?"

34 But they would not answer him, because on the road they had been arguing among themselves about who was the greatest. 35 Jesus sat down, called the twelve disciples, and said to them, "Whoever wants to be first must place himself last of all and be the servant of all." 36 Then he took a child and had him stand in front of them. He put his arms around him and said to them, 37 "Whoever welcomes in my name one of these children, welcomes me; and whoever

welcomes me, welcomes not only me but also the one who sent me."

Whoever Is Not against Us Is for Us
(Luke 9.49, 50)

38 John said to him, "Teacher, we saw a man who was driving out demons in your name, and we told him to stop, because he doesn't belong to our group."

39 "Do not try to stop him," Jesus told them, "because no one who performs a miracle in my name will be able soon afterward to say evil things about me. 40 For whoever is not against us is for us. 41 I assure you that anyone who gives you a drink of water because you belong to me will certainly receive a reward.

Temptations to Sin
(Matthew 18.6-9; Luke 17.1, 2)

42 "If anyone should cause one of these little ones to lose faith in me, it would be better for that person to have a large millstone tied around the neck and be thrown into the sea. 43 So if your hand makes you lose your faith, cut it off! It is better for you to enter life without a hand than to keep both hands and go off to hell, to the fire that never goes out.o 45 And if your foot makes you lose your faith, cut it off! It is better for you to enter life without a foot than to keep both feet and be thrown into hell.p 47 And if your eye makes you lose your faith, take it out! It is better for you to enter the Kingdom of God with only one eye than to keep both eyes and be thrown into hell. 48 There 'the worms that eat them never die, and the fire that burns them is never put out.'

49 "Everyone will be purified by fire as a sacrifice is purified by salt.

50 "Salt is good; but if it loses its saltiness, how can you make it salty again?

"Have the salt of friendship among yourselves, and live in peace with one another."

Jesus Teaches about Divorce
(Matthew 19.1-12; Luke 16.18)

10 Then Jesus left that place, went to the province of Judea, and crossed the Jordan River. Crowds came flocking to him again, and he taught them, as he always did.

o Some manuscripts add verse 44: There 'the worms that eat them never die, and the fire that burns them is never put out' (see verse 48).   p Some manuscripts add verse 46: There 'the worms that eat them never die, and the fire that burns them is never put out' (see verse 48).

2 Some Pharisees came to him and tried to trap him. "Tell us," they asked, "does our Law allow a man to divorce his wife?"

3 Jesus answered with a question, "What law did Moses give you?"

4 Their answer was, "Moses gave permission for a man to write a divorce notice and send his wife away."

5 Jesus said to them, "Moses wrote this law for you because you are so hard to teach. 6 But in the beginning, at the time of creation, 'God made them male and female,' as the scripture says. 7 'And for this reason a man will leave his father and mother and unite with his wife,^q 8 and the two will become one.' So they are no longer two, but one. 9 No human being must separate, then, what God has joined together."

10 When they went back into the house, the disciples asked Jesus about this matter. 11 He said to them, "A man who divorces his wife and marries another woman commits adultery against his wife. 12 In the same way, a woman who divorces her husband and marries another man commits adultery."

Jesus Blesses Little Children
(Matthew 19.13-15; Luke 18.15-17)

13 Some people brought children to Jesus for him to place his hands on them, but the disciples scolded the people. 14 When Jesus noticed this, he was angry and said to his disciples, "Let the children come to me, and do not stop them, because the Kingdom of God belongs to such as these. 15 I assure you that whoever does not receive the Kingdom of God like a child will never enter it." 16 Then he took the children in his arms, placed his hands on each of them, and blessed them.

The Rich Man
(Matthew 19.16-30; Luke 18.18-30)

17 As Jesus was starting on his way again, a man ran up, knelt before him, and asked him, "Good Teacher, what must I do to receive eternal life?"

18 "Why do you call me good?" Jesus asked him. "No one is good except God alone. 19 You know the commandments: 'Do not commit murder; do not commit adultery; do not steal; do not accuse

anyone falsely; do not cheat; respect your father and your mother.' "

20 "Teacher," the man said, "ever since I was young, I have obeyed all these commandments."

21 Jesus looked straight at him with love and said, "You need only one thing. Go and sell all you have and give the money to the poor, and you will have riches in heaven; then come and follow me." 22 When the man heard this, gloom spread over his face, and he went away sad, because he was very rich.

23 Jesus looked around at his disciples and said to them, "How hard it will be for rich people to enter the Kingdom of God!"

24 The disciples were shocked at these words, but Jesus went on to say, "My children, how hard it is to enter the Kingdom of God! 25 It is much harder for a rich person to enter the Kingdom of God than for a camel to go through the eye of a needle."

26 At this the disciples were completely amazed and asked one another, "Who, then, can be saved?"

27 Jesus looked straight at them and answered, "This is impossible for human beings but not for God; everything is possible for God."

28 Then Peter spoke up, "Look, we have left everything and followed you."

29 "Yes," Jesus said to them, "and I tell you that those who leave home or brothers or sisters or mother or father or children or fields for me and for the gospel, 30 will receive much more in this present age. They will receive a hundred times more houses, brothers, sisters, mothers, children, and fields—and persecutions as well; and in the age to come they will receive eternal life. 31 But many who are now first will be last, and many who are now last will be first."

Jesus Speaks a Third Time about His Death
(Matthew 20.17-19; Luke 18.31-34)

32 Jesus and his disciples were now on the road going up to Jerusalem. Jesus was going ahead of the disciples, who were filled with alarm; the people who followed behind were afraid. Once again Jesus took the twelve disciples aside and spoke of the things that were going to

^q *Some manuscripts do not have* and unite with his wife.

M
A
R
K

happen to him. 33"Listen," he told them, "we are going up to Jerusalem where the Son of Man will be handed over to the chief priests and the teachers of the Law. They will condemn him to death and then hand him over to the Gentiles, 34who will make fun of him, spit on him, whip him, and kill him; but three days later he will rise to life."

The Request of James and John
(Matthew 20.20-28)

35Then James and John, the sons of Zebedee, came to Jesus. "Teacher," they said, "there is something we want you to do for us."

36"What is it?" Jesus asked them.

37They answered, "When you sit on your throne in your glorious Kingdom, we want you to let us sit with you, one at your right and one at your left."

38Jesus said to them, "You don't know what you are asking for. Can you drink the cup of suffering that I must drink? Can you be baptized in the way I must be baptized?"

39"We can," they answered.

Jesus said to them, "You will indeed drink the cup I must drink and be baptized in the way I must be baptized. 40But I do not have the right to choose who will sit at my right and my left. It is God who will give these places to those for whom he has prepared them."

41When the other ten disciples heard about it, they became angry with James and John. 42So Jesus called them all together to him and said, "You know that those who are considered rulers of the heathen have power over them, and the leaders have complete authority. 43This, however, is not the way it is among you. If one of you wants to be great, you must be the servant of the rest; 44and if one of you wants to be first, you must be the slave of all. 45For even the Son of Man did not come to be served; he came to serve and to give his life to redeem many people."

Jesus Heals Blind Bartimaeus
(Matthew 20.29-34; Luke 18.35-43)

46They came to Jericho, and as Jesus was leaving with his disciples and a large crowd, a blind beggar named Bartimaeus son of Timaeus was sitting by the road. 47When he heard that it was Jesus of Nazareth, he began to shout, "Jesus! Son of David! Have mercy on me!"

48Many of the people scolded him and told him to be quiet. But he shouted even more loudly, "Son of David, have mercy on me!"

49Jesus stopped and said, "Call him." So they called the blind man. "Cheer up!" they said. "Get up, he is calling you."

50So he threw off his cloak, jumped up, and came to Jesus.

51"What do you want me to do for you?" Jesus asked him.

"Teacher," the blind man answered, "I want to see again."

52"Go," Jesus told him, "your faith has made you well."

At once he was able to see and followed Jesus on the road.

The Triumphant Entry into Jerusalem
(Matthew 21.1-11; Luke 19.28-40; John 12.12-19)

11 As they approached Jerusalem, near the towns of Bethphage and Bethany, they came to the Mount of Olives. Jesus sent two of his disciples on ahead 2with these instructions: "Go to the village there ahead of you. As soon as you get there, you will find a colt tied up that has never been ridden. Untie it and bring it here. 3And if someone asks you why you are doing that, say that the Master' needs it and will send it back at once."

4So they went and found a colt out in the street, tied to the door of a house. As they were untying it, 5some of the bystanders asked them, "What are you doing, untying that colt?"

6They answered just as Jesus had told them, and the crowd let them go. 7They brought the colt to Jesus, threw their cloaks over the animal, and Jesus got on. 8Many people spread their cloaks on the road, while others cut branches in the field and spread them on the road. 9The people who were in front and those who followed behind began to shout, "Praise God! God bless him who comes in the name of the Lord! 10God bless the coming kingdom of King David, our father! Praise be to God!"

11Jesus entered Jerusalem, went into

---

r the Master; *or its owner.*

the Temple, and looked around at everything. But since it was already late in the day, he went out to Bethany with the twelve disciples.

Jesus Curses the Fig Tree
(Matthew 21.18, 19)

12 The next day, as they were coming back from Bethany, Jesus was hungry. 13 He saw in the distance a fig tree covered with leaves, so he went to see if he could find any figs on it. But when he came to it, he found only leaves, because it was not the right time for figs. 14 Jesus said to the fig tree, "No one shall ever eat figs from you again!"

And his disciples heard him.

Jesus Goes to the Temple
(Matthew 21.12-17; Luke 19.45-48; John 2.13-22)

15 When they arrived in Jerusalem, Jesus went to the Temple and began to drive out all those who were buying and selling. He overturned the tables of the moneychangers and the stools of those who sold pigeons, 16 and he would not let anyone carry anything through the Temple courtyards. 17 He then taught the people: "It is written in the Scriptures that God said, 'My Temple will be called a house of prayer for the people of all nations.' But you have turned it into a hideout for thieves!"

18 The chief priests and the teachers of the Law heard of this, so they began looking for some way to kill Jesus. They were afraid of him, because the whole crowd was amazed at his teaching.

19 When evening came, Jesus and his disciples left the city.

The Lesson from the Fig Tree
(Matthew 21.20-22)

20 Early next morning, as they walked along the road, they saw the fig tree. It was dead all the way down to its roots. 21 Peter remembered what had happened and said to Jesus, "Look, Teacher, the fig tree you cursed has died!"

22 Jesus answered them, "Have faith in God. 23 I assure you that whoever tells this hill to get up and throw itself in the sea and does not doubt in his heart, but believes that what he says will happen, it

will be done for him. 24 For this reason I tell you: When you pray and ask for something, believe that you have received it, and you will be given whatever you ask for. 25 And when you stand and pray, forgive anything you may have against anyone, so that your Father in heaven will forgive the wrongs you have done."s

The Question about Jesus' Authority
(Matthew 21.23-27; Luke 20.1-8)

27 They arrived once again in Jerusalem. As Jesus was walking in the Temple, the chief priests, the teachers of the Law, and the elders came to him 28 and asked him, "What right do you have to do these things? Who gave you such right?"

29 Jesus answered them, "I will ask you just one question, and if you give me an answer, I will tell you what right I have to do these things. 30 Tell me, where did John's right to baptize come from: was it from God or from human beings?"

31 They started to argue among themselves: "What shall we say? If we answer, 'From God,' he will say, 'Why, then, did you not believe John?' 32 But if we say, 'From human beings ...'" (They were afraid of the people, because everyone was convinced that John had been a prophet.) 33 So their answer to Jesus was, "We don't know."

Jesus said to them, "Neither will I tell you, then, by what right I do these things."

The Parable of the Tenants in the Vineyard
(Matthew 21.33-46; Luke 20.9-19)

12 Then Jesus spoke to them in parables: "Once there was a man who planted a vineyard, put a fence around it, dug a hole for the wine press, and built a watchtower. Then he rented the vineyard to tenants and left home on a trip. 2 When the time came to gather the grapes, he sent a slave to the tenants to receive from them his share of the harvest. 3 The tenants grabbed the slave, beat him, and sent him back without a thing. 4 Then the owner sent another

s Some manuscripts add verse 26: If you do not forgive others, your Father in heaven will not forgive the wrongs you have done (see Mt 6.15).

M
A
R
K

slave; the tenants beat him over the head and treated him shamefully. 5 The owner sent another slave, and they killed him; and they treated many others the same way, beating some and killing others. 6 The only one left to send was the man's own dear son. Last of all, then, he sent his son to the tenants. 'I am sure they will respect my son,' he said. 7 But those tenants said to one another, 'This is the owner's son. Come on, let's kill him, and his property will be ours!' 8 So they grabbed the son and killed him and threw his body out of the vineyard.

9 "What, then, will the owner of the vineyard do?" asked Jesus. "He will come and kill those tenants and turn the vineyard over to others. 10 Surely you have read this scripture?

'The stone which the builders
    rejected as worthless
turned out to be the most
    important of all.
11 This was done by the Lord;
    what a wonderful sight it is!' "

12 The Jewish leaders tried to arrest Jesus, because they knew that he had told this parable against them. But they were afraid of the crowd, so they left him and went away.

The Question about Paying Taxes
(Matthew 22.15-22; Luke 20.20-26)

13 Some Pharisees and some members of Herod's party were sent to Jesus to trap him with questions. 14 They came to him and said, "Teacher, we know that you tell the truth, without worrying about what people think. You pay no attention to anyone's status, but teach the truth about God's will for people. Tell us, is it against our Law to pay taxes to the Roman Emperor? Should we pay them or not?"

15 But Jesus saw through their trick and answered, "Why are you trying to trap me? Bring a silver coin, and let me see it."

16 They brought him one, and he asked, "Whose face and name are these?"

"The Emperor's," they answered.

17 So Jesus said, "Well, then, pay to the Emperor what belongs to the Emperor, and pay to God what belongs to God."

And they were amazed at Jesus.

The Question about Rising from Death
(Matthew 22.23-33; Luke 20.27-40)

18 Then some Sadducees, who say that people will not rise from death, came to Jesus and said, 19 "Teacher, Moses wrote this law for us: 'If a man dies and leaves a wife but no children, that man's brother must marry the widow so that they can have children who will be considered the dead man's children.' 20 Once there were seven brothers; the oldest got married and died without having children. 21 Then the second one married the woman, and he also died without having children. The same thing happened to the third brother, 22 and then to the rest: all seven brothers married the woman and died without having children. Last of all, the woman died. 23 Now, when all the dead rise to life on the day of resurrection, whose wife will she be? All seven of them had married her."

24 Jesus answered them, "How wrong you are! And do you know why? It is because you don't know the Scriptures or God's power. 25 For when the dead rise to life, they will be like the angels in heaven and will not marry. 26 Now, as for the dead being raised: haven't you ever read in the Book of Moses the passage about the burning bush? There it is written that God said to Moses, 'I am the God of Abraham, the God of Isaac, and the God of Jacob.' 27 He is the God of the living, not of the dead. You are completely wrong!"

The Great Commandment
(Matthew 22.34-40; Luke 10.25-28)

28 A teacher of the Law was there who heard the discussion. He saw that Jesus had given the Sadducees a good answer, so he came to him with a question: "Which commandment is the most important of all?"

29 Jesus replied, "The most important one is this: 'Listen, Israel! The Lord our God is the only Lord.*t* 30 Love the Lord your God with all your heart, with all your soul, with all your mind, and with all your strength.' 31 The second most important commandment is this: 'Love your neighbor as you love yourself.' There is no other commandment more important than these two."

t The Lord our God is the only Lord; or The Lord is our God, the Lord alone.

32 The teacher of the Law said to Jesus, "Well done, Teacher! It is true, as you say, that only the Lord is God and that there is no other god but he. 33 And you must love God with all your heart and with all your mind and with all your strength; and you must love your neighbor as you love yourself. It is more important to obey these two commandments than to offer on the altar animals and other sacrifices to God."

34 Jesus noticed how wise his answer was, and so he told him, "You are not far from the Kingdom of God."

After this nobody dared to ask Jesus any more questions.

The Question about the Messiah
(Matthew 22.41-46; Luke 20.41-44)

35 As Jesus was teaching in the Temple, he asked the question, "How can the teachers of the Law say that the Messiah will be the descendant of David? 36 The Holy Spirit inspired David to say:

'The Lord said to my Lord:
Sit here at my right side
until I put your enemies under
    your feet.'

37 David himself called him 'Lord'; so how can the Messiah be David's descendant?"

Jesus Warns against the Teachers of the Law
(Matthew 23.1-36; Luke 20.45-47)

A large crowd was listening to Jesus gladly. 33 As he taught them, he said, "Watch out for the teachers of the Law, who like to walk around in their long robes and be greeted with respect in the marketplace, 39 who choose the reserved seats in the synagogues and the best places at feasts. 40 They take advantage of widows and rob them of their homes, and then make a show of saying long prayers. Their punishment will be all the worse!"

The Widow's Offering
(Luke 21.1-4)

41 As Jesus sat near the Temple treasury, he watched the people as they dropped in their money. Many rich men dropped in a lot of money; 42 then a poor widow came along and dropped in two little copper coins, worth about a penny. 43 He called his disciples together and said to them, "I tell you that this poor widow put more in the offering box than all the others. 44 For the others put in what they had to spare of their riches; but she, poor as she is, put in all she had—she gave all she had to live on."

Jesus Speaks of the Destruction of the Temple
(Matthew 24.1, 2; Luke 21.5, 6)

13 As Jesus was leaving the Temple, one of his disciples said, "Look, Teacher! What wonderful stones and buildings!"

2 Jesus answered, "You see these great buildings? Not a single stone here will be left in its place; every one of them will be thrown down."

Troubles and Persecutions
(Matthew 24.3-14; Luke 21.7-19)

3 Jesus was sitting on the Mount of Olives, across from the Temple, when Peter, James, John, and Andrew came to him in private. 4 "Tell us when this will be," they said, "and tell us what will happen to show that the time has come for all these things to take place."

5 Jesus said to them, "Watch out, and don't let anyone fool you. 6 Many men, claiming to speak for me, will come and say, 'I am he!' and they will fool many people. 7 And don't be troubled when you hear the noise of battles close by and news of battles far away. Such things must happen, but they do not mean that the end has come. 8 Countries will fight each other; kingdoms will attack one another. There will be earthquakes everywhere, and there will be famines. These things are like the first pains of childbirth.

9 "You yourselves must watch out. You will be arrested and taken to court. You will be beaten in the synagogues; you will stand before rulers and kings for my sake to tell them the Good News. 10 But before the end comes, the gospel must be preached to all peoples. 11 And when you are arrested and taken to court, do not worry ahead of time about what you are going to say; when the time comes, say whatever is then given to you. For the words you speak will not be yours; they will come from the Holy Spirit.

MARK

12 Men will hand over their own brothers to be put to death, and fathers will do the same to their children. Children will turn against their parents and have them put to death. 13 Everyone will hate you because of me. But whoever holds out to the end will be saved.

The Awful Horror
(Matthew 24.15-28; Luke 21.20-24)

14 "You will see 'The Awful Horror' standing in the place where he should not be." (Note to the reader: understand what this means!) "Then those who are in Judea must run away to the hills. 15 Someone who is on the roof of a house must not lose time by going down into the house to get anything to take along. 16 Someone who is in the field must not go back to the house for a cloak. 17 How terrible it will be in those days for women who are pregnant and for mothers with little babies! 18 Pray to God that these things will not happen in the winter! 19 For the trouble of those days will be far worse than any the world has ever known from the very beginning when God created the world until the present time. Nor will there ever be anything like it again. 20 But the Lord has reduced the number of those days; if he had not, nobody would survive. For the sake of his chosen people, however, he has reduced those days.

21 "Then, if anyone says to you, 'Look, here is the Messiah!' or, 'Look, there he is!' — do not believe it. 22 For false Messiahs and false prophets will appear. They will perform miracles and wonders in order to deceive even God's chosen people, if possible. 23 Be on your guard! I have told you everything ahead of time.

The Coming of the Son of Man
(Matthew 24.29-31; Luke 21.25-28)

24 "In the days after that time of trouble the sun will grow dark, the moon will no longer shine, 25 the stars will fall from heaven, and the powers in space will be driven from their courses. 26 Then the Son of Man will appear, coming in the clouds with great power and glory. 27 He will send the angels out to the four corners of the earth to gather God's chosen people from one end of the world to the other.

The Lesson of the Fig Tree
(Matthew 24.32-35; Luke 21.29-33)

28 "Let the fig tree teach you a lesson. When its branches become green and tender and it starts putting out leaves, you know that summer is near. 29 In the same way, when you see these things happening, you will know that the time is near, ready to begin. *u* 30 Remember that all these things will happen before the people now living have all died. 31 Heaven and earth will pass away, but my words will never pass away.

No One Knows the Day or Hour
(Matthew 24.36-44)

32 "No one knows, however, when that day or hour will come — neither the angels in heaven, nor the Son; only the Father knows. 33 Be on watch, be alert, for you do not know when the time will come. 34 It will be like a man who goes away from home on a trip and leaves his servants in charge, after giving to each one his own work to do and after telling the doorkeeper to keep watch. 35 Watch, then, because you do not know when the master of the house is coming — it might be in the evening or at midnight or before dawn or at sunrise. 36 If he comes suddenly, he must not find you asleep. 37 What I say to you, then, I say to all: Watch!"

The Plot against Jesus
(Matthew 26.1-5; Luke 22.1, 2; John 11.45-53)

14 It was now two days before the Festival of Passover and Unleavened Bread. The chief priests and the teachers of the Law were looking for a way to arrest Jesus secretly and put him to death. 2 "We must not do it during the festival," they said, "or the people might riot."

Jesus Is Anointed at Bethany
(Matthew 26.6-13; John 12.1-8)

3 Jesus was in Bethany at the house of Simon, a man who had suffered from a dreaded skin disease. While Jesus was eating, a woman came in with an alabaster jar full of a very expensive perfume made of pure nard. She broke the jar and poured the perfume on Jesus' head. 4 Some of the people there became angry and said to one another, "What was the

---

u the time is near, ready to begin; *or* he is near, ready to come.

EVENTS OF HOLY WEEK

The gospel writers devoted many pages to the events leading up to the crucifixion of Jesus. The final week of his earthly ministry began with the triumphal entry into Jerusalem and the shouting of "Praise God" from the crowd that changed to cries of "Crucify him" before the week was over. Jesus apparently spent most of the week teaching in the Temple area during the day. His evenings were spent in the home of Mary, Martha, and Lazarus in Bethany. Significant events during this week included the plot of the Council, Jesus' betrayal and arrest, the trials of Jesus, his journey to Golgotha down the Jerusalem street, known today as the Via Dolorosa, and the resurrection. After his resurrection, Jesus ministered another forty days before his ascension.

Day	Event	Biblical Reference
Sunday	The triumphal entry into Jerusalem	Mk 11.1–11
Monday	Cleanses the Temple in Jerusalem	Mk 11.15–19
Tuesday	The chief priests, teachers of the Law, and elders challenge Jesus' authority	Lk 20.1–8
	Jesus foretells the destruction of Jerusalem and his second coming	Mt 24; 25
	Mary anoints Jesus at Bethany	Jn 12.2–8
	Judas bargains with the Jewish rulers to betray Jesus	Lk 22.3–6
Thursday	Jesus eats the Passover meal with his disciples and institutes the Lord's Supper	Jn 13.1–30; Mk 14.22–26
	Prays in Gethsemane for his disciples	Jn 17
Friday	His betrayal and arrest in the Garden of Gethsemane	Mk 14.43–50
	Jesus questioned by Annas, the former high priest	Jn 18.12–24
	Condemned by Caiaphas and the Council	Mt 26.57–67
	Peter denies Jesus three times	Jn 18.15–27
	Jesus is formally condemned by the Council	Lk 22.66–71
	Judas commits suicide	Mt 27.3–10
	The trial of Jesus before Pilate	Lk 23.1–5
	Jesus' appearance before Herod	Lk 23.6–12
	Formally sentenced to death by Pilate	Lk 23.13–25
	Jesus is mocked and crucified between two bandits	Mk 15.16–27
	The curtain in the Temple is torn as Jesus dies	Mt 27.51–56
	His burial in the tomb by Joseph of Arimathea	Jn 19.38–42
Sunday	Jesus is raised from the dead	Lk 24.1–9

M
A
R
K

use of wasting the perfume? 5 It could have been sold for more than three hundred silver coins[v] and the money given to the poor!" And they criticized her harshly.

6 But Jesus said, "Leave her alone! Why are you bothering her? She has done a fine and beautiful thing for me. 7 You will always have poor people with you, and any time you want to, you can help them. But you will not always have me. 8 She did what she could; she poured perfume on my body to prepare it ahead of time for burial. 9 Now, I assure you that wherever the gospel is preached all over the world, what she has done will be told in memory of her."

Judas Agrees to Betray Jesus
(Matthew 26.14-16; Luke 22.3-6)

10 Then Judas Iscariot, one of the twelve disciples, went off to the chief priests in order to betray Jesus to them. 11 They were pleased to hear what he had to say, and promised to give him money. So Judas started looking for a good chance to hand Jesus over to them.

Jesus Eats the Passover Meal with His Disciples
(Matthew 26.17-25; Luke 22.7-14, 21-23; John 13.21-30)

12 On the first day of the Festival of Unleavened Bread, the day the lambs for the Passover meal were killed, Jesus' disciples asked him, "Where do you want us to go and get the Passover meal ready for you?"

13 Then Jesus sent two of them with these instructions: "Go into the city, and a man carrying a jar of water will meet you. Follow him 14 to the house he enters, and say to the owner of the house: 'The Teacher says, Where is the room where my disciples and I will eat the Passover meal?' 15 Then he will show you a large upstairs room, fixed up and furnished, where you will get everything ready for us."

16 The disciples left, went to the city, and found everything just as Jesus had told them; and they prepared the Passover meal.

17 When it was evening, Jesus came with the twelve disciples. 18 While they were at the table eating, Jesus said, "I tell you that one of you will betray me — one who is eating with me."

19 The disciples were upset and began to ask him, one after the other, "Surely you don't mean me, do you?"

20 Jesus answered, "It will be one of you twelve, one who dips his bread in the dish with me. 21 The Son of Man will die as the Scriptures say he will; but how terrible for that man who will betray the Son of Man! It would have been better for that man if he had never been born!"

The Lord's Supper
(Matthew 26.26-30; Luke 22.14-20; 1 Corinthians 11.23-25)

22 While they were eating, Jesus took a piece of bread, gave a prayer of thanks, broke it, and gave it to his disciples. "Take it," he said, "this is my body."

23 Then he took a cup, gave thanks to God, and handed it to them; and they all drank from it. 24 Jesus said, "This is my blood which is poured out for many, my blood which seals God's covenant. 25 I tell you, I will never again drink this wine until the day I drink the new wine in the Kingdom of God."

26 Then they sang a hymn and went out to the Mount of Olives.

Jesus Predicts Peter's Denial
(Matthew 26.31-35; Luke 22.31-34; John 13.36-38)

27 Jesus said to them, "All of you will run away and leave me, for the scripture says, 'God will kill the shepherd, and the sheep will all be scattered.' 28 But after I am raised to life, I will go to Galilee ahead of you."

29 Peter answered, "I will never leave you, even though all the rest do!"

30 Jesus said to Peter, "I tell you that before the rooster crows two times tonight, you will say three times that you do not know me."

31 Peter answered even more strongly, "I will never say that, even if I have to die with you!"

And all the other disciples said the same thing.

Jesus Prays in Gethsemane
(Matthew 26.36-46; Luke 22.39-46)

32 They came to a place called Gethsemane, and Jesus said to his disciples,

"Sit here while I pray." 33 He took Peter, James, and John with him. Distress and anguish came over him, 34 and he said to them. "The sorrow in my heart is so great that it almost crushes me. Stay here and keep watch."

35 He went a little farther on, threw himself on the ground, and prayed that, if possible, he might not have to go through that time of suffering. 36 "Father," he prayed, "my Father! All things are possible for you. Take this cup of suffering away from me. Yet not what I want, but what you want."

37 Then he returned and found the three disciples asleep. He said to Peter, "Simon, are you asleep? Weren't you able to stay awake for even one hour?" 38 And he said to them, "Keep watch, and pray that you will not fall into temptation. The spirit is willing, but the flesh is weak."

39 He went away once more and prayed, saying the same words. 40 Then he came back to the disciples and found them asleep; they could not keep their eyes open. And they did not know what to say to him.

41 When he came back the third time, he said to them, "Are you still sleeping and resting? Enough! The hour has come! Look, the Son of Man is now being handed over to the power of sinners. 42 Get up, let us go. Look, here is the man who is betraying me!"

The Arrest of Jesus
(Matthew 26.47-56; Luke 22.47-53; John 18.3-12)

43 Jesus was still speaking when Judas, one of the twelve disciples, arrived. With him was a crowd armed with swords and clubs and sent by the chief priests, the teachers of the Law, and the elders. 44 The traitor had given the crowd a signal: "The man I kiss is the one you want. Arrest him and take him away under guard."

45 As soon as Judas arrived, he went up to Jesus and said, "Teacher!" and kissed him. 46 So they arrested Jesus and held him tight. 47 But one of those standing there drew his sword and struck at the High Priest's slave, cutting off his ear. 48 Then Jesus spoke up and said to them, "Did you have to come with swords and clubs to capture me, as though I were an outlaw? 49 Day after day I was with you teaching in the Temple, and you did not arrest me. But the Scriptures must come true."

50 Then all the disciples left him and ran away.

51 A certain young man, dressed only in a linen cloth, was following Jesus. They tried to arrest him, 52 but he ran away naked, leaving the cloth behind.

Jesus before the Council
(Matthew 26.57-68; Luke 22.54, 55, 63-71; John 18.13, 14, 19-24)

53 Then Jesus was taken to the High Priest's house, where all the chief priests, the elders, and the teachers of the Law were gathering. 54 Peter followed from a distance and went into the courtyard of the High Priest's house. There he sat down with the guards, keeping himself warm by the fire. 55 The chief priests and the whole Council tried to find some evidence against Jesus in order to put him to death, but they could not find any. 56 Many witnesses told lies against Jesus, but their stories did not agree.

57 Then some men stood up and told this lie against Jesus: 58 "We heard him say, 'I will tear down this Temple which men have made, and after three days I will build one that is not made by men.'" 59 Not even they, however, could make their stories agree.

60 The High Priest stood up in front of them all and questioned Jesus, "Have you no answer to the accusation they bring against you?"

61 But Jesus kept quiet and would not say a word. Again the High Priest questioned him, "Are you the Messiah, the Son of the Blessed God?"

62 "I am," answered Jesus, "and you will all see the Son of Man seated at the right side of the Almighty and coming with the clouds of heaven!"

63 The High Priest tore his robes and said, "We don't need any more witnesses! 64 You heard his blasphemy. What is your decision?"

They all voted against him: he was guilty and should be put to death.

65 Some of them began to spit on Jesus, and they blindfolded him and hit him. "Guess who hit you!" they said. And the guards took him and slapped him.

Peter Denies Jesus
(Matthew 26.69-75; Luke 22.56-62; John 18.15-18, 25-27)

66 Peter was still down in the courtyard when one of the High Priest's servant women came by. **67** When she saw Peter warming himself, she looked straight at him and said, "You, too, were with Jesus of Nazareth."

68 But he denied it. "I don't know . . . I don't understand what you are talking about," he answered, and went out into the passageway. Just then a rooster crowed.ʷ

69 The servant woman saw him there and began to repeat to the bystanders, "He is one of them!" **70** But Peter denied it again.

A little while later the bystanders accused Peter again, "You can't deny that you are one of them, because you, too, are from Galilee."

71 Then Peter said, "I swear that I am telling the truth! May God punish me if I am not! I do not know the man you are talking about!"

72 Just then a rooster crowed a second time, and Peter remembered how Jesus had said to him, "Before the rooster crows two times, you will say three times that you do not know me." And he broke down and cried.

Jesus before Pilate
(Matthew 27.1, 2, 11-14; Luke 23.1-5; John 18.28-38)

15 Early in the morning the chief priests met hurriedly with the elders, the teachers of the Law, and the whole Council, and made their plans. They put Jesus in chains, led him away, and handed him over to Pilate. **2** Pilate questioned him, "Are you the king of the Jews?"

Jesus answered, "So you say."

3 The chief priests were accusing Jesus of many things, **4** so Pilate questioned him again, "Aren't you going to answer? Listen to all their accusations!"

5 Again Jesus refused to say a word, and Pilate was amazed.

Jesus Is Sentenced to Death
(Matthew 27.15-26; Luke 23.13-25; John 18.39 — 19.16)

6 At every Passover Festival Pilate was in the habit of setting free any one prisoner the people asked for. **7** At that time a man named Barabbas was in prison with the rebels who had committed murder in the riot. **8** When the crowd gathered and began to ask Pilate for the usual favor, **9** he asked them, "Do you want me to set free for you the king of the Jews?" **10** He knew very well that the chief priests had handed Jesus over to him because they were jealous.

11 But the chief priests stirred up the crowd to ask, instead, that Pilate set Barabbas free for them. **12** Pilate spoke again to the crowd, "What, then, do you want me to do with the one you call the king of the Jews?"

13 They shouted back, "Crucify him!"

14 "But what crime has he committed?" Pilate asked.

They shouted all the louder, "Crucify him!"

15 Pilate wanted to please the crowd, so he set Barabbas free for them. Then he had Jesus whipped and handed him over to be crucified.

The Soldiers Make Fun of Jesus
(Matthew 27.27-31; John 19.2, 3)

16 The soldiers took Jesus inside to the courtyard of the governor's palace and called together the rest of the company. **17** They put a purple robe on Jesus, made a crown out of thorny branches, and put it on his head. **18** Then they began to salute him: "Long live the King of the Jews!" **19** They beat him over the head with a stick, spat on him, fell on their knees, and bowed down to him. **20** When they had finished making fun of him, they took off the purple robe and put his own clothes back on him. Then they led him out to crucify him.

Jesus Is Crucified
(Matthew 27.32-44; Luke 23.26-43; John 19.17-27)

21 On the way they met a man named Simon, who was coming into the city from the country, and the soldiers forced him to carry Jesus' cross. (Simon was from Cyrene and was the father of Alexander and Rufus.) **22** They took Jesus to a place called Golgotha, which means "The Place of the Skull." **23** There they tried to give him wine mixed with a drug called myrrh, but Jesus would not drink it. **24** Then they crucified him and divided his clothes among themselves, throwing

---

ʷ *Some manuscripts do not have* Just then a rooster crowed.

dice to see who would get which piece of clothing. 25 It was nine o'clock in the morning when they crucified him. 26 The notice of the accusation against him said: "The King of the Jews." 27 They also crucified two bandits with Jesus, one on his right and the other on his left.x

29 People passing by shook their heads and hurled insults at Jesus: "Aha! You were going to tear down the Temple and build it back up in three days! 30 Now come down from the cross and save yourself!"

31 In the same way the chief priests and the teachers of the Law made fun of Jesus, saying to one another, "He saved others, but he cannot save himself! 32 Let us see the Messiah, the king of Israel, come down from the cross now, and we will believe in him!"

And the two who were crucified with Jesus insulted him also.

The Death of Jesus
(Matthew 27.45-56; Luke 23.44-49; John 19.28-30)

33 At noon the whole country was covered with darkness, which lasted for three hours. 34 At three o'clock Jesus cried out with a loud shout, *"Eloi, Eloi, lema sabachthani?"* which means, "My God, my God, why did you abandon me?"

35 Some of the people there heard him and said, "Listen, he is calling for Elijah!" 36 One of them ran up with a sponge, soaked it in cheap wine, and put it on the end of a stick. Then he held it up to Jesus' lips and said, "Wait! Let us see if Elijah is coming to bring him down from the cross!"

37 With a loud cry Jesus died.

38 The curtain hanging in the Temple was torn in two, from top to bottom. 39 The army officer who was standing there in front of the cross saw how Jesus had died.y "This man was really the Son of God!" he said.

40 Some women were there, looking on from a distance. Among them were Mary Magdalene, Mary the mother of the younger James and of Joseph, and Salome. 41 They had followed Jesus while he was in Galilee and had helped him. Many other women who had come to Jerusalem with him were there also.

The Burial of Jesus
(Matthew 27.57-61; Luke 23.50-56; John 19.38-42)

42-43 It was toward evening when Joseph of Arimathea arrived. He was a respected member of the Council, who was waiting for the coming of the Kingdom of God. It was Preparation day (that is, the day before the Sabbath), so Joseph went boldly into the presence of Pilate and asked him for the body of Jesus. 44 Pilate was surprised to hear that Jesus was already dead. He called the army officer and asked him if Jesus had been dead a long time. 45 After hearing the officer's report, Pilate told Joseph he could have the body. 46 Joseph bought a linen sheet, took the body down, wrapped it in the sheet, and placed it in a tomb which had been dug out of solid rock. Then he rolled a large stone across the entrance to the tomb. 47 Mary Magdalene and Mary the mother of Joseph were watching and saw where the body of Jesus was placed.

The Resurrection
(Matthew 28.1-8; Luke 24.1-12; John 20.1-10)

16 After the Sabbath was over, Mary Magdalene, Mary the mother of James, and Salome bought spices to go and anoint the body of Jesus. 2 Very early on Sunday morning, at sunrise, they went to the tomb. 3-4 On the way they said to one another, "Who will roll away the stone for us from the entrance to the tomb?" (It was a very large stone.) Then they looked up and saw that the stone had already been rolled back. 5 So they entered the tomb, where they saw a young man sitting at the right, wearing a white robe — and they were alarmed.

6 "Don't be alarmed," he said. "I know you are looking for Jesus of Nazareth, who was crucified. He is not here — he has been raised! Look, here is the place where he was placed. 7 Now go and give this message to his disciples, including Peter: 'He is going to Galilee ahead of you; there you will see him, just as he told you.'"

8 So they went out and ran from the tomb, distressed and terrified. They said

---

x *Some manuscripts add verse 28:* In this way the scripture came true which says, "He shared the fate of criminals" *(see Lk 22.37).*   y had died; *some manuscripts have* had cried out and died.

nothing to anyone, because they were afraid.

AN OLD ENDING TO THE GOSPEL z

Jesus Appears to Mary Magdalene
(Matthew 28.9, 10; John 20.11-18)

[9 After Jesus rose from death early on Sunday, he appeared first to Mary Magdalene, from whom he had driven out seven demons. 10 She went and told his companions. They were mourning and crying; 11 and when they heard her say that Jesus was alive and that she had seen him, they did not believe her.

Jesus Appears to Two Followers
(Luke 24.13-35)

12 After this, Jesus appeared in a different manner to two of them while they were on their way to the country. 13 They returned and told the others, but these would not believe it.

Jesus Appears to the Eleven
(Matthew 28.16-20; Luke 24.36-49; John 20.19-23; Acts 1.6-8)

14 Last of all, Jesus appeared to the eleven disciples as they were eating. He scolded them, because they did not have faith and because they were too stubborn to believe those who had seen him alive. 15 He said to them, "Go throughout the whole world and preach the gospel to all people. 16 Whoever believes and is baptized will be saved; whoever does not believe will be condemned. 17 Believers will be given the power to perform miracles: they will drive out demons in my name; they will speak in strange tongues; 18 if they pick up snakes or drink any poison, they will not be harmed; they will place their hands on sick people, and these will get well."

Jesus Is Taken Up to Heaven
(Luke 24.50-53; Acts 1.9-11)

19 After the Lord Jesus had talked with them, he was taken up to heaven and sat at the right side of God. 20 The disciples went and preached everywhere, and the Lord worked with them and proved that their preaching was true by the miracles that were performed.]

ANOTHER OLD ENDING a

[9 The women went to Peter and his friends and gave them a brief account of all they had been told. 10 After this, Jesus himself sent out through his disciples from the east to the west the sacred and everliving message of eternal salvation.]

z Some manuscripts and ancient translations do not have this ending to the Gospel (verses 9-20).
a Some manuscripts and ancient translations have this shorter ending to the Gospel in addition to the longer ending (verses 9-20).

The Gospel according to
LUKE

Introduction

The Gospel according to Luke *presents Jesus as both the promised Savior of Israel and as the Savior of all people. Luke records that Jesus was called by the Spirit of the Lord to "bring good news to the poor," and this Gospel is filled with a concern for people with all kinds of need. The note of joy is also prominent in Luke, especially in the opening chapters that announce the coming of Jesus, and again at the conclusion, when Jesus ascends to heaven. The story of the growth and spread of the Christian faith after the ascension of Jesus is told by the same writer in the book of Acts.*

Parts 2 and 6 (see the outline below) contain much material that is found only in this Gospel, such as the stories about the song of the angels and the shepherds' visit at the birth of Jesus, Jesus in the Temple as a boy, and the parables of the Good Samaritan and the Lost Son. Throughout the Gospel great emphasis is placed on prayer, the Holy Spirit, the role of women in the ministry of Jesus, and God's forgiveness of sins.

Outline of Contents

Introduction

1 Dear Theophilus:
Many people have done their best to write a report of the things that have taken place among us. ²They wrote what we have been told by those who saw these things from the beginning and who proclaimed the message. ³And so, Your Excellency, because I have carefully studied all these matters from their beginning, I thought it would be good to write an orderly account for you. ⁴I do this so that you will know the full truth about everything which you have been taught.

The Birth of John the Baptist Is Announced

⁵During the time when Herod was king of Judea,ᵃ there was a priest named Zechariah, who belonged to the priestly order of Abijah. His wife's name was Elizabeth; she also belonged to a priestly family. ⁶They both lived good lives in God's sight and obeyed fully all the Lord's laws and commands. ⁷They

had no children because Elizabeth could not have any, and she and Zechariah were both very old.

⁸One day Zechariah was doing his work as a priest in the Temple, taking his turn in the daily service. ⁹According to the custom followed by the priests, he was chosen by lot to burn incense on the altar. So he went into the Temple of the Lord, ¹⁰while the crowd of people outside prayed during the hour when the incense was burned. ¹¹An angel of the Lord appeared to him, standing at the right side of the altar where the incense was burned. ¹²When Zechariah saw him, he was alarmed and felt afraid. ¹³But the angel said to him, "Don't be afraid, Zechariah! God has heard your prayer, and your wife Elizabeth will bear you a son. You are to name him John. ¹⁴How glad and happy you will be, and how happy many others will be when he is born! ¹⁵John will be great in the Lord's sight. He must not drink any wine or strong drink. From his very birth he will be filled with the Holy

---

ᵃ JUDEA: *The term here refers to the whole land of Palestine.*

LUKE

Spirit, 16 and he will bring back many of the people of Israel to the Lord their God. 17 He will go ahead of the Lord, strong and mighty like the prophet Elijah. He will bring fathers and children together again; he will turn disobedient people back to the way of thinking of the righteous; he will get the Lord's people ready for him."

18 Zechariah said to the angel, "How shall I know if this is so? I am an old man, and my wife is old also."

19 "I am Gabriel," the angel answered. "I stand in the presence of God, who sent me to speak to you and tell you this good news. 20 But you have not believed my message, which will come true at the right time. Because you have not believed, you will be unable to speak; you will remain silent until the day my promise to you comes true."

21 In the meantime the people were waiting for Zechariah and wondering why he was spending such a long time in the Temple. 22 When he came out, he could not speak to them, and so they knew that he had seen a vision in the Temple. Unable to say a word, he made signs to them with his hands.

23 When his period of service in the Temple was over, Zechariah went back home. 24 Some time later his wife Elizabeth became pregnant and did not leave the house for five months. 25 "Now at last the Lord has helped me," she said. "He has taken away my public disgrace!"

The Birth of Jesus Is Announced

26 In the sixth month of Elizabeth's pregnancy God sent the angel Gabriel to a town in Galilee named Nazareth. 27 He had a message for a young woman promised in marriage to a man named Joseph, who was a descendant of King David. Her name was Mary. 28 The angel came to her and said, "Peace be with you! The Lord is with you and has greatly blessed you!"

29 Mary was deeply troubled by the angel's message, and she wondered what his words meant. 30 The angel said to her, "Don't be afraid, Mary; God has been gracious to you. 31 You will become pregnant and give birth to a son, and you will name him Jesus. 32 He will be great and will be called the Son of the Most High God. The Lord God will make him a king, as his ancestor David was,

33 and he will be the king of the descendants of Jacob forever; his kingdom will never end!"

34 Mary said to the angel, "I am a virgin. How, then, can this be?"

35 The angel answered, "The Holy Spirit will come on you, and God's power will rest upon you. For this reason the holy child will be called the Son of God. 36 Remember your relative Elizabeth. It is said that she cannot have children, but she herself is now six months pregnant, even though she is very old. 37 For there is nothing that God cannot do."

38 "I am the Lord's servant," said Mary; "may it happen to me as you have said." And the angel left her.

Mary Visits Elizabeth

39 Soon afterward Mary got ready and hurried off to a town in the hill country of Judea. 40 She went into Zechariah's house and greeted Elizabeth. 41 When Elizabeth heard Mary's greeting, the baby moved within her. Elizabeth was filled with the Holy Spirit 42 and said in a loud voice, "You are the most blessed of all women, and blessed is the child you will bear! 43 Why should this great thing happen to me, that my Lord's mother comes to visit me? 44 For as soon as I heard your greeting, the baby within me jumped with gladness. 45 How happy you are to believe that the Lord's message to you will come true!"

Mary's Song of Praise

46 Mary said,
"My heart praises the Lord;
47 my soul is glad because of God
      my Savior,
48 for he has remembered me, his
      lowly servant!
   From now on all people will call
      me happy,
49 because of the great things the
      Mighty God has done for me.
   His name is holy;
50 from one generation to another
      he shows mercy to those who
      honor him.
51 He has stretched out his
      mighty arm
   and scattered the proud with all
      their plans.
52 He has brought down mighty
      kings from their thrones,

and lifted up the lowly.
53 He has filled the hungry with good
    things,
    and sent the rich away with
    empty hands.
54 He has kept the promise he made
    to our ancestors,
    and has come to the help of his
    servant Israel.
55 He has remembered to show
    mercy to Abraham
    and to all his descendants
    forever!"

56 Mary stayed about three months
with Elizabeth and then went back
home.

The Birth of John the Baptist

57 The time came for Elizabeth to have
her baby, and she gave birth to a son.
58 Her neighbors and relatives heard
how wonderfully good the Lord had
been to her, and they all rejoiced
with her. 59 When the baby was a week old, they
came to circumcise him, and they were
going to name him Zechariah, after his
father. 60 But his mother said, "No! His
name is to be John."

61 They said to her, "But you don't
have any relative with that name!"
62 Then they made signs to his father,
asking him what name he would like the
boy to have. 63 Zechariah asked for a writing pad
and wrote, "His name is John." How surprised they all were! 64 At that moment
Zechariah was able to speak again, and
he started praising God. 65 The neighbors were all filled with fear, and the
news about these things spread through
all the hill country of Judea. 66 Everyone
who heard of it thought about it and
asked, "What is this child going to be?"
For it was plain that the Lord's power
was upon him.

Zechariah's Prophecy

67 John's father Zechariah was filled
with the Holy Spirit, and he spoke God's
message:
68 "Let us praise the Lord, the God
    of Israel!
    He has come to the help of his
    people and has set them free.
69 He has provided for us a mighty
    Savior,

a descendant of his servant
    David.
70 He promised through his holy
    prophets long ago
71 that he would save us from our
    enemies,
    from the power of all those who
    hate us.
72 He said he would show mercy to
    our ancestors
    and remember his sacred
    covenant.
73-74 With a solemn oath to our
    ancestor Abraham
    he promised to rescue us from
    our enemies
    and allow us to serve him
    without fear,
75 so that we might be holy and
    righteous before him
    all the days of our life.

76 "You, my child, will be called a
    prophet of the Most High God.
    You will go ahead of the Lord
    to prepare his road for him,
77 to tell his people that they will be
    saved
    by having their sins forgiven.
78 Our God is merciful and tender.
    He will cause the bright dawn of
    salvation to rise on us
79 and to shine from heaven on all
    those who live in the dark
    shadow of death,
    to guide our steps into the path
    of peace."

80 The child grew and developed in
body and spirit. He lived in the desert
until the day when he appeared publicly
to the people of Israel.

The Birth of Jesus
(Matthew 1.18-25)

2 At that time Emperor Augustus ordered a census to be taken throughout the Roman Empire. 2 When this first
census took place, Quirinius was the
governor of Syria. 3 Everyone, then,
went to register himself, each to his own
hometown.

4 Joseph went from the town of Nazareth in Galilee to the town of Bethlehem
in Judea, the birthplace of King David.
Joseph went there because he was a
descendant of David. 5 He went to register with Mary, who was promised in
marriage to him. She was pregnant,

6and while they were in Bethlehem, the time came for her to have her baby. 7She gave birth to her first son, wrapped him in cloths and laid him in a manger — there was no room for them to stay in the inn.

The Shepherds and the Angels

8There were some shepherds in that part of the country who were spending the night in the fields, taking care of their flocks. 9An angel of the Lord appeared to them, and the glory of the Lord shone over them. They were terribly afraid, 10but the angel said to them, "Don't be afraid! I am here with good news for you, which will bring great joy to all the people. 11This very day in David's town your Savior was born — Christ the Lord! 12And this is what will prove it to you: you will find a baby wrapped in cloths and lying in a manger."

13Suddenly a great army of heaven's angels appeared with the angel, singing praises to God:

14"Glory to God in the highest heaven,
    and peace on earth to those with whom he is pleased!"

15When the angels went away from them back into heaven, the shepherds said to one another, "Let's go to Bethlehem and see this thing that has happened, which the Lord has told us."

16So they hurried off and found Mary and Joseph and saw the baby lying in the manger. 17When the shepherds saw him, they told them what the angel had said about the child. 18All who heard it were amazed at what the shepherds said. 19Mary remembered all these things and thought deeply about them. 20The shepherds went back, singing praises to God for all they had heard and seen; it had been just as the angel had told them.

Jesus Is Named

21A week later, when the time came for the baby to be circumcised, he was named Jesus, the name which the angel had given him before he had been conceived.

Jesus Is Presented in the Temple

22The time came for Joseph and Mary to perform the ceremony of purification, as the Law of Moses commanded. So they took the child to Jerusalem to present him to the Lord, 23as it is written in the law of the Lord: "Every first-born male is to be dedicated to the Lord." 24They also went to offer a sacrifice of a pair of doves or two young pigeons, as required by the law of the Lord.

25At that time there was a man named Simeon living in Jerusalem. He was a good, God-fearing man and was waiting for Israel to be saved. The Holy Spirit was with him 26and had assured him that he would not die before he had seen the Lord's promised Messiah. 27Led by the Spirit, Simeon went into the Temple. When the parents brought the child Jesus into the Temple to do for him what the Law required, 28Simeon took the child in his arms and gave thanks to God:

29"Now, Lord, you have kept your promise,
    and you may let your servant go in peace.
30With my own eyes I have seen your salvation,
31   which you have prepared in the presence of all peoples:
32A light to reveal your will to the Gentiles
    and bring glory to your people Israel."

33The child's father and mother were amazed at the things Simeon said about him. 34Simeon blessed them and said to Mary, his mother, "This child is chosen by God for the destruction and the salvation of many in Israel. He will be a sign from God which many people will speak against 35and so reveal their secret thoughts. And sorrow, like a sharp sword, will break your own heart."

36-37There was a very old prophet, a widow named Anna, daughter of Phanuel of the tribe of Asher. She had been married for only seven years and was now eighty-four years old.b She never left the Temple; day and night she worshiped God, fasting and praying. 38That very same hour she arrived and gave thanks to God and spoke about the child

b was now eighty-four years old; or had been a widow eighty-four years.

to all who were waiting for God to set Jerusalem free.

The Return to Nazareth

39 When Joseph and Mary had finished doing all that was required by the Law of the Lord, they returned to their hometown of Nazareth in Galilee. 40 The child grew and became strong; he was full of wisdom, and God's blessings were upon him.

The Boy Jesus in the Temple

41 Every year the parents of Jesus went to Jerusalem for the Passover Festival. 42 When Jesus was twelve years old, they went to the festival as usual. 43 When the festival was over, they started back home, but the boy Jesus stayed in Jerusalem. His parents did not know this; 44 they thought that he was with the group, so they traveled a whole day and then started looking for him among their relatives and friends. 45 They did not find him, so they went back to Jerusalem looking for him. 46 On the third day they found him in the Temple, sitting with the Jewish teachers, listening to them and asking questions. 47 All who heard him were amazed at his intelligent answers. 48 His parents were astonished when they saw him, and his mother said to him, "Son, why have you done this to us? Your father and I have been terribly worried trying to find you."

49 He answered them, "Why did you have to look for me? Didn't you know that I had to be in my Father's house?" 50 But they did not understand his answer.

51 So Jesus went back with them to Nazareth, where he was obedient to them. His mother treasured all these things in her heart. 52 Jesus grew both in body and in wisdom, gaining favor with God and people.

The Preaching of John the Baptist
(Matthew 3.1-12; Mark 1.1-8; John 1.19-28)

3 It was the fifteenth year of the rule of Emperor Tiberius; Pontius Pilate was governor of Judea, Herod was ruler of Galilee, and his brother Philip was ruler of the territory of Iturea and Trachonitis; Lysanias was ruler of Abilene, 2 and Annas and Caiaphas were High Priests. At that time the word of God came to John son of Zechariah in the desert. 3 So John went throughout the whole territory of the Jordan River, preaching, "Turn away from your sins and be baptized, and God will forgive your sins." 4 As it is written in the book of the prophet Isaiah:

"Someone is shouting in the
    desert:
'Get the road ready for the Lord;
    make a straight path for him to
      travel!
5 Every valley must be filled up,
    every hill and mountain
      leveled off.
The winding roads must be made
    straight,
    and the rough paths made
      smooth.
6 The whole human race will see
    God's salvation!' "

7 Crowds of people came out to John to be baptized by him. "You snakes!" he said to them. "Who told you that you could escape from the punishment God is about to send? 8 Do those things that will show that you have turned from your sins. And don't start saying among yourselves that Abraham is your ancestor. I tell you that God can take these rocks and make descendants for Abraham! 9 The ax is ready to cut down the trees at the roots; every tree that does not bear good fruit will be cut down and thrown in the fire."

10 The people asked him, "What are we to do, then?"

11 He answered, "Whoever has two shirts must give one to the man who has none, and whoever has food must share it."

12 Some tax collectors came to be baptized, and they asked him, "Teacher, what are we to do?"

13 "Don't collect more than is legal," he told them.

14 Some soldiers also asked him, "What about us? What are we to do?"

He said to them, "Don't take money from anyone by force or accuse anyone falsely. Be content with your pay."

15 People's hopes began to rise, and they began to wonder whether John perhaps might be the Messiah. 16 So John said to all of them, "I baptize you with water, but someone is coming who is much greater than I am. I am not good enough even to untie his sandals. He will baptize you with the Holy Spirit and fire.

17He has his winnowing shovel with him, to thresh out all the grain and gather the wheat into his barn; but he will burn the chaff in a fire that never goes out."

18In many different ways John preached the Good News to the people and urged them to change their ways. 19But John reprimanded Governor Herod, because he had married Herodias, his brother's wife, and had done many other evil things. 20Then Herod did an even worse thing by putting John in prison.

The Baptism of Jesus
(Matthew 3.13-17; Mark 1.9-11)

21After all the people had been baptized, Jesus also was baptized. While he was praying, heaven was opened, 22and the Holy Spirit came down upon him in bodily form like a dove. And a voice came from heaven, "You are my own dear Son. I am pleased with you."

The Ancestors of Jesus
(Matthew 1.1-17)

23When Jesus began his work, he was about thirty years old. He was the son, so people thought, of Joseph, who was the son of Heli, 24the son of Matthat, the son of Levi, the son of Melchi, the son of Jannai, the son of Joseph, 25the son of Mattathias, the son of Amos, the son of Nahum, the son of Esli, the son of Naggai, 26the son of Maath, the son of Mattathias, the son of Semein, the son of Josech, the son of Joda, 27the son of Joanan, the son of Rhesa, the son of Zerubbabel, the son of Shealtiel, the son of Neri, 28the son of Melchi, the son of Addi, the son of Cosam, the son of Elmadam, the son of Er, 29the son of Joshua, the son of Eliezer, the son of Jorim, the son of Matthat, the son of Levi, 30the son of Simeon, the son of Judah, the son of Joseph, the son of Jonam, the son of Eliakim, 31the son of Melea, the son of Menna, the son of Mattatha, the son of Nathan, the son of David, 32the son of Jesse, the son of Obed, the son of Boaz, the son of Salmon, the son of Nahshon, 33the son of Amminadab, the son of Admin, the son of Arni, the son of Hezron, the son of Perez, the son of Judah, 34the son of Jacob, the son of Isaac, the son of Abraham, the son of Terah, the son of Nahor, 35the son of Serug, the son of

Reu, the son of Peleg, the son of Eber, the son of Shelah, 36the son of Cainan, the son of Arphaxad, the son of Shem, the son of Noah, the son of Lamech, 37the son of Methuselah, the son of Enoch, the son of Jared, the son of Mahalaleel, the son of Kenan, 38the son of Enosh, the son of Seth, the son of Adam, the son of God.

The Temptation of Jesus
(Matthew 4.1-11; Mark 1.12, 13)

4 Jesus returned from the Jordan full of the Holy Spirit and was led by the Spirit into the desert, 2where he was tempted by the Devil for forty days. In all that time he ate nothing, so that he was hungry when it was over.

3The Devil said to him, "If you are God's Son, order this stone to turn into bread."

4But Jesus answered, "The scripture says, 'Human beings cannot live on bread alone.' "

5Then the Devil took him up and showed him in a second all the kingdoms of the world. 6"I will give you all this power and all this wealth," the Devil told him. "It has all been handed over to me, and I can give it to anyone I choose. 7All this will be yours, then, if you worship me."

8Jesus answered, "The scripture says, 'Worship the Lord your God and serve only him!' "

9Then the Devil took him to Jerusalem and set him on the highest point of the Temple, and said to him, "If you are God's Son, throw yourself down from here. 10For the scripture says, 'God will order his angels to take good care of you.' 11It also says, 'They will hold you up with their hands so that not even your feet will be hurt on the stones.' "

12But Jesus answered, "The scripture says, 'Do not put the Lord your God to the test.' "

13When the Devil finished tempting Jesus in every way, he left him for a while.

Jesus Begins His Work in Galilee
(Matthew 4.12-17; Mark 1.14, 15)

14Then Jesus returned to Galilee, and the power of the Holy Spirit was with him. The news about him spread throughout all that territory. 15He taught

THE SYNAGOGUE

The synagogue as a Jewish religious institution probably arose after the Israelites returned from exile in Babylon. The public readings of the Law by Ezra the priest after the exiles resettled in Jerusalem (Ne 8) may have signaled the beginning of the movement that led to the development of the synagogue system.

The synagogue, as distinguished from the Tent and the Temple with their sacrifices, was a local gathering place where Jews of all ages met for prayer and study of the Law of Moses. Scores of these synagogues sprang up in Jerusalem and surrounding cities during the two hundred years or so before the New Testament era. They were organized wherever ten or more men showed interest in preserving their Jewish customs and learning and obeying the Law.

Synagogue worship included readings from the Law, prayers, and a commentary or sermon on the Bible passage. Any competent member of the congregation might be asked to read the Scriptures or bring the sermon. This privilege was apparently extended to Jesus in the synagogue at Nazareth early in his ministry. He read from the prophet Isaiah, identifying himself as the Messiah whom Isaiah had prophesied hundreds of years before (Lk 4.16–30).

Several synagogue buildings, including one at the city of Capernaum, have been uncovered by archaeologists. These were generally rectangular structures with a large central seating area, much like a modern church building. The congregation sat on stone benches along the walls or cross-legged on the floor. The main piece of furniture in a synagogue was the Covenant Box, where the sacred scrolls with the Law were kept. The Box was placed along the wall nearest to the city of Jerusalem—the direction which the people faced during a synagogue service.

Synagogue life, as influenced by the rabbis who attached themselves to these local Jewish centers, came to dominate the religious thinking of the Jewish people during New Testament times. Each local synagogue had its own ruling group, which governed religious behavior among the Jews in that community.

The apostle Paul regularly proclaimed Christ at synagogues on his missionary journeys (Ac 13.5; 14.1). The emphasis of the synagogue on Scripture, prayer, and a sermon in worship has influenced the order of service used in most Christian churches today.

in the synagogues and was praised by everyone.

Jesus Is Rejected at Nazareth
(Matthew 13.53-58; Mark 6.1-6)

16 Then Jesus went to Nazareth, where he had been brought up, and on the Sabbath he went as usual to the synagogue. He stood up to read the Scriptures 17 and was handed the book of the prophet Isaiah. He unrolled the scroll and found the place where it is written,

18 "The Spirit of the Lord is upon me,
    because he has chosen me to
        bring good news to the poor.
He has sent me to proclaim liberty
    to the captives
  and recovery of sight to the
    blind,
to set free the oppressed
19   and announce that the time has
    come
  when the Lord will save his
    people."

20 Jesus rolled up the scroll, gave it back to the attendant, and sat down. All the people in the synagogue had their eyes fixed on him, 21 as he said to them, "This passage of scripture has come true today, as you heard it being read."

22 They were all well impressed with him and marveled at the eloquent words that he spoke. They said, "Isn't he the son of Joseph?"

23 He said to them, "I am sure that you will quote this proverb to me, 'Doctor, heal yourself.' You will also tell me to do here in my hometown the same things you heard were done in Capernaum. 24 I tell you this," Jesus added, "prophets are never welcomed in their hometown. 25 Listen to me: it is true that there were many widows in Israel during the time of Elijah, when there was no rain for three and a half years and a severe famine spread throughout the whole land. 26 Yet Elijah was not sent to anyone in Israel, but only to a widow living in Zarephath in the territory of Sidon. 27 And there were many people suffering from a dreaded skin disease who lived in Israel during the time of the prophet Elisha; yet not one of them was healed, but only Naaman the Syrian."

28 When the people in the synagogue heard this, they were filled with anger. 29 They rose up, dragged Jesus out of town, and took him to the top of the hill on which their town was built. They meant to throw him over the cliff, 30 but he walked through the middle of the crowd and went his way.

A Man with an Evil Spirit
(Mark 1.21-28)

31 Then Jesus went to Capernaum, a town in Galilee, where he taught the people on the Sabbath. 32 They were all amazed at the way he taught, because he spoke with authority. 33 In the synagogue was a man who had the spirit of an evil demon in him; he screamed out in a loud voice, 34 "Ah! What do you want with us, Jesus of Nazareth? Are you here to destroy us? I know who you are: you are God's holy messenger!"

35 Jesus ordered the spirit, "Be quiet and come out of the man!" The demon threw the man down in front of them and went out of him without doing him any harm.

36 The people were all amazed and said to one another, "What kind of words are these? With authority and power this man gives orders to the evil spirits, and they come out!" 37 And the report about Jesus spread everywhere in that region.

Jesus Heals Many People
(Matthew 8.14-17; Mark 1.29-34)

38 Jesus left the synagogue and went to Simon's home. Simon's mother-in-law was sick with a high fever, and they spoke to Jesus about her. 39 He went and stood at her bedside and ordered the fever to leave her. The fever left her, and she got up at once and began to wait on them.

40 After sunset all who had friends who were sick with various diseases brought them to Jesus; he placed his hands on every one of them and healed them all. 41 Demons also went out from many people, screaming, "You are the Son of God!"

Jesus gave the demons an order and would not let them speak, because they knew he was the Messiah.

Jesus Preaches in the Synagogues
(Mark 1.35-39)

42 At daybreak Jesus left the town and went off to a lonely place. The people started looking for him, and when they found him, they tried to keep him from

leaving. 43But he said to them, "I must preach the Good News about the Kingdom of God in other towns also, because that is what God sent me to do."

44So he preached in the synagogues throughout the country.

Jesus Calls the First Disciples
(Matthew 4.18-22; Mark 1.16-20)

5 One day Jesus was standing on the shore of Lake Gennesaret while the people pushed their way up to him to listen to the word of God. 2He saw two boats pulled up on the beach; the fishermen had left them and were washing the nets. 3Jesus got into one of the boats—it belonged to Simon—and asked him to push off a little from the shore. Jesus sat in the boat and taught the crowd.

4When he finished speaking, he said to Simon, "Push the boat out further to the deep water, and you and your partners let down your nets for a catch."

5"Master," Simon answered, "we worked hard all night long and caught nothing. But if you say so, I will let down the nets." 6They let them down and caught such a large number of fish that the nets were about to break. 7So they motioned to their partners in the other boat to come and help them. They came and filled both boats so full of fish that the boats were about to sink. 8When Simon Peter saw what had happened, he fell on his knees before Jesus and said, "Go away from me, Lord! I am a sinful man!"

9He and the others with him were all amazed at the large number of fish they had caught. 10The same was true of Simon's partners, James and John, the sons of Zebedee. Jesus said to Simon, "Don't be afraid; from now on you will be catching people."

11They pulled the boats up on the beach, left everything, and followed Jesus.

Jesus Heals a Man
(Matthew 8.1-4; Mark 1.40-45)

12Once Jesus was in a town where there was a man who was suffering from a dreaded skin disease. When he saw Jesus, he threw himself down and begged him, "Sir, if you want to, you can make me clean!"c

13Jesus reached out and touched him. "I do want to," he answered. "Be clean!" At once the disease left the man. 14Jesus ordered him, "Don't tell anyone, but go straight to the priest and let him examine you; then to prove to everyone that you are cured, offer the sacrifice as Moses ordered."

15But the news about Jesus spread all the more widely, and crowds of people came to hear him and be healed from their diseases. 16But he would go away to lonely places, where he prayed.

Jesus Heals a Paralyzed Man
(Matthew 9.1-8; Mark 2.1-12)

17One day when Jesus was teaching, some Pharisees and teachers of the Law were sitting there who had come from every town in Galilee and Judea and from Jerusalem. The power of the Lord was present for Jesus to heal the sick. 18Some men came carrying a paralyzed man on a bed, and they tried to carry him into the house and put him in front of Jesus. 19Because of the crowd, however, they could find no way to take him in. So they carried him up on the roof, made an opening in the tiles, and let him down on his bed into the middle of the group in front of Jesus. 20When Jesus saw how much faith they had, he said to the man, "Your sins are forgiven, my friend."

21The teachers of the Law and the Pharisees began to say to themselves, "Who is this man who speaks such blasphemy! God is the only one who can forgive sins!"

22Jesus knew their thoughts and said to them, "Why do you think such things? 23Is it easier to say, 'Your sins are forgiven you,' or to say, 'Get up and walk'? 24I will prove to you, then, that the Son of Man has authority on earth to forgive sins." So he said to the paralyzed man, "I tell you, get up, pick up your bed, and go home!"

25At once the man got up in front of them all, took the bed he had been lying on, and went home, praising God. 26They were all completely amazed! Full of fear, they praised God, saying, "What marvelous things we have seen today!"

c MAKE ME CLEAN: *This disease was considered to make a person ritually unclean.*

Jesus Calls Levi
(Matthew 9.9-13; Mark 2.13-17)

27 After this, Jesus went out and saw a tax collector named Levi, sitting in his office. Jesus said to him, "Follow me." 28 Levi got up, left everything, and followed him.

29 Then Levi had a big feast in his house for Jesus, and among the guests was a large number of tax collectors and other people. 30 Some Pharisees and some teachers of the Law who belonged to their group complained to Jesus' disciples. "Why do you eat and drink with tax collectors and other outcasts?" they asked.

31 Jesus answered them, "People who are well do not need a doctor, but only those who are sick. 32 I have not come to call respectable people to repent, but outcasts."

The Question about Fasting
(Matthew 9.14-17; Mark 2.18-22)

33 Some people said to Jesus, "The disciples of John fast frequently and offer prayers, and the disciples of the Pharisees do the same; but your disciples eat and drink."

34 Jesus answered, "Do you think you can make the guests at a wedding party go without food as long as the bridegroom is with them? Of course not! 35 But the day will come when the bridegroom will be taken away from them, and then they will fast."

36 Jesus also told them this parable: "You don't tear a piece off a new coat to patch up an old coat. If you do, you will have torn the new coat, and the piece of new cloth will not match the old. 37 Nor do you pour new wine into used wineskins, because the new wine will burst the skins, the wine will pour out, and the skins will be ruined. 38 Instead, new wine must be poured into fresh wineskins! 39 And you don't want new wine after drinking old wine. 'The old is better,' you say."

The Question about the Sabbath
(Matthew 12.1-8; Mark 2.23-28)

6 Jesus was walking through some wheat fields on a Sabbath. His disciples began to pick the heads of wheat, rub them in their hands, and eat the grain. 2 Some Pharisees asked, "Why are you doing what our Law says you cannot do on the Sabbath?"

3 Jesus answered them, "Haven't you read what David did when he and his men were hungry? 4 He went into the house of God, took the bread offered to God, ate it, and gave it also to his men. Yet it is against our Law for anyone except the priests to eat that bread."

5 And Jesus concluded, "The Son of Man is Lord of the Sabbath."

The Man with a Paralyzed Hand
(Matthew 12.9-14; Mark 3.1-6)

6 On another Sabbath Jesus went into a synagogue and taught. A man was there whose right hand was paralyzed. 7 Some teachers of the Law and some Pharisees wanted a reason to accuse Jesus of doing wrong, so they watched him closely to see if he would heal on the Sabbath. 8 But Jesus knew their thoughts and said to the man, "Stand up and come here to the front." The man got up and stood there. 9 Then Jesus said to them, "I ask you: What does our Law allow us to do on the Sabbath? To help or to harm? To save someone's life or destroy it?" 10 He looked around at them all; then he said[d] to the man, "Stretch out your hand." He did so, and his hand became well again.

11 They were filled with rage and began to discuss among themselves what they could do to Jesus.

Jesus Chooses the Twelve Apostles
(Matthew 10.1-4; Mark 3.13-19)

12 At that time Jesus went up a hill to pray and spent the whole night there praying to God. 13 When day came, he called his disciples to him and chose twelve of them, whom he named apostles: 14 Simon (whom he named Peter) and his brother Andrew; James and John, Philip and Bartholomew, 15 Matthew and Thomas, James son of Alphaeus, and Simon (who was called the Patriot), 16 Judas son of James, and Judas Iscariot, who became the traitor.

Jesus Teaches and Heals
(Matthew 4.23-25)

17 When Jesus had come down from the hill with the apostles, he stood on a

---

d said; *some manuscripts have* said angrily.

level place with a large number of his disciples. A large crowd of people was there from all over Judea and from Jerusalem and from the coast cities of Tyre and Sidon; 18 they had come to hear him and to be healed of their diseases. Those who were troubled by evil spirits also came and were healed. 19 All the people tried to touch him, for power was going out from him and healing them all.

Happiness and Sorrow
(Matthew 5.1-12)

20 Jesus looked at his disciples and said,

"Happy are you poor;
the Kingdom of God is yours!

21 "Happy are you who are
hungry now;
you will be filled!

"Happy are you who weep now;
you will laugh!

22 "Happy are you when people hate you, reject you, insult you, and say that you are evil, all because of the Son of Man! 23 Be glad when that happens and dance for joy, because a great reward is kept for you in heaven. For their ancestors did the very same things to the prophets.

24 "But how terrible for you who are
rich now;
you have had your easy life!

25 "How terrible for you who are
full now;
you will go hungry!

"How terrible for you who
laugh now;
you will mourn and weep!

26 "How terrible when all people speak well of you; their ancestors said the very same things about the false prophets."

Love for Enemies
(Matthew 5.38-48; 7.12a)

27 "But I tell you who hear me: Love your enemies, do good to those who hate you, 28 bless those who curse you, and pray for those who mistreat you. 29 If anyone hits you on one cheek, let him hit the other one too; if someone takes your coat, let him have your shirt as well. 30 Give to everyone who asks you for something, and when someone takes what is yours, do not ask for it back. 31 Do for others just what you want them to do for you.

32 "If you love only the people who love you, why should you receive a blessing? Even sinners love those who love them! 33 And if you do good only to those who do good to you, why should you receive a blessing? Even sinners do that! 34 And if you lend only to those from whom you hope to get it back, why should you receive a blessing? Even sinners lend to sinners, to get back the same amount! 35 No! Love your enemies and do good to them; lend and expect nothing back. You will then have a great reward, and you will be children of the Most High God. For he is good to the ungrateful and the wicked. 36 Be merciful just as your Father is merciful.

Judging Others
(Matthew 7.1-5)

37 "Do not judge others, and God will not judge you; do not condemn others, and God will not condemn you; forgive others, and God will forgive you. 38 Give to others, and God will give to you. Indeed, you will receive a full measure, a generous helping, poured into your hands—all that you can hold. The measure you use for others is the one that God will use for you."

39 And Jesus told them this parable: "One blind man cannot lead another one; if he does, both will fall into a ditch. 40 No pupils are greater than their teacher; but all pupils, when they have completed their training, will be like their teacher.

41 "Why do you look at the speck in your brother's eye, but pay no attention to the log in your own eye? 42 How can you say to your brother, 'Please, brother, let me take that speck out of your eye,' yet cannot even see the log in your own eye? You hypocrite! First take the log out of your own eye, and then you will be able to see clearly to take the speck out of your brother's eye.

A Tree and Its Fruit
(Matthew 7.16-20; 12.33-35)

43 "A healthy tree does not bear bad fruit, nor does a poor tree bear good fruit. 44 Every tree is known by the fruit it bears; you do not pick figs from thorn bushes or gather grapes from bramble bushes. 45 A good person brings good out of the treasure of good things in his heart; a bad person brings bad out of his

treasure of bad things. For the mouth speaks what the heart is full of.

The Two House Builders
(Matthew 7.24-27)

46 "Why do you call me, 'Lord, Lord,' and yet don't do what I tell you? 47 Anyone who comes to me and listens to my words and obeys them—I will show you what he is like. 48 He is like a man who, in building his house, dug deep and laid the foundation on rock. The river flooded over and hit that house but could not shake it, because it was well built. 49 But anyone who hears my words and does not obey them is like a man who built his house without laying a foundation; when the flood hit that house it fell at once—and what a terrible crash that was!"

Jesus Heals a Roman Officer's Servant
(Matthew 8.5-13)

7 When Jesus had finished saying all these things to the people, he went to Capernaum. 2 A Roman officer there had a servant who was very dear to him; the man was sick and about to die. 3 When the officer heard about Jesus, he sent some Jewish elders to ask him to come and heal his servant. 4 They came to Jesus and begged him earnestly, "This man really deserves your help. 5 He loves our people and he himself built a synagogue for us."

6 So Jesus went with them. He was not far from the house when the officer sent friends to tell him, "Sir, don't trouble yourself. I do not deserve to have you come into my house, 7 neither do I consider myself worthy to come to you in person. Just give the order, and my servant will get well. 8 I, too, am a man placed under the authority of superior officers, and I have soldiers under me. I order this one, 'Go!' and he goes; I order that one, 'Come!' and he comes; and I order my slave, 'Do this!' and he does it."

9 Jesus was surprised when he heard this; he turned around and said to the crowd following him, "I tell you, I have never found faith like this, not even in Israel!"

10 The messengers went back to the officer's house and found his servant well.

Jesus Raises a Widow's Son

11 Soon afterward[e] Jesus went to a town named Nain, accompanied by his disciples and a large crowd. 12 Just as he arrived at the gate of the town, a funeral procession was coming out. The dead man was the only son of a woman who was a widow, and a large crowd from the town was with her. 13 When the Lord saw her, his heart was filled with pity for her, and he said to her, "Don't cry." 14 Then he walked over and touched the coffin, and the men carrying it stopped. Jesus said, "Young man! Get up, I tell you!" 15 The dead man sat up and began to talk, and Jesus gave him back to his mother.

16 They all were filled with fear and praised God. "A great prophet has appeared among us!" they said; "God has come to save his people!"

17 This news about Jesus went out through all the country and the surrounding territory.

The Messengers from John the Baptist
(Matthew 11.2-19)

18 When John's disciples told him about all these things, he called two of them 19 and sent them to the Lord to ask him, "Are you the one John said was going to come, or should we expect someone else?"

20 When they came to Jesus, they said, "John the Baptist sent us to ask if you are the one he said was going to come, or should we expect someone else?"

21 At that very time Jesus healed many people from their sicknesses, diseases, and evil spirits, and gave sight to many blind people. 22 He answered John's messengers, "Go back and tell John what you have seen and heard: the blind can see, the lame can walk, those who suffer from dreaded skin diseases are made clean,[f] the deaf can hear, the dead are raised to life, and the Good News is preached to the poor. 23 How happy are those who have no doubts about me!"

---

[e] *Soon afterward; some manuscripts have* The next day.   [f] MADE CLEAN: *See 5.12.*

NEW TESTAMENT WOMEN

Mary, the virgin mother of Jesus, has a place of honor among the women of the New Testament. As the first member of the human race to accept Christ, she stands as the first of the redeemed throughout Christian history. She is an enduring example of faith, humility, and service (Lk 1.26–56).

Other notable women of the New Testament include the following:

Name	Description	Biblical Reference
Anna	Recognized Jesus as the long-awaited Messiah	Lk 2.36–38
Bernice	Sister of Agrippa before whom Paul made his defense	Ac 25.13
Chloe	Woman who knew of divisions in the church at Corinth	1 Co 1.11
Claudia	Christian of Rome	2 Ti 4.21
Damaris	Woman of Athens converted under Paul's ministry	Ac 17.34
Dorcas (Tabitha)	Christian in Joppa who was raised from the dead by Peter	Ac 9.36–41
Drusilla	Wife of Felix, governor of Judea	Ac 24.24
Elizabeth	Mother of John the Baptist	Lk 1.5, 13
Eunice	Mother of Timothy	2 Ti 1.5
Herodias	Queen who demanded the execution of John the Baptist	Mt 14.3–10
Joanna	Provided for the material needs of Jesus	Lk 8.3
Lois	Grandmother of Timothy	2 Ti 1.5
Lydia	Convert under Paul's ministry in Philippi	Ac 16.14
Martha and Mary	Sisters of Lazarus; friends of Jesus	Lk 10.38–42
Mary Magdalene	Woman present at Jesus' burial and from whom Jesus cast out demons	Mt 27.56–61; Mk 16.9
Phoebe	A servant in the church at Cenchreae	Ro 16.1, 2
Priscilla	Wife of Aquila; laborer with Paul at Corinth and Ephesus	Ac 18.2, 18, 19
Salome	Accompanied Mary Magdalene and Mary to anoint Jesus' body	Mk 16.1
Sapphira	Held back goods from the early Christian community	Ac 5.1
Susanna	Provided for the material needs of Jesus	Lk 8.3

24 After John's messengers had left, Jesus began to speak about him to the crowds: "When you went out to John in the desert, what did you expect to see? A blade of grass bending in the wind? 25 What did you go out to see? A man dressed up in fancy clothes? People who dress like that and live in luxury are found in palaces! 26 Tell me, what did you go out to see? A prophet? Yes indeed, but you saw much more than a prophet. 27 For John is the one of whom the scripture says: 'God said, I will send my messenger ahead of you to open the way for you.' 28 I tell you," Jesus added, "John is greater than anyone who has ever lived. But the one who is least in the Kingdom of God is greater than John."

29 All the people heard him; they and especially the tax collectors were the ones who had obeyed God's righteous demands and had been baptized by John. 30 But the Pharisees and the teachers of the Law rejected God's purpose for themselves and refused to be baptized by John.

31 Jesus continued, "Now to what can I compare the people of this day? What are they like? 32 They are like children sitting in the marketplace. One group shouts to the other, 'We played wedding music for you, but you wouldn't dance! We sang funeral songs, but you wouldn't cry!' 33 John the Baptist came, and he fasted and drank no wine, and you said, 'He has a demon in him!' 34 The Son of Man came, and he ate and drank, and you said, 'Look at this man! He is a glutton and wine drinker, a friend of tax collectors and other outcasts!' 35 God's wisdom, however, is shown to be true by all who accept it."

Jesus at the Home of Simon the Pharisee

36 A Pharisee invited Jesus to have dinner with him, and Jesus went to his house and sat down to eat. 37 In that town was a woman who lived a sinful life. She heard that Jesus was eating in the Pharisee's house, so she brought an alabaster jar full of perfume 38 and stood behind Jesus, by his feet, crying and wetting his feet with her tears. Then she dried his feet with her hair, kissed them, and poured the perfume on them. 39 When the Pharisee saw this, he said to himself, "If this man really were a prophet, he would know who this woman is who is touching him; he would know what kind of sinful life she lives!"

40 Jesus spoke up and said to him, "Simon, I have something to tell you."

"Yes, Teacher," he said, "tell me."

41 "There were two men who owed money to a moneylender," Jesus began. "One owed him five hundred silver coins, and the other owed him fifty. 42 Neither of them could pay him back, so he canceled the debts of both. Which one, then, will love him more?"

43 "I suppose," answered Simon, "that it would be the one who was forgiven more."

"You are right," said Jesus. 44 Then he turned to the woman and said to Simon, "Do you see this woman? I came into your home, and you gave me no water for my feet, but she has washed my feet with her tears and dried them with her hair. 45 You did not welcome me with a kiss, but she has not stopped kissing my feet since I came. 46 You provided no olive oil for my head, but she has covered my feet with perfume. 47 I tell you, then, the great love she has shown proves that her many sins have been forgiven. But whoever has been forgiven little shows only a little love."

48 Then Jesus said to the woman, "Your sins are forgiven."

49 The others sitting at the table began to say to themselves, "Who is this, who even forgives sins?"

50 But Jesus said to the woman, "Your faith has saved you; go in peace."

Women Who Accompanied Jesus

8 Some time later Jesus traveled through towns and villages, preaching the Good News about the Kingdom of God. The twelve disciples went with him, 2 and so did some women who had been healed of evil spirits and diseases: Mary (who was called Magdalene), from whom seven demons had been driven out; 3 Joanna, whose husband Chuza was an officer in Herod's court; and Susanna, and many other women who used their own resources to help Jesus and his disciples.

The Parable of the Sower
(Matthew 13.1-9; Mark 4.1-9)

4 People kept coming to Jesus from one town after another; and when a great crowd gathered, Jesus told this parable:

5 "Once there was a man who went out to sow grain. As he scattered the seed in the field, some of it fell along the path, where it was stepped on, and the birds ate it up. 6 Some of it fell on rocky ground, and when the plants sprouted, they dried up because the soil had no moisture. 7 Some of the seed fell among thorn bushes, which grew up with the plants and choked them. 8 And some seeds fell in good soil; the plants grew and bore grain, one hundred grains each."

And Jesus concluded, "Listen, then, if you have ears!"

The Purpose of the Parables
(Matthew 13.10-17; Mark 4.10-12)

9 His disciples asked Jesus what this parable meant, 10 and he answered, "The knowledge of the secrets of the Kingdom of God has been given to you, but to the rest it comes by means of parables, so that they may look but not see, and listen but not understand.

Jesus Explains the Parable of the Sower
(Matthew 13.18-23; Mark 4.13-20)

11 "This is what the parable means: the seed is the word of God. 12 The seeds that fell along the path stand for those who hear; but the Devil comes and takes the message away from their hearts in order to keep them from believing and being saved. 13 The seeds that fell on rocky ground stand for those who hear the message and receive it gladly. But it does not sink deep into them; they believe only for a while but when the time of testing comes, they fall away. 14 The seeds that fell among thorn bushes stand for those who hear; but the worries and riches and pleasures of this life crowd in and choke them, and their fruit never ripens. 15 The seeds that fell in good soil stand for those who hear the message and retain it in a good and obedient heart, and they persist until they bear fruit.

A Lamp under a Bowl
(Mark 4.21-25)

16 "No one lights a lamp and covers it with a bowl or puts it under a bed. Instead, it is put on the lampstand, so that people will see the light as they come in.

17 "Whatever is hidden away will be brought out into the open, and whatever is covered up will be found and brought to light.

18 "Be careful, then, how you listen; because those who have something will be given more, but whoever has nothing will have taken away from them even the little they think they have."

Jesus' Mother and Brothers
(Matthew 12.46-50; Mark 3.31-35)

19 Jesus' mother and brothers came to him, but were unable to join him because of the crowd. 20 Someone said to Jesus, "Your mother and brothers are standing outside and want to see you."

21 Jesus said to them all, "My mother and brothers are those who hear the word of God and obey it."

Jesus Calms a Storm
(Matthew 8.23-27; Mark 4.35-41)

22 One day Jesus got into a boat with his disciples and said to them, "Let us go across to the other side of the lake." So they started out. 23 As they were sailing, Jesus fell asleep. Suddenly a strong wind blew down on the lake, and the boat began to fill with water, so that they were all in great danger. 24 The disciples went to Jesus and woke him up, saying, "Master, Master! We are about to die!"

Jesus got up and gave an order to the wind and to the stormy water; they quieted down, and there was a great calm. 25 Then he said to the disciples, "Where is your faith?"

But they were amazed and afraid, and said to one another, "Who is this man? He gives orders to the winds and waves, and they obey him!"

Jesus Heals a Man with Demons
(Matthew 8.28-34; Mark 5.1-20)

26 Jesus and his disciples sailed on over to the territory of Gerasa,g which

g Gerasa; some manuscripts have Gadara (see Mt 8.28); others have Gergesa.

is across the lake from Galilee. 27 As Jesus stepped ashore, he was met by a man from the town who had demons in him. For a long time this man had gone without clothes and would not stay at home, but spent his time in the burial caves. 28 When he saw Jesus, he gave a loud cry, threw himself down at his feet, and shouted, "Jesus, Son of the Most High God! What do you want with me? I beg you, don't punish me!" 29 He said this because Jesus had ordered the evil spirit to go out of him. Many times it had seized him, and even though he was kept a prisoner, his hands and feet tied with chains, he would break the chains and be driven by the demon out into the desert.

30 Jesus asked him, "What is your name?"

"My name is 'Mob,' " he answered — because many demons had gone into him. 31 The demons begged Jesus not to send them into the abyss. h

32 There was a large herd of pigs near by, feeding on a hillside. So the demons begged Jesus to let them go into the pigs, and he let them. 33 They went out of the man and into the pigs. The whole herd rushed down the side of the cliff into the lake and was drowned.

34 The men who had been taking care of the pigs saw what happened, so they ran off and spread the news in the town and among the farms. 35 People went out to see what had happened, and when they came to Jesus, they found the man from whom the demons had gone out sitting at the feet of Jesus, clothed and in his right mind; and they were all afraid. 36 Those who had seen it told the people how the man had been cured. 37 Then all the people from that territory asked Jesus to go away, because they were terribly afraid. So Jesus got into the boat and left. 38 The man from whom the demons had gone out begged Jesus, "Let me go with you."

But Jesus sent him away, saying, 39 "Go back home and tell what God has done for you."

The man went through the town, telling what Jesus had done for him.

Jairus' Daughter and the Woman Who Touched Jesus' Cloak

(Matthew 9.18-26; Mark 5.21-43)

40 When Jesus returned to the other side of the lake, the people welcomed him, because they had all been waiting for him. 41 Then a man named Jairus arrived; he was an official in the local synagogue. He threw himself down at Jesus' feet and begged him to go to his home, 42 because his only daughter, who was twelve years old, was dying.

As Jesus went along, the people were crowding him from every side. 43 Among them was a woman who had suffered from severe bleeding for twelve years; she had spent all she had on doctors, i but no one had been able to cure her. 44 She came up in the crowd behind Jesus and touched the edge of his cloak, and her bleeding stopped at once. 45 Jesus asked, "Who touched me?"

Everyone denied it, and Peter said, "Master, the people are all around you and crowding in on you."

46 But Jesus said, "Someone touched me, for I knew it when power went out of me." 47 The woman saw that she had been found out, so she came trembling and threw herself at Jesus' feet. There in front of everybody, she told him why she had touched him and how she had been healed at once. 48 Jesus said to her, "My daughter, your faith has made you well. Go in peace."

49 While Jesus was saying this, a messenger came from the official's house. "Your daughter has died," he told Jairus; "don't bother the Teacher any longer."

50 But Jesus heard it and said to Jairus, "Don't be afraid; only believe, and she will be well."

51 When he arrived at the house, he would not let anyone go in with him except Peter, John, and James, and the child's father and mother. 52 Everyone there was crying and mourning for the child. Jesus said, "Don't cry; the child is not dead — she is only sleeping!"

53 They all made fun of him, because they knew that she was dead. 54 But Jesus took her by the hand and called out, "Get up, child!" 55 Her life returned, and she got up at once, and Jesus ordered them to give her something to eat.

---

h ABYSS: *It was thought that the demons were to be imprisoned in the depths of the earth until their final punishment.*   i *Some manuscripts do not have* she had spent all she had on doctors.

JESUS AND THE TWELVE

Jesus chose twelve apostles to serve with him during his ministry and to provide leadership for the church after his ascension.

Chosen by Jesus after he prayed all night (Lk 6.12-16), the twelve included two sets of fishermen brothers, a tax collector, and a traitor. Among the twelve, Peter, James, and John were particularly close to Jesus.

The terms *disciple* and *apostle* are often used interchangeably in referring to these men. But a disciple is a learner or follower, while an apostle generally refers to a person who is sent with a special message or commission (Jn 13.16). The twelve were definitely apostles; when Jesus called them, he had a specific mission in mind for them—to carry on his work after he ended his earthly ministry.

The original twelve were chosen from among those people whom Jesus knew personally (Ac 1.21, 22). They had an inadequate understanding of Jesus' mission and the necessity for his death (Mt 15.16). Jesus was patient with the immature apostles, although he occasionally rebuked them (Lk 9.55). After they were empowered by the Holy Spirit at Pentecost, the apostles were filled with new boldness and understanding. They became powerful witnesses in Jerusalem and surrounding regions, in spite of harsh persecution. Many were martyred for their faith.

The Twelve Apostles

1. Simon Peter, son of Jonah; from Bethsaida, then Capernaum

2. Andrew; brother of Simon Peter; both were fishermen

3. James, son of Zebedee; from Bethsaida; brother of John

4. John; gospel writer; fisherman with brother James

5. Philip; from Bethsaida

6. Bartholomew; from Cana in Galilee

7. Thomas; from Galilee

8. Matthew; gospel writer; from Capernaum; tax collector

9. James, son of Alphaeus; from Galilee

10. Thaddaeus; brother of James from Galilee

11. Simon the Patriot; from Galilee

12. Judas Iscariot; betrayed Jesus; replaced by Matthias (Ac 1.26)

56 Her parents were astounded, but Jesus commanded them not to tell anyone what had happened.

Jesus Sends Out the Twelve Disciples

(Matthew 10.5-15; Mark 6.7-13)

9 Jesus called the twelve disciples together and gave them power and authority to drive out all demons and to cure diseases. 2 Then he sent them out to preach the Kingdom of God and to heal the sick, 3 after saying to them, "Take nothing with you for the trip: no walking stick, no beggar's bag, no food, no money, not even an extra shirt. 4 Wherever you are welcomed, stay in the same house until you leave that town; 5 wherever people don't welcome you, leave that town and shake the dust off your feet as a warning to them."

6 The disciples left and traveled through all the villages, preaching the Good News and healing people everywhere.

Herod's Confusion

(Matthew 14.1-12; Mark 6.14-29)

7 When Herod, the ruler of Galilee, heard about all the things that were happening, he was very confused, because some people were saying that John the Baptist had come back to life. 8 Others were saying that Elijah had appeared, and still others that one of the prophets of long ago had come back to life. 9 Herod said, "I had John's head cut off; but who is this man I hear these things about?" And he kept trying to see Jesus.

Jesus Feeds Five Thousand

(Matthew 14.13-21; Mark 6.30-44; John 6.1-14)

10 The apostles came back and told Jesus everything they had done. He took them with him, and they went off by themselves to a town named Bethsaida. 11 When the crowds heard about it, they followed him. He welcomed them, spoke to them about the Kingdom of God, and healed those who needed it.

12 When the sun was beginning to set, the twelve disciples came to him and said, "Send the people away so that they can go to the villages and farms around here and find food and lodging, because this is a lonely place."

13 But Jesus said to them, "You yourselves give them something to eat."

They answered, "All we have are five loaves and two fish. Do you want us to go and buy food for this whole crowd?" 14 (There were about five thousand men there.)

Jesus said to his disciples, "Make the people sit down in groups of about fifty each."

15 After the disciples had done so, 16 Jesus took the five loaves and two fish, looked up to heaven, thanked God for them, broke them, and gave them to the disciples to distribute to the people. 17 They all ate and had enough, and the disciples took up twelve baskets of what was left over.

Peter's Declaration about Jesus

(Matthew 16.13-19; Mark 8.27-29)

18 One day when Jesus was praying alone, the disciples came to him. "Who do the crowds say I am?" he asked them.

19 "Some say that you are John the Baptist," they answered. "Others say that you are Elijah, while others say that one of the prophets of long ago has come back to life."

20 "What about you?" he asked them. "Who do you say I am?"

Peter answered, "You are God's Messiah."

Jesus Speaks about His Suffering and Death

(Matthew 16.20-28; Mark 8.30 — 9.1)

21 Then Jesus gave them strict orders not to tell this to anyone. 22 He also told them, "The Son of Man must suffer much and be rejected by the elders, the chief priests, and the teachers of the Law. He will be put to death, but three days later he will be raised to life."

23 And he said to them all, "If you want to come with me, you must forget yourself, take up your cross every day, and follow me. 24 For if you want to save your own life, you will lose it, but if you lose your life for my sake, you will save it. 25 Will you gain anything if you win the whole world but are yourself lost or defeated? Of course not! 26 If you are ashamed of me and of my teaching, then the Son of Man will be ashamed of you when he comes in his glory and in the glory of the Father and of the holy angels. 27 I assure you that there are some here who will not die until they have seen the Kingdom of God."

The Transfiguration
(Matthew 17.1-8; Mark 9.2-8)

28 About a week after he had said these things, Jesus took Peter, John, and James with him and went up a hill to pray. 29 While he was praying, his face changed its appearance, and his clothes became dazzling white. 30 Suddenly two men were there talking with him. They were Moses and Elijah, 31 who appeared in heavenly glory and talked with Jesus about the way in which he would soon fulfill God's purpose by dying in Jerusalem. 32 Peter and his companions were sound asleep, but they woke up and saw Jesus' glory and the two men who were standing with him. 33 As the men were leaving Jesus, Peter said to him, "Master, how good it is that we are here! We will make three tents, one for you, one for Moses, and one for Elijah." (He did not really know what he was saying.)

34 While he was still speaking, a cloud appeared and covered them with its shadow; and the disciples were afraid as the cloud came over them. 35 A voice said from the cloud, "This is my Son, whom I have chosen—listen to him!"

36 When the voice stopped, there was Jesus all alone. The disciples kept quiet about all this and told no one at that time anything they had seen.

Jesus Heals a Boy with an Evil Spirit
(Matthew 17.14-18; Mark 9.14-27)

37 The next day Jesus and the three disciples went down from the hill, and a large crowd met Jesus. 38 A man shouted from the crowd, "Teacher! I beg you, look at my son—my only son! 39 A spirit attacks him with a sudden shout and throws him into a fit, so that he foams at the mouth; it keeps on hurting him and will hardly let him go! 40 I begged your disciples to drive it out, but they couldn't."

41 Jesus answered, "How unbelieving and wrong you people are! How long must I stay with you? How long do I have to put up with you?" Then he said to the man, "Bring your son here."

42 As the boy was coming, the demon knocked him to the ground and threw him into a fit. Jesus gave a command to the evil spirit, healed the boy, and gave him back to his father. 43 All the people were amazed at the mighty power of God.

Jesus Speaks Again about His Death
(Matthew 17.22, 23; Mark 9.30-32)

The people were still marveling at everything Jesus was doing, when he said to his disciples, 44 "Don't forget what I am about to tell you! The Son of Man is going to be handed over to the power of human beings." 45 But the disciples did not know what this meant. It had been hidden from them so that they could not understand it, and they were afraid to ask him about the matter.

Who Is the Greatest?
(Matthew 18.1-5; Mark 9.33-37)

46 An argument broke out among the disciples as to which one of them was the greatest. 47 Jesus knew what they were thinking, so he took a child, stood him by his side, 48 and said to them, "Whoever welcomes this child in my name, welcomes me; and whoever welcomes me, also welcomes the one who sent me. For the one who is least among you all is the greatest."

Whoever Is Not against You Is for You
(Mark 9.38-40)

49 John spoke up, "Master, we saw a man driving out demons in your name, and we told him to stop, because he doesn't belong to our group."

50 "Do not try to stop him," Jesus said to him and to the other disciples, "because whoever is not against you is for you."

A Samaritan Village Refuses to Receive Jesus

51 As the time drew near when Jesus would be taken up to heaven, he made up his mind and set out on his way to Jerusalem. 52 He sent messengers ahead of him, who went into a village in Samaria to get everything ready for him. 53 But the people there would not receive him, because it was clear that he was on his way to Jerusalem. 54 When the disciples James and John saw this, they said, "Lord, do you want us to call fire down from heaven to destroy them?"*i*

i Some manuscripts add as Elijah did.

55 Jesus turned and rebuked them.[k] **56** Then Jesus and his disciples went on to another village.

The Would-Be Followers of Jesus
(Matthew 8.19-22)

57 As they went on their way, a man said to Jesus, "I will follow you wherever you go." **58** Jesus said to him, "Foxes have holes, and birds have nests, but the Son of Man has no place to lie down and rest."

59 He said to another man, "Follow me."

But that man said, "Sir, first let me go back and bury my father."

60 Jesus answered, "Let the dead bury their own dead. You go and proclaim the Kingdom of God."

61 Someone else said, "I will follow you, sir; but first let me go and say goodbye to my family."

62 Jesus said to him, "Anyone who starts to plow and then keeps looking back is of no use for the Kingdom of God."

Jesus Sends Out the Seventy-Two

10 After this the Lord chose another seventy-two[l] men and sent them out two by two, to go ahead of him to every town and place where he himself was about to go. **2** He said to them, "There is a large harvest, but few workers to gather it in. Pray to the owner of the harvest that he will send out workers to gather in his harvest. **3** Go! I am sending you like lambs among wolves. **4** Don't take a purse or a beggar's bag or shoes; don't stop to greet anyone on the road. **5** Whenever you go into a house, first say, 'Peace be with this house.' **6** If someone who is peace-loving lives there, let your greeting of peace remain on that person; if not, take back your greeting of peace. **7** Stay in that same house, eating and drinking whatever they offer you, for workers should be given their pay. Don't move around from one house to another. **8** Whenever you go into a town and are made welcome, eat what is set before you, **9** heal the sick in that town, and say to the peo-

ple there, 'The Kingdom of God has come near you.' **10** But whenever you go into a town and are not welcomed, go out in the streets and say, **11** 'Even the dust from your town that sticks to our feet we wipe off against you. But remember that the Kingdom of God has come near you!' **12** I assure you that on the Judgment Day God will show more mercy to Sodom than to that town!

The Unbelieving Towns
(Matthew 11.20-24)

13 "How terrible it will be for you, Chorazin! How terrible for you too, Bethsaida! If the miracles which were performed in you had been performed in Tyre and Sidon, the people there would have long ago sat down, put on sackcloth, and sprinkled ashes on themselves, to show that they had turned from their sins! **14** God will show more mercy on the Judgment Day to Tyre and Sidon than to you. **15** And as for you, Capernaum! Did you want to lift yourself up to heaven? You will be thrown down to hell!"

16 Jesus said to his disciples, "Whoever listens to you listens to me; whoever rejects you rejects me; and whoever rejects me rejects the one who sent me."

The Return of the Seventy-Two

17 The seventy-two[m] men came back in great joy. "Lord," they said, "even the demons obeyed us when we gave them a command in your name!"

18 Jesus answered them, "I saw Satan fall like lightning from heaven. **19** Listen! I have given you authority, so that you can walk on snakes and scorpions and overcome all the power of the Enemy, and nothing will hurt you. **20** But don't be glad because the evil spirits obey you; rather be glad because your names are written in heaven."

Jesus Rejoices
(Matthew 11.25-27; 13.16, 17)

21 At that time Jesus was filled with joy by the Holy Spirit[n] and said, "Father, Lord of heaven and earth! I thank you because you have shown to the un-

---

[k] *Some manuscripts add* and said, "You don't know what kind of a Spirit you belong to; for the Son of Man did not come to destroy human lives, but to save them."
[l] seventy-two; *some manuscripts have* seventy.   [m] seventy-two; *some manuscripts have* seventy *(see verse 1)*.   [n] by the Holy Spirit; *some manuscripts have* by the Spirit; *others have* in his spirit.

learned what you have hidden from the wise and learned. Yes, Father, this was how you were pleased to have it happen. 22 "My Father has given me all things. No one knows who the Son is except the Father, and no one knows who the Father is except the Son and those to whom the Son chooses to reveal him." 23 Then Jesus turned to the disciples and said to them privately, "How fortunate you are to see the things you see! 24 I tell you that many prophets and kings wanted to see what you see, but they could not, and to hear what you hear, but they did not."

The Parable of the Good Samaritan

25 A teacher of the Law came up and tried to trap Jesus. "Teacher," he asked, "what must I do to receive eternal life?" 26 Jesus answered him, "What do the Scriptures say? How do you interpret them?"

27 The man answered, " 'Love the Lord your God with all your heart, with all your soul, with all your strength, and with all your mind'; and 'Love your neighbor as you love yourself.' "

28 "You are right," Jesus replied; "do this and you will live."

29 But the teacher of the Law wanted to justify himself, so he asked Jesus, "Who is my neighbor?"

30 Jesus answered, "There was once a man who was going down from Jerusalem to Jericho when robbers attacked him, stripped him, and beat him up, leaving him half dead. 31 It so happened that a priest was going down that road; but when he saw the man, he walked on by on the other side. 32 In the same way a Levite also came there, went over and looked at the man, and then walked on by on the other side. 33 But a Samaritan who was traveling that way came upon the man, and when he saw him, his heart was filled with pity. 34 He went over to him, poured oil and wine on his wounds and bandaged them; then he put the man on his own animal and took him to an inn, where he took care of him. 35 The next day he took out two silver coins and gave them to the innkeeper. 'Take care of him,' he told the innkeeper, 'and when I come back this way, I will pay you whatever else you spend on him.' "

36 And Jesus concluded, "In your opinion, which one of these three acted like a neighbor toward the man attacked by the robbers?"

37 The teacher of the Law answered, "The one who was kind to him."

Jesus replied, "You go, then, and do the same."

Jesus Visits Martha and Mary

38 As Jesus and his disciples went on their way, he came to a village where a woman named Martha welcomed him in her home. 39 She had a sister named Mary, who sat down at the feet of the Lord and listened to his teaching. 40 Martha was upset over all the work she had to do, so she came and said, "Lord, don't you care that my sister has left me to do all the work by myself? Tell her to come and help me!"

41 The Lord answered her, "Martha, Martha! You are worried and troubled over so many things, 42 but just one is needed. Mary has chosen the right thing, and it will not be taken away from her."

Jesus' Teaching on Prayer
(Matthew 6.9-13; 7.7-11)

11 One day Jesus was praying in a certain place. When he had finished, one of his disciples said to him, "Lord, teach us to pray, just as John taught his disciples."

2 Jesus said to them, "When you pray, say this:

'Father:
　　May your holy name be
　　　honored;
　　may your Kingdom come.
3　Give us day by day the food we
　　　need.o
4　Forgive us our sins,
　　for we forgive everyone who
　　　does us wrong.
　　And do not bring us to hard
　　　testing.' "

5 And Jesus said to his disciples, "Suppose one of you should go to a friend's house at midnight and say, 'Friend, let me borrow three loaves of bread. 6 A friend of mine who is on a trip has just come to my house, and I don't have any food for him!' 7 And suppose your friend should answer from inside, 'Don't bother me! The door is already locked,

---

o the food we need; or food for the next day.

and my children and I are in bed. I can't get up and give you anything.' 8 Well, what then? I tell you that even if he will not get up and give you the bread because you are his friend, yet he will get up and give you everything you need because you are not ashamed to keep on asking. 9 And so I say to you: Ask, and you will receive; seek, and you will find; knock, and the door will be opened to you. 10 For those who ask will receive, and those who seek will find, and the door will be opened to anyone who knocks. 11 Would any of you who are fathers give your son a snake when he asks for fish? 12 Or would you give him a scorpion when he asks for an egg? 13 As bad as you are, you know how to give good things to your children. How much more, then, will the Father in heaven give the Holy Spirit to those who ask him!"

Jesus and Beelzebul
(Matthew 12.22-30; Mark 3.20-27)

14 Jesus was driving out a demon that could not talk; and when the demon went out, the man began to talk. The crowds were amazed, 15 but some of the people said, "It is Beelzebul, the chief of the demons, who gives him the power to drive them out."

16 Others wanted to trap Jesus, so they asked him to perform a miracle to show that God approved of him. 17 But Jesus knew what they were thinking, so he said to them, "Any country that divides itself into groups which fight each other will not last very long; a family divided against itself falls apart. 18 So if Satan's kingdom has groups fighting each other, how can it last? You say that I drive out demons because Beelzebul gives me the power to do so. 19 If this is how I drive them out, how do your followers drive them out? Your own followers prove that you are wrong! 20 No, it is rather by means of God's power that I drive out demons, and this proves that the Kingdom of God has already come to you.

21 "When a strong man, with all his weapons ready, guards his own house, all his belongings are safe. 22 But when a stronger man attacks him and defeats him, he carries away all the weapons the owner was depending on and divides up what he stole.

23 "Anyone who is not for me is really against me; anyone who does not help me gather is really scattering.

The Return of the Evil Spirit
(Matthew 12.43-45)

24 "When an evil spirit goes out of a person, it travels over dry country looking for a place to rest. If it can't find one, it says to itself, 'I will go back to my house.' 25 So it goes back and finds the house clean and all fixed up. 26 Then it goes out and brings seven other spirits even worse than itself, and they come and live there. So when it is all over, that person is in worse shape than at the beginning."

True Happiness

27 When Jesus had said this, a woman spoke up from the crowd and said to him, "How happy is the woman who bore you and nursed you!"

28 But Jesus answered, "Rather, how happy are those who hear the word of God and obey it!"

The Demand for a Miracle
(Matthew 12.38-42)

29 As the people crowded around Jesus, he went on to say, "How evil are the people of this day! They ask for a miracle, but none will be given them except the miracle of Jonah. 30 In the same way that the prophet Jonah was a sign for the people of Nineveh, so the Son of Man will be a sign for the people of this day. 31 On the Judgment Day the Queen of Sheba will stand up and accuse the people of today, because she traveled all the way from her country to listen to King Solomon's wise teaching; and there is something here, I tell you, greater than Solomon. 32 On the Judgment Day the people of Nineveh will stand up and accuse you, because they turned from their sins when they heard Jonah preach; and I assure you that there is something here greater than Jonah!

The Light of the Body
(Matthew 5.15; 6.22, 23)

33 "No one lights a lamp and then hides it or puts it under a bowl;p instead, it is

---

p *Some manuscripts do not have* or puts it under a bowl.

put on the lampstand, so that people may see the light as they come in. ³⁴Your eyes are like a lamp for the body. When your eyes are sound, your whole body is full of light; but when your eyes are no good, your whole body will be in darkness. ³⁵Make certain, then, that the light in you is not darkness. ³⁶If your whole body is full of light, with no part of it in darkness, it will be bright all over, as when a lamp shines on you with its brightness."

Jesus Accuses the Pharisees and the Teachers of the Law
(Matthew 23.1-36; Mark 12.38-40)

³⁷When Jesus finished speaking, a Pharisee invited him to eat with him; so he went in and sat down to eat. ³⁸The Pharisee was surprised when he noticed that Jesus had not washed before eating. ³⁹So the Lord said to him, "Now then, you Pharisees clean the outside of your cup and plate, but inside you are full of violence and evil. ⁴⁰Fools! Did not God, who made the outside, also make the inside? ⁴¹But give what is in your cups and plates to the poor, and everything will be ritually clean for you.

⁴²"How terrible for you Pharisees! You give to God one tenth of the seasoning herbs, such as mint and rue and all the other herbs, but you neglect justice and love for God. These you should practice, without neglecting the others.

⁴³"How terrible for you Pharisees! You love the reserved seats in the synagogues and to be greeted with respect in the marketplaces. ⁴⁴How terrible for you! You are like unmarked graves which people walk on without knowing it."

⁴⁵One of the teachers of the Law said to him, "Teacher, when you say this, you insult us too!"

⁴⁶Jesus answered, "How terrible also for you teachers of the Law! You put onto people's backs loads which are hard to carry, but you yourselves will not stretch out a finger to help them carry those loads. ⁴⁷How terrible for you! You make fine tombs for the prophets—the very prophets your ancestors murdered. ⁴⁸You yourselves admit, then, that you approve of what your ancestors did; they murdered the prophets, and you build their tombs. ⁴⁹For this reason the Wisdom of God said, 'I will send them prophets and messengers; they will kill some of them and persecute others.' ⁵⁰So the people of this time will be punished for the murder of all the prophets killed since the creation of the world, ⁵¹from the murder of Abel to the murder of Zechariah, who was killed between the altar and the Holy Place. Yes, I tell you, the people of this time will be punished for them all!

⁵²"How terrible for you teachers of the Law! You have kept the key that opens the door to the house of knowledge; you yourselves will not go in, and you stop those who are trying to go in!"

⁵³When Jesus left that place, the teachers of the Law and the Pharisees began to criticize him bitterly and ask him questions about many things, ⁵⁴trying to lay traps for him and catch him saying something wrong.

A Warning against Hypocrisy
(Matthew 10.26, 27)

12 As thousands of people crowded together, so that they were stepping on each other, Jesus said first to his disciples, "Be on guard against the yeast of the Pharisees—I mean their hypocrisy. ²Whatever is covered up will be uncovered, and every secret will be made known. ³So then, whatever you have said in the dark will be heard in broad daylight, and whatever you have whispered in private in a closed room will be shouted from the housetops.

Whom to Fear
(Matthew 10.28-31)

⁴"I tell you, my friends, do not be afraid of those who kill the body but cannot afterward do anything worse. ⁵I will show you whom to fear: fear God, who, after killing, has the authority to throw into hell. Believe me, he is the one you must fear!

⁶"Aren't five sparrows sold for two pennies? Yet not one sparrow is forgotten by God. ⁷Even the hairs of your head have all been counted. So do not be afraid; you are worth much more than many sparrows!

Confessing and Rejecting Christ
(Matthew 10.32, 33; 12.32; 10.19, 20)

⁸"I assure you that those who declare publicly that they belong to me, the Son

of Man will do the same for them before the angels of God. 9 But those who reject me publicly, the Son of Man will also reject them before the angels of God.

10 "Whoever says a word against the Son of Man can be forgiven; but whoever says evil things against the Holy Spirit will not be forgiven.

11 "When they bring you to be tried in the synagogues or before governors or rulers, do not be worried about how you will defend yourself or what you will say. 12 For the Holy Spirit will teach you at that time what you should say."

The Parable of the Rich Fool

13 A man in the crowd said to Jesus, "Teacher, tell my brother to divide with me the property our father left us."

14 Jesus answered him, "Friend, who gave me the right to judge or to divide the property between you two?" 15 And he went on to say to them all, "Watch out and guard yourselves from every kind of greed; because your true life is not made up of the things you own, no matter how rich you may be."

16 Then Jesus told them this parable: "There was once a rich man who had land which bore good crops. 17 He began to think to himself, 'I don't have a place to keep all my crops. What can I do? 18 This is what I will do,' he told himself; 'I will tear down my barns and build bigger ones, where I will store the grain and all my other goods. 19 Then I will say to myself, Lucky man! You have all the good things you need for many years. Take life easy, eat, drink, and enjoy yourself!' 20 But God said to him, 'You fool! This very night you will have to give up your life; then who will get all these things you have kept for yourself?' "

21 And Jesus concluded, "This is how it is with those who pile up riches for themselves but are not rich in God's sight."

Trust in God
(Matthew 6.25-34)

22 Then Jesus said to the disciples, "And so I tell you not to worry about the food you need to stay alive or about the clothes you need for your body. 23 Life is much more important than food, and the body much more important than clothes. 24 Look at the crows: they don't plant seeds or gather a harvest; they don't have storage rooms or barns; God feeds them! You are worth so much more than birds! 25 Can any of you live a bit longer[q] by worrying about it? 26 If you can't manage even such a small thing, why worry about the other things? 27 Look how the wild flowers grow: they don't work or make clothes for themselves. But I tell you that not even King Solomon with all his wealth had clothes as beautiful as one of these flowers. 28 It is God who clothes the wild grass — grass that is here today and gone tomorrow, burned up in the oven. Won't he be all the more sure to clothe you? What little faith you have!

29 "So don't be all upset, always concerned about what you will eat and drink. 30 (For the pagans of this world are always concerned about all these things.) Your Father knows that you need these things. 31 Instead, be concerned with his Kingdom, and he will provide you with these things.

Riches in Heaven
(Matthew 6.19-21)

32 "Do not be afraid, little flock, for your Father is pleased to give you the Kingdom. 33 Sell all your belongings and give the money to the poor. Provide for yourselves purses that don't wear out, and save your riches in heaven, where they will never decrease, because no thief can get to them, and no moth can destroy them. 34 For your heart will always be where your riches are.

Watchful Servants

35 "Be ready for whatever comes, dressed for action and with your lamps lit, 36 like servants who are waiting for their master to come back from a wedding feast. When he comes and knocks, they will open the door for him at once. 37 How happy are those servants whose master finds them awake and ready when he returns! I tell you, he will take off his coat, have them sit down, and will wait on them. 38 How happy they are if he finds them ready, even if he should come at midnight or even later! 39 And you can be sure that if the owner of a

q live a bit longer; *or* grow a bit taller.

house knew the time when the thief would come, he would not let the thief break into his house. 40 And you, too, must be ready, because the Son of Man will come at an hour when you are not expecting him."

The Faithful or the Unfaithful Servant
(Matthew 24.45-51)

41 Peter said, "Lord, does this parable apply to us, or do you mean it for everyone?"

42 The Lord answered, "Who, then, is the faithful and wise servant? He is the one that his master will put in charge, to run the household and give the other servants their share of the food at the proper time. 43 How happy that servant is if his master finds him doing this when he comes home! 44 Indeed, I tell you, the master will put that servant in charge of all his property. 45 But if that servant says to himself that his master is taking a long time to come back and if he begins to beat the other servants, both the men and the women, and eats and drinks and gets drunk, 46 then the master will come back one day when the servant does not expect him and at a time he does not know. The master will cut him in pieces[r] and make him share the fate of the disobedient.

47 "The servant who knows what his master wants him to do, but does not get himself ready and do it, will be punished with a heavy whipping. 48 But the servant who does not know what his master wants, and yet does something for which he deserves a whipping, will be punished with a light whipping. Much is required from the person to whom much is given; much more is required from the person to whom much more is given.

Jesus the Cause of Division
(Matthew 10.34-36)

49 "I came to set the earth on fire, and how I wish it were already kindled! 50 I have a baptism to receive, and how distressed I am until it is over! 51 Do you suppose that I came to bring peace to the world? No, not peace, but division. 52 From now on a family of five will be divided, three against two and two against three. 53 Fathers will be against

their sons, and sons against their fathers; mothers will be against their daughters, and daughters against their mothers; mothers-in-law will be against their daughters-in-law, and daughters-in-law against their mothers-in-law."

Understanding the Time
(Matthew 16.2, 3)

54 Jesus said also to the people, "When you see a cloud coming up in the west, at once you say that it is going to rain — and it does. 55 And when you feel the south wind blowing, you say that it is going to get hot — and it does. 56 Hypocrites! You can look at the earth and the sky and predict the weather; why, then, don't you know the meaning of this present time?

Settle with Your Opponent
(Matthew 5.25, 26)

57 "Why do you not judge for yourselves the right thing to do? 58 If someone brings a lawsuit against you and takes you to court, do your best to settle the dispute before you get to court. If you don't, you will be dragged before the judge, who will hand you over to the police, and you will be put in jail. 59 There you will stay, I tell you, until you pay the last penny of your fine."

Turn from Your Sins or Die

13 At that time some people were there who told Jesus about the Galileans whom Pilate had killed while they were offering sacrifices to God. 2 Jesus answered them, "Because those Galileans were killed in that way, do you think it proves that they were worse sinners than all other Galileans? 3 No indeed! And I tell you that if you do not turn from your sins, you will all die as they did. 4 What about those eighteen people in Siloam who were killed when the tower fell on them? Do you suppose this proves that they were worse than all the other people living in Jerusalem? 5 No indeed! And I tell you that if you do not turn from your sins, you will all die as they did."

_____
r cut him in pieces; or throw him out.

LUKE

The Parable of the Unfruitful Fig Tree

6 Then Jesus told them this parable: "There was once a man who had a fig tree growing in his vineyard. He went looking for figs on it but found none. 7 So he said to his gardener, 'Look, for three years I have been coming here looking for figs on this fig tree, and I haven't found any. Cut it down! Why should it go on using up the soil?' 8 But the gardener answered, 'Leave it alone, sir, just one more year; I will dig around it and put in some fertilizer. 9 Then if the tree bears figs next year, so much the better; if not, then you can have it cut down.'"

Jesus Heals a Crippled Woman on the Sabbath

10 One Sabbath Jesus was teaching in a synagogue. 11 A woman there had an evil spirit that had kept her sick for eighteen years; she was bent over and could not straighten up at all. 12 When Jesus saw her, he called out to her, "Woman, you are free from your sickness!" 13 He placed his hands on her, and at once she straightened herself up and praised God.

14 The official of the synagogue was angry that Jesus had healed on the Sabbath, so he spoke up and said to the people, "There are six days in which we should work; so come during those days and be healed, but not on the Sabbath!"

15 The Lord answered him, "You hypocrites! Any one of you would untie your ox or your donkey from the stall and take it out to give it water on the Sabbath. 16 Now here is this descendant of Abraham whom Satan has kept in bonds for eighteen years; should she not be released on the Sabbath?" 17 His answer made his enemies ashamed of themselves, while the people rejoiced over all the wonderful things that he did.

The Parable of the Mustard Seed

(Matthew 13.31, 32; Mark 4.30-32)

18 Jesus asked, "What is the Kingdom of God like? What shall I compare it with? 19 It is like this. A man takes a mustard seed and plants it in his field. The plant grows and becomes a tree, and the birds make their nests in its branches."

The Parable of the Yeast

(Matthew 13.33)

20 Again Jesus asked, "What shall I compare the Kingdom of God with? 21 It is like this. A woman takes some yeast and mixes it with a bushel of flour until the whole batch of dough rises."

The Narrow Door

(Matthew 7.13, 14, 21-23)

22 Jesus went through towns and villages, teaching the people and making his way toward Jerusalem. 23 Someone asked him, "Sir, will just a few people be saved?"

Jesus answered them, 24 "Do your best to go in through the narrow door; because many people will surely try to go in but will not be able. 25 The master of the house will get up and close the door; then when you stand outside and begin to knock on the door and say, 'Open the door for us, sir!' he will answer you, 'I don't know where you come from!' 26 Then you will answer, 'We ate and drank with you; you taught in our town!' 27 But he will say again, 'I don't know where you come from. Get away from me, all you wicked people!' 28 How you will cry and gnash your teeth when you see Abraham, Isaac, and Jacob, and all the prophets in the Kingdom of God, while you are thrown out! 29 People will come from the east and the west, from the north and the south, and sit down at the feast in the Kingdom of God. 30 Then those who are now last will be first, and those who are now first will be last."

Jesus' Love for Jerusalem

(Matthew 23.37-39)

31 At that same time some Pharisees came to Jesus and said to him, "You must get out of here and go somewhere else, because Herod wants to kill you." 32 Jesus answered them, "Go and tell that fox: 'I am driving out demons and performing cures today and tomorrow, and on the third day I shall finish my work.' 33 Yet I must be on my way today, tomorrow, and the next day; it is not right for a prophet to be killed anywhere except in Jerusalem.

34 "Jerusalem, Jerusalem! You kill the prophets, you stone the messengers God has sent you! How many times I wanted to put my arms around all your people, just as a hen gathers her chicks under

her wings, but you would not let me!
35 And so your Temple will be abandoned. I assure you that you will not see
me until the time comes when you say,
'God bless him who comes in the name
of the Lord.'"

Jesus Heals a Sick Man

14 One Sabbath Jesus went to eat a
meal at the home of one of the
leading Pharisees; and people were
watching Jesus closely. 2 A man whose
legs and arms were swollen came to
Jesus. 3 and Jesus spoke up and asked
the teachers of the Law and the Pharisees, "Does our Law allow healing on
the Sabbath or not?"

4 But they would not say a thing. Jesus
took the man, healed him, and sent him
away. 5 Then he said to them, "If any one
of you had a child or an ox that happened to fall in a well on a Sabbath,
would you not pull it out at once on the
Sabbath itself?"

6 But they were not able to answer him
about this.

Humility and Hospitality

7 Jesus noticed how some of the guests
were choosing the best places, so he told
this parable to all of them: 8 "When
someone invites you to a wedding feast,
do not sit down in the best place. It could
happen that someone more important
than you has been invited, 9 and your
host, who invited both of you, would
have to come and say to you, 'Let him
have this place.' Then you would be embarrassed and have to sit in the lowest
place. 10 Instead, when you are invited,
go and sit in the lowest place, so that
your host will come to you and say,
'Come on up, my friend, to a better
place.' This will bring you honor in the
presence of all the other guests. 11 For
those who make themselves great will
be humbled, and those who humble
themselves will be made great."

12 Then Jesus said to his host, "When
you give a lunch or a dinner, do not invite your friends or your brothers or
your relatives or your rich neighbors—
for they will invite you back, and in this
way you will be paid for what you did.
13 When you give a feast, invite the poor,
the crippled, the lame, and the blind;
14 and you will be blessed, because they
are not able to pay you back. God will

repay you on the day the good people
rise from death."

The Parable of the Great Feast
(Matthew 22.1-10)

15 When one of the guests sitting at the
table heard this, he said to Jesus, "How
happy are those who will sit down at the
feast in the Kingdom of God!"

16 Jesus said to him, "There was once a
man who was giving a great feast to
which he invited many people. 17 When
it was time for the feast, he sent his servant to tell his guests, 'Come, everything
is ready!' 18 But they all began, one after
another, to make excuses. The first one
told the servant, 'I have bought a field
and must go and look at it; please accept
my apologies.' 19 Another one said, 'I
have bought five pairs of oxen and am
on my way to try them out; please accept
my apologies.' 20 Another one said, 'I
have just gotten married, and for that
reason I cannot come.' 21 The servant
went back and told all this to his master.
The master was furious and said to his
servant, 'Hurry out to the streets and alleys of the town, and bring back the
poor, the crippled, the blind, and the
lame.' 22 Soon the servant said, 'Your order has been carried out, sir, but there is
room for more.' 23 So the master said to
the servant, 'Go out to the country roads
and lanes and make people come in, so
that my house will be full. 24 I tell you all
that none of those who were invited will
taste my dinner!'"

The Cost of Being a Disciple
(Matthew 10.37, 38)

25 Once when large crowds of people
were going along with Jesus, he turned
and said to them, 26 "Those who come to
me cannot be my disciples unless they
love me more than they love father and
mother, wife and children, brothers and
sisters, and themselves as well. 27 Those
who do not carry their own cross and
come after me cannot be my disciples.
28 If one of you is planning to build a
tower, you sit down first and figure out
what it will cost, to see if you have
enough money to finish the job. 29 If you
don't, you will not be able to finish the
tower after laying the foundation; and
all who see what happened will make
fun of you. 30 'You began to build but
can't finish the job!' they will say. 31 If a

king goes out with ten thousand men to fight another king who comes against him with twenty thousand men, he will sit down first and decide if he is strong enough to face that other king. 32 If he isn't, he will send messengers to meet the other king to ask for terms of peace while he is still a long way off. 33 In the same way," concluded Jesus, "none of you can be my disciple unless you give up everything you have.

Worthless Salt
(Matthew 5.13; Mark 9.50)

34 "Salt is good, but if it loses its saltiness, there is no way to make it salty again. 35 It is no good for the soil or for the manure pile; it is thrown away. Listen, then, if you have ears!"

The Lost Sheep
(Matthew 18.12-14)

15 One day when many tax collectors and other outcasts came to listen to Jesus, 2 the Pharisees and the teachers of the Law started grumbling, "This man welcomes outcasts and even eats with them!" 3 So Jesus told them this parable:
4 "Suppose one of you has a hundred sheep and loses one of them — what do you do? You leave the other ninety-nine sheep in the pasture and go looking for the one that got lost until you find it. 5 When you find it, you are so happy that you put it on your shoulders 6 and carry it back home. Then you call your friends and neighbors together and say to them, 'I am so happy I found my lost sheep. Let us celebrate!' 7 In the same way, I tell you, there will be more joy in heaven over one sinner who repents than over ninety-nine respectable people who do not need to repent.

The Lost Coin

8 "Or suppose a woman who has ten silver coins loses one of them — what does she do? She lights a lamp, sweeps her house, and looks carefully everywhere until she finds it. 9 When she finds it, she calls her friends and neighbors together, and says to them, 'I am so happy I found the coin I lost. Let us celebrate!' 10 In the same way, I tell you, the angels of God rejoice over one sinner who repents."

The Lost Son

11 Jesus went on to say, "There was once a man who had two sons. 12 The younger one said to him, 'Father, give me my share of the property now.' So the man divided his property between his two sons. 13 After a few days the younger son sold his part of the property and left home with the money. He went to a country far away, where he wasted his money in reckless living. 14 He spent everything he had. Then a severe famine spread over that country, and he was left without a thing. 15 So he went to work for one of the citizens of that country, who sent him out to his farm to take care of the pigs. 16 He wished he could fill himself with the bean pods the pigs ate, but no one gave him anything to eat. 17 At last he came to his senses and said, 'All my father's hired workers have more than they can eat, and here I am about to starve! 18 I will get up and go to my father and say, "Father, I have sinned against God and against you. 19 I am no longer fit to be called your son; treat me as one of your hired workers." ' 20 So he got up and started back to his father.

"He was still a long way from home when his father saw him; his heart was filled with pity, and he ran, threw his arms around his son, and kissed him. 21 'Father,' the son said, 'I have sinned against God and against you. I am no longer fit to be called your son.' 22 But the father called to his servants. 'Hurry!' he said. 'Bring the best robe and put it on him. Put a ring on his finger and shoes on his feet. 23 Then go and get the prize calf and kill it, and let us celebrate with a feast! 24 For this son of mine was dead, but now he is alive; he was lost, but now he has been found.' And so the feasting began.

25 "In the meantime the older son was out in the field. On his way back, when he came close to the house, he heard the music and dancing. 26 So he called one of the servants and asked him, 'What's going on?' 27 'Your brother has come back home,' the servant answered, 'and your father has killed the prize calf, because he got him back safe and sound.' 28 The older brother was so angry that he would not go into the house; so his father came out and begged him to come

in. 29But he spoke back to his father, 'Look, all these years I have worked for you like a slave, and I have never disobeyed your orders. What have you given me? Not even a goat for me to have a feast with my friends! 30But this son of yours wasted all your property on prostitutes, and when he comes back home, you kill the prize calf for him!' 31'My son,' the father answered, 'you are always here with me, and everything I have is yours. 32But we had to celebrate and be happy, because your brother was dead, but now he is alive; he was lost, but now he has been found.' "

The Shrewd Manager

16 Jesus said to his disciples, "There was once a rich man who had a servant who managed his property. The rich man was told that the manager was wasting his master's money, 2so he called him in and said, 'What is this I hear about you? Turn in a complete account of your handling of my property, because you cannot be my manager any longer.' 3The servant said to himself, 'My master is going to dismiss me from my job. What shall I do? I am not strong enough to dig ditches, and I am ashamed to beg. 4Now I know what I will do! Then when my job is gone, I shall have friends who will welcome me in their homes.' 5So he called in all the people who were in debt to his master. He asked the first one, 'How much do you owe my master?' 6'One hundred barrels of olive oil,' he answered. 'Here is your account,' the manager told him; 'sit down and write fifty.' 7Then he asked another one, 'And you—how much do you owe?' 'A thousand bushels of wheat,' he answered. 'Here is your account,' the manager told him; 'write eight hundred.' 8As a result the master of this dishonest manager praised him for doing such a shrewd thing; because the people of this world are much more shrewd in handling their affairs than the people who belong to the light."

9And Jesus went on to say, "And so I tell you: make friends for yourselves with worldly wealth, so that when it gives out, you will be welcomed in the eternal home. 10Whoever is faithful in small matters will be faithful in large ones; whoever is dishonest in small matters will be dishonest in large ones. 11If, then, you have not been faithful in handling worldly wealth, how can you be trusted with true wealth? 12And if you have not been faithful with what belongs to someone else, who will give you what belongs to you?

13"No servant can be the slave of two masters; such a slave will hate one and love the other or will be loyal to one and despise the other. You cannot serve both God and money."

Some Sayings of Jesus
(Matthew 11.12, 13; 5.31, 32; Mark 10.11, 12)

14When the Pharisees heard all this, they made fun of Jesus, because they loved money. 15Jesus said to them, "You are the ones who make yourselves look right in other people's sight, but God knows your hearts. For the things that are considered of great value by people are worth nothing in God's sight.

16"The Law of Moses and the writings of the prophets were in effect up to the time of John the Baptist; since then the Good News about the Kingdom of God is being told, and everyone forces their way in. 17But it is easier for heaven and earth to disappear than for the smallest detail of the Law to be done away with.

18"Any man who divorces his wife and marries another woman commits adultery; and the man who marries a divorced woman commits adultery.

The Rich Man and Lazarus

19"There was once a rich man who dressed in the most expensive clothes and lived in great luxury every day. 20There was also a poor man named Lazarus, covered with sores, who used to be brought to the rich man's door, 21hoping to eat the bits of food that fell from the rich man's table. Even the dogs would come and lick his sores. 22The poor man died and was carried by the angels to sit beside Abraham at the feast in heaven. The rich man died and was buried, 23and in Hades,s where he was in great pain, he looked up and saw Abraham, far away, with Lazarus at his side. 24So he called out, 'Father Abraham! Take pity on me, and send Lazarus to dip his finger in some water and cool

s HADES: *The world of the dead.*

off my tongue, because I am in great pain in this fire!' 25 But Abraham said, 'Remember, my son, that in your lifetime you were given all the good things, while Lazarus got all the bad things. But now he is enjoying himself here, while you are in pain. 26 Besides all that, there is a deep pit lying between us, so that those who want to cross over from here to you cannot do so, nor can anyone cross over to us from where you are.' 27 The rich man said, 'Then I beg you, father Abraham, send Lazarus to my father's house, 28 where I have five brothers. Let him go and warn them so that they, at least, will not come to this place of pain.' 29 Abraham said, 'Your brothers have Moses and the prophets to warn them; your brothers should listen to what they say.' 30 The rich man answered, 'That is not enough, father Abraham! But if someone were to rise from death and go to them, then they would turn from their sins.' 31 But Abraham said, 'If they will not listen to Moses and the prophets, they will not be convinced even if someone were to rise from death.' "

Sin
(Matthew 18.6, 7, 21, 22; Mark 9.42)

17 Jesus said to his disciples, "Things that make people fall into sin are bound to happen, but how terrible for the one who makes them happen! 2 It would be better for him if a large millstone were tied around his neck and he were thrown into the sea than for him to cause one of these little ones to sin. 3 So watch what you do!

"If your brother sins, rebuke him, and if he repents, forgive him. 4 If he sins against you seven times in one day, and each time he comes to you saying, 'I repent,' you must forgive him."

Faith

5 The apostles said to the Lord, "Make our faith greater."

6 The Lord answered, "If you had faith as big as a mustard seed, you could say to this mulberry tree, 'Pull yourself up by the roots and plant yourself in the sea!' and it would obey you.

A Servant's Duty

7 "Suppose one of you has a servant who is plowing or looking after the sheep. When he comes in from the field, do you tell him to hurry along and eat his meal? 8 Of course not! Instead, you say to him, 'Get my supper ready, then put on your apron and wait on me while I eat and drink; after that you may have your meal.' 9 The servant does not deserve thanks for obeying orders, does he? 10 It is the same with you; when you have done all you have been told to do, say, 'We are ordinary servants; we have only done our duty.' "

Jesus Heals Ten Men

11 As Jesus made his way to Jerusalem, he went along the border between Samaria and Galilee. 12 He was going into a village when he was met by ten men suffering from a dreaded skin disease. They stood at a distance 13 and shouted, "Jesus! Master! Have pity on us!"

14 Jesus saw them and said to them, "Go and let the priests examine you." On the way they were made clean.ᵗ

15 When one of them saw that he was healed, he came back, praising God in a loud voice. 16 He threw himself to the ground at Jesus' feet and thanked him. The man was a Samaritan. 17 Jesus spoke up, "There were ten who were healed; where are the other nine? 18 Why is this foreigner the only one who came back to give thanks to God?" 19 And Jesus said to him, "Get up and go; your faith has made you well."

The Coming of the Kingdom
(Matthew 24.23-28, 37-41)

20 Some Pharisees asked Jesus when the Kingdom of God would come. His answer was, "The Kingdom of God does not come in such a way as to be seen. 21 No one will say, 'Look, here it is!' or, 'There it is!'; because the Kingdom of God is within you."ᵘ

22 Then he said to the disciples, "The time will come when you will wish you could see one of the days of the Son of Man, but you will not see it. 23 There will be those who will say to you, 'Look, over there!' or, 'Look, over here!' But don't go out looking for it. 24 As the lightning

ᵗ MADE CLEAN: See 5.12.   ᵘ within you; or among you, or will suddenly appear among you.

flashes across the sky and lights it up from one side to the other, so will the Son of Man be in his day. 25 But first he must suffer much and be rejected by the people of this day. 26 As it was in the time of Noah so shall it be in the days of the Son of Man. 27 Everybody kept on eating and drinking, and men and women married, up to the very day Noah went into the boat and the flood came and killed them all. 28 It will be as it was in the time of Lot. Everybody kept on eating and drinking, buying and selling, planting and building. 29 On the day Lot left Sodom, fire and sulfur rained down from heaven and killed them all. 30 That is how it will be on the day the Son of Man is revealed.

31 "On that day someone who is on the roof of a house must not go down into the house to get any belongings; in the same way anyone who is out in the field must not go back to the house. 32 Remember Lot's wife! 33 Those who try to save their own life will lose it; those who lose their life will save it. 34 On that night, I tell you, there will be two people sleeping in the same bed: one will be taken away, the other will be left behind. 35 Two women will be grinding meal together: one will be taken away, the other will be left behind."*v*

37 The disciples asked him, "Where, Lord?"

Jesus answered, "Wherever there is a dead body, the vultures will gather."

The Parable of the Widow and the Judge

18 Then Jesus told his disciples a parable to teach them that they should always pray and never become discouraged. 2 "In a certain town there was a judge who neither feared God nor respected people. 3 And there was a widow in that same town who kept coming to him and pleading for her rights, saying, 'Help me against my opponent!' 4 For a long time the judge refused to act, but at last he said to himself, 'Even though I don't fear God or respect people, 5 yet because of all the trouble this widow is giving me, I will see to it that she gets her rights. If I don't, she will keep on coming and finally wear me out!'"

6 And the Lord continued, "Listen to what that corrupt judge said. 7 Now, will God not judge in favor of his own people who cry to him day and night for help? Will he be slow to help them? 8 I tell you, he will judge in their favor and do it quickly. But will the Son of Man find faith on earth when he comes?"

The Parable of the Pharisee and the Tax Collector

9 Jesus also told this parable to people who were sure of their own goodness and despised everybody else. 10 "Once there were two men who went up to the Temple to pray: one was a Pharisee, the other a tax collector. 11 The Pharisee stood apart by himself and prayed,*w* 'I thank you, God, that I am not greedy, dishonest, or an adulterer, like everybody else. I thank you that I am not like that tax collector over there. 12 I fast two days a week, and I give you one tenth of all my income.' 13 But the tax collector stood at a distance and would not even raise his face to heaven, but beat on his breast and said, 'God, have pity on me, a sinner!' 14 I tell you," said Jesus, "the tax collector, and not the Pharisee, was in the right with God when he went home. For those who make themselves great will be humbled, and those who humble themselves will be made great."

Jesus Blesses Little Children
(Matthew 19.13-15; Mark 10.13-16)

15 Some people brought their babies to Jesus for him to place his hands on them. The disciples saw them and scolded them for doing so, 16 but Jesus called the children to him and said, "Let the children come to me and do not stop them, because the Kingdom of God belongs to such as these. 17 Remember this! Whoever does not receive the Kingdom of God like a child will never enter it."

The Rich Man
(Matthew 19.16-30; Mark 10.17-31)

18 A Jewish leader asked Jesus, "Good Teacher, what must I do to receive eternal life?"

19 "Why do you call me good?" Jesus

---

v Some manuscripts add verse 36: Two men will be working in a field: one will be taken away, the other will be left behind (see Mt 24.40).   *w stood apart by himself and prayed; some manuscripts have stood up and prayed to himself.*

asked him. "No one is good except God alone. 20 You know the commandments: 'Do not commit adultery; do not commit murder; do not steal; do not accuse anyone falsely; respect your father and your mother.' "

21 The man replied, "Ever since I was young, I have obeyed all these commandments."

22 When Jesus heard this, he said to him, "There is still one more thing you need to do. Sell all you have and give the money to the poor, and you will have riches in heaven; then come and follow me." 23 But when the man heard this, he became very sad, because he was very rich.

24 Jesus saw that he was sad and said, "How hard it is for rich people to enter the Kingdom of God! 25 It is much harder for a rich person to enter the Kingdom of God than for a camel to go through the eye of a needle."

26 The people who heard him asked, "Who, then, can be saved?"

27 Jesus answered, "What is humanly impossible is possible for God."

28 Then Peter said, "Look! We have left our homes to follow you."

29 "Yes," Jesus said to them, "and I assure you that anyone who leaves home or wife or brothers or parents or children for the sake of the Kingdom of God 30 will receive much more in this present age and eternal life in the age to come."

Jesus Speaks a Third Time about His Death
(Matthew 20.17-19; Mark 10.32-34)

31 Jesus took the twelve disciples aside and said to them, "Listen! We are going to Jerusalem where everything the prophets wrote about the Son of Man will come true. 32 He will be handed over to the Gentiles, who will make fun of him, insult him, and spit on him. 33 They will whip him and kill him, but three days later he will rise to life."

34 But the disciples did not understand any of these things; the meaning of the words was hidden from them, and they did not know what Jesus was talking about.

Jesus Heals a Blind Beggar
(Matthew 20.29-34; Mark 10.46-52)

35 As Jesus was coming near Jericho, there was a blind man sitting by the road, begging. 36 When he heard the crowd passing by, he asked, "What is this?"

37 "Jesus of Nazareth is passing by," they told him.

38 He cried out, "Jesus! Son of David! Have mercy on me!"

39 The people in front scolded him and told him to be quiet. But he shouted even more loudly, "Son of David! Have mercy on me!"

40 So Jesus stopped and ordered the blind man to be brought to him. When he came near, Jesus asked him, 41 "What do you want me to do for you?"

"Sir," he answered, "I want to see again."

42 Jesus said to him, "Then see! Your faith has made you well."

43 At once he was able to see, and he followed Jesus, giving thanks to God. When the crowd saw it, they all praised God.

Jesus and Zacchaeus

19 Jesus went on into Jericho and was passing through. 2 There was a chief tax collector there named Zacchaeus, who was rich. 3 He was trying to see who Jesus was, but he was a little man and could not see Jesus because of the crowd. 4 So he ran ahead of the crowd and climbed a sycamore tree to see Jesus, who was going to pass that way. 5 When Jesus came to that place, he looked up and said to Zacchaeus, "Hurry down, Zacchaeus, because I must stay in your house today."

6 Zacchaeus hurried down and welcomed him with great joy. 7 All the people who saw it started grumbling, "This man has gone as a guest to the home of a sinner!"

8 Zacchaeus stood up and said to the Lord, "Listen, sir! I will give half my belongings to the poor, and if I have cheated anyone, I will pay back four times as much."

9 Jesus said to him, "Salvation has come to this house today, for this man, also, is a descendant of Abraham. 10 The Son of Man came to seek and to save the lost."

The Parable of the Gold Coins
(Matthew 25.14-30)

11 While the people were listening to this, Jesus continued and told them a

parable. He was now almost at Jerusalem, and they supposed that the Kingdom of God was just about to appear. 12 So he said, "There was once a man of high rank who was going to a country far away to be made king, after which he planned to come back home. 13 Before he left, he called his ten servants and gave them each a gold coin and told them, 'See what you can earn with this while I am gone.' 14 Now, his own people hated him, and so they sent messengers after him to say, 'We don't want this man to be our king.'

15 "The man was made king and came back. At once he ordered his servants to appear before him, in order to find out how much they had earned. 16 The first one came and said, 'Sir, I have earned ten gold coins with the one you gave me.' 17 'Well done,' he said; 'you are a good servant! Since you were faithful in small matters, I will put you in charge of ten cities.' 18 The second servant came and said, 'Sir, I have earned five gold coins with the one you gave me.' 19 To this one he said, 'You will be in charge of five cities.' 20 Another servant came and said, 'Sir, here is your gold coin; I kept it hidden in a handkerchief. 21 I was afraid of you, because you are a hard man. You take what is not yours and reap what you did not plant.' 22 He said to him, 'You bad servant! I will use your own words to condemn you! You know that I am a hard man, taking what is not mine and reaping what I have not planted. 23 Well, then, why didn't you put my money in the bank? Then I would have received it back with interest when I returned.' 24 Then he said to those who were standing there, 'Take the gold coin away from him and give it to the servant who has ten coins.' 25 But they said to him, 'Sir, he already has ten coins!' 26 'I tell you,' he replied, 'that to those who have something, even more will be given; but those who have nothing, even the little that they have will be taken away from them. 27 Now, as for those enemies of mine who did not want me to be their king, bring them here and kill them in my presence!' "

The Triumphant Approach to Jerusalem

(Matthew 21.1-11; Mark 11.1-11; John 12.12-19)

28 After Jesus said this, he went on in front of them toward Jerusalem. 29 As he came near Bethphage and Bethany at the Mount of Olives, he sent two disciples ahead 30 with these instructions: "Go to the village there ahead of you; as you go in, you will find a colt tied up that has never been ridden. Untie it and bring it here. 31 If someone asks you why you are untying it, tell him that the Master^x needs it."

32 They went on their way and found everything just as Jesus had told them. 33 As they were untying the colt, its owners said to them, "Why are you untying it?"

34 "The Master needs it," they answered, 35 and they took the colt to Jesus. Then they threw their cloaks over the animal and helped Jesus get on. 36 As he rode on, people spread their cloaks on the road.

37 When he came near Jerusalem, at the place where the road went down the Mount of Olives, the large crowd of his disciples began to thank God and praise him in loud voices for all the great things that they had seen: 38 "God bless the king who comes in the name of the Lord! Peace in heaven and glory to God!"

39 Then some of the Pharisees in the crowd spoke to Jesus. "Teacher," they said, "command your disciples to be quiet!"

40 Jesus answered, "I tell you that if they keep quiet, the stones themselves will start shouting."

Jesus Weeps over Jerusalem

41 He came closer to the city, and when he saw it, he wept over it, 42 saying, "If you only knew today what is needed for peace! But now you cannot see it! 43 The time will come when your enemies will surround you with barricades, blockade you, and close in on you from every side. 44 They will completely destroy you and the people within your walls; not a single stone will they leave in its place, because you did not recognize the time when God came to save you!"

x the Master. *or* its owner.

Jesus Goes to the Temple

(Matthew 21.12-17; Mark 11.15-19; John 2.13-22)

45 Then Jesus went into the Temple and began to drive out the merchants, 46 saying to them, "It is written in the Scriptures that God said, 'My Temple will be a house of prayer.' But you have turned it into a hideout for thieves!"

47 Every day Jesus taught in the Temple. The chief priests, the teachers of the Law, and the leaders of the people wanted to kill him, 48 but they could not find a way to do it, because all the people kept listening to him, not wanting to miss a single word.

The Question about Jesus' Authority

(Matthew 21.23-27; Mark 11.27-33)

20 One day when Jesus was in the Temple teaching the people and preaching the Good News, the chief priests and the teachers of the Law, together with the elders, came 2 and said to him, "Tell us, what right do you have to do these things? Who gave you such right?"

3 Jesus answered them, "Now let me ask you a question. Tell me, 4 did John's right to baptize come from God or from human beings?"

5 They started to argue among themselves, "What shall we say? If we say, 'From God,' he will say, 'Why, then, did you not believe John?' 6 But if we say, 'From human beings,' this whole crowd here will stone us, because they are convinced that John was a prophet." 7 So they answered, "We don't know where it came from."

8 And Jesus said to them, "Neither will I tell you, then, by what right I do these things."

The Parable of the Tenants in the Vineyard

(Matthew 21.33-46; Mark 12.1-12)

9 Then Jesus told the people this parable: "There was once a man who planted a vineyard, rented it out to tenants, and then left home for a long time. 10 When the time came to gather the grapes, he sent a slave to the tenants to receive from them his share of the harvest. But the tenants beat the slave and sent him back without a thing. 11 So he sent another slave; but the tenants beat him also, treated him shamefully, and sent

him back without a thing. 12 Then he sent a third slave; the tenants wounded him, too, and threw him out. 13 Then the owner of the vineyard said, 'What shall I do? I will send my own dear son; surely they will respect him!' 14 But when the tenants saw him, they said to one another, 'This is the owner's son. Let's kill him, and his property will be ours!' 15 So they threw him out of the vineyard and killed him.

"What, then, will the owner of the vineyard do to the tenants?" Jesus asked. 16 "He will come and kill those men, and turn the vineyard over to other tenants."

When the people heard this, they said, "Surely not!"

17 Jesus looked at them and asked, "What, then, does this scripture mean?

'The stone which the builders
    rejected as worthless
turned out to be the most
    important of all.'

18 Everyone who falls on that stone will be cut to pieces; and if that stone falls on someone, that person will be crushed to dust."

The Question about Paying Taxes

(Matthew 22.15-22; Mark 12.13-17)

19 The teachers of the Law and the chief priests tried to arrest Jesus on the spot, because they knew that he had told this parable against them; but they were afraid of the people. 20 So they looked for an opportunity. They bribed some men to pretend they were sincere, and they sent them to trap Jesus with questions, so that they could hand him over to the authority and power of the Roman Governor. 21 These spies said to Jesus, "Teacher, we know that what you say and teach is right. We know that you pay no attention to anyone's status, but teach the truth about God's will for people. 22 Tell us, is it against our Law for us to pay taxes to the Roman Emperor, or not?"

23 But Jesus saw through their trick and said to them, 24 "Show me a silver coin. Whose face and name are these on it?"

"The Emperor's," they answered.

25 So Jesus said, "Well, then, pay to the Emperor what belongs to the Emperor, and pay to God what belongs to God."

26 There before the people they could

not catch him in a thing, so they kept quiet, amazed at his answer.

The Question about Rising from Death

(Matthew 22.23-33; Mark 12.18-27)

27 Then some Sadducees, who say that people will not rise from death, came to Jesus and said, 28 "Teacher, Moses wrote this law for us: 'If a man dies and leaves a wife but no children, that man's brother must marry the widow so that they can have children who will be considered the dead man's children.' 29 Once there were seven brothers; the oldest got married and died without having children. 30 Then the second one married the woman, 31 and then the third. The same thing happened to all seven—they died without having children. 32 Last of all, the woman died. 33 Now, on the day when the dead rise to life, whose wife will she be? All seven of them had married her."

34 Jesus answered them, "The men and women of this age marry, 35 but the men and women who are worthy to rise from death and live in the age to come will not then marry. 36 They will be like angels and cannot die. They are the children of God, because they have risen from death. 37 And Moses clearly proves that the dead are raised to life. In the passage about the burning bush he speaks of the Lord as 'the God of Abraham, the God of Isaac, and the God of Jacob.' 38 He is the God of the living, not of the dead, for to him all are alive."

39 Some of the teachers of the Law spoke up, "A good answer, Teacher!" 40 For they did not dare ask him any more questions.

The Question about the Messiah

(Matthew 22.41-46; Mark 12.35-37)

41 Jesus asked them, "How can it be said that the Messiah will be the descendant of David? 42 For David himself says in the book of Psalms:

'The Lord said to my Lord:
Sit here at my right side
43   until I put your enemies as a
footstool under your feet.'

44 David called him 'Lord'; how, then, can the Messiah be David's descendant?"

Jesus Warns against the Teachers of the Law

(Matthew 23.1-36; Mark 12.38-40)

45 As all the people listened to him, Jesus said to his disciples, 46 "Be on your guard against the teachers of the Law, who like to walk around in their long robes and love to be greeted with respect in the marketplace; who choose the reserved seats in the synagogues and the best places at feasts; 47 who take advantage of widows and rob them of their homes, and then make a show of saying long prayers! Their punishment will be all the worse!"

The Widow's Offering

(Mark 12.41-44)

21 Jesus looked around and saw rich people dropping their gifts in the Temple treasury, 2 and he also saw a very poor widow dropping in two little copper coins. 3 He said, "I tell you that this poor widow put in more than all the others. 4 For the others offered their gifts from what they had to spare of their riches; but she, poor as she is, gave all she had to live on."

Jesus Speaks of the Destruction of the Temple

(Matthew 24.1, 2; Mark 13.1, 2)

5 Some of the disciples were talking about the Temple, how beautiful it looked with its fine stones and the gifts offered to God. Jesus said, 6 "All this you see—the time will come when not a single stone here will be left in its place; every one will be thrown down."

Troubles and Persecutions

(Matthew 24.3-14; Mark 13.3-13)

7 "Teacher," they asked, "when will this be? And what will happen in order to show that the time has come for it to take place?"

8 Jesus said, "Watch out; don't be fooled. Many men, claiming to speak for me, will come and say, 'I am he!' and, 'The time has come!' But don't follow them. 9 Don't be afraid when you hear of wars and revolutions; such things must happen first, but they do not mean that the end is near."

10 He went on to say, "Countries will fight each other; kingdoms will attack one another. 11 There will be terrible

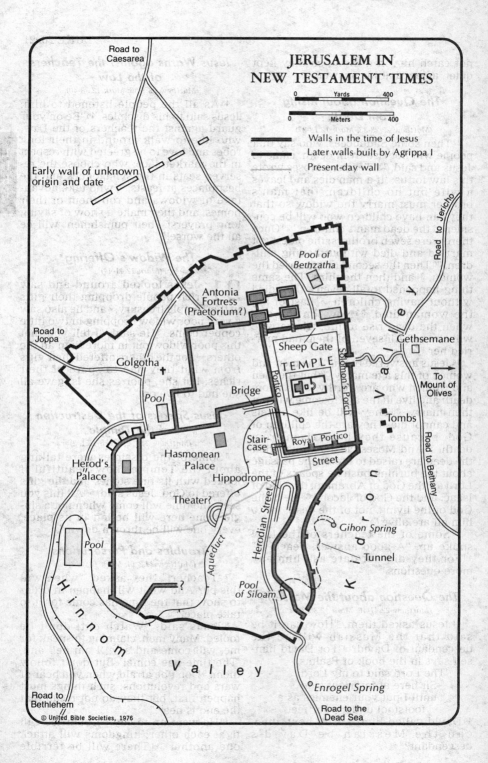

JERUSALEM IN
NEW TESTAMENT TIMES

Yards 0 — 400
Meters 0 — 400

Walls in the time of Jesus
Later walls built by Agrippa I
Present-day wall

Road to Caesarea

Early wall of unknown
origin and date

Road to Joppa

Road to Jericho

Pool of Bethzatha

Antonia Fortress (Praetorium?)

Sheep Gate

Golgotha

TEMPLE

Solomon's Porch

Gethsemane

To Mount of Olives

Pool

Bridge

Portico

Tombs

Staircase

Royal Portico

Street

Herod's Palace

Hasmonean Palace

Hippodrome

Theater?

Herodian Street

Gihon Spring

Tunnel

Aqueduct

Pool

?

Pool of Siloam

Kidron Valley

Hinnom Valley

Enrogel Spring

Road to Bethlehem

© United Bible Societies, 1976

Road to the Dead Sea

Road to Bethany

earthquakes, famines, and plagues everywhere; there will be strange and terrifying things coming from the sky. 12 Before all these things take place, however, you will be arrested and persecuted; you will be handed over to be tried in synagogues and be put in prison; you will be brought before kings and rulers for my sake. 13 This will be your chance to tell the Good News. 14 Make up your minds ahead of time not to worry about how you will defend yourselves, 15 because I will give you such words and wisdom that none of your enemies will be able to refute or contradict what you say. 16 You will be handed over by your parents, your brothers, your relatives, and your friends; and some of you will be put to death. 17 Everyone will hate you because of me. 18 But not a single hair from your heads will be lost. 19 Stand firm, and you will save yourselves.

Jesus Speaks of the Destruction of Jerusalem
(Matthew 24.15-21; Mark 13.14-19)

20 "When you see Jerusalem surrounded by armies, then you will know that it will soon be destroyed. 21 Then those who are in Judea must run away to the hills; those who are in the city must leave, and those who are out in the country must not go into the city. 22 For those will be 'The Days of Punishment,' to make come true all that the Scriptures say. 23 How terrible it will be in those days for women who are pregnant and for mothers with little babies! Terrible distress will come upon this land, and God's punishment will fall on this people. 24 Some will be killed by the sword, and others will be taken as prisoners to all countries; and the heathen will trample over Jerusalem until their time is up.

The Coming of the Son of Man
(Matthew 24.29-31; Mark 13.24-27)

25 "There will be strange things happening to the sun, the moon, and the stars. On earth whole countries will be in despair, afraid of the roar of the sea and the raging tides. 26 People will faint from fear as they wait for what is coming over the whole earth, for the powers in space will be driven from their courses. 27 Then the Son of Man will appear, coming in a cloud with great power and glory. 28 When these things

begin to happen, stand up and raise your heads, because your salvation is near."

The Lesson of the Fig Tree
(Matthew 24.32-35; Mark 13.28-31)

29 Then Jesus told them this parable: "Think of the fig tree and all the other trees. 30 When you see their leaves beginning to appear, you know that summer is near. 31 In the same way, when you see these things happening, you will know that the Kingdom of God is about to come.

32 "Remember that all these things will take place before the people now living have all died. 33 Heaven and earth will pass away, but my words will never pass away.

The Need to Watch

34 "Be careful not to let yourselves become occupied with too much feasting and drinking and with the worries of this life, or that Day may suddenly catch you 35 like a trap. For it will come upon all people everywhere on earth. 36 Be on watch and pray always that you will have the strength to go safely through all those things that will happen and to stand before the Son of Man."

37 Jesus spent those days teaching in the Temple, and when evening came, he would go out and spend the night on the Mount of Olives. 38 Early each morning all the people went to the Temple to listen to him.

The Plot against Jesus
(Matthew 26.1-5; Mark 14.1, 2; John 11.45-53)

22 The time was near for the Festival of Unleavened Bread, which is called the Passover. 2 The chief priests and the teachers of the Law were afraid of the people, and so they were trying to find a way of putting Jesus to death secretly.

Judas Agrees to Betray Jesus
(Matthew 26.14-16; Mark 14.10, 11)

3 Then Satan entered into Judas, called Iscariot, who was one of the twelve disciples. 4 So Judas went off and spoke with the chief priests and the officers of the Temple guard about how he could betray Jesus to them. 5 They were pleased and offered to pay him money. 6 Judas agreed to it and started looking for a good chance to hand Jesus over to

LUKE

them without the people knowing about it.

Jesus Prepares to Eat the Passover Meal

(Matthew 26.17-25; Mark 14.12-21; John 13.21-30)

7 The day came during the Festival of Unleavened Bread when the lambs for the Passover meal were to be killed. 8 Jesus sent Peter and John with these instructions: "Go and get the Passover meal ready for us to eat."

9 "Where do you want us to get it ready?" they asked him.

10 He answered, "As you go into the city, a man carrying a jar of water will meet you. Follow him into the house that he enters, 11 and say to the owner of the house: 'The Teacher says to you, Where is the room where my disciples and I will eat the Passover meal?' 12 He will show you a large furnished room upstairs, where you will get everything ready."

13 They went off and found everything just as Jesus had told them, and they prepared the Passover meal.

The Lord's Supper

(Matthew 26.26-30; Mark 14.22-26; 1 Corinthians 11.23-25)

14 When the hour came, Jesus took his place at the table with the apostles. 15 He said to them, "I have wanted so much to eat this Passover meal with you before I suffer! 16 For I tell you, I will never eat it until it is given its full meaning in the Kingdom of God."

17 Then Jesus took a cup, gave thanks to God, and said, "Take this and share it among yourselves. 18 I tell you that from now on I will not drink this wine until the Kingdom of God comes."

19 Then he took a piece of bread, gave thanks to God, broke it, and gave it to them, saying, "This is my body, which is given for you. Do this in memory of me." 20 In the same way, he gave them the cup after the supper, saying, "This cup is God's new covenant sealed with my blood, which is poured out for you.ʸ

21 "But, look! The one who betrays me is here at the table with me! 22 The Son of Man will die as God has decided, but how terrible for that man who betrays him!"

23 Then they began to ask among themselves which one of them it could be who was going to do this.

The Argument about Greatness

24 An argument broke out among the disciples as to which one of them should be thought of as the greatest. 25 Jesus said to them, "The kings of the pagans have power over their people, and the rulers claim the title 'Friends of the People,' 26 But this is not the way it is with you; rather, the greatest one among you must be like the youngest, and the leader must be like the servant. 27 Who is greater, the one who sits down to eat or the one who serves? The one who sits down, of course. But I am among you as one who serves.

28 "You have stayed with me all through my trials; 29 and just as my Father has given me the right to rule, so I will give you the same right. 30 You will eat and drink at my table in my Kingdom, and you will sit on thrones to rule over the twelve tribes of Israel.

Jesus Predicts Peter's Denial

(Matthew 26.31-35; Mark 14.27-31; John 13.36-38)

31 "Simon, Simon! Listen! Satan has received permission to test all of you, to separate the good from the bad, as a farmer separates the wheat from the chaff. 32 But I have prayed for you, Simon, that your faith will not fail. And when you turn back to me, you must strengthen your brothers."

33 Peter answered, "Lord, I am ready to go to prison with you and to die with you!"

34 "I tell you, Peter," Jesus said, "the rooster will not crow tonight until you have said three times that you do not know me."

Purse, Bag, and Sword

35 Then Jesus asked his disciples, "When I sent you out that time without purse, bag, or shoes, did you lack anything?"

"Not a thing," they answered.

36 "But now," Jesus said, "whoever has a purse or a bag must take it; and whoever does not have a sword must sell his coat and buy one. 37 For I tell you that the scripture which says, 'He shared the fate

ʸ *Some manuscripts do not have the words of Jesus after* This is my body *in verse 19, and all of verse 20.*

of criminals,' must come true about me, because what was written about me is coming true."

38 The disciples said, "Look! Here are two swords, Lord!"

"That is enough!"z he replied.

Jesus Prays on the Mount of Olives
(Matthew 26.36-46; Mark 14.32-42)

39 Jesus left the city and went, as he usually did, to the Mount of Olives; and the disciples went with him. 40 When he arrived at the place, he said to them, "Pray that you will not fall into temptation."

41 Then he went off from them about the distance of a stone's throw and knelt down and prayed. 42 "Father," he said, "if you will, take this cup of suffering away from me. Not my will, however, but your will be done." 43 An angel from heaven appeared to him and strengthened him. 44 In great anguish he prayed even more fervently; his sweat was like drops of blood falling to the ground.a

45 Rising from his prayer, he went back to the disciples and found them asleep, worn out by their grief. 46 He said to them, "Why are you sleeping? Get up and pray that you will not fall into temptation."

The Arrest of Jesus
(Matthew 26.47-56; Mark 14.43-50; John 18.3-11)

47 Jesus was still speaking when a crowd arrived, led by Judas, one of the twelve disciples. He came up to Jesus to kiss him. 48 But Jesus said, "Judas, is it with a kiss that you betray the Son of Man?"

49 When the disciples who were with Jesus saw what was going to happen, they asked, "Shall we use our swords, Lord?" 50 And one of them struck the High Priest's slave and cut off his right ear.

51 But Jesus said, "Enough of this!" He touched the man's ear and healed him. 52 Then Jesus said to the chief priests and the officers of the Temple guard and the elders who had come there to get him, "Did you have to come with swords and clubs, as though I were an outlaw? 53 I was with you in the Temple every day, and you did not try to arrest me. But this is your hour to act, when the power of darkness rules."

Peter Denies Jesus
(Matthew 26.57, 58, 69-75; Mark 14.53, 54, 66-72; John 18.12-18, 25-27)

54 They arrested Jesus and took him away into the house of the High Priest; and Peter followed at a distance. 55 A fire had been lit in the center of the courtyard, and Peter joined those who were sitting around it. 56 When one of the servant women saw him sitting there at the fire, she looked straight at him and said, "This man too was with Jesus!"

57 But Peter denied it, "Woman, I don't even know him!"

58 After a little while a man noticed Peter and said, "You are one of them, too!"

But Peter answered, "Man, I am not!"

59 And about an hour later another man insisted strongly, "There isn't any doubt that this man was with Jesus, because he also is a Galilean!"

60 But Peter answered, "Man, I don't know what you are talking about!"

At once, while he was still speaking, a rooster crowed. 61 The Lord turned around and looked straight at Peter, and Peter remembered that the Lord had said to him, "Before the rooster crows tonight, you will say three times that you do not know me." 62 Peter went out and wept bitterly.

Jesus Is Mocked and Beaten
(Matthew 26.67, 68; Mark 14.65)

63 The men who were guarding Jesus made fun of him and beat him. 64 They blindfolded him and asked him, "Who hit you? Guess!" 65 And they said many other insulting things to him.

Jesus before the Council
(Matthew 26.59-66; Mark 14.55-64; John 18.19-24)

66 When day came, the elders, the chief priests, and the teachers of the Law met together, and Jesus was brought before the Council. 67 "Tell us," they said, "are you the Messiah?"

He answered, "If I tell you, you will not believe me; 68 and if I ask you a question, you will not answer. 69 But from now on the Son of Man will be seated at the right side of Almighty God."

70 They all said, "Are you, then, the Son of God?"

---

z *That is enough; or Enough of this.*   a *Some manuscripts do not have verses 43-44.*

He answered them, "You say that I am."

71 And they said, "We don't need any witnesses! We ourselves have heard what he said!"

Jesus before Pilate
(Matthew 27.1, 2, 11-14; Mark 15.1-5; John 18.28-38)

23 The whole group rose up and took Jesus before Pilate, 2 where they began to accuse him: "We caught this man misleading our people, telling them not to pay taxes to the Emperor and claiming that he himself is the Messiah, a king."

3 Pilate asked him, "Are you the king of the Jews?"

"So you say," answered Jesus.

4 Then Pilate said to the chief priests and the crowds, "I find no reason to condemn this man."

5 But they insisted even more strongly, "With his teaching he is starting a riot among the people all through Judea. He began in Galilee and now has come here."

Jesus before Herod

6 When Pilate heard this, he asked, "Is this man a Galilean?" 7 When he learned that Jesus was from the region ruled by Herod, he sent him to Herod, who was also in Jerusalem at that time. 8 Herod was very pleased when he saw Jesus, because he had heard about him and had been wanting to see him for a long time. He was hoping to see Jesus perform some miracle. 9 So Herod asked Jesus many questions, but Jesus made no answer. 10 The chief priests and the teachers of the Law stepped forward and made strong accusations against Jesus. 11 Herod and his soldiers made fun of Jesus and treated him with contempt; then they put a fine robe on him and sent him back to Pilate. 12 On that very day Herod and Pilate became friends; before this they had been enemies.

Jesus Is Sentenced to Death
(Matthew 27.15-26; Mark 15.6-15; John 18.39 — 19.16)

13 Pilate called together the chief priests, the leaders, and the people, 14 and said to them, "You brought this man to me and said that he was misleading the people. Now, I have examined him here in your presence, and I have not found him guilty of any of the crimes you accuse him of. 15 Nor did Herod find him guilty, for he sent him back to us. There is nothing this man has done to deserve death. 16 So I will have him whipped and let him go."b

18 The whole crowd cried out, "Kill him! Set Barabbas free for us!" (19 Barabbas had been put in prison for a riot that had taken place in the city, and for murder.)

20 Pilate wanted to set Jesus free, so he appealed to the crowd again. 21 But they shouted back, "Crucify him! Crucify him!"

22 Pilate said to them the third time, "But what crime has he committed? I cannot find anything he has done to deserve death! I will have him whipped and set him free."

23 But they kept on shouting at the top of their voices that Jesus should be crucified, and finally their shouting succeeded. 24 So Pilate passed the sentence on Jesus that they were asking for. 25 He set free the man they wanted, the one who had been put in prison for riot and murder, and he handed Jesus over for them to do as they wished.

Jesus Is Crucified
(Matthew 27.32-44; Mark 15.21-32; John 19.17-27)

26 The soldiers led Jesus away, and as they were going, they met a man from Cyrene named Simon who was coming into the city from the country. They seized him, put the cross on him, and made him carry it behind Jesus.

27 A large crowd of people followed him; among them were some women who were weeping and wailing for him. 28 Jesus turned to them and said, "Women of Jerusalem! Don't cry for me, but for yourselves and your children. 29 For the days are coming when people will say, 'How lucky are the women who never had children, who never bore babies, who never nursed them!' 30 That will be the time when people will say to the mountains, 'Fall on us!' and to the hills, 'Hide us!' 31 For if such things as these are done when the wood is green, what will happen when it is dry?"

32 Two other men, both of them crimi-

b *Some manuscripts add verse 17: At every Passover Festival Pilate had to set free one prisoner for them (see Mk 15.6).*

nals, were also led out to be put to death with Jesus. 33 When they came to the place called "The Skull," they crucified Jesus there, and the two criminals, one on his right and the other on his left. 34 Jesus said, "Forgive them, Father! They don't know what they are doing."c

They divided his clothes among themselves by throwing dice. 35 The people stood there watching while the Jewish leaders made fun of him: "He saved others; let him save himself if he is the Messiah whom God has chosen!"

36 The soldiers also made fun of him: they came up to him and offered him cheap wine, 37 and said, "Save yourself if you are the king of the Jews!"

38 Above him were written these words: "This is the King of the Jews."

39 One of the criminals hanging there hurled insults at him: "Aren't you the Messiah? Save yourself and us!"

40 The other one, however, rebuked him, saying, "Don't you fear God? You received the same sentence he did. 41 Ours, however, is only right, because we are getting what we deserve for what we did; but he has done no wrong." 42 And he said to Jesus, "Remember me, Jesus, when you come as King!"

43 Jesus said to him, "I promise you that today you will be in Paradise with me."

The Death of Jesus
(Matthew 27.45-56; Mark 15.33-41; John 19.28-30)

44-45 It was about twelve o'clock when the sun stopped shining and darkness covered the whole country until three o'clock; and the curtain hanging in the Temple was torn in two. 46 Jesus cried out in a loud voice, "Father! In your hands I place my spirit!" He said this and died.

47 The army officer saw what had happened, and he praised God, saying, "Certainly he was a good man!"

48 When the people who had gathered there to watch the spectacle saw what happened, they all went back home, beating their breasts in sorrow. 49 All those who knew Jesus personally, including the women who had followed him from Galilee, stood at a distance to watch.

The Burial of Jesus
(Matthew 27.57-61; Mark 15.42-47; John 19.38-42)

50-51 There was a man named Joseph from Arimathea, a town in Judea. He was a good and honorable man, who was waiting for the coming of the Kingdom of God. Although he was a member of the Council, he had not agreed with their decision and action. 52 He went into the presence of Pilate and asked for the body of Jesus. 53 Then he took the body down, wrapped it in a linen sheet, and placed it in a tomb which had been dug out of solid rock and which had never been used. 54 It was Friday, and the Sabbath was about to begin.

55 The women who had followed Jesus from Galilee went with Joseph and saw the tomb and how Jesus' body was placed in it. 56 Then they went back home and prepared the spices and perfumes for the body.

On the Sabbath they rested, as the Law commanded.

The Resurrection
(Matthew 28.1-10; Mark 16.1-8; John 20.1-10)

24 Very early on Sunday morning the women went to the tomb, carrying the spices they had prepared. 2 They found the stone rolled away from the entrance to the tomb, 3 so they went in; but they did not find the body of the Lord Jesus. 4 They stood there puzzled about this, when suddenly two men in bright shining clothes stood by them. 5 Full of fear, the women bowed down to the ground, as the men said to them, "Why are you looking among the dead for one who is alive? 6 He is not here; he has been raised. Remember what he said to you while he was in Galilee: 7 'The Son of Man must be handed over to sinners, be crucified, and three days later rise to life.' "

8 Then the women remembered his words, 9 returned from the tomb, and told all these things to the eleven disciples and all the rest. 10 The women were Mary Magdalene, Joanna, and Mary the mother of James; they and the other women with them told these things to the apostles. 11 But the apostles thought that what the women said was nonsense, and they did not believe them. 12 But Pe-

c *Some manuscripts do not have* Jesus said, "Forgive them, Father! They don't know what they are doing."

L
U
K
E

ter got up and ran to the tomb; he bent down and saw the grave cloths but nothing else. Then he went back home amazed at what had happened.d

The Walk to Emmaus
(Mark 16.12, 13)

13 On that same day two of Jesus' followers were going to a village named Emmaus, about seven miles from Jerusalem, 14 and they were talking to each other about all the things that had happened. 15 As they talked and discussed, Jesus himself drew near and walked along with them; 16 they saw him, but somehow did not recognize him. 17 Jesus said to them, "What are you talking about to each other, as you walk along?"

They stood still, with sad faces. 18 One of them, named Cleopas, asked him, "Are you the only visitor in Jerusalem who doesn't know the things that have been happening there these last few days?"

19 "What things?" he asked.

"The things that happened to Jesus of Nazareth," they answered. "This man was a prophet and was considered by God and by all the people to be powerful in everything he said and did. 20 Our chief priests and rulers handed him over to be sentenced to death, and he was crucified. 21 And we had hoped that he would be the one who was going to set Israel free! Besides all that, this is now the third day since it happened. 22 Some of the women of our group surprised us; they went at dawn to the tomb, 23 but could not find his body. They came back saying they had seen a vision of angels who told them that he is alive. 24 Some of our group went to the tomb and found it exactly as the women had said, but they did not see him."

25 Then Jesus said to them, "How foolish you are, how slow you are to believe everything the prophets said! 26 Was it not necessary for the Messiah to suffer these things and then to enter his glory?" 27 And Jesus explained to them what was said about himself in all the Scriptures, beginning with the books of Moses and the writings of all the prophets.

28 As they came near the village to which they were going, Jesus acted as if he were going farther; 29 but they held him back, saying, "Stay with us; the day is almost over and it is getting dark." So he went in to stay with them. 30 He sat down to eat with them, took the bread, and said the blessing; then he broke the bread and gave it to them. 31 Then their eyes were opened and they recognized him, but he disappeared from their sight. 32 They said to each other, "Wasn't it like a fire burning in us when he talked to us on the road and explained the Scriptures to us?"

33 They got up at once and went back to Jerusalem, where they found the eleven disciples gathered together with the others 34 and saying, "The Lord is risen indeed! He has appeared to Simon!"

35 The two then explained to them what had happened on the road, and how they had recognized the Lord when he broke the bread.

Jesus Appears to His Disciples
(Matthew 28.16-20; Mark 16.14-18; John 20.19-23; Acts 1.6-8)

36 While the two were telling them this, suddenly the Lord himself stood among them and said to them, "Peace be with you."e

37 They were terrified, thinking that they were seeing a ghost. 38 But he said to them, "Why are you alarmed? Why are these doubts coming up in your minds? 39 Look at my hands and my feet, and see that it is I myself. Feel me, and you will know, for a ghost doesn't have flesh and bones, as you can see I have."

40 He said this and showed them his hands and his feet.f 41 They still could not believe, they were so full of joy and wonder; so he asked them, "Do you have anything here to eat?" 42 They gave him a piece of cooked fish, 43 which he took and ate in their presence.

44 Then he said to them, "These are the very things I told you about while I was still with you: everything written about me in the Law of Moses, the writings of the prophets, and the Psalms had to come true."

45 Then he opened their minds to understand the Scriptures, 46 and said to

---

d Some manuscripts do not have verse 12.   e Some manuscripts do not have and said to them, "Peace be with you."   f Some manuscripts do not have verse 40.

them, "This is what is written: the Messiah must suffer and must rise from death three days later, 47 and in his name the message about repentance and the forgiveness of sins must be preached to all nations, beginning in Jerusalem. 48 You are witnesses of these things. 49 And I myself will send upon you what my Father has promised. But you must wait in the city until the power from above comes down upon you."

Jesus Is Taken Up to Heaven
(Mark 16.19, 20; Acts 1.9-11)

50 Then he led them out of the city as far as Bethany, where he raised his hands and blessed them. 51 As he was blessing them, he departed from them and was taken up into heaven.g 52 They worshiped him and went back into Jerusalem, filled with great joy; 53 and spent all their time in the Temple giving thanks to God.

g *Some manuscripts do not have* and was taken up into heaven.

The Gospel according to

JOHN

Introduction

The Gospel according to John *presents Jesus as the eternal Word of God, who "became a human being and lived among us."* As the book itself says, this Gospel was written so that its readers might believe that Jesus is the promised Savior, the Son of God, and that through their faith in him they may have life (20.31).

After an introduction that identifies the eternal Word of God with Jesus, the first part of the Gospel presents various miracles which show that Jesus is the promised Savior, the Son of God. These are followed by discourses that explain what is revealed by the miracles. This part of the book tells how some people believed in Jesus and became his followers, while others opposed him and refused to believe. Chapters 13–17 record at length the close fellowship of Jesus with his disciples on the night of his arrest, and his words of preparation and encouragement to them on the eve of his crucifixion. The closing chapters tell of Jesus' arrest and trial, his crucifixion and resurrection, and his appearances to his disciples after the resurrection.

The story of the woman caught in adultery (8.1-11) is placed in brackets because many manuscripts and early translations omit it, while others include it in other places.

John emphasizes the gift of eternal life through Christ, a gift which begins now and which comes to those who respond to Jesus as the way, the truth, and the life. A striking feature of John is the symbolic use of common things from everyday life to point to spiritual realities, such as water, bread, light, the shepherd and his sheep, and the grapevine and its fruit.

Outline of Contents

The Word of Life

1 In the beginning the Word already existed; the Word was with God, and the Word was God. ² From the very beginning the Word was with God. ³ Through him God made all things; not one thing in all creation was made without him. ⁴ The Word was the source of life,ᵃ and this life brought light to people. ⁵ The light shines in the darkness, and the darkness has never put it out.

⁶ God sent his messenger, a man named John, ⁷ who came to tell people about the light, so that all should hear the message and believe. ⁸ He himself was not the light; he came to tell about the light. ⁹ This was the real light — the light that comes into the world and shines on all people.

¹⁰ The Word was in the world, and though God made the world through him, yet the world did not recognize him. ¹¹ He came to his own country, but his own people did not receive him. ¹² Some, however, did receive him and believed in him; so he gave them the right to become God's children. ¹³ They did not become God's children by natural means, that is, by being born as the children of a human father; God himself was their Father.

¹⁴ The Word became a human being and, full of grace and truth, lived among us. We saw his glory, the glory which he received as the Father's only Son.

¹⁵ John spoke about him. He cried out, "This is the one I was talking about when I said, 'He comes after me, but he is greater than I am, because he existed before I was born.'"

¹⁶ Out of the fullness of his grace he has blessed us all, giving us one blessing

---

ᵃ The Word was the source of life; or What was made had life in union with the Word.

after another. 17 God gave the Law through Moses, but grace and truth came through Jesus Christ. 18 No one has ever seen God. The only Son, who is the same as God and is at the Father's side, he has made him known.

John the Baptist's Message
(Matthew 3.1-12; Mark 1.1-8; Luke 3.1-18)

19 The Jewish authorities in Jerusalem sent some priests and Levites to John to ask him, "Who are you?"

20 John did not refuse to answer, but spoke out openly and clearly, saying: "I am not the Messiah."

21 "Who are you, then?" they asked. "Are you Elijah?"

"No, I am not," John answered.

"Are you the Prophet?"*b* they asked.

"No," he replied.

22 "Then tell us who you are," they said. "We have to take an answer back to those who sent us. What do you say about yourself?"

23 John answered by quoting the prophet Isaiah:

"I am 'the voice of someone
shouting in the desert:
Make a straight path for the
Lord to travel!' "

24 The messengers, who had been sent by the Pharisees, 25 then*c* asked John, "If you are not the Messiah nor Elijah nor the Prophet, why do you baptize?"

26 John answered, "I baptize with water, but among you stands the one you do not know. 27 He is coming after me, but I am not good enough even to untie his sandals."

28 All this happened in Bethany on the east side of the Jordan River, where John was baptizing.

The Lamb of God

29 The next day John saw Jesus coming to him, and said, "There is the Lamb of God, who takes away the sin of the world! 30 This is the one I was talking about when I said, 'A man is coming after me, but he is greater than I am, because he existed before I was born.' 31 I did not know who he would be, but I came baptizing with water in order to

make him known to the people of Israel."

32 And John gave this testimony: "I saw the Spirit come down like a dove from heaven and stay on him. 33 I still did not know that he was the one, but God, who sent me to baptize with water, had said to me, 'You will see the Spirit come down and stay on a man; he is the one who baptizes with the Holy Spirit.' 34 I have seen it," said John, "and I tell you that he is the Son of God."

The First Disciples of Jesus

35 The next day John was standing there again with two of his disciples, 36 when he saw Jesus walking by. "There is the Lamb of God!" he said.

37 The two disciples heard him say this and went with Jesus. 38 Jesus turned, saw them following him, and asked, "What are you looking for?"

They answered, "Where do you live, Rabbi?" (This word means "Teacher.")

39 "Come and see," he answered. (It was then about four o'clock in the afternoon.) So they went with him and saw where he lived, and spent the rest of that day with him.

40 One of them was Andrew, Simon Peter's brother. 41 At once he found his brother Simon and told him, "We have found the Messiah." (This word means "Christ.") 42 Then he took Simon to Jesus.

Jesus looked at him and said, "Your name is Simon son of John, but you will be called Cephas." (This is the same as Peter and means "a rock.")

Jesus Calls Philip and Nathanael

43 The next day Jesus decided to go to Galilee. He found Philip and said to him, "Come with me!" (44 Philip was from Bethsaida, the town where Andrew and Peter lived.) 45 Philip found Nathanael and told him, "We have found the one whom Moses wrote about in the book of the Law and whom the prophets also wrote about. He is Jesus son of Joseph, from Nazareth."

46 "Can anything good come from Nazareth?" Nathanael asked.

"Come and see," answered Philip.

b THE PROPHET: *The one who was expected to appear and announce the coming of the Messiah.*
c The messengers, who had been sent by the Pharisees, then; *or* Those who had been sent were Pharisees; they.

47 When Jesus saw Nathanael coming to him, he said about him, "Here is a real Israelite; there is nothing false in him!" 48 Nathanael asked him, "How do you know me?"

Jesus answered, "I saw you when you were under the fig tree before Philip called you."

49 "Teacher," answered Nathanael, "you are the Son of God! You are the King of Israel!"

50 Jesus said, "Do you believe just because I told you I saw you when you were under the fig tree? You will see much greater things than this!" 51 And he said to them, "I am telling you the truth: you will see heaven open and God's angels going up and coming down on the Son of Man."

The Wedding in Cana

2 Two days later there was a wedding in the town of Cana in Galilee. Jesus' mother was there, 2 and Jesus and his disciples had also been invited to the wedding. 3 When the wine had given out, Jesus' mother said to him, "They are out of wine."

4 "You must not tell me what to do," Jesus replied. "My time has not yet come."

5 Jesus' mother then told the servants, "Do whatever he tells you."

6 The Jews have rules about ritual washing, and for this purpose six stone water jars were there, each one large enough to hold between twenty and thirty gallons. 7 Jesus said to the servants, "Fill these jars with water." They filled them to the brim, 8 and then he told them, "Now draw some water out and take it to the man in charge of the feast." They took him the water, 9 which now had turned into wine, and he tasted it. He did not know where this wine had come from (but, of course, the servants who had drawn out the water knew); so he called the bridegroom 10 and said to him, "Everyone else serves the best wine first, and after the guests have drunk a lot, he serves the ordinary wine. But you have kept the best wine until now!"

11 Jesus performed this first miracle in Cana in Galilee; there he revealed his glory, and his disciples believed in him.

12 After this, Jesus and his mother, brothers, and disciples went to Capernaum and stayed there a few days.

Jesus Goes to the Temple

(Matthew 21.12, 13; Mark 11.15-17; Luke 19.45, 46)

13 It was almost time for the Passover Festival, so Jesus went to Jerusalem. 14 There in the Temple he found people selling cattle, sheep, and pigeons, and also the moneychangers sitting at their tables. 15 So he made a whip from cords and drove all the animals out of the Temple, both the sheep and the cattle; he overturned the tables of the moneychangers and scattered their coins; 16 and he ordered those who sold the pigeons, "Take them out of here! Stop making my Father's house a marketplace!" 17 His disciples remembered that the scripture says, "My devotion to your house, O God, burns in me like a fire."

18 The Jewish authorities came back at him with a question, "What miracle can you perform to show us that you have the right to do this?"

19 Jesus answered, "Tear down this Temple, and in three days I will build it again."

20 "Are you going to build it again in three days?" they asked him. "It has taken forty-six years to build this Temple!"

21 But the temple Jesus was speaking about was his body. 22 So when he was raised from death, his disciples remembered that he had said this, and they believed the scripture and what Jesus had said.

Jesus' Knowledge of Human Nature

23 While Jesus was in Jerusalem during the Passover Festival, many believed in him as they saw the miracles he performed. 24 But Jesus did not trust himself to them, because he knew them all. 25 There was no need for anyone to tell him about them, because he himself knew what was in their hearts.

Jesus and Nicodemus

3 There was a Jewish leader named Nicodemus, who belonged to the party of the Pharisees. 2 One night he went to Jesus and said to him, "Rabbi, we know that you are a teacher sent by God. No one could perform the miracles you are doing unless God were with him."

3 Jesus answered, "I am telling you the

truth: no one can see the Kingdom of God without being born again."[d]

4 "How can a grown man be born again?" Nicodemus asked. "He certainly cannot enter his mother's womb and be born a second time!"

5 "I am telling you the truth," replied Jesus, "that no one can enter the Kingdom of God without being born of water and the Spirit. 6 A person is born physically of human parents, but is born spiritually of the Spirit. 7 Do not be surprised because I tell you that you must all be born again.[d] 8 The wind blows wherever it wishes; you hear the sound it makes, but you do not know where it comes from or where it is going. It is like that with everyone who is born of the Spirit."

9 "How can this be?" asked Nicodemus.

10 Jesus answered, "You are a great teacher in Israel, and you don't know this? 11 I am telling you the truth: we speak of what we know and report what we have seen, yet none of you is willing to accept our message. 12 You do not believe me when I tell you about the things of this world; how will you ever believe me, then, when I tell you about the things of heaven? 13 And no one has ever gone up to heaven except the Son of Man, who came down from heaven."[e]

14 As Moses lifted up the bronze snake on a pole in the desert, in the same way the Son of Man must be lifted up, 15 so that everyone who believes in him may have eternal life. 16 For God loved the world so much that he gave his only Son, so that everyone who believes in him may not die but have eternal life. 17 For God did not send his Son into the world to be its judge, but to be its savior.

18 Those who believe in the Son are not judged; but those who do not believe have already been judged, because they have not believed in God's only Son. 19 This is how the judgment works: the light has come into the world, but people love the darkness rather than the light, because their deeds are evil. 20 Those who do evil things hate the light and will not come to the light, because they do not want their evil deeds to be shown up. 21 But those who do what is true come to the light in order that the light may show

that what they did was in obedience to God.

Jesus and John

22 After this, Jesus and his disciples went to the province of Judea, where he spent some time with them and baptized. 23 John also was baptizing in Aenon, not far from Salim, because there was plenty of water in that place. People were going to him, and he was baptizing them. (24 This was before John had been put in prison.)

25 Some of John's disciples began arguing with a Jew[f] about the matter of ritual washing. 26 So they went to John and told him, "Teacher, you remember the man who was with you on the east side of the Jordan, the one you spoke about? Well, he is baptizing now, and everyone is going to him!"

27 John answered, "No one can have anything unless God gives it. 28 You yourselves are my witnesses that I said, 'I am not the Messiah, but I have been sent ahead of him.' 29 The bridegroom is the one to whom the bride belongs; but the bridegroom's friend, who stands by and listens, is glad when he hears the bridegroom's voice. This is how my own happiness is made complete. 30 He must become more important while I become less important."

He Who Comes from Heaven

31 He who comes from above is greater than all. He who is from the earth belongs to the earth and speaks about earthly matters, but he who comes from heaven is above all. 32 He tells what he has seen and heard, yet no one accepts his message. 33 But whoever accepts his message confirms by this that God is truthful. 34 The one whom God has sent speaks God's words, because God gives him the fullness of his Spirit. 35 The Father loves his Son and has put everything in his power. 36 Whoever believes in the Son has eternal life; whoever disobeys the Son will not have life, but will remain under God's punishment.

Jesus and the Samaritan Woman

4 The Pharisees heard that Jesus was winning and baptizing more disciples than John. (2 Actually, Jesus him-

---

d again; or from above.   e The quotation may continue through verse 21.   f a Jew; some manuscripts have some Jews.

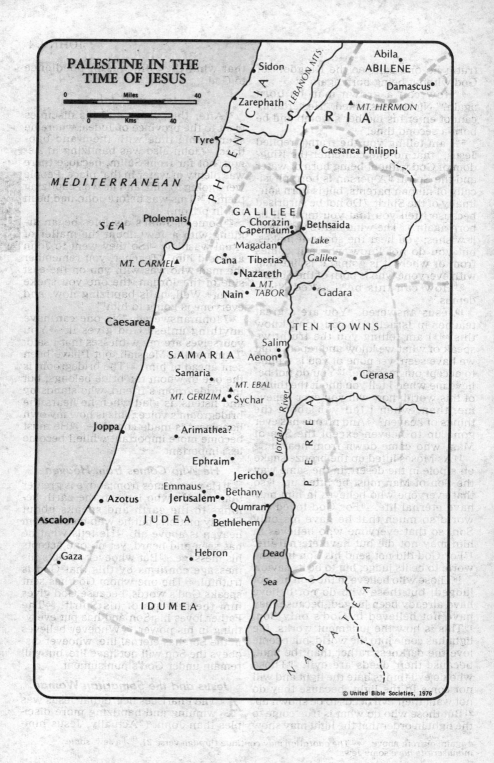

PALESTINE IN THE
TIME OF JESUS

Miles 0 — 40

Kms 0 — 40

Abila •
ABILENE

Sidon •

Damascus •

PHOENICIA

LEBANON MTS.

Zarephath •

▲ MT. HERMON

SYRIA

Tyre •

Caesarea Philippi •

MEDITERRANEAN

SEA

Ptolemais •

GALILEE

Chorazin •
Capernaum • Bethsaida •

Lake

Magadan •

Cana • Tiberias

Galilee

MT. CARMEL ▲

• Nazareth

▲ MT.
Nain • TABOR

Gadara •

Caesarea •

TEN TOWNS

Salim •

SAMARIA

Aenon •

Samaria •

Gerasa •

MT. EBAL ▲

MT. GERIZIM ▲ Sychar •

Jordan River

Joppa •

PEREA

• Arimathea?

Ephraim •

Jericho •

Emmaus • Bethany •

Azotus •

Jerusalem •

Qumran •

JUDEA

Bethlehem •

Ascalon •

Hebron •

Dead

Gaza •

Sea

IDUMEA

NABATEA

© United Bible Societies, 1976

self did not baptize anyone; only his disciples did.) ³ So when Jesus heard what was being said, he left Judea and went back to Galilee; ⁴ on his way there he had to go through Samaria.

⁵ In Samaria he came to a town named Sychar, which was not far from the field that Jacob had given to his son Joseph. ⁶ Jacob's well was there, and Jesus, tired out by the trip, sat down by the well. It was about noon.

⁷ A Samaritan woman came to draw some water, and Jesus said to her, "Give me a drink of water." (⁸ His disciples had gone into town to buy food.)

⁹ The woman answered, "You are a Jew, and I am a Samaritan—so how can you ask me for a drink?" (Jews will not use the same cups and bowls that Samaritans use.)ᵍ

¹⁰ Jesus answered, "If you only knew what God gives and who it is that is asking you for a drink, you would ask him, and he would give you life-giving water."

¹¹ "Sir," the woman said, "you don't have a bucket, and the well is deep. Where would you get that life-giving water? ¹² It was our ancestor Jacob who gave us this well; he and his children and his flocks all drank from it. You don't claim to be greater than Jacob, do you?"

¹³ Jesus answered, "Those who drink this water will get thirsty again, ¹⁴ but those who drink the water that I will give them will never be thirsty again. The water that I will give them will become in them a spring which will provide them with life-giving water and give them eternal life."

¹⁵ "Sir," the woman said, "give me that water! Then I will never be thirsty again, nor will I have to come here to draw water."

¹⁶ "Go and call your husband," Jesus told her, "and come back."

¹⁷ "I don't have a husband," she answered.

Jesus replied, "You are right when you say you don't have a husband. ¹⁸ You have been married to five men, and the man you live with now is not really your husband. You have told me the truth."

¹⁹ "I see you are a prophet, sir," the woman said. ²⁰ "My Samaritan ancestors worshiped God on this mountain, but you Jews say that Jerusalem is the place where we should worship God."

²¹ Jesus said to her, "Believe me, woman, the time will come when people will not worship the Father either on this mountain or in Jerusalem. ²² You Samaritans do not really know whom you worship; but we Jews know whom we worship, because it is from the Jews that salvation comes. ²³ But the time is coming and is already here, when by the power of God's Spirit people will worship the Father as he really is, offering him the true worship that he wants. ²⁴ God is Spirit, and only by the power of his Spirit can people worship him as he really is."

²⁵ The woman said to him, "I know that the Messiah will come, and when he comes, he will tell us everything."

²⁶ Jesus answered, "I am he, I who am talking with you."

²⁷ At that moment Jesus' disciples returned, and they were greatly surprised to find him talking with a woman. But none of them said to her, "What do you want?" or asked him, "Why are you talking with her?"

²⁸ Then the woman left her water jar, went back to the town, and said to the people there, ²⁹ "Come and see the man who told me everything I have ever done. Could he be the Messiah?" ³⁰ So they left the town and went to Jesus.

³¹ In the meantime the disciples were begging Jesus, "Teacher, have something to eat!"

³² But he answered, "I have food to eat that you know nothing about."

³³ So the disciples started asking among themselves, "Could somebody have brought him food?"

³⁴ "My food," Jesus said to them, "is to obey the will of the one who sent me and to finish the work he gave me to do. ³⁵ You have a saying, 'Four more months and then the harvest.' But I tell you, take a good look at the fields; the crops are now ripe and ready to be harvested! ³⁶ The one who reaps the harvest is being paid and gathers the crops for eternal life; so the one who plants and the one who reaps will be glad together. ³⁷ For

ᵍ Jews will not use the same cups and bowls that Samaritans use; *or* Jews will have nothing to do with Samaritans.

the saying is true, 'Someone plants, someone else reaps.' 38 I have sent you to reap a harvest in a field where you did not work; others worked there, and you profit from their work."

39 Many of the Samaritans in that town believed in Jesus because the woman had said, "He told me everything I have ever done." 40 So when the Samaritans came to him, they begged him to stay with them, and Jesus stayed there two days.

41 Many more believed because of his message, 42 and they told the woman, "We believe now, not because of what you said, but because we ourselves have heard him, and we know that he really is the Savior of the world."

Jesus Heals an Official's Son

43 After spending two days there, Jesus left and went to Galilee. 44 For he himself had said, "Prophets are not respected in their own country." 45 When he arrived in Galilee, the people there welcomed him, because they had gone to the Passover Festival in Jerusalem and had seen everything that he had done during the festival.

46 Then Jesus went back to Cana in Galilee, where he had turned the water into wine. A government official was there whose son was sick in Capernaum. 47 When he heard that Jesus had come from Judea to Galilee, he went to him and asked him to go to Capernaum and heal his son, who was about to die. 48 Jesus said to him, "None of you will ever believe unless you see miracles and wonders."

49 "Sir," replied the official, "come with me before my child dies."

50 Jesus said to him, "Go; your son will live!"

The man believed Jesus' words and went. 51 On his way home his servants met him with the news, "Your boy is going to live!"

52 He asked them what time it was when his son got better, and they answered, "It was one o'clock yesterday afternoon when the fever left him." 53 Then the father remembered that it was at that very hour when Jesus had told him, "Your son will live." So he and all his family believed.

54 This was the second miracle that Jesus performed after coming from Judea to Galilee.

The Healing at the Pool

5 After this, Jesus went to Jerusalem for a religious festival. 2 Near the Sheep Gate in Jerusalem there is a pool h with five porches; in Hebrew it is called Bethzatha.ⁱ 3 A large crowd of sick people were lying on the porches — the blind, the lame, and the paralyzed.ʲ 5 A man was there who had been sick for thirty-eight years. 6 Jesus saw him lying there, and he knew that the man had been sick for such a long time; so he asked him, "Do you want to get well?"

7 The sick man answered, "Sir, I don't have anyone here to put me in the pool when the water is stirred up; while I am trying to get in, somebody else gets there first."

8 Jesus said to him, "Get up, pick up your mat, and walk." 9 Immediately the man got well; he picked up his mat and started walking.

The day this happened was a Sabbath, 10 so the Jewish authorities told the man who had been healed, "This is a Sabbath, and it is against our Law for you to carry your mat."

11 He answered, "The man who made me well told me to pick up my mat and walk."

12 They asked him, "Who is the man who told you to do this?"

13 But the man who had been healed did not know who Jesus was, for there was a crowd in that place, and Jesus had slipped away.

14 Afterward, Jesus found him in the Temple and said, "Listen, you are well now; so stop sinning or something worse may happen to you."

15 Then the man left and told the Jewish authorities that it was Jesus who had healed him. 16 So they began to persecute Jesus, because he had done this healing on a Sabbath. 17 Jesus answered

---

h Near the Sheep Gate . . . a pool; or Near the Sheep Pool . . . a place.
i Bethzatha; some manuscripts have Bethesda. ʲ Some manuscripts add verses 3b-4: They were waiting for the water to move, 4because every now and then an angel of the Lord went down into the pool and stirred up the water. The first sick person to go into the pool after the water was stirred up was healed from whatever disease he had.

them, "My Father is always working, and I too must work."

18 This saying made the Jewish authorities all the more determined to kill him; not only had he broken the Sabbath law, but he had said that God was his own Father and in this way had made himself equal with God.

The Authority of the Son

19 So Jesus answered them, "I tell you the truth: the Son can do nothing on his own; he does only what he sees his Father doing. What the Father does, the Son also does. 20 For the Father loves the Son and shows him all that he himself is doing. He will show him even greater things to do than this, and you will all be amazed. 21 Just as the Father raises the dead and gives them life, in the same way the Son gives life to those he wants to. 22 Nor does the Father himself judge anyone. He has given his Son the full right to judge, 23 so that all will honor the Son in the same way as they honor the Father. Whoever does not honor the Son does not honor the Father who sent him.

24 "I am telling you the truth: those who hear my words and believe in him who sent me have eternal life. They will not be judged, but have already passed from death to life. 25 I am telling you the truth: the time is coming—the time has already come—when the dead will hear the voice of the Son of God, and those who hear it will come to life. 26 Just as the Father is himself the source of life, in the same way he has made his Son to be the source of life. 27 And he has given the Son the right to judge, because he is the Son of Man. 28 Do not be surprised at this; the time is coming when all the dead will hear his voice 29 and come out of their graves: those who have done good will rise and live, and those who have done evil will rise and be condemned.

Witnesses to Jesus

30 "I can do nothing on my own authority; I judge only as God tells me, so my judgment is right, because I am not trying to do what I want, but only what he who sent me wants.

31 "If I testify on my own behalf, what I say is not to be accepted as real proof. 32 But there is someone else who testifies on my behalf, and I know that what he says about me is true. 33 John is the one to whom you sent your messengers, and he spoke on behalf of the truth. 34 It is not that I must have a human witness; I say this only in order that you may be saved. 35 John was like a lamp, burning and shining, and you were willing for a while to enjoy his light. 36 But I have a witness on my behalf which is even greater than the witness that John gave: what I do, that is, the deeds my Father gave me to do, these speak on my behalf and show that the Father has sent me. 37 And the Father, who sent me, also testifies on my behalf. You have never heard his voice or seen his face, 38 and you do not keep his message in your hearts, for you do not believe in the one whom he sent. 39 You study the Scriptures, because you think that in them you will find eternal life. And these very Scriptures speak about me! 40 Yet you are not willing to come to me in order to have life.

41 "I am not looking for human praise. 42 But I know what kind of people you are, and I know that you have no love for God in your hearts. 43 I have come with my Father's authority, but you have not received me; when, however, someone comes with his own authority, you will receive him. 44 You like to receive praise from one another, but you do not try to win praise from the one who alone is God; how, then, can you believe me? 45 Do not think, however, that I am the one who will accuse you to my Father. Moses, in whom you have put your hope, is the very one who will accuse you. 46 If you had really believed Moses, you would have believed me, because he wrote about me. 47 But since you do not believe what he wrote, how can you believe what I say?"

Jesus Feeds Five Thousand

(Matthew 14.13-21; Mark 6.30-44; Luke 9.10-17)

6 After this, Jesus went across Lake Galilee (or, Lake Tiberias, as it is also called). 2 A large crowd followed him, because they had seen his miracles of healing the sick. 3 Jesus went up a hill and sat down with his disciples. 4 The time for the Passover Festival was near. 5 Jesus looked around and saw that a large crowd was coming to him, so he asked Philip, "Where can we buy enough food to feed all these people?"

J
O
H
N

(6 He said this to test Philip; actually he already knew what he would do.)

7 Philip answered, "For everyone to have even a little, it would take more than two hundred silver coins *k* to buy enough bread."

8 Another one of his disciples, Andrew, who was Simon Peter's brother, said, 9 "There is a boy here who has five loaves of barley bread and two fish. But they will certainly not be enough for all these people."

10 "Make the people sit down," Jesus told them. (There was a lot of grass there.) So all the people sat down; there were about five thousand men. 11 Jesus took the bread, gave thanks to God, and distributed it to the people who were sitting there. He did the same with the fish, and they all had as much as they wanted. 12 When they were all full, he said to his disciples, "Gather the pieces left over; let us not waste a bit." 13 So they gathered them all and filled twelve baskets with the pieces left over from the five barley loaves which the people had eaten.

14 Seeing this miracle that Jesus had performed, the people there said, "Surely this is the Prophet*l* who was to come into the world!" 15 Jesus knew that they were about to come and seize him in order to make him king by force; so he went off again to the hills by himself.

Jesus Walks on the Water
(Matthew 14.22-33; Mark 6.45-52)

16 When evening came, Jesus' disciples went down to the lake, 17 got into a boat, and went back across the lake toward Capernaum. Night came on, and Jesus still had not come to them. 18 By then a strong wind was blowing and stirring up the water. 19 The disciples had rowed about three or four miles when they saw Jesus walking on the water, coming near the boat, and they were terrified. 20 "Don't be afraid," Jesus told them, "it is I!" 21 Then they willingly took him into the boat, and immediately the boat reached land at the place they were heading for.

The People Seek Jesus

22 Next day the crowd which had stayed on the other side of the lake realized that there had been only one boat there. They knew that Jesus had not gone in it with his disciples, but that they had left without him. 23 Other boats, which were from Tiberias, came to shore near the place where the crowd had eaten the bread after the Lord had given thanks. 24 When the crowd saw that Jesus was not there, nor his disciples, they got into those boats and went to Capernaum, looking for him.

Jesus the Bread of Life

25 When the people found Jesus on the other side of the lake, they said to him, "Teacher, when did you get here?"

26 Jesus answered, "I am telling you the truth: you are looking for me because you ate the bread and had all you wanted, not because you understood my miracles. 27 Do not work for food that spoils; instead, work for the food that lasts for eternal life. This is the food which the Son of Man will give you, because God, the Father, has put his mark of approval on him."

28 So they asked him, "What can we do in order to do what God wants us to do?"

29 Jesus answered, "What God wants you to do is to believe in the one he sent."

30 They replied, "What miracle will you perform so that we may see it and believe you? What will you do? 31 Our ancestors ate manna in the desert, just as the scripture says, 'He gave them bread from heaven to eat.' "

32 "I am telling you the truth," Jesus said. "What Moses gave you was not*m* the bread from heaven; it is my Father who gives you the real bread from heaven. 33 For the bread that God gives is he who comes down from heaven and gives life to the world."

34 "Sir," they asked him, "give us this bread always."

35 "I am the bread of life," Jesus told them. "Those who come to me will never be hungry; those who believe in me will never be thirsty. 36 Now, I told you that you have seen me but will not believe. 37 Everyone whom my Father gives me will come to me. I will never turn away anyone who comes to me, 38 because I have come down from heaven to do not

---

k SILVER COINS: *A silver coin was the daily wage of a rural worker (see Mt 20.2).*
l THE PROPHET: *See 1.21.*   *m* What Moses gave you was not; *or* It was not Moses who gave you.

my own will but the will of him who sent me. 39 And it is the will of him who sent me that I should not lose any of all those he has given me, but that I should raise them all to life on the last day. 40 For what my Father wants is that all who see the Son and believe in him should have eternal life. And I will raise them to life on the last day."

41 The people started grumbling about him, because he said, "I am the bread that came down from heaven." 42 So they said, "This man is Jesus son of Joseph, isn't he? We know his father and mother. How, then, does he now say he came down from heaven?"

43 Jesus answered, "Stop grumbling among yourselves. 44 People cannot come to me unless the Father who sent me draws them to me; and I will raise them to life on the last day. 45 The prophets wrote, 'Everyone will be taught by God.' Anyone who hears the Father and learns from him comes to me. 46 This does not mean that anyone has seen the Father; he who is from God is the only one who has seen the Father. 47 I am telling you the truth: he who believes has eternal life. 48 I am the bread of life. 49 Your ancestors ate manna in the desert, but they died. 50 But the bread that comes down from heaven is of such a kind that whoever eats it will not die. 51 I am the living bread that came down from heaven. If you eat this bread, you will live forever. The bread that I will give you is my flesh, which I give so that the world may live."

52 This started an angry argument among them. "How can this man give us his flesh to eat?" they asked.

53 Jesus said to them, "I am telling you the truth: if you do not eat the flesh of the Son of Man and drink his blood, you will not have life in yourselves. 54 Those who eat my flesh and drink my blood have eternal life, and I will raise them to life on the last day. 55 For my flesh is the real food; my blood is the real drink. 56 Those who eat my flesh and drink my blood live in me, and I live in them. 57 The living Father sent me, and because of him I live also. In the same way whoever eats me will live because of me. 58 This, then, is the bread that came down from heaven; it is not like the bread that your ancestors ate, but then

later died. Those who eat this bread will live forever."

59 Jesus said this as he taught in the synagogue in Capernaum.

The Words of Eternal Life

60 Many of his followers heard this and said, "This teaching is too hard. Who can listen to it?"

61 Without being told, Jesus knew that they were grumbling about this, so he said to them, "Does this make you want to give up? 62 Suppose, then, that you should see the Son of Man go back up to the place where he was before? 63 What gives life is God's Spirit; human power is of no use at all. The words I have spoken to you bring God's life-giving Spirit. 64 Yet some of you do not believe." (Jesus knew from the very beginning who were the ones that would not believe and which one would betray him.) 65 And he added, "This is the very reason I told you that no people can come to me unless the Father makes it possible for them to do so."

66 Because of this, many of Jesus' followers turned back and would not go with him any more. 67 So he asked the twelve disciples, "And you—would you also like to leave?"

68 Simon Peter answered him, "Lord, to whom would we go? You have the words that give eternal life. 69 And now we believe and know that you are the Holy One who has come from God."

70 Jesus replied, "I chose the twelve of you, didn't I? Yet one of you is a devil!" 71 He was talking about Judas, the son of Simon Iscariot. For Judas, even though he was one of the twelve disciples, was going to betray him.

Jesus and His Brothers

7 After this, Jesus traveled in Galilee; he did not want to travel in Judea, because the Jewish authorities there were wanting to kill him. 2 The time for the Festival of Shelters was near, 3 so Jesus' brothers said to him, "Leave this place and go to Judea, so that your followers will see the things that you are doing. 4 People don't hide what they are doing if they want to be well known. Since you are doing these things, let the whole world know about you!" (5 Not even his brothers believed in him.)

6 Jesus said to them, "The right time

for me has not yet come. Any time is right for you. [7] The world cannot hate you, but it hates me, because I keep telling it that its ways are bad. [8] You go on to the festival. I am not going[n] to this festival, because the right time has not come for me." [9] He said this and then stayed on in Galilee.

Jesus at the Festival of Shelters

[10] After his brothers had gone to the festival, Jesus also went; however, he did not go openly, but secretly. [11] The Jewish authorities were looking for him at the festival. "Where is he?" they asked.

[12] There was much whispering about him in the crowd. "He is a good man," some people said. "No," others said, "he fools the people." [13] But no one talked about him openly, because they were afraid of the Jewish authorities.

[14] The festival was nearly half over when Jesus went to the Temple and began teaching. [15] The Jewish authorities were greatly surprised and said, "How does this man know so much when he has never been to school?"

[16] Jesus answered, "What I teach is not my own teaching, but it comes from God, who sent me. [17] Whoever is willing to do what God wants will know whether what I teach comes from God or whether I speak on my own authority. [18] Those who speak on their own authority are trying to gain glory for themselves. But he who wants glory for the one who sent him is honest, and there is nothing false in him. [19] Moses gave you the Law, didn't he? But not one of you obeys the Law. Why are you trying to kill me?"

[20] "You have a demon in you!" the crowd answered. "Who is trying to kill you?"

[21] Jesus answered, "I performed one miracle, and you were all surprised. [22] Moses ordered you to circumcise your sons (although it was not Moses but your ancestors who started it), and so you circumcise a boy on the Sabbath. [23] If a boy is circumcised on the Sabbath so that Moses' Law is not broken, why are you angry with me because I made a man completely well on the Sabbath?

[24] Stop judging by external standards, and judge by true standards."

Is He the Messiah?

[25] Some of the people of Jerusalem said, "Isn't this the man the authorities are trying to kill? [26] Look! He is talking in public, and they say nothing against him! Can it be that they really know that he is the Messiah? [27] But when the Messiah comes, no one will know where he is from. And we all know where this man comes from."

[28] As Jesus taught in the Temple, he said in a loud voice, "Do you really know me and know where I am from? I have not come on my own authority. He who sent me, however, is truthful. You do not know him, [29] but I know him, because I come from him and he sent me."

[30] Then they tried to seize him, but no one laid a hand on him, because his hour had not yet come. [31] But many in the crowd believed in him and said, "When the Messiah comes, will he perform more miracles than this man has?"

Guards Are Sent to Arrest Jesus

[32] The Pharisees heard the crowd whispering these things about Jesus, so they and the chief priests sent some guards to arrest him. [33] Jesus said, "I shall be with you a little while longer, and then I shall go away to him who sent me. [34] You will look for me, but you will not find me, because you cannot go where I will be."

[35] The Jewish authorities said among themselves, "Where is he about to go so that we shall not find him? Will he go to the Greek cities where our people live, and teach the Greeks? [36] He says that we will look for him but will not find him, and that we cannot go where he will be. What does he mean?"

Streams of Life-Giving Water

[37] On the last and most important day of the festival Jesus stood up and said in a loud voice, "Whoever is thirsty should come to me, and [38] whoever believes in me should drink. As the scripture says, 'Streams of life-giving water will pour out from his side.' "[o] [39] Jesus said this about the Spirit, which those who be-

---

[n] *I am not going; some manuscripts have* I am not yet going.   [o] *Jesus' words in verses 37-38 may be translated:* "Whoever is thirsty should come to me and drink. [38] As the scripture says, 'Streams of life-giving water will pour out from within anyone who believes in me.' "

lieved in him were going to receive. At that time the Spirit had not yet been given, because Jesus had not been raised to glory.

Division among the People

40 Some of the people in the crowd heard him say this and said, "This man is really the Prophet!"*p*

41 Others said, "He is the Messiah!"

But others said, "The Messiah will not come from Galilee! 42 The scripture says that the Messiah will be a descendant of King David and will be born in Bethlehem, the town where David lived." 43 So there was a division in the crowd because of Jesus. 44 Some wanted to seize him, but no one laid a hand on him.

The Unbelief of the Jewish Authorities

45 When the guards went back, the chief priests and Pharisees asked them, "Why did you not bring him?"

46 The guards answered, "Nobody has ever talked the way this man does!"

47 "Did he fool you, too?" the Pharisees asked them. 48 "Have you ever known one of the authorities or one Pharisee to believe in him? 49 This crowd does not know the Law of Moses, so they are under God's curse!"

50 One of the Pharisees there was Nicodemus, the man who had gone to see Jesus before. He said to the others, 51 "According to our Law we cannot condemn people before hearing them and finding out what they have done."

52 "Well," they answered, "are you also from Galilee? Study the Scriptures and you will learn that no prophet ever comes *q* from Galilee."

The Woman Caught in Adultery

8 [Then everyone went home, but Jesus went to the Mount of Olives. 2 Early the next morning he went back to the Temple. All the people gathered around him, and he sat down and began to teach them. 3 The teachers of the Law and the Pharisees brought in a woman who had been caught committing adultery, and they made her stand before them all. 4 "Teacher," they said to Jesus, "this woman was caught in the very act

of committing adultery. 5 In our Law Moses commanded that such a woman must be stoned to death. Now, what do you say?" 6 They said this to trap Jesus, so that they could accuse him. But he bent over and wrote on the ground with his finger. 7 As they stood there asking him questions, he straightened up and said to them, "Whichever one of you has committed no sin may throw the first stone at her." 8 Then he bent over again and wrote on the ground. 9 When they heard this, they all left, one by one, the older ones first. Jesus was left alone, with the woman still standing there. 10 He straightened up and said to her, "Where are they? Is there no one left to condemn you?"

11 "No one, sir," she answered.

"Well, then," Jesus said, "I do not condemn you either. Go, but do not sin again."]*r*

Jesus the Light of the World

12 Jesus spoke to the Pharisees again. "I am the light of the world," he said. "Whoever follows me will have the light of life and will never walk in darkness."

13 The Pharisees said to him, "Now you are testifying on your own behalf; what you say proves nothing."

14 "No," Jesus answered, "even though I do testify on my own behalf, what I say is true, because I know where I came from and where I am going. You do not know where I came from or where I am going. 15 You make judgments in a purely human way; I pass judgment on no one. 16 But if I were to do so, my judgment would be true, because I am not alone in this; the Father who sent me is with me. 17 It is written in your Law that when two witnesses agree, what they say is true. 18 I testify on my own behalf, and the Father who sent me also testifies on my behalf."

19 "Where is your father?" they asked him.

"You know neither me nor my Father," Jesus answered. "If you knew me, you would know my Father also."

20 Jesus said all this as he taught in the Temple, in the room where the offering boxes were placed. And no one arrested him, because his hour had not come.

You Cannot Go Where I Am Going

21 Again Jesus said to them, "I will go away; you will look for me, but you will die in your sins. You cannot go where I am going."

22 So the Jewish authorities said, "He says that we cannot go where he is going. Does this mean that he will kill himself?"

23 Jesus answered, "You belong to this world here below, but I come from above. You are from this world, but I am not from this world. 24 That is why I told you that you will die in your sins. And you will die in your sins if you do not believe that 'I Am Who I Am'."

25 "Who are you?" they asked him.

Jesus answered, "What I have told you from the very beginning.s 26 I have much to say about you, much to condemn you for. The one who sent me, however, is truthful, and I tell the world only what I have heard from him."

27 They did not understand that Jesus was talking to them about the Father. 28 So he said to them, "When you lift up the Son of Man, you will know that 'I Am Who I Am'; then you will know that I do nothing on my own authority, but I say only what the Father has instructed me to say. 29 And he who sent me is with me; he has not left me alone, because I always do what pleases him."

30 Many who heard Jesus say these things believed in him.

The Truth Will Set You Free

31 So Jesus said to those who believed in him, "If you obey my teaching, you are really my disciples; 32 you will know the truth, and the truth will set you free."

33 "We are the descendants of Abraham," they answered, "and we have never been anybody's slaves. What do you mean, then, by saying, 'You will be free'?"

34 Jesus said to them, "I am telling you the truth: everyone who sins is a slave of sin. 35 A slave does not belong to a family permanently, but a son belongs there forever. 36 If the Son sets you free, then you will be really free. 37 I know you are Abraham's descendants. Yet you are trying to kill me, because you will not accept my teaching. 38 I talk about what my Father has shown me, but you do what your father has told you."

39 They answered him, "Our father is Abraham."

"If you really were Abraham's children," Jesus replied, "you would dot the same things that he did. 40 All I have ever done is to tell you the truth I heard from God, yet you are trying to kill me. Abraham did nothing like this! 41 You are doing what your father did."

"God himself is the only Father we have," they answered, "and we are his true children."

42 Jesus said to them, "If God really were your Father, you would love me, because I came from God and now I am here. I did not come on my own authority, but he sent me. 43 Why do you not understand what I say? It is because you cannot bear to listen to my message. 44 You are the children of your father, the Devil, and you want to follow your father's desires. From the very beginning he was a murderer and has never been on the side of truth, because there is no truth in him. When he tells a lie, he is only doing what is natural to him, because he is a liar and the father of all lies. 45 But I tell the truth, and that is why you do not believe me. 46 Which one of you can prove that I am guilty of sin? If I tell the truth, then why do you not believe me? 47 He who comes from God listens to God's words. You, however, are not from God, and that is why you will not listen."

Jesus and Abraham

48 They asked Jesus, "Were we not right in saying that you are a Samaritan and have a demon in you?"

49 "I have no demon," Jesus answered. "I honor my Father, but you dishonor me. 50 I am not seeking honor for myself. But there is one who is seeking it and who judges in my favor. 51 I am telling you the truth: whoever obeys my teaching will never die."

52 They said to him, "Now we know for sure that you have a demon! Abraham died, and the prophets died, yet you say that whoever obeys your teaching will never die. 53 Our father Abraham died; you do not claim to be greater than

---

s What I have told you from the very beginning; *or* Why should I speak to you at all?
t If you really were . . . you would do; *some manuscripts have* If you are . . . do.

Abraham, do you? And the prophets also died. Who do you think you are?"

54 Jesus answered, "If I were to honor myself, that honor would be worth nothing. The one who honors me is my Father—the very one you say is your God. 55 You have never known him, but I know him. If I were to say that I do not know him, I would be a liar like you. But I do know him, and I obey his word. 56 Your father Abraham rejoiced that he was to see the time of my coming; he saw it and was glad."

57 They said to him, "You are not even fifty years old—and you have seen Abraham?"[u]

58 "I am telling you the truth," Jesus replied. "Before Abraham was born, 'I Am'."

59 Then they picked up stones to throw at him, but Jesus hid himself and left the Temple.

Jesus Heals a Man Born Blind

9 As Jesus was walking along, he saw a man who had been born blind. 2 His disciples asked him, "Teacher, whose sin caused him to be born blind? Was it his own or his parents' sin?"

3 Jesus answered, "His blindness has nothing to do with his sins or his parents' sins. He is blind so that God's power might be seen at work in him. 4 As long as it is day, we must do the work of him who sent me; night is coming when no one can work. 5 While I am in the world, I am the light for the world."

6 After he said this, Jesus spat on the ground and made some mud with the spittle; he rubbed the mud on the man's eyes 7 and told him, "Go and wash your face in the Pool of Siloam." (This name means "Sent.") So the man went, washed his face, and came back seeing.

8 His neighbors, then, and the people who had seen him begging before this, asked, "Isn't this the man who used to sit and beg?"

9 Some said, "He is the one," but others said, "No he isn't; he just looks like him."

So the man himself said, "I am the man."

10 "How is it that you can now see?" they asked him.

11 He answered, "The man called Jesus made some mud, rubbed it on my eyes, and told me to go to Siloam and wash my face. So I went, and as soon as I washed, I could see."

12 "Where is he?" they asked.

"I don't know," he answered.

The Pharisees Investigate the Healing

13 Then they took to the Pharisees the man who had been blind. 14 The day that Jesus made the mud and cured him of his blindness was a Sabbath. 15 The Pharisees, then, asked the man again how he had received his sight. He told them, "He put some mud on my eyes; I washed my face, and now I can see."

16 Some of the Pharisees said, "The man who did this cannot be from God, for he does not obey the Sabbath law."

Others, however, said, "How could a man who is a sinner perform such miracles as these?" And there was a division among them.

17 So the Pharisees asked the man once more, "You say he cured you of your blindness—well, what do you say about him?"

"He is a prophet," the man answered.

18 The Jewish authorities, however, were not willing to believe that he had been blind and could now see, until they called his parents 19 and asked them, "Is this your son? You say that he was born blind; how is it, then, that he can now see?"

20 His parents answered, "We know that he is our son, and we know that he was born blind. 21 But we do not know how it is that he is now able to see, nor do we know who cured him of his blindness. Ask him; he is old enough, and he can answer for himself!" 22 His parents said this because they were afraid of the Jewish authorities, who had already agreed that anyone who said he believed that Jesus was the Messiah would be expelled from the synagogue. 23 That is why his parents said, "He is old enough; ask him!"

24 A second time they called back the man who had been born blind, and said to him, "Promise before God that you

_____

u you have seen Abraham?; *some manuscripts have* has Abraham seen you?

will tell the truth! We know that this man who cured you is a sinner."

25 "I do not know if he is a sinner or not," the man replied. "One thing I do know: I was blind, and now I see."

26 "What did he do to you?" they asked. "How did he cure you of your blindness?"

27 "I have already told you," he answered, "and you would not listen. Why do you want to hear it again? Maybe you, too, would like to be his disciples?"

28 They insulted him and said, "You are that fellow's disciple; but we are Moses' disciples. 29 We know that God spoke to Moses; as for that fellow, however, we do not even know where he comes from!"

30 The man answered, "What a strange thing that is! You do not know where he comes from, but he cured me of my blindness! 31 We know that God does not listen to sinners; he does listen to people who respect him and do what he wants them to do. 32 Since the beginning of the world nobody has ever heard of anyone giving sight to a person born blind. 33 Unless this man came from God, he would not be able to do a thing."

34 They answered, "You were born and brought up in sin—and you are trying to teach us?" And they expelled him from the synagogue.

Spiritual Blindness

35 When Jesus heard what had happened, he found the man and asked him, "Do you believe in the Son of Man?"

36 The man answered, "Tell me who he is, sir, so that I can believe in him!"

37 Jesus said to him, "You have already seen him, and he is the one who is talking with you now."

38 "I believe, Lord!" the man said, and knelt down before Jesus.

39 Jesus said, "I came to this world to judge, so that the blind should see and those who see should become blind."

40 Some Pharisees who were there with him heard him say this and asked him, "Surely you don't mean that we are blind, too?"

41 Jesus answered, "If you were blind, then you would not be guilty; but since you claim that you can see, this means that you are still guilty."

The Parable of the Shepherd

10 Jesus said, "I am telling you the truth: the man who does not enter the sheep pen by the gate, but climbs in some other way, is a thief and a robber. 2 The man who goes in through the gate is the shepherd of the sheep. 3 The gatekeeper opens the gate for him; the sheep hear his voice as he calls his own sheep by name, and he leads them out. 4 When he has brought them out, he goes ahead of them, and the sheep follow him, because they know his voice. 5 They will not follow someone else; instead, they will run away from such a person, because they do not know his voice."

6 Jesus told them this parable, but they did not understand what he meant.

Jesus the Good Shepherd

7 So Jesus said again, "I am telling you the truth: I am the gate for the sheep. 8 All others who came before me are thieves and robbers, but the sheep did not listen to them. 9 I am the gate. Those who come in by me will be saved; they will come in and go out and find pasture. 10 The thief comes only in order to steal, kill, and destroy. I have come in order that you might have life—life in all its fullness.

11 "I am the good shepherd, who is willing to die for the sheep. 12 When the hired man, who is not a shepherd and does not own the sheep, sees a wolf coming, he leaves the sheep and runs away; so the wolf snatches the sheep and scatters them. 13 The hired man runs away because he is only a hired man and does not care about the sheep. 14-15 I am the good shepherd. As the Father knows me and I know the Father, in the same way I know my sheep and they know me. And I am willing to die for them. 16 There are other sheep which belong to me that are not in this sheep pen. I must bring them, too; they will listen to my voice, and they will become*v* one flock with one shepherd.

17 "The Father loves me because I am willing to give up my life, in order that I may receive it back again. 18 No one takes my life away from me. I give it up of my own free will. I have the right to give it up, and I have the right to take it

---

v they will become; *some manuscripts have* there will be.

back. This is what my Father has commanded me to do."

19 Again there was a division among the people because of these words. 20 Many of them were saying, "He has a demon! He is crazy! Why do you listen to him?"

21 But others were saying, "A man with a demon could not talk like this! How could a demon give sight to blind people?"

Jesus Is Rejected

22 It was winter, and the Festival of the Dedication of the Temple was being celebrated in Jerusalem. 23 Jesus was walking in Solomon's Porch in the Temple, 24 when the people gathered around him and asked, "How long are you going to keep us in suspense? Tell us the plain truth: are you the Messiah?"

25 Jesus answered, "I have already told you, but you would not believe me. The deeds I do by my Father's authority speak on my behalf; 26 but you will not believe, for you are not my sheep. 27 My sheep listen to my voice; I know them, and they follow me. 28 I give them eternal life, and they shall never die. No one can snatch them away from me. 29 What my Father has given me is greaterᵂ than everything, and no one can snatch them away from the Father's care. 30 The Father and I are one."

31 Then the people again picked up stones to throw at him. 32 Jesus said to them, "I have done many good deeds in your presence which the Father gave me to do; for which one of these do you want to stone me?"

33 They answered, "We do not want to stone you because of any good deeds, but because of your blasphemy! You are only a man, but you are trying to make yourself God!"

34 Jesus answered, "It is written in your own Law that God said, 'You are gods.' 35 We know that what the scripture says is true forever; and God called those people gods, the people to whom his message was given. 36 As for me, the Father chose me and sent me into the world. How, then, can you say that I blaspheme because I said that I am the Son of God? 37 Do not believe me, then, if

I am not doing the things my Father wants me to do. 38 But if I do them, even though you do not believe me, you should at least believe my deeds, in order that you may know once and for all that the Father is in me and that I am in the Father."

39 Once more they tried to seize Jesus, but he slipped out of their hands.

40 Jesus then went back again across the Jordan River to the place where John had been baptizing, and he stayed there. 41 Many people came to him. "John performed no miracles," they said, "but everything he said about this man was true." 42 And many people there believed in him.

The Death of Lazarus

11 A man named Lazarus, who lived in Bethany, became sick. Bethany was the town where Mary and her sister Martha lived. (2 This Mary was the one who poured the perfume on the Lord's feet and wiped them with her hair; it was her brother Lazarus who was sick.) 3 The sisters sent Jesus a message: "Lord, your dear friend is sick."

4 When Jesus heard it, he said, "The final result of this sickness will not be the death of Lazarus; this has happened in order to bring glory to God, and it will be the means by which the Son of God will receive glory."

5 Jesus loved Martha and her sister and Lazarus. 6 Yet when he received the news that Lazarus was sick, he stayed where he was for two more days. 7 Then he said to the disciples, "Let us go back to Judea."

8 "Teacher," the disciples answered, "just a short time ago the people there wanted to stone you; and are you planning to go back?"

9 Jesus said, "A day has twelve hours, doesn't it? So those who walk in broad daylight do not stumble, for they see the light of this world. 10 But if they walk during the night they stumble, because they have no light." 11 Jesus said this and then added, "Our friend Lazarus has fallen asleep, but I will go and wake him up."

12 The disciples answered, "If he is asleep, Lord, he will get well."

ᵂ What my Father has given me is greater; *some manuscripts have* My Father, who gave them to me, is greater.

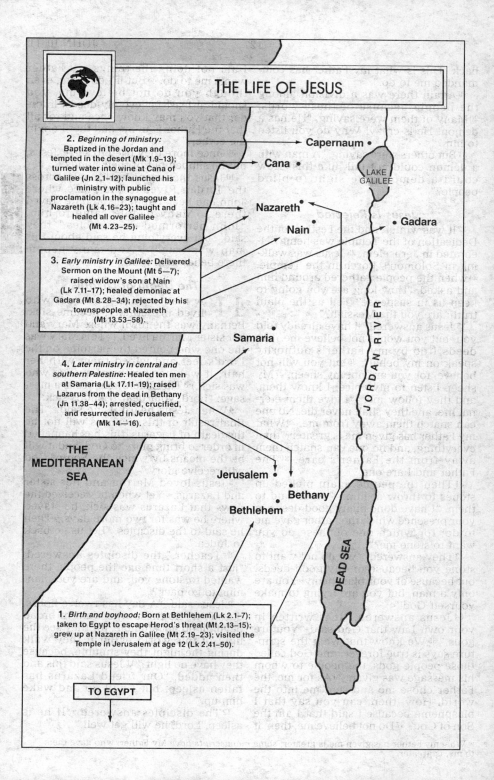

THE LIFE OF JESUS

2. *Beginning of ministry:* Baptized in the Jordan and tempted in the desert (Mk 1.9–13); turned water into wine at Cana of Galilee (Jn 2.1–12); launched his ministry with public proclamation in the synagogue at Nazareth (Lk 4.16–23); taught and healed all over Galilee (Mt 4.23–25).

3. *Early ministry in Galilee:* Delivered Sermon on the Mount (Mt 5–7); raised widow's son at Nain (Lk 7.11–17); healed demoniac at Gadara (Mt 8.28–34); rejected by his townspeople at Nazareth (Mt 13.53–58).

4. *Later ministry in central and southern Palestine:* Healed ten men at Samaria (Lk 17.11–19); raised Lazarus from the dead in Bethany (Jn 11.38–44); arrested, crucified, and resurrected in Jerusalem (Mk 14—16).

1. *Birth and boyhood:* Born at Bethlehem (Lk 2.1–7); taken to Egypt to escape Herod's threat (Mt 2.13–15); grew up at Nazareth in Galilee (Mt 2.19–23); visited the Temple in Jerusalem at age 12 (Lk 2.41–50).

Capernaum •

Cana •

LAKE GALILEE

Nazareth •

Nain •

• Gadara

JORDAN RIVER

Samaria •

THE MEDITERRANEAN SEA

Jerusalem •

• Bethany

Bethlehem •

DEAD SEA

TO EGYPT

13 Jesus meant that Lazarus had died, but they thought he meant natural sleep. 14 So Jesus told them plainly, "Lazarus is dead. 15 but for your sake I am glad that I was not with him, so that you will believe. Let us go to him."

16 Thomas (called the Twin) said to his fellow disciples, "Let us all go along with the Teacher, so that we may die with him!"

Jesus the Resurrection and the Life

17 When Jesus arrived, he found that Lazarus had been buried four days before. 18 Bethany was less than two miles from Jerusalem, 19 and many Judeans had come to see Martha and Mary to comfort them about their brother's death.

20 When Martha heard that Jesus was coming, she went out to meet him, but Mary stayed in the house. 21 Martha said to Jesus, "If you had been here, Lord, my brother would not have died! 22 But I know that even now God will give you whatever you ask him for."

23 "Your brother will rise to life," Jesus told her.

24 "I know," she replied, "that he will rise to life on the last day."

25 Jesus said to her, "I am the resurrection and the life. Those who believe in me will live, even though they die; 26 and those who live and believe in me will never die. Do you believe this?"

27 "Yes, Lord!" she answered. "I do believe that you are the Messiah, the Son of God, who was to come into the world."

Jesus Weeps

28 After Martha said this, she went back and called her sister Mary privately. "The Teacher is here," she told her, "and is asking for you." 29 When Mary heard this, she got up and hurried out to meet him. (30 Jesus had not yet arrived in the village, but was still in the place where Martha had met him.) 31 The people who were in the house with Mary comforting her followed her when they saw her get up and hurry out. They thought that she was going to the grave to weep there.

32 Mary arrived where Jesus was, and as soon as she saw him, she fell at his feet. "Lord," she said, "if you had been here, my brother would not have died!"

33 Jesus saw her weeping, and he saw how the people with her were weeping also; his heart was touched, and he was deeply moved. 34 "Where have you buried him?" he asked them.

"Come and see, Lord," they answered. 35 Jesus wept. 36 "See how much he loved him!" the people said.

37 But some of them said, "He gave sight to the blind man, didn't he? Could he not have kept Lazarus from dying?"

Lazarus Is Brought to Life

38 Deeply moved once more, Jesus went to the tomb, which was a cave with a stone placed at the entrance. 39 "Take the stone away!" Jesus ordered.

Martha, the dead man's sister, answered, "There will be a bad smell, Lord. He has been buried four days!"

40 Jesus said to her, "Didn't I tell you that you would see God's glory if you believed?" 41 They took the stone away. Jesus looked up and said, "I thank you, Father, that you listen to me. 42 I know that you always listen to me, but I say this for the sake of the people here, so that they will believe that you sent me."

43 After he had said this, he called out in a loud voice, "Lazarus, come out!" 44 He came out, his hands and feet wrapped in grave cloths, and with a cloth around his face. "Untie him," Jesus told them, "and let him go."

The Plot against Jesus

(Matthew 26.1-5; Mark 14.1, 2; Luke 22.1, 2)

45 Many of the people who had come to visit Mary saw what Jesus did, and they believed in him. 46 But some of them returned to the Pharisees and told them what Jesus had done. 47 So the Pharisees and the chief priests met with the Council and said, "What shall we do? Look at all the miracles this man is performing! 48 If we let him go on in this way, everyone will believe in him, and the Roman authorities will take action and destroy our Temple and our nation!"

49 One of them, named Caiaphas, who was High Priest that year, said, "What fools you are! 50 Don't you realize that it is better for you to have one man die for the people, instead of having the whole nation destroyed?" 51 Actually, he did not say this of his own accord; rather, as he was High Priest that year, he was prophesying that Jesus was going to die

for the Jewish people, 52and not only for them, but also to bring together into one body all the scattered people of God.

53From that day on the Jewish authorities made plans to kill Jesus. 54So Jesus did not travel openly in Judea, but left and went to a place near the desert, to a town named Ephraim, where he stayed with the disciples.

55The time for the Passover Festival was near, and many people went up from the country to Jerusalem to perform the ritual of purification before the festival. 56They were looking for Jesus, and as they gathered in the Temple, they asked one another, "What do you think? Surely he will not come to the festival, will he?" 57The chief priests and the Pharisees had given orders that if anyone knew where Jesus was, he must report it, so that they could arrest him.

Jesus Is Anointed at Bethany
(Matthew 26.6-13; Mark 14.3-9)

12 Six days before the Passover, Jesus went to Bethany, the home of Lazarus, the man he had raised from death. 2They prepared a dinner for him there, which Martha helped serve; Lazarus was one of those who were sitting at the table with Jesus. 3Then Mary took a whole pint of a very expensive perfume made of pure nard, poured it on Jesus' feet, and wiped them with her hair. The sweet smell of the perfume filled the whole house. 4One of Jesus' disciples, Judas Iscariot—the one who was going to betray him—said, 5"Why wasn't this perfume sold for three hundred silver coinsˣ and the money given to the poor?" 6He said this, not because he cared about the poor, but because he was a thief. He carried the money bag and would help himself from it.

7But Jesus said, "Leave her alone! Let her keep what she has for the day of my burial. 8You will always have poor people with you, but you will not always have me."

The Plot against Lazarus
9A large number of people heard that Jesus was in Bethany, so they went there, not only because of Jesus but also to see Lazarus, whom Jesus had raised from death. 10So the chief priests made plans to kill Lazarus too, 11because on his account many Jews were rejecting them and believing in Jesus.

The Triumphant Entry into Jerusalem
(Matthew 21.1-11; Mark 11.1-11; Luke 19.28-40)

12The next day the large crowd that had come to the Passover Festival heard that Jesus was coming to Jerusalem. 13So they took branches of palm trees and went out to meet him, shouting, "Praise God! God bless him who comes in the name of the Lord! God bless the King of Israel!"

14Jesus found a donkey and rode on it, just as the scripture says,
15"Do not be afraid, city of Zion!
   Here comes your king,
      riding on a young donkey."
16His disciples did not understand this at the time; but when Jesus had been raised to glory, they remembered that the scripture said this about him and that they had done this for him.

17The people who had been with Jesus when he called Lazarus out of the grave and raised him from death had reported what had happened. 18That was why the crowd met him—because they heard that he had performed this miracle. 19The Pharisees then said to one another, "You see, we are not succeeding at all! Look, the whole world is following him!"

Some Greeks Seek Jesus
20Some Greeks were among those who had gone to Jerusalem to worship during the festival. 21They went to Philip (he was from Bethsaida in Galilee) and said, "Sir, we want to see Jesus." 22Philip went and told Andrew, and the two of them went and told Jesus. 23Jesus answered them, "The hour has now come for the Son of Man to receive great glory. 24I am telling you the truth: a grain of wheat remains no more than a single grain unless it is dropped into the ground and dies. If it does die, then it produces many grains. 25Those who love their own life will lose it; those who hate their own life in this world will keep it for life eternal. 26Whoever wants to serve me must follow me, so that my servant will be with me where I am. And

ˣ SILVER COINS: *See 6.7.*

my Father will honor anyone who serves me.

Jesus Speaks about His Death

27 "Now my heart is troubled — and what shall I say? Shall I say, 'Father, do not let this hour come upon me'? But that is why I came — so that I might go through this hour of suffering. 28 Father, bring glory to your name!"

Then a voice spoke from heaven, "I have brought glory to it, and I will do so again."

29 The crowd standing there heard the voice, and some of them said it was thunder, while others said, "An angel spoke to him!"

30 But Jesus said to them, "It was not for my sake that this voice spoke, but for yours. 31 Now is the time for this world to be judged; now the ruler of this world will be overthrown. 32 When I am lifted up from the earth, I will draw everyone to me." (33 In saying this he indicated the kind of death he was going to suffer.)

34 The crowd answered, "Our Law tells us that the Messiah will live forever. How, then, can you say that the Son of Man must be lifted up? Who is this Son of Man?"

35 Jesus answered, "The light will be among you a little longer. Continue on your way while you have the light, so that the darkness will not come upon you; for the one who walks in the dark does not know where he is going. 36 Believe in the light, then, while you have it, so that you will be the people of the light."

The Unbelief of the People

After Jesus said this, he went off and hid himself from them. 37 Even though he had performed all these miracles in their presence, they did not believe in him, 38 so that what the prophet Isaiah had said might come true:

"Lord, who believed the message
    we told?
  To whom did the Lord reveal his
    power?"

39 And so they were not able to believe, because Isaiah also said,

40 "God has blinded their eyes
  and closed their minds,
  so that their eyes would not see,

and their minds would not
    understand,
  and they would not turn to me,
    says God,
  for me to heal them."

41 Isaiah said this because he saw Jesus' glory and spoke about him.

42 Even then, many Jewish authorities believed in Jesus; but because of the Pharisees they did not talk about it openly, so as not to be expelled from the synagogue. 43 They loved human approval rather than the approval of God.

Judgment by Jesus' Words

44 Jesus said in a loud voice, "Whoever believes in me believes not only in me but also in him who sent me. 45 Whoever sees me sees also him who sent me. 46 I have come into the world as light, so that everyone who believes in me should not remain in the darkness. 47 If people hear my message and do not obey it, I will not judge them. I came, not to judge the world, but to save it. 48 Those who reject me and do not accept my message have one who will judge them. The words I have spoken will be their judge on the last day! 49 This is true, because I have not spoken on my own authority, but the Father who sent me has commanded me what I must say and speak. 50 And I know that his command brings eternal life. What I say, then, is what the Father has told me to say."

Jesus Washes His Disciples' Feet

13 It was now the day before the Passover Festival. Jesus knew that the hour had come for him to leave this world and go to the Father. He had always loved those in the world who were his own, and he loved them to the very end.

2 Jesus and his disciples were at supper. The Devil had already put into the heart of Judas, the son of Simon Iscariot, the thought of betraying Jesus.y 3 Jesus knew that the Father had given him complete power; he knew that he had come from God and was going to God. 4 So he rose from the table, took off his outer garment, and tied a towel around his waist. 5 Then he poured some water into a washbasin and began to wash the disciples' feet and dry them with the

y The Devil . . . betraying Jesus; or The Devil had already decided that Judas, the son of Simon Iscariot, would betray Jesus.

towel around his waist. 6 He came to Simon Peter, who said to him, "Are you going to wash my feet, Lord?"

7 Jesus answered him, "You do not understand now what I am doing, but you will understand later."

8 Peter declared, "Never at any time will you wash my feet!"

"If I do not wash your feet," Jesus answered, "you will no longer be my disciple."

9 Simon Peter answered, "Lord, do not wash only my feet, then! Wash my hands and head, too!"

10 Jesus said, "Those who have taken a bath are completely clean and do not have to wash themselves, except for their feet.ᶻ All of you are clean—all except one." (11 Jesus already knew who was going to betray him; that is why he said, "All of you, except one, are clean.")

12 After Jesus had washed their feet, he put his outer garment back on and returned to his place at the table. "Do you understand what I have just done to you?" he asked. 13 "You call me Teacher and Lord, and it is right that you do so, because that is what I am. 14 I, your Lord and Teacher, have just washed your feet. You, then, should wash one another's feet. 15 I have set an example for you, so that you will do just what I have done for you. 16 I am telling you the truth: no slaves are greater than their master, and no messengers are greater than the one who sent them. 17 Now that you know this truth, how happy you will be if you put it into practice!

18 "I am not talking about all of you; I know those I have chosen. But the scripture must come true that says, 'The man who shared my food turned against me.' 19 I tell you this now before it happens, so that when it does happen, you will believe that 'I Am Who I Am.' 20 I am telling you the truth: whoever receives anyone I send receives me also; and whoever receives me receives him who sent me."

Jesus Predicts His Betrayal

(Matthew 26.20-25; Mark 14.17-21; Luke 22.21-23)

21 After Jesus had said this, he was deeply troubled and declared openly, "I am telling you the truth: one of you is going to betray me."

22 The disciples looked at one another, completely puzzled about whom he meant. 23 One of the disciples, the one whom Jesus loved, was sitting next to Jesus. 24 Simon Peter motioned to him and said, "Ask him whom he is talking about."

25 So that disciple moved closer to Jesus' side and asked, "Who is it, Lord?"

26 Jesus answered, "I will dip some bread in the sauce and give it to him; he is the man." So he took a piece of bread, dipped it, and gave it to Judas, the son of Simon Iscariot. 27 As soon as Judas took the bread, Satan entered into him. Jesus said to him, "Hurry and do what you must!" 28 None of the others at the table understood why Jesus said this to him. 29 Since Judas was in charge of the money bag, some of the disciples thought that Jesus had told him to go and buy what they needed for the festival, or to give something to the poor.

30 Judas accepted the bread and went out at once. It was night.

The New Commandment

31 After Judas had left, Jesus said, "Now the Son of Man's glory is revealed; now God's glory is revealed through him. 32 And if God's glory is revealed through him, then God will reveal the glory of the Son of Man in himself, and he will do so at once. 33 My children, I shall not be with you very much longer. You will look for me; but I tell you now what I told the Jewish authorities, 'You cannot go where I am going.' 34 And now I give you a new commandment: love one another. As I have loved you, so you must love one another. 35 If you have love for one another, then everyone will know that you are my disciples."

Jesus Predicts Peter's Denial

(Matthew 26.31-35; Mark 14.27-31; Luke 22.31-34)

36 "Where are you going, Lord?" Simon Peter asked him.

"You cannot follow me now where I am going," answered Jesus; "but later you will follow me."

37 "Lord, why can't I follow you now?" asked Peter. "I am ready to die for you!"

38 Jesus answered, "Are you really ready to die for me? I am telling you the truth: before the rooster crows you

---

ᶻ *Some manuscripts do not have* except for their feet.

will say three times that you do not
know me.

Jesus the Way to the Father

14 "Do not be worried and upset,"
Jesus told them. "Believe[a] in
God and believe also in me. 2 There are
many rooms in my Father's house, and I
am going to prepare a place for you. I
would not tell you this if it were not so.[b]
3 And after I go and prepare a place for
you, I will come back and take you to
myself, so that you will be where I am.
4 You know the way that leads to the
place where I am going."

5 Thomas said to him, "Lord, we do not
know where you are going; so how can
we know the way to get there?"

6 Jesus answered him, "I am the way,
the truth, and the life; no one goes to the
Father except by me. 7 Now that you
have known me," he said to them, "you
will know[c] my Father also, and from
now on you do know him and you have
seen him."

8 Philip said to him, "Lord, show us the
Father; that is all we need."

9 Jesus answered, "For a long time I
have been with you all; yet you do not
know me, Philip? Whoever has seen me
has seen the Father. Why, then, do you
say, 'Show us the Father'? 10 Do you not
believe, Philip, that I am in the Father
and the Father is in me? The words that
I have spoken to you," Jesus said to his
disciples, "do not come from me. The
Father, who remains in me, does his own
work. 11 Believe me when I say that I am
in the Father and the Father is in me. If
not, believe because of the things I do.
12 I am telling you the truth: those who
believe in me will do what I do — yes,
they will do even greater things, because
I am going to the Father. 13 And I will do
whatever you ask for in my name, so
that the Father's glory will be shown
through the Son. 14 If you ask me[d] for
anything in my name, I will do it.

The Promise of the Holy Spirit

15 "If you love me, you will obey my
commandments. 16 I will ask the Father,
and he will give you another Helper,
who will stay with you forever. 17 He is
the Spirit, who reveals the truth about
God. The world cannot receive him, because it cannot see him or know him.
But you know him, because he remains
with you and is[e] in you.

18 "When I go, you will not be left all
alone; I will come back to you. 19 In a
little while the world will see me no
more, but you will see me; and because
I live, you also will live. 20 When that day
comes, you will know that I am in my
Father and that you are in me, just as I
am in you.

21 "Those who accept my commandments and obey them are the ones who
love me. My Father will love those who
love me; I too will love them and reveal
myself to them."

22 Judas (not Judas Iscariot) said,
"Lord, how can it be that you will reveal
yourself to us and not to the world?"

23 Jesus answered him, "Those who
love me will obey my teaching. My
Father will love them, and my Father
and I will come to them and live with
them. 24 Those who do not love me do
not obey my teaching. And the teaching
you have heard is not mine, but comes
from the Father, who sent me.

25 "I have told you this while I am still
with you. 26 The Helper, the Holy Spirit,
whom the Father will send in my name,
will teach you everything and make you
remember all that I have told you.

27 "Peace is what I leave with you; it is
my own peace that I give you. I do not
give it as the world does. Do not be worried and upset; do not be afraid. 28 You
heard me say to you, 'I am leaving, but I
will come back to you.' If you loved me,
you would be glad that I am going to the
Father; for he is greater than I. 29 I have
told you this now before it all happens,
so that when it does happen, you will
believe. 30 I cannot talk with you much
longer, because the ruler of this world is
coming. He has no power over me, 31 but
the world must know that I love the
Father; that is why I do everything as he
commands me.

"Come, let us go from this place.

---

a Believe; or You believe.   b There are ... were not so; or There are many rooms in my
Father's house; if it were not so, would I tell you that I am going to prepare a place for you?
c Now that you have known me ... you will know; some manuscripts have If you had known
me ... you would know.   d Some manuscripts do not have me.   e is; some manuscripts have
will be.

Jesus the Real Vine

15 "I am the real vine, and my Father is the gardener. 2 He breaks off every branch in me that does not bear fruit, and he prunes every branch that does bear fruit, so that it will be clean and bear more fruit. 3 You have been made clean already by the teaching I have given you. 4 Remain united to me, and I will remain united to you. A branch cannot bear fruit by itself; it can do so only if it remains in the vine. In the same way you cannot bear fruit unless you remain in me.

5 "I am the vine, and you are the branches. Those who remain in me, and I in them, will bear much fruit; for you can do nothing without me. 6 Those who do not remain in me are thrown out like a branch and dry up; such branches are gathered up and thrown into the fire, where they are burned. 7 If you remain in me and my words remain in you, then you will ask for anything you wish, and you shall have it. 8 My Father's glory is shown by your bearing much fruit; and in this way you become my disciples. 9 I love you just as the Father loves me; remain in my love. 10 If you obey my commands, you will remain in my love, just as I have obeyed my Father's commands and remain in his love.

11 "I have told you this so that my joy may be in you and that your joy may be complete. 12 My commandment is this: love one another, just as I love you. 13 The greatest love you can have for your friends is to give your life for them. 14 And you are my friends if you do what I command you. 15 I do not call you servants any longer, because servants do not know what their master is doing. Instead, I call you friends, because I have told you everything I heard from my Father. 16 You did not choose me; I chose you and appointed you to go and bear much fruit, the kind of fruit that endures. And so the Father will give you whatever you ask of him in my name. 17 This, then, is what I command you: love one another.

The World's Hatred

18 "If the world hates you, just remember that it has hated me first. 19 If you belonged to the world, then the world would love you as its own. But I chose you from this world, and you do not belong to it; that is why the world hates you. 20 Remember what I told you: 'Slaves are not greater than their master.' If people persecuted me, they will persecute you too; if they obeyed my teaching, they will obey yours too. 21 But they will do all this to you because you are mine; for they do not know the one who sent me. 22 They would not have been guilty of sin if I had not come and spoken to them; as it is, they no longer have any excuse for their sin. 23 Whoever hates me hates my Father also. 24 They would not have been guilty of sin if I had not done among them the things that no one else ever did; as it is, they have seen what I did, and they hate both me and my Father. 25 This, however, was bound to happen so that what is written in their Law may come true: 'They hated me for no reason at all.'

26 "The Helper will come—the Spirit, who reveals the truth about God and who comes from the Father. I will send him to you from the Father, and he will speak about me. 27 And you, too, will speak about me, because you have been with me from the very beginning.

16 "I have told you this, so that you will not give up your faith. 2 You will be expelled from the synagogues, and the time will come when those who kill you will think that by doing this they are serving God. 3 People will do these things to you because they have not known either the Father or me. 4 But I have told you this, so that when the time comes for them to do these things, you will remember what I told you.

The Work of the Holy Spirit

"I did not tell you these things at the beginning, for I was with you. 5 But now I am going to him who sent me, yet none of you asks me where I am going. 6 And now that I have told you, your hearts are full of sadness. 7 But I am telling you the truth: it is better for you that I go away, because if I do not go, the Helper will not come to you. But if I do go away, then I will send him to you. 8 And when he comes, he will prove to the people of the world that they are wrong about sin and about what is right and about God's judgment. 9 They are wrong about sin, because they do not believe in me; 10 they are wrong about what is right, because I am going to the Father and you will not see me any more; [11] and they are wrong about judgment, because the ruler of this world has already been judged.

[12] "I have much more to tell you, but now it would be too much for you to bear. [13] When, however, the Spirit comes, who reveals the truth about God, he will lead you into all the truth. He will not speak on his own authority, but he will speak of what he hears and will tell you of things to come. [14] He will give me glory, because he will take what I say and tell it to you. [15] All that my Father has is mine; that is why I said that the Spirit will take what I give him and tell it to you.

Sadness and Gladness

[16] "In a little while you will not see me any more, and then a little while later you will see me."

[17] Some of his disciples asked among themselves, "What does this mean? He tells us that in a little while we will not see him, and then a little while later we will see him; and he also says, 'It is because I am going to the Father.' [18] What does this 'a little while' mean? We don't know what he is talking about!"

[19] Jesus knew that they wanted to question him, so he said to them, "I said, 'In a little while you will not see me, and then a little while later you will see me.' Is this what you are asking about among yourselves? [20] I am telling you the truth: you will cry and weep, but the world will be glad; you will be sad, but your sadness will turn into gladness. [21] When a woman is about to give birth, she is sad because her hour of suffering has come; but when the baby is born, she forgets her suffering, because she is happy that a baby has been born into the world. [22] That is how it is with you: now you are sad, but I will see you again, and your hearts will be filled with gladness, the kind of gladness that no one can take away from you.

[23] "When that day comes, you will not ask me for anything. I am telling you the truth: the Father will give you whatever you ask of him in my name.[f] [24] Until now you have not asked for anything in my name; ask and you will receive, so that your happiness may be complete.

Victory over the World

[25] "I have used figures of speech to tell you these things. But the time will come when I will not use figures of speech, but will speak to you plainly about the Father. [26] When that day comes, you will ask him in my name; and I do not say that I will ask him on your behalf, [27] for the Father himself loves you. He loves you because you love me and have believed that I came from God. [28] I did come from the Father, and I came into the world; and now I am leaving the world and going to the Father,"

[29] Then his disciples said to him, "Now you are speaking plainly, without using figures of speech. [30] We know now that you know everything; you do not need to have someone ask you questions. This makes us believe that you came from God."

[31] Jesus answered them, "Do you believe now? [32] The time is coming, and is already here, when all of you will be scattered, each of you to your own home, and I will be left all alone. But I am not really alone, because the Father is with me. [33] I have told you this so that you will have peace by being united to me. The world will make you suffer. But be brave! I have defeated the world!"

Jesus Prays for His Disciples

17 After Jesus finished saying this, he looked up to heaven and said, "Father, the hour has come. Give glory to your Son, so that the Son may give glory to you. [2] For you gave him authority over all people, so that he might give eternal life to all those you gave him. [3] And eternal life means to know you, the only true God, and to know Jesus Christ, whom you sent. [4] I have shown your glory on earth; I have finished the work you gave me to do. [5] Father! Give me glory in your presence now, the same glory I had with you before the world was made.

[6] "I have made you known to those you gave me out of the world. They belonged to you, and you gave them to me. They have obeyed your word, [7] and now they know that everything you gave me

---

[f] the Father will give you whatever you ask of him in my name; *some manuscripts have* if you ask the Father for anything, he will give it to you in my name.

comes from you. [8]I gave them the message that you gave me, and they received it; they know that it is true that I came from you, and they believe that you sent me.

[9]"I pray for them. I do not pray for the world but for those you gave me, for they belong to you. [10]All I have is yours, and all you have is mine; and my glory is shown through them. [11]And now I am coming to you; I am no longer in the world, but they are in the world. Holy Father! Keep them safe by the power of your name, the name you gave me,[g] so that they may be one just as you and I are one. [12]While I was with them, I kept them safe by the power of your name, the name you gave me.[h] I protected them, and not one of them was lost, except the man who was bound to be lost — so that the scripture might come true. [13]And now I am coming to you, and I say these things in the world so that they might have my joy in their hearts in all its fullness. [14]I gave them your message, and the world hated them, because they do not belong to the world, just as I do not belong to the world. [15]I do not ask you to take them out of the world, but I do ask you to keep them safe from the Evil One. [16]Just as I do not belong to the world, they do not belong to the world. [17]Dedicate them to yourself by means of the truth; your word is truth. [18]I sent them into the world, just as you sent me into the world. [19]And for their sake I dedicate myself to you, in order that they, too, may be truly dedicated to you.

[20]"I pray not only for them, but also for those who believe in me because of their message. [21]I pray that they may all be one. Father! May they be in us, just as you are in me and I am in you. May they be one, so that the world will believe that you sent me. [22]I gave them the same glory you gave me, so that they may be one, just as you and I are one: [23]I in them and you in me, so that they may be completely one, in order that the world may know that you sent me and that you love them as you love me.

[24]"Father! You have given them to me, and I want them to be with me where I am, so that they may see my glory, the glory you gave me; for you loved me before the world was made. [25]Righteous Father! The world does not know you, but I know you, and these know that you sent me. [26]I made you known to them, and I will continue to do so, in order that the love you have for me may be in them, and so that I also may be in them."

The Arrest of Jesus

(Matthew 26.47-56; Mark 14.43-50; Luke 22.47-53)

18 After Jesus had said this prayer, he left with his disciples and went across Kidron Brook. There was a garden in that place, and Jesus and his disciples went in. [2]Judas, the traitor, knew where it was, because many times Jesus had met there with his disciples. [3]So Judas went to the garden, taking with him a group of Roman soldiers, and some Temple guards sent by the chief priests and the Pharisees; they were armed and carried lanterns and torches. [4]Jesus knew everything that was going to happen to him, so he stepped forward and asked them, "Who is it you are looking for?"

[5]"Jesus of Nazareth," they answered.

"I am he," he said.

Judas, the traitor, was standing there with them. [6]When Jesus said to them, "I am he," they moved back and fell to the ground. [7]Again Jesus asked them, "Who is it you are looking for?"

"Jesus of Nazareth," they said.

[8]"I have already told you that I am he," Jesus said. "If, then, you are looking for me, let these others go." ([9]He said this so that what he had said might come true: "Father, I have not lost even one of those you gave me.")

[10]Simon Peter, who had a sword, drew it and struck the High Priest's slave, cutting off his right ear. The name of the slave was Malchus. [11]Jesus said to Peter, "Put your sword back in its place! Do you think that I will not drink the cup of suffering which my Father has given me?"

Jesus before Annas

[12]Then the Roman soldiers with their commanding officer and the Jewish guards arrested Jesus, tied him up,

---

[g] Keep them safe by the power of your name, the name you gave me; *some manuscripts have* By the power of your name keep safe those you have given me.   [h] I kept them safe by the power of your name, the name you gave me; *some manuscripts have* By the power of your name I kept safe those you have given me.

THE JEWISH COUNCIL

The Jewish Council was the highest ruling body among the Jews in New Testament times. This group probably evolved from the council of advisors to the high priest during the years when the Jewish people lived under the domination of the Persians and the Greeks.

The Council originally was composed of leading priests and distinguished aristocrats among the Jewish people, but later scribes and Pharisees and Sadducees were added to the group.

With an assembly of seventy-one members, the Council was headed by the high priest. The body was granted limited authority over certain religious, civil, and criminal matters by the Romans during their years of dominance in Palestine. Most of the day-to-day business was left to the Council, which was permitted to have its own police force. However, the Council was denied the right to exercise the death penalty (Jn 18.31). In spite of these restrictions, the Council exercised considerable influence in religious matters.

The Council played a prominent role in the arrest and trial of Jesus, although it is not clear whether he was formally tried by the Council or given preliminary hearings. Christ was arrested by the temple police in the Garden of Gethsemane and subjected to false accusations before the high priest (Mt 26.46, 59). Several of the apostles, including Peter, John, and Paul, were charged before the Council (Ac 4.1–23; 5.17–41; 22—24) in later years.

Prominent members of the Council mentioned in a favorable light in the New Testament were Joseph of Arimathea (Mk 15.43); Gamaliel (Ac 5.34); and Nicodemus (Jn 3.1; 7.50).

During most of its history, the Council met at Jerusalem. But after A.D. 150, it convened at Tiberias, a Roman city on the shores of Lake Galilee.

13 and took him first to Annas. He was the father-in-law of Caiaphas, who was High Priest that year. 14 It was Caiaphas who had advised the Jewish authorities that it was better that one man should die for all the people.

Peter Denies Jesus
(Matthew 26.69, 70; Mark 14.66-68; Luke 22.55-57)

15 Simon Peter and another disciple followed Jesus. That other disciple was well known to the High Priest, so he went with Jesus into the courtyard of the High Priest's house, 16 while Peter stayed outside by the gate. Then the other disciple went back out, spoke to the girl at the gate, and brought Peter inside. 17 The girl at the gate said to Peter, "Aren't you also one of the disciples of that man?"

"No, I am not," answered Peter.

18 It was cold, so the servants and guards had built a charcoal fire and were standing around it, warming themselves. So Peter went over and stood with them, warming himself.

The High Priest Questions Jesus
(Matthew 26.59-66; Mark 14.55-64; Luke 22.66-71)

19 The High Priest questioned Jesus about his disciples and about his teaching. 20 Jesus answered, "I have always spoken publicly to everyone; all my teaching was done in the synagogues and in the Temple, where all the people come together. I have never said anything in secret. 21 Why, then, do you question me? Question the people who heard me. Ask them what I told them — they know what I said."

22 When Jesus said this, one of the guards there slapped him and said, "How dare you talk like that to the High Priest!"

23 Jesus answered him, "If I have said anything wrong, tell everyone here what it was. But if I am right in what I have said, why do you hit me?"

24 Then Annas sent him, still tied up, to Caiaphas the High Priest.

Peter Denies Jesus Again
(Matthew 26.71-75; Mark 14.69-72; Luke 22.58-62)

25 Peter was still standing there keeping himself warm. So the others said to him, "Aren't you also one of the disciples of that man?"

But Peter denied it. "No, I am not," he said.

26 One of the High Priest's slaves, a relative of the man whose ear Peter had cut off, spoke up. "Didn't I see you with him in the garden?" he asked.

27 Again Peter said "No" — and at once a rooster crowed.

Jesus before Pilate
(Matthew 27.1, 2, 11-14; Mark 15.1-5; Luke 23.1-5)

28 Early in the morning Jesus was taken from Caiaphas' house to the governor's palace. The Jewish authorities did not go inside the palace, for they wanted to keep themselves ritually clean, in order to be able to eat the Passover meal. 29 So Pilate went outside to them and asked, "What do you accuse this man of?"

30 Their answer was, "We would not have brought him to you if he had not committed a crime."

31 Pilate said to them, "Then you yourselves take him and try him according to your own law."

They replied, "We are not allowed to put anyone to death." (32 This happened in order to make come true what Jesus had said when he indicated the kind of death he would die.)

33 Pilate went back into the palace and called Jesus. "Are you the king of the Jews?" he asked him.

34 Jesus answered, "Does this question come from you or have others told you about me?"

35 Pilate replied, "Do you think I am a Jew? It was your own people and the chief priests who handed you over to me. What have you done?"

36 Jesus said, "My kingdom does not belong to this world; if my kingdom belonged to this world, my followers would fight to keep me from being handed over to the Jewish authorities. No, my kingdom does not belong here!"

37 So Pilate asked him, "Are you a king, then?"

Jesus answered, "You say that I am a king. I was born and came into the world for this one purpose, to speak about the truth. Whoever belongs to the truth listens to me."

38 "And what is truth?" Pilate asked.

Jesus Is Sentenced to Death
(Matthew 27.15-31; Mark 15.6-20; Luke 23.13-25)

Then Pilate went back outside to the people and said to them, "I cannot find any reason to condemn him. 39 But according to the custom you have, I always set free a prisoner for you during the Passover. Do you want me to set free for you the king of the Jews?"

40 They answered him with a shout, "No, not him! We want Barabbas!" (Barabbas was a bandit.)

19 Then Pilate took Jesus and had him whipped. 2 The soldiers made a crown out of thorny branches and put it on his head; then they put a purple robe on him 3 and came to him and said, "Long live the King of the Jews!" And they went up and slapped him.

4 Pilate went back out once more and said to the crowd, "Look, I will bring him out here to you to let you see that I cannot find any reason to condemn him." 5 So Jesus came out, wearing the crown of thorns and the purple robe. Pilate said to them, "Look! Here is the man!"

6 When the chief priests and the Temple guards saw him, they shouted, "Crucify him! Crucify him!"

Pilate said to them, "You take him, then, and crucify him. I find no reason to condemn him."

7 The crowd answered back, "We have a law that says he ought to die, because he claimed to be the Son of God."

8 When Pilate heard this, he was even more afraid. 9 He went back into the palace and asked Jesus, "Where do you come from?"

But Jesus did not answer. 10 Pilate said to him, "You will not speak to me? Remember, I have the authority to set you free and also to have you crucified."

11 Jesus answered, "You have authority over me only because it was given to you by God. So the man who handed me over to you is guilty of a worse sin."

12 When Pilate heard this, he tried to find a way to set Jesus free. But the crowd shouted back, "If you set him free, that means that you are not the Emperor's friend! Anyone who claims to be a king is a rebel against the Emperor!"

13 When Pilate heard these words, he took Jesus outside and sat down on the judge's seat in the place called "The Stone Pavement." (In Hebrew the name is "Gabbatha.") 14 It was then almost noon of the day before the Passover. Pilate said to the people, "Here is your king!"

15 They shouted back, "Kill him! Kill him! Crucify him!"

Pilate asked them, "Do you want me to crucify your king?"

The chief priests answered, "The only king we have is the Emperor!"

16 Then Pilate handed Jesus over to them to be crucified.

Jesus Is Crucified

(Matthew 27.32-44; Mark 15.21-32; Luke 23.26-43)

So they took charge of Jesus. 17 He went out, carrying his cross, and came to "The Place of the Skull," as it is called. (In Hebrew it is called "Golgotha.") 18 There they crucified him; and they also crucified two other men, one on each side, with Jesus between them. 19 Pilate wrote a notice and had it put on the cross. "Jesus of Nazareth, the King of the Jews," is what he wrote. 20 Many people read it, because the place where Jesus was crucified was not far from the city. The notice was written in Hebrew, Latin, and Greek. 21 The chief priests said to Pilate, "Do not write 'The King of the Jews,' but rather, 'This man said, I am the King of the Jews.' "

22 Pilate answered, "What I have written stays written."

23 After the soldiers had crucified Jesus, they took his clothes and divided them into four parts, one part for each soldier. They also took the robe, which was made of one piece of woven cloth without any seams in it. 24 The soldiers said to one another, "Let's not tear it; let's throw dice to see who will get it." This happened in order to make the scripture come true:

"They divided my clothes among themselves
        and gambled for my robe."

And this is what the soldiers did.

25 Standing close to Jesus' cross were his mother, his mother's sister, Mary the wife of Clopas, and Mary Magdalene. 26 Jesus saw his mother and the disciple he loved standing there; so he said to his mother, "He is your son."

27 Then he said to the disciple, "She is your mother." From that time the disciple took her to live in his home.

The Death of Jesus

(Matthew 27.45-56; Mark 15.33-41; Luke 23.44-49)

28 Jesus knew that by now everything had been completed; and in order to

make the scripture come true, he said, "I am thirsty."

29 A bowl was there, full of cheap wine; so a sponge was soaked in the wine, put on a stalk of hyssop, and lifted up to his lips. 30 Jesus drank the wine and said, "It is finished!"

Then he bowed his head and gave up his spirit.

Jesus' Side Is Pierced

31 Then the Jewish authorities asked Pilate to allow them to break the legs of the men who had been crucified, and to take the bodies down from the crosses. They requested this because it was Friday, and they did not want the bodies to stay on the crosses on the Sabbath, since the coming Sabbath was especially holy. 32 So the soldiers went and broke the legs of the first man and then of the other man who had been crucified with Jesus. 33 But when they came to Jesus, they saw that he was already dead, so they did not break his legs. 34 One of the soldiers, however, plunged his spear into Jesus' side, and at once blood and water poured out. (35 The one who saw this happen has spoken of it, so that you also may believe.ⁱ What he said is true, and he knows that he speaks the truth.) 36 This was done to make the scripture come true: "Not one of his bones will be broken." 37 And there is another scripture that says, "People will look at him whom they pierced."

The Burial of Jesus
(Matthew 27.57-61; Mark 15.42-47; Luke 23.50-56)

38 After this, Joseph, who was from the town of Arimathea, asked Pilate if he could take Jesus' body. (Joseph was a follower of Jesus, but in secret, because he was afraid of the Jewish authorities.) Pilate told him he could have the body, so Joseph went and took it away. 39 Nicodemus, who at first had gone to see Jesus at night, went with Joseph, taking with him about one hundred pounds of spices, a mixture of myrrh and aloes. 40 The two men took Jesus' body and wrapped it in linen cloths with the spices according to the Jewish custom of preparing a body for burial. 41 There was a garden in the place where Jesus had been put to death, and in it there was a new tomb where no one had ever been buried. 42 Since it was the day before the Sabbath and because the tomb was close by, they placed Jesus' body there.

The Empty Tomb
(Matthew 28.1-8; Mark 16.1-8; Luke 24.1-12)

20 Early on Sunday morning, while it was still dark, Mary Magdalene went to the tomb and saw that the stone had been taken away from the entrance. 2 She went running to Simon Peter and the other disciple, whom Jesus loved, and told them, "They have taken the Lord from the tomb, and we don't know where they have put him!"

3 Then Peter and the other disciple went to the tomb. 4 The two of them were running, but the other disciple ran faster than Peter and reached the tomb first. 5 He bent over and saw the linen cloths, but he did not go in. 6 Behind him came Simon Peter, and he went straight into the tomb. He saw the linen cloths lying there 7 and the cloth which had been around Jesus' head. It was not lying with the linen cloths but was rolled up by itself. 8 Then the other disciple, who had reached the tomb first, also went in; he saw and believed. (9 They still did not understand the scripture which said that he must rise from death.) 10 Then the disciples went back home.

Jesus Appears to Mary Magdalene
(Matthew 28.9, 10; Mark 16.9-11)

11 Mary stood crying outside the tomb. While she was still crying, she bent over and looked in the tomb 12 and saw two angels there dressed in white, sitting where the body of Jesus had been, one at the head and the other at the feet. 13 "Woman, why are you crying?" they asked her.

She answered, "They have taken my Lord away, and I do not know where they have put him!"

14 Then she turned around and saw Jesus standing there; but she did not know that it was Jesus. 15 "Woman, why are you crying?" Jesus asked her. "Who is it that you are looking for?"

She thought he was the gardener, so she said to him, "If you took him away, sir, tell me where you have put him, and I will go and get him."

ⁱ believe; *some manuscripts have* continue to believe.

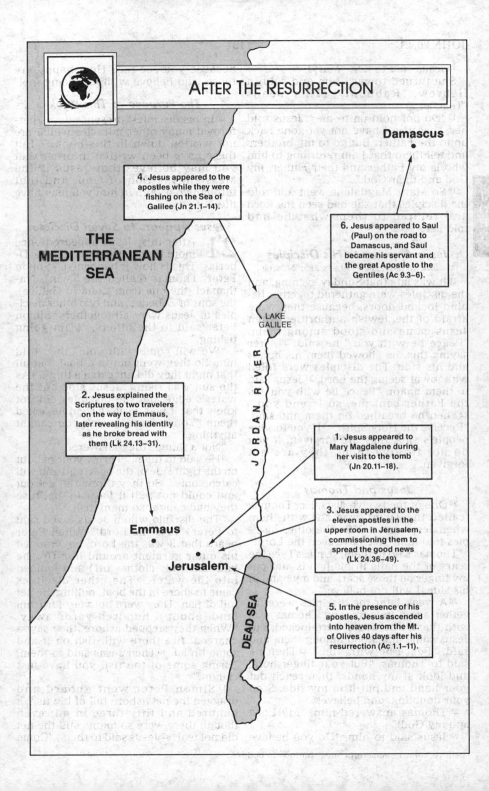

AFTER THE RESURRECTION

THE MEDITERRANEAN SEA

Damascus

4. Jesus appeared to the apostles while they were fishing on the Sea of Galilee (Jn 21.1–14).

6. Jesus appeared to Saul (Paul) on the road to Damascus, and Saul became his servant and the great Apostle to the Gentiles (Ac 9.3–6).

LAKE GALILEE

JORDAN RIVER

2. Jesus explained the Scriptures to two travelers on the way to Emmaus, later revealing his identity as he broke bread with them (Lk 24.13–31).

1. Jesus appeared to Mary Magdalene during her visit to the tomb (Jn 20.11–18).

3. Jesus appeared to the eleven apostles in the upper room in Jerusalem, commissioning them to spread the good news (Lk 24.36–49).

Emmaus

Jerusalem

DEAD SEA

5. In the presence of his apostles, Jesus ascended into heaven from the Mt. of Olives 40 days after his resurrection (Ac 1.1–11).

16 Jesus said to her, "Mary!"

She turned toward him and said in Hebrew, "Rabboni!" (This means "Teacher.")

17 "Do not hold on to me," Jesus told her, "because I have not yet gone back up to the Father. But go to my brothers and tell them that I am returning to him who is my Father and their Father, my God and their God."

18 So Mary Magdalene went and told the disciples that she had seen the Lord and related to them what he had told her.

Jesus Appears to His Disciples

(Matthew 28.16-20; Mark 16.14-18; Luke 24.36-49)

19 It was late that Sunday evening, and the disciples were gathered together behind locked doors, because they were afraid of the Jewish authorities. Then Jesus came and stood among them. "Peace be with you," he said. 20 After saying this, he showed them his hands and his side. The disciples were filled with joy at seeing the Lord. 21 Jesus said to them again, "Peace be with you. As the Father sent me, so I send you." 22 Then he breathed on them and said, "Receive the Holy Spirit. 23 If you forgive people's sins, they are forgiven; if you do not forgive them, they are not forgiven."

Jesus and Thomas

24 One of the twelve disciples, Thomas (called the Twin), was not with them when Jesus came. 25 So the other disciples told him, "We have seen the Lord!"

Thomas said to them, "Unless I see the scars of the nails in his hands and put my finger on those scars and my hand in his side, I will not believe."

26 A week later the disciples were together again indoors, and Thomas was with them. The doors were locked, but Jesus came and stood among them and said, "Peace be with you." 27 Then he said to Thomas, "Put your finger here, and look at my hands; then reach out your hand and put it in my side. Stop your doubting, and believe!"

28 Thomas answered him, "My Lord and my God!"

29 Jesus said to him, "Do you believe because you see me? How happy are those who believe without seeing me!"

The Purpose of This Book

30 In his disciples' presence Jesus performed many other miracles which are not written down in this book. 31 But these have been written in order that you may believe *f* that Jesus is the Messiah, the Son of God, and that through your faith in him you may have life.

Jesus Appears to Seven Disciples

21 After this, Jesus appeared once more to his disciples at Lake Tiberias. This is how it happened. 2 Simon Peter, Thomas (called the Twin), Nathanael (the one from Cana in Galilee), the sons of Zebedee, and two other disciples of Jesus were all together. 3 Simon Peter said to the others, "I am going fishing."

"We will come with you," they told him. So they went out in a boat, but all that night they did not catch a thing. 4 As the sun was rising, Jesus stood at the water's edge, but the disciples did not know that it was Jesus. 5 Then he asked them, "Young men, haven't you caught anything?"

"Not a thing," they answered.

6 He said to them, "Throw your net out on the right side of the boat, and you will catch some." So they threw the net out and could not pull it back in, because they had caught so many fish.

7 The disciple whom Jesus loved said to Peter, "It is the Lord!" When Peter heard that it was the Lord, he wrapped his outer garment around him (for he had taken his clothes off) and jumped into the water. 8 The other disciples came to shore in the boat, pulling the net full of fish. They were not very far from land, about a hundred yards away. 9 When they stepped ashore, they saw a charcoal fire there with fish on it and some bread. 10 Then Jesus said to them, "Bring some of the fish you have just caught."

11 Simon Peter went aboard and dragged the net ashore full of big fish, a hundred and fifty-three in all; even though there were so many, still the net did not tear. 12 Jesus said to them, "Come

f believe; some manuscripts have continue to believe.

and eat." None of the disciples dared ask him, "Who are you?" because they knew it was the Lord. 13 So Jesus went over, took the bread, and gave it to them; he did the same with the fish.

14 This, then, was the third time Jesus appeared to the disciples after he was raised from death.

Jesus and Peter

15 After they had eaten, Jesus said to Simon Peter, "Simon son of John, do you love me more than these others do?"

"Yes, Lord," he answered, "you know that I love you."

Jesus said to him, "Take care of my lambs." 16 A second time Jesus said to him, "Simon son of John, do you love me?"

"Yes, Lord," he answered, "you know that I love you."

Jesus said to him, "Take care of my sheep." 17 A third time Jesus said, "Simon son of John, do you love me?"

Peter became sad because Jesus asked him the third time, "Do you love me?" and so he said to him, "Lord, you know everything; you know that I love you!"

Jesus said to him, "Take care of my sheep. 18 I am telling you the truth: when you were young, you used to get ready and go anywhere you wanted to; but when you are old, you will stretch out your hands and someone else will tie you up and take you where you don't want to go." 19 (In saying this, Jesus was indicating the way in which Peter would die and bring glory to God.) Then Jesus said to him, "Follow me!"

Jesus and the Other Disciple

20 Peter turned around and saw behind him that other disciple, whom Jesus loved—the one who had leaned close to Jesus at the meal and had asked, "Lord, who is going to betray you?" 21 When Peter saw him, he asked Jesus, "Lord, what about this man?"

22 Jesus answered him, "If I want him to live until I come, what is that to you? Follow me!"

23 So a report spread among the followers of Jesus that this disciple would not die. But Jesus did not say he would not die; he said, "If I want him to live until I come, what is that to you?"

24 He is the disciple who spoke of these things, the one who also wrote them down; and we know that what he said is true.

Conclusion

25 Now, there are many other things that Jesus did. If they were all written down one by one, I suppose that the whole world could not hold the books that would be written.

JOHN

THE ACTS OF THE APOSTLES

Acts is a unique book in the Scripture. It is a continuation of Luke's work and tells the story of the beginnings of the church. It begins with the ascension of Jesus, has the record of the giving of the Holy Spirit at Pentecost, and the life of the early church.

It is not, however, the story of the whole church, or even of all the apostles. It focuses on the beginnings of the church, then on the work of Peter, and finally on the work of Paul. Luke wanted to show how the church spread from Jerusalem to all over Palestine and then to the Gentiles.

Luke reports a series of episodes in the life and faith of the early church to show how Christianity rose out of Judaism and has deep roots in the Jewish faith. He shows something of the struggle the disciples felt in moving out in a mission to Gentiles.

One of the major themes in the book is the role of the Holy Spirit in guiding and strengthening the church as it spread across the Mediterranean world. Another theme is the message that Christianity is not dangerous to the authority or power of the Roman Empire. More than one-half of Acts is devoted to the ministry of Paul and his travels to preach the Good News.

THE ACTS
of the Apostles

Introduction

The Acts of the Apostles *is a continuation of* The Gospel according to Luke. *Its chief purpose is to tell how Jesus' early followers, led by the Holy Spirit, spread the Good News about him "in Jerusalem, in all of Judea and Samaria, and to the ends of the earth" (1.8). It is the story of the Christian movement as it began among the Jewish people and went on to become a faith for the whole world. The writer was also concerned to reassure his readers that the Christians were not a subversive political threat to the Roman Empire, and that the Christian faith was the fulfillment of the Jewish religion.*

Acts may be divided into three principal parts, reflecting the ever widening area in which the Good News about Jesus was proclaimed and the church established: (1) the beginning of the Christian movement in Jerusalem following the ascension of Jesus; (2) expansion into other parts of Palestine; and (3) further expansion, into the Mediterranean world as far as Rome.

An important feature of Acts is the activity of the Holy Spirit, who comes with power upon the believers in Jerusalem on the day of Pentecost and continues to guide and strengthen the church and its leaders throughout the events reported in the book. The early Christian message is summarized in a number of sermons, and the events recorded in Acts show the power of this message in the lives of the believers and in the fellowship of the church.

Outline of Contents

---

1 Dear Theophilus:
In my first book I wrote about all the things that Jesus did and taught from the time he began his work ²until the day he was taken up to heaven. Before he was taken up, he gave instructions by the power of the Holy Spirit to the men he had chosen as his apostles. ³For forty days after his death he appeared to them many times in ways that proved beyond doubt that he was alive. They saw him, and he talked with them about the Kingdom of God. ⁴And when they came together,ᵃ he gave them this order: "Do not leave Jerusalem, but wait for the gift I told you about, the gift my Father promised. ⁵John baptized with water, but in a few days you will be baptized with the Holy Spirit."

Jesus Is Taken Up to Heaven

⁶When the apostles met together with Jesus, they asked him, "Lord, will you at this time give the Kingdom back to Israel?"

⁷Jesus said to them, "The times and occasions are set by my Father's own authority, and it is not for you to know when they will be. ⁸But when the Holy Spirit comes upon you, you will be filled with power, and you will be witnesses for me in Jerusalem, in all of Judea and Samaria, and to the ends of the earth." ⁹After saying this, he was taken up to

---

ᵃ *when they came together;* or *while he was staying with them,* or *while he was eating with them.*

heaven as they watched him, and a cloud hid him from their sight.

¹⁰They still had their eyes fixed on the sky as he went away, when two men dressed in white suddenly stood beside them ¹¹and said, "Galileans, why are you standing there looking up at the sky? This Jesus, who was taken from you into heaven, will come back in the same way that you saw him go to heaven."

Judas' Successor

¹²Then the apostles went back to Jerusalem from the Mount of Olives, which is about half a mile away from the city. ¹³They entered the city and went up to the room where they were staying: Peter, John, James and Andrew, Philip and Thomas, Bartholomew and Matthew, James son of Alphaeus, Simon the Patriot, and Judas son of James. ¹⁴They gathered frequently to pray as a group, together with the women and with Mary the mother of Jesus and with his brothers.

¹⁵A few days later there was a meeting of the believers, about a hundred and twenty in all, and Peter stood up to speak. ¹⁶"My friends," he said, "the scripture had to come true in which the Holy Spirit, speaking through David, made a prediction about Judas, who was the guide for those who arrested Jesus. ¹⁷Judas was a member of our group, for he had been chosen to have a part in our work."

(¹⁸ With the money that Judas got for his evil act he bought a field, where he fell to his death; he burst open and all his insides spilled out. ¹⁹All the people living in Jerusalem heard about it, and so in their own language they call that field Akeldama, which means "Field of Blood.")

²⁰"For it is written in the book of Psalms,

'May his house become empty;
    may no one live in it.'

It is also written,

'May someone else take his place
    of service.'

²¹⁻²²"So then, someone must join us as a witness to the resurrection of the Lord Jesus. He must be one of the men who were in our group during the whole time

that the Lord Jesus traveled about with us, beginning from the time John preached his message of baptismᵇ until the day Jesus was taken up from us to heaven."

²³So they proposed two men: Joseph, who was called Barsabbas (also known as Justus), and Matthias. ²⁴Then they prayed, "Lord, you know the thoughts of everyone, so show us which of these two you have chosen ²⁵to serve as an apostle in the place of Judas, who left to go to the place where he belongs." ²⁶Then they drew lots to choose between the two men, and the one chosen was Matthias, who was added to the group of eleven apostles.

The Coming of the Holy Spirit

2 When the day of Pentecost came, all the believers were gathered together in one place. ²Suddenly there was a noise from the sky which sounded like a strong wind blowing, and it filled the whole house where they were sitting. ³Then they saw what looked like tongues of fire which spread out and touched each person there. ⁴They were all filled with the Holy Spirit and began to talk in other languages, as the Spirit enabled them to speak.

⁵There were Jews living in Jerusalem, religious people who had come from every country in the world. ⁶When they heard this noise, a large crowd gathered. They were all excited, because all of them heard the believers talking in their own languages. ⁷In amazement and wonder they exclaimed, "These people who are talking like this are Galileans! ⁸How is it, then, that all of us hear them speaking in our own native languages? ⁹We are from Parthia, Media, and Elam; from Mesopotamia, Judea, and Cappadocia; from Pontus and Asia, ¹⁰from Phrygia and Pamphylia, from Egypt and the regions of Libya near Cyrene. Some of us are from Rome, ¹¹both Jews and Gentiles converted to Judaism, and some of us are from Crete and Arabia — yet all of us hear them speaking in our own languages about the great things that God has done!" ¹²Amazed and confused, they kept asking each other, "What does this mean?"

ᵇ John preached his message of baptism; or John baptized him.

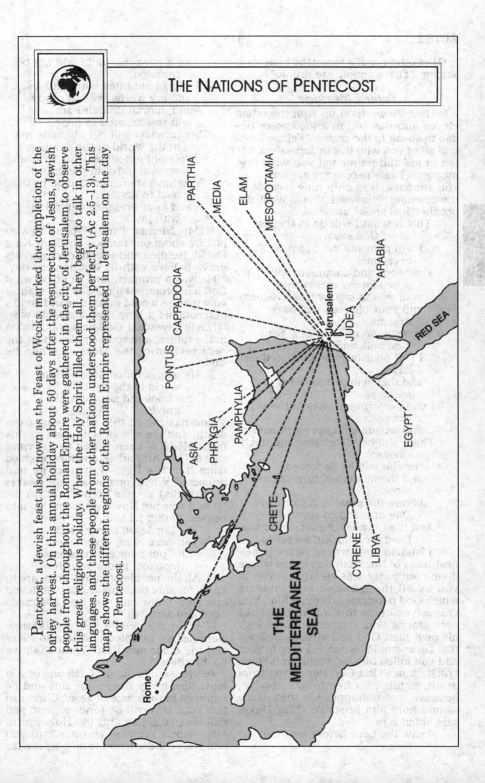

THE NATIONS OF PENTECOST

Pentecost, a Jewish feast also known as the Feast of Weeks, marked the completion of the barley harvest. On this annual holiday about 50 days after the resurrection of Jesus, Jewish people from throughout the Roman Empire were gathered in the city of Jerusalem to observe this great religious holiday. When the Holy Spirit filled them all, they began to talk in other languages, and these people from other nations understood them perfectly (Ac 2.5–13). This map shows the different regions of the Roman Empire represented in Jerusalem on the day of Pentecost.

PARTHIA

MEDIA

ELAM

MESOPOTAMIA

ARABIA

Jerusalem

JUDEA

RED SEA

CAPPADOCIA

PONTUS

PAMPHYLIA

PHRYGIA

ASIA

EGYPT

CRETE

CYRENE

LIBYA

THE MEDITERRANEAN SEA

Rome

13 But others made fun of the believers, saying, "These people are drunk!"

Peter's Message

14 Then Peter stood up with the other eleven apostles and in a loud voice began to speak to the crowd: "Fellow Jews and all of you who live in Jerusalem, listen to me and let me tell you what this means. 15 These people are not drunk, as you suppose; it is only nine o'clock in the morning. 16 Instead, this is what the prophet Joel spoke about:

17 'This is what I will do in the last days, God says:
I will pour out my Spirit on everyone.
Your sons and daughters will proclaim my message;
your young men will see visions,
and your old men will have dreams.
18 Yes, even on my servants, both men and women,
I will pour out my Spirit in those days,
and they will proclaim my message.
19 I will perform miracles in the sky above
and wonders on the earth below.
There will be blood, fire, and thick smoke;
20 the sun will be darkened,
and the moon will turn red as blood,
before the great and glorious Day of the Lord comes.
21 And then, whoever calls out to the Lord for help will be saved.'

22 "Listen to these words, fellow Israelites! Jesus of Nazareth was a man whose divine authority was clearly proven to you by all the miracles and wonders which God performed through him. You yourselves know this, for it happened here among you. 23 In accordance with his own plan God had already decided that Jesus would be handed over to you; and you killed him by letting sinful men crucify him. 24 But God raised him from death, setting him free from its power, because it was impossible that death should hold him prisoner. 25 For David said about him,
'I saw the Lord before me at all times;

he is near me, and I will not be troubled.
26 And so I am filled with gladness,
and my words are full of joy.
And I, mortal though I am,
will rest assured in hope,
27 because you will not abandon me in the world of the dead;
you will not allow your faithful servant to rot in the grave.
28 You have shown me the paths that lead to life,
and your presence will fill me with joy.'

29 "My friends, I must speak to you plainly about our famous ancestor King David. He died and was buried, and his grave is here with us to this very day. 30 He was a prophet, and he knew what God had promised him: God had made a vow that he would make one of David's descendants a king, just as David was. 31 David saw what God was going to do in the future, and so he spoke about the resurrection of the Messiah when he said,
'He was not abandoned in the world of the dead;
his body did not rot in the grave.'
32 God has raised this very Jesus from death, and we are all witnesses to this fact. 33 He has been raised to the right side of God, his Father, and has received from him the Holy Spirit, as he had promised. What you now see and hear is his gift that he has poured out on us. 34 For it was not David who went up into heaven; rather he said,
'The Lord said to my Lord:
Sit here at my right side
35 until I put your enemies as a footstool under your feet.'
36 "All the people of Israel, then, are to know for sure that this Jesus, whom you crucified, is the one that God has made Lord and Messiah!"

37 When the people heard this, they were deeply troubled and said to Peter and the other apostles, "What shall we do, brothers?"

38 Peter said to them, "Each one of you must turn away from your sins and be baptized in the name of Jesus Christ, so that your sins will be forgiven; and you will receive God's gift, the Holy Spirit. 39 For God's promise was made to you and your children, and to all who are far

away—all whom the Lord our God calls to himself."

40 Peter made his appeal to them and with many other words he urged them, saying, "Save yourselves from the punishment coming on this wicked people!" 41 Many of them believed his message and were baptized, and about three thousand people were added to the group that day. 42 They spent their time in learning from the apostles, taking part in the fellowship, and sharing in the fellowship meals and the prayers.

Life among the Believers

43 Many miracles and wonders were being done through the apostles, and everyone was filled with awe. 44 All the believers continued together in close fellowship and shared their belongings with one another. 45 They would sell their property and possessions, and distribute the money among all, according to what each one needed. 46 Day after day they met as a group in the Temple, and they had their meals together in their homes, eating with glad and humble hearts, 47 praising God, and enjoying the good will of all the people. And every day the Lord added to their group those who were being saved.

A Lame Beggar Is Healed

3 One day Peter and John went to the Temple at three o'clock in the afternoon, the hour for prayer. 2 There at the Beautiful Gate, as it was called, was a man who had been lame all his life. Every day he was carried to the gate to beg for money from the people who were going into the Temple. 3 When he saw Peter and John going in, he begged them to give him something. 4 They looked straight at him, and Peter said, "Look at us!" 5 So he looked at them, expecting to get something from them. 6 But Peter said to him, "I have no money at all, but I give you what I have: in the name of Jesus Christ of Nazareth I order you to get up and walk!" 7 Then he took him by his right hand and helped him up. At once the man's feet and ankles became strong; 8 he jumped up, stood on his feet, and started walking around. Then he went into the Temple with them, walking and jumping and praising

God. 9 The people there saw him walking and praising God, 10 and when they recognized him as the beggar who had sat at the Beautiful Gate, they were all surprised and amazed at what had happened to him.

Peter's Message in the Temple

11 As the man held on to Peter and John in Solomon's Porch, as it was called, the people were amazed and ran to them. 12 When Peter saw the people, he said to them, "Fellow Israelites, why are you surprised at this, and why do you stare at us? Do you think that it was by means of our own power or godliness that we made this man walk? 13 The God of Abraham, Isaac, and Jacob, the God of our ancestors, has given divine glory to his Servant Jesus. But you handed him over to the authorities, and you rejected him in Pilate's presence, even after Pilate had decided to set him free. 14 He was holy and good, but you rejected him, and instead you asked Pilate to do you the favor of turning loose a murderer. 15 You killed the one who leads to life, but God raised him from death—and we are witnesses to this. 16 It was the power of his name that gave strength to this lame man. What you see and know was done by faith in his name; it was faith in Jesus that has made him well, as you can all see.

17 "And now, my friends, I know that what you and your leaders did to Jesus was due to your ignorance. 18 God announced long ago through all the prophets that his Messiah had to suffer; and he made it come true in this way. 19 Repent, then, and turn to God, so that he will forgive your sins. If you do, 20 times of spiritual strength will come from the Lord, and he will send Jesus, who is the Messiah he has already chosen for you. 21 He must remain in heaven until the time comes for all things to be made new, as God announced through his holy prophets of long ago. 22 For Moses said, 'The Lord your God will send you a prophet, just as he sent me,c and he will be one of your own people. You are to obey everything that he tells you to do. 23 Anyone who does not obey that prophet shall be separated from God's people and destroyed.' 24 And all the

c just as he sent me; or like me.

prophets who had a message, including Samuel and those who came after him, also announced what has been happening these days. 25 The promises of God through his prophets are for you, and you share in the covenant which God made with your ancestors. As he said to Abraham, 'Through your descendants I will bless all the people on earth.' 26 And so God chose his Servant and sent him to you first, to bless you by making every one of you turn away from your wicked ways."

Peter and John before the Council

4 Peter and John were still speaking to the people when some priests,d the officer in charge of the Temple guards, and some Sadducees arrived. 2 They were annoyed because the two apostles were teaching the people that Jesus had risen from death, which proved that the dead will rise to life. 3 So they arrested them and put them in jail until the next day, since it was already late. 4 But many who heard the message believed; and the number grew to about five thousand.

5 The next day the Jewish leaders, the elders, and the teachers of the Law gathered in Jerusalem. 6 They met with the High Priest Annas and with Caiaphas, John, Alexander, and the others who belonged to the High Priest's family. 7 They made the apostles stand before them and asked them, "How did you do this? What power do you have or whose name did you use?"

8 Peter, full of the Holy Spirit, answered them, "Leaders of the people and elders: 9 if we are being questioned today about the good deed done to the lame man and how he was healed, 10 then you should all know, and all the people of Israel should know, that this man stands here before you completely well through the power of the name of Jesus Christ of Nazareth—whom you crucified and whom God raised from death. 11 Jesus is the one of whom the scripture says,

'The stone that you the builders
      despised
   turned out to be the most
      important of all.'

12 Salvation is to be found through him alone; in all the world there is no one else whom God has given who can save us."

13 The members of the Council were amazed to see how bold Peter and John were and to learn that they were ordinary men of no education. They realized then that they had been companions of Jesus. 14 But there was nothing that they could say, because they saw the man who had been healed standing there with Peter and John. 15 So they told them to leave the Council room, and then they started discussing among themselves. 16 "What shall we do with these men?" they asked. "Everyone in Jerusalem knows that this extraordinary miracle has been performed by them, and we cannot deny it. 17 But to keep this matter from spreading any further among the people, let us warn these men never again to speak to anyone in the name of Jesus."

18 So they called them back in and told them that under no condition were they to speak or to teach in the name of Jesus. 19 But Peter and John answered them, "You yourselves judge which is right in God's sight—to obey you or to obey God. 20 For we cannot stop speaking of what we ourselves have seen and heard." 21 So the Council warned them even more strongly and then set them free. They saw that it was impossible to punish them, because the people were all praising God for what had happened. 22 The man on whom this miracle of healing had been performed was over forty years old.

The Believers Pray for Boldness

23 As soon as Peter and John were set free, they returned to their group and told them what the chief priests and the elders had said. 24 When the believers heard it, they all joined together in prayer to God: "Master and Creator of heaven, earth, and sea, and all that is in them! 25 By means of the Holy Spirit you spoke through our ancestor David, your servant, when he said,

'Why were the Gentiles furious;
   why did people make their
      useless plots?
26 The kings of the earth prepared
      themselves,
   and the rulers met together

d priests; *some manuscripts have* chief priests.

against the Lord and his Messiah.'

27 For indeed Herod and Pontius Pilate met together in this city with the Gentiles and the people of Israel against Jesus, your holy Servant, whom you made Messiah. 28 They gathered to do everything that you by your power and will had already decided would happen. 29 And now, Lord, take notice of the threats they have made, and allow us, your servants, to speak your message with all boldness. 30 Reach out your hand to heal, and grant that wonders and miracles may be performed through the name of your holy Servant Jesus."

31 When they finished praying, the place where they were meeting was shaken. They were all filled with the Holy Spirit and began to proclaim God's message with boldness.

The Believers Share Their Possessions

32 The group of believers was one in mind and heart. None of them said that any of their belongings were their own, but they all shared with one another everything they had. 33 With great power the apostles gave witness to the resurrection of the Lord Jesus, and God poured rich blessings on them all. 34 There was no one in the group who was in need. Those who owned fields or houses would sell them, bring the money received from the sale, 35 and turn it over to the apostles; and the money was distributed according to the needs of the people.

36 And so it was that Joseph, a Levite born in Cyprus, whom the apostles called Barnabas (which means "One who Encourages"), 37 sold a field he owned, brought the money, and turned it over to the apostles.

Ananias and Sapphira

5 But there was a man named Ananias, who with his wife Sapphira sold some property that belonged to them. 2 But with his wife's agreement he kept part of the money for himself and turned the rest over to the apostles. 3 Peter said to him, "Ananias, why did you let Satan take control of you and make you lie to the Holy Spirit by keeping part of the money you received for the property? 4 Before you sold the property, it belonged to you; and after you sold it, the money was yours. Why, then, did you decide to do such a thing? You have not lied to people — you have lied to God!" 5 As soon as Ananias heard this, he fell down dead; and all who heard about it were terrified. 6 The young men came in, wrapped up his body, carried him out, and buried him.

7 About three hours later his wife, not knowing what had happened, came in. 8 Peter asked her, "Tell me, was this the full amount you and your husband received for your property?"

"Yes," she answered, "the full amount."

9 So Peter said to her, "Why did you and your husband decide to put the Lord's Spirit to the test? The men who buried your husband are at the door right now, and they will carry you out too!" 10 At once she fell down at his feet and died. The young men came in and saw that she was dead, so they carried her out and buried her beside her husband. 11 The whole church and all the others who heard of this were terrified.

Miracles and Wonders

12 Many miracles and wonders were being performed among the people by the apostles. All the believers met together in Solomon's Porch. 13 Nobody outside the group dared join them, even though the people spoke highly of them. 14 But more and more people were added to the group — a crowd of men and women who believed in the Lord. 15 As a result of what the apostles were doing, sick people were carried out into the streets and placed on beds and mats so that at least Peter's shadow might fall on some of them as he passed by. 16 And crowds of people came in from the towns around Jerusalem, bringing those who were sick or who had evil spirits in them; and they were all healed.

The Apostles Are Persecuted

17 Then the High Priest and all his companions, members of the local party of the Sadducees, became extremely jealous of the apostles; so they decided to take action. 18 They arrested the apostles and put them in the public jail. 19 But that night an angel of the Lord opened the prison gates, led the apostles out, and said to them, 20 "Go and stand in the

Temple, and tell the people all about this new life." 21 The apostles obeyed, and at dawn they entered the Temple and started teaching.

The High Priest and his companions called together all the Jewish elders for a full meeting of the Council; then they sent orders to the prison to have the apostles brought before them. 22 But when the officials arrived, they did not find the apostles in prison, so they returned to the Council and reported, 23 "When we arrived at the jail, we found it locked up tight and all the guards on watch at the gates; but when we opened the gates, we found no one inside!" 24 When the chief priests and the officer in charge of the Temple guards heard this, they wondered what had happened to the apostles. 25 Then a man came in and said to them, "Listen! The men you put in prison are in the Temple teaching the people!" 26 So the officer went off with his men and brought the apostles back. They did not use force, however, because they were afraid that the people might stone them.

27 They brought the apostles in, made them stand before the Council, and the High Priest questioned them. 28 "We gave you strict orders not to teach in the name of this man," he said; "but see what you have done! You have spread your teaching all over Jerusalem, and you want to make us responsible for his death!"

29 Peter and the other apostles answered, "We must obey God, not men. 30 The God of our ancestors raised Jesus from death, after you had killed him by nailing him to a cross. 31 God raised him to his right side as Leader and Savior, to give the people of Israel the opportunity to repent and have their sins forgiven. 32 We are witnesses to these things — we and the Holy Spirit, who is God's gift to those who obey him."

33 When the members of the Council heard this, they were so furious that they wanted to have the apostles put to death. 34 But one of them, a Pharisee named Gamaliel, who was a teacher of the Law and was highly respected by all the people, stood up in the Council. He ordered the apostles to be taken out for a while, 35 and then he said to the Council, "Fellow Israelites, be careful what you do to these men. 36 You remember that Theudas appeared some time ago, claiming to be somebody great, and about four hundred men joined him. But he was killed, all his followers were scattered, and his movement died out. 37 After that, Judas the Galilean appeared during the time of the census; he drew a crowd after him, but he also was killed, and all his followers were scattered. 38 And so in this case, I tell you, do not take any action against these men. Leave them alone! If what they have planned and done is of human origin, it will disappear, 39 but if it comes from God, you cannot possibly defeat them. You could find yourselves fighting against God!"

The Council followed Gamaliel's advice. 40 They called the apostles in, had them whipped, and ordered them never again to speak in the name of Jesus; and then they set them free. 41 As the apostles left the Council, they were happy, because God had considered them worthy to suffer disgrace for the sake of Jesus. 42 And every day in the Temple and in people's homes they continued to teach and preach the Good News about Jesus the Messiah.

The Seven Helpers

6 Some time later, as the number of disciples kept growing, there was a quarrel between the Greek-speaking Jews and the native Jews. The Greek-speaking Jews claimed that their widows were being neglected in the daily distribution of funds. 2 So the twelve apostles called the whole group of believers together and said, "It is not right for us to neglect the preaching of God's word in order to handle finances. 3 So then, friends, choose seven men among you who are known to be full of the Holy Spirit and wisdom, and we will put them in charge of this matter. 4 We ourselves, then, will give our full time to prayer and the work of preaching."

5 The whole group was pleased with the apostles' proposal, so they chose Stephen, a man full of faith and the Holy Spirit, and Philip, Prochorus, Nicanor, Timon, Parmenas, and Nicolaus, a Gentile from Antioch who had earlier been converted to Judaism. 6 The group presented them to the apostles, who prayed and placed their hands on them.

7 And so the word of God continued to spread. The number of disciples in

Jerusalem grew larger and larger, and a great number of priests accepted the faith.

The Arrest of Stephen

8 Stephen, a man richly blessed by God and full of power, performed great miracles and wonders among the people. 9 But he was opposed by some men who were members of the synagogue of the Freedmen*e* (as it was called), which had Jews from Cyrene and Alexandria. They and other Jews from the provinces of Cilicia and Asia started arguing with Stephen. 10 But the Spirit gave Stephen such wisdom that when he spoke, they could not refute him. 11 So they bribed some men to say, "We heard him speaking against Moses and against God!" 12 In this way they stirred up the people, the elders, and the teachers of the Law. They seized Stephen and took him before the Council. 13 Then they brought in some men to tell lies about him. "This man," they said, "is always talking against our sacred Temple and the Law of Moses. 14 We heard him say that this Jesus of Nazareth will tear down the Temple and change all the customs which have come down to us from Moses!" 15 All those sitting in the Council fixed their eyes on Stephen and saw that his face looked like the face of an angel.

Stephen's Speech

7 The High Priest asked Stephen, "Is this true?"

2 Stephen answered, "Brothers and fathers, listen to me! Before our ancestor Abraham had gone to live in Haran, the God of glory appeared to him in Mesopotamia 3 and said to him, 'Leave your family and country and go to the land that I will show you.' 4 And so he left his country and went to live in Haran. After Abraham's father died, God made him move to this land where you now live. 5 God did not then give Abraham any part of it as his own, not even a square foot of ground, but God promised to give it to him, and that it would belong to him and to his descendants. At the time God made this promise, Abraham had no children. 6 This is what God said to him: 'Your descendants will live in a foreign country, where they will be slaves and

will be badly treated for four hundred years. 7 But I will pass judgment on the people that they will serve, and afterward your descendants will come out of that country and will worship me in this place.' 8 Then God gave to Abraham the ceremony of circumcision as a sign of the covenant. So Abraham circumcised Isaac a week after he was born; Isaac circumcised his son Jacob, and Jacob circumcised his twelve sons, the famous ancestors of our race.

9 "Jacob's sons became jealous of their brother Joseph and sold him to be a slave in Egypt. But God was with him 10 and brought him safely through all his troubles. When Joseph appeared before the king of Egypt, God gave him a pleasing manner and wisdom, and the king made Joseph governor over the country and the royal household. 11 Then there was a famine all over Egypt and Canaan, which caused much suffering. Our ancestors could not find any food, 12 and when Jacob heard that there was grain in Egypt, he sent his sons, our ancestors, on their first visit there. 13 On the second visit Joseph made himself known to his brothers, and the king of Egypt came to know about Joseph's family. 14 So Joseph sent a message to his father Jacob, telling him and the whole family, seventy-five people in all, to come to Egypt. 15 Then Jacob went to Egypt, where he and his sons died. 16 Their bodies were taken to Shechem, where they were buried in the grave which Abraham had bought from the clan of Hamor for a sum of money.

17 "When the time drew near for God to keep the promise he had made to Abraham, the number of our people in Egypt had grown much larger. 18 At last a king who did not know about Joseph began to rule in Egypt. 19 He tricked our ancestors and was cruel to them, forcing them to put their babies out of their homes, so that they would die. 20 It was at this time that Moses was born, a very beautiful child. He was cared for at home for three months, 21 and when he was put out of his home, the king's daughter adopted him and brought him up as her own son. 22 He was taught all the wisdom of the Egyptians and became a great man in words and deeds.

e FREEDMEN: *These were Jews who had been slaves, but had bought or been given their freedom.*

23 "When Moses was forty years old, he decided to find out how his fellow Israelites were being treated. 24 He saw one of them being mistreated by an Egyptian, so he went to his help and took revenge on the Egyptian by killing him. (25 He thought that his own people would understand that God was going to use him to set them free, but they did not understand.) 26 The next day he saw two Israelites fighting, and he tried to make peace between them. 'Listen, men,' he said, 'you are fellow Israelites; why are you fighting like this?' 27 But the one who was mistreating the other pushed Moses aside. 'Who made you ruler and judge over us?' he asked. 28 'Do you want to kill me, just as you killed that Egyptian yesterday?' 29 When Moses heard this, he fled from Egypt and went to live in the land of Midian. There he had two sons.

30 "After forty years had passed, an angel appeared to Moses in the flames of a burning bush in the desert near Mount Sinai. 31 Moses was amazed by what he saw, and went near the bush to get a better look. But he heard the Lord's voice: 32 'I am the God of your ancestors, the God of Abraham, Isaac, and Jacob.' Moses trembled with fear and dared not look. 33 The Lord said to him, 'Take your sandals off, for the place where you are standing is holy ground. 34 I have seen the cruel suffering of my people in Egypt. I have heard their groans, and I have come down to set them free. Come now; I will send you to Egypt.'

35 "Moses is the one who was rejected by the people of Israel. 'Who made you ruler and judge over us?' they asked. He is the one whom God sent to rule the people and set them free with the help of the angel who appeared to him in the burning bush. 36 He led the people out of Egypt, performing miracles and wonders in Egypt and at the Red Sea and for forty years in the desert. 37 Moses is the one who said to the people of Israel, 'God will send you a prophet, just as he sent me,f and he will be one of your own people.' 38 He is the one who was with the people of Israel assembled in the desert; he was there with our ancestors and with the angel who spoke to

him on Mount Sinai, and he received God's living messages to pass on to us.

39 "But our ancestors refused to obey him; they pushed him aside and wished that they could go back to Egypt. 40 So they said to Aaron, 'Make us some gods who will lead us. We do not know what has happened to that man Moses, who brought us out of Egypt.' 41 It was then that they made an idol in the shape of a bull, offered sacrifice to it, and had a feast in honor of what they themselves had made. 42 So God turned away from them and gave them over to worship the stars of heaven, as it is written in the book of the prophets:

'People of Israel! It was not to me
  that you slaughtered and
    sacrificed animals
  for forty years in the desert.
43 It was the tent of the god Molech
    that you carried,
  and the image of Rephan, your
    star god;
  they were idols that you had
    made to worship.
And so I will send you into exile
    beyond Babylon.'

44 "Our ancestors had the Tent of God's presence with them in the desert. It had been made as God had told Moses to make it, according to the pattern that Moses had been shown. 45 Later on, our ancestors who received the tent from their fathers carried it with them when they went with Joshua and took over the land from the nations that God drove out as they advanced. And it stayed there until the time of David. 46 He won God's favor and asked God to allow him to provide a dwelling place for the God of Jacob.g 47 But it was Solomon who built him a house.

48 "But the Most High God does not live in houses built by human hands; as the prophet says,

49 'Heaven is my throne, says the
    Lord,
  and the earth is my footstool.
What kind of house would you
    build for me?
  Where is the place for me to
    live in?
50 Did not I myself make all these
    things?'

---

f just as he sent me; or like me.   g the God of Jacob; some manuscripts have the people of Israel.

51"How stubborn you are!" Stephen went on to say. "How heathen your hearts, how deaf you are to God's message! You are just like your ancestors: you too have always resisted the Holy Spirit! 52Was there any prophet that your ancestors did not persecute? They killed God's messengers, who long ago announced the coming of his righteous Servant. And now you have betrayed and murdered him. 53You are the ones who received God's law, that was handed down by angels—yet you have not obeyed it!"

The Stoning of Stephen

54As the members of the Council listened to Stephen, they became furious and ground their teeth at him in anger. 55But Stephen, full of the Holy Spirit, looked up to heaven and saw God's glory and Jesus standing at the right side of God. 56"Look!" he said. "I see heaven opened and the Son of Man standing at the right side of God!"

57With a loud cry the Council members covered their ears with their hands. Then they all rushed at him at once, 58threw him out of the city, and stoned him. The witnesses left their cloaks in the care of a young man named Saul. 59They kept on stoning Stephen as he called out to the Lord, "Lord Jesus, receive my spirit!" 60He knelt down and cried out in a loud voice, "Lord! Do not remember this sin against them!" He said this and died.

8 And Saul approved of his murder.

Saul Persecutes the Church

That very day the church in Jerusalem began to suffer cruel persecution. All the believers, except the apostles, were scattered throughout the provinces of Judea and Samaria. 2Some devout men buried Stephen, mourning for him with loud cries.

3But Saul tried to destroy the church; going from house to house, he dragged out the believers, both men and women, and threw them into jail.

The Gospel Is Preached in Samaria

4The believers who were scattered went everywhere, preaching the message. 5Philip went to the principal city[h]

h the principal city; some manuscripts have a city.

in Samaria and preached the Messiah to the people there. 6The crowds paid close attention to what Philip said, as they listened to him and saw the miracles that he performed. 7Evil spirits came out from many people with a loud cry, and many paralyzed and lame people were healed. 8So there was great joy in that city.

9A man named Simon lived there, who for some time had astounded the Samaritans with his magic. He claimed that he was someone great, 10and everyone in the city, from all classes of society, paid close attention to him. "He is that power of God known as 'The Great Power,'" they said. 11They paid this attention to him because for such a long time he had astonished them with his magic. 12But when they believed Philip's message about the good news of the Kingdom of God and about Jesus Christ, they were baptized, both men and women. 13Simon himself also believed; and after being baptized, he stayed close to Philip and was astounded when he saw the great wonders and miracles that were being performed.

14The apostles in Jerusalem heard that the people of Samaria had received the word of God, so they sent Peter and John to them. 15When they arrived, they prayed for the believers that they might receive the Holy Spirit. 16For the Holy Spirit had not yet come down on any of them; they had only been baptized in the name of the Lord Jesus. 17Then Peter and John placed their hands on them, and they received the Holy Spirit.

18Simon saw that the Spirit had been given to the believers when the apostles placed their hands on them. So he offered money to Peter and John, 19and said, "Give this power to me too, so that anyone I place my hands on will receive the Holy Spirit."

20But Peter answered him, "May you and your money go to hell, for thinking that you can buy God's gift with money! 21You have no part or share in our work, because your heart is not right in God's sight. 22Repent, then, of this evil plan of yours, and pray to the Lord that he will forgive you for thinking such a thing as this. 23For I see that you are full of bitter envy and are a prisoner of sin."

THE SPREAD OF THE GOSPEL

Philip and Peter, two of the original apostles of Jesus, were the first to preach the gospel throughout Palestine in the cities around Jerusalem in response to the command of Jesus, "You will be witnesses for me in Jerusalem, in all Judea and Samaria, and to the end of the earth" (Ac 1.8). In later years, the apostle Paul became the great missionary to the Gentiles, proclaiming Christ in other nations throughout the Roman Empire.

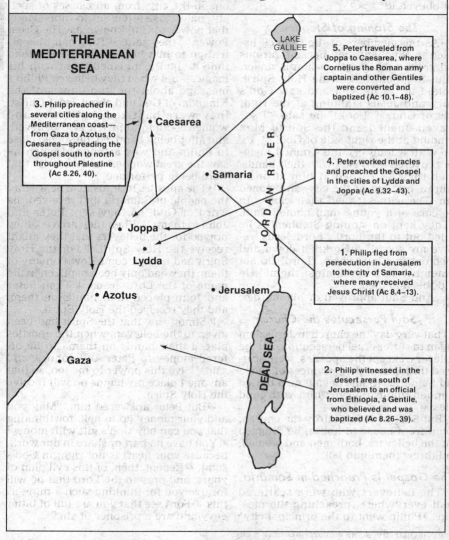

THE MEDITERRANEAN SEA

LAKE GALILEE

JORDAN RIVER

DEAD SEA

• Caesarea

• Samaria

• Joppa

• Lydda

• Jerusalem

• Azotus

• Gaza

3. Philip preached in several cities along the Mediterranean coast—from Gaza to Azotus to Caesarea—spreading the Gospel south to north throughout Palestine (Ac 8.26, 40).

5. Peter traveled from Joppa to Caesarea, where Cornelius the Roman army captain and other Gentiles were converted and baptized (Ac 10.1–48).

4. Peter worked miracles and preached the Gospel in the cities of Lydda and Joppa (Ac 9.32–43).

1. Philip fled from persecution in Jerusalem to the city of Samaria, where many received Jesus Christ (Ac 8.4–13).

2. Philip witnessed in the desert area south of Jerusalem to an official from Ethiopia, a Gentile, who believed and was baptized (Ac 8.26–39).

24 Simon said to Peter and John, "Please pray to the Lord for me, so that none of these things you spoke of will happen to me."

25 After they had given their testimony and proclaimed the Lord's message, Peter and John went back to Jerusalem. On their way they preached the Good News in many villages of Samaria.

Philip and the Ethiopian Official

26 An angel of the Lord said to Philip, "Get ready and go south[i] to the road that goes from Jerusalem to Gaza." (This road is not used nowadays.)[j] 27-28 So Philip got ready and went. Now an Ethiopian eunuch, who was an important official in charge of the treasury of the queen of Ethiopia, was on his way home. He had been to Jerusalem to worship God and was going back home in his carriage. As he rode along, he was reading from the book of the prophet Isaiah. 29 The Holy Spirit said to Philip, "Go over to that carriage and stay close to it." 30 Philip ran over and heard him reading from the book of the prophet Isaiah. He asked him, "Do you understand what you are reading?"

31 The official replied, "How can I understand unless someone explains it to me?" And he invited Philip to climb up and sit in the carriage with him. 32 The passage of scripture which he was reading was this:

"He was like a sheep that is taken
    to be slaughtered,
like a lamb that makes no sound
    when its wool is cut off.
He did not say a word.
33 He was humiliated, and justice
    was denied him.
No one will be able to tell about
    his descendants,
because his life on earth has
    come to an end."

34 The official asked Philip, "Tell me, of whom is the prophet saying this? Of himself or of someone else?" 35 Then Philip began to speak; starting from this passage of scripture, he told him the Good News about Jesus. 36 As they traveled down the road, they came to a place where there was some water, and the of-

ficial said, "Here is some water. What is to keep me from being baptized?"[k]

38 The official ordered the carriage to stop, and both Philip and the official went down into the water, and Philip baptized him. 39 When they came up out of the water, the Spirit of the Lord took Philip away. The official did not see him again, but continued on his way, full of joy. 40 Philip found himself in Azotus; he went on to Caesarea, and on the way he preached the Good News in every town.

The Conversion of Saul
(Acts 22.6-16; 26.12-18)

9 In the meantime Saul kept up his violent threats of murder against the followers of the Lord. He went to the High Priest 2 and asked for letters of introduction to the synagogues in Damascus, so that if he should find there any followers of the Way of the Lord, he would be able to arrest them, both men and women, and bring them back to Jerusalem.

3 As Saul was coming near the city of Damascus, suddenly a light from the sky flashed around him. 4 He fell to the ground and heard a voice saying to him, "Saul, Saul! Why do you persecute me?"

5 "Who are you, Lord?" he asked.

"I am Jesus, whom you persecute," the voice said. 6 "But get up and go into the city, where you will be told what you must do."

7 The men who were traveling with Saul had stopped, not saying a word; they heard the voice but could not see anyone. 8 Saul got up from the ground and opened his eyes, but could not see a thing. So they took him by the hand and led him into Damascus. 9 For three days he was not able to see, and during that time he did not eat or drink anything.

10 There was a believer in Damascus named Ananias. He had a vision, in which the Lord said to him, "Ananias!"

"Here I am, Lord," he answered.

11 The Lord said to him, "Get ready and go to Straight Street, and at the house of Judas ask for a man from Tarsus named Saul. He is praying, 12 and in a vision he has seen a man named Ananias come in and place his hands on him so that he might see again."

---

i south; *or* at midday.   j This road is not used nowadays; *or* This is the desert road.
k *Some manuscripts add verse 37:* Philip said to him, "You may be baptized if you believe with all your heart." "I do," he answered; "I believe that Jesus Christ is the Son of God."

THE CITY OF DAMASCUS

Damascus is the oldest continually inhabited city in the world. As the current capital of Syria, the city is located on the border of some of the most important highways in the ancient Near Eastern world. Because of its ideal location, the city has always been an important trade center. Its name may be derived from a patterned cloth known as damask, its most important export item in Old Testament times (Ez 27.18).

According to Josephus, the founder of Damascus was Uz, grandson of Shem (Gn 5.32; 10.21, 23). Its strategic location as a trading center brought Damascus into conflict with Israel on numerous occasions as it sought to regulate the flow of trade into all parts of the ancient Near East.

After periods of dominance by the Assyrians and the Persians, Damascus was conquered by Alexander the Great in 333 B.C. Later it became the capital of the Roman province of Syria. In the early years of Roman influence in Syria, many Jews from Judea moved to Damascus. The city had a large Jewish community during New Testament times.

All references to Damascus in the New Testament are associated with the apostle Paul's conversion and early ministry. He was blinded in a vision while traveling to Damascus to persecute early Christians (Ac 9.1–8). After his conversion, Paul went to the house of Judas on Straight Street in Damascus. There he met Ananias, a Christian citizen of the city who healed Paul's blindness (Ac 9.10–22). After regaining his sight, Paul preached in the Jewish synagogue in Damascus, astonishing those who remembered him as a persecutor of the Christian faith. Eventually Paul was forced to flee Damascus because of threats on his life.

Damascus is still a trading center filled with open-air markets and crowded streets, some of which are very similar to those which Paul might have visited.

13Ananias answered, "Lord, many people have told me about this man and about all the terrible things he has done to your people in Jerusalem. 14And he has come to Damascus with authority from the chief priests to arrest all who worship you."

15The Lord said to him, "Go, because I have chosen him to serve me, to make my name known to Gentiles and kings and to the people of Israel. 16And I myself will show him all that he must suffer for my sake."

17So Ananias went, entered the house where Saul was, and placed his hands on him. "Brother Saul," he said, "the Lord has sent me — Jesus himself, who appeared to you on the road as you were coming here. He sent me so that you might see again and be filled with the Holy Spirit." 18At once something like fish scales fell from Saul's eyes, and he was able to see again. He stood up and was baptized; 19and after he had eaten, his strength came back.

Saul Preaches in Damascus

Saul stayed for a few days with the believers in Damascus. 20He went straight to the synagogues and began to preach that Jesus was the Son of God.

21All who heard him were amazed and asked, "Isn't he the one who in Jerusalem was killing those who worship that man Jesus? And didn't he come here for the very purpose of arresting those people and taking them back to the chief priests?"

22But Saul's preaching became even more powerful, and his proofs that Jesus was the Messiah were so convincing that the Jews who lived in Damascus could not answer him.

23After many days had gone by, the Jews met together and made plans to kill Saul, 24but he was told of their plan. Day and night they watched the city gates in order to kill him. 25But one night Saul's followers took him and let him down through an opening in the wall, lowering him in a basket.

Saul in Jerusalem

26Saul went to Jerusalem and tried to join the disciples. But they would not believe that he was a disciple, and they were all afraid of him. 27Then Barnabas came to his help and took him to the apostles. He explained to them how Saul had seen the Lord on the road and that the Lord had spoken to him. He also told them how boldly Saul had preached in the name of Jesus in Damascus. 28And so Saul stayed with them and went all over Jerusalem, preaching boldly in the name of the Lord. 29He also talked and disputed with the Greek-speaking Jews, but they tried to kill him. 30When the believers found out about this, they took Saul to Caesarea and sent him away to Tarsus.

31And so it was that the church throughout Judea, Galilee, and Samaria had a time of peace. Through the help of the Holy Spirit it was strengthened and grew in numbers, as it lived in reverence for the Lord.

Peter in Lydda and Joppa

32Peter traveled everywhere, and on one occasion he went to visit God's people who lived in Lydda. 33There he met a man named Aeneas, who was paralyzed and had not been able to get out of bed for eight years. 34"Aeneas," Peter said to him, "Jesus Christ makes you well. Get up and make your bed." At once Aeneas got up. 35All the people living in Lydda and Sharon saw him, and they turned to the Lord.

36In Joppa there was a woman named Tabitha, who was a believer. (Her name in Greek is Dorcas, meaning "a deer.") She spent all her time doing good and helping the poor. 37At that time she got sick and died. Her body was washed and laid in a room upstairs. 38Joppa was not very far from Lydda, and when the believers in Joppa heard that Peter was in Lydda, they sent two men to him with the message, "Please hurry and come to us." 39So Peter got ready and went with them. When he arrived, he was taken to the room upstairs, where all the widows crowded around him, crying and showing him all the shirts and coats that Dorcas had made while she was alive. 40Peter put them all out of the room, and knelt down and prayed; then he turned to the body and said, "Tabitha, get up!" She opened her eyes, and when she saw Peter, she sat up. 41Peter reached over and helped her get up. Then he called all the believers, including the widows, and presented her alive to them. 42The news about this spread all over Joppa, and many people believed in the Lord. 43 Peter stayed on in Joppa for many days with a tanner of leather named Simon.

Peter and Cornelius

10 There was a man in Caesarea named Cornelius, who was a captain in the Roman army regiment called "The Italian Regiment." 2 He was a religious man; he and his whole family worshiped God. He also did much to help the Jewish poor people and was constantly praying to God. 3 It was about three o'clock one afternoon when he had a vision, in which he clearly saw an angel of God come in and say to him, "Cornelius!"

4 He stared at the angel in fear and said, "What is it, sir?"

The angel answered, "God is pleased with your prayers and works of charity, and is ready to answer you. 5 And now send some men to Joppa for a certain man whose full name is Simon Peter. 6 He is a guest in the home of a tanner of leather named Simon, who lives by the sea." 7 Then the angel went away, and Cornelius called two of his house servants and a soldier, a religious man who was one of his personal attendants. 8 He told them what had happened and sent them off to Joppa.

9 The next day, as they were on their way and coming near Joppa, Peter went up on the roof of the house about noon in order to pray. 10 He became hungry and wanted something to eat; while the food was being prepared, he had a vision. 11 He saw heaven opened and something coming down that looked like a large sheet being lowered by its four corners to the earth. 12 In it were all kinds of animals, reptiles, and wild birds. 13 A voice said to him, "Get up, Peter; kill and eat!"

14 But Peter said, "Certainly not, Lord! I have never eaten anything ritually unclean or defiled."

15 The voice spoke to him again, "Do not consider anything unclean that God has declared clean." 16 This happened three times, and then the thing was taken back up into heaven.

17 While Peter was wondering about the meaning of this vision, the men sent by Cornelius had learned where Simon's house was, and they were now standing in front of the gate. 18 They called out and asked, "Is there a guest here by the name of Simon Peter?"

19 Peter was still trying to understand what the vision meant, when the Spirit said, "Listen! Three*l* men are here looking for you. 20 So get ready and go down, and do not hesitate to go with them, for I have sent them." 21 So Peter went down and said to the men, "I am the man you are looking for. Why have you come?"

22 "Captain Cornelius sent us," they answered. "He is a good man who worships God and is highly respected by all the Jewish people. An angel of God told him to invite you to his house, so that he could hear what you have to say." 23 Peter invited the men in and had them spend the night there.

The next day he got ready and went with them; and some of the believers from Joppa went along with him. 24 The following day he arrived in Caesarea, where Cornelius was waiting for him, together with relatives and close friends that he had invited. 25 As Peter was about to go in, Cornelius met him, fell at his feet, and bowed down before him. 26 But Peter made him rise. "Stand up," he said, "I myself am only a man." 27 Peter kept on talking to Cornelius as he went into the house, where he found many people gathered. 28 He said to them, "You yourselves know very well that a Jew is not allowed by his religion to visit or associate with Gentiles. But God has shown me that I must not consider any person ritually unclean or defiled. 29 And so when you sent for me, I came without any objection. I ask you, then, why did you send for me?"

30 Cornelius said, "It was about this time three days ago that I was praying*m* in my house at three o'clock in the afternoon. Suddenly a man dressed in shining clothes stood in front of me 31 and said: 'Cornelius! God has heard your prayer and has taken notice of your works of charity. 32 Send someone to Joppa for a man whose full name is Simon Peter. He is a guest in the home of Simon the tanner of leather, who lives by the sea.' 33 And so I sent for you at

---

l Three; *some manuscripts have* Some; *one manuscript has* Two.
m praying; *some manuscripts have* fasting and praying.

once, and you have been good enough to come. Now we are all here in the presence of God, waiting to hear anything that the Lord has instructed you to say."

Peter's Speech

34 Peter began to speak: "I now realize that it is true that God treats everyone on the same basis. 35 Those who fear him and do what is right are acceptable to him, no matter what race they belong to. 36 You know the message he sent to the people of Israel, proclaiming the Good News of peace through Jesus Christ, who is Lord of all. 37 You know of the great event that took place throughout the land of Israel, beginning in Galilee after John preached his message of baptism. 38 You know about Jesus of Nazareth and how God poured out on him the Holy Spirit and power. He went everywhere, doing good and healing all who were under the power of the Devil, for God was with him. 39 We are witnesses of everything that he did in the land of Israel and in Jerusalem. Then they put him to death by nailing him to a cross. 40 But God raised him from death three days later and caused him to appear, 41 not to everyone, but only to the witnesses that God had already chosen, that is, to us who ate and drank with him after he rose from death. 42 And he commanded us to preach the gospel to the people and to testify that he is the one whom God has appointed judge of the living and the dead. 43 All the prophets spoke about him, saying that all who believe in him will have their sins forgiven through the power of his name."

The Gentiles Receive the Holy Spirit

44 While Peter was still speaking, the Holy Spirit came down on all those who were listening to his message. 45 The Jewish believers who had come from Joppa with Peter were amazed that God had poured out his gift of the Holy Spirit on the Gentiles also. 46 For they heard them speaking in strange tongues and praising God's greatness. Peter spoke up: 47 "These people have received the Holy Spirit, just as we also did. Can anyone, then, stop them from being baptized with water?" 48 So he ordered them to be baptized in the name of Jesus

Christ. Then they asked him to stay with them for a few days.

Peter's Report to the Church at Jerusalem

11 The apostles and the other believers throughout Judea heard that the Gentiles also had received the word of God. 2 When Peter went to Jerusalem, those who were in favor of circumcising Gentiles criticized him, saying, 3 "You were a guest in the home of uncircumcised Gentiles, and you even ate with them!" 4 So Peter gave them a complete account of what had happened from the very beginning:

5 "While I was praying in the city of Joppa, I had a vision. I saw something coming down that looked like a large sheet being lowered by its four corners from heaven, and it stopped next to me. 6 I looked closely inside and saw domesticated and wild animals, reptiles, and wild birds. 7 Then I heard a voice saying to me, 'Get up, Peter; kill and eat!' 8 But I said, 'Certainly not, Lord! No ritually unclean or defiled food has ever entered my mouth.' 9 The voice spoke again from heaven, 'Do not consider anything unclean that God has declared clean.' 10 This happened three times, and finally the whole thing was drawn back up into heaven. 11 At that very moment three men who had been sent to me from Caesarea arrived at the house where I was[n] staying. 12 The Spirit told me to go with them without hesitation. These six fellow believers from Joppa accompanied me to Caesarea, and we all went into the house of Cornelius. 13 He told us how he had seen an angel standing in his house, who said to him, 'Send someone to Joppa for a man whose full name is Simon Peter. 14 He will speak words to you by which you and all your family will be saved.' 15 And when I began to speak, the Holy Spirit came down on them just as on us at the beginning. 16 Then I remembered what the Lord had said: 'John baptized with water, but you will be baptized with the Holy Spirit.' 17 It is clear that God gave those Gentiles the same gift that he gave us when we believed in the Lord Jesus Christ; who was I, then, to try to stop God!"

18 When they heard this, they stopped

_____

n I was; some manuscripts have we were.

THE CITY OF ANTIOCH

Situated on the most important trade routes of the day, Antioch was an ideal city for a flourishing missions-minded church that was destined to play a key role in the expansion of early Christianity. Seleuchus I founded the city about 300 B.C. and named it for his father, Antiochus. Antioch served as the capital of the Roman province of Syria during the New Testament times.

Located on the east bank of the Orontes River, Antioch was about 16 miles from the Mediterranean Sea and about 300 miles north of Jerusalem. With a population of more than half a million, it was the third largest city of the Roman Empire, ranking behind only Rome and Alexandria.

Under the Roman rulers, Antioch became one of the most beautiful cities of the Roman Empire. Its main street, about two miles long, was paved with marble and flanked on both sides by hundreds of columns, which supported ornamented porches and balconies. Its cultural splendor and beautiful buildings, including the temple of Artemis, the amphitheater, and royal palaces, contributed to its reputation as the "Paris of the Ancient World" among scholars and researchers.

Antioch was also a city of many philosophies and cults. It prided itself on its toleration. But many citizens sought a more significant religious experience than the old Greek and Roman gods offered. Many accepted the gospel and committed themselves to Christ. Because this church was made up of both Gentiles and Jews, city officials sought a name that would distinguish them from other religious groups. According to the Book of Acts, "It was at Antioch that the believers were first called Christians" (Ac 11.26).

Except for Jerusalem, Antioch played a larger part in the early life of the Christian church than any other city of the Roman Empire. It became the birthplace of foreign missions as Paul used the Antioch church as a base of operations for his missionary tours into Asia Minor.

their criticism and praised God, saying, "Then God has given to the Gentiles also the opportunity to repent and live!"

The Church at Antioch

19 Some of the believers who were scattered by the persecution which took place when Stephen was killed went as far as Phoenicia, Cyprus, and Antioch, telling the message to Jews only. 20 But other believers, who were from Cyprus and Cyrene, went to Antioch and proclaimed the message to Gentiles° also, telling them the Good News about the Lord Jesus. 21 The Lord's power was with them, and a great number of people believed and turned to the Lord.

22 The news about this reached the church in Jerusalem, so they sent Barnabas to Antioch. 23 When he arrived and saw how God had blessed the people, he was glad and urged them all to be faithful and true to the Lord with all their hearts. 24 Barnabas was a good man, full of the Holy Spirit and faith, and many people were brought to the Lord.

25 Then Barnabas went to Tarsus to look for Saul. 26 When he found him, he took him to Antioch, and for a whole year the two met with the people of the church and taught a large group. It was at Antioch that the believers were first called Christians.

27 About that time some prophets went from Jerusalem to Antioch. 28 One of them, named Agabus, stood up and by the power of the Spirit predicted that a severe famine was about to come over all the earth. (It came when Claudius was emperor.) 29 The disciples decided that they each would send as much as they could to help their fellow believers who lived in Judea. 30 They did this, then, and sent the money to the church elders by Barnabas and Saul.

More Persecution

12 About this time King Herod[p] began to persecute some members of the church. 2 He had James, the brother of John, put to death by the sword. 3 When he saw that this pleased the Jews, he went ahead and had Peter arrested. (This happened during the time of the Festival of Unleavened Bread.) 4 After his arrest Peter was put in jail, where he was handed over to be guarded by four groups of four soldiers each. Herod planned to put him on trial in public after Passover. 5 So Peter was kept in jail, but the people of the church were praying earnestly to God for him.

Peter Is Set Free from Prison

6 The night before Herod was going to bring him out to the people, Peter was sleeping between two guards. He was tied with two chains, and there were guards on duty at the prison gate. 7 Suddenly an angel of the Lord stood there, and a light shone in the cell. The angel shook Peter by the shoulder, woke him up, and said, "Hurry! Get up!" At once the chains fell off Peter's hands. 8 Then the angel said, "Tighten your belt and put on your sandals." Peter did so, and the angel said, "Put your cloak around you and come with me." 9 Peter followed him out of the prison, not knowing, however, if what the angel was doing was real; he thought he was seeing a vision. 10 They passed by the first guard station and then the second, and came at last to the iron gate that opens into the city. The gate opened for them by itself, and they went out. They walked down a street, and suddenly the angel left Peter.

11 Then Peter realized what had happened to him, and said, "Now I know that it is really true! The Lord sent his angel to rescue me from Herod's power and from everything the Jewish people expected to happen."

12 Aware of his situation, he went to the home of Mary, the mother of John Mark, where many people had gathered and were praying. 13 Peter knocked at the outside door, and a servant named Rhoda came to answer it. 14 She recognized Peter's voice and was so happy that she ran back in without opening the door, and announced that Peter was standing outside. 15 "You are crazy!" they told her. But she insisted that it was true. So they answered, "It is his angel."

16 Meanwhile Peter kept on knocking. At last they opened the door, and when they saw him, they were amazed. 17 He motioned with his hand for them to be quiet, and he explained to them how the Lord had brought him out of prison.

_o_ Gentiles; _some manuscripts have_ Greek-speaking Jews _or_ Greek-speaking people.
_p_ KING HEROD: _Herod Agrippa I, ruler of all Palestine._

"Tell this to James and the rest of the believers," he said; then he left and went somewhere else.

18 When morning came, there was a tremendous confusion among the guards—what had happened to Peter? 19 Herod gave orders to search for him, but they could not find him. So he had the guards questioned and ordered them put to death.

After this, Herod left Judea and spent some time in Caesarea.

The Death of Herod

20 Herod was very angry with the people of Tyre and Sidon, so they went in a group to see him. First they convinced Blastus, the man in charge of the palace, that he should help them. Then they went to Herod and asked him for peace, because their country got its food supplies from the king's country. 21 On a chosen day Herod put on his royal robes, sat on his throne, and made a speech to the people. 22 "It isn't a man speaking, but a god!" they shouted. 23 At once the angel of the Lord struck Herod down, because he did not give honor to God. He was eaten by worms and died. 24 Meanwhile the word of God continued to spread and grow.

25 Barnabas and Saul finished their mission and returned from q Jerusalem, taking John Mark with them.

Barnabas and Saul Are Chosen and Sent

13 In the church at Antioch there were some prophets and teachers: Barnabas, Simeon (called the Black), Lucius (from Cyrene), Manaen (who had been brought up with Governor Herod r), and Saul. 2 While they were serving the Lord and fasting, the Holy Spirit said to them, "Set apart for me Barnabas and Saul, to do the work to which I have called them."

3 They fasted and prayed, placed their hands on them, and sent them off.

In Cyprus

4 Having been sent by the Holy Spirit, Barnabas and Saul went to Seleucia and sailed from there to the island of Cyprus. 5 When they arrived at Salamis, they preached the word of God in the synagogues. They had John Mark with them to help in the work.

6 They went all the way across the island to Paphos, where they met a certain magician named Bar-Jesus, a Jew who claimed to be a prophet. 7 He was a friend of the governor of the island, Sergius Paulus, who was an intelligent man. The governor called Barnabas and Saul before him because he wanted to hear the word of God. 8 But they were opposed by the magician Elymas (that is his name in Greek), who tried to turn the governor away from the faith. 9 Then Saul—also known as Paul—was filled with the Holy Spirit; he looked straight at the magician 10 and said, "You son of the Devil! You are the enemy of everything that is good. You are full of all kinds of evil tricks, and you always keep trying to turn the Lord's truths into lies! 11 The Lord's hand will come down on you now; you will be blind and will not see the light of day for a time."

At once Elymas felt a dark mist cover his eyes, and he walked around trying to find someone to lead him by the hand. 12 When the governor saw what had happened, he believed; for he was greatly amazed at the teaching about the Lord.

In Antioch in Pisidia

13 Paul and his companions sailed from Paphos and came to Perga, a city in Pamphylia, where John Mark left them and went back to Jerusalem. 14 They went on from Perga and arrived in Antioch in Pisidia, and on the Sabbath they went into the synagogue and sat down. 15 After the reading from the Law of Moses and from the writings of the prophets, the officials of the synagogue sent them a message: "Friends, we want you to speak to the people if you have a message of encouragement for them." 16 Paul stood up, motioned with his hand, and began to speak:

"Fellow Israelites and all Gentiles here who worship God: hear me! 17 The God of the people of Israel chose our ancestors and made the people a great nation during the time they lived as foreigners in Egypt. God brought them out of Egypt by his great power, 18 and for forty years

---

q from; *some manuscripts have to.*   r HEROD: *Herod Antipas, ruler of Galilee (see Lk 3.1).*

he endured[s] them in the desert. 19 He destroyed seven nations in the land of Canaan and made his people the owners of the land. 20 All of this took about 450 years.

"After this[t] he gave them judges until the time of the prophet Samuel. 21 And when they asked for a king, God gave them Saul son of Kish from the tribe of Benjamin, to be their king for forty years. 22 After removing him, God made David their king. This is what God said about him: 'I have found that David son of Jesse is the kind of man I like, a man who will do all I want him to do.' 23 It was Jesus, a descendant of David, whom God made the Savior of the people of Israel, as he had promised. 24 Before Jesus began his work, John preached to all the people of Israel that they should turn from their sins and be baptized. 25 And as John was about to finish his mission, he said to the people, 'Who do you think I am? I am not the one you are waiting for. But listen! He is coming after me, and I am not good enough to take his sandals off his feet.'

26 "My fellow Israelites, descendants of Abraham, and all Gentiles here who worship God: it is to us that this message of salvation has been sent! 27 For the people who live in Jerusalem and their leaders did not know that he is the Savior, nor did they understand the words of the prophets that are read every Sabbath. Yet they made the prophets' words come true by condemning Jesus. 28 And even though they could find no reason to pass the death sentence on him, they asked Pilate to have him put to death. 29 And after they had done everything that the Scriptures say about him, they took him down from the cross and placed him in a tomb. 30 But God raised him from death, 31 and for many days he appeared to those who had traveled with him from Galilee to Jerusalem. They are now witnesses for him to the people of Israel. 32-33 And we are here to bring the Good News to you: what God promised our ancestors he would do, he has now done for us, who are their descendants, by raising Jesus to life. As it is written in the second Psalm,

'You are my Son;
    today I have become your
        Father.'

34 And this is what God said about raising him from death, never to rot away in the grave:

'I will give you the sacred and
    sure blessings
    that I promised to David.'

35 As indeed he says in another passage,

'You will not allow your faithful
    servant to rot in the grave.'

36 For David served God's purposes in his own time, and then he died, was buried with his ancestors, and his body rotted in the grave. 37 But this did not happen to the one whom God raised from death. 38-39 All of you, my fellow Israelites, are to know for sure that it is through Jesus that the message about forgiveness of sins is preached to you; you are to know that everyone who believes in him is set free from all the sins from which the Law of Moses could not set you free. 40 Take care, then, so that what the prophets said may not happen to you:[u]

41 'Look, you scoffers! Be astonished
        and die!
    For what I am doing today
        is something that you will not
            believe,
        even when someone explains it
            to you!' "

42 As Paul and Barnabas were leaving the synagogue, the people invited them to come back the next Sabbath and tell them more about these things. 43 After the people had left the meeting, Paul and Barnabas were followed by many Jews and by many Gentiles who had been converted to Judaism. The apostles spoke to them and encouraged them to keep on living in the grace of God.

44 The next Sabbath nearly everyone in the town came to hear the word of the Lord. 45 When the Jews saw the crowds, they were filled with jealousy; they disputed what Paul was saying and insulted him. 46 But Paul and Barnabas spoke out even more boldly: "It was necessary that the word of God should be spoken first to you. But since you reject it and do not consider yourselves worthy of eternal life, we will leave you and go to the

Gentiles. 47 For this is the commandment that the Lord has given us:

'I have made you a light for the Gentiles,
so that all the world may be saved.' "

48 When the Gentiles heard this, they were glad and praised the Lord's message; and those who had been chosen for eternal life became believers.

49 The word of the Lord spread everywhere in that region. 50 But the Jews stirred up the leading men of the city and the Gentile women of high social standing who worshiped God. They started a persecution against Paul and Barnabas and threw them out of their region. 51 The apostles shook the dust off their feet in protest against them and went on to Iconium. 52 The believers in Antioch were full of joy and the Holy Spirit.

In Iconium

14 The same thing happened in Iconium: Paul and Barnabas went to the synagogue and spoke in such a way that a great number of Jews and Gentiles became believers. 2 But the Jews who would not believe stirred up the Gentiles and turned them against the believers. 3 The apostles stayed there for a long time, speaking boldly about the Lord, who proved that their message about his grace was true by giving them the power to perform miracles and wonders. 4 The people of the city were divided: some were for the Jews, others for the apostles.

5 Then some Gentiles and Jews, together with their leaders, decided to mistreat the apostles and stone them. 6 When the apostles learned about it, they fled to the cities of Lystra and Derbe in Lycaonia and to the surrounding territory. 7 There they preached the Good News.

In Lystra and Derbe

8 In Lystra there was a crippled man who had been lame from birth and had never been able to walk. 9 He sat there and listened to Paul's words. Paul saw that he believed and could be healed, so he looked straight at him 10 and said in a loud voice, "Stand up straight on your feet!" The man jumped up and started walking around. 11 When the crowds saw what Paul had done, they started shouting in their own Lycaonian language, "The gods have become like men and have come down to us!" 12 They gave Barnabas the name Zeus, and Paul the name Hermes, because he was the chief speaker. 13 The priest of the god Zeus, whose temple stood just outside the town, brought bulls and flowers to the gate, for he and the crowds wanted to offer sacrifice to the apostles.

14 When Barnabas and Paul heard what they were about to do, they tore their clothes and ran into the middle of the crowd, shouting, 15 "Why are you doing this? We ourselves are only human beings like you! We are here to announce the Good News, to turn you away from these worthless things to the living God, who made heaven, earth, sea, and all that is in them. 16 In the past he allowed all people to go their own way. 17 But he has always given evidence of his existence by the good things he does: he gives you rain from heaven and crops at the right times; he gives you food and fills your hearts with happiness." 18 Even with these words the apostles could hardly keep the crowd from offering a sacrifice to them.

19 Some Jews came from Antioch in Pisidia and from Iconium; they won the crowds over to their side, stoned Paul and dragged him out of the town, thinking that he was dead. 20 But when the believers gathered around him, he got up and went back into the town. The next day he and Barnabas went to Derbe.

The Return to Antioch in Syria

21 Paul and Barnabas preached the Good News in Derbe and won many disciples. Then they went back to Lystra, to Iconium, and on to Antioch in Pisidia. 22 They strengthened the believers and encouraged them to remain true to the faith. "We must pass through many troubles to enter the Kingdom of God," they taught. 23 In each church they appointed elders, and with prayers and fasting they commended them to the Lord, in whom they had put their trust.

24 After going through the territory of Pisidia, they came to Pamphylia. 25 There they preached the message in Perga and then went to Attalia, 26 and from there they sailed back to Antioch, the place where they had been com-

PALESTINE AND SYRIA

PISIDIA — Antioch, Iconium, Lystra, Derbe

CILICIA — Tarsus

PAMPHYLIA — Attalia, Perga

LYCIA — Patara, Myra

CYPRUS — Salamis, Paphos

MEDITERRANEAN SEA

SYRIA — Seleucia, Antioch, Damascus

Euphrates R.

PHOENICIA — Sidon, Tyre, Ptolemais, Caesarea, Samaria, Joppa, Lydda, Azotus, Jerusalem, Gaza

JUDEA

Alexandria

Miles 0 — 200

Kms 0 — 200

mended to the care of God's grace for the work they had now completed.

27 When they arrived in Antioch, they gathered the people of the church together and told them about all that God had done with them and how he had opened the way for the Gentiles to believe. 28 And they stayed a long time there with the believers.

The Meeting at Jerusalem

15 Some men came from Judea to Antioch and started teaching the believers, "You cannot be saved unless you are circumcised as the Law of Moses requires." 2 Paul and Barnabas got into a fierce argument with them about this, so it was decided that Paul and Barnabas and some of the others in Antioch should go to Jerusalem and see the apostles and elders about this matter.

3 They were sent on their way by the church; and as they went through Phoenicia and Samaria, they reported how the Gentiles had turned to God; this news brought great joy to all the believers. 4 When they arrived in Jerusalem, they were welcomed by the church, the apostles, and the elders, to whom they told all that God had done through them. 5 But some of the believers who belonged to the party of the Pharisees stood up and said, "The Gentiles must be circumcised and told to obey the Law of Moses."

6 The apostles and the elders met together to consider this question. 7 After a long debate Peter stood up and said, "My friends, you know that a long time ago God chose me from among you to preach the Good News to the Gentiles, so that they could hear and believe. 8 And God, who knows the thoughts of everyone, showed his approval of the Gentiles by giving the Holy Spirit to them, just as he had to us. 9 He made no difference between us and them; he forgave their sins because they believed. 10 So then, why do you now want to put God to the test by laying a load on the backs of the believers which neither our ancestors nor we ourselves were able to carry? 11 No! We believe and are saved by the grace of the Lord Jesus, just as they are."

12 The whole group was silent as they heard Barnabas and Paul report all the miracles and wonders that God had performed through them among the Gentiles. 13 When they had finished speaking, James spoke up: "Listen to me, my friends! 14 Simon has just explained how God first showed his care for the Gentiles by taking from among them a people to belong to him. 15 The words of the prophets agree completely with this. As the scripture says,

16 'After this I will return, says the
    Lord,
    and restore the kingdom of
    David.
 I will rebuild its ruins
    and make it strong again.
17 And so all the rest of the human
    race will come to me,
    all the Gentiles whom I have
    called to be my own.
18 So says the Lord, who made this
    known long ago.'

19 "It is my opinion," James went on, "that we should not trouble the Gentiles who are turning to God. 20 Instead, we should write a letter telling them not to eat any food that is ritually unclean because it has been offered to idols; to keep themselves from sexual immorality; and not to eat any animal that has been strangled, or any blood. 21 For the Law of Moses has been read for a very long time in the synagogues every Sabbath, and his words are preached in every town."

The Letter to the Gentile Believers

22 Then the apostles and the elders, together with the whole church, decided to choose some men from the group and send them to Antioch with Paul and Barnabas. They chose two men who were highly respected by the believers, Judas, called Barsabbas, and Silas, 23 and they sent the following letter by them:

"We, the apostles and the elders, your brothers, send greetings to all our brothers of Gentile birth who live in Antioch, Syria, and Cilicia. 24 We have heard that some who went from our group have troubled and upset you by what they said; they had not, however, received any instruction from us. 25 And so we have met together and have all agreed to choose some messengers and send them to you. They will go with our dear friends Barnabas and Paul, 26 who have risked their lives in the service of our Lord Jesus Christ. 27We send you, then, Judas and Silas, who will tell you in person the same things we are writing. 28The Holy Spirit and we have agreed not to put any other burden on you besides these necessary rules: 29eat no food that has been offered to idols; eat no blood; eat no animal that has been strangled; and keep yourselves from sexual immorality. You will do well if you take care not to do these things. With our best wishes."

30The messengers were sent off and went to Antioch, where they gathered the whole group of believers and gave them the letter. 31When the people read it, they were filled with joy by the message of encouragement. 32Judas and Silas, who were themselves prophets, spoke a long time with them, giving them courage and strength. 33After spending some time there, they were sent off in peace by the believers and went back to those who had sent them.v

35Paul and Barnabas spent some time in Antioch, and together with many others they taught and preached the word of the Lord.

Paul and Barnabas Separate

36Some time later Paul said to Barnabas, "Let us go back and visit the believers in every town where we preached the word of the Lord, and let us find out how they are getting along." 37Barnabas wanted to take John Mark with them, 38but Paul did not think it was right to take him, because he had not stayed with them to the end of their mission, but had turned back and left them in Pamphylia. 39There was a sharp argument, and they separated: Barnabas took Mark and sailed off for Cyprus, 40while Paul chose Silas and left, commended by the believers to the care of the Lord's grace. 41He went through Syria and Cilicia, strengthening the churches.

Timothy Goes with Paul and Silas

16 Paul traveled on to Derbe and Lystra, where a Christian named Timothy lived. His mother, who was also a Christian, was Jewish, but his father

was a Greek. 2All the believers in Lystra and Iconium spoke well of Timothy. 3Paul wanted to take Timothy along with him, so he circumcised him. He did so because all the Jews who lived in those places knew that Timothy's father was Greek. 4As they went through the towns, they delivered to the believers the rules decided upon by the apostles and elders in Jerusalem, and they told them to obey those rules. 5So the churches were made stronger in the faith and grew in numbers every day.

In Troas: Paul's Vision

6They traveled through the region of Phrygia and Galatia because the Holy Spirit did not let them preach the message in the province of Asia. 7When they reached the border of Mysia, they tried to go into the province of Bithynia, but the Spirit of Jesus did not allow them. 8So they traveled right on throughw Mysia and went to Troas. 9That night Paul had a vision in which he saw a Macedonian standing and begging him, "Come over to Macedonia and help us!" 10As soon as Paul had this vision, we got ready to leave for Macedonia, because we decided that God had called us to preach the Good News to the people there.

In Philippi: the Conversion of Lydia

11We left by ship from Troas and sailed straight across to Samothrace, and the next day to Neapolis. 12From there we went inland to Philippi, a city of the first district of Macedonia;x it is also a Roman colony. We spent several days there. 13On the Sabbath we went out of the city to the riverside, where we thought there would be a place where Jews gathered for prayer. We sat down and talked to the women who gathered there. 14One of those who heard us was Lydia from Thyatira, who was a dealer in purple cloth. She was a woman who worshiped God, and the Lord opened her mind to pay attention to what Paul was saying. 15After she and the people of her house had been baptized, she invited us, "Come and stay in my house if you have decided that I am a true believer in the Lord." And she persuaded us to go.

In Prison at Philippi

16 One day as we were going to the place of prayer, we were met by a young servant woman who had an evil spirit that enabled her to predict the future. She earned a lot of money for her owners by telling fortunes. 17 She followed Paul and us, shouting, "These men are servants of the Most High God! They announce to you how you can be saved!" 18 She did this for many days, until Paul became so upset that he turned around and said to the spirit, "In the name of Jesus Christ I order you to come out of her!" The spirit went out of her that very moment. 19 When her owners realized that their chance of making money was gone, they seized Paul and Silas and dragged them to the authorities in the public square. 20 They brought them before the Roman officials and said, "These men are Jews, and they are causing trouble in our city. 21 They are teaching customs that are against our law; we are Roman citizens, and we cannot accept these customs or practice them."
22 And the crowd joined in the attack against Paul and Silas.

Then the officials tore the clothes off Paul and Silas and ordered them to be whipped. 23 After a severe beating, they were thrown into jail, and the jailer was ordered to lock them up tight. 24 Upon receiving this order, the jailer threw them into the inner cell and fastened their feet between heavy blocks of wood.

25 About midnight Paul and Silas were praying and singing hymns to God, and the other prisoners were listening to them. 26 Suddenly there was a violent earthquake, which shook the prison to its foundations. At once all the doors opened, and the chains fell off all the prisoners. 27 The jailer woke up, and when he saw the prison doors open, he thought that the prisoners had escaped; so he pulled out his sword and was about to kill himself. 28 But Paul shouted at the top of his voice, "Don't harm yourself! We are all here!"

29 The jailer called for a light, rushed in, and fell trembling at the feet of Paul and Silas. 30 Then he led them out and asked, "Sirs, what must I do to be saved?"

31 They answered, "Believe in the Lord Jesus, and you will be saved—you and your family." 32 Then they preached the word of the Lord to him and to all the others in the house. 33 At that very hour of the night the jailer took them and washed their wounds; and he and all his family were baptized at once. 34 Then he took Paul and Silas up into his house and gave them some food to eat. He and his family were filled with joy, because they now believed in God.

35 The next morning the Roman authorities sent police officers with the order, "Let those men go."

36 So the jailer told Paul, "The officials have sent an order for you and Silas to be released. You may leave, then, and go in peace."

37 But Paul said to the police officers, "We were not found guilty of any crime, yet they whipped us in public—and we are Roman citizens! Then they threw us in prison. And now they want to send us away secretly? Not at all! The Roman officials themselves must come here and let us out."

38 The police officers reported these words to the Roman officials; and when they heard that Paul and Silas were Roman citizens, they were afraid. 39 So they went and apologized to them; then they led them out of the prison and asked them to leave the city. 40 Paul and Silas left the prison and went to Lydia's house. There they met the believers, spoke words of encouragement to them, and left.

In Thessalonica

17 Paul and Silas traveled on through Amphipolis and Apollonia and came to Thessalonica, where there was a synagogue. 2 According to his usual habit Paul went to the synagogue. There during three Sabbaths he held discussions with the people, quoting 3 and explaining the Scriptures, and proving from them that the Messiah had to suffer and rise from death. "This Jesus whom I announce to you," Paul said, "is the Messiah." 4 Some of them were convinced and joined Paul and Silas; so did many of the leading women and a large group of Greeks who worshiped God.

5 But some Jews were jealous and gathered worthless loafers from the streets and formed a mob. They set the

THE CITY OF ATHENS

As the capital city of the ancient Greek state of Attica, Athens dates to before 3000 B.C. It has a long history of famous and successful military campaigns. Athens was the center of art, architecture, literature, and politics during the golden age of the Greeks (fifth century B.C.). Many famous philosophers, playwrights, and other artists lived in Athens during this time. The city is recognized even today as the birthplace of western civilization and culture. Modern visitors to Athens are impressed by the city's ancient glory, with the ruins of the Parthenon and several other massive buildings that were devoted to pagan worship.

The apostle Paul visited Athens during his second missionary journey (Ac 17.15—18.1). While waiting in the city for Silas and Timothy, he spent some time sightseeing. He noticed the Athenians erected statues to all the gods, and even to "an Unknown God" (Ac 17.23). Paul described Athens as a city "full of idols" (Ac 17.16).

During his visit, Paul met "certain Epicurean and Stoic teachers" (Ac 17.18) and preached to them about Jesus. This led them to bring him before the city council, the Areopagus. This council met upon the hill called Areopagus. Its purpose was to decide religious matters. Members of the court were curious about Paul's proclamation of the god they worshiped without knowing (Ac 17.23).

Paul's speech to the court (Ac 17.22-31) provides a model for communicating the gospel to a group that has no Bible background. He drew from his surroundings by mentioning the Athenians' love for religion, demonstrated by their many idols. He then made his plea for Christianity by declaring that God does not dwell in man-made temples.

In spite of this approach, most of the Athenians were not responsive to Paul's preaching. They could not accept Paul's statement about the resurrection of Jesus (Ac 17.32).

whole city in an uproar and attacked the home of a man named Jason, in an attempt to find Paul and Silas and bring them out to the people. 6 But when they did not find them, they dragged Jason and some other believers before the city authorities and shouted, "These men have caused trouble everywhere! Now they have come to our city, 7 and Jason has kept them in his house. They are all breaking the laws of the Emperor, saying that there is another king, whose name is Jesus." 8 With these words they threw the crowd and the city authorities in an uproar. 9 The authorities made Jason and the others pay the required amount of money to be released, and then let them go.

In Berea

10 As soon as night came, the believers sent Paul and Silas to Berea. When they arrived, they went to the synagogue. 11 The people there were more open-minded than the people in Thessalonica. They listened to the message with great eagerness, and every day they studied the Scriptures to see if what Paul said was really true. 12 Many of them believed; and many Greek women of high social standing and many Greek men also believed. 13 But when the Jews in Thessalonica heard that Paul had preached the word of God in Berea also, they came there and started exciting and stirring up the mobs. 14 At once the believers sent Paul away to the coast; but both Silas and Timothy stayed in Berea. 15 The men who were taking Paul went with him as far as Athens and then returned to Berea with instructions from Paul that Silas and Timothy should join him as soon as possible.

In Athens

16 While Paul was waiting in Athens for Silas and Timothy, he was greatly upset when he noticed how full of idols the city was. 17 So he held discussions in the synagogue with the Jews and with the Gentiles who worshiped God, and also in the public square every day with the people who happened to come by. 18 Certain Epicurean and Stoic teachers also debated with him. Some of them asked, "What is this ignorant show-off trying to say?"

Others answered, "He seems to be talking about foreign gods." They said this because Paul was preaching about Jesus and the resurrection.y 19 So they took Paul, brought him before the city council, the Areopagus, and said, "We would like to know what this new teaching is that you are talking about. 20 Some of the things we hear you say sound strange to us, and we would like to know what they mean." (21 For all the citizens of Athens and the foreigners who lived there liked to spend all their time telling and hearing the latest new thing.)

22 Paul stood up in front of the city council and said, "I see that in every way you Athenians are very religious. 23 For as I walked through your city and looked at the places where you worship, I found an altar on which is written, 'To an Unknown God.' That which you worship, then, even though you do not know it, is what I now proclaim to you. 24 God, who made the world and everything in it, is Lord of heaven and earth and does not live in temples made by human hands. 25 Nor does he need anything that we can supply by working for him, since it is he himself who gives life and breath and everything else to everyone. 26 From one human being he created all races of people and made them live throughout the whole earth. He himself fixed beforehand the exact times and the limits of the places where they would live. 27 He did this so that they would look for him, and perhaps find him as they felt around for him. Yet God is actually not far from any one of us; 28 as someone has said,

'In him we live and move and exist.'

It is as some of your poets have said,
'We too are his children.'

29 Since we are God's children, we should not suppose that his nature is anything like an image of gold or silver or stone, shaped by human art and skill. 30 God has overlooked the times when people did not know him, but now he commands all of them everywhere to turn away from their evil ways. 31 For he has fixed a day in which he will judge

y JESUS AND THE RESURRECTION: In Greek, the feminine noun "resurrection" could be understood to be the name of a goddess.

the whole world with justice by means of a man he has chosen. He has given proof of this to everyone by raising that man from death!"

32 When they heard Paul speak about a raising from death, some of them made fun of him, but others said, "We want to hear you speak about this again." 33 And so Paul left the meeting. 34 Some men joined him and believed, among whom was Dionysius, a member of the council; there was also a woman named Damaris, and some other people.

In Corinth

18 After this, Paul left Athens and went on to Corinth. 2 There he met a Jew named Aquila, born in Pontus, who had recently come from Italy with his wife Priscilla, for Emperor Claudius had ordered all the Jews to leave Rome. Paul went to see them, 3 and stayed and worked with them, because he earned his living by making tents, just as they did. 4 He held discussions in the synagogue every Sabbath, trying to convince both Jews and Greeks.

5 When Silas and Timothy arrived from Macedonia, Paul gave his whole time to preaching the message, testifying to the Jews that Jesus is the Messiah. 6 When they opposed him and said evil things about him, he protested by shaking the dust from his clothes and saying to them, "If you are lost, you yourselves must take the blame for it! I am not responsible. From now on I will go to the Gentiles." 7 So he left them and went to live in the house of a Gentile named Titius Justus, who worshiped God; his house was next to the synagogue. 8 Crispus, who was the leader of the synagogue, believed in the Lord, together with all his family; and many other people in Corinth heard the message, believed, and were baptized.

9 One night Paul had a vision in which the Lord said to him, "Do not be afraid, but keep on speaking and do not give up, 10 for I am with you. No one will be able to harm you, for many in this city are my people." 1 So Paul stayed there for a year and a half, teaching the people the word of God.

12 When Gallio was made the Roman governor of Achaia, Jews there got together, seized Paul, and took him into court. 13 "This man," they said, "is trying to persuade people to worship God in a way that is against the law!"

14 Paul was about to speak when Gallio said to the Jews, "If this were a matter of some evil crime or wrong that has been committed, it would be reasonable for me to be patient with you Jews. 15 But since it is an argument about words and names and your own law, you yourselves must settle it. I will not be the judge of such things!" 16 And he drove them out of the court. 17 They all grabbed Sosthenes, the leader of the synagogue, and beat him in front of the court. But that did not bother Gallio a bit.

The Return to Antioch

18 Paul stayed on with the believers in Corinth for many days, then left them and sailed off with Priscilla and Aquila for Syria. Before sailing from Cenchreae he had his head shaved because of a vow he had taken.z 19 They arrived in Ephesus, where Paul left Priscilla and Aquila. He went into the synagogue and held discussions with the Jews. 20 The people asked him to stay longer, but he would not consent. 21 Instead, he told them as he left, "If it is the will of God, I will come back to you." And so he sailed from Ephesus.

22 When he arrived at Caesarea, he went to Jerusalem and greeted the church, and then went to Antioch. 23 After spending some time there, he left and went through the region of Galatia and Phrygia, strengthening all the believers.

Apollos in Ephesus and Corinth

24 At that time a Jew named Apollos, who had been born in Alexandria, came to Ephesus. He was an eloquent speaker and had a thorough knowledge of the Scriptures. 25 He had been instructed in the Way of the Lord, and with great enthusiasm he proclaimed and taught correctly the facts about Jesus. However, he knew only the baptism of John. 26 He began to speak boldly in the synagogue. When Priscilla and Aquila heard him, they took him home with them and explained to him more correctly the Way of God. 27 Apollos then decided to go to

---

z A VOW HE HAD TAKEN: *This refers to the Jewish custom of shaving the head as a sign that a vow has been kept.*

NEW TESTAMENT JOURNEYS

The most famous traveler of the New Testament was the apostle Paul. The account of his journey to Rome in a Roman grain ship gives many insights into sea travel in New Testament times (Ac 27). Caught in a winter storm, the ship and its passengers ran aground on the island of Malta off the coast of Sicily. After three months and a break in the bad weather, they continued to Rome in a second ship which sailed from Alexandria, Egypt (Ac 28.11).

Other famous journeys of New Testament personalities include the following:

Personality(ies)	Description of Journey	Biblical Reference
Visitors from the East	From the East to Bethlehem to worship the newborn Jesus	Mt 2.1-12
Joseph and Mary	From Nazareth to Bethlehem, where Jesus was born	Lk 2.4
Mary, Joseph, and Jesus	Fled to Egypt to escape Herod's threat; returned to Nazareth after Herod's death	Mt 2.13-23
Philip	From Jerusalem to Samaria to preach to the Samaritans; from Samaria into the desert to witness to the Ethiopian eunuch; from the desert to Caesarea	Ac 8.5 Ac 8.26 Ac 8.40
Paul	From Jerusalem to Damascus to arrest the early Christians	Ac 9
Peter	From Joppa to Caesarea to meet Cornelius and preach to the Gentiles	Ac 10
Barnabas	From Jerusalem to Antioch to work with the Gentile converts	Ac 11.19-26
Paul and Barnabas	Paul's first missionary tour from Antioch to numerous places, including the island of Cyprus and the cities of Attalia, Perga, Antioch of Pisidia, Iconium, Lystra, and Derbe	Ac 13; 14
Paul and Silas	Paul's second missionary tour from Antioch to numerous cities, including Tarsus, Troas, Neapolis, Philippi, Apollonia, Thessalonica, Berea, Athens, Corinth, and Ephesus	Ac 15—18
Paul	Paul's third missionary tour from Antioch to numerous cities; new locations visited on this tour included Assos, Mitylene, Miletus, Cos, Patara, and the island of Rhodes in the Aegean Sea off the coast of Asia Minor	Ac 18—21

Achaia, so the believers in Ephesus helped him by writing to the believers in Achaia, urging them to welcome him. When he arrived, he was a great help to those who through God's grace had become believers. 28 For with his strong arguments he defeated the Jews in public debates by proving from the Scriptures that Jesus is the Messiah.

Paul in Ephesus

19 While Apollos was in Corinth, Paul traveled through the interior of the province and arrived in Ephesus. There he found some disciples 2 and asked them, "Did you receive the Holy Spirit when you became believers?"

"We have not even heard that there is a Holy Spirit," they answered.

3 "Well, then, what kind of baptism did you receive?" Paul asked.

"The baptism of John," they answered.

4 Paul said, "The baptism of John was for those who turned from their sins; and he told the people of Israel to believe in the one who was coming after him—that is, in Jesus."

5 When they heard this, they were baptized in the name of the Lord Jesus. 6 Paul placed his hands on them, and the Holy Spirit came upon them; they spoke in strange tongues and also proclaimed God's message. 7 They were about twelve men in all.

8 Paul went into the synagogue and for three months spoke boldly with the people, holding discussions with them and trying to convince them about the Kingdom of God. 9 But some of them were stubborn and would not believe, and before the whole group they said evil things about the Way of the Lord. So Paul left them and took the believers with him, and every day a he held discussions in the lecture hall of Tyrannus. 10 This went on for two years, so that all the people who lived in the province of Asia, both Jews and Gentiles, heard the word of the Lord.

The Sons of Sceva

11 God was performing unusual miracles through Paul. 12 Even handkerchiefs and aprons he had used were taken to the sick, and their diseases would be driven

away, and the evil spirits would go out of them. 13 Some Jews who traveled around and drove out evil spirits also tried to use the name of the Lord Jesus to do this. They said to the evil spirits, "I command you in the name of Jesus, whom Paul preaches." 14 Seven brothers, who were the sons of a Jewish High Priest named Sceva, were doing this.

15 But the evil spirit said to them, "I know Jesus, and I know about Paul; but you—who are you?"

16 The man who had the evil spirit in him attacked them with such violence that he overpowered them all. They ran away from his house, wounded and with their clothes torn off. 17 All the Jews and Gentiles who lived in Ephesus heard about this; they were all filled with fear, and the name of the Lord Jesus was given greater honor. 18 Many of the believers came, publicly admitting and revealing what they had done. 19 Many of those who had practiced magic brought their books together and burned them in public. They added up the price of the books, and the total came to fifty thousand silver coins. b 20 In this powerful way the word of the Lord c kept spreading and growing stronger.

The Riot in Ephesus

21 After these things had happened, Paul made up his mind d to travel through Macedonia and Achaia and go on to Jerusalem. "After I go there," he said, "I must also see Rome." 22 So he sent Timothy and Erastus, two of his helpers, to Macedonia, while he spent more time in the province of Asia.

23 It was at this time that there was serious trouble in Ephesus because of the Way of the Lord. 24 A certain silversmith named Demetrius made silver models of the temple of the goddess Artemis, and his business brought a great deal of profit to the workers. 25 So he called them all together with others whose work was like theirs and said to them, "Men, you know that our prosperity comes from this work. 26 Now, you can see and hear for yourselves what this fellow Paul is doing. He says that handmade gods are not gods at all, and he has succeeded in convincing many people,

a Some manuscripts add from 11:00 a.m. until 4:00 p.m.   b SILVER COINS: A silver coin was the daily wage of a rural worker (see Mt 20.2).   c In this . . . Lord; or And so, by the power of the Lord, the message.   d Paul made up his mind; or Paul, led by the Spirit, decided.

both here in Ephesus and in nearly the whole province of Asia. 27 There is the danger, then, that this business of ours will get a bad name. Not only that, but there is also the danger that the temple of the great goddess Artemis will come to mean nothing and that her greatness will be destroyed—the goddess worshiped by everyone in Asia and in all the world!"

28 As the crowd heard these words, they became furious and started shouting, "Great is Artemis of Ephesus!" 29 The uproar spread throughout the whole city. The mob grabbed Gaius and Aristarchus, two Macedonians who were traveling with Paul, and rushed with them to the theater. 30 Paul himself wanted to go before the crowd, but the believers would not let him. 31 Some of the provincial authorities, who were his friends, also sent him a message begging him not to show himself in the theater. 32 Meanwhile the whole meeting was in an uproar: some people were shouting one thing, others were shouting something else, because most of them did not even know why they had come together. 33 Some of the people concluded that Alexander was responsible, since the Jews made him go up to the front. Then Alexander motioned with his hand for the people to be silent, and he tried to make a speech of defense. 34 But when they recognized that he was a Jew, they all shouted together the same thing for two hours: "Great is Artemis of Ephesus!"

35 At last the city clerk was able to calm the crowd. "Fellow Ephesians!" he said. "Everyone knows that the city of Ephesus is the keeper of the temple of the great Artemis and of the sacred stone that fell down from heaven. 36 Nobody can deny these things. So then, you must calm down and not do anything reckless. 37 You have brought these men here even though they have not robbed temples or said evil things about our goddess. 38 If Demetrius and his workers have an accusation against anyone, we have the authorities and the regular days for court; charges can be made there. 39 But if there is something more that you want, it will have to be settled in a legal meeting of citizens. 40 For after what has happened today, there is the danger that we will be accused of a riot. There is no excuse for all this uproar, and we would not be able to give a good reason for it." 41 After saying this, he dismissed the meeting.

To Macedonia and Achaia

20 After the uproar died down, Paul called together the believers and with words of encouragement said goodbye to them. Then he left and went on to Macedonia. 2 He went through those regions and encouraged the people with many messages. Then he came to Achaia, 3 where he stayed three months. He was getting ready to go to Syria when he discovered that there were Jews plotting against him; so he decided to go back through Macedonia. 4 Sopater son of Pyrrhus, from Berea, went with him; so did Aristarchus and Secundus, from Thessalonica; Gaius, from Derbe; Tychicus and Trophimus, from the province of Asia; and Timothy. 5 They went ahead and waited for us in Troas. 6 We sailed from Philippi after the Festival of Unleavened Bread, and five days later we joined them in Troas, where we spent a week.

Paul's Last Visit to Troas

7 On Saturday[e] evening we gathered together for the fellowship meal. Paul spoke to the people and kept on speaking until midnight, since he was going to leave the next day. 8 Many lamps were burning in the upstairs room where we were meeting. 9 A young man named Eutychus was sitting in the window, and as Paul kept on talking, Eutychus got sleepier and sleepier, until he finally went sound asleep and fell from the third story to the ground. When they picked him up, he was dead. 10 But Paul went down and threw himself on him and hugged him. "Don't worry," he said, "he is still alive!" 11 Then he went back upstairs, broke bread, and ate. After talking with them for a long time, even until sunrise, Paul left. 12 They took the young man home alive and were greatly comforted.

From Troas to Miletus

13 We went on ahead to the ship and sailed off to Assos, where we were going

e Saturday; or Sunday.

to take Paul aboard. He had told us to do this, because he was going there by land. 14When he met us in Assos, we took him aboard and went on to Mitylene. 15We sailed from there and arrived off Chios the next day. A day later we came to Samos, and the following day we reached Miletus. 16Paul had decided to sail on by Ephesus, so as not to lose any time in the province of Asia. He was in a hurry to arrive in Jerusalem by the day of Pentecost if at all possible.

Paul's Farewell Speech to the Elders of Ephesus

17From Miletus Paul sent a message to Ephesus, asking the elders of the church to meet him. 18When they arrived, he said to them, "You know how I spent the whole time I was with you, from the first day I arrived in the province of Asia. 19With all humility and many tears I did my work as the Lord's servant during the hard times that came to me because of the plots of some Jews. 20You know that I did not hold back anything that would be of help to you as I preached and taught in public and in your homes. 21To Jews and Gentiles alike I gave solemn warning that they should turn from their sins to God and believe in our Lord Jesus. 22And now, in obedience to the Holy Spirit I am going to Jerusalem, not knowing what will happen to me there. 23I only know that in every city the Holy Spirit has warned me that prison and troubles wait for me. 24But I reckon my own life to be worth nothing to me; I only want to complete my mission and finish the work that the Lord Jesus gave me to do, which is to declare the Good News about the grace of God.

25"I have gone about among all of you, preaching the Kingdom of God. And now I know that none of you will ever see me again. 26So I solemnly declare to you this very day: if any of you should be lost, I am not responsible. 27For I have not held back from announcing to you the whole purpose of God. 28So keep watch over yourselves and over all the flock which the Holy Spirit has placed in your care. Be shepherds of the church of God,f which he made his own through the blood of his Son.g 29I know

that after I leave, fierce wolves will come among you, and they will not spare the flock. 30The time will come when some men from your own group will tell lies to lead the believers away after them. 31Watch, then, and remember that with many tears, day and night, I taught every one of you for three years.

32"And now I commend you to the care of God and to the message of his grace, which is able to build you up and give you the blessings God has for all his people. 33I have not wanted anyone's silver or gold or clothing. 34You yourselves know that I have worked with these hands of mine to provide everything that my companions and I have needed. 35I have shown you in all things that by working hard in this way we must help the weak, remembering the words that the Lord Jesus himself said, 'There is more happiness in giving than in receiving.' "

36When Paul finished, he knelt down with them and prayed. 37They were all crying as they hugged him and kissed him good-bye. 38They were especially sad because he had said that they would never see him again. And so they went with him to the ship.

Paul Goes to Jerusalem

21 We said good-bye to them and left. After sailing straight across, we came to Cos; the next day we reached Rhodes, and from there we went on to Patara. 2There we found a ship that was going to Phoenicia, so we went aboard and sailed away. 3We came to where we could see Cyprus, and then sailed south of it on to Syria. We went ashore at Tyre, where the ship was going to unload its cargo. 4There we found some believers and stayed with them a week. By the power of the Spirit they told Paul not to go to Jerusalem. 5But when our time with them was over, we left and went on our way. All of them, together with their wives and children, went with us out of the city to the beach, where we all knelt down and prayed. 6Then we said good-bye to one another, and we went on board the ship while they went back home.

7We continued our voyage, sailing

---

f God; *some manuscripts have* the Lord.   g through the blood of his Son; *or* through the sacrificial death of his Son; *or* through his own blood.

from Tyre to Ptolemais, where we greeted the believers and stayed with them for a day. 8 On the following day we left and arrived in Caesarea. There we stayed at the house of Philip the evangelist, one of the seven men who had been chosen as helpers in Jerusalem. 9 He had four unmarried daughters who proclaimed God's message. 10 We had been there for several days when a prophet named Agabus arrived from Judea. 11 He came to us, took Paul's belt, tied up his own feet and hands with it, and said, "This is what the Holy Spirit says: The owner of this belt will be tied up in this way by the Jews in Jerusalem, and they will hand him over to the Gentiles."

12 When we heard this, we and the others there begged Paul not to go to Jerusalem. 13 But he answered, "What are you doing, crying like this and breaking my heart? I am ready not only to be tied up in Jerusalem but even to die there for the sake of the Lord Jesus."

14 We could not convince him, so we gave up and said, "May the Lord's will be done."

15 After spending some time there, we got our things ready and left for Jerusalem. 16 Some of the disciples from Caesarea also went with us and took us to the house of the man we were going to stay with h — Mnason, from Cyprus, who had been a believer since the early days.

Paul Visits James

17 When we arrived in Jerusalem, the believers welcomed us warmly. 18 The next day Paul went with us to see James; and all the church elders were present. 19 Paul greeted them and gave a complete report of everything that God had done among the Gentiles through his work. 20 After hearing him, they all praised God. Then they said, "Brother Paul, you can see how many thousands of Jews have become believers, and how devoted they all are to the Law. 21 They have been told that you have been teaching all the Jews who live in Gentile countries to abandon the Law of Moses, telling them not to circumcise their children or follow the Jewish customs. 22 They are sure to hear that you have arrived. What should be done, then? 23 This is what we want you to do. There are four men here who have taken a vow. 24 Go along with them and join them in the ceremony of purification and pay their expenses; then they will be able to shave their heads. i In this way everyone will know that there is no truth in any of the things that they have been told about you, but that you yourself live in accordance with the Law of Moses. 25 But as for the Gentiles who have become believers, we have sent them a letter telling them we decided that they must not eat any food that has been offered to idols, or any blood, or any animal that has been strangled, and that they must keep themselves from sexual immorality."

26 So Paul took the men and the next day performed the ceremony of purification with them. Then he went into the Temple and gave notice of how many days it would be until the end of the period of purification, when a sacrifice would be offered for each one of them.

Paul Is Arrested in the Temple

27 But just when the seven days were about to come to an end, some Jews from the province of Asia saw Paul in the Temple. They stirred up the whole crowd and grabbed Paul. 28 "People of Israel!" they shouted. "Help! This is the man who goes everywhere teaching everyone against the people of Israel, the Law of Moses, and this Temple. And now he has even brought some Gentiles into the Temple and defiled this holy place!" (29 They said this because they had seen Trophimus from Ephesus with Paul in the city, and they thought that Paul had taken him into the Temple.)

30 Confusion spread through the whole city, and the people all ran together, grabbed Paul, and dragged him out of the Temple. At once the Temple doors were closed. 31 The mob was trying to kill Paul, when a report was sent up to the commander of the Roman troops that all of Jerusalem was rioting. 32 At once the commander took some officers

h and took us to the house of the man we were going to stay with; or bringing with them the man at whose house we were going to stay. i SHAVE THEIR HEADS: See 18.18.

and soldiers and rushed down to the crowd. When the people saw him with the soldiers, they stopped beating Paul. 33 The commander went over to Paul, arrested him, and ordered him to be bound with two chains. Then he asked, "Who is this man, and what has he done?" 34 Some in the crowd shouted one thing, others something else. There was such confusion that the commander could not find out exactly what had happened, so he ordered his men to take Paul up into the fort. 35 They got as far as the steps with him, and then the soldiers had to carry him because the mob was so wild. 36 They were all coming after him and screaming, "Kill him!"

Paul Defends Himself

37 As the soldiers were about to take Paul into the fort, he spoke to the commander: "May I say something to you?"

"You speak Greek, do you?" the commander asked. 38 "Then you are not that Egyptian fellow who some time ago started a revolution and led four thousand armed terrorists out into the desert?"

39 Paul answered, "I am a Jew, born in Tarsus in Cilicia, a citizen of an important city. Please let me speak to the people."

40 The commander gave him permission, so Paul stood on the steps and motioned with his hand for the people to be silent. When they were quiet, Paul spoke to them in Hebrew:

22 "My fellow Jews, listen to me as I make my defense before you!" 2 When they heard him speaking to them in Hebrew, they became even quieter; and Paul went on:

3 "I am a Jew, born in Tarsus in Cilicia, but brought up here in Jerusalem as a student of Gamaliel. I received strict instruction in the Law of our ancestors and was just as dedicated to God as are all of you who are here today. 4 I persecuted to the death the people who followed this Way. I arrested men and women and threw them into prison. 5 The High Priest and the whole Council can prove that I am telling the truth. I received from them letters written to fellow Jews in Damascus, so I went there to arrest these people and bring them back in chains to Jerusalem to be punished.

Paul Tells of His Conversion
(Acts 9.1-19; 26.12-18)

6 "As I was traveling and coming near Damascus, about midday a bright light from the sky flashed suddenly around me. 7 I fell to the ground and heard a voice saying to me, 'Saul, Saul! Why do you persecute me?' 8 'Who are you, Lord?' I asked. 'I am Jesus of Nazareth, whom you persecute,' he said to me. 9 The men with me saw the light, but did not hear the voice of the one who was speaking to me. 10 I asked, 'What shall I do, Lord?' and the Lord said to me, 'Get up and go into Damascus, and there you will be told everything that God has determined for you to do.' 11 I was blind because of the bright light, and so my companions took me by the hand and led me into Damascus.

12 "In that city was a man named Ananias, a religious man who obeyed our Law and was highly respected by all the Jews living there. 13 He came to me, stood by me, and said, 'Brother Saul, see again!' At that very moment I saw again and looked at him. 14 He said, 'The God of our ancestors has chosen you to know his will, to see his righteous Servant, and to hear him speaking with his own voice. 15 For you will be a witness for him to tell everyone what you have seen and heard. 16 And now, why wait any longer? Get up and be baptized and have your sins washed away by praying to him.'

Paul's Call to Preach to the Gentiles

17 "I went back to Jerusalem, and while I was praying in the Temple, I had a vision, 18 in which I saw the Lord, as he said to me, 'Hurry and leave Jerusalem quickly, because the people here will not accept your witness about me.' 19 'Lord,' I answered, 'they know very well that I went to the synagogues and arrested and beat those who believe in you. 20 And when your witness Stephen was put to death, I myself was there, approving of his murder and taking care of the cloaks of his murderers.' 21 'Go,' the Lord said to me, 'for I will send you far away to the Gentiles.'"

22 The people listened to Paul until he said this; but then they started shouting at the top of their voices, "Away with him! Kill him! He's not fit to live!" 23 They were screaming, waving their

clothes, and throwing dust up in the air. 24 The Roman commander ordered his men to take Paul into the fort, and he told them to whip him in order to find out why the Jews were screaming like this against him. 25 But when they had tied him up to be whipped, Paul said to the officer standing there, "Is it lawful for you to whip a Roman citizen who hasn't even been tried for any crime?"

26 When the officer heard this, he went to the commander and asked him, "What are you doing? That man is a Roman citizen!"

27 So the commander went to Paul and asked him, "Tell me, are you a Roman citizen?"

"Yes," answered Paul.

28 The commander said, "I became one by paying a large amount of money."

"But I am one by birth," Paul answered.

29 At once the men who were going to question Paul drew back from him; and the commander was frightened when he realized that Paul was a Roman citizen and that he had put him in chains.

Paul before the Council

30 The commander wanted to find out for sure what the Jews were accusing Paul of; so the next day he had Paul's chains taken off and ordered the chief priests and the whole Council to meet. Then he took Paul and made him stand before them.

23 Paul looked straight at the Council and said, "My fellow Israelites! My conscience is perfectly clear about the way in which I have lived before God to this very day." 2 The High Priest Ananias ordered those who were standing close to Paul to strike him on the mouth. 3 Paul said to him, "God will certainly strike you — you whitewashed wall! You sit there to judge me according to the Law, yet you break the Law by ordering them to strike me!"

4 The men close to Paul said to him, "You are insulting God's High Priest!"

5 Paul answered, "My fellow Israelites, I did not know that he was the High Priest. The scripture says, 'You must not speak evil of the ruler of your people.' "

6 When Paul saw that some of the group were Sadducees and the others were Pharisees, he called out in the Council, "Fellow Israelites! I am a Pharisee, the son of Pharisees. I am on trial here because of the hope I have that the dead will rise to life!"

7 As soon as he said this, the Pharisees and Sadducees started to quarrel, and the group was divided. (8 For the Sadducees say that people will not rise from death and that there are no angels or spirits; but the Pharisees believe in all three.) 9 The shouting became louder, and some of the teachers of the Law who belonged to the party of the Pharisees stood up and protested strongly: "We cannot find a thing wrong with this man! Perhaps a spirit or an angel really did speak to him!"

10 The argument became so violent that the commander was afraid that Paul would be torn to pieces. So he ordered his soldiers to go down into the group, get Paul away from them, and take him into the fort.

11 That night the Lord stood by Paul and said, "Don't be afraid! You have given your witness for me here in Jerusalem, and you must also do the same in Rome."

The Plot against Paul's Life

12 The next morning some Jews met together and made a plan. They took a vow that they would not eat or drink anything until they had killed Paul. 13 There were more than forty who planned this together. 14 Then they went to the chief priests and elders and said, "We have taken a solemn vow together not to eat a thing until we have killed Paul. 15 Now then, you and the Council send word to the Roman commander to bring Paul down to you, pretending that you want to get more accurate information about him. But we will be ready to kill him before he ever gets here."

16 But the son of Paul's sister heard about the plot; so he went to the fort and told Paul. 17 Then Paul called one of the officers and said to him, "Take this young man to the commander; he has something to tell him." 18 The officer took him, led him to the commander, and said, "The prisoner Paul called me and asked me to bring this young man to you, because he has something to say to you."

19 The commander took him by the hand, led him off by himself, and asked him, "What do you have to tell me?"

20 He said, "The Jewish authorities have agreed to ask you tomorrow to take Paul down to the Council, pretending that the Council wants to get more accurate information about him. 21 But don't listen to them, because there are more than forty men who will be hiding and waiting for him. They have taken a vow not to eat or drink until they have killed him. They are now ready to do it and are waiting for your decision."

22 The commander said, "Don't tell anyone that you have reported this to me." And he sent the young man away.

Paul Is Sent to Governor Felix

23 Then the commander called two of his officers and said, "Get two hundred soldiers ready to go to Caesarea, together with seventy horsemen and two hundred spearmen, and be ready to leave by nine o'clock tonight. 24 Provide some horses for Paul to ride and get him safely through to Governor Felix." 25 Then the commander wrote a letter that went like this:

26 "Claudius Lysias to His Excellency, Governor Felix: Greetings. 27 The Jews seized this man and were about to kill him. I learned that he is a Roman citizen, so I went with my soldiers and rescued him. 28 I wanted to know what they were accusing him of, so I took him down to their Council. 29 I found out that he had not done a thing for which he deserved to die or be put in prison; the accusation against him had to do with questions about their own law. 30 And when I was informed that there was a plot against him, at once I decided to send him to you. I have told his accusers to make their charges against him before you."

31 The soldiers carried out their orders. They got Paul and took him that night as far as Antipatris. 32 The next day the foot soldiers returned to the fort and left the horsemen to go on with him. 33 They took him to Caesarea, delivered the letter to the governor, and turned Paul over to him. 34 The governor read the letter and asked Paul what province he was from. When he found out that he was from Cilicia, 35 he said, "I will hear you

when your accusers arrive." Then he gave orders for Paul to be kept under guard in the governor's headquarters.

The Case Against Paul

24 Five days later the High Priest Ananias went to Caesarea with some elders and a lawyer named Tertullus. They appeared before Governor Felix and made their charges against Paul. 2 Then Paul was called in, and Tertullus began to make his accusation, as follows:

"Your Excellency! Your wise leadership has brought us a long period of peace, and many necessary reforms are being made for the good of our country. 3 We welcome this everywhere and at all times, and we are deeply grateful to you. 4 I do not want to take up too much of your time, however, so I beg you to be kind and listen to our brief account. 5 We found this man to be a dangerous nuisance; he starts riots among Jews all over the world and is a leader of the party of the Nazarenes. 6 He also tried to defile the Temple, and we arrested him.j 8 If you question this man, you yourself will be able to learn from him all the things that we are accusing him of." 9 The Jews joined in the accusation and said that all this was true.

Paul's Defense before Felix

10 The governor then motioned to Paul to speak, and Paul said,

"I know that you have been a judge over this nation for many years, and so I am happy to defend myself before you. 11 As you can find out for yourself, it was no more than twelve days ago that I went to Jerusalem to worship. 12 The Jews did not find me arguing with anyone in the Temple, nor did they find me stirring up the people, either in the synagogues or anywhere else in the city. 13 Nor can they give you proof of the accusations they now bring against me. 14 I do admit this to you: I worship the God of our ancestors by following that Way which they say is false. But I also believe in everything written in the Law of Moses and the books of the prophets. 15 I have the same hope in God that these themselves have, namely, that all peo-

---

j Some manuscripts add verses 6b-8a: We planned to judge him according to our own law, 7 but the commander Lysias came, and with great violence took him from us. 8 Then Lysias gave orders that his accusers should come before you.

ple, both the good and the bad, will rise from death. 16 And so I do my best always to have a clear conscience before God and people.

17 "After being away from Jerusalem for several years, I went there to take some money to my own people and to offer sacrifices. 18 It was while I was doing this that they found me in the Temple after I had completed the ceremony of purification. There was no crowd with me and no disorder. 19 But some Jews from the province of Asia were there; they themselves ought to come before you and make their accusations if they have anything against me. 20 Or let these who are here tell what crime they found me guilty of when I stood before the Council — 21 except for the one thing I called out when I stood before them: 'I am being tried by you today for believing that the dead will rise to life.' "

22 Then Felix, who was well informed about the Way, brought the hearing to a close. "When the commander Lysias arrives," he told them, "I will decide your case." 23 He ordered the officer in charge of Paul to keep him under guard, but to give him some freedom and allow his friends to provide for his needs.

Paul before Felix and Drusilla

24 After some days Felix came with his wife Drusilla, who was Jewish. He sent for Paul and listened to him as he talked about faith in Christ Jesus. 25 But as Paul went on discussing about goodness, self-control, and the coming Day of Judgment, Felix was afraid and said, "You may leave now. I will call you again when I get the chance." 26 At the same time he was hoping that Paul would give him some money; and for this reason he would call for him often and talk with him.

27 After two years had passed, Porcius Festus succeeded Felix as governor. Felix wanted to gain favor with the Jews so he left Paul in prison.

Paul Appeals to the Emperor

25 Three days after Festus arrived in the province, he went from Caesarea to Jerusalem, 2 where the chief priests and the Jewish leaders brought their charges against Paul. They begged Festus 3 to do them the favor of having Paul come to Jerusalem, for they had made a plot to kill him on the way. 4 Festus answered, "Paul is being kept a prisoner in Caesarea, and I myself will be going back there soon. 5 Let your leaders go to Caesarea with me and accuse the man if he has done anything wrong."

6 Festus spent another eight or ten days with them and then went to Caesarea. On the next day he sat down in the judgment court and ordered Paul to be brought in. 7 When Paul arrived, the Jews who had come from Jerusalem stood around him and started making many serious charges against him, which they were not able to prove. 8 But Paul defended himself: "I have done nothing wrong against the Law of the Jews or against the Temple or against the Roman Emperor."

9 But Festus wanted to gain favor with the Jews, so he asked Paul, "Would you be willing to go to Jerusalem and be tried on these charges before me there?"

10 Paul said, "I am standing before the Emperor's own judgment court, where I should be tried. I have done no wrong to the Jews, as you yourself well know. 11 If I have broken the law and done something for which I deserve the death penalty, I do not ask to escape it. But if there is no truth in the charges they bring against me, no one can hand me over to them. I appeal to the Emperor."

12 Then Festus, after conferring with his advisers, answered, "You have appealed to the Emperor, so to the Emperor you will go."

Paul before Agrippa and Bernice

13 Some time later King Agrippa and Bernice came to Caesarea to pay a visit of welcome to Festus. 14 After they had been there several days, Festus explained Paul's situation to the king: "There is a man here who was left a prisoner by Felix; 15 and when I went to Jerusalem, the Jewish chief priests and elders brought charges against him and asked me to condemn him. 16 But I told them that we Romans are not in the habit of handing over any who are accused of a crime before they have met their accusers face-to-face and have had the chance of defending themselves against the accusation. 17 When they came here, then, I lost no time, but on the very next day I sat in the judgment court and ordered the man to be brought

SERMONS IN ACTS

One of the most eloquent sermons in the Book of Acts is Paul's speech to the Athenian philosophers from the Areopagus, or Mars' Hill, a stony point named for the Greek god of war Ares (Roman god Mars). This hill overlooked the city of Athens. In his speech, Paul declared that God will hold all people accountable for their response to his Son (Ac 17).

Several other important sermons and speeches, including the following, occur in the Book of Acts.

Speech	Theme	Biblical Reference
Peter to crowds at Pentecost	Peter's explanation of the meaning of Pentecost	Ac 2.14–40
Peter to crowds at the Temple	The Jewish people should repent for crucifying the Messiah	Ac 3.12–26
Peter to the Council	Testimony that a lame man was healed by the power of Jesus	Ac 4.5–12
Stephen to the Council	Stephen's rehearsal of Jewish history, accusing the Jews of killing the Messiah	Ac 7
Peter to Gentiles	Gentiles can be saved in the same manner as Jews	Ac 10.28–47
Peter to church at Jerusalem	Peter's testimony of his experiences at Joppa and a defense of his ministry to the Gentiles	Ac 11.4–18
Paul to synagogue at Antioch	Jesus was the Messiah in fulfillment of Old Testament prophecies	Ac 13.16–41
Peter to Jerusalem council	Salvation by grace available to all	Ac 15.7–11
James to Jerusalem council	Gentile converts do not require circumcision	Ac 15.13–21
Paul to Ephesian elders	Remain faithful in spite of false teachers and persecution	Ac 20.17–35
Paul to crowd at Jerusalem	Paul's statement of his conversion and his mission to the Gentiles	Ac 22.1–21
Paul to Council	Paul's defense, declaring himself a Pharisee	Ac 23.1–6
Paul to King Agrippa	Paul's statement of his conversion and his zeal for the gospel	Ac 26
Paul to Jewish leaders at Rome	Paul's statement about his Jewish heritage	Ac 28.17–20

in. 18His opponents stood up, but they did not accuse him of any of the evil crimes that I thought they would. 19All they had were some arguments with him about their own religion and about a man named Jesus, who has died; but Paul claims that he is alive. 20I was undecided about how I could get information on these matters, so I asked Paul if he would be willing to go to Jerusalem and be tried there on these charges. 21But Paul appealed; he asked to be kept under guard and to let the Emperor decide his case. So I gave orders for him to be kept under guard until I could send him to the Emperor."

22Agrippa said to Festus, "I would like to hear this man myself."

"You will hear him tomorrow," Festus answered.

23The next day Agrippa and Bernice came with great pomp and ceremony and entered the audience hall with the military chiefs and the leading men of the city. Festus gave the order, and Paul was brought in. 24Festus said, "King Agrippa and all who are here with us: You see this man against whom all the Jewish people, both here and in Jerusalem, have brought complaints to me. They scream that he should not live any longer. 25But I could not find that he had done anything for which he deserved the death sentence. And since he himself made an appeal to the Emperor, I have decided to send him. 26But I have nothing definite about him to write to the Emperor. So I have brought him here before you — and especially before you, King Agrippa! — so that, after investigating his case, I may have something to write. 27For it seems unreasonable to me to send a prisoner without clearly indicating the charges against him."

Paul Defends Himself before Agrippa

26 Agrippa said to Paul, "You have permission to speak on your own behalf." Paul stretched out his hand and defended himself as follows:

2"King Agrippa! I consider myself fortunate that today I am to defend myself before you from all the things these Jews accuse me of, 3particularly since you know so well all the Jewish customs

and disputes. I ask you, then, to listen to me with patience.

4"All the Jews know how I have lived ever since I was young. They know how I have spent my whole life, at first in my own country and then in Jerusalem. 5They have always known, if they are willing to testify, that from the very first I have lived as a member of the strictest party of our religion, the Pharisees. 6And now I stand here to be tried because of the hope I have in the promise that God made to our ancestors — 7the very thing that the twelve tribes of our people hope to receive, as they worship God day and night. And it is because of this hope, Your Majesty, that I am being accused by these Jews! 8Why do you who are here find it impossible to believe that God raises the dead?

9"I myself thought that I should do everything I could against the cause of Jesus of Nazareth. 10That is what I did in Jerusalem. I received authority from the chief priests and put many of God's people in prison; and when they were sentenced to death, I also voted against them. 11Many times I had them punished in the synagogues and tried to make them deny their faith. I was so furious with them that I even went to foreign cities to persecute them.

Paul Tells of His Conversion
(Acts 9.1-19; 22.6-16)

12"It was for this purpose that I went to Damascus with authority and orders from the chief priests. 13It was on the road at midday, Your Majesty, that I saw a light much brighter than the sun, coming from the sky and shining around me and the men traveling with me. 14All of us fell to the ground, and I heard a voice say to me in Hebrew, 'Saul, Saul! Why are you persecuting me? You are hurting yourself by hitting back, like an ox kicking against its owner's stick.' 15'Who are you, Lord?' I asked. And the Lord answered, 'I am Jesus, whom you persecute. 16But get up and stand on your feet. I have appeared to you to appoint you as my servant. You are to tell others what you have seen of mek today and what I will show you in the future. 17I will rescue you from the people of Israel and from the Gentiles to whom I will send

k *Some manuscripts do not have* of me.

you. 18 You are to open their eyes and turn them from the darkness to the light and from the power of Satan to God, so that through their faith in me they will have their sins forgiven and receive their place among God's chosen people.'

Paul Tells of His Work

19 "And so, King Agrippa, I did not disobey the vision I had from heaven. 20 First in Damascus and in Jerusalem and then in the whole country of Israel and among the Gentiles, I preached that they must repent of their sins and turn to God and do the things that would show they had repented. 21 It was for this reason that these Jews seized me while I was in the Temple, and they tried to kill me. 22 But to this very day I have been helped by God, and so I stand here giving my witness to all, to small and great alike. What I say is the very same thing which the prophets and Moses said was going to happen: 23 that the Messiah must suffer and be the first one to rise from death, to announce the light of salvation to the Jews and to the Gentiles."

24 As Paul defended himself in this way, Festus shouted at him, "You are mad, Paul! Your great learning is driving you mad!"

25 Paul answered, "I am not mad, Your Excellency! I am speaking the sober truth. 26 King Agrippa! I can speak to you with all boldness, because you know about these things. I am sure that you have taken notice of every one of them, for this thing has not happened hidden away in a corner. 27 King Agrippa, do you believe the prophets? I know that you do!"

28 Agrippa said to Paul, "In this short time do you think you will make me a Christian?"

29 "Whether a short time or a long time," Paul answered, "my prayer to God is that you and all the rest of you who are listening to me today might become what I am — except, of course, for these chains!"

30 Then the king, the governor, Bernice, and all the others got up, 31 and after leaving they said to each other, "This man has not done anything for which he should die or be put in prison." 32 And

Agrippa said to Festus, "This man could have been released if he had not appealed to the Emperor."

Paul Sails for Rome

27 When it was decided that we should sail to Italy, they handed Paul and some other prisoners over to Julius, an officer in the Roman army regiment called "The Emperor's Regiment." 2 We went aboard a ship from Adramyttium, which was ready to leave for the seaports of the province of Asia, and we sailed away. Aristarchus, a Macedonian from Thessalonica, was with us. 3 The next day we arrived at Sidon. Julius was kind to Paul and allowed him to go and see his friends, to be given what he needed. 4 We went on from there, and because the winds were blowing against us, we sailed on the sheltered side of the island of Cyprus. 5 We crossed over the sea off Cilicia and Pamphylia and came to Myra in Lycia. 6 There the officer found a ship from Alexandria that was going to sail for Italy, so he put us aboard.

7 We sailed slowly for several days and with great difficulty finally arrived off the town of Cnidus. The wind would not let us go any farther in that direction, so we sailed down the sheltered side of the island of Crete, passing by Cape Salmone. 8 We kept close to the coast and with great difficulty came to a place called Safe Harbors, not far from the town of Lasea.

9 We spent a long time there, until it became dangerous to continue the voyage, for by now the Day of Atonement[l] was already past. So Paul gave them this advice: 10 "Men, I see that our voyage from here on will be dangerous; there will be great damage to the cargo and to the ship, and loss of life as well." 11 But the army officer was convinced by what the captain and the owner of the ship said, and not by what Paul said. 12 The harbor was not a good one to spend the winter in; so almost everyone was in favor of putting out to sea and trying to reach Phoenix, if possible, in order to spend the winter there. Phoenix is a harbor in Crete that faces southwest and northwest.[m]

---

[l] DAY OF ATONEMENT: *This was celebrated toward the end of September or beginning of October, at which time bad weather made sailing dangerous.* [m] *southwest and northwest; or northeast and southeast.*

The Storm at Sea

13 A soft wind from the south began to blow, and the men thought that they could carry out their plan, so they pulled up the anchor and sailed as close as possible along the coast of Crete. 14 But soon a very strong wind — the one called "Northeaster" — blew down from the island. 15 It hit the ship, and since it was impossible to keep the ship headed into the wind, we gave up trying and let it be carried along by the wind. 16 We got some shelter when we passed to the south of the little island of Cauda. There, with some difficulty we managed to make the ship's boat secure. 17 They pulled it aboard and then fastened some ropes tight around the ship. They were afraid that they might run into the sandbanks off the coast of Libya, so they lowered the sail and let the ship be carried by the wind. 18 The violent storm continued, so on the next day they began to throw some of the ship's cargo overboard, 19 and on the following day they threw part of the ship's equipment overboard. 20 For many days we could not see the sun or the stars, and the wind kept on blowing very hard. We finally gave up all hope of being saved.

21 After everyone had gone a long time without food, Paul stood before them and said, "You should have listened to me and not have sailed from Crete; then we would have avoided all this damage and loss. 22 But now I beg you, take courage! Not one of you will lose your life; only the ship will be lost. 23 For last night an angel of the God to whom I belong and whom I worship came to me 24 and said, 'Don't be afraid, Paul! You must stand before the Emperor. And God in his goodness to you has spared the lives of all those who are sailing with you.' 25 So take courage, men! For I trust in God that it will be just as I was told. 26 But we will be driven ashore on some island."

27 It was the fourteenth night, and we were being driven in the Mediterranean by the storm. About midnight the sailors suspected that we were getting close to land. 28 So they dropped a line with a weight tied to it and found that the water was one hundred and twenty feet deep; a little later they did the same and found that it was ninety feet deep. 29 They were afraid that the ship would go on the rocks, so they lowered four anchors from the back of the ship and prayed for daylight. 30 Then the sailors tried to escape from the ship; they lowered the boat into the water and pretended that they were going to put out some anchors from the front of the ship. 31 But Paul said to the army officer and soldiers, "If the sailors don't stay on board, you have no hope of being saved." 32 So the soldiers cut the ropes that held the boat and let it go.

33 Just before dawn, Paul begged them all to eat some food: "You have been waiting for fourteen days now, and all this time you have not eaten a thing. 34 I beg you, then, eat some food; you need it in order to survive. Not even a hair of your heads will be lost." 35 After saying this, Paul took some bread, gave thanks to God before them all, broke it, and began to eat. 36 They took courage, and every one of them also ate some food. 37 There was a total of 276[n] of us on board. 38 After everyone had eaten enough, they lightened the ship by throwing all the wheat into the sea.

The Shipwreck

39 When day came, the sailors did not recognize the coast, but they noticed a bay with a beach and decided that, if possible, they would run the ship aground there. 40 So they cut off the anchors and let them sink in the sea, and at the same time they untied the ropes that held the steering oars. Then they raised the sail at the front of the ship so that the wind would blow the ship forward, and we headed for shore. 41 But the ship hit a sandbank and went aground; the front part of the ship got stuck and could not move, while the back part was being broken to pieces by the violence of the waves.

42 The soldiers made a plan to kill all the prisoners, in order to keep them from swimming ashore and escaping. 43 But the army officer wanted to save Paul, so he stopped them from doing this. Instead, he ordered everyone who could swim to jump overboard first and swim ashore; 44 the rest were to follow, holding on to the planks or to some bro-

[n] 276; *some manuscripts have* 275; *others have* about 76.

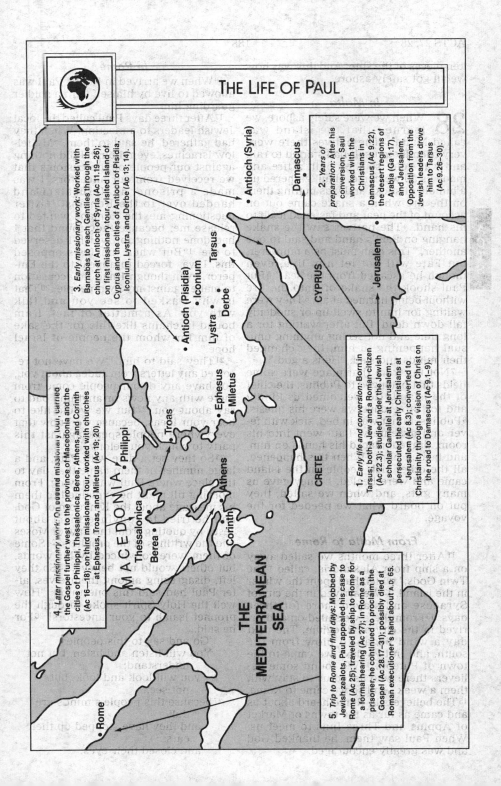

THE LIFE OF PAUL

2. Years of preparation: After his conversion, Saul worked with the Christians in Damascus (Ac 9.22), the desert regions of Arabia (Ga 1.17), and Jerusalem. Opposition from the Jewish leaders drove him to Tarsus (Ac 9.26–30).

3. Early missionary work: Worked with Barnabas to reach Gentiles at Antioch of Syria (Ac 11.19–26); on first missionary tour, visited island of Cyprus and the cities of Antioch of Pisidia, Iconium, Lystra, and Derbe (Ac 13: 14).

4. Later missionary work: On second missionary tour, carried the Gospel further west to the province of Macedonia and the cities of Philippi, Thessalonica, Berea, Athens, and Corinth (Ac 16–18); on third missionary tour, worked with churches at Ephesus, Troas, and Miletus (Ac 19; 20).

1. Early life and conversion: Born in Tarsus; both a Jew and a Roman citizen (Ac 22.3); studied under the Jewish scholar Gamaliel at Jerusalem; persecuted the early Christians at Jerusalem (Ac 8.3); converted to Christianity through a vision of Christ on the road to Damascus (Ac 9.1–9).

5. Trip to Rome and final days: Mobbed by Jewish zealots, Paul appealed his case to Rome (Ac 25); traveled by ship to Rome for a formal hearing (Ac 27); in Rome as a prisoner, he continued to proclaim the Gospel (Ac 28.17–31); possibly died at Roman executioner's hand about A.D. 65.

Damascus

Antioch (Syria)

Jerusalem

CYPRUS

Tarsus

Iconium

Antioch (Pisidia)

Lystra

Derbe

Ephesus

Miletus

Troas

Philippi

MACEDONIA

Thessalonica

Berea

Athens

Corinth

CRETE

Rome

THE MEDITERRANEAN SEA

ken pieces of the ship. And this was how we all got safely ashore.

In Malta

28 When we were safely ashore, we learned that the island was called Malta. ²The natives there were very friendly to us. It had started to rain and was cold, so they built a fire and made us all welcome. ³Paul gathered up a bundle of sticks and was putting them on the fire when a snake came out on account of the heat and fastened itself to his hand. ⁴The natives saw the snake hanging on Paul's hand and said to one another, "This man must be a murderer, but Fate will not let him live, even though he escaped from the sea." ⁵But Paul shook the snake off into the fire without being harmed at all. ⁶They were waiting for him to swell up or suddenly fall down dead. But after waiting for a long time and not seeing anything unusual happening to him, they changed their minds and said, "He is a god!"

⁷Not far from that place were some fields that belonged to Publius, the chief of the island. He welcomed us kindly and for three days we were his guests. ⁸Publius' father was in bed, sick with fever and dysentery. Paul went into his room, prayed, placed his hands on him, and healed him. ⁹When this happened, all the other sick people on the island came and were healed. ¹⁰They gave us many gifts, and when we sailed, they put on board what we needed for the voyage.

From Malta to Rome

¹¹After three months we sailed away on a ship from Alexandria, called "The Twin Gods," which had spent the winter in the island. ¹²We arrived in the city of Syracuse and stayed there for three days. ¹³From there we sailed on and arrived in the city of Rhegium. The next day a wind began to blow from the south, and in two days we came to the town of Puteoli. ¹⁴We found some believers there who asked us to stay with them a week. And so we came to Rome. ¹⁵The believers in Rome heard about us and came as far as the towns of Market of Appius and Three Inns to meet us. When Paul saw them, he thanked God and was greatly encouraged.

In Rome

¹⁶When we arrived in Rome, Paul was allowed to live by himself with a soldier guarding him.

¹⁷After three days Paul called the local Jewish leaders to a meeting. When they had gathered, he said to them, "My fellow Israelites, even though I did nothing against our people or the customs that we received from our ancestors, I was made a prisoner in Jerusalem and handed over to the Romans. ¹⁸After questioning me, the Romans wanted to release me, because they found that I had done nothing for which I deserved to die. ¹⁹But when the Jews opposed this, I was forced to appeal to the Emperor, even though I had no accusation to make against my own people. ²⁰That is why I asked to see you and talk with you. As a matter of fact, I am bound in chains like this for the sake of him for whom the people of Israel hope."

²¹They said to him, "We have not received any letters from Judea about you, nor have any of our people come from there with any news or anything bad to say about you. ²²But we would like to hear your ideas, because we know that everywhere people speak against this party to which you belong."

²³So they set a date with Paul, and a large number of them came that day to the place where Paul was staying. From morning till night he explained to them his message about the Kingdom of God, and he tried to convince them about Jesus by quoting from the Law of Moses and the writings of the prophets. ²⁴Some of them were convinced by his words, but others would not believe. ²⁵So they left, disagreeing among themselves, after Paul had said this one thing: "How well the Holy Spirit spoke through the prophet Isaiah to your ancestors! ²⁶For he said,

'Go and say to this people:
You will listen and listen, but not
    understand;
  you will look and look, but
    not see,
²⁷because this people's minds are
    dull,
  and they have stopped up their
    ears
  and closed their eyes.

Otherwise, their eyes would see,
  their ears would hear,
  their minds would understand,
and they would turn to me,
  says God,
  and I would heal them.' "
28 And Paul concluded: "You are to
know, then, that God's message of salvation has been sent to the Gentiles. They
will listen!"o
  30 For two years Paul lived in a place
he rented for himself, and there he welcomed all who came to see him. 31 He
preached about the Kingdom of God and
taught about the Lord Jesus Christ,
speaking with all boldness and freedom.

o *Some manuscripts add verse 29*: After Paul said this, the Jews left, arguing violently among
themselves.

THE LETTERS OF PAUL

Paul's letters are the oldest Christian documents we have. These letters are the largest collection of writings by any one person in the New Testament. They are in order of length, with the longest letter to a church first, and the letters to individuals last.

We can learn from Paul's letters a great deal about Paul's faith and his understanding of what Jesus Christ means for the life of the ordinary Christian. We can learn some of the problems that churches and persons were facing because of their faith and what Paul said was an answer to the problem.

Romans was written to pave the way for Paul's visit to a church he had never seen, but whose help he needed as he began to preach the gospel in the western Mediterranean world. Romans is one of the fullest statements of Paul's faith. He tries to show how Christianity is a faith for all of humanity.

1 and 2 Corinthians are the most typical of Paul's letters. They were written in response to specific concerns, in this case division in the church and how Christians are called to live a way of life different from pagans. The accounts of the resurrection and of the Lord's Supper in 1 Corinthians are the oldest written accounts of those events we have. 2 Corinthians is a combination of harsh differences and rejoicing over reconciliation.

Galatians contains important information about Paul's own life and about the beginnings of the church. It is also a key to understanding Paul's faith in Christ, justification, and the relationship between Judaism and Christianity.

Ephesians is a meditation on the purpose of God in reconciling all things in Christ. The church is a part of the purpose of God, called to bring unity to the world, as Christ brought unity to the church.

Philippians is a warm, personal letter giving thanks for a gift from the church and encouraging the church to be faithful. The hymn quoted in 2.5–11 is a powerful statement about Christ coming into the world for salvation.

Colossians was written to a church confused by false teaching. He says that Christ is the ruling power in the universe. He also gives guidance for the true spiritual life.

1 and 2 Thessalonians are possibly the earliest writings of the New Testament. Persecution has compelled Paul to leave Thessalonica, and in his letters he tells Christians there how they ought to live, and to await the Lord's return with constant diligence.

1 and 2 Timothy and Titus are known as the Pastoral Epistles, since they are concerned about the care of the church. They reflect the beginnings of organizational life in the church. Paul wants to show how true faith results in a way of life in both the church and the world.

Philemon is the only surviving private letter of Paul. It is a plea for Philemon to forgive the runaway slave Onesimus and receive him back as a brother in Christ.

Paul's Letter to the
ROMANS

Introduction

Paul's Letter to the Romans was written to prepare the way for a visit Paul planned to make to the church at Rome. His plan was to work among the Christians there for a while and then, with their support, to go on to Spain. He wrote to explain his understanding of the Christian faith and its practical implications for the lives of Christians. The book contains Paul's most complete statement of his message.

After greeting the people of the church at Rome and telling them of his prayers for them, Paul states the theme of the letter: "The gospel reveals how God puts people right with himself: it is through faith from beginning to end" (1.17).

Paul then develops this theme. All people, both Jews and Gentiles, need to be put right with God, for all alike are under the power of sin. People are put right with God through faith in Jesus Christ. Next Paul describes the new life in union with Christ that results from this new relation with God. The believer has peace with God and is set free by God's Spirit from the power of sin and death. In chapters 5–8 Paul also discusses the purpose of the Law of God and the power of God's Spirit in the believer's life. Then the apostle wrestles with the question of how Jews and Gentiles fit into the plan of God for all people. He concludes that the Jewish rejection of Jesus is part of God's plan for bringing all people within the reach of God's grace in Jesus Christ, and he believes that the Jews will not always reject Jesus. Finally Paul writes about how the Christian life should be lived, especially about the way of love in relations with others. He takes up such themes as service to God, the duty of Christians to the state and to one another, and questions of conscience. He ends the letter with personal messages and with words of praise to God.

Outline of Contents

---

1 From Paul, a servant of Christ Jesus and an apostle chosen and called by God to preach his Good News.

2 The Good News was promised long ago by God through his prophets, as written in the Holy Scriptures. 3 It is about his Son, our Lord Jesus Christ: as to his humanity, he was born a descendant of David; 4 as to his divine holiness, he was shown with great power to be the Son of God by being raised from death. 5 Through him God gave me the privilege of being an apostle for the sake of Christ, in order to lead people of all nations to believe and obey. 6 This also includes you who are in Rome, whom God has called to belong to Jesus Christ.

7 And so I write to all of you in Rome whom God loves and has called to be his own people:

May God our Father and the Lord Jesus Christ give you grace and peace.

Prayer of Thanksgiving

8 First, I thank my God through Jesus Christ for all of you, because the whole world is hearing about your faith. 9 God is my witness that what I say is true — the God whom I serve with all my heart by preaching the Good News about his Son. God knows that I remember you 10 every time I pray. I ask that God in his good will may at last make it possible for me to visit you now. 11 For I want very much to see you, in order to share a spiritual blessing with you to make you strong. 12 What I mean is that both you and I will be helped at the same time, you by my faith and I by yours.

13 You must remember, my friends,

that many times I have planned to visit you, but something has always kept me from doing so. I want to win converts among you also, as I have among other Gentiles. 14 For I have an obligation to all peoples, to the civilized and to the savage, to the educated and to the ignorant. 15 So then, I am eager to preach the Good News to you also who live in Rome.

The Power of the Gospel

16 I have complete confidence in the gospel; it is God's power to save all who believe, first the Jews and also the Gentiles. 17 For the gospel reveals how God puts people right with himself: it is through faith from beginning to end. As the scripture says, "The person who is put right with God through faith shall live."*a*

Human Guilt

18 God's anger is revealed from heaven against all the sin and evil of the people whose evil ways prevent the truth from being known. 19 God punishes them, because what can be known about God is plain to them, for God himself made it plain. 20 Ever since God created the world, his invisible qualities, both his eternal power and his divine nature, have been clearly seen; they are perceived in the things that God has made. So those people have no excuse at all! 21 They know God, but they do not give him the honor that belongs to him, nor do they thank him. Instead, their thoughts have become complete nonsense, and their empty minds are filled with darkness. 22 They say they are wise, but they are fools; 23 instead of worshiping the immortal God, they worship images made to look like mortals or birds or animals or reptiles.

24 And so God has given those people over to do the filthy things their hearts desire, and they do shameful things with each other. 25 They exchange the truth about God for a lie; they worship and serve what God has created instead of the Creator himself, who is to be praised forever! Amen.

26 Because they do this, God has given them over to shameful passions. Even the women pervert the natural use of their sex by unnatural acts. 27 In the same way the men give up natural sexual relations with women and burn with passion for each other. Men do shameful things with each other, and as a result they bring upon themselves the punishment they deserve for their wrongdoing.

28 Because those people refuse to keep in mind the true knowledge about God, he has given them over to corrupted minds, so that they do the things that they should not do. 29 They are filled with all kinds of wickedness, evil, greed, and vice; they are full of jealousy, murder, fighting, deceit, and malice. They gossip 30 and speak evil of one another; they are hateful to God, insolent,*b* proud, and boastful; they think of more ways to do evil; they disobey their parents; 31 they have no conscience; they do not keep their promises, and they show no kindness or pity for others. 32 They know that God's law says that people who live in this way deserve death. Yet, not only do they continue to do these very things, but they even approve of others who do them.

God's Judgment

2 Do you, my friend, pass judgment on others? You have no excuse at all, whoever you are. For when you judge others and then do the same things which they do, you condemn yourself. 2 We know that God is right when he judges the people who do such things as these. 3 But you, my friend, do those very things for which you pass judgment on others! Do you think you will escape God's judgment? 4 Or perhaps you despise his great kindness, tolerance, and patience. Surely you know that God is kind, because he is trying to lead you to repent. 5 But you have a hard and stubborn heart, and so you are making your own punishment even greater on the Day when God's anger and righteous judgments will be revealed. 6 For God will reward each of us according to what we have done. 7 Some people keep on doing good, and seek glory, honor, and immortal life; to them God will give eternal life. 8 Other people are selfish and reject what is right, in order to follow what is wrong; on them God will pour out his anger and fury. 9 There will

---

a put right with God through faith shall live; *or* put right with God shall live through faith.
b are hateful to God, insolent; *or* hate God, and are insolent.

be suffering and pain for all those who do what is evil, for the Jews first and also for the Gentiles. 10 But God will give glory, honor, and peace to all who do what is good, to the Jews first and also to the Gentiles. 11 For God judges everyone by the same standard.

12 The Gentiles do not have the Law of Moses; they sin and are lost apart from the Law. The Jews have the Law; they sin and are judged by the Law. 13 For it is not by hearing the Law that people are put right with God, but by doing what the Law commands. 14 The Gentiles do not have the Law; but whenever they do by instinct what the Law commands, they are their own law, even though they do not have the Law. 15 Their conduct shows that what the Law commands is written in their hearts. Their consciences also show that this is true, since their thoughts sometimes accuse them and sometimes defend them. 16 And so, according to the Good News I preach, this is how it will be on that Day when God through Jesus Christ will judge the secret thoughts of all.

The Jews and the Law

17 What about you? You call yourself a Jew; you depend on the Law and boast about God; 18 you know what God wants you to do, and you have learned from the Law to choose what is right; 19 you are sure that you are a guide for the blind, a light for those who are in darkness, 20 an instructor for the foolish, and a teacher for the ignorant. You are certain that in the Law you have the full content of knowledge and of truth. 21 You teach others—why don't you teach yourself? You preach, "Do not steal"—but do you yourself steal? 22 You say, "Do not commit adultery"—but do you commit adultery? You detest idols—but do you rob temples? 23 You boast about having God's law—but do you bring shame on God by breaking his law? 24 The scripture says, "Because of you Jews, the Gentiles speak evil of God."

25 If you obey the Law, your circumcision is of value; but if you disobey the Law, you might as well never have been circumcised. 26 If the Gentile, who is not circumcised, obeys the commands of the Law, will not God regard him as though he were circumcised? 27 And so you Jews will be condemned by the Gentiles because you break the Law, even though you have it written down and are circumcised; but they obey the Law, even though they are not physically circumcised. 28 After all, who is a real Jew, truly circumcised? It is not the man who is a Jew on the outside, whose circumcision is a physical thing. 29 Rather, the real Jew is the person who is a Jew on the inside, that is, whose heart has been circumcised, and this is the work of God's Spirit, not of the written Law. Such a person receives praise from God, not from human beings.

3 Do the Jews then have any advantage over the Gentiles? Or is there any value in being circumcised? 2 Much, indeed, in every way! In the first place, God trusted his message to the Jews. 3 But what if some of them were not faithful? Does this mean that God will not be faithful? 4 Certainly not! God must be true, even though all human beings are liars. As the scripture says,

"You must be shown to be right
  when you speak;
  you must win your case when
    you are being tried."

5 But what if our doing wrong serves to show up more clearly God's doing right? Can we say that God does wrong when he punishes us? (This would be the natural question to ask.) 6 By no means! If God is not just, how can he judge the world?

7 But what if my untruth serves God's glory by making his truth stand out more clearly? Why should I still be condemned as a sinner? 8 Why not say, then, "Let us do evil so that good may come"? Some people, indeed, have insulted me by accusing me of saying this very thing! They will be condemned, as they should be.

No One Is Righteous

9 Well then, are we Jews in any better condition than the Gentiles? Not at all! c I have already shown that Jews and Gentiles alike are all under the power of sin. 10 As the Scriptures say:

c any better condition than the Gentiles? Not at all!; or any worse condition than the Gentiles? Not altogether.

"There is no one who is righteous,
11 no one who is wise
   or who worships God.
12 All have turned away from God;
   they have all gone wrong;
   no one does what is right, not
      even one.
13 Their words are full of deadly
      deceit;
   wicked lies roll off their tongues,
   and dangerous threats, like
      snake's poison, from their lips;
14 their speech is filled with bitter
      curses.
15 They are quick to hurt and kill;
16 they leave ruin and destruction
      wherever they go.
17 They have not known the path of
      peace,
18 nor have they learned reverence
      for God."

19 Now we know that everything in the Law applies to those who live under the Law, in order to stop all human excuses and bring the whole world under God's judgment. 20 For no one is put right in God's sight by doing what the Law requires; what the Law does is to make us know that we have sinned.

How We Are Put Right with God

21 But now God's way of putting people right with himself has been revealed. It has nothing to do with law, even though the Law of Moses and the prophets gave their witness to it. 22 God puts people right through their faith in Jesus Christ. God does this to all who believe in Christ, because there is no difference at all: 23 everyone has sinned and is far away from God's saving presence. 24 But by the free gift of God's grace all are put right with him through Christ Jesus, who sets them free. 25-26 God offered him, so that by his blood[d] he should become the means by which people's sins are forgiven through their faith in him. God did this in order to demonstrate that he is righteous. In the past he was patient and overlooked people's sins; but in the present time he deals with their sins, in order to demonstrate his righteousness. In this way God shows that he himself is righteous and that he puts right everyone who believes in Jesus. 27 What, then, can we boast about?

Nothing! And what is the reason for this? Is it that we obey the Law? No, but that we believe. 28 For we conclude that a person is put right with God only through faith, and not by doing what the Law commands. 29 Or is God the God of the Jews only? Is he not the God of the Gentiles also? Of course he is. 30 God is one, and he will put the Jews right with himself on the basis of their faith, and will put the Gentiles right through their faith. 31 Does this mean that by this faith we do away with the Law? No, not at all; instead, we uphold the Law.

The Example of Abraham

4 What shall we say, then, of Abraham, the father of our race? What was his experience? 2 If he was put right with God by the things he did, he would have something to boast about—but not in God's sight. 3 The scripture says, "Abraham believed God, and because of his faith God accepted him as righteous." 4 A person who works is paid wages, but they are not regarded as a gift; they are something that has been earned. 5 But those who depend on faith, not on deeds, and who believe in the God who declares the guilty to be innocent, it is this faith that God takes into account in order to put them right with himself. 6 This is what David meant when he spoke of the happiness of the person whom God accepts as righteous, apart from anything that person does:
7 "Happy are those whose wrongs
      are forgiven,
   whose sins are pardoned!
8 Happy is the person whose sins
      the Lord will not keep
      account of!"
9 Does this happiness that David spoke of belong only to those who are circumcised? No indeed! It belongs also to those who are not circumcised. For we have quoted the scripture, "Abraham believed God, and because of his faith God accepted him as righteous." 10 When did this take place? Was it before or after Abraham was circumcised? It was before, not after. 11 He was circumcised later, and his circumcision was a sign to show that because of his faith God had accepted him as righteous before he had been circumcised. And so Abraham is

---

d by his blood; or by his sacrificial death.

the spiritual father of all who believe in God and are accepted as righteous by him, even though they are not circumcised. 12 He is also the father of those who are circumcised, that is, of those who, in addition to being circumcised, also live the same life of faith that our father Abraham lived before he was circumcised.

God's Promise Is Received through Faith

13 When God promised Abraham and his descendants that the world would belong to him, he did so, not because Abraham obeyed the Law, but because he believed and was accepted as righteous by God. 14 For if what God promises is to be given to those who obey the Law, then faith means nothing and God's promise is worthless. 15 The Law brings down God's anger; but where there is no law, there is no disobeying of the law.

16 And so the promise was based on faith, in order that the promise should be guaranteed as God's free gift to all of Abraham's descendants — not just to those who obey the Law, but also to those who believe as Abraham did. For Abraham is the spiritual father of us all; 17 as the scripture says, "I have made you father of many nations." So the promise is good in the sight of God, in whom Abraham believed — the God who brings the dead to life and whose command brings into being what did not exist. 18 Abraham believed and hoped, even when there was no reason for hoping, and so became "the father of many nations." Just as the scripture says, "Your descendants will be as many as the stars." 19 He was then almost one hundred years old; but his faith did not weaken when he thought of his body, which was already practically dead, or of the fact that Sarah could not have children. 20 His faith did not leave him, and he did not doubt God's promise; his faith filled him with power, and he gave praise to God. 21 He was absolutely sure that God would be able to do what he had promised. 22 That is why Abraham, through faith, "was accepted as righteous by God." 23 The words "he was accepted as righteous" were not written for

him alone. 24 They were written also for us who are to be accepted as righteous, who believe in him who raised Jesus our Lord from death. 25 Because of our sins he was given over to die, and he was raised to life in order to put us right with God.

Right with God

5 Now that we have been put right with God through faith, we have^e peace with God through our Lord Jesus Christ. 2 He has brought us by faith into this experience of God's grace, in which we now live. And so we boast^f of the hope we have of sharing God's glory! 3 We also boast^g of our troubles, because we know that trouble produces endurance, 4 endurance brings God's approval, and his approval creates hope. 5 This hope does not disappoint us, for God has poured out his love into our hearts by means of the Holy Spirit, who is God's gift to us.

6 For when we were still helpless, Christ died for the wicked at the time that God chose. 7 It is a difficult thing for someone to die for a righteous person. It may even be that someone might dare to die for a good person. 8 But God has shown us how much he loves us — it was while we were still sinners that Christ died for us! 9 By his blood^h we are now put right with God; how much more, then, will we be saved by him from God's anger! 10 We were God's enemies, but he made us his friends through the death of his Son. Now that we are God's friends, how much more will we be saved by Christ's life! 11 But that is not all; we rejoice because of what God has done through our Lord Jesus Christ, who has now made us God's friends.

Adam and Christ

12 Sin came into the world through one man, and his sin brought death with it. As a result, death has spread to the whole human race because everyone has sinned. 13 There was sin in the world before the Law was given; but where there is no law, no account is kept of sins. 14 But from the time of Adam to the time of Moses, death ruled over all human beings, even over those who did not

---

e we have, some manuscripts have let us have.   *f we boast; or let us boast.*   *g We also boast; or Let us also boast.*   *h By his blood; or By his sacrificial death.*

sin in the same way that Adam did when he disobeyed God's command.

Adam was a figure of the one who was to come. 15 But the two are not the same, because God's free gift is not like Adam's sin. It is true that many people died because of the sin of that one man. But God's grace is much greater, and so is his free gift to so many people through the grace of the one man, Jesus Christ. 16 And there is a difference between God's gift and the sin of one man. After the one sin, came the judgment of "Guilty"; but after so many sins, comes the undeserved gift of "Not guilty!" 17 It is true that through the sin of one man death began to rule because of that one man. But how much greater is the result of what was done by the one man, Jesus Christ! All who receive God's abundant grace and are freely put right with him will rule in life through Christ.

18 So then, as the one sin condemned all people, in the same way the one righteous act sets all people free and gives them life. 19 And just as all people were made sinners as the result of the disobedience of one man, in the same way they will all be put right with God as the result of the obedience of the one man.

20 Law was introduced in order to increase wrongdoing; but where sin increased, God's grace increased much more. 21 So then, just as sin ruled by means of death, so also God's grace rules by means of righteousness, leading us to eternal life through Jesus Christ our Lord.

Dead to Sin but Alive in Union with Christ

6 What shall we say, then? Should we continue to live in sin so that God's grace will increase? 2 Certainly not! We have died to sin — how then can we go on living in it? 3 For surely you know that when we were baptized into union with Christ Jesus, we were baptized into union with his death. 4 By our baptism, then, we were buried with him and shared his death, in order that, just as Christ was raised from death by the glorious power of the Father, so also we might live a new life.

5 For since we have become one with him in dying as he did, in the same way we shall be one with him by being raised to life as he was. 6 And we know that our old being has been put to death with Christ on his cross, in order that the power of the sinful self might be destroyed, so that we should no longer be the slaves of sin. 7 For when we die, we are set free from the power of sin. 8 Since we have died with Christ, we believe that we will also live with him. 9 For we know that Christ has been raised from death and will never die again — death will no longer rule over him. 10 And so, because he died, sin has no power over him; and now he lives his life in fellowship with God. 11 In the same way you are to think of yourselves as dead, so far as sin is concerned, but living in fellowship with God through Christ Jesus.

12 Sin must no longer rule in your mortal bodies, so that you obey the desires of your natural self. 13 Nor must you surrender any part of yourselves to sin to be used for wicked purposes. Instead, give yourselves to God, as those who have been brought from death to life, and surrender your whole being to him to be used for righteous purposes. 14 Sin must not be your master; for you do not live under law but under God's grace.

Slaves of Righteousness

15 What, then? Shall we sin, because we are not under law but under God's grace? By no means! 16 Surely you know that when you surrender yourselves as slaves to obey someone, you are in fact the slaves of the master you obey — either of sin, which results in death, or of obedience, which results in being put right with God. 17 But thanks be to God! For though at one time you were slaves to sin, you have obeyed with all your heart the truths found in the teaching you received. 18 You were set free from sin and became the slaves of righteousness. 19 (I use everyday language because of the weakness of your natural selves.) At one time you surrendered yourselves entirely as slaves to impurity and wickedness for wicked purposes. In the same way you must now surrender yourselves entirely as slaves of righteousness for holy purposes.

20 When you were the slaves of sin, you were free from righteousness. 21 What did you gain from doing the things that you are now ashamed of?

The result of those things is death! 22But now you have been set free from sin and are the slaves of God. Your gain is a life fully dedicated to him, and the result is eternal life. 23For sin pays its wage—death; but God's free gift is eternal life in union with Christ Jesus our Lord.

An Illustration from Marriage

7 Certainly you will understand what I am about to say, my friends, because all of you know about law. The law rules over people only as long as they live. 2A married woman, for example, is bound by the law to her husband as long as he lives; but if he dies, then she is free from the law that bound her to him. 3So then, if she lives with another man while her husband is alive, she will be called an adulteress; but if her husband dies, she is legally a free woman and does not commit adultery if she marries another man. 4That is how it is with you, my friends. As far as the Law is concerned, you also have died because you are part of the body of Christ; and now you belong to him who was raised from death in order that we might be useful in the service of God. 5For when we lived according to our human nature the sinful desires stirred up by the Law were at work in our bodies, and all we did ended in death. 6Now, however, we are free from the Law, because we died to that which once held us prisoners. No longer do we serve in the old way of a written law, but in the new way of the Spirit.

Law and Sin

7Shall we say, then, that the Law itself is sinful? Of course not! But it was the Law that made me know what sin is. If the Law had not said, "Do not desire what belongs to someone else," I would not have known such a desire. 8But by means of that commandment sin found its chance to stir up all kinds of selfish desires in me. Apart from law, sin is a dead thing. 9I myself was once alive apart from law; but when the commandment came, sin sprang to life, 10and I died. And the commandment which was meant to bring life, in my case brought death. 11Sin found its chance, and by

means of the commandment it deceived me and killed me.

12So then, the Law itself is holy, and the commandment is holy, right, and good. 13But does this mean that what is good caused my death? By no means! It was sin that did it; by using what is good, sin brought death to me, in order that its true nature as sin might be revealed. And so, by means of the commandment sin is shown to be even more terribly sinful.

The Conflict in Us

14We know that the Law is spiritual; but I am a mortal, sold as a slave to sin. 15I do not understand what I do; for I don't do what I would like to do, but instead I do what I hate. 16Since what I do is what I don't want to do, this shows that I agree that the Law is right. 17So I am not really the one who does this thing; rather it is the sin that lives in me. 18I know that good does not live in me—that is, in my human nature. For even though the desire to do good is in me, I am not able to do it. 19I don't do the good I want to do; instead, I do the evil that I do not want to do. 20If I do what I don't want to do, this means that I am no longer the one who does it; instead, it is the sin that lives in me.

21So I find that this law is at work: when I want to do what is good, what is evil is the only choice I have. 22My inner being delights in the law of God. 23But I see a different law at work in my body—a law that fights against the law which my mind approves of. It makes me a prisoner to the law of sin which is at work in my body. 24What an unhappy man I am! Who will rescue me from this body that is taking me to death? 25Thanks be to God, who does this through our Lord Jesus Christ!

This, then, is my condition: on my own I can serve God's law only with my mind, while my human nature serves the law of sin.

Life in the Spirit

8 There is no condemnation now for those who live in union with Christ Jesus. 2For the law of the Spirit, which brings us life in union with Christ Jesus, has set me i free from the law of sin and

i me; some manuscripts have you; others have us.

death. ³What the Law could not do, because human nature was weak, God did. He condemned sin in human nature by sending his own Son, who came with a nature like our sinful nature, to do away with sin. ⁴God did this so that the righteous demands of the Law might be fully satisfied in us who live according to the Spirit, and not according to human nature. ⁵Those who live as their human nature tells them to, have their minds controlled by what human nature wants. Those who live as the Spirit tells them to, have their minds controlled by what the Spirit wants. ⁶To be controlled by human nature results in death; to be controlled by the Spirit results in life and peace. ⁷And so people become enemies of God when they are controlled by their human nature; for they do not obey God's law, and in fact they cannot obey it. ⁸Those who obey their human nature cannot please God.

⁹But you do not live as your human nature tells you to; instead, you live as the Spirit tells you to—if, in fact, God's Spirit lives in you. Whoever does not have the Spirit of Christ does not belong to him. ¹⁰But if Christ lives in you, the Spirit is life for you*ʲ* because you have been put right with God, even though your bodies are going to die because of sin. ¹¹If the Spirit of God, who raised Jesus from death, lives in you, then he who raised Christ from death will also give life to your mortal bodies by the presence of his Spirit in you.

¹²So then, my friends, we have an obligation, but it is not to live as our human nature wants us to. ¹³For if you live according to your human nature, you are going to die; but if by the Spirit you put to death your sinful actions, you will live. ¹⁴Those who are led by God's Spirit are God's children. ¹⁵For the Spirit that God has given you does not make you slaves and cause you to be afraid; instead, the Spirit makes you God's children, and by the Spirit's power we cry out to God, "Father! my Father!" ¹⁶God's Spirit joins himself to our spirits to declare that we are God's children. ¹⁷Since we are his children, we will possess the blessings he keeps for his people, and we will also possess with Christ what

God has kept for him; for if we share Christ's suffering, we will also share his glory.

The Future Glory

¹⁸I consider that what we suffer at this present time cannot be compared at all with the glory that is going to be revealed to us. ¹⁹All of creation waits with eager longing for God to reveal his children. ²⁰For creation was condemned to lose its purpose, not of its own will, but because God willed it to be so. Yet there was the hope ²¹that creation itself would one day be set free from its slavery to decay and would share the glorious freedom of the children of God. ²²For we know that up to the present time all of creation groans with pain, like the pain of childbirth. ²³But it is not just creation alone which groans; we who have the Spirit as the first of God's gifts also groan within ourselves as we wait for God to make us his children and*ᵏ* set our whole being free. ²⁴For it was by hope that we were saved; but if we see what we hope for, then it is not really hope. For who of us hopes for something we see? ²⁵But if we hope for what we do not see, we wait for it with patience.

²⁶In the same way the Spirit also comes to help us, weak as we are. For we do not know how we ought to pray; the Spirit himself pleads with God for us in groans that words cannot express. ²⁷And God, who sees into our hearts, knows what the thought of the Spirit is; because the Spirit pleads with God on behalf of his people and in accordance with his will.

²⁸We know that in all things God works for good with those who love him,*ˡ* those whom he has called according to his purpose. ²⁹Those whom God had already chosen he also set apart to become like his Son, so that the Son would be the first among many believers. ³⁰And so those whom God set apart, he called; and those he called, he put right with himself, and he shared his glory with them.

God's Love in Christ Jesus

³¹In view of all this, what can we say? If God is for us, who can be against us?

ʲ the Spirit is life for you; *or* your spirit is alive.   *ᵏ Some manuscripts do not have* make us his children and.   *ˡ* in all things God works for good with those who love him; *some manuscripts have* all things work for good for those who love God.

32 Certainly not God, who did not even keep back his own Son, but offered him for us all! He gave us his Son—will he not also freely give us all things? 33 Who will accuse God's chosen people? God himself declares them not guilty! 34 Who, then, will condemn them? Not Christ Jesus, who died, or rather, who was raised to life and is at the right side of God, pleading with him for us! 35 Who, then, can separate us from the love of Christ? Can trouble do it, or hardship or persecution or hunger or poverty or danger or death? 36 As the scripture says,

"For your sake we are in danger of
    death at all times;
we are treated like sheep that
    are going to be slaughtered."

37 No, in all these things we have complete victory through him who loved us! 38 For I am certain that nothing can separate us from his love: neither death nor life, neither angels nor other heavenly rulers or powers, neither the present nor the future, 39 neither the world above nor the world below—there is nothing in all creation that will ever be able to separate us from the love of God which is ours through Christ Jesus our Lord.

God and His People

9 I am speaking the truth; I belong to Christ and I do not lie. My conscience, ruled by the Holy Spirit, also assures me that I am not lying 2 when I say how great is my sorrow, how endless the pain in my heart 3 for my people, my own flesh and blood! For their sake I could wish that I myself were under God's curse and separated from Christ. 4 They are God's people; he made them his children and revealed his glory to them; he made his covenants m with them and gave them the Law; they have the true worship; they have received God's promises; 5 they are descended from the famous Hebrew ancestors; and Christ, as a human being, belongs to their race. May God, who rules over all, be praised forever! n Amen.

6 I am not saying that the promise of God has failed; for not all the people of Israel are the people of God. 7 Nor are all of Abraham's descendants the children

of God. God said to Abraham, "It is through Isaac that you will have the descendants I promised you." 8 This means that the children born in the usual way o are not the children of God; instead, the children born as a result of God's promise are regarded as the true descendants. 9 For God's promise was made in these words: "At the right time p I will come back, and Sarah will have a son."

10 And this is not all. For Rebecca's two sons had the same father, our ancestor Isaac. 11-12 But in order that the choice of one son might be completely the result of God's own purpose, God said to her, "The older will serve the younger." He said this before they were born, before they had done anything either good or bad; so God's choice was based on his call, and not on anything they had done. 13 As the scripture says, "I loved Jacob, but I hated Esau."

14 Shall we say, then, that God is unjust? Not at all. 15 For he said to Moses, "I will have mercy on anyone I wish; I will take pity on anyone I wish." 16 So then, everything depends, not on what we humans want or do, but only on God's mercy. 17 For the scripture says to the king of Egypt, "I made you king in order to use you to show my power and to spread my fame over the whole world." 18 So then, God has mercy on anyone he wishes, and he makes stubborn anyone he wishes.

God's Anger and Mercy

19 But one of you will say to me, "If this is so, how can God find fault with anyone? Who can resist God's will?" 20 But who are you, my friend, to talk back to God? A clay pot does not ask the man who made it, "Why did you make me like this?" 21 After all, the man who makes the pots has the right to use the clay as he wishes, and to make two pots from the same lump of clay, one for special occasions and the other for ordinary use.

22 And the same is true of what God has done. He wanted to show his anger and to make his power known. But he was very patient in enduring those who

were the objects of his anger, who were doomed to destruction. 23 And he also wanted to reveal his abundant glory, which was poured out on us who are the objects of his mercy, those of us whom he has prepared to receive his glory. 24 For we are the people he called, not only from among the Jews but also from among the Gentiles. 25 This is what he says in the book of Hosea:

"The people who were not mine
    I will call 'My People.'
The nation that I did not love
    I will call 'My Beloved.'
26 And in the very place where they
        were told, 'You are not my
        people,'
    there they will be called the
        children of the living God."

27 And Isaiah exclaims about Israel: "Even if the people of Israel are as many as the grains of sand by the sea, yet only a few of them will be saved; 28 for the Lord will quickly settle his full account with the world." 29 It is as Isaiah had said before, "If the Lord Almighty had not left us some descendants, we would have become like Sodom, we would have been like Gomorrah."

Israel and the Gospel

30 So we say that the Gentiles, who were not trying to put themselves right with God, were put right with him through faith; 31 while God's people, who were seeking a law that would put them right with God, did not find it. 32 And why not? Because they did not depend on faith but on what they did. And so they stumbled over the "stumbling stone" 33 that the scripture speaks of:

"Look, I place in Zion a stone
    that will make people stumble,
    a rock that will make them fall.
But whoever believes in him will
        not be disappointed."

10 My friends, how I wish with all my heart that my own people might be saved! How I pray to God for them! 2 I can assure you that they are deeply devoted to God; but their devotion is not based on true knowledge. 3 They have not known the way in which God puts people right with himself, and instead, they have tried to set up their own way; and so they did not submit themselves to God's way of putting people right. 4 For Christ has brought the Law to an end, so that everyone who believes is put right with God.

Salvation Is for All

5 Moses wrote this about being put right with God by obeying the Law: "Whoever obeys the commands of the Law will live." 6 But what the scripture says about being put right with God through faith is this: "You are not to ask yourself, Who will go up into heaven?" (that is, to bring Christ down). 7 "Nor are you to ask, Who will go down into the world below?" (that is, to bring Christ up from death). 8 What it says is this: "God's message is near you, on your lips and in your heart"—that is, the message of faith that we preach. 9 If you confess that Jesus is Lord and believe that God raised him from death, you will be saved. 10 For it is by our faith that we are put right with God; it is by our confession that we are saved. 11 The scripture says, "Whoever believes in him will not be disappointed." 12 This includes everyone, because there is no difference between Jews and Gentiles; God is the same Lord of all and richly blesses all who call to him. 13 As the scripture says, "Everyone who calls out to the Lord for help will be saved."

14 But how can they call to him for help if they have not believed? And how can they believe if they have not heard the message? And how can they hear if the message is not proclaimed? 15 And how can the message be proclaimed if the messengers are not sent out? As the scripture says, "How wonderful is the coming of messengers who bring good news!" 16 But not all have accepted the Good News. Isaiah himself said, "Lord, who believed our message?" 17 So then, faith comes from hearing the message, and the message comes through preaching Christ.

18 But I ask: Is it true that they did not hear the message? Of course they did—for as the scripture says:

"The sound of their voice went out
        to all the world;
    their words reached the ends of
        the earth."

19 Again I ask: Did the people of Israel not understand? Moses himself is the first one to answer:

"I will use a so-called nation
    to make my people jealous;

and by means of a nation of fools
  I will make my people angry."
20 And Isaiah is even bolder when he says,
  "I was found by those who were
    not looking for me;
  I appeared to those who were
    not asking for me."
21 But concerning Israel he says, "All day long I held out my hands to welcome a disobedient and rebellious people."

God's Mercy on Israel

11 I ask, then: Did God reject his own people? Certainly not! I myself am an Israelite, a descendant of Abraham, a member of the tribe of Benjamin. 2 God has not rejected his people, whom he chose from the beginning. You know what the scripture says in the passage where Elijah pleads with God against Israel: 3 "Lord, they have killed your prophets and torn down your altars; I am the only one left, and they are trying to kill me." 4 What answer did God give him? "I have kept for myself seven thousand men who have not worshiped the false god Baal." 5 It is the same way now: there is a small number left of those whom God has chosen because of his grace. 6 His choice is based on his grace, not on what they have done. For if God's choice were based on what people do, then his grace would not be real grace.

7 What then? The people of Israel did not find what they were looking for. It was only the small group that God chose who found it; the rest grew deaf to God's call. 8 As the scripture says, "God made their minds and hearts dull; to this very day they cannot see or hear." 9 And David says,

  "May they be caught and trapped
    at their feasts;
  may they fall, may they be
    punished!
10 May their eyes be blinded so that
    they cannot see;
  and make them bend under their
    troubles at all times."

11 I ask, then: When the Jews stumbled, did they fall to their ruin? By no means! Because they sinned, salvation has come to the Gentiles, to make the Jews jealous of them. 12 The sin of the Jews brought rich blessings to the world, and their spiritual poverty brought rich blessings to the Gentiles. Then, how much greater the blessings will be when the complete number of Jews is included!

The Salvation of the Gentiles

13 I am speaking now to you Gentiles: As long as I am an apostle to the Gentiles, I will take pride in my work. 14 Perhaps I can make the people of my own race jealous, and so be able to save some of them. 15 For when they were rejected, all other people were changed from God's enemies into his friends. What will it be, then, when they are accepted? It will be life for the dead!

16 If the first piece of bread is given to God, then the whole loaf is his also; and if the roots of a tree are offered to God, the branches are his also. 17 Some of the branches of the cultivated olive tree have been broken off, and a branch of a wild olive tree has been joined to it. You Gentiles are like that wild olive tree, and now you share the strong spiritual life of the Jews. 18 So then, you must not despise those who were broken off like branches. How can you be proud? You are just a branch; you don't support the roots — the roots support you.

19 But you will say, "Yes, but the branches were broken off to make room for me." 20 That is true. They were broken off because they did not believe, while you remain in place because you do believe. But do not be proud of it; instead, be afraid. 21 God did not spare the Jews, who are like natural branches; do you think he will spare you? 22 Here we see how kind and how severe God is. He is severe toward those who have fallen, but kind to you — if you continue in his kindness. But if you do not, you too will be broken off. 23 And if the Jews abandon their unbelief, they will be put back in the place where they were; for God is able to do that. 24 You Gentiles are like the branch of a wild olive tree that is broken off and then, contrary to nature, is joined to a cultivated olive tree. The Jews are like this cultivated tree; and it will be much easier for God to join these broken-off branches to their own tree again.

God's Mercy on All

25 There is a secret truth, my friends, which I want you to know, for it will

THE CITY OF ROME

The seat of the mighty Roman Empire, Rome was the largest and most magnificent city of its day, with a population of more than 1,000,000 people in New Testament times. Situated near where the Tiber River meets the Mediterranean Sea, it was called *Urbs Septicollis* (City of the Seven Hills) because of the seven hills upon which it was built.

When the apostle Paul entered Rome as a prisoner, the city boasted of a history extending back more than 800 years. According to the legends of the Romans, the city was founded in 753 B.C. by Romulus, son of the Roman god Mars. The city grew over the years as the Roman Empire expanded its power and influence throughout the ancient world.

Rome reached the height of its splendor under the emperor Augustus. Especially notable was the Forum, the center of the city with roads leading off in all directions, and the great outdoor theater known as the Colosseum, where Roman games and public events were held. The city featured more than 400 temples dedicated to worship of pagan gods. It was also noted for its public buildings, baths, aqueducts, arches, temples, and roads.

To keep from being killed by hostile Jews at Jerusalem, and because he was a Roman citizen (Ac 22.27), Paul appealed to Caesar, an act that ultimately brought him to Rome as a prisoner to await trial. Paul must have seen many of Rome's pagan temples and spectacular public buildings when he entered the city on the famous road known as the Via Appia (Appian Way). He was kept at first under house arrest, and later, according to tradition, as a condemned prisoner in a dungeon near the Forum.

The great missionary to the Gentiles proclaimed the gospel to all classes of people while in Rome, especially to Greek-speaking easterners and Jews. According to tradition, he was executed outside the city at a spot on the Via Ostia.

Paul's first known connection with Rome had occurred several years before he actually visited the city. During his ministry at Corinth, he worked with Priscilla and Aquila, who had left Rome when the emperor Claudius expelled all Jews from the city (Ac 18.2). An active Christian church also existed at Rome several years before Paul arrived in the city; these were the Christians to whom Paul addressed his letter known as the epistle to the Romans.

In Paul's time the houses of the wealthy people of Rome were elaborately constructed and situated on the various hills of the city. But the common people lived in tenements, much like the crowded inner city of a modern metropolis. Thousands of people were crowded into these tenements, which were surrounded by narrow, noisy streets with a constant flow of traffic.

The citizens of Rome received food and entertainment from the government. Wine was cheap and plentiful. Admission to the Roman games was free. Thousands of people attended these games, which included contests among the gladiators, chariot races, and theatrical performances.

The Emperors of Rome

The Roman empire was the world superpower when Jesus was born. People in areas all around the Mediterranean Sea had to pay taxes to Rome. The only army or navy in the area was Rome's. Here is a list of the Roman emperors during New Testament times with the years they reigned.

Augustus	31 B.C. to A.D. 14 (see Luke 2.1)
Tiberius	A.D. 14 to 37 (See Luke 3.1; Matthew 22.17; John 19.12)
Caligula	37 to 41
Claudius	41 to 54 (see Acts 11.28; 17.7)
Nero	54 to 68 (see Acts 25.11; 27.24; 28.19)
Galba	68 to 69
Otho	69
Vitellius	69
Vespasian	69 to 79
Titus	79 to 81 (invaded Jerusalem A.D. 70; see Matthew 24.2)
Domitian	81 to 96 (had John sent to Patmos; see Revelation 1.9)

keep you from thinking how wise you are. It is that the stubbornness of the people of Israel is not permanent, but will last only until the complete number of Gentiles comes to God. 26 And this is how all Israel will be saved. As the scripture says,

"The Savior will come from Zion
  and remove all wickedness from
    the descendants of Jacob.
27 I will make this covenant with
  them
    when I take away their sins."

28 Because they reject the Good News, the Jews are God's enemies for the sake of you Gentiles. But because of God's choice, they are his friends because of their ancestors. 29 For God does not change his mind about whom he chooses and blesses. 30 As for you Gentiles, you disobeyed God in the past; but now you have received God's mercy because the Jews were disobedient. 31 In the same way, because of the mercy that you have received, the Jews now disobey God, in order that they also may now q receive God's mercy. 32 For God has made all people prisoners of disobedience, so that he might show mercy to them all.

Praise to God

33 How great are God's riches! How deep are his wisdom and knowledge! Who can explain his decisions? Who can understand his ways? 34 As the scripture says,

"Who knows the mind of the
  Lord?
Who is able to give him advice?
35 Who has ever given him anything,
  so that he had to pay it back?"

36 For all things were created by him, and all things exist through him and for him. To God be the glory forever! Amen.

Life in God's Service

12 So then, my friends, because of God's great mercy to us I appeal to you: Offer yourselves as a living sacrifice to God, dedicated to his service and pleasing to him. This is the true worship that you should offer. 2 Do not conform yourselves to the standards of this world, but let God transform you inwardly by a complete change of your mind. Then you will be able to know the will of God—what is good and is pleasing to him and is perfect.

3 And because of God's gracious gift to me I say to every one of you: Do not think of yourself more highly than you should. Instead, be modest in your thinking, and judge yourself according to the amount of faith that God has given you. 4 We have many parts in the one body, and all these parts have different functions. 5 In the same way, though we are many, we are one body in union with Christ, and we are all joined to each other as different parts of one body. 6 So we are to use our different gifts in accordance with the grace that God has given us. If our gift is to speak God's message, we should do it according to the faith that we have; 7 if it is to serve, we should serve; if it is to teach, we should teach; 8 if it is to encourage others, we should do so. Whoever shares with others should do it generously; whoever has authority should work hard; whoever shows kindness to others should do it cheerfully.

9 Love must be completely sincere. Hate what is evil, hold on to what is good. 10 Love one another warmly as Christians, and be eager to show respect for one another. 11 Work hard and do not be lazy. Serve the Lord with a heart full of devotion. 12 Let your hope keep you joyful, be patient in your troubles, and pray at all times. 13 Share your belongings with your needy fellow Christians, and open your homes to strangers.

14 Ask God to bless those who persecute you—yes, ask him to bless, not to curse. 15 Be happy with those who are happy, weep with those who weep. 16 Have the same concern for everyone. Do not be proud, but accept humble duties. r Do not think of yourselves as wise.

17 If someone has done you wrong, do not repay him with a wrong. Try to do what everyone considers to be good. 18 Do everything possible on your part to live in peace with everybody. 19 Never take revenge, my friends, but instead let God's anger do it. For the scripture says, "I will take revenge, I will pay back, says the Lord." 20 Instead, as the scripture

---

q Some manuscripts do not have now.   r accept humble duties; or make friends with humble people.

says: "If your enemies are hungry, feed them; if they are thirsty, give them a drink for by doing this you will make them burn with shame." 21 Do not let evil defeat you; instead, conquer evil with good.

Duties toward State Authorities

13 Everyone must obey state authorities, because no authority exists without God's permission, and the existing authorities have been put there by God. 2 Whoever opposes the existing authority opposes what God has ordered; and anyone who does so will bring judgment on himself. 3 For rulers are not to be feared by those who do good, but by those who do evil. Would you like to be unafraid of those in authority? Then do what is good, and they will praise you, 4 because they are God's servants working for your own good. But if you do evil, then be afraid of them, because their power to punish is real. They are God's servants and carry out God's punishment on those who do evil. 5 For this reason you must obey the authorities — not just because of God's punishment, but also as a matter of conscience.

6 That is also why you pay taxes, because the authorities are working for God when they fulfill their duties. 7 Pay, then, what you owe them; pay them your personal and property taxes, and show respect and honor for them all.

Duties toward One Another

8 Be under obligation to no one — the only obligation you have is to love one another. Whoever does this has obeyed the Law. 9 The commandments, "Do not commit adultery; do not commit murder; do not steal; do not desire what belongs to someone else" — all these, and any others besides, are summed up in the one command, "Love your neighbor as you love yourself." 10 If you love others, you will never do them wrong; to love, then, is to obey the whole Law.

11 You must do this, because you know that the time has come for you to wake up from your sleep. For the moment when we will be saved is closer now than it was when we first believed. 12 The night is nearly over, day is almost here. Let us stop doing the things that belong to the dark, and let us take up weapons for fighting in the light. 13 Let us conduct ourselves properly, as people who live in the light of day — no orgies or drunkenness, no immorality or indecency, no fighting or jealousy. 14 But take up the weapons of the Lord Jesus Christ, and stop paying attention to your sinful nature and satisfying its desires.

Do Not Judge Others

14 Welcome those who are weak in faith, but do not argue with them about their personal opinions. 2 Some people's faith allows them to eat anything, but the person who is weak in the faith eats only vegetables. 3 The person who will eat anything is not to despise the one who doesn't; while the one who eats only vegetables is not to pass judgment on the one who will eat anything; for God has accepted that person. 4 Who are you to judge the servants of someone else? It is their own Master who will decide whether they succeed or fail. And they will succeed, because the Lord is able to make them succeed.

5 Some people think that a certain day is more important than other days, while others think that all days are the same. We each should firmly make up our own minds. 6 Those who think highly of a certain day do so in honor of the Lord; those who will eat anything do so in honor of the Lord, because they give thanks to God for the food. Those who refuse to eat certain things do so in honor of the Lord, and they give thanks to God. 7 We do not live for ourselves only, and we do not die for ourselves only. 8 If we live, it is for the Lord that we live, and if we die, it is for the Lord that we die. So whether we live or we die, we belong to the Lord. 9 For Christ died and rose to life in order to be the Lord of the living and of the dead. 10 You then, who eat only vegetables — why do you pass judgment on others? And you who eat anything — why do you despise other believers? All of us will stand before God to be judged by him. 11 For the scripture says,

"As surely as I am the living God, says the Lord,
everyone will kneel before me,
and everyone will confess that I am God."

12 Every one of us, then, will have to give an account to God.

ROMANS

Do Not Make Others Fall

13 So then, let us stop judging one another. Instead, you should decide never to do anything that would make others stumble or fall into sin. 14 My union with the Lord Jesus makes me certain that no food is of itself ritually unclean; but if you believe that some food is unclean, then it becomes unclean for you. 15 If you hurt others because of something you eat, then you are no longer acting from love. Do not let the food that you eat ruin the person for whom Christ died! 16 Do not let what you regard as good get a bad name. 17 For God's Kingdom is not a matter of eating and drinking, but of the righteousness, peace, and joy which the Holy Spirit gives. 18 And when you serve Christ in this way, you please God and are approved by others.

19 So then, we must always aim[s] at those things that bring peace and that help strengthen one another. 20 Do not, because of food, destroy what God has done. All foods may be eaten, but it is wrong to eat anything that will cause someone else to fall into sin. 21 The right thing to do is to keep from eating meat, drinking wine, or doing anything else that will make other believers fall. 22 Keep what you believe about this matter, then, between yourself and God. Happy are those who do not feel guilty when they do something they judge is right! 23 But if they have doubts about what they eat, God condemns them when they eat it, because their action is not based on faith. And anything that is not based on faith is sin.

Please Others, Not Yourselves

15 We who are strong in the faith ought to help the weak to carry their burdens. We should not please ourselves. 2 Instead, we should all please other believers for their own good, in order to build them up in the faith. 3 For Christ did not please himself. Instead, as the scripture says, "The insults which are hurled at you have fallen on me." 4 Everything written in the Scriptures was written to teach us, in order that we might have hope through the patience and encouragement which the Scriptures give us. 5 And may God, the source of patience and encouragement, enable you to have the same point of view among yourselves by following the example of Christ Jesus, 6 so that all of you together may praise with one voice the God and Father of our Lord Jesus Christ.

The Gospel to the Gentiles

7 Accept one another, then, for the glory of God, as Christ has accepted you. 8 For I tell you that Christ's life of service was on behalf of the Jews, to show that God is faithful, to make his promises to their ancestors come true, 9 and to enable even the Gentiles to praise God for his mercy. As the scripture says,

"And so I will praise you among
     the Gentiles;
   I will sing praises to you."
10 Again it says,
   "Rejoice, Gentiles, with God's
     people!"
11 And again,
   "Praise the Lord, all Gentiles;
     praise him, all peoples!"
12 And again, Isaiah says,
   "A descendant of Jesse will
     appear;
   he will come to rule the Gentiles,
     and they will put their hope
     in him."

13 May God, the source of hope, fill you with all joy and peace by means of your faith in him, so that your hope will continue to grow by the power of the Holy Spirit.

Paul's Reason for Writing So Boldly

14 My friends: I myself feel sure that you are full of goodness, that you have all knowledge, and that you are able to teach one another. 15 But in this letter I have been quite bold about certain subjects of which I have reminded you. I have been bold because of the privilege God has given me 16 of being a servant of Christ Jesus to work for the Gentiles. I serve like a priest in preaching the Good News from God, in order that the Gentiles may be an offering acceptable to God, dedicated to him by the Holy Spirit. 17 In union with Christ Jesus, then, I can be proud of my service for God. 18 I will be bold and speak only about what Christ has done through me to lead the Gentiles to obey God. He has done this by means of words and deeds, 19 by the

---

[s] we must always aim; *some manuscripts have* we always aim.

power of miracles and wonders, and by the power of the Spirit of God. And so, in traveling all the way from Jerusalem to Illyricum, I have proclaimed fully the Good News about Christ. 20 My ambition has always been to proclaim the Good News in places where Christ has not been heard of, so as not to build on a foundation laid by someone else. 21 As the scripture says,

"Those who were not told about
    him will see,
and those who have not heard
    will understand."

Paul's Plan to Visit Rome

22 And so I have been prevented many times from coming to you. 23 But now that I have finished my work in these regions and since I have been wanting for so many years to come to see you, 24 I hope to do so now. I would like to see you on my way to Spain, and be helped by you to go there, after I have enjoyed visiting you for a while. 25 Right now, however, I am going to Jerusalem in the service of God's people there. 26 For the churches in Macedonia and Achaia have freely decided to give an offering to help the poor among God's people in Jerusalem. 27 That decision was their own; but, as a matter of fact, they have an obligation to help them. Since the Jews shared their spiritual blessings with the Gentiles, the Gentiles ought to use their material blessings to help the Jews. 28 When I have finished this task and have turned over to them all the money that has been raised for them, I shall leave for Spain and visit you on my way there. 29 When I come to you, I know that I shall come with a full measure of the blessing of Christ.

30 I urge you, friends, by our Lord Jesus Christ and by the love that the Spirit gives: join me in praying fervently to God for me. 31 Pray that I may be kept safe from the unbelievers in Judea and that my service in Jerusalem may be acceptable to God's people there. 32 And so I will come to you full of joy, if it is God's will, and enjoy a refreshing visit with you. 33 May God, our source of peace, be with all of you. Amen.

Personal Greetings

16 I recommend to you our sister Phoebe, who serves the church at Cenchreae. 2 Receive her in the Lord's name, as God's people should, and give her any help she may need from you; for she herself has been a good friend to many people and also to me.

3 I send greetings to Priscilla and Aquila, my fellow workers in the service of Christ Jesus; 4 they risked their lives for me. I am grateful to them — not only I, but all the Gentile churches as well. 5 Greetings also to the church that meets in their house.

Greetings to my dear friend Epaenetus, who was the first in the province of Asia to believe in Christ. 6 Greetings to Mary, who has worked so hard for you. 7 Greetings also to Andronicus and Junia,[t] fellow Jews who were in prison with me; they are well known among the apostles, and they became Christians before I did.

8 My greetings to Ampliatus, my dear friend in the fellowship of the Lord. 9 Greetings also to Urbanus, our fellow worker in Christ's service, and to Stachys, my dear friend. 10 Greetings to Apelles, whose loyalty to Christ has been proved. Greetings to those who belong to the family of Aristobulus. 11 Greetings to Herodion, a fellow Jew, and to the Christians in the family of Narcissus.

12 My greetings to Tryphaena and Tryphosa, who work in the Lord's service, and to my dear friend Persis, who has done so much work for the Lord. 13 I send greetings to Rufus, that outstanding worker in the Lord's service, and to his mother, who has always treated me like a son. 14 My greetings to Asyncritus, Phlegon, Hermes, Patrobas, Hermas, and all the other Christians with them. 15 Greetings to Philologus and Julia, to Nereus and his sister, to Olympas and to all of God's people who are with them.

16 Greet one another with the kiss of peace. All the churches of Christ send you their greetings.

Final Instructions

17 I urge you, my friends: watch out for those who cause divisions and upset

---

t Junia; or Junias; *some manuscripts have* Julia.

PAUL'S JOURNEY TO ROME

© United Bible Societies 1978

people's faith and go against the teaching which you have received. Keep away from them! 18 For those who do such things are not serving Christ our Lord, but their own appetites. By their fine words and flattering speech they deceive innocent people. 19 Everyone has heard of your loyalty to the gospel, and for this reason I am happy about you. I want you to be wise about what is good, but innocent in what is evil. 20 And God, our source of peace, will soon crush Satan under your feet.

The grace of our Lord Jesus be with you.u

21 Timothy, my fellow worker, sends you his greetings; and so do Lucius, Jason, and Sosipater, fellow Jews.

22 I, Tertius, the writer of this letter, send you Christian greetings.

23 My host Gaius, in whose house the church meets, sends you his greetings; Erastus, the city treasurer, and our brother Quartus send you their greetings.v

Concluding Prayer of Praise

25 Let us give glory to God! He is able to make you stand firm in your faith, according to the Good News I preach about Jesus Christ and according to the revelation of the secret truth which was hidden for long ages in the past. 26 Now, however, that truth has been brought out into the open through the writings of the prophets; and by the command of the eternal God it is made known to all nations, so that all may believe and obey.

27 To the only God, who alone is all-wise, be glory through Jesus Christ forever! Amen.w

u Some manuscripts omit this sentence.   v Some manuscripts add verse 24: The grace of our Lord Jesus Christ be with you all. Amen; others add this after verse 27.
w Some manuscripts have verses 25-27 here and after 14.23; others have them only after 14.23; one has them after 15.33.

Paul's First Letter to the
CORINTHIANS

Introduction

Paul's First Letter to the Corinthians was written to deal with problems of Christian life and faith that had arisen in the church which Paul had established at Corinth. At that time Corinth was a great cosmopolitan Greek city, the capital of the Roman province of Achaia. It was noted for its thriving commerce, proud culture, widespread immorality, and variety of religions.

The apostle's chief concerns are with problems such as divisions and immorality in the church, and with questions about sex and marriage, matters of conscience, church order, gifts of the Holy Spirit, and the resurrection. With deep insight he shows how the Good News speaks to these questions.

Chapter 13, which presents love as the best of God's gifts to his people, is probably the most widely known passage in the book.

Outline of Contents

1 From Paul, who was called by the will of God to be an apostle of Christ Jesus, and from our brother Sosthenes—

2 To the church of God which is in Corinth, to all who are called to be God's holy people, who belong to him in union with Christ Jesus, together with all people everywhere who worship our Lord Jesus Christ, their Lord and ours: 3 May God our Father and the Lord Jesus Christ give you grace and peace.

Blessings in Christ

4 I always give thanks to my God for you because of the grace he has given you through Christ Jesus. 5 For in union with Christ you have become rich in all things, including all speech and all knowledge. 6 The message about Christ has become so firmly established in you 7 that you have not failed to receive a single blessing, as you wait for our Lord Jesus Christ to be revealed. 8 He will also keep you firm to the end, so that you will be faultless on the Day of our Lord Jesus Christ. 9 God is to be trusted, the God who called you to have fellowship with his Son Jesus Christ, our Lord.

Divisions in the Church

10 By the authority of our Lord Jesus Christ I appeal to all of you, my friends, to agree in what you say, so that there will be no divisions among you. Be completely united, with only one thought and one purpose. 11 For some people from Chloe's family have told me quite plainly, my friends, that there are quarrels among you. 12 Let me put it this way: each one of you says something different. One says, "I follow Paul"; another, "I follow Apollos"; another, "I follow Peter"; and another, "I follow Christ." 13 Christ has been divided[a] into groups! Was it Paul who died on the cross for you? Were you baptized as Paul's disciples?

14 I thank God that I did not baptize any of you except Crispus and Gaius. 15 No one can say, then, that you were baptized as my disciples. (16 Oh yes, I also baptized Stephanas and his family; but I can't remember whether I baptized anyone else.) 17 Christ did not send me to baptize. He sent me to tell the Good News, and to tell it without using the language of human wisdom, in order to make sure that Christ's death on the cross is not robbed of its power.

Christ the Power and the Wisdom of God

18 For the message about Christ's death on the cross is nonsense to those who are being lost; but for us who are being saved it is God's power. 19 The scripture says,

"I will destroy the wisdom of the wise
and set aside the understanding of the scholars."

20 So then, where does that leave the wise? or the scholars? or the skillful debaters of this world? God has shown that this world's wisdom is foolishness!

21 For God in his wisdom made it impossible for people to know him by means of their own wisdom. Instead, by means of the so-called "foolish" message we preach, God decided to save those who believe. 22 Jews want miracles for proof, and Greeks look for wisdom. 23 As for us, we proclaim the crucified Christ, a message that is offensive to the Jews and nonsense to the Gentiles; 24 but for those whom God has called, both Jews and Gentiles, this message is Christ, who is the power of God and the wisdom of God. 25 For what seems to be God's foolishness is wiser than human wisdom, and what seems to be God's weakness is stronger than human strength.

26 Now remember what you were, my friends, when God called you. From the human point of view few of you were wise or powerful or of high social standing. 27 God purposely chose what the world considers nonsense in order to shame the wise, and he chose what the world considers weak in order to shame the powerful. 28 He chose what the world looks down on and despises and thinks is nothing, in order to destroy what the world thinks is important. 29 This means that no one can boast in God's presence. 30 But God has brought you into union with Christ Jesus, and God has made Christ to be our wisdom. By him we are put right with God; we become God's holy people and are set free. 31 So then, as the scripture says, "Whoever wants to

---

a Christ has been divided; *some manuscripts have* Christ cannot be divided.

boast must boast of what the Lord has done."

The Message about the Crucified Christ

2 When I came to you, my friends, to preach God's secret truth,[b] I did not use big words and great learning. [2]For while I was with you, I made up my mind to forget everything except Jesus Christ and especially his death on the cross. [3]So when I came to you, I was weak and trembled all over with fear, [4]and my teaching and message were not delivered with skillful words of human wisdom, but with convincing proof of the power of God's Spirit. [5]Your faith, then, does not rest on human wisdom but on God's power.

God's Wisdom

[6]Yet I do proclaim a message of wisdom to those who are spiritually mature. But it is not the wisdom that belongs to this world or to the powers that rule this world—powers that are losing their power. [7]The wisdom I proclaim is God's secret wisdom, which is hidden from human beings, but which he had already chosen for our glory even before the world was made. [8]None of the rulers of this world knew this wisdom. If they had known it, they would not have crucified the Lord of glory. [9]However, as the scripture says,

"What no one ever saw or heard,
　　what no one ever thought could
　　　happen,
is the very thing God prepared
　　for those who love him."

[10]But[c] it was to us that God made known his secret by means of his Spirit. The Spirit searches everything, even the hidden depths of God's purposes. [11]It is only our own spirit within us that knows all about us; in the same way, only God's Spirit knows all about God. [12]We have not received this world's spirit; instead, we have received the Spirit sent by God, so that we may know all that God has given us. [13]So then, we do not speak in words taught by human wisdom, but in words taught by the Spirit, as we explain spiritual truths to those who have the Spirit.[d]

[14]Whoever does not have the Spirit cannot receive the gifts that come from God's Spirit. Such a person really does not understand them, and they seem to be nonsense, because their value can be judged only on a spiritual basis. [15]Whoever has the Spirit, however, is able to judge the value of everything, but no one is able to judge him. [16]As the scripture says,

"Who knows the mind of the
　　Lord?
　　Who is able to give him advice?"
We, however, have the mind of Christ.

Servants of God

3 As a matter of fact, my friends, I could not talk to you as I talk to people who have the Spirit; I had to talk to you as though you belonged to this world, as children in the Christian faith. [2]I had to feed you milk, not solid food, because you were not ready for it. And even now you are not ready for it, [3]because you still live as the people of this world live. When there is jealousy among you and you quarrel with one another, doesn't this prove that you belong to this world, living by its standards? [4]When one of you says, "I follow Paul," and another, "I follow Apollos"—aren't you acting like worldly people?

[5]After all, who is Apollos? And who is Paul? We are simply God's servants, by whom you were led to believe. Each one of us does the work which the Lord gave him to do: [6]I planted the seed, Apollos watered the plant, but it was God who made the plant grow. [7]The one who plants and the one who waters really do not matter. It is God who matters, because he makes the plant grow. [8]There is no difference between the one who plants and the one who waters; God will reward each one according to the work each has done. [9]For we are partners working together for God, and you are God's field.

You are also God's building. [10]Using the gift that God gave me, I did the work of an expert builder and laid the foundation, and someone else is building on it. But each of you must be careful how you build. [11]For God has already placed Jesus Christ as the one and only founda-

[b] God's secret truth; some manuscripts have the testimony about God.
[c] But; some manuscripts have For.　　[d] to those who have the Spirit; or with words given by the Spirit.

tion, and no other foundation can be laid. 12 Some will use gold or silver or precious stones in building on the foundation; others will use wood or grass or straw. 13 And the quality of each person's work will be seen when the Day of Christ exposes it. For on that Day fire will reveal everyone's work; the fire will test it and show its real quality. 14 If what was built on the foundation survives the fire, the builder will receive a reward. 15 But if your work is burnt up, then you will lose it; but you yourself will be saved, as if you had escaped through the fire.

16 Surely you know that you are God's temple and that God's Spirit lives in you! 17 God will destroy anyone who destroys God's temple. For God's temple is holy, and you yourselves are his temple.

18 You should not fool yourself. If any of you think that you are wise by this world's standards, you should become a fool, in order to be really wise. 19 For what this world considers to be wisdom is nonsense in God's sight. As the scripture says, "God traps the wise in their cleverness"; 20 and another scripture says, "The Lord knows that the thoughts of the wise are worthless." 21 No one, then, should boast about what human beings can do. Actually everything belongs to you: 22 Paul, Apollos, and Peter; this world, life and death, the present and the future — all these are yours, 23 and you belong to Christ, and Christ belongs to God.

Apostles of Christ

4 You should think of us as Christ's servants, who have been put in charge of God's secret truths. 2 The one thing required of such servants is that they be faithful to their master. 3 Now, I am not at all concerned about being judged by you or by any human standard; I don't even pass judgment on myself. 4 My conscience is clear, but that does not prove that I am really innocent. The Lord is the one who passes judgment on me. 5 So you should not pass judgment on anyone before the right time comes. Final judgment must wait until the Lord comes; he will bring to light the dark secrets and expose the hidden purposes of people's minds. And then all will receive from God the praise they deserve.

6 For your sake, my friends, I have applied all this to Apollos and me, using the two of us as an example, so that you may learn what the saying means, "Observe the proper rules." None of you should be proud of one person and despise another. 7 Who made you superior to others? Didn't God give you everything you have? Well, then, how can you boast, as if what you have were not a gift?

8 Do you already have everything you need? Are you already rich? Have you become kings, even though we are not? Well, I wish you really were kings, so that we could be kings together with you. 9 For it seems to me that God has given the very last place to us apostles, like people condemned to die in public as a spectacle for the whole world of angels and of human beings. 10 For Christ's sake we are fools; but you are wise in union with Christ! We are weak, but you are strong! We are despised, but you are honored! 11 To this very moment we go hungry and thirsty; we are clothed in rags; we are beaten; we wander from place to place; 12 we wear ourselves out with hard work. When we are cursed, we bless; when we are persecuted, we endure; 13 when we are insulted, we answer back with kind words. We are no more than this world's garbage; we are the scum of the earth to this very moment!

14 I write this to you, not because I want to make you feel ashamed, but to instruct you as my own dear children. 15 For even if you have ten thousand guardians in your Christian life, you have only one father. For in your life in union with Christ Jesus I have become your father by bringing the Good News to you. 16 I beg you, then, to follow my example. 17 For this purpose I am sending to you Timothy, who is my own dear and faithful son in the Christian life. He will remind you of the principles which I follow in the new life in union with Christ Jesus and which I teach in all the churches everywhere.

18 Some of you have become proud because you have thought that I would not be coming to visit you. 19 If the Lord is willing, however, I will come to you soon, and then I will find out for myself the power which these proud people have, and not just what they say. 20 For

the Kingdom of God is not a matter of words but of power. 21 Which do you prefer? Shall I come to you with a whip, or in a spirit of love and gentleness?

Immorality in the Church

5 Now, it is actually being said that there is sexual immorality among you so terrible that not even the heathen would be guilty of it. I am told that a man is sleeping with his stepmother! 2 How, then, can you be proud? On the contrary, you should be filled with sadness, and the man who has done such a thing should be expelled from your fellowship. 3-4 And even though I am far away from you in body, still I am there with you in spirit; and as though I were there with you, I have in the name of our Lord Jesus already passed judgment on the man who has done this terrible thing. As you meet together, and I meet with you in my spirit, by the power of our Lord Jesus present with us, 5 you are to hand this man over to Satan for his body to be destroyed, so that his spirit may be saved in the Day of the Lord.

6 It is not right for you to be proud! You know the saying, "A little bit of yeast makes the whole batch of dough rise." 7 You must remove the old yeast of sin so that you will be entirely pure. Then you will be like a new batch of dough without any yeast, as indeed I know you actually are. For our Passover Festival is ready, now that Christ, our Passover lamb, has been sacrificed. 8 Let us celebrate our Passover, then, not with bread having the old yeast of sin and wickedness, but with the bread that has no yeast, the bread of purity and truth.

9 In the letter that I wrote you I told you not to associate with immoral people. 10 Now I did not mean pagans who are immoral or greedy or are thieves, or who worship idols. To avoid them you would have to get out of the world completely. 11 What I meant was that you should not associate with a person who calls himself a believer but is immoral or greedy or worships idols or is a slanderer or a drunkard or a thief. Don't even sit down to eat with such a person.

12-13 After all, it is none of my business to judge outsiders. God will judge them. But should you not judge the members of your own fellowship? As the scripture says, "Remove the evil person from your group."

Lawsuits against Fellow Christians

6 If any of you have a dispute with another Christian, how dare you go before heathen judges instead of letting God's people settle the matter? 2 Don't you know that God's people will judge the world? Well, then, if you are to judge the world, aren't you capable of judging small matters? 3 Do you not know that we shall judge the angels? How much more, then, the things of this life! 4 If such matters come up, are you going to take them to be settled by people who have no standing in the church? 5 Shame on you! Surely there is at least one wise person in your fellowship who can settle a dispute between fellow Christians. 6 Instead, one Christian goes to court against another and lets unbelievers judge the case!

7 The very fact that you have legal disputes among yourselves shows that you have failed completely. Would it not be better for you to be wronged? Would it not be better for you to be robbed? 8 Instead, you yourselves wrong one another and rob one another, even other believers! 9 Surely you know that the wicked will not possess God's Kingdom. Do not fool yourselves; people who are immoral or who worship idols or are adulterers or homosexual perverts 10 or who steal or are greedy or are drunkards or who slander others or are thieves — none of these will possess God's Kingdom. 11 Some of you were like that. But you have been purified from sin; you have been dedicated to God; you have been put right with God by the Lord Jesus Christ and by the Spirit of our God.

Use Your Bodies for God's Glory

12 Someone will say, "I am allowed to do anything." Yes; but not everything is good for you. I could say that I am allowed to do anything, but I am not going to let anything make me its slave. 13 Someone else will say, "Food is for the stomach, and the stomach is for food." Yes; but God will put an end to both. The body is not to be used for sexual immorality, but to serve the Lord; and the Lord provides for the body. 14 God raised

the Lord from death, and he will also raise us by his power.

15 You know that your bodies are parts of the body of Christ. Shall I take a part of Christ's body and make it part of the body of a prostitute? Impossible! 16 Or perhaps you don't know that the man who joins his body to a prostitute becomes physically one with her? The scripture says quite plainly, "The two will become one body." 17 But he who joins himself to the Lord becomes spiritually one with him.

18 Avoid immorality. Any other sin a man commits does not affect his body; but the man who is guilty of sexual immorality sins against his own body. 19 Don't you know that your body is the temple of the Holy Spirit, who lives in you and who was given to you by God? You do not belong to yourselves but to God; 20 he bought you for a price. So use your bodies for God's glory.

Questions about Marriage

7 Now, to deal with the matters you wrote about.

A man does well not to marry.e 2 But because there is so much immorality, every man should have his own wife, and every woman should have her own husband. 3 A man should fulfill his duty as a husband, and a woman should fulfill her duty as a wife, and each should satisfy the other's needs. 4 A wife is not the master of her own body, but her husband is; in the same way a husband is not the master of his own body, but his wife is. 5 Do not deny yourselves to each other, unless you first agree to do so for a while in order to spend your time in prayer; but then resume normal marital relations. In this way you will be kept from giving in to Satan's temptation because of your lack of self-control.

6 I tell you this not as an order, but simply as a permission. 7 Actually I would prefer that all of you were as I am; but each one has a special gift from God, one person this gift, another one that gift.

8 Now, to the unmarried and to the widows I say that it would be better for you to continue to live alone as I do. 9 But

if you cannot restrain your desires, go ahead and marry—it is better to marry than to burn with passion.

10 For married people I have a command which is not my own but the Lord's: a wife must not leave her husband; 11 but if she does, she must remain single or else be reconciled to her husband; and a husband must not divorce his wife.

12 To the others I say (I, myself, not the Lord): if a Christian man has a wife who is an unbeliever and she agrees to go on living with him, he must not divorce her. 13 And if a Christian woman is married to a man who is an unbeliever and he agrees to go on living with her, she must not divorce him. 14 For the unbelieving husband is made acceptable to God by being united to his wife, and the unbelieving wife is made acceptable to God by being united to her Christian husband. If this were not so, their children would be like pagan children; but as it is, they are acceptable to God. 15 However, if the one who is not a believer wishes to leave the Christian partner, let it be so. In such cases the Christian partner, whether husband or wife, is free to act. God has called you to live in peace. 16 How can you be sure, Christian wife, that you will not savef your husband? Or how can you be sure, Christian husband, that you will not savef your wife?

Live As God Called You

17 Each of you should go on living according to the Lord's gift to you, and as you were when God called you. This is the rule I teach in all the churches. 18 If a circumcised man has accepted God's call, he should not try to remove the marks of circumcision; if an uncircumcised man has accepted God's call, he should not get circumcised. 19 For whether or not a man is circumcised means nothing; what matters is to obey God's commandments. 20 Each of you should remain as you were when you accepted God's call. 21 Were you a slave when God called you? Well, never mind; but if you have a chance to become free, use it.g 22 For a slave who has been called by the Lord is the Lord's free

---

e A man does well not to marry; or You say that a man does well not to marry.
f How can you be sure . . . that you will not save; or How do you know . . . that you will save.
g but if you have a chance to become free, use it; or but even if you have a chance to become free, choose rather to make the best of your condition as a slave.

THE CITY OF CORINTH

Corinth was a busy commercial city in ancient Greece, strategically located on the narrow strip of land connecting the peninsula to the mainland. The city had two excellent harbors, Cenchreae and Lechaeum. A cosmopolitan center of about 500,000 people when Paul arrived, this metropolis has dwindled to only a small city in modern times.

In Paul's view, Corinth was an ideal city for a church. The constant movement of travelers, merchants, and pilgrims as they practiced their trades through Corinth made it possible for the gospel to influence people from every part of the Roman world.

In addition to its commercial importance, Corinth was a center of idolatry with numerous pagan temples dedicated to worship of the Greek and Roman gods. The infamous temple of Aphrodite, a fertility goddess, had a poisonous effect on the city's culture and morals. Paul must have been moved by the godless masses that were consumed with the pursuit of profit and pleasure.

With the Corinthian church made up of people from these backgrounds, learning to live together in harmony was most difficult. Paul's two letters to the young church at Corinth (1 and 2 Corinthians) contain instruction on Christian living in a pagan environment.

But along with these struggles, the Corinthian church also experienced significant Christian victories (Ac 18.8). One noted convert may have been the city treasurer, Erastus, mentioned in Romans 16.23. A bronze plaque, known as the Erastus Inscription, found near the ruins of a large amphitheater, mentions a generous patron by this name.

Paul labored with the church at Corinth for about eighteen months. After he left the city, a Christian community apparently was established at Corinth's eastern port of Cenchreae (Ro 16.1).

person; in the same way a free person who has been called by Christ is his slave. 23 God bought you for a price; so do not become slaves of people. 24 My friends, each of you should remain in fellowship with God in the same condition that you were when you were called.

Questions about the Unmarried and the Widows

25 Now, concerning what you wrote about unmarried people: I do not have a command from the Lord, but I give my opinion as one who by the Lord's mercy is worthy of trust.

26 Considering the present distress, I think it is better for a man to stay as he is. 27 Do you have a wife? Then don't try to get rid of her. Are you unmarried? Then don't look for a wife. 28 But if you do marry, you haven't committed a sin; and if an unmarried woman marries, she hasn't committed a sin. But I would rather spare you the everyday troubles that married people will have.

29 What I mean, my friends, is this: there is not much time left, and from now on married people should live as though they were not married; 30 those who weep, as though they were not sad; those who laugh, as though they were not happy; those who buy, as though they did not own what they bought; 31 those who deal in material goods, as though they were not fully occupied with them. For this world, as it is now, will not last much longer.

32 I would like you to be free from worry. An unmarried man concerns himself with the Lord's work, because he is trying to please the Lord. 33 But a married man concerns himself with worldly matters, because he wants to please his wife; 34 and so he is pulled in two directions. An unmarried woman or a virgin concerns herself with the Lord's work, because she wants to be dedicated both in body and spirit; but a married woman concerns herself with worldly matters, because she wants to please her husband.

35 I am saying this because I want to help you. I am not trying to put restric-

tions on you. Instead, I want you to do what is right and proper, and to give yourselves completely to the Lord's service without any reservation.

36 In the case of an engaged couple who have decided not to marry: if the man feels that he is not acting properly toward the young woman and if his passions are too strong and he feels that they ought to marry, then they should get married, as he wants to.h There is no sin in this. 37 But if a man, without being forced to do so, has firmly made up his mind not to marry,i and if he has his will under complete control and has already decided in his own mind what to do — then he does well not to marry the young woman.j 38 So the man who marriesk does well, but the one who doesn't marryl does even better.

39 A married woman is not free as long as her husband lives; but if her husband dies, then she is free to be married to any man she wishes, but only if he is a Christian. 40 She will be happier, however, if she stays as she is. That is my opinion, and I think that I too have God's Spirit.

The Question about Food Offered to Idols

8 Now, concerning what you wrote about food offered to idols.

It is true, of course, that "all of us have knowledge," as they say. Such knowledge, however, puffs a person up with pride; but love builds up. 2 Those who think they know something really don't know as they ought to know. 3 But the person who loves God is known by him.

4 So then, about eating the food offered to idols: we know that an idol stands for something that does not really exist; we know that there is only the one God. 5 Even if there are so-called "gods," whether in heaven or on earth, and even though there are many of these "gods" and "lords," 6 yet there is for us only one God, the Father, who is the Creator of all things and for whom we live; and there is only one Lord, Jesus Christ, through whom all things were created and through whom we live.

7 But not everyone knows this truth.

---

h an engaged couple . . . as he wants to; or a man and his unmarried daughter: if he feels that he is not acting properly toward her, and if she is at the right age to marry, then he should do as he wishes and let her get married.   i not to marry; or not to let his daughter get married.
j marry the young woman; or let her get married.   k marries; or lets his daughter get married.
l doesn't marry; or doesn't let her get married.

Some people have been so used to idols that to this day when they eat such food they still think of it as food that belongs to an idol; their conscience is weak, and they feel they are defiled by the food. 8Food, however, will not improve our relation with God; we shall not lose anything if we do not eat, nor shall we gain anything if we do eat.

9Be careful, however, not to let your freedom of action make those who are weak in the faith fall into sin. 10Suppose a person whose conscience is weak in this matter sees you, who have so-called "knowledge," eating in the temple of an idol; will not this encourage him to eat food offered to idols? 11And so this weak person, your brother for whom Christ died, will perish because of your "knowledge" 12And in this way you will be sinning against Christ by sinning against other Christians and wounding their weak conscience. 13So then, if food makes a believer sin, I will never eat meat again, so as not to make a believer fall into sin.

Rights and Duties of an Apostle

9 Am I not a free man? Am I not an apostle? Haven't I seen Jesus our Lord? And aren't you the result of my work for the Lord? 2Even if others do not accept me as an apostle, surely you do! Because of your life in union with the Lord you yourselves are proof of the fact that I am an apostle.

3When people criticize me, this is how I defend myself: 4Don't I have the right to be given food and drink for my work? 5Don't I have the right to follow the example of the other apostles and the Lord's brothers and Peter, by taking a Christian wife with me on my trips? 6Or are Barnabas and I the only ones who have to work for our living? 7What soldiers ever have to pay their own expenses in the army? What farmers do not eat the grapes from their own vineyard? What shepherds do not use the milk from their own sheep?

8I don't have to limit myself to these everyday examples, because the Law says the same thing. 9We read in the Law of Moses, "Do not muzzle an ox when you are using it to thresh grain." Now, is God concerned about oxen? 10Didn't he really mean us when he said that? Of course that was written for us.

Anyone who plows and anyone who reaps should do their work in the hope of getting a share of the crop. 11We have sown spiritual seed among you. Is it too much if we reap material benefits from you? 12If others have the right to expect this from you, don't we have an even greater right?

But we haven't made use of this right. Instead, we have endured everything in order not to put any obstacle in the way of the Good News about Christ. 13Surely you know that the men who work in the Temple get their food from the Temple and that those who offer the sacrifices on the altar get a share of the sacrifices. 14In the same way, the Lord has ordered that those who preach the gospel should get their living from it.

15But I haven't made use of any of these rights, nor am I writing this now in order to claim such rights for myself. I would rather die first! Nobody is going to turn my rightful boast into empty words! 16I have no right to boast just because I preach the gospel. After all, I am under orders to do so. And how terrible it would be for me if I did not preach the gospel! 17If I did my work as a matter of free choice, then I could expect to be paid; but I do it as a matter of duty, because God has entrusted me with this task. 18What pay do I get, then? It is the privilege of preaching the Good News without charging for it, without claiming my rights in my work for the gospel.

19I am a free man, nobody's slave; but I make myself everybody's slave in order to win as many people as possible. 20While working with the Jews, I live like a Jew in order to win them; and even though I myself am not subject to the Law of Moses, I live as though I were when working with those who are, in order to win them. 21In the same way, when working with Gentiles, I live like a Gentile, outside the Jewish Law, in order to win Gentiles. This does not mean that I don't obey God's law; I am really under Christ's law. 22Among the weak in faith I become weak like one of them, in order to win them. So I become all things to all people, that I may save some of them by whatever means are possible.

23All this I do for the gospel's sake, in order to share in its blessings. 24Surely you know that many runners take part in a race, but only one of them wins the prize. Run, then, in such a way as to win the prize. 25 Every athlete in training submits to strict discipline, in order to be crowned with a wreath that will not last; but we do it for one that will last forever. 26 That is why I run straight for the finish line; that is why I am like a boxer who does not waste his punches. 27 I harden my body with blows and bring it under complete control, to keep myself from being disqualified after having called others to the contest.

Warnings against Idols

10 I want you to remember, my friends, what happened to our ancestors who followed Moses. They were all under the protection of the cloud, and all passed safely through the Red Sea. 2 In the cloud and in the sea they were all baptized as followers of Moses. 3 All ate the same spiritual bread 4 and drank the same spiritual drink. They drank from the spiritual rock that went with them; and that rock was Christ himself. 5 But even then God was not pleased with most of them, and so their dead bodies were scattered over the desert.

6 Now, all of this is an example for us, to warn us not to desire evil things, as they did, 7 nor to worship idols, as some of them did. As the scripture says, "The people sat down to a feast which turned into an orgy of drinking and sex." 8 We must not be guilty of sexual immorality, as some of them were — and in one day twenty-three thousand of them fell dead. 9 We must not put the Lord[m] to the test, as some of them did — and they were killed by snakes. 10 We must not complain, as some of them did — and they were destroyed by the Angel of Death.

11 All these things happened to them as examples for others, and they were written down as a warning for us. For we live at a time when the end is about to come.

12 If you think you are standing firm you had better be careful that you do not fall. 13 Every test that you have experienced is the kind that normally comes to people. But God keeps his promise, and he will not allow you to be tested beyond your power to remain firm; at the time you are put to the test, he will give you the strength to endure it, and so provide you with a way out.

14 So then, my dear friends, keep away from the worship of idols. 15 I speak to you as sensible people; judge for yourselves what I say. 16 The cup we use in the Lord's Supper and for which we give thanks to God: when we drink from it, we are sharing in the blood of Christ. And the bread we break: when we eat it, we are sharing in the body of Christ. 17 Because there is the one loaf of bread, all of us, though many, are one body, for we all share the same loaf.

18 Consider the people of Israel; those who eat what is offered in sacrifice share in the altar's service to God. 19 Do I imply, then, that an idol or the food offered to it really amounts to anything? 20 No! What I am saying is that what is sacrificed on pagan altars is offered to demons, not to God. And I do not want you to be partners with demons. 21 You cannot drink from the Lord's cup and also from the cup of demons; you cannot eat at the Lord's table and also at the table of demons. 22 Or do we want to make the Lord jealous? Do we think that we are stronger than he?

23 "We are allowed to do anything," so they say. That is true, but not everything is good. "We are allowed to do anything" — but not everything is helpful. 24 None of you should be looking out for your own interests, but for the interests of others.

25 You are free to eat anything sold in the meat market, without asking any questions because of your conscience. 26 For, as the scripture says, "The earth and everything in it belong to the Lord." 27 If an unbeliever invites you to a meal and you decide to go, eat what is set before you, without asking any questions because of your conscience. 28 But if someone tells you, "This food was offered to idols," then do not eat that food, for the sake of the one who told you and for conscience' sake — 29 that is, not your own conscience, but the other person's conscience.

"Well, then," someone asks, "why should my freedom to act be limited by another person's conscience? 30 If I thank God for my food, why should any-

---

m the Lord; *some manuscripts have* Christ.

one criticize me about food for which I give thanks?" ³¹ Well, whatever you do, whether you eat or drink, do it all for God's glory. ³² Live in such a way as to cause no trouble either to Jews or Gentiles or to the church of God. ³³ Just do as I do; I try to please everyone in all that I do, not thinking of my own good, but of the good of all, so that they might be saved.

11 Imitate me, then, just as I imitate Christ.

Covering the Head in Worship

² I praise you because you always remember me and follow the teachings that I have handed on to you. ³ But I want you to understand that Christ is supreme over every man, the husband is supreme over his wife, and God is supreme over Christ. ⁴ So a man who prays or proclaims God's message in public worship with his head covered disgraces Christ. ⁵ And any woman who prays or proclaims God's message in public worship with nothing on her head disgraces her husband; there is no difference between her and a woman whose head has been shaved. ⁶ If the woman does not cover her head, she might as well cut her hair. And since it is a shameful thing for a woman to shave her head or cut her hair, she should cover her head. ⁷ A man has no need to cover his head, because he reflects the image and glory of God. But woman reflects the glory of man; ⁸ for man was not created from woman, but woman from man. ⁹ Nor was man created for woman's sake, but woman was created for man's sake. ¹⁰ On account of the angels, then, a woman should have a covering over her head to show that she is under her husband's authority. ¹¹ In our life in the Lord, however, woman is not independent of man, nor is man independent of woman. ¹² For as woman was made from man, in the same way man is born of woman; and it is God who brings everything into existence.

¹³ Judge for yourselves whether it is proper for a woman to pray to God in public worship with nothing on her head. ¹⁴ Why, nature itself teaches you that long hair on a man is a disgrace, ¹⁵ but on a woman it is a thing of beauty. Her long hair has been given her to serve as a covering. ¹⁶ But if anyone wants to argue about it, all I have to say is that neither we nor the churches of God have any other custom in worship.

The Lord's Supper

(Matthew 26.26-29; Mark 14.22-25; Luke 22.14-20)

¹⁷ In the following instructions, however, I do not praise you, because your meetings for worship actually do more harm than good. ¹⁸ In the first place, I have been told that there are opposing groups in your meetings; and this I believe is partly true. (¹⁹ No doubt there must be divisions among you so that the ones who are in the right may be clearly seen.) ²⁰ When you meet together as a group, it is not the Lord's Supper that you eat. ²¹ For as you eat, you each go ahead with your own meal, so that some are hungry while others get drunk. ²² Don't you have your own homes in which to eat and drink? Or would you rather despise the church of God and put to shame the people who are in need? What do you expect me to say to you about this? Shall I praise you? Of course I don't!

²³ For I received from the Lord the teaching that I passed on to you: that the Lord Jesus, on the night he was betrayed, took a piece of bread, ²⁴ gave thanks to God, broke it, and said, "This is my body, which is for you. Do this in memory of me." ²⁵ In the same way, after the supper he took the cup and said, "This cup is God's new covenant, sealed with my blood. Whenever you drink it, do so in memory of me."

²⁶ This means that every time you eat this bread and drink from this cup you proclaim the Lord's death until he comes. ²⁷ It follows that if one of you eats the Lord's bread or drinks from his cup in a way that dishonors him, you are guilty of sin against the Lord's body and blood. ²⁸ So then, you should each examine yourself first, and then eat the bread and drink from the cup. ²⁹ For if you do not recognize the meaning of the Lord's body when you eat the bread and drink from the cup, you bring judgment on yourself as you eat and drink. ³⁰ That is why many of you are sick and weak, and several have died. ³¹ If we would examine ourselves first, we would not come under God's judgment. ³² But we are judged and punished by the Lord, so that

we shall not be condemned together with the world.

33 So then, my friends, when you gather together to eat the Lord's Supper, wait for one another. 34 And if any of you are hungry, you should eat at home, so that you will not come under God's judgment as you meet together. As for the other matters, I will settle them when I come.

Gifts from the Holy Spirit

12 Now, concerning what you wrote about the gifts from the Holy Spirit.

I want you to know the truth about them, my friends. 2 You know that while you were still heathen, you were led astray in many ways to the worship of lifeless idols. 3 I want you to know that no one who is led by God's Spirit can say "A curse on Jesus!" and no one can confess "Jesus is Lord," without being guided by the Holy Spirit.

4 There are different kinds of spiritual gifts, but the same Spirit gives them. 5 There are different ways of serving, but the same Lord is served. 6 There are different abilities to perform service, but the same God gives ability to all for their particular service. 7 The Spirit's presence is shown in some way in each person for the good of all. 8 The Spirit gives one person a message full of wisdom, while to another person the same Spirit gives a message full of knowledge. 9 One and the same Spirit gives faith to one person, while to another person he gives the power to heal. 10 The Spirit gives one person the power to work miracles; to another, the gift of speaking God's message; and to yet another, the ability to tell the difference between gifts that come from the Spirit and those that do not. To one person he gives the ability to speak in strange tongues, and to another he gives the ability to explain what is said. 11 But it is one and the same Spirit who does all this; as he wishes, he gives a different gift to each person.

One Body with Many Parts

12 Christ is like a single body, which has many parts; it is still one body, even though it is made up of different parts. 13 In the same way, all of us, whether Jews or Gentiles, whether slaves or free, have been baptized into the one body by

the same Spirit, and we have all been given the one Spirit to drink.

14 For the body itself is not made up of only one part, but of many parts. 15 If the foot were to say, "Because I am not a hand, I don't belong to the body," that would not keep it from being a part of the body. 16 And if the ear were to say, "Because I am not an eye, I don't belong to the body," that would not keep it from being a part of the body. 17 If the whole body were just an eye, how could it hear? And if it were only an ear, how could it smell? 18 As it is, however, God put every different part in the body just as he wanted it to be. 19 There would not be a body if it were all only one part! 20 As it is, there are many parts but one body.

21 So then, the eye cannot say to the hand, "I don't need you!" Nor can the head say to the feet, "Well, I don't need you!" 22 On the contrary, we cannot do without the parts of the body that seem to be weaker; 23 and those parts that we think aren't worth very much are the ones which we treat with greater care; while the parts of the body which don't look very nice are treated with special modesty, 24 which the more beautiful parts do not need. God himself has put the body together in such a way as to give greater honor to those parts that need it. 25 And so there is no division in the body, but all its different parts have the same concern for one another. 26 If one part of the body suffers, all the other parts suffer with it; if one part is praised, all the other parts share its happiness.

27 All of you are Christ's body, and each one is a part of it. 28 In the church God has put all in place: in the first place apostles, in the second place prophets, and in the third place teachers; then those who perform miracles, followed by those who are given the power to heal or to help others or to direct them or to speak in strange tongues. 29 They are not all apostles or prophets or teachers. Not everyone has the power to work miracles 30 or to heal diseases or to speak in strange tongues or to explain what is said. 31 Set your hearts, then, on the more important gifts.

Best of all, however, is the following way.

Love

13 I may be able to speak the languages of human beings and even of angels, but if I have no love, my speech is no more than a noisy gong or a clanging bell. 2I may have the gift of inspired preaching; I may have all knowledge and understand all secrets; I may have all the faith needed to move mountains—but if I have no love, I am nothing. 3I may give away everything I have, and even give up my body to be burned*n*—but if I have no love, this does me no good.

4Love is patient and kind; it is not jealous or conceited or proud; 5love is not ill-mannered or selfish or irritable; love does not keep a record of wrongs; 6love is not happy with evil, but is happy with the truth. 7Love never gives up; and its faith, hope, and patience never fail.

8Love is eternal. There are inspired messages, but they are temporary; there are gifts of speaking in strange tongues, but they will cease; there is knowledge, but it will pass. 9For our gifts of knowledge and of inspired messages are only partial; 10but when what is perfect comes, then what is partial will disappear.

11When I was a child, my speech, feelings, and thinking were all those of a child; now that I am an adult, I have no more use for childish ways. 12What we see now is like a dim image in a mirror; then we shall see face-to-face. What I know now is only partial; then it will be complete—as complete as God's knowledge of me.

13Meanwhile these three remain: faith, hope, and love; and the greatest of these is love.

More about Gifts from the Spirit

14 It is love, then, that you should strive for. Set your hearts on spiritual gifts, especially the gift of proclaiming God's message. 2Those who speak in strange tongues do not speak to others but to God, because no one understands them. They are speaking secret truths by the power of the Spirit. 3But those who proclaim God's message speak to people and give them help, encouragement, and comfort. 4Those who speak in strange tongues help only themselves, but those who proclaim God's message help the whole church.

5I would like for all of you to speak in strange tongues; but I would rather that you had the gift of proclaiming God's message. For the person who proclaims God's message is of greater value than the one who speaks in strange tongues—unless there is someone present who can explain what is said, so that the whole church may be helped. 6So when I come to you, my friends, what use will I be to you if I speak in strange tongues? Not a bit, unless I bring you some revelation from God or some knowledge or some inspired message or some teaching.

7Take such lifeless musical instruments as the flute or the harp—how will anyone know the tune that is being played unless the notes are sounded distinctly? 8And if the one who plays the bugle does not sound a clear call, who will prepare for battle? 9In the same way, how will anyone understand what you are talking about if your message given in strange tongues is not clear? Your words will vanish in the air! 10There are many different languages in the world, yet none of them is without meaning. 11But if I do not know the language being spoken, those who use it will be foreigners to me and I will be a foreigner to them. 12Since you are eager to have the gifts of the Spirit, you must try above everything else to make greater use of those which help to build up the church.

13The person who speaks in strange tongues, then, must pray for the gift to explain what is said. 14For if I pray in this way, my spirit prays indeed, but my mind has no part in it. 15What should I do, then? I will pray with my spirit, but I will pray also with my mind; I will sing with my spirit, but I will sing also with my mind. 16When you give thanks to God in spirit only, how can ordinary people taking part in the meeting say "Amen" to your prayer of thanksgiving? They have no way of knowing what you are saying. 17Even if your prayer of thanks to God is quite good, other people are not helped at all.

18I thank God that I speak in strange tongues much more than any of you.

n to be burned; some manuscripts have in order to boast.

1 CORINTHIANS

19 But in church worship I would rather speak five words that can be understood, in order to teach others, than speak thousands of words in strange tongues.

20 Do not be like children in your thinking, my friends; be children so far as evil is concerned, but be grown up in your thinking. 21 In the Scriptures it is written,

"By means of people speaking
    strange languages
I will speak to my people, says
    the Lord.
I will speak through lips of
    foreigners,
but even then my people will not
    listen to me."

22 So then, the gift of speaking in strange tongues is proof for unbelievers, not for believers, while the gift of proclaiming God's message is proof for believers, not for unbelievers.

23 If, then, the whole church meets together and everyone starts speaking in strange tongues — and if some ordinary people or unbelievers come in, won't they say that you are all crazy? 24 But if everyone is proclaiming God's message when some unbelievers or ordinary people come in, they will be convinced of their sin by what they hear. They will be judged by all they hear, 25 their secret thoughts will be brought into the open, and they will bow down and worship God, confessing, "Truly God is here among you!"

Order in the Church

26 This is what I mean, my friends. When you meet for worship, one person has a hymn, another a teaching, another a revelation from God, another a message in strange tongues, and still another the explanation of what is said. Everything must be of help to the church. 27 If someone is going to speak in strange tongues, two or three at the most should speak, one after the other, and someone else must explain what is being said. 28 But if no one is there who can explain, then the one who speaks in strange tongues must be quiet and speak only to himself and to God. 29 Two or three who are given God's message should speak, while the others are to judge what they say. 30 But if someone sitting in the meeting receives a message

from God, the one who is speaking should stop. 31 All of you may proclaim God's message, one by one, so that everyone will learn and be encouraged. 32 The gift of proclaiming God's message should be under the speaker's control, 33 because God does not want us to be in disorder but in harmony and peace.

As in all the churches of God's people, 34 the women should keep quiet in the meetings. They are not allowed to speak; as the Jewish Law says, they must not be in charge. 35 If they want to find out about something, they should ask their husbands at home. It is a disgraceful thing for a woman to speak in a church meeting.

36 Or could it be that the word of God came from you? Or are you the only ones to whom it came? 37 If anyone supposes he is God's messenger or has a spiritual gift, he must realize that what I am writing to you is the Lord's command. 38 But if he does not pay attention to this, pay no attention to him.

39 So then, my friends, set your heart on proclaiming God's message, but do not forbid the speaking in strange tongues. 40 Everything must be done in a proper and orderly way.

The Resurrection of Christ

15 And now I want to remind you, my friends, of the Good News which I preached to you, which you received, and on which your faith stands firm. 2 That is the gospel, the message that I preached to you. You are saved by the gospel if you hold firmly to it — unless it was for nothing that you believed.

3 I passed on to you what I received, which is of the greatest importance: that Christ died for our sins, as written in the Scriptures; 4 that he was buried and that he was raised to life three days later, as written in the Scriptures; 5 that he appeared to Peter and then to all twelve apostles. 6 Then he appeared to more than five hundred of his followers at once, most of whom are still alive, although some have died. 7 Then he appeared to James, and afterward to all the apostles.

8 Last of all he appeared also to me — even though I am like someone whose

birth was abnormal.o 9For I am the least of all the apostles—I do not even deserve to be called an apostle, because I persecuted God's church. 10But by God's grace I am what I am, and the grace that he gave me was not without effect. On the contrary, I have worked harder than any of the other apostles, although it was not really my own doing, but God's grace working with me. 11So then, whether it came from me or from them, this is what we all preach, and this is what you believe.

Our Resurrection

12Now, since our message is that Christ has been raised from death, how can some of you say that the dead will not be raised to life? 13If that is true, it means that Christ was not raised; 14and if Christ has not been raised from death, then we have nothing to preach and you have nothing to believe. 15More than that, we are shown to be lying about God, because we said that he raised Christ from death—but if it is true that the dead are not raised to life, then he did not raise Christ. 16For if the dead are not raised, neither has Christ been raised. 17And if Christ has not been raised, then your faith is a delusion and you are still lost in your sins. 18It would also mean that the believers in Christ who have died are lost. 19If our hope in Christ is good for this life only and no more,p then we deserve more pity than anyone else in all the world.

20But the truth is that Christ has been raised from death, as the guarantee that those who sleep in death will also be raised. 21For just as death came by means of a man, in the same way the rising from death comes by means of a man. 22For just as all people die because of their union with Adam, in the same way all will be raised to life because of their union with Christ. 23But each one will be raised in proper order: Christ, first of all; then, at the time of his coming, those who belong to him. 24Then the end will come; Christ will overcome all spiritual rulers, authorities, and powers, and will hand over the Kingdom to God the Father. 25For Christ must rule until God defeats all enemies and puts them

under his feet. 26The last enemy to be defeated will be death. 27For the scripture says, "God put all things under his feet." It is clear, of course, that the words "all things" do not include God himself, who puts all things under Christ. 28But when all things have been placed under Christ's rule, then he himself, the Son, will place himself under God, who placed all things under him; and God will rule completely over all.

29Now, what about those people who are baptized for the dead? What do they hope to accomplish? If it is true, as some claim, that the dead are not raised to life, why are those people being baptized for the dead? 30And as for us—why would we run the risk of danger every hour? 31My friends, I face death every day! The pride I have in you, in our life in union with Christ Jesus our Lord, makes me declare this. 32If I have, as it were, fought "wild beasts" here in Ephesus simply from human motives, what have I gained? But if the dead are not raised to life, then, as the saying goes, "Let us eat and drink, for tomorrow we will die."

33Do not be fooled. "Bad companions ruin good character." 34Come back to your right senses and stop your sinful ways. I declare to your shame that some of you do not know God.

The Resurrection Body

35Someone will ask, "How can the dead be raised to life? What kind of body will they have?" 36You fool! When you plant a seed in the ground, it does not sprout to life unless it dies. 37And what you plant is a bare seed, perhaps a grain of wheat or some other grain, not the full-bodied plant that will later grow up. 38God provides that seed with the body he wishes; he gives each seed its own proper body.

39And the flesh of living beings is not all the same kind of flesh; human beings have one kind of flesh, animals another, birds another, and fish another.

40And there are heavenly bodies and earthly bodies; the beauty that belongs to heavenly bodies is different from the beauty that belongs to earthly bodies. 41The sun has its own beauty, the moon another beauty, and the stars a different

o whose birth was abnormal; or who was born at the wrong time.   p If our hope in Christ is good for this life only and no more; or If all we have in this life is our hope in Christ.

beauty; and even among stars there are different kinds of beauty.

42 This is how it will be when the dead are raised to life. When the body is buried, it is mortal; when raised, it will be immortal. **43** When buried, it is ugly and weak; when raised, it will be beautiful and strong. **44** When buried, it is a physical body; when raised, it will be a spiritual body. There is, of course, a physical body, so there has to be a spiritual body. **45** For the scripture says, "The first man, Adam, was created a living being"; but the last Adam is the life-giving Spirit. **46** It is not the spiritual that comes first, but the physical, and then the spiritual. **47** The first Adam, made of earth, came from the earth; the second Adam came from heaven. **48** Those who belong to the earth are like the one who was made of earth; those who are of heaven are like the one who came from heaven. **49** Just as we wear the likeness of the man made of earth, so we will wear *q* the likeness of the Man from heaven.

50 What I mean, friends, is that what is made of flesh and blood cannot share in God's Kingdom, and what is mortal cannot possess immortality. **51-52** Listen to this secret truth: we shall not all die, but when the last trumpet sounds, we shall all be changed in an instant, as quickly as the blinking of an eye. For when the trumpet sounds, the dead will be raised, never to die again, and we shall all be changed. **53** For what is mortal must be changed into what is immortal; what will die must be changed into what cannot die. **54** So when this takes place, and the mortal has been changed into the immortal, then the scripture will come true: "Death is destroyed; victory is complete!"

55 "Where, Death, is your victory?
　Where, Death, is your power to
　　hurt?"

56 Death gets its power to hurt from sin, and sin gets its power from the Law. **57** But thanks be to God who gives us the victory through our Lord Jesus Christ! **58** So then, my dear friends, stand firm and steady. Keep busy always in your work for the Lord, since you know that nothing you do in the Lord's service is ever useless.

The Offering for Needy Believers

16 Now, concerning what you wrote about the money to be raised to help God's people in Judea. You must do what I told the churches in Galatia to do. **2** Every Sunday each of you must put aside some money, in proportion to what you have earned, and save it up, so that there will be no need to collect money when I come. **3** After I come, I shall give letters of introduction to those you have approved, and send them to take your gift to Jerusalem. **4** If it seems worthwhile for me to go, then they can go along with me.

Paul's Plans

5 I shall come to you after I have gone through Macedonia—for I have to go through Macedonia. **6** I shall probably spend some time with you, perhaps the whole winter, and then you can help me to continue my trip, wherever it is I shall go next. **7** I want to see you more than just briefly in passing; I hope to spend quite a long time with you, if the Lord allows.

8 I will stay here in Ephesus until the day of Pentecost. **9** There is a real opportunity here for great and worthwhile work, even though there are many opponents.

10 If Timothy comes your way, be sure to make him feel welcome among you, because he is working for the Lord, just as I am. **11** No one should look down on him, but you must help him continue his trip in peace, so that he will come back to me; for I am expecting him back with the believers.

12 Now, about brother Apollos. I have often encouraged him to visit you with the other believers, but he is not completely convinced*r* that he should go at this time. When he gets the chance, however, he will go.

Final Words

13 Be alert, stand firm in the faith, be brave, be strong. **14** Do all your work in love.

15 You know about Stephanas and his family; they are the first Christian converts in Achaia and have given them-

---

q we will wear; *some manuscripts have* let us wear. *r* he is not completely convinced; *or* it is
not at all God's will.

selves to the service of God's people. I beg you, my friends, 16to follow the leadership of such people as these, and of anyone else who works and serves with them

17I am happy about the coming of Stephanas, Fortunatus, and Achaicus; they have made up for your absence 18and have cheered me up, just as they cheered you up. Such men as these deserve notice.

19The churches in the province of Asia send you their greetings; Aquila and Priscilla and the church that meets in

their house send warm Christian greetings. 20All the believers here send greetings.

Greet one another with the kiss of peace.

21With my own hand I write this: *Greetings from Paul.*

22Whoever does not love the Lord—a curse on him!

Marana tha—Our Lord, come!

23The grace of the Lord Jesus be with you.

24My love be with you all in Christ Jesus.

Paul's Second Letter to the
CORINTHIANS

Introduction
Paul's Second Letter to the Corinthians *was written during a difficult period in his relation with the church at Corinth. Some members of the church had evidently made strong attacks against Paul, but he shows his deep longing for reconciliation and expresses his great joy when this is brought about.*

In the first part of the letter Paul discusses his relationship with the church at Corinth, explaining why he had responded with severity to insult and opposition in the church and expressing his joy that this severity had resulted in repentance and reconciliation. Then he appeals to the church for a generous offering to help the needy Christians in Judea. In the final chapters Paul defends his apostleship against a few people at Corinth who had set themselves up as true apostles, while accusing Paul of being a false one.

Outline of Contents

1 From Paul, an apostle of Christ Jesus by God's will, and from our brother Timothy—

To the church of God in Corinth, and to all God's people throughout Achaia: 2May God our Father and the Lord Jesus Christ give you grace and peace.

Paul Gives Thanks to God
3Let us give thanks to the God and Father of our Lord Jesus Christ, the merciful Father, the God from whom all help comes! 4He helps us in all our troubles, so that we are able to help others who

have all kinds of troubles, using the same help that we ourselves have received from God. 5Just as we have a share in Christ's many sufferings, so also through Christ we share in God's great help. 6If we suffer, it is for your help and salvation; if we are helped, then you too are helped and given the strength to endure with patience the same sufferings that we also endure. 7So our hope in you is never shaken; we know that just as you share in our sufferings, you also share in the help we receive.

8 We want to remind you, friends, of the trouble we had in the province of Asia. The burdens laid upon us were so great and so heavy that we gave up all hope of staying alive. 9 We felt that the death sentence had been passed on us. But this happened so that we should rely, not on ourselves, but only on God, who raises the dead. 10 From such terrible dangers of death*a* he saved us, and will save us; and we have placed our hope in him that he will save us again, 11 as you help us by means of your prayers for us. So it will be that the many prayers for us will be answered, and God will bless us; and many will raise their voices to him in thanksgiving for us.

The Change in Paul's Plans

12 We are proud that our conscience assures us that our lives in this world, and especially our relations with you, have been ruled by God-given frankness*b* and sincerity, by the power of God's grace and not by human wisdom. 13-14 We write to you only what you can read and understand. But even though you now understand us only in part, I hope that you will come to understand us completely, so that in the Day of our Lord Jesus you can be as proud of us as we shall be of you.

15 I was so sure of all this that I made plans at first to visit you, in order that you might be blessed twice. 16 For I planned to visit you on my way to Macedonia and again on my way back, in order to get help from you for my trip to Judea. 17 In planning this, did I appear fickle? When I make my plans, do I make them from selfish motives, ready to say "Yes, yes" and "No, no" at the same time? 18 As surely as God speaks the truth, my promise to you was not a "Yes" and a "No." 19 For Jesus Christ, the Son of God, who was preached among you by Silas, Timothy, and myself, is not one who is "Yes" and "No." On the contrary, he is God's "Yes"; 20 for it is he who is the "Yes" to all of God's promises. This is why through Jesus Christ our "Amen" is said to the glory of God. 21 It is God himself who makes us, together with you, sure of our life in union

with Christ; it is God himself who has set us apart, 22 who has placed his mark of ownership upon us, and who has given us the Holy Spirit in our hearts as the guarantee of all that he has in store for us.

23 I call God as my witness—he knows my heart! It was in order to spare you that I decided not to go to Corinth. 24 We are not trying to dictate to you what you must believe; we know that you stand firm in the faith. Instead, we are working with you for your own happiness.

2 So I made up my mind not to come to you again to make you sad. 2 For if I were to make you sad, who would be left to cheer me up? Only the very persons I had made sad. 3 That is why I wrote that letter to you—I did not want to come to you and be made sad by the very people who should make me glad. For I am convinced that when I am happy, then all of you are happy too. 4 I wrote you with a greatly troubled and distressed heart and with many tears; my purpose was not to make you sad, but to make you realize how much I love you all.

Forgiveness for the Offender

5 Now, if anyone has made somebody sad, he has not done it to me but to all of you—in part, at least. (I say this because I do not want to be too hard on him.) 6 It is enough that this person has been punished in this way by most of you. 7 Now, however, you should forgive him and encourage him, in order to keep him from becoming so sad as to give up completely. 8 And so I beg you to let him know that you really do love him. 9 I wrote you that letter because I wanted to find out how well you had stood the test and whether you are always ready to obey my instructions. 10 When you forgive people for what they have done, I forgive them too. For when I forgive—if, indeed, I need to forgive anything—I do it in Christ's presence because of you, 11 in order to keep Satan from getting the upper hand over us; for we know what his plans are.

Paul's Anxiety in Troas

12 When I arrived in Troas to preach the Good News about Christ, I found

---

a terrible dangers of death; *some manuscripts have* terrible death.
b frankness; *some manuscripts have* holiness.

that the Lord had opened the way for the work there. 13 But I was deeply worried, because I could not find our brother Titus. So I said good-bye to the people there and went on to Macedonia.

Victory through Christ

14 But thanks be to God! For in union with Christ we are always led by God as prisoners in Christ's victory procession. God uses us to make the knowledge about Christ spread everywhere like a sweet fragrance. 15 For we are like a sweet-smelling incense offered by Christ to God, which spreads among those who are being saved and those who are being lost. 16 For those who are being lost, it is a deadly stench that kills; but for those who are being saved, it is a fragrance that brings life. Who, then, is capable for such a task? 17 We are not like so many others, who handle God's message as if it were cheap merchandise; but because God has sent us, we speak with sincerity in his presence, as servants of Christ.

Servants of the New Covenant

3 Does this sound as if we were again boasting about ourselves? Could it be that, like some other people, we need letters of recommendation to you or from you? 2 You yourselves are the letter we have, written on our hearts for everyone to know and read. 3 It is clear that Christ himself wrote this letter and sent it by us. It is written, not with ink but with the Spirit of the living God, and not on stone tablets but on human hearts.

4 We say this because we have confidence in God through Christ. 5 There is nothing in us that allows us to claim that we are capable of doing this work. The capacity we have comes from God; 6 it is he who made us capable of serving the new covenant, which consists not of a written law but of the Spirit. The written law brings death, but the Spirit gives life.

7 The Law was carved in letters on stone tablets, and God's glory appeared when it was given. Even though the brightness on Moses' face was fading, it was so strong that the people of Israel could not keep their eyes fixed on him. If the Law, which brings death when it is in force, came with such glory, 8 how

much greater is the glory that belongs to the activity of the Spirit! 9 The system which brings condemnation was glorious; how much more glorious is the activity which brings salvation! 10 We may say that because of the far brighter glory now the glory that was so bright in the past is gone. 11 For if there was glory in that which lasted for a while, how much more glory is there in that which lasts forever!

12 Because we have this hope, we are very bold. 13 We are not like Moses, who had to put a veil over his face so that the people of Israel would not see the brightness fade and disappear. 14 Their minds, indeed, were closed; and to this very day their minds are covered with the same veil as they read the books of the old covenant. The veil is removed only when a person is joined to Christ. 15 Even today, whenever they read the Law of Moses, the veil still covers their minds. 16 But it can be removed, as the scripture says about Moses: "His veil was removed when he turned to the Lord."c 17 Now, "the Lord" in this passage is the Spirit; and where the Spirit of the Lord is present, there is freedom. 18 All of us, then, reflect the glory of the Lord with uncovered faces; and that same glory, coming from the Lord, who is the Spirit, transforms us into his likeness in an ever greater degree of glory.

Spiritual Treasure in Clay Pots

4 God in his mercy has given us this work to do, and so we do not become discouraged. 2 We put aside all secret and shameful deeds; we do not act with deceit, nor do we falsify the word of God. In the full light of truth we live in God's sight and try to commend ourselves to everyone's good conscience. 3 For if the gospel we preach is hidden, it is hidden only from those who are being lost. 4 They do not believe, because their minds have been kept in the dark by the evil god of this world. He keeps them from seeing the light shining on them, the light that comes from the Good News about the glory of Christ, who is the exact likeness of God. 5 For it is not ourselves that we preach; we preach Jesus Christ as Lord, and ourselves as your servants for Jesus' sake. 6 The God who

---

c Verse 16 may be translated: But the veil is removed whenever someone turns to the Lord.

said, "Out of darkness the light shall shine!" is the same God who made his light shine in our hearts, to bring us the knowledge of God's glory shining in the face of Christ.

7 Yet we who have this spiritual treasure are like common clay pots, in order to show that the supreme power belongs to God, not to us. 8 We are often troubled, but not crushed; sometimes in doubt, but never in despair; 9 there are many enemies, but we are never without a friend; and though badly hurt at times, we are not destroyed. 10 At all times we carry in our mortal bodies the death of Jesus, so that his life also may be seen in our bodies. 11 Throughout our lives we are always in danger of death for Jesus' sake, in order that his life may be seen in this mortal body of ours. 12 This means that death is at work in us, but life is at work in you.

13 The scripture says, "I spoke because I believed." In the same spirit of faith we also speak because we believe. 14 We know that God, who raised the Lord Jesus to life, will also raise us up with Jesus and take us, together with you, into his presence. 15 All this is for your sake; and as God's grace reaches more and more people, they will offer to the glory of God more prayers of thanksgiving.

Living by Faith

16 For this reason we never become discouraged. Even though our physical being is gradually decaying, yet our spiritual being is renewed day after day. 17 And this small and temporary trouble we suffer will bring us a tremendous and eternal glory, much greater than the trouble. 18 For we fix our attention, not on things that are seen, but on things that are unseen. What can be seen lasts only for a time, but what cannot be seen lasts forever.

5 For we know that when this tent we live in — our body here on earth — is torn down, God will have a house in heaven for us to live in, a home he himself has made, which will last forever. 2 And now we sigh, so great is our desire that our home which comes from heaven should be put on over us; 3 by being clothed with it we shall not be without a body. 4 While we live in this earthly tent, we groan with a feeling of oppression; it is not that we want to get rid of our earthly body, but that we want to have the heavenly one put on over us, so that what is mortal will be transformed by life. 5 God is the one who has prepared us for this change, and he gave us his Spirit as the guarantee of all that he has in store for us.

6 So we are always full of courage. We know that as long as we are at home in the body we are away from the Lord's home. 7 For our life is a matter of faith, not of sight. 8 We are full of courage and would much prefer to leave our home in the body and be at home with the Lord. 9 More than anything else, however, we want to please him, whether in our home here or there. 10 For all of us must appear before Christ, to be judged by him. We will each receive what we deserve, according to everything we have done, good or bad, in our bodily life.

Friendship with God through Christ

11 We know what it means to fear the Lord, and so we try to persuade others. God knows us completely, and I hope that in your hearts you know me as well. 12 We are not trying again to recommend ourselves to you; rather, we are trying to give you a good reason to be proud of us, so that you will be able to answer those who boast about people's appearance and not about their character. 13 Are we really insane? It is for God's sake. Or are we sane? Then it is for your sake. 14 We are ruled by the love of Christ, now that we recognize that one man died for everyone, which means that they all share in his death. 15 He died for all, so that those who live should no longer live for themselves, but only for him who died and was raised to life for their sake.

16 No longer, then, do we judge anyone by human standards. Even if at one time we judged Christ according to human standards, we no longer do so. 17 Anyone who is joined to Christ is a new being; the old is gone, the new has come. 18 All this is done by God, who through Christ changed us from enemies into his friends and gave us the task of making others his friends also. 19 Our message is that God was making all human beings

his friends through Christ.[d] God did not keep an account of their sins, and he has given us the message which tells how he makes them his friends.

20 Here we are, then, speaking for Christ, as though God himself were making his appeal through us. We plead on Christ's behalf: let God change you from enemies into his friends! 21 Christ was without sin, but for our sake God made him share our sin in order that in union with him we might share the righteousness of God.

6 In our work together with God, then, we beg you who have received God's grace not to let it be wasted. 2 Hear what God says:

"When the time came for me to
     show you favor,
   I heard you;
when the day arrived for me to
     save you,
   I helped you."

Listen! This is the hour to receive God's favor; today is the day to be saved!

3 We do not want anyone to find fault with our work, so we try not to put obstacles in anyone's way. 4 Instead, in everything we do we show that we are God's servants by patiently enduring troubles, hardships, and difficulties. 5 We have been beaten, jailed, and mobbed; we have been overworked and have gone without sleep or food. 6 By our purity, knowledge, patience, and kindness we have shown ourselves to be God's servants—by the Holy Spirit, by our true love, 7 by our message of truth, and by the power of God. We have righteousness as our weapon, both to attack and to defend ourselves. 8 We are honored and disgraced; we are insulted and praised. We are treated as liars, yet we speak the truth; 9 as unknown, yet we are known by all; as though we were dead, but, as you see, we live on. Although punished, we are not killed; 10 although saddened, we are always glad; we seem poor, but we make many people rich; we seem to have nothing, yet we really possess everything.

11 Dear friends in Corinth! We have spoken frankly to you; we have opened our hearts wide. 12 It is not we who have closed our hearts to you; it is you who have closed your hearts to us. 13 I speak now as though you were my children: show us the same feelings that we have for you. Open your hearts wide!

Warning against Pagan Influences

14 Do not try to work together as equals with unbelievers, for it cannot be done. How can right and wrong be partners? How can light and darkness live together? 15 How can Christ and the Devil agree? What does a believer have in common with an unbeliever? 16 How can God's temple come to terms with pagan idols? For we are the temple of the living God! As God himself has said,

"I will make my home with my
     people
   and live among them;
I will be their God,
   and they shall be my people."

17 And so the Lord says,

"You must leave them
   and separate yourselves from
     them.
Have nothing to do with what is
     unclean,
   and I will accept you.
18 I will be your father,
   and you shall be my sons and
     daughters,
   says the Lord Almighty."

7 All these promises are made to us, my dear friends. So then, let us purify ourselves from everything that makes body or soul unclean, and let us be completely holy by living in awe of God.

Paul's Joy

2 Make room for us in your hearts. We have wronged no one; we have ruined no one, nor tried to take advantage of anyone. 3 I do not say this to condemn you; for, as I have said before, you are so dear to us that we are always together, whether we live or die. 4 I am so sure of you; I take such pride in you! In all our troubles I am still full of courage; I am running over with joy.

5 Even after we arrived in Macedonia, we did not have any rest. There were troubles everywhere, quarrels with others, fears in our hearts. 6 But God, who encourages the downhearted, encouraged us with the coming of Titus. 7 It was

___

[d] God was making all human beings his friends through Christ; or God was in Christ making all human beings his friends.

not only his coming that cheered us, but also his report of how you encouraged him. He told us how much you want to see me, how sorry you are, how ready you are to defend me; and so I am even happier now.

8 For even if that letter of mine made you sad, I am not sorry I wrote it. I could have been sorry when I saw that it made you sad for a while. 9 But now I am happy — not because I made you sad, but because your sadness made you change your ways. That sadness was used by God, and so we caused you no harm. 10 For the sadness that is used by God brings a change of heart that leads to salvation — and there is no regret in that! But sadness that is merely human causes death. 11 See what God did with this sadness of yours: how earnest it has made you, how eager to prove your innocence! Such indignation, such alarm, such feelings, such devotion, such readiness to punish wrongdoing! You have shown yourselves to be without fault in the whole matter.

12 So, even though I wrote that letter, it was not because of the one who did wrong or the one who was wronged. Instead, I wrote it to make plain to you, in God's sight, how deep your devotion to us really is. 13 That is why we were encouraged.

Not only were we encouraged; how happy Titus made us with his happiness over the way in which all of you helped to cheer him up! 14 I did boast of you to him, and you have not disappointed me. We have always spoken the truth to you, and in the same way the boast we made to Titus has proved true. 15 And so his love for you grows stronger, as he remembers how all of you were ready to obey his instructions, how you welcomed him with fear and trembling. 16 How happy I am that I can depend on you completely!

Christian Giving

8 Our friends, we want you to know what God's grace has accomplished in the churches in Macedonia. 2 They have been severely tested by the troubles they went through; but their joy was so great that they were extremely generous in their giving, even though they are very poor. 3 I can assure you that they gave as much as they could, and even more than they could. Of their own free will 4 they begged us and pleaded for the privilege of having a part in helping God's people in Judea. 5 It was more than we could have hoped for! First they gave themselves to the Lord; and then, by God's will they gave themselves to us as well. 6 So we urged Titus, who began this work, to continue it and help you complete this special service of love. 7 You are so rich in all you have: in faith, speech, and knowledge, in your eagerness to help and in your love for us.e And so we want you to be generous also in this service of love.

8 I am not laying down any rules. But by showing how eager others are to help, I am trying to find out how real your own love is. 9 You know the grace of our Lord Jesus Christ; rich as he was, he made himself poor for your sake, in order to make you rich by means of his poverty.

10 My opinion is that it is better for you to finish now what you began last year. You were the first, not only to act, but also to be willing to act. 11 On with it, then, and finish the job! Be as eager to finish it as you were to plan it, and do it with what you now have. 12 If you are eager to give, God will accept your gift on the basis of what you have to give, not on what you don't have.

13-14 I am not trying to relieve others by putting a burden on you; but since you have plenty at this time, it is only fair that you should help those who are in need. Then, when you are in need and they have plenty, they will help you. In this way both are treated equally. 15 As the scripture says, "The one who gathered much did not have too much, and the one who gathered little did not have too little."

Titus and His Companions

16 How we thank God for making Titus as eager as we are to help you! 17 Not only did he welcome our request; he was so eager to help that of his own free will he decided to go to you. 18 With him we are sending the brother who is highly respected in all the churches for his work in preaching the gospel. 19 And be-

e your love for us; some manuscripts have our love for you.

sides that, he has been chosen and appointed by the churches to travel with us as we carry out this service of love for the sake of the Lord's glory and in order to show that we want to help.

20 We are being careful not to stir up any complaints about the way we handle this generous gift. 21 Our purpose is to do what is right, not only in the sight of the Lord, but also in the sight of others.

22 So we are sending our brother with them; we have tested him many times and found him always very eager to help. And now that he has so much confidence in you, he is all the more eager to help. 23 As for Titus, he is my partner and works with me to help you; as for the other brothers who are going with him, they represent the churches and bring glory to Christ. 24 Show your love to them, so that all the churches will be sure of it and know that we are right in boasting about you.

Help for Needy Believers

9 There is really no need for me to write you about the help being sent to God's people in Judea. 2 I know that you are willing to help, and I have boasted of you to the people in Macedonia. "The believers in Achaia," I said, "have been ready to help since last year.' Your eagerness has stirred up most of them. 3 Now I am sending these believers, so that our boasting about you in this matter may not turn out to be empty words. But, just as I said, you will be ready with your help. 4 However, if the people from Macedonia should come with me and find out that you are not ready how ashamed we would be — not to speak of your shame — for feeling so sure of you! 5 So I thought it was necessary to urge these believers to go to you ahead of me and get ready in advance the gift you promised to make. Then it will be ready when I arrive, and it will show that you give because you want to, not because you have to.

6 Remember that the person who plants few seeds will have a small crop; the one who plants many seeds will have a large crop. 7 You should each give, then, as you have decided, not with regret or out of a sense of duty; for God loves the one who gives gladly. 8 And God is able to give you more than you need, so that you will always have all

you need for yourselves and more than enough for every good cause. 9 As the scripture says,

"He gives generously to the needy; his kindness lasts forever."

10 And God, who supplies seed for the sower and bread to eat, will also supply you with all the seed you need and will make it grow and produce a rich harvest from your generosity. 11 He will always make you rich enough to be generous at all times, so that many will thank God for your gifts which they receive from us. 12 For this service you perform not only meets the needs of God's people, but also produces an outpouring of gratitude to God. 13 And because of the proof which this service of yours brings, many will give glory to God for your loyalty to the gospel of Christ, which you profess, and for your generosity in sharing with them and everyone else. 14 And so with deep affection they will pray for you because of the extraordinary grace God has shown you. 15 Let us thank God for his priceless gift!

Paul Defends His Ministry

10 I, Paul, make a personal appeal to you — I who am said to be meek and mild when I am with you, but harsh with you when I am away. By the gentleness and kindness of Christ 2 I beg you not to force me to be harsh when I come; for I am sure I can deal harshly with those who say that we act from worldly motives. 3 It is true that we live in the world, but we do not fight from worldly motives. 4 The weapons we use in our fight are not the world's weapons but God's powerful weapons, which we use to destroy strongholds. We destroy false arguments; 5 we pull down every proud obstacle that is raised against the knowledge of God; we take every thought captive and make it obey Christ. 6 And after you have proved your complete loyalty, we will be ready to punish any act of disloyalty.

7 You are looking at the outward appearance of things. Are there some there who reckon themselves to belong to Christ? Well, let them think again about themselves, because we belong to Christ just as much as they do. 8 For I am not ashamed, even if I have boasted somewhat too much about the authority that the Lord has given us — authority to

build you up, not to tear you down. 9 I do not want it to appear that I am trying to frighten you with my letters. 10 Someone will say, "Paul's letters are severe and strong, but when he is with us in person, he is weak, and his words are nothing!" 11 Such a person must understand that there is no difference between what we write in our letters when we are away and what we will do when we are there with you.

12 Of course we would not dare classify ourselves or compare ourselves with those who rate themselves so highly. How stupid they are! They make up their own standards to measure themselves by, and they judge themselves by their own standards! 13 As for us, however, our boasting will not go beyond certain limits; it will stay within the limits of the work which God has set for us, and this includes our work among you. 14 And since you are within those limits, we were not going beyond them when we came to you, bringing the Good News about Christ. 15 So we do not boast about the work that others have done beyond the limits God set for us. Instead, we hope that your faith may grow and that we may be able to do a much greater work among you, always within the limits that God has set. 16 Then we can preach the Good News in other countries beyond you and shall not have to boast about work already done in someone else's field.

17 But as the scripture says, "Whoever wants to boast must boast about what the Lord has done." 18 For it is when the Lord thinks well of us that we are really approved, and not when we think well of ourselves.

Paul and the False Apostles

11 I wish you would tolerate me, even when I am a bit foolish. Please do! 2 I am jealous for you, just as God is; you are like a pure virgin whom I have promised in marriage to one man only, Christ himself. 3 I am afraid that your minds will be corrupted and that you will abandon your full and pure devotion to Christ—in the same way that Eve was deceived by the snake's clever lies. 4 For you gladly tolerate anyone who comes to you and preaches a different Jesus, not the one we preached; and you accept a spirit and a gospel com-

pletely different from the Spirit and the gospel you received from us!

5 I do not think that I am the least bit inferior to those very special so-called "apostles" of yours! 6 Perhaps I am an amateur in speaking, but certainly not in knowledge; we have made this clear to you at all times and in all conditions.

7 I did not charge you a thing when I preached the Good News of God to you; I humbled myself in order to make you important. Was that wrong of me? 8 While I was working among you, I was paid by other churches. I was robbing them, so to speak, in order to help you. 9 And during the time I was with you I did not bother you for help when I needed money; the believers who came from Macedonia brought me everything I needed. As in the past, so in the future: I will never be a burden to you! 10 By Christ's truth in me, I promise that this boast of mine will not be silenced anywhere in all of Achaia. 11 Do I say this because I don't love you? God knows I love you!

12 I will go on doing what I am doing now, in order to keep those other "apostles" from having any reason for boasting and saying that they work in the same way that we do. 13 Those men are not true apostles—they are false apostles, who lie about their work and disguise themselves to look like real apostles of Christ. 14 Well, no wonder! Even Satan can disguise himself to look like an angel of light! 15 So it is no great thing if his servants disguise themselves to look like servants of righteousness. In the end they will get exactly what their actions deserve.

Paul's Sufferings as an Apostle

16 I repeat: no one should think that I am a fool. But if you do, at least accept me as a fool, just so I will have a little to boast of. 17 Of course what I am saying now is not what the Lord would have me say; in this matter of boasting I am really talking like a fool. 18 But since there are so many who boast for merely human reasons, I will do the same. 19 You yourselves are so wise, and so you gladly tolerate fools! 20 You tolerate anyone who orders you around or takes advantage of you or traps you or looks down on you or slaps you in the face. 21 I am ashamed

to admit that we were too timid to do those things!

But if anyone dares to boast about something—I am talking like a fool—I will be just as daring. 22 Are they Hebrews? So am I. Are they Israelites? So am I. Are they Abraham's descendants? So am I. 23 Are they Christ's servants? I sound like a madman—but I am a better servant than they are! I have worked much harder, I have been in prison more times, I have been whipped much more, and I have been near death more often. 24 Five times I was given the thirty-nine lashes by the Jews; 25 three times I was whipped by the Romans; and once I was stoned. I have been in three shipwrecks, and once I spent twenty-four hours in the water. 26 In my many travels I have been in danger from floods and from robbers, in danger from my own people and from Gentiles; there have been dangers in the cities, dangers in the wilds, dangers on the high seas, and dangers from false friends. 27 There has been work and toil; often I have gone without sleep; I have been hungry and thirsty; I have often been without enough food, shelter, or clothing. 28 And not to mention other things, every day I am under the pressure of my concern for all the churches. 29 When someone is weak, then I feel weak too; when someone is led into sin, I am filled with distress.

30 If I must boast, I will boast about things that show how weak I am. 31 The God and Father of the Lord Jesus—blessed be his name forever!—knows that I am not lying. 32 When I was in Damascus, the governor under King Aretas placed guards at the city gates to arrest me. 33 But I was let down in a basket through an opening in the wall and escaped from him.

Paul's Visions and Revelations

12 I have to boast, even though it doesn't do any good. But I will now talk about visions and revelations given me by the Lord. 2 I know a certain Christian man who fourteen years ago was snatched up to the highest heaven (I do not know whether this actually happened or whether he had a vision—only God knows). 3-4 I repeat, I know that this man was snatched to Paradise (again, I do not know whether this actually happened or whether it was a vision—only

God knows), and there he heard things which cannot be put into words, things that human lips may not speak. 5 So I will boast about this man—but I will not boast about myself, except the things that show how weak I am. 6 If I wanted to boast, I would not be a fool, because I would be telling the truth. But I will not boast, because I do not want any of you to have a higher opinion of me than you have as a result of what you have seen me do and heard me say.

7 But to keep me from being puffed up with pride because of the many wonderful things I saw, I was given a painful physical ailment, which acts as Satan's messenger to beat me and keep me from being proud. 8 Three times I prayed to the Lord about this and asked him to take it away. 9 But his answer was: "My grace is all you need, for my power is greatest when you are weak." I am most happy, then, to be proud of my weaknesses, in order to feel the protection of Christ's power over me. 10 I am content with weaknesses, insults, hardships, persecutions, and difficulties for Christ's sake. For when I am weak, then I am strong.

Paul's Concern for the Corinthians

11 I am acting like a fool—but you have made me do it. You are the ones who ought to show your approval of me. For even if I am nothing, I am in no way inferior to those very special "apostles" of yours. 12 The many miracles and wonders that prove that I am an apostle were performed among you with much patience. 13 How were you treated any worse than the other churches, except that I did not bother you for financial help? Please forgive me for being so unfair!

14 This is now the third time that I am ready to come to visit you—and I will not make any demands on you. It is you I want, not your money. After all, children should not have to provide for their parents, but parents should provide for their children. 15 I will be glad to spend all I have, and myself as well, in order to help you. Will you love me less because I love you so much?

16 You will agree, then, that I was not a burden to you. But someone will say that I was tricky, and trapped you with lies. 17 How? Did I take advantage of you

through any of the messengers I sent? 18I begged Titus to go, and I sent the other believer with him. Would you say that Titus took advantage of you? Do not he and I act from the very same motives and behave in the same way?

19Perhaps you think that all along we have been trying to defend ourselves before you. No! We speak as Christ would have us speak in the presence of God, and everything we do, dear friends, is done to help you. 20I am afraid that when I get there I will find you different from what I would like you to be and you will find me different from what you would like me to be. I am afraid that I will find quarreling and jealousy, hot tempers and selfishness, insults and gossip, pride and disorder. 21I am afraid that the next time I come my God will humiliate me in your presence, and I shall weep over many who sinned in the past and have not repented of the immoral things they have done—their lust and their sexual sins.

Final Warnings and Greetings

13 This is now the third time that I am coming to visit you. "Any accusation must be upheld by the evidence of two or more witnesses"—as the scripture says. 2I want to tell those of you who have sinned in the past, and all the others; I said it before during my second visit to you, but I will say it again now that I am away: the next time I come nobody will escape punishment. 3You will have all the proof you want that Christ speaks through me. When he deals with

you, he is not weak; instead, he shows his power among you. 4For even though it was in weakness that he was put to death on the cross, it is by God's power that he lives. In union with him we also are weak; but in our relations with you we shall share God's power in his life.

5Put yourselves to the test and judge yourselves, to find out whether you are living in faith. Surely you know that Christ Jesus is in you?—unless you have completely failed. 6I trust you will know that we are not failures. 7We pray to God that you will do no wrong—not in order to show that we are a success, but so that you may do what is right, even though we may seem to be failures. 8For we cannot do a thing against the truth, but only for it. 9We are glad when we are weak but you are strong. And so we also pray that you will become perfect. 10That is why I write this while I am away from you; it is so that when I arrive I will not have to deal harshly with you in using the authority that the Lord has given me—authority to build you up, not to tear you down.

11And now, my friends, good-bye! Strive for perfection; listen to my appeals; agree with one another; live in peace. And the God of love and peace will be with you.

12Greet one another with the kiss of peace.

All of God's people send you their greetings.

13The grace of the Lord Jesus Christ, the love of God, and the fellowship of the Holy Spirit be with you all.

Paul's Letter to the
GALATIANS

Introduction

As the good news about Jesus began to be preached and welcomed among people who were not Jews, the question arose as to whether a person must obey the Law of Moses in order to be a true Christian. Paul had argued that this was not necessary — that in fact, the only sound basis for life in Christ was faith, by which all are put right with God. But among the churches of Galatia, a Roman province in Asia Minor, there had come people who opposed Paul and claimed that one must also observe the Law of Moses in order to be right with God.

Paul's Letter to the Galatians *was written in order to bring back to true faith and practice those people who were being misled by this false teaching. Paul begins by defending his right to be called an apostle of Jesus Christ. He insists that his call to be an apostle came from God, not from any human authority, and that his mission was especially to the non-Jews. Then he develops the argument that it is by faith alone that people are put right with God. In the concluding chapters Paul shows that Christian conduct flows naturally from the love that results from faith in Christ.*

Outline of Contents

1 From Paul, whose call to be an apostle did not come from human beings or by human means, but from Jesus Christ and God the Father, who raised him from death. ²All the believers who are here join me in sending greetings to the churches of Galatia:

³May God our Father and the Lord Jesus Christ give you grace and peace.

⁴In order to set us free from this present evil age, Christ gave himself for our sins, in obedience to the will of our God and Father. ⁵To God be the glory forever and ever! Amen.

The One Gospel

⁶I am surprised at you! In no time at all you are deserting the one who called you by the grace of Christ,ᵃ and are accepting another gospel. ⁷Actually, there is no "other gospel," but I say this because there are some people who are upsetting you and trying to change the gospel of Christ. ⁸But even if we or an angel from heaven should preach to you a gospel that is different from the one we preached to you, may he be condemned to hell! ⁹We have said it before, and now I say it again: if anyone preaches to you

a gospel that is different from the one you accepted, may he be condemned to hell!

¹⁰Does this sound as if I am trying to win human approval? No indeed! What I want is God's approval! Am I trying to be popular with people? If I were still trying to do so, I would not be a servant of Christ.

How Paul Became an Apostle

¹¹Let me tell you, my friends, that the gospel I preach is not of human origin. ¹²I did not receive it from any human being, nor did anyone teach it to me. It was Jesus Christ himself who revealed it to me.

¹³You have been told how I used to live when I was devoted to the Jewish religion, how I persecuted without mercy the church of God and did my best to destroy it. ¹⁴I was ahead of most other Jews of my age in my practice of the Jewish religion, and was much more devoted to the traditions of our ancestors.

¹⁵But God in his grace chose me even before I was born, and called me to serve him. And when he decided ¹⁶to reveal

---

ᵃ by the grace of Christ; *some manuscripts have* by his grace.

GALATIANS

his Son to me, so that I might preach the Good News about him to the Gentiles, I did not go to anyone for advice, 17nor did I go to Jerusalem to see those who were apostles before me. Instead, I went at once to Arabia, and then I returned to Damascus. 18It was three years later that I went to Jerusalem to obtain information from Peter, and I stayed with him for two weeks. 19I did not see any other apostle except James,b the Lord's brother.

20What I write is true. God knows that I am not lying!

21Afterward I went to places in Syria and Cilicia. 22At that time the members of the churches in Judea did not know me personally. 23They knew only what others were saying: "The man who used to persecute us is now preaching the faith that he once tried to destroy!" 24And so they praised God because of me.

Paul and the Other Apostles

2 Fourteen years later I went back to Jerusalem with Barnabas, taking Titus along with me. 2I went because God revealed to me that I should go. In a private meeting with the leaders I explained the gospel message that I preach to the Gentiles. I did not want my work in the past or in the present to be a failure. 3My companion Titus, even though he is Greek, was not forced to be circumcised, 4although some wanted it done. Pretending to be believers, these men slipped into our group as spies, in order to find out about the freedom we have through our union with Christ Jesus. They wanted to make slaves of us, 5but in order to keep the truth of the gospel safe for you, we did not give in to them for a minute.

6But those who seemed to be the leaders—I say this because it makes no difference to me what they were; God does not judge by outward appearances—those leaders, I say, made no new suggestions to me. 7On the contrary, they saw that God had given me the task of preaching the gospel to the Gentiles, just as he had given Peter the task of preaching the gospel to the

Jews. 8For by God's power I was made an apostle to the Gentiles, just as Peter was made an apostle to the Jews. 9James, Peter, and John, who seemed to be the leaders, recognized that God had given me this special task; so they shook hands with Barnabas and me, as a sign that we were all partners. We agreed that Barnabas and I would work among the Gentiles and they among the Jews. 10All they asked was that we should remember the needy in their group, which is the very thing I havec been eager to do.

Paul Rebukes Peter at Antioch

11But when Peter came to Antioch, I opposed him in public, because he was clearly wrong. 12Before some men who had been sent by James arrived there, Peter had been eating with the Gentile believers. But after these men arrived, he drew back and would not eat with the Gentiles, because he was afraid of those who were in favor of circumcising them. 13The other Jewish believers also started acting like cowards along with Peter; and even Barnabas was swept along by their cowardly action. 14When I saw that they were not walking a straight path in line with the truth of the gospel, I said to Peter in front of them all, "You are a Jew, yet you have been living like a Gentile, not like a Jew. How, then, can you try to force Gentiles to live like Jews?"

Jews and Gentiles Are Saved by Faith

15Indeed, we are Jews by birth and not "Gentile sinners," as they are called. 16Yet we know that a person is put right with God only through faith in Jesus Christ, never by doing what the Law requires. We, too, have believed in Christ Jesus in order to be put right with God through our faith in Christ, and not by doing what the Law requires. For no one is put right with God by doing what the Law requires. 17If, then, as we try to be put right with God by our union with Christ, we are found to be sinners, as much as the Gentiles are—does this mean that Christ is serving the cause of sin? By no means! 18If I start to rebuild

b any other apostle except James; or any other apostle; the only other person I saw was James.
c have; or had.

the system of Law that I tore down, then I show myself to be someone who breaks the Law. 19 So far as the Law is concerned, however, I am dead—killed by the Law itself—in order that I might live for God. I have been put to death with Christ on his cross, 20 so that it is no longer I who live, but it is Christ who lives in me. This life that I live now, I live by faith in the Son of God, who loved me and gave his life for me. 21 I refuse to reject the grace of God. But if a person is put right with God through the Law, it means that Christ died for nothing!

Law or Faith

3 You foolish Galatians! Who put a spell on you? Before your very eyes you had a clear description of the death of Jesus Christ on the cross! 2 Tell me this one thing: did you receive God's Spirit by doing what the Law requires or by hearing the gospel and believing it? 3 How can you be so foolish! You began by God's Spirit; do you now want to finish by your own power? 4 Did all your experience mean nothing at all? Surely it meant something! 5 Does God give you the Spirit and work miracles among you because you do what the Law requires or because you hear the gospel and believe it?

6 Consider the experience of Abraham; as the scripture says, "He believed God, and because of his faith God accepted him as righteous." 7 You should realize, then, that the real descendants of Abraham are the people who have faith. 8 The scripture predicted that God would put the Gentiles right with himself through faith. And so the scripture announced the Good News to Abraham: "Through you God will bless all people." 9 Abraham believed and was blessed; so all who believe are blessed as he was.

10 Those who depend on obeying the Law live under a curse. For the scripture says, "Whoever does not always obey everything that is written in the book of the Law is under God's curse!" 11 Now, it is clear that no one is put right with God by means of the Law, because the scripture says, "Only the person who is put right with God through faith shall live."d 12 But the Law has nothing to do

with faith. Instead, as the scripture says, "Whoever does everything the Law requires will live."

13 But by becoming a curse for us Christ has redeemed us from the curse that the Law brings; for the scripture says, "Anyone who is hanged on a tree is under God's curse." 14 Christ did this in order that the blessing which God promised to Abraham might be given to the Gentiles by means of Christ Jesus, so that through faith we might receive the Spirit promised by God.

The Law and the Promise

15 My friends, I am going to use an everyday example: when two people agree on a matter and sign an agreement, no one can break it or add anything to it. 16 Now, God made his promises to Abraham and to his descendant. The scripture does not use the plural "descendants," meaning many people, but the singular "descendant," meaning one person only, namely, Christ. 17 What I mean is that God made a covenant with Abraham and promised to keep it. The Law, which was given four hundred and thirty years later, cannot break that covenant and cancel God's promise. 18 For if God's gift depends on the Law, then it no longer depends on his promise. However, it was because of his promise that God gave that gift to Abraham.

19 What, then, was the purpose of the Law? It was added in order to show what wrongdoing is, and it was meant to last until the coming of Abraham's descendant, to whom the promise was made. The Law was handed down by angels, with a man acting as a go-between. 20 But a go-between is not needed when only one person is involved; and God is one.e

The Purpose of the Law

21 Does this mean that the Law is against God's promises? No, not at all! For if human beings had received a law that could bring life, then everyone could be put right with God by obeying it. 22 But the scripture says that the whole world is under the power of sin; and so the gift which is promised on the basis of

d put right with God through faith shall live; or put right with God shall live through faith.
e and God is one; or and God acts alone.

faith in Jesus Christ is given to those who believe.

23 But before the time for faith came, the Law kept us all locked up as prisoners until this coming faith should be revealed. 24 And so the Law was in charge of us until Christ came, in order that we might then be put right with God through faith. 25 Now that the time for faith is here, the Law is no longer in charge of us.

26 It is through faith that all of you are God's children in union with Christ Jesus. 27 You were baptized into union with Christ, and now you are clothed, so to speak, with the life of Christ himself. 28 So there is no difference between Jews and Gentiles, between slaves and free people, between men and women; you are all one in union with Christ Jesus. 29 If you belong to Christ, then you are the descendants of Abraham and will receive what God has promised.

4 But now to continue—the son who will receive his father's property is treated just like a slave while he is young, even though he really owns everything. 2 While he is young, there are men who take care of him and manage his affairs until the time set by his father. 3 In the same way, we too were slaves of the ruling spirits of the universe before we reached spiritual maturity. 4 But when the right time finally came, God sent his own Son. He came as the son of a human mother and lived under the Jewish Law, 5 to redeem those who were under the Law, so that we might become God's children.

6 To show that you are f his children, God sent the Spirit of his Son into our hearts, the Spirit who cries out, "Father, my Father." 7 So then, you are no longer a slave but a child. And since you are his child, God will give you all that he has for his children.

Paul's Concern for the Galatians

8 In the past you did not know God, and so you were slaves of beings who are not gods. 9 But now that you know God—or, I should say, now that God knows you—how is it that you want to turn back to those weak and pitiful ruling spirits? Why do you want to become

their slaves all over again? 10 You pay special attention to certain days, months, seasons, and years. 11 I am worried about you! Can it be that all my work for you has been for nothing?

12 I beg you, my friends, be like me. After all, I am like you. You have not done me any wrong. 13 You remember why I preached the gospel to you the first time; it was because I was sick. 14 But even though my physical condition was a great trial to you, you did not despise or reject me. Instead, you received me as you would an angel from heaven; you received me as you would Christ Jesus. 15 You were so happy! What has happened? I myself can say that you would have taken out your own eyes, if you could, and given them to me. 16 Have I now become your enemy by telling you the truth?

17 Those other people show a deep interest in you, but their intentions are not good. All they want is to separate you from me, so that you will have the same interest in them as they have in you. 18 Now, it is good to have such a deep interest if the purpose is good—this is true always, and not merely when I am with you. 19 My dear children! Once again, just like a mother in childbirth, I feel the same kind of pain for you until Christ's nature is formed in you. 20 How I wish I were with you now, so that I could take a different attitude toward you. I am so worried about you!

The Example of Hagar and Sarah

21 Let me ask those of you who want to be subject to the Law: do you not hear what the Law says? 22 It says that Abraham had two sons, one by a slave woman, the other by a free woman. 23 His son by the slave woman was born in the usual way, but his son by the free woman was born as a result of God's promise. 24 These things can be understood as a figure: the two women represent two covenants. The one whose children are born in slavery is Hagar, and she represents the covenant made at Mount Sinai. 25 Hagar, who stands for Mount Sinai in Arabia, is g a figure of the present city of Jerusalem, in slavery with all its people. 26 But the heavenly

---

f To show that you are; or Because you are.   g Hagar . . . is; some manuscripts have Sinai is a mountain in Arabia, and it is.

Jerusalem is free, and she is our mother. [27]For the scripture says,

"Be happy, you childless woman!
    Shout and cry with joy, you who
        never felt the pains of
        childbirth!
For the woman who was deserted
    will have more children
    than the woman whose husband
        never left her."

[28]Now, you, my friends, are God's children as a result of his promise, just as Isaac was. [29]At that time the son who was born in the usual way persecuted the one who was born because of God's Spirit; and it is the same now. [30]But what does the scripture say? It says, "Send the slave woman and her son away; for the son of the slave woman will not have a part of the father's property along with the son of the free woman." [31]So then, my friends, we are not the children of a slave woman but of a free woman.

Preserve Your Freedom

5 Freedom is what we have—Christ has set us free! Stand, then, as free people, and do not allow yourselves to become slaves again.

[2]Listen! I, Paul, tell you that if you allow yourselves to be circumcised, it means that Christ is of no use to you at all. [3]Once more I warn any man who allows himself to be circumcised that he is obliged to obey the whole Law. [4]Those of you who try to be put right with God by obeying the Law have cut yourselves off from Christ. You are outside God's grace. [5]As for us, our hope is that God will put us right with him; and this is what we wait for by the power of God's Spirit working through our faith. [6]For when we are in union with Christ Jesus, neither circumcision nor the lack of it makes any difference at all; what matters is faith that works through love.

[7]You were doing so well! Who made you stop obeying the truth? How did he persuade you? [8]It was not done by God, who calls you. [9]"It takes only a little yeast to make the whole batch of dough rise," as they say. [10]But I still feel confident about you. Our life in union with the Lord makes me confident that you will not take a different view and that whoever is upsetting you will be punished by God.

[11]But as for me, my friends, if I continue to preach that circumcision is necessary, why am I still being persecuted? If that were true, then my preaching about the cross of Christ would cause no trouble. [12]I wish that the people who are upsetting you would go all the way; let them go on and castrate themselves!

[13]As for you, my friends, you were called to be free. But do not let this freedom become an excuse for letting your physical desires control you. Instead, let love make you serve one another. [14]For the whole Law is summed up in one commandment: "Love your neighbor as you love yourself." [15]But if you act like wild animals, hurting and harming each other, then watch out, or you will completely destroy one another.

The Spirit and Human Nature

[16]What I say is this: let the Spirit direct your lives, and you will not satisfy the desires of the human nature. [17]For what our human nature wants is opposed to what the Spirit wants, and what the Spirit wants is opposed to what our human nature wants. These two are enemies, and this means that you cannot do what you want to do. [18]If the Spirit leads you, then you are not subject to the Law.

[19]What human nature does is quite plain. It shows itself in immoral, filthy, and indecent actions; [20]in worship of idols and witchcraft. People become enemies and they fight; they become jealous, angry, and ambitious. They separate into parties and groups; [21]they are envious, get drunk, have orgies, and do other things like these. I warn you now as I have before: those who do these things will not possess the Kingdom of God.

[22]But the Spirit produces love, joy, peace, patience, kindness, goodness, faithfulness, [23]humility, and self-control. There is no law against such things as these. [24]And those who belong to Christ Jesus have put to death their human nature with all its passions and desires. [25]The Spirit has given us life; he must also control our lives. [26]We must not be proud or irritate one another or be jealous of one another.

Bear One Another's Burdens

6 My friends, if someone is caught in any kind of wrongdoing, those of you who are spiritual should set him

right; but you must do it in a gentle way. And keep an eye on yourselves, so that you will not be tempted, too. 2 Help carry one another's burdens, and in this way you will obey[h] the law of Christ. 3 If you think you are something when you really are nothing, you are only deceiving yourself. 4 You should each judge your own conduct. If it is good, then you can be proud of what you yourself have done, without having to compare it with what someone else has done. 5 For each of you have to carry your own load.

6 If you are being taught the Christian message, you should share all the good things you have with your teacher.

7 Do not deceive yourselves; no one makes a fool of God. You will reap exactly what you plant. 8 If you plant in the field of your natural desires, from it you will gather the harvest of death; if you plant in the field of the Spirit, from the Spirit you will gather the harvest of eternal life. 9 So let us not become tired of doing good; for if we do not give up, the time will come when we will reap the harvest. 10 So then, as often as we have the chance, we should do good to everyone, and especially to those who belong to our family in the faith.

h you will obey; some manuscripts have obey.

Final Warning and Greeting

11 See what big letters I make as I write to you now with my own hand! 12 The people who are trying to force you to be circumcised are the ones who want to show off and boast about external matters. They do it, however, only so that they may not be persecuted for the cross of Christ. 13 Even those who practice circumcision do not obey the Law; they want you to be circumcised so that they can boast that you submitted to this physical ceremony. 14 As for me, however, I will boast only about the cross of our Lord Jesus Christ; for by means of his cross the world is dead to me, and I am dead to the world. 15 It does not matter at all whether or not one is circumcised; what does matter is being a new creature. 16 As for those who follow this rule in their lives, may peace and mercy be with them—with them and with all of God's people!

17 To conclude: let no one give me any more trouble, because the scars I have on my body show that I am the slave of Jesus.

18 May the grace of our Lord Jesus Christ be with you all, my friends. Amen.

Paul's Letter to the
EPHESIANS

Introduction

Paul's Letter to the Ephesians is concerned first of all with "God's plan . . . to bring all creation together, everything in heaven and on earth, with Christ as head" (1.10). It is also an appeal to God's people to live out the meaning of this great plan for the unity of the whole human race through oneness with Jesus Christ.

In the first part of Ephesians the writer develops the theme of unity by speaking of the way in which God the Father has chosen his people, how they are forgiven and set free from their sins through Jesus Christ the Son, and how God's great promise is guaranteed by the Holy Spirit. In the second part he appeals to the readers to live in such a way that their oneness in Christ may become real in their life together.

Several figures of speech are used to show the oneness of God's people in union with Christ: the church is like a body, with Christ as the head; or like a building, with Christ as the cornerstone; or like a wife, with Christ as the husband. This letter rises to great heights of expression as the writer is moved by the thought of God's grace in Christ. Everything is seen in the light of Christ's love, sacrifice, forgiveness, grace, and purity.

Outline of Contents
Introduction   1.1-2
Christ and the church   1.3 — 3.21
The new life in Christ   4.1 — 6.20
Conclusion   6.21-24

---

1 From Paul, who by God's will is an apostle of Christ Jesus —

To God's people in Ephesus,*a* who are faithful in their life in union with Christ Jesus:

2 May God our Father and the Lord Jesus Christ give you grace and peace.

Spiritual Blessings in Christ

3 Let us give thanks to the God and Father of our Lord Jesus Christ! For in our union with Christ he has blessed us by giving us every spiritual blessing in the heavenly world. 4 Even before the world was made, God had already chosen us to be his through our union with Christ, so that we would be holy and without fault before him.

Because of his love 5 God*b* had already decided that through Jesus Christ he would make us his children — this was his pleasure and purpose. 6 Let us praise God for his glorious grace, for the free gift he gave us in his dear Son! 7 For by the blood of Christ*c* we are set free, that is, our sins are forgiven. How great is the grace of God, 8 which he gave to us in such large measure!

In all his wisdom and insight 9 God did what he had purposed, and made known to us the secret plan he had already decided to complete by means of Christ. 10 This plan, which God will complete when the time is right, is to bring all creation together, everything in heaven and on earth, with Christ as head.

11 All things are done according to God's plan and decision; and God chose us to be his own people in union with Christ because of his own purpose, based on what he had decided from the very beginning. 12 Let us, then, who were the first to hope in Christ, praise God's glory!

13 And you also became God's people when you heard the true message, the Good News that brought you salvation. You believed in Christ, and God put his stamp of ownership on you by giving you the Holy Spirit he had promised. 14 The Spirit is the guarantee that we shall receive what God has promised his people, and this assures us that God will give complete freedom to those who are his. Let us praise his glory!

Paul's Prayer

15 For this reason, ever since I heard of your faith in the Lord Jesus and your love for all of God's people, 16 I have not stopped giving thanks to God for you. I remember you in my prayers 17 and ask the God of our Lord Jesus Christ, the glorious Father, to give you the Spirit, who will make you wise and reveal God to you, so that you will know him. 18 I ask that your minds may be opened to see his light, so that you will know what is the hope to which he has called you, how rich are the wonderful blessings he promises his people, 19 and how very great is his power at work in us who believe. This power working in us is the same as the mighty strength 20 which he used when he raised Christ from death and seated him at his right side in the heavenly world. 21 Christ rules there above all heavenly rulers, authorities, powers, and lords; he has a title superior to all titles of authority in this world and in the next. 22 God put all things under Christ's feet and gave him to the church as supreme Lord over all things. 23 The church is Christ's body, the completion of him who himself completes all things everywhere.*d*

E
P
H
E
S
I
A
N
S

---

a Some manuscripts do not have in Ephesus.   *b* before him. Because of his love God; *or* before him, and to live in love. God.   *c* by the blood of Christ; *or* by the sacrificial death of Christ.
d who himself completes all things everywhere; *or* who is himself completely filled with God's fullness.

From Death to Life

2 In the past you were spiritually dead because of your disobedience and sins. 2 At that time you followed the world's evil way; you obeyed the ruler of the spiritual powers in space, the spirit who now controls the people who disobey God. 3 Actually all of us were like them and lived according to our natural desires, doing whatever suited the wishes of our own bodies and minds. In our natural condition we, like everyone else, were destined to suffer God's anger.

4 But God's mercy is so abundant, and his love for us is so great, 5 that while we were spiritually dead in our disobedience he brought us to life with Christ. It is by God's grace that you have been saved. 6 In our union with Christ Jesus he raised us up with him to rule with him in the heavenly world. 7 He did this to demonstrate for all time to come the extraordinary greatness of his grace in the love he showed us in Christ Jesus. 8-9 For it is by God's grace that you have been saved through faith. It is not the result of your own efforts, but God's gift, so that no one can boast about it. 10 God has made us what we are, and in our union with Christ Jesus he has created us for a life of good deeds, which he has already prepared for us to do.

One in Christ

11 You Gentiles by birth—called "the uncircumcised" by the Jews, who call themselves the circumcised (which refers to what men do to their bodies)—remember what you were in the past. 12 At that time you were apart from Christ. You were foreigners and did not belong to God's chosen people. You had no part in the covenants, which were based on God's promises to his people, and you lived in this world without hope and without God. 13 But now, in union with Christ Jesus you, who used to be far away, have been brought near by the blood of Christ.[e] 14 For Christ himself has brought us peace by making Jews and Gentiles one people. With his own body he broke down the wall that separated them and kept them enemies. 15 He abolished the Jewish Law with its commandments and rules, in order to create out of the two races one new people in union with himself, in this way making peace. 16 By his death on the cross Christ destroyed their enmity; by means of the cross he united both races into one body and brought them back to God. 17 So Christ came and preached the Good News of peace to all—to you Gentiles, who were far away from God, and to the Jews, who were near to him. 18 It is through Christ that all of us, Jews and Gentiles, are able to come in the one Spirit into the presence of the Father.

19 So then, you Gentiles are not foreigners or strangers any longer; you are now citizens together with God's people and members of the family of God. 20 You, too, are built upon the foundation laid by the apostles and prophets,[f] the cornerstone being Christ Jesus himself. 21 He is the one who holds the whole building together and makes it grow into a sacred temple dedicated to the Lord. 22 In union with him you too are being built together with all the others into a place where God lives through his Spirit.

Paul's Work for the Gentiles

3 For this reason I, Paul, the prisoner of Christ Jesus for the sake of you Gentiles, pray to God. 2 Surely you have heard that God in his grace has given me this work to do for your good. 3 God revealed his secret plan and made it known to me. (I have written briefly about this, 4 and if you will read what I have written, you can learn about my understanding of the secret of Christ.) 5 In past times human beings were not told this secret, but God has revealed it now by the Spirit to his holy apostles and prophets. 6 The secret is that by means of the gospel the Gentiles have a part with the Jews in God's blessings; they are members of the same body and share in the promise that God made through Christ Jesus.

7 I was made a servant of the gospel by God's special gift, which he gave me through the working of his power. 8 I am less than the least of all God's people; yet God gave me this privilege of taking to the Gentiles the Good News about the

---

e by the blood of Christ; or by the sacrificial death of Christ.   f the foundation laid by the apostles and prophets; or the foundation, that is, the apostles and prophets.

infinite riches of Christ, 9and of making all people see how God's secret plan is to be put into effect. God, who is the Creator of all things, kept his secret hidden through all the past ages, 10in order that at the present time, by means of the church, the angelic rulers and powers in the heavenly world might learn of his wisdom in all its different forms. 11God did this according to his eternal purpose, which he achieved through Christ Jesus our Lord. 12In union with Christ and through our faith in him we have the boldness to go into God's presence with all confidence. 13I beg you, then, not to be discouraged because I am suffering for you; it is all for your benefit.

The Love of Christ

14For this reason I fall on my knees before the Father, 15from whom every family in heaven and on earth receives its true name. 16I ask God from the wealth of his glory to give you power through his Spirit to be strong in your inner selves, 17and I pray that Christ will make his home in your hearts through faith. I pray that you may have your roots and foundation in love, 18so that you, together with all God's people, may have the power to understand how broad and long, how high and deep, is Christ's love. 19Yes, may you come to know his love—although it can never be fully known—and so be completely filled with the very nature of God.

20To him who by means of his power working in us is able to do so much more than we can ever ask for, or even think of: 21to God be the glory in the church and in Christ Jesus for all time, forever and ever! Amen.

The Unity of the Body

4 I urge you, then—I who am a prisoner because I serve the Lord: live a life that measures up to the standard God set when he called you. 2Be always humble, gentle, and patient. Show your love by being tolerant with one another. 3Do your best to preserve the unity which the Spirit gives by means of the peace that binds you together. 4There is one body and one Spirit, just as there is one hope to which God has called you.

5There is one Lord, one faith, one baptism; 6there is one God and Father of all people, who is Lord of all, works through all, and is in all.

7Each one of us has received a special gift in proportion to what Christ has given. 8As the scripture says,

"When he went up to the very
　heights,
　he took many captives with him;
　he gave gifts to people."

9Now, what does "he went up" mean? It means that first he came down to the lowest depths of the earth.g 10So the one who came down is the same one who went up, above and beyond the heavens, to fill the whole universe with his presence. 11It was he who "gave gifts to people"; he appointed some to be apostles, others to be prophets, others to be evangelists, others to be pastors and teachers. 12He did this to prepare all God's people for the work of Christian service, in order to build up the body of Christ. 13And so we shall all come together to that oneness in our faith and in our knowledge of the Son of God; we shall become mature people, reaching to the very height of Christ's full stature. 14Then we shall no longer be children, carried by the waves and blown about by every shifting wind of the teaching of deceitful people, who lead others into error by the tricks they invent. 15Instead, by speaking the truth in a spirit of love, we must grow up in every way to Christ, who is the head. 16Under his control all the different parts of the body fit together, and the whole body is held together by every joint with which it is provided. So when each separate part works as it should, the whole body grows and builds itself up through love.

The New Life in Christ

17In the Lord's name, then, I warn you: do not continue to live like the heathen, whose thoughts are worthless 18and whose minds are in the dark. They have no part in the life that God gives, for they are completely ignorant and stubborn. 19They have lost all feeling of shame; they give themselves over to vice and do all sorts of indecent things without restraint.

20That was not what you learned

E
P
H
E
S
I
A
N
S

---

g the lowest depths of the earth; or the lower depths, the earth itself.

about Christ! 21 You certainly heard about him, and as his followers you were taught the truth that is in Jesus. 22 So get rid of your old self, which made you live as you used to — the old self that was being destroyed by its deceitful desires. 23 Your hearts and minds must be made completely new, 24 and you must put on the new self, which is created in God's likeness and reveals itself in the true life that is upright and holy.

25 No more lying, then! Each of you must tell the truth to the other believer, because we are all members together in the body of Christ. 26 If you become angry, do not let your anger lead you into sin, and do not stay angry all day. 27 Don't give the Devil a chance. 28 If you used to rob, you must stop robbing and start working, in order to earn an honest living for yourself and to be able to help the poor. 29 Do not use harmful words, but only helpful words, the kind that build up and provide what is needed, so that what you say will do good to those who hear you. 30 And do not make God's Holy Spirit sad; for the Spirit is God's mark of ownership on you, a guarantee that the Day will come when God will set you free. 31 Get rid of all bitterness, passion, and anger. No more shouting or insults, no more hateful feelings of any sort. 32 Instead, be kind and tenderhearted to one another, and forgive one another, as God has forgiven you through Christ.

Living in the Light

5 Since you are God's dear children, you must try to be like him. 2 Your life must be controlled by love, just as Christ loved us and gave his life for us as a sweet-smelling offering and sacrifice that pleases God.

3 Since you are God's people, it is not right that any matters of sexual immorality or indecency or greed should even be mentioned among you. 4 Nor is it fitting for you to use language which is obscene, profane, or vulgar. Rather you should give thanks to God. 5 You may be sure that no one who is immoral, indecent, or greedy (for greed is a form of idolatry) will ever receive a share in the Kingdom of Christ and of God.

6 Do not let anyone deceive you with foolish words; it is because of these very things that God's anger will come upon those who do not obey him. 7 So have nothing at all to do with such people. 8 You yourselves used to be in the darkness, but since you have become the Lord's people, you are in the light. So you must live like people who belong to the light, 9 for it is the light h that brings a rich harvest of every kind of goodness, righteousness, and truth. 10 Try to learn what pleases the Lord. 11 Have nothing to do with the worthless things that people do, things that belong to the darkness. Instead, bring them out to the light. (12 It is really too shameful even to talk about the things they do in secret.) 13 And when all things are brought out to the light, then their true nature is clearly revealed; 14 for anything that is clearly revealed becomes light. i That is why it is said,

"Wake up, sleeper,
   and rise from death,
   and Christ will shine on you."

15 So be careful how you live. Don't live like ignorant people, but like wise people. 16 Make good use of every opportunity you have, because these are evil days. 17 Don't be fools, then, but try to find out what the Lord wants you to do.

18 Do not get drunk with wine, which will only ruin you; instead, be filled with the Spirit. 19 Speak to one another with the words of psalms, hymns, and sacred songs; sing hymns and psalms to the Lord with praise in your hearts. 20 In the name of our Lord Jesus Christ, always give thanks for everything to God the Father.

Wives and Husbands

21 Submit yourselves to one another because of your reverence for Christ. 22 Wives, submit yourselves to your husbands as to the Lord. 23 For a husband has authority over his wife just as Christ has authority over the church; and Christ is himself the Savior of the church, his body. 24 And so wives must submit themselves completely to their husbands just as the church submits itself to Christ.

---

h the light; *some manuscripts have* the Spirit.   i anything that is clearly revealed becomes light; *or* it is light that clearly reveals everything.

25 Husbands, love your wives just as Christ loved the church and gave his life for it. 26 He did this to dedicate the church to God by his word, after making it clean by washing it in water, 27 in order to present the church to himself in all its beauty—pure and faultless, without spot or wrinkle or any other imperfection. 28 Men ought to love their wives just as they love their own bodies. A man who loves his wife loves himself. (29 None of us ever hate our own bodies. Instead, we feed them, and take care of them, just as Christ does the church; 30 for we are members of his body.) 31 As the scripture says, "For this reason a man will leave his father and mother and unite with his wife, and the two will become one." 32 There is a deep secret truth revealed in this scripture, which I understand as applying to Christ and the church. 33 But it also applies to you: every husband must love his wife as himself, and every wife must respect her husband.

Children and Parents

6 Children, it is your Christian duty to obey your parents, for this is the right thing to do. 2 "Respect your father and mother" is the first commandment that has a promise added: 3 "so that all may go well with you, and you may live a long time in the land."

4 Parents, do not treat your children in such a way as to make them angry. Instead, raise them with Christian discipline and instruction.

Slaves and Masters

5 Slaves, obey your human masters with fear and trembling; and do it with a sincere heart, as though you were serving Christ. 6 Do this not only when they are watching you, because you want to gain their approval; but with all your heart do what God wants, as slaves of Christ. 7 Do your work as slaves cheerfully, as though you served the Lord, and not merely human beings. 8 Remember that the Lord will reward each of us, whether slave or free, for the good work we do.

9 Masters, behave in the same way toward your slaves and stop using threats. Remember that you and your slaves belong to the same Master in heaven, who judges everyone by the same standard.

The Whole Armor of God

10 Finally, build up your strength in union with the Lord and by means of his mighty power. 11 Put on all the armor that God gives you, so that you will be able to stand up against the Devil's evil tricks. 12 For we are not fighting against human beings but against the wicked spiritual forces in the heavenly world, the rulers, authorities, and cosmic powers of this dark age. 13 So put on God's armor now! Then when the evil day comes, you will be able to resist the enemy's attacks; and after fighting to the end, you will still hold your ground.

14 So stand ready, with truth as a belt tight around your waist, with righteousness as your breastplate, 15 and as your shoes the readiness to announce the Good News of peace. 16 At all times carry faith as a shield; for with it you will be able to put out all the burning arrows shot by the Evil One. 17 And accept salvation as a helmet, and the word of God as the sword which the Spirit gives you. 18 Do all this in prayer, asking for God's help. Pray on every occasion, as the Spirit leads. For this reason keep alert and never give up; pray always for all God's people. 19 And pray also for me, that God will give me a message when I am ready to speak, so that I may speak boldly and make known the gospel's secret. 20 For the sake of this gospel I am an ambassador, though now I am in prison. Pray that I may be bold in speaking about the gospel as I should.

Final Greetings

21 Tychicus, our dear brother and faithful servant in the Lord's work, will give you all the news about me, so that you may know how I am getting along. 22 That is why I am sending him to you— to tell you how all of us are getting along and to encourage you.

23 May God the Father and the Lord Jesus Christ give to all Christians peace and love with faith. 24 May God's grace be with all those who love our Lord Jesus Christ with undying love.

E
P
H
E
S
I
A
N
S

Some manuscripts do not have it is your Christian duty to.

Paul's Letter to the
PHILIPPIANS

Introduction

Paul's Letter to the Philippians *was written to the first church that Paul established on European soil, in the Roman province of Macedonia. It was written while the apostle was in prison, and at a time when he was troubled by the opposition of other Christian workers toward himself and was distressed by false teaching in the church at Philippi. Yet this letter breathes a joy and confidence that can be explained only by Paul's deep faith in Jesus Christ.*

The immediate reason for writing the letter was to thank the Philippian Christians for the gift which they had sent to help him in his time of need. He uses this opportunity to reassure them, so that they may have courage and confidence in spite of all his troubles and their own as well. He pleads with them to have the humble attitude of Jesus, rather than to be controlled by selfish ambition and pride. He reminds them that their life in union with Christ is a gift of God's grace which they have received through faith, not through obedience to the ceremonies of the Jewish Law. He writes of the joy and peace that God gives to those who live in union with Christ.

This letter is marked by its emphasis on joy, confidence, unity, and perseverance in the Christian faith and life. It also reveals the deep affection Paul had for the church at Philippi.

Outline of Contents

1 From Paul and Timothy, servants of Christ Jesus—

To all God's people in Philippi who are in union with Christ Jesus, including the church leaders and helpers:

2 May God our Father and the Lord Jesus Christ give you grace and peace.

Paul's Prayer for His Readers

3 I thank my God for you every time I think of you; 4 and every time I pray for you all, I pray with joy 5 because of the way in which you have helped me in the work of the gospel from the very first day until now. 6 And so I am sure that God, who began this good work in you, will carry it on until it is finished on the Day of Christ Jesus. 7 You are always in my heart! And so it is only right for me to feel as I do about you. For you have all shared with me in this privilege that God has given me, both now that I am in prison and also while I was free to defend the gospel and establish it firmly.

8 God is my witness that I tell the truth when I say that my deep feeling for you all comes from the heart of Christ Jesus himself.

9 I pray that your love will keep on growing more and more, together with true knowledge and perfect judgment, 10 so that you will be able to choose what is best. Then you will be free from all impurity and blame on the Day of Christ. 11 Your lives will be filled with the truly good qualities which only Jesus Christ can produce, for the glory and praise of God.

To Live Is Christ

12 I want you to know, my friends, that the things that have happened to me have really helped the progress of the gospel. 13 As a result, the whole palace guard and all the others here know that I am in prison because I am a servant of Christ. 14 And my being in prison has given most of the believers more confidence in the Lord, so that they grow

bolder all the time to preach the message [a] fearlessly.

15 Of course some of them preach Christ because they are jealous and quarrelsome, but others from genuine good will. 16 These do so from love, because they know that God has given me the work of defending the gospel. 17 The others do not proclaim Christ sincerely, but from a spirit of selfish ambition; they think that they will make more trouble for me while I am in prison.

18 It does not matter! I am happy about it — just so Christ is preached in every way possible, whether from wrong or right motives. And I will continue to be happy, 19 because I know that by means of your prayers and the help which comes from the Spirit of Jesus Christ I shall be set free. 20 My deep desire and hope is that I shall never fail in my duty, but that at all times, and especially right now, I shall be full of courage, so that with my whole being I shall bring honor to Christ, whether I live or die. 21 For what is life? To me, it is Christ. Death, then, will bring more. 22 But if by continuing to live I can do more worthwhile work, then I am not sure which I should choose. 23 I am pulled in two directions. I want very much to leave this life and be with Christ, which is a far better thing; 24 but for your sake it is much more important that I remain alive. 25 I am sure of this, and so I know that I will stay. I will stay on with you all, to add to your progress and joy in the faith, 26 so that when I am with you again, you will have even more reason to be proud of me in your life in union with Christ Jesus.

27 Now, the important thing is that your way of life should be as the gospel of Christ requires, so that, whether or not I am able to go and see you, I will hear that you are standing firm with one common purpose and that with only one desire you are fighting together for the faith of the gospel. 28 Don't be afraid of your enemies; always be courageous, and this will prove to them that they will lose and that you will win, because it is God who gives you the victory. 29 For you have been given the privilege of serving Christ, not only by believing in him, but also by suffering for him. 30 Now you can take part with me in the battle. It is the same battle you saw me fighting in the past, and as you hear, the one I am fighting still.

Christ's Humility and Greatness

2 Your life in Christ makes you strong, and his love comforts you. You have fellowship with the Spirit, [b] and you have kindness and compassion for one another. 2 I urge you, then, to make me completely happy by having the same thoughts, sharing the same love, and being one in soul and mind. 3 Don't do anything from selfish ambition or from a cheap desire to boast, but be humble toward one another, always considering others better than yourselves. 4 And look out for one another's interests, not just for your own. 5 The attitude you should have is the one that Christ Jesus had:

6 He always had the nature of God,
    but he did not think that by
        force he should try to remain [c]
        equal with God.
7 Instead of this, of his own free will
    he gave up all he had,
    and took the nature of a servant.
He became like a human being
    and appeared in human likeness.
8 He was humble and walked the
        path of obedience all the way
        to death —
    his death on the cross.
9 For this reason God raised him to
        the highest place above
    and gave him the name that is
        greater than any other name.
10 And so, in honor of the name of
    Jesus
    all beings in heaven, on earth,
        and in the world below [d]
    will fall on their knees,
11 and all will openly proclaim that
    Jesus Christ is Lord,
    to the glory of God the Father.

Shining as Lights in the World

12 So then, dear friends, as you always obeyed me when I was with you, it is even more important that you obey me now while I am away from you. Keep on

---

[a] the message; some manuscripts have God's message.   [b] You have fellowship with the Spirit; or The Spirit has brought you into fellowship with one another.   [c] remain; or become.
[d] WORLD BELOW: It was thought that the dead continued to exist in a dark world under the ground.

working with fear and trembling to complete your salvation, 13because God is always at work in you to make you willing and able to obey his own purpose.

14Do everything without complaining or arguing, 15so that you may be innocent and pure as God's perfect children, who live in a world of corrupt and sinful people. You must shine among them like stars lighting up the sky, 16as you offer them the message of life. If you do so, I shall have reason to be proud of you on the Day of Christ, because it will show that all my effort and work have not been wasted.

17Perhaps my life's blood is to be poured out like an offering on the sacrifice that your faith offers to God. If that is so, I am glad and share my joy with you all. 18In the same way, you too must be glad and share your joy with me.

Timothy and Epaphroditus

19If it is the Lord's will, I hope that I will be able to send Timothy to you soon, so that I may be encouraged by news about you. 20He is the only one who shares my feelings and who really cares about you. 21Everyone else is concerned only with their own affairs, not with the cause of Jesus Christ. 22And you yourselves know how he has proved his worth, how he and I, like a son and his father, have worked together for the sake of the gospel. 23So I hope to send him to you as soon as I know how things are going to turn out for me. 24And I trust in the Lord that I myself will be able to come to you soon.

25I have thought it necessary to send to you our brother Epaphroditus, who has worked and fought by my side and who has served as your messenger in helping me. 26He is anxious to see you all and is very upset because you had heard that he was sick. 27Indeed he was sick and almost died. But God had pity on him, and not only on him but on me, too, and spared me an even greater sorrow. 28I am all the more eager, then, to send him to you, so that you will be glad again when you see him, and my own sorrow will disappear. 29Receive him, then, with joy, as a believer in the Lord. Show respect to all such people as he, 30because he risked his life and nearly died for the sake of the work of Christ, in order to give me the help that you yourselves could not give.

The True Righteousness

3 In conclusion, my friends, be joyful in your union with the Lord. I don't mind repeating what I have written before, and you will be safer if I do so. 2Watch out for those who do evil things, those dogs, those who insist on cutting the body. 3It is we, not they, who have received the true circumcision, for we worship God by means of his Spirit and rejoice in our life in union with Christ Jesus. We do not put any trust in external ceremonies. 4I could, of course, put my trust in such things. If any of you think you can trust in external ceremonies, I have even more reason to feel that way. 5I was circumcised when I was a week old. I am an Israelite by birth, of the tribe of Benjamin, a pure-blooded Hebrew. As far as keeping the Jewish Law is concerned, I was a Pharisee, 6and I was so zealous that I persecuted the church. As far as a person can be righteous by obeying the commands of the Law, I was without fault. 7But all those things that I might count as profit I now reckon as loss for Christ's sake. 8Not only those things; I reckon everything as complete loss for the sake of what is so much more valuable, the knowledge of Christ Jesus my Lord. For his sake I have thrown everything away; I consider it all as mere garbage, so that I may gain Christ 9and be completely united with him. I no longer have a righteousness of my own, the kind that is gained by obeying the Law. I now have the righteousness that is given through faith in Christ, the righteousness that comes from God and is based on faith. 10All I want is to know Christ and to experience the power of his resurrection, to share in his sufferings and become like him in his death, 11in the hope that I myself will be raised from death to life.

Running toward the Goal

12I do not claim that I have already succeeded or have already become perfect. I keep striving to win the prize for which Christ Jesus has already won me to himself. 13Of course, my friends, I really do not[e] think that I have already won it; the one thing I do, however, is to forget what is behind me and do my best to reach what is ahead. 14 So I run straight toward the goal in order to win the prize, which is God's call through Christ Jesus to the life above.

15 All of us who are spiritually mature should have this same attitude. But if some of you have a different attitude, God will make this clear to you. 16 However that may be, let us go forward according to the same rules we have followed until now.

17 Keep on imitating me, my friends. Pay attention to those who follow the right example that we have set for you. 18 I have told you this many times before, and now I repeat it with tears: there are many whose lives make them enemies of Christ's death on the cross. 19 They are going to end up in hell, because their god is their bodily desires. They are proud of what they should be ashamed of, and they think only of things that belong to this world. 20 We, however, are citizens of heaven, and we eagerly wait for our Savior, the Lord Jesus Christ, to come from heaven. 21 He will change our weak mortal bodies and make them like his own glorious body, using that power by which he is able to bring all things under his rule.

Instructions

4 So then, my friends, how dear you are to me and how I miss you! How happy you make me, and how proud I am of you! — this, dear friends, is how you should stand firm in your life in the Lord.

2 Euodia and Syntyche, please, I beg you, try to agree as sisters in the Lord. 3 And you too, my faithful partner, I want you to help these women; for they have worked hard with me to spread the gospel, together with Clement and all my other fellow workers, whose names are in God's book of the living.

4 May you always be joyful in your union with the Lord. I say it again: rejoice!

5 Show a gentle attitude toward everyone. The Lord is coming soon. 6 Don't worry about anything, but in all your prayers ask God for what you need, always asking him with a thankful heart. 7 And God's peace, which is far beyond human understanding, will keep your hearts and minds safe in union with Christ Jesus.

8 In conclusion, my friends, fill your minds with those things that are good and that deserve praise: things that are true, noble, right, pure, lovely, and honorable. 9 Put into practice what you learned and received from me, both from my words and from my actions. And the God who gives us peace will be with you.

Thanks for the Gift

10 In my life in union with the Lord it is a great joy to me that after so long a time you once more had the chance of showing that you care for me. I don't mean that you had stopped caring for me — you just had no chance to show it. 11 And I am not saying this because I feel neglected, for I have learned to be satisfied with what I have. 12 I know what it is to be in need and what it is to have more than enough. I have learned this secret, so that anywhere, at any time, I am content, whether I am full or hungry, whether I have too much or too little. 13 I have the strength to face all conditions by the power that Christ gives me.

14 But it was very good of you to help me in my troubles. 15 You Philippians know very well that when I left Macedonia in the early days of preaching the Good News, you were the only church to help me; you were the only ones who shared my profits and losses. 16 More than once when I needed help in Thessalonica, you sent it to me. 17 It is not that I just want to receive gifts; rather, I want to see profit added to your account. 18 Here, then, is my receipt for everything you have given me — and it has been more than enough! I have all I need now that Epaphroditus has brought me all your gifts. They are like a sweet-smelling offering to God, a sacrifice which is acceptable and pleasing to him. 19 And with all his abundant wealth through Christ Jesus, my God will supply all your needs. 20 To our God and

PHILIPPIANS

---

e not; some manuscripts have not yet.

Father be the glory forever and ever! Amen.

Final Greetings

21 Greetings to each one of God's people who belong to Christ Jesus. The believers here with me send you their greetings. 22 All God's people here send greetings, especially those who belong to the Emperor's palace.

23 May the grace of the Lord Jesus Christ be with you all.

Paul's Letter to the
COLOSSIANS

Introduction

Paul's Letter to the Colossians was written to the church at Colossae, a town in Asia Minor east of Ephesus. This church had not been established by Paul, but was in an area for which Paul felt responsible, as he sent out workers from Ephesus, the capital of the Roman province of Asia. Paul had learned that there were false teachers in the church at Colossae who insisted that in order to know God and have full salvation one must worship certain "spiritual rulers and authorities." In addition, these teachers said, one must submit to special rites such as circumcision and must observe strict rules about foods and other matters.

Paul writes to oppose these teachings with the true Christian message. The heart of his reply is that Jesus Christ is able to give full salvation and that these other beliefs and practices actually lead away from him. Through Christ, God created the world and through him he is bringing it back to himself. Only in union with Christ is there hope of salvation for the world. Paul then spells out the implications of this great teaching for the lives of believers.

It is noteworthy that Tychicus, who took this letter to Colossae for Paul, was accompanied by Onesimus, the slave on whose behalf Paul wrote Philemon.

Outline of Contents

1 From Paul, who by God's will is an apostle of Christ Jesus, and from our brother Timothy —

2 To God's people in Colossae, who are our faithful friends in union with Christ:

May God our Father give you grace and peace.

Prayer of Thanksgiving

3 We always give thanks to God, the Father of our Lord Jesus Christ, when we pray for you. 4 For we have heard of your faith in Christ Jesus and of your love for all God's people. 5 When the true message, the Good News, first came to you, you heard about the hope it offers. So your faith and love are based on what you hope for, which is kept safe for you in heaven. 6 The gospel keeps bringing blessings and is spreading throughout the world, just as it has among you ever since the day you first heard about the grace of God and came to know it as it really is. 7 You learned of God's grace from Epaphras, our dear fellow servant, who is Christ's faithful worker on our a behalf. 8 He has told us of the love that the Spirit has given you.

9 For this reason we have always prayed for you, ever since we heard about you. We ask God to fill you with the knowledge of his will, with all the

a our; some manuscripts have your.

wisdom and understanding that his Spirit gives. 10 Then you will be able to live as the Lord wants and will always do what pleases him. Your lives will produce all kinds of good deeds, and you will grow in your knowledge of God. 11-12 May you be made strong with all the strength which comes from his glorious power, so that you may be able to endure everything with patience. And with joy give thanks to b the Father, who has made you fit to have your share of what God has reserved for his people in the kingdom of light. 13 He rescued us from the power of darkness and brought us safe into the kingdom of his dear Son, 14 by whom we are set free, that is, our sins are forgiven.

The Person and Work of Christ

15 Christ is the visible likeness of the invisible God. He is the first-born Son, superior to all created things. 16 For through him God created everything in heaven and on earth, the seen and the unseen things, including spiritual powers, lords, rulers, and authorities. God created the whole universe through him and for him. 17 Christ existed before all things, and in union with him all things have their proper place. 18 He is the head of his body, the church; he is the source of the body's life. He is the first-born Son, who was raised from death, in order that he alone might have the first place in all things. 19 For it was by God's own decision that the Son has in himself the full nature of God. 20 Through the Son, then, God decided to bring the whole universe back to himself. God made peace through his Son's blood c on the cross and so brought back to himself all things, both on earth and in heaven.

21 At one time you were far away from God and were his enemies because of the evil things you did and thought. 22 But now, by means of the physical death of his Son, God has made you his friends, in order to bring you, holy, pure, and faultless, into his presence. 23 You must, of course, continue faithful on a firm and sure foundation, and must not

allow yourselves to be shaken from the hope you gained when you heard the gospel. It is of this gospel that I, Paul, became a servant — this gospel which has been preached to everybody in the world.

Paul's Work as a Servant of the Church

24 And now I am happy about my sufferings for you, for by means of my physical sufferings I am helping to complete what still remains of Christ's sufferings on behalf of his body, the church. 25 And I have been made a servant of the church by God, who gave me this task to perform for your good. It is the task of fully proclaiming his message, 26 which is the secret he hid through all past ages from all human beings but has now revealed to his people. 27 God's plan is to make known his secret to his people, this rich and glorious secret which he has for all peoples. And the secret is that Christ is in you, which means that you will share in the glory of God. 28 So we preach Christ to everyone. With all possible wisdom we warn and teach them in order to bring each one into God's presence as a mature individual in union with Christ. 29 To get this done I toil and struggle, using the mighty strength which Christ supplies and which is at work in me.

2 Let me tell you how hard I have worked for you and for the people in Laodicea and for all others who do not know me personally. 2 I do this in order that they may be filled with courage and may be drawn together in love, and so have the full wealth of assurance which true understanding brings. In this way they will know God's secret, which is Christ himself. d 3 He is the key that opens all the hidden treasures of God's wisdom and knowledge.

4 I tell you, then, do not let anyone deceive you with false arguments, no matter how good they seem to be. 5 For even though I am absent in body, yet I am with you in spirit, and I am glad as I see the resolute firmness with which you stand together in your faith in Christ.

b with patience. And with joy give thanks to; or with patience and joy. And give thanks to.
c his Son's blood; or his Son's sacrificial death. d God's secret, which is Christ himself; some manuscripts have God's secret; others have the secret of God the Father of Christ; others have the secret of the God and Father, and of Christ.

COLOSSIANS

Fullness of Life in Christ

6 Since you have accepted Christ Jesus as Lord, live in union with him. 7 Keep your roots deep in him, build your lives on him, and become stronger in your faith, as you were taught. And be filled with thanksgiving.

8 See to it, then, that no one enslaves you by means of the worthless deceit of human wisdom, which comes from the teachings handed down by human beings and from the ruling spirits of the universe, and not from Christ. 9 For the full content of divine nature lives in Christ, in his humanity, 10 and you have been given full life in union with him. He is supreme over every spiritual ruler and authority.

11 In union with Christ you were circumcised, not with the circumcision that is made by human beings, but with the circumcision made by Christ, which consists of being freed from the power of this sinful self. 12 For when you were baptized, you were buried with Christ, and in baptism you were also raised with Christ through your faith in the active power of God, who raised him from death. 13 You were at one time spiritually dead because of your sins and because you were Gentiles without the Law. But God has now brought you to life with Christ. God forgave us all our sins; 14 he canceled the unfavorable record of our debts with its binding rules and did away with it completely by nailing it to the cross. 15 And on that cross Christ freed himself from the power of the spiritual rulers and authorities;ᵉ he made a public spectacle of them by leading them as captives in his victory procession.

16 So let no one make rules about what you eat or drink or about holy days or the New Moon Festival or the Sabbath. 17 All such things are only a shadow of things in the future; the reality is Christ. 18 Do not allow yourselves to be condemned by anyone who claims to be superior because of special visions and who insists on false humility and the worship of angels. For no reason at all, such people are all puffed up by their human way of thinking 19 and have

stopped holding on to Christ, who is the head of the body. Under Christ's control the whole body is nourished and held together by its joints and ligaments, and it grows as God wants it to grow.

Dying and Living with Christ

20 You have died with Christ and are set free from the ruling spirits of the universe. Why, then, do you live as though you belonged to this world? Why do you obey such rules as 21 "Don't handle this," "Don't taste that," "Don't touch the other"? 22 All these refer to things which become useless once they are used; they are only human rules and teachings. 23 Of course such rules appear to be based on wisdom in their forced worship of angels, and false humility, and severe treatment of the body; but they have no real value in controlling physical passions.

3 You have been raised to life with Christ, so set your hearts on the things that are in heaven, where Christ sits on his throne at the right side of God. 2 Keep your minds fixed on things there, not on things here on earth. 3 For you have died, and your life is hidden with Christ in God. 4 Your real life is Christ and when he appears, then you too will appear with him and share his glory!

The Old Life and the New

5 You must put to death, then, the earthly desires at work in you, such as sexual immorality, indecency, lust, evil passions, and greed (for greed is a form of idolatry). 6 Because of such things God's anger will come upon those who do not obey him.ᶠ 7 At one time you yourselves used to live according to such desires, when your life was dominated by them.

8 But now you must get rid of all these things: anger, passion, and hateful feelings. No insults or obscene talk must ever come from your lips. 9 Do not lie to one another, for you have put off the old self with its habits 10 and have put on the new self. This is the new being which God, its Creator, is constantly renewing

---

ᵉ Christ freed himself from the power of the spiritual rulers and authorities; or Christ stripped the spiritual rulers and authorities of their power.   ᶠ Some manuscripts do not have upon those who do not obey him.

in his own image, in order to bring you to a full knowledge of himself. 11As a result, there is no longer any distinction between Gentiles and Jews, circumcised and uncircumcised, barbarians, savages, slaves, and free, but Christ is all, Christ is in all.

12You are the people of God; he loved you and chose you for his own. So then, you must clothe yourselves with compassion, kindness, humility, gentleness, and patience. 13Be tolerant with one another and forgive one another whenever any of you has a complaint against someone else. You must forgive one another just as the Lord has forgiven you. 14And to all these qualities add love, which binds all things together in perfect unity. 15The peace that Christ gives is to guide you in the decisions you make; for it is to this peace that God has called you together in the one body. And be thankful. 16Christ's message in all its richness must live in your hearts. Teach and instruct one another with all wisdom. Sing psalms, hymns, and sacred songs; sing to God with thanksgiving in your hearts. 17Everything you do or say, then, should be done in the name of the Lord Jesus, as you give thanks through him to God the Father.

Personal Relations in the New Life

18Wives, submit yourselves to your husbands, for that is what you should do as Christians.

19Husbands, love your wives and do not be harsh with them.

20Children, it is your Christian duty to obey your parents always, for that is what pleases God.

21Parents, do not irritate your children, or they will become discouraged.

22Slaves, obey your human masters in all things, not only when they are watching you because you want to gain their approval; but do it with a sincere heart because of your reverence for the Lord. 23Whatever you do, work at it with all your heart, as though you were working for the Lord and not for people. 24Remember that the Lord will give you as a reward what he has kept for his people. For Christ is the real Master you serve. 25And all wrongdoers will be repaid for the wrong things they do, because God judges everyone by the same standard.

4 Masters, be fair and just in the way you treat your slaves. Remember that you too have a Master in heaven.

Instructions

2Be persistent in prayer, and keep alert as you pray, giving thanks to God. 3At the same time pray also for us, so that God will give us a good opportunity to preach his message about the secret of Christ. For that is why I am now in prison. 4Pray, then, that I may speak, as I should, in such a way as to make it clear.

5Be wise in the way you act toward those who are not believers, making good use of every opportunity you have. 6Your speech should always be pleasant and interesting, and you should know how to give the right answer to everyone.

Final Greetings

7Our dear friend Tychicus, who is a faithful worker and fellow servant in the Lord's work, will give you all the news about me. 8That is why I am sending him to you, in order to cheer you up by telling you how all of us are getting along. 9With him goes Onesimus, that dear and faithful friend, who belongs to your group. They will tell you everything that is happening here.

10Aristarchus, who is in prison with me, sends you greetings, and so does Mark, the cousin of Barnabas. (You have already received instructions to welcome Mark if he comes your way.) 11Joshua, also called Justus, sends greetings too. These three are the only Jewish believers who work with me for the Kingdom of God, and they have been a great help to me.

12Greetings from Epaphras, another member of your group and a servant of Christ Jesus. He always prays fervently for you, asking God to make you stand firm, as mature and fully convinced Christians, in complete obedience to God's will. 13I can personally testify to his hard work for you and for the people in Laodicea and Hierapolis. 14Luke, our dear doctor, and Demas send you their greetings.

15Give our best wishes to the believers in Laodicea and to Nympha and the

COLOSSIANS

church that meets in her house.g 16After you read this letter, make sure that it is read also in the church at Laodicea. At the same time, you are to read the letter that the believers in Laodicea will send you. 17And tell Archippus, "Be sure to finish the task you were given in the Lord's service."

18With my own hand I write this: *Greetings from Paul. Do not forget my chains!*

May God's grace be with you.

g *Nympha . . . her house; some manuscripts have* Nymphas . . . his house.

Paul's First Letter to the
THESSALONIANS

Introduction

Thessalonica was the capital city of the Roman province of Macedonia. Paul established a church there after he left Philippi. Soon, however, there was opposition from Jews who were jealous of Paul's success in preaching the Christian message among the non-Jews who had become interested in Judaism. Paul was forced to leave Thessalonica and go on to Berea. Later on, after he reached Corinth, Paul received a personal report from his companion and fellow worker Timothy about the situation in the church at Thessalonica.

Paul's First Letter to the Thessalonians was then written to encourage and reassure the Christians there. He gives thanks for the news about their faith and love; he reminds them of the kind of life he had lived while he was with them, and then answers questions that had arisen in the church about the return of Christ: Could a believer who died before Christ's return still share in the eternal life that his return will bring? And when will Christ come again? Paul takes this occasion to tell them to go on working quietly while waiting in hope for Christ's return.

Outline of Contents

1 From Paul, Silas, and Timothy —
To the people of the church in Thessalonica, who belong to God the Father and the Lord Jesus Christ;
May grace and peace be yours.

The Life and Faith of the Thessalonians

2We always thank God for you all and always mention you in our prayers. 3For we remember before our God and Father how you put your faith into practice, how your love made you work so hard, and how your hope in our Lord Jesus Christ is firm. 4Our friends, we know that God loves you and has chosen you to be his own. 5For we brought the Good News to you, not with words only, but also with power and the Holy Spirit, and with complete conviction of its truth. You know how we lived when we were with you; it was for your own good. 6You imitated us and the Lord; and even though you suffered much, you received the message with the joy that comes from the Holy Spirit. 7So you became an example to all believers in Macedonia and Achaia. 8For not only did the message about the Lord go out from you throughout Macedonia and Achaia, but the news about your faith in God has gone everywhere. There is nothing, then, that we need to say. 9All those people speak about how you received us

THE CITY OF THESSALONICA

Thessalonica was founded in 315 B.C. by the Macedonian king Cassander. He named the city after his wife Thessalonica, sister of the Greek military conqueror, Alexander the Great. The apostle Paul worked for several months in Thessalonica and later addressed two letters (1 and 2 Thessalonians) to the church in this city.

Paul visited Thessalonica in the early fifties during his second missionary journey through the Roman province of Macedonia (Ac 17.1–9). The church that he worked with here consisted of former members of the Jewish synagogue, as well as non-Jews from pagan backgrounds. The tender words with which Paul addressed the Thessalonians make it clear that he developed strong affection for the Thessalonian church (1 Th 2.1–12).

Thessalonica's natural harbor made it a vital trading center, which brought in people from many places. This may have been why it was selected as the site for a church. At the time of his visit, Thessalonica was the most populous city in the entire Roman province of Macedonia.

Roman influence on Thessalonica is evident in the city's physical structure. Vital to the city's prosperity was the Egnatian Way, a Roman military highway which provided a route to the empire's eastern provinces. This route still serves as one of the main streets for modern Thessalonica (known as Salonika). Roman arches stood at Thessalonica's two entrances to the Egnatian Way. The one built in A.D. 297 to honor the Roman emperor Galerius remains intact.

Thessalonica's importance is also demonstrated by the great wall that surrounded the city, portions of which are still standing. The modern wall was built after Paul's time, but it was constructed on the foundations of the old city wall from the New Testament era.

when we visited you, and how you turned away from idols to God, to serve the true and living God [10] and to wait for his Son to come from heaven—his Son Jesus, whom he raised from death and who rescues us from God's anger that is coming.

Paul's Work in Thessalonica

2 Our friends, you yourselves know that our visit to you was not a failure. [2] You know how we had already been mistreated and insulted in Philippi before we came to you in Thessalonica. And even though there was much opposition, our God gave us courage to tell you the Good News that comes from him. [3] Our appeal to you is not based on error or impure motives, nor do we try to trick anyone. [4] Instead, we always speak as God wants us to, because he has judged us worthy to be entrusted with the Good News. We do not try to please people, but to please God, who tests our motives. [5] You know very well that we did not come to you with flattering talk, nor did we use words to cover up greed—God is our witness! [6] We did not try to get praise from anyone, either from you or from others, [7] even though as apostles of Christ we could have made demands on you. But we were gentle when we were with you, like a mother [a] taking care of her children. [8] Because of our love for you we were ready to share with you not only the Good News from God but even our own lives. You were so dear to us! [9] Surely you remember, our friends, how we worked and toiled! We worked day and night so that we would not be any trouble to you as we preached to you the Good News from God.

[10] You are our witnesses, and so is God, that our conduct toward you who believe was pure, right, and without fault. [11] You know that we treated each one of you just as parents treat their own children. [12] We encouraged you, we comforted you, and we kept urging you to live the kind of life that pleases God, who calls you to share in his own Kingdom and glory.

[13] And there is another reason why we always give thanks to God. When we brought you God's message, you heard it and accepted it, not as a message from human beings but as God's message, which indeed it is. For God is at work in you who believe. [14] Our friends, the same things happened to you that happened to the churches of God in Judea, to the people there who belong to Christ Jesus. You suffered the same persecutions from your own people that they suffered from the Jews, [15] who killed the Lord Jesus and the prophets, and persecuted us. How displeasing they are to God! How hostile they are to everyone! [16] They even tried to stop us from preaching to the Gentiles the message that would bring them salvation. In this way they have brought to completion all the sins they have always committed. And now God's anger has at last come down on them!

Paul's Desire to Visit Them Again

[17] As for us, friends, when we were separated from you for a little while— not in our thoughts, of course, but only in body—how we missed you and how hard we tried to see you again! [18] We wanted to return to you. I myself tried to go back more than once, but Satan would not let us. [19] After all, it is you— you, no less than others!—who are our hope, our joy, and our reason for boasting of our victory in the presence of our Lord Jesus when he comes. [20] Indeed, you are our pride and our joy!

3 Finally, we could not bear it any longer. So we decided to stay on alone in Athens [2] while we sent Timothy, our brother who works with us for God in preaching the Good News about Christ. We sent him to strengthen you and help your faith, [3] so that none of you should turn back because of these persecutions. You yourselves know that such persecutions are part of God's will for us. [4] For while we were still with you, we told you ahead of time that we were going to be persecuted; and as you well know, that is exactly what happened. [5] That is why I had to send Timothy. I could not bear it any longer, so I sent him to find out about your faith. Surely it could not be that the Devil had

---

[a] we were gentle when we were with you, like a mother; *some manuscripts have* we were like children when we were with you; we were like a mother.

tempted you and all our work had been for nothing!

6 Now Timothy has come back, and he has brought us the welcome news about your faith and love. He has told us that you always think well of us and that you want to see us just as much as we want to see you. 7 So, in all our trouble and suffering we have been encouraged about you, friends. It was your faith that encouraged us, 8 because now we really live if you stand firm in your life in union with the Lord. 9 Now we can give thanks to our God for you. We thank him for the joy we have in his presence because of you. 10 Day and night we ask him with all our heart to let us see you personally and supply what is needed in your faith.

11 May our God and Father himself and our Lord Jesus prepare the way for us to come to you! 12 May the Lord make your love for one another and for all people grow more and more and become as great as our love for you. 13 In this way he will strengthen you, and you will be perfect and holy in the presence of our God and Father when our Lord Jesus comes with all who belong to him.*b*

A Life That Pleases God

4 Finally, our friends, you learned from us how you should live in order to please God. This is, of course, the way you have been living. And now we beg and urge you in the name of the Lord Jesus to do even more. 2 For you know the instructions we gave you by the authority of the Lord Jesus. 3 God wants you to be holy and completely free from sexual immorality. 4 Each of you should know how to live with your wife*c* in a holy and honorable way, 5 not with a lustful desire, like the heathen who do not know God. 6 In this matter, then, none of you should do wrong to other Christians or take advantage of them. We have told you this before, and we strongly warned you that the Lord will punish those who do that. 7 God did not call us to live in immorality, but in holiness. 8 So then, whoever rejects this teaching is not rejecting a human being, but God, who gives you his Holy Spirit.

9 There is no need to write you about love for each other. You yourselves have been taught by God how you should love

one another. 10 And you have, in fact, behaved like this toward all the believers in all of Macedonia. So we beg you, our friends, to do even more. 11 Make it your aim to live a quiet life, to mind your own business, and to earn your own living, just as we told you before. 12 In this way you will win the respect of those who are not believers, and you will not have to depend on anyone for what you need.

The Lord's Coming

13 Our friends, we want you to know the truth about those who have died, so that you will not be sad, as are those who have no hope. 14 We believe that Jesus died and rose again, and so we believe that God will take back with Jesus those who have died believing in him.

15 What we are teaching you now is the Lord's teaching: we who are alive on the day the Lord comes will not go ahead of those who have died. 16 There will be the shout of command, the archangel's voice, the sound of God's trumpet, and the Lord himself will come down from heaven. Those who have died believing in Christ will rise to life first; 17 then we who are living at that time will be gathered up along with them in the clouds to meet the Lord in the air. And so we will always be with the Lord. 18 So then, encourage one another with these words.

Be Ready for the Lord's Coming

5 There is no need to write you, friends, about the times and occasions when these things will happen. 2 For you yourselves know very well that the Day of the Lord will come as a thief comes at night. 3 When people say, "Everything is quiet and safe," then suddenly destruction will hit them! It will come as suddenly as the pains that come upon a woman in labor, and people will not escape. 4 But you, friends, are not in the darkness, and the Day should not take you by surprise like a thief. 5 All of you are people who belong to the light, who belong to the day. We do not belong to the night or to the darkness. 6 So then, we should not be sleeping like the others; we should be awake and sober. 7 It is at night when people sleep; it is at night when they get drunk. 8 But we belong to

---

b all who belong to him; *or* all his angels.   *c* live with your wife; *or* control your body.

1 THESSALONIANS

the day, and we should be sober. We must wear faith and love as a breastplate, and our hope of salvation as a helmet. ⁹God did not choose us to suffer his anger, but to possess salvation through our Lord Jesus Christ, ¹⁰who died for us in order that we might live together with him, whether we are alive or dead when he comes. ¹¹And so encourage one another and help one another, just as you are now doing.

Final Instructions and Greetings

¹²We beg you, our friends, to pay proper respect to those who work among you, who guide and instruct you in the Christian life. ¹³Treat them with the greatest respect and love because of the work they do. Be at peace among yourselves.

¹⁴We urge you, our friends, to warn the idle, encourage the timid, help the weak, be patient with everyone. ¹⁵See that no one pays back wrong for wrong, but at all times make it your aim to do good to one another and to all people.

¹⁶Be joyful always, ¹⁷pray at all times, ¹⁸be thankful in all circumstances. This is what God wants from you in your life in union with Christ Jesus.

¹⁹Do not restrain the Holy Spirit; ²⁰do not despise inspired messages. ²¹Put all things to the test: keep what is good ²²and avoid every kind of evil.

²³May the God who gives us peace make you holy in every way and keep your whole being—spirit, soul, and body—free from every fault at the coming of our Lord Jesus Christ. ²⁴He who calls you will do it, because he is faithful.

²⁵Pray also for us, friends.

²⁶Greet all the believers with the kiss of peace.

²⁷I urge you by the authority of the Lord to read this letter to all the believers.

²⁸The grace of our Lord Jesus Christ be with you.

Paul's Second Letter to the
THESSALONIANS

Introduction

Confusion over the expected return of Christ continued to cause disturbances in the church at Thessalonica. Paul's Second Letter to the Thessalonians deals with the belief that the day of the Lord's coming had already arrived. Paul corrects this idea, pointing out that before Christ returns, evil and wickedness will reach a climax under the leadership of a mysterious figure called "the Wicked One," who would be opposed to Christ.

The apostle emphasizes the need for his readers to remain steady in their faith in spite of trouble and suffering, to work for a living as did Paul and his fellow workers, and to persevere in doing good.

Outline of Contents

1 From Paul, Silas, and Timothy—
To the people of the church in Thessalonica, who belong to God our Father and the Lord Jesus Christ:

²May God our Father and the Lord Jesus Christ give you grace and peace.

The Judgment at Christ's Coming

3 Our friends, we must thank God at all times for you. It is right for us to do so, because your faith is growing so much and the love each of you has for the others is becoming greater. 4 That is why we ourselves boast about you in the churches of God. We boast about the way you continue to endure and believe through all the persecutions and sufferings you are experiencing.

5 All of this proves that God's judgment is just and as a result you will become worthy of his Kingdom, for which you are suffering. 6 God will do what is right: he will bring suffering on those who make you suffer, 7 and he will give relief to you who suffer and to us as well. He will do this when the Lord Jesus appears from heaven with his mighty angels, 8 with a flaming fire, to punish those who reject God and who do not obey the Good News about our Lord Jesus. 9 They will suffer the punishment of eternal destruction, separated from the presence of the Lord and from his glorious might, 10 when he comes on that Day to receive glory from all his people and honor from all who believe. You too will be among them, because you have believed the message that we told you.

11 That is why we always pray for you. We ask our God to make you worthy of the life he has called you to live. May he fulfill by his power all your desire for goodness and complete your work of faith 12 In this way the name of our Lord Jesus will receive glory from you, and you from him, by the grace of our God and of the Lord[a] Jesus Christ.

The Wicked One

2 Concerning the coming of our Lord Jesus Christ and our being gathered together to be with him: I beg you, my friends, 2 not to be so easily confused in your thinking or upset by the claim that the Day of the Lord has come. Perhaps it is thought that we said this while prophesying or preaching, or that we wrote it in a letter. 3 Do not let anyone deceive you in any way. For the Day will not come until the final Rebellion takes place and the Wicked One appears, who is destined to hell. 4 He will oppose every so-called god or object of worship and will put himself above them all. He will even go in and sit down in God's Temple and claim to be God.

5 Don't you remember? I told you all this while I was with you. 6 Yet there is something that keeps this from happening now, and you know what it is. At the proper time, then, the Wicked One will appear. 7 The Mysterious Wickedness is already at work, but what is going to happen will not happen until the one who holds it back is taken out of the way. 8 Then the Wicked One will be revealed, but when the Lord Jesus comes, he will kill him with the breath from his mouth and destroy him with his dazzling presence. 9 The Wicked One will come with the power of Satan and perform all kinds of false miracles and wonders, 10 and use every kind of wicked deceit on those who will perish. They will perish because they did not welcome and love the truth so as to be saved. 11 And so God sends the power of error to work in them so that they believe what is false. 12 The result is that all who have not believed the truth, but have taken pleasure in sin, will be condemned.

You Are Chosen for Salvation

13 We must thank God at all times for you, friends, you whom the Lord loves. For God chose you as the first[b] to be saved by the Spirit's power to make you his holy people and by your faith in the truth. 14 God called you to this through the Good News we preached to you; he called you to possess your share of the glory of our Lord Jesus Christ. 15 So then, our friends, stand firm and hold on to those truths which we taught you, both in our preaching and in our letter.

16 May our Lord Jesus Christ himself and God our Father, who loved us and in his grace gave us unfailing courage and a firm hope, 17 encourage you and strengthen you to always do and say what is good.

Pray for Us

3 Finally, our friends, pray for us that the Lord's message may continue to spread rapidly and be received with honor, just as it was among you. 2 Pray

---

a our God and of the Lord; or our God and Lord.
the beginning.

b as the first; some manuscripts have from

also that God will rescue us from wicked and evil people; for not everyone believes the message.

3 But the Lord is faithful, and he will strengthen you and keep you safe from the Evil One. 4 And the Lord gives us confidence in you, and we are sure that you are doing and will continue to do what we tell you.

5 May the Lord lead you into a greater understanding of God's love and the endurance that is given by Christ.

The Obligation to Work

6 Our friends, we command you in the name of our Lord Jesus Christ to keep away from all believers who are living a lazy life and who do not follow the instructions that we gave them. 7 You yourselves know very well that you should do just what we did. We were not lazy when we were with you. 8 We did not accept anyone's support without paying for it. Instead, we worked and toiled; we kept working day and night so as not to be an expense to any of you. 9 We did this, not because we do not have the right to demand our support; we did it to be an example for you to follow. 10 While we were with you, we used to tell you, "Whoever refuses to work is not allowed to eat."

11 We say this because we hear that there are some people among you who live lazy lives and who do nothing except meddle in other people's business. 12 In the name of the Lord Jesus Christ we command these people and warn them to lead orderly lives and work to earn their own living.

13 But you, friends, must not become tired of doing good. 14 It may be that some there will not obey the message we send you in this letter. If so, take note of them and have nothing to do with them, so that they will be ashamed. 15 But do not treat them as enemies; instead, warn them as believers.

Final Words

16 May the Lord himself, who is our source of peace, give you peace at all times and in every way. The Lord be with you all.

17 With my own hand I write this: *Greetings from Paul.* This is the way I sign every letter; this is how I write.

18 May the grace of our Lord Jesus Christ be with you all.

Paul's First Letter to
TIMOTHY

Introduction

Timothy, a young Christian from Asia Minor, was the son of a Jewish mother and a Greek father. He became a companion and assistant to Paul in his missionary work. Paul's First Letter to Timothy deals with three main concerns.

The letter is first of all a warning against false teaching in the church. This teaching, a mixture of Jewish and non-Jewish ideas, was based on the belief that the physical world is evil and that one can attain salvation only by special secret knowledge and by practices such as avoiding certain foods and not marrying. The letter also contains instructions about church administration and worship, with a description of the kind of character that church leaders and helpers should have. Finally, Timothy is advised how to be a good servant of Jesus Christ and about the responsibilities that he has toward various groups of believers.

Outline of Contents

1 From Paul, an apostle of Christ Jesus by order of God our Savior and Christ Jesus our hope —

2 To Timothy, my true son in the faith: May God the Father and Christ Jesus our Lord give you grace, mercy, and peace.

Warnings against False Teaching

3 I want you to stay in Ephesus, just as I urged you when I was on my way to Macedonia. Some people there are teaching false doctrines, and you must order them to stop. 4 Tell them to give up those legends and those long lists of ancestors, which only produce arguments; they do not serve God's plan, which is known by faith. 5 The purpose of this order is to arouse the love that comes from a pure heart, a clear conscience, and a genuine faith. 6 Some people have turned away from these and have lost their way in foolish discussions. 7 They want to be teachers of God's law, but they do not understand their own words or the matters about which they speak with so much confidence.

8 We know that the Law is good if it is used as it should be used. 9 It must be remembered, of course, that laws are made, not for good people, but for lawbreakers and criminals, for the godless and sinful, for those who are not religious or spiritual, for those who kill their fathers or mothers, for murderers, 10 for the immoral, for sexual perverts, for kidnappers, for those who lie and give false testimony or who do anything else contrary to sound doctrine. 11 That teaching is found in the gospel that was entrusted to me to announce, the Good News from the glorious and blessed God.

Gratitude for God's Mercy

12 I give thanks to Christ Jesus our Lord, who has given me strength for my work. I thank him for considering me worthy and appointing me to serve him, 13 even though in the past I spoke evil of him and persecuted and insulted him. But God was merciful to me because I did not yet have faith and so did not know what I was doing. 14 And our Lord poured out his abundant grace on me and gave me the faith and love which are ours in union with Christ Jesus. 15 This is a true saying, to be completely accepted and believed: Christ Jesus came into the world to save sinners. I am the worst of them, 16 but God was merciful to me in order that Christ Jesus might show his full patience in dealing with me, the worst of sinners, as an example for all those who would later believe in him and receive eternal life. 17 To the eternal King, immortal and invisible, the only God — to him be honor and glory forever and ever! Amen.

18 Timothy, my child, I entrust to you this command, which is in accordance with the words of prophecy spoken in the past about you. Use those words as weapons in order to fight well, 19 and keep your faith and a clear conscience. Some people have not listened to their conscience and have made a ruin of their faith. 20 Among them are Hymenaeus and Alexander, whom I have punished by handing them over to the power of Satan; this will teach them to stop their blasphemy.

Church Worship

2 First of all, then, I urge that petitions, prayers, requests, and thanksgivings be offered to God for all people; 2 for kings and all others who are in authority, that we may live a quiet and peaceful life with all reverence toward God and with proper conduct. 3 This is good and it pleases God our Savior, 4 who wants everyone to be saved and to come to know the truth. 5 For there is one God, and there is one who brings God and human beings together, the man Christ Jesus, 6 who gave himself to redeem the whole human race. That was the proof at the right time that God wants everyone to be saved, 7 and that is why I was sent as an apostle and teacher of the Gentiles, to proclaim the message of faith and truth. I am not lying; I am telling the truth!

8 In every church service I want the men to pray, men who are dedicated to God and can lift up their hands in prayer without anger or argument. 9 I also want the women to be modest and sensible about their clothes and to dress properly; not with fancy hair styles or with gold ornaments or pearls or expensive dresses, 10 but with good deeds, as is proper for women who claim to be religious. 11 Women should learn in silence and all humility. 12 I do not allow them to

teach or to have authority over men; they must keep quiet. 13 For Adam was created first, and then Eve. 14 And it was not Adam who was deceived; it was the woman who was deceived and broke God's law. 15 But a woman will be saved through having children,*a* if she perseveres*b* in faith and love and holiness, with modesty.

Leaders in the Church

3 This is a true saying: If a man is eager to be a church leader, he desires an excellent work. 2 A church leader must be without fault; he must have only one wife,*c* be sober, self-controlled, and orderly; he must welcome strangers in his home; he must be able to teach; 3 he must not be a drunkard or a violent man, but gentle and peaceful; he must not love money; 4 he must be able to manage his own family well and make his children obey him with all respect. 5 For if a man does not know how to manage his own family, how can he take care of the church of God? 6 He must be mature in the faith, so that he will not swell up with pride and be condemned, as the Devil was. 7 He should be a man who is respected by the people outside the church, so that he will not be disgraced and fall into the Devil's trap.

Helpers in the Church

8 Church helpers must also have a good character and be sincere; they must not drink too much wine or be greedy for money; 9 they should hold to the revealed truth of the faith with a clear conscience. 10 They should be tested first, and then, if they pass the test, they are to serve. 11 Their wives*d* also must be of good character and must not gossip; they must be sober and honest in everything. 12 A church helper must have only one wife,*e* and be able to manage his children and family well. 13 Those helpers who do their work well win for themselves a good standing and are able to speak boldly about their faith in Christ Jesus.

The Great Secret

14 As I write this letter to you, I hope to come and see you soon. 15 But if I delay, this letter will let you know how we should conduct ourselves in God's household, which is the church of the living God, the pillar and support of the truth. 16 No one can deny how great is the secret of our religion:

He appeared in human form,
    was shown to be right by the
        Spirit,*f*
    and was seen by angels.
He was preached among the
        nations,
    was believed in throughout
        the world,
    and was taken up to
        heaven.

False Teachers

4 The Spirit says clearly that some people will abandon the faith in later times; they will obey lying spirits and follow the teachings of demons. 2 Such teachings are spread by deceitful liars, whose consciences are dead, as if burnt with a hot iron. 3 Such people teach that it is wrong to marry and to eat certain foods. But God created those foods to be eaten, after a prayer of thanks, by those who are believers and have come to know the truth. 4 Everything that God has created is good; nothing is to be rejected, but everything is to be received with a prayer of thanks, 5 because the word of God and the prayer make it acceptable to God.

A Good Servant of Christ Jesus

6 If you give these instructions to the believers, you will be a good servant of Christ Jesus, as you feed yourself spiritually on the words of faith and of the true teaching which you have followed. 7 But keep away from those godless legends, which are not worth telling. Keep yourself in training for a godly life. 8 Physical exercise has some value, but spiritual exercise is valuable in every way, because it promises life both for the present and for the future. 9 This is a true saying, to be completely accepted

---

a will be saved through having children; *or* will be kept safe through childbirth.
b if she perseveres; *or* if they persevere.   *c* have only one wife; *or* be married only once.
d Their wives; *or* Women helpers.   *e* have only one wife; *or* be married only once.
f was shown to be right by the Spirit; *or* and, in spiritual form, was shown to be right.

and believed. 10 We struggle[g] and work hard, because we have placed our hope in the living God, who is the Savior of all and especially of those who believe.

11 Give them these instructions and these teachings. 12 Do not let anyone look down on you because you are young, but be an example for the believers in your speech, your conduct, your love, faith, and purity. 13 Until I come, give your time and effort to the public reading of the Scriptures and to preaching and teaching. 14 Do not neglect the spiritual gift that is in you, which was given to you when the prophets spoke and the elders laid their hands on you. 15 Practice these things and devote yourself to them, in order that your progress may be seen by all. 16 Watch yourself and watch your teaching. Keep on doing these things, because if you do, you will save both yourself and those who hear you.

Responsibilities toward Believers

5 Do not rebuke an older man, but appeal to him as if he were your father. Treat the younger men as your brothers, 2 the older women as mothers, and the younger women as sisters, with all purity.

3 Show respect for widows who really are all alone. 4 But if a widow has children or grandchildren, they should learn first to carry out their religious duties toward their own family and in this way repay their parents and grandparents, because that is what pleases God. 5 A widow who is all alone, with no one to take care of her, has placed her hope in God and continues to pray and ask him for his help night and day. 6 But a widow who gives herself to pleasure has already died, even though she lives. 7 Give them these instructions, so that no one will find fault with them. 8 But if any do not take care of their relatives, especially the members of their own family, they have denied the faith and are worse than an unbeliever.

9 Do not add any widow to the list of widows unless she is over sixty years of age. In addition, she must have been married only once[h] 10 and have a reputation for good deeds: a woman who

brought up her children well, received strangers in her home, performed humble duties for other Christians, helped people in trouble, and devoted herself to doing good.

11 But do not include younger widows in the list; because when their desires make them want to marry, they turn away from Christ, 12 and so become guilty of breaking their earlier promise to him. 13 They also learn to waste their time in going around from house to house; but even worse, they learn to be gossips and busybodies, talking of things they should not. 14 So I would prefer that the younger widows get married, have children, and take care of their homes, so as to give our enemies no chance of speaking evil of us. 15 For some widows have already turned away to follow Satan. 16 But if any Christian woman has widows in her family, she must take care of them and not put the burden on the church, so that it may take care of the widows who are all alone.

17 The elders who do good work as leaders should be considered worthy of receiving double pay, especially those who work hard at preaching and teaching. 18 For the scripture says, "Do not muzzle an ox when you are using it to thresh grain" and "Workers should be given their pay." 19 Do not listen to an accusation against an elder unless it is brought by two or more witnesses. 20 Rebuke publicly all those who commit sins, so that the rest may be afraid.

21 In the presence of God and of Christ Jesus and of the holy angels I solemnly call upon you to obey these instructions without showing any prejudice or favor to anyone in anything you do. 22 Be in no hurry to lay hands on people to dedicate them to the Lord's service. Take no part in the sins of others; keep yourself pure.

23 Do not drink water only, but take a little wine to help your digestion, since you are sick so often.

24 The sins of some people are plain to see, and their sins go ahead of them to judgment; but the sins of others are seen only later. 25 In the same way good deeds are plainly seen, and even those that are not so plain cannot be hidden.

---

[g] struggle; *some manuscripts have* are reviled.   [h] married only once; *or* faithful to her husband.

6 Those who are slaves must consider their masters worthy of all respect, so that no one will speak evil of the name of God and of our teaching. [2] Slaves belonging to Christian masters must not despise them, for they are believers too. Instead, they are to serve them even better, because those who benefit from their work are believers whom they love.

False Teaching and True Riches

You must teach and preach these things. [3] Whoever teaches a different doctrine and does not agree with the true words of our Lord Jesus Christ and with the teaching of our religion [4] is swollen with pride and knows nothing. He has an unhealthy desire to argue and quarrel about words, and this brings on jealousy, disputes, insults, evil suspicions, [5] and constant arguments from people whose minds do not function and who no longer have the truth. They think that religion is a way to become rich.

[6] Well, religion does make us very rich, if we are satisfied with what we have. [7] What did we bring into the world? Nothing! What can we take out of the world? Nothing! [8] So then, if we have food and clothes, that should be enough for us. [9] But those who want to get rich fall into temptation and are caught in the trap of many foolish and harmful desires, which pull them down to ruin and destruction. [10] For the love of money is a source of all kinds of evil. Some have been so eager to have it that they have wandered away from the faith and have broken their hearts with many sorrows.

Personal Instructions

[11] But you, man of God, avoid all these things. Strive for righteousness, godliness, faith, love, endurance, and gentleness. [12] Run your best in the race of faith, and win eternal life for yourself; for it was to this life that God called you when you firmly professed your faith before many witnesses. [13] Before God, who gives life to all things, and before Christ Jesus, who firmly professed his faith before Pontius Pilate, I command you [14] to obey your orders and keep them faithfully until the Day when our Lord Jesus Christ will appear. [15] His appearing will be brought about at the right time by God, the blessed and only Ruler, the King of kings and the Lord of lords. [16] He alone is immortal; he lives in the light that no one can approach. No one has ever seen him; no one can ever see him. To him be honor and eternal power! Amen.

[17] Command those who are rich in the things of this life not to be proud, but to place their hope, not in such an uncertain thing as riches, but in God, who generously gives us everything for our enjoyment. [18] Command them to do good, to be rich in good works, to be generous and ready to share with others. [19] In this way they will store up for themselves a treasure which will be a solid foundation for the future. And then they will be able to win the life which is true life.

[20] Timothy, keep safe what has been entrusted to your care. Avoid the profane talk and foolish arguments of what some people wrongly call "Knowledge." [21] For some have claimed to possess it, and as a result they have lost the way of faith.

God's grace be with you all.

Paul's Second Letter to
TIMOTHY

Introduction

Paul's Second Letter to Timothy *consists largely of personal advice to Timothy, as a younger colleague and assistant. The main theme is endurance. Timothy is advised and encouraged to keep on witnessing faithfully to Jesus Christ, to hold to the true teaching of the Good News and the Old Testament, and to do his duty as teacher and evangelist, all in the face of suffering and opposition.*

Timothy is especially warned about the dangers of becoming involved in "foolish and ignorant arguments" that do no good, but only ruin the people who listen to them.

In all this, Timothy is reminded of the example of the writer's own life and purpose—his faith, patience, love, endurance, and suffering in persecution.

Outline of Contents

1 From Paul, an apostle of Christ Jesus by God's will, sent to proclaim the promised life which we have in union with Christ Jesus—

2 To Timothy, my dear son:

May God the Father and Christ Jesus our Lord give you grace, mercy, and peace.

Thanksgiving and Encouragement

3 I give thanks to God, whom I serve with a clear conscience, as my ancestors did. I thank him as I remember you always in my prayers night and day. 4 I remember your tears, and I want to see you very much, so that I may be filled with joy. 5 I remember the sincere faith you have, the kind of faith that your grandmother Lois and your mother Eunice also had. I am sure that you have it also. 6 For this reason I remind you to keep alive the gift that God gave you when I laid my hands on you. 7 For the Spirit that God has given us does not make us timid; instead, his Spirit fills us with power, love, and self-control.

8 Do not be ashamed, then, of witnessing for our Lord; neither be ashamed of me, a prisoner for Christ's sake. Instead, take your part in suffering for the Good News, as God gives you the strength for it. 9 He saved us and called us to be his

own people, not because of what we have done, but because of his own purpose and grace. He gave us this grace by means of Christ Jesus before the beginning of time, 10 but now it has been revealed to us through the coming of our Savior, Christ Jesus. He has ended the power of death and through the gospel has revealed immortal life.

11 God has appointed me as an apostle and teacher to proclaim the Good News, 12 and it is for this reason that I suffer these things. But I am still full of confidence, because I know whom I have trusted, and I am sure that he is able to keep safe until that Day what he has entrusted to me.*a* 13 Hold firmly to the true words that I taught you, as the example for you to follow, and remain in the faith and love that are ours in union with Christ Jesus. 14 Through the power of the Holy Spirit, who lives in us, keep the good things that have been entrusted to you.

15 You know that everyone in the province of Asia, including Phygelus and Hermogenes, has deserted me. 16 May the Lord show mercy to the family of Onesiphorus, because he cheered me up many times. He was not ashamed that I am in prison, 17 but as soon as he arrived in Rome, he started looking for me until

a what he has entrusted to me; or what I have entrusted to him.

he found me. 18 May the Lord grant him his mercy on that Day! And you know very well how much he did for me in Ephesus.

A Loyal Soldier of Christ Jesus

2 As for you, my son, be strong through the grace that is ours in union with Christ Jesus. 2 Take the teachings that you heard me proclaim in the presence of many witnesses, and entrust them to reliable people, who will be able to teach others also.

3 Take your part in suffering, as a loyal soldier of Christ Jesus. 4 A soldier on active duty wants to please his commanding officer and so does not get mixed up in the affairs of civilian life. 5 An athlete who runs in a race cannot win the prize unless he obeys the rules. 6 The farmer who has done the hard work should have the first share of the harvest. 7 Think about what I am saying, because the Lord will enable you to understand it all.

8 Remember Jesus Christ, who was raised from death, who was a descendant of David, as is taught in the Good News I preach. 9 Because I preach the Good News, I suffer and I am even chained like a criminal. But the word of God is not in chains, 10 and so I endure everything for the sake of God's chosen people, in order that they too may obtain the salvation that comes through Christ Jesus and brings eternal glory. 11 This is a true saying:
"If we have died with him,
    we shall also live with him.
12 If we continue to endure,
    we shall also rule with him.
If we deny him,
    he also will deny us.
13 If we are not faithful,
    he remains faithful,
    because he cannot be false to
    himself."

An Approved Worker

14 Remind your people of this, and give them a solemn warning in God's presence not to fight over words. It does no good, but only ruins the people who listen. 15 Do your best to win full approval in God's sight, as a worker who is not ashamed of his work, one who correctly teaches the message of God's truth. 16 Keep away from profane and foolish discussions, which only drive people farther away from God. 17 Such teaching is like an open sore that eats away the flesh. Two men who have taught such things are Hymenaeus and Philetus. 18 They have left the way of truth and are upsetting the faith of some believers by saying that our resurrection has already taken place. 19 But the solid foundation that God has laid cannot be shaken; and on it are written these words: "The Lord knows those who are his" and "Those who say that they belong to the Lord must turn away from wrongdoing."

20 In a large house there are dishes and bowls of all kinds: some are made of silver and gold, others of wood and clay; some are for special occasions, others for ordinary use. 21 Those who make themselves clean from all those evil things, will be used for special purposes, because they are dedicated and useful to their Master, ready to be used for every good deed. 22 Avoid the passions of youth, and strive for righteousness, faith, love, and peace, together with those who with a pure heart call out to the Lord for help. 23 But keep away from foolish and ignorant arguments; you know that they end up in quarrels. 24 As the Lord's servant, you must not quarrel. You must be kind toward all, a good and patient teacher, 25 who is gentle as you correct your opponents, for it may be that God will give them the opportunity to repent and come to know the truth. 26 And then they will come to their senses and escape from the trap of the Devil, who had caught them and made them obey his will.

The Last Days

3 Remember that there will be difficult times in the last days. 2 People will be selfish, greedy, boastful, and conceited; they will be insulting, disobedient to their parents, ungrateful, and irreligious; 3 they will be unkind, merciless, slanderers, violent, and fierce; they will hate the good; 4 they will be treacherous, reckless, and swollen with pride; they will love pleasure rather than God; 5 they will hold to the outward form of our religion, but reject its real power. Keep away from such people. 6 Some of them go into people's houses and gain control over weak women who are burdened by the guilt of their sins and

driven by all kinds of desires, 7 women who are always trying to learn but who can never come to know the truth. 8 As Jannes and Jambres were opposed to Moses, so also these people are opposed to the truth—people whose minds do not function and who are failures in the faith. 9 But they will not get very far, because everyone will see how stupid they are. That is just what happened to Jannes and Jambres.

Last Instructions

10 But you have followed my teaching, my conduct, and my purpose in life; you have observed my faith, my patience, my love, my endurance, 11 my persecutions, and my sufferings. You know all that happened to me in Antioch, Iconium, and Lystra, the terrible persecutions I endured! But the Lord rescued me from them all. 12 Everyone who wants to live a godly life in union with Christ Jesus will be persecuted; 13 and evil persons and impostors will keep on going from bad to worse, deceiving others and being deceived themselves. 14 But as for you, continue in the truths that you were taught and firmly believe. You know who your teachers were, 15 and you remember that ever since you were a child, you have known the Holy Scriptures, which are able to give you the wisdom that leads to salvation through faith in Christ Jesus. 16 All Scripture is inspired by God and is useful[b] for teaching the truth, rebuking error, correcting faults, and giving instruction for right living, 7 so that the person who serves God may be fully qualified and equipped to do every kind of good deed.

4 In the presence of God and of Christ Jesus, who will judge the living and the dead, and because he is coming to rule as King, I solemnly urge you 2 to preach the message, to insist upon proclaiming it (whether the time is right or not), to convince, reproach, and encourage, as you teach with all patience. 3 The time will come when people will not listen to sound doctrine, but will follow their own desires and will collect for themselves more and more teachers who will tell them what they are itching to hear. 4 They will turn away from lis-

tening to the truth and give their attention to legends. 5 But you must keep control of yourself in all circumstances; endure suffering, do the work of a preacher of the Good News, and perform your whole duty as a servant of God.

6 As for me, the hour has come for me to be sacrificed; the time is here for me to leave this life. 7 I have done my best in the race, I have run the full distance, and I have kept the faith.[c] 8 And now there is waiting for me the victory prize of being put right with God, which the Lord, the righteous Judge, will give me on that Day—and not only to me, but to all those who wait with love for him to appear.

Personal Words

9 Do your best to come to me soon. 10 Demas fell in love with this present world and has deserted me, going off to Thessalonica. Crescens went to Galatia, and Titus to Dalmatia. 11 Only Luke is with me. Get Mark and bring him with you, because he can help me in the work. 12 I sent Tychicus to Ephesus. 13 When you come, bring my coat that I left in Troas with Carpus; bring the books too, and especially the ones made of parchment.

14 Alexander the metalworker did me great harm; the Lord will reward him according to what he has done. 15 Be on your guard against him yourself, because he was violently opposed to our message.

16 No one stood by me the first time I defended myself; all deserted me. May God not count it against them! 17 But the Lord stayed with me and gave me strength, so that I was able to proclaim the full message for all the Gentiles to hear; and I was rescued from being sentenced to death. 18 And the Lord will rescue me from all evil and take me safely into his heavenly Kingdom. To him be the glory forever and ever! Amen.

Final Greetings

19 I send greetings to Priscilla and Aquila and to the family of Onesiphorus. 20 Erastus stayed in Corinth, and I left

---

b All Scripture is inspired by God and is useful; or Every scripture inspired by God is also useful.   c kept the faith; or been true to my promise.

Trophimus in Miletus, because he was sick. 21 Do your best to come before winter.

Eubulus, Pudens, Linus, and Claudia send their greetings, and so do all the other Christians.

22 The Lord be with your spirit.

God's grace be with you all.

Paul's Letter to
TITUS

Introduction

Titus was a Gentile convert to Christianity who became a fellow worker and assistant to Paul in his missionary work. Paul's Letter to Titus is addressed to his young helper in Crete, who had been left there to supervise the work of the church. The letter expresses three main concerns.

First, Titus is reminded of the kind of character that church leaders should have, especially in view of the bad character of many Cretans. Next, Titus is advised how to teach the various groups in the church, the older men, the older women (who are, in turn, to teach the younger women), the young men, and the slaves. Finally, the writer gives Titus advice regarding Christian conduct, especially the need to be peaceful and friendly, and to avoid hatred, argument, and division in the church.

Outline of Contents

1 From Paul, a servant of God and an apostle of Jesus Christ.

I was chosen and sent to help the faith of God's chosen people and to lead them to the truth taught by our religion, 2 which is based on the hope for eternal life. God, who does not lie, promised us this life before the beginning of time, 3 and at the right time he revealed it in his message. This was entrusted to me, and I proclaim it by order of God our Savior.

4 I write to Titus, my true son in the faith that we have in common.

May God the Father and Christ Jesus our Savior give you grace and peace.

Titus' Work in Crete

5 I left you in Crete, so that you could put in order the things that still needed doing and appoint church elders in every town. Remember my instructions: 6 an elder must be without fault; he must have only one wife,a and his children must be believers and not have the reputation of being wild or disobedient. 7 For since a church leader is in charge of God's work, he should be without fault. He must not be arrogant or quick-tempered, or a drunkard or violent or greedy for money, 8 He must be hospitable and love what is good. He must be self-controlled, upright, holy, and disciplined. 9 He must hold firmly to the message which can be trusted and which agrees with the doctrine. In this way he will be able to encourage others with the true teaching and also to show the error of those who are opposed to it.

10 For there are many, especially the converts from Judaism, who rebel and deceive others with their nonsense. 11 It is necessary to stop their talk, because they are upsetting whole families by teaching what they should not, and all for the shameful purpose of making money. 12-13 It was a Cretan himself, one of their own prophets, who spoke the

a have only one wife; or be married only once.

truth when he said, "Cretans are always liars, wicked beasts, and lazy gluttons." For this reason you must rebuke them sharply, so that they may have a healthy faith [14] and no longer hold on to Jewish legends and to human commandments which come from people who have rejected the truth. [15] Everything is pure to those who are themselves pure; but nothing is pure to those who are defiled and unbelieving, for their minds and consciences have been defiled. [16] They claim that they know God, but their actions deny it. They are hateful and disobedient, not fit to do anything good.

Sound Doctrine

2 But you must teach what agrees with sound doctrine. [2] Instruct the older men to be sober, sensible, and self-controlled; to be sound in their faith, love, and endurance. [3] In the same way instruct the older women to behave as women should who live a holy life. They must not be slanderers or slaves to wine. They must teach what is good, [4] in order to train the younger women to love their husbands and children, [5] to be self-controlled and pure, and to be good housewives who submit themselves to their husbands, so that no one will speak evil of the message that comes from God.

[6] In the same way urge the young men to be self-controlled. [7] In all things you yourself must be an example of good behavior. Be sincere and serious in your teaching. [8] Use sound words that cannot be criticized, so that your enemies may be put to shame by not having anything bad to say about us.

[9] Slaves are to submit themselves to their masters and please them in all things. They must not talk back to them [10] or steal from them. Instead, they must show that they are always good and faithful, so as to bring credit to the teaching about God our Savior in all they do.

[11] For God has revealed his grace for the salvation of all people. [12] That grace instructs us to give up ungodly living and worldly passions, and to live self-controlled, upright, and godly lives in this world, [13] as we wait for the blessed Day we hope for, when the glory of our great God and Savior Jesus Christ[b] will appear. [14] He gave himself for us, to rescue us from all wickedness and to make us a pure people who belong to him alone and are eager to do good.

[15] Teach these things and use your full authority as you encourage and rebuke your hearers. Let none of them look down on you.

Christian Conduct

3 Remind your people to submit to rulers and authorities, to obey them, and to be ready to do good in every way. [2] Tell them not to speak evil of anyone, but to be peaceful and friendly, and always to show a gentle attitude toward everyone. [3] For we ourselves were once foolish, disobedient, and wrong. We were slaves to passions and pleasures of all kinds. We spent our lives in malice and envy; others hated us and we hated them. [4] But when the kindness and love of God our Savior was revealed, [5] he saved us. It was not because of any good deeds that we ourselves had done, but because of his own mercy that he saved us, through the Holy Spirit, who gives us new birth and new life by washing us. [6] God poured out the Holy Spirit abundantly on us through Jesus Christ our Savior, [7] so that by his grace we might be put right with God and come into possession of the eternal life we hope for. [8] This is a true saying.

I want you to give special emphasis to these matters, so that those who believe in God may be concerned with giving their time to doing good deeds, which are good and useful for everyone. [9] But avoid stupid arguments, long lists of ancestors, quarrels, and fights about the Law. They are useless and worthless. [10] Give at least two warnings to those who cause divisions, and then have nothing more to do with them. [11] You know that such people are corrupt, and their sins prove that they are wrong.

Final Instructions

[12] When I send Artemas or Tychicus to you, do your best to come to me in Nicopolis, because I have decided to spend the winter there. [13] Do your best to help

[b] our great God and Savior Jesus Christ; *or* the great God and our Savior Jesus Christ.

Zenas the lawyer and Apollos to get started on their travels, and see to it that they have everything they need. 14 Our people must learn to spend their time doing good, in order to provide for real

needs; they should not live useless lives. 15 All who are with me send you greetings. Give our greetings to our friends in the faith.

God's grace be with you all.

Paul's Letter to
PHILEMON

Introduction

Philemon was a prominent Christian, probably a member of the church at Colossae and the owner of a slave named Onesimus. This slave had run away from his master, and then somehow he had come in contact with Paul, who was then in prison. Through Paul, Onesimus became a Christian. Paul's Letter to Philemon is an appeal to Philemon to be reconciled to his slave, whom Paul is sending back to him, and to welcome him not only as a forgiven slave but as a Christian brother.

1 From Paul, a prisoner for the sake of Christ Jesus, and from our brother Timothy—

To our friend and fellow worker Philemon, 2 and the church that meets in your house, and our sister Apphia, and our fellow soldier Archippus:

3 May God our Father and the Lord Jesus Christ give you grace and peace.

Philemon's Love and Faith

4 Brother Philemon, every time I pray, I mention you and give thanks to my God. 5 For I hear of your love for all of God's people and the faith you have in the Lord Jesus. 6 My prayer is that our fellowship with you as believers will bring about a deeper understanding of every blessing which we have in our life in union with Christ. 7 Your love, dear brother, has brought me great joy and much encouragement! You have cheered the hearts of all of God's people.

A Request for Onesimus

8 For this reason I could be bold enough, as your brother in Christ, to order you to do what should be done. 9 But because I love you, I make a request instead. I do this even though I am Paul, the ambassador of Christ Jesus, and at present also a prisoner for his sake.a 10 So I make a request to you on behalf of Onesimus, who is my own son in Christ; for while in prison I have become his spiritual father. 11 At one time he was of no use to you, but now he is usefulb both to you and to me.

12 I am sending him back to you now, and with him goes my heart. 13 I would like to keep him here with me, while I am in prison for the gospel's sake, so that he could help me in your place. 14 However, I do not want to force you to help me; rather, I would like for you to do it of your own free will. So I will not do anything unless you agree,

a the ambassador of Christ Jesus, and at present also a prisoner for his sake; or an old man, and at present a prisoner for the sake of Christ Jesus.   b The Greek name Onesimus means "useful."

15 It may be that Onesimus was away from you for a short time so that you might have him back for all time. 16 And now he is not just a slave, but much more than a slave: he is a dear brother in Christ. How much he means to me! And how much more he will mean to you, both as a slave and as a brother in the Lord!

17 So, if you think of me as your partner, welcome him back just as you would welcome me. 18 If he has done you any wrong or owes you anything, charge it to my account. 19 Here, I will write this with my own hand: *I, Paul, will pay you back.* (I should not have to remind you, of course, that you owe your very self to me.) 20 So, my brother, please do me this favor for the Lord's sake; as a brother in Christ, cheer me up!

21 I am sure, as I write this, that you will do what I ask—in fact I know that you will do even more. 22 At the same time, get a room ready for me, because I hope that God will answer the prayers of all of you and give me back to you.

Final Greetings

23 Epaphras, who is in prison with me for the sake of Christ Jesus, sends you his greetings, 24 and so do my co-workers Mark, Aristarchus, Demas, and Luke.

25 May the grace of the Lord Jesus Christ be with you all.

P
H
I
L
E
M
O
N

THE GENERAL EPISTLES AND REVELATION

Hebrews was written to Christians, saying that Jesus Christ is the true and final revelation of God. Hebrews emphasizes the humanity of Jesus more than any other book in the New Testament, except the gospels. It also emphasizes the role of Jesus as the mediator between God and humanity, the one who brings forgiveness once and for all.

James was written to Christians to remind them that faith, if it is real faith, leads to faithful living. We are to show our faith in the little acts of daily living. Church tradition says the book was written by James the Lord's brother.

1 Peter was written to encourage the church in Asia Minor in a time of persecution. The key idea of the book is hope in Christ. It is this hope that sees us through tough times. Because we have hope in Christ, we are called to live a life of hope and love in the world.

2 Peter is addressed to a wide circle of early Christians. It calls the church to be faithful and continue to expect Jesus to return.

1, 2, and 3 John are (1) a sermon, (2) a letter to a church, and (3) a letter to an individual. 1 John has two main purposes: to encourage its readers to live in fellowship with God and with his Son, Jesus Christ, and to warn them against following false teaching. The writer says that believers experience eternal life now, that to know God is to obey God's commandments, and that the mark of eternal life is love. 2 John was written to a church to emphasize the commandment of love. 3 John is a letter to a church leader warning against a false teacher.

Jude was written to warn against a doctrine that said God's grace is an excuse for immoral living.

Revelation is a book about the struggle between good and evil and the ultimate triumph of Christ. It was written in a time of persecution. Writing in code, the author encourages his readers to stand fast in the face of persecution, for only the faithful will share in the final triumph of Christ. Yes, he says, things are bad and they will get worse, but Christ will triumph. Some of the great hymns and prayers of the early church are found in this book.

The Letter to the
HEBREWS

Introduction

The Letter to the Hebrews was written to a group of Christians who, faced with increasing opposition, were in danger of abandoning the Christian faith. The writer encourages them in their faith primarily by showing that Jesus Christ is the true and final revelation of God. In doing this he emphasizes three truths: (1) Jesus is the eternal Son of God, who learned true obedience to the Father through the suffering that he endured. As the Son of God, Jesus is superior to the prophets of the Old Testament, to the angels, and to Moses himself. (2) Jesus has been declared by God to be an eternal priest, superior to the priests of the Old Testament. (3) Through Jesus the believer is saved from sin, fear, and death; and Jesus, as High Priest, provides the true salvation, which was only fore-shadowed by the rituals and animal sacrifices of the Hebrew religion.

By citing the example of the faith of some famous persons in Israel's history (chapter 11), the writer appeals to his readers to remain faithful, and in chapter 12 he urges his readers to continue faithful to the end, with eyes fixed on Jesus, and to endure whatever suffering and persecution may come to them. The book closes with words of advice and warning.

Outline of Contents

God's Word through His Son

1 In the past God spoke to our ancestors many times and in many ways through the prophets, 2 but in these last days he has spoken to us through his Son. He is the one through whom God created the universe, the one whom God has chosen to possess all things at the end. 3 He reflects the brightness of God's glory and is the exact likeness of God's own being, sustaining the universe with his powerful word. After achieving forgiveness for the sins of all human beings, he sat down in heaven at the right side of God, the Supreme Power.

The Greatness of God's Son

4 The Son was made greater than the angels, just as the name that God gave

him is greater than theirs. 5 For God never said to any of his angels,

"You are my Son;
    today I have become your
        Father."

Nor did God say about any angel,

"I will be his Father,
    and he will be my Son."

6 But when God was about to send his first-born Son into the world, he said,

"All of God's angels must
    worship him."

7 But about the angels God said,

"God makes his angels winds,
    and his servants flames of fire."

8 About the Son, however, God said:

"Your kingdom, O God, will last[a]
    forever and ever!
You rule over your[b] people with
    justice.

---

[a] Your kingdom, O God, will last; or God is your kingdom.   [b] your; some manuscripts have his.

9 You love what is right and hate
what is wrong.
That is why God, your God, has
chosen you
and has given you the joy of an
honor far greater
than he gave to your
companions."
10 He also said,
"You, Lord, in the beginning
created the earth,
and with your own hands you
made the heavens.
11 They will disappear, but you will
remain;
they will all wear out like
clothes.
12 You will fold them up like a coat,
and they will be changed like
clothes.
But you are always the same,
and your life never ends."
13 God never said to any of his angels:
"Sit here at my right side
until I put your enemies
as a footstool under your feet."
14 What are the angels, then? They are
spirits who serve God and are sent by
him to help those who are to receive
salvation.

The Great Salvation

2 That is why we must hold on all the
more firmly to the truths we have
heard, so that we will not be carried
away. 2 The message given to our ancestors by the angels was shown to be true,
and those who did not follow it or obey
it received the punishment they deserved. 3 How, then, shall we escape if
we pay no attention to such a great salvation? The Lord himself first announced this salvation, and those who
heard him proved to us that it is true. 4 At
the same time God added his witness to
theirs by performing all kinds of miracles and wonders and by distributing the
gifts of the Holy Spirit according to his
will.

The One Who Leads Us to Salvation

5 God has not placed the angels as rulers over the new world to come—the
world of which we speak. 6 Instead, as it
is said somewhere in the Scriptures:

"What are human beings, O God,
that you should think of them;
mere human beings, that you
should care for them?
7 You made them for a little while
lower than the angels;
you crowned them with glory
and honor,c
8 and made them rulers over all
things."

It says that God made them "rulers over
all things"; this clearly includes everything. We do not, however, see human
beings ruling over all things now. 9 But
we do see Jesus, who for a little while
was made lower than the angels, so that
through God's grace he should die for
everyone. We see him now crowned
with glory and honor because of the
death he suffered. 10 It was only right
that God, who creates and preserves all
things, should make Jesus perfect
through suffering, in order to bring
many children to share his glory. For
Jesus is the one who leads them to
salvation.

11 He purifies people from their sins,
and both he and those who are made
pure all have the same Father. That is
why Jesus is not ashamed to call them
his family. 12 He says to God,

"I will tell my people what you
have done;
I will praise you in their
meeting."

13 He also says, "I will put my trust in
God." And he also says, "Here I am with
the children that God has given me."

14 Since the children, as he calls them,
are people of flesh and blood, Jesus himself became like them and shared their
human nature. He did this so that
through his death he might destroy the
Devil, who has the power over death,
15 and in this way set free those who
were slaves all their lives because of
their fear of death. 16 For it is clear that it
is not the angels that he helps. Instead,
he helps the descendants of Abraham.
17 This means that he had to become like
his people in every way, in order to be
their faithful and merciful High Priest in
his service to God, so that the people's
sins would be forgiven. 18 And now he
can help those who are tempted, be-

---

c *Many manuscripts add:* You made them rulers over everything you made (see Ps 8.6).

cause he himself was tempted and suffered.

Jesus Is Greater than Moses

3 My Christian friends, who also have been called by God! Think of Jesus, whom God sent to be the High Priest of the faith we profess. 2 He was faithful to God, who chose him to do this work, just as Moses was faithful in his work in God's house. 3 A man who builds a house receives more honor than the house itself. In the same way Jesus is worthy of much greater honor than Moses. 4 Every house, of course, is built by someone—and God is the one who has built all things. 5 Moses was faithful in God's house as a servant, and he spoke of the things that God would say in the future. 6 But Christ is faithful as the Son in charge of God's house. We are his house if we keep up our courage and our confidence in what we hope for.

A Rest for God's People

7 So then, as the Holy Spirit says,
  "If you hear God's voice today,
8   do not be stubborn, as your
      ancestors were when they
      rebelled against God,
    as they were that day in the
      desert when they put him to
      the test.
9 There they put me to the test and
      tried me, says God,
    although they had seen what I
      did for forty years.
10 And so I was angry with those
      people and said,
    'They are always disloyal
    and refuse to obey my
      commands.'
11 I was angry and made a solemn
      promise:
    'They will never enter the land
      where I would have given
      them rest!' "

12 My friends, be careful that none of you have a heart so evil and unbelieving that you will turn away from the living God. 13 Instead, in order that none of you be deceived by sin and become stubborn, you must help one another every day, as long as the word "Today" in the scripture applies to us. 14 For we are all partners with Christ if we hold firmly to the end the confidence we had at the beginning.

15 This is what the scripture says:
  "If you hear God's voice today,
    do not be stubborn, as your
      ancestors were
    when they rebelled
      against God."
16 Who were the people who heard God's voice and rebelled against him? All those who were led out of Egypt by Moses. 17 With whom was God angry for forty years? With the people who sinned, who fell down dead in the desert. 18 When God made his solemn promise, "They will never enter the land where I would have given them rest"—of whom was he speaking? Of those who rebelled. 19 We see, then, that they were not able to enter the land, because they did not believe.

4 Now, God has offered us the promise that we may receive that rest he spoke about. Let us take care, then, that none of you will be found to have failed to receive that promised rest. 2 For we have heard the Good News, just as they did. They heard the message, but it did them no good, because when they heard it, they did not accept it with faith. 3 We who believe, then, do receive that rest which God promised. It is just as he said,
  "I was angry and made a solemn
      promise:
    'They will never enter the land
      where I would have given
      them rest!' "
He said this even though his work had been finished from the time he created the world. 4 For somewhere in the Scriptures this is said about the seventh day: "God rested on the seventh day from all his work." 5 This same matter is spoken of again: "They will never enter that land where I would have given them rest." 6 Those who first heard the Good News did not receive that rest, because they did not believe. There are, then, others who are allowed to receive it. 7 This is shown by the fact that God sets another day, which is called "Today." Many years later he spoke of it through David in the scripture already quoted:
  "If you hear God's voice today,
    do not be stubborn."
8 If Joshua had given the people the rest that God had promised, God would not have spoken later about another day. 9 As it is, however, there still remains for God's people a rest like God's

HEBREWS

resting on the seventh day. 10 For those who receive that rest which God promised will rest from their own work, just as God rested from his. 11 Let us, then, do our best to receive that rest, so that no one of us will fail as they did because of their lack of faith.

12 The word of God is alive and active, sharper than any double-edged sword. It cuts all the way through, to where soul and spirit meet, to where joints and marrow come together. It judges the desires and thoughts of the heart. 13 There is nothing that can be hid from God; everything in all creation is exposed and lies open before his eyes. And it is to him that we must all give an account of ourselves.

Jesus the Great High Priest

14 Let us, then, hold firmly to the faith we profess. For we have a great High Priest who has gone into the very presence of God — Jesus, the Son of God. 15 Our High Priest is not one who cannot feel sympathy for our weaknesses. On the contrary, we have a High Priest who was tempted in every way that we are, but did not sin. 16 Let us have confidence, then, and approach God's throne, where there is grace. There we will receive mercy and find grace to help us just when we need it.

5 Every high priest is chosen from his fellow-men and appointed to serve God on their behalf, to offer sacrifices and offerings for sins. 2 Since he himself is weak in many ways, he is able to be gentle with those who are ignorant and make mistakes. 3 And because he is himself weak, he must offer sacrifices not only for the sins of the people but also for his own sins. 4 No one chooses for himself the honor of being a high priest. It is only by God's call that a man is made a high priest — just as Aaron was.

5 In the same way, Christ did not take upon himself the honor of being a high priest. Instead, God said to him,

"You are my Son;
today I have become your
Father."

6 He also said in another place,

"You will be a priest forever,

in the priestly order of
Melchizedek."d

7 In his life on earth Jesus made his prayers and requests with loud cries and tears to God, who could save him from death. Because he was humble and devoted, God heard him. 8 But even though he was God's Son, he learned through his sufferings to be obedient. 9 When he was made perfect, he became the source of eternal salvation for all those who obey him, 10 and God declared him to be high priest, in the priestly order of Melchizedek.d

Warning against Abandoning the Faith

11 There is much we have to say about this matter, but it is hard to explain to you, because you are so slow to understand. 12 There has been enough time for you to be teachers — yet you still need someone to teach you the first lessons of God's message. Instead of eating solid food, you still have to drink milk. 13 Anyone who has to drink milk is still a child, without any experience in the matter of right and wrong. 14 Solid food, on the other hand, is for adults, who through practice are able to distinguish between good and evil.

6 Let us go forward, then, to mature teaching and leave behind us the first lessons of the Christian message. We should not lay again the foundation of turning away from useless works and believing in God; 2 of the teaching about baptisms e and the laying on of hands; of the resurrection of the dead and the eternal judgment. 3 Let us go forward! And this is what we will do, if God allows.

4 For how can those who abandon their faith be brought back to repent again? They were once in God's light; they tasted heaven's gift and received their share of the Holy Spirit; 5 they knew from experience that God's word is good, and they had felt the powers of the coming age. 6 And then they abandoned their faith! It is impossible to bring them back to repent again, because they are again crucifying the Son of God and exposing him to public shame.

d in the priestly order of Melchizedek; or like Melchizedek; or in the line of succession to Melchizedek.   e baptisms; or purification ceremonies.

7God blesses the soil which drinks in the rain that often falls on it and which grows plants that are useful to those for whom it is cultivated. 8But if it grows thorns and weeds, it is worth nothing; it is in danger of being cursed by God and will be destroyed by fire.

9But even if we speak like this, dear friends, we feel sure about you. We know that you have the better blessings that belong to your salvation. 10God is not unfair. He will not forget the work you did or the love you showed for him in the help you gave and are still giving to other Christians. 11Our great desire is that each of you keep up your eagerness to the end, so that the things you hope for will come true. 12We do not want you to become lazy, but to be like those who believe and are patient, and so receive what God has promised.

God's Sure Promise

13When God made his promise to Abraham, he made a vow to do what he had promised. Since there was no one greater than himself, he used his own name when he made his vow. 14He said, "I promise you that I will bless you and give you many descendants." 15Abraham was patient, and so he received what God had promised. 16When we make a vow, we use the name of someone greater than ourselves, and the vow settles all arguments. 17To those who were to receive what he promised, God wanted to make it very clear that he would never change his purpose; so he added his vow to the promise. 18There are these two things, then, that cannot change and about which God cannot lie. So we who have found safety with him are greatly encouraged to hold firmly to the hope placed before us. 19We have this hope as an anchor for our lives. It is safe and sure, and goes through the curtain of the heavenly temple into the inner sanctuary. 20On our behalf Jesus has gone in there before us and has become a high priest forever, in the priestly order of Melchizedek.f

The Priest Melchizedek

7 This Melchizedek was king of Salem and a priest of the Most High God. As Abraham was coming back from the battle in which he defeated the four kings, Melchizedek met him and blessed him, 2and Abraham gave him one tenth of all he had taken. (The first meaning of Melchizedek's name is "King of Righteousness"; and because he was king of Salem, his name also means "King of Peace.") 3There is no record of Melchizedek's father or mother or of any of his ancestors; no record of his birth or of his death. He is like the Son of God; he remains a priest forever.

4You see, then, how great he was. Abraham, our famous ancestor, gave him one tenth of all he got in the battle. 5And those descendants of Levi who are priests are commanded by the Law to collect one tenth from the people of Israel, that is, from their own people, even though they are also descendants of Abraham. 6Melchizedek was not descended from Levi, but he collected one tenth from Abraham and blessed him, the man who received God's promises. 7There is no doubt that the one who blesses is greater than the one who is blessed. 8In the case of the priests the tenth is collected by men who die; but as for Melchizedek the tenth was collected by one who lives, as the scripture says. 9And, so to speak, when Abraham paid the tenth, Levi (whose descendants collect the tenth) also paid it. 10For Levi had not yet been born, but was, so to speak, in the body of his ancestor Abraham when Melchizedek met him.

11It was on the basis of the levitical priesthood that the Law was given to the people of Israel. Now, if the work of the levitical priests had been perfect, there would have been no need for a different kind of priest to appear, one who is in the priestly order of Melchizedek,f not of Aaron. 12For when the priesthood is changed, there also has to be a change in the law. 13And our Lord, of whom these things are said, belonged to a different tribe, and no member of his tribe ever served as a priest. 14It is well known that he was born a member of the tribe of Judah; and Moses did not mention this tribe when he spoke of priests.

f in the priestly order of Melchizedek (see 5.6).

Another Priest, like Melchizedek

15 The matter becomes even plainer; a different priest has appeared, who is like Melchizedek. 16 He was made a priest, not by human rules and regulations, but through the power of a life which has no end. 17 For the scripture says, "You will be a priest forever, in the priestly order of Melchizedek."*f* 18 The old rule, then, is set aside, because it was weak and useless. 19 For the Law of Moses could not make anything perfect. And now a better hope has been provided through which we come near to God.

20 In addition, there is also God's vow. There was no such vow when the others were made priests. 21 But Jesus became a priest by means of a vow when God said to him,

"The Lord has made a solemn
     promise
   and will not take it back:
 'You will be a priest forever.' "

22 This difference, then, also makes Jesus the guarantee of a better covenant.

23 There is another difference: there were many of those other priests, because they died and could not continue their work. 24 But Jesus lives on forever, and his work as priest does not pass on to someone else. 25 And so he is able, now and always, to save those who come to God through him, because he lives forever to plead with God for them. 26 Jesus, then, is the High Priest that meets our needs. He is holy; he has no fault or sin in him; he has been set apart from sinners and raised above the heavens. 27 He is not like other high priests; he does not need to offer sacrifices every day for his own sins first and then for the sins of the people. He offered one sacrifice, once and for all, when he offered himself. 28 The Law of Moses appoints men who are imperfect to be high priests; but God's promise made with the vow, which came later than the Law, appoints the Son, who has been made perfect forever.

Jesus Our High Priest

8 The whole point of what we are saying is that we have such a High Priest, who sits at the right of the throne of the Divine Majesty in heaven. 2 He serves as high priest in the Most Holy Place, that is, in the real tent which was put up by the Lord, not by human hands.

3 Every high priest is appointed to present offerings and animal sacrifices to God, and so our High Priest must also have something to offer. 4 If he were on earth, he would not be a priest at all, since there are priests who offer the gifts required by the Jewish Law. 5 The work they do as priests is really only a copy and a shadow of what is in heaven. It is the same as it was with Moses. When he was about to build the Sacred Tent, God told him, "Be sure to make everything according to the pattern you were shown on the mountain." 6 But now, Jesus has been given priestly work which is superior to theirs, just as the covenant which he arranged between God and his people is a better one, because it is based on promises of better things.

7 If there had been nothing wrong with the first covenant, there would have been no need for a second one. 8 But God finds fault with his people when he says,

"The days are coming, says the
     Lord,
   when I will draw up a new
     covenant with the people of
     Israel and with the people of
     Judah.
9 It will not be like the covenant
     that I made with their
     ancestors
   on the day I took them by the
     hand and led them out of
     Egypt.
 They were not faithful to the
     covenant I made with them,
   and so I paid no attention to
     them.
10 Now, this is the covenant that I
     will make with the people
     of Israel
   in the days to come, says the
     Lord:
 I will put my laws in their minds
   and write them on their hearts.
 I will be their God,
   and they will be my people.
11 None of them will have to teach
     their friends
   or tell their neighbors,
     'Know the Lord.'
 For they will all know me,

f in the priestly order of Melchizedek (see 5.6).

from the least to the greatest. 12 I will forgive their sins and will no longer remember their wrongs."

13 By speaking of a new covenant, God has made the first one old; and anything that becomes old and worn out will soon disappear.

Earthly and Heavenly Worship

9 The first covenant had rules for worship and a place made for worship as well. 2 A tent was put up, the outer one, which was called the Holy Place. In it were the lampstand and the table with the bread offered to God. 3 Behind the second curtain was the tent called the Most Holy Place. 4 In it were the gold altar for the burning of incense and the Covenant Box all covered with gold and containing the gold jar with the manna in it, Aaron's stick that had sprouted leaves, and the two stone tablets with the commandments written on them. 5 Above the Box were the winged creatures representing God's presence, with their wings spread over the place where sins were forgiven. But now is not the time to explain everything in detail.

6 This is how those things have been arranged. The priests go into the outer tent every day to perform their duties, 7 but only the high priest goes into the inner tent, and he does so only once a year. He takes with him blood which he offers to God on behalf of himself and for the sins which the people have committed without knowing they were sinning. 8 The Holy Spirit clearly teaches from all these arrangements that the way into the Most Holy Place has not yet been opened as long as the outer tent still stands. 9 This is a symbol which points to the present time. It means that the offerings and animal sacrifices presented to God cannot make the worshiper's heart perfect, 10 since they have to do only with food, drink, and various purification ceremonies. These are all outward rules, which apply only until the time when God will establish the new order.

11 But Christ has already come as the High Priest of the good things that are already here.g The tent in which he serves is greater and more perfect; it is not a tent made by human hands, that is, it is not a part of this created world. 12 When Christ went through the tent and entered once and for all into the Most Holy Place, he did not take the blood of goats and bulls to offer as a sacrifice; rather, he took his own blood and obtained eternal salvation for us. 13 The blood of goats and bulls and the ashes of a burnt calf are sprinkled on the people who are ritually unclean, and this purifies them by taking away their ritual impurity. 14 Since this is true, how much more is accomplished by the blood of Christ! Through the eternal Spirit he offered himself as a perfect sacrifice to God. His blood will purify our consciences from useless rituals, so that we may serve the living God.

15 For this reason Christ is the one who arranges a new covenant, so that those who have been called by God may receive the eternal blessings that God has promised. This can be done because there has been a death which sets people free from the wrongs they did while the first covenant was in effect. 16 In the case of a will it is necessary to prove that the person who made it has died, 17 for a will means nothing while the person who made it is alive; it goes into effect only after his death. 18 That is why even the first covenanth went into effect only with the use of blood. 19 First, Moses proclaimed to the people all the commandments as set forth in the Law. Then he took the blood of bulls and goats, mixed it with water, and sprinkled it on the book of the Law and all the people, using a sprig of hyssop and some red wool. 20 He said, "This is the blood which seals the covenant that God has commanded you to obey." 21 In the same way Moses also sprinkled the blood on the Sacred Tent and over all the things used in worship. 22 Indeed, according to the Law almost everything is purified by blood, and sins are forgiven only if blood is poured out.

Christ's Sacrifice Takes Away Sins

23 Those things, which are copies of the heavenly originals, had to be purified in that way. But the heavenly things

g already here; some manuscripts have coming. "will" and "covenant."   h COVENANT: In Greek the same word means

themselves require much better sacri-fices. 24For Christ did not go into a Holy Place made by human hands, which was a copy of the real one. He went into heaven itself, where he now appears on our behalf in the presence of God. 25The Jewish high priest goes into the Most Holy Place every year with the blood of an animal. But Christ did not go in to offer himself many times, 26for then he would have had to suffer many times ever since the creation of the world. In-stead, now when all ages of time are nearing the end, he has appeared once and for all, to remove sin through the sacrifice of himself. 27Everyone must die once, and after that be judged by God. 28In the same manner Christ also was offered in sacrifice once to take away the sins of many. He will appear a sec-ond time, not to deal with sin, but to save those who are waiting for him.

10 The Jewish Law is not a full and faithful model of the real things; it is only a faint outline of the good things to come. The same sacrifices are offered forever, year after year. How can the Law, then, by means of these sacrifices make perfect the people who come to God? 2If the people worshiping God had really been purified from their sins, they would not feel guilty of sin any more, and all sacrifices would stop. 3As it is, however, the sacrifices serve year after year to remind people of their sins. 4For the blood of bulls and goats can never take away sins.

5For this reason, when Christ was about to come into the world, he said to God:

"You do not want sacrifices and offerings,
but you have prepared a body for me.
6You are not pleased with animals burned whole on the altar
or with sacrifices to take away sins.
7Then I said, 'Here I am,
to do your will, O God,
just as it is written of me in the book of the Law.'"

8First he said, "You neither want nor are you pleased with sacrifices and offer-ings or with animals burned on the altar and the sacrifices to take away sins." He said this even though all these sacrifices are offered according to the Law. 9Then he said, "Here I am, O God, to do your will." So God does away with all the old sacrifices and puts the sacrifice of Christ in their place. 10Because Jesus Christ did what God wanted him to do, we are all purified from sin by the offering that he made of his own body once and for all.

11Every Jewish priest performs his services every day and offers the same sacrifices many times; but these sacri-fices can never take away sins. 12Christ, however, offered one sacrifice for sins, an offering that is effective forever, and then he sat down at the right side of God. 13There he now waits until God puts his enemies as a footstool under his feet. 14With one sacrifice, then, he has made perfect forever those who are purified from sin.

15And the Holy Spirit also gives us his witness. First he says,
16"This is the covenant that I will
make with them
in the days to come, says the
Lord:
I will put my laws in their hearts
and write them on their minds."
17And then he says, "I will not remember their sins and evil deeds any longer." 18So when these have been forgiven, an offering to take away sins is no longer needed.

Let Us Come Near to God

19We have, then, my friends, complete freedom to go into the Most Holy Place by means of the death of Jesus. 20He opened for us a new way, a living way, through the curtain—that is, through his own body. 21We have a great priest in charge of the house of God. 22So let us come near to God with a sincere heart and a sure faith, with hearts that have been purified from a guilty conscience and with bodies washed with clean wa-ter. 23Let us hold on firmly to the hope we profess, because we can trust God to keep his promise. 24Let us be concerned for one another, to help one another to show love and to do good. 25Let us not give up the habit of meeting together, as some are doing. Instead, let us encour-age one another all the more, since you see that the Day of the Lord is coming nearer.

26For there is no longer any sacrifice that will take away sins if we purposely go on sinning after the truth has been made known to us. 27 Instead, all that is left is to wait in fear for the coming Judgment and the fierce fire which will destroy those who oppose God! 28 Anyone who disobeys the Law of Moses is put to death without any mercy when judged guilty from the evidence of two or more witnesses. 29 What, then, of those who despise the Son of God? who treat as a cheap thing the blood of God's covenant which purified them from sin? who insult the Spirit of grace? Just think how much worse is the punishment they will deserve! 30 For we know who said, "I will take revenge, I will repay"; and who also said, "The Lord will judge his people." 31 It is a terrifying thing to fall into the hands of the living God!

32 Remember how it was with you in the past. In those days, after God's light had shone on you, you suffered many things, yet were not defeated by the struggle. 33 You were at times publicly insulted and mistreated, and at other times you were ready to join those who were being treated in this way. 34 You shared the sufferings of prisoners, and when all your belongings were seized, you endured your loss gladly, because you knew that you still possessed something much better, which would last forever. 35 Do not lose your courage, then, because it brings with it a great reward. 36 You need to be patient, in order to do the will of God and receive what he promises. 37 For, as the scripture says,

"Just a little while longer,
 and he who is coming will come;
 he will not delay.
38 My righteous people, however, will
    believe and live;
 but if any of them turns back,
 I will not be pleased with them."

39 We are not people who turn back and are lost. Instead, we have faith and are saved.

Faith

11 To have faith is to be sure of the things we hope for, to be certain of the things we cannot see. 2 It was by their faith that people of ancient times won God's approval.

3 It is by faith that we understand that the universe was created by God's word, so that what can be seen was made out of what cannot be seen.

4 It was faith that made Abel offer to God a better sacrifice than Cain's. Through his faith he won God's approval as a righteous man, because God himself approved of his gifts. By means of his faith Abel still speaks, even though he is dead.

5 It was faith that kept Enoch from dying. Instead, he was taken up to God, and nobody could find him, because God had taken him up. The scripture says that before Enoch was taken up, he had pleased God. 6 No one can please God without faith, for whoever comes to God must have faith that God exists and rewards those who seek him.

7 It was faith that made Noah hear God's warnings about things in the future that he could not see. He obeyed God and built a boat in which he and his family were saved. As a result, the world was condemned, and Noah received from God the righteousness that comes by faith.

8 It was faith that made Abraham obey when God called him to go out to a country which God had promised to give him. He left his own country without knowing where he was going. 9 By faith he lived as a foreigner in the country that God had promised him. He lived in tents, as did Isaac and Jacob, who received the same promise from God. 10 For Abraham was waiting for the city which God has designed and built, the city with permanent foundations.

11 It was faith that made Abraham able to become a father, even though he was too old and Sarah herself could not have children. He[i] trusted God to keep his promise. 12 Though Abraham was practically dead, from this one man came as many descendants as there are stars in the sky, as many as the numberless grains of sand on the seashore.

13 It was in faith that all these persons died. They did not receive the things God had promised, but from a long way off they saw them and welcomed them, and admitted openly that they were foreigners and refugees on earth. 14 Those who say such things make it clear that

---

i It was faith . . . children. He; *some manuscripts have* It was faith that made Sarah herself able to conceive, even though she was too old to have children. She.

they are looking for a country of their own. 15 They did not keep thinking about the country they had left; if they had, they would have had the chance to return. 16 Instead, it was a better country they longed for, the heavenly country. And so God is not ashamed for them to call him their God, because he has prepared a city for them.

17 It was faith that made Abraham offer his son Isaac as a sacrifice when God put Abraham to the test. Abraham was the one to whom God had made the promise, yet he was ready to offer his only son as a sacrifice. 18 God had said to him, "It is through Isaac that you will have the descendants I promised." 19 Abraham reckoned that God was able to raise Isaac from death—and, so to speak, Abraham did receive Isaac back from death.

20 It was faith that made Isaac promise blessings for the future to Jacob and Esau.

21 It was faith that made Jacob bless each of the sons of Joseph just before he died. He leaned on the top of his walking stick and worshiped God.

22 It was faith that made Joseph, when he was about to die, speak of the departure of the Israelites from Egypt, and leave instructions about what should be done with his body.

23 It was faith that made the parents of Moses hide him for three months after he was born. They saw that he was a beautiful child, and they were not afraid to disobey the king's order.

24 It was faith that made Moses, when he had grown up, refuse to be called the son of the king's daughter. 25 He preferred to suffer with God's people rather than to enjoy sin for a little while. 26 He reckoned that to suffer scorn for the Messiah was worth far more than all the treasures of Egypt, for he kept his eyes on the future reward.

27 It was faith that made Moses leave Egypt without being afraid of the king's anger. As though he saw the invisible God, he refused to turn back. 28 It was faith that made him establish the Passover and order the blood to be sprinkled on the doors, so that the Angel of Death would not kill the first-born sons of the Israelites.

29 It was faith that made the Israelites able to cross the Red Sea as if on dry land; when the Egyptians tried to do it, the water swallowed them up.

30 It was faith that made the walls of Jericho fall down after the Israelites had marched around them for seven days. 31 It was faith that kept the prostitute Rahab from being killed with those who disobeyed God, for she gave the Israelite spies a friendly welcome.

32 Should I go on? There isn't enough time for me to speak of Gideon, Barak, Samson, Jephthah, David, Samuel, and the prophets. 33 Through faith they fought whole countries and won. They did what was right and received what God had promised. They shut the mouths of lions, 34 put out fierce fires, escaped being killed by the sword. They were weak, but became strong; they were mighty in battle and defeated the armies of foreigners. 35 Through faith women received their dead relatives raised back to life.

Others, refusing to accept freedom, died under torture in order to be raised to a better life. 36 Some were mocked and whipped, and others were put in chains and taken off to prison. 37 They were stoned, they were sawed in two, they were killed by the sword. They went around clothed in skins of sheep or goats—poor, persecuted, and mistreated. 38 The world was not good enough for them! They wandered like refugees in the deserts and hills, living in caves and holes in the ground.

39 What a record all of these have won by their faith! Yet they did not receive what God had promised, 40 because God had decided on an even better plan for us. His purpose was that only in company with us would they be made perfect.

God Our Father

12 As for us, we have this large crowd of witnesses around us. So then, let us rid ourselves of everything that gets in the way, and of the sin which holds on to us so tightly, and let us run with determination the race that lies before us. 2 Let us keep our eyes fixed on Jesus, on whom our faith depends from beginning to end. He did not give up because of the cross! On the contrary, because of the joy that was waiting for him, he thought nothing of the disgrace of dying on the cross, and he is

now seated at the right side of God's throne.

3 Think of what he went through; how he put up with so much hatred from sinners! So do not let yourselves become discouraged and give up. 4 For in your struggle against sin you have not yet had to resist to the point of being killed. 5 Have you forgotten the encouraging words which God speaks to you as his children?

"My child, pay attention when the
Lord corrects you,
and do not be discouraged when
he rebukes you.
6 Because the Lord corrects
everyone he loves,
and punishes everyone he
accepts as a child."

7 Endure what you suffer as being a father's punishment; your suffering shows that God is treating you as his children. Was there ever a child who was not punished by his father? 8 If you are not punished, as all his children are, it means you are not real children, but bastards. 9 In the case of our human fathers, they punished us and we respected them. How much more, then, should we submit to our spiritual Father and live! 10 Our human fathers punished us for a short time, as it seemed right to them; but God does it for our own good, so that we may share his holiness. 11 When we are punished, it seems to us at the time something to make us sad, not glad. Later, however, those who have been disciplined by such punishment reap the peaceful reward of a righteous life.

Instructions and Warnings

12 Lift up your tired hands, then, and strengthen your trembling knees! 13 Keep walking on straight paths, so that the lame foot may not be disabled, but instead be healed.

14 Try to be at peace with everyone, and try to live a holy life, because no one will see the Lord without it. 15 Guard against turning back from the grace of God. Let no one become like a bitter plant that grows up and causes many troubles with its poison. 16 Let no one become immoral or unspiritual like Esau, who for a single meal sold his rights as

the older son. 17 Afterward, you know, he wanted to receive his father's blessing; but he was turned back, because he could not find any way to change what he had done, even though in tears he looked for it.*j*

18 You have not come, as the people of Israel came, to what you can feel, to Mount Sinai with its blazing fire, the darkness and the gloom, the storm, 19 the blast of a trumpet, and the sound of a voice. When the people heard the voice, they begged not to hear another word, 20 because they could not bear the order which said, "If even an animal touches the mountain, it must be stoned to death." 21 The sight was so terrifying that Moses said, "I am trembling and afraid!"

22 Instead, you have come to Mount Zion and to the city of the living God, the heavenly Jerusalem, with its thousands of angels. 23 You have come to the joyful gathering of God's first-born, whose names are written in heaven. You have come to God, who is the judge of all people, and to the spirits of good people made perfect. 24 You have come to Jesus, who arranged the new covenant, and to the sprinkled blood that promises much better things than does the blood of Abel.

25 Be careful, then, and do not refuse to hear him who speaks. Those who refused to hear the one who gave the divine message on earth did not escape. How much less shall we escape, then, if we turn away from the one who speaks from heaven! 26 His voice shook the earth at that time, but now he has promised, "I will once more shake not only the earth but heaven as well." 27 The words "once more" plainly show that the created things will be shaken and removed, so that the things that cannot be shaken will remain.

28 Let us be thankful, then, because we receive a kingdom that cannot be shaken. Let us be grateful and worship God in a way that will please him, with reverence and awe; 29 because our God is indeed a destroying fire.

How to Please God

13 Keep on loving one another as Christians. 2 Remember to welcome strangers in your homes. There

j he looked for it; *or* he tried to get the blessing.

were some who did that and welcomed angels without knowing it. ³Remember those who are in prison, as though you were in prison with them. Remember those who are suffering, as though you were suffering as they are.

⁴Marriage is to be honored by all, and husbands and wives must be faithful to each other. God will judge those who are immoral and those who commit adultery.

⁵Keep your lives free from the love of money, and be satisfied with what you have. For God has said, "I will never leave you; I will never abandon you." ⁶Let us be bold, then, and say,

"The Lord is my helper,
    I will not be afraid.
What can anyone do to me?"

⁷Remember your former leaders, who spoke God's message to you. Think back on how they lived and died, and imitate their faith. ⁸Jesus Christ is the same yesterday, today, and forever. ⁹Do not let all kinds of strange teachings lead you from the right way. It is good to receive inner strength from God's grace, and not by obeying rules about foods; those who obey these rules have not been helped by them.

¹⁰The priests who serve in the Jewish place of worship have no right to eat any of the sacrifice on our altar. ¹¹The Jewish high priest brings the blood of the animals into the Most Holy Place to offer it as a sacrifice for sins; but the bodies of the animals are burned outside the camp. ¹²For this reason Jesus also died outside the city, in order to purify the people from sin with his own blood. ¹³Let us, then, go to him outside the camp and share his shame. ¹⁴For there is no permanent city for us here on earth; we are looking for the city which is to come. ¹⁵Let us, then, always offer praise

k his blood; or his sacrificial death.

to God as our sacrifice through Jesus, which is the offering presented by lips that confess him as Lord. ¹⁶Do not forget to do good and to help one another, because these are the sacrifices that please God.

¹⁷Obey your leaders and follow their orders. They watch over your souls without resting, since they must give to God an account of their service. If you obey them, they will do their work gladly; if not, they will do it with sadness, and that would be of no help to you.

¹⁸Keep on praying for us. We are sure we have a clear conscience, because we want to do the right thing at all times. ¹⁹And I beg you even more earnestly to pray that God will send me back to you soon.

Closing Prayer

²⁰⁻²¹God has raised from death our Lord Jesus, who is the Great Shepherd of the sheep as the result of his blood,ᵏ by which the eternal covenant is sealed. May the God of peace provide you with every good thing you need in order to do his will, and may he, through Jesus Christ, do in us what pleases him. And to Christ be the glory forever and ever! Amen.

Final Words

²²I beg you, my friends, to listen patiently to this message of encouragement; for this letter I have written you is not very long. ²³I want you to know that our brother Timothy has been let out of prison. If he comes soon enough, I will have him with me when I see you.

²⁴Give our greetings to all your leaders and to all God's people. The believers from Italy send you their greetings.

²⁵May God's grace be with you all.

The Letter from
JAMES

Introduction

The Letter from James *is a collection of practical instructions, written to "all God's people scattered over the whole world." The writer uses many vivid figures of speech to present instructions regarding practical wisdom and guidance for Christian attitudes and conduct. From the Christian perspective he deals with a variety of topics such as riches and poverty, temptation, good conduct, prejudice, faith and actions, the use of the tongue, wisdom, quarreling, pride and humility, judging others, boasting, patience, and prayer.*

The letter emphasizes the importance of actions along with faith, in the practice of the Christian religion.

Outline of Contents

1 From James, a servant of God and of the Lord Jesus Christ:
Greetings to all God's people scattered over the whole world.

Faith and Wisdom

2 My friends, consider yourselves fortunate when all kinds of trials come your way, 3 for you know that when your faith succeeds in facing such trials, the result is the ability to endure. 4 Make sure that your endurance carries you all the way without failing, so that you may be perfect and complete, lacking nothing. 5 But if any of you lack wisdom, you should pray to God, who will give it to you; because God gives generously and graciously to all. 6 But when you pray, you must believe and not doubt at all. Whoever doubts is like a wave in the sea that is driven and blown about by the wind. 7-8 If you are like that, unable to make up your mind and undecided in all you do, you must not think that you will receive anything from the Lord.

Poverty and Riches

9 Those Christians who are poor must be glad when God lifts them up, 10 and the rich Christians must be glad when God brings them down. For the rich will pass away like the flower of a wild plant. 11 The sun rises with its blazing heat and burns the plant; its flower falls off, and its beauty is destroyed. In the same way the rich will be destroyed while they go about their business.

Testing and Tempting

12 Happy are those who remain faithful under trials, because when they succeed in passing such a test, they will receive as their reward the life which God has promised to those who love him. 13 If we are tempted by such trials, we must not say, "This temptation comes from God." For God cannot be tempted by evil, and he himself tempts no one. 14 But we are tempted when we are drawn away and trapped by our own evil desires. 15 Then our evil desires conceive and give birth to sin; and sin, when it is full-grown, gives birth to death.

16 Do not be deceived, my dear friends! 17 Every good gift and every perfect present comes from heaven; it comes down from God, the Creator of the heavenly lights, who does not change or

cause darkness by turning. 18 By his own will he brought us into being through the word of truth, so that we should have first place among all his creatures.

Hearing and Doing

19 Remember this, my dear friends! Everyone must be quick to listen, but slow to speak and slow to become angry. 20 Human anger does not achieve God's righteous purpose. 21 So get rid of every filthy habit and all wicked conduct. Submit to God and accept the word that he plants in your hearts, which is able to save you.

22 Do not deceive yourselves by just listening to his word; instead, put it into practice. 23 If you listen to the word, but do not put it into practice you are like people who look in a mirror and see themselves as they are. 24 They take a good look at themselves and then go away and at once forget what they look like. 25 But if you look closely into the perfect law that sets people free, and keep on paying attention to it and do not simply listen and then forget it, but put it into practice — you will be blessed by God in what you do.

26 Do any of you think you are religious? If you do not control your tongue, your religion is worthless and you deceive yourself. 27 What God the Father considers to be pure and genuine religion is this: to take care of orphans and widows in their suffering and to keep oneself from being corrupted by the world.

Warning against Prejudice

2 My friends, as believers in our Lord Jesus Christ, the Lord of glory, you must never treat people in different ways according to their outward appearance. 2 Suppose a rich man wearing a gold ring and fine clothes comes to your meeting, and a poor man in ragged clothes also comes. 3 If you show more respect to the well-dressed man and say to him, "Have this best seat here," but say to the poor man, "Stand over there, or sit here on the floor by my feet," 4 then you are guilty of creating distinctions among yourselves and of making judgments based on evil motives.

5 Listen, my dear friends! God chose the poor people of this world to be rich in faith and to possess the kingdom which he promised to those who love him. 6 But you dishonor the poor! Who are the ones who oppress you and drag you before the judges? The rich! 7 They are the ones who speak evil of that good name which has been given to you.

8 You will be doing the right thing if you obey the law of the Kingdom, which is found in the scripture, "Love your neighbor as you love yourself." 9 But if you treat people according to their outward appearance, you are guilty of sin, and the Law condemns you as a lawbreaker. 10 Whoever breaks one commandment is guilty of breaking them all. 11 For the same one who said, "Do not commit adultery," also said, "Do not commit murder." Even if you do not commit adultery, you have become a lawbreaker if you commit murder. 12 Speak and act as people who will be judged by the law that sets us free. 13 For God will not show mercy when he judges the person who has not been merciful; but mercy triumphs over judgment.

Faith and Actions

14 My friends, what good is it for one of you to say that you have faith if your actions do not prove it? Can that faith save you? 15 Suppose there are brothers or sisters who need clothes and don't have enough to eat. 16 What good is there in your saying to them, "God bless you! Keep warm and eat well!" — if you don't give them the necessities of life? 17 So it is with faith: if it is alone and includes no actions, then it is dead.

18 But someone will say, "One person has faith, another has actions." My answer is, "Show me how anyone can have faith without actions. I will show you my faith by my actions." 19 Do you believe that there is only one God? Good! The demons also believe — and tremble with fear. 20 You fool! Do you want to be shown that faith without actions is useless?_a_ 21 How was our ancestor Abraham put right with God? It was through his actions, when he offered his son Isaac on the altar. 22 Can't you see? His faith and his actions worked together; his faith was made perfect through his

a useless; some manuscripts have dead.

actions. 23 And the scripture came true that said, "Abraham believed God, and because of his faith God accepted him as righteous." And so Abraham was called God's friend. 24 You see, then, that it is by our actions that we are put right with God, and not by our faith alone.

25 It was the same with the prostitute Rahab. She was put right with God through her actions, by welcoming the Israelite spies and helping them to escape by a different road.

26 So then, as the body without the spirit is dead, also faith without actions is dead.

The Tongue

3 My friends, not many of you should become teachers. As you know, we teachers will be judged with greater strictness than others. 2 All of us often make mistakes. But if a person never makes a mistake in what he says, he is perfect and is also able to control his whole being. 3 We put a bit into the mouth of a horse to make it obey us, and we are able to make it go where we want. 4 Or think of a ship: big as it is and driven by such strong winds, it can be steered by a very small rudder, and it goes wherever the pilot wants it to go. 5 So it is with the tongue: small as it is, it can boast about great things.

Just think how large a forest can be set on fire by a tiny flame! 6 And the tongue is like a fire. It is a world of wrong, occupying its place in our bodies and spreading evil through our whole being. It sets on fire the entire course of our existence with the fire that comes to it from hell itself. 7 We humans are able to tame and have tamed all other creatures — wild animals and birds, reptiles and fish. 8 But no one has ever been able to tame the tongue. It is evil and uncontrollable, full of deadly poison. 9 We use it to give thanks to our Lord and Father and also to curse other people, who are created in the likeness of God. 10 Words of thanksgiving and cursing pour out from the same mouth. My friends, this should not happen! 11 No spring of water pours out sweet water and bitter water from the same opening. 12 A fig tree, my friends, cannot bear ol-

ives; a grapevine cannot bear figs, nor can a salty spring produce sweet water.

The Wisdom from Above

13 Are there any of you who are wise and understanding? You are to prove it by your good life, by your good deeds performed with humility and wisdom. 14 But if in your heart you are jealous, bitter, and selfish, don't sin against the truth by boasting of your wisdom. 15 Such wisdom does not come down from heaven; it belongs to the world, it is unspiritual and demonic. 16 Where there is jealousy and selfishness, there is also disorder and every kind of evil. 17 But the wisdom from above is pure first of all; it is also peaceful, gentle, and friendly; it is full of compassion and produces a harvest of good deeds; it is free from prejudice and hypocrisy. 18 And goodness is the harvest that is produced from the seeds the peacemakers plant in peace.

Friendship with the World

4 Where do all the fights and quarrels among you come from? They come from your desires for pleasure, which are constantly fighting within you. 2 You want things, but you cannot have them, so you are ready to kill; you strongly desire things, but you cannot get them, so you quarrel and fight. You do not have what you want because you do not ask God for it. 3 And when you ask, you do not receive it, because your motives are bad; you ask for things to use for your own pleasures. 4 Unfaithful people! Don't you know that to be the world's friend means to be God's enemy? If you want to be the world's friend, you make yourself God's enemy. 5 Don't think that there is no truth in the scripture that says, "The spirit that God placed in us is filled with fierce desires."*b* 6 But the grace that God gives is even stronger. As the scripture says, "God resists the proud, but gives grace to the humble." 7 So then, submit yourselves to God. Resist the Devil, and he will run away from you. 8 Come near to God, and he will come near to you. Wash your hands, you sinners! Purify your hearts, you hypocrites! 9 Be sorrowful, cry, and weep; change your laughter into crying,

---

The spirit ... fierce desires; or God yearns jealously over the spirit that he placed in us.

your joy into gloom! 10 Humble yourselves before the Lord, and he will lift you up.

Warning against Judging One Another

11 Do not criticize one another, my friends. If you criticize or judge another Christian, you criticize and judge the Law. If you judge the Law, then you are no longer one who obeys the Law, but one who judges it. 12 God is the only lawgiver and judge. He alone can save and destroy. Who do you think you are, to judge someone else?

Warning against Boasting

13 Now listen to me, you that say, "Today or tomorrow we will travel to a certain city, where we will stay a year and go into business and make a lot of money." 14 You don't even know what your life tomorrow will be! You are like a puff of smoke, which appears for a moment and then disappears. 15 What you should say is this: "If the Lord is willing, we will live and do this or that." 16 But now you are proud, and you boast; all such boasting is wrong.

17 So then, if we do not do the good we know we should do, we are guilty of sin.

Warning to the Rich

5 And now, you rich people, listen to me! Weep and wail over the miseries that are coming upon you! 2 Your riches have rotted away, and your clothes have been eaten by moths. 3 Your gold and silver are covered with rust, and this rust will be a witness against you and will eat up your flesh like fire. You have piled up riches in these last days. 4 You have not paid any wages to those who work in your fields. Listen to their complaints! The cries of those who gather in your crops have reached the ears of God, the Lord Almighty. 5 Your life here on earth has been full of luxury and pleasure. You have made yourselves fat for the day of slaughter. 6 You have condemned and murdered innocent people, and they do not resist you.c

Patience and Prayer

7 Be patient, then, my friends, until the Lord comes. See how patient farmers are as they wait for their land to produce precious crops. They wait patiently for the autumn and spring rains. 8 You also must be patient. Keep your hopes high, for the day of the Lord's coming is near.

9 Do not complain against one another, my friends, so that God will not judge you. The Judge is near, ready to appear. 10 My friends, remember the prophets who spoke in the name of the Lord. Take them as examples of patient endurance under suffering. 11 We call them happy because they endured. You have heard of Job's patience, and you know how the Lord provided for him in the end. For the Lord is full of mercy and compassion.

12 Above all, my friends, do not use an oath when you make a promise. Do not swear by heaven or by earth or by anything else. Say only "Yes" when you mean yes, and "No" when you mean no, and then you will not come under God's judgment.

13 Are any among you in trouble? They should pray. Are any among you happy? They should sing praises. 14 Are any among you sick? They should send for the church elders, who will pray for them and rub olive oil on them in the name of the Lord. 15 This prayer made in faith will heal the sick; the Lord will restore them to health, and the sins they have committed will be forgiven. 16 So then, confess your sins to one another and pray for one another, so that you will be healed. The prayer of a good person has a powerful effect. 17 Elijah was the same kind of person as we are. He prayed earnestly that there would be no rain, and no rain fell on the land for three and a half years. 18 Once again he prayed, and the sky poured out its rain and the earth produced its crops.

19 My friends, if any of you wander away from the truth and another one brings you back again, 20 remember this: whoever turns a sinner back from the wrong way will save that sinner's sould from death and bring about the forgiveness of many sins.

c people, and they do not resist you; or people. Will God not resist you?   d that sinner's soul; or his own soul.

The First Letter from
PETER

Introduction

The First Letter from Peter *was addressed to Christians, here called "God's chosen people," who were scattered throughout the northern part of Asia Minor. The main purpose of the letter is to encourage the readers, who were facing persecution and suffering for their faith. The writer does this by reminding his readers of the Good News about Jesus Christ, whose death, resurrection, and promised coming gave them hope. In the light of this they are to accept and endure their suffering, confident that it is a test of the genuineness of their faith and that they will be rewarded on "the Day when Jesus Christ is revealed."*

Along with his encouragement in time of trouble, the writer also urges his readers to live as people who belong to Christ.

Outline of Contents

1

From Peter, apostle of Jesus Christ —

To God's chosen people who live as refugees scattered throughout the provinces of Pontus, Galatia, Cappadocia, Asia, and Bithynia. ²You were chosen according to the purpose of God the Father and were made a holy people by his Spirit, to obey Jesus Christ and be purified by his blood.

May grace and peace be yours in full measure.

A Living Hope

³Let us give thanks to the God and Father of our Lord Jesus Christ! Because of his great mercy he gave us new life by raising Jesus Christ from death. This fills us with a living hope, ⁴and so we look forward to possessing the rich blessings that God keeps for his people. He keeps them for you in heaven, where they cannot decay or spoil or fade away. ⁵They are for you, who through faith are kept safe by God's power for the salvation which is ready to be revealed at the end of time.

⁶Be glad about this, even though it may now be necessary for you to be sad for a while because of the many kinds of trials you suffer. ⁷Their purpose is to prove that your faith is genuine. Even gold, which can be destroyed, is tested by fire; and so your faith, which is much more precious than gold, must also be tested, so that it may endure. Then you will receive praise and glory and honor on the Day when Jesus Christ is revealed. ⁸You love him, although you have not seen him, and you believe in him, although you do not now see him. So you rejoice with a great and glorious joy which words cannot express, ⁹because you are receiving the salvation of your souls, which is the purpose of your faith in him.

¹⁰It was concerning this salvation that the prophets made careful search and investigation, and they prophesied about this gift which God would give you. ¹¹They tried to find out when the time would be and how it would come.ᵃ This was the time to which Christ's Spirit in them was pointing, in predicting the sufferings that Christ would have to endure and the glory that would follow. ¹²God revealed to these prophets that their work was not for their own

---

ᵃ when the time would be and how it would come; *or* who the person would be and when he would come.

benefit, but for yours, as they spoke about those things which you have now heard from the messengers who announced the Good News by the power of the Holy Spirit sent from heaven. These are things which even the angels would like to understand.

A Call to Holy Living

13 So then, have your minds ready for action. Keep alert and set your hope completely on the blessing which will be given you when Jesus Christ is revealed. 14 Be obedient to God, and do not allow your lives to be shaped by those desires you had when you were still ignorant. 15 Instead, be holy in all that you do, just as God who called you is holy. 16 The scripture says, "Be holy because I am holy."

17 You call him Father, when you pray to God, who judges all people by the same standard, according to what each one has done; so then, spend the rest of your lives here on earth in reverence for him. 18 For you know what was paid to set you free from the worthless manner of life handed down by your ancestors. It was not something that can be destroyed, such as silver or gold; 19 it was the costly sacrifice of Christ, who was like a lamb without defect or flaw. 20 He had been chosen by God before the creation of the world and was revealed in these last days for your sake. 21 Through him you believe in God, who raised him from death and gave him glory; and so your faith and hope are fixed on God.

22 Now that by your obedience to the truth you have purified yourselves and have come to have a sincere love for other believers, love one another earnestly with all your heart.b 23 For through the living and eternal word of God you have been born again as the children of a parent who is immortal, not mortal. 24 As the scripture says,

"All human beings are like grass,
   and all their glory is like wild
     flowers.
The grass withers, and the flowers
     fall,
25   but the word of the Lord
     remains forever."

This word is the Good News that was proclaimed to you.

The Living Stone and the Holy Nation

2 Rid yourselves, then, of all evil; no more lying or hypocrisy or jealousy or insulting language. 2 Be like newborn babies, always thirsty for the pure spiritual milk, so that by drinking it you may grow up and be saved. 3 As the scripture says, "You have found out for yourselves how kind the Lord is."

4 Come to the Lord, the living stone rejected by people as worthless but chosen by God as valuable. 5 Come as living stones, and let yourselves be used in building the spiritual temple, where you will serve as holy priests to offer spiritual and acceptable sacrifices to God through Jesus Christ. 6 For the scripture says,

"I chose a valuable stone,
   which I am placing as the
     cornerstone in Zion;
   and whoever believes in him will
     never be disappointed."

7 This stone is of great value for you that believe; but for those who do not believe:

"The stone which the builders
   rejected as worthless
   turned out to be the most
     important of all."

8 And another scripture says,

"This is the stone that will make
     people stumble,
   the rock that will make them
     fall."

They stumbled because they did not believe in the word; such was God's will for them.

9 But you are the chosen race, the King's priests, the holy nation, God's own people, chosen to proclaim the wonderful acts of God, who called you out of darkness into his own marvelous light. 10 At one time you were not God's people, but now you are his people; at one time you did not know God's mercy, but now you have received his mercy.

Slaves of God

11 I appeal to you, my friends, as strangers and refugees in this world! Do not give in to bodily passions, which are al-

b with all your heart; some manuscripts have with a pure heart.

ways at war against the soul. 12 Your conduct among the heathen should be so good that when they accuse you of being evildoers, they will have to recognize your good deeds and so praise God on the Day of his coming.

13 For the sake of the Lord submit yourselves to every human authority: to the Emperor, who is the supreme authority, 14 and to the governors, who have been appointed by him to punish the evildoers and to praise those who do good. 15 For God wants you to silence the ignorant talk of foolish people by the good things you do. 16 Live as free people; do not, however, use your freedom to cover up any evil, but live as God's slaves. 17 Respect everyone, love other believers, honor God, and respect the Emperor.

The Example of Christ's Suffering

18 You servants must submit yourselves to your masters and show them complete respect, not only to those who are kind and considerate, but also to those who are harsh. 19 God will bless you for this, if you endure the pain of undeserved suffering because you are conscious of his will. 20 For what credit is there if you endure the beatings you deserve for having done wrong? But if you endure suffering even when you have done right, God will bless you for it. 21 It was to this that God called you, for Christ himself suffered for you and left you an example, so that you would follow in his steps. 22 He committed no sin, and no one ever heard a lie come from his lips. 23 When he was insulted, he did not answer back with an insult; when he suffered, he did not threaten, but placed his hopes in God, the righteous Judge. 24 Christ himself carried our sins in his body to the cross, so that we might die to sin and live for righteousness. It is by his wounds that you have been healed. 25 You were like sheep that had lost their way, but now you have been brought back to follow the Shepherd and Keeper of your souls.

Wives and Husbands

3 In the same way you wives must submit yourselves to your husbands, so that if any of them do not believe God's word, your conduct will win them over to believe. It will not be neces-

sary for you to say a word, 2 because they will see how pure and reverent your conduct is. 3 You should not use outward aids to make yourselves beautiful, such as the way you fix your hair, or the jewelry you put on, or the dresses you wear. 4 Instead, your beauty should consist of your true inner self, the ageless beauty of a gentle and quiet spirit, which is of the greatest value in God's sight. 5 For the devout women of the past who placed their hope in God used to make themselves beautiful by submitting themselves to their husbands. 6 Sarah was like that; she obeyed Abraham and called him her master. You are now her daughters if you do good and are not afraid of anything.

7 In the same way you husbands must live with your wives with the proper understanding that they are more delicate than you. Treat them with respect, because they also will receive, together with you, God's gift of life. Do this so that nothing will interfere with your prayers.

Suffering for Doing Right

8 To conclude: you must all have the same attitude and the same feelings; love one another, and be kind and humble with one another. 9 Do not pay back evil with evil or cursing with cursing; instead, pay back with a blessing, because a blessing is what God promised to give you when he called you. 10 As the scripture says,

"If you want to enjoy life
    and wish to see good times,
    you must keep from speaking
        evil
    and stop telling lies.
11 You must turn away from evil and
        do good;
    you must strive for peace with
        all your heart.
12 For the Lord watches over the
        righteous
    and listens to their prayers;
    but he opposes those who do
        evil."

13 Who will harm you if you are eager to do what is good? 14 But even if you should suffer for doing what is right, how happy you are! Do not be afraid of anyone, and do not worry. 15 But have reverence for Christ in your hearts, and honor him as Lord. Be ready at all times

1 PETER

to answer anyone who asks you to explain the hope you have in you, 16 but do it with gentleness and respect. Keep your conscience clear, so that when you are insulted, those who speak evil of your good conduct as followers of Christ will become ashamed of what they say. 17 For it is better to suffer for doing good, if this should be God's will, than for doing evil. 18 For Christ died c for sins once and for all, a good man on behalf of sinners, in order to lead you to God. He was put to death physically, but made alive spiritually, 19 and in his spiritual existence he went and preached to the imprisoned spirits. 20 These were the spirits of those who had not obeyed God when he waited patiently during the days that Noah was building his boat. The few people in the boat — eight in all — were saved by the water, 21 which was a symbol pointing to baptism, which now saves you. It is not the washing off of bodily dirt, but the promise made to God from a good conscience. It saves you through the resurrection of Jesus Christ, 22 who has gone to heaven and is at the right side of God, ruling over all angels and heavenly authorities and powers.

Changed Lives

4 Since Christ suffered physically, you too must strengthen yourselves with the same way of thinking that he had; because whoever suffers physically is no longer involved with sin. 2 From now on, then, you must live the rest of your earthly lives controlled by God's will and not by human desires. 3 You have spent enough time in the past doing what the heathen like to do. Your lives were spent in indecency, lust, drunkenness, orgies, drinking parties, and the disgusting worship of idols. 4 And now the heathen are surprised when you do not join them in the same wild and reckless living, and so they insult you. 5 But they will have to give an account of themselves to God, who is ready to judge the living and the dead. 6 That is why the Good News was preached also to the dead, to those who had been judged in their physical existence as everyone is judged; it was preached to them so that in their spiritual existence they may live as God lives.

Good Managers of God's Gifts

7 The end of all things is near. You must be self-controlled and alert, to be able to pray. 8 Above everything, love one another earnestly, because love covers over many sins. 9 Open your homes to each other without complaining. 10 Each one, as a good manager of God's different gifts, must use for the good of others the special gift he has received from God. 11 Those who preach must preach God's messages; those who serve must serve with the strength that God gives them, so that in all things praise may be given to God through Jesus Christ, to whom belong glory and power forever and ever. Amen.

Suffering as a Christian

12 My dear friends, do not be surprised at the painful test you are suffering, as though something unusual were happening to you. 13 Rather be glad that you are sharing Christ's sufferings, so that you may be full of joy when his glory is revealed. 14 Happy are you if you are insulted because you are Christ's followers; this means that the glorious Spirit, the Spirit of God, is resting on you. 15 If you suffer, it must not be because you are a murderer or a thief or a criminal or a meddler in other people's affairs. 16 However, if you suffer because you are a Christian, don't be ashamed of it, but thank God that you bear Christ's name.

17 The time has come for judgment to begin, and God's own people are the first to be judged. If it starts with us, how will it end with those who do not believe the Good News from God? 18 As the scripture says,

"It is difficult for good people to be saved;
what, then, will become of godless sinners?"

19 So then, those who suffer because it is God's will for them, should by their good actions trust themselves completely to their Creator, who always keeps his promise.

The Flock of God

5 I, who am an elder myself, appeal to the church elders among you. I am a witness of Christ's sufferings, and I

c died; many manuscripts have suffered.

will share in the glory that will be revealed. I appeal to you ²to be shepherds of the flock that God gave you and to take care of it willingly, as God wants you to, and not unwillingly. Do your work, not for mere pay, but from a real desire to serve. ³Do not try to rule over those who have been put in your care, but be examples to the flock. ⁴And when the Chief Shepherd appears, you will receive the glorious crown which will never lose its brightness.

⁵In the same way you younger people must submit yourselves to your elders. And all of you must put on the apron of humility, to serve one another; for the scripture says, "God resists the proud, but shows favor to the humble." ⁶Humble yourselves, then, under God's mighty hand, so that he will lift you up in his own good time. ⁷Leave all your worries with him, because he cares for you.

⁸Be alert, be on watch! Your enemy, the Devil, roams around like a roaring lion, looking for someone to devour. ⁹Be firm in your faith and resist him, because you know that other believers in all the world are going through the same kind of sufferings. ¹⁰But after you have suffered for a little while, the God of all grace, who calls you to share his eternal glory in union with Christ, will himself perfect you and give you firmness, strength, and a sure foundation. ¹¹To him be the power forever! Amen.

Final Greetings

¹²I write you this brief letter with the help of Silas, whom I regard as a faithful Christian. I want to encourage you and give my testimony that this is the true grace of God. Stand firm in it.

¹³Your sister church in Babylon,ᵈ also chosen by God, sends you greetings, and so does my son Mark. ¹⁴Greet one another with the kiss of Christian love.

May peace be with all of you who belong to Christ.

ᵈ BABYLON: As in the book of Revelation, this probably refers to Rome.

The Second Letter from
PETER

Introduction

The Second Letter from Peter is addressed to a wide circle of early Christians. Its main concern is to combat the work of false teachers and the immorality which results from such teaching. The answer to these problems is found in holding to the true knowledge of God and of the Lord Jesus Christ, knowledge which has been conveyed by persons who themselves have seen Jesus and have heard him teach. The writer is especially concerned with the teaching of those who claim that Christ will not return again. He says that the apparent delay in Christ's return is due to the fact that God "does not want anyone to be destroyed, but wants all to turn away from their sins."

Outline of Contents

1 From Simon Peter, a servant and apostle of Jesus Christ—
To those who through the righteousness of our God and Savior Jesus Christ have been given a faith as precious as ours:

2 May grace and peace be yours in full measure through your knowledge of God and of Jesus our Lord.

God's Call and Choice

3 God's divine power has given us everything we need to live a truly religious life through our knowledge of the one who called us to share in his own[a] glory and goodness. 4 In this way he has given us the very great and precious gifts he promised, so that by means of these gifts you may escape from the destructive lust that is in the world, and may come to share the divine nature. 5 For this very reason do your best to add goodness to your faith; to your goodness add knowledge; 6 to your knowledge add self-control; to your self-control add endurance; to your endurance add godliness; 7 to your godliness add Christian affection; and to your Christian affection add love. 8 These are the qualities you need, and if you have them in abundance, they will make you active and effective in your knowledge of our Lord Jesus Christ. 9 But if you do not have them, you are so shortsighted that you cannot see and have forgotten that you have been purified from your past sins.

10 So then, my friends, try even harder to make God's call and his choice of you a permanent experience; if you do so, you will never abandon your faith.[b] 11 In this way you will be given the full right to enter the eternal Kingdom of our Lord and Savior Jesus Christ.

12 And so I will always remind you of these matters, even though you already know them and are firmly grounded in the truth you have received. 13 I think it only right for me to stir up your memory of these matters as long as I am still alive. 14 I know that I shall soon put off this mortal body, as our Lord Jesus Christ plainly told me. 15 I will do my best, then, to provide a way for you to remember these matters at all times after my death.

Eyewitnesses of Christ's Glory

16 We have not depended on made-up stories in making known to you the mighty coming of our Lord Jesus Christ. With our own eyes we saw his great-ness. 17 We were there when he was given honor and glory by God the Father, when the voice came to him from the Supreme Glory, saying, "This is my own dear Son, with whom I am pleased!" 18 We ourselves heard this voice coming from heaven, when we were with him on the holy mountain.

19 So we are even more confident of the message proclaimed by the prophets. You will do well to pay attention to it, because it is like a lamp shining in a dark place until the Day dawns and the light of the morning star shines in your hearts. 20 Above all else, however, remember that none of us can explain by ourselves a prophecy in the Scriptures. 21 For no prophetic message ever came just from the human will, but people were under the control of the Holy Spirit as they spoke the message that came from God.

False Teachers

2 False prophets appeared in the past among the people, and in the same way false teachers will appear among you. They will bring in destructive, untrue doctrines, and will deny the Master who redeemed them, and so they will bring upon themselves sudden destruction. 2 Even so, many will follow their immoral ways; and because of what they do, others will speak evil of the Way of truth. 3 In their greed these false teachers will make a profit out of telling you made-up stories. For a long time now their Judge has been ready, and their Destroyer has been wide awake!

4 God did not spare the angels who sinned, but threw them into hell, where they are kept chained in darkness,[c] waiting for the Day of Judgment. 5 God did not spare the ancient world, but brought the flood on the world of godless people; the only ones he saved were Noah, who preached righteousness, and seven other people. 6 God condemned the cities of Sodom and Gomorrah, destroying them with fire, and made them an example of what will happen to the godless. 7 He rescued Lot, a good man, who was distressed by the immoral conduct of lawless people. 8 That good man lived among them, and day after day he

---

a to share in his own; *some manuscripts have* through his.   b abandon your faith; *or* fall into sin.   c chained in darkness; *some manuscripts have* in dark pits.

suffered agony as he saw and heard their evil actions. 9 And so the Lord knows how to rescue godly people from their trials and how to keep the wicked under punishment for the Day of Judgment, 10 especially those who follow their filthy bodily lusts and despise God's authority.

These false teachers are bold and arrogant, and show no respect for the glorious beings above; instead, they insult them. 11 Even the angels, who are so much stronger and mightier than these false teachers, do not accuse them with insults in the presence of the Lord. 12 But these people act by instinct, like wild animals born to be captured and killed; they attack with insults anything they do not understand. They will be destroyed like wild animals, 13 and they will be paid with suffering for the suffering they have caused. Pleasure for them is to do anything in broad daylight that will satisfy their bodily appetites; they are a shame and a disgrace as they join you in your meals, all the while enjoying their deceitful ways! 14 They want to look for nothing but the chance to commit adultery; their appetite for sin is never satisfied. They lead weak people into a trap. Their hearts are trained to be greedy. They are under God's curse! 15 They have left the straight path and have lost their way; they have followed the path taken by Balaam son of Beor, who loved the money he would get for doing wrong 16 and was rebuked for his sin. His donkey spoke with a human voice and stopped the prophet's insane action.

17 These people are like dried-up springs, like clouds blown along by a storm; God has reserved a place for them in the deepest darkness. 18 They make proud and stupid statements, and use immoral bodily lusts to trap those who are just beginning to escape from among people who live in error. 19 They promise them freedom while they themselves are slaves of destructive habits — for we are slaves of anything that has conquered us. 20 If people have escaped from the corrupting forces of the world through their knowledge of our Lord and Savior Jesus Christ, and then are again caught and conquered by them, such people are in worse condition at the end than they were at the beginning. 21 It

would have been much better for them never to have known the way of righteousness than to know it and then turn away from the sacred command that was given them. 22 What happened to them shows that the proverbs are true: "A dog goes back to what it has vomited" and "A pig that has been washed goes back to roll in the mud."

The Promise of the Lord's Coming

3 My dear friends, this is now the second letter I have written you. In both letters I have tried to arouse pure thoughts in your minds by reminding you of these things. 2 I want you to remember the words that were spoken long ago by the holy prophets, and the command from the Lord and Savior which was given you by your apostles. 3 First of all, you must understand that in the last days some people will appear whose lives are controlled by their own lusts. They will make fun of you 4 and will ask, "He promised to come, didn't he? Where is he? Our ancestors have already died, but everything is still the same as it was since the creation of the world!" 5 They purposely ignore the fact that long ago God gave a command, and the heavens and earth were created. The earth was formed out of water and by water, 6 and it was also by water, the water of the flood, that the old world was destroyed. 7 But the heavens and the earth that now exist are being preserved by the same command of God, in order to be destroyed by fire. They are being kept for the day when godless people will be judged and destroyed.

8 But do not forget one thing, my dear friends! There is no difference in the Lord's sight between one day and a thousand years; to him the two are the same. 9 The Lord is not slow to do what he has promised, as some think. Instead, he is patient with you, because he does not want anyone to be destroyed, but wants all to turn away from their sins.

10 But the Day of the Lord will come like a thief. On that Day the heavens will disappear with a shrill noise, the heavenly bodies will burn up and be destroyed, and the earth with everything

2 PETER

in it will vanish.*d* 11 Since all these things will be destroyed in this way, what kind of people should you be? Your lives should be holy and dedicated to God, 12 as you wait for the Day of God and do your best to make it come soon—the Day when the heavens will burn up and be destroyed, and the heavenly bodies will be melted by the heat. 13 But we wait for what God has promised: new heavens and a new earth, where righteousness will be at home.

14 And so, my friends, as you wait for that Day, do your best to be pure and faultless in God's sight and to be at peace with him. 15 Look on our Lord's patience as the opportunity he is giving you to be saved, just as our dear friend Paul wrote to you, using the wisdom that God gave him. 16 This is what he says in all his letters when he writes on the subject. There are some difficult things in his letters which ignorant and unstable people explain falsely, as they do with other passages of the Scriptures. So they bring on their own destruction.

17 But you, my friends, already know this. Be on your guard, then, so that you will not be led away by the errors of lawless people and fall from your safe position. 18 But continue to grow in the grace and knowledge of our Lord and Savior Jesus Christ. To him be the glory, now and forever! Amen.

d vanish; *some manuscripts have* be found; *others have* be burned up; *one has* be found destroyed.

The First Letter of
JOHN

Introduction

The First Letter of John *has two main purposes: to encourage its readers to live in fellowship with God and with his Son, Jesus Christ, and to warn them against following false teaching that would destroy this fellowship. This teaching was based on the belief that evil results from contact with the physical world, and so Jesus, the Son of God, could not really have been a human being. Those teachers claimed that to be saved was to be set free from concern with life in this world; and they also taught that salvation had nothing to do with matters of morality or of love for others.*

In opposition to this teaching the writer clearly states that Jesus Christ was a real human being, and he emphasizes that all who believe in Jesus and love God must also love one another.

Outline of Contents

The Word of Life

1 We write to you about the Word of life, which has existed from the very beginning. We have heard it, and we have seen it with our eyes; yes, we have seen it, and our hands have touched it. 2 When this life became visible, we saw it; so we speak of it and tell you about the eternal life which was with the Father and was made known to us. 3 What we have seen and heard we announce to you also, so that you will join with us in the fellowship that we have with the Father and with his Son Jesus Christ. 4 We write this in order that our *a* joy may be complete.

a our; *some manuscripts have* your.

God Is Light

5 Now the message that we have heard from his Son and announce is this: God is light, and there is no darkness at all in him. 6 If, then, we say that we have fellowship with him, yet at the same time live in the darkness, we are lying both in our words and in our actions. 7 But if we live in the light—just as he is in the light—then we have fellowship with one another, and the blood of Jesus, his Son, purifies us from every sin.

8 If we say that we have no sin, we deceive ourselves, and there is no truth in us. 9 But if we confess our sins to God, he will keep his promise and do what is right: he will forgive us our sins and purify us from all our wrongdoing. 10 If we say that we have not sinned, we make a liar out of God, and his word is not in us.

Christs Our Helper

2 I am writing this to you, my children, so that you will not sin; but if anyone does sin, we have someone who pleads with the Father on our behalf—Jesus Christ, the righteous one. 2 And Christ himself is the means by which our sins are forgiven, and not our sins only, but also the sins of everyone.

3 If we obey God's commands, then we are sure that we know him. 4 If we say that we know him, but do not obey his commands, we are liars and there is no truth in us. 5 But if we obey his word, we are the ones whose love for God has really been made perfect. This is how we can be sure that we are in union with God: 6 if we say that we remain in union with God, we should live just as Jesus Christ did.

The New Command

7 My dear friends, this command I am writing you is not new; it is the old command, the one you have had from the very beginning. The old command is the message you have already heard. 8 However, the command I now write you is new, because its truth is seen in Christ and also in you. For the darkness is passing away, and the real light is already shining.

9 If we say that we are in the light, yet hate others, we are in the darkness to this very hour. 10 If we love others, we live in the light, and so there is nothing in us that will cause someone else[b] to sin. 11 But if we hate others, we are in the darkness; we walk in it and do not know where we are going, because the darkness has made us blind.

12 I write to you, my children, because your sins are forgiven for the sake of Christ. 13 I write to you, fathers, because you know him who has existed from the beginning. I write to you, young people, because you have defeated the Evil One.

14 I write to you, my children, because you know the Father. I write to you, fathers, because you know him who has existed from the beginning. I write to you, young people, because you are strong; the word of God lives in you, and you have defeated the Evil One.

15 Do not love the world or anything that belongs to the world. If you love the world, you do not love the Father. 16 Everything that belongs to the world—what the sinful self desires, what people see and want, and everything in this world that people are so proud of—none of this comes from the Father; it all comes from the world. 17 The world and everything in it that people desire is passing away; but those who do the will of God live forever.

The Enemy of Christ

18 My children, the end is near! You were told that the Enemy of Christ would come; and now many enemies of Christ have already appeared, and so we know that the end is near. 19 These people really did not belong to our fellowship, and that is why they left us; if they had belonged to our fellowship, they would have stayed with us. But they left so that it might be clear that none of them really belonged to us.

20 But you have had the Holy Spirit poured out on you by Christ, and so all of you know the truth. 21 I write you, then, not because you do not know the truth; instead, it is because you do know it, and you also know that no lie ever comes from the truth.

22 Who, then, is the liar? It is those who say that Jesus is not the Messiah. Such people are the Enemy of Christ—they reject both the Father and the Son. 23 For those who reject the Son reject also the

b someone else; or us.

Father; those who accept the Son have the Father also.

24 Be sure, then, to keep in your hearts the message you heard from the beginning. If you keep that message, then you will always live in union with the Son and the Father. 25 And this is what Christ himself promised to give us — eternal life.

26 I am writing this to you about those who are trying to deceive you. 27 But as for you, Christ has poured out his Spirit on you. As long as his Spirit remains in you, you do not need anyone to teach you. For his Spirit teaches you about everything, and what he teaches is true, not false. Obey the Spirit's teaching, then, and remain in union with Christ.

28 Yes, my children, remain in union with him, so that when he appears we may be full of courage and need not hide in shame from him on the Day he comes. 29 You know that Christ is righteous; you should know, then, that everyone who does what is right is God's child.

Children of God

3 See how much the Father has loved us! His love is so great that we are called God's children — and so, in fact, we are. This is why the world does not know us: it has not known God. 2 My dear friends, we are now God's children, but it is not yet clear what we shall become. But we know that when Christ appears, we shall be like him, because we shall see him as he really is. 3 Everyone who has this hope in Christ keeps himself pure, just as Christ is pure.

4 Whoever sins is guilty of breaking God's law, because sin is a breaking of the law. 5 You know that Christ appeared in order to take away sins,c and that there is no sin in him. 6 So everyone who lives in union with Christ does not continue to sin; but whoever continues to sin has never seen him or known him.

7 Let no one deceive you, my children! Whoever does what is right is righteous, just as Christ is righteous. 8 Whoever continues to sin belongs to the Devil, because the Devil has sinned from the very beginning. The Son of God appeared for this very reason, to destroy what the Devil had done.

9 Those who are children of God do not continue to sin, for God's very nature is in them; and because God is their Father, they cannot continue to sin. 10 Here is the clear difference between God's children and the Devil's children: those who do not do what is right or do not love others are not God's children.

Love One Another

11 The message you heard from the very beginning is this: we must love one another. 12 We must not be like Cain; he belonged to the Evil One and murdered his own brother Abel. Why did Cain murder him? Because the things he himself did were wrong, and the things his brother did were right.

13 So do not be surprised, my friends, if the people of the world hate you. 14 We know that we have left death and come over into life; we know it because we love others. Those who do not love are still under the power of death. 15 Those who hate others are murderers, and you know that murderers do not have eternal life in them. 16 This is how we know what love is: Christ gave his life for us. We too, then, ought to give our lives for others! 17 If we are rich and see others in need, yet close our hearts against them, how can we claim that we love God? 18 My children, our love should not be just words and talk; it must be true love, which shows itself in action.

Courage before God

19 This, then, is how we will know that we belong to the truth; this is how we will be confident in God's presence. 20 If our conscience condemns us, we know that God is greater than our conscience and that he knows everything. 21 And so, my dear friends, if our conscience does not condemn us, we have courage in God's presence. 22 We receive from him whatever we ask, because we obey his commands and do what pleases him. 23 What he commands is that we believe in his Son Jesus Christ and love one another, just as Christ commanded us. 24 Those who obey God's commands live in union with God and God lives in union with them. And because of the Spirit that God has given us we know that God lives in union with us.

The True Spirit and the False Spirit

4 My dear friends, do not believe all who claim to have the Spirit, but test them to find out if the spirit they have comes from God. For many false prophets have gone out everywhere. 2 This is how you will be able to know whether it is God's Spirit: anyone who acknowledges that Jesus Christ came as a human being has the Spirit who comes from God. 3 But anyone who denies this about Jesus does not have the Spirit from God. The spirit that he has is from the Enemy of Christ; you heard that it would come, and now it is here in the world already.

4 But you belong to God, my children, and have defeated the false prophets, because the Spirit who is in you is more powerful than the spirit in those who belong to the world. 5 Those false prophets speak about matters of the world, and the world listens to them because they belong to the world. 6 But we belong to God. Whoever knows God listens to us; whoever does not belong to God does not listen to us. This, then, is how we can tell the difference between the Spirit of truth and the spirit of error.

God Is Love

7 Dear friends, let us love one another, because love comes from God. Whoever loves is a child of God and knows God. 8 Whoever does not love does not know God, for God is love. 9 And God showed his love for us by sending his only Son into the world, so that we might have life through him. 10 This is what love is: it is not that we have loved God, but that he loved us and sent his Son to be the means by which our sins are forgiven. 11 Dear friends, if this is how God loved us, then we should love one another. 12 No one has ever seen God, but if we love one another, God lives in union with us, and his love is made perfect in us.

13 We are sure that we live in union with God and that he lives in union with us, because he has given us his Spirit. 14 And we have seen and tell others that the Father sent his Son to be the Savior of the world. 15 If we declare that Jesus is the Son of God, we live in union with God and God lives in union with us. 16 And we ourselves know and believe the love which God has for us.

God is love, and those who live in love live in union with God and God lives in union with them. 17 Love is made perfect in us in order that we may have courage on the Judgment Day; and we will have it because our life in this world is the same as Christ's. 18 There is no fear in love; perfect love drives out all fear. So then, love has not been made perfect in anyone who is afraid, because fear has to do with punishment.

19 We love because God first loved us. 20 If we say we love God, but hate others, we are liars. For we cannot love God, whom we have not seen, if we do not love others, whom we have seen. 21 The command that Christ has given us is this: whoever loves God must love others also.

Our Victory over the World

5 Whoever believes that Jesus is the Messiah is a child of God; and whoever loves a father loves his child also. 2 This is how we know that we love God's children: it is by loving God and obeying his commands. 3 For our love for God means that we obey his commands. And his commands are not too hard for us, 4 because every child of God is able to defeat the world. And we win the victory over the world by means of our faith. 5 Who can defeat the world? Only the person who believes that Jesus is the Son of God.

The Witness about Jesus Christ

6 Jesus Christ is the one who came with the water of his baptism and the blood of his death. He came not only with the water, but with both the water and the blood. And the Spirit himself testifies that this is true, because the Spirit is truth. 7 There are three witnesses: 8 the Spirit, the water, and the blood; and all three give the same testimony. 9 We believe human testimony; but God's testimony is much stronger, and he has given this testimony about his Son. 10 So those who believe in the Son of God have this testimony in their own heart; but those who do not believe

1 JOHN

God, have made a liar of him, because they have not believed what God has said about his son. 11 The testimony is this: God has given us eternal life, and this life has its source in his Son. 12 Whoever has the Son has this life; whoever does not have the Son of God does not have life.

Eternal Life

13 I am writing this to you so that you may know that you have eternal life— you that believe in the Son of God. 14 We have courage in God's presence, because we are sure that he hears us if we ask him for anything that is according to his will. 15 He hears us whenever we ask him; and since we know this is true, we know also that he gives us what we ask from him.

16 If you see a believer commit a sin that does not lead to death, you should pray to God, who will give that person life. This applies to those whose sins do not lead to death. But there is sin which leads to death, and I do not say that you should pray to God about that. 17 All wrongdoing is sin, but there is sin which does not lead to death.

18 We know that no children of God keep on sinning, for the Son of God keeps them safe, and the Evil One cannot harm them.

19 We know that we belong to God even though the whole world is under the rule of the Evil One.

20 We know that the Son of God has come and has given us understanding, so that we know the true God. We live in union with the true God—in union with his Son Jesus Christ. This is the true God, and this is eternal life.

21 My children, keep yourselves safe from false gods!

The Second Letter of
JOHN

Introduction
The Second Letter of John *was written by "the Elder" to "the dear Lady and to her children," probably meaning a local church and its members. The brief message is an appeal to love one another and a warning against false teachers and their teachings.*

Outline of Contents
Introduction 1-3
The primacy of love 4-6
Warning against false doctrine 7-11
Conclusion 12-13

1 From the Elder—

To the dear Lady and to her children,[a] whom I truly love. And I am not the only one, but all who know the truth love you, 2 because the truth remains in us and will be with us forever.

3 May God the Father and Jesus Christ, the Father's Son, give us grace, mercy, and peace; may they be ours in truth and love.

Truth and Love

4 How happy I was to find that some of your children live in the truth, just as the Father commanded us. 5 And so I ask you, dear Lady: let us all love one another. This is no new command I am writing you; it is the command which we have had from the beginning. 6 This love I speak of means that we must live in obedience to God's commands. The

[a] LADY AND . . . HER CHILDREN: *This probably refers to a church and its members (also in verses 4, 5).*

command, as you have all heard from the beginning, is that you must all live in love.

7 Many deceivers have gone out over the world, people who do not acknowledge that Jesus Christ came as a human being. Such a person is a deceiver and the Enemy of Christ. 8 Be on your guard, then, so that you will not lose what we[b] have worked for, but will receive your reward in full.

9 Anyone who does not stay with the teaching of Christ, but goes beyond it, does not have God. Whoever does stay with the teaching has both the Father and the Son. 10 So then, if some come to you who do not bring this teaching, do not welcome them in your homes; do not even say, "Peace be with you." 11 For anyone who wishes them peace becomes their partner in the evil things they do.

Final Words

12 I have so much to tell you, but I would rather not do it with paper and ink; instead, I hope to visit you and talk with you personally, so that we shall be completely happy.

13 The children of your dear Sister[c] send you their greetings.

[b] we; some manuscripts have you. [c] CHILDREN OF YOUR DEAR SISTER: This probably refers to the members of the church to which the writer belonged.

The Third Letter of
JOHN

Introduction

The Third Letter of John was written by "the Elder" to a church leader named Gaius. The writer praises Gaius because of his help to other Christians, and warns against a man named Diotrephes.

Outline of Contents

1 From the Elder—
To my dear Gaius, whom I truly love.
2 My dear friend, I pray that everything may go well with you and that you may be in good health—as I know you are well in spirit. 3 I was so happy when some Christians arrived and told me how faithful you are to the truth—just as you always live in the truth. 4 Nothing makes me happier than to hear that my children live in the truth.

Gaius Is Praised

5 My dear friend, you are so faithful in the work you do for other Christians, even when they are strangers. 6 They have spoken to the church here about your love. Please help them to continue their trip in a way that will please God. 7 For they set out on their trip in the service of Christ without accepting any help from unbelievers. 8 We Christians, then, must help these people, so that we may share in their work for the truth.

Diotrephes and Demetrius

9 I wrote a short letter to the church; but Diotrephes, who likes to be their leader, will not pay any attention to what I say. 10 When I come, then, I will

bring up everything he has done: the terrible things he says about us and the lies he tells! But that is not enough for him; he will not receive the Christians when they come, and even stops those who want to receive them and tries to drive them out of the church!

11 My dear friend, do not imitate what is bad, but imitate what is good. Whoever does good belongs to God; whoever does what is bad has not seen God.

12 Everyone speaks well of Demetrius; truth itself speaks well of him. And we add our testimony, and you know that what we say is true.

Final Greetings

13 I have so much to tell you, but I do not want to do it with pen and ink. 14 I hope to see you soon, and then we will talk personally.

15 Peace be with you.

All your friends send greetings. Greet all our friends personally.

The Letter from

JUDE

Introduction

The Letter from Jude *was written to warn against false teachers who claimed to be believers. In this brief letter, which is similar in content to* 2 Peter, *the writer encourages his readers "to fight on for the faith which once and for all God has given to his people."*

Outline of Contents

1 From Jude, servant of Jesus Christ, and brother of James —

To those who have been called by God, who live in the love of God the Father and the protection of Jesus Christ:

2 May mercy, peace, and love be yours in full measure.

False Teachers

3 My dear friends, I was doing my best to write to you about the salvation we share in common, when I felt the need of writing at once to encourage you to fight on for the faith which once and for all God has given to his people. 4 For some godless people have slipped in unnoticed among us, persons who distort the message about the grace of our God in order to excuse their immoral ways, and who reject Jesus Christ, our only Master and Lord. Long ago the Scriptures predicted the condemnation they have received.

5 For even though you know all this, I want to remind you of how the Lord[a] once rescued the people of Israel from Egypt, but afterward destroyed those who did not believe. 6 Remember the angels who did not stay within the limits of their proper authority, but abandoned their own dwelling place: they are bound with eternal chains in the darkness below, where God is keeping them for that great Day on which they will be condemned. 7 Remember Sodom and Gomorrah, and the nearby towns, whose people acted as those angels did and indulged in sexual immorality and perversion: they suffer the punishment of eternal fire as a plain warning to all.

8 In the same way also, these people have visions which make them sin

a the Lord; *some manuscripts have* Jesus, *which in Greek is the same as* Joshua.

against their own bodies; they despise God's authority and insult the glorious beings above. 9 Not even the chief angel Michael did this. In his quarrel with the Devil, when they argued about who would have the body of Moses, Michael did not dare condemn the Devil with insulting words, but said, "The Lord rebuke you!" 10 But these people attack with insults anything they do not understand; and those things that they know by instinct, like wild animals, are the very things that destroy them. 11 How terrible for them! They have followed the way that Cain took. For the sake of money they have given themselves over to the error that Balaam committed. They have rebelled as Korah rebelled, and like him they are destroyed. 12 With their shameless carousing they are like dirty spots in your fellowship meals. They take care only of themselves. They are like clouds carried along by the wind, but bringing no rain. They are like trees that bear no fruit, even in autumn, trees that have been pulled up by the roots and are completely dead. 13 They are like wild waves of the sea, with their shameful deeds showing up like foam. They are like wandering stars, for whom God has reserved a place forever in the deepest darkness.

14 It was Enoch, the seventh[b] direct descendant from Adam, who long ago prophesied this about them: "The Lord will come with many thousands of his holy angels 15 to bring judgment on all, to condemn them all for the godless deeds they have performed and for all the terrible words that godless sinners have spoken against him!"

16 These people are always grumbling and blaming others; they follow their own evil desires; they brag about themselves and flatter others in order to get their own way.

Warnings and Instructions

17 But remember, my friends, what you were told in the past by the apostles of our Lord Jesus Christ. 18 They said to you, "When the last days come, people will appear who will make fun of you, people who follow their own godless desires." 19 These are the people who cause divisions, who are controlled by their natural desires, who do not have the Spirit. 20 But you, my friends, keep on building yourselves up on your most sacred faith. Pray in the power of the Holy Spirit, 21 and keep yourselves in the love of God, as you wait for our Lord Jesus Christ in his mercy to give you eternal life.

22 Show mercy toward those who have doubts; 23 save others by snatching them out of the fire; and to others show mercy mixed with fear, but hate their very clothes, stained by their sinful lusts.

Prayer of Praise

24 To him who is able to keep you from falling and to bring you faultless and joyful before his glorious presence — 25 to the only God our Savior, through Jesus Christ our Lord, be glory, majesty, might, and authority, from all ages past, and now, and forever and ever! Amen.

b SEVENTH: *This numbering includes both the first and the last in the series of seven names from Adam to Enoch.*

THE REVELATION
to John

Introduction

The Revelation to John *was written at a time when Christians were being persecuted because of their faith in Jesus Christ as Lord. The writer's main concern is to give his readers hope and encouragement, and to urge them to remain faithful during times of suffering and persecution.*

For the most part the book consists of several series of revelations and visions presented in symbolic language that would have been understood by Christians of that day, but would have remained a mystery to all others. As with the themes of a symphony, the themes of this book are repeated again and again in different ways through the various series of visions. Although there are differences of opinion regarding the details of interpretation of the book, the central theme is clear: through Christ the Lord, God will finally and totally defeat all of his enemies, including Satan, and will reward his faithful people with the blessings of a new heaven and a new earth when this victory is complete.

Outline of Contents

---

1 This book is the record of the events that Jesus Christ revealed. God gave him this revelation in order to show to his servants what must happen very soon. Christ made these things known to his servant John by sending his angel to him, 2 and John has told all that he has seen. This is his report concerning the message from God and the truth revealed by Jesus Christ. 3 Happy is the one who reads this book, and happy are those who listen to the words of this prophetic message and obey what is written in this book! For the time is near when all these things will happen.

Greetings to the Seven Churches

4 From John to the seven churches in the province of Asia:

Grace and peace be yours from God, who is, who was, and who is to come, and from the seven spirits in front of his throne, 5 and from Jesus Christ, the faithful witness, the first to be raised from death and who is also the ruler of the kings of the world.

He loves us, and by his sacrificial death he has freed us from our sins 6 and made us a kingdom of priests to serve his God and Father. To Jesus Christ be the glory and power forever and ever! Amen.

7 Look, he is coming on the clouds! Everyone will see him, including those who pierced him. All peoples on earth will mourn over him. So shall it be!

8 "I am the first and the last," says the Lord God Almighty, who is, who was, and who is to come.

A Vision of Christ

9 I am John, your brother, and as a follower of Jesus I am your partner in patiently enduring the suffering that comes to those who belong to his Kingdom. I was put on the island of Patmos because I had proclaimed God's word and the truth that Jesus revealed. 10 On the

Lord s day the Spirit took control of me, and I heard a loud voice, that sounded like a trumpet, speaking behind me. 11 It said, "Write down what you see, and send the book to the churches in these seven cities: Ephesus, Smyrna, Pergamum, Thyatira, Sardis, Philadelphia, and Laodicea."

12 I turned around to see who was talking to me, and I saw seven gold lampstands, 13 and among them there was what looked like a human being, wearing a robe that reached to his feet, and a gold band around his chest. 14 His hair was white as wool, or as snow, and his eyes blazed like fire; 15 his feet shone like brass that has been refined and polished, and his voice sounded like a roaring waterfall. 16 He held seven stars in his right hand, and a sharp two-edged sword came out of his mouth. His face was as bright as the midday sun. 17 When I saw him, I fell down at his feet like a dead man. He placed his right hand on me and said, "Don't be afraid! I am the first and the last. 18 I am the living one! I was dead, but now I am alive forever and ever. I have authority over death and the world of the dead. 19 Write, then, the things you see, both the things that are now and the things that will happen afterward. 20 Here is the secret meaning of the seven stars that you see in my right hand, and of the seven gold lampstands: the seven stars are the angels of the seven churches, and the seven lampstands are the seven churches.

The Message to Ephesus

2 "To the angel of the church in Ephesus write:

"This is the message from the one who holds the seven stars in his right hand and who walks among the seven gold lampstands. 2 I know what you have done; I know how hard you have worked and how patient you have been. I know that you cannot tolerate evil people and that you have tested those who say they are apostles but are not, and have found out that they are liars. 3 You are patient, you have suffered for my sake, and you have not given up. 4 But this is what I have against you: you do not love me now as you did at first. 5 Think how far you have fallen! Turn

from your sins and do what you did at first. If you don't turn from your sins, I will come to you and take your lampstand from its place. 6 But this is what you have in your favor: you hate what the Nicolaitans do, as much as I do.

7 "If you have ears, then, listen to what the Spirit says to the churches!

"To those who win the victory I will give the right to eat the fruit of the tree of life that grows in the Garden of God.

The Message to Smyrna

8 "To the angel of the church in Smyrna write:

"This is the message from the one who is the first and the last, who died and lived again. 9 I know your troubles; I know that you are poor—but really you are rich! I know the evil things said against you by those who claim to be Jews but are not; they are a group that belongs to Satan! 10 Don't be afraid of anything you are about to suffer. Listen! The Devil will put you to the test by having some of you thrown into prison, and your troubles will last ten days. Be faithful to me, even if it means death, and I will give you life as your prize of victory.

11 "If you have ears, then, listen to what the Spirit says to the churches!

"Those who win the victory will not be hurt by the second death.

The Message to Pergamum

12 "To the angel of the church in Pergamum write:

"This is the message from the one who has the sharp two-edged sword. 13 I know where you live, there where Satan has his throne. You are true to me, and you did not abandon your faith in me even during the time when Antipas, my faithful witness, was killed there where Satan lives. 14 But there are a few things I have against you: there are some among you who follow the teaching of Balaam, who taught Balak how to lead the people of Israel into sin by persuading them to eat food that had been offered to idols and to practice sexual immorality. 15 In the same way you have people among you who follow the teaching of the Nicolaitans. 16 Now turn from your sins! If you don't, I will come to you soon and fight against those people with the sword that comes out of my mouth.

R
E
V
E
L
A
T
I
O
N

17 "If you have ears, then, listen to what the Spirit says to the churches!

"To those who win the victory I will give some of the hidden manna. I will also give each of them a white stone on which is written a new name that no one knows except the one who receives it.

The Message to Thyatira

18 "To the angel of the church in Thyatira write:

"This is the message from the Son of God, whose eyes blaze like fire, whose feet shine like polished brass. 19 I know what you do. I know your love, your faithfulness, your service, and your patience. I know that you are doing more now than you did at first. 20 But this is what I have against you: you tolerate that woman Jezebel, who calls herself a messenger of God. By her teaching she misleads my servants into practicing sexual immorality and eating food that has been offered to idols. 21 I have given her time to repent of her sins, but she does not want to turn from her immorality. 22 And so I will throw her on a bed where she and those who committed adultery with her will suffer terribly. I will do this now unless they repent of the wicked things they did with her. 23 I will also kill her followers, and then all the churches will know that I am the one who knows everyone's thoughts and wishes. I will repay each of you according to what you have done.

24 "But the rest of you in Thyatira have not followed this evil teaching; you have not learned what the others call 'the deep secrets of Satan.' I say to you that I will not put any other burden on you. 25 But until I come, you must hold firmly to what you have. 26-28 To those who win the victory, who continue to the end to do what I want, I will give the same authority that I received from my Father: I will give them authority over the nations, to rule them with an iron rod and to break them to pieces like clay pots. I will also give them the morning star.

29 "If you have ears, then, listen to what the Spirit says to the churches!

The Message to Sardis

3 "To the angel of the church in Sardis write:

"This is the message from the one who has the seven spirits of God and the seven stars. I know what you are doing; I know that you have the reputation of being alive, even though you are dead! 2 So wake up, and strengthen what you still have before it dies completely. For I find that what you have done is not yet perfect in the sight of my God. 3 Remember, then, what you were taught and what you heard; obey it and turn from your sins. If you do not wake up, I will come upon you like a thief, and you will not even know the time when I will come. 4 But a few of you there in Sardis have kept your clothes clean. You will walk with me, clothed in white, because you are worthy to do so. 5 Those who win the victory will be clothed like this in white, and I will not remove their names from the book of the living. In the presence of my Father and of his angels I will declare openly that they belong to me.

6 "If you have ears, then, listen to what the Spirit says to the churches!

The Message to Philadelphia

7 "To the angel of the church in Philadelphia write:

"This is the message from the one who is holy and true. He has the key that belonged to David, and when he opens a door, no one can close it, and when he closes it, no one can open it. 8 I know what you do; I know that you have a little power; you have followed my teaching and have been faithful to me. I have opened a door in front of you, which no one can close. 9 Listen! As for that group that belongs to Satan, those liars who claim that they are Jews but are not, I will make them come and bow down at your feet. They will all know that I love you. 10 Because you have kept my command to endure, I will also keep you safe from the time of trouble which is coming upon the world to test all the people on earth. 11 I am coming soon. Keep safe what you have, so that no one will rob you of your victory prize. 12 I will make those who are victorious pillars in the temple of my God, and they will never leave it. I will write on them the name of my God and the name of the city of my God, the new Jerusalem, which will come down out of heaven from my God. I will also write on them my new name.

13 "If you have ears, then, listen to what the Spirit says to the churches!

The Message to Laodicea

14 "To the angel of the church in Laodicea write:

"This is the message from the Amen, the faithful and true witness, who is the origin*a* of all that God has created. 15 I know what you have done; I know that you are neither cold nor hot. How I wish you were either one or the other! 16 But because you are lukewarm, neither hot nor cold, I am going to spit you out of my mouth! 17 You say, 'I am rich and well off; I have all I need.' But you do not know how miserable and pitiful you are! You are poor, naked, and blind. 18 I advise you, then, to buy gold from me, pure gold, in order to be rich. Buy also white clothing to dress yourself and cover up your shameful nakedness. Buy also some ointment to put on your eyes, so that you may see. 19 I rebuke and punish all whom I love. Be in earnest, then, and turn from your sins. 20 Listen! I stand at the door and knock; if any hear my voice and open the door, I will come into their house and eat with them, and they will eat with me. 21 To those who win the victory I will give the right to sit beside me on my throne, just as I have been victorious and now sit by my Father on his throne.

22 "If you have ears, then, listen to what the Spirit says to the churches!"

Worship in Heaven

4 At this point I had another vision and saw an open door in heaven. And the voice that sounded like a trumpet, which I had heard speaking to me before, said, "Come up here, and I will show you what must happen after this." 2 At once the Spirit took control of me. There in heaven was a throne with someone sitting on it. 3 His face gleamed like such precious stones as jasper and carnelian, and all around the throne there was a rainbow the color of an emerald. 4 In a circle around the throne were twenty-four other thrones, on which were seated twenty-four elders dressed in white and wearing crowns of gold. 5 From the throne came flashes of lightning, rumblings, and peals of thunder. In front of the throne seven lighted torches were burning, which are the seven spirits of God. 6 Also in front of the

throne there was what looked like a sea of glass, clear as crystal.

Surrounding the throne on each of its sides, were four living creatures covered with eyes in front and behind. 7 The first one looked like a lion; the second looked like a bull; the third had a face like a human face; and the fourth looked like an eagle in flight. 8 Each one of the four living creatures had six wings, and they were covered with eyes, inside and out. Day and night they never stop singing:

"Holy, holy, holy, is the Lord God
    Almighty,
    who was, who is, and who is to
    come."

9 The four living creatures sing songs of glory and honor and thanks to the one who sits on the throne, who lives forever and ever. When they do so, 10 the twenty-four elders fall down before the one who sits on the throne, and worship him who lives forever and ever. They throw their crowns down in front of the throne and say,

11 "Our Lord and God! You are
    worthy
    to receive glory, honor, and
    power.
For you created all things,
    and by your will they were
    given existence and life."

The Scroll and the Lamb

5 I saw a scroll in the right hand of the one who sits on the throne; it was covered with writing on both sides and was sealed with seven seals. 2 And I saw a mighty angel, who announced in a loud voice, "Who is worthy to break the seals and open the scroll?" 3 But there was no one in heaven or on earth or in the world below *b* who could open the scroll and look inside it. 4 I cried bitterly because no one could be found who was worthy to open the scroll or look inside it. 5 Then one of the elders said to me, "Don't cry. Look! The Lion from Judah's tribe, the great descendant of David, has won the victory, and he can break the seven seals and open the scroll."

6 Then I saw a Lamb standing in the center of the throne, surrounded by the four living creatures and the elders. The Lamb appeared to have been killed. It had seven horns and seven eyes, which

---

a origin; *or* ruler.   *b* WORLD BELOW: *The world of the dead (see 1.18).*

are the seven spirits of God that have been sent through the whole earth. 7 The Lamb went and took the scroll from the right hand of the one who sits on the throne. 8 As he did so, the four living creatures and the twenty-four elders fell down before the Lamb. Each had a harp and gold bowls filled with incense, which are the prayers of God's people. 9 They sang a new song:

"You are worthy to take the scroll
    and to break open its seals.
For you were killed, and by your
        sacrificial death you bought
        for God
    people from every tribe,
        language, nation, and race.
10 You have made them a kingdom
        of priests to serve our God,
    and they shall rule on earth."

11 Again I looked, and I heard angels, thousands and millions of them! They stood around the throne, the four living creatures, and the elders, 12 and sang in a loud voice:

"The Lamb who was killed is
        worthy
    to receive power, wealth,
        wisdom, and strength,
    honor, glory, and praise!"

13 And I heard every creature in heaven, on earth, in the world below, and in the sea — all living beings in the universe — and they were singing:

"To him who sits on the throne
    and to the Lamb,
    be praise and honor, glory and
        might,
    forever and ever!"

14 The four living creatures answered, "Amen!" And the elders fell down and worshiped.

The Seals

6 Then I saw the Lamb break open the first of the seven seals, and I heard one of the four living creatures say in a voice that sounded like thunder, "Come!" 2 I looked, and there was a white horse. Its rider held a bow, and he was given a crown. He rode out as a conqueror to conquer.

3 Then the Lamb broke open the second seal; and I heard the second living creature say, "Come!" 4 Another horse came out, a red one. Its rider was given the power to bring war on the earth, so that people should kill each other. He was given a large sword.

5 Then the Lamb broke open the third seal; and I heard the third living creature say, "Come!" I looked, and there was a black horse. Its rider held a pair of scales in his hand. 6 I heard what sounded like a voice coming from among the four living creatures, which said, "A quart of wheat for a day's wages, and three quarts of barley for a day's wages. But do not damage the olive trees and the vineyards!"

7 Then the Lamb broke open the fourth seal; and I heard the fourth living creature say, "Come!" 8 I looked, and there was a pale-colored horse. Its rider was named Death, and Hades[c] followed close behind. They were given authority over one fourth of the earth, to kill by means of war, famine, disease, and wild animals.

9 Then the Lamb broke open the fifth seal. I saw underneath the altar the souls of those who had been killed because they had proclaimed God's word and had been faithful in their witnessing. 10 They shouted in a loud voice, "Almighty Lord, holy and true! How long will it be until you judge the people on earth and punish them for killing us?" 11 Each of them was given a white robe, and they were told to rest a little while longer, until the complete number of other servants and believers were killed, as they had been.

12 And I saw the Lamb break open the sixth seal. There was a violent earthquake, and the sun became black like coarse black cloth, and the moon turned completely red like blood. 13 The stars fell down to the earth, like unripe figs falling from the tree when a strong wind shakes it. 14 The sky disappeared like a scroll being rolled up, and every mountain and island was moved from its place. 15 Then the kings of the earth, the rulers and the military chiefs, the rich and the powerful, and all other people, slave and free, hid themselves in caves and under rocks on the mountains. 16 They called out to the mountains and to the rocks, "Fall on us and hide us from the eyes of the one who sits on the throne and from the anger of the Lamb!

c HADES: *The world of the dead (see 1.18).*

17 The terrible day of their anger is here, and who can stand up against it?"

The 144,000 People of Israel

7 After this I saw four angels standing at the four corners of the earth, holding back the four winds so that no wind should blow on the earth or the sea or against any tree. 2 And I saw another angel coming up from the east with the seal of the living God. He called out in a loud voice to the four angels to whom God had given the power to damage the earth and the sea. 3 The angel said, "Do not harm the earth, the sea, or the trees, until we mark the servants of our God with a seal on their foreheads." 4 And I was told that the number of those who were marked with God's seal on their foreheads was 144,000. They were from the twelve tribes of Israel, 5-8 twelve thousand from each tribe: Judah, Reuben, Gad, Asher, Naphtali, Manasseh, Simeon, Levi, Issachar, Zebulun, Joseph, and Benjamin.

The Enormous Crowd

9 After this I looked, and there was an enormous crowd—no one could count all the people! They were from every race, tribe, nation, and language, and they stood in front of the throne and of the Lamb, dressed in white robes and holding palm branches in their hands. 10 They called out in a loud voice: "Salvation comes from our God, who sits on the throne, and from the Lamb!" 11 All the angels stood around the throne, the elders, and the four living creatures. Then they threw themselves face downward in front of the throne and worshiped God, 12 saying, "Amen! Praise, glory, wisdom, thanksgiving, honor, power, and might belong to our God forever and ever! Amen!"

13 One of the elders asked me, "Who are these people dressed in white robes, and where do they come from?"

14 "I don't know, sir. You do," I answered.

He said to me, "These are the people who have come safely through the terrible persecution. They have washed their robes and made them white with the blood of the Lamb. 15 That is why they stand before God's throne and serve him day and night in his temple. He who sits on the throne will protect them with his presence. 16 Never again will they hunger or thirst; neither sun nor any scorching heat will burn them, 17 because the Lamb, who is in the center of the throne, will be their shepherd, and he will guide them to springs of life-giving water. And God will wipe away every tear from their eyes."

The Seventh Seal

8 When the Lamb broke open the seventh seal, there was silence in heaven for about half an hour. 2 Then I saw the seven angels who stand before God, and they were given seven trumpets.

3 Another angel, who had a gold incense container, came and stood at the altar. He was given a lot of incense to add to the prayers of all God's people and to offer it on the gold altar that stands before the throne. 4 The smoke of the burning incense went up with the prayers of God's people from the hands of the angel standing before God. 5 Then the angel took the incense container, filled it with fire from the altar, and threw it on the earth. There were rumblings and peals of thunder, flashes of lightning, and an earthquake.

The Trumpets

6 Then the seven angels with the seven trumpets prepared to blow them.

7 The first angel blew his trumpet. Hail and fire, mixed with blood, came pouring down on the earth. A third of the earth was burned up, a third of the trees, and every blade of green grass.

8 Then the second angel blew his trumpet. Something that looked like a huge mountain on fire was thrown into the sea. A third of the sea was turned into blood, 9 a third of the living creatures in the sea died, and a third of the ships were destroyed.

10 Then the third angel blew his trumpet. A large star, burning like a torch, dropped from the sky and fell on a third of the rivers and on the springs of water. 11 (The name of the star is "Bitterness.") A third of the water turned bitter, and many people died from drinking the water, because it had turned bitter.

12 Then the fourth angel blew his trumpet. A third of the sun was struck, and a third of the moon, and a third of the stars, so that their light lost a third of its

brightness; there was no light during a third of the day and a third of the night also.

13 Then I looked, and I heard an eagle that was flying high in the air say in a loud voice, "O horror! horror! How horrible it will be for all who live on earth when the sound comes from the trumpets that the other three angels must blow!"

9 Then the fifth angel blew his trumpet. I saw a star which had fallen down to the earth, and it was given the key to the abyss.d 2 The star opened the abyss, and smoke poured out of it, like the smoke from a large furnace; the sunlight and the air were darkened by the smoke from the abyss. 3 Locusts came down out of the smoke upon the earth, and they were given the same kind of power that scorpions have. 4 They were told not to harm the grass or the trees or any other plant; they could harm only the people who did not have the mark of God's seal on their foreheads. 5 The locusts were not allowed to kill these people, but only to torture them for five months. The pain caused by the torture is like the pain caused by a scorpion's sting. 6 During those five months they will seek death, but will not find it; they will want to die, but death will flee from them.

7 The locusts looked like horses ready for battle; on their heads they had what seemed to be crowns of gold, and their faces were like human faces. 8 Their hair was like women's hair, their teeth were like lions' teeth. 9 Their chests were covered with what looked like iron breastplates, and the sound made by their wings was like the noise of many horse-drawn chariots rushing into battle. 10 They have tails and stings like those of a scorpion, and it is with their tails that they have the power to hurt people for five months. 11 They have a king ruling over them, who is the angel in charge of the abyss. His name in Hebrew is Abaddon; in Greek the name is Apollyon (meaning "The Destroyer").

12 The first horror is over; after this there are still two more horrors to come.

13 Then the sixth angel blew his trumpet. I heard a voice coming from the four corners of the gold altar standing before God. 14 The voice said to the sixth angel, "Release the four angels who are bound at the great Euphrates River!" 15 The four angels were released; for this very hour of this very day of this very month and year they had been kept ready to kill a third of all the human race. 16 I was told the number of the mounted troops: it was two hundred million. 17 And in my vision I saw the horses and their riders: they had breastplates red as fire, blue as sapphire, and yellow as sulfur. The horses' heads were like lions' heads, and from their mouths came out fire, smoke, and sulfur. 18 A third of the human race was killed by those three plagues: the fire, the smoke, and the sulfur coming out of the horses' mouths. 19 For the power of the horses is in their mouths and also in their tails. Their tails are like snakes with heads, and they use them to hurt people.

20 The rest of the human race, all those who had not been killed by these plagues, did not turn away from what they themselves had made. They did not stop worshiping demons, nor the idols of gold, silver, bronze, stone, and wood, which cannot see, hear, or walk. 21 Nor did they repent of their murders, their magic, their sexual immorality, or their stealing.

The Angel and the Little Scroll

10 Then I saw another mighty angel coming down out of heaven. He was wrapped in a cloud and had a rainbow around his head; his face was like the sun, and his legs were like columns of fire. 2 He had a small scroll open in his hand. He put his right foot on the sea and his left foot on the land, 3 and called out in a loud voice that sounded like the roar of lions. After he had called out, the seven thunders answered with a roar. 4 As soon as they spoke, I was about to write. But I heard a voice speak from heaven, "Keep secret what the seven thunders have said; do not write it down!"

5 Then the angel that I saw standing on the sea and on the land raised his right hand to heaven 6 and took a vow in the name of God, who lives forever and

---

d ABYSS: The place in the depths of the earth where the demons were imprisoned until their final punishment.

ever, who created heaven, earth, and the sea, and everything in them. The angel said, "There will be no more delay! 7 But when the seventh angel blows his trumpet, then God will accomplish his secret plan, as he announced to his servants, the prophets."

8 Then the voice that I had heard speaking from heaven spoke to me again, saying, "Go and take the open scroll which is in the hand of the angel standing on the sea and on the land."

9 I went to the angel and asked him to give me the little scroll. He said to me, "Take it and eat it; it will turn sour in your stomach, but in your mouth it will be sweet as honey."

10 I took the little scroll from his hand and ate it, and it tasted sweet as honey in my mouth. But after I swallowed it, it turned sour in my stomach. 11 Then I was told, "Once again you must proclaim God's message about many nations, races, languages, and kings."

The Two Witnesses

11 I was then given a stick that looked like a measuring-rod, and was told, "Go and measure the temple of God and the altar, and count those who are worshiping in the temple. 2 But do not measure the outer courts, because they have been given to the heathen, who will trample on the Holy City for forty-two months. 3 I will send my two witnesses dressed in sackcloth, and they will proclaim God's message during those 1,260 days."

4 The two witnesses are the two olive trees and the two lamps that stand before the Lord of the earth. 5 If anyone tries to harm them, fire comes out of their mouths and destroys their enemies; and in this way whoever tries to harm them will be killed. 6 They have authority to shut up the sky so that there will be no rain during the time they proclaim God's message. They have authority also over the springs of water, to turn them into blood; they have authority also to strike the earth with every kind of plague as often as they wish.

7 When they finish proclaiming their message, the beast that comes up out of the abyss will fight against them. He will defeat them and kill them, 8 and their bodies will lie in the street of the great city, where their Lord was crucified. The symbolic name of that city is Sodom, or Egypt. 9 People from all nations, tribes, languages, and races will look at their bodies for three and a half days and will not allow them to be buried. 10 The people of the earth will be happy because of the death of these two. They will celebrate and send presents to each other, because those two prophets brought much suffering upon the whole human race. 11 After three and a half days a life-giving breath came from God and entered them, and they stood up; and all who saw them were terrified. 12 Then the two prophets heard a loud voice say to them from heaven, "Come up here!" As their enemies watched, they went up into heaven in a cloud. 13 At that very moment there was a violent earthquake; a tenth of the city was destroyed, and seven thousand people were killed. The rest of the people were terrified and praised the greatness of the God of heaven.

14 The second horror is over, but the third horror will come soon!

The Seventh Trumpet

15 Then the seventh angel blew his trumpet, and there were loud voices in heaven, saying, "The power to rule over the world belongs now to our Lord and his Messiah, and he will rule forever and ever!" 16 Then the twenty-four elders who sit on their thrones in front of God threw themselves face downward and worshiped God, 17 saying:

"Lord God Almighty, the one who is and who was!
We thank you that you have taken your great power
and have begun to rule!
18 The heathen were filled with rage,
because the time for your anger has come,
the time for the dead to be judged.
The time has come to reward your servants, the prophets,
and all your people, all who have reverence for you,
great and small alike.
The time has come to destroy those who destroy the earth!"

19 God's temple in heaven was opened, and the Covenant Box was seen there. Then there were flashes of lightning,

rumblings and peals of thunder, an earthquake, and heavy hail.

The Woman and the Dragon

12 Then a great and mysterious sight appeared in the sky. There was a woman, whose dress was the sun and who had the moon under her feet and a crown of twelve stars on her head. 2 She was soon to give birth, and the pains and suffering of childbirth made her cry out.

3 Another mysterious sight appeared in the sky. There was a huge red dragon with seven heads and ten horns and a crown on each of his heads. 4 With his tail he dragged a third of the stars out of the sky and threw them down to the earth. He stood in front of the woman, in order to eat her child as soon as it was born. 5 Then she gave birth to a son, who will rule over all nations with an iron rod. But the child was snatched away and taken to God and his throne. 6 The woman fled to the desert, to a place God had prepared for her, where she will be taken care of for 1,260 days.

7 Then war broke out in heaven. Michael and his angels fought against the dragon, who fought back with his angels; 8 but the dragon was defeated, and he and his angels were not allowed to stay in heaven any longer. 9 The huge dragon was thrown out—that ancient serpent, named the Devil, or Satan, that deceived the whole world. He was thrown down to earth, and all his angels with him.

10 Then I heard a loud voice in heaven saying, "Now God's salvation has come! Now God has shown his power as King! Now his Messiah has shown his authority! For the one who stood before our God and accused believers day and night has been thrown out of heaven. 11 They won the victory over him by the blood of the Lamb and by the truth which they proclaimed; and they were willing to give up their lives and die. 12 And so be glad, you heavens, and all you that live there! But how terrible for the earth and the sea! For the Devil has come down to you, and he is filled with rage, because he knows that he has only a little time left."

13 When the dragon realized that he had been thrown down to the earth, he began to pursue the woman who had given birth to the boy. 14 She was given the two wings of a large eagle in order to fly to her place in the desert, where she will be taken care of for three and a half years, safe from the dragon's attack. 15 And then from his mouth the dragon poured out a flood of water after the woman, so that it would carry her away. 16 But the earth helped the woman; it opened its mouth and swallowed the water that had come from the dragon's mouth. 17 The dragon was furious with the woman and went off to fight against the rest of her descendants, all those who obey God's commandments and are faithful to the truth revealed by Jesus. 18 And the dragon stood[e] on the seashore.

The Two Beasts

13 Then I saw a beast coming up out of the sea. It had ten horns and seven heads; on each of its horns there was a crown, and on each of its heads there was a name that was insulting to God. 2 The beast looked like a leopard, with feet like a bear's feet and a mouth like a lion's mouth. The dragon gave the beast his own power, his throne, and his vast authority. 3 One of the heads of the beast seemed to have been fatally wounded, but the wound had healed. The whole earth was amazed and followed the beast. 4 Everyone worshiped the dragon because he had given his authority to the beast. They worshiped the beast also, saying, "Who is like the beast? Who can fight against it?"

5 The beast was allowed to make proud claims which were insulting to God, and it was permitted to have authority for forty-two months. 6 It began to curse God, his name, the place where he lives, and all those who live in heaven. 7 It was allowed to fight against God's people and to defeat them, and it was given authority over every tribe, nation, language, and race. 8 All people living on earth will worship it, except those whose names were written before the creation of the world in the book of the

e And the dragon stood; *some manuscripts have* And I stood, *connecting this verse with what follows.*

living which belongs to the Lamb that was killed.

9 "Listen, then, if you have ears! 10 Whoever is meant to be captured will surely be captured; whoever is meant to be killed by the sword will surely be killed by the sword. This calls for endurance and faith on the part of God's people."

11 Then I saw another beast, which came up out of the earth. It had two horns like a lamb's horns, and it spoke like a dragon. 12 It used the vast authority of the first beast in its presence. It forced the earth and all who live on it to worship the first beast, whose wound had healed. 13 This second beast performed great miracles; it made fire come down out of heaven to earth in the sight of everyone. 14 And it deceived all the people living on earth by means of the miracles which it was allowed to perform in the presence of the first beast. The beast told them to build an image in honor of the beast that had been wounded by the sword and yet lived. 15 The second beast was allowed to breathe life into the image of the first beast, so that the image could talk and put to death all those who would not worship it. 16 The beast forced all the people, small and great, rich and poor, slave and free, to have a mark placed on their right hands or on their foreheads. 17 No one could buy or sell without this mark, that is, the beast's name or the number that stands for the name.

18 This calls for wisdom. Whoever is intelligent can figure out the meaning of the number of the beast, because the number stands for the name of someone. Its number is 666.

The Lamb and His People

14 Then I looked, and there was the Lamb standing on Mount Zion; with him were 144,000 people who have his name and his Father's name written on their foreheads. 2 And I heard a voice from heaven that sounded like a roaring waterfall, like a loud peal of thunder. It sounded like the music made by musicians playing their harps. 3 The 144,000 people stood before the throne, the four living creatures, and the elders; they were singing a new song, which only they could learn. Of the whole human race they are the only ones who have

been redeemed. 4 They are the men who have kept themselves pure by not having sexual relations with women; they are virgins. They follow the Lamb wherever he goes. They have been redeemed from the rest of the human race and are the first ones to be offered to God and to the Lamb. 5 They have never been known to tell lies; they are faultless.

The Three Angels

6 Then I saw another angel flying high in the air, with an eternal message of Good News to announce to the peoples of the earth, to every race, tribe, language, and nation. 7 He said in a loud voice, "Honor God and praise his greatness! For the time has come for him to judge all people. Worship him who made heaven, earth, sea, and the springs of water!"

8 A second angel followed the first one, saying, "She has fallen! Great Babylon has fallen! She made all peoples drink her wine—the strong wine of her immoral lust!"

9 A third angel followed the first two, saying in a loud voice, "Those who worship the beast and its image and receive the mark on their forehead or on their hand 10 will themselves drink God's wine, the wine of his fury, which he has poured at full strength into the cup of his anger! All who do this will be tormented in fire and sulfur before the holy angels and the Lamb. 11 The smoke of the fire that torments them goes up forever and ever. There is no relief day or night for those who worship the beast and its image, for anyone who has the mark of its name."

12 This calls for endurance on the part of God's people, those who obey God's commandments and are faithful to Jesus.

13 Then I heard a voice from heaven saying, "Write this: Happy are those who from now on die in the service of the Lord!"

"Yes indeed!" answers the Spirit. "They will enjoy rest from their hard work, because the results of their service go with them."

The Harvest of the Earth

14 Then I looked, and there was a white cloud, and sitting on the cloud was what looked like a human being, with a crown

of gold on his head and a sharp sickle in his hand. 15 Then another angel came out from the temple and cried out in a loud voice to the one who was sitting on the cloud, "Use your sickle and reap the harvest, because the time has come; the earth is ripe for the harvest!" 16 Then the one who sat on the cloud swung his sickle on the earth, and the earth's harvest was reaped.

17 Then I saw another angel come out of the temple in heaven, and he also had a sharp sickle.

18 Then another angel, who is in charge of the fire, came from the altar. He shouted in a loud voice to the angel who had the sharp sickle, "Use your sickle, and cut the grapes from the vineyard of the earth, because the grapes are ripe!" 19 So the angel swung his sickle on the earth, cut the grapes from the vine, and threw them into the wine press of God's furious anger. 20 The grapes were squeezed out in the wine press outside the city, and blood came out of the wine press in a flood two hundred miles long and about five feet deep.

The Angels with the Last Plagues

15 Then I saw in the sky another mysterious sight, great and amazing. There were seven angels with seven plagues, which are the last ones, because they are the final expression of God's anger.

2 Then I saw what looked like a sea of glass mixed with fire. I also saw those who had won the victory over the beast and its image and over the one whose name is represented by a number. They were standing by the sea of glass, holding harps that God had given them 3 and singing the song of Moses, the servant of God, and the song of the Lamb:

"Lord God Almighty,
  how great and wonderful are
    your deeds!
King of the nations,f
  how right and true are your
    ways!
4 Who will not stand in awe of you,
    Lord?
Who will refuse to declare your
    greatness?
You alone are holy.
All the nations will come

and worship you,
  because your just actions are
    seen by all."

5 After this I saw the temple in heaven open, with the Sacred Tent in it. 6 The seven angels who had the seven plagues came out of the temple, dressed in clean shining linen and with gold bands tied around their chests. 7 Then one of the four living creatures gave the seven angels seven gold bowls full of the anger of God, who lives forever and ever. 8 The temple was filled with smoke from the glory and power of God, and no one could go into the temple until the seven plagues brought by the seven angels had come to an end.

The Bowls of God's Anger

16 Then I heard a loud voice speaking from the temple to the seven angels: "Go and pour out the seven bowls of God's anger on the earth!"

2 The first angel went and poured out his bowl on the earth. Terrible and painful sores appeared on those who had the mark of the beast and on those who had worshiped its image.

3 Then the second angel poured out his bowl on the sea. The water became like the blood of a dead person, and every living creature in the sea died.

4 Then the third angel poured out his bowl on the rivers and the springs of water, and they turned into blood. 5 I heard the angel in charge of the waters say, "The judgments you have made are just, O Holy One, you who are and who were! 6 They poured out the blood of God's people and of the prophets, and so you have given them blood to drink. They are getting what they deserve!" 7 Then I heard a voice from the altar saying, "Lord God Almighty! True and just indeed are your judgments!"

8 Then the fourth angel poured out his bowl on the sun, and it was allowed to burn people with its fiery heat. 9 They were burned by the fierce heat, and they cursed the name of God, who has authority over these plagues. But they would not turn from their sins and praise his greatness.

10 Then the fifth angel poured out his bowl on the throne of the beast. Darkness fell over the beast's kingdom, and

people bit their tongues because of their pain, 11 and they cursed the God of heaven for their pains and sores. But they did not turn from their evil ways.

12 Then the sixth angel poured out his bowl on the great Euphrates River. The river dried up, to provide a way for the kings who come from the east. 13 Then I saw three unclean spirits that looked like frogs. They were coming out of the mouth of the dragon, the mouth of the beast, and the mouth of the false prophet. 14 They are the spirits of demons that perform miracles. These three spirits go out to all the kings of the world, to bring them together for the battle on the great Day of Almighty God.

15 "Listen! I am coming like a thief! Happy is he who stays awake and guards his clothes, so that he will not walk around naked and be ashamed in public!"

16 Then the spirits brought the kings together in the place that in Hebrew is called Armageddon.

17 Then the seventh angel poured out his bowl in the air. A loud voice came from the throne in the temple, saying, "It is done!" 18 There were flashes of lightning, rumblings and peals of thunder, and a terrible earthquake. There has never been such an earthquake since the creation of human beings; this was the worst earthquake of all! 19 The great city was split into three parts, and the cities of all countries were destroyed. God remembered great Babylon and made her drink the wine from his cup—the wine of his furious anger. 20 All the islands disappeared, all the mountains vanished. 21 Huge hailstones, each weighing as much as a hundred pounds, fell from the sky on people, who cursed God on account of the plague of hail, because it was such a terrible plague.

The Famous Prostitute

17 Then one of the seven angels who had the seven bowls came to me and said, "Come, and I will show you how the famous prostitute is to be punished, that great city that is built near many rivers. 2 The kings of the earth practiced sexual immorality with her, and the people of the world became drunk from drinking the wine of her immorality."

3 The Spirit took control of me, and the angel carried me to a desert. There I saw a woman sitting on a red beast that had names insulting to God written all over it; the beast had seven heads and ten horns. 4 The woman was dressed in purple and scarlet, and covered with gold ornaments, precious stones, and pearls. In her hand she held a gold cup full of obscene and filthy things, the result of her immorality. 5 On her forehead was written a name that has a secret meaning: "Great Babylon, the mother of all prostitutes and perverts in the world." 6 And I saw that the woman was drunk with the blood of God's people and the blood of those who were killed because they had been loyal to Jesus.

When I saw her, I was completely amazed. 7 "Why are you amazed?" the angel asked me. "I will tell you the secret meaning of the woman and of the beast that carries her, the beast with seven heads and ten horns. 8 That beast was once alive, but lives no longer; it is about to come up from the abyss and will go off to be destroyed. The people living on earth whose names have not been written before the creation of the world in the book of the living, will all be amazed as they look at the beast. It was once alive; now it no longer lives, but it will reappear.

9 "This calls for wisdom and understanding. The seven heads are seven hills, on which the woman sits. They are also seven kings: 10 five of them have fallen, one still rules, and the other one has not yet come; when he comes, he must rule only a little while. 11 And the beast that was once alive, but lives no longer, is itself an eighth king who is one of the seven and is going off to be destroyed.

12 "The ten horns you saw are ten kings who have not yet begun to rule, but who will be given authority to rule as kings for one hour with the beast. 13 These ten all have the same purpose, and they give their power and authority to the beast. 14 They will fight against the Lamb; but the Lamb, together with his called, chosen, and faithful followers, will defeat them, because he is Lord of lords and King of kings."

15 The angel also said to me, "The waters you saw, on which the prostitute sits, are nations, peoples, races, and

languages. 16 The ten horns you saw and the beast will hate the prostitute; they will take away everything she has and leave her naked; they will eat her flesh and destroy her with fire. 17 For God has placed in their hearts the will to carry out his purpose by acting together and giving to the beast their power to rule until God's words come true.

18 "The woman you saw is the great city that rules over the kings of the earth."

The Fall of Babylon

18 After this I saw another angel coming down out of heaven. He had great authority, and his splendor brightened the whole earth. 2 He cried out in a loud voice: "She has fallen! Great Babylon has fallen! She is now haunted by demons and unclean spirits; all kinds of filthy and hateful birds live in her. 3 For all the nations have drunk her wine—the strong wine of her immoral lust. The kings of the earth practiced sexual immorality with her, and the merchants of the world grew rich from her unrestrained lust."

4 Then I heard another voice from heaven, saying,

"Come out, my people! Come out from her!
You must not take part in her sins;
you must not share in her punishment!
5 For her sins are piled up as high as heaven,
and God remembers her wicked ways.
6 Treat her exactly as she has treated you;
pay her back double for all she has done.
Fill her cup with a drink twice as strong
as the drink she prepared for you.
7 Give her as much suffering and grief
as the glory and luxury she gave herself.
For she keeps telling herself:
'Here I sit, a queen!
I am no widow,
I will never know grief!'
8 Because of this, in one day she will be struck with plagues—

disease, grief, and famine.
And she will be burned with fire,
because the Lord God, who judges her, is mighty."

9 The kings of the earth who took part in her immorality and lust will cry and weep over the city when they see the smoke from the flames that consume her. 10 They stand a long way off, because they are afraid of sharing in her suffering. They say, "How terrible! This great and mighty city Babylon! In just one hour you have been punished!"

11 The merchants of the earth also cry and mourn for her, because no one buys their goods any longer; 12 no one buys their gold, silver, precious stones, and pearls; their goods of linen, purple cloth, silk, and scarlet cloth; all kinds of rare woods and all kinds of objects made of ivory and of expensive wood, of bronze, iron, and marble; 13 and cinnamon, spice, incense, myrrh, and frankincense; wine and oil, flour and wheat, cattle and sheep, horses and carriages, slaves, and even human lives. 14 The merchants say to her, "All the good things you longed to own have disappeared, and all your wealth and glamor are gone, and you will never find them again!" 15 The merchants, who became rich from doing business in that city, will stand a long way off, because they are afraid of sharing in her suffering. They will cry and mourn, 16 and say, "How terrible! How awful for the great city! She used to dress herself in linen, purple, and scarlet, and cover herself with gold ornaments, precious stones, and pearls! 17 And in one hour she has lost all this wealth!"

All the ships' captains and passengers, the sailors and all others who earn their living on the sea, stood a long way off, 18 and cried out as they saw the smoke from the flames that consumed her: "There never has been another city like this great city!" 19 They threw dust on their heads, they cried and mourned, saying, "How terrible! How awful for the great city! She is the city where all who have ships sailing the seas became rich on her wealth! And in one hour she has lost everything!"

20 Be glad, heaven, because of her destruction! Be glad, God's people and the

apostles and prophets! For God has condemned her for what she did to you!

21 Then a mighty angel picked up a stone the size of a large millstone and threw it into the sea, saying, "This is how the great city Babylon will be violently thrown down and will never be seen again. 22 The music of harps and of human voices, of players of the flute and the trumpet, will never be heard in you again! No workman in any trade will ever be found in you again; and the sound of the millstone will be heard no more! 23 Never again will the light of a lamp be seen in you; no more will the voices of brides and grooms be heard in you. Your merchants were the most powerful in all the world, and with your false magic you deceived all the peoples of the world!"

24 Babylon was punished because the blood of prophets and of God's people was found in the city; yes, the blood of all those who have been killed on earth.

19 After this I heard what sounded like the roar of a large crowd of people in heaven, saying, "Praise God! Salvation, glory, and power belong to our God! 2 True and just are his judgments! He has condemned the prostitute who was corrupting the earth with her immorality. God has punished her because she killed his servants." 3 Again they shouted, "Praise God! The smoke from the flames that consume the great city goes up forever and ever!" 4 The twenty-four elders and the four living creatures fell down and worshiped God, who was seated on the throne. They said, "Amen! Praise God!"

The Wedding Feast of the Lamb

5 Then there came from the throne the sound of a voice, saying, "Praise our God, all his servants and all people, both great and small, who have reverence for him!" 6 Then I heard what sounded like a crowd, like the sound of a roaring waterfall, like loud peals of thunder. I heard them say, "Praise God! For the Lord, our Almighty God, is King! 7 Let us rejoice and be glad; let us praise his greatness! For the time has come for the wedding of the Lamb, and his bride has prepared herself for it. 8 She has been given clean shining linen to wear." (The linen is the good deeds of God's people.)

9 Then the angel said to me, "Write this: Happy are those who have been invited to the wedding feast of the Lamb." And the angel added, "These are the true words of God."

10 I fell down at his feet to worship him, but he said to me, "Don't do it! I am a servant together with you and with other believers, all those who hold to the truth that Jesus revealed. Worship God!"

For the truth that Jesus revealed is what inspires the prophets.

The Rider on the White Horse

11 Then I saw heaven open, and there was a white horse. Its rider is called Faithful and True; it is with justice that he judges and fights his battles. 12 His eyes were like a flame of fire, and he wore many crowns on his head. He had a name written on him, but no one except himself knows what it is. 13 The robe he wore was covered with blood. His name is "The Word of God." 14 The armies of heaven followed him, riding on white horses and dressed in clean white linen. 15 Out of his mouth came a sharp sword, with which he will defeat the nations. He will rule over them with a rod of iron, and he will trample out the wine in the wine press of the furious anger of the Almighty God. 16 On his robe and on his thigh was written the name: "King of kings and Lord of lords."

17 Then I saw an angel standing on the sun. He shouted in a loud voice to all the birds flying in midair: "Come and gather together for God's great feast! 18 Come and eat the flesh of kings, generals, and soldiers, the flesh of horses and their riders, the flesh of all people, slave and free, great and small!"

19 Then I saw the beast and the kings of the earth and their armies gathered to fight against the one who was riding the horse and against his army. 20 The beast was taken prisoner, together with the false prophet who had performed miracles in his presence. (It was by those miracles that he had deceived those who had the mark of the beast and those who had worshiped the image of the beast.) The beast and the false prophet were both thrown alive into the lake of fire that burns with sulfur. 21 Their armies were killed by the sword that comes out of the mouth of the one who was riding

the horse; and all the birds ate all they could of their flesh.

The Thousand Years

20 Then I saw an angel coming down from heaven, holding in his hand the key of the abyss and a heavy chain. 2 He seized the dragon, that ancient serpent — that is, the Devil, or Satan — and chained him up for a thousand years. 3 The angel threw him into the abyss, locked it, and sealed it, so that he could not deceive the nations any more until the thousand years were over. After that he must be set loose for a little while.

4 Then I saw thrones, and those who sat on them were given the power to judge. I also saw the souls of those who had been executed because they had proclaimed the truth that Jesus revealed and the word of God. They had not worshiped the beast or its image, nor had they received the mark of the beast on their foreheads or their hands. They came to life and ruled as kings with Christ for a thousand years. 5 (The rest of the dead did not come to life until the thousand years were over.) This is the first raising of the dead. 6 Happy and greatly blessed are those who are included in this first raising of the dead. The second death has no power over them; they shall be priests of God and of Christ, and they will rule with him for a thousand years.

The Defeat of Satan

7 After the thousand years are over, Satan will be set loose from his prison, 8 and he will go out to deceive the nations scattered over the whole world, that is, Gog and Magog. Satan will bring them all together for battle, as many as the grains of sand on the seashore. 9 They spread out over the earth and surrounded the camp of God's people and the city that he loves. But fire came down from heaven and destroyed them. 10 Then the Devil, who deceived them, was thrown into the lake of fire and sulfur, where the beast and the false prophet had already been thrown; and they will be tormented day and night forever and ever.

The Final Judgment

11 Then I saw a great white throne and the one who sits on it. Earth and heaven fled from his presence and were seen no more. 12 And I saw the dead, great and small alike, standing before the throne. Books were opened, and then another book was opened, the book of the living. The dead were judged according to what they had done, as recorded in the books. 13 Then the sea gave up its dead. Death and the world of the dead also gave up the dead they held. And all were judged according to what they had done. 14 Then death and the world of the dead were thrown into the lake of fire. (This lake of fire is the second death.) 15 Those who did not have their name written in the book of the living were thrown into the lake of fire.

The New Heaven and the New Earth

21 Then I saw a new heaven and a new earth. The first heaven and the first earth disappeared, and the sea vanished. 2 And I saw the Holy City, the new Jerusalem, coming down out of heaven from God, prepared and ready, like a bride dressed to meet her husband. 3 I heard a loud voice speaking from the throne: "Now God's home is with people! He will live with them, and they shall be his people. God himself will be with them, and he will be their God. 4 He will wipe away all tears from their eyes. There will be no more death, no more grief or crying or pain. The old things have disappeared."

5 Then the one who sits on the throne said, "And now I make all things new!" He also said to me, "Write this, because these words are true and can be trusted." 6 And he said, "It is done! I am the first and the last, the beginning and the end. To anyone who is thirsty I will give the right to drink from the spring of the water of life without paying for it. 7 Those who win the victory will receive this from me: I will be their God, and they will be my children. 8 But cowards, traitors, perverts, murderers, the immoral, those who practice magic, those who worship idols, and all liars — the place for them is the lake burning with fire and sulfur, which is the second death."

The New Jerusalem

9 One of the seven angels who had the seven bowls full of the seven last plagues came to me and said, "Come, and I will show you the Bride, the wife of the Lamb." 10 The Spirit took control of me, and the angel carried me to the top of a very high mountain. He showed me Jerusalem, the Holy City, coming down out of heaven from God 11 and shining with the glory of God. The city shone like a precious stone, like a jasper, clear as crystal. 12 It had a great, high wall with twelve gates and with twelve angels in charge of the gates. On the gates were written the names of the twelve tribes of the people of Israel. 13 There were three gates on each side: three on the east, three on the south, three on the north, and three on the west. 14 The city's wall was built on twelve foundation stones on which were written the names of the twelve apostles of the Lamb. 15 The angel who spoke to me had a gold measuring stick to measure the city, its gates, and its wall. 16 The city was perfectly square, as wide as it was long. The angel measured the city with his measuring stick: it was fifteen hundred miles long and was as wide and as high as it was long. 17 The angel also measured the wall, and it was 216 feet high,g according to the standard unit of measure which he was using.h 18 The wall was made of jasper, and the city itself was made of pure gold, as clear as glass. 19 The foundation stones of the city wall were adorned with all kinds of precious stones. The first foundation stone was jasper, the second sapphire, the third agate, the fourth emerald, 20 the fifth onyx, the sixth carnelian, the seventh yellow quartz, the eighth beryl, the ninth topaz, the tenth chalcedony, the eleventh turquoise, the twelfth amethyst. 21 The twelve gates were twelve pearls; each gate was made from a single pearl. The street of the city was of pure gold, transparent as glass.

22 I did not see a temple in the city, because its temple is the Lord God Almighty and the Lamb. 23 The city has no need of the sun or the moon to shine on it, because the glory of God shines on it, and the Lamb is its lamp. 24 The peoples of the world will walk by its light, and the kings of the earth will bring their wealth into it. 25 The gates of the city will stand open all day; they will never be closed, because there will be no night there. 26 The greatness and the wealth of the nations will be brought into the city. 27 But nothing that is impure will enter the city, nor anyone who does shameful things or tells lies. Only those whose names are written in the Lamb's book of the living will enter the city.

22 The angel also showed me the river of the water of life, sparkling like crystal, and coming from the throne of God and of the Lamb 2 and flowing down the middle of the city's street. On each side of the river was the tree of life, which bears fruit twelve times a year, once each month; and its leaves are for the healing of the nations. 3 Nothing that is under God's curse will be found in the city.

The throne of God and of the Lamb will be in the city, and his servants will worship him. 4 They will see his face, and his name will be written on their foreheads. 5 There shall be no more night, and they will not need lamps or sunlight, because the Lord God will be their light, and they will rule as kings forever and ever.

The Coming of Jesus

6 Then the angel said to me, "These words are true and can be trusted. And the Lord God, who gives his Spirit to the prophets, has sent his angel to show his servants what must happen very soon."

7 "Listen!" says Jesus. "I am coming soon! Happy are those who obey the prophetic words in this book!"

8 I, John, have heard and seen all these things. And when I finished hearing and seeing them, I fell down at the feet of the angel who had shown me these things, and I was about to worship him. 9 But he said to me, "Don't do it! I am a servant together with you and with your brothers the prophets and of all those who obey the words in this book. Worship

---

g high; or thick.   h In verses 16 and 17 the Greek text speaks of "12,000 furlongs" and "144 cubits" which may have symbolic significance.

God!" 10 And he said to me, "Do not keep the prophetic words of this book a secret, because the time is near when all this will happen. 11 Whoever is evil must go on doing evil, and whoever is filthy must go on being filthy; whoever is good must go on doing good, and whoever is holy must go on being holy."

12 "Listen!" says Jesus. "I am coming soon! I will bring my rewards with me, to give to each one according to what he has done. 13 I am the first and the last, the beginning and the end."

14 Happy are those who wash their robes clean and so have the right to eat the fruit from the tree of life and to go through the gates into the city. 15 But outside the city are the perverts and those who practice magic, the immoral and the murderers, those who worship idols and those who are liars both in words and deeds.

16 "I, Jesus, have sent my angel to announce these things to you in the churches. I am descended from the family of David; I am the bright morning star."

17 The Spirit and the Bride say, "Come!"

Everyone who hears this must also say, "Come!"

Come, whoever is thirsty; accept the water of life as a gift, whoever wants it.

Conclusion

18 I, John, solemnly warn everyone who hears the prophetic words of this book: if any add anything to them, God will add to their punishment the plagues described in this book. 19 And if any take anything away from the prophetic words of this book, God will take away from them their share of the fruit of the tree of life and of the Holy City, which are described in this book.

20 He who gives his testimony to all this says, "Yes indeed! I am coming soon!"

So be it. Come, Lord Jesus!

21 May the grace of the Lord Jesus be with everyone.i

i everyone; *some manuscripts have* God's people; *others have* all of God's people.

Word List

WORD LIST

This Word List identifies many objects or cultural features whose meaning may not be known to all readers.

Abib The first month of the Hebrew calendar, corresponding to the period from about mid-March to about mid-April. This month is also called Nisan.

Abyss The place in the depths of the earth where the demons were imprisoned until their final punishment.

Acacia A flowering tree, a type of mimosa, with hard and durable wood.

Adar The twelfth month of the Hebrew calendar, corresponding to the period from about mid-February to about mid-March.

Agate A semiprecious stone of various colors, but usually white and brown.

Alabaster A soft stone of usually light creamy color, from which vases and jars were made.

Aloes A sweet-smelling substance, derived from a plant. It was used medicinally and as a perfume.

Amen A Hebrew word which means "it is so" or "may it be so." It can also be translated "certainly," "truly," or "surely." In Revelation 3.14 it is used as a title for Christ.

Amethyst A semiprecious stone, usually purple or violet in color.

Anoint To pour or rub olive oil on someone in order to honor him or to appoint him to some special work. The Israelite kings were anointed as a sign of their taking office, and so the king could be called "the anointed one." In a figurative sense, "The Anointed One" is the title of the one whom God chose and appointed as Savior and Lord.

Apostle Principally one of the group of twelve men whom Jesus chose to be his special followers and helpers. It is also used in the New Testament to refer to Paul and other Christian workers. The word may have the sense of "messenger."

Areopagus A hill in Athens where the city council used to meet. For this reason the council itself was called Areopagus, even after it no longer met on the hill.

Artemis The Greek name of an ancient goddess of fertility, worshiped especially in Asia Minor.

Asherah A goddess of fertility worshiped by the Canaanites; her male counterpart was Baal. After the Hebrews invaded Canaan, many of them began worshiping these two gods.

Astarte A goddess of fertility and war who was widely worshiped in the ancient Near East.

Atonement, Day of The most important of Israel's holy days, when the High Priest would offer sacrifice for the sins of the people of Israel (Leviticus 16). It was held on the 10th day of the seventh month of the Hebrew calendar (around October 1). The Jewish name for this day is Yom Kippur.

Baal The god of fertility worshiped by the Canaanites; his female counterpart was Asherah. After the Hebrews invaded Canaan, many of them began worshiping these two gods.

Baal-of-the-Covenant A name by which the god Baal was known by the people of Shechem.

Balsam A tree from which sweet-smelling resin was obtained; the resin was used for perfume and medicine.

Barley A cultivated grain similar to wheat, grown as a food crop.

Beelzebul A New Testament name given to the Devil as the chief of the evil spirits.

Beryl A semiprecious stone, usually green or bluish green in color.

Breastplate Part of a soldier's armor, made of leather or metal; it covered the chest and sometimes the back as a protection against arrows and the blows of a sword.

Bul The eighth month of the Hebrew calendar, corresponding to the period from about mid-October to about mid-November.

Burnt offering A type of sacrifice in which all the parts of the animal were completely burned on the altar; in other sacrifices only certain parts of the animal were burned.

Calamus A sweet-smelling reed-like plant.

Capital The top part of a column supporting a roof.

Carnelian A semiprecious stone, usually red in color.

Cassia A spice made from the bark of a tree; it closely resembles cinnamon.

Chalcedony A semiprecious stone, usually milky or gray in color.

Christ Originally a title, the Greek equivalent of the Hebrew word "Messiah." It means "the anointed one." Jesus was called the Christ because he was the one whom God chose and sent as Savior and Lord.

Circumcise To cut off the foreskin of the penis. As a sign of God's covenant with his people Israelite boys were circumcised eight days after they were born (Genesis 17.9-14).

Concubine A servant woman who, although not a wife, had sexual relations with her master. She had important legal rights, and her master was referred to as her husband.

Coral A brightly colored stony substance found in the sea; it was used as jewelry.

Council The supreme religious court of the Jews, composed of seventy leaders of the Jewish people and presided over by the High Priest.

Covenant An agreement, either between persons or between God and a person or a people. God made a covenant with Noah (Genesis 9.8-17) and with Abraham (Genesis 17.1-8), but in the Old Testament the term usually refers to the covenant made between God and the people of Israel at the time of Moses (Exodus 24.4-8).

Covenant Box The wooden chest covered with gold, in which were kept the two stone tablets on which were written the Ten Commandments. It has traditionally been called the Ark of the Covenant.

Cumin A small plant whose seeds are ground up and used for seasoning foods.

Cush The term "Cush" in the Old Testament Hebrew text normally designates the territory extending south from the First Cataract of the Nile River at Aswan. It was known in Graeco-Roman times as Ethiopia (Gk., *Aithiopia*), and later as Nubia. This extensive region included within its borders most of modern Sudan and some of present-day Ethiopia (Abyssinia). In Genesis 10, the Table of Nations, verses 8-12 are included under the genealogy of Egyptian Cush, yet all the peoples named are in Mesopotamia. Apparently the Hebrew designation for the Babylonian Kassites was "Cush" as well, thus resulting in the mixing of the two regions. Genesis 2.13 may be another reference to Babylonian Cush.

Cymbals A pair of thin pieces of metal held in the hands and struck together rhythmically in music.

David's City In the Old Testament the reference is generally to that part of the city of Jerusalem which was captured from the Jebusites by King David. In the New Testament the reference is to the town of Bethlehem, David's boyhood home, where Jesus was born.

Dedication, Festival of The Jewish festival, lasting eight days, which celebrated the restoration and rededication in 165 B.C. of the Temple altar by the Jewish patriot Judas Maccabeus. The festival began on the 25th day of the month Kislev (around December 10). The Jewish name for this festival is Hanukkah.

Defile To make ritually unclean or impure. Certain foods and practices were prohibited by the Law of Moses because they were thought to make a person ritually or ceremonially unclean. Such a person could not take part in the public worship until he had performed certain rituals which would remove the defilement.

Demon An evil spirit with the power to harm people; it was regarded as a messenger and servant of the Devil.

Dill A small garden plant whose stems, leaves, and seeds are used for seasoning food.

Dipper: Big Dipper and **Little Dipper** Two groups of stars which in the Northern Hemisphere are visible in the northern sky. The star at the end of the "handle" of the Little Dipper is Polaris, the North Star.

Disciple A person who follows and learns from someone else. In the New Testament the word is used of the followers of John the Baptist and especially of the followers of Jesus, particularly the twelve apostles.

Divination The attempt to discover a message from God or the gods by examining such things as marked stones or the liver of a sacrificed animal.

Dragon A legendary beast, thought to be like a huge lizard. It is also called a serpent and appears as a figure of the Devil (Revelation 12.3—13.4; 20.2, 3).

Elders In the Old Testament this is a name given to certain respected leaders of a tribe, nation, or city. In the New Testament three different groups are called elders: (1) in the Gospels the elders are influential Jewish religious leaders, some of whom were members of the supreme Council; (2) in Acts 11—21 and the Letters the elders are Christian church officers who had general responsibility for the work of the church; (3) in Revelation the twenty-four elders are part of God's court in heaven, perhaps as representatives of God's people.

Elul The sixth month of the Hebrew calendar, corresponding to the period from about mid-August to about mid-September.

Ephod The Hebrew term traditionally transliterated as "ephod" is of uncertain meaning in a number of contexts. Generally it refers to some type of priestly garment which was worn over the shoulder by the High Priest and with which the Urim and Thummim were associated. In certain contexts, however, the Hebrew term refers to an object of worship, and in some other passages, it evidently refers to an object used to foretell future events.

Epicureans Those who followed the teaching of Epicurus (died 270 B.C.), a Greek philosopher who taught that happiness is the highest good in life.

Epileptic A person who suffers from a nervous disease causing convulsions and fainting.

Ethanim The seventh month of the Hebrew calendar, corresponding to the period from about mid-September to about mid-October; it was later called Tishri.

Ethiopia See "Cush."

Eunuch A man who has been made physically incapable of having normal sexual relations. Eunuchs were often important officials in the courts of ancient kings, and the term may have come to be used of such officials in general, regardless of their sexual condition.

Fast To go without food for a while as a religious duty.

Feldspar A colorful, rather hard rock, often glassy in appearance.

Fellowship offerings A type of sacrifice offered to insure a right relationship with God. Only a portion of the animal was burned on the altar; the rest was eaten by the worshipers or the priests.

Flax A small cultivated plant; the fibers of its stem are spun into thread used in making linen cloth.

Frankincense A valuable incense, made from the sap of a certain tree. This incense was probably imported from Arabia.

Garnet A semiprecious stone, usually red in color.

Gazelle A kind of antelope, known for its beauty and gracefulness.

Gentile A person who is not a Jew.

Hades The Greek name used in the New Testament to refer to the world of the dead.

Harrow A farm implement used to break up the ground and level it after plowing.

Harvest Festival The Israelite festival celebrating the wheat harvest, held in the latter part of May, fifty days after Passover. The Jewish name for this festival is Shavuoth (the Feast of Weeks). It has also been called Pentecost.

Hermes The name of a Greek god who served as messenger of the gods.

Herod's party A political party in New Testament times composed of Jews who favored being ruled by one of the descendants of Herod the Great rather than by the Roman governor.

High Priest The priest who occupied the highest office in the Jewish priestly system and was president of the supreme Council of the Jews. Once a year (on the Day of Atonement) he would enter the Most Holy Place in the Temple and offer sacrifice for himself and for the sins of the people of Israel.

Hyssop A small bushy plant, used in religious ceremonies to sprinkle liquids.

Incense Material which is burned in order to produce a pleasant smell. The Israelites used it in their worship.

Jackal A small wild animal resembling a fox.

Jasper A semiprecious stone of various colors. The jasper mentioned in the Bible was probably green, or else clear.

Javelin A short, light spear used by soldiers in ancient times.

Kislev The ninth month of the Hebrew calendar, corresponding to the period from about mid-November to about mid-December.

Law The name which the Jews applied to the first five books of the Old Testament, also called "The Books of Moses." Sometimes, however, the name is applied in a more general way to the entire Old Testament.

Leviathan A legendary animal associated with water, in some passages identified by some scholars as the crocodile. In a figurative sense it may represent the chaos that existed before God created the world (Isaiah 27.1; Psalm 74.14).

Levite (1) A member of the tribe of Levi; (2) a man who assisted the priest in the performance of religious duties.

Levitical priest A Hebrew priest descended from the tribe of Levi. All priests were supposed to be members of the tribe of Levi, but in later times not all members of the tribe of Levi were priests.

Living creatures (also referred to as "winged creatures" and traditionally called "cherubim") symbols of God's majesty and associated with his presence. For a description of such creatures see Exodus 25.18-20; Ezekiel 1.5-13; 10; Revelation 4.6-9.

Lord in this translation represents the Hebrew name Yahweh (traditionally represented by Jehovah), corresponding either to the occurrence of the name itself or to a pronoun standing for the name.

Lyre A kind of harp.

Mandrake A small plant; it was believed that eating its root or fruit would make a woman more easily able to have children.

Manna A food eaten by the Israelites during their travels in the wilderness. It was white and flaky and looked like small seeds (Exodus 16.14-21; Numbers 11.7-9).

Medium A person who believes that he or she can communicate with the dead.

Messiah A Hebrew title (meaning "the anointed one") given to the promised Savior, whose coming was foretold by the Hebrew prophets; the corresponding Greek term "the Christ" has the same meaning.

Mildew A fungus that appears on various objects, especially in damp weather.

Millet A cultivated grain that was grown as a food crop.

Molech One of the gods of the ancient people of Canaan.

Most Holy Place The innermost room of the Tent of the LORD's presence or the Temple. The Covenant Box was kept there. Only the High Priest could enter the Most Holy Place, and he did so only once a year, on the Day of Atonement.

Mustard A large plant which grows from a very small seed. The seeds were ground into powder and used as spice on food.

Myrrh A sweet-smelling resin that was highly prized. It served as a medicine (Mark 15.23) and was used by the Jews in preparing bodies for burial (John 19.39).

Myrtle A kind of evergreen shrub or tree.

Nard An expensive perfume made from a plant.

Nazarene Someone from the town of Nazareth. The name was used as a title for Jesus and also as a name for the early Christians (Acts 24.5).

Nazirite A person who took a special vow of self-dedication. Such a person was not to drink beer or wine, cut his hair, or touch a dead body (Numbers 6.1-21). The vow could be taken for a certain period of time, but some persons were dedicated to God as Nazirites from their birth.

New Moon Festival A religious observance held by the Israelites on the day of each new moon.

New Year Festival The Jewish name for this festival is "Rosh Hashanah."

Nisan The first month of the Hebrew calendar, corresponding to the period from about mid-March to about mid-April. The month is also called Abib.

Onyx A semiprecious stone of various colors.

Orion A group of prominent stars visible during winter evenings.

Outcasts In the Gospels this name, which in many translations appears as "sinners," refers to those Jews who had been excluded from synagogue worship because they violated rules about foods that should not be eaten and about associating with people who were not Jews. Such outcasts were despised by

many of their fellow Jews, and Jesus was criticized for associating with them (Mark 2.15-17; Luke 7.34; 15.1, 2).

Parable A story which teaches spiritual truth; it was often used by Jesus.

Paradise A name for heaven (Luke 23.43; 2 Corinthians 12.3).

Paralytic Someone who suffers from a disease that prevents him from moving part or all of his body.

Passover The Israelite festival, on the 14th day of the month Nisan (around April 1), which celebrated the deliverance of the ancient Hebrews from their captivity in Egypt. The Angel of Death killed the firstborn in the Egyptian homes but passed over the Hebrew homes (Exodus 12.23-27). The Jewish name for this festival is Pesach.

Pentecost, Day of The Greek name for the Israelite festival of wheat harvest (see Harvest Festival). The name Pentecost (meaning "fiftieth") comes from the fact that the feast was held fifty days after Passover.

Pervert One who commits unnatural sexual acts.

Pharisees A Jewish religious party during the time of Jesus. They were strict in obeying the Law of Moses and other regulations which had been added to it through the centuries.

Pistachio nut A small greenish nut.

Pleiades A small group of stars visible during winter evenings.

Pomegranate A reddish fruit about the size of a large apple; it has a hard rind and is full of tasty seeds.

Preparation, Day of The sixth day of the week (Friday), on which the Jews made the required preparations to observe the Sabbath (Saturday).

Prophet A person who proclaims a message from God. The term usually refers to certain men in the Old Testament, but the New Testament speaks of prophets in the early church. John the Baptist is also called a prophet.

Purim The Jewish religious holiday

held on the 14th day of the month Adar (around March 1), celebrating the deliverance of the Jews from Haman by Esther and Mordecai. The story is told in the book of Esther.

Quartz A semiprecious stone of various colors, but usually clear.

Rabbi A Hebrew word which means "my teacher."

Red Sea Evidently referred originally to (1) a series of lakes and marshes between the head of the Gulf of Suez and the Mediterranean, the region generally regarded as the site of the events described in Exodus 13, and was also used to designate (2) the Gulf of Suez, (3) the Gulf of Aqaba.

Rephan The name of an ancient god that was worshiped as the ruler of the planet Saturn.

Resin A fragrant, gummy substance produced from the sap of certain trees and shrubs.

Restoration, Year of The year, coming every fifty years, when the ancient Israelites returned to the original owner any property they were holding, freed their Israelite slaves, and did not cultivate their fields.

Sabbath The seventh day of the Jewish week (from sundown on Friday to sundown on Saturday), a holy day on which no work was permitted.

Sackcloth A coarse cloth made of goats' hair, which was worn as a sign of mourning or distress.

Sadducees A small Jewish religious party in New Testament times, composed largely of priests. They based their beliefs primarily on the first five books of the Old Testament and differed in several matters of belief and practice from the larger party of the Pharisees.

Samaritan A name used to refer to a native of Samaria, the region between Judea and Galilee. Because of differences in politics, race, customs, and religion (including especially the central place of worship), there was much bad feeling between the Jews and the Samaritans.

Sanctuary A building dedicated to the worship of God. Sometimes the word refers to the central place of worship and not to the whole building.

Sapphire A very valuable stone, usually blue in color.

Scepter A short rod held by kings to symbolize their authority.

Scorpion A small creature which has eight legs and a long tail with a poisonous sting. It can inflict a very painful, and sometimes fatal, wound.

Scribe A person whose business it was to write documents for others or to copy written material. Some scribes were employed by ancient kings to prepare official documents, and some of them became important officials.

Scriptures In the New Testament the word refers to the collected body of Hebrew sacred writings, known to Christians as the Old Testament. Various names are used: the Law (or the Law of Moses) and the prophets (Matthew 5.17; 7.12; Luke 2.22; 24.44; Acts 13.15; 28.23); the Holy Scriptures (Romans 1.2; 2 Timothy 3.15); the old covenant (2 Corinthians 3.14). The singular "scripture" refers to a single passage of the Old Testament.

Serpent A name given to the dragon, which appears in the New Testament as a figure of the Devil (Revelation 12.3-17; 20.2, 3).

Seventh year The year, coming every seventh year, when the ancient Israelites did not cultivate their fields and when debts were canceled.

Shebat The eleventh month of the Hebrew calendar, corresponding to the period from about mid-January to about mid-February.

Shelters, Festival of A joyous festival celebrated by the Israelites in the fall after the completion of the harvest. In order to help them remember the years when their ancestors wandered through the wilderness, the Israelites constructed rough shelters to live in during the festival. The Jewish name for this festival is Sukkoth. It has been traditionally called the Feast of Tabernacles or the Feast of Booths.

Sickle A tool consisting of a curved

metal blade and a wooden handle, used for cutting wheat and other crops.

Sivan The third month of the Hebrew calendar, corresponding to the period from about mid-May to about mid-June.

Snuffer The Hebrew word translated "snuffer" apparently identifies an implement used to trim the oil lamps used in the Tent of the LORD's presence or the Temple.

Sorcerer A person who works magic for evil purposes.

Stoics Those who followed the teachings of the Greek philosopher Zeno (died 265 B.C.), who taught that happiness is to be found in being free from pleasure and pain.

Sulfur In the Bible this refers to a sulfur compound which burns with great heat and produces an unpleasant smell.

Synagogue A place where Jews met every Sabbath day for their public worship. It probably also served as a center for Jewish social life and a school for Jewish children.

Tambourine A small drum with pieces of metal in the rim, held in the hand and shaken. In biblical times it was generally used by women.

Tassel A group of threads or cords, fastened together at one end and loose at the other. The Israelites were commanded to wear these on their clothes (Numbers 15.37-41).

Teachers of the Law Men who in New Testament times taught and interpreted the teachings of the Old Testament, especially the first five books.

Tebeth The tenth month of the Hebrew calendar, corresponding to the period from about mid-December to about mid-January.

Tenant A man who grows crops on land owned by someone else, and turns over a part of the harvest to the owner to pay for the use of his land.

Tent of the LORD's presence The large tent described in detail in Exodus 26, where the Israelites worshiped God until Solomon built the Temple.

It has traditionally been called the Tabernacle or Tent of meeting.

Tithe A tenth part of a person's produce or income, given for religious purposes.

Topaz A semiprecious stone, usually yellow in color.

Turban A head covering worn by men, made of cloth wrapped around the head.

Turquoise A semiprecious stone, blue or bluish green in color.

Unleavened Bread, Festival of The Israelite festival, lasting seven days after Passover; it also celebrated the deliverance of the ancient Hebrews from Egypt. The name came from the practice of not using leaven (yeast) in making bread during that week (Exodus 12.14-20). It was held from the 15th to the 22nd day of the month Nisan (around the first week of April).

Urim and Thummim Two small objects used by Israelite priests to determine God's will.

Vow A strong declaration or promise, usually made while calling upon God to punish the speaker if the statement should prove to be not true or if the promise were not kept.

Winged creatures (also referred to as "living creatures" and traditionally called "cherubim") symbols of God's majesty and associated with his presence. For a description of such creatures see Exodus 25.18-20; Ezekiel 1.5-13; 10; Revelation 4.6-9.

Winnowing shovel A tool like a shovel or a large fork, used to separate the wheat from the chaff.

Wreath Flowers or leaves arranged in a circle, to be placed on a person's head. In ancient times a wreath of leaves was the prize given to winners in athletic contests.

Yeast A substance, also called leaven, which is added to dough made from the flour of wheat or barley to make it rise before being baked into bread.

Yoke A heavy bar of wood fitted over

the necks of two oxen to make it possible for them to pull a plow or a cart. The word is used figuratively to describe the moral lessons that a teacher passes on to his pupils.

Zeus The name of the supreme god of the Greeks.

Zion Originally a designation for "David's City," the Jebusite stronghold captured by King David's forces. The term "Zion" was later extended in meaning to refer to the hill on which the Temple stood.

Ziv The second month of the Hebrew calendar, corresponding to the period from about mid-April to about mid-May.

Chronology of the Bible

CHRONOLOGY OF THE BIBLE

DATE   Time scales represent varied number of years.
   B.C. = Before Christ
   c. = circa (around)*

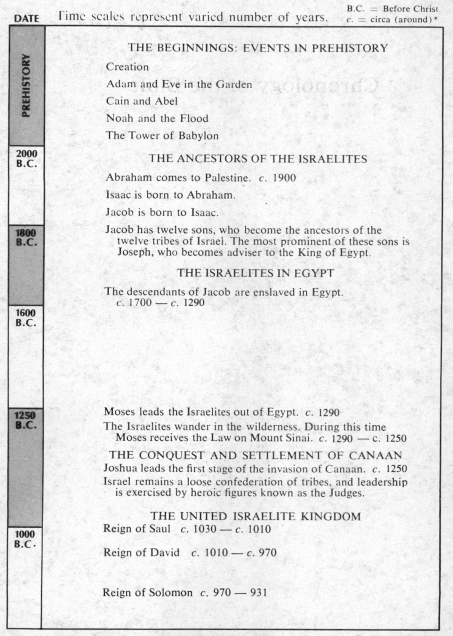

PREHISTORY

THE BEGINNINGS: EVENTS IN PREHISTORY

Creation

Adam and Eve in the Garden

Cain and Abel

Noah and the Flood

The Tower of Babylon

2000 B.C.

THE ANCESTORS OF THE ISRAELITES

Abraham comes to Palestine. *c.* 1900

Isaac is born to Abraham.

Jacob is born to Isaac.

1800 B.C.

Jacob has twelve sons, who become the ancestors of the twelve tribes of Israel. The most prominent of these sons is Joseph, who becomes adviser to the King of Egypt.

THE ISRAELITES IN EGYPT

The descendants of Jacob are enslaved in Egypt. *c.* 1700 — *c.* 1290

1600 B.C.

1250 B.C.

Moses leads the Israelites out of Egypt. *c.* 1290

The Israelites wander in the wilderness. During this time Moses receives the Law on Mount Sinai. *c.* 1290 — *c.* 1250

THE CONQUEST AND SETTLEMENT OF CANAAN

Joshua leads the first stage of the invasion of Canaan. *c.* 1250

Israel remains a loose confederation of tribes, and leadership is exercised by heroic figures known as the Judges.

THE UNITED ISRAELITE KINGDOM

Reign of Saul   *c.* 1030 — *c.* 1010

1000 B.C.

Reign of David   *c.* 1010 — *c.* 970

Reign of Solomon   *c.* 970 — 931

*A circa date is only an approximation. Generally speaking, the earlier the time, the less precise is the dating. From the time of the death of Solomon in 931 B.C. to the Edict of Cyrus in 538 B.C., the dates given are fairly accurate, but even in this epoch a possible error of a year or two must be allowed for.

CHRONOLOGY OF THE BIBLE

DATE

950 B.C.

THE TWO ISRAELITE KINGDOMS

JUDAH (Southern Kingdom)	ISRAEL (Northern Kingdom)
Kings	*Kings*
Rehoboam 931-913	Jeroboam 931-910
Abijah 913-911	Nadab 910-909

900 B.C.

Asa 911-870	Baasha 909-886

Jehoshaphat 870-848	*Prophets*	Elah 886-885
		Zimri 7 days in 885
		Omri 885-874
	Elijah	Ahab 874-853

850 B.C.

Jehoram 848-841	Ahaziah 853-852
Ahaziah 841	Joram 852-841
Queen Athaliah 841-835	Jehu 841-814
	Elisha
Joash 835-796	Jehoahaz 814-798

800 B.C.

Amaziah 796-781	Jehoash 798-783
Uzziah 781-740	Jeroboam II 783-743

Jonah
Amos

750 B.C.

Jotham 740-736	Zechariah 6 mo. in 743
	Shallum 1 mo. in 743
Ahaz 736-716	Menahem 743-738
Hosea	Pekahiah 738-737
Micah Isaiah	Pekah 737-732
Hezekiah 716-687	Hoshea 732-723
	Fall of Samaria 722

700 B.C.

THE LAST YEARS OF THE KINGDOM OF JUDAH

Manasseh 687-642

650 B.C.

Amon 642-640

Josiah 640-609

Joahaz 3 mo. in 609

Prophets

Zephaniah

Nahum

Jehoiakim 609-598

Jeremiah

Habakkuk?

600 B.C.

Jehoiachin 3 mo. in 598

Zedekiah 598-587

Ezekiel

Fall of Jerusalem July 587 or 586

CHRONOLOGY OF THE BIBLE

DATE	
550 B.C.	**THE EXILE AND THE RESTORATION** The Jews taken into exile in Babylonia after the fall of Jerusalem Persian rule begins. 539 *Prophets* Edict of Cyrus allows Jews to return. 538 Haggai Zechariah Foundations of New Temple laid. 520 Obadiah Daniel Restoration of the walls of Jerusalem Malachi 445-443 Joel?

400 B.C.	**THE TIME BETWEEN THE TESTAMENTS**
	Alexander the Great establishes Greek rule in Palestine. 333
	
	Palestine is ruled by the Ptolemies, descendants of one of
	     Alexander's generals, who had been given the position of
	     ruler over Egypt. 323 to 198

200 B.C.	Palestine is ruled by the Seleucids, descendants of one of
	     Alexander's generals, who had acquired the rule of
	     Syria. 198 to 166
	
	Jewish revolt under Judas Maccabeus reestablishes Jewish
	     independence. Palestine is ruled by Judas' family and
	     descendants, the Hasmoneans. 166 to 63
	
	The Roman general Pompey takes Jerusalem 63 B.C.
	     Palestine is ruled by puppet kings appointed by Rome. One of
	     these is Herod the Great, who rules from 37 B.C. to 4 B.C.
	THE TIME OF THE NEW TESTAMENT

A.D. 1	Birth of Jesus*
	Ministry of John the Baptist; baptism of Jesus and beginning of his public ministry
A.D. 30	Death and resurrection of Jesus Conversion of Paul (Saul of Tarsus) *c.* A.D. 37 Ministry of Paul *c.* A.D. 41 to A.D. 65 Final imprisonment of Paul *c.* A.D. 65

*The present era was calculated to begin with the birth of Jesus Christ, that is, in A.D. 1 (A.D. standing for *Anno Domini* 'in the year of the Lord'). However, the original calculation was later found to be wrong by a few years, so that the birth of Christ took place perhaps about 6 B.C.

Maps

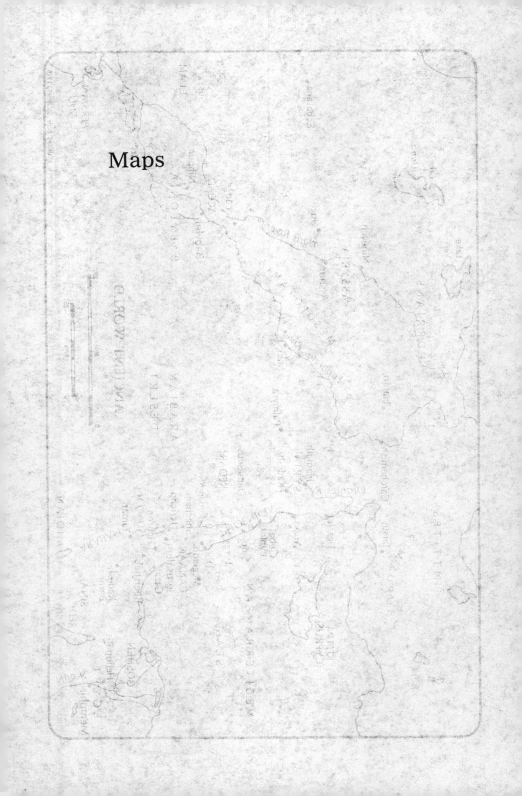

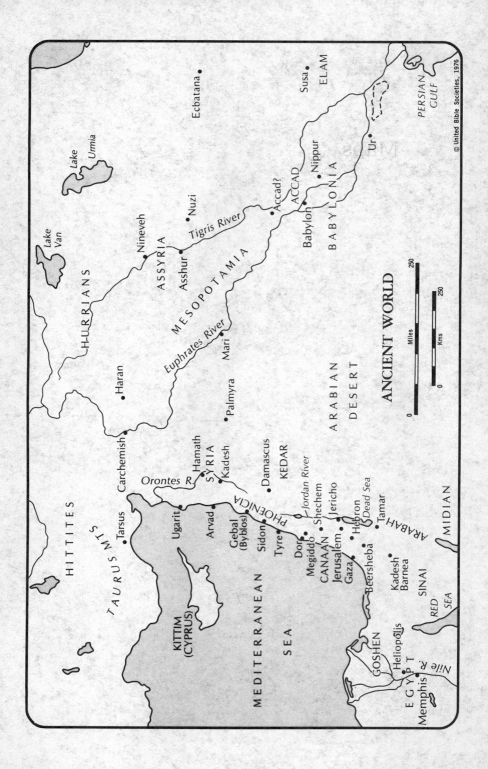

ANCIENT WORLD

© United Bible Societies, 1976

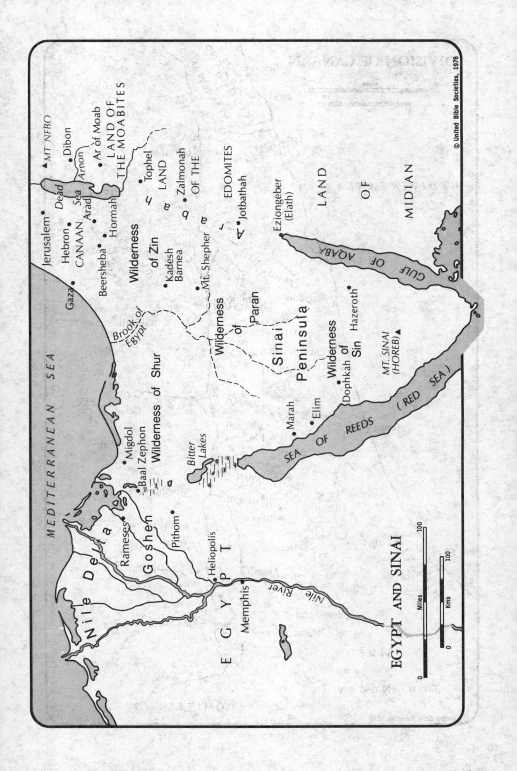

EGYPT AND SINAI

© United Bible Societies, 1976

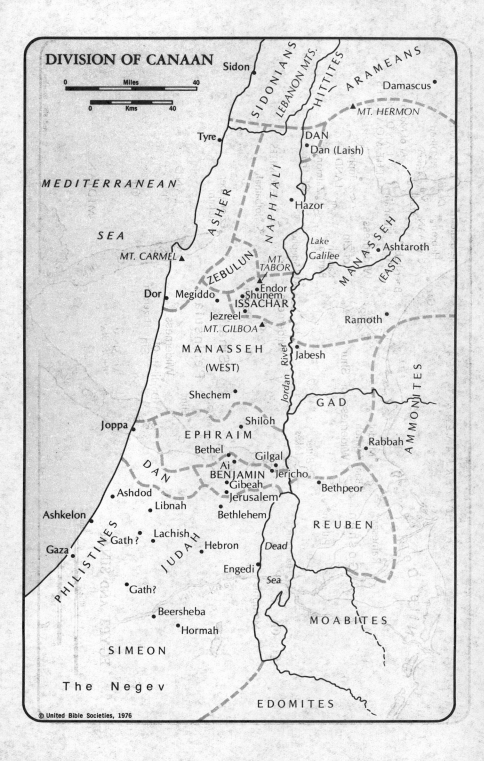

DIVISION OF CANAAN

0 Miles 40
0 Kms 40

Sidon

SIDONIANS
LEBANON MTS.
HITTITES
ARAMEANS
Damascus

MT. HERMON

Tyre

DAN
Dan (Laish)

MEDITERRANEAN

ASHER

NAPHTALI

Hazor

SEA

MT. CARMEL ▲

Lake
Galilee

MANASSEH
(EAST)

Ashtaroth

ZEBULUN

MT.
TABOR ▲

Dor

Megiddo

Endor
Shunem
ISSACHAR

Jezreel
MT. GILBOA ▲

Ramoth

MANASSEH

(WEST)

Jordan River

Jabesh

Shechem

GAD

AMMONITES

Joppa

Shiloh

EPHRAIM

Bethel

Gilgal

DAN

Ai
BENJAMIN
Gibeah
Jerusalem

Jericho

Rabbah

Bethpeor

Ashdod

Libnah

Bethlehem

Ashkelon

Gath?

Lachish

JUDAH

Hebron

REUBEN

Gaza

Dead

PHILISTINES

Gath?

Engedi

Sea

Beersheba

Hormah

SIMEON

MOABITES

The Negev

EDOMITES

© United Bible Societies, 1976

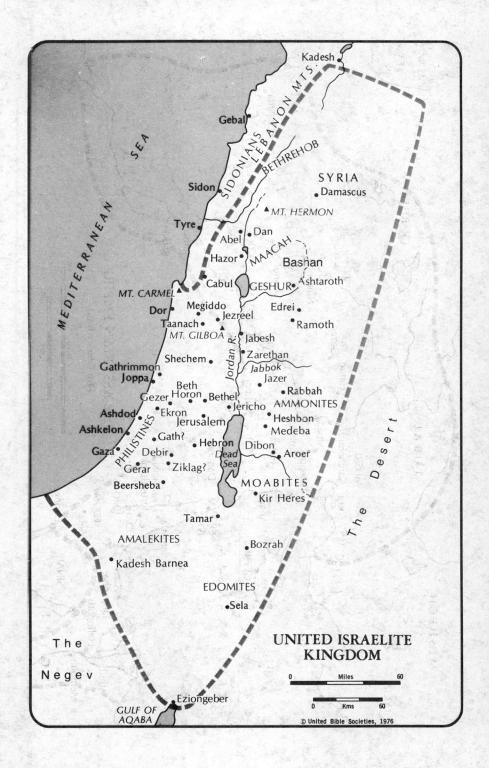

UNITED ISRAELITE
KINGDOM

© United Bible Societies, 1976

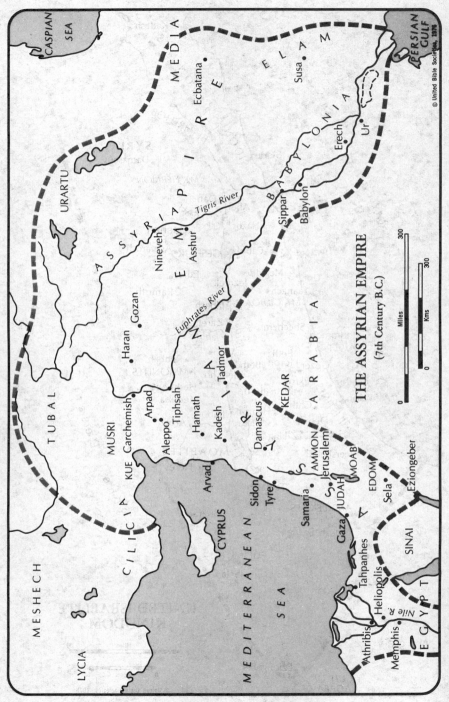

THE ASSYRIAN EMPIRE
(7th Century B.C.)

© United Bible Societies, 1976

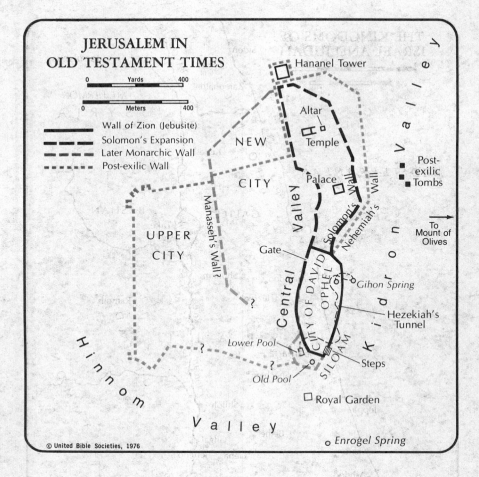

JERUSALEM IN OLD TESTAMENT TIMES

0 Yards 400
0 Meters 400

—— Wall of Zion (Jebusite)
– – Solomon's Expansion
– – Later Monarchic Wall
····· Post-exilic Wall

Hananel Tower

NEW CITY

Altar
Temple
Palace

Solomon's Wall

Nehemiah's Wall

Manasseh's Wall?

UPPER CITY

Central Valley

Gate

CITY OF DAVID

OPHEL

Gihon Spring

Hezekiah's Tunnel

Kidron Valley

To Mount of Olives

Post-exilic Tombs

Lower Pool
?
?
Old Pool

SILOAM

Steps

Royal Garden

Hinnom Valley

Enrogel Spring

© United Bible Societies, 1976

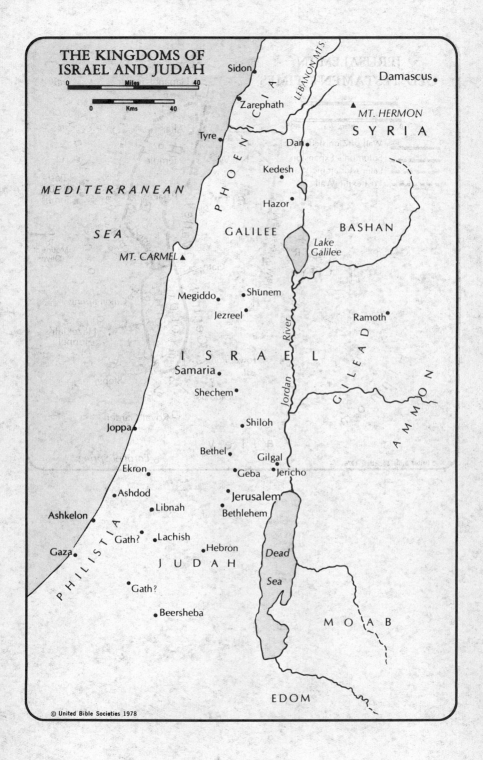

THE KINGDOMS OF ISRAEL AND JUDAH

Miles 0 — 40

Kms 0 — 40

MEDITERRANEAN

SEA

MT. CARMEL ▲

Sidon

Zarephath

Tyre

PHOENICIA

LEBANON MTS.

Damascus

MT. HERMON ▲

SYRIA

Dan

Kedesh

Hazor

GALILEE

BASHAN

Lake Galilee

Megiddo

Shunem

Jezreel

Ramoth

I S R A E L

Samaria

Shechem

Jordan River

GILEAD

AMMON

Shiloh

Joppa

Bethel

Gilgal

Ekron

Geba

Jericho

Ashdod

Jerusalem

Ashkelon

Libnah

Bethlehem

Gath?

Lachish

Gaza

Hebron

Dead

Sea

PHILISTIA

J U D A H

Gath?

Beersheba

M O A B

EDOM

© United Bible Societies 1978

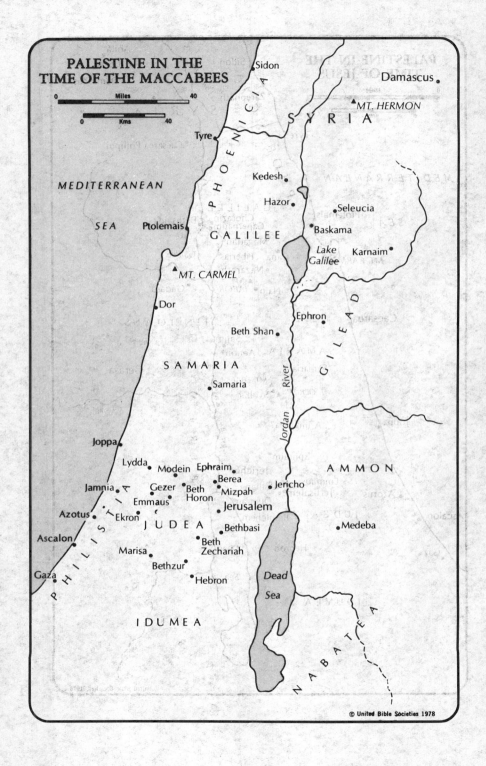

PALESTINE IN THE TIME OF THE MACCABEES

Miles 0 — 40
Kms 0 — 40

MEDITERRANEAN

SEA

Sidon

Damascus

SYRIA

▲ MT. HERMON

PHOENICIA

Tyre

Kedesh

Hazor

Seleucia

Ptolemais

GALILEE

Baskama

Lake Galilee

Karnaim

▲ MT. CARMEL

Dor

Ephron

Beth Shan

GILEAD

SAMARIA

Samaria

Jordan River

Joppa

Lydda

Modein

Ephraim

Berea

AMMON

Jamnia

Gezer

Beth Horon

Mizpah

Jericho

Emmaus

Jerusalem

Azotus

Ekron

JUDEA

Bethbasi

Medeba

Ascalon

Marisa

Beth Zechariah

Gaza

Bethzur

PHILISTIA

Hebron

Dead Sea

IDUMEA

NABATEA

© United Bible Societies 1978

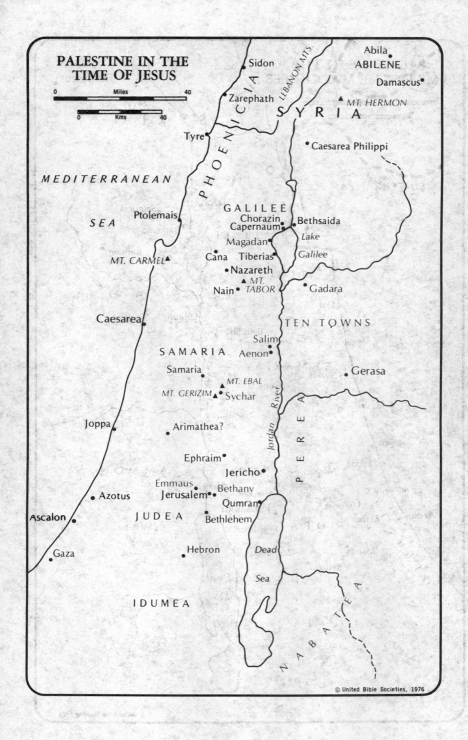

PALESTINE IN THE TIME OF JESUS

Miles
0   40

Kms
0   40

MEDITERRANEAN

SEA

Abila
ABILENE

Damascus

Sidon

Zarephath

LEBANON MTS.

S Y R I A

▲ *MT. HERMON*

Tyre

PHOENICIA

• Caesarea Philippi

Ptolemais

G A L I L E E

Chorazin
Capernaum • Bethsaida

Magadan
Lake

Cana   Tiberias
Galilee

MT. CARMEL ▲

• Nazareth
▲ MT.
TABOR

Nain •
• Gadara

Caesarea

T E N   T O W N S

Salim

S A M A R I A   Aenon •

Samaria •
• Gerasa

MT. EBAL ▲
MT. GERIZIM ▲ • Sychar

Jordan River

P
E
R
E
A

Joppa
• Arimathea?

Ephraim •
• Jericho

Emmaus
Jerusalem • • Bethany

• Azotus
• Qumran

Ascalon

J U D E A   • Bethlehem

• Gaza
• Hebron
Dead

Sea

I D U M E A

N
A
B
A
T
E
A

© United Bible Societies, 1976

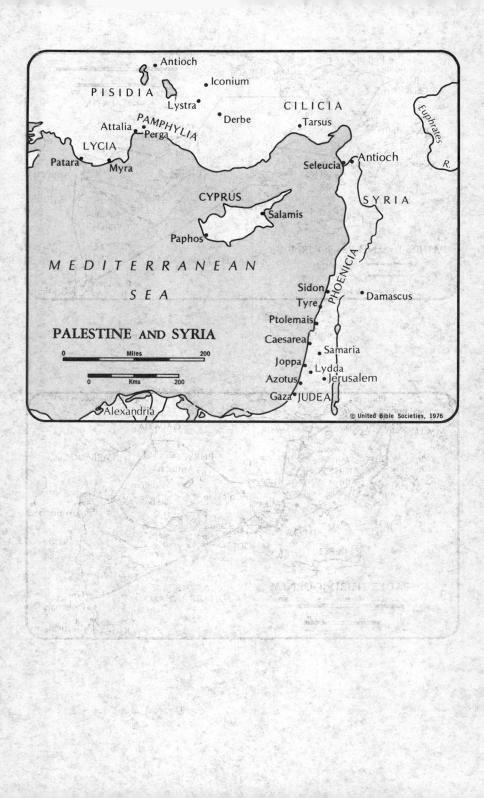

PALESTINE AND SYRIA

© United Bible Societies, 1976

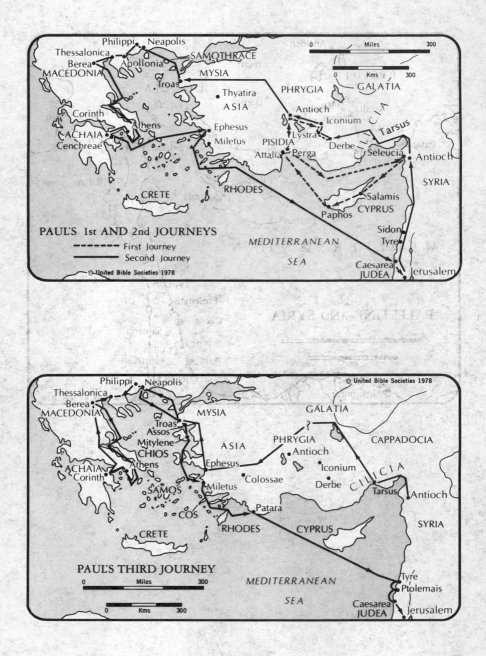

PAUL'S 1st AND 2nd JOURNEYS

‑ ‑ ‑ First Journey
——— Second Journey

© United Bible Societies 1978

Philippi · Neapolis
Thessalonica
Berea · Apollonia SAMOTHRACE
MACEDONIA
Troas MYSIA
Thyatira
ASIA PHRYGIA GALATIA
Corinth Antioch
Athens Ephesus Iconium C I L I C I A
ACHAIA Miletus Lystra Tarsus
Cenchreae PISIDIA Derbe Seleucia
Attalia Perga Antioch
SYRIA
CRETE RHODES
Salamis
Paphos CYPRUS
Sidon
MEDITERRANEAN Tyre
SEA
Caesarea
JUDEA Jerusalem

Miles 300
Kms 300

PAUL'S THIRD JOURNEY

© United Bible Societies 1978

Philippi · Neapolis
Thessalonica
Berea GALATIA
MACEDONIA MYSIA
Troas
Assos CAPPADOCIA
Mitylene ASIA PHRYGIA
CHIOS Ephesus Antioch
Athens Iconium C I L I C I A
ACHAIA Derbe
Corinth Colossae Tarsus
SAMOS Miletus Antioch
COS Patara SYRIA
CRETE RHODES CYPRUS
Tyre
MEDITERRANEAN Ptolemais
SEA Caesarea
JUDEA Jerusalem

Miles 300
Kms 300

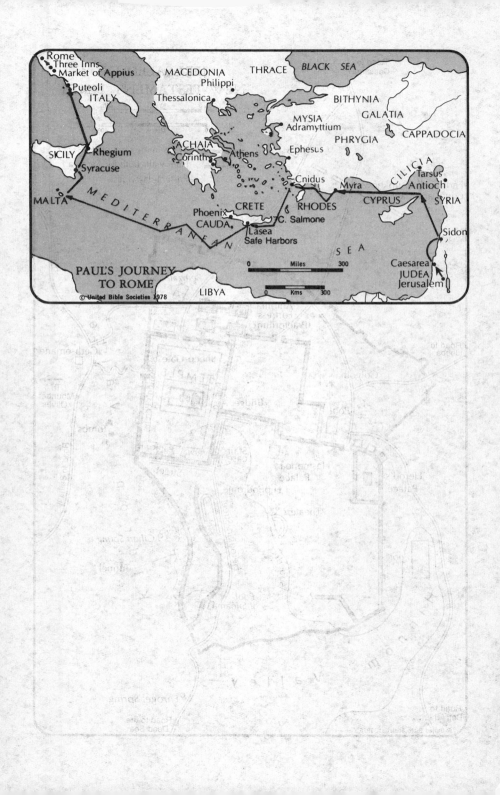

PAUL'S JOURNEY TO ROME

© United Bible Societies 1978

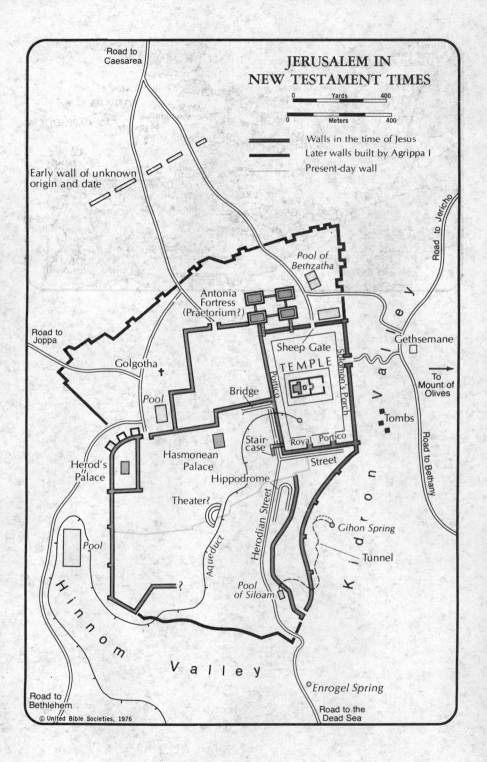

JERUSALEM IN NEW TESTAMENT TIMES

Yards 0 — 400
Meters 0 — 400

Walls in the time of Jesus
Later walls built by Agrippa I
Present-day wall

Road to Caesarea

Early wall of unknown origin and date

Road to Joppa

Road to Jericho

Pool of Bethzatha

Antonia Fortress (Praetorium?)

Sheep Gate

Golgotha

TEMPLE

Solomon's Porch

Gethsemane

To Mount of Olives

Pool

Bridge

Portico

Tombs

Staircase

Royal Portico

Hasmonean Palace

Street

Herod's Palace

Hippodrome

Theater?

Herodian Street

Gihon Spring

Tunnel

Kidron Valley

Road to Bethany

Pool

Aqueduct

?

Pool of Siloam

Hinnom Valley

Enrogel Spring

Road to Bethlehem

Road to the Dead Sea

© United Bible Societies, 1976